1999
SPORTS
COLLECTORS
Almanac

From The Editors Of

Sports *Voice for the Hobby*
Collectors
Digest
The hobby's oldest and largest publication

Published by

**krause
publications**

700 E. State Street • Iola, WI 54990-0001
Telephone: 715/445-2214

Please call or write for our free catalog.
Our toll-free number to place an order or obtain a free catalog is 800-258-0929
or please use our regular business telephone 715-445-2214
for editorial comment and further information.

ISBN: 0-87341-744-5

Printed in the United States of America

TABLE OF CONTENTS

FOOTBALL

Events that shaped sports collecting in 1998

Baseball's great home run chase the top story of the year

By Tom Mortenson

John Elway and the Denver Broncos won their first world title on Jan. 25 with a thrilling upset victory over the Green Bay Packers in Super Bowl XXXII.

After setting a record with 114 regular season victories, the New York Yankees won their 24th Championship in October by defeating the San Diego Padres in the 1998 World Series.

In June, the Chicago Bulls, behind Michael Jordan, Scottie Pippen, Dennis Rodman and company, claimed their sixth NBA title.

The Detroit Red Wings swept the Washington Capitals to gain their ninth Stanley Cup crown.

As exciting as these events were, the year 1998 in sports will be remembered as the year of the great home run race — the year of Mark McGwire and Sammy Sosa. It was the year that one of the most revered records in all sports — Roger Maris' single-season home run record that stood for 37 years — was shattered.

The year of the home run provided a boost for the baseball collectibles industry. Interest in baseball memorabilia — particularly home run baseballs — was at an all-time high. McGwire and Sosa collectibles were produced and offered everywhere. Relatively older McGwire material came out of the woodwork, too. A McGwire rookie card rated at a perfect gem mint by one of the card grading service companies — a card that had been printed in quantities of perhaps one million specimens in 1985 by Topps — went for an astounding $2,750 at the National Sports Collectors Convention auction in Chicago in August, 1998.

Fittingly, the home run chase, and all the drama that surrounded it, became the top story of the year in sports.

That was the good news. While Major League Baseball enjoyed a banner campaign, there were some casualties in the collecting industry. Two major players in the sports trading card and memorabilia industry filed for Chapter 11 bankruptcy protection in 1998. New Jersey-based Score Board Inc., and Texas-based Pinnacle Brands Inc., are no longer in business. Along with producing cards and card-related products, Score Board was also deeply active in the autographed memorabilia market. Pinnacle Brands, which produced Pinnacle, Score, Donruss andLeaf trading cards, also closed shop last summer.

On a brighter note, interest in football cards was high among collectors. That interest was fueled initially by new cards of rookie quarterbacks Peyton Manning of the Indianapolis Colts and Ryan Leaf of the San Diego Chargers, the first two players chosen in the NFL draft. Later, as the football season progressed, interest in cards of the Minnesota Vikings' sensational rookie receiver Randy Moss boosted football card sales.

On the other hand, sales of 1998-99 basketball cards took a hit due to the turbulent labor situation in the NBA.

In sports collecting, 1998 was certainly an interesting year. It was a topsy-turvy year with plenty of peaks and valleys.

Along with a comprehensive listing of new card sets that came out in 1998 and their pricing, the following pages of this *1999 Sports Collecting Almanac* includes an assortment of some of the top stories in sports collecting for 1998. Taken from the pages of *Sports Collectors Digest* and *Sports Cards* magazine, this compilation of articles are a capsulized history of the year. Among the reprinted articles, you'll find market reports for baseball, basketball, football and hockey cards and figurines. There are also interesting features on McGwire, Moss, Bill Russell, the Beanie Baby phenomenon, SportsFest, the National Sports Collectors Convention and much more.

We hope this bonus will add to your enjoyment of the *1999 Sports Collecting Almanac.*

The hottest names in 1998

The ten hottest active players to collect in 1998 were:

1. Mark McGwire
2. Sammy Sosa
3. Randy Moss
4. Terrell Davis
5. Barry Sanders
6. Michael Jordan
7. Kerry Wood
8. Peyton Manning
9. John Elway
10. Wayne Gretzky

Mark McGwire realizes one person can't clean up the autograph industry. Still, he intends to try.

Baseball's all-time HR king worked with *Sports Collectors Digest* throughout the 1998 baseball season in an investigation of McGwire-autographed sports collectibles. The unfortunate finding: None of the McGwire autographs purchased by *SCD* was authentic.

"Some of these autographs are ridiculous," McGwire told *SCD* during a meeting prior to a Brewers-Cardinals game in early August. "I just can't believe a person would knowingly sell something that is as phony as what I've seen. This stuff isn't even close."

As part of its investigation, *SCD* showed McGwire five autographed 8x10s purchased from hobby retailers during the summer. McGwire declared four signatures to be forgeries; one, he said, was legitimate. The sole authentic photograph was provided, without the first baseman's knowledge, by a business advisor.

"That's too bad," McGwire responded. "I was hoping at least one of those you bought was the real deal."

SCD's McGwire test case contributed to intense national scrutiny of McGwire-signed collectibles. McGwire was asked to serve as *SCD's* test subject due to his infrequent signing (he hasn't signed for money or participated in a private signing in 10 years), his marketability, his one-year tenure with the Cardinals (only National League materials and Cardinal-specific items were included in the sampling program) and his unique desire to preserve the purity of sports autographs among America's youth.

"I know a lot of guys don't want to bother with this, but I feel I have to," McGwire said. "For some reason, children seem to be drawn to me. I know the parents, or the children themselves, are buying these bogus autographs, and that really bothers me. It's just sad to think that a child is working somewhere this summer only to spend his hard-earned money on a forgery."

Big Mac Attack:

St. Louis slugger works with *Sports Collectors Digest* to improve the hobby

McGwire admits he signs almost daily at the ballpark and also signs individual items for teammates, opponents and friends. Some of those signatures, he admits, find their way into the hobby. *SCD* viewed more than a dozen authentic McGwire signatures for sale at the 1998 Chicago National, for example. The

majority of those signatures, though, are placed in a specific, consistent position, often away from the item's "sweet spot," to discourage resale and to provide an added element of control.

"Sure, I do autographs, but I don't do them in bulk or for money," McGwire said. "There is not enough to go around. It's not possible for any dealer to have enough to sell them in any quantity."

In its research on McGwire autographs, *SCD* talked with several hobby

retailers who each reported selling more than 50 McGwire-autographed items during the past six months. *SCD* has researched the sources of several bogus autograph lots, tracking transactions across multiple state lines. Several retailers, apprised of the convincing results of *SCD's* investigation, have agreed to offer refunds to consumers concerned about the authenticity of their McGwire-signed items.

McGwire also advised consumers to be cautious regarding letters of authenticity. Each of the McGwire autographs purchased came with an LOA, signed either by the individual retailer or a third-party service. In each case, the letter authenticated a forged signature. While authenticating services can certainly be an asset, the McGwire example indicates that not all LOAs serve to protect consumers.

"If they haven't witnessed me signing it – and they haven't, because I don't do signings – how can these people say this stuff is my signature?" McGwire said.

SCD confirmed at the time of this probe that several law enforcement agencies are investigating forged McGwire signatures. In mid-August, Missouri Attorney General Jay Nixon filed consent orders against businesses based in Boca Raton, Fla., Doylestown, Pa., and St. Peters, Mo. The Missouri investigation is ongoing and will focus on the origin of forged McGwire items.

Should the McGwire forgery situation turn collectors away from autographed items? Not at all. But collectors must use common sense in making autograph purchases. For example:

If you are offered a McGwire-signed ball for $20, be very wary. If you can buy 50 balls at that price, the decision is obvious: Don't.

ABOUT THIS REPORT

A business struggling for legitimacy amid persistent authenticity issues.

That is the unsettling result of what *SCD*, in keeping with its leadership role in the sports collectible industry, found during its three-month study of the sports autograph market.

Here are some of the trends *SCD's* study uncovered:

*A large percentage of consumers still choose low price over authenticity.

If you could buy a McGwire-signed ball for $20 or $50, how much would you pay?

Before you decide, consider this: The ball costs about $12 and a top star will charge at least $20 per signature (McGwire doesn't sign for money). That doesn't factor in any profit for the dealer, or the expense of an authenticating procedure.

When the cost of goods is $32, one has to wonder about a $20 retail price on a star-signed baseball.

Yet, many consumers ignore logic and opt for the lower-priced item. Until consumers decline to purchase ridiculously underpriced merchandise, sports forgers will continue to profit from this industry.

Pricing on the 8-by-10 photos we purchased, purportedly signed by McGwire, ranged from $25 to $32. None was authentic. *SCD* did find one authentic McGwire signature on an 8-by-10 photo at the Chicago National. Price tag: $50.

*Bad merchandise is directly proportional to on-field success.

McGwire hadn't held a public signing for 10 years when large quantities of signed memorabilia turned up in the hobby in the wake of the home run craze. A measure of McGwire's increased popularity: Photo File, a baseball-licensed manufacturer, reports that nearly half of all McGwire photos sold since early 1997 have been purchased in the past three months.

*Seemingly reputable dealers can't source their product.

SCD tracked one lot of nearly 150 items supposedly autographed by McGwire through dealers in three states. Two of the dealers now say they were misled, having thought they were purchasing from a "good source: One who had given us good autographed product in the past." The third dealer said his source was a San Francisco-area charity (McGwire hasn't signed in quantity for any charity, including his own). The dealer refused to provide any purchase orders or other confirming data to *SCD*.

Many dealers are addressing the authenticity issue by scheduling private signings with top athletes. Said veteran dealer Darren Prince: "It's to the point where, if I haven't seen it signed, I really can't be comfortable selling it."

*The hobby is mobilizing against bad autographs.

Information is power, and the mass media has certainly publicized the autograph industry's darker issues, initially with Michael Jordan forgeries, and now with bad McGwire sigs.

While negative media reports are unpleasant for all who work in the hobby, they do play the important role of educating the consumer/collector.

When the majority of collectors finally understand that good autographs cost more than forgeries, legitimate dealers will see a boost in sales.

Thanks to McGwire and concerned athletes like him, the autograph business is undergoing a necessary change.

As legitimate retailers use their access to athletes through private signings as a selling point, dealers who can't account for the origin of their product will continue to lose sales.

Also, the industry is aware that law enforcement officials are very willing to pursue forgers – which only serves to strengthen reputable hobby dealers.

Clearly, the combination of informed collectors, authenticity-minded dealers and the threat of law enforcement is ultimately good news for everyone involved in the sports autograph hobby.

METHODS VARY FOR AUTOGRAPH DEALERS

The autograph market these days brings out the cliches in full force:

"Buyer beware."

"If it's too good to be true, it probably isn't."

"Better safe than sorry."

Hopefully, the cliches associated with autographs will turn around in the next few years.

"Safe and sound."

"More fun than a barrel of monkeys."

"That 70 percent figure is completely bogus."

OK, that last one isn't a cliche; it's an editorial. But there's no doubt that collectors, dealers and the media need to be educated to the point that they can easily dismiss the FBI's ridiculous claim that 70 percent of all sports autographs in the market are fraudulent.

The autograph market has taken such a hit in the past decade, you'd think it isn't possible to collect sports autographs without filling your mantle with Mantle fakes. Nothing could be further from the truth, of course, but you wouldn't know it from watching or reading the national media.

How is it possible to collect sports autographs safely and inexpensively? Well, that inexpensive thing is getting more and more difficult all the time, but you can still find legitimate autographs, and there are still thousands of trustworthy dealers across the country. You just have to know where to find them.

One of the best places is *Sports Collectors Digest*. Is *SCD* completely free of fakes? We can't make that claim. But *SCD* continues to take industry-leading steps to help the consumer buy from its pages with confidence and security.

SCD requires its advertisers to offer a money-back guarantee if buyers can establish questions about an item's authenticity. Advertisers who do not resolve issues with collectors lose their advertising privileges.

Many dealers we contacted – not all of them are *SCD* advertisers – expressed concern about the policy, arguing that collectors could switch product on them.

"I would need a third-party authentication if it was several months later," said dealer Arthur Gottheim of New York. "There's too much room for finagling to go on. Who knows if you're getting the same thing back?"

Other dealers gave similar sentiments.

"Once something leaves your hands, some people try to return something that you didn't sell them," said Bill Vizas of Bill's Sports Collectibles in Denver, Colo.

Said show dealer Barry Krizan of K-2 Sports in Columbia, Ill., "If a customer is gone awhile and then they come back, then we're very skeptical," Krizan said. "We've always been customer-friendly, but you have to be careful (about product being switched)." Added Mike Darwish of M.D.'s Sports Connection in Wilder, Ky., "There are switches."

Of course, dealers can employ a system using unique stickers, holograms or initializing that will curtail the potential for switched product. A unique, num-

SCD'S ADVICE FOR COLLECTORS•

- Buy autographs from a publication that has a money-back guarantee policy. Autographs purchased on-line or at shows from somebody you don't know are often going to be yours to keep, whether or not you like the autograph after you receive it. Always ask a dealer about his return policy prior to paying for an item.

- Purchase autographs from a dealer you can trust. That sounds obvious, but in many cases, a collector will try to convince himself or herself that an autograph is real because its price is right, especially from an anonymous Internet seller. Don't let your wallet overcome your conscience.

- If you can't see the autograph signed yourself, get the autograph from somebody who did see it signed. That means finding a dealer who was at a show with the player, or ideally had a private signing with the player. The best source for finding player signings are the advertisements in SCD.

- Find a dealer who can document his/her sources. Every fake autograph has a story behind it. If you have documentation behind the story, i.e. copies of contracts or better yet a UDA-like authentication system, you greatly increase your odds of finding a real autograph.

- Don't put an overemphasis on a certificate of authenticity. Most fakes come with one.

- Do your homework in terms of finding out what an autograph should look like. This doesn't mean you'll become an authenticator yourself, but you should know enough about a Brett Favre signature, for example, to know that he almost always signs his name with a "4" except occasionally when he signs a jersey. Become somewhat acquainted with a player's autograph before you pay money for it, to avoid patently obvious fakes.

- If you collect expensive, vintage autographs, develop a network of dealers and authenticators who can help you authenticate your purchases.

SCD'S ADVICE FOR DEALERS

- Ask yourself the following question: "Am I basing a retail business around the ability to trick an athlete or entertainer into signing a free autograph for me?" If the answer is yes, ask yourself what that does to the autograph market and the relationship between celebrities and fans.

- Develop a dealer, distributor and show promoter network that can not only supply you with real autographs, but can back up those autographs with paperwork and verification that you can pass along to your customers.

- Develop a computerized or index card system so that you can track autographs you've obtained yourself in the future.

- If you hold private signings, develop a method of identifying which product is yours. That might mean initializing or signing the item itself, or developing a sticker or hologram to put on the item. The extra work will save you headaches down the road.

- Become familiar with the authentication services, both those that authenticate autographs after they've been signed and those that authenticate at the time of signing. There are services available for dealers who hold private signings that can supply you with the ability to authenticate and document your autographs at the signing.

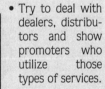

- Try to deal with dealers, distributors and show promoters who utilize those types of services.

- Monitor the pages of SCD to stay informed on the different services that are available, and also look for articles in the future that can help you help the autograph industry.

- Watch for upcoming signings at both private and public events and call those promoters/dealers in advance to order autographs.

- Ensure your autographs are valid on the front end so you won't need authenticators on the back end. If you have an autograph obtained at a signing that was documented, you won't need a return policy.

14

bered sticker system isn't cost effective to duplicate, and provides the seller with a method for identifying his products and tracking their resale.

While *SCD's* policy may increase the responsibility level for some dealers, that's where much of the opportunity lies for cleaning up the autograph industry. Much has been written about how collectors should protect themselves, but autograph dealers haven't been asked, industry-wide, to alter their business plan accordingly.

From a time when autographs were a hobby, not a business, athletes are now being paid for their autographs. However, many dealers are still selling autographs that the athlete or entertainer wasn't paid for. While most of those autographs are legitimate, that situation creates problems.

"We need to get dealers away from using runners," said Bill Vizas. "Dealers shouldn't be buying from people they don't know. Some kids will buy 50 (unsigned) photos from us."

Many dealers have perfectly legitimate autographs, but they were obtained in less-than-legitimate ways. And the informality of the process leaves the door open for fakes and frauds.

For a perfect case study, let's look at an entertainment/celebrity autograph business that is based around runners.

This company's autographs are real. The owner and his handful of runners utilize contacts with restaurant owners, limousine drivers, etc., and a fleet of cellular phones to track down celebrities. The six people who track down the autographs know nothing about forging signatures; they couldn't do it if they tried. And the company's autographs are immediately authenticated with the owner's initials on the back of the item. There is also a system, either a sticker or a number, put on the item so the origination can be tracked. The company keeps all of its autographs' provenance on computer so it can be tracked later.

On the surface, it's a very good system. The company sees 100 percent of its autographs signed. It guarantees its autographs 100 percent, with no time limit

because of the number and initial on the item. You can feel very safe buying an autograph from a dealer who uses this supplier. But in many ways, companies like this are exactly what is hurting the autograph industry.

What's the problem? The athlete is not paid, and therefore there are no contracts involved. What's to keep a forger from saying he has a similar system? If a dealer holds a private signing with a celebrity or obtains autographs at a public signing, that celebrity has exerted some control over the authenticity of that particular autograph market. In this instance, the celebrity is at the mercy of a company he/she most likely has never heard of.

When the owner of this business was asked if his livelihood is based around the ability to trick an entertainer into signing a free autograph, he said, "I have guys that work for me that will do anything for one. I don't do that. But celebrities get hounded a lot."

That doesn't really answer the question. The answer, of course, is yes. Dealers who use runners are basing a retail business around the ability to obtain free autographs from unsuspecting celebrities, including athletes, so they can sell them for nearly 100 percent profit. This same autograph supplier estimated that

at least 70 percent of all entertainment autographs are forgeries. But when asked what could be done to clean up that market, he said, "Nothing. Well, every item that's sold has to come with a 30-day, money-back guarantee and has to have a stamp or sticker saying when and where it was signed."

His original answer – nothing – stems from the fact that, at heart, a dealer who uses runners knows that system is not perfect. Selling an autograph that was signed for free is not a service to the collector; it's a disservice to the legitimate autograph market.

We asked 20 autograph dealers how they obtained their autographs, and most of them went about their business in ways that help the industry. Krizan and his K-2 Sports obtains 95 percent of its autographs at shows that it attends, or shows that its dealer friends attended. The other 5 percent of its autographs are of the vintage variety. Obviously a dealer has to rely on his/her expertise when dealing in those autographs.

Krizan said he would never sell an autograph that wasn't obtained through an organized signing. He said the way to clean up the autograph industry is to maintain a level of formality that is fair to everybody involved. That means that the athlete knows it's real because he was paid to sign it, the dealer knows it's real because it was obtained at a signing, and therefore the collector can know it is real. Unfortunately, Krizan said, enforcement is very difficult.

"We need to get more agents involved, like McGwire's," he said. "That's the best thing that can happen. I don't know that the industry itself has a lot of control over the situation."

Many dealers encouraged *SCD* to take an increasingly hard line on fake autographs. Said Darwish of M.D.'s Sports Connection, "We need firmer punishments for people who get caught (making or selling forgeries). They get caught and they get a slap on the wrist. I think *SCD* could crack down harder." Said Harlan Werner, owner of Art of the Game stationed in Dodger Stadium, "Krause holds most of the power – cut off advertising privileges. *(SCD)* must take a stance."

Hugh McAloon, *SCD's* publisher, said the magazine has been and will continue to be vigilant in policing autograph dealers. *SCD* has the industry's most stringent customer service policy: Advertisers who do not resolve disputes with collectors lose their advertising privileges, a policy that McAloon has enforced many times in recent years.

"We do much more to police advertisers than the other publishers in this industry," McAloon said. "Our money-back-guarantee is an enhancement of our long-standing effort to protect *SCD's* collector readers.

"But our efforts aren't alone to curb the questionable segment of this business. We need the industry to work together and take responsibility for protecting consumers interested in buying autographs."

SCD asked several dealers what industry efforts they suggest for policing the autograph industry:

B&E Collectibles, Joe Esposito: "Everybody should have a lifetime guarantee."

Jeff Bassman, Bassman Collectibles, Beverly Hills: "Patrol shows for fakes."

Chuck Dandrea, Shooting Star Hockey Memorabilia: "There needs to be some licensing body. Every dealer should be licensed. There is an opinion that dealers are like used-car salesmen. We need a licensing body in which if a dealer is caught, the license is revoked."

David Stuart, Wichita, Kan.: "If there's a deal that's too good to be true, it's not a true deal. That's my advice for the average collector."

SCD's advice for the autograph collector is to make the line as short as possible from the athlete to the collector. One of the ways to do that is to utilize a dealer who saw the autograph signed himself, or got the autograph from somebody who saw it signed. And the way to ensure that somebody actually saw it signed is to have the person running the signing use an Upper Deck Authenticated-style procedure to label the item, so it can't be confused with a fake at a later time.

All of this is unfortunate and, in many ways, discouraging. Unfortunately, it's the way autographs are headed. Collectors can still find good autographs. It's just a lot more harrowing than it used to be.

SCD'S AUTOGRAPH POLL

Staffers at *SCD* polled 20 prominent autograph dealers to ask them about their inventory, the state of the autograph market and what can be done to improve it. Here are the results:

1. *What percentage of your business involves autographs?*
Half said 75 percent of their business or more is in autographs, one-quarter said half of their business and one-quarter said less than 30 percent.

2. *For what percentage of your signed inventory did you witness the signing?*
30 percent said they've witnessed 95 percent of their inventory or more, 10 percent said they've witnessed 50-70 percent and the other 60 percent were witnesses in 25 percent or less.

3. *List the athletes you see with the most questionable material on the market.*
Half of those answering said Michael Jordan, and nearly half said Mark McGwire. Other popular answers were Brett Favre, Dan Marino, Ken Griffey Jr., Wayne Gretzky, Tiger Woods, Muhammad Ali and Mickey Mantle. Most dealers said any autograph that's expensive, while one dealer added, "Anybody who's died recently."

4. *What is your return policy for you retail customers?*
70 percent have a lifetime guarantee, no questions asked. Another 15 percent said 30 days no questions asked, while the other 15 dealt mainly at shows and were hesitant about a return policy.

5. *Would you be comfortable with Krause's new 30 days, no-questions-asked policy?*
Surprisingly after the previous answers, only 55 percent said yes. 25 percent said that's too stringent, while it didn't apply to the other 30 percent.

6. *Has the recent widespread media coverage of fraudulent merchandise hurt your business?*
65 percent said no, while 35 percent said yes. One of those answering yes said anybody who answered no "is a liar."

7. *What percentage of autographed material in the marketplace do you believe is fake?*
15 percent had no guess. 15 percent said 70 percent or more for stars, but much lower for others. 15 percent said one-half to one-third are fakes. 55 percent of those answering said 15 percent or less are fakes.

8. *Offer percentages of the sources for your autographed material.*
40 percent obtain all of their autographs themselves. Another 40 percent obtain at least 80 percent of their autographs from private signings, public signings, or dealers or promoters who attended private signings. 20 percent obtain at least half of their material from people they don't know — runners or collectors.

9. *What can be done to address the problem of fake autographs?*
Some answers: Get agents involved, require dealers to have guarantees, firmer punishment, start a licensing body. 60 percent said there isn't much that can be done, and most added that collectors must use their collecting savvy.

The chase for Roger Maris's single-season home run record turned into a lovefest between baseball fans who came back to the game and sluggers Mark McGwire and Sammy Sosa. Along the way, the baseball card industry enjoyed a captivating ride.

McGwire's record-breaking performance produced positive feelings for the game that were buried since the players' strike in 1994. The Cardinals' massive slugger not only eclipsed Maris's 37-year-old record of 61 homers, he did so in dramatic fashion. McGwire did everything right along the way, from hugging the six siblings of Maris after his 62nd homer to donating the record-breaking ball to the Baseball Hall of Fame.

"To be honest, I realize what I have done and I know how special it is," McGwire said after his 62nd home run. "It's been quite amazing. I think I have amazed myself. I think I have amazed other people. So it is hard not to have emotions for this. It's an unbelievable feat."

62

Some people have compared the emotions generated from this historic feat to Cal Ripken breaking Lou Gehrig's consecutive games streak in 1995. After the negative feelings generated from the baseball strike the previous year, Ripken's record-breaking feat brought baseball out of the doldrums. But McGwire's record-breaking performance – and the way Sosa matched him homer for homer down the stretch – made this season the most memorable in several decades.

"We're going to look back on this season like people look back on 1927," said Rich Donnelly, Florida Marlins hitting coach. "This might be the greatest thing that's ever happened in baseball."

St. Louis's love affair with McGwire began on July 31, 1997 when he was traded from Oakland to St. Louis. He hit 24 homers over

the last 51 games of the season to finish with 58 and the slugfest continued this year, when he hit three homers on Opening Day, including a grand slam. He became the first player to collect 50 or more homers in three consecutive seasons and blasted the longest home runs in seven different ballparks, adding a 545-foot blast at Busch Stadium for good measure.

McGwire didn't even bother going through the free-agent process after last season. He signed a three-year, $28.5 million deal with the Cardinals and then announced that he was donating $1 million a year to form the Mark McGwire Foundation for Children, which fights child abuse. The lovefest with Cardinals fans was just beginning.

"Ever since he was traded to St. Louis last summer, I've been asked, 'What's he really like?' The sentiment I've repeated most often is that he's a better person than he is a player," said St. Louis manager Tony LaRussa.

That's what has made McGwire so likeable during this run to the record books. His massive home runs have become mythic in nature, yet he gets teary-eyed when talking about his past personal troubles. He hit his

Mark McGwire's Record-Breaking Season United Baseball Fans And Reignited The Baseball Card Market

By Greg Ambrosius

61st home run on his dad's 61st birthday and pumped his chest and pointed toward the sky as a tribute to Roger Maris after his 61st and 62nd home runs. His outward emotions toward his 10-year-old son, Matthew, who was a batboy for several Cardinals' games this summer, has also endeared him to parents everywhere. Heck, he even thanked his ex-wife during the post-game ceremonies after his 62nd home run.

So with this lovefest in full force and 43,688 fans in attendance on Sept. 8 at Busch Stadium, it wasn't surprising that McGwire was given the record-breaking baseball by a Cardinals' grounds-crew member despite estimates that the ball would be worth $1 million in an open auction.

"That ball doesn't belong to me or anyone else," said Tim Forneris, the 22-year-old grounds keeper who tracked down the 62nd homer. "That's why you have a Hall of Fame."

The six previous home run balls were also returned to McGwire, who was adamant about giving the 62nd home run ball to the Hall of Fame. He gave the ball, bat, full uniform, hat and his son Mathew's jersey to Don Marr, the Hall's president, for display.

"Just think," McGwire told his son, "your jersey is going to be in the Hall of Fame."

"It's refreshing," Marr said. "People shortchange America. These baseball fans are showing their true colors."

Two teenagers who caught numbers 58 and 59 in Miami turned down $5,000 offers for the baseballs and returned the balls to McGwire in exchange for meeting the superstar and getting signed balls, bats and jerseys. Deni Allen, who caught No. 60 in St. Louis, also received autographed items in exchange for the ball and took batting practice with the Cardinals before a game. Mike Davidson, who nabbed No. 61 in St. Louis, gave it back to McGwire with no strings attached.

Before the record-breaking feat, the hobby was abuzz with speculation about what the 62nd home run ball would be worth. Sports memorabilia experts agreed that the home run ball would be worth $1 million if McGwire hit it. Sosa's 62nd home run ball was caught by a Chicago fan and will likely be auctioned for hundreds of thousands of dollars. Shop At Home first offered $250,000 for McGwire's 62nd home run ball, but it never got to that point.

"He's been extremely lucky to get all of these balls back," said Mark Jordan of Mark Jordan, Inc., Arlington, Texas. "I think people are caught up in the positive feeling toward McGwire."

While plenty of attention was given to the record-breaking ball, the final home run ball could create the most excitement. Two prominent dealers offered $1 million for the final home run ball even before the final number was established.

"I think there's a lot of hoopla for No. 62 now, but I think down the line the final ball will be worth more," added Jordan. "I think people are excited about the record-breaker, but the new standard is going to be the new standard and that makes that ball worth more."

McGwire was intent on staying focused on the home run chase during the season and didn't sign any commercial endorsements, although that will certainly change during the offseason. He still doesn't have an autograph and memorabilia agreement, although Upper Deck Authenticated has tried to lure McGwire into its stable of superstar signers. But as of press-time McGwire was still a free agent signer.

Because of the scarcity of legitimate McGwire autographed baseballs, values have risen from $50 to $200 this season, while a

Sosa autographed baseball sells for around $150. Demand is so intense for McGwire autographed balls right now that dealers have become frustrated with the lack of available items.

"It seems like I've been getting about 50 calls a day for McGwire and I just don't have them," Jordan said. "I'm lucky if I've had 15 all year."

Collectors have had no problem finding McGwire's top cards, however. His 1985 Topps rookie card (#401) has been the hottest card in the market over the last four months and has seen an unprecedented rise in value. Priced at $20 a year ago, it is now at $175 and still heading up. PSA-9 examples have sold for over $550 in recent auctions, with an SGC-100 McGwire selling for $2,750 in August.

Other McGwire cards on the rise include his 1987 Donruss (#46, up $7 this month to $15), 1998 Bowman Golden Anniversary (#5, up $100 to $400), 1998 Stadium Club One of a Kind (#203, up $50 to $175) and 1998 Flair Showcase Legacy (#9, up $150 to $600).

There's also been huge interest in his minor league cards. McGwire is pictured on seven minor league cards: 1985 Modesto A's (name misspelled as McGuire $800; corrected version $650), 1986 Burger King Huntsville Stars ($45), 1986 Southern League All-Stars ($65), 1988 "1982" Glacier Pilots ($350), 1989 Modesto A's ($45) and 1989 Tacoma Tigers Pro Card ($30).

Sosa's top cards are also in great demand. His 1990 Leaf rookie card (#220) doubled this past month to $60, while his 1998 Stadium Club One of a Kind (#16) has risen to $60.

Now the key for the industry is to capitalize on baseball's renewed relationship with the fans and bring back collectors to the industry. Look for several commemorative insert sets in upcoming '99 sets, along with a few specially produced boxed sets. McGwire and Sosa's home run chase has been good for baseball in 1998, but it will likely produce even better results for the card industry in 1999.

"All current memorabilia – all current licensed products – are really at the mercy of how people feel about the game," said Marty Appel, spokesman for Topps. "We just follow along and there's little we can do about things that are out of our control. The strike was out of our control and McGwire was out of our control, but this is a real good thing."

So good that history may look back at this accomplishment as baseball's turning point after the strike of 1994.

"It may not be overstating it, and time will tell, that what Babe Ruth did for the game after the Black Sox scandal Mark McGwire may go down as having done after the strike," Appel said. "This transcends what Cal Ripken did with the consecutive games streak in 1995. McGwire is like a super hero."

A super hero indeed.

The thrilling 1998 baseball season — by the numbers

By Greg Ambrosius

There's no question that 1998 will be remembered as the season of historic numbers. It starts with number 70, the single-season home run record set by the Cardinals' Mark McGwire, and continues all the way to Cal Ripken's consecutive games played streak, which concluded at 2,632.

Major League Baseball fans began concentrating on numbers from Opening Day as the assault on Roger Maris's single-season home run record of 61 first came into focus. McGwire hit three home runs on Opening Day – including a grand slam – and from that point on number 61 was brought up on a daily basis. Maris held that record for 37 years and now it will be interesting to see how long McGwire's record will last.

But McGwire wasn't the only player making history in 1998. Here's a quick look at other historic milestones accomplished during the memorable '98 season:

1 Games needed to decide this year's National League wild card team. The Chicago Cubs defeated the San Francisco Giants 5-3 in the one-game playoff, with the New York Mets finishing one game behind both teams after losing their last five games of the season.

2 The number of players who reached the 50-homer mark, the first time four players had accomplished that during the same season. Mark McGwire, Sammy Sosa, Ken Griffey Jr. and Greg Vaughn reached that plateau in 1998.

5 Roger Clemens will likely become the first pitcher in major league history to win five Cy Young Awards after posting a 20-6 record with a 2.65 ERA and 271 strikeouts.

7 The number of consecutive post-season appearances by the Atlanta Braves, the most in major league history.

10 The number of years between 20 win seasons for David Cone – the longest span in major league history – who went 20-7 this year after going 20-3 in 1988 with the New York Mets.

15 Barry Bonds and John Olerud set the major league record for reaching base in 15 consecutive plate appearances.

20 The number of strikeouts by Cubs' rookie Kerry Wood, tying a major league record on May 6 against Houston.

21 The number of runs scored in the highest-scoring All-Star Game in history (13-8, won by the American League at Coors Field in Denver).

22 Roger Clemens was undefeated in his last 22 starts of the season, the longest streak since Dave McNally went 26 games without a loss for Baltimore in 1969.

27 David Wells retired 27 straight Minnesota Twins on May 17 for the Yankees' first perfect game in two decades.

40 Alex Rodriguez became the third player in major league history to hit 40 home runs and steal 40 bases in the same season, joining Jose Canseco and Barry Bonds.

42 Consecutive saves by Tom Gordon, breaking the major league record of 40 by Rod Beck and Trevor Hoffman.

50-50 Craig Biggio became only the second player this century to finish a season with at least 50 doubles and 50 stolen bases.

50 Mark McGwire became the first player in major league history with three consecutive seasons of 50 or more home runs.

50-20 Ken Griffey Jr. became the third player in major league history to hit at least 50 homers and have at least 20 stolen bases in a single season, joining Willie Mays and Brady Anderson.

53 Trevor Hoffman set the National League record with 53 saves and Rod Beck had 51, becoming the fourth and fifth relievers in major league history to record 50 or more saves in a season.

66 The number of home runs by Sammy Sosa, who broke Roger Maris's major-league record, but still finished second in the National League home run race to Mark McGwire.

70 Single season home run record by Mark McGwire, who shattered Roger Maris's mark of 61 set in 1961.

108 Number of losses by the defending world champion Florida Marlins, the most losses by any team since 1969.

114 The number of wins posted by the New York Yankees, the most wins by a team in the last half century. The Yankees won the AL East with a 114-48 record.

179 The number of hits by Tampa Bay's Quinton McCracken, the most for an expansion team player.

300 Ken Griffey Jr. became the fifth youngest player and Juan Gonzalez was the sixth youngest player to reach the 300 home run mark.

300 Number of strikeouts by Curt Schilling, becoming the fifth pitcher in major-league history with consecutive 300 strikeout seasons.

400 Barry Bonds became the first player in major league history to accumulate 400 career home runs and 400 stolen bases.

2,632 Consecutive games played by Cal Ripken, whose streak was snapped on Sept. 13 when he voluntarily stepped out of the lineup for the first time since May 30, 1982.

2,878 Number of career hits for Baltimore's Cal Ripken Jr., one of the players with a shot at 3,000 this season.

2,922 Number of career hits for Tampa Bay's Wade Boggs heading into the 1999 season.

2,928 Number of career hits by San Diego's Tony Gwynn after the 1998 season.

3,319 Paul Molitor concluded his amazing 21-year career with 3,319 hits, eighth best in history. Molitor became only the third player in major league history to collect 3,000 hits, 600 doubles and 500 stolen bases.

Methods vary widely for dealers in the business of autographs

Collectors and dealers alike need to arm themselves with the knowledge needed

By Rocky Landsverk

The autograph market is in a shape that brings out the clinches in full force:

"Buyer beware."

"If it's too good to be true, it probably isn't."

"Better safe than sorry."

Hopefully, the cliches associated with autographs will turn around in the next few years.

"Safe and sound."

"More fun than a barrel of monkeys."

:That 70 percent figure is completely bogus."

OK, that last one isn't a cliche; it's an editorial. But there's no doubt that collectors, dealers and the media need to be educated to the point that they can easily dismiss the FBI's ridiculous claim that 70 percent of all sports autographs in the market are fraudulent.

The autograph market has taken such a hit in the past decade, you'd think it isn't possible to collect sports autographs without filling your mantel with Mantle fakes. Nothing could be further from the truth, of course, but you wouldn't know it from watching or reading the national media.

How is it possible to collect sports autographs safely and inexpensively? Well, that inexpensive thing is getting more and more difficult all the time, but you can still find legitimate autographs, and there are still thousands of dealers across the country who you can trust completely. You just have to know where to find them.

One of the best places is *Sports Collectors Digest*. Is *SCD* completely free of fakes? We can't make that claim. But *SCD* continues to take industry-leading steps to help the consumer buy from its pates with confidence and security.

SCD requires its advertisers to offer a money-back guarantee if buyers can establish questions about an item's authenticity. Advertisers who do not resolve issues with collectors lose their advertising privileges.

Many dealers we contacted — not all of them are *SCD* advertisers — expressed concern about the policy, arguing that collectors could switch product on them.

"I would need a third-party authentication if it was Vizas of Bill's Sports Collectibles in Denver, Colo.

Said show dealer Barry Krizan of K-2 Sports in Columbia, Ill., "If a customer is gone a while and then they come back, then we're very skeptical," Krizan said. "We've always been customer-friendly, but you have to be careful (about product being switched)." Added Mike Darwish of

M.D.'s Sports Connection in Wilder, KY., "There are switches."

Of course, dealers can employ a system using unique stickers, holograms or initializing that will curtail the potential for switched product. A unique, numbered sticker system isn't cost effective to duplicate, and provides the seller with a method for identifying his products and tracking their resale.

While *SCD*'s policy may increase the responsibility level for some dealers, that's where much of the opportunity lies for cleaning up the autograph industry. Much has been written about how collectors should protect themselves, but autograph dealers business plan accordingly.

From a time when autographs were a hobby, not a business, athletes are now being paid for their autographs. However, many dealers are still selling autographs that the athlete or entertainer wasn't paid for. While most of those autographs are legitimate, that situation creates problems.

"We need to get dealers away from using runners," said Bill Vizas. "Dealers shouldn't be buying from people they don't know. Some kids will buy 50 (unsigned) photos from us."

Many dealers have perfectly legitimate autographs, but they were obtained in less-than-legitimate ways. And the informality of the process leaves the door open for fakes and frauds.

For a perfect case study, let's look at an entertainment/celebrity autograph business that is based around runners.

This company's autographs are real. The owner and his handful of runners utilize contacts with restaurant owners, limousine

Autograph "runners" ruined what had been a pleasant event at the NFL Quarterback Challenge this spring in Orlando. After three days of relaxed atmosphere and pleasant interaction between the QBs and lucky fans at the hotel, the local paper ran an article naming the site. The following morning, autograph sharks descended, forcing security to lock the doors and escort the athletes everywhere they went, while leaving a terrible taste in the QBs' mouths.

drivers, etc., and a fleet of cellular phones to track down celebrities. The six people who track down the autographs know nothing about forging signatures; they couldn't do it if they tried. And the company's autographs are immediately authenticated with the owner's initials on the back of the item. There is also a system, either a sticker or a number, put on the item so the origination can be tracked. The company keeps all of its autographs' provenance on computer so it can be tracked later.

On the face value, it's a very good system. The company sees 100 percent of its autographs signed. It guarantees, its autographs 100 percent, with no time limit because of the number and initial on the item. You can feel very safe buying an autograph from a dealer who uses this supplier. But in many ways, companies like this are exactly what is hurting the autograph industry.

What's the problem? The athlete is not paid, and therefore there are no contracts involved. What's to keep a forger from saying he has a similar system? If a dealer holds a private signing with a celebrity or obtains autographs at a public signing, that celebrity has exerted some control over the authenticity of that particular autograph market. In this instance, the celebrity is a the mercy of a company he/she most likely has never heard of.

When the owner of this business was asked if his livelihood is based around the ability to trick an entertainer into signing a free autograph, he said, "I have guys that work for me that will do anything for one. I don't do that. But celebrities get hounded a lot."

That doesn't really answer the question. The answer, of course, is yes. Dealers who use runners are basing a retail business around the ability to obtain free autographs from unsuspecting celebrities, including athletes, so they can sell them for nearly 100 percent profit. This same autograph supplier estimated that at least 70 percent of all entertainment autographs are forgeries. But when asked what could be done to clean up that market, he said, "Nothing. Well, every item that's sold has to come with a 30-day, money-back guarantee and has to have a stamp or sticker saying when and where it was signed."

His original answer — nothing — stems from the fact that, at heart, a dealer who uses runners knows that system is not perfect. Selling an autograph that was signed for free is not a service to the collector; it's a disservice to the legitimate autograph market.

We asked 20 autograph dealers how they obtained their autographs, and most of them went about their business in ways that help the industry. Krizan and his K-2 Sports obtains 95 percent of its autographs at shows that it attends, or shows that its dealer friends attended. The other 5 percent of its autographs are of the vintage variety. Obviously a dealer has to rely on his/her expertise when dealing in those autographs.

> "We need to get dealers away from using runners. Dealers shouldn't be buying from people they don't know."
> — Bill Vizas, Bill's Sports Collectibles

Krizan said he would never sell an autograph that wasn't obtained through an organized signing. He said the way to clean up the autograph industry is to maintain a level of formality that is fair to everybody involved. That means that the athlete knows it's real because he was paid to sign it, the dealer knows it's real because it was obtained at a signing, and therefore the collector can know it is real. Unfortunately, Krizan said, enforcement is very difficult.

"We need to get more agents involved, like McGwire's" he said. "That's the best thing that can happen. I don't know that the industry itself has a lot of control over the situation."

Many dealers encouraged *Sports Collectors Digest* to take an increasingly hard line on fake autographs. Said Darwish of M.D.'s Sports Connection, "We need firmer punishments for people who get caught (making or selling forgeries). They get caught and they get a slap on the wrist. I think *SCD* could crack down harder." Said Harlan Werner, owner of Art of the Game stationed in Dodger Stadium, "Krause holds most of the power — cut off advertising privileges. (*SCD*) must take a stance."

Hugh McAloon *SCD's* publisher, said the magazine has been and will continue to be vigilant in policing autograph dealers. *SCD* has the industry's most stringent customer service policy: Advertisers who do not resolve disputes with collectors lose their advertising privileges, a policy that McAloon has enforced many times in recent years.

"We do much more to police advertisers than the other publishers in this industry," McAloon said. "Our money-back-guarantee is an enhancement of our long-standing effort to protect *SCD's* collector readers.

"But our efforts aren't alone to curb the questionable segment of this business. We need the industry to work together and take responsibility for protecting consumers interested in buying autographs."

SCD asked several dealers what industry efforts they suggest for policing the autograph industry:

B&E Collectibles, Joe Esposito: "Everybody should have a lifetime guarantee."

Jeff Bassman, Bassman Collectibles, Beverly Hills: "Patrol shows for fakes."

Chuck Dandrea, Shooting Star Hockey Memorabilia: "There needs to be some licensing body. Every dealer should be licenses. There is an opinion that dealers are like used-car salesmen. We need a licensing body in which if a dealer is caught, the license is revoked."

David Stuart, Wichita, Kan.: "If there's a deal that's too good to be true, it's not a true deal. That's my advice for the average collector."

SCD's advice for the autograph collector is to make the line as short as possible from the athlete to the collector. One of the ways to do that is to utilize a dealer who saw the autograph signed himself, or got the autograph from somebody who saw it signed. And the way to ensure that somebody actually saw it singed is to have the person running the signing use an Upper Deck Authenticated-style procedure to label the item, so it can't be confused with a fake at a later time.

All of this is unfortunate and, in many ways, discouraging. Unfortunately, it's the way autographs are headed. Collectors can still find goo autographs. It's just a lot more harrowing than it used to be. Dealers, distributors and promoters have the ball in their court.

SLABBED & GRADED

Things heat up in the card grading arena...

By T.S. O'Connell

Under the heading of "Everything old is new again," one of the pioneers in the card grading and slabbing business has resurfaced, this time as president of Sportscard Guaranty Corp. Joe Merkel, a man who might be regarded as having been a bit ahead of this time, has revived his 100-point grading scale and dusted off his unique card holder for another try at the lucrative card-grading market.

It was a little more than 10 years ago that he launched Superlative Baseball Card Certification (SBCC), which lasted a couple of years and, by his own admission, cost him "a lot of money." While there can be some argument about why it didn't work at the time (Merkel is convinced it was, simply, just a bit too soon for graded cards to catch on), he is just as certain that the Merkel card holder and that 100-point grading scale deserve another time at bat.

And the stakes seem to have escalated. Regardless of your views about graded and slabbed cards, the marketplace seems to have announced quite firmly that premium grades of vintage cards were, quite probably, underpriced in the years before grading services.

How else to explain both the staggering prices announced for some of the highest-grade cards and the dramatic expansion in the numbers of cards being "slabbed?".

PSA, with a seven-year head start, has profited from boatloads of positive publicity from reported auction and sales prices of some of the most famous cards in the hobby, prices that have made many long-time hobbyists scratch their heads.

When a PSA-10 Andy Pafko card from the coveted 1952 Topps set was auctioned for a reported $83,000 a couple of months ago, it wound up getting a couple of weeks-worth of national media attention, the kind of nuzzling from the big boys that the hobby hasn't seen since the late 1970s or early 1980s.

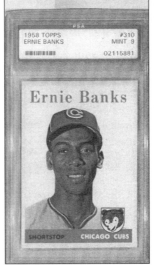

So it may be no coincidence that PSA officials reported a quantum leap in business from around 15,000 to 18,000 cards per month to a staggering 30,000 or so in June, similar numbers for July and more than 35,000 for August. "Everything has exploded in the last couple of months," said PSA President Steve Rocchi, whose staff has grown to more than 25 full-time employees. He also noted that in the last year the number of PSA-authorized dealers has nearly tripled to 250 and the two-year-old PSA Collectors Club is expected to top 3,000 members by the end of the summer.

And while such gaudy numbers have, no doubt, caught the attention of Merkel, he insists that this re-entrance into the card-grading field was prompted by the urging of veteran dealers who came to him insisting that his expertise was needed.

"The market needs somebody who's a card expert and a paper expert," said the 32-year-old Merkel, who has been a regular on the card show circuit since he was in college in the mid-1980s.

He concedes that when he first tried this venture in the spring of 1988, it may have been too soon. "Initially, some dealers fought against grading because they felt they could grade their own cards," said Merkel.

He added that there was also some resistance because there was, at the time, a lot of "bad material" in the hobby, including trimmed, bleached and doctored cards, and some dealers were less than eager to have it exposed.

With his return to the card grading field in 1998, Merkel unveils his card holder that offers 46 different interior sizes and a grading system that utilizes almost two dozen different categories and a multi-step process that he designed to eliminate the usual bias of grading, where possible. Points are deducted according to his system on a weighted basis, with the information fed into a computer program. Somebody still has to make a final determination about a grade. That's where Merkel comes in.

"I finalize all of the cards," said the president. That likely provides a good deal of comfort to some veteran dealers who have known him over the years, a group that includes Alan "Mr. Mint" Rosen, who has worked with Merkel and consulted with him on numerous occasions. Rosen thinks enough of Merkel's abilities that he has even agreed to serve as a spokesman for SGC, ending a very vocal and decade-long opposition to the very idea of third-party grading.

With a full-time staff of five and several part-timers, Merkel understands he faces an uphill battle against the entrenched PSA. Both companies have connections to the coin-grading hobby that gave life to the idea of entombing a collectible in plastic and assigning it a grade: PSA is owned by David Hall, who also owns Professional Coin Grading Service, and the principal investors of Numismatic Guaranty Corp. of America have an interest in the newly created SGC.

And as PSA approaches the grading of card No. 1 million (expected sometime before the arrival of the new millennium), Merkel is counting on that "revolutionary" holder and the 1-100 grading scale to close some of that gap. "The proof is how fast our cards are selling," said Merkel, adding that he understands the difficulty initially until the SGC name gets broader recognition within the hobby. Still, they have as many as 5,000 cards in-house waiting to be graded, and expect eventually to create a population report, though that will be a ways down the road, since Merkel is convinced that printing one is too soon with only a small number of cards graded offers too much potential for abuse within the hobby.

PSA expansion

PSA founder David Hall is in the middle of a good deal of expansion of his own company, and he appears unfazed by the arrival of yet another competitor. "Our attitude has always been that there is a lot of room and a lot of cards to grade. We never thought we would be the only grading service," said Hall.

And along with the impressive growth in its monthly numbers, PSA is looking around for other ways to expand its reach, including possible ventures into vintage authentication, signed-in-presence opportunities and even the recent creation of a "Universal Rarities Scale."

At a press conference in August at the National, PSA officials announced that the company has teamed with DNA Technologies to create PSA/DNA Authenticated. Each item authenticated by the service will bear a tamper-evident sticker displaying a certification number, as well as the logo of the service. Also, all of the items certified will be tagged with a DNA trace unique to PSA/DNA Authenticated.fs

The invisible mark will be used to identify authenticated signatures without detracting from the item. The authenticity of the item can be instantly verified with a hand held detector.

CSA ENJOYING RECORD GROWTH SPURT AS WELL

Certified Sports Authentication (CSA), founded in 1996 by Sean and Wayne Moore, is currently grading between 4,000 and 7,000 cards per month and enjoying an average growth rate of 125 percent per month for the past year.

Sean Moore calls the grading scale used by the London, Ohio company "the most accurate and easiest to understand." CSA uses the 1 to 10 scale, but starting at CSA-7 (near-mint) the scale includes .5 gradiations up to CSA-10 (gem mint).

The company employs two full-time graders, both with extensive backgrounds in paper restoration. CSA's customer base is largely made up of collectors, and relatively few dealers, a configuration that Moore says reflects their belief that the majority of ungraded cards are being held by collectors.

Moore also pointed out that a T-206 Ty Cobb red background card graded CSA-10 was recently sold by Walker Quality Auctions for nearly $20,000, a record price for the card.

Who says professional grading killed the coin hobby?

Joe Merkel is familiar with the frequently repeated chorus that the arrival of professional grading dealt a serious blow to the coin hobby years ago, a charge that Merkel dismisses. "It isn't true, (grading) didn't ruin the coin hobby," he insisted. While he agrees that some hobbyists were lost because of the prices increases, the overall affect was beneficial. "More money was actually brought into the hobby, because (grading) allowed for people to enter the hobby with little or no knowledge."

No less of an authority than Cliff Mishler, the president of Krause Publications, the largest publisher of hobby periodicals in the nation, also disputes the idea that slabbing and grading dealt a crippling blow to the coin collecting hobby. "The total dollars in the coin market is probably bigger than its ever been. The hobby is not "ruined," it's different," said Mishler.

Mishler added that there is a negative to the expansion of grading services. "A collector likes to feel that he can have "the best," but slabbing puts the best out of reach of the average collector." Like Merkel, he concedes that there probably are some collectors who were turned off to the hobby because of it.

"When people say that the coin market is ruined today compared to 10 years ago, they are comparing apples to oranges." Mishler explained that coin collectors, like their sports cards counterparts, tended to be "generalists," and over time evolved to collecting more in specific areas.

Mishler also pointed out that the doom sayers in the sports cards hobby seem to forget the enormous hold that sports has on the populace. "Cards, because of the connection to the individual players and teams, enjoys a closer attachment to collectors than in stamps and coins and other hobbies. And that's a real strength."

"PSA/DNA Authenticated hopes to eliminate the problem of counterfeits by labeling items in such a way that they can be sold time after time with each new buyer confident that the or she is spending money on an authentic item," PSA President Steve Rocchi said.

Meanwhile, Topps and PSA will begin a joint program beginning with the release of 1998 Topps Finest Football Series II.

Included in approximately 10,000 boxes of the product will be redemption cards good for free grading and authentication of any Finest sports cards issued by Topps, covering all years, and all sports.

In addition, Topps and PSA are having on-going discussions regarding expansion of the relationship into several other programs, including autograph authentication.

Hall is also excited about the recent creation of the "Universal Rarities Scale," which he describes as "a shorthand, comparative method for indicating the number of known specimens of specific items."

The 1 to 10 sale describes whether a particular rare coin, postage stamp, vintage toy, autograph, musical record, sports card or any other collectible is unique or easily available in large quantity. For example, an item listed as UR-1 is believed by experts to be readily available with over 10,000 surviving specimens. At the other end of the Universal Rarity Scale, an item described as UR-10 is believed to be unique, with only one known example.

According to Hall, the 20 experts involved in created of the scale said they immediately will begin using the comparative numbers in their price guides, auction catalogs and product offerings. For his part, he said he expects the scale will play a role in price reporting and how card specimens (in PSA's case) will be described, but he conceded that it would likely take some time for it to become widely accepted.

He added that while it might also be included in some fashion in PSA's Population Report, the report itself, obviously, would not be based on the estimates from the Rarities Scale, since the figures wouldn't be valid over the passage of time.

Hall is intrigued by the possibilities of developing a data base that would offer estimates of card rarity for a vast number of cards, an undertaking he admits would "take years to do." In the meantime, PSA will look at possibly increasing its presence in the memorabilia market. "There are some things that we might be able to help with," said Hall, who noted that his company had even looked at the possibility of a ball holder suitable for authenticating single-signed baseballs.

That one's on hold for the moment, but with all those Mark McGwire baseballs flying out of the ballpark, one wonders how long.

Football's new Saviors

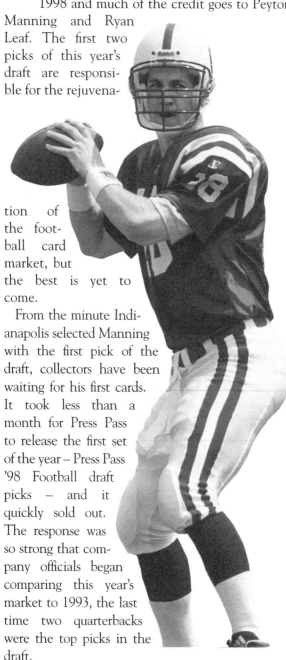

The football card market, coming off two sub-par selling seasons, is off to a strong start in 1998 and much of the credit goes to Peyton Manning and Ryan Leaf. The first two picks of this year's draft are responsible for the rejuvena-tion of the foot-ball card market, but the best is yet to come.

From the minute Indianapolis selected Manning with the first pick of the draft, collectors have been waiting for his first cards. It took less than a month for Press Pass to release the first set of the year – Press Pass '98 Football draft picks – and it quickly sold out. The response was so strong that company officials began comparing this year's market to 1993, the last time two quarterbacks were the top picks in the draft.

"We're sold out and a lot of distributors have called to reorder," said Bill Surdock of Press Pass. "This is blowing the (Drew) Bledsoe and (Rick) Mirer year away. The last draft I'd compare this to was 1983 with Dan Marino."

That's the story throughout the football card market. When Ultra Football from Fleer/SkyBox hit the hobby in early July, packs quickly went above the suggested retail price. Ultra featured short-printed rookie cards as part of its base set and they had collectors scurrying for Manning and Leaf singles. Packs were moving for $4 (SRP $2.69), with boxes going for $90. The Manning single initially was selling at $25-$40, while the Leaf rookie was going for $20-$30.

Manning and Leaf are also the driving forces behind the new super-premium Playoff Prestige brand. While not short-printed, the rookies in the product have packs going for $6-$7 each.

But Manning and Leaf aren't the only top prospects from this year's talented rookie class. Don't be surprised if Chicago RB Curtis Enis, Minnesota WR Randy Moss, New England RB Robert Edwards, Jacksonville RB Fred Taylor and Tennessee WR Kevin Dyson also make big impacts during their rookie seasons.

"There is a lot of talent at the skill positions from this year's class and that generates excitement," said Dawn Ridley, assistant vice president at Players Inc. "There has been so much discussion about this class of rookies as it relates to trading cards, so you naturally wonder if they can live up to that hype, or will they drown."

Although collectors aren't looking for any downsides to this rookie class right now, it should be noted that very few quarterbacks excel during their rookie seasons. The only QB to ever be named NFL Offensive Rookie of the Year was Buffalo's Dennis Shaw, who earned the award in 1970 when he had 10 TDs and 20 interceptions.

Collectors need to look no further than Bledsoe and Mirer to see what can happen to heralded rookie quarterbacks. Bledsoe was the first pick of the 1993 draft out of Washington State, while Mirer was selected second out of Notre Dame. Both QBs became starters as rookies and both had mixed results. Bledsoe started 12 games as a rookie for New England and completed 214 of 429 passes for 2,494 yards with 15 TDs and 15 INTs. Mirer started all 16 games for Seattle during his rookie season and had similar success, completing 274 of 486 passes for 2,833 yards with 12 TDs and 17 INTs.

Despite their early struggles, collectors were convinced that both quarterbacks were on their way to stardom. Their first super-premium rookie cards, 1993 Upper Deck SP, quickly jumped to $14 for each player. But by the next year, the careers of the two players were headed in opposite directions.

Bledsoe had a stellar sophomore season with the Patriots, leading the NFL in completions (400), attempts (691) and passing

yards (4,555), while throwing 25 TDs and 27 INTs. Mirer, on the other hand, missed the last three games of the season to injury after completing only 195 of 381 passes for 2,151 yards, 11 TDs and seven INTs. During the '94 off-season, Bledsoe's Upper Deck SP rookie card (#9) shot up to $70, with Mirer's rookie card (#16) remaining at $14. Today, with Bledsoe throwing for 18,348 yards and 108 TDs through five seasons, his Upper Deck SP lists for $75, while Mirer's career is in jeopardy, as is his SP rookie card at $6.

It will be interesting to see how collectors handle cards of Manning and Leaf if they struggle this year. And it's almost inevitable that they will struggle.

"They're going to stink it up, everybody does," said Tampa Bay QB Trent Dilfer, who knows something about the subject first-hand. "They'll have their flashes, but it's going to be too much for them. The game is so fast, it's so difficult right now for quarterbacks. They'll have their games — each of them will throw for 300 yards a couple times this season. But can they win games consistently? It's going to be very difficult. And that's just history talking."

Yes, history has a way of chewing up and spitting out quarterbacks who fail early in their careers. But collectors would be wise to be patient with Manning and Leaf because they should have long, successful careers.

"The best advice I've gotten so far is to be patient," Manning said at the Quarterback Challenge in Orlando in April. "You see some guys that have bad experiences early on and just haven't overcome it. If it goes bad early, as long as I keep coming back, week after week, I'll be okay in the long run."

But just in case the going gets tough, Manning and Leaf can feel better knowing that other star QBs struggled during their rookie seasons only to go on to Hall of Fame careers.

NATIONAL PROVES STRENGTH OF THE HOBBY

Collectors Convention in Chicago

Collectors, Dealers All Smiles At The 19th National In Chicago

By Tom Hultman

It was tough to find anyone who was disappointed at the 19th National Sports Collectors Convention in Chicago Aug. 6-9 at the Rosemont Convention Center.

Dealers, corporate executives and collectors were all smiles when asked about this year's show. It was a positive that couldn't have happened at a better time for the hobby.

Questions about the strength of the hobby were definitely answered at this National.

Adam Martin of Dave and Adam's Card World of Tonawanda, N.Y., who was working his sixth National, said his company's booth was constantly busy even though it was set up in the back corner of the convention center.

"Every year we do more and more business at the National," he said. "It's by far our best show ever."

National organizers did not disclose attendance figures, but many dealers estimated the crowds were in the 30,000 range, which was in line with pre-show estimates.

"Super crowds. I've done a ton of business. I have no complaints," Ohio dealer Kevin Savage said. "I would rank this one in the top three or four Nationals. That's pretty good considering the market conditions the way they are."

Ryne Sandberg, Nolan Ryan, Joe Montana and Dick Butkus were among the celebrities signing at the 19th National in Chicago Aug. 6-9. Dealers estimate nearly 30,000 collectors came through the doors.

By the way, the 1999 National will be held in Atlanta at the Georgia World Congress Center July 22-25.

Martin Glisinski of Longmont, Colo., said he has been to several Nationals, including the 1993 National at McCormick Place.

"I'm just like an older kid in Toys R Us," he said. "This National met my expectations. They go all out and have a lot of dealers and have a lot of opportunities to buy. It's actually quite dangerous, you could overspend very easily if you're not careful."

"Amazing" is how Dennis Fikert of Bolingbrook, Ill., described the National.

"There are a lot more people than I thought would be here," he said. "I primarily collect baseball. I collect old, hard to find items, things from the Chicago Cubs and Sox. So far I have found them here. There's a lot of neat stuff here."

Fikert picked up a 1945 Cubs World Series pennant, a baseball lapel pin and programs from the 1962 All-Star Game at Wrigley Field.

Of course, this National – like the previous 18 – was the place to be for collectors who were in search of high-ticket vintage material. This year was no different with 1950s and 1960s Topps and Bowman cards, along with tobacco baseball cards being sought after by collectors and dealers.

Autographed memorabilia and game-used jerseys also took center stage among collectors.

Bob Pressley of BP Sports Collectibles, Marietta, Ga., said memorabilia sold very well at his booth.

"The more unusual stuff has done well for me like the Jimmie Foxx pieces and team-signed balls and Braves material, Chipper Jones and Andres Galarraga game-used bats," he said. "We sold a Michael Jordan Upper Deck Authenticated replica autographed baseball jersey for $1,750."

And because of Jordan and the Bulls, Chicago most likely is the best collectibles market in the country.

"It's got a lot of tradition, but show-wise over the past couple of years most people would rank Chicago as one of the better cities, if not the best city, because of its strong market," Pressley said.

Interest in rookie cards of McGwire and Sammy Sosa dominated the show. Depending on condition, McGwire's 1985 Topps card was selling for $75-$200, with some PSA-9 versions priced as high as $500.

Sosa's 1990 Leaf rookie card topped out in the $18-$25 range. Dealers also reported strong interest in new football products, while the fallout from the NBA lockout virtually crippled basketball card sales, despite the fact Chicago has been a strong basketball card market. In addition, cards of current and past Chicago Bears weren't a high priority on collectors' lists at the National.

However, Jordan cards still sold well at the tables, despite the current NBA lockout. Even during down times, Michael Jordan still sells very well in Chicago.

"Jordan collectors have deep pockets and are willing to spend the money," Martin said.

Other National Notes

AUTOGRAPH NOTES: The most popular autograph guests to sign at the National were Nolan Ryan and Joe Montana, who each rarely sign at shows, and Chicago favorite Dick Butkus, who sold out for his appearance.

Each of the three signed more than 1,000 items for their Saturday, Aug. 8, appearances. Ryan was so popular that he also signed for collectors on Sunday.

NATIONAL AUCTION NOTE: Michael Jordan's 1992-93 Chicago Bulls game-worn road jersey sold for $26,400 to top all items at the National Auction Wednesday night, Aug. 5. What's interesting about the Jordan jersey is that it was purchased by Upper Deck. The rare jersey – Jordan has kept virtually all of his jerseys for his family – will be cut into 138 pieces (each will be signed), with 23 being inserted in each of UD's six basketball products for release the rest of the year.

The six products include SP Finite (hobby only, October), MJ Living Legend (retail/hobby, October), Upper Deck Series I (hobby/retail, November), Ovation (retail/hobby, November), MJ (hobby only, December) and UD³ (retail/hobby, December). Each of the products will receive their own photo and the cards will be in packs, not redemption cards.

SPORTSFEST '98

Krause Publications' Inaugural Sports Collectibles Show Brought In Thousands Of New Collectors.

By Greg Ambrosius

If there was ever any question that the trading card industry had a promising future, SportsFest '98 provided an answer that any hobbyist will celebrate.

SportsFest '98's innovative mix of NFL interactive games, promotional card giveaways, popular autograph guests and the special Field of Dreams KidStore youth shopping area combined to put smiles on the faces of dealers, manufacturers, collectors – and most critically – potential new collectors.

"We accomplished our goals," said Hugh McAloon, Krause Publications' sports publisher. "I personally had two goals for SportsFest. One, I wanted SportsFest to dress up our industry. SportsFest needed to portray all that was good. And the second goal was to make sure we attracted kids and new collectors, and that every collector/fan who attended SportsFest left with

an appreciation of our industry and wanted to come back for more. We accomplished both goals."

The show also set a new standard for the sports card industry, with a fully carpeted show floor, easy move-in and move-out for dealers and an educational trade show before the main event.

"This show was without a doubt one of the best organized and managed shows I have done in the past 10 years," said Mike Caffey, Wholesale Card Company of Franklin, Tenn. "Thanks to all of the manufacturers, distributors, dealers, and above all, the customers, who made this an overwhelming success. With this type of event we are sure to grow our industry and expand our customer base. What a success."

Perhaps the brightest point of the show was kids receiving free cards donated by all industry manufacturers either as prizes in the 30,000 square foot interactive area or at the high-traffic KidStore location, which featured appearances by the Philly Fanatic and Ronald McDonald. Thou-

JEROME BETTIS

OSCAR ROBERTSON

JOE MORGAN

sands of charitable dollars were raised for the Philadelphia Ronald McDonald House as kids 12 and under purchased product at a significantly reduced price.

"I think this was a wonderful event for the children," said Susan Lonker, a volunteer worker who manned the KidStore booth. "The best part about this is that the money is going to an excellent cause. The kids were in heaven the whole time and I

Favre, Wilt Chamberlain, Johnny Unitas and Pete Rose, an NFL interactive area, free giveaways from the manufacturers, a live auction, and a dealer lineup that included the biggest names in the industry.

"It was one of our top five shows all-time. This was the best show we've ever done other than the National," said Adam Martin of Dave & Adam's Card World of Tonawanda, N.Y. "Do you know what it

The show's biggest day was Saturday when the autograph lineup included Favre, Chamberlain, Rose, Oscar Robertson, Frank Robinson, Johnny Bench and Joe Morgan. Each attendee also received a free autograph ticket when they entered SportsFest '98, which entitled them to one autograph of former players such as Lou Groza, Leon Spinks, Gerry Cooney, Don Maynard and Ron Swoboda.

"The way the autograph pavilion was set

Fun In Philly: From the frenzied activity at the show booths (left) to the lovable atmosphere at the KidStore (bottom), collectors had plenty to do at SportsFest '98.

felt like Santa Claus. It's something the manufacturers didn't have to do. They'll all go to sports heaven. People have even given us donations and told us to keep the change."

The KidStore was just one of the innovative additions to SportsFest '98 which made this show unique. Billed as "not just another card show," SportsFest '98 lived up to its promise in many ways. The event included a trade show for dealers, a national sponsor (Nabisco), an all-star autograph lineup that included Brett

was? It was FanFest meets the National. You had some serious heavy hitters who walked around and spent money and you had some first timers to a show. It was half people who had been to shows before and were there to spend serious money and the other half were people who hadn't been to a show before and hopefully will be coming back. It brought a lot of new people into the hobby and it also brought in the big hitters."

up and run, I don't think it's ever run smoother," said Ross Tannenbaum of Mounted Memories, which coordinated the autograph pavilion. "We got nothing but compliments from the people who attended. Every single player was in a great mood and they were all great with the people. That was very positive."

PETE ROSE

BRETT FAVRE

WILLIE STARGELL

30

Autograph tickets for Favre were $125, while Chamberlain autographs went for between $79 and $125, and Rose autographs went for $28 for a flat item or ball and $65 for a jersey or bat. Sunday's autograph lineup included Unitas ($35 to $75), Paul Hornung ($20-$25) and Ryne Sandberg ($38 and $65), with Sandberg attracting the most interest.

"People loved to see Favre and Chamberlain, but the Big Red Machine (Rose, Bench, Morgan and Tony Perez) did extremely well," added Tannenbaum. "Pete Rose sold more tickets than anyone. Pete Rose being the spokesman of SportsFest was the most popular guest. Price is also an issue because you have to remember that Rose autographs are more inexpensive than Favre or Chamberlain.

"The free autograph guests were well received. Everyone managed to get the autograph they wanted and got what they were looking for. They got a free ticket for whomever they wanted, and if that line was too long, they got their second choice."

Tannenbaum also stated that SportsFest '98 produced the most mail-order requests in the company's history, with hobbyists sending in their items to get signed by their favorite athletes. Upper Deck Authenticated also was on hand to authenticate all paid autographs.

"The fact that UDA was authenticating any and all athlete signatures signed at the show just added to the professionalism of the event," said Terry Melia, hobby media manager at Upper Deck.

"My opinion of what Krause's did with the autograph pavilion, with Upper Deck Authenticated authenticating the autographs, was just an excellent idea," added

John O'Brien of Midwest Sports & Collectibles of Wheeler, Ill.

Along with the Mounted Memories Autograph Pavilion, attendees also had the chance to meet athletes at the corporate booths. Free autographs and special guests included Bernie Parent at Pinnacle, Richard Ashburn Jr. at Upper Deck, Marvin Harrison and Mike Alstott at NFL Players Inc, Danny Mantle at Fleer/SkyBox, Joe Frazier at Darren Prince's booth, NFL Hall of Famers Ron Mix and Lenny Moore at Hall of Fame Signature Series, and seven ex-Green Bay Packer Super Bowl I and II stars, including Herb Adderley, at Tom Brown's Rookie League.

The innovative KidStore allowed youngsters to purchase packs of cards for as little as 25 cents.

"This was the perfect venue for manufacturers to meet new collectors," said Mike Monson, director of media relations for Pacific Trading Cards. "For a first time event, it was incredibly successful. Dealers on the show floor sold 685 boxes of Paramount – by far the highest total ever for a Pacific product at a show – so I know our dealers had a good show."

"We were pleased with all of our activity surrounding SportsFest," added Doug Drotman, spokesman for Fleer/SkyBox.

"We were very aggressive in creating programs to benefit dealers, collectors and our Authorized Distributors. We redeemed more than 10,000 packs in the Scott Rolen wrapper redemption, our Spin & Win had non-stop lines of activity at our booth and Danny Mantle signing at the booth helped us promote Fleer's relationship with Mickey Mantle. We noticed a strong family atmosphere and that's what Krause promised. We think shows like this are great for exposing new people to the hobby."

There's no doubt that SportsFest '98 attracted new collectors to the hobby. Kids 12 and under were allowed to enter the show free if accompanied by an adult, which produced a rare sight nowadays: Fathers and sons, grandmas and grandkids, and mothers and daughters walking hand-in-hand at a sports card show.

"My feeling of SportsFest '98 was that it was very well run, very well thought of, well attended by large groups of families, who in my opinion, were first time goers to a show," said Alan "Mr. Mint" Rosen, one of the most recognizable dealers in the hobby, of Montvale, N.J. "From your extensive advertising program, you brought in thousands of people who had never been to a show before. I know that for a fact because people were coming up to me left and right and asking me if I was a ballplayer or a retired player (as he signed Mr. Mint hats at his booth). I know for a fact that there were a ton of people who had never been to a card show before."

McAloon said he was encouraged by the family atmosphere of SportsFest. While attendance numbers still weren't finalized by presstime, McAloon said the numbers

JOE FRAZIER

JOHNNY BENCH

LEON SPINKS

aren't the critical measuring stick of the show's success.

"Rather than give you a number, let me tell you what I saw," McAloon said. "I saw kids and their parents getting a positive introduction to collecting. I saw dealers with the right products and the right enthusiasm making a lot of money. I saw great promotion and great investment in our industry from our corporate partners, and I saw a great experience for every consumer who attended SportsFest '98. From a long-term industry perspective, I liked what I saw."

The KidStore was designed with the young new collector in mind. Corporate sponsors donated product, allowing kids 12 and under to buy packs of cards and other sports memorabilia product for between 25 cents and $2, with some items even being free.

"I like the KidStore because the prices are reasonable and I can buy cards that I like," said Danny Vorski, 10, of Oldrige N.J., who was there with his mom.

"My husband is the biggest kid here," said Angie Vorski. "This has been fun for the whole family. We'll definitely be back next year."

"The KidStore was a great idea," added Ann Scheinduer of Stoney Point, N.Y., who was buying items with her eight-year-old son, Matthew. "It's a great place for the kids and it gets them into collecting."

"I came down to the show a couple of days ago and saw the KidStore and came back today," Marge Holmes of Philadelphia said on the show's final day, toting seven-year-old cousins Jonathon Baker and Jamie Holmes at her side. "It was great for the corporate sponsors to donate the items and I like the fact that the money is going to a great cause, the Ronald McDonald House."

While the KidStore was designed with the young, new collector in mind, it allowed the serious collector to also bring his entire family to the show.

"There was so much for all of us to do here," said Maria Haubrich of Newark, Del. "My husband's a big collector and he's out on the show floor looking for his stuff and we're in here at KidStore buying all of this. It's been great for the whole family."

Adding Nabisco as a corporate sponsor helped to bring in many of the new collectors. Sports fans in the Philadelphia area heard first-hand about the show through Nabisco's extensive promotional campaign.

But new collectors weren't the only ones benefitting from SportsFest '98. The show featured many of the industry's most recognizable dealers and dealer-to-dealer sales were brisk during the first two days of the show. In fact, Mark Lewis of Mark Lewis Sports Memorabilia, Centereach, N.Y., made $50,000 in transactions with dealers. Included in his sales were a 1970-71 Roberto Clemente jersey for $27,000 and a single-signed Mickey Mantle baseball from 1951 or '52 (Will Harridge ball) for $3,600.

Alan Rosen's live 100-lot auction also produced 98 sold items, including a 1962 Topps Presentation Set for $9,300 and a Babe Ruth single-signed baseball for $3,740.

All in all, SportsFest '98 provided something for everyone, while cultivating a new generation of collectors. Next year, hobbyists will get the chance to double their pleasure as SportsFest will appear in Philadelphia June 16-21, while also debuting in Chicago August 25-30.

"I feel very confident that this past week we helped to expand the collecting base in the greater Philadelphia area and I can't wait to get back to Philadelphia and Chicago in 1999," said McAloon.

Namath's Super Bowl guarantee was believed by entire 1969 Jets squad

30-year reunion autograph show allows players to relive victory

By Michael Stadnicki

Joe Namath's guarantee the New York Jets would beat Baltimore in Super Bowl III was a remark that was taken lightly by football fans and also the Colts.

On Jan. 12, 1969, the Jets backed up "Broadway Joe's" boast as they beat the Colts 16-7.

Though Namath made the comment, he wasn't the only one on the team who felt that way.

To hear the players talk about the Super Bowl victory 30 years later at the 1969 Jets Reunion Show Oct. 16-18 in Atlantic City, N.J., it was a feeling that ran throughout the team.

"It was a foregone conclusion that we were going to win," said former linebacker Larry Grantham. "We all felt that way. We knew that Joe and the offense would get some points. We analyzed our opponent, the Baltimore Colts.

"Earl Morrall was their quarterback. Tom Matte in the backfield couldn't outrun our defense. He was a three-yard-and-a-cloud-of-dust type of runner.

"Jimmy Orr was older and he wasn't coming across the middle. We knew John Mackey, the tight end, could beat us so we double covered him. I think he caught two or three passes. We were the better ballclub that day and showed it."

"If we had watched the films anymore then we would have been overconfident," said Jets running back Bill Mathis.

"The 1969 season was a year of over-achievement for us," recalled former linebacker George Atkinson. "We were a talented bunch of guys who loved to win. We won 13 of 16 and 10 of our last 11. We were confident."

Wide receiver George Sauer said the Jets were a confident bunch at the end of the season, but the team didn't start the year out that way.

"We were not consistent at the start of the year," he said. "We didn't start out so well. We did lose to Buffalo and they were the worst team. They had the first pick in the draft the following year and took O.J. Simpson."

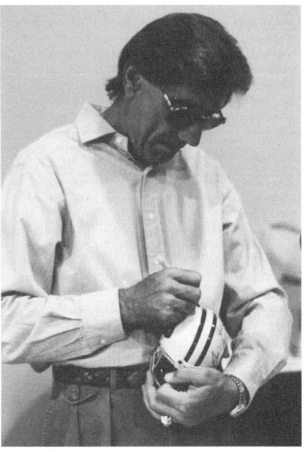

Hall of Famer Joe Namath signs a New York Jets mini-helmet for a fan.

Ralph Baker, who played linebacker, summed up the experience.

"A lot of guys worked hard for a common purpose," he said. "We were fortunate to win the big one."

"I don't know how the heck we did it," recalled John Elliott. "We were in the right place at the right time."

"It's weird that they still talk about the 1969 New York Jets," said fullback Matt Snell.

Snell ran the "19 Straight" play many times that day on his way to 121 yards rushing.

"It just seemed like it was our day," he said. "We were not a great team, but we got it done

'69 Jets reunion show fails to hit paydirt

By Mike Stadnicki

While the 1969 Super Bowl III Champion New York Jets drew the attention of the football world with their Super Bowl win, the reunion autograph show held in Atlantic City, N.J., Oct. 16-18 failed to draw a large crowd.

Attendance for the three-day event – which was promoted by Pastime Productions in association with Steiner Sports Marketing at Bally's Park Place – was estimated at under 1,000.

Football and Atlantic City just can't connect. An all football lineup of great running backs in April 19, 1997, drew less than 1,000 collectors.

Dealers seemed to sense this at this year's show, as there were fewer dealers than at a normal Pastime event.

Former Jets coach Weeb Ewbank and ex-Brooklyn Dodger shortstop Pee Wee Reese did not attend due to illness.

Artist Doo S. Oh created a poster which was given to those in attendance at the show. Each of the 1969 Jets are featured on the lithograph, which is offered by All American Collectibles.

Autographed and framed, the litho is priced at $1,295. To order, call (800) WOODY-64.

Stephen Hisler of Pastime Productions said it was his most disappointing show.

"Had the show been in northern New Jersey, it would have been more successful," he said. "This does not make me want to change my direction. There is tremendous thought into putting a show together. We are in the public service business and we want to keep them happy."

Hisler said he has learned something from this show.

"Football is a popular sport, but baseball is the number one collectible," Hisler said.

when we had to. I know the AFL was glad we won. I think they (the NFL and AFL) would have merged without us winning."

Snell, who currently runs a construction company, recalls beating Oakland for the AFL championship at Shea Stadium one of the highlights of his career.

"The Super Bowl was not the extravaganza it is today," Snell said. "Green Bay won the first two and they beat everybody."

"We are so lucky that game has never ended for us," said former offensive guard Dave Herman. "We were so different. We had this long haired, white-shoed quarterback. Joe was never critical of how you did."

His former teammates spoke fondly of Joe Willie's white shoes.

"Joe's a great friend," said former defensive back Cornell Gordon. "We're all close family. Curley Johnson keeps everybody together. He's still the life of the party."

Gordon also has been inducted into the Afro-American Hall of Fame.

"I chose to come here, that's saying a lot for this team," he said.

Grantham said, "We lived and died together. We were always a team. We really care about each other."

"We were good friends playing together," said Bill Mathis.

Mathis, Grantham and Don Maynard were members of the New York Titans before the team became the Jets.

"We were the stepchild of the New York Giants," Mathis said. "All three of us were captains when we played them. The Giants were not the championship powerhouse of the 1960s when they met.

"We won. I'd rather give back my Super Bowl ring than lose to the Giants."

Mathis had another Giant connection. He roomed with Tucker Frederickson who played for the Giants.

"I'd go from the Polo Grounds to Yankee Stadium to watch the Giants play," he said.

Denver hosts All-Star Game, FanFest

By Tom Mortenson

The biggest sporting event to ever take place in the city of Denver occurred at this year's All-Star Baseball Game July 7. A total of 51,267 fans were in attendance to witness the American League beat the National League 13-8 in the highest scoring All-Star Game in history.

The All-Star Game is Major League Baseball's midsummer party event that comes closes to rivaling the festivities of NFL's Super Bowl. In reality, nothing will ever be equivalent to the Super Bowl in terms of hype and party atmosphere. But Denver, once known as a cowtown of the old west, was decked out in fine form. And, as the slogan goes, Denver lived true to the All-Star tradition, "Where Baseball is Everything."

Hosting this year's game also meant that Pinnacle's All-Star FanFest — the eighth annual — would come to Denver. FanFest was held at the Colorado Convention Center over the Independence Day holiday weekend and days prior the All-Star Game, July 3-7.

According to Pinnacle Vice-President Laurie Goldberg, more than 75,000 baseballs fans attended this year's FanFest. That figure is close to Pinnacle and MLB's attendance expectations. Last year in Cleveland, attendance was reported to have been around 90,000. In 1996, 103,000 reportedly attended FanFest in Philadelphia.

Although a new attendance record wasn't set this year, it doesn't mean fans didn't have a lot of fun. With dozens of interactive events, clinics, free autographs, memorabilia displays and entertainment, there was something anyone would enjoy. You don't even have to be a baseball fan to enjoy All-Star FanFest.

Speaking of free autographs, there were 40 (mostly former) stars signing. For the second consecutive year, Topps sponsored the free autograph pavilion. On hand to sign, in alphabetical order, were Luis Aparicio, Joe Black, Ralph Branca, George Brett, Lou Brock, BErt Campaneris, Dave Campbell, Steve Carlton, Orlando Cepeda, Rick Cerone, Chris Chambliss, Tommy Davis, Andrew Dawson, Larry Doby, Carl Erskin, Rollie Fingers, George Foster, Joe Garagiola, Steve Gavey, Bob Gibson, Joe Girardi, Goose Gossage, Keith Hernandez, Doc Horn, Fergie Jenkins, Tommy John, Don Johnson, Don Larsen, Joe Scott, Verdell "Lefty" Mathis, Robin Roberts, Brooks Robinson, Enos Slaughter, Al "Slick" Suratt, Bobby Thomson, Frank Torre, Dick Williams, Earl Wilson, Maury Wills and Robin Yount.

The good part of the autographs at FanFest is that they are free. A possible downside is that when you are standing in line there are no guarantees you'll get the autograph or autographs you really want the most. Monday morning's lineup of autograph guests that included Brett, Yount, Robinson, Fingers and Dawson drew the longest lines. Since Brett and Yount make relatively few card show signings appearances and are future Hall of Famers and members of the 3,000 Hit Club, this was a popular session.

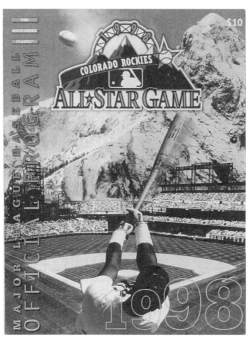

Among the souvenirs from the 1998 All-Stat Game at Coors Field in Denver were official game programs.

Any time during FanFest you might run into a celebrity. Among the visitors to the Krause Publications/*SCD* booth were Jay Johnstone, Steve Garvey and ESPN's Roy Firestone. Also seen in the Collector's Showcase area was Toronto Blue Jays ace Roger Clemens and his family. Maryland dealer/player rep Dick Gordon and Aparicio and Williams visit his booth.

Traffic in the Collector's Showcase area was brisk, especially on Sunday, July 5, when attendance at FanFest was reported as 22,000. Most dealers were pleased with the amount of business they were doing. Memorabilia dealer Jim Fick of Littleton, Colo., gave *SCD* the following report of the show. "This is the best show I've ever done," he said. "I'm very impressed with the way the show has been run. Kudos to Ray Schulte and his staff and Major League Baseball."

Schulte, coordinator of the Collector's Showcase, said he was pleased with the mix of dealers and the variety of collectible items vendors brought to sell.

One item that was strictly not allowed on dealer tables was Beanie Babies. Dealers were aware of this rule in advance and officials from MLB were out and about enforcing the ban. Schulte said the reason for the ban on the little stuffed toy critters was because he felt it was better for customers at a baseball/sports related event to spend money on sports related material. He said that last year at the National Convention in Cleveland a lot of money was being spent on Beanies that could have been spent on sports material. This sounds reasonable to me.

Ironically, MLB executed a Beanie Baby giveaway at Tuesday's All-Star Game. Ticketed fans entering Coors Field were give a red, white and blue beanie baby bear named "Glory." Dealers were outside the stadium buying the bears for $60-$150. One dealer brought $30,000 to buy as many bears as he could.

During Monday's All-Star Workout and home run contest, while Ken Griffey Jr., Jim Thome, Vinnie Castilla, Mark McGwire and company were smashing balls out of the park, the Jumbotron scoreboard screen was showing highlights of the original Home Run Derby TV program from 1959. Scenes picturing Mickey Mantle, Willie Mays, Bob Allison and Ernie Banks appeared on the screen to the delight of old-timers like me.

One thing about Colorado fans is they are very enthusiastic and supportive of their teams. Last year, *The Sporting News* named Denver the No. 1 Sports City in the USA. *The Sporting News* ranked cities based on their overall sports climate, fan fervor and over all sports atmosphere.

However, when it comes to big league baseball history, Denver — with he Rockies — is still in its infant stages. That's why it was necessary to have Lou Brock — a baseball great normally associated with the city of St. Louis — as the selected player in the card companies' redemption offer this year.

Next year, the All-Star Game and FanFest will return to the East Coast. It'll be in Boston, a city with a long tradition of big league baseball and collecting. It's not too early to begin making your plans.

Ali was the in-person star, but McGwire stole the show

By T.S. O'Connell

While patiently waiting for my rental car in San Francisco the other day en route to the Tri-Star Labor Day Show, an unnamed American League umpire was getting the royal treatment from four or five employees of the rental car company. After all the obsequious treatment from the staffers, the ump dutifully offers' free tickets to the A's/Tampa Bay game that evening. Sorry, no takers.

Presumably he would have fared a bit better had Oakland not traded away one Mark McGwire to St. Louis just over a year ago. During a weekend when the most famous baseball player in the world was making history (in the ballfield, he did a pretty good job of having an impact in the hobby even when he was a couple of time zones removed.

At a show where about 20 percent of the floor space was devoted to cute little stuffed animals, The Missouri Mauler managed to steal the show even from the Beanie Babies. McGwire material was everywhere, though most of it seemed to be of the pasteboard variety, after recent *Sports Collectors Digest* articles had suggested that the historic assault on the all-time home run record had yielded an avalanche of phony McGwire signatures in the marketplace. Still, there were plenty of McGwire cards available, especially that 1985 rookie card that is making so much news.

Tri-Star's president, Jeff Rosenberg, speculated that the four-day show might, have drawn as many as 10,000 to 12,000 collectors. "It's been a great crowd," said Rosenberg. "People are happy that we are back downtown where this show originated and where most people feel it should be.

"We think that (McGwire and Sosa) have impacted this show in the hundreds of thousands of dollars just in terms of product that changed hands," Rosenberg noted. "I saw a PSA-10 that sold here for $2,000. (The dealer) came with two, sold one for $2,000 and offered the other for $2,250. It's a good sign for our hobby that there has been a lot of business done at this show."

STAR OF THE SHOW: As is always the case, Muhammad Ali proved to be the major attraction at the Tri-Star Labor Day Show shown above hugging a youngster in the autograph line.

"This is one of the best things that could be happening in the baseball world," said veteran hobbyist Ted Forsberg of Howard's Sports Collectibles. "It's fabulous for the game. It's stimulated the hobby, not just the sale of McGwire cards, but also Maris cards, Ruth cards and the other great home run hitters."

Having said that, Forsberg was still a tad dismayed when a fellow dealer offered him a PSA-10 McGwire at a wholesale cost of $2,200. That seems a bit steep, especially in light of uncut 1985 Topps sheets (with the McGwire rookie) that were available on the show floor for $500 or so, and would presumably yield a killer McGwire if professionally cut.

One dealer reported selling eight McGwire rookies in the first 20 minutes of the show; at $125 per, and another had almost 100 of them available on his table, ranging from middle grades and offered from $125 to $200.

SHOW NOTES: There was more that reminded you of a traditional card show, including lots of sharp material that you don't see every day. Louis Bollman was sporting a PSA-10 1953 Topps Mickey Mantle that is headed for his Oct. 2 auction and another dealer was sporting a 1956 Topps unopened pack with a $2,100 price tag. Dealer Bill Waite had an imposing stash of R312s, 1936 Goudey premiums, the classic black and white photos with the soft pastel colors added and one of the tougher issues in the hobby. You don't see those three items every day, no matter what side of the Mississippi you are on.

Speaking of unopened material, Chris Weber of Strike Zone Sports in Pomona was offering what remained of the largest quantity of unopened material from the 1960s that he had ever purchased, about $80,000. That purchase included 'the largest quantity of penny packs that I had ever seen,' said Weber.

Some of the cool stuff that was at the show wasn't necessarily all that old, With Muhammad Ali as the featured guest, National Sports Distributors of San Rafael, Calif., created a really neat 'bell' that looks for all the world like the real thing and even rings loudly enough to scare the heck out of the family cat. They made only 220 bells, and Ali signed them all in gold ($450).

Wood makes first show appearance in Chicago

Sun Times show draws more than 12,000 fans

By Rob Steva

Chicago Cubs fans had their first opportunity to congratulate newly crowned, National League Rookie of the Year Kerry Wood at the 16th annual Chicago *Sun Times* Sports and Toy Collectible Convention Nov. 20-22 in Rosemont, Ill.

The three-day extravaganza drew an estimated crowd of 12,000-13,000 collectors.

"We are excited that so many people turned out for the show," said Sports News Productions' George Johnson, who noted that approximately 2,000 collectors showed up for the opening on Friday evening at the show which featured 450 tables on the second floor of the Rosemont Convention Center.

Saturday's lineup opened with Robin Yount, Rollie Fingers, Bob Lilly, Richard Dent and Hank Aaron, who drew the most autograph seekers.

Aaron, however, caused a blip on the screen when he departed almost an hour early, citing the need to catch a plane to meet his wife.

While a number of collectors were quite disappointed (an estimated 100 were still in line when Aaron departed), Johnson offered refunds or assurances of future arrangements to get the materials autographed.

A much larger crowd on Sunday saw Walt Frazier, Dave DeBusschere, Brad Park, Jim Rice and Stan Musial, along with hometown favorites Luis Aparicio, Carlton Fisk and Wood.

"We knew Sunday was going to be the big day," said Johnson. "It was Kerry Wood's first show appearance and right now he is probably the hottest player in the hobby."

Johnson has been promoting the *Sun Times* Convention for eight years and feels the Chicago market is the best in the country.

"The team loyalty and having Michael Jordan make Chicago the premier city for this hobby," he said.

Collectors were able to purchase a VIP membership package for $59. It included admission to each of the three days, early entry into the show, one free autograph, a complimentary Sammy Sosa or Mark McGwire Bamm Beano Bear, trading cards from Fleer, Upper Deck, Collector's Edge and Pacific.

On top of that, fans who purchased the VIP pack received unlimited autographs from the following guests – Don Maynard, Ken Morrow, Bill Lee, Dock Ellis, Jay Johnstone and Ron Jackson.

Over the years Johnson's shows have featured an eclectic variety of athletes, including Joe DiMaggio to Dennis Rodman to Emmitt Smith.

"We have a strong clientele and customers return year after year, mostly because we have some of the biggest names in professional sports," said Johnson.

Two of those big names who really enjoyed mingling with the fans were Musial and Fingers.

> ## "The team loyalty and having Michael Jordan make Chicago the premier city for this hobby."
>
> — George Johnson, show promoter

Wood signs for more than 1,000 collectors at show

Kerry Wood

After tying the record for most strikeouts in a single game, helping the Cubs reach the playoffs for the first time since 1989 and winning the National League Rookie of the Year, what else was left for Kerry Wood to do? He capped off an unbelievable 1998 season for Cubs fans by making his first sports collectible convention appearance.

The 21-year-old was more than generous, as he posed for photos, shook hands and personalized autographs for more than 1,000 persons who purchased tickets.

"It's always fun to meet and greet fans," Musial said. "As an old-timer I remember going to hospitals to see fans and sign autographs. I think it's important to pay back the fans."

Most of the celebrities try to make at least three to five appearances as autograph guests per year at card shows.

"It's good to see such a large turnout for events like these," Fingers said. "I think it's a good indication that fans have forgiven baseball."

Sports News Productions presents more than 50 smaller shows per year in conjunction with the much larger *Sun Times* Convention.

"Ninety-percent of the dealers at the *Sun Times* show return for every show we do, which should indicate that Chicago is a very strong market," said Johnson.

"This is one of the best and well-attended shows in the country," veteran dealer Alan Rosen said. "There is always a constant flow of people and quality merchandise out there."

Some of Rosen's purchases at the show included a collection of 1951 and 1953 Bowman cards, containing several Mickey Mantle and Willie Mays rookies. He also bought a 1931 New York Yankees autographed baseball.

Among the show's hottest collectibles included cards of Sosa, McGwire, Roger Maris and Terrell Davis, and anything with Wood's name on it.

"Babe Ruth cards and Maris cards are moving well," said Levi Bleam of 707 Sportscards. "Our business as a whole has prospered from the Sosa-McGwire episode."

Despite the large number of Beanie Baby dealers the interest level has tapered off.

"Beanies just aren't as hot as they were a year or so ago," Johnson said. "There are just too many and the market is becoming saturated."

Much like the baseball strike in 1994-95, many dealers said the basketball lockout has had a major impact on the hobby.

"People just aren't interested in basketball merchandise, which is why baseball stuff is still going so strong," Johnson said.

The next *Sun Times* Convention is slated for April. Confirmed autograph guests include Jerry Rice and Terrell Davis. For details, call 630-551-1975.

Barry Halper's collection auctioned by Sotheby's

MLB buys $5 million grouping for the HOF

By T.S. O'Connell

The most famous baseball memorabilia collection on the planet, the treasured accumulation of Barry Halper, is headed for auction, opening up for thousands of hobbyists the opportunity to bid on some of the most famous signed pieces extant. In addition, Major League Baseball has purchased a portion of the collection for a reported $5 million, with all of the items earmarked for eventual permanent display at the HOF in Cooperstown.

On Nov. 5 Halper signed an agreement with representatives of Sotheby's to auction his collection, which had been evaluated for insurance purposes at $40 million. Details have not yet been released by Sotheby's, but Halper said he expects the vast horde will be offered in at least two separate live auctions, and Sotheby's press spokesman Matt Robbins noted that a portion of the collection will be offered over the Internet. He added that Sotheby's officials expect to have the entire collection liquidated by the end of next year.

"This collection has been a labor of love for most of my life, and I doubt any private collection will ever approach it," said Halper. "I had hoped along the way to sell the collection intact, perhaps for the establishment of a museum, but this has now become the best approach for the collection."

The announcement of the plans for the famed Halper Collection came almost simultaneously with word that a portion of the collection, including Halper's T206 Honus Wagner card thought to be the second-best in the hobby and jerseys from many turn-of-the-century greats, have been sold to Major League Baseball for $5 million, according to sources close to the negotiations. MLB in turn will make the material available to the Hall of Fame in Cooperstown. According to Halper, the items obtained by MLB are currently in the process of being transfered to the Hall of Fame.

Barry Halper

He added that details about the sale, including the price, would have to be supplied by MLB officials. "I cannot confirm the amount paid, but I would say that the sale represents only a portion of the collection," said Halper. "Representatives of Major League Baseball spent many hours reviewing the collection and selected what they felt were the most essential items to transfer to the Hall of Fame."

The New York Daily News reported that the items headed to Cooperstown include Shoeless Joe Jackson's famed "Black Betsey" bat, the last MLB contract

38

he ever signed and the jersey he wore in the 1919 World Series, along with the sale papers that transferred Babe Ruth to the Yankees from the Red Sox. The sale to MLB also included Ruth's 500th home run ball, game-used bats from two other Black Sox, Chick Gandil and Buck Weaver, and a ball from the 1889 Albert Spalding tour of Egypt. The Hall of Fame will also receive 85 uniforms from Halper's legendary collection, including those of Satchel Paige, Tony Lazzeri and pre-1900 HOFers like Bobby Lowe, John Clarkson and Hoss Radbourn.

And while that sounds like an imposing pile of uniforms, it still leaves perhaps 900 uniforms, 1,800 signed balls, 400 bats, 30,000 cards, 4,000 photographs, 1,000 contracts, 4,500 personal papers, 500 rings and pins and nearly 3,000 miscellaneous pieces, a vast grouping that includes everything from movies posters, trophies and awards to All-Star and World Series programs, scorecards, ticket stubs and cigar boxes.

Veteran dealer Rob Lifson of Robert Edward Auctions, another noted name in the hobby and a longtime friend of

Halper's, is assisting in the cataloging of the material.

"This is not a painful decision, but a practical one, given my stage of life and the realities of estate planning and concern for my family," continued Halper. "I've had decades of enjoyment and hundreds of stories from the acquisition process, and from the old ballplayers I've met. I'm 58, and I am in relatively good health, but I have had heart trouble in the past, and I know it is wise to make decisions while you can, in the best interests of my family."

Auction looms of incredible Ruth-signed ball given to dying boy

By T.S. O'Connell

Babe Ruth's legend includes so many moments that blur the line between reality and fantasy that sometimes the former gets confused with the latter. In such instances, it helps to have some tangible piece of memorabilia to bolster your case. Corroborating evidence such as photographs, newspaper articles and letters from the principals can be a nice touch, too.

When you have all of that, plus a story of a dying child that sounds like it came from the handiwork of a Hollywood screenwriter, there would seen to be the potential for the kind of memorabilia magic that has created some of the priciest artifacts in the hobby. An organization called "Hearts & Hands," in Mattapoisett, Mass., has a Babe Ruth-signed baseball that can lay claim to all of the above. It is being auctioned in that city on the evening of Aug. 8, and officials of the non-profit "Hearts & Hands" are hopeful that the baseball in question can work the kind of miracle that is so entwined in Ruthian lore.

Indeed, in one of the most famous of all the Ruth stories, the recovery of young Johnny Sylvester after Ruth promised to hit a home run for him the next day (in fact, he hit three) was duly recreated in the features film

"The Babe Ruth Story." It happened during the 1926 World Series, and though it seems an apocryphal tale, it is true, and duly recorded in the major newspapers of the day.

The story of this incredible baseball is also true.

Five years later, while Ruth was recovering in a Boston hospital from an injury suffered in a game, he met an 11-year-old boy in the ward who was afflicted with a brain tumor. Walter Kent had already been in the hospital for five weeks when the great slugger introduced himself. "How are you?" said Ruth, as he shook the boy's hand.

"I am just fine," Walter replied." Ruth promised to send him some fruit and candy, and did so later the same day. Three days later, a Sunday, the day Ruth was scheduled to leave the hospital, he and young Walter met a second time, and the youngster thanked him for the candy. Walter

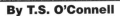

Ron Stark artwork

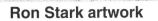

A MOVING STORY — Walter Kent is shown above holding the baseball that meant so much to him. At the left is the ball itself, showing the clear and well-preserved signature of The Babe. Kent also received a ball from Hall of Famer Rabbit Maranville (facing page), though the story surrounding it is unknown.

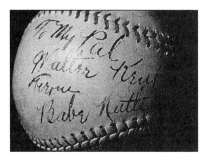

told Ruth he hoped he would be better soon. "You look out for yourself," said Ruth. "Never mind about me. You get better right away."

Then he signed a baseball, "To my pal, Walter Kent. From Babe Ruth," and handed it to the boy. With the ball tightly gripped in his hand, Walter returned to the ward and told other patients of his meeting with the Babe.

That afternoon, while a police escort and a huge crowd waited for Ruth outside the hospital, the Hall of Famer stopped to see Walter a final time. "Well, good-bye, Sonny," he said to Kent as they shook hands once again. "I hope I see you again sometime. And I hope you'll be much better when I do."

The boy kept the treasured ball at the side of his bed, and told reporters who covered the story at the time that he was going to keep the ball "all of his life."

Walter Kent Jr. died almost seven years later after yet another operation to half the growing blindness caused by the deadly march of the brain tumor. The ball was at his bedside when he died at his home in Boston.

Sixty-five years after that meeting in the hospital, Walter Kent's niece, Janice Morrissette, gave the ball and another signed by Hall of Famer Rabbit Maranville to Hearts & Hands "because she felt it was the right place for them." The baseballs had been left to her by her mother, who had told her stories about the famous uncle that she never knew. "It was an intuitive kind of thing. I knew Hearts &Hands was the right place for them. They help children with illnesses like Buddy (Walter) had, and I just know it was the right place for them."

The ball had been in a safety deposit box for 65 years.

In our hobby it's hard to beat a really nice piece of memorabilia that comes with: a) Babe Ruth; b) a good story; and c) ironclad provenance. This amaz-

ing ball seems to have all three.

The ball is an official American League ball, with the blue and red stitching used until 1934. The provenance includes several notarized letters from the family and a host of newspaper articles from 1931 when Ruth gave him the ball and from nearly seven years later when Kent died. Plus there is the remarkable photo (shown on the facing page) which clearly shows the distinctive writing on the ball.

Heart & Hands officials note that they have had the ball looked at by experts, who have accorded it an "8" or "9" in terms of the quality of the signature.

All that's left is the auction, which includes dozens of items from big-name sports stars, with an understandable emphasis on former Boston-area stars. The lineup includes signed color photos from Hall of Famers like Ted Williams, Henry Aaron, Joe DiMaggio, Whitey Ford, Yogi Berra, Mickey Mantle, Willie Mays and a couple of dozen more, plus signed baseballs and basketballs (Bob Cousy and Tom Heinsohn). There also will be autographed photos from football stars like Troy Aikman, Michael Irvin and Reggie White, and basketball prints of Dennis Rodman, Michael Jordan, Shaquille O'Neal and Scottie Pippen.

But in the end, the spotlight is going to be on that Ruth ball. Alan "Mr. Mint" Rosen, perhaps the most famous dealer in the country, noted that though single-signed balls usually bring the highest prices, this particular ball might jostle that notion. "If it were my choice, I'd rather have that one, because of the provenance that comes with it," said Rosen, adding that the ball, as described to him, would be "one

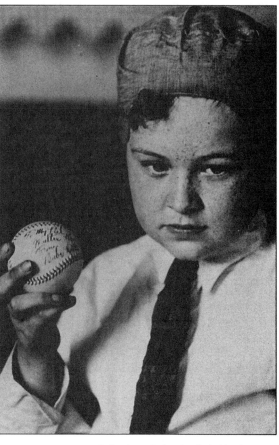

of the best Babe Ruth balls that you could have."

For those who would like to bid on the ball or learn more about the details of the auction, call the Hearts & Hands organization at (508) 758-1300.

Some of the most memorable pieces in the history of the hobby include fascinating stories that are passed on (and occasionally embellished or even revised) from generation to generation. One need only think of the story surrounding the famous Honus Wagner T206, the sleight-of-hand by the Goudey company in not including a Lajoie card in 1933, and even the chilling recounting of Sy Berger's brief venture out to the Atlantic Ocean when he unceremoniously consigned a barge full of 1952 Topps stories take on a life of their own, but mostly they instill in the hobby a sense of history and connection with the past.

A ball with a story this good and a cause this noble deserves a spectacular price to go with it. It makes for a better story, even if it is true.

Mastro's auction tops record $5.4 million

Staggering prices for graded cards help pass Copeland

By T.S. O'Connell

• • • • •

The Mastro Fine Sports Auction Nov. 19-20 in Chicago figured to be a whopper, but few in the hobby were prepared for a record $5.4 million total (including 15 percent premium) that would eclipse the $4.6 million sale total of the famed Copeland Collection in 1991.

Still, in a record-setting year it seems fitting that another seemingly insurmountable mark would fall, and in this case it was Sotheby's record auction total. "I figured we had a shot at $5 million," a weary but elated Bill Mastro told SCD in the early morning hours on Saturday, "but it would have been a big disappointment if we hadn't beaten Sotheby's 1991 record."

And the record fell with the help of more than 100 lots that totaled $10,000 or more, including pristine cards and rare memorabilia that set a host of individual records as well, often selling for prices three, four or five times and even higher than particular cards had ever enjoyed. The list includes: Mickey Mantle 1951 rookie year jersey ($73,386); Lou Gehrig bat ($61,034); a 1933 Sport Kings Ty Cobb ($50,600); a pair of PSA-8s 1933 Goudey Lajoies ($61,226 and $56,026); a PSA-9 1951 Bowman Mickey Mantle rookie ($56,023); a 1952 Topps Andy Pafko ($49,302); 1933 Goudey Benny Bengough (PSA-8, $46,000); and a 1952 Topps Mantle ($46,302).

Also: 1938 Goudey Heads Up DiMaggio (PSA-9, $40,250); 1941 Play Ball DiMaggio (PSA-8, $41,745); Babe Ruth game-worn hat ($39,637); Mark McGwire All-Star uniform ($27,782, proceeds to Baseball Assistance Team, BAT); 1903 World Series program ($43,671); Lou Gehrig signed ball ($37,950); Dan Brouthers signed ball ($36,991); and Steve Carlton's 1977 Cy Young Award ($32,754).

And it's worth noting that the McGwire jersey mentioned above was part of a run of 51 lots of MLB All-Star uniforms that raised a total of $95,500 for BAT.

It's not all that unusual in really swanky offices to find golf clubs and bag belonging to the chairman of the board tucked into a corner of the room and at the ready. Such was the case of the front reception area of Mastro Fine Sports Auctions' elegant new digs in suburban Chicago last week, with one rather significant difference. This particular set of clubs belonged to the Chairman of the Board. As in Sinatra.

Aside from noticing the plush offices and Wall Street-worthy furniture, I was struck by the fact that the items didn't seem to take up as much space as I would have expected. Cards and memorabilia pieces were tucked into virtually every usable corner of the main offices, not unlike a ship where every nook and cranny winds up being home to something or other.

But once I started looking closer at the various lots, and even moreso during the bidding and afterwards when it became apparent that high-grade cards, thousands of them, were carrying the day. A quick check of the highlights (see sidebar) shows that almost three-quarters of the highest prices were cards.

In the area that Mastro affectionately calls "the War Room," a dozen or more staffers handle the phones, now with the help of computers that have brought the phone auction a couple of generations ahead of where it was three or four years ago.

The efficiency factor with the all-encompassing computer program is such that the weary "operators standing by" were able to conduct a baby shower in the middle of the second day of bidding. I'm not sure if that would have worked in the "old days" when every bid was recorded manually on a series of bid boards around the room.

There is still some of the occasionally high-spirited banter that is found when a close-knit group has been working long hours for an extended period. When informed that a certain bidder might go to bed and miss out on an opportunity for a particular card, Mastro loudly proclaimed, "Nobody that bids $13,000 on a baseball card is going to bed." Coming from Mastro, it sounded like an order, but I think it was merely an observation. He's probably speaking from personal experience.

Mastro can be forgiven for his exuberance. A veteran of nearly 30 years in the hobby and a former consultant at Sotheby's, he was understandably excited as the extraordinary record of that famous 1991 auction was passed.

"In 1991 when the Copeland Collection was sold by Sotheby's there were no other auctions," said Mastro. "The only avenue for collectors to buy things was through the trade papers and at card shows. Today, there's an auction every

> ## "Nobody that bids $13,000 on a baseball card is going to bed."
> — Bill Mastro

day in the various publications and on the Internet."

He also pointed out that in the previous three weeks there had been three major auctions that totaled about $4 million. "You wonder how that is going to affect our auction." The answer: "This auction did more money than those other three combined."

"Bats are real strong, they've had a big resurgence. Big ticket uniforms are soft right now. That Mantle jersey should have been at least $100,000," he continued.

Mastro also noted that literally hundreds of lots in the auction sold for what would be considered double and triple

Highlighted Items

MEMORABILIA
1951 Mickey Mantle rookie jersey . $73,386
Babe Ruth letter 45,920
Lou Gehrig bat 61,034
Ruth cap 39,637
1977 Carlton Cy Young Award 32,754
1968 Steve Carlton jersey 12,234
1937 Joe Louis champ. belt 23,000
Mark McGwire 65½HR ball 22,417
Jim Brown 1964 NFL Champ. ring. 21,656
1903 World Series programs
.... $43,671 & 11,624
NBA-50 signed lithograph 30,560
Roger Maris jersey 26,847
1942 Pee Wee Reese jersey 11,094
1954 Gil Hodges jersey 8,419
1955 Sandy Koufax jersey 24,019
1967 Bobby Orr jersey 9,490
Ted Williams signed bat 9,169
Game-used Mantle bat 6,889
Brooks Robinson 1970 flannel 9,598
Nolan Ryan signed jersey 8,205
1950s Ted Williams Moxie ad decal 9,286
Complete Hartland Statue set 3,061
Spalding Guides collection (56) 6,325
All-Star Game program run 1933-84 ... 8,149
Boxing advertising piece 8,419
Cassius Clay boxing license 5,372
1955 Bob Cousy AS uniform 5,603
Jack Nicklaus Ryder Cup sweater 4,600
Frank Sinatra golf clubs and bag 11,132
1926 Beech Nut triptych 9,608
1922 Coca-Cola baseball calendar 8,419
Inscribed *Big Six* book 5,604
Autographed Gehrig photo 14,790
Vintage baseball cigar cutter 17,942
Christy Mathewson contract 11,486
1940 Reds World Series ring 7,959
1998 All-Star McGwire jersey (proceeds to
BAT) 27,782
1998 All-Star Cal Ripken jersey (proceeds to
BAT) 11,646
1998 All-Star Derek Jeter jersey (proceeds to
BAT) 4,804

SIGNED BASEBALLS
Lou Gehrig signed ball $37,950
Dan Brouthers signed ball 36,991
Babe Ruth signed balls
.... $24,020, 17,869, 13,214 & 9,936
Ruth/Gehrig signed ball 10,441
Jack Chesbro signed ball 24,033
Tris Speaker signed ball 6,197
Cy Young signed ball 6,193
Walter Johnson signed ball 5,966
Connie Mack signed ball 4,074
Grover Alexander signed ball 6,962
Mickey Cochrane signed ball 16,421
Roger Bresnahan signed ball 15,481
KiKi Cuyler signed ball 5,282
1933 All-Star signed ball 18,490
1934 All-Star signed ball 6,780
1918 Reds team-signed ball 6,325
1934 Tour of Japan baseball 9,023

EARLY TOBACCO AND GUM CARDS
Collection of (41) high-grade T204 Ramlys
.... $37,042

1915 Cracker Jack PSA8 Joe Jackson
.... 27,830
Uncut sheet N172 Old Judges 23,051
1915 Cracker Jack PSA8 Cobb 15,813
E93 1910 Standard Caramel Cobb 10,441
M101-5 Sporting News PSA8 Joe Jackson
.... 17,250
Set nr-mt B18 Blankets 14,571
T4 Obak Premiums (23) 8,737
Sporting News Premiums 8,628
T205 Gold Border PSA8 Mathewson 9,611
T205 Gold Border PSA8 Johnson 7,941
T205 Gold Border PSA8 Young 6,561
Four high-grade T206 Cobbs 17,897
T206 Eddie Plank (restored) 9,488
Five (5) T206 near sets (500+ cards each) ..
$18,185/$16,669/$14,830/$12,106/$10,013

PREWAR SETS AND SINGLES
1933 Sport Kings Cobb PSA10 ...... $50,600
1933 Sport Kings Ruth PSA8 18,049
1933 Delong Gehrig PSA7 18,048
1933 R333 Delong Collection, all slabbed
...................................27,118
1933 Goudey PSA8 Nap Lajoies (2) $61,226
& 56,026
1933 Goudey Benny Bengough PSA8
.... 46,000
1933 Goudey Bengough PSA7 9,492
1933 Goudey Ruth No. 149 PSA8 27,830
1933 Goudey Ruth No. 181 PSA8 14,611
1933 Goudey Ruth No. 92 PSA8..........8,050
High-grade 1933 Goudeys (63) 18,046
PSA-graded 1933 Goudeys (44) 11,485
R319 1933 Goudey uncut sheet............5,098
1933 Goudey near set of 230 autographed
...................................12,688
1933-35 National Chicle ex-mt set......14,914
1933 Tattoo Orbit set 9,929
1934 Goudey set..............................6,903
1934 Goudey near set 9,861
1934 Goudey Gehrig No. 37, PSA7........7,942
1934 Goudey Gehrig No. 61, PSA8......10,187
1938 Goudey DiMaggio PSA9.........40,250
1938 Goudey DiMaggio PSA8 16,837
1938 Goudey DiMaggio PSA7...............4,210
1940 Play Ball set 10,187
1940 Play Ball Williams PSA8 6,553
1941 Play Ball set 8,630
1941 Play Ball DiMaggio PSA8 41,745
1941 Play Ball Williams PSA8 6,784
1933 Sport King Eddie Shore PSA9.....5,766
1933 Sport Kings (15) PSA graded 6,779
R73 Goudey Indian Gum set 7,132
1936-37 G-Men set 8,335

POST-WAR SETS AND SINGLES
1948 Leaf Baseball set......................$7,412
1948-52 Bowman Baseball run............20,373
1951 Bowman Mantle PSA9...........56,026
1951 Bowman Mantle PSA8 20,169
1951 Bowman Mantle PSA7 9,024
1952 Bowman Mantle PSA9 10,846
1952 Bowman Mantle PSA8 4,074
1953 Bowman Color nr-mt set 31,373
1954 Bowman Williams PSA8 10,830
1954 Bowman Williams PSA7 2,780
1955 Bowman nr-mt to mt set 13,559
1950 Bowman set.............................8,047
1951 Bowman set.............................4,993
1954 Dan Dee Potato Chips set 6,900

1953 Glendale Meats set 8,956
1954 Wilson Weiner set 5,556
1989 Upper Deck Ken Griffey rookies 12,161
1948 Bowman Football set, nr-mt 11,786
1951 Bowman Football set 8,735
1952 Bowman Football Small set 16,269
1952 Bowman Football Large sets
.... $22,225 & 7,458
1948 Bowman George Mikan rookie 9,026
1948 Bowman Basketball sets
............................$7,458 & 7,271
1948 Leaf Boxing set PSA graded 8,735
1961 Fleer Basketball set 3,056
1986 Fleer Basketball set, mint 7,132

TOPPS SETS AND SINGLES
1951 Current All-Stars sets, (2) mint
.... $7,844 & 7,394
1951 Connie Mack All-Stars set 9,860
1952 Baseball set 24,477
1952 Baseball near set (385) autographed
.... 11,912
1952 Mantle PSA9 46,302
1952 Mantle PSA8 29,095
1952 Mantle PSA5 6,484
1952 Andy Pafko PSA8 49,302
1952 Andy Pafko PSA7 5,603
1952 Andy Pafko PSA7 4,075
1952 Jackie Robinson PSA9 9,960
1952 Roy Campanella PSA9 10,846
1953 Baseball near set, signed 3,954
1953 Mantle PSA9 14,914
1953 Mantle PSA8 7,130
1953 Mantle PSA8 3,334
1953 Robinson PSA9 13,559
1953 Robinson PSA8........................ 1,459
1953 Willie Mays PSA8 5,093
1954 Baseball sets .... $16,298 & 8,725
1954 Baseball near set, signed 3,704
1954 Ted Williams No. 250 PSA9 27,830
1954 Ted Williams No. 250 PSA8......... 3,974
1954 Henry Aaron PSA9 11,500
1954 Henry Aaron PSA8 3,367
1955 Baseball set 20,169
1955 Baseball near set, signed 3,367
1955 Sandy Koufax PSA8 1,804
1955 Roberto Clemente PSA8 3,701
1956 Baseball, four sets
.... $8,735/$7,843/$6,316 & $3,057
1957 Baseball sets .... $5,704 & 4,477
1957 Baseball near set, signed 5,358
1958 Baseball set 8,737
1958 Baseball near set, signed 4,485
1958 Mantle PSA9 13,915
1959 Baseball sets .... $9,611 & 7,643
1959 Baseball near set, signed 3,795
1959 Mantle PSA9 7,220
1960 Baseball near set, signed 4,934
1961 Baseball sets .... $8,205 & 4,482
1961 Baseball near set, signed 5,423
1962 Baseball set........................7,459
1962 Baseball set (spanish)................ 3,288
1962 Baseball near set, signed 5,427
1963 Baseball sets ....$5,414 & 3,697
1965 Baseball set 5,413
1967 Baseball set........................8,720
1969 Topps Supers set, all PSA-9-10 except
two 15,290
1969 Topps Supers set 7,220
1985 Mark McGwire PSA8-9 rookies (12)
....3,212

BILL MASTRO (at left) is getting pretty adept at putting millions of dollars-worth of collectibles in a relatively tight space (above).

retail, and in many cases even more than that. Some of the prices for slabbed and graded cards were nothing short of incredible, like $27,830 for a 1954 Topps No. 250 Ted Williams. A couple of months ago I wrote a column listing the Top 25 Cards of All Time, putting that particular card at No. 1. I figure that explains the amazing price for the Williams card, that and the fact that it was a PSA9.

"High-grade PSA cards are extremely strong. It was inevitable that it would happen," said Mastro. "Within the next 10 years, the vast majority of cards that have any value at all will be in some kind of a holder. They will be in tombs. We will no longer touch cardboard. We did that to ourselves, because we did nothing to police ourselves."

As he traditionally does with his auctions, some of his biggest bidders flew in for the festivities, giving a genuine air of camaraderie to the proceedings, to say nothing of a pile of cash. That group includes John Brigandi, Steve Rotman,

Marshall Fogel, Scott Bradshaw, David Forman and perhaps a dozen others who were in and out of the offices during the week of the auction.

Each auction, Mastro hears from a roster that includes several MLB owners, an impressive array of players who are active and occasionally notable collectors and even an actor of considerable reknown who bids under the name of one of his most famous movie characters. As I frequently scanned some of the computer screens during the course of the auction's final hours Friday evening, I never did see any suspicious names, like maybe Ratso Rizzo or Pee Wee Herman.

The rest of the "action" comes via that bank of 10 phones and 10 comput-

ers, thanks to list of perhaps 10,000 registered bidders and a mailing of perhaps 6,000 or 7,000 catalogs. That last is no minor undertaking, since the latest catalog topped 300 pages, every one in color and on glossy paper.

And not a Beanie Baby anywhere to be found, even in the hobby's first phone auction/baby shower.

Aaron's Last Home Run Ball Is Back

Although he initially intended to give the ball back to Aaron in person, Arndt was fired from his job

By Tom Mortenson

With so much interest in significant home run baseballs lately, the agent for the owner of Hank Aaron's final home run ball thinks it's a good time to take offers.

Yes, the owner of Aaron's 755th home run ball, Richard Arndt of Albuquerque, N.M., is back in the news. He's been successful recently in generating national publicity in the Milwaukee Journal-Sentinel, USA Today and the Chicago Tribune.

Arndt's agent is Tim "Shoe" Sullivan, a freelance writer from Stevens Point, Wis, who wrote about the historic ball for Sports Collectors Digest in 1988.

"The whole thing started on July 20, 1976, when Henry took Dick Drago over the wall," wrote Sullivan. "A member of the Brewers' ground crew, Dick Arndt, was sitting with two other workers way down the left field line. Arndt was assigned to be a spotter for the bullpen. He was supposed to watch for a pitching change. Once a change was made, he'd open the gate so another guy could drive a car to the bullpen and get the relief pitcher.

"Anyway, Aaron's homer, a line drive, went about 10 feet over Arndt's head. It hit the seats and fell back down. Arndt went over, picked it up and took it back to where he had been sitting."

After that point, the story of the famous ball has taken some strange bounces.

Since it was July when Aaron hit home run No. 755, there was no way of knowing it would be the final blast by the all-time home run champ. Arndt simply wanted to give the ball to Aaron – one of his heroes. After the game, Arndt was told by his boss, the late Harry Gill, the team's head grounds keeper, that the Brewers wanted the ball and that Arndt should turn over the ball to the team. Arndt asked Gill if he could give the ball back to Aaron himself, and Gill agreed.

When he went to the Brewers' dugout hoping to find Aaron to give him the ball, Aaron wasn't there. Arndt was confronted by the equipment manager, who told him he couldn't meet with Aaron because the team was busy packing for a road trip to Kansas City. The equipment manager said Arndt should give him the ball and after they returned from their road trip they'd take a photo of Arndt giving the ball to Aaron and he'd get one of Aaron's signed bats and an autographed ball in return.

Not thinking it was a big deal, Arndt decided to take the ball home with him.

The next day, Arndt was fired by the Brewers for leaving the stadium with club property. The team deducted $5 from his final paycheck for the ball.

Fast forward to the 1980s. The boom in memorabilia collecting is sweeping the country and Arndt decides it's time to sell the prized ball. Through the years there have been a series of on-again, off-again offers from potential buyers of the ball, including Aaron himself.

A few years ago Arndt, who works at an office supply and furniture outlet in Albuquerque, took the ball to a Phoenix card show and bought an autograph ticket to have the slugger sign it. Aaron wasn't aware that he was signing such an important piece of history. Arndt didn't tell him either, because he wasn't sure how Aaron would react. Other than Aaron's autograph on the 755th ball, an official Spalding American League ball with Lee MacPhail's stamped signature, there's no way of proving it's any other 1970s-era ball.

However, in Aaron's 1991 autobiography with Lonnie Wheeler, I had a Hammer, the Hall of Famer acknowledges Arndt is the owner of the ball. "There was only one more home run in me," wrote Aaron. "It came in Milwaukee on July 20 against Dick Drago of the California Angels, my 10th of 1976 and 755th over 23 seasons. A kid on the ground crew named Dick Arndt picked up the ball, and he wouldn't give it to me. The Brewers fired him over it, but he still wouldn't give me the ball. Every few years I call him and try to buy it from him – I've offered him as much as $10,000 – but he won't part with it. To me, that ball is just as important as the one from number 715, because it's the one that established the record. The record is 755, not 715."

And now, Arndt is again seeking offers for the 755th ball.

"He's a huge Aaron fan and he'd really like to see Aaron end up with the ball," said Sullivan of his client. "We've proposed an offer to the Milwaukee Brewers that we think would be a win-win situation for everyone. We proposed that the Brewers buy the ball from Dick at a fair price. They could display it at the stadium for a specified amount of time. At some point in time they would have a ceremony and give the ball to Aaron. That scenario would be ideal for everyone."

Sullivan and Arndt have given the Brewers until Thanksgiving to respond to their proposal. They have had one six-figure offer from a collector, but have decided to honor their self-imposed Thanksgiving deadline in order to give the Brewers ample time to respond.

Sullivan admits that he's not holding his breath in the hopes some sort of deal can be worked out with the Brewers. If an arrangement with the team can't be worked out, Arndt will hang on to the sacred ball until he gets another offer he's satisfied with.

The Battle Over Beanies

Bean toys: Friend or foe of the sports collectibles hobby? You decide

By Andy Heimerman

You walk into your local card shop on a leisurely Saturday afternoon, intent on purchasing a few packs (or cans) of cards to add to your collection, and what do you see on the shelves: Little balls of fluff called Beanie Babies, Bamm Beanos, Puffkins or Cushy Critters, in flamboyant colors, some with cute poems on their tags and others wearing Ken Griffey Jr.'s name and number. What in tarnation is going on here?

Hobby shops, card shows and even professional ball games are being inundated with the seemingly endless parade of stuffed animal toys that have popped up in the past year. Their appearance has ruffled the feathers of some dealers who have watched the show dollars they count on being spent in the Beanie Baby

Ty Beanie Babies have been big hits at sporting events, drawing people who would otherwise not attend games. Pictured here (bottom row) are Beanie giveaways Daisy the Cow, Pugsly the Pug Dog, Lucky the Ladybug and Mystic the Unicorn. The top row has Rocket the Blue Jay, Cubbie the Bear and Valentino the Bear.

pavilion. Others are simply distressed with having to share their space with stuffed animals that having nothing to do with sports.

But with the Ty Inc. Beanie Baby Valentino the Bear in the Baseball Hall of Fame, how long can dealers and collectors ignore the relevance bean toys have in the sports collectible hobby? When Street & Smith's SportsBusiness Journal finds that the attendance at Major League Baseball games increased by an average of 37.4% on Beanie Baby giveaway days, can they be dismissed as not legitimate sports collectibles?

The History

"Sports bears have been around since I was a kid," Wayne Salvino, vice president of Salvino Inc., said. Salvino produces Bamm Beanos sports bean bear collectibles. "There were bears with logos of sports teams on them when I was a kid. We thought on a limited basis we would sell (in the hobby) but we didn't realize what the market was going to be."

Illinois-based Ty Inc. started the Beanie Baby craze. H. Ty Warner formed Ty Inc. in the mid-1980s and began producing stuffed animal toys. In 1993, his company debuted its Beanie Baby line at a trade show. In 1994, Ty unleashed the first nine Beanie Babies on the public. The under-stuffed animals were designed to be cheap toys for children, with a suggested retail price around $5. Each animal was given a name and birthdate and had a heart tag with a unique poem.

The toys became a hit in the Chicago area and soon expanded around the country. The toys were successful, but it

wasn't until Ty teamed with McDonald's for a Happy Meal promotion in 1997 that they became a phenomenon.

Ty produced 10 Teenie Beanie Babies for the promotion and people went insane. The miniature versions of regular issue Beanies became a national sensation. Mobs of people lined up outside McDonald's restaurants hours before opening. Collectors walked out with armloads of Happy Meals which were promptly dumped because they were not the main objective. Dealers and collectors loitered outside restaurants, offering quick cash to people lucky enough to get their hands on a Teenie Beanie. Today, those Beanies carry market values of $20-40. Even the in-store displays have become hot collectibles, priced at $350. The two companies teamed for a second promotion in May, with similar results.

A contributing factor to the activity on Beanie Babies is the Internet. Not just dealers, but collectors as well had a quick way to contact and deal with each other. The access made it easy for people to not only trade, but make money in Beanie Babies.

Ty Inc. considers Beanie Babies to be children's toys, but the large collector demand and secondary market prices brought the realization that collectors needed to be encouraged. To that end, Ty began "retiring" Beanies in 1995. Retired Beanie Babies were taken out of production, thus making them difficult to find and heightening collector interest. Production numbers on Beanies are unknown, but some are more rare than others. Both these factors contribute to a healthy secondary market, while current (i.e. non-retired) Beanies provide kids with a cheap, enjoyable toy. Ty seems to have achieved a tenuous balance with the two markets.

Valentino the Bear was a giveaway at Canadian Special Olympics events and the May 17, 1998 New York Yankees game. Ten thousand Valentinos contributed to a sell out for David Wells' perfect game. Valentino is now in the Baseball Hall of Fame.

Recently, due to high demand, Ty was forced to institute a new shipping policy. The company will ship Beanie Babies to its most supportive accounts first, with the remaining Ty accounts getting whatever product is left over. This could potentially regionalize product, increase prices on the secondary market and upset the balance.

As with every hot collectible, more companies decided to enter the market. The bean toy line to make the biggest splash in the sports collectibles hobby is Salvino's Bamm Beanos. Salvino was in the sports figurine market for 11 years before delving into bean toys in 1998. The Salvino produces bears which feature the name and number of a Major League Baseball player and are decorated in his team's colors.

Salvino's first release, the Commemorative Gold Series, sold out in a matter of days. A follow-up series featuring three Colorado Rockies was released in the Denver area and was also gone quickly. A hockey release that is upcoming and is rumored to include Wayne Gretzky will certainly be another big success.

"We didn't think (Bamm Beanos) would be accepted the way they have been accepted," Salvino said. "We've always tried to expand our figurine market. It seemed like the sports collectibles hobby was selling beanie-type products, but nobody seemed to be doing anything with players."

Tri-Star Productions brought beanies into the sports collecting mainstream when it introduced the Beanie Expo at its Houston sports card show in January. A separate area was set aside for beanie dealers at the show. The Beanie Expo has been a part of Tri-Star shows all year.

"It was an enormous part of the show," Tri-Star spokesperson Mandy Fuerst said. "It really added to the family atmosphere in a big way. We've seen that continuously throughout the year."

Sports card collectors should be able to understand the draw of these unique collectibles, for much in the plush toy collecting hobby is similar to the card collecting hobby. The different production runs on bean toys fuels collector interest in those perceived as scarce or rare. Other Beanie Babies are distributed regionally, specifically the ones available at special functions and professional sports events. The thrill of the chase is a large part of the draw these toys have on collectors.

The Good

The upside for sports collectibles dealers who carried bean toys the past two years has been tremendous. Store owners use them to draw different consumers into their stores – families, women, children – who normally would not enter a sports card store. Dealers strategically place beanies in the back of their shop so potential customers must walk past all the rows of sports collectibles to get to the bean toys, hopefully creating interest in their other products. The profit and traffic that bean toys now bring to stores is significant. Some stores would not have open doors if not for Beanie Babies and Bamm Beanos.

Although the small sacks of bean animals have ballooned into a big business, dealers and collectors still enjoy it because, for them, it is fun.

According to a posting on Ty Inc.'s web site, that is the reason the company started producing Beanie Babies in the first place. The statement reads: "We take pride in creating and distributing a non-violent, creative toy for boys and girls that they can afford to collect. It is upsetting and intolerable to us when the 'short-term greed' of some of our customers takes over."

Illinois-based dealer Sally Grace sold sports cards since the mid-1980s before switching to Beanie Babies two years ago. She claims that dealing in beanies is more profitable and fun than sports cards

"I love the trading card industry and I love beanie babies," Grace said. "It's a great mixture when you combine the two at shows and in shops because now you have something the whole family can do. Before, the wives would stay home saying they didn't want to go to a card show, and now the wives, husbands and kids all come together."

Fuerst estimates that with the Beanie Expos, traffic has increased as much as 30% at some shows this year. "We've definitely seen the jump in our numbers this year, as far as attendance," Fuerst said. "At first we met a little bit of resistance from dealers, but what they see now is that it's bringing in more attendance."

The Bad

The speculation and greed that hurt the trading card industry does rear its ugly head in Beanie Baby collecting as well. Some dealers compare it to the insert craze of the early '90s, when people opened pack after pack looking for a quick payout. "Beanie shows this year look like the Anaheim National of '91 did with the inserts," Grace said.

Speculators have driven the prices of some Beanie Babies through the roof, with absolutely no reason to back it up. When the Beanie Baby Tabasco the Bull was retired, a rumor started that Chicago Bulls' fans would pay any price for the red-and-white stuffed critter. Ads were placed in Chicago-area newspapers offering the toy for $1,500, a slight increase over the actual market value at the time, which was approximately $50.

Following this year's MLB All-Star Game in Colorado, dealers and collectors surrounded the stadium and offered hundreds of dollars for the Glory the Bear toy which was given to game attendees. Glory is currently commanding around $300.

Ty has also had problems with its direct accounts selling Beanies at secondary market rates to other dealers and collectors. Ty's policy has always been that direct accounts must put all current Beanie Babies on the shelf for around $5. Ty recently put a message on its web site to inform collectors of the policy and reinforce the point with its direct accounts, who pay approximately $2.60 for a Beanie.

Forgeries of Ty Beanie Babies have also popped up. A shipment of over 8,500 fake Beanies was confiscated at O'Hare Airport in Chicago in March. Ty reached agreements with customs officials in Canada and China to block shipments of Beanies headed for the USA due to a fear of forged goods reaching the market.

Of course, lawsuits were bound to occur in this hot and crowded market. In October, Ty sought a temporary restraining order in Illinois Northern District Court to prevent Salvino from selling their Series Two Bamm Beanos. Ty alleged that Salvino infringed on its copyright due to the similarity in the appearance of each companies' bears.

Judge Elaine E. Bucklo denied Ty's request, but admitted there are similarities in the products. "Clearly there was some copying here on the part of Salvino," Bucklo stated in her decision, while citing previous rulings. "However, not all copying ... is copyright infringement. An ordinary, reasonable person would not overlook the differences in the two products."

Ty asked for reconsideration of the decision but was denied. The company is now seeking an injunction, but the hearing is scheduled for January 23, meaning Salvino's Series Two can be completely distributed. Salvino's two November releases, Holiday and Home Run Kings Sets, and a hockey release that is TBA should also experience no court-related delays to shipping.

> ## "Store owners will tell you their traffic has increased because of the Beanie Babies. They do help expose people to the trading cards, which is good."
> — Sally Grace, Beanie Baby dealer

"We feel confident in the product we are producing," Salvino said. "We don't feel we are infringing on anybody's copyright. It's just business as usual."

Many dealers do feel that bean toys take collectors and sales away from sports cards at shows and in shops. Eddie Silard, owner of Eddie's Sports Den in Greenwich, CT, has sold sports cards for 13 years. He added Beanie Babies and Bamm Beanos to his shelves six months ago.

"What I've noticed is a lot of people who were dealing in sports cards have turned away," Silard said. "About 30% of the people that buy sports cards are looking to sell and are now buying Bamm Beanos and Beanie Babies. The beanies are taking away from sports cards in my store. I think within six months you'll find more and more Beanie Baby dealers just giving it up and hopefully sports card people will get back into it."

Bean toys will not disappear from sports events any time soon. Although no one can predict how long they will remain a hot collectible, they have established a successful presence that should keep them around well into 1999.

The number of dealers carrying bean toys at card shows has grown marketedly in the past year. Beanie Babies were easily the biggest drawing promotion at Major League Baseball games this season. Beanie Baby giveaway days produced an average ticket sale increase of 9,175 on the 18 dates, a trend that will ensure more Beanie days in 1999.

A Beanie Baby even contributed to one of the more memorable moments in recent baseball history. Valentino the Bear was given away at the May 17 New York Yankees' game versus the Minnesota Twins. Ten thousand bears were distributed, resulting in a sold out Yankee Stadium. The larger-than-normal

crowd witnessed David Wells' perfect game. The combination of the accomplishment and the crowd made for a magical baseball moment – and, like it or not, a Beanie Baby was a major cause.

The problem that most dealers who don't sell bean toys have with the varmints is the belief that they steal money from "legitimate" sports dealers pockets. The argument is that they may help ticket sales go up at stadiums on Beanie Baby Days, but many of those collectors walk through the gate, grab their Beanie and head for home. Many do not stay to watch the true sports product or care about sports in the least. At shows, Beanie pavilions draw families, women and children who would not normally attend a card show, but their attention is focused on bean toys and card dealers are left twiddling their thumbs while show dollars are being spent elsewhere. Are dealers simply not finding ways to capitalize on the increased traffic beanies create at shows? Do these toys provide real benefit to the sports collectibles hobby?

"There is a definite crossover," Grace said. "Store owners will tell you their traffic has increased because of the Beanie Babies. When you bring a whole family in, the mother might be interested in the Beanie Babies and the son would look at the sports cards. But they do help expose people to the trading cards, which is good."

So beanies may be good for the hobby, but do all dealers feel good about selling them?

"I did not want to get into it," Silard said. "It just seemed like you had to in order to survive. It's helped my shop, but it's not what I want it to be. I'd prefer doing just sports cards."

Sports Promotions Beanie Baby and Salvino Bamm Beano Price Guide

Those not released by press time are listed with the date and sporting event at which they are available. The pricing is designated n/a.

Ty Beanie Baby Sports Promotions

Baldy the Eagle (Phila. 76ers)	200.00
Batty the Bat (Brewers, Mets)	125.00
Blackie the Bear (Boston Bruins)	150.00
Blackie the Bear (Chi. Bears)	75.00
Blizzard the Tiger (Chi. White Sox)	150.00
Bones the Dog (Yankees)	200.00
Bones the Dog (Blackhawks 10/24)	n/a
Bongo the Monkey (Cleve. Cavaliers)	180.00
Chip the Cat (Atlanta Braves)	100.00
Chocolate the Moose (Den. Nuggets)	200.00
Chocolate the Moose (Tenn. Oilers 10/18)	n/a
Chocolate the Moose (S. Mariners)	60.00
Chocolate the Moose (Cowboys)	90.00
Cubbie the Bear (Cubs Convention)	400.00
Curly the Bear (Chi. Bears 12/20)	n/a
Curly the Bear (N.Y. Mets)	70.00
Curly the Bear (San Antonio Spurs)	200.00
Daisy the Cow (Chi. Cubs)	400.00
Derby the Horse (Hous. Astros)	100.00
Ears the Rabbit (Oakland A's)	250.00
Glory the Bear (BB All-Star Game)	300.00
Gobbles the Turkey (S.L. Blues 11/24)	n/a
Gracie the Swan (Chi. Cubs)	150.00
Hissy the Snake (Az. Diamondbacks)	150.00
Lucky the Ladybug (Minn. Twins)	100.00
Maple the Bear (Can. Spec Olympics)	400.00
Mel the Koala (Anaheim Angels)	75.00
Mystic the Unicorn (L.A. Sparks)	120.00
Mystic the Unicorn (Wash. Mystics)	160.00
Peanut the Elephant (Oakland A's)	75.00
Pinky the Flamingo (S.A. Spurs)	200.00
Pinky the Flamingo (T.B. Devil Rays)	75.00
Pugsly the Pug (Atlanta Braves)	75.00
Pugsly the Pug (Texas Rangers)	150.00
Roary the Lion (K.C. Royals)	100.00
Rocket the Blue Jay (Tor. Blue Jays)	100.00
Rover the Dog (Cincinnati Reds)	90.00

Scoop the Pelican (Houston Comets)	150.00
Sly the Fox (Az. Diamondbacks)	75.00
Smoochy the Frog (S.L. Cardinals)	100.00
Spunky the C. Spaniel (B. Sabres 10/23)	n/a
Stretch the Ostrich (Yankees)	120.00
Stretch the Ostrich (S.L. Cardinals)	150.00
Stripes the Tiger (Det. Tigers)	100.00
Strut the Rooster (Ind. Pacers)	120.00
Tuffy the Terrier (N.J. Devils 10/24)	n/a
Tuffy the Terrier (San Fran. Giants)	60.00
Valentino the Bear (Can. Spec. Olymp)	220.00
Valentino the Bear (Yankees)	275.00
Waddle the Penguin (P. Penguins 10/24)	n/a
Weenie the Dachshund (T.B. D. Rays)	150.00

Salvino Bamm Beanos

Gold Commemorative Set (12):	**350.00**
Frank Thomas	40.00
Ken Griffey Jr.	50.00
Dante Bichette	15.00
Derek Jeter	40.00
Tony Gwynn	30.00
Gary Sheffield	15.00
Mike Piazza	40.00
Cal Ripken	40.00
Juan Gonzalez	35.00
Mark McGwire	100.00
Kerry Wood	35.00
Greg Maddux	40.00
Complete Series II set (12):	**100.00**
Dave Justice	8.00
Sammy Sosa	15.00
Ivan Rodriguez	10.00
Tino Martinez	10.00
Mark McGwire/Cal Ripken	15.00
Roger Clemens	12.00
Barry Bonds	10.00
Chipper Jones	10.00
Ken Griffey Jr.	15.00
Alex Rodriguez	12.00
Jim Edmonds	8.00

---

if you collect it – you'll find it

COLLECTit™ .net
www.collectit.net

Introducing: Collectit.net
SCD gives collectors online avenue for buying, selling

By Andrew Brawner

In a way, Collectit.net was born on a kitchen table in rural Wisconsin in 1952. That's where Chet Krause, founder of Krause Publications, first assembled his then-newsletter *Numismatic News*.

Nearly 50 years and thousands of publications later, the people who bring you *SCD* have extended their business into cyberspace with Collectit.net, an online auction.

The online auction – a website where collectors meet to electronically buy and sell their wares – is yet another example of the way computers have changed sports collecting. If you break down "sports collecting," you arrive at the notion that "collecting" involves what one might describe as "getting stuff." And the newest, most convenient way to get stuff has to be the Internet.

Online auctions were born in 1995 when a software developer wanting to help his girlfriend collect her beloved PEZ dispensers designed a primitive Internet auction. That particular small auction became eBay, now worth a billion dollars. Other opportunistic, Internet-savvy collectors followed suit, and what was once a quirky invention is now a full-fledged industry.

There are hundreds of Internet auction sites, and the trend is gaining momentum.

Mainstream media such as The Atlantic Monthly are picking up on the newsworthiness of the situation; the online version of the esteemed magazine recently ran an overview of the online auction phenomenon. A week later, USA Today was analyzing the trend.

It seemed only natural that the publishers of *Sports Collectors Digest* take a leading role. Said Krause executive vice president Roger Case, "We are looking at continuing to expand our services to hobbyists in a variety of ways, and it will be exciting for enthusiasts to watch our services grow."

SCD on the web

SCD
www.krause.com/periodicals/html/sd.html
Learn more about the bible of sports collecting

auctions
www.collectit.net/
Join the online auction revolution with the only site truly designed for collectors

periodicals
www.krause.com/periodicals/
Browse the many titles in the Krause Publications periodicals roster

shows
www.krause.com/shows/
Find out more about SportsFest '99 and other important shows

books
books.krause.com/
Don't forget the Krause books list; here you'll find such key reference guides as the *Standard Catalog*

THE COLLECTIT.NET HOW-TO GUIDE

Registration

There is a free, one-time registration to bid on or list items for auction on Collectit.net Auctions. You can register to bid only or to bid and list items for auction.

1. Go to http://www.collectit.net and click on "Auctions."
2. Under "User Services" on the right, click on "Register."
3. Complete the secure registration form and click on "Submit Registration" at the bottom of the page.

If you registered to bid only, your registration will take only a few minutes to process. If you registered to bid and list items for auction, you will receive a confirmation via e-mail within 48 hours of registering. This e-mail will confirm your password and handle, and give you a customer service number. You will need these when you sign onto the site, so keep them in a safe place. After you receive this confirmation, you can list items for auction.

List an item for sale

There is no fee to list an item on Collectit.net Auctions. If your item receives no bids or if your reserve price is not met, you pay nothing. If bids are received and any reserve price is met, you will be charged a simple commission of 2.5 percent of the highest bid received (minimum charge of 50 cents per transaction and $1 per monthly charge-card billing cycle). There are no confusing sliding rates based on the amount of the highest bid. This charge will be automatically billed to your charge-card number, which you are required to provide when registering to list items for auction.

Here is how to list an item for auction on Collectit.net Auctions:
1. Go to http://www.collectit.net and click on "Auctions."
2. Click on "Seller Administration" in the row of red buttons on the left.
3. Type in your customer number and password in the resulting form.
4. Click on "Enter Seller Administration Area."
5. In the resulting form under the "Submit Data" column, click on "Create."
6. Complete the form.
7. Click on "Enter This Item" at the bottom.

Images

If your browser software is Netscape Navigator 3.0 or greater or Microsoft Internet Explorer 4.0 or greater, you can also upload an image from your computer to accompany your listing. Click on the "Browse" button in the "Picture" section of the "Create Auction Item" form and follow the directions. Or, if the image is stored on a web site, you can include a link to the image in your listing by completing the URL field in the "Picture" section. You can use this linking feature with any browser, for no additional charge. There is a $2 charge per image for images you upload to Collectit.net Auctions from your computer.

Duration

You can run your auction for three, five, seven, 10 or 14 days by filling in the "Duration" field near the bottom of the auction listing form. Collectit.net will not close your auction until five minutes after the last bid. For example, if your auction is scheduled to close at 10:00 and a bid is received at 9:58, your auction will remain open until 10:03. If another bid is received at 10:02, the auction will extend to 10:07, and so on. This allows you to get maximum dollar for your item and helps prevent last-second bid manipulation. You will be automatically notified by Collectit.net as soon as your auction ends. Collectit.net will tell you if the item sold, the winning bid, buyer's name and how to contact him or her, and other pertinent information.

Bid on an item for sale

1. Go to http://www.collectit.net and click on "Auctions."
2. On the Collectit.net Auctions home page, click on one of the auction categories that interests you.
3. Click on a subcategory to see a list of items available in that subcategory, or click on MultiBid (see below) to bid on multiple items within the category you selected.
4. Click on an item's title to view bidding activity for the item and other details about it.
5. To bid on the item, enter your customer number, password, and bid amount under "Place Your Bid" on the right. Bids must be made in 5-percent increments.
6. Click on the "Bid Now" button.

Collectit.net Auctions will confirm via e-mail that your bid has been received. It will also notify you if you have been outbid or if you submitted the winning bid.

In addition, Collectit.net Auctions offers several handy bidding features:

Keyword search: Instead of clicking on a category, you can also search for items by entering one or more key words.

AutoBid: This feature allows a bidder to enter a maximum bid for an item. If your current bid is topped by another bidder, AutoBid will automatically raise your bid. If you're outbid again, AutoBid will continue to raise your bid up to the maximum that you indicate.

MultiBid: This feature allows you to bid easily on multiple items from the category and search pages.

AuctionWatch: This feature allows you to view your past bidding activity or to monitor bidding activity on items you add to your personal AuctionWatch page.

AuctionRate: This feature allows you to submit feedback on other buyers and sellers. If a seller gives you good service, you can give him or her a pat on the back by submitting a positive rating through AuctionRate.

Krause webmaster Eric Senf put it another way: "There are a lot of other auction sites that came up with a technical solution and looked at gathering the market, whereas we *had* the market and were able to create a solution tailored to something that's already known. Though many of the startups offer a lot of glitz, nobody else out there has 45 years of experience doing business with their audience in this industry. We're bringing some very unique things to the table that have the potential of redefining the way things happen."

While Collectit.net will function much in the same way as other auction sites, it will offer improvements such as the ability to extend an auction if bids come in strong and go high; a bidder's passport allowing single sign-on and quick navigation through the site; a multi-bid feature allowing bids to be placed on multiple items from a single screen; and user-friendly uploading of graphics and descriptions for sellers offering one or multiple items.

And then, there's perhaps the most attractive feature: It's free. The only time you pay with Collectit.net is when and if you sell your item.

As with other sites, Collectit.net's prospective buyers can log on, peruse auction listings, and make bids. The auctions are live, interactive and ongoing. The site is updated in real time so bidders can follow each auction, and participants can search the histories of sellers before bidding. If they buy an item, bidders can contact a seller directly to finalize details. Bidders will be notified immediately, via e-mail, if they have been outbid or won an auction.

While those features are not necessarily unique to our site, our technology and hobby expertise allow us to simply execute them better.

"Selling collectibles online is a perfect match for the Internet. It's quick and easy," said Case. "The Web auction is a phenomenon that is raising online retail to new heights. Online auctions infuse the buying process with fun, competition, and community – the same as physical auctions."

Added Case, "The larger Collectit.net becomes, the more it will establish itself as *the* place on the Internet to buy and sell collectibles and hobby-related items."

While there is plenty of positivity surrounding Internet auctions, there is also a fair amount of skepticism aimed at the still-developing sales device, mostly due to fraud. "Problems with online auction transactions are the No. 1 Internet fraud reported to us," said Susan Grant, director of the Internet fraud watch program of the National Consumers League. The problem shouldn't be overly-amplified though, said Grant: "Whatever the number is, it's the minority of transactions that are fraudulent. But, for individual consumers, we see transactions of thousands of dollars for one item. So, in that sense, it's a significant problem because consumers stand to lose a lot of money if they're dealing with somebody who's crooked."

Grant said there are plenty of steps consumers can take to protect themselves, such as:

* Get a physical address and other identifying information from sellers. You'll need the seller's name, street address and telephone number to check them out or follow up if there is a problem. Don't do business with sellers who won't provide that information

* Ask about delivery, returns, warranties and service. Get a definite delivery time and insist that the shipment is insured

* Since you can't examine a collectible item or have it appraised until after the sale, you can't assume that claims made about it are valid. Insist on getting a written statement describing the item and its value before you pay

* Use common sense to guide you. Ask yourself: Is what the seller promises realistic? Is this the best way to buy this item? What is the most I am willing to bid for it?

* Pay the safest way. Requesting cash is a clear sign of fraud. If possible, pay by credit card because you can dispute the charges if the goods are misrepresented or never arrive. Another option is cash on delivery. Pay by check made out to the seller, not the post office, so you can stop payment if necessary.

While some auction sites are safer than others, *SCD* publisher Hugh McAloon said Collectit.net – much like *SCD* itself – will offer added security for sports collectors. "The *SCD* Guarantee will certainly apply to Collectit.net," McAloon said. "We will listen to the buyers: If they call in legitimate complaints, we will pull the seller's rights immediately."

Because they carefully observed the online auction phenomenon for two years, the makers of Collectit.net can ensure that their service will provide the best auction experience for collectors. Krause has proven for nearly 50 years that it knows how to bring collectors, buyers and sellers together, and the company plans to keep up the tradition with Collectit.net. "By simply keeping with Chet Krause's vision and extending it into the expanding arena of cyber-commerce," said McAloon, "we've given *SCD* readers and collecting enthusiasts of all kinds a high-quality, collector-friendly place to meet and do business on the Internet. As we celebrate the 25th anniversary of *SCD*, we find it exciting to consider the added value Collectit.net will give collecting over the next 25 years."

1998 - The Year in Sports Figurines

By Andy Heimerman

For the sports figurine market, just like sports cards, 1998 was the "Year of McGwire." His very large presence was felt in new releases from Kenner, Headliners and SAM, with his earlier figurine issues experiencing a surge in interest. McGwire's home run compatriot, Sammy Sosa, was also a driving force in this market and they easily topped all other players in terms of popularity. Ken Griffey Jr. remained a strong seller. For football, running backs like Barry Sanders and Terrell Davis led the way, while the Great One continues to top the hockey charts.

By sport, baseball led the other sports in number of releases. Hockey figurines continue to have a strong following and football sales were also good. Basketball lagged behind the other major sports in terms of number of issues.

Here is a company-by-company rundown of the year in sports figurines:

Kenner

The biggest Starting Lineup release of 1998 was the Extended Baseball series. This set contained all the right players and released them at the right time. McGwire's first SLU in a St. Louis Cardinal uniform was the top prize, reaching prices of $100. Sosa was also included in the set, with his piece being one of the rarer finds. The home run chase and scarcity of the figure pushed its value into the $60 range.

Other top pieces from the set included the first SLUs of 1997 National League Rookie of the Year Scott Rolen and the Yankees' Hideki Irabu.

Nomar Garciaparra, the 1997 AL ROY, headlined the regular Baseball series. His first figure remained hot throughout the summer and could be found for $40. Darin Erstad and Mariano Rivera were the other top first-time pieces, both demanding $20.

The biggest story involving Kenner this year was the loss of its NBA license. Just when collectors thought they had purchased their last NBA SLUs though, Kenner released a final basketball series before the license expired. The 16-figure set did not contain any first figures, but it sold well as collectors scrambled to finish their NBASLU collections.

The 1997-98 Extended Basketball series did very well behind strong debut issues of Tim Duncan and Keith Van Horn. Little did collectors know at the time that the rookie SLUs of these young stars would likely be their last.

Headliners

Headliners were originally a product of Corinthian Marketing, but Corinthian was purchased by Equity Marketing this year. The sale did not slow down the release of the many lines of Headliners.

Besides issuing products for the NHL, MLBand NFL in the standard 3.5-inch format, the company debuted its Headliners XL line. The 5.5-inch figures

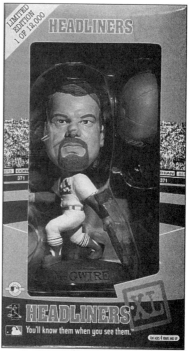

Mark McGwire XL Headliners were one of the top selling figurines of 1998.

debuted with the XL baseball series this past summer. The set sold well with a top roster of baseball stars, including McGwire and KenGriffey Jr.

Perhaps the Headliner product to make the biggest splash was the special XL Home Run Two-Pack, featuring McGwire and Griffey in their All-Star Home Run Derby jerseys. The set sold well in all outlets, sparked by the Maris chase.

The company also made a push into the college football figure market. The Heroes of the Gridiron line featured NFL stars in their college uniforms. Both regular and XLseries were produced, with Terrell Davis leading the way.

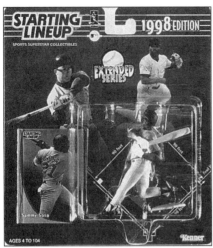

Sammy Sosa's Extended Baseball SLU was one of the most chased pieces of the year.

Romito

Romito more than doubled its figurine line by releasing five new pieces this year. The company released a figure of Bill Mazeroski depicting him rounding second base after his legendary home run in the 1960 World Series. A total of 500 were produced.

Romito also debuted its Hall of Fame Series. With the ambitious goal of someday producing a figure for every player in the Hall, the company issued its first four pieces – Al Kaline, Bob Feller, Rollie Fingers and Willie Stargell. They were produced in an edition of 100 unsigned and 400 signed figures.

Sports, Accessories and Memorabilia

SAM added a number of new Bobbing Head figures to its product list. The company obtained a license from MLBPA to produce Bobbers of baseball players in 1998 and 1999.

Their top figure of the year was a McGwire Bobber, released just weeks before he broke Maris' record. SAM sold out of the 5,000 pieces it produced. SAM also issued Bobbing Head figures of Larry Walker, Chipper Jones, Mike Piazza and Alex Rodriguez.

The company produced Rollie Fingers, Bob Griese and Luis Aparicio early in the year, with each limited to 3,000. Other releases included signed Bobbers of Derek Jeter and Mark Messier (limited to 100 each).

SAM took a rest from Bobbing Heads to produce a Nolan Ryan figurine. Issued in April, the figurine stands 10-inches high and weighs 10 pounds. Ryan is pictured in his Texas Rangers' uniform. Production was limited to 500 pieces.

Playmates Toys

Playmates Toys produces NHL-Pro Zone figures. The sculpted 12.5-inch figures feature cloth jerseys and removable pads, helmets and sticks. Twelve fully articulated figures were released in the past year, with Patrick Roy, Eric Lindros and Paul Kariya leading the list.

Southland Plastics

Southland Plastics debuted in the marketplace in 1998. The company produces figures in the style of the Hartland statues from the '50s and '60s. The first release was a signed Nolan Ryan statue limited to 1,000 pieces. The company also has contracts with Griffey, Greg Maddux and Tony Gwynn.

Prime Time

Another new company on the block is Prime Time. The company obtained licenses from the NHLPA and several national hockey federations to produce two lines of hockey action figures. The 20-figure Heroes of the Ice set consisted of 7.25-inch figures in NHLPA uniforms, while Heroes of the Ice: Teams of the World featured 27 players in their national uniforms.

The Rise and Fall of Pinnacle Brands

Dallas-based manufacturer emerged as an innovator during the hobby's turbulent last half-decade

By Kevin Isaacson

It you were recently dropped onto this planet and first exposed to the sports collecting hobby in, say, August 1998, you'd think Pinnacle were a dirty word or a punch line.

Then you'd do your homework and learn that in an industry where shrinkage has been the rule of late, Pinnacle was long the exception.

Under innovative, risk-taking leadership, Pinnacle affected the sports trading card industry in ways unthinkable when CEO Jerry Meyer assumed control and changed the company's name in July 1993.

Then an also-ran manufacturer best known to the hobby as "Score," Pinnacle Brands blossomed into an industry leader in baseball, hockey, racing and football card sales. While competitors such as Topps, Fleer and Upper Deck benefitted from fond history, Pinnacle made more news than all those heavyweights combined during the past half-decade, watching its market share multiply in the process. For a company that entered 1993 as the No. 6 card manufacturer, Pinnacle and Meyer have compiled an impressive number of "firsts." Consider:

* The first hobby-only product (Score Select, 1993).

* The first industry use of sub-brands – Score II became Summit, Pinnacle II became Zenith, Select II became Certified – which, for a time, dramatically increased the impact of second-series releases.

* The first huge off-season NFL product, 1995's Pinnacle Zenith, which cemented football cards' status as a year-round offering.

* The first "major" to delve into the NASCAR market.

* The first to hire a celebrity photographer (Christie Brinkley).

* The first to strategically target the mass media (frequent mentions in *USA Today*, plus prominent appearances on Nightline and CNN).

* The first to maintain high-profile title sponsorships in three sports: All-Star FanFest, NHL Fantasy, the NFL's Quarterback Challenge.

* The first to issue "cards in a can" and other unique packages, creating renewed retail interest in trading card-related products.

* The first to break away from national hobby distribution to an organized, regional system.

Combine these "firsts" with Pinnacle's acquisition of two competitors – Action Packed in 1995 and Donruss in 1996 – and it becomes evident how profoundly Meyer & Co. enhanced the standing of Pinnacle Brands Inc. in the sports collectible industry.

"It has always been our goal to be innovative, to make a change that makes a difference," Meyer said in an interview before Pinnacle's collapse. "Certainly, we are not perfect. We have screwed up from time to time. But we'll continue to do whatever we can, try whatever we can, to make this business better for the customer."

Pinnacle's total market share in 1997 was comparable to that of Topps, Fleer/SkyBox and Upper Deck, an improvement made more impressive given the new card business' shrinkage of an estimated 50 percent during the past five years. Meyer's high standing among his peers was evident in his election as the first chairman of the Sports Cards Association.

"You have to give Jerry credit – he's always been willing to speak his mind, and he's always been available to the hobby," said Laurie Goldberg, a one-time competitor who served as Pinnacle's VP/public relations. "Unfortunately, his willingness to answer the tough question and put himself forward has made him a target for some who, for whatever reason, don't like where the business is going today."

Pinnacle was the hobby's darling for about 18 months during late 1993, 1994 and early 1995. But its acquisitions of Action Packed and Donruss, then an aborted attempt to

JERRY MEYER

become publicly traded, didn't always help Pinnacle adhere to the principles that made it successful to that point. Where Pinnacle was once able to focus on one line each of football, baseball and hockey cards, it suddenly was attempting to manage two lines in each sport *and* a difficult-to-integrate NASCAR business while key executives were participating in a "road show" to increase interest in Pinnacle's stock offering. Transition and training issues in late 1996 sometimes kept Pinnacle and Donruss from producing their best products, an admission Meyer made in mid-1997.

In that same interview, though, Meyer promised that "the focus of our entire company now is where it should be: Squarely on the hobby."

To that end, the Pinnacle and Donruss card companies in late 1997 issued a flurry of diverse products featuring coins, interactive opportunities and easily the most creative packaging in the industry. "Cards in a can" piqued the interest of retail consumers, metal baseball cards in diamond-shaped packaging gave retailers a $29.95 item to offer, and a new CD-ROM baseball product drew notice in *Time* and *Newsweek.*

Of course, not all of Pinnacle's "news" was positively received by the hobby. Pinnacle and Donruss did not eliminate any products in their merger, which continued to add to the industry's product proliferation. Included: A reported nine product releases during a two-week stretch in late 1997.

Though Meyer accepted responsibility for some shipping irregularities, he expressed surprise that his companies were blamed for the card industry's product proliferation.

"If someone takes a look at it, maybe they'll find that Upper Deck and Topps combined for 10, 12, maybe 14 products during a given time period. To say Pinnacle and Donruss are responsible...well, then someone should combine Topps and Upper Deck products and see how that compares. Honestly, there won't be a lot of difference."

Pinnacle also drew criticism for implementing a landmark regional system of distribution in late 1997. The change resulted in breaks with four long-time hobby distributors, three of whom filed suit against Pinnacle. The suits and initial uncertainty about Pinnacle's new distribution program limited its impact in late 1997, though several participants were impressed with the company's attempts to promote products on a regional basis.

"It was clear in my mind that someone had to take a bold move to help the customer, and that's why we put our distribution program in place," Meyer said. I think, as this distribution program matures, you will see the great things we can do to service both the dealer and the consumer."

Though *SCD* speculated that Pinnacle's innovative distribution plan could help propel the company into the next century, things, of course, did not turn out that way. Part of Pinnacle's downfall was likely its lack of a basketball card license. Meyer in 1995 said Pinnacle needed an NBA licensing agreement to "be a true, viable player" in the card market.

But it wasn't just the lack of an NBA license that killed Pinnacle. Other Pinnacle problems:1) The hobby, at some point, stopped responding to Pinnacle's innovations. It is unclear whether this was due to a decrease in quality on Pinnacle's end or a simple loss of interest on the collector side; 2) The regional distribution system failed to move enough product; 3) Sales dropped industry-wide. Pinnacle's collapse quickly followed the rumors of late summer 1998; by fall, Meyer and COO Michael Cleary had left the company and assets were being liquidated.

Nonetheless, Pinnacle will be remembered for the pioneer it was.

When asked about the future, an optimistic Meyer replied "If we can get more and more people interested in collecting, everyone in this business can benefit." Perhaps the unfortunate lesson of the Pinnacle saga is that good intentions don't always produce the best results.

Tom Marmalich of Wood Craftsmen in Newbury Park, Calif., cuts up the vintage Babe Ruth bat for Upper Deck's "Piece of History" insert set.

By Greg Ambrosius

Is it sacrilegious to cut up a piece of history like a Babe Ruth game-used bat or just savvy marketing by an innovative card company?

That's the question collectors and sports fans across the country are asking after The

GOING BATTY

Upper Deck Has Received Plenty Of Attention - Not All Of It Good - Through Its Latest Innovations: A Cut-Up Babe Ruth Bat.

Upper Deck Company received national attention with the announcement of its latest promotion. Upper Deck recently purchased a game-used Babe Ruth bat from 1923-31 for $23,000 and cut it up into hundreds of slivers for a special insert

set. The mounted slivers will highlight approximately 200 "Piece of History" cards that will be randomly inserted into 1999 Upper Deck Baseball Series I packs.

"This is another first," said Richard McWilliam, Upper Deck CEO. "We're commemorating Ruth's legacy on trading cards in a way that has never been done before, because these rare cards feature authentic memorabilia."

There's no denying that Upper Deck has succeeded with its game-used insert card theme. Starting with 1996 Upper Deck Football, UD began inserting Game Jerseys, featuring swatches of actual game-used jerseys from top stars such as Joe

Montana, Barry Sanders and Jerry Rice. That 10-card set was an instant hit and now lists for $4,000.

After its successful debut, Upper Deck expanded the game-used jersey concept to baseball, basketball and hockey in 1997 and '98, featuring Game Jersey inserts of Michael Jordan, Grant Hill, Ken Griffey Jr., Alex Rodriguez, Wayne Gretzky and Patrick Roy. The Game Jerseys, which included a pair of Brett Favre inserts in 1997, continue to be among the hottest in the industry in all sports, with secondary values continually on the rise.

Then in '98 Upper Deck Baseball, company officials expanded the game-used theme to include portions of bats in the 14-card "A Piece of the Action" insert set. Like its predecessors, this innovative idea was an instant hit.

Now Upper Deck is taking this concept to the next level, including a game-used item from an era that some consider sacred. The cracked, 40-ounce, 35-inch bat was purchased from Mastro Fine Sports Auction in June, along with Ruth "cut" signatures from two of the industry's leading autograph experts.

"Our product development team is gutsy with their ideas," said Mary Mancera, Upper Deck manager of corporate communications. "Part of the deal with this indus-

57

try is coming up with something that's innovative enough to capture collectors' attention, while at the same time being collectible. I think we hit both notes with this release."

To no one's surprise, not all collectors feel grateful to Upper Deck for the chance to get a sliver of one of Ruth's bats. Instead, some are downright upset with the company for cutting up a great piece of baseball history.

"Talk about desecration," said Barry Halper, an esteemed collector who owns eight autographed Ruth bats, including two game-used models. "I can't believe it. I'm sorry to see it come to this. Why would something like this be so important to splinter up a bat into hundreds of pieces?"

Well-known hobby dealer Alan Rosen was also disconcerted to learn of the fate of the bat. "It's an absolute travesty for collectors," said Rosen.

New York Daily News columnist Bill Madden called the promotion a "revolting example yet of collector exploitation...a disgraceful act by an MLB licensee and a desecration of a true baseball artifact."

While veteran hobbyists are understandably upset about the hallowed wood chips, the fact remains that one less Babe Ruth bat isn't catastrophic to the industry.

"We know that memorabilia buffs have cringed a bit with the idea, but trading card collectors seem to be very excited. Obviously there are two camps, but I think overall we've received favorable reviews."
Mary Mancera of Upper Deck

Hobby experts agree that there are between 50 and 100 game-used Ruth bats in existence today and this promotion has already brought national publicity to the hobby, including write-ups in USAToday and the New York Times.

"It's not like it's the only game-used Babe Ruth bat out there," said Terry Melia, Upper Deck media manager. "It's not the bat he used to hit his 60th home run in 1927 or the one he used to hit his 714th home run."

"There are at least 50 Ruth game-used bats in existence and more likely around 100," added Dave Bushing, memorabilia expert. "They are quite common compared

to other Hall of Famers' bats from that era. Do I think it is a waste? Yes, but it's not like it's a (rare) Lou Gehrig or Honus Wagner, or even a Hack Wilson game bat."

But does that make it right for Upper Deck to cut up a historic item like the Sultan of Swat's bat?

"We know that memorabilia buffs have cringed a bit with the idea, but trading card collectors seem to be very excited," said Mancera. "Obviously there are two camps, but I think overall we've received favorable reviews."

The Ruth signatures will be used in two different Upper Deck products this year. Along with the approximately 200 "Piece of History" Ruth bat inserts in Upper Deck Series I, scheduled for a Nov. 9 release, there will be three additional "Signed Piece of History" insert cards that contain both a Ruth signature and a piece of his bat. Two of the signatures sport "Babe Ruth," while the third signature is signed "GH Ruth."

UD Retro was released in late October and contained the first inserts of Ruth's signature. There are three cards in the "Legendary Cuts" insert, each with a different photo to create a unique card.

The Ruth promotions were made possible through an agreement with Curtis Management. With Mark McGwire and Sammy Sosa drawing national attention for their historic home run chase, and the New York Yankees setting a new American League record for most wins during the regular season, it seemed like the perfect time to feature Ruth in a mainstream card product

"Internally, the feeling is that we're striking a chord with innovation and that's what we wanted to do," said Mancera. "The timing is right in terms of the home run chase and we're definitely looking to seize some of this publicity over the period of time when these products hit the hobby. So from that standpoint it's been good."

Upper Deck will continue the bat theme in its inaugural 1999 UD Black Dia-

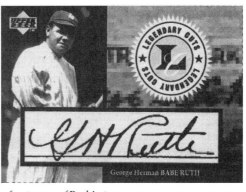

> **"I'm sorry to see it come to this. Why would something like this be so important to splinter up a bat into hundreds of pieces?"**
> *Barry Halper, esteemed collector*

mond Baseball product, set for an early December release. Although not as controversial as the Ruth cutup, Upper Deck purchased a McGwire 1988 World Series bat and cut it up into hundreds of slivers. The end result is an 86-card insert set called "Mark McGwire Bat Cards."

The 86 McGwire Bat Cards will be broken down into four levels: 50 Single Black Diamond McGwire Bat Cards, featuring one sliver of McGwire's bat; 25 Double Black Diamond McGwire Bat Cards, featuring two slivers of his bat; 10 Triple Black Diamond McGwire Bat Cards, featuring three slivers of his bat; and a 1-of-1 Black Diamond McGwire card, featuring four slivers of his bat.

Is this just the start of unique game-used memorabilia themes for Upper Deck or the end of the line? Although some of the feedback from the Ruth bat promotion has been negative, don't expect Upper Deck officials to end this unique idea of combining game-used memorabilia with trading cards.

"I think there are a lot of untapped areas that Upper Deck is starting to chip away at," said Melia. "We've accomplished a lot with the Game Jersey cards and now the next step is to bring something else into the picture."

That something else could include pieces of game-used hockey sticks and other memorabilia. Along the way you will see more from the Babe, as that 40-ounce bat surely produced more than just 200 slivers.

"It's safe to say there are additional pieces of that bat under lock and key," said Melia. "Our product development team is still deciding what to do with that."

Veteran hobbyists will continue to cry foul with this latest promotion, but it looks like the Sultan of Swat has hit another home run for the hobby. And remember, he did it with a cracked bat.

Ryan Is On Cooperstown's Doorstep

Baseball's all-time strikeout king should be a first-ballot inductee

By Scott Kelnhofer

I It's not a question of if Nolan Ryan will be enshrined in baseball's Hall of Fame, it's only a matter of when.

If the Baseball Writers Association of America – the panel responsible for choosing the members of Cooperstown – has any common sense at all, Ryan will be among the Hall's Class of 1999, the first year in which he is eligible for induction. The results will be announced in January.

While baseball's all-time strikeout king admits it will be a thrill to be a Hall of Famer, he's much too busy to worry about his Hall of Fame chances. In addition to being a cattle rancher and a banker, Ryan has also been involved in local politics. During the most recent political campaign in Texas, Ryan helped win voter approval for a new baseball stadium in Round Rock that will house the Double-A affiliate of the Houston Astros. Ryan's son, Reid, is one of the team's executives.

Ryan is also busy enjoying his new role as a spokesman for Topps. In anticipation of Ryan's election to the Hall, the card company will be inserting reprints of each of Ryan's 27 regular-issue Topps cards from his career into packs of 1999 Topps Baseball.

Ryan joins an elite group of major league legends – Mickey Mantle, Willie Mays and Roberto Clemente – who have had their careers honored by Topps in the last four years.

While each of those players had a memorable career, none was longer than Ryan's. He made his major league debut on Sept. 11, 1966 as a reliever for the New York Mets. He retired from the game 27 seasons later, with 324 wins, 5,714 strikeouts and an amazing seven no-hitters. In 807 major league appearances, opposing hitters could only muster a .204 batting average against Ryan and his blazing fastball.

Despite his amazing achievements, there are some who feel that Ryan is not a lock for induction into Cooperstown this

> ### "One of the things I get a lot of satisfaction out of was my longevity. There was no way that I ever anticipated playing as long as I did."
> — Nolan Ryan

year. They point to the fact that Ryan only won 20 games twice in his career (1973 & '74) and never won a Cy Young award.

But while Ryan was blessed with an outstanding fastball, he wasn't always blessed with great talent around him. Ryan only appeared in nine post-season games in his career.

While he may never have had a dominating season from a wins-and-losses perspective, few hitters would argue that there was another pitcher who had the potential to dominate a game each time he took the mound like Ryan did. He lead the majors in strikeouts in 11 of his seasons, including seven times between 1972-79.

Topps arranged for Ryan to speak to us from his home in Alvin, Texas, where he reminisced about his career and his early baseball card collection.

SCD: Tell us how you got involved with Topps?

Ryan: Topps has been in the business for my entire baseball career. They have a complete series of cards from my rookie year all the way through. It's interesting to look at those cards from when I broke into the big leagues until I retired with the Rangers. I see how I changed physically over the years, but I also noticed that my delivery seemed pretty consistent over those years.

SCD: As you look back at all of those cards, is there one that you consider your favorite, or that brings back some special memories for you?

Ryan: There's a couple from the years that I spent with the Angels that I really like. Those were really some fun years for me. It was the early stage of my career and I will always look back on that as a very exciting time.

Ryan's major league career spanned 27 seasons with four different teams – the Mets, Angels, Astros and Rangers. It was with Texas that Ryan recorded his 300th career victory, 5,000th strikeout and two of his seven career no-hitters. No other player in major league history has ever thrown more than four no-hitters.

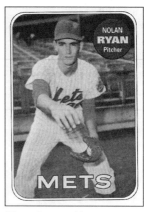

Ryan began his career with the Mets as a relief pitcher. He was traded to California after the 1971 season.

SCD: Was that a big deal amongst the players back then to make it onto a baseball card?

Ryan: It was. As a kid, you grew up listening to baseball and playing with baseball cards. So as a youngster, baseball cards were a big deal. You had your favorite teams and your favorite players, so I think for every player, back when I broke in, it was a big deal when you got your own baseball card. It was all part of earning your stripes, so to speak.

SCD: Were you a big collector of cards when you were younger?

Ryan: I remember buying cards for two reasons – one was the bubble gum and the second was the cards. We always chewed the bubble gum, then we saved the cards. We usually tried to trade for players or teams we really liked.

SCD: Did you have a favorite team or player that you followed when you were growing up?

Ryan: I was always a Yankees fan, but in the middle to late '50s I became a Milwaukee Braves fan. That's when I started following Henry Aaron. But it always seemed like the Yankees were the team you always heard about.

SCD: What memorabilia have you saved from your career?

Ryan: The thing I saved were the baseballs from the no-hitters, and some of the strikeout balls in increments of 500. I also kept some jerseys from each club that I played for. But I wasn't a big memorabilia collector until later in my career, when I started thinking about saving things that I could pass on to my kids in later years.

SCD: Is there any one item of memorabilia that you cherish more than any of the others?

Ryan: I'd say my World Series ring, because it only happened one time. It's very near and dear to my heart. I've kept the jerseys from my no-hitters, thinking they might be something my kids will want sometime.

SCD: Many people are anticipating that you will be elected to baseball's Hall of Fame this January in your first year of eligibility. How much are you looking forward to getting the word that you'll be heading for Cooperstown?

Ryan: I think my attitude is that this is something that's not in my control. It will be voted on by other people. It never really crosses my mind unless it's brought up by someone.

Obviously, it would be something that will be very exciting and one of the highlights of my career. If it happens, it will really be a neat honor. If it doesn't, then I'll just go on.

SCD: You played with four different teams in your career, so a lot of people are curious which cap you will wear on your induction plaque for Cooperstown. Have you given any thought to that?

Ryan: No, I really haven't. I guess it will be one of two teams – either the Angels or the Rangers. I guess off the top of my head, that would be my response.

SCD: The numbers you accumulated during your career, such as the seven no-hitters and the 5,714 strikeouts, are truly amazing. Is there one statistic that you're most proud of?

Ryan: I think one of the things I get a lot of satisfaction out of was my longevity. There was no way that I ever anticipated playing as long as I did, so I'm very proud of that.

SCD: Between 1972 and 1979, when you were with the Angels, you threw 156 complete games. I know there's an emphasis on closers and set-up men today, but why is it that so many of today's starters seem to struggle just to make it through six or seven innings?

Ryan: I think it's a combination of two things. One, they don't have the mindset to go nine innings. Two, they're not conditioned to do that. The way managers use starters and the way starters are looked at, they're not expected to go nine innings.

During the first 15 to 18 years of my career, I never thought about NOT completing my game. That was my attitude; I was a starter and I was planning on going out and pitching nine innings. But the game's changed and the way pitchers are used has changed.

SCD: Did they count pitches during your career, or ever try to hold you to a certain pitch count?

Ryan: They counted them. I can remember throwing over 200 pitches in one game, and that was when I was part of a four-day rotation. I certainly didn't think about taking an extra day of rest; that was just part of the game.

SCD: When you were with the Rangers, a lot of attention was paid to the extensive conditioning program that you put yourself through. Was that something that you worked on during your whole career, or just during the latter stages of it?

Ryan: I started my weight program when I was with the Angels, but we didn't have conditioning coaches in those days, so we didn't have a program that was designed specifically for baseball players or pitchers. It was kind of a trial-and-error thing – there was a weight room in the stadium that had been left there from some football league. I would go down there and use it because I felt there had to be some things I could do to improve myself physically to become a better pitcher. When I got to the Astros, they actually had a conditioning coach. He was the first one who had specific exercises for throwing and pitching, as well as a complete body program with the weight training.

SCD: And you never really had any major arm trouble, correct?

Ryan: No I didn't. I was very fortunate to stay away from any type of career-threatening injuries like a rotator cuff injury or having the tendon in my elbow go. I did have some tendon problems, and also had some bone chips removed in 1975, but it never threatened my career.

SCD: You led the majors in strikeouts 11 times during your career. Do you have to have a certain mindset to be a strikeout pitcher?

Ryan: Well, I was just a strikeout-style of pitcher. I pitched a lot of innings, which is something you have to do to lead the league in strikeouts. And when you're a hard thrower and throw a lot of innings, it's more conducive to accumulating a lot of strikeouts.

SCD: There are a number of great players who are also eligible for the Hall of Fame this year, including Robin Yount, George Brett and Carlton Fisk. If it were up to you, would each of those players be inducted into the Hall of Fame this year as well?

Ryan: No doubt about it. Each of them were terrific ballplayers. The one that gave me the most trouble was Brett, because he was a left-handed hitter. Being a right-handed pitcher, my breaking ball broke into him, so for that reason it was a bigger challenge to face him than Yount or Fisk.

SCD: Over the years, you've had a reputation for being a very willing autograph signer. Has the demand for your autograph changed at all since you retired?

Ryan: There must still be a demand, because we're still getting quite a few requests. What we've done is set up the Nolan Ryan Foundation to try and accommodate the industry. The funds go to the Nolan Ryan Center at Alvin Community College, where we built a continuing education facility and a special community room. We're using the center as a vehicle to continue education on the adult level here. It's been interesting to see the interest in autographs grow from the time I came into the big leagues until the time I left. It was quite a phenomenon that I think grew as the electronic media started to make more people aware of the game and its stars.

SCD: What were your thoughts on some of the incredible events that took place in Major League Baseball in 1998?

Ryan: I thought it was an extremely good year for baseball, and a great fan year for baseball. The Cubs getting into the playoffs, Kerry Wood's performance, David Wells' perfect game, and of course the home run race all got a lot of people interested in baseball that don't really follow the game. Anytime something of that nature happens, it's good for the game.

SCD: You mentioned Kerry Wood. He's a Texas native who has said that he was a big fan of yours when he was growing up. Have you had the chance to meet him yet?

Ryan: No, I haven't. I've had the opportunity to watch him on TV a few times. I do think he's the next up-and-coming strikeout pitcher, with the stuff and the command he has. It's going to be real interesting to watch how he develops during his career.

Ultimate Champion

NBA great Bill Russell hopes to extend his legacy through autograph market

By Kevin Isaacson

Imagine the irony: You are Bill Russell, sports' ultimate winner during the 20th century, and your grandchildren have just compiled their Christmas wish lists. At the top: A Michael Jordan jersey.

"I had to laugh a bit," Russell admits.

While clearly a Jordan fan, Russell understandably cringes when universal credit for basketball's prominence is heaped upon the Chicago Bulls' six NBA championships. When your Boston Celtics won 11 NBA titles in 13 years, that's allowed.

"What I did is the standard," Russell told SCD. "I find it amusing that every time a player shows something, he's 'The best who ever played.' Then, five years later, there's another guy that is the 'best that ever played.' Still, I'm the standard by which they're all judged."

As Russell approaches his 65th birthday and the 30th anniversary of his 11th Celtics championship, he has experienced an epiphany of sorts: He believes that through reflection on Celtics basketball circa 1960, today's youth can learn to celebrate cooperation and teamwork rather than the individual pursuits that seem to predominate today's game.

"I'm trying to make a connection with the kids today, with their folks and their grandparents, about the history of basketball and what teamwork is all about," Russell said. "As we reach the end of the millennium, I'm getting kind of sentimental

about certain things. I'd like for kids to know that basketball was built on teams, and not individuals.

"For example, I happen to think that the Celtics were the greatest team in the 20th century. We won eight straight championships and 11 out of 13. That was teamwork. That was individuals working together.

"It's my hope that we all might get back to understanding the concept of team play, because it is a great lesson regarding being part of an organized society. We're all out there together, and we've got to make it work together."

As part of his initiative, Russell has entered into an exclusive autograph agreement with Rich Altman's Hollywood Collectibles. Why has perhaps the most infrequent signer of modern sports decided, at age 65, to avail himself to autograph collectors? Russell explains in this Q&A session.

Q: We've talked about your grandkids and today's youth, but do today's NBA players know what you accomplished?

A: No. But let me qualify that. There are 10- and 12-year-old kids in our society who don't know what the Vietnam War was about. Because of where our society is, yesterday's news is yesterday's news, and the historical values are lost. If you don't know where you've been, you cannot possibly know where you're going. This autograph program is my small way of attacking that issue.

Q: Why did you stay away from the autograph field for so long?

A: Certain things belong to me. My autograph is one of them – for over 30 years, there was not one single Bill Russell autograph available. That goes back to the early 1960s. They used to bring basketballs into the Celtics locker room for us to sign ... (laughs) .. we voted (Tom) Heinsohn the best at giving a Bill Russell autograph.

In the early 1960s, I had basically stopped signing. I abstained. I decided I just was not going to do it anymore.

Russell: Career At A Glance

FULL NAME: William Felton Russell
BORN: 2-12-34 in Monroe, La.
COLLEGE: San Francisco
DRAFTED: Selected by the St. Louis Hawks in the first round of the 1956 NBA Draft (third pick overall). Draft rights traded by Hawks to Celtics for Ed Macauley and rights to Cliff Hagan.

HIGHLIGHTS:

- Member of NCAA championship teams in 1955, 1956
- Member of 1956 gold-medal-winning U.S. Olympic basketball team
- Member of 11 NBA championship teams (1957, 1959, 1960-66, 1968, 1969)
- 12-time NBA all-star
- Holds NBA single-game record for most rebounds in one half (32; Nov. 16, 1957)
- Holds Celtics all-time rebounding record with 21,620 (22.5 per game average)
- Holds NBA career playoff record for most rebounds (4,104)
- Elected to Basketball Hall of Fame in 1974
- Named to NBA 25th Anniversary All-Time Team (1970), 35th Anniversary All-Time Team (1980) and 50th Anniversary All-Time Team (1996)
- Won two NBA championships as Celtics' player-coach (1968, 1969)

I felt it was a totally and completely impersonal process. It created an illusion of contact, where someone could say, "I was something to Bill Russell, and here's the proof," when I never even got a chance to say hello to that person.

Since then, one of the rewards has been a tremendous amount of great conversations with people about autographs. People will say, "You won't sign them?" and I say, "No, there's a difference between 'won't' and 'don't.'" 'Won't' is a personal thing, and 'don't' is a policy thing. I always felt kind of strange doing it, and the more I did it, the less comfortable I felt. This was something I had to deal with every day, and, being selfish, I decided I didn't want to do it.

To me, it was dishonest, because over the years I saw guys sign autographs, and they were saying the meanest thing to kids, yet they signed their autograph. I thought

that was strange.

Q: Why are you willing to sign autographs now?

A: I'm extraordinarily proud of my achievements in basketball in high school, college and the NBA, and I believe each of us who has had success in basketball needs to serve as a facility for the institution. I want

---

"Over the years I saw guys … saying the meanest things to kids, yet they signed their autograph. I thought that was strange."
— Bill Russell

---

kids to know and respect this game. I always have. In the 1960s, I went to Africa to do basketball clinics with kids who didn't speak the same language, trying to make a connection. With this program, a lot of the grandparents are my contemporaries, and they've told their kids about

me and the time and I played. My goal now is to provide these autographs – in the right place, at the right time, at the right price – that will allow grandparents and parents to share their knowledge of my time in basketball with today's kids.

Q: Why did you decide to try to reach kids through the autograph industry?

A: If you're going to teach, you have to go where the students are. You have to look at where they're getting information and the trading card business is one of those places. Since a lot of kids collect trading cards and other sports items, you work through that medium, and present the information in a way kids can appreciate it.

Q: Any discussion of the Celtics will include speculation on a team's ability to match or exceed those 11 championships. Does today's free agency system eliminate the possibility of another Celtics dynasty?

A: We only made one trade during the entire time I played with Boston. We had a core of players who were only Celtics – that's the only place they had played. But what Red (Auerbach) was also able to do was to pick up guys who had played for other teams – like Wayne Embry, Emmitt Bryant, Don Nelson, Clyde Lovelette – but were at the end of their careers. Red would supplement the core group with those type of veteran players, and we'd get another one or two good years out of them.

It's similar to what Chicago has done with Michael and Scottie Pippen – moving players like Paxson and Kerr, Cartwright and Longley, in and out to supplement the core group.

The difference, though, is that in my core group, all four guards – Cousy, Sharman, K.C. and Sam Jones – are in the Hall of Fame. That's a core group that's hard to beat.

It is interesting, though, how the game evolves. When Michael Jordan was a young guy, he was winning scoring championships but Isiah, Bird and Magic were winning the rings. Slowly, we're getting back to the concept of this being a team game. Michael wanted a ring, and he adjusted his game to get them.

Q: Let's talk about coaching. Do you think it's possible for another high-profile player to succeed as a player-coach?

A: Let me tell you the truth: I was getting bored. We had won eight straight championships, and it seemed like the first minute after we won a championship, some reporter would say, "Do you think you can do it again?" I was like, "Hello! Do you realize what we just accomplished?"

But I was getting bored. Then Red, who is one of the best friends I've ever had, said he was retiring. He knew I was getting bored, and he also cared enough to not hire a coach that I didn't approve of, because of what I had done for the franchise. I started thinking about

Russell Names Altman As Autograph Agent

Bill Russell has selected veteran dealer Rich Altman (Hollywood Collectibles, Hollywood, Fla.) as his exclusive autograph agent. Altman is planning to offer three introductory Russell-signed products, including:

- 1962-63 Celtics jersey.300 "home" and "away" jerseys have been manufactured, using the same production techniques and fabric of the original jersey. Price:$475.
- Spalding NBA game ball, with "Bill Russell, HOF-1974" laser-printed into the panel; 300 have been produced. Price:$350
- 1965 NBA archive photo, showing Russell starting at Celtics fast break, in 8x10 or 16x20 format ($150 and $195).

Among the unique attributes of Russell's autograph program:

Price point: "When I played, anybody could've seen the Celtics," Russell said. "Now, very few people can afford to go to professional games. With this in mind, we're going to put these things out at below market prices. The few autographs that I did previously, well, only the guys who owned the private planes had access to them."

Russell's signing had been limited to a short-term agreement with Field of Dreams, for whom he signed jerseys that retailed at $995.

"What I want to do in this situation is limit the number, but also limit the price so a person who is not necessarily a "serious" collector can afford one. My primary goal is connecting with the people who were fans when I was playing."

Authenticity: "Each item will come with a certificate that I will personally sign with the name my mother gave me. The autographed item will be Bill Russell, but the certificate will hold the signature of William F. Russell, so you know it's something that I've signed."

coaches I'd want to play for ... and I ended up with me. It really did get me re-energized into thinking about the game differently. The really great players, you know, have a tremendous amount of energy. Michael Jordan can go out and play golf, then play in a championship-level game. The normal player can't do that, because they won't have enough energy. Jordan has the most energy of anybody on the planet right now. I was that way, too – but to continue to be dedicated to what I was doing, I had to take some additional responsibility. You might not know that I never had an assistant coach while I coached the Celtics, either.

Q: If Michael Jordan asked for your advice on the matter, would you recommend he become a player-coach?

A: I would never presume to recommend anything to him. He's doing pretty well by himself.

If he wanted to talk about it with

me, I'd ask him what his issues were. It's not a yes or no answer. It depends on why he would want to do it.

Q: Who, in your opinion, is the all-time greatest basketball coach?

A: Red obviously did a great job with the Celtics, and I thought Johnny Wooden did a great job at UCLA. Johnny did it with different teams. On his first teams, the biggest guys were 6-foot-6; then he had Walton and Kareem, and that was a different style of play all together. But I think Auerbach was the greatest coach of the 20th century, besides, of course (laughs), me.

Q: What do you want young people to know about basketball?

A: That playing winning, team basketball is FUN!!

Sometimes, in my career, I couldn't sleep because I was awaiting the next game. I wasn't worried about winning or losing. I just wanted to play.

Growing Moss

Minnesota Randy Moss is so good that he's lifted the football card market to new heights.

By Jim Smith

Everyone had a pretty good idea that Randy Moss could spark a franchise, but save a hobby?

That was the farthest thing from football collectors' minds when Moss came to the Minnesota Vikings last spring with a rap sheet and a reputation that had scared other potential suitors away.

Most of the early action in 1998 trading card sets was focused on Peyton Manning and Ryan Leaf, a pair of promising quarterbacks with "can't miss" tags who went 1-2 in the NFL Draft and were promised immediate playing time on their respective teams, Indianapolis and San Diego.

So low was Moss' stock on Draft Day that one team – Cincinnati – passed on him twice in the first round, despite the stunning numbers he had put up in two seasons at Marshall University. Minnesota, however, wasn't scared away. When the sleek, speedy receiver was still available on the 21st pick, Vikings coach Dennis Green didn't flinch, immediately selecting the flashy wide receiver.

"It took us two seconds to pull the trigger," said Green, who wanted Moss to know how badly the Vikings wanted him.

The only people flinching now are the defensive backs who are assigned to cover Moss. Despite breaking in on a team that already features the great pass-catching tandem of Cris Carter and Jake Reed, Moss has been nothing short of magnificent, putting up Pro Bowl numbers while drawing comparisons to San Francisco's Jerry Rice in his early years.

Midway through the season, Moss led a team that is threatening the league record for most points scored in a season while averaging over 19 yards per catch. Moss' incredible rookie output – which included five touchdowns in his first five games – surprised even the coach who chose him, knowing that his team's primary needs were on the defensive side of the ball.

"He can do things that you don't realize a guy can do," said Green. "He's probably a better player than I realized he was."

THE MOSS FILE

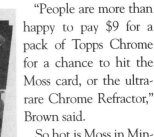

Full Name: Randy Gene Moss
Born: Feb. 13, 1977 in Rand, W. Va.
Height: 6'4"
Weight: 194
High School: DuPont (Rand W.Va.)
College: Marshall
Drafted: Selected after sophomore season by Minnesota Vikings in first round of 1998 NFL draft (21st pick overall).
Honors: Winner of the Fred Biletnikoff Award (1997); named to *The Sporting News* college All-America first team (1997).

Imagine being Brian Billick, Minnesota's offensive coordinator, who acts like a mad scientist with an overpowering new potion. "Every day (in practice) he does something that makes you go, 'Gosh, that's something special,'" he said. Those goshes have a way of winding up in the Vikings' lethal playbook.

To say that Moss has had an impact on the trading card business would be like saying the Vikings are capable of advancing the football down the field. A colossal understatement.

"It's Moss, more Moss and nothing but Moss," said Steve Brown, vice-president of Shinder's, a chain of 14 hobby and magazine stores in the Twin Cities, where Moss-mania took off with the Vikings' electric 7-0 start. "People keep buying packs, and that's why pack prices keep going up."

With Manning and Leaf taking the lumps common to rookie quarterbacks on rebuilding teams, Moss has become a hobby lightning rod from coast to coast. But nowhere have things become as crazy as in the homeland that now embraces No. 84 of the purple.

"Nobody cares about (rookie running backs) Fred Taylor or Robert Edwards," Brown said. "We can't even get low book on Leaf or Manning. It's Moss and only Moss."

Even an inexpensive base brand such as Topps has gone from $1.50 to $2 to $2.50 a pack as Moss' rookie cards have rocketed into orbit. You can't find a Moss single for under $10, and his inserts run as high as $600 for his Playoff Prestige Gold, of which only 25 exist.

Brown acknowledged the move by manufacturers to short-print rookie cards has contributed to the surging interest in football. The rare rookies have created a lottery mentality that feeds the current pack-opening frenzy.

"People are more than happy to pay $9 for a pack of Topps Chrome for a chance to hit the Moss card, or the ultra-rare Chrome Refractor," Brown said.

So hot is Moss in Minnesota that Shinder's pays near high book for his cards and sells them for well above posted values. Still, it's difficult to keep all but the highest-priced Moss cards in stock.

With the NBA players' lockout taking the air out of basketball sales, Moss has triggered a resurgence in football that has been a timely blessing for many hobby outlets. The numbers don't lie: "Last year football pack sales were maybe 25 percent of our total sales," said Brown. "This year, it's 60, maybe 70 percent."

Moss' numbers in two seasons at Marshall were eye-popping: 145 receptions for 2,720 yards and 44 touchdowns in the regular season, plus 29 catches for 809 yards and 10 TDs in the playoffs, where he led the Thundering Herd to the Division I-AA national title in 1996.

A splendid pre-season eliminated any notion that the kid might have problems adjusting to pro defenses. He led the Vikings with 14 receptions for 223 yards and four touchdowns. And then came the regular season.

Moss started his pro career with a bang, becoming the first Viking to score two touchdowns in his debut. His TD receptions of 48 and 31 yards led the Vikings to a 31-7 victory over Tampa Bay at the Metrodome that set the tone for a year of offensive fireworks. The first catch, on a ball tipped first by a defender and then by Moss, was a stunning combination of concentration and acrobatics that left Buccaneers safety Floyd Young shaking

"I fear no team. With the talent we have on this side of the ball, it's scary."

his head in the endzone. After the game, quarterback Brad Johnson served warning to the league that Moss was a force to be reckoned with.

"Leave Randy one-on-one," said Johnson, "and you are going to pay the price."

Carter, who believes he has few equals in the NFL, has been similarly impressed while mentoring his star pupil. "Randy probably has more raw talent than Jake and myself," Carter said. "What he's capable of doing in this offense is unlimited. Plus, he'll always be single covered."

Meanwhile, Moss, whose past includes charges of domestic abuse and a marijuana conviction, has been behaving like a model citizen. On the field, though, he is a pure terror.

"I fear no team," said Moss. "If you're going to try to take me out of the game, hey, fine with me. With the talent we have on this side of the ball, it's scary. Take me out and we'll just beat you other ways."

In early October, ABC Monday Night Football provided Moss an opportunity to showcase his incredible skills before a national audience. He didn't disappoint. With veteran quarterback Randall Cunningham steering the offense in place of the injured Johnson, Moss caught five passes for 190 yards and two touchdowns in the Vikings' stunning 37-24 victory over division rival Green Bay at Lambeau Field, ending the Packers' 25-game home winning streak.

"Every time he scores a touchdown, the price of his cards goes up," said Bob Debnar of Atlanta, Ga., a longtime collector who switched his attention from older sets to new issues after watching Moss' coming out party in Green Bay. "I can't remember the last time I paid more than book value for a football card."

Even when Moss isn't scoring touchdowns, he's contributing to the Vikings' attack. In consecutive victories against Washington and Detroit in which he failed to strike paydirt, Moss drew defensive holding calls that set up touchdowns. Lined up opposite Redskins cornerback Darrell Green, a future Hall of Famer, Moss had five catches for 64 yards and called it an "off day."

Such games do not bother collectors like James Sobeski, 23, of St. Paul, who collects only Moss, all the time. "I have 27 Moss cards and I want to have them all," said Sobeski. "But it's nuts trying to collect them. The prices are crazy. You expect to pay more here, but it's the same in California. It's like this everywhere. I've never seen anything like it."

Even Garth Brooks stoked Moss-mania when he visited Minnesota in October for a week of sold-out shows at the Target Center. When the country singer introduced his mother on stage, she came out wearing a purple jersey, No. 84. It has replaced blaze orange as the most popular apparel in Minnesota.

Yes, Moss-mania is growing, and it's likely to spread beyond the Minnesota borders.

Will The Real Randy Moss Please Stand Up?

Everyone knows that Randy Moss' rookie cards are among the hottest in the football card industry. But did you know that you can find Moss pictured with four different jerseys on his rookie cards?

Moss is pictured in his Marshall University #88 uniform on such early releases as Ultra, Finest, Fleer, Metal Universe, SkyBox Thunder, Playoff Prestige and Press Pass.

Moss was given #18 early in training camp and is also pictured on a few sets in that uniform. Moss pictured as #18 can be found on his Bowman, SkyBox Premium, Pacific Aurora and Upper Deck rookie cards.

He then changed to his old college number during the pre-season and is pictured as #88 on the following rookie cards: Topps, Topps Chrome and Topps Season Opener (which all use the same photo), Stadium Club and Topps Stars.

But #88 has been retired for Hall of Famer Alan Page, so when WR Tony Bland was cut in pre-season, Moss took #84, the jersey that is now the fastest seller in the Twin Cities area. Expect to see Moss pictured as #84 on most of the late season card releases and in future releases for years to come.

— Greg Ambrosius

66

Baseball Market Report

All Signs Are Pointing Toward A Big Season For 1999 Baseball Card Releases

Baseball card sales are considered to be a lagging indicator of baseball's popularity throughout the country. If that's true, then card sales should surge in 1999.

So far, early indications are that they will. Dealers and distributors are reporting great interest for the early '99 releases and that trend should carry into the premium and super-premium releases later on.

"Our '99 baseball pre-orders have been out of this world," said Emil Picchi of All-Sports Marketing in St. Charles, Ill. "Two really strong products are out early – Ultra and Upper Deck – and dealers are anticipating a lot of interest in those products."

The renewed interest in baseball that was generated from the explosive 1998 season is one factor in the success of baseball's '99 releases, but there are other factors as well. The NBA lockout, for one, is changing the buying habits of some collectors today.

"We're definitely seeing some dollars shifting from basketball to baseball, plus the products themselves have improved," Picchi said.

Among the 1999 baseball products set to be released in '98 are Upper Deck and Upper Deck Black Diamond, Fleer Ultra, Topps, Topps Stars 'N Steel and Pacific. The loss of late-season 1998 and early-season 1999 brands for Pinnacle/Donruss/Leaf has also cleared the way for other brands.

"The first brands of the year always do very well," said Red Barnes of Baseline Sports in Norfolk, Va. "Out of the pack, Upper Deck looks very strong with the 10th anniversary, but all of the brands are strong. We're short a few products, including a shortage of late-season Pinnacle/Donruss product. There's not a whole

lot of baseball out there. Overall, I'm encouraged."

Upper Deck Series I kicked off the '99 season with the release of its 10th anniversary set in early November. The set includes autographed Ken Griffey Jr. rookie cards and the Babe Ruth Piece of History bat inserts. Topps and Ultra followed with solid releases in late November. Topps (see Thumbs Up) has Nolan Ryan Reprints, while Ultra is seeding 25 Prospect cards, which should create a buzz for rookie cards in baseball.

Speaking of hot rookies, St. Louis' J.D. Drew has already caused quite a stir in the hobby with the release of 1998 Fleer Traditions. Fleer beat the other manufacturers to the punch by including Drew in its first Update set since 1994. The Drew card debuted at $30, with Traditions already selling for $50.

Yes, the '99 baseball season will have something for everyone. Along with the chase for rookie cards, collectors should also realize that three future Hall of Famers – Cal Ripken, Tony Gwynn and Wade Boggs – will all likely surpass the 3,000-hit mark in '99. And don't forget about the Hall of Fame vote, which could include former stars Nolan Ryan, George Brett, Robin Yount and Carlton Fisk.

Wow, what a way to end the millennium. Baseball is back and better than ever.

BASEBALL

1997 Bowman Chrome

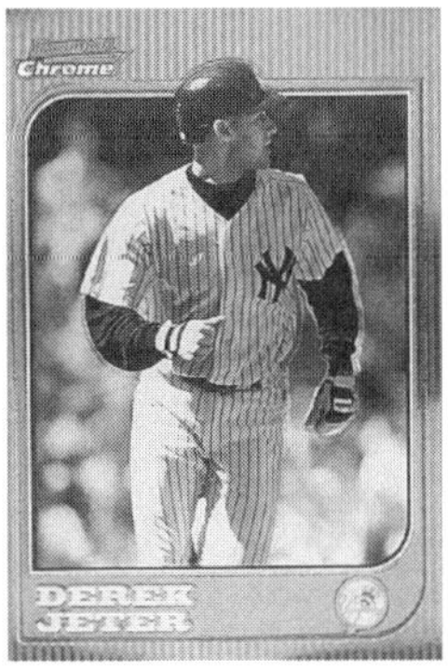

Bowman Chrome was released in the winter after the conclusion of the 1997 season in one 300-card set. Packs contained four cards and carried an SRP of $3. Each card is simply a reprint of the regular Bowman set, with a chromium finish added to it. Key rookies include: Kerry Wood, Adrian Beltre, Travis Lee, Jose Cruz Jr., and Aramis Ramirez. Inserts include: International parallels (1:4 packs), Internation Refractors (1:24), Refractors (1:12), Rookie of the Year Favorites (1:24), ROY Favorites (1:72), Scout's Honor Roll (1:12) and Scout's Honor Roll Refractors (1:36).

		MT
Complete Set (300):		375.00
Common Player:		.25
Internationals:		1.5x to 2.5x
Wax Box:		275.00
1	Derek Jeter	4.00
2	Chipper Jones	4.00
3	Hideo Nomo	1.25
4	Tim Salmon	.60
5	Robin Ventura	.40
6	Tony Clark	1.00
7	Barry Larkin	.75
8	Paul Molitor	1.00
9	Andy Benes	.25
10	Ryan Klesko	.50
11	Mark McGwire	8.00
12	Ken Griffey Jr.	7.00
13	Robb Nen	.25
14	Cal Ripken Jr.	5.00
15	John Valentin	.25
16	Ricky Bottalico	.25
17	Mike Lansing	.25
18	Ryne Sandberg	2.00
19	Carlos Delgado	.50
20	Craig Biggio	.50
21	Eric Karros	.40
22	Kevin Appier	.25
23	Mariano Rivera	.50
24	Vinny Castilla	.40
25	Juan Gonzalez	3.00
26	Al Martin	.25
27	Jeff Cirillo	.25
28	Ray Lankford	.25
29	Manny Ramirez	1.50
30	Roberto Alomar	1.25
31	Will Clark	.75
32	Chuck Knoblauch	.75
33	Harold Baines	.25
34	Edgar Martinez	.40
35	Mike Mussina	1.25
36	Kevin Brown	.40
37	Dennis Eckersley	.40
38	Tino Martinez	.75
39	Raul Mondesi	.50
40	Sammy Sosa	5.00
41	John Smoltz	.50
42	Billy Wagner	.25
43	Ken Caminiti	.50
44	Wade Boggs	.50
45	Andres Galarraga	.75
46	Roger Clemens	2.50
47	Matt Williams	.75
48	Albert Belle	1.50
49	Jeff King	.25
50	John Wetteland	.25
51	Deion Sanders	.75
52	Ellis Burks	.25
53	Pedro Martinez	.75
54	Kenny Lofton	1.50
55	Randy Johnson	1.00
56	Bernie Williams	1.00
57	Marquis Grissom	.40
58	Gary Sheffield	.75
59	Curt Schilling	.50
60	Reggie Sanders	.25
61	Bobby Higginson	.25
62	Moises Alou	.40
63	Tom Glavine	.50
64	Mark Grace	.75
65	Rafael Palmeiro	.60
66	John Olerud	.50
67	Dante Bichette	.50
68	Jeff Bagwell	2.50
69	Barry Bonds	1.50
70	Pat Hentgen	.25
71	Jim Thome	1.00
72	Andy Pettitte	1.00
73	Jay Bell	.25
74	Jim Edmonds	.40
75	Ron Gant	.40
76	David Cone	.40
77	Jose Canseco	.75
78	Jay Buhner	.50
79	Greg Maddux	4.00
80	Lance Johnson	.25
81	Travis Fryman	.40
82	Paul O'Neill	.50
83	Ivan Rodriguez	1.50
84	Fred McGriff	.50
85	Mike Piazza	4.00
86	Brady Anderson	.40
87	Marty Cordova	.25
88	Joe Carter	.40
89	Brian Jordan	.25
90	David Justice	.75
91	Tony Gwynn	3.50
92	Larry Walker	.75
93	Mo Vaughn	1.50
94	Sandy Alomar	.40
95	Rusty Greer	.40
96	Roberto Hernandez	.25
97	Hal Morris	.25
98	Todd Hundley	.25
99	Rondell White	.50
100	Frank Thomas	5.00
101	*Bubba Trammell*	2.50
102	*Sidney Ponson*	2.00
103	*Ricky Ledee*	8.00
104	Brett Tomko	.25
105	*Braden Looper*	1.00
106	Jason Dickson	.40
107	*Chad Green*	3.00
108	*R.A. Dickey*	.75
109	Jeff Liefer	.40
110	Richard Hidalgo	.25
111	*Chad Hermansen*	12.00
112	Felix Martinez	.25
113	J.J. Johnson	.25
114	Todd Dunwoody	1.50
115	Katsuhiro Maeda	.25
116	Darin Erstad	2.50
117	Elieser Marrero	.25
118	Bartolo Colon	.25
119	Ugueth Urbina	.25
120	Jaime Bluma	.25
121	*Seth Greisinger*	2.00
122	*Jose Cruz Jr.*	20.00
123	Todd Dunn	.25
124	*Justin Towle*	4.00
125	Brian Rose	1.50
126	Jose Guillen	1.50
127	Andruw Jones	3.50
128	*Mark Kotsay*	12.00
129	Wilton Guerrero	.25
130	Jacob Cruz	.25
131	Mike Sweeney	.25
132	Matt Morris	.50
133	John Thomson	.25
134	*Javier Valentin*	.40
135	*Mike Drumright*	1.50
136	Michael Barrett	.25
137	*Tony Saunders*	3.00
138	Kevin Brown	.25
139	*Anthony Sanders*	4.00
140	Jeff Abbott	.25
141	Eugene Kingsale	.25
142	Paul Konerko	2.00
143	*Randall Simon*	6.00
144	Freddy Garcia	.25
145	Karim Garcia	.40
146	Carlos Guillen	.25
147	Aaron Boone	.25
148	Donnie Sadler	.25
149	Brooks Kieschnick	.25
150	Scott Spiezio	.25
151	Kevin Orie	.25
152	Russ Johnson	.25
153	Livan Hernandez	.40
154	*Vladimir Nunez*	3.00
155	Calvin Reese	.25
156	Chris Carpenter	.25
157	*Eric Milton*	8.00
158	Richie Sexson	.40
159	Carl Pavano	1.50
160	Pat Cline	.25
161	Ron Wright	.25
162	Dante Powell	.25
163	Mark Bellhorn	.25
164	George Lombard	1.00
165	*Paul Wilder*	4.00
166	Brad Fullmer	.50
167	*Kris Benson*	7.00
168	Torii Hunter	.25
169	D.T. Cromer	.25
170	Nelson Figueroa	1.00
171	*Hiram Bocachica*	2.50
172	Shane Monahan	.25
173	Juan Melo	.25
174	*Calvin Pickering*	8.00
175	Reggie Taylor	.25
176	Geoff Jenkins	.50
177	Steve Rain	1.00
178	Nerio Rodriguez	1.00
179	Derrick Gibson	1.00
180	Darin Blood	.25
181	Ben Davis	.25
182	*Adrian Beltre*	30.00
183	*Kerry Wood*	75.00
184	Nate Rolison	3.00
185	Fernando Tatis	8.00
186	Jake Westbrook	2.00
187	Edwin Diaz	.25
188	Joe Fontenot	2.00
189	Matt Halloran	1.00
190	*Matt Clement*	8.00
191	Todd Greene	.25
192	*Eric Chavez*	18.00
193	Edgard Velazquez	.25
194	*Bruce Chen*	6.00
195	Jason Brester	.25
196	*Chris Reitsma*	1.50
197	Neifi Perez	.25
198	*Hideki Irabu*	15.00
199	*Don Denbow*	.25
200	Derrek Lee	.25
201	Todd Walker	.75
202	Scott Rolen	4.00
203	Wes Helms	2.00
204	Bob Abreu	.25
205	*John Patterson*	4.00
206	*Alex Gonzalez*	3.00
207	*Grant Roberts*	4.00
208	Jeff Suppan	.25
209	Luke Wilcox	.25
210	Marlon Anderson	.25
211	*Mike Caruso*	5.00
212	*Roy Halladay*	3.00
213	*Jeremi Gonzalez*	3.00
214	*Aramis Ramirez*	20.00
215	*Dermal Brown*	10.00
216	Justin Thompson	.25
217	Danny Clyburn	.25
218	Bruce Aven	.25
219	Keith Foulke	.25
220	Shannon Stewart	.25
221	Larry Barnes	.25
222	Mark Johnson	.75
223	Randy Winn	.25
224	Nomar Garciaparra	5.00
225	*Jacque Jones*	5.00
226	Chris Clemons	.25
227	Todd Helton	3.00
228	*Ryan Brannan*	1.50
229	*Alex Sanchez*	2.00
230	Russell Branyan	1.50
231	Daryle Ward	3.00
232	Kevin Witt	5.00
233	Gabby Martinez	.25
234	Preston Wilson	.25
235	*Donzell McDonald*	2.00
236	*Orlando Cabrera*	2.00
237	Brian Banks	.25
238	Robbie Bell	2.00
239	Brad Rigby	.25
240	Scott Elarton	.25
241	*Donny Leon*	.75
242	*Abraham Nunez*	3.00
243	*Adam Eaton*	.75
244	*Octavio Dotel*	.75
245	Sean Casey	6.00
246	*Joe Lawrence*	.75
247	*Adam Johnson*	2.50
248	*Ronnie Belliard*	1.00
249	Bobby Estalella	.25
250	*Corey Lee*	1.50
251	Mike Cameron	.75
252	*Kerry Robinson*	1.50
253	*A.J. Zapp*	6.00
254	Jarrod Washburn	.25
255	Ben Grieve	4.00
256	*Javier Vazquez*	2.00
257	*Travis Lee*	35.00
258	*Dennis Reyes*	3.00
259	Danny Buxbaum	.25
260	*Kelvim Escobar*	1.00
261	Danny Klassen	.35
262	*Ken Cloude*	5.00
263	Gabe Alvarez	.25
264	*Clayton Brunner*	1.50
265	*Jason Marquis*	3.00
266	Jamey Wright	.25
267	*Matt Snyder*	.75
268	*Josh Garrett*	3.00
269	Juan Encarnacion	1.00
270	Heath Murray	.25
271	*Brent Butler*	8.00
272	*Danny Peoples*	3.00
273	*Miguel Tejada*	10.00
274	Jim Pittsley	.25
275	Dmitri Young	.25
276	Vladimir Guerrero	2.50
277	*Cole Liniak*	6.00
278	Ramon Hernandez	.75
279	*Cliff Politte*	2.00
280	*Mel Rosario*	.75
281	*Jorge Carrion*	1.00
282	*John Barnes*	3.00
283	*Chris Stowe*	1.50
284	*Vernon Wells*	10.00
285	*Brett Caradonna*	5.00
286	*Scott Hodges*	2.00
287	*Jon Garland*	5.00
288	*Nathan Haynes*	2.00
289	*Geoff Goetz*	3.00
290	*Adam Kennedy*	3.00
291	*T.J. Tucker*	.75
292	*Aaron Akin*	1.50
293	*Jayson Werth*	10.00
294	*Glenn Davis*	3.00
295	*Mark Mangum*	1.50
296	*Troy Cameron*	5.00
297	*J.J. Davis*	7.00
298	*Lance Berkman*	20.00
299	*Jason Standridge*	3.00
300	*Jason Dellaero*	3.00

1997 Bowman Chrome Refractors

All 300 cards in Bowman Chrome were reprinted in Refractor versions and inserted one per 12 packs. The cards are very similar to the base cards, but feature a refrative foil finish.

		MT
Common Player:		5.00
1	Derek Jeter	50.00
2	Chipper Jones	60.00
3	Hideo Nomo	20.00
4	Tim Salmon	15.00
5	Robin Ventura	8.00
6	Tony Clark	15.00
7	Barry Larkin	15.00
8	Paul Molitor	20.00
9	Andy Benes	5.00
10	Ryan Klesko	15.00
11	Mark McGwire	125.00
12	Ken Griffey Jr.	100.00
13	Robb Nen	5.00
14	Cal Ripken Jr.	80.00
15	John Valentin	5.00
16	Ricky Bottalico	5.00
17	Mike Lansing	5.00
18	Ryne Sandberg	30.00
19	Carlos Delgado	10.00
20	Craig Biggio	10.00
21	Eric Karros	8.00
22	Kevin Appier	5.00
23	Mariano Rivera	8.00
24	Vinny Castilla	8.00
25	Juan Gonzalez	50.00
26	Al Martin	5.00
27	Jeff Cirillo	5.00
28	Ray Lankford	5.00
29	Manny Ramirez	25.00
30	Roberto Alomar	20.00
31	Will Clark	15.00
32	Chuck Knoblauch	15.00
33	Harold Baines	5.00
34	Edgar Martinez	8.00
35	Mike Mussina	20.00
36	Kevin Brown	8.00
37	Dennis Eckersley	8.00
38	Tino Martinez	15.00
39	Raul Mondesi	12.00
40	Sammy Sosa	60.00
41	John Smoltz	8.00
42	Billy Wagner	5.00
43	Ken Caminiti	8.00
44	Wade Boggs	12.00
45	Andres Galarraga	15.00
46	Roger Clemens	40.00
47	Matt Williams	15.00
48	Albert Belle	25.00
49	Jeff King	5.00
50	John Wetteland	5.00
51	Deion Sanders	10.00
52	Ellis Burks	5.00
53	Pedro Martinez	15.00
54	Kenny Lofton	25.00
55	Randy Johnson	20.00
56	Bernie Williams	20.00
57	Marquis Grissom	8.00
58	Gary Sheffield	15.00
59	Curt Schilling	10.00
60	Reggie Sanders	5.00
61	Bobby Higginson	5.00
62	Moises Alou	10.00
63	Tom Glavine	10.00
64	Mark Grace	15.00
65	Rafael Palmeiro	10.00
66	John Olerud	10.00
67	Dante Bichette	10.00
68	Jeff Bagwell	35.00
69	Barry Bonds	25.00
70	Pat Hentgen	5.00
71	Jim Thome	20.00
72	Andy Pettitte	20.00
73	Jay Bell	5.00
74	Jim Edmonds	5.00
75	Ron Gant	8.00
76	David Cone	8.00
77	Jose Canseco	15.00
78	Jay Buhner	12.00
79	Greg Maddux	60.00
80	Lance Johnson	5.00
81	Travis Fryman	8.00
82	Paul O'Neill	10.00
83	Ivan Rodriguez	25.00
84	Fred McGriff	10.00
85	Mike Piazza	60.00
86	Brady Anderson	8.00
87	Marty Cordova	5.00
88	Joe Carter	8.00
89	Brian Jordan	5.00
90	David Justice	15.00
91	Tony Gwynn	50.00
92	Larry Walker	15.00
93	Mo Vaughn	25.00
94	Sandy Alomar	8.00
95	Rusty Greer	8.00
96	Roberto Hernandez	5.00
97	Hal Morris	5.00
98	Todd Hundley	5.00
99	Rondell White	10.00
100	Frank Thomas	70.00
101	*Bubba Trammell*	25.00
102	*Sidney Ponson*	20.00
103	*Ricky Ledee*	40.00
104	Brett Tomko	5.00
105	*Braden Looper*	15.00
106	Jason Dickson	5.00
107	*Chad Green*	25.00
108	*R.A. Dickey*	10.00
109	Jeff Liefer	5.00
110	Richard Hidalgo	5.00
111	*Chad Hermansen*	50.00
112	Felix Martinez	5.00
113	J.J. Johnson	5.00
114	Todd Dunwoody	10.00
115	Katsuhiro Maeda	5.00
116	Darin Erstad	30.00
117	Elieser Marrero	5.00
118	Bartolo Colon	10.00
119	Ugueth Urbina	5.00
120	Jaime Bluma	5.00
121	Seth Greisinger	20.00
122	Jose Cruz Jr.	80.00
123	Todd Dunn	5.00
124	Justin Towle	25.00
125	Brian Rose	10.00
126	Jose Guillen	15.00
127	Andruw Jones	25.00
128	*Mark Kotsay*	40.00
129	Wilton Guerrero	5.00
130	Jacob Cruz	5.00
131	Mike Sweeney	5.00
132	Matt Morris	10.00
133	John Thomson	5.00
134	*Javier Valentin*	8.00
135	*Mike Drumright*	15.00
136	Michael Barrett	5.00
137	*Tony Saunders*	20.00
138	Kevin Brown	5.00
139	*Anthony Sanders*	20.00
140	Jeff Abbott	5.00
141	Eugene Kingsale	5.00
142	Paul Konerko	25.00
143	*Randall Simon*	40.00
144	Freddy Garcia	5.00
145	Karim Garcia	5.00
146	Carlos Guillen	5.00
147	Aaron Boone	5.00

148	Donnie Sadler	5.00
149	Brooks Kieschnick	5.00
150	Scott Spiezio	5.00
151	Kevin Orie	5.00
152	Russ Johnson	5.00
153	Livan Hernandez	8.00
154	Vladimir Nunez	20.00
155	Calvin Reese	5.00
156	Chris Carpenter	5.00
157	*Eric Milton*	30.00
158	Richie Sexson	5.00
159	Carl Pavano	15.00
160	Pat Cline	5.00
161	Ron Wright	8.00
162	Dante Powell	5.00
163	Mark Bellhorn	5.00
164	George Lombard	5.00
165	*Paul Wilder*	25.00
166	Brad Fullmer	10.00
167	*Kris Benson*	40.00
168	Torii Hunter	5.00
169	D.T. Cromer	5.00
170	Nelson Figueroa	10.00
171	*Hiram Bocachica*	20.00
172	Shane Monahan	5.00
173	Juan Melo	5.00
174	*Calvin Pickering*	50.00
175	Reggie Taylor	5.00
176	Geoff Jenkins	8.00
177	Steve Rain	8.00
178	Nerio Rodriguez	8.00
179	Derrick Gibson	8.00
180	Darin Blood	5.00
181	Ben Davis	5.00
182	Adrian Beltre	90.00
183	*Kerry Wood*	200.00
184	Nate Rolison	20.00
185	Fernando Tatis	40.00
186	Jake Westbrook	12.00
187	Edwin Diaz	5.00
188	Joe Fontenot	10.00
189	Matt Halloran	8.00
190	*Matt Clement*	25.00
191	Todd Greene	5.00
192	Eric Chavez	50.00
193	Edgard Velazquez	5.00
194	*Bruce Chen*	30.00
195	Jason Brester	5.00
196	*Chris Reitsma*	10.00
197	Neifi Perez	5.00
198	*Hideki Irabu*	50.00
199	*Don Denbow*	5.00
200	Derrek Lee	5.00
201	Todd Walker	12.00
202	Scott Rolen	40.00
203	Wes Helms	12.00
204	Bob Abreu	5.00
205	*John Patterson*	20.00
206	*Alex Gonzalez*	20.00
207	*Grant Roberts*	25.00
208	Jeff Suppan	5.00
209	Luke Wilcox	5.00
210	Marlon Anderson	5.00
211	*Mike Caruso*	30.00
212	*Roy Halladay*	20.00
213	*Jeremi Gonzalez*	20.00
214	Aramis Ramirez	75.00
215	*Dermal Brown*	40.00
216	Justin Thompson	5.00
217	Danny Clyburn	5.00
218	Bruce Aven	5.00
219	Keith Foulke	5.00
220	Shannon Stewart	5.00
221	Larry Barnes	5.00
222	Mark Johnson	8.00
223	Randy Winn	5.00
224	Nomar Garciaparra	60.00
225	*Jacque Jones*	25.00
226	Chris Clemons	5.00
227	Todd Helton	30.00
228	*Ryan Brannan*	10.00
229	*Alex Sanchez*	12.00
230	Russell Branyan	10.00
231	Daryle Ward	15.00
232	Kevin Witt	30.00
233	Gabby Martinez	5.00
234	Preston Wilson	5.00
235	*Donzell McDonald*	10.00
236	*Orlando Cabrera*	10.00
237	Brian Banks	5.00
238	Robbie Bell	10.00
239	Brad Rigby	5.00
240	Scott Elarton	5.00
241	*Donny Leon*	8.00
242	*Abraham Nunez*	20.00
243	*Adam Eaton*	8.00
244	*Octavio Dotel*	8.00
245	Sean Casey	40.00
246	*Joe Lawrence*	8.00
247	*Adam Johnson*	15.00
248	*Ronnie Belliard*	10.00
249	Bobby Estalella	5.00
250	*Corey Lee*	10.00
251	Mike Cameron	10.00
252	*Kerry Robinson*	10.00
253	*A.J. Zapp*	40.00
254	Jarrod Washburn	10.00
255	Ben Grieve	40.00
256	*Javier Vazquez*	10.00
257	*Travis Lee*	150.00
258	*Dennis Reyes*	20.00
259	Danny Buxbaum	5.00
260	*Kelvim Escobar*	8.00
261	Danny Klassen	5.00
262	*Ken Cloude*	30.00
263	Gabe Alvarez	5.00
264	*Clayton Brunner*	10.00
265	*Jason Marquis*	20.00
266	Jamey Wright	5.00
267	*Matt Snyder*	8.00
268	*Josh Garrett*	20.00
269	Juan Encarnacion	8.00
270	Heath Murray	5.00
271	*Brent Butler*	40.00
272	*Danny Peoples*	20.00
273	*Miguel Tejada*	50.00
274	Jim Pittsley	5.00
275	Dmitri Young	5.00
276	Vladimir Guerrero	25.00
277	*Cole Liniak*	40.00
278	Ramon Hernandez	5.00
279	*Cliff Politte*	10.00
280	*Mel Rosario*	5.00
281	*Jorge Carrion*	8.00
282	*John Barnes*	20.00
283	*Chris Stowe*	10.00
284	*Vernon Wells*	50.00
285	*Brett Caradonna*	30.00
286	*Scott Hodges*	10.00
287	*Jon Garland*	30.00
288	*Nathan Haynes*	15.00
289	*Geoff Goetz*	20.00
290	*Adam Kennedy*	20.00
291	*T.J. Tucker*	5.00
292	*Aaron Akin*	10.00
293	*Jayson Werth*	50.00
294	Glenn Davis	20.00
295	*Mark Mangum*	10.00
296	*Troy Cameron*	30.00
297	*J.J. Davis*	40.00
298	*Lance Berkman*	80.00
299	*Jason Standridge*	10.00
300	*Jason Dellaero*	12.00

1997 Bowman Chrome International

Internationals paralleled all 300 cards in the base set with a flag from the player's native country in the background. These inserts were seeded one per four packs.

	MT
Complete Set (300):	
Common Player:	1.5x to 2.5x
Inserted 1:4	

1997 Bowman Chrome International Refractors

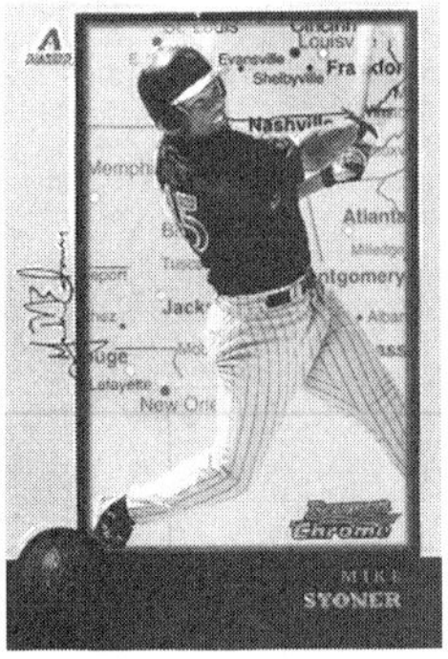

Each International parallel card was also reprinted in a Refractor version. International Refractors were seeded one per 24 packs.

	MT
Common Player:	5.00
Star Refractors:	6x to 12x
Yng Stars & RC's:	3x to 6x
Inserted 1:24	

1997 Bowman Chrome ROY Candidates

This 15-card insert set features color action photos of 1998 Rookie of the Year candidates printed on chromium finish cards. Card backs are numbered with a "ROY" prefix and were inserted one per 24 packs of Bowman Chrome. Refractor versions are seeded one per 72 packs.

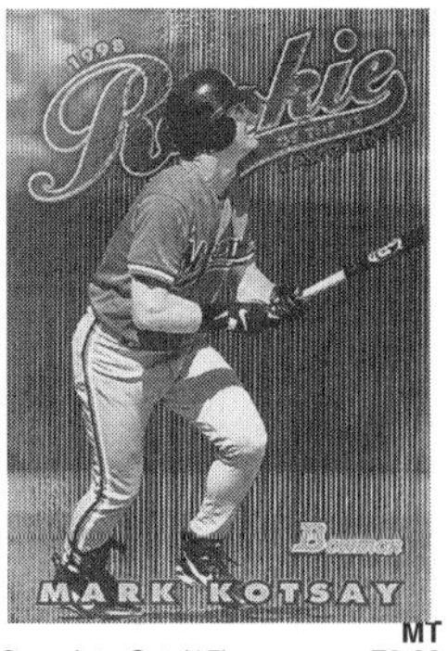

		MT
Complete Set (15):		70.00
Common Player:		2.00
Refractors:		1.5x to 2.5x
ROY1	Jeff Abbott	2.00
ROY2	Karim Garcia	2.50
ROY3	Todd Helton	7.00
ROY4	Richard Hidalgo	2.00
ROY5	Geoff Jenkins	2.00
ROY6	Russ Johnson	2.00
ROY7	Paul Konerko	8.00
ROY8	Mark Kotsay	10.00
ROY9	Ricky Ledee	8.00
ROY10	Travis Lee	30.00
ROY11	Derrek Lee	2.00
ROY12	Elieser Marrero	2.00
ROY13	Juan Melo	2.00
ROY14	Brian Rose	3.00
ROY15	Fernando Tatis	8.00

1997 Bowman Chrome Scout's Honor Roll

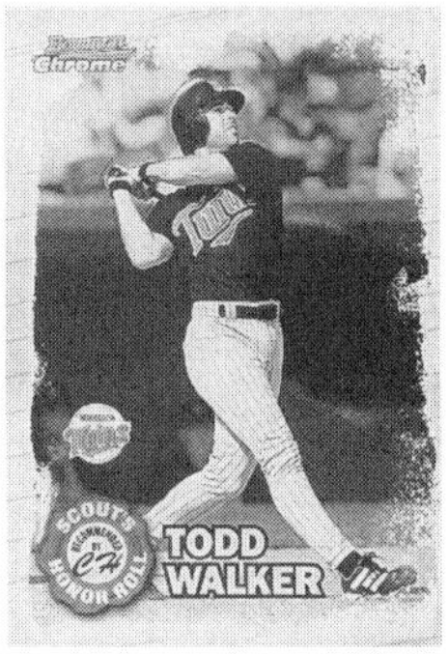

This 15-card set featured top prospects and rookies as selected by the Bowman Scouts. These chromium cards are numbered with a "SHR" prefix and were inserted one per 12 packs, while Refractor versions are seeded one per 36 packs.

		MT
Complete Set (15):		70.00
Common Player:		1.50
Refractors:		1.5x to 2.5x
SHR1	Dmitri Young	1.50
SHR2	Bob Abreu	1.50
SHR3	Vladimir Guerrero	5.00
SHR4	Paul Konerko	4.00
SHR5	Kevin Orie	1.50
SHR6	Todd Walker	2.00
SHR7	Ben Grieve	6.00
SHR8	Darin Erstad	4.00
SHR9	Derrek Lee	1.50
SHR10	Jose Cruz, Jr.	12.00
SHR11	Scott Rolen	8.00
SHR12	Travis Lee	20.00
SHR13	Andruw Jones	6.00
SHR14	Wilton Guerrero	1.50
SHR15	Nomar Garciaparra	10.00

1998 Bowman

Bowman arrived in a 440-card set released in two, 220-card series in 1998. Within each series, there were 150 prospects printed on a silver and blue design and 70 veterans printed on a silver and red design. The cards feature a Bowman stamp, and in cases where its the player's first Bowman card a "Bowman Rookie Card" stamp is included. The player's facsimile signature from their first Bowman contract runs down the side. The entire set was paralleled twice in a Bowman International parallel (one per pack) and a Golden Anniversary parallel (numbered to 50). Inserts in Series I include Autographs, Scout's Choice, and Japanese Rookies. Inserts in Series II include: Autographs, 1999 Rookie of the Year Favorites, Minor League MVPs and Japanese Rookies.

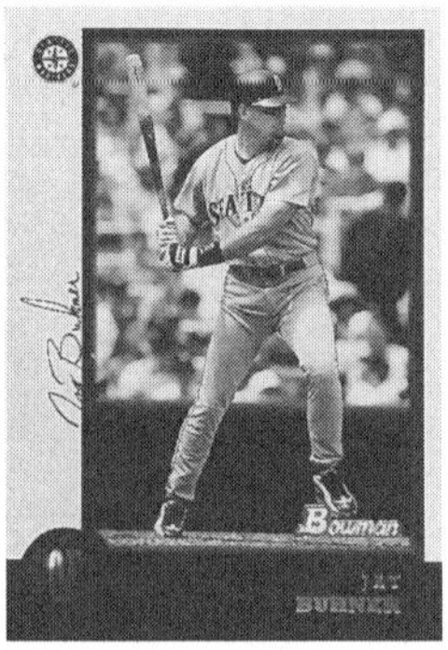

		MT
Complete Set (441):		160.00
Complete Series I set (221):		90.00
Complete Series II set (220):		75.00
Common Player:		.20
Inserted 1:1		
Wax Box:		85.00
1	Nomar Garciaparra	2.50
2	Scott Rolen	1.50
3	Andy Pettitte	.75
4	Ivan Rodriguez	1.00
5	Mark McGwire	5.00
6	Jason Dickson	.20
7	Jose Cruz Jr.	1.50
8	Jeff Kent	.20
9	Mike Mussina	.75
10	Jason Kendall	.20
11	Brett Tomko	.20
12	Jeff King	.20
13	Brad Radke	.20
14	Robin Ventura	.30
15	Jeff Bagwell	1.50
16	Greg Maddux	2.50
17	John Jaha	.20
18	Mike Piazza	2.50
19	Edgar Martinez	.20
20	David Justice	.40
21	Todd Hundley	.20
22	Tony Gwynn	2.00
23	Larry Walker	.60
24	Bernie Williams	.75
25	Edgar Renteria	.20
26	Rafael Palmeiro	.40
27	Tim Salmon	.50
28	Matt Morris	.40
29	Shawn Estes	.20
30	Vladimir Guerrero	1.00
31	Fernando Tatis	.20
32	Justin Thompson	.20
33	Ken Griffey Jr.	4.00
34	Edgardo Alfonzo	.20
35	Mo Vaughn	1.00
36	Marty Cordova	.20
37	Craig Biggio	.40
38	Roger Clemens	1.50
39	Mark Grace	.50
40	Ken Caminiti	.40
41	Tony Womack	.20
42	Albert Belle	1.00
43	Tino Martinez	.75
44	Sandy Alomar	.40
45	Jeff Cirillo	.20
46	Jason Giambi	.20
47	Darin Erstad	1.00
48	Livan Hernandez	.20
49	Mark Grudzielanek	.20
50	Sammy Sosa	2.00
51	Curt Schilling	.40
52	Brian Hunter	.20
53	Neifi Perez	.20
54	Todd Walker	.40
55	Jose Guillen	.40
56	Jim Thome	.75
57	Tom Glavine	.40
58	Todd Greene	.20
59	Rondell White	.40
60	Roberto Alomar	.75
61	Tony Clark	.60
62	Vinny Castilla	.40
63	Barry Larkin	.50
64	Hideki Irabu	1.00
65	Johnny Damon	.20
66	Juan Gonzalez	2.00
67	John Olerud	.40
68	Gary Sheffield	.50
69	Raul Mondesi	.40
70	Chipper Jones	2.50
71	David Ortiz	.75
72	*Warren Morris*	.50
73	Alex Gonzalez	.40
74	Nick Bierbrodt	.20
75	Roy Halladay	.40
76	Danny Buxbaum	.20
77	Adam Kennedy	.40
78	*Jared Sandberg*	1.50
79	Michael Barrett	.20
80	Gil Meche	.40
81	Jayson Werth	.50
82	Abraham Nunez	.50
83	Ben Petrick	.20
84	Brett Caradonna	.40
85	*Mike Lowell*	2.00
86	*Clay Bruner*	1.00
87	*John Curtice*	1.00
88	Bobby Estalella	.20
89	Juan Melo	.20
90	Arnold Gooch	.20
91	*Kevin Millwood*	6.00
92	Richie Sexson	.20
93	Orlando Cabrera	.40
94	Pat Cline	.20
95	Anthony Sanders	.50
96	Russ Johnson	.20
97	Ben Grieve	1.50
98	Kevin McGlinchy	.20
99	Paul Wilder	.20
100	Russ Ortiz	.20
101	*Ryan Jackson*	2.00
102	Heath Murray	.20
103	Brian Rose	.40
104	*Ryan Radmanovich*	1.00
105	Ricky Ledee	1.00
106	*Jeff Wallace*	.50
107	*Ryan Minor*	5.00
108	Dennis Reyes	.50
109	*James Manias*	1.00
110	Chris Carpenter	.20
111	Daryle Ward	.20
112	Vernon Wells	.75
113	Chad Green	.40
114	*Mike Stoner*	5.00
115	Brad Fullmer	.20
116	Adam Eaton	.20
117	Jeff Liefer	.20
118	*Corey Koskie*	2.00
119	Todd Helton	.75
120	*Jaime Jones*	1.00
121	Mel Rosario	.20
122	Geoff Goetz	.20
123	Adrian Beltre	3.00
124	Jason Dellaero	.50
125	*Gabe Kapler*	5.00
126	Scott Schoeneweis	.20
127	Ryan Brannan	.20
128	Aaron Akin	.20
129	*Ryan Anderson*	6.00
130	Brad Penny	.20
131	Bruce Chen	.50
132	Eli Marrero	.20
133	Eric Chavez	1.50
134	*Troy Glaus*	10.00
135	Troy Cameron	.50
136	*Brian Sikorski*	.75
137	*Mike Kinkade*	2.00
138	Braden Looper	.20
139	Mark Mangum	.20
140	Danny Peoples	.50
141	J.J. Davis	.75
142	Ben Davis	.20
143	Jacque Jones	.50
144	Derrick Gibson	.20
145	Bronson Arroyo	.50
146	*Cristian Guzman*	.50
147	Jeff Abbott	.20
148	*Mike Cuddyer*	6.00
149	Jason Romano	.75
150	Shane Monahan	.20
151	*Ntema Ndungidi*	1.00
152	Alex Sanchez	.40
153	*Jack Cust*	2.00
154	Brent Butler	1.00
155	Ramon Hernandez	.20
156	Norm Hutchins	.20
157	Jason Marquis	.20
158	Jacob Cruz	.20
159	*Rob Burger*	1.50
160	Eric Milton	.75
161	Preston Wilson	.20
162	*Jason Fitzgerald*	1.00
163	Dan Serafini	.20
164	Peter Munro	.20
165	Trot Nixon	.20
166	Homer Bush	.20
167	Dermal Brown	1.00
168	Chad Hermansen	1.50
169	*Julio Moreno*	.75
170	*John Roskos*	1.00
171	Grant Roberts	1.00
172	Ken Cloude	.50
173	Jason Brester	.20
174	Jason Conti	.20
175	Jon Garland	.50
176	Robbie Bell	.20
177	Nathan Haynes	.20
178	*Ramon Ortiz*	5.00
179	Shannon Stewart	.20
180	Pablo Ortega	.20
181	*Jimmy Rollins*	1.00
182	Sean Casey	.50
183	*Ted Lilly*	.50
184	*Chris Enochs*	2.50
185	*Magglio Ordonez*	3.00
186	Mike Drumright	.20
187	Aaron Boone	.20
188	Matt Clement	.20
189	Todd Dunwoody	.40
190	Larry Rodriguez	.20

191	Todd Noel	.20
192	Geoff Jenkins	.20
193	George Lombard	.20
194	Lance Berkman	2.00
195	*Marcus McCain*	.50
196	Ryan McGuire	.20
197	*Jhensy Sandoval*	2.00
198	Corey Lee	.20
199	Mario Valdez	.20
200	*Robert Fick*	1.00
201	Donnie Sadler	.20
202	Marc Kroon	.20
203	David Miller	.20
204	Jarrod Washburn	.20
205	Miguel Tejada	1.50
206	Raul Ibanez	.20
207	John Patterson	.50
208	Calvin Pickering	.75
209	Felix Martinez	.20
210	Mark Redman	.20
211	Scott Elarton	.20
212	*Jose Amado*	.75
213	Kerry Wood	8.00
214	Dante Powell	.20
215	Aramis Ramirez	2.50
216	A.J. Hinch	1.50
217	*Dustin Carr*	.50
218	Mark Kotsay	1.50
219	Jason Standridge	.20
220	Luis Ordaz	.20
221	*Orlando Hernandez*	8.00
222	Cal Ripken Jr.	3.00
223	Paul Molitor	.75
224	Derek Jeter	2.50
225	Barry Bonds	1.00
226	Jim Edmonds	.20
227	John Smoltz	.40
228	Eric Karros	.30
229	Ray Lankford	.20
230	Rey Ordonez	.20
231	Kenny Lofton	1.00
232	Alex Rodriguez	2.50
233	Dante Bichette	.40
234	Pedro Martinez	.75
235	Carlos Delgado	.20
236	Rod Beck	.20
237	Matt Williams	.50
238	Charles Johnson	.20
239	Rico Brogna	.20
240	Frank Thomas	2.50
241	Paul O'Neill	.50
242	Jaret Wright	1.00
243	Brant Brown	.20
244	Ryan Klesko	.40
245	Chuck Finley	.20
246	Derek Bell	.20
247	Delino DeShields	.20
248	Chan Ho Park	.40
249	Wade Boggs	.40
250	Jay Buhner	.50
251	Butch Huskey	.20
252	Steve Finley	.20
253	Will Clark	.50
254	John Valentin	.20
255	Bobby Higginson	.20
256	Darryl Strawberry	.40
257	Randy Johnson	.75
258	Al Martin	.20
259	Travis Fryman	.20
260	Fred McGriff	.40
261	Jose Valentin	.20
262	Andruw Jones	1.00
263	Kenny Rogers	.20
264	Moises Alou	.40
265	Denny Neagle	.20
266	Ugueth Urbina	.20
267	Derrek Lee	.20
268	Ellis Burks	.20
269	Mariano Rivera	.40
270	Dean Palmer	.20
271	Eddie Taubensee	.20
272	Brady Anderson	.20
273	Brian Giles	.20
274	Quinton McCracken	.20
275	Henry Rodriguez	.20
276	Andres Galarraga	.50
277	Jose Canseco	.60
278	David Segui	.20
279	Bret Saberhagen	.20
280	Kevin Brown	.40
281	Chuck Knoblauch	.60
282	Jeromy Burnitz	.20
283	Jay Bell	.20
284	Manny Ramirez	1.00
285	Rick Helling	.20
286	Francisco Cordova	.20
287	Bob Abreu	.20
288	J.T. Snow Jr.	.20
289	Hideo Nomo	.60
290	Brian Jordan	.20
291	Javy Lopez	.20
292	Travis Lee	2.00
293	Russell Branyan	.20
294	Paul Konerko	.40
295	*Masato Yoshii*	1.50
296	Kris Benson	.40
297	Juan Encarnacion	.20
298	Eric Milton	.20
299	Mike Caruso	.20
300	*Ricardo Aramboles*	2.50
301	Bobby Smith	.20
302	Billy Koch	.20
303	Richard Hidalgo	.20
304	*Justin Baughman*	1.00
305	Chris Gissell	.20
306	*Donnie Bridges*	1.50
307	*Nelson Lara*	1.00
308	*Randy Wolf*	.75
309	*Jason LaRue*	1.00
310	*Jason Gooding*	.50
311	*Edgar Clemente*	.50
312	Andrew Vessel	.20
313	Chris Reitsma	.20
314	*Jesus Sanchez*	1.00
315	*Buddy Carlyle*	.75
316	Randy Winn	.20
317	Luis Rivera	2.50
318	*Marcus Thames*	1.50
319	A.J. Pierzynski	.20
320	Scott Randall	.20
321	Damian Sapp	.20
322	*Eddie Yarnell*	3.00
323	*Luke Allen*	1.50
324	J.D. Smart	.20
325	Willie Martinez	.20
326	Alex Ramirez	.20
327	*Eric DuBose*	1.00
328	Kevin Witt	.20
329	*Dan McKinley*	.75
330	Cliff Politte	.20
331	Vladimir Nunez	.20
332	*John Halama*	.50
333	Nerio Rodriguez	.20
334	Desi Relaford	.20
335	Robinson Checo	.20
336	*John Nicholson*	1.00
337	*Tom LaRosa*	.75
338	*Kevin Nicholson*	2.00
339	Javier Vazquez	.20
340	A.J. Zapp	.20
341	Tom Evans	.20
342	Kerry Robinson	.20
343	*Gabe Gonzalez*	.75
344	Ralph Milliard	.20
345	Enrique Wilson	.20
346	Elvin Hernandez	.20
347	*Mike Lincoln*	1.50
348	*Cesar King*	2.00
349	*Cristian Guzman*	1.00
350	Donzell McDonald	.20
351	*Jim Parque*	1.00
352	*Mike Saipe*	1.00
353	*Carlos Febles*	.75
354	*Dernell Stenson*	2.00
355	*Mark Osborne*	1.50
356	*Odalis Perez*	1.50
357	*Jason Dewey*	1.00
358	Joe Fontenot	.20
359	*Jason Grilli*	1.50
360	*Kevin Haverbusch*	1.50
361	*Jay Yennaco*	.50
362	Brian Buchanan	.20
363	John Barnes	.20
364	Chris Fussell	.20
365	*Kevin Gibbs*	.75
366	Joe Lawrence	.20
367	DaRond Stovall	.20
368	*Brian Fuentes*	2.00
369	Jimmy Anderson	.20
370	*Laril Gonzalez*	1.00
371	*Scott Williamson*	1.00
372	Milton Bradley	.20
373	*Jason Halper*	.75
374	*Brent Billingsley*	.75
375	*Joe DePastino*	.20
376	Jake Westbrook	.20
377	Octavio Dotel	.20
378	*Jason Williams*	.50
379	*Julio Ramirez*	1.50
380	Seth Greisinger	.20
381	*Mike Judd*	1.00
382	*Ben Ford*	.50
383	Tom Bennett	.20
384	*Adam Butler*	.50
385	*Wade Miller*	.75
386	*Kyle Peterson*	.75
387	*Tommy Peterman*	1.00
388	Onan Masaoka	.20
389	*Jason Rakers*	.75
390	Rafael Medina	.20
391	Luis Lopez	.20
392	Jeff Yoder	.20
393	*Vance Wilson*	.75
394	*Fernando Seguignol*	2.00
395	Ron Wright	.20
396	*Ruben Mateo*	4.00
397	*Steve Lomasney*	.75
398	Damian Jackson	.20
399	*Mike Jerzembeck*	.75
400	*Luis Rivas*	1.50
401	*Kevin Burford*	1.50
402	Glenn Davis	.20
403	*Robert Luce*	.75
404	Cole Liniak	.20
405	*Matthew LeCroy*	1.00
406	*Jeremy Giambi*	2.50
407	Shawn Chacon	.20
408	*Dewayne Wise*	1.50
409	*Steve Woodard*	.75
410	*Francisco Cordero*	.50
411	*Damon Minor*	.75
412	Lou Collier	.20
413	Justin Towle	.20
414	Juan LeBron	.20
415	Michael Coleman	.20
416	Felix Rodriguez	.20
417	*Paul Ah Yat*	.75
418	*Kevin Barker*	1.50
419	Brian Meadows	.20
420	*Darnell McDonald*	3.00
421	*Matt Kinney*	.75
422	*Mike Vavrek*	.75
423	*Courtney Duncan*	.75
424	*Kevin Millar*	.75
425	Ruben Rivera	.20
426	*Steve Shoemaker*	.50
427	*Dan Reichert*	.75
428	*Carlos Lee*	2.00
429	*Rod Barajas*	.75
430	*Pablo Ozuna*	2.00
431	*Todd Belitz*	.50
432	Sidney Ponson	.20
433	*Steve Carver*	1.00
434	Esteban Yan	1.50
435	*Cedrick Bowers*	.75
436	Marlon Anderson	.20
437	Carl Pavano	.20
438	*Jae Weong Seo*	1.00
439	*Jose Taveras*	1.50
440	*Matt Anderson*	2.50
441	*Darron Ingram*	1.00

1998 Bowman Internationals

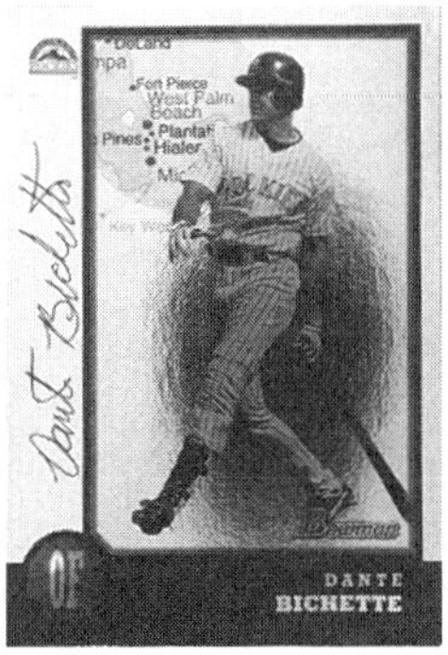

All 441 cards in Bowman Series I and II were reprinted in International versions, with the player's native country highlighted. Background map designs and vital information were translated into the player's native language on these one per pack parallel cards.

	MT
Internationals:	1.5x to 2.5x
Inserted 1:1	

1998 Bowman Autographs

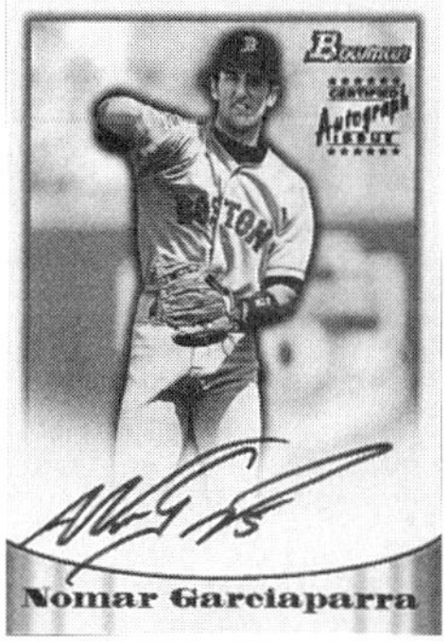

Seventy different players autographed cards in Bowman, with 35 in Series I and 35 in Series II. Card rarity was determined by the color of the Certified Autographs Issue foil stamp, with three different colors available. Series I odds were 1:149 for blue, 1:992 for silver and 1:2,976 for gold, while Series II odds were 1:122 for blue, 1:815 for silver and 1:2,445 for gold.

		MT
Complete Set (70):		
Common Player:		15.00
Inserted 1:149		
Silvers:		1.5x to 2.5x
Inserted 1:992		
Golds:		2x to 3x
Inserted 1:2,976		
1	Adrian Beltre	50.00
2	Brad Fullmer	25.00
3	Ricky Ledee	25.00
4	David Ortiz	25.00
5	Fernando Tatis	20.00
6	Kerry Wood	90.00
7	Mel Rosario	15.00
8	Cole Liniak	20.00
9	A.J. Hinch	25.00
10	Jhensy Sandoval	15.00
11	Jose Cruz Jr.	40.00
12	Richard Hidalgo	20.00
13	Geoff Jenkins	15.00
14	Carl Pavano	25.00
15	Richie Sexson	25.00
16	Tony Womack	20.00
17	Scott Rolen	60.00
18	Ryan Minor	50.00
19	Elieser Marrero	15.00
20	Jason Marquis	15.00
21	Mike Lowell	25.00
22	Todd Helton	35.00
23	Chad Green	15.00
24	Scott Elarton	15.00
25	Russell Branyan	20.00
26	Mike Drumright	15.00
27	Ben Grieve	60.00
28	Jacque Jones	25.00
29	Jared Sandberg	20.00
30	Grant Roberts	25.00
31	Mike Stoner	40.00
32	Brian Rose	15.00
33	Randy Winn	15.00
34	Justin Towle	25.00
35	Anthony Sanders	15.00
36	Rafael Medina	15.00
37	Corey Lee	15.00
38	Mike Kinkade	15.00
39	Norm Hutchins	15.00
40	Jason Brester	15.00
41	Ben Davis	15.00
42	Nomar Garciaparra	80.00
43	Jeff Liefer	15.00
44	Eric Milton	20.00
45	Preston Wilson	20.00
46	Miguel Tejada	30.00
47	Luis Ordaz	15.00
48	Travis Lee	80.00
49	Kris Benson	25.00
50	Jacob Cruz	20.00
51	Dermal Brown	25.00
52	Marc Kroon	15.00
53	Chad Hermansen	40.00
54	Roy Halladay	15.00
55	Eric Chavez	50.00
56	Jason Conti	15.00
57	Juan Encarnacion	20.00
58	Paul Wilder	25.00
59	Aramis Ramirez	50.00
60	Cliff Politte	15.00
61	Todd Dunwoody	15.00
62	Paul Konerko	30.00
63	Shane Monahan	15.00
64	Alex Sanchez	15.00
65	Jeff Abbott	25.00
66	John Patterson	15.00
67	Peter Munro	15.00
68	Jarrod Washburn	30.00
69	Derrek Lee	15.00
70	Ramon Hernandez	15.00

1998 Bowman Minor League MVP's

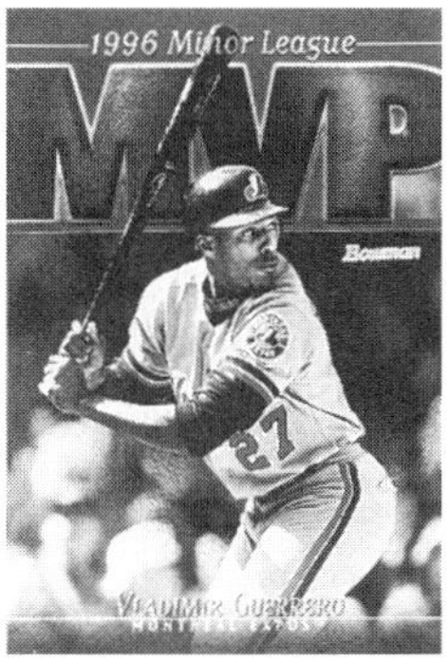

This 10-card insert set features players who are former Minor League MVPs and are now playing in the majors. Minor League MVPs were seeded one per 12 packs of Series II.

	MT
Complete Set (11):	40.00
Common Player:	1.50
MVP1Jeff Bagwell	6.00
MVP2Andres Galarraga	2.50
MVP3Juan Gonzalez	8.00
MVP4Tony Gwynn	8.00
MVP5Vladimir Guerrero	4.00
MVP6Derek Jeter	8.00
MVP7Andruw Jones	4.00
MVP8Tino Martinez	2.50
MVP9Manny Ramirez	4.00
MVP10Gary Sheffield	1.50
MVP11Jim Thome	2.50

1998 Bowman Scout's Choice

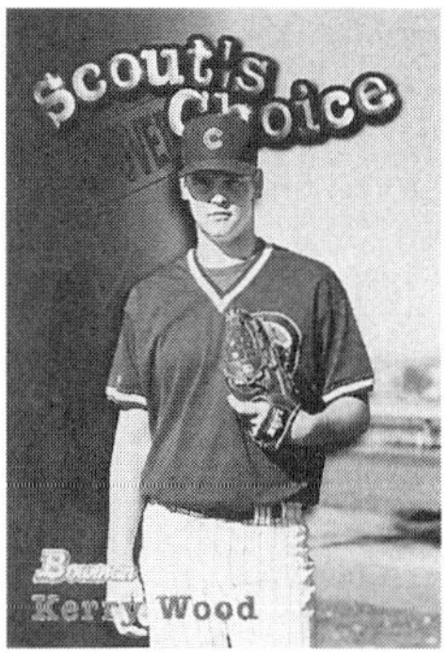

This 20-card insert had players with major potential and could win the Rookie of the Year award. Scout's Choice inserts were seeded one per 12 packs of Series I.

	MT
Complete Set (21):	75.00
Common Player:	1.50
Inserted 1:12	
SC1 Paul Konerko	4.00
SC2 Richard Hidalgo	1.50
SC3 Mark Kotsay	3.00
SC4 Ben Grieve	6.00
SC5 Chad Hermansen	4.00
SC6 Matt Clement	1.50
SC7 Brad Fullmer	3.00
SC8 Eli Marrero	1.50
SC9 Kerry Wood	20.00
SC10Adrian Beltre	5.00
SC11Ricky Ledee	1.50
SC12Travis Lee	10.00
SC13Abraham Nunez	1.50
SC14Ryan Anderson	10.00
SC15Dermal Brown	1.50
SC16Juan Encarnacion	1.50
SC17Aramis Ramirez	10.00
SC18Todd Helton	4.00
SC19Kris Benson	5.00
SC20Russell Branyan	1.50
SC21Mike Stoner	5.00

1998 Bowman Golden Anniversary

This 441-card parallel set celebrated Bowman's 50th anniversary with a gold-stamped facsimile autograph on each card. Golden Anniversary cards were inserted into both Series I (1:237) and Series II (1:194) packs and were sequentially numbered to 50.

		MT
Common Player:		15.00
Production 50 sets		
1	Nomar Garciaparra	200.00
2	Scott Rolen	125.00
3	Andy Pettitte	60.00
4	Ivan Rodriguez	100.00
5	Mark McGwire	450.00
6	Jason Dickson	15.00
7	Jose Cruz Jr.	75.00
8	Jeff Kent	15.00
9	Mike Mussina	75.00
10	Jason Kendall	15.00
11	Brett Tomko	15.00
12	Jeff King	15.00
13	Brad Radke	15.00
14	Robin Ventura	25.00
15	Jeff Bagwell	125.00
16	Greg Maddux	250.00
17	John Jaha	15.00
18	Mike Piazza	250.00
19	Edgar Martinez	15.00
20	David Justice	40.00
21	Todd Hundley	15.00
22	Tony Gwynn	200.00
23	Larry Walker	60.00
24	Bernie Williams	60.00
25	Edgar Renteria	15.00
26	Rafael Palmeiro	40.00
27	Tim Salmon	40.00
28	Matt Morris	15.00
29	Shawn Estes	15.00
30	Vladimir Guerrero	100.00
31	Fernando Tatis	15.00
32	Justin Thompson	15.00
33	Ken Griffey Jr.	400.00
34	Edgardo Alfonzo	15.00
35	Mo Vaughn	100.00
36	Marty Cordova	15.00
37	Craig Biggio	30.00
38	Roger Clemens	150.00

39	Mark Grace	40.00
40	Ken Caminiti	30.00
41	Tony Womack	15.00
42	Albert Belle	100.00
43	Tino Martinez	60.00
44	Sandy Alomar	40.00
45	Jeff Cirillo	15.00
46	Jason Giambi	15.00
47	Darin Erstad	100.00
48	Livan Hernandez	15.00
49	Mark Grudzielanek	15.00
50	Sammy Sosa	200.00
51	Curt Schilling	40.00
52	Brian Hunter	15.00
53	Neifi Perez	15.00
54	Todd Walker	40.00
55	Jose Guillen	40.00
56	Jim Thome	60.00
57	Tom Glavine	40.00
58	Todd Greene	15.00
59	Rondell White	30.00
60	Roberto Alomar	75.00
61	Tony Clark	60.00
62	Vinny Castilla	25.00
63	Barry Larkin	40.00
64	Hideki Irabu	60.00
65	Johnny Damon	15.00
66	Juan Gonzalez	200.00
67	John Olerud	40.00
68	Gary Sheffield	50.00
69	Raul Mondesi	40.00
70	Chipper Jones	250.00
71	David Ortiz	25.00
72	*Warren Morris*	20.00
73	Alex Gonzalez	15.00
74	Nick Bierbrodt	15.00
75	Roy Halladay	20.00
76	Danny Buxbaum	15.00
77	Adam Kennedy	20.00
78	*Jared Sandberg*	30.00
79	Michael Barrett	15.00
80	Gil Meche	15.00
81	Jayson Werth	20.00
82	Abraham Nunez	20.00
83	Ben Petrick	15.00
84	Brett Caradonna	20.00
85	Mike Lowell	25.00
86	*Clay Bruner*	20.00
87	*John Curtice*	20.00
88	Bobby Estalella	15.00
89	Juan Melo	15.00
90	Arnold Gooch	15.00
91	Kevin Millwood	100.00
92	Richie Sexson	15.00
93	Orlando Cabrera	15.00
94	Pat Cline	15.00
95	Anthony Sanders	20.00
96	Russ Johnson	15.00
97	Ben Grieve	125.00
98	Kevin McGlinchy	15.00
99	Paul Wilder	15.00
100	Russ Ortiz	15.00
101	Ryan Jackson	35.00
102	Heath Murray	15.00
103	Brian Rose	20.00
104	*Ryan Radmanovich*	20.00
105	Ricky Ledee	25.00
106	*Jeff Wallace*	20.00
107	Ryan Minor	90.00
108	Dennis Reyes	15.00
109	*James Manias*	20.00
110	Chris Carpenter	15.00
111	Daryle Ward	15.00
112	Vernon Wells	20.00
113	Chad Green	15.00
114	*Mike Stoner*	80.00
115	Brad Fullmer	20.00
116	Adam Eaton	15.00
117	Jeff Liefer	15.00
118	Corey Koskie	20.00
119	Todd Helton	50.00
120	*Jaime Jones*	25.00
121	Mel Rosario	15.00
122	Geoff Goetz	15.00
123	Adrian Beltre	120.00
124	Jason Dellaero	20.00
125	Gabe Kapler	100.00
126	Scott Schoeneweis	15.00
127	Ryan Brannan	15.00
128	Aaron Akin	15.00
129	Ryan Anderson	100.00
130	Brad Penny	15.00
131	Bruce Chen	20.00
132	Eli Marrero	15.00
133	Eric Chavez	30.00
134	Troy Glaus	160.00
135	Troy Cameron	20.00
136	*Brian Sikorski*	20.00
137	Mike Kinkade	20.00
138	Braden Looper	15.00
139	Mark Mangum	15.00
140	Danny Peoples	15.00
141	J.J. Davis	20.00
142	Ben Davis	15.00
143	Jacque Jones	15.00
144	Derrick Gibson	15.00
145	Bronson Arroyo	15.00
146	*Cristian Guzman*	15.00
147	Jeff Abbott	15.00
148	*Mike Cuddyer*	30.00
149	Jason Romano	20.00
150	Shane Monahan	15.00
151	*Ntema Ndungidi*	20.00
152	Alex Sanchez	15.00
153	*Jack Cust*	35.00
154	Brent Butler	20.00
155	Ramon Hernandez	15.00
156	Norm Hutchins	15.00
157	Jason Marquis	15.00
158	Jacob Cruz	15.00
159	*Rob Burger*	30.00
160	Eric Milton	20.00
161	Preston Wilson	15.00
162	*Jason Fitzgerald*	20.00
163	Dan Serafini	15.00
164	Peter Munro	15.00
165	Trot Nixon	20.00
166	Homer Bush	15.00
167	Dermal Brown	20.00
168	Chad Hermansen	25.00
169	*Julio Moreno*	20.00
170	*John Roskos*	20.00
171	Grant Roberts	20.00
172	Ken Cloude	15.00
173	Jason Brester	15.00
174	Jason Conti	15.00
175	Jon Garland	15.00
176	Robbie Bell	15.00
177	Nathan Haynes	15.00
178	Ramon Ortiz	40.00
179	Shannon Stewart	15.00
180	Pablo Ortega	15.00
181	*Jimmy Rollins*	20.00
182	Sean Casey	20.00
183	*Ted Lilly*	15.00
184	*Chris Enochs*	40.00
185	*Magglio Ordonez*	60.00
186	Mike Drumright	15.00
187	Aaron Boone	15.00
188	Matt Clement	15.00
189	Todd Dunwoody	15.00
190	Larry Rodriguez	15.00
191	Todd Noel	15.00
192	Geoff Jenkins	15.00
193	George Lombard	15.00
194	Lance Berkman	60.00
195	*Marcus McCain*	20.00
196	Ryan McGuire	15.00
197	*Jhensy Sandoval*	20.00
198	Corey Lee	15.00
199	Mario Valdez	15.00
200	*Robert Fick*	20.00
201	Donnie Sadler	15.00
202	Marc Kroon	15.00
203	David Miller	15.00
204	Jarrod Washburn	15.00
205	Miguel Tejada	25.00
206	Raul Ibanez	15.00
207	John Patterson	15.00
208	Calvin Pickering	15.00
209	Felix Martinez	15.00
210	Mark Redman	15.00
211	Scott Elarton	15.00
212	*Jose Amado*	20.00
213	Kerry Wood	250.00
214	Dante Powell	15.00
215	Aramis Ramirez	100.00
216	A.J. Hinch	30.00
217	*Dustin Carr*	15.00
218	Mark Kotsay	25.00
219	Jason Standridge	15.00
220	Luis Ordaz	15.00
221	Orlando Hernandez	125.00
222	Cal Ripken Jr.	275.00
223	Paul Molitor	75.00
224	Derek Jeter	200.00
225	Barry Bonds	100.00
226	Jim Edmonds	25.00
227	John Smoltz	25.00
228	Eric Karros	25.00
229	Ray Lankford	15.00
230	Rey Ordonez	15.00
231	Kenny Lofton	100.00
232	Alex Rodriguez	250.00
233	Dante Bichette	40.00
234	Pedro Martinez	75.00
235	Carlos Delgado	15.00
236	Rod Beck	15.00
237	Matt Williams	40.00
238	Charles Johnson	15.00
239	Rico Brogna	15.00
240	Frank Thomas	250.00
241	Paul O'Neill	40.00
242	Jaret Wright	75.00
243	Brant Brown	25.00
244	Ryan Klesko	25.00
245	Chuck Finley	20.00
246	Derek Bell	15.00
247	Delino DeShields	15.00
248	Chan Ho Park	40.00
249	Wade Boggs	50.00
250	Jay Buhner	50.00
251	Butch Huskey	15.00
252	Steve Finley	15.00
253	Will Clark	50.00
254	John Valentin	15.00
255	Bobby Higginson	15.00
256	Darryl Strawberry	40.00
257	Randy Johnson	75.00
258	Al Martin	15.00
259	Travis Fryman	15.00
260	Fred McGriff	30.00
261	Jose Valentin	15.00
262	Andruw Jones	100.00
263	Kenny Rogers	15.00
264	Moises Alou	40.00
265	Denny Neagle	15.00
266	Ugueth Urbina	15.00
267	Derrek Lee	15.00
268	Ellis Burks	15.00
269	Mariano Rivera	30.00
270	Dean Palmer	15.00
271	Eddie Taubensee	15.00
272	Brady Anderson	15.00
273	Brian Giles	15.00
274	Quinton McCracken	15.00
275	Henry Rodriguez	15.00
276	Andres Galarraga	60.00
277	Jose Canseco	60.00
278	David Segui	15.00
279	Bret Saberhagen	15.00
280	Kevin Brown	30.00
281	Chuck Knoblauch	50.00
282	Jeromy Burnitz	15.00
283	Jay Bell	15.00
284	Manny Ramirez	100.00
285	Rick Helling	15.00
286	Francisco Cordova	15.00
287	Bob Abreu	15.00
288	J.T. Snow Jr.	15.00
289	Hideo Nomo	60.00
290	Brian Jordan	15.00
291	Javy Lopez	15.00
292	Travis Lee	125.00
293	Russell Branyan	15.00
294	Paul Konerko	25.00
295	*Masato Yoshii*	50.00
296	Kris Benson	30.00
297	Juan Encarnacion	15.00
298	Eric Milton	15.00
299	Mike Caruso	15.00
300	*Ricardo Aramboles*	75.00
301	Bobby Smith	15.00
302	Billy Koch	15.00
303	Richard Hidalgo	15.00
304	*Justin Baughman*	20.00
305	Chris Gissell	15.00
306	*Donnie Bridges*	25.00
307	*Nelson Lara*	20.00
308	*Randy Wolf*	20.00
309	*Jason LaRue*	20.00
310	*Jason Gooding*	20.00
311	*Edgar Clemente*	20.00
312	Andrew Vessel	15.00
313	Chris Reitsma	15.00
314	*Jesus Sanchez*	25.00
315	*Buddy Carlyle*	20.00
316	Randy Winn	15.00
317	Luis Rivera	30.00
318	*Marcus Thames*	25.00
319	A.J. Pierzynski	15.00
320	Scott Randall	15.00
321	Damian Sapp	15.00
322	*Eddie Yarnell*	50.00
323	*Luke Allen*	25.00
324	J.D. Smart	15.00
325	Willie Martinez	15.00
326	Alex Ramirez	15.00
327	*Eric DuBose*	25.00
328	Kevin Witt	15.00
329	*Dan McKinley*	20.00
330	Cliff Politte	15.00
331	Vladimir Nunez	15.00
332	*John Halama*	20.00
333	Nerio Rodriguez	15.00
334	Desi Relaford	15.00
335	Robinson Checo	15.00
336	*John Nicholson*	20.00
337	*Tom LaRosa*	20.00
338	*Kevin Nicholson*	30.00
339	Javier Vazquez	15.00
340	A.J. Zapp	15.00
341	Tom Evans	15.00
342	Kerry Robinson	15.00
343	*Gabe Gonzalez*	20.00
344	Ralph Milliard	15.00
345	Enrique Wilson	15.00
346	Elvin Hernandez	15.00
347	*Mike Lincoln*	25.00
348	*Cesar King*	30.00
349	*Cristian Guzman*	20.00
350	Donzell McDonald	15.00
351	*Jim Parque*	25.00
352	*Mike Saipe*	20.00
353	*Carlos Febles*	20.00
354	*Dernell Stenson*	30.00
355	*Mark Osborne*	25.00
356	*Odalis Perez*	25.00
357	*Jason Dewey*	20.00
358	Joe Fontenot	15.00
359	*Jason Grilli*	25.00
360	*Kevin Haverbusch*	25.00
361	*Jay Yennaco*	20.00
362	Brian Buchanan	15.00
363	John Barnes	15.00
364	Chris Fussell	15.00
365	*Kevin Gibbs*	20.00
366	Joe Lawrence	15.00
367	DaRond Stovall	15.00
368	*Brian Fuentes*	25.00
369	Jimmy Anderson	15.00
370	*Laril Gonzalez*	30.00
371	*Scott Williamson*	20.00
372	Milton Bradley	15.00
373	*Jason Halper*	20.00
374	*Brent Billingsley*	20.00
375	*Joe DePastino*	15.00
376	Jake Westbrook	15.00
377	Octavio Dotel	15.00
378	*Jason Williams*	20.00
379	*Julio Ramirez*	25.00
380	Seth Greisinger	15.00
381	*Mike Judd*	20.00
382	*Ben Ford*	20.00
383	Tom Bennett	15.00
384	*Adam Butler*	20.00
385	*Wade Miller*	20.00
386	*Kyle Peterson*	20.00
387	*Tommy Peterman*	20.00
388	Onan Masaoka	15.00
389	*Jason Rakers*	20.00
390	Rafael Medina	15.00
391	Luis Lopez	15.00
392	Jeff Yoder	15.00
393	*Vance Wilson*	20.00
394	*Fernando Seguignol*	30.00
395	Ron Wright	15.00
396	*Ruben Mateo*	60.00
397	*Steve Lomasney*	20.00
398	Damian Jackson	15.00
399	*Mike Jerzembeck*	20.00
400	*Luis Rivas*	25.00
401	*Kevin Burford*	25.00
402	Glenn Davis	15.00
403	*Robert Luce*	20.00
404	Cole Liniak	15.00
405	*Matthew LeCroy*	20.00
406	*Jeremy Giambi*	35.00
407	Shawn Chacon	15.00
408	*Dewayne Wise*	25.00
409	*Steve Woodard*	20.00
410	*Francisco Cordero*	20.00
411	*Damon Minor*	20.00
412	Lou Collier	15.00
413	Justin Towle	15.00
414	Juan LeBron	15.00
415	Michael Coleman	15.00
416	Felix Rodriguez	15.00
417	*Paul Ah Yat*	20.00
418	*Kevin Barker*	25.00
419	Brian Meadows	15.00
420	*Darnell McDonald*	30.00
421	*Matt Kinney*	20.00
422	*Mike Vavrek*	20.00
423	*Courtney Duncan*	20.00
424	*Kevin Millar*	20.00
425	Ruben Rivera	15.00
426	*Steve Shoemaker*	20.00
427	*Dan Reichert*	20.00
428	*Carlos Lee*	30.00
429	*Rod Barajas*	20.00
430	*Pablo Ozuna*	30.00
431	*Todd Belitz*	15.00
432	Sidney Ponson	20.00
433	*Steve Carver*	20.00
434	Esteban Yan	25.00
435	*Cedrick Bowers*	20.00
436	Marlon Anderson	15.00
437	Carl Pavano	15.00
438	*Jae Weong Seo*	20.00
439	*Jose Taveras*	25.00
440	*Matt Anderson*	30.00
441	*Darron Ingram*	20.00

1998 Bowman Japanese Rookies

Bowman offered collectors a chance to receive original BBM Japanese rookie cards of three players. Series I had rookie cards of Hideo Nomo and Shigetoshi Hasegawa inserted in one per 2,685 packs, while Series II offered Hideki Irabu seeded one per 4,411 packs.

	MT
Complete Set (2):	50.00
Common Player:	10.00
BBM11Hideo Nomo	40.00
BBM17Shigetosi Hasegawa	10.00

1998 Bowman ROY Favorites

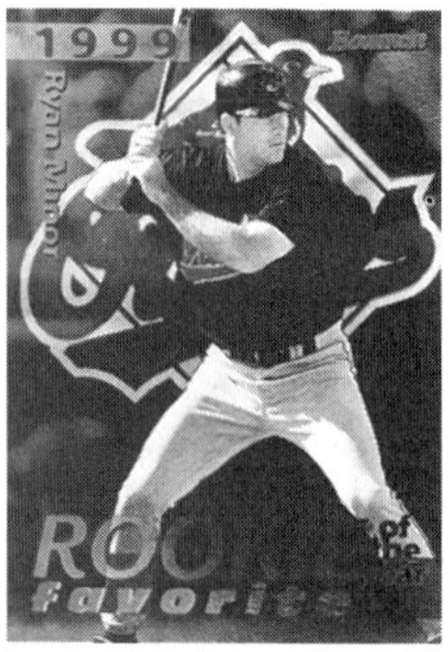

Rookie of the Year Favorites displayed 20 players who had a legitimate shot at the 1999 Rookie of the Year award as selected by the Bowman Scouts. The insert was seeded per 12 packs of Series II.

	MT
Complete Set (10):	25.00
Common Player:	1.00
ROY1Adrian Beltre	3.00
ROY2Troy Glaus	10.00
ROY3Chad Hermansen	1.00
ROY4Matt Clement	2.50
ROY5Eric Chavez	6.00
ROY6Kris Benson	1.00
ROY7Richie Sexson	2.00
ROY8Randy Wolf	1.00
ROY9Ryan Minor	5.00
ROY10Alex Gonzalez	1.00

1998 Bowman Chrome

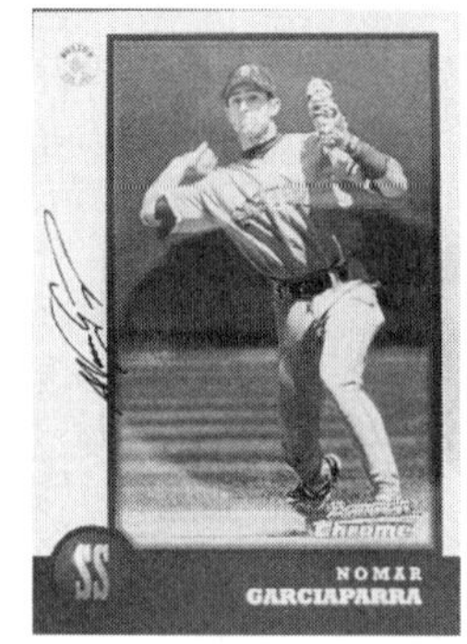

All 440 cards in Bowman I and II have been reprinted with a chromium finish for Bowman Chrome. Issue in two Series, it contained International and Golden Anniversary parallels, similar to Bowman. International parallels were seeded one per four packs, with Refractor versions every 24 packs. Golden Anniversary parallels were exclusive to hobby packs and inserted one per 164 packs and sequentially numbered to 50 sets. Refractor versions were seeded one per 1,279 packs and numbered to just five sets. In addition, 50 Bowman Chrome Reprints were inserted with 25 in each series.

		MT
Complete Set (441):		300.00
Complete Series I Set (221):		180.00
Complete Series II Set (220):		120.00
Wax Box:		110.00
1	Nomar Garciaparra	5.00
2	Scott Rolen	3.00
3	Andy Pettitte	1.50
4	Ivan Rodriguez	2.00
5	Mark McGwire	10.00
6	Jason Dickson	.40
7	Jose Cruz Jr.	2.00
8	Jeff Kent	.40
9	Mike Mussina	1.50
10	Jason Kendall	.40
11	Brett Tomko	.40
12	Jeff King	.40
13	Brad Radke	.40
14	Robin Ventura	.50
15	Jeff Bagwell	3.00
16	Greg Maddux	5.00
17	John Jaha	.40
18	Mike Piazza	5.00
19	Edgar Martinez	.40
20	David Justice	.75
21	Todd Hundley	.40
22	Tony Gwynn	4.00
23	Larry Walker	1.00
24	Bernie Williams	1.50
25	Edgar Renteria	.40
26	Rafael Palmeiro	.75
27	Tim Salmon	1.00
28	Matt Morris	.50
29	Shawn Estes	.40
30	Vladimir Guerrero	2.00
31	Fernando Tatis	.60
32	Justin Thompson	.40
33	Ken Griffey Jr.	8.00
34	Edgardo Alfonzo	.40
35	Mo Vaughn	2.00
36	Marty Cordova	.40
37	Craig Biggio	.75
38	Roger Clemens	3.00
39	Mark Grace	.75
40	Ken Caminiti	.60
41	Tony Womack	.40
42	Albert Belle	2.00
43	Tino Martinez	1.00
44	Sandy Alomar	.60
45	Jeff Cirillo	.40
46	Jason Giambi	.40
47	Darin Erstad	2.00
48	Livan Hernandez	.40
49	Mark Grudzielanek	.40
50	Sammy Sosa	5.00
51	Curt Schilling	.60
52	Brian Hunter	.40

53	Neifi Perez	.40
54	Todd Walker	.60
55	Jose Guillen	.60
56	Jim Thome	1.00
57	Tom Glavine	.60
58	Todd Greene	.40
59	Rondell White	.50
60	Roberto Alomar	1.50
61	Tony Clark	1.25
62	Vinny Castilla	.50
63	Barry Larkin	.75
64	Hideki Irabu	1.50
65	Johnny Damon	.40
66	Juan Gonzalez	4.00
67	John Olerud	.60
68	Gary Sheffield	.75
69	Raul Mondesi	.60
70	Chipper Jones	5.00
71	David Ortiz	1.50
72	*Warren Morris*	3.00
73	Alex Gonzalez	.40
74	Nick Bierbrodt	.40
75	Roy Halladay	.40
76	Danny Buxbaum	.40
77	Adam Kennedy	.40
78	*Jared Sandberg*	5.00
79	Michael Barrett	.40
80	Gil Meche	.40
81	Jayson Werth	2.50
82	Abraham Nunez	.75
83	Ben Petrick	.40
84	Brett Caradonna	.40
85	*Mike Lowell*	4.00
86	*Clay Bruner*	2.00
87	*John Curtice*	4.00
88	Bobby Estalella	.40
89	Juan Melo	.40
90	Arnold Gooch	.40
91	*Kevin Millwood*	15.00
92	Richie Sexson	.40
93	Orlando Cabrera	.40
94	Pat Cline	.40
95	Anthony Sanders	.50
96	Russ Johnson	.40
97	Ben Grieve	3.00
98	Kevin McGlinchy	.40
99	Paul Wilder	.40
100	Russ Ortiz	.40
101	*Ryan Jackson*	4.00
102	Heath Murray	.40
103	Brian Rose	.40
104	*Ryan Radmanovich*	2.00
105	Ricky Ledee	1.50
106	*Jeff Wallace*	2.00
107	*Ryan Minor*	10.00
108	Dennis Reyes	.50
109	*James Manias*	2.00
110	Chris Carpenter	.40
111	Daryle Ward	.50
112	Vernon Wells	2.50
113	Chad Green	.40
114	*Mike Stoner*	10.00
115	Brad Fullmer	.60
116	Adam Eaton	.40
117	Jeff Liefer	.40
118	*Corey Koskie*	4.00
119	Todd Helton	2.00
120	*Jaime Jones*	2.00
121	Mel Rosario	.40
122	Geoff Goetz	.40
123	Adrian Beltre	3.00
124	Jason Dellaero	.50
125	*Gabe Kapler*	10.00
126	Scott Schoeneweis	.40
127	Ryan Brannan	.40
128	Aaron Akin	.40
129	*Ryan Anderson*	18.00
130	Brad Penny	.40
131	Bruce Chen	.50
132	Eli Marrero	.40
133	Eric Chavez	3.00
134	*Troy Glaus*	30.00
135	Troy Cameron	.50
136	*Brian Sikorski*	1.50
137	*Mike Kinkade*	4.00
138	Braden Looper	.40
139	Mark Mangum	.40
140	Danny Peoples	.50
141	J.J. Davis	1.50
142	Ben Davis	.40
143	Jacque Jones	.50
144	Derrick Gibson	.40
145	Bronson Arroyo	.50
146	*Luis DeLosSantos*	3.00
147	Jeff Abbott	.40
148	*Mike Cuddyer*	8.00
149	Jason Romano	1.50
150	Shane Monahan	.40
151	*Ntema Ndungidi*	4.00
152	Alex Sanchez	.40
153	*Jack Cust*	6.00
154	Brent Butler	2.00
155	Ramon Hernandez	.40
156	Norm Hutchins	.40
157	Jason Marquis	.40
158	Jacob Cruz	.40
159	*Rob Burger*	2.50
160	Eric Milton	1.50
161	Preston Wilson	.40
162	*Jason Fitzgerald*	2.50
163	Dan Serafini	.40
164	Peter Munro	.40
165	Trot Nixon	.40
166	Homer Bush	.40
167	Dermal Brown	2.00
168	Chad Hermansen	3.00
169	*Julio Moreno*	2.00
170	*John Roskos*	2.00

171	Grant Roberts	1.50
172	Ken Cloude	.50
173	Jason Brester	.40
174	Jason Conti	.40
175	Jon Garland	.50
176	Robbie Bell	.40
177	Nathan Haynes	.40
178	*Ramon Ortiz*	6.00
179	Shannon Stewart	.40
180	Pablo Ortega	.40
181	*Jimmy Rollins*	4.00
182	Sean Casey	1.00
183	*Ted Lilly*	.75
184	*Chris Enochs*	6.00
185	*Magglio Ordonez*	8.00
186	Mike Drumright	.40
187	Aaron Boone	.40
188	Matt Clement	.40
189	Todd Dunwoody	.40
190	Larry Rodriguez	.40
191	Todd Noel	.40
192	Geoff Jenkins	.40
193	George Lombard	.50
194	Lance Berkman	4.00
195	*Marcus McCain*	.75
196	Ryan McGuire	.40
197	*Jhensy Sandoval*	7.00
198	Corey Lee	.40
199	Mario Valdez	.40
200	*Robert Fick*	3.00
201	Donnie Sadler	.40
202	Marc Kroon	.40
203	David Miller	.40
204	Jarrod Washburn	.40
205	Miguel Tejada	3.00
206	Raul Ibanez	.40
207	John Patterson	.60
208	Calvin Pickering	2.00
209	Felix Martinez	.40
210	Mark Redman	.40
211	Scott Elarton	.40
212	*Jose Amado*	1.50
213	Kerry Wood	10.00
214	Dante Powell	.40
215	Aramis Ramirez	4.00
216	A.J. Hinch	3.00
217	*Dustin Carr*	2.00
218	Mark Kotsay	3.00
219	Jason Standridge	.40
220	Luis Ordaz	.40
221	*Orlando Hernandez*	30.00
222	Cal Ripken Jr.	6.00
223	Paul Molitor	1.50
224	Derek Jeter	5.00
225	Barry Bonds	2.00
226	Jim Edmonds	.40
227	John Smoltz	.40
228	Eric Karros	.40
229	Ray Lankford	.20
230	Rey Ordonez	.20
231	Kenny Lofton	2.00
232	Alex Rodriguez	5.00
233	Dante Bichette	.50
234	Pedro Martinez	1.50
235	Carlos Delgado	.20
236	Rod Beck	.20
237	Matt Williams	.50
238	Charles Johnson	.20
239	Rico Brogna	.20
240	Frank Thomas	5.00
241	Paul O'Neill	.75
242	Jaret Wright	2.00
243	Brant Brown	.20
244	Ryan Klesko	.50
245	Chuck Finley	.20
246	Derek Bell	.20
247	Delino DeShields	.20
248	Chan Ho Park	.50
249	Wade Boggs	.50
250	Jay Buhner	.75
251	Butch Huskey	.20
252	Steve Finley	.20
253	Will Clark	.75
254	John Valentin	.20
255	Bobby Higginson	.20
256	Darryl Strawberry	.50
257	Randy Johnson	1.50
258	Al Martin	.20
259	Travis Fryman	.20
260	Fred McGriff	.50
261	Jose Valentin	.20
262	Andruw Jones	2.00
263	Kenny Rogers	.20
264	Moises Alou	.50
265	Denny Neagle	.20
266	Ugueth Urbina	.20
267	Derrek Lee	.20
268	Ellis Burks	.20
269	Mariano Rivera	.50
270	Dean Palmer	.20
271	Eddie Taubensee	.20
272	Brady Anderson	.20
273	Brian Giles	.20
274	Quinton McCracken	.20
275	Henry Rodriguez	.20
276	Andres Galarraga	.75
277	Jose Canseco	1.00
278	David Segui	.20
279	Bret Saberhagen	.20
280	Kevin Brown	.50
281	Chuck Knoblauch	.75
282	Jeromy Burnitz	.20
283	Jay Bell	.20
284	Manny Ramirez	2.00
285	Rick Helling	.20
286	Francisco Cordova	.20
287	Bob Abreu	.20
288	J.T. Snow Jr.	.20

289	Hideo Nomo	1.50
290	Brian Jordan	.20
291	Javy Lopez	.20
292	Travis Lee	4.00
293	Russell Branyan	.20
294	Paul Konerko	.50
295	*Masato Yoshii*	3.00
296	Kris Benson	.75
297	Juan Encarnacion	.20
298	Eric Milton	.20
299	Mike Caruso	.20
300	*Ricardo Aramboles*	6.00
301	Bobby Smith	.20
302	Billy Koch	.20
303	Richard Hidalgo	.20
304	*Justin Baughman*	2.00
305	Chris Gissell	.20
306	*Donnie Bridges*	3.00
307	*Nelson Lara*	2.00
308	*Randy Wolf*	2.00
309	*Jason LaRue*	2.00
310	*Jason Gooding*	1.00
311	*Edgar Clemente*	1.00
312	Andrew Vessel	.20
313	Chris Reitsma	.20
314	*Jesus Sanchez*	2.00
315	*Buddy Carlyle*	2.00
316	Randy Winn	.20
317	Luis Rivera	5.00
318	*Marcus Thames*	3.00
319	A.J. Pierzynski	.20
320	Scott Randall	.20
321	Damian Sapp	.20
322	*Eddie Yarnell*	6.00
323	*Luke Allen*	3.00
324	J.D. Smart	.20
325	Willie Martinez	.20
326	Alex Ramirez	.20
327	*Eric DuBose*	2.00
328	Kevin Witt	.20
329	*Dan McKinley*	1.50
330	Cliff Politte	.20
331	Vladimir Nunez	.20
332	*John Halama*	1.00
333	Nerio Rodriguez	.20
334	Desi Relaford	.20
335	Robinson Checo	.20
336	*John Nicholson*	2.00
337	*Tom LaRosa*	1.50
338	*Kevin Nicholson*	4.00
339	Javier Vazquez	.20
340	A.J. Zapp	.20
341	Tom Evans	.20
342	Kerry Robinson	.20
343	*Gabe Gonzalez*	1.50
344	Ralph Milliard	.20
345	Enrique Wilson	.20
346	Elvin Hernandez	.20
347	*Mike Lincoln*	3.00
348	*Cesar King*	4.00
349	Cristian Guzman	2.00
350	Donzell McDonald	.20
351	*Jim Parque*	3.00
352	*Mike Saipe*	2.00
353	*Carlos Febles*	2.00
354	*Dernell Stenson*	5.00
355	*Mark Osborne*	3.00
356	*Odalis Perez*	4.00
357	*Jason Dewey*	2.00
358	Joe Fontenot	.20
359	*Jason Grilli*	3.00
360	*Kevin Haverbusch*	3.00
361	*Jay Yennaco*	1.00
362	Brian Buchanan	.20
363	John Barnes	.20
364	Chris Fussell	.20
365	*Kevin Gibbs*	1.50
366	Joe Lawrence	.20
367	DaRond Stovall	.20
368	*Brian Fuentes*	2.00
369	Jimmy Anderson	.20
370	*Laril Gonzalez*	2.00
371	*Scott Williamson*	2.00
372	Milton Bradley	.20
373	*Jason Halper*	1.50
374	*Brent Billingsley*	1.50
375	*Joe DePastino*	.20
376	Jake Westbrook	.20
377	Octavio Dotel	.20
378	*Jason Williams*	1.00
379	*Julio Ramirez*	3.00
380	Seth Greisinger	.20
381	*Mike Judd*	2.00
382	*Ben Ford*	1.00
383	Tom Bennett	.20
384	*Adam Butler*	1.00
385	*Wade Miller*	2.00
386	*Kyle Peterson*	2.00
387	*Tommy Peterman*	2.00
388	Onan Masaoka	.20
389	*Jason Rakers*	1.50
390	Rafael Medina	.20
391	Luis Lopez	.20
392	Jeff Yoder	.20
393	*Vance Wilson*	1.50
394	*Fernando Seguignol*	5.00
395	Ron Wright	.20
396	*Ruben Mateo*	8.00
397	*Steve Lomasney*	2.00
398	Damian Jackson	.20
399	*Mike Jerzembeck*	1.50
400	*Luis Rivas*	3.00
401	*Kevin Burford*	3.00
402	Glenn Davis	.20
403	*Robert Luce*	1.50
404	Cole Liniak	.20
405	*Matthew LeCroy*	2.00
406	*Jeremy Giambi*	5.00

407	Shawn Chacon	.20
408	*Dewayne Wise*	3.00
409	*Steve Woodard*	1.50
410	*Francisco Cordero*	1.00
411	*Damon Minor*	2.00
412	Lou Collier	.20
413	Justin Towle	.20
414	Juan LeBron	.20
415	Michael Coleman	.20
416	Felix Rodriguez	.20
417	*Paul Ah Yat*	2.00
418	*Kevin Barker*	2.00
419	Brian Meadows	.20
420	*Darnell McDonald*	6.00
421	*Matt Kinney*	2.00
422	*Mike Vavrek*	2.00
423	*Courtney Duncan*	1.50
424	*Kevin Millar*	2.00
425	Ruben Rivera	.20
426	*Steve Shoemaker*	1.00
427	*Dan Reichert*	1.50
428	*Carlos Lee*	4.00
429	Rod Barajas	2.00
430	*Pablo Ozuna*	5.00
431	*Todd Belitz*	1.00
432	Sidney Ponson	.20
433	*Steve Carver*	2.00
434	Esteban Yan	2.00
435	*Cedrick Bowers*	2.00
436	Marlon Anderson	.20
437	Carl Pavano	.20
438	*Jae Weong Seo*	3.00
439	*Jose Taveras*	3.00
440	*Matt Anderson*	4.00
441	*Darron Ingram*	3.00

1998 Bowman Chrome Internationals

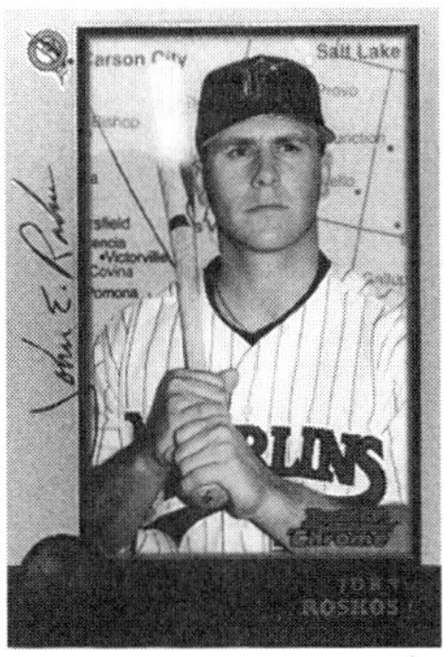

All 441 cards throughout Bowman Chrome Series I and II were paralleled in International versions. The cards were identified by the background regional map denoting the player's birthplace and written in the player's native language. Regular versions were inserted one per four packs while Refractor versions arrived every 24 packs.

Internationals:	1.5x to 2.5x
Inserted: 1:4	

1998 Bowman Chrome Refractors

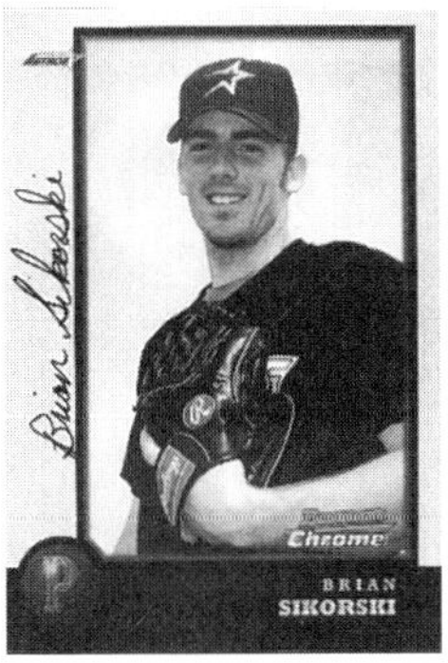

Refractor versions for all 441 cards in Bowman Chrome Series I and II were inserted one per 12 packs. The cards contained the word "Refractor" on the back in black letters directly under the card number.

	MT
Common Player:	4.00
Stars:	5x to 10x
Yng. Stars & RC's:	3x to 6x
Inserted 1:12	
International Refractors:	8x to 15x
Yng. Stars & RC's:	4x to 10x
Inserted 1:24	

1998 Bowman Chrome Golden Anniversary

Golden Anniversary parallels were printed for all 440 cards in Bowman Chrome I and II. They were exclusive to hobby packs, seeded one per 164 packs and sequentially numbered to 50 sets. Refractor versions were also available, numbered to just five sets and inserted one per 1,279 packs.

		MT
Common Player:		15.00
Production 50 sets		
1	Nomar Garciaparra	200.00
2	Scott Rolen	125.00
3	Andy Pettitte	60.00
4	Ivan Rodriguez	100.00
5	Mark McGwire	450.00
6	Jason Dickson	15.00
7	Jose Cruz Jr.	75.00
8	Jeff Kent	15.00
9	Mike Mussina	75.00
10	Jason Kendall	15.00
11	Brett Tomko	15.00
12	Jeff King	15.00
13	Brad Radke	15.00
14	Robin Ventura	25.00
15	Jeff Bagwell	125.00
16	Greg Maddux	250.00
17	John Jaha	15.00
18	Mike Piazza	250.00
19	Edgar Martinez	15.00
20	David Justice	40.00
21	Todd Hundley	15.00
22	Tony Gwynn	200.00
23	Larry Walker	60.00
24	Bernie Williams	60.00
25	Edgar Renteria	15.00
26	Rafael Palmeiro	40.00
27	Tim Salmon	40.00
28	Matt Morris	15.00
29	Shawn Estes	15.00
30	Vladimir Guerrero	100.00
31	Fernando Tatis	15.00
32	Justin Thompson	15.00
33	Ken Griffey Jr.	400.00
34	Edgardo Alfonzo	15.00
35	Mo Vaughn	100.00
36	Marty Cordova	15.00
37	Craig Biggio	30.00
38	Roger Clemens	150.00
39	Mark Grace	40.00
40	Ken Caminiti	30.00
41	Tony Womack	15.00
42	Albert Belle	100.00
43	Tino Martinez	60.00
44	Sandy Alomar	40.00
45	Jeff Cirillo	15.00
46	Jason Giambi	15.00
47	Darin Erstad	100.00
48	Livan Hernandez	15.00
49	Mark Grudzielanek	15.00
50	Sammy Sosa	200.00
51	Curt Schilling	40.00
52	Brian Hunter	15.00
53	Neifi Perez	15.00
54	Todd Walker	40.00
55	Jose Guillen	40.00
56	Jim Thome	60.00
57	Tom Glavine	40.00
58	Todd Greene	15.00
59	Rondell White	30.00
60	Roberto Alomar	75.00
61	Tony Clark	60.00
62	Vinny Castilla	25.00
63	Barry Larkin	40.00
64	Hideki Irabu	60.00
65	Johnny Damon	15.00
66	Juan Gonzalez	200.00
67	John Olerud	40.00
68	Gary Sheffield	50.00
69	Raul Mondesi	40.00
70	Chipper Jones	250.00
71	David Ortiz	25.00
72	*Warren Morris*	20.00
73	Alex Gonzalez	15.00
74	Nick Bierbrodt	15.00
75	Roy Halladay	20.00
76	Danny Buxbaum	15.00
77	Adam Kennedy	20.00
78	*Jared Sandberg*	30.00
79	Michael Barrett	15.00
80	Gil Meche	15.00
81	Jayson Werth	20.00
82	Abraham Nunez	20.00
83	Ben Petrick	15.00
84	Brett Caradonna	20.00
85	Mike Lowell	25.00
86	*Clay Bruner*	20.00
87	*John Curtice*	20.00

88	Bobby Estalella	15.00
89	Juan Melo	15.00
90	Arnold Gooch	15.00
91	Kevin Millwood	100.00
92	Richie Sexson	15.00
93	Orlando Cabrera	15.00
94	Pat Cline	15.00
95	Anthony Sanders	20.00
96	Russ Johnson	15.00
97	Ben Grieve	125.00
98	Kevin McGlinchy	15.00
99	Paul Wilder	15.00
100	Russ Ortiz	15.00
101	Ryan Jackson	35.00
102	Heath Murray	15.00
103	Brian Rose	20.00
104	*Ryan Radmanovich*	20.00
105	Ricky Ledee	25.00
106	*Jeff Wallace*	20.00
107	Ryan Minor	90.00
108	Dennis Reyes	15.00
109	*James Manias*	20.00
110	Chris Carpenter	15.00
111	Daryle Ward	15.00
112	Vernon Wells	20.00
113	Chad Green	15.00
114	*Mike Stoner*	80.00
115	Brad Fullmer	20.00
116	Adam Eaton	15.00
117	Jeff Liefer	15.00
118	Corey Koskie	20.00
119	Todd Helton	50.00
120	*Jaime Jones*	25.00
121	Mel Rosario	15.00
122	Geoff Goetz	15.00
123	Adrian Beltre	120.00
124	Jason Dellaero	20.00
125	Gabe Kapler	100.00
126	Scott Schoeneweis	15.00
127	Ryan Brannan	15.00
128	Aaron Akin	15.00
129	Ryan Anderson	100.00
130	Brad Penny	15.00
131	Bruce Chen	20.00
132	Eli Marrero	15.00
133	Eric Chavez	30.00
134	Troy Glaus	180.00
135	Troy Cameron	20.00
136	*Brian Sikorski*	20.00
137	Mike Kinkade	20.00
138	Braden Looper	15.00
139	Mark Mangum	15.00
140	Danny Peoples	15.00
141	J.J. Davis	20.00
142	Ben Davis	15.00
143	Jacque Jones	15.00
144	Derrick Gibson	15.00
145	Bronson Arroyo	15.00
146	*Cristian Guzman*	15.00
147	Jeff Abbott	15.00
148	*Mike Cuddyer*	30.00
149	Jason Romano	20.00
150	Shane Monahan	15.00
151	*Ntema Ndungidi*	20.00
152	Alex Sanchez	15.00
153	*Jack Cust*	35.00
154	Brent Butler	20.00
155	Ramon Hernandez	15.00
156	Norm Hutchins	15.00
157	Jason Marquis	15.00
158	Jacob Cruz	15.00
159	*Rob Burger*	30.00
160	Eric Milton	20.00
161	Preston Wilson	15.00
162	*Jason Fitzgerald*	20.00
163	Dan Serafini	15.00
164	Peter Munro	15.00
165	Trot Nixon	20.00
166	Homer Bush	15.00
167	Dermal Brown	20.00
168	Chad Hermansen	25.00
169	*Julio Moreno*	20.00
170	*John Roskos*	20.00
171	Grant Roberts	20.00
172	Ken Cloude	15.00
173	Jason Brester	15.00
174	Jason Conti	15.00
175	Jon Garland	15.00
176	Robbie Bell	15.00
177	Nathan Haynes	15.00
178	Ramon Ortiz	40.00
179	Shannon Stewart	15.00
180	Pablo Ortega	15.00
181	*Jimmy Rollins*	20.00
182	Sean Casey	20.00
183	*Ted Lilly*	15.00
184	*Chris Enochs*	40.00
185	*Magglio Ordonez*	60.00
186	Mike Drumright	15.00
187	Aaron Boone	15.00
188	Matt Clement	15.00
189	Todd Dunwoody	15.00
190	Larry Rodriguez	15.00
191	Todd Noel	15.00
192	Geoff Jenkins	15.00
193	George Lombard	15.00
194	Lance Berkman	60.00
195	*Marcus McCain*	20.00
196	Ryan McGuire	15.00
197	*Jhensy Sandoval*	20.00
198	Corey Lee	15.00
199	Mario Valdez	15.00
200	*Robert Fick*	20.00
201	Donnie Sadler	15.00
202	Marc Kroon	15.00
203	David Miller	15.00
204	Jarrod Washburn	15.00
205	Miguel Tejada	25.00
206	Raul Ibanez	15.00
207	John Patterson	15.00
208	Calvin Pickering	15.00
209	Felix Martinez	15.00
210	Mark Redman	15.00
211	Scott Elarton	15.00
212	*Jose Amado*	20.00
213	Kerry Wood	250.00
214	Dante Powell	15.00
215	Aramis Ramirez	100.00
216	A.J. Hinch	30.00
217	*Dustin Carr*	15.00
218	Mark Kotsay	25.00
219	Jason Standridge	15.00
220	Luis Ordaz	15.00
221	Orlando Hernandez	125.00
222	Cal Ripken Jr.	300.00
223	Paul Molitor	50.00
224	Derek Jeter	225.00
225	Barry Bonds	100.00
226	Jim Edmonds	30.00
227	John Smoltz	30.00
228	Eric Karros	20.00
229	Ray Lankford	15.00
230	Rey Ordonez	15.00
231	Kenny Lofton	80.00
232	Alex Rodriguez	250.00
233	Dante Bichette	30.00
234	Pedro Martinez	75.00
235	Carlos Delgado	25.00
236	Rod Beck	15.00
237	Matt Williams	40.00
238	Charles Johnson	15.00
239	Rico Brogna	15.00
240	Frank Thomas	250.00
241	Paul O'Neill	40.00
242	Jaret Wright	75.00
243	Brant Brown	15.00
244	Ryan Klesko	30.00
245	Chuck Finley	15.00
246	Derek Bell	15.00
247	Delino DeShields	15.00
248	Chan Ho Park	30.00
249	Wade Boggs	50.00
250	Jay Buhner	30.00
251	Butch Huskey	15.00
252	Steve Finley	15.00
253	Will Clark	40.00
254	John Valentin	15.00
255	Bobby Higginson	15.00
256	Darryl Strawberry	25.00
257	Randy Johnson	75.00
258	Al Martin	15.00
259	Travis Fryman	15.00
260	Fred McGriff	30.00
261	Jose Valentin	15.00
262	Andruw Jones	100.00
263	Kenny Rogers	15.00
264	Moises Alou	25.00
265	Denny Neagle	15.00
266	Ugueth Urbina	15.00
267	Derrek Lee	15.00
268	Ellis Burks	15.00
269	Mariano Rivera	25.00
270	Dean Palmer	15.00
271	Eddie Taubensee	15.00
272	Brady Anderson	15.00
273	Brian Giles	15.00
274	Quinton McCracken	15.00
275	Henry Rodriguez	15.00
276	Andres Galarraga	50.00
277	Jose Canseco	40.00
278	David Segui	15.00
279	Bret Saberhagen	15.00
280	Kevin Brown	25.00
281	Chuck Knoblauch	40.00
282	Jeromy Burnitz	15.00
283	Jay Bell	15.00
284	Manny Ramirez	100.00
285	Rick Helling	15.00
286	Francisco Cordova	15.00
287	Bob Abreu	15.00
288	J.T. Snow Jr.	15.00
289	Hideo Nomo	60.00
290	Brian Jordan	15.00
291	Javy Lopez	25.00
292	Travis Lee	150.00
293	Russell Branyan	15.00
294	Paul Konerko	25.00
295	*Masato Yoshii*	40.00
296	Kris Benson	30.00
297	Juan Encarnacion	15.00
298	Eric Milton	15.00
299	Mike Caruso	15.00
300	*Ricardo Aramboles*	75.00
301	Bobby Smith	15.00
302	Billy Koch	15.00
303	Richard Hidalgo	15.00
304	Justin Baughman	25.00
305	Chris Gissell	15.00
306	*Donnie Bridges*	25.00
307	*Nelson Lara*	25.00
308	*Randy Wolf*	25.00
309	*Jason LaRue*	25.00
310	*Jason Gooding*	20.00
311	*Edgar Clemente*	20.00
312	Andrew Vessel	15.00
313	Chris Reitsma	15.00
314	*Jesus Sanchez*	25.00
315	*Buddy Carlyle*	25.00
316	Randy Winn	15.00
317	Luis Rivera	60.00
318	*Marcus Thames*	30.00
319	A.J. Pierzynski	15.00
320	Scott Randall	15.00
321	Damian Sapp	15.00
322	*Eddie Yarnell*	75.00
323	*Luke Allen*	30.00
324	J.D. Smart	15.00
325	Willie Martinez	15.00
326	Alex Ramirez	15.00
327	*Eric DuBose*	25.00
328	Kevin Witt	15.00
329	*Dan McKinley*	25.00
330	Cliff Politte	15.00
331	Vladimir Nunez	15.00
332	*John Halama*	20.00
333	Nerio Rodriguez	15.00
334	Desi Relaford	15.00
335	Robinson Checo	15.00
336	*John Nicholson*	25.00
337	*Tom LaRosa*	25.00
338	*Kevin Nicholson*	40.00
339	Javier Vazquez	15.00
340	A.J. Zapp	15.00
341	Tom Evans	15.00
342	Kerry Robinson	15.00
343	*Gabe Gonzalez*	25.00
344	Ralph Milliard	15.00
345	Enrique Wilson	15.00
346	Elvin Hernandez	15.00
347	*Mike Lincoln*	30.00
348	*Cesar King*	50.00
349	Cristian Guzman	25.00
350	Donzell McDonald	15.00
351	Jim Parque	30.00
352	*Mike Saipe*	25.00
353	*Carlos Febles*	25.00
354	*Dernell Stenson*	60.00
355	*Mark Osborne*	30.00
356	*Odalis Perez*	50.00
357	*Jason Dewey*	25.00
358	Joe Fontenot	15.00
359	*Jason Grilli*	35.00
360	*Kevin Haverbusch*	35.00
361	*Jay Yennaco*	20.00
362	Brian Buchanan	15.00
363	John Barnes	15.00
364	Chris Fussell	15.00
365	*Kevin Gibbs*	25.00
366	Joe Lawrence	15.00
367	DaRond Stovall	15.00
368	*Brian Fuentes*	25.00
369	Jimmy Anderson	15.00
370	*Laril Gonzalez*	25.00
371	*Scott Williamson*	25.00
372	Milton Bradley	15.00
373	*Jason Halper*	25.00
374	*Brent Billingsley*	25.00
375	*Joe DePastino*	15.00
376	Jake Westbrook	15.00
377	Octavio Dotel	15.00
378	*Jason Williams*	20.00
379	*Julio Ramirez*	30.00
380	Seth Greisinger	15.00
381	*Mike Judd*	25.00
382	*Ben Ford*	20.00
383	Tom Bennett	15.00
384	*Adam Butler*	20.00
385	*Wade Miller*	25.00
386	*Kyle Peterson*	25.00
387	*Tommy Peterman*	25.00
388	Onan Masaoka	15.00
389	*Jason Rakers*	25.00
390	Rafael Medina	15.00
391	Luis Lopez	15.00
392	Jeff Yoder	15.00
393	*Vance Wilson*	25.00
394	*Fernando Seguignol*	70.00
395	Ron Wright	15.00
396	*Ruben Mateo*	90.00
397	*Steve Lomasney*	25.00
398	Damian Jackson	15.00
399	*Mike Jerzembeck*	25.00
400	*Luis Rivas*	35.00
401	*Kevin Burford*	35.00
402	Glenn Davis	15.00
403	*Robert Luce*	25.00
404	Cole Liniak	15.00
405	*Matthew LeCroy*	25.00
406	Jeremy Giambi	60.00
407	Shawn Chacon	15.00
408	*Dewayne Wise*	35.00
409	*Steve Woodard*	25.00
410	*Francisco Cordero*	20.00
411	*Damon Minor*	25.00
412	Lou Collier	15.00
413	Justin Towle	15.00
414	Juan LeBron	15.00
415	Michael Coleman	15.00
416	Felix Rodriguez	15.00
417	*Paul Ah Yat*	25.00
418	*Kevin Barker*	25.00
419	Brian Meadows	15.00
420	*Darnell McDonald*	60.00
421	*Matt Kinney*	25.00
422	*Mike Vavrek*	25.00
423	*Courtney Duncan*	25.00
424	*Kevin Millar*	25.00
425	Ruben Rivera	15.00
426	*Steve Shoemaker*	20.00
427	*Dan Reichert*	25.00
428	*Carlos Lee*	40.00
429	Rod Barajas	25.00
430	*Pablo Ozuna*	50.00
431	*Todd Belitz*	20.00
432	Sidney Ponson	15.00
433	*Steve Carver*	25.00
434	Esteban Yan	25.00
435	*Cedrick Bowers*	25.00
436	Marlon Anderson	15.00
437	Carl Pavano	15.00
438	*Jae Weong Seo*	30.00
439	*Jose Taveras*	30.00
440	Matt Anderson	40.00
441	*Darron Ingram*	35.00

1998 Bowman Chrome Reprints

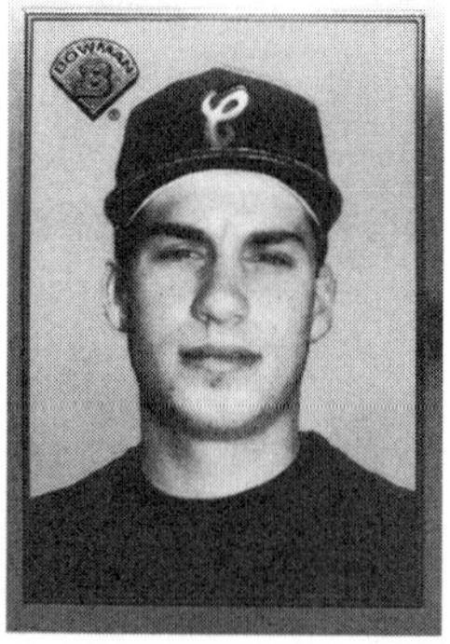

Bowman Chrome Reprints showcased 50 of the most popular Bowman rookie cards to appear in the brand. Regular versions were seeded one per 12, while Refractor versions were seeded one per 36. There were 25 cards from this set inserted into each series.

		MT
Complete Set (50):		130.00
Common Player:		1.00
Inserted 1:12		
Refractors:		1.5x to 2.5x
Inserted 1:36		
BC1	Yogi Berra	6.00
BC2	Jackie Robinson	15.00
BC3	Don Newcombe	1.00
BC4	Don Newcombe	1.00
BC5	Willie Mays	8.00
BC6	Gil McDougald	1.00
BC7	Don Larsen	3.00
BC8	Elston Howard	1.50
BC9	Robin Ventura	1.00
BC10	Brady Anderson	1.00
BC11	Gary Sheffield	2.00
BC12	Tino Martinez	2.50
BC13	Ken Griffey Jr.	18.00
BC14	John Smoltz	1.00
BC15	Sandy Alomar Jr.	1.00
BC16	Larry Walker	2.50
BC17	Todd Hundley	1.00
BC18	Mo Vaughn	5.00
BC19	Sammy Sosa	10.00
BC20	Frank Thomas	12.00
BC21	Chuck Knoblauch	2.50
BC22	Bernie Williams	3.00
BC23	Juan Gonzalez	8.00
BC24	Mike Mussina	4.00
BC25	Mike Mussina	3.00
BC26	Tim Salmon	2.50
BC27	Ivan Rodriguez	5.00
BC28	Kenny Lofton	5.00
BC29	Chipper Jones	12.00
BC30	Javier Lopez	1.00
BC31	Ryan Klesko	2.00
BC32	Raul Mondesi	2.00
BC33	Raul Mondesi	2.00
BC34	Carlos Delgado	1.00
BC35	Mike Piazza	12.00
BC36	Manny Ramirez	5.00
BC37	Andy Pettitte	3.00
BC38	Derek Jeter	12.00
BC39	Brad Fullmer	2.00
BC40	Richard Hidalgo	1.00
BC41	Tony Clark	3.00
BC42	Andruw Jones	5.00
BC43	Vladimir Guerrero	6.00
BC44	Nomar Garciaparra	12.00
BC45	Paul Konerko	2.00
BC46	Ben Grieve	6.00
BC47	Hideo Nomo	4.00
BC48	Scott Rolen	5.00
BC49	Jose Guillen	1.00
BC50	Livan Hernandez	1.00

1998 Bowman's Best

Bowman's Best was issued in a single 200-card series in 1998 and contained 100 prospects and 100 veterans. The prospects were shown on a silver design, while the veterans were shown on gold. The set was paralleled twice - once in a Refractor version seeded one per 20 packs and sequentially numbered to 400, and next in an Atomic Refractor version inserted one per 82 packs and numbered to 100 sets. Inserts include regular, Refractor and Atomic Refractor versions of: Autographs, Double- Sided Mirror Image Fusion and Performers.

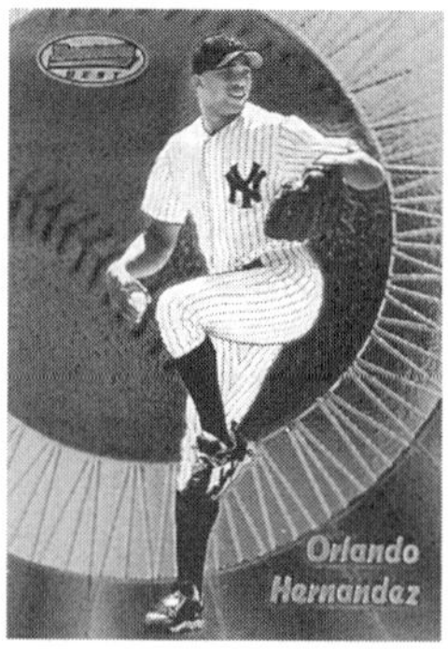

		MT
Complete Set (200):		90.00
Common Player:		.25
Wax Box:		100.00
1	Mark McGwire	6.00
2	Hideo Nomo	.75
3	Barry Bonds	1.25
4	Dante Bichette	.50
5	Chipper Jones	3.00
6	Frank Thomas	4.00
7	Kevin Brown	.40
8	Juan Gonzalez	2.50
9	Jay Buhner	.50
10	Chuck Knoblauch	.50
11	Cal Ripken Jr.	4.00
12	Matt Williams	.50
13	Jim Edmonds	.25
14	Manny Ramirez	1.25
15	Tony Clark	.75
16	Mo Vaughn	1.25
17	Bernie Williams	1.00
18	Scott Rolen	1.50
19	Gary Sheffield	.60
20	Albert Belle	1.25
21	Mike Piazza	3.00
22	John Olerud	.50
23	Tony Gwynn	2.50
24	Jay Bell	.25
25	Jose Cruz Jr.	1.25
26	Justin Thompson	.25
27	Ken Griffey Jr.	5.00
28	Sandy Alomar	.40
29	Mark Grudzielanek	.25
30	Mark Grace	.50
31	Ron Gant	.40
32	Javy Lopez	.25
33	Jeff Bagwell	2.00
34	Fred McGriff	.50
35	Rafael Palmeiro	.50
36	Vinny Castilla	.40
37	Andy Benes	.25
38	Pedro Martinez	1.00
39	Andy Pettitte	.75
40	Marty Cordova	.25
41	Rusty Greer	.25
42	Kevin Orie	.25
43	Chan Ho Park	.75
44	Ryan Klesko	.50
45	Alex Rodriguez	3.00
46	Travis Fryman	.25
47	Jeff King	.25
48	Roger Clemens	2.00
49	Darin Erstad	1.25
50	Brady Anderson	.25
51	Jason Kendall	.25
52	John Valentin	.25
53	Ellis Burks	.25
54	Brian Hunter	.25
55	Paul O'Neill	.50
56	Ken Caminiti	.50
57	David Justice	.60
58	Eric Karros	.40
59	Pat Hentgen	.25
60	Greg Maddux	3.00
61	Craig Biggio	.50
62	Edgar Martinez	.25
63	Mike Mussina	1.00
64	Larry Walker	.75
65	Tino Martinez	.75
66	Jim Thome	1.00
67	Tom Glavine	.50
68	Raul Mondesi	.50
69	Marquis Grissom	.25
70	Randy Johnson	1.00
71	Steve Finley	.25
72	Jose Guillen	.50
73	Nomar Garciaparra	3.00
74	Wade Boggs	.75
75	Bobby Higginson	.25
76	Robin Ventura	.40
77	Derek Jeter	2.50
78	Andruw Jones	1.25
79	Ray Lankford	.25
80	Vladimir Guerrero	1.25
81	Kenny Lofton	1.25
82	Ivan Rodriguez	1.25
83	Neifi Perez	.25
84	John Smoltz	.40
85	Tim Salmon	.50
86	Carlos Delgado	.25

87	Sammy Sosa	4.00
88	Jaret Wright	1.25
89	Roberto Alomar	.75
90	Paul Molitor	.75
91	Dean Palmer	.25
92	Barry Larkin	.50
93	Jason Giambi	.25
94	Curt Schilling	.40
95	Eric Young	.25
96	Denny Neagle	.25
97	Moises Alou	.40
98	Livan Hernandez	.25
99	Todd Hundley	.25
100	Andres Galarraga	.50
101	Travis Lee	3.00
102	Lance Berkman	2.00
103	Orlando Cabrera	.40
104	*Mike Lowell*	2.50
105	Ben Grieve	2.00
106	*Jae Weong Seo*	.75
107	Richie Sexson	.25
108	Eli Marrero	.25
109	Aramis Ramirez	2.50
110	Paul Konerko	.50
111	Carl Pavano	.25
112	Brad Fullmer	.50
113	Matt Clement	.40
114	Donzell McDonald	.25
115	Todd Helton	1.25
116	Mike Caruso	.25
117	Donnie Sadler	.25
118	Bruce Chen	.50
119	Jarrod Washburn	.25
120	Adrian Beltre	3.00
121	*Ryan Jackson*	2.50
122	*Kevin Millar*	.50
123	*Corey Koskie*	2.50
124	Dermal Brown	1.00
125	Kerry Wood	6.00
126	Juan Melo	.25
127	Ramon Hernandez	.25
128	Roy Halladay	.25
129	Ron Wright	.25
130	*Darnell McDonald*	3.00
131	*Odaliz Perez*	2.00
132	*Alex Cora*	.75
133	Justin Towle	.50
134	Juan Encarnacion	.25
135	Brian Rose	.40
136	Russell Branyan	.25
137	*Cesar King*	.75
138	Ruben Rivera	.25
139	Ricky Ledee	.25
140	Vernon Wells	1.00
141	*Luis Rivas*	.75
142	Brent Butler	1.00
143	Karim Garcia	.25
144	George Lombard	.40
145	*Masato Yoshii*	1.50
146	Braden Looper	.25
147	Alex Sanchez	.40
148	Kris Benson	1.00
149	Mark Kotsay	1.50
150	Richard Hidalgo	.25
151	Scott Elarton	.25
152	*Ryan Minor*	6.00
153	*Troy Glaus*	15.00
154	*Carlos Lee*	3.00
155	Michael Coleman	.25
156	*Jason Grilli*	.75
157	*Julio Ramirez*	1.50
158	Preston Wilson	.25
159	Ryan Brannan	.25
160	*Edgar Clemente*	.50
161	Miguel Tejada	1.50
162	Chad Hermansen	1.50
163	*Ryan Anderson*	8.00
164	Ben Petrick	.25
165	Alex Gonzalez	.40
166	Ben Davis	.25
167	John Patterson	.50
168	Cliff Politte	.25
169	Randall Simon	1.50
170	Javier Vazquez	.25
171	Kevin Witt	.50
172	Geoff Jenkins	.25
173	David Ortiz	1.00
174	Derrick Gibson	.25
175	Abraham Nunez	.50
176	A.J. Hinch	1.50
177	*Ruben Mateo*	6.00
178	*Magglio Ordonez*	4.00
179	Todd Dunwoody	.25
180	Daryle Ward	.50
181	*Mike Kinkade*	2.50
182	Willie Martinez	.25
183	*Orlando Hernandez*	15.00
184	Eric Milton	.75
185	Eric Chavez	1.50
186	Damian Jackson	.25
187	*Jim Parque*	1.50
188	*Dan Reichert*	1.00
189	Mike Drumright	.25
190	Todd Walker	.50
191	Shane Monahan	.25
192	Derrek Lee	.25
193	*Jeremy Giambi*	3.00
194	*Dan McKinley*	.75
195	*Tony Armas*	1.50
196	*Matt Anderson*	3.00
197	*Jim Chamblee*	.75
198	*Francisco Cordero*	.75
199	Calvin Pickering	1.00
200	Reggie Taylor	.25

1998 Bowman's Best Refractors

Refractor versions for all 200 cards in Bowman's Best were available. Fronts featured a reflective finish, while backs were numbered to 400 and inserted one per 20 packs.

	MT
Complete Set (200):	
Common Player:	5.00
Stars:	15x to 25x
Yng Stars & RC's:	8x to 15x
Production 400 sets	

1998 Bowman's Best Atomic Refractors

Atomic Refractor versions were available for all 200 cards in Bowman's Best. The cards were printed in a prismatic foil on the front, sequentially numbered to 100 sets on the back and inserted one per 82 packs.

	MT
Common Player:	15.00
Stars:	40x to 75x
Yng Stars & RCs:	25x to 50x
Production 100 sets	

1998 Bowman's Best Autographs

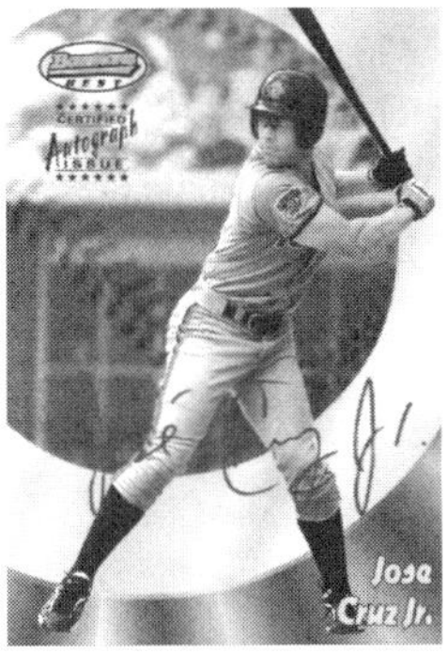

This 10-card set included autographed cards from five prospects and five veterans. Each card contained the Topps "Certified Autograph Issue" logo for authentication. Regular versions were seeded one per 180 packs, Refractor versions were seeded one per 2,158 packs and Atomic Refractor versions were seeded one per 6,437 packs.

		MT
Complete Set (10):		450.00
Common Player:		25.00
Inserted 1:180		
Refractors:		1.5x to 2.5x
Inserted 1:2,158		
Atomics:		2x to 4x
Inserted1:6,437		
5	Chipper Jones	90.00
10	Chuck Knoblauch	35.00
15	Tony Clark	35.00
20	Albert Belle	50.00
25	Jose Cruz Jr.	45.00
105	Ben Grieve	75.00
110	Paul Konerko	25.00
115	Todd Helton	40.00
120	Adrian Beltre	40.00
125	Kerry Wood	100.00

1998 Bowman's Best Mirror Image

This 20-card die-cut insert features a veteran star on one side and a young player of the same position on the other. Regular versions are seeded one per 12 packs, while Refractor versions are seeded one per 809 packs and numbered to 100 and Atomic Refractors were seeded one per 3,237 packs and numbered to 25.

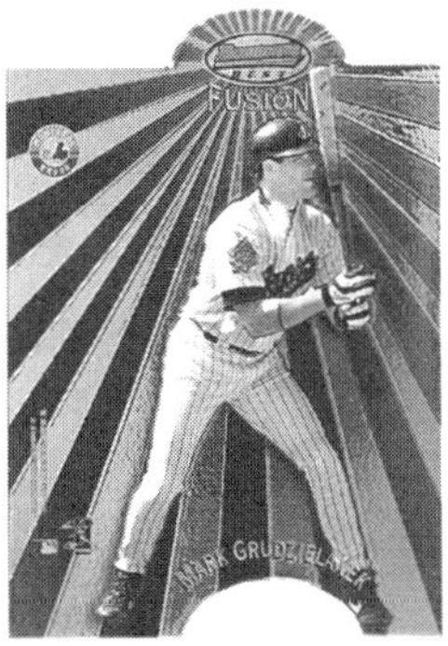

		MT
Complete Set (20):		100.00
Common Player:		1.50
Inserted 1:12		
MI1	Frank Thomas, David Ortiz	12.00
MI2	Chuck Knoblauch, Enrique Wilson	1.50
MI3	Nomar Garciaparra, Miguel Tejada	8.00
MI4	Alex Rodriguez, Mike Caruso	8.00
MI5	Cal Ripken Jr., Ryan Minor	12.00
MI6	Ken Griffey Jr., Ben Grieve	15.00
MI7	Juan Gonzalez, Juan Encarnacion	8.00
MI8	Jose Cruz Jr., Ruben Mateo	4.00
MI9	Randy Johnson, Ryan Anderson	3.00
MI10	Ivan Rodriguez, A.J. Hinch	4.00
MI11	Jeff Bagwell, Paul Konerko	5.00
MI12	Mark McGwire, Travis Lee	15.00
MI13	Craig Biggio, Chad Hermanson	1.50
MI14	Mark Grudzielanek, Alex Gonzalez	1.50
MI15	Chipper Jones, Adrian Beltre	10.00
MI16	Larry Walker, Mark Kotsay	2.00
MI17	Tony Gwynn, Preston Wilson	7.00
MI18	Barry Bonds, Richard Hidalgo	4.00
MI19	Greg Maddux, Kerry Wood	15.00
MI20	Mike Piazza, Ben Petrick	10.00

1998 Bowman's Best Mirror Image Refractors

All 20 cards in the Mirror Image insert were reprinted in both Refractor and Atomic Refractor versions. Refractors were seeded one per 809 packs and numbered to 100 sets, while Atomic Refractors were seeded one per 3,237 packs and numbered to 25 sets.

		MT
Complete Set (20):		2500.
Common Player:		25.00
Production 100 sets		
Atomic Refractors:		1.5x to 2.5x
Production 25 sets		
MI1	Frank Thomas, David Ortiz	250.00
MI2	Chuck Knoblauch, Enrique Wilson	40.00
MI3	Nomar Garciaparra, Miguel Tejada	200.00
MI4	Alex Rodriguez, Mike Caruso	200.00
MI5	Cal Ripken Jr., Ryan Minor	250.00
MI6	Ken Griffey Jr., Ben Grieve	350.00
MI7	Juan Gonzalez, Juan Encarnacion	180.00
MI8	Jose Cruz Jr., Ruben Mateo	75.00
MI9	Randy Johnson, Ryan Anderson	60.00
MI10	Ivan Rodriguez, A.J. Hinch	80.00
MI11	Jeff Bagwell, Paul Konerko	125.00
MI12	Mark McGwire, Travis Lee	300.00
MI13	Craig Biggio, Chad Hermanson	40.00
MI14	Mark Grudzielanek, Alex Gonzalez	25.00
MI15	Chipper Jones, Adrian Beltre	200.00
MI16	Larry Walker, Mark Kotsay	40.00
MI17	Tony Gwynn, Preston Wilson	180.00
MI18	Barry Bonds, Richard Hidalgo	75.00
MI19	Greg Maddux, Kerry Wood	300.00
MI20	Mike Piazza, Ben Petrick	200.00

1998 Bowman's Best Performers

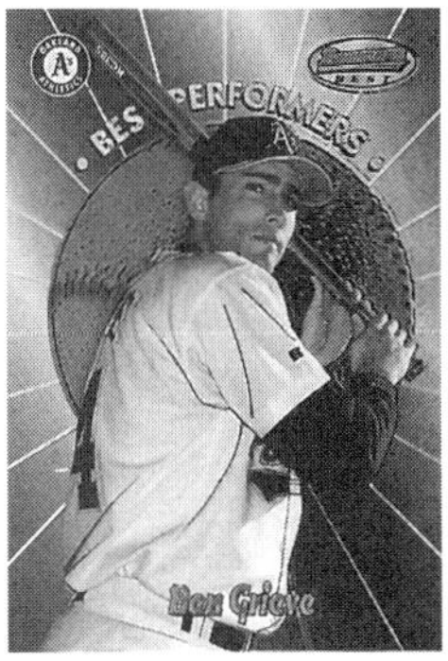

Performers contained 10 players who had the best minor league stats in 1997. Regular versions were inserted one per six packs, while Refractors were seeded one per 809 packs and numbered to 200 and Atomic Refractors were inserted one per 3,237 and numbered to 50 sets.

		MT
Complete Set (10):		20.00
Common Player:		1.00
BP1	Ben Grieve	4.00
BP2	Travis Lee	8.00
BP3	Ryan Minor	3.00
BP4	Todd Helton	2.00
BP5	Brad Fullmer	1.50
BP6	Paul Konerko	1.00
BP7	Adrian Beltre	3.00
BP8	Richie Sexson	1.00
BP9	Aramis Ramirez	2.50
BP10	Russell Branyan	1.00

1998 Bowman's Best Performers Refractors

All 10 cards in the Performers insert also arrived in Refractor and Atomic Refractor versions. Refractors were seeded one per 809 packs and numbered to 200 sets, while Atomic Refractors are seeded one per 3,237 packs and numbered to 50 on the back.

		MT
Complete Set (10):		500.00
Common Player:		1.00
Production 200 sets		
Atomic Refractors:		1.5x to 2.5x
Production 50 sets		
BP1	Ben Grieve	100.00
BP2	Travis Lee	150.00
BP3	Ryan Minor	100.00
BP4	Todd Helton	60.00
BP5	Brad Fullmer	15.00
BP6	Paul Konerko	25.00
BP7	Adrian Beltre	90.00
BP8	Richie Sexson	10.00
BP9	Aramis Ramirez	40.00
BP10	Russell Branyan	10.00

1998 Donruss

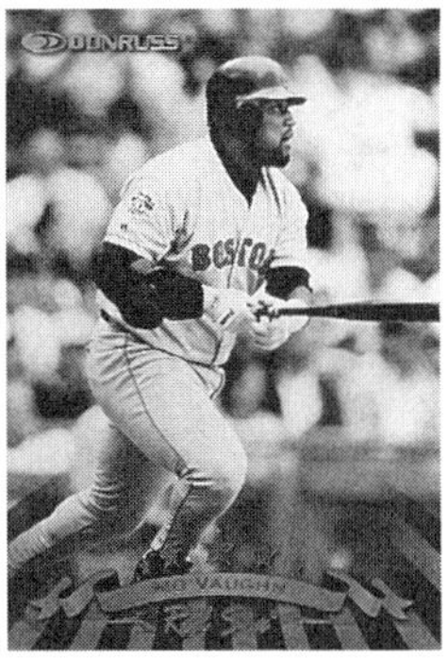

This 170-card set includes 155 regular player cards, the 10-card Fan Club subset and five checklists. The cards have color photos and the player's name listed at the bottom. The backs have a horizontal layout with stats and a biography on the left and another photo on the right. The base set is paralleled twice. Silver Press Proofs is a silver foil and die-cut parallel numbered "1 of 1,500." Gold Press Proofs is die-cut, has gold foil and is numbered "1 of 500." The inserts are Crusade, Diamond Kings, Longball Leaders, Production Line and Rated Rookies.

		MT
Complete Set (420):		45.00
Complete Series I Set (170):		20.00
Complete Update II Set (250):		25.00
Common Player:		.10
Wax Box:		45.00
1	Paul Molitor	.50
2	Juan Gonzalez	1.50
3	Darryl Kile	.10
4	Randy Johnson	.40
5	Tom Glavine	.20
6	Pat Hentgen	.10
7	David Justice	.25
8	Kevin Brown	.10
9	Mike Mussina	.60
10	Ken Caminiti	.20
11	Todd Hundley	.20
12	Frank Thomas	2.50
13	Ray Lankford	.10
14	Justin Thompson	.10
15	Jason Dickson	.10
16	Kenny Lofton	.75
17	Ivan Rodriguez	.60
18	Pedro Martinez	.25
19	Brady Anderson	.20
20	Barry Larkin	.20
21	Chipper Jones	2.00
22	Tony Gwynn	1.50
23	Roger Clemens	1.00
24	Sandy Alomar Jr.	.10
25	Tino Martinez	.20
26	Jeff Bagwell	1.25
27	Shawn Estes	.10
28	Ken Griffey Jr.	3.00
29	Javier Lopez	.20
30	Denny Neagle	.10
31	Mike Piazza	2.00
32	Andres Galarraga	.20
33	Larry Walker	.25
34	Alex Rodriguez	2.50
35	Greg Maddux	2.00
36	Albert Belle	.75
37	Barry Bonds	.75
38	Mo Vaughn	.75
39	Kevin Appier	.10
40	Wade Boggs	.25
41	Garret Anderson	.10
42	Jeffrey Hammonds	.10
43	Marquis Grissom	.10
44	Jim Edmonds	.10
45	Brian Jordan	.10
46	Raul Mondesi	.20
47	John Valentin	.10
48	Brad Radke	.10
49	Ismael Valdes	.10
50	Matt Stairs	.10
51	Matt Williams	.20
52	Reggie Jefferson	.10
53	Alan Benes	.10
54	Charles Johnson	.10
55	Chuck Knoblauch	.25
56	Edgar Martinez	.10
57	Nomar Garciaparra	2.00
58	Craig Biggio	.20
59	Bernie Williams	.50
60	David Cone	.20
61	Cal Ripken Jr.	2.50
62	Mark McGwire	4.00

63	Roberto Alomar	.50
64	Fred McGriff	.20
65	Eric Karros	.10
66	Robin Ventura	.10
67	Darin Erstad	.75
68	Michael Tucker	.10
69	Jim Thome	.40
70	Mark Grace	.25
71	Lou Collier	.10
72	Karim Garcia	.20
73	Alex Fernandez	.10
74	J.T. Snow	.10
75	Reggie Sanders	.10
76	John Smoltz	.10
77	Tim Salmon	.25
78	Paul O'Neill	.20
79	Vinny Castilla	.10
80	Rafael Palmeiro	.20
81	Jaret Wright	1.00
82	Jay Buhner	.20
83	Brett Butler	.10
84	Todd Greene	.10
85	Scott Rolen	1.50
86	Sammy Sosa	1.50
87	Jason Giambi	.10
88	Carlos Delgado	.10
89	Deion Sanders	.25
90	Wilton Guerrero	.10
91	Andy Pettitte	.50
92	Brian Giles	.10
93	Dmitri Young	.10
94	Ron Coomer	.10
95	Mike Cameron	.10
96	Edgardo Alfonzo	.10
97	Jimmy Key	.10
98	Ryan Klesko	.25
99	Andy Benes	.10
100	Derek Jeter	2.00
101	Jeff Fassero	.10
102	Neifi Perez	.10
103	Hideo Nomo	.60
104	Andruw Jones	1.50
105	Todd Helton	.75
106	Livan Hernandez	.20
107	Brett Tomko	.10
108	Shannon Stewart	.10
109	Bartolo Colon	.10
110	Matt Morris	.10
111	Miguel Tejada	.50
112	Pokey Reese	.10
113	Fernando Tatis	.25
114	Todd Dunwoody	.10
115	Jose Cruz Jr.	1.50
116	Chan Ho Park	.10
117	Kevin Young	.10
118	Rickey Henderson	.10
119	Hideki Irabu	.75
120	Francisco Cordova	.10
121	Al Martin	.10
122	Tony Clark	.30
123	Curt Schilling	.10
124	Rusty Greer	.10
125	Jose Canseco	.25
126	Edgar Renteria	.10
127	Todd Walker	.20
128	Wally Joyner	.10
129	Bill Mueller	.10
130	Jose Guillen	.40
131	Manny Ramirez	.50
132	Bobby Higginson	.10
133	Kevin Orie	.10
134	Will Clark	.20
135	Dave Nilsson	.10
136	Jason Kendall	.10
137	Ivan Cruz	.10
138	Gary Sheffield	.25
139	Bubba Trammell	.20
140	Vladimir Guerrero	1.00
141	Dennis Reyes	.25
142	Bobby Bonilla	.20
143	Ruben Rivera	.10
144	Ben Grieve	1.00
145	Moises Alou	.20
146	Tony Womack	.10
147	Eric Young	.10
148	Paul Konerko	1.00
149	Dante Bichette	.20
150	Joe Carter	.15
151	Rondell White	.20
152	Chris Holt	.10
153	Shawn Green	.10
154	Mark Grudzielanek	.10
155	Jermaine Dye	.10
156	Ken Griffey Jr. (Fan Club)	1.50
157	Frank Thomas (Fan Club)	1.25
158	Chipper Jones (Fan Club)	1.00
159	Mike Piazza (Fan Club)	1.00
160	Cal Ripken Jr. (Fan Club)	1.25
161	Greg Maddux (Fan Club)	1.00
162	Juan Gonzalez (Fan Club)	.75
163	Alex Rodriguez (Fan Club)	1.25
164	Mark McGwire (Fan Club)	1.50
165	Derek Jeter (Fan Club)	1.00
166	Larry Walker CL	.20
167	Tony Gwynn CL	.75
168	Tino Martinez CL	.15
169	Scott Rolen CL	.75
170	Nomar Garciaparra CL	1.00
171	Mike Sweeney	.10
172	Dustin Hermanson	.10
173	Darren Dreifort	.10
174	Ron Gant	.20
175	Todd Hollandsworth	.10
176	John Jaha	.10
177	Kerry Wood	4.00
178	Chris Stynes	.10
179	Kevin Elster	.10
180	Derek Bell	.10
181	Darryl Strawberry	.20
182	Damion Easley	.10
183	Jeff Cirillo	.10
184	John Thomson	.10
185	Dan Wilson	.10
186	Jay Bell	.10
187	Bernard Gilkey	.10
188	Marc Valdes	.10
189	Ramon Martinez	.20
190	Charles Nagy	.10
191	Derek Lowe	.10
192	Andy Benes	.10
193	Delino DeShields	.10
194	*Ryan Jackson*	.40
195	Kenny Lofton	.75
196	Chuck Knoblauch	.25
197	Andres Galarraga	.30
198	Jose Canseco	.25
199	John Olerud	.20
200	Lance Johnson	.10
201	Darryl Kile	.10
202	Luis Castillo	.10
203	Joe Carter	.20
204	Dennis Eckersley	.20
205	Steve Finley	.10
206	Esteban Loaiza	.10
207	*Ryan Christenson*	.25
208	Deivi Cruz	.10
209	Mariano Rivera	.10
210	*Mike Judd*	.20
211	Billy Wagner	.10
212	Scott Spiezio	.10
213	Russ Davis	.10
214	Jeff Suppan	.10
215	Doug Glanville	.10
216	Dmitri Young	.10
217	Rey Ordonez	.10
218	Cecil Fielder	.20
219	*Masato Yoshii*	.50
220	Raul Casanova	.10
221	*Rolando Arrojo*	.40
222	Ellis Burks	.10
223	Butch Huskey	.10
224	Brian Hunter	.10
225	Marquis Grissom	.10
226	Kevin Brown	.10
227	Joe Randa	.10
228	Henry Rodriguez	.10
229	Omar Vizquel	.10
230	Fred McGriff	.25
231	Matt Williams	.25
232	Moises Alou	.20
233	Travis Fryman	.20
234	Wade Boggs	.25
235	Pedro Martinez	.40
236	Rickey Henderson	.20
237	Bubba Trammell	.10
238	Mike Caruso	.20
239	Wilson Alvarez	.10
240	Geronimo Berroa	.10
241	Eric Milton	.10
242	Scott Erickson	.10
243	*Todd Erdos*	.20
244	Bobby Hughes	.10
245	Dave Hollins	.10
246	Dean Palmer	.10
247	Carlos Baerga	.10
248	Jose Silva	.10
249	*Jose Cabrera*	.20
250	Tom Evans	.10
251	Marty Cordova	.10
252	*Hanley Frias*	.20
253	Javier Valentin	.10
254	Mario Valdez	.10
255	Joey Cora	.10
256	Mike Lansing	.10
257	Jeff Kent	.10
258	*David Dellucci*	.50
259	*Curtis King*	.10
260	David Segui	.10
261	Royce Clayton	.10
262	Jeff Blauser	.10
263	*Manny Aybar*	.20
264	*Mike Cather*	.20
265	Todd Zeile	.10
266	Richard Hidalgo	.10
267	Dante Powell	.10
268	*Mike DeJean*	.10
269	Ken Cloude	.10
270	Danny Klassen	.20
271	Sean Casey	.25
272	A.J. Hinch	.50
273	*Rich Butler*	.50
274	*Ben Ford*	.10
275	Billy McMillon	.10
276	Wilson Delgado	.10
277	Orlando Cabrera	.10
278	Geoff Jenkins	.10
279	Enrique Wilson	.10
280	Derrek Lee	.10
281	*Marc Pisciotta*	.10
282	Abraham Nunez	.20
283	Aaron Boone	.10
284	Brad Fullmer	.20
285	*Rob Stanifer*	.25
286	Preston Wilson	.10
287	Greg Norton	.10
288	Bobby Smith	.10
289	Josh Booty	.10
290	Russell Branyan	.10
291	Jeremi Gonzalez	.10
292	Michael Coleman	.10
293	Cliff Politte	.10
294	Eric Ludwick	.10
295	Rafael Medina	.10
296	Jason Varitek	.10
297	Ron Wright	.10
298	Mark Kotsay	.25
299	David Ortiz	.25
300	*Frank Catalanotto*	.20
301	Robinson Checo	.10
302	*Kevin Millwood*	1.00
303	Jacob Cruz	.10
304	Javier Vazquez	.10
305	*Magglio Ordonez*	.75
306	Kevin Witt	.10
307	Derrick Gibson	.10
308	Shane Monahan	.10
309	Brian Rose	.10
310	Bobby Estalella	.10
311	Felix Heredia	.10
312	Desi Relaford	.10
313	*Esteban Yan*	.20
314	Ricky Ledee	.10
315	*Steve Woodard*	.25
316	Pat Watkins	.10
317	Damian Moss	.10
318	Bob Abreu	.10
319	Jeff Abbott	.10
320	Miguel Cairo	.10
321	*Rigo Beltran*	.10
322	Tony Saunders	.10
323	Randall Simon	.25
324	Hiram Bocachica	.10
325	Richie Sexson	.10
326	Karim Garcia	.10
327	*Mike Lowell*	.40
328	Pat Cline	.10
329	Matt Clement	.10
330	Scott Elarton	.10
331	*Manuel Barrios*	.10
332	Bruce Chen	.20
333	Juan Encarnacion	.10
334	Travis Lee	2.00
335	Wes Helms	.10
336	*Chad Fox*	.10
337	Donnie Sadler	.10
338	*Carlos Mendoza*	.25
339	Damian Jackson	.10
340	*Julio Ramirez*	.50
341	*John Halama*	.30
342	Edwin Diaz	.10
343	Felix Martinez	.10
344	Eli Marrero	.10
345	Carl Pavano	.10
346	Vladimir Guerrero (Hit List)	.40
347	Barry Bonds (Hit List)	.40
348	Darin Erstad (Hit List)	.40
349	Albert Belle (Hit List)	.40
350	Kenny Lofton (Hit List)	.40
351	Mo Vaughn (Hit List)	.40
352	Jose Cruz Jr. (Hit List)	.30
353	Tony Clark (Hit List)	.25
354	Roberto Alomar (Hit List)	.25
355	Manny Ramirez (Hit List)	.40
356	Paul Molitor (Hit List)	.25
357	Jim Thome (Hit List)	.25
358	Tino Martinez (Hit List)	.20
359	Tim Salmon (Hit List)	.20
360	David Justice (Hit List)	.20
361	Raul Mondesi (Hit List)	.10
362	Mark Grace (Hit List)	.10
363	Craig Biggio (Hit List)	.10
364	Larry Walker (Hit List)	.10
365	Mark McGwire (Hit List)	1.50
366	Juan Gonzalez (Hit List)	.75
367	Derek Jeter (Hit List)	.75
368	Chipper Jones (Hit List)	1.00
369	Frank Thomas (Hit List)	1.00
370	Alex Rodriguez (Hit List)	1.00
371	Mike Piazza (Hit List)	1.00
372	Tony Gwynn (Hit List)	.75
373	Jeff Bagwell (Hit List)	.50
374	Nomar Garciaparra (Hit List)	1.00
375	Ken Griffey Jr. (Hit List)	1.50
376	Livan Hernandez (Untouchables)	.10
377	Chan Ho Park (Untouchables)	.10
378	Mike Mussina (Untouchables)	.25
379	Andy Pettitte (Untouchables)	.25
380	Greg Maddux (Untouchables)	1.00
381	Hideo Nomo (Untouchables)	.25
382	Roger Clemens (Untouchables)	.50
383	Randy Johnson (Untouchables)	.25
384	Pedro Martinez (Untouchables)	.25
385	Jaret Wright (Untouchables)	.40
386	Ken Griffey Jr. (Spirit of the Game)	1.50
387	Todd Helton (Spirit of the Game)	.40
388	Paul Konerko (Spirit of the Game)	.10
389	Cal Ripken Jr. (Spirit of the Game)	1.25
390	Larry Walker (Spirit of the Game)	.10
391	Ken Caminiti (Spirit of the Game)	.10
392	Jose Guillen (Spirit of the Game)	.10
393	Jim Edmonds (Spirit of the Game)	.10
394	Barry Larkin (Spirit of the Game)	.10
395	Bernie Williams (Spirit of the Game)	.25
396	Tony Clark (Spirit of the Game)	.20
397	Jose Cruz Jr. (Spirit of the Game)	.30
398	Ivan Rodriguez (Spirit of the Game)	.40
399	Darin Erstad (Spirit of the Game)	.40
400	Scott Rolen (Spirit of the Game)	.50
401	Mark McGwire (Spirit of the Game)	1.50
402	Andruw Jones (Spirit of the Game)	.40
403	Juan Gonzalez (Spirit of the Game)	.75
404	Derek Jeter (Spirit of the Game)	.75
405	Chipper Jones (Spirit of the Game)	1.00
406	Greg Maddux (Spirit of the Game)	1.00
407	Frank Thomas (Spirit of the Game)	1.00
408	Alex Rodriguez (Spirit of the Game)	1.00
409	Mike Piazza (Spirit of the Game)	1.00
410	Tony Gwynn (Spirit of the Game)	.75
411	Jeff Bagwell (Spirit of the Game)	.50
412	Nomar Garciaparra (Spirit of the Game)	1.00
413	Hideo Nomo (Spirit of the Game)	.25
414	Barry Bonds (Spirit of the Game)	.40
415	Ben Grieve (Spirit of the Game)	.50
416	Checklist (Barry Bonds)	.25
417	Checklist (Mark McGwire)	1.00
418	Checklist (Roger Clemens)	.40
419	Checklist (Livan Hernandez)	.10
420	Checklist (Ken Griffey Jr.)	1.00

1998 Donruss Silver Press Proofs

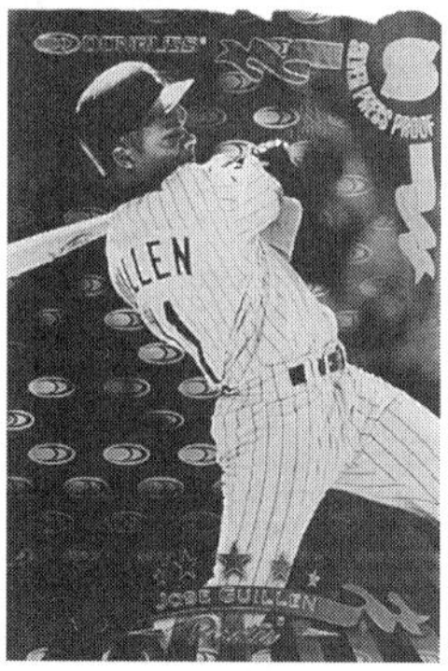

Silver Press Proofs paralleled all 420 cards in the Donruss and Donruss Update Baseball. Cards featured silver foil stamping and a die-cut top right corner. Backs had a silver tint and were numbered "1 of 1500" in the bottom left corner.

	MT
Complete Set (420):	1500.
Common Player:	1.50
Stars:	6x to 12x
Yng Stars & RCs:	4x to 8x
Production 1,500 sets	

1998 Donruss Gold Press Proofs

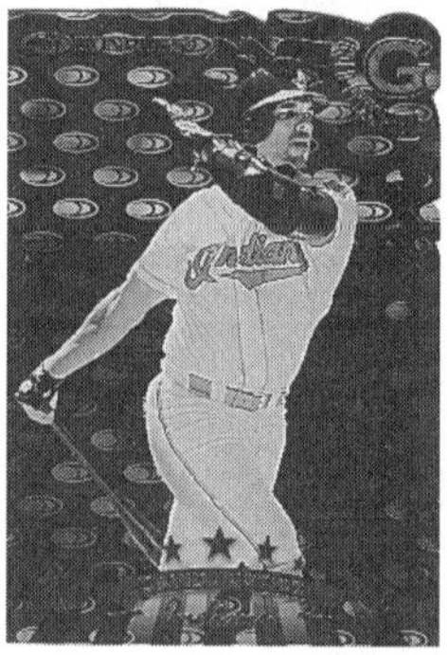

All 420 cards in Donruss and Donruss Update were also issued in Gold Press Proofs. These cards were die-cut on the top right corner and contained gold foil stamping. Backs featured a gold tint and "1 of 500" was printed in black in the bottome left corner.

	MT
Complete Set (420):	4000.
Common Player:	4.00
Stars:	20x to 40x
Yng Stars & RCs:	12x to 25x
Production 500 sets	

1998 Donruss Crusade Green

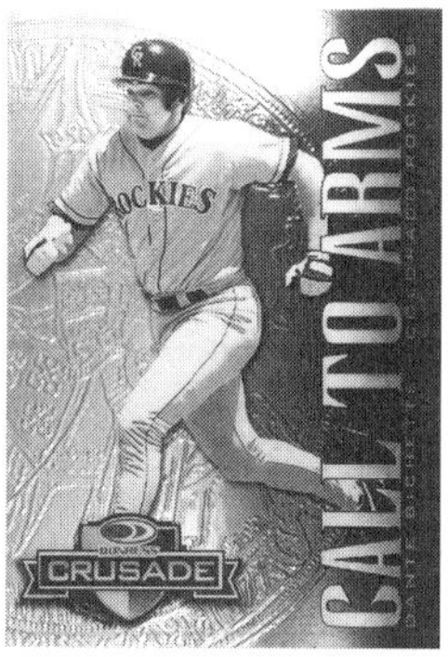

This 100-card insert was included in 1998 Donruss (40 cards), Leaf (30) and Donruss Update (30). The cards use refractive technology and the background features Crusades era dragons. The cards are sequentially numbered to 250. Crusade Purple (numbered to 100) and Red (25) parallels were also inserted in the three products.

		MT
Complete Set (40):		
Common Player:		10.00
Production 250 sets		
Purples:		1.5x
Production 100 sets		
Reds:		4x to 6x
Production 25 sets		
5	Jason Dickson	10.00
6	Todd Greene	20.00
7	Roberto Alomar	30.00
8	Cal Ripken Jr.	150.00
12	Mo Vaughn	50.00
13	Nomar Garciaparra	120.00
16	Mike Cameron	20.00
20	Sandy Alomar Jr.	20.00
21	David Justice	25.00
25	Justin Thompson	10.00
27	Kevin Appier	10.00
33	Tino Martinez	30.00
36	Hideki Irabu	20.00
37	Jose Canseco	25.00
39	Ken Griffey Jr.	200.00

42	Edgar Martinez	20.00
45	Will Clark	25.00
47	Rusty Greer	20.00
50	Shawn Green	10.00
51	Jose Cruz Jr.	50.00
52	Kenny Lofton	40.00
53	Chipper Jones	120.00
62	Kevin Orie	10.00
65	Deion Sanders	20.00
67	Larry Walker	30.00
68	Dante Bichette	20.00
71	Todd Helton	50.00
74	Bobby Bonilla	15.00
75	Kevin Brown	20.00
78	Craig Biggio	20.00
82	Wilton Guerrero	10.00
85	Pedro J. Martinez	40.00
86	Edgardo Alfonzo	15.00
88	Scott Rolen	75.00
89	Francisco Cordova	10.00
90	Jose Guillen	20.00
92	Ray Lankford	20.00
93	Mark McGwire	250.00
94	Matt Morris	15.00
100	Shawn Estes	15.00

1998 Donruss Diamond Kings

Diamond Kings is a 20-card insert featuring a color portrait of the player on the card front. The backs have a ghosted image of the portrait with a player biography and the card's number printed over it. A total of 10,000 sets were produced with the first 500 of each card printed on canvas. A Frank Thomas sample card was also created.

		MT
Complete Set (20):		150.00
Common Player:		4.00
Production 9,500 sets		
1	Cal Ripken Jr.	20.00
2	Greg Maddux	15.00
3	Ivan Rodriguez	6.00
4	Tony Gwynn	12.00
5	Paul Molitor	4.00
6	Kenny Lofton	6.00
7	Andy Pettitte	5.00
8	Darin Erstad	8.00
9	Randy Johnson	4.00
10	Derek Jeter	15.00
11	Hideo Nomo	5.00
12	David Justice	4.00
13	Bernie Williams	5.00
14	Roger Clemens	8.00
15	Barry Larkin	4.00
16	Andruw Jones	12.00
17	Mike Piazza	15.00
18	Frank Thomas	20.00
19	Alex Rodriguez	20.00
20	Ken Griffey Jr.	25.00

1998 Donruss Diamond Kings Canvas

The first 500 numbered sets of Diamond Kings were printed on canvas. The 20-card set featured artwork by Dan Gardiner and 10,000 total numbered sets were printed.

	MT
Complete Set (20):	450.00
Common Player:	10.00
Canvas Cards:	2x to 3x
Production 500 sets	

1998 Donruss Longball Leaders

Longball Leaders features 24 top home run hitters. The right border features a home run meter with zero at the bottom, 61 at the top and the player's 1997 home run total marked. Each card is sequentially numbered to 5,000.

		MT
Complete Set (24):		260.00
Common Player:		6.00
Production 5,000 sets		
1	Ken Griffey Jr.	40.00
2	Mark McGwire	50.00
3	Tino Martinez	6.00
4	Barry Bonds	10.00
5	Frank Thomas	30.00
6	Albert Belle	10.00
7	Mike Piazza	25.00
8	Chipper Jones	25.00
9	Vladimir Guerrero	12.00
10	Matt Williams	6.00
11	Sammy Sosa	20.00
12	Tim Salmon	6.00
13	Raul Mondesi	6.00
14	Jeff Bagwell	15.00
15	Mo Vaughn	10.00
16	Manny Ramirez	8.00
17	Jim Thome	8.00
18	Jim Edmonds	6.00
19	Tony Clark	8.00
20	Nomar Garciaparra	25.00
21	Juan Gonzalez	20.00
22	Scott Rolen	20.00
23	Larry Walker	8.00
24	Andres Galarraga	6.00

1998 Donruss Production Line-ob

This 20-card insert was printed on holographic foil board. Inserted in magazine packs, this insert features player's with a high on-base percentage in 1997. Each player's card is sequentially numbered to his on-base percentage from that season. The card back has a player photo and a list of the 20 players with their stat.

		MT
Complete Set (20):		1000.
Common Player:		15.00
1	Frank Thomas (456)	150.00
2	Edgar Martinez (456)	15.00
3	Barry Bonds (446)	40.00
4	Barry Larkin (440)	20.00
5	Mike Piazza (431)	140.00
6	Jeff Bagwell (425)	80.00
7	Gary Sheffield (424)	25.00
8	Mo Vaughn (420)	40.00
9	Craig Biggio (415)	20.00
10	Kenny Lofton (409)	40.00
11	Tony Gwynn (409)	100.00
12	Bernie Williams (408)	30.00
13	Rusty Greer (405)	15.00
14	Brady Anderson (393)	15.00
15	Mark McGwire (393)	200.00
16	Chuck Knoblauch (390)	25.00
17	Roberto Alomar (390)	30.00
18	Ken Griffey Jr. (382)	220.00
19	Chipper Jones (371)	140.00
20	Derek Jeter (370)	125.00

1998 Donruss Production Line-sg

This 20-card insert was printed on holographic board. It featured players with high slugging percentages in 1997. Each card is sequentially numbered to the player's slugging percentage from that season.

		MT
Complete Set (20):		1000.
Common Player:		15.00
1	Larry Walker (720)	20.00
2	Ken Griffey Jr. (646)	150.00
3	Mark McGwire (646)	150.00
4	Mike Piazza (638)	90.00
5	Frank Thomas (611)	125.00
6	Jeff Bagwell (592)	60.00
7	Juan Gonzalez (589)	70.00
8	Andres Galarraga (585)	15.00
9	Barry Bonds (585)	40.00
10	Jim Thome (579)	25.00
11	Tino Martinez (577)	15.00
12	Mo Vaughn (560)	40.00
13	Raul Mondesi (541)	20.00
14	Manny Ramirez (538)	35.00
15	Nomar Garciaparra (534)	90.00
16	Tim Salmon (517)	20.00
17	Tony Clark (500)	25.00
18	Jose Cruz Jr. (499)	50.00
19	Alex Rodriguez (496)	100.00
20	Cal Ripken Jr. (402)	110.00

1998 Donruss Production Line-PI

This 20-card insert was printed on holographic board. The set features players with a high power index from 1997. Each card is sequentially numbered to that player's power index from that season.

		MT
Complete Set (20):		600.00
Common Player:		10.00
1	Larry Walker (1,172)	15.00
2	Mike Piazza (1,070)	60.00
3	Frank Thomas (1,067)	80.00
4	Mark McGwire (1,039)	100.00
5	Barry Bonds (1,031)	25.00
6	Ken Griffey Jr. (1,028)	100.00
7	Jeff Bagwell (1,017)	40.00
8	David Justice (1,013)	10.00
9	Jim Thome (1,001)	20.00
10	Mo Vaughn (980)	25.00
11	Tony Gwynn (957)	50.00
12	Manny Ramirez (953)	20.00
13	Bernie Williams (952)	20.00
14	Tino Martinez (948)	10.00
15	Brady Anderson (863)	10.00
16	Chipper Jones (850)	60.00
17	Scott Rolen (846)	50.00
18	Alex Rodriguez (846)	70.00
19	Vladimir Guerrero (833)	25.00
20	Albert Belle (823)	25.00

1998 Donruss Rated Rookies

This 30-card insert features top young players. The fronts have a color player photo in front of a stars and stripes background, with "Rated Rookies" and the player's name printed on the right. The backs have another photo, basic player information and career highlights.

		MT
Complete Set (30):		70.00
Common Player:		2.00
Medalists (250 sets):		8x to 15x
1	Mark Kotsay	5.00
2	Neifi Perez	2.00
3	Paul Konerko	4.00
4	Jose Cruz Jr.	10.00
5	Hideki Irabu	3.00
6	Mike Cameron	2.00
7	Jeff Suppan	2.00
8	Kevin Orie	2.00
9	Pokey Reese	2.00
10	Todd Dunwoody	2.00
11	Miguel Tejada	4.00
12	Jose Guillen	3.00
13	Bartolo Colon	2.00
14	Derrek Lee	2.00
15	Antone Williamson	2.00
16	Wilton Guerrero	2.00
17	Jaret Wright	4.00
18	Todd Helton	4.00
19	Shannon Stewart	2.00
20	Nomar Garciaparra	10.00
21	Brett Tomko	2.00
22	Fernando Tatis	4.00
23	Raul Ibanez	2.00
24	Dennis Reyes	2.00
25	Bobby Estalella	2.00
26	Lou Collier	2.00
27	Bubba Trammell	2.00
28	Ben Grieve	5.00
29	Ivan Cruz	2.00
30	Karim Garcia	3.00

1998 Donruss Update Dominators

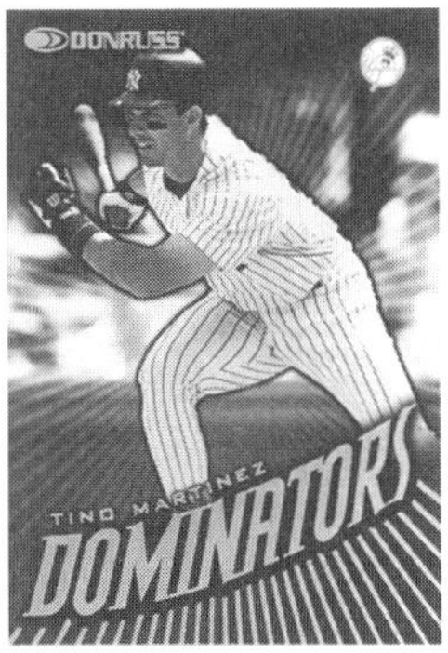

This 30-card insert features color player photos and holographic foil.

		MT
Complete Set (30):		200.00
Common Player:		2.50
Approx. 1:12		
1	Roger Clemens	10.00
2	Tony Clark	4.00
3	Darin Erstad	6.00
4	Jeff Bagwell	10.00
5	Ken Griffey Jr.	25.00
6	Andruw Jones	6.00
7	Juan Gonzalez	12.00
8	Ivan Rodriguez	6.00
9	Randy Johnson	4.00
10	Tino Martinez	3.00
11	Mark McGwire	30.00
12	Chuck Knoblauch	3.00
13	Jim Thome	6.00
14	Alex Rodriguez	15.00
15	Hideo Nomo	6.00
16	Jose Cruz Jr.	5.00
17	Chipper Jones	15.00
18	Tony Gwynn	12.00
19	Barry Bonds	6.00
20	Mo Vaughn	6.00
21	Cal Ripken Jr.	20.00
22	Greg Maddux	15.00
23	Manny Ramirez	6.00
24	Andres Galarraga	3.00
25	Vladimir Guerrero	6.00
26	Albert Belle	6.00
27	Nomar Garciaparra	15.00
28	Kenny Lofton	6.00
29	Mike Piazza	15.00
30	Frank Thomas	20.00

1998 Donruss Update Elite

This 20-card insert features color player photos in a diamond-shaped border at the top with the Elite Series logo and player's name at the bottom. The fronts have a cream-colored border. The cards are sequentially numbered to 2,500.

		MT
Complete Set (20):		400.00
Common Player:		5.00
Production 2,500 sets		
1	Jeff Bagwell	20.00
2	Andruw Jones	12.00
3	Ken Griffey Jr.	50.00
4	Derek Jeter	25.00
5	Juan Gonzalez	25.00
6	Mark McGwire	60.00
7	Ivan Rodriguez	15.00
8	Paul Molitor	10.00
9	Hideo Nomo	10.00
10	Mo Vaughn	15.00
11	Chipper Jones	30.00
12	Nomar Garciaparra	30.00
13	Mike Piazza	30.00
14	Frank Thomas	40.00
15	Greg Maddux	30.00
16	Cal Ripken Jr.	40.00
17	Alex Rodriguez	30.00
18	Scott Rolen	18.00
19	Barry Bonds	15.00
20	Tony Gwynn	25.00

1998 Donruss Update FANtasy Team

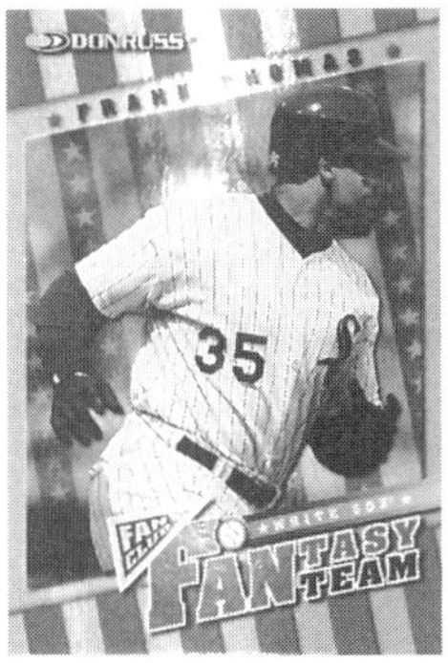

This 20-card set features the top vote getters from the Donruss online Fan Club ballot box. The top ten make up the 1st Team FANtasy Team and are sequentially numbered to 2,000. The other players are included in the 2nd Team FANtasy Team and are numbered to 4,000. The first 250 cards of each player are die-cut. The front of the cards feature a color photo inside a stars and stripes border.

		MT
Complete Set (20):		250.00
Common Player (1-10):		8.00
Common Player (11-20):		4.00
Production 1-10 1,750 sets		
Production 11-20 3,750 sets		
1	Frank Thomas	30.00
2	Ken Griffey Jr.	40.00
3	Cal Ripken Jr.	30.00
4	Jose Cruz Jr.	8.00
5	Travis Lee	25.00
6	Greg Maddux	25.00
7	Alex Rodriguez	25.00
8	Mark McGwire	50.00
9	Chipper Jones	25.00
10	Andruw Jones	10.00
11	Mike Piazza	15.00
12	Tony Gwynn	12.00
13	Larry Walker	4.00
14	Nomar Garciaparra	15.00
15	Jaret Wright	6.00
16	Livan Hernandez	4.00
17	Roger Clemens	10.00
18	Derek Jeter	12.00
19	Scott Rolen	8.00
20	Jeff Bagwell	10.00

1998 Donruss Update FANtasy Team Die-Cuts

This 20-card set paralleled the regular FANtasy Team insert, with only the first 250 numbered sets of 1st and 2nd team available in die-cut versions.

	MT
Complete Set (20):	600.00
Common Player:	15.00
1st Teams (1-10):	1.5x to 3x
2nd Teams (11-20):	2x to 4x
Production 250 sets	

1998 Donruss Update Rookie Diamond Kings

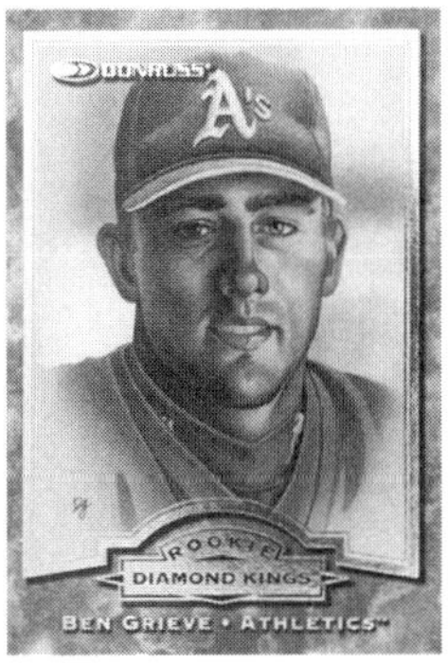

The Rookie Diamond Kings insert features color portraits of young players inside a golden border. The player's name, team and Rookie Diamond Kings logo are listed at the bottom. Each card is sequentially numbered to 10,000 with the first 500 printed on canvas.

		MT
Complete Set (12):		80.00
Common Player:		4.00
Production 9,500 sets		
1	Travis Lee	25.00
2	Fernando Tatis	4.00
3	Livan Hernandez	4.00
4	Todd Helton	10.00
5	Derrek Lee	4.00
6	Jaret Wright	10.00
7	Ben Grieve	15.00
8	Paul Konerko	6.00
9	Jose Cruz Jr.	8.00
10	Mark Kotsay	6.00
11	Todd Greene	4.00
12	Brad Fullmer	6.00

1998 Donruss Update Rookie Diamond Kings Die-Cuts

This insert featured the 12 Rookie Diamond Kings, but included the first 500 numbered sets (of 10,000) and were printed on canvas.

	MT
Complete Set (12):	200.00
Common Player:	8.00
Die-Cuts:	3x to 5x
Production 500 sets	

1998 Donruss Update Signature Series Preview

This 29-card insert was a surprise addition to Donruss Update. The set features autographs from top rookies and stars. The number of cards produced varies for each player. The card fronts have a color player photo in front of a checkered border with the signature in a white area near the bottom.

	MT
Common Player:	25.00
Sandy Alomar Jr. (96)	50.00
Andy Benes (135)	40.00
Russell Branyan (188)	40.00
Tony Clark (188)	60.00
Juan Encarnacion (193)	30.00
Brad Fullmer (396)	40.00
Juan Gonzalez (108)	250.00
Ben Grieve (100)	150.00
Todd Helton (101)	90.00
Richard Hidalgo (380)	25.00
A.J. Hinch (400)	35.00
Damian Jackson (15)	200.00
Chipper Jones (112)	300.00
Chuck Knoblauch (98)	80.00
Travis Lee (101)	175.00
Mike Lowell (450)	25.00
Greg Maddux (92)	350.00
Kevin Millwood (395)	75.00
Magglio Ordonez (420)	40.00
David Ortiz (393)	25.00
Rafael Palmeiro (107)	75.00
Cal Ripken Jr. (22)	1200.
Alex Rodriguez (23)	1000.
Curt Schilling (100)	75.00
Randall Simon (380)	25.00
Fernando Tatis (400)	25.00
Miguel Tejada (375)	40.00
Robin Ventura (95)	50.00
Kerry Wood (373)	150.00

1998 Donruss Update Sony MLB 99

This 20-card set promotes the MLB '99 game for Sony PlayStation systems. The card front has a color player photo with a red border on two

sides. The Donruss, PlayStation and MLB '99 logos appear on the front as well. The backs have a MLB '99 Tip and instructions on entering the PlayStation MLB '99 Sweepstakes.

		MT
Complete Set (20):		10.00
Common Player:		.25
1	Cal Ripken Jr.	2.00
2	Nomar Garciaparra	1.50
3	Barry Bonds	.60
4	Mike Mussina	.50
5	Pedro Martinez	.40
6	Derek Jeter	1.25
7	Andruw Jones	.60
8	Kenny Lofton	.60
9	Gary Sheffield	.25
10	Raul Mondesi	.25
11	Jeff Bagwell	.75
12	Tim Salmon	.25
13	Tom Glavine	.25
14	Ben Grieve	.75
15	Matt Williams	.25
16	Juan Gonzalez	1.25
17	Mark McGwire	2.00
18	Bernie Williams	.40
19	Andres Galarraga	.25
20	Jose Cruz Jr.	.40

1998 Donruss Elite

Donruss Elite consists of a 150-card base set with two parallels and five inserts. The base cards feature a bordered player photo on the front and another photo on the back with stats and basic player information. The Aspirations parallel is numbered to 750 and the Status parallel is numbered to 100. The base set also includes the 30-card Generations subset and three checklists. The inserts are Back to the Future, Back to the Future Autographs, Craftsmen, Prime Numbers and Prime Numbers Die-Cuts.

		MT
Complete Set (150):		35.00
Common Player:		.15
Wax Box:		65.00
1	Ken Griffey Jr.	4.00
2	Frank Thomas	3.00
3	Alex Rodriguez	2.50
4	Mike Piazza	2.50
5	Greg Maddux	2.50
6	Cal Ripken Jr.	3.00
7	Chipper Jones	2.50
8	Derek Jeter	2.50
9	Tony Gwynn	2.00
10	Andruw Jones	2.00
11	Juan Gonzalez	2.00
12	Jeff Bagwell	1.50
13	Mark McGwire	5.00
14	Roger Clemens	1.50
15	Albert Belle	1.00
16	Barry Bonds	1.00
17	Kenny Lofton	1.00
18	Ivan Rodriguez	.75
19	Manny Ramirez	.75
20	Jim Thome	.50
21	Chuck Knoblauch	.40
22	Paul Molitor	.60
23	Barry Larkin	.30
24	Andy Pettitte	.60
25	John Smoltz	.25
26	Randy Johnson	.50
27	Bernie Williams	.75
28	Larry Walker	.30
29	Mo Vaughn	1.00
30	Bobby Higginson	.15
31	Edgardo Alfonzo	.15
32	Justin Thompson	.15
33	Jeff Suppan	.15
34	Roberto Alomar	.75
35	Hideo Nomo	1.00
36	Rusty Greer	.15
37	Tim Salmon	.30
38	Jim Edmonds	.15
39	Gary Sheffield	.30
40	Ken Caminiti	.25
41	Sammy Sosa	2.00
42	Tony Womack	.15
43	Matt Williams	.30
44	Andres Galarraga	.30
45	Garret Anderson	.15
46	Rafael Palmeiro	.25
47	Mike Mussina	.75
48	Craig Biggio	.25
49	Wade Boggs	.30
50	Tom Glavine	.25
51	Jason Giambi	.15
52	Will Clark	.25
53	David Justice	.25
54	Sandy Alomar Jr.	.15
55	Edgar Martinez	.15
56	Brady Anderson	.25
57	Eric Young	.15
58	Ray Lankford	.15
59	Kevin Brown	.25
60	Raul Mondesi	.30
61	Bobby Bonilla	.20
62	Javier Lopez	.15
63	Fred McGriff	.25
64	Rondell White	.25
65	Todd Hundley	.25
66	Mark Grace	.30
67	Alan Benes	.25
68	Jeff Abbott	.15
69	Bob Abreu	.15
70	Deion Sanders	.30
71	Tino Martinez	.30
72	Shannon Stewart	.15
73	Homer Bush	.15
74	Carlos Delgado	.25
75	Raul Ibanez	.15
76	Hideki Irabu	1.00
77	Jose Cruz Jr.	1.50
78	Tony Clark	.60
79	Wilton Guerrero	.15
80	Vladimir Guerrero	1.25
81	Scott Rolen	2.00
82	Nomar Garciaparra	2.50
83	Darin Erstad	1.00
84	Chan Ho Park	.25
85	Mike Cameron	.15
86	Todd Walker	.25
87	Todd Dunwoody	.15
88	Neifi Perez	.15
89	Brett Tomko	.15
90	Jose Guillen	.40
91	Matt Morris	.15
92	Bartolo Colon	.15
93	Jaret Wright	1.50
94	Shawn Estes	.15
95	Livan Hernandez	.25
96	Bobby Estalella	.15
97	Ben Grieve	1.50
98	Paul Konerko	1.25
99	David Ortiz	.75
100	Todd Helton	1.00
101	Juan Encarnacion	.30
102	Bubba Trammell	.15
103	Miguel Tejada	.75
104	Jacob Cruz	.15
105	Todd Greene	.15
106	Kevin Orie	.15
107	Mark Kotsay	.60
108	Fernando Tatis	.30
109	Jay Payton	.15
110	Pokey Reese	.15
111	Derrek Lee	.25
112	Richard Hidalgo	.15
113	Ricky Ledee	.75
114	Lou Collier	.15
115	Ruben Rivera	.15
116	Shawn Green	.15
117	Moises Alou	.25
118	Ken Griffey Jr. (Generations)	2.00
119	Frank Thomas (Generations)	1.50
120	Alex Rodriguez (Generations)	1.25
121	Mike Piazza (Generations)	1.25
122	Greg Maddux (Generations)	1.25
123	Cal Ripken Jr. (Generations)	1.50
124	Chipper Jones (Generations)	1.25
125	Derek Jeter (Generations)	1.25
126	Tony Gwynn (Generations)	1.00
127	Andruw Jones (Generations)	1.00
128	Juan Gonzalez (Generations)	1.00
129	Jeff Bagwell (Generations)	.75
130	Mark McGwire (Generations)	2.50
131	Roger Clemens (Generations)	.75
132	Albert Belle (Generations)	.50
133	Barry Bonds (Generations)	.50
134	Kenny Lofton (Generations)	.50
135	Ivan Rodriguez (Generations)	.40
136	Manny Ramirez (Generations)	.40
137	Jim Thome (Generations)	.30
138	Chuck Knoblauch (Generations)	.25
139	Paul Molitor (Generations)	.30
140	Barry Larkin (Generations)	.15
141	Mo Vaughn (Generations)	.50
142	Hideki Irabu (Generations)	.50
143	Jose Cruz Jr. (Generations)	1.00
144	Tony Clark (Generations)	.40
145	Vladimir Guerrero (Generations)	.60
146	Scott Rolen (Generations)	1.00
147	Nomar Garciaparra (Generations)	1.25
148	Checklist (Garciaparra) (Hit Streaks)	.75
149	Checklist (Walker) (Long HR-Coors)	.15
150	Checklist (Martinez) (3 HR in game)	.15

1998 Donruss Elite Aspirations

A parallel edition of 750 of each player is found in this die-cut set. Cards have a scalloped treatment cut into the top and sides and red, rather than silver metallic borders. The word "ASPIRATIONS" in printed on front at bottom-right. Backs have the notation "1 of 750".

	MT
Complete Set (150):	550.00
Common Player:	2.00
Aspirations:	15x to 25x
Yng. Stars & RCs:	8x to 15x
Production 750 sets	

1998 Donruss Elite Status

Just 100 serially numbered cards of each player are found in this die-cut parallel set. Cards have a scalloped treatment cut into the top and sides and red, rather than silver metallic borders.

	MT
Common Player:	9.00
Gold Status Stars:	60x to 80x
Status Yng Stars & RCs:	40x to 60x
Production: 100 sets	

1998 Donruss Elite Back to the Future

These double-front cards feature a veteran or retired star on one side and a young player on the other. The player's name, team and "Back to the Future" are printed in the border. The cards are numbered to 1,500, with the first 100 of each card signed by both players. Exceptions are cards #1 and #6. Ripken and Konerko did not sign the same cards and Frank Thomas did not sign his Back to the Future card. Thomas instead signed 100 copies of his base set card.

		MT
Complete Set (8):		450.00
Common Player:		15.00
Production 1,400 sets		
1	Cal Ripken Jr., Paul Konerko	75.00
2	Jeff Bagwell, Todd Helton	40.00
3	Eddie Mathews, Chipper Jones	50.00
4	Juan Gonzalez, Ben Grieve	60.00
5	Hank Aaron, Jose Cruz Jr.	60.00
6	Frank Thomas, David Ortiz	80.00
7	Nolan Ryan, Greg Maddux	80.00
8	Alex Rodriguez, Nomar Garciaparra	70.00

1998 Donruss Elite Back to the Future Autographs

The first 100 of each card in the Back to the Future insert was autographed by both players. Exceptions are cards #1 and #6. Ripken and Konerko did not sign the same cards and Frank Thomas did not sign his Back to the Future card. Thomas instead signed 100 copies of his base set card.

		MT
Common Autograph:		125.00
F. Thomas Redemption:		450.00
C. Ripken Redemption:		450.00
Production 100 sets		
1	Paul Konerko	125.00
2	Jeff Bagwell, Todd Helton	350.00
3	Eddie Mathews, Chipper Jones	400.00
4	Juan Gonzalez, Ben Grieve	600.00
5	Hank Aaron, Jose Cruz Jr.	500.00
7	Nolan Ryan, Greg Maddux	1000.
8	Alex Rodriguez, Nomar Garciaparra	600.00

1998 Donruss Elite Craftsmen

This 30-card insert has color player photos on the front and back. The set is sequentially numbered to 3,500. The Master Craftsmen parallel is numbered to 100.

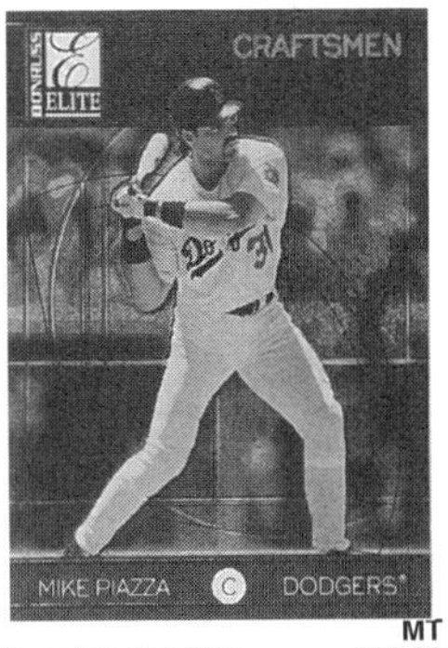

		MT
Complete Set (30):		300.00
Common Player:		4.00
Production 3,500 sets		
1	Ken Griffey Jr.	30.00
2	Frank Thomas	20.00
3	Alex Rodriguez	20.00
4	Cal Ripken Jr.	20.00
5	Greg Maddux	20.00
6	Mike Piazza	20.00
7	Chipper Jones	20.00
8	Derek Jeter	15.00
9	Tony Gwynn	15.00
10	Nomar Garciaparra	20.00
11	Scott Rolen	10.00
12	Jose Cruz Jr.	10.00
13	Tony Clark	5.00
14	Vladimir Guerrero	10.00
15	Todd Helton	6.00
16	Ben Grieve	10.00
17	Andruw Jones	10.00
18	Jeff Bagwell	10.00
19	Mark McGwire	30.00
20	Juan Gonzalez	15.00
21	Roger Clemens	12.00
22	Albert Belle	8.00
23	Barry Bonds	8.00
24	Kenny Lofton	8.00
25	Ivan Rodriguez	8.00
26	Paul Molitor	6.00
27	Barry Larkin	4.00
28	Mo Vaughn	8.00
29	Larry Walker	5.00
30	Tino Martinez	4.00

1998 Donruss Elite Master Craftsmen

The first 100 sequentially numbered sets of Craftsmen inserts were printed on holographic board. Master Craftsmen includes the same 30 players, with the regular versions numbered to 3,500.

	MT
Complete Set (30):	2200.
Common Player:	20.00
Master Craftsmen:	6x to 10x
Production 100 sets	

1998 Donruss Elite Prime Numbers

This 36-card insert includes three cards for each of 12 players. Each card has a single number in the background. The three numbers for each player represent a key statistic for the player (ex. Mark McGwire's cards are 3-8-7; his career home run total at the time was 387). Each card in the set is sequentially numbered. The total is dependent upon the player's statistic.

		MT
Common Player:		30.00
1A	Ken Griffey Jr. (94)	350.00
1B	Ken Griffey Jr. (204)	175.00
1C	Ken Griffey Jr. (290)	140.00
2A	Frank Thomas (56)	400.00
2B	Frank Thomas (406)	100.00
2C	Frank Thomas (450)	100.00
3A	Mark McGwire (87)	350.00
3B	Mark McGwire (307)	150.00
3C	Mark McGwire (380)	150.00
4A	Cal Ripken Jr. (17)	1000.
4B	Cal Ripken Jr. (507)	100.00
4C	Cal Ripken Jr. (510)	100.00
5A	Mike Piazza (76)	225.00
5B	Mike Piazza (506)	75.00
5C	Mike Piazza (570)	75.00
6A	Chipper Jones (89)	180.00
6B	Chipper Jones (409)	50.00
6C	Chipper Jones (480)	50.00
7A	Tony Gwynn (72)	200.00
7B	Tony Gwynn (302)	75.00
7C	Tony Gwynn (370)	75.00
8A	Barry Bonds (74)	100.00
8B	Barry Bonds (304)	40.00
8C	Barry Bonds (370)	40.00
9A	Jeff Bagwell (25)	375.00
9B	Jeff Bagwell (405)	50.00
9C	Jeff Bagwell (420)	50.00
10A	Juan Gonzalez (89)	180.00
10B	Juan Gonzalez (509)	60.00
10C	Juan Gonzalez (580)	60.00
11A	Alex Rodriguez (34)	375.00
11B	Alex Rodriguez (504)	75.00
11C	Alex Rodriguez (530)	75.00
12A	Kenny Lofton (54)	120.00
12B	Kenny Lofton (304)	40.00
12C	Kenny Lofton (350)	40.00

1998 Donruss Elite Prime Numbers Die-Cuts

This set is a die-cut parallel of the Prime Numbers insert. Each card is sequentially numbered. The production run for each player is the number featured on his first card times 100, his second card times 10 and his third card is sequentially numbered to the number featured on the card.

		MT
Common Player:		30.00
1A	Ken Griffey Jr. (200)	175.00
1B	Ken Griffey Jr. (90)	400.00
1C	Ken Griffey Jr. (4)	30.00
2A	Frank Thomas (400)	100.00
2B	Frank Thomas (50)	400.00
2C	Frank Thomas (6)	30.00
3A	Mark McGwire (300)	150.00
3B	Mark McGwire (80)	400.00
3C	Mark McGwire (7)	40.00
4A	Cal Ripken Jr. (500)	100.00
4B	Cal Ripken Jr. (10)	30.00
4C	Cal Ripken Jr. (7)	30.00
5A	Mike Piazza (500)	75.00
5B	Mike Piazza (70)	200.00
5C	Mike Piazza (6)	30.00
6A	Chipper Jones (400)	50.00
6B	Chipper Jones (80)	200.00
6C	Chipper Jones (9)	30.00
7A	Tony Gwynn (300)	75.00
7B	Tony Gwynn (70)	180.00
7C	Tony Gwynn (2)	30.00
8A	Barry Bonds (300)	40.00
8B	Barry Bonds (70)	100.00
8C	Barry Bonds (4)	30.00
9A	Jeff Bagwell (400)	50.00
9B	Jeff Bagwell (20)	400.00
9C	Jeff Bagwell (5)	30.00
10A	Juan Gonzalez (500)	60.00
10B	Juan Gonzalez (80)	180.00
10C	Juan Gonzalez (9)	30.00
11A	Alex Rodriguez (500)	75.00
11B	Alex Rodriguez (30)	450.00
11C	Alex Rodriguez (4)	30.00
12A	Kenny Lofton (300)	40.00
12B	Kenny Lofton (50)	120.00
12C	Kenny Lofton (4)	30.00

1998 Donruss Preferred

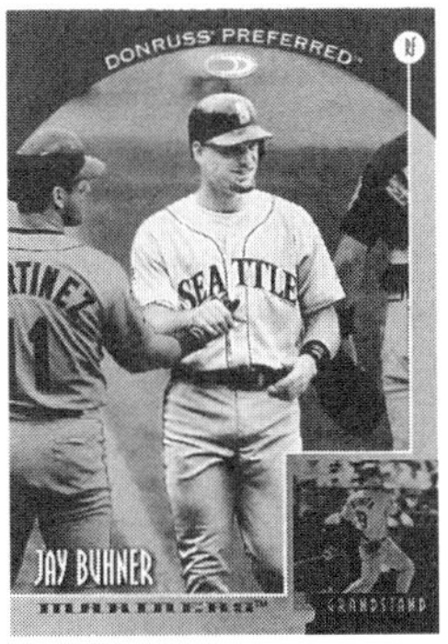

The Donruss Preferred 200-card base set is broken down into five subsets: 100 Grand Stand cards (5:1), 40 Mezzanine (1:6), 30 Club Level (1:12), 20 Field Box (1:23) and 10 Executive Suite (1:65). The base set is paralleled in the Preferred Seating set. Each subset has a different die-cut in the parallel. Inserts in this product include Great X-Pectations, Precious Metals and Title Waves.

		MT
Complete Set (200):		900.00
Common Grand Stand:		.20
Common Mezzanine:		1.50
Mezz. Inserted 1:6		
Common Club Level:		2.00
C.L. Inserted 1:12		
Common Field Box:		3.00
F.B. Inserted 1:23		
Common Executive Suite:		30.00
E.S. Inserted 1:65		
Wax Box:		100.00
1	Ken Griffey Jr. EX	90.00
2	Frank Thomas EX	75.00
3	Cal Ripken Jr. EX	60.00
4	Alex Rodriguez EX	50.00
5	Greg Maddux EX	50.00
6	Mike Piazza EX	50.00
7	Chipper Jones EX	50.00
8	Tony Gwynn FB	40.00
9	Derek Jeter FB	30.00
10	Jeff Bagwell EX	35.00
11	Juan Gonzalez EX	40.00
12	Nomar Garciaparra EX	50.00
13	Andruw Jones FB	15.00
14	Hideo Nomo FB	15.00
15	Roger Clemens FB	25.00
16	Mark McGwire FB	60.00
17	Scott Rolen FB	20.00
18	Vladimir Guerrero FB	15.00
19	Barry Bonds FB	15.00
20	Darin Erstad FB	15.00
21	Albert Belle FB	15.00
22	Kenny Lofton FB	15.00
23	Mo Vaughn FB	15.00
24	Tony Clark FB	8.00
25	Ivan Rodriguez FB	15.00
26	Larry Walker CL	5.00
27	Eddie Murray CL	4.00
28	Andy Pettitte CL	8.00
29	Roberto Alomar CL	8.00
30	Randy Johnson CL	8.00
31	Manny Ramirez CL	10.00
32	Paul Molitor FB	12.00
33	Mike Mussina CL	8.00
34	Jim Thome FB	10.00
35	Tino Martinez CL	5.00
36	Gary Sheffield CL	5.00
37	Chuck Knoblauch CL	5.00
38	Bernie Williams CL	8.00
39	Tim Salmon CL	6.00
40	Sammy Sosa CL	20.00
41	Wade Boggs MZ	3.00
42	Will Clark GS	.50
43	Andres Galarraga CL	5.00
44	Raul Mondesi CL	5.00
45	Rickey Henderson GS	.20
46	Jose Canseco GS	.50
47	Pedro Martinez GS	.75
48	Jay Buhner GS	.50
49	Ryan Klesko GS	.50
50	Barry Larkin CL	5.00
51	Charles Johnson GS	.20
52	Tom Glavine GS	.50
53	Edgar Martinez CL	2.00
54	Fred McGriff GS	.50
55	Moises Alou MZ	1.50
56	Dante Bichette GS	.50
57	Jim Edmonds CL	2.00
58	Mark Grace MZ	2.50
59	Chan Ho Park MZ	2.50
60	Justin Thompson MZ	1.50
61	John Smoltz MZ	2.50
62	Craig Biggio CL	4.00
63	Ken Caminiti MZ	2.50
64	Deion Sanders MZ	2.50
65	Carlos Delgado GS	.50
66	David Justice CL	4.00
67	J.T. Snow GS	.20
68	Jason Giambi CL	2.00
69	Garret Anderson MZ	.20
70	Rondell White MZ	.50
71	Matt Williams MZ	.60
72	Brady Anderson MZ	.40
73	Eric Karros GS	.50
74	Javier Lopez GS	.40
75	Pat Hentgen GS	.40
76	Todd Hundley GS	.20
77	Ray Lankford GS	.20
78	Denny Neagle GS	.20
79	Henry Rodriguez GS	.20
80	Sandy Alomar Jr. MZ	1.50
81	Rafael Palmeiro MZ	2.50
82	Robin Ventura GS	.40
83	John Olerud GS	.40
84	Omar Vizquel GS	.20
85	Joe Randa GS	.20
86	Lance Johnson GS	.20
87	Kevin Brown GS	.40
88	Curt Schilling GS	.50
89	Ismael Valdes GS	.20
90	Francisco Cordova GS	.20
91	David Cone GS	.40
92	Paul O'Neill GS	.40
93	Jimmy Key GS	.20
94	Brad Radke GS	.20
95	Kevin Appier GS	.20
96	Al Martin GS	.20
97	Rusty Greer MZ	1.50
98	Reggie Jefferson GS	.20
99	Ron Coomer GS	.20
100	Vinny Castilla GS	.40
101	Bobby Bonilla MZ	1.50
102	Eric Young GS	.20
103	Tony Womack GS	.20
104	Jason Kendall GS	.20
105	Jeff Suppan GS	.20
106	Shawn Estes MZ	1.50
107	Shawn Green GS	.20
108	Edgardo Alfonzo MZ	1.50
109	Alan Benes MZ	1.50
110	Bobby Higginson GS	.20
111	Mark Grudzielanek GS	.20
112	Wilton Guerrero GS	.20
113	Todd Greene MZ	1.50
114	Pokey Reese GS	.20
115	Jose Guillen CL	2.00
116	Neifi Perez MZ	1.50
117	Luis Castillo GS	.20
118	Edgar Renteria GS	.20
119	Karim Garcia GS	.20
120	Butch Huskey GS	.20
121	Michael Tucker GS	.20
122	Jason Dickson GS	.20
123	Todd Walker MZ	2.50
124	Brian Jordan GS	.20
125	Joe Carter GS	.20
126	Matt Morris MZ	1.50
127	Brett Tomko MZ	1.50
128	Mike Cameron CL	3.00
129	Russ Davis GS	.20
130	Shannon Stewart MZ	1.50
131	Kevin Orie GS	.20
132	Scott Spiezio GS	.20
133	Brian Giles GS	.20
134	Raul Casanova GS	.20
135	Jose Cruz Jr. CL	10.00
136	Hideki Irabu GS	1.00
137	Bubba Trammell GS	.20
138	Richard Hidalgo CL	2.00
139	Paul Konerko CL	6.00
140	Todd Helton FB	15.00
141	Miguel Tejada CL	8.00
142	Fernando Tatis MZ	1.50
143	Ben Grieve FB	25.00
144	Travis Lee FB	40.00
145	Mark Kotsay CL	8.00
146	Eli Marrero MZ	1.50
147	David Ortiz CL	5.00
148	Juan Encarnacion MZ	1.50
149	Jaret Wright MZ	10.00
150	Livan Hernandez CL	4.00
151	Ruben Rivera GS	.20
152	Brad Fullmer MZ	4.00
153	Dennis Reyes GS	.20
154	Enrique Wilson MZ	1.50
155	Todd Dunwoody MZ	1.50
156	Derrick Gibson MZ	1.50
157	Aaron Boone MZ	1.50
158	Ron Wright MZ	1.50
159	Preston Wilson MZ	1.50
160	Abraham Nunez GS	.20
161	Shane Monahan GS	.20
162	Carl Pavano GS	.50
163	Derrek Lee GS	.50
164	Jeff Abbott GS	.20
165	Wes Helms MZ	.20
166	Brian Rose GS	.50
167	Bobby Estalella GS	.20
168	Ken Griffey Jr. GS	3.00
169	Frank Thomas GS	3.00
170	Cal Ripken Jr. GS	2.50
171	Alex Rodriguez GS	2.00
172	Greg Maddux GS	2.00
173	Mike Piazza GS	2.00
174	Chipper Jones GS	2.00
175	Tony Gwynn GS	1.50
176	Derek Jeter GS	1.50
177	Jeff Bagwell GS	1.00
178	Juan Gonzalez GS	1.50
179	Nomar Garciaparra GS	2.00
180	Andruw Jones GS	.75
181	Hideo Nomo GS	.75
182	Roger Clemens GS	1.25
183	Mark McGwire GS	4.00
184	Scott Rolen GS	1.00
185	Barry Bonds GS	.75
186	Darin Erstad GS	.75
187	Mo Vaughn GS	.75
188	Ivan Rodriguez GS	.75
189	Larry Walker MZ	4.00
190	Andy Pettitte GS	.50
191	Randy Johnson MZ	4.00
192	Paul Molitor GS	.60
193	Jim Thome GS	.50
194	Tino Martinez MZ	4.00
195	Gary Sheffield GS	.40
196	Albert Belle GS	.75
197	Jose Cruz Jr. GS	1.00
198	Todd Helton GS	.75
199	Ben Grieve GS	1.25
200	Paul Konerko GS	.75

1998 Donruss Preferred Seating

Preferred Seating is a die-cut parallel of the base set. Each section of the base set has a different die-cut.

		MT
Complete Set (200):		4000.
Comp. Grand Stand (100):		400.00
Common Grand Stand:		1.50
Comp. Mezzanine (40):		275.00
Common Mezzanine:		5.00
Comp. Club Level (30):		600.00
Common Club Level:		8.00
Comp. Field Box (20):		1000.
Common Field Box:		10.00
Comp. Executive Suite (10):		1800.
Common Executive Suite:		100.00
1	Ken Griffey Jr. EX	300.00
2	Frank Thomas EX	200.00
3	Cal Ripken Jr. EX	220.00
4	Alex Rodriguez EX	200.00
5	Greg Maddux EX	200.00
6	Mike Piazza EX	200.00
7	Chipper Jones EX	200.00
8	Tony Gwynn FB	100.00
9	Derek Jeter FB	100.00
10	Jeff Bagwell EX	125.00
11	Juan Gonzalez EX	150.00
12	Nomar Garciaparra EX	200.00
13	Andruw Jones FB	50.00
14	Hideo Nomo FB	50.00
15	Roger Clemens FB	80.00
16	Mark McGwire FB	200.00
17	Scott Rolen FB	70.00
18	Vladimir Guerrero FB	50.00
19	Barry Bonds FB	50.00
20	Darin Erstad FB	50.00
21	Albert Belle FB	50.00
22	Kenny Lofton FB	50.00
23	Mo Vaughn FB	50.00
24	Tony Clark FB	30.00
25	Ivan Rodriguez FB	50.00
26	Larry Walker CL	30.00
27	Eddie Murray CL	25.00
28	Andy Pettitte CL	30.00
29	Roberto Alomar CL	35.00
30	Randy Johnson CL	30.00
31	Manny Ramirez CL	35.00
32	Paul Molitor FB	40.00
33	Mike Mussina CL	30.00
34	Jim Thome FB	40.00
35	Tino Martinez CL	25.00
36	Gary Sheffield CL	30.00
37	Chuck Knoblauch CL	25.00
38	Bernie Williams CL	30.00
39	Tim Salmon CL	25.00
40	Sammy Sosa CL	75.00
41	Wade Boggs MZ	15.00
42	Will Clark GS	5.00
43	Andres Galarraga CL	25.00
44	Raul Mondesi CL	20.00
45	Rickey Henderson GS	4.00
46	Jose Canseco GS	6.00
47	Pedro Martinez GS	10.00
48	Jay Buhner GS	8.00
49	Ryan Klesko GS	10.00
50	Barry Larkin CL	15.00
51	Charles Johnson GS	2.00
52	Tom Glavine GS	4.00
53	Edgar Martinez CL	15.00
54	Fred McGriff GS	5.00
55	Moises Alou MZ	8.00
56	Dante Bichette GS	6.00
57	Jim Edmonds CL	15.00
58	Mark Grace MZ	15.00
59	Chan Ho Park MZ	15.00
60	Justin Thompson MZ	10.00
61	John Smoltz MZ	15.00
62	Craig Biggio CL	20.00
63	Ken Caminiti MZ	15.00
64	Deion Sanders MZ	15.00
65	Carlos Delgado GS	5.00
66	David Justice CL	25.00
67	J.T. Snow GS	2.00
68	Jason Giambi CL	8.00
69	Garret Anderson MZ	5.00
70	Rondell White MZ	8.00
71	Matt Williams MZ	20.00
72	Brady Anderson MZ	15.00
73	Eric Karros GS	5.00
74	Javier Lopez GS	5.00
75	Pat Hentgen GS	4.00
76	Todd Hundley GS	2.00
77	Ray Lankford GS	2.00
78	Denny Neagle GS	4.00
79	Henry Rodriguez GS	2.00
80	Sandy Alomar Jr. MZ	8.00
81	Rafael Palmeiro MZ	15.00
82	Robin Ventura GS	4.00
83	John Olerud GS	4.00
84	Omar Vizquel GS	2.00
85	Joe Randa GS	2.00
86	Lance Johnson GS	2.00
87	Kevin Brown GS	5.00
88	Curt Schilling GS	5.00
89	Ismael Valdes GS	2.00
90	Francisco Cordova GS	2.00
91	David Cone GS	5.00
92	Paul O'Neill GS	5.00
93	Jimmy Key GS	2.00
94	Brad Radke GS	2.00
95	Kevin Appier GS	2.00
96	Al Martin GS	2.00
97	Rusty Greer MZ	10.00
98	Reggie Jefferson GS	2.00
99	Ron Coomer GS	2.00
100	Vinny Castilla GS	5.00
101	Bobby Bonilla MZ	10.00
102	Eric Young GS	2.00
103	Tony Womack GS	2.00
104	Jason Kendall GS	2.00
105	Jeff Suppan GS	2.00
106	Shawn Estes MZ	5.00
107	Shawn Green GS	2.00
108	Edgardo Alfonzo MZ	5.00
109	Alan Benes MZ	5.00
110	Bobby Higginson GS	2.00

111	Mark Grudzielanek GS	2.00
112	Wilton Guerrero GS	2.00
113	Todd Greene MZ	5.00
114	Pokey Reese GS	2.00
115	Jose Guillen CL	15.00
116	Neifi Perez MZ	5.00
117	Luis Castillo GS	2.00
118	Edgar Renteria GS	2.00
119	Karim Garcia GS	2.00
120	Butch Huskey GS	2.00
121	Michael Tucker GS	2.00
122	Jason Dickson GS	2.00
123	Todd Walker MZ	10.00
124	Brian Jordan GS	2.00
125	Joe Carter GS	4.00
126	Matt Morris MZ	5.00
127	Brett Tomko MZ	5.00
128	Mike Cameron CL	15.00
129	Russ Davis GS	2.00
130	Shannon Stewart MZ	5.00
131	Kevin Orie GS	2.00
132	Scott Spiezio GS	2.00
133	Brian Giles GS	2.00
134	Raul Casanova GS	2.00
135	Jose Cruz Jr. CL	40.00
136	Hideki Irabu GS	10.00
137	Bubba Trammell GS	2.00
138	Richard Hidalgo CL	8.00
139	Paul Konerko CL	12.00
140	Todd Helton FB	20.00
141	Miguel Tejada CL	12.00
142	Fernando Tatis MZ	10.00
143	Ben Grieve FB	25.00
144	Travis Lee FB	100.00
145	Mark Kotsay CL	20.00
146	Eli Marrero MZ	5.00
147	David Ortiz CL	12.00
148	Juan Encarnacion MZ	5.00
149	Jaret Wright MZ	30.00
150	Livan Hernandez CL	8.00
151	Ruben Rivera GS	2.00
152	Brad Fullmer MZ	12.00
153	Dennis Reyes GS	2.00
154	Enrique Wilson MZ	5.00
155	Todd Dunwoody MZ	5.00
156	Derrick Gibson MZ	5.00
157	Aaron Boone MZ	5.00
158	Ron Wright MZ	5.00
159	Preston Wilson MZ	5.00
160	Abraham Nunez GS	2.00
161	Shane Monahan GS	2.00
162	Carl Pavano GS	5.00
163	Derrek Lee GS	5.00
164	Jeff Abbott GS	2.00
165	Wes Helms MZ	5.00
166	Brian Rose GS	5.00
167	Bobby Estalella GS	2.00
168	Ken Griffey Jr. GS	40.00
169	Frank Thomas GS	30.00
170	Cal Ripken Jr. GS	30.00
171	Alex Rodriguez GS	25.00
172	Greg Maddux GS	25.00
173	Mike Piazza GS	25.00
174	Chipper Jones GS	25.00
175	Tony Gwynn GS	20.00
176	Derek Jeter GS	20.00
177	Jeff Bagwell GS	15.00
178	Juan Gonzalez GS	20.00
179	Nomar Garciaparra GS	25.00
180	Andruw Jones GS	12.00
181	Hideo Nomo GS	12.00
182	Roger Clemens GS	15.00
183	Mark McGwire GS	40.00
184	Scott Rolen GS	12.00
185	Barry Bonds GS	10.00
186	Darin Erstad GS	10.00
187	Mo Vaughn GS	10.00
188	Ivan Rodriguez GS	10.00
189	Larry Walker MZ	20.00
190	Andy Pettitte GS	8.00
191	Randy Johnson MZ	15.00
192	Paul Molitor GS	8.00
193	Jim Thome GS	8.00
194	Tino Martinez MZ	15.00
195	Gary Sheffield GS	5.00
196	Albert Belle GS	10.00
197	Jose Cruz Jr. GS	15.00
198	Todd Helton GS	6.00
199	Ben Grieve GS	10.00
200	Paul Konerko GS	8.00

1998 Donruss Preferred Great X-pectations

This 26-card insert features a veteran player on one side and a young player on the other. A large "GX" appears in the background on each side. The cards are sequentially numbered to 2,700, with the first 300 of each die-cut around the "GX".

		MT
Complete Set (26):		450.00
Common Player:		6.00
Production 2,700 sets		
Die-Cuts:		3x to 5x
Production 300 sets		
1	Jeff Bagwell, Travis Lee	25.00
2	Jose Cruz Jr., Ken Griffey Jr.	40.00
3	Larry Walker, Ben Grieve	20.00
4	Frank Thomas, Todd Helton	35.00
5	Jim Thome, Paul Konerko	8.00
6	Alex Rodriguez, Miguel Tejada	30.00
7	Greg Maddux, Livan Hernandez	30.00
8	Roger Clemens, Jaret Wright	20.00
9	Albert Belle, Juan Encarnacion	12.00
10	Mo Vaughn, David Ortiz	12.00
11	Manny Ramirez, Mark Kotsay	10.00
12	Tim Salmon, Brad Fullmer	6.00
13	Cal Ripken Jr., Fernando Tatis	40.00
14	Hideo Nomo, Hideki Irabu	10.00
15	Mike Piazza, Todd Greene	30.00
16	Gary Sheffield, Richard Hidalgo	8.00
17	Paul Molitor, Darin Erstad	12.00
18	Ivan Rodriguez, Eli Marrero	12.00
19	Ken Caminiti, Todd Walker	8.00
20	Tony Gwynn, Jose Guillen	25.00
21	Derek Jeter, Nomar Garciaparra	30.00
22	Chipper Jones, Scott Rolen	30.00
23	Juan Gonzalez, Andruw Jones	25.00
24	Barry Bonds, Vladimir Guerrero	12.00
25	Mark McGwire, Tony Clark	50.00
26	Bernie Williams, Mike Cameron	10.00

1998 Donruss Preferred Great X-pectations Die-Cuts

While regular versions of Great X-pectations were numbered to 3,000, the first 300 sets of this 26-card insert were die-cut.

	MT
Complete Set (26):	900.00
Common Player:	12.00
Die-Cuts:	2x to 3x
Production 300 sets	

1998 Donruss Preferred Precious Metals

Precious Metals is a 30-card partial parallel of the Preferred base set. Each card was printed on stock using real silver, gold or platinum. Fifty complete sets were produced.

		MT
Complete Set (30):		7000.
Common Player:		80.00
Production 50 sets		
1	Ken Griffey Jr.	700.00
2	Frank Thomas	600.00
3	Cal Ripken Jr.	500.00
4	Alex Rodriguez	400.00
5	Greg Maddux	400.00
6	Mike Piazza	400.00
7	Chipper Jones	400.00
8	Tony Gwynn	350.00
9	Derek Jeter	350.00
10	Jeff Bagwell	300.00
11	Juan Gonzalez	350.00
12	Nomar Garciaparra	400.00
13	Andruw Jones	200.00
14	Hideo Nomo	175.00
15	Roger Clemens	300.00
16	Mark McGwire	600.00
17	Scott Rolen	200.00
18	Barry Bonds	150.00
19	Darin Erstad	125.00
20	Kenny Lofton	150.00
21	Mo Vaughn	150.00
22	Ivan Rodriguez	150.00
23	Randy Johnson	100.00
24	Paul Molitor	125.00
25	Jose Cruz Jr.	200.00
26	Paul Konerko	125.00
27	Todd Helton	150.00
28	Ben Grieve	250.00
29	Travis Lee	250.00
30	Mark Kotsay	80.00

1998 Donruss Preferred Tins

Donruss Preferred was packaged in collectible tins. Each tin contained five cards and featured one of 24 players on the top. Silver (numbered to 999) and gold (199) parallel tins were also produced and included in hobby-only boxes. The hobby boxes were actually large tins that held 24 tin packs. The 24 tin boxes came in green (numbered to 999) and gold (199) versions. Five-card retail packs came in one of 12 double-wide tins featuring two players on the top.

		MT
Complete Set (26):		20.00
Common Player:		.50
1	Todd Helton	.75
2	Ben Grieve	1.00
3	Cal Ripken Jr.	2.00
4	Alex Rodriguez	1.50
5	Greg Maddux	1.50
6	Mike Piazza	1.50
7	Chipper Jones	1.50
8	Travis Lee	1.50
9	Derek Jeter	1.25
10	Jeff Bagwell	1.00
11	Juan Gonzalez	1.25
12	Mark McGwire	2.00
13	Hideo Nomo	.75
14	Roger Clemens	1.00
15	Andruw Jones	.75
16	Paul Molitor	.50
17	Vladimir Guerrero	.75
18	Jose Cruz Jr.	1.50
19	Nomar Garciaparra	1.50
20	Scott Rolen	1.00
21	Ken Griffey Jr.	2.50
22	Larry Walker	.50
25	Frank Thomas	2.00
26	Tony Gwynn	1.25

1998 Donruss Preferred Tins Gold

All 24 tins in Donruss Preferred were available in gold versions. These tins were sequentially numbered to 199 sets.

	MT
Complete Gold Set (26):	300.00
Common Gold Tin:	5.00
Golds:	10x to 20x
Production 199 sets	
Silver & Green:	4x to 8x
Production 999 sets	

1998 Donruss Preferred Title Waves

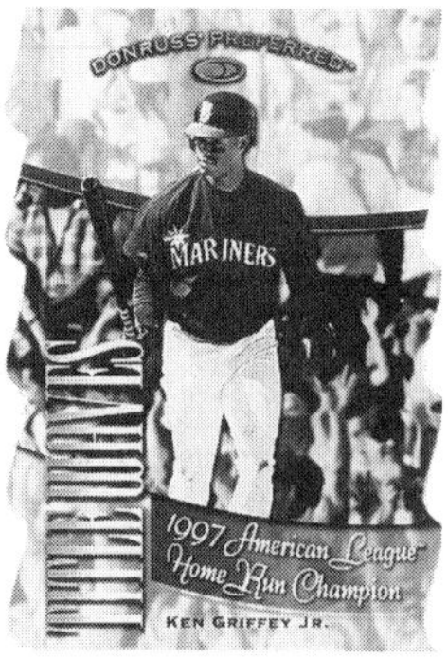

This 30-card set features players who won awards or titles between 1993-1997. Printed on plastic stock, each card is sequentially numbered to the year the player won the award. The card fronts feature the Title Waves logo, a color player photo in front of a background of fans and the name of the award the player won.

		MT
Complete Set (30):		700.00
Common Player:		8.00
#'d to year award was won		
1	Nomar Garciaparra	40.00
2	Scott Rolen	25.00
3	Roger Clemens	30.00
4	Gary Sheffield	8.00
5	Jeff Bagwell	30.00
6	Cal Ripken Jr.	50.00
7	Frank Thomas	50.00
8	Ken Griffey Jr.	70.00
9	Larry Walker	10.00
10	Derek Jeter	35.00
11	Juan Gonzalez	35.00
12	Bernie Williams	12.00
13	Andruw Jones	25.00
14	Andy Pettitte	12.00
15	Ivan Rodriguez	15.00
16	Alex Rodriguez	40.00
17	Mark McGwire	80.00
18	Andres Galarraga	10.00
19	Hideo Nomo	15.00
20	Mo Vaughn	15.00
21	Randy Johnson	12.00
22	Chipper Jones	40.00
23	Greg Maddux	40.00
24	Manny Ramirez	15.00
25	Tony Gwynn	35.00
26	Albert Belle	15.00
27	Kenny Lofton	15.00
28	Mike Piazza	40.00
29	Paul Molitor	12.00
30	Barry Bonds	15.00

1998 Donruss Studio

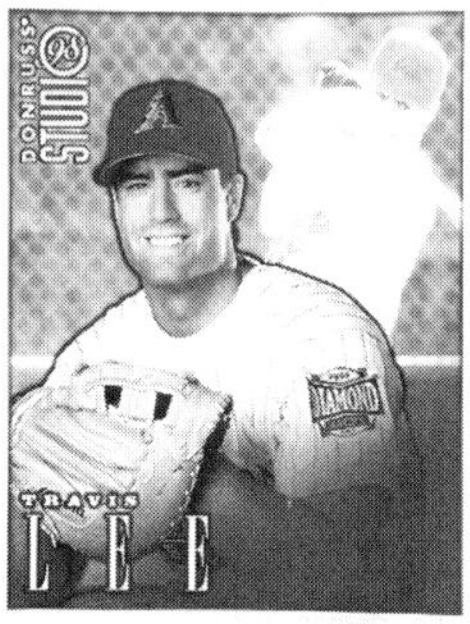

The Donruss Studio base set consists of 220 regular-sized cards and 36 8-x-10 portraits. The base cards feature a posed photo with an action shot in the background, surrounded by a white border. Silver Studio Proofs (numbered to 1,000) and Gold Studio Proofs (300) parallel the regular-size base set. Inserts included Freeze Frame, Hit Parade and Masterstrokes.

		MT
Complete Set (220):		35.00
Common Player:		.15
Wax Box:		50.00
1	Tony Clark	.40
2	Jose Cruz Jr.	.75
3	Ivan Rodriguez	.75
4	Mo Vaughn	.75
5	Kenny Lofton	.75
6	Will Clark	.25
7	Barry Larkin	.25
8	Jay Bell	.15
9	Kevin Young	.15
10	Francisco Cordova	.15
11	Justin Thompson	.15
12	Paul Molitor	.50
13	Jeff Bagwell	1.25
14	Jose Canseco	.30
15	Scott Rolen	1.00
16	Wilton Guerrero	.15
17	Shannon Stewart	.15
18	Hideki Irabu	.50
19	Michael Tucker	.15
20	Joe Carter	.15
21	Gabe Alvarez	.15
22	Ricky Ledee	.40
23	Karim Garcia	.15
24	Eli Marrero	.15
25	Scott Elarton	.15
26	Mario Valdez	.15
27	Ben Grieve	1.00
28	Paul Konerko	.40
29	*Esteban Yan*	.25
30	Esteban Loaiza	.15
31	Delino DeShields	.15
32	Bernie Williams	.50
33	Joe Randa	.15
34	Randy Johnson	.50
35	Brett Tomko	.15
36	*Todd Erdos*	.25
37	Bobby Higginson	.15
38	Jason Kendall	.15
39	Ray Lankford	.15
40	Mark Grace	.30
41	Andy Pettitte	.50
42	Alex Rodriguez	2.00
43	Hideo Nomo	.50
44	Sammy Sosa	1.50
45	J.T. Snow	.15
46	Jason Varitek	.25
47	Vinny Castilla	.15
48	Neifi Perez	.15
49	Todd Walker	.15
50	Mike Cameron	.15
51	Jeffrey Hammonds	.15
52	Deivi Cruz	.15
53	Brian Hunter	.15
54	Al Martin	.15
55	Ron Coomer	.15
56	Chan Ho Park	.15
57	Pedro Martinez	.40
58	Darin Erstad	.75
59	Albert Belle	.75
60	Nomar Garciaparra	2.00
61	Tony Gwynn	1.50
62	Mike Piazza	2.00
63	Todd Helton	.75
64	David Ortiz	.40
65	Todd Dunwoody	.15
66	Orlando Cabrera	.15
67	Ken Cloude	.15
68	Andy Benes	.25
69	Mariano Rivera	.25
70	Cecil Fielder	.25
71	Brian Jordan	.15
72	Darryl Kile	.15
73	Reggie Jefferson	.15
74	Shawn Estes	.15
75	Bobby Bonilla	.15
76	Denny Neagle	.25
77	Robin Ventura	.25
78	Omar Vizquel	.15
79	Craig Biggio	.30
80	Moises Alou	.25
81	Garret Anderson	.15
82	Eric Karros	.25
83	Dante Bichette	.30
84	Charles Johnson	.15
85	Rusty Greer	.15
86	Travis Fryman	.15
87	Fernando Tatis	.25
88	Wilson Alvarez	.15
89	Carl Pavano	.15
90	Brian Rose	.15
91	Geoff Jenkins	.15
92	*Magglio Ordonez*	.75
93	David Segui	.15
94	David Cone	.25
95	John Smoltz	.15
96	Jim Thome	.50
97	Gary Sheffield	.40
98	Barry Bonds	.75
99	Andres Galarraga	.40
100	Brad Fullmer	.40
101	Bobby Estalella	.15
102	Enrique Wilson	.15
103	*Frank Catalanotto*	.20
104	*Mike Lowell*	.40
105	Kevin Orie	.15
106	Matt Morris	.15
107	Pokey Reese	.15
108	Shawn Green	.15
109	Tony Womack	.15
110	Ken Caminiti	.25
111	Roberto Alomar	.50
112	Ken Griffey Jr.	3.00
113	Cal Ripken Jr.	2.50
114	Lou Collier	.15
115	Larry Walker	.40
116	Fred McGriff	.30
117	Jim Edmonds	.25
118	Edgar Martinez	.15
119	Matt Williams	.40
120	Ismael Valdes	.15
121	Bartolo Colon	.15
122	Jeff Cirillo	.15
123	*Steve Woodard*	.25
124	*Kevin Millwood*	1.00
125	Derrick Gibson	.15
126	Jacob Cruz	.15
127	Russell Branyan	.15
128	Sean Casey	.40
129	Derrek Lee	.15
130	Paul O'Neill	.25
131	Brad Radke	.15
132	Kevin Appier	.15
133	John Olerud	.25
134	Alan Benes	.25
135	Todd Greene	.15
136	*Carlos Mendoza*	.25
137	Wade Boggs	.30
138	Jose Guillen	.25
139	Tino Martinez	.30
140	Aaron Boone	.15
141	Abraham Nunez	.15
142	Preston Wilson	.15
143	Randall Simon	.20
144	Dennis Reyes	.15
145	Mark Kotsay	.30
146	Richard Hidalgo	.15
147	Travis Lee	2.00
148	*Hanley Frias*	.15
149	Ruben Rivera	.15
150	Rafael Medina	.15
151	Dave Nilsson	.15
152	Curt Schilling	.25
153	Brady Anderson	.15
154	Carlos Delgado	.15
155	Jason Giambi	.15
156	Pat Hentgen	.15
157	Tom Glavine	.25

158 Ryan Klesko .30
159 Chipper Jones 2.00
160 Juan Gonzalez 1.50
161 Mark McGwire 4.00
162 Vladimir Guerrero .75
163 Derek Jeter 1.50
164 Manny Ramirez .75
165 Mike Mussina .60
166 Rafael Palmeiro .30
167 Henry Rodriguez .15
168 Jeff Suppan .15
169 Eric Milton .15
170 Scott Spiezio .15
171 Wilson Delgado .15
172 Bubba Trammell .15
173 Ellis Burks .15
174 Jason Dickson .15
175 Butch Huskey .15
176 Edgardo Alfonzo .15
177 Eric Young .15
178 Marquis Grissom .15
179 Lance Johnson .15
180 Kevin Brown .25
181 Sandy Alomar Jr. .25
182 Todd Hundley .15
183 Rondell White .25
184 Javier Lopez .25
185 Damian Jackson .15
186 Raul Mondesi .40
187 Rickey Henderson .25
188 David Justice .40
189 Jay Buhner .30
190 Jaret Wright 1.00
191 Miguel Tejada .40
192 Ron Wright .15
193 Livan Hernandez .15
194 A.J. Hinch .50
195 Richie Sexson .15
196 Bob Abreu .15
197 Luis Castillo .15
198 Michael Coleman .15
199 Greg Maddux 2.00
200 Frank Thomas 2.50
201 Andruw Jones .75
202 Roger Clemens 1.25
203 Tim Salmon .40
204 Chuck Knoblauch .40
205 Wes Helms .15
206 Juan Encarnacion .15
207 Russ Davis .15
208 John Valentin .15
209 Tony Saunders .15
210 Mike Sweeney .15
211 Steve Finley .15
212 *David Dellucci* .50
213 Edgar Renteria .15
214 Jeremi Gonzalez .15
215 Checklist (Jeff Bagwell) .60
216 Checklist (Mike Piazza) 1.00
217 Checklist (Greg Maddux) 1.00
218 Checklist (Cal Ripken Jr.) 1.25
219 Checklist (Frank Thomas) 1.25
220 Checklist (Ken Griffey Jr.) 1.50

1998 Donruss Studio Silver Proofs

This parallel set included all 220 cards in Studio Baseball. Cards were identified by a silver holographic strip around the outside of the card. Silver versions were limited to 1,000 sets.

	MT
Silver Stars:	8x to 12x
Yng Stars & RCs:	5x to 10x
Production 1,000 sets	

1998 Donruss Studio Gold Proofs

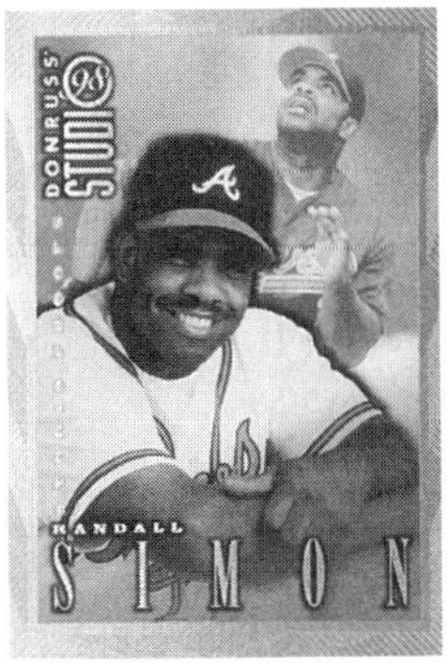

Gold Proofs is a parallel of the 220-card base set. The cards feature gold holo-foil treatments and are sequentially numbered to 300.

	MT
Common Player:	5.00
Semistars:	25.00
Production 300 sets	

1 Tony Clark 30.00
2 Jose Cruz Jr. 40.00
3 Ivan Rodriguez 50.00
4 Mo Vaughn 50.00
5 Kenny Lofton 50.00
6 Will Clark 25.00
7 Barry Larkin 25.00
8 Jay Bell 5.00
9 Kevin Young 5.00
10 Francisco Cordova 5.00
11 Justin Thompson 5.00
12 Paul Molitor 40.00
13 Jeff Bagwell 75.00
14 Jose Canseco 25.00
15 Scott Rolen 60.00
16 Wilton Guerrero 5.00
17 Shannon Stewart 5.00
18 Hideki Irabu 25.00
19 Michael Tucker 5.00
20 Joe Carter 10.00
21 Gabe Alvarez 5.00
22 Ricky Ledee 15.00
23 Karim Garcia 5.00
24 Eli Marrero 5.00
25 Scott Elarton 5.00
26 Mario Valdez 5.00
27 Ben Grieve 60.00
28 Paul Konerko 15.00
29 *Esteban Yan* 5.00
30 Esteban Loaiza 5.00
31 Delino DeShields 5.00
32 Bernie Williams 40.00
33 Joe Randa 5.00
34 Randy Johnson 35.00
35 Brett Tomko 5.00
36 Todd Erdos 5.00
37 Bobby Higginson 5.00
38 Jason Kendall 5.00
39 Ray Lankford 5.00
40 Mark Grace 25.00
41 Andy Pettitte 35.00
42 Alex Rodriguez 120.00
43 Hideo Nomo 40.00
44 Sammy Sosa 75.00
45 J.T. Snow 5.00
46 Jason Varitek 5.00
47 Vinny Castilla 15.00
48 Neifi Perez 5.00
49 Todd Walker 5.00
50 Mike Cameron 5.00
51 Jeffrey Hammonds 5.00
52 Deivi Cruz 5.00
53 Brian Hunter 5.00
54 Al Martin 5.00
55 Ron Coomer 5.00
56 Chan Ho Park 15.00
57 Pedro Martinez 40.00
58 Darin Erstad 50.00
59 Albert Belle 50.00
60 Nomar Garciaparra 120.00
61 Tony Gwynn 100.00
62 Mike Piazza 120.00
63 Todd Helton 30.00
64 David Ortiz 15.00
65 Todd Dunwoody 5.00
66 Orlando Cabrera 5.00
67 Ken Cloude 5.00
68 Andy Benes 15.00
69 Mariano Rivera 15.00
70 Cecil Fielder 15.00
71 Brian Jordan 15.00
72 Darryl Kile 5.00
73 Reggie Jefferson 5.00
74 Shawn Estes 5.00
75 Bobby Bonilla 15.00
76 Denny Neagle 15.00
77 Robin Ventura 15.00
78 Omar Vizquel 5.00
79 Craig Biggio 20.00
80 Moises Alou 15.00
81 Garret Anderson 5.00
82 Eric Karros 15.00
83 Dante Bichette 25.00
84 Charles Johnson 15.00
85 Rusty Greer 5.00
86 Travis Fryman 5.00
87 Fernando Tatis 15.00
88 Wilson Alvarez 5.00
89 Carl Pavano 5.00
90 Brian Rose 5.00
91 Geoff Jenkins 5.00
92 Magglio Ordonez 25.00
93 David Segui 5.00
94 David Cone 15.00
95 John Smoltz 15.00
96 Jim Thome 40.00
97 Gary Sheffield 25.00
98 Barry Bonds 50.00
99 Andres Galarraga 25.00
100 Brad Fullmer 25.00
101 Bobby Estalella 5.00
102 Enrique Wilson 5.00
103 Frank Catalanotto 5.00
104 Mike Lowell 5.00
105 Kevin Orie 5.00
106 Matt Morris 5.00
107 Pokey Reese 5.00
108 Shawn Green 5.00
109 Tony Womack 5.00
110 Ken Caminiti 15.00
111 Roberto Alomar 40.00
112 Ken Griffey Jr. 200.00
113 Cal Ripken Jr. 150.00
114 Lou Collier 5.00
115 Larry Walker 30.00
116 Fred McGriff 20.00
117 Jim Edmonds 15.00
118 Edgar Martinez 5.00
119 Matt Williams 25.00
120 Ismael Valdes 5.00
121 Bartolo Colon 5.00
122 Jeff Cirillo 5.00
123 Steve Woodard 5.00
124 *Kevin Millwood* 40.00
125 Derrick Gibson 5.00
126 Jacob Cruz 5.00
127 Russell Branyan 5.00
128 Sean Casey 15.00
129 Derrek Lee 5.00
130 Paul O'Neill 15.00
131 Brad Radke 5.00
132 Kevin Appier 5.00
133 John Olerud 15.00
134 Alan Benes 15.00
135 Todd Greene 5.00
136 Carlos Mendoza 5.00
137 Wade Boggs 25.00
138 Jose Guillen 15.00
139 Tino Martinez 25.00
140 Aaron Boone 5.00
141 Abraham Nunez 5.00
142 Preston Wilson 5.00
143 Randall Simon 5.00
144 Dennis Reyes 5.00
145 Mark Kotsay 15.00
146 Richard Hidalgo 5.00
147 Travis Lee 120.00
148 Hanley Frias 5.00
149 Ruben Rivera 5.00
150 Rafael Medina 5.00
151 Dave Nilsson 5.00
152 Curt Schilling 15.00
153 Brady Anderson 5.00
154 Carlos Delgado 15.00
155 Jason Giambi 5.00
156 Pat Hentgen 5.00
157 Tom Glavine 15.00
158 Ryan Klesko 25.00
159 Chipper Jones 120.00
160 Juan Gonzalez 100.00
161 Mark McGwire 220.00
162 Vladimir Guerrero 50.00
163 Derek Jeter 100.00
164 Manny Ramirez 50.00
165 Mike Mussina 40.00
166 Rafael Palmeiro 25.00
167 Henry Rodriguez 5.00
168 Jeff Suppan 5.00
169 Eric Milton 5.00
170 Scott Spiezio 5.00
171 Wilson Delgado 5.00
172 Bubba Trammell 5.00
173 Ellis Burks 5.00
174 Jason Dickson 5.00
175 Butch Huskey 5.00
176 Edgardo Alfonzo 5.00
177 Eric Young 5.00
178 Marquis Grissom 5.00
179 Lance Johnson 5.00
180 Kevin Brown 15.00
181 Sandy Alomar Jr. 15.00
182 Todd Hundley 5.00
183 Rondell White 15.00
184 Javier Lopez 15.00
185 Damian Jackson 5.00
186 Raul Mondesi 20.00
187 Rickey Henderson 15.00
188 David Justice 25.00
189 Jay Buhner 20.00
190 Jaret Wright 50.00
191 Miguel Tejada 15.00
192 Ron Wright 5.00
193 Livan Hernandez 5.00
194 A.J. Hinch 5.00
195 Richie Sexson 5.00
196 Bob Abreu 5.00
197 Luis Castillo 5.00
198 Michael Coleman 5.00
199 Greg Maddux 120.00
200 Frank Thomas 150.00
201 Andruw Jones 50.00
202 Roger Clemens 75.00
203 Tim Salmon 25.00
204 Chuck Knoblauch 25.00
205 Wes Helms 5.00
206 Juan Encarnacion 5.00
207 Russ Davis 5.00
208 John Valentin 5.00
209 Tony Saunders 5.00
210 Mike Sweeney 5.00
211 Steve Finley 5.00
212 David Dellucci 5.00
213 Edgar Renteria 5.00
214 Jeremi Gonzalez 5.00
215 Checklist (Jeff Bagwell) 40.00
216 Checklist (Mike Piazza) 60.00
217 Checklist (Greg Maddux) 60.00
218 Checklist (Cal Ripken Jr.) 75.00
219 Checklist (Frank Thomas) 75.00
220 Checklist (Ken Griffey Jr.) 100.00

1998 Donruss Studio Autographs

Three top rookies (Ben Grieve, Travis Lee and Todd Helton) signed a number of 8-x-10s for this product. Lee signed 500 while the other two autographed 1,000 each.

	MT
Travis Lee (500):	100.00
Todd Helton (1,000):	40.00
Ben Grieve (1,000):	50.00

1998 Donruss Studio Freeze Frame

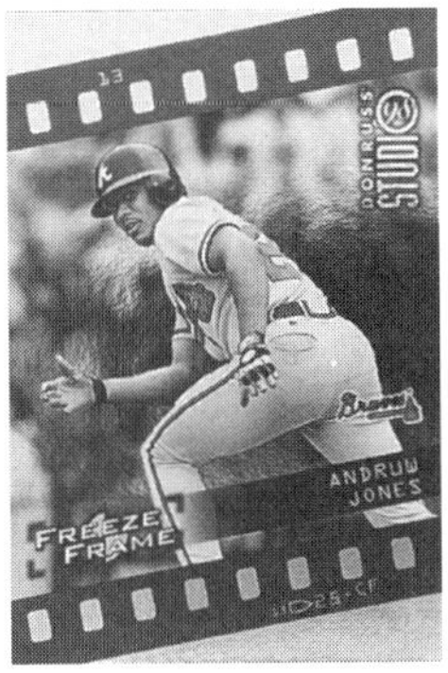

Freeze Frame is a 30-card insert sequentially numbered to 5,000. The cards are designed to look like a piece of film with a color action photo. The first 500 of each card are die-cut.

	MT
Complete Set (30):	325.00
Common Player:	4.00
Production 4,500 sets	
Die-Cuts:	2x to 4x
Production 500 sets	

1 Ken Griffey Jr. 30.00
2 Derek Jeter 15.00
3 Ben Grieve 10.00
4 Cal Ripken Jr. 25.00
5 Alex Rodriguez 20.00
6 Greg Maddux 20.00
7 David Justice 6.00
8 Mike Piazza 20.00
9 Chipper Jones 20.00
10 Randy Johnson 6.00
11 Jeff Bagwell 12.00
12 Nomar Garciaparra 20.00
13 Andruw Jones 8.00
14 Frank Thomas 25.00
15 Scott Rolen 10.00
16 Barry Bonds 8.00
17 Kenny Lofton 8.00
18 Ivan Rodriguez 8.00
19 Chuck Knoblauch 6.00
20 Jose Cruz Jr. 8.00
21 Bernie Williams 6.00
22 Tony Gwynn 15.00
23 Juan Gonzalez 15.00
24 Gary Sheffield 4.00
25 Roger Clemens 12.00
26 Travis Lee 25.00
27 Brad Fullmer 8.00
28 Tim Salmon 6.00
29 Raul Mondesi 4.00
30 Roberto Alomar 6.00

1998 Donruss Studio Hit Parade

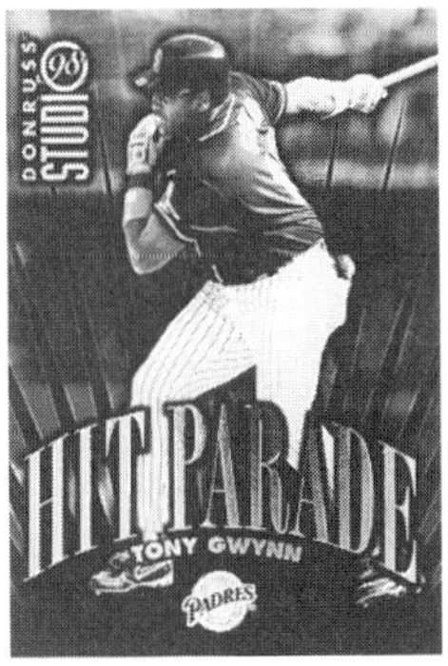

These 20 cards are printed on micro-etched foil board. This set honors baseball's top hitters and is sequentially numbered to 5,000.

	MT
Complete Set (20):	140.00
Common Player:	4.00
Production 5,000 sets	

1 Tony Gwynn 12.00
2 Larry Walker 4.00
3 Mike Piazza 15.00
4 Frank Thomas 20.00
5 Manny Ramirez 6.00
6 Ken Griffey Jr. 25.00
7 Todd Helton 6.00
8 Vladimir Guerrero 6.00
9 Albert Belle 6.00
10 Jeff Bagwell 10.00
11 Juan Gonzalez 12.00
12 Jim Thome 4.00
13 Scott Rolen 8.00
14 Tino Martinez 4.00
15 Mark McGwire 30.00
16 Barry Bonds 6.00
17 Tony Clark 4.00
18 Mo Vaughn 6.00
19 Darin Erstad 6.00
20 Paul Konerko 4.00

1998 Donruss Studio Masterstrokes

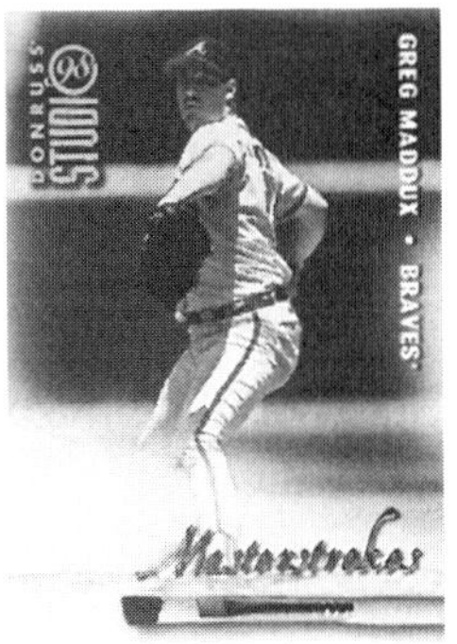

Printed on a canvas-like material, these 20 cards are numbered to 1,000.

	MT
Complete Set (20):	850.00
Common Player:	15.00
Production 1,000 sets	

1 Travis Lee 65.00
2 Kenny Lofton 25.00
3 Mo Vaughn 25.00
4 Ivan Rodriguez 25.00
5 Roger Clemens 40.00
6 Mark McGwire 120.00
7 Hideo Nomo 20.00
8 Andruw Jones 25.00
9 Nomar Garciaparra 60.00
10 Juan Gonzalez 50.00
11 Jeff Bagwell 40.00
12 Derek Jeter 50.00
13 Tony Gwynn 50.00
14 Chipper Jones 60.00
15 Mike Piazza 60.00
16 Greg Maddux 60.00
17 Alex Rodriguez 60.00
18 Cal Ripken Jr. 80.00
19 Frank Thomas 80.00
20 Ken Griffey Jr. 100.00

1998 Donruss Studio 8x10 Portraits

One Studio 8-x-10 was included in each pack. The cards were blown-up versions of the regular-size base cards, which were inserted seven per pack. The large portraits are paralleled in the Gold Proofs set, which adds gold holo-foil to the cards. Gold Proofs are numbered to 300.

	MT
Complete Set (36):	50.00
Common Player:	.50
Inserted 1:1	

1 Travis Lee 4.00
2 Todd Helton 1.25
3 Ben Grieve 1.50
4 Paul Konerko .50
5 Jeff Bagwell 2.00
6 Derek Jeter 2.50
7 Ivan Rodriguez 1.50
8 Cal Ripken Jr. 4.00

9	Mike Piazza	3.00
10	Chipper Jones	3.00
11	Frank Thomas	4.00
12	Tony Gwynn	2.50
13	Nomar Garciaparra	3.00
14	Juan Gonzalez	2.50
15	Greg Maddux	3.00
16	Hideo Nomo	1.00
17	Scott Rolen	1.50
18	Barry Bonds	1.50
19	Ken Griffey Jr.	5.00
20	Alex Rodriguez	3.00
21	Roger Clemens	2.00
22	Mark McGwire	6.00
23	Jose Cruz Jr.	1.50
24	Andruw Jones	1.50
25	Tino Martinez	.50
26	Mo Vaughn	1.50
27	Vladimir Guerrero	1.50
28	Tony Clark	1.00
29	Andy Pettitte	1.00
30	Jaret Wright	1.50
31	Paul Molitor	1.00
32	Darin Erstad	1.50
33	Larry Walker	.50
34	Chuck Knoblauch	.50
35	Barry Larkin	.50
36	Kenny Lofton	1.50

1998 Donruss Studio 8x10 Portraits Gold Proofs

This parallel of the 8-x-10 base set adds gold holo-foil treatments to the 36 cards, which are sequentially numbered to 300.

		MT
Common Player:		25.00
Unlisted Stars:		40.00
Production 300 sets		
1	Travis Lee	100.00
2	Todd Helton	40.00
3	Ben Grieve	50.00
4	Paul Konerko	25.00
5	Jeff Bagwell	60.00
6	Derek Jeter	75.00
7	Ivan Rodriguez	40.00
8	Cal Ripken Jr.	120.00
9	Mike Piazza	100.00
10	Chipper Jones	100.00
11	Frank Thomas	120.00
12	Tony Gwynn	75.00
13	Nomar Garciaparra	100.00
14	Juan Gonzalez	75.00
15	Greg Maddux	100.00
16	Hideo Nomo	30.00
17	Scott Rolen	50.00
18	Barry Bonds	40.00
19	Ken Griffey Jr.	150.00
20	Alex Rodriguez	100.00
21	Roger Clemens	60.00
22	Mark McGwire	175.00
23	Jose Cruz Jr.	40.00
24	Andruw Jones	40.00
25	Tino Martinez	25.00
26	Mo Vaughn	40.00
27	Vladimir Guerrero	40.00
28	Tony Clark	25.00
29	Andy Pettitte	25.00
30	Jaret Wright	40.00
31	Paul Molitor	40.00
32	Darin Erstad	40.00
33	Larry Walker	25.00
34	Chuck Knoblauch	25.00
35	Barry Larkin	25.00
36	Kenny Lofton	40.00

1998 Donruss Studio Sony MLB 99

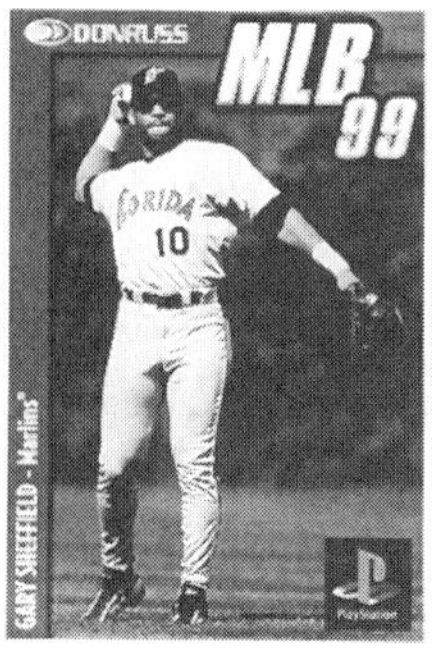

Twenty Sony MLB '99 sweepstakes cards were inserted one per two Studio packs. The fronts feature a color action shot and the backs have sweepstakes rules and a MLB '99 tip.

		MT
Complete Set (20):		10.00
Common Player:		.25
1	Cal Ripken Jr.	2.00
2	Nomar Garciaparra	1.50
3	Barry Bonds	.60
4	Mike Mussina	.50
5	Pedro Martinez	.40
6	Derek Jeter	1.25
7	Andruw Jones	.60
8	Kenny Lofton	.60
9	Gary Sheffield	.25
10	Raul Mondesi	.25
11	Jeff Bagwell	.75
12	Tim Salmon	.25
13	Tom Glavine	.25
14	Ben Grieve	.75
15	Matt Williams	.25
16	Juan Gonzalez	1.25
17	Mark McGwire	3.00
18	Bernie Williams	.40
19	Andres Galarraga	.25
20	Jose Cruz Jr.	.40

1998 Finest

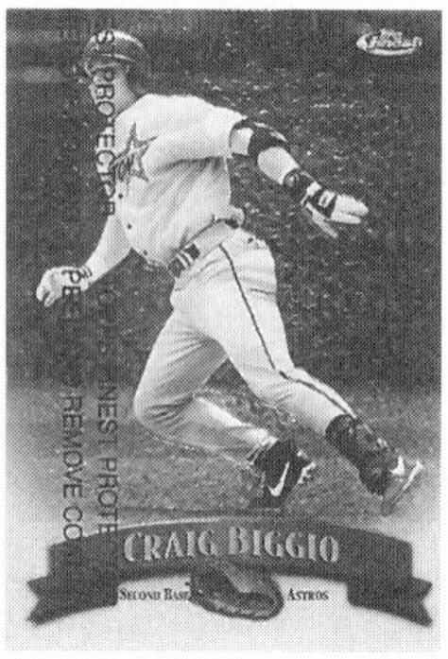

Finest dropped its three-tiered format in 1998 and produced a 275-card set with a thicker 26-point stock, with 150 cards in Series I and 125 in Series II. The catch in 1998 was that each card arrived in Protector, No-Protector, Protector Refractor and No-Protector Refractor versions. Six-card packs sold for a suggested retail price of $5. Finest also included insert sets for the first time since 1995. Included in Series I packs were Centurions, Mystery Finest and Power Zone inserts. Series II had Mystery Finest, Stadium Stars and The Man. Throughout Series I and II, Finest Protector cards are considered base cards, while No-Protector are inserted one per two packs (HTA odds 1:1), No-Protector Refractors are seeded 1:24 packs (HTA odds 1:10) and Finest Refractors are seeded 1:12 packs (HTA odds 1:5).

		MT
Complete Set (275):		90.00
Complete Series I Set (150):		50.00
Complete Series II Set (125):		40.00
Common Player:		.25
No-Protector:		2x to 4x
Inserted 1:2		
Wax Box:		100.00
1	Larry Walker	1.00
2	Andruw Jones	1.75
3	Ramon Martinez	.25
4	Geronimo Berroa	.25
5	David Justice	.60
6	Rusty Greer	.40
7	Chad Ogea	.25
8	Tom Goodwin	.25
9	Tino Martinez	.75
10	Jose Guillen	.50
11	Jeffrey Hammonds	.25
12	Brian McRae	.25
13	Jeremi Gonzalez	.25
14	Craig Counsell	.25
15	Mike Piazza	4.00
16	Greg Maddux	4.00
17	Todd Greene	.25
18	Rondell White	.50
19	Kirk Rueter	.25
20	Tony Clark	1.00
21	Brad Radke	.25
22	Jaret Wright	3.00
23	Carlos Delgado	.25
24	Dustin Hermanson	.50
25	Gary Sheffield	.75
26	Jose Canseco	.50
27	Kevin Young	.25
28	David Wells	.25
29	Mariano Rivera	.50
30	Reggie Sanders	.25
31	Mike Cameron	.50
32	Bobby Witt	.25
33	Kevin Orie	.25
34	Royce Clayton	.25
35	Edgar Martinez	.40
36	Neifi Perez	.25
37	Kevin Appier	.25
38	Darryl Hamilton	.25
39	Michael Tucker	.25
40	Roger Clemens	2.50
41	Carl Everett	.25
42	Mike Sweeney	.25
43	Pat Meares	.25
44	Brian Giles	.25
45	Matt Morris	.25
46	Jason Dickson	.25
47	Rich Loiselle	.25
48	Joe Girardi	.25
49	Steve Trachsel	.25
50	Ben Grieve	3.00
51	Jose Vizcaino	.25
52	Hideki Irabu	1.00
53	J.T. Snow	.25
54	Mike Hampton	.25
55	Dave Nilsson	.25
56	Alex Fernandez	.25
57	Brett Tomko	.25
58	Wally Joyner	.25
59	Kelvim Escobar	.25
60	Roberto Alomar	1.25
61	Todd Jones	.25
62	Paul O'Neill	.50
63	Jamie Moyer	.25
64	Mark Wohlers	.25
65	Jose Cruz Jr.	2.50
66	Troy Percival	.25
67	Rick Reed	.25
68	Will Clark	.50
69	Jamey Wright	.25
70	Mike Mussina	1.25
71	David Cone	.50
72	Ryan Klesko	.75
73	Scott Hatteberg	.25
74	James Baldwin	.25
75	Tony Womack	.25
76	Carlos Perez	.25
77	Charles Nagy	.25
78	Jeromy Burnitz	.25
79	Shane Reynolds	.25
80	Cliff Floyd	.25
81	Jason Kendall	.25
82	Chad Curtis	.25
83	Matt Karchner	.25
84	Ricky Bottalico	.25
85	Sammy Sosa	4.00
86	Javy Lopez	.40
87	Jeff Kent	.25
88	Shawn Green	.25
89	Devon White	.25
90	Tony Gwynn	3.00
91	Bob Tewksbury	.25
92	Derek Jeter	4.00
93	Eric Davis	.25
94	Jeff Fassero	.25
95	Denny Neagle	.50
96	Ismael Valdes	.25
97	Tim Salmon	1.00
98	Mark Grudzielanek	.25
99	Curt Schilling	.75
100	Ken Griffey Jr.	6.00
101	Edgardo Alfonzo	.25
102	Vinny Castilla	.25
103	Jose Rosado	.25
104	Scott Erickson	.25
105	Alan Benes	.50
106	Shannon Stewart	.25
107	Delino DeShields	.25
108	Mark Loretta	.25
109	Todd Hundley	.50
110	Chuck Knoblauch	.75
111	Quinton McCracken	.25
112	F.P. Santangelo	.25
113	Gerald Williams	.25
114	Omar Vizquel	.25
115	John Valentin	.25
116	Damion Easley	.25
117	Matt Lawton	.25
118	Jim Thome	1.00
119	Sandy Alomar	.50
120	Albert Belle	1.50
121	Chris Stynes	.25
122	Butch Huskey	.25
123	Shawn Estes	.25
124	Terry Adams	.25
125	Ivan Rodriguez	1.50
126	Ron Gant	.50
127	John Mabry	.25
128	Jeff Shaw	.25
129	Jeff Montgomery	.25
130	Justin Thompson	.50
131	Livan Hernandez	.50
132	Ugueth Urbina	.25
133	Doug Glanville	.25
134	Troy O'Leary	.25
135	Cal Ripken Jr.	5.00
136	Quilvio Veras	.25
137	Pedro Astacio	.25
138	Willie Greene	.25
139	Lance Johnson	.25
140	Nomar Garciaparra	4.00
141	Jose Offerman	.25
142	Scott Rolen	2.50
143	Derek Bell	.25
144	Johnny Damon	.25
145	Mark McGwire	8.00
146	Chan Ho Park	.50
147	Edgar Renteria	.25
148	Eric Young	.25
149	Craig Biggio	.50
150	Checklist 1-150	.25
151	Frank Thomas	5.00
152	John Wetteland	.25
153	Mike Lansing	.25
154	Pedro Martinez	1.00
155	Rico Brogna	.25
156	Kevin Brown	.40
157	Alex Rodriguez	3.00
158	Wade Boggs	.50
159	Richard Hidalgo	.25
160	Mark Grace	.50
161	Jose Mesa	.25
162	John Olerud	.50
163	Tim Belcher	.25
164	Chuck Finley	.25
165	Brian Hunter	.25
166	Joe Carter	.40
167	Stan Javier	.25
168	Jay Bell	.25
169	Ray Lankford	.25
170	John Smoltz	.40
171	Ed Sprague	.25
172	Jason Giambi	.25
173	Todd Walker	.50
174	Paul Konerko	.75
175	Rey Ordonez	.25
176	Dante Bichette	.50
177	Bernie Williams	1.00
178	Jon Nunnally	.25
179	Rafael Palmeiro	.75
180	Jay Buhner	.50
181	Devon White	.25
182	Jeff D'Amico	.25
183	Walt Weiss	.25
184	Scott Spiezio	.25
185	Moises Alou	.50
186	Carlos Baerga	.25
187	Todd Zeile	.25
188	Gregg Jefferies	.25
189	Mo Vaughn	1.50
190	Terry Steinbach	.25
191	Ray Durham	.25
192	Robin Ventura	.40
193	Jeff Reed	.25
194	Ken Caminiti	.50
195	Eric Karros	.40
196	Wilson Alvarez	.25
197	Gary Gaetti	.25
198	Andres Galarraga	.75
199	Alex Gonzalez	.25
200	Garret Anderson	.25
201	Andy Benes	.25
202	Harold Baines	.25
203	Ron Coomer	.25
204	Dean Palmer	.25
205	Reggie Jefferson	.25
206	John Burkett	.25
207	Jermaine Allensworth	.25
208	Bernard Gilkey	.25
209	Jeff Bagwell	2.00
210	Kenny Lofton	1.50
211	Bobby Jones	.25
212	Bartolo Colon	.50
213	Jim Edmonds	.40
214	Pat Hentgen	.25
215	Matt Williams	.75
216	Bob Abreu	.25
217	Jorge Posada	.25
218	Marty Cordova	.25
219	Ken Hill	.25
220	Steve Finley	.25
221	Jeff King	.25
222	Quinton McCracken	.25
223	Matt Stairs	.25
224	Darin Erstad	1.50
225	Fred McGriff	.50
226	Marquis Grissom	.25
227	Doug Glanville	.25
228	Tom Glavine	.40
229	John Franco	.25
230	Darren Bragg	.25
231	Barry Larkin	.50
232	Trevor Hoffman	.25
233	Brady Anderson	.25
234	Al Martin	.25
235	B.J. Surhoff	.25
236	Ellis Burks	.25
237	Randy Johnson	1.00
238	Mark Clark	.25
239	Tony Saunders	.25
240	Hideo Nomo	.75
241	Brad Fullmer	.50
242	Chipper Jones	4.00
243	Jose Valentin	.25
244	Manny Ramirez	1.50
245	Derrek Lee	.25
246	Jimmy Key	.25
247	Tim Naehring	.25
248	Bobby Higginson	.25
249	Charles Johnson	.25
250	Chili Davis	.25
251	Tom Gordon	.25
252	Mike Lieberthal	.25
253	Billy Wagner	.25
254	Juan Guzman	.25
255	Todd Stottlemyre	.25
256	Brian Jordan	.25
257	Barry Bonds	1.50
258	Dan Wilson	.25
259	Paul Molitor	1.00
260	Juan Gonzalez	3.00
261	Francisco Cordova	.25
262	Cecil Fielder	.50
263	Travis Lee	4.00
264	Kevin Tapani	.25
265	Raul Mondesi	.50
266	Travis Fryman	.25
267	Armando Benitez	.25
268	Pokey Reese	.25
269	Rick Aguilera	.25
270	Andy Pettitte	1.00
271	Jose Vizcaino	.25
272	Kerry Wood	8.00
273	Vladimir Guerrero	1.50
274	John Smiley	.25
275	Checklist 151-275	.25

1998 Finest Refractors

All 275 cards from Finest Series I and II were available in both Protector Refractor versions and No-Protector Refractor versions. Protector versions were seeded one per 12 packs, while No-Protector versions were every 24 packs.

	MT
Star Refractors:	10x to 20x
Yng Stars & RCs:	8x to 15x
Inserted 1:12	
No protector Refract:	15x to 30x
Inserted 1:24	

1998 Finest Centurions

Centurions was a 20-card insert found only Series I hobby (1:153) and Home Team Advantage packs (1:71). The theme of the insert to top players who will lead the game into the next century. Each card is sequentially numbered on the back to 500, while Refractor versions are numbered to 75.

		MT
Complete Set (20):		900.00
Common Player:		25.00
Production 500 sets		
Refractors:		2x to 3x
Production 75 sets		
C1	Andruw Jones	30.00
C2	Vladimir Guerrero	30.00
C3	Nomar Garciaparra	75.00
C4	Scott Rolen	40.00
C5	Ken Griffey Jr.	120.00
C6	Jose Cruz Jr.	25.00
C7	Barry Bonds	30.00
C8	Mark McGwire	140.00
C9	Juan Gonzalez	60.00
C10	Jeff Bagwell	40.00
C11	Frank Thomas	90.00
C12	Paul Konerko	20.00
C13	Alex Rodriguez	120.00
C14	Mike Piazza	75.00
C15	Travis Lee	90.00
C16	Chipper Jones	75.00
C17	Larry Walker	20.00
C18	Mo Vaughn	30.00
C19	Livan Hernandez	15.00
C20	Jaret Wright	40.00

1998 Finest Mystery Finest

This 50-card insert was seeded one per 36 Series I packs and one per 15 HTA packs. The set included 20 top players, each matched on double sided card with three other players and once with himself. Each side of the card is printed on a chromium finish and arrives with a black opaque protector. Mystery Finest inserts are numbered with a "M" prefix. Refractor versions were seeded one per 64 packs (HTA odds 1:15).

		MT
Complete Set (50):		1000.
Common Player:		8.00
Inserted 1:36		
Refractors:		1.5x to 2.5x
Inserted 1:144		
M1	Frank Thomas, Ken Griffey Jr.	60.00
M2	Frank Thomas, Mike Piazza	50.00

M3	Frank Thomas, Mark McGwire	50.00
M4	Frank Thomas, Frank Thomas	50.00
M5	Ken Griffey Jr., Mike Piazza	50.00
M6	Ken Griffey Jr., Mark McGwire	60.00
M7	Ken Griffey Jr., Ken Griffey Jr.	65.00
M8	Mike Piazza, Mark McGwire	40.00
M9	Mike Piazza, Mike Piazza	40.00
M10	Mark McGwire, Mark McGwire	60.00
M11	Nomar Garciaparra, Jose Cruz Jr.	25.00
M12	Nomar Garciaparra, Derek Jeter	40.00
M13	Nomar Garciaparra, Andruw Jones	35.00
M14	Nomar Garciaparra, Nomar Garciaparra	40.00
M15	Jose Cruz Jr., Derek Jeter	25.00
M16	Jose Cruz Jr., Andruw Jones	25.00
M17	Jose Cruz Jr., Jose Cruz Jr.	25.00
M18	Derek Jeter, Andruw Jones	35.00
M19	Derek Jeter, Derek Jeter	40.00
M20	Andruw Jones, Andruw Jones	20.00
M21	Cal Ripken Jr., Tony Gwynn	50.00
M22	Cal Ripken Jr., Barry Bonds	45.00
M23	Cal Ripken Jr., Greg Maddux	50.00
M24	Cal Ripken Jr., Cal Ripken Jr.	50.00
M25	Tony Gwynn, Barry Bonds	30.00
M26	Tony Gwynn, Greg Maddux	35.00
M27	Tony Gwynn, Tony Gwynn	30.00
M28	Barry Bonds, Greg Maddux	35.00
M29	Barry Bonds, Barry Bonds	20.00
M30	Greg Maddux, Greg Maddux	40.00
M31	Juan Gonzalez, Larry Walker	30.00
M32	Juan Gonzalez, Andres Galarraga	30.00
M33	Juan Gonzalez, Chipper Jones	35.00
M34	Juan Gonzalez, Juan Gonzalez	30.00
M35	Larry Walker, Andres Galarraga	15.00
M36	Larry Walker, Chipper Jones	20.00
M37	Larry Walker, Larry Walker	15.00
M38	Andres Galarraga, Chipper Jones	20.00
M39	Andres Galarraga, Andres Galarraga	10.00
M40	Chipper Jones, Chipper Jones	40.00
M41	Gary Sheffield, Sammy Sosa	25.00
M42	Gary Sheffield, Jeff Bagwell	20.00
M43	Gary Sheffield, Tino Martinez	15.00
M44	Gary Sheffield, Gary Sheffield	15.00
M45	Sammy Sosa, Jeff Bagwell	25.00
M46	Sammy Sosa, Tino Martinez	15.00
M47	Sammy Sosa, Sammy Sosa	15.00
M48	Jeff Bagwell, Tino Martinez	25.00
M49	Jeff Bagwell, Jeff Bagwell	25.00
M50	Tino Martinez, Tino Martinez	10.00

1998 Finest II Mystery Finest

Fifty more Mystery Finest inserts were seeded in Series II packs at a rate of one per 36 packs (HTA odds 1:15), with Refrators every 1:144 packs (HTA odds 1:64). As with Series I, 20 players are in the insert, with each player featured with three different players on the back or by himself on each side.

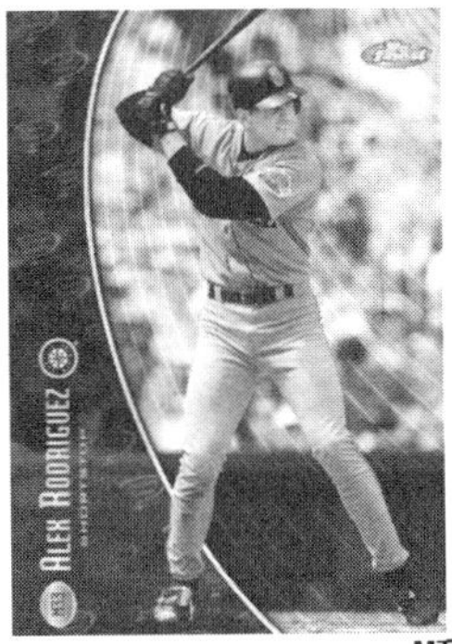

		MT
Complete Set (40):		1000.
Common Player:		6.00
Inserted 1:36		
Refractors:		1.5x to 3x
Inserted 1:144		
M1	Nomar Garciaparra, Frank Thomas	45.00
M2	Nomar Garciaparra, Albert Belle	40.00
M3	Nomar Garciaparra, Scott Rolen	40.00
M4	Frank Thomas, Albert Belle	45.00
M5	Frank Thomas, Scott Rolen	45.00
M6	Albert Belle, Scott Rolen	20.00
M7	Ken Griffey Jr., Jose Cruz	50.00
M8	Ken Griffey Jr., Alex Rodriguez	60.00
M9	Ken Griffey Jr., Roger Clemens	60.00
M10	Jose Cruz, Alex Rodriguez	35.00
M11	Jose Cruz, Roger Clemens	20.00
M12	Alex Rodriguez, Roger Clemens	40.00
M13	Mike Piazza, Barry Bonds	40.00
M14	Mike Piazza, Derek Jeter	40.00
M15	Mike Piazza, Bernie Williams	35.00
M16	Barry Bonds, Derek Jeter	30.00
M17	Barry Bonds, Bernie Williams	15.00
M18	Derek Jeter, Bernie Williams	25.00
M19	Mark McGwire, Jeff Bagwell	50.00
M20	Mark McGwire, Mo Vaughn	45.00
M21	Mark McGwire, Jim Thome	45.00
M22	Jeff Bagwell, Mo Vaughn	20.00
M23	Jeff Bagwell, Jim Thome	20.00
M24	Mo Vaughn, Jim Thome	15.00
M25	Juan Gonzalez, Travis Lee	35.00
M26	Juan Gonzalez, Ben Grieve	30.00
M27	Juan Gonzalez, Fred McGriff	25.00
M28	Travis Lee, Ben Grieve	35.00
M29	Travis Lee, Fred McGriff	30.00
M30	Ben Grieve, Fred McGriff	20.00
M31	Albert Belle, Albert Belle	15.00
M32	Scott Rolen, Scott Rolen	20.00
M33	Alex Rodriguez, Alex Rodriguez	40.00
M34	Roger Clemens, Roger Clemens	20.00
M35	Bernie Williams, Bernie Williams	10.00
M36	Mo Vaughn, Mo Vaughn	15.00
M37	Jim Thome, Jim Thome	10.00
M38	Travis Lee, Travis Lee	30.00
M39	Fred McGriff, Fred McGriff	6.00
M40	Ben Grieve, Ben Grieve	20.00

1998 Finest Oversize

Eight oversized cards were inserted into both Series I and Series II boxes as box toppers. The cards measure 3" x 5" and were inserted one per three boxes, with Refractor versions every six boxes. The oversized cards are similar to the regular-issed cards except for the numbering.

		MT
Complete Set (16):		180.00
Complete Series 1 (8):		120.00
Complete Series 2 (8):		75.00
Common Player:		5.00
Refractors:		1x to 2x
A1	Mark McGwire	25.00
A2	Cal Ripken Jr.	25.00
A3	Nomar Garciaparra	20.00
A4	Mike Piazza	20.00
A5	Greg Maddux	20.00
A6	Jose Cruz Jr.	8.00
A7	Roger Clemens	10.00
A8	Ken Griffey Jr.	30.00
B1	Frank Thomas	25.00
B2	Bernie Williams	6.00
B3	Randy Johnson	6.00
B4	Chipper Jones	20.00
B5	Manny Ramirez	8.00
B6	Barry Bonds	8.00
B7	Juan Gonzalez	15.00
B8	Jeff Bagwell	10.00

1998 Finest Power Zone

This Series I insert feature Topps' new printing technology which actually changes the color of the card depending on what angle you are viewing it from. This 20-card set was inserted one per 72 packs (HTA odds 1:32).

		MT
Complete Set (20):		500.00
Common Player:		10.00
Inserted 1:72 hobby packs		
P1	Ken Griffey Jr.	80.00
P2	Jeff Bagwell	35.00
P3	Jose Cruz Jr.	35.00
P4	Barry Bonds	20.00
P5	Mark McGwire	90.00
P6	Jim Thome	15.00
P7	Mo Vaughn	20.00
P8	Gary Sheffield	12.00
P9	Andres Galarraga	10.00
P10	Nomar Garciaparra	50.00
P11	Rafael Palmeiro	10.00
P12	Sammy Sosa	40.00
P13	Jay Buhner	10.00
P14	Tony Clark	15.00
P15	Mike Piazza	50.00
P16	Larry Walker	12.00
P17	Albert Belle	20.00
P18	Tino Martinez	12.00
P19	Juan Gonzalez	40.00
P20	Frank Thomas	70.00

1998 Finest Stadium Stars

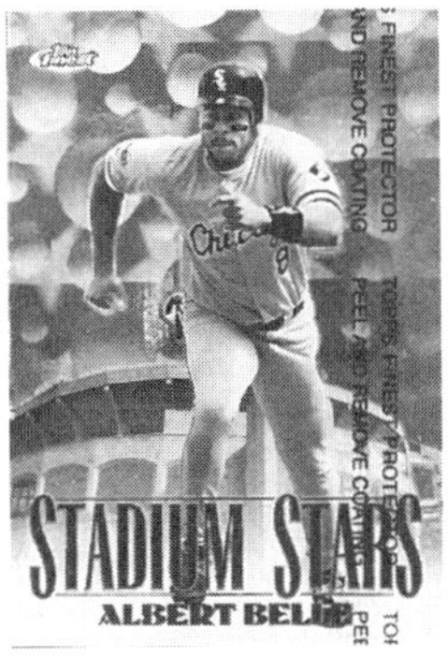

Stadium Stars was a 24-card insert that featured Topps' new lenticular holographic chromium technology. These were exclusive to Series II packs and carried an insertion rate of one per 72 packs (HTA odds 1:32).

		MT
Complete Set (24):		600.00
Common Player:		8.00
Inserted 1:72		
SS1	Ken Griffey Jr.	70.00
SS2	Alex Rodriguez	45.00
SS3	Mo Vaughn	18.00
SS4	Nomar Garciaparra	45.00
SS5	Frank Thomas	50.00
SS6	Albert Belle	18.00
SS7	Derek Jeter	35.00
SS8	Chipper Jones	45.00
SS9	Cal Ripken Jr.	50.00
SS10	Jim Thome	15.00
SS11	Mike Piazza	45.00
SS12	Juan Gonzalez	35.00
SS13	Jeff Bagwell	25.00
SS14	Sammy Sosa	40.00
SS15	Jose Cruz Jr.	15.00
SS16	Gary Sheffield	10.00
SS17	Larry Walker	12.00
SS18	Tony Gwynn	35.00
SS19	Mark McGwire	80.00
SS20	Barry Bonds	18.00
SS21	Tino Martinez	10.00
SS22	Manny Ramirez	18.00
SS23	Ken Caminiti	8.00
SS24	Andres Galarraga	10.00

1998 Finest The Man

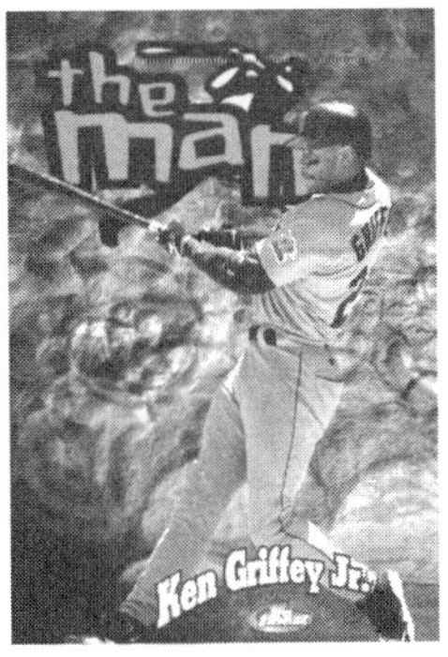

This 20-card insert featured the top players in baseball and was exlusive inserted into Series II packs. Regular versions were sequentially numbered to 500 and inserted one per 119 packs, while Refractor versions were numbered to 75 and inserted one per 793 packs.

		MT
Complete Set (20):		1000.
Common Player:		15.00
Production 500 sets		
Refractors:		2x to 3x
Production 75 sets		
TM1	Ken Griffey Jr.	125.00
TM2	Barry Bonds	30.00
TM3	Frank Thomas	90.00
TM4	Chipper Jones	75.00
TM5	Cal Ripken Jr.	90.00
TM6	Nomar Garciaparra	75.00
TM7	Mark McGwire	125.00
TM8	Mike Piazza	75.00
TM9	Derek Jeter	60.00
TM10	Alex Rodriguez	75.00
TM11	Jose Cruz Jr.	25.00
TM12	Larry Walker	15.00
TM13	Jeff Bagwell	40.00
TM14	Tony Gwynn	60.00
TM15	Travis Lee	40.00
TM16	Juan Gonzalez	60.00
TM17	Scott Rolen	40.00
TM18	Randy Johnson	25.00
TM19	Roger Clemens	40.00
TM20	Greg Maddux	75.00

1998 Flair Showcase Row 3

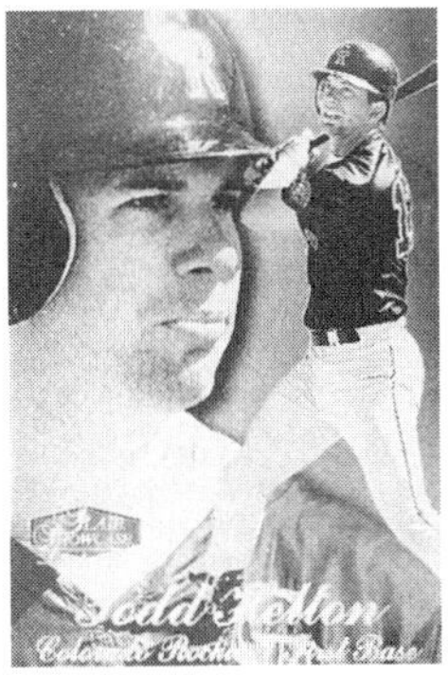

Row 3, or Flair, cards were considered the base cards of Flair Showcase. These featured a close-up shot of the player on the right side with an action shot on the right, all over a silver foil background. Flair (front)/Showtime (back) cards were inserted 1:.9 packs, Flair/Showstopper cards were inserted 1:1.1 packs, Flair/Showdown cards were inserted 1:1.5 packs and Flair/Showdown cards were inserted 1:2 packs.

		MT
Complete Set (120):		70.00
Common Player:		.25
Unlisted Stars:		1.00 to 2.00
1	Ken Griffey Jr.	10.00
2	Travis Lee	6.00
3	Frank Thomas	8.00
4	Ben Grieve	3.00
5	Nomar Garciaparra	6.00
6	Jose Cruz Jr.	2.00
7	Alex Rodriguez	6.00
8	Cal Ripken Jr.	8.00
9	Mark McGwire	12.00
10	Chipper Jones	6.00
11	Paul Konerko	1.50
12	Todd Helton	2.50
13	Greg Maddux	6.00
14	Derek Jeter	5.00
15	Jaret Wright	2.50
16	Livan Hernandez	.25
17	Mike Piazza	6.00
18	Juan Encarnacion	.25
19	Tony Gwynn	5.00
20	Scott Rolen	3.00
21	Roger Clemens	3.00
22	Tony Clark	1.50
23	Albert Belle	2.50
24	Mo Vaughn	2.50
25	Andruw Jones	2.50
26	Jason Dickson	.25
27	Fernando Tatis	.50
28	Ivan Rodriguez	2.50
29	Ricky Ledee	.50
30	Darin Erstad	2.50
31	Brian Rose	.25
32	*Magglio Ordonez*	2.50
33	Larry Walker	1.00
34	Bobby Higginson	.25
35	Chili Davis	.25
36	Barry Bonds	2.50
37	Vladimir Guerrero	2.50
38	Jeff Bagwell	3.00
39	Kenny Lofton	2.50
40	Ryan Klesko	.75
41	Mike Cameron	.25
42	Charles Johnson	.25
43	Andy Pettitte	1.50
44	Juan Gonzalez	5.00
45	Tim Salmon	1.00
46	Hideki Irabu	1.00
47	Paul Molitor	2.00
48	Edgar Renteria	.25
49	Manny Ramirez	2.50
50	Jim Edmonds	.50
51	Bernie Williams	2.00
52	Roberto Alomar	2.00
53	David Justice	.75
54	Rey Ordonez	.25
55	Ken Caminiti	.50
56	Jose Guillen	.50
57	Randy Johnson	1.50
58	Brady Anderson	.25
59	Hideo Nomo	1.50
60	Tino Martinez	1.00
61	John Smoltz	.50
62	Joe Carter	.50
63	Matt Williams	.75
64	Robin Ventura	.50
65	Barry Larkin	.75
66	Dante Bichette	.75
67	Travis Fryman	.25
68	Gary Sheffield	1.00
69	Eric Karros	.40
70	Matt Stairs	.25
71	Al Martin	.25
72	Jay Buhner	.75
73	Ray Lankford	.25
74	Carlos Delgado	.50
75	Edgardo Alfonzo	.25
76	Rondell White	.50
77	Chuck Knoblauch	.75
78	Raul Mondesi	.50
79	Johnny Damon	.25
80	Matt Morris	.25
81	Tom Glavine	.50
82	Kevin Brown	.50
83	Garret Anderson	.25
84	Mike Mussina	2.00
85	Pedro Martinez	1.50
86	Craig Biggio	.50
87	Darryl Kile	.25
88	Rafael Palmeiro	.75
89	Jim Thome	1.50
90	Andres Galarraga	1.00
91	Sammy Sosa	5.00
92	Willie Greene	.25
93	Vinny Castilla	.50
94	Justin Thompson	.25
95	Jeff King	.25
96	Jeff Cirillo	.25
97	Mark Grudzielanek	.25
98	Brad Radke	.25
99	John Olerud	.50
100	Curt Schilling	.50
101	Steve Finley	.25

102	J.T. Snow	.25
103	Edgar Martinez	.25
104	Wilson Alvarez	.25
105	Rusty Greer	.25
106	Pat Hentgen	.25
107	David Cone	.50
108	Fred McGriff	.50
109	Jason Giambi	.25
110	Tony Womack	.25
111	Bernard Gilkey	.25
112	Alan Benes	.50
113	Mark Grace	.75
114	Reggie Sanders	.25
115	Moises Alou	.50
116	John Jaha	.25
117	Henry Rodriguez	.25
118	Dean Palmer	.25
119	Mike Lieberthal	.25
120	Shawn Estes	.25

1998 Flair Showcase Row 2

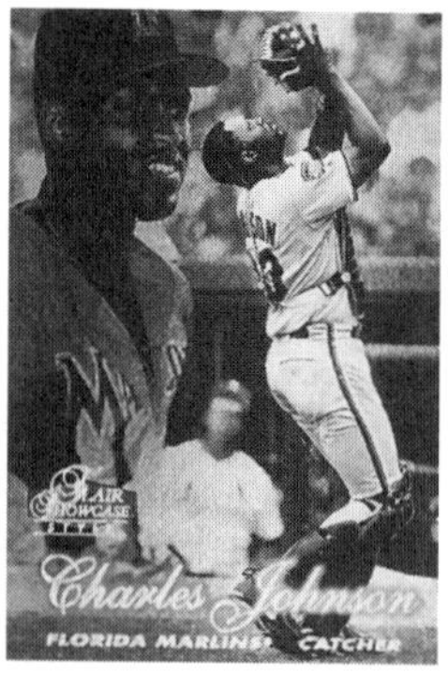

All 120 players were featured on Row 2, or Style cards in Flair Showcase. These were the second easiest type of card to pull from packs and pictured a still shot of the player on the right side with an action shot on the rest of the card. Style (front)/Showtime (back) cards were inserted one per 2.5 packs, Style/Showstopper cards were inserted one per three packs, Style/Showdown cards were inserted one per 3.5 packs and Style/Showpiece cards were inserted one per four packs.

		MT
Complete Set (120):		140.00
Common Player:		.50
Stars:		1x to 2x Row 3
1	Ken Griffey Jr.	20.00
2	Travis Lee	12.00
3	Frank Thomas	15.00
4	Ben Grieve	6.00
5	Nomar Garciaparra	12.00
6	Jose Cruz Jr.	4.00
7	Alex Rodriguez	12.00
8	Cal Ripken Jr.	15.00
9	Mark McGwire	25.00
10	Chipper Jones	12.00
11	Paul Konerko	2.50
12	Todd Helton	5.00
13	Greg Maddux	12.00
14	Derek Jeter	10.00
15	Jaret Wright	5.00
16	Livan Hernandez	.50
17	Mike Piazza	12.00
18	Juan Encarnacion	.50
19	Tony Gwynn	10.00
20	Scott Rolen	6.00
21	Roger Clemens	6.00
22	Tony Clark	2.50
23	Albert Belle	5.00
24	Mo Vaughn	5.00
25	Andruw Jones	5.00
26	Jason Dickson	.50
27	Fernando Tatis	1.00
28	Ivan Rodriguez	5.00
29	Ricky Ledee	1.00
30	Darin Erstad	5.00
31	Brian Rose	.50
32	Magglio Ordonez	5.00
33	Larry Walker	2.00
34	Bobby Higginson	.50
35	Chili Davis	.50
36	Barry Bonds	5.00
37	Vladimir Guerrero	5.00
38	Jeff Bagwell	6.00
39	Kenny Lofton	5.00
40	Ryan Klesko	1.50
41	Mike Cameron	.50
42	Charles Johnson	.50
43	Andy Pettitte	3.00
44	Juan Gonzalez	10.00
45	Tim Salmon	1.50
46	Hideki Irabu	2.00
47	Paul Molitor	4.00
48	Edgar Renteria	.50
49	Manny Ramirez	5.00
50	Jim Edmonds	.75
51	Bernie Williams	4.00
52	Roberto Alomar	4.00
53	David Justice	1.50
54	Rey Ordonez	.50
55	Ken Caminiti	.75
56	Jose Guillen	1.00
57	Randy Johnson	3.00
58	Brady Anderson	.50
59	Hideo Nomo	3.00
60	Tino Martinez	2.00
61	John Smoltz	.75
62	Joe Carter	.50
63	Matt Williams	1.50
64	Robin Ventura	.75
65	Barry Larkin	1.50
66	Dante Bichette	1.50
67	Travis Fryman	.50
68	Gary Sheffield	2.00
69	Eric Karros	.50
70	Matt Stairs	.50
71	Al Martin	.50
72	Jay Buhner	1.25
73	Ray Lankford	.50
74	Carlos Delgado	.50
75	Edgardo Alfonzo	.50
76	Rondell White	.75
77	Chuck Knoblauch	1.50
78	Raul Mondesi	.75
79	Johnny Damon	.50
80	Matt Morris	.50
81	Tom Glavine	.75
82	Kevin Brown	.75
83	Garret Anderson	.50
84	Mike Mussina	4.00
85	Pedro Martinez	3.00
86	Craig Biggio	.75
87	Darryl Kile	.50
88	Rafael Palmeiro	1.25
89	Jim Thome	3.00
90	Andres Galarraga	2.00
91	Sammy Sosa	10.00
92	Willie Greene	.50
93	Vinny Castilla	.75
94	Justin Thompson	.50
95	Jeff King	.50
96	Jeff Cirillo	.50
97	Mark Grudzielanek	.50
98	Brad Radke	.50
99	John Olerud	.75
100	Curt Schilling	.75
101	Steve Finley	.50
102	J.T. Snow	.50
103	Edgar Martinez	.50
104	Wilson Alvarez	.50
105	Rusty Greer	.50
106	Pat Hentgen	.50
107	David Cone	.75
108	Fred McGriff	.75
109	Jason Giambi	.50
110	Tony Womack	.50
111	Bernard Gilkey	.50
112	Alan Benes	.75
113	Mark Grace	1.25
114	Reggie Sanders	.50
115	Moises Alou	.75
116	John Jaha	.50
117	Henry Rodriguez	.50
118	Dean Palmer	.50
119	Mike Lieberthal	.50
120	Shawn Estes	.50

1998 Flair Showcase Row 1

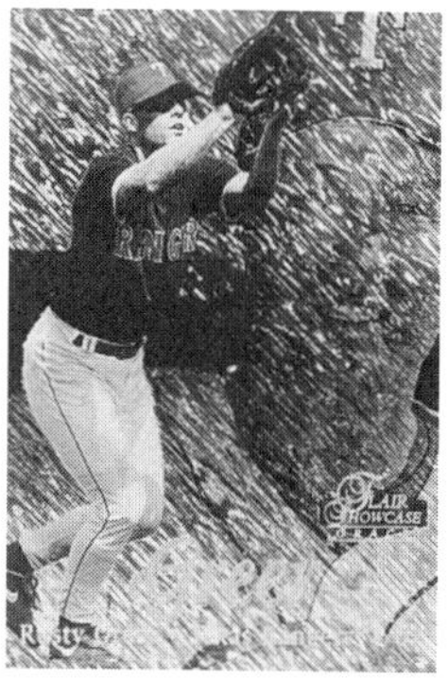

Row 1, also referred to as Grace, was the second most difficult type of card to pull from Flair Showcase. All 120 players were featured on this design that contained a foil patterned background. Grace (front)/ Showtime (back) cards were seeded one per six packs, Grace/Showstopper cards were seeded one per 10 packs, Grace/Showdown cards were seeded one per 16 packs and Grace/Showpiece cards were seeded one per 24 packs.

		MT
Commons (1-30):		3.00
Stars (1-30):		2.5x to 5x Row 3
Commons (31-60):		2.00
Stars (31-60):		3x to 6x Row 3
Commons (61-90):		1.00
Stars (61-90):		1.5x to 2.5x Row 3
Commons (91-120):		1.00
Stars (91-120):		2x to 4x Row 3
1	Ken Griffey Jr.	50.00
2	Travis Lee	30.00
3	Frank Thomas	40.00
4	Ben Grieve	15.00
5	Nomar Garciaparra	30.00
6	Jose Cruz Jr.	8.00
7	Alex Rodriguez	30.00
8	Cal Ripken Jr.	40.00
9	Mark McGwire	60.00
10	Chipper Jones	30.00
11	Paul Konerko	6.00
12	Todd Helton	12.00
13	Greg Maddux	30.00
14	Derek Jeter	25.00
15	Jaret Wright	12.00
16	Livan Hernandez	3.00
17	Mike Piazza	30.00
18	Juan Encarnacion	3.00
19	Tony Gwynn	25.00
20	Scott Rolen	15.00
21	Roger Clemens	15.00
22	Tony Clark	6.00
23	Albert Belle	12.00
24	Mo Vaughn	12.00
25	Andruw Jones	12.00
26	Jason Dickson	3.00
27	Fernando Tatis	4.00
28	Ivan Rodriguez	12.00
29	Ricky Ledee	5.00
30	Darin Erstad	12.00
31	Brian Rose	2.00
32	Magglio Ordonez	12.00
33	Larry Walker	6.00
34	Bobby Higginson	2.00
35	Chili Davis	2.00
36	Barry Bonds	15.00
37	Vladimir Guerrero	15.00
38	Jeff Bagwell	20.00
39	Kenny Lofton	15.00
40	Ryan Klesko	4.00
41	Mike Cameron	2.00
42	Charles Johnson	2.00
43	Andy Pettitte	8.00
44	Juan Gonzalez	30.00
45	Tim Salmon	6.00
46	Hideki Irabu	6.00
47	Paul Molitor	12.00
48	Edgar Renteria	2.00
49	Manny Ramirez	15.00
50	Jim Edmonds	3.00
51	Bernie Williams	12.00
52	Roberto Alomar	12.00
53	David Justice	4.00
54	Rey Ordonez	2.00
55	Ken Caminiti	3.00
56	Jose Guillen	3.00
57	Randy Johnson	8.00
58	Brady Anderson	2.00
59	Hideo Nomo	8.00
60	Tino Martinez	6.00
61	John Smoltz	1.50
62	Joe Carter	1.50
63	Matt Williams	2.00
64	Robin Ventura	1.00
65	Barry Larkin	2.00
66	Dante Bichette	2.00
67	Travis Fryman	1.00
68	Gary Sheffield	2.00
69	Eric Karros	1.00
70	Matt Stairs	1.00
71	Al Martin	1.00
72	Jay Buhner	2.00
73	Ray Lankford	1.00
74	Carlos Delgado	1.50
75	Edgardo Alfonzo	1.00
76	Rondell White	1.50
77	Chuck Knoblauch	2.00
78	Raul Mondesi	1.50
79	Johnny Damon	1.00
80	Matt Morris	1.00
81	Tom Glavine	1.50
82	Kevin Brown	1.50
83	Garret Anderson	1.00
84	Mike Mussina	6.00
85	Pedro Martinez	4.00
86	Craig Biggio	1.50
87	Darryl Kile	1.00
88	Rafael Palmeiro	2.00
89	Jim Thome	4.00
90	Andres Galarraga	3.00
91	Sammy Sosa	25.00
92	Willie Greene	1.00
93	Vinny Castilla	1.50
94	Justin Thompson	1.00
95	Jeff King	1.00
96	Jeff Cirillo	1.00
97	Mark Grudzielanek	1.00
98	Brad Radke	1.00
99	John Olerud	1.50
100	Curt Schilling	1.50
101	Steve Finley	1.00
102	J.T. Snow	1.00
103	Edgar Martinez	1.00
104	Wilson Alvarez	1.00
105	Rusty Greer	1.00
106	Pat Hentgen	1.00
107	David Cone	1.50
108	Fred McGriff	1.50
109	Jason Giambi	1.00
110	Tony Womack	1.00
111	Bernard Gilkey	1.00
112	Alan Benes	1.50
113	Mark Grace	3.00
114	Reggie Sanders	1.00
115	Moises Alou	1.50
116	John Jaha	1.00
117	Henry Rodriguez	1.00
118	Dean Palmer	1.00
119	Mike Lieberthal	1.00
120	Shawn Estes	1.00

1998 Flair Showcase Row 0

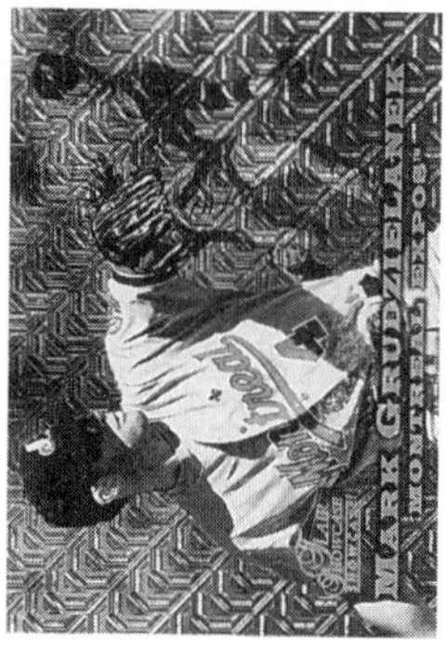

Row 0 was the most difficult of the four Rows to obtain from packs. Each of these were printed on a horizontal format and featured a prismatic foil background. The first 30 cards were numbered to 250, 30-60 were numbered to 500, 61-90 were numbered to 1,000 and 91-120 were numbered to 2,000.

		MT
Common Player (1-30):		20.00
Production 250 sets		
Common Player (31-60):		6.00
Production 500 sets		
Common Player (61-90):		4.00
Production 1,000 sets		
Common Player (91-120):		2.00
Production 2,000 sets		
1	Ken Griffey Jr.	250.00
2	Travis Lee	125.00
3	Frank Thomas	180.00
4	Ben Grieve	75.00
5	Nomar Garciaparra	150.00
6	Jose Cruz Jr.	50.00
7	Alex Rodriguez	150.00
8	Cal Ripken Jr.	180.00
9	Mark McGwire	300.00
10	Chipper Jones	150.00
11	Paul Konerko	35.00
12	Todd Helton	60.00
13	Greg Maddux	150.00
14	Derek Jeter	125.00
15	Jaret Wright	60.00
16	Livan Hernandez	20.00
17	Mike Piazza	150.00
18	Juan Encarnacion	20.00
19	Tony Gwynn	125.00
20	Scott Rolen	75.00
21	Roger Clemens	85.00
22	Tony Clark	45.00
23	Albert Belle	60.00
24	Mo Vaughn	60.00
25	Andruw Jones	60.00
26	Jason Dickson	20.00
27	Fernando Tatis	25.00
28	Ivan Rodriguez	60.00
29	Ricky Ledee	40.00
30	Darin Erstad	60.00
31	Brian Rose	6.00
32	Magglio Ordonez	30.00
33	Larry Walker	20.00
34	Bobby Higginson	6.00
35	Chili Davis	6.00
36	Barry Bonds	40.00
37	Vladimir Guerrero	40.00
38	Jeff Bagwell	50.00
39	Kenny Lofton	40.00
40	Ryan Klesko	15.00
41	Mike Cameron	6.00
42	Charles Johnson	6.00
43	Andy Pettitte	25.00
44	Juan Gonzalez	75.00
45	Tim Salmon	20.00
46	Hideki Irabu	20.00
47	Paul Molitor	30.00
48	Edgar Renteria	6.00
49	Manny Ramirez	40.00
50	Jim Edmonds	6.00
51	Bernie Williams	30.00
52	Roberto Alomar	30.00
53	David Justice	15.00
54	Rey Ordonez	6.00
55	Ken Caminiti	12.00
56	Jose Guillen	12.00
57	Randy Johnson	25.00
58	Brady Anderson	6.00
59	Hideo Nomo	25.00
60	Tino Martinez	20.00
61	John Smoltz	8.00
62	Joe Carter	8.00
63	Matt Williams	12.00
64	Robin Ventura	6.00
65	Barry Larkin	12.00
66	Dante Bichette	12.00
67	Travis Fryman	4.00
68	Gary Sheffield	15.00
69	Eric Karros	6.00
70	Matt Stairs	4.00
71	Al Martin	4.00
72	Jay Buhner	12.00
73	Ray Lankford	4.00
74	Carlos Delgado	6.00
75	Edgardo Alfonzo	4.00
76	Rondell White	6.00
77	Chuck Knoblauch	12.00
78	Raul Mondesi	8.00
79	Johnny Damon	4.00
80	Matt Morris	4.00
81	Tom Glavine	8.00
82	Kevin Brown	8.00
83	Garret Anderson	4.00
84	Mike Mussina	25.00
85	Pedro Martinez	20.00
86	Craig Biggio	10.00
87	Darryl Kile	4.00
88	Rafael Palmeiro	12.00
89	Jim Thome	20.00
90	Andres Galarraga	15.00
91	Sammy Sosa	40.00
92	Willie Greene	2.00
93	Vinny Castilla	4.00
94	Justin Thompson	2.00
95	Jeff King	2.00
96	Jeff Cirillo	2.00
97	Mark Grudzielanek	2.00
98	Brad Radke	2.00
99	John Olerud	4.00
100	Curt Schilling	4.00
101	Steve Finley	2.00
102	J.T. Snow	2.00
103	Edgar Martinez	2.00
104	Wilson Alvarez	2.00
105	Rusty Greer	2.00
106	Pat Hentgen	2.00
107	David Cone	4.00
108	Fred McGriff	4.00
109	Jason Giambi	2.00
110	Tony Womack	2.00
111	Bernard Gilkey	2.00
112	Alan Benes	4.00
113	Mark Grace	8.00
114	Reggie Sanders	2.00
115	Moises Alou	4.00
116	John Jaha	2.00
117	Henry Rodriguez	2.00
118	Dean Palmer	2.00
119	Mike Lieberthal	2.00
120	Shawn Estes	2.00

1998 Flair Showcase Legacy

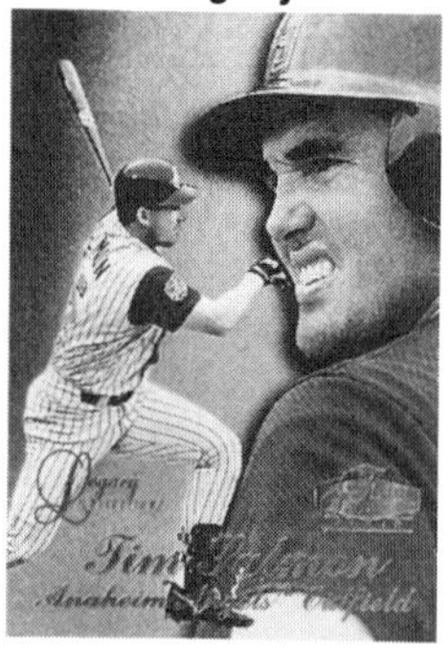

Legacy Collection and Legacy Masterpieces both paralleled all 480 cards in the Flair Showcase set. Each Legacy Collection card displayed the player's name in black plate laminated on the back, with the cards sequential numbering to 100 in gold foil. Each Masterpiece arrived with special foil overstamps on the front and "The Only 1 of 1 Masterpiece" stamped on the back.

		MT
Common Player:		10.00
Semistars:		40.00
Each Player Has Four Different Cards		
Production 100 sets		
1	Ken Griffey Jr.	600.00
2	Travis Lee	300.00
3	Frank Thomas	450.00
4	Ben Grieve	200.00
5	Nomar Garciaparra	400.00
6	Jose Cruz Jr.	120.00
7	Alex Rodriguez	400.00
8	Cal Ripken Jr.	450.00
9	Mark McGwire	600.00
10	Chipper Jones	400.00
11	Paul Konerko	50.00
12	Todd Helton	125.00
13	Greg Maddux	400.00
14	Derek Jeter	300.00
15	Jaret Wright	150.00
16	Livan Hernandez	10.00
17	Mike Piazza	400.00
18	Juan Encarnacion	10.00
19	Tony Gwynn	300.00
20	Scott Rolen	180.00
21	Roger Clemens	200.00
22	Tony Clark	100.00
23	Albert Belle	150.00
24	Mo Vaughn	150.00
25	Andruw Jones	150.00
26	Jason Dickson	10.00
27	Fernando Tatis	20.00
28	Ivan Rodriguez	150.00
29	Ricky Ledee	40.00
30	Darin Erstad	150.00
31	Brian Rose	10.00
32	Magglio Ordonez	100.00
33	Larry Walker	75.00
34	Bobby Higginson	10.00
35	Chili Davis	10.00
36	Barry Bonds	150.00
37	Vladimir Guerrero	150.00
38	Jeff Bagwell	200.00
39	Kenny Lofton	150.00
40	Ryan Klesko	40.00
41	Mike Cameron	10.00
42	Charles Johnson	10.00
43	Andy Pettitte	100.00
44	Juan Gonzalez	300.00
45	Tim Salmon	75.00
46	Hideki Irabu	75.00
47	Paul Molitor	125.00
48	Edgar Renteria	10.00
49	Manny Ramirez	150.00
50	Jim Edmonds	40.00
51	Bernie Williams	125.00
52	Roberto Alomar	125.00
53	David Justice	50.00
54	Rey Ordonez	10.00
55	Ken Caminiti	40.00
56	Jose Guillen	40.00
57	Randy Johnson	100.00
58	Brady Anderson	10.00
59	Hideo Nomo	100.00
60	Tino Martinez	75.00
61	John Smoltz	40.00
62	Joe Carter	40.00
63	Matt Williams	50.00
64	Robin Ventura	25.00
65	Barry Larkin	50.00
66	Dante Bichette	50.00
67	Travis Fryman	25.00
68	Gary Sheffield	75.00
69	Eric Karros	25.00
70	Matt Stairs	10.00
71	Al Martin	10.00
72	Jay Buhner	50.00
73	Ray Lankford	10.00
74	Carlos Delgado	25.00
75	Edgardo Alfonzo	10.00
76	Rondell White	25.00
77	Chuck Knoblauch	50.00
78	Raul Mondesi	40.00
79	Johnny Damon	10.00
80	Matt Morris	10.00
81	Tom Glavine	40.00
82	Kevin Brown	40.00
83	Garret Anderson	10.00
84	Mike Mussina	125.00
85	Pedro Martinez	100.00
86	Craig Biggio	40.00
87	Darryl Kile	10.00
88	Rafael Palmeiro	50.00
89	Jim Thome	100.00
90	Andres Galarraga	75.00
91	Sammy Sosa	300.00
92	Willie Greene	10.00
93	Vinny Castilla	25.00
94	Justin Thompson	10.00
95	Jeff King	10.00
96	Jeff Cirillo	10.00
97	Mark Grudzielanek	10.00
98	Brad Radke	10.00
99	John Olerud	25.00
100	Curt Schilling	25.00
101	Steve Finley	10.00
102	J.T. Snow	10.00
103	Edgar Martinez	10.00
104	Wilson Alvarez	10.00
105	Rusty Greer	10.00
106	Pat Hentgen	10.00
107	David Cone	25.00
108	Fred McGriff	40.00
109	Jason Giambi	10.00
110	Tony Womack	10.00
111	Bernard Gilkey	10.00
112	Alan Benes	25.00
113	Mark Grace	50.00
114	Reggie Sanders	10.00
115	Moises Alou	25.00
116	John Jaha	10.00
117	Henry Rodriguez	10.00
118	Dean Palmer	10.00
119	Mike Lieberthal	10.00
120	Shawn Estes	10.00

1998 Flair Showcase Wave of the Future

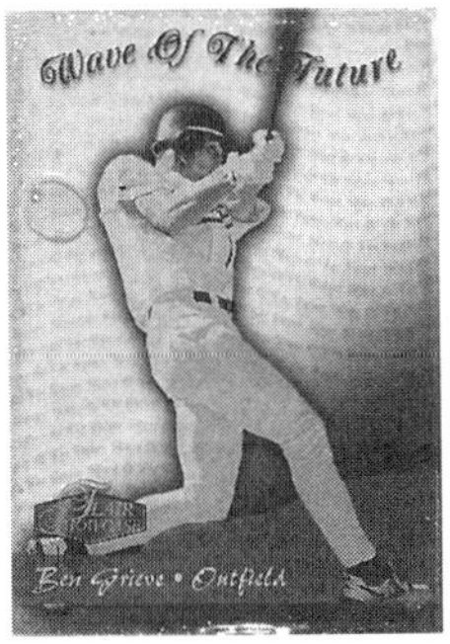

Twelve up-and-coming players whose minor league stats and Major League potential are displayed in Wave of the Future. The cards actually contain a plastic card inside a plastic covering that is filled with vegetable oil inside. These were inserted one per 20 packs and are numbered with a "WF" prefix.

	MT
Complete Set (12):	50.00
Common Player:	2.00
Inserted 1:20	
WF1 Travis Lee	20.00
WF2 Todd Helton	6.00
WF3 Ben Grieve	15.00
WF4 Juan Encarnacion	2.00
WF5 Brad Fullmer	4.00
WF6 Ruben Rivera	2.00
WF7 Paul Konerko	4.00
WF8 Derrek Lee	2.00
WF9 Mike Lowell	2.00
WF10Magglio Ordonez	6.00
WF11Rich Butler	4.00
WF12Eli Marrero	2.00

1998 Flair Showcase Perfect 10

Perfect 10 features 10 of the game's most popular players on a silk-screen technology design. The cards were serial numbered to 10 on the back and were inserted into packs of Flair Showcase. Due to production being limited to only 10 sets, these are unable to be priced at this time.

		MT
Complete Set (10):		
Common Player:		
Production 10 sets		
1	Ken Griffey Jr.	—
2	Cal Ripken Jr.	—
3	Frank Thomas	—
4	Mike Piazza	—
5	Greg Maddux	—
6	Nomar Garciaparra	—
7	Mark McGwire	—
8	Scott Rolen	—
9	Alex Rodriguez	—
10	Roger Clemens	—

1998 Fleer

Fleer was issued in two series in 1998, with 350 cards in Series I and 250 in Series II. Each card featured a borderless color action shot, with backs containing player information. Subsets in Series I included Smoke 'N Heat (301-310), Golden Memories (311-320) and Tale of the Tape (321-340). Golden Memories (1:6 packs) and Tale of the Tape (1:4) were shortprinted. Series II subsets included 25 Unforgetable Moments (571-595). Inserts in Series I were Vintage '63, Vintage '63 Classic, Decade of Excellence, Decade of Excellence Rare Traditions, Diamond Ink, Diamond Standouts, Lumber Company, Power Game, Rookie Sensations and Zone. Inserts in Series II include: Vintage '63, Vintage '63 Classic, Promising Forecast, In the Clutch, Mickey Mantle: Monumental Moments, Mickey Mantle: Monumental Moments Gold Edition, Diamond Tribute and Diamond Ink. Card No. 7 in the regular set pictures Mickey Mantle.

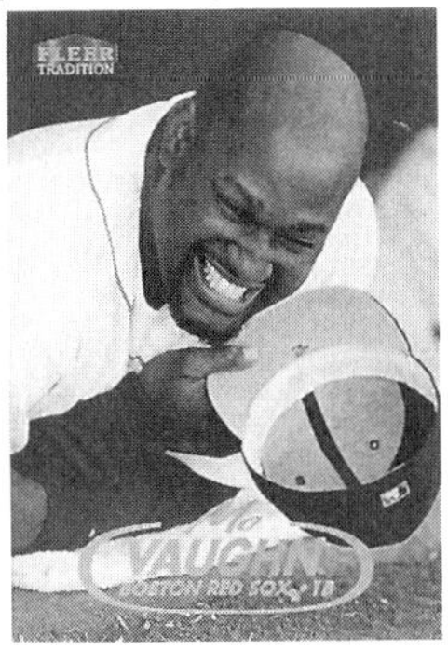

		MT
Complete Set (600):		75.00
Complete Series I Set (350):		30.00
Complete Series II Set (250):		45.00
Common Player:		.10
Wax Box:		50.00
1	Ken Griffey Jr.	3.00
2	Derek Jeter	2.00
3	Gerald Williams	.10
4	Carlos Delgado	.10
5	Nomar Garciaparra	2.00
6	Gary Sheffield	.30
7	Jeff King	.10
8	Cal Ripken Jr.	2.50
9	Matt Williams	.25
10	Chipper Jones	2.00
11	Chuck Knoblauch	.25
12	Mark Grudzielanek	.10
13	Edgardo Alfonzo	.10
14	Andres Galarraga	.20
15	Tim Salmon	.25
16	Reggie Sanders	.10
17	Tony Clark	.40
18	Jason Kendall	.10
19	Juan Gonzalez	1.50
20	Ben Grieve	1.00
21	Roger Clemens	1.00
22	Raul Mondesi	.20
23	Robin Ventura	.10
24	Derrek Lee	.10
25	Mark McGwire	4.00
26	Luis Gonzalez	.10
27	Kevin Brown	.20
28	Kirk Rueter	.10
29	Bobby Estalella	.10
30	Shawn Green	.10
31	Greg Maddux	2.00
32	Jorge Velandia	.10
33	Larry Walker	.25
34	Joey Cora	.10
35	Frank Thomas	2.50
36	*Curtis King*	.10
37	Aaron Boone	.10
38	Curt Schilling	.10
39	Bruce Aven	.10
40	Ben McDonald	.10
41	Andy Ashby	.10
42	Jason McDonald	.10
43	Eric Davis	.10
44	Mark Grace	.25
45	Pedro Martinez	.25
46	Lou Collier	.10
47	Chan Ho Park	.10
48	Shane Halter	.10
49	Brian Hunter	.10
50	Jeff Bagwell	1.25
51	Bernie Williams	.50
52	J.T. Snow	.10
53	Todd Greene	.10
54	Shannon Stewart	.10
55	Darren Bragg	.10
56	Fernando Tatis	.20
57	Darryl Kile	.10
58	Chris Stynes	.10
59	Javier Valentin	.10
60	Brian McRae	.10
61	Tom Evans	.10
62	Randall Simon	.20
63	Darrin Fletcher	.10
64	Jaret Wright	1.50
65	Luis Ordaz	.10
66	Jose Canseco	.20
67	Edgar Renteria	.10
68	Jay Buhner	.20
69	Paul Konerko	1.00
70	Adrian Brown	.10
71	Chris Carpenter	.10
72	Mike Lieberthal	.10
73	Dean Palmer	.10
74	Jorge Fabregas	.10
75	Stan Javier	.10
76	Damion Easley	.10
77	David Cone	.20
78	Aaron Sele	.10
79	Antonio Alfonseca	.10
80	Bobby Jones	.10
81	David Justice	.25
82	Jeffrey Hammonds	.10
83	Doug Glanville	.10
84	Jason Dickson	.10
85	Brad Radke	.10
86	David Segui	.10
87	Greg Vaughn	.10
88	*Mike Cather*	.20
89	Alex Fernandez	.10
90	Billy Taylor	.10
91	Jason Schmidt	.10
92	*Mike DeJean*	.10
93	Domingo Cedeno	.10
94	Jeff Cirillo	.10
95	*Manny Aybar*	.20
96	Jaime Navarro	.10
97	Dennis Reyes	.10
98	Barry Larkin	.20
99	Troy O'Leary	.10
100	Alex Rodriguez	2.50
101	Pat Hentgen	.10
102	Bubba Trammell	.20
103	Glendon Rusch	.10
104	Kenny Lofton	.75
105	Craig Biggio	.20
106	Kelvim Escobar	.10
107	Mark Kotsay	.40
108	Rondell White	.20
109	Darren Oliver	.10
110	Jim Thome	.40
111	Rich Becker	.10
112	Chad Curtis	.10
113	Dave Hollins	.10
114	Bill Mueller	.10
115	Antone Williamson	.10
116	Tony Womack	.10
117	Randy Myers	.10
118	Rico Brogna	.10
119	Pat Watkins	.10
120	Eli Marrero	.10
121	Jay Bell	.10
122	Kevin Tapani	.10
123	*Todd Erdos*	.20
124	Neifi Perez	.10
125	Todd Hundley	.10
126	Jeff Abbott	.10
127	Todd Zeile	.10
128	Travis Fryman	.10
129	Sandy Alomar	.10
130	Fred McGriff	.20
131	Richard Hidalgo	.10
132	Scott Spiezio	.10
133	John Valentin	.10
134	Quilvio Veras	.10
135	Mike Lansing	.10
136	Paul Molitor	.50
137	Randy Johnson	.40
138	Harold Baines	.10
139	Doug Jones	.10
140	Abraham Nunez	.25
141	Alan Benes	.20
142	Matt Perisho	.10
143	Chris Clemons	.10
144	Andy Pettitte	.50
145	Jason Giambi	.10
146	Moises Alou	.20
147	*Chad Fox*	.25
148	Felix Martinez	.10
149	*Carlos Mendoza*	.20
150	Scott Rolen	1.50
151	*Jose Cabrera*	.20
152	Justin Thompson	.10
153	Ellis Burks	.10
154	Pokey Reese	.10
155	Bartolo Colon	.10
156	Ray Durham	.10
157	Ugueth Urbina	.10
158	Tom Goodwin	.10
159	*David Dellucci*	.50
160	Rod Beck	.10
161	Ramon Martinez	.10
162	Joe Carter	.15
163	Kevin Orie	.10
164	Trevor Hoffman	.10
165	Emil Brown	.10
166	Robb Nen	.10
167	Paul O'Neill	.20
168	Ryan Long	.10
169	Ray Lankford	.10
170	Ivan Rodriguez	.60
171	Rick Aguilera	.10
172	Deivi Cruz	.10
173	Ricky Bottalico	.10
174	Garret Anderson	.10
175	Jose Vizcaino	.10
176	Omar Vizquel	.10
177	Jeff Blauser	.10
178	Orlando Cabrera	.10
179	Russ Johnson	.10
180	Matt Stairs	.10
181	Will Cunnane	.10
182	Adam Riggs	.10
183	Matt Morris	.10
184	Mario Valdez	.10
185	Larry Sutton	.10
186	*Marc Pisciotta*	.10
187	Dan Wilson	.10
188	John Franco	.10
189	Darren Daulton	.10
190	Todd Helton	.75
191	Brady Anderson	.20
192	Ricardo Rincon	.10
193	Kevin Stocker	.10
194	Jose Valentin	.10
195	Ed Sprague	.10
196	Ryan McGuire	.10
197	*Scott Eyre*	.25
198	Steve Finley	.10
199	T.J. Mathews	.10
200	Mike Piazza	2.00
201	Mark Wohlers	.10
202	Brian Giles	.10
203	Eduardo Perez	.10
204	Shigetosi Hasegawa	.10
205	Mariano Rivera	.20
206	Jose Rosado	.10
207	Michael Coleman	.10
208	James Baldwin	.10
209	Russ Davis	.10
210	Billy Wagner	.10
211	Sammy Sosa	1.50
212	*Frank Catalanotto*	.25
213	Delino DeShields	.10
214	John Olerud	.10
215	Heath Murray	.10
216	Jose Vidro	.10
217	Jim Edmonds	.20
218	Shawon Dunston	.10
219	Homer Bush	.10
220	Midre Cummings	.10
221	Tony Saunders	.20
222	Jeromy Burnitz	.10
223	Enrique Wilson	.10
224	Chili Davis	.10
225	Jerry DiPoto	.10
226	Dante Powell	.10
227	Javier Lopez	.20
228	*Kevin Polcovich*	.20
229	Deion Sanders	.25
230	Jimmy Key	.10
231	Rusty Greer	.10
232	Reggie Jefferson	.10
233	Ron Coomer	.10
234	Bobby Higginson	.20
235	*Magglio Ordonez*	.75
236	Miguel Tejada	.50
237	Rick Gorecki	.10
238	Charles Johnson	.10
239	Lance Johnson	.10
240	Derek Bell	.10
241	Will Clark	.20
242	Brady Raggio	.10
243	Orel Hershiser	.10
244	Vladimir Guerrero	1.25
245	John LeRoy	.10
246	Shawn Estes	.10
247	Brett Tomko	.10
248	Dave Nilsson	.10
249	Edgar Martinez	.10
250	Tony Gwynn	1.50
251	Mark Bellhorn	.10
252	Jed Hansen	.10
253	Butch Huskey	.10
254	Eric Young	.10
255	Vinny Castilla	.10
256	Hideki Irabu	.75
257	Mike Cameron	.10
258	Juan Encarnacion	.25
259	Brian Rose	.25
260	Brad Ausmus	.10
261	Dan Serafini	.10
262	Willie Greene	.10
263	Troy Percival	.10
264	*Jeff Wallace*	.20
265	Richie Sexson	.10
266	Rafael Palmeiro	.20
267	Brad Fullmer	.10
268	Jeremi Gonzalez	.10
269	*Rob Stanifer*	.25
270	Mickey Morandini	.10
271	Andruw Jones	1.50
272	Royce Clayton	.10
273	Takashi Kashiwada	.40
274	*Steve Woodard*	.25
275	Jose Cruz Jr.	1.50
276	Keith Foulke	.10
277	Brad Rigby	.10
278	Tino Martinez	.20
279	Todd Jones	.10
280	John Wetteland	.10
281	Alex Gonzalez	.10
282	Ken Cloude	.25
283	Jose Guillen	.40
284	Danny Clyburn	.10
285	David Ortiz	.40
286	John Thomson	.10
287	Kevin Appier	.10
288	Ismael Valdes	.10
289	Gary DiSarcina	.10
290	Todd Dunwoody	.10
291	Wally Joyner	.10
292	Charles Nagy	.10
293	Jeff Shaw	.10
294	*Kevin Millwood*	1.00
295	*Rigo Beltran*	.20
296	Jeff Frye	.10
297	Oscar Henriquez	.10
298	Mike Thurman	.10
299	Garrett Stephenson	.10
300	Barry Bonds	.75
301	Roger Clemens (Smoke 'N Heat)	.50

302 David Cone (Smoke 'N Heat) .15
303 Hideki Irabu (Smoke 'N Heat) .40
304 Randy Johnson (Smoke 'N Heat) .20
305 Greg Maddux (Smoke 'N Heat) 1.00
306 Pedro Martinez (Smoke 'N Heat) .15
307 Mike Mussina (Smoke 'N Heat) .30
308 Andy Pettitte (Smoke 'N Heat) .25
309 Curt Schilling (Smoke 'N Heat) .10
310 John Smoltz (Smoke 'N Heat) .15
311 Roger Clemens (Golden Memories) .50
312 Jose Cruz Jr. (Golden Memories) .75
313 Nomar Garciaparra (Golden Memories) 1.00
314 Ken Griffey Jr. (Golden Memories) 1.50
315 Tony Gwynn (Golden Memories) .75
316 Hideki Irabu (Golden Memories) .40
317 Randy Johnson (Golden Memories) .20
318 Mark McGwire (Golden Memories) 2.00
319 Curt Schilling (Golden Memories) .10
320 Larry Walker (Golden Memories) .15
321 Jeff Bagwell (Tale of the Tape) .60
322 Albert Belle (Tale of the Tape) .40
323 Barry Bonds (Tale of the Tape) .40
324 Jay Buhner (Tale of the Tape) .15
325 Tony Clark (Tale of the Tape) .20
326 Jose Cruz Jr. (Tale of the Tape) .75
327 Andres Galarraga (Tale of the Tape) .15
328 Juan Gonzalez (Tale of the Tape) .75
329 Ken Griffey Jr. (Tale of the Tape) 1.50
330 Andruw Jones (Tale of the Tape) .75
331 Tino Martinez (Tale of the Tape) .15
332 Mark McGwire (Tale of the Tape) 2.00
333 Rafael Palmeiro (Tale of the Tape) .15
334 Mike Piazza (Tale of the Tape) 1.00
335 Manny Ramirez (Tale of the Tape) .25
336 Alex Rodriguez (Tale of the Tape) 1.25
337 Frank Thomas (Tale of the Tape) 1.25
338 Jim Thome (Tale of the Tape) .20
339 Mo Vaughn (Tale of the Tape) .40
340 Larry Walker (Tale of the Tape) .15
341 Checklist (Jose Cruz Jr.) .50
342 Checklist (Ken Griffey Jr.) 1.00
343 Checklist (Derek Jeter) .60
344 Checklist (Andruw Jones) .50
345 Checklist (Chipper Jones) .60
346 Checklist (Greg Maddux) .60
347 Checklist (Mike Piazza) .60
348 Checklist (Cal Ripken Jr.) .75
349 Checklist (Alex Rodriguez) .75
350 Checklist (Frank Thomas) 1.00
351 Mo Vaughn .75
352 Andres Galarraga .25
353 Roberto Alomar .50
354 Darin Erstad .75
355 Albert Belle .75
356 Matt Williams .25
357 Darryl Kile .10
358 Kenny Lofton .75
359 Orel Hershiser .10
360 Bob Abreu .10
361 Chris Widger .10
362 Glenallen Hill .10
363 Chili Davis .10
364 Kevin Brown .15
365 Marquis Grissom .15
366 Livan Hernandez .10
367 Moises Alou .20
368 Matt Lawton .10
369 Rey Ordonez .10
370 Kenny Rogers .10
371 Lee Stevens .10
372 Wade Boggs .20
373 Luis Gonzalez .10
374 Jeff Conine .10
375 Esteban Loaiza .10
376 Jose Canseco .25
377 Henry Rodriguez .10
378 Dave Burba .10
379 Todd Hollandsworth .10
380 Ron Gant .20
381 Pedro Martinez .40
382 Ryan Klesko .30
383 Derrek Lee .10
384 Doug Glanville .10
385 David Wells .10
386 Ken Caminiti .20
387 Damon Hollins .10
388 Manny Ramirez .75
389 Mike Mussina .60
390 Jay Bell .10
391 Mike Piazza .40
392 Mike Lansing .10
393 Mike Hampton .10
394 Geoff Jenkins .10
395 Jimmy Haynes .10
396 Scott Servais .10
397 Kent Mercker .10
398 Jeff Kent .10
399 Kevin Elster .10
400 *Masato Yoshii* .40
401 Jose Vizcaino .10
402 Javier Martinez .10
403 David Segui .10
404 Tony Saunders .10
405 Karim Garcia .10
406 Armando Benitez .10
407 Joe Randa .10
408 Vic Darensbourg .10
409 Sean Casey .20
410 Eric Milton .20
411 Trey Moore .10
412 Mike Stanley .10
413 Tom Gordon .10
414 Hal Morris .10
415 Braden Looper .10
416 Mike Kelly .10
417 John Smoltz .10
418 Roger Cedeno .10
419 Al Leiter .20
420 Chuck Knoblauch .30
421 Felix Rodriguez .10
422 Bip Roberts .10
423 Ken Hill .10
424 Jermaine Allensworth .10
425 Esteban Yan .10
426 Scott Karl .10
427 Sean Berry .10
428 Rafael Medina .10
429 Javier Vazquez .10
430 Rickey Henderson .20
431 *Adam Butler* .10
432 Todd Stottlemyre .10
433 Yamil Benitez .10
434 Sterling Hitchcock .10
435 Paul Sorrento .10
436 Bobby Ayala .10
437 Tim Raines .10
438 Chris Hoiles .10
439 Rod Beck .10
440 Donnie Sadler .10
441 Charles Johnson .10
442 Russ Ortiz .10
443 Pedro Astacio .10
444 Wilson Alvarez .10
445 Mike Blowers .10
446 Todd Zeile .10
447 Mel Rojas .10
448 F.P. Santangelo .10
449 Dmitri Young .10
450 Brian Anderson .10
451 Cecil Fielder .20
452 Roberto Hernandez .10
453 Todd Walker .20
454 Tyler Green .10
455 Jorge Posada .10
456 Geronimo Berroa .10
457 Jose Silva .10
458 Bobby Bonilla .20
459 Walt Weiss .10
460 Darren Dreifort .10
461 B.J. Surhoff .10
462 Quinton McCracken .10
463 Derek Lowe .10
464 Jorge Fabregas .10
465 Joey Hamilton .10
466 Brian Jordan .10
467 Allen Watson .10
468 John Jaha .10
469 Heathcliff Slocumb .10
470 Gregg Jefferies .10
471 Scott Brosius .10
472 Chad Ogea .10
473 A.J. Hinch .20
474 Bobby Smith .10
475 Brian Moehler .10
476 DaRond Stovall .10
477 Kevin Young .10
478 Jeff Suppan .10
479 Marty Cordova .10
480 *John Halama* .25
481 Bubba Trammell .10
482 Mike Caruso .10
483 Eric Karros .20
484 Jamey Wright .10
485 Mike Sweeney .10
486 Aaron Sele .10
487 Cliff Floyd .10
488 Jeff Brantley .10
489 Jim Leyritz .10
490 Denny Neagle .20
491 Travis Fryman .10
492 Carlos Baerga .10
493 Eddie Taubensee .10
494 Darryl Strawberry .20
495 Brian Johnson .10
496 Randy Myers .10
497 Jeff Blauser .10
498 Jason Wood .10
499 *Rolando Arrojo* .40
500 Johnny Damon .10
501 Jose Mercedes .10
502 Tony Batista .10
503 Mike Piazza 2.00
504 Hideo Nomo .50
505 Chris Gomez .10
506 *Jesus Sanchez* .25
507 Al Martin .10
508 Brian Edmondson .10
509 Joe Girardi .10
510 Shayne Bennett .10
511 Joe Carter .15
512 Dave Mlicki .10
513 *Rich Butler* .50
514 Dennis Eckersley .10
515 Travis Lee 2.00
516 John Mabry .10
517 Jose Mesa .10
518 Phil Nevin .10
519 Raul Casanova .10
520 Mike Fetters .10
521 Gary Sheffield .25
522 Terry Steinbach .10
523 Steve Trachsel .10
524 Josh Booty .10
525 Darryl Hamilton .10
526 Mark McLemore .10
527 Kevin Stocker .10
528 Bret Boone .10
529 Shane Andrews .10
530 Robb Nen .10
531 Carl Everett .10
532 LaTroy Hawkins .10
533 Fernando Vina .10
534 Michael Tucker .10
535 Mark Langston .10
536 Mickey Mantle 5.00
537 Bernard Gilkey .10
538 Francisco Cordova .10
539 Mike Bordick .10
540 Fred McGriff .20
541 Cliff Politte .10
542 Jason Varitek .10
543 Shawon Dunston .10
544 Brian Meadows .10
545 Pat Meares .10
546 Carlos Perez .10
547 Desi Relaford .10
548 Antonio Osuna .10
549 Devon White .10
550 Sean Runyan .10
551 Mickey Morandini .10
552 Dave Martinez .10
553 Jeff Fassero .10
554 *Ryan Jackson* .25
555 Stan Javier .10
556 Jaime Navarro .10
557 Jose Offerman .10
558 *Mike Lowell* .40
559 Darrin Fletcher .10
560 Mark Lewis .10
561 Dante Bichette .25
562 Chuck Finley .10
563 Kerry Wood 5.00
564 Andy Benes .10
565 Freddy Garcia .10
566 Tom Glavine .20
567 Jon Nunnally .10
568 Miguel Cairo .10
569 Shane Reynolds .10
570 Roberto Kelly .10
571 Checklist (Jose Cruz Jr.) .50
572 Checklist (Ken Griffey Jr.) 1.50
573 Checklist (Mark McGwire) 1.50
574 Checklist (Cal Ripken Jr.) 1.00
575 Checklist (Frank Thomas) 1.00
576 Jeff Bagwell (Unforgettable Moments) 1.50
577 Barry Bonds (Unforgettable Moments) 1.00
578 Tony Clark (Unforgettable Moments) .75
579 Roger Clemens (Unforgettable Moments) 1.50
580 Jose Cruz Jr. (Unforgettable Moments) 1.00
581 Nomar Garciaparra (Unforgettable Moments) 2.50
582 Juan Gonzalez (Unforgettable Moments) 2.00
583 Ben Grieve (Unforgettable Moments) 1.50
584 Ken Griffey Jr. (Unforgettable Moments) 4.00
585 Tony Gwynn (Unforgettable Moments) 2.00
586 Derek Jeter (Unforgettable Moments) 2.50
587 Randy Johnson (Unforgettable Moments) .75
588 Chipper Jones (Unforgettable Moments) 2.50
589 Greg Maddux (Unforgettable Moments) 2.50
590 Mark McGwire (Unforgettable Moments) 5.00
591 Andy Pettitte (Unforgettable Moments) .60
592 Paul Molitor (Unforgettable Moments) .50
593 Cal Ripken Jr. (Unforgettable Moments) 3.00
594 Alex Rodriguez (Unforgettable Moments) 2.50
595 Scott Rolen (Unforgettable Moments) 1.25
596 Curt Schilling (Unforgettable Moments) .40
597 Frank Thomas (Unforgettable Moments) 2.50
598 Jim Thome (Unforgettable Moments) .75
599 Larry Walker (Unforgettable Moments) .50
600 Bernie Williams (Unforgettable Moments) .75

1998 Fleer Decade of Excellence

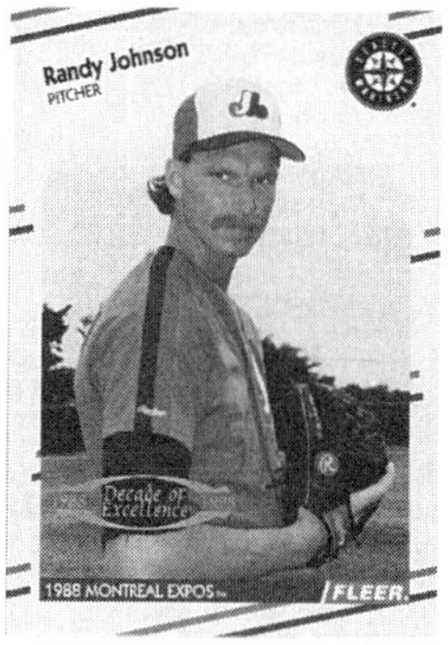

Decade of Excellence inserts were found in one per 72 Series I hobby packs of Fleer Tradition. The 12-card set features 1988 season photos in Fleer's 1988 card design. The set includes only those current players who have been in baseball for ten years or more.

		MT
Complete Set (12):		100.00
Common Player:		4.00
Inserted 1:72		
Rare Traditions: 3x to 5x		
Inserted 1:720		
1	Roberto Alomar	8.00
2	Barry Bonds	10.00
3	Roger Clemens	12.00
4	David Cone	4.00
5	Andres Galarraga	5.00
6	Mark Grace	4.00
7	Tony Gwynn	16.00
8	Randy Johnson	6.00
9	Greg Maddux	24.00
10	Mark McGwire	35.00
11	Paul O'Neill	4.00
12	Cal Ripken Jr.	30.00

1998 Fleer Diamond Ink

These one-per-pack inserts offer collectors a chance to acquire genuine autographed baseballs. Issued in denominations of 1, 5 and 10 points, the cards had to be accumulated to a total of 500 points of the same player to be redeemed for an autographed ball of that player. Cards are the standard 3-1/2" x 2-1/2" and are printed in black and purple on front and black and yellow on back. The point value of each card is embossed at center to prevent counterfeiting. The rules of the exchange program are printed on back. The deadline for redemption was Dec. 31, 1998. Values shown are for 1-pt. cards, and the unnumbered players in the series are listed alphabetically.

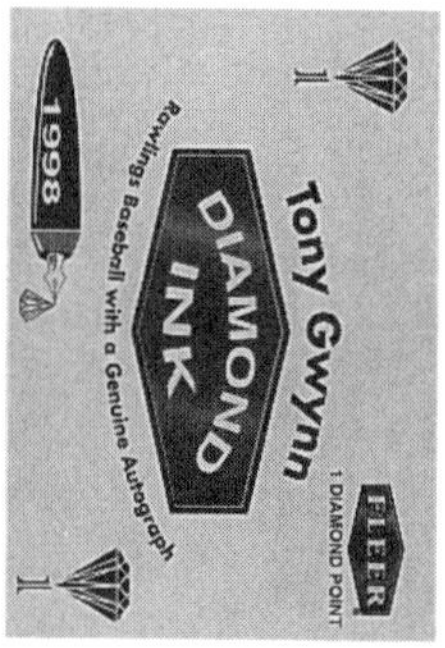

		MT
Complete Set, 1 pt. (11):		1.25
Common Player, 1 pt.:		.05
5-pt. cards:		5X
10-pt. cards:		12X
(1)	Jay Buhner	.05
(2)	Roger Clemens	.10
(3)	Jose Cruz Jr.	.15
(4)	Nomar Garciaparra	.10
(5)	Tony Gwynn	.10
(6)	Roberto Hernandez	.05
(7)	Greg Maddux	.10
(8)	Cal Ripken Jr.	.20
(9)	Alex Rodriguez	.20
(10)	Scott Rolen	.10
(11)	Tony Womack	.05

1998 Fleer Diamond Standouts

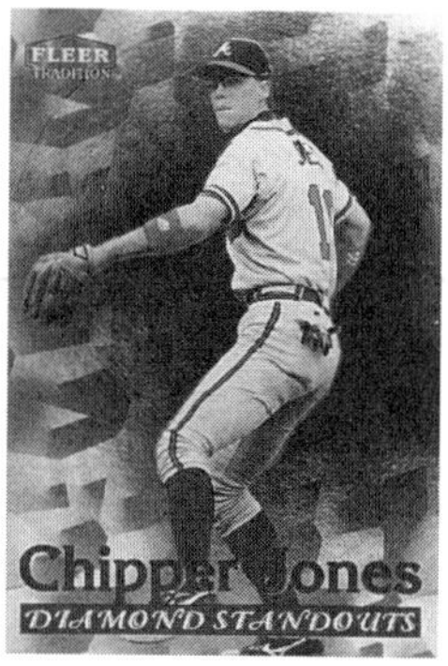

Diamond Standouts were inserted into Series I packs at a rate of one per 12. The 20-card insert set features players over a diamond design silver foil background.

		MT
Complete Set (20):		75.00
Common Player:		1.50
Inserted 1:12		
1	Jeff Bagwell	5.00
2	Barry Bonds	3.00
3	Roger Clemens	5.00
4	Jose Cruz Jr.	5.00
5	Andres Galarraga	1.50
6	Nomar Garciaparra	8.00
7	Juan Gonzalez	6.00
8	Ken Griffey Jr.	12.00
9	Derek Jeter	7.00
10	Randy Johnson	2.00
11	Chipper Jones	8.00
12	Kenny Lofton	3.00
13	Greg Maddux	8.00
14	Pedro Martinez	1.50

15	Mark McGwire	15.00
16	Mike Piazza	8.00
17	Alex Rodriguez	10.00
18	Curt Schilling	1.50
19	Frank Thomas	10.00
20	Larry Walker	2.00

1998 Fleer Diamond Tribute

This 10-card insert was exclusive to Series II packs and seeded one per 300 packs. Cards were printed on a leather-like laminated stock and had silver holofoil stamping.

		MT
Complete Set (10):		400.00
Common Player:		30.00
Inserted 1:300		
DT1	Jeff Bagwell	35.00
DT2	Roger Clemens	35.00
DT3	Nomar Garciaparra	50.00
DT4	Juan Gonzalez	40.00
DT5	Ken Griffey Jr.	80.00
DT6	Mark McGwire	90.00
DT7	Mike Piazza	50.00
DT8	Cal Ripken Jr.	60.00
DT9	Alex Rodriguez	50.00
DT10	Frank Thomas	60.00

1998 Fleer In the Clutch

This Series 2 insert features stars who can stand up to pressure of big league ball. Fronts have embossed action photos on a prismatic metallic foil background. Backs have a portrait photo and a few words about the player. Stated insertion rate for the inserts was one per 20 packs on average.

		MT
Complete Set (15):		75.00
Common Player:		1.50
Inserted 1:20		
IC1	Jeff Bagwell	5.00
IC2	Barry Bonds	3.00
IC3	Roger Clemens	5.00
IC4	Jose Cruz Jr.	3.00
IC5	Nomar Garciaparra	8.00
IC6	Juan Gonzalez	6.00
IC7	Ken Griffey Jr.	12.00
IC8	Tony Gwynn	6.00
IC9	Derek Jeter	6.00
IC10	Chipper Jones	8.00
IC11	Greg Maddux	8.00
IC12	Mark McGwire	15.00
IC13	Mike Piazza	8.00
IC14	Frank Thomas	10.00
IC15	Larry Walker	1.50

1998 Fleer Lumber Company

This 15-card set was exclusive to Series I retail packs and inserted one per 36 packs. It included power hitters and featured the insert name in large letters across the top.

		MT
Complete Set (15):		200.00
Common Player:		3.00
Inserted 1:36 retail		
1	Jeff Bagwell	12.00
2	Barry Bonds	7.00
3	Jose Cruz Jr.	10.00
4	Nomar Garciaparra	20.00
5	Juan Gonzalez	15.00
6	Ken Griffey Jr.	30.00
7	Tony Gwynn	15.00
8	Chipper Jones	20.00
9	Tino Martinez	3.00
10	Mark McGwire	35.00
11	Mike Piazza	20.00
12	Cal Ripken Jr.	25.00
13	Alex Rodriguez	25.00
14	Frank Thomas	25.00
15	Larry Walker	4.00

1998 Fleer Mickey Mantle Monumental Moments

This 10-card insert set honored Hall of Famer Mickey Mantle legendary career and was seeded one per 68 packs of Series II. Fleer/SkyBox worked closely with Mantle's family with each photo in the set personally selected by them.

	MT
Complete Set (10):	150.00
Common Mantle:	20.00
Inserted 1:68	
Golds (51 sets)	3x to 5x

1998 Fleer Promising Forecast

Potential future stars are showcased in this Series 2 insert. Both front and back have a background of a colorful weather map. Fronts have a glossy player action photo on a matte-finish background. Backs are all-glossy and have a second photo and a few words about the player's po-

tential. Average odds of pulling a Promising Forecast card were stated as one per 12 packs.

		MT
Complete Set (20):		30.00
Common Player:		.50
Inserted 1:12		
PF1	Rolando Arrojo	1.00
PF2	Sean Casey	1.50
PF3	Brad Fullmer	2.00
PF4	Karim Garcia	.50
PF5	Ben Grieve	4.00
PF6	Todd Helton	3.00
PF7	Richard Hidalgo	.50
PF8	A.J. Hinch	.50
PF9	Paul Konerko	1.50
PF10	Mark Kotsay	1.00
PF11	Derrek Lee	.50
PF12	Travis Lee	5.00
PF13	Eric Milton	.50
PF14	Magglio Ordonez	1.50
PF15	David Ortiz	1.50
PF16	Brian Rose	.50
PF17	Miguel Tejada	1.50
PF18	Jason Varitek	.50
PF19	Enrique Wilson	.50
PF20	Kerry Wood	8.00

1998 Fleer Rookie Sensation

Rookie Sensations included 20 gray-bordered cards of the 1997 most promising players who were eligible for the Rookie of the Year award. Each card contained a multicolored background and was inserted one per 18 packs.

		MT
Complete Set (20):		60.00
Common Player:		2.00
Inserted 1:18		
1	Mike Cameron	2.00
2	Jose Cruz Jr.	10.00
3	Jason Dickson	2.00
4	Kelvim Escobar	2.00
5	Nomar Garciaparra	12.00
6	Ben Grieve	5.00
7	Vladimir Guerrero	5.00
8	Wilton Guerrero	2.00
9	Jose Guillen	3.00
10	Todd Helton	4.00
11	Livan Hernandez	2.00
12	Hideki Irabu	4.00
13	Andruw Jones	6.00
14	Matt Morris	2.00
15	Magglio Ordonez	2.00
16	Neifi Perez	2.00
17	Scott Rolen	8.00
18	Fernando Tatis	4.00
19	Brett Tomko	2.00
20	Jaret Wright	4.00

1998 Fleer The Power Game

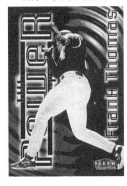

Pitchers and hitters are pictured over a purple metallic background with UV coating in this 20-card insert. Power Game inserts were exclusive to Series I and seeded one per 36 packs.

		MT
Complete Set (20):		175.00
Common Player:		3.00
Inserted 1:36		
1	Jeff Bagwell	12.00
2	Albert Belle	7.00
3	Barry Bonds	7.00
4	Tony Clark	5.00
5	Roger Clemens	10.00
6	Jose Cruz Jr.	10.00
7	Andres Galarraga	3.00
8	Nomar Garciaparra	20.00
9	Juan Gonzalez	15.00
10	Ken Griffey Jr.	30.00
11	Randy Johnson	5.00
12	Greg Maddux	20.00
13	Pedro Martinez	3.00
14	Tino Martinez	3.00
15	Mark McGwire	35.00
16	Mike Piazza	20.00
17	Curt Schilling	3.00
18	Frank Thomas	25.00
19	Jim Thome	5.00
20	Larry Walker	4.00

1998 Fleer Vintage '63

MARK McGWIRE
St. Louis Cardinals.—1B

Vintage featured 126 different players, with 63 in Series I and 63 in Series II, on the design of 1963 Fleer cards. The insert commemorated the 35th anniversary of Fleer and was seeded one per hobby pack. In addition, Series II featured Mickey Mantle on card No. 67, which completed the original 1963 Fleer set that ended at card No. 66 and wasn't able to include Mantle for licensing reasons. The Mantle card was printed in vintage looking stock and was purposely made to look and feel like the originals. Fleer also printed a Classic parallel version to this insert that contained gold foil on the front and was sequentially numbered to 63 with a "C" prefix on the back.

		MT
Complete Set (126):		35.00
Complete Series I Set (63):		20.00
Complete Series II Set (63):		15.00
Common Player:		.25
Inserted 1:1		
1	Jason Dickson	.25
2	Tim Salmon	.40
3	Andruw Jones	1.00
4	Chipper Jones	1.50
5	Kenny Lofton	.75
6	Greg Maddux	1.50
7	Rafael Palmeiro	.30
8	Cal Ripken Jr.	2.00
9	Nomar Garciaparra	1.50
10	Mark Grace	.40
11	Sammy Sosa	1.50
12	Frank Thomas	2.50
13	Deion Sanders	.30
14	Sandy Alomar	.25
15	David Justice	.40
16	Jim Thome	.50
17	Matt Williams	.30
18	Jaret Wright	1.50
19	Vinny Castilla	.25
20	Andres Galarraga	.40
21	Todd Helton	.75
22	Larry Walker	.40
23	Tony Clark	.40
24	Moises Alou	.25
25	Kevin Brown	.25
26	Charles Johnson	.25
27	Edgar Renteria	.25
28	Gary Sheffield	.40
29	Jeff Bagwell	1.00
30	Craig Biggio	.25
31	Raul Mondesi	.25
32	Mike Piazza	1.50
33	Chuck Knoblauch	.40
34	Paul Molitor	.50
35	Vladimir Guerrero	1.00
36	Pedro J. Martinez	.40
37	Todd Hundley	.25
38	Derek Jeter	1.50
39	Tino Martinez	.40
40	Paul O'Neill	.25
41	Andy Pettitte	.50
42	Mariano Rivera	.25
43	Bernie Williams	.50
44	Ben Grieve	1.50
45	Scott Rolen	1.00
46	Curt Schilling	.25
47	Jason Kendall	.25
48	Tony Womack	.25
49	Ray Lankford	.25
50	Mark McGwire	4.00
51	Matt Morris	.25
52	Tony Gwynn	1.50
53	Barry Bonds	.75
54	Jay Buhner	.25
55	Ken Griffey Jr.	3.00
56	Randy Johnson	.40
57	Edgar Martinez	.25
58	Alex Rodriguez	2.00
59	Juan Gonzalez	1.50
60	Rusty Greer	.25
61	Ivan Rodriguez	.75
62	Roger Clemens	1.25
63	Jose Cruz Jr.	1.50
	Checklist (Vintage '63)	.25
64	Darin Erstad	.75
65	Jay Bell	.25
66	Andy Benes	.25
67	Mickey Mantle	5.00
68	Travis Lee	3.00
69	Matt Williams	.40
70	Andres Galarraga	.40
71	Tom Glavine	.40
72	Ryan Klesko	.40
73	Denny Neagle	.25
74	John Smoltz	.25
75	Roberto Alomar	.50
76	Joe Carter	.25
77	Mike Mussina	.60
78	B.J. Surhoff	.25
79	Dennis Eckersley	.25
80	Pedro Martinez	.40
81	Mo Vaughn	.75
82	Jeff Blauser	.25
83	Henry Rodriguez	.25
84	Albert Belle	.75
85	Sean Casey	.50
86	Travis Fryman	.25
87	Kenny Lofton	.75
88	Darryl Kile	.25
89	Mike Lansing	.25
90	Bobby Bonilla	.25
91	Cliff Floyd	.25
92	Livan Hernandez	.25
93	Derek Lee	.25
94	Moises Alou	.25
95	Shane Reynolds	.25
96	Jeff Conine	.25
97	Johnny Damon	.25
98	Eric Karros	.25
99	Hideo Nomo	.50
100	Marquis Grissom	.25
101	Matt Lawton	.25
102	Todd Walker	.25
103	Carlos Baerga	.25
104	Bernard Gilkey	.25
105	Rey Ordonez	.25
106	Chili Davis	.25
107	Jason Giambi	.40
108	Chuck Knoblauch	.40
109	Tim Raines	.25
110	Rickey Henderson	.25
111	Bob Abreu	.25
112	Doug Glanville	.25
113	Gregg Jefferies	.25
114	Al Martin	.25
115	Kevin Young	.25
116	Ron Gant	.25
117	Kevin Brown	.25
118	Ken Caminiti	.25
119	Joey Hamilton	.25
120	Jeff Kent	.25
121	Wade Boggs	.50
122	Quinton McCracken	.25
123	Fred McGriff	.40
124	Paul Sorrento	.25
125	Jose Canseco	.40
126	Randy Myers	.25

1998 Fleer Vintage '63 Classic

Vintage '63 Classic paralleled all 126 Vintage '63 inserts throughout Series I and II, plus the checklist. These cards contained foil stamping on the front, specifically around the diamond in the lower left corner, and were sequentailly numbered to 63 sets.

	MT
Stars:	50x to 100x
Yng Stars & RCs:	40x to 75x
Production 63 sets	

1998 Fleer Zone

Inserted in one per 288 packs of Series I Fleer Tradition, Zone featured 15 top players printed on rainbow foil and etching.

		MT
Complete Set (15):		800.00
Common Player:		15.00
Inserted 1:288		
1	Jeff Bagwell	50.00
2	Barry Bonds	30.00
3	Roger Clemens	50.00
4	Jose Cruz Jr.	40.00
5	Nomar Garciaparra	75.00
6	Juan Gonzalez	60.00
7	Ken Griffey Jr.	125.00
8	Tony Gwynn	60.00
9	Chipper Jones	75.00
10	Greg Maddux	75.00
11	Mark McGwire	125.00
12	Mike Piazza	75.00
13	Alex Rodriguez	90.00
14	Frank Thomas	90.00
15	Larry Walker	15.00

1998 Fleer Sports Illustrated

The second of three Sports Illustrated releases of 1998 from Fleer contained 200 cards and featured exclusive Sports Illustrated photography and commentary. Cards arrived in six-card packs and carried a Sports Illustrated logo in a top corner. The set included a Travis Lee One to Watch cards (#201) that was inserted just before going to press. Subsets included: Baseball's Best (129-148), One to Watch (149-176), and '97 in Review (177-200). Inserts sets include: Extra Edition and First Edition parallels, Autographs, Covers, Editor's Choice and Opening Day Mini Posters.

		MT
Complete Set (201):		25.00
Common Player:		.10
Wax Box:		42.00
1	Edgardo Alfonzo	.10
2	Roberto Alomar	.50
3	Sandy Alomar	.10
4	Moises Alou	.20
5	Brady Anderson	.20
6	Garret Anderson	.10
7	Kevin Appier	.10
8	Jeff Bagwell	1.00
9	Jay Bell	.10
10	Albert Belle	.75
11	Dante Bichette	.25
12	Craig Biggio	.20
13	Barry Bonds	.75
14	Bobby Bonilla	.20
15	Kevin Brown	.20
16	Jay Buhner	.25
17	Ellis Burks	.20
18	Mike Cameron	.20
19	Ken Caminiti	.20
20	Jose Canseco	.25
21	Joe Carter	.20
22	Vinny Castilla	.10
23	Jeff Cirillo	.10
24	Tony Clark	.50
25	Will Clark	.25
26	Roger Clemens	1.00
27	David Cone	.20
28	Jose Cruz Jr.	1.00
29	Carlos Delgado	.10
30	Jason Dickson	.10
31	Dennis Eckersley	.10
32	Jim Edmonds	.20
33	Scott Erickson	.10
34	Darin Erstad	.75
35	Shawn Estes	.10
36	Jeff Fassero	.10
37	Alex Fernandez	.10
38	Chuck Finley	.10
39	Steve Finley	.10
40	Travis Fryman	.10
41	Andres Galarraga	.25
42	Ron Gant	.20
43	Nomar Garciaparra	1.50
44	Jason Giambi	.10
45	Tom Glavine	.20
46	Juan Gonzalez	1.50
47	Mark Grace	.25
48	Willie Green	.10
49	Rusty Greer	.20
50	Ben Grieve	1.25
51	Ken Griffey Jr.	3.00
52	Mark Grudzielanek	.10
53	Vladimir Guerrero	.75
54	Juan Guzman	.10
55	Tony Gwynn	1.50
56	Joey Hamilton	.10
57	Rickey Henderson	.10
58	Pat Hentgen	.20
59	Livan Hernandez	.20
60	Bobby Higginson	.10
61	Todd Hundley	.20
62	Hideki Irabu	.35
63	John Jaha	.10
64	Derek Jeter	1.50
65	Charles Johnson	.10
66	Randy Johnson	.50
67	Andruw Jones	.75
68	Bobby Jones	.10
69	Chipper Jones	2.00
70	Brian Jordan	.10
71	David Justice	.25
72	Eric Karros	.10
73	Jeff Kent	.10
74	Jimmy Key	.10
75	Darryl Kile	.10
76	Jeff King	.10
77	Ryan Klesko	.30
78	Chuck Knoblauch	.25
79	Ray Lankford	.10
80	Barry Larkin	.20
81	Kenny Lofton	.75
82	Greg Maddux	2.00
83	Al Martin	.10
84	Edgar Martinez	.20
85	Pedro Martinez	.25
86	Tino Martinez	.25
87	Mark McGwire	4.00
88	Paul Molitor	.40
89	Raul Mondesi	.25
90	Jamie Moyer	.10
91	Mike Mussina	.60
92	Tim Naehring	.10
93	Charles Nagy	.10
94	Denny Neagle	.20
95	Dave Nilsson	.10
96	Hideo Nomo	.60
97	Rey Ordonez	.10
98	Dean Palmer	.10
99	Rafael Palmeiro	.20
100	Andy Pettitte	.50
101	Mike Piazza	2.00
102	Brad Radke	.10
103	Manny Ramirez	.60
104	Edgar Renteria	.10
105	Cal Ripken Jr.	2.50
106	Alex Rodriguez	2.00
107	Henry Rodriguez	.10
108	Ivan Rodriguez	.75
109	Scott Rolen	1.00
110	Tim Salmon	.30
111	Curt Schilling	.25
112	Gary Sheffield	.25
113	John Smoltz	.20
114	J.T. Snow	.10
115	Sammy Sosa	1.50
116	Matt Stairs	.10
117	Shannon Stewart	.10
118	Frank Thomas	2.50
119	Jim Thome	.40
120	Justin Thompson	.20
121	Mo Vaughn	.75
122	Robin Ventura	.20
123	Larry Walker	.40
124	Rondell White	.20
125	Bernie Williams	.60
126	Matt Williams	.25
127	Tony Womack	.10
128	Jaret Wright	1.75
129	Edgar Renteria (Baseball's Best)	.10
130	Kenny Lofton (Baseball's Best)	.40
131	Tony Gwynn (Baseball's Best)	.75
132	Mark McGwire (Baseball's Best)	2.00
133	Craig Biggio (Baseball's Best)	.10
134	Charles Johnson (Baseball's Best)	.10
135	J.T. Snow (Baseball's Best)	.10
136	Ken Caminiti (Baseball's Best)	.10
137	Vladimir Guerrero (Baseball's Best)	.40
138	Jim Edmonds (Baseball's Best)	.10
139	Randy Johnson (Baseball's Best)	.25
140	Darryl Kile (Baseball's Best)	.10
141	John Smoltz (Baseball's Best)	.10
142	Greg Maddux (Baseball's Best)	1.00
143	Andy Pettitte (Baseball's Best)	.25
144	Ken Griffey Jr. (Baseball's Best)	1.50
145	Mike Piazza (Baseball's Best)	1.00
146	Todd Greene (Baseball's Best)	.10
147	Vinny Castilla (Baseball's Best)	.10
148	Derek Jeter (Baseball's Best)	.75
149	Travis Lee (One to Watch)	5.00
150	Mike Gulan (One to Watch)	.10
151	Randall Simon (One to Watch)	.20
152	Michael Coleman (One to Watch)	.10
153	Brian Rose (One to Watch)	.25
154	*Scott Eyre* (One to Watch)	.25
155	*Magglio Ordonez* (One to Watch)	.75
156	Todd Helton (One to Watch)	.75
157	Juan Encarnacion (One to Watch)	.10
158	Mark Kotsay (One to Watch)	.50
159	Josh Booty (One to Watch)	.10
160	*Melvin Rosario* (One to Watch)	.25
161	Shane Halter (One to Watch)	.10
162	Paul Konerko (One to Watch)	1.00
163	*Henry Blanco* (One to Watch)	.20
164	Antone Williamson (One to Watch)	.10
165	Brad Fullmer (One to Watch)	.20
166	Ricky Ledee (One to Watch)	.50
167	Ben Grieve (One to Watch)	.60
168	*Frank Catalanotto* (One to Watch)	.20
169	Bobby Estalella (One to Watch)	.10
170	Dennis Reyes (One to Watch)	.10
171	Kevin Polcovich (One to Watch)	.10
172	Jacob Cruz (One to Watch)	.10
173	Ken Cloude (One to Watch)	.10
174	Eli Marrero (One to Watch)	.10
175	Fernando Tatis (One to Watch)	.10
176	Tom Evans (One to Watch)	.10
177	Everett, Garciaparra (97 in Review)	.75
178	Eric Davis (97 in Review)	.10
179	Roger Clemens (97 in Review)	.50
180	Butler, Murray (97 in Review)	.10
181	Frank Thomas (97 in Review)	1.25
182	Curt Schilling (97 in Review)	.10
183	Jeff Bagwell (97 in Review)	.50
184	McGwire, Griffey (97 in Review)	1.50
185	Kevin Brown (97 in Review)	.10
186	Cordova, Rincon (97 in Review)	.10
187	Charles Johnson (97 in Review)	.10
188	Hideki Irabu (97 in Review)	.20
189	Tony Gwynn (97 in Review)	.75
190	Sandy Alomar (97 in Review)	.10
191	Ken Griffey Jr. (97 in Review)	1.50
192	Larry Walker (97 in Review)	.20
193	Roger Clemens (97 in Review)	.50
194	Pedro Martinez (97 in Review)	.20
195	Nomar Garciaparra (97 in Review)	.75
196	Scott Rolen (97 in Review)	.50
197	Brian Anderson (97 in Review)	.10
198	Tony Saunders (97 in Review)	.10
199	Fla. Celebration (97 in Review)	.10
200	Livan Hernandez (97 in Review)	.10
201	Travis Lee	4.00

1998 Fleer Sports Illustrated Extra Edition

Extra Edition was a 201-card parallel set that included a holofoil stamp on the front and sequential numbering to 250 on the back. There was also a First Edition version of these that was identical on the front, but contained the text "The Only 1 of 1 First Edition" written in purple lettering on the card back.

		MT
Common Player:		8.00
Semistars:		20.00
Production 250 sets		
1	Edgardo Alfonzo	8.00
2	Roberto Alomar	40.00
3	Sandy Alomar	8.00
4	Moises Alou	12.00
5	Brady Anderson	12.00
6	Garret Anderson	8.00
7	Kevin Appier	8.00
8	Jeff Bagwell	80.00
9	Jay Bell	8.00
10	Albert Belle	50.00
11	Dante Bichette	15.00
12	Craig Biggio	15.00
13	Barry Bonds	50.00
14	Bobby Bonilla	12.00
15	Kevin Brown	12.00
16	Jay Buhner	15.00
17	Ellis Burks	.20
18	Mike Cameron	15.00
19	Ken Caminiti	15.00
20	Jose Canseco	15.00
21	Joe Carter	12.00
22	Vinny Castilla	8.00
23	Jeff Cirillo	8.00
24	Tony Clark	35.00
25	Will Clark	20.00
26	Roger Clemens	80.00
27	David Cone	12.00
28	Jose Cruz Jr.	60.00
29	Carlos Delgado	8.00
30	Jason Dickson	8.00
31	Dennis Eckersley	8.00
32	Jim Edmonds	12.00
33	Scott Erickson	8.00
34	Darin Erstad	50.00
35	Shawn Estes	8.00
36	Jeff Fassero	8.00
37	Alex Fernandez	8.00
38	Chuck Finley	8.00
39	Steve Finley	8.00
40	Travis Fryman	12.00
41	Andres Galarraga	20.00
42	Ron Gant	12.00
43	Nomar Garciaparra	100.00
44	Jason Giambi	8.00
45	Tom Glavine	15.00
46	Juan Gonzalez	100.00
47	Mark Grace	15.00
48	Willie Green	8.00
49	Rusty Greer	12.00
50	Ben Grieve	75.00
51	Ken Griffey Jr.	200.00
52	Mark Grudzielanek	8.00
53	Vladimir Guerrero	50.00
54	Juan Guzman	8.00
55	Tony Gwynn	100.00
56	Joey Hamilton	8.00
57	Rickey Henderson	8.00
58	Pat Hentgen	12.00
59	Livan Hernandez	12.00
60	Bobby Higginson	8.00
61	Todd Hundley	12.00
62	Hideki Irabu	20.00
63	John Jaha	8.00
64	Derek Jeter	100.00
65	Charles Johnson	8.00
66	Randy Johnson	40.00
67	Andruw Jones	50.00
68	Bobby Jones	8.00
69	Chipper Jones	120.00
70	Brian Jordan	8.00
71	David Justice	20.00
72	Eric Karros	8.00
73	Jeff Kent	8.00
74	Jimmy Key	8.00
75	Darryl Kile	8.00
76	Jeff King	8.00
77	Ryan Klesko	25.00
78	Chuck Knoblauch	20.00
79	Ray Lankford	8.00
80	Barry Larkin	15.00
81	Kenny Lofton	50.00
82	Greg Maddux	120.00
83	Al Martin	8.00
84	Edgar Martinez	12.00
85	Pedro Martinez	25.00
86	Tino Martinez	20.00
87	Mark McGwire	250.00
88	Paul Molitor	35.00
89	Raul Mondesi	20.00
90	Jamie Moyer	8.00
91	Mike Mussina	40.00
92	Tim Naehring	8.00
93	Charles Nagy	8.00
94	Denny Neagle	12.00
95	Dave Nilsson	8.00
96	Hideo Nomo	40.00
97	Rey Ordonez	8.00
98	Dean Palmer	8.00
99	Rafael Palmeiro	15.00
100	Andy Pettitte	35.00
101	Mike Piazza	120.00
102	Brad Radke	8.00
103	Manny Ramirez	40.00
104	Edgar Renteria	8.00
105	Cal Ripken Jr.	160.00
106	Alex Rodriguez	120.00
107	Henry Rodriguez	8.00
108	Ivan Rodriguez	50.00
109	Scott Rolen	60.00
110	Tim Salmon	25.00
111	Curt Schilling	15.00
112	Gary Sheffield	20.00
113	John Smoltz	12.00
114	J.T. Snow	8.00
115	Sammy Sosa	120.00
116	Matt Stairs	8.00
117	Shannon Stewart	8.00
118	Frank Thomas	150.00
119	Jim Thome	30.00
120	Justin Thompson	15.00
121	Mo Vaughn	50.00
122	Robin Ventura	15.00
123	Larry Walker	25.00
124	Rondell White	15.00
125	Bernie Williams	40.00
126	Matt Williams	20.00
127	Tony Womack	8.00
128	Jaret Wright	100.00
129	Edgar Renteria (Baseball's Best)	8.00
130	Kenny Lofton (Baseball's Best)	25.00
131	Tony Gwynn (Baseball's Best)	50.00
132	Mark McGwire (Baseball's Best)	100.00
133	Craig Biggio (Baseball's Best)	12.00
134	Charles Johnson (Baseball's Best)	8.00
135	J.T. Snow (Baseball's Best)	8.00
136	Ken Caminiti (Baseball's Best)	12.00
137	Vladimir Guerrero (Baseball's Best)	25.00
138	Jim Edmonds (Baseball's Best)	12.00
139	Randy Johnson (Baseball's Best)	20.00
140	Darryl Kile (Baseball's Best)	8.00
141	John Smoltz (Baseball's Best)	12.00
142	Greg Maddux (Baseball's Best)	60.00
143	Andy Pettitte (Baseball's Best)	20.00
144	Ken Griffey Jr. (Baseball's Best)	100.00
145	Mike Piazza (Baseball's Best)	60.00
146	Todd Greene (Baseball's Best)	8.00
147	Vinny Castilla (Baseball's Best)	8.00
148	Derek Jeter (Baseball's Best)	25.00

149 Travis Lee 125.00 (One to Watch)
150 Mike Gulan 8.00 (One to Watch)
151 Randall Simon 12.00 (One to Watch)
152 Michael Coleman 8.00 (One to Watch)
153 Brian Rose 15.00 (One to Watch)
154 *Scott Eyre* 12.00 (One to Watch)
155 Magglio Ordonez 25.00 (One to Watch)
156 Todd Helton 35.00 (One to Watch)
157 Juan Encarnacion 8.00 (One to Watch)
158 Mark Kotsay 20.00 (One to Watch)
159 Josh Booty 8.00 (One to Watch)
160 *Melvin Rosario* 12.00 (One to Watch)
161 Shane Halter 8.00 (One to Watch)
162 Paul Konerko 35.00 (One to Watch)
163 *Henry Blanco* 8.00 (One to Watch)
164 Antone Williamson 8.00 (One to Watch)
165 Brad Fullmer 15.00 (One to Watch)
166 Ricky Ledee 20.00 (One to Watch)
167 Ben Grieve 35.00 (One to Watch)
168 Frank Catalanotto 8.00 (One to Watch)
169 Bobby Estalella 8.00 (One to Watch)
170 Dennis Reyes 8.00 (One to Watch)
171 Kevin Polcovich 8.00 (One to Watch)
172 Jacob Cruz 8.00 (One to Watch)
173 Ken Cloude 8.00 (One to Watch)
174 Eli Marrero 8.00 (One to Watch)
175 Fernando Tatis 8.00 (One to Watch)
176 Tom Evans 8.00 (One to Watch)
177 Everett, Garciaparra 25.00 (97 in Review)
178 Eric Davis 8.00 (97 in Review)
179 Roger Clemens 40.00 (97 in Review)
180 Butler, Murray 8.00 (97 in Review)
181 Frank Thomas 75.00 (97 in Review)
182 Curt Schilling 8.00 (97 in Review)
183 Jeff Bagwell 40.00 (97 in Review)
184 McGwire, Griffey 80.00 (97 in Review)
185 Kevin Brown 8.00 (97 in Review)
186 Cordova, Rincon 8.00 (97 in Review)
187 Charles Johnson 8.00 (97 in Review)
188 Hideki Irabu 12.00 (97 in Review)
189 Tony Gwynn 40.00 (97 in Review)
190 Sandy Alomar 8.00 (97 in Review)
191 Ken Griffey Jr. 100.00 (97 in Review)
192 Larry Walker 15.00 (97 in Review)
193 Roger Clemens 40.00 (97 in Review)
194 Pedro Martinez 20.00 (97 in Review)
195 Nomar Garciaparra 40.00 (97 in Review)
196 Scott Rolen 30.00 (97 in Review)
197 Brian Anderson 8.00 (97 in Review)
198 Tony Saunders 8.00 (97 in Review)
199 Fla. Celebration 15.00 (97 in Review)
200 Livan Hernandez 12.00 (97 in Review)

1998 Fleer Sports Illustrated Autographs

This six-card insert featured autographs of players with the following production: Brock 500, Cruz Jr. 250, Fingers 500, Grieve 250, Konerko 250 and Robinson 500.

The Konerko and Greive cards were available through redemptions.

	MT
Complete Set (6):	400.00
Common Player:	30.00
Jose Cruz Jr. (250)	100.00
Ben Grieve (250)	90.00
Paul Konerko (250)	60.00
Lou Brock (500)	75.00
Rollie Fingers (500)	30.00
Brooks Robinson (250)	75.00

1998 Fleer Sports Illustrated Covers

This 10-card insert set pictures actual Sports Illustrated covers on trading cards. The cards are numbered with a "C" prefix and inserted one per nine packs.

	MT
Complete Set (10):	45.00
Common Player:	2.50
Inserted 1:9	
C1 Griffey, Piazza	10.00
C2 Derek Jeter	6.00
C3 Ken Griffey Jr.	12.00
C4 Cal Ripken Jr.	10.00
C5 Manny Ramirez	4.00
C6 Jay Buhner	2.50
C7 Matt Williams	3.00
C8 Randy Johnson	4.00
C9 Deion Sanders	2.50
C10 Jose Canseco	2.50

1998 Fleer Sports Illustrated Editor's Choice

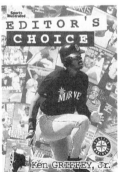

Editor's Choice includes 10 top players in 1998 as profiled by the editors of Sports Illustrated. Cards are numbered with an "EC" prefix and seeded one per 24 packs.

	MT
Complete Set (10):	100.00
Common Player:	4.00
Inserted 1:24	
EP1 Ken Griffey Jr.	20.00
EP2 Alex Rodriguez	12.00
EP3 Frank Thomas	15.00
EP4 Mark McGwire	25.00
EP5 Greg Maddux	12.00
EP6 Derek Jeter	12.00
EP7 Cal Ripken Jr.	15.00
EP8 Nomar Garciaparra	12.00
EP9 Jeff Bagwell	8.00
EP10 Jose Cruz Jr.	8.00

1998 Fleer Sports Illustrated Mini-Posters

Thirty 5" x 7" mini-posters were available at a rate of one per pack. The posters took the top player or two from each team and added their 1998 schedule. Backs were blank so the cards are numbered on the front with a "OD" prefix.

	MT
Complete Set (30):	8.00
Common Player:	.15
Inserted 1:1	
OD1 Tim Salmon	.25
OD2 Travis Lee	1.50
OD3 Smoltz, Maddux	.75
OD4 Cal Ripken Jr.	1.00
OD5 Nomar Garciaparra	.75
OD6 Sammy Sosa	.50
OD7 Frank Thomas	1.25
OD8 Barry Larkin	.15
OD9 David Justice	.15
OD10 Larry Walker	.25
OD11 Tony Clark	.40
OD12 Livan Hernandez	.15
OD13 Jeff Bagwell	.60
OD14 Kevin Appier	.15
OD15 Mike Piazza	1.00
OD16 Fernando Vina	.15
OD17 Chuck Knoblauch	.25
OD18 Vladimir Guerrero	.40
OD19 Rey Ordonez	.15
OD20 Bernie Williams	.40
OD21 Matt Stairs	.15
OD22 Curt Schilling	.15
OD23 Tony Womack	.15
OD24 Mark McGwire	2.00
OD25 Tony Gwynn	.75
OD26 Barry Bonds	.50
OD27 Ken Griffey Jr.	1.50
OD28 Fred McGriff	.25
OD29 Gonzalez, Rodriguez	.75
OD30 Roger Clemens	.75

1998 Fleer Sports Illustrated Then & Now

Then and Now was the first of three Sports Illustrated Baseball releases in 1998. It contained 150 cards and sold in six-card packs, with five cards and a mini- poster. Fronts carried photos of active and retired players, as well as rookies. There was only one subset - A Place in History (37-53) - and it compared statistics between current players and retired greats. The product arrived with an Extra Edition parallel set, Art of the Game, Autograph Redemptions, Covers and Great Shots inserts. There was also an Alex Rodriguez checklist/mini-poster seeded every 12th pack.

	MT
Complete Set (150):	25.00
Common Player:	.10
Wax Box:	45.00
1 Luis Aparicio (Legends of the Game)	.10
2 Richie Ashburn (Legends of the Game)	.10
3 Ernie Banks (Legends of the Game)	.75
4 Yogi Berra (Legends of the Game)	.75
5 Lou Boudreau (Legends of the Game)	.10
6 Lou Brock (Legends of the Game)	.25
7 Jim Bunning (Legends of the Game)	.10
8 Rod Carew (Legends of the Game)	.25
9 Bob Feller (Legends of the Game)	.25
10 Rollie Fingers (Legends of the Game)	.10
11 Bob Gibson (Legends of the Game)	.50
12 Fergie Jenkins (Legends of the Game)	.10
13 Al Kaline (Legends of the Game)	.25
14 George Kell (Legends of the Game)	.10
15 Harmon Killebrew (Legends of the Game)	.50
16 Ralph Kiner (Legends of the Game)	.10
17 Tommy Lasorda (Legends of the Game)	.10
18 Juan Marichal (Legends of the Game)	.10
19 Eddie Mathews (Legends of the Game)	.40
20 Willie Mays (Legends of the Game)	1.50
21 Willie McCovey (Legends of the Game)	.10
22 Joe Morgan (Legends of the Game)	.10
23 Gaylord Perry (Legends of the Game)	.10
24 Kirby Puckett (Legends of the Game)	1.00
25 Pee Wee Reese (Legends of the Game)	.10
26 Phil Rizzuto (Legends of the Game)	.25
27 Robin Roberts (Legends of the Game)	.10
28 Brooks Robinson (Legends of the Game)	.75
29 Frank Robinson (Legends of the Game)	.50
30 Red Schoendienst (Legends of the Game)	.10
31 Enos Slaughter (Legends of the Game)	.10
32 Warren Spahn (Legends of the Game)	.50
33 Willie Stargell (Legends of the Game)	.20
34 Earl Weaver (Legends of the Game)	.10
35 Billy Williams (Legends of the Game)	.20
36 Early Wynn (Legends of the Game)	.10
37 Rickey Henderson (A Place in History)	.10
38 Greg Maddux (A Place in History)	1.50
39 Mike Mussina (A Place in History)	.50
40 Cal Ripken Jr. (A Place in History)	2.00
41 Albert Belle (A Place in History)	.60
42 Frank Thomas (A Place in History)	2.00
43 Jeff Bagwell (A Place in History)	.75
44 Paul Molitor (A Place in History)	.40
45 Chuck Knoblauch (A Place in History)	.25
46 Todd Hundley (A Place in History)	.10
47 Bernie Williams (A Place in History)	.40
48 Tony Gwynn (A Place in History)	1.00
49 Barry Bonds (A Place in History)	.60
50 Ken Griffey Jr. (A Place in History)	2.50
51 Randy Johnson (A Place in History)	.50
52 Mark McGwire (A Place in History)	3.00
53 Roger Clemens (A Place in History)	.75
54 Jose Cruz Jr. (A Place in History)	1.00
55 Roberto Alomar (Legends of Today)	.50
56 Sandy Alomar (Legends of Today)	.10
57 Brady Anderson (Legends of Today)	.10
58 Kevin Appier (Legends of Today)	.10
59 Jeff Bagwell (Legends of Today)	.75
60 Albert Belle (Legends of Today)	.60
61 Dante Bichette (Legends of Today)	.20
62 Craig Biggio (Legends of Today)	.20
63 Barry Bonds (Legends of Today)	.60
64 Kevin Brown (Legends of Today)	.10
65 Jay Buhner (Legends of Today)	.20
66 Ellis Burks (Legends of Today)	.10
67 Ken Caminiti (Legends of Today)	.25
68 Jose Canseco (Legends of Today)	.25
69 Joe Carter (Legends of Today)	.10
70 Vinny Castilla (Legends of Today)	.10
71 Tony Clark (Legends of Today)	.40
72 Roger Clemens (Legends of Today)	.75
73 David Cone (Legends of Today)	.20
74 Jose Cruz Jr. (Legends of Today)	1.00
75 Jacon Dickson (Legends of Today)	.10
76 Jim Edmonds (Legends of Today)	.10
77 Scott Erickson (Legends of Today)	.10
78 Darin Erstad (Legends of Today)	.60
79 Alex Fernandez (Legends of Today)	.10
80 Steve Finley (Legends of Today)	.10
81 Travis Fryman (Legends of Today)	.10
82 Andres Galarraga (Legends of Today)	.25
83 Nomar Garciaparra (Legends of Today)	2.00
84 Tom Glavine (Legends of Today)	.20
85 Juan Gonzalez (Legends of Today)	1.50
86 Mark Grace (Legends of Today)	.25
87 Willie Greene (Legends of Today)	.10
88 Ken Griffey Jr. (Legends of Today)	2.50
89 Vladimir Guerrero (Legends of Today)	.75
90 Tony Gwynn (Legends of Today)	1.00
91 Livan Hernandez (Legends of Today)	.10
92 Bobby Higginson (Legends of Today)	.10
93 Derek Jeter (Legends of Today)	1.50
94 Charles Johnson (Legends of Today)	.10
95 Randy Johnson (Legends of Today)	.40
96 Andruw Jones (Legends of Today)	1.00
97 Chipper Jones (Legends of Today)	1.50
98 David Justice (Legends of Today)	.25
99 Eric Karros (Legends of Today)	.10

100	Jason Kendall (Legends of Today)	.10
101	Jimmy Key (Legends of Today)	.10
102	Darryl Kile (Legends of Today)	.10
103	Chuck Knoblauch (Legends of Today)	.25
104	Ray Lankford (Legends of Today)	.10
105	Barry Larkin (Legends of Today)	.20
106	Kenny Lofton (Legends of Today)	.60
107	Greg Maddux (Legends of Today)	1.50
108	Al Martin (Legends of Today)	.10
109	Edgar Martinez (Legends of Today)	.10
110	Pedro Martinez (Legends of Today)	.25
111	Ramon Martinez (Legends of Today)	.10
112	Tino Martinez (Legends of Today)	.25
113	Mark McGwire (Legends of Today)	3.00
114	Raul Mondesi (Legends of Today)	.25
115	Matt Morris (Legends of Today)	.10
116	Charles Nagy (Legends of Today)	.10
117	Denny Neagle (Legends of Today)	.10
118	Hideo Nomo (Legends of Today)	.75
119	Dean Palmer (Legends of Today)	.10
120	Andy Pettitte (Legends of Today)	.50
121	Mike Piazza (Legends of Today)	1.50
122	Manny Ramirez (Legends of Today)	.50
123	Edgar Renteria (Legends of Today)	.10
124	Cal Ripken Jr. (Legends of Today)	2.00
125	Alex Rodriguez (Legends of Today)	1.50
126	Henry Rodriguez (Legends of Today)	.10
127	Ivan Rodriguez (Legends of Today)	.60
128	Scott Rolen (Legends of Today)	1.00
129	Tim Salmon (Legends of Today)	.25
130	Curt Schilling (Legends of Today)	.10
131	Gary Sheffield (Legends of Today)	.25
132	John Smoltz (Legends of Today)	.20
133	Sammy Sosa (Legends of Today)	1.50
134	Frank Thomas (Legends of Today)	2.50
135	Jim Thome (Legends of Today)	.50
136	Mo Vaughn (Legends of Today)	.60
137	Robin Ventura (Legends of Today)	.10
138	Larry Walker (Legends of Today)	.25
139	Bernie Williams (Legends of Today)	.40
140	Matt Williams (Legends of Today)	.25
141	Jaret Wright (Legends of Today)	1.00
142	Michael Coleman (Legends of the Future)	.10
143	Juan Encarnacion (Legends of the Future)	.20
144	Brad Fullmer (Legends of the Future)	.25
145	Ben Grieve (Legends of the Future)	1.00
146	Todd Helton (Legends of the Future)	.75
147	Paul Konerko (Legends of the Future)	.75
148	Derrek Lee (Legends of the Future)	.20
149	*Magglio Ordonez* (Legends of the Future)	.75
150	Enrique Wilson (Legends of the Future)	.10

1998 Fleer Sports Illustrated Then & Now Extra Edition

This 150-card set paralleled the base set and was distinguished by an "Extra Edition" foil stamp on the front. There were 500 sets of Extra Edition and the cards were individually numbered on the back.

	MT
Extra Edition Stars:	25x to 40x
Yng Stars & RCs:	15x to 25x
Production 500 sets	

1998 Fleer Sports Illustrated Then & Now Art of the Game

"Brooks"

Art of the Game was an eight-card insert featuring reproductions of original artwork of current and retired baseball stars done by eight popular sports artists, including world renowned T.S. O'Connell. They are numbered with a "AG" prefix and inserted one per nine packs.

	MT
Complete Set (8):	45.00
Common Player:	3.00
Inserted 1:9	
AG1 It's Gone	10.00
AG2 Alex Rodriguez	8.00
AG3 Mike Piazza	8.00
AG4 Brooks Robinson	5.00
AG5 David Justice (All-Star)	4.00
AG6 Cal Ripken Jr.	10.00
AG7 The Prospect and the Prospector	3.00
AG8 Barry Bonds	5.00

1998 Fleer Sports Illustrated Then & Now Autographs

Six autograph redemption cards were randomly inserted into packs of Then & Now and could be exchanged prior to the Nov. 1, 1999. The signed cards were produced in the following quantities: Clemens 250, Gibson 500, Gwynn 250, Killebrew 500, Mays 250 and Rolen 250. Four of the six

cards, excluding Gibson and Rolen, used the same fronts as the Covers insert. Gibson and Rolen cards both featured unique card fronts.

	MT
Complete Set (6):	600.00
Common Autograph:	70.00
Bob Gibson (500)	70.00
Tony Gwynn (250)	200.00
Roger Clemens (250)	200.00
Scott Rolen (250)	125.00
Willie Mays (250)	175.00
Harmon Killebrew (500)	70.00

1998 Fleer Sports Illustrated Then & Now Covers

This 12-card insert features color shots of six actual Sports Illustrated covers, including six current players and six retired players. The cards are numbered with a "C" prefix and were seeded one per 18 packs.

		MT
Complete Set (12):		75.00
Common Player:		4.00
Inserted 1:18		
C1	Lou Brock (10/16/67)	4.00
C2	Kirby Puckett (4/6/92)	8.00
C3	Harmon Killebrew (4/8/63 - inside)	4.00
C4	Eddie Mathews (8/16/54)	10.00
C5	Willie Mays (5/22/72)	10.00
C6	Frank Robinson (10/6/69)	8.00
C7	Cal Ripken Jr. (9/11/95)	12.00
C8	Roger Clemens (5/12/86)	8.00
C9	Ken Griffey Jr. (10/16/95)	15.00
C10	Mark McGwire (6/1/92)	20.00
C11	Tony Gwynn (7/28/97)	8.00
C12	Ivan Rodriguez (8/11/97)	5.00

1998 Fleer Sports Illustrated Then & Now Great Shots!

This 25-card set featured 5" x 7" fold-out mini-posters using Sports Illustrated photos. Great Shots were inserted

one per pack and contained a mix of retired and current players.

		MT
Complete Set (25):		5.00
Common Player:		.10
Inserted 1:1		
1	Ken Griffey Jr.	1.00
2	Frank Thomas	1.00
3	Alex Rodriguez	.60
4	Andruw Jones	.40
5	Chipper Jones	.60
6	Cal Ripken Jr.	.75
7	Mark McGwire	2.00
8	Derek Jeter	.60
9	Greg Maddux	.60
10	Jeff Bagwell	.40
11	Mike Piazza	.60
12	Scott Rolen	.40
13	Nomar Garciaparra	.60
14	Jose Cruz Jr.	.50
15	Charles Johnson	.10
16	Fergie Jenkins	.10
17	Lou Brock	.10
18	Bob Gibson	.10
19	Harmon Killebrew	.10
20	Juan Marichal	.10
21	Brooks Robinson	.25
22	Rod Carew	.20
23	Yogi Berra	.25
24	Willie Mays	.50
25	Kirby Puckett	.50

1998 Fleer Sports Illustrated Then & Now Road to Cooperstown

Road to Cooperstown features 10 current players who are having Hall of Fame careers. The insert name is printed across the back in bold, gold letters. Cards are numbered with a "RC" prefix and were inserted one per 24 packs.

		MT
Complete Set (10):		80.00
Common Player:		2.00
Inserted 1:24		
RC1	Barry Bonds	5.00
RC2	Roger Clemens	8.00
RC3	Ken Griffey Jr.	20.00
RC4	Tony Gwynn	10.00
RC5	Rickey Henderson	2.00
RC6	Greg Maddux	12.00
RC7	Paul Molitor	4.00
RC8	Mike Piazza	12.00
RC9	Cal Ripken Jr.	15.00
RC10	Frank Thomas	20.00

1998 Fleer Sports Illustrated World Series Fever

The third and final Sports Illustrated release of 1998 contained 150 cards and focused on the World Series while recapping memorable moments from the season. The set also included many stars of tomorrow, like Kerry Wood, Orlando Hernandez, Ben Grieve and Travis Lee. Once again, all the photos were taken from Sports Illustrated archives. The set has two subsets - 10 Magnificent Moments and 20 Cover Collection. The set is paralleled twice in Extra and First Edition parallel sets, and has three insert sets - MVP Collection, Reggie Jackson's Picks and Autumn Excellence.

		MT
Complete Set (150):		25.00
Common Player:		.10
Wax Box:		42.00
1	Mickey Mantle (Covers)	2.00
2	1957 World Series Preview (Covers)	.20
3	1958 World Series Preview (Covers)	.20
4	1959 World Series Preview (Covers)	.20
5	1962 World Series (Covers)	.20
6	Lou Brock (Covers)	.40
7	Brooks Robinson (Covers)	.75
8	Frank Robinson (Covers)	.50
9	1974 World Series (Covers)	.20
10	Reggie Jackson (Covers)	.50
11	1985 World Series (Covers)	.20
12	1987 World Series (Covers)	.20
13	Orel Hershiser (Covers)	.10
14	Rickey Henderson (Covers)	.10
15	1991 World Series (Covers)	.20
16	1992 World Series (Covers)	.10
17	Joe Carter (Covers)	.10
18	1995 World Series (Covers)	.20
19	1996 World Series (Covers)	.40
20	Edgar Renteria (Covers)	.10
21	Bill Mazeroski (Magnificent Moments)	.10
22	Joe Carter (Magnificent Moments)	.10
23	Carlton Fisk (Magnificent Moments)	.10
24	Bucky Dent (Magnificent Moments)	.10
25	Mookie Wilson (Magnificent Moments)	.10
26	Enos Slaughter (Magnificent Moments)	.10
27	Mickey Lolich (Magnificent Moments)	.10
28	Bobby Richardson (Magnificent Moments)	.10
29	Kirk Gibson (Magnificent Moments)	.10
30	Edgar Renteria (Magnificent Moments)	.10
31	Albert Belle	.75
32	Kevin Brown	.10
33	Brian Rose	.10
34	Ron Gant	.20
35	Jeromy Burnitz	.10
36	Andres Galarraga	.40
37	Jim Edmonds	.10
38	Jose Cruz Jr.	.75
39	Mark Grudzielanek	.10
40	Shawn Estes	.10
41	Mark Grace	.25
42	Nomar Garciaparra	2.00
43	Juan Gonzalez	1.50
44	Tom Glavine	.20
45	Brady Anderson	.10
46	Tony Clark	.50
47	Jeff Cirillo	.10
48	Dante Bichette	.25
49	Ben Grieve	1.00
50	Ken Griffey Jr.	3.00

51	Edgardo Alfonzo	.10
52	Roger Clemens	1.00
53	Pat Hentgen	.10
54	Todd Helton	.75
55	Andy Benes	.10
56	Tony Gwynn	1.50
57	Andruw Jones	.75
58	Bobby Higginson	.10
59	Bobby Jones	.10
60	Darryl Kile	.10
61	Chan Ho Park	.25
62	Charles Johnson	.10
63	Rusty Greer	.10
64	Travis Fryman	.10
65	Derek Jeter	1.50
66	Jay Buhner	.25
67	Chuck Knoblauch	.40
68	David Justice	.40
69	Brian Hunter	.10
70	Eric Karros	.20
71	Edgar Martinez	.10
72	Chipper Jones	2.00
73	Barry Larkin	.25
74	Mike Lansing	.10
75	Craig Biggio	.25
76	Al Martin	.10
77	Barry Bonds	.75
78	Randy Johnson	.50
79	Ryan Klesko	.25
80	Mark McGwire	4.00
81	Fred McGriff	.25
82	Javy Lopez	.10
83	Kenny Lofton	.75
84	Sandy Alomar Jr.	.10
85	Matt Morris	.10
86	Paul Konerko	.25
87	Ray Lankford	.10
88	Kerry Wood	4.00
89	Roberto Alomar	.50
90	Greg Maddux	2.00
91	Travis Lee	2.00
92	Moises Alou	.25
93	Dean Palmer	.10
94	Hideo Nomo	.50
95	Ken Caminiti	.20
96	Pedro Martinez	.75
97	Raul Mondesi	.25
98	Denny Neagle	.20
99	Tino Martinez	.30
100	Mike Mussina	.60
101	Kevin Appier	.10
102	Vinny Castilla	.20
103	Jeff Bagwell	1.00
104	Paul O'Neill	.20
105	Rey Ordonez	.10
106	Vladimir Guerrero	.75
107	Rafael Palmeiro	.25
108	Alex Rodriguez	2.00
109	Andy Pettitte	.50
110	Carl Pavano	.20
111	Henry Rodriguez	.10
112	Gary Sheffield	.25
113	Curt Schilling	.20
114	John Smoltz	.20
115	Reggie Sanders	.10
116	Scott Rolen	1.00
117	Mike Piazza	2.00
118	Manny Ramirez	.75
119	Cal Ripken Jr.	2.50
120	Brad Radke	.10
121	Tim Salmon	.30
122	Brett Tomko	.10
123	Robin Ventura	.10
124	Mo Vaughn	.75
125	A.J. Hinch	.10
126	Derrek Lee	.10
127	*Orlando Hernandez*	3.00
128	Aramis Ramirez	.75
129	Frank Thomas	2.50
130	J.T. Snow	.10
131	*Magglio Ordonez*	.75
132	Bobby Bonilla	.20
133	Marquis Grissom	.10
134	Jim Thome	.50
135	Justin Thompson	.10
136	Matt Williams	.30
137	Matt Stairs	.10
138	Wade Boggs	.25
139	Chuck Finley	.10
140	Jaret Wright	.75
141	Ivan Rodriguez	.75
142	Brad Fullmer	.25
143	Bernie Williams	.50
144	Jason Giambi	.10
145	Larry Walker	.40
146	Tony Womack	.10
147	Sammy Sosa	1.50
148	Rondell White	.20
149	Todd Stottlemyre	.10
150	Shane Reynolds	.10

1998 Fleer Sports Illustrated WS Fever Extra Edition

Extra Edition paralleled the entire 150-card base set and were identified by a gold foil stamp on the card front and sequential numbering to 98 sets on the back. World Series Fever also included one-of-one parallel versions called First Edition. These had the same fronts, but were numbered 1 of 1 on the back.

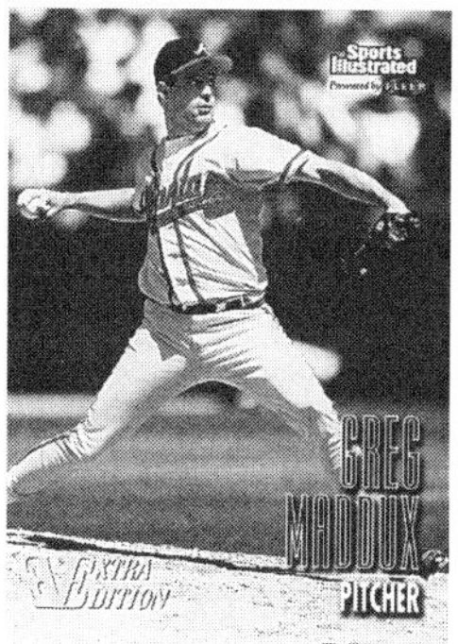

		MT
Common Player:		15.00
Semistars:		40.00
Extra Edition Stars:		50x to 80x
Extra Edition Yng Stars & RC:		30x to 50x
Production 98 sets		
1	Mickey Mantle (Covers)	75.00
2	1957 World Series Preview (Covers)	25.00
3	1958 World Series Preview (Covers)	25.00
4	1959 World Series Preview (Covers)	25.00
5	1962 World Series (Covers)	20.00
6	Lou Brock (Covers)	30.00
7	Brooks Robinson (Covers)	40.00
8	Frank Robinson (Covers)	40.00
9	1974 World Series (Covers)	25.00
10	Reggie Jackson (Covers)	50.00
11	1985 World Series (Covers)	20.00
12	1987 World Series (Covers)	25.00
13	Orel Hershiser (Covers)	15.00
14	Rickey Henderson (Covers)	15.00
15	1991 World Series (Covers)	25.00
16	1992 World Series (Covers)	15.00
17	Joe Carter (Covers)	15.00
18	1995 World Series (Covers)	25.00
19	1996 World Series (Covers)	40.00
20	Edgar Renteria (Covers)	15.00
21	Bill Mazeroski (Magnificent Moments)	15.00
22	Joe Carter (Magnificent Moments)	15.00
23	Carlton Fisk (Magnificent Moments)	15.00
24	Bucky Dent (Magnificent Moments)	15.00
25	Mookie Wilson (Magnificent Moments)	15.00
26	Enos Slaughter (Magnificent Moments)	15.00
27	Mickey Lolich (Magnificent Moments)	15.00
28	Bobby Richardson (Magnificent Moments)	15.00
29	Kirk Gibson (Magnificent Moments)	15.00
30	Edgar Renteria (Magnificent Moments)	15.00
31	Albert Belle	60.00
32	Kevin Brown	15.00
33	Brian Rose	15.00
34	Ron Gant	20.00
35	Jeromy Burnitz	15.00
36	Andres Galarraga	30.00
37	Jim Edmonds	15.00
38	Jose Cruz Jr.	60.00
39	Mark Grudzielanek	15.00
40	Shawn Estes	15.00
41	Mark Grace	25.00
42	Nomar Garciaparra	150.00
43	Juan Gonzalez	125.00
44	Tom Glavine	20.00
45	Brady Anderson	15.00
46	Tony Clark	40.00
47	Jeff Cirillo	15.00
48	Dante Bichette	25.00
49	Ben Grieve	80.00
50	Ken Griffey Jr.	250.00
51	Edgardo Alfonzo	15.00
52	Roger Clemens	90.00
53	Pat Hentgen	15.00
54	Todd Helton	50.00
55	Andy Benes	15.00
56	Tony Gwynn	125.00
57	Andruw Jones	60.00
58	Bobby Higginson	15.00
59	Bobby Jones	15.00
60	Darryl Kile	15.00
61	Chan Ho Park	30.00
62	Charles Johnson	15.00
63	Rusty Greer	15.00
64	Travis Fryman	15.00
65	Derek Jeter	120.00
66	Jay Buhner	30.00
67	Chuck Knoblauch	35.00
68	David Justice	30.00
69	Brian Hunter	15.00
70	Eric Karros	20.00
71	Edgar Martinez	15.00
72	Chipper Jones	150.00
73	Barry Larkin	25.00
74	Mike Lansing	15.00
75	Craig Biggio	25.00
76	Al Martin	15.00
77	Barry Bonds	60.00
78	Randy Johnson	40.00
79	Ryan Klesko	25.00
80	Mark McGwire	275.00
81	Fred McGriff	25.00
82	Javy Lopez	15.00
83	Kenny Lofton	60.00
84	Sandy Alomar Jr.	15.00
85	Matt Morris	15.00
86	Paul Konerko	25.00
87	Ray Lankford	15.00
88	Kerry Wood	180.00
89	Roberto Alomar	40.00
90	Greg Maddux	150.00
91	Travis Lee	150.00
92	Moises Alou	25.00
93	Dean Palmer	15.00
94	Hideo Nomo	40.00
95	Ken Caminiti	20.00
96	Pedro Martinez	60.00
97	Raul Mondesi	25.00
98	Denny Neagle	20.00
99	Tino Martinez	30.00
100	Mike Mussina	50.00
101	Kevin Appier	15.00
102	Vinny Castilla	20.00
103	Jeff Bagwell	75.00
104	Paul O'Neill	20.00
105	Rey Ordonez	15.00
106	Vladimir Guerrero	60.00
107	Rafael Palmeiro	25.00
108	Alex Rodriguez	150.00
109	Andy Pettitte	40.00
110	Carl Pavano	20.00
111	Henry Rodriguez	15.00
112	Gary Sheffield	25.00
113	Curt Schilling	20.00
114	John Smoltz	20.00
115	Reggie Sanders	15.00
116	Scott Rolen	75.00
117	Mike Piazza	150.00
118	Manny Ramirez	60.00
119	Cal Ripken Jr.	200.00
120	Brad Radke	15.00
121	Tim Salmon	25.00
122	Brett Tomko	15.00
123	Robin Ventura	15.00
124	Mo Vaughn	60.00
125	A.J. Hinch	15.00
126	Derrek Lee	15.00
127	Orlando Hernandez	100.00
128	Aramis Ramirez	30.00
129	Frank Thomas	200.00
130	J.T. Snow	15.00
131	Magglio Ordonez	35.00
132	Bobby Bonilla	20.00
133	Marquis Grissom	15.00
134	Jim Thome	40.00
135	Justin Thompson	15.00
136	Matt Williams	30.00
137	Matt Stairs	15.00
138	Wade Boggs	25.00
139	Chuck Finley	15.00
140	Jaret Wright	50.00
141	Ivan Rodriguez	60.00
142	Brad Fullmer	25.00
143	Bernie Williams	40.00
144	Jason Giambi	15.00
145	Larry Walker	40.00
146	Tony Womack	15.00
147	Sammy Sosa	125.00
148	Rondell White	20.00
149	Todd Stottlemyre	15.00
150	Shane Reynolds	15.00

1998 Fleer Sports Illustrated WS Fever Autumn Excellence

Autumn Excellence honors players with the most select World Series records. The 10-card set was seeded one per 24 packs, while rarer Gold versions were seeded one per 240 packs.

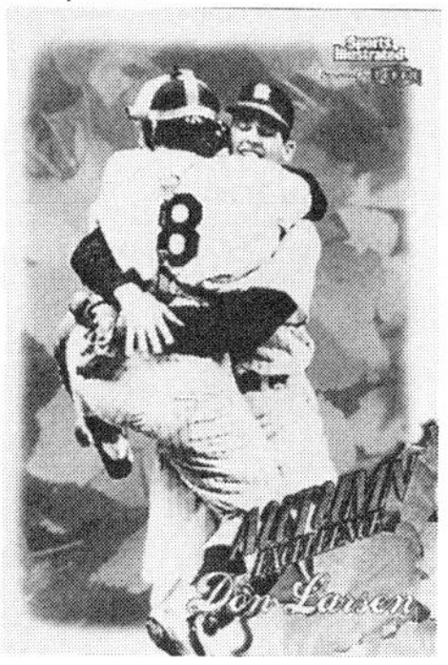

		MT
Complete Set (10):		60.00
Common Player:		2.00
Inserted 1:24		
Golds:		3x to 5x
Inserted 1:240		
AE1	Willie Mays	6.00
AE2	Kirby Puckett	8.00
AE3	Babe Ruth	25.00
AE4	Reggie Jackson	4.00
AE5	Whitey Ford	2.00
AE6	Lou Brock	4.00
AE7	Mickey Mantle	15.00
AE8	Yogi Berra	5.00
AE9	Bob Gibson	4.00
AE10	Don Larsen	2.00

1998 Fleer Sports Illustrated WS Fever MVP Collection

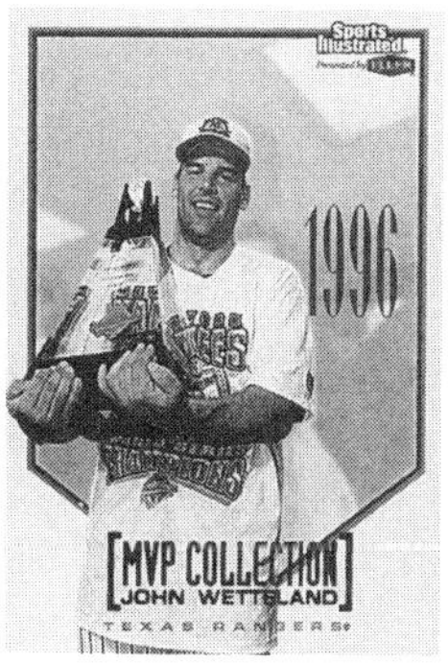

This 10-card insert set features select MVPs from the World Series. Card fronts contain a shot of the player over a white border with the year in black letters and the insert and player's name in blue foil. MVP Collection inserts were seeded one per four packs and numbered with a "MC" prefix.

		MT
Complete Set (10):		15.00
Common Player:		1.50
Inserted 1:4		
MC1	Frank Robinson	3.00
MC2	Brooks Robinson	4.00
MC3	Willie Stargell	1.50
MC4	Bret Saberhagen	1.50
MC5	Rollie Fingers	1.50
MC6	Orel Hershiser	1.50
MC7	Paul Molitor	4.00
MC8	Tom Glavine	1.50
MC9	John Wetteland	1.50
MC10	Livan Hernandez	1.50

1998 Fleer Sports Illustrated WS Fever Reggie Jackson Picks

Reggie Jackson's Picks contains top players that Jackson believes have what it takes to perform on center stage in the World Series. Fronts have a shot of the player with his name in the background, and a head shot of Reggie Jackson in the bottom right corner. These were numbered with a "RP" prefix and inserted one per 12 packs.

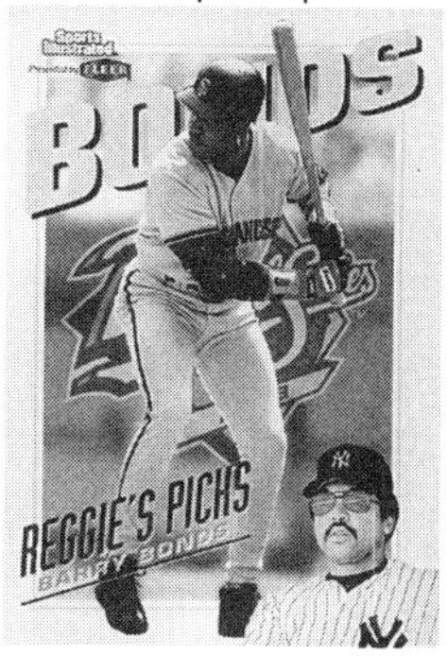

		MT
Complete Set (15):		140.00
Common Player:		3.00
Inserted 1:12		
R1	Paul O'Neill	3.00
R2	Barry Bonds	6.00
R3	Ken Griffey Jr.	25.00
R4	Juan Gonzalez	12.00
R5	Greg Maddux	15.00
R6	Mike Piazza	15.00
R7	Larry Walker	4.00
R8	Mo Vaughn	6.00
R9	Roger Clemens	8.00
R10	John Smoltz	3.00
R11	Alex Rodriguez	15.00
R12	Frank Thomas	20.00
R13	Mark McGwire	30.00
R14	Jeff Bagwell	8.00
R15	Randy Johnson	5.00

1998 Leaf

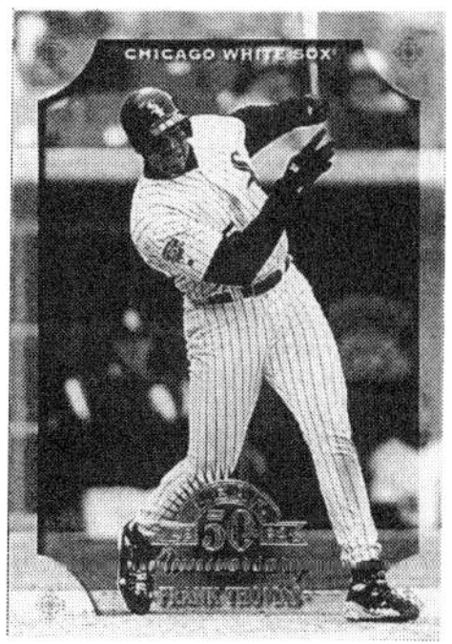

The 50th Anniversary edition of Leaf Baseball consists of a 200-card base set with three subsets, three parallels and four inserts. The base set has 147 regular cards, a 10-card Curtain Calls subset, Gold Leaf Stars subset (20 cards), Gold Leaf Rookies subset (20 cards) and three checklists. Card #42 does not exist because Leaf retired the number in honor of Jackie Robinson. The base set was paralleled in Fractal Matrix, Fractal Matrix Die-Cuts and Fractal Diamond Axis. Inserts include Crusade, Heading for the Hall, State Representatives and Statistical Standouts.

		MT
Complete Set (200):		200.00
Common Player:		.10
Wax Box:		65.00
1	Rusty Greer	.10
2	Tino Martinez	.25
3	Bobby Bonilla	.15
4	Jason Giambi	.10
5	Matt Morris	.20
6	Craig Counsell	.10
7	Reggie Jefferson	.10
8	Brian Rose	.25
9	Ruben Rivera	.10
10	Shawn Estes	.10
11	Tony Gwynn	1.50
12	Jeff Abbott	.10
13	Jose Cruz Jr.	1.50
14	Francisco Cordova	.10
15	Ryan Klesko	.30
16	Tim Salmon	.30
17	Brett Tomko	.10
18	Matt Williams	.25

19 Joe Carter .20
20 Harold Baines .10
21 Gary Sheffield .25
22 Charles Johnson .20
23 Aaron Boone .20
24 Eddie Murray .20
25 Matt Stairs .10
26 David Cone .20
27 Jon Nunnally .10
28 Chris Stynes .10
29 Enrique Wilson .10
30 Randy Johnson .50
31 Garret Anderson .10
32 Manny Ramirez .60
33 Jeff Suppan .10
34 Rickey Henderson .10
35 Scott Spiezio .10
36 Rondell White .20
37 Todd Greene .20
38 Delino DeShields .10
39 Kevin Brown .20
40 Chili Davis .10
41 Jimmy Key .10
42 .10
43 Mike Mussina .60
44 Joe Randa .10
45 Chan Ho Park .20
46 Brad Radke .10
47 Geronimo Berroa .10
48 Wade Boggs .25
49 Kevin Appier .10
50 Moises Alou .20
51 David Justice .25
52 Ivan Rodriguez .75
53 J.T. Snow .20
54 Brian Giles .10
55 Will Clark .25
56 Justin Thompson .10
57 Javier Lopez .20
58 Hideki Irabu .30
59 Mark Grudzielanek .10
60 Abraham Nunez .10
61 Todd Hollandsworth .10
62 Jay Bell .10
63 Nomar Garciaparra 2.00
64 Vinny Castilla .10
65 Lou Collier .10
66 Kevin Orie .10
67 John Valentin .10
68 Robin Ventura .20
69 Denny Neagle .20
70 Tony Womack .10
71 Dennis Reyes .10
72 Wally Joyner .10
73 Kevin Brown .20
74 Ray Durham .10
75 Mike Cameron .20
76 Dante Bichette .25
77 Jose Guillen .25
78 Carlos Delgado .20
79 Paul Molitor .40
80 Jason Kendall .10
81 Mark Belhorn .10
82 Damian Jackson .10
83 Bill Mueller .10
84 Kevin Young .10
85 Curt Schilling .20
86 Jeffrey Hammonds .10
87 Sandy Alomar Jr. .20
88 Bartolo Colon .10
89 Wilton Guerrero .10
90 Bernie Williams .50
91 Deion Sanders .25
92 Mike Piazza 2.00
93 Butch Huskey .10
94 Edgardo Alfonzo .10
95 Alan Benes .20
96 Craig Biggio .20
97 Mark Grace .25
98 Shawn Green .10
99 Derrek Lee .25
100 Ken Griffey Jr. 3.00
101 Tim Raines .10
102 Pokey Reese .10
103 Lee Stevens .10
104 Shannon Stewart .10
105 John Smoltz .20
106 Frank Thomas 2.50
107 Jeff Fassero .10
108 Jay Buhner .20
109 Jose Canseco .25
110 Omar Vizquel .10
111 Travis Fryman .10
112 Dave Nilsson .10
113 John Olerud .10
114 Larry Walker .25
115 Jim Edmonds .20
116 Bobby Higginson .20
117 Todd Hundley .10
118 Paul O'Neill .20
119 Bip Roberts .10
120 Ismael Valdes .10
121 Pedro Martinez .25
122 Jeff Cirillo .10
123 Andy Benes .20
124 Bobby Jones .10
125 Brian Hunter .10
126 Darryl Kile .10
127 Pat Hentgen .10
128 Marquis Grissom .10
129 Eric Davis .10
130 Chipper Jones 2.00
131 Edgar Martinez .10
132 Andy Pettitte .50
133 Cal Ripken Jr. 2.50
134 Scott Rolen 1.50
135 Ron Coomer .10
136 Luis Castillo .10
137 Fred McGriff .20
138 Neifi Perez .10
139 Eric Karros .20
140 Alex Fernandez .10
141 Jason Dickson .10
142 Lance Johnson .10
143 Ray Lankford .10
144 Sammy Sosa 2.00
145 Eric Young .10
146 Bubba Trammell .20
147 Todd Walker .20
148 Mo Vaughn (Curtain Calls) 3.00
149 Jeff Bagwell (Curtain Calls) 5.00
150 Kenny Lofton (Curtain Calls) 3.00
151 Raul Mondesi (Curtain Calls) 1.50
152 Mike Piazza (Curtain Calls) 10.00
153 Chipper Jones (Curtain Calls) 8.00
154 Larry Walker (Curtain Calls) 1.50
155 Greg Maddux (Curtain Calls) 10.00
156 Ken Griffey Jr. (Curtain Calls) 15.00
157 Frank Thomas (Curtain Calls) 12.00
158 Darin Erstad (Gold Leaf Stars) 3.00
159 Roberto Alomar (Gold Leaf Stars) 2.00
160 Albert Belle (Gold Leaf Stars) 3.00
161 Jim Thome (Gold Leaf Stars) 1.50
162 Tony Clark (Gold Leaf Stars) 2.00
163 Chuck Knoblauch (Gold Leaf Stars) 1.50
164 Derek Jeter (Gold Leaf Stars) 8.00
165 Alex Rodriguez (Gold Leaf Stars) 8.00
166 Tony Gwynn (Gold Leaf Stars) 6.00
167 Roger Clemens (Gold Leaf Stars) 5.00
168 Barry Larkin (Gold Leaf Stars) 1.00
169 Andres Galarraga (Gold Leaf Stars) 1.00
170 Vladimir Guerrero (Gold Leaf Stars) 3.00
171 Mark McGwire (Gold Leaf Stars) 20.00
172 Barry Bonds (Gold Leaf Stars) 3.00
173 Juan Gonzalez (Gold Leaf Stars) 6.00
174 Andruw Jones (Gold Leaf Stars) 6.00
175 Paul Molitor (Gold Leaf Stars) 2.00
176 Hideo Nomo (Gold Leaf Stars) 3.00
177 Cal Ripken Jr. (Gold Leaf Stars) 12.00
178 Brad Fullmer (Gold Leaf Rookies) 1.50
179 Jaret Wright (Gold Leaf Rookies) 8.00
180 Bobby Estalella (Gold Leaf Rookies) .75
181 Ben Grieve (Gold Leaf Rookies) 5.00
182 Paul Konerko (Gold Leaf Rookies) 4.00
183 David Ortiz (Gold Leaf Rookies) 1.00
184 Todd Helton (Gold Leaf Rookies) 3.00
185 Juan Encarnacion (Gold Leaf Rookies) .75
186 Miguel Tejada (Gold Leaf Rookies) 3.00
187 Jacob Cruz (Gold Leaf Rookies) 1.00
188 Mark Kotsay (Gold Leaf Rookies) 1.50
189 Fernando Tatis (Gold Leaf Rookies) 1.00
190 Ricky Ledee (Gold Leaf Rookies) 1.00
191 Richard Hidalgo (Gold Leaf Rookies) .75
192 Richie Sexson (Gold Leaf Rookies) .75
193 Luis Ordaz (Gold Leaf Rookies) .75
194 Eli Marrero (Gold Leaf Rookies) .75
195 Livan Hernandez (Gold Leaf Rookies) 1.50
196 Homer Bush (Gold Leaf Rookies) .75
197 Raul Ibanez (Gold Leaf Rookies) .75
198 Checklist (Nomar Garciaparra) 1.50
199 Checklist (Scott Rolen) 1.00
200 Checklist (Jose Cruz Jr.) .25

1998 Fleer Leaf Diamond Axis

As part of the 50th anniversary for Leaf Baseball, a special Diamond Axis parallel was created. The parallel reprints each card in the set (1-41, 43-201) on a Diamond Axis die-cut, with only 50 sequentially numbered sets available.

	MT
Common Player:	15.00
Diamond Axis Stars:	60x to 100x
Yng Stars & RCs:	30x to 60x
SP (148-177):	15x to 25x

1998 Leaf Fractal Matrix

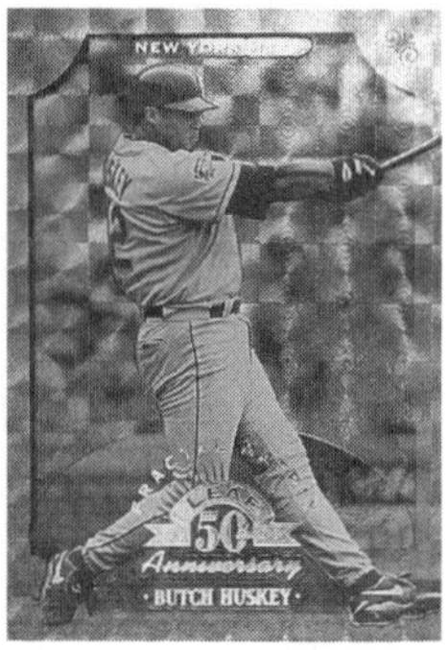

Fractal Matrix parallels the 1998 Leaf set. The cards have a metallic-colored finish, with 100 done in bronze, 60 in silver and 40 in gold.

	MT
Complete Set (200):	
Common Bronze:	1.50
Bronze Semistars:	4.00
Common Silver:	5.00
Silver Semistars:	10.00
Common Gold:	10.00
Common G/X Axis:	40.00
Gold Semistars:	20.00

1 Rusty Greer G/Z 10.00
2 Tino Martinez G/Z 20.00
3 Bobby Bonilla S/Y 8.00
4 Jason Giambi S/Y 5.00
5 Matt Morris S/Y 5.00
6 Craig Counsell B/X 1.50
7 Reggie Jefferson B/X 1.50
8 Brian Rose S/Y 15.00
9 Ruben Rivera B/X 3.00
10 Shawn Estes S/Y 5.00
11 Tony Gwynn G/Z 80.00
12 Jeff Abbott B/Y 1.50
13 Jose Cruz Jr. G/Z 80.00
14 Francisco Cordova B/X 1.50
15 Ryan Klesko B/X 8.00
16 Tim Salmon G/Y 30.00
17 Brett Tomko B/X 1.50
18 Matt Williams S/Y 12.00
19 Joe Carter B/X 3.00
20 Harold Baines B/X 1.50
21 Gary Sheffield S/Z 20.00
22 Charles Johnson S/X 5.00
23 Aaron Boone B/X 4.00
24 Eddie Murray G/Y 20.00
25 Matt Stairs B/X 1.50
26 David Cone B/X 4.00
27 Jon Nunnally B/X 1.50
28 Chris Stynes B/X 1.50
29 Enrique Wilson B/Y 1.50
30 Randy Johnson S/Z 30.00
31 Garret Anderson S/Y 5.00
32 Manny Ramirez G/Z 35.00
33 Jeff Suppan S/X 5.00
34 Rickey Henderson B/X 1.50
35 Scott Spiezio B/X 1.50
36 Rondell White S/Y 10.00
37 Todd Greene S/Z 10.00
38 Delino DeShields B/X 1.50
39 Kevin Brown S/X 8.00
40 Chili Davis B/X 1.50
41 Jimmy Key B/X 1.50
42 Not Issued 1.50
43 Mike Mussina G/Y 40.00
44 Joe Randa B/X 1.50
45 Chan Ho Park S/Z 10.00
46 Brad Radke B/X 1.50
47 Geronimo Berroa B/X 1.50
48 Wade Boggs S/Y 10.00
49 Kevin Appier B/X 1.50
50 Moises Alou S/Y 10.00
51 David Justice G/Y 20.00
52 Ivan Rodriguez G/Z 40.00
53 J.T. Snow B/X 3.00
54 Brian Giles B/X 1.50
55 Will Clark B/Y 5.00
56 Justin Thompson S/Y 5.00
57 Javier Lopez S/X 8.00
58 Hideki Irabu B/Z 10.00
59 Mark Grudzielanek B/X 1.50
60 Abraham Nunez S/X 10.00
61 Todd Hollandsworth B/X 1.50
62 Jay Bell B/X 1.50
63 Nomar Garciaparra G/Z 100.00
64 Vinny Castilla B/Y 1.50
65 Lou Collier B/Y 1.50
66 Kevin Orie S/X 5.00
67 John Valentin B/X 1.50
68 Robin Ventura B/X 3.00
69 Denny Neagle B/X 3.00
70 Tony Womack S/Y 5.00
71 Dennis Reyes S/Y 5.00
72 Wally Joyner B/X 1.50
73 Kevin Brown B/Y 3.00
74 Ray Durham B/X 1.50
75 Mike Cameron S/Z 10.00
76 Dante Bichette B/X 4.00
77 Jose Guillen G/Y 20.00
78 Carlos Delgado B/Y 1.50
79 Paul Molitor G/Z 30.00
80 Jason Kendall B/X 1.50
81 Mark Belhorn B/X 1.50
82 Damian Jackson B/X 1.50
83 Bill Mueller B/X 1.50
84 Kevin Young B/X 1.50
85 Curt Schilling B/X 4.00
86 Jeffrey Hammonds B/X 1.50
87 Sandy Alomar Jr. S/Y 10.00
88 Bartolo Colon B/Y 1.50
89 Wilton Guerrero B/Y 1.50
90 Bernie Williams G/Y 40.00
91 Deion Sanders S/Y 12.00
92 Mike Piazza G/X 300.00
93 Butch Huskey B/X 1.50
94 Edgardo Alfonzo S/X 5.00
95 Alan Benes S/Y 10.00
96 Craig Biggio S/Y 10.00
97 Mark Grace S/Y 12.00
98 Shawn Green S/Y 5.00
99 Derrek Lee S/Y 10.00
100 Ken Griffey Jr. G/Z 160.00
101 Tim Raines B/X 1.50
102 Pokey Reese S/X 5.00
103 Lee Stevens B/X 1.50
104 Shannon Stewart S/Y 5.00
105 John Smoltz S/Y 10.00
106 Frank Thomas G/X 350.00
107 Jeff Fassero B/X 1.50
108 Jay Buhner B/Y 4.00
109 Jose Canseco B/X 4.00
110 Omar Vizquel B/X 1.50
111 Travis Fryman B/X 1.50
112 Dave Nilsson B/X 1.50
113 John Olerud B/X 1.50
114 Larry Walker G/Z 25.00
115 Jim Edmonds S/Y 10.00
116 Bobby Higginson S/X 10.00
117 Todd Hundley S/X 8.00
118 Paul O'Neill B/X 3.00
119 Bip Roberts B/X 1.50
120 Ismael Valdes B/X 1.50
121 Pedro Martinez S/Y 15.00
122 Jeff Cirillo B/X 1.50
123 Andy Benes B/X 1.50
124 Bobby Jones B/X 1.50
125 Brian Hunter B/X 1.50
126 Darryl Kile B/X 1.50
127 Pat Hentgen B/X 1.50
128 Marquis Grissom B/X 1.50
129 Eric Davis B/X 1.50
130 Chipper Jones G/Z 100.00
131 Edgar Martinez S/Z 5.00
132 Andy Pettitte G/Z 30.00
133 Cal Ripken Jr. G/X 400.00
134 Scott Rolen G/Z 75.00
135 Ron Coomer B/X 1.50
136 Luis Castillo B/Y 1.50
137 Fred McGriff B/Y 4.00
138 Neifi Perez S/Y 5.00
139 Eric Karros B/X 3.00
140 Alex Fernandez B/X 1.50
141 Jason Dickson B/X 1.50
142 Lance Johnson B/X 1.50
143 Ray Lankford B/Y 1.50
144 Sammy Sosa G/Y 75.00
145 Eric Young B/Y 1.50
146 Bubba Trammell S/Y 10.00
147 Todd Walker S/Y 10.00
148 Mo Vaughn S/X (Curtain Calls) 20.00
149 Jeff Bagwell S/X (Curtain Calls) 30.00
150 Kenny Lofton S/X (Curtain Calls) 20.00
151 Raul Mondesi S/X (Curtain Calls) 10.00
152 Mike Piazza S/X (Curtain Calls) 50.00
153 Chipper Jones S/X (Curtain Calls) 50.00
154 Larry Walker S/X (Curtain Calls) 10.00
155 Greg Maddux S/X (Curtain Calls) 50.00
156 Ken Griffey Jr. S/X (Curtain Calls) 80.00
157 Frank Thomas S/X (Curtain Calls) 60.00
158 Darin Erstad B/Z (Gold Leaf Stars) 8.00
159 Roberto Alomar B/Y (Gold Leaf Stars) 5.00
160 Albert Belle G/Y (Gold Leaf Stars) 25.00
161 Jim Thome G/Y (Gold Leaf Stars) 18.00
162 Tony Clark G/Y (Gold Leaf Stars) 18.00
163 Chuck Knoblauch B/Y (Gold Leaf Stars) 4.00
164 Derek Jeter G/Z (Gold Leaf Stars) 50.00
165 Alex Rodriguez G/Z (Gold Leaf Stars) 50.00
166 Tony Gwynn B/X (Gold Leaf Stars) 25.00
167 Roger Clemens G/Z (Gold Leaf Stars) 30.00
168 Barry Larkin B/Y (Gold Leaf Stars) 4.00
169 Andres Galarraga B/Y (Gold Leaf Stars) 4.00
170 Vladimir Guerrero G/Z (Gold Leaf Stars) 25.00
171 Mark McGwire B/Z (Gold Leaf Stars) 30.00
172 Barry Bonds B/Z (Gold Leaf Stars) 12.00
173 Juan Gonzalez G/Z (Gold Leaf Stars) 40.00
174 Andruw Jones G/Z (Gold Leaf Stars) 40.00
175 Paul Molitor B/X (Gold Leaf Stars) 5.00
176 Hideo Nomo B/Z (Gold Leaf Stars) 15.00
177 Cal Ripken Jr. B/X (Gold Leaf Stars) 20.00
178 Brad Fullmer S/Z (Gold Leaf Rookies) 12.00
179 Jaret Wright G/Z (Gold Leaf Rookies) 50.00
180 Bobby Estalella B/Y (Gold Leaf Rookies) 1.50
181 Ben Grieve G/X (Gold Leaf Rookies) 120.00
182 Paul Konerko G/Z (Gold Leaf Rookies) 30.00
183 David Ortiz G/Z (Gold Leaf Rookies) 15.00
184 Todd Helton G/X (Gold Leaf Rookies) 80.00
185 Juan Encarnacion G/Z (Gold Leaf Rookies) 20.00
186 Miguel Tejada G/Z (Gold Leaf Rookies) 25.00
187 Jacob Cruz B/Y (Gold Leaf Rookies) 3.00
188 Mark Kotsay G/Z (Gold Leaf Rookies) 20.00
189 Fernando Tatis S/Z (Gold Leaf Rookies) 10.00
190 Ricky Ledee S/Y (Gold Leaf Rookies) 12.00
191 Richard Hidalgo S/Y (Gold Leaf Rookies) 5.00
192 Richie Sexson S/Y (Gold Leaf Rookies) 5.00
193 Luis Ordaz B/X (Gold Leaf Rookies) 1.50
194 Eli Marrero S/Z (Gold Leaf Rookies) 8.00
195 Livan Hernandez S/Z (Gold Leaf Rookies) 10.00
196 Homer Bush B/X (Gold Leaf Rookies) 1.50
197 Raul Ibanez B/X (Gold Leaf Rookies) 1.50
198 Checklist (Nomar Garciaparra B/X) 15.00
199 Checklist (Scott Rolen B/X) 10.00
200 Checklist (Jose Cruz Jr. B/X) 15.00

1998 Leaf Fractal Matrix Die-Cut

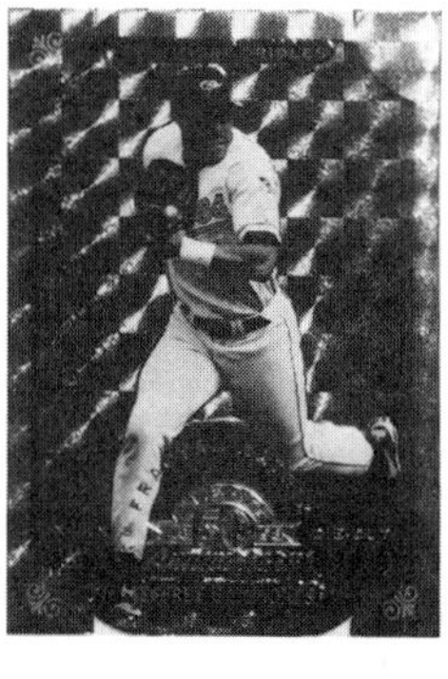

fsThis parallel set adds a die-cut to the Fractal Matrix set. Three different die-cut versions were created: x-axis, y-axis and z-axis. An x-axis die-cut was added to 75 bronze, 20 silver and five gold cards. A y-axis die-cut was added to 20 bronze, 30 silver and 10 gold cards. Of the 40 z-axis cards, five are bronze, 10 silver and 25 gold.

		MT
	Common X-Axis:	6.00
	Common Y-Axis:	10.00
	Y-Axis Semistars:	20.00
	Common Z-Axis:	20.00
	Z-Axis Semistars:	30.00
1	Rusty Greer G/Z	20.00
2	Tino Martinez G/Z	30.00
3	Bobby Bonilla S/Y	15.00
4	Jason Giambi S/Y	12.00
5	Matt Morris S/Y	15.00
6	Craig Counsell B/X	6.00
7	Reggie Jefferson B/X	6.00
8	Brian Rose S/Y	20.00
9	Ruben Rivera B/X	10.00
10	Shawn Estes S/Y	10.00
11	Tony Gwynn G/Z	150.00
12	Jeff Abbott B/Y	10.00
13	Jose Cruz Jr. G/Z	150.00
14	Francisco Cordova B/X	6.00
15	Ryan Klesko B/X	15.00
16	Tim Salmon G/Y	25.00
17	Brett Tomko B/X	6.00
18	Matt Williams S/Y	20.00
19	Joe Carter B/X	10.00
20	Harold Baines B/X	6.00
21	Gary Sheffield S/Z	40.00
22	Charles Johnson S/X	8.00
23	Aaron Boone B/X	8.00
24	Eddie Murray G/Y	20.00
25	Matt Stairs B/X	6.00
26	David Cone B/X	10.00
27	Jon Nunnally B/X	6.00
28	Chris Stynes B/X	6.00
29	Enrique Wilson B/Y	10.00
30	Randy Johnson S/Z	50.00
31	Garret Anderson S/Y	10.00
32	Manny Ramirez G/Z	60.00
33	Jeff Suppan S/X	6.00
34	Rickey Henderson B/X	6.00
35	Scott Spiezio B/X	6.00
36	Rondell White S/Y	20.00
37	Todd Greene S/Z	30.00
38	Delino DeShields B/X	6.00
39	Kevin Brown S/X	8.00
40	Chili Davis B/X	6.00
41	Jimmy Key B/X	6.00
42	Not Issued	6.00
43	Mike Mussina G/Y	40.00
44	Joe Randa B/X	6.00
45	Chan Ho Park S/Z	30.00
46	Brad Radke B/X	6.00
47	Geronimo Berroa B/X	6.00
48	Wade Boggs S/Y	25.00
49	Kevin Appier B/X	6.00
50	Moises Alou S/Y	15.00
51	David Justice G/Y	25.00
52	Ivan Rodriguez G/Z	75.00
53	J.T. Snow B/X	8.00
54	Brian Giles B/X	6.00
55	Will Clark B/Y	20.00
56	Justin Thompson S/Y	10.00
57	Javier Lopez S/X	8.00
58	Hideki Irabu B/Z	50.00
59	Mark Grudzielanek B/X	6.00
60	Abraham Nunez S/X	10.00
61	Todd Hollandsworth B/X	6.00
62	Jay Bell B/X	6.00
63	Nomar Garciaparra G/Z	200.00
64	Vinny Castilla B/Y	10.00
65	Lou Collier B/Y	10.00
66	Kevin Orie S/X	6.00
67	John Valentin B/X	6.00
68	Robin Ventura B/X	8.00
69	Denny Neagle B/X	8.00
70	Tony Womack S/Y	10.00
71	Dennis Reyes S/Y	10.00
72	Wally Joyner B/X	6.00
73	Kevin Brown B/Y	15.00
74	Ray Durham B/X	6.00
75	Mike Cameron S/Z	30.00
76	Dante Bichette B/X	10.00
77	Jose Guillen G/Y	20.00
78	Carlos Delgado B/Y	15.00
79	Paul Molitor G/Z	60.00
80	Jason Kendall B/X	6.00
81	Mark Belhorn B/X	6.00
82	Damian Jackson B/X	6.00
83	Bill Mueller B/X	6.00
84	Kevin Young B/X	6.00
85	Curt Schilling B/X	10.00
86	Jeffrey Hammonds B/X	6.00
87	Sandy Alomar Jr. S/Y	20.00
88	Bartolo Colon B/Y	6.00
89	Wilton Guerrero B/Y	6.00
90	Bernie Williams G/Y	40.00
91	Deion Sanders S/Y	20.00
92	Mike Piazza G/X	75.00
93	Butch Huskey B/X	6.00
94	Edgardo Alfonzo S/X	6.00
95	Alan Benes S/Y	15.00
96	Craig Biggio S/Y	20.00
97	Mark Grace S/Y	25.00
98	Shawn Green S/Y	10.00
99	Derrek Lee S/Y	20.00
100	Ken Griffey Jr. G/Z	300.00
101	Tim Raines B/X	6.00
102	Pokey Reese S/X	6.00
103	Lee Stevens B/X	6.00
104	Shannon Stewart S/Y	10.00
105	John Smoltz S/Y	20.00
106	Frank Thomas G/X	90.00
107	Jeff Fassero B/X	6.00
108	Jay Buhner B/Y	20.00
109	Jose Canseco B/X	10.00
110	Omar Vizquel B/X	6.00
111	Travis Fryman B/X	8.00
112	Dave Nilsson B/X	6.00
113	John Olerud B/X	8.00
114	Larry Walker G/Z	40.00
115	Jim Edmonds S/Y	20.00
116	Bobby Higginson S/X	10.00
117	Todd Hundley S/X	8.00
118	Paul O'Neill B/X	10.00
119	Bip Roberts B/X	6.00
120	Ismael Valdes B/X	6.00
121	Pedro Martinez S/Y	25.00
122	Jeff Cirillo B/X	6.00
123	Andy Benes B/X	6.00
124	Bobby Jones B/X	6.00
125	Brian Hunter B/X	6.00
126	Darryl Kile B/X	6.00
127	Pat Hentgen B/X	6.00
128	Marquis Grissom B/X	6.00
129	Eric Davis B/X	6.00
130	Chipper Jones G/Z	200.00
131	Edgar Martinez S/Z	20.00
132	Andy Pettitte G/Z	60.00
133	Cal Ripken Jr. G/X	100.00
134	Scott Rolen G/Z	150.00
135	Ron Coomer B/X	6.00
136	Luis Castillo B/Y	10.00
137	Fred McGriff B/Y	20.00
138	Neifi Perez S/Y	10.00
139	Eric Karros B/X	8.00
140	Alex Fernandez B/X	6.00
141	Jason Dickson B/X	6.00
142	Lance Johnson B/X	6.00
143	Ray Lankford B/Y	10.00
144	Sammy Sosa G/Y	75.00
145	Eric Young B/Y	10.00
146	Bubba Trammell S/Y	15.00
147	Todd Walker S/Y	20.00
148	Mo Vaughn S/X (Curtain Calls)	15.00
149	Jeff Bagwell S/X (Curtain Calls)	25.00
150	Kenny Lofton S/X (Curtain Calls)	15.00
151	Raul Mondesi S/X (Curtain Calls)	10.00
152	Mike Piazza S/X (Curtain Calls)	40.00
153	Chipper Jones S/X (Curtain Calls)	40.00
154	Larry Walker S/X (Curtain Calls)	10.00
155	Greg Maddux S/X (Curtain Calls)	40.00
156	Ken Griffey Jr. S/X (Curtain Calls)	75.00
157	Frank Thomas S/X (Curtain Calls)	60.00
158	Darin Erstad B/Z (Gold Leaf Stars)	40.00
159	Roberto Alomar B/Y (Gold Leaf Stars)	20.00
160	Albert Belle G/Y (Gold Leaf Stars)	25.00
161	Jim Thome G/Y (Gold Leaf Stars)	18.00
162	Tony Clark G/Y (Gold Leaf Stars)	18.00
163	Chuck Knoblauch B/Y (Gold Leaf Stars)	20.00
164	Derek Jeter G/Z (Gold Leaf Stars)	100.00
165	Alex Rodriguez G/Z (Gold Leaf Stars)	100.00
166	Tony Gwynn B/X (Gold Leaf Stars)	35.00
167	Roger Clemens G/Z (Gold Leaf Stars)	60.00
168	Barry Larkin B/Y (Gold Leaf Stars)	20.00
169	Andres Galarraga B/Y (Gold Leaf Stars)	20.00
170	Vladimir Guerrero G/Z (Gold Leaf Stars)	50.00
171	Mark McGwire B/Z (Gold Leaf Stars)	100.00
172	Barry Bonds B/Z (Gold Leaf Stars)	40.00
173	Juan Gonzalez G/Z (Gold Leaf Stars)	75.00
174	Andruw Jones G/Z (Gold Leaf Stars)	75.00
175	Paul Molitor B/X (Gold Leaf Stars)	15.00
176	Hideo Nomo B/Z (Gold Leaf Stars)	80.00
177	Cal Ripken Jr. B/X (Gold Leaf Stars)	50.00
178	Brad Fullmer S/Z (Gold Leaf Rookies)	35.00
179	Jaret Wright G/Z (Gold Leaf Rookies)	80.00
180	Bobby Estalella B/Y (Gold Leaf Rookies)	10.00
181	Ben Grieve G/X (Gold Leaf Rookies)	30.00
182	Paul Konerko G/Z (Gold Leaf Rookies)	50.00
183	David Ortiz G/Z (Gold Leaf Rookies)	30.00
184	Todd Helton G/X (Gold Leaf Rookies)	15.00
185	Juan Encarnacion G/Z (Gold Leaf Rookies)	30.00
186	Miguel Tejada G/Z (Gold Leaf Rookies)	40.00
187	Jacob Cruz B/Y (Gold Leaf Rookies)	15.00
188	Mark Kotsay G/Z (Gold Leaf Rookies)	35.00
189	Fernando Tatis S/Z (Gold Leaf Rookies)	25.00
190	Ricky Ledee S/Y (Gold Leaf Rookies)	20.00
191	Richard Hidalgo S/Y (Gold Leaf Rookies)	10.00
192	Richie Sexson S/Y (Gold Leaf Rookies)	10.00
193	Luis Ordaz B/X (Gold Leaf Rookies)	6.00
194	Eli Marrero S/Z (Gold Leaf Rookies)	20.00
195	Livan Hernandez S/Z (Gold Leaf Rookies)	30.00
196	Homer Bush B/X (Gold Leaf Rookies)	6.00
197	Raul Ibanez B/X (Gold Leaf Rookies)	6.00
198	Checklist (Nomar Garciaparra B/X)	40.00
199	Checklist (Scott Rolen B/X)	30.00
200	Checklist (Jose Cruz Jr. B/X)	40.00

1998 Leaf Heading for the Hall

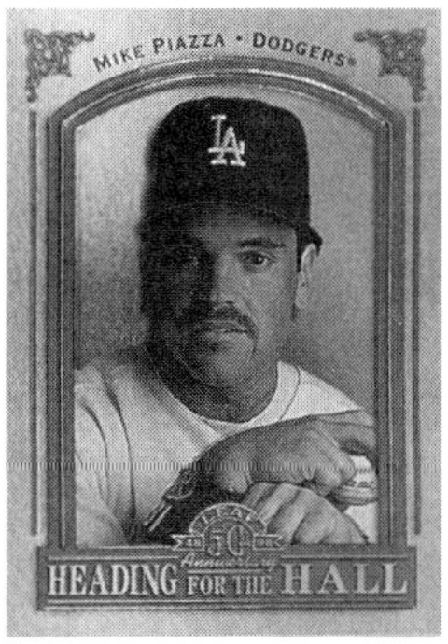

This 20-card insert features players destined for the Hall of Fame. The set is sequentially numbered to 3,500.

		MT
	Complete Set (20):	250.00
	Common Player:	6.00
1	Roberto Alomar	8.00
2	Jeff Bagwell	15.00
3	Albert Belle	10.00
4	Wade Boggs	6.00
5	Barry Bonds	10.00
6	Roger Clemens	15.00
7	Juan Gonzalez	20.00
8	Ken Griffey Jr.	35.00
9	Tony Gwynn	20.00
10	Barry Larkin	6.00
11	Kenny Lofton	10.00
12	Greg Maddux	25.00
13	Mark McGwire	40.00
14	Paul Molitor	8.00
15	Eddie Murray	6.00
16	Mike Piazza	25.00
17	Cal Ripken Jr.	30.00
18	Ivan Rodriguez	10.00
19	Ryne Sandberg	10.00
20	Frank Thomas	30.00

1998 Leaf State Representatives

This 30-card insert features top players. The background has a picture of the state in which he plays. "State Representatives" is printed at the top with the player's name at the bottom. This set is sequentially numbered to 5,000.

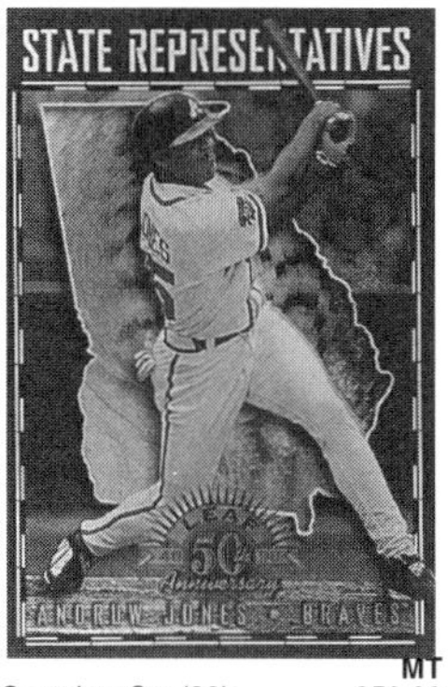

		MT
	Complete Set (30):	250.00
	Common Player:	4.00
1	Ken Griffey Jr.	25.00
2	Frank Thomas	20.00
3	Alex Rodriguez	15.00
4	Cal Ripken Jr.	20.00
5	Chipper Jones	15.00
6	Andruw Jones	12.00
7	Scott Rolen	12.00
8	Nomar Garciaparra	15.00
9	Tim Salmon	6.00
10	Manny Ramirez	8.00
11	Jose Cruz Jr.	10.00
12	Vladimir Guerrero	10.00
13	Tino Martinez	6.00
14	Larry Walker	6.00
15	Mo Vaughn	8.00
16	Jim Thome	6.00
17	Tony Clark	6.00
18	Derek Jeter	15.00
19	Juan Gonzalez	12.00
20	Jeff Bagwell	10.00
21	Ivan Rodriguez	8.00
22	Mark McGwire	30.00
23	David Justice	4.00
24	Chuck Knoblauch	6.00
25	Andy Pettitte	6.00
26	Raul Mondesi	6.00
27	Randy Johnson	6.00
28	Greg Maddux	15.00
29	Bernie Williams	6.00
30	Rusty Greer	4.00

1998 Leaf Statistical Standouts

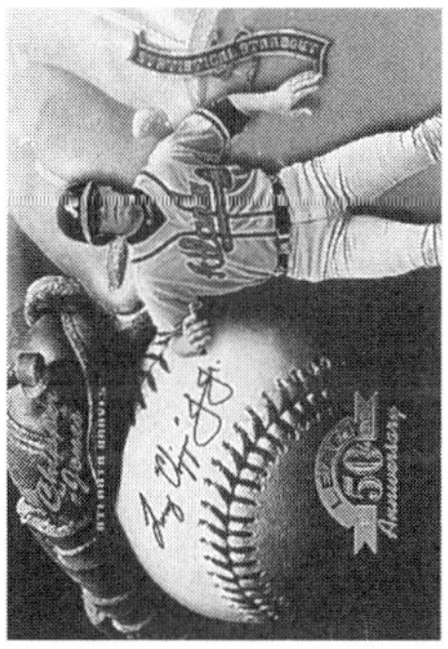

This 24-card insert features players with impressive statistics. The cards have a horizontal layout and the feel of leather. The background has a ball and glove with the player's facsimile signature on the ball. Statistical Standouts is numbered to 2,500.

		MT
	Complete Set (24):	600.00
	Common Player:	10.00
1	Frank Thomas	50.00
2	Ken Griffey Jr.	60.00
3	Alex Rodriguez	40.00
4	Mike Piazza	40.00
5	Greg Maddux	40.00
6	Cal Ripken Jr.	50.00
7	Chipper Jones	40.00
8	Juan Gonzalez	30.00
9	Jeff Bagwell	25.00
10	Mark McGwire	60.00
11	Tony Gwynn	30.00
12	Mo Vaughn	15.00
13	Nomar Garciaparra	40.00
14	Jose Cruz Jr.	25.00
15	Vladimir Guerrero	20.00
16	Scott Rolen	30.00
17	Andy Pettitte	12.00
18	Randy Johnson	12.00
19	Larry Walker	10.00
20	Kenny Lofton	15.00
21	Tony Clark	12.00
22	David Justice	12.00
23	Derek Jeter	35.00
24	Barry Bonds	15.00

1998 Leaf Fractal Foundation

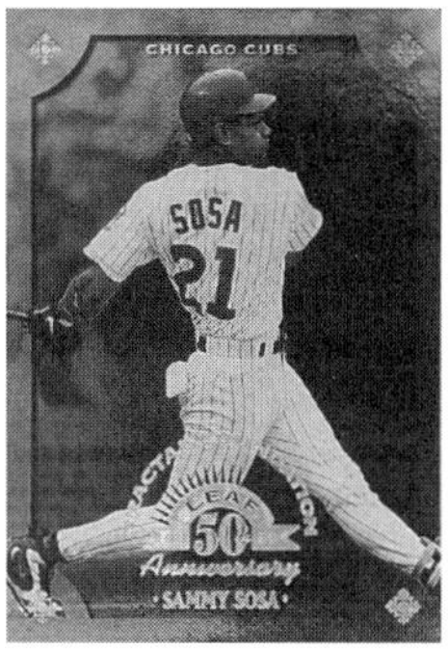

Fractal Foundations is a stand-alone product but it parallels the 1998 Leaf set. It contains the Curtain Calls, Gold Leaf Stars and Gold Leaf Rookies subsets and is missing card #42 which Leaf retired in honor of Jackie Robinson. The set was printed on foil board and each card is numbered to 3,999. The set is paralleled in Fractal Materials, Fractal Materials Die-Cuts and Fractal Materials Z2 Axis.

		MT
	Complete Set (200):	500.00
	Common Player:	1.00
	Wax Box:	125.00
1	Rusty Greer	1.00
2	Tino Martinez	3.00
3	Bobby Bonilla	2.00
4	Jason Giambi	1.00
5	Matt Morris	2.00
6	Craig Counsell	1.00
7	Reggie Jefferson	1.00
8	Brian Rose	3.00
9	Ruben Rivera	1.00
10	Shawn Estes	1.00
11	Tony Gwynn	10.00
12	Jeff Abbott	1.00
13	Jose Cruz Jr.	8.00
14	Francisco Cordova	1.00
15	Ryan Klesko	3.00
16	Tim Salmon	3.00
17	Brett Tomko	1.00
18	Matt Williams	3.00
19	Joe Carter	2.00
20	Harold Baines	1.00
21	Gary Sheffield	3.00
22	Charles Johnson	2.00
23	Aaron Boone	1.00
24	Eddie Murray	3.00
25	Matt Stairs	1.00
26	David Cone	2.00
27	Jon Nunnally	1.00
28	Chris Stynes	1.00
29	Enrique Wilson	1.00
30	Randy Johnson	4.00
31	Garret Anderson	1.00
32	Manny Ramirez	5.00
33	Jeff Suppan	1.00
34	Rickey Henderson	1.00
35	Scott Spiezio	1.00
36	Rondell White	2.00
37	Todd Greene	1.00
38	Delino DeShields	1.00
39	Kevin Brown	2.00
40	Chili Davis	1.00
41	Jimmy Key	1.00
42	Not Issued	1.00
43	Mike Mussina	5.00
44	Joe Randa	1.00
45	Chan Ho Park	2.00
46	Brad Radke	1.00
47	Geronimo Berroa	1.00
48	Wade Boggs	3.00
49	Kevin Appier	1.00
50	Moises Alou	2.00
51	David Justice	3.00
52	Ivan Rodriguez	5.00
53	J.T. Snow	1.00
54	Brian Giles	1.00
55	Will Clark	3.00
56	Justin Thompson	1.00
57	Javier Lopez	2.00
58	Hideki Irabu	3.00
59	Mark Grudzielanek	1.00
60	Abraham Nunez	1.00
61	Todd Hollandsworth	1.00
62	Jay Bell	1.00
63	Nomar Garciaparra	12.00
64	Vinny Castilla	2.00
65	Lou Collier	1.00
66	Kevin Orie	1.00

67 John Valentin 1.00
68 Robin Ventura 2.00
69 Denny Neagle 2.00
70 Tony Womack 1.00
71 Dennis Reyes 1.00
72 Wally Joyner 1.00
73 Kevin Brown 2.00
74 Ray Durham 1.00
75 Mike Cameron 2.00
76 Dante Bichette 3.00
77 Jose Guillen 3.00
78 Carlos Delgado 2.00
79 Paul Molitor 4.00
80 Jason Kendall 1.00
81 Mark Belhorn 1.00
82 Damian Jackson 1.00
83 Bill Mueller 1.00
84 Kevin Young 1.00
85 Curt Schilling 2.00
86 Jeffrey Hammonds 1.00
87 Sandy Alomar Jr. 2.00
88 Bartolo Colon 1.00
89 Wilton Guerrero 1.00
90 Bernie Williams 4.00
91 Deion Sanders 3.00
92 Mike Piazza 12.00
93 Butch Huskey 1.00
94 Edgardo Alfonzo 1.00
95 Alan Benes 2.00
96 Craig Biggio 2.00
97 Mark Grace 2.50
98 Shawn Green 1.00
99 Derrek Lee 3.00
100 Ken Griffey Jr. 20.00
101 Tim Raines 1.00
102 Pokey Reese 1.00
103 Lee Stevens 1.00
104 Shannon Stewart 1.00
105 John Smoltz 2.00
106 Frank Thomas 15.00
107 Jeff Fassero 1.00
108 Jay Buhner 3.00
109 Jose Canseco 3.00
110 Omar Vizquel 1.00
111 Travis Fryman 1.00
112 Dave Nilsson 1.00
113 John Olerud 1.00
114 Larry Walker 3.00
115 Jim Edmonds 2.00
116 Bobby Higginson 2.00
117 Todd Hundley 1.00
118 Paul O'Neill 2.00
119 Bip Roberts 1.00
120 Ismael Valdes 1.00
121 Pedro Martinez 4.00
122 Jeff Cirillo 1.00
123 Andy Benes 2.00
124 Bobby Jones 1.00
125 Brian Hunter 1.00
126 Darryl Kile 1.00
127 Pat Hentgen 1.00
128 Marquis Grissom 1.00
129 Eric Davis 1.00
130 Chipper Jones 12.00
131 Edgar Martinez 1.00
132 Andy Pettitte 3.00
133 Cal Ripken Jr. 15.00
134 Scott Rolen 8.00
135 Ron Coomer 1.00
136 Luis Castillo 1.00
137 Fred McGriff 2.00
138 Neifi Perez 1.00
139 Eric Karros 2.00
140 Alex Fernandez 1.00
141 Jason Dickson 1.00
142 Lance Johnson 1.00
143 Ray Lankford 1.00
144 Sammy Sosa 10.00
145 Eric Young 1.00
146 Bubba Trammell 2.00
147 Todd Walker 2.00
148 Mo Vaughn (Curtain Calls) 6.00
149 Jeff Bagwell (Curtain Calls) 8.00
150 Kenny Lofton (Curtain Calls) 5.00
151 Raul Mondesi (Curtain Calls) 2.00
152 Mike Piazza (Curtain Calls) 12.00
153 Chipper Jones (Curtain Calls) 12.00
154 Larry Walker (Curtain Calls) 3.00
155 Greg Maddux (Curtain Calls) 12.00
156 Ken Griffey Jr. (Curtain Calls) 20.00
157 Frank Thomas (Curtain Calls) 15.00
158 Darin Erstad (Gold Leaf Stars) 5.00
159 Roberto Alomar (Gold Leaf Stars) 4.00
160 Albert Belle (Gold Leaf Stars) 5.00
161 Jim Thome (Gold Leaf Stars) 3.00
162 Tony Clark (Gold Leaf Stars) 3.00
163 Chuck Knoblauch (Gold Leaf Stars) 2.50
164 Derek Jeter (Gold Leaf Stars) 10.00
165 Alex Rodriguez (Gold Leaf Stars) 12.00
166 Tony Gwynn (Gold Leaf Stars) 10.00
167 Roger Clemens (Gold Leaf Stars) 8.00
168 Barry Larkin (Gold Leaf Stars) 3.00
169 Andres Galarraga (Gold Leaf Stars) 3.00
170 Vladimir Guerrero (Gold Leaf Stars) 5.00
171 Mark McGwire (Gold Leaf Stars) 25.00
172 Barry Bonds (Gold Leaf Stars) 5.00
173 Juan Gonzalez (Gold Leaf Stars) 10.00
174 Andruw Jones (Gold Leaf Stars) 6.00
175 Paul Molitor (Gold Leaf Stars) 4.00
176 Hideo Nomo (Gold Leaf Stars) 5.00
177 Cal Ripken Jr. (Gold Leaf Stars) 15.00
178 Brad Fullmer (Gold Leaf Rookies) 3.00
179 Jaret Wright (Gold Leaf Rookies) 8.00
180 Bobby Estalella (Gold Leaf Rookies) 1.00
181 Ben Grieve (Gold Leaf Rookies) 8.00
182 Paul Konerko (Gold Leaf Rookies) 4.00
183 David Ortiz (Gold Leaf Rookies) 2.00
184 Todd Helton (Gold Leaf Rookies) 5.00
185 Juan Encarnacion (Gold Leaf Rookies) 1.00
186 Miguel Tejada (Gold Leaf Rookies) 4.00
187 Jacob Cruz (Gold Leaf Rookies) 1.00
188 Mark Kotsay (Gold Leaf Rookies) 2.00
189 Fernando Tatis (Gold Leaf Rookies) 1.00
190 Ricky Ledee (Gold Leaf Rookies) 2.00
191 Richard Hidalgo (Gold Leaf Rookies) 1.00
192 Richie Sexson (Gold Leaf Rookies) 1.00
193 Luis Ordaz (Gold Leaf Rookies) 1.00
194 Eli Marrero (Gold Leaf Rookies) 1.00
195 Livan Hernandez (Gold Leaf Rookies) 2.00
196 Homer Bush (Gold Leaf Rookies) 1.00
197 Raul Ibanez (Gold Leaf Rookies) 1.00
198 Checklist (Nomar Garciaparra) 6.00
199 Checklist (Scott Rolen) 4.00
200 Checklist (Jose Cruz Jr.) 4.00

1998 Leaf Fractal Materials

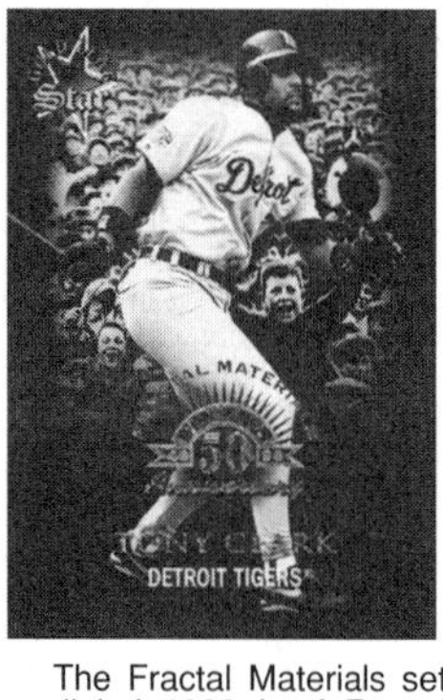

The Fractal Materials set paralleled 1998 Leaf Fractal Foundations. Every card in the set is sequentially numbered. The 200 card set was printed on four different materials: 100 plastic cards (numbered to 3,250), 50 leather (numbered to 1,000), 30 nylon (500) and 20 wood (250). This set was inserted one per pack.

	MT
Common Plastic (3,250):	1.00
Common Leather (1,000):	4.00
Common Nylon (500):	10.00
Common Wood (250):	25.00
Wax Box:	120.00

1 Rusty Greer N 10.00
2 Tino Martinez W 30.00
3 Bobby Bonilla N 15.00
4 Jason Giambi N 10.00
5 Matt Morris L 8.00
6 Craig Counsell P 1.00
7 Reggie Jefferson P 1.00
8 Brian Rose P 2.00
9 Ruben Rivera L 4.00
10 Shawn Estes L 8.00
11 Tony Gwynn W 100.00
12 Jeff Abbott P 1.00
13 Jose Cruz Jr. W 80.00
14 Francisco Cordova P 1.00
15 Ryan Klesko L 15.00
16 Tim Salmon W 30.00
17 Brett Tomko L 4.00
18 Matt Williams N 20.00
19 Joe Carter P 2.00
20 Harold Baines P 1.00
21 Gary Sheffield N 25.00
22 Charles Johnson L 8.00
23 Aaron Boone P 1.00
24 Eddie Murray N 25.00
25 Matt Stairs P 1.00
26 David Cone P 2.00
27 Jon Nunnally P 1.00
28 Chris Stynes P 1.00
29 Enrique Wilson P 1.00
30 Randy Johnson W 40.00
31 Garret Anderson N 10.00
32 Manny Ramirez W 50.00
33 Jeff Suppan L 4.00
34 Rickey Henderson N 20.00
35 Scott Spiezio P 1.00
36 Rondell White L 8.00
37 Todd Greene N 10.00
38 Delino DeShields P 1.00
39 Kevin Brown L 8.00
40 Chili Davis P 1.00
41 Jimmy Key P 1.00
43 Mike Mussina N 30.00
44 Joe Randa P 1.00
45 Chan Ho Park N 15.00
46 Brad Radke P 1.00
47 Geronimo Berroa P 1.00
48 Wade Boggs N 25.00
49 Kevin Appier P 1.00
50 Moises Alou N 15.00
51 David Justice N 20.00
52 Ivan Rodriguez W 50.00
53 J.T. Snow L 6.00
54 Brian Giles P 1.00
55 Will Clark L 15.00
56 Justin Thompson N 10.00
57 Javier Lopez P 2.00
58 Hideki Irabu L 20.00
59 Mark Grudzielanek P 1.00
60 Abraham Nunez P 1.00
61 Todd Hollandsworth P 1.00
62 Jay Bell P 1.00
63 Nomar Garciaparra W 125.00
64 Vinny Castilla P 2.00
65 Lou Collier P 1.00
66 Kevin Orie L 4.00
67 John Valentin P 1.00
68 Robin Ventura P 2.00
69 Denny Neagle P 2.00
70 Tony Womack L 4.00
71 Dennis Reyes L 4.00
72 Wally Joyner P 1.00
73 Kevin Brown P 2.00
74 Ray Durham P 1.00
75 Mike Cameron N 15.00
76 Dante Bichette L 12.00
77 Jose Guillen N 15.00
78 Carlos Delgado L 8.00
79 Paul Molitor W 40.00
80 Jason Kendall P 1.00
81 Mark Belhorn L 4.00
82 Damian Jackson P 1.00
83 Bill Mueller P 1.00
84 Kevin Young P 1.00
85 Curt Schilling P 2.00
86 Jeffrey Hammonds P 1.00
87 Sandy Alomar Jr. L 8.00
88 Bartolo Colon P 2.00
89 Wilton Guerrero L 4.00
90 Bernie Williams N 30.00
91 Deion Sanders N 20.00
92 Mike Piazza W 125.00
93 Butch Huskey L 4.00
94 Edgardo Alfonzo L 4.00
95 Alan Benes L 8.00
96 Craig Biggio N 20.00
97 Mark Grace L 12.00
98 Shawn Green L 4.00
99 Derrek Lee L 10.00
100 Ken Griffey Jr. W 200.00
101 Tim Raines P 1.00
102 Pokey Reese P 1.00
103 Lee Stevens P 1.00
104 Shannon Stewart N 10.00
105 John Smoltz L 10.00
106 Frank Thomas W 160.00
107 Jeff Fassero P 1.00
108 Jay Buhner L 12.00
109 Jose Canseco L 15.00
110 Omar Vizquel P 1.00
111 Travis Fryman P 1.00
112 Dave Nilsson P 1.00
113 John Olerud P 1.00
114 Larry Walker W 30.00
115 Jim Edmonds N 15.00
116 Bobby Higginson L 4.00
117 Todd Hundley L 8.00
118 Paul O'Neill P 2.00
119 Bip Roberts P 1.00
120 Ismael Valdes P 1.00
121 Pedro Martinez N 25.00
122 Jeff Cirillo P 1.00
123 Andy Benes P 1.00
124 Bobby Jones P 1.00
125 Brian Hunter P 1.00
126 Darryl Kile P 1.00
127 Pat Hentgen P 1.00
128 Marquis Grissom P 1.00
129 Eric Davis P 1.00
130 Chipper Jones W 125.00
131 Edgar Martinez N 15.00
132 Andy Pettitte W 40.00
133 Cal Ripken Jr. W 150.00
134 Scott Rolen W 80.00
135 Ron Coomer P 1.00
136 Luis Castillo L 4.00
137 Fred McGriff L 12.00
138 Neifi Perez L 4.00
139 Eric Karros P 2.00
140 Alex Fernandez P 1.00
141 Jason Dickson P 1.00
142 Lance Johnson P 1.00
143 Ray Lankford P 1.00
144 Sammy Sosa N 50.00
145 Eric Young P 1.00
146 Bubba Trammell L 8.00
147 Todd Walker L 8.00
148 Mo Vaughn P (Curtain Calls) 6.00
149 Jeff Bagwell P (Curtain Calls) 8.00
150 Kenny Lofton P (Curtain Calls) 6.00
151 Raul Mondesi P (Curtain Calls) 2.00
152 Mike Piazza P (Curtain Calls) 15.00
153 Chipper Jones P (Curtain Calls) 15.00
154 Larry Walker P (Curtain Calls) 4.00
155 Greg Maddux P (Curtain Calls) 15.00
156 Ken Griffey Jr. P (Curtain Calls) 25.00
157 Frank Thomas P (Curtain Calls) 25.00
158 Darin Erstad L (Gold Leaf Stars) 20.00
159 Roberto Alomar P (Gold Leaf Stars) 5.00
160 Albert Belle L (Gold Leaf Stars) 6.00
161 Jim Thome L (Gold Leaf Stars) 4.00
162 Tony Clark L (Gold Leaf Stars) 5.00
163 Chuck Knoblauch L (Gold Leaf Stars) 4.00
164 Derek Jeter P (Gold Leaf Stars) 12.00
165 Alex Rodriguez P (Gold Leaf Stars) 15.00
166 Tony Gwynn P (Gold Leaf Stars) 12.00
167 Roger Clemens L (Gold Leaf Stars) 35.00
168 Barry Larkin P (Gold Leaf Stars) 3.00
169 Andres Galarraga P (Gold Leaf Stars) 3.00
170 Vladimir Guerrero L (Gold Leaf Stars) 15.00
171 Mark McGwire L (Gold Leaf Stars) 75.00
172 Barry Bonds L (Gold Leaf Stars) 25.00
173 Juan Gonzalez P (Gold Leaf Stars) 12.00
174 Andruw Jones P (Gold Leaf Stars) 8.00
175 Paul Molitor P (Gold Leaf Stars) 5.00
176 Hideo Nomo L (Gold Leaf Stars) 25.00
177 Cal Ripken Jr. P (Gold Leaf Stars) 20.00
178 Brad Fullmer P (Gold Leaf Rookies) 3.00
179 Jaret Wright N (Gold Leaf Rookies) 60.00
180 Bobby Estalella P (Gold Leaf Rookies) 1.00
181 Ben Grieve W (Gold Leaf Rookies) 60.00
182 Paul Konerko W (Gold Leaf Rookies) 25.00
183 David Ortiz N (Gold Leaf Rookies) 12.00
184 Todd Helton W (Gold Leaf Rookies) 40.00
185 Juan Encarnacion N (Gold Leaf Rookies) 10.00
186 Miguel Tejada N (Gold Leaf Rookies) 25.00
187 Jacob Cruz P (Gold Leaf Rookies) 1.00
188 Mark Kotsay N (Gold Leaf Rookies) 25.00
189 Fernando Tatis L (Gold Leaf Rookies) 10.00
190 Ricky Ledee P (Gold Leaf Rookies) 2.00
191 Richard Hidalgo P (Gold Leaf Rookies) 1.00
192 Richie Sexson P (Gold Leaf Rookies) 1.00
193 Luis Ordaz P (Gold Leaf Rookies) 1.00
194 Eli Marrero L (Gold Leaf Rookies) 8.00
195 Livan Hernandez L (Gold Leaf Rookies) 8.00
196 Homer Bush P (Gold Leaf Rookies) 1.00
197 Raul Ibanez P (Gold Leaf Rookies) 1.00
198 Checklist (Nomar Garciaparra P) 10.00
199 Checklist (Scott Rolen P) 5.00
200 Checklist (Jose Cruz Jr. P) 10.00

1998 Leaf Fractal Materials Die-Cut

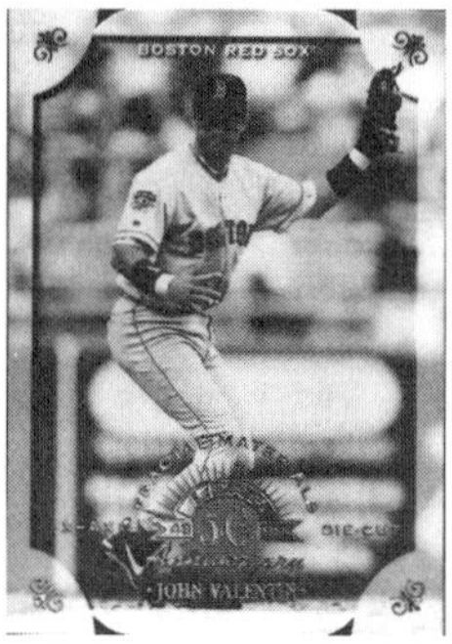

This parallel set adds a die-cut to the Fractal Materials set. The first 200 of 75 plastic, 15 Leather, five nylon and five wood cards have an x-axis die-cut. The first 100 of 20 plastic, 25 leather, 10 nylon and five wood cards have a y-axis die-cut. The first 50 of five plastic, 10 leather, 15 nylon and 10 wood cards have a z-axis die-cut.

	MT
Common X (200 of each):	8.00
Common Y (100):	20.00
Common Z (50):	40.00

1 Rusty Greer Z 40.00
2 Tino Martinez Y 40.00
3 Bobby Bonilla Y 30.00
4 Jason Giambi Z 40.00
5 Matt Morris Y 30.00
6 Craig Counsell X 8.00
7 Reggie Jefferson X 8.00
8 Brian Rose X 25.00
9 Ruben Rivera Y 20.00
10 Shawn Estes Y 20.00
11 Tony Gwynn X 100.00
12 Jeff Abbott Y 20.00
13 Jose Cruz Jr. Z 200.00
14 Francisco Cordova Y 20.00
15 Ryan Klesko X 25.00
16 Tim Salmon Y 40.00
17 Brett Tomko Y 20.00
18 Matt Williams Y 40.00
19 Joe Carter X 20.00
20 Harold Baines X 8.00
21 Gary Sheffield Z 80.00
22 Charles Johnson Y 30.00
23 Aaron Boone Y 20.00
24 Eddie Murray Y 40.00
25 Matt Stairs X 8.00
26 David Cone X 20.00
27 Jon Nunnally X 8.00
28 Chris Stynes X 8.00
29 Enrique Wilson Y 20.00
30 Randy Johnson Y 40.00
31 Garret Anderson Y 20.00
32 Manny Ramirez Y 75.00
33 Jeff Suppan Y 20.00
34 Rickey Henderson X 15.00
35 Scott Spiezio Y 20.00
36 Rondell White Y 30.00
37 Todd Greene Z 60.00
38 Delino DeShields Y 20.00
39 Kevin Brown X 15.00
40 Chili Davis X 8.00
41 Jimmy Key X 8.00
42 Not Issued .10
43 Mike Mussina Z 120.00
44 Joe Randa X 8.00
45 Chan Ho Park Y 25.00
46 Brad Radke X 8.00
47 Geronimo Berroa X 8.00
48 Wade Boggs Y 30.00
49 Kevin Appier X 8.00
50 Moises Alou X 15.00
51 David Justice Z 75.00
52 Ivan Rodriguez X 40.00

53 J.T. Snow X 15.00
54 Brian Giles Y 20.00
55 Will Clark X 20.00
56 Justin Thompson Y 25.00
57 Javier Lopez Y 25.00
58 Hideki Irabu X 25.00
59 Mark Grudzielanek X 8.00
60 Abraham Nunez Z 40.00
61 Todd Hollandsworth X 8.00
62 Jay Bell X 8.00
63 Nomar Garciaparra Z 350.00
64 Vinny Castilla Y 25.00
65 Lou Collier Y 20.00
66 Kevin Orie X 8.00
67 John Valentin X 8.00
68 Robin Ventura X 15.00
69 Denny Neagle X 15.00
70 Tony Womack X 8.00
71 Dennis Reyes Y 20.00
72 Wally Joyner X 8.00
73 Kevin Brown X 8.00
74 Ray Durham X 8.00
75 Mike Cameron Y 30.00
76 Dante Bichette X 25.00
77 Jose Guillen Z 60.00
78 Carlos Delgado Y 30.00
79 Paul Molitor X 40.00
80 Jason Kendall X 8.00
81 Mark Belhorn X 8.00
82 Damian Jackson Y 20.00
83 Bill Mueller X 8.00
84 Kevin Young X 8.00
85 Curt Schilling X 20.00
86 Jeffrey Hammonds X 8.00
87 Sandy Alomar Jr. Y 30.00
88 Bartolo Colon Y 20.00
89 Wilton Guerrero Y 20.00
90 Bernie Williams Z 125.00
91 Deion Sanders Y 30.00
92 Mike Piazza Z 400.00
93 Butch Huskey X 8.00
94 Edgardo Alfonzo Y 20.00
95 Alan Benes Z 40.00
96 Craig Biggio X 20.00
97 Mark Grace Y 40.00
98 Shawn Green Y 20.00
99 Derrek Lee Y 30.00
100 Ken Griffey Jr. Z 600.00
101 Tim Raines X 8.00
102 Pokey Reese Y 20.00
103 Lee Stevens X 8.00
104 Shannon Stewart X 8.00
105 John Smoltz Y 30.00
106 Frank Thomas Z 500.00
107 Jeff Fassero X 8.00
108 Jay Buhner Y 40.00
109 Jose Canseco X 25.00
110 Omar Vizquel X 8.00
111 Travis Fryman X 8.00
112 Dave Nilsson X 8.00
113 John Olerud X 15.00
114 Larry Walker X 30.00
115 Jim Edmonds Z 40.00
116 Bobby Higginson Y 20.00
117 Todd Hundley Z 40.00
118 Paul O'Neill X 20.00
119 Bip Roberts X 8.00
120 Ismael Valdes X 15.00
121 Pedro Martinez X 25.00
122 Jeff Cirillo X 8.00
123 Andy Benes X 20.00
124 Bobby Jones X 8.00
125 Brian Hunter X 8.00
126 Darryl Kile X 8.00
127 Pat Hentgen X 8.00
128 Marquis Grissom X 8.00
129 Eric Davis X 8.00
130 Chipper Jones Z 400.00
131 Edgar Martinez Z 60.00
132 Andy Pettitte Y 60.00
133 Cal Ripken Jr. Z 450.00
134 Scott Rolen X 80.00
135 Ron Coomer X 8.00
136 Luis Castillo X 8.00
137 Fred McGriff X 25.00
138 Neifi Perez Y 20.00
139 Eric Karros X 20.00
140 Alex Fernandez X 8.00
141 Jason Dickson X 8.00
142 Lance Johnson X 8.00
143 Ray Lankford Y 20.00
144 Sammy Sosa Y 80.00
145 Eric Young Y 20.00
146 Bubba Trammell Z 40.00
147 Todd Walker Z 60.00
148 Mo Vaughn X (Curtain Calls) 40.00
149 Jeff Bagwell X (Curtain Calls) 75.00
150 Kenny Lofton X (Curtain Calls) 40.00
151 Raul Mondesi X (Curtain Calls) 20.00
152 Mike Piazza X (Curtain Calls) 120.00
153 Chipper Jones X (Curtain Calls) 120.00
154 Larry Walker X (Curtain Calls) 30.00
155 Greg Maddux X (Curtain Calls) 120.00
156 Ken Griffey Jr. X (Curtain Calls) 200.00
157 Frank Thomas X (Curtain Calls) 160.00
158 Darin Erstad Y (Gold Leaf Stars) 75.00
159 Roberto Alomar X (Gold Leaf Stars) 40.00
160 Albert Belle X (Gold Leaf Stars) 40.00
161 Jim Thome X (Gold Leaf Stars) 30.00
162 Tony Clark Z (Gold Leaf Stars) 100.00
163 Chuck Knoblauch Z (Gold Leaf Stars) 75.00
164 Derek Jeter X (Gold Leaf Stars) 100.00
165 Alex Rodriguez Y (Gold Leaf Stars) 180.00
166 Tony Gwynn X (Gold Leaf Stars) 100.00
167 Roger Clemens Y (Gold Leaf Stars) 120.00
168 Barry Larkin Y (Gold Leaf Stars) 40.00
169 Andres Galarraga Y (Gold Leaf Stars) 40.00
170 Vladimir Guerrero Y (Gold Leaf Stars) 60.00
171 Mark McGwire Z (Gold Leaf Stars) 400.00
172 Barry Bonds Y (Gold Leaf Stars) 75.00
173 Juan Gonzalez Y (Gold Leaf Stars) 150.00
174 Andruw Jones X (Gold Leaf Stars) 40.00
175 Paul Molitor X (Gold Leaf Stars) 35.00
176 Hideo Nomo Z (Gold Leaf Stars) 125.00
177 Cal Ripken Jr. X (Gold Leaf Stars) 150.00
178 Brad Fullmer Z (Gold Leaf Rookies) 60.00
179 Jaret Wright Z (Gold Leaf Rookies) 240.00
180 Bobby Estalella Y (Gold Leaf Rookies) 20.00
181 Ben Grieve Z (Gold Leaf Rookies) 180.00
182 Paul Konerko Z (Gold Leaf Rookies) 100.00
183 David Ortiz Z (Gold Leaf Rookies) 60.00
184 Todd Helton Z (Gold Leaf Rookies) 125.00
185 Juan Encarnacion Z (Gold Leaf Rookies) 40.00
186 Miguel Tejada Z (Gold Leaf Rookies) 80.00
187 Jacob Cruz X (Gold Leaf Rookies) 8.00
188 Mark Kotsay Z (Gold Leaf Rookies) 80.00
189 Fernando Tatis Y (Gold Leaf Rookies) 40.00
190 Ricky Ledee X (Gold Leaf Rookies) 25.00
191 Richard Hidalgo Z (Gold Leaf Rookies) 40.00
192 Richie Sexson Z (Gold Leaf Rookies) 40.00
193 Luis Ordaz X (Gold Leaf Rookies) 8.00
194 Eli Marrero Z (Gold Leaf Rookies) 40.00
195 Livan Hernandez Z (Gold Leaf Rookies) 75.00
196 Homer Bush X (Gold Leaf Rookies) 8.00
197 Raul Ibanez X (Gold Leaf Rookies) 8.00
198 Checklist (Nomar Garciaparra X) 60.00
199 Checklist (Scott Rolen Z) 125.00
200 Checklist (Jose Cruz Jr. X) 50.00

1998 Leaf Fractal Foundation Z2 Axis

This 200-card set parallels Leaf Fractal Materials and was numbered to 20 sets.

	MT
Z2 Stars:	25x to 50x
Yng Stars & RCs:	15x to 30x
Production 20 sets	

1998 Metal Universe

This 220-card single series release captured players over a foil etched, art background that related in some way to them or the city they played in. Metal Universe included a 15-card Hardball Galaxy subset and dealers and media were given an Alex Rodriguez promo card that was identical the base card except for the words "Promotional Sample" written across the back. The set arrived with a parallel called Precious Metal Gems, and included the following insert sets: All-Galactic Team, Diamond Heroes, Platinum Portraits, Titanium and Universal Language.

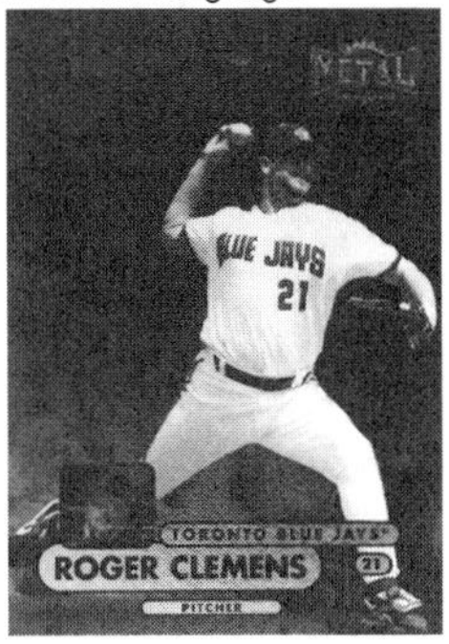

	MT
Complete Set (220):	30.00
Common Player:	.10
Wax Box:	55.00

1 Jose Cruz Jr. 1.00
2 Jeff Abbott .10
3 Rafael Palmeiro .25
4 Ivan Rodriguez .75
5 Jaret Wright .75
6 Derek Bell .10
7 Chuck Finley .10
8 Travis Fryman .10
9 Randy Johnson .50
10 Derrek Lee .20
11 Bernie Williams .50
12 Carlos Baerga .10
13 Ricky Bottalico .10
14 Ellis Burks .10
15 Russ Davis .10
16 Nomar Garciaparra 2.00
17 Joey Hamilton .10
18 Jason Kendall .20
19 Darryl Kile .10
20 Edgardo Alfonzo .10
21 Moises Alou .20
22 Bobby Bonilla .20
23 Jim Edmonds .20
24 Jose Guillen .25
25 Chuck Knoblauch .40
26 Javy Lopez .20
27 Billy Wagner .10
28 Kevin Appier .10
29 Joe Carter .20
30 Todd Dunwoody .10
31 Gary Gaetti .10
32 Juan Gonzalez 1.50
33 Jeffrey Hammonds .10
34 Roberto Hernandez .10
35 Dave Nilsson .10
36 Manny Ramirez .60
37 Robin Ventura .20
38 Rondell White .20
39 Vinny Castilla .20
40 Will Clark .25
41 Scott Hatteberg .10
42 Russ Johnson .10
43 Ricky Ledee .50
44 Kenny Lofton .75
45 Paul Molitor .50
46 Justin Thompson .20
47 Craig Biggio .20
48 Damion Easley .10
49 Brad Radke .10
50 Ben Grieve 1.00
51 Mark Bellhorn .10
52 *Henry Blanco* .10
53 Mariano Rivera .20
54 Reggie Sanders .10
55 Paul Sorrento .10
56 Terry Steinbach .10
57 Mo Vaughn .75
58 Brady Anderson .20
59 Tom Glavine .20
60 Sammy Sosa 1.50
61 Larry Walker .30
62 Rod Beck .10
63 Jose Canseco .25
64 Steve Finley .10
65 Pedro Martinez .50
66 John Olerud .20
67 Scott Rolen 1.00
68 Ismael Valdes .10
69 Andrew Vessel .10
70 Mark Grudzielanek .10
71 Eric Karros .10
72 Jeff Shaw .10
73 Lou Collier .10
74 Edgar Martinez .10
75 Vladimir Guerrero 1.00
76 Paul Konerko .50
77 Kevin Orie .10
78 Kevin Polcovich .10
79 Brett Tomko .10
80 Jeff Bagwell 1.00
81 Barry Bonds .75
82 David Justice .25
83 Hideo Nomo .60
84 Ryne Sandberg .75
85 Shannon Stewart .10
86 Derek Wallace .10
87 Tony Womack .10
88 Jason Giambi .10
89 Mark Grace .25
90 Pat Hentgen .10
91 Raul Mondesi .25
92 Matt Morris .20
93 Matt Perisho .10
94 Tim Salmon .25
95 Jeremi Gonzalez .10
96 Shawn Green .10
97 Todd Greene .10
98 Ruben Rivera .10
99 Deion Sanders .20
100 Alex Rodriguez 2.00
101 Will Cunnane .10
102 Ray Lankford .10
103 Ryan McGuire .10
104 Charles Nagy .10
105 Rey Ordonez .10
106 Mike Piazza 2.00
107 Tony Saunders .10
108 Curt Schilling .20
109 Fernando Tatis .10
110 Mark McGwire 4.00
111 *David Dellucci* .50
112 Garret Anderson .10
113 Shane Bowers .10
114 David Cone .20
115 Jeff King .10
116 Matt Williams .25
117 Aaron Boone .10
118 Dennis Eckersley .20
119 Livan Hernandez .20
120 Richard Hidalgo .10
121 Bobby Higginson .10
122 Tino Martinez .40
123 Tim Naehring .10
124 Jose Vidro .10
125 John Wetteland .10
126 Jay Bell .10
127 Albert Belle .75
128 Marty Cordova .10
129 Chili Davis .10
130 Jason Dickson .10
131 Rusty Greer .20
132 Hideki Irabu .40
133 Greg Maddux 2.00
134 Billy Taylor .10
135 Jim Thome .50
136 Gerald Williams .10
137 Jeff Cirillo .10
138 Delino DeShields .10
139 Andres Galarraga .40
140 Willie Greene .10
141 John Jaha .10
142 Charles Johnson .20
143 Ryan Klesko .40
144 Paul O'Neill .20
145 Robinson Checo .10
146 Roberto Alomar .50
147 Wilson Alvarez .10
148 Bobby Jones .10
149 Raul Casanova .10
150 Andruw Jones 1.00
151 Mike Lansing .10
152 Mickey Morandini .10
153 Neifi Perez .10
154 Pokey Reese .10
155 Edgar Renteria .10
156 Eric Young .10
157 Darin Erstad 1.00
158 Kelvim Escobar .10
159 Carl Everett .10
160 Tom Gordon .10
161 Ken Griffey Jr. 3.00
162 Al Martin .10
163 Bubba Trammell .20
164 Carlos Delgado .10
165 Kevin Brown .20
166 Ken Caminiti .20
167 Roger Clemens 1.00
168 Ron Gant .20
169 Jeff Kent .10
170 Mike Mussina .60
171 Dean Palmer .10
172 Henry Rodriguez .10
173 Matt Stairs .10
174 Jay Buhner .25
175 Frank Thomas 2.50
176 Mike Cameron .10
177 Johnny Damon .10
178 Tony Gwynn 1.50
179 John Smoltz .20
180 B.J. Surhoff .10
181 Antone Williamson .10
182 Alan Benes .20
183 Jeromy Burnitz .10
184 Tony Clark .40
185 Shawn Estes .10
186 Todd Helton .75
187 Todd Hundley .10
188 Chipper Jones 2.00
189 Mark Kotsay .25
190 Barry Larkin .25
191 Mike Lieberthal .10
192 Andy Pettitte .50
193 Gary Sheffield .30
194 Jeff Suppan .10
195 Mark Wohlers .10
196 Dante Bichette .25
197 Trevor Hoffman .10
198 J.T. Snow .20
199 Derek Jeter 2.00
200 Cal Ripken Jr. 2.50
201 *Steve Woodard* .40
202 Ray Durham .10
203 Barry Bonds (Hardball Galaxy) .40
204 Tony Clark (Hardball Galaxy) .20
205 Roger Clemens (Hardball Galaxy) .50
206 Ken Griffey Jr. (Hardball Galaxy) 1.50
207 Tony Gwynn (Hardball Galaxy) .75
208 Derek Jeter (Hardball Galaxy) 1.00
209 Randy Johnson (Hardball Galaxy) .20
210 Mark McGwire (Hardball Galaxy) 2.00
211 Hideo Nomo (Hardball Galaxy) .40
212 Mike Piazza (Hardball Galaxy) 1.00
213 Cal Ripken Jr. (Hardball Galaxy) 1.25
214 Alex Rodriguez (Hardball Galaxy) 1.00
215 Frank Thomas (Hardball Galaxy) 1.25
216 Mo Vaughn (Hardball Galaxy) .40
217 Larry Walker (Hardball Galaxy) .15
218 Checklist (Ken Griffey Jr.) 1.00
219 Checklist (Alex Rodriguez) .60
220 Checklist (Frank Thomas) .75

1998 Metal Universe Precious Metal Gems

Precious Metal Gems included 217 (220 minus three checklist cards) cards from Metal Universe and were serial numbered to 50 sets. Because there were five Ultimate Metal Gems redemption cards (good for a complete set of Metal Gems) available, only serial numberes 1-45 were found in packs (46-50 were held back for the exchage program).

	MT
Common Player:	20.00
Semistars:	60.00

1 Jose Cruz Jr. 100.00
2 Jeff Abbott 20.00
3 Rafael Palmeiro 40.00
4 Ivan Rodriguez 100.00
5 Jaret Wright 100.00
6 Derek Bell 20.00
7 Chuck Finley 20.00
8 Travis Fryman 30.00
9 Randy Johnson 75.00
10 Derrek Lee 20.00
11 Bernie Williams 75.00
12 Carlos Baerga 20.00
13 Ricky Bottalico 20.00
14 Ellis Burks 20.00
15 Russ Davis 20.00
16 Nomar Garciaparra 250.00
17 Joey Hamilton 20.00
18 Jason Kendall 30.00
19 Darryl Kile 20.00
20 Edgardo Alfonzo 20.00
21 Moises Alou 35.00
22 Bobby Bonilla 30.00
23 Jim Edmonds 30.00
24 Jose Guillen 30.00
25 Chuck Knoblauch 40.00
26 Javy Lopez 30.00
27 Billy Wagner 20.00
28 Kevin Appier 20.00
29 Joe Carter 30.00
30 Todd Dunwoody 20.00
31 Gary Gaetti 20.00
32 Juan Gonzalez 200.00
33 Jeffrey Hammonds 20.00
34 Roberto Hernandez 20.00
35 Dave Nilsson 20.00
36 Manny Ramirez 100.00
37 Robin Ventura 30.00
38 Rondell White 30.00
39 Vinny Castilla 30.00
40 Will Clark 40.00
41 Scott Hatteberg 20.00
42 Russ Johnson 20.00
43 Ricky Ledee 35.00
44 Kenny Lofton 100.00
45 Paul Molitor 75.00
46 Justin Thompson 20.00
47 Craig Biggio 40.00
48 Damion Easley 20.00
49 Brad Radke 20.00
50 Ben Grieve 125.00
51 Mark Bellhorn 20.00
52 *Henry Blanco* 20.00

53	Mariano Rivera	30.00
54	Reggie Sanders	20.00
55	Paul Sorrento	20.00
56	Terry Steinbach	20.00
57	Mo Vaughn	100.00
58	Brady Anderson	25.00
59	Tom Glavine	30.00
60	Sammy Sosa	150.00
61	Larry Walker	60.00
62	Rod Beck	20.00
63	Jose Canseco	40.00
64	Steve Finley	20.00
65	Pedro Martinez	75.00
66	John Olerud	40.00
67	Scott Rolen	150.00
68	Ismael Valdes	20.00
69	Andrew Vessel	20.00
70	Mark Grudzielanek	20.00
71	Eric Karros	30.00
72	Jeff Shaw	20.00
73	Lou Collier	20.00
74	Edgar Martinez	30.00
75	Vladimir Guerrero	100.00
76	Paul Konerko	40.00
77	Kevin Orie	20.00
78	Kevin Polcovich	20.00
79	Brett Tomko	20.00
80	Jeff Bagwell	75.00
81	Barry Bonds	100.00
82	David Justice	40.00
83	Hideo Nomo	75.00
84	Ryne Sandberg	100.00
85	Shannon Stewart	20.00
86	Derek Wallace	20.00
87	Tony Womack	20.00
88	Jason Giambi	20.00
89	Mark Grace	40.00
90	Pat Hentgen	20.00
91	Raul Mondesi	40.00
92	Matt Morris	30.00
93	Matt Perisho	20.00
94	Tim Salmon	40.00
95	Jeremi Gonzalez	20.00
96	Shawn Green	20.00
97	Todd Greene	20.00
98	Ruben Rivera	20.00
99	Deion Sanders	30.00
100	Alex Rodriguez	250.00
101	Will Cunnane	20.00
102	Ray Lankford	20.00
103	Ryan McGuire	20.00
104	Charles Nagy	20.00
105	Rey Ordonez	20.00
106	Mike Piazza	250.00
107	Tony Saunders	20.00
108	Curt Schilling	30.00
109	Fernando Tatis	30.00
110	Mark McGwire	400.00
111	*David Dellucci*	30.00
112	Garret Anderson	20.00
113	Shane Bowers	20.00
114	David Cone	30.00
115	Jeff King	20.00
116	Matt Williams	50.00
117	Aaron Boone	20.00
118	Dennis Eckersley	20.00
119	Livan Hernandez	20.00
120	Richard Hidalgo	20.00
121	Bobby Higginson	20.00
122	Tino Martinez	60.00
123	Tim Naehring	20.00
124	Jose Vidro	20.00
125	John Wetteland	20.00
126	Jay Bell	20.00
127	Albert Belle	100.00
128	Marty Cordova	20.00
129	Chili Davis	20.00
130	Jason Dickson	20.00
131	Rusty Greer	20.00
132	Hideki Irabu	50.00
133	Greg Maddux	250.00
134	Billy Taylor	20.00
135	Jim Thome	60.00
136	Gerald Williams	20.00
137	Jeff Cirillo	20.00
138	Delino DeShields	20.00
139	Andres Galarraga	50.00
140	Willie Greene	20.00
141	John Jaha	20.00
142	Charles Johnson	20.00
143	Ryan Klesko	40.00
144	Paul O'Neill	30.00
145	Robinson Checo	20.00
146	Roberto Alomar	75.00
147	Wilson Alvarez	20.00
148	Bobby Jones	20.00
149	Raul Casanova	20.00
150	Andruw Jones	100.00
151	Mike Lansing	20.00
152	Mickey Morandini	20.00
153	Neifi Perez	20.00
154	Pokey Reese	20.00
155	Edgar Renteria	20.00
156	Eric Young	20.00
157	Darin Erstad	100.00
158	Kelvim Escobar	20.00
159	Carl Everett	20.00
160	Tom Gordon	20.00
161	Ken Griffey Jr.	400.00
162	Al Martin	20.00
163	Bubba Trammell	20.00
164	Carlos Delgado	20.00
165	Kevin Brown	30.00
166	Ken Caminiti	30.00
167	Roger Clemens	150.00
168	Ron Gant	20.00
169	Jeff Kent	20.00
170	Mike Mussina	75.00
171	Dean Palmer	20.00
172	Henry Rodriguez	20.00
173	Matt Stairs	20.00
174	Jay Buhner	40.00
175	Frank Thomas	300.00
176	Mike Cameron	20.00
177	Johnny Damon	20.00
178	Tony Gwynn	200.00
179	John Smoltz	30.00
180	B.J. Surhoff	20.00
181	Antone Williamson	20.00
182	Alan Benes	30.00
183	Jeromy Burnitz	20.00
184	Tony Clark	60.00
185	Shawn Estes	20.00
186	Todd Helton	80.00
187	Todd Hundley	20.00
188	Chipper Jones	225.00
189	Mark Kotsay	30.00
190	Barry Larkin	40.00
191	Mike Lieberthal	20.00
192	Andy Pettitte	60.00
193	Gary Sheffield	50.00
194	Jeff Suppan	20.00
195	Mark Wohlers	20.00
196	Dante Bichette	40.00
197	Trevor Hoffman	20.00
198	J.T. Snow	20.00
199	Derek Jeter	200.00
200	Cal Ripken Jr.	300.00
201	Steve Woodard	30.00
202	Ray Durham	20.00
203	Barry Bonds (Hardball Galaxy)	50.00
204	Tony Clark (Hardball Galaxy)	40.00
205	Roger Clemens (Hardball Galaxy)	75.00
206	Ken Griffey Jr. (Hardball Galaxy)	200.00
207	Tony Gwynn (Hardball Galaxy)	100.00
208	Derek Jeter (Hardball Galaxy)	100.00
209	Randy Johnson (Hardball Galaxy)	40.00
210	Mark McGwire (Hardball Galaxy)	200.00
211	Hideo Nomo (Hardball Galaxy)	40.00
212	Mike Piazza (Hardball Galaxy)	125.00
213	Cal Ripken Jr. (Hardball Galaxy)	150.00
214	Alex Rodriguez (Hardball Galaxy)	125.00
215	Frank Thomas (Hardball Galaxy)	150.00
216	Mo Vaughn (Hardball Galaxy)	50.00
217	Larry Walker (Hardball Galaxy)	30.00

1998 Metal Universe All-Galactic Team

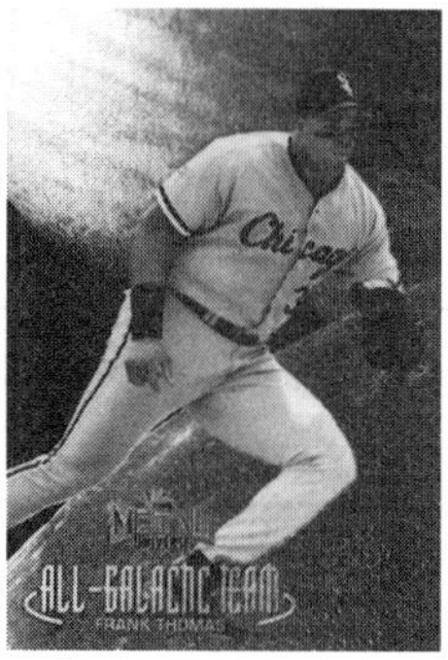

This 18-card insert captures players over a planet holofoil background. Cards were inserted one per 192 packs.

		MT
Complete Set (18):		750.00
Common Player:		20.00
1	Ken Griffey Jr.	100.00
2	Frank Thomas	75.00
3	Chipper Jones	60.00
4	Albert Belle	25.00
5	Juan Gonzalez	50.00
6	Jeff Bagwell	30.00
7	Andruw Jones	25.00
8	Cal Ripken Jr.	75.00
9	Derek Jeter	50.00
10	Nomar Garciaparra	60.00
11	Darin Erstad	30.00
12	Greg Maddux	60.00
13	Alex Rodriguez	60.00
14	Mike Piazza	60.00
15	Vladimir Guerrero	25.00
16	Jose Cruz Jr.	25.00
17	Mark McGwire	120.00
18	Scott Rolen	30.00

1998 Metal Universe Diamond Heroes

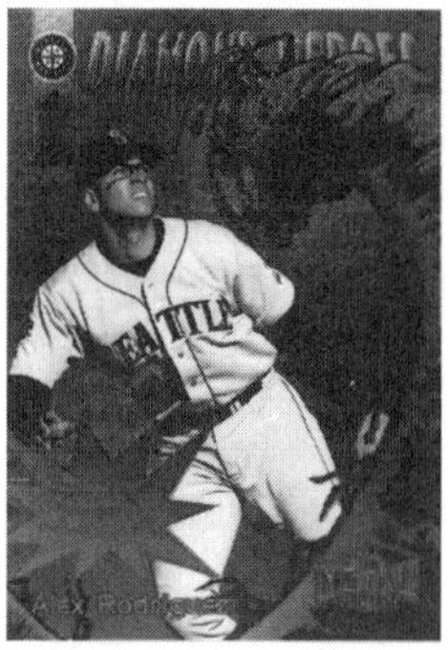

Diamond Heroes displayed six players in a comic book setting. This insert was seeded one per 18 packs and contained a foil etched image of a Marvel comic in the background.

		MT
Complete Set (6):		35.00
Common Player:		1.50
1	Ken Griffey Jr.	10.00
2	Frank Thomas	8.00
3	Andruw Jones	4.00
4	Alex Rodriguez	6.00
5	Jose Cruz Jr.	4.00
6	Cal Ripken Jr.	8.00

1998 Metal Universe Platinum Portraits

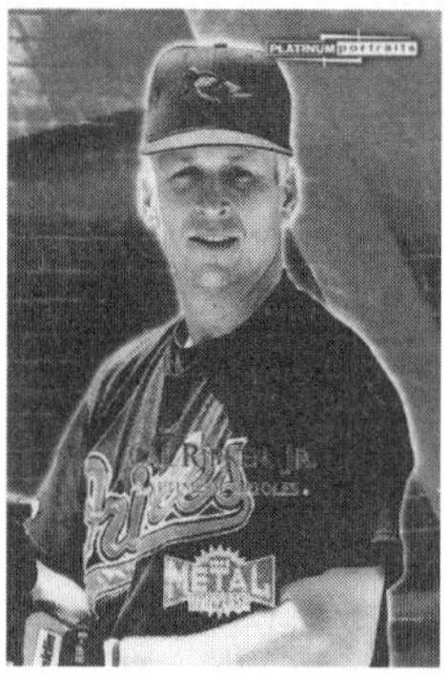

This 12-card insert set featured color portraits of top players highlighted with a platinum-colored etched foil frame over it. Platinum Portraits are seeded one per 360 packs of Metal Universe.

		MT
Complete Set (12):		700.00
Common Player:		25.00
1	Ken Griffey Jr.	120.00
2	Frank Thomas	90.00
3	Chipper Jones	75.00
4	Jose Cruz Jr.	25.00
5	Andruw Jones	30.00
6	Cal Ripken Jr.	90.00
7	Derek Jeter	60.00
8	Darin Erstad	30.00
9	Greg Maddux	75.00
10	Alex Rodriguez	90.00
11	Mike Piazza	75.00
12	Vladimir Guerrero	30.00

1998 Metal Universe Titanium

This die-cut 15-card insert contained color photos printed on embossed, sculpted cards on etched foil. Titanium inserts were seeded one per 96 packs.

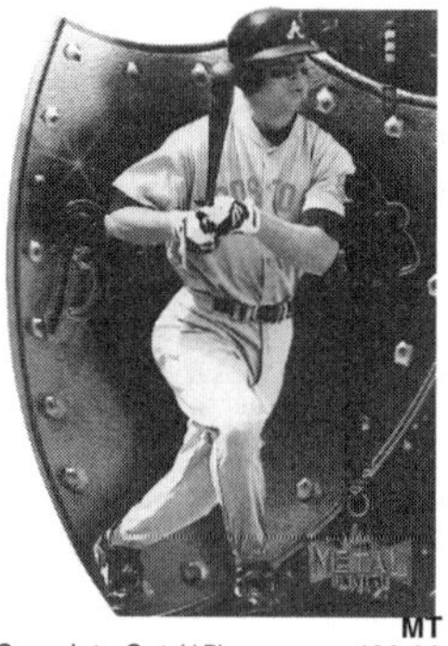

		MT
Complete Set (15):		400.00
Common Player:		8.00
1	Ken Griffey Jr.	50.00
2	Frank Thomas	40.00
3	Chipper Jones	30.00
4	Jose Cruz Jr.	20.00
5	Juan Gonzalez	25.00
6	Scott Rolen	20.00
7	Andruw Jones	20.00
8	Cal Ripken Jr.	40.00
9	Derek Jeter	30.00
10	Nomar Garciaparra	30.00
11	Darin Erstad	15.00
12	Greg Maddux	30.00
13	Alex Rodriguez	30.00
14	Mike Piazza	30.00
15	Vladimir Guerrero	15.00

1998 Metal Universe Universal Language

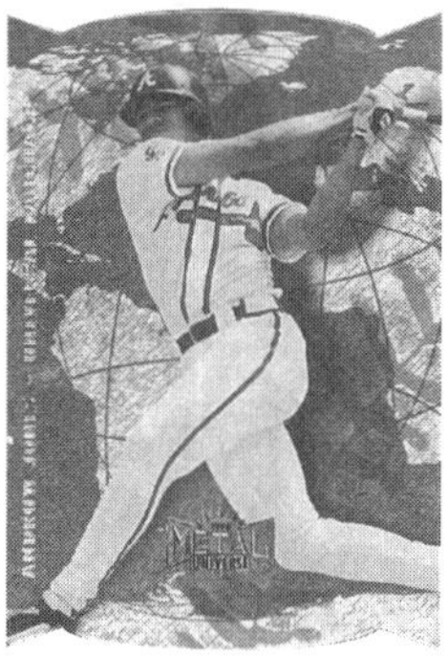

This 20-card insert features illustration and copy done in the player's native language. Cards were die-cut and inserted one per six packs.

		MT
Complete Set (20):		75.00
Common Player:		1.00
1	Ken Griffey Jr.	10.00
2	Frank Thomas	8.00
3	Chipper Jones	6.00
4	Albert Belle	2.50
5	Juan Gonzalez	5.00
6	Jeff Bagwell	4.00
7	Andruw Jones	4.00
8	Cal Ripken Jr.	8.00
9	Derek Jeter	6.00
10	Nomar Garciaparra	6.00
11	Darin Erstad	3.00
12	Greg Maddux	6.00
13	Alex Rodriguez	6.00
14	Mike Piazza	6.00
15	Vladimir Guerrero	3.00
16	Jose Cruz Jr.	4.00
17	Hideo Nomo	2.50
18	Kenny Lofton	2.50
19	Tony Gwynn	5.00
20	Scott Rolen	5.00

1998 Pacific

1998 Pacific Baseball is a 450-card, bilingual set. The base set features full-bleed photos with the Pacific Crown Collection logo in the upper left and the player's name, position and team at the bottom. Inserts include Cramer's Choice Awards, In The Cage Laser-Cuts, Home Run Hitters, Team Checklist Laser-Cuts, Gold Crown Die-Cuts and Latinos of the Major Leagues.

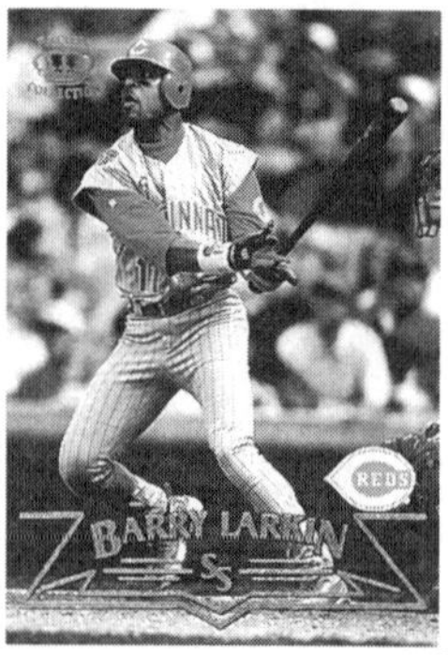

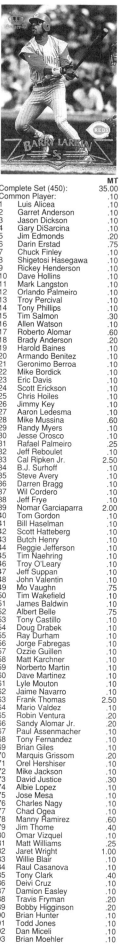

		MT
Complete Set (450):		35.00
Common Player:		.10
1	Luis Alicea	.10
2	Garret Anderson	.10
3	Jason Dickson	.10
4	Gary DiSarcina	.10
5	Jim Edmonds	.20
6	Darin Erstad	.75
7	Chuck Finley	.10
8	Shigetosi Hasegawa	.10
9	Rickey Henderson	.10
10	Dave Hollins	.10
11	Mark Langston	.10
12	Orlando Palmeiro	.10
13	Troy Percival	.10
14	Tony Phillips	.10
15	Tim Salmon	.30
16	Allen Watson	.10
17	Roberto Alomar	.60
18	Brady Anderson	.20
19	Harold Baines	.10
20	Armando Benitez	.10
21	Geronimo Berroa	.10
22	Mike Bordick	.10
23	Eric Davis	.10
24	Scott Erickson	.10
25	Chris Hoiles	.10
26	Jimmy Key	.10
27	Aaron Ledesma	.10
28	Mike Mussina	.60
29	Randy Myers	.10
30	Jesse Orosco	.10
31	Rafael Palmeiro	.25
32	Jeff Reboulet	.10
33	Cal Ripken Jr.	2.50
34	B.J. Surhoff	.10
35	Steve Avery	.10
36	Darren Bragg	.10
37	Wil Cordero	.10
38	Jeff Frye	.10
39	Nomar Garciaparra	2.00
40	Tom Gordon	.10
41	Bill Haselman	.10
42	Scott Hatteberg	.10
43	Butch Henry	.10
44	Reggie Jefferson	.10
45	Tim Naehring	.10
46	Troy O'Leary	.10
47	Jeff Suppan	.10
48	John Valentin	.10
49	Mo Vaughn	.75
50	Tim Wakefield	.10
51	James Baldwin	.10
52	Albert Belle	.75
53	Tony Castillo	.10
54	Doug Drabek	.10
55	Ray Durham	.10
56	Jorge Fabregas	.10
57	Ozzie Guillen	.10
58	Matt Karchner	.10
59	Norberto Martin	.10
60	Dave Martinez	.10
61	Lyle Mouton	.10
62	Jaime Navarro	.10
63	Frank Thomas	2.50
64	Mario Valdez	.10
65	Robin Ventura	.20
66	Sandy Alomar Jr.	.20
67	Paul Assenmacher	.10
68	Tony Fernandez	.10
69	Brian Giles	.10
70	Marquis Grissom	.20
71	Orel Hershiser	.10
72	Mike Jackson	.10
73	David Justice	.30
74	Albie Lopez	.10
75	Jose Mesa	.10
76	Charles Nagy	.10
77	Chad Ogea	.10
78	Manny Ramirez	.60
79	Jim Thome	.40
80	Omar Vizquel	.10
81	Matt Williams	.25
82	Jaret Wright	1.00
83	Willie Blair	.10
84	Raul Casanova	.10
85	Tony Clark	.40
86	Deivi Cruz	.10
87	Damion Easley	.10
88	Travis Fryman	.20
89	Bobby Higginson	.20
90	Brian Hunter	.10
91	Todd Jones	.10
92	Dan Miceli	.10
93	Brian Moehler	.10

94	Melvin Nieves	.10
95	Jody Reed	.10
96	Justin Thompson	.10
97	Bubba Trammell	.20
98	Kevin Appier	.10
99	Jay Bell	.10
100	Yamil Benitez	.10
101	Johnny Damon	.10
102	Chili Davis	.10
103	Jermaine Dye	.10
104	Jed Hansen	.10
105	Jeff King	.10
106	Mike Macfarlane	.10
107	Felix Martinez	.10
108	Jeff Montgomery	.10
109	Jose Offerman	.10
110	Dean Palmer	.20
111	Hipolito Pichardo	.10
112	Jose Rosado	.10
113	Jeromy Burnitz	.10
114	Jeff Cirillo	.10
115	Cal Eldred	.10
116	John Jaha	.10
117	Doug Jones	.10
118	Scott Karl	.10
119	Jesse Levis	.10
120	Mark Loretta	.10
121	Ben McDonald	.10
122	Jose Mercedes	.10
123	Matt Mieske	.10
124	Dave Nilsson	.10
125	Jose Valentin	.10
126	Fernando Vina	.10
127	Gerald Williams	.10
128	Rick Aguilera	.10
129	Rich Becker	.10
130	Ron Coomer	.10
131	Marty Cordova	.10
132	Eddie Guardado	.10
133	LaTroy Hawkins	.10
134	Denny Hocking	.10
135	Chuck Knoblauch	.30
136	Matt Lawton	.10
137	Pat Meares	.10
138	Paul Molitor	.50
139	David Ortiz	.40
140	Brad Radke	.10
141	Terry Steinbach	.10
142	Bob Tewksbury	.10
143	Javier Valentin	.10
144	Wade Boggs	.25
145	David Cone	.20
146	Chad Curtis	.10
147	Cecil Fielder	.20
148	Joe Girardi	.10
149	Dwight Gooden	.20
150	Hideki Irabu	.75
151	Derek Jeter	2.00
152	Tino Martinez	.25
153	Ramiro Mendoza	.10
154	Paul O'Neill	.20
155	Andy Pettitte	.60
156	Jorge Posada	.10
157	Mariano Rivera	.20
158	Rey Sanchez	.10
159	Luis Sojo	.10
160	David Wells	.10
161	Bernie Williams	.50
162	Rafael Bournigal	.10
163	Scott Brosius	.10
164	Jose Canseco	.20
165	Jason Giambi	.10
166	Ben Grieve	1.00
167	Dave Magadan	.10
168	Brent Mayne	.10
169	Jason McDonald	.10
170	Izzy Molina	.10
171	Ariel Prieto	.10
172	Carlos Reyes	.10
173	Scott Spiezio	.10
174	Matt Stairs	.10
175	Bill Taylor	.10
176	Dave Telgheder	.10
177	Steve Wojciechowski	.10
178	Rich Amaral	.10
179	Bobby Ayala	.10
180	Jay Buhner	.25
181	Rafael Carmona	.10
182	Ken Cloude	.10
183	Joey Cora	.10
184	Russ Davis	.10
185	Jeff Fassero	.10
186	Ken Griffey Jr.	3.00
187	Raul Ibanez	.10
188	Randy Johnson	.50
189	Roberto Kelly	.10
190	Edgar Martinez	.20
191	Jamie Moyer	.10
192	Omar Olivares	.10
193	Alex Rodriguez	2.00
194	Heathcliff Slocumb	.10
195	Paul Sorrento	.10
196	Dan Wilson	.10
197	Scott Bailes	.10
198	John Burkett	.10
199	Domingo Cedeno	.10
200	Will Clark	.25
	Hanley Frias	.10
202	Juan Gonzalez	1.50
203	Tom Goodwin	.10
204	Rusty Greer	.20
205	Wilson Heredia	.10
206	Darren Oliver	.10
207	Billy Ripken	.10
208	Ivan Rodriguez	.60
209	Lee Stevens	.10
210	Fernando Tatis	.25
211	John Wetteland	.10
212	Bobby Witt	.10
213	Jacob Brumfield	.10
214	Joe Carter	.20
215	Roger Clemens	1.00
216	Felipe Crespo	.10
217	Jose Cruz Jr.	1.00
218	Carlos Delgado	.20
219	Mariano Duncan	.10
220	Carlos Garcia	.10
221	Alex Gonzalez	.10
222	Juan Guzman	.10
223	Pat Hentgen	.10
224	Orlando Merced	.10
225	Tomas Perez	.10
226	Paul Quantrill	.10
227	Benito Santiago	.10
228	Woody Williams	.10
229	Rafael Belliard	.10
230	Jeff Blauser	.10
231	Pedro Borbon	.10
232	Tom Glavine	.20
233	Tony Graffanino	.10
234	Andruw Jones	1.50
235	Chipper Jones	2.00
236	Ryan Klesko	.30
237	Mark Lemke	.10
238	Kenny Lofton	.75
239	Javier Lopez	.20
240	Fred McGriff	.25
241	Greg Maddux	2.00
242	Denny Neagle	.10
243	John Smoltz	.20
244	Michael Tucker	.10
245	Mark Wohlers	.10
246	Manny Alexander	.10
247	Miguel Batista	.10
248	Mark Clark	.10
249	Doug Glanville	.10
250	Jeremi Gonzalez	.10
251	Mark Grace	.25
252	Jose Hernandez	.10
253	Lance Johnson	.10
254	Brooks Kieschnick	.10
255	Kevin Orie	.10
256	Ryne Sandberg	.75
257	Scott Servais	.10
258	Sammy Sosa	1.50
259	Kevin Tapani	.10
260	Ramon Tatis	.10
261	Bret Boone	.10
262	Dave Burba	.10
263	Brook Fordyce	.10
264	Willie Greene	.10
265	Barry Larkin	.25
266	Pedro A. Martinez	.10
267	Hal Morris	.10
268	Joe Oliver	.10
269	Eduardo Perez	.10
270	Pokey Reese	.10
271	Felix Rodriguez	.10
272	Deion Sanders	.25
273	Reggie Sanders	.10
274	Jeff Shaw	.10
275	Scott Sullivan	.10
276	Brett Tomko	.10
277	Roger Bailey	.10
278	Dante Bichette	.25
279	Ellis Burks	.10
280	Vinny Castilla	.20
281	Frank Castillo	.10
282	*Mike DeJean*	.10
283	Andres Galarraga	.25
284	Darren Holmes	.10
285	Kirt Manwaring	.10
286	Quinton McCracken	.10
287	Neifi Perez	.10
288	Steve Reed	.10
289	John Thomson	.10
290	Larry Walker	.30
291	Walt Weiss	.10
292	Kurt Abbott	.10
293	Antonio Alfonseca	.10
294	Moises Alou	.20
295	Alex Arias	.10
296	Bobby Bonilla	.20
297	Kevin Brown	.20
298	Craig Counsell	.10
299	Darren Daulton	.10
300	Jim Eisenreich	.10
301	Alex Fernandez	.10
302	Felix Heredia	.10
303	Livan Hernandez	.20
304	Charles Johnson	.20
305	Al Leiter	.10
306	Robb Nen	.10
307	Edgar Renteria	.10
308	Gary Sheffield	.30
309	Devon White	.10
310	Bob Abreu	.10
311	Brad Ausmus	.10
312	Jeff Bagwell	1.25
313	Derek Bell	.10
314	Sean Berry	.10
315	Craig Biggio	.20
316	Ramon Garcia	.10
317	Luis Gonzalez	.10
318	Ricky Gutierrez	.10
319	Mike Hampton	.10
320	Richard Hidalgo	.10
321	Thomas Howard	.10
322	Darryl Kile	.10
323	Jose Lima	.10
324	Shane Reynolds	.10
325	Bill Spiers	.10
326	Tom Candiotti	.10
327	Roger Cedeno	.10
328	Greg Gagne	.10
329	Karim Garcia	.10
330	Wilton Guerrero	.10
331	Todd Hollandsworth	.10
332	Eric Karros	.20
333	Ramon Martinez	.10
334	Raul Mondesi	.25
335	Otis Nixon	.10
336	Hideo Nomo	.75
337	Antonio Osuna	.10
338	Chan Ho Park	.20
339	Mike Piazza	2.00
340	Dennis Reyes	.10
341	Ismael Valdes	.10
342	Todd Worrell	.10
343	Todd Zeile	.10
344	Darrin Fletcher	.10
345	Mark Grudzielanek	.10
346	Vladimir Guerrero	1.00
347	Dustin Hermanson	.10
348	Mike Lansing	.10
349	Pedro J. Martinez	.25
350	Ryan McGuire	.10
351	Jose Paniagua	.10
352	Carlos Perez	.10
353	Henry Rodriguez	.10
354	F.P. Santangelo	.10
355	David Segui	.10
356	Ugueth Urbina	.10
357	Marc Valdes	.10
358	Jose Vidro	.10
359	Rondell White	.20
360	Juan Acevedo	.10
361	Edgardo Alfonzo	.10
362	Carlos Baerga	.10
363	Carl Everett	.10
364	John Franco	.10
365	Bernard Gilkey	.10
366	Todd Hundley	.20
367	Butch Huskey	.10
368	Bobby Jones	.10
369	Takashi Kashiwada	.40
370	Greg McMichael	.10
371	Brian McRae	.10
372	Alex Ochoa	.10
373	John Olerud	.10
374	Rey Ordonez	.10
375	Turk Wendell	.10
376	Ricky Bottalico	.10
377	Rico Brogna	.10
378	Lenny Dykstra	.10
379	Bobby Estalella	.10
380	Wayne Gomes	.10
381	Tyler Green	.10
382	Gregg Jefferies	.10
383	Mark Leiter	.10
384	Mike Lieberthal	.10
385	Mickey Morandini	.10
386	Scott Rolen	1.50
387	Curt Schilling	.20
388	Kevin Stocker	.10
389	Danny Tartabull	.10
390	Jermaine Allensworth	.10
391	Adrian Brown	.10
392	Jason Christiansen	.10
393	Steve Cooke	.10
394	Francisco Cordova	.10
395	Jose Guillen	.40
396	Jason Kendall	.10
397	Jon Lieber	.10
398	Esteban Loaiza	.10
399	Al Martin	.10
400	*Kevin Polcovich*	.20
401	Joe Randa	.10
402	Ricardo Rincon	.10
403	Tony Womack	.10
404	Kevin Young	.10
405	Andy Benes	.10
406	Royce Clayton	.10
407	Delino DeShields	.10
408	Mike Difelice	.10
409	Dennis Eckersley	.20
410	John Frascatore	.10
411	Gary Gaetti	.10
412	Ron Gant	.20
413	Brian Jordan	.10
414	Ray Lankford	.10
415	Willie McGee	.10
416	Mark McGwire	4.00
417	Matt Morris	.10
418	Luis Ordaz	.10
419	Todd Stottlemyre	.10
420	Andy Ashby	.10
421	Jim Bruske	.10
422	Ken Caminiti	.25
423	Will Cunnane	.10
424	Steve Finley	.10
425	John Flaherty	.10
426	Chris Gomez	.10
427	Tony Gwynn	1.50
428	Joey Hamilton	.20
429	Carlos Hernandez	.10
430	Sterling Hitchcock	.10
431	Trevor Hoffman	.10
432	Wally Joyner	.10
433	Greg Vaughn	.10
434	Quilvio Veras	.10
435	Wilson Alvarez	.10
436	Rod Beck	.10
437	Barry Bonds	.75
438	Jacob Cruz	.10
439	Shawn Estes	.10
440	Darryl Hamilton	.10
441	Roberto Hernandez	.10
442	Glenallen Hill	.10
443	Stan Javier	.10
444	Brian Johnson	.10
445	Jeff Kent	.10
446	Bill Mueller	.10
447	Kirk Rueter	.10
448	J.T. Snow	.10
449	Julian Tavarez	.10
450	Jose Vizcaino	.10

1998 Pacific Red/Silver

Red and Silver parallels reprinted all 450 cards in Pacific, with the gold foil used on base cards replaced by red or silver foil. Red foil versions were inserted one per Wal-Mart pack (retail), while Silver versions were inserted one per hobby pack.

	MT
Reds:	2x to 4x
Inserted 1:1 Retail	
Silvers:	2x to 4x
Inserted 1:1 Hobby	

1998 Pacific Platinum Blue

This 450-card parallel set reprinted each card in Pacific, but used a platinum blue foil on the front instead of the gold foil used on base cards. These were inserted one per 73 packs.

	MT
Platinum Blue Stars:	40x to 80x
Yng Stars & RCs:	30x to 60x
Inserted 1:73	

1998 Pacific Cramer's Choice

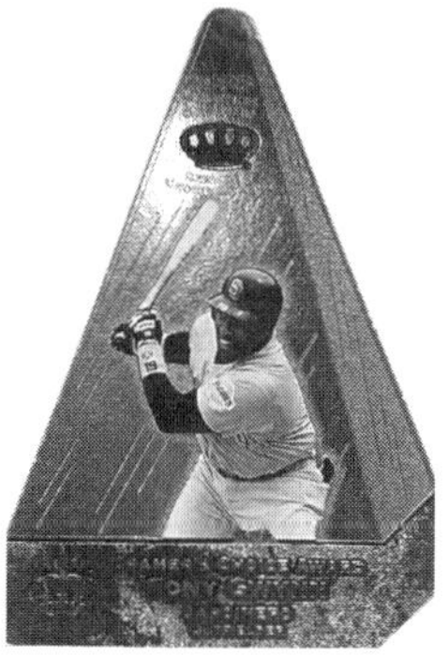

Cramer's Choice Awards is a 10-card die-cut insert. The cards feature the top player at each position as selected by Pacific CEO Mike Cramer. Each card is shaped like a trophy. Cramer's Choice Awards were inserted one per 721 packs of 1998 Pacific Baseball.

		MT
Complete Set (10):		900.00
Common Player:		40.00
Inserted 1:721		
1	Greg Maddux	120.00
2	Roberto Alomar	40.00
3	Cal Ripken Jr.	150.00
4	Nomar Garciaparra	120.00
5	Larry Walker	40.00
6	Mike Piazza	120.00
7	Mark McGwire	200.00
8	Tony Gwynn	100.00
9	Ken Griffey Jr.	200.00
10	Roger Clemens	75.00

1998 Pacific Gold Crown Die-Cuts

Gold Crown Die-Cuts is a 36-card insert seeded one per 37 packs. Each card has a holographic silver foil background and gold etching. The cards are die-cut around a crown design at the top.

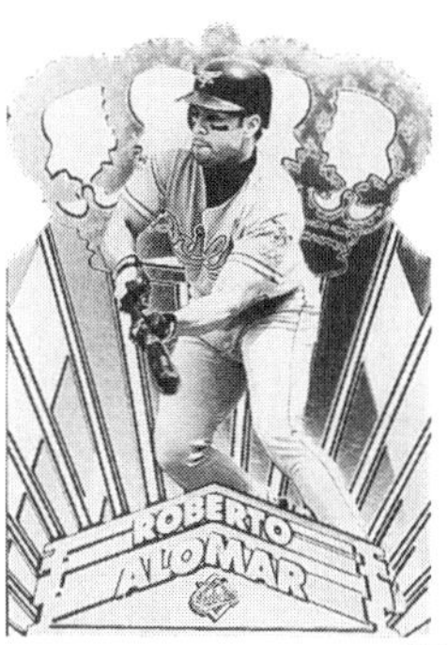

		MT
Complete Set (36):		400.00
Common Player:		4.00
1	Chipper Jones	25.00
2	Greg Maddux	25.00
3	Denny Neagle	4.00
4	Roberto Alomar	8.00
5	Rafael Palmeiro	6.00
6	Cal Ripken Jr.	30.00
7	Nomar Garciaparra	25.00
8	Mo Vaughn	10.00
9	Frank Thomas	40.00
10	Sandy Alomar Jr.	4.00
11	David Justice	5.00
12	Manny Ramirez	8.00
13	Andres Galarraga	5.00
14	Larry Walker	6.00
15	Moises Alou	4.00
16	Livan Hernandez	4.00
17	Gary Sheffield	6.00
18	Jeff Bagwell	15.00
19	Raul Mondesi	6.00
20	Hideo Nomo	10.00
21	Mike Piazza	25.00
22	Derek Jeter	25.00
23	Tino Martinez	5.00
24	Bernie Williams	8.00
25	Ben Grieve	12.00
26	Mark McGwire	45.00
27	Tony Gwynn	20.00
28	Barry Bonds	10.00
29	Ken Griffey Jr.	40.00
30	Randy Johnson	8.00
31	Edgar Martinez	4.00
32	Alex Rodriguez	25.00
33	Juan Gonzalez	20.00
34	Ivan Rodriguez	8.00
35	Roger Clemens	15.00
36	Jose Cruz Jr.	12.00

1998 Pacific Home Run Hitters

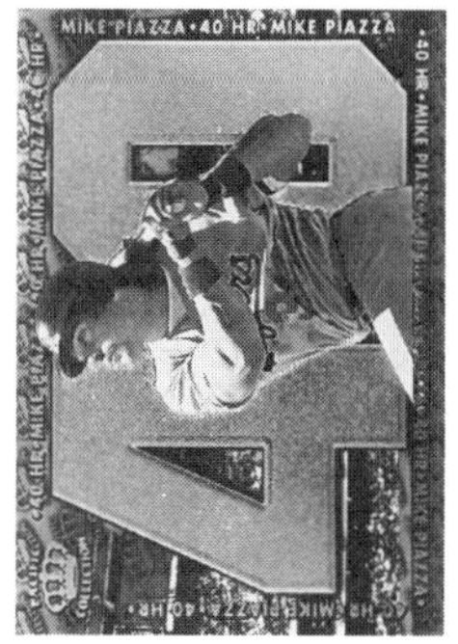

This 20-card set was inserted one per 73 packs. The full-foil cards feature a color player photo with their home run total from 1997 embossed in the background.

		MT
Complete Set (20):		220.00
Common Player:		6.00
1	Rafael Palmeiro	6.00
2	Mo Vaughn	10.00
3	Sammy Sosa	25.00
4	Albert Belle	10.00
5	Frank Thomas	40.00
6	David Justice	6.00
7	Jim Thome	8.00
8	Matt Williams	6.00
9	Vinny Castilla	6.00
10	Andres Galarraga	6.00
11	Larry Walker	8.00
12	Jeff Bagwell	15.00
13	Mike Piazza	25.00
14	Tino Martinez	6.00
15	Mark McGwire	45.00
16	Barry Bonds	10.00
17	Jay Buhner	6.00
18	Ken Griffey Jr.	40.00
19	Alex Rodriguez	25.00
20	Juan Gonzalez	20.00

1998 Pacific In the Cage

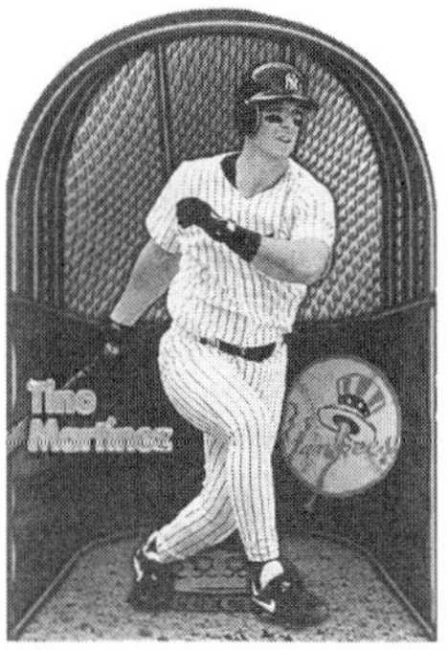

This 20-card insert features top players in a die-cut batting cage. The netting on the cage is laser-cut. In The Cage Laser-Cuts were inserted one per 145 packs.

		MT
Complete Set (20):		550.00
Common Player:		10.00
1	Chipper Jones	50.00
2	Roberto Alomar	15.00
3	Cal Ripken Jr.	60.00
4	Nomar Garciaparra	50.00
5	Frank Thomas	70.00
6	Sandy Alomar Jr.	10.00
7	David Justice	10.00
8	Larry Walker	12.00
9	Bobby Bonilla	10.00
10	Mike Piazza	50.00
11	Tino Martinez	10.00
12	Bernie Williams	15.00
13	Mark McGwire	80.00
14	Tony Gwynn	40.00
15	Barry Bonds	20.00
16	Ken Griffey Jr.	80.00
17	Edgar Martinez	10.00
18	Alex Rodriguez	50.00
19	Juan Gonzalez	40.00
20	Ivan Rodriguez	15.00

1998 Pacific Latinos of the Major Leagues

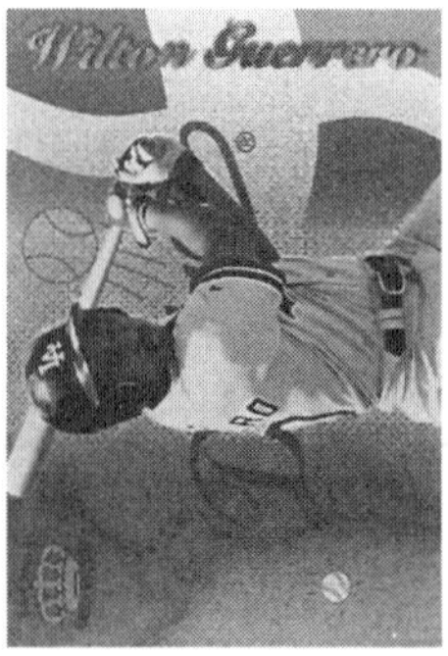

This 36-card set (2:37) features Major League players of Hispanic descent. The background has a world map on the left, the player's team logo in the center and an American flag on the right.

		MT
Complete Set (36):		75.00
Common Player:		1.50
Inserted 2:37		
1	Andruw Jones	8.00
2	Javier Lopez	1.50
3	Roberto Alomar	4.00
4	Geronimo Berroa	1.50
5	Rafael Palmeiro	2.00
6	Nomar Garciaparra	10.00
7	Sammy Sosa	10.00
8	Ozzie Guillen	1.50
9	Sandy Alomar Jr.	1.50
10	Manny Ramirez	4.00
11	Omar Vizquel	1.50
12	Vinny Castilla	1.50
13	Andres Galarraga	2.50
14	Moises Alou	1.50
15	Bobby Bonilla	1.50
16	Livan Hernandez	1.50
17	Edgar Renteria	1.50
18	Wilton Guerrero	1.50
19	Raul Mondesi	2.50
20	Ismael Valdes	1.50
21	Fernando Vina	1.50
22	Pedro Martinez	2.00
23	Edgardo Alfonzo	1.50
24	Carlos Baerga	1.50
25	Rey Ordonez	1.50
26	Tino Martinez	2.00
27	Mariano Rivera	1.50
28	Bernie Williams	4.00
29	Jose Canseco	2.50
30	Joey Cora	1.50
31	Roberto Kelly	1.50
32	Edgar Martinez	1.50
33	Alex Rodriguez	10.00
34	Juan Gonzalez	8.00
35	Ivan Rodriguez	5.00
36	Jose Cruz Jr.	6.00

1998 Pacific Team Checklists

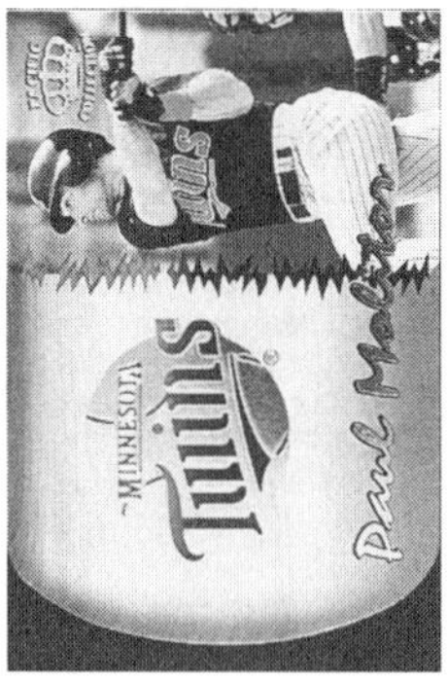

Team Checklists is a 30-card insert in the bilingual Pacific Baseball set. One card was created for each team. A player photo is featured on the right with the team logo laser-cut into a bat barrel design on the left.

		MT
Complete Set (30):		240.00
Common Player:		3.00
1	Tim Salmon, Jim Edmonds	4.00
2	Cal Ripken Jr., Roberto Alomar	25.00
3	Nomar Garciaparra, Mo Vaughn	20.00
4	Frank Thomas, Albert Belle	30.00
5	Sandy Alomar Jr., Manny Ramirez	5.00
6	Justin Thompson, Tony Clark	5.00
7	Johnny Damon, Jermaine Dye	3.00
8	Dave Nilsson, Jeff Cirillo	3.00
9	Paul Molitor, Chuck Knoblauch	5.00
10	Tino Martinez, Derek Jeter	8.00
11	Ben Grieve, Jose Canseco	10.00
12	Ken Griffey Jr., Alex Rodriguez	30.00
13	Juan Gonzalez, Ivan Rodriguez	15.00
14	Jose Cruz Jr., Roger Clemens	10.00
15	Greg Maddux, Chipper Jones	20.00
16	Sammy Sosa, Mark Grace	10.00
17	Barry Larkin, Deion Sanders	4.00
18	Larry Walker, Andres Galarraga	4.00
19	Moises Alou, Bobby Bonilla	3.00
20	Jeff Bagwell, Craig Biggio	12.00
21	Mike Piazza, Hideo Nomo	20.00
22	Pedro Martinez, Henry Rodriguez	4.00
23	Rey Ordonez, Carlos Baerga	3.00
24	Curt Schilling, Scott Rolen	8.00
25	Al Martin, Tony Womack	3.00
26	Mark McGwire, Dennis Eckersley	30.00
27	Tony Gwynn, Wally Joyner	15.00
28	Barry Bonds, J.T. Snow	8.00
29	Matt Williams, Jay Bell	5.00
30	Fred McGriff, Roberto Hernandez	4.00

1998 Pacific Aurora

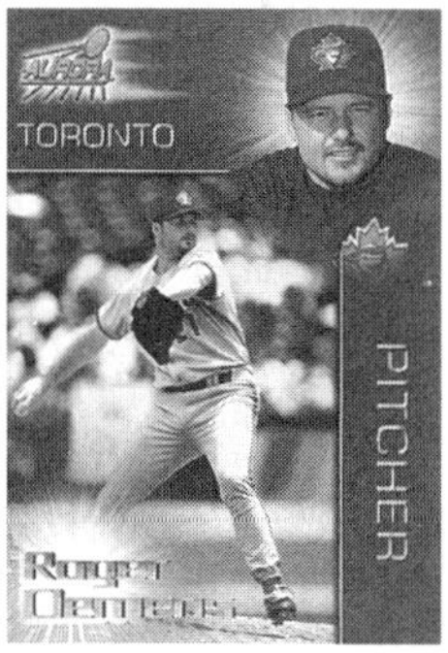

The Aurora base set consists of 200 cards printed on 24-point board. The cards have a color photo bordered on two sides by a thick green border. A headshot of the player appears in the corner of the border. Inserts include Pennant Fever (with three parallels), Hardball Cel-Fusions, Kings of the Major Leagues, On Deck Laser-Cuts and Pacific Cubes.

		MT
Complete Set (200):		40.00
Common Player:		.15
Wax Box:		90.00
1	Garret Anderson	.15
2	Jim Edmonds	.25
3	Darin Erstad	.75
4	Cecil Fielder	.25
5	Chuck Finley	.15
6	Todd Greene	.15
7	Ken Hill	.15
8	Tim Salmon	.40
9	Roberto Alomar	.60
10	Brady Anderson	.15
11	Joe Carter	.25
12	Mike Mussina	.60
13	Rafael Palmeiro	.25
14	Cal Ripken Jr.	2.50
15	B.J. Surhoff	.15
16	Steve Avery	.15
17	Nomar Garciaparra	2.00
18	Pedro Martinez	.50
19	John Valentin	.15
20	Jason Varitek	.15
21	Mo Vaughn	.75
22	Albert Belle	.75
23	Ray Durham	.15
24	*Magglio Ordonez*	.75
25	Frank Thomas	2.50
26	Robin Ventura	.25
27	Sandy Alomar Jr.	.25
28	Travis Fryman	.15
29	Dwight Gooden	.25
30	David Justice	.50
31	Kenny Lofton	.75
32	Manny Ramirez	.75
33	Jim Thome	.50
34	Omar Vizquel	.15
35	Enrique Wilson	.15
36	Jaret Wright	1.00
37	Tony Clark	.50
38	Bobby Higginson	.15
39	Brian Hunter	.15
40	Bip Roberts	.15
41	Justin Thompson	.15
42	Jeff Conine	.15
43	Johnny Damon	.15
44	Jermaine Dye	.15
45	Jeff King	.15
46	Jeff Montgomery	.15
47	Hal Morris	.15
48	Dean Palmer	.15
49	Terry Pendleton	.15
50	Rick Aguilera	.15
51	Marty Cordova	.15
52	Paul Molitor	.50
53	Otis Nixon	.15
54	Brad Radke	.15
55	Terry Steinbach	.15
56	Todd Walker	.40
57	Chili Davis	.15
58	Derek Jeter	1.50
59	Chuck Knoblauch	.40
60	Tino Martinez	.40
61	Paul O'Neill	.40
62	Andy Pettitte	.60
63	Mariano Rivera	.25
64	Bernie Williams	.60
65	Jason Giambi	.15
66	Ben Grieve	1.00
67	Rickey Henderson	.25
68	A.J. Hinch	.40
69	Kenny Rogers	.15
70	Jay Buhner	.40
71	Joey Cora	.15
72	Ken Griffey Jr.	3.00
73	Randy Johnson	.60
74	Edgar Martinez	.25
75	Jamie Moyer	.15
76	Alex Rodriguez	2.00
77	David Segui	.15
78	*Rolando Arrojo*	.50
79	Wade Boggs	.40
80	Roberto Hernandez	.15
81	Dave Martinez	.15
82	Fred McGriff	.40
83	Paul Sorrento	.15
84	Kevin Stocker	.15
85	Will Clark	.40
86	Juan Gonzalez	1.50
87	Tom Goodwin	.15
88	Rusty Greer	.25
89	Ivan Rodriguez	.75
90	John Wetteland	.15
91	Jose Canseco	.40
92	Roger Clemens	1.00
93	Jose Cruz Jr.	.75
94	Carlos Delgado	.25
95	Pat Hentgen	.15
96	Jay Bell	.15
97	Andy Benes	.25
98	Karim Garcia	.15
99	Travis Lee	2.00
100	Devon White	.15
101	Matt Williams	.40
102	Andres Galarraga	.40
103	Tom Glavine	.25
104	Andruw Jones	.75
105	Chipper Jones	2.00
106	Ryan Klesko	.40
107	Javy Lopez	.25
108	Greg Maddux	2.00
109	Walt Weiss	.15
110	Rod Beck	.15
111	Jeff Blauser	.15
112	Mark Grace	.40
113	Lance Johnson	.15
114	Mickey Morandini	.15
115	Henry Rodriguez	.15
116	Sammy Sosa	1.50
117	Kerry Wood	4.00
118	Lenny Harris	.15
119	Damian Jackson	.15
120	Barry Larkin	.40
121	Reggie Sanders	.15
122	Brett Tomko	.15
123	Dante Bichette	.40
124	Ellis Burks	.15
125	Vinny Castilla	.25
126	Todd Helton	.75
127	Darryl Kile	.15
128	Larry Walker	.40
129	Bobby Bonilla	.25
130	Livan Hernandez	.25
131	Charles Johnson	.15
132	Derrek Lee	.15
133	Edgar Renteria	.15
134	Gary Sheffield	.50
135	Moises Alou	.25
136	Jeff Bagwell	1.00
137	Derek Bell	.15
138	Craig Biggio	.40
139	*John Halama*	.40
140	Mike Hampton	.15
141	Richard Hidalgo	.15
142	Wilton Guerrero	.15
143	Todd Hollandsworth	.15
144	Eric Karros	.25
145	Paul Konerko	.40
146	Raul Mondesi	.40
147	Hideo Nomo	.60
148	Chan Ho Park	.40
149	Mike Piazza	2.00
150	Jeromy Burnitz	.15
151	Todd Dunn	.15
152	Marquis Grissom	.15
153	John Jaha	.15
154	Dave Nilsson	.15
155	Fernando Vina	.15
156	Mark Grudzielanek	.15
157	Vladimir Guerrero	.75
158	F.P. Santangelo	.15
159	Jose Vidro	.15
160	Rondell White	.25
161	Edgardo Alfonzo	.15
162	Carlos Baerga	.15
163	John Franco	.15
164	Todd Hundley	.15
165	Brian McRae	.15
166	John Olerud	.25
167	Rey Ordonez	.15
168	*Masato Yoshii*	.50
169	Ricky Bottalico	.15
170	Doug Glanville	.15
171	Gregg Jefferies	.15
172	Desi Relaford	.15
173	Scott Rolen	1.00
174	Curt Schilling	.25
175	Jose Guillen	.25
176	Jason Kendall	.15
177	Al Martin	.15
178	Abraham Nunez	.15
179	Kevin Young	.15
180	Royce Clayton	.15
181	Delino DeShields	.15
182	Gary Gaetti	.15
183	Ron Gant	.25
184	Brian Jordan	.15
185	Ray Lankford	.15
186	Willie McGee	.15
187	Mark McGwire	4.00
188	Kevin Brown	.15
189	Ken Caminiti	.25
190	Steve Finley	.15
191	Tony Gwynn	1.50
192	Wally Joyner	.15
193	Ruben Rivera	.15
194	Quilvio Veras	.15
195	Barry Bonds	.75
196	Shawn Estes	.15
197	Orel Hershiser	.15
198	Jeff Kent	.15
199	Robb Nen	.15
200	J.T. Snow	.15

1998 Pacific Aurora Cubes

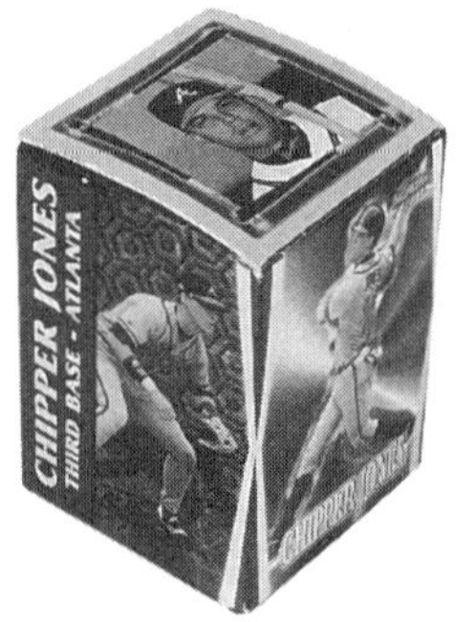

A cardboard cube presenting player photos on top and three sides, plus a side of stats was created as a hobby-only insert for Pacific Aurora. The assembled, shrink-wrapped cubes were packed one per box.

		MT
Complete Set (20):		140.00
Common Player:		3.00
Inserted 1:box		
1	Travis Lee	6.00
2	Chipper Jones	12.00
3	Greg Maddux	12.00
4	Cal Ripken Jr.	15.00
5	Nomar Garciaparra	12.00
6	Frank Thomas	15.00
7	Manny Ramirez	5.00
8	Larry Walker	2.50
9	Hideo Nomo	4.00
10	Mike Piazza	12.00
11	Derek Jeter	10.00
12	Ben Grieve	6.00
13	Mark McGwire	20.00
14	Tony Gwynn	10.00
15	Barry Bonds	5.00
16	Ken Griffey Jr.	20.00
17	Alex Rodriguez	12.00
18	Wade Boggs	2.50
19	Juan Gonzalez	10.00
20	Jose Cruz Jr.	5.00

1998 Pacific Aurora Hardball

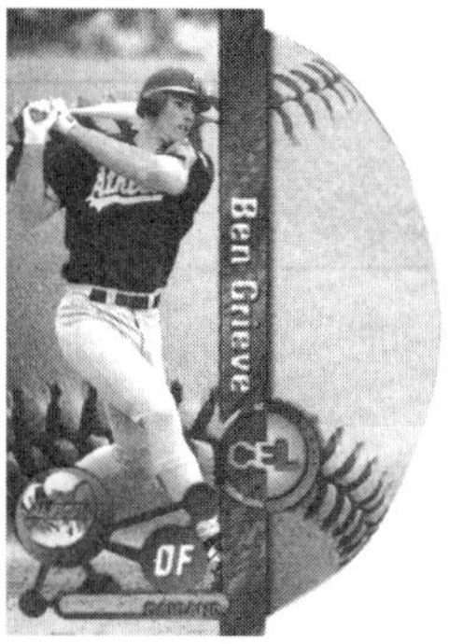

Hardball Cel-Fusions is a 20-card insert seeded one per 73 packs. The cards feature a die-cut cel baseball fused to a foiled and etched card.

		MT
Complete Set (20):		500.00
Common Player:		10.00
Inserted 1:73		
1	Travis Lee	40.00
2	Chipper Jones	40.00
3	Greg Maddux	40.00
4	Cal Ripken Jr.	50.00
5	Nomar Garciaparra	40.00
6	Frank Thomas	50.00
7	David Justice	10.00
8	Jeff Bagwell	20.00
9	Hideo Nomo	15.00
10	Mike Piazza	40.00

11	Derek Jeter	40.00
12	Ben Grieve	20.00
13	Scott Rolen	20.00
14	Mark McGwire	60.00
15	Tony Gwynn	30.00
16	Ken Griffey Jr.	60.00
17	Alex Rodriguez	40.00
18	Ivan Rodriguez	15.00
19	Roger Clemens	20.00
20	Jose Cruz Jr.	15.00

1998 Pacific Aurora Kings of the Major Leagues

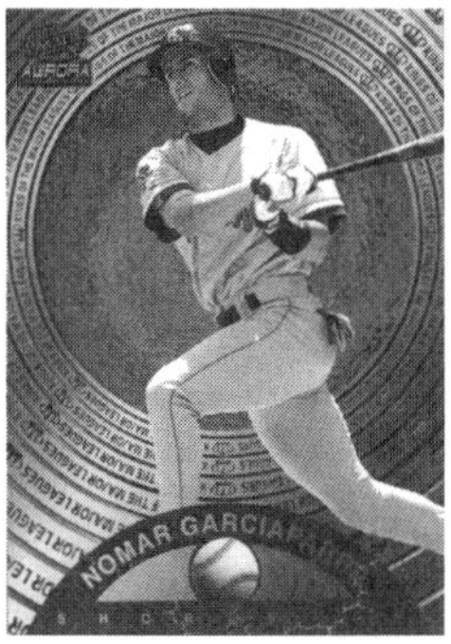

This 10-card insert features star players on fully-foiled cards. Kings of the Major Leagues was seeded one per 361 packs.

		MT
Complete Set (10):		850.00
Common Player:		20.00
Inserted 1:361		
1	Chipper Jones	90.00
2	Greg Maddux	90.00
3	Cal Ripken Jr.	110.00
4	Nomar Garciaparra	90.00
5	Frank Thomas	110.00
6	Mike Piazza	90.00
7	Mark McGwire	150.00
8	Tony Gwynn	75.00
9	Ken Griffey Jr.	150.00
10	Alex Rodriguez	90.00

1998 Pacific Aurora On Deck Laser-Cut

On Deck Laser-Cuts is a 20-card insert seeded four per 37 packs of 1998 Pacific Aurora Baseball.

		MT
Complete Set (20):		70.00
Common Player:		1.00
Inserted 1:9		
1	Travis Lee	3.00
2	Chipper Jones	6.00
3	Greg Maddux	6.00
4	Cal Ripken Jr.	8.00
5	Nomar Garciaparra	6.00
6	Frank Thomas	8.00
7	Manny Ramirez	2.50
8	Larry Walker	1.00
9	Hideo Nomo	2.00
10	Mike Piazza	6.00
11	Derek Jeter	6.00
12	Ben Grieve	4.00
13	Mark McGwire	12.00
14	Tony Gwynn	5.00
15	Barry Bonds	2.50
16	Ken Griffey Jr.	10.00
17	Alex Rodriguez	8.00
18	Wade Boggs	1.00
19	Juan Gonzalez	5.00
20	Jose Cruz Jr.	2.50

1998 Pacific Aurora Pennant Fever

Pennant Fever is a 50-card insert seeded one per pack. Each card is fully foiled and etched. The color player image is duplicated in the upper left corner with an image stamped in gold foil. Pennant Fever has three parallels. The Silver retail parallel is numbered to 250, Platinum Blue is numbered to 100 and the Copper hobby parallel is numbered to 20. Tony Gwynn signed his card serially numbered one in each insert.

		MT
Complete Set (50):		20.00
Common Player:		.25
Inserted 1:1		
Silvers:		40x to 75x
Production 250 sets		
Platinum Blues:		60x to 100x
Production 100 sets		
1	Tony Gwynn	1.00
2	Derek Jeter	1.25
3	Alex Rodriguez	1.25
4	Paul Molitor	.40
5	Nomar Garciaparra	1.25
6	Jeff Bagwell	.75
7	Ivan Rodriguez	.50
8	Cal Ripken Jr.	1.50
9	Matt Williams	.25
10	Chipper Jones	1.25
11	Edgar Martinez	.25
12	Wade Boggs	.25
13	Paul Konerko	.25
14	Ben Grieve	.75
15	Sandy Alomar Jr.	.25
16	Travis Lee	.75
17	Scott Rolen	.75
18	Ryan Klesko	.25
19	Juan Gonzalez	1.00
20	Albert Belle	.50
21	Roger Clemens	.75
22	Javy Lopez	.25
23	Jose Cruz Jr.	.50
24	Ken Griffey Jr.	2.00
25	Mark McGwire	2.50
26	Brady Anderson	.25
27	Jaret Wright	1.00
28	Roberto Alomar	.40
29	Joe Carter	.25
30	Hideo Nomo	.40
31	Mike Piazza	1.25
32	Andres Galarraga	.25
33	Larry Walker	.25
34	Tim Salmon	.25
35	Frank Thomas	1.50
36	Moises Alou	.25
37	David Justice	.40
38	Manny Ramirez	.50
39	Jim Edmonds	.25
40	Barry Bonds	.50
41	Jim Thome	.40
42	Mo Vaughn	.50
43	Rafael Palmeiro	.25
44	Darin Erstad	.50
45	Pedro Martinez	.40
46	Greg Maddux	1.25
47	Jose Canseco	.25
48	Vladimir Guerrero	.50
49	Bernie Williams	.40
50	Randy Johnson	.40

1998 Pacific Crown Royale

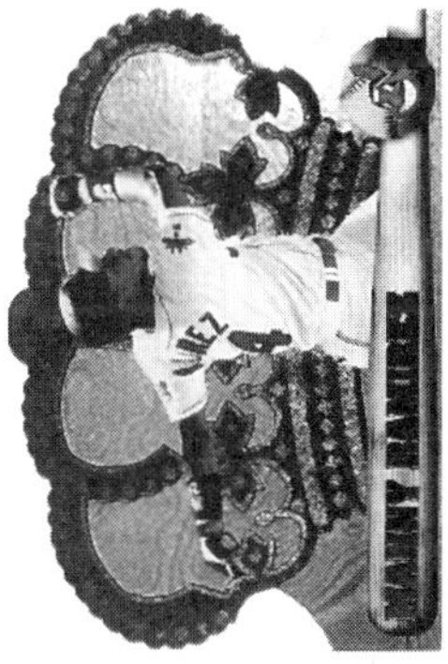

The Crown Royale base set consists of 144 die-cut cards. The cards have a horizontal layout and are die-cut around a crown design at the top. The cards are double-foiled and etched. Inserts include Diamond Knights, Pillars of the Game, Race to the Record, All-Star Die-Cuts, Firestone on Baseball and Cramer's Choice Awards.

		MT
Complete Set (144):		125.00
Common Player:		.50
1	Garret Anderson	.50
2	Jim Edmonds	.75
3	Darin Erstad	2.50
4	Tim Salmon	1.00
5	Jarrod Washburn	.50
6	David Dellucci	.50
7	Travis Lee	6.00
8	Devon White	.50
9	Matt Williams	1.00
10	Andres Galarraga	1.00
11	Tom Glavine	.75
12	Andruw Jones	2.50
13	Chipper Jones	6.00
14	Ryan Klesko	1.00
15	Javy Lopez	.75
16	Greg Maddux	6.00
17	Walt Weiss	.50
18	Roberto Alomar	1.50
19	Harold Baines	.50
20	Eric Davis	.50
21	Mike Mussina	2.00
22	Rafael Palmeiro	1.00
23	Cal Ripken Jr.	8.00
24	Nomar Garciaparra	6.00
25	Pedro Martinez	2.50
26	Troy O'Leary	.50
27	Mo Vaughn	2.50
28	Tim Wakefield	.50
29	Mark Grace	1.00
30	Mickey Morandini	.50
31	Sammy Sosa	8.00
32	Kerry Wood	10.00
33	Albert Belle	2.50
34	Mike Caruso	.50
35	Ray Durham	.50
36	Frank Thomas	8.00
37	Robin Ventura	.75
38	Bret Boone	.50
39	Sean Casey	.50
40	Barry Larkin	.75
41	Reggie Sanders	.50
42	Sandy Alomar Jr.	.50
43	David Justice	1.00
44	Kenny Lofton	2.50
45	Manny Ramirez	2.50
46	Jim Thome	1.50
47	Omar Vizquel	.50
48	Jaret Wright	2.50
49	Dante Bichette	.75
50	Ellis Burks	.50
51	Vinny Castilla	.75
52	Todd Helton	2.00
53	Larry Walker	1.00
54	Tony Clark	1.50
55	Damion Easley	.50
56	Bobby Higginson	.50
57	Cliff Floyd	.50
58	Livan Hernandez	.50
59	Derrek Lee	.50
60	Edgar Renteria	.50
61	Moises Alou	.75
62	Jeff Bagwell	3.00
63	Derek Bell	.50
64	Craig Biggio	.75
65	Johnny Damon	.50
66	Jeff King	.50
67	Hal Morris	.50
68	Dean Palmer	.50
69	Bobby Bonilla	.50
70	Eric Karros	.75
71	Raul Mondesi	.75
72	Gary Sheffield	.75
73	Jeromy Burnitz	.50
74	Jeff Cirillo	.50
75	Marquis Grissom	.50
76	Fernando Vina	.50
77	Marty Cordova	.50
78	Pat Meares	.50
79	Paul Molitor	1.50
80	Terry Steinbach	.50
81	Todd Walker	.75
82	Brad Fullmer	1.00
83	Vladimir Guerrero	2.50
84	Carl Pavano	.50
85	Rondell White	.75
86	Carlos Baerga	.50
87	Hideo Nomo	1.50
88	John Olerud	.75
89	Rey Ordonez	.50
90	Mike Piazza	6.00
91	*Masato Yoshii*	1.50
92	*Orlando Hernandez*	10.00
93	Hideki Irabu	1.50
94	Derek Jeter	5.00
95	Chuck Knoblauch	1.00
96	Ricky Ledee	.75
97	Tino Martinez	1.00
98	Paul O'Neill	.75
99	Bernie Williams	2.00
100	Jason Giambi	.50
101	Ben Grieve	3.00
102	Rickey Henderson	.50
103	Matt Stairs	.50
104	Bob Abreu	.50
105	Doug Glanville	.50
106	Scott Rolen	3.00
107	Curt Schilling	.50
108	Jose Guillen	.50
109	Jason Kendall	.75
110	Jason Schmidt	.50
111	Kevin Young	.50
112	Delino DeShields	.50
113	Brian Jordan	.50
114	Ray Lankford	.75
115	Mark McGwire	12.00
116	Tony Gwynn	5.00
117	Wally Joyner	.50
118	Ruben Rivera	.50
119	Greg Vaughn	.75
120	Rich Aurilia	.50
121	Barry Bonds	2.50
122	Bill Mueller	.50
123	Robb Nen	.50
124	Jay Buhner	1.00
125	Ken Griffey Jr.	10.00
126	Edgar Martinez	.75
127	Shane Monahan	.50
128	Alex Rodriguez	8.00
129	David Segui	.50
130	*Rolando Arrojo*	2.00
131	Wade Boggs	.75
132	Quinton McCracken	.50
133	Fred McGriff	.75
134	Bobby Smith	.50
135	Will Clark	1.00
136	Juan Gonzalez	5.00
137	Rusty Greer	.75
138	Ivan Rodriguez	2.50
139	Aaron Sele	.50
140	John Wetteland	.50
141	Jose Canseco	1.00
142	Roger Clemens	4.00
143	Carlos Delgado	.50
144	Shawn Green	.50

1998 Pacific Crown Royale All-Star

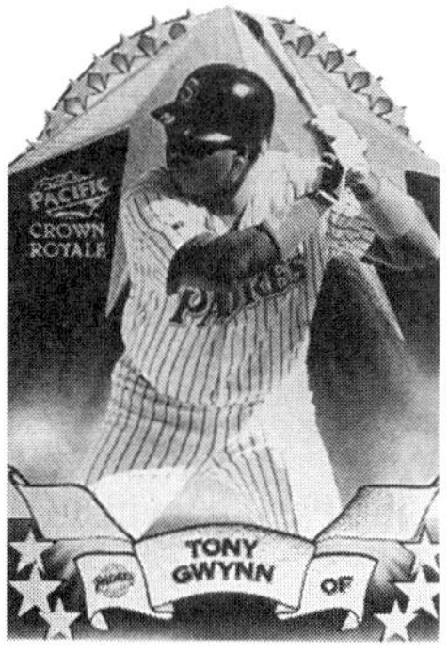

This 20-card insert was seeded one per 25 packs. The featured players all participated in the 1998 All-Star Game. The background features the sun rising over a mountain with a die-cut at the top of the card.

		MT
Complete Set (20):		350.00
Common Player:		5.00
Inserted 1:25		
1	Roberto Alomar	10.00
2	Cal Ripken Jr.	40.00
3	Kenny Lofton	15.00
4	Jim Thome	8.00
5	Derek Jeter	25.00
6	David Wells	5.00
7	Ken Griffey Jr.	50.00
8	Alex Rodriguez	40.00
9	Juan Gonzalez	25.00
10	Ivan Rodriguez	15.00
11	Gary Sheffield	5.00
12	Chipper Jones	30.00
13	Greg Maddux	30.00
14	Walt Weiss	5.00
15	Larry Walker	8.00
16	Craig Biggio	5.00
17	Mike Piazza	30.00
18	Mark McGwire	50.00
19	Tony Gwynn	25.00
20	Barry Bonds	15.00

1998 Pacific Crown Royale Cramer's Choice Awards

Premium-sized Cramer's Choice Awards were inserted one per box. The ten players in the set are featured on a die-cut card designed to resemble a trophy. Pacific CEO Mike Cramer signed and hand-numbered ten sets of Cramer's Choice Awards.

		MT
Complete Set (10):		100.00
Common Player:		5.00
Inserted 1:box		
1	Cal Ripken Jr.	15.00
2	Ken Griffey Jr.	20.00
3	Alex Rodriguez	15.00
4	Juan Gonzalez	10.00
5	Travis Lee	12.00
6	Chipper Jones	12.00
7	Greg Maddux	12.00
8	Kerry Wood	20.00
9	Mark McGwire	20.00
10	Tony Gwynn	10.00

1998 Pacific Crown Royale Diamond Knights

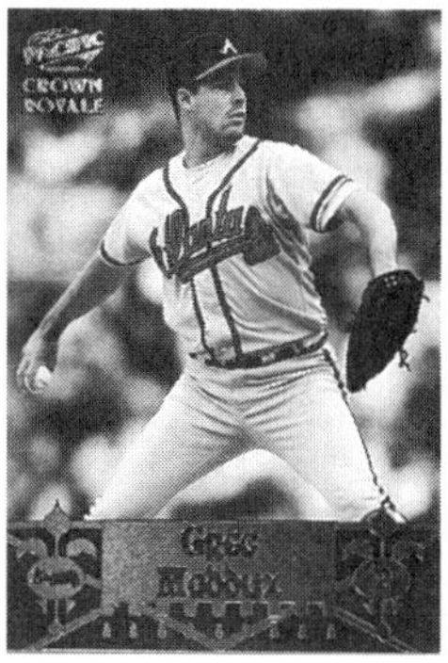

Diamond Knights is a 25-card, one per pack insert. Each card features a color action photo and the player's name, team and position listed in a Medieval-type border at the bottom.

		MT
Complete Set (25):		40.00
Common Player:		.75
Inserted 1:1		
1	Andres Galarraga	1.00
2	Chipper Jones	3.00
3	Greg Maddux	3.00
4	Cal Ripken Jr.	4.00
5	Nomar Garciaparra	3.00
6	Mo Vaughn	1.25
7	Kerry Wood	5.00
8	Frank Thomas	4.00
9	Vinny Castilla	.75
10	Jeff Bagwell	1.50
11	Craig Biggio	.75
12	Paul Molitor	1.00
13	Mike Piazza	3.00
14	Orlando Hernandez	4.00
15	Derek Jeter	2.50
16	Ricky Ledee	.75
17	Mark McGwire	6.00
18	Tony Gwynn	2.50
19	Barry Bonds	1.25
20	Ken Griffey Jr.	5.00
21	Alex Rodriguez	4.00
22	Wade Boggs	.75
23	Juan Gonzalez	2.50
24	Ivan Rodriguez	1.25
25	Jose Canseco	1.00

1998 Pacific Crown Royale Firestone on Baseball

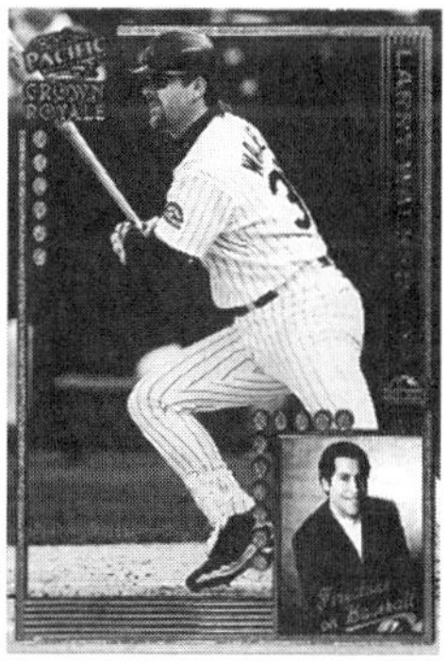

This 26-card insert features star players with commentary by sports personality Roy Firestone. The fronts have a color photo of the player and a portrait of Firestone in the lower right corner. The card backs have text by Firestone on what makes the featured player great. Firestone signed a total of 300 cards in this insert.

		MT
Complete Set (26):		400.00
Common Player:		4.00
Inserted 1:12		
1	Travis Lee	25.00
2	Chipper Jones	25.00
3	Greg Maddux	25.00

4	Cal Ripken Jr.	30.00
5	Nomar Garciaparra	25.00
6	Mo Vaughn	10.00
7	Kerry Wood	40.00
8	Frank Thomas	30.00
9	Manny Ramirez	10.00
10	Larry Walker	6.00
11	Gary Sheffield	4.00
12	Paul Molitor	8.00
13	Hideo Nomo	6.00
14	Mike Piazza	25.00
15	Ben Grieve	15.00
16	Mark McGwire	40.00
17	Tony Gwynn	20.00
18	Barry Bonds	10.00
19	Ken Griffey Jr.	40.00
20	Randy Johnson	8.00
21	Alex Rodriquez	30.00
22	Wade Boggs	4.00
23	Juan Gonzalez	20.00
24	Ivan Rodriguez	10.00
25	Roger Clemens	18.00
26	Roy Firestone	4.00

1998 Pacific Crown Royale HomeRun Fever

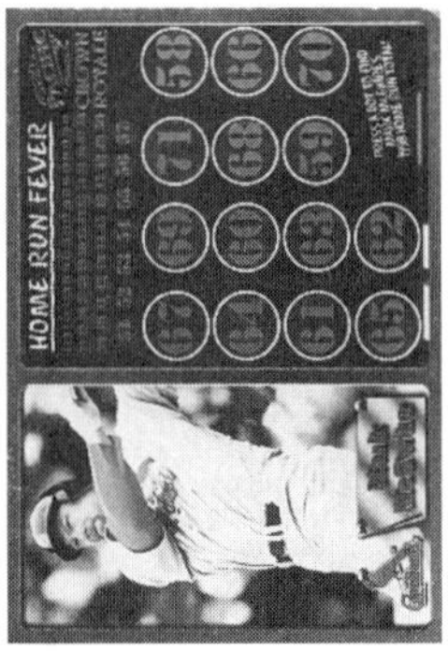

Home Run Fever (10 cards, 1:73) features players who had a shot at breaking Roger Maris' home run record in 1998. The card fronts have a player photo on the left and a blackboard with numbers from 1 to 60 on the right. Ten circles featuring disappearing ink contained numbers 61 through 70. Collectors could rub the circles to reveal the player's potential record home run total.

		MT
Complete Set (10):		450.00
Common Player:		15.00
Inserted 1:73		
1	Andres Galarraga	20.00
2	Sammy Sosa	75.00
3	Albert Belle	30.00
4	Jim Thome	20.00
5	Mark McGwire	120.00
6	Greg Vaughn	15.00
7	Ken Griffey Jr.	120.00
8	Alex Rodriguez	100.00
9	Juan Gonzalez	60.00
10	Jose Canseco	20.00

1998 Pacific Crown Royale Pillars of the Game

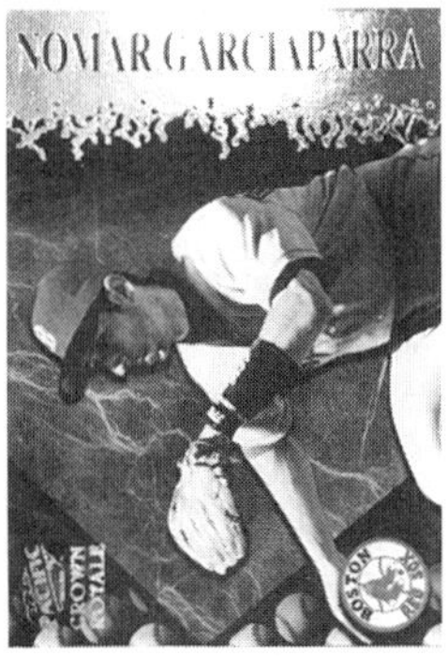

This 25-card insert was seeded one per pack. Each card features a star player with a background of holographic silver foil.

		MT
Complete Set (25):		40.00
Common Player:		.75
Inserted 1:1		
1	Jim Edmonds	.75
2	Travis Lee	3.00
3	Chipper Jones	3.00
4	Tom Glavine, John Smoltz, Greg Maddux	2.00
5	Cal Ripken Jr.	4.00
6	Nomar Garciaparra	3.00
7	Mo Vaughn	1.25
8	Sammy Sosa	4.00
9	Kerry Wood	5.00
10	Frank Thomas	4.00
11	Jim Thome	1.00
12	Larry Walker	1.00
13	Moises Alou	.75
14	Raul Mondesi	1.00
15	Mike Piazza	3.00
16	Hideki Irabu	1.00
17	Bernie Williams	1.00
18	Ben Grieve	1.50
19	Scott Rolen	1.50
20	Mark McGwire	6.00
21	Tony Gwynn	2.50
22	Ken Griffey Jr.	5.00
23	Alex Rodriguez	4.00
24	Juan Gonzalez	2.50
25	Roger Clemens	2.00

1998 Pacific Invincible

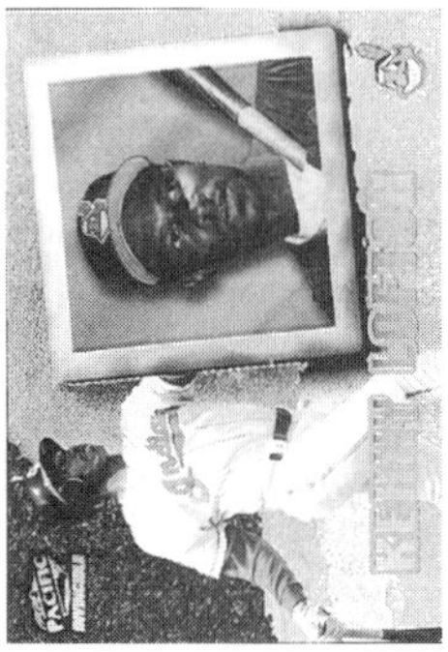

Invincible Baseball consists of a 150-card base set. The base cards have a horizontal layout and feature a player photo on the left and a headshot in a cel window on the right. The regular cards were inserted one per five-card pack. Silver (2:37) and Platinum Blue (1:73) parallels were also created. Inserts include Moments in Time, Team Checklists, Photoengravings, Interleague Players, Gems of the Diamond and Cramer's Choice Awards.

		MT
Complete Set (150):		175.00
Common Player:		1.00
Silvers:		2x to 4x
Inserted 2:37		
Wax Box:		90.00
1	Garret Anderson	1.00
2	Jim Edmonds	1.50
3	Darin Erstad	4.00
4	Chuck Finley	1.00
5	Tim Salmon	2.00
6	Roberto Alomar	3.00
7	Brady Anderson	1.50
8	Geronimo Berroa	1.00
9	Eric Davis	1.00
10	Mike Mussina	3.00
11	Rafael Palmeiro	2.00
12	Cal Ripken Jr.	12.00
13	Steve Avery	1.00
14	Nomar Garciaparra	9.00
15	John Valentin	1.00
16	Mo Vaughn	4.00
17	Albert Belle	4.00
18	Ozzie Guillen	1.00
19	Norberto Martin	1.00
20	Frank Thomas	12.00
21	Robin Ventura	1.00
22	Sandy Alomar Jr.	1.00
23	David Justice	1.50
24	Kenny Lofton	4.00
25	Manny Ramirez	3.00
26	Jim Thome	2.50
27	Omar Vizquel	1.00
28	Matt Williams	2.00
29	Jaret Wright	8.00
30	Raul Casanova	1.00
31	Tony Clark	2.50
32	Deivi Cruz	1.00
33	Bobby Higginson	1.00
34	Justin Thompson	1.00
35	Yamil Benitez	1.00
36	Johnny Damon	1.00
37	Jermaine Dye	1.00
38	Jed Hansen	1.00
39	Larry Sutton	1.00
40	Jeromy Burnitz	1.00
41	Jeff Cirillo	1.00
42	Dave Nilsson	1.00
43	Jose Valentin	1.00
44	Fernando Vina	1.00
45	Marty Cordova	1.00
46	Chuck Knoblauch	2.00
47	Paul Molitor	3.00
48	Brad Radke	1.00
49	Terry Steinbach	1.00
50	Wade Boggs	1.50
51	Hideki Irabu	2.00
52	Derek Jeter	9.00
53	Tino Martinez	2.00
54	Andy Pettitte	3.00
55	Mariano Rivera	1.50
56	Bernie Williams	3.00
57	Jose Canseco	1.50
58	Jason Giambi	1.00
59	Ben Grieve	6.00
60	Aaron Small	1.00
61	Jay Buhner	2.00
62	Ken Cloude	1.00
63	Joey Cora	1.00
64	Ken Griffey Jr.	15.00
65	Randy Johnson	3.00
66	Edgar Martinez	1.50
67	Alex Rodriguez	9.00
68	Will Clark	1.50
69	Juan Gonzalez	8.00
70	Rusty Greer	1.00
71	Ivan Rodriguez	4.00
72	Joe Carter	1.50
73	Roger Clemens	5.00
74	Jose Cruz Jr.	5.00
75	Carlos Delgado	1.00
76	Andruw Jones	7.00
77	Chipper Jones	9.00
78	Ryan Klesko	2.00
79	Javier Lopez	1.50
80	Greg Maddux	9.00
81	Miguel Batista	1.00
82	Jeremi Gonzalez	1.00
83	Mark Grace	2.00
84	Kevin Orie	1.00
85	Sammy Sosa	8.00
86	Barry Larkin	1.50
87	Deion Sanders	1.50
88	Reggie Sanders	1.00
89	Chris Stynes	1.00
90	Dante Bichette	1.50
91	Vinny Castilla	1.00
92	Andres Galarraga	2.00
93	Neifi Perez	1.00
94	Larry Walker	2.00
95	Moises Alou	1.00
96	Bobby Bonilla	1.00
97	Kevin Brown	1.00
98	Craig Counsell	1.00
99	Livan Hernandez	2.00
100	Edgar Renteria	1.00
101	Gary Sheffield	2.00
102	Jeff Bagwell	7.00
103	Craig Biggio	1.50
104	Luis Gonzalez	1.00
105	Darryl Kile	1.00
106	Wilton Guerrero	1.00
107	Eric Karros	1.50
108	Ramon Martinez	1.50
109	Raul Mondesi	2.00
110	Hideo Nomo	4.00
111	Chan Ho Park	1.50
112	Mike Piazza	9.00
113	Mark Grudzielanek	1.00
114	Vladimir Guerrero	4.00
115	Pedro Martinez	2.00
116	Henry Rodriguez	1.00
117	David Segui	1.00
118	Edgardo Alfonzo	1.00
119	Carlos Baerga	1.00
120	John Franco	1.00
121	John Olerud	1.00
122	Rey Ordonez	1.00
123	Ricky Bottalico	1.00
124	Gregg Jefferies	1.00
125	Mickey Morandini	1.00
126	Scott Rolen	6.00
127	Curt Schilling	1.50
128	Jose Guillen	2.00
129	Esteban Loaiza	1.00
130	Al Martin	1.00
131	Tony Womack	1.00
132	Dennis Eckersley	1.00
133	Gary Gaetti	1.00
134	Curtis King	1.00
135	Ray Lankford	1.00
136	Mark McGwire	15.00
137	Ken Caminiti	1.50
138	Steve Finley	1.00
139	Tony Gwynn	7.00
140	Carlos Hernandez	1.00
141	Wally Joyner	1.00
142	Barry Bonds	4.00
143	Jacob Cruz	1.00
144	Shawn Estes	1.00
145	Stan Javier	1.00
146	J.T. Snow	1.50
147	Nomar Garciaparra	6.00
148	Scott Rolen	4.00
149	Ken Griffey Jr.	10.00
150	Larry Walker	1.50

1998 Pacific Invincible Platinum Blue

This parallel set included all 150 cards from Pacific Invincible printed with a blue foil vs. the gold foil used on base cards. Platinum Blues were inserted one per 73 packs.

	MT
Platinum Blue Stars:	8x to 15x
Yng Stars & RCs	: 5x to 10x
Inserted 1:73	

1998 Pacific Invincible Cramer's Choice

The 10-card Cramer's Choice Awards insert features top players on cards with a die-cut trophy design. This set has six different foil variations, each with a different production number. Green (99 hand-numbered sets), Dark Blue (80), Light Blue (50), Red (25), Gold (15) and Purple (10) versions were included in Invincible.

		MT
Complete Green Set (10):		1100.
Common Green (99 sets):		50.00
Dark Blues (80 sets):		.8x to 1.25x
Light Blues (50 sets):		1x to 1.5x
Reds (25 sets):		1.5x to 3x
Golds (15 sets):		2.5x to 5x
Purples (10 sets):		3x to 6x
1	Greg Maddux	150.00
2	Roberto Alomar	50.00
3	Cal Ripken Jr.	200.00
4	Nomar Garciaparra	150.00
5	Larry Walker	50.00
6	Mike Piazza	150.00
7	Mark McGwire	250.00
8	Tony Gwynn	125.00
9	Ken Griffey Jr.	250.00
10	Roger Clemens	100.00

1998 Pacific Invincible Gems of the Diamond

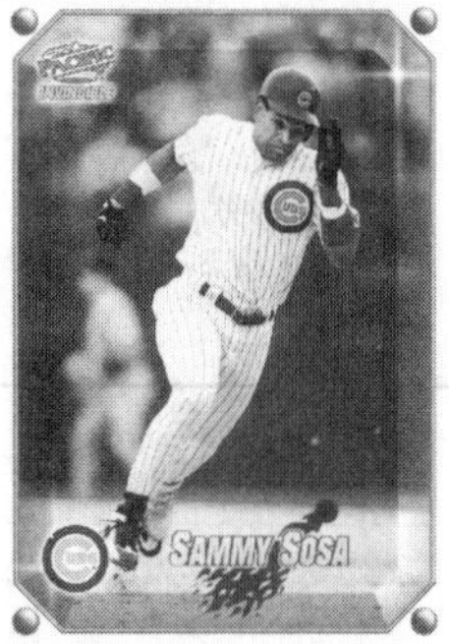

Gems of the Diamond is a 220-card insert seeded four per pack. The cards feature a color photo inside a white border.

		MT
Complete Set (220):		30.00
Common Player:		.10
1	Jim Edmonds	.20
2	Todd Greene	.20
3	Ken Hill	.10
4	Mike Holtz	.10
5	Mike James	.10
6	Chad Kreuter	.10
7	Tim Salmon	.30
8	Roberto Alomar	.60
9	Brady Anderson	.20
10	David Dellucci	.10
11	Jeffrey Hammonds	.10
12	Mike Mussina	.60
13	Rafael Palmeiro	.25
14	Arthur Rhodes	.10
15	Cal Ripken Jr.	2.50
16	Nerio Rodriguez	.10
17	Tony Tarasco	.10
18	Lenny Webster	.10
19	Mike Benjamin	.10
20	Rich Garces	.10
21	Nomar Garciaparra	2.00
22	Shane Mack	.10
23	Jose Malave	.10
24	Jesus Tavarez	.10
25	Mo Vaughn	.75
26	John Wasdin	.10
27	Jeff Abbott	.10
28	Albert Belle	.75
29	Mike Cameron	.25
30	Al Levine	.10
31	Robert Machado	.10
32	Greg Norton	.10
33	Magglio Ordonez	.75
34	Mike Sirotka	.10
35	Frank Thomas	2.50
36	Mario Valdez	.10
37	Sandy Alomar Jr.	.20
38	David Justice	.25
39	Jack McDowell	.10
40	Eric Plunk	.10
41	Manny Ramirez	.60
42	Kevin Seitzer	.10
43	Paul Shuey	.10
44	Omar Vizquel	.10
45	Kimera Bartee	.10
46	Glenn Dishman	.10
47	Orlando Miller	.10
48	Mike Myers	.10
49	Phil Nevin	.10
50	A.J. Sager	.10
51	Ricky Bones	.10
52	Scott Cooper	.10
53	Shane Halter	.10
54	David Howard	.10
55	Glendon Rusch	.10
56	Joe Vitiello	.10
57	Jeff D'Amico	.10
58	Mike Fetters	.10
59	Mike Matheny	.10
60	Jose Mercedes	.10
61	Ron Villone	.10
62	Jack Voigt	.10
63	Brent Brede	.10
64	Chuck Knoblauch	.25
65	Paul Molitor	.50
66	Todd Ritchie	.10
67	Frankie Rodriguez	.10
68	Scott Stahoviak	.10
69	Greg Swindell	.10
70	Todd Walker	.20
71	Wade Boggs	.20
72	Hideki Irabu	.30
73	Derek Jeter	1.75
74	Pat Kelly	.10
75	Graeme Lloyd	.10
76	Tino Martinez	.25
77	Jeff Nelson	.10
78	Scott Pose	.10
79	Mike Stanton	.10
80	Darryl Strawberry	.10
81	Bernie Williams	.60
82	Tony Batista	.10
83	Mark Bellhorn	.10
84	Ben Grieve	1.25
85	Pat Lennon	.10
86	Brian Lesher	.10
87	Miguel Tejada	.75
88	George Williams	.10
89	Joey Cora	.10
90	Rob Ducey	.10
91	Ken Griffey Jr.	3.00
92	Randy Johnson	.50
93	Edgar Martinez	.10
94	John Marzano	.10
95	Greg McCarthy	.10
96	Alex Rodriguez	2.00
97	Andy Sheets	.10
98	Mike Timlin	.10
99	Lee Tinsley	.10
100	Damon Buford	.10
101	Alex Diaz	.10
102	Benji Gil	.10
103	Juan Gonzalez	1.50
104	Eric Gunderson	.10
105	Danny Patterson	.10
106	Ivan Rodriguez	.75
107	Mike Simms	.10
108	Luis Andujar	.10
109	Joe Carter	.20
110	Roger Clemens	1.00
111	Jose Cruz Jr.	1.50
112	Shawn Green	.10
113	Robert Perez	.10
114	Juan Samuel	.10
115	Ed Sprague	.10
116	Shannon Stewart	.10
117	Danny Bautista	.10
118	Chipper Jones	2.00
119	Ryan Klesko	.30
120	Keith Lockhart	.10
121	Javier Lopez	.10
122	Greg Maddux	2.00
123	Kevin Millwood	.75
124	Mike Mordecai	.10
125	Eddie Perez	.10
126	Randall Simon	.25
127	Miguel Cairo	.10
128	Dave Clark	.10
129	Kevin Foster	.10
130	Mark Grace	.25
131	Tyler Houston	.10
132	Mike Hubbard	.10
133	Kevin Orie	.10
134	Ryne Sandberg	.75
135	Sammy Sosa	1.00
136	Lenny Harris	.10
137	Kent Mercker	.10
138	Mike Morgan	.10

139	Deion Sanders	.20
140	Chris Stynes	.10
141	Gabe White	.10
142	Jason Bates	.10
143	Vinny Castilla	.10
144	Andres Galarraga	.25
145	Curtis Leskanic	.10
146	Jeff McCurry	.10
147	Mike Munoz	.10
148	Larry Walker	.30
149	Jamey Wright	.10
150	Moises Alou	.20
151	Bobby Bonilla	.10
152	Kevin Brown	.10
153	John Cangelosi	.10
154	Jeff Conine	.10
155	Cliff Floyd	.10
156	Jay Powell	.10
157	Edgar Renteria	.10
158	Tony Saunders	.10
159	Gary Sheffield	.25
160	Jeff Bagwell	1.25
161	Tim Bogar	.10
162	Tony Eusebio	.10
163	Chris Holt	.10
164	Ray Montgomery	.10
165	Luis Rivera	.10
166	Eric Anthony	.10
167	Brett Butler	.10
168	Juan Castro	.10
169	Tripp Cromer	.10
170	Raul Mondesi	.25
171	Hideo Nomo	.75
172	Mike Piazza	2.00
173	Tom Prince	.10
174	Adam Riggs	.10
175	Shane Andrews	.10
176	Shayne Bennett	.10
177	Raul Chavez	.10
178	Pedro Martinez	.30
179	Sherman Obando	.10
180	Andy Stankiewicz	.10
181	Alberto Castillo	.10
182	Shawn Gilbert	.10
183	Luis Lopez	.10
184	Roberto Petagine	.10
185	Armando Reynoso	.10
186	Midre Cummings	.10
187	Kevin Jordan	.10
188	Desi Relaford	.10
189	Scott Rolen	1.25
190	Ken Ryan	.10
191	Kevin Sefcik	.10
192	Emil Brown	.10
193	Lou Collier	.10
194	Francisco Cordova	.10
195	Kevin Elster	.10
196	Mark Smith	.10
197	Marc Wilkins	.10
198	Manny Aybar	.10
199	Jose Bautista	.10
200	David Bell	.10
201	Rigo Beltran	.10
202	Delino DeShields	.10
203	Dennis Eckersley	.10
204	John Mabry	.10
205	Eli Marrero	.10
206	Willie McGee	.10
207	Mark McGwire	4.00
208	Ken Caminiti	.20
209	Tony Gwynn	1.50
210	Chris Jones	.10
211	Craig Shipley	.10
212	Pete Smith	.10
213	Jorge Velandia	.10
214	Dario Veras	.10
215	Rich Aurilia	.10
216	Damon Berryhill	.10
217	Barry Bonds	.75
218	Osvaldo Fernandez	.10
219	Dante Powell	.10
220	Rich Rodriguez	.10

1998 Pacific Invincible Interleague Players

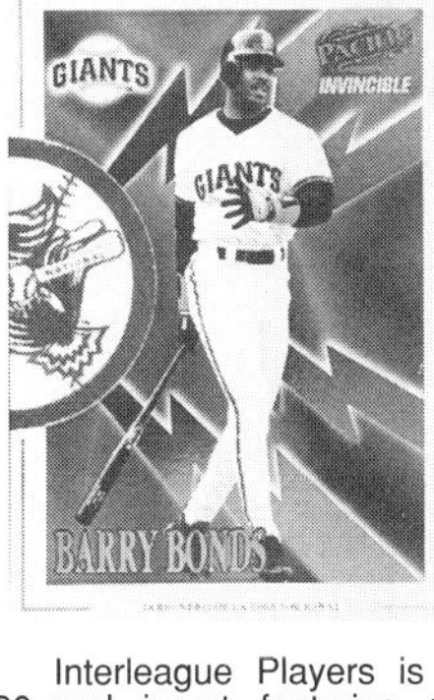

Interleague Players is a 30-card insert featuring 15 sets of players - one National League and one American League player. The dark blue backgrounds have red lightning bolts and the white borders are made of a leather-like material. When a set of players is placed next to each other, they form the MLB Interleague logo in the center. Interleague Players cards were inserted one per 73 packs.

		MT
Complete Set (30):		950.00
Common Player:		8.00
Inserted 1:73		
1A	Roberto Alomar	20.00
1N	Craig Biggio	10.00
2A	Cal Ripken Jr.	80.00
2N	Chipper Jones	60.00
3A	Nomar Garciaparra	60.00
3N	Scott Rolen	40.00
4A	Mo Vaughn	25.00
4N	Andres Galarraga	12.00
5A	Frank Thomas	80.00
5N	Tony Gwynn	50.00
6A	Albert Belle	25.00
6N	Barry Bonds	25.00
7A	Hideki Irabu	15.00
7N	Hideo Nomo	25.00
8A	Derek Jeter	60.00
8N	Rey Ordonez	8.00
9A	Tino Martinez	15.00
9N	Mark McGwire	100.00
10A	Alex Rodriguez	60.00
10N	Edgar Renteria	8.00
11A	Ken Griffey Jr.	100.00
11N	Larry Walker	15.00
12A	Randy Johnson	20.00
12N	Greg Maddux	60.00
13A	Ivan Rodriguez	25.00
13N	Mike Piazza	60.00
14A	Roger Clemens	40.00
14N	Pedro Martinez	15.00
15A	Jose Cruz Jr.	30.00
15N	Wilton Guerrero	8.00

1998 Pacific Invincible Moments in Time

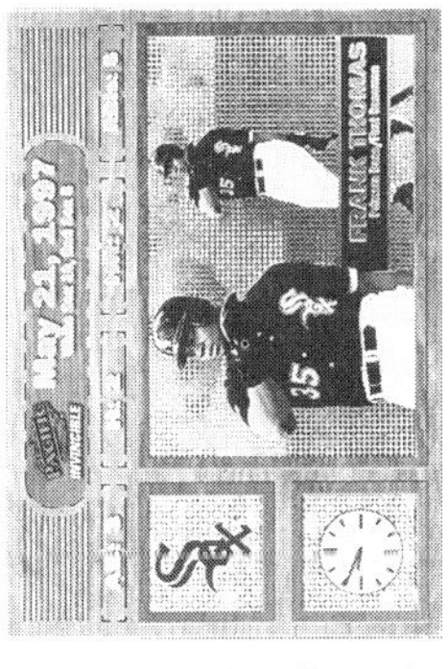

Moments in Time (20 cards, 1:145) is designed as a baseball scoreboard. The cards have a horizontal layout with the date of an important game in the player's career at the top. The player's stats from the game are featured and a picture is located on the scoreboard screen.

		MT
Complete Set (20):		900.00
Common Player:		15.00
Inserted 1:145		
1	Chipper Jones	70.00
2	Cal Ripken Jr.	100.00
3	Frank Thomas	80.00
4	David Justice	15.00
5	Andres Galarraga	20.00
6	Larry Walker	25.00
7	Livan Hernandez	20.00
8	Wilton Guerrero	15.00
9	Hideo Nomo	35.00
10	Mike Piazza	70.00
11	Pedro Martinez	25.00
12	Bernie Williams	25.00
13	Ben Grieve	50.00
14	Scott Rolen	45.00
15	Mark McGwire	120.00
16	Tony Gwynn	60.00
17	Ken Griffey Jr.	120.00
18	Alex Rodriguez	70.00
19	Juan Gonzalez	60.00
20	Jose Cruz Jr.	50.00

1998 Pacific Invincible Photoengravings

Photoengravings is an 18-card insert seeded one per 37 packs. Each card has a unique "old-style" design with a player photo in a frame in the center.

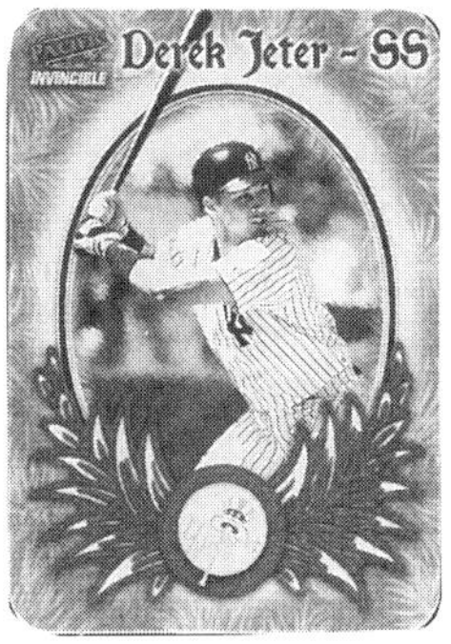

		MT
Complete Set (18):		300.00
Common Player:		4.00
Inserted 1:37		
1	Greg Maddux	25.00
2	Cal Ripken Jr.	30.00
3	Nomar Garciaparra	25.00
4	Frank Thomas	30.00
5	Larry Walker	8.00
6	Mike Piazza	25.00
7	Hideo Nomo	10.00
8	Pedro Martinez	6.00
9	Derek Jeter	25.00
10	Tino Martinez	6.00
11	Mark McGwire	40.00
12	Tony Gwynn	20.00
13	Barry Bonds	10.00
14	Ken Griffey Jr.	40.00
15	Alex Rodriguez	25.00
16	Ivan Rodriguez	10.00
17	Roger Clemens	15.00
18	Jose Cruz Jr.	15.00

1998 Pacific Invincible Team Checklists

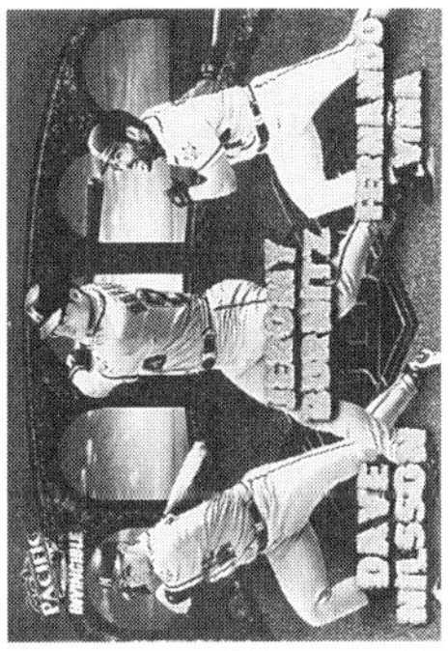

Team Checklists is a 30-card insert seeded 2:37. The fronts feature a player collage with the team logo in the background. The back has a complete checklist for that team in Invincible.

		MT
Complete Set (30):		200.00
Common Player:		3.00
Inserted 2:37		
1	Anaheim Angels	6.00
2	Atlanta Braves	15.00
3	Baltimore Orioles	20.00
4	Boston Red Sox	15.00
5	Chicago Cubs	4.00
6	Chicago White Sox	20.00
7	Cincinnati Reds	3.00
8	Cleveland Indians	5.00
9	Colorado Rockies	4.00
10	Detroit Tigers	5.00
11	Florida Marlins	4.00
12	Houston Astros	10.00
13	Kansas City Royals	3.00
14	Los Angeles Dodgers	15.00
15	Milwaukee Brewers	3.00
16	Minnesota Twins	5.00
17	Montreal Expos	6.00
18	New York Mets	3.00
19	New York Yankees	15.00
20	Oakland Athletics	10.00
21	Philadelphia Phillies	10.00
22	Pittsburgh Pirates	3.00
23	St. Louis Cardinals	10.00
24	San Diego Padres	12.00
25	San Francisco Giants	6.00
26	Seattle Mariners	25.00
27	Texas Rangers	12.00
28	Toronto Blue Jays	15.00
29	Arizona Diamondbacks	5.00
30	Tampa Bay Devil Rays	5.00

1998 Pacific Omega

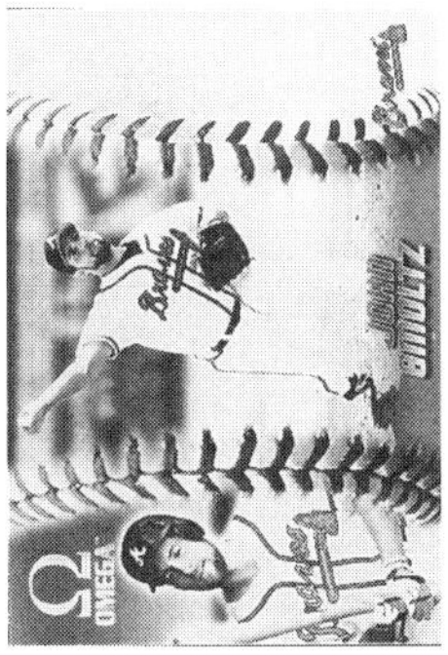

The Omega base set consists of 250 three-image cards. The horizontal cards feature a color player photo in the center with the image duplicated in foil on the right. Another color photo is on the left. The photos are divided by a baseball seam design. Inserts in the set include Prisms, Face to Face, EO Portraits, Online and Rising Stars.

		MT
Complete Set (250):		35.00
Common Player:		.10
Wax Box:		60.00
1	Garret Anderson	.10
2	Gary DiSarcina	.10
3	Jim Edmonds	.20
4	Darin Erstad	.75
5	Cecil Fielder	.20
6	Chuck Finley	.10
7	Shigetosi Hasegawa	.10
8	Tim Salmon	.25
9	Brian Anderson	.10
10	Jay Bell	.10
11	Andy Benes	.10
12	Yamil Benitez	.10
13	Jorge Fabregas	.10
14	Travis Lee	2.00
15	Devon White	.10
16	Matt Williams	.30
17	Andres Galarraga	.25
18	Tom Glavine	.20
19	Andruw Jones	.75
20	Chipper Jones	2.00
21	Ryan Klesko	.25
22	Javy Lopez	.10
23	Greg Maddux	2.00
24	*Kevin Millwood*	1.00
25	Denny Neagle	.10
26	John Smoltz	.20
27	Roberto Alomar	.60
28	Brady Anderson	.10
29	Joe Carter	.20
30	Eric Davis	.10
31	Jimmy Key	.10
32	Mike Mussina	.60
33	Rafael Palmeiro	.25
34	Cal Ripken Jr.	2.50
35	B.J. Surhoff	.10
36	Dennis Eckersley	.10
37	Nomar Garciaparra	2.00
38	Reggie Jefferson	.10
39	Derek Lowe	.10
40	Pedro Martinez	.50
41	Brian Rose	.10
42	John Valentin	.10
43	Jason Varitek	.10
44	Mo Vaughn	.75
45	Jeff Blauser	.10
46	Jeremi Gonzalez	.10
47	Mark Grace	.25
48	Lance Johnson	.10
49	Kevin Orie	.10
50	Henry Rodriguez	.10
51	Sammy Sosa	1.50
52	Kerry Wood	4.00
53	Albert Belle	.75
54	Mike Cameron	.10
55	Mike Caruso	.10
56	Ray Durham	.10
57	Jaime Navarro	.10
58	Greg Norton	.10
59	*Magglio Ordonez*	.75
60	Frank Thomas	2.50
61	Robin Ventura	.20
62	Bret Boone	.10
63	Willie Greene	.10
64	Barry Larkin	.25
65	Jon Nunnally	.10
66	Eduardo Perez	.10
67	Reggie Sanders	.10
68	Brett Tomko	.10
69	Sandy Alomar Jr.	.20
70	Travis Fryman	.10
71	David Justice	.25
72	Kenny Lofton	.75
73	Charles Nagy	.10
74	Manny Ramirez	.75
75	Jim Thome	.40
76	Omar Vizquel	.10
77	Enrique Wilson	.10
78	Jaret Wright	.75
79	Dante Bichette	.25
80	Ellis Burks	.10
81	Vinny Castilla	.20
82	Todd Helton	.75
83	Darryl Kile	.10
84	Mike Lansing	.10
85	Neifi Perez	.10
86	Larry Walker	.40
87	Raul Casanova	.10
88	Tony Clark	.50
89	Luis Gonzalez	.10
90	Bobby Higginson	.10
91	Brian Hunter	.10
92	Bip Roberts	.10
93	Justin Thompson	.10
94	Josh Booty	.10
95	Craig Counsell	.10
96	Livan Hernandez	.10
97	*Ryan Jackson*	.50
98	Mark Kotsay	.25
99	Derrek Lee	.10
100	Mike Piazza	2.00
101	Edgar Renteria	.10
102	Cliff Floyd	.10
103	Moises Alou	.20
104	Jeff Bagwell	1.00
105	Derrick Bell	.10
106	Sean Berry	.10
107	Craig Biggio	.20
108	*John Halama*	.25
109	Richard Hidalgo	.10
110	Shane Reynolds	.10
111	Tim Belcher	.10
112	Brian Bevil	.10
113	Jeff Conine	.10
114	Johnny Damon	.10
115	Jeff King	.10
116	Jeff Montgomery	.10
117	Dean Palmer	.10
118	Terry Pendleton	.10
119	Bobby Bonilla	.20
120	Wilton Guerrero	.10
121	Todd Hollandsworth	.10
122	Charles Johnson	.10
123	Eric Karros	.20
124	Paul Konerko	.25
125	Ramon Martinez	.10
126	Raul Mondesi	.25
127	Hideo Nomo	.50
128	Gary Sheffield	.30
129	Ismael Valdes	.10
130	Jeromy Burnitz	.10
131	Jeff Cirillo	.10
132	Todd Dunn	.10
133	Marquis Grissom	.10
134	John Jaha	.10
135	Scott Karl	.10
136	Dave Nilsson	.10
137	Jose Valentin	.10
138	Fernando Vina	.10
139	Rick Aguilera	.10
140	Marty Cordova	.10
141	Pat Meares	.10
142	Paul Molitor	.50
143	David Ortiz	.20
144	Brad Radke	.10
145	Terry Steinbach	.10
146	Todd Walker	.20
147	Shane Andrews	.10
148	Brad Fullmer	.25
149	Mark Grudzielanek	.10
150	Vladimir Guerrero	.75
151	F.P. Santangelo	.10
152	Jose Vidro	.10
153	Rondell White	.20
154	Carlos Baerga	.10
155	Bernard Gilkey	.10
156	Todd Hundley	.10
157	Butch Huskey	.10
158	Bobby Jones	.10
159	Brian McRae	.10
160	John Olerud	.20
161	Rey Ordonez	.10
162	*Masato Yoshii*	.50
163	David Cone	.20
164	Hideki Irabu	.50
165	Derek Jeter	1.50
166	Chuck Knoblauch	.30
167	Tino Martinez	.30
168	Paul O'Neill	.20
169	Andy Pettitte	.50
170	Mariano Rivera	.20
171	Darryl Strawberry	.20
172	David Wells	.10
173	Bernie Williams	.50
174	*Ryan Christenson*	.20
175	Jason Giambi	.10
176	Ben Grieve	1.00
177	Rickey Henderson	.10
178	A.J. Hinch	.30
179	Kenny Rogers	.10
180	Ricky Bottalico	.10
181	Rico Brogna	.10
182	Doug Glanville	.10
183	Gregg Jefferies	.10
184	Mike Lieberthal	.10
185	Scott Rolen	1.00
186	Curt Shilling	.20
187	Jermaine Allensworth	.10
188	Lou Collier	.10
189	Jose Guillen	.25
190	Jason Kendall	.10
191	Al Martin	.10
192	Tony Womack	.10
193	Kevin Young	.10

194	Royce Clayton	.10
195	Delino DeShields	.10
196	Gary Gaetti	.10
197	Ron Gant	.20
198	Brian Jordan	.10
199	Ray Lankford	.10
200	Mark McGwire	4.00
201	Todd Stottlemyre	.10
202	Kevin Brown	.20
203	Ken Caminiti	.20
204	Steve Finley	.10
205	Tony Gwynn	1.50
206	Carlos Hernandez	.10
207	Wally Joyner	.10
208	Greg Vaughn	.25
209	Barry Bonds	.75
210	Shawn Estes	.10
211	Orel Hershiser	.10
212	Stan Javier	.10
213	Jeff Kent	.10
214	Bill Mueller	.10
215	Robb Nen	.10
216	J.T. Snow	.10
217	Jay Buhner	.25
218	Ken Cloude	.25
219	Joey Cora	.10
220	Ken Griffey Jr.	3.00
221	Glenallen Hill	.10
222	Randy Johnson	.50
223	Edgar Martinez	.10
224	Jamie Moyer	.10
225	Alex Rodriguez	2.00
226	David Segui	.10
227	Dan Wilson	.10
228	*Rolando Arrojo*	.40
229	Wade Boggs	.25
230	Miguel Cairo	.10
231	Roberto Hernandez	.10
232	Quinton McCracken	.10
233	Fred McGriff	.20
234	Paul Sorrento	.10
235	Kevin Stocker	.10
236	Will Clark	.20
237	Juan Gonzalez	1.50
238	Rusty Greer	.10
239	Rick Helling	.10
240	Roberto Kelly	.10
241	Ivan Rodriguez	.75
242	Aaron Sele	.10
243	John Wetteland	.10
244	Jose Canseco	.25
245	Roger Clemens	1.00
246	Jose Cruz Jr.	.50
247	Carlos Delgado	.10
248	Alex Gonzalez	.10
249	Ed Sprague	.10
250	Shannon Stewart	.10

1998 Pacific Omega EO Portraits

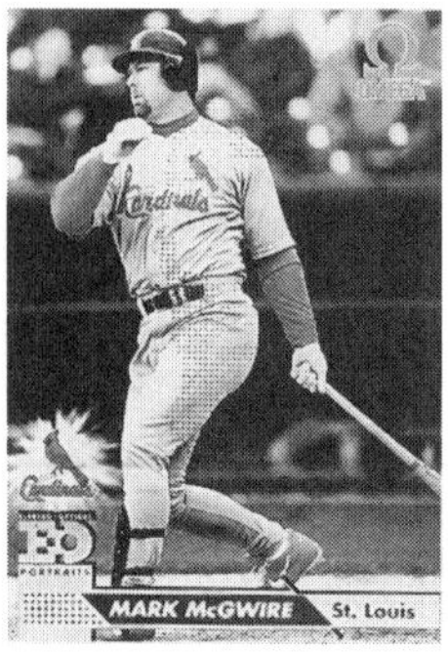

EO Portraits is a 20-card insert seeded 1:73. Each card has a color player photo with a player portrait laser-cut into the card. A "1-of-1" parallel features a laser-cut number on the card as well.

		MT
Complete Set (20):		350.00
Common Player:		5.00
Inserted 1:73		
1	Cal Ripken Jr.	30.00
2	Nomar Garciaparra	25.00
3	Mo Vaughn	10.00
4	Frank Thomas	30.00
5	Manny Ramirez	10.00
6	Ben Grieve	15.00
7	Ken Griffey Jr.	40.00
8	Alex Rodriguez	25.00
9	Juan Gonzalez	20.00
10	Ivan Rodriguez	10.00
11	Travis Lee	20.00
12	Greg Maddux	25.00
13	Chipper Jones	25.00
14	Kerry Wood	35.00
15	Larry Walker	5.00
16	Jeff Bagwell	15.00
17	Mike Piazza	25.00
18	Mark McGwire	40.00
19	Tony Gwynn	20.00
20	Barry Bonds	10.00

1998 Pacific Omega Face to Face

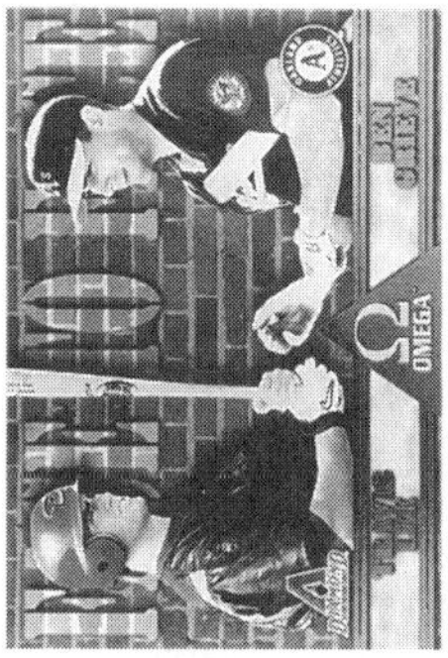

Face to Face features two star players on each card. It is a 10-card insert seeded one per 145 packs.

		MT
Complete Set (10):		200.00
Common Player:		8.00
Inserted 1:145		
1	Alex Rodriguez, Nomar Garciaparra	25.00
2	Mark McGwire, Ken Griffey Jr.	60.00
3	Mike Piazza, Sandy Alomar Jr.	25.00
4	Kerry Wood, Roger Clemens	35.00
5	Cal Ripken Jr., Paul Molitor	30.00
6	Tony Gwynn, Wade Boggs	20.00
7	Frank Thomas, Chipper Jones	30.00
8	Travis Lee, Ben Grieve	20.00
9	Hideo Nomo, Hideki Irabu	8.00
10	Juan Gonzalez, Manny Ramirez	20.00

1998 Pacific Omega Online

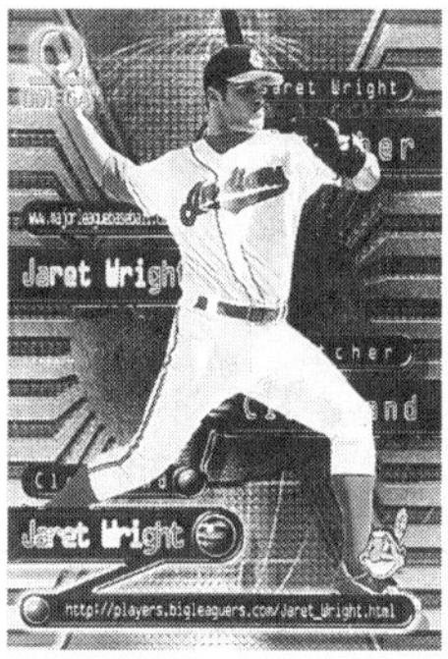

Online is a 36-card insert seeded four per 37 packs. The foiled and etched cards feature a color player photo in front of a hi-tech designed background. The card fronts also include the internet address for the player's web site on bigleaguers.com.

		MT
Complete Set (36):		140.00
Common Player:		1.00
Inserted 1:9		
1	Cal Ripken Jr.	10.00
2	Nomar Garciaparra	8.00
3	Pedro Martinez	2.00
4	Mo Vaughn	3.00
5	Frank Thomas	10.00
6	Sandy Alomar Jr.	1.00
7	Manny Ramirez	3.00
8	Jaret Wright	3.00
9	Paul Molitor	2.50
10	Derek Jeter	6.00
11	Bernie Williams	2.00
12	Ben Grieve	4.00
13	Ken Griffey Jr.	12.00
14	Edgar Martinez	1.00
15	Alex Rodriguez	8.00
16	Wade Boggs	1.50
17	Juan Gonzalez	6.00
18	Ivan Rodriguez	3.00
19	Roger Clemens	4.00
20	Travis Lee	6.00
21	Matt Williams	1.50
22	Andres Galarraga	1.50
23	Chipper Jones	8.00
24	Greg Maddux	8.00
25	Sammy Sosa	6.00
26	Kerry Wood	15.00
27	Barry Larkin	1.50
28	Larry Walker	2.00
29	Derrek Lee	1.00
30	Jeff Bagwell	4.00
31	Hideo Nomo	2.00
32	Mike Piazza	8.00
33	Scott Rolen	4.00
34	Mark McGwire	15.00
35	Tony Gwynn	6.00
36	Barry Bonds	3.00

1998 Pacific Omega Prism

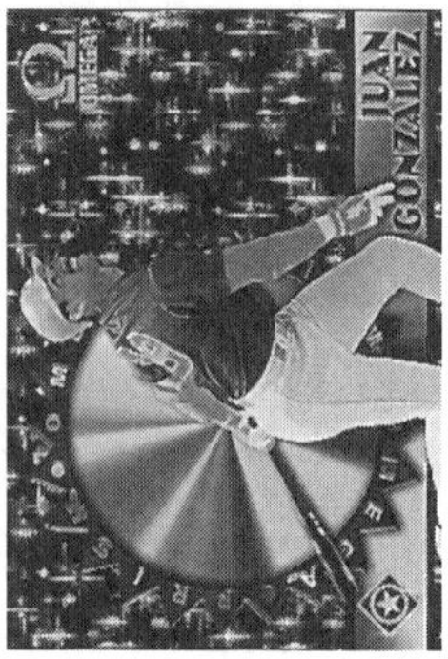

This 20-card insert was seeded one per 37 packs. The card fronts feature prismatic foil technology.

		MT
Complete Set (20):		220.00
Common Player:		3.00
Inserted 1:37		
1	Cal Ripken Jr.	20.00
2	Nomar Garciaparra	15.00
3	Pedro Martinez	4.00
4	Frank Thomas	20.00
5	Manny Ramirez	6.00
6	Brian Giles	3.00
7	Derek Jeter	12.00
8	Ben Grieve	8.00
9	Ken Griffey Jr.	25.00
10	Alex Rodriguez	15.00
11	Juan Gonzalez	12.00
12	Travis Lee	12.00
13	Chipper Jones	15.00
14	Greg Maddux	15.00
15	Kerry Wood	25.00
16	Larry Walker	4.00
17	Hideo Nomo	5.00
18	Mike Piazza	15.00
19	Mark McGwire	25.00
20	Tony Gwynn	12.00

1998 Pacific Omega Rising Stars

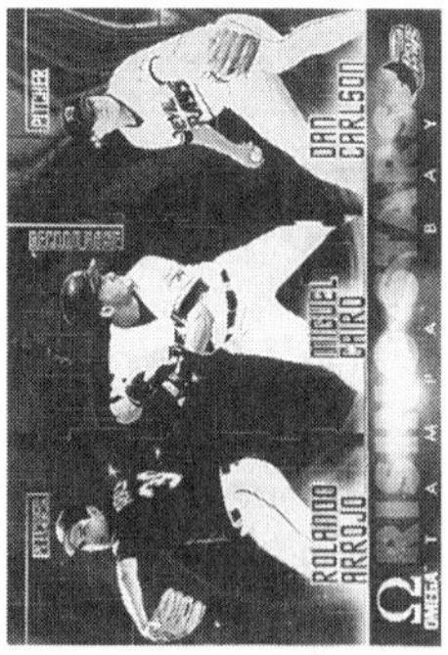

Rising Stars is a four-tiered hobby-only insert. The 20 cards were seeded four per 37 packs. Each card featured three rookies and each tier has a different foil color. A parallel of the insert is sequentially numbered. Tier One cards are numbered to 100, Tier Two to 50, Tier Three to 25 and Tier 4 to one.

		MT
Complete Set (30):		55.00
Common Player:		1.00
Inserted 1:9		
1	Nerio Rodriguez, Sidney Ponson	1.00
2	Frank Catalanotto, Roberto Duran, Sean Runyan	1.00
3	Kevin L. Brown, Carlos Almanzar	1.00
4	Aaron Boone, Pat Watkins, Scott Winchester	1.00
5	Brian Meadows, Andy Larkin, Antonio Alfonseca	1.00
6	DaRond Stovall, Trey Moore, Shayne Bennett	1.00
7	Felix Martinez, Larry Sutton, Brian Bevil	1.00
8	Homer Bush, Mike Buddie	1.00
9	Rich Butler, Esteban Yan	2.50
10	Damon Hollins, Brian Edmondson	1.00
11	Lou Collier, Jose Silva, Javier Martinez	1.00
12	Steve Sinclair, Mark Dalesandro	1.00
13	Jason Varitek, Brian Rose, Brian Shouse	2.00
14	Mike Caruso, Jeff Abbott, Tom Fordham	2.00
15	Jason Johnson, Bobby Smith	1.00
16	Dave Berg, Mark Kotsay, Jesus Sanchez	3.00
17	Richard Hidalgo, John Halama, Trever Miller	2.00
18	Geoff Jenkins, Bobby Hughes, Steve Woodard	2.00
19	Eli Marrero, Cliff Politte, Mike Busby	1.00
20	Desi Relaford, Darrin Winston	1.00
21	Todd Helton, Bobby Jones	4.00
22	Rolando Arrojo, Miguel Cairo, Dan Carlson	3.00
23	David Ortiz, Javier Valentin, Eric Milton	2.00
24	Magglio Ordonez, Greg Norton	3.00
25	Brad Fullmer, Javier Vazquez, Rick DeHart	2.00
26	Paul Konerko, Matt Luke	3.00
27	Derrek Lee, Ryan Jackson, John Roskos	2.00
28	Ben Grieve, A.J. Hinch, Ryan Christenson	5.00
29	Travis Lee, Karim Garcia, David Dellucci	8.00
30	Kerry Wood, Marc Pisciotta	12.00

1998 Pacific Online

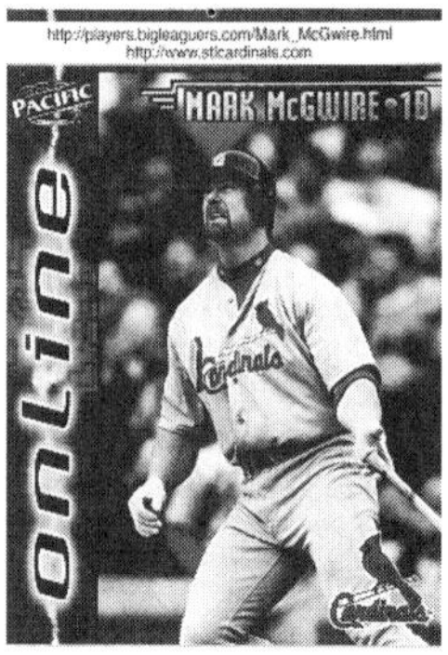

Online Baseball consists of an 800-card base set with one parallel. The base set features 750 players on cards that list the internet address of the player's home page on the bigleaguers.com web site. Twenty players have two cards and each of the 30 teams has a checklist that lists the team's web site. The Web Cards set parallels the 750 player cards. It has a serial number that can be entered at the bigleaguers.com web site to determine if a prize has been won.

		MT
Complete Set (780):		100.00
Common Player:		.15
1	Garret Anderson	.15
2	*Rich DeLucia*	.40
3	Jason Dickson	.15
4	Gary DiSarcina	.15
5	Jim Edmonds	.15
6	Darin Erstad	1.50
7	Cecil Fielder	.25
8	Chuck Finley	.15
9	Carlos Carcia	.15
10	Shigetosi Hasegawa	.15
11	Ken Hill	.15
12	Dave Hollins	.15
13	Mike Holtz	.15
14	Mike James	.15
15	Norberto Martin	.15
16	Damon Mashore	.15
17	Jack McDowell	.15
18	Phil Nevin	.15
19	Omar Olivares	.15
20	Troy Percival	.15
21	Rich Robertson	.15
22	Tim Salmon	.30
23	Craig Shipley	.15
24	Matt Walbeck	.15
25	Allen Watson	.15
26	Jim Edmonds	.15
27	Brian Anderson	.15
28	Tony Batista	.15
29	Jay Bell	.15
30	Andy Benes	.15
31	Yamil Benitez	.15
32	Willie Blair	.15
33	Brent Brede	.15
34	Scott Brow	.15
35	Omar Daal	.15
36	David Dellucci	.15
37	Edwin Diaz	.15
38	Jorge Fabregas	.15
39	Andy Fox	.15
40	Karim Garcia	.15
41	Travis Lee	2.00
42	Barry Manuel	.15
43	Gregg Olson	.15
44	Felix Rodriguez	.15
45	Clint Sodowsky	.15
46	Russ Springer	.15
47	Andy Stankiewicz	.15
48	Kelly Stinnett	.15
49	Jeff Suppan	.15
50	Devon White	.15
51	Matt Williams	.15
52	Travis Lee	1.00
53	Danny Bautista	.15
54	Rafael Belliard	.15
55	*Adam Butler*	.30
56	Mike Cather	.15
57	Brian Edmondson	.15
58	Alan Embree	.15
59	Andres Galarraga	.40
60	Tom Glavine	.30
61	Tony Graffanino	.15
62	Andruw Jones	1.00
63	Chipper Jones	2.00
64	Ryan Klesko	.30
65	Keith Lockhart	.15
66	Javy Lopez	.15
67	Greg Maddux	2.50
68	Dennis Martinez	.15
69	*Kevin Millwood*	2.00
70	Denny Neagle	.15
71	Eddie Perez	.15
72	Curtis Pride	.15
73	John Smoltz	.25
74	Michael Tucker	.15
75	Walt Weiss	.15
76	Gerald Williams	.15
77	Mark Wohlers	.15
78	Chipper Jones	1.00
79	Roberto Alomar	.40
80	Brady Anderson	.15
81	Harold Baines	.15
82	Armando Benitez	.15
83	Mike Bordick	.15
84	Joe Carter	.15
85	Norm Charlton	.15
86	Eric Davis	.15
87	Doug Drabek	.15
88	Scott Erickson	.15
89	Jeffrey Hammonds	.15
90	Chris Hoiles	.15
91	Scott Kamieniecki	.15
92	Jimmy Key	.15
93	Terry Mathews	.15
94	Alan Mills	.15
95	Mike Mussina	.75
96	Jesse Orosco	.15
97	Rafael Palmeiro	.25
98	Sidney Ponson	.15
99	Jeff Reboulet	.15
100	Arthur Rhodes	.15
101	Cal Ripken Jr.	2.50
102	Nerio Rodriguez	.15
103	B.J. Surhoff	.15
104	Lenny Webster	.15
105	Cal Ripken Jr.	3.00
106	Steve Avery	.15
107	Mike Benjamin	.15

108	Darren Bragg	.15
109	Damon Buford	.15
110	Jim Corsi	.15
111	Dennis Eckersley	.15
112	Rich Garces	.15
113	Nomar Garciaparra	2.50
114	Tom Gordon	.15
115	Scott Hatteberg	.15
116	Butch Henry	.15
117	Reggie Jefferson	.15
118	Mark Lemke	.15
119	Darren Lewis	.15
120	Jim Leyritz	.15
121	Derek Lowe	.15
122	Pedro Martinez	.75
123	Troy O'Leary	.15
124	Brian Rose	.15
125	Bret Saberhagen	.15
126	Donnie Sadler	.15
127	Brian Shouse	.15
128	John Valentin	.15
129	Jason Varitek	.15
130	Mo Vaughn	1.00
131	Tim Wakefield	.15
132	John Wasdin	.15
133	Nomar Garciaparra	2.50
134	Terry Adams	.15
135	Manny Alexander	.15
136	Rod Beck	.15
137	Jeff Blauser	.15
138	Brant Brown	.15
139	Mark Clark	.15
140	Jeremi Gonzalez	.15
141	Mark Grace	.25
142	Jose Hernandez	.15
143	Tyler Houston	.15
144	Lance Johnson	.15
145	Sandy Martinez	.15
146	Matt Mieske	.15
147	Mickey Morandini	.15
148	Terry Mulholland	.15
149	Kevin Orie	.15
150	Bob Patterson	.15
151	Marc Pisciotta	.15
152	Henry Rodriguez	.15
153	Scott Servais	.15
154	Sammy Sosa	2.50
155	Kevin Tapani	.15
156	Steve Trachsel	.15
157	Kerry Wood	4.00
158	Kerry Wood	4.00
159	Jeff Abbott	.15
160	James Baldwin	.15
161	Albert Belle	1.00
162	Jason Bere	.15
163	Mike Cameron	.15
164	Mike Caruso	.15
165	Carlos Castillo	.15
166	Tony Castillo	.15
167	Ray Durham	.15
168	Scott Eyre	.15
169	Tom Fordham	.15
170	Keith Foulke	.15
171	Lou Frazier	.15
172	Matt Karchner	.15
173	Chad Kreuter	.15
174	Jaime Navarro	.15
175	Greg Norton	.15
176	Charlie O'Brien	.15
177	Magglio Ordonez	.75
178	Ruben Sierra	.15
179	Bill Simas	.15
180	Mike Sirotka	.15
181	Chris Snopek	.15
182	Frank Thomas	2.50
183	Robin Ventura	.15
184	Frank Thomas	1.50
185	Stan Belinda	.15
186	Aaron Boone	.15
187	Bret Boone	.15
188	Brook Fordyce	.15
189	Willie Greene	.15
190	Pete Harnisch	.15
191	Lenny Harris	.15
192	Mark Hutton	.15
193	Damian Jackson	.15
194	Ricardo Jordan	.15
195	Barry Larkin	.30
196	Eduardo Perez	.15
197	Pokey Reese	.15
198	Mike Remlinger	.15
199	Reggie Sanders	.15
200	Jeff Shaw	.15
201	Chris Stynes	.15
202	Scott Sullivan	.15
203	Eddie Taubensee	.15
204	Brett Tomko	.15
205	Pat Watkins	.15
206	David Weathers	.15
207	Gabe White	.15
208	Scott Winchester	.15
209	Barry Larkin	.25
210	Sandy Alomar Jr.	.15
211	Paul Assenmacher	.15
212	Geronimo Berroa	.15
213	Pat Borders	.15
214	Jeff Branson	.15
215	Dave Burba	.15
216	Bartolo Colon	.30
217	Shawon Dunston	.15
218	Travis Fryman	.15
219	Brian Giles	.15
220	Dwight Gooden	.15
221	Mike Jackson	.15
222	David Justice	.40
223	Kenny Lofton	1.00
224	Jose Mesa	.15
225	Alvin Morman	.15
226	Charles Nagy	.15
227	Chad Ogea	.15
228	Eric Plunk	.15
229	Manny Ramirez	1.00
230	Paul Shuey	.15
231	Jim Thome	.60
232	Ron Villone	.15
233	Omar Vizquel	.15
234	Enrique Wilson	.15
235	Jaret Wright	1.00
236	Manny Ramirez	1.00
237	Pedro Astacio	.15
238	Jason Bates	.15
239	Dante Bichette	.30
240	Ellis Burks	.15
241	Vinny Castilla	.25
242	Greg Colbrunn	.15
243	Mike DeJean	.15
244	Jerry Dipoto	.15
245	Curtis Goodwin	.15
246	Todd Helton	.75
247	Bobby Jones	.15
248	Darryl Kile	.15
249	Mike Lansing	.15
250	Curtis Leskanic	.15
251	Nelson Liriano	.15
252	Kirt Manwaring	.15
253	Chuck McElroy	.15
254	Mike Munoz	.15
255	Neifi Perez	.15
256	Jeff Reed	.15
257	Mark Thompson	.15
258	John Vander Wal	.15
259	Dave Veres	.15
260	Larry Walker	.40
261	Jamey Wright	.15
262	Larry Walker	.25
263	Kimera Bartee	.15
264	Doug Brocail	.15
265	Raul Casanova	.15
266	Frank Castillo	.15
267	Frank Catalanotto	.15
268	Tony Clark	.75
269	Deivi Cruz	.15
270	Roberto Duran	.15
271	Damion Easley	.15
272	Bryce Florie	.15
273	Luis Gonzalez	.15
274	Bob Higginson	.15
275	Brian Hunter	.15
276	Todd Jones	.15
277	Greg Keagle	.15
278	Jeff Manto	.15
279	Brian Moehler	.15
280	Joe Oliver	.15
281	Joe Randa	.15
282	Billy Ripken	.15
283	Bip Roberts	.15
284	Sean Runyan	.15
285	A.J. Sager	.15
286	Justin Thompson	.15
287	Tony Clark	.50
288	Antonio Alfonseca	.15
289	Dave Berg	.15
290	Josh Booty	.15
291	John Cangelosi	.15
292	Craig Counsell	.15
293	Vic Darensbourg	.15
294	Cliff Floyd	.15
295	Oscar Henriquez	.15
296	Felix Heredia	.15
297	*Ryan Jackson*	.15
298	Mark Kotsay	.40
299	Andy Larkin	.15
300	Derrek Lee	.15
301	Brian Meadows	.15
302	Rafael Medina	.15
303	Jay Powell	.15
304	Edgar Renteria	.15
305	*Jesus Sanchez*	.30
306	Rob Stanifer	.15
307	Greg Zaun	.15
308	Derrek Lee	.15
309	Moises Alou	.25
310	Brad Ausmus	.15
311	Jeff Bagwell	1.50
312	Derek Bell	.15
313	Sean Bergman	.15
314	Sean Berry	.15
315	Craig Biggio	.25
316	Tim Bogar	.15
317	Jose Cabrera	.15
318	Dave Clark	.15
319	Tony Eusebio	.15
320	Carl Everett	.15
321	Ricky Gutierrez	.15
322	John Halama	.15
323	Mike Hampton	.15
324	Doug Henry	.15
325	Richard Hidalgo	.15
326	Jack Howell	.15
327	Jose Lima	.15
328	Mike Magnante	.15
329	Trever Miller	.15
330	C.J. Nitkowski	.15
331	Shane Reynolds	.15
332	Bill Spiers	.15
333	Billy Wagner	.15
334	Jeff Bagwell	.75
335	Tim Belcher	.15
336	Brian Bevil	.15
337	Johnny Damon	.15
338	Jermaine Dye	.15
339	Sal Fasano	.15
340	Shane Halter	.15
341	Chris Haney	.15
342	Jed Hansen	.15
343	Jeff King	.15
344	Jeff Montgomery	.15
345	Hal Morris	.15
346	Jose Offerman	.15
347	Dean Palmer	.15
348	Terry Pendleton	.15
349	Hipolito Pichardo	.15
350	Jim Pittsley	.15
351	Pat Rapp	.15
352	Jose Rosado	.15
353	Glendon Rusch	.15
354	Scott Service	.15
355	Larry Sutton	.15
356	Mike Sweeney	.15
357	Joe Vitiello	.15
358	Matt Whisenant	.15
359	Ernie Young	.15
360	Jeff King	.15
361	Bobby Bonilla	.15
362	Jim Bruske	.15
363	Juan Castro	.15
364	Roger Cedeno	.15
365	Mike Devereaux	.15
366	Darren Dreifort	.15
367	Jim Eisenreich	.15
368	Wilton Guerrero	.15
369	Mark Guthrie	.15
370	Darren Hall	.15
371	Todd Hollandsworth	.15
372	Thomas Howard	.15
373	Trenidad Hubbard	.15
374	Charles Johnson	.15
375	Eric Karros	.15
376	Paul Konerko	.40
377	Matt Luke	.15
378	Ramon Martinez	.15
379	Raul Mondesi	.30
380	Hideo Nomo	.75
381	Antonio Osuna	.15
382	Chan Ho Park	.30
383	Tom Prince	.15
384	Scott Radinsky	.15
385	Gary Sheffield	.40
386	Ismael Valdes	.15
387	Jose Vizcaino	.15
388	Eric Young	.15
389	Gary Sheffield	.40
390	Jeromy Burnitz	.15
391	Jeff Cirillo	.15
392	Cal Eldred	.15
393	Chad Fox	.15
394	Marquis Grissom	.15
395	Bob Hamelin	.15
396	Bobby Hughes	.15
397	Darrin Jackson	.15
398	John Jaha	.15
399	Geoff Jenkins	.15
400	Doug Jones	.15
401	Jeff Juden	.15
402	Scott Karl	.15
403	Jesse Levis	.15
404	Mark Loretta	.15
405	Mike Matheny	.15
406	Jose Mercedes	.15
407	Mike Myers	.15
408	Marc Newfield	.15
409	Dave Nilsson	.15
410	Al Reyes	.15
411	Jose Valentin	.15
412	Fernando Vina	.15
413	Paul Wagner	.15
414	Bob Wickman	.15
415	Steve Woodard	.15
416	Marquis Grissom	.15
417	Rick Aguilera	.15
418	Ron Coomer	.15
419	Marty Cordova	.15
420	Brent Gates	.15
421	Eddie Guardado	.15
422	Denny Hocking	.15
423	Matt Lawton	.15
424	Pat Meares	.15
425	Orlando Merced	.15
426	Eric Milton	.15
427	Paul Molitor	.75
428	Mike Morgan	.15
429	Dan Naulty	.15
430	Otis Nixon	.15
431	Alex Ochoa	.15
432	David Ortiz	.15
433	Brad Radke	.15
434	Todd Ritchie	.15
435	Frank Rodriguez	.15
436	Terry Steinbach	.15
437	Greg Swindell	.15
438	Bob Tewksbury	.15
439	Mike Trombley	.15
440	Javier Valentin	.15
441	Todd Walker	.40
442	Paul Molitor	.40
443	Shane Andrews	.15
444	Miguel Batista	.15
445	Shayne Bennett	.15
446	Rick DeHart	.15
447	Brad Fullmer	.40
448	Mark Grudzielanek	.15
449	Vladimir Guerrero	1.25
450	Dustin Hermanson	.15
451	Steve Kline	.15
452	Scott Livingstone	.15
453	Mike Maddux	.15
454	Derrick May	.15
455	Ryan McGuire	.15
456	Trey Moore	.15
457	Mike Mordecai	.15
458	Carl Pavano	.15
459	Carlos Perez	.15
460	F.P. Santangelo	.15
461	DaRond Stovall	.15
462	Anthony Telford	.15
463	Ugueth Urbina	.15
464	Marc Valdes	.15
465	Jose Vidro	.15
466	Rondell White	.25
467	Chris Widger	.15
468	Vladimir Guerrero	.60
469	Edgardo Alfonzo	.15
470	Carlos Baerga	.15
471	Rich Becker	.15
472	Brian Bohanon	.15
473	Alberto Castillo	.15
474	Dennis Cook	.15
475	John Franco	.15
476	Matt Franco	.15
477	Bernard Gilkey	.15
478	John Hudek	.15
479	Butch Huskey	.15
480	Bobby Jones	.15
481	Al Leiter	.25
482	Luis Lopez	.15
483	Brian McRae	.15
484	Dave Mlicki	.15
485	John Olerud	.25
486	Rey Ordonez	.15
487	Craig Paquette	.15
488	Mike Piazza	2.50
489	Todd Pratt	.15
490	Mel Rojas	.15
491	Tim Spehr	.15
492	Turk Wendell	.15
493	*Masato Yoshii*	.40
494	Mike Piazza	1.25
495	Willie Banks	.15
496	Scott Brosius	.15
497	Mike Buddie	.15
498	Homer Bush	.15
499	David Cone	.15
500	Chad Curtis	.15
501	Chili Davis	.15
502	Joe Girardi	.15
503	Darren Holmes	.15
504	Hideki Irabu	.40
505	Derek Jeter	2.50
506	Chuck Knoblauch	.50
507	Graeme Lloyd	.15
508	Tino Martinez	.40
509	Ramiro Mendoza	.15
510	Jeff Nelson	.15
511	Paul O'Neill	.40
512	Andy Pettitte	.60
513	Jorge Posada	.25
514	Tim Raines	.15
515	Mariano Rivera	.25
516	Luis Sojo	.15
517	Mike Stanton	.15
518	Darryl Strawberry	.25
519	Dale Sveum	.15
520	David Wells	.15
521	Bernie Williams	.75
522	Bernie Williams	.40
523	Kurt Abbott	.15
524	Mike Blowers	.15
525	Rafael Bournigal	.15
526	Tom Candiotti	.15
527	Ryan Christenson	.15
528	Mike Fetters	.15
529	Jason Giambi	.15
530	Ben Grieve	1.25
531	Buddy Groom	.15
532	Jimmy Haynes	.15
533	Rickey Henderson	.15
534	A.J. Hinch	.15
535	Mike Macfarlane	.15
536	Dave Magadan	.15
537	T.J. Mathews	.15
538	Jason McDonald	.15
539	Kevin Mitchell	.15
540	Mike Mohler	.15
541	Mike Oquist	.15
542	Ariel Prieto	.15
543	Kenny Rogers	.15
544	Aaron Small	.15
545	Scott Spiezio	.15
546	Matt Stairs	.15
547	Bill Taylor	.15
548	Dave Telgheder	.15
549	Jack Voigt	.15
550	Ben Grieve	.60
551	Bob Abreu	.15
552	Ruben Amaro	.15
553	Alex Arias	.15
554	Matt Beech	.15
555	Ricky Bottalico	.15
556	Billy Brewer	.15
557	Rico Brogna	.15
558	Doug Glanville	.15
559	Wayne Gomes	.15
560	Mike Grace	.15
561	Tyler Green	.15
562	Rex Hudler	.15
563	Gregg Jefferies	.15
564	Kevin Jordan	.15
565	Mark Leiter	.15
566	Mark Lewis	.15
567	Mike Lieberthal	.15
568	Mark Parent	.15
569	Yorkis Perez	.15
570	Desi Relaford	.15
571	Scott Rolen	1.25
572	Curt Schilling	.25
573	Kevin Sefcik	.15
574	Jerry Spradlin	.15
575	Garrett Stephenson	.15
576	Darrin Winston	.15
577	Scott Rolen	.60
578	Jermaine Allensworth	.15
579	Jason Christiansen	.15
580	Lou Collier	.15
581	Francisco Cordova	.15
582	Elmer Dessens	.15
583	Freddy Garcia	.15
584	Jose Guillen	.25
585	Jason Kendall	.15
586	Jon Lieber	.15
587	Esteban Loaiza	.15
588	Al Martin	.15
589	Javier Martinez	.15
590	Chris Peters	.15
591	Kevin Polcovich	.15
592	Ricardo Rincon	.15
593	Jason Schmidt	.15
594	Jose Silva	.15
595	Mark Smith	.15
596	Doug Strange	.15
597	Turner Ward	.15
598	Marc Wilkins	.15
599	Mike Williams	.15
600	Tony Womack	.15
601	Kevin Young	.15
602	Tony Womack	.15
603	Manny Aybar	.15
604	Kent Bottenfield	.15
605	Jeff Brantley	.15
606	Mike Busby	.15
607	Royce Clayton	.15
608	Delino DeShields	.15
609	John Frascatore	.15
610	Gary Gaetti	.15
611	Ron Gant	.15
612	David Howard	.15
613	Brian Hunter	.15
614	Brian Jordan	.15
615	Tom Lampkin	.15
616	Ray Lankford	.15
617	Braden Looper	.15
618	John Mabry	.15
619	Eli Marrero	.15
620	Willie McGee	.15
621	Mark McGwire	5.00
622	Kent Mercker	.15
623	Matt Morris	.15
624	Donovan Osborne	.15
625	Tom Pagnozzi	.15
626	Lance Painter	.15
627	Mark Petkovsek	.15
628	Todd Stottlemyre	.15
629	Mark McGwire	2.50
630	Andy Ashby	.15
631	Brian Boehringer	.15
632	Kevin Brown	.25
633	Ken Caminiti	.25
634	Steve Finley	.15
635	Ed Giovanola	.15
636	Chris Gomez	.15
637	Tony Gwynn	2.00
638	Joey Hamilton	.15
639	Carlos Hernandez	.15
640	Sterling Hitchcock	.15
641	Trevor Hoffman	.15
642	Wally Joyner	.15
643	Dan Miceli	.15
644	James Mouton	.15
645	Greg Myers	.15
646	Carlos Reyes	.15
647	Andy Sheets	.15
648	Pete Smith	.15
649	Mark Sweeney	.15
650	Greg Vaughn	.15
651	Quilvio Veras	.15
652	Tony Gwynn	1.00
653	Rich Aurilla	.15
654	Marvin Benard	.15
655	Barry Bonds	1.00
656	Danny Darwin	.15
657	Shawn Estes	.15
658	Mark Gardner	.15
659	Darryl Hamilton	.15
660	Charlie Hayes	.15
661	Orel Hershiser	.15
662	Stan Javier	.15
663	Brian Johnson	.15
664	John Johnstone	.15
665	Jeff Kent	.15
666	Brent Mayne	.15
667	Bill Mueller	.15
668	Robb Nen	.15
669	Jim Poole	.15
670	Steve Reed	.15
671	Rich Rodriguez	.15
672	Kirk Rueter	.15
673	Rey Sanchez	.15
674	J.T. Snow	.15
675	Julian Tavarez	.15
676	Barry Bonds	.50
677	Rich Amaral	.15
678	Bobby Ayala	.15
679	Jay Buhner	.30
680	Ken Cloude	.15
681	Joey Cora	.15
682	Russ Davis	.15
683	Rob Ducey	.15
684	Jeff Fassero	.15
685	Tony Fossas	.15
686	Ken Griffey Jr.	4.00
687	Glenallen Hill	.15
688	Jeff Huson	.15
689	Randy Johnson	.75
690	Edgar Martinez	.15
691	John Marzano	.15
692	Jamie Moyer	.15
693	Alex Rodriguez	2.50
694	David Segui	.15
695	Heathcliff Slocumb	.15
696	Paul Spoljaric	.15
697	Bill Swift	.15

698 Mike Timlin .15
699 Bob Wells .15
700 Dan Wilson .15
701 Ken Griffey Jr. 2.00
702 Wilson Alvarez .15
703 *Rolando Arrojo* .75
704 Wade Boggs .30
705 Rich Butler .25
706 Miguel Cairo .15
707 Mike Difelice .15
708 John Flaherty .15
709 Roberto Hernandez .15
710 Mike Kelly .15
711 Aaron Ledesma .15
712 Albie Lopez .15
713 Dave Martinez .15
714 Quinton McCracken .15
715 Fred McGriff .25
716 Jim Mecir .15
717 Tony Saunders .15
718 Bobby Smith .15
719 Paul Sorrento .15
720 Dennis Springer .15
721 Kevin Stocker .15
722 Ramon Tatis .15
723 Bubba Trammell .15
724 Esteban Yan .15
725 Wade Boggs .30
726 Luis Alicea .15
727 Scott Bailes .15
728 John Burkett .15
729 Domingo Cedeno .15
730 Will Clark .40
731 Kevin Elster .15
732 Juan Gonzalez 2.00
733 Tom Goodwin .15
734 Rusty Greer .15
735 Eric Gunderson .15
736 Bill Haselman .15
737 Rick Helling .15
738 Roberto Kelly .15
739 Mark McLemore .15
740 Darren Oliver .15
741 Danny Patterson .15
742 Roger Pavlik .15
743 Ivan Rodriguez 1.00
744 Aaron Sele .15
745 Mike Simms .15
746 Lee Stevens .15
747 Fernando Tatis .15
748 John Wetteland .15
749 Bobby Witt .15
750 Juan Gonzalez 1.00
751 Carlos Almanzar .15
752 Kevin Brown .25
753 Jose Canseco .40
754 Chris Carpenter .15
755 Roger Clemens 1.50
756 Felipe Crespo .15
757 Jose Cruz Jr. 1.00
758 Mark Dalesandro .15
759 Carlos Delgado .15
760 Kelvim Escobar .15
761 Tony Fernandez .15
762 Darrin Fletcher .15
763 Alex Gonzalez .15
764 Craig Grebeck .15
765 Shawn Green .15
766 Juan Guzman .15
767 Erik Hanson .15
768 Pat Hentgen .15
769 Randy Myers .15
770 Robert Person .15
771 Dan Plesac .15
772 Paul Quantrill .15
773 Bill Risley .15
774 Juan Samuel .15
775 Steve Sinclair .15
776 Ed Sprague .15
777 Mike Stanley .15
778 Shannon Stewart .15
779 Woody Williams .15
780 Roger Clemens .75

1998 Pacific Online Web Cards

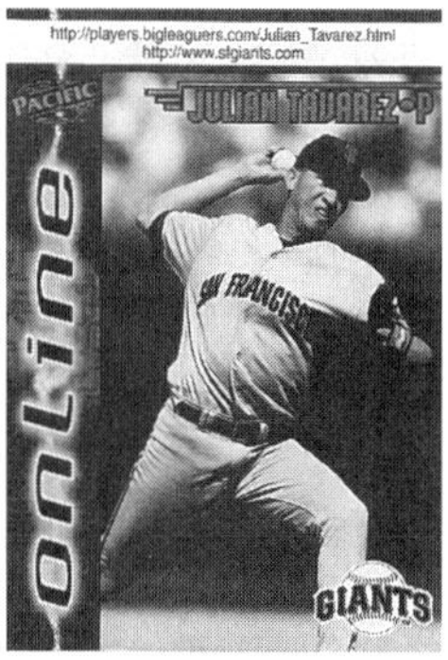

This 800-card parallel set allowed collectors to use Pacific's web site to find out the prize they had won. The cards used gold foil on the front instead of the silver foil used on base cards, and contained an eight-digit code on the left side that was the claim number. These were inserted one per pack in Online Baseball.

	MT
Web Stars:	2x to 3x
Yng Stars & RCs:	1.5x to 2x
Inserted 1:1	

1998 Pacific Paramount

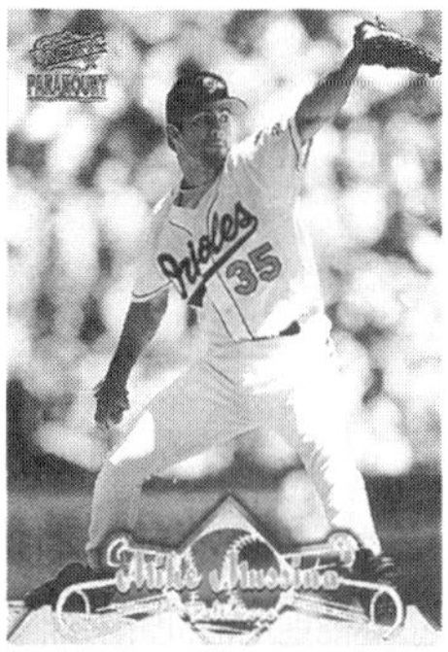

Paramount was Pacific's first fully-licensed baseball card product. The 250 base cards feature full-bleed photos with the player's name and team listed at the bottom. The base set is paralleled three times. Gold retail (1:1), Copper hobby (1:1) and Platinum Blue (1:73) versions were included. Inserts in the product are Special Delivery Die-Cuts, Team Checklist Die-Cuts, Cooperstown Bound, Fielder's Choice Laser-Cuts and Inaugural Issue.

	MT
Complete Set (250):	20.00
Common Player:	.10
Wax Box:	48.00

1 Garret Anderson .10
2 Gary DiSarcina .10
3 Jim Edmonds .20
4 Darin Erstad .50
5 Cecil Fielder .20
6 Chuck Finley .10
7 Todd Greene .10
8 Shigetosi Hasegawa .10
9 Tim Salmon .30
10 Roberto Alomar .50
11 Brady Anderson .20
12 Joe Carter .20
13 Eric Davis .10
14 Ozzie Guillen .10
15 Mike Mussina .50
16 Rafael Palmeiro .25
17 Cal Ripken Jr. 2.00
18 B.J. Surhoff .10
19 Steve Avery .10
20 Nomar Garciaparra 1.50
21 Reggie Jefferson .10
22 Pedro Martinez .25
23 Tim Naehring .10
24 John Valentin .10
25 Mo Vaughn .60
26 James Baldwin .10
27 Albert Belle .60
28 Ray Durham .10
29 Benji Gil .10
30 Jaime Navarro .10
31 *Magglio Ordonez* .75
32 Frank Thomas 2.00
33 Robin Ventura .20
34 Sandy Alomar Jr. .20
35 Geronimo Berroa .10
36 Travis Fryman .10
37 David Justice .25
38 Kenny Lofton .60
39 Charles Nagy .10
40 Manny Ramirez .60
41 Jim Thome .40
42 Omar Vizquel .10
43 Jaret Wright 1.25
44 Raul Casanova .10
45 *Frank Catalanotto* .20
46 Tony Clark .40
47 Bobby Higginson .10
48 Brian Hunter .10
49 Todd Jones .10
50 Bip Roberts .10
51 Justin Thompson .10
52 Kevin Appier .10
53 Johnny Damon .10
54 Jermaine Dye .10
55 Jeff King .10
56 Jeff Montgomery .10
57 Dean Palmer .10
58 Jose Rosado .10
59 Larry Sutton .10
60 Rick Aguilera .10
61 Marty Cordova .10
62 Pat Meares .10
63 Paul Molitor .40
64 Otis Nixon .10
65 Brad Radke .10
66 Terry Steinbach .10
67 Todd Walker .25
68 Hideki Irabu .50
69 Derek Jeter 1.25
70 Chuck Knoblauch .30
71 Tino Martinez .40
72 Paul O'Neill .20
73 Andy Pettitte .40
74 Mariano Rivera .25
75 Bernie Williams .50
76 Mark Bellhorn .10
77 Tom Candiotti .10
78 Jason Giambi .10
79 Ben Grieve 1.00
80 Rickey Henderson .10
81 Jason McDonald .10
82 Aaron Small .10
83 Miguel Tejada .10
84 Jay Buhner .25
85 Joey Cora .10
86 Jeff Fassero .10
87 Ken Griffey Jr. 2.50
88 Randy Johnson .40
89 Edgar Martinez .20
90 Alex Rodriguez 1.50
91 David Segui .10
92 Dan Wilson .10
93 Wilson Alvarez .10
94 Wade Boggs .25
95 Miguel Cairo .10
96 John Flaherty .10
97 Dave Martinez .10
98 Quinton McCracken .10
99 Fred McGriff .25
100 Paul Sorrento .10
101 Kevin Stocker .10
102 John Burkett .10
103 Will Clark .25
104 Juan Gonzalez 1.25
105 Rusty Greer .20
106 Roberto Kelly .10
107 Ivan Rodriguez .60
108 Fernando Tatis .10
109 John Wetteland .10
110 Jose Canseco .25
111 Roger Clemens 1.00
112 Jose Cruz Jr. .50
113 Carlos Delgado .20
114 Alex Gonzalez .10
115 Pat Hentgen .10
116 Ed Sprague .10
117 Shannon Stewart .10
118 Brian Anderson .10
119 Jay Bell .10
120 Andy Benes .20
121 Yamil Benitez .10
122 Jorge Fabregas .10
123 Travis Lee 2.00
124 Devon White .10
125 Matt Williams .25
126 Bob Wolcott .10
127 Andres Galarraga .25
128 Tom Glavine .20
129 Andruw Jones .60
130 Chipper Jones 1.50
131 Ryan Klesko .30
132 Javy Lopez .10
133 Greg Maddux 1.50
134 Denny Neagle .20
135 John Smoltz .20
136 Rod Beck .10
137 Jeff Blauser .10
138 Mark Grace .25
139 Lance Johnson .10
140 Mickey Morandini .10
141 Kevin Orie .10
142 Sammy Sosa 1.50
143 Aaron Boone .10
144 Bret Boone .10
145 Dave Burba .10
146 Lenny Harris .10
147 Barry Larkin .25
148 Reggie Sanders .10
149 Brett Tomko .10
150 Pedro Astacio .10
151 Dante Bichette .20
152 Ellis Burks .10
153 Vinny Castilla .20
154 Todd Helton .50
155 Darryl Kile .10
156 Jeff Reed .10
157 Larry Walker .30
158 Bobby Bonilla .20
159 Todd Dunwoody .10
160 Livan Hernandez .20
161 Charles Johnson .20
162 Mark Kotsay .50
163 Derrek Lee .10
164 Edgar Renteria .10
165 Gary Sheffield .30
166 Moises Alou .20
167 Jeff Bagwell 1.00
168 Derek Bell .10
169 Craig Biggio .20
170 Mike Hampton .10
171 Richard Hidalgo .10
172 Chris Holt .10
173 Shane Reynolds .10
174 Wilton Guerrero .10
175 Eric Karros .20
176 Paul Konerko .25
177 Ramon Martinez .20
178 Raul Mondesi .25
179 Hideo Nomo .50
180 Chan Ho Park .20
181 Mike Piazza 1.50
182 Ismael Valdes .10
183 Jeromy Burnitz .10
184 Jeff Cirillo .10
185 Todd Dunn .10
186 Marquis Grissom .10
187 John Jaha .10
188 Doug Jones .10
189 Dave Nilsson .10
190 Jose Valentin .10
191 Fernando Vina .10
192 Orlando Cabrera .10
193 Steve Falteisek .10
194 Mark Grudzielanek .10
195 Vladimir Guerrero .50
196 Carlos Perez .10
197 F.P. Santangelo .10
198 Jose Vidro .10
199 Rondell White .20
200 Edgardo Alfonzo .10
201 Carlos Baerga .10
202 John Franco .10
203 Bernard Gilkey .10
204 Todd Hundley .20
205 Butch Huskey .10
206 Bobby Jones .10
207 Brian McRae .10
208 John Olerud .20
209 Rey Ordonez .10
210 Ricky Bottalico .10
211 Bobby Estalella .10
212 Doug Glanville .10
213 Gregg Jefferies .10
214 Mike Lieberthal .10
215 Desi Relaford .10
216 Scott Rolen .75
217 Curt Schilling .25
218 Adrian Brown .10
219 Emil Brown .10
220 Francisco Cordova .10
221 Jose Guillen .40
222 Al Martin .10
223 Abraham Nunez .10
224 Tony Womack .10
225 Kevin Young .10
226 Alan Benes .20
227 Royce Clayton .10
228 Gary Gaetti .10
229 Ron Gant .20
230 Brian Jordan .20
231 Ray Lankford .10
232 Mark McGwire 3.00
233 Todd Stottlemyre .10
234 Kevin Brown .20
235 Ken Caminiti .20
236 Steve Finley .10
237 Tony Gwynn 1.25
238 Wally Joyner .10
239 Ruben Rivera .10
240 Greg Vaughn .10
241 Quilvio Veras .10
242 Barry Bonds .60
243 Jacob Cruz .10
244 Shawn Estes .20
245 Orel Hershiser .10
246 Stan Javier .10
247 Brian Johnson .10
248 Jeff Kent .10
249 Robb Nen .10
250 J.T. Snow .10

1998 Pacific Paramount Gold/Copper/Red

Gold, Copper and Red foil versions of all 250 cards in Paramount were reprinted and inserted at a rate of one per pack. Gold versions were retail exclusive, Copper versions were hobby exclusive and Red versions were ANCO pack exclusive. The only different was these parallels used a different color foil than the base cards.

	MT
Golds & Coppers:	1.5x to 3x
Inserted 1:1	
Reds:	2x to 3x
Inserted 1:ANCO pack	

1998 Pacific Paramount Platinum Blue

This paralle set reprinted all 250 cards in Paramount using blue foil stamping on the card front. These were inserted one per 73 packs.

	MT
Platinum Blue Stars:	40x to 80x
Yng Stars & RCs:	25x to 50x
Inserted 1:73	

1998 Pacific Paramount Holographic Silver

Holographics Silver parallel cards were issued for all 250 cards in the Paramount set. These were inserted into hobby packs, while only 99 sets were produced.

	MT
Holographic Stars:	50x to 100x
Yng Stars & RCs:	30x to 60x
Production 99 sets	

1998 Pacific Paramount Inaugural Issue

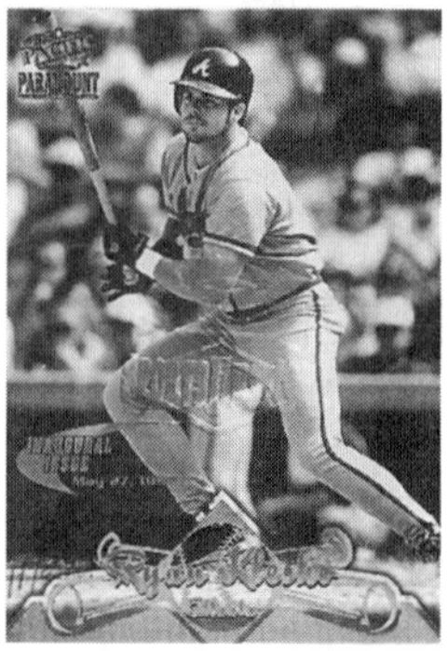

A special edition of Pacific's premiere Paramount issue was created to mark the new brand's introduction on May 27 at the debut SportsFest '98 show in Philadelphia. Each of the cards from the Paramount issue was printed with a gold-foil "INAUGURAL ISSUE May 27, 1998" logo, was embossed with Pacific and SportsFest logos at center and hand-numbered at bottom from within an edition of just 20 cards each.

	MT
Common Player:	6.00
(Stars and rookies valued at 50-75X regular Paramount version.)	

1998 Pacific Paramount Cooperstown Bound

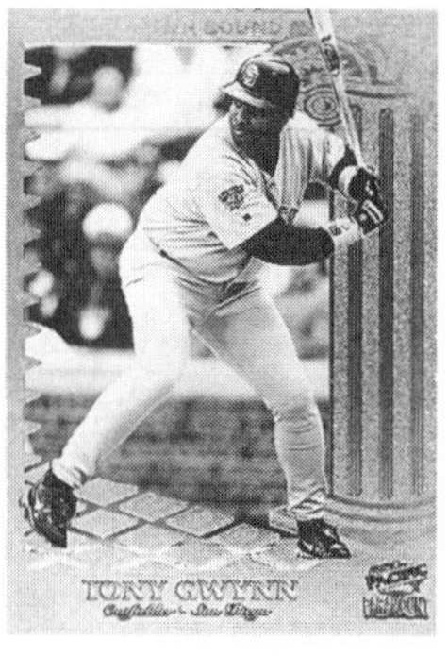

Cooperstown Bound is a 10-card insert seeded one per 361 packs. Each card features a color player photo with a silver foil column on the left. The cards are fully foiled and etched.

	MT
Complete Set (10):	450.00
Common Player:	15.00
Inserted 1:361	
Pacific Proofs:	5x to 8x
Production 20 sets	
1 Greg Maddux	60.00

2	Cal Ripken Jr.	80.00
3	Frank Thomas	80.00
4	Mike Piazza	60.00
5	Paul Molitor	20.00
6	Mark McGwire	100.00
7	Tony Gwynn	50.00
8	Barry Bonds	25.00
9	Ken Griffey Jr.	100.00
10	Wade Boggs	15.00

1998 Pacific Paramount Fielder's Choice

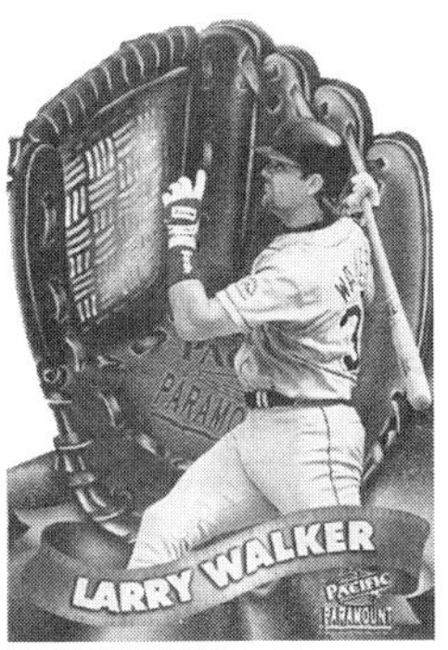

Fielder's Choice Laser-Cuts is a 20-card insert seeded one per 73 packs. Each card is die-cut around a baseball glove that appears in the background. The webbing of the glove is laser-cut.

		MT
Complete Set (20):		400.00
Common Player:		5.00
Inserted 1:73		
1	Chipper Jones	30.00
2	Greg Maddux	30.00
3	Cal Ripken Jr.	40.00
4	Nomar Garciaparra	30.00
5	Frank Thomas	40.00
6	David Justice	5.00
7	Larry Walker	8.00
8	Jeff Bagwell	20.00
9	Hideo Nomo	10.00
10	Mike Piazza	30.00
11	Derek Jeter	25.00
12	Ben Grieve	20.00
13	Mark McGwire	50.00
14	Tony Gwynn	25.00
15	Barry Bonds	15.00
16	Ken Griffey Jr	50.00
17	Alex Rodriguez	30.00
18	Wade Boggs	5.00
19	Ivan Rodriguez	15.00
20	Jose Cruz Jr.	12.00

1998 Pacific Paramount Special Delivery

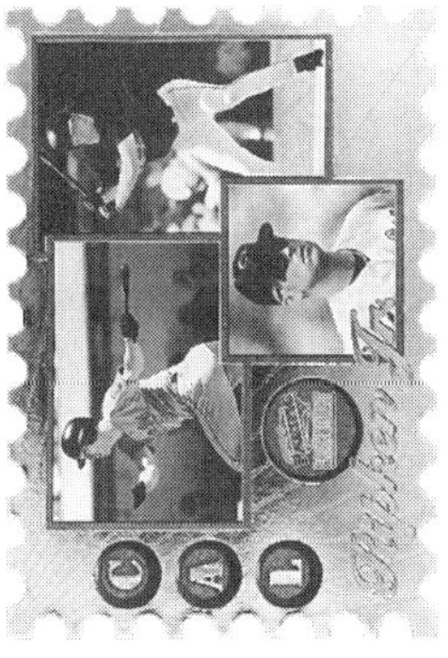

Special Delivery cards are die-cut to resemble a postage stamp. Each card front is foiled and etched and features three photos of the player. Special Delivery is a 20-card insert seeded one per 37 packs.

		MT
Complete Set (20):		240.00
Common Player:		3.00
Inserted 1:37		
1	Chipper Jones	20.00
2	Greg Maddux	20.00
3	Cal Ripken Jr.	25.00
4	Nomar Garciaparra	20.00
5	Pedro Martinez	6.00
6	Frank Thomas	25.00
7	David Justice	4.00
8	Larry Walker	5.00
9	Jeff Bagwell	12.00
10	Hideo Nomo	6.00
11	Mike Piazza	20.00
12	Vladimir Guerrero	8.00
13	Derek Jeter	15.00
14	Ben Grieve	10.00
15	Mark McGwire	30.00
16	Tony Gwynn	15.00
17	Barry Bonds	8.00
18	Ken Griffey Jr.	30.00
19	Alex Rodriguez	20.00
20	Jose Cruz Jr.	6.00

1998 Pacific Paramount Team Checklist

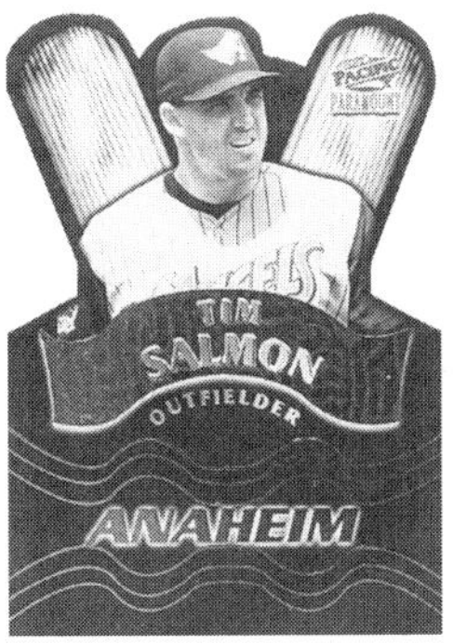

Team Checklists (30 cards, 2:37) feature a player photo surrounded by two bats. The card is die-cut around the photo and the bats at the top. The bottom has the player's name, position and team.

		MT
Complete Set (30):		150.00
Common Player:		1.50
Inserted 1:18		
1	Tim Salmon	3.00
2	Cal Ripken Jr.	15.00
3	Nomar Garciaparra	12.00
4	Frank Thomas	15.00
5	Manny Ramirez	5.00
6	Tony Clark	4.00
7	Dean Palmer	1.50
8	Paul Molitor	4.00
9	Derek Jeter	12.00
10	Ben Grieve	8.00
11	Ken Griffey Jr.	20.00
12	Wade Boggs	2.00
13	Ivan Rodriguez	5.00
14	Roger Clemens	8.00
15	Matt Williams	2.50
16	Chipper Jones	12.00
17	Sammy Sosa	10.00
18	Barry Larkin	2.00
19	Larry Walker	3.00
20	Livan Hernandez	1.50
21	Jeff Bagwell	8.00
22	Mike Piazza	12.00
23	John Jaha	1.50
24	Vladimir Guerrero	5.00
25	Todd Hundley	1.50
26	Scott Rolen	8.00
27	Kevin Young	1.50
28	Mark McGwire	25.00
29	Tony Gwynn	10.00
30	Barry Bonds	5.00

1998 Pacific Revolution

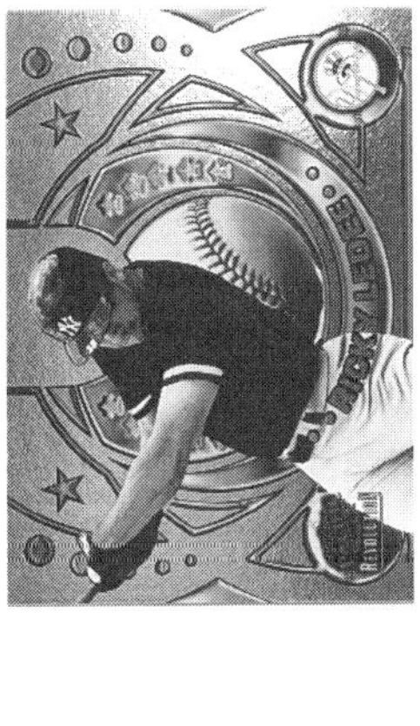

Pacific Revolution Baseball consists of a 150-card base set. The base cards are dual-foiled, etched and embossed. Inserts include Showstoppers, Prime Time Performers Laser-Cuts, Foul Pole Laser-Cuts, Major League Icons and Shadow Series.

		MT
Complete Set (150):		
Common Player:		.40
Wax Box:		80.00
1	Garret Anderson	.40
2	Jim Edmonds	.40
3	Darin Erstad	2.50
4	Chuck Finley	.40
5	Tim Salmon	1.00
6	Jay Bell	.40
7	Travis Lee	6.00
8	Devon White	.40
9	Matt Williams	1.00
10	Andres Galarraga	1.00
11	Tom Glavine	.60
12	Andruw Jones	2.50
13	Chipper Jones	6.00
14	Ryan Klesko	1.00
15	Javy Lopez	.60
16	Greg Maddux	6.00
17	Walt Weiss	.40
18	Roberto Alomar	2.00
19	Joe Carter	.60
20	Mike Mussina	2.00
21	Rafael Palmeiro	1.00
22	Cal Ripken Jr.	8.00
23	B.J. Surhoff	.40
24	Nomar Garciaparra	6.00
25	Reggie Jefferson	.40
26	Pedro Martinez	2.00
27	Troy O'Leary	.40
28	Mo Vaughn	2.50
29	Mark Grace	1.00
30	Mickey Morandini	.40
31	Henry Rodriguez	.40
32	Sammy Sosa	5.00
33	Kerry Wood	12.00
34	Albert Belle	2.50
35	Ray Durham	.40
36	*Magglio Ordonez*	2.50
37	Frank Thomas	8.00
38	Robin Ventura	.40
39	Bret Boone	.40
40	Barry Larkin	.75
41	Reggie Sanders	.40
42	Brett Tomko	.40
43	Sandy Alomar	.60
44	David Justice	.75
45	Kenny Lofton	2.50
46	Manny Ramirez	2.50
47	Jim Thome	1.50
48	Omar Vizquel	.40
49	Jaret Wright	2.50
50	Dante Bichette	.75
51	Ellis Burks	.40
52	Vinny Castilla	.40
53	Todd Helton	2.50
54	Larry Walker	1.50
55	Tony Clark	1.50
56	Deivi Cruz	.40
57	Damion Easley	.40
58	Bobby Higginson	.40
59	Brian Hunter	.40
60	Cliff Floyd	.40
61	Livan Hernandez	.40
62	Derrek Lee	.40
63	Edgar Renteria	.40
64	Moises Alou	.75
65	Jeff Bagwell	3.00
66	Derek Bell	.40
67	Craig Biggio	.75
68	Richard Hidalgo	.40
69	Johnny Damon	.40
70	Jeff King	.40
71	Hal Morris	.40
72	Dean Palmer	.40
73	Bobby Bonilla	.60
74	Charles Johnson	.40
75	Paul Konerko	.75
76	Raul Mondesi	.75
77	Gary Sheffield	1.00
78	Jeromy Burnitz	.40
79	Marquis Grissom	.40
80	Dave Nilsson	.40
81	Fernando Vina	.40
82	Marty Cordova	.40
83	Pat Meares	.40
84	Paul Molitor	2.00
85	Brad Radke	.40
86	Terry Steinbach	.40
87	Todd Walker	.75
88	Brad Fullmer	.75
89	Vladimir Guerrero	2.50
90	Carl Pavano	.40
91	Rondell White	.75
92	Bernard Gilkey	.40
93	Hideo Nomo	2.00
94	John Olerud	.75
95	Rey Ordonez	.40
96	Mike Piazza	6.00
97	*Masato Yoshii*	1.50
98	Hideki Irabu	1.50
99	Derek Jeter	5.00
100	Chuck Knoblauch	1.00
101	Tino Martinez	1.00
102	Paul O'Neill	.75
103	Darryl Strawberry	.60
104	Bernie Williams	2.00
105	Jason Giambi	.40
106	Ben Grieve	3.00
107	Rickey Henderson	.40
108	Matt Stairs	.40
109	Doug Glanville	.40
110	Desi Relaford	.40
111	Scott Rolen	3.00
112	Curt Schilling	.75
113	Jason Kendall	.75
114	Al Martin	.40
115	Jason Schmidt	.40
116	Kevin Young	.40
117	Delino DeShields	.40
118	Gary Gaetti	.40
119	Brian Jordan	.40
120	Ray Lankford	.40
121	Mark McGwire	12.00
122	Kevin Brown	.60
123	Steve Finley	.40
124	Tony Gwynn	5.00
125	Wally Joyner	.40
126	Greg Vaughn	.40
127	Barry Bonds	2.50
128	Orel Hershiser	.40
129	Jeff Kent	.40
130	Bill Mueller	.40
131	Jay Buhner	1.00
132	Ken Griffey Jr.	10.00
133	Randy Johnson	2.00
134	Edgar Martinez	.40
135	Alex Rodriguez	6.00
136	David Segui	.40
137	*Rolando Arrojo*	4.00
138	Wade Boggs	.75
139	Quinton McCracken	.40
140	Fred McGriff	.60
141	Will Clark	.75
142	Juan Gonzalez	5.00
143	Tom Goodwin	.40
144	Ivan Rodriguez	2.50
145	Aaron Sele	.40
146	John Wetteland	.40
147	Jose Canseco	1.00
148	Roger Clemens	3.00
149	Jose Cruz Jr.	2.50
150	Carlos Delgado	.40

1998 Pacific Revolution Shadows

Shadows is a full parallel of the Revolution base set. Limited to 99 sequentially numbered sets, each card is embossed with a special "Shadow Series" stamp.

		MT
Complete Set (150):		
Common Player:		15.00
Production 99 sets		
1	Garret Anderson	15.00
2	Jim Edmonds	15.00
3	Darin Erstad	60.00
4	Chuck Finley	15.00
5	Tim Salmon	30.00
6	Jay Bell	15.00
7	Travis Lee	125.00
8	Devon White	15.00
9	Matt Williams	30.00
10	Andres Galarraga	30.00
11	Tom Glavine	25.00
12	Andruw Jones	60.00
13	Chipper Jones	150.00
14	Ryan Klesko	30.00
15	Javy Lopez	20.00
16	Greg Maddux	150.00
17	Walt Weiss	15.00
18	Roberto Alomar	50.00
19	Joe Carter	20.00
20	Mike Mussina	50.00
21	Rafael Palmeiro	30.00
22	Cal Ripken Jr.	200.00
23	B.J. Surhoff	15.00
24	Nomar Garciaparra	150.00
25	Reggie Jefferson	15.00
26	Pedro Martinez	50.00
27	Troy O'Leary	15.00
28	Mo Vaughn	60.00
29	Mark Grace	30.00
30	Mickey Morandini	15.00
31	Henry Rodriguez	15.00
32	Sammy Sosa	125.00
33	Kerry Wood	150.00
34	Albert Belle	60.00
35	Ray Durham	15.00
36	*Magglio Ordonez*	40.00
37	Frank Thomas	200.00
38	Robin Ventura	15.00
39	Bret Boone	15.00
40	Barry Larkin	25.00
41	Reggie Sanders	15.00
42	Brett Tomko	15.00
43	Sandy Alomar	20.00
44	David Justice	25.00
45	Kenny Lofton	60.00
46	Manny Ramirez	60.00
47	Jim Thome	40.00
48	Omar Vizquel	15.00
49	Jaret Wright	60.00
50	Dante Bichette	30.00
51	Ellis Burks	15.00
52	Vinny Castilla	15.00
53	Todd Helton	60.00
54	Larry Walker	40.00
55	Tony Clark	40.00
56	Deivi Cruz	15.00
57	Damion Easley	15.00
58	Bobby Higginson	15.00
59	Brian Hunter	15.00
60	Cliff Floyd	15.00
61	Livan Hernandez	15.00
62	Derrek Lee	15.00
63	Edgar Renteria	15.00
64	Moises Alou	25.00
65	Jeff Bagwell	80.00
66	Derek Bell	15.00
67	Craig Biggio	25.00
68	Richard Hidalgo	15.00
69	Johnny Damon	15.00
70	Jeff King	15.00
71	Hal Morris	15.00
72	Dean Palmer	15.00
73	Bobby Bonilla	20.00
74	Charles Johnson	15.00
75	Paul Konerko	25.00
76	Raul Mondesi	25.00
77	Gary Sheffield	40.00
78	Jeromy Burnitz	15.00
79	Marquis Grissom	15.00
80	Dave Nilsson	15.00
81	Fernando Vina	15.00
82	Marty Cordova	15.00
83	Pat Meares	15.00
84	Paul Molitor	50.00
85	Brad Radke	15.00
86	Terry Steinbach	15.00
87	Todd Walker	25.00
88	Brad Fullmer	25.00
89	Vladimir Guerrero	60.00
90	Carl Pavano	15.00
91	Rondell White	20.00
92	Bernard Gilkey	15.00
93	Hideo Nomo	50.00
94	John Olerud	25.00
95	Rey Ordonez	15.00
96	Mike Piazza	150.00
97	*Masato Yoshii*	30.00
98	Hideki Irabu	30.00
99	Derek Jeter	125.00
100	Chuck Knoblauch	30.00
101	Tino Martinez	40.00
102	Paul O'Neill	25.00
103	Darryl Strawberry	25.00
104	Bernie Williams	50.00
105	Jason Giambi	15.00
106	Ben Grieve	80.00
107	Rickey Henderson	15.00
108	Matt Stairs	15.00
109	Doug Glanville	15.00
110	Desi Relaford	15.00
111	Scott Rolen	80.00
112	Curt Schilling	25.00
113	Jason Kendall	25.00
114	Al Martin	15.00
115	Jason Schmidt	15.00
116	Kevin Young	15.00
117	Delino DeShields	15.00
118	Gary Gaetti	15.00
119	Brian Jordan	15.00
120	Ray Lankford	15.00
121	Mark McGwire	250.00
122	Kevin Brown	25.00
123	Steve Finley	15.00
124	Tony Gwynn	125.00
125	Wally Joyner	15.00
126	Greg Vaughn	15.00
127	Barry Bonds	60.00
128	Orel Hershiser	15.00
129	Jeff Kent	15.00
130	Bill Mueller	15.00
131	Jay Buhner	30.00
132	Ken Griffey Jr.	250.00
133	Randy Johnson	50.00
134	Edgar Martinez	20.00
135	Alex Rodriguez	150.00
136	David Segui	15.00
137	*Rolando Arrojo*	30.00
138	Wade Boggs	25.00
139	Quinton McCracken	15.00
140	Fred McGriff	25.00
141	Will Clark	25.00
142	Juan Gonzalez	125.00
143	Tom Goodwin	15.00
144	Ivan Rodriguez	60.00
145	Aaron Sele	15.00
146	John Wetteland	15.00
147	Jose Canseco	30.00
148	Roger Clemens	90.00
149	Jose Cruz Jr.	60.00
150	Carlos Delgado	15.00

1998 Pacific Revolution Foul Pole

Foul Pole Laser-Cuts is a 20-card insert seeded one per 49 packs. Each card features a color player photo on the left and a foul pole on the right. The foul pole design includes netting that is laser cut.

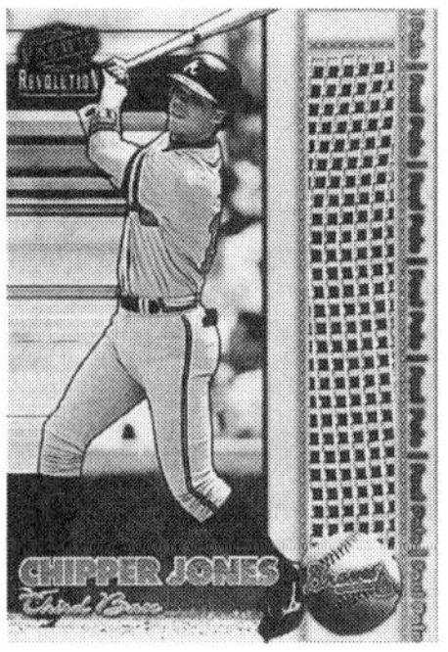

		MT
Complete Set (20):		350.00
Common Player:		6.00
Inserted 1:49		
1	Cal Ripken Jr.	35.00
2	Nomar Garciaparra	30.00
3	Mo Vaughn	12.00
4	Frank Thomas	35.00
5	Manny Ramirez	12.00
6	Bernie Williams	10.00
7	Ben Grieve	15.00
8	Ken Griffey Jr.	50.00
9	Alex Rodriguez	30.00
10	Juan Gonzalez	25.00
11	Ivan Rodriguez	12.00
12	Travis Lee	25.00
13	Chipper Jones	30.00
14	Sammy Sosa	25.00
15	Vinny Castilla	6.00
16	Moises Alou	6.00
17	Gary Sheffield	6.00
18	Mike Piazza	30.00
19	Mark McGwire	60.00
20	Barry Bonds	12.00

1998 Pacific Revolution Major League Icons

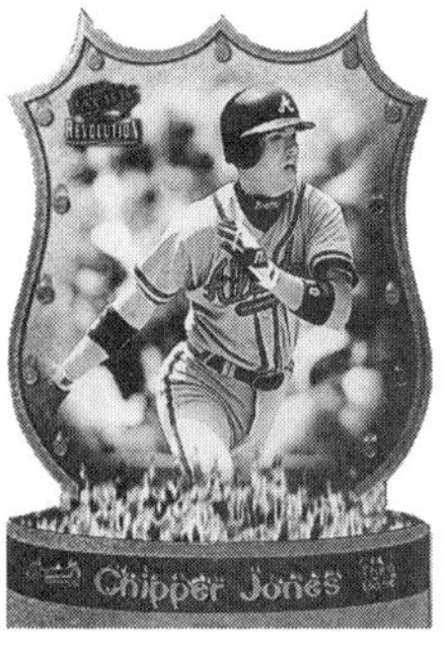

Major League Icons is a 10-card insert seeded one per 121 packs. Each card features a player photo on a die-cut shield, with the shield on a flaming stand.

		MT
Complete Set (10):		500.00
Common Player:		30.00
Inserted 1:121		
1	Cal Ripken Jr.	60.00
2	Nomar Garciaparra	50.00
3	Frank Thomas	60.00
4	Ken Griffey Jr.	80.00
5	Alex Rodriguez	50.00
6	Chipper Jones	50.00
7	Kerry Wood	50.00
8	Mike Piazza	50.00
9	Mark McGwire	90.00
10	Tony Gwynn	40.00

1998 Pacific Revolution Prime Time Performers

Prime Time Performers is a 20-card insert seeded one per 25 packs. The cards are designed like a TV program guide with the team logo laser-cut on the TV screen. The color player photo is located on the left.

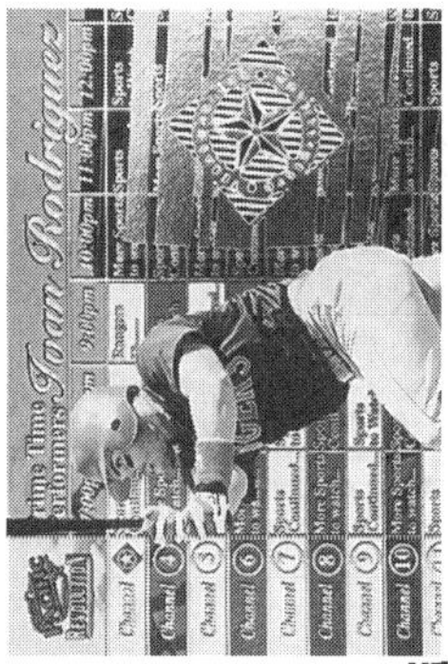

		MT
Complete Set (20):		350.00
Common Player:		6.00
Inserted 1:25		
1	Cal Ripken Jr.	30.00
2	Nomar Garciaparra	25.00
3	Frank Thomas	30.00
4	Jim Thome	6.00
5	Hideki Irabu	8.00
6	Derek Jeter	20.00
7	Ben Grieve	15.00
8	Ken Griffey Jr.	35.00
9	Alex Rodriguez	25.00
10	Juan Gonzalez	20.00
11	Ivan Rodriguez	10.00
12	Travis Lee	20.00
13	Chipper Jones	25.00
14	Greg Maddux	25.00
15	Kerry Wood	30.00
16	Larry Walker	6.00
17	Jeff Bagwell	15.00
18	Mike Piazza	25.00
19	Mark McGwire	40.00
20	Tony Gwynn	20.00

1998 Pacific Revolution Rookies and Hardball Heroes

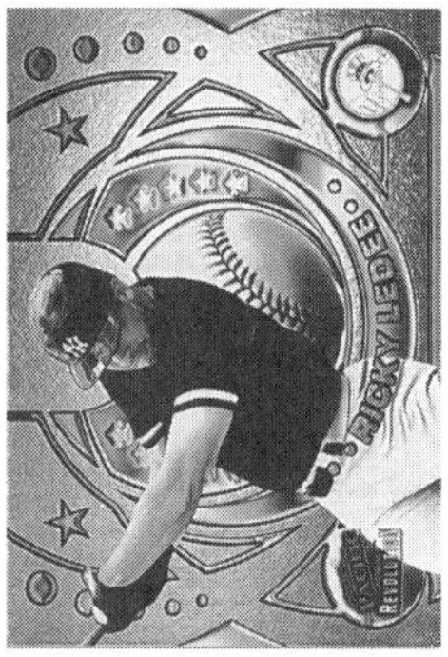

This 30-card hobby-only insert set was seeded one per six packs of Revolution. It contained a mix of top rookies and top veterans on a horizontal foil card. Gold versions of this insert are also available and numbered to 50 sets.

		MT
Complete Set (30):		100.00
Common Player:		.50
Inserted 1:6		
Gold (1-20):		8x to 15x
Gold (1-20) Production 50 sets		
1	Justin Baughman	.50
2	Jarrod Washburn	.50
3	Travis Lee	5.00
4	Kerry Wood	10.00
5	Magglio Ordonez	2.00
6	Todd Helton	2.50
7	Derrek Lee	1.50
8	Richard Hidalgo	1.00
9	Mike Caruso	1.00
10	David Ortiz	2.00
11	Brad Fullmer	2.00
12	Masato Yoshii	1.00
13	Orlando Hernandez	8.00
14	Ricky Ledee	1.00
15	Ben Grieve	5.00
16	Carlton Loewer	1.00
17	Desi Relaford	.50
18	Ruben Rivera	.50
19	Rolando Arrojo	3.00
20	Matt Perisho	.50
21	Chipper Jones	8.00
22	Greg Maddux	8.00
23	Cal Ripken Jr.	10.00
24	Nomar Garciaparra	8.00
25	Frank Thomas	8.00
26	Mark McGwire	15.00
27	Tony Gwynn	6.00
28	Ken Griffey Jr.	12.00
29	Alex Rodriguez	8.00
30	Juan Gonzalez	6.00

1998 Pacific Revolution Showstoppers

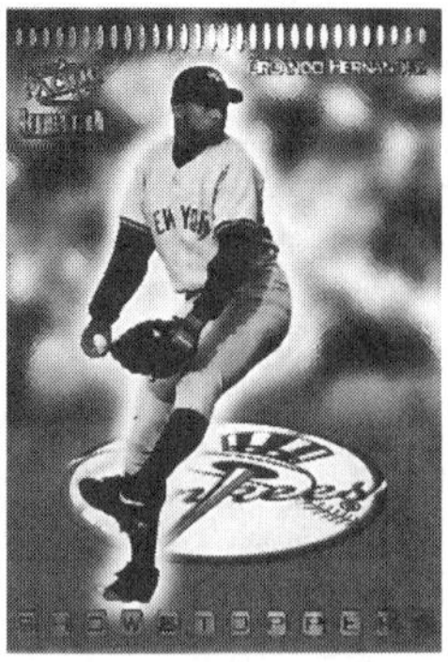

This 36-card insert was seeded two per 25 packs. The cards feature holographic foil. The color photo is centered above the team logo and the Showstoppers logo.

		MT
Complete Set (36):		275.00
Common Player:		2.00
Inserted 1:12		
1	Cal Ripken Jr.	20.00
2	Nomar Garciaparra	15.00
3	Pedro Martinez	5.00
4	Mo Vaughn	6.00
5	Frank Thomas	20.00
6	Manny Ramirez	6.00
7	Jim Thome	5.00
8	Jaret Wright	6.00
9	Paul Molitor	6.00
10	Orlando Hernandez	12.00
11	Derek Jeter	12.00
12	Bernie Williams	6.00
13	Ben Grieve	8.00
14	Ken Griffey Jr.	25.00
15	Alex Rodriguez	15.00
16	Wade Boggs	3.00
17	Juan Gonzalez	12.00
18	Ivan Rodriguez	6.00
19	Jose Canseco	4.00
20	Roger Clemens	10.00
21	Travis Lee	15.00
22	Andres Galarraga	4.00
23	Chipper Jones	15.00
24	Greg Maddux	15.00
25	Sammy Sosa	12.00
26	Kerry Wood	20.00
27	Vinny Castilla	2.00
28	Larry Walker	4.00
29	Moises Alou	2.00
30	Raul Mondesi	3.00
31	Gary Sheffield	4.00
32	Hideo Nomo	5.00
33	Mike Piazza	15.00
34	Mark McGwire	25.00
35	Tony Gwynn	12.00
36	Barry Bonds	6.00

1998 Pinnacle

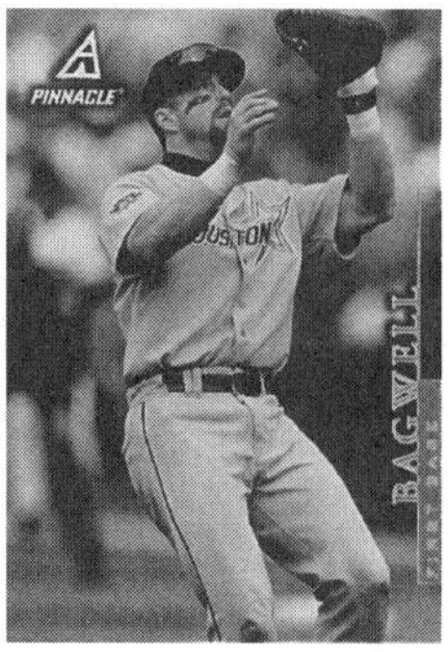

Pinnacle Baseball consists of a 200-card base set. The regular cards feature full-bleed photos on the front. Three different backs were produced for each card: home stats, away stats and seasonal stats. The set includes 157 regular cards, 24 Rookies, six Field of Vision, 10 Goin' Jake cards and three checklists. Parallel sets include Artist's Proofs, Press Plates and Museum Collection. Inserts include Epix, Hit it Here, Spellbound and Uncut.

		MT
Complete Set (200):		20.00
Common Player:		.10
1	Tony Gwynn (All-Star)	1.50
2	Pedro Martinez (All-Star)	.25
3	Kenny Lofton (All-Star)	.75
4	Curt Schilling (All-Star)	.10
5	Shawn Estes (All-Star)	.10
6	Tom Glavine (All-Star)	.20
7	Mike Piazza (All-Star)	2.00
8	Ray Lankford (All-Star)	.10
9	Barry Larkin (All-Star)	.20
10	Tony Womack (All-Star)	.10
11	Jeff Blauser (All-Star)	.10
12	Rod Beck (All-Star)	.10
13	Larry Walker (All-Star)	.30
14	Greg Maddux (All-Star)	2.00
15	Mark Grace (All-Star)	.20
16	Ken Caminiti (All-Star)	.20
17	Bobby Jones (All-Star)	.10
18	Chipper Jones (All-Star)	2.00
19	Javier Lopez (All-Star)	.10
20	Moises Alou (All-Star)	.20
21	Royce Clayton (All-Star)	.10
22	Darryl Kile (All-Star)	.10
23	Barry Bonds (All-Star)	.75
24	Steve Finley (All-Star)	.10
25	Andres Galarraga (All-Star)	.25
26	Denny Neagle (All-Star)	.10
27	Todd Hundley (All-Star)	.15
28	Jeff Bagwell	.75
29	Andy Pettitte	.35
30	Darin Erstad	.75
31	Carlos Delgado	.15
32	Matt Williams	.25
33	Will Clark	.20
34	Vinny Castilla	.15
35	Brad Radke	.10
36	John Olerud	.20
37	Andruw Jones	1.50
38	Jason Giambi	.10
39	Scott Rolen	1.50
40	Gary Sheffield	.30
41	Jimmy Key	.10
42	Kevin Appier	.10
43	Wade Boggs	.25
44	Hideo Nomo	.60
45	Manny Ramirez	.60
46	Wilton Guerrero	.10
47	Travis Fryman	.15
48	Chili Davis	.10
49	Jeromy Burnitz	.10
50	Craig Biggio	.20
51	Tim Salmon	.25
52	Jose Cruz Jr.	1.50
53	Sammy Sosa	1.50
54	Hideki Irabu	1.00
55	Chan Ho Park	.20
56	Robin Ventura	.10
57	Jose Guillen	.30
58	Deion Sanders	.25
59	Jose Canseco	.20
60	Jay Buhner	.20
61	Rafael Palmeiro	.20
62	Vladimir Guerrero	1.00
63	Mark McGwire	4.00
64	Derek Jeter	2.00
65	Bobby Bonilla	.20
66	Raul Mondesi	.20
67	Paul Molitor	.40
68	Joe Carter	.15
69	Marquis Grissom	.10
70	Juan Gonzalez	1.50
71	Kevin Orie	.10
72	Rusty Greer	.10
73	Henry Rodriguez	.10
74	Fernando Tatis	.25
75	John Valentin	.10
76	Matt Morris	.10
77	Ray Durham	.10
78	Geronimo Berroa	.10
79	Scott Brosius	.10
80	Willie Greene	.10
81	Rondell White	.20
82	Doug Drabek	.10
83	Derek Bell	.10
84	Butch Huskey	.10
85	Doug Jones	.10
86	Jeff Kent	.10
87	Jim Edmonds	.10
88	Mark McLemore	.10
89	Todd Zeile	.10
90	Edgardo Alfonzo	.10
91	Carlos Baerga	.10
92	Jorge Fabregas	.10
93	Alan Benes	.20
94	Troy Percival	.10
95	Edgar Renteria	.10
96	Jeff Fassero	.10
97	Reggie Sanders	.10
98	Dean Palmer	.10
99	J.T. Snow	.20
100	Dave Nilsson	.10
101	Dan Wilson	.10
102	Robb Nen	.10
103	Damion Easley	.10
104	Kevin Foster	.10
105	Jose Offerman	.10
106	Steve Cooke	.10
107	Matt Stairs	.10
108	Darryl Hamilton	.10
109	Steve Karsay	.10
110	Gary DiSarcina	.10
111	Dante Bichette	.25
112	Billy Wagner	.10
113	David Segui	.10
114	Bobby Higginson	.10
115	Jeffrey Hammonds	.10
116	Kevin Brown	.20
117	Paul Sorrento	.10
118	Mark Leiter	.10
119	Charles Nagy	.10
120	Danny Patterson	.10
121	Brian McRae	.10
122	Jay Bell	.10
123	Jamie Moyer	.10
124	Carl Everett	.10
125	Greg Colbrunn	.10
126	Jason Kendall	.10
127	Luis Sojo	.10
128	Mike Lieberthal	.10
129	Reggie Jefferson	.10
130	Cal Eldred	.10
131	Orel Hershiser	.10
132	Doug Glanville	.10
133	Willie Blair	.10
134	Neifi Perez	.10
135	Sean Berry	.10
136	Chuck Finley	.10
137	Alex Gonzalez	.10
138	Dennis Eckersley	.20
139	Kenny Rogers	.10
140	Troy O'Leary	.10
141	Roger Bailey	.10
142	Yamil Benitez	.10
143	Wally Joyner	.10
144	Bobby Witt	.10
145	Pete Schourek	.10
146	Terry Steinbach	.10
147	B.J. Surhoff	.10
148	Esteban Loaiza	.10
149	Heathcliff Slocumb	.10
150	Ed Sprague	.10
151	Gregg Jefferies	.10
152	Scott Erickson	.10
153	Jaime Navarro	.10
154	David Wells	.10
155	Alex Fernandez	.10
156	Tim Belcher	.10
157	Mark Grudzielanek	.10
158	Scott Hatteberg	.10
159	Paul Konerko	1.00
160	Ben Grieve	1.00
161	Abraham Nunez	.25
162	Shannon Stewart	.10
163	Jaret Wright	1.00
164	Derrek Lee	.10
165	Todd Dunwoody	.10
166	*Steve Woodard*	.25
167	Ryan McGuire	.10
168	Jeremi Gonzalez	.10
169	Mark Kotsay	.50
170	Brett Tomko	.10
171	Bobby Estalella	.10
172	Livan Hernandez	.20
173	Todd Helton	.75
174	Garrett Stephenson	.10
175	Pokey Reese	.10
176	Tony Saunders	.20
177	Antone Williamson	.10
178	Bartolo Colon	.10
179	Karim Garcia	.10
180	Juan Encarnacion	.25
181	Jacob Cruz	.10
182	Alex Rodriguez (Field of Vision)	1.00
183	Cal Ripken Jr., Roberto Alomar (Field of Vision)	1.00
184	Roger Clemens (Field of Vision)	.50
185	Derek Jeter (Field of Vision)	1.00
186	Frank Thomas (Field of Vision)	1.50
187	Ken Griffey Jr. (Field of Vision)	1.50
188	Mark McGwire (Goin' Jake)	2.00
189	Tino Martinez (Goin' Jake)	.10
190	Larry Walker (Goin' Jake)	.15
191	Brady Anderson (Goin' Jake)	.10

192	Jeff Bagwell (Goin' Jake)	.50
193	Ken Griffey Jr. (Goin' Jake)	1.50
194	Chipper Jones (Goin' Jake)	1.00
195	Ray Lankford (Goin' Jake)	.10
196	Jim Thome (Goin' Jake)	.20
197	Nomar Garciaparra (Goin' Jake)	1.00
198	Checklist (1997 HR Contest)	.10
199	Checklist (1997 HR Contest Winner)	.10
200	Checklist (Overall View of the Park)	.10

1998 Pinnacle Museum Collection

One hundred of the most popular players and hot prospects were selected for inclusion in the Pinnacle Museum Collection. Fronts differ from regular cards in the use of textured silver foil as a background and gold foil, instead of silver, for the player surname and position and the Pinnacle logo. Backs include a Museum Collection logo at bottom center and are numbered differently from the regular version. Museum Collection card numbers have a "PP" prefix.

	MT
Complete Set (100):	400.00
Common Player:	1.50
Museums:	5x to 10x

1998 Pinnacle Artist's Proofs

Artist's Proof is a 100-card partial parallel of the Pinnacle base set. The gold-foil Dufex cards were renumbered and inserted one per 39 packs.

		MT
Complete Set (100):		800.00
Common Player:		3.00
Inserted 1:39		
1	Tony Gwynn (All-Star)	30.00
2	Pedro J. Martinez (All-Star)	8.00
3	Kenny Lofton (All-Star)	15.00
4	Curt Schilling (All-Star)	3.00

5	Shawn Estes (All-Star)	3.00
6	Tom Glavine (All-Star)	6.00
7	Mike Piazza (All-Star)	40.00
8	Ray Lankford (All-Star)	3.00
9	Barry Larkin (All-Star)	6.00
10	Tony Womack (All-Star)	3.00
11	Jeff Blauser (All-Star)	3.00
12	Rod Beck (All-Star)	3.00
13	Larry Walker (All-Star)	8.00
14	Greg Maddux (All-Star)	40.00
15	Mark Grace (All-Star)	6.00
16	Ken Caminiti (All-Star)	6.00
17	Bobby Jones (All-Star)	3.00
18	Chipper Jones (All-Star)	40.00
19	Javier Lopez (All-Star)	4.00
20	Moises Alou (All-Star)	4.00
21	Royce Clayton (All-Star)	3.00
22	Darryl Kile (All-Star)	3.00
23	Barry Bonds (All-Star)	15.00
24	Steve Finley (All-Star)	3.00
25	Andres Galarraga (All-Star)	8.00
26	Denny Neagle (All-Star)	4.00
27	Todd Hundley (All-Star)	4.00
28	Jeff Bagwell	25.00
29	Andy Pettitte	12.00
30	Darin Erstad	12.00
31	Carlos Delgado	3.00
32	Matt Williams	5.00
33	Will Clark	5.00
34	Brad Radke	3.00
35	John Olerud	4.00
36	Andruw Jones	30.00
37	Scott Rolen	30.00
38	Gary Sheffield	8.00
39	Jimmy Key	3.00
40	Wade Boggs	5.00
41	Hideo Nomo	15.00
42	Manny Ramirez	12.00
43	Wilton Guerrero	3.00
44	Travis Fryman	3.00
45	Craig Biggio	5.00
46	Tim Salmon	6.00
47	Jose Cruz Jr.	30.00
48	Sammy Sosa	40.00
49	Hideki Irabu	12.00
50	Jose Guillen	6.00
51	Deion Sanders	5.00
52	Jose Canseco	5.00
53	Jay Buhner	5.00
54	Rafael Palmeiro	5.00
55	Vladimir Guerrero	20.00
56	Mark McGwire	75.00
57	Derek Jeter	40.00
58	Bobby Bonilla	4.00
59	Raul Mondesi	6.00
60	Paul Molitor	10.00
61	Joe Carter	4.00
62	Marquis Grissom	4.00
63	Juan Gonzalez	30.00
64	Dante Bichette	5.00
65	Shannon Stewart (Rookie)	3.00
66	Jaret Wright (Rookie)	25.00
67	Derrek Lee (Rookie)	3.00
68	Todd Dunwoody (Rookie)	3.00
69	Steve Woodard (Rookie)	3.00
70	Ryan McGuire (Rookie)	3.00
71	Jeremi Gonzalez (Rookie)	5.00
72	Mark Kotsay (Rookie)	10.00
73	Brett Tomko (Rookie)	3.00
74	Bobby Estalella (Rookie)	5.00
75	Livan Hernandez (Rookie)	5.00
76	Todd Helton (Rookie)	15.00
77	Garrett Stephenson (Rookie)	3.00
78	Pokey Reese (Rookie)	3.00
79	Tony Saunders (Rookie)	5.00
80	Antone Williamson (Rookie)	3.00
81	Bartolo Colon (Rookie)	3.00
82	Karim Garcia (Rookie)	5.00
83	Juan Encarnacion (Rookie)	8.00
84	Jacob Cruz (Rookie)	6.00
85	Alex Rodriguez (Field of Vision)	25.00
86	Cal Ripken Jr., Roberto Alomar (Field of Vision)	25.00
87	Roger Clemens (Field of Vision)	12.00
88	Derek Jeter (Field of Vision)	20.00

89	Frank Thomas (Field of Vision)	30.00
90	Ken Griffey Jr. (Field of Vision)	35.00
91	Mark McGwire (Goin' Jake)	40.00
92	Tino Martinez (Goin' Jake)	4.00
93	Larry Walker (Goin' Jake)	5.00
94	Brady Anderson (Goin' Jake)	3.00
95	Jeff Bagwell (Goin' Jake)	12.00
96	Ken Griffey Jr. (Goin' Jake)	35.00
97	Chipper Jones (Goin' Jake)	20.00
98	Ray Lankford (Goin' Jake)	3.00
99	Jim Thome (Goin' Jake)	6.00
100	Nomar Garciaparra (Goin' Jake)	20.00

1998 Pinnacle Epix

This cross-brand insert was included in Pinnacle, Score, Pinnacle Certified and Zenith. Twenty-four cards were seeded in Pinnacle packs (1:21). The four-tiered set highlights a memorable Game, Season, Moment and Play in a player's career. The dot matrix hologram cards came in three colors: orange, purple and emerald.

	MT
Common Game & Play:	6.00
Common Season (7-12):	15.00
Common Moment (13-18):	30.00
Purples:	1.5x
Emeralds:	2x to 3x
1	Ken Griffey Jr. G	40.00
2	Juan Gonzalez G	20.00
3	Jeff Bagwell G	15.00
4	Ivan Rodriguez G	8.00
5	Nomar Garciaparra G	25.00
6	Ryne Sandberg G	10.00
7	Frank Thomas S	100.00
8	Derek Jeter S	60.00
9	Tony Gwynn S	50.00
10	Albert Belle S	25.00
11	Scott Rolen S	50.00
12	Barry Larkin S	15.00
13	Alex Rodriguez M	120.00
14	Cal Ripken Jr. M	150.00
15	Chipper Jones M	120.00
16	Roger Clemens M	75.00
17	Mo Vaughn M	50.00
18	Mark McGwire M	175.00
19	Mike Piazza P	25.00
20	Andruw Jones P	20.00
21	Greg Maddux P	25.00
22	Barry Bonds P	12.00
23	Paul Molitor P	8.00
24	Eddie Murray P	6.00

1998 Pinnacle Hit it Here

Hit it Here is a 10-card insert seeded one per 17 packs. The micro-etched silver foil cards feature a color player photo with a red "Hit it Here" target on the left. Each card has a serial number. If the pictured player hit for the cycle on Opening Day 1998, the collector with the correct serially numbered card would win $1 million.

	MT
Complete Set (10):	75.00
Common Player:	3.00
Inserted 1:17	
1	Larry Walker	3.00
2	Ken Griffey Jr.	20.00
3	Mike Piazza	12.00
4	Frank Thomas	15.00
5	Barry Bonds	5.00
6	Albert Belle	5.00
7	Tino Martinez	3.00
8	Mark McGwire	25.00
9	Juan Gonzalez	10.00
10	Jeff Bagwell	8.00

1998 Pinnacle Spellbound

Spellbound is a 50-card insert seeded one per 17 packs of Pinnacle Baseball. Nine players were featured in the set. The cards featured a photo of the player with a letter from his first or last name in the background. Each player had enough cards to spell either his first or last name.

	MT
Complete Set (50):	500.00
Com. Mark McGwire (1MM-7MM)	25.00
Com. Roger Clemens (1RC-6RC)	10.00
Com. Frank Thomas (1FT-7FT)	20.00
Com. Scott Rolen (1SR-5SR)	12.00
Com. Ken Griffey Jr. (1KG-7KG)	25.00
Com. Larry Walker (1LW-6LW)	5.00
Com. Nomar Garciaparra (1NG-5NG)	15.00
Com. Cal Ripken Jr. (1CR-3CR)	20.00
Com. Tony Gwynn (1TG-4TG)	12.00
Inserted 1:17	

1998 Pinnacle Inside

Pinnacle Inside Baseball featured cards in a can. The 150 base cards featured full-bleed photos on the front with stats on the right and the player's name and position at the bottom. The Club Edition parallel (1:7) is printed on silver foil board and the Diamond Edition parallel (1:67) is printed on prismatic foil board. Each pack of cards was packaged inside a collectible can. Inserts include Behind the Numbers and Stand Up Guys.

		MT
Complete Set (150):		40.00
Common Player:		.15
1	Darin Erstad	1.00
2	Derek Jeter	2.50
3	Alex Rodriguez	2.50
4	Bobby Higginson	.15
5	Nomar Garciaparra	2.50
6	Kenny Lofton	1.00
7	Ivan Rodriguez	1.00
8	Cal Ripken Jr.	3.00
9	Todd Hundley	.15
10	Chipper Jones	2.50
11	Barry Larkin	.40
12	Roberto Alomar	.75
13	Mo Vaughn	1.00
14	Sammy Sosa	2.00
15	Sandy Alomar Jr.	.25
16	Albert Belle	1.00
17	Scott Rolen	1.50
18	Pokey Reese	.15
19	Ryan Klesko	.30
20	Andres Galarraga	.40
21	Justin Thompson	.25
22	Gary Sheffield	.40
23	David Justice	.40
24	Ken Griffey Jr.	4.00
25	Andruw Jones	2.00
26	Jeff Bagwell	1.50
27	Vladimir Guerrero	1.25
28	Mike Piazza	2.50
29	Chuck Knoblauch	.40
30	Rondell White	.40
31	Greg Maddux	2.50
32	Andy Pettitte	.75
33	Larry Walker	.40
34	Bobby Estalella	.15
35	Frank Thomas	3.00
36	Tony Womack	.15
37	Tony Gwynn	2.00
38	Barry Bonds	1.00
39	Randy Johnson	.75
40	Mark McGwire	5.00
41	Juan Gonzalez	2.00
42	Tim Salmon	.40
43	John Smoltz	.25
44	Rafael Palmeiro	.40
45	Mark Grace	.40
46	Mike Cameron	.25
47	Jim Thome	.50
48	Neifi Perez	.15
49	Kevin Brown	.40
50	Craig Biggio	.40
51	Bernie Williams	.75
52	Hideo Nomo	.75
53	Bob Abreu	.15
54	Edgardo Alfonzo	.15
55	Wade Boggs	.40
56	Jose Guillen	.40
57	Ken Caminiti	.40
58	Paul Molitor	.75
59	Shawn Estes	.15
60	Edgar Martinez	.15
61	Livan Hernandez	.40
62	Ray Lankford	.15
63	Rusty Greer	.25
64	Jim Edmonds	.25
65	Tom Glavine	.25
66	Alan Benes	.15
67	Will Clark	.25
68	Garret Anderson	.15
69	Javier Lopez	.25
70	Mike Mussina	.75
71	Kevin Orie	.15
72	Matt Williams	.40
73	Bobby Bonilla	.25
74	Ruben Rivera	.25
75	Jason Giambi	.15
76	Todd Walker	.40
77	Tino Martinez	.40
78	Matt Morris	.15
79	Fernando Tatis	.25
80	Todd Greene	.15
81	Fred McGriff	.25
82	Brady Anderson	.25
83	Mark Kotsay	.40
84	Raul Mondesi	.40
85	Moises Alou	.25
86	Roger Clemens	1.50
87	Wilton Guerrero	.15
88	Shannon Stewart	.15
89	Chan Ho Park	.25
90	Carlos Delgado	.15
91	Jose Cruz Jr.	1.50
92	Shawn Green	.15
93	Robin Ventura	.25
94	Reggie Sanders	.15

95	Orel Hershiser	.15
96	Dante Bichette	.25
97	Charles Johnson	.15
98	Pedro Martinez	.40
99	Mariano Rivera	.40
100	Joe Randa	.15
101	Jeff Kent	.15
102	Jay Buhner	.30
103	Brian Jordan	.15
104	Jason Kendall	.15
105	Scott Spiezio	.15
106	Desi Relaford	.15
107	Bernard Gilkey	.15
108	Manny Ramirez	.75
109	Tony Clark	.75
110	Eric Young	.15
111	Johnny Damon	.15
112	Glendon Rusch	.15
113	Ben Grieve	2.00
114	Homer Bush	.15
115	Miguel Tejada	1.00
116	Lou Collier	.15
117	Derrek Lee	.15
118	Jacob Cruz	.15
119	Raul Ibanez	.15
120	Ryan McGuire	.15
121	Antone Williamson	.15
122	Abraham Nunez	.15
123	Jeff Abbott	.15
124	Brett Tomko	.15
125	Richie Sexson	.15
126	Todd Helton	1.00
127	Juan Encarnacion	.15
128	Richard Hidalgo	.15
129	Paul Konerko	1.00
130	Brad Fullmer	1.00
131	Jeremi Gonzalez	.15
132	Jaret Wright	2.50
133	Derek Jeter (Inside Tips)	1.00
134	Frank Thomas (Inside Tips)	1.50
135	Nomar Garciaparra (Inside Tips)	1.00
136	Kenny Lofton (Inside Tips)	.50
137	Jeff Bagwell (Inside Tips)	.75
138	Todd Hundley (Inside Tips)	.15
139	Alex Rodriguez (Inside Tips)	1.00
140	Ken Griffey Jr. (Inside Tips)	2.00
141	Sammy Sosa (Inside Tips)	1.00
142	Greg Maddux (Inside Tips)	1.00
143	Albert Belle (Inside Tips)	.50
144	Cal Ripken Jr. (Inside Tips)	1.50
145	Mark McGwire (Inside Tips)	2.50
146	Chipper Jones (Inside Tips)	1.00
147	Charles Johnson (Inside Tips)	.15
148	Checklist (Ken Griffey Jr.)	1.50
149	Checklist (Jose Cruz Jr.)	.75
150	Checklist (Larry Walker)	.20

1998 Pinnacle Inside Club Edition

This parallel set is virtually identical to the regular Inside cards, except for the addition of a "CLUB EDITION" notice to the right of the player's first name, and the use of gold foil highlights instead of silver on front.

	MT
Complete Set (xx):	400.00
Common Player:	1.00
Club Editions: 5x to 10x	
Inserted 1:7	
(Stars and rookies valued 6-10X regular version.)	

1998 Pinnacle Inside Diamond Edition

Diamond Edition cards paralleled all 150 cards in Pinnacle Inside. The fronts had the insert name and they were printed on a prismatic foil and inserted one per 67 packs.

	MT
Diamond Edition Stars:	40x to 70x
Yng Stars & RCs:	25x to 50x
Inserted 1:67	

1998 Pinnacle Inside Behind the Numbers

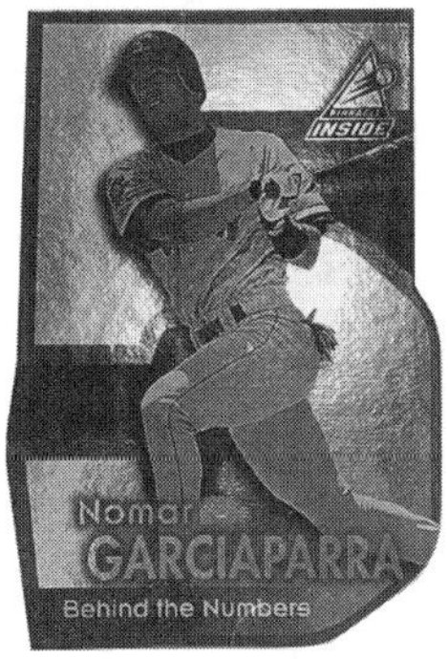

Behind the Numbers is a 20-card insert seeded one per 23 cans. The card front features the player's number in the background and the card is die-cut around it. The back has text explaining why the player wears that number.

		MT
Complete Set (20):		500.00
Common Player:		8.00
Inserted 1:23		
1	Ken Griffey Jr.	60.00
2	Cal Ripken Jr.	50.00
3	Alex Rodriguez	40.00
4	Jose Cruz Jr.	25.00
5	Mike Piazza	40.00
6	Nomar Garciaparra	40.00
7	Scott Rolen	25.00
8	Andruw Jones	25.00
9	Frank Thomas	50.00
10	Mark McGwire	70.00
11	Ivan Rodriguez	15.00
12	Greg Maddux	40.00
13	Roger Clemens	25.00
14	Derek Jeter	30.00
15	Tony Gwynn	30.00
16	Ben Grieve	25.00
17	Jeff Bagwell	25.00
18	Chipper Jones	40.00
19	Hideo Nomo	15.00
20	Sandy Alomar Jr.	8.00

1998 Pinnacle Inside Cans

Ten-card packs of Pinnacle Inside were packaged in collectible cans. The 24 cans featured a player photo or team logo. Cans were created to honor the Florida Marlins' world championship and the expansion Arizona and Tampa Bay teams. Gold parallel versions of the cans were found one every 47 cans.

		MT
Complete Set (23):		25.00
Common Can:		.40
Sealed Cans:		2x to 3x
Gold Cans:		10x
1	Ken Griffey Jr.	2.50
2	Frank Thomas	2.50
3	Alex Rodriguez	1.50
4	Andruw Jones	1.25
5	Mike Piazza	1.50
6	Ben Grieve	1.00
7	Hideo Nomo	.50
8	Vladimir Guerrero	.60
9	Roger Clemens	1.00
10	Tony Gwynn	1.25
11	Mark McGwire	3.00
12	Cal Ripken Jr.	2.00
13	Jose Cruz Jr.	1.00
14	Greg Maddux	1.50
15	Chipper Jones	1.50
16	Derek Jeter	1.50
17	Juan Gonzalez	1.25
18	Nomar Garciaparra (AL ROY)	1.50
19	Scott Rolen (NL ROY)	1.00
20	World Series Winner	.50
21	Larry Walker (NL MVP)	.50
22	Tampa Bay Devil Rays	.40
23	Arizona Diamondbacks	.40

1998 Pinnacle Inside Stand Up Guys

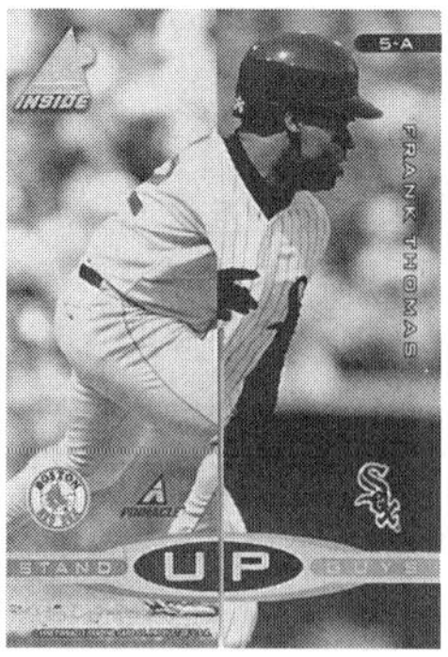

This 50-card insert was seeded one per can. Each card has a match. The two cards join together in the center to form a stand up collectible featuring four Major League players.

		MT
Complete Set (100):		40.00
Common Player:		.25
Inserted 1:1		
1a	Ken Griffey Jr.	2.00
1b	Cal Ripken Jr.	1.50
1c	Tony Gwynn	1.00
1d	Mike Piazza	1.25
2a	Andruw Jones	.75
2b	Alex Rodriguez	1.25
2c	Scott Rolen	.75
2d	Nomar Garciaparra	1.25
3a	Andruw Jones	.75
3b	Greg Maddux	1.25
3c	Javier Lopez	.25
3d	Chipper Jones	1.25
4a	Jay Buhner	.25
4b	Randy Johnson	.40
4c	Ken Griffey Jr.	2.00
4d	Alex Rodriguez	1.25
5a	Frank Thomas	2.00
5b	Jeff Bagwell	.75
5c	Mark McGwire	2.00
5d	Mo Vaughn	.50
6a	Nomar Garciaparra	1.25
6b	Derek Jeter	1.00
6c	Alex Rodriguez	1.25
6d	Barry Larkin	.25
7a	Mike Piazza	1.25
7b	Ivan Rodriguez	.50
7c	Charles Johnson	.25
7d	Javier Lopez	.25
8a	Cal Ripken Jr.	1.50
8b	Chipper Jones	1.25
8c	Ken Caminiti	.25
8d	Scott Rolen	.75
9a	Jose Cruz Jr.	.75
9b	Vladimir Guerrero	.50
9c	Andruw Jones	.75
9d	Jose Guillen	.25
10a	Larry Walker	.40
10b	Dante Bichette	.25
10c	Ellis Burks	.25
10d	Neifi Perez	.25
11a	Juan Gonzalez	1.00
11b	Sammy Sosa	1.50
11c	Vladimir Guerrero	.50
11d	Manny Ramirez	.40
12a	Greg Maddux	1.25
12b	Roger Clemens	.75
12c	Hideo Nomo	.50
12d	Randy Johnson	.50
13a	Ben Grieve	.60
13b	Paul Konerko	.50
13c	Jose Cruz Jr.	.75
13d	Fernando Tatis	.25
14a	Ryne Sandberg	.50
14b	Chuck Knoblauch	.40
14c	Roberto Alomar	.40
14d	Craig Biggio	.25
15a	Cal Ripken Jr.	1.50
15b	Brady Anderson	.25
15c	Rafael Palmeiro	.25
15d	Roberto Alomar	.40
16a	Darin Erstad	.50
16b	Jim Edmonds	.25
16c	Tim Salmon	.40
16d	Garret Anderson	.25
17a	Mike Piazza	1.25
17b	Hideo Nomo	.40
17c	Raul Mondesi	.25
17d	Eric Karros	.25
18a	Ivan Rodriguez	.50
18b	Juan Gonzalez	1.00
18c	Will Clark	.40
18d	Rusty Greer	.25
19a	Derek Jeter	1.00
19b	Bernie Williams	.40
19c	Tino Martinez	.40
19d	Andy Pettitte	.40
20a	Kenny Lofton	.50
20b	Ken Griffey Jr.	2.00
20c	Brady Anderson	.25
20d	Bernie Williams	.40
21a	Paul Molitor	.40
21b	Eddie Murray	.25
21c	Ryne Sandberg	.50
21d	Rickey Henderson	.25
22a	Tony Clark	.40
22b	Frank Thomas	2.00
22c	Jeff Bagwell	.75
22d	Mark McGwire	2.00
23a	Manny Ramirez	.40
23b	Jim Thome	.40
23c	David Justice	.25
23d	Sandy Alomar Jr.	.25
24a	Barry Bonds	.50
24b	Albert Belle	.50
24c	Jeff Bagwell	.75
24d	Dante Bichette	.25
25a	Ken Griffey Jr.	2.00
25b	Frank Thomas	2.00
25c	Alex Rodriguez	1.25
25d	Andruw Jones	.75

1998 Pinnacle Mint Collection

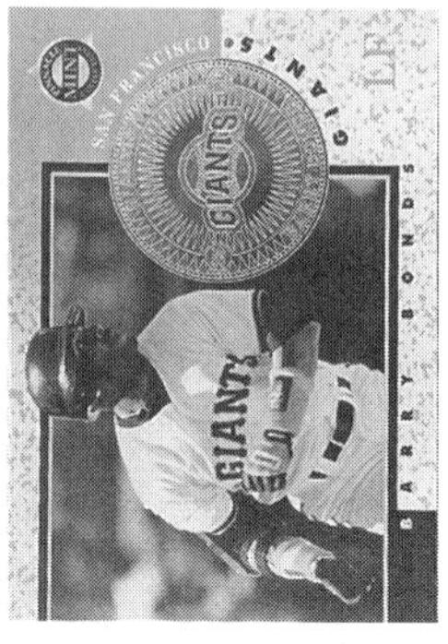

Mint Collection consists of 30 cards and 30 matching coins with numerous parallels of each. The horizontal cards come in four different versions. The base card features a player photo on the left with a circular bronze foil team logo on the right. The base cards were inserted one per hobby pack and two per retail pack. Die-cut versions removed the team logo and were inserted two per hobby and one per retail packs. Silver Mint Team (1:15 hobby, 1:23 retail) and Gold Mint Team (1:47 hobby, 1:71 retail) parallels were printed on silver foil and gold foil board, respectively.

		MT
Complete Set (30):		20.00
Common Die-Cut:		.25
Bronze:		1.5x to 2x
Inserted 1:1 H		
Silver:		4x to 8x
Inserted 1:15 H		
Gold:		8x to 15x
Inserted 1:47 H		
Wax Box:		80.00
1	Jeff Bagwell	1.00
2	Albert Belle	.75
3	Barry Bonds	.75
4	Tony Clark	.50
5	Roger Clemens	1.00
6	Juan Gonzalez	1.25
7	Ken Griffey Jr.	2.50
8	Tony Gwynn	1.25
9	Derek Jeter	1.50
10	Randy Johnson	.40
11	Chipper Jones	1.50
12	Greg Maddux	1.50
13	Tino Martinez	.40
14	Mark McGwire	3.00
15	Hideo Nomo	.75
16	Andy Pettitte	.50
17	Mike Piazza	1.50
18	Cal Ripken Jr.	2.00
19	Alex Rodriguez	1.50
20	Ivan Rodriguez	.75
21	Sammy Sosa	1.50
22	Frank Thomas	2.00
23	Mo Vaughn	.75
24	Larry Walker	.40
25	Jose Cruz Jr.	1.00
26	Nomar Garciaparra	1.50
27	Vladimir Guerrero	.75
28	Livan Hernandez	.25
29	Andruw Jones	1.25
30	Scott Rolen	1.00

1998 Pinnacle Mint Collection Coins

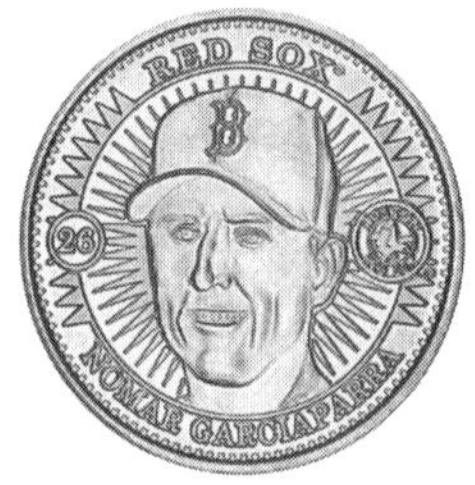

Two base coins were included in each pack of Mint Collection. The coins feature the player's image, name and number on the front along with his team's name and logo. The back has the Mint Collection logo. Seven parallels were included: Nickel-Silver (1:41), Bronze Proof (numbered to 500), Silver Proof (numbered to 250), Gold Proof (numbered to 100), Gold-Plated (1:199), Solid Silver (1:288 hobby, 1:960 retail) and Solid Gold by redemption (1-of-1).

		MT
Complete Set (30):		60.00
Common Brass Coin:		.75
Nickel:		3x to 6x
Inserted 1:41		
Silver:		12x to 25x
Inserted 1:288 H, 1:960 R		
Gold:		10x to 25x
Inserted 1:199		
1	Jeff Bagwell	2.50
2	Albert Belle	1.50
3	Barry Bonds	1.50
4	Tony Clark	1.00
5	Roger Clemens	2.50
6	Juan Gonzalez	3.00
7	Ken Griffey Jr.	6.00
8	Tony Gwynn	3.00
9	Derek Jeter	4.00
10	Randy Johnson	1.00
11	Chipper Jones	4.00
12	Greg Maddux	4.00
13	Tino Martinez	1.00
14	Mark McGwire	6.00
15	Hideo Nomo	1.50
16	Andy Pettitte	1.00
17	Mike Piazza	4.00
18	Cal Ripken Jr.	5.00
19	Alex Rodriguez	4.00
20	Ivan Rodriguez	1.50
21	Sammy Sosa	3.00
22	Frank Thomas	5.00
23	Mo Vaughn	1.50
24	Larry Walker	1.00
25	Jose Cruz Jr.	2.50
26	Nomar Garciaparra	4.00
27	Vladimir Guerrero	1.50
28	Livan Hernandez	.75
29	Andruw Jones	3.00
30	Scott Rolen	2.50

1998 Pinnacle Mint Collection Mint Gems

Mint Gems is a six-card insert printed on silver foil board. The cards were inserted 1:31 hobby packs and 1:47 retail. The oversized Mint Gems coins are twice the size of the regular coins. The six coins were inserted 1:31 hobby packs.

		MT
Complete Set (6)		50.00
Common Player:		4.00
Coins:		.5x to 1x
1	Ken Griffey Jr.	20.00
2	Larry Walker	4.00
3	Roger Clemens	8.00
4	Pedro Martinez	4.00
5	Nomar Garciaparra	12.00
6	Scott Rolen	10.00

1998 Pinnacle Performers

Pinnacle Performers consists of a 150-card base set. The Peak Performers parallel adds silver foil to the base cards and was inserted 1:7. Inserts in the home run-themed product include Big Bang, Launching Pad, Player's Card and Power Trip.

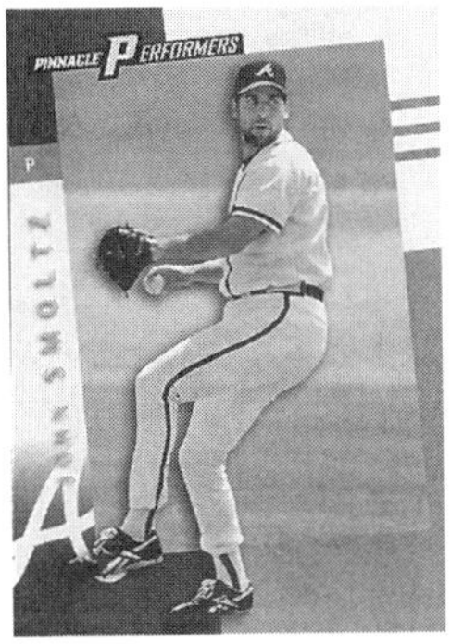

		MT
Complete Set (150):		20.00
Common Player:		.10
1	Ken Griffey Jr.	2.50
2	Frank Thomas	2.00
3	Cal Ripken Jr.	2.00
4	Alex Rodriguez	1.50
5	Greg Maddux	1.50
6	Mike Piazza	1.50
7	Chipper Jones	1.50
8	Tony Gwynn	1.25
9	Derek Jeter	1.25
10	Jeff Bagwell	.75
11	Juan Gonzalez	1.25
12	Nomar Garciaparra	1.50
13	Andruw Jones	.60
14	Hideo Nomo	.40
15	Roger Clemens	.75
16	Mark McGwire	3.00
17	Scott Rolen	.75
18	Vladimir Guerrero	.60
19	Barry Bonds	.60
20	Darin Erstad	.60
21	Albert Belle	.60
22	Kenny Lofton	.60
23	Mo Vaughn	.60
24	Tony Clark	.40
25	Ivan Rodriguez	.60
26	Jose Cruz Jr.	.50
27	Larry Walker	.30
28	Jaret Wright	.60
29	Andy Pettitte	.50
30	Roberto Alomar	.50
31	Randy Johnson	.40
32	Manny Ramirez	.60
33	Paul Molitor	.40
34	Mike Mussina	.50
35	Jim Thome	.40
36	Tino Martinez	.25
37	Gary Sheffield	.25
38	Chuck Knoblauch	.25
39	Bernie Williams	.50
40	Tim Salmon	.20
41	Sammy Sosa	1.00
42	Wade Boggs	.20
43	Will Clark	.20
44	Andres Galarraga	.25
45	Raul Mondesi	.20
46	Rickey Henderson	.10
47	Jose Canseco	.25
48	Pedro Martinez	.50
49	Jay Buhner	.20
50	Ryan Klesko	.25
51	Barry Larkin	.25
52	Charles Johnson	.10
53	Tom Glavine	.20
54	Edgar Martinez	.10
55	Fred McGriff	.20
56	Moises Alou	.20
57	Dante Bichette	.20
58	Jim Edmonds	.20
59	Mark Grace	.25
60	Chan Ho Park	.20
61	Justin Thompson	.10
62	John Smoltz	.20
63	Craig Biggio	.20
64	Ken Caminiti	.20
65	Richard Hidalgo	.10
66	Carlos Delgado	.10
67	David Justice	.25
68	J.T. Snow	.10
69	Jason Giambi	.10
70	Garret Anderson	.10
71	Rondell White	.20
72	Matt Williams	.25
73	Brady Anderson	.10
74	Eric Karros	.20
75	Javier Lopez	.10
76	Pat Hentgen	.10
77	Todd Hundley	.10
78	Ray Lankford	.10
79	Denny Neagle	.10
80	Sandy Alomar Jr.	.20
81	Jason Kendall	.10
82	Omar Vizquel	.10
83	Kevin Brown	.20
84	Kevin Appier	.10
85	Al Martin	.10
86	Rusty Greer	.10
87	Bobby Bonilla	.20
88	Shawn Estes	.10
89	Rafael Palmeiro	.25
90	Edgar Renteria	.10
91	Alan Benes	.20
92	Bobby Higginson	.10
93	Mark Grudzielanek	.10
94	Jose Guillen	.20
95	Neifi Perez	.10
96	Jeff Abbott	.10
97	Todd Walker	.25
98	Eric Young	.10
99	Brett Tomko	.10
100	Mike Cameron	.10
101	Karim Garcia	.10
102	Brian Jordan	.10
103	Jeff Suppan	.10
104	Robin Ventura	.20
105	Henry Rodriguez	.10
106	Shannon Stewart	.10
107	Kevin Orie	.10
108	Bartolo Colon	.20
109	Bob Abreu	.10
110	Vinny Castilla	.20
111	Livan Hernandez	.10
112	Derrek Lee	.10
113	Mark Kotsay	.25
114	Todd Greene	.10
115	Edgardo Alfonzo	.10
116	A.J. Hinch	.40
117	Paul Konerko	.30
118	Todd Helton	.60
119	Miguel Tejada	.30
120	Fernando Tatis	.20
121	Ben Grieve	.75
122	Travis Lee	1.50
123	Kerry Wood	3.00
124	Eli Marrero	.10
125	David Ortiz	.10
126	Juan Encarnacion	.10
127	Brad Fullmer	.25
128	Richie Sexson	.10
129	Aaron Boone	.10
130	Enrique Wilson	.10
131	Javier Valentin	.10
132	Abraham Nunez	.10
133	Ricky Ledee	.25
134	Carl Pavano	.10
135	Bobby Estalella	.10
136	Homer Bush	.10
137	Brian Rose	.10
138	Ken Griffey Jr. (Far and Away)	1.25
139	Frank Thomas (Far and Away)	1.00
140	Cal Ripken Jr. (Far and Away)	1.00
141	Alex Rodriguez (Far and Away)	.75
142	Greg Maddux (Far and Away)	.75
143	Chipper Jones (Far and Away)	.75
144	Mike Piazza (Far and Away)	.75
145	Tony Gwynn (Far and Away)	.60
146	Derek Jeter (Far and Away)	.60
147	Jeff Bagwell (Far and Away)	.40
148	Checklist (Hideo Nomo)	.20
149	Checklist (Roger Clemens)	.40
150	Checklist (Greg Maddux)	.60

1998 Pinnacle Performers Peak Performers

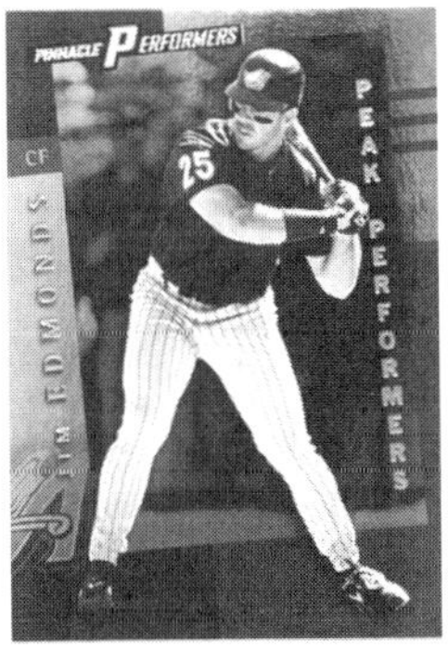

This 150-card parallel set is printed on silver foil vs. the white cardboard stock used on regular-issue cards. The parallel set name is printed down the right side in gold letters and they were seeded one per seven packs.

	MT
Peak Performers Stars:	3x to 6x
Yng Stars & RCs:	2x to 4x
Inserted 1:7	

1998 Pinnacle Performers Big Bang

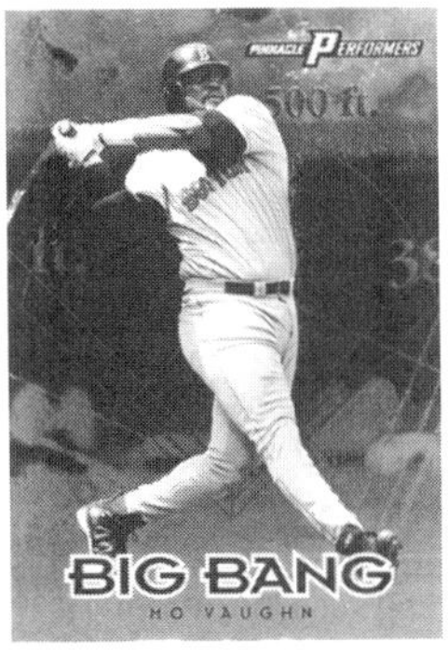

This 20-card insert features top power hitters. The micro-etched cards are sequentially numbered to 2,500. Each player has a Seasonal Outburst parallel, with a red overlay and numbered to that player's best seasonal home run total.

		MT
Complete Set (20):		175.00
Common Player:		4.00
Production 5,000 sets		
1	Ken Griffey Jr.	25.00
2	Frank Thomas	18.00
3	Mike Piazza	15.00
4	Chipper Jones	15.00
5	Alex Rodriguez	15.00
6	Nomar Garciaparra	15.00
7	Jeff Bagwell	8.00
8	Cal Ripken Jr.	18.00
9	Albert Belle	6.00
10	Mark McGwire	30.00
11	Juan Gonzalez	12.00
12	Larry Walker	4.00
13	Tino Martinez	4.00
14	Jim Thome	5.00
15	Manny Ramirez	6.00
16	Barry Bonds	6.00
17	Mo Vaughn	6.00
18	Jose Cruz Jr.	5.00
19	Tony Clark	5.00
20	Andruw Jones	6.00

1998 Pinnacle Performers Big Bang Season Outburst

Season Outburst parallels the Big Bang insert. The cards have a red overlay and are sequentially numbered to each player's season-high home run total.

		MT
Common Player:		40.00
#'d to players home run total from 1997		
1	Ken Griffey Jr. (56)	250.00
2	Frank Thomas (35)	220.00
3	Mike Piazza (40)	175.00
4	Chipper Jones (21)	220.00
5	Alex Rodriguez (23)	250.00
6	Nomar Garciaparra (30)	200.00
7	Jeff Bagwell (43)	140.00
8	Cal Ripken Jr. (17)	350.00
9	Albert Belle (30)	80.00
10	Mark McGwire (58)	275.00
11	Juan Gonzalez (42)	150.00
12	Larry Walker (49)	40.00
13	Tino Martinez (44)	40.00
14	Jim Thome (40)	40.00
15	Manny Ramirez (26)	80.00
16	Barry Bonds (40)	70.00
17	Mo Vaughn (35)	75.00
18	Jose Cruz Jr. (26)	100.00
19	Tony Clark (32)	50.00
20	Andruw Jones (18)	125.00

1998 Pinnacle Performers Launching Pad

Launching Pad is a 20-card insert seeded one per nine packs. It features top sluggers on foil-on-foil cards with an outer space background.

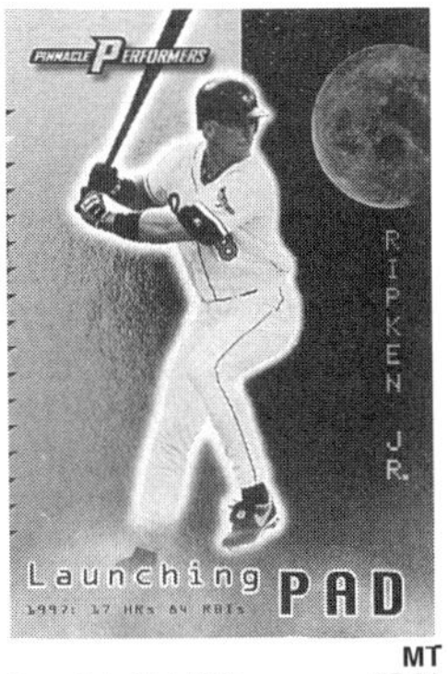

		MT
Complete Set (20):		75.00
Common Player:		1.50
Inserted 1:9		
1	Ben Grieve	3.00
2	Ken Griffey Jr.	10.00
3	Derek Jeter	5.00
4	Frank Thomas	8.00
5	Travis Lee	6.00
6	Vladimir Guerrero	2.50
7	Tony Gwynn	5.00
8	Jose Cruz Jr.	2.00
9	Cal Ripken Jr.	8.00
10	Chipper Jones	6.00
11	Scott Rolen	3.00
12	Andruw Jones	2.50
13	Ivan Rodriguez	2.50
14	Todd Helton	2.50
15	Nomar Garciaparra	6.00
16	Mark McGwire	12.00
17	Gary Sheffield	1.50
18	Bernie Williams	2.00
19	Alex Rodriguez	6.00
20	Mike Piazza	6.00

1998 Pinnacle Performers Power Trip

This 10-card insert was seeded 1:21. Printed on silver foil, each card is sequentially-numbered to 10,000.

		MT
Complete Set (10):		80.00
Common Player:		2.50
Production 10,000 sets		
1	Frank Thomas	12.00
2	Alex Rodriguez	10.00
3	Nomar Garciaparra	10.00
4	Jeff Bagwell	5.00
5	Cal Ripken Jr.	12.00
6	Mike Piazza	10.00
7	Chipper Jones	10.00
8	Ken Griffey Jr.	15.00
9	Mark McGwire	18.00
10	Juan Gonzalez	8.00

1998 Pinnacle Performers Swing for the Fences

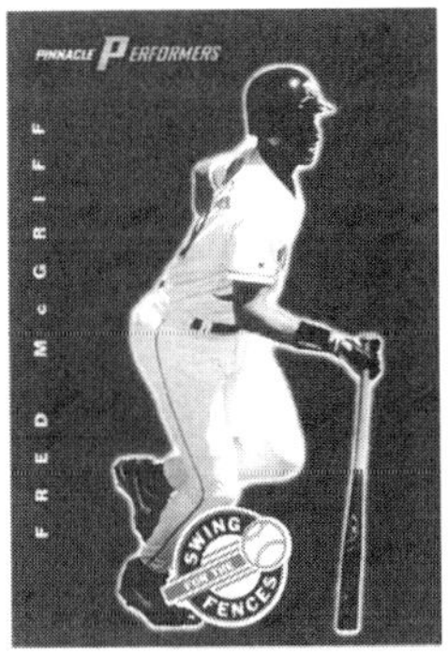

Pinnacle Performers included the "Swing for the Fences" sweepstakes. Fifty players were featured on cards with numbers on an all-red background. Fifty Home Run Points cards were also inserted, with each card featuring a point total on the front. Collectors who found the player cards of the AL and NL home run leaders, as well as enough point cards to match each of their season totals, were eligible to win prizes. A player or point card was inserted in each pack.

		MT
Complete Set (50):		20.00
Common Player:		.20
Inserted 1:1		
1	Brady Anderson	.20
2	Albert Belle	.60
3	Jay Buhner	.30
4	Jose Canseco	.30
5	Tony Clark	.50
6	Jose Cruz Jr.	.50
7	Jim Edmonds	.20
8	Cecil Fielder	.20
9	Travis Fryman	.20
10	Nomar Garciaparra	1.50
11	Juan Gonzalez	1.25
12	Ken Griffey Jr.	2.50
13	David Justice	.30
14	Travis Lee	1.50
15	Edgar Martinez	.20
16	Tino Martinez	.30
17	Rafael Palmeiro	.30
18	Manny Ramirez	.60
19	Cal Ripken Jr.	2.00
20	Alex Rodriguez	1.50
21	Tim Salmon	.30
22	Frank Thomas	2.00
23	Jim Thome	.40
24	Mo Vaughn	.60
25	Bernie Williams	.50
26	Fred McGriff	.25
27	Jeff Bagwell	.75
28	Dante Bichette	.30
29	Barry Bonds	.60
30	Ellis Burks	.20
31	Ken Caminiti	.20
32	Vinny Castilla	.20
33	Andres Galarraga	.30
34	Vladimir Guerrero	.60
35	Todd Helton	.60
36	Todd Hundley	.20
37	Andruw Jones	.60
38	Chipper Jones	1.50
39	Eric Karros	.20
40	Ryan Klesko	.30
41	Ray Lankford	.20
42	Mark McGwire	2.50
43	Raul Mondesi	.25
44	Mike Piazza	1.50
45	Scott Rolen	.75
46	Gary Sheffield	.30
47	Sammy Sosa	1.00
48	Larry Walker	.40
49	Matt Williams	.30
50	WILDCARD	.20

1998 Pinnacle Plus

Pinnacle Plus consists of a 200-card base set. Five subsets are included: Field of Vision, Naturals, All-Stars, Devil Rays and Diamondbacks. Artist's Proof is a 60-card partial parallel of the base set, inserted 1:35 packs. Gold Artist's Proof cards are numbered to 100 and Mirror Artist's Proofs are 1-of-1 inserts. Inserts include Lasting Memories, Yardwork, A Piece of the Game, All-Star Epix, Team Pinnacle, Gold Team Pinnacle, Pinnabilia and Certified Souvenir.

		MT
Complete Set (200):		25.00
Common Player:		.10
Nolan Ryan Auto. Baseball (1,000)		85.00
1	Roberto Alomar (All-star)	.50
2	Sandy Alomar Jr. (All-star)	.15
3	Brady Anderson (All-star)	.10
4	Albert Belle (All-star)	.75
5	Jeff Cirillo (All-star)	.10
6	Roger Clemens (All-star)	1.00
7	David Cone (All-star)	.20
8	Nomar Garciaparra (All-star)	2.00
9	Ken Griffey Jr. (All-star)	3.00
10	Jason Dickson (All-star)	.10
11	Edgar Martinez (All-star)	.10
12	Tino Martinez (All-star)	.25
13	Randy Johnson (All-star)	.50

14	Mark McGwire (All-star)	3.00
15	David Justice (All-star)	.25
16	Mike Mussina (All-star)	.50
17	Chuck Knoblauch (All-star)	.30
18	Joey Cora (All-star)	.10
19	Pat Hentgen (All-star)	.10
20	Randy Myers (All-star)	.10
21	Cal Ripken Jr. (All-star)	2.50
22	Mariano Rivera (All-star)	.20
23	Jose Rosado (All-star)	.10
24	Frank Thomas (All-star)	2.00
25	Alex Rodriguez (All-star)	2.00
26	Justin Thompson (All-star)	.10
27	Ivan Rodriguez (All-star)	.75
28	Bernie Williams (All-star)	.50
29	Pedro Martinez	.50
30	Tony Clark	.40
31	Garret Anderson	.10
32	Travis Fryman	.10
33	Mike Piazza	2.00
34	Carl Pavano	.10
35	*Kevin Millwood*	1.25
36	Miguel Tejada	.20
37	Willie Blair	.10
38	Devon White	.10
39	Andres Galarraga	.30
40	Barry Larkin	.20
41	Al Leiter	.20
42	Moises Alou	.20
43	Eric Young	.10
44	John Jaha	.10
45	Bernard Gilkey	.10
46	Freddy Garcia	.10
47	Ruben Rivera	.10
48	Robb Nen	.10
49	Ray Lankford	.10
50	Kenny Lofton	.75
51	Joe Carter	.10
52	Jason McDonald	.10
53	Quinton McCracken	.10
54	Kerry Wood	3.00
55	Mike Lansing	.10
56	Chipper Jones	1.50
57	Barry Bonds	.75
58	Brad Fullmer	.25
59	Jeff Bagwell	1.00
60	Rondell White	.20
61	Geronimo Berroa	.10
62	*Magglio Ordonez*	.50
63	Dwight Gooden	.10
64	Brian Hunter	.10
65	Todd Walker	.20
66	*Frank Catalanotto*	.20
67	Tony Saunders	.10
68	Travis Lee	1.00
69	Michael Tucker	.10
70	Reggie Sanders	.10
71	Derrek Lee	.10
72	Larry Walker	.25
73	Marquis Grissom	.10
74	Craig Biggio	.10
75	Kevin Brown	.20
76	J.T. Snow	.10
77	Eric Davis	.10
78	Jeff Abbott	.10
79	Jermaine Dye	.10
80	Otis Nixon	.10
81	Curt Schilling	.20
82	Enrique Wilson	.10
83	Tony Gwynn	1.50
84	Orlando Cabrera	.10
85	Ramon Martinez	.10
86	Greg Vaughn	.20
87	Alan Benes	.10
88	Dennis Eckersley	.10
89	Jim Thome	.40
90	Juan Encarnacion	.25
91	Jeff King	.10
92	Shannon Stewart	.10
93	Roberto Hernandez	.10
94	Raul Ibanez	.10
95	Darryl Kile	.10
96	Charles Johnson	.10
97	Rich Becker	.10
98	Hal Morris	.10
99	Ismael Valdes	.10
100	Orel Hershiser	.10
101	Mo Vaughn	.75
102	Aaron Boone	.10
103	Jeff Conine	.10
104	Paul O'Neill	.25
105	Tom Candiotti	.10
106	Wilson Alvarez	.10
107	Mike Stanley	.10
108	Carlos Delgado	.10
109	Tony Batista	.10
110	Dante Bichette	.25
111	Henry Rodriguez	.10
112	Karim Garcia	.10
113	Shane Reynolds	.10
114	Ken Caminiti	.20
115	Jose Silva	.10
116	Juan Gonzalez	1.50
117	Brian Jordan	.10
118	Jim Leyritz	.10
119	Manny Ramirez	.75
120	Fred McGriff	.20
121	Brooks Kieschnick	.10
122	Sean Casey	.25
123	John Smoltz	.20
124	Rusty Greer	.10
125	Cecil Fielder	.10
126	Mike Cameron	.20
127	Reggie Jefferson	.10
128	Bobby Higginson	.10
129	Kevin Appier	.10
130	Robin Ventura	.10
131	Ben Grieve	1.00
132	Wade Boggs	.25
133	Jose Cruz Jr.	.75
134	Jeff Suppan	.10
135	Vinny Castilla	.20
136	Sammy Sosa	2.00
137	Mark Wohlers	.10
138	Jay Bell	.10
139	Brett Tomko	.10
140	Gary Sheffield	.25
141	Tim Salmon	.25
142	Jaret Wright	.75
143	Kenny Rogers	.10
144	Brian Anderson	.10
145	Darrin Fletcher	.10
146	John Flaherty	.10
147	Dmitri Young	.10
148	Andruw Jones	.75
149	Matt Williams	.25
150	Bobby Bonilla	.20
151	Mike Hampton	.10
152	Al Martin	.10
153	Mark Grudzielanek	.10
154	Dave Nilsson	.10
155	Roger Cedeno	.10
156	Greg Maddux	2.00
157	Mark Kotsay	.40
158	Steve Finley	.10
159	Wilson Delgado	.10
160	Ron Gant	.10
161	Jim Edmonds	.10
162	Jeff Blauser	.10
163	Dave Burba	.10
164	Pedro Astacio	.10
165	Livan Hernandez	.10
166	Neifi Perez	.10
167	Ryan Klesko	.20
168	Fernando Tatis	.10
169	Richard Hidalgo	.10
170	Carlos Perez	.10
171	Bob Abreu	.10
172	Francisco Cordova	.10
173	Todd Helton	.40
174	Doug Glanville	.10
175	Brian Rose	.10
176	Yamil Benitez	.10
177	Darin Erstad	.75
178	Scott Rolen	.75
179	John Wetteland	.10
180	Paul Sorrento	.10
181	Walt Weiss	.10
182	Vladimir Guerrero	.75
183	Ken Griffey Jr. (The Naturals)	1.50
184	Alex Rodriguez (The Naturals)	1.00
185	Cal Ripken Jr. (The Naturals)	1.00
186	Frank Thomas (The Naturals)	1.00
187	Chipper Jones (The Naturals)	.75
188	Hideo Nomo (The Naturals)	.30
189	Nomar Garciaparra (The Naturals)	1.00
190	Mike Piazza (The Naturals)	1.00
191	Greg Maddux (The Naturals)	1.00
192	Tony Gwynn (The Naturals)	.75
193	Mark McGwire (The Naturals)	1.50
194	Roger Clemens (The Naturals)	.50
195	Mike Piazza (Field of Vision)	1.00
196	Mark McGwire (Field of Vision)	1.50
197	Chipper Jones (Field of Vision)	.75
198	Larry Walker (Field of Vision)	.20
199	Hideo Nomo (Field of Vision)	.30
200	Barry Bonds (Field of Vision)	.40

1998 Pinnacle Plus Artist's Proofs

Artist's Proofs is a 60-card partial parallel of the Pinnacle Plus base set. The dot matrix hologram cards were inserted 1:35. Gold Artist's Proofs added a gold finish and are sequentially numbered to 100. Mirror Artist's Proofs are a "1-of-1" insert.

		MT
Complete Set (60):		500.00
Common Player:		2.50
Inserted 1:35		
1	Roberto Alomar (All-Star)	12.00
2	Albert Belle (All-Star)	15.00
3	Roger Clemens (All-Star)	25.00
4	Nomar Garciaparra (All-Star)	40.00
5	Ken Griffey Jr. (All-Star)	60.00
6	Tino Martinez (All-Star)	6.00
7	Randy Johnson (All-Star)	10.00
8	Mark McGwire (All-Star)	75.00
9	David Justice (All-Star)	4.00
10	Chuck Knoblauch (All-Star)	5.00
11	Cal Ripken Jr. (All-Star)	50.00
12	Frank Thomas (All-Star)	40.00
13	Alex Rodriguez (All-Star)	40.00
14	Ivan Rodriguez (All-Star)	15.00
15	Bernie Williams (All-Star)	12.00
16	Pedro Martinez	10.00
17	Tony Clark	10.00
18	Mike Piazza	40.00
19	Miguel Tejada	4.00
20	Andres Galarraga	5.00
21	Barry Larkin	4.00
22	Kenny Lofton	15.00
23	Chipper Jones	30.00
24	Barry Bonds	15.00
25	Brad Fullmer	4.00
26	Jeff Bagwell	20.00
27	Todd Walker	4.00
28	Travis Lee	20.00
29	Larry Walker	5.00
30	Craig Biggio	2.50
31	Tony Gwynn	30.00
32	Jim Thome	5.00
33	Juan Encarnacion	4.00
34	Mo Vaughn	15.00
35	Karim Garcia	4.00
36	Ken Caminiti	4.00
37	Juan Gonzalez	30.00
38	Manny Ramirez	15.00
39	Fred McGriff	4.00
40	Rusty Greer	2.50
41	Bobby Higginson	2.50
42	Ben Grieve	15.00
43	Wade Boggs	4.00
44	Jose Cruz Jr.	12.00
45	Sammy Sosa	40.00
46	Gary Sheffield	4.00
47	Tim Salmon	4.00
48	Jaret Wright	12.00
49	Andruw Jones	15.00
50	Matt Williams	4.00
51	Greg Maddux	40.00
52	Jim Edmonds	2.50
53	Livan Hernandez	2.50
54	Neifi Perez	2.50
55	Fernando Tatis	2.50
56	Richard Hidalgo	2.50
57	Todd Helton	12.00
58	Darin Erstad	15.00
59	Scott Rolen	15.00
60	Vladimir Guerrero	18.00

1998 Pinnacle Plus Artist's Proofs Gold

This 60-card parallel repeated a sampling of the Pinnacle Plus set. They were identified by a gold foil finish and an Artist's Proofs logo. Cards were sequentially numbered to 100.

	MT
Gold Stars: 3x to 5x Art. Proof prices	
Yng Stars & RCs:	2x to 4x
Production 100 sets	

1998 Pinnacle Plus All-Star Epix

The All-Star Epix insert is part of the cross-brand Epix set. This 12-card set honors the All-Star Game achievements of baseball's stars on cards with dot matrix holograms. All-Star Epix was seeded 1:21.

		MT
Complete Set (12):		160.00
Common Player:		5.00
Purples:		.75x to 1.5x
Emeralds:		2x to 3x
Overall Odds 1:21		
13	Alex Rodriguez	30.00
14	Cal Ripken Jr.	30.00
15	Chipper Jones	15.00
16	Roger Clemens	15.00
17	Mo Vaughn	10.00
18	Mark McGwire	40.00
19	Mike Piazza	20.00
20	Andruw Jones	8.00
21	Greg Maddux	20.00
22	Barry Bonds	10.00
23	Paul Molitor	8.00
24	Hideo Nomo	5.00

1998 Pinnacle Plus Lasting Memories

Lasting Memories is a 30-card insert seeded 1:5. Printed on foil board, the cards feature a player photo with a sky background.

		MT
Complete Set (30):		40.00
Common Player:		.50
Inserted 1:5		
1	Nomar Garciaparra	3.00
2	Ken Griffey Jr.	5.00
3	Livan Hernandez	.50
4	Hideo Nomo	.75
5	Ben Grieve	1.50
6	Scott Rolen	1.50
7	Roger Clemens	2.00
8	Cal Ripken Jr.	4.00
9	Mo Vaughn	1.25
10	Frank Thomas	3.00
11	Mark McGwire	6.00
12	Barry Larkin	.50
13	Matt Williams	.50
14	Jose Cruz Jr.	1.00
15	Andruw Jones	1.25
16	Mike Piazza	3.00
17	Jeff Bagwell	1.50
18	Chipper Jones	3.00
19	Juan Gonzalez	2.50
20	Kenny Lofton	1.25
21	Greg Maddux	3.00
22	Ivan Rodriguez	1.25
23	Alex Rodriguez	4.00
24	Derek Jeter	3.00
25	Albert Belle	1.25
26	Barry Bonds	1.25
27	Larry Walker	.75
28	Sammy Sosa	4.00
29	Tony Gwynn	2.50
30	Randy Johnson	1.00

1998 Pinnacle Plus A Piece of the Game

Inserted 1:17 hoby packs (1:19 retail), this 10-card insert features baseball's top players on micro-etched foil cards.

		MT
Complete Set (10):		75.00
Common Player:		3.00
Inserted 1:19		
1	Ken Griffey Jr.	15.00
2	Frank Thomas	10.00
3	Alex Rodriguez	10.00
4	Chipper Jones	8.00
5	Cal Ripken Jr.	10.00
6	Mike Piazza	10.00
7	Greg Maddux	10.00
8	Juan Gonzalez	8.00
9	Nomar Garciaparra	10.00
10	Larry Walker	3.00

1998 Pinnacle Plus Team Pinnacle

Team Pinnacle is a 15-card, double-sided insert. Printed on mirror-mylar, the cards were inserted 1:71. The hobby-only Gold Team Pinnacle parallel was inserted 1:199 packs.

		MT
Complete Set (15):		300.00
Common Player:		10.00
Inserted 1:71		
Golds:		1.5x to 2x
Inserted 1:199		
1	Mike Piazza, Ivan Rodriguez	30.00
2	Mark McGwire, Mo Vaughn	60.00
3	Roberto Alomar, Craig Biggio	10.00
4	Alex Rodriguez, Barry Larkin	30.00
5	Cal Ripken Jr., Chipper Jones	40.00
6	Ken Griffey Jr., Larry Walker	50.00
7	Juan Gonzalez, Tony Gwynn	25.00
8	Albert Belle, Barry Bonds	12.00
9	Kenny Lofton, Andruw Jones	12.00
10	Tino Martinez, Jeff Bagwell	15.00
11	Frank Thomas, Andres Galarraga	30.00
12	Roger Clemens, Greg Maddux	30.00
13	Pedro Martinez, Hideo Nomo	10.00
14	Nomar Garciaparra, Scott Rolen	30.00
15	Ben Grieve, Paul Konerko	15.00

1998 Pinnacle Plus Yardwork

Yardwork is a 15-card insert seeded one per 19 packs. It features the top home run hitters in Major League Baseball.

		MT
Complete Set (15):		30.00
Common Player:		.75
Inserted 1:9		
1	Mo Vaughn	1.50
2	Frank Thomas	4.00
3	Albert Belle	1.50
4	Nomar Garciaparra	4.00
5	Tony Clark	1.00
6	Tino Martinez	.75
7	Ken Griffey Jr.	6.00
8	Juan Gonzalez	3.00
9	Sammy Sosa	4.00
10	Jose Cruz Jr.	1.25
11	Jeff Bagwell	2.00
12	Mike Piazza	4.00
13	Larry Walker	.75
14	Mark McGwire	8.00
15	Barry Bonds	1.50

1998 Pinnacle Zenith

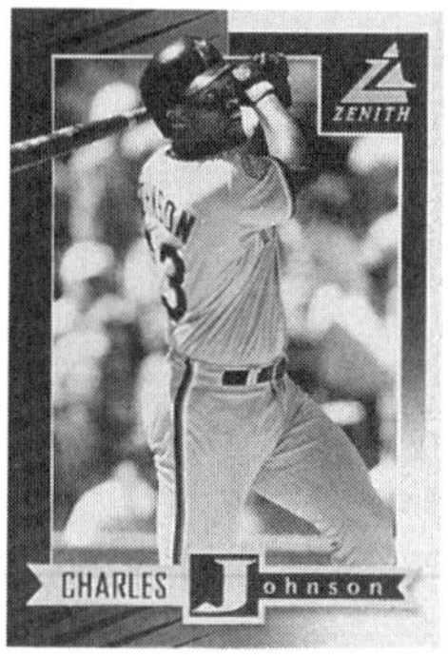

Zenith Baseball was part of Pinnacle's "Dare to Tear" program. Sold in three-card packs, the set consisted of 5"-x-7" cards, each with a standard-size card inside. Collectors had to decide whether to keep the large cards or tear them open to get the smaller card inside. Eighty 5"-x-7" cards and 100 regular cards made up the set. The regular, or Z2, cards were paralleled twice - Z-Silver (1:7) and Z-Gold (numbered to 100). The large cards also had two parallels - Impulse (1:7) and Gold Impulse (numbered to 100). Inserts include Raising the Bar, Rookie Thrills, Epix, 5x7 Z Team, Z Team, Gold Z Team, Rookie Z Team and Gold Rookie Z Team.

		MT
Complete Set (100):		75.00
Common Player:		.25
Wax Box:		80.00
1	Larry Walker	.50
2	Ken Griffey Jr.	6.00
2p	Ken Griffey Jr. (SAMPLE)	.25
3	Cal Ripken Jr.	5.00

4	Sammy Sosa	3.00
5	Andruw Jones	1.50
6	Frank Thomas	5.00
7	Tony Gwynn	3.00
8	Rafael Palmeiro	.40
9	Tim Salmon	.50
10	Randy Johnson	1.00
11	Juan Gonzalez	3.00
12	Greg Maddux	4.00
13	Vladimir Guerrero	1.50
14	Mike Piazza	4.00
15	Andres Galarraga	.50
16	Alex Rodriguez	4.00
17	Derek Jeter	4.00
18	Nomar Garciaparra	4.00
19	Ivan Rodriguez	1.50
20	Chipper Jones	4.00
21	Barry Larkin	.40
22	Mo Vaughn	1.50
23	Albert Belle	1.50
24	Scott Rolen	2.00
25	Sandy Alomar Jr.	.40
26	Roberto Alomar	1.00
27	Andy Pettitte	1.00
28	Chuck Knoblauch	.50
29	Jeff Bagwell	2.50
30	Mike Mussina	1.00
31	Fred McGriff	.40
32	Roger Clemens	2.50
33	Rusty Greer	.25
34	Edgar Martinez	.25
35	Paul Molitor	1.00
36	Mark Grace	.50
37	Darin Erstad	1.50
38	Kenny Lofton	1.50
39	Tom Glavine	.40
40	Javier Lopez	.25
41	Will Clark	.50
42	Tino Martinez	.50
43	Raul Mondesi	.50
44	Brady Anderson	.25
45	Chan Ho Park	.40
46	Jason Giambi	.25
47	Manny Ramirez	1.25
48	Jay Buhner	.50
49	Dante Bichette	.40
50	Jose Cruz Jr.	1.50
51	Charles Johnson	.25
52	Bernard Gilkey	.25
53	Johnny Damon	.25
54	David Justice	.40
55	Justin Thompson	.25
56	Bobby Higginson	.25
57	Todd Hundley	.25
58	Gary Sheffield	.50
59	Barry Bonds	1.50
60	Mark McGwire	8.00
61	John Smoltz	.40
62	Tony Clark	1.00
63	Brian Jordan	.25
64	Jason Kendall	.25
65	Mariano Rivera	.50
66	Pedro Martinez	.75
67	Jim Thome	1.00
68	Neifi Perez	.25
69	Kevin Brown	.25
70	Hideo Nomo	1.25
71	Craig Biggio	.40
72	Bernie Williams	1.00
73	Jose Guillen	.40
74	Ken Caminiti	.40
75	Livan Hernandez	.40
76	Ray Lankford	.25
77	Jim Edmonds	.40
78	Matt Williams	.50
79	Mark Kotsay	1.00
80	Moises Alou	.40
81	Antone Williamson	.25
82	Jaret Wright	3.00
83	Jacob Cruz	.25
84	Abraham Nunez	.25
85	Raul Ibanez	.25
86	Miguel Tejada	.25
87	Derek Lee	.25
88	Juan Encarnacion	.25
89	Todd Helton	1.50
90	Travis Lee	5.00
91	Ben Grieve	2.50
92	Ryan McGuire	.25
93	Richard Hidalgo	.25
94	Paul Konerko	.50
95	Shannon Stewart	.25
96	Homer Bush	.25
97	Lou Collier	.25
98	Jeff Abbott	.25
99	Brett Tomko	.25
100	Fernando Tatis	.25

1998 Pinnacle Zenith Silver

This parallel set reprinted all 100 standard sized cards in Zenith on silver foilboard, with a "Z-Silver" logo across the bottom center. Z-Silvers were inserted one per seven packs.

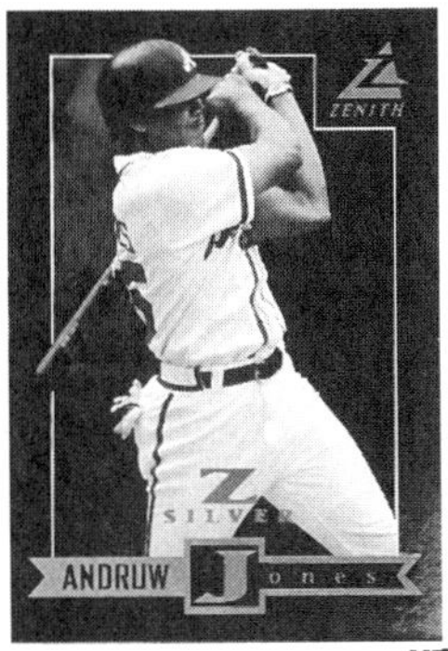

	MT
Silver Stars:	2x to 4x
Yng Stars & RCs:	1.5x to 3x
Inserted 1:7	

1998 Pinnacle Zenith Gold

The Z-Gold set parallels the Z2 base set. The 100-card set adds gold coloring to the border on the right side of the cards. The parallel is sequentially numbered to 100.

		MT
Common Player:		25.00
Semistars:		50.00
Production 100 sets		
1	Larry Walker	60.00
2	Ken Griffey Jr.	400.00
3	Cal Ripken Jr.	300.00
4	Sammy Sosa	200.00
5	Andruw Jones	100.00
6	Frank Thomas	300.00
7	Tony Gwynn	200.00
8	Rafael Palmeiro	40.00
9	Tim Salmon	40.00
10	Randy Johnson	80.00
11	Juan Gonzalez	200.00
12	Greg Maddux	250.00
13	Vladimir Guerrero	100.00
14	Mike Piazza	250.00
15	Andres Galarraga	40.00
16	Alex Rodriguez	250.00
17	Derek Jeter	200.00
18	Nomar Garciaparra	250.00
19	Ivan Rodriguez	100.00
20	Chipper Jones	225.00
21	Barry Larkin	40.00
22	Mo Vaughn	100.00
23	Albert Belle	100.00
24	Scott Rolen	150.00
25	Sandy Alomar Jr.	40.00
26	Roberto Alomar	80.00
27	Andy Pettitte	80.00
28	Chuck Knoblauch	50.00
29	Jeff Bagwell	150.00
30	Mike Mussina	80.00
31	Fred McGriff	40.00
32	Roger Clemens	150.00
33	Rusty Greer	25.00
34	Edgar Martinez	25.00
35	Paul Molitor	80.00
36	Mark Grace	50.00
37	Darin Erstad	125.00
38	Kenny Lofton	100.00
39	Tom Glavine	40.00
40	Javier Lopez	25.00
41	Will Clark	40.00
42	Tino Martinez	40.00
43	Raul Mondesi	40.00
44	Brady Anderson	25.00
45	Chan Ho Park	40.00
46	Jason Giambi	25.00
47	Manny Ramirez	100.00
48	Jay Buhner	40.00
49	Dante Bichette	40.00
50	Jose Cruz Jr.	90.00
51	Charles Johnson	25.00
52	Bernard Gilkey	25.00
53	Johnny Damon	25.00
54	David Justice	50.00
55	Justin Thompson	25.00
56	Bobby Higginson	25.00
57	Todd Hundley	25.00
58	Gary Sheffield	50.00
59	Barry Bonds	100.00
60	Mark McGwire	400.00
61	John Smoltz	30.00
62	Tony Clark	70.00
63	Brian Jordan	25.00
64	Jason Kendall	25.00
65	Mariano Rivera	40.00
66	Pedro Martinez	80.00
67	Jim Thome	70.00
68	Neifi Perez	25.00
69	Kevin Brown	30.00
70	Hideo Nomo	90.00
71	Craig Biggio	40.00
72	Bernie Williams	80.00
73	Jose Guillen	40.00
74	Ken Caminiti	40.00
75	Livan Hernandez	25.00
76	Ray Lankford	25.00
77	Jim Edmonds	30.00
78	Matt Williams	50.00
79	Mark Kotsay	50.00
80	Moises Alou	40.00
81	Antone Williamson	25.00
82	Jaret Wright	125.00
83	Jacob Cruz	25.00
84	Abraham Nunez	25.00
85	Raul Ibanez	25.00
86	Miguel Tejada	40.00
87	Derek Lee	25.00
88	Juan Encarnacion	25.00
89	Todd Helton	100.00
90	Travis Lee	200.00
91	Ben Grieve	150.00
92	Ryan McGuire	25.00
93	Richard Hidalgo	25.00
94	Paul Konerko	50.00
95	Shannon Stewart	25.00
96	Homer Bush	25.00
97	Lou Collier	25.00
98	Jeff Abbott	25.00
99	Brett Tomko	25.00
100	Fernando Tatis	35.00

1998 Pinnacle Zenith 5x7

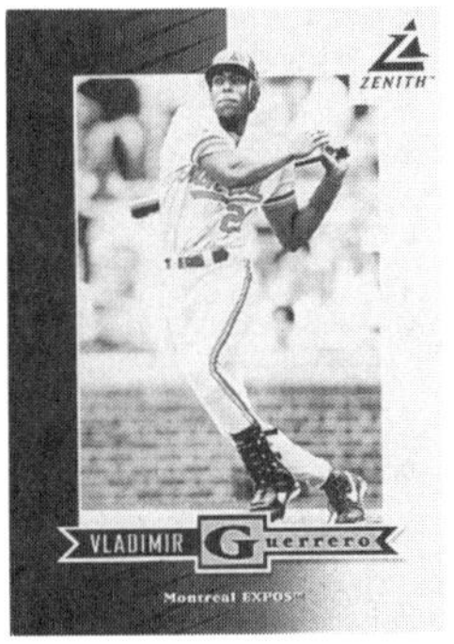

The 80 Zenith 5x7 cards all contained a regular-size card. Collectors could tear open the 5x7 to get at the smaller card inside. The set has two parallels: 5x7 Impulse (1:7) and 5x7 Gold Impulse (1:43).

		MT
Complete Set (80):		100.00
Common Player:		.50
1	Nomar Garciaparra	5.00
2	Andres Galarraga	1.00
3	Greg Maddux	5.00
4	Frank Thomas	6.00
5	Mark McGwire	8.00
6	Rafael Palmeiro	1.00
7	John Smoltz	.50
8	Jeff Bagwell	3.00
9	Andruw Jones	2.00
10	Rusty Greer	.50
11	Paul Molitor	1.50
12	Bernie Williams	1.50
13	Kenny Lofton	2.00
14	Alex Rodriguez	5.00
15	Derek Jeter	4.00
16	Scott Rolen	3.00
17	Albert Belle	2.00
18	Mo Vaughn	2.00
19	Chipper Jones	5.00
20	Chuck Knoblauch	.75
21	Mike Piazza	5.00
22	Tony Gwynn	4.00
23	Juan Gonzalez	4.00
24	Andy Pettitte	1.00
25	Tim Salmon	1.00
26	Brady Anderson	.50
27	Mike Mussina	1.50
28	Edgar Martinez	.50
29	Jose Guillen	.50
30	Hideo Nomo	1.50
31	Jim Thome	1.00
32	Mark Grace	.75
33	Darin Erstad	2.00
34	Bobby Higginson	.50
35	Ivan Rodriguez	2.00
36	Todd Hundley	.50
37	Sandy Alomar Jr.	.50
38	Gary Sheffield	.75
39	David Justice	.75
40	Ken Griffey Jr.	8.00
41	Vladimir Guerrero	2.00
42	Larry Walker	.75
43	Barry Bonds	2.00
44	Randy Johnson	1.00
45	Roger Clemens	3.00
46	Raul Mondesi	.75
47	Tino Martinez	.75
48	Jason Giambi	.50
49	Matt Williams	.75
50	Cal Ripken Jr.	6.00
51	Barry Larkin	.75
52	Jim Edmonds	.50
53	Ken Caminiti	.75
54	Sammy Sosa	3.00
55	Tony Clark	1.00
56	Manny Ramirez	1.50
57	Bernard Gilkey	.50
58	Jose Cruz Jr.	2.00
59	Brian Jordan	.50
60	Kevin Brown	.50
61	Craig Biggio	.75
62	Javier Lopez	.50
63	Jay Buhner	.75
64	Roberto Alomar	1.50
65	Justin Thompson	.50
66	Todd Helton	2.00
67	Travis Lee	6.00
68	Paul Konerko	.75
69	Jaret Wright	4.00
70	Ben Grieve	3.00
71	Juan Encarnacion	.50
72	Ryan McGuire	.50
73	Derrek Lee	.50
74	Abraham Nunez	.50
75	Richard Hidalgo	.50
76	Miguel Tejada	.50
77	Jacob Cruz	.50
78	Homer Bush	.50
79	Jeff Abbott	.50
80	Lou Collier	.50
	Checklist	.50

1998 Pinnacle Zenith 5x7 Silvers

These silver parallels reprinted each of the 80 cards in the 5" x 7" set. Cards were called Impulse and carried that logo on the front and were inserted one per seven packs. Since these cards contained other cards inside them, they are condition sensitive and only worth full price if left in mint condition and not cut open.

	MT
Silver Stars:	2x to 4x
Yng Stars & RCs:	1.5x to 3x
Inserted 1:7	

1998 Pinnacle Zenith 5x7 Gold

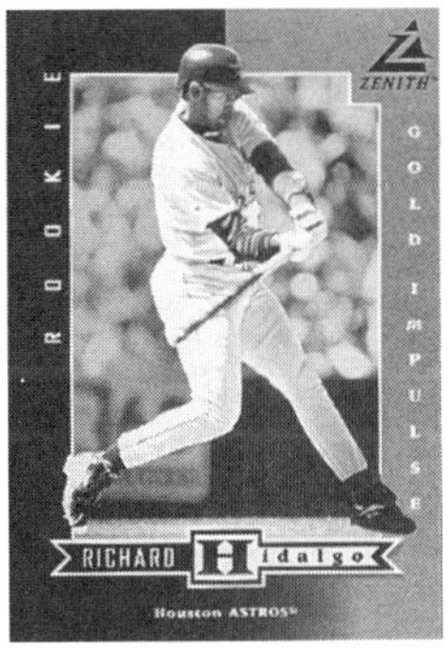

The 5x7 Gold Impulse set parallels the 80-card 5x7 base set. The cards were inserted one per 43 packs.

		MT
Common Player:		25.00
Semistars:		50.00
Production 100 sets		
1	Nomar Garciaparra	300.00
2	Andres Galarraga	50.00
3	Greg Maddux	300.00
4	Frank Thomas	400.00
5	Mark McGwire	500.00
6	Rafael Palmeiro	50.00
7	John Smoltz	40.00
8	Jeff Bagwell	200.00
9	Andruw Jones	125.00
10	Rusty Greer	25.00
11	Paul Molitor	100.00
12	Bernie Williams	100.00
13	Kenny Lofton	150.00
14	Alex Rodriguez	300.00
15	Derek Jeter	250.00
16	Scott Rolen	180.00
17	Albert Belle	150.00
18	Mo Vaughn	150.00
19	Chipper Jones	275.00
20	Chuck Knoblauch	50.00
21	Mike Piazza	300.00
22	Tony Gwynn	250.00
23	Juan Gonzalez	250.00
24	Andy Pettitte	100.00
25	Tim Salmon	50.00
26	Brady Anderson	25.00
27	Mike Mussina	100.00
28	Edgar Martinez	25.00
29	Jose Guillen	40.00
30	Hideo Nomo	125.00
31	Jim Thome	80.00
32	Mark Grace	50.00
33	Darin Erstad	125.00
34	Bobby Higginson	25.00
35	Ivan Rodriguez	150.00
36	Todd Hundley	25.00
37	Sandy Alomar Jr.	40.00
38	Gary Sheffield	50.00
39	David Justice	50.00
40	Ken Griffey Jr.	500.00
41	Vladimir Guerrero	125.00
42	Larry Walker	60.00
43	Barry Bonds	150.00
44	Randy Johnson	80.00
45	Roger Clemens	200.00
46	Raul Mondesi	50.00
47	Tino Martinez	50.00
48	Jason Giambi	25.00
49	Matt Williams	60.00
50	Cal Ripken Jr.	400.00
51	Barry Larkin	50.00
52	Jim Edmonds	25.00
53	Ken Caminiti	40.00
54	Sammy Sosa	200.00
55	Tony Clark	100.00
56	Manny Ramirez	125.00
57	Bernard Gilkey	25.00
58	Jose Cruz Jr.	150.00
59	Brian Jordan	25.00
60	Kevin Brown	25.00
61	Craig Biggio	40.00
62	Javier Lopez	25.00
63	Jay Buhner	50.00
64	Roberto Alomar	100.00
65	Justin Thompson	25.00
66	Todd Helton	125.00
67	Travis Lee	250.00
68	Paul Konerko	50.00
69	Jaret Wright	150.00
70	Ben Grieve	150.00
71	Juan Encarnacion	25.00
72	Ryan McGuire	25.00
73	Derrek Lee	25.00
74	Abraham Nunez	25.00
75	Richard Hidalgo	25.00
76	Miguel Tejada	40.00
77	Jacob Cruz	25.00
78	Homer Bush	25.00
79	Jeff Abbott	25.00
80	Lou Collier	25.00
	Checklist	25.00

1998 Pinnacle Zenith Raising the Bar

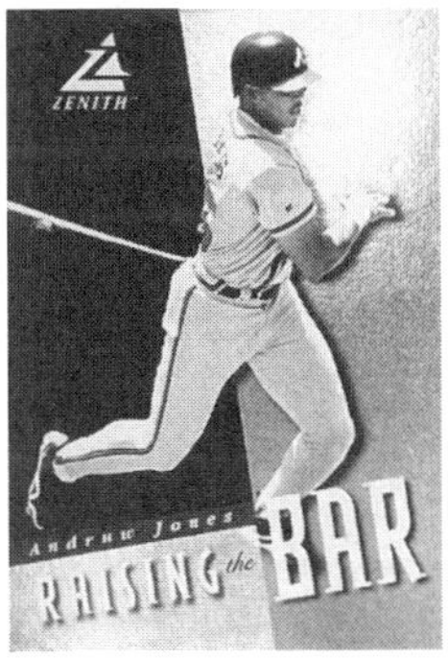

Raising the Bar is a 15-card insert seeded 1:25. The set features players who have set high standards for other players to follow.

		MT
Complete Set (15):		350.00
Common Player:		6.00
Inserted 1:25		
1	Ken Griffey Jr.	50.00
2	Frank Thomas	40.00
3	Alex Rodriguez	30.00
4	Tony Gwynn	30.00
5	Mike Piazza	30.00
6	Ivan Rodriguez	15.00
7	Cal Ripken Jr.	40.00
8	Greg Maddux	30.00
9	Hideo Nomo	12.00
10	Mark McGwire	50.00
11	Juan Gonzalez	25.00
12	Andruw Jones	15.00
13	Jeff Bagwell	20.00
14	Chipper Jones	30.00
15	Nomar Garciaparra	30.00

1998 Pinnacle Zenith Rookie Thrills

Rookie Thrills is a 15-card insert seeded 1:25. The set features many of the top rookies of 1998.

		MT
Complete Set (15):		75.00
Common Player:		5.00
Inserted 1:25		
1	Travis Lee	25.00
2	Juan Encarnacion	4.00
3	Derrek Lee	4.00
4	Raul Ibanez	4.00
5	Ryan McGulre	4.00
6	Todd Helton	10.00
7	Jacob Cruz	4.00
8	Abraham Nunez	4.00
9	Paul Konerko	8.00
10	Ben Grieve	15.00
11	Jeff Abbott	4.00
12	Richard Hidalgo	4.00
13	Jaret Wright	10.00
14	Lou Collier	4.00
15	Miguel Tejada	6.00

1998 Pinnacle Zenith Z-Team

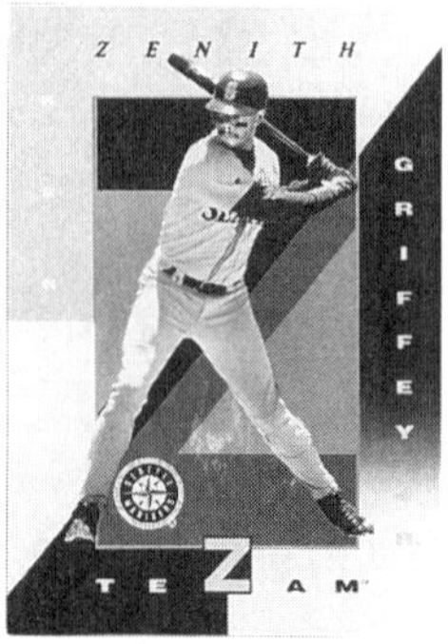

The Z Team insert was created in 5x7 and standard-size versions. The 5x7 Z Team insert consisted of nine cards and was inserted 1:35. The standard-size Z Team also had nine cards and was inserted 1:35. The nine Rookie Z Team cards were seeded 1:58 and gold versions of both were found 1:175.

		MT
Complete Set (18):		550.00
Common Player:		20.00
#'s 1-9 1:35		
#'s 10-18 1:58		
Golds:		1.5x to 3x
Inserted 1:175		
1	Frank Thomas	50.00
2	Ken Griffey Jr.	60.00
3	Mike Piazza	40.00
4	Cal Ripken Jr.	50.00
5	Alex Rodriguez	40.00
6	Greg Maddux	40.00
7	Derek Jeter	30.00
8	Chipper Jones	40.00
9	Roger Clemens	20.00
10	Ben Grieve	30.00
11	Derrek Lee	8.00
12	Jose Cruz Jr.	15.00
13	Nomar Garciaparra	50.00
14	Travis Lee	50.00
15	Todd Helton	25.00
16	Paul Konerko	15.00
17	Miguel Tejada	15.00
18	Scott Rolen	25.00

1998 Score

The cards in the 270-card base set feature a color photo inside a black and white border. The player's name is printed in the left border. The entire base set is paralleled in the silver-foil Showcase Series (1:5). The Artist's Proof partial parallel gives a prismatic foil treatment to 165 base cards and was seeded 1:23. Inserts included All-Stars, Complete Players and Epix.

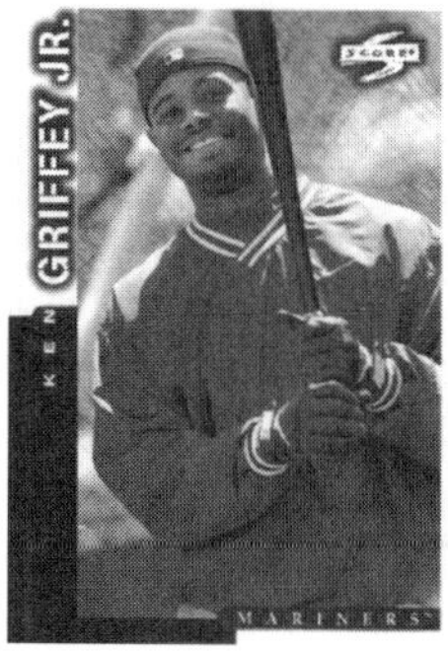

		MT
Complete Set (270):		15.00
Common Player:		.05
Wax Box:		32.00
1	Andruw Jones	1.00
2	Dan Wilson	.05
3	Hideo Nomo	.40
4	Chuck Carr	.05
5	Barry Bonds	.50
6	Jack McDowell	.05
7	Albert Belle	.50
8	Francisco Cordova	.05
9	Greg Maddux	1.25
10	Alex Rodriguez	1.50
11	Steve Avery	.05
12	Chuck McElroy	.05
13	Larry Walker	.20
14	Hideki Irabu	.75
15	Roberto Alomar	.40
16	Neifi Perez	.05
17	Jim Thome	.30
18	Rickey Henderson	.05
19	Andres Galarraga	.20
20	Jeff Fassero	.05
21	Kevin Young	.05
22	Derek Jeter	1.25
23	Andy Benes	.05
24	Mike Piazza	1.25
25	Todd Stottlemyre	.05
26	Michael Tucker	.05
27	Denny Neagle	.05
28	Javier Lopez	.10
29	Aaron Sele	.05
30	Ryan Klesko	.25
31	Dennis Eckersley	.10
32	Quinton McCracken	.05
33	Brian Anderson	.05
34	Ken Griffey Jr.	2.00
35	Shawn Estes	.05
36	Tim Wakefield	.05
37	Jimmy Key	.05
38	Jeff Bagwell	.75
39	Edgardo Alfonzo	.05
40	Mike Cameron	.05
41	Mark McGwire	2.50
42	Tino Martinez	.15
43	Cal Ripken Jr.	1.50
44	Curtis Goodwin	.05
45	Bobby Ayala	.05
46	Sandy Alomar Jr.	.10
47	Bobby Jones	.05
48	Omar Vizquel	.05
49	Roger Clemens	.60
50	Tony Gwynn	1.00
51	Chipper Jones	1.25
52	Ron Coomer	.05
53	Dmitri Young	.05
54	Brian Giles	.05
55	Steve Finley	.05
56	David Cone	.10
57	Andy Pettitte	.50
58	Wilton Guerrero	.05
59	Deion Sanders	.15
60	Carlos Delgado	.05
61	Jason Giambi	.05
62	Ozzie Guillen	.05
63	Jay Bell	.05
64	Barry Larkin	.15
65	Sammy Sosa	1.00
66	Bernie Williams	.40
67	Terry Steinbach	.05
68	Scott Rolen	1.00
69	Melvin Nieves	.05
70	Craig Biggio	.10
71	Todd Greene	.05
72	Greg Gagne	.05
73	Shigetosi Hasegawa	.05
74	Mark McLemore	.05
75	Darren Bragg	.05
76	Brett Butler	.05
77	Ron Gant	.10
78	Mike Difelice	.05
79	Charles Nagy	.05
80	Scott Hatteberg	.05
81	Brady Anderson	.15
82	Jay Buhner	.15
83	Todd Hollandsworth	.05
84	Geronimo Berroa	.05
85	Jeff Suppan	.05
86	Pedro Martinez	.20
87	Roger Cedeno	.05
88	Ivan Rodriguez	.40
89	Jaime Navarro	.05
90	Chris Hoiles	.05
91	Nomar Garciaparra	1.25
92	Rafael Palmeiro	.15
93	Darin Erstad	.75
94	Kenny Lofton	.50
95	Mike Timlin	.05
96	Chris Clemons	.05
97	Vinny Castilla	.10
98	Charlie Hayes	.05
99	Lyle Mouton	.05
100	Jason Dickson	.05
101	Justin Thompson	.05
102	Pat Kelly	.05
103	Chan Ho Park	.05
104	Ray Lankford	.05
105	Frank Thomas	1.50
106	Jermaine Allensworth	.05
107	Doug Drabek	.05
108	Todd Hundley	.15
109	Carl Everett	.05
110	Edgar Martinez	.05
111	Robin Ventura	.05
112	John Wetteland	.05
113	Mariano Rivera	.15
114	Jose Rosado	.05
115	Ken Caminiti	.15
116	Paul O'Neill	.15
117	Tim Salmon	.20
118	Eduardo Perez	.05
119	Mike Jackson	.05
120	John Smoltz	.10
121	Brant Brown	.05
122	John Mabry	.05
123	Chuck Knoblauch	.20
124	Reggie Sanders	.05
125	Ken Hill	.05
126	Mike Mussina	.40
127	Chad Curtis	.05
128	Todd Worrell	.05
129	Chris Widger	.05
130	Damon Mashore	.05
131	Kevin Brown	.10
132	Bip Roberts	.05
133	Tim Naehring	.05
134	Dave Martinez	.05
135	Jeff Blauser	.05
136	David Justice	.20
137	Dave Hollins	.05
138	Pat Hentgen	.05
139	Darren Daulton	.05
140	Ramon Martinez	.05
141	Raul Casanova	.05
142	Tom Glavine	.15
143	J.T. Snow	.05
144	Tony Graffanino	.05
145	Randy Johnson	.35
146	Orlando Merced	.05
147	Jeff Juden	.05
148	Darryl Kile	.05
149	Ray Durham	.05
150	Alex Fernandez	.05
151	Joey Cora	.05
152	Royce Clayton	.05
153	Randy Myers	.05
154	Charles Johnson	.05
155	Alan Benes	.05
156	Mike Bordick	.05
157	Heathcliff Slocumb	.05
158	Roger Bailey	.05
159	Reggie Jefferson	.05
160	Ricky Bottalico	.05
161	Scott Erickson	.05
162	Matt Williams	.20
163	Robb Nen	.05
164	Matt Stairs	.05
165	Ismael Valdes	.05
166	Lee Stevens	.05
167	Gary DiSarcina	.05
168	Brad Radke	.05
169	Mike Lansing	.05
170	Armando Benitez	.05
171	Mike James	.05
172	Russ Davis	.05
173	Lance Johnson	.05
174	Joey Hamilton	.05
175	John Valentin	.05
176	David Segui	.05
177	David Wells	.05
178	Delino DeShields	.05
179	Eric Karros	.10
180	Jim Leyritz	.05
181	Raul Mondesi	.15
182	Travis Fryman	.05
183	Todd Zeile	.05
184	Brian Jordan	.05
185	Rey Ordonez	.05
186	Jim Edmonds	.05
187	Terrell Wade	.05
188	Marquis Grissom	.10
189	Chris Snopek	.05
190	Shane Reynolds	.05
191	Jeff Frye	.05
192	Paul Sorrento	.05
193	James Baldwin	.05
194	Brian McRae	.05
195	Fred McGriff	.15
196	Troy Percival	.05
197	Rich Amaral	.05
198	Juan Guzman	.05
199	Cecil Fielder	.10
200	Willie Blair	.05
201	Chili Davis	.05
202	Gary Gaetti	.05
203	B.J. Surhoff	.05
204	Steve Cooke	.05
205	Chuck Finley	.05
206	Jeff Kent	.05
207	Ben McDonald	.05
208	Jeffrey Hammonds	.05
209	Tom Goodwin	.05
210	Billy Ashley	.05
211	Wil Cordero	.05
212	Shawon Dunston	.05
213	Tony Phillips	.05
214	Jamie Moyer	.05
215	John Jaha	.05
216	Troy O'Leary	.05
217	Brad Ausmus	.05
218	Garret Anderson	.05
219	Wilson Alvarez	.05
220	Kent Mercker	.05
221	Wade Boggs	.15
222	Mark Wohlers	.05
223	Kevin Appier	.05
224	Tony Fernandez	.05
225	Ugueth Urbina	.05
226	Gregg Jefferies	.05
227	Mo Vaughn	.50
228	Arthur Rhodes	.05
229	Jorge Fabregas	.05
230	Mark Gardner	.05
231	Shane Mack	.05
232	Jorge Posada	.05
233	Jose Cruz Jr.	.75
234	Paul Konerko	.60
235	Derrek Lee	.05
236	*Steve Woodard*	.15
237	Todd Dunwoody	.05
238	Fernando Tatis	.20
239	Jacob Cruz	.05
240	*Pokey Reese*	.05
241	Mark Kotsay	.30
242	Matt Morris	.05
243	*Antone Williamson*	.05
244	Ben Grieve	.60
245	Ryan McGuire	.05
246	*Lou Collier*	.05
247	*Shannon Stewart*	.05
248	*Brett Tomko*	.05
249	Bobby Estalella	.05
250	*Livan Hernandez*	.05
251	Todd Helton	.40
252	Jaret Wright	.75
253	Darryl Hamilton (Interleague Moments)	.05
254	Stan Javier (Interleague Moments)	.05
255	Glenallen Hill (Interleague Moments)	.05
256	Mark Gardner (Interleague Moments)	.05
257	Cal Ripken Jr. (Interleague Moments)	.75
258	Mike Mussina (Interleague Moments)	.20
259	Mike Piazza (Interleague Moments)	.60
260	Sammy Sosa (Interleague Moments)	.50
261	Todd Hundley (Interleague Moments)	.05
262	Eric Karros (Interleague Moments)	.05
263	Denny Neagle (Interleague Moments)	.05
264	Jeromy Burnitz (Interleague Moments)	.05
265	Greg Maddux (Interleague Moments)	.60
266	Tony Clark (Interleague Moments)	.20
267	Vladimir Guerrero (Interleague Moments)	.40
268	Checklist	.05
269	Checklist	.05
270	Checklist	.05

1998 Score Showcase

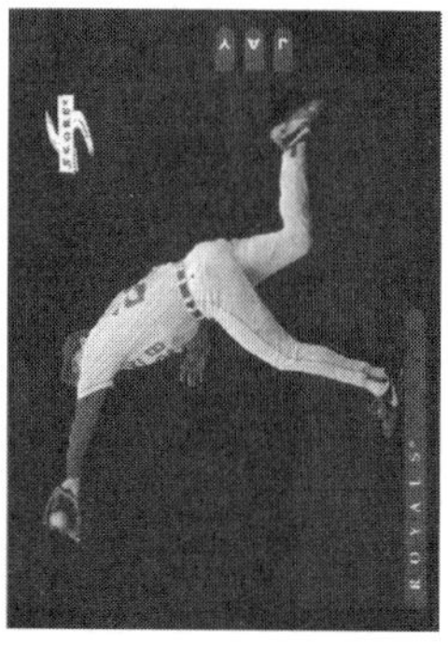

This partial parallel reprinted 160 of the 270 cards in Score Baseball on a foil surface. They were marked on the back and renumbered within the 160-card set. Showcase parallels were inserted one per seven packs.

	MT
Showcase Stars:	3x to 6x
Yng Stars & RCs:	2x to 4x
Inserted 1:7	

1998 Score Artist's Proofs

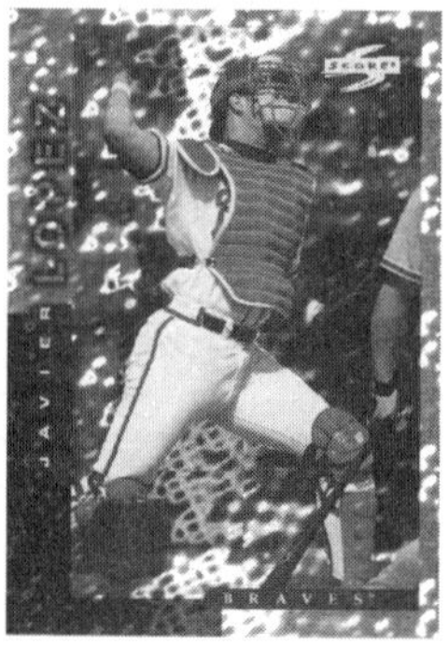

This partial parallel reprinted 160 of the 270 cards in Score Baseball on a foil background with an Artist's Proof logo on the front. The cards were renumbered within the 160 cards set and inserted one per 35 packs.

	MT
Artist's Proof Stars:	10x to 20x
Yng Stars & RCs:	8x to 15x
Inserted 1:35	

1998 Score All-Stars

All-Stars is a 20-card insert featuring the top players in baseball. The cards were inserted one per 35 packs.

		MT
Complete Set (20):		125.00
Common Player:		2.00
Inserted 1:35		
1	Mike Piazza	15.00
2	Ivan Rodriguez	6.00
3	Frank Thomas	20.00
4	Mark McGwire	30.00
5	Ryne Sandberg	6.00
6	Roberto Alomar	4.00
7	Cal Ripken Jr.	20.00
8	Barry Larkin	2.00
9	Paul Molitor	3.00
10	Travis Fryman	2.00
11	Kirby Puckett	6.00
12	Tony Gwynn	12.00
13	Ken Griffey Jr.	25.00
14	Juan Gonzalez	12.00
15	Barry Bonds	6.00
16	Andruw Jones	10.00
17	Roger Clemens	10.00
18	Randy Johnson	4.00
19	Greg Maddux	15.00
20	Dennis Eckersley	2.00

1998 Score Complete Players

Complete Players is a 30-card insert featuring 10 players who can do it all. Each player had three cards displaying their variety of skills. The cards feature holographic foil stamping and were inserted 1:5.

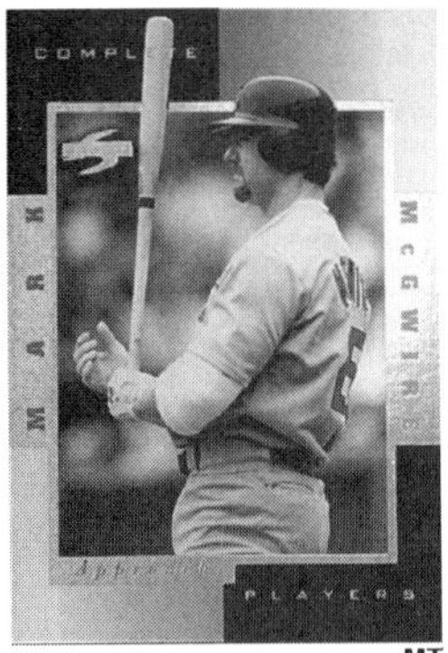

	MT
Complete Set (10):	60.00
Common Player:	1.50
Inserted 1:23	

1	Ken Griffey Jr.	12.00
2	Mark McGwire	15.00
3	Derek Jeter	8.00
4	Cal Ripken Jr.	10.00
5	Mike Piazza	8.00
6	Darin Erstad	4.00
7	Frank Thomas	10.00
8	Andruw Jones	6.00
9	Nomar Garciaparra	8.00
10	Manny Ramirez	3.00

1998 Score First Pitch

This 20-card set was exclusive to All-Star Edition packs of Score Baseball. First Pitch inserts were seeded one per 11 packs.

	MT
Complete Set (20):	60.00
Common Player:	1.50
Inserted 1:11 All-Star Edition	

1	Ken Griffey Jr.	8.00
2	Frank Thomas	5.00
3	Alex Rodriguez	5.00
4	Cal Ripken Jr.	6.00
5	Chipper Jones	5.00
6	Juan Gonzalez	4.00
7	Derek Jeter	4.00
8	Mike Piazza	5.00
9	Andruw Jones	2.00
10	Nomar Garciaparra	5.00
11	Barry Bonds	2.00
12	Jeff Bagwell	3.00
13	Scott Rolen	3.00
14	Hideo Nomo	1.50
15	Roger Clemens	3.00
16	Mark McGwire	10.00
17	Greg Maddux	5.00
18	Albert Belle	2.00
19	Ivan Rodriguez	2.00
20	Mo Vaughn	2.00

1998 Score Loaded Lineup

	MT
Complete Set (10):	60.00
Common Player:	2.50
Inserted 1:45 All-Star Edition	

LL1	Chuck Knoblauch	2.50
LL2	Tony Gwynn	8.00
LL3	Frank Thomas	10.00
LL4	Ken Griffey Jr.	15.00
LL5	Mike Piazza	10.00
LL6	Barry Bonds	4.00
LL7	Cal Ripken Jr.	12.00
LL8	Paul Molitor	3.00
LL9	Nomar Garciaparra	10.00
LL10	Greg Maddux	10.00

1998 Score New Season

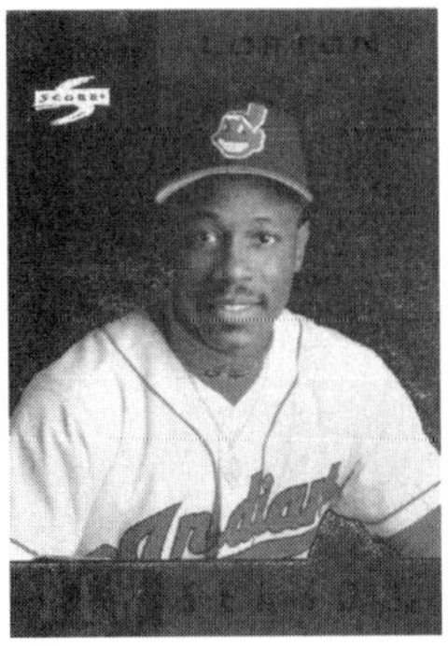

	MT
Complete Set (15):	60.00
Common Player:	2.00
Inserted 1:23 All-Star Edition	

NS1	Kenny Lofton	3.00
NS2	Nomar Garciaparra	8.00
NS3	Todd Helton	2.50
NS4	Miguel Tejada	2.00
NS5	Jaret Wright	4.00
NS6	Alex Rodriguez	8.00
NS7	Vladimir Guerrero	3.00
NS8	Ken Griffey Jr.	12.00
NS9	Ben Grieve	4.00
NS10	Travis Lee	6.00
NS11	Jose Cruz Jr.	3.00
NS12	Paul Konerko	2.00
NS13	Frank Thomas	8.00
NS14	Chipper Jones	8.00
NS15	Cal Ripken Jr.	10.00

1998 Score Rookie & Traded

Score Rookie/Traded consists of a 270-card base set. The base cards have a white and gray border with the player's name on the left. The Showcase Series parallels 110 base cards and was inserted 1:7. Artist's Proofs is a 50-card partial parallel done on prismatic foil and inserted 1:35. Inserts included All-Star Epix, Complete Players and Star Gazing.

	MT
Complete Set (270):	25.00
Common SP (1-50):	.25
Common Player (51-270):	.10
Paul Konerko Auto. (500):	50.00
Wax Box:	28.00

1	Tony Clark	.50
2	Juan Gonzalez	1.50
3	Frank Thomas	2.50
4	Greg Maddux	2.00
5	Barry Larkin	.40
6	Derek Jeter	1.50
7	Randy Johnson	.50
8	Roger Clemens	1.00
9	Tony Gwynn	1.50
10	Barry Bonds	.75
11	Jim Edmonds	.25
12	Bernie Williams	.50
13	Ken Griffey Jr.	3.00
14	Tim Salmon	.40
15	Mo Vaughn	.75
16	David Justice	.40
17	Jose Cruz Jr.	.50
18	Andruw Jones	.75
19	Sammy Sosa	1.25
20	Jeff Bagwell	1.00
21	Scott Rolen	1.00
22	Darin Erstad	.75
23	Andy Pettitte	.50
24	Mike Mussina	.50
25	Mark McGwire	3.00
26	Hideo Nomo	.50
27	Chipper Jones	2.00
28	Cal Ripken Jr.	2.50
29	Chuck Knoblauch	.40
30	Alex Rodriguez	2.00
31	Jim Thome	.50
32	Mike Piazza	2.00
33	Ivan Rodriguez	.75
34	Roberto Alomar	.50
35	Nomar Garciaparra	2.00
36	Albert Belle	.75
37	Vladimir Guerrero	.75
38	Raul Mondesi	.25
39	Larry Walker	.40
40	Manny Ramirez	.75
41	Tino Martinez	.40
42	Craig Biggio	.25
43	Jay Buhner	.40
44	Kenny Lofton	.75
45	Pedro Martinez	.60
46	Edgar Martinez	.25
47	Gary Sheffield	.30
48	Jose Guillen	.25
49	Ken Caminiti	.25
50	Bobby Higginson	.25
51	Alan Benes	.20
52	Shawn Green	.10
53	Ron Coomer	.10
54	Charles Nagy	.10
55	Steve Karsay	.10
56	Matt Morris	.10
57	Bobby Jones	.10
58	Jason Kendall	.10
59	Jeff Conine	.10
60	Joe Girardi	.10
61	Mark Kotsay	.30
62	Eric Karros	.20
63	Bartolo Colon	.10
64	Mariano Rivera	.20
65	Alex Gonzalez	.10
66	Scott Spiezio	.10
67	Luis Castillo	.10
68	Joey Cora	.10
69	Mark McLemore	.10
70	Reggie Jefferson	.10
71	Lance Johnson	.10
72	Damian Jackson	.10
73	Jeff D'Amico	.10
74	David Ortiz	.10
75	J.T. Snow	.10
76	Todd Hundley	.10
77	Billy Wagner	.10
78	Vinny Castilla	.20
79	Ismael Valdes	.10
80	Neifi Perez	.10
81	Derek Bell	.10
82	Ryan Klesko	.30
83	Rey Ordonez	.10
84	Carlos Garcia	.10
85	Curt Schilling	.20
86	Robin Ventura	.20
87	Pat Hentgen	.10
88	Glendon Rusch	.10
89	Hideki Irabu	.40
90	Antone Williamson	.10
91	Denny Neagle	.10
92	Kevin Orie	.10
93	Reggie Sanders	.10
94	Brady Anderson	.10
95	Andy Benes	.10
96	John Valentin	.10
97	Bobby Bonilla	.20
98	Walt Weiss	.10
99	Robin Jennings	.10
100	Marty Cordova	.10
101	Brad Ausmus	.10
102	Brian Rose	.10
103	Calvin Maduro	.10
104	Raul Casanova	.10
105	Jeff King	.10
106	Sandy Alomar	.20
107	Tim Naehring	.10
108	Mike Cameron	.10
109	Omar Vizquel	.10
110	Brad Radke	.10
111	Jeff Fassero	.10
112	Deivi Cruz	.10
113	Dave Hollins	.10
114	Dean Palmer	.10
115	Esteban Loaiza	.10
116	Brian Giles	.10
117	Steve Finley	.10
118	Jose Canseco	.25
119	Al Martin	.10
120	Eric Young	.10
121	Curtis Goodwin	.10
122	Ellis Burks	.10
123	Mike Hampton	.10
124	Lou Collier	.10
125	John Olerud	.20
126	Ramon Martinez	.10
127	Todd Dunwoody	.10
128	Jermaine Allensworth	.10
129	Eduardo Perez	.10
130	Dante Bichette	.25
131	Edgar Renteria	.10
132	Bob Abreu	.10
133	Rondell White	.20
134	Michael Coleman	.10
135	Jason Giambi	.10
136	Brant Brown	.10
137	Michael Tucker	.10
138	Dave Nilsson	.10
139	Benito Santiago	.10
140	Ray Durham	.10
141	Jeff Kent	.10
142	Matt Stairs	.10
143	Kevin Young	.10
144	Eric Davis	.10
145	John Wetteland	.10
146	Esteban Yan	.10
147	Wilton Guerrero	.10
148	Moises Alou	.20
149	Edgardo Alfonzo	.10
150	Andy Ashby	.10
151	Todd Walker	.20
152	Jermaine Dye	.10
153	Brian Hunter	.10
154	Shawn Estes	.10
155	Bernard Gilkey	.10
156	Tony Womack	.10
157	John Smoltz	.20
158	Delino DeShields	.10
159	Jacob Cruz	.10
160	Javier Valentin	.10
161	Chris Hoiles	.10
162	Garret Anderson	.10
163	Dan Wilson	.10
164	Paul O'Neill	.20
165	Matt Williams	.25
166	Travis Fryman	.10
167	Javier Lopez	.10
168	Ray Lankford	.10
169	Bobby Estalella	.10
170	Henry Rodriguez	.10
171	Quinton McCracken	.10
172	Jaret Wright	.50
173	Darryl Kile	.10
174	Wade Boggs	.25
175	Orel Hershiser	.10
176	B.J. Surhoff	.10
177	Fernando Tatis	.20
178	Carlos Delgado	.10
179	Jorge Fabregas	.10
180	Tony Saunders	.10
181	Devon White	.10
182	Dmitri Young	.10
183	Ryan McGuire	.10
184	Mark Bellhorn	.10
185	Joe Carter	.20
186	Kevin Stocker	.10
187	Mike Lansing	.10
188	Jason Dickson	.10
189	Charles Johnson	.10
190	Will Clark	.25
191	Shannon Stewart	.10
192	Johnny Damon	.10
193	Todd Greene	.10
194	Carlos Baerga	.10
195	David Cone	.20
196	Pokey Reese	.10
197	Livan Hernandez	.10
198	Tom Glavine	.20
199	Geronimo Berroa	.10
200	Darryl Hamilton	.10
201	Terry Steinbach	.10
202	Robb Nen	.10
203	Ron Gant	.10
204	Rafael Palmeiro	.25
205	Rickey Henderson	.10
206	Justin Thompson	.10
207	Jeff Suppan	.10
208	Kevin Brown	.20
209	Jimmy Key	.10
210	Brian Jordan	.10
211	Aaron Sele	.10
212	Fred McGriff	.20
213	Jay Bell	.10
214	Andres Galarraga	.25
215	Mark Grace	.25
216	Brett Tomko	.10
217	Francisco Cordova	.10
218	Rusty Greer	.10
219	Bubba Trammell	.10
220	Derrek Lee	.10
221	Brian Anderson	.10
222	Mark Grudzielanek	.10
223	Marquis Grissom	.10
224	Gary DiSarcina	.10
225	Jim Leyritz	.10
226	Jeffrey Hammonds	.10
227	Karim Garcia	.10
228	Chan Ho Park	.30
229	Brooks Kieschnick	.10
230	Trey Beamon	.10
231	Kevin Appier	.10
232	Wally Joyner	.10
233	Richie Sexson	.10
234	*Frank Catalanotto*	.20
235	Rafael Medina	.10
236	Travis Lee	1.50
237	Eli Marrero	.10
238	Carl Pavano	.25
239	Enrique Wilson	.10
240	Richard Hidalgo	.10
241	Todd Helton	.50
242	Ben Grieve	.75
243	Mario Valdez	.10
244	*Magglio Ordonez*	.50
245	Juan Encarnacion	.10
246	Russell Branyan	.10
247	Sean Casey	.20
248	Abraham Nunez	.10
249	Brad Fullmer	.25
250	Paul Konerko	.25
251	Miguel Tejada	.30
252	*Mike Lowell*	.30
253	Ken Griffey Jr. (Spring Training)	1.00
254	Frank Thomas (Spring Training)	.75
255	Alex Rodriguez (Spring Training)	.60
256	Jose Cruz Jr. (Spring Training)	.25
257	Jeff Bagwell (Spring Training)	.30
258	Chipper Jones (Spring Training)	.60
259	Mo Vaughn (Spring Training)	.25
260	Nomar Garciaparra (Spring Training)	.60
261	Jim Thome (Spring Training)	.20
262	Derek Jeter (Spring Training)	.50
263	Mike Piazza (Spring Training)	.60
264	Tony Gwynn (Spring Training)	.50
265	Scott Rolen (Spring Training)	.30
266	Andruw Jones (Spring Training)	.25
267	Cal Ripken Jr. (Spring Training)	.75
268	Checklist (Ken Griffey Jr.)	.75
269	Checklist (Cal Ripken Jr.)	.50
270	Checklist (Jose Cruz Jr.)	.20

1998 Score Rookie & Traded Showcase

Showcase partial parallel reprinted 160 of the 270 cards in Rookie & Traded. The cards were printed on a foil surface, marked on the back and renumbered within the 160-card set. Showcase parallels were inserted one per seven packs.

	MT
Showcase (1-50):	1.5x to 3x
Showcase (51-270):	2.5x to 4x
Inserted 1:7	

1998 Score Rookie & Traded Artist's Proofs

This partial parallel reprinted 160 of the 270 cards in Score Rookie & Traded. The cards were printed on a foil surface and featured an Artist's Proofs logo on the front. The cards were renumbered within the 160-card set and inserted one per 35 packs.

	MT
Artist's Proofs (1-50):	5x to 10x
A-P (51-270):	10x to 20x
Inserted 1:35	

1998 Score Rookie & Traded Complete Players

Complete Players is a 30-card insert seeded one per 11 packs. The set highlights 10 players who can do it all on the field. Each player has three cards showcasing one of their talents. The cards feature holographic foil stamping.

	MT
Complete Set (30):	90.00
Common Player:	1.50
3 cards per player	
Inserted 1:11	

1	Ken Griffey Jr.	8.00
2	Larry Walker	1.50
3	Alex Rodriguez	5.00
4	Jose Cruz	1.50
5	Jeff Bagwell	3.00
6	Greg Maddux	5.00
7	Ivan Rodriguez	2.50
8	Roger Clemens	3.00
9	Chipper Jones	5.00
10	Hideo Nomo	1.50

1998 Score Rookie & Traded Star Gazing

Printed on micro-etched foil board, Star Gazing features 20 top players and was seeded 1:35.

	MT
Complete Set (20):	150.00
Common Player:	3.00
Inserted 1:35	

1	Ken Griffey Jr.	20.00
2	Frank Thomas	15.00
3	Chipper Jones	12.00
4	Mark McGwire	25.00
5	Cal Ripken Jr.	15.00
6	Mike Piazza	12.00
7	Nomar Garciaparra	12.00
8	Derek Jeter	10.00
9	Juan Gonzalez	10.00
10	Vladimir Guerrero	5.00
11	Alex Rodriguez	12.00
12	Tony Gwynn	10.00
13	Andruw Jones	5.00
14	Scott Rolen	7.00
15	Jose Cruz	4.00
16	Mo Vaughn	5.00
17	Bernie Williams	4.00
18	Greg Maddux	12.00
19	Tony Clark	3.00
20	Ben Grieve	6.00

1998 Skybox Circa Thunder

The 1998 Circa Thunder set was issued as one series of 300 cards and sold in eight-card packs for $1.59. This set marked SkyBox's brand transition from Circa to Thunder so it named this product with both names. There are two card No. 8 in the set, but Marquis Grissom should be No. 280 (Cal Ripken is No. 8). There is also a Cal Ripken promo card that was sent to dealers and media. The card is identical to the base card, but has the words "Promotional Sample" written across the back. Inserts include: Rave and Super Rave parallels, Boss, Fast Track, Quick Strike, Limited Access, Rave Review and Thunder Boomers.

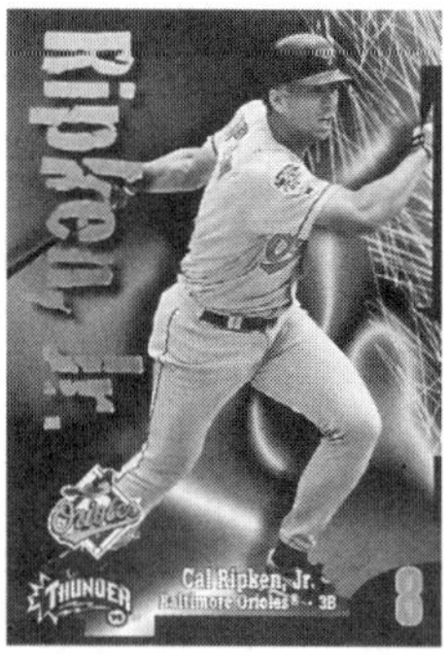

		MT
Complete Set (300):		25.00
Common Player:		.15
Wax Box:		50.00
1	Ben Grieve	1.25
2	Derek Jeter	2.00
3	Alex Rodriguez	2.00
4	Paul Molitor	.50
5	Nomar Garciaparra	2.00
6	Fred McGriff	.25
7	Kenny Lofton	.75
8	Cal Ripken Jr.	2.50
9	Matt Williams	.30
10	Chipper Jones	2.00
11	Barry Larkin	.25
12	Steve Finley	.15
13	Billy Wagner	.15
14	Rico Brogna	.15
15	Tim Salmon	.30
16	Hideo Nomo	.60
17	Tony Clark	.50
18	Jason Kendall	.15
19	Juan Gonzalez	1.50
20	Jeromy Burnitz	.15
21	Roger Clemens	1.00
22	Mark Grace	.30
23	Robin Ventura	.25
24	Manny Ramirez	.75
25	Mark McGwire	4.00
26	Gary Sheffield	.30
27	Vladimir Guerrero	.75
28	Butch Huskey	.15
29	Cecil Fielder	.25
30	Roderick Myers	.15
31	Greg Maddux	2.00
32	Bill Mueller	.15
33	Larry Walker	.30
34	Henry Rodriguez	.15
35	Mike Mussina	.60
36	Ricky Ledee	.25
37	Bobby Bonilla	.25
38	Curt Schilling	.30
39	Luis Gonzalez	.15
40	Troy Percival	.15
41	Eric Milton	.40
42	Mo Vaughn	.75
43	Raul Mondesi	.30
44	Kenny Rogers	.15
45	Frank Thomas	2.50
46	Jose Canseco	.30
47	Tom Glavine	.25
48	*Rich Butler*	.40
49	Jay Buhner	.25
50	Jose Cruz Jr.	1.00
51	Bernie Williams	.50
52	Doug Glanville	.15
53	Travis Fryman	.15
54	Rey Ordonez	.15
55	Jeff Conine	.15
56	Trevor Hoffman	.15
57	Kirk Rueter	.15
58	Ron Gant	.25
59	Carl Everett	.15
60	Joe Carter	.25
61	Livan Hernandez	.25
62	John Jaha	.15
63	Ivan Rodriguez	.75
64	Willie Blair	.15
65	Todd Helton	.75
66	Kevin Young	.15
67	Mike Caruso	.15
68	Steve Trachsel	.15
69	Marty Cordova	.15
70	Alex Fernandez	.15
71	Eric Karros	.25
72	Reggie Sanders	.15
73	Russ Davis	.15
74	Roberto Hernandez	.15
75	Barry Bonds	.75
76	Alex Gonzalez	.15
77	Roberto Alomar	.50
78	Troy O'Leary	.15
79	Bernard Gilkey	.15
80	Ismael Valdes	.15
81	Travis Lee	3.00
82	Brant Brown	.15
83	Gary DiSarcina	.15
84	Joe Randa	.15
85	Jaret Wright	1.50
86	Quilvio Veras	.15
87	Rickey Henderson	.15
88	Randall Simon	.25
89	Mariano Rivera	.25
90	Ugueth Urbina	.15
91	Fernando Vina	.15
92	Alan Benes	.25
93	Dante Bichette	.25
94	Karim Garcia	.15
95	A.J. Hinch	.75
96	Shane Reynolds	.15
97	Kevin Stocker	.15
98	John Wetteland	.15
99	Terry Steinbach	.15
100	Ken Griffey Jr.	3.00
101	Mike Cameron	.25
102	Damion Easley	.15
103	Randy Myers	.15
104	Jason Schmidt	.15
105	Jeff King	.15
106	Gregg Jefferies	.15
107	Sean Casey	.40
108	Mark Kotsay	.40
109	Brad Fullmer	.15
110	Wilson Alvarez	.15
111	Sandy Alomar Jr.	.25
112	Walt Weiss	.15
113	Doug Jones	.15
114	Andy Benes	.25
115	Paul O'Neill	.25
116	Dennis Eckersley	.15
117	Todd Greene	.15
118	Bobby Jones	.15
119	Darrin Fletcher	.15
120	Eric Young	.15
121	Jeffrey Hammonds	.15
122	Mickey Morandini	.15
123	Chuck Knoblauch	.40
124	Moises Alou	.25
125	Miguel Tejada	.50
126	Brian Anderson	.15
127	Edgar Renteria	.15
128	Mike Lansing	.15
129	Quinton McCracken	.15
130	Ray Lankford	.15
131	Andy Ashby	.15
132	Kelvim Escobar	.15
133	*Mike Lowell*	.25
134	Randy Johnson	.50
135	Andres Galarraga	.35
136	Armando Benitez	.15
137	Rusty Greer	.15
138	Jose Guillen	.25
139	Paul Konerko	.75
140	Edgardo Alfonzo	.15
141	Jim Leyritz	.15
142	Mark Clark	.15
143	Brian Johnson	.15
144	Scott Rolen	1.00
145	David Cone	.25
146	Jeff Shaw	.15
147	Shannon Stewart	.15
148	Brian Hunter	.15
149	Garret Anderson	.15
150	Jeff Bagwell	1.00
151	James Baldwin	.15
152	Devon White	.15
153	Jim Thome	.40
154	Wally Joyner	.15
155	Mark Wohlers	.15
156	Jeff Cirillo	.15
157	Jason Giambi	.15
158	Royce Clayton	.15
159	Dennis Reyes	.15
160	Raul Casanova	.15
161	Pedro Astacio	.15
162	Todd Dunwoody	.15
163	Sammy Sosa	1.50
164	Todd Hundley	.15
165	Wade Boggs	.25
166	Robb Nen	.15
167	Dan Wilson	.15
168	Hideki Irabu	.50
169	B.J. Surhoff	.15
170	Carlos Delgado	.15
171	Fernando Tatis	.15
172	Bob Abreu	.15
173	David Ortiz	.25
174	Tony Womack	.15
175	*Magglio Ordonez*	.75
176	Aaron Boone	.15
177	Brian Giles	.15
178	Kevin Appier	.15
179	Chuck Finley	.15
180	Brian Rose	.25
181	Ryan Klesko	.30
182	Mike Stanley	.15
183	Dave Nilsson	.15
184	Carlos Perez	.15
185	Jeff Blauser	.15
186	Richard Hidalgo	.15
187	Charles Johnson	.25
188	Vinny Castilla	.25
189	Joey Hamilton	.15
190	Bubba Trammell	.15
191	Eli Marrero	.15
192	Scott Erickson	.15
193	Pat Hentgen	.15
194	Jorge Fabregas	.15
195	Tino Martinez	.30
196	Bobby Higginson	.15
197	Dave Hollins	.15
198	*Rolando Arrojo*	.40
199	Joey Cora	.15
200	Mike Piazza	2.00
201	Reggie Jefferson	.15
202	John Smoltz	.25
203	Bobby Smith	.15
204	Tom Goodwin	.15
205	Omar Vizquel	.15
206	John Olerud	.25
207	Matt Stairs	.15
208	Bobby Estalella	.15
209	Miguel Cairo	.15
210	Shawn Green	.15
211	Jon Nunnally	.15
212	Al Leiter	.15
213	Matt Lawton	.15
214	Brady Anderson	.15
215	Jeff Kent	.15
216	Ray Durham	.15
217	Al Martin	.15
218	Jeff D'Amico	.15
219	Kevin Tapani	.15
220	Jim Edmonds	.25
221	Jose Vizcaino	.15
222	Jay Bell	.15
223	Ken Caminiti	.25
224	Craig Biggio	.30
225	Bartolo Colon	.25
226	Neifi Perez	.15
227	Delino DeShields	.15
228	Javier Lopez	.15
229	David Wells	.15
230	Brad Rigby	.15
231	John Franco	.15
232	Michael Coleman	.15
233	Edgar Martinez	.25
234	Francisco Cordova	.15
235	Johnny Damon	.15
236	Deivi Cruz	.15
237	J.T. Snow	.15
238	Enrique Wilson	.15
239	Rondell White	.25
240	Aaron Sele	.25
241	Tony Saunders	.15
242	Ricky Bottalico	.15
243	Cliff Floyd	.15
244	Chili Davis	.15
245	Brian McRae	.15
246	Brad Radke	.15
247	Chan Ho Park	.25
248	Lance Johnson	.15
249	Rafael Palmeiro	.25
250	Tony Gwynn	1.50
251	Denny Neagle	.15
252	Dean Palmer	.15
253	Jose Valentin	.15
254	Matt Morris	.15
255	Ellis Burks	.15
256	Jeff Suppan	.15
257	Jimmy Key	.15
258	Justin Thompson	.15
259	Brett Tomko	.15
260	Mark Grudzielanek	.15
261	Mike Hampton	.15
262	Jeff Fassero	.15
263	Charles Nagy	.15
264	Pedro Martinez	.40
265	Todd Zeile	.15
266	Will Clark	.30
267	Abraham Nunez	.15
268	Dave Martinez	.15
269	Jason Dickson	.15
270	Eric Davis	.15
271	Kevin Orie	.15
272	Derrek Lee	.25
273	Andruw Jones	.75
274	Juan Encarnacion	.15
275	Carlos Baerga	.15
276	Andy Pettitte	.50
277	Brent Brede	.15
278	Paul Sorrento	.15
279	Mike Lieberthal	.15
280	Marquis Grissom	.15
281	Darin Erstad	.75
282	Willie Greene	.15
283	Derek Bell	.15
284	Scott Spiezio	.15
285	David Segui	.15
286	Albert Belle	.75
287	Ramon Martinez	.15
288	Jeremi Gonzalez	.15
289	Shawn Estes	.15
290	Ron Coomer	.15
291	John Valentin	.15
292	Kevin Brown	.15
293	Michael Tucker	.15
294	Brian Jordan	.15
295	Darryl Kile	.15
296	David Justice	.30
297	Jose Cruz Jr. CL	.50
298	Ken Griffey Jr. CL	1.50
299	Alex Rodriguez CL	1.00
300	Frank Thomas CL	1.25

1998 Skybox Circa Thunder Rave

Rave paralleled each card in Circa Thunder except for the four checklist cards. A special silver sparkling foil is used on the player's name and the Thunder logo on the card front. This 296-card set was inserted approximately one per 36 packs and sequentially numbered to 150 sets on the back.

		MT
Common Player:		10.00
Semistars:		25.00
Production 150 sets		
1	Ben Grieve	60.00
2	Derek Jeter	100.00
3	Alex Rodriguez	120.00
4	Paul Molitor	40.00
5	Nomar Garciaparra	120.00
6	Fred McGriff	25.00
7	Kenny Lofton	50.00
8	Cal Ripken Jr.	150.00
9	Matt Williams	25.00
10	Chipper Jones	120.00
11	Barry Larkin	25.00
12	Steve Finley	10.00
13	Billy Wagner	10.00
14	Rico Brogna	10.00
15	Tim Salmon	25.00
16	Hideo Nomo	40.00
17	Tony Clark	40.00
18	Jason Kendall	10.00
19	Juan Gonzalez	100.00
20	Jeromy Burnitz	10.00
21	Roger Clemens	80.00
22	Mark Grace	25.00
23	Robin Ventura	20.00
24	Manny Ramirez	50.00
25	Mark McGwire	200.00
26	Gary Sheffield	25.00
27	Vladimir Guerrero	50.00
28	Butch Huskey	10.00
29	Cecil Fielder	20.00
30	Roderick Myers	10.00
31	Greg Maddux	120.00
32	Bill Mueller	10.00
33	Larry Walker	30.00
34	Henry Rodriguez	10.00
35	Mike Mussina	40.00
36	Ricky Ledee	20.00
37	Bobby Bonilla	20.00
38	Curt Schilling	20.00
39	Luis Gonzalez	10.00
40	Troy Percival	10.00
41	Eric Milton	25.00
42	Mo Vaughn	50.00
43	Raul Mondesi	25.00
44	Kenny Rogers	10.00
45	Frank Thomas	150.00
46	Jose Canseco	25.00
47	Tom Glavine	20.00
48	Rich Butler	10.00
49	Jay Buhner	20.00
50	Jose Cruz Jr.	50.00
51	Bernie Williams	40.00
52	Doug Glanville	10.00
53	Travis Fryman	10.00
54	Rey Ordonez	10.00
55	Jeff Conine	10.00
56	Trevor Hoffman	10.00
57	Kirk Rueter	10.00
58	Ron Gant	20.00
59	Carl Everett	10.00
60	Joe Carter	20.00
61	Livan Hernandez	20.00
62	John Jaha	10.00
63	Ivan Rodriguez	50.00
64	Willie Blair	10.00
65	Todd Helton	40.00
66	Kevin Young	10.00
67	Mike Caruso	10.00
68	Steve Trachsel	10.00
69	Marty Cordova	10.00
70	Alex Fernandez	10.00
71	Eric Karros	20.00
72	Reggie Sanders	10.00
73	Russ Davis	10.00
74	Roberto Hernandez	10.00
75	Barry Bonds	50.00
76	Alex Gonzalez	10.00
77	Roberto Alomar	40.00
78	Troy O'Leary	10.00
79	Bernard Gilkey	10.00
80	Ismael Valdes	10.00
81	Travis Lee	125.00
82	Brant Brown	10.00
83	Gary DiSarcina	10.00
84	Joe Randa	10.00
85	Jaret Wright	75.00
86	Quilvio Veras	10.00
87	Rickey Henderson	10.00
88	Randall Simon	10.00
89	Mariano Rivera	20.00
90	Ugueth Urbina	10.00
91	Fernando Vina	10.00
92	Alan Benes	20.00
93	Dante Bichette	25.00
94	Karim Garcia	10.00
95	A.J. Hinch	25.00
96	Shane Reynolds	10.00
97	Kevin Stocker	10.00
98	John Wetteland	10.00
99	Terry Steinbach	10.00
100	Ken Griffey Jr.	200.00
101	Mike Cameron	10.00
102	Damion Easley	10.00
103	Randy Myers	10.00
104	Jason Schmidt	10.00
105	Jeff King	10.00
106	Gregg Jefferies	10.00
107	Sean Casey	25.00
108	Mark Kotsay	30.00
109	Brad Fullmer	20.00
110	Wilson Alvarez	10.00
111	Sandy Alomar Jr.	20.00
112	Walt Weiss	10.00
113	Doug Jones	10.00
114	Andy Benes	20.00
115	Paul O'Neill	20.00
116	Dennis Eckersley	20.00
117	Todd Greene	10.00
118	Bobby Jones	10.00
119	Darrin Fletcher	10.00
120	Eric Young	10.00
121	Jeffrey Hammonds	10.00
122	Mickey Morandini	10.00
123	Chuck Knoblauch	25.00
124	Moises Alou	20.00
125	Miguel Tejada	30.00
126	Brian Anderson	10.00
127	Edgar Renteria	10.00
128	Mike Lansing	10.00
129	Quinton McCracken	10.00
130	Ray Lankford	10.00
131	Andy Ashby	10.00
132	Kelvim Escobar	10.00
133	Mike Lowell	10.00
134	Randy Johnson	40.00
135	Andres Galarraga	25.00
136	Armando Benitez	10.00
137	Rusty Greer	10.00
138	Jose Guillen	20.00
139	Paul Konerko	25.00
140	Edgardo Alfonzo	10.00
141	Jim Leyritz	10.00
142	Mark Clark	10.00
143	Brian Johnson	10.00
144	Scott Rolen	75.00
145	David Cone	20.00
146	Jeff Shaw	10.00
147	Shannon Stewart	10.00
148	Brian Hunter	10.00
149	Garret Anderson	10.00
150	Jeff Bagwell	80.00
151	James Baldwin	10.00
152	Devon White	10.00
153	Jim Thome	40.00
154	Wally Joyner	10.00
155	Mark Wohlers	10.00
156	Jeff Cirillo	10.00
157	Jason Giambi	10.00
158	Royce Clayton	10.00
159	Dennis Reyes	10.00
160	Raul Casanova	10.00
161	Pedro Astacio	10.00
162	Todd Dunwoody	10.00
163	Sammy Sosa	100.00
164	Todd Hundley	10.00
165	Wade Boggs	20.00
166	Robb Nen	10.00
167	Dan Wilson	10.00
168	Hideki Irabu	40.00
169	B.J. Surhoff	10.00
170	Carlos Delgado	10.00
171	Fernando Tatis	10.00
172	Bob Abreu	10.00
173	David Ortiz	10.00
174	Tony Womack	10.00
175	Magglio Ordonez	25.00
176	Aaron Boone	10.00
177	Brian Giles	10.00
178	Kevin Appier	10.00
179	Chuck Finley	10.00
180	Brian Rose	20.00
181	Ryan Klesko	25.00
182	Mike Stanley	10.00
183	Dave Nilsson	10.00
184	Carlos Perez	10.00
185	Jeff Blauser	10.00
186	Richard Hidalgo	10.00
187	Charles Johnson	20.00
188	Vinny Castilla	20.00
189	Joey Hamilton	10.00
190	Bubba Trammell	10.00
191	Eli Marrero	10.00
192	Scott Erickson	10.00
193	Pat Hentgen	10.00
194	Jorge Fabregas	10.00
195	Tino Martinez	25.00
196	Bobby Higginson	10.00
197	Dave Hollins	10.00
198	Rolando Arrojo	10.00
199	Joey Cora	10.00
200	Mike Piazza	120.00
201	Reggie Jefferson	10.00
202	John Smoltz	20.00
203	Bobby Smith	10.00
204	Tom Goodwin	10.00
205	Omar Vizquel	10.00
206	John Olerud	20.00
207	Matt Stairs	10.00
208	Bobby Estalella	10.00
209	Miguel Cairo	10.00
210	Shawn Green	10.00
211	Jon Nunnally	10.00
212	Al Leiter	10.00
213	Matt Lawton	10.00
214	Brady Anderson	10.00
215	Jeff Kent	10.00
216	Ray Durham	10.00
217	Al Martin	10.00
218	Jeff D'Amico	10.00
219	Kevin Tapani	10.00
220	Jim Edmonds	20.00
221	Jose Vizcaino	10.00

222	Jay Bell	10.00
223	Ken Caminiti	20.00
224	Craig Biggio	25.00
225	Bartolo Colon	20.00
226	Neifi Perez	10.00
227	Delino DeShields	10.00
228	Javier Lopez	20.00
229	David Wells	10.00
230	Brad Rigby	10.00
231	John Franco	10.00
232	Michael Coleman	10.00
233	Edgar Martinez	20.00
234	Francisco Cordova	10.00
235	Johnny Damon	10.00
236	Deivi Cruz	10.00
237	J.T. Snow	10.00
238	Enrique Wilson	10.00
239	Rondell White	20.00
240	Aaron Sele	10.00
241	Tony Saunders	10.00
242	Ricky Bottalico	10.00
243	Cliff Floyd	10.00
244	Chili Davis	10.00
245	Brian McRae	10.00
246	Brad Radke	10.00
247	Chan Ho Park	25.00
248	Lance Johnson	10.00
249	Rafael Palmeiro	25.00
250	Tony Gwynn	100.00
251	Denny Neagle	10.00
252	Dean Palmer	10.00
253	Jose Valentin	10.00
254	Matt Morris	10.00
255	Ellis Burks	10.00
256	Jeff Suppan	10.00
257	Jimmy Key	10.00
258	Justin Thompson	10.00
259	Brett Tomko	10.00
260	Mark Grudzielanek	10.00
261	Mike Hampton	10.00
262	Jeff Fassero	10.00
263	Charles Nagy	10.00
264	Pedro Martinez	30.00
265	Todd Zeile	10.00
266	Will Clark	25.00
267	Abraham Nunez	10.00
268	Dave Martinez	10.00
269	Jason Dickson	10.00
270	Eric Davis	10.00
271	Kevin Orie	10.00
272	Derrek Lee	10.00
273	Andruw Jones	50.00
274	Juan Encarnacion	10.00
275	Carlos Baerga	10.00
276	Andy Pettitte	40.00
277	Brent Brede	10.00
278	Paul Sorrento	10.00
279	Mike Lieberthal	10.00
280	Marquis Grissom	10.00
281	Darin Erstad	50.00
282	Willie Greene	10.00
283	Derek Bell	10.00
284	Scott Spiezio	10.00
285	David Segui	10.00
286	Albert Belle	50.00
287	Ramon Martinez	10.00
288	Jeremi Gonzalez	10.00
289	Shawn Estes	10.00
290	Ron Coomer	10.00
291	John Valentin	10.00
292	Kevin Brown	10.00
293	Michael Tucker	10.00
294	Brian Jordan	10.00
295	Darryl Kile	10.00
296	David Justice	25.00
297	Jose Cruz Jr. CL	25.00
298	Ken Griffey Jr. CL	100.00
299	Alex Rodriguez CL	60.00
300	Frank Thomas CL	75.00

1998 Skybox Circa Thunder Super Rave

Only 25 Super Rave parallel sets were printed and they were inserted approximately one per 216 packs. The set contains 296 cards in total, which is 300 minus the four checklist cards. Fronts are identified by sparkling gold foil on the player's name and the Thunder logo, with sequential numbering on the back to 25.

		MT
Common Player:		40.00
Semistars:		80.00
Production 25 sets		
1	Ben Grieve	250.00
2	Derek Jeter	500.00
3	Alex Rodriguez	600.00
4	Paul Molitor	160.00
5	Nomar Garciaparra	500.00
6	Fred McGriff	80.00
7	Kenny Lofton	250.00
8	Cal Ripken Jr.	750.00
9	Matt Williams	80.00
10	Chipper Jones	500.00
11	Barry Larkin	80.00
12	Steve Finley	40.00
13	Billy Wagner	40.00
14	Rico Brogna	40.00
15	Tim Salmon	125.00
16	Hideo Nomo	200.00
17	Tony Clark	150.00
18	Jason Kendall	40.00
19	Juan Gonzalez	500.00
20	Jeromy Burnitz	40.00
21	Roger Clemens	400.00
22	Mark Grace	80.00
23	Robin Ventura	60.00
24	Manny Ramirez	200.00
25	Mark McGwire	800.00
26	Gary Sheffield	80.00
27	Vladimir Guerrero	200.00
28	Butch Huskey	40.00
29	Cecil Fielder	60.00
30	Roderick Myers	40.00
31	Greg Maddux	600.00
32	Bill Mueller	40.00
33	Larry Walker	100.00
34	Henry Rodriguez	40.00
35	Mike Mussina	200.00
36	Ricky Ledee	60.00
37	Bobby Bonilla	60.00
38	Curt Schilling	60.00
39	Luis Gonzalez	40.00
40	Troy Percival	40.00
41	Eric Milton	60.00
42	Mo Vaughn	250.00
43	Raul Mondesi	80.00
44	Kenny Rogers	40.00
45	Frank Thomas	750.00
46	Jose Canseco	80.00
47	Tom Glavine	60.00
48	Rich Butler	40.00
49	Jay Buhner	80.00
50	Jose Cruz Jr.	250.00
51	Bernie Williams	175.00
52	Doug Glanville	40.00
53	Travis Fryman	60.00
54	Rey Ordonez	40.00
55	Jeff Conine	40.00
56	Trevor Hoffman	40.00
57	Kirk Rueter	40.00
58	Ron Gant	60.00
59	Carl Everett	40.00
60	Joe Carter	60.00
61	Livan Hernandez	60.00
62	John Jaha	40.00
63	Ivan Rodriguez	250.00
64	Willie Blair	40.00
65	Todd Helton	200.00
66	Kevin Young	40.00
67	Mike Caruso	40.00
68	Steve Trachsel	40.00
69	Marty Cordova	40.00
70	Alex Fernandez	40.00
71	Eric Karros	60.00
72	Reggie Sanders	40.00
73	Russ Davis	40.00
74	Roberto Hernandez	40.00
75	Barry Bonds	250.00
76	Alex Gonzalez	40.00
77	Roberto Alomar	180.00
78	Troy O'Leary	40.00
79	Bernard Gilkey	40.00
80	Ismael Valdes	40.00
81	Travis Lee	500.00
82	Brant Brown	40.00
83	Gary DiSarcina	40.00
84	Joe Randa	40.00
85	Jaret Wright	350.00
86	Quilvio Veras	40.00
87	Rickey Henderson	60.00
88	Randall Simon	40.00
89	Mariano Rivera	60.00
90	Ugueth Urbina	40.00
91	Fernando Vina	40.00
92	Alan Benes	60.00
93	Dante Bichette	80.00
94	Karim Garcia	40.00
95	A.J. Hinch	60.00
96	Shane Reynolds	40.00
97	Kevin Stocker	40.00
98	John Wetteland	40.00
99	Terry Steinbach	40.00
100	Ken Griffey Jr.	1000.
101	Mike Cameron	40.00
102	Damion Easley	40.00
103	Randy Myers	40.00
104	Jason Schmidt	40.00
105	Jeff King	40.00
106	Gregg Jefferies	40.00
107	Sean Casey	75.00
108	Mark Kotsay	75.00
109	Brad Fullmer	75.00
110	Wilson Alvarez	40.00
111	Sandy Alomar Jr.	60.00
112	Walt Weiss	40.00
113	Doug Jones	40.00
114	Andy Benes	60.00
115	Paul O'Neill	70.00
116	Dennis Eckersley	60.00
117	Todd Greene	40.00
118	Bobby Jones	40.00
119	Darrin Fletcher	40.00
120	Eric Young	40.00
121	Jeffrey Hammonds	40.00
122	Mickey Morandini	40.00
123	Chuck Knoblauch	80.00
124	Moises Alou	60.00
125	Miguel Tejada	80.00
126	Brian Anderson	40.00
127	Edgar Renteria	40.00
128	Mike Lansing	40.00
129	Quinton McCracken	40.00
130	Ray Lankford	40.00
131	Andy Ashby	40.00
132	Kelvim Escobar	40.00
133	Mike Lowell	40.00
134	Randy Johnson	200.00
135	Andres Galarraga	80.00
136	Armando Benitez	40.00
137	Rusty Greer	40.00
138	Jose Guillen	60.00
139	Paul Konerko	60.00
140	Edgardo Alfonzo	40.00
141	Jim Leyritz	40.00
142	Mark Clark	40.00
143	Brian Johnson	40.00
144	Scott Rolen	300.00
145	David Cone	60.00
146	Jeff Shaw	40.00
147	Shannon Stewart	40.00
148	Brian Hunter	40.00
149	Garret Anderson	40.00
150	Jeff Bagwell	400.00
151	James Baldwin	40.00
152	Devon White	40.00
153	Jim Thome	150.00
154	Wally Joyner	40.00
155	Mark Wohlers	40.00
156	Jeff Cirillo	40.00
157	Jason Giambi	40.00
158	Royce Clayton	40.00
159	Dennis Reyes	40.00
160	Raul Casanova	40.00
161	Pedro Astacio	40.00
162	Todd Dunwoody	40.00
163	Sammy Sosa	300.00
164	Todd Hundley	40.00
165	Wade Boggs	80.00
166	Robb Nen	40.00
167	Dan Wilson	40.00
168	Hideki Irabu	100.00
169	B.J. Surhoff	40.00
170	Carlos Delgado	40.00
171	Fernando Tatis	40.00
172	Bob Abreu	40.00
173	David Ortiz	40.00
174	Tony Womack	40.00
175	Magglio Ordonez	80.00
176	Aaron Boone	40.00
177	Brian Giles	40.00
178	Kevin Appier	40.00
179	Chuck Finley	40.00
180	Brian Rose	60.00
181	Ryan Klesko	80.00
182	Mike Stanley	40.00
183	Dave Nilsson	40.00
184	Carlos Perez	40.00
185	Jeff Blauser	40.00
186	Richard Hidalgo	40.00
187	Charles Johnson	60.00
188	Vinny Castilla	80.00
189	Joey Hamilton	40.00
190	Bubba Trammell	40.00
191	Eli Marrero	40.00
192	Scott Erickson	40.00
193	Pat Hentgen	40.00
194	Jorge Fabregas	40.00
195	Tino Martinez	80.00
196	Bobby Higginson	40.00
197	Dave Hollins	40.00
198	Rolando Arrojo	40.00
199	Joey Cora	40.00
200	Mike Piazza	600.00
201	Reggie Jefferson	40.00
202	John Smoltz	60.00
203	Bobby Smith	40.00
204	Tom Goodwin	40.00
205	Omar Vizquel	60.00
206	John Olerud	60.00
207	Matt Stairs	40.00
208	Bobby Estalella	40.00
209	Miguel Cairo	40.00
210	Shawn Green	40.00
211	Jon Nunnally	40.00
212	Al Leiter	40.00
213	Matt Lawton	40.00
214	Brady Anderson	60.00
215	Jeff Kent	40.00
216	Ray Durham	40.00
217	Al Martin	40.00
218	Jeff D'Amico	40.00
219	Kevin Tapani	40.00
220	Jim Edmonds	60.00
221	Jose Vizcaino	40.00
222	Jay Bell	40.00
223	Ken Caminiti	60.00
224	Craig Biggio	80.00
225	Bartolo Colon	60.00
226	Neifi Perez	40.00
227	Delino DeShields	40.00
228	Javier Lopez	60.00
229	David Wells	40.00
230	Brad Rigby	40.00
231	John Franco	40.00
232	Michael Coleman	40.00
233	Edgar Martinez	60.00
234	Francisco Cordova	40.00
235	Johnny Damon	40.00
236	Deivi Cruz	40.00
237	J.T. Snow	40.00
238	Enrique Wilson	40.00
239	Rondell White	60.00
240	Aaron Sele	40.00
241	Tony Saunders	40.00
242	Ricky Bottalico	40.00
243	Cliff Floyd	40.00
244	Chili Davis	40.00
245	Brian McRae	40.00
246	Brad Radke	40.00
247	Chan Ho Park	80.00
248	Lance Johnson	40.00
249	Rafael Palmeiro	80.00
250	Tony Gwynn	500.00
251	Denny Neagle	40.00
252	Dean Palmer	40.00
253	Jose Valentin	40.00
254	Matt Morris	40.00
255	Ellis Burks	40.00
256	Jeff Suppan	40.00
257	Jimmy Key	40.00
258	Justin Thompson	40.00
259	Brett Tomko	40.00
260	Mark Grudzielanek	40.00
261	Mike Hampton	40.00
262	Jeff Fassero	40.00
263	Charles Nagy	40.00
264	Pedro Martinez	100.00
265	Todd Zeile	40.00
266	Will Clark	80.00
267	Abraham Nunez	40.00
268	Dave Martinez	40.00
269	Jason Dickson	40.00
270	Eric Davis	40.00
271	Kevin Orie	40.00
272	Derrek Lee	40.00
273	Andruw Jones	200.00
274	Juan Encarnacion	40.00
275	Carlos Baerga	40.00
276	Andy Pettitte	150.00
277	Brent Brede	40.00
278	Paul Sorrento	40.00
279	Mike Lieberthal	40.00
280	Marquis Grissom	40.00
281	Darin Erstad	200.00
282	Willie Greene	40.00
283	Derek Bell	40.00
284	Scott Spiezio	40.00
285	David Segui	40.00
286	Albert Belle	250.00
287	Ramon Martinez	40.00
288	Jeremi Gonzalez	40.00
289	Shawn Estes	40.00
290	Ron Coomer	40.00
291	John Valentin	40.00
292	Kevin Brown	40.00
293	Michael Tucker	40.00
294	Brian Jordan	40.00
295	Darryl Kile	40.00
296	David Justice	80.00
297	Jose Cruz Jr. CL	125.00
298	Ken Griffey Jr. CL	500.00
299	Alex Rodriguez CL	300.00
300	Frank Thomas CL	350.00

1998 Skybox Circa Thunder Boss

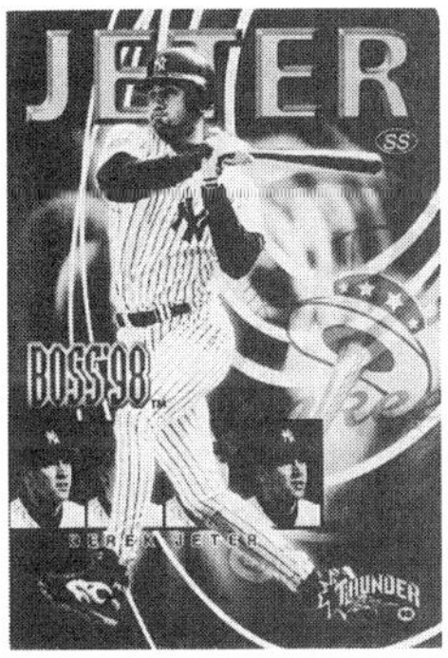

This 20-card insert set was seeded one per six packs of Circa Thunder. Cards are embossed with the player's last name printed in large letters across the top.

		MT
Complete Set (20):		50.00
Common Player:		1.00
Inserted 1:6		
1B	Jeff Bagwell	2.50
2B	Barry Bonds	1.50
3B	Roger Clemens	2.50
4B	Jose Cruz Jr.	2.00
5B	Nomar Garciaparra	4.00
6B	Juan Gonzalez	3.00
7B	Ken Griffey Jr.	6.00
8B	Tony Gwynn	3.00
9B	Derek Jeter	3.00
10B	Chipper Jones	4.00
11B	Travis Lee	4.00
12B	Greg Maddux	4.00
13B	Pedro Martinez	1.00
14B	Mark McGwire	8.00
15B	Mike Piazza	4.00
16B	Cal Ripken Jr.	5.00
17B	Alex Rodriguez	4.00
18B	Scott Rolen	2.00
19B	Frank Thomas	5.00
20B	Larry Walker	1.00

1998 Skybox Circa Thunder Fast Track

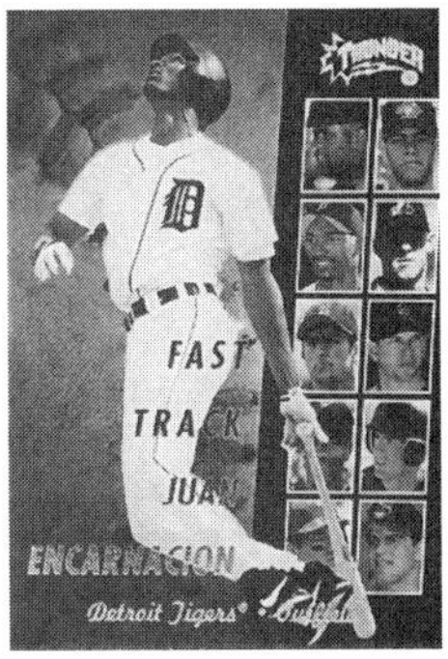

This 10-card insert showcases some of the top young stars in baseball and was seeded one per 24 packs of Circa. Card fronts picture the player over a closeup of a gold foil baseball on the left. The right side has smaller head shots of all 10 players with the featured player's head in gold foil.

		MT
Complete Set (10):		35.00
Common Player:		1.50
Inserted 1:24		
1FT	Jose Cruz Jr.	5.00
2FT	Juan Encarnacion	1.50
3FT	Brad Fullmer	3.00
4FT	Nomar Garciaparra	6.00
5FT	Todd Helton	3.00
6FT	Livan Hernandez	1.50
7FT	Travis Lee	10.00
8FT	Neifi Perez	1.50
9FT	Scott Rolen	4.00
10FT	Jaret Wright	5.00

1998 Skybox Circa Thunder Limited Access

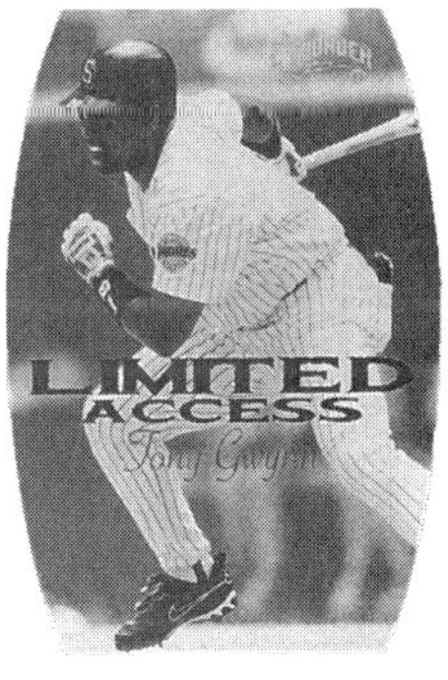

This 15-card, retail exclusive insert was seeded one per 18 packs. The cards were bi-fold and die-cut with foil stamping on the front. The theme of the insert was to provide an in-depth statistical scouting analysis of each player.

		MT
Complete Set (15):		90.00
Common Player:		2.00
Inserted 1:18		
1LA	Jeff Bagwell	6.00
2LA	Roger Clemens	6.00
3LA	Jose Cruz Jr.	6.00
4LA	Nomar Garciaparra	10.00
5LA	Juan Gonzalez	8.00
6LA	Ken Griffey Jr.	15.00
7LA	Tony Gwynn	8.00
8LA	Derek Jeter	8.00
9LA	Greg Maddux	10.00
10LA	Pedro Martinez	2.00
11LA	Mark McGwire	20.00
12LA	Mike Piazza	10.00
13LA	Alex Rodriguez	10.00
14LA	Frank Thomas	12.00
15LA	Larry Walker	2.00

1998 Skybox Circa Thunder Quick Strike

This insert pictures 12 different players over a colorful foil-board front that is die-cut. Quick Strikes were seeded one per 36 packs of Circa Thunder.

		MT
Complete Set (12):		90.00
Common Player:		3.00
Inserted 1:36		
1QS	Jeff Bagwell	8.00
2QS	Roger Clemens	8.00
3QS	Jose Cruz Jr.	8.00
4QS	Nomar Garciaparra	12.00
5QS	Ken Griffey Jr.	20.00
6QS	Greg Maddux	12.00
7QS	Pedro Martinez	3.00
8QS	Mark McGwire	25.00
9QS	Mike Piazza	12.00
10QS	Alex Rodriguez	12.00
11QS	Frank Thomas	15.00
12QS	Larry Walker	3.00

1998 Skybox Circa Thunder Rave Reviews

Rave Reviews were inserted at one per 288 packs of Circa Thunder. The cards were die-cut in a horizontal design with bronze foil etching and the image of a ball field in the background. This was the most difficult insert to pull from packs of Circa Thunder at one per 288 packs.

		MT
Complete Set (15):		500.00
Common Player:		15.00
Inserted 1:288		
1RR	Jeff Bagwell	30.00
2RR	Barry Bonds	20.00
3RR	Roger Clemens	35.00
4RR	Jose Cruz Jr.	20.00
5RR	Nomar Garciaparra	50.00
6RR	Juan Gonzalez	40.00
7RR	Ken Griffey Jr.	80.00
8RR	Tony Gwynn	40.00
9RR	Derek Jeter	50.00
10RR	Greg Maddux	50.00
11RR	Mark McGwire	100.00
12RR	Mike Piazza	50.00
13RR	Alex Rodriguez	50.00
14RR	Frank Thomas	50.00
15RR	Larry Walker	15.00

1998 Skybox Circa Thunder Thunder Boomers

Thunder Boomers featured top power hitters imposed over a see-through cloud-like plastic center with the imagery of a wooden fence with a large hole blasted through the middle of it. This 12-card set was inserted one per 96 packs of Circa Thunder.

		MT
Complete Set (12):		150.00
Common Player:		5.00
Inserted 1:96		
1TB	Jeff Bagwell	15.00
2TB	Barry Bonds	10.00
3TB	Jay Buhner	5.00
4TB	Andres Galarraga	5.00
5TB	Juan Gonzalez	20.00
6TB	Ken Griffey Jr.	40.00
7TB	Tino Martinez	5.00
8TB	Mark McGwire	45.00
9TB	Mike Piazza	25.00
10TB	Frank Thomas	30.00
11TB	Jim Thome	6.00
12TB	Larry Walker	5.00

1998 SkyBox Dugout Axcess

Dugout Axcess was a 150-card set that attempted to provide collectors with an inside look at baseball. The cards were printed on "playing card" quality stock and used unique information and photography. The product arrived in 12-card packs with an Inside Axcess parallel set that was individually numbered to 50 sets. Six different inserts sets were available, including Double Header, Frequent Flyers, Dishwashers, Superheroes, Gronks and Autograph Redemptions.

		MT
Complete Set (150):		20.00
Common Player:		.10
Wax Box:		45.00
1	Travis Lee	1.00
2	Matt Williams	.25
3	Andy Benes	.15
4	Chipper Jones	1.50
5	Ryan Klesko	.25
6	Greg Maddux	1.50
7	Sammy Sosa	1.25
8	Henry Rodriguez	.10

9	Mark Grace	.25
10	Barry Larkin	.20
11	Bret Boone	.10
12	Reggie Sanders	.10
13	Vinny Castilla	.10
14	Larry Walker	.30
15	Darryl Kile	.10
16	Charles Johnson	.10
17	Edgar Renteria	.10
18	Gary Sheffield	.30
19	Jeff Bagwell	.75
20	Craig Biggio	.20
21	Moises Alou	.20
22	Mike Piazza	1.50
23	Hideo Nomo	.40
24	Raul Mondesi	.20
25	John Jaha	.10
26	Jeff Cirillo	.10
27	Jeromy Burnitz	.10
28	Mark Grudzielanek	.10
29	Vladimir Guerrero	.60
30	Rondell White	.20
31	Edgardo Alfonzo	.10
32	Rey Ordonez	.10
33	Bernard Gilkey	.10
34	Scott Rolen	.75
35	Curt Schilling	.20
36	Ricky Bottalico	.10
37	Tony Womack	.10
38	Al Martin	.10
39	Jason Kendall	.10
40	Ron Gant	.20
41	Mark McGwire	3.00
42	Ray Lankford	.10
43	Tony Gwynn	1.25
44	Ken Caminiti	.20
45	Kevin Brown	.10
46	Barry Bonds	.60
47	J.T. Snow	.10
48	Shawn Estes	.10
49	Jim Edmonds	.10
50	Tim Salmon	.30
51	Jason Dickson	.10
52	Cal Ripken Jr.	2.00
53	Mike Mussina	.50
54	Roberto Alomar	.50
55	Mo Vaughn	.60
56	Pedro Martinez	.50
57	Nomar Garciaparra	1.50
58	Albert Belle	.60
59	Frank Thomas	2.00
60	Robin Ventura	.20
61	Jim Thome	.40
62	Sandy Alomar Jr.	.20
63	Jaret Wright	.75
64	Bobby Higginson	.10
65	Tony Clark	.30
66	Justin Thompson	.10
67	Dean Palmer	.10
68	Kevin Appier	.10
69	Johnny Damon	.10
70	Paul Molitor	.40
71	Marty Cordova	.10
72	Brad Radke	.10
73	Derek Jeter	1.50
74	Bernie Williams	.40
75	Andy Pettitte	.40
76	Matt Stairs	.10
77	Ben Grieve	.75
78	Jason Giambi	.10
79	Randy Johnson	.40
80	Ken Griffey Jr.	2.50
81	Alex Rodriguez	1.50
82	Fred McGriff	.20
83	Wade Boggs	.20
84	Wilson Alvarez	.10
85	Juan Gonzalez	1.25
86	Ivan Rodriguez	.60
87	Fernando Tatis	.20
88	Roger Clemens	.75
89	Jose Cruz Jr.	.50
90	Shawn Green	.10
91	Jeff Suppan (Little Dawgs)	.10
92	Eli Marrero (Little Dawgs)	.10
93	*Mike Lowell* (Little Dawgs)	.30
94	Ben Grieve (Little Dawgs)	.75
95	Cliff Politte (Little Dawgs)	.10
96	*Rolando Arrojo* (Little Dawgs)	.40
97	Mike Caruso (Little Dawgs)	.10
98	Miguel Tejada (Little Dawgs)	.20
99	Rod Myers (Little Dawgs)	.10
100	Juan Encarnacion (Little Dawgs)	.10
101	Enrique Wilson (Little Dawgs)	.10
102	Brian Giles (Little Dawgs)	.10
103	*Magglio Ordonez* (Little Dawgs)	.50
104	Brian Rose (Little Dawgs)	.10
105	*Ryan Jackson* (Little Dawgs)	.25
106	Mark Kotsay (Little Dawgs)	.30
107	Desi Relaford (Little Dawgs)	.10
108	A.J. Hinch (Little Dawgs)	.10

109	Eric Milton (Little Dawgs)	.10
110	Ricky Ledee (Little Dawgs)	.25
111	Karim Garcia (Little Dawgs)	.10
112	Derrek Lee (Little Dawgs)	.10
113	Brad Fullmer (Little Dawgs)	.20
114	Travis Lee (Little Dawgs)	1.00
115	Greg Norton (Little Dawgs)	.10
116	Rich Butler (Little Dawgs)	.10
117	*Masato Yoshii* (Little Dawgs)	.40
118	Paul Konerko (Little Dawgs)	.25
119	Richard Hidalgo (Little Dawgs)	.10
120	Todd Helton (Little Dawgs)	.40
121	Nomar Garciaparra (7th Inning Sketch)	.75
122	Scott Rolen (7th Inning Sketch)	.40
123	Cal Ripken Jr. (7th Inning Sketch)	1.00
124	Derek Jeter (7th Inning Sketch)	.60
125	Mike Piazza (7th Inning Sketch)	.75
126	Tony Gwynn (7th Inning Sketch)	.60
127	Mark McGwire (7th Inning Sketch)	1.50
128	Kenny Lofton (7th Inning Sketch)	.30
129	Greg Maddux (7th Inning Sketch)	.75
130	Jeff Bagwell (7th Inning Sketch)	.40
131	Randy Johnson (7th Inning Sketch)	.25
132	Alex Rodriguez (7th Inning Sketch)	.75
133	Mo Vaughn (Name Plates)	.30
134	Chipper Jones (Name Plates)	.75
135	Juan Gonzalez (Name Plates)	.60
136	Tony Clark (Name Plates)	.20
137	Fred McGriff (Name Plates)	.10
138	Roger Clemens (Name Plates)	.40
139	Ken Griffey Jr. (Name Plates)	1.25
140	Ivan Rodriguez (Name Plates)	.30
141	Vinny Castilla (Trivia Card)	.10
142	Livan Hernandez (Trivia Card)	.10
143	Jose Cruz Jr. (Trivia Card)	.25
144	Andruw Jones (Trivia Card)	.30
145	Rafael Palmeiro (Trivia Card)	.20
146	Chuck Knoblauch (Trivia Card)	.10
147	Jay Buhner (Trivia Card)	.10
148	Andres Galarraga (Trivia Card)	.10
149	Frank Thomas (Trivia Card)	1.00
150	Todd Hundley (Trivia Card)	.10

1998 SkyBox Dugout Axcess Inside Axcess

This parallel set reprinted all 150 cards in Dugout Axcess. Cards in this parallel were sequetially numbered to 50.

	MT
Inside Axcess Stars:	100x to 150x
Yng Stars & RCs:	50x to 100x

1998 SkyBox Dugout Axcess Autograph Redemptions

This 150-card parallel set was sequentially numbered to 50 sets, with each card containing a stamped logo on the front and serial numbering on the back.

		MT
Common Ball:		15.00
Common Glove:		50.00
Inserted 1:96		
1	Jay Buhner (Ball)	25.00
2	Roger Clemens (Ball)	120.00
3	Jose Cruz Jr. (Ball)	40.00
4	Darin Erstad (Glove)	220.00
5	Nomar Garciaparra (Ball)	100.00
6	Tony Gwynn (Ball)	100.00
7	Roberto Hernandez (Ball)	15.00
8	Todd Hollandsworth (Glove)	50.00
9	Greg Maddux (Ball)	180.00
10	Alex Ochoa (Glove)	50.00
11	Alex Rodriguez (Ball)	160.00
12	Scott Rolen (Ball)	250.00
13	Scott Rolen (Ball)	80.00
14	Todd Walker (Glove)	75.00
15	Tony Womack (Ball)	15.00

1998 SkyBox Dugout Axcess Dishwashers

This 10-card set was a tribute to the game's best pitchers who "clean the home plate of opposing batters." Cards were inserted one per eight packs.

		MT
Complete Set (10):		6.00
Common Player:		.10
Inserted 1:8		
D1	Greg Maddux	3.00
D2	Kevin Brown	.10
D3	Pedro Martinez	1.00
D4	Randy Johnson	.75
D5	Curt Schilling	.40
D6	John Smoltz	.10
D7	Darryl Kile	.10
D8	Roger Clemens	2.00
D9	Andy Pettitte	.75
D10	Mike Mussina	1.00

1998 SkyBox Dugout Axcess Double Header

Double Header featured 20 players on cards that doubled as game pieces. The game instructions were on the card and required two dice to play. These were inserted at a rate of two per pack.

		MT
Complete Set (20):		5.00
Common Player:		.10
Inserted 2:1		
DH1	Jeff Bagwell	.30

DH2	Albert Belle	.25
DH3	Barry Bonds	.25
DH4	Derek Jeter	.50
DH5	Tony Clark	.20
DH6	Nomar Garciaparra	.60
DH7	Juan Gonzalez	.50
DH8	Ken Griffey Jr.	1.00
DH9	Chipper Jones	.60
DH10	Kenny Lofton	.25
DH11	Mark McGwire	1.00
DH12	Mo Vaughn	.25
DH13	Mike Piazza	.60
DH14	Cal Ripken Jr.	.75
DH15	Ivan Rodriguez	.25
DH16	Scott Rolen	.30
DH17	Frank Thomas	.75
DH18	Tony Gwynn	.50
DH19	Travis Lee	.50
DH20	Jose Cruz Jr.	.20

1998 SkyBox Dugout Axcess Frequent Flyers

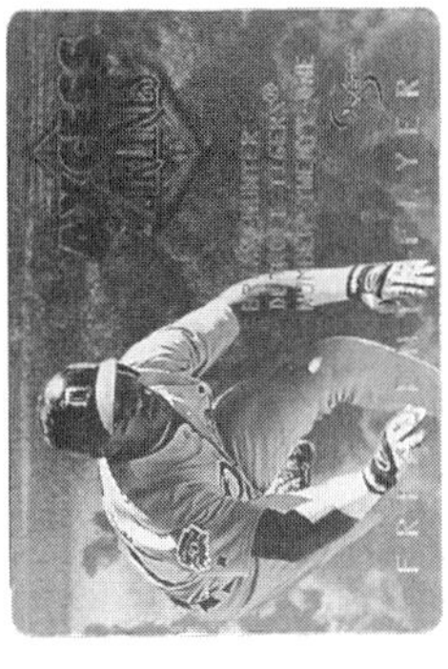

The game's top 10 base stealers were included in Frequent Flyers. This insert was designed to look like airline frequent flyer cards and was inserted one per four packs.

		MT
Complete Set (10):		3.00
Common Player:		.25
Inserted 1:4		
FF1	Brian Hunter	.25
FF2	Kenny Lofton	.75
FF3	Chuck Knoblauch	.40
FF4	Tony Womack	.25
FF5	Marquis Grissom	.25
FF6	Craig Biggio	.25
FF7	Barry Bonds	.75
FF8	Tom Goodwin	.25
FF9	Delino DeShields	.25
FF10	Eric Young	.25

1998 SkyBox Dugout Axcess Gronks

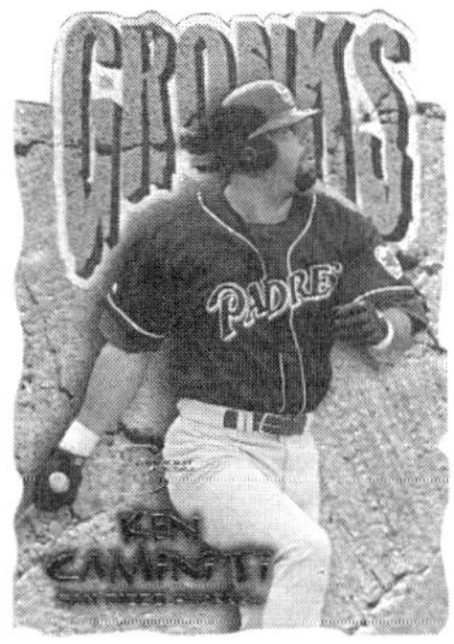

Gronks featured 10 of the top home run hitters and was a hobby exclusive insert. The name of the insert originated from shortstop Greg Gagne, and the cards were inserted in one per 72 packs.

		MT
Complete Set (10):		150.00
Common Player:		6.00
Inserted 1:72		
G1	Jeff Bagwell	15.00
G2	Albert Belle	10.00
G3	Juan Gonzalez	20.00
G4	Ken Griffey Jr.	40.00
G5	Mark McGwire	40.00
G6	Mike Piazza	25.00
G7	Frank Thomas	30.00
G8	Mo Vaughn	10.00
G9	Ken Caminiti	6.00
G10	Tony Clark	6.00

1998 SkyBox Dugout Axcess SuperHeroes

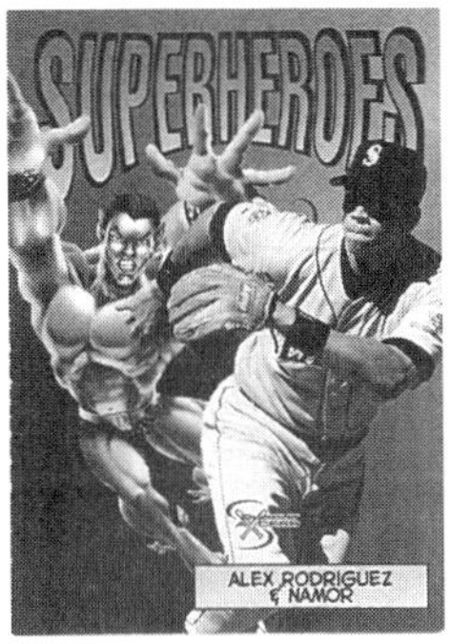

SuperHeroes combined 10 top superstars with the Marvel Comics superhero with whom they share a common trait in this 10-card insert set. Cards were inserted at a rate of one per 20 packs.

		MT
Complete Set (10):		60.00
Common Player:		2.00
Inserted 1:20		
SH1	Barry Bonds	4.00
SH2	Andres Galarraga	2.00
SH3	Ken Griffey Jr.	15.00
SH4	Chipper Jones	10.00
SH5	Andruw Jones	4.00
SH6	Hideo Nomo	2.50
SH7	Cal Ripken Jr.	12.00
SH8	Alex Rodriguez	10.00
SH9	Frank Thomas	12.00
SH10	Mo Vaughn	4.00

1998 SkyBox E-X2001

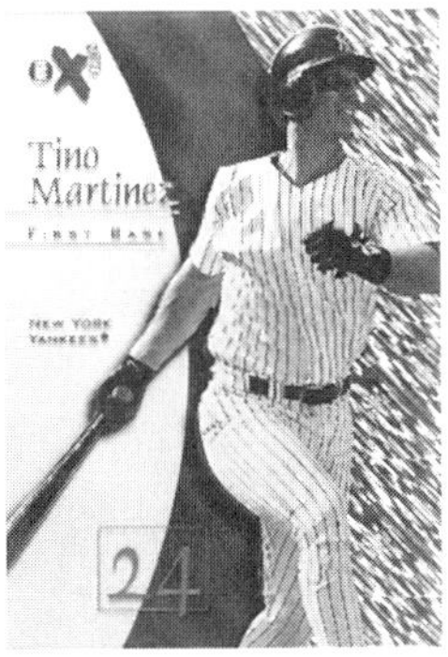

This super-premium set featured 100 players on a layered, die-cuct design utilizing mirror-image silhouetted photography and etched holofoil treatment over a clear, 20-point plastic card.

		MT
Complete Set (100):		90.00
Common Player:		.75
Kerry Wood Exchange:		15.00
Wax Box:		100.00
1	Alex Rodriguez	6.00
2	Barry Bonds	2.50
3	Greg Maddux	6.00
4	Roger Clemens	4.00
5	Juan Gonzalez	5.00
6	Chipper Jones	6.00
7	Derek Jeter	5.00
8	Frank Thomas	8.00
9	Cal Ripken Jr.	8.00
10	Ken Griffey Jr.	10.00
11	Mark McGwire	12.00
12	Hideo Nomo	2.00
13	Tony Gwynn	5.00
14	Ivan Rodriguez	2.50
15	Mike Piazza	6.00
16	Roberto Alomar	2.00
17	Jeff Bagwell	4.00
18	Andruw Jones	2.50
19	Albert Belle	2.50
20	Mo Vaughn	2.50
21	Kenny Lofton	2.50
22	Gary Sheffield	.75
23	Tony Clark	1.50
24	Mike Mussina	2.00
25	Barry Larkin	.75
26	Moises Alou	.75
27	Brady Anderson	.75
28	Andy Pettitte	1.50
29	Sammy Sosa	6.00
30	Raul Mondesi	.75
31	Andres Galarraga	1.00
32	Chuck Knoblauch	1.00
33	Jim Thome	1.50
34	Craig Biggio	.75
35	Jay Buhner	.75
36	Rafael Palmeiro	.75
37	Curt Schilling	.75
38	Tino Martinez	1.00
39	Pedro Martinez	1.50
40	Jose Canseco	1.00
41	Jeff Cirillo	.75
42	Dean Palmer	.75
43	Tim Salmon	1.50
44	Jason Giambi	.75
45	Bobby Higginson	.75
46	Jim Edmonds	.75
47	David Justice	1.00
48	John Olerud	.75
49	Ray Lankford	.75
50	Al Martin	.75
51	Mike Lieberthal	.75
52	Henry Rodriguez	.75
53	Edgar Renteria	.75
54	Eric Karros	.75
55	Marquis Grissom	.75
56	Wilson Alvarez	.75
57	Darryl Kile	.75
58	Jeff King	.75
59	Shawn Estes	.75
60	Tony Womack	.75
61	Willie Greene	.75
62	Ken Caminiti	1.00
63	Vinny Castilla	.75
64	Mark Grace	1.00
65	Ryan Klesko	1.00
66	Robin Ventura	.75
67	Todd Hundley	.75
68	Travis Fryman	.75
69	Edgar Martinez	.75
70	Matt Williams	1.00
71	Paul Molitor	1.50
72	Kevin Brown	.75
73	Randy Johnson	1.50
74	Bernie Williams	1.50
75	Manny Ramirez	2.50
76	Fred McGriff	.75
77	Tom Glavine	.75
78	Carlos Delgado	.75
79	Larry Walker	1.00
80	Hideki Irabu	1.50
81	Ryan McGuire	.75
82	Justin Thompson	.75
83	Kevin Orie	.75
84	Jon Nunnally	.75
85	Mark Kotsay	2.00
86	Todd Walker	.75
87	Jason Dickson	.75
88	Fernando Tatis	.75
89	Karim Garcia	.75
90	Ricky Ledee	1.50
91	Paul Konerko	1.50
92	Jaret Wright	3.00
93	Darin Erstad	2.50
94	Livan Hernandez	1.00
95	Nomar Garciaparra	6.00
96	Jose Cruz Jr.	2.00
97	Scott Rolen	4.00
98	Ben Grieve	3.00
99	Vladimir Guerrero	2.50
100	Travis Lee	4.00

1998 SkyBox E-X2001 Essential Credentials "Future"

Essential Credentials Future, along with Essential Credentials Now, paralleled all 100 cards in the base set. Production varied depending on the card number, with the exact production number of each player determined by subtracting his card number from 101. Since Essential Credentials Now was numbered to that player's card number, the two equalled production of 101.

		MT
Complete Set (100):		
Common Player:		20.00
1	Alex Rodriguez (100)	250.00
2	Barry Bonds (99)	100.00
3	Greg Maddux (98)	250.00
4	Roger Clemens (97)	150.00
5	Juan Gonzalez (96)	200.00
6	Chipper Jones (95)	200.00
7	Derek Jeter (94)	200.00
8	Frank Thomas (93)	300.00
9	Cal Ripken Jr. (92)	300.00
10	Ken Griffey Jr. (91)	400.00
11	Mark McGwire (90)	450.00
12	Hideo Nomo (89)	125.00
13	Tony Gwynn (88)	200.00
14	Ivan Rodriguez (87)	100.00
15	Mike Piazza (86)	250.00
16	Roberto Alomar (85)	75.00
17	Jeff Bagwell (84)	150.00
18	Andruw Jones (83)	100.00
19	Albert Belle (82)	90.00
20	Mo Vaughn (81)	100.00
21	Kenny Lofton (80)	90.00
22	Gary Sheffield (79)	50.00
23	Tony Clark (78)	50.00
24	Mike Mussina (77)	75.00
25	Barry Larkin (76)	50.00
26	Moises Alou (75)	30.00
27	Brady Anderson (74)	25.00
28	Andy Pettitte (73)	60.00
29	Sammy Sosa (72)	75.00
30	Raul Mondesi (71)	40.00
31	Andres Galarraga (70)	75.00
32	Chuck Knoblauch (69)	60.00
33	Jim Thome (68)	100.00
34	Craig Biggio (67)	50.00
35	Jay Buhner (66)	50.00
36	Rafael Palmeiro (65)	50.00
37	Curt Schilling (64)	40.00
38	Tino Martinez (63)	75.00
39	Pedro Martinez (62)	125.00
40	Jose Canseco (61)	75.00
41	Jeff Cirillo (60)	20.00
42	Dean Palmer (59)	20.00
43	Tim Salmon (58)	75.00
44	Jason Giambi (57)	30.00
45	Bobby Higginson (56)	40.00
46	Jim Edmonds (55)	40.00
47	David Justice (54)	75.00
48	John Olerud (53)	30.00
49	Ray Lankford (52)	35.00
50	Al Martin (51)	20.00
51	Mike Lieberthal (50)	20.00
52	Henry Rodriguez (49)	30.00
53	Edgar Renteria (48)	30.00
54	Eric Karros (47)	40.00
55	Marquis Grissom (46)	30.00
56	Wilson Alvarez (45)	20.00
57	Darryl Kile (44)	25.00
58	Jeff King (43)	20.00
59	Shawn Estes (42)	25.00
60	Tony Womack (41)	20.00
61	Willie Greene (40)	25.00
62	Ken Caminiti (39)	75.00
63	Vinny Castilla (38)	50.00
64	Mark Grace (37)	75.00
65	Ryan Klesko (36)	60.00
66	Robin Ventura (35)	50.00
67	Todd Hundley (34)	40.00
68	Travis Fryman (33)	40.00
69	Edgar Martinez (32)	80.00
70	Matt Williams (31)	90.00
71	Paul Molitor (30)	180.00
72	Kevin Brown (29)	60.00
73	Randy Johnson (28)	180.00
74	Bernie Williams (27)	150.00
75	Manny Ramirez (26)	200.00
76	Fred McGriff (25)	120.00
77	Tom Glavine (24)	100.00
78	Carlos Delgado (23)	75.00
79	Larry Walker (22)	250.00
80	Hideki Irabu (21)	125.00
81	Ryan McGuire (20)	50.00
82	Justin Thompson (19)	80.00
83	Kevin Orie (18)	75.00
84	Jon Nunnally (17)	50.00
85	Mark Kotsay (16)	180.00
86	Todd Walker (15)	150.00
87	Jason Dickson (14)	80.00
88	Fernando Tatis (13)	120.00
89	Karim Garcia (12)	100.00
90	Ricky Ledee (11)	120.00
91	Paul Konerko (10)	150.00
92	Jaret Wright (9)	300.00
93	Darin Erstad (8)	20.00
94	Livan Hernandez (7)	20.00
95	Nomar Garciaparra (6)	20.00
96	Jose Cruz (5)	20.00
97	Scott Rolen (4)	20.00
98	Ben Grieve (3)	20.00
99	Vladimir Guerrero (2)	20.00
100	Travis Lee (1)	20.00

1998 SkyBox E-X2001 Essential Credentials "Now"

Essential Credentials Now, along with Essential Credentials Future, paralleled all 100 cards in the base set. Production for each card was limited to that player's card number so that together with Essential Credentials Furture, production equalled 101.

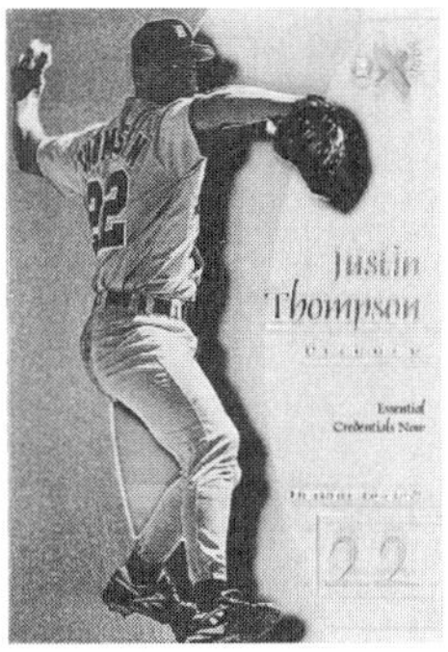

		MT
Complete Set (100):		
Common Player:		20.00
1	Alex Rodriguez (1)	20.00
2	Barry Bonds (2)	20.00
3	Greg Maddux (3)	20.00
4	Roger Clemens (4)	20.00
5	Juan Gonzalez (5)	20.00
6	Chipper Jones (6)	20.00
7	Derek Jeter (7)	20.00
8	Frank Thomas (8)	20.00
9	Cal Ripken Jr. (9)	20.00
10	Ken Griffey Jr. (10)	20.00
11	Mark McGwire (11)	20.00
12	Hideo Nomo (12)	350.00
13	Tony Gwynn (13)	550.00
14	Ivan Rodriguez (14)	350.00
15	Mike Piazza (15)	600.00
16	Roberto Alomar (16)	250.00
17	Jeff Bagwell (17)	450.00
18	Andruw Jones (18)	300.00
19	Albert Belle (19)	250.00
20	Mo Vaughn (20)	275.00
21	Kenny Lofton (21)	275.00
22	Gary Sheffield (22)	175.00
23	Tony Clark (23)	150.00
24	Mike Mussina (24)	220.00
25	Barry Larkin (25)	150.00
26	Moises Alou (26)	75.00
27	Brady Anderson (27)	60.00
28	Andy Pettitte (28)	150.00
29	Sammy Sosa (29)	250.00
30	Raul Mondesi (30)	100.00
31	Andres Galarraga (31)	120.00
32	Chuck Knoblauch (32)	120.00
33	Jim Thome (33)	150.00
34	Craig Biggio (34)	80.00
35	Jay Buhner (35)	100.00
36	Rafael Palmeiro (36)	75.00
37	Curt Schilling (37)	50.00
38	Tino Martinez (38)	100.00
39	Pedro Martinez (39)	150.00
40	Jose Canseco (40)	100.00
41	Jeff Cirillo (41)	25.00
42	Dean Palmer (42)	25.00
43	Tim Salmon (43)	75.00
44	Jason Giambi (44)	40.00
45	Bobby Higginson (45)	40.00
46	Jim Edmonds (46)	50.00
47	David Justice (47)	75.00
48	John Olerud (48)	35.00
49	Ray Lankford (49)	35.00
50	Al Martin (50)	25.00
51	Mike Lieberthal (51)	20.00
52	Henry Rodriguez (52)	25.00
53	Edgar Renteria (53)	30.00
54	Eric Karros (54)	40.00
55	Marquis Grissom (55)	30.00
56	Wilson Alvarez (56)	20.00
57	Darryl Kile (57)	25.00
58	Jeff King (58)	25.00
59	Shawn Estes (59)	25.00
60	Tony Womack (60)	25.00
61	Willie Greene (61)	25.00
62	Ken Caminiti (62)	50.00
63	Vinny Castilla (63)	40.00
64	Mark Grace (64)	50.00
65	Ryan Klesko (65)	50.00
66	Robin Ventura (66)	40.00
67	Todd Hundley (67)	30.00
68	Travis Fryman (68)	35.00
69	Edgar Martinez (69)	40.00
70	Matt Williams (70)	60.00
71	Paul Molitor (71)	75.00
72	Kevin Brown (72)	25.00
73	Randy Johnson (73)	75.00
74	Bernie Williams (74)	60.00
75	Manny Ramirez (75)	75.00
76	Fred McGriff (76)	40.00
77	Tom Glavine (77)	40.00
78	Carlos Delgado (78)	25.00
79	Larry Walker (79)	75.00
80	Hideki Irabu (80)	50.00
81	Ryan McGuire (81)	20.00
82	Justin Thompson (82)	30.00
83	Kevin Orie (83)	25.00
84	Jon Nunnally (84)	20.00
85	Mark Kotsay (85)	50.00
86	Todd Walker (86)	40.00
87	Jason Dickson (87)	30.00
88	Fernando Tatis (88)	30.00
89	Karim Garcia (89)	30.00
90	Ricky Ledee (90)	40.00
91	Paul Konerko (91)	75.00

92	Jaret Wright (92)	120.00
93	Darin Erstad (93)	75.00
94	Livan Hernandez (94)	30.00
95	Nomar Garciaparra (95)	180.00
96	Jose Cruz Jr. (96)	100.00
97	Scott Rolen (97)	140.00
98	Ben Grieve (98)	120.00
99	Vladimir Guerrero (99)	100.00
100	Travis Lee (100)	200.00

1998 SkyBox E-X2001 Cheap Seat Treats

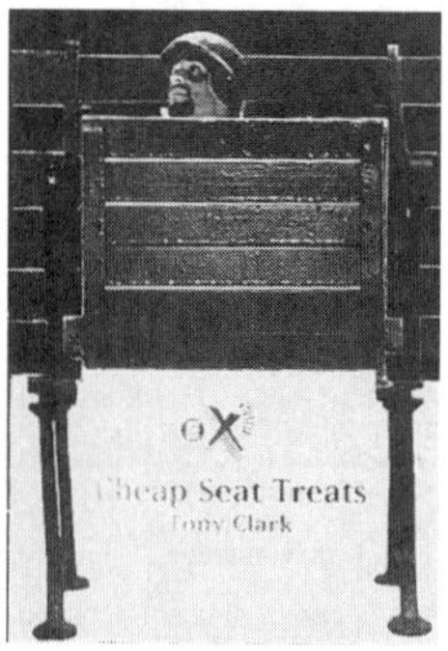

This 20-card die-cut insert arrived in the shape of a stadium seat. Inserted at one per 24 packs, Cheap Seat Treats included some of the top home run hitters and were numbered with a "CS" prefix.

	MT
Complete Set (20):	325.00
Common Player:	4.00
Inserted 1:24	
CS1 Frank Thomas	50.00
CS2 Ken Griffey Jr.	60.00
CS3 Mark McGwire	70.00
CS4 Tino Martinez	8.00
CS5 Larry Walker	10.00
CS6 Juan Gonzalez	30.00
CS7 Mike Piazza	40.00
CS8 Jeff Bagwell	25.00
CS9 Tony Clark	10.00
CS10Albert Belle	15.00
CS11Andres Galarraga	8.00
CS12Jim Thome	10.00
CS13Mo Vaughn	15.00
CS14Barry Bonds	15.00
CS15Vladimir Guerrero	15.00
CS16Scott Rolen	20.00
CS17Travis Lee	40.00
CS18David Justice	4.00
CS19Jose Cruz Jr.	15.00
CS20Andruw Jones	15.00

1998 SkyBox E-X2001 Destination: Cooperstown

Destination: Cooperstown captured a mixture of rising young stars and top veterans on die-cut cards that were inserted one per 720 packs. This insert included 15 players and was numbered with a "DC" prefix.

	MT
Complete Set (15):	2500.
Common Player:	60.00
Inserted 1:720	
DC1 Alex Rodriguez	250.00
DC2 Frank Thomas	300.00
DC3 Cal Ripken Jr.	300.00
DC4 Roger Clemens	160.00
DC5 Greg Maddux	250.00
DC6 Chipper Jones	250.00
DC7 Ken Griffey Jr.	400.00
DC8 Mark McGwire	450.00
DC9 Tony Gwynn	200.00
DC10Mike Piazza	250.00
DC11Jeff Bagwell	160.00
DC12Jose Cruz Jr.	100.00
DC13Derek Jeter	200.00
DC14Hideo Nomo	90.00
DC15Ivan Rodriguez	100.00

1998 SkyBox E-X2001 Signature 2001

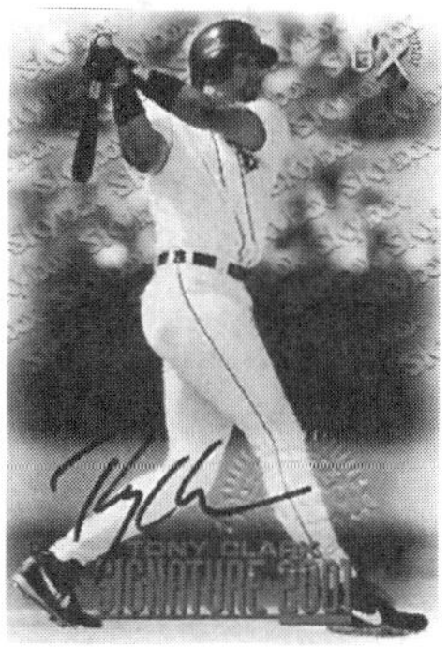

Seventeen top young and future stars signed cards for Signature 2001 inserts in E-X2001. The cards featured the player over a blue and white, sky-like background, with an embossed SkyBox seal of authenticity. Backs were horizontal and also included a Certificate of Authenticity. These cards were unnumbered and inserted one per 60 packs.

		MT
Complete Set (17):		400.00
Common Player:		15.00
Inserted 1:60		
1	Ricky Ledee	15.00
2	Derrick Gibson	15.00
3	Mark Kotsay	25.00
4	Kevin Millwood	40.00
5	Brad Fullmer	25.00
6	Todd Walker	20.00
7	Ben Grieve	50.00
8	Tony Clark	20.00
9	Jaret Wright	25.00
10	Randall Simon	15.00
11	Paul Konerko	20.00
12	Todd Helton	25.00
13	David Ortiz	15.00
14	Alex Gonzalez	15.00
15	Bobby Estalella	15.00
16	Alex Rodriguez	120.00
17	Mike Lowell	20.00

1998 SkyBox E-X2001 Star Date 2001

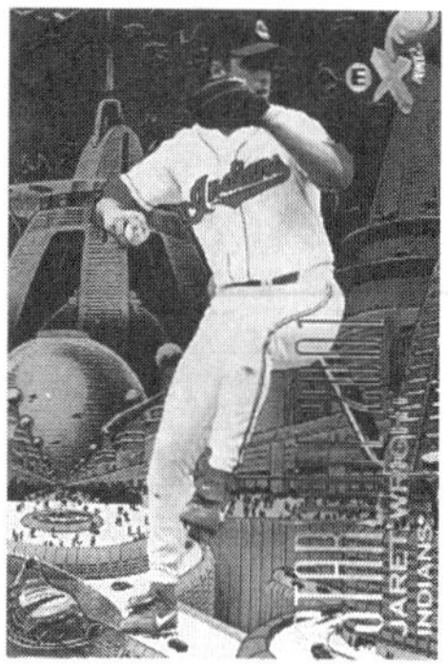

Star Date 2001 displayed 15 of the top rising stars on a space/planet background. This insert was seeded one per 12 packs and was numbered with a "SD" prefix.

	MT
Complete Set (15):	60.00
Common Player:	2.00
Inserted 1:12	
SD1 Travis Lee	20.00
SD2 Jose Cruz Jr.	6.00
SD3 Paul Konerko	4.00
SD4 Bobby Estalella	2.00
SD5 Magglio Ordonez	5.00
SD6 Juan Encarnacion	2.00
SD7 Richard Hidalgo	2.00
SD8 Abraham Nunez	2.00
SD9 Sean Casey	4.00
SD10Todd Helton	5.00
SD11Brad Fullmer	4.00
SD12Ben Grieve	15.00
SD13Livan Hernandez	2.00
SD14Jaret Wright	10.00
SD15Todd Dunwoody	2.00

1998 SP Authentic

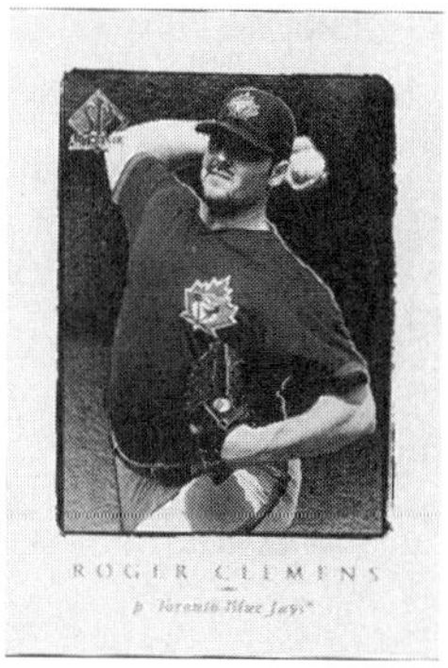

The SP Authentic base set consists of 198 cards, including the 30-card Future Watch subset and one checklist card. The base cards have a color photo inside a thick white border. Inserts include Chirography, Sheer Dominance and SP Authentics.

		MT
Complete Set (198):		50.00
Common Player:		.25
Wax Box:		110.00
1	Travis Lee (Future Watch)	3.00
2	Mike Caruso (Future Watch)	.40
3	Kerry Wood (Future Watch)	6.00
4	Mark Kotsay (Future Watch)	.50
5	*Magglio Ordonez* (Future Watch)	1.50
6	Scott Elarton (Future Watch)	.25
7	Carl Pavano (Future Watch)	.25
8	A.J. Hinch (Future Watch)	.25
9	*Rolando Arrojo* (Future Watch)	.75
10	Ben Grieve (Future Watch)	1.50
11	Gabe Alvarez (Future Watch)	.25
12	*Mike Kinkade* (Future Watch)	1.50
13	Bruce Chen (Future Watch)	.25
14	Juan Encarnacion (Future Watch)	.25
15	Todd Helton (Future Watch)	1.25
16	Aaron Boone (Future Watch)	.25
17	Sean Casey (Future Watch)	.50
18	Ramon Hernandez (Future Watch)	.25
19	Daryle Ward (Future Watch)	.25
20	Paul Konerko (Future Watch)	.50
21	David Ortiz (Future Watch)	.25
22	Derrek Lee (Future Watch)	.25
23	Brad Fullmer (Future Watch)	.40
24	Javier Vazquez (Future Watch)	.25
25	Miguel Tejada (Future Watch)	.75
26	David Delluchi (Future Watch)	.25
27	Alex Gonzalez (Future Watch)	.25
28	Matt Clement (Future Watch)	.25
29	Eric Milton (Future Watch)	.25
30	Russell Branyan (Future Watch)	.25
31	Chuck Finley	.25
32	Jim Edmonds	.25
33	Darren Erstad	1.25
34	Jason Dickson	.25
35	Tim Salmon	.50
36	Cecil Fielder	.40
37	Todd Greene	.25
38	Andy Benes	.25
39	Jay Bell	.25
40	Matt Williams	.50
41	Brian Anderson	.25
42	Karim Garcia	.25
43	Javy Lopez	.25
44	Tom Glavine	.50
45	Greg Maddux	3.00
46	Andruw Jones	1.25
47	Chipper Jones	3.00
48	Ryan Klesko	.50
49	John Smoltz	.40
50	Andres Galarraga	.50
51	Rafael Palmeiro	.50
52	Mike Mussina	1.00
53	Roberto Alomar	1.00
54	Joe Carter	.25
55	Cal Ripken Jr.	4.00
56	Brady Anderson	.25
57	Mo Vaughn	1.25
58	John Valentin	.25
59	Dennis Eckersley	.25
60	Nomar Garciaparra	3.00
61	Pedro J. Martinez	1.00
62	Jeff Blauser	.25
63	Kevin Orie	.25
64	Henry Rodriguez	.25
65	Mark Grace	.50
66	Albert Belle	1.25
67	Mike Cameron	.25
68	Robin Ventura	.25
69	Frank Thomas	4.00
70	Barry Larkin	.50
71	Brett Tomko	.25
72	Willie Greene	.25
73	Reggie Sanders	.25
74	Sandy Alomar Jr.	.40
75	Kenny Lofton	1.25
76	Jaret Wright	1.25
77	David Justice	.25
78	Omar Vizquel	.25
79	Manny Ramirez	1.25
80	Jim Thome	.75
81	Travis Fryman	.25
82	Neifi Perez	.25
83	Mike Lansing	.25
84	Vinny Castilla	.25
85	Larry Walker	.75
86	Dante Bichette	.50
87	Darryl Kile	.25
88	Justin Thompson	.25
89	Damion Easley	.25
90	Tony Clark	.75
91	Bobby Higginson	.25
92	Brian L. Hunter	.25
93	Edgar Renteria	.25
94	Craig Counsell	.25
95	Mike Piazza	3.00
96	Livan Hernandez	.25
97	Todd Zeile	.25
98	Richard Hidalgo	.25
99	Moises Alou	.50
100	Jeff Bagwell	1.50
101	Mike Hampton	.25
102	Craig Biggio	.50
103	Dean Palmer	.25
104	Tim Belcher	.25
105	Jeff King	.25
106	Jeff Conine	.25
107	Johnny Damon	.25
108	Hideo Nomo	1.00
109	Raul Mondesi	.50
110	Gary Sheffield	.75
111	Ramon Martinez	.40
112	Chan Ho Park	.50
113	Eric Young	.25
114	Charles Johnson	.25
115	Eric Karros	.40
116	Bobby Bonilla	.40
117	Jeromy Burnitz	.25
118	Carl Eldred	.25
119	Jeff D'Amico	.25
120	Marquis Grissom	.25
121	Dave Nilsson	.25
122	Brad Radke	.25
123	Marty Cordova	.25
124	Ron Coomer	.25
125	Paul Molitor	1.00
126	Todd Walker	.50
127	Rondell White	.40
128	Mark Grudzielanek	.25
129	Carlos Perez	.25
130	Vladimir Guerrero	1.25
131	Dustin Hermanson	.25
132	Butch Huskey	.25
133	John Franco	.25
134	Rey Ordonez	.25
135	Todd Hundley	.25
136	Edgardo Alfonzo	.25
137	Bobby Jones	.25
138	John Olerud	.40
139	Chili Davis	.25
140	Tino Martinez	.75
141	Andy Pettitte	.75
142	Chuck Knoblauch	.50
143	Bernie Williams	1.00
144	David Cone	.40
145	Derek Jeter	2.50
146	Paul O'Neill	.50
147	Rickey Henderson	.40
148	Jason Giambi	.25
149	Kenny Rogers	.25
150	Scott Rolen	1.50
151	Curt Schilling	.40
152	Ricky Bottalico	.25
153	Mike Lieberthal	.25
154	Francisco Cordova	.25
155	Jose Guillen	.50
156	Jason Schmidt	.25
157	Jason Kendall	.25
158	Kevin Young	.25
159	Delino DeShields	.25
160	Mark McGwire	5.00
161	Ray Lankford	.25
162	Brian Jordan	.25
163	Ron Gant	.25
164	Todd Stottlemyre	.25
165	Ken Caminiti	.50
166	Kevin Brown	.40
167	Trevor Hoffman	.25
168	Steve Finley	.25
169	Wally Joyner	.25
170	Tony Gwynn	2.50
171	Shawn Estes	.25
172	J.T. Snow	.25
173	Jeff Kent	.25
174	Robb Nen	.25
175	Barry Bonds	1.25
176	Randy Johnson	1.00
177	Edgar Martinez	.40
178	Jay Buhner	.75
179	Alex Rodriguez	3.00
180	Ken Griffey Jr.	5.00
181	Ken Cloude	.25
182	Wade Boggs	.50
183	Tony Saunders	.25
184	Wilson Alvarez	.25
185	Fred McGriff	.40
186	Roberto Hernandez	.25
187	Kevin Stocker	.25
188	Fernando Tatis	.40
189	Will Clark	.50
190	Juan Gonzalez	2.50
191	Rusty Greer	.25
192	Ivan Rodriguez	1.25
193	Jose Canseco	.50
194	Carlos Delgado	.25
195	Roger Clemens	1.75
196	Pat Hentgen	.25
197	Randy Myers	.25
198	Checklist (Ken Griffey Jr.)	2.00

1998 SP Authentic SP Authentics

The 15 SP Authentics cards can be redeemed for autographed memorabilia. Each card was good for a different signed item from a Major League player. The cards were inserted one per 320 packs.

	MT
Complete Set (15):	
Common Player:	
TC1 Ken Griffey Jr. Card (1,000.)	40.00
TC2 Ken Griffey Jr. Auto. Glove (30)	NA
TC3 Robin Ventura Ball (50)	40.00
TC4 Raul Mondesi Ball (100)	50.00
TC5 Albert Belle Ball (100)	75.00
TC6 Brian Jordan Ball (50)	40.00
TC7 Roberto Alomar Ball (100)	65.00
TC8 Ken Griffey Jr. Jersey (30)	NA
TC9 Ken Griffey Jr. Jersey Card (125)	450.00
TC10Tony Gwynn Jersey Card (415)	120.00
TC11Greg Maddux Jersey Card (125)	250.00
TC12Alex Rodriguez Jersey Card (125)	250.00
TC13Gary Sheffield Jersey Card (125)	80.00
TC14Jay Buhner Jersey Card (125	80.00
TC15Ken Griffey Jr. Standee (200)	75.00

1998 SP Authentic Chirography

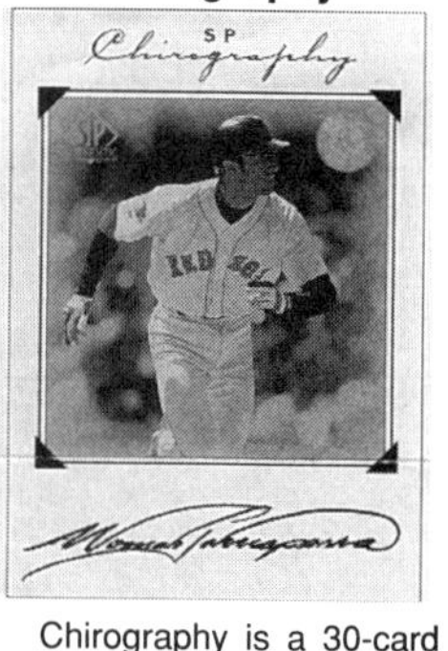

Chirography is a 30-card insert seeded one per 25 packs. The featured player signed his cards in the white border at the bottom.

	MT
Complete Set (30):	1,700.00
Common autograph:	15.00

Inserted 1:25
RA Roberto Alomar 75.00
RB Russell Branyan 15.00
SC Sean Casey 25.00
TC Tony Clark 30.00
RC Roger Clemens 160.00
JC Jose Cruz Jr. 60.00
DE Darin Erstad 60.00
NG Nomar Garciaparra 150.00
BG Ben Grieve 60.00
KG Ken Griffey Jr. 300.00
VG Vladimir Guerrero 60.00
TG Tony Gwynn 160.00
TH Todd Helton 50.00
LH Livan Hernandez 25.00
CJ Charles Johnson 25.00
AJ Andruw Jones 60.00
CHIP Chipper Jones 160.00
PK Paul Konerko 40.00
MK Mark Kotsay 40.00
RL Ray Lankford 25.00
TL Travis Lee 110.00
PM Paul Molitor 75.00
MM Mike Mussina 70.00
AR Alex Rodriguez 180.00
IR Ivan Rodriguez 80.00
SR Scott Rolen 75.00
DL Gary Sheffield 35.00
MT Miguel Tejada 40.00
JW Jaret Wright 75.00
MV Mo Vaughn 80.00

1998 SP Authentic Sheer Dominance

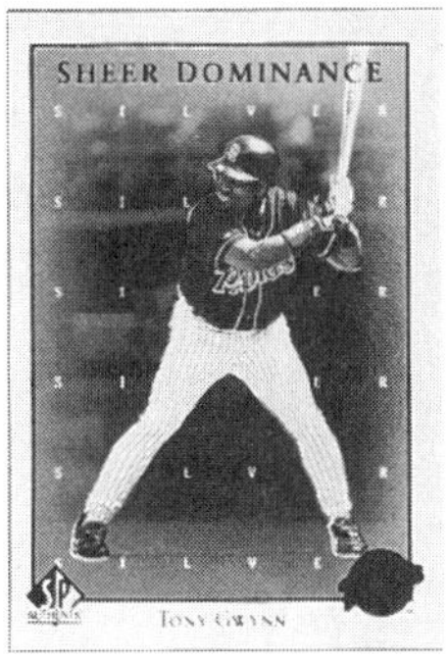

Sheer Dominance is a 42-card insert. The base set is inserted one per three packs. The Sheer Dominance Gold parallel is sequentially numbered to 2,000 and the Titanium parallel is numbered to 100. The cards feature a player photo inside a white border. The background color corresponds to the level of the insert.

	MT
Complete Set (42):	120.00
Common Player:	1.00
Inserted 1:3	
Golds:	3x
Production 2,000 sets	
SD1 Ken Griffey Jr.	12.00
SD2 Rickey Henderson	1.00
SD3 Jaret Wright	3.00
SD4 Craig Biggio	1.50
SD5 Travis Lee	8.00
SD6 Kenny Lofton	3.00
SD7 Raul Mondesi	1.50
SD8 Cal Ripken Jr.	10.00
SD9 Matt Williams	2.00
SD10 Mark McGwire	12.00
SD11 Alex Rodriguez	8.00
SD12 Fred McGriff	1.00
SD13 Scott Rolen	4.00
SD14 Paul Molitor	2.50
SD15 Nomar Garciaparra	8.00
SD16 Vladimir Guerrero	3.00
SD17 Andruw Jones	3.00
SD18 Manny Ramirez	3.00
SD19 Tony Gwynn	6.00
SD20 Barry Bonds	3.00
SD21 Ben Grieve	4.00
SD22 Ivan Rodriguez	3.00
SD23 Jose Cruz Jr.	3.00
SD24 Pedro J. Martinez	2.50
SD25 Chipper Jones	8.00
SD26 Albert Belle	3.00
SD27 Todd Helton	3.00
SD28 Paul Konerko	1.50
SD29 Sammy Sosa	6.00
SD30 Frank Thomas	10.00
SD31 Greg Maddux	8.00
SD32 Randy Johnson	2.50
SD33 Larry Walker	2.00
SD34 Roberto Alomar	2.50
SD35 Roger Clemens	4.00
SD36 Mo Vaughn	3.00
SD37 Jim Thome	2.00
SD38 Jeff Bagwell	4.00
SD39 Tino Martinez	2.00
SD40 Mike Piazza	8.00
SD41 Derek Jeter	6.00
SD42 Juan Gonzalez	6.00

1998 SP Authentic Sheer Dominance Titanium

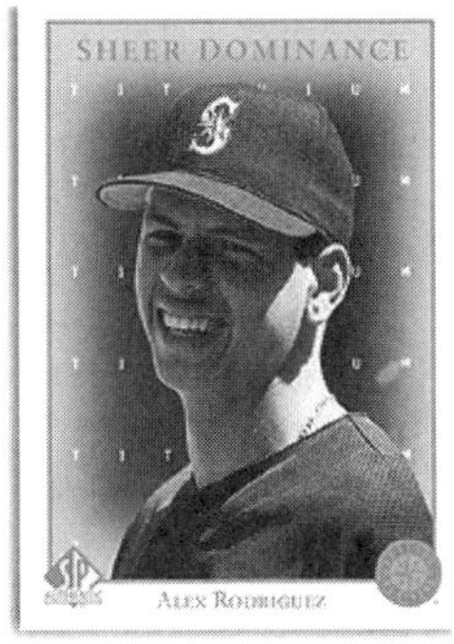

Sheer Dominance Titanium is a parallel of the 42-card Sheer Dominance insert. The cards are numbered to 100 and have a gray background with "Titanium" printed across it.

	MT
Common Player:	20.00
Semistars:	50.00
Production 100 sets	
SD1 Ken Griffey Jr.	300.00
SD2 Rickey Henderson	20.00
SD3 Jaret Wright	75.00
SD4 Craig Biggio	40.00
SD5 Travis Lee	180.00
SD6 Kenny Lofton	75.00
SD7 Raul Mondesi	40.00
SD8 Cal Ripken Jr.	225.00
SD9 Matt Williams	40.00
SD10 Mark McGwire	250.00
SD11 Alex Rodriguez	200.00
SD12 Fred McGriff	25.00
SD13 Scott Rolen	100.00
SD14 Paul Molitor	60.00
SD15 Nomar Garciaparra	180.00
SD16 Vladimir Guerrero	75.00
SD17 Andruw Jones	75.00
SD18 Manny Ramirez	75.00
SD19 Tony Gwynn	150.00
SD20 Barry Bonds	75.00
SD21 Ben Grieve	100.00
SD22 Ivan Rodriguez	75.00
SD23 Jose Cruz Jr.	75.00
SD24 Pedro J. Martinez	60.00
SD25 Chipper Jones	200.00
SD26 Albert Belle	75.00
SD27 Todd Helton	75.00
SD28 Paul Konerko	30.00
SD29 Sammy Sosa	150.00
SD30 Frank Thomas	225.00
SD31 Greg Maddux	200.00
SD32 Randy Johnson	60.00
SD33 Larry Walker	50.00
SD34 Roberto Alomar	60.00
SD35 Roger Clemens	100.00
SD36 Mo Vaughn	75.00
SD37 Jim Thome	50.00
SD38 Jeff Bagwell	100.00
SD39 Tino Martinez	50.00
SD40 Mike Piazza	200.00
SD41 Derek Jeter	150.00
SD42 Juan Gonzalez	150.00

1998 SPx Finite

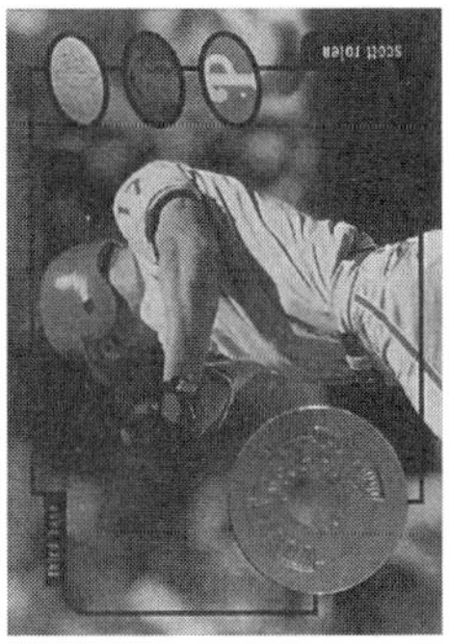

SPx Finite is an all-sequentially numbered set that was released in two 180-card series. The base set for the first series consisted of five subsets: 90 regular cards (numbered to 9,000), 30 Star Focus (7,000), 30 Youth Movement (5,000), 20 Power Explosion (4,000) and 10 Heroes of the Game (2,000). The set is paralleled in the Radiance and Spectrum sets. Radiance regular cards are numbered to 4,500, Star Focus to 3,500, Youth Movement to 2,500, Power Explosion to 1,000 and Heroes of the Game to 100. Spectrum regular cards are numbered to 2,250, Star Focus to 1,750, Youth Movement to 1,250, Power Explosion to 50 and Heroes of the Game to 1. The Series Two base set had 90 regular cards (numbered to 9,000), 30 Power Passion (7,000), 30 Youth Movement (5,000), 20 Tradewinds (4,000) and 10 Cornerstones of the Game (2,000). Series Two also had the Radiance and Spectrum parallel. Radiance regular cards are numbered to 4,500, Power Passion to 3,500, Youth Movement to 2,500, Tradewinds to 1,000 and Cornerstones of the Game to 100. Spectrum regular cards are numbered to 2,250, Power Passion to 1,750, Youth Movement to 1,250, Tradewinds to 50 and Cornerstones of the Game to 1. The only insert is Home Run Hysteria.

	MT
Complete Set (360):	2000.
Common Youth Movement (1-30), (181-210):	1.00
Radiance Youth Movement (2,500):	2x
Spectrum Youth Movement (1,250):	4x
Common Power Explosion (31-50):	3.00
Radiance Power Explosion (1,000):	4x
Common Reg. Card (51-140), (241-330):	1.00
Radiance Regular Card (4,500):	2x
Spectrum Regular Card (2,250):	4x
Common Star Focus (141-170):	1.50
Radiance Star Focus (3,500):	2x
Spectrum Star Focus (1,750):	4x
Common Heroes of the Game (171-180):	12.00
Common Power Passion (211-240):	1.50
Radiance Power Passion (3,500)	2x
Spectrum Power Passion (1,750)	4x
Common Tradewinds (331-350):	2.50
Radiance Tradewinds (1,000)	4x
Common Cornerstones (351-360):	12.00
Wax Box:	95.00
1 Nomar Garciaparra (Youth Movement)	15.00
2 Miguel Tejada (Youth Movement)	2.50
3 Mike Cameron (Youth Movement)	1.00
4 Ken Cloude (Youth Movement)	2.00
5 Jaret Wright (Youth Movement)	10.00
6 Mark Kotsay (Youth Movement)	2.50
7 Craig Counsell (Youth Movement)	1.00
8 Jose Guillen (Youth Movement)	2.00
9 Neifi Perez (Youth Movement)	1.00
10 Jose Cruz Jr. (Youth Movement)	6.00
11 Brett Tomko (Youth Movement)	1.00
12 Matt Morris (Youth Movement)	1.50
13 Justin Thompson (Youth Movement)	1.00
14 Jeremi Gonzalez (Youth Movement)	1.00
15 Scott Rolen (Youth Movement)	10.00
16 Vladimir Guerrero (Youth Movement)	6.00
17 Brad Fullmer (Youth Movement)	2.50
18 Brian Giles (Youth Movement)	1.00
19 Todd Dunwoody (Youth Movement)	1.00
20 Ben Grieve (Youth Movement)	8.00
21 Juan Encarnacion (Youth Movement)	1.00
22 Aaron Boone (Youth Movement)	1.00
23 Richie Sexson (Youth Movement)	1.00
24 Richard Hidalgo (Youth Movement)	1.00
25 Andruw Jones (Youth Movement)	6.00
26 Todd Helton (Youth Movement)	6.00
27 Paul Konerko (Youth Movement)	3.00
28 Dante Powell (Youth Movement)	1.00
29 Elieser Marrero (Youth Movement)	1.00
30 Derek Jeter (Youth Movement)	15.00
31 Mike Piazza (Power Explosion)	15.00
32 Tony Clark (Power Explosion)	4.00
33 Larry Walker (Power Explosion)	3.00
34 Jim Thome (Power Explosion)	4.00
35 Juan Gonzalez (Power Explosion)	12.00
36 Jeff Bagwell (Power Explosion)	10.00
37 Jay Buhner (Power Explosion)	3.00
38 Tim Salmon (Power Explosion)	3.00
39 Albert Belle (Power Explosion)	6.00
40 Mark McGwire (Power Explosion)	12.00
41 Sammy Sosa (Power Explosion)	8.00
42 Mo Vaughn (Power Explosion)	6.00
43 Manny Ramirez (Power Explosion)	6.00
44 Tino Martinez (Power Explosion)	3.00
45 Frank Thomas (Power Explosion)	20.00
46 Nomar Garciaparra (Power Explosion)	15.00
47 Alex Rodriguez (Power Explosion)	15.00
48 Chipper Jones (Power Explosion)	15.00
49 Barry Bonds (Power Explosion)	6.00
50 Ken Griffey Jr. (Power Explosion)	25.00
51 Jason Dickson	1.00
52 Jim Edmonds	1.50
53 Darin Erstad	4.00
54 Tim Salmon	2.00
55 Chipper Jones	10.00
56 Ryan Klesko	2.00
57 Tom Glavine	1.50
58 Denny Neagle	1.00
59 John Smoltz	1.00
60 Javy Lopez	1.00
61 Roberto Alomar	3.00
62 Rafael Palmeiro	1.50
63 Mike Mussina	4.00
64 Cal Ripken Jr.	12.00
65 Mo Vaughn	4.00
66 Tim Naehring	1.00
67 John Valentin	1.00
68 Mark Grace	2.00
69 Kevin Orie	1.00
70 Sammy Sosa	6.00
71 Albert Belle	4.00
72 Frank Thomas	12.00
73 Robin Ventura	1.50
74 David Justice	2.00
75 Kenny Lofton	4.00
76 Omar Vizquel	1.00
77 Manny Ramirez	4.00
78 Jim Thome	2.50
79 Dante Bichette	2.00
80 Larry Walker	2.00
81 Vinny Castilla	1.50
82 Ellis Burks	1.00
83 Bobby Higginson	1.00
84 Brian L. Hunter	1.00
85 Tony Clark	2.50
86 Mike Hampton	1.00
87 Jeff Bagwell	6.00
88 Craig Biggio	2.00
89 Derek Bell	1.00
90 Mike Piazza	10.00
91 Ramon Martinez	1.00
92 Raul Mondesi	2.00
93 Hideo Nomo	3.00
94 Eric Karros	1.50
95 Paul Molitor	3.00
96 Marty Cordova	1.00
97 Brad Radke	1.00
98 Mark Grudzielanek	1.00
99 Carlos Perez	1.00
100 Rondell White	1.50
101 Todd Hundley	1.00
102 Edgardo Alfonzo	1.00
103 John Franco	1.00
104 John Olerud	1.50
105 Tino Martinez	2.00
106 David Cone	1.50
107 Paul O'Neill	1.50
108 Andy Pettitte	2.50
109 Bernie Williams	3.00
110 Rickey Henderson	1.50
111 Jason Giambi	1.00
112 Matt Stairs	1.00
113 Gregg Jefferies	1.00
114 Rico Brogna	1.00
115 Curt Schilling	1.50
116 Jason Schmidt	1.00
117 Jose Guillen	2.00
118 Kevin Young	1.00
119 Ray Lankford	1.00
120 Mark McGwire	8.00
121 Delino DeShields	1.00
122 Ken Caminiti	2.00
123 Tony Gwynn	8.00
124 Trevor Hoffman	1.00
125 Barry Bonds	4.00
126 Jeff Kent	1.00
127 Shawn Estes	1.00
128 J.T. Snow	1.00
129 Jay Buhner	2.00
130 Ken Griffey Jr.	15.00
131 Dan Wilson	1.00
132 Edgar Martinez	1.00
133 Alex Rodriguez	10.00
134 Rusty Greer	1.00
135 Juan Gonzalez	8.00
136 Fernando Tatis	1.00
137 Ivan Rodriguez	4.00
138 Carlos Delgado	1.50
139 Pat Hentgen	1.00
140 Roger Clemens	6.00
141 Chipper Jones (Star Focus)	12.00
142 Greg Maddux (Star Focus)	12.00
143 Rafael Palmeiro (Star Focus)	2.00
144 Mike Mussina (Star Focus)	4.00
145 Cal Ripken Jr. (Star Focus)	14.00
146 Nomar Garciaparra (Star Focus)	12.00
147 Mo Vaughn (Star Focus)	5.00
148 Sammy Sosa (Star Focus)	6.00
149 Albert Belle (Star Focus)	5.00
150 Frank Thomas (Star Focus)	14.00
151 Jim Thome (Star Focus)	4.00
152 Kenny Lofton (Star Focus)	5.00
153 Manny Ramirez (Star Focus)	5.00
154 Larry Walker (Star Focus)	2.50
155 Jeff Bagwell (Star Focus)	8.00
156 Craig Biggio (Star Focus)	1.50
157 Mike Piazza (Star Focus)	12.00
158 Paul Molitor (Star Focus)	4.00
159 Derek Jeter (Star Focus)	10.00
160 Tino Martinez (Star Focus)	2.50
161 Curt Schilling (Star Focus)	1.50
162 Mark McGwire (Star Focus)	10.00
163 Tony Gwynn (Star Focus)	10.00
164 Barry Bonds (Star Focus)	5.00
165 Ken Griffey Jr. (Star Focus)	18.00
166 Randy Johnson (Star Focus)	3.00
167 Alex Rodriguez (Star Focus)	12.00
168 Juan Gonzalez (Star Focus)	10.00
169 Ivan Rodriguez (Star Focus)	5.00
170 Roger Clemens (Star Focus)	8.00
171 Greg Maddux (Heroes of the Game)	30.00
172 Cal Ripken Jr. (Heroes of the Game)	40.00
173 Frank Thomas (Heroes of the Game)	40.00
174 Jeff Bagwell (Heroes of the Game)	20.00
175 Mike Piazza (Heroes of the Game)	30.00

176	Mark McGwire (Heroes of the Game)	25.00
177	Barry Bonds (Heroes of the Game)	12.00
178	Ken Griffey Jr. (Heroes of the Game)	50.00
179	Alex Rodriguez (Heroes of the Game)	30.00
180	Roger Clemens (Heroes of the Game)	20.00
181	Mike Caruso	1.00
182	David Ortiz	2.00
183	Gabe Alvarez	1.00
184	Gary Matthews Jr.	1.00
185	Kerry Wood	20.00
186	Carl Pavano	1.00
187	Alex Gonzalez	1.00
188	Masato Yoshii	2.00
189	Larry Sutton	1.00
190	Russell Branyan	1.00
191	Bruce Chen	1.00
192	Rolando Arrojo	2.50
193	Ryan Christenson	1.00
194	Cliff Politte	1.00
195	A.J. Hinch	1.00
196	Kevin Witt	1.00
197	Daryle Ward	1.00
198	Corey Koskie	1.00
199	Mike Lowell	1.00
200	Travis Lee	10.00
201	Kevin Millwood	1.00
202	Robert Smith	1.00
203	Magglio Ordonez	1.00
204	Eric Milton	1.00
205	Geoff Jenkins	1.00
206	Rich Butler	1.00
207	*Mike Kinkade*	1.00
208	Braden Looper	1.00
209	Matt Clement	1.00
210	Derrek Lee	1.00
211	Randy Johnson	3.00
212	John Smoltz	1.50
213	Roger Clemens	5.00
214	Curt Schilling	2.00
215	Pedro J. Martinez	4.00
216	Vinny Castilla	1.00
217	Jose Cruz Jr.	4.00
218	Jim Thome	2.50
219	Alex Rodriguez	10.00
220	Frank Thomas	10.00
221	Tim Salmon	2.00
222	Larry Walker	2.50
223	Albert Belle	4.00
224	Manny Ramirez	4.00
225	Mark McGwire	18.00
226	Mo Vaughn	4.00
227	Andres Galarraga	2.00
228	Scott Rolen	4.00
229	Travis Lee	8.00
230	Mike Piazza	10.00
231	Nomar Garciaparra	10.00
232	Andruw Jones	4.00
233	Barry Bonds	4.00
234	Jeff Bagwell	5.00
235	Juan Gonzalez	8.00
236	Tino Martinez	2.00
237	Vladimir Guerrero	4.00
238	Rafael Palmeiro	2.00
239	Russell Branyan	1.00
240	Ken Griffey Jr.	15.00
241	Cecil Fielder	1.00
242	Chuck Finley	1.00
243	Jay Bell	1.00
244	Andy Benes	1.00
245	Matt Williams	1.50
246	Brian Anderson	1.00
247	David Dellucci	1.00
248	Andres Galarraga	2.00
249	Andruw Jones	2.50
250	Greg Maddux	6.00
251	Brady Anderson	1.00
252	Joe Carter	1.00
253	Eric Davis	1.00
254	Pedro J. Martinez	2.50
255	Nomar Garciaparra	6.00
256	Dennis Eckersley	1.00
257	Henry Rodriguez	1.00
258	Jeff Blauser	1.00
259	Jaime Navarro	1.00
260	Ray Durham	1.00
261	Chris Stynes	1.00
262	Willie Greene	1.00
263	Reggie Sanders	1.00
264	Bret Boone	1.00
265	Barry Larkin	1.50
266	Travis Fryman	1.00
267	Charles Nagy	1.00
268	Sandy Alomar Jr.	1.00
269	Darryl Kile	1.00
270	Mike Lansing	1.00
271	Pedro Astacio	1.00
272	Damion Easley	1.00
273	Joe Randa	1.00
274	Luis Gonzalez	1.00
275	Mike Piazza	6.00
276	Todd Zeile	1.00
277	Edgar Renteria	1.00
278	Livan Hernandez	1.00
279	Cliff Floyd	1.00
280	Moises Alou	1.50
281	Billy Wagner	1.00
282	Jeff King	1.00
283	Hal Morris	1.00
284	Johnny Damon	1.00
285	Dean Palmer	1.00
286	Tim Belcher	1.00
287	Eric Young	1.00
288	Bobby Bonilla	1.00
289	Gary Sheffield	1.50
290	Chan Ho Park	1.50
291	Charles Johnson	1.00
292	Jeff Cirillo	1.00
293	Jeromy Burnitz	1.00
294	Jose Valentin	1.00
295	Marquis Grissom	1.00
296	Todd Walker	1.00
297	Terry Steinbach	1.00
298	Rick Aguilera	1.00
299	Vladimir Guerrero	2.50
300	Rey Ordonez	1.00
301	Butch Huskey	1.00
302	Bernard Gilkey	1.00
303	Mariano Rivera	1.50
304	Chuck Knoblauch	1.50
305	Derek Jeter	5.00
306	Ricky Bottalico	1.00
307	Bob Abreu	1.00
308	Scott Rolen	3.00
309	Al Martin	1.00
310	Jason Kendall	1.00
311	Brian Jordan	1.00
312	Ron Gant	1.00
313	Todd Stottlemyre	1.00
314	Greg Vaughn	1.00
315	J. Kevin Brown	1.00
316	Wally Joyner	1.00
317	Robb Nen	1.00
318	Orel Hershiser	1.00
319	Russ Davis	1.00
320	Randy Johnson	2.00
321	Quinton McCracken	1.00
322	Tony Saunders	1.00
323	Wilson Alvarez	1.00
324	Wade Boggs	1.50
325	Fred McGriff	1.50
326	Lee Stevens	1.00
327	John Wetteland	1.00
328	Jose Canseco	1.50
329	Randy Myers	1.00
330	Jose Cruz Jr.	2.50
331	Matt Williams	3.00
332	Andres Galarraga	4.00
333	Walt Weiss	2.50
334	Joe Carter	2.50
335	Pedro J. Martinez	5.00
336	Henry Rodriguez	2.50
337	Travis Fryman	2.50
338	Darryl Kile	2.50
339	Mike Lansing	2.50
340	Mike Piazza	12.00
341	Moises Alou	3.00
342	Charles Johnson	2.50
343	Chuck Knoblauch	4.00
344	Rickey Henderson	2.50
345	J. Kevin Brown	3.00
346	Orel Hershiser	2.50
347	Wade Boggs	3.00
348	Fred McGriff	3.00
349	Jose Canseco	3.00
350	Gary Sheffield	3.00
351	Travis Lee	20.00
352	Nomar Garciaparra	25.00
353	Frank Thomas	30.00
354	Cal Ripken Jr.	30.00
355	Mark McGwire	50.00
356	Mike Piazza	30.00
357	Alex Rodriguez	30.00
358	Barry Bonds	10.00
359	Tony Gwynn	20.00
360	Ken Griffey Jr.	40.00

1998 SPx Finite Home Run Hysteria

Home Run Hysteria is a 10-card insert in SPx Finite Series Two. The cards were sequentially numbered to 62.

		MT
Common Player:		75.00
Production 62 sets		
HR1	Ken Griffey Jr.	350.00
HR2	Mark McGwire	450.00
HR3	Sammy Sosa	300.00
HR4	Albert Belle	120.00
HR5	Alex Rodriguez	250.00
HR6	Greg Vaughn	75.00
HR7	Andres Galarraga	90.00
HR8	Vinny Castilla	75.00
HR9	Juan Gonzalez	200.00
HR10	Chipper Jones	250.00

1998 SPx Finite Radiance Cornerstones

Radiance Cornerstones of the Game is a parallel of the 10-card subset. The cards have two images of the player on the front and are numbered to 100.

		MT
Common Player (100 sets):		40.00
351	Travis Lee	100.00
352	Nomar Garciaparra	200.00
353	Frank Thomas	175.00
354	Cal Ripken Jr.	225.00
355	Mark McGwire	350.00
356	Mike Piazza	200.00
357	Alex Rodriguez	200.00
358	Barry Bonds	75.00
359	Tony Gwynn	150.00
360	Ken Griffey Jr.	300.00

1998 SPx Finite Radiance Heroes of the Game

Radiance Heroes of the Game is a parallel of the 10-card subset. The cards have a horizontal layout and are numbered to 100.

		MT
Common Player:		100.00
Production 100 sets		
171	Greg Maddux	175.00
172	Cal Ripken Jr.	225.00
173	Frank Thomas	225.00
174	Jeff Bagwell	100.00
175	Mike Piazza	175.00
176	Mark McGwire	150.00
177	Barry Bonds	75.00
178	Ken Griffey Jr.	300.00
179	Alex Rodriguez	175.00
180	Roger Clemens	100.00

1998 SPx Finite Spectrum Power Explosion

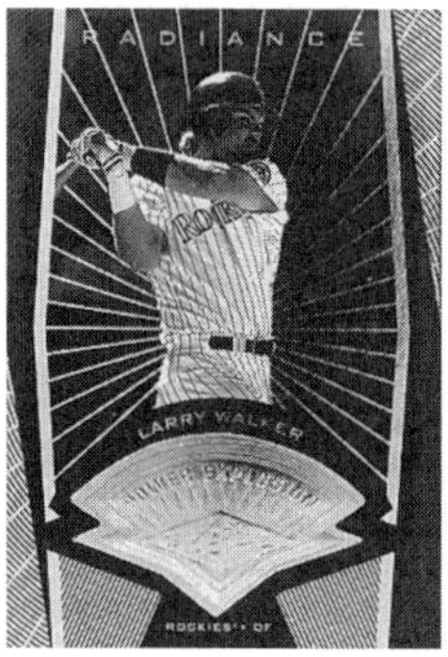

Spectrum Power Explosion is a parallel of the 20-card subset in Series One. The horizontal cards have two images of the player and are numbered to 50.

		MT
Common Player:		50.00
Semistars:		100.00
Production 50 sets		
31	Mike Piazza	350.00
32	Tony Clark	100.00
33	Larry Walker	75.00
34	Jim Thome	100.00
35	Juan Gonzalez	300.00
36	Jeff Bagwell	200.00
37	Jay Buhner	75.00
38	Tim Salmon	40.00
39	Albert Belle	150.00
40	Mark McGwire	300.00
41	Sammy Sosa	250.00
42	Mo Vaughn	150.00
43	Manny Ramirez	100.00
44	Tino Martinez	75.00
45	Frank Thomas	450.00
46	Nomar Garciaparra	300.00
47	Alex Rodriguez	350.00
48	Chipper Jones	300.00
49	Barry Bonds	150.00
50	Ken Griffey Jr.	600.00

1998 SPx Finite Spectrum Tradewinds

Spectrum Tradewinds is a parallel of the 20-card subset in Series Two. The horizontal cards have two images of the player and are numbered to 50.

		MT
Common Player (50 sets):		40.00
331	Matt Williams	60.00
332	Andres Galarraga	80.00
333	Walt Weiss	40.00
334	Joe Carter	60.00
335	Pedro J. Martinez	150.00
336	Henry Rodriguez	40.00
337	Travis Fryman	50.00
338	Darryl Kile	40.00
339	Mike Lansing	40.00
340	Mike Piazza	300.00
341	Moises Alou	60.00
342	Charles Johnson	40.00
343	Chuck Knoblauch	80.00
344	Rickey Henderson	50.00
345	Kevin Brown	60.00
346	Orel Hershiser	40.00
347	Wade Boggs	60.00
348	Fred McGriff	60.00
349	Jose Canseco	80.00
350	Gary Sheffield	80.00

1998 Stadium Club

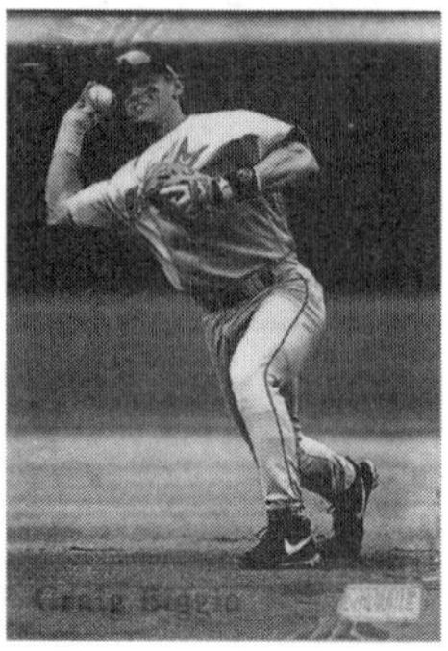

Stadium Club was issued in two separate series for 1998, with 200 odd-numbered cards in Series I and 200 even- numbered cards in Series II. Retail packs contained six cards and an SRP of $2, hobby packs contained nine cards and an SRP of $3 and HTA packs contained 15 cards and an SRP of $5. Three subets were included in the set, with Future Stars (361-379) and Draft Picks (381-399) both being odd-numbered and Traded (356-400) being even- numbered. Inserts in Series I include: First Day Issue parallels (retail), One of a Kind parallels (hobby), Printing Plates parallels (HTA), Bowman Previews, Co-Signers (hobby), In the Wings, Never Compromise, and Triumvirates (retail). Inserts in Series II include: First Day Issue parallels (retail), One of a Kind parallels (hobby), Printing Plates parallels (HTA), Bowman Prospect Previews, Co-Signers (hobby), Playing with Passion, Royal Court and Triumvirates (retail).

		MT
Complete Set (400):		75.00
Complete Series I (200):		40.00
Complete Series II (200):		35.00
Common Player:		.10
Cal Ripken Screen Play Sound Chip:		20.00
Wax Box:		65.00
1	Chipper Jones	2.00
2	Frank Thomas	2.50
3	Vladimir Guerrero	1.00
4	Ellis Burks	.10
5	John Franco	.10
6	Paul Molitor	.50
7	Rusty Greer	.10
8	Todd Hundley	.10
9	Brett Tomko	.10
10	Eric Karros	.20
11	Mike Cameron	.10
12	Jim Edmonds	.10
13	Bernie Williams	.50
14	Denny Neagle	.20
15	Jason Dickson	.10
16	Sammy Sosa	2.00
17	Brian Jordan	.10
18	Jose Vidro	.10
19	Scott Spiezio	.10
20	Jay Buhner	.25
21	Jim Thome	.40
22	Sandy Alomar	.20
23	Devon White	.10
24	Roberto Alomar	.60
25	John Flaherty	.10
26	John Wetteland	.10
27	Willie Greene	.10
28	Gregg Jefferies	.10
29	Johnny Damon	.10
30	Barry Larkin	.25
31	Chuck Knoblauch	.25
32	Mo Vaughn	.75
33	Tony Clark	.40
34	Marty Cordova	.10
35	Vinny Castilla	.10
36	Jeff King	.10
37	Reggie Jefferson	.10
38	Mariano Rivera	.20
39	Jermaine Allensworth	.10
40	Livan Hernandez	.10
41	Heathcliff Slocumb	.10
42	Jacob Cruz	.10
43	Barry Bonds	.75
44	Dave Magadan	.10
45	Chan Ho Park	.10
46	Jeremi Gonzalez	.10
47	Jeff Cirillo	.10
48	Delino DeShields	.10
49	Craig Biggio	.20
50	Benito Santiago	.10
51	Mark Clark	.10
52	Fernando Vina	.10
53	F.P. Santangelo	.10
54	*Pep Harris*	.25
55	Edgar Renteria	.10
56	Jeff Bagwell	1.25
57	Jimmy Key	.10
58	Bartolo Colon	.10
59	Curt Schilling	.20
60	Steve Finley	.10
61	Andy Ashby	.10
62	John Burkett	.10
63	Orel Hershiser	.10
64	Pokey Reese	.10
65	Scott Servais	.10
66	Todd Jones	.10
67	Javy Lopez	.20
68	Robin Ventura	.20
69	Miguel Tejada	.50
70	Raul Casanova	.10
71	Reggie Sanders	.10
72	Edgardo Alfonzo	.10
73	Dean Palmer	.10
74	Todd Stottlemyre	.10
75	David Wells	.10
76	Troy Percival	.10
77	Albert Belle	.75
78	Pat Hentgen	.20
79	Brian Hunter	.10
80	Richard Hidalgo	.10
81	Darren Oliver	.10
82	Mark Wohlers	.10
83	Cal Ripken Jr.	2.50
84	Hideo Nomo	.60
85	Derrek Lee	.20
86	Stan Javier	.10
87	Rey Ordonez	.10
88	Randy Johnson	.60
89	Jeff Kent	.10
90	Brian McRae	.10
91	Manny Ramirez	.60
92	Trevor Hoffman	.10
93	Doug Glanville	.10
94	Todd Walker	.20
95	Andy Benes	.10
96	Jason Schmidt	.10
97	Mike Matheny	.10
98	Tim Naehring	.10
99	Jeff Blauser	.10
100	Jose Rosado	.10
101	Roger Clemens	1.00
102	Pedro Astacio	.10
103	Mark Bellhorn	.10
104	Paul O'Neill	.20
105	Darin Erstad	.75
106	Mike Lieberthal	.10
107	Wilson Alvarez	.10
108	Mike Mussina	.60
109	George Williams	.10
110	Cliff Floyd	.10
111	Shawn Estes	.10
112	Mark Grudzielanek	.10
113	Tony Gwynn	1.50
114	Alan Benes	.20
115	Terry Steinbach	.10
116	Greg Maddux	2.00
117	Andy Pettitte	.50
118	Dave Nilsson	.10
119	Deivi Cruz	.10
120	Carlos Delgado	.10
121	Scott Hatteberg	.10
122	John Olerud	.20
123	Moises Alou	.20
124	Garret Anderson	.10
125	Royce Clayton	.10
126	Dante Powell	.10
127	Tom Glavine	.20
128	Gary DiSarcina	.10
129	Terry Adams	.10
130	Raul Mondesi	.30
131	Dan Wilson	.10
132	Al Martin	.10
133	Mickey Morandini	.10
134	Rafael Palmeiro	.25
135	Juan Encarnacion	.25
136	Jim Pittsley	.10
137	*Magglio Ordonez*	.75
138	Will Clark	.30
139	Todd Helton	1.00
140	Kelvin Escobar	.10
141	Esteban Loaiza	.10

142	John Jaha	.10
143	Jeff Fassero	.10
144	Harold Baines	.10
145	Butch Huskey	.10
146	Pat Meares	.10
147	Brian Giles	.10
148	Ramiro Mendoza	.10
149	John Smoltz	.20
150	Felix Martinez	.10
151	Jose Valentin	.10
152	Brad Rigby	.10
153	Ed Sprague	.10
154	Mike Hampton	.10
155	Mike Lansing	.10
156	Ray Lankford	.10
157	Bobby Bonilla	.20
158	Bill Mueller	.10
159	Jeffrey Hammonds	.10
160	Charles Nagy	.10
161	Rich Loiselle	.10
162	Al Leiter	.10
163	Larry Walker	.25
164	Chris Hoiles	.10
165	Jeff Montgomery	.10
166	Francisco Cordova	.10
167	James Baldwin	.10
168	Mark McLemore	.10
169	Kevin Appier	.10
170	Jamey Wright	.10
171	Nomar Garciaparra	2.00
172	Matt Franco	.10
173	Armando Benitez	.10
174	Jeromy Burnitz	.10
175	Ismael Valdes	.10
176	Lance Johnson	.10
177	Paul Sorrento	.10
178	Rondell White	.20
179	Kevin Elster	.10
180	Jason Giambi	.10
181	Carlos Baerga	.10
182	Russ Davis	.10
183	Ryan McGuire	.10
184	Eric Young	.10
185	Ron Gant	.10
186	Manny Alexander	.10
187	Scott Karl	.10
188	Brady Anderson	.10
189	Randall Simon	.10
190	Tim Belcher	.10
191	Jaret Wright	1.00
192	Dante Bichette	.25
193	John Valentin	.10
194	Darren Bragg	.10
195	Mike Sweeney	.10
196	Craig Counsell	.10
197	Jaime Navarro	.10
198	Todd Dunn	.10
199	Ken Griffey Jr.	3.00
200	Juan Gonzalez	1.50
201	Billy Wagner	.10
202	Jeff D'Amico	.10
203	Mark McGwire	4.00
204	Jeff D'Amico	.10
205	Rico Brogna	.10
206	Todd Hollandsworth	.10
207	Chad Curtis	.10
208	Tom Goodwin	.10
209	Neifi Perez	.10
210	Derek Bell	.10
211	Quilvio Veras	.10
212	Greg Vaughn	.10
213	Roberto Hernandez	.10
214	Arthur Rhodes	.10
215	Cal Eldred	.10
216	Bill Taylor	.10
217	Todd Greene	.10
218	Mario Valdez	.10
219	Ricky Bottalico	.10
220	Frank Rodriguez	.10
221	Rich Becker	.10
222	Roberto Duran	.10
223	Ivan Rodriguez	.75
224	Mike Jackson	.10
225	Deion Sanders	.25
226	Tony Womack	.10
227	Mark Kotsay	.50
228	Steve Trachsel	.10
229	Ryan Klesko	.35
230	Ken Cloude	.25
231	Luis Gonzalez	.10
232	Gary Gaetti	.10
233	Michael Tucker	.10
234	Shawn Green	.10
235	Ariel Prieto	.10
236	Kirt Manwaring	.10
237	Omar Vizquel	.10
238	Matt Beech	.10
239	Justin Thompson	.20
240	Bret Boone	.10
241	Derek Jeter	2.00
242	Ken Caminiti	.25
243	Jay Bell	.10
244	Kevin Tapani	.10
245	Jason Kendall	.10
246	Jose Guillen	.20
247	Mike Bordick	.10
248	Dustin Hermanson	.10
249	Darrin Fletcher	.10
250	Dave Hollins	.10
251	Ramon Martinez	.20
252	Hideki Irabu	.50
253	Mark Grace	.25
254	Jason Isringhausen	.10
255	Jose Cruz Jr.	1.50
256	Brian Johnson	.10
257	Brad Ausmus	.10
258	Andruw Jones	.75
259	Doug Jones	.10
260	Jeff Shaw	.10
261	Chuck Finley	.10
262	Gary Sheffield	.30
263	David Segui	.10
264	John Smiley	.10
265	Tim Salmon	.25
266	J.T. Snow Jr.	.10
267	Alex Fernandez	.10
268	Matt Stairs	.10
269	B.J. Surhoff	.10
270	Keith Foulke	.10
271	Edgar Martinez	.10
272	Shannon Stewart	.10
273	Eduardo Perez	.10
274	Wally Joyner	.10
275	Kevin Young	.10
276	Eli Marrero	.10
277	Brad Radke	.10
278	Jamie Moyer	.10
279	Joe Girardi	.10
280	Troy O'Leary	.10
281	Aaron Sele	.10
282	Jose Offerman	.10
283	Scott Erickson	.10
284	Sean Berry	.10
285	Shigetosi Hasegawa	.10
286	Felix Heredia	.10
287	Willie McGee	.10
288	Alex Rodriguez	3.00
289	Ugueth Urbina	.10
290	Jon Lieber	.10
291	Fernando Tatis	.10
292	Chris Stynes	.10
293	Bernard Gilkey	.10
294	Joey Hamilton	.10
295	Matt Karchner	.10
296	Paul Wilson	.10
297	Mel Nieves	.10
298	*Kevin Millwood*	1.50
299	Quinton McCracken	.10
300	Jerry DiPoto	.10
301	Jermaine Dye	.10
302	Travis Lee	2.50
303	Ron Coomer	.10
304	Matt Williams	.25
305	Bobby Higginson	.10
306	Jorge Fabregas	.10
307	Hal Morris	.10
308	Jay Bell	.10
309	Joe Randa	.10
310	Andy Benes	.10
311	Sterling Hitchcock	.10
312	Jeff Suppan	.10
313	Shane Reynolds	.10
314	Willie Blair	.10
315	Scott Rolen	1.50
316	Wilson Alvarez	.10
317	David Justice	.25
318	Fred McGriff	.25
319	Bobby Jones	.10
320	Wade Boggs	.30
321	Tim Wakefield	.10
322	Tony Saunders	.10
323	David Cone	.20
324	Roberto Hernandez	.10
325	Jose Canseco	.25
326	Kevin Stocker	.10
327	Gerald Williams	.10
328	Quinton McCracken	.10
329	Mark Gardner	.10
330	Ben Grieve (Prime Rookie)	1.50
331	Kevin Brown	.20
332	*Mike Lowell* (Prime Rookie)	.40
333	Jed Hansen	.10
334	Abraham Nunez (Prime Rookie)	.25
335	John Thomson	.10
336	Derrek Lee (Prime Rookie)	.10
337	Mike Piazza	2.00
338	Brad Fullmer (Prime Rookie)	.10
339	Ray Durham	.10
340	Kerry Wood (Prime Rookie)	5.00
341	*Kevin Polcovich*	.10
342	Russ Johnson (Prime Rookie)	.10
343	Darryl Hamilton	.10
344	David Ortiz (Prime Rookie)	.40
345	Kevin Orie	.10
346	Sean Casey (Prime Rookie)	.50
347	Juan Guzman	.10
348	Ruben Rivera (Prime Rookie)	.10
349	Rick Aguilera	.10
350	Bobby Estalella (Prime Rookie)	.10
351	Bobby Witt	.10
352	Paul Konerko (Prime Rookie)	.50
353	Matt Morris	.10
354	Carl Pavano (Prime Rookie)	.20
355	Todd Zeile	.10
356	Kevin Brown (Transaction)	.10
357	Alex Gonzalez	.10
358	Chuck Knoblauch (Transaction)	.40
359	Joey Cora	.10
360	Mike Lansing (Transaction)	.10
361	Adrian Beltre (Future Stars)	3.00
362	Dennis Eckersley (Transaction)	.10
363	A.J. Hinch (Future Stars)	1.50
364	Kenny Lofton (Transaction)	.75
365	Alex Gonzalez (Future Stars)	.10
366	Henry Rodriguez (Transaction)	.10
367	*Mike Stoner* (Future Stars)	2.00
368	Darryl Kile (Transaction)	.10
369	Carl Pavano (Future Stars)	.50
370	Walt Weiss (Transaction)	.10
371	Kris Benson (Future Stars)	.75
372	Cecil Fielder (Transaction)	.10
373	Dermal Brown (Future Stars)	1.50
374	Rod Beck (Transaction)	.10
375	Eric Milton (Future Stars)	1.00
376	Travis Fryman (Transaction)	.10
377	Preston Wilson (Future Stars)	.10
378	Chili Davis (Transaction)	.10
379	Travis Lee (Future Stars)	5.00
380	Jim Leyritz (Transaction)	.10
381	Vernon Wells (Draft Picks)	1.50
382	Joe Carter (Transaction)	.10
383	J.J. Davis (Draft Picks)	1.00
384	Marquis Grissom (Transaction)	.10
385	*Mike Cuddyer* (Draft Picks)	1.50
386	Rickey Henderson (Transaction)	.10
387	*Chris Enochs* (Draft Picks)	1.00
388	Andres Galarraga (Transaction)	.40
389	Jason Dellaero (Draft Picks)	.20
390	Robb Nen (Transaction)	.10
391	Mark Mangum (Draft Picks)	.10
392	Jeff Blauser (Transaction)	.10
393	Adam Kennedy (Draft Picks)	.20
394	Bob Abreu (Transaction)	.10
395	*Jack Cust* (Draft Picks)	1.00
396	Jose Vizcaino (Transaction)	.10
397	Jon Garland (Draft Picks)	.50
398	Pedro Martinez (Transaction)	.40
399	Aaron Akin (Draft Picks)	.10
400	Jeff Conine (Transaction)	.10

1998 Stadium Club First Day Issue

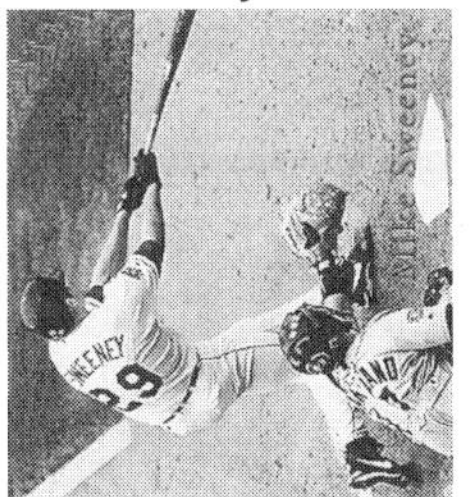

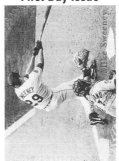

This retail-only parallel set was individually numbered to 200 and inserted through both series. First Day Issue cards were inserted in one per 44 Series I packs and one per 47 Series II packs.

		MT
	Common Player:	8.00
	Production 200 sets	
1	Chipper Jones	75.00
2	Frank Thomas	125.00
3	Vladimir Guerrero	30.00
4	Ellis Burks	8.00
5	John Franco	8.00
6	Paul Molitor	25.00
7	Rusty Greer	15.00
8	Todd Hundley	15.00
9	Brett Tomko	8.00
10	Eric Karros	15.00
11	Mike Cameron	15.00
12	Jim Edmonds	8.00
13	Bernie Williams	25.00
14	Denny Neagle	15.00
15	Jason Dickson	8.00
16	Sammy Sosa	80.00
17	Brian Jordan	8.00
18	Jose Vidro	8.00
19	Scott Spiezio	8.00
20	Jay Buhner	20.00
21	Jim Thome	25.00
22	Sandy Alomar	15.00
23	Devon White	8.00
24	Roberto Alomar	30.00
25	John Flaherty	8.00
26	John Wetteland	8.00
27	Willie Greene	8.00
28	Gregg Jefferies	8.00
29	Johnny Damon	8.00
30	Barry Larkin	15.00
31	Chuck Knoblauch	20.00
32	Mo Vaughn	40.00
33	Tony Clark	25.00
34	Marty Cordova	8.00
35	Vinny Castilla	12.00
36	Jeff King	8.00
37	Reggie Jefferson	8.00
38	Mariano Rivera	15.00
39	Jermaine Allensworth	8.00
40	Livan Hernandez	15.00
41	Heathcliff Slocumb	8.00
42	Jacob Cruz	8.00
43	Barry Bonds	40.00
44	Dave Magadan	8.00
45	Chan Ho Park	20.00
46	Jeremi Gonzalez	8.00
47	Jeff Cirillo	8.00
48	Delino DeShields	8.00
49	Craig Biggio	15.00
50	Benito Santiago	8.00
51	Mark Clark	8.00
52	Fernando Vina	8.00
53	F.P. Santangelo	8.00
54	*Pep Harris*	8.00
55	Edgar Renteria	8.00
56	Jeff Bagwell	60.00
57	Jimmy Key	8.00
58	Bartolo Colon	8.00
59	Curt Schilling	15.00
60	Steve Finley	8.00
61	Andy Ashby	8.00
62	John Burkett	8.00
63	Orel Hershiser	8.00
64	Pokey Reese	8.00
65	Scott Servais	8.00
66	Todd Jones	8.00
67	Javy Lopez	15.00
68	Robin Ventura	15.00
69	Miguel Tejada	20.00
70	Raul Casanova	8.00
71	Reggie Sanders	8.00
72	Edgardo Alfonzo	8.00
73	Dean Palmer	8.00
74	Todd Stottlemyre	12.00
75	David Wells	8.00
76	Troy Percival	8.00
77	Albert Belle	40.00
78	Pat Hentgen	8.00
79	Brian Hunter	8.00
80	Richard Hidalgo	8.00
81	Darren Oliver	8.00
82	Mark Wohlers	8.00
83	Cal Ripken Jr.	100.00
84	Hideo Nomo	40.00
85	Derrek Lee	15.00
86	Stan Javier	8.00
87	Rey Ordonez	8.00
88	Randy Johnson	30.00
89	Jeff Kent	8.00
90	Brian McRae	8.00
91	Manny Ramirez	35.00
92	Trevor Hoffman	8.00
93	Doug Glanville	8.00
94	Todd Walker	15.00
95	Andy Benes	8.00
96	Jason Schmidt	8.00
97	Mike Matheny	8.00
98	Tim Naehring	8.00
99	Jeff Blauser	8.00
100	Jose Rosado	8.00
101	Roger Clemens	70.00
102	Pedro Astacio	8.00
103	Mark Bellhorn	8.00
104	Paul O'Neill	15.00
105	Darin Erstad	25.00
106	Mike Lieberthal	8.00
107	Wilson Alvarez	8.00
108	Mike Mussina	30.00
109	George Williams	8.00
110	Cliff Floyd	8.00
111	Shawn Estes	8.00
112	Mark Grudzielanek	8.00
113	Tony Gwynn	70.00
114	Alan Benes	15.00
115	Terry Steinbach	8.00
116	Greg Maddux	80.00
117	Andy Pettitte	25.00
118	Dave Nilsson	8.00
119	Deivi Cruz	8.00
120	Carlos Delgado	15.00
121	Scott Hatteberg	8.00
122	John Olerud	15.00
123	Moises Alou	15.00
124	Garret Anderson	8.00
125	Royce Clayton	8.00
126	Dante Powell	8.00
127	Tom Glavine	15.00
128	Gary DiSarcina	8.00
129	Terry Adams	8.00
130	Raul Mondesi	20.00
131	Dan Wilson	8.00
132	Al Martin	8.00
133	Mickey Morandini	8.00
134	Rafael Palmeiro	15.00
135	Juan Encarnacion	12.00
136	Jim Pittsley	8.00
137	Magglio Ordonez	20.00
138	Will Clark	20.00
139	Todd Helton	30.00
140	Kelvim Escobar	8.00
141	Esteban Loaiza	8.00
142	John Jaha	8.00
143	Jeff Fassero	8.00
144	Harold Baines	8.00
145	Butch Huskey	8.00
146	Pat Meares	8.00
147	Brian Giles	8.00
148	Ramiro Mendoza	8.00
149	John Smoltz	15.00
150	Felix Martinez	8.00
151	Jose Valentin	8.00
152	Brad Rigby	8.00
153	Ed Sprague	8.00
154	Mike Hampton	8.00
155	Mike Lansing	8.00
156	Ray Lankford	8.00
157	Bobby Bonilla	15.00
158	Bill Mueller	8.00
159	Jeffrey Hammonds	8.00
160	Charles Nagy	8.00
161	Rich Loiselle	8.00
162	Al Leiter	8.00
163	Larry Walker	20.00
164	Chris Hoiles	8.00
165	Jeff Montgomery	8.00
166	Francisco Cordova	8.00
167	James Baldwin	8.00
168	Mark McLemore	8.00
169	Kevin Appier	8.00
170	Jamey Wright	8.00
171	Nomar Garciaparra	80.00
172	Matt Franco	8.00
173	Armando Benitez	8.00
174	Jeromy Burnitz	8.00
175	Ismael Valdes	8.00
176	Lance Johnson	8.00
177	Paul Sorrento	8.00
178	Rondell White	15.00
179	Kevin Elster	8.00
180	Jason Giambi	8.00
181	Carlos Baerga	8.00
182	Russ Davis	8.00
183	Ryan McGuire	8.00
184	Eric Young	8.00
185	Ron Gant	15.00
186	Manny Alexander	8.00
187	Scott Karl	8.00
188	Brady Anderson	12.00
189	Randall Simon	15.00
190	Tim Belcher	8.00
191	Jaret Wright	40.00
192	Dante Bichette	15.00
193	John Valentin	8.00
194	Darren Bragg	8.00
195	Mike Sweeney	8.00
196	Craig Counsell	8.00
197	Jaime Navarro	8.00
198	Todd Dunn	8.00
199	Ken Griffey Jr.	150.00
200	Juan Gonzalez	70.00
201	Billy Wagner	8.00
202	Jeff D'Amico	8.00
203	Mark McGwire	160.00
204	Jeff D'Amico	8.00
205	Rico Brogna	8.00
206	Todd Hollandsworth	8.00
207	Chad Curtis	8.00
208	Tom Goodwin	8.00
209	Neifi Perez	8.00
210	Derek Bell	8.00
211	Quilvio Veras	8.00
212	Greg Vaughn	8.00
213	Roberto Hernandez	8.00
214	Arthur Rhodes	8.00
215	Cal Eldred	8.00
216	Bill Taylor	8.00
217	Todd Greene	8.00
218	Mario Valdez	8.00
219	Ricky Bottalico	8.00
220	Frank Rodriguez	8.00
221	Rich Becker	8.00
222	Roberto Duran	8.00
223	Ivan Rodriguez	40.00
224	Mike Jackson	8.00
225	Deion Sanders	15.00
226	Tony Womack	8.00
227	Mark Kotsay	15.00
228	Steve Trachsel	8.00
229	Ryan Klesko	20.00
230	Ken Cloude	12.00
231	Luis Gonzalez	8.00
232	Gary Gaetti	8.00
233	Michael Tucker	8.00
234	Shawn Green	8.00
235	Ariel Prieto	8.00
236	Kirt Manwaring	8.00

237 Omar Vizquel 8.00
238 Matt Beech 8.00
239 Justin Thompson 8.00
240 Bret Boone 8.00
241 Derek Jeter 75.00
242 Ken Caminiti 15.00
243 Jay Bell 8.00
244 Kevin Tapani 8.00
245 Jason Kendall 8.00
246 Jose Guillen 15.00
247 Mike Bordick 8.00
248 Dustin Hermanson 8.00
249 Darrin Fletcher 8.00
250 Dave Hollins 8.00
251 Ramon Martinez 15.00
252 Hideki Irabu 25.00
253 Mark Grace 20.00
254 Jason Isringhausen 8.00
255 Jose Cruz Jr. 60.00
256 Brian Johnson 8.00
257 Brad Ausmus 8.00
258 Andruw Jones 35.00
259 Doug Jones 8.00
260 Jeff Shaw 8.00
261 Chuck Finley 8.00
262 Gary Sheffield 20.00
263 David Segui 8.00
264 John Smiley 8.00
265 Tim Salmon 20.00
266 J.T. Snow Jr. 8.00
267 Alex Fernandez 8.00
268 Matt Stairs 8.00
269 B.J. Surhoff 8.00
270 Keith Foulke 8.00
271 Edgar Martinez 12.00
272 Shannon Stewart 8.00
273 Eduardo Perez 8.00
274 Wally Joyner 8.00
275 Kevin Young 8.00
276 Eli Marrero 8.00
277 Brad Radke 8.00
278 Jamie Moyer 8.00
279 Joe Girardi 8.00
280 Troy O'Leary 8.00
281 Aaron Sele 12.00
282 Jose Offerman 8.00
283 Scott Erickson 8.00
284 Sean Berry 8.00
285 Shigetosi Hasegawa 8.00
286 Felix Heredia 8.00
287 Willie McGee 8.00
288 Alex Rodriguez 100.00
289 Ugueth Urbina 8.00
290 Jon Lieber 8.00
291 Fernando Tatis 8.00
292 Chris Stynes 8.00
293 Bernard Gilkey 8.00
294 Joey Hamilton 8.00
295 Matt Karchner 8.00
296 Paul Wilson 8.00
297 Mel Nieves 8.00
298 Kevin Millwood 30.00
299 Quinton McCracken 8.00
300 Jerry DiPoto 8.00
301 Jermaine Dye 8.00
302 Travis Lee 60.00
303 Ron Coomer 8.00
304 Matt Williams 20.00
305 Bobby Higginson 8.00
306 Jorge Fabregas 8.00
307 Hal Morris 8.00
308 Jay Bell 8.00
309 Joe Randa 8.00
310 Andy Benes 8.00
311 Sterling Hitchcock 8.00
312 Jeff Suppan 8.00
313 Shane Reynolds 8.00
314 Willie Blair 8.00
315 Scott Rolen 50.00
316 Wilson Alvarez 8.00
317 David Justice 20.00
318 Fred McGriff 15.00
319 Bobby Jones 8.00
320 Wade Boggs 15.00
321 Tim Wakefield 8.00
322 Tony Saunders 8.00
323 David Cone 15.00
324 Roberto Hernandez 8.00
325 Jose Canseco 20.00
326 Kevin Stocker 8.00
327 Gerald Williams 8.00
328 Quinton McCracken 8.00
329 Mark Gardner 8.00
330 Ben Grieve (Prime Rookie) 65.00
331 Kevin Brown 8.00
332 Mike Lowell (Prime Rookie) 8.00
333 Jed Hansen 8.00
334 Abraham Nunez (Prime Rookie) 8.00
335 John Thomson 8.00
336 Derrek Lee (Prime Rookie) 15.00
337 Mike Piazza 90.00
338 Brad Fullmer (Prime Rookie) 20.00
339 Ray Durham 8.00
340 Kerry Wood (Prime Rookie) 100.00
341 *Kevin Polcovich* 8.00
342 Russ Johnson (Prime Rookie) 8.00
343 Darryl Hamilton 8.00
344 David Ortiz (Prime Rookie) 10.00
345 Kevin Orie 8.00
346 Sean Casey (Prime Rookie) 25.00
347 Juan Guzman 8.00
348 Ruben Rivera (Prime Rookie) 8.00
349 Rick Aguilera 8.00
350 Bobby Estalella (Prime Rookie) 8.00
351 Bobby Witt 8.00
352 Paul Konerko (Prime Rookie) 25.00
353 Matt Morris 8.00
354 Carl Pavano (Prime Rookie) 15.00
355 Todd Zeile 8.00
356 Kevin Brown (Transaction) 8.00
357 Alex Gonzalez 8.00
358 Chuck Knoblauch (Transaction) 20.00
359 Joey Cora 8.00
360 Mike Lansing (Transaction) 8.00
361 Adrian Beltre (Future Stars) 40.00
362 Dennis Eckersley (Transaction) 8.00
363 A.J. Hinch (Future Stars) 8.00
364 Kenny Lofton (Transaction) 20.00
365 Alex Gonzalez (Future Stars) 8.00
366 Henry Rodriguez (Transaction) 8.00
367 *Mike Stoner* (Future Stars) 35.00
368 Darryl Kile (Transaction) 8.00
369 Carl Pavano (Future Stars) 8.00
370 Walt Weiss (Transaction) 8.00
371 Kris Benson (Future Stars) 25.00
372 Cecil Fielder (Transaction) 12.00
373 Dermal Brown (Future Stars) 35.00
374 Rod Beck (Transaction) 8.00
375 Eric Milton (Future Stars) 25.00
376 Travis Fryman (Transaction) 8.00
377 Preston Wilson (Future Stars) 8.00
378 Chili Davis (Transaction) 8.00
379 Travis Lee (Future Stars) 60.00
380 Jim Leyritz (Transaction) 8.00
381 Vernon Wells (Draft Picks) 20.00
382 Joe Carter (Transaction) 8.00
383 J.J. Davis (Draft Picks) 15.00
384 Marquis Grissom (Transaction) 8.00
385 *Mike Cuddyer* (Draft Picks) 25.00
386 Rickey Henderson (Transaction) 8.00
387 *Chris Enochs* (Draft Picks) 15.00
388 Andres Galarraga (Transaction) 20.00
389 Jason Dellaero (Draft Picks) 8.00
390 Robb Nen (Transaction) 8.00
391 Mark Mangum (Draft Picks) 8.00
392 Jeff Blauser (Transaction) 8.00
393 Adam Kennedy (Draft Picks) 8.00
394 Bob Abreu (Transaction) 8.00
395 *Jack Cust* (Draft Picks) 15.00
396 Jose Vizcaino (Transaction) 8.00
397 Jon Garland (Draft Picks) 12.00
398 Pedro Martinez (Transaction) 25.00
399 Aaron Akin (Draft Picks) 8.00
400 Jeff Conine (Transaction) 8.00

1998 Stadium Club One of a Kind

This hobby-only parallel set included all 400 cards from Series I and II printed on a silver mirrorboard stock. Cards were sequentially numbered to 150 and inserted one per 21 Series I packs and one per 24 Series II packs.

		MT
	Common Player:	8.00
	Semistars:	15.00
	Production 150 sets	
1	Chipper Jones	90.00
2	Frank Thomas	160.00
3	Vladimir Guerrero	40.00
4	Ellis Burks	8.00
5	John Franco	8.00
6	Paul Molitor	30.00
7	Rusty Greer	15.00
8	Todd Hundley	15.00
9	Brett Tomko	8.00
10	Eric Karros	15.00
11	Mike Cameron	15.00
12	Jim Edmonds	8.00
13	Bernie Williams	30.00
14	Denny Neagle	15.00
15	Jason Dickson	8.00
16	Sammy Sosa	100.00
17	Brian Jordan	8.00
18	Jose Vidro	8.00
19	Scott Spiezio	8.00
20	Jay Buhner	20.00
21	Jim Thome	25.00
22	Sandy Alomar	15.00
23	Devon White	8.00
24	Roberto Alomar	30.00
25	John Flaherty	8.00
26	John Wetteland	8.00
27	Willie Greene	8.00
28	Gregg Jefferies	8.00
29	Johnny Damon	8.00
30	Barry Larkin	20.00
31	Chuck Knoblauch	20.00
32	Mo Vaughn	40.00
33	Tony Clark	25.00
34	Marty Cordova	8.00
35	Vinny Castilla	12.00
36	Jeff King	8.00
37	Reggie Jefferson	8.00
38	Mariano Rivera	15.00
39	Jermaine Allensworth	8.00
40	Livan Hernandez	15.00
41	Heathcliff Slocumb	8.00
42	Jacob Cruz	8.00
43	Barry Bonds	40.00
44	Dave Magadan	8.00
45	Chan Ho Park	20.00
46	Jeremi Gonzalez	8.00
47	Jeff Cirillo	8.00
48	Delino DeShields	8.00
49	Craig Biggio	15.00
50	Benito Santiago	8.00
51	Mark Clark	8.00
52	Fernando Vina	8.00
53	F.P. Santangelo	8.00
54	*Pep Harris*	8.00
55	Edgar Renteria	8.00
56	Jeff Bagwell	60.00
57	Jimmy Key	8.00
58	Bartolo Colon	8.00
59	Curt Schilling	15.00
60	Steve Finley	8.00
61	Andy Ashby	8.00
62	John Burkett	8.00
63	Orel Hershiser	8.00
64	Pokey Reese	8.00
65	Scott Servais	8.00
66	Todd Jones	8.00
67	Javy Lopez	15.00
68	Robin Ventura	15.00
69	Miguel Tejada	20.00
70	Raul Casanova	8.00
71	Reggie Sanders	8.00
72	Edgardo Alfonzo	8.00
73	Dean Palmer	8.00
74	Todd Stottlemyre	12.00
75	David Wells	8.00
76	Troy Percival	8.00
77	Albert Belle	40.00
78	Pat Hentgen	8.00
79	Brian Hunter	8.00
80	Richard Hidalgo	8.00
81	Darren Oliver	8.00
82	Mark Wohlers	8.00
83	Cal Ripken Jr.	125.00
84	Hideo Nomo	40.00
85	Derrek Lee	15.00
86	Stan Javier	8.00
87	Rey Ordonez	8.00
88	Randy Johnson	30.00
89	Jeff Kent	8.00
90	Brian McRae	8.00
91	Manny Ramirez	40.00
92	Trevor Hoffman	8.00
93	Doug Glanville	8.00
94	Todd Walker	15.00
95	Andy Benes	8.00
96	Jason Schmidt	8.00
97	Mike Matheny	8.00
98	Tim Naehring	8.00
99	Jeff Blauser	8.00
100	Jose Rosado	8.00
101	Roger Clemens	70.00
102	Pedro Astacio	8.00
103	Mark Bellhorn	8.00
104	Paul O'Neill	15.00
105	Darin Erstad	25.00
106	Mike Lieberthal	8.00
107	Wilson Alvarez	8.00
108	Mike Mussina	30.00
109	George Williams	8.00
110	Cliff Floyd	8.00
111	Shawn Estes	8.00
112	Mark Grudzielanek	8.00
113	Tony Gwynn	80.00
114	Alan Benes	15.00
115	Terry Steinbach	8.00
116	Greg Maddux	90.00
117	Andy Pettitte	30.00
118	Dave Nilsson	8.00
119	Deivi Cruz	8.00
120	Carlos Delgado	15.00
121	Scott Hatteberg	8.00
122	John Olerud	15.00
123	Moises Alou	15.00
124	Garret Anderson	8.00
125	Royce Clayton	8.00
126	Dante Powell	8.00
127	Tom Glavine	15.00
128	Gary DiSarcina	8.00
129	Terry Adams	8.00
130	Raul Mondesi	20.00
131	Dan Wilson	8.00
132	Al Martin	8.00
133	Mickey Morandini	8.00
134	Rafael Palmeiro	15.00
135	Juan Encarnacion	15.00
136	Jim Pittsley	8.00
137	Magglio Ordonez	20.00
138	Will Clark	20.00
139	Todd Helton	40.00
140	Kelvim Escobar	8.00
141	Esteban Loaiza	8.00
142	John Jaha	8.00
143	Jeff Fassero	8.00
144	Harold Baines	8.00
145	Butch Huskey	8.00
146	Pat Meares	8.00
147	Brian Giles	8.00
148	Ramiro Mendoza	8.00
149	John Smoltz	15.00
150	Felix Martinez	8.00
151	Jose Valentin	8.00
152	Brad Rigby	8.00
153	Ed Sprague	8.00
154	Mike Hampton	8.00
155	Mike Lansing	8.00
156	Ray Lankford	8.00
157	Bobby Bonilla	15.00
158	Bill Mueller	8.00
159	Jeffrey Hammonds	8.00
160	Charles Nagy	8.00
161	Rich Loiselle	8.00
162	Al Leiter	8.00
163	Larry Walker	25.00
164	Chris Hoiles	8.00
165	Jeff Montgomery	8.00
166	Francisco Cordova	8.00
167	James Baldwin	8.00
168	Mark McLemore	8.00
169	Kevin Appier	8.00
170	Jamey Wright	8.00
171	Nomar Garciaparra	90.00
172	Matt Franco	8.00
173	Armando Benitez	8.00
174	Jeromy Burnitz	8.00
175	Ismael Valdes	8.00
176	Lance Johnson	8.00
177	Paul Sorrento	8.00
178	Rondell White	15.00
179	Kevin Elster	8.00
180	Jason Giambi	8.00
181	Carlos Baerga	8.00
182	Russ Davis	8.00
183	Ryan McGuire	8.00
184	Eric Young	8.00
185	Ron Gant	15.00
186	Manny Alexander	8.00
187	Scott Karl	8.00
188	Brady Anderson	12.00
189	Randall Simon	15.00
190	Tim Belcher	8.00
191	Jaret Wright	40.00
192	Dante Bichette	20.00
193	John Valentin	8.00
194	Darren Bragg	8.00
195	Mike Sweeney	8.00
196	Craig Counsell	8.00
197	Jaime Navarro	8.00
198	Todd Dunn	8.00
199	Ken Griffey Jr.	180.00
200	Juan Gonzalez	80.00
201	Billy Wagner	8.00
202	Jeff D'Amico	8.00
203	Mark McGwire	200.00
204	Jeff D'Amico	8.00
205	Rico Brogna	8.00
206	Todd Hollandsworth	8.00
207	Chad Curtis	8.00
208	Tom Goodwin	8.00
209	Neifi Perez	8.00
210	Derek Bell	8.00
211	Quilvio Veras	8.00
212	Greg Vaughn	8.00
213	Roberto Hernandez	8.00
214	Arthur Rhodes	8.00
215	Cal Eldred	8.00
216	Bill Taylor	8.00
217	Todd Greene	8.00
218	Mario Valdez	8.00
219	Ricky Bottalico	8.00
220	Frank Rodriguez	8.00
221	Rich Becker	8.00
222	Roberto Duran	8.00
223	Ivan Rodriguez	40.00
224	Mike Jackson	8.00
225	Deion Sanders	15.00
226	Tony Womack	8.00
227	Mark Kotsay	15.00
228	Steve Trachsel	8.00
229	Ryan Klesko	25.00
230	Ken Cloude	15.00
231	Luis Gonzalez	8.00
232	Gary Gaetti	8.00
233	Michael Tucker	8.00
234	Shawn Green	8.00
235	Ariel Prieto	8.00
236	Kirt Manwaring	8.00
237	Omar Vizquel	8.00
238	Matt Beech	8.00
239	Justin Thompson	8.00
240	Bret Boone	8.00
241	Derek Jeter	90.00
242	Ken Caminiti	20.00
243	Jay Bell	8.00
244	Kevin Tapani	8.00
245	Jason Kendall	8.00
246	Jose Guillen	15.00
247	Mike Bordick	8.00
248	Dustin Hermanson	8.00
249	Darrin Fletcher	8.00
250	Dave Hollins	8.00
251	Ramon Martinez	15.00
252	Hideki Irabu	25.00
253	Mark Grace	20.00
254	Jason Isringhausen	8.00
255	Jose Cruz Jr.	75.00
256	Brian Johnson	8.00
257	Brad Ausmus	8.00
258	Andruw Jones	40.00
259	Doug Jones	8.00
260	Jeff Shaw	8.00
261	Chuck Finley	8.00
262	Gary Sheffield	20.00
263	David Segui	8.00
264	John Smiley	8.00
265	Tim Salmon	20.00
266	J.T. Snow Jr.	8.00
267	Alex Fernandez	8.00
268	Matt Stairs	8.00
269	B.J. Surhoff	8.00
270	Keith Foulke	8.00
271	Edgar Martinez	12.00
272	Shannon Stewart	8.00
273	Eduardo Perez	8.00
274	Wally Joyner	8.00
275	Kevin Young	8.00
276	Eli Marrero	8.00
277	Brad Radke	8.00
278	Jamie Moyer	8.00
279	Joe Girardi	8.00
280	Troy O'Leary	8.00
281	Aaron Sele	15.00
282	Jose Offerman	8.00
283	Scott Erickson	8.00
284	Sean Berry	8.00
285	Shigetosi Hasegawa	8.00
286	Felix Heredia	8.00
287	Willie McGee	8.00
288	Alex Rodriguez	150.00
289	Ugueth Urbina	8.00
290	Jon Lieber	8.00
291	Fernando Tatis	8.00
292	Chris Stynes	8.00
293	Bernard Gilkey	8.00
294	Joey Hamilton	8.00
295	Matt Karchner	8.00
296	Paul Wilson	8.00
297	Mel Nieves	8.00
298	Kevin Millwood	40.00
299	Quinton McCracken	8.00
300	Jerry DiPoto	8.00
301	Jermaine Dye	8.00
302	Travis Lee	70.00
303	Ron Coomer	8.00
304	Matt Williams	20.00
305	Bobby Higginson	8.00
306	Jorge Fabregas	8.00
307	Hal Morris	8.00
308	Jay Bell	8.00
309	Joe Randa	8.00
310	Andy Benes	8.00
311	Sterling Hitchcock	8.00
312	Jeff Suppan	8.00
313	Shane Reynolds	8.00
314	Willie Blair	8.00
315	Scott Rolen	70.00
316	Wilson Alvarez	8.00
317	David Justice	25.00
318	Fred McGriff	20.00
319	Bobby Jones	8.00
320	Wade Boggs	15.00
321	Tim Wakefield	8.00
322	Tony Saunders	8.00
323	David Cone	15.00
324	Roberto Hernandez	8.00
325	Jose Canseco	20.00
326	Kevin Stocker	8.00
327	Gerald Williams	8.00
328	Quinton McCracken	8.00
329	Mark Gardner	8.00
330	Ben Grieve (Prime Rookie)	75.00
331	Kevin Brown	8.00
332	Mike Lowell (Prime Rookie)	8.00
333	Jed Hansen	8.00
334	Abraham Nunez (Prime Rookie)	8.00
335	John Thomson	8.00
336	Derrek Lee (Prime Rookie)	15.00
337	Mike Piazza	90.00

338	Brad Fullmer (Prime Rookie)	20.00
339	Ray Durham	8.00
340	Kerry Wood (Prime Rookie)	125.00
341	*Kevin Polcovich*	8.00
342	Russ Johnson (Prime Rookie)	8.00
343	Darryl Hamilton	8.00
344	David Ortiz (Prime Rookie)	10.00
345	Kevin Orie	8.00
346	Sean Casey (Prime Rookie)	30.00
347	Juan Guzman	8.00
348	Ruben Rivera (Prime Rookie)	8.00
349	Rick Aguilera	8.00
350	Bobby Estalella (Prime Rookie)	8.00
351	Bobby Witt	8.00
352	Paul Konerko (Prime Rookie)	30.00
353	Matt Morris	8.00
354	Carl Pavano (Prime Rookie)	15.00
355	Todd Zeile	8.00
356	Kevin Brown (Transaction)	8.00
357	Alex Gonzalez	8.00
358	Chuck Knoblauch (Transaction)	25.00
359	Joey Cora	8.00
360	Mike Lansing (Transaction)	8.00
361	Adrian Beltre (Future Stars)	50.00
362	Dennis Eckersley (Transaction)	8.00
363	A.J. Hinch (Future Stars)	8.00
364	Kenny Lofton (Transaction)	20.00
365	Alex Gonzalez (Future Stars)	8.00
366	Henry Rodriguez (Transaction)	8.00
367	*Mike Stoner* (Future Stars)	40.00
368	Darryl Kile (Transaction)	8.00
369	Carl Pavano (Future Stars)	8.00
370	Walt Weiss (Transaction)	8.00
371	Kris Benson (Future Stars)	25.00
372	Cecil Fielder (Transaction)	15.00
373	Dermal Brown (Future Stars)	40.00
374	Rod Beck (Transaction)	8.00
375	Eric Milton (Future Stars)	30.00
376	Travis Fryman (Transaction)	8.00
377	Preston Wilson (Future Stars)	8.00
378	Chili Davis (Transaction)	8.00
379	Travis Lee (Future Stars)	75.00
380	Jim Leyritz (Transaction)	8.00
381	Vernon Wells (Draft Picks)	25.00
382	Joe Carter (Transaction)	8.00
383	J.J. Davis (Draft Picks)	20.00
384	Marquis Grissom (Transaction)	8.00
385	*Mike Cuddyer* (Draft Picks)	30.00
386	Rickey Henderson (Transaction)	8.00
387	*Chris Enochs* (Draft Picks)	20.00
388	Andres Galarraga (Transaction)	20.00
389	Jason Dellaero (Draft Picks)	8.00
390	Robb Nen (Transaction)	8.00
391	Mark Mangum (Draft Picks)	8.00
392	Jeff Blauser (Transaction)	8.00
393	Adam Kennedy (Draft Picks)	8.00
394	Bob Abreu (Transaction)	8.00
395	*Jack Cust* (Draft Picks)	20.00
396	Jose Vizcaino (Transaction)	8.00
397	Jon Garland (Draft Picks)	15.00
398	Pedro Martinez (Transaction)	30.00
399	Aaron Akin (Draft Picks)	8.00
400	Jeff Conine (Transaction)	8.00

1998 Stadium Club 98 Bowman Preview

This Series I insert gave collectors a sneak peak at Bowman's 50th anniversary set, with 10 top veterans displayed on the 1998 Bowman design. The cards were inserted one per 12 packs and numbered with a "BP" prefix.

		MT
Complete Set (10):		50.00
Common Player:		1.00
Inserted 1:12		
BP1	Nomar Garciaparra	8.00
BP2	Scott Rolen	6.00
BP3	Ken Griffey Jr.	12.00
BP4	Frank Thomas	10.00
BP5	Larry Walker	1.50
BP6	Mike Piazza	8.00
BP7	Chipper Jones	8.00
BP8	Tino Martinez	1.00
BP9	Mark McGwire	15.00
BP10	Barry Bonds	3.00

1998 Stadium Club Bowman Prospect Preview

Bowman Prospect Previews were inserted into Series II retail and hobby packs at a rate of one per 12 and HTA packs at one per four. The 10-card insert previews the upcoming 1998 Bowman set and includes top prospects that are expected to make an impact in 1998.

		MT
Complete Set (10):		20.00
Common Player:		1.00
Inserted 1:12		
BP1	Ben Grieve	8.00
BP2	Brad Fullmer	2.50
BP3	Ryan Anderson	6.00
BP4	Mark Kotsay	2.00
BP5	Bobby Estalella	1.00
BP6	Juan Encarnacion	2.00
BP7	Todd Helton	3.00
BP8	Mike Lowell	1.00
BP9	A.J. Hinch	2.00
BP10	Richard Hidalgo	1.00

1998 Stadium Club Co-Signers

Co-Signers were inserted into both Series I and II hobby and HTA packs. The complete set is 36 cards and contains two top players one side along with both autographs. The were available in three levels of scarcity - Groups A, B and C. Seeding is as follows: Series I Group A 1:4,372 hobby and 1:2,623 HTA, Series I Group B 1:1,457 hobby and HTA 1:874, Series I Group C 1:121 hobby and 1:73 HTA, Series II Group A 1:4,702 hobby and 1:2,821 HTA, Series II Group B 1:1,567 hobby and 1:940 HTA, Series II Group C 1:1:131 hobby and 1:78 HTA.

		MT
Common Player:		50.00
Group A 1:4,372		
Group B 1:1,457		
Group C 1:121		
CS1	Nomar Garciaparra, Scott Rolen	50.00
CS2	Nomar Garciaparra, Derek Jeter	250.00
CS3	Nomar Garciaparra, Eric Karros	120.00
CS4	Scott Rolen, Derek Jeter	150.00
CS5	Scott Rolen, Eric Karros	150.00
CS6	Derek Jeter, Eric Karros	50.00
CS7	Travis Lee, Jose Cruz Jr.	250.00
CS8	Travis Lee, Mark Kotsay	125.00
CS9	Travis Lee, Paul Konerko	50.00
CS10	Jose Cruz Jr., Mark Kotsay	50.00
CS11	Jose Cruz Jr., Paul Konerko	150.00
CS12	Mark Kotsay, Paul Konerko	125.00
CS13	Tony Gwynn, Larry Walker	50.00
CS14	Tony Gwynn, Mark Grudzielanek	125.00
CS15	Tony Gwynn, Andres Galarraga	200.00
CS16	Larry Walker, Mark Grudzielanek	100.00
CS17	Larry Walker, Andres Galarraga	50.00
CS18	Mark Grudzielanek, Andres Galarraga	50.00
CS19	Sandy Alomar, Roberto Alomar	50.00
CS20	Sandy Alomar, Andy Pettitte	50.00
CS21	Sandy Alomar, Tino Martinez	80.00
CS22	Roberto Alomar, Andy Pottitte	125.00
CS23	Roberto Alomar, Tino Martinez	75.00
CS24	Andy Pettitte, Tino Martinez	50.00
CS25	Tony Clark, Todd Hundley	50.00
CS26	Tony Clark, Tim Salmon	100.00
CS27	Tony Clark, Robin Ventura	50.00
CS28	Todd Hundley, Tim Salmon	50.00
CS29	Todd Hundley, Robin Ventura	50.00
CS30	Tim Salmon, Robin Ventura	50.00
CS31	Roger Clemens, Randy Johnson	200.00
CS32	Roger Clemens, Jaret Wright	50.00
CS33	Roger Clemens, Matt Morris	100.00
CS34	Randy Johnson, Jaret Wright	100.00
CS35	Randy Johnson, Matt Morris	50.00
CS36	Jaret Wright, Matt Morris	125.00

1998 Stadium Club In the Wings

In the Wings was a Series I insert found every 36 packs. It included 15 future stars on uniluster technology.

		MT
Complete Set (15):		90.00
Common Player:		3.00
Inserted 1:36		
W1	Juan Encarnacion	5.00
W2	Brad Fullmer	6.00
W3	Ben Grieve	20.00
W4	Todd Helton	15.00
W5	Richard Hidalgo	3.00
W6	Russ Johnson	3.00
W7	Paul Konerko	15.00
W8	Mark Kotsay	8.00
W9	Derek Lee	6.00
W10	Travis Lee	25.00
W11	Eli Marrero	3.00
W12	David Ortiz	3.00
W13	Randall Simon	5.00
W14	Shannon Stewart	3.00
W15	Fernando Tatis	5.00

1998 Stadium Club Never Compromise

Never Compromise was a 20-card insert found in packs of Series I. Cards were inserted one per 12 packs and numbered with a "NC" prefix.

		MT
Complete Set (20):		120.00
Common Player:		1.00
Inserted 1:12		
NC1	Cal Ripken Jr.	15.00
NC2	Ivan Rodriguez	5.00
NC3	Ken Griffey Jr.	20.00
NC4	Frank Thomas	15.00
NC5	Tony Gwynn	10.00
NC6	Mike Piazza	12.00
NC7	Randy Johnson	3.00
NC8	Greg Maddux	12.00
NC9	Roger Clemens	8.00
NC10	Derek Jeter	12.00
NC11	Chipper Jones	12.00
NC12	Barry Bonds	5.00
NC13	Larry Walker	2.00
NC14	Jeff Bagwell	8.00
NC15	Barry Larkin	1.00
NC16	Ken Caminiti	1.00
NC17	Mark McGwire	25.00
NC18	Manny Ramirez	4.00
NC19	Tim Salmon	2.00
NC20	Paul Molitor	3.00

1998 Stadium Club Playing with Passion

This Series II insert displayed 10 players with a strong desire to win. The cards were inserted one per 12 packs and numbered with a "P" prefix.

		MT
Complete Set (10):		40.00
Common Player:		1.50
Inserted 1:12		
P1	Bernie Williams	2.00
P2	Jim Edmonds	1.50
P3	Chipper Jones	6.00
P4	Cal Ripken Jr.	8.00
P5	Craig Biggio	1.50
P6	Juan Gonzalez	5.00
P7	Alex Rodriguez	6.00
P8	Tino Martinez	2.00
P9	Mike Piazza	6.00
P10	Ken Griffey Jr.	10.00

1998 Stadium Club Royal Court

Fifteen players were showcased on uniluster technology for this Series II insert. The set is broken up into 10 Kings (veterans) and five Princes (rookies) and inserted one per 36 packs.

		MT
Complete Set (15):		180.00
Common Player:		3.00
Inserted 1:36		
RC1	Ken Griffey Jr.	35.00
RC2	Frank Thomas	30.00
RC3	Mike Piazza	20.00
RC4	Chipper Jones	20.00
RC5	Mark McGwire	40.00
RC6	Cal Ripken Jr.	25.00
RC7	Jeff Bagwell	10.00
RC8	Barry Bonds	8.00
RC9	Juan Gonzalez	15.00
RC10	Alex Rodriguez	20.00
RC11	Travis Lee	15.00
RC12	Paul Konerko	5.00
RC13	Todd Helton	5.00
RC14	Ben Grieve	10.00
RC15	Mark Kotsay	3.00

1998 Stadium Club Triumvirate

Triumvirates were included in both series of Stadium Club and were available only in retail packs. Series I had 24 players, with three players from eight different teams, while Series II had 30 players, with three players from 10 different positions. The cards were all die-cut and fit together to form one three-card panel. Three different versions of each card were available - Luminous (regular) versions were seeded one per 48 packs, Luminescent versions were seeded one per 192 packs and Illuminator versions were seeded one per 384 packs.

	MT
Complete Set (54):	700.00
Complete Series I (24):	300.00
Complete Series II (30):	400.00
Common Player:	4.00
Luminous 1:48	
Luminescents 1:192:	1.5x to 3x
Illuminators 1:384:	3x to 5x
T1a Chipper Jones	30.00
T1b Andruw Jones	20.00
T1c Kenny Lofton	12.00
T2a Derek Jeter	30.00
T2b Bernie Williams	10.00
T2c Tino Martinez	4.00
T3a Jay Buhner	6.00
T3b Edgar Martinez	4.00
T3c Ken Griffey Jr.	50.00
T4a Albert Belle	12.00
T4b Robin Ventura	4.00
T4c Frank Thomas	40.00
T5a Brady Anderson	4.00
T5b Cal Ripken Jr.	40.00
T5c Rafael Palmeiro	6.00
T6a Mike Piazza	30.00
T6b Raul Mondesi	6.00
T6c Eric Karros	4.00
T7a Vinny Castilla	4.00
T7b Andres Galarraga	6.00
T7c Larry Walker	6.00
T8a Jim Thome	8.00
T8b Manny Ramirez	10.00
T8c David Justice	6.00
T9a Mike Mussina	10.00
T9b Greg Maddux	30.00
T9c Randy Johnson	10.00
T10a Mike Piazza	30.00
T10b Sandy Alomar	4.00
T10c Ivan Rodriguez	12.00
T11a Mark McGwire	40.00
T11b Tino Martinez	6.00
T11c Frank Thomas	40.00
T12a Roberto Alomar	10.00
T12b Chuck Knoblauch	8.00
T12c Craig Biggio	4.00
T13a Cal Ripken Jr.	40.00
T13b Chipper Jones	30.00
T13c Ken Caminiti	4.00
T14a Derek Jeter	30.00
T14b Nomar Garciaparra	30.00
T14c Alex Rodriguez	30.00
T15a Barry Bonds	12.00
T15b David Justice	6.00
T15c Albert Belle	12.00
T16a Bernie Williams	8.00
T16b Ken Griffey Jr.	50.00
T16c Ray Lankford	4.00
T17a Tim Salmon	6.00
T17b Larry Walker	6.00
T17c Tony Gwynn	25.00
T18a Paul Molitor	10.00
T18b Edgar Martinez	4.00
T18c Juan Gonzalez	25.00

1998 Topps

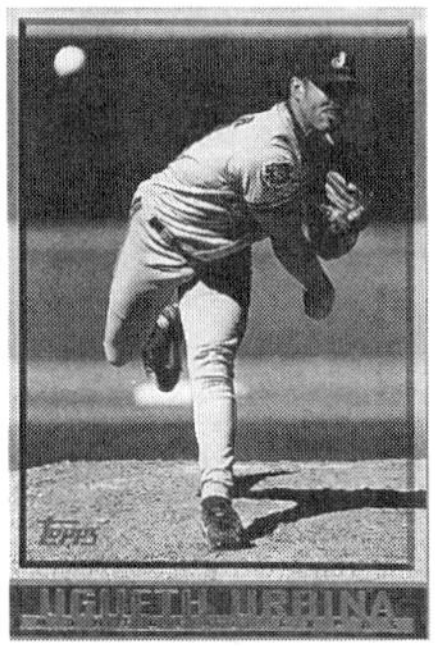

Topps was issued in two series in 1998 that totalled 503 cards, with 282 in Series I and 220 in Series II. Cards featured a gold border instead of the traditional white used in past years and the product featured Roberto Clemente inserts and a tribute card No. 21 in the base set. Series Highlights, Expansion Team Prospects, Interleague Highlights, Season Highlights, Prospects and Draft Picks. Subsets in Series II included: Expansion Teams, InterLeague Preview, Season Highlights, Prospects and Draft Picks. Every card in the set is paralleled in a Minted in Cooperstown insert that was stamped on-site at the Baseball Hall of Fame in Cooperstown. Inserts in Series I include: Roberto Clemente Reprints, Clemente Finest, Clemente Tribute, Memorabilia Madness, Etch a Sketch, Mystery Finest, Flashback and Baby Boomers. Inserts in Series II included: Clemente Reprints, Clemente Finest, 1998 Rookie Class, Mystery Finest, Milestones, Focal Points, and Clout 9.

		MT
Complete Set (503):		40.00
Complete Series I Set (282):		20.00
Complete Series II Set (220):		20.00
Common Player:		.05
Wax Box:		45.00
1	Tony Gwynn	1.25
2	Larry Walker	.25
3	Billy Wagner	.05
4	Denny Neagle	.05
5	Vladimir Guerrero	.75
6	Kevin Brown	.10
7	NOT ISSUED	
8	Mariano Rivera	.15
9	Tony Clark	.50
10	Deion Sanders	.15
11	Francisco Cordova	.05
12	Matt Williams	.20
13	Carlos Baerga	.05
14	Mo Vaughn	.60
15	Bobby Witt	.05
16	Matt Stairs	.05
17	Chan Ho Park	.10
18	Mike Bordick	.05
19	Michael Tucker	.05
20	Frank Thomas	2.00
21	Roberto Clemente	2.00
22	Dmitri Young	.05
23	Steve Trachsel	.05
24	Jeff Kent	.05
25	Scott Rolen	1.25
26	John Thomson	.05
27	Joe Vitiello	.05
28	Eddie Guardado	.05
29	Charlie Hayes	.05
30	Juan Gonzalez	1.25
31	Garret Anderson	.05
32	John Jaha	.05
33	Omar Vizquel	.05
34	Brian Hunter	.05
35	Jeff Bagwell	1.00
36	Mark Lemke	.05
37	Doug Glanville	.05
38	Dan Wilson	.05
39	Steve Cooke	.05
40	Chili Davis	.05
41	Mike Cameron	.05
42	F.P. Santangelo	.05
43	Brad Ausmus	.05
44	Gary DiSarcina	.05
45	Pat Hentgen	.05
46	Wilton Guerrero	.05
47	Devon White	.05
48	Danny Patterson	.05
49	Pat Meares	.05
50	Rafael Palmeiro	.15
51	Mark Gardner	.05
52	Jeff Blauser	.05
53	Dave Hollins	.05
54	Carlos Garcia	.05
55	Ben McDonald	.05
56	John Mabry	.05
57	Trevor Hoffman	.05
58	Tony Fernandez	.05
59	Rich Loiselle	.05
60	Mark Leiter	.05
61	Pat Kelly	.05
62	John Flaherty	.05
63	Roger Bailey	.05
64	Tom Gordon	.05
65	Ryan Klesko	.25
66	Darryl Hamilton	.05
67	Jim Eisenreich	.05
68	Butch Huskey	.05
69	Mark Grudzielanek	.05
70	Marquis Grissom	.15
71	Mark McLemore	.05
72	Gary Gaetti	.05
73	Greg Gagne	.05
74	Lyle Mouton	.05
75	Jim Edmonds	.15
76	Shawn Green	.05
77	Greg Vaughn	.05
78	Terry Adams	.05
79	*Kevin Polcovich*	.20
80	Troy O'Leary	.05
81	Jeff Shaw	.05
82	Rich Becker	.05
83	David Wells	.05
84	Steve Karsay	.05
85	Charles Nagy	.05
86	B.J. Surhoff	.05
87	Jamey Wright	.05
88	James Baldwin	.05
89	Edgardo Alfonzo	.05
90	Jay Buhner	.15
91	Brady Anderson	.15
92	Scott Servais	.05
93	Edgar Renteria	.05
94	Mike Lieberthal	.05
95	Rick Aguilera	.05
96	Walt Weiss	.05
97	Deivi Cruz	.05
98	Kurt Abbott	.05
99	Henry Rodriguez	.05
100	Mike Piazza	1.50
101	Bill Taylor	.05
102	Todd Zeile	.05
103	Rey Ordonez	.05
104	Willie Greene	.05
105	Tony Womack	.05
106	Mike Sweeney	.05
107	Jeffrey Hammonds	.05
108	Kevin Orie	.05
109	Alex Gonzalez	.05
110	Jose Canseco	.20
111	Paul Sorrento	.05
112	Joey Hamilton	.05
113	Brad Radke	.05
114	Steve Avery	.05
115	Esteban Loaiza	.05
116	Stan Javier	.05
117	Chris Gomez	.05
118	Royce Clayton	.05
119	Orlando Merced	.05
120	Kevin Appier	.05
121	Mel Nieves	.05
122	Joe Girardi	.05
123	Rico Brogna	.05
124	Kent Mercker	.05
125	Manny Ramirez	.50
126	Jeromy Burnitz	.05
127	Kevin Foster	.05
128	Matt Morris	.05
129	Jason Dickson	.05
130	Tom Glavine	.15
131	Wally Joyner	.05
132	Rick Reed	.05
133	Todd Jones	.05
134	Dave Martinez	.05
135	Sandy Alomar	.05
136	Mike Lansing	.05
137	Sean Berry	.05
138	Doug Jones	.05
139	Todd Stottlemyre	.05
140	Jay Bell	.05
141	Jaime Navarro	.05
142	Chris Hoiles	.05
143	Joey Cora	.05
144	Scott Spiezio	.05
145	Joe Carter	.15
146	Jose Guillen	.50
147	Damion Easley	.05
148	Lee Stevens	.05
149	Alex Fernandez	.05
150	Randy Johnson	.40
151	J.T. Snow	.15
152	Chuck Finley	.05
153	Bernard Gilkey	.05
154	David Segui	.05
155	Dante Bichette	.15
156	Kevin Stocker	.05
157	Carl Everett	.05
158	Jose Valentin	.05
159	Pokey Reese	.05
160	Derek Jeter	1.50
161	Roger Pavlik	.05
162	Mark Wohlers	.05
163	Ricky Bottalico	.05
164	Ozzie Guillen	.05
165	Mike Mussina	.50
166	Gary Sheffield	.20
167	Hideo Nomo	.50
168	Mark Grace	.20
169	Aaron Sele	.05
170	Darryl Kile	.10
171	Shawn Estes	.05
172	Vinny Castilla	.10
173	Ron Coomer	.05
174	Jose Rosado	.05
175	Kenny Lofton	.60
176	Jason Giambi	.10
177	Hal Morris	.05
178	Darren Bragg	.05
179	Orel Hershiser	.05
180	Ray Lankford	.10
181	Hideki Irabu	.75
182	Kevin Young	.05
183	Javy Lopez	.15
184	Jeff Montgomery	.05
185	Mike Holtz	.05
186	George Williams	.05
187	Cal Eldred	.05
188	Tom Candiotti	.05
189	Glenallen Hill	.05
190	Brian Giles	.05
191	Dave Mlicki	.05
192	Garrett Stephenson	.05
193	Jeff Frye	.05
194	Joe Oliver	.05
195	Bob Hamelin	.05
196	Luis Sojo	.05
197	LaTroy Hawkins	.05
198	Kevin Elster	.05
199	Jeff Reed	.05
200	Dennis Eckersley	.15
201	Bill Mueller	.05
202	Russ Davis	.05
203	Armando Benitez	.05
204	Quilvio Veras	.05
205	Tim Naehring	.05
206	Quinton McCracken	.05
207	Raul Casanova	.05
208	Matt Lawton	.05
209	Luis Alicea	.05
210	Luis Gonzalez	.05
211	Allen Watson	.05
212	Gerald Williams	.05
213	David Bell	.05
214	Todd Hollandsworth	.05
215	Wade Boggs	.15
216	Jose Mesa	.05
217	Jamie Moyer	.05
218	Darren Daulton	.10
219	Mickey Morandini	.05
220	Rusty Greer	.15
221	Jim Bullinger	.05
222	Jose Offerman	.05
223	Matt Karchner	.05
224	Woody Williams	.05
225	Mark Loretta	.05
226	Mike Hampton	.05
227	Willie Adams	.05
228	Scott Hatteberg	.05
229	Rich Amaral	.05
230	Terry Steinbach	.05
231	Glendon Rusch	.05
232	Bret Boone	.05
233	Robert Person	.05
234	Jose Hernandez	.05
235	Doug Drabek	.05
236	Jason McDonald	.05
237	Chris Widger	.05
238	*Tom Martin*	.05
239	Dave Burba	.05
240	Pete Rose	.05
241	Bobby Ayala	.05
242	Tim Wakefield	.05
243	Dennis Springer	.05
244	Tim Belcher	.05
245	Jon Garland, Geoff Goetz (Draft Pick)	.15
246	Glenn Davis, Lance Berkman (Draft Pick)	.50
247	Vernon Wells, Aaron Akin (Draft Pick)	.25
248	Adam Kennedy, Jason Romano (Draft Pick)	.10
249	Jason Dellaero, Troy Cameron (Draft Pick)	.20
250	Alex Sanchez, *Jared Sandberg* (Expansion Team Prospects)	.20
251	Pablo Ortega, Jim Manias (Expansion Team Prospects)	.15
252	Jason Conti, *Mike Stoner* (Expansion Team Prospects)	.50
253	John Patterson, Larry Rodriguez (Expansion Team Prospects)	.20
254	Adrian Beltre, *Ryan Minor* Aaron Boone (Prospect)	1.00
255	Ben Grieve, Brian Buchanan, Dermal Brown (Prospect)	1.00
256	Carl Pavano, Kerry Wood, Gil Meche (Prospect)	3.00
257	David Ortiz, Daryle Ward, Richie Sexson (Prospect)	.35
258	Randy Winn, Juan Encarnacion, Andrew Vessel (Prospect)	.25
259	Kris Benson, Travis Smith, Courtney Duncan (Prospect)	.40
260	Chad Hermansen, Brent Butler, *Warren Morris* (Prospect)	.50
261	Ben Davis, Elieser Marrero, Ramon Hernandez (Prospect)	.05
262	Eric Chavez, Russell Branyan, Russ Johnson (Prospect)	.40
263	Todd Dunwoody, John Barnes, *Ryan Jackson* (Prospect)	.25
264	Matt Clement, Roy Halladay ,*Brian Fuentes* (Prospect)	.40
265	Randy Johnson (Season Highlight)	.25
266	Kevin Brown (Season Highlight)	.05
267	Ricardo Rincon, Cordova, Rincon (Season Highlight)	.05
268	Nomar Garciaparra (Season Highlight)	.75
269	Tino Martinez (Season Highlight)	.10
270	Chuck Knoblauch (Interleague)	.15
271	Pedro Martinez (Interleague)	.10
272	Denny Neagle (Interleague)	.05
273	Juan Gonzalez (Interleague)	.60
274	Andres Galarraga (Interleague)	.10
275	Checklist	.05
276	Checklist	.05
277	(World Series)	.05
278	(World Series)	.05
279	(World Series)	.05
280	(World Series)	.05
281	(World Series)	.05
282	(World Series)	.05
283	(World Series)	.05
284	Tino Martinez	.20
285	Roberto Alomar	.50
286	Jeff King	.05
287	Brian Jordan	.05
288	Darin Erstad	.60
289	Ken Caminiti	.20
290	Jim Thome	.40
291	Paul Molitor	.50
292	Ivan Rodriguez	.60
293	Bernie Williams	.50
294	Todd Hundley	.15
295	Andres Galarraga	.20
296	Greg Maddux	1.50
297	Edgar Martinez	.10
298	Ron Gant	.15
299	Derek Bell	.05
300	Roger Clemens	1.00
301	Rondell White	.15
302	Barry Larkin	.15
303	Robin Ventura	.10
304	Jason Kendall	.05
305	Chipper Jones	1.50
306	John Franco	.05
307	Sammy Sosa	1.50
308	Troy Percival	.05
309	Chuck Knoblauch	.25
310	Ellis Burks	.15
311	Al Martin	.05
312	Tim Salmon	.25
313	Moises Alou	.15
314	Lance Johnson	.05
315	Justin Thompson	.15
316	Will Clark	.20
317	Barry Bonds	.60
318	Craig Biggio	.20
319	John Smoltz	.15
320	Cal Ripken Jr.	2.00
321	Ken Griffey Jr.	2.50
322	Paul O'Neill	.15
323	Todd Helton	.60
324	John Olerud	.15
325	Mark McGwire	3.00
326	Jose Cruz Jr.	1.50
327	Jeff Cirillo	.05
328	Dean Palmer	.05
329	John Wetteland	.05
330	Steve Finley	.05
331	Albert Belle	.60
332	Curt Schilling	.15
333	Raul Mondesi	.20
334	Andruw Jones	.75
335	Nomar Garciaparra	1.50
336	David Justice	.20
337	Andy Pettitte	.40
338	Pedro Martinez	.25
339	Travis Miller	.05
340	Chris Stynes	.05
341	Gregg Jefferies	.05
342	Jeff Fassero	.05
343	Craig Counsell	.05
344	Wilson Alvarez	.05
345	Bip Roberts	.05
346	Kelvim Escobar	.05
347	Mark Bellhorn	.05
348	Rickey Henderson	.05
349	Fred McGriff	.15
350	Chuck Carr	.05
351	Bob Abreu	.05
352	Juan Guzman	.05
353	Fernando Vina	.05
354	Andy Benes	.05
355	Dave Nilsson	.05
356	Bobby Bonilla	.10
357	Ismael Valdes	.05
358	Carlos Perez	.05
359	Kirk Rueter	.05
360	Bartolo Colon	.05
361	Mel Rojas	.05
362	Johnny Damon	.05
363	Geronimo Berroa	.05
364	Reggie Sanders	.05
365	Jermaine Allensworth	.05
366	Orlando Cabrera	.05
367	Jorge Fabregas	.05
368	Scott Stahoviak	.05
369	Ken Cloude	.05
370	Donovan Osborne	.05
371	Roger Cedeno	.05
372	Neifi Perez	.05
373	Chris Holt	.05
374	Cecil Fielder	.15
375	Marty Cordova	.05
376	Tom Goodwin	.05
377	Jeff Suppan	.05
378	Jeff Brantley	.05
379	Mark Langston	.05
380	Shane Reynolds	.05

381	Mike Fetters	.05
382	Todd Greene	.05
383	Ray Durham	.05
384	Carlos Delgado	.05
385	Jeff D'Amico	.05
386	Brian McRae	.05
387	Alan Benes	.15
388	Heathcliff Slocumb	.05
389	Eric Young	.05
390	Travis Fryman	.05
391	David Cone	.15
392	Otis Nixon	.05
393	Jeremi Gonzalez	.05
394	Jeff Juden	.05
395	Jose Vizcaino	.05
396	Ugueth Urbina	.05
397	Ramon Martinez	.10
398	Robb Nen	.05
399	Harold Baines	.10
400	Delino DeShields	.05
401	John Burkett	.05
402	Sterling Hitchcock	.05
403	Mark Clark	.05
404	Mariano Duncan	.05
405	Scott Brosius	.05
406	Chad Curtis	.05
407	Brian Johnson	.05
408	Roberto Kelly	.05
409	Rey Sanchez	.05
410	Michael Tucker	.05
411	Mark Kotsay	.20
412	Mark Lewis	.05
413	Ryan McGuire	.05
414	Shawon Dunston	.10
415	Brad Rigby	.05
416	Scott Erickson	.05
417	Bobby Jones	.05
418	Darren Oliver	.05
419	John Smiley	.05
420	T.J. Mathews	.05
421	Dustin Hermanson	.05
422	Mike Timlin	.05
423	Willie Blair	.05
424	Manny Alexander	.05
425	Bob Tewksbury	.05
426	Pete Schourek	.05
427	Reggie Jefferson	.05
428	Ed Sprague	.05
429	Jeff Conine	.05
430	Roberto Hernandez	.05
431	Tom Pagnozzi	.05
432	Jaret Wright	1.50
433	Livan Hernandez	.20
434	Andy Ashby	.05
435	Todd Dunn	.05
436	Bobby Higginson	.05
437	Jack McDowell	.05
438	Jim Leyritz	.05
439	Matt Williams	.20
440	Brett Tomko	.05
441	Joe Randa	.05
442	Chris Carpenter	.05
443	Dennis Reyes	.05
444	Al Leiter	.05
445	Jason Schmidt	.05
446	Ken Hill	.05
447	Shannon Stewart	.05
448	Enrique Wilson	.05
449	Fernando Tatis	.05
450	Jimmy Key	.05
451	Darrin Fletcher	.05
452	John Valentin	.05
453	Kevin Tapani	.05
454	Eric Karros	.05
455	Jay Bell	.05
456	Walt Weiss	.05
457	Devon White	.05
458	Carl Pavano	.05
459	Mike Lansing	.05
460	John Flaherty	.05
461	Richard Hidalgo	.05
462	Quinton McCracken	.05
463	Karim Garcia	.15
464	Miguel Cairo	.05
465	Edwin Diaz	.05
466	Bobby Smith	.05
467	Yamil Benitez	.05
468	*Rich Butler*	.25
469	*Ben Ford*	.05
470	Bubba Trammell	.05
471	Brent Brede	.05
472	Brooks Kieschnick	.05
473	Carlos Castillo	.05
474	Brad Radke (Season Highlight)	.05
475	Roger Clemens (Season Highlight)	.50
476	Curt Schilling (Season Highlight)	.10
477	John Olerud (Season Highlight)	.05
478	Mark McGwire (Season Highlight)	1.50
479	Mike Piazza, Ken Griffey Jr. (Interleague)	1.00
480	Jeff Bagwell, Frank Thomas (Interleague)	1.00
481	Chipper Jones, Nomar Garciaparra (Interleague)	.75
482	Larry Walker, Juan Gonzalez (Interleague)	.60
483	Gary Sheffield, Tino Martinez (Interleague)	.15
484	Derrick Gibson, Michael Coleman, Norm Hutchins (Prospect)	.05
485	Braden Looper, Cliff Politte, Brian Rose (Prospect)	.25
486	Eric Milton, Jason Marquis, Corey Lee (Prospect)	.15
487	A.J. Hinch, Mark Osborne, *Robert Fick* (Prospect)	.50
488	Aramis Ramirez, Alex Gonzalez, Sean Casey (Prospect)	1.00
489	*Donnie Bridges,* *Tim Drew* (Draft Pick)	.40
490	*Ntema Ndungidi,* *Darnell McDonald* (Draft Pick)	.50
491	*Ryan Anderson,* Mark Mangum (Draft Pick)	1.50
492	J.J. Davis, *Troy Glaus* (Draft Pick)	1.50
493	Jayson Werth, *Dan Reichert* (Draft Pick)	.25
494	*John Curtice,* *Mike Cuddyer* (Draft Pick)	.50
495	*Jack Cust,* Jason Standridge (Draft Pick)	.40
496	Brian Anderson (Expansion Team Prospect)	.05
497	Tony Saunders (Expansion Team Prospect)	.05
498	Vladimir Nunez, *Jhensy Sandoval* (Expansion Team Prospect)	.05
499	Brad Penny, Nick Bierbrodt (Expansion Team Prospect)	.05
500	*Dustin Carr,Luis Cruz* (Expansion Team Prospect)	.25
501	*Marcus McCain,* *Cedrick Bowers* (Expansion Team Prospect)	.40
502	Checklist	.05
503	Checklist	.05
504	Alex Rodriguez	2.00

1998 Topps Opening Day

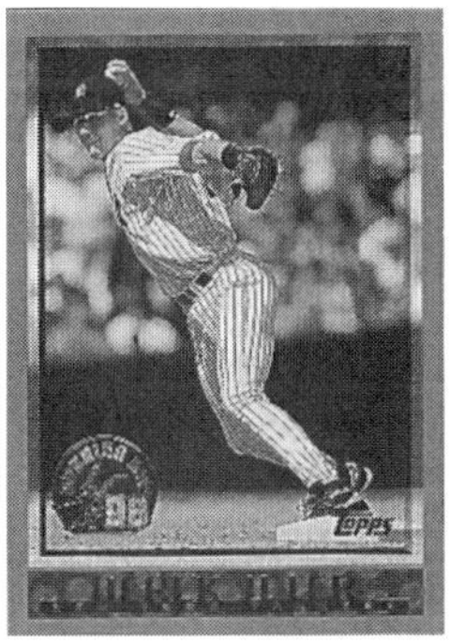

Topps Opening Day was a retail exclusive product included 165 cards, with 110 from Series I and 55 from Series II. The 55 cards from Series II were available in this product prior to the cards being released. Opening Day cards featured a silver border vs. the gold border in the base set, and included a silver Opening Day stamp.

		MT
Complete Set (165):		15.00
Common Player:		.05
1	Tony Gwynn	1.00
2	Larry Walker	.25
3	Billy Wagner	.05
4	Denny Neagle	.15
5	Vladimir Guerrero	.60
6	Kevin Brown	.15
7	Mariano Rivera	.15
8	Tony Clark	.40
9	Deion Sanders	.15
10	Matt Williams	.15
11	Carlos Baerga	.05
12	Mo Vaughn	.50
13	Chan Ho Park	.15
14	Frank Thomas	1.50
15	John Jaha	.05
16	Steve Trachsel	.05
17	Jeff Kent	.05
18	Scott Rolen	.60
19	Juan Gonzalez	1.00
20	Garret Anderson	.05
21	Roberto Clemente	1.50
22	Omar Vizquel	.05
23	Brian Hunter	.05
24	Jeff Bagwell	.75
25	Chili Davis	.05
26	Mike Cameron	.15
27	Pat Hentgen	.15
28	Wilton Guerrero	.05
29	Devon White	.05
30	Rafael Palmeiro	.20
31	Jeff Blauser	.05
32	Dave Hollins	.05
33	Trevor Hoffman	.10
34	Ryan Klesko	.25
35	Butch Huskey	.05
36	Mark Grudzielanek	.05
37	Marquis Grissom	.05
38	Jim Edmonds	.15
39	Greg Vaughn	.05
40	David Wells	.05
41	Charles Nagy	.05
42	B.J. Surhoff	.05
43	Edgardo Alfonzo	.05
44	Jay Buhner	.15
45	Brady Anderson	.15
46	Edgar Renteria	.05
47	Rick Aguilera	.05
48	Henry Rodriguez	.05
49	Mike Piazza	1.25
50	Todd Zeile	.05
51	Rey Ordonez	.05
52	Tony Womack	.05
53	Mike Sweeney	.05
54	Jeffrey Hammonds	.05
55	Kevin Orie	.05
56	Alex Gonzalez	.05
57	Jose Canseco	.20
58	Joey Hamilton	.05
59	Brad Radke	.05
60	Kevin Appier	.05
61	Manny Ramirez	.40
62	Jeromy Burnitz	.05
63	Matt Morris	.05
64	Jason Dickson	.05
65	Tom Glavine	.15
66	Wally Joyner	.05
67	Todd Jones	.05
68	Sandy Alomar	.10
69	Mike Lansing	.05
70	Todd Stottlemyre	.05
71	Jay Bell	.05
72	Joey Cora	.05
73	Scott Spiezio	.05
74	Joe Carter	.10
75	Jose Guillen	.20
76	Damion Easley	.05
77	Alex Fernandez	.05
78	Randy Johnson	.40
79	J.T. Snow	.15
80	Bernard Gilkey	.05
81	David Segui	.05
82	Dante Bichette	.15
83	Derek Jeter	1.25
84	Mark Wohlers	.05
85	Ricky Bottalico	.05
86	Mike Mussina	.40
87	Gary Sheffield	.20
88	Hideo Nomo	.40
89	Mark Grace	.15
90	Darryl Kile	.05
91	Shawn Estes	.15
92	Vinny Castilla	.10
93	Jose Rosado	.05
94	Kenny Lofton	.50
95	Jason Giambi	.05
96	Ray Lankford	.05
97	Hideki Irabu	.25
98	Javy Lopez	.05
99	Jeff Montgomery	.05
100	Dennis Eckersley	.05
101	Armando Benitez	.05
102	Tim Naehring	.05
103	Luis Gonzalez	.05
104	Todd Hollandsworth	.05
105	Wade Boggs	.15
106	Mickey Morandini	.05
107	Rusty Greer	.15
108	Terry Steinbach	.05
109	Pete Rose	.25
110	Checklist	.05
111	Tino Martinez	.25
112	Roberto Alomar	.40
113	Jeff King	.05
114	Brian Jordan	.05
115	Darin Erstad	.50
116	Ken Caminiti	.15
117	Jim Thome	.30
118	Paul Molitor	.40
119	Ivan Rodriguez	.50
120	Bernie Williams	.40
121	Todd Hundley	.15
122	Andres Galarraga	.20
123	Greg Maddux	1.25
124	Edgar Martinez	.05
125	Ron Gant	.05
126	Derek Bell	.05
127	Roger Clemens	.75
128	Rondell White	.15
129	Barry Larkin	.15
130	Robin Ventura	.05
131	Jason Kendall	.05
132	Chipper Jones	1.25
133	John Franco	.05
134	Sammy Sosa	1.00
135	Chuck Knoblauch	.20
136	Ellis Burks	.05
137	Al Martin	.05
138	Tim Salmon	.25
139	Moises Alou	.15
140	Lance Johnson	.05
141	Justin Thompson	.05
142	Will Clark	.15
143	Barry Bonds	.50
144	Craig Biggio	.20
145	John Smoltz	.15
146	Cal Ripken Jr.	1.50
147	Ken Griffey Jr.	2.00
148	Paul O'Neill	.15
149	Todd Helton	.60
150	John Olerud	.05
151	Mark McGwire	2.50
152	Jose Cruz Jr.	.75
153	Jeff Cirillo	.05
154	Dean Palmer	.05
155	John Wetteland	.05
156	Eric Karros	.05
157	Steve Finley	.05
158	Albert Belle	.50
159	Curt Schilling	.15
160	Raul Mondesi	.20
161	Andruw Jones	.60
162	Nomar Garciaparra	1.25
163	David Justice	.15
164	Andy Pettitte	.40
165	Pedro Martinez	.25

1998 Topps Minted in Cooperstown

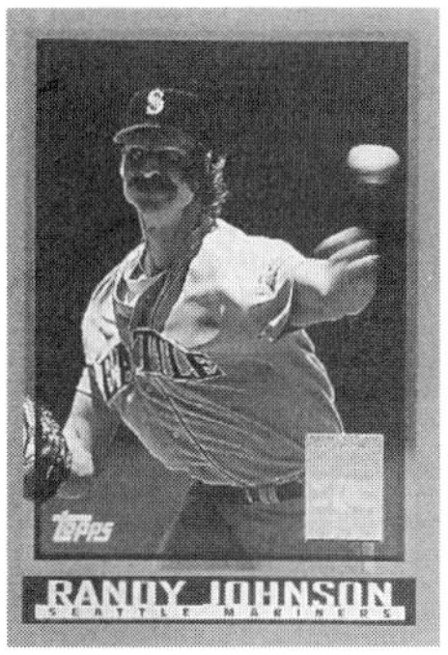

As part of an effort to promote interest in the various major sports' halls of fame, Topps produced this parallel version of its Series 1 baseball set. A special embossing machine was set up at the National Baseball Hall of Fame in Cooperstown to apply a bronze-foil "MINTED IN COOPERSTOWN" logo to cards. Twenty-card sheets of the logoed cards were sold on the premises and single cards were inserted into foil packs.

	MT
Common Card: (Star cards valued at 2.5X-4X corresponding card in regular issue)	.25

1998 Topps Baby Boomers

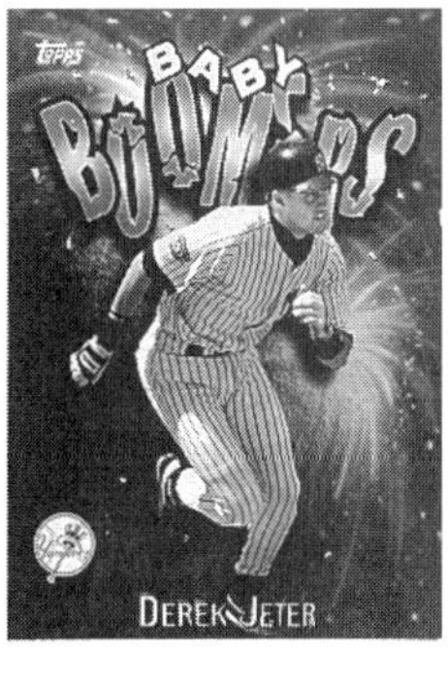

This 15-card retail exclusive insert was seeded one per 36 packs of Series I. It featured some of the top young players in the game and was numbered with a "BB" prefix.

		MT
Complete Set (15):		60.00
Common Player:		2.00
Inserted 1:36 retail		
BB1	Derek Jeter	10.00
BB2	Scott Rolen	8.00
BB3	Nomar Garciaparra	10.00
BB4	Jose Cruz Jr.	6.00
BB5	Darin Erstad	6.00
BB6	Todd Helton	4.00
BB7	Tony Clark	3.00
BB8	Jose Guillen	3.00
BB9	Andruw Jones	8.00
BB10	Vladimir Guerrero	5.00
BB11	Mark Kotsay	3.00
BB12	Todd Greene	2.00
BB13	Andy Pettitte	4.00
BB14	Justin Thompson	2.00
BB15	Alan Benes	2.00

1998 Topps Roberto Clemente Finest

Clemente Finest inserts were included in both Series I and II at a rate of one per 72 packs. There were a total of 19 different, with odd numbers in Series I and even numbers in Series II. The insert helped honor the memory of the 25th anniversary of his death.

		MT
Complete Set (19):		150.00
Common Clemente:		10.00
Inserted 1:72		
Common Refractor:		25.00
Refractors:		2x to 3x
Inserted 1:288		
1	1955	20.00
2	1956	10.00
3	1957	10.00
4	1958	10.00
5	1959	10.00
6	1960	10.00
7	1961	10.00
8	1962	10.00
9	1963	10.00
10	1964	10.00
11	1965	10.00
12	1966	10.00
14	1968	10.00
15	1969	10.00
16	1970	10.00
17	1971	10.00
18	1972	10.00
19	1973	10.00

1998 Topps Roberto Clemente Reprints

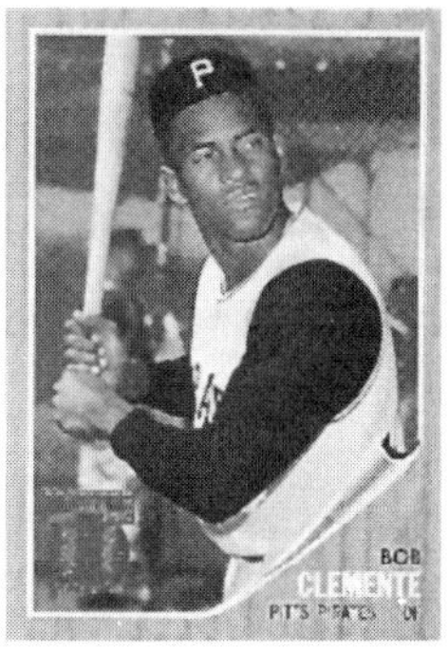

Nineteen different Topps Clemente cards were reprinted with a gold foil stamp and included 1998 Topps. Odd numbers were included in Series I, while even numbers were inserted into Series II, both at a rate of one per 18 packs. The insert was created to honor the memory of the 25th anniversary of Clemente's death.

	MT
Complete Set (19):	70.00

Common Clemente:		4.00
Inserted 1:18		
1	1955	10.00
2	1956	4.00
3	1957	4.00
4	1958	4.00
5	1959	4.00
6	1960	4.00
7	1961	4.00
8	1962	4.00
9	1963	4.00
10	1964	4.00
11	1965	4.00
12	1966	4.00
13	1967	4.00
14	1968	4.00
15	1969	4.00
16	1970	4.00
17	1971	4.00
18	1972	4.00
19	1973	4.00

1998 Topps Roberto Clemente Tribute

Five Clemente Tribute cards were produced for Series I and inserted in one per 12 packs. The set features some classic photos of Clemente and honor his memory in the 25th anniversary of his death. Clemente Tribute cards are numbered with a "RC" prefix.

		MT
Complete Set (5):		12.00
Common Clemente:		3.00
Inserted 1:12		
RC1	Roberto Clemente	3.00
RC2	Roberto Clemente	3.00
RC3	Roberto Clemente	3.00
RC4	Roberto Clemente	3.00
RC5	Roberto Clemente	3.00

1998 Topps Clout 9

Clout 9 captured nine players known for their statistical supremacy. Cards were numbered with a "C" prefix and inserted one per 72 packs of Series II.

		MT
Complete Set (9):		75.00
Common Player:		3.00
Inserted 1:72		
C1	Edgar Martinez	3.00
C2	Mike Piazza	15.00
C3	Frank Thomas	20.00
C4	Craig Biggio	4.00
C5	Vinny Castilla	4.00
C6	Jeff Blauser	3.00
C7	Barry Bonds	6.00
C8	Ken Griffey Jr.	25.00
C9	Larry Walker	5.00

1998 Topps Etch-A-Sketch

Etch a Sketch featured nine different players depicted by nationally acclaimed artist George Vlosich III. Known as "The Etch a Sketch Kid," Vlosich created each one of these Series I inserts, which were inserted at a rate of one per 36 packs.

		MT
Complete Set (9):		50.00
Common Player:		2.00
Inserted 1:36		
ES1	Albert Belle	4.00
ES2	Barry Bonds	3.00
ES3	Ken Griffey Jr.	12.00
ES4	Greg Maddux	8.00
ES5	Hideo Nomo	2.50
ES6	Mike Piazza	8.00
ES7	Cal Ripken Jr.	10.00
ES8	Frank Thomas	10.00
ES9	Mo Vaughn	3.00

1998 Topps Flashback

This double-sided insert showed "then and now" photos of 10 top major leaguers. One side contained a shot of the player in 1998, while the other side showed him at the beginning of his major league career. Flashback inserts were seeded one per 72 packs and numbered with a "FB" prefix.

		MT
Complete Set (10):		70.00
Common Player:		3.00
Inserted 1:72		
FB1	Barry Bonds	6.00
FB2	Ken Griffey Jr.	25.00
FB3	Paul Molitor	4.00
FB4	Randy Johnson	4.00
FB5	Cal Ripken Jr.	20.00
FB6	Tony Gwynn	12.00
FB7	Kenny Lofton	6.00
FB8	Gary Sheffield	4.00
FB9	Deion Sanders	3.00
FB10	Brady Anderson	3.00

1998 Topps Focal Point

This hobby exclusive insert contained 15 top players and focused on the skills that have made that player great. Focal Point inserts were available in Series II packs and

seeded one per 36 packs, and were numbered with a "FP" prefix.

		MT
Complete Set (15):		120.00
Common Player:		2.00
Inserted 1:36		
FP1	Juan Gonzalez	10.00
FP2	Nomar Garciaparra	12.00
FP3	Jose Cruz Jr.	8.00
FP4	Cal Ripken Jr.	15.00
FP5	Ken Griffey Jr.	20.00
FP6	Ivan Rodriguez	5.00
FP7	Larry Walker	4.00
FP8	Barry Bonds	5.00
FP9	Roger Clemens	8.00
FP10	Frank Thomas	15.00
FP11	Chuck Knoblauch	3.00
FP12	Mike Piazza	12.00
FP13	Greg Maddux	12.00
FP14	Vladimir Guerrero	6.00
FP15	Andruw Jones	6.00

1998 Topps Hallbound

Hall Bound featured 15 top players who are considered locks to be inducted into the Hall of Fame when their career is over. This insert was exclusive to Series I hobby packs and seeded one per 36 packs.

		MT
Complete Set (15):		100.00
Common Player:		2.00
HB1	Paul Molitor	3.50
HB2	Tony Gwynn	8.00
HB3	Wade Boggs	2.50
HB4	Roger Clemens	7.00
HB5	Dennis Eckersley	2.00
HB6	Cal Ripken Jr.	14.00
HB7	Greg Maddux	10.00
HB8	Rickey Henderson	2.00
HB9	Ken Griffey Jr.	18.00
HB10	Frank Thomas	15.00
HB11	Mark McGwire	20.00
HB12	Barry Bonds	5.00
HB13	Mike Piazza	10.00
HB14	Juan Gonzalez	8.00
HB15	Randy Johnson	4.00

1998 Topps Inter-League Mystery Finest

Five of the 1997 season's most intriguing inter-league matchups are showcased with four cards each in Inter-League Mystery Finest. Regular versions of this Series I insert are seeded one per 36

packs, while Refractor versions are seeded one per 144 packs.

		MT
Complete Set (20):		100.00
Common Player:		2.00
Inserted 1:36		
Refractors:		2x to 3x
Inserted 1:144		
ILM1	Chipper Jones	12.00
ILM2	Cal Ripken Jr.	15.00
ILM3	Greg Maddux	12.00
ILM4	Rafael Palmeiro	2.50
ILM5	Todd Hundley	2.00
ILM6	Derek Jeter	10.00
ILM7	John Olerud	2.00
ILM8	Tino Martinez	3.00
ILM9	Larry Walker	4.00
ILM10	Ken Griffey Jr.	20.00
ILM11	Andres Galarraga	3.00
ILM12	Randy Johnson	4.00
ILM13	Mike Piazza	12.00
ILM14	Jim Edmonds	2.00
ILM15	Eric Karros	2.00
ILM16	Tim Salmon	3.00
ILM17	Sammy Sosa	10.00
ILM18	Frank Thomas	15.00
ILM19	Mark Grace	3.00
ILM20	Albert Belle	5.00

1998 Topps Milestones

Milestones features 10 records that could be broken in during the 1998 season and the player's who have the best shot at breaking them. This retail exclusive insert is seeded one per 36 packs and is numbered with a "MS" prefix.

		MT
Complete Set (10):		60.00
Common Player:		1.50
MS1	Barry Bonds	4.00
MS2	Roger Clemens	5.00
MS3	Dennis Eckersley	1.50
MS4	Juan Gonzalez	7.50
MS5	Ken Griffey Jr.	15.00
MS6	Tony Gwynn	7.50
MS7	Greg Maddux	10.00
MS8	Mark McGwire	15.00
MS9	Cal Ripken Jr.	12.50
MS10	Frank Thomas	12.50

1998 Topps Mystery Finest

This 20-card insert set features top players on bordered and borderless designs, with Refractor versions of each. Exclusive to Series II packs, bordered cards are seeded 1:36 packs, border-

less are seeded 1:72 packs, bordered Refractors are 1:108 and borderless Refractors are seeded 1:288 packs. Mystery Finest inserts are numbered with a "M" prefix.

		MT
Complete Set (20):		200.00
Common Player:		2.50
Inserted 1:36		
Borderless 1:72:		1x to 1.5x
Bordered Refractors 1:108:		2x
Borderless Refractors 1:288:		
		4x to 5x
M1	Nomar Garciaparra	15.00
M2	Chipper Jones	15.00
M3	Scott Rolen	10.00
M4	Albert Belle	6.00
M5	Mo Vaughn	6.00
M6	Jose Cruz Jr.	10.00
M7	Mark McGwire	20.00
M8	Derek Jeter	15.00
M9	Tony Gwynn	12.00
M10	Frank Thomas	20.00
M11	Tino Martinez	4.00
M12	Greg Maddux	15.00
M13	Juan Gonzalez	12.00
M14	Larry Walker	4.00
M15	Mike Piazza	15.00
M16	Cal Ripken Jr.	20.00
M17	Jeff Bagwell	10.00
M18	Andruw Jones	6.00
M19	Barry Bonds	6.00
M20	Ken Griffey Jr.	25.00

1998 Topps 98 Rookie Class

Rookie Class features 10 young stars from 1998 and was exclusive to Series II packs. The cards were inserted one per 12 packs and numbered with a "R" prefix.

		MT
Complete Set (10):		20.00
Common Player:		1.00
Inserted 1:12		
R1	Travis Lee	8.00
R2	Richard Hidalgo	1.00
R3	Todd Helton	3.00
R4	Paul Konerko	3.00
R5	Mark Kotsay	2.00
R6	Derrek Lee	1.50
R7	Eli Marrero	1.00
R8	Fernando Tatis	1.00
R9	Juan Encarnacion	1.00
R10	Ben Grieve	4.00

1998 Topps Chrome

All 502 cards from Topps Series I and II were reprinted in chromium versions for Topps Chrome. Chrome was released in two series, with Series I containing 282 cards and Series II including 220 cards. Four-card packs were sold for a suggested retail price of $3, while cards included a Topps Chrome logo. Chrome also included a sampling of the inserts from Topps, along with Refractor versions of every card and insert. Series I inserts included: Flashbacks, Baby Boomers and Hall Bound. Series II inserts included: Milestones, '98 Rookie Class and Clout 9.

		MT
Complete Set (502):		250.00
Complete Series I Set (282)		160.00
Complete Series II Set (220)		90.00
Common Player:		.25
Wax Box:		100.00
1	Tony Gwynn	4.00
2	Larry Walker	1.00
3	Billy Wagner	.25
4	Denny Neagle	.25
5	Vladimir Guerrero	2.50
6	Kevin Brown	.50
8	Mariano Rivera	.75
9	Tony Clark	1.50
10	Deion Sanders	.75
11	Francisco Cordova	.25
12	Matt Williams	1.00
13	Carlos Baerga	.25
14	Mo Vaughn	2.00
15	Bobby Witt	.25
16	Matt Stairs	.25
17	Chan Ho Park	.50
18	Mike Bordick	.25
19	Michael Tucker	.25
20	Frank Thomas	6.00
21	Roberto Clemente (Tribute)	6.00
22	Dmitri Young	.25
23	Steve Trachsel	.25
24	Jeff Kent	.25
25	Scott Rolen	4.00
26	John Thomson	.25
27	Joe Vitiello	.25
28	Eddie Guardado	.25
29	Charlie Hayes	.25
30	Juan Gonzalez	4.00
31	Garret Anderson	.25
32	John Jaha	.25
33	Omar Vizquel	.25
34	Brian Hunter	.25
35	Jeff Bagwell	3.00
36	Mark Lemke	.25
37	Doug Glanville	.25
38	Dan Wilson	.25
39	Steve Cooke	.25
40	Chili Davis	.25
41	Mike Cameron	.25
42	F.P. Santangelo	.25
43	Brad Ausmus	.25
44	Gary DiSarcina	.25
45	Pat Hentgen	.25
46	Wilton Guerrero	.25
47	Devon White	.25
48	Danny Patterson	.25
49	Pat Meares	.25
50	Rafael Palmeiro	.75
51	Mark Gardner	.25
52	Jeff Blauser	.25
53	Dave Hollins	.25
54	Carlos Garcia	.25
55	Ben McDonald	.25
56	John Mabry	.25
57	Trevor Hoffman	.25
58	Tony Fernandez	.25
59	Rich Loiselle	.25
60	Mark Leiter	.25
61	Pat Kelly	.25
62	John Flaherty	.25
63	Roger Bailey	.25
64	Tom Gordon	.25
65	Ryan Klesko	1.00
66	Darryl Hamilton	.25
67	Jim Eisenreich	.25
68	Butch Huskey	.25
69	Mark Grudzielanek	.25
70	Marquis Grissom	.25
71	Mark McLemore	.25
72	Gary Gaetti	.25
73	Greg Gagne	.25
74	Lyle Mouton	.25
75	Jim Edmonds	.25
76	Shawn Green	.25
77	Terry Vaughn	.25
78	Terry Adams	.25
79	*Kevin Polcovich*	.60
80	Troy O'Leary	.25
81	Jeff Shaw	.25
82	Rich Becker	.25
83	David Wells	.25
84	Steve Karsay	.25
85	Charles Nagy	.25
86	B.J. Surhoff	.25
87	Jamey Wright	.25
88	James Baldwin	.25
89	Edgardo Alfonzo	.50
90	Jay Buhner	.75
91	Brady Anderson	.50
92	Scott Servais	.25
93	Edgar Renteria	.25
94	Mike Lieberthal	.25
95	Rick Aguilera	.25
96	Walt Weiss	.25
97	Deivi Cruz	.25
98	Kurt Abbott	.25
99	Henry Rodriguez	.25
100	Mike Piazza	5.00
101	Bill Taylor	.25
102	Todd Zeile	.25
103	Rey Ordonez	.25
104	Willie Greene	.25
105	Tony Womack	.25
106	Mike Sweeney	.25
107	Jeffrey Hammonds	.25
108	Kevin Orie	.25
109	Alex Gonzalez	.25
110	Jose Canseco	.75
111	Paul Sorrento	.25
112	Joey Hamilton	.25
113	Brad Radke	.25
114	Steve Avery	.25
115	Esteban Loaiza	.25
116	Stan Javier	.25
117	Chris Gomez	.25
118	Royce Clayton	.25
119	Orlando Merced	.25
120	Kevin Appier	.25
121	Mel Nieves	.25
122	Joe Girardi	.25
123	Rico Brogna	.25
124	Kent Mercker	.25
125	Manny Ramirez	1.50
126	Jeromy Burnitz	.25
127	Kevin Foster	.25
128	Matt Morris	.50
129	Jason Dickson	.25
130	Tom Glavine	.50
131	Wally Joyner	.25
132	Rick Reed	.25
133	Todd Jones	.25
134	Dave Martinez	.25
135	Sandy Alomar	.50
136	Mike Lansing	.25
137	Sean Berry	.25
138	Doug Jones	.25
139	Todd Stottlemyre	.25
140	Jay Bell	.25
141	Jaime Navarro	.25
142	Chris Hoiles	.25
143	Joey Cora	.25
144	Scott Spiezio	.25
145	Joe Carter	.50
146	Jose Guillen	.75
147	Damion Easley	.25
148	Lee Stevens	.25
149	Alex Fernandez	.25
150	Randy Johnson	1.50
151	J.T. Snow	.50
152	Chuck Finley	.25
153	Bernard Gilkey	.25
154	David Segui	.25
155	Dante Bichette	.75
156	Kevin Stocker	.25
157	Carl Everett	.25
158	Jose Valentin	.50
159	Pokey Reese	.25
160	Derek Jeter	5.00
161	Roger Pavlik	.25
162	Mark Wohlers	.25
163	Ricky Bottalico	.25
164	Ozzie Guillen	.25
165	Mike Mussina	1.50
166	Gary Sheffield	1.00
167	Hideo Nomo	2.00
168	Mark Grace	.75
169	Aaron Sele	.25
170	Darryl Kile	.25
171	Shawn Estes	.25
172	Vinny Castilla	.50
173	Ron Coomer	.25
174	Jose Rosado	.25
175	Kenny Lofton	2.00
176	Jason Giambi	.25
177	Hal Morris	.25
178	Darren Bragg	.25
179	Orel Hershiser	.25
180	Ray Lankford	.25
181	Hideki Irabu	1.00
182	Kevin Young	.25
183	Javy Lopez	.25
184	Jeff Montgomery	.25
185	Mike Holtz	.25
186	George Williams	.25
187	Cal Eldred	.25
188	Tom Candiotti	.25
189	Glenallen Hill	.25
190	Brian Giles	.25
191	Dave Mlicki	.25
192	Garrett Stephenson	.25
193	Jeff Frye	.25
194	Joe Oliver	.25
195	Bob Hamelin	.25
196	Luis Sojo	.25
197	LaTroy Hawkins	.25
198	Kevin Elster	.25
199	Jeff Reed	.25
200	Dennis Eckersley	.50
201	Bill Mueller	.25
202	Russ Davis	.25
203	Armando Benitez	.25
204	Quilvio Veras	.25
205	Tim Naehring	.25
206	Quinton McCracken	.25
207	Raul Casanova	.25
208	Matt Lawton	.25
209	Luis Alicea	.25
210	Luis Gonzalez	.25
211	Allen Watson	.25
212	Gerald Williams	.25
213	David Bell	.25
214	Todd Hollandsworth	.25
215	Wade Boggs	.75
216	Jose Mesa	.25
217	Jamie Moyer	.25
218	Darren Daulton	.25
219	Mickey Morandini	.25
220	Rusty Greer	.50
221	Jim Bullinger	.25
222	Jose Offerman	.25
223	Matt Karchner	.25
224	Woody Williams	.25
225	Mark Loretta	.25
226	Mike Hampton	.25
227	Willie Adams	.25
228	Scott Hatteberg	.25
229	Rich Amaral	.25
230	Terry Steinbach	.25
231	Glendon Rusch	.25
232	Bret Boone	.25
233	Robert Person	.25
234	Jose Hernandez	.25
235	Doug Drabek	.25
236	Jason McDonald	.25
237	Chris Widger	.25
238	*Tom Martin*	.25
239	Dave Burba	.25
240	Pete Rose	.25
241	Bobby Ayala	.25
242	Tim Wakefield	.25
243	Dennis Springer	.25
244	Tim Belcher	.25
245	Jon Garland, Geoff Goetz (Draft Pick)	3.00
246	Glenn Davis, Lance Berkman (Draft Pick)	6.00
247	Vernon Wells, Aaron Akin (Draft Pick)	4.00
248	Adam Kennedy, Jason Romano (Draft Pick)	3.00
249	Jason Dellaero, Troy Cameron (Draft Pick)	3.00
250	Alex Sanchez, *Jared Sandberg* (Expansion)	3.00
251	Pablo Ortega, *James Manias* (Expansion)	2.00
252	Jason Conti, *Mike Stoner* (Expansion)	8.00
253	John Patterson, Larry Rodriguez (Expansion)	1.50
254	Adrian Beltre, *Ryan Minor*, Aaron Boone (Prospect)	12.00
255	Ben Grieve, Brian Buchanan, Dermal Brown (Prospect)	6.00
256	Carl Pavano, Kerry Wood, Gil Meche (Prospect)	15.00
257	David Ortiz, Daryle Ward, Richie Sexson (Prospect)	4.00
258	Randy Winn, Juan Encarnacion, Andrew Vessel (Prospect)	1.00
259	Kris Benson, Travis Smith, Courtney Duncan (Prospect)	2.50
260	Chad Hermansen, Brent Butler, *Warren Morris* (Prospect)	5.00
261	Ben Davis, Elieser Marrero, Ramon Hernandez (Prospect)	2.50
262	Eric Chavez, Russell Branyan, Russ Johnson (Prospect)	4.00
263	Todd Dunwoody, John Barnes, *Ryan Jackson* (Prospect)	2.50
264	Matt Clement, Roy Halladay, Brian Fuentes (Prospect)	4.00
265	Randy Johnson (Season Highlight)	.75
266	Kevin Brown (Season Highlight)	.40
267	Francisco Cordova, Ricardo Rincon (Season Highlight)	.25
268	Nomar Garciaparra (Season Highlight)	3.00
269	Tino Martinez (Season Highlight)	.50
270	Chuck Knoblauch (Inter-League)	.50
271	Pedro Martinez (Inter-League)	.50
272	Denny Neagle (Inter-League)	.25
273	Juan Gonzalez (Inter-League)	2.00
274	Andres Galarraga (Inter-League)	.50
275	Checklist	.25
276	Checklist	.25
277	Moises Alou (World Series)	.25
278	Sandy Alomar (World Series)	.25
279	Gary Sheffield (World Series)	.50
280	Matt Williams (World Series)	.50
281	Livan Hernandez (World Series)	.50
282	Chad Ogea (World Series)	.25
283	Celebration (World Series)	.75
284	Tino Martinez	.75
285	Roberto Alomar	1.50
286	Jeff King	.25
287	Brian Jordan	.25
288	Darin Erstad	2.00
289	Ken Caminiti	.50
290	Jim Thome	1.00
291	Paul Molitor	1.50
292	Ivan Rodriguez	2.00
293	Bernie Williams	1.50
294	Todd Hundley	.50
295	Andres Galarraga	.75
296	Greg Maddux	5.00
297	Edgar Martinez	.50
298	Ron Gant	.50
299	Derek Bell	.25
300	Roger Clemens	3.00
301	Rondell White	.50
302	Barry Larkin	.75
303	Robin Ventura	.50
304	Jason Kendall	.25
305	Chipper Jones	5.00
306	John Franco	.25
307	Sammy Sosa	4.00
308	Troy Percival	.25
309	Chuck Knoblauch	.75
310	Ellis Burks	.25
311	Al Martin	.25
312	Tim Salmon	.75
313	Moises Alou	.50
314	Lance Johnson	.25
315	Justin Thompson	.25
316	Will Clark	.75
317	Barry Bonds	2.00
318	Craig Biggio	.50
319	John Smoltz	.50
320	Cal Ripken Jr.	6.00
321	Ken Griffey Jr.	8.00
322	Paul O'Neill	.50
323	Todd Helton	2.00
324	John Olerud	.25
325	Mark McGwire	10.00
326	Jose Cruz Jr.	2.00
327	Jeff Cirillo	.25
328	Dean Palmer	.25
329	John Wetteland	.25
330	Steve Finley	.25
331	Albert Belle	2.00
332	Curt Schilling	.50
333	Raul Mondesi	.50
334	Andruw Jones	2.00
335	Nomar Garciaparra	5.00
336	David Justice	.75
337	Andy Pettitte	1.00
338	Pedro Martinez	1.00
339	Travis Miller	.25
340	Chris Stynes	.25
341	Gregg Jefferies	.25
342	Jeff Fassero	.25
343	Craig Counsell	.25
344	Wilson Alvarez	.25
345	Bip Roberts	.25
346	Kelvim Escobar	.25
347	Mark Bellhorn	.25
348	Rickey Henderson	.25
349	Fred McGriff	.50
350	Chuck Carr	.25
351	Bob Abreu	.25
352	Juan Guzman	.25
353	Fernando Vina	.25
354	Andy Benes	.50
355	Dave Nilsson	.25
356	Bobby Bonilla	.50
357	Ismael Valdes	.25
358	Carlos Perez	.25
359	Kirk Rueter	.25
360	Bartolo Colon	.25
361	Mel Rojas	.25
362	Johnny Damon	.25
363	Geronimo Berroa	.25
364	Reggie Sanders	.25
365	Jermaine Allensworth	.25
366	Orlando Cabrera	.25
367	Jorge Fabregas	.25
368	Scott Stahoviak	.25
369	Ken Cloude	.50
370	Donovan Osborne	.25
371	Roger Cedeno	.25
372	Neifi Perez	.25
373	Chris Holt	.25
374	Cecil Fielder	.50
375	Marty Cordova	.25
376	Tom Goodwin	.25
377	Jeff Suppan	.25
378	Jeff Brantley	.25
379	Mark Langston	.25
380	Shane Reynolds	.25
381	Mike Fetters	.25
382	Todd Greene	.25
383	Ray Durham	.25
384	Carlos Delgado	.25
385	Jeff D'Amico	.25
386	Brian McRae	.25
387	Alan Benes	.50
388	Heathcliff Slocumb	.25
389	Eric Young	.25
390	Travis Fryman	.25
391	David Cone	.50
392	Otis Nixon	.25
393	Jeremi Gonzalez	.25
394	Jeff Juden	.25
395	Jose Vizcaino	.25
396	Ugueth Urbina	.25
397	Ramon Martinez	.50
398	Robb Nen	.25
399	Harold Baines	.25
400	Delino DeShields	.25
401	John Burkett	.25
402	Sterling Hitchcock	.25
403	Mark Clark	.25
404	Mariano Duncan	.25
405	Scott Brosius	.25
406	Chad Curtis	.25
407	Brian Johnson	.25
408	Roberto Kelly	.25
409	Rey Sanchez	.25
410	Michael Tucker	.25
411	Mark Kotsay	.75
412	Mark Lewis	.25
413	Ryan McGuire	.25
414	Shawon Dunston	.25
415	Brad Rigby	.25
416	Scott Erickson	.25
417	Bobby Jones	.25
418	Darren Oliver	.25
419	John Smiley	.25
420	T.J. Mathews	.25
421	Dustin Hermanson	.25
422	Mike Timlin	.25
423	Willie Blair	.25
424	Manny Alexander	.25
425	Bob Tewksbury	.25
426	Pete Schourek	.25
427	Reggie Jefferson	.25
428	Ed Sprague	.25
429	Jeff Conine	.25
430	Roberto Hernandez	.25
431	Tom Pagnozzi	.25
432	Jaret Wright	2.50
433	Livan Hernandez	.25
434	Andy Ashby	.25
435	Todd Dunn	.25
436	Bobby Higginson	.25
437	Jack McDowell	.25
438	Jim Leyritz	.25
439	Matt Williams	.75
440	Brett Tomko	.25
441	Joe Randa	.25
442	Chris Carpenter	.25
443	Dennis Reyes	.25
444	Al Leiter	.25
445	Jason Schmidt	.25
446	Ken Hill	.25
447	Shannon Stewart	.25
448	Enrique Wilson	.25
449	Fernando Tatis	.50
450	Jimmy Key	.25
451	Darrin Fletcher	.25
452	John Valentin	.25
453	Kevin Tapani	.25
454	Eric Karros	.50
455	Jay Bell	.25
456	Walt Weiss	.25
457	Devon White	.25
458	Carl Pavano	.50
459	Mike Lansing	.25
460	John Flaherty	.25
461	Richard Hidalgo	.25
462	Quinton McCracken	.25
463	Karim Garcia	.50
464	Miguel Cairo	.25
465	Edwin Diaz	.25
466	Bobby Smith	.25
467	Yamil Benitez	.25
468	*Rich Butler*	1.50
469	*Ben Ford*	.50
470	Bubba Trammell	.25
471	Brent Brede	.25
472	Brooks Kieschnick	.25
473	Carlos Castillo	.25
474	Brad Radke (Season Highlight)	.25
475	Roger Clemens (Season Highlight)	1.50
476	Curt Schilling (Season Highlight)	.25
477	John Olerud (Season Highlight)	.25
478	Mark McGwire (Season Highlight)	5.00
479	Mike Piazza, Ken Griffey Jr. (Interleague)	5.00
480	Jeff Bagwell, Frank Thomas (Interleague)	3.00
481	Chipper Jones, Nomar Garciaparra (Interleague)	3.00

482	Larry Walker, Juan Gonzalez (Interleague)	2.50
483	Gary Sheffield, Tino Martinez (Interleague)	.50
484	Derrick Gibson, Michael Coleman, Norm Hutchins (Prospect)	.50
485	Braden Looper, Cliff Politte, Brian Rose (Prospect)	2.00
486	Eric Milton, Jason Marquis, Corey Lee (Prospect)	1.00
487	A.J. Hinch, Mark Osborne, *Robert Fick* (Prospect)	6.00
488	Aramis Ramirez, Alex Gonzalez, Sean Casey (Prospect)	8.00
489	*Donnie Bridges, Tim Drew* (Draft Pick)	2.00
490	*Ntema Ndungidi, Darnell McDonald* (Draft Pick)	6.00
491	*Ryan Anderson, Mark Mangum* (Draft Pick)	8.00
492	*J.J. Davis,Troy Glaus* (Draft Pick)	6.00
493	Jayson Werth, Dan Reichert (Draft Pick)	2.00
494	*John Curtice, Mike Cuddyer* (Draft Pick)	2.00
495	*Jack Cust,* Jason Standridge (Draft Pick)	1.50
496	Brian Anderson (Expansion Team Prospect)	.25
497	Tony Saunders (Expansion Team Prospect)	.50
498	Vladimir Nunez, *Jhensy Sandoval* (Expansion Team Prospect)	.50
499	Brad Penny, Nick Bierbrodt (Expansion Team Prospect)	.25
500	*Dustin Carr,Luis Cruz* (Expansion Team Prospect)	1.00
501	*Marcus McCain, Cedrick Bowers* (Expansion Team Prospect)	.25
502	Checklist	.25
503	Checklist	.25
504	Alex Rodriguez	5.00
		.25

1998 Topps Chrome Refractors

Each card in the regular Topps Series 1 and Series 2 Chrome issue could also be found in a refractor version seeded approximately one per 12 packs. Refractor versions are so designated above the card number of back.

	MT
Common Player:	4.00
(Stars and rookies valued at 5-15X regular Chrome version)	

1998 Topps Chrome Baby Boomers

This 15-card insert featured players with less than three years of experience. Cards were inserted one per 24 packs, with Refractor versions found every 72 packs of Series I. Cards were numbered with a "BB" prefix.

		MT
Complete Set (15):		90.00
Common Player:		2.00
Inserted 1:24		
Refractors:		2x to 3x
Inserted 1:72		
BB1	Derek Jeter	15.00
BB2	Scott Rolen	12.00
BB3	Nomar Garciaparra	15.00
BB4	Jose Cruz Jr.	10.00
BB5	Darin Erstad	6.00
BB6	Todd Helton	6.00
BB7	Tony Clark	4.00
BB8	Jose Guillen	4.00
BB9	Andruw Jones	12.00
BB10	Vladimir Guerrero	8.00
BB11	Mark Kotsay	4.00
BB12	Todd Greene	2.00
BB13	Andy Pettitte	4.00
BB14	Justin Thompson	2.00
BB15	Alan Benes	2.00

1998 Topps Chrome Clout 9

This nine-card insert included players for their statistical supremacy. Clout 9 cards were found in Series II packs at a rate of one per 24 packs, with Refractor versions every 72 packs.

		MT
Complete Set (9):		75.00
Common Player:		3.00
Inserted 1:24		
Refractors:		1.5x to 2x
Inserted 1:72		
C1	Edgar Martinez	3.00
C2	Mike Piazza	20.00
C3	Frank Thomas	25.00
C4	Craig Biggio	4.00
C5	Vinny Castilla	4.00
C6	Jeff Blauser	3.00
C7	Barry Bonds	8.00
C8	Ken Griffey Jr.	30.00
C9	Larry Walker	6.00

1998 Topps Chrome Flashback

This 10-card double-sided insert features top players as they looked in 1998 on one side, and how they looked when they first appeared in the majors on the other side. Flashback inserts were seeded one per 24 packs of Series I, with Refractors every 72 packs. This insert was numbered with a "FB" prefix.

		MT
Complete Set (10):		60.00
Common Player:		3.00
Inserted 1:24		
Refractors:		2x to 3x
Inserted 1:72		
FB1	Barry Bonds	5.00
FB2	Ken Griffey Jr.	20.00
FB3	Paul Molitor	4.00
FB4	Randy Johnson	4.00
FB5	Cal Ripken Jr.	15.00
FB6	Tony Gwynn	10.00
FB7	Kenny Lofton	5.00
FB8	Gary Sheffield	4.00
FB9	Deion Sanders	3.00
FB10	Brady Anderson	3.00

1998 Topps Chrome Hallbound

Hall Bound highlighted 15 players destined for the Hall of Fame on die-cut cards. Inserted at a rate of one per 24 packs of Series I, with Refractors every 72 packs, these were numbered with a "HB" prefix.

		MT
Complete Set (15):		125.00
Common Player:		3.00
Inserted 1:24		
Refractors:		2x to 3x
Inserted 1:72		
HB1	Paul Molitor	3.00
HB2	Tony Gwynn	12.00
HB3	Wade Boggs	4.00
HB4	Roger Clemens	10.00
HB5	Dennis Eckersley	3.00
HB6	Cal Ripken Jr.	20.00
HB7	Greg Maddux	15.00
HB8	Rickey Henderson	3.00
HB9	Ken Griffey Jr.	25.00
HB10	Frank Thomas	20.00
HB11	Mark McGwire	30.00
HB12	Barry Bonds	6.00
HB13	Mike Piazza	15.00
HB14	Juan Gonzalez	12.00
HB15	Randy Johnson	5.00

1998 Topps Chrome Milestones

Ten superstars who were within reach of major records for the 1998 season are featured in Milestones. This Series II insert was seeded one per 24 packs, with Refractor versions seeded one per 72 packs. Milestones were numbered with a "MS" prefix.

		MT
Complete Set (10):		125.00
Common Player:		3.00
Inserted 1:24		
Refractors:		1.5x to 2x
Inserted 1:72		
MS1	Barry Bonds	8.00
MS2	Roger Clemens	10.00
MS3	Dennis Eckersley	3.00
MS4	Juan Gonzalez	15.00
MS5	Ken Griffey Jr.	30.00
MS6	Tony Gwynn	15.00
MS7	Greg Maddux	20.00
MS8	Mark McGwire	35.00
MS9	Cal Ripken Jr.	25.00
MS10	Frank Thomas	25.00

1998 Topps Chrome 98 Rookie Class

This insert featured 10 players with less than one year of major league experience. Inserted in Series II packs at a rate of one per 12 packs, with Refractors every 24 packs, '98 Rookie Class inserts were numbered with a "R" prefix.

		MT
Complete Set (10):		30.00
Common Player:		1.50
Inserted 1:12		
Refractors:		1x to 1.5x
Inserted 1:24		
R1	Travis Lee	12.00
R2	Richard Hidalgo	1.50
R3	Todd Helton	5.00
R4	Paul Konerko	4.00
R5	Mark Kotsay	3.00
R6	Derrek Lee	3.00
R7	Eli Marrero	1.50
R8	Fernando Tatis	1.50
R9	Juan Encarnacion	1.50
R10	Ben Grieve	10.00

1998 Topps Gallery

Gallery returned in 1998 with a 150-card set broken up into five different subsets - Ex-hibitions, Impressions, Ex-pressionists, Portraits and Permanent Collection. The set was paralleled twice - first in a Player's Private Issue set and, second in Gallery Proofs. Gallery cards were made to look like works of art instead of simply a photo of the player on cardboard, and were sold in six-card packs. Inserts in this single-series product include: Photo Gallery, Gallery of Heroes and Awards Gallery.

		MT
Complete Set (150):		50.00
Common Player:		.20
Wax Box:		65.00
1	Andruw Jones	1.25
2	Fred McGriff	.40
3	Wade Boggs	.40
4	Pedro Martinez	.75
5	Matt Williams	.50
6	Wilson Alvarez	.20
7	Henry Rodriguez	.20
8	Jay Bell	.20
9	Marquis Grissom	.20
10	Darryl Kile	.20
11	Chuck Knoblauch	.50
12	Kenny Lofton	1.25
13	Quinton McCracken	.20
14	Andres Galarraga	.50
15	Brian Jordan	.20
16	Mike Lansing	.20
17	Travis Fryman	.20
18	Tony Saunders	.20
19	Moises Alou	.40
20	Travis Lee	4.00
21	Garret Anderson	.20
22	Ken Caminiti	.40
23	Pedro Astacio	.20
24	Ellis Burks	.20
25	Albert Belle	1.25
26	Alan Benes	.40
27	Jay Buhner	.50
28	Derek Bell	.20
29	Jeromy Burnitz	.20
30	Kevin Appier	.20
31	Jeff Cirillo	.20
32	Bernard Gilkey	.20
33	David Cone	.40
34	Jason Dickson	.20
35	Jose Cruz Jr.	.75
36	Marty Cordova	.20
37	Ray Durham	.20
38	Jaret Wright	1.25
39	Billy Wagner	.20
40	Roger Clemens	2.00
41	Juan Gonzalez	2.50
42	Jeremi Gonzalez	.20
43	Mark Grudzielanek	.20
44	Tom Glavine	.40
45	Barry Larkin	.40
46	Lance Johnson	.20
47	Bobby Higginson	.20
48	Mike Mussina	1.00
49	Al Martin	.20
50	Mark McGwire	6.00
51	Todd Hundley	.20
52	Ray Lankford	.20
53	Jason Kendall	.20
54	Javy Lopez	.40
55	Ben Grieve	2.00
56	Randy Johnson	.75
57	Jeff King	.20
58	Mark Grace	.50
59	Rusty Greer	.40
60	Greg Maddux	3.00
61	Jeff Kent	.20
62	Rey Ordonez	.20
63	Hideo Nomo	.75
64	Charles Nagy	.20
65	Rondell White	.40
66	Todd Helton	1.25
67	Jim Thome	.75
68	Denny Neagle	.20
69	Ivan Rodriguez	1.25
70	Vladimir Guerrero	1.25
71	Jorge Posada	.20
72	J.T. Snow Jr.	.20
73	Reggie Sanders	.20
74	Scott Rolen	2.00
75	Robin Ventura	.40

76	Mariano Rivera	.40
77	Cal Ripken Jr.	4.00
78	Justin Thompson	.20
79	Mike Piazza	3.00
80	Kevin Brown	.20
81	Sandy Alomar	.40
82	Craig Biggio	.40
83	Vinny Castilla	.40
84	Eric Young	.20
85	Bernie Williams	.75
86	Brady Anderson	.20
87	Bobby Bonilla	.20
88	Tony Clark	.75
89	Dan Wilson	.20
90	John Wetteland	.20
91	Barry Bonds	1.25
92	Chan Ho Park	.50
93	Carlos Delgado	.40
94	David Justice	.50
95	Chipper Jones	3.00
96	Shawn Estes	.20
97	Jason Giambi	.20
98	Ron Gant	.40
99	John Olerud	.40
100	Frank Thomas	4.00
101	Jose Guillen	.40
102	Brad Radke	.20
103	Troy Percival	.20
104	John Smoltz	.40
105	Edgardo Alfonzo	.20
106	Dante Bichette	.40
107	Larry Walker	.50
108	John Valentin	.20
109	Roberto Alomar	1.00
110	Mike Cameron	.20
111	Eric Davis	.20
112	Johnny Damon	.20
113	Darin Erstad	1.25
114	Omar Vizquel	.20
115	Derek Jeter	2.50
116	Tony Womack	.20
117	Edgar Renteria	.20
118	Raul Mondesi	.40
119	Tony Gwynn	2.50
120	Ken Griffey Jr.	5.00
121	Jim Edmonds	.20
122	Brian Hunter	.20
123	Neifi Perez	.20
124	Dean Palmer	.20
125	Alex Rodriguez	3.00
126	Tim Salmon	.50
127	Curt Schilling	.40
128	Kevin Orie	.20
129	Andy Pettitte	.75
130	Gary Sheffield	.50
131	Jose Rosado	.20
132	Manny Ramirez	1.25
133	Rafael Palmeiro	.50
134	Sammy Sosa	3.00
135	Jeff Bagwell	2.00
136	Delino DeShields	.20
137	Ryan Klesko	.50
138	Mo Vaughn	1.25
139	Steve Finley	.20
140	Nomar Garciaparra	3.00
141	Paul Molitor	.75
142	Pat Hentgen	.20
143	Eric Karros	.40
144	Bobby Jones	.20
145	Tino Martinez	.50
146	Matt Morris	.20
147	Livan Hernandez	.40
148	Edgar Martinez	.20
149	Paul O'Neill	.40
150	Checklist	.20

1998 Topps Gallery Players Private Issue

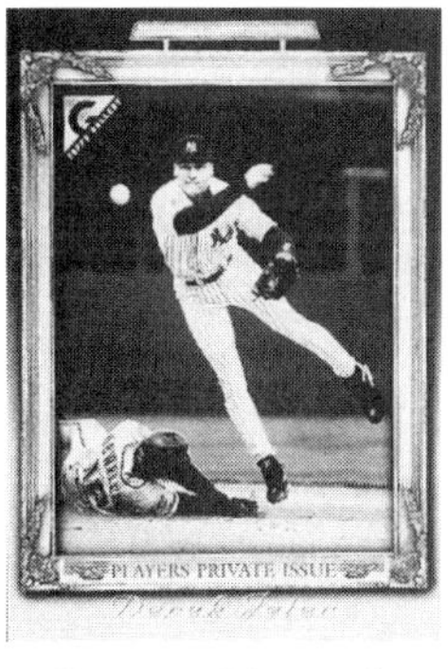

Player's Private Issue cards paralleled the 150-card base set with a distinct design and embossing. These parallel cards were inserted one per 12 packs.

		MT
Common Player:		8.00
Semistars:		20.00
Unlisted Stars:		30.00
Production 250 sets		
1	Andruw Jones	35.00
2	Fred McGriff	15.00
3	Wade Boggs	15.00
4	Pedro Martinez	25.00
5	Matt Williams	20.00
6	Wilson Alvarez	8.00
7	Henry Rodriguez	8.00
8	Jay Bell	8.00
9	Marquis Grissom	8.00
10	Darryl Kile	8.00
11	Chuck Knoblauch	20.00
12	Kenny Lofton	35.00
13	Quinton McCracken	8.00
14	Andres Galarraga	25.00
15	Brian Jordan	8.00
16	Mike Lansing	8.00
17	Travis Fryman	8.00
18	Tony Saunders	8.00
19	Moises Alou	15.00
20	Travis Lee	100.00
21	Garret Anderson	8.00
22	Ken Caminiti	15.00
23	Pedro Astacio	8.00
24	Ellis Burks	8.00
25	Albert Belle	35.00
26	Alan Benes	12.00
27	Jay Buhner	20.00
28	Derek Bell	8.00
29	Jeromy Burnitz	8.00
30	Kevin Appier	8.00
31	Jeff Cirillo	8.00
32	Bernard Gilkey	8.00
33	David Cone	15.00
34	Jason Dickson	8.00
35	Jose Cruz Jr.	30.00
36	Marty Cordova	8.00
37	Ray Durham	8.00
38	Jaret Wright	40.00
39	Billy Wagner	8.00
40	Roger Clemens	50.00
41	Juan Gonzalez	75.00
42	Jeremi Gonzalez	8.00
43	Mark Grudzielanek	8.00
44	Tom Glavine	15.00
45	Barry Larkin	15.00
46	Lance Johnson	8.00
47	Bobby Higginson	8.00
48	Mike Mussina	30.00
49	Al Martin	8.00
50	Mark McGwire	160.00
51	Todd Hundley	8.00
52	Ray Lankford	8.00
53	Jason Kendall	8.00
54	Javy Lopez	12.00
55	Ben Grieve	50.00
56	Randy Johnson	30.00
57	Jeff King	8.00
58	Mark Grace	20.00
59	Rusty Greer	15.00
60	Greg Maddux	90.00
61	Jeff Kent	8.00
62	Rey Ordonez	8.00
63	Hideo Nomo	30.00
64	Charles Nagy	8.00
65	Rondell White	15.00
66	Todd Helton	40.00
67	Jim Thome	30.00
68	Denny Neagle	8.00
69	Ivan Rodriguez	40.00
70	Vladimir Guerrero	40.00
71	Jorge Posada	8.00
72	J.T. Snow Jr.	8.00
73	Reggie Sanders	8.00
74	Scott Rolen	50.00
75	Robin Ventura	15.00
76	Mariano Rivera	15.00
77	Cal Ripken Jr.	120.00
78	Justin Thompson	8.00
79	Mike Piazza	90.00
80	Kevin Brown	8.00
81	Sandy Alomar	15.00
82	Craig Biggio	15.00
83	Vinny Castilla	15.00
84	Eric Young	8.00
85	Bernie Williams	30.00
86	Brady Anderson	8.00
87	Bobby Bonilla	15.00
88	Tony Clark	25.00
89	Dan Wilson	8.00
90	John Wetteland	8.00
91	Barry Bonds	40.00
92	Chan Ho Park	20.00
93	Carlos Delgado	15.00
94	David Justice	20.00
95	Chipper Jones	90.00
96	Shawn Estes	8.00
97	Jason Giambi	8.00
98	Ron Gant	15.00
99	John Olerud	15.00
100	Frank Thomas	120.00
101	Jose Guillen	15.00
102	Brad Radke	8.00
103	Troy Percival	8.00
104	John Smoltz	15.00
105	Edgardo Alfonzo	8.00
106	Dante Bichette	15.00
107	Larry Walker	20.00
108	John Valentin	8.00
109	Roberto Alomar	30.00
110	Mike Cameron	8.00
111	Eric Davis	8.00
112	Johnny Damon	8.00
113	Darin Erstad	40.00
114	Omar Vizquel	8.00
115	Derek Jeter	75.00
116	Tony Womack	8.00
117	Edgar Renteria	8.00
118	Raul Mondesi	15.00
119	Tony Gwynn	75.00
120	Ken Griffey Jr.	150.00
121	Jim Edmonds	8.00
122	Brian Hunter	8.00
123	Neifi Perez	8.00
124	Dean Palmer	8.00
125	Alex Rodriguez	100.00
126	Tim Salmon	20.00
127	Curt Schilling	15.00
128	Kevin Orie	8.00
129	Andy Pettitte	30.00
130	Gary Sheffield	25.00
131	Jose Rosado	8.00
132	Manny Ramirez	40.00
133	Rafael Palmeiro	20.00
134	Sammy Sosa	80.00
135	Jeff Bagwell	50.00
136	Delino DeShields	8.00
137	Ryan Klesko	20.00
138	Mo Vaughn	40.00
139	Steve Finley	8.00
140	Nomar Garciaparra	90.00
141	Paul Molitor	30.00
142	Pat Hentgen	8.00
143	Eric Karros	15.00
144	Bobby Jones	8.00
145	Tino Martinez	20.00
146	Matt Morris	8.00
147	Livan Hernandez	12.00
148	Edgar Martinez	8.00
149	Paul O'Neill	15.00
150	Checklist	8.00

1998 Topps Gallery Gallery Proofs

This hobby-only parallel set included all 150 cards in the base set. Gallery Proofs were sequentially numbered to 125 sets.

	MT
Gallery Proof Stars:	25x to 50x
Yng Stars & RCs:	15x to 30x
Production 125 sets	

1998 Topps Gallery of Heroes

Gallery of Heroes was a 15-card insert printed on colored, die-cut plastic that resembled a stained glass window. Cards were inserted one per 24 packs and numbered with a "GH" prefix.

		MT
Complete Set (15):		250.00
Common Player:		3.00
Inserted 1:24		
GH1	Ken Griffey Jr.	40.00
GH2	Derek Jeter	20.00
GH3	Barry Bonds	10.00
GH4	Alex Rodriguez	25.00
GH5	Frank Thomas	30.00
GH6	Nomar Garciaparra	25.00
GH7	Mark McGwire	40.00
GH8	Mike Piazza	25.00
GH9	Cal Ripken Jr.	30.00
GH10	Jose Cruz Jr.	6.00
GH11	Jeff Bagwell	15.00
GH12	Chipper Jones	25.00
GH13	Juan Gonzalez	20.00
GH14	Hideo Nomo	8.00
GH15	Greg Maddux	25.00

1998 Topps Gallery Awards Gallery

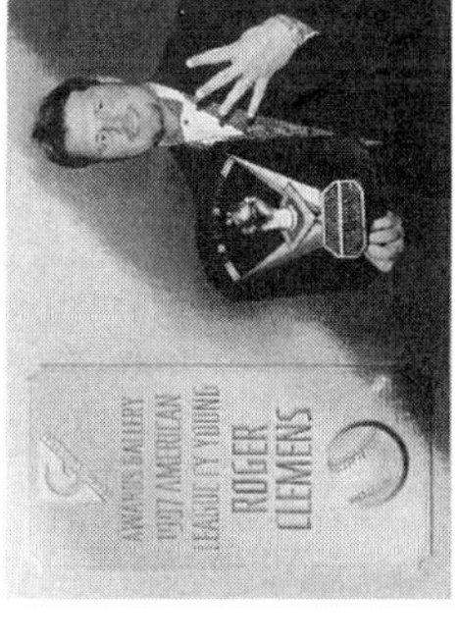

Awards Gallery featured 10 players who earned the highest honors in the game on a horizontal design. Fronts featured a shot of the player and the award he won on silver foilboard. These were inserted every 24 packs and numbered with an "AG" prefix.

		MT
Complete Set (10):		75.00
Common Player:		3.00
Inserted 1:24		
AG1	Ken Griffey Jr.	25.00
AG2	Larry Walker	4.00
AG3	Roger Clemens	8.00
AG4	Pedro Martinez	4.00
AG5	Nomar Garciaparra	15.00
AG6	Scott Rolen	8.00
AG7	Frank Thomas	20.00
AG8	Tony Gwynn	12.00
AG9	Mark McGwire	30.00
AG10	Livan Hernandez	3.00

1998 Topps Gallery Photo Gallery

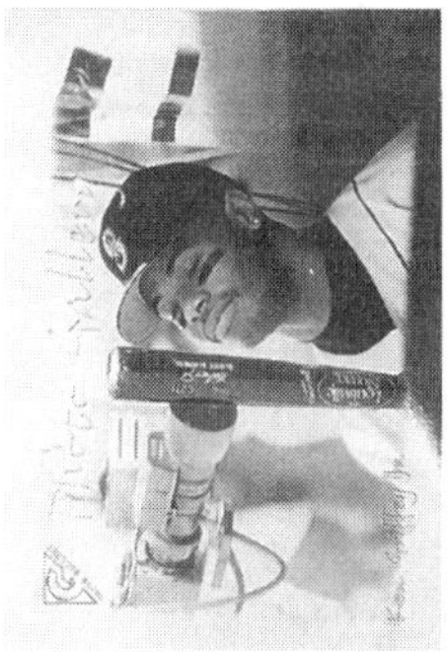

This 10-card insert captured unique shots of players on a silver foilboard design. Photo Gallery inserts were seeded one per 24 packs and numbered with a "PG" prefix.

		MT
Complete Set (10):		100.00
Common Player:		3.00
Inserted 1:24		
PG1	Alex Rodriguez	15.00
PG2	Frank Thomas	20.00
PG3	Derek Jeter	12.00
PG4	Cal Ripken Jr.	20.00
PG5	Ken Griffey Jr.	25.00
PG6	Mike Piazza	15.00
PG7	Nomar Garciaparra	15.00
PG8	Tim Salmon	4.00
PG9	Jeff Bagwell	8.00
PG10	Barry Bonds	6.00

1998 Topps Gold Label

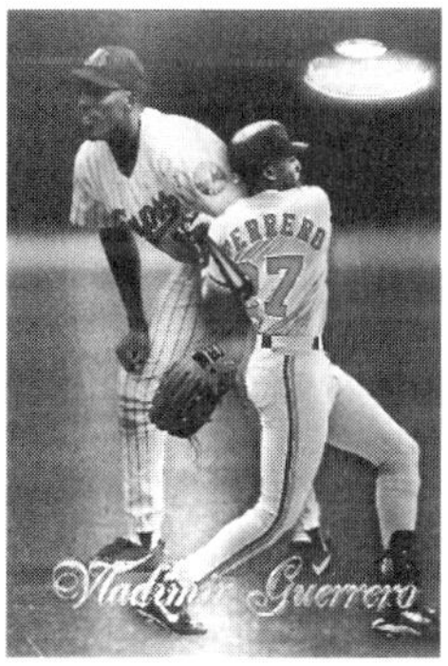

Topps debuted its Gold Label Baseball in 1998 with 100 card printed on 30-point "spectral-reflective stock" with gold foil stamping and two shots of the player on each card front. Cards arrived in Gold Label, Black Label and Red Label versions, all with varying levels of insertion. The rarity of the cards was determined by the photo and foil stamping of the cards. In the foreground of each card, the photograph is the same, but in the background one of three shots is featured. Variation 1: fielding are considered base cards, Variation 2: running (inserted 1:4 packs) and Variation 3: hitting (inserted 1:8 packs) are seeded levels. For pitching the levels are: Variation 1: ready (regular), Variation 2: pitch (inserted 1:4 packs) and Variation 3: follow-through (inserted 1:8 packs). Black Label cards are the second-most rare, while Red Label cards are third. Only one insert is issued in Gold Label, called Home Run Race of '98, and it is also available Gold, Red and Black versions.

		MT
Complete Set (100):		75.00
Common Player:		.25
Variation 2:		2x
Inserted 1:4		
Variation 3:		4x
Inserted 1:8		
1	Kevin Brown	.50
2	Greg Maddux	4.00
3	Albert Belle	1.50
4	Andres Galarraga	.75
5	Craig Biggio	.40
6	Matt Williams	.75
7	Derek Jeter	3.00
8	Randy Johnson	1.00
9	Jay Bell	.25
10	Jim Thome	.75
11	Roberto Alomar	1.00
12	Tom Glavine	.50
13	Reggie Sanders	.25
14	Tony Gwynn	3.00
15	Mark McGwire	8.00
16	Jeromy Burnitz	.25
17	Andruw Jones	1.50
18	Jay Buhner	.75
19	Robin Ventura	.40
20	Jeff Bagwell	2.00
21	Roger Clemens	2.50
22	*Masato Yoshii*	.75
23	Travis Fryman	.25
24	Rafael Palmeiro	.50
25	Alex Rodriguez	4.00
26	Sandy Alomar	.25
27	Chipper Jones	4.00
28	Rusty Greer	.25
29	Cal Ripken Jr.	5.00
30	Tony Clark	1.00
31	Derek Bell	.25
32	Fred McGriff	.50
33	Paul O'Neill	.75
34	Moises Alou	.50
35	Henry Rodriguez	.25
36	Steve Finley	.25
37	Marquis Grissom	.25
38	Jason Giambi	.25
39	Javy Lopez	.40
40	Damion Easley	.25
41	Mariano Rivera	.50
42	Mo Vaughn	1.50
43	Mike Mussina	1.00
44	Jason Kendall	.25
45	Pedro Martinez	1.50
46	Frank Thomas	4.00
47	Jim Edmonds	.25
48	Hideki Irabu	.75
49	Eric Karros	.40
50	Juan Gonzalez	3.00
51	Ellis Burks	.25
52	Dean Palmer	.25
53	Scott Rolen	1.50
54	Raul Mondesi	.50
55	Quinton McCraken	.25
56	John Olerud	.50
57	Ken Caminiti	.50
58	Brian Jordan	.25
59	Wade Boggs	.50
60	Mike Piazza	4.00
61	Darin Erstad	1.50
62	Curt Schilling	.50
63	David Justice	.75
64	Kenny Lofton	1.50
65	Barry Bonds	1.50
66	Ray Lankford	.25
67	Brian Hunter	.25
68	Chuck Knoblauch	.75
69	Vinny Castilla	.25
70	Vladimir Guerrero	1.50
71	Tim Salmon	.75
72	Larry Walker	.75
73	Paul Molitor	1.00
74	Barry Larkin	.75
75	Edgar Martinez	.25
76	Bernie Williams	1.00
77	Dante Bichette	.75
78	Nomar Garciaparra	4.00
79	Ben Grieve	2.00
80	Ivan Rodriguez	1.50
81	Todd Helton	1.00
82	Ryan Klesko	.50
83	Sammy Sosa	4.00
84	Travis Lee	3.00
85	Jose Cruz	1.50
86	Mark Kotsay	.25
87	Richard Hidalgo	.25
88	Rondell White	.50
89	Greg Vaughn	.50
90	Gary Sheffield	.50
91	Paul Konerko	.50
92	Mark Grace	.50
93	*Kevin Millwood*	4.00
94	Manny Ramirez	1.50
95	Tino Martinez	.75
96	Brad Fullmer	.50
97	Todd Walker	.25
98	Carlos Delgado	.25
99	Kerry Wood	6.00
100	Ken Griffey Jr.	6.00

1998 Topps Gold Label Black

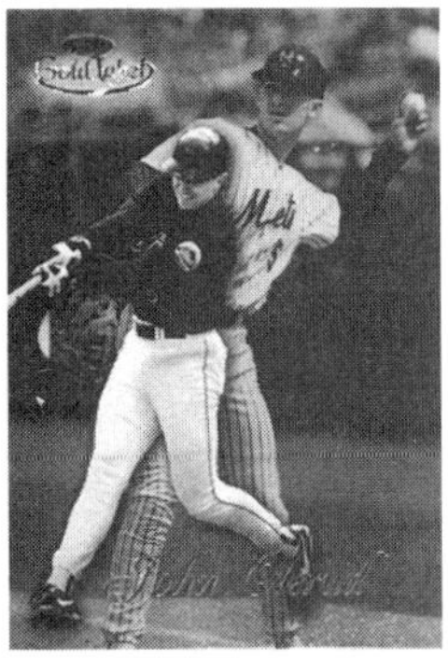

Black Label cards were the second parallel tier of Gold Label and featured black foil stamping. Insert rates were as follows: Variation 1: fielding (1:12 packs), Variation 2: running (1:24 packs) and Variation 3: hitting (1:48 packs).

	MT
Variation 1: 5x-6x Gold Label prices	
Inserted 1:12	
Variation 2:	10x to 12x
Inserted 1:24	
Variation 3:	15x to 20x
Inserted 1:48	

1998 Topps Gold Label Red

Red Label cards were the third highest tier of Topps Gold Label and featured red foil stamping. Red Label cards were sequentially numbered as follows: Variation 1 cards were numbered to 100 and inserted 1:165 packs, Variation 2 cards were numbered to 50 and inserted 1:330 packs and Variation 3 cards are numbered to 25 and inserted 1:660 packs.

		MT
Common Player:		15.00
Variation 2:		1.5x to 2x
Production 50 sets		
Variation 3:		3x to 4x
Production 25 sets		
1	Kevin Brown	30.00
2	Greg Maddux	200.00
3	Albert Belle	80.00
4	Andres Galarraga	40.00
5	Craig Biggio	25.00
6	Matt Williams	30.00
7	Derek Jeter	175.00
8	Randy Johnson	60.00
9	Jay Bell	15.00
10	Jim Thome	50.00
11	Roberto Alomar	60.00
12	Tom Glavine	40.00
13	Reggie Sanders	15.00
14	Tony Gwynn	150.00
15	Mark McGwire	400.00
16	Jeromy Burnitz	15.00
17	Andruw Jones	80.00
18	Jay Buhner	40.00
19	Robin Ventura	25.00
20	Jeff Bagwell	120.00
21	Roger Clemens	140.00
22	Masato Yoshii	40.00
23	Travis Fryman	15.00
24	Rafael Palmeiro	30.00
25	Alex Rodriguez	200.00
26	Sandy Alomar	15.00
27	Chipper Jones	200.00
28	Rusty Greer	15.00
29	Cal Ripken Jr.	250.00
30	Tony Clark	40.00
31	Derek Bell	15.00
32	Fred McGriff	25.00
33	Paul O'Neill	40.00
34	Moises Alou	30.00
35	Henry Rodriguez	15.00
36	Steve Finley	15.00
37	Marquis Grissom	15.00
38	Jason Giambi	15.00
39	Javy Lopez	25.00
40	Damion Easley	15.00
41	Mariano Rivera	30.00
42	Mo Vaughn	80.00
43	Mike Mussina	60.00
44	Jason Kendall	15.00
45	Pedro Martinez	70.00
46	Frank Thomas	200.00
47	Jim Edmonds	15.00
48	Hideki Irabu	30.00
49	Eric Karros	25.00
50	Juan Gonzalez	150.00
51	Ellis Burks	15.00
52	Dean Palmer	15.00
53	Scott Rolen	90.00
54	Raul Mondesi	25.00
55	Quinton McCraken	15.00
56	John Olerud	25.00
57	Ken Caminiti	25.00
58	Brian Jordan	15.00
59	Wade Boggs	30.00
60	Mike Piazza	200.00
61	Darin Erstad	80.00
62	Curt Schilling	30.00
63	David Justice	30.00
64	Kenny Lofton	80.00
65	Barry Bonds	80.00
66	Ray Lankford	15.00
67	Brian Hunter	15.00
68	Chuck Knoblauch	50.00
69	Vinny Castilla	15.00
70	Vladimir Guerrero	80.00
71	Tim Salmon	40.00
72	Larry Walker	50.00
73	Paul Molitor	60.00
74	Barry Larkin	25.00
75	Edgar Martinez	15.00
76	Bernie Williams	60.00
77	Dante Bichette	30.00
78	Nomar Garciaparra	200.00
79	Ben Grieve	100.00
80	Ivan Rodriguez	80.00
81	Todd Helton	40.00
82	Ryan Klesko	25.00
83	Sammy Sosa	200.00
84	Travis Lee	140.00
85	Jose Cruz Jr.	80.00
86	Mark Kotsay	30.00
87	Richard Hidalgo	15.00
88	Rondell White	30.00
89	Greg Vaughn	30.00
90	Gary Sheffield	30.00
91	Paul Konerko	30.00
92	Mark Grace	40.00
93	Kevin Millwood	90.00
94	Manny Ramirez	80.00
95	Tino Martinez	50.00
96	Brad Fullmer	30.00
97	Todd Walker	15.00
98	Carlos Delgado	15.00
99	Kerry Wood	200.00
100	Ken Griffey Jr.	300.00

1998 Topps Gold Label Home Run Race

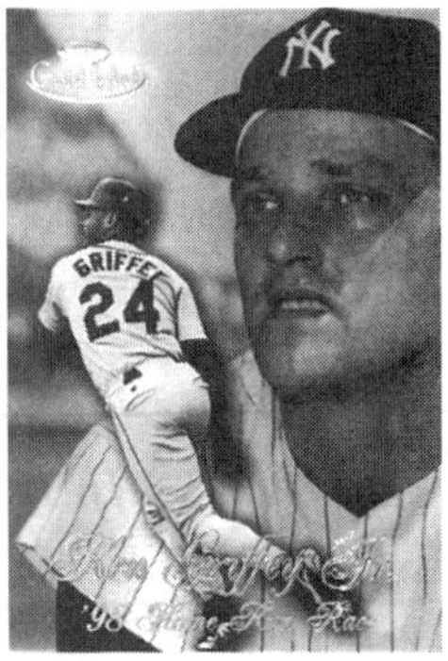

Home Run Race of '98 was a four-card set containing Mark McGwire, Sammy Sosa, Ken Griffey Jr. and Roger Maris. Each of the current player feature a background photo of Maris, while the fourth card features two shots of Maris. Gold, Black and Red Label versions were identified by the different foil-stamp logos. Gold cards were inserted 1:12 packs, Black Label cards were inserted 1:48 packs and Red Label cards were sequentially numbered to 61 and inserted 1:4,055 packs.

		MT
Complete Set (4):		60.00
Common Player:		10.00
Inserted 1:12		
Blacks:		2x to 3x
Inserted 1:48		
HR1	Roger Maris	10.00
HR2	Mark McGwire	30.00
HR3	Ken Griffey Jr.	20.00
HR4	Sammy Sosa	20.00

1998 Topps Stars

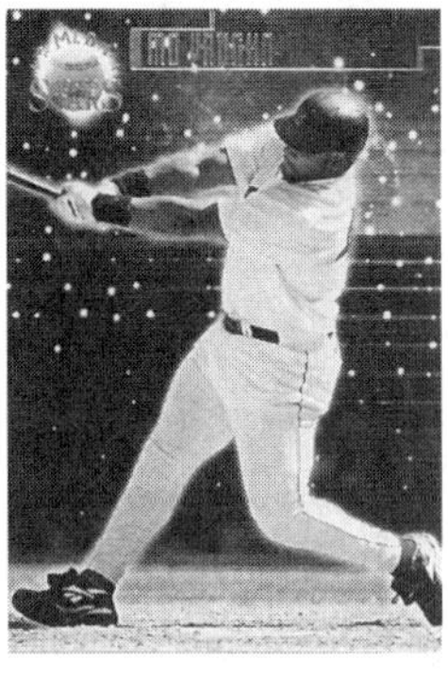

Topps Stars adopted an all-sequential numbering format in 1998 with a 150-card set. Every card was available in a bronze (numbered to 9,799), red (9,799), silver (4,399), gold (2,299) and gold rainbow format (99) with different color foil to distinquish between the groups. Players were each judged in five categories: arm strength, hit for average, power, defense and speed. Inserts in the product include: Galaxy, Luminaries, Supernovas, Rookie Reprints and Rookie Reprint Autographs. All regular-issue cards and inserts were individually numbered except the Rookie Reprints.

		MT
Complete Set (150):		125.00
Common Player:		.25
Production 9,799 sets		
1	Greg Maddux	6.00
2	Darryl Kile	.25
3	Rod Beck	.25
4	Ellis Burks	.25
5	Gary Sheffield	.75
6	David Ortiz	.25
7	Marquis Grissom	.40
8	Tony Womack	.25
9	Mike Mussina	2.00
10	Bernie Williams	2.00
11	Andy Benes	.25
12	Rusty Greer	.50
13	Carlos Delgado	.25
14	Jim Edmonds	.50
15	Raul Mondesi	.75
16	Andres Galarraga	1.00
17	Wade Boggs	.50
18	Paul O'Neill	.75
19	Edgar Renteria	.25
20	Tony Clark	1.50
21	Vladimir Guerrero	2.50
22	Moises Alou	.50
23	Bernard Gilkey	.25
24	Lance Johnson	.25
25	Ben Grieve	3.00
26	Sandy Alomar	.25
27	Ray Durham	.25
28	Shawn Estes	.25
29	David Segui	.25
30	Javy Lopez	.40
31	Steve Finley	.25
32	Rey Ordonez	.25
33	Derek Jeter	5.00
34	Henry Rodriguez	.25
35	Mo Vaughn	2.50
36	Richard Hidalgo	.25
37	Omar Vizquel	.25
38	Johnny Damon	.25
39	Brian Hunter	.25
40	Matt Williams	1.00
41	Chuck Finley	.25
42	Jeromy Burnitz	.25
43	Livan Hernandez	.25
44	Delino DeShields	.25
45	Charles Nagy	.25
46	Scott Rolen	3.00
47	Neifi Perez	.25
48	John Wetteland	.25
49	Eric Milton	.25
50	Mike Piazza	6.00
51	Cal Ripken Jr.	8.00
52	Mariano Rivera	.50
53	Butch Huskey	.25
54	Quinton McCracken	.25
55	Jose Cruz Jr.	2.50
56	Brian Jordan	.25
57	Hideo Nomo	1.50
58	Masato Yoshii	.25
59	Cliff Floyd	.25
60	Jose Guillen	.50
61	Jeff Shaw	.25
62	Edgar Martinez	.25
63	Rondell White	.50
64	Hal Morris	.25
65	Barry Larkin	.75
66	Eric Young	.25
67	Ray Lankford	.25
68	Derek Bell	.25
69	Charles Johnson	.25
70	Robin Ventura	.50
71	Chuck Knoblauch	.75
72	Kevin Brown	.75
73	Jose Valentin	.25
74	Jay Buhner	.75
75	Tony Gwynn	5.00
76	Andy Pettitte	1.50
77	Edgardo Alfonzo	.25
78	Kerry Wood	12.00
79	Darin Erstad	2.50
80	Paul Konerko	.50
81	Jason Kendall	.25
82	Tino Martinez	1.00
83	Brad Radke	.25
84	Jeff King	.25
85	Travis Lee	5.00
86	Jeff Kent	.25
87	Trevor Hoffman	.25
88	David Cone	.50
89	Jose Canseco	1.00
90	Juan Gonzalez	5.00
91	Todd Hundley	.25
92	John Valentin	.25
93	Sammy Sosa	6.00
94	Jason Giambi	.25
95	Chipper Jones	6.00
96	Jeff Blauser	.25
97	Brad Fullmer	.50
98	Derrek Lee	.25
99	Denny Neagle	.25
100	Ken Griffey Jr.	10.00
101	David Justice	.75
102	Tim Salmon	.75
103	J.T. Snow	.25
104	Fred McGriff	.50
105	Brady Anderson	.25
106	Larry Walker	1.00
107	Jeff Cirillo	.25
108	Andruw Jones	2.50
109	Manny Ramirez	2.50
110	Justin Thompson	.25
111	Vinny Castilla	.50
112	Chan Ho Park	.50
113	Mark Grudzielanek	.25
114	Mark Grace	.75
115	Ken Caminiti	.50
116	Ryan Klesko	.75
117	Rafael Palmeiro	.75
118	Pat Hentgen	.25
119	Eric Karros	.50
120	Randy Johnson	1.50
121	Roberto Alomar	1.50
122	John Olerud	.75
123	Paul Molitor	1.50
124	Dean Palmer	.25
125	Nomar Garciaparra	6.00
126	Curt Schilling	.50
127	Jay Bell	.25
128	Craig Biggio	.50
129	Marty Cordova	.25
130	Ivan Rodriguez	2.50
131	Todd Helton	2.00
132	Jim Thome	1.50
133	Albert Belle	2.50
134	Mike Lansing	.25
135	Mark McGwire	12.00
136	Roger Clemens	4.00
137	Tom Glavine	.50
138	Ron Gant	.25
139	Alex Rodriguez	8.00
140	Jeff Bagwell	3.00
141	John Smoltz	.50
142	Kenny Lofton	2.50
143	Dante Bichette	.50
144	Pedro Martinez	2.00
145	Barry Bonds	2.50
146	Travis Fryman	.25
147	Bobby Jones	.25
148	Bobby Higginson	.25
149	Reggie Sanders	.25
150	Frank Thomas	8.00

1998 Topps Stars Silver

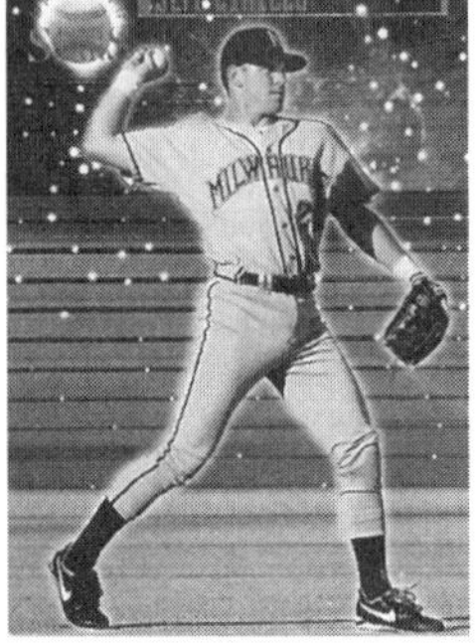

Silver versions of all 150 Topps Stars cards were available and seeded one per pack. They were distingished by silver foil on the front and sequentail numbering to 4,399 on the back.

		MT
Complete Set (150):		350.00
Common Player:		.75
Production 4,399 sets		
1	Greg Maddux	15.00
2	Darryl Kile	.75
3	Rod Beck	.75
4	Ellis Burks	.75
5	Gary Sheffield	1.50
6	David Ortiz	.75
7	Marquis Grissom	1.00
8	Tony Womack	.75
9	Mike Mussina	5.00
10	Bernie Williams	5.00
11	Andy Benes	.75
12	Rusty Greer	1.00
13	Carlos Delgado	.75
14	Jim Edmonds	1.00
15	Raul Mondesi	1.50
16	Andres Galarraga	3.00
17	Wade Boggs	1.50
18	Paul O'Neill	1.50
19	Edgar Renteria	.75
20	Tony Clark	4.00
21	Vladimir Guerrero	6.00
22	Moises Alou	1.00
23	Bernard Gilkey	.75
24	Lance Johnson	.75
25	Ben Grieve	8.00
26	Sandy Alomar	1.00
27	Ray Durham	.75
28	Shawn Estes	.75
29	David Segui	.75
30	Javy Lopez	1.00
31	Steve Finley	.75
32	Rey Ordonez	.75
33	Derek Jeter	12.00
34	Henry Rodriguez	.75
35	Mo Vaughn	6.00
36	Richard Hidalgo	.75
37	Omar Vizquel	.75
38	Johnny Damon	.75
39	Brian Hunter	.75
40	Matt Williams	3.00
41	Chuck Finley	.75
42	Jeromy Burnitz	.75
43	Livan Hernandez	.75
44	Delino DeShields	.75
45	Charles Nagy	.75
46	Scott Rolen	8.00
47	Neifi Perez	.75
48	John Wetteland	.75
49	Eric Milton	1.50
50	Mike Piazza	15.00
51	Cal Ripken Jr.	18.00
52	Mariano Rivera	1.00
53	Butch Huskey	.75
54	Quinton McCracken	.75
55	Jose Cruz Jr.	6.00
56	Brian Jordan	.75
57	Hideo Nomo	4.00
58	Masato Yoshii	1.50
59	Cliff Floyd	.75
60	Jose Guillen	1.00
61	Jeff Shaw	.75
62	Edgar Martinez	1.00
63	Rondell White	1.00
64	Hal Morris	.75
65	Barry Larkin	1.50
66	Eric Young	.75
67	Ray Lankford	.75
68	Derek Bell	.75
69	Charles Johnson	.75
70	Robin Ventura	1.00
71	Chuck Knoblauch	1.50
72	Kevin Brown	1.50
73	Jose Valentin	.75
74	Jay Buhner	1.50
75	Tony Gwynn	12.00
76	Andy Pettitte	4.00
77	Edgardo Alfonzo	.75
78	Kerry Wood	25.00
79	Darin Erstad	6.00
80	Paul Konerko	1.00
81	Jason Kendall	.75
82	Tino Martinez	3.00
83	Brad Radke	.75
84	Jeff King	.75
85	Travis Lee	12.00
86	Jeff Kent	.75
87	Trevor Hoffman	.75
88	David Cone	1.00
89	Jose Canseco	3.00
90	Juan Gonzalez	12.00
91	Todd Hundley	.75
92	John Valentin	.75
93	Sammy Sosa	15.00
94	Jason Giambi	.75
95	Chipper Jones	15.00
96	Jeff Blauser	.75
97	Brad Fullmer	1.00
98	Derrek Lee	.75
99	Denny Neagle	.75
100	Ken Griffey Jr.	25.00
101	David Justice	1.50
102	Tim Salmon	1.50
103	J.T. Snow	.75
104	Fred McGriff	1.00
105	Brady Anderson	.75
106	Larry Walker	3.00
107	Jeff Cirillo	.75
108	Andruw Jones	6.00

109	Manny Ramirez	6.00
110	Justin Thompson	.75
111	Vinny Castilla	1.00
112	Chan Ho Park	1.00
113	Mark Grudzielanek	.75
114	Mark Grace	1.50
115	Ken Caminiti	1.00
116	Ryan Klesko	1.50
117	Rafael Palmeiro	1.50
118	Pat Hentgen	.75
119	Eric Karros	1.00
120	Randy Johnson	4.00
121	Roberto Alomar	4.00
122	John Olerud	1.50
123	Paul Molitor	4.00
124	Dean Palmer	.75
125	Nomar Garciaparra	15.00
126	Curt Schilling	1.00
127	Jay Bell	.75
128	Craig Biggio	1.00
129	Marty Cordova	.75
130	Ivan Rodriguez	6.00
131	Todd Helton	5.00
132	Jim Thome	4.00
133	Albert Belle	6.00
134	Mike Lansing	.75
135	Mark McGwire	25.00
136	Roger Clemens	10.00
137	Tom Glavine	1.00
138	Ron Gant	.75
139	Alex Rodriguez	18.00
140	Jeff Bagwell	8.00
141	John Smoltz	1.00
142	Kenny Lofton	6.00
143	Dante Bichette	1.00
144	Pedro Martinez	5.00
145	Barry Bonds	6.00
146	Travis Fryman	.75
147	Bobby Jones	.75
148	Bobby Higginson	.75
149	Reggie Sanders	.75
150	Frank Thomas	18.00

1998 Topps Stars Gold

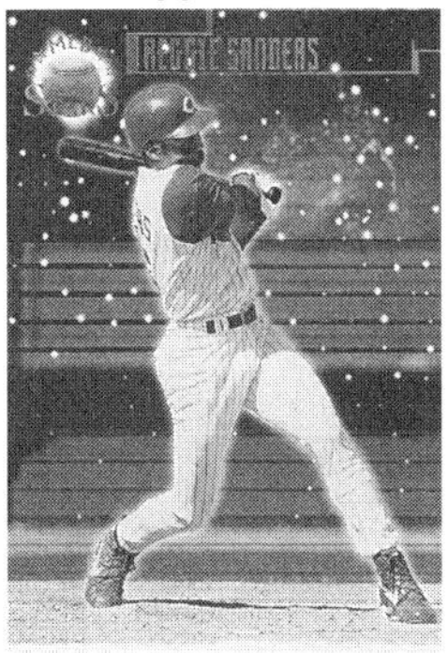

All 150 cards were paralelled in Gold Star versions. This was the second rarest version of each card and was numbered to 2,299. Gold Star versions featured gold foil and were seeded every two packs.

		MT
Complete Set (150):		700.00
Common Player:		2.50
Production 2,299 sets		
1	Greg Maddux	25.00
2	Darryl Kile	2.50
3	Rod Beck	2.50
4	Ellis Burks	2.50
5	Gary Sheffield	5.00
6	David Ortiz	2.50
7	Marquis Grissom	2.50
8	Tony Womack	2.50
9	Mike Mussina	8.00
10	Bernie Williams	8.00
11	Andy Benes	2.50
12	Rusty Greer	4.00
13	Carlos Delgado	2.50
14	Jim Edmonds	4.00
15	Raul Mondesi	5.00
16	Andres Galarraga	6.00
17	Wade Boggs	5.00
18	Paul O'Neill	5.00
19	Edgar Renteria	2.50
20	Tony Clark	6.00
21	Vladimir Guerrero	10.00
22	Moises Alou	4.00
23	Bernard Gilkey	2.50
24	Lance Johnson	2.50
25	Ben Grieve	12.00
26	Sandy Alomar	4.00
27	Ray Durham	2.50
28	Shawn Estes	2.50
29	David Segui	2.50
30	Javy Lopez	4.00
31	Steve Finley	2.50
32	Rey Ordonez	2.50
33	Derek Jeter	20.00
34	Henry Rodriguez	2.50
35	Mo Vaughn	10.00
36	Richard Hidalgo	2.50
37	Omar Vizquel	2.50
38	Johnny Damon	2.50
39	Brian Hunter	2.50
40	Matt Williams	5.00
41	Chuck Finley	2.50
42	Jeromy Burnitz	2.50
43	Livan Hernandez	2.50
44	Delino DeShields	2.50
45	Charles Nagy	2.50
46	Scott Rolen	12.00
47	Neifi Perez	2.50
48	John Wetteland	2.50
49	Eric Milton	5.00
50	Mike Piazza	25.00
51	Cal Ripken Jr.	30.00
52	Mariano Rivera	4.00
53	Butch Huskey	2.50
54	Quinton McCracken	2.50
55	Jose Cruz Jr.	10.00
56	Brian Jordan	2.50
57	Hideo Nomo	6.00
58	Masato Yoshii	5.00
59	Cliff Floyd	2.50
60	Jose Guillen	4.00
61	Jeff Shaw	2.50
62	Edgar Martinez	4.00
63	Rondell White	4.00
64	Hal Morris	2.50
65	Barry Larkin	5.00
66	Eric Young	2.50
67	Ray Lankford	2.50
68	Derek Bell	2.50
69	Charles Johnson	2.50
70	Robin Ventura	4.00
71	Chuck Knoblauch	5.00
72	Kevin Brown	4.00
73	Jose Valentin	2.50
74	Jay Buhner	5.00
75	Tony Gwynn	20.00
76	Andy Pettitte	8.00
77	Edgardo Alfonzo	2.50
78	Kerry Wood	40.00
79	Darin Erstad	10.00
80	Paul Konerko	4.00
81	Jason Kendall	2.50
82	Tino Martinez	5.00
83	Brad Radke	2.50
84	Jeff King	2.50
85	Travis Lee	20.00
86	Jeff Kent	2.50
87	Trevor Hoffman	2.50
88	David Cone	4.00
89	Jose Canseco	6.00
90	Juan Gonzalez	20.00
91	Todd Hundley	2.50
92	John Valentin	2.50
93	Sammy Sosa	25.00
94	Jason Giambi	2.50
95	Chipper Jones	25.00
96	Jeff Blauser	2.50
97	Brad Fullmer	4.00
98	Derrek Lee	2.50
99	Denny Neagle	2.50
100	Ken Griffey Jr.	40.00
101	David Justice	5.00
102	Tim Salmon	5.00
103	J.T. Snow	2.50
104	Fred McGriff	4.00
105	Brady Anderson	2.50
106	Larry Walker	6.00
107	Jeff Cirillo	2.50
108	Andruw Jones	10.00
109	Manny Ramirez	10.00
110	Justin Thompson	2.50
111	Vinny Castilla	4.00
112	Chan Ho Park	4.00
113	Mark Grudzielanek	2.50
114	Mark Grace	5.00
115	Ken Caminiti	4.00
116	Ryan Klesko	5.00
117	Rafael Palmeiro	5.00
118	Pat Hentgen	2.50
119	Eric Karros	4.00
120	Randy Johnson	8.00
121	Roberto Alomar	8.00
122	John Olerud	5.00
123	Paul Molitor	8.00
124	Dean Palmer	2.50
125	Nomar Garciaparra	25.00
126	Curt Schilling	4.00
127	Jay Bell	2.50
128	Craig Biggio	4.00
129	Marty Cordova	2.50
130	Ivan Rodriguez	10.00
131	Todd Helton	8.00
132	Jim Thome	8.00
133	Albert Belle	10.00
134	Mike Lansing	2.50
135	Mark McGwire	40.00
136	Roger Clemens	15.00
137	Tom Glavine	4.00
138	Ron Gant	4.00
139	Alex Rodriguez	30.00
140	Jeff Bagwell	12.00
141	John Smoltz	4.00
142	Kenny Lofton	10.00
143	Dante Bichette	4.00
144	Pedro Martinez	8.00
145	Barry Bonds	10.00
146	Travis Fryman	2.50
147	Bobby Jones	2.50
148	Bobby Higginson	2.50
149	Reggie Sanders	2.50
150	Frank Thomas	30.00

1998 Topps Stars Gold Rainbow

Each card in Topps Stars was available in a Gold Rainbow version. This was the most limited of the five parallels and was numbered to 99. Cards featured gold prismatic foil on the front and were seeded every 46 packs.

		MT
Common Player:		15.00
Semistars:		40.00
Production 99 sets		
1	Greg Maddux	125.00
2	Darryl Kile	15.00
3	Rod Beck	15.00
4	Ellis Burks	15.00
5	Gary Sheffield	25.00
6	David Ortiz	15.00
7	Marquis Grissom	15.00
8	Tony Womack	15.00
9	Mike Mussina	40.00
10	Bernie Williams	40.00
11	Andy Benes	15.00
12	Rusty Greer	20.00
13	Carlos Delgado	15.00
14	Jim Edmonds	20.00
15	Raul Mondesi	25.00
16	Andres Galarraga	30.00
17	Wade Boggs	25.00
18	Paul O'Neill	25.00
19	Edgar Renteria	15.00
20	Tony Clark	30.00
21	Vladimir Guerrero	50.00
22	Moises Alou	20.00
23	Bernard Gilkey	15.00
24	Lance Johnson	15.00
25	Ben Grieve	60.00
26	Sandy Alomar	20.00
27	Ray Durham	15.00
28	Shawn Estes	15.00
29	David Segui	15.00
30	Javy Lopez	20.00
31	Steve Finley	15.00
32	Rey Ordonez	15.00
33	Derek Jeter	100.00
34	Henry Rodriguez	15.00
35	Mo Vaughn	50.00
36	Richard Hidalgo	15.00
37	Omar Vizquel	15.00
38	Johnny Damon	15.00
39	Brian Hunter	15.00
40	Matt Williams	25.00
41	Chuck Finley	15.00
42	Jeromy Burnitz	15.00
43	Livan Hernandez	15.00
44	Delino DeShields	15.00
45	Charles Nagy	15.00
46	Scott Rolen	60.00
47	Neifi Perez	15.00
48	John Wetteland	15.00
49	Eric Milton	20.00
50	Mike Piazza	125.00
51	Cal Ripken Jr.	150.00
52	Mariano Rivera	20.00
53	Butch Huskey	15.00
54	Quinton McCracken	15.00
55	Jose Cruz Jr.	50.00
56	Brian Jordan	15.00
57	Hideo Nomo	30.00
58	Masato Yoshii	20.00
59	Cliff Floyd	15.00
60	Jose Guillen	20.00
61	Jeff Shaw	15.00
62	Edgar Martinez	20.00
63	Rondell White	20.00
64	Hal Morris	15.00
65	Barry Larkin	25.00
66	Eric Young	15.00
67	Ray Lankford	15.00
68	Derek Bell	15.00
69	Charles Johnson	15.00
70	Robin Ventura	20.00
71	Chuck Knoblauch	25.00
72	Kevin Brown	20.00
73	Jose Valentin	15.00
74	Jay Buhner	25.00
75	Tony Gwynn	100.00
76	Andy Pettitte	40.00
77	Edgardo Alfonzo	15.00
78	Kerry Wood	150.00
79	Darin Erstad	50.00
80	Paul Konerko	20.00
81	Jason Kendall	15.00
82	Tino Martinez	25.00
83	Brad Radke	15.00
84	Jeff King	15.00
85	Travis Lee	100.00
86	Jeff Kent	15.00
87	Trevor Hoffman	15.00
88	David Cone	20.00
89	Jose Canseco	30.00
90	Juan Gonzalez	100.00
91	Todd Hundley	15.00
92	John Valentin	15.00
93	Sammy Sosa	125.00
94	Jason Giambi	15.00
95	Chipper Jones	125.00
96	Jeff Blauser	15.00
97	Brad Fullmer	20.00
98	Derrek Lee	15.00
99	Denny Neagle	15.00
100	Ken Griffey Jr.	200.00
101	David Justice	25.00
102	Tim Salmon	25.00
103	J.T. Snow	15.00
104	Fred McGriff	20.00
105	Brady Anderson	15.00
106	Larry Walker	30.00
107	Jeff Cirillo	15.00
108	Andruw Jones	50.00
109	Manny Ramirez	50.00
110	Justin Thompson	15.00
111	Vinny Castilla	20.00
112	Chan Ho Park	20.00
113	Mark Grudzielanek	15.00
114	Mark Grace	25.00
115	Ken Caminiti	20.00
116	Ryan Klesko	25.00
117	Rafael Palmeiro	25.00
118	Pat Hentgen	15.00
119	Eric Karros	20.00
120	Randy Johnson	40.00
121	Roberto Alomar	40.00
122	John Olerud	25.00
123	Paul Molitor	40.00
124	Dean Palmer	15.00
125	Nomar Garciaparra	125.00
126	Curt Schilling	20.00
127	Jay Bell	15.00
128	Craig Biggio	20.00
129	Marty Cordova	15.00
130	Ivan Rodriguez	50.00
131	Todd Helton	40.00
132	Jim Thome	40.00
133	Albert Belle	50.00
134	Mike Lansing	15.00
135	Mark McGwire	250.00
136	Roger Clemens	75.00
137	Tom Glavine	20.00
138	Ron Gant	20.00
139	Alex Rodriguez	150.00
140	Jeff Bagwell	60.00
141	John Smoltz	20.00
142	Kenny Lofton	50.00
143	Dante Bichette	20.00
144	Pedro Martinez	40.00
145	Barry Bonds	50.00
146	Travis Fryman	15.00
147	Bobby Jones	15.00
148	Bobby Higginson	15.00
149	Reggie Sanders	15.00
150	Frank Thomas	125.00

1998 Topps Stars Galaxy

Galaxy featured 10 players who possess all five skills featured in Topps Stars Baseball. Four versions were available and sequentially numbered, including: Bronze (numbered to 100, inserted 1:682 packs), Silver (numbered to 75, inserted 1:910), Gold (numbered to 50, inserted 1:1,364) and Gold Rainbow (numbered to 5, inserted 1:13,643).

		MT
Complete Set (10):		800.00
Common Player:		25.00
Production 100 sets		
Silvers:		1x to 1.5x
Production 75 sets		
Golds:		1.5x to 2x
Production 50 sets		
G1	Barry Bonds	50.00
G2	Jeff Bagwell	75.00
G3	Nomar Garciaparra	125.00
G4	Chipper Jones	100.00
G5	Ken Griffey Jr.	200.00
G6	Sammy Sosa	125.00
G7	Larry Walker	40.00
G8	Alex Rodriguez	140.00
G9	Craig Biggio	25.00
G10	Raul Mondesi	25.00

1998 Topps Stars Luminaries

Luminaries featured three top players in each tool group in Topps Stars. The 15-card insert arrived in four different versions and were sequentially numbered. They were inserted as follows: bronze (numbered to 100, inserted 1:455), silver (numbered to 75, inserted 1:606), gold (numbered to 50, inserted 1:910) and gold rainbow (numbered to 5, inserted 1:9,095).

		MT
Complete Set (15):		1000.
Common Player:		25.00
Production 100 sets		
Silvers:		1x to 1.5x
Production 75 sets		
Golds:		1.5x to 2x
Production 50 sets		
L1	Ken Griffey Jr.	200.00
L2	Mark McGwire	250.00
L3	Juan Gonzalez	100.00
L4	Tony Gwynn	100.00
L5	Frank Thomas	125.00
L6	Mike Piazza	125.00
L7	Chuck Knoblauch	30.00
L8	Kenny Lofton	50.00
L9	Barry Bonds	50.00
L10	Matt Williams	30.00
L11	Raul Mondesi	25.00
L12	Ivan Rodriguez	50.00
L13	Alex Rodriguez	140.00
L14	Nomar Garciaparra	125.00
L15	Ken Caminiti	25.00

1998 Topps Stars Rookie Reprints

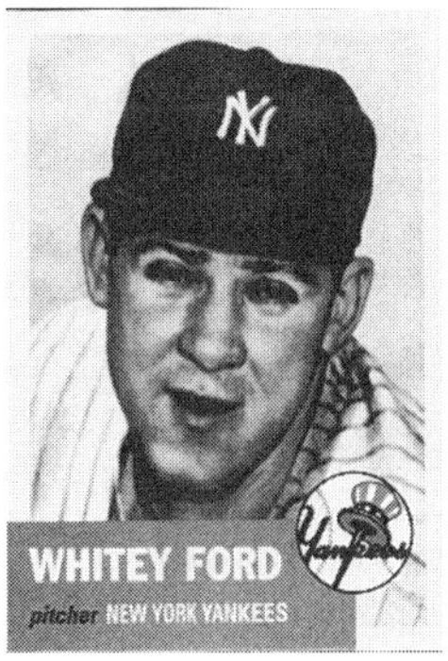
WHITEY FORD
pitcher NEW YORK YANKEES

Topps reprinted the rookie cards of five Hall of Famers in Rookie Reprints. The cards are inserted one per 24 packs and have UV coating.

	MT
Complete Set (5):	20.00
Common Player:	3.00
Johnny Bench	6.00
Whitey Ford	3.00
Joe Morgan	3.00
Mike Schmidt	8.00
Carl Yastrzemski	4.00

1998 Topps Stars Rookie Reprints Autographs

Autographed versions of all five Rookie Reprint inserts were available and seeded one per 273 packs. Each card arrive with a Topps "Certified Autograph Issue" stamp to ensure its authenticity.

	MT
Complete Set (5):	120.00
Common Player:	25.00
Johnny Bench	40.00
Whitey Ford	25.00
Joe Morgan	25.00
Mike Schmidt	60.00
Carl Yastrzemski	40.00

1998 Topps Stars Supernovas

Supernovas was a 10-card insert in Topps Stars and included rookies and prospects who either have all five tools focused on in the product, or excel dramatically in one of the five. Four sequentially numbered levels were available, with insert rates as follows: bronze (numbered to 100, inserted 1:682), silver (numbered to 75, inserted 1:910), gold (numbered to 50, inserted 1:1,364) and gold rainbow (numbered to 5, inserted 1:13,643).

	MT
Complete Set (10):	400.00
Common Player:	20.00
Production 100 sets	
Silvers:	1x to 1.5x
Production 75 sets	
Golds:	1.5x to 2x
Production 50 sets	
S1 Ben Grieve	60.00
S2 Travis Lee	100.00
S3 Todd Helton	50.00
S4 Adrian Beltre	30.00
S5 Derrek Lee	20.00
S6 David Ortiz	20.00
S7 Brad Fullmer	30.00
S8 Mark Kotsay	20.00
S9 Paul Konerko	20.00
S10 Kerry Wood	120.00

1998 Topps Stars N' Steel

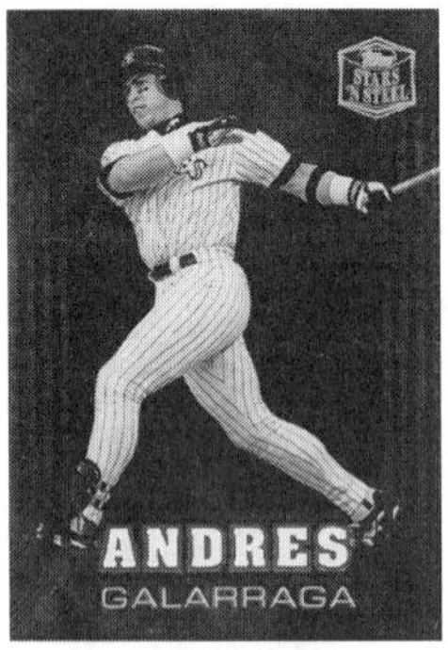

Stars 'N Steel was a 44-card set printed on four-colored textured film laminate bonded to a sheet of 25-gauge metal. Regular cards featured a silver colored border while gold versions were also available and seeded one per 12 packs. Stars 'N Steel was available only to Home Team Advantage members and was packaged in three-card packs that arrived in sturdy, tri-fold stand-up display unit. A second parallel version was also available featuring gold holographic technology and was seeded one per 40 packs.

		MT
Complete Set (44):		150.00
Common Player:		2.00
Golds		: 2x to 4x
Refractors:		6x to 12x
Wax Box:		100.00
1	Roberto Alomar	5.00
2	Jeff Bagwell	10.00
3	Albert Belle	6.00
4	Dante Bichette	2.00
5	Barry Bonds	6.00
6	Jay Buhner	3.00
7	Ken Caminiti	2.00
8	Vinny Castilla	2.00
9	Roger Clemens	10.00
10	Jose Cruz Jr.	10.00
11	Andres Galarraga	3.00
12	Nomar Garciaparra	15.00
13	Juan Gonzalez	12.00
14	Mark Grace	3.00
15	Ken Griffey Jr.	25.00
16	Tony Gwynn	12.00
17	Todd Hundley	2.00
18	Derek Jeter	12.00
19	Randy Johnson	4.00
20	Andruw Jones	10.00
21	Chipper Jones	15.00
22	David Justice	2.00
23	Ray Lankford	2.00
24	Barry Larkin	3.00
25	Kenny Lofton	6.00
26	Greg Maddux	15.00
27	Edgar Martinez	2.00
28	Tino Martinez	3.00
29	Mark McGwire	30.00
30	Paul Molitor	5.00
31	Rafael Palmeiro	3.00
32	Mike Piazza	15.00
33	Manny Ramirez	5.00
34	Cal Ripken Jr.	18.00
35	Ivan Rodriguez	6.00
36	Scott Rolen	10.00
37	Tim Salmon	3.00
38	Gary Sheffield	3.00
39	Sammy Sosa	12.00
40	Frank Thomas	20.00
41	Jim Thome	4.00
42	Mo Vaughn	6.00
43	Larry Walker	3.00
44	Bernie Williams	4.00

1998 Topps Super Chrome

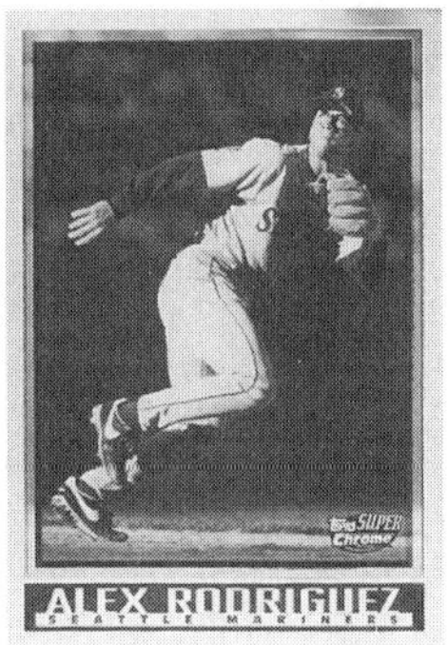

This 36-card oversized set featured some of the top players from Chrome on 4-1/8" x 5-3/4" cards. The product sold in three-card packs and featured similar photography as Topps and Topps Chrome before it, but added a Super Chrome logo. Refractor versions of each card were also available.

		MT
Complete Set (36):		60.00
Common Player:		.50
1	Tony Gwynn	3.00
2	Larry Walker	1.00
3	Vladimir Guerrero	1.50
4	Mo Vaughn	1.50
5	Frank Thomas	4.00
6	Barry Larkin	.75
7	Scott Rolen	2.00
8	Juan Gonzalez	3.00
9	Jeff Bagwell	2.00
10	Ryan Klesko	.75
11	Mike Piazza	4.00
12	Randy Johnson	1.00
13	Derek Jeter	3.00
14	Gary Sheffield	.75
15	Hideo Nomo	1.00
16	Tino Martinez	.75
17	Ivan Rodriguez	1.50
18	Bernie Williams	1.00
19	Greg Maddux	4.00
20	Roger Clemens	3.00
21	Roberto Clemente	2.50
22	Chipper Jones	4.00
23	Sammy Sosa	5.00
24	Tony Clark	1.00
25	Barry Bonds	1.50
26	Craig Biggio	.50
27	Cal Ripken Jr.	5.00
28	Ken Griffey Jr.	6.00
29	Todd Helton	1.50
30	Mark McGwire	8.00
31	Jose Cruz	1.50
32	Albert Belle	1.50
33	Andruw Jones	1.50
34	Nomar Garciaparra	4.00
35	Andy Pettitte	1.00
36	Alex Rodriguez	4.00

1998 Topps Super Chrome Refractors

All 36 cards in Topps Super Chrome Baseball were also featured in Refractor parallel set. Refractors were seeded one per 12 packs.

	MT
Refractors:	4x to 8x
Inserted 1:12	

1998 Ultra

Ultra was released in two series and contained a total of 501 cards, with 250 in Series I and 251 in Series II. The product sold in 10-card packs for an SRP of $2.59 and three parallel sets - Gold Medallion, Platinum Medallion and Masterpieces. Series I has 210 regular cards, 25 Prospects (seeded 1:4 packs), 10 Season's Crowns (seeded 1:12) and five Checklists (1:8). Series II had 202 regular cards, 25 Pizzazz (seeded 1:4), 20 New Horizons and three checklists. Series II also added a Mike Piazza N.Y. Mets cards that was added to the set as card No. 501 and inserted every 20 packs. Inserts in Series I include: Big Shots, Double Trouble, Kid Gloves, Back to the Future, Artistic Talents, Fall Classics, Power Plus, Prime Leather, Diamond Producers, Diamond Ink and Million Dollar Moments. Series II included: Notables, Rocket to Stardom, Millennium Men, Win Now, Ticket Studs, Diamond Immortals, Diamond Ink, Top 30 and 750 sequentially numbered Alex Rodriguez autographed cards.

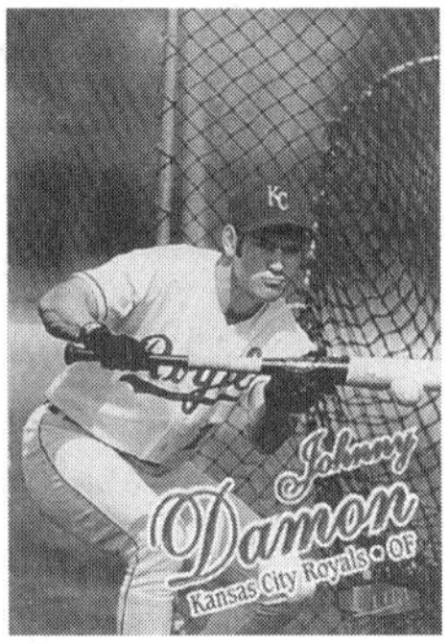

		MT
Complete Set (501):		150.00
Complete Series I Set (250):		80.00
Complete Series II Set (250):		70.00
Common Player:		.10
A. Rodriguez Auto. Sample (750)		125.00
Wax Box:		55.00
1	Ken Griffey Jr.	3.00
2	Matt Morris	.10
3	Roger Clemens	1.00
4	Matt Williams	.25
5	Roberto Hernandez	.10
6	Rondell White	.10
7	Tim Salmon	.20
8	Brad Radke	.10
9	Brett Butler	.10
10	Carl Everett	.10
11	Chili Davis	.10
12	Chuck Finley	.10
13	Darryl Kile	.10
14	Deivi Cruz	.10
15	Gary Gaetti	.10
16	Matt Stairs	.10
17	Pat Meares	.10
18	Will Cunnane	.10
19	*Steve Woodard*	.30
20	Andy Ashby	.10
21	Bobby Higginson	.20
22	Brian Jordan	.10
23	Craig Biggio	.20
24	Jim Edmonds	.20
25	Ryan McGuire	.10
26	Scott Hatteberg	.10
27	Willie Greene	.10
28	Albert Belle	.75
29	Ellis Burks	.10
30	Hideo Nomo	.60
31	Jeff Bagwell	1.25
32	Kevin Brown	.10
33	Nomar Garciaparra	2.00
34	Pedro Martinez	.25
35	Raul Mondesi	.25
36	Ricky Bottalico	.10
37	Shawn Estes	.10
38	Shawon Dunston	.10
39	Terry Steinbach	.10
40	Tom Glavine	.20
41	Todd Dunwoody	.10
42	Deion Sanders	.25
43	Gary Sheffield	.35
44	Mike Lansing	.10
45	Mike Lieberthal	.10
46	Paul Sorrento	.10
47	Paul O'Neill	.20
48	Tom Goodwin	.10
49	Andruw Jones	1.50
50	Barry Bonds	.75
51	Bernie Williams	.50
52	Jeremi Gonzalez	.20
53	Mike Piazza	2.00
54	Russ Davis	.10
55	Vinny Castilla	.10
56	Rod Beck	.10
57	Andres Galarraga	.20
58	Ben McDonald	.10
59	Billy Wagner	.10
60	Charles Johnson	.10
61	Fred McGriff	.25
62	Dean Palmer	.10
63	Frank Thomas	2.50
64	Ismael Valdes	.10
65	Mark Bellhorn	.10
66	Jeff King	.10
67	John Wetteland	.10
68	Mark Grace	.25
69	Mark Kotsay	.50
70	Scott Rolen	1.50
71	Todd Hundley	.20
72	Todd Worrell	.10
73	Wilson Alvarez	.10
74	Bobby Jones	.10
75	Jose Canseco	.25
76	Kevin Appier	.10
77	Neifi Perez	.10
78	Paul Molitor	.50
79	Quilvio Veras	.10
80	Randy Johnson	.50
81	Glendon Rusch	.10
82	Curt Schilling	.10
83	Alex Rodriguez	2.50
84	Rey Ordonez	.10
85	Jeff Juden	.10
86	Mike Cameron	.10
87	Ryan Klesko	.25
88	Trevor Hoffman	.10
89	Chuck Knoblauch	.25
90	Larry Walker	.30
91	Mark McLemore	.10
92	B.J. Surhoff	.10
93	Darren Daulton	.10
94	Ray Durham	.10
95	Sammy Sosa	1.50
96	Eric Young	.10
97	Gerald Williams	.10
98	Javy Lopez	.15
99	John Smiley	.10
100	Juan Gonzalez	1.50
101	Shawn Green	.10
102	Charles Nagy	.10
103	David Justice	.25
104	Joey Hamilton	.10
105	Pat Hentgen	.10
106	Raul Casanova	.10
107	Tony Phillips	.10
108	Tony Gwynn	1.50
109	Will Clark	.25
110	Jason Giambi	.10
111	Jay Bell	.10
112	Johnny Damon	.10
113	Alan Benes	.10
114	Jeff Suppan	.10
115	*Kevin Polcovich*	.25
116	Shigetosi Hasegawa	.10
117	Steve Finley	.10
118	Tony Clark	.40
119	David Cone	.20
120	Jose Guillen	.40
121	*Kevin Millwood*	1.00
122	Greg Maddux	2.00
123	Dave Nilsson	.10
124	Hideki Irabu	.75
125	Jason Kendall	.10
126	Jim Thome	.40
127	Delino DeShields	.10
128	Edgar Renteria	.20
129	Edgardo Alfonzo	.10
130	J.T. Snow	.10
131	Jeff Abbott	.10
132	Jeffrey Hammonds	.10
133	Rich Loiselle	.10
134	Vladimir Guerrero	1.00
135	Jay Buhner	.20
136	Jeff Cirillo	.10
137	Jeromy Burnitz	.10
138	Mickey Morandini	.10
139	Tino Martinez	.25
140	Jeff Shaw	.10
141	Rafael Palmeiro	.20
142	Bobby Bonilla	.20
143	Cal Ripken Jr.	2.50
144	*Chad Fox*	.25
145	Dante Bichette	.20
146	Dennis Eckersley	.20
147	Mariano Rivera	.20
148	Mo Vaughn	.75
149	Reggie Sanders	.10
150	Derek Jeter	1.75
151	Rusty Greer	.20
152	Brady Anderson	.20
153	Brett Tomko	.10
154	Jaime Navarro	.10
155	Kevin Orie	.10
156	Roberto Alomar	.60
157	Edgar Martinez	.10
158	John Olerud	.10
159	John Smoltz	.20
160	Ryne Sandberg	.75
161	Billy Taylor	.10
162	Chris Holt	.10
163	Damion Easley	.10
164	Darin Erstad	.75
165	Joe Carter	.20
166	Kelvim Escobar	.10
167	Ken Caminiti	.25
168	Pokey Reese	.10
169	Ray Lankford	.10
170	Livan Hernandez	.20
171	Steve Kline	.10
172	Tom Gordon	.10
173	Travis Fryman	.10
174	Al Martin	.10
175	Andy Pettitte	.50
176	Jeff Kent	.10
177	Jimmy Key	.10
178	Mark Grudzielanek	.10
179	Tony Saunders	.20
180	Barry Larkin	.25
181	Bubba Trammell	.20
182	Carlos Delgado	.10
183	Carlos Baerga	.10
184	Derek Bell	.10
185	Henry Rodriguez	.10
186	Jason Dickson	.10
187	Ron Gant	.10
188	Tony Womack	.10
189	Justin Thompson	.10
190	Fernando Tatis	.30
191	Mark Wohlers	.10
192	Takashi Kashiwada	.50
193	Garret Anderson	.10
194	Jose Cruz, Jr.	1.00
195	Ricardo Rincon	.10
196	Tim Naehring	.10
197	Moises Alou	.20
198	Eric Karros	.10
199	John Jaha	.10
200	Marty Cordova	.10
201	Travis Lee	3.00
202	Mark Davis	.10
203	Vladimir Nunez	.10
204	Stanton Cameron	.10
205	*Mike Stoner*	1.00
206	*Rolando Arrojo*	.40
207	Rick White	.10
208	Luis Polonia	.10
209	Greg Blosser	.10
210	Cesar Devarez	.10
211	Jeff Bagwell (Season Crown)	4.00
212	Barry Bonds (Season Crown)	2.50
213	Roger Clemens (Season Crown)	4.00
214	Nomar Garciaparra (Season Crown)	7.00
215	Ken Griffey Jr. (Season Crown)	10.00
216	Tony Gwynn (Season Crown)	5.00
217	Randy Johnson (Season Crown)	1.50
218	Mark McGwire (Season Crown)	12.00
219	Scott Rolen (Season Crown)	5.00
220	Frank Thomas (Season Crown)	8.00
221	Matt Perisho (Prospect)	.10
222	Wes Helms (Prospect)	1.00
223	*David Dellucci* (Prospect)	2.00
224	Todd Helton (Prospect)	3.00
225	Brian Rose (Prospect)	1.00
226	Aaron Boone (Prospect)	.25
227	Keith Foulke (Prospect)	.50
228	Homer Bush (Prospect)	.40
229	Shannon Stewart (Prospect)	.25
230	Richard Hidalgo (Prospect)	1.00
231	Russ Johnson (Prospect)	.50
232	*Henry Blanco* (Prospect)	.40
233	Paul Konerko (Prospect)	5.00
234	Antone Williamson (Prospect)	.50
235	*Shane Bowers* (Prospect)	.50
236	Jose Vidro (Prospect)	.25
237	Derek Wallace (Prospect)	.25
238	Ricky Ledee (Prospect)	1.50
239	Kris Benson (Prospect)	5.00
240	Lou Collier (Prospect)	.50
241	Derrek Lee (Prospect)	1.00
242	Ruben Rivera (Prospect)	.50
243	Jorge Velandia (Prospect)	.25
244	Andrew Vessel (Prospect)	.40
245	Chris Carpenter (Prospect)	.50
246	Checklist (Ken Griffey Jr.)	1.50
247	Checklist (Andruw Jones)	.75
248	Checklist (Alex Rodriguez)	1.00
249	Checklist (Frank Thomas)	1.25
250	Checklist (Cal Ripken Jr.)	1.00
251	Carlos Perez	.10
252	Larry Sutton	.10
253	Brad Rigby	.10
254	Wally Joyner	.10
255	Todd Stottlemyre	.10
256	Nerio Rodriguez	.10
257	Jeff Frye	.10
258	Pedro Astacio	.10
259	Cal Eldred	.10

260	Chili Davis	.10
261	Freddy Garcia	.10
262	Bobby Witt	.10
263	Michael Coleman	.10
264	Mike Caruso	.20
265	Mike Lansing	.10
266	Dennis Reyes	.10
267	F.P. Santangelo	.10
268	Darryl Hamilton	.10
269	Mike Fetters	.10
270	Charlie Hayes	.10
271	Royce Clayton	.10
272	Doug Drabek	.10
273	James Baldwin	.10
274	Brian Hunter	.10
275	Chan Ho Park	.20
276	John Franco	.10
277	David Wells	.10
278	Eli Marrero	.10
279	Kerry Wood	5.00
280	Donnie Sadler	.10
281	*Scott Winchester*	.25
282	Hal Morris	.10
283	Brad Fullmer	.25
284	Bernard Gilkey	.10
285	Ramiro Mendoza	.10
286	Kevin Brown	.20
287	David Segui	.10
288	Willie McGee	.10
289	Darren Oliver	.10
290	Antonio Alfonseca	.10
291	Eric Davis	.10
292	Mickey Morandini	.10
293	*Frank Catalanotto*	.20
294	Derrek Lee	.10
295	Todd Zeile	.10
296	Chuck Knoblauch	.25
297	Wilson Delgado	.10
298	Raul Ibanez	.10
299	Orel Hershiser	.10
300	Ozzie Guillen	.10
301	Aaron Sele	.10
302	Joe Carter	.20
303	Darryl Kile	.10
304	Shane Reynolds	.10
305	Todd Dunn	.10
306	Bob Abreu	.10
307	Doug Strange	.10
308	Jose Canseco	.30
309	Lance Johnson	.10
310	Harold Baines	.10
311	Todd Pratt	.10
312	Greg Colbrunn	.10
313	*Masato Yoshii*	.50
314	Felix Heredia	.10
315	Dennis Martinez	.10
316	Geronimo Berroa	.10
317	Darren Lewis	.10
318	Billy Ripken	.10
319	Enrique Wilson	.10
320	Alex Ochoa	.10
321	Doug Glanville	.10
322	Mike Stanley	.10
323	Gerald Williams	.10
324	Pedro Martinez	.50
325	Jaret Wright	1.00
326	Terry Pendleton	.10
327	LaTroy Hawkins	.10
328	Emil Brown	.10
329	Walt Weiss	.10
330	Omar Vizquel	.10
331	Carl Everett	.10
332	Fernando Vina	.10
333	Mike Blowers	.10
334	Dwight Gooden	.20
335	Mark Lewis	.10
336	Jim Leyritz	.10
337	Kenny Lofton	.75
338	*John Halama*	.30
339	Jose Valentin	.10
340	Desi Relaford	.10
341	Dante Powell	.10
342	Ed Sprague	.10
343	Reggie Jefferson	.10
344	Mike Hampton	.10
345	Marquis Grissom	.10
346	Heathcliff Slocumb	.10
347	Francisco Cordova	.10
348	Ken Cloude	.25
349	Benito Santiago	.10
350	Denny Neagle	.10
351	Sean Casey	.25
352	Robb Nen	.10
353	Orlando Merced	.10
354	Adrian Brown	.10
355	Gregg Jefferies	.10
356	Otis Nixon	.10
357	Michael Tucker	.10
358	Eric Milton	.25
359	Travis Fryman	.10
360	Gary DiSarcina	.10
361	Mario Valdez	.10
362	Craig Counsell	.10
363	Jose Offerman	.10
364	Tony Fernandez	.10
365	Jason McDonald	.10
366	Sterling Hitchcock	.10
367	Donovan Osborne	.10
368	Troy Percival	.10
369	Henry Rodriguez	.10
370	Dmitri Young	.10
371	Jay Powell	.10
372	Jeff Conine	.10
373	Orlando Cabrera	.10
374	Butch Huskey	.10
375	*Mike Lowell*	.10
376	Kevin Young	.10
377	Jamie Moyer	.10
378	Jeff D'Amico	.10
379	Scott Erickson	.10
380	*Magglio Ordonez*	.75
381	Melvin Nieves	.10
382	Ramon Martinez	.20
383	A.J. Hinch	.50
384	Jeff Brantley	.10
385	Kevin Elster	.10
386	Allen Watson	.10
387	Moises Alou	.20
388	Jeff Blauser	.10
389	Pete Harnisch	.10
390	Shane Andrews	.10
391	Rico Brogna	.10
392	Stan Javier	.10
393	David Howard	.10
394	Darryl Strawberry	.20
395	Kent Mercker	.10
396	Juan Encarnacion	.25
397	Sandy Alomar	.20
398	Al Leiter	.20
399	Tony Graffanino	.10
400	Terry Adams	.10
401	Bruce Aven	.10
402	Derrick Gibson	.10
403	Jose Cabrera	.10
404	Rich Becker	.10
405	David Ortiz	.40
406	Brian McRae	.10
407	Bobby Estalella	.10
408	Bill Mueller	.10
409	Dennis Eckersley	.20
410	Sandy Martinez	.10
411	Jose Vizcaino	.10
412	Jermaine Allensworth	.10
413	Miguel Tejada	.40
414	Turner Ward	.10
415	Glenallen Hill	.10
416	Lee Stevens	.10
417	Cecil Fielder	.25
418	Ruben Sierra	.10
419	Jon Nunnally	.10
420	Rod Myers	.10
421	Dustin Hermanson	.10
422	James Mouton	.10
423	Dan Wilson	.10
424	Roberto Kelly	.10
425	Antonio Osuna	.10
426	Jacob Cruz	.10
427	Brent Mayne	.10
428	Matt Karchner	.10
429	Damian Jackson	.10
430	Roger Cedeno	.10
431	Rickey Henderson	.10
432	Joe Randa	.10
433	Greg Vaughn	.10
434	Andres Galarraga	.40
435	Rod Beck	.10
436	Curtis Goodwin	.10
437	Brad Ausmus	.10
438	Bob Hamelin	.10
439	Todd Walker	.30
440	Scott Brosius	.10
441	Lenny Dykstra	.10
442	Abraham Nunez	.10
443	Brian Johnson	.10
444	Randy Myers	.10
445	Bret Boone	.10
446	Oscar Henriquez	.10
447	Mike Sweeney	.10
448	Kenny Rogers	.10
449	Mark Langston	.10
450	Luis Gonzalez	.10
451	John Burkett	.10
452	Bip Roberts	.10
453	Travis Lee (New Horizons)	1.00
454	Felix Rodriguez (New Horizons)	.10
455	Andy Benes (New Horizons)	.10
456	Willie Blair (New Horizons)	.10
457	Brian Anderson (New Horizons)	.10
458	Jay Bell (New Horizons)	.10
459	Matt Williams (New Horizons)	.25
460	Devon White (New Horizons)	.10
461	Karim Garcia (New Horizons)	.10
462	Jorge Fabregas (New Horizons)	.10
463	Wilson Alvarez (New Horizons)	.10
464	Roberto Hernandez (New Horizons)	.10
465	Tony Saunders (New Horizons)	.10
466	Rolando Arrojo (New Horizons)	.40
467	Wade Boggs (New Horizons)	.25
468	Fred McGriff (New Horizons)	.25
469	Paul Sorrento (New Horizons)	.10
470	Kevin Stocker (New Horizons)	.10
471	Bubba Trammell (New Horizons)	.25
472	Quinton McCracken (New Horizons)	.10
473	Checklist (Ken Griffey Jr.)	1.00
474	Checklist (Cal Ripken Jr.)	.75
475	Checklist (Frank Thomas)	.60
476	Ken Griffey Jr. (Pizzazz)	6.00
477	Cal Ripken Jr. (Pizzazz)	5.00
478	Frank Thomas (Pizzazz)	5.00
479	Alex Rodriguez (Pizzazz)	4.00
480	Nomar Garciaparra (Pizzazz)	4.00
481	Derek Jeter (Pizzazz)	3.00
482	Andruw Jones (Pizzazz)	1.50
483	Chipper Jones (Pizzazz)	4.00
484	Greg Maddux (Pizzazz)	4.00
485	Mike Piazza (Pizzazz)	4.00
486	Juan Gonzalez (Pizzazz)	3.00
487	Jose Cruz (Pizzazz)	1.00
488	Jaret Wright (Pizzazz)	2.50
489	Hideo Nomo (Pizzazz)	1.00
490	Scott Rolen (Pizzazz)	2.00
491	Tony Gwynn (Pizzazz)	3.00
492	Roger Clemens (Pizzazz)	2.00
493	Darin Erstad (Pizzazz)	1.50
494	Mark McGwire (Pizzazz)	8.00
495	Jeff Bagwell (Pizzazz)	2.00
496	Mo Vaughn (Pizzazz)	1.50
497	Albert Belle (Pizzazz)	1.50
498	Kenny Lofton (Pizzazz)	1.50
499	Ben Grieve (Pizzazz)	2.00
500	Barry Bonds (Pizzazz)	1.50
501	Mike Piazza (mets)	3.00

1998 Ultra Gold Medallion Edition

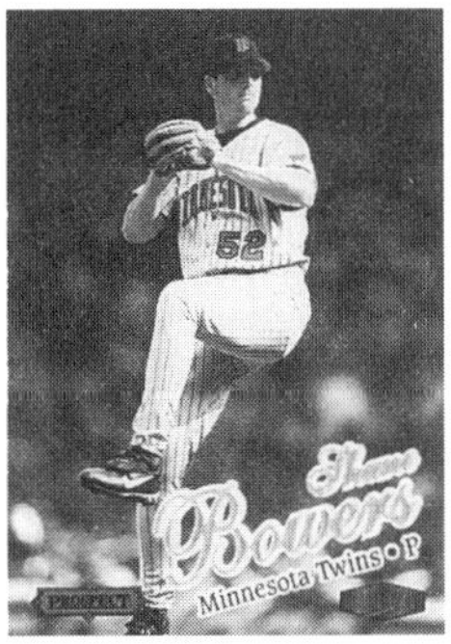

This parallel to the basic Ultra set is found seeded on a one per pack ratio. Cards are similar to the regular-issue Ultra except for a gold presentation of the embossed player name on front and a shower of gold specks in the photo background. Backs have a "G" suffix to the card number and a "GOLD MEDALLION EDITION" notation at bottom.

	MT
Complete Set (250):	75.00
Common Player:	.25
Inserted 1:1	
(Star cards 2X-4X regular Ultra)	

1998 Ultra Platinum Medallion

Insertion odds on this super-scarce insert set are not given but each card is produced and serially numbered in an edition of only 100. Fronts are similar to regular Ultra cards except the photo is black-and-white and the name is rendered in silver prismatic foil. Backs are in color with the serial number printed in silver foil at bottom.

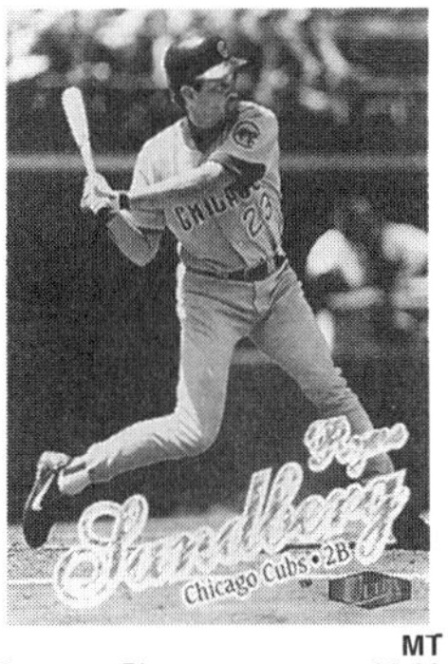

	MT
Common Player:	30.00
(Star cards 50X-75X regular Ultra)	

1998 Ultra Artistic Talents

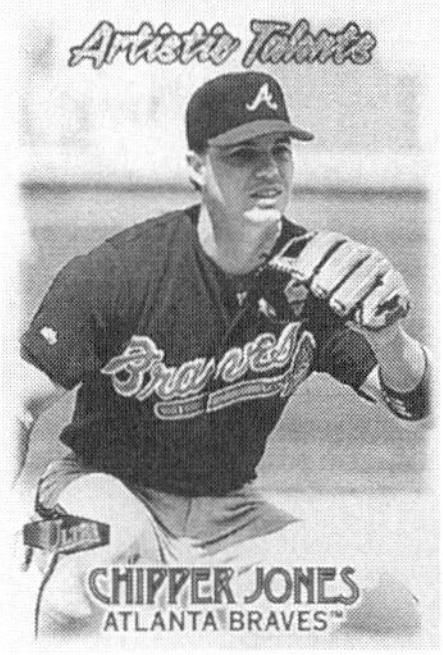

This 18-card insert featured top players in the game on a canvas-like surface with the insert name in silver holographic letters across the top. The backs are done in black and white and numbered with an "AT" suffix. Artistic Talents are inserted one per eight packs.

		MT
Complete Set (18):		60.00
Common Player:		.75
Inserted 1:8		
1	Ken Griffey Jr.	8.00
2	Andruw Jones	4.00
3	Alex Rodriguez	6.00
4	Frank Thomas	6.00
5	Cal Ripken Jr.	6.00
6	Derek Jeter	5.00
7	Chipper Jones	5.00
8	Greg Maddux	5.00
9	Mike Piazza	5.00
10	Albert Belle	2.50
11	Darin Erstad	3.00
12	Juan Gonzalez	4.00
13	Jeff Bagwell	3.00
14	Tony Gwynn	4.00
15	Mark McGwire	10.00
16	Scott Rolen	4.00
17	Barry Bonds	2.50
18	Kenny Lofton	2.50

1998 Ultra Back to the Future

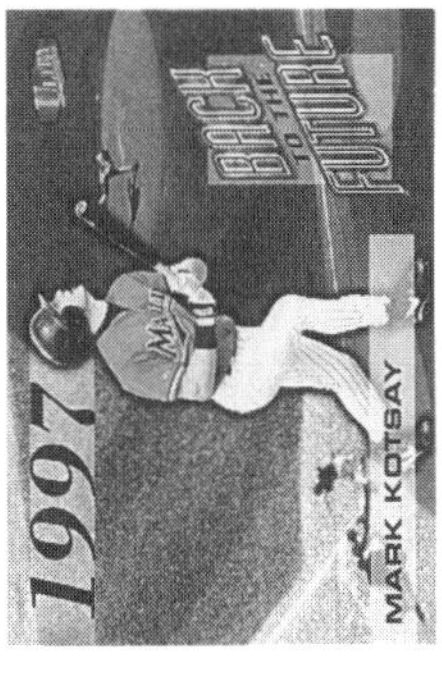

This 15-card insert was printed in a horizontal format with a baseball field background. Cards were numbered with a "BF" suffix and seeded one per six packs.

		MT
Complete Set (15):		20.00
Common Player:		.50
Inserted 1:6		
1	Andruw Jones	2.50
2	Alex Rodriguez	4.00
3	Derek Jeter	3.00
4	Darin Erstad	2.00
5	Mike Cameron	.50
6	Scott Rolen	2.50
7	Nomar Garciaparra	3.00
8	Hideki Irabu	1.50
9	Jose Cruz, Jr.	2.00
10	Vladimir Guerrero	1.50
11	Mark Kotsay	1.00
12	Tony Womack	.50
13	Jason Dickson	.50
14	Jose Guillen	.75
15	Tony Clark	1.00

1998 Ultra Big Shots

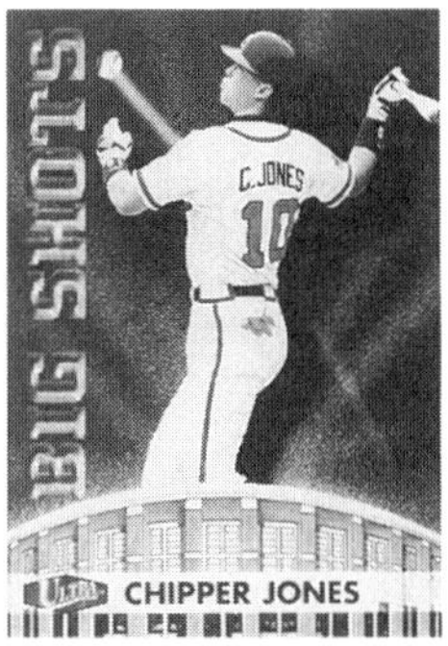

Big Shots was a 15-card insert displaying some of the top home run hitters in baseball. A generic stadium is pictured across the bottom with the insert name running up the left side. Cards were numbered with a "BS" suffix and inserted one per four Series I packs.

		MT
Complete Set (15):		15.00
Common Player:		.25
Inserted 1:4		
1	Ken Griffey Jr.	4.00
2	Frank Thomas	3.00
3	Chipper Jones	2.50
4	Albert Belle	1.25
5	Juan Gonzalez	2.00
6	Jeff Bagwell	1.50
7	Mark McGwire	5.00
8	Barry Bonds	1.00
9	Manny Ramirez	.75
10	Mo Vaughn	1.00
11	Matt Williams	.25
12	Jim Thome	.50
13	Tino Martinez	.25
14	Mike Piazza	2.50
15	Tony Clark	.75

1998 Ultra Diamond Immortals

This Series II insert showcased 15 top player on an intricate silver holographic foil design that frames each player. Cards were numbered with a "DI" suffix and inserted one per 288 packs.

		MT
Complete Set (15):		850.00
Common Player:		20.00
Inserted 1:288		
1	Ken Griffey Jr.	125.00
2	Frank Thomas	75.00
3	Alex Rodriguez	75.00
4	Cal Ripken Jr.	90.00
5	Mike Piazza	75.00
6	Mark McGwire	140.00
7	Greg Maddux	75.00
8	Andruw Jones	30.00
9	Chipper Jones	75.00
10	Derek Jeter	60.00
11	Tony Gwynn	60.00
12	Juan Gonzalez	60.00
13	Jose Cruz	20.00
14	Roger Clemens	40.00
15	Barry Bonds	30.00

1998 Ultra Diamond Producers

This 15-card insert captured players on a prismatic silver design, with a wood backdrop and a black felt frame around the border. Cards were seeded one per 288 Series I packs and numbered with a "DP" suffix.

		MT
Complete Set (15):		800.00
Common Player:		20.00
Inserted 1:288		
1	Ken Griffey Jr.	125.00
2	Andruw Jones	60.00
3	Alex Rodriguez	80.00
4	Frank Thomas	90.00
5	Cal Ripken Jr.	80.00
6	Derek Jeter	60.00
7	Chipper Jones	60.00
8	Greg Maddux	60.00
9	Mike Piazza	60.00
10	Juan Gonzalez	50.00
11	Jeff Bagwell	40.00
12	Tony Gwynn	50.00
13	Mark McGwire	125.00
14	Barry Bonds	25.00
15	Jose Cruz, Jr.	40.00

1998 Ultra Double Trouble

Double Trouble includes 20 cards and pairs two teammates on a horizontal format with the team's logo and the insert name featured in a silver holographic circle in the middle. These were numbered with a "DT" suffix and exclusive to Series I packs at a rate of one per four.

		MT
Complete Set (20):		20.00
Common Player:		.25
Inserted 1:4		
1	Ken Griffey Jr., Alex Rodriguez	4.00
2	Vladimir Guerrero, Pedro Martinez	1.50
3	Andruw Jones, Kenny Lofton	2.00
4	Chipper Jones, Greg Maddux	2.50
5	Derek Jeter, Tino Martinez	2.00
6	Frank Thomas, Albert Belle	3.00
7	Cal Ripken Jr., Roberto Alomar	2.50
8	Mike Piazza, Hideo Nomo	2.00

9	Darin Erstad, Jason Dickson	1.00
10	Juan Gonzalez, Ivan Rodriguez	1.50
11	Jeff Bagwell, Darryl Kile	1.50
12	Tony Gwynn, Steve Finley	1.50
13	Mark McGwire, Ray Lankford	4.00
14	Barry Bonds, Jeff Kent	.75
15	Andy Pettitte, Bernie Williams	.50
16	Mo Vaughn, Nomar Garciaparra	1.50
17	Matt Williams, Jim Thome	.25
18	Hideki Irabu, Mariano Rivera	1.50
19	Roger Clemens, Jose Cruz, Jr.	1.50
20	Manny Ramirez, David Justice	.50

1998 Ultra Fall Classics

This Series I insert pictures 15 stars over a green holographic bacground that contains the insert name in script. Fall Classics were inserted one per 18 packs and numbered with a "FC" suffix.

		MT
Complete Set (15):		100.00
Common Player:		2.00
Inserted 1:18		
1	Ken Griffey Jr.	15.00
2	Andruw Jones	8.00
3	Alex Rodriguez	12.00
4	Frank Thomas	12.00
5	Cal Ripken Jr.	12.00
6	Derek Jeter	9.00
7	Chipper Jones	9.00
8	Greg Maddux	9.00
9	Mike Piazza	9.00
10	Albert Belle	4.00
11	Juan Gonzalez	7.50
12	Jeff Bagwell	6.00
13	Tony Gwynn	7.50
14	Mark McGwire	20.00
15	Barry Bonds	3.50

1998 Ultra Kid Gloves

Kid Gloves featured top fielders in the game over an embossed glove background. Exclusive to Series I packs, they were inserted in one per eight packs and numbered with a "KG" suffix.

		MT
Complete Set (12):		30.00
Common Player:		.75
Inserted 1:8		
1	Andruw Jones	3.00
2	Alex Rodriguez	5.00
3	Derek Jeter	4.00
4	Chipper Jones	4.00
5	Darin Erstad	2.00
6	Todd Walker	1.00
7	Scott Rolen	3.00
8	Nomar Garciaparra	4.00
9	Jose Cruz, Jr.	3.00
10	Charles Johnson	.75
11	Rey Ordonez	.75
12	Vladimir Guerrero	2.00

1998 Ultra Millennium Men

Millenium Men was a 15-card hobby-only insert exclusive to Series II packs. These tri-fold cards featured an embossed wax seal design and could be unfolded to reveal another shot of the player, team logo and statistics. They were numbered with a "MM" suffix and inserted every 35 packs.

		MT
Complete Set (15):		200.00
Common Player:		4.00
Inserted 1:35		
1	Jose Cruz	6.00
2	Ken Griffey Jr.	30.00
3	Cal Ripken Jr.	25.00
4	Derek Jeter	15.00
5	Andruw Jones	8.00
6	Alex Rodriguez	20.00
7	Chipper Jones	20.00
8	Scott Rolen	10.00
9	Nomar Garciaparra	20.00
10	Frank Thomas	20.00
11	Mike Piazza	20.00
12	Greg Maddux	20.00
13	Juan Gonzalez	15.00
14	Ben Grieve	10.00
15	Jaret Wright	8.00

1998 Ultra Notables

This 20-card insert pictured a player over a holographic background with either an American League or National League logo in the background. Notables were seeded one per four Series II packs and numbered with a "N" suffix.

		MT
Complete Set (20):		25.00
Common Player:		.25
Inserted 1:4		
1	Frank Thomas	3.00
2	Ken Griffey Jr.	4.00
3	Edgar Renteria	.25
4	Albert Belle	1.00
5	Juan Gonzalez	2.00
6	Jeff Bagwell	1.50
7	Mark McGwire	5.00
8	Barry Bonds	1.00
9	Scott Rolen	1.50
10	Mo Vaughn	1.00
11	Andruw Jones	1.00
12	Chipper Jones	2.50
13	Tino Martinez	.50
14	Mike Piazza	2.50
15	Tony Clark	.50
16	Jose Cruz	.75
17	Nomar Garciaparra	2.50
18	Cal Ripken Jr.	3.00
19	Alex Rodriguez	2.50
20	Derek Jeter	2.00

1998 Ultra Power Plus

This 10-card insert was exclusive to Series I packs and seeded one per 36 packs. Cards pictured the player over an embossed blue background featuring plus signs. These were numbered with a "PP" suffix.

		MT
Complete Set (10):		120.00
Common Player:		3.00
Inserted 1:36		
1	Ken Griffey Jr.	25.00
2	Andruw Jones	12.00
3	Alex Rodriguez	20.00
4	Frank Thomas	20.00
5	Mike Piazza	15.00
6	Albert Belle	7.00
7	Juan Gonzalez	12.00
8	Jeff Bagwell	10.00
9	Barry Bonds	6.00
10	Jose Cruz, Jr.	8.00

1998 Ultra Prime Leather

This 18-card insert features top fielders on a leather-like card stock, with a large baseball in the background. Cards are seeded one per 144 Series I packs and numbered with a "PL" suffix.

		MT
Complete Set (18):		550.00
Common Player:		10.00
Inserted 1:144		
1	Ken Griffey Jr.	75.00
2	Andruw Jones	35.00
3	Alex Rodriguez	50.00
4	Frank Thomas	50.00
5	Cal Ripken Jr.	50.00
6	Derek Jeter	40.00
7	Chipper Jones	40.00
8	Greg Maddux	40.00
9	Mike Piazza	40.00
10	Albert Belle	20.00
11	Darin Erstad	25.00
12	Juan Gonzalez	35.00
13	Jeff Bagwell	30.00
14	Tony Gwynn	35.00
15	Roberto Alomar	15.00
16	Barry Bonds	20.00
17	Kenny Lofton	20.00
18	Jose Cruz, Jr.	25.00

1998 Ultra Rocket to Stardom

This 15-card insert set was exclusive to Series II packs and inserted in one per 20 packs. Cards were in black-and-white and were die-cut and embossed. The insert contained a collection of top young stars and was numbered with a "RS" suffix.

		MT
Complete Set (15):		45.00
Common Player:		2.00
Inserted 1:20		
1	Ben Grieve	8.00
2	Magglio Ordonez	4.00
3	Travis Lee	12.00
4	Carl Pavano	2.00
5	Brian Rose	2.00
6	Brad Fullmer	4.00
7	Michael Coleman	2.00
8	Juan Encarnacion	2.00
9	Karim Garcia	2.00
10	Todd Helton	4.00
11	Richard Hildalgo	2.00
12	Paul Konerko	4.00
13	Rod Myers	2.00
14	Jaret Wright	6.00
15	Miguel Tejada	4.00

1998 Ultra Ticket Studs

Fifteen players are featured on fold-out game ticket-like cards in Ticket Studs. The cards arrived folded across the middle and open to reveal a full-length shot of the player with prismatic team color stripes in over a white background that has section, seat and row numbers. Cards were inserted one per 144 Series II packs and are numbered with a "TS" suffix.

		MT
Complete Set (15):		500.00
Common Player:		10.00
Inserted 1:144		
1	Travis Lee	25.00
2	Tony Gwynn	35.00
3	Scott Rolen	25.00
4	Nomar Garciaparra	50.00
5	Mike Piazza	50.00
6	Mark McGwire	100.00
7	Ken Griffey Jr.	75.00
8	Juan Gonzalez	40.00
9	Jose Cruz	15.00
10	Frank Thomas	50.00
11	Derek Jeter	40.00
12	Chipper Jones	50.00
13	Cal Ripken Jr.	60.00
14	Andruw Jones	18.00
15	Alex Rodriguez	50.00

1998 Ultra Top 30

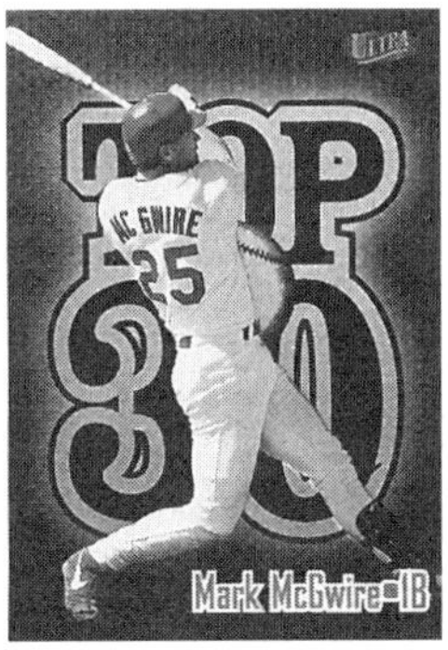

This 30-card insert was exclusive to Series II packs and inserted one per retail pack. Cards featured the player over a silver and black background with a large "Top 30" logo. Card backs were numbered with a "T3" suffix.

		MT
Complete Set (30):		35.00
Common Player:		.25
Inserted 1:1 R		
1	Barry Bonds	1.00
2	Ivan Rodriguez	1.00
3	Kenny Lofton	1.00
4	Albert Belle	1.00
5	Mo Vaughn	1.00
6	Jeff Bagwell	1.50
7	Mark McGwire	5.00
8	Darin Erstad	1.00
9	Roger Clemens	2.00
10	Tony Gwynn	2.00
11	Scott Rolen	1.00
12	Hideo Nomo	.50
13	Juan Gonzalez	2.00
14	Mike Piazza	2.50
15	Greg Maddux	2.50
16	Chipper Jones	2.50
17	Andruw Jones	1.00
18	Derek Jeter	2.00
19	Nomar Garciaparra	2.50
20	Alex Rodriguez	2.50
21	Frank Thomas	2.50
22	Cal Ripken Jr.	3.00
23	Ken Griffey Jr.	4.00
24	Jose Cruz Jr.	1.00
25	Jaret Wright	1.00
26	Travis Lee	1.50
27	Wade Boggs	.40
28	Chuck Knoblauch	.40
29	Joe Carter	.25
30	Ben Grieve	1.50

1998 Ultra Win Now

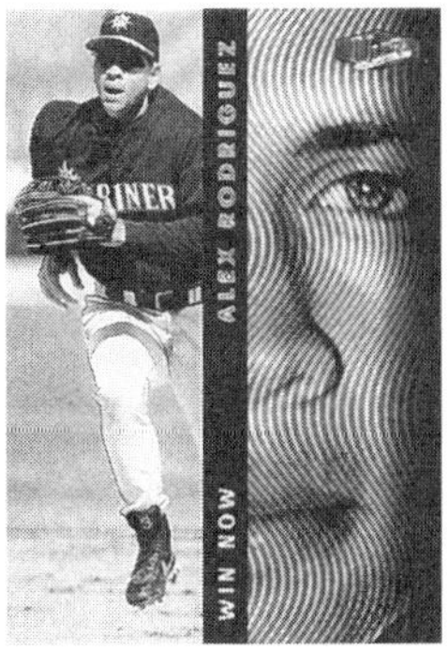

This Series II insert has 20 top players printed on plastic card stock, with a color shot of the player on the left side and a close-up shot on the right with black lines through it. Win Now cards were seeded one per 72 packs and numbered with a "WN" suffix.

		MT
Complete Set (20):		425.00
Common Player:		6.00
Inserted 1:72		
1	Alex Rodriguez	30.00
2	Andruw Jones	12.00
3	Cal Ripken Jr.	40.00
4	Chipper Jones	30.00
5	Darin Erstad	15.00
6	Derek Jeter	25.00
7	Frank Thomas	35.00
8	Greg Maddux	30.00
9	Hideo Nomo	10.00
10	Jeff Bagwell	15.00
11	Jose Cruz	10.00
12	Juan Gonzalez	25.00
13	Ken Griffey Jr.	50.00
14	Mark McGwire	60.00
15	Mike Piazza	30.00
16	Mo Vaughn	12.00
17	Nomar Garciaparra	30.00
18	Roger Clemens	15.00
19	Scott Rolen	15.00
20	Tony Gwynn	25.00

1998 Upper Deck

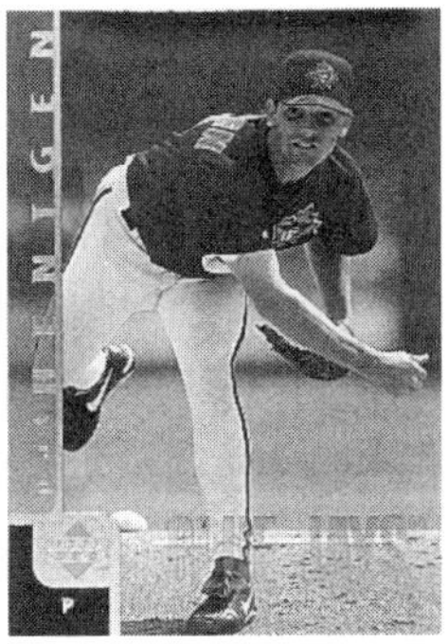

Upper Deck Baseball was released in three series. Series One consisted of 270 base cards, with five subsets. Inserts included A Piece of the Action, Amazing Greats, National Pride, Ken Griffey Jr.'s Home Run Chronicles and 10th Anniversary Preview. The 270-card second series also had five subsets. Inserts include Prime Nine, Ken Griffey Jr.'s Home Run Chronicles, Tape Measure Titans, Blue Chip Prospects, Clearly Dominant and A Piece of the Action. The third series, Upper Deck Rookie Edition, had a 210-card base set. Insert sets were Ken Griffey Jr. Game Jersey, Game Jersey Rookie Cards, Unparalleled, Destination Stardom, All-Star Credentials and Retrospectives.

		MT
Complete Set (750):		135.00
Complete Series I Set (270):		25.00
Complete Series II Set (270):		25.00
Complete Series III Set (210):		85.00
Common Emminent Prestige (601-630):		1.00
Common Player:		.10
Series I,II & III Box:		55.00
1	Tino Martinez (History in the Making)	.15
2	Jimmy Key (History in the Making)	.10
3	Jay Buhner (History in the Making)	.15
4	Mark Gardner (History in the Making)	.10
5	Greg Maddux (History in the Making)	1.00
6	Pedro J. Martinez (History in the Making)	.15
7	Hideo Nomo, Shigetosi Hasegawa (History in the Making)	.25
8	Sammy Sosa (History in the Making)	.75
9	Mark McGwire (Griffey Hot List)	1.50
10	Ken Griffey Jr. (Griffey Hot List)	1.50
11	Larry Walker (Griffey Hot List)	.20
12	Tino Martine (Griffey Hot List)	.15
13	Mike Piazz (Griffey Hot List)	1.00
14	Jose Cruz, Jr. (Griffey Hot List)	.75
15	Tony Gwynn (Griffey Hot List)	.75
16	Greg Maddux (Griffey Hot List)	1.00
17	Roger Clemens (Griffey Hot List)	.50
18	Alex Rodriguez (Griffey Hot List)	1.00
19	Shigetosi Hasegawa	.10
20	Eddie Murray	.25
21	Jason Dickson	.10
22	Darin Erstad	.75
23	Chuck Finley	.10
24	Dave Hollins	.10
25	Garret Anderson	.10
26	Michael Tucker	.10
27	Kenny Lofton	.75
28	Javier Lopez	.20
29	Fred McGriff	.25
30	Greg Maddux	2.00
31	Jeff Blauser	.10
32	John Smoltz	.20
33	Mark Wohlers	.10
34	Scott Erickson	.10
35	Jimmy Key	.10
36	Harold Baines	.10
37	Randy Myers	.10
38	B.J. Surhoff	.10
39	Eric Davis	.10
40	Rafael Palmeiro	.20
41	Jeffrey Hammonds	.10
42	Mo Vaughn	.75
43	Tom Gordon	.10
44	Tim Naehring	.10
45	Darren Bragg	.10
46	Aaron Sele	.10
47	Troy O'Leary	.10
48	John Valentin	.10
49	Doug Glanville	.10
50	Ryne Sandberg	.75
51	Steve Trachsel	.10
52	Mark Grace	.25
53	Kevin Foster	.10
54	Kevin Tapani	.10
55	Kevin Orie	.10
56	Lyle Mouton	.10
57	Ray Durham	.10
58	Jaime Navarro	.10
59	Mike Cameron	.10
60	Albert Belle	.75
61	Doug Drabek	.10
62	Chris Snopek	.10
63	Eddie Taubensee	.10
64	Terry Pendleton	.10
65	Barry Larkin	.20
66	Willie Greene	.10
67	Deion Sanders	.20
68	Pokey Reese	.10
69	Jeff Shaw	.10
70	Jim Thome	.40
71	Orel Hershiser	.10
72	Omar Vizquel	.10
73	Brian Giles	.10
74	David Justice	.25
75	Bartolo Colon	.10
76	Sandy Alomar Jr.	.20
77	Neifi Perez	.10
78	Eric Young	.10
79	Vinny Castilla	.10
80	Dante Bichette	.20
81	Quinton McCracken	.10
82	Jamey Wright	.10
83	John Thomson	.10
84	Damion Easley	.10
85	Justin Thompson	.10
86	Willie Blair	.10
87	Raul Casanova	.10
88	Bobby Higginson	.10
89	Bubba Trammell	.20
90	Tony Clark	.50
91	Livan Hernandez	.20
92	Charles Johnson	.10
93	Edgar Renteria	.10
94	Alex Fernandez	.10
95	Gary Sheffield	.30
96	Moises Alou	.20
97	Tony Saunders	.20
98	Robb Nen	.10
99	Darryl Kile	.10
100	Craig Biggio	.20
101	Chris Holt	.10
102	Bob Abreu	.10
103	Luis Gonzalez	.10
104	Billy Wagner	.10
105	Brad Ausmus	.10
106	Chili Davis	.10
107	Tim Belcher	.10
108	Dean Palmer	.10
109	Jeff King	.10
110	Jose Rosado	.10
111	Mike Macfarlane	.10
112	Jay Bell	.10
113	Todd Worrell	.10
114	Chan Ho Park	.10
115	Raul Mondesi	.25
116	Brett Butler	.10
117	Greg Gagne	.10
118	Hideo Nomo	.50
119	Todd Zeile	.10
120	Eric Karros	.20
121	Cal Eldred	.10
122	Jeff D'Amico	.10
123	Antone Williamson	.10
124	Doug Jones	.10
125	Dave Nilsson	.10
126	Gerald Williams	.10
127	Fernando Vina	.10
128	Ron Coomer	.10
129	Matt Lawton	.10
130	Paul Molitor	.40
131	Todd Walker	.10
132	Rick Aguilera	.10
133	Brad Radke	.10
134	Bob Tewksbury	.10
135	Vladimir Guerrero	1.00
136	Tony Gwynn (Define The Game)	.75
137	Roger Clemens (Define The Game)	.50
138	Dennis Eckersley (Define The Game)	.10
139	Brady Anderson (Define The Game)	.10
140	Ken Griffey Jr. (Define The Game)	1.50
141	Derek Jeter (Define The Game)	1.00
142	Ken Camini (Define The Game)	.15
143	Frank Thomas (Define The Game)	1.25
144	Barry Bonds (Define The Game)	.40
145	Cal Ripken Jr. (Define The Game)	1.25
146	Alex Rodriguez (Define The Game)	1.25
147	Greg Maddux (Define The Game)	1.00
148	Kenny Lofton (Define The Game)	.40
149	Mike Piazza (Define The Game)	1.00
150	Mark McGwire (Define The Game)	1.50
151	Andruw Jones (Define The Game)	.75
152	Rusty Greer (Define The Game)	.10
153	F.P. Santangelo (Define The Game)	.10
154	Mike Lansing	.10
155	Lee Smith	.10
156	Carlos Perez	.10
157	Pedro J. Martinez	.20
158	Ryan McGuire	.10
159	F.P. Santangelo	.10
160	Rondell White	.20
161	Takashi Kashiwada	.50
162	Butch Huskey	.10
163	Edgardo Alfonzo	.10
164	John Franco	.10
165	Todd Hundley	.20
166	Rey Ordonez	.10
167	Armando Reynoso	.10
168	John Olerud	.10
169	Bernie Williams	.50
170	Andy Pettitte	.50
171	Wade Boggs	.25
172	Paul O'Neill	.20
173	Cecil Fielder	.20
174	Charlie Hayes	.10
175	David Cone	.20
176	Hideki Irabu	.75
177	Mark Bellhorn	.10
178	Steve Karsay	.10
179	Damon Mashore	.10
180	Jason McDonald	.10
181	Scott Spiezio	.10
182	Ariel Prieto	.10
183	Jason Giambi	.10
184	Wendell Magee	.10
185	Rico Brogna	.10
186	Garrett Stephenson	.10
187	Wayne Gomes	.10
188	Ricky Bottalico	.10
189	Mickey Morandini	.10
190	Mike Lieberthal	.10
191	*Kevin Polcovich*	.25
192	Francisco Cordova	.10
193	Kevin Young	.10
194	Jon Lieber	.10
195	Kevin Elster	.10
196	Tony Womack	.10
197	Lou Collier	.10
198	*Mike Defelice*	.20
199	Gary Gaetti	.10
200	Dennis Eckersley	.10
201	Alan Benes	.10
202	Willie McGee	.10
203	Ron Gant	.10
204	Fernando Valenzuela	.10
205	Mark McGwire	4.00
206	Archi Cianfrocco	.10
207	Andy Ashby	.10
208	Steve Finley	.10
209	Quilvio Veras	.10
210	Ken Caminiti	.25
211	Rickey Henderson	.10
212	Joey Hamilton	.10
213	Derrek Lee	.10
214	Bill Mueller	.10
215	Shawn Estes	.10
216	J.T. Snow	.10
217	Mark Gardner	.10
218	Terry Mulholland	.10
219	Dante Powell	.10
220	Jeff Kent	.10
221	Jamie Moyer	.10
222	Joey Cora	.10
223	Jeff Fassero	.10
224	Dennis Martinez	.10
225	Ken Griffey Jr.	3.00
226	Edgar Martinez	.10
227	Russ Davis	.10
228	Dan Wilson	.10
229	Will Clark	.20
230	Ivan Rodriguez	.60
231	Benji Gil	.10
232	Lee Stevens	.10
233	Mickey Tettleton	.10
234	Julio Santana	.10
235	Rusty Greer	.20
236	Bobby Witt	.10
237	Ed Sprague	.10
238	Pat Hentgen	.10
239	Kevin Escobar	.10
240	Joe Carter	.20
241	Carlos Delgado	.10
242	Shannon Stewart	.10
243	Benito Santiago	.10
244	Tino Martinez (Season Highlights)	.15
245	Ken Griffey Jr. (Season Highlights)	1.50
246	Kevin Brown (Season Highlights)	.10
247	Ryne Sandberg (Season Highlights)	.40
248	Mo Vaughn (Season Highlights)	.40
249	Darryl Hamilton (Season Highlights)	.10
250	Randy Johnson (Season Highlights)	.30
251	Steve Finley (Season Highlights)	.10
252	Bobby Higginson (Season Highlights)	.10
253	Brett Tomk (Star Rookie)	.10
254	Mark Kotsay (Star Rookie)	.50
255	Jose Guillen (Star Rookie)	.40
256	Elieser Marrero (Star Rookie)	.10
257	Dennis Reyes (Star Rookie)	.25
258	Richie Sexson (Star Rookie)	.10
259	Pat Cline (Star Rookie)	.10
260	Todd Helton (Star Rookie)	.75
261	Juan Melo (Star Rookie)	.10
262	Matt Morris (Star Rookie)	.10
263	Jeremi Gonzalez (Star Rookie)	.20
264	Jeff Abbot (Star Rookie)	.10
265	Aaron Boone (Star Rookie)	.10
266	Todd Dunwoody (Star Rookie)	.10
267	Jaret Wright (Star Rookie)	1.50
268	Derrick Gibson (Star Rookie)	.10
269	Mario Valdez (Star Rookie)	.10
270	Fernando Tatis (Star Rookie)	.25
271	Craig Counsell (Star Rookie)	.10
272	Brad Rigby (Star Rookie)	.10
273	Danny Clyburn (Star Rookie)	.10
274	Brian Rose (Star Rookie)	.25
275	Miguel Tejada (Star Rookie)	.60
276	Jason Varitek (Star Rookie)	.20
277	*David Dellucci* (Star Rookie)	.50
278	Michael Coleman (Star Rookie)	.10
279	Adam Riggs (Star Rookie)	.10
280	Ben Grieve (Star Rookie)	1.25
281	Brad Fullmer (Star Rookie)	.10
282	Ken Cloude (Star Rookie)	.25
283	Tom Evans (Star Rookie)	.10
284	*Kevin Millwood* (Star Rookie)	1.00
285	Paul Konerko (Star Rookie)	.75

286	Juan Encarnacion (Star Rookie)	.10
287	Chris Carpenter (Star Rookie)	.10
288	Tom Fordham (Star Rookie)	.10
289	Gary DiSarcina	.10
290	Tim Salmon	.30
291	Troy Percival	.10
292	Todd Greene	.10
293	Ken Hill	.10
294	Dennis Springer	.10
295	Jim Edmonds	.20
296	Allen Watson	.10
297	Brian Anderson	.10
298	Keith Lockhart	.10
299	Tom Glavine	.20
300	Chipper Jones	2.00
301	Randall Simon	.20
302	Mark Lemke	.10
303	Ryan Klesko	.30
304	Denny Neagle	.10
305	Andruw Jones	1.25
306	Mike Mussina	.60
307	Brady Anderson	.20
308	Chris Hoiles	.10
309	Mike Bordick	.10
310	Cal Ripken Jr.	2.50
311	Geronimo Berroa	.10
312	Armando Benitez	.10
313	Roberto Alomar	.60
314	Tim Wakefield	.10
315	Reggie Jefferson	.10
316	Jeff Frye	.10
317	Scott Hatteberg	.10
318	Steve Avery	.10
319	Robinson Checo	.10
320	Nomar Garciaparra	2.00
321	Lance Johnson	.10
322	Tyler Houston	.10
323	Mark Clark	.10
324	Terry Adams	.10
325	Sammy Sosa	2.00
326	Scott Servais	.10
327	Manny Alexander	.10
328	Norberto Martin	.10
329	*Scott Eyre*	.25
330	Frank Thomas	2.50
331	Robin Ventura	.10
332	Matt Karchner	.10
333	Keith Foulke	.10
334	James Baldwin	.10
335	Chris Stynes	.10
336	Bret Boone	.10
337	Jon Nunnally	.10
338	Dave Burba	.10
339	Eduardo Perez	.10
340	Reggie Sanders	.10
341	Mike Remlinger	.10
342	Pat Watkins	.10
343	Chad Ogea	.10
344	John Smiley	.10
345	Kenny Lofton	.75
346	Jose Mesa	.10
347	Charles Nagy	.10
348	Bruce Aven	.10
349	Enrique Wilson	.10
350	Manny Ramirez	.60
351	Jerry DiPoto	.10
352	Ellis Burks	.10
353	Kirt Manwaring	.10
354	Vinny Castilla	.20
355	Larry Walker	.30
356	Kevin Ritz	.10
357	Pedro Astacio	.10
358	Scott Sanders	.10
359	Deivi Cruz	.10
360	Brian L. Hunter	.10
361	Pedro J. Martinez (History in the Making)	.20
362	Tom Glavine (History in the Making)	.10
363	Willie McGee (History in the Making)	.10
364	J.T. Snow (History in the Making)	.10
365	Rusty Greer (History in the Making)	.10
366	Mike Grace (History in the Making)	.10
367	Tony Clark (History in the Making)	.25
368	Ben Grieve (History in the Making)	.75
369	Gary Sheffield (History in the Making)	.20
370	Joe Oliver	.10
371	Todd Jones	.10
372	*Frank Catalanotto*	.20
373	Brian Moehler	.10
374	Cliff Floyd	.10
375	Bobby Bonilla	.15
376	Al Leiter	.10
377	Josh Booty	.10
378	Darren Daulton	.10
379	Jay Powell	.10
380	Felix Heredia	.10
381	Jim Eisenreich	.10
382	Richard Hidalgo	.10
383	Mike Hampton	.10
384	Shane Reynolds	.10
385	Jeff Bagwell	1.25
386	Derek Bell	.10
387	Ricky Gutierrez	.10
388	Bill Spiers	.10
389	Jose Offerman	.10
390	Johnny Damon	.10
391	Jermaine Dye	.10
392	Jeff Montgomery	.10
393	Glendon Rusch	.10
394	Mike Sweeney	.10
395	Kevin Appier	.10
396	Joe Vitiello	.10
397	Ramon Martinez	.20
398	Darren Dreifort	.10
399	Wilton Guerrero	.10
400	Mike Piazza	2.00
401	Eddie Murray	.25
402	Ismael Valdes	.10
403	Todd Hollandsworth	.10
404	Mark Loretta	.10
405	Jeromy Burnitz	.10
406	Jeff Cirillo	.10
407	Scott Karl	.10
408	Mike Matheny	.10
409	Jose Valentin	.10
410	John Jaha	.10
411	Terry Steinbach	.10
412	Torii Hunter	.10
413	Pat Meares	.10
414	Marty Cordova	.10
415	Jaret Wright (Postseason Headliners)	1.00
416	Mike Mussina (Postseason Headliners)	.30
417	John Smoltz (Postseason Headliners)	.10
418	Devon White (Postseason Headliners)	.10
419	Denny Neagle (Postseason Headliners)	.10
420	Livan Hernandez (Postseason Headliners)	.20
421	Kevin Brown (Postseason Headliners)	.10
422	Marquis Grissom (Postseason Headliners)	.10
423	Mike Mussina (Postseason Headliners)	.30
424	Eric Davis (Postseason Headliners)	.10
425	Tony Fernandez (Postseason Headliners)	.10
426	Moises Alou (Postseason Headliners)	.10
427	Sandy Alomar Jr. (Postseason Headliners)	.10
428	Gary Sheffield (Postseason Headliners)	.20
429	Jaret Wright (Postseason Headliners)	1.00
430	Livan Hernandez (Postseason Headliners)	.20
431	Chad Ogea (Postseason Headliners)	.10
432	Edgar Renteria (Postseason Headliners)	.10
433	LaTroy Hawkins	.10
434	Rich Robertson	.10
435	Chuck Knoblauch	.25
436	Jose Vidro	.10
437	Dustin Hermanson	.10
438	Jim Bullinger	.10
439	Orlando Cabrera (Star Rookie)	.10
440	Vladimir Guerrero	.75
441	Ugueth Urbina	.10
442	Brian McRae	.10
443	Matt Franco	.10
444	Bobby Jones	.10
445	Bernard Gilkey	.10
446	Dave Mlicki	.10
447	Brian Bohanon	.10
448	Mel Rojas	.10
449	Tim Raines	.10
450	Derek Jeter	2.00
451	Roger Clemens (Upper Echelon)	.60
452	Nomar Garciaparra (Upper Echelon)	1.00
453	Mike Piazza (Upper Echelon)	1.00
454	Mark McGwire (Upper Echelon)	1.50
455	Ken Griffey Jr. (Upper Echelon)	1.50
456	Larry Walker (Upper Echelon)	.20
457	Alex Rodriguez (Upper Echelon)	1.00
458	Tony Gwynn (Upper Echelon)	.60
459	Frank Thomas (Upper Echelon)	1.25
460	Tino Martinez	.25
461	Chad Curtis	.10
462	Ramiro Mendoza	.10
463	Joe Girardi	.10
464	David Wells	.10
465	Mariano Rivera	.20
466	Willie Adams	.10
467	George Williams	.10
468	Dave Telgheder	.10
469	Dave Magadan	.10
470	Matt Stairs	.10
471	Billy Taylor	.10
472	Jimmy Haynes	.10
473	Gregg Jefferies	.10
474	Midre Cummings	.10
475	Curt Schilling	.20
476	Mike Grace	.10
477	Mark Leiter	.10
478	Matt Beech	.10
479	Scott Rolen	1.25
480	Jason Kendall	.10
481	Esteban Loaiza	.10
482	Jermaine Allensworth	.10
483	Mark Smith	.10
484	Jason Schmidt	.10
485	Jose Guillen	.25
486	Al Martin	.10
487	Delino DeShields	.10
488	Todd Stottlemyre	.10
489	Brian Jordan	.10
490	Ray Lankford	.10
491	Matt Morris	.10
492	Royce Clayton	.10
493	John Mabry	.10
494	Wally Joyner	.10
495	Trevor Hoffman	.10
496	Chris Gomez	.10
497	Sterling Hitchcock	.10
498	Pete Smith	.10
499	Greg Vaughn	.10
500	Tony Gwynn	1.50
501	Will Cunnane	.10
502	Darryl Hamilton	.10
503	Brian Johnson	.10
504	Kirk Rueter	.10
505	Barry Bonds	.75
506	Osvaldo Fernandez	.10
507	Stan Javier	.10
508	Julian Tavarez	.10
509	Rich Aurilia	.10
510	Alex Rodriguez	2.00
511	David Segui	.10
512	Rich Amaral	.10
513	Raul Ibanez	.10
514	Jay Buhner	.20
515	Randy Johnson	.50
516	Heathcliff Slocumb	.10
517	Tony Saunders	.10
518	Kevin Elster	.10
519	John Burkett	.10
520	Juan Gonzalez	1.50
521	John Wetteland	.10
522	Domingo Cedeno	.10
523	Darren Oliver	.10
524	Roger Pavlik	.10
525	Jose Cruz Jr.	1.00
526	Woody Williams	.10
527	Alex Gonzalez	.10
528	Robert Person	.10
529	Juan Guzman	.10
530	Roger Clemens	1.00
531	Shawn Green	.10
532	Cordova, Ricon, Smith (Season Highlights)	.10
533	Nomar Garciaparra (Season Highlights)	1.00
534	Roger Clemens (Season Highlights)	.60
535	Mark McGwire (Season Highlights)	1.50
536	Larry Walker (Season Highlights)	.20
537	Mike Piazza (Season Highlights)	1.00
538	Curt Schilling (Season Highlights)	.10
539	Tony Gwynn (Season Highlights)	.75
540	Ken Griffey Jr. (Season Highlights)	1.50
541	Carl Pavano (Star Rookies)	.10
542	Shane Monahan (Star Rookies)	.10
543	*Gabe Kapler* (Star Rookies)	2.00
544	Eric Milton (Star Rookies)	.25
545	*Gary Matthews Jr.* (Star Rookies)	.50
546	*Mike Kinkade* (Star Rookies)	.50
547	*Ryan Christenson* (Star Rookies)	.25
548	*Corey Koskie* (Star Rookies)	.50
549	Norm Hutchins (Star Rookies)	.10
550	Russell Branyan (Star Rookies)	.10
551	*Masato Yoshii* (Star Rookies)	.50
552	*Jesus Sanchez* (Star Rookies)	.25
553	Anthony Sanders (Star Rookies)	.20
554	Edwin Diaz (Star Rookies)	.10
555	Gabe Alvarez (Star Rookies)	.10
556	*Carlos Lee* (Star Rookies)	.75
557	Mike Darr (Star Rookies)	.10
558	Kerry Wood (Star Rookies)	5.00
559	Carlos Guillen (Star Rookies)	.10
560	Sean Casey (Star Rookies)	.30
561	*Manny Aybar* (Star Rookies)	.25
562	Octavio Dotel (Star Rookies)	.10
563	Jarrod Washburn (Star Rookies)	.10
564	Mark L. Johnson (Star Rookies)	.10
565	Ramon Hernandez (Star Rookies)	.10
566	*Rich Butler* (Star Rookies)	.50
567	Mike Caruso (Star Rookies)	.25
568	Cliff Politte (Star Rookies)	.10
569	Scott Elarton (Star Rookies)	.10
570	*Magglio Ordonez* (Star Rookies)	.75
571	*Adam Butler* (Star Rookies)	.25
572	Marlon Anderson (Star Rookies)	.10
573	*Julio Ramirez* (Star Rookies)	.50
574	*Darron Ingram* (Star Rookies)	.20
575	Bruce Chen (Star Rookies)	.10
576	*Steve Woodard* (Star Rookies)	.25
577	Hiram Bocachica (Star Rookies)	.10
578	Kevin Witt (Star Rookies)	.10
579	Javier Vazquez (Star Rookies)	.10
580	Alex Gonzalez (Star Rookies)	.10
581	Brian Powell (Star Rookies)	.10
582	Wes Helms (Star Rookies)	.10
583	Ron Wright (Star Rookies)	.10
584	Rafael Medina (Star Rookies)	.10
585	Daryle Ward (Star Rookies)	.15
586	Geoff Jenkins (Star Rookies)	.10
587	Preston Wilson (Star Rookies)	.10
588	*Jim Chamblee* (Star Rookies)	.25
589	*Mike Lowell* (Star Rookies)	.40
590	A.J. Hinch (Star Rookies)	.50
591	*Francisco Cordero* (Star Rookies)	.25
592	*Rolando Arrojo* (Star Rookies)	.50
593	Braden Looper (Star Rookies)	.10
594	Sidney Ponson (Star Rookies)	.10
595	Matt Clement (Star Rookies)	.10
596	Carlton Loewer (Star Rookies)	.10
597	Brian Meadows (Star Rookies)	.10
598	Danny Klassen (Star Rookies)	.20
599	Larry Sutton (Star Rookies)	.10
600	Travis Lee (Star Rookies)	2.50
601	Randy Johnson (Eminent Prestige)	2.00
602	Greg Maddux (Eminent Prestige)	6.00
603	Roger Clemens (Eminent Prestige)	3.00
604	Jaret Wright (Eminent Prestige)	2.50
605	Mike Piazza (Eminent Prestige)	6.00
606	Tino Martinez (Eminent Prestige)	1.00
607	Frank Thomas (Eminent Prestige)	8.00
608	Mo Vaughn (Eminent Prestige)	2.50
609	Todd Helton (Eminent Prestige)	2.50
610	Mark McGwire (Eminent Prestige)	12.00
611	Jeff Bagwell (Eminent Prestige)	3.00
612	Travis Lee (Eminent Prestige)	5.00
613	Scott Rolen (Eminent Prestige)	3.00
614	Cal Ripken Jr. (Eminent Prestige)	8.00
615	Chipper Jones (Eminent Prestige)	6.00
616	Nomar Garciaparra (Eminent Prestige)	6.00
617	Alex Rodriguez (Eminent Prestige)	6.00
618	Derek Jeter (Eminent Prestige)	5.00
619	Tony Gwynn (Eminent Prestige)	5.00
620	Ken Griffey Jr. (Eminent Prestige)	10.00
621	Kenny Lofton (Eminent Prestige)	2.50
622	Juan Gonzalez (Eminent Prestige)	5.00
623	Jose Cruz Jr. (Eminent Prestige)	2.00
624	Larry Walker (Eminent Prestige)	1.00
625	Barry Bonds (Eminent Prestige)	2.50
626	Ben Grieve (Eminent Prestige)	3.00
627	Andruw Jones (Eminent Prestige)	2.50
628	Vladimir Guerrero (Eminent Prestige)	2.50
629	Paul Konerko (Eminent Prestige)	1.00
630	Paul Molitor (Eminent Prestige)	2.00
631	Cecil Fielder	.20
632	Jack McDowell	.10
633	Mike James	.10
634	Brian Anderson	.10
635	Jay Bell	.10
636	Devon White	.10
637	Andy Stankiewicz	.10
638	Tony Batista	.10
639	Omar Daal	.10
640	Matt Williams	.25
641	Brent Brede	.10
642	Jorge Fabregas	.10
643	Karim Garcia	.10
644	Felix Rodriguez	.10
645	Andy Benes	.10
646	Willie Blair	.10
647	Jeff Suppan	.10
648	Yamil Benitez	.10
649	Walt Weiss	.10
650	Andres Galarraga	.25
651	Doug Drabek	.10
652	Ozzie Guillen	.10
653	Joe Carter	.10
654	Dennis Eckersley	.10
655	Pedro J. Martinez	.30
656	Jim Leyritz	.10
657	Henry Rodriguez	.10
658	Rod Beck	.10
659	Mickey Morandini	.10
660	Jeff Blauser	.10
661	Ruben Sierra	.10
662	Mike Sirotka	.10
663	Pete Harnisch	.10
664	Damian Jackson	.10
665	Dmitri Young	.10
666	Steve Cooke	.10
667	Geronimo Berroa	.10
668	Shawon Dunston	.10
669	Mike Jackson	.10
670	Travis Fryman	.10
671	Dwight Gooden	.10
672	Paul Assenmacher	.10
673	Eric Plunk	.10
674	Mike Lansing	.10
675	Darryl Kile	.10
676	Luis Gonzalez	.10
677	Frank Castillo	.10
678	Joe Randa	.10
679	Bip Roberts	.10
680	Derrek Lee	.10
681	Mike Piazza	2.00
682	Sean Berry	.10
683	Ramon Garcia	.10
684	Carl Everett	.10
685	Moises Alou	.10
686	Hal Morris	.10
687	Jeff Conine	.10
688	Gary Sheffield LA	.35
689	Jose Vizcaino	.10
690	Charles Johnson	.10
691	Bobby Bonilla LA	.20
692	Marquis Grissom	.10
693	Alex Ochoa	.10
694	Mike Morgan	.10
695	Orlando Merced	.10
696	David Ortiz	.30
697	Brent Gates	.10
698	Otis Nixon	.10
699	Trey Moore	.10
700	Derrick May	.10
701	Rich Becker	.10
702	Al Leiter	.20
703	Chili Davis	.10
704	Scott Brosius	.10
705	Chuck Knoblauch	.30
706	Kenny Rogers	.10
707	Mike Blowers	.10
708	Mike Fetters	.10
709	Tom Candiotti	.10
710	Rickey Henderson	.10
711	Bob Abreu	.10
712	Mark Lewis	.10
713	Doug Glanville	.10
714	Desi Relaford	.10

715	Kent Mercker	.10
716	J. Kevin Brown	.20
717	James Mouton	.10
718	Mark Langston	.10
719	Greg Myers	.10
720	Orel Hershiser	.10
721	Charlie Hayes	.10
722	Robb Nen	.10
723	Glenallen Hill	.10
724	Tony Saunders	.10
725	Wade Boggs	.25
726	Kevin Stocker	.10
727	Wilson Alvarez	.10
728	Albie Lopez	.10
729	Dave Martinez	.10
730	Fred McGriff	.20
731	Quinton McCracken	.10
732	Bryan Rekar	.10
733	Paul Sorrento	.10
734	Roberto Hernandez	.10
735	Bubba Trammell	.10
736	Miguel Cairo	.10
737	John Flaherty	.10
738	Terrell Wade	.10
739	Roberto Kelly	.10
740	Mark Mclemore (McLemore)	.10
741	Danny Patterson	.10
742	Aaron Sele	.10
743	Tony Fernandez	.10
744	Randy Myers	.10
745	Jose Canseco	.30
746	Darrin Fletcher	.10
747	Mike Stanley	.10
748	Marquis Grissom (Season Highlights)	.10
749	Fred McGriff (Season Highlights)	.20
750	Travis Lee (Season Highlights)	1.00

1998 Upper Deck A Piece of the Action

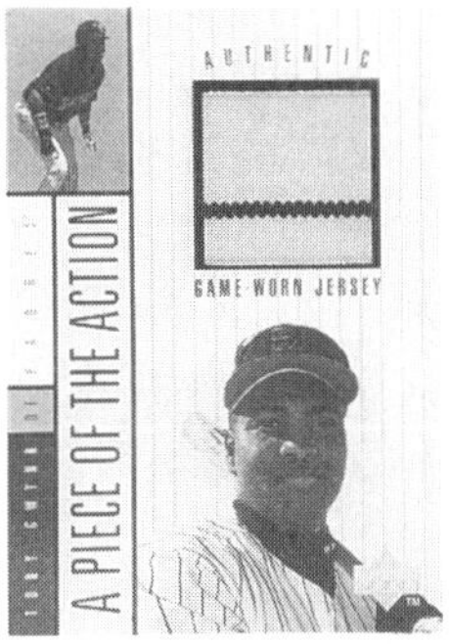

A Piece of the Action was inserted in both Series One and Series Two packs. Series One featured 10 cards: five with a piece of game-used jersey and five with a piece of game-used bat. Series Two offered a piece of game-used bat and jersey on four cards. The cards were inserted one per 2,500 packs in both series.

		MT
Complete Set (14):		2100.
Complete Series 1 Set (10):		1700.
Complete Series 2 Set (4):		450.00
Common Player:		75.00
Inserted 1:2,500		
(1)	Tony Gwynn (Jersey)	300.00
(2)	Tony Gwynn (Bat)	225.00
(3)	Alex Rodriguez (Jersey)	400.00
(4)	Alex Rodriguez (Bat)	300.00
(5)	Gary Sheffield (Jersey)	100.00
(6)	Gary Sheffield (Bat)	75.00
(7)	Todd Hollandsworth (Jersey)	100.00
(8)	Todd Hollandsworth (Bat)	75.00
(9)	Greg Maddux (Jersey)	400.00
(10)	Jay Buhner (Bat)	90.00
(11)	Roberto Alomar	200.00
(12)	Jay Buhner	125.00
(13)	Andruw Jones	250.00
(14)	Gary Sheffield	125.00

1998 Upper Deck Amazing Greats

The 30-card Amazing Greats insert is printed on acetate. The cards are numbered to 2,000. A die-cut parallel was sequentially numbered to 250. Amazing Greats was an insert in Upper Deck Series One packs.

		MT
Complete Set (30):		550.00
Common Player:		6.00
Die-Cuts (250):		3x to 4x
AG1	Ken Griffey Jr.	60.00
AG2	Derek Jeter	30.00
AG3	Alex Rodriguez	40.00
AG4	Paul Molitor	12.00
AG5	Jeff Bagwell	20.00
AG6	Larry Walker	8.00
AG7	Kenny Lofton	12.00
AG8	Cal Ripken Jr.	40.00
AG9	Juan Gonzalez	25.00
AG10	Chipper Jones	30.00
AG11	Greg Maddux	30.00
AG12	Roberto Alomar	10.00
AG13	Mike Piazza	30.00
AG14	Andres Galarraga	8.00
AG15	Barry Bonds	12.00
AG16	Andy Pettitte	10.00
AG17	Nomar Garciaparra	30.00
AG18	Hideki Irabu	8.00
AG19	Tony Gwynn	25.00
AG20	Frank Thomas	50.00
AG21	Roger Clemens	20.00
AG22	Sammy Sosa	30.00
AG23	Jose Cruz, Jr.	25.00
AG24	Manny Ramirez	10.00
AG25	Mark McGwire	70.00
AG26	Randy Johnson	10.00
AG27	Mo Vaughn	12.00
AG28	Gary Sheffield	8.00
AG29	Andruw Jones	20.00
AG30	Albert Belle	12.00

1998 Upper Deck Blue Chip Prospects

Inserted in Series Two packs, Blue Chip Prospects is printed on die-cut acetate. The cards are sequentially numbered to 2,000.

		MT
Complete Set (30):		600.00
Common Player:		8.00
BC1	Nomar Garciaparra	60.00
BC2	Scott Rolen	40.00
BC3	Jason Dickson	8.00
BC4	Darin Erstad	20.00
BC5	Brad Fullmer	12.00
BC6	Jaret Wright	40.00
BC7	Justin Thompson	8.00
BC8	Matt Morris	8.00
BC9	Fernando Tatis	8.00
BC10	Alex Rodriguez	60.00
BC11	Todd Helton	25.00
BC12	Andy Pettitte	15.00
BC13	Jose Cruz Jr.	50.00
BC14	Mark Kotsay	15.00
BC15	Derek Jeter	50.00
BC16	Paul Konerko	20.00
BC17	Todd Dunwoody	8.00
BC18	Vladimir Guerrero	20.00
BC19	Miguel Tejada	20.00
BC20	Chipper Jones	60.00
BC21	Kevin Orie	8.00
BC22	Juan Encarnacion	8.00
BC23	Brian Rose	20.00
BC24	Andruw Jones	25.00
BC25	Livan Hernandez	15.00
BC26	Brian Giles	8.00
BC27	Brett Tomko	8.00
BC28	Jose Guillen	12.00
BC29	Aaron Boone	8.00
BC30	Ben Grieve	35.00

1998 Upper Deck Clearly Dominant

Clearly Dominant was an insert in Series Two. Printed on Light F/X plastic stock, the 30-card set is sequentially numbered to 250.

		MT
Common Player:		25.00
Production 250 sets		
CD1	Mark McGwire	250.00
CD2	Derek Jeter	150.00
CD3	Alex Rodriguez	150.00
CD4	Paul Molitor	40.00
CD5	Jeff Bagwell	100.00
CD6	Ivan Rodriguez	60.00
CD7	Kenny Lofton	60.00
CD8	Cal Ripken Jr.	200.00
CD9	Albert Belle	60.00
CD10	Chipper Jones	150.00
CD11	Gary Sheffield	40.00
CD12	Roberto Alomar	50.00
CD13	Mo Vaughn	60.00
CD14	Andres Galarraga	30.00
CD15	Nomar Garciaparra	150.00
CD16	Randy Johnson	40.00
CD17	Mike Mussina	50.00
CD18	Greg Maddux	150.00
CD19	Tony Gwynn	120.00
CD20	Frank Thomas	200.00
CD21	Roger Clemens	80.00
CD22	Dennis Eckersley	25.00
CD23	Juan Gonzalez	120.00
CD24	Tino Martinez	40.00
CD25	Andruw Jones	80.00
CD26	Larry Walker	40.00
CD27	Ken Caminiti	30.00
CD28	Mike Piazza	150.00
CD29	Barry Bonds	60.00
CD30	Ken Griffey Jr.	240.00

1998 Upper Deck Ken Griffey's HR Chronicles

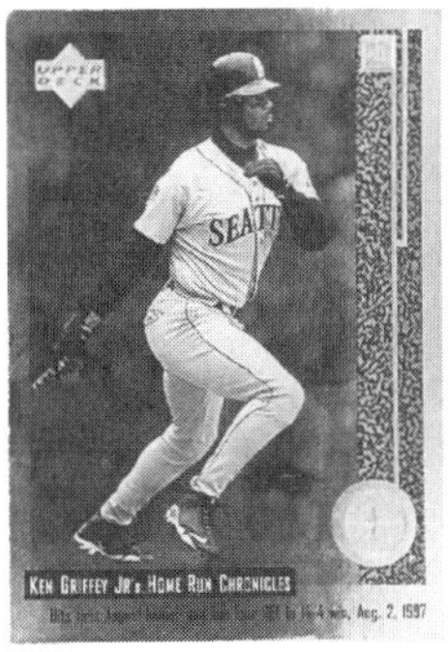

Griffey's Home Run Chronicles was inserted in both Series One and Two packs. Series One had 30 cards, each spotlighting one of Ken Griffey Jr.'s first 30 home runs of the 1997 season. Series Two had 26 cards highlighting the rest of his 1997 home run output. In both series, the cards were inserted one per nine packs.

		MT
Complete Set (56):		190.00
Common Griffey Jr.:		4.00
Inserted 1:9		
KG1	Ken Griffey Jr.	5.00
KG2	Ken Griffey Jr.	5.00
KG3	Ken Griffey Jr.	5.00
KG4	Ken Griffey Jr.	5.00
KG5	Ken Griffey Jr.	5.00
KG6	Ken Griffey Jr.	5.00
KG7	Ken Griffey Jr.	5.00
KG8	Ken Griffey Jr.	5.00
KG9	Ken Griffey Jr.	5.00
KG10	Ken Griffey Jr.	5.00
KG11	Ken Griffey Jr.	5.00
KG12	Ken Griffey Jr.	5.00
KG13	Ken Griffey Jr.	5.00
KG14	Ken Griffey Jr.	5.00
KG15	Ken Griffey Jr.	5.00
KG16	Ken Griffey Jr.	5.00
KG17	Ken Griffey Jr.	5.00
KG18	Ken Griffey Jr.	5.00
KG19	Ken Griffey Jr.	5.00
KG20	Ken Griffey Jr.	5.00
KG21	Ken Griffey Jr.	5.00
KG22	Ken Griffey Jr.	5.00
KG23	Ken Griffey Jr.	5.00
KG24	Ken Griffey Jr.	5.00
KG25	Ken Griffey Jr.	5.00
KG26	Ken Griffey Jr.	5.00
KG27	Ken Griffey Jr.	5.00
KG28	Ken Griffey Jr.	5.00
KG29	Ken Griffey Jr.	5.00
KG30	Ken Griffey Jr.	5.00

1998 Upper Deck National Pride

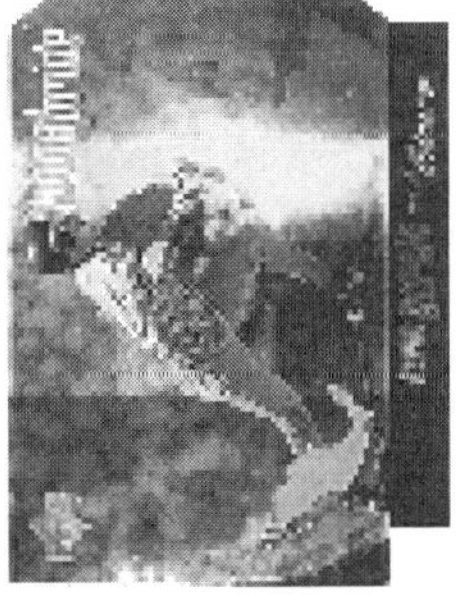

National Pride is a 42-card insert printed on die-cut rainbow foil. The set honors the nationality of the player with their country's flag in the background. The cards were inserted one per 24 packs.

		MT
Complete Set (42):		350.00
Common Player:		3.00
NP1	Dave Nilsson	3.00
NP2	Larry Walker	5.00
NP3	Edgar Renteria	3.00
NP4	Jose Canseco	4.00
NP5	Rey Ordonez	3.00
NP6	Rafael Palmeiro	4.00
NP7	Livan Hernandez	3.00
NP8	Andruw Jones	20.00
NP9	Manny Ramirez	12.00
NP10	Sammy Sosa	25.00
NP11	Raul Mondesi	5.00
NP12	Moises Alou	3.00
NP13	Pedro J. Martinez	3.00
NP14	Vladimir Guerrero	15.00
NP15	Chili Davis	3.00
NP16	Hideo Nomo	10.00
NP17	Hideki Irabu	8.00
NP18	Shigetosi Hasegawa	3.00
NP19	Takashi Kashiwada	3.00
NP20	Chan Ho Park	3.00
NP21	Fernando Valenzuela	3.00
NP22	Vinny Castilla	3.00
NP23	Armando Reynoso	3.00
NP24	Karim Garcia	4.00
NP25	Marvin Benard	3.00
NP26	Mariano Rivera	3.00
NP27	Juan Gonzalez	25.00
NP28	Roberto Alomar	10.00
NP29	Ivan Rodriguez	10.00
NP30	Carlos Delgado	3.00
NP31	Bernie Williams	10.00
NP32	Edgar Martinez	3.00
NP33	Frank Thomas	50.00
NP34	Barry Bonds	12.00
NP35	Mike Piazza	30.00
NP36	Chipper Jones	30.00
NP37	Cal Ripken Jr.	40.00
NP38	Alex Rodriguez	40.00
NP39	Ken Griffey Jr.	60.00
NP40	Andres Galarraga	4.00
NP41	Omar Vizquel	3.00
NP42	Ozzie Guillen	3.00

1998 Upper Deck Prime Nine

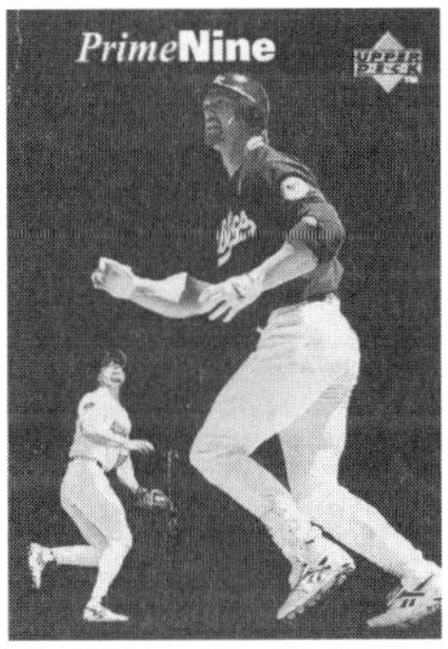

Nine of the most popular players are featured in this insert set. The cards are printed on silver foil stock and inserted 1:5.

	MT
Complete Set (60):	175.00
Common Griffey (PN1-PN7):	6.00
Common Piazza (PN8-PN14):	4.00
Common Thomas (PN15-PN21):	6.00
Common McGwire (PN22-PN28):	8.00
Common Ripken (PN29-PN35)	5.00
Common Gonzalez (PN36-PN42):	3.00
Common Gwynn (PN43-PN49):	3.00
Common Bonds (PN50-PN55):	1.50
Common Maddux (PN56-PN60):	4.00
Inserted 1:5	

1998 Upper Deck Rookie Edition Preview

This 10-card set contained topy young players in the game. It was issued in Upper Deck Series II packs to preview the upcoming Rookie Edition product.

		MT
Complete Set (10):		25.00
Common Player:		1.00
1	Nomar Garciaparra	6.00
2	Scott Rolen	5.00
3	Mark Kotsay	2.00
4	Todd Helton	3.00
5	Paul Konerko	4.00
6	Juan Encarnacion	1.00
7	Brad Fullmer	1.50
8	Miguel Tejada	2.00
9	Richard Hidalgo	1.00
10	Ben Grieve	5.00

1998 Upper Deck Tape Measure Titans

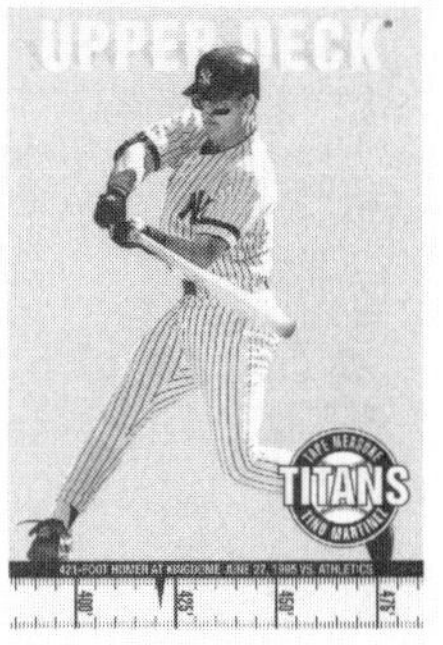

Tape Measure Titans is a 30-card insert seeded 1:23. The set honors the game's top home run hitters.

		MT
Complete Set (30):		240.00
Common Player:		2.50
Inserted 1:23		
1	Mark McGwire	35.00
2	Andres Galarraga	4.00
3	Jeff Bagwell	12.00
4	Larry Walker	5.00
5	Frank Thomas	25.00
6	Rafael Palmeiro	4.00
7	Nomar Garciaparra	20.00
8	Mo Vaughn	8.00
9	Albert Belle	8.00
10	Ken Griffey Jr.	30.00
11	Manny Ramirez	6.00
12	Jim Thome	5.00
13	Tony Clark	5.00
14	Juan Gonzalez	15.00
15	Mike Piazza	20.00
16	Jose Canseco	2.50
17	Jay Buhner	3.00
18	Alex Rodriguez	20.00
19	Jose Cruz Jr.	8.00
20	Tino Martinez	4.00
21	Carlos Delgado	2.50
22	Andruw Jones	8.00
23	Chipper Jones	20.00
24	Fred McGriff	4.00
25	Matt Williams	4.00
26	Sammy Sosa	15.00
27	Vinny Castilla	2.50
28	Tim Salmon	5.00
29	Ken Caminiti	4.00
30	Barry Bonds	8.00

1998 Upper Deck 10th Anniversary Preview

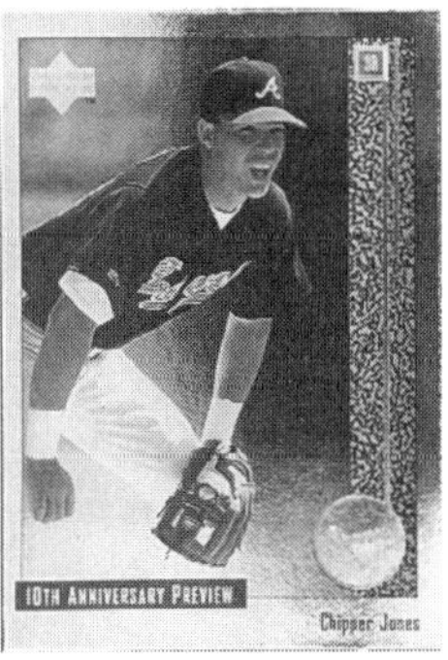

10th Anniversary Preview is a 60-card set. The foil cards have the same design as the 1989 Upper Deck base cards. The set was inserted one per five packs.

		MT
Complete Set (60):		120.00
Common Player:		.75
1	Greg Maddux	8.00
2	Mike Mussina	2.50
3	Roger Clemens	4.00
4	Hideo Nomo	2.50
4	David Cone	.75
6	Tom Glavine	.75
7	Andy Pettitte	2.50
8	Jimmy Key	.75
9	Randy Johnson	2.50
10	Dennis Eckersley	.75
11	Lee Smith	.75
12	John Franco	.75
13	Randy Myers	.75
14	Mike Piazza	8.00
15	Ivan Rodriguez	3.00
16	Todd Hundley	1.00
17	Sandy Alomar Jr.	.75
18	Frank Thomas	10.00
19	Rafael Palmeiro	1.00
20	Mark McGwire	15.00
21	Mo Vaughn	3.00
22	Fred McGriff	1.25
23	Andres Galarraga	1.25
24	Mark Grace	1.25
25	Jeff Bagwell	5.00
26	Roberto Alomar	2.50
27	Chuck Knoblauch	1.50
28	Ryne Sandberg	3.00
29	Eric Young	.75
30	Craig Biggio	1.00
31	Carlos Baerga	.75
32	Robin Ventura	.75
33	Matt Williams	1.25
34	Wade Boggs	1.00
35	Dean Palmer	.75
36	Chipper Jones	8.00
37	Vinny Castilla	.75
38	Ken Caminiti	1.25
39	Omar Vizquel	.75
40	Cal Ripken Jr.	10.00
41	Derek Jeter	8.00
42	Alex Rodriguez	10.00
43	Barry Larkin	1.25
44	Mark Grudzielanek	.75
45	Albert Belle	3.00
46	Manny Ramirez	3.00
47	Jose Canseco	1.25
48	Ken Griffey Jr.	12.00
49	Juan Gonzalez	6.00
50	Kenny Lofton	3.00
51	Sammy Sosa	5.00
52	Larry Walker	1.50
53	Gary Sheffield	1.50
54	Rickey Henderson	.75
55	Tony Gwynn	6.00
56	Barry Bonds	3.00
57	Paul Molitor	2.50
58	Edgar Martinez	.75
59	Chili Davis	.75
60	Eddie Murray	1.25

1998 Upper Deck Rookie Edition A Piece of the Action

A Piece of the Action consists of five Game Jersey cards. Three rookie Game Jersey cards were sequentially numbered to 200, while a Ken Griffey Jr. Game Jersey card was numbered to 300. Griffey also signed and hand-numbered 24 Game Jersey cards.

		MT
Common Card:		200.00
KG	Ken Griffey Jr. (300)	750.00
KGS	Ken Griffey Jr. (24) (Signed)	3000.
BG	Ben Grieve (200)	300.00
JC	Jose Cruz Jr. (200)	200.00
TL	Travis Lee (200)	400.00

1998 Upper Deck Rookie Edition All-Star Credentials

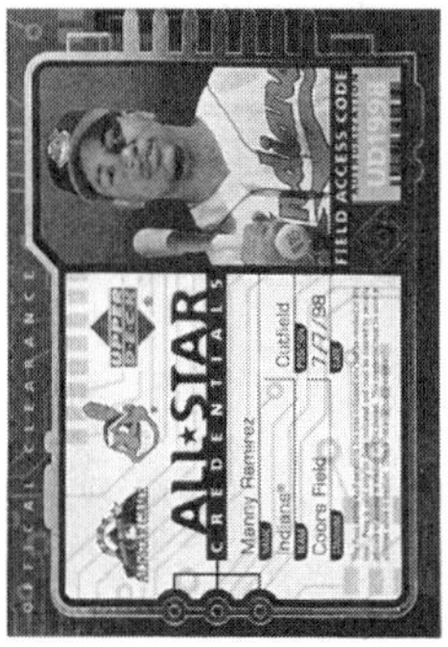

All-Star Credentials is a 30-card insert seeded 1:9. It features the game's top players.

		MT
Complete Set (30):		100.00
Common Player:		.75
Inserted 1:9		
AS1	Ken Griffey Jr.	12.00
AS2	Travis Lee	8.00
AS3	Ben Grieve	4.00
AS4	Jose Cruz Jr.	2.50
AS5	Andruw Jones	3.00
AS6	Craig Biggio	.75
AS7	Hideo Nomo	2.00
AS8	Cal Ripken Jr.	10.00
AS9	Jaret Wright	3.00
AS10	Mark McGwire	10.00
AS11	Derek Jeter	6.00
AS12	Scott Rolen	5.00
AS13	Jeff Bagwell	4.00
AS14	Manny Ramirez	3.00
AS15	Alex Rodriguez	8.00
AS16	Chipper Jones	8.00
AS17	Larry Walker	1.00
AS18	Barry Bonds	3.00
AS19	Tony Gwynn	6.00
AS20	Mike Piazza	8.00
AS21	Roger Clemens	4.00
AS22	Greg Maddux	8.00
AS23	Jim Thome	2.00
AS24	Tino Martinez	1.00
AS25	Nomar Garciaparra	8.00
AS26	Juan Gonzalez	6.00
AS27	Kenny Lofton	3.00
AS28	Randy Johnson	1.50
AS29	Todd Helton	3.00
AS30	Frank Thomas	10.00

1998 Upper Deck Rookie Edition Destination Stardom

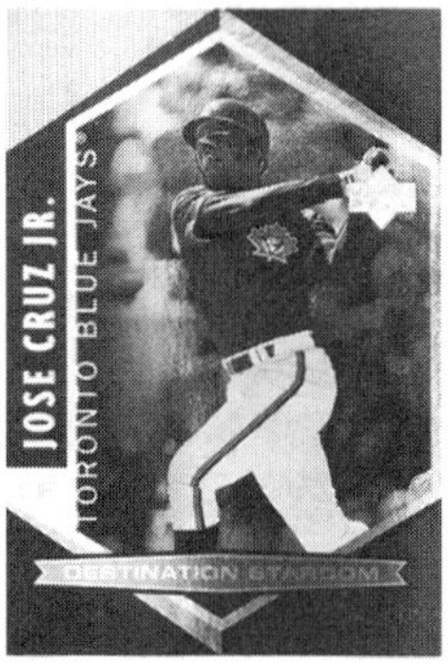

This 60-card insert features top young players. The cards are die-cut and foil-enhanced. The insertion rate was one card per five packs.

		MT
Complete Set (60):		75.00
Common Player:		.50
Inserted 1:5		
DS1	Travis Lee	10.00
DS2	Nomar Garciaparra	10.00
DS3	Alex Gonzalez	.50
DS4	Richard Hidalgo	.50
DS5	Jaret Wright	4.00
DS6	Mike Kinkade	.50
DS7	Matt Morris	.50
DS8	Gary Mathews Jr.	.50
DS9	Brett Tomko	.50
DS10	Todd Helton	3.00
DS11	Scott Elarton	.50
DS12	Scott Rolen	4.00
DS13	Jose Cruz Jr.	2.00
DS14	Jarrod Washburn	.50
DS15	Sean Casey	1.50
DS16	Magglio Ordonez	2.00
DS17	Gabe Alvarez	.50
DS18	Todd Dunwoody	.50
DS19	Kevin Witt	.50
DS20	Ben Grieve	5.00
DS21	Daryle Ward	.60
DS22	Matt Clement	.50
DS23	Carlton Loewer	.50
DS24	Javier Vazquez	.50
DS25	Paul Konerko	2.00
DS26	Preston Wilson	.50
DS27	Wes Helms	.50
DS28	Derek Jeter	6.00
DS29	Corey Koskie	.50
DS30	Russell Branyan	.50
DS31	Vladimir Guerrero	3.00
DS32	Ryan Christenson	.50
DS33	Carlos Lee	.50
DS34	David Dellucci	.50
DS35	Bruce Chen	.50
DS36	Ricky Ledee	1.00
DS37	Ron Wright	.50
DS38	Derrek Lee	.50
DS39	Miguel Tejada	2.00
DS40	Brad Fullmer	2.00
DS41	Rich Butler	2.50
DS42	Chris Carpenter	.50
DS43	Alex Rodriguez	10.00
DS44	Darron Ingram	.50
DS45	Kerry Wood	15.00
DS46	Jason Varitek	.50
DS47	Ramon Hernandez	.50
DS48	Aaron Boone	.50
DS49	Juan Encarnacion	.50
DS50	A.J. Hinch	1.50
DS51	Mike Lowell	.50
DS52	Fernando Tatis	1.00
DS53	Jose Guillen	1.50
DS54	Mike Caruso	.50
DS55	Carl Pavano	.50
DS56	Chris Clemons	.50
DS57	Mark L. Johnson	.50
DS58	Ken Cloude	.50
DS59	Rolando Arrojo	2.50
DS60	Mark Kotsay	2.50

1998 Upper Deck Rookie Edition Retrospectives

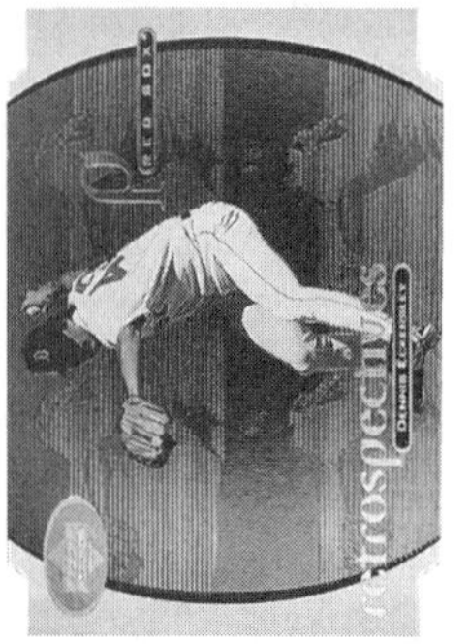

Retrospectives is a 30-card insert seeded 1:24. The cards offer a look back at the careers of baseball's top stars.

		MT
Complete Set (30):		200.00
Common Player:		2.50
Inserted 1:24		
1	Dennis Eckersley	2.50
2	Rickey Henderson	2.50
3	Harold Baines	2.50
4	Cal Ripken Jr.	25.00
5	Tony Gwynn	15.00
6	Wade Boggs	2.50
7	Orel Hershiser	2.50
8	Joe Carter	2.50
9	Roger Clemens	10.00
10	Barry Bonds	8.00
11	Mark McGwire	35.00
12	Greg Maddux	20.00
13	Fred McGriff	2.50
14	Rafael Palmeiro	3.00
15	Craig Biggio	2.50
16	Brady Anderson	2.50
17	Randy Johnson	5.00
18	Gary Sheffield	4.00
19	Albert Belle	8.00
20	Ken Griffey Jr.	30.00
21	Juan Gonzalez	15.00
22	Larry Walker	4.00
23	Tino Martinez	4.00
24	Frank Thomas	25.00
25	Jeff Bagwell	10.00
26	Kenny Lofton	8.00
27	Mo Vaughn	8.00
28	Mike Piazza	20.00
29	Alex Rodriguez	20.00
30	Chipper Jones	20.00

1998 Upper Deck Rookie Edition Unparalleled

Unparalleled is a 20-card, hobby-only insert. The set consists of holo-pattern foil-stamped cards. They were inserted one per 72 packs.

		MT
Complete Set (20):		400.00
Common Player:		5.00
Inserted 1:72		
1	Ken Griffey Jr.	50.00
2	Travis Lee	30.00
3	Ben Grieve	15.00
4	Jose Cruz Jr.	10.00
5	Nomar Garciaparra	30.00
6	Hideo Nomo	10.00
7	Kenny Lofton	12.00
8	Cal Ripken Jr.	40.00
9	Roger Clemens	20.00
10	Mike Piazza	30.00
11	Jeff Bagwell	20.00
12	Chipper Jones	30.00
13	Greg Maddux	30.00
14	Randy Johnson	10.00
15	Alex Rodriguez	30.00
16	Barry Bonds	12.00
17	Frank Thomas	40.00
18	Juan Gonzalez	25.00
19	Tony Gwynn	25.00
20	Mark McGwire	60.00

1998 Upper Deck Collector's Choice

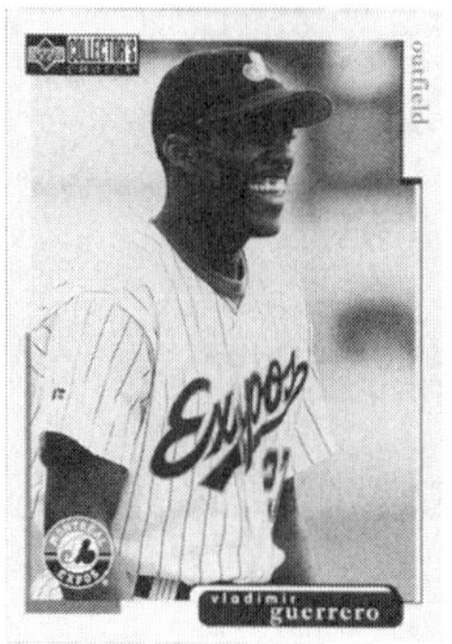

The 530-card Collectors Choice set was issued in two 265-card series. Series One featured 197-regular cards, five checklists and four subsets. Cover Story features 18 of the league's top stars, Rookie Class has 27 young players, the nine-card Top of the Charts subset honors 1997's statistical leaders and Masked Marauders is a nine-card subset. The inserts in Series One are Super Action Stick-Ums, Evolution Revolution and StarQuest. Series Two has 233 regular cards, five checklist cards, an 18-card Rookie Class subset and the nine-card Golden Jubilee subset. Inserts in Series Two include Mini Bobbing Head Cards, You Crash the Game and StarQuest.

		MT
Complete Set (530):		30.00
Complete Series I Set (265):		15.00
Complete Series II Set (265):		15.00
Common Player:		.05
Wax Box:		40.00
1	Nomar Garciaparra (Cover Glory)	.60
2	Roger Clemens (Cover Glory)	.30
3	Larry Walker (Cover Glory)	.10
4	Mike Piazza (Cover Glory)	.60
5	Mark McGwire (Cover Glory)	1.00
6	Tony Gwynn (Cover Glory)	.50
7	Jose Cruz Jr. (Cover Glory)	.50
8	Frank Thomas (Cover Glory)	.75
9	Tino Martinez (Cover Glory)	.10
10	Ken Griffey Jr. (Cover Glory)	1.00
11	Barry Bonds (Cover Glory)	.25
12	Scott Rolen (Cover Glory)	.50
13	Randy Johnson (Cover Glory)	.15
14	Ryne Sandberg (Cover Glory)	.25
15	Eddie Murray (Cover Glory)	.10
16	Kevin Brown (Cover Glory)	.05
17	Greg Maddux (Cover Glory)	.60
18	Sandy Alomar Jr. (Cover Glory)	.05
19	Checklist (Ken Griffey Jr.), (Adam Riggs)	.50
20	Checklist (Nomar Garciaparra), (Charlie O'Brien)	.30
21	Checklist (Ben Grieve), (Ken Griffey Jr.), (Larry Walker), (Mark McGwire)	1.00
22	Checklist (Mark McGwire), (Cal Ripken Jr.)	1.00
23	Checklist (Tino Martinez)	.05
24	Jason Dickson	.05
25	Darin Erstad	.60
26	Todd Greene	.15
27	Chuck Finley	.05
28	Garret Anderson	.05
29	Dave Hollins	.05
30	Rickey Henderson	.05
31	John Smoltz	.15
32	Michael Tucker	.05
33	Jeff Blauser	.05
34	Javier Lopez	.10
35	Andruw Jones	1.00
36	Denny Neagle	.05
37	Randall Simon	.15
38	Mark Wohlers	.05
39	Harold Baines	.05
40	Cal Ripken Jr.	1.50
41	Mike Bordick	.05
42	Jimmy Key	.05
43	Armando Benitez	.05
44	Scott Erickson	.05
45	Eric Davis	.05
46	Bret Saberhagen	.05
47	Darren Bragg	.05
48	Steve Avery	.05
49	Jeff Frye	.05
50	Aaron Sele	.05
51	Scott Hatteberg	.05
52	Tom Gordon	.05
53	Kevin Orie	.05
54	Kevin Foster	.05
55	Ryne Sandberg	.50
56	Doug Glanville	.05
57	Tyler Houston	.05
58	Steve Trachsel	.05
59	Mark Grace	.15
60	Frank Thomas	1.50
61	*Scott Eyre*	.15
62	Jeff Abbott	.05
63	Chris Clemons	.05
64	Jorge Fabregas	.05
65	Robin Ventura	.10
66	Matt Karchner	.05
67	Jon Nunnally	.05
68	Aaron Boone	.05
69	Pokey Reese	.05
70	Deion Sanders	.15
71	Jeff Shaw	.05
72	Eduardo Perez	.05
73	Brett Tomko	.05
74	Bartolo Colon	.05
75	Manny Ramirez	.40
76	Jose Mesa	.05
77	Brian Giles	.05
78	Richie Sexson	.05
79	Orel Hershiser	.05
80	Matt Williams	.20
81	Walt Weiss	.05
82	Jerry DiPoto	.05
83	Quinton McCracken	.05
84	Neifi Perez	.05
85	Vinny Castilla	.10
86	Ellis Burks	.05
87	John Thomson	.05
88	Willie Blair	.05
89	Bob Hamelin	.05
90	Tony Clark	.35
91	Todd Jones	.05
92	Deivi Cruz	.05
93	*Frank Catalanotto*	.15
94	Justin Thompson	.05
95	Gary Sheffield	.25
96	Kevin Brown	.15
97	Charles Johnson	.10
98	Bobby Bonilla	.10
99	Livan Hernandez	.05
100	Paul Konerko (Rookie Class)	.60
101	Craig Counsell (Rookie Class)	.05
102	*Magglio Ordonez* (Rookie Class)	.50
103	Garrett Stephenson (Rookie Class)	.05
104	Ken Cloude (Rookie Class)	.15
105	Miguel Tejada (Rookie Class)	.40
106	Juan Encarnacion (Rookie Class)	.20
107	Dennis Reyes (Rookie Class)	.15
108	Orlando Cabrera (Rookie Class)	.05
109	Kelvim Escobar (Rookie Class)	.05
110	Ben Grieve (Rookie Class)	.75
111	Brian Rose (Rookie Class)	.05
112	Fernando Tatis (Rookie Class)	.20
113	Tom Evans (Rookie Class)	.05
114	Tom Fordham (Rookie Class)	.05
115	Mark Kotsay (Rookie Class)	.40

116 Mario Valdez (Rookie Class) .05
117 Jeremi Gonzalez (Rookie Class) .05
118 Todd Dunwoody (Rookie Class) .05
119 Javier Valentin (Rookie Class) .05
120 Todd Helton (Rookie Class) .50
121 Jason Varitek (Rookie Class) .05
122 Chris Carpenter (Rookie Class) .05
123 *Kevin Millwood* (Rookie Class) .50
124 Brad Fullmer (Rookie Class) .05
125 Jaret Wright (Rookie Class) 1.00
126 Brad Rigby (Rookie Class) .05
127 Edgar Renteria .05
128 Robb Nen .05
129 Tony Pena .05
130 Craig Biggio .15
131 Brad Ausmus .05
132 Shane Reynolds .05
133 Mike Hampton .05
134 Billy Wagner .05
135 Richard Hidalgo .05
136 Jose Rosado .05
137 Yamil Benitez .05
138 Felix Martinez .05
139 Jeff King .05
140 Jose Offerman .05
141 Joe Vitiello .05
142 Tim Belcher .05
143 Brett Butler .05
144 Greg Gagne .05
145 Mike Piazza 1.25
146 Ramon Martinez .10
147 Raul Mondesi .20
148 Adam Riggs .05
149 Eddie Murray .20
150 Jeff Cirillo .05
151 Scott Karl .05
152 Mike Fetters .05
153 Dave Nilsson .05
154 Antone Williamson .05
155 Jeff D'Amico .05
156 Jose Valentin .05
157 Brad Radke .05
158 Torii Hunter .05
159 Chuck Knoblauch .15
160 Paul Molitor .35
161 Travis Miller .05
162 Rich Robertson .05
163 Ron Coomer .05
164 Mark Grudzielanek .05
165 Lee Smith .05
166 Vladimir Guerrero .60
167 Dustin Hermanson .05
168 Ugueth Urbina .05
169 F.P. Santangelo .05
170 Rondell White .15
171 Bobby Jones .05
172 Edgardo Alfonzo .15
173 John Franco .05
174 Carlos Baerga .05
175 Butch Huskey .05
176 Rey Ordonez .10
177 Matt Franco .05
178 Dwight Gooden .15
179 Chad Curtis .05
180 Tino Martinez .15
181 Charlie O'Brien (Masked Marauders) .05
182 Sandy Alomar Jr. (Masked Marauders) .05
183 Raul Casanova (Masked Marauders) .05
184 Jim Leyritz (Masked Marauders) .05
185 Mike Piazza (Masked Marauders) .60
186 Ivan Rodriguez (Masked Marauders) .25
187 Charles Johnson (Masked Marauders) .10
188 Brad Ausmus (Masked Marauders) .05
189 Brian Johnson (Masked Marauders) .05
190 Wade Boggs .20
191 David Wells .05
192 Tim Raines .05
193 Ramiro Mendoza .05
194 Willie Adams .05
195 Matt Stairs .05
196 Jason McDonald .05
197 Dave Magadan .05
198 Mark Bellhorn .05
199 Ariel Prieto .05
200 Jose Canseco .20
201 Bobby Estalella .05
202 *Tony Barron* .05
203 Midre Cummings .05
204 Ricky Bottalico .05
205 Mike Grace .05
206 Rico Brogna .05
207 Mickey Morandini .05
208 Lou Collier .05
209 *Kevin Polcovich* .05
210 Kevin Young .05
211 Jose Guillen .25
212 Esteban Loaiza .05
213 Marc Wilkins .05
214 Jason Schmidt .05
215 Gary Gaetti .05
216 Fernando Valenzuela .05
217 Willie McGee .05
218 Alan Benes .15
219 Eli Marrero .05
220 Mark McGwire 2.50
221 Matt Morris .05
222 Trevor Hoffman .05
223 Will Cunnane .05
224 Joey Hamilton .05
225 Ken Caminiti .15
226 Derrek Lee .15
227 Mark Sweeney .05
228 Carlos Hernandez .05
229 Brian Johnson .05
230 Jeff Kent .05
231 Kirk Rueter .05
232 Bill Mueller .05
233 Dante Powell .05
234 J.T. Snow .15
235 Shawn Estes .05
236 Dennis Martinez .05
237 Jamie Moyer .05
238 Dan Wilson .05
239 Joey Cora .05
240 Ken Griffey Jr. 2.00
241 Paul Sorrento .05
242 Jay Buhner .20
243 *Hanley Frias* .05
244 John Burkett .05
245 Juan Gonzalez 1.00
246 Rick Helling .05
247 Darren Oliver .05
248 Mickey Tettleton .05
249 Ivan Rodriguez .50
250 Joe Carter .15
251 Pat Hentgen .05
252 Marty Janzen .05
253 Frank Thomas, Tony Gwynn (Top of the Charts) .50
254 Mark McGwire, Ken Griffey Jr., Larry Walker (Top of the Charts) 1.00
255 Ken Griffey Jr., Andres Galarraga (Top of the Charts) .50
256 Brian Hunter, Tony Womack (Top of the Charts) .05
257 Roger Clemens, Denny Neagle (Top of the Charts) .20
258 Roger Clemens, Curt Schilling (Top of the Charts) .20
259 Roger Clemens, Pedro J. Martinez (Top of the Charts) .20
260 Randy Myers, Jeff Shaw (Top of the Charts) .05
261 Nomar Garciaparra, Scott Rolen (Top of the Charts) .30
262 Charlie O'Brien .05
263 Shannon Stewart .05
264 Robert Person .05
265 Carlos Delgado .05
266 Checklist (Matt Williams), (Travis Lee) .40
267 Checklist (Nomar Garciaparra), (Cal Ripken Jr.) .40
268 Checklist (Mark McGwire), (Mike Piazza) .75
269 Checklist (Tony Gwynn), (Ken Griffey Jr.) .50
270 Checklist (Fred McGriff), (Jose Cruz Jr.) .15
271 Andruw Jones (Golden Jubilee) .25
272 Alex Rodriguez (Golden Jubilee) .60
273 Juan Gonzalez (Golden Jubilee) .50
274 Nomar Garciaparra (Golden Jubilee) .60
275 Ken Griffey Jr. (Golden Jubilee) 1.00
276 Tino Martinez (Golden Jubilee) .15
277 Roger Clemens (Golden Jubilee) .40
278 Barry Bonds (Golden Jubilee) .25
279 Mike Piazza (Golden Jubilee) .60
280 Tim Salmon (Golden Jubilee) .15
281 Gary DiSarcina .05
282 Cecil Fielder .15
283 Ken Hill .05
284 Troy Percival .05
285 Jim Edmonds .05
286 Allen Watson .05
287 Brian Anderson .05
288 Jay Bell .05
289 Jorge Fabregas .05
290 Devon White .05
291 Yamil Benitez .05
292 Jeff Suppan .05
293 Tony Batista .05
294 Brent Brede .05
295 Andy Benes .15
296 Felix Rodriguez .05
297 Karim Garcia .05
298 Omar Daal .05
299 Andy Stankiewicz .05
300 Matt Williams .25
301 Willie Blair .05
302 Ryan Klesko .20
303 Tom Glavine .15
304 Walt Weiss .05
305 Greg Maddux 1.25
306 Chipper Jones 1.25
307 Keith Lockhart .05
308 Andres Galarraga .20
309 Chris Hoiles .05
310 Roberto Alomar .40
311 Joe Carter .15
312 Doug Drabek .05
313 Jeffrey Hammonds .05
314 Rafael Palmeiro .20
315 Mike Mussina .40
316 Brady Anderson .05
317 B.J. Surhoff .05
318 Dennis Eckersley .05
319 Jim Leyritz .05
320 Mo Vaughn .50
321 Nomar Garciaparra 1.25
322 Reggie Jefferson .05
323 Tim Naehring .05
324 Troy O'Leary .05
325 Pedro J. Martinez .25
326 John Valentin .05
327 Mark Clark .05
328 Rod Beck .05
329 Mickey Morandini .05
330 Sammy Sosa 1.00
331 Jeff Blauser .05
332 Lance Johnson .05
333 Scott Servais .05
334 Kevin Tapani .05
335 Henry Rodriguez .05
336 Jaime Navarro .05
337 Benji Gil .05
338 James Baldwin .05
339 Mike Cameron .05
340 Ray Durham .05
341 Chris Snopek .05
342 Eddie Taubensee .05
343 Bret Boone .05
344 Willie Greene .05
345 Barry Larkin .15
346 Chris Stynes .05
347 Pete Harnisch .05
348 Dave Burba .05
349 Sandy Alomar Jr. .15
350 Kenny Lofton .50
351 Geronimo Berroa .05
352 Omar Vizquel .05
353 Travis Fryman .05
354 Dwight Gooden .05
355 Jim Thome .40
356 David Justice .25
357 Charles Nagy .05
358 Chad Ogea .05
359 Pedro Astacio .05
360 Larry Walker .25
361 Mike Lansing .05
362 Kirt Manwaring .05
363 Dante Bichette .15
364 Jamey Wright .05
365 Darryl Kile .05
366 Luis Gonzalez .05
367 Joe Randa .05
368 Raul Casanova .05
369 Damion Easley .05
370 Brian L. Hunter .05
371 Bobby Higginson .05
372 Brian Moehler .05
373 Scott Sanders .05
374 Jim Eisenreich .05
375 Derrek Lee .05
376 Jay Powell .05
377 Cliff Floyd .05
378 Alex Fernandez .05
379 Felix Heredia .05
380 Jeff Bagwell .75
381 Bill Spiers .05
382 Chris Holt .05
383 Carl Everett .05
384 Derek Bell .05
385 Moises Alou .15
386 Ramon Garcia .05
387 Mike Sweeney .05
388 Glendon Rusch .05
389 Kevin Appier .05
390 Dean Palmer .05
391 Jeff Conine .05
392 Johnny Damon .05
393 Jose Vizcaino .05
394 Todd Hollandsworth .05
395 Eric Karros .05
396 Todd Zeile .05
397 Chan Ho Park .15
398 Ismael Valdes .05
399 Eric Young .05
400 Hideo Nomo .40
401 Mark Loretta .05
402 Doug Jones .05
403 Jeromy Burnitz .05
404 John Jaha .05
405 Marquis Grissom .05
406 Mike Matheny .05
407 Todd Walker .05
408 Marty Cordova .05
409 Matt Lawton .05
410 Terry Steinbach .05
411 Pat Meares .05
412 Rick Aguilera .05
413 Otis Nixon .05
414 Derrick May .05
415 Carl Pavano (Rookie Class) .05
416 A.J. Hinch (Rookie Class) .15
417 *David Dellucci* (Rookie Class) .25
418 Bruce Chen (Rookie Class) .05
419 *Darron Ingram* (Rookie Class) .05
420 Sean Casey (Rookie Class) .05
421 Mark L. Johnson (Rookie Class) .05
422 Gabe Alvarez (Rookie Class) .05
423 Alex Gonzalez (Rookie Class) .05
424 Daryle Ward (Rookie Class) .15
425 Russell Branyan (Rookie Class) .05
426 Mike Caruso (Rookie Class) .05
427 *Mike Kinkade* (Rookie Class) .25
428 Ramon Hernandez (Rookie Class) .05
429 Matt Clement (Rookie Class) .10
430 Travis Lee (Rookie Class) 1.50
431 Shane Monahan (Rookie Class) .05
432 *Rich Butler* (Rookie Class) .25
433 Chris Widger .05
434 Jose Vidro .05
435 Carlos Perez .05
436 Ryan McGuire .05
437 Brian McRae .05
438 Al Leiter .05
439 Rich Becker .05
440 Todd Hundley .05
441 Dave Mlicki .05
442 Bernard Gilkey .05
443 John Olerud .15
444 Paul O'Neill .15
445 Andy Pettitte .40
446 David Cone .15
447 Chili Davis .05
448 Bernie Williams .40
449 Joe Girardi .05
450 Derek Jeter 1.00
451 Mariano Rivera .15
452 George Williams .05
453 Kenny Rogers .05
454 Tom Candiotti .05
455 Rickey Henderson .05
456 Jason Giambi .05
457 Scott Spiezio .05
458 Doug Glanville .05
459 Desi Relaford .05
460 Curt Schilling .15
461 Bob Abreu .05
462 Gregg Jefferies .05
463 Scott Rolen .75
464 Mike Lieberthal .05
465 Tony Womack .05
466 Jermaine Allensworth .05
467 Francisco Cordova .05
468 Jon Lieber .05
469 Al Martin .05
470 Jason Kendall .05
471 Todd Stottlemyre .05
472 Royce Clayton .05
473 Brian Jordan .05
474 John Mabry .05
475 Ray Lankford .05
476 Delino DeShields .05
477 Ron Gant .05
478 Mark Langston .05
479 Steve Finley .05
480 Tony Gwynn 1.00
481 Andy Ashby .05
482 Wally Joyner .05
483 Greg Vaughn .05
484 Sterling Hitchcock .05
485 J. Kevin Brown .05
486 Orel Hershiser .05
487 Charlie Hayes .05
488 Darryl Hamilton .05
489 Mark Gardner .05
490 Barry Bonds .50
491 Robb Nen .05
492 Kirk Rueter .05
493 Randy Johnson .40
494 Jeff Fassero .05
495 Alex Rodriguez 1.25
496 David Segui .05
497 Rich Amaral .05
498 Russ Davis .05
499 Bubba Trammell .05
500 Wade Boggs .20
501 Roberto Hernandez .05
502 Dave Martinez .05
503 Dennis Springer .05
504 Paul Sorrento .05
505 Wilson Alvarez .05
506 Mike Kelly .05
507 Albie Lopez .05
508 Tony Saunders .05
509 John Flaherty .05
510 Fred McGriff .15
511 Quinton McCracken .05
512 Terrell Wade .05
513 Kevin Stocker .05
514 Kevin Elster .05
515 Will Clark .20
516 Bobby Witt .05
517 Tom Goodwin .05
518 Aaron Sele .05
519 Lee Stevens .05
520 Rusty Greer .05
521 John Wetteland .05
522 Darrin Fletcher .05
523 Jose Canseco .25
524 Randy Myers .05
525 Jose Cruz Jr. .50
526 Shawn Green .05
527 Tony Fernandez .05
528 Alex Gonzalez .05
529 Ed Sprague .05
530 Roger Clemens .75

1998 Upper Deck Collector's Choice Cover Glory 5x7

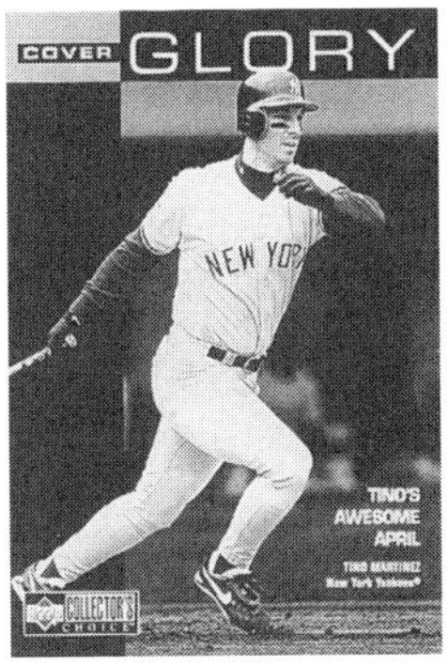

		MT
Complete Set (8):		12.00
Common Player:		1.00
1	Nomar Garciaparra	2.00
2	Roger Clemens	1.50
3	Larry Walker	1.00
4	Mike Piazza	2.00
5	Mark McGwire	3.00
6	Tony Gwynn	1.50
7	Jose Cruz Jr.	1.50
8	Frank Thomas	2.50
9	Tino Martinez	1.00
10	Ken Griffey Jr.	3.50

1998 Upper Deck Collector's Choice Evolution Revolution

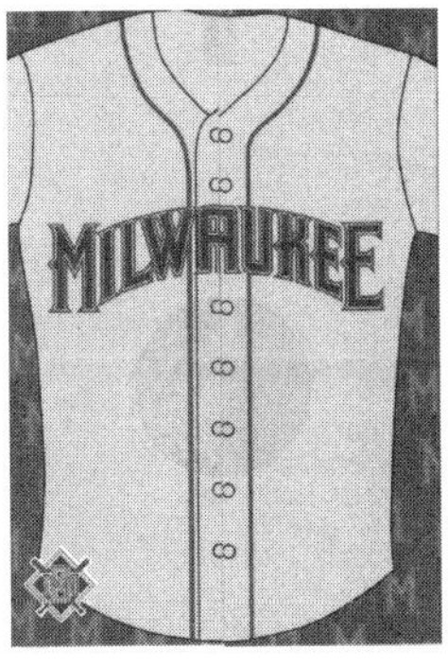

This 28-card insert features one player from each Major League team. The fronts have the team jersey and fold out to reveal the player's top 1997 accomplishment. Evolution Revolution was inserted one per 13 Series One packs.

		MT
Complete Set (28):		60.00
Common Player:		.75
Inserted 1:13		
ER1	Tim Salmon	1.25
ER2	Greg Maddux	6.00

ER3	Cal Ripken Jr.	8.00
ER4	Mo Vaughn	2.50
ER5	Sammy Sosa	4.00
ER6	Frank Thomas	8.00
ER7	Barry Larkin	1.00
ER8	Jim Thome	1.50
ER9	Larry Walker	1.25
ER10	Travis Fryman	.75
ER11	Gary Sheffield	1.50
ER12	Jeff Bagwell	4.00
ER13	Johnny Damon	.75
ER14	Mike Piazza	6.00
ER15	Jeff Cirillo	.75
ER16	Paul Molitor	2.00
ER17	Vladimir Guerrero	3.00
ER18	Todd Hundley	.75
ER19	Tino Martinez	.75
ER20	Jose Canseco	1.00
ER21	Scott Rolen	5.00
ER22	Al Martin	.75
ER23	Mark McGwire	12.00
ER24	Tony Gwynn	5.00
ER25	Barry Bonds	2.50
ER26	Ken Griffey Jr.	10.00
ER27	Juan Gonzalez	5.00
ER28	Roger Clemens	4.00

1998 Upper Deck Collector's Choice Mini Bobbing Heads

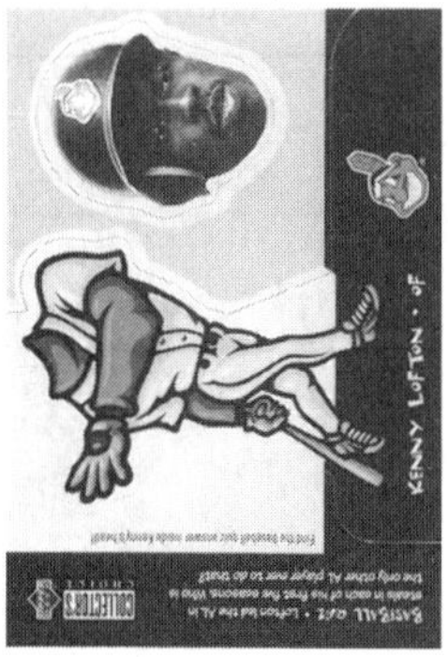

The cards in this 30-card insert fold into a stand-up figure with a removable bobbing head. They were inserted 1:3 in Series Two packs.

		MT
Complete Set (30):		20.00
Common Player:		.25
Inserted 1:3		
1	Tim Salmon	.40
2	Travis Lee	2.00
3	Matt Williams	.25
4	Chipper Jones	1.50
5	Greg Maddux	1.50
6	Cal Ripken Jr.	2.00
7	Nomar Garciaparra	1.50
8	Mo Vaughn	.75
9	Sammy Sosa	1.00
10	Frank Thomas	2.00
11	Kenny Lofton	.75
12	Jaret Wright	.75
13	Larry Walker	.40
14	Tony Clark	.50
15	Edgar Renteria	.25
16	Jeff Bagwell	1.00
17	Mike Piazza	1.50
18	Vladimir Guerrero	.75
19	Derek Jeter	1.25
20	Ben Grieve	.75
21	Scott Rolen	.75
22	Mark McGwire	3.00
23	Tony Gwynn	1.25
24	Barry Bonds	.75
25	Ken Griffey Jr.	2.50
26	Alex Rodriguez	1.50
27	Fred McGriff	.40
28	Juan Gonzalez	1.25
29	Roger Clemens	1.00
30	Jose Cruz Jr.	.75

1998 Upper Deck Collector's Choice Rookie Class: Prime Choice

This 18-card set is a parallel of the Rookie Class subset. Each card is foil-stamped with the words "Prime Choice Reserve." This hobby-only set is sequentially numbered to 500 and was inserted in Series Two packs.

		MT
Complete Set (18):		200.00
Common Player:		5.00
415	Carl Pavano	15.00
416	A.J. Hinch	15.00
417	David Dellucci	25.00
418	Bruce Chen	20.00
419	Darron Ingram	5.00
420	Sean Casey	20.00
421	Mark L. Johnson	5.00
422	Gabe Alvarez	5.00
423	Alex Gonzalez	15.00
424	Daryle Ward	10.00
425	Russell Branyan	10.00
426	Mike Caruso	15.00
427	Mike Kinkade	5.00
428	Ramon Hernandez	5.00
429	Matt Clement	5.00
430	Travis Lee	60.00
431	Shane Monahan	5.00
432	Rich Butler	20.00

1998 Upper Deck Collector's Choice StarQuest

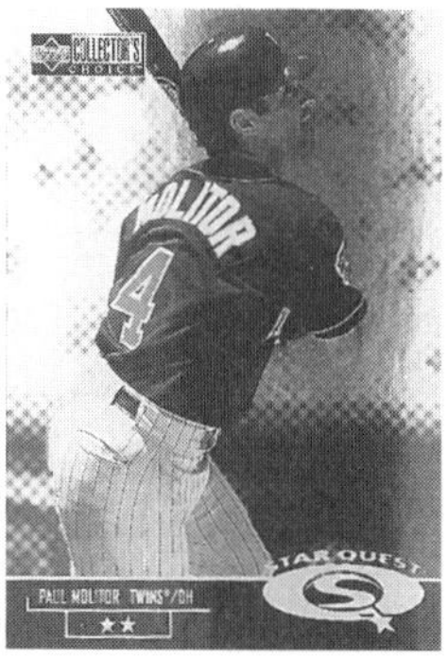

The StarQuest insert in Series One consisted of 90 cards with four tiers. Special Delivery (one star, 45 cards) was inserted 1:1, Students of the Game (two stars, 20 cards) 1:21, Super Powers (three stars, 15 cards) 1:71 and Super Star Domain (four stars, 10 cards) 1:145.

		MT
Complete Set (90):		500.00
Common Special Delivery (1-45):		.20
Inserted 1:1		
Common Student of the Game (46-65):		1.50
Inserted 1:21		
Common Super Power (66-80):		5.00
Inserted 1:71		
Common Superstar Domain (81-90):		10.00
Inserted 1:145		
SQ1	Nomar Garciaparra	2.00
SQ2	Scott Rolen	1.50
SQ3	Jason Dickson	.20
SQ4	Jaret Wright	1.50
SQ5	Kevin Orie	.20
SQ6	Jose Guillen	.50
SQ7	Matt Morris	.20
SQ8	Mike Cameron	.30
SQ9	Kevin Polcovich	.20
SQ10	Jose Cruz Jr.	1.50
SQ11	Miguel Tejada	.50
SQ12	Fernando Tatis	.40
SQ13	Todd Helton	.75
SQ14	Ken Cloude	.20
SQ15	Ben Grieve	1.00
SQ16	Dante Powell	.20
SQ17	Bubba Trammell	.30
SQ18	Juan Encarnacion	.40
SQ19	Derrek Lee	.20
SQ20	Paul Konerko	1.00
SQ21	Richard Hidalgo	.20
SQ22	Denny Neagle	.20
SQ23	David Justice	.40
SQ24	Pedro J. Martinez	.40
SQ25	Greg Maddux	2.00
SQ26	Edgar Martinez	.20
SQ27	Cal Ripken Jr.	2.50
SQ28	Tim Salmon	.40
SQ29	Shawn Estes	.20
SQ30	Ken Griffey Jr.	3.00
SQ31	Brad Radke	.20
SQ32	Andy Pettitte	.50
SQ33	Curt Schilling	.20
SQ34	Raul Mondesi	.40
SQ35	Alex Rodriguez	2.00
SQ36	Jeff Kent	.20
SQ37	Jeff Bagwell	1.25
SQ38	Juan Gonzalez	1.50
SQ39	Barry Bonds	.75
SQ40	Mark McGwire	4.00
SQ41	Frank Thomas	2.50
SQ42	Ray Lankford	.20
SQ43	Tony Gwynn	1.50
SQ44	Mike Piazza	2.00
SQ45	Tino Martinez	.20
SQ46	Nomar Garciaparra	10.00
SQ47	Paul Molitor	3.00
SQ48	Chuck Knoblauch	2.00
SQ49	Rusty Greer	1.50
SQ50	Cal Ripken Jr.	12.00
SQ51	Roberto Alomar	3.00
SQ52	Scott Rolen	7.00
SQ53	Derek Jeter	10.00
SQ54	Mark Grace	2.00
SQ55	Randy Johnson	2.50
SQ56	Craig Biggio	1.50
SQ57	Kenny Lofton	4.00
SQ58	Eddie Murray	2.00
SQ59	Ryne Sandberg	4.00
SQ60	Rickey Henderson	1.50
SQ61	Darin Erstad	4.00
SQ62	Jim Edmonds	1.50
SQ63	Ken Caminiti	2.00
SQ64	Ivan Rodriguez	3.00
SQ65	Tony Gwynn	8.00
SQ66	Tony Clark	8.00
SQ67	Andres Galarraga	6.00
SQ68	Rafael Palmeiro	6.00
SQ69	Manny Ramirez	8.00
SQ70	Albert Belle	10.00
SQ71	Jay Buhner	5.00
SQ72	Mo Vaughn	10.00
SQ73	Barry Bonds	10.00
SQ74	Chipper Jones	25.00
SQ75	Jeff Bagwell	18.00
SQ76	Jim Thome	8.00
SQ77	Sammy Sosa	12.00
SQ78	Todd Hundley	5.00
SQ79	Matt Williams	6.00
SQ80	Vinny Castilla	5.00
SQ81	Jose Cruz Jr.	25.00
SQ82	Frank Thomas	50.00
SQ83	Juan Gonzalez	30.00
SQ84	Mike Piazza	40.00
SQ85	Alex Rodriguez	40.00
SQ86	Larry Walker	12.00
SQ87	Tino Martinez	10.00
SQ88	Greg Maddux	40.00
SQ89	Mark McGwire	70.00
SQ90	Ken Griffey Jr.	65.00

1998 Upper Deck Collector's Choice Star Quest

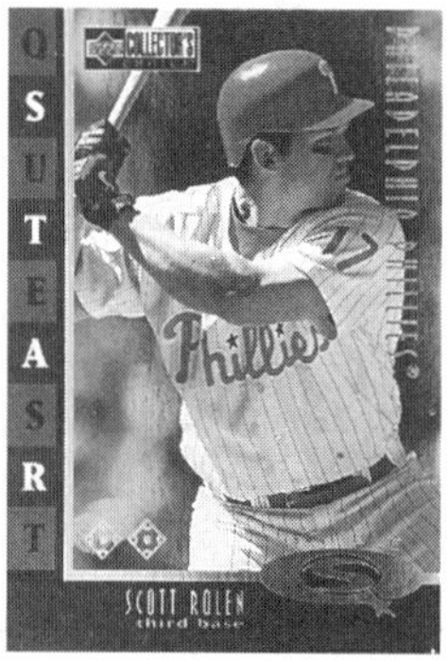

The 30-card StarQuest insert was included in Series Two packs. The insert has four 30-card tiers - Single, Double, Triple and Home Run. The tier is designated by the number of baseball diamond icons on the card front. Single cards were inserted 1:1, Doubles 1:21, Triples 1:71 and Home Runs are sequentially numbered to 100.

		MT
Complete Set (30):		18.00
Common Player:		.25
Singles 1:1		
Doubles 1:21		4x to 8x
Triples 1:71		12x to 20x
1	Ken Griffey Jr.	2.00
2	Jose Cruz Jr.	.50
3	Cal Ripken Jr.	1.50
4	Roger Clemens	.75
5	Frank Thomas	1.50
6	Derek Jeter	1.00
7	Alex Rodriguez	1.25
8	Andruw Jones	.50
9	Vladimir Guerrero	.50
10	Mark McGwire	3.00
11	Kenny Lofton	.50
12	Pedro J. Martinez	.25
13	Greg Maddux	1.25
14	Larry Walker	.25
15	Barry Bonds	.50
16	Chipper Jones	1.25
17	Jeff Bagwell	.75
18	Juan Gonzalez	1.00
19	Tony Gwynn	1.00
20	Mike Piazza	1.25
21	Tino Martinez	.25
22	Mo Vaughn	.50
23	Ben Grieve	.60
24	Scott Rolen	.60
25	Nomar Garciaparra	1.25
26	Paul Konerko	.25
27	Jaret Wright	.50
28	Gary Sheffield	.25
29	Travis Lee	1.50
30	Todd Helton	.50

1998 Upper Deck Collector's Choice Star Quest Home Run

StarQuest Home Run cards are the fourth tier of the insert in Series Two. The cards have four baseball diamond icons to designate their level. Home Run cards are sequentially numbered to 100.

		MT
Common Player:		10.00
Semistars:		25.00
Production 100 sets		
1	Ken Griffey Jr.	150.00
2	Jose Cruz Jr.	40.00
3	Cal Ripken Jr.	120.00
4	Roger Clemens	60.00
5	Frank Thomas	120.00
6	Derek Jeter	75.00
7	Alex Rodriguez	100.00
8	Andruw Jones	40.00
9	Vladimir Guerrero	40.00
10	Mark McGwire	150.00
11	Kenny Lofton	40.00
12	Pedro J. Martinez	20.00
13	Greg Maddux	100.00
14	Larry Walker	25.00
15	Barry Bonds	40.00
16	Chipper Jones	90.00
17	Jeff Bagwell	60.00
18	Juan Gonzalez	75.00
19	Tony Gwynn	75.00
20	Mike Piazza	100.00
21	Tino Martinez	20.00
22	Mo Vaughn	40.00
23	Ben Grieve	50.00
24	Scott Rolen	50.00
25	Nomar Garciaparra	90.00
26	Paul Konerko	10.00
27	Jaret Wright	40.00
28	Gary Sheffield	20.00
29	Travis Lee	100.00
30	Todd Helton	40.00

1998 Upper Deck Collector's Choice Stickums

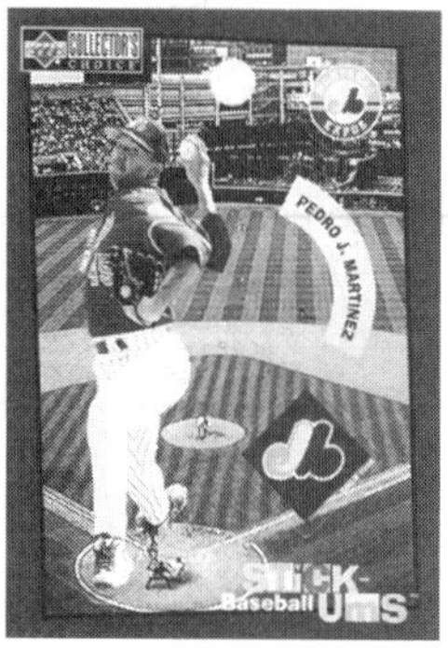

This 30-card insert was seeded 1:3 Series One packs. The stickers can be peeled off the card.

		MT
Complete Set (30):		20.00
Common Player:		.25
Inserted 1:3		
1	Andruw Jones	.60
2	Chipper Jones	1.50
3	Cal Ripken Jr.	2.00
4	Nomar Garciaparra	1.50
5	Mo Vaughn	.60
6	Ryne Sandberg	.60
7	Sammy Sosa	1.25
8	Frank Thomas	2.00
9	Albert Belle	.60
10	Jim Thome	.40
11	Manny Ramirez	.60
12	Larry Walker	.40
13	Gary Sheffield	.40
14	Jeff Bagwell	.75
15	Mike Piazza	1.50
16	Paul Molitor	.50
17	Pedro J. Martinez	.50
18	Todd Hundley	.25
19	Derek Jeter	1.25
20	Tino Martinez	.50
21	Curt Schilling	.25
22	Mark McGwire	3.00
23	Tony Gwynn	1.25
24	Barry Bonds	.60
25	Ken Griffey Jr.	2.50
26	Alex Rodriguez	1.50
27	Juan Gonzalez	1.25
28	Ivan Rodriguez	.60
29	Roger Clemens	1.25
30	Jose Cruz Jr.	.75

1998 Upper Deck Collector's Choice You Crash the Game

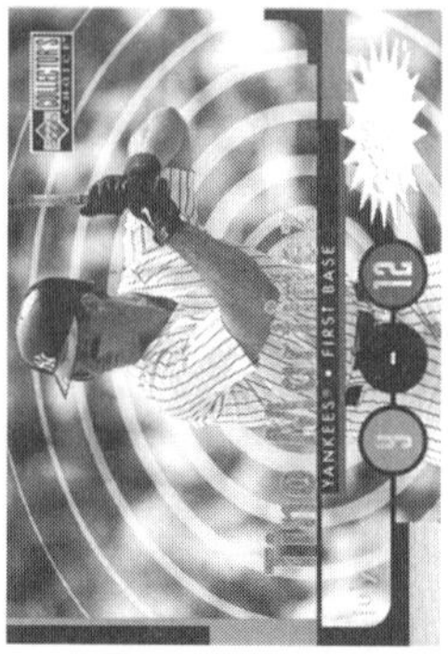

These 30 game cards were inserted one per five Series Two packs. Each card features a player and a list of dates. If the pictured player hit a home run on one of those days, collectors with the card won a prize.

		MT
Complete Set (30):		30.00
Common Player:		.50
Inserted 1:5		
CG1	Ken Griffey Jr.	4.00
CG2	Travis Lee	3.00
CG3	Larry Walker	.75
CG4	Tony Clark	.75
CG5	Cal Ripken Jr.	3.00
CG6	Tim Salmon	.50
CG7	Vinny Castilla	.50
CG8	Fred McGriff	.50
CG9	Matt Williams	.75
CG10	Mark McGwire	2.50
CG11	Albert Belle	1.00
CG12	Jay Buhner	.50
CG13	Vladimir Guerrero	1.00
CG14	Andruw Jones	1.00
CG15	Nomar Garciaparra	2.50
CG16	Ken Caminiti	.50
CG17	Sammy Sosa	1.00
CG18	Ben Grieve	1.00
CG19	Mo Vaughn	1.00
CG20	Frank Thomas	3.00
CG21	Manny Ramirez	1.00
CG22	Jeff Bagwell	1.50
CG23	Jose Cruz Jr.	1.00
CG24	Alex Rodriguez	2.50
CG25	Mike Piazza	2.50
CG26	Tino Martinez	.75
CG27	Chipper Jones	2.50
CG28	Juan Gonzalez	2.00
CG29	Jim Thome	.75
CG30	Barry Bonds	1.00

1998 Upper Deck Collector's Choice Crash Winners

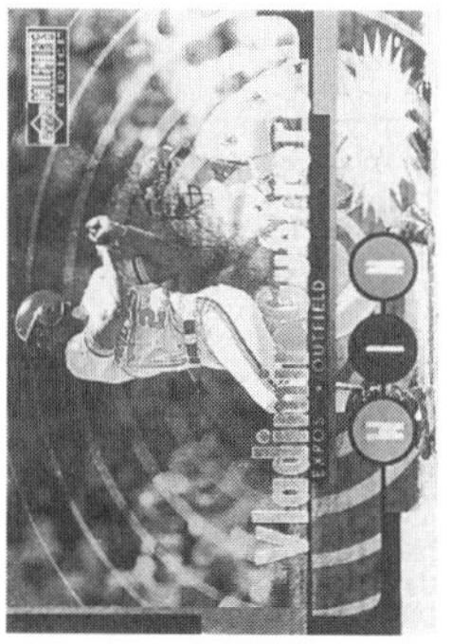

Collectors who redeemed winning "Crash" cards prior to the Dec. 1, 1998, deadline received an upgraded version of that player's card. Similar in format, the winners' cards have an action photo on front (different than the game card), with a metallic foil background. Instead of dates in the three circles at bottom are the letters "W I N". Backs hae a career summary and stats, instead of the redemption instructions found on the game cards. The cards are numbered with a "CG" prefix.

	MT
Complete Set (30):	90.00
Common Player:	1.50
CG1 Ken Griffey Jr.	12.00
CG2 Travis Lee	9.00
CG3 Larry Walker	2.25
CG4 Tony Clark	2.25
CG5 Cal Ripken Jr.	9.00
CG6 Tim Salmon	1.50
CG7 Vinny Castilla	1.50
CG8 Fred McGriff	1.50
CG9 Matt Williams	2.25
CG10Mark McGwire	8.00
CG11Albert Belle	3.00
CG12Jay Buhner	1.50
CG13Vladimir Guerrero	3.00
CG14Andruw Jones	3.00
CG15Nomar Garciaparra	7.50
CG16Ken Caminiti	1.50
CG17Sammy Sosa	3.00
CG18Ben Grieve	3.00
CG19Mo Vaughn	3.00
CG20Frank Thomas	8.00
CG21Manny Ramirez	3.00
CG22Jeff Bagwell	4.50
CG23Jose Cruz Jr.	3.00
CG24Alex Rodriguez	7.50
CG25Mike Piazza	7.50
CG26Tino Martinez	2.25
CG27Chipper Jones	7.50
CG28Juan Gonzalez	6.00
CG29Jim Thome	2.25
CG30Barry Bonds	3.00

1998 Upper Deck UD 3

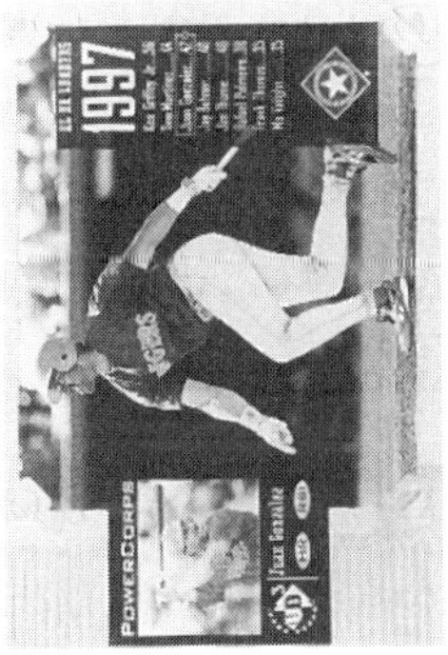

UD Cubed Baseball consists of a 270-card base set built from three 30-card subsets: Future Impact, Power Corps and The Establishment.Each subset is printed on three different technologies: Light F/X, Embossed andRainbow Foil. Future Impact Light F/X cards are seeded 1:12, Future Impact Embossed are seeded 1:6 and Future Impact Rainbow Foil cards are inserted 1:1. Power Corps Light F/X cards are seeded 1:1, Embossed are found 1:4 andRainbow Foil are inserted 1:12. TheEstablishment LightF/X cards are found 1:6, Embossed are seeded 1:1 and Rainbow Foil are inserted 1:24 . Each card also has a numbered die-cut parallel.

		MT
Complete Set (270):		700.00
Comm. Fut. Impacts (1-30):		.50
Inserted 1:12		
Comm. Pow. Corps (31-60):		.25
Inserted 1:1.5		
Comm. Establ. (61-90):		.50
Inserted 1:6		
Comm. Fut. Impact (91-120):		.40
Inserted 1:6		
Comm. Pow Corps (121-150):		.25
Inserted 1:4		
Comm. Estab. (151-180):		.25
Inserted 1:1		
Comm. Fut. Impact (181-210):		.25
Inserted 1:1		
Comm. Pow Corps (211-240):		1.50
Inserted 1:12		
Comm. Establ. (241-270):		2.00
Inserted 1:24		
1	Travis Lee	12.00
2	A.J. Hinch	.50
3	Mike Caruso	.50
4	Miguel Tejada	1.50
5	Brad Fullmer	1.50
6	Eric Milton	.50
7	Mark Kotsay	2.00
8	Darin Erstad	6.00
9	Magglio Ordonez	1.50
10	Ben Grieve	8.00
11	Brett Tomko	.50
12	*Mike Kinkade*	1.00
13	Rolando Arrojo	5.00
14	Todd Helton	1.50
15	Scott Rolen	4.00
16	Bruce Chen	.50
17	Daryle Ward	.50
18	Jaret Wright	4.00
19	Cliff Politte	.50
20	Paul Konerko	.75
21	Kerry Wood	25.00
22	Russell Branyan	.50
23	Gabe Alvarez	.50
24	Juan Encarnacion	.50
25	Andruw Jones	4.00
26	Vladimir Guerrero	5.00
27	Eli Marrero	.25
28	Matt Clement	.25
29	Gary Matthews Jr.	1.00
30	Derrek Lee	.50
31	Ken Caminiti	.75
32	Gary Sheffield	1.00
33	Jay Buhner	.75
34	Ryan Klesko	.75
35	Nomar Garciaparra	5.00
36	Vinny Castilla	.25
37	Tony Clark	.75
38	Sammy Sosa	5.00
39	Tino Martinez	.75
40	Mike Piazza	5.00
41	Manny Ramirez	2.00
42	Larry Walker	.75
43	Jose Cruz Jr.	2.00
44	Matt Williams	.75
45	Frank Thomas	5.00
46	Jim Edmonds	.25
47	Raul Mondesi	.50
48	Alex Rodriguez	5.00
49	Albert Belle	2.00
50	Mark McGwire	10.00
51	Tim Salmon	.75
52	Andres Galarraga	.75
53	Jeff Bagwell	3.00
54	Jim Thome	1.00
55	Barry Bonds	2.00
56	Carlos Delgado	.25
57	Mo Vaughn	2.00
58	Chipper Jones	4.00
59	Juan Gonzalez	4.00
60	Ken Griffey Jr.	8.00
61	David Cone	.40
62	Hideo Nomo	3.00
63	Edgar Martinez	.25
64	Fred McGriff	1.00
65	Cal Ripken Jr.	10.00
66	Todd Hundley	.25
67	Barry Larkin	.75
68	Dennis Eckersley	.25
69	Randy Johnson	3.00
70	Paul Molitor	3.00
71	Eric Karros	.25
72	Rafael Palmeiro	.75
73	Chuck Knoblauch	2.00
74	Ivan Rodriguez	4.00
75	Greg Maddux	8.00
76	Dante Bichette	1.50
77	Brady Anderson	.25
78	Craig Biggio	.75
79	Derek Jeter	7.00
80	Roger Clemens	6.00
81	Roberto Alomar	2.50
82	Wade Boggs	.75
83	Charles Johnson	.25
84	Mark Grace	.75
85	Kenny Lofton	4.00
86	Mike Mussina	3.00
87	Pedro J. Martinez	3.00
88	Curt Schilling	.50
89	Bernie Williams	2.50
90	Tony Gwynn	6.00
91	Travis Lee	6.00
92	A.J. Hinch	.50
93	Mike Caruso	.40
94	Miguel Tejada	1.00
95	Brad Fullmer	1.50
96	Eric Milton	.25
97	Mark Kotsay	1.50
98	Darin Erstad	3.00
99	Magglio Ordonez	1.50
100	Ben Grieve	5.00
101	Brett Tomko	.40
102	Mike Kinkade	.40
103	Rolando Arrojo	4.00
104	Todd Helton	2.50
105	Scott Rolen	4.00
106	Bruce Chen	.40
107	Daryle Ward	.40
108	Jaret Wright	3.00
109	Sean Casey	.50
110	Paul Konerko	.75
111	Kerry Wood	12.00
112	Russell Branyan	.40
113	Gabe Alvarez	.40
114	Juan Encarnacion	.40
115	Andruw Jones	3.00
116	Vladimir Guerrero	4.00
117	Eli Marrero	.40
118	Matt Clement	.40
119	Gary Matthews Jr.	1.00
120	Derrek Lee	.25
121	Ken Caminiti	.50
122	Gary Sheffield	.75
123	Jay Buhner	.50
124	Ryan Klesko	.50
125	Nomar Garciaparra	5.00
126	Vinny Castilla	.25
127	Tony Clark	1.00
128	Sammy Sosa	5.00
129	Tino Martinez	1.00
130	Mike Piazza	5.00
131	Manny Ramirez	2.00
132	Larry Walker	1.00
133	Jose Cruz Jr.	2.00
134	Matt Williams	.75
135	Frank Thomas	5.00
136	Jim Edmonds	.25
137	Raul Mondesi	.40
138	Alex Rodriguez	5.00
139	Albert Belle	2.00
140	Mark McGwire	10.00
141	Tim Salmon	.50
142	Andres Galarraga	.75
143	Jeff Bagwell	2.50
144	Jim Thome	.75
145	Barry Bonds	2.00
146	Carlos Delgado	.25
147	Mo Vaughn	2.00
148	Chipper Jones	4.00
149	Juan Gonzalez	4.00
150	Ken Griffey Jr.	8.00
151	David Cone	.40
152	Hideo Nomo	.75
153	Edgar Martinez	.25
154	Fred McGriff	.25
155	Cal Ripken Jr.	3.00
156	Todd Hundley	.25
157	Barry Larkin	.40
158	Dennis Eckersley	.25
159	Randy Johnson	1.00
160	Paul Molitor	1.00
161	Eric Karros	.40
162	Rafael Palmeiro	.40
163	Chuck Knoblauch	.75
164	Ivan Rodriguez	1.25
165	Greg Maddux	2.50
166	Dante Bichette	.50
167	Brady Anderson	.25
168	Craig Biggio	.25
169	Derek Jeter	2.50
170	Roger Clemens	2.00
171	Roberto Alomar	1.00
172	Wade Boggs	.50
173	Charles Johnson	.25
174	Mark Grace	.50
175	Kenny Lofton	1.25
176	Mike Mussina	1.00
177	Pedro J. Martinez	1.00
178	Curt Schilling	.40
179	Bernie Williams	.75
180	Tony Gwynn	2.00
181	Travis Lee	3.00
182	A.J. Hinch	.25
183	Mike Caruso	.40
184	Miguel Tejada	.75
185	Brad Fullmer	.75
186	Eric Milton	.25
187	Mark Kotsay	.75
188	Darin Erstad	1.50
189	Maggio Ordonez	1.00
190	Ben Grieve	2.00
191	Brett Tomko	.25
192	Mike Kinkade	.25
193	Rolando Arrojo	2.00
194	Todd Helton	1.00
195	Scott Rolen	1.50
196	Bruce Chen	.25
197	Daryle Ward	.25
198	Jaret Wright	1.25
199	Cliff Politte	.25
200	Paul Konerko	.50
201	Kerry Wood	6.00
202	Russell Branyan	.25
203	Gabe Alvarez	.25
204	Juan Encarnacion	.25
205	Andruw Jones	1.00
206	Vladimir Guerrero	1.50
207	Eli Marrero	.25
208	Matt Clement	.25
209	Gary Matthews Jr.	.25
210	Derrek Lee	.25
211	Ken Caminiti	1.50
212	Gary Sheffield	2.50
213	Jay Buhner	2.50
214	Ryan Klesko	2.50
215	Nomar Garciaparra	15.00
216	Vinny Castilla	1.50
217	Tony Clark	4.00
218	Sammy Sosa	15.00
219	Tino Martinez	3.00
220	Mike Piazza	15.00
221	Manny Ramirez	6.00
222	Larry Walker	3.00
223	Jose Cruz Jr.	6.00
224	Matt Williams	2.50
225	Frank Thomas	15.00
226	Jim Edmonds	1.50
227	Raul Mondesi	2.00
228	Alex Rodriguez	15.00
229	Albert Belle	6.00
230	Mark McGwire	30.00
231	Tim Salmon	2.50
232	Andres Galarraga	3.00
233	Jeff Bagwell	8.00
234	Jim Thome	4.00
235	Barry Bonds	6.00
236	Carlos Delgado	1.50
267	Mo Vaughn	6.00
238	Chipper Jones	12.00
239	Juan Gonzalez	12.00
240	Ken Griffey Jr.	25.00
241	David Cone	2.50
242	Hideo Nomo	6.00
243	Edgar Martinez	2.00
244	Fred McGriff	2.50
245	Cal Ripken Jr.	30.00
246	Todd Hundley	2.00
247	Barry Larkin	2.50
248	Dennis Eckersley	2.00
249	Randy Johnson	8.00
250	Paul Molitor	8.00
251	Eric Karros	2.00
252	Rafael Palmeiro	3.00
253	Chuck Knoblauch	4.00
254	Ivan Rodriguez	10.00
255	Greg Maddux	25.00
256	Dante Bichette	3.00
257	Brady Anderson	2.00
258	Craig Biggio	2.00
259	Derek Jeter	25.00
260	Roger Clemens	20.00
261	Roberto Alomar	8.00
262	Wade Boggs	4.00
263	Charles Johnson	2.00
264	Mark Grace	3.00
265	Kenny Lofton	10.00
266	Mike Mussina	8.00
267	Pedro J. Martinez	8.00
268	Curt Schilling	2.00
269	Bernie Williams	6.00
270	Tony Gwynn	20.00

1998 Upper Deck UD 3 Die-Cut

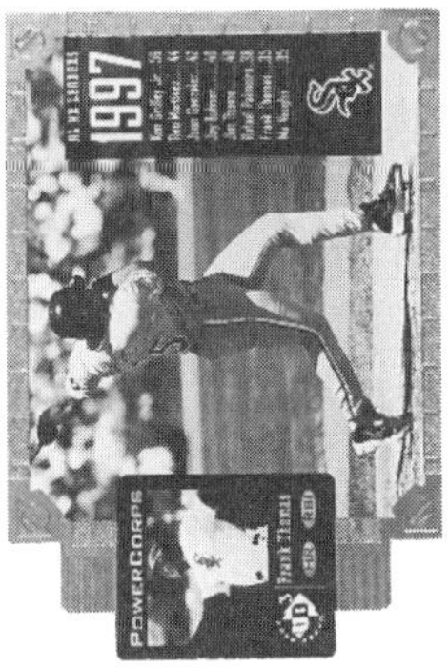

Die-cut versions of all 270 cards in UD 3 were available and sequentially numbered. FX subset cards (1-90) were numbered to 2,000 sets, Embossed cards (91-180) were numbered to 1,000 and Rainbow foil cards (181-270) were numbered to 100.

	MT
Future Impacts (1-30):	1x to 1.5x
Production 2,000 sets	
Power Corps (31-60):	3x to 4x
Production 2,000 sets	
Establishment (61-90):	2x to 3x
Production 2,000 sets	
Future Impact (91-120):	3x to 5x
Production 1,000 sets	
Power Corps (121-150):	6x to 10x
Production 1,000 sets	
Establishment (151-180):	12x to 20x
Production 1,000 sets	
Future Impact (181-210):	25x to 40x
Production 100 sets	
Power Corps (211-240):	8x to 15x
Production 100 sets	
Establishment (241-270):	5x to 8x
Production 100 sets	

1998 Upper Deck Special F/X

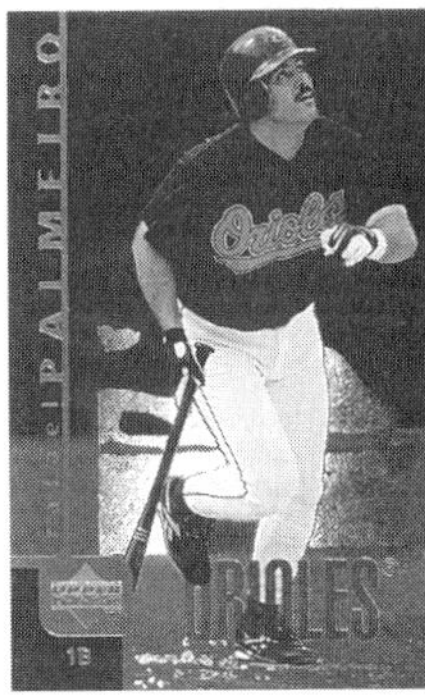

Special F/X is a retail-only product. The 150-card set consists of 125 regular cards, the 15-card Star Rookies subset and a 10-card subset called Ken Griffey Jr.'s Hot List. The base cards are printed on 20-point stock. The only insert is Power Zone which has four levels: Level One, Level Two - Octoberbest, Level Three - Power Driven and Level Four - Superstar Xcitement.

		MT
Complete Set (150):		50.00
Common Player:		.25
Unlisted Stars: .75 to 1.00		
1	Ken Griffey Jr. (Griffey Hot List)	5.00
2	Mark McGwire (Griffey Hot List)	3.00
3	Alex Rodriguez (Griffey Hot List)	3.00
4	Larry Walker (Griffey Hot List)	.75
5	Tino Martinez (Griffey Hot List)	.75
6	Mike Piazza (Griffey Hot List)	3.00
7	Jose Cruz Jr. (Griffey Hot List)	1.00
8	Greg Maddux (Griffey Hot List)	3.00
9	Tony Gwynn (Griffey Hot List)	2.50
10	Roger Clemens (Griffey Hot List)	2.00
11	Jason Dickson	.25
12	Darin Erstad	1.50
13	Chuck Finley	.25
14	Dave Hollins	.25
15	Garret Anderson	.25
16	Michael Tucker	.25
17	Javier Lopez	.40
18	John Smoltz	.40
19	Mark Wohlers	.25
20	Greg Maddux	3.00
21	Scott Erickson	.25
22	Jimmy Key	.25
23	B.J. Surhoff	.25
24	Eric Davis	.25
25	Rafael Palmeiro	.50
26	Tim Naehring	.25
27	Darren Bragg	.25
28	Troy O'Leary	.25
29	John Valentin	.25
30	Mo Vaughn	1.50
31	Mark Grace	.75
32	Kevin Foster	.25
33	Kevin Tapani	.25
34	Kevin Orie	.25
35	Albert Belle	1.50
36	Ray Durham	.25
37	Jaime Navarro	.25
38	Mike Cameron	.25
39	Eddie Taubensee	.25
40	Barry Larkin	.75
41	Willie Greene	.25
42	Jeff Shaw	.25
43	Omar Vizquel	.25
44	Brian Giles	.25
45	Jim Thome	1.00
46	David Justice	.75
47	Sandy Alomar Jr.	.50
48	Neifi Perez	.25
49	Dante Bichette	.50
50	Vinny Castilla	.50
51	John Thomson	.25
52	Damion Easley	.25
53	Justin Thompson	.25
54	Bobby Higginson	.25
55	Tony Clark	1.00
56	Charles Johnson	.25
57	Edgar Renteria	.25
58	Alex Fernandez	.25
59	Gary Sheffield	.75
60	Livan Hernandez	.25

61	Craig Biggio	.75
62	Chris Holt	.25
63	Billy Wagner	.25
64	Brad Ausmus	.25
65	Dean Palmer	.25
66	Tim Belcher	.25
67	Jeff King	.25
68	Jose Rosado	.25
69	Chan Ho Park	.75
70	Raul Mondesi	.50
71	Hideo Nomo	1.00
72	Todd Zeile	.25
73	Eric Karros	.40
74	Cal Eldred	.25
75	Jeff D'Amico	.25
76	Doug Jones	.25
77	Dave Nilsson	.25
78	Todd Walker	.25
79	Rick Aguilera	.25
80	Paul Molitor	1.00
81	Brad Radke	.25
82	Vladimir Guerrero	1.50
83	Carlos Perez	.25
84	F.P. Santangelo	.25
85	Rondell White	.40
86	Butch Huskey	.25
87	Edgardo Alfonzo	.25
88	John Franco	.25
89	John Olerud	.40
90	Todd Hundley	.25
91	Bernie Williams	1.00
92	Andy Pettitte	1.00
93	Paul O'Neill	.50
94	David Cone	.40
95	Jason Giambi	.25
96	Damon Mashore	.25
97	Scott Spiezio	.25
98	Ariel Prieto	.25
99	Rico Brogna	.25
100	Mike Lieberthal	.25
101	Garrett Stephenson	.25
102	Ricky Bottalico	.25
103	Kevin Polcovich	.25
104	Jon Lieber	.25
105	Kevin Young	.25
106	Tony Womack	.25
107	Gary Gaetti	.25
108	Alan Benes	.50
109	Willie McGee	.25
110	Mark McGwire	3.00
111	Ron Gant	.40
112	Andy Ashby	.25
113	Steve Finley	.25
114	Quilvio Veras	.25
115	Ken Caminiti	.50
116	Joey Hamilton	.25
117	Bill Mueller	.25
118	Mark Gardner	.25
119	Shawn Estes	.25
120	J.T. Snow	.25
121	Dante Powell	.25
122	Jeff Kent	.25
123	Jamie Moyer	.25
124	Joey Cora	.25
125	Ken Griffey Jr.	5.00
126	Jeff Fassero	.25
127	Edgar Martinez	.40
128	Will Clark	.50
129	Lee Stevens	.25
130	Ivan Rodriguez	1.50
131	Rusty Greer	.50
132	Ed Sprague	.25
133	Pat Hentgen	.25
134	Shannon Stewart	.25
135	Carlos Delgado	.40
136	Brett Tomko (Star Rookie)	.25
137	Jose Guillen (Star Rookie)	.50
138	Elieser Marrero (Star Rookie)	.25
139	Dennis Reyes (Star Rookie)	.25
140	Mark Kotsay (Star Rookie)	.75
141	Richie Sexson (Star Rookie)	.25
142	Todd Helton (Star Rookie)	1.50
143	Jeremi Gonzalez (Star Rookie)	.25
144	Jeff Abbott (Star Rookie)	.25
145	Matt Morris (Star Rookie)	.25
146	Aaron Boone (Star Rookie)	.25
147	Todd Dunwoody (Star Rookie)	.25
148	Mario Valdez (Star Rookie)	.25
149	Fernando Tatis (Star Rookie)	.25
150	Jaret Wright (Star Rookie)	2.00

1998 Upper Deck Special F/X OctoberBest

OctoberBest is Level Two of the Power Zone insert. This 20-card insert is die-cut and printed on silver foil. Inserted one per 34 packs, the set features the postseason exploits of 20 players from Power Zone Level One.

		MT
Complete Set (15):		160.00
Common Player:		4.00
Inserted 1:34		
PZ1	Frank Thomas	25.00
PZ2	Juan Gonzalez	15.00
PZ3	Mike Piazza	20.00
PZ4	Mark McGwire	40.00
PZ5	Jeff Bagwell	12.00
PZ6	Barry Bonds	8.00
PZ7	Ken Griffey Jr.	30.00
PZ8	John Smoltz	4.00
PZ9	Andruw Jones	8.00
PZ10	Greg Maddux	20.00
PZ11	Sandy Alomar Jr.	4.00
PZ12	Roberto Alomar	6.00
PZ13	Chipper Jones	20.00
PZ14	Kenny Lofton	8.00
PZ15	Tom Glavine	4.00

1998 Upper Deck Special F/X Power Driven

Power Driven is Level Three of the Power Zone insert. Inserted 1:69, the set features the top 10 power hitters from Power Zone Level Two. The cards feature gold Light F/X.

		MT
Complete Set (10):		150.00
Common Player:		6.00
Inserted 1:69		
PZ1	Frank Thomas	30.00
PZ2	Juan Gonzalez	20.00
PZ3	Mike Piazza	25.00
PZ4	Larry Walker	6.00
PZ5	Mark McGwire	50.00
PZ6	Jeff Bagwell	15.00
PZ7	Mo Vaughn	10.00
PZ8	Barry Bonds	10.00
PZ9	Tino Martinez	6.00
PZ10	Ken Griffey Jr.	40.00

1998 Upper Deck Special F/X Power Zone

Power Zone Level One is a 30-card insert seeded one per seven packs. The cards are printed using silver Light F/X technology.

		MT
Complete Set (20):		50.00
Common Player:		.75
Inserted 1:7		
PZ1	Jose Cruz Jr.	2.00
PZ2	Frank Thomas	8.00
PZ3	Juan Gonzalez	5.00
PZ4	Mike Piazza	6.00
PZ5	Mark McGwire	12.00
PZ6	Barry Bonds	2.50
PZ7	Greg Maddux	6.00
PZ8	Alex Rodriguez	6.00
PZ9	Nomar Garciaparra	6.00
PZ10	Ken Griffey Jr.	10.00
PZ11	John Smoltz	.75
PZ12	Andruw Jones	2.50
PZ13	Sandy Alomar Jr.	.75
PZ14	Roberto Alomar	2.00
PZ15	Chipper Jones	6.00
PZ16	Kenny Lofton	2.50
PZ17	Larry Walker	1.50
PZ18	Jeff Bagwell	4.00
PZ19	Mo Vaughn	2.50
PZ20	Tom Glavine	.75

1998 Upper Deck Special F/X Superstar Xcitement

Printed on Light F/X gold foil, this 10-card set features the same players as the Power Driven insert. This set is Power Zone Level Four and is sequentially numbered to 250.

		MT
Complete Set (10):		1000.
Common Player:		20.00
Production 250 sets		
PZ1	Jose Cruz Jr.	40.00
PZ2	Frank Thomas	150.00
PZ3	Juan Gonzalez	100.00
PZ4	Mike Piazza	120.00
PZ5	Mark McGwire	220.00
PZ6	Barry Bonds	50.00
PZ7	Greg Maddux	120.00
PZ8	Alex Rodriguez	120.00
PZ9	Nomar Garciaparra	120.00
PZ10	Ken Griffey Jr.	200.00

Basketball Market Report

The Basketball Card Market Faces A Tough Battle Even After The Lockout Is Settled

As Yogi Berra once said, "It's deja vu all over again."

Haven't sports fans seen this labor war before? Haven't sports fans been held hostage by lawyers in suits representing greedy owners against greedy players before? It seems all too familiar and yet all too silly.

The lockout has wiped out the first two months of the NBA season and was threatening the season altogether by presstime. The game's popularity was at an all-time high before the lockout, but now most sports fans could care less if the season is saved or not. It's gotten to that point.

Unfortunately, the labor dispute has long arms and the fallout has reached all the way to the basketball card market. Baseball card sales fell 45 percent the year after the baseball strike ended in 1995 and this lockout could have the same effect on basketball card sales. Sales of early season releases were down 25 percent from a year ago, prompting some companies to make lineup changes.

Fleer/SkyBox was scheduled to release Ultra in late November,

but that rookie-driven set has been postponed until the lockout is resolved. The card manufacturers can't picture any of the rookies until they sign contracts, so look for Ultra to be released once the rookies are signed.

Upper Deck became the first company to cancel a product due to the lockout. UD3 was scheduled for a late November release with 23 Michael Jordan-signed, game-used jersey cards, but the project was scrapped altogether once the labor war carried into the regular season.

"Fewer products eliminates confusion for the collector overall," said Richard McWilliam, CEO of Upper Deck. "A limited number of products enables collectors to focus their efforts on products which truly excite them and offer something special."

The 23 Jordan Autographed Game Jerseys that were scheduled for UD3 will be added to a 1999 product, most likely Upper Deck II, which is slated for a Feb. 19 release. The lockout has taken some of the lustre off this insert set that carries into all of Upper Deck's 1998-99 products, but not enough to discourage UD officials.

"When the lockout was first talked about, it was our plan to combat the lockout by spicing up each one of our products with 23 Michael Jordan Autographed Game Jersey cards," said Terry Melia, media relations manager for Upper Deck. "We still believe it's a great incentive for our products, but no doubt the lockout has hurt."

That's an understatement, indeed. The lockout has hurt every manufacturer and it will be interesting to see if the NBA helps its licensees if the lockout substantially interrupts the season. The three licensees – Topps, Upper Deck and Fleer/SkyBox – can't afford another repeat of what happened after the baseball strike.

"We learned during the 1994 Major League Baseball strike that it can take years for the category to recover from a situation like this," said Ruby Randall, VP/marketing at Upper Deck. "The NBA's support and cooperation is vital to our efforts to minimize the immediate impact and rebuild interest in the sports and players."

No matter how this plays out, it will take a long time for the league to win back its fans – which is bad news for our industry.

BASKETBALL

1997-98 Bowman's Best

Bowman's Best consisted of 125 cards including 90 current stars printed on a gold design, 25 draft picks printed on a silver design and 10 Bowman's Best Performers printed on gold, borderless cards. Card backs are horizontal with a closeup of the player on the left and stats on the right. Inserts include: Best Techniques, Best Cuts, Mirror Image and Best Picks. Every card in the regular set and inserts is available in both a Refractor and Atomic Refractor version.

		MT
Complete Set (125):		80.00
Common Player:		.20
Wax Box:		175.00
1	Scottie Pippen	1.50
2	Michael Finley	.40
3	David Wesley	.20
4	Brent Barry	.20
5	Gary Payton	.75
6	Christian Laettner	.40
7	Grant Hill	3.00
8	Glenn Robinson	.40
9	Reggie Miller	.40
10	Tyus Edney	.20
11	Jim Jackson	.20
12	John Stockton	.50
13	Karl Malone	.50
14	Samaki Walker	.20
15	Bryant Stith	.20
16	Clyde Drexler	.50
17	Danny Ferry	.20
18	Shawn Bradley	.20
19	Bryant Reeves	.20
20	John Starks	.20
21	Joe Dumars	.20
22	Latrell Sprewell	.40
23	Antonio McDyess	.50
24	Jeff Hornacek	.20
25	Terrell Brandon	.40
26	Kendall Gill	.20
27	LaPhonso Ellis	.20
28	Shaquille O'Neal	2.00
29	Mahmoud Abdul-Rauf	.20
30	Eric Williams	.20
31	Lorenzen Wright	.20
32	Shareef Abdur-Rahim	1.50
33	Avery Johnson	.20
34	Juwan Howard	.50
35	Vin Baker	.50
36	Dikembe Mutombo	.40
37	Patrick Ewing	.40
38	Allen Iverson	2.50
39	Alonzo Mourning	.40
40	Travis Knight	.20
41	Ray Allen	.75
42	Detlef Schrempf	.20
43	Kevin Johnson	.20
44	David Robinson	.75
45	Tim Hardaway	.40
46	Shawn Kemp	1.50
47	Marcus Camby	.50
48	Rony Seikaly	.20
49	Eddie Jones	.50
50	Rik Smits	.20
51	Jayson Williams	.20
52	Malik Sealy	.20
53	Chris Mullin	.20
54	Larry Johnson	.40
55	Isaiah Rider	.20
56	Dennis Rodman	1.75
57	Bob Sura	.20
58	Hakeem Olajuwon	1.00
59	Steve Smith	.20
60	Michael Jordan	6.00
61	Jerry Stackhouse	.50
62	Joe Smith	.50
63	Walt Williams	.20
64	Anthony Peeler	.20
65	Charles Barkley	.75
66	Erick Dampier	.40
67	Horace Grant	.20
68	Anthony Mason	.20
69	Anfernee Hardaway	2.00
70	Elden Campbell	.20
71	Cedric Ceballos	.20
72	Allan Houston	.20
73	Kerry Kittles	.20
74	Antoine Walker	2.50
75	Sean Elliott	.20
76	Jamal Mashburn	.40
77	Mitch Richmond	.40
78	Damon Stoudamire	.75
79	Tom Gugliotta	.20
80	Jason Kidd	.75
81	Chris Webber	1.00
82	Glen Rice	.40
83	Loy Vaught	.20
84	Olden Polynice	.20
85	Kenny Anderson	.20
86	Stephon Marbury	2.50
87	Calbert Cheaney	.20
88	Kobe Bryant	4.00
89	Arvydas Sabonis	.20
90	Kevin Garnett	3.00
91	Grant Hill BP	1.50
92	Clyde Drexler BP	.20
93	Patrick Ewing BP	.20
94	Shawn Kemp BP	.75
95	Shaquille O'Neal BP	1.00
96	Michael Jordan BP	3.00
97	Karl Malone BP	.20
98	Allen Iverson BP	1.25
99	Shareef Abdur-Rahim BP	.75
100	Dikembe Mutombo BP	.20
101	*Bobby Jackson*	5.00
102	*Tony Battie*	3.00
103	*Keith Booth*	.40
104	*Keith Van Horn*	20.00
105	*Paul Grant*	1.00
106	*Tim Duncan*	25.00
107	*Scot Pollard*	.40
108	*Maurice Taylor*	3.00
109	*Antonio Daniels*	5.00
110	*Austin Croshere*	1.50
111	*Tracy McGrady*	7.00
112	*Charles O'Bannon*	.40
113	*Rodrick Rhodes*	2.00
114	*Johnny Taylor*	.40
115	*Danny Fortson*	1.00
116	*Chauncey Billups*	6.00
117	*Tim Thomas*	7.00
118	*Derek Anderson*	6.00
119	*Ed Gray*	.40
120	*Jacque Vaughn*	1.50
121	*Kelvin Cato*	1.00
122	*Tariq Abdul-Wahad*	1.50
123	*Ron Mercer*	10.00
124	*Brevin Knight*	6.00
125	*Adonal Foyle*	1.50

1997-98 Bowman's Best Refractors

Refractors versions of all 125 cards were produced and inserted one per 12 packs. Cards featured a holographic rainbow look to the card front and the word "Refractor" was typed on the back near the card number.

	MT
Refractor Stars:	6x-12x
Refractor Rookies:	2x-4x

1997-98 Bowman's Best Atomic Refractors

Atomic Refrators paralleled all 125 cards in Bowman's Best. These prismatic Refractors cards were inserted one per 24 packs and the words "Atomic Refractor" were typed on the back by the card number.

	MT
Atomic Refractor Stars:	15x-30x
Atomic Refractor Rookies:	5x-10x

1997-98 Bowman's Best Autographs

Five gold veterans and five silver rookies signed cards, along with a special Karl Malone MVP card were signed and inserted into Bowman's Best packs. Each card arrived with a Topps "Certified Autograph Issue" stamp, with regular versions seeded one per 373 packs, Refractors seeded one per 1,987 packs and Atomic Refractor versions seeded one per 5,961 packs.

		MT
Complete Set (11):		700.00
Common Player:		25.00
Inserted 1:373		
Refractors:		2x
Inserted 1:1,987		
Atomic Refractors:		3x
Inserted 1:5,961		
8	Glenn Robinson	50.00
13	Karl Malone	75.00
36	Dikembe Mutombo	25.00
59	Steve Smith	25.00
77	Mitch Richmond	50.00
102	Tony Battie	50.00
104	Keith Van Horn	200.00
116	Chauncey Billups	75.00
123	Ron Mercer	125.00
125	Adonal Foyle	25.00
KM	Karl Malone (MVP)	100.00

1997-98 Bowman's Best Cuts

Best Cuts was a 10-card insert set featuring intricate laser cutting and a psychadelic square pattern on the front. Backs were numbered with a "BC" prefix and were yellow with a similar square pattern. Regular versions were seeded one per 24 packs, Refractors were seeded every 48 packs and Atomic Refractors were inserted every 96 packs.

	MT
Complete Set (10):	50.00
Common Player:	1.00

1997-98 Bowman's Best Mirror Image

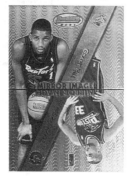

Mirror Image was a 10-card insert that showcased the top four players at each position, two from each conference all on one double-sided card. Fronts were split diagonally by a wide strip that included both players' names, while backs were numbered with a "M" prefix. Regular versions were seeded one per 48 packs, Refractors one per 96 and Atomic Refractors every 192 packs.

		MT
Complete Set (10):		150.00
Common Player:		5.00
Refractors:		1x-2x
Atomic Refractors:		2x-4x
M1	Michael Jordan, Ron Mercer, Stephon Marbury, Gary Payton	50.00
M2	Tim Thomas, Chris Webber, Shaquille O'Neal, Adonal Foyle	20.00
M3	Tim Hardaway, Allen Iverson, Bobby Jackson, Jason Kidd	20.00
M4	Scottie Pippen, Keith Van Horn, Kobe Bryant, Cedric Ceballos	30.00
M5	Grant Hill, Tracy McGrady, Shareef Abdur Rahim, Kevin Garnett	30.00
M6	Shawn Kemp, Marcus Camby, Tim Duncan, David Robinson	25.00
M7	Ray Allen, Steve Smith, Shandon Anderson, Sean Elliott	5.00
M8	Chauncey Billups, Terrell Brandon, Antonio Daniels, Kevin Johnson	15.00
M9	Kerry Kittles, Reggie Miller, Tony Battie, Hakeem Olajuwon	5.00
M10	Larry Johnson, Antoine Walker, Maurice Taylor, Vin Baker	15.00

	MT
Refractors:	1x-2x
Atomic Refractors:	2x-4x
BC1	Vin Baker	3.00
BC2	Patrick Ewing	1.00
BC3	Scottie Pippen	7.00
BC4	Karl Malone	3.00
BC5	Kevin Garnett	14.00
BC6	Anfernee Hardaway	10.00
BC7	Shawn Kemp	7.00
BC8	Charles Barkley	3.00
BC9	Stephon Marbury	14.00
BC10	Shaquille O'Neal	10.00

1997-98 Bowman's Best Picks

Best Picks are printd on a similar background as the Best Cuts with intricate laser-cutting and a psychadelic background. This 10-card insert set featured top picks from the 1997 NBA Draft and was numbered with a "BP" prefix.

		MT
Complete Set (10):		60.00
Common Player:		1.00
Refractors:		1x-2x
Atomic Refractors:		2x-4x
BP1	Adonal Foyle	1.00
BP2	Maurice Taylor	3.00
BP3	Austin Croshere	1.00
BP4	Tracy McGrady	7.00
BP5	Antonio Daniels	5.00
BP6	Tony Battie	3.00
BP7	Chauncey Billups	6.00
BP8	Tim Duncan	20.00
BP9	Ron Mercer	10.00
BP10	Keith Van Horn	20.00

1997-98 Bowman's Best Techniques

This 10-card insert set captured players over a spiral, foil background. The cards were numbered with a "T" prefix, with regular versions seeded one per 12 packs, Refractors every 48 packs and Atomic Refractors every 96 packs.

		MT
Complete Set (10):		60.00
Common Player:		2.50
Refractors:		1x-2x
Atomic Refractors:		2x-4x
T1	Dikembe Mutombo	2.50
T2	Michael Jordan	20.00
T3	Grant Hill	10.00
T4	Kobe Bryant	14.00
T5	Gary Payton	3.00
T6	Glen Rice	2.50

T7	Dennis Rodman	7.00
T8	Hakeem Olajuwon	4.00
T9	Allen Iverson	8.00
T10	John Stockton	2.50

1997 Collector's Edge Promos

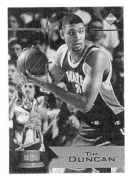

This six-card set was distributed to promote Collector's Edge Impulse Basketball in 1997. The cards similar to the base cards, but are numbered "of 6" with the word "Promo" printed above it.

		MT
Complete Set (6):		7.00
Common Player:		.50
1	Tim Duncan	2.00
2	Scottie Pippen	1.00
3	Ron Mercer	1.00
4	Keith Van Horn	1.50
5	Antonio Daniels	.50
6	Kobe Bryant	2.50

1997 Collector's Edge Impulse

The 45-card set appeared in three versions, including base cards, Die-Cut Parallel (1:1 pack) and Impulse Metal Parallel (1:1). The base cards have a full-bleed photo on the front, with a gold-foil pulse line at the top. The Edge Impulse "award" logo is in the lower left. The player's name is printed inside a gold-foil banner in the lower right. The backs have the player's name and bio printed in the upper left. The card number is printed inside a red diamond in the upper right, while his stats and highlights are printed at the bottom. All the information is printed over a full-bleed photo of the player. The Die-Cut Parallel has the photo superimposed over a basketball at the top and a purple and white "groovy" mixture of colors beneath it. The player's name and draft pick status are printed inside a silver foil banner at the bottom of the front. The backs include the player's photo inside a basketball at the top, along with his name. His bio, stats and highlights are printed inside a rectangle

at the bottom of the card back. The Metal Parallel has a player photo superimposed over a foil background of a basketball. The player's name and draft status are printed inside a gold-foil banner at the bottom. The card backs are identical to the base card's.

		MT
Complete Set (45):		15.00
Common Player:		.10
Die-Cut Cards:		1.5x
Metal Cards:		1.5x
Wax Box:		60.00
1	Tim Duncan	3.00
2	Keith Van Horn	1.50
3	Kebu Stewart	.20
4	Antonio Daniels	1.00
5	Tony Battie	1.25
6	Ron Mercer	1.50
7	Tim Thomas	.75
8	Adonal Foyle	.75
9	Chauncey Billups	1.25
10	Danny Fortson	.75
11	Austin Croshere	.50
12	Derek Anderson	.75
13	Antoine Walker	.50
14	Kobe Bryant	1.00
15	Shareef Abdur-Rahim	.50
16	Stephon Marbury	.75
17	Scottie Pippen	.30
18	Kelvin Cato	.75
19	Scot Pollard	.20
20	Paul Grant	.10
21	Anthony Parker	.10
22	Ed Gray	.10
23	Bobby Jackson	.50
24	John Thomas	.10
25	Charles Smith	.20
26	Jacque Vaughn	.50
27	Keith Booth	.10
28	Charles O'Bannon	.50
29	James Collins	.10
30	Marc Jackson	.10
31	Anthony Johnson	.10
32	Jason Lawson	.10
33	Alvin Williams	.10
34	DeJuan Wheat	.10
35	Nate Erdmann	.10
36	Olivier Saint-Jean	1.00
37	Serge Zwikker	.10
38	Antoine Walker	.50
39	Kobe Bryant	1.00
40	Shareef Abdur-Rahim	.50
41	Stephon Marbury	.75
42	Scottie Pippen	.30
43	Checklist 1	.10
44	Checklist 2	.10
45	Checklist 3	.10

1997 Collector's Edge Air Apparent

Inserted 1:72 packs, the 15-card set features two players on both the front and back of the cards. "Air Apparent" is printed at the top, while the player's name appears vertically along the left border. Both photos are superimposed over a basketball background. The card number is printed in the upper left inside a red diamond.

		MT
Complete Set (16):		150.00
Common Player:		8.00
1	Duncan, Pippen	40.00
2	Van Horn, Bryant	30.00
3	Saint-Jean, Abdur-Rahim	8.00
4	Daniels, Marbury	15.00
5	Battie, Pippen	10.00
6	Mercer, Marbury	15.00
7	T. Thomas, Bryant	15.00
8	Foyle, Abdur-Rahim	8.00

9	Billups, Marbury	15.00
10	Fortson, Pippen	10.00
11	Walker, A. Walker	8.00
12	Anderson, Bryant	15.00
13	Cato, Abdur-Rahim	8.00
14	A. Walker, A. Walker	8.00
15	A. Walker, Walker	8.00
NNO	Checklist	8.00

1997 Collector's Edge Energy

Danny Fortson

Inserted 1:12 packs, the 25-card set features a player photo superimposed over a motion background of a backboard being shattered by a basketball. The player's name is printed inside a yellow stripe at the bottom of the front. The backs have the card number in the upper right. The player photo dominates the back, with his name and bio printed in the lower left. "Edge Energy" appears in the lower right.

		MT
Complete Set (13):		30.00
Common Player:		.50
1	Antonio Daniels	4.00
2	Austin Croshere	3.00
3	Charles O'Bannon	.50
4	Scot Pollard	.50
5	Paul Grant	.50
6	Danny Fortson	2.00
7	Keith Van Horn	6.00
8	Kelvin Cato	2.00
9	Ron Mercer	5.00
10	Tim Duncan	8.00
11	Tim Thomas	3.00
12	Chauncey Billups	3.00
NNO	Checklist	.50

1997 Collector's Edge Extra

Inserted 1:48 packs, the 12-card set has a photo of the player "coming out" of a newspaper design background on the front. The player's name and his draft status are printed beneath the player photo in the lower left. The backs have "Edge Sports" printed at the top, with a photo, the player's name, bio, highlights and card number rounding out the back.

		MT
Complete Set (13):		100.00
Common Player:		1.50
1	Tim Duncan	25.00
2	Keith Van Horn	18.00

3	Olivier Saint-Jean	6.00
4	Antonio Daniels	12.00
5	Tony Battie	8.00
6	Ron Mercer	15.00
7	Tim Thomas	8.00
8	Antoine Walker	1.50
9	Kobe Bryant	15.00
10	Shareef Abdur-Rahim	1.50
11	Stephon Marbury	10.00
12	Scottie Pippen	8.00
NNO	Checklist	1.50

1997 Collector's Edge Game-Used Ball

Inserted 1:36 packs, the five-card set boasts a circular piece of a game-used basketball on the front. The player photo is printed over a basketball floor background. "Authentic game-used ball" is printed at the top. The player's name is printed at the bottom center below a pulse line.

		MT
Complete Set (5):		90.00
Common Player:		15.00
1	Antoine Walker	15.00
2	Kobe Bryant	30.00
3	Shareef Abdur-Rahim	15.00
4	Stephon Marbury	25.00
5	Scottie Pippen	20.00

1997 Collector's Edge Hardcourt Force

Inserted 1:36 packs, the 25-card set features a player photo superimposed over a parquet floor background. "Hard Court Force" is printed vertically along the left border. The player's name, position and draft status are printed at the bottom center inside a basketball floor design. The card back has a player photo inside a basketball at the top center of the back. The card number is inside a red diamond in the upper right. The player's name and bio are printed at the bottom center of the backs.

		MT
Complete Set (25):		200.00
Common Player:		2.00
1	Chauncey Billups	15.00
2	Tony Battie	15.00
3	Tim Duncan	30.00
4	Paul Grant	2.00
5	John Thomas	2.00
6	Scottie Pippen	8.00
7	Scot Pollard	2.00
8	Ron Mercer	20.00
9	Tim Thomas	10.00
10	Kobe Bryant	15.00
11	Antonio Daniels	10.00
12	Kelvin Cato	10.00
13	Danny Fortson	8.00
14	Ed Gray	2.00
15	Derek Anderson	10.00
16	Bobby Jackson	8.00
17	Antoine Walker	10.00
18	Anthony Parker	2.00
19	Shareef Abdur-Rahim	10.00
20	Olivier Saint-Jean	6.00
21	Stephon Marbury	12.00
22	Keith Van Horn	20.00
23	Austin Croshere	6.00
24	Adonal Foyle	6.00
25	Serge Zwikker	2.00

1997 Collector's Edge Swoosh

TIM DUNCAN

Inserted 1:24 packs, the 12-card set features a player photo superimposed over a background of basketballs on the front of the acetate cards. "Swoosh" is printed vertically along the left border of the front. The player's name appears at the bottom center of the front. The backs have the card number in the upper left inside a red diamond. The player's name and bio is printed at the bottom center of the backs.

		MT
Complete Set (13):		50.00
Common Player:		.75
1	Adonal Foyle	.75
2	Keith Booth	.75
3	Danny Fortson	3.00
4	Derek Anderson	4.00
5	Jacque Vaughn	3.00
6	Keith Van Horn	10.00
7	Kelvin Cato	4.00
8	Ron Mercer	8.00
9	Tim Duncan	15.00
10	Tony Battie	5.00
11	Chauncey Billups	6.00
12	Charles O'Bannon	2.00
13	Checklist	.75

1997-98 Finest Promos

Allen Iverson

This six-card set was issued to dealers and members of the media to promote the 1997-98 Finest set. The cards were exactly like regular-issue cards except the words "Promotional Sample Not For Resale" printed in red letters across the back.

		MT
Complete Set (6):		7.00
Common Player:		.50
27	Chris Webber	1.00
45	Vin Baker	1.00
57	Allen Iverson	2.50
67	Eddie Jones	2.00
68	Joe Smith	.50
80	Gary Payton	1.00

1997-98 Finest

Finest Basketball was released in two series and contained 326 cards in 1997-98.

The first series had 173 cards, with commons 1-120 (101-120 was a 1997 NBA Draft Picks subset), 121-153 uncommons (1:4 packs) and 154-173 rare (1:24 packs). Themed subsets included Debuts, BallHawks, Catalysts, Finishers, Force and Masters. Series II had 153 cards, with 174-273 commons, 274-306 uncommons (1:4) and 307-326 rares (1:24). Themed subsets in Series II included Showstoppers, Masters, Creators, Defenders and Arrivals. While commons were only paralleled in Refractor versions, all uncommons were paralleled in both Refractors and embossed versions, while rares were paralleled in both Refractors and die-cut embossed versions. Cards are numbered within the set and within each theme.

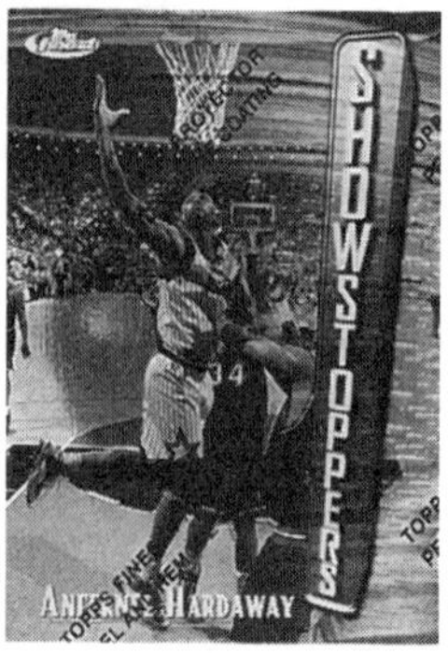

		MT
	Complete Set (326):	975.00
	Complete Bronze 1 (120):	120.00
	Complete Bronze 2 (100):	40.00
	Common Bronze Player:	.25
	Complete Silver 1 (33):	100.00
	Complete Silver 2 (33):	100.00
	Common Silver Player:	1.00
	Complete Gold 1 (20):	225.00
	Complete Gold 2 (20):	400.00
	Common Gold Player:	5.00
	Series 1 Wax Box:	220.00
	Series 2 Wax Box:	120.00
1	Scottie Pippen	2.00
2	Tim Hardaway	.50
3	Charles Outlaw	.25
4	Rik Smits	.25
5	Dale Ellis	.25
6	Clyde Drexler	.75
7	Steve Smith	.25
8	Nick Anderson	.25
9	Juwan Howard	1.00
10	Cedric Ceballos	.25
11	Shawn Bradley	.50
12	Loy Vaught	.25
13	Todd Day	.25
14	Glen Rice	.50
15	Bryant Stith	.25
16	Bob Sura	.25
17	Derrick McKey	.25
18	Ray Allen	1.00
19	Stephon Marbury	3.00
20	David Robinson	1.00
21	Anthony Peeler	.25
22	Isaiah Rider	.25
23	Mookie Blaylock	.25
24	Damon Stoudamire	1.00
25	Rod Strickland	.25
26	Glenn Robinson	.75
27	Chris Webber	1.25
28	Christian Laettner	.50
29	Joe Dumars	.25
30	Mark Price	.25
31	Jamal Mashburn	.50
32	Danny Manning	.25
33	John Stockton	.75
34	Detlef Schrempf	.25
35	Tyus Edney	.25
36	Chris Childs	.25
37	Dana Barros	.25
38	Bobby Phills	.25
39	Michael Jordan	8.00
40	Grant Hill	4.00
41	Brent Barry	.50
42	Rony Seikaly	.25
43	Shareef Abdur-Rahim	2.00
44	Dominique Wilkins	.25
45	Vin Baker	.75
46	Kendall Gill	.25
47	Muggsy Bogues	.25
48	Hakeem Olajuwon	1.50
49	Reggie Miller	.75
50	Shaquille O'Neal	3.00
51	Antonio McDyess	.50
52	Michael Finley	.50
53	Jerry Stackhouse	.75
54	Brian Grant	.25
55	Greg Anthony	.25
56	Patrick Ewing	.75
57	Allen Iverson	3.00
58	Rasheed Wallace	.25
59	Shawn Kemp	2.00
60	Bryant Reeves	.50
61	Kevin Garnett	4.00
62	Allan Houston	.50
63	Stacey Augmon	.25
64	Rick Fox	.25
65	Derek Harper	.25
66	Lindsey Hunter	.25
67	Eddie Jones	1.25
68	Joe Smith	.75
69	Alonzo Mourning	.50
70	LaPhonso Ellis	.25
71	Tyrone Hill	.25
72	Charles Barkley	1.00
73	Malik Sealy	.25
74	Shandon Anderson	.25
75	Arvydas Sabonis	.25
76	Tom Gugliotta	.50
77	Anfernee Hardaway	3.00
78	Sean Elliott	.25
79	Marcus Camby	1.75
80	Gary Payton	1.00
81	Kerry Kittles	1.00
82	Dikembe Mutombo	.50
83	Antoine Walker	3.00
84	Terrell Brandon	.50
85	Otis Thorpe	.25
86	Mark Jackson	.25
87	A.C. Green	.25
88	John Starks	.25
89	Kenny Anderson	.25
90	Karl Malone	1.00
91	Mitch Richmond	.50
92	Derrick Coleman	.25
93	Horace Grant	.25
94	John Williams	.25
95	Jason Kidd	1.00
96	Mahmoud Abdul-Rauf	.25
97	Walt Williams	.25
98	Anthony Mason	.25
99	Latrell Sprewell	.50
100	Checklist	.25
101	*Tim Duncan*	45.00
102	*Keith Van Horn*	30.00
103	*Chauncey Billups*	8.00
104	*Antonio Daniels*	5.00
105	*Tony Battie*	4.00
106	*Tim Thomas*	12.00
107	*Tracy McGrady*	10.00
108	*Adonal Foyle*	2.00
109	*Maurice Taylor*	8.00
110	*Austin Croshere*	2.00
111	*Bobby Jackson*	6.00
112	*Olivier Saint-Jean*	2.00
113	*John Thomas*	1.00
114	*Derek Anderson*	8.00
115	*Brevin Knight*	8.00
116	*Charles Smith*	1.00
117	*Johnny Taylor*	1.00
118	*Jacque Vaughn*	2.00
119	*Anthony Parker*	1.00
120	*Paul Grant*	1.00
121	Stephon Marbury S	12.00
122	Terrell Brandon S	2.00
123	Dikembe Mutombo S	1.00
124	Patrick Ewing S	2.00
125	Scottie Pippen S	6.00
126	Antoine Walker S	12.00
127	Karl Malone S	2.00
128	Sean Elliott S	1.00
129	Chris Webber S	4.00
130	Shawn Kemp S	6.00
131	Hakeem Olajuwon S	4.00
132	Tim Hardaway S	2.00
133	Glen Rice S	2.00
134	Vin Baker S	3.00
135	Jim Jackson S	1.00
136	Kevin Garnett S	12.00
137	Kobe Bryant S	20.00
138	Damon Stoudamire S	3.00
139	Larry Johnson S	2.00
140	Latrell Sprewell S	2.00
141	Lorenzen Wright S	1.00
142	Toni Kukoc S	2.00
143	Allen Iverson S	12.00
144	Elden Campbell S	1.00
145	Tom Gugliotta S	2.00
146	David Robinson S	3.00
147	Jayson Williams S	1.00
148	Shaquille O'Neal S	8.00
149	Grant Hill S	14.00
150	Reggie Miller S	2.00
151	Clyde Drexler S	3.00
152	Ray Allen S	4.00
153	Eddie Jones S	4.00
154	Michael Jordan G	90.00
155	Dominique Wilkins G	5.00
156	Charles Barkley G	15.00
157	Jerry Stackhouse G	10.00
158	Juwan Howard G	12.00
159	Marcus Camby G	12.00
160	Christian Laettner G	5.00
161	Anthony Mason G	5.00
162	Joe Smith G	10.00
163	Kerry Kittles G	10.00
164	Mitch Richmond G	10.00
165	Shareef Abdur-Rahim G	25.00
166	Alonzo Mourning G	10.00
167	Dennis Rodman G	30.00
168	Antonio McDyess G	10.00
169	Shawn Bradley G	5.00
170	Anfernee Hardaway G	30.00
171	Jason Kidd G	12.00
172	Gary Payton G	12.00
173	John Stockton G	10.00
174	Allan Houston	.50
175	Bob Sura	.25
176	Clyde Drexler	.75
177	Glenn Robinson	.75
178	Joe Smith	.75
179	Larry Johnson	.50
180	Mitch Richmond	.50
181	Rony Seikaly	.25
182	Tyrone Hill	.25
183	Allen Iverson	2.50
184	Brent Barry	.25
185	Damon Stoudamire	1.00
186	Grant Hill	3.00
187	John Stockton	.75
188	Latrell Sprewell	.50
189	Mookie Blaylock	.25
190	Samaki Walker	.25
191	Vin Baker	.75
192	Alonzo Mourning	.75
193	Brevin Knight	2.00
194	Danny Manning	.25
195	Hakeem Olajuwon	1.25
196	Johnny Taylor	.25
197	Lorenzen Wright	.25
198	Olden Polynice	.25
199	Scottie Pippen	1.50
200	Lindsey Hunter	.25
201	Anfernee Hardaway	2.50
202	Greg Anthony	.25
203	David Robinson	.75
204	Horace Grant	.25
205	Calbert Cheaney	.25
206	Loy Vaught	.25
207	Tariq Abdul-Wahad	.75
208	Sean Elliott	.25
209	Rodney Rogers	.25
210	Anthony Mason	.25
211	Bryant Reeves	.25
212	David Wesley	.25
213	Isaiah Rider	.25
214	Karl Malone	.75
215	Mahmoud Abdul-Rauf	.25
216	Patrick Ewing	.50
217	Shaquille O'Neal	2.00
218	Antoine Walker	2.50
219	Charles Barkley	.75
220	Dennis Rodman	2.00
221	Jamal Mashburn	.50
222	Kendall Gill	.25
223	Malik Sealy	.25
224	Rasheed Wallace	.25
225	Shareef Abdur-Rahim	1.50
226	Antonio Daniels	1.50
227	Charles Oakley	.25
228	Derek Anderson	2.00
229	Jason Kidd	.75
230	Kenny Anderson	.25
231	Marcus Camby	.75
232	Ray Allen	.75
233	Shawn Bradley	.25
234	Antonio McDyess	.75
235	Chauncey Billups	2.00
236	Detlef Schrempf	.25
237	Jayson Williams	.25
238	Kerry Kittles	.75
239	Jalen Rose	.25
240	Reggie Miller	.50
241	Shawn Kemp	1.50
242	Arvydas Sabonis	.25
243	Tom Gugliotta	.50
244	Dikembe Mutombo	.50
245	Jeff Hornacek	.25
246	Kevin Garnett	3.00
247	Matt Maloney	.25
248	Rex Chapman	.25
249	Stephon Marbury	2.50
250	Austin Croshere	.75
251	Chris Childs	.25
252	Eddie Jones	.75
253	Jerry Stackhouse	.75
254	Kevin Johnson	.50
255	Maurice Taylor	1.00
256	Chris Mullin	.50
257	Terrell Brandon	.50
258	Avery Johnson	.25
259	Chris Webber	1.00
260	Gary Payton	.75
261	Jim Jackson	.50
262	Kobe Bryant	4.00
263	Michael Finley	.50
264	Rod Strickland	.25
265	Tim Hardaway	.50
266	B.J. Armstrong	.25
267	Christian Laettner	.50
268	Glen Rice	.50
269	Joe Dumars	.25
270	LaPhonso Ellis	.25
271	Michael Jordan	6.00
272	*Ron Mercer*	20.00
273	Checklist	.25
274	Anfernee Hardaway S	8.00
275	Dennis Rodman S	8.00
276	Gary Payton S	3.00
277	Jamal Mashburn S	2.00
278	Shareef Abdur-Rahim S	8.00
279	Steve Smith S	1.00
280	Tony Battie S	3.00
281	Alonzo Mourning S	2.00
282	Bobby Jackson S	3.00
283	Christian Laettner S	2.00
284	Jerry Stackhouse S	2.00
285	Terrell Brandon S	2.00
286	Chauncey Billups S	5.00
287	Michael Jordan S	25.00
288	Glenn Robinson S	3.00
289	Jason Kidd S	3.00
290	Joe Smith S	2.00
291	Michael Finley S	2.00
292	Rod Strickland S	1.00
293	Ron Mercer S	10.00
294	Tracy McGrady S	8.00
295	Adonal Foyle S	3.00
296	Marcus Camby S	3.00
297	John Stockton S	3.00
298	Kerry Kittles S	3.00
299	Mitch Richmond S	2.00
300	Shawn Bradley S	1.00
301	Anthony Mason S	1.00
302	Antonio Daniels S	4.00
303	Antonio McDyess S	3.00
304	Charles Barkley S	3.00
305	Keith Van Horn S	12.00
306	Tim Duncan S	16.00
307	Dikembe Mutombo G	5.00
308	Grant Hill G	50.00
309	Shaquille O'Neal G	30.00
310	Keith Van Horn G	35.00
311	Shawn Kemp G	20.00
312	Antoine Walker G	35.00
313	Hakeem Olajuwon G	15.00
314	Vin Baker G	12.00
315	Patrick Ewing G	10.00
316	Tracy McGrady G	25.00
317	Glen Rice G	12.00
318	Reggie Miller G	12.00
319	Kevin Garnett G	50.00
320	Allen Iverson G	35.00
321	Karl Malone G	12.00
322	Scottie Pippen G	20.00
323	Kobe Bryant G	70.00
324	Stephon Marbury G	35.00
325	Tim Duncan G	50.00
326	Chris Webber G	15.00

1997-98 Finest Refractors

Refractor versions were made for all 326 cards in Finest Basketball. Common Refractors were seeded one per 12 packs, Uncommon Refractors were seeded 1:48 packs and rare Refractors were seeded 1:288 packs. Uncommon embossed Refractors were seeded 1:192 packs and rare embossed die-cut Refactors were inserted 1:1,152 packs. Regular uncommon Refractors were sequentially numbered to 1,090, uncommon ebossed Refractors were numbered to 192, rare Refractors were numbered to 289 and rare embossed die-cut Refractors were numbered to 74 sets. All Refractors are labeled on the card back near the number.

		MT
	Comp. Bronze 1 (120):	1500.
	Comp. Bronze 2 (100):	800.00
	Common Bronze Player:	3.00
	Complete Silver 1 (33):	400.00
	Complete Silver 2 (33):	400.00
	Common Silver Player:	4.00
	Complete Gold 1 (20):	1700.
	Complete Gold 2 (20):	2500.
	Common Gold Player:	30.00
1	Scottie Pippen	25.00
2	Tim Hardaway	6.00
3	Charles Outlaw	3.00
4	Rik Smits	3.00
5	Dale Ellis	3.00
6	Clyde Drexler	8.00
7	Steve Smith	3.00
8	Nick Anderson	3.00
9	Juwan Howard	8.00
10	Cedric Ceballos	3.00
11	Shawn Bradley	6.00
12	Loy Vaught	3.00
13	Todd Day	3.00
14	Glen Rice	8.00
15	Bryant Stith	3.00
16	Bob Sura	3.00
17	Derrick McKey	3.00
18	Ray Allen	10.00
19	Stephon Marbury	35.00
20	David Robinson	10.00
21	Anthony Peeler	3.00
22	Isaiah Rider	3.00
23	Mookie Blaylock	3.00
24	Damon Stoudamire	12.00
25	Rod Strickland	3.00
26	Glenn Robinson	6.00
27	Chris Webber	12.00
28	Christian Laettner	6.00
29	Joe Dumars	3.00
30	Mark Price	3.00
31	Jamal Mashburn	6.00
32	Danny Manning	3.00
33	John Stockton	8.00
34	Detlef Schrempf	3.00
35	Tyus Edney	3.00
36	Chris Childs	3.00
37	Dana Barros	3.00
38	Bobby Phills	3.00
39	Michael Jordan	90.00
40	Grant Hill	45.00
41	Brent Barry	6.00
42	Rony Seikaly	3.00
43	Shareef Abdur-Rahim	25.00
44	Dominique Wilkins	3.00
45	Vin Baker	10.00
46	Kendall Gill	3.00
47	Muggsy Bogues	3.00
48	Hakeem Olajuwon	15.00
49	Reggie Miller	8.00
50	Shaquille O'Neal	30.00
51	Antonio McDyess	8.00
52	Michael Finley	6.00
53	Jerry Stackhouse	6.00
54	Brian Grant	3.00
55	Greg Anthony	3.00
56	Patrick Ewing	8.00
57	Allen Iverson	35.00
58	Rasheed Wallace	3.00
59	Shawn Kemp	25.00
60	Bryant Reeves	6.00
61	Kevin Garnett	45.00
62	Allan Houston	6.00
63	Stacey Augmon	3.00
64	Rick Fox	3.00
65	Derek Harper	3.00
66	Lindsey Hunter	3.00
67	Eddie Jones	12.00
68	Joe Smith	6.00
69	Alonzo Mourning	6.00
70	LaPhonso Ellis	3.00
71	Tyrone Hill	3.00
72	Charles Barkley	10.00
73	Malik Sealy	3.00
74	Shandon Anderson	3.00
75	Arvydas Sabonis	3.00
76	Tom Gugliotta	6.00
77	Anfernee Hardaway	30.00
78	Sean Elliott	3.00
79	Marcus Camby	8.00
80	Gary Payton	10.00
81	Kerry Kittles	8.00
82	Dikembe Mutombo	6.00
83	Antoine Walker	35.00
84	Terrell Brandon	6.00
85	Otis Thorpe	3.00
86	Mark Jackson	3.00
87	A.C. Green	3.00
88	John Starks	3.00
89	Kenny Anderson	3.00
90	Karl Malone	8.00
91	Mitch Richmond	8.00
92	Derrick Coleman	3.00
93	Horace Grant	3.00
94	John Williams	3.00
95	Jason Kidd	12.00
96	Mahmoud Abdul-Rauf	3.00
97	Walt Williams	3.00
98	Anthony Mason	3.00
99	Latrell Sprewell	6.00
100	Checklist	3.00
101	Tim Duncan	220.00
102	Keith Van Horn	175.00
103	Chauncey Billups	70.00
104	Antonio Daniels	45.00
105	Tony Battie	35.00
106	Tim Thomas	75.00
107	Tracy McGrady	80.00
108	Adonal Foyle	20.00
109	Maurice Taylor	60.00
110	Austin Croshere	15.00
111	Bobby Jackson	50.00
112	Olivier Saint-Jean	20.00
113	John Thomas	10.00
114	Derek Anderson	60.00
115	Brevin Knight	60.00
116	Charles Smith	10.00
117	Johnny Taylor	10.00
118	Jacque Vaughn	15.00
119	Anthony Parker	10.00
120	Paul Grant	10.00
121	Stephon Marbury S	45.00
122	Terrell Brandon S	8.00
123	Dikembe Mutombo S	8.00
124	Patrick Ewing S	8.00
125	Scottie Pippen S	30.00
126	Antoine Walker S	45.00
127	Karl Malone S	10.00
128	Sean Elliott S	4.00
129	Chris Webber S	15.00
130	Shawn Kemp S	25.00
131	Hakeem Olajuwon S	20.00
132	Tim Hardaway S	10.00
133	Glen Rice S	10.00
134	Vin Baker S	15.00
135	Jim Jackson S	8.00
136	Kevin Garnett S	60.00
137	Kobe Bryant S	70.00
138	Damon Stoudamire S	15.00
139	Larry Johnson S	8.00
140	Latrell Sprewell S	8.00
141	Lorenzen Wright S	4.00
142	Toni Kukoc S	8.00
143	Allen Iverson S	45.00
144	Elden Campbell S	4.00
145	Tom Gugliotta S	8.00
146	David Robinson S	12.00

147	Jayson Williams S	4.00
148	Shaquille O'Neal S	35.00
149	Grant Hill S	60.00
150	Reggie Miller S	8.00
151	Clyde Drexler S	10.00
152	Ray Allen S	10.00
153	Eddie Jones S	15.00
154	Michael Jordan G	700.00
155	Dominique Wilkins G	30.00
156	Charles Barkley G	60.00
157	Jerry Stackhouse G	30.00
158	Juwan Howard G	40.00
159	Marcus Camby G	40.00
160	Christian Laettner G	30.00
161	Anthony Mason G	30.00
162	Joe Smith G	40.00
163	Kerry Kittles G	40.00
164	Mitch Richmond G	40.00
165	Shareef Abdur-Rahim G	130.00
166	Alonzo Mourning G	40.00
167	Dennis Rodman G	150.00
168	Antonio McDyess G	40.00
169	Shawn Bradley G	30.00
170	Anfernee Hardaway G	160.00
171	Jason Kidd G	75.00
172	Gary Payton G	50.00
173	John Stockton G	40.00
174	Allan Houston	6.00
175	Bob Sura	3.00
176	Clyde Drexler	8.00
177	Glenn Robinson	6.00
178	Joe Smith	6.00
179	Larry Johnson	6.00
180	Mitch Richmond	6.00
181	Rony Seikaly	3.00
182	Tyrone Hill	3.00
183	Allen Iverson	35.00
184	Brent Barry	3.00
185	Damon Stoudamire	12.00
186	Grant Hill	45.00
187	John Stockton	6.00
188	Latrell Sprewell	6.00
189	Mookie Blaylock	3.00
190	Samaki Walker	3.00
191	Vin Baker	10.00
192	Alonzo Mourning	6.00
193	Brevin Knight	15.00
194	Danny Manning	3.00
195	Hakeem Olajuwon	15.00
196	Johnny Taylor	3.00
197	Lorenzen Wright	3.00
198	Olden Polynice	3.00
199	Scottie Pippen	20.00
200	Lindsey Hunter	3.00
201	Anfernee Hardaway	30.00
202	Greg Anthony	3.00
203	David Robinson	10.00
204	Horace Grant	3.00
205	Calbert Cheaney	3.00
206	Loy Vaught	3.00
207	Tariq Abdul-Wahad	8.00
208	Sean Elliott	3.00
209	Rodney Rogers	3.00
210	Anthony Mason	3.00
211	Bryant Reeves	3.00
212	David Wesley	3.00
213	Isaiah Rider	3.00
214	Karl Malone	8.00
215	Mahmoud Abdul-Rauf	3.00
216	Patrick Ewing	6.00
217	Shaquille O'Neal	30.00
218	Antoine Walker	35.00
219	Charles Barkley	10.00
220	Dennis Rodman	30.00
221	Jamal Mashburn	6.00
222	Kendall Gill	3.00
223	Malik Sealy	3.00
224	Rasheed Wallace	3.00
225	Shareef Abdur-Rahim	20.00
226	Antonio Daniels	10.00
227	Charles Oakley	3.00
228	Derek Anderson	15.00
229	Jason Kidd	12.00
230	Kenny Anderson	3.00
231	Marcus Camby	8.00
232	Ray Allen	8.00
233	Shawn Bradley	3.00
234	Antonio McDyess	8.00
235	Chauncey Billups	12.00
236	Detlef Schrempf	3.00
237	Jayson Williams	3.00
238	Kerry Kittles	8.00
239	Jalen Rose	3.00
240	Reggie Miller	8.00
241	Shawn Kemp	20.00
242	Arvydas Sabonis	3.00
243	Tom Gugliotta	6.00
244	Dikembe Mutombo	6.00
245	Jeff Hornacek	3.00
246	Kevin Garnett	45.00
247	Matt Maloney	3.00
248	Rex Chapman	3.00
249	Stephon Marbury	35.00
250	Austin Croshere	6.00
251	Chris Childs	3.00
252	Eddie Jones	12.00
253	Jerry Stackhouse	6.00
254	Kevin Johnson	6.00
255	Maurice Taylor	18.00
256	Chris Mullin	6.00
257	Terrell Brandon	6.00
258	Avery Johnson	3.00
259	Chris Webber	12.00
260	Gary Payton	8.00
261	Jim Jackson	6.00
262	Kobe Bryant	70.00
263	Michael Finley	6.00
264	Rod Strickland	3.00
265	Tim Hardaway	6.00
266	B.J. Armstrong	3.00
267	Christian Laettner	6.00
268	Glen Rice	6.00
269	Joe Dumars	3.00
270	LaPhonso Ellis	3.00
271	Michael Jordan	90.00
272	Ron Mercer	120.00
273	Checklist	3.00
274	Anfernee Hardaway S	35.00
275	Dennis Rodman S	35.00
276	Gary Payton S	10.00
277	Jamal Mashburn S	8.00
278	Shareef Abdur-Rahim S	30.00
279	Steve Smith S	4.00
280	Tony Battie S	8.00
281	Alonzo Mourning S	8.00
282	Bobby Jackson S	10.00
283	Christian Laettner S	8.00
284	Jerry Stackhouse S	8.00
285	Terrell Brandon S	8.00
286	Chauncey Billups S	15.00
287	Michael Jordan S	100.00
288	Glenn Robinson S	8.00
289	Jason Kidd S	14.00
290	Joe Smith S	8.00
291	Michael Finley S	8.00
292	Rod Strickland S	4.00
293	Ron Mercer S	30.00
294	Tracy McGrady S	30.00
295	Adonal Foyle S	8.00
296	Marcus Camby S	8.00
297	John Stockton S	8.00
298	Kerry Kittles S	8.00
299	Mitch Richmond S	8.00
300	Shawn Bradley S	4.00
301	Anthony Mason S	4.00
302	Antonio Daniels S	10.00
303	Antonio McDyess S	10.00
304	Charles Barkley S	12.00
305	Keith Van Horn S	45.00
306	Tim Duncan S	60.00
307	Dikembe Mutombo G	30.00
308	Grant Hill G	275.00
309	Shaquille O'Neal G	175.00
310	Keith Van Horn G	220.00
311	Shawn Kemp G	125.00
312	Antoine Walker G	200.00
313	Hakeem Olajuwon G	100.00
314	Vin Baker G	70.00
315	Patrick Ewing G	40.00
316	Tracy McGrady G	125.00
317	Glen Rice G	40.00
318	Reggie Miller G	40.00
319	Kevin Garnett G	275.00
320	Allen Iverson G	220.00
321	Karl Malone G	50.00
322	Scottie Pippen G	125.00
323	Kobe Bryant G	325.00
324	Stephon Marbury G	220.00
325	Tim Duncan G	250.00
326	Chris Webber G	100.00

1997-98 Finest Embossed Silvers

Embossed Silver or uncommons were available in both series, with cards 121-153 in Series I and 274-306 in Series II. This 66-card set featured embossed versions of each silver card and was inserted one per 16 packs, while Refractor versions were seeded one per 192 packs and sequentially numbered to 263. Only Silver versions arrived in an embossed only verions - Embossed Gold cards were all die-cut.

	MT
Silver Cards:	2x
Silver Refractors:	4x-8x

1997-98 Finest Embossed Golds

The rare cards from both Series I and II were also available in embossed/die-cut versions. In Series I, the rare cards were 154-173, while in Series II they were numbered 307-326. Only these rare or gold versions were available in this format, with regular embossed/die-cut versions seeded one per 96 packs, while Refractor versions were seeded one per 1,152 packs. Series II embossed/die-cut cards were sequentially numbered to 74 on the back.

	MT
Gold Cards:	2x
Gold Refractors:	5x-10x

1997-98 Flair Showcase Promo Sheet

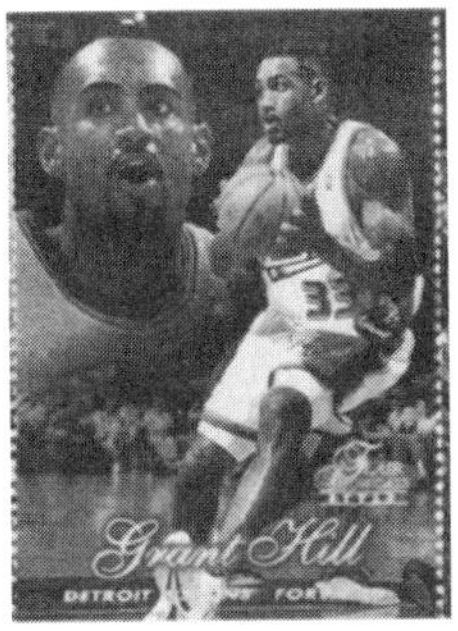

This four-card promo sheet pictured Grant Hill on four different Flair Showcase cards, including one from each of the four different rows. The sheet was issued to promote the 1997-98 set.

		MT
Complete Set (4):		
Common Player:		
2	Grant Hill (Flair - Row 0)	
2	Grant Hill (Style - Row 1)	
2	Grant Hill (Grace - Row 2)	
2	Grant Hill (Showcase - Row 3)	

1997-98 Flair Showcase Row 3

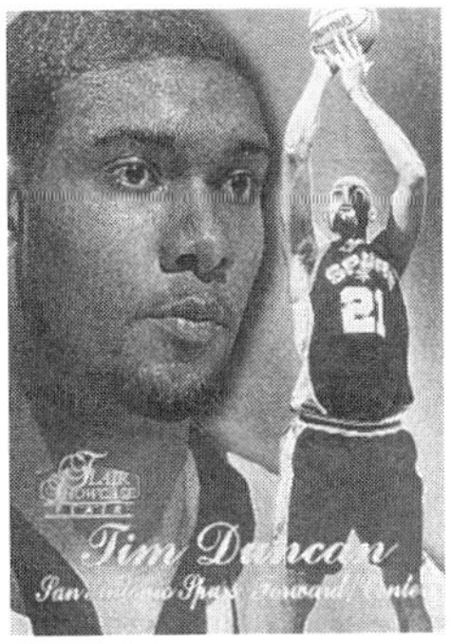

All 80 cards in Flair Showcase arrived in a Flair, or Row 3 front, with one of four different backs. Flair fronts with Showtime backs were inserted slightly less than one per pack, Flair/Showstopper one per 1.1, Flair/ Showdown 1:1.5 and Flair Showpiece one per two packs. Flair fronts have a very close shot of the player on the left, with an action shot over it and a silver foil background.

		MT
Complete Set (80):		70.00
Common Player:		.25
Wax Box:		175.00
1	Michael Jordan	10.00
2	Grant Hill	5.00
3	Allen Iverson	4.00
4	Kevin Garnett	5.00
5	*Tim Duncan*	20.00
6	Shawn Kemp	2.00
7	Shaquille O'Neal	3.00
8	Antoine Walker	5.00
9	Shareef Abdur-Rahim	2.50
10	Damon Stoudamire	1.50
11	Anfernee Hardaway	3.00
12	*Keith Van Horn*	15.00
13	Dennis Rodman	3.00
14	*Ron Mercer*	10.00
15	Stephon Marbury	5.00
16	Scottie Pippen	2.50
17	Kerry Kittles	.75
18	Kobe Bryant	7.00
19	Marcus Camby	.75
20	*Chauncey Billups*	5.00
21	*Tracy McGrady*	8.00
22	Joe Smith	.50
23	*Brevin Knight*	5.00
24	*Danny Fortson*	2.00
25	*Tim Thomas*	8.00
26	Gary Payton	1.00
27	David Robinson	1.00
28	Hakeem Olajuwon	1.50
29	*Antonio Daniels*	3.00
30	Antonio McDyess	.75
31	Eddie Jones	1.00
32	*Adonal Foyle*	.50
33	Glenn Robinson	.50
34	Charles Barkley	1.00
35	Vin Baker	1.00
36	Jerry Stackhouse	.50
37	Ray Allen	.75
38	*Derek Anderson*	5.00
39	Isaac Austin	.25
40	*Tony Battie*	2.00
41	*Tariq Abdul-Wahad*	1.50
42	Dikembe Mutombo	.50
43	Clyde Drexler	.75
44	Chris Mullin	.50
45	Tim Hardaway	.75
46	Terrell Brandon	.50
47	John Stockton	.50
48	Patrick Ewing	.50
49	Horace Grant	.25
50	Tom Gugliotta	.50
51	Mookie Blaylock	.25
52	Mitch Richmond	.50
53	Anthony Mason	.25
54	Michael Finley	.50
55	Jason Kidd	1.00
56	Karl Malone	1.00
57	Reggie Miller	.50
58	Steve Smith	.25
59	Glen Rice	.50
60	Bryant Stith	.25
61	Loy Vaught	.25
62	Brian Grant	.25
63	Joe Dumars	.25
64	Juwan Howard	.75
65	Rik Smits	.25
66	Alonzo Mourning	.50
67	Allan Houston	.50
68	Chris Webber	1.00
69	Kendall Gill	.25
70	Rony Seikaly	.25
71	Kenny Anderson	.25
72	John Wallace	.25
73	Bryant Reeves	.25
74	Brian Williams	.25
75	Larry Johnson	.50
76	Shawn Bradley	.25
77	Kevin Johnson	.25
78	Rod Strickland	.25
79	Rodney Rogers	.25
80	Rasheed Wallace	.25

1997-98 Flair Showcase Row 2

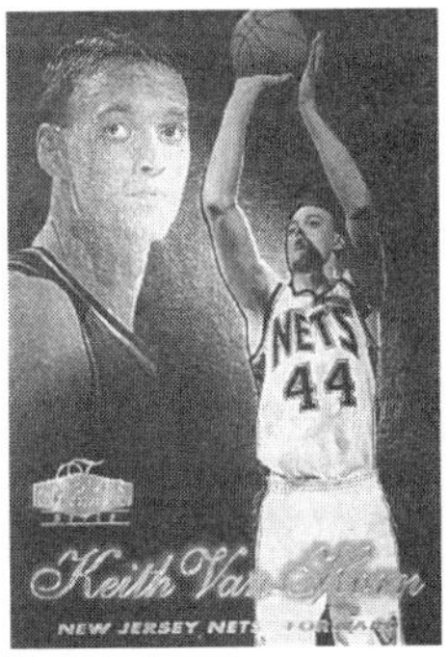

All 80 cards in Flair Showcase arrived in Row 2, or Style fronts, with four different backs to match. Style fronts with a Showtime back were inserted one per 2.5 packs, Style/Showstopper one per three, Style/Showdown one per 3.5 and Style/Showpiece cards were inserted one per four packs. The Row 2 fronts feature two shots of the player on a darkened, glossy background.

		MT
Complete Set (80):		175.00
Common Player:		.50
1	Michael Jordan	15.00
2	Grant Hill	7.50
3	Allen Iverson	6.00
4	Kevin Garnett	7.50
5	Tim Duncan	30.00
6	Shawn Kemp	3.00
7	Shaquille O'Neal	4.50
8	Antoine Walker	7.50
9	Shareef Abdur-Rahim	4.00
10	Damon Stoudamire	2.00
11	Anfernee Hardaway	4.50
12	Keith Van Horn	22.00
13	Dennis Rodman	4.50
14	Ron Mercer	15.00
15	Stephon Marbury	7.50
16	Scottie Pippen	4.00
17	Kerry Kittles	1.25
18	Kobe Bryant	10.00
19	Marcus Camby	1.25
20	Chauncey Billups	7.50
21	Tracy McGrady	12.00
22	Joe Smith	1.00
23	Brevin Knight	7.50
24	Danny Fortson	3.00
25	Tim Thomas	12.00
26	Gary Payton	1.50
27	David Robinson	1.50
28	Hakeem Olajuwon	2.50
29	Antonio Daniels	4.50
30	Antonio McDyess	1.25
31	Eddie Jones	1.50
32	Adonal Foyle	1.00
33	Glenn Robinson	1.00
34	Charles Barkley	1.50
35	Vin Baker	1.50
36	Jerry Stackhouse	1.00
37	Ray Allen	1.25
38	Derek Anderson	7.50
39	Isaac Austin	.50
40	Tony Battie	3.00
41	Tariq Abdul-Wahad	2.50
42	Dikembe Mutombo	1.00
43	Clyde Drexler	1.25
44	Chris Mullin	1.00
45	Tim Hardaway	1.25
46	Terrell Brandon	1.00
47	John Stockton	1.00
48	Patrick Ewing	1.00
49	Horace Grant	.50
50	Tom Gugliotta	1.00
51	Mookie Blaylock	.50
52	Mitch Richmond	1.00
53	Anthony Mason	.50
54	Michael Finley	1.00
55	Jason Kidd	1.50
56	Karl Malone	1.50
57	Reggie Miller	1.00
58	Steve Smith	.50
59	Glen Rice	1.00
60	Bryant Stith	.50
61	Loy Vaught	.50
62	Brian Grant	.50
63	Joe Dumars	.50
64	Juwan Howard	1.25
65	Rik Smits	.50
66	Alonzo Mourning	1.00
67	Allan Houston	1.00
68	Chris Webber	1.50
69	Kendall Gill	.50
70	Rony Seikaly	.50
71	Kenny Anderson	.50
72	John Wallace	.50
73	Bryant Reeves	.50
74	Brian Williams	.50
75	Larry Johnson	1.00
76	Shawn Bradley	.50
77	Kevin Johnson	.50
78	Rod Strickland	.50
79	Rodney Rogers	.50
80	Rasheed Wallace	.50

1997-98 Flair Showcase Row 1

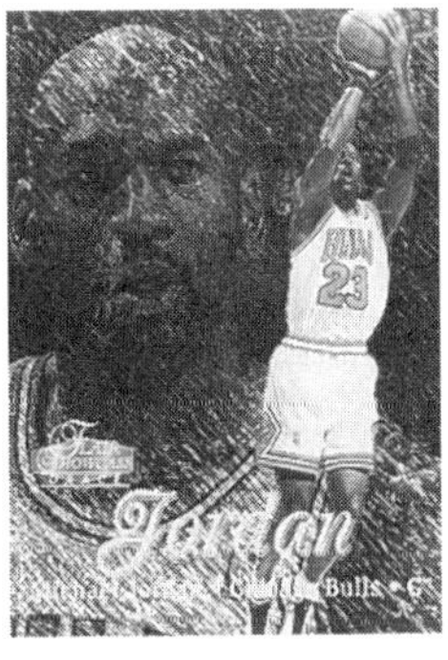

All 80 cards in Flair Showcase arrived in Grace, or Row 1 versions, with four different backs to match. Grace fronts with Showtime backs were inserted one per six packs, Grace/Showstopper were seeded one per 10, Grace/ Showdown one per 16 and Grace/Showpiece were seeded one per 24 packs. The Row 1 cards have a prismatic foil background and feature two shots of the player.

		MT
Complete Set (80):		800.00
Common Player (1-20):		5.00
Common Player (21-40):		10.00
Common Player (41-60):		.50
Common Player (61-80):		2.00
1	Michael Jordan	80.00
2	Grant Hill	40.00
3	Allen Iverson	30.00
4	Kevin Garnett	40.00
5	Tim Duncan	60.00
6	Shawn Kemp	15.00
7	Shaquille O'Neal	25.00
8	Antoine Walker	40.00
9	Shareef Abdur-Rahim	20.00
10	Damon Stoudamire	12.00
11	Anfernee Hardaway	25.00
12	Keith Van Horn	45.00
13	Dennis Rodman	25.00
14	Ron Mercer	30.00
15	Stephon Marbury	40.00
16	Scottie Pippen	20.00
17	Kerry Kittles	10.00
18	Kobe Bryant	50.00
19	Marcus Camby	10.00
20	Chauncey Billups	15.00
21	Tracy McGrady	50.00
22	Joe Smith	10.00
23	Brevin Knight	35.00
24	Danny Fortson	15.00
25	Tim Thomas	55.00
26	Gary Payton	15.00
27	David Robinson	15.00
28	Hakeem Olajuwon	22.00
29	Antonio Daniels	20.00
30	Antonio McDyess	12.00
31	Eddie Jones	15.00
32	Adonal Foyle	10.00
33	Glenn Robinson	10.00
34	Charles Barkley	15.00
35	Vin Baker	15.00
36	Jerry Stackhouse	10.00
37	Ray Allen	12.00
38	Derek Anderson	35.00
39	Isaac Austin	10.00
40	Tony Battie	15.00
41	Tariq Abdul-Wahad	3.00
42	Dikembe Mutombo	1.00
43	Clyde Drexler	1.50
44	Chris Mullin	1.00
45	Tim Hardaway	1.50
46	Terrell Brandon	1.00
47	John Stockton	1.00
48	Patrick Ewing	1.00
49	Horace Grant	.50
50	Tom Gugliotta	1.00
51	Mookie Blaylock	.50
52	Mitch Richmond	1.00
53	Anthony Mason	.50
54	Michael Finley	1.00
55	Jason Kidd	3.00
56	Karl Malone	3.00
57	Reggie Miller	1.00
58	Steve Smith	.50
59	Glen Rice	1.00
60	Bryant Stith	.50
61	Loy Vaught	2.00
62	Brian Grant	2.00
63	Joe Dumars	2.00
64	Juwan Howard	5.00
65	Rik Smits	2.00
66	Alonzo Mourning	4.00
67	Allan Houston	4.00
68	Chris Webber	6.00
69	Kendall Gill	2.00
70	Rony Seikaly	2.00
71	Kenny Anderson	2.00
72	John Wallace	2.00
73	Bryant Reeves	2.00
74	Brian Williams	2.00
75	Larry Johnson	4.00
76	Shawn Bradley	2.00
77	Kevin Johnson	2.00
78	Rod Strickland	2.00
79	Rodney Rogers	2.00
80	Rasheed Wallace	2.00

1997-98 Flair Showcase Row 0

All 80 players in Flair Showcase horizontal, prismatic foil verions called Row 0. Each card in Row 0 was sequentially numbered, with cards 1-20 numbered to 250, 21-40 numbered to 500, cards 41-60 numbered to 1,000 and cards 61-80 numbered to 2,000. Parallel Legacy Collection versions of each also exist, but are distinguished by blue foil and numbering to 100 on the back.

		MT
Common Player (1-20):		25.00
Production 250 Sets		
Common Player (21-40):		5.00
Production 500 Sets		
Common Player (41-60):		4.00
Production 1,000 Sets		
Common Player (61-80):		3.00
Production 2,000 Sets		
1	Michael Jordan	300.00
2	Grant Hill	150.00
3	Allen Iverson	100.00
4	Kevin Garnett	150.00
5	Tim Duncan	150.00
6	Shawn Kemp	75.00
7	Shaquille O'Neal	100.00
8	Antoine Walker	125.00
9	Shareef Abdur-Rahim	75.00
10	Damon Stoudamire	50.00
11	Anfernee Hardaway	100.00
12	Keith Van Horn	125.00
13	Dennis Rodman	100.00
14	Ron Mercer	100.00
15	Stephon Marbury	125.00
16	Scottie Pippen	75.00
17	Kerry Kittles	25.00
18	Kobe Bryant	200.00
19	Marcus Camby	25.00
20	Chauncey Billups	50.00
21	Tracy McGrady	50.00
22	Joe Smith	10.00
23	Brevin Knight	25.00
24	Danny Fortson	10.00
25	Tim Thomas	50.00
26	Gary Payton	25.00
27	David Robinson	25.00
28	Hakeem Olajuwon	30.00
29	Antonio Daniels	20.00
30	Antonio McDyess	15.00
31	Eddie Jones	35.00
32	Adonal Foyle	10.00
33	Glenn Robinson	10.00
34	Charles Barkley	25.00
35	Vin Baker	25.00
36	Jerry Stackhouse	10.00
37	Ray Allen	20.00
38	Derek Anderson	25.00
39	Isaac Austin	5.00
40	Tony Battie	10.00
41	Tariq Abdul-Wahad	4.00
42	Dikembe Mutombo	8.00
43	Clyde Drexler	12.00
44	Chris Mullin	8.00
45	Tim Hardaway	12.00
46	Terrell Brandon	8.00
47	John Stockton	8.00
48	Patrick Ewing	8.00
49	Horace Grant	4.00
50	Tom Gugliotta	8.00
51	Mookie Blaylock	4.00
52	Mitch Richmond	8.00
53	Anthony Mason	4.00
54	Michael Finley	8.00
55	Jason Kidd	20.00
56	Karl Malone	15.00
57	Reggie Miller	8.00
58	Steve Smith	4.00
59	Glen Rice	8.00
60	Bryant Stith	4.00
61	Loy Vaught	3.00
62	Brian Grant	3.00
63	Joe Dumars	6.00
64	Juwan Howard	6.00
65	Rik Smits	3.00
66	Alonzo Mourning	6.00
67	Allan Houston	6.00
68	Chris Webber	12.00
69	Kendall Gill	3.00
70	Rony Seikaly	3.00
71	Kenny Anderson	3.00
72	John Wallace	3.00
73	Bryant Reeves	3.00
74	Brian Williams	3.00
75	Larry Johnson	6.00
76	Shawn Bradley	3.00
77	Kevin Johnson	3.00
78	Rod Strickland	3.00
79	Rodney Rogers	3.00
80	Rasheed Wallace	3.00

1997-98 Flair Showcase Legacy

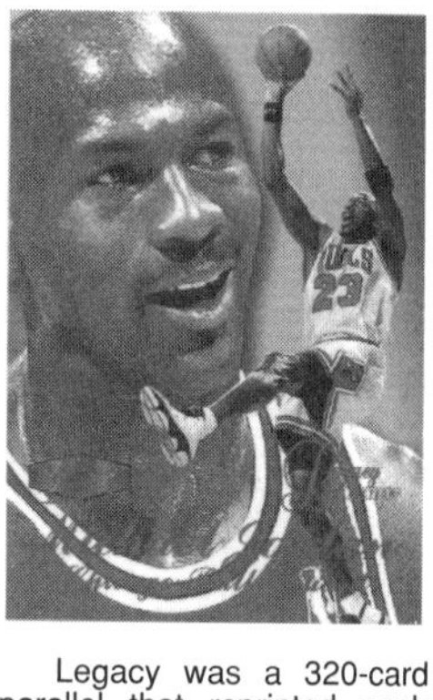

Legacy was a 320-card parallel that reprinted each card in all versions of Flair Showcase. A blue foil was added to the front, while the glossy finish was taken away from the back. The matte finish on the back was sequentially numbered to 100 sets. Rarer versions, called Legacy Masterpieces, were also produced and limited to only one set. Masterpieces used a purple foil versus the blue used in Legacy.

		MT
Common Player:		10.00
Each Player Has Four Different Cards.		
1	Michael Jordan	600.00
2	Grant Hill	250.00
3	Allen Iverson	200.00
4	Kevin Garnett	250.00
5	Tim Duncan	350.00
6	Shawn Kemp	100.00
7	Shaquille O'Neal	175.00
8	Antoine Walker	200.00
9	Shareef Abdur-Rahim	125.00
10	Damon Stoudamire	75.00
11	Anfernee Hardaway	175.00
12	Keith Van Horn	250.00
13	Dennis Rodman	175.00
14	Ron Mercer	175.00
15	Stephon Marbury	200.00
16	Scottie Pippen	125.00
17	Kerry Kittles	35.00
18	Kobe Bryant	325.00
19	Marcus Camby	35.00
20	Chauncey Billups	100.00
21	Tracy McGrady	150.00
22	Joe Smith	35.00
23	Brevin Knight	100.00
24	Danny Fortson	50.00
25	Tim Thomas	150.00
26	Gary Payton	75.00
27	David Robinson	75.00
28	Hakeem Olajuwon	90.00
29	Antonio Daniels	70.00
30	Antonio McDyess	50.00
31	Eddie Jones	80.00
32	Adonal Foyle	35.00
33	Glenn Robinson	40.00
34	Charles Barkley	75.00
35	Vin Baker	80.00
36	Jerry Stackhouse	35.00
37	Ray Allen	35.00
38	Derek Anderson	100.00
39	Isaac Austin	10.00
40	Tony Battie	50.00
41	Tariq Abdul-Wahad	40.00
42	Dikembe Mutombo	20.00
43	Clyde Drexler	50.00
44	Chris Mullin	20.00
45	Tim Hardaway	40.00
46	Terrell Brandon	20.00
47	John Stockton	40.00
48	Patrick Ewing	40.00
49	Horace Grant	10.00
50	Tom Gugliotta	20.00
51	Mookie Blaylock	10.00
52	Mitch Richmond	40.00
53	Anthony Mason	10.00
54	Michael Finley	20.00
55	Jason Kidd	80.00
56	Karl Malone	50.00
57	Reggie Miller	40.00
58	Steve Smith	10.00
59	Glen Rice	40.00
60	Bryant Stith	10.00
61	Loy Vaught	10.00
62	Brian Grant	10.00
63	Joe Dumars	10.00
64	Juwan Howard	50.00
65	Rik Smits	10.00
66	Alonzo Mourning	40.00
67	Allan Houston	20.00
68	Chris Webber	90.00
69	Kendall Gill	10.00
70	Rony Seikaly	10.00
71	Kenny Anderson	10.00
72	John Wallace	10.00
73	Bryant Reeves	10.00
74	Brian Williams	10.00
75	Larry Johnson	20.00
76	Shawn Bradley	10.00
77	Kevin Johnson	10.00
78	Rod Strickland	10.00
79	Rodney Rogers	10.00
80	Rasheed Wallace	10.00

1997-98 Flair Showcase Wave of the Future

Wave of the Future inserts showcases 12 different rookies not included in the set. The cards feature one cardboard card in plastic inside another outer coating of plastic, with the inner area filled with an oil substance and glitter. Backs are numbered with a "WF" prefix and the cards were inserted one per 20 packs.

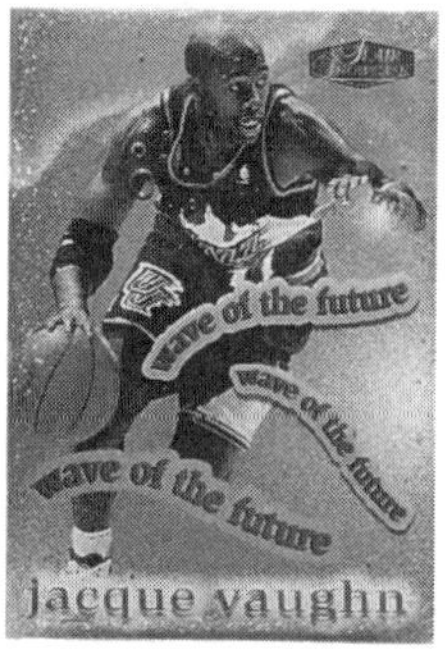

		MT
Complete Set (12):		90.00
Common Player:		5.00
WF1	Corey Beck	5.00
WF2	Maurice Taylor	25.00
WF3	Chris Antsey	8.00
WF4	Keith Booth	5.00
WF5	Anthony Parker	5.00
WF6	Austin Croshere	8.00
WF7	Jacque Vaughn	10.00
WF8	God Shammgod	5.00
WF9	Bobby Jackson	16.00
WF10	Johnny Taylor	5.00
WF11	Ed Gray	8.00
WF12	Kelvin Cato	8.00

1997-98 Fleer II

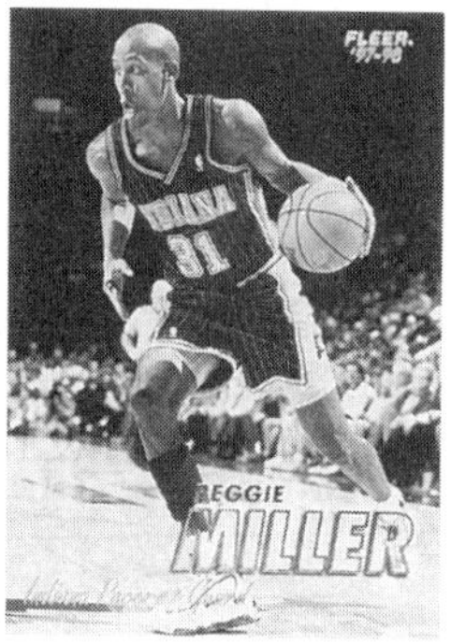

Fleer's 1997-98 set contained 350 cards, with 200 in Series I and 150 in Series II. Every base card was printed on matte finish. The fronts have full-bleed photos with the player's name, team and position printed in gold foil across the bottom and the Fleer logo in the upper right corner. Backs are white with a color photo at the top and statistics filling up the remainder. Inserts in Series I include: Fleer NBA Million Dollar Moments, Key Ingredients, Rookie Rewind, Flair Hardwood Legends, Decade of Excellence, Franchise Futures and Game Breakers, as well as two parallel sets called Tiffany Collection and Crystal Collection. Inserts in Series II include: Soaring Stars, Goudey Greats, Rookie Sensations, Total "O", Towers of Power, High Flying Soaring Stars, Zone, Thrill Seekers, Million Dollar Moments, Diamond Ink and Crystal and Tiffany Collection parallels.

		MT
Complete Series 2 (150):		20.00
Common Player:		.05
Series 2 Wax Box:		45.00
201	*Tim Duncan*	3.00
202	*Tim Thomas*	1.00
203	Clifford Rozier	.05
204	Bryant Reeves	.05
205	Glen Rice	.20
206	Darrell Armstrong	.05
207	Juwan Howard	.30
208	John Stockton	.30
209	Antonio McDyess	.30
210	*James Cotton*	.10
211	Brian Grant	.05
212	Chris Whitney	.05
213	Antonio Davis	.05
214	Kendall Gill	.05
215	*Adonal Foyle*	.50
216	Dean Garrett	.05
217	Dennis Scott	.05
218	Zydrunas Ilgauskas	.40
219	*Antonio Daniels*	1.00
220	Derek Harper	.05
221	Travis Knight	.05
222	Bobby Hurley	.05
223	Greg Anderson	.05
224	Rod Strickland	.05
225	David Benoit	.05
226	*Tracy McGrady*	1.00
227	Brian Williams	.05
228	James Robinson	.05
229	Randy Brown	.05
230	Greg Foster	.05
231	Reggie Miller	.25
232	Eric Montross	.05
233	Malik Rose	.05
234	Charles Barkley	.30
235	*Tony Battie*	1.00
236	Terry Mills	.05
237	*Jerald Honeycutt*	.10
238	*Bubba Wells*	.10
239	John Wallace	.10
240	Jason Kidd	.30
241	Mark Price	.05
242	*Ron Mercer*	1.50
243	Derrick Coleman	.10
244	Fred Hoiberg	.05
245	Wesley Person	.05
246	Eddie Jones	.40
247	Allan Houston	.10
248	*Keith Van Horn*	3.00
249	Johnny Newman	.05
250	Kevin Garnett	1.50
251	Latrell Sprewell	.20
252	Tracy Murray	.05
253	Charles O'Bannon	.05
254	Lamond Murray	.05
255	Jerry Stackhouse	.30
256	Rik Smits	.05
257	Alan Henderson	.05
258	*Tariq Abdul-Wahad*	.20
259	Nick Anderson	.05
260	Calbert Cheaney	.05
261	Scottie Pippen	.75
262	*Rodrick Rhodes*	.75
263	*Derek Anderson*	1.00
264	Dana Barros	.05
265	Todd Day	.05
266	Michael Finley	.20
267	Kevin Edwards	.05
268	Terrell Brandon	.10
269	Bobby Phills	.05
270	*Kelvin Cato*	.20
271	Vin Baker	.30
272	*Eric Washington*	.10
273	Jim Jackson	.05
274	Joe Dumars	.05
275	David Robinson	.30
276	Jayson Williams	.05
277	Travis Best	.05
278	Kurt Thomas	.05
279	Otis Thorpe	.05
280	Damon Stoudamire	.40
281	John Williams	.05
282	Loy Vaught	.05
283	Charles Outlaw	.05
284	Todd Fuller	.05
285	Terry Dehere	.05
286	Clarence Weatherspoon	.05
287	*Danny Fortson*	.50
288	Howard Eisley	.05
289	Steve Smith	.05
290	Chris Webber	.50
291	Shawn Kemp	.75
292	Sam Cassell	.05
293	Rick Fox	.05
294	Walter McCarty	.05
295	Mark Jackson	.05
296	Chris Mills	.05
297	*Jacque Vaughn*	.50
298	Shawn Respert	.05
299	Scott Burrell	.05
300	Allen Iverson	1.25
301	*Charles Smith*	.05
302	Ervin Johnson	.05
303	*Hubert Davis*	.05
304	*Eddie Johnson*	.05
305	Erick Dampier	.05
306	Eric Williams	.05
307	*Anthony Johnson*	.10
308	David Wesley	.05
309	Eric Piatkowski	.05
310	*Austin Croshere*	.50
311	Malik Sealy	.05
312	George McCloud	.05
313	*Anthony Parker*	.10
314	*Cedric Henderson*	.40
315	*John Thomas*	.10
316	Cory Alexander	.05
317	*Johnny Taylor*	.10
318	Chris Mullin	.10
319	J.R. Reid	.05
320	George Lynch	.05
321	*Lawrence Funderburke*	.10
322	*God Shammgod*	.10
323	*Bobby Jackson*	1.00
324	Khalid Reeves	.05
325	Zan Tabak	.05
326	Chris Gatling	.05

		MT
327	*Alvin Williams*	.10
328	*Scot Pollard*	.10
329	Kerry Kittles	.30
330	Tim Hardaway	.10
331	*Maurice Taylor*	.75
332	Keith Booth	.10
333	Chris Morris	.05
334	Bryant Stith	.05
335	Terry Cummings	.05
336	Ed Gray	.10
337	Eric Snow	.05
338	Clifford Robinson	.05
339	Chris Dudley	.05
340	*Chauncey Billups*	1.50
341	Paul Grant	.10
342	Tyrone Hill	.05
343	Joe Smith	.30
344	Sean Rooks	.05
345	Harvey Grant	.05
346	Dale Davis	.05
347	*Brevin Knight*	1.25
348	*Serge Zwikker*	.10
349	Checklist	.05
350	Checklist	.05

1997-98 Fleer Crystal

Crystal Collection paralleled the regular-issue Fleer set, and was inserted every two hobby packs. Crystal Collection contains silver foil printing and a small logo that reads "Traditions Crystal" in the upper right corner. The set includes 345 cards, which is minus the five checklists from the 350-card Fleer set.

	MT
Complete Set (200):	120.00
Crystal Cards:	3x-6x

1997-98 Fleer Tiffany

This parallel set of Fleer was inserted at a rate of one per 20 hobby packs and contains each regular-issue card printed in holographic silver foil. The cards are identified by a Traditions Tiffany logo in the upper right corner. The set contained 345 of the 350 cards in the Fleer set minus five checklist cards.

	MT
Complete Set (200):	1000.
Tiffany Cards:	25x-50x

1997-98 Fleer Diamond Ink

Diamond Ink cards were inserted at a rate of one per pack in various Fleer Basketball products throughout the 1997-98 season. Fleer II, Ultra II and Flair Showcase all contained these cards which held either one, five or 10 points. When a prescribed point total was reached, collectors could redeem the points for an autographed mini-basketball from a group of around 10 players.

	MT
Kobe Bryant	.75
Grant Hill	1.00
Kevin Garnett	.40
Joe Smith	.10
Antoine Walker	.30
Antonio McDyess	.10
Danny Fortson	.10
Tim Thomas	.10
Tracy McGrady	.15
Tony Battie	.10
Stephon Marbury	.30
Chauncey Billups	.20

1997-98 Fleer Goudey Greats

Goudey Greats was a 15-card set utilizing the design from 1934 Goudey, including the famous Goudey "Says" spotlighting Hall of Fame point guard Nate "Tiny" Archibald's analysis of today's players. These mini cards were inserted every four packs. Card fronts feature an old-time look, with the player's image larger and the bottom portion featuring Archibald. The back also resembles the 1934 Goudey look and is numbered "x of 15GG." These were found in Series II packs only.

		MT
Complete Set (15):		20.00
Common Player:		.50
1	Ray Allen	1.00
2	Clyde Drexler	1.50
3	Patrick Ewing	.50
4	Anfernee Hardaway	5.00
5	Grant Hill	6.00
6	Stephon Marbury	5.00
7	Alonzo Mourning	1.00
8	Shaquille O'Neal	4.00
9	Gary Payton	2.00
10	Scottie Pippen	2.50
11	David Robinson	1.50
12	Joe Smith	1.00
13	John Stockton	1.00
14	Damon Stoudamire	1.50
15	Antoine Walker	4.00

1997-98 Fleer Rookie Sensations

This 10-card insert set was seeded one per eight packs of Fleer Series II. The set included some of the top players chosen in the 1997 NBA Draft.

		MT
Complete Set (10):		30.00
Common Player:		.75
1	Derek Anderson	3.00
2	Tony Battie	2.00
3	Chauncey Billups	5.00
4	Austin Croshere	.75
5	Antonio Daniels	4.00
6	Tim Duncan	10.00
7	Tracy McGrady	5.00
8	Ron Mercer	5.00
9	Tim Thomas	3.00
10	Keith Van Horn	8.00

1997-98 Fleer Soaring Stars

This 20-card insert was found exclusively in Series II retail packs at a rate of one per two packs. Fronts had the words "Soaring Stars" down the left side outlined in red. The cards are numbered on the back with an "SS" suffix. High Flying versions were also made and contain silver foil instead of the red outlined letters.

		MT
Complete Set (20):		12.00
Common Player:		.25
Soaring Stars:		4x-8x
1	Shareef Abdur-Rahim	1.25
2	Ray Allen	.50
3	Charles Barkley	.75
4	Kobe Bryant	3.00
5	Marcus Camby	.50
6	Kevin Garnett	2.00
7	Tim Hardaway	.25
8	Eddie Jones	.75
9	Michael Jordan	4.00
10	Shawn Kemp	1.00
11	Jason Kidd	.50
12	Kerry Kittles	.50
13	Karl Malone	.50
14	Antonio McDyess	.25
15	Glen Rice	.25
16	Mitch Richmond	.25
17	Latrell Sprewell	.50
18	Jerry Stackhouse	.50
19	Antoine Walker	1.50
20	Chris Webber	.75

1997-98 Fleer Thrill Seekers

This 10-card insert set was found in one per 288 packs of Series II. Cards featured a framed look, with prismatic foil in the background in back of the player's cut-out image. Cards were numbered with a "TS" suffix.

		MT
Complete Set (10):		425.00
Common Player:		12.00
1	Shareef Abdur-Rahim	30.00
2	Kobe Bryant	80.00
3	Tim Duncan	60.00
4	Anfernee Hardaway	50.00
5	Grant Hill	60.00
6	Allen Iverson	60.00
7	Michael Jordan	120.00
8	Stephon Marbury	50.00
9	Dennis Rodman	35.00
10	Joe Smith	12.00

1997-98 Fleer Total "O"

Total "O" was found exclusively in retail packs at a rate of one per 18. Card fronts pictured a top offensive star over the free-throw lane of a basketball court. Card backs included a closeup and were numbered with a "TO" suffix. This insert included 10 cards.

		MT
Complete Set (10):		70.00
Common Player:		1.00
1	Anfernee Hardaway	10.00
2	Grant Hill	15.00
3	Juwan Howard	1.00
4	Allen Iverson	12.00
5	Michael Jordan	30.00
6	Karl Malone	1.00
7	Stephon Marbury	10.00
8	Hakeem Olajuwon	6.00
9	Shaquille O'Neal	10.00
10	Damon Stoudamire	4.00

1997-98 Fleer Towers of Power

Towers of Power was a unique, 12-card insert that featured a die-cut front and back and opened up into a 10-inch shot of the player. Inserted one per 18 packs, each card had the insert name on the front (closed card) and across the bottom when the card was opened, and carried a "TP" suffix on the card number on back.

		MT
Complete Set (12):		60.00
Common Player:		1.50
1	Shareef Abdur-Rahim	8.00
2	Marcus Camby	1.50
3	Patrick Ewing	1.50
4	Kevin Garnett	15.00
5	Shawn Kemp	8.00
6	Karl Malone	3.00
7	Hakeem Olajuwon	6.00
8	Shaquille O'Neal	10.00
9	Dennis Rodman	10.00
10	Joe Smith	3.00
11	Antoine Walker	10.00
12	Chris Webber	4.00

1997-98 Fleer Zone

Zone featured 15 NBA stars over a holographic green patterned background, with the name printed within circles in the top right corner. Backs were numbered with a "Z" suffix, with cards inserted every 36 hobby packs.

		MT
Complete Set (15):		130.00
Common Player:		1.50
1	Shareef Abdur-Rahim	8.00
2	Kobe Bryant	20.00
3	Marcus Camby	1.50
4	Tim Duncan	15.00
5	Kevin Garnett	15.00
6	Anfernee Hardaway	12.00
7	Grant Hill	15.00
8	Juwan Howard	1.50
9	Allen Iverson	15.00
10	Michael Jordan	30.00
11	Hakeem Olajuwon	6.00
12	Gary Payton	4.00
13	Scottie Pippen	8.00
14	Glen Rice	1.50
15	Keith Van Horn	15.00

1997 Genuine Article

The 27-card set comes in seven-card packs, in 12-pack boxes. Produced by General Article Inc., the set consists of 27 cards. Each pack contains an autographed and insert card. On each card, "Hardwood Signature Series" is written in gold foil.

		MT
Complete Set (27):		10.00
Common Player:		.10
1	Derek Anderson UER	.75
2	Keith Booth	.25
3	Bobby Jackson	.75
4	Antonio Daniels	.75
5	Harold Deane	.10
6	Ya-Ya Dia	.10
7	Lee Wilson	.10
8	Kebu Stewart	.10
9	Adonal Foyle	.50
10	Othella Harrington	.10
11	Alvin Sims	.10
12	Brevin Knight	.75
13	Walter McCarty	.25
14	Victor Page	.25

15	Lorenzen Wright	.10
16	Scot Pollard	.25
17	Vitaly Potapenko	.10
18	Jamal Robinson	.10
19	Roy Rogers	.25
20	Shea Seals	.25
21	Carmelo Travieso	.25
22	Jacque Vaughn	.75
23	DeJuan Wheat	.25
24	Allen Iverson	1.00
25	Damon Stoudamire	.75
26	Ron Mercer	1.25
27	Keith Van Horn	1.50

1997 Genuine Article Autographs

This set is a parallel of the base set, with each player autographing 7,500 hand-numbered cards, with Ron Mercer and Keith Van Horn signing 200. The autographs are inserted one per pack.

		MT
Complete Set (27):		275.00
Common Player:		2.50
1	Derek Anderson UER	12.00
2	Keith Booth	2.50
3	Bobby Jackson	10.00
4	Antonio Daniels	12.00
5	Harold Deane	2.50
6	Ya-Ya Dia	2.50
7	Lee Wilson	2.50
8	Kebu Stewart	2.50
9	Adonal Foyle	10.00
10	Othella Harrington	2.50
11	Alvin Sims	2.50
12	Brevin Knight	12.00
13	Walter McCarty	2.50
14	Victor Page	2.50
15	Lorenzen Wright	2.50
16	Scot Pollard	2.50
17	Vitaly Potapenko	2.50
18	Jamal Robinson	2.50
19	Roy Rogers	2.50
20	Shea Seals	2.50
21	Carmelo Travieso	2.50
22	Jacque Vaughn	10.00
23	DeJuan Wheat	2.50
24	Allen Iverson	25.00
25	Damon Stoudamire	20.00
26	Ron Mercer	60.00
27	Keith Van Horn	90.00

1997 Genuine Article Double Cards

This three-card set is randonmly inserted and contains pros in their college uniforms.

		MT
Complete Set (3):		10.00
Common Player:		4.00
D1S	Antoine Walker, Ron Mercer, Derek Anderson	5.00
D2S	Allen Iverson, Damon Stoudamire	4.00
D3S	Ron Mercer, Keith Van Horn	5.00

1997 Genuine Article Double Cards Autographs

This set is an exact parallel to the insert set, with the cards now being autographed by the three players. The set is five cards and randomly inserted.

		MT
Complete Set (3):		325.00
Common Player:		35.00
D1S	Antoine Walker, Ron Mercer, Derek Anderson AU/200	150.00
D2S	Damon Stoudamire AU/200	35.00
D2S	Allen Iverson AU/200	80.00
D3S	Keith Van Horn AU 200	80.00
D3S	Ron Mercer AU/200	50.00

1997 Genuine Article Duo-Sport Preview

The five-card set portrays five football players in their college uniforms, and are numbered with a "DS" prefix.

		MT
Complete Set (5):		12.00
Common Player:		2.00
DS1	Eddie George	5.00
DS2	Karim Abdul-Jabbar	3.00
DS3	Jim Druckenmiller	4.00
DS4	Orlando Pace	2.00
DS5	Yatil Green	2.50

1997 Genuine Article Hometown Heroes

The set features eight players in the 15-card set. The fronts have a photo of a player with a background map indicating where they played, in college or in the pros.

		MT
Complete Set (13):		20.00
Common Player:		1.00
HH1	Ray Allen	2.00
HH2	Ray Allen	2.00
HH3	Allen Iverson	3.00
HH4	Kerry Kittles	2.00
HH5	Kerry Kittles	2.00
HH6	Bryant Reeves	1.50
HH7	Glen Rice	2.50
HH8	Damon Stoudamire	2.00
HH9	Damon Stoudamire	2.00
HH10	Antoine Walker	4.00
HH11	Antoine Walker	4.00
HH12	Lorenzen Wright	1.00
HH13	Lorenzen Wright	1.00

1997 Genuine Article Hometown Heroes Autographs

This set is the same at the original Hometown Heroes set except the cards are autographed.

		MT
Complete Set (13):		250.00
Common Player:		10.00
HH1	Ray Allen	20.00
HH2	Ray Allen	20.00
HH3	Allen Iverson	50.00
HH4	Kerry Kittles	20.00
HH5	Kerry Kittles	20.00
HH6	Bryant Reeves	20.00
HH7	Glen Rice	40.00
HH8	Damon Stoudamire	30.00
HH9	Damon Stoudamire	30.00
HH10	Antoine Walker	50.00
HH11	Antoine Walker	50.00
HH12	Lorenzen Wright	10.00
HH13	Lorenzen Wright	10.00

1997 Genuine Article Lottery Connection

The five-card set features five NBA players in the uniforms. The player's last name only is used in gold foil.

		MT
Complete Set (5):		8.00
Common Player:		1.00
LC1	Derek Anderson	2.00
LC2	Bobby Jackson	2.00
LC3	Brevin Knight	3.00
LC4	Jacque Vaughn	2.00
LC5	Lorenzen Wright	1.00

1997 Genuine Article Lottery Connection Autographs

The set is the same as the base Lottery Connection set, only the cards are now autographed on the front.

		MT
Complete Set (5):		80.00
Common Player:		12.00
LC1	Derek Anderson	25.00
LC2	Bobby Jackson	20.00
LC3	Brevin Knight	25.00
LC4	Jacque Vaughn	20.00
LC5	Lorenzen Wright	12.00

1997 Genuine Article Lottery Gems

The five-card set contains five of the top picks in the 1997 draft. The player's name is in gold foil on the bottom.

		MT
Complete Set (5):		12.00
Common Player:		2.50
LG1	Antonio Daniels	2.50
LG2	Adonal Foyle	2.50
LG3	Danny Fortson	2.50
LG4	Ron Mercer	4.00
LG5	Keith Van Horn	5.00

1997 Genuine Article Lottery Gems Autographs

The same as the base set Lottery Gems, except the cards are autographed on the front.

		MT
Complete Set (5):		125.00
Common Player:		25.00
LG1	Antonio Daniels	25.00
LG2	Adonal Foyle	25.00
LG3	Danny Fortson	25.00
LG4	Ron Mercer	40.00
LG5	Keith Van Horn	50.00

1997-98 Hoops II

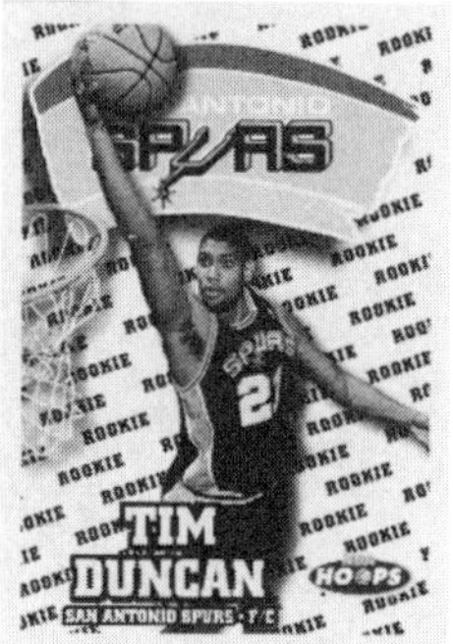

Hoops was issued in two, 165-card series in 1997-98. The first series had 155 base cards, eight League Leaders and two checklists, while the Series II had 125 veterans and 40 Rookies. Series I marked the first release for the second season of Autographics. Cards had a white border, with the player shown over a large team logo. Backs had another large shot of the player, with stats on the right side over a white background. Inserts in Series I included: Talkin' Hoops, Dish N Swish, Chill with Hill, Frequent Flyer Club, Rookie Headliners, Autographics and Hooperstars. Inserts in Series II included: Great Shots, Chairmen of the Boards, Rock the House, High Voltage, Top of the World, 9-1-1, Autographics and High Voltage 500 Volts.

		MT
Complete Series 2 (165):		18.00
Common Player:		.05
Series 2 Wax Box:		30.00
166	*Tim Duncan*	3.00
167	*Chauncey Billups*	1.50
168	*Keith Van Horn*	3.00
169	*Tracy McGrady*	1.50
170	*John Thomas*	.05
171	*Tim Thomas*	1.25
172	*Ron Mercer*	1.50
173	*Scot Pollard*	.05
174	*Jason Lawson*	.05
175	*Keith Booth*	.05
176	*Adonal Foyle*	.50
177	*Bubba Wells*	.05
178	*Derek Anderson*	1.00
179	*Rodrick Rhodes*	.50
180	*Kelvin Cato*	.25
181	*Serge Zwikker*	.05
182	*Ed Gray*	.25
183	*Brevin Knight*	1.00
184	*Alvin Williams*	.05
185	*Paul Grant*	.05
186	*Austin Croshere*	.30
187	*Chris Crawford*	.05
188	*Anthony Johnson*	.05
189	*James Cotton*	.05
190	*James Collins*	.05
191	*Tony Battie*	.75
192	*Tariq Abdul-Wahad*	.50
193	*Danny Fortson*	.50
194	*Maurice Taylor*	.75
195	*Bobby Jackson*	1.00
196	*Charles Smith*	.05
197	*Johnny Taylor*	.05
198	*Jerald Honeycutt*	.05
199	*Marko Milic*	.10
200	*Anthony Parker*	.05
201	*Jacque Vaughn*	.50
202	*Antonio Daniels*	1.25
203	*Charles O'Bannon*	.10
204	*God Shammgod*	.10
205	*Kebu Stewart*	.10
206	Mookie Blaylock	.05
207	Chucky Brown	.05
208	Alan Henderson	.05
209	Dana Barros	.05
210	Tyus Edney	.05
211	Travis Knight	.05
212	Walter McCarty	.05
213	Vlade Divac	.05
214	Matt Geiger	.05
215	Bobby Phills	.05
216	J.R. Reid	.05
217	David Wesley	.05
218	Scott Burrell	.05
219	Ron Harper	.05
220	Michael Jordan	3.00
221	Bill Wennington	.05
222	Mitchell Butler	.05
223	Zydrunas Ilgauskas	.50
224	Shawn Kemp	.75
225	Wesley Person	.05
226	Shawnelle Scott	.05
227	Bob Sura	.05
228	Hubert Davis	.05
229	Michael Finley	.10
230	Dennis Scott	.05
231	Erick Strickland	.05
232	Samaki Walker	.05
233	Dean Garrett	.05
234	Priest Lauderdale	.05
235	Eric Williams	.05
236	Grant Long	.05
237	Malik Sealy	.05
238	Brian Williams	.05
239	Muggsy Bogues	.05
240	Bimbo Coles	.05
241	Brian Shaw	.05
242	Joe Smith	.25
243	Donyell Marshall	.05
244	Charles Barkley	.30
245	Emanuel Davis	.05
246	Brent Price	.05
247	Reggie Miller	.25
248	Chris Mullin	.10
249	Jalen Rose	.05
250	Rik Smits	.05
251	Mark West	.05
252	Lamond Murray	.05
253	Pooh Richardson	.05
254	Rodney Rogers	.05
255	Stojko Vrankovic	.05
256	Jon Barry	.05
257	Corie Blount	.05
258	Elden Campbell	.05
259	Rick Fox	.05
260	Nick Van Exel	.20
261	Isaac Austin	.05
262	Dan Majerle	.05
263	Terry Mills	.05
264	Mark Strickland	.05
265	Terrell Brandon	.10
266	Tyrone Hill	.05
267	Ervin Johnson	.05
268	Andrew Lang	.05
269	Elliot Perry	.05
270	Chris Carr	.05
271	Reggie Jordan	.05
272	Sam Mitchell	.05
273	Stanley Roberts	.05
274	Michael Cage	.05
275	Sam Cassell	.05
276	Lucious Harris	.05
277	Kerry Kittles	.25
278	Don MacLean	.05
279	Chris Dudley	.05
280	Chris Mills	.05
281	Charlie Ward	.05
282	Buck Williams	.05
283	Herb Williams	.05
284	Derek Harper	.05
285	Mark Price	.05
286	Gerald Wilkins	.05
287	Allen Iverson	1.25
288	Jim Jackson	.05
289	Eric Montross	.05
290	Jerry Stackhouse	.25
291	Clarence Weatherspoon	.05
292	Tom Chambers	.05
293	Rex Chapman	.05
294	Danny Manning	.05
295	Antonio McDyess	.25
296	Clifford Robinson	.05
297	Stacey Augmon	.05
298	Brian Grant	.05
299	Rasheed Wallace	.05
300	Mahmoud Abdul-Rauf	.05
301	Terry Dehere	.05
302	Billy Owens	.05
303	Michael Smith	.05
304	Cory Alexander	.05
305	Chuck Person	.05
306	David Robinson	.30
307	Charles Smith	.05
308	Monty Williams	.05
309	Vin Baker	.20
310	Jerome Kersey	.05
311	Nate McMillan	.05
312	Gary Payton	.30
313	Eric Snow	.05
314	Carlos Rogers	.05
315	Zan Tabak	.05
316	John Wallace	.05
317	Sharone Wright	.05
318	Shandon Anderson	.05
319	Antoine Carr	.05
320	Howard Eisley	.05
321	Chris Morris	.05
322	Pete Chilcutt	.05
323	George Lynch	.05
324	Chris Robinson	.05
325	Otis Thorpe	.05
326	Harvey Grant	.05
327	Darvin Ham	.05
328	Juwan Howard	.25
329	Ben Wallace	.05
330	Chris Webber	.50

1997-98 Hoops Chairman of the Boards

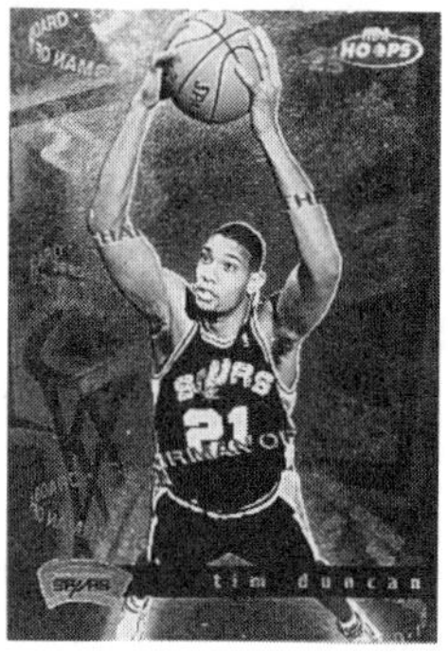

Chairmen of the Boards was a 10-card set that highlighted the league's top rebounders over a foil background that highlighted that player's various rebounding achievements. These cards were inserted in one per nine Series II packs and were numbered with a "CB" suffix.

		MT
Complete Set (10):		30.00
Common Player:		.75
CB1	Shaquille O'Neal	8.00
CB2	Dikembe Mutombo	.75
CB3	Dennis Rodman	5.00
CB4	Patrick Ewing	1.50
CB5	Charles Barkley	2.50
CB6	Karl Malone	2.00
CB7	Rasheed Wallace	.75
CB8	Chris Webber	4.00
CB9	Tim Duncan	10.00
CB10	Kevin Garnett	10.00

1997-98 Hoops Great Shot

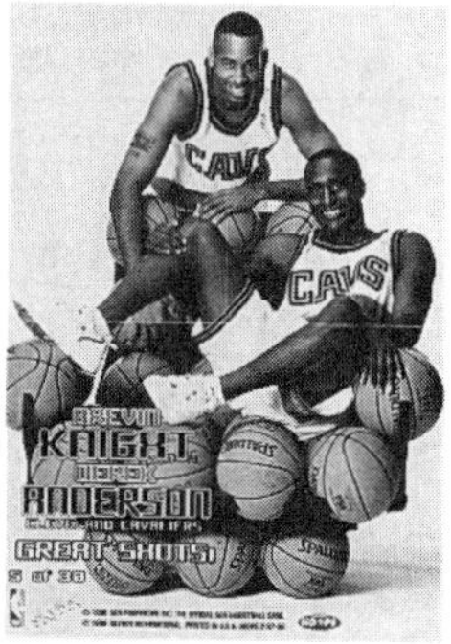

Great Shots higlighted 30 different players on 5" x 7" mini-posters. These inserts were seeded one per pack in Series II Hoops and featured a full-color shot on one side and a plain white back.

		MT
Complete Set (30):		15.00
Common Player:		.10
1	Dikembe Mutombo	.10
2	Antoine Walker	1.50
3	Glen Rice	.30
4	Dennis Rodman	1.00
5	Anderson, Knight	.75
6	Michael Finley	.20
7	Fortson, Battie, Jackson	.50
8	Grant Hill	2.00
9	Joe Smith	.30
10	Charles Barkley	.40
11	Reggie Miller	.30
12	Lamond Murray	.10
13	Kobe Bryant	2.50
14	Alonzo Mourning	.30
15	Ray Allen	.75
16	Kevin Garnett	2.00
17	Stephon Marbury	1.25
18	Kerry Kittles	.30
19	Patrick Ewing	.30
20	Anfernee Hardaway	1.25
21	Allen Iverson	1.50
22	Jason Kidd	.40
23	Rasheed Wallace	.10
24	Mitch Richmond	.25
25	David Robinson	.40
26	Gary Payton	.40
27	Damon Stoudamire	.50
28	John Stockton	.30
29	Shareef Abdur-Rahim	1.00
30	Chris Webber	.75

1997-98 Hoops High Voltage

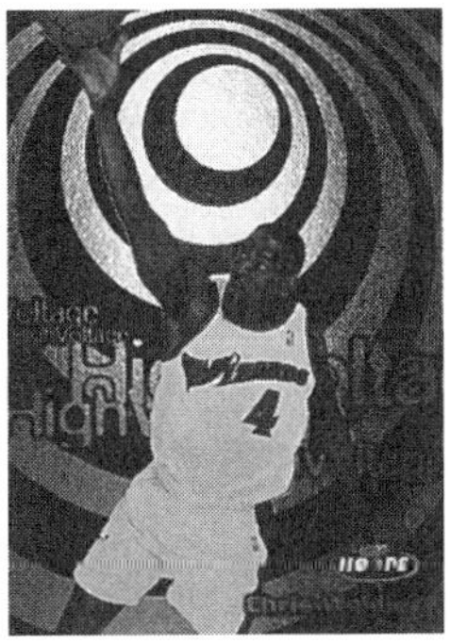

This 20-card insert was exclusive to Series II hobby packs. Card fronts featured an all-foil backgroud with black and silver bullseye stripes. Inserted at a rate of one per 36 packs, this insert is numbered with a "HV" suffix. Parallel 500 Voltage versions of each card were also produced and numbered sequentially to 500.

		MT
Complete Set (20):		150.00
Common Player:		1.50
HV1	Kobe Bryant	20.00
HV2	Eddie Jones	5.00
HV3	Ray Allen	3.00
HV4	Anfernee Hardaway	12.00
HV5	Grant Hill	15.00
HV6	Shareef Abdur-Rahim	8.00
HV7	Marcus Camby	3.00
HV8	Allen Iverson	15.00
HV9	Kerry Kittles	3.00
HV10	Kevin Garnett	15.00
HV11	Stephon Marbury	12.00
HV12	Chris Webber	5.00
HV13	Antoine Walker	12.00
HV14	Michael Jordan	30.00
HV15	Tim Duncan	15.00
HV16	Dennis Rodman	10.00
HV17	Scottie Pippen	7.50
HV18	Shawn Kemp	7.50
HV19	Hakeem Olajuwon	6.00
HV20	Karl Malone	1.50

1997-98 Hoops 911

This 10-card insert set featured a card within a sleeve that could be pulled out to reveal the player. Each sleeve was laser engraved "9-1-1," and was fitted around the inner card. These cards were seeded one per 288 packs of Series II and numbered with a "N" suffix.

		MT
Complete Set (10):		400.00
Common Player:		12.00
N1	Michael Jordan	125.00
N2	Grant Hill	60.00
N3	Shawn Kemp	30.00
N4	Stephon Marbury	50.00
N5	Damon Stoudamire	12.00
N6	Shaquille O'Neal	45.00
N7	Shareef Abdur-Rahim	30.00
N8	Allen Iverson	50.00
N9	Antoine Walker	50.00
N10	Anfernee Hardaway	50.00

1997-98 Hoops Rock the House

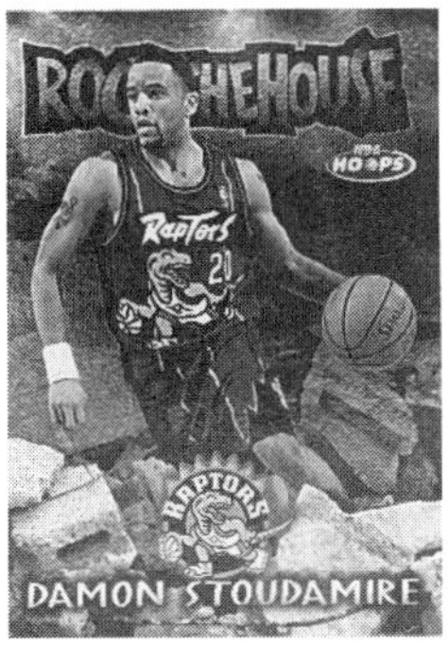

Rock the House was a 10-card, one per 18 retail exclusive insert found in Series II packs. Fronts captured the player over a foil background of rocks, with the insert name printed across the top. Backs were numbered with a "RTH" suffix.

		MT
Complete Set (10):		70.00
Common Player:		1.25
RH1	Anfernee Hardaway	12.00
RH2	Stephon Marbury	10.00
RH3	Grant Hill	15.00
RH4	Shaquille O'Neal	10.00
RH5	Kerry Kittles	1.25
RH6	Michael Jordan	30.00
RH7	Ray Allen	5.00
RH8	Damon Stoudimire	3.00
RH9	Kevin Garnett	15.00
RH10	Shawn Kemp	7.50

1997-98 Hoops Top of the World

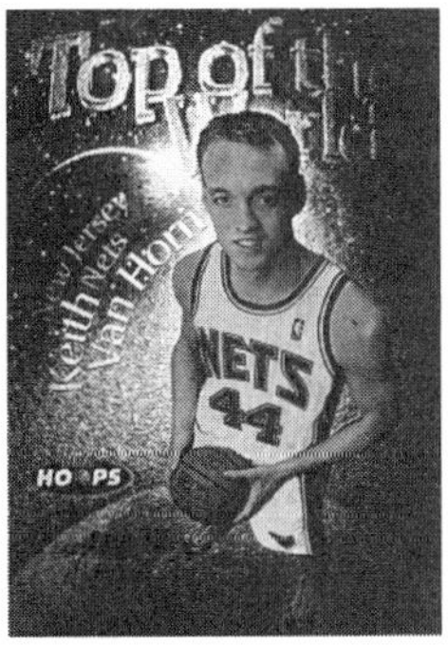

This 15-card insert set was seeded one per 48 packs of Series II. Each player is photographed and superimposed on a globe background, while cards are numbered with a "TW" suffix.

		MT
Complete Set (15):		85.00
Common Player:		1.50
TW1	Tim Duncan	25.00
TW2	Tim Thomas	8.00
TW3	Tony Battie	6.00
TW4	Keith Van Horn	25.00
TW5	Antonio Daniels	8.00
TW6	Derek Anderson	6.00
TW7	Chauncey Billups	12.00
TW8	Tracy McGrady	12.00
TW9	Danny Fortson	3.00
TW10	Austin Croshere	3.00
TW11	Tariq Abdul-Wahad	3.00
TW12	Adonal Foyle	3.00
TW13	Rodrick Rhodes	3.00
TW14	Ron Mercer	12.00
TW15	Charles Smith	1.50

1997-98 Metal Universe

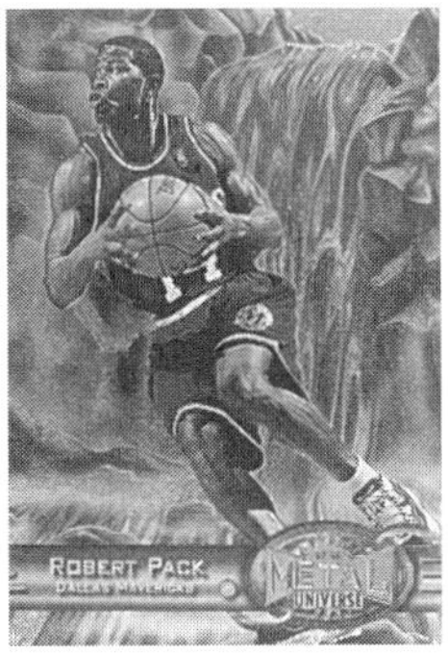

The first series of Metal Universe contained 125 cards, including two checklists. Cards featured comic-art illustrations on 100 percent etched foil fronts. The set included some rookies, like Tim Duncan, Keith Van Horn, Tracy McGrady and Ron Mercer, and sold in eight-card packs. A Series II issue arrived later in the season, but was called Championship Series. Insert sets in Series I included: Silver Slams, Planet Metal, Titanium, Autographics, Gold Universe, Platinum Portraits and Reebok, as well as a 123-card parallel set called Precious Metal Gems.

		MT
Complete Set (125):		25.00
Common Player:		.10
Wax Box:		60.00
1	Charles Barkley	.50
2	Dell Curry	.10
3	Derek Fisher	.10
4	Derek Harper	.10
5	Avery Johnson	.10
6	Steve Smith	.10
7	Alonzo Mourning	.20
8	Rod Strickland	.10
9	Chris Mullin	.20
10	Rony Seikaly	.10
11	Vin Baker	.30
12	*Austin Croshere*	1.00
13	Vinny Del Negro	.10
14	Sherman Douglas	.10
15	Priest Lauderdale	.10
16	Cedric Ceballos	.10
17	LaPhonso Ellis	.10
18	Luc Longley	.10
19	Brian Grant	.10
20	Allen Iverson	1.50
21	Anthony Mason	.10
22	Bryant Reeves	.20
23	Michael Jordan	4.00
24	Dale Ellis	.10
25	Terrell Brandon	.20
26	Patrick Ewing	.30
27	Allan Houston	.10
28	Damon Stoudamire	.50
29	Loy Vaught	.10
30	Walt Williams	.10
31	Shareef Abdur-Rahim	.75
32	Mario Elie	.10
33	Juwan Howard	.40
34	Tom Gugliotta	.10
35	Glen Rice	.20
36	Isaiah Rider	.10
37	Arvydas Sabonis	.10
38	Derrick Coleman	.10
39	Kevin Willis	.10
40	Kendall Gill	.10
41	John Wallace	.20
42	*Tracy McGrady*	2.00
43	Travis Best	.10
44	Malik Rose	.10
45	Anfernee Hardaway	1.75
46	Roy Rogers	.10
47	Kerry Kittles	.40
48	Matt Maloney	.20
49	Antonio McDyess	.30
50	Shaquille O'Neal	1.50
51	George McCloud	.10
52	Wesley Person	.10
53	Shawn Bradley	.10
54	Antonio Davis	.10
55	P.J. Brown	.10
56	Joe Dumars	.10
57	Horace Grant	.10
58	Steve Kerr	.10
59	Hakeem Olajuwon	.75
60	Tim Hardaway	.20
61	Toni Kukoc	.20
62	*Ron Mercer*	3.00
63	Gary Payton	.40
64	Grant Hill	2.00
65	Detlef Schrempf	.10
66	*Tim Duncan*	5.00
67	Shawn Kemp	1.00
68	Voshon Lenard	.10
69	Othella Harrington	.10
70	Hersey Hawkins	.10
71	Lindsey Hunter	.10
72	Antoine Walker	2.00
73	Jamal Mashburn	.20
74	Kenny Anderson	.10
75	Todd Day	.10
76	Todd Fuller	.10
77	Jermaine O'Neal	.20
78	David Robinson	.50
79	Erick Dampier	.10
80	*Keith Van Horn*	4.00
81	Kobe Bryant	3.00
82	Chris Childs	.10
83	Scottie Pippen	1.00
84	Marcus Camby	.75
85	Danny Ferry	.10
86	Jeff Hornacek	.10
87	Charles Outlaw	.10
88	Larry Johnson	.20
89	Tony Delk	.10
90	Stephon Marbury	1.25
91	Robert Pack	.10
92	Chris Webber	.75
93	Clyde Drexler	.40
94	Eddie Jones	.50
95	Jerry Stackhouse	.40
96	Tyrone Hill	.10
97	Karl Malone	.40
98	Reggie Miller	.30
99	Bryan Russell	.10
100	Dale Davis	.10
101	Steve Nash	.10
102	Vitaly Potapenko	.10
103	Nick Anderson	.10
104	Ray Allen	.40
105	Sean Elliott	.10
106	Dikembe Mutombo	.10
107	Dennis Rodman	1.00
108	Lorenzen Wright	.10
109	Kevin Garnett	2.00
110	Christian Laettner	.20
111	Mitch Richmond	.20
112	Joe Smith	.40
113	Jason Kidd	.30
114	Glenn Robinson	.30
115	Mark Price	.10
116	Mark Jackson	.10
117	Bobby Phills	.10
118	John Starks	.10
119	John Stockton	.30
120	Mookie Blaylock	.10
121	Dean Garrett	.10
122	Olden Polynice	.10
123	Latrell Sprewell	.30
124	Checklist	.10
125	Checklist	.10

1997-98 Metal Universe Precious Metal Gems

Precious Metal Gems paralleled the first 123 cards in Metal Universe, excluding the two checklists. The cards are sequentially numbered to 100 and were inserted only into hobby packs. The first 10 numbered sets are printed with green foil, while the rest are printed on red foil.

	MT
Metal Gem Stars:	75x-150x
Metal Gem Rookies:	25x-50x
Production 100 Sets	
Metal Gem Green Stars:	5x-10x
Metal Gem Green Rookies:	3x-6x
First 10 Cards Are Green	

1997-98 Metal Universe Gold Universe

Gold Universe was a 10-card insert set that was found in one per 120 retail packs of Metal Universe. Fronts featured a color shot of the player over a gold-etched, solar system background. Card backs were horizontal with a closeup of the player on the left and text on the right. Cards were numbered "x of 10" and carried a "GU" suffix.

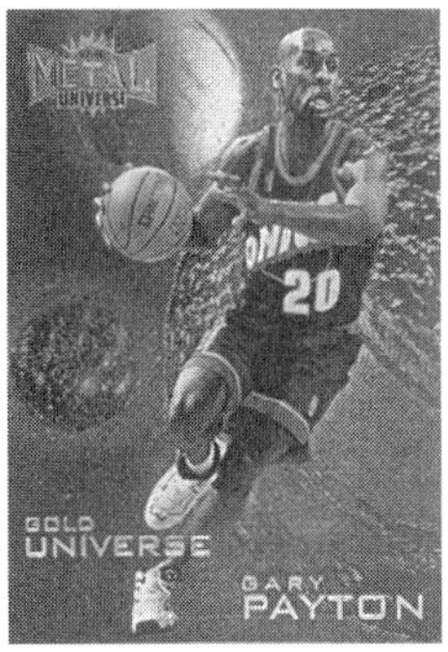

		MT
Complete Set (10):		140.00
Common Player:		10.00
1	Damon Stoudamire	30.00
2	Shawn Kemp	40.00
3	John Stockton	10.00
4	Jerry Stackhouse	20.00
5	John Wallace	10.00
6	Juwan Howard	20.00
7	David Robinson	20.00
8	Gary Payton	20.00
9	Joe Smith	20.00
10	Charles Barkley	20.00

1997-98 Metal Universe Planet Metal

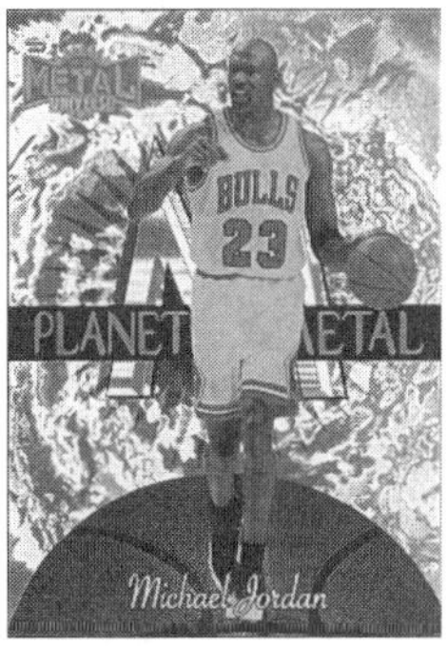

Planet Metal was a 15-card insert set that was found every 24 packs of Metal Universe. Cards feature a color shot of the player over a silver-etched background, with a basketball at his feet and a black strip across the middle containing the insert's name. Backs were horizontal and numbered "x of 15" with a "PM" suffix.

		MT
Complete Set (15):		120.00
Common Player:		3.00
1	Michael Jordan	30.00
2	Allen Iverson	15.00
3	Kobe Bryant	20.00
4	Shaquille O'Neal	10.00
5	Stephon Marbury	12.00
6	Marcus Camby	8.00
7	Anfernee Hardaway	12.00
8	Kevin Garnett	15.00
9	Shareef Abdur-Rahim	8.00
10	Dennis Rodman	10.00
11	Grant Hill	15.00
12	Hakeem Olajuwon	6.00
13	David Robinson	3.00
14	Charles Barkley	3.00
15	Gary Payton	3.00

1997-98 Metal Universe Platinum Portraits

This 15-card insert was seeded only one per 288 packs of Series I. It includes a laser-cut closeup shot of the player on a platinum card. The player's name runs up the left side along the insert's name. Backs capture the reverse shot of the player, with card numbers in the upper right with a "PP" suffix.

		MT
Complete Set (15):		700.00
Common Player:		25.00
1	Michael Jordan	180.00
2	Allen Iverson	90.00
3	Kobe Bryant	120.00
4	Shaquille O'Neal	75.00
5	Stephon Marbury	75.00
6	Marcus Camby	35.00
7	Anfernee Hardaway	75.00
8	Kevin Garnett	90.00
9	Shareef Abdur-Rahim	35.00
10	Dennis Rodman	75.00
11	Ray Allen	25.00
12	Grant Hill	90.00
13	Kerry Kittles	25.00
14	Antoine Walker	70.00
15	Scottie Pippen	35.00

1997-98 Metal Universe Reebok Value

This 15-card insert arrived in bronze, silver and gold versions and included Reebok spokesmen. The versions are virtually identical to regular-issue cards of the players, except for a Reebok logo on the back and a website address to Reebok's web page.

		MT
Complete Set (15):		3.00
Common Player:		.10
Silver Cards:		1.5x
Gold Cards:		2x
5	Avery Johnson	.10
6	Steve Smith	.10
13	Vinny Del Negro	.10
16	Cedric Ceballos	.10
20	Allen Iverson	1.00
32	Mario Elie	.10
50	Shaquille O'Neal	1.00
67	Shawn Kemp	.50
68	Voshon Lenard	.10
74	Kenny Anderson	.10
91	Robert Pack	.10
93	Clyde Drexler	.25
96	Tyrone Hill	.10
114	Glenn Robinson	.20
116	Mark Jackson	.10

1997-98 Metal Universe Silver Slams

Silver Slams was a 20-card insert that was seeded one per 12 packs of Series I.

The cards featured a color shot of the player over a holographic bronze/silver background depending on the angle the light is hitting. Horizontal backs include a black-and-white shot of the player on the left, with text in white letters on the right. Cards are numbered "x of 20" and carry a "SS" suffix.

		MT
Complete Set (20):		45.00
Common Player:		.75
1	Ray Allen	2.50
2	Kerry Kittles	2.00
3	Antoine Walker	6.00
4	Scottie Pippen	5.00
5	Damon Stoudamire	3.00
6	Shawn Kemp	5.00
7	Jerry Stackhouse	2.00
8	John Wallace	.75
9	Juwan Howard	3.00
10	Gary Payton	2.00
11	Joe Smith	2.00
12	Terrell Brandon	.75
13	Hakeem Olajuwon	4.00
14	Tom Gugliotta	.75
15	Glen Rice	.75
16	Charles Barkley	2.50
17	David Robinson	2.50
18	Patrick Ewing	1.50
19	Christian Laettner	.75
20	Chris Webber	4.00

1997-98 Metal Universe Titanium

These die-cut plastic cards were printed on a horizontal design and included holgraphic highlights within the plastic. The set contains 20 cards and was seeded one per 72 hobby packs. Backs are numbered "x of 20" and contain a "T" suffix.

		MT
Complete Set (20):		525.00
Common Player:		6.00
1	Michael Jordan	100.00
2	Allen Iverson	50.00
3	Kobe Bryant	70.00
4	Shaquille O'Neal	40.00
5	Stephon Marbury	40.00
6	Marcus Camby	20.00
7	Anfernee Hardaway	40.00
8	Kevin Garnett	50.00
9	Shareef Abdur-Rahim	25.00
10	Dennis Rodman	40.00
11	Ray Allen	6.00
12	Grant Hill	50.00
13	Kerry Kittles	6.00
14	Antoine Walker	40.00
15	Scottie Pippen	25.00
16	Damon Stoudamire	20.00

17	Shawn Kemp	25.00
18	Hakeem Olajuwon	20.00
19	Jerry Stackhouse	15.00
20	Juwan Howard	12.00

1997-98 Metal Universe Promo Sheet

This six-card perforated sheet was distributed to dealers, distributors and media members to promote the 1997-98 Metal Universe Basketball set. The sheet was geared toward the younger players, with Kobe Bryant, Tim Duncan and Kevin Garnett, and also included spokesman Grant Hill. All six cards were base cards.

		MT
Complete Set (6):		5.00
Common Player:		.50
9	Keith Van Horn	.75
26	Allen Iverson	.50
33	Grant Hill	1.00
41	Kevin Garnett	1.00
72	Tim Duncan	1.00
86	Kobe Bryant	1.50

1997-98 Metal Universe Championship

This 100-card set was essentially the Series II release for 1997-98. It included 98 regular player cards and two checklists and was oriented toward the playoffs. Each regular-issue card featured the veterans superimposed on an Earth landscape, while the rookies are featured over an intergalactic background. The full set is paralleled (minus the two checklists) in a Precious Metals insert. Other inserts include: All Millenium Team, Future Champions, Trophy Case, Championship Galaxy, Hardware and Autographics.

		MT
Complete Set (100):		30.00
Common Player:		.10
Wax Box:		55.00
1	Shaquille O'Neal	1.50
2	Chris Mills	.10
3	Tariq Abdul-Wahad	.50
4	Adonal Foyle	.75
5	Kendall Gill	.10

6	Vin Baker	.30
7	Chauncey Billups	2.00
8	Bobby Jackson	1.50
9	Keith Van Horn	4.00
10	Avery Johnson	.10
11	Juwan Howard	.40
12	Steve Smith	.10
13	Alonzo Mourning	.20
14	Anfernee Hardaway	1.50
15	Sean Elliott	.10
16	Danny Fortson	.75
17	John Stockton	.30
18	John Thomas	.20
19	Lorenzen Wright	.10
20	Mark Price	.10
21	Rasheed Wallace	.10
22	Ray Allen	.40
23	Michael Jordan	4.00
24	John Wallace	.10
25	Bryant Reeves	.10
26	Allen Iverson	1.50
27	Antoine Walker	2.00
28	Terrell Brandon	.20
29	Damon Stoudamire	.50
30	Antonio Daniels	1.50
31	Corey Beck	.10
32	Tyrone Hill	.10
33	Grant Hill	2.00
34	Tim Thomas	2.00
35	Clifford Robinson	.10
36	Tracy McGrady	2.50
37	Chris Webber	.75
38	Austin Croshere	.50
39	Reggie Miller	.30
40	Derek Anderson	1.00
41	Kevin Garnett	2.00
42	Kevin Johnson	.20
43	Antonio McDyess	.30
44	Brevin Knight	1.50
45	Charles Barkley	.50
46	Tom Gugliotta	.20
47	Jason Kidd	.50
48	Marcus Camby	.50
49	God Shammgod	.20
50	Wesley Person	.10
51	Clyde Drexler	.40
52	Paul Grant	.10
53	Rod Strickland	.10
54	Tony Delk	.10
55	Stephon Marbury	1.50
56	Detlef Schrempf	.10
57	Joe Smith	.40
58	Sam Cassell	.10
59	Gary Payton	.40
60	Chris Crawford	.10
61	Hakeem Olajuwon	.75
62	Dennis Rodman	1.25
63	Eddie Jones	.50
64	Mitch Richmond	.30
65	David Wesley	.10
66	Tony Battie	1.00
67	Isaac Austin	.10
68	Isaiah Rider	.10
69	Jacque Vaughn	.50
70	Tim Hardaway	.20
71	Darrell Armstrong	.10
72	Tim Duncan	5.00
73	Glen Rice	.30
74	Bubba Wells	.10
75	Maurice Taylor	.75
76	Kelvin Cato	.20
77	Shareef Abdur-Rahim	1.00
78	Shawn Kemp	1.00
79	Michael Finley	.20
80	Chris Mullin	.20
81	Ron Mercer	3.00
82	Brian Williams	.10
83	Kerry Kittles	.30
84	David Robinson	.50
85	Scottie Pippen	1.00
86	Kobe Bryant	3.00
87	Anthony Johnson	.10
88	Karl Malone	.30
89	Mookie Blaylock	.10
90	Joe Dumars	.10
91	Patrick Ewing	.30
92	Bobby Phills	.10
93	Dennis Scott	.10
94	Rodney Rogers	.10
95	Jim Jackson	.10
96	Kenny Anderson	.10
97	Jerry Stackhouse	.40
98	Larry Johnson	.20
99	Checklist	.10
100	Checklist	.10

1997-98 Metal Universe Championship Precious Metal Gems

Precious Metal Gems paralleled 98 of the 100 cards in Metal Universe Championship, excluding the two checklists. The stated print run for this parallel is 50 sequentially numbered sets..

	MT
Metal Gem Stars:	75x-150x
Metal Gem Rookies:	40x-80x
Production 50 Sets	

1997-98 Metal Universe Championship All-Millenium Team

All-Millenium Team included 20 young stars over a gold foil etched Spalding basketball background. These cards are seeded one per six packs, while card backs are numbered with a "AM" suffix.

		MT
Complete Set (20):		40.00
Common Player:		.50
1	Stephon Marbury	6.00
2	Shareef Abdur-Rahim	3.00
3	Karl Malone	1.00
4	Scottie Pippen	3.00
5	Michael Jordan	12.00
6	Marcus Camby	.50
7	Kobe Bryant	8.00
8	Allen Iverson	6.00
9	Kerry Kittles	1.00
10	Ray Allen	1.00
11	Dennis Rodman	4.00
12	Damon Stoudamire	1.50
13	Antoine Walker	6.00
14	Anfernee Hardaway	6.00
15	Hakeem Olajuwon	2.50
16	Shawn Kemp	3.00
17	Antonio Daniels	.50
18	Juwan Howard	1.50
19	Gary Payton	1.50
20	Tim Duncan	6.00

1997-98 Metal Universe Championship Championship Galaxy

This 20-card insert highlights players who have won NBA Championships. Fronts are presented in three layers - a foil background, double-etched player image and brushed silver foil frame with embossed rivets. Cards were inserted one per 192 packs and carry a "CG" suffix.

		MT
Complete Set (15):		525.00
Common Player:		8.00
1	Michael Jordan	120.00
2	Allen Iverson	45.00
3	Kobe Bryant	80.00
4	Shaquille O'Neal	40.00
5	Stephon Marbury	45.00
6	Marcus Camby	8.00
7	Anfernee Hardaway	45.00
8	Kevin Garnett	60.00

9	Shareef Abdur-Rahim	30.00
10	Dennis Rodman	40.00
11	Grant Hill	60.00
12	Kerry Kittles	8.00
13	Antoine Walker	45.00
14	Scottie Pippen	30.00
15	Damon Stoudamire	12.00

1997-98 Metal Universe Championship Future Champions

Fifteen rookies from the 1997 NBA Draft are included in the Future Champions insert set. The cards give off a three-dimensional look with an action photo of the player encased in a copper from that appears to be hanging from the sky. Each die-cut card is inserted one per 18 packs and carries a "FC" suffix.

		MT
Complete Set (15):		85.00
Common Player:		2.00
1	Tim Duncan	20.00
2	Tony Battie	5.00
3	Keith Van Horn	18.00
4	Antonio Daniels	6.00
5	Chauncey Billups	8.00
6	Ron Mercer	12.00
7	Tracy McGrady	10.00
8	Danny Fortson	3.00
9	Brevin Knight	8.00
10	Derek Anderson	6.00
11	Bobby Jackson	6.00
12	Jacque Vaughn	2.00
13	Tim Thomas	8.00
14	Austin Croshere	2.00
15	Kelvin Cato	2.00

1997-98 Metal Universe Championship Hardware

This one-per-360-pack insert set captures 15 players who have the best shot to win top NBA awards. Fronts offer dual foil including an embossed background and a gold rainbow holographic background. Cards are inserted one per 360 packs and are numbered with a "H" suffix.

	MT
Complete Set (15):	800.00
Common Player:	15.00

1	Stephon Marbury	70.00
2	Shareef Abdur-Rahim	50.00
3	Shaquille O'Neal	60.00
4	Scottie Pippen	50.00
5	Michael Jordan	180.00
6	Marcus Camby	15.00
7	Kobe Bryant	120.00
8	Kevin Garnett	100.00
9	Kerry Kittles	15.00
10	Grant Hill	100.00
11	Dennis Rodman	60.00
12	Tim Duncan	100.00
13	Antonio Daniels	50.00
14	Anfernee Hardaway	70.00
15	Allen Iverson	70.00

1997-98 Metal Universe Championship Trophy Case

Trophy Case includes 10 players on a gold foil sculpted embossed background. The insert's name runs across the top of the card, while the player's name runs across the bottom. Cards are inserted every 96 packs and numbered with a "TC" suffix.

		MT
Complete Set (10):		120.00
Common Player:		4.00
1	Kevin Garnett	30.00
2	Grant Hill	30.00
3	Damon Stoudamire	10.00
4	Shaquille O'Neal	20.00
5	Ray Allen	4.00
6	Gary Payton	8.00
7	Shawn Kemp	15.00
8	Hakeem Olajuwon	12.00
9	John Stockton	4.00
10	Antoine Walker	25.00

1997 Pinnacle Inside WNBA

Pinnacle Inside WNBA arrived in cans that featured a player on the outside, and when opened, yielded a pack of cards. It was the inaugural edition of WNBA cards and celebrated the first season of the new league. The set contained 81 cards and was paralleled in both Court Collection and Executive Collection sets. My Town and Team Development were the names of the two insert sets available.

		MT
Complete Set (82):		45.00
Common Player:		.10
1	Lisa Leslie	3.00
2	Cynthia Cooper	3.00
3	Rebecca Lobo	2.50
4	Michele Timms	1.00
5	Ruthie Bolton-Holifield	2.00
6	Michelle Edwards	.75
7	Vicky Bullett	.30
8	Tammi Reiss	.50
9	Penny Toler	.10
10	Tia Jackson	.10
11	Rhonda Mapp	.10
12	Elena Baranova	.75
13	Tina Thompson	.75
14	Merlakia Jones	.30
15	Tora Suber	.10
16	Sophia Witherspoon	.30
17	Tajama Abraham	.10
18	Jessie Hicks	.10
19	Tina Nicholson	.10
20	Tiffany Woosley	.10
21	Chantel Tremitiere	.10
22	Daedra Charles	.10
23	Nancy Lieberman-Cline	2.00
24	Denique Graves	.10
25	Toni Foster	.10
26	Sheryl Swoopes	3.00
27	Kym Hampton	.30
28	Sharon Manning	.10
29	Janice Lawrence Braxton	.10
30	Sue Wicks	.10
31	Lady Hardmon	.10
32	Jamila Wideman	.10
33	Bridgette Gordon	.10
34	Lynette Woodard	1.00
35	Kim Perrot	.30
36	Teresa Weatherspoon	.30
37	Andrea Stinson	1.00
38	Janeth Arcain	.10
39	Pamela McGee	.10
40	Tamecka Dixon	.30
41	Wendy Palmer	1.00
42	Umeki Webb	.10
43	Isabelle Fijalkowski	.10
44	Jennifer Gillom	1.00
45	Latasha Byears	.30
46	Zheng Haixia	.10
47	Kisha Ford	.10
48	Eva Nemcova	.10
49	Penny Moore	.30
50	Mwadi Mabika	.10
51	Kim Williams	.10
52	Wanda Guyton	.10
53	Vickie Johnson	.30
54	Deborah Carter	.10
55	Bridget Pettis	.10
56	Andrea Congreaves	.10
57	Zheng Haixia (Hoop Scoops)	.10
58	Tammi Reiss (Hoop Scoops)	.30
59	Jennifer Gillom (Hoop Scoops)	.50
60	Bridgette Gordon (Hoop Scoops)	.10
61	Janice Lawrence Braxton (Hoop Scoops)	.10
62	Cynthia Cooper (Hoop Scoops)	1.50
63	Teresa Weatherspoon (Hoop Scoops)	.10
64	Elena Baranova (Hoop Scoops)	.30
65	Nancy Lieberman-Cline (Hoop Scoops)	.75
66	Andrea Congreaves (Hoop Scoops)	.10
67	Sophia Witherspoon (Hoop Scoops)	.10
68	Vicky Bullett (Hoop Scoops)	.10
69	Ruthie Bolton-Holifield (Hoop Scoops)	1.00
70	Tina Thompson (Hoop Scoops)	.30
71	Lynette Woodard (Hoop Scoops)	.30
72	Jamila Wideman (Hoop Scoops)	.10
73	Lisa Leslie (Style & Grace)	1.50
74	Wendy Palmer (Style & Grace)	.30
75	Michele Timms (Style & Grace)	.30
76	Ruthie Bolton-Holifield (Style & Grace)	1.00
77	Andrea Stinson (Style & Grace)	.30
78	Lynette Woodard (Style & Grace)	.30
79	Cynthia Cooper (Style & Grace)	1.50
80	Rebecca Lobo (Style & Grace)	1.00
81	Checklist	.10
82	Checklist	.10

1997 Pinnacle Inside WNBA Court

Court Collection was an 81-card parallel set that included the insert name in foil across the bottom. These were inserted into one per seven packs.

	MT
Court Cards:	3x-6x

1997 Pinnacle Inside WNBA Executive Collection

Executive Collection was an 81-card parallel set that included a prismatic foil finish to the front of the card along with the insert name in foil letters. These were seeded one per 47 packs.

	MT
Executive Cards:	25x-50x

1997 Pinnacle Inside WNBA Cans

Pinnacle WNBA cards arrived in Cans that featured a shot of a player, the WNBA logo, team logo and information about the product on the outside. When opened with a can opener, a 10-card pack of cards were inside a foil wrapper. Seventeen different Cans were available.

		MT
Complete Set (17):		15.00
Common Player:		.50
1	Andrea Stinson	1.00
2	Vicky Bullett	1.00
3	Lynette Woodard	1.00
4	Michelle Edwards	1.00
5	Cynthia Cooper	3.00
6	Tina Thompson	1.00
7	Lisa Leslie	3.00
8	Jamila Wideman	.50
9	Teresa Weatherspoon	1.00
10	Rebecca Lobo	2.00
11	Michele Timms	1.00
12	Bridget Pettis	.50
13	Bridgette Gordon	.50
14	Ruthie Bolton-Holifield	2.00
15	Wendy Palmer	1.00
16	Elena Baranova	1.00
17	WNBA League	2.00

1997 Pinnacle Inside WNBA My Town

My Town featured eight top players on a horizontal, foil background that featured the skyline from the city she played in. These inserts were numbered "of 8" on the back and seeded one per 19 packs.

		MT
Complete Set (8):		120.00
Common Player:		5.00
1	Lisa Leslie	45.00
2	Lady Hardmon	5.00
3	Michele Timms	10.00
4	Ruthie Bolton-Holifield	25.00
5	Andrea Stinson	10.00
6	Michelle Edwards	10.00
7	Cynthia Cooper	45.00
8	Rebecca Lobo	30.00

1997 Pinnacle Inside WNBA Team Development

Team Development featured eight young stars on a silver foil background with a swoosh of the player's team color. These were numbered "of 8" on the back and inserted one per 19 packs.

		MT
Complete Set (8):		50.00
Common Player:		5.00
1	Tina Thompson	20.00
2	Pamela McGee	5.00
3	Jamila Wideman	5.00
4	Eva Nemcova	10.00
5	Tammi Reiss	15.00
6	Sue Wicks	5.00
7	Tora Suber	5.00
8	Toni Foster	5.00

1997 Press Pass Double Threat

Press Pass Double Threat marked the company's second release of the year. The base set contained 45 cards that included the player's name up the left side in gold foil and the team that drafted him and the pick he was drafted with in the lower right. Double Threat added professional players like Karl Malone and David Robinson to its college star checklist. Inserts included: Certified Autographs, Double Threat Autographs, Double Thread Jersey Cards, Rookie Jersey Cards, Double Threat Nitrokrome, Light it up, Retro-active, Showdown and Lottery Club.

		MT
Complete Set (45):		15.00
Common Player:		.10
Wax Box:		60.00
1	Tim Duncan	2.50
2	Keith Van Horn	1.75
3	Chauncey Billups	1.00
4	Antonio Daniels	1.00
5	Tony Battie	.75
6	Ron Mercer	1.50
7	Tim Thomas	.75
8	Adonal Foyle	.50
9	Tracy McGrady	1.50
10	Danny Fortson	.75
11	Olivier Saint-Jean	.50
12	Austin Croshere	.50
13	Derek Anderson	1.00
14	Maurice Taylor	.50
15	Kelvin Cato	.50
16	Brevin Knight	1.00
17	Johnny Taylor	.10
18	Chris Anstey	.10
19	Scot Pollard	.10
20	Paul Grant	.10
21	Anthony Parker	.10
22	Ed Gray	.50
23	Bobby Jackson	.75
24	John Thomas	.10
25	Charles Smith	.10
26	Jacque Vaughn	.50
27	Keith Booth	.10
28	Serge Zwikker	.20
29	Charles O'Bannon	.50
30	Bubba Wells	.10
31	Kebu Stewart	.25
32	James Collins	.10
33	Eddie Elisma	.10
34	Tim Duncan, David Robinson	1.25
35	Chauncey Billups, Antoine Walker	.75
36	Tony Battie, Antonio McDyess	.75
37	Ron Mercer, Antoine Walker	.75
38	Antonio Daniels, Shareef Abdur-Rahim	.75
39	Danny Fortson, Antonio McDyess	.20
40	Jacque Vaughn, Karl Malone	.20
41	Adonal Foyle, Joe Smith	.20
42	Paul Grant, Stephon Marbury	.20
43	Keith Booth, Scottie Pippen	.20
44	Charles Smith, Alonzo Mourning	.10
45	Checklist Tim Duncan, David Robinson	.50

1997 Press Pass Double Threat Silver

Double Threat arrived with a silver foil verions of each card in the regular-issue set. Where base cards had gold

foil, these had silver, and they were seeded one per pack.

	MT
Silver Cards:	1.5x

1997 Press Pass Double Threat Retroactive

Retroactive was a 36-card insert that was seeded one per pack of Double Threat. These featured top new draftees on the look of older cards that measured 2 3/8" x 2 7/8" and had a matte finish.

	MT
Retroactive Cards:	1.5x

1997 Press Pass Double Threat Autographs

Thirty players signed cards for Double Threat, with one per 18 hobby packs and one per 36 retail packs. Some of the autographs are duplicates of those inserted in Press Pass Draft Picks sets, while others were specifically created for Double Threats.

		MT
Complete Set (29):		450.00
Common Player:		7.00
	Tim Duncan	100.00
	Keith Van Horn	60.00
	Chauncey Billups	35.00
	Antonio Daniels	35.00
	Tony Battie	30.00
	Tim Thomas	30.00
	Adonal Foyle	12.00
	Tracy McGrady	40.00
	Danny Fortson	20.00
	Olivier Saint-Jean	20.00
	Austin Croshere	20.00
	Derek Anderson	25.00
	Kelvin Cato	20.00
	Brevin Knight	20.00
	Johnny Taylor	7.00
	Chris Anstey	7.00
	Scot Pollard	7.00
	Paul Grant	7.00
	Anthony Parker	7.00
	Bobby Jackson	30.00
	John Thomas	7.00
	Charles Smith	7.00
	Jacque Vaughn	20.00
	Serge Zwikker	7.00
	Charles O'Bannon	15.00
	Bubba Wells	7.00
	Kebu Stewart	15.00
	James Collins	7.00
	Eddie Elisma	7.00

1997 Press Pass Double Threat Autograph Combos

This five-card insert set highlights five matchups on double-sided cards, with a rookie on one side and a veteran on the other. Both sides are autographed and all cards are individually numbered, with varying production numbers for each. Autograph Combos were inserted one per 432 packs of Double Threat.

	MT
Complete Set (5):	750.00
Common Player:	40.00
Tim Duncan, David Robinson	450.00
Jacque Vaughn, Karl Malone	125.00
Tony Battie, Antonio McDyess	40.00
Ron Mercer, Antoine Walker	150.00
Chauncey Billups, Antoine Walker	70.00

1997 Press Pass Double Threat Double-Threads

Double Threads combine a top draft pick with a veteran star from the NBA and includes a piece of game-worn jersey from each player on the card. The stated print run for each card was 325, with an insertion rate of one per 720 packs.

	MT
Complete Set (5):	800.00
Common Player:	125.00
DD1 Tim Duncan, David Robinson	300.00
DD2 Chauncey Billups, Antoine Walker	175.00
DD3 Ron Mercer, Antoine Walker	200.00
DD4 Tony Battie, Antonio McDyess	125.00
DD5 Jacque Vaughn, Karl Malone	150.00

1997 Press Pass Double Threat Jersey Cards

Four rookie Jersey Cards were included in Double Threat with an insertion rate of one per 720 packs. The Mercer and Van Horn cards were numbered with a "JC" prefix, while Duncan and Battie were considered Bonus cards.

	MT
Complete Set (4):	550.00
Common Player:	100.00
JC2 Ron Mercer	150.00
JC3 Keith Van Horn	175.00
Bonus Tony Battie	100.00
Bonus Tim Duncan	250.00

1997 Press Pass Double Threat Light it Up

This 25-card insert was seeded one per nine packs of Double Threat and was numbered with a "LU" prefix. These inserts featured a die-cut design in the shape of a basketball hoop, with the player's image over it.

	MT
Complete Set (25):	160.00
Common Player:	4.00
LU1 Tim Duncan	30.00
LU2 Keith Van Horn	20.00
LU3 Chauncey Billups	12.00
LU4 Antonio Daniels	12.00
LU5 Tony Battie	12.00
LU6 Ron Mercer	15.00
LU7 Tim Thomas	10.00
LU8 Adonal Foyle	8.00
LU9 Tracy McGrady	15.00
LU10 Danny Fortson	10.00
LU11 Jacque Vaughn	8.00
LU12 Austin Croshere	8.00
LU13 Derek Anderson	10.00
LU14 Maurice Taylor	4.00
LU15 Kelvin Cato	4.00
LU16 Brevin Knight	12.00
LU17 Alonzo Mourning	4.00
LU18 Joe Smith	4.00
LU19 Shareef Abdur-Rahim	8.00
LU20 Scottie Pippen	4.00
LU21 David Robinson	4.00
LU22 Karl Malone	4.00
LU23 Stephon Marbury	10.00
LU24 Antonio McDyess	4.00
LU25 Checklist Antoine Walker	4.00

1997 Press Pass Double Threat Lottery Club

This eigth-card insert set was randomly inserted into packs of Double Threat, with two high draft picks - one current, one veteran - matched up by position. Card No. 1A was seeded 1:720, 1B was seeded 1:360, 2A was seeded 1:180, 2B seeded 1:90, 3A and 3B seeded 1:45 and 4A and 4B seeded 1:36.

	MT
Complete Set (8):	200.00
Common Player:	10.00
LC1a Tim Duncan	80.00
LC1b David Robinson	50.00
LC2a Keith Van Horn	40.00
LC2b Antonio McDyess	20.00
LC3a Antonio Daniels	15.00
LC3b Stephon Marbury	15.00
LC4a Ron Mercer	10.00
LC4b Antoine Walker	10.00

1997 Press Pass Double Threat Nitrokrome

This nine-card insert featured an NBA veteran with a top draft choice that resembles that player on a foil etched card. Double Threat Nitrokrome inserts were seeded one per 18 packs and were numbered with a "DT" prefix.

	MT
Complete Set (9):	40.00
Common Player:	2.00
DT1 Tim Duncan, David Robinson	14.00
DT2 Jacque Vaughn, Karl Malone	4.00
DT3 Tony Battie, Antonio McDyess	6.00
DT4 Ron Mercer, Antoine Walker	8.00
DT5 Paul Grant, Stephon Marbury	4.00
DT6 Chauncey Billups, Antoine Walker	6.00
DT7 Antonio Daniels, Shareef Abdur-Rahim	6.00
DT8 Alonzo Mourning, Charles Smith	2.00
DT9 Joe Smith, Adonal Foyle	2.00

1997 Press Pass Double Threat Showdown

This six-card back-to-back insert features some of the newest rivalries between veterans and rookies. Showdown inserts were seeded one per 36 hobby packs and were numbered with a "S" prefix.

	MT
Complete Set (6):	75.00
Common Player:	8.00
S1 Alonzo Mourning, Tim Duncan	25.00
S2 Karl Malone, Danny Fortson	8.00
S3 Joe Smith, Tony Battie	12.00
S4 Antonio McDyess, Keith Van Horn	18.00
S5 Scottie Pippen, Ron Mercer	18.00
S6 David Robinson, Adonal Foyle	8.00

1997-98 SkyBox

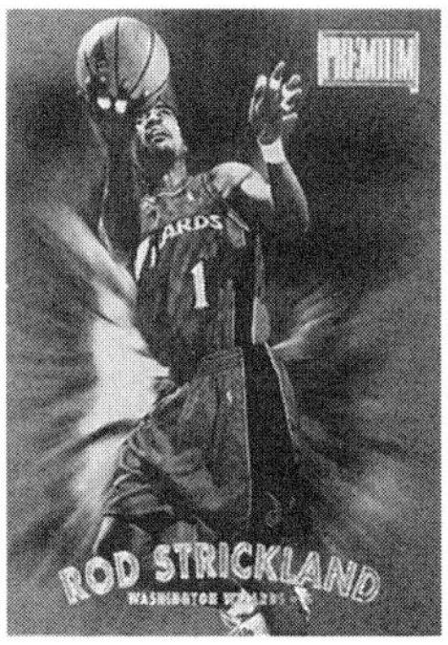

SkyBox Basketball in 1997-98 consisted of two, 125-card series. Series I had 123 regular cards and two checklists, while Series II had 98 veterans and rookies, a 25-card Team SkyBox insert (1:4 packs) and two checklists. Base card featured a color shot of the player on a borderless design with a colored, blurred background done with computer graphics. Star Rubies parallels ran through both series, with 246 cards (250 minus four checklists) numbered to only 50 sets. Inserts in Series I include: Next Game, Rock 'N Fire, And One..., Premium Players and Silky Smooth. Inserts in Series II include: Star Search, Jam Pack, Competitive Advantage, Thunder & Lightning and Golden Touch. Autographics cards were also inserted into both series.

	MT
Complete Set (250):	65.00
Complete Series 1 (125):	30.00
Complete Series 2 (125):	35.00
Common Player:	.10
Common Player (224-248):	.50
Series 1 Wax Box:	60.00
Series 2 Wax Box:	60.00

1	Grant Hill	2.00
2	Matt Maloney	.20
3	Vinny Del Negro	.10
4	Bobby Phills	.10
5	Mark Jackson	.10
6	Ray Allen	.25
7	Derrick Coleman	.10
8	Isaiah Rider	.10
9	Rod Strickland	.10
10	Danny Ferry	.10
11	Antonio Davis	.10
12	Glenn Robinson	.25
13	Cedric Ceballos	.10
14	Sean Elliott	.10
15	Walt Williams	.10
16	Glen Rice	.20
17	Clyde Drexler	.30
18	Sherman Douglas	.10
19	Brian Grant	.10
20	John Stockton	.30
21	Priest Lauderdale	.10
22	Khalid Reeves	.10
23	Kobe Bryant	3.00
24	Vin Baker	.25
25	Steve Nash	.10
26	Jeff Hornacek	.10
27	Malik Rose	.10
28	Charles Barkley	.40
29	Michael Jordan	4.00
30	Latrell Sprewell	.30
31	Anfernee Hardaway	1.50
32	Steve Kerr	.10
33	Joe Smith	.30
34	Jermaine O'Neal	.20
35	*Ron Mercer*	3.00
36	Antonio McDyess	.30
37	Patrick Ewing	.25
38	Avery Johnson	.10
39	Toni Kukoc	.10
40	Chris Mullin	.10
41	Voshon Lenard	.10
42	Detlef Schrempf	.10
43	Horace Grant	.10
44	Luc Longley	.10
45	Todd Fuller	.10
46	Tim Hardaway	.20
47	Nick Anderson	.10
48	Scottie Pippen	1.00
49	Lindsey Hunter	.10
50	Shawn Kemp	1.00
51	Larry Johnson	.20
52	Shawn Bradley	.10
53	Charles Outlaw	.10
54	Jamal Mashburn	.20
55	John Starks	.10
56	Rony Seikaly	.10
57	Gary Payton	.30
58	Juwan Howard	.30
59	Vitaly Potapenko	.10
60	Reggie Miller	.25
61	Alonzo Mourning	.20
62	Roy Rogers	.10
63	Antoine Walker	2.00
64	Joe Dumars	.10
65	Allan Houston	.10
66	Hersey Hawkins	.10
67	Dell Curry	.10
68	Tony Delk	.10
69	Mookie Blaylock	.10
70	Derek Harper	.10
71	Loy Vaught	.10
72	Tom Gugliotta	.20
73	Mitch Richmond	.20
74	Dikembe Mutombo	.10
75	*Tony Battie*	2.00
76	Derek Fisher	.10
77	Jason Kidd	.30
78	Shareef Abdur-Rahim	.75
79	*Tracy McGrady*	2.00
80	Anthony Mason	.10
81	Mario Elie	.10
82	Karl Malone	.30
83	Dean Garrett	.10
84	Steve Smith	.10
85	LaPhonso Ellis	.10
86	Robert Horry	.10
87	Wesley Person	.10
88	Marcus Camby	.50
89	*Antonio Daniels*	2.00
90	Eddie Jones	.50
91	Todd Day	.10
92	*Danny Fortson*	1.75
93	Chris Childs	.10
94	David Robinson	.40
95	Bryant Reeves	.10
96	Chris Webber	.40
97	P.J. Brown	.10
98	Tyrone Hill	.10
99	Dale Davis	.10
100	Allen Iverson	2.00
101	Jerry Stackhouse	.30
102	Arvydas Sabonis	.10
103	Damon Stoudamire	.40
104	*Tim Thomas*	2.00
105	Christian Laettner	.20
106	Robert Pack	.10
107	Lorenzen Wright	.10
108	Olden Polynice	.10
109	Terrell Brandon	.20
110	Erick Dampier	.10
111	Kevin Garnett	2.00
112	*Tim Duncan*	5.00
113	Bryon Russell	.10
114	*Chauncey Billups*	2.00
115	Dale Ellis	.10
116	Shaquille O'Neal	1.50
117	*Keith Van Horn*	4.00
118	Kenny Anderson	.10
119	Dennis Rodman	1.00
120	Hakeem Olajuwon	.75
121	Stephon Marbury	1.50
122	Kendall Gill	.10
123	Kerry Kittles	.30
124	Checklist	.10
125	Checklist	.10
126	Anthony Johnson	.10
127	*Chris Anstey*	.20
128	Dean Garrett	.10
129	Rik Smits	.10
130	Tracy Murray	.10
131	Charles O'Bannon	.10
132	Eldridge Recasner	.10
133	Johnny Taylor	.10
134	Priest Lauderdale	.10
135	Rod Strickland	.10
136	Alan Henderson	.10
137	*Austin Croshere*	.50
138	Buck Williams	.10
139	Clifford Robinson	.10
140	Darrell Armstrong	.10
141	Dennis Scott	.10
142	Carl Herrera	.10
143	*Maurice Taylor*	.75
144	Chris Gatling	.10
145	Alvin Williams	.10
146	Antonio McDyess	.50
147	Chauncey Billups	1.00
148	George McCloud	.10
149	George Lynch	.10
150	John Thomas	.10
151	Jayson Williams	.10
152	Otis Thorpe	.10
153	Serge Zwikker	.10
154	Chris Crawford	.10
155	Muggsy Bogues	.10
156	Mark Jackson	.10
157	Dontonio Wingfield	.10
158	*Rodrick Rhodes*	.50
159	Sam Cassell	.10
160	Hubert Davis	.10
161	Clarence Weatherspoon	.10
162	Eddie Johnson	.10
163	*Jacque Vaughn*	.30
164	Mark Price	.10
165	Terry Dehere	.10
166	Travis Knight	.10
167	Charles Smith	.10
168	David Wesley	.10
169	David Wingate	.10
170	Todd Day	.10
171	*Adonal Foyle*	.50
172	Chris Mills	.10
173	Paul Grant	.10
174	Adam Keefe	.10
175	Erick Dampier	.10
176	Ervin Johnson	.10
177	Lamond Murray	.10
178	Vlade Divac	.10
179	Bobby Phills	.10
180	Brian Williams	.10
181	Chris Dudley	.10
182	Tyrone Hill	.10
183	Donyell Marshall	.10
184	Kevin Gamble	.10
185	Scot Pollard	.10
186	Cherokee Parks	.10
187	Terry Mills	.10
188	Glen Rice	.30
189	Shawn Respert	.10
190	Terrell Brandon	.20
191	Keith Closs	.10
192	*Tariq Abdul-Wahad*	.50
193	Wesley Person	.10
194	Chuck Person	.10
195	*Derek Anderson*	1.50
196	Jon Barry	.10
197	Chris Mullin	.20
198	Ed Gray	.10
199	Charlie Ward	.10
200	*Kelvin Cato*	.20
201	Michael Finley	.20
202	Rick Fox	.10
203	Scott Burrell	.10
204	Vin Baker	.50
205	Eric Snow	.10
206	Isaac Austin	.10
207	Keith Booth	.10
208	Brian Grant	.10
209	Chris Webber	.75
210	Eric Williams	.10
211	Jim Jackson	.20
212	Anthony Parker	.10
213	*Brevin Knight*	1.00
214	Cory Alexander	.10
215	James Robinson	.10
216	*Bobby Jackson*	1.00
217	Charles Outlaw	.10
218	*God Shammgod*	.50
219	James Cotton	.10
220	Jud Buechler	.10
221	Shandon Anderson	.10
222	Kevin Johnson	.10
223	Chris Morris	.10
224	Shareef Abdur-Rahim	2.00
225	Ray Allen	.75
226	Kobe Bryant	5.00
227	Marcus Camby	.50
228	Antonio Daniels	1.50
229	Tim Duncan	4.00
230	Kevin Garnett	4.00
231	Anfernee Hardaway	3.00
232	Grant Hill	4.00
233	Allen Iverson	3.00
234	Bobby Jackson	.75
235	Michael Jordan	8.00
236	Shawn Kemp	2.00
237	Karl Malone	.50
238	Stephon Marbury	3.00
239	Hakeem Olajuwon	1.50
240	Shaquille O'Neal	3.00
241	Gary Payton	.75
242	Scottie Pippen	2.00
243	David Robinson	.75
244	Dennis Rodman	2.50
245	Jerry Stackhouse	.75
246	Damon Stoudamire	1.25
247	Keith Van Horn	2.00
248	Antoine Walker	.75
249	Grant Hill	1.25
250	Hakeem Olajuwon	.50

1997-98 SkyBox Rubies

Rubies featured all 250 cards from Series I and II with red foil stamping on the front vs. the gold used on regular cards. These parallel versions were found in hobby packs only and sequentially numbered to 50 sets. In addition, the short-printed Team SkyBox subset is not short-printed in Rubies; it is numbered to 50 like the other cards.

	MT
Ruby Stars:	100x-200x
Ruby Rookies:	50x-100x

1997-98 SkyBox and One

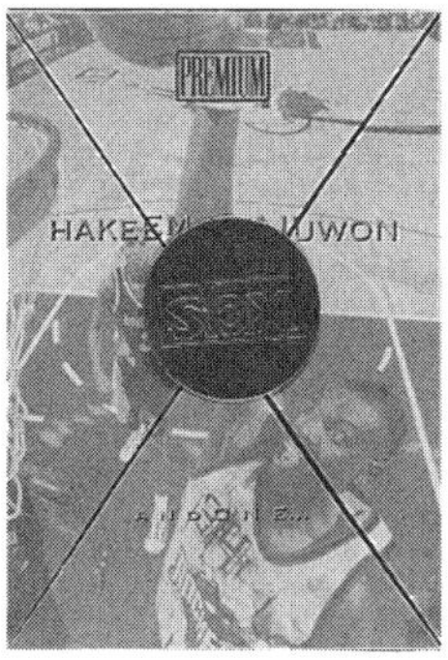

This 10-card features an outer layer that opens in four directions to reveal a larger photo in a diamond-shaped "poster" that is highighted in silver and gold. In addition, there's an extra bonus card inside that is printed in silver foil. And One inserts were seeded every 96 packs of Series I and are numbered on the innermost card with an "AO" suffix.

		MT
Complete Set (10):		200.00
Common Player:		8.00
1	Shawn Kemp	15.00
2	Hakeem Olajuwon	12.00
3	Charles Barkley	8.00
4	Antoine Walker	30.00
5	Dennis Rodman	20.00
6	Tim Duncan	40.00
7	Marcus Camby	10.00
8	Keith Van Horn	30.00
9	Shareef Abdur-Rahim	15.00
10	Michael Jordan	70.00

1997-98 SkyBox Autographics

Autographics returned for a second season with around 150 player's signatures in all. The inserts were included in packs of Hoops I and II (1:240 packs), SkyBox I and II (1:72 packs), Z-Force I and II (1:120 packs) and E-X2001 (1:60 packs). Rarer versions of each card were also available and included prismatic foil on the front and individual, hand numbering.

	MT
Common Player:	15.00
Century Marks:	2x-3x
Shareef Abdur-Rahim	150.00
Cory Alexander	15.00
Kenny Anderson	25.00
Nick Anderson	20.00
Stacey Augmon	15.00
Isaac Austin	20.00
Vin Baker	100.00
Charles Barkley	300.00
Dana Barros	15.00
Brent Barry	25.00
Tony Battie	40.00
Travis Best	15.00
Corie Blount	15.00
P.J. Brown	20.00
Randy Brown	20.00
Jud Buechler	20.00
Marcus Camby	75.00
Elden Campbell	25.00
Antoine Carr	15.00
Chris Carr	15.00
Duane Causwell	15.00
Rex Chapman	30.00
Calbert Cheaney	20.00
Randolph Childress	15.00
Derrick Coleman	35.00
Austin Croshere	25.00
Dell Curry	15.00
Ben Davis	15.00
Mark Davis	15.00
Andrew DeClercq	20.00
Tony Delk	30.00
Vlade Divac	25.00
Clyde Drexler	120.00
Joe Dumars	50.00
Howard Eisley	15.00
Danny Ferry	15.00
Michael Finley	30.00
Derek Fisher	25.00
Danny Fortson	30.00
Todd Fuller	15.00
Chris Gatling	15.00
Matt Geiger	15.00
Brian Grant	20.00
Tom Gugliotta	70.00
Tim Hardaway	75.00
Ron Harper	25.00
Othella Harrington	15.00
Grant Hill	325.00
Tyrone Hill	15.00
Allan Houston	40.00
Juwan Howard	100.00
Lindsey Hunter	35.00
Bobby Hurley	15.00
Jimmy Jackson	25.00
Avery Johnson	15.00
Eddie Johnson	15.00
Ervin Johnson	15.00
Larry Johnson	50.00
Popeye Jones	15.00
Adam Keefe	15.00
Steve Kerr	25.00
Kerry Kittles	75.00
Brevin Knight	70.00
Travis Knight	25.00
George Lynch	15.00
Don MacLean	15.00
Stephon Marbury	175.00
Donny Marshall	20.00
Walter McCarty	30.00
Antonio McDyess	70.00
Tracy McGrady CM	325.00
Ron Mercer	175.00
Reggie Miller	200.00
Chris Mills	15.00
Sam Mitchell	15.00
Chris Morris	15.00
Alonzo Mourning	125.00
Chris Mullin	30.00
Dikembe Mutombo	50.00
Sam Perkins	20.00
Elliot Perry	15.00
Bobby Phills	15.00
Eric Piatkowski	20.00
Scottie Pippen	275.00
Vitaly Potapenko	15.00
Brent Price	15.00
Theo Ratliff	25.00
Glen Rice	60.00
Glenn Robinson	75.00
Dennis Rodman	500.00
Roy Rogers	15.00
Malik Rose	15.00
Joe Smith	75.00
Tony Smith	15.00
Eric Snow	15.00
Jerry Stackhouse Det.	75.00
Jerry Stackhouse Phi.	75.00
John Starks	25.00
Bryant Stith	15.00
Erick Strickland	20.00
Rod Strickland	45.00
Nick Van Exel	85.00
Keith Van Horn	325.00
David Vaughn	15.00
Jacque Vaughn	40.00
Antoine Walker	150.00
John Wallace	15.00
Rasheed Wallace CM	75.00
Clarence Weatherspoon	15.00
David Wesley	15.00
Dominique Wilkins	60.00
Gerald Wilkins	15.00
Erik Williams	15.00
John Williams	15.00
Lorenzo Williams	15.00
Monty Williams	15.00
Scott Williams	15.00
Walt Williams	25.00
Lorenzen Wright	30.00

1997-98 SkyBox Competitive Advantage

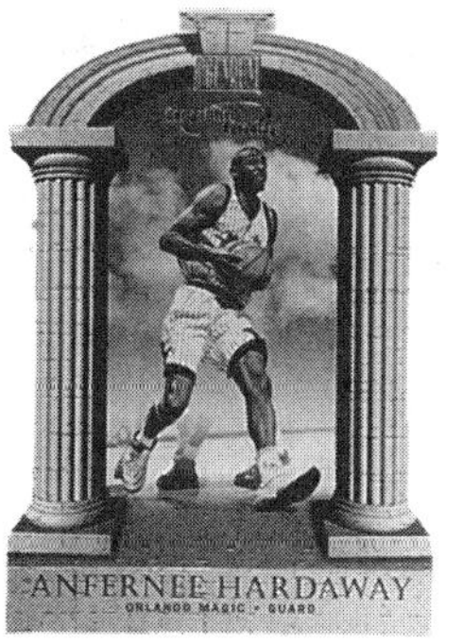

This 15-card insert set highlights players between the arches of stone columns on a die-cut format. Competitive Advantage inserts were seeded one per 96 packs of Series II and numbered with a "CA" suffix.

		MT
Complete Set (15):		275.00
Common Player:		7.00
CA1	Allen Iverson	30.00
CA2	Kobe Bryant	45.00
CA3	Michael Jordan	70.00
CA4	Shaquille O'Neal	25.00
CA5	Stephon Marbury	35.00
CA6	Shareef Abdur-Rahim	25.00
CA7	Marcus Camby	7.00
CA8	Kevin Garnett	35.00
CA9	Dennis Rodman	20.00
CA10	Anfernee Hardaway	25.00
CA11	Ray Allen	14.00
CA12	Scottie Pippen	17.00
CA13	Shawn Kemp	17.00
CA14	Hakeem Olajuwon	15.00
CA15	John Stockton	7.00

1997-98 SkyBox Golden Touch

Golden Touch is a 15-card insert set that was seeded one per 360 packs of Series II. Each card featured the color image of the player on a gold foil, die-cut card with the insert name in bold, gold letters across the top and bottom. Golden Touch inserts were numbered with a "GT" suffix.

		MT
Complete Set (15):		1000.
Common Player:		25.00
GT1	Michael Jordan	250.00
GT2	Allen Iverson	100.00
GT3	Kobe Bryant	150.00
GT4	Shaquille O'Neal	75.00
GT5	Stephon Marbury	125.00
GT6	Marcus Camby	25.00
GT7	Anfernee Hardaway	100.00
GT8	Kevin Garnett	125.00
GT9	Shareef Abdur-Rahim	60.00
GT10	Dennis Rodman	75.00
GT11	Grant Hill	125.00
GT12	Kerry Kittles	35.00
GT13	Antoine Walker	125.00
GT14	Scottie Pippen	60.00
GT15	Damon Stoudamire	35.00

1997-98 SkyBox Jam Pack

Fifteen of the top young players in the NBA were included in the Jam Pack insert. Card fronts feature the player on a silver foil, scenery background. Jam Pack inserts were seeded one per 18 packs of Series II and numbered with a "JP" suffix.

		MT
Complete Set (15):		60.00
Common Player:		2.00
JP1	Ray Allen	4.00
JP2	Damon Stoudamire	6.00
JP3	Shawn Kemp	10.00
JP4	Hakeem Olajuwon	8.00
JP5	Jerry Stackhouse	4.00
JP6	John Wallace	2.00
JP7	Juwan Howard	4.00
JP8	David Robinson	5.00
JP9	Gary Payton	4.00
JP10	Joe Smith	4.00
JP11	Charles Barkley	5.00
JP12	Terrell Brandon	2.00
JP13	Vin Baker	4.00
JP14	Antonio McDyess	4.00
JP15	Tim Duncan	20.00

1997-98 SkyBox Next Game

Next Game was a 15-card insert set that was seeded one per six packs of Series I. Card fronts are done with an original art background, with backs chronicling the player's college career. These inserts were numbered with "NG" suffix.

		MT
Complete Set (15):		40.00
Common Player:		1.00
1	Derek Anderson	3.00
2	Tony Battie	3.00
3	Chauncey Billups	4.00
4	Kelvin Cato	1.00
5	Austin Croshere	1.00
6	Antonio Daniels	4.00
7	Tim Duncan	8.00
8	Danny Fortson	2.00
9	Adonal Foyle	2.00
10	Tracy McGrady	4.00
11	Ron Mercer	4.00
12	Olivier Saint-Jean	2.00
13	Maurice Taylor	1.00
14	Tim Thomas	3.00
15	Keith Van Horn	7.00

1997-98 SkyBox Premium Players

Premium Players was a 15-card insert set that was seeded one per 192 packs of Series I. Fronts are done in a silver holographic rainbow foil and include a montage of action photos of that player. Backs include another shot of the player on the left, with bio information on the right and are numbered with a "PP" suffix.

		MT
Complete Set (15):		600.00
Common Player:		8.00
1	Michael Jordan	120.00
2	Allen Iverson	60.00
3	Kobe Bryant	75.00
4	Shaquille O'Neal	45.00
5	Stephon Marbury	45.00
6	Marcus Camby	15.00
7	Anfernee Hardaway	50.00
8	Kevin Garnett	60.00
9	Shareef Abdur-Rahim	30.00
10	Dennis Rodman	35.00
11	Ray Allen	8.00
12	Grant Hill	60.00
13	Kerry Kittles	8.00
14	Karl Malone	8.00
15	Scottie Pippen	25.00

1997-98 SkyBox Reebok Value

This insert contained 15 card and was included in each pack of Series I. It includes the same photos from regular-issue cards, but slightly different background photos and three color variations. Backs featured the Reebok logo and web page address.

		MT
Complete Set (15):		4.00
Common Player:		.25
	Steve Smith	.25
	Tyrone Hill	.25
	Robert Pack	.25
	Clyde Drexler	.50
	Mario Elie	.25
	Mark Jackson	.25
	Shaquille O'Neal	1.00
	Voshon Lenard	.25
	Glenn Robinson	.40
	Allen Iverson	.50
	Cedric Ceballos	.25
	Kenny Anderson	.25
	Vinny Del Negro	.25
	Avery Johnson	.25
	Shawn Kemp	.75

1997-98 SkyBox Rock n' Fire

Rock 'N Fire includes 10 rising stars with a mini-card that pulls out of a black outer frame through the top or bottom. These are inserted one per 18 packs of Series I and are numbered with a "RF" suffix.

		MT
Complete Set (10):		100.00
Common Player:		3.00
1	Allen Iverson	18.00
2	Kobe Bryant	25.00
3	Shaquille O'Neal	12.00
4	Stephon Marbury	15.00
5	Marcus Camby	8.00
6	Anfernee Hardaway	12.00
7	Kevin Garnett	18.00
8	Shareef Abdur-Rahim	10.00
9	Damon Stoudamire	3.00
10	Grant Hill	18.00

1997-98 SkyBox Silky Smooth

Silky Smooth was a 10-card insert set that was seeded one per 360 packs of Series I. Each card featured a white die-cut basketball net that could be opened like a book to reveal a full-color shot of the player. Backs were primarily black, contained a portrait of the player and were numbered with a "SS" suffix.

		MT
Complete Set (10):		750.00
Common Player:		20.00
1	Michael Jordan	175.00
2	Allen Iverson	85.00
3	Kobe Bryant	140.00
4	Shaquille O'Neal	60.00
5	Stephon Marbury	75.00
6	Gary Payton	20.00
7	Anfernee Hardaway	75.00
8	Kevin Garnett	100.00
9	Scottie Pippen	45.00
10	Grant Hill	100.00

1997-98 SkyBox Star Search

Star Search was a 15-card insert set that was inserted one per six packs of Series II. The front features a reddish wood grain flap with a small picture of the player near the bottom. The flap opens up to reveal a color action shot of the player, with the insert name and the player's name in the lower right corner. Card backs are numbered with a "SS" suffix.

		MT
Complete Set (15):		30.00
Common Player:		.50
SS1	Tim Duncan	8.00
SS2	Tony Battie	2.00
SS3	Keith Van Horn	8.00
SS4	Antonio Daniels	3.00
SS5	Chauncey Billups	4.00
SS6	Ron Mercer	5.00
SS7	Tracy McGrady	4.00
SS8	Danny Fortson	1.00
SS9	Brevin Knight	2.00
SS10	Derek Anderson	3.00
SS11	Bobby Jackson	2.00
SS12	Jacque Vaughn	1.00
SS13	Tim Thomas	3.00
SS14	Austin Croshere	1.00
SS15	Kelvin Cato	.50

1997-98 SkyBox Thunder & Lightning

Thunder and Lightning captured 15 players and was included one per 192 packs of Series II. Each card had a holographic front and was numbered with a "TL" suffix.

		MT
Complete Set (15):		500.00
Common Player:		8.00
TL1	Stephon Marbury	40.00
TL2	Shareef Abdur-Rahim	25.00
TL3	Shaquille O'Neal	30.00
TL4	Scottie Pippen	25.00
TL5	Michael Jordan	100.00
TL6	Marcus Camby	8.00
TL7	Kobe Bryant	60.00
TL8	Kevin Garnett	50.00
TL9	Kerry Kittles	12.00
TL10	Grant Hill	50.00
TL11	Dennis Rodman	30.00
TL12	Damon Stoudamire	12.00
TL13	Antoine Walker	40.00
TL14	Anfernee Hardaway	40.00
TL15	Allen Iverson	40.00

1997-98 SkyBox E-X2001

E-X2001 was an 80-card, super-premium set that was available to hobby stores only. The base cards arrived two per pack and were two layered, with one layer containing a die-cut image of the player over a prismatic background, with the other layer consisting of thick plastic that is clear on the right side, but in team color as it fades behind the player. E-X2001 arrived with an Essential Credentials Now and Future parallel sets, as well as Stardate 2001, Gravity Denied, Jam-Balaya and Autographics inserts.

		MT
Complete Set (80):		125.00
Common Player:		.50
Wax Box:		125.00
1	Grant Hill	6.00
2	Kevin Garnett	6.00
3	Allen Iverson	5.00
4	Anfernee Hardaway	4.00
5	Dennis Rodman	4.00
6	Shawn Kemp	3.00
7	Shaquille O'Neal	4.00
8	Kobe Bryant	10.00
9	Michael Jordan	15.00

10	Marcus Camby	1.00
11	Scottie Pippen	3.00
12	Antoine Walker	5.00
13	Stephon Marbury	5.00
14	Shareef Abdur-Rahim	3.00
15	Jerry Stackhouse	1.00
16	Eddie Jones	2.00
17	Charles Barkley	1.50
18	David Robinson	1.50
19	Karl Malone	1.25
20	Damon Stoudamire	2.00
21	Patrick Ewing	1.00
22	Kerry Kittles	1.00
23	Gary Payton	1.25
24	Glenn Robinson	1.00
25	Hakeem Olajuwon	2.00
26	John Starks	.50
27	John Stockton	1.00
28	Vin Baker	1.50
29	Reggie Miller	1.00
30	Clyde Drexler	1.25
31	Alonzo Mourning	1.00
32	Juwan Howard	1.25
33	Ray Allen	1.25
34	Christian Laettner	1.00
35	Terrell Brandon	1.00
36	Sean Elliott	.50
37	Rod Strickland	1.00
38	Rodney Rogers	.50
39	Donyell Marshall	.50
40	David Wesley	.50
41	Sam Cassell	.50
42	Cedric Ceballos	.50
43	Mahmoud Abdul-Rauf	.50
44	Rik Smits	.50
45	Lindsey Hunter	.50
46	Michael Finley	1.00
47	Steve Smith	.50
48	Larry Johnson	1.00
49	Dikembe Mutombo	.50
50	Tom Gugliotta	1.00
51	Joe Dumars	.50
52	Glen Rice	1.00
53	Bryant Reeves	.50
54	Tim Hardaway	1.00
55	Isaiah Rider	.50
56	Rasheed Wallace	.50
57	Jason Kidd	1.50
58	Joe Smith	1.00
59	Chris Webber	2.00
60	Mitch Richmond	1.00
61	Antonio McDyess	1.00
62	*Bobby Jackson*	5.00
63	*Derek Anderson*	5.00
64	*Kelvin Cato*	1.50
65	*Jacque Vaughn*	1.50
66	*Tariq Abdul-Wahad*	1.00
67	*Johnny Taylor*	1.00
68	*Chris Anstey*	1.00
69	*Maurice Taylor*	4.00
70	*Antonio Daniels*	4.00
71	*Chauncey Billups*	5.00
72	*Austin Croshere*	1.50
73	*Brevin Knight*	5.00
74	*Keith Van Horn*	20.00
75	*Tim Duncan*	30.00
76	*Danny Fortson*	2.00
77	*Tim Thomas*	10.00
78	*Tony Battie*	2.00
79	*Tracy McGrady*	8.00
80	*Ron Mercer*	15.00

1997-98 SkyBox E-X2001 Essential Credentials Future

Essential Credentials Future cards were parallel to the 80-card E-X2001 set. The cards were printed on a pinkish red color plastic, with a holographic cardboard strip on the left side and the parallels name in small letters above his number on the plastic part. Cards were sequentially numbered to 81 minus the card number. For example, Shareef Abdur-Rahim is card No. 14 so his Future card is numbered to 67 (81-14). Together with the Now parallel, the total number of cards equally 81. The set is called Future because the rookies in the set, numbers 62-80 are the shortest printed cards.

		MT
Common Player:		50.00
Unable To Price #70-80		
1	Grant Hill	450.00
2	Kevin Garnett	450.00
3	Allen Iverson	350.00
4	Anfernee Hardaway	250.00
5	Dennis Rodman	250.00
6	Shawn Kemp	200.00
7	Shaquille O'Neal	250.00
8	Kobe Bryant	700.00
9	Michael Jordan	1000.
10	Marcus Camby	50.00
11	Scottie Pippen	200.00
12	Antoine Walker	300.00
13	Stephon Marbury	300.00
14	Shareef Abdur-Rahim	225.00
15	Jerry Stackhouse	75.00
16	Eddie Jones	125.00
17	Charles Barkley	100.00
18	David Robinson	100.00
19	Karl Malone	100.00
20	Damon Stoudamire	120.00
21	Patrick Ewing	75.00
22	Kerry Kittles	75.00
23	Gary Payton	100.00
24	Glenn Robinson	75.00
25	Hakeem Olajuwon	150.00
26	John Starks	50.00
27	John Stockton	75.00
28	Vin Baker	100.00
29	Reggie Miller	75.00
30	Clyde Drexler	100.00
31	Alonzo Mourning	75.00
32	Juwan Howard	75.00
33	Ray Allen	75.00
34	Christian Laettner	50.00
35	Terrell Brandon	50.00
36	Sean Elliott	50.00
37	Rod Strickland	50.00
38	Rodney Rogers	50.00
39	Donyell Marshall	50.00
40	David Wesley	50.00
41	Sam Cassell	50.00
42	Cedric Ceballos	50.00
43	Mahmoud Abdul-Rauf	50.00
44	Rik Smits	50.00
45	Lindsey Hunter	50.00
46	Michael Finley	100.00
47	Steve Smith	75.00
48	Larry Johnson	75.00
49	Dikembe Mutombo	75.00
50	Tom Gugliotta	75.00
51	Joe Dumars	75.00
52	Glen Rice	100.00
53	Bryant Reeves	75.00
54	Tim Hardaway	150.00
55	Isaiah Rider	75.00
56	Rasheed Wallace	75.00
57	Jason Kidd	300.00
58	Joe Smith	100.00
59	Chris Webber	300.00
60	Mitch Richmond	125.00
61	Antonio McDyess	150.00
62	*Bobby Jackson*	100.00
63	*Derek Anderson*	225.00
64	*Kelvin Cato*	100.00
65	*Jacque Vaughn*	120.00
66	*Tariq Abdul-Wahad*	100.00
67	*Johnny Taylor*	120.00
68	*Chris Anstey*	120.00
69	*Maurice Taylor*	250.00
70	*Antonio Daniels*	300.00

1997-98 SkyBox E-X2001 Essential Credentials Now

Essential Credentials Now was a parallel set that reprinted all 80 cards on a greenish yellow plastic stock. The cards also had a holographic cardboard strip up the left side and the insert name printed in small letters above his number. Cards were sequentially numbered to the player's card number in the set. For example, Shareef Abdur-Rahim is card No. 14, so he would have 14 Now cards. Together with the Future parallel, the total parallel cards for each player added up to 81.

		MT
Common Player:		50.00
Unable To Price #1-10		
11	Scottie Pippen	600.00
12	Antoine Walker	800.00
13	Stephon Marbury	800.00
14	Shareef Abdur-Rahim	600.00
15	Jerry Stackhouse	175.00
16	Eddie Jones	400.00
17	Charles Barkley	300.00
18	David Robinson	300.00
19	Karl Malone	300.00
20	Damon Stoudamire	250.00
21	Patrick Ewing	175.00
22	Kerry Kittles	150.00
23	Gary Payton	175.00
24	Glenn Robinson	100.00
25	Hakeem Olajuwon	225.00
26	John Starks	50.00
27	John Stockton	175.00
28	Vin Baker	200.00
29	Reggie Miller	200.00
30	Clyde Drexler	175.00
31	Alonzo Mourning	100.00
32	Juwan Howard	100.00
33	Ray Allen	100.00
34	Christian Laettner	50.00
35	Terrell Brandon	75.00
36	Sean Elliott	50.00
37	Rod Strickland	50.00
38	Rodney Rogers	50.00
39	Donyell Marshall	50.00
40	David Wesley	50.00
41	Sam Cassell	50.00
42	Cedric Ceballos	50.00
43	Mahmoud Abdul-Rauf	50.00
44	Rik Smits	50.00
45	Lindsey Hunter	50.00
46	Michael Finley	75.00
47	Steve Smith	50.00
48	Larry Johnson	75.00
49	Dikembe Mutombo	75.00
50	Tom Gugliotta	75.00
51	Joe Dumars	50.00
52	Glen Rice	75.00
53	Bryant Reeves	50.00
54	Tim Hardaway	100.00
55	Isaiah Rider	50.00
56	Rasheed Wallace	50.00
57	Jason Kidd	125.00
58	Joe Smith	75.00
59	Chris Webber	175.00
60	Mitch Richmond	75.00
61	Antonio McDyess	75.00
62	*Bobby Jackson*	75.00
63	*Derek Anderson*	100.00
64	*Kelvin Cato*	50.00
65	*Jacque Vaughn*	50.00
66	*Tariq Abdul-Wahad*	50.00
67	*Johnny Taylor*	50.00
68	*Chris Anstey*	50.00
69	*Maurice Taylor*	100.00
70	*Antonio Daniels*	100.00
71	*Chauncey Billups*	100.00
72	*Austin Croshere*	50.00
73	*Brevin Knight*	100.00
74	*Keith Van Horn*	300.00
75	*Tim Duncan*	400.00
76	*Danny Fortson*	50.00
77	*Tim Thomas*	200.00
78	*Tony Battie*	75.00
79	*Tracy McGrady*	200.00
80	*Ron Mercer*	250.00

1997-98 SkyBox E-X2001 Gravity Denied

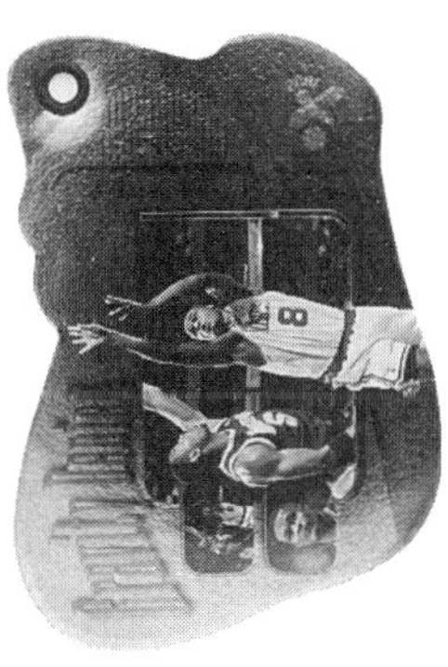

Gravity Denied was a 20-card insert set that was inserted one per 24 packs of E-X2001. It featured a clear plastic layer with a color image of the player that was hinged over a silver foil card. When the two cards were moved over each other, the pictures lined up with each other. An actual metal hinge was placed in the top right corner, while card backs were numbered with a "GD" suffix.

		MT
Complete Set (20):		275.00
Common Player:		3.00
1	Vin Baker	8.00
2	Charles Barkley	8.00
3	Tony Battie	6.00
4	Kobe Bryant	45.00
5	Patrick Ewing	3.00
6	Kevin Garnett	35.00
7	Anfernee Hardaway	25.00
8	Grant Hill	35.00
9	Michael Jordan	70.00
10	Shawn Kemp	20.00
11	Kerry Kittles	3.00
12	Karl Malone	6.00
13	Tracy McGrady	12.00
14	Hakeem Olajuwon	12.00
15	Shaquille O'Neal	25.00
16	Scottie Pippen	20.00
17	Jerry Stackhouse	6.00
18	Tim Thomas	12.00
19	Antoine Walker	30.00
20	Chris Webber	10.00

1997-98 SkyBox E-X2001 Jam-Balaya

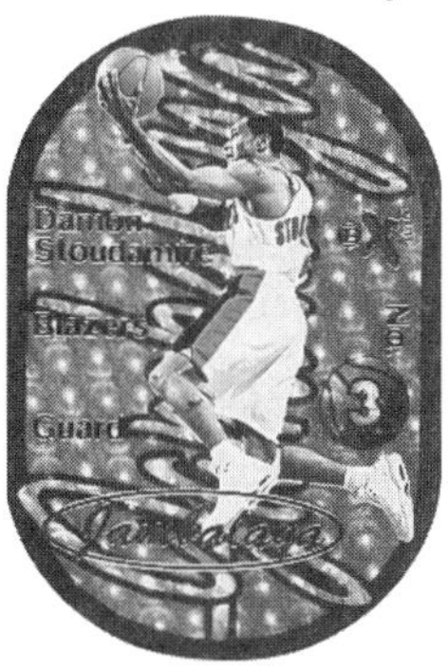

Jam-Balaya was a 15-card die-cut insert set that was limited to only one per 720 packs of E-X2001. Each card was die-cut with a prismatic, three-dimensional background to it and the insert's name written up the middle. Fronts and backs had a black border around the perimeter and was numbered with a "JB" suffix.

		MT
Complete Set (15):		1600.
Common Player:		40.00
1	Allen Iverson	150.00
2	Anfernee Hardaway	125.00
3	Dennis Rodman	125.00
4	Grant Hill	200.00
5	Kevin Garnett	200.00
6	Michael Jordan	400.00
7	Shaquille O'Neal	125.00
8	Tim Duncan	200.00
9	Keith Van Horn	150.00
10	Stephon Marbury	150.00
11	Shareef Abdur-Rahim	100.00
12	Kobe Bryant	250.00
13	Damon Stoudamire	40.00
14	Scottie Pippen	100.00
15	Eddie Jones	75.00

1997-98 SkyBox E-X2001 Star Date 2001

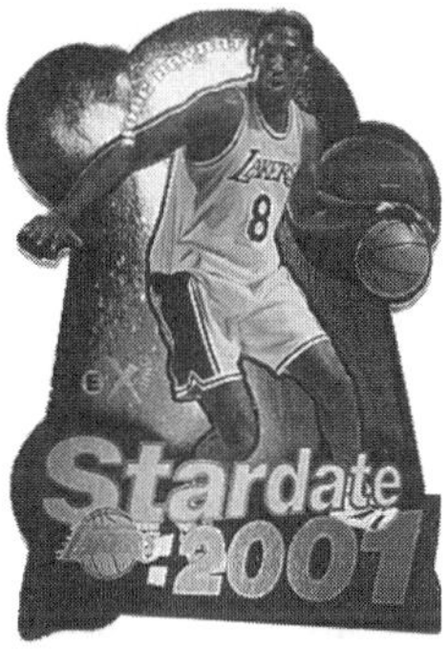

This 15-card insert set captured the top rookies from the 1997 NBA Draft and was inserted one per 12 packs. Each card was die-cut with the player's image over a space background and the insert's name across the bottom. A closer image of the player was pictured on the back and the card was numbered with a "SD" suffix.

		MT
Complete Set (15):		100.00
Common Player:		2.00
1	Shareef Abdur-Rahim	8.00
2	Tony Battie	4.00
3	Kobe Bryant	20.00
4	Antonio Daniels	6.00
5	Tim Duncan	20.00
6	Adonal Foyle	4.00
7	Allen Iverson	12.00
8	Matt Maloney	2.00
9	Stephon Marbury	12.00
10	Tracy McGrady	8.00
11	Ron Mercer	10.00
12	Tim Thomas	8.00
13	Keith Van Horn	15.00
14	Jacque Vaughn	2.00
15	Antoine Walker	12.00

1997-98 SkyBox Z-Force II

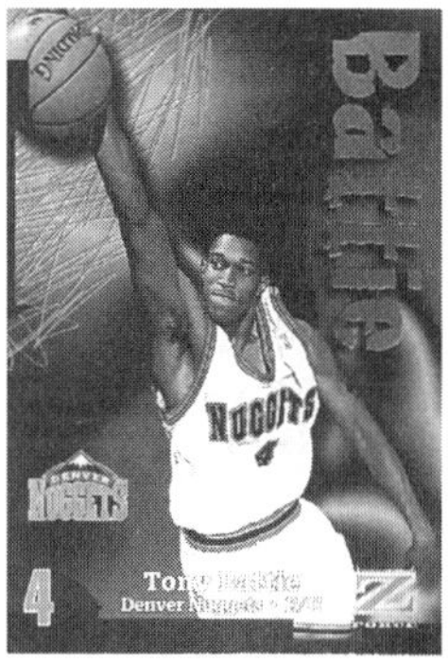

This 110-card set included 108 player cards and two checklists in Series I, while Series II included 98 cards and two checklists. Fronts featured the player over an artsy, spiral background, with the player's name running down the right side in foil. The player's team, uniform number, position and the Z-Force logo run across the bottom. The back is white with another shot of the player, statistics and the card number in the lower right corner. Card No. 143 does not exist in the set or any of the parallels. Vin Baker and Tracy McGrady were both numbered as card No. 172. Inserts in Series I include: Boss, Super Boss, Limited Access, Rave Reviews, Total Impact, Fast Track, Autographics and the parallel Raves. Inserts in Series II included: Zensations, Star Gazing, Zebut, Slam Cam, Quick Strike, Autographics and BMOC as well as Rave and Super Rave parallels.

		MT
Complete Series 2 (100):		15.00
Common Player:		.10
Series 2 Wax Box:		45.00
111	*Tim Duncan*	2.50
112	Joe Smith	.30
113	Shawn Kemp	.75
114	Terry Mills	.10
115	*Jacque Vaughn*	.20
116	*Ron Mercer*	1.25
117	Brian Williams	.10
118	Rik Smits	.10
119	Eric Williams	.10
120	*Tim Thomas*	.75
121	Damon Stoudamire	.40
122	*God Shammgod*	.20
123	Tyrone Hill	.10
124	Elden Campbell	.10
125	*Keith Van Horn*	2.50
126	Brian Grant	.10
127	Antonio McDyess	.30
128	Darrell Armstrong	.10
129	Sam Perkins	.10
130	Chris Mills	.10
131	Reggie Miller	.20
132	Chris Gatling	.10
133	Ed Gray	.10
134	Hakeem Olajuwon	.50
135	Chris Webber	.40
136	Kendall Gill	.10
137	Wesley Person	.10
138	Derrick Coleman	.10
139	Dana Barros	.10
140	Dennis Scott	.10
141	*Paul Grant*	.20
142	Scott Burrell	.10
143	*Tracy McGrady*	1.25
144	*Austin Croshere*	.30
145	*Maurice Taylor*	.40
146	Kevin Johnson	.10
147	*Tony Battie*	.50
148	*Tariq Abdul-Wahad*	.20
149	Johnny Taylor	.10
150	Allen Iverson	1.25
151	Terrell Brandon	.10
152	*Derek Anderson*	.50

153	Calbert Cheaney	.10
154	Jayson Williams	.10
155	Rick Fox	.10
156	John Thomas	.10
157	David Wesley	.10
158	*Bobby Jackson*	.50
159	*Kelvin Cato*	.20
160	Vinny Del Negro	.10
161	*Adonal Foyle*	.30
162	Larry Johnson	.20
163	*Brevin Knight*	.50
164	Rod Strickland	.10
165	*Rodrick Rhodes*	.30
166	*Scot Pollard*	.20
167	Sam Cassell	.10
168	Jerry Stackhouse	.30
169	Mark Jackson	.10
170	John Wallace	.20
171	Horace Grant	.10
172	Vin Baker	.30
173	Eddie Jones	.40
174	Kerry Kittles	.25
175	*Antonio Daniels*	.75
176	Alan Henderson	.10
177	Sean Elliott	.10
178	John Starks	.10
179	*Chauncey Billups*	1.00
180	Juwan Howard	.30
181	Bobby Phills	.10
182	Latrell Sprewell	.20
183	Jim Jackson	.10
184	*Danny Fortson*	.30
185	*Zydrunas Ilgauskas*	.50
186	Clifford Robinson	.10
187	Chris Mullin	.10
188	Greg Ostertag	.10
189	Antoine Walker (Zupermen)	.60
190	Michael Jordan (Zupermen)	1.50
191	Scottie Pippen (Zupermen)	.30
192	Dennis Rodman (Zupermen)	.50
193	Grant Hill (Zupermen)	.75
194	Clyde Drexler (Zupermen)	.10
195	Kobe Bryant (Zupermen)	1.00
196	Shaquille O'Neal (Zupermen)	.60
197	Alonzo Mourning (Zupermen)	.10
198	Ray Allen (Zupermen)	.10
199	Kevin Garnett (Zupermen)	.75
200	Stephon Marbury (Zupermen)	.60
201	Anfernee Hardaway (Zupermen)	.60
202	Jason Kidd (Zupermen)	
203	David Robinson (Zupermen)	.10
204	Gary Payton (Zupermen)	.10
205	Marcus Camby (Zupermen)	.10
206	Karl Malone (Zupermen)	.10
207	John Stockton (Zupermen)	.10
208	Shareef Abdur-Rahim (Zupermen)	.40
209	Checklist Charles Barkley	.10
210	Checklist Gary Payton	.10

1997-98 SkyBox Z-Force Raves

This 206-card parallel set (210 minus the four checklists) included prismatic silver foil on the front, and individual numbering to 399 on the back. No odds for Rave inserts were given, but it is estimated that they are seeded one per 60-80 packs. Once again, card No. 143 does not exist; both Baker and McGrady are numbered as card 172.

	MT
Rave Stars:	30x-60x
Rave Rookies:	15x-30x

1997-98 SkyBox Z-Force Super Raves

Super Raves was a second level of parallel set and was numbered to only 50 sets. Super Raves featured purple prismatic foil on the front in contrast to the gold used on base cards and silver prismat-

ic foil used on Raves. Once again, card No. 143 does not exist; both Baker and McGrady are numbered as card No. 172.

	MT
Super Rave Stars:	125x-250x
Super Rave Rookies:	60x-120x

1997-98 SkyBox Z-Force B.M.O.C.

This 15-card insert was inserted into one per 288 packs of Series II. Each card is printed on a multi-dimensional thermo plastic card stock, with the NBA's elite players included in the set.

		MT
Complete Set (15):		675.00
Common Player:		25.00
B1	Shareef Abdur-Rahim	40.00
B2	Kobe Bryant	100.00
B3	Marcus Camby	25.00
B4	Tim Duncan	70.00
B5	Kevin Garnett	70.00
B6	Anfernee Hardaway	60.00
B7	Grant Hill	70.00
B8	Allen Iverson	60.00
B9	Michael Jordan	140.00
B10	Shawn Kemp	35.00
B11	Stephon Marbury	60.00
B12	Shaquille O'Neal	50.00
B13	Scottie Pippen	35.00
B14	Dennis Rodman	50.00
B15	Antoine Walker	60.00

1997-98 SkyBox Z-Force Quick Strike

Quickstrike consisted of 12 cards and was seeded one per 96 packs of Series II. The cards were printed on holographic silver plastic, with a clear oval window in the middle that included the insert name. The player's image was cast over this background. Cards were numbered with a "QS" suffix.

		MT
Complete Set (12):		200.00
Common Player:		5.00
QS1	Shareef Abdur-Rahim	20.00
QS2	Anfernee Hardaway	25.00
QS3	Grant Hill	35.00
QS4	Allen Iverson	25.00
QS5	Michael Jordan	70.00
QS6	Stephon Marbury	25.00
QS7	Hakeem Olajuwon	12.00
QS8	Scottie Pippen	18.00
QS9	Damon Stoudamire	5.00
QS10	Keith Van Horn	35.00
QS11	Antoine Walker	25.00
QS12	Chris Webber	10.00

1997-98 SkyBox Z-Force Slam Cam

Slam Cam featured 12 highlight film players on a horizontal format. Each card was made to look like a piece of film and was printed on black plastic. The player's closeup was placed on the left of the card, while a shot of him dunking and the insert's name was on the right. Slam Cam inserts were seeded one per 36 packs of Series II and numbered with a "SC" suffix.

		MT
Complete Set (12):		75.00
Common Player:		2.00
SC1	Kobe Bryant	18.00
SC2	Marcus Camby	2.00
SC3	Tim Duncan	18.00
SC4	Kevin Garnett	12.00
SC5	Michael Jordan	25.00
SC6	Shawn Kemp	6.00
SC7	Karl Malone	2.00
SC8	Antonio McDyess	4.00
SC9	Shaquille O'Neal	10.00
SC10	Joe Smith	4.00
SC11	Jerry Stackhouse	4.00
SC12	Chris Webber	5.00

1997-98 SkyBox Z-Force Star Gazing

This 15-card insert set was seeded one per 18 retail packs in Series II. Star Gazing captured the player over a dark, foil background with gold rings going around the basketball. Star Gazing were numbered with a "SG" suffix.

		MT
Complete Set (15):		100.00
Common Player:		2.50
SG1	Shareef Abdur-Rahim	7.00
SG2	Kobe Bryant	15.00
SG3	Marcus Camby	2.50
SG4	Kevin Garnett	12.00
SG5	Anfernee Hardaway	8.00
SG6	Grant Hill	12.00
SG7	Allen Iverson	8.00
SG8	Stephon Marbury	10.00
SG9	Hakeem Olajuwon	5.00
SG10	Shaquille O'Neal	8.00
SG11	Scottie Pippen	6.00
SG12	Dennis Rodman	8.00
SG13	Damon Stoudamire	4.00
SG14	Keith Van Horn	10.00
SG15	Antoine Walker	10.00

1997-98 SkyBox Z-Force Zebut

This 12-card insert set highlighted the top rookies from the 1997 NBA Draft and was seeded one per 24 Series II packs. Each card is printed on gold foil and die-cut around the bottom, with a large "Z" in the background and the word "Force" under it. Cards are numbered on the back with a "ZB" suffix.

		MT
Complete Set (12):		50.00
Common Player:		2.00
ZE1	Derek Anderson	6.00
ZE2	Tony Battie	4.00
ZE3	Chauncey Billups	8.00
ZE4	Austin Croshere	2.00
ZE5	Antonio Daniels	6.00
ZE6	Tim Duncan	15.00
ZE7	Danny Fortson	2.00
ZE8	Tracy McGrady	8.00
ZE9	Ron Mercer	8.00
ZE10	Tariq Abdul-Wahad	2.00
ZE11	Tim Thomas	8.00
ZE12	Keith Van Horn	15.00

1997-98 SkyBox Z-Force Zensations

Zensations consisted of 25 cards and was inserted into one per six Series II packs. Fronts contain four different blocks of wild colored patterns, with the insert's name across the top in gold foil. Zensations are numbered on the back with a "ZN" suffix.

		MT
Complete Set (25):		25.00
Common Player:		.50
Z1	Ray Allen	1.25
Z2	Vin Baker	1.00
Z3	Charles Barkley	1.50
Z4	Clyde Drexler	1.25
Z5	Patrick Ewing	1.00
Z6	Juwan Howard	1.50
Z7	Eddie Jones	1.75
Z8	Shawn Kemp	3.00
Z9	Jason Kidd	1.50
Z10	Kerry Kittles	1.00
Z11	Karl Malone	1.00
Z12	Antonio McDyess	1.00
Z13	Hakeem Olajuwon	2.50
Z14	Gary Payton	1.50
Z15	Glen Rice	1.00
Z16	Mitch Richmond	1.00
Z17	David Robinson	1.50
Z18	Dennis Rodman	4.00
Z19	Joe Smith	1.25
Z20	Latrell Sprewell	1.00
Z21	Jerry Stackhouse	1.25
Z22	John Stockton	1.00
Z23	Damon Stoudamire	1.75
Z24	Rasheed Wallace	.50
Z25	Chris Webber	2.00

1997-98 SP Authentic

A 176-card set that has 156 veterans and 20 cards of rising stars. Also included is six inserts, with redemption cards. The inserts include: NBA Profiles (three tiers), Sign of the Times, SP Buybacks, Premium Portraits and SP Authentics. The base cards have a color action photo on the front, with another on the back along with career statistics.

		MT
Complete Set (176):		100.00
Common Player:		.25
Wax Box:		100.00
1	Steve Smith	.25
2	Dikembe Mutombo	.50
3	Christian Laettner	.50
4	Mookie Blaylock	.25
5	Alan Henderson	.25
6	Antoine Walker	2.50
7	*Ron Mercer*	10.00
8	Walter McCarty	.25
9	Kenny Anderson	.25
10	Travis Knight	.25
11	Dana Barros	.25
12	Glen Rice	.75
13	Vlade Divac	.25
14	Dell Curry	.25
15	David Wesley	.25
16	Bobby Phills	.25
17	Anthony Mason	.25
18	Toni Kukoc	.25
19	Dennis Rodman	2.00
20	Ron Harper	.25
21	Steve Kerr	.25
22	Scottie Pippen	1.50
23	Michael Jordan	6.00
24	Shawn Kemp	1.50
25	Wesley Person	.25
26	*Derek Anderson*	4.00
27	Zydrunas Ilgauskas	.50
28	*Brevin Knight*	4.00
29	Michael Finley	.50
30	Shawn Bradley	.25
31	A.C. Green	.25
32	Hubert Davis	.25
33	Dennis Scott	.25
34	*Tony Battie*	2.00
35	*Bobby Jackson*	4.00
36	LaPhonso Ellis	.25
37	Bryant Stith	.25
38	Dean Garrett	.25
39	*Danny Fortson*	2.00
40	Grant Hill	3.00
41	Brian Williams	.25
42	Lindsey Hunter	.25
43	Malik Sealy	.25
44	Jerry Stackhouse	.50
45	Muggsy Bogues	.25
46	Joe Smith	.50
47	Donyell Marshall	.25
48	Erick Dampier	.25
49	Bimbo Coles	.25
50	Charles Barkley	.75
51	Hakeem Olajuwon	1.25
52	Clyde Drexler	.75
53	Kevin Willis	.25
54	Mario Elie	.25
55	Reggie Miller	.50
56	Rik Smits	.25
57	Chris Mullin	.25
58	Antonio Davis	.25
59	Dale Davis	.25
60	Mark Jackson	.25

61	Brent Barry	.25
62	Loy Vaught	.25
63	Rodney Rogers	.25
64	Lamond Murray	.25
65	*Maurice Taylor*	3.00
66	Shaquille O'Neal	2.00
67	Eddie Jones	1.00
68	Kobe Bryant	4.00
69	Nick Van Exel	.50
70	Robert Horry	.25
71	Tim Hardaway	.50
72	Jamal Mashburn	.25
73	Alonzo Mourning	.50
74	Isaac Austin	.25
75	P.J. Brown	.25
76	Ray Allen	.75
77	Glenn Robinson	.50
78	Ervin Johnson	.25
79	Terrell Brandon	.50
80	Tyrone Hill	.25
81	Stephon Marbury	2.50
82	Kevin Garnett	3.00
83	Tom Gugliotta	.50
84	Chris Carr	.25
85	Cherokee Parks	.25
86	Sam Cassell	.25
87	Chris Gatling	.25
88	Kendall Gill	.25
89	*Keith Van Horn*	15.00
90	Jayson Williams	.25
91	Kerry Kittles	.75
92	Patrick Ewing	.50
93	Larry Johnson	.50
94	Chris Childs	.25
95	John Starks	.25
96	Charles Oakley	.25
97	Allan Houston	.25
98	Mark Price	.25
99	Anfernee Hardaway	2.00
100	Rony Seikaly	.25
101	Horace Grant	.25
102	Charles Outlaw	.25
103	Clarence Weatherspoon	.25
104	Allen Iverson	2.50
105	Jim Jackson	.25
106	Theo Ratliff	.25
107	*Tim Thomas*	8.00
108	Danny Manning	.25
109	Jason Kidd	1.00
110	Kevin Johnson	.25
111	Rex Chapman	.25
112	Clifford Robinson	.25
113	Antonio McDyess	.50
114	Damon Stoudamire	.75
115	Isaiah Rider	.25
116	Arvydas Sabonis	.25
117	Rasheed Wallace	.25
118	Brian Grant	.25
119	Gary Trent	.25
120	Mitch Richmond	.75
121	Corliss Williamson	.25
122	*Lawrence Funderburke*	.50
123	Olden Polynice	.25
124	Billy Owens	.25
125	Avery Johnson	.25
126	Sean Elliott	.25
127	David Robinson	.75
128	*Tim Duncan*	20.00
129	Jaren Jackson	.25
130	Detlef Schrempf	.25
131	Gary Payton	.75
132	Vin Baker	.75
133	Hersey Hawkins	.25
134	Dale Ellis	.25
135	Sam Perkins	.25
136	Marcus Camby	.50
137	John Wallace	.25
138	Doug Christie	.25
139	*Chauncey Billups*	4.00
140	Walt Williams	.25
141	Karl Malone	.75
142	Bryon Russell	.25
143	Jeff Hornacek	.25
144	Greg Ostertag	.25
145	John Stockton	.50
146	Shandon Anderson	.25
147	Shareef Abdur-Rahim	1.50
148	Bryant Reeves	.25
149	*Antonio Daniels*	3.00
150	Otis Thorpe	.25
151	Blue Edwards	.25
152	Chris Webber	1.00
153	Juwan Howard	.75
154	Rod Strickland	.25
155	Calbert Cheaney	.25
156	Tracy Murray	.25
157	Chauncey Billups	2.00
158	*Ed Gray*	.50
159	Tony Battie	1.00
160	Keith Van Horn	7.50
161	*Cedric Henderson*	1.50
162	*Kelvin Cato*	.50
163	*Tariq Abdul-Wahad*	.50
164	Derek Anderson	2.00
165	Tim Duncan	10.00
166	*Tracy McGrady*	6.00
167	Ron Mercer	5.00
168	Bobby Jackson	2.00
169	Antonio Daniels	1.50
170	Zydrunas Ilgauskas	.25
171	Maurice Taylor	1.50
172	Tim Thomas	4.00
173	Brevin Knight	2.00
174	Lawrence Funderburke	.25
175	*Jacque Vaughn*	.50
176	Danny Fortson	1.00

1997-98 SP Authentic Authentics

Authentics was a redemption insert that included four different Anfernee Hardaway items, eight Michael Jordan, three Shawn Kemp and one SP uncut sheet. Collectors could send in their Authentics card for the corresponding Upper Deck Authenticated item ranging from a special card set to autographed jerseys, balls and photos. The Jordan Game Night listing includes five different cards all numbered to 100. The number of items given away for each piece is listed in parentheses. Authentics were seeded one per 288 packs.

		MT
Common Player:		30.00
AH1	Anfernee Hardaway/ AU Blk. Jrsy	550.00
AH2	Anfernee Hardaway/ AU Blue Jrsy	450.00
AH3	Anfernee Hardaway/ AU SI Cover	80.00
AH4	Anfernee Hardaway/ 8x10 Photo	30.00
MJ1	Michael Jordan/AU Jersey	2500.
MJ2	Michael Jordan/AU 16x20	750.00
MJ3	Michael Jordan/2-card	75.00
MJ4	Michael Jordan/8x10	75.00
MJ5	Michael Jordan/Gold Card	85.00
MJ6	Michael Jordan/ Game	500.00
MJ6	Michael Jordan/ Poster	100.00
MJ8	Michael Jordan/AU Game	8500.
SK1	Shawn Kemp/AU Jersey	400.00
SK2	Shawn Kemp/AU Photo	100.00
SK3	Shawn Kemp/AU Mini-ball	100.00
NNO	SP Uncut Sheet	125.00

1997-98 SP Authentic BuyBack

The basketball segment of Upper Deck Authenticated involved old SP cards that were purchased and autographed through UDA, then inserted into packs. The cards were inserted at a rate of one per 309 packs and contained UDA's holographic seal with an identification number.

		MT
Common Player:		50.00
1	Shareef Abdur-Rahim '96/7	100.00
2	Vin Baker '94/5	125.00
3	Vin Baker '95/6	100.00
4	Vin Baker '95/6AS	100.00
5	Clyde Drexler '94/5	100.00
6	Clyde Drexler '95/6	100.00
7	Clyde Drexler '96/7	120.00
8	Anfernee Hardaway '94/5	200.00
9	Anfernee Hardaway '95/6	180.00
10	Anfernee Hardaway '96/7	180.00
11	Tim Hardaway Exchange	75.00
14	Juwan Howard '94/5	100.00
15	Juwan Howard '95/6	75.00
16	Juwan Howard '95/ 6AS	100.00
17	Juwan Howard '96/7	100.00
18	Eddie Jones '94/5	125.00
19	Eddie Jones '95/6	100.00
20	Eddie Jones '96/7	100.00
21	Michael Jordan '94/ 5MJ1R	4000.
22	Jason Kidd Exchange	100.00
26	Kerry Kittles '96/7	75.00
27	Karl Malone '94/5	125.00
28	Karl Malone '95/6	125.00
29	Glen Rice '95/6AS	50.00
30	Glen Rice '96/7	75.00
31	Mitch Richmond '94/5	50.00
32	Mitch Richmond '95/6	50.00
33	Mitch Richmond '96/7	75.00
34	Damon Stoudamire '95/6	75.00
35	Damon Stoudamire '96/7	75.00
36	Antoine Walker '96/7	150.00

1997-98 SP Authentic Premium Portraits

The seven-card set features autographed cards of the league's stars. Inserted at 1:1,528, the cards have a color portrait of the player on the front.

		MT
Complete Set (7):		1100.00
Common Player:		100.00
TP	Tim Hardaway	175.00
EP	Eddie Jones	275.00
JP	Jason Kidd	275.00
KP	Kerry Kittles	125.00
RP	Glen Rice	150.00
DP	Damon Stoudamire	150.00
MP	Dikembe Mutombo	100.00

1997-98 SP Authentic Profiles

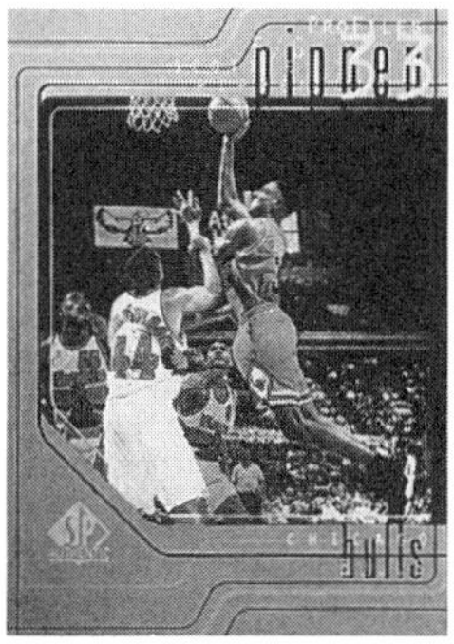

A 40-card set, it divides itself into three subsets. The front show a color photo of the athlete, bordered in red. The first subset is inserted 1:3, the second 1:12. The third is 100 sequentially-numbered die-cut cards.

		MT
Complete Set (40):		100.00
Common Player:		.50
P1	Michael Jordan	16.00
P2	Glen Rice	1.00
P3	Brent Barry	.50
P4	LaPhonso Ellis	.50
P5	Allen Iverson	6.00
P6	Dikembe Mutombo	.50
P7	Charles Barkley	2.00
P8	Antoine Walker	6.00
P9	Karl Malone	2.00
P10	Jason Kidd	2.00
P11	Gary Payton	2.00
P12	Kevin Garnett	8.00
P13	Keith Van Horn	6.00
P14	Glenn Robinson	1.00
P15	Michael Finley	1.00
P16	Hakeem Olajuwon	3.00
P17	Chris Webber	3.00
P18	Mitch Richmond	1.00
P19	Marcus Camby	1.00
P20	Tim Hardaway	1.00
P21	Shawn Kemp	4.00
P22	Reggie Miller	1.00
P23	Shaquille O'Neal	5.00
P24	Chauncey Billups	2.00
P25	Grant Hill	8.00
P26	Shareef Abdur-Rahim	4.00
P27	David Robinson	2.00
P28	Scottie Pippen	4.00
P29	Juwan Howard	1.00
P30	Anfernee Hardaway	5.00
P31	Jerry Stackhouse	1.00
P32	Kobe Bryant	10.00
P33	Patrick Ewing	.50
P34	Alonzo Mourning	1.00
P35	John Stockton	1.00
P36	Kenny Anderson	.50
P37	Tim Duncan	8.00
P38	Stephon Marbury	6.00
P39	Dennis Rodman	5.00
P40	Joe Smith	1.00

1997-98 SP Authentic Profiles II

Profiles II was a parallel set to Profiles, but adds embossing and is marked "Profiles 2" on the front. These are inserted every 12 packs.

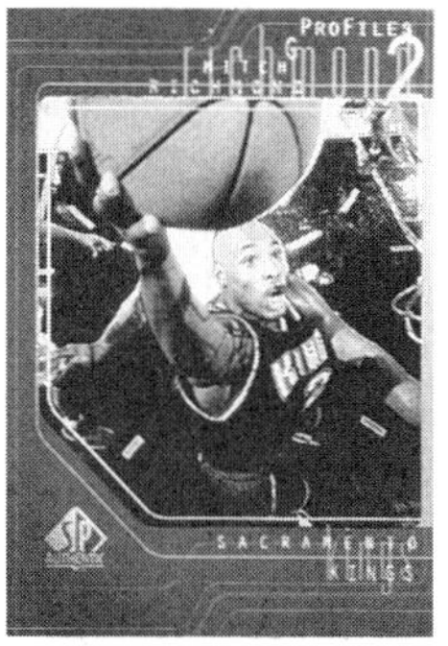

	MT
Profiles II Cards:	3x

1997-98 SP Authentic Profiles III

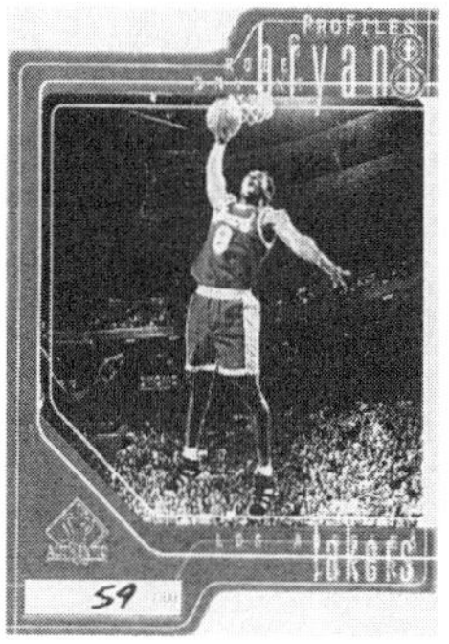

Profiles III was scarcest tier of Profiles and paralleled all 40 cards in the insert on a die-cut design that was individually numbered to 100 on the front.

	MT
Profiles III Cards:	20x-40x

1997-98 SP Authentic Sign of the Times

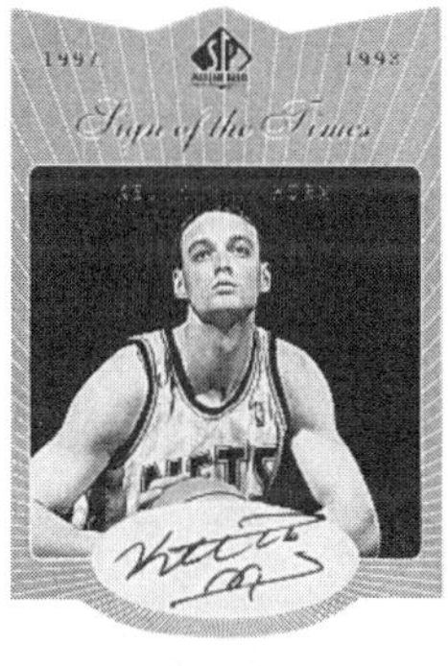

The 11-card set features the young and old stars of the NBA. The featured players have autographed randomly inserted cards. Insertion rate is 1:42.

		MT
Complete Set (33):		600.00
Common Player:		12.00
TB	Tony Battie	12.00
BW	Brian Williams	12.00
TH	Tim Hardaway	60.00
AH	Allan Houston	20.00
HW	Juwan Howard	50.00
KJ	Kevin Johnson	20.00
EJ	Eddie Jones	75.00
KK	Kerry Kittles	30.00
DM	Dikembe Mutombo	20.00
GR	Glen Rice	40.00
DS	Damon Stoudamire	40.00
TG	Tom Gugliotta	40.00
TE	Terrell Brandon	30.00
GM	Gheorghe Muresan	12.00
MB	Mookie Blaylock	12.00
CM	Chris Mullin	15.00
SC	Sam Cassell	12.00
BB	Brent Barry	12.00
SE	Sean Elliott	12.00
AJ	Avery Johnson	12.00
MR	Mitch Richmond	30.00
VB	Vin Baker	50.00

1997-98 Stadium Club

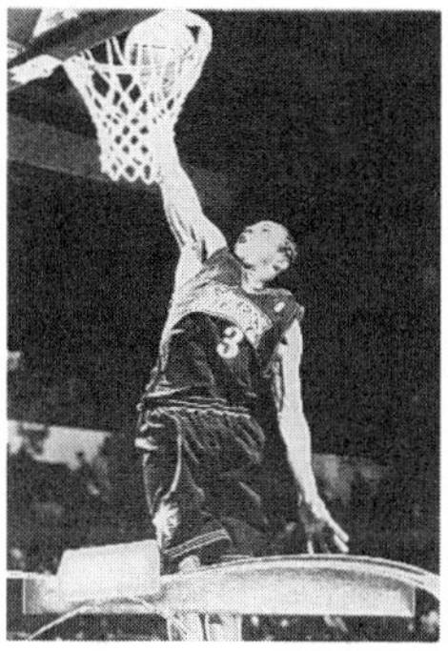

Stadium Club Basketball was released in two, 120-card series in 1997-98, with each series containing 100 base cards and a 20-card Rookies subset. The cards clearly focused on photography, with a full-bleed, glossy photo on each card, with a silver Stadium Club logo and a blue foil strip across the bottom that contained the player's name. Inserts in Series I included: Printing Plates, Bowman's Best Veteran Preview, Hoop Screams, Hardwood Hopefuls, Co-Signers, Triumvirates and Hardcourt Heroics, along with One of a Kind and First Day Issue parallels. Series II included: Printing Plates, Co-Signers, Bowman's Best Rookie Preview, Triumvirate, Never Compromise and Royal Court, along with One of a Kind and First Day Issue parallel sets.

		MT
Complete Set (240):		55.00
Complete Series 1 (120):		35.00
Complete Series 2 (120):		20.00
Common Player:		.10
Series 1 Wax Box:		60.00
Series 2 Wax Box:		60.00
1	Scottie Pippen	1.00
2	Bryon Russell	.10
3	Muggsy Bogues	.10
4	Gary Payton	.50
5	Team of the 90's	2.00
6	Corliss Williamson	.10
7	Samaki Walker	.20
8	Allan Houston	.10
9	Ray Allen	.30
10	Nick Van Exel	.30
11	Chris Mullin	.20
12	Popeye Jones	.10
13	Horace Grant	.10
14	Rik Smits	.10
15	Wayman Tisdale	.10
16	Donny Marshall	.10
17	Rod Strickland	.10
18	Rod Strickland	.10
19	Greg Anthony	.10
20	Lindsey Hunter	.10
21	Glen Rice	.20
22	Anthony Goldwire	.10
23	Mahmoud Abdul-Rauf	.10
24	Sean Elliott	.10
25	Cory Alexander	.10
26	Tyrone Corbin	.10
27	Sam Perkins	.10
28	Brian Shaw	.10
29	Doug Christie	.10
30	Mark Jackson	.10
31	Christian Laettner	.20
32	Damon Stoudamire	.75
33	Eric Williams	.10
34	Glenn Robinson	.30
35	Brooks Thompson	.10
36	Derrick Coleman	.10
37	Theo Ratliff	.20
38	Ron Harper	.10
39	Hakeem Olajuwon	.75
40	Mitch Richmond	.30
41	Reggie Miller	.20
42	Reggie Miller	.20
43	Shaquille O'Neal	1.50
44	Zydrunas Ilgauskas	.10
45	Jamal Mashburn	.20
46	Isaiah Rider	.10

47	Tom Gugliotta	.20
48	Rex Chapman	.10
49	Lorenzen Wright	.10
50	Pooh Richardson	.10
51	Armon Gilliam	.10
52	Kevin Johnson	.20
53	Kerry Kittles	.40
54	Kerry Kittles	.40
55	Charles Oakley	.10
56	Dennis Rodman	1.50
57	Greg Ostertag	.10
58	Todd Fuller	.10
59	Mark Davis	.10
60	Erick Strickland	.10
61	Clifford Robinson	.10
62	Nate McMillan	.10
63	Steve Kerr	.10
64	Bob Sura	.10
65	Danny Ferry	.10
66	Loy Vaught	.10
67	A.C. Green	.10
68	John Stockton	.40
69	Terry Mills	.10
70	Voshon Lenard	.10
71	Matt Maloney	.20
72	Charlie Ward	.10
73	Brent Barry	.10
74	Chris Webber	1.00
75	Stephon Marbury	1.50
76	Bryant Stith	.10
77	Shareef Abdur-Rahim	1.00
78	Sean Rooks	.10
79	Rony Seikaly	.10
80	Brent Price	.10
81	Wesley Person	.10
82	Michael Smith	.10
83	Gary Trent	.10
84	Dan Majerle	.10
85	Rex Walters	.10
86	Clarence Weatherspoon	.10
87	Patrick Ewing	.30
88	B.J. Armstrong	.10
89	Travis Best	.10
90	Steve Smith	.10
91	Vitaly Potapenko	.10
92	Derek Strong	.10
93	Michael Finley	.20
94	Will Perdue	.10
95	Antoine Walker	2.00
96	Chuck Person	.10
97	Mookie Blaylock	.10
98	Eric Snow	.10
99	Tony Delk	.10
100	Mario Elie	.10
101	Terrell Brandon	.20
102	Shawn Bradley	.10
103	Latrell Sprewell	.20
104	Latrell Sprewell	.20
105	Tim Hardaway	.20
106	Terry Porter	.10
107	Darrell Armstrong	.10
108	Rasheed Wallace	.10
109	Vinny Del Negro	.10
110	Gheorghe Muresan	.10
111	Lawrence Moten	.10
112	Lamond Murray	.10
113	Juwan Howard	.30
114	Juwan Howard	.30
115	Karl Malone	.40
116	Kurt Thomas	.10
117	Shawn Respert	.10
118	Michael Jordan	5.00
119	Shawn Kemp	1.00
120	Arvydas Sabonis	.10
121	Tyus Edney	.10
122	Bryant Reeves	.20
123	Jason Kidd	.40
124	Dikembe Mutombo	.20
125	Allen Iverson	2.00
126	Allen Iverson	2.00
127	Larry Johnson	.20
128	Jerry Stackhouse	.50
129	Kendall Gill	.10
130	Kendall Gill	.10
131	Vin Baker	.30
132	Joe Dumars	.10
133	Calbert Cheaney	.10
134	Alonzo Mourning	.30
135	Isaac Austin	.10
136	Joe Smith	.50
137	Elden Campbell	.10
138	Kevin Garnett	2.50
139	Malik Sealy	.10
140	John Starks	.10
141	Clyde Drexler	.40
142	Matt Geiger	.10
143	Mark Price	.10
144	Buck Williams	.10
145	Grant Hill	2.50
146	Kobe Bryant	3.00
147	Dale Ellis	.10
148	Jason Caffey	.10
149	Toni Kukoc	.10
150	Avery Johnson	.10
151	Alan Henderson	.10
152	Walt Williams	.10
153	Greg Minor	.10
154	Calbert Cheaney	.10
155	Vlade Divac	.10
156	Greg Foster	.10
157	LaPhonso Ellis	.10
158	Charles Barkley	.50
159	Antonio Davis	.10
160	Roy Rogers	.10
161	Robert Horry	.10
162	Chris Gatling	.10
163	Chris Carr	.10
164	Robert Pack	.10
165	Sam Cassell	.10
166	Rodney Rogers	.10
167	Chris Childs	.10
168	Shandon Anderson	.10
169	Kenny Anderson	.10
170	Anthony Mason	.10
171	Olden Polynice	.10
172	David Wingate	.10
173	David Robinson	.40
174	Billy Owens	.10
175	Detlef Schrempf	.10
176	Carlos Rogers	.10
177	Marcus Camby	.75
178	Dana Barros	.10
179	Shandon Anderson	.10
180	Jayson Williams	.10
181	Eldridge Recasner	.10
182	Doug West	.10
183	Kevin Willis	.10
184	Eddie Johnson	.10
185	Derek Fisher	.10
186	Eddie Jones	.50
187	Sherman Douglas	.10
188	Anthony Peeler	.10
189	Danny Manning	.10
190	Walter McCarty	.10
191	Hersey Hawkins	.10
192	Micheal Williams	.10
193	Jeff Hornacek	.10
194	Anfernee Hardaway	2.00
195	Harvey Grant	.10
196	Nick Anderson	.10
197	Luc Longley	.10
198	Andrew Lang	.10
199	P.J. Brown	.10
200	Cedric Ceballos	.10
201	*Tim Duncan*	5.00
202	Ervin Johnson	.10
203	*Keith Van Horn*	4.00
204	David Wesley	.10
205	*Chauncey Billups*	2.50
206	Jim Jackson	.20
207	*Antonio Daniels*	2.50
208	Travis Knight	.10
209	*Tony Battie*	2.50
210	Bobby Phills	.10
211	*Bobby Jackson*	2.50
212	Otis Thorpe	.10
213	*Tim Thomas*	3.00
214	Chris Mullin	.20
215	*Adonal Foyle*	2.00
216	Brian Williams	.10
217	*Tracy McGrady*	2.50
218	Tyus Edney	.10
219	*Danny Fortson*	2.00
220	Clifford Robinson	.10
221	*Olivier Saint-Jean*	2.00
222	Vin Baker	.40
223	*Austin Croshere*	.50
224	Brian Grant	.10
225	*Derek Anderson*	3.00
226	Kelvin Cato	.20
227	*Maurice Taylor*	.50
228	Scot Pollard	.10
229	*John Thomas*	.20
230	Dean Garrett	.10
231	*Brevin Knight*	3.00
232	*Ron Mercer*	2.00
233	*Johnny Taylor*	.20
234	Antonio McDyess	.40
235	*Ed Gray*	.20
236	Terrell Brandon	.20
237	*Anthony Parker*	.20
238	Shawn Kemp	1.00
239	*Paul Grant*	.20
240	Terry Mills	.10

1997-98 Stadium Club Promos

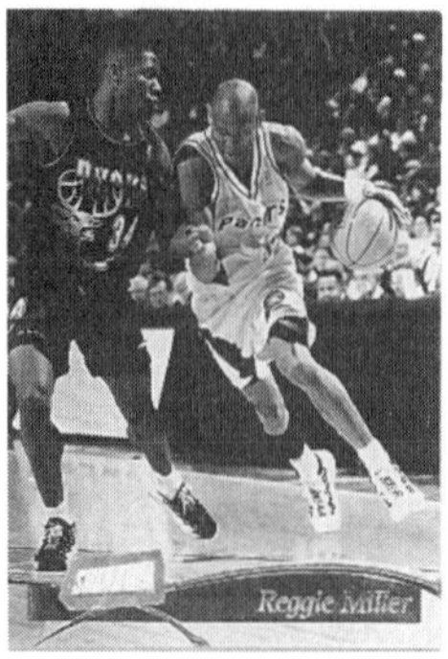

This six-card set was a promo for the 1997-98 Stadium Club set. The card fronts feature a color player photo and a foil-embossed logo. The backs have biographical information, three-year player stats and a ranking based on those stats and the position he playes.

		MT
Complete Set (6):		5.00
Common Player:		.50
21	Glen Rice	1.00
41	Reggie Miller	1.00
87	Patrick Ewing	1.00
95	Antoine Walker	3.00
115	Karl Malone	1.00
169	Kenny Anderson	.50

1997-98 Stadium Club First Day Issue

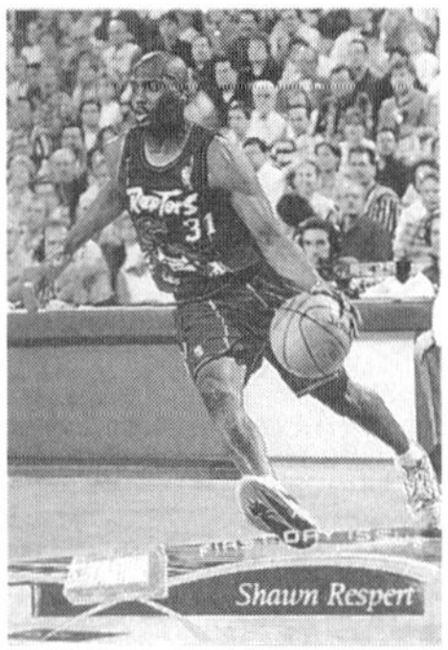

First Day Issue cards paralleled all 240 cards in Stadium Club Series I and II. The cards contained a First Day Issue stamp on the front and were sequentially numbered to 200 sets. They were inserted in retail packs only and seeded one per 24.

	MT
F.D.I. Stars:	15x-30x
F.D.I. Rookies:	8x-16x

1997-98 Stadium Club One Of A Kind

One of a Kind was a hobby-only parallel that mirrored all 240 cards in Series I and II. Cards were printed on a foilboard stock and sequentially numbered on the back to 150. They were seeded one per 86 packs in Series I and one per 69 packs in Series II.

	MT
One Of A Kind Stars:	30x-60x
One Of A Kind Rookies:	15x-30x

1997-98 Stadium Club Bowman's Best Veteran Preview

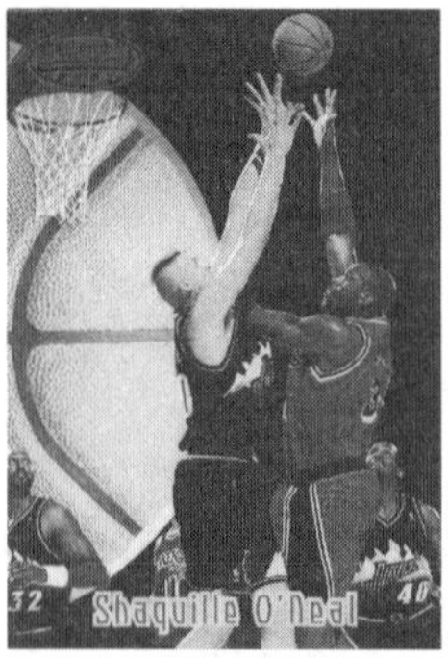

This 10-card set was inserted into packs of Series I, with regular versions every 24 packs, Refractor versions every 96 packs and Atomic Refractors every 192 packs. The cards are identified by a "BBP" prefix on the card number and a gold color to the Bowman's Best design on the front.

	MT
Complete Set (10):	60.00
Common Player:	2.00
Refractors:	2x-3x
Atomic Refractors:	3x-6x
BBP1Allen Iverson	12.00
BBP2Gary Payton	4.00
BBP3Greg Hill	12.00
BBP4Anfernee Hardaway	10.00
BBP5Karl Malone	3.00
BBP6Glen Rice	2.00
BBP7Antoine Walker	8.00
BBP8Alonzo Mourning	2.00
BBP9Shareef Abdur-Rahim	6.00
BBP10Shaquille O'Neal	8.00

1997-98 Stadium Club Bowman's Best Rookie Preview

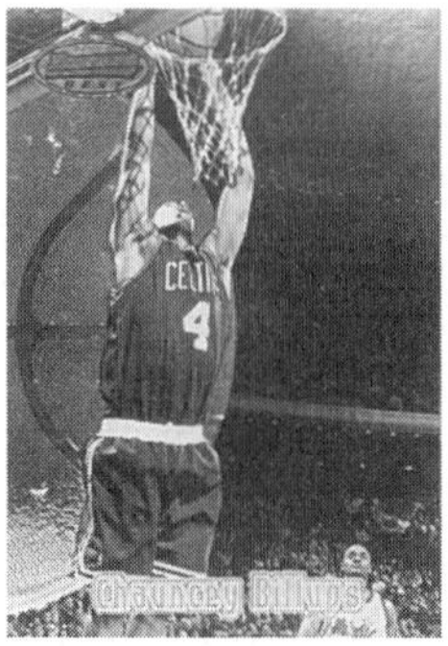

This 10-card set was inserted into packs of Stadium Club Series II packs. Regular versions were seeded one per 24 packs, Refractors were seeded one per 96 packs and Atomic Refractors every 192 packs. These were identified by a "BBP" prefix on the card number and a silver design to the Bowman's Best card on the front.

	MT
Complete Set (10):	30.00
Common Player:	1.50
Refractors:	2x-3x
Atomic Refractors:	3x-6x
BBP11Maurice Taylor	4.00
BBP12Chauncey Billups	10.00
BBP13Paul Grant	1.50
BBP14Tony Battie	8.00
BBP15Austin Croshere	3.00
BBP16Brevin Knight	6.00
BBP17Bobby Jackson	6.00
BBP18Johnny Taylor	1.50
BBP19Scot Pollard	1.50
BBP20Olivier Saint-Jean	3.00

1997-98 Stadium Club Co-Signers

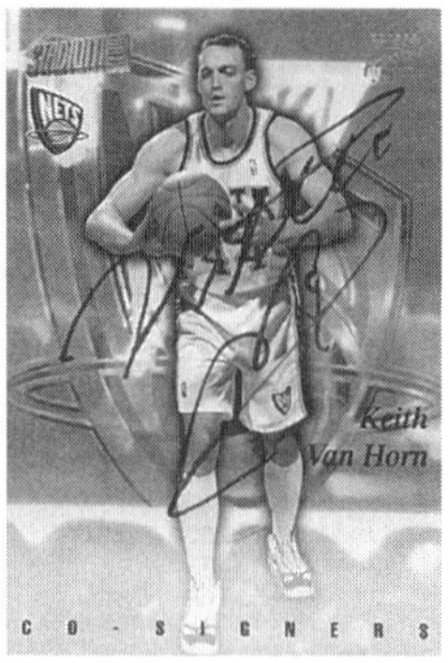

This 24-card insert ran through Series I and II of Stadium Club and was inserted one per 309 hobby packs. These double-sided cards featured two NBA stars, one per side, with both players autographs and were numbered with a "CO" prefix.

	MT
Common Player:	75.00
CO1 Karl Malone, Kobe Bryant	1200.
CO2 Juwan Howard, Hakeem Olajuwon	325.00
CO3 John Starks, Joe Smith	225.00
CO4 Clyde Drexler, Tim Hardaway	400.00
CO5 Kobe Bryant, John Starks	425.00
CO6 Hakeem Olajuwon, Clyde Drexler	180.00
CO7 Tim Hardaway, Juwan Howard	125.00
CO8 Joe Smith, Karl Malone	125.00
CO9 Juwan Howard, Clyde Drexler	125.00
CO10Hakeem Olajuwon, Tim Hardaway	125.00
CO11Joe Smith, Kobe Bryant	225.00
CO12Karl Malone, John Starks	75.00
CO13Dikembe Mutombo, Chauncey Billups	175.00
CO14Keith Van Horn, Chris Webber	550.00
CO15Karl Malone, Kerry Kittles	275.00
CO16Ron Mercer, Antoine Walker	600.00
CO17Chris Webber, Karl Malone	150.00
CO18Antoine Walker, Dikembe Mutombo	125.00
CO19Kerry Kittles, Keith Van Horn	300.00
CO20Chauncey Billups, Ron Mercer	225.00
CO21Antoine Walker, Chauncey Billups	175.00
CO22Dikembe Mutombo, Ron Mercer	100.00
CO23Keith Van Horn, Karl Malone	250.00
CO24Chris Webber, Kerry Kittles	125.00

1997-98 Stadium Club Hardcourt Heroics

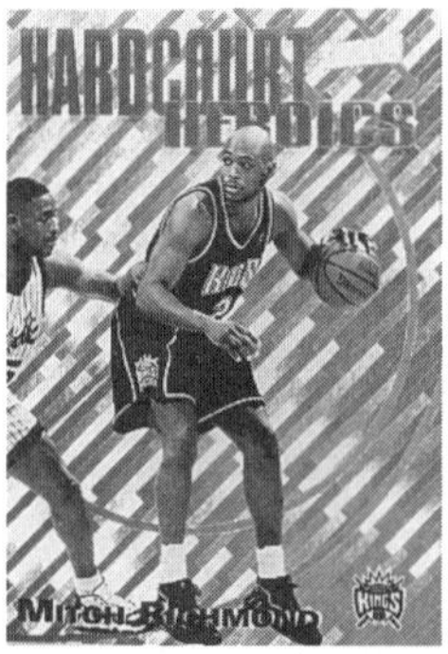

This 10-card insert set was found in Series I packs at a rate of one per 12 packs. The cards were printed on a silver unilustre technology and numbered with a "H" prefix.

		MT
Complete Set (10):		50.00
Common Player:		1.50
H1	Michael Jordan	20.00
H2	Gary Payton	3.00
H3	Charles Barkley	3.00
H4	Mitch Richmond	1.50
H5	Shawn Kemp	4.00
H6	Anfernee Hardaway	8.00
H7	Vin Baker	3.00
H8	Shaquille O'Neal	6.00
H9	Scottie Pippen	4.00
H10	Grant Hill	10.00

1997-98 Stadium Club Hardwood Hopefuls

Hardcourt Hopefuls was a 10-card insert set that was seeded one per 36 packs of Series I. The insert features 1997 NBA Draft Picks on a textured, metalized plastic card that carries a "HH" prefix.

		MT
Complete Set (10):		100.00
Common Player:		3.00
HH1	Brevin Knight	8.00
HH2	Adonal Foyle	8.00
HH3	Keith Van Horn	25.00
HH4	Tim Duncan	30.00
HH5	Danny Fortson	8.00

		MT
HH6	Tracy McGrady	15.00
HH7	Tony Battie	12.00
HH8	Chauncey Billups	15.00
HH9	Austin Croshere	3.00
HH10	Antonio Daniels	15.00

1997-98 Stadium Club Hoop Screams

This 10-card set is inserted one per 12 packs of Series I. The cards capture each player on a metallized look done in blue and silver and are numbered with a "HS" prefix.

		MT
Complete Set (10):		50.00
Common Player:		1.00
HS1	Shaquille O'Neal	6.00
HS2	Cedric Ceballos	1.00
HS3	Kevin Garnett	10.00
HS4	Shawn Kemp	4.00
HS5	Jerry Stackhouse	3.00
HS6	Anfernee Hardaway	10.00
HS7	Patrick Ewing	3.00
HS8	Marcus Camby	4.00
HS9	Kobe Bryant	12.00
HS10	Michael Jordan	20.00

1997-98 Stadium Club Never Compromise

This Series II exclusive included 10 veterans and 10 rookies on a glossy card featuring the insert name printed repeatedly across the background. These were found every 36 packs and numbered with a "NC" prefix.

		MT
Complete Set (20):		175.00
Common Player:		2.00
NC1	Michael Jordan	40.00
NC2	Karl Malone	4.00
NC3	Hakeem Olajuwon	8.00
NC4	Kevin Garnett	20.00
NC5	Dikembe Mutombo	2.00
NC6	Gary Payton	5.00
NC7	Grant Hill	20.00
NC8	Charles Barkley	2.00
NC9	Shaquille O'Neal	15.00
NC10	Anfernee Hardaway	15.00
NC11	Tim Duncan	25.00
NC12	Keith Van Horn	25.00
NC13	Tracy McGrady	12.00
NC14	Tim Thomas	10.00
NC15	Austin Croshere	2.00
NC16	Maurice Taylor	6.00
NC17	Chauncey Billups	12.00
NC18	Adonal Foyle	2.00
NC19	Tony Battie	8.00
NC20	Bobby Jackson	6.00

1997-98 Stadium Club Royal Court

Grant Hill

Ten rookies and 10 veterans are included in this insert that highlights each player coming out of a silver foil background. Inserted one per 12 packs of Series II, these cards are numbered with a "RC" prefix.

		MT
Complete Set (20):		100.00
Common Player:		1.00
RC1	Scottie Pippen	5.00
RC2	Karl Malone	2.00
RC3	Gary Payton	3.00
RC4	Kobe Bryant	15.00
RC5	Antoine Walker	8.00
RC6	Michael Jordan	20.00
RC7	Shaquille O'Neal	8.00
RC8	Dikembe Mutombo	1.00
RC9	Hakeem Olajuwon	4.00
RC10	Grant Hill	10.00
RC11	Tim Duncan	15.00
RC12	Keith Van Horn	15.00
RC13	Chauncey Billups	8.00
RC14	Antonio Daniels	6.00
RC15	Tony Battie	6.00
RC16	Bobby Jackson	5.00
RC17	Tim Thomas	6.00
RC18	Adonal Foyle	1.00
RC19	Tracy McGrady	8.00
RC20	Danny Fortson	2.00

1997-98 Stadium Club Triumvirate

TRACY McGRADY

This 48-card, retail only insert was distributed in both Series I and II packs with half the set in each. Three players from eight different teams were included in each series on Finest technology cards that fit together to form a three card panel. Within each series, Triumvirates were seeded 1:48 (luminous), 1:192 (luminescent) and 1:384 (illuminator) and numbered with a "T" prefix and a "A," "B," or "C" suffix.

		MT
Complete Set (48):		525.00
Complete Series 1 (24):		225.00
Complete Series 2 (24):		300.00
Common Player:		2.00
Luminescent Cards:		3x
Illuminator Cards:		3x-6x
T1A	Scottie Pippen	15.00
T1B	Michael Jordan	60.00
T1C	Dennis Rodman	20.00
T2A	Ray Allen	6.00
T2B	Vin Baker	8.00

		MT
T2C	Glenn Robinson	4.00
T3A	Juwan Howard	4.00
T3B	Chris Webber	10.00
T3C	Rod Strickland	2.00
T4A	Christian Laettner	2.00
T4B	Dikembe Mutombo	2.00
T4C	Steve Smith	2.00
T5A	Tom Gugliotta	2.00
T5B	Kevin Garnett	30.00
T5C	Stephon Marbury	25.00
T6A	Charles Barkley	8.00
T6B	Hakeem Olajuwon	12.00
T6C	Clyde Drexler	6.00
T7A	John Stockton	4.00
T7B	Karl Malone	6.00
T7C	Bryon Russell	2.00
T8A	Larry Johnson	2.00
T8B	Patrick Ewing	4.00
T8C	Allan Houston	2.00
T9A	Tim Hardaway	4.00
T9B	Michael Jordan	50.00
T9C	Anfernee Hardaway	20.00
T10A	Glen Rice	4.00
T10B	Scottie Pippen	12.00
T10C	Grant Hill	25.00
T11A	Dikembe Mutombo	2.00
T11B	Patrick Ewing	4.00
T11C	Alonzo Mourning	4.00
T12A	Ron Mercer	15.00
T12B	Keith Van Horn	25.00
T12C	Tracy McGrady	12.00
T13A	Gary Payton	6.00
T13B	John Stockton	4.00
T13C	Stephon Marbury	20.00
T14A	Karl Malone	5.00
T14B	Charles Barkley	6.00
T14C	Kevin Garnett	25.00
T15A	David Robinson	6.00
T15B	Hakeem Olajuwon	10.00
T15C	Shaquille O'Neal	10.00
T16A	Antonio Daniels	8.00
T16B	Tim Duncan	25.00
T16C	Adonal Foyle	2.00

1997-98 Topps II

Topps 1997-98 consisted of 220 cards, with 110 in each Series. Card fronts featured a color shot of the player surrounded by a white border on all sides. The featured player's image was glossy, with the rest of the background slightly dulled, with two color strips up the left side and one color strip across the bottom with the player's name in gold foil stamped in it. Inserts in Series I included: Minted in Springfield parallel cards, Autographs, Rock Stars, Fantastic 15, Topps 40, Rookie Redemption, Season's Best and Bound for Glory. Inserts in Series II included: Minted in Springfield, New School, Topps 40, Generations Finest, Inside Stuff, Destiny and Clutch Time.

		MT
Complete Series 2 (110):		20.00
Common Player:		.05
Series 2 Wax Box:		45.00
111	Antonio McDyess	.20
112	Bob Sura	.10
113	Terrell Brandon	.10
114	*Tim Thomas*	2.00
115	*Tim Duncan*	4.00
116	*Antonio Daniels*	2.00
117	Bryant Reeves	.05
118	*Keith Van Horn*	3.00
119	Loy Vaught	.05
120	Rasheed Wallace	.05
121	*Bobby Jackson*	1.50
122	Kevin Johnson	.10
123	Michael Jordan	3.00
124	*Ron Mercer*	2.00
125	*Tracy McGrady*	2.00

		MT
126	Antoine Walker	1.25
127	Carlos Rogers	.05
128	Isaac Austin	.05
129	Mookie Blaylock	.05
130	*Rodrick Rhodes*	.50
131	Dennis Scott	.05
132	Chris Mullin	.10
133	P.J. Brown	.05
134	Rex Chapman	.05
135	Sean Elliott	.05
136	Alan Henderson	.05
137	*Austin Croshere*	.50
138	Nick Van Exel	.20
139	Derek Strong	.05
140	Glenn Robinson	.25
141	Avery Johnson	.05
142	Calbert Cheaney	.05
143	Mahmoud Abdul-Rauf	.05
144	Stojko Vrankovic	.05
145	Chris Childs	.05
146	Danny Manning	.05
147	Jeff Hornacek	.05
148	Kevin Garnett	1.50
149	Joe Dumars	.10
150	*Johnny Taylor*	.20
151	Mark Price	.05
152	Toni Kukoc	.10
153	Erick Dampier	.05
154	Lorenzen Wright	.05
155	Matt Geiger	.05
156	Tim Hardaway	.20
157	Charles Smith	.05
158	Hersey Hawkins	.05
159	Michael Finley	.20
160	Tyus Edney	.05
161	Christian Laettner	.10
162	Doug West	.05
163	Jim Jackson	.20
164	Larry Johnson	.20
165	Vin Baker	.30
166	Karl Malone	.30
167	*Kelvin Cato*	.50
168	Luc Longley	.05
169	Dale Davis	.05
170	Joe Smith	.20
171	Kobe Bryant	2.00
172	Scot Pollard	.05
173	*Derek Anderson*	1.50
174	Erick Strickland	.05
175	Olden Polynice	.05
176	Chris Whitney	.05
177	Anthony Parker	.05
178	Armon Gilliam	.05
179	Gary Payton	.30
180	Glen Rice	.25
181	*Chauncey Billups*	2.00
182	Derek Fisher	.05
183	John Starks	.05
184	Mario Elie	.05
185	Chris Webber	.40
186	Shawn Kemp	.60
187	Greg Ostertag	.05
188	*Olivier Saint-Jean*	.50
189	Eric Snow	.05
190	Isaiah Rider	.05
191	*Paul Grant*	.20
192	Samaki Walker	.05
193	Cory Alexander	.05
194	Eddie Jones	.40
195	John Thomas	.05
196	Otis Thorpe	.05
197	Rod Strickland	.05
198	David Wesley	.05
199	*Jacque Vaughn*	.20
200	Rik Smits	.05
201	*Brevin Knight*	1.50
202	Clifford Robinson	.05
203	Hakeem Olajuwon	.50
204	Jerry Stackhouse	.20
205	Tyrone Hill	.05
206	Kendall Gill	.05
207	Marcus Camby	.30
208	*Tony Battie*	1.50
209	Brent Price	.05
210	*Danny Fortson*	1.00
211	Jerome Williams	.05
212	*Maurice Taylor*	.75
213	Brian Williams	.05
214	Keith Booth	.05
215	Nick Anderson	.05
216	Travis Knight	.05
217	*Adonal Foyle*	.50
218	Anfernee Hardaway	1.25
219	Kerry Kittles	.25
220	Checklist	.05

1997-98 Topps Mint

This 220-card parallel set was gold foil stamped at the Basketball Hall of Fame in Springfield, Mass., and inserted one per six packs. Minted in Springfield inserts were identical to the base cards, except for a gold foil Basketball Hall of Fame stamp in the lower left corner. Minted in Springfield parallel cards were inserted one per nine packs.

Minted Cards: MT 4x-8x

1997-98 Topps Clutch Time

Allen Iverson

This 20-card insert was exclusive to hobby packs and seeded at a rate of one per 36 packs. The cards have a silver dot pattern in the background and the words "Clutch Time" in gold dots across the top. The cards are numbered with a "CT" prefix.

		MT
Complete Set (20):		130.00
Common Player:		2.00
CT1	Michael Jordan	40.00
CT2	Christian Laettner	2.00
CT3	Patrick Ewing	2.00
CT4	Glen Rice	4.00
CT5	Stephon Marbury	15.00
CT6	Tim Hardaway	4.00
CT7	Reggie Miller	4.00
CT8	Gary Payton	5.00
CT9	Charles Barkley	5.00
CT10	Grant Hill	20.00
CT11	Karl Malone	4.00
CT12	Dikembe Mutombo	2.00
CT13	Hakeem Olajuwon	8.00
CT14	Shawn Kemp	10.00
CT15	John Stockton	4.00
CT16	Anfernee Hardaway	15.00
CT17	Glenn Robinson	4.00
CT18	Chris Webber	8.00
CT19	Allen Iverson	20.00
CT20	Scottie Pippen	10.00

1997-98 Topps Destiny

ANTONIO McDYESS

Destiny was a 15-card insert set displaying some of the top players under the age 27. The insert name was printed in large silver foil embossed letters across the top and cards were numbered with a "D" prefix. Destiny inserts were found one per 18 retail packs of Series II.

		MT
Complete Set (15):		75.00
Common Player:		2.00
D1	Grant Hill	10.00
D2	Kevin Garnett	10.00
D3	Vin Baker	2.00
D4	Antoine Walker	10.00
D5	Kobe Bryant	14.00
D6	Tracy McGrady	6.00
D7	Keith Van Horn	10.00
D8	Tim Duncan	12.00
D9	Eddie Jones	3.00
D10	Stephon Marbury	8.00
D11	Marcus Camby	2.00
D12	Antonio McDyess	2.00
D13	Shareef Abdur-Rahim	6.00
D14	Allen Iverson	8.00
D15	Shaquille O'Neal	6.00

1997-98 Topps Generations

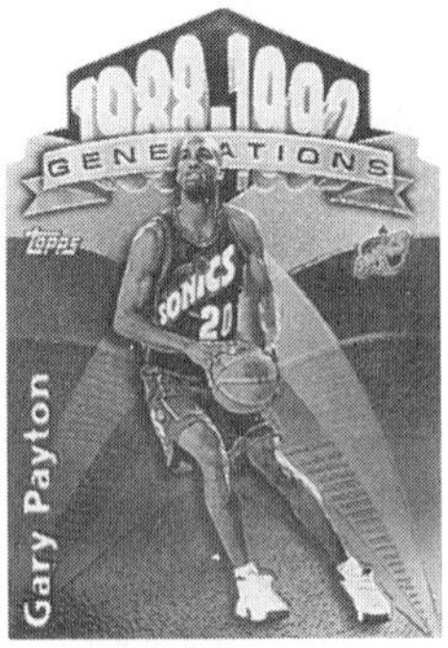

Generations features 30 players from three categories of draft years - 1983-1987, 1988-1992 and 1993-1997. Inserts were printed on die-cut, borderless Finest stock and insert one per 36 packs, with Refractor versions every 144 packs. Generations inserts were numbered with a "G" prefix and only inserted into Series II packs.

		MT
Complete Set (30):		250.00
Common Player:		2.00
Refractors:		2x-4x
G1	Clyde Drexler	4.00
G2	Michael Jordan	50.00
G3	Charles Barkley	5.00
G4	Hakeem Olajuwon	10.00
G5	John Stockton	4.00
G6	Patrick Ewing	2.00
G7	Karl Malone	5.00
G8	Dennis Rodman	15.00
G9	Scottie Pippen	12.00
G10	David Robinson	5.00
G11	Mitch Richmond	2.00
G12	Glen Rice	2.00
G13	Shawn Kemp	12.00
G14	Gary Payton	4.00
G15	Dikembe Mutombo	2.00
G16	Steve Smith	2.00
G17	Christian Laettner	2.00
G18	Shaquille O'Neal	15.00
G19	Alonzo Mourning	2.00
G20	Tom Gugliotta	2.00
G21	Anfernee Hardaway	15.00
G22	Grant Hill	25.00
G23	Kevin Garnett	25.00
G24	Kobe Bryant	30.00
G25	Stephon Marbury	20.00
G26	Antoine Walker	20.00
G27	Shareef Abdur-Rahim	15.00
G28	Tim Duncan	25.00
G29	Keith Van Horn	25.00
G30	Tracy McGrady	15.00

1997-98 Topps Inside Stuff

This 10-card insert was found in one per 36 packs of Topps Series II and numbered with a "IS" prefix. The cards were printed on silver foilboard and highlighted the NBC show Inside Stuff.

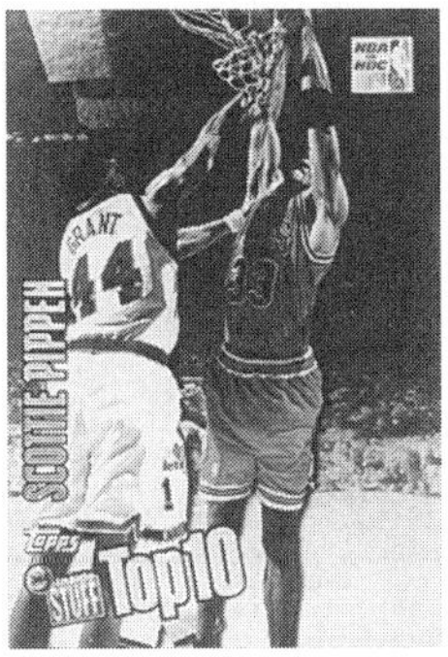

		MT
Complete Set (10):		60.00
Common Player:		1.50
IS1	Michael Jordan	25.00
IS2	Eddie Johnson	1.50
IS3	John Stockton	3.00
IS4	Patrick Ewing	1.50
IS5	Shaquille O'Neal	10.00
IS6	Rex Chapman	1.50
IS7	Shawn Kemp	6.00
IS8	Scottie Pippen	6.00
IS9	Kobe Bryant	15.00
IS10	Anfernee Hardaway	10.00

1997-98 Topps New School

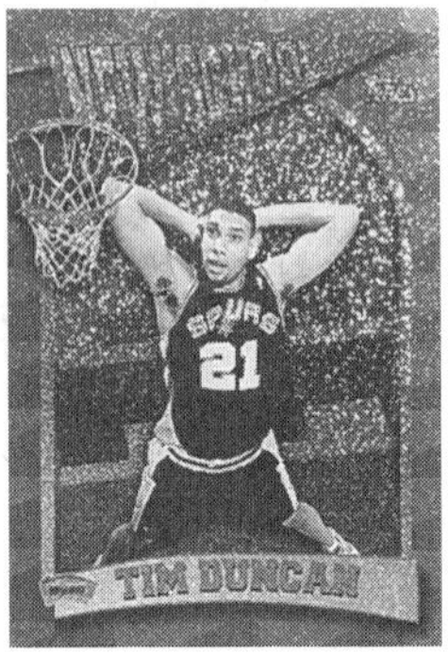

This 15-card set was seeded one per 36 Series II hobby and retail packs. It featured 1997 NBA Draft picks and included a sparkling background with the insert name printed in a pennant. Card backs were numbered with a "NS" prefix.

		MT
Complete Set (15):		85.00
Common Player:		1.50
NS1	Austin Croshere	3.00
NS2	Antonio Daniels	10.00
NS3	Tim Thomas	10.00
NS4	Keith Van Horn	20.00
NS5	Bobby Jackson	6.00
NS6	Derek Anderson	10.00
NS7	Adonal Foyle	3.00
NS8	Johnny Taylor	1.50
NS9	Jacque Vaughn	3.00
NS10	Chauncey Billups	10.00
NS11	Brevin Knight	10.00
NS12	Tracy McGrady	10.00
NS13	Tony Battie	8.00
NS14	Scot Pollard	1.50
NS15	Tim Duncan	25.00

1997-98 Topps 40

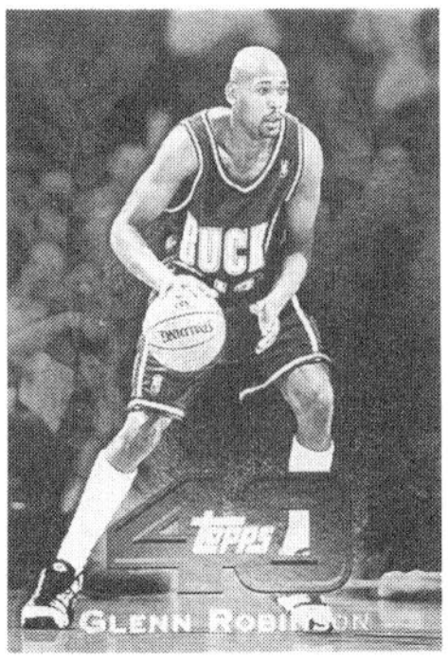

This insert includes selections from NBA players, writers and coaches to come up with the top 40 players in the NBA. Series I has 20 cards, with the other 20 found in Series II, both with insertion rates of one per 12 packs and numbered "T40-x". The cards are printed on reflective, foil-stamped mirrorboard cards, with a large number 40 across the bottom.

		MT
Complete Set (20):		35.00
Common Player:		.50
21	Tom Gugliotta	1.00
22	Allen Iverson	8.00
23	David Robinson	2.00
24	Dikembe Mutombo	.50
25	John Stockton	1.00
26	Charles Barkley	2.00
27	Mitch Richmond	1.00
28	Damon Stoudamire	2.00
29	Anthony Mason	.50
30	Shaquille O'Neal	6.00
31	Glenn Robinson	1.00
32	Juwan Howard	2.00
33	Shawn Kemp	4.00
34	Dennis Rodman	6.00
35	Grant Hill	8.00
36	Kevin Johnson	.50
37	Alonzo Mourning	1.00
38	Hakeem Olajuwon	3.00
39	Joe Dumars	.50
40	Scottie Pippen	4.00

1997-98 Topps Chrome

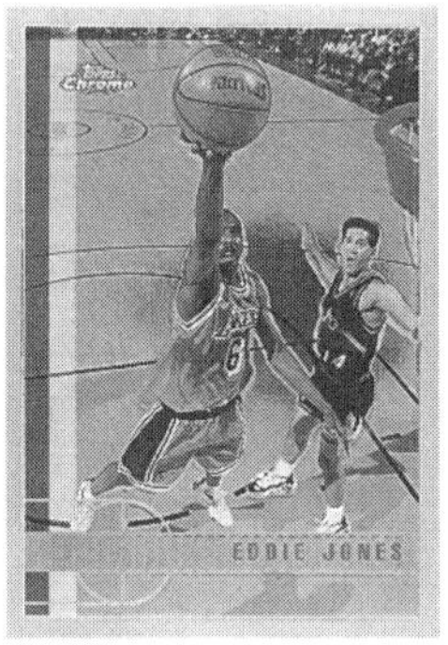

Chrome included all 220 cards from Topps Series I and II and added a chromium finish to each card. The cards identical to regular-issue Topps cards, except for the Topps Chrome logo in the upper left corner and the finish. Each card was also available in a Refractor version, while three inserts from Topps - Season's Best, Top 40 and Destiny - were also available in Refractor versions. This season's Chrome product followed up the extremely popular retail-only product of 1996-97, but was available in both retail and hobby locations.

		MT
Complete Set (220):		400.00
Common Player:		.25
Wax Box:		175.00
1	Scottie Pippen	2.00
2	Nate McMillan	.25
3	Byron Scott	.25
4	Mark Davis	.25
5	Rod Strickland	.50
6	Brian Grant	.25
7	Damon Stoudamire	1.50
8	John Stockton	.75
9	Grant Long	.25
10	Darrell Armstrong	.25
11	Anthony Mason	.25
12	Travis Best	.25
13	Stephon Marbury	4.00
14	Jamal Mashburn	.25
15	Detlef Schrempf	.25
16	Terrell Brandon	.50
17	Charles Barkley	1.00
18	Vin Baker	1.50
19	Gary Trent	.25
20	Vinny Del Negro	.25
21	Todd Day	.25
22	Malik Sealy	.25
23	Wesley Person	.25
24	Reggie Miller	.75
25	Dan Majerle	.25
26	Todd Fuller	.25
27	Juwan Howard	.75
28	Clarence Weatherspoon	.25
29	Grant Hill	5.00
30	John Williams	.25
31	Ken Norman	.25
32	Patrick Ewing	.50
33	Bryon Russell	.25
34	Tony Smith	.25
35	Andrew Lang	.25
36	Rony Seikaly	.25
37	Billy Owens	.25
38	Dino Radja	.25
39	Chris Gatling	.25
40	Dale Davis	.25
41	Arvydas Sabonis	.25
42	Chris Mills	.25
43	A.C. Green	.25
44	Tyrone Hill	.25
45	Tracy Murray	.25
46	David Robinson	1.00
47	Lee Mayberry	.25
48	Jayson Williams	.25
49	Jason Kidd	1.50
50	Bryant Stith	.25
51	Bulls	4.00
52	Brent Barry	.25
53	Henry James	.25
54	Allen Iverson	4.00
55	Shandon Anderson	.25
56	Mitch Richmond	.75
57	Allan Houston	.50
58	Ron Harper	.25
59	Gheorghe Muresan	.25
60	Vincent Askew	.25
61	Ray Allen	1.25
62	Kenny Anderson	.50
63	Dikembe Mutombo	.50
64	Sam Perkins	.25
65	Walt Williams	.25
66	Chris Carr	.25
67	Vlade Divac	.25
68	LaPhonso Ellis	.25
69	B.J. Armstrong	.25
70	Jim Jackson	.50
71	Clyde Drexler	.75
72	Lindsey Hunter	.25
73	Sasha Danilovic	.25
74	Elden Campbell	.25
75	Robert Pack	.25
76	Dennis Scott	.25
77	Will Perdue	.25
78	Anthony Peeler	.25
79	Steve Smith	.25
80	Steve Kerr	.25
81	Buck Williams	.25
82	Terry Mills	.25
83	Michael Smith	.25
84	Adam Keefe	.25
85	Kevin Willis	.25
86	David Wesley	.25
87	Muggsy Bogues	.25
88	Bimbo Coles	.25
89	Tom Gugliotta	.50
90	Jermaine O'Neal	.50
91	Cedric Ceballos	.25
92	Shawn Kemp	2.00
93	Horace Grant	.25
94	Shareef Abdur-Rahim	2.50
95	Robert Horry	.25
96	Vitaly Potapenko	.25
97	Pooh Richardson	.25
98	Doug Christie	.25
99	Voshon Lenard	.25
100	Dominique Wilkins	.25
101	Alonzo Mourning	.50
102	Sam Cassell	.25
103	Sherman Douglas	.25
104	Shawn Bradley	.25
105	Mark Jackson	.25
106	Dennis Rodman	2.50
107	Charles Oakley	.25
108	Matt Maloney	.50
109	Shaquille O'Neal	3.00
110	Checklist	.25
111	Antonio McDyess	.50
112	Bob Sura	.25
113	Terrell Brandon	.50
114	*Tim Thomas*	30.00
115	*Tim Duncan*	100.00
116	*Antonio Daniels*	12.00
117	Bryant Reeves	.25
118	*Keith Van Horn*	70.00
119	Loy Vaught	.25
120	Rasheed Wallace	.25
121	*Bobby Jackson*	15.00
122	Kevin Johnson	.50
123	Michael Jordan	25.00
124	*Ron Mercer*	50.00
125	*Tracy McGrady*	25.00
126	Antoine Walker	4.00
127	Carlos Rogers	.25
128	Isaac Austin	.25
129	Mookie Blaylock	.25
130	*Rodrick Rhodes*	5.00
131	Dennis Scott	.25
132	Chris Mullin	.50
133	P.J. Brown	.25
134	Rex Chapman	.25
135	Sean Elliott	.25
136	Alan Henderson	.25
137	*Austin Croshere*	5.00
138	Nick Van Exel	.50
139	Derek Strong	.25
140	Glenn Robinson	.75
141	Avery Johnson	.25
142	Calbert Cheaney	.25
143	Mahmoud Abdul-Rauf	.25
144	Stojko Vrankovic	.25
145	Chris Childs	.25
146	Danny Manning	.25
147	Jeff Hornacek	.25
148	Kevin Garnett	5.00
149	Joe Dumars	.25
150	*Johnny Taylor*	.50
151	Mark Price	.25
152	Toni Kukoc	.50
153	Erick Dampier	.25
154	Lorenzen Wright	.25
155	Matt Geiger	.25
156	Tim Hardaway	.50
157	Charles Smith	.25
158	Hersey Hawkins	.25
159	Michael Finley	.50
160	Tyus Edney	.25
161	Christian Laettner	.50
162	Doug West	.25
163	Jim Jackson	.50
164	Larry Johnson	.50
165	Vin Baker	1.50
166	Karl Malone	.75
167	*Kelvin Cato*	5.00
168	Luc Longley	.25
169	Dale Davis	.25
170	Joe Smith	.50
171	Kobe Bryant	10.00
172	Scot Pollard	.25
173	*Derek Anderson*	20.00
174	Erick Strickland	.25
175	Olden Polynice	.25
176	Chris Whitney	.25
177	*Anthony Parker*	.50
178	Armon Gilliam	.25
179	Gary Payton	1.00
180	Glen Rice	.75
181	*Chauncey Billups*	20.00
182	Derek Fisher	.50
183	John Starks	.25
184	Mario Elie	.25
185	Chris Webber	1.25
186	Shawn Kemp	2.00
187	Greg Ostertag	.25
188	*Olivier Saint-Jean*	.50
189	Eric Snow	.25
190	Isaiah Rider	.50
191	*Paul Grant*	.50
192	Samaki Walker	.25
193	Cory Alexander	.25
194	Eddie Jones	1.25
195	John Thomas	.25
196	Otis Thorpe	.25
197	Rod Strickland	.50
198	David Wesley	.25
199	*Jacque Vaughn*	5.00
200	Rik Smits	.25
201	*Brevin Knight*	20.00
202	Clifford Robinson	.25
203	Hakeem Olajuwon	1.50
204	Jerry Stackhouse	.50
205	Tyrone Hill	.25
206	Kendall Gill	.25
207	Marcus Camby	1.00
208	*Tony Battie*	8.00
209	Brent Price	.25
210	*Danny Fortson*	8.00
211	Jerome Williams	.25
212	*Maurice Taylor*	15.00
213	Brian Williams	.25
214	Keith Booth	.25
215	Nick Anderson	.25
216	Travis Knight	.25
217	*Adonal Foyle*	4.00
218	Anfernee Hardaway	2.50
219	Kerry Kittles	1.00
220	Checklist	.25

1997-98 Topps Chrome Refractors

Refractors of all 220 cards in Topps Chrome were available in these parallel versions. The cards contained the word "Refractor" on the back and were inserted one per 12 packs.

	MT
Refractor Stars:	7x-14x
Refractor Rookies:	2x-4x

1997-98 Topps Chrome Destiny

Destiny featured 15 players under the age of 27 and were seeded one per 12 packs with a Refractor version every 48 packs. This insert was identical to the regular Topps version, except added the chromium finish to each card.

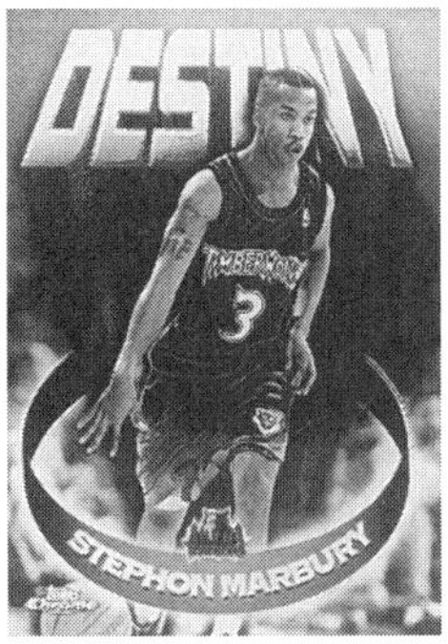

		MT
Complete Set (15):		120.00
Common Player:		1.50
Refractors:		3x
D1	Grant Hill	15.00
D2	Kevin Garnett	15.00
D3	Vin Baker	4.00
D4	Antoine Walker	12.00
D5	Kobe Bryant	20.00
D6	Tracy McGrady	10.00
D7	Keith Van Horn	15.00
D8	Tim Duncan	25.00
D9	Eddie Jones	4.00
D10	Stephon Marbury	12.00
D11	Marcus Camby	1.50
D12	Antonio McDyess	1.50
D13	Shareef Abdur-Rahim	8.00
D14	Allen Iverson	12.00
D15	Shaquille O'Neal	10.00

1997-98 Topps Chrome Season's Best

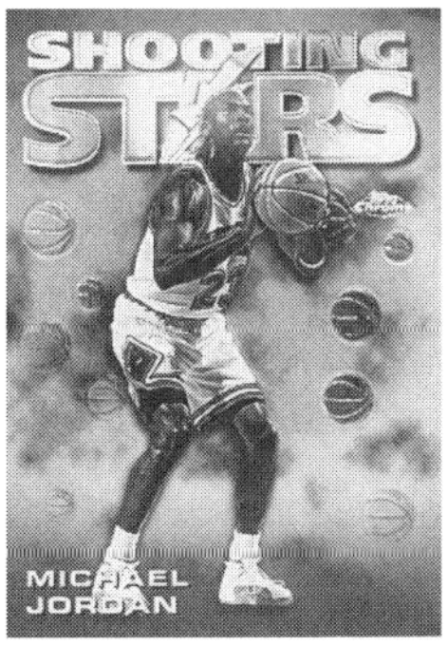

All 30 Season's Best inserts from Topps were reprinted with a chromium finish and inserted into packs of Chome. The Chrome logo appeared in either top corner, with the cards seeded one per eight packs and Refractor versions seeded every 24 packs.

		MT
Complete Set (29):		100.00
Common Player:		1.00
Refractors:		3x
SB1	Gary Payton	3.00
SB2	Kevin Johnson	1.00
SB3	Tim Hardaway	2.00
SB4	John Stockton	2.00
SB5	Damon Stoudamire	3.00
SB6	Michael Jordan	25.00
SB7	Mitch Richmond	2.00
SB9	Reggie Miller	2.00
SB10	Clyde Drexler	2.00
SB11	Grant Hill	12.00
SB12	Scottie Pippen	6.00
SB13	Kendall Gill	1.00
SB14	Glen Rice	2.00
SB15	LaPhonso Ellis	1.00
SB16	Karl Malone	2.00
SB17	Charles Barkley	3.00
SB18	Vin Baker	4.00
SB19	Chris Webber	5.00
SB20	Tom Gugliotta	1.00
SB21	Shaquille O'Neal	8.00
SB22	Patrick Ewing	2.00
SB23	Hakeem Olajuwon	5.00
SB24	Alonzo Mourning	2.00
SB25	Dikembe Mutombo	1.00
SB26	Allen Iverson	10.00
SB27	Antoine Walker	10.00
SB28	Shareef Abdur-Rahim	6.00
SB29	Stephon Marbury	10.00
SB30	Kerry Kittles	2.00

1997-98 Topps Chrome Topps 40

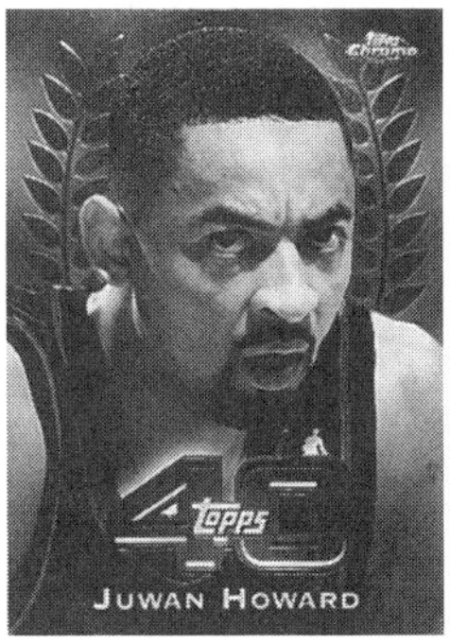

The same 39 cards that were inserted into Topps Series I and II packs were reprinted with a chromium finish and inserted into Chrome. The logo could be found in either upper corner and regular versions were seeded every six packs, with Refractor versions every 18 packs.

		MT
Complete Set (39):		110.00
Common Player:		.75
Refractors:		3x
T40-1	Glen Rice	1.50
T40-2	Patrick Ewing	1.50
T40-3	Terrell Brandon	.75
T40-4	Jerry Stackhouse	1.50
T40-5	Michael Jordan	25.00
T40-6	Christian Laettner	.75
T40-8	Reggie Miller	1.50
T40-9	Gary Payton	3.00
T40-10	Detlef Schrempf	.75
T40-11	Kevin Garnett	12.00
T40-12	Eddie Jones	4.00
T40-13	Clyde Drexler	2.00
T40-14	Anfernee Hardaway	8.00
T40-15	Chris Webber	4.00
T40-16	Jayson Williams	.75
T40-17	Joe Smith	1.50
T40-18	Karl Malone	2.00
T40-19	Tim Hardaway	1.50
T40-20	Vin Baker	3.00
T40-21	Tom Gugliotta	.75
T40-22	Allen Iverson	10.00
T40-23	David Robinson	3.00
T40-24	Dikembe Mutombo	.75
T40-25	John Stockton	1.50
T40-26	Charles Barkley	3.00
T40-27	Mitch Richmond	1.50
T40-28	Damon Stoudamire	3.00
T40-29	Anthony Mason	.75
T40-30	Shaquille O'Neal	8.00
T40-31	Glenn Robinson	1.50
T40-32	Juwan Howard	2.00
T40-33	Shawn Kemp	6.00
T40-34	Dennis Rodman	8.00
T40-35	Grant Hill	12.00
T40-36	Kevin Johnson	.75
T40-37	Alonzo Mourning	1.50
T40-38	Hakeem Olajuwon	5.00
T40-39	Joe Dumars	.75
T40-40	Scottie Pippen	6.00

1997-98 Ultra

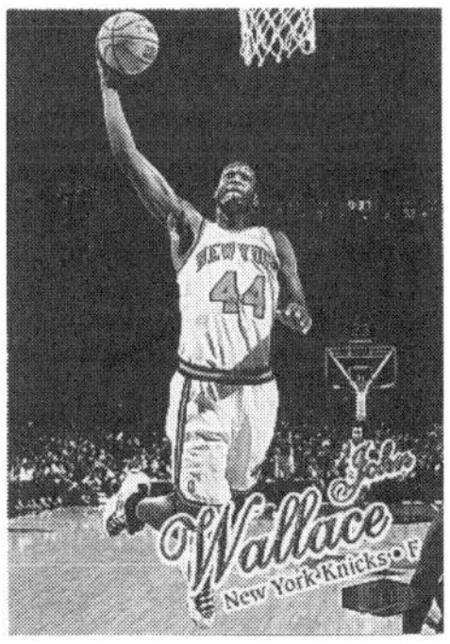

Ultra Basketball was issued in two series in 1997-98, with Series I containing 150 cards and Series II including 125 cards. Series I had 123 base cards, two checklists and a 25-card Rookies insert that was seeded one per four packs. Series II had 97 base cards, three checklists and a 25-card '98 Greats subset that was seeded one per four packs. Cards featured a full-bleed glossy photo, with his name, team, position and the Ultra logo in the lower right corner. Each card in each series was paralleled three times (minus the five checklists), with Gold Medallions inserted one per pack, Platinum cards numbered to 100 and Masterpieces numbered one of one. Inserts in Series I include: Big Shots, Quick Picks, Inside/Outside, Jam City, Heir to the Throne, Ultrabilities, Ultra Stars, Diamond Ink and Million Dollar Moments. Inserts in Series II include: All Rookies, Sweet Deal, Rim Rockers, Neat Feats, View to a Thrill, Court Masters, Star Power, Diamond Ink and Million Dollar Moments.

		MT
Complete Set (275):		240.00
Complete Series 1 (150):		200.00
Complete Series 2 (125):		40.00
Common Player:		.10
Common Player (249-273):		.50
Common Rookie (124-148):		1.00
Series 1 Wax Box:		200.00
Series 2 Wax Box:		60.00
1	Kobe Bryant	4.00
2	Charles Barkley	.50
3	Joe Dumars	.10
4	Wesley Person	.10
5	Walt Williams	.10
6	Vlade Divac	.10
7	Mookie Blaylock	.10
8	Jason Kidd	.50
9	Ron Harper	.10
10	Sherman Douglas	.10
11	Cedric Ceballos	.10
12	Karl Malone	.40
13	Antonio McDyess	.40
14	Steve Kerr	.10
15	Matt Maloney	.20
16	Glenn Robinson	.30
17	Rony Seikaly	.10
18	Derrick Coleman	.10
19	Jermaine O'Neal	.20
20	Scott Burrell	.10
21	Glen Rice	.30
22	Dale Ellis	.10
23	Michael Jordan	5.00
24	Anfernee Hardaway	2.00
25	Bryon Russell	.10
26	Toni Kukoc	.20
27	Theo Ratliff	.10
28	Tom Gugliotta	.20
29	Dennis Rodman	1.50
30	John Stockton	.40
31	Priest Lauderdale	.10
32	Luc Longley	.10
33	Grant Hill	2.50
34	Antonio Davis	.10
35	Eddie Jones	.50
36	Nick Anderson	.10
37	Shareef Abdur-Rahim	1.25
38	Stephon Marbury	2.00
39	Todd Day	.10
40	Tim Hardaway	.30
41	Larry Johnson	.20
42	Sam Perkins	.10
43	Dikembe Mutombo	.20
44	Charles Outlaw	.10
45	Mitch Richmond	.30
46	Bryant Reeves	.20
47	P.J. Brown	.10
48	Steve Smith	.10
49	Martin Muursepp	.10
50	Jamal Mashburn	.20
51	Kendall Gill	.10
52	Vinny Del Negro	.10
53	Roy Rogers	.10
54	Khalid Reeves	.10
55	Scottie Pippen	1.25
56	Joe Smith	.50
57	Mark Jackson	.10
58	Voshon Lenard	.10
59	Dan Majerle	.10
60	Alonzo Mourning	.30
61	Kerry Kittles	.30
62	Chris Childs	.10
63	Patrick Ewing	.30
64	Allan Houston	.20
65	Marcus Camby	.75
66	Christian Laettner	.20
67	Loy Vaught	.10
68	Jayson Williams	.10
69	Avery Johnson	.10
70	Damon Stoudamire	.75
71	Kevin Johnson	.20
72	Gheorghe Muresan	.10
73	Reggie Miller	.30
74	John Wallace	.30
75	Terrell Brandon	.20
76	Dale Davis	.10
77	Latrell Sprewell	.20
78	Lorenzen Wright	.10
79	Rod Strickland	.10
80	Kenny Anderson	.10
81	Anthony Mason	.10
82	Hakeem Olajuwon	1.00
83	Kevin Garnett	2.50
84	Isaiah Rider	.10
85	Mark Price	.10
86	Shawn Bradley	.20
87	Vin Baker	.40
88	Steve Nash	.20
89	Jeff Hornacek	.10
90	Tony Delk	.20
91	Horace Grant	.10
92	Othella Harrington	.20
93	Arvydas Sabonis	.10
94	Antoine Walker	2.00
95	Todd Fuller	.10
96	John Starks	.10
97	Olden Polynice	.10
98	Sean Elliott	.10
99	Travis Best	.10
100	Chris Gatling	.10
101	Derek Harper	.10
102	LaPhonso Ellis	.10
103	Dean Garrett	.10
104	Hersey Hawkins	.10
105	Jerry Stackhouse	.50
106	Ray Allen	.50
107	Allen Iverson	2.50
108	Chris Webber	.75
109	Robert Pack	.10
110	Gary Payton	.50
111	Mario Elie	.10
112	Dell Curry	.10
113	Lindsey Hunter	.10
114	Robert Horry	.10
115	David Robinson	.50
116	Kevin Willis	.10
117	Tyrone Hill	.10
118	Vitaly Potapenko	.10
119	Clyde Drexler	.40
120	Derek Fisher	.20
121	Detlef Schrempf	.10
122	Gary Trent	.10
123	Danny Ferry	.10
124	*Derek Anderson*	10.00
125	*Chris Anstey*	1.00
126	*Tony Battie*	4.00
127	*Chauncey Billups*	12.00
128	*Kelvin Cato*	2.00
129	*Austin Croshere*	2.00
130	*Antonio Daniels*	6.00
131	*Tim Duncan*	70.00
132	*Danny Fortson*	3.00
133	*Adonal Foyle*	3.00
134	*Paul Grant*	1.00
135	*Ed Gray*	2.00
136	*Bobby Jackson*	8.00
137	*Brevin Knight*	10.00
138	*Tracy McGrady*	15.00
139	*Ron Mercer*	25.00
140	*Anthony Parker*	1.00
141	*Scot Pollard*	1.00
142	*Rodrick Rhodes*	3.00
143	*Olivier Saint-Jean*	2.00
144	*Maurice Taylor*	10.00
145	*Johnny Taylor*	1.00
146	*Tim Thomas*	20.00
147	*Keith Van Horn*	40.00
148	*Jacque Vaughn*	3.00
149	Checklist	.10
150	Checklist	.10
151	Scott Burrell	.10
152	Brian Williams	.10
153	Terry Mills	.10
154	Jim Jackson	.10
155	Michael Finley	.20
156	*Jeff Nordgaard*	.20
157	Carl Herrera	.10
158	Otis Thorpe	.10
159	Wesley Person	.10
160	Tyrone Hill	.10
161	*Charles O'Bannon*	.20
162	Greg Anthony	.10
163	*Rusty LaRue*	.10
164	David Wesley	.10
165	*Chris Garner*	.10
166	George McCloud	.10
167	Mark Price	.10
168	*God Shammgod*	.20
169	Isaac Austin	.10
170	Alan Henderson	.10
171	*Eric Washington*	.10
172	Darrell Armstrong	.10
173	Calbert Cheaney	.10
174	*Cedric Henderson*	.75
175	Bryant Stith	.10
176	Sean Rooks	.10
177	Chris Mills	.10
178	Eldridge Recasner	.10
179	Priest Lauderdale	.10
180	Rick Fox	.10
181	*Keith Closs*	.10
182	Chris Dudley	.10
183	*Lawrence Funderburke*	.20
184	*Michael Stewart*	.20
185	*Alvin Williams*	.10
186	Adam Keefe	.10
187	*Chauncey Billups*	1.75
188	Jon Barry	.10
189	*Bobby Jackson*	1.25
190	Sam Cassell	.10
191	Dee Brown	.10
192	Travis Knight	.10
193	Dean Garrett	.10
194	David Benoit	.10
195	Chris Morris	.10
196	*Bubba Wells*	.10
197	James Robinson	.10
198	*Anthony Johnson*	.10
199	Dennis Scott	.10
200	*DeJuan Wheat*	.10
201	Rodney Rogers	.10
202	*Tariq Abdul-Wahad*	.10
203	Cherokee Parks	.10
204	*Jacque Vaughn*	.20
205	Cory Alexander	.10
206	*Kevin Ollie*	.10
207	George Lynch	.10
208	Lamond Murray	.10
209	Jud Buechler	.10
210	Erick Dampier	.10
211	*Malcolm Huckaby*	.10
212	Chris Webber	.75
213	*Chris Crawford*	.10
214	J.R. Reid	.10
215	Eddie Johnson	.10
216	Nick Van Exel	.25
217	Antonio McDyess	.40
218	David Wingate	.10
219	Malik Sealy	.10
220	Charles Outlaw	.10
221	*Serge Zwikker*	.20
222	Bobby Phills	.10
223	*Shea Seals*	.10
224	Clifford Robinson	.10
225	*Zydrunas Ilgauskas*	1.50
226	*John Thomas*	.10
227	Rik Smits	.10
228	Rasheed Wallace	.10
229	John Wallace	.10
230	Bob Sura	.10
231	Ervin Johnson	.10
232	*Keith Booth*	.10
233	Chuck Person	.10
234	Brian Shaw	.10
235	Todd Day	.10
236	Clarence Weatherspoon	.10
237	Charlie Ward	.10
238	Rod Strickland	.10
239	Shawn Kemp	1.00
240	Terrell Brandon	.20
241	*Corey Beck*	.10
242	Vin Baker	.50
243	*Fred Hoiberg*	.40
244	Chris Mullin	.20
245	Brian Grant	.10
246	*Derek Anderson*	1.00
247	Zan Tabak	.10
248	*Charles Smith*	.10
249	Shareef Abdur-Rahim	2.50
250	Ray Allen	1.00
251	Charles Barkley	1.25
252	Kobe Bryant	6.00
253	Marcus Camby	1.00
254	Kevin Garnett	5.00
255	Anfernee Hardaway	4.00
256	Grant Hill	5.00
257	Juwan Howard	1.00
258	Allen Iverson	4.00
259	Michael Jordan	10.00
260	Shawn Kemp	2.50
261	Kerry Kittles	1.00
262	Karl Malone	.10
263	Stephon Marbury	4.00
264	Hakeem Olajuwon	2.00
265	Shaquille O'Neal	3.00
266	Gary Payton	1.50
267	Scottie Pippen	2.50
268	David Robinson	1.25
269	Dennis Rodman	3.00
270	Joe Smith	1.00
271	Jerry Stackhouse	1.00
272	Damon Stoudamire	1.50
273	Antoine Walker	4.00
274	Checklist	.10
275	Checklist	.10

1997-98 Ultra Gold

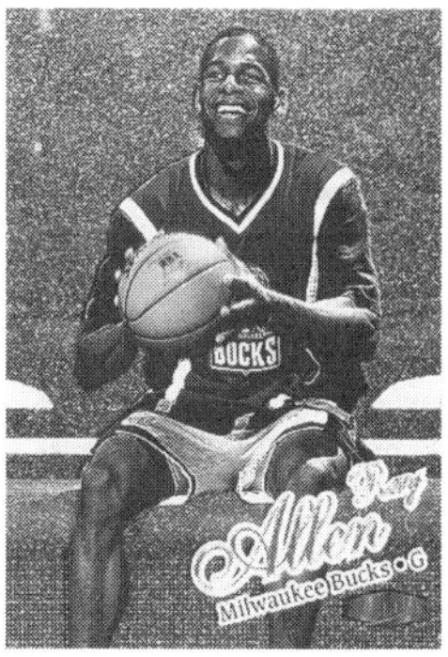

Gold Medallion versions were produced 271 of the 275 cards in Ultra Series I and II, excluding the four checklist cards. These were identified by a gold sparkling background and were inserted one per hobby pack in both series.

	MT
Gold Cards:	2x-3x
Gold Rookies:	.5x

1997-98 Ultra Platinum

This 270-card parallel set reprinted each card in the Ultra Series I and II base set, minus the five checklists. Platinum versions were identified by a platinum colored shade added to the card front and the player shot was in black-and-white. Card backs were individually numbered up to 100 of each card.

		MT
Common Player:		15.00
1	Kobe Bryant	400.00
2	Charles Barkley	60.00
3	Joe Dumars	15.00
4	Wesley Person	15.00
5	Walt Williams	15.00
6	Vlade Divac	15.00
7	Mookie Blaylock	15.00
8	Jason Kidd	75.00
9	Ron Harper	15.00
10	Sherman Douglas	15.00
11	Cedric Ceballos	15.00
12	Karl Malone	50.00
13	Antonio McDyess	40.00
14	Steve Kerr	15.00
15	Matt Maloney	30.00
16	Glenn Robinson	40.00
17	Rony Seikaly	15.00
18	Derrick Coleman	15.00
19	Jermaine O'Neal	30.00
20	Scott Burrell	15.00
21	Glen Rice	40.00
22	Dale Ellis	15.00
23	Michael Jordan	625.00
24	Anfernee Hardaway	200.00
25	Bryon Russell	15.00
26	Toni Kukoc	15.00
27	Theo Ratliff	15.00
28	Tom Gugliotta	30.00
29	Dennis Rodman	150.00
30	John Stockton	40.00
31	Priest Lauderdale	15.00
32	Luc Longley	15.00
33	Grant Hill	250.00
34	Antonio Davis	15.00
35	Eddie Jones	75.00
36	Nick Anderson	15.00
37	Shareef Abdur-Rahim	130.00
38	Stephon Marbury	200.00
39	Todd Day	15.00
40	Tim Hardaway	40.00
41	Larry Johnson	30.00
42	Sam Perkins	15.00
43	Dikembe Mutombo	30.00
44	Charles Outlaw	15.00
45	Mitch Richmond	40.00
46	Bryant Reeves	15.00
47	P.J. Brown	15.00
48	Steve Smith	15.00
49	Martin Muursepp	15.00
50	Jamal Mashburn	30.00
51	Kendall Gill	15.00
52	Vinny Del Negro	15.00
53	Roy Rogers	15.00
54	Khalid Reeves	15.00
55	Scottie Pippen	125.00
56	Joe Smith	50.00
57	Mark Jackson	15.00
58	Voshon Lenard	15.00
59	Dan Majerle	15.00
60	Alonzo Mourning	40.00
61	Kerry Kittles	40.00
62	Chris Childs	15.00
63	Patrick Ewing	40.00
64	Allan Houston	30.00
65	Marcus Camby	60.00
66	Christian Laettner	30.00
67	Loy Vaught	15.00
68	Jayson Williams	15.00
69	Avery Johnson	15.00
70	Damon Stoudamire	75.00
71	Kevin Johnson	30.00
72	Gheorghe Muresan	15.00
73	Reggie Miller	40.00
74	John Wallace	30.00
75	Terrell Brandon	30.00
76	Dale Davis	15.00
77	Latrell Sprewell	30.00
78	Lorenzen Wright	15.00
79	Rod Strickland	15.00
80	Kenny Anderson	15.00
81	Anthony Mason	15.00
82	Hakeem Olajuwon	100.00
83	Kevin Garnett	250.00
84	Isaiah Rider	15.00
85	Mark Price	15.00
86	Shawn Bradley	15.00
87	Vin Baker	40.00
88	Steve Nash	30.00
89	Jeff Hornacek	15.00
90	Tony Delk	15.00
91	Horace Grant	15.00
92	Othella Harrington	15.00
93	Arvydas Sabonis	15.00
94	Antoine Walker	200.00
95	Todd Fuller	15.00
96	John Starks	15.00
97	Olden Polynice	15.00
98	Sean Elliott	15.00
99	Travis Best	15.00
100	Chris Gatling	15.00
101	Derek Harper	15.00
102	LaPhonso Ellis	15.00
103	Dean Garrett	15.00
104	Hersey Hawkins	15.00
105	Jerry Stackhouse	50.00
106	Ray Allen	50.00
107	Allen Iverson	200.00
108	Chris Webber	100.00
109	Robert Pack	15.00
110	Gary Payton	50.00
111	Mario Elie	15.00
112	Dell Curry	15.00
113	Lindsey Hunter	15.00
114	Robert Horry	15.00
115	David Robinson	60.00
116	Kevin Willis	15.00
117	Tyrone Hill	15.00
118	Vitaly Potapenko	15.00
119	Clyde Drexler	50.00
120	Derek Fisher	15.00
121	Detlef Schrempf	15.00
122	Gary Trent	15.00
123	Danny Ferry	15.00
124	Derek Anderson	60.00
125	Chris Anstey	15.00
126	Tony Battie	60.00
127	Chauncey Billups	125.00
128	Kelvin Cato	15.00
129	Austin Croshere	30.00
130	Antonio Daniels	80.00
131	Tim Duncan	275.00
132	Danny Fortson	40.00
133	Adonal Foyle	40.00
134	Paul Grant	15.00
135	Ed Gray	15.00
136	Bobby Jackson	60.00
137	Brevin Knight	60.00
138	Tracy McGrady	125.00
139	Ron Mercer	150.00
140	Anthony Parker	15.00
141	Scot Pollard	15.00
142	Rodrick Rhodes	40.00
143	Olivier Saint-Jean	30.00
144	Maurice Taylor	40.00
145	Johnny Taylor	15.00
146	Tim Thomas	100.00
147	Keith Van Horn	250.00
148	Jacque Vaughn	30.00
151	Scott Burrell	15.00
152	Brian Williams	15.00
153	Terry Mills	15.00
154	Jim Jackson	15.00
155	Michael Finley	30.00
156	*Jeff Nordgaard*	30.00
157	Carl Herrera	15.00
158	Otis Thorpe	15.00
159	Wesley Person	15.00
160	Tyrone Hill	15.00
161	*Charles O'Bannon*	30.00
162	Greg Anthony	15.00
163	*Rusty LaRue*	15.00
164	David Wesley	15.00
165	*Chris Garner*	15.00
166	George McCloud	15.00
167	Mark Price	15.00
168	*God Shammgod*	30.00
169	Isaac Austin	15.00
170	Alan Henderson	15.00
171	*Eric Washington*	15.00
172	Darrell Armstrong	15.00
173	Calbert Cheaney	15.00
174	*Cedric Henderson*	45.00
175	Bryant Stith	15.00
176	Sean Rooks	15.00
177	Chris Mills	15.00
178	Eldridge Recasner	15.00
179	Priest Lauderdale	15.00
180	Rick Fox	15.00
181	*Keith Closs*	15.00
182	Chris Dudley	15.00
183	*Lawrence Funderburke*	30.00
184	*Michael Stewart*	30.00
185	*Alvin Williams*	15.00
186	Adam Keefe	15.00
187	*Chauncey Billups*	85.00
188	Jon Barry	15.00
189	*Bobby Jackson*	50.00
190	Sam Cassell	15.00
191	Dee Brown	15.00
192	Travis Knight	15.00
193	Dean Garrett	15.00
194	David Benoit	15.00
195	Chris Morris	15.00
196	*Bubba Wells*	15.00
197	James Robinson	15.00
198	*Anthony Johnson*	15.00
199	Dennis Scott	15.00
200	*DeJuan Wheat*	15.00
201	Rodney Rogers	15.00
202	*Tariq Abdul-Wahad*	15.00
203	Cherokee Parks	15.00
204	*Jacque Vaughn*	30.00
205	Cory Alexander	15.00
206	*Kevin Ollie*	15.00
207	George Lynch	15.00
208	Lamond Murray	15.00
209	Jud Buechler	15.00
210	Erick Dampier	15.00
211	*Malcolm Huckaby*	15.00
212	Chris Webber	100.00
213	*Chris Crawford*	15.00
214	J.R. Reid	15.00
215	Eddie Johnson	15.00
216	Nick Van Exel	35.00
217	Antonio McDyess	40.00
218	David Wingate	15.00
219	Malik Sealy	15.00
220	Charles Outlaw	15.00
221	*Serge Zwikker*	30.00
222	Bobby Phills	15.00
223	*Shea Seals*	15.00
224	Clifford Robinson	15.00
225	*Zydrunas Ilgauskas*	60.00
226	*John Thomas*	15.00
227	Rik Smits	15.00
228	Rasheed Wallace	15.00
229	John Wallace	15.00
230	Bob Sura	15.00
231	Ervin Johnson	15.00
232	*Keith Booth*	15.00
233	Chuck Person	15.00
234	Brian Shaw	15.00
235	Todd Day	15.00
236	Clarence Weatherspoon	15.00
237	Charlie Ward	15.00
238	Rod Strickland	15.00
239	Shawn Kemp	125.00
240	Terrell Brandon	30.00
241	*Corey Beck*	15.00
242	Vin Baker	40.00
243	*Fred Hoiberg*	30.00
244	Chris Mullin	30.00
245	Brian Grant	15.00
246	*Derek Anderson*	50.00
247	Zan Tabak	15.00
248	*Charles Smith*	15.00
249	Shareef Abdur-Rahim	60.00
250	Ray Allen	30.00
251	Charles Barkley	30.00
252	Kobe Bryant	200.00
253	Marcus Camby	30.00
254	Kevin Garnett	125.00
255	Anfernee Hardaway	100.00
256	Grant Hill	125.00
257	Juwan Howard	15.00
258	Allen Iverson	100.00
259	Michael Jordan	300.00
260	Shawn Kemp	60.00
261	Kerry Kittles	15.00
262	Karl Malone	15.00
263	Stephon Marbury	100.00
264	Hakeem Olajuwon	50.00
265	Shaquille O'Neal	100.00
266	Gary Payton	30.00
267	Scottie Pippen	60.00
268	David Robinson	30.00
269	Dennis Rodman	75.00
270	Joe Smith	15.00
271	Jerry Stackhouse	15.00
272	Damon Stoudamire	40.00
273	Antoine Walker	100.00

1997-98 Ultra All-Rookie

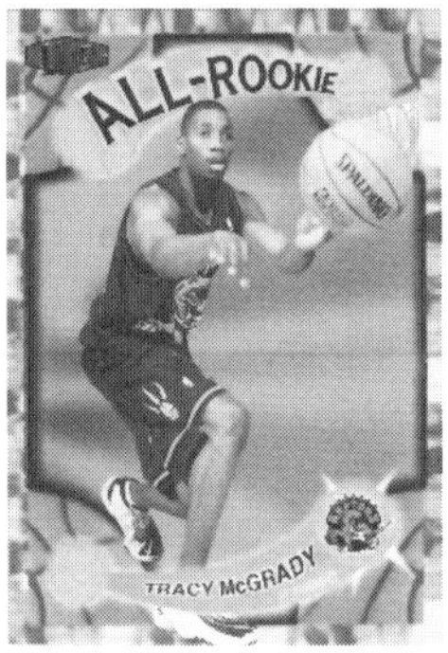

All-Rookies was a 15-card insert set featuring the top rookies from the 1997 NBA Draft. Cards were inserted one per four packs of Series II and were numbered with an "AR" suffix.

		MT
Complete Set (15):		20.00
Common Player:		.50
AR1	Tim Duncan	6.00
AR2	Tony Battie	1.50
AR3	Keith Van Horn	6.00
AR4	Antonio Daniels	2.00
AR5	Chauncey Billups	2.50
AR6	Ron Mercer	4.00
AR7	Tracy McGrady	3.00
AR8	Danny Fortson	1.00
AR9	Brevin Knight	2.00
AR10	Derek Anderson	2.00
AR11	Cedric Henderson	1.50
AR12	Jacque Vaughn	1.00
AR13	Tim Thomas	2.50
AR14	Austin Croshere	1.00
AR15	Kelvin Cato	.50

1997-98 Ultra Big Shots

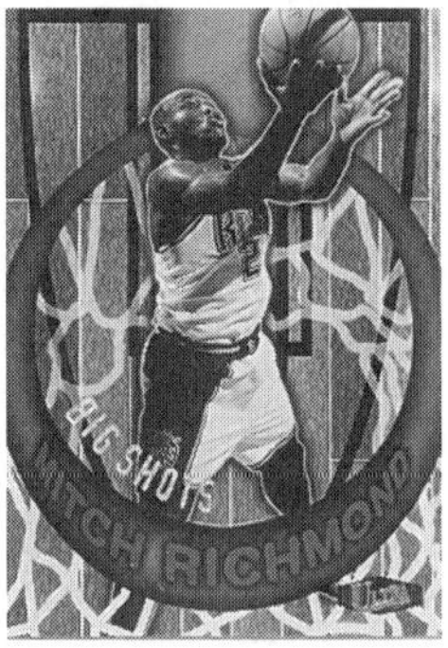

Big Shots was a 15-card insert featuring a wood background and an embossed red basketball rim with a net hanging from it that included the player's name. The words "Big Shots" was printed just above the bottom of the circle in silver holographic type. These inserts were seeded one per four packs of Series II and are numbered with a "BS" suffix.

		MT
Complete Set (15):		30.00
Common Player:		.50
1	Michael Jordan	10.00
2	Allen Iverson	5.00
3	Shaquille O'Neal	3.00
4	Anfernee Hardaway	4.00
5	Dennis Rodman	3.00
6	Grant Hill	5.00
7	Juwan Howard	1.50
8	David Robinson	1.50
9	Gary Payton	1.50
10	Joe Smith	1.00
11	Charles Barkley	1.50
12	Terrell Brandon	.50
13	John Stockton	1.00
14	Mitch Richmond	1.00
15	Vin Baker	1.00

1997-98 Ultra Court Masters

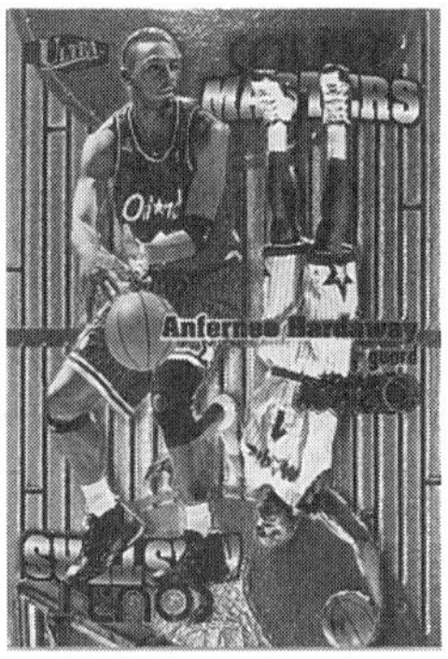

Court Masters is a 20-card insert set that features two photos of each player - one his home jersey and one in his away jersey - on flip sides of the front. The holographic foil inserts are were seeded one per 144 packs of Series II, and numbered with a "CM" suffix.

		MT
Complete Set (20):		600.00
Common Player:		5.00
CM1	Michael Jordan	100.00
CM2	Allen Iverson	40.00
CM3	Kobe Bryant	60.00
CM4	Shaquille O'Neal	30.00
CM5	Stephon Marbury	40.00
CM6	Shawn Kemp	25.00
CM7	Anfernee Hardaway	35.00
CM8	Kevin Garnett	50.00
CM9	Shareef Abdur-Rahim	25.00
CM10	Dennis Rodman	30.00
CM11	Grant Hill	50.00
CM12	Kerry Kittles	5.00
CM13	Antoine Walker	40.00
CM14	Scottie Pippen	25.00
CM15	Damon Stoudamire	12.00
CM16	Marcus Camby	5.00
CM17	Hakeem Olajuwon	20.00
CM18	Tim Duncan	50.00
CM19	Keith Van Horn	50.00
CM20	Chauncey Billups	25.00

1997-98 Ultra Heirs to the Throne

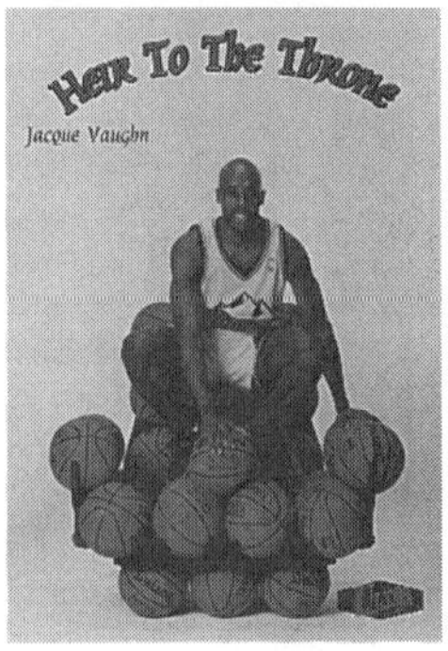

This 15-card insert showcases the top rookies, with each sitting in a special throne of basketballs created by Fleer for the NBA rookie photo shoot. Each rookie autographed a basketball, which was then secured into a throne and given away at the 1998 SportsFest show. These inserts were seeded one per 18 packs and are numbered with a "HT" suffix.

		MT
Complete Set (15):		100.00
Common Player:		2.00
1	Derek Anderson	8.00
2	Tony Battie	8.00
3	Chauncey Billups	12.00
4	Kelvin Cato	2.00
5	Austin Croshere	2.00
6	Antonio Daniels	12.00
7	Tim Duncan	25.00
8	Danny Fortson	6.00
9	Jacque Vaughn	4.00
10	Tracy McGrady	12.00
11	Ron Mercer	12.00
12	Olivier Saint-Jean	2.00
13	Maurice Taylor	4.00
14	Tim Thomas	10.00
15	Keith Van Horn	20.00

1997-98 Ultra Inside/Outside

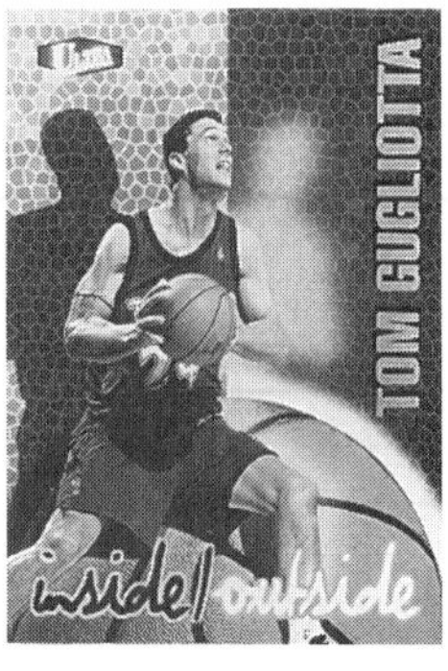

This 15-card insert set was seeded one per six packs of Ultra Series I. The set featured versatile players who can play under the basket or out on the perimeter. Card fronts show the player over a basketball with the insert's name printed across the bottom. Cards are numbered with a "I/O" suffix.

		MT
Complete Set (15):		12.00
Common Player:		.50
1	Shareef Abdur-Rahim	2.00
2	Juwan Howard	1.00
3	David Robinson	1.25
4	Joe Smith	1.00
5	Charles Barkley	1.25
6	Tom Gugliotta	.50
7	Glenn Robinson	.50

8	Patrick Ewing	.50
9	Chris Webber	1.50
10	Glen Rice	.50
11	Shawn Kemp	2.00
12	Antonio McDyess	.50
13	Clyde Drexler	1.00
14	Eddie Jones	1.50
15	Jason Kidd	1.25

1997-98 Ultra Jam City

Jam City was an 18-card insert set that was seeded one per eight packs of Series I. Fronts featured a color shot of the player over a black-and-white sketched city background, with the words "Jam City" across the bottom in silver foil. Cards were numbered on the back with a "JC" suffix.

		MT
Complete Set (18):		50.00
Common Player:		.75
1	Kevin Garnett	8.00
2	Antoine Walker	6.00
3	Scottie Pippen	4.00
4	Shawn Kemp	4.00
5	Hakeem Olajuwon	3.00
6	Jerry Stackhouse	2.00
7	Karl Malone	2.00
8	Shaquille O'Neal	5.00
9	John Wallace	.75
10	Marcus Camby	2.00
11	Juwan Howard	2.00
12	David Robinson	2.00
13	Gary Payton	2.00
14	Dennis Rodman	5.00
15	Joe Smith	2.00
16	Charles Barkley	2.00
17	Terrell Brandon	.75
18	Kobe Bryant	10.00

1997-98 Ultra Neat Feats

This 18-card insert set picture an embossed color shot of the player over a split color background, with the left side having a blue tint and the right side having a red tint. Neat Feats were seeded one per eight packs of Series II and are numbered with a "NF" suffix.

		MT
Complete Set (18):		18.00
Common Player:		.50
NF1	Michael Finley	.50
NF2	Jason Kidd	1.75
NF3	Rasheed Wallace	.50
NF4	Shaquille O'Neal	4.00
NF5	Tom Gugliotta	.50
NF6	Marcus Camby	1.25
NF7	Jerry Stackhouse	1.25
NF8	John Wallace	.50
NF9	Juwan Howard	1.25
NF10	David Robinson	1.50
NF11	Gary Payton	1.50
NF12	Joe Smith	1.25
NF13	Charles Barkley	1.50
NF14	Terrell Brandon	.75
NF15	John Stockton	1.00
NF16	Vin Baker	1.25
NF17	Antonio McDyess	1.25
NF18	Antonio Daniels	1.50

1997-98 Ultra Quick Picks

Quick Picks featured players in front of an outdoor, metal fence over a blue holographic background. This 12-card insert set was seeded one per eight packs and were numbered with a "QP" suffix.

		MT
Complete Set (12):		12.00
Common Player:		.50
1	Stephon Marbury	4.00
2	Ray Allen	1.25
3	Damon Stoudamire	2.00
4	Kerry Kittles	1.00
5	Gary Payton	1.50
6	Terrell Brandon	1.00
7	John Stockton	1.00
8	Mookie Blaylock	.50
9	Eddie Jones	3.00
10	Nick Van Exel	.50
11	Kenny Anderson	.50
12	Tim Hardaway	1.00

1997-98 Ultra Rim Rocker

This 12-card insert set was seeded one per eight packs of Series II. Each card is die-cut around the player's body and contains a holographic background. Cards are numbered with a "RR" suffix.

		MT
Complete Set (12):		10.00
Common Player:		.25
RR1	Ron Mercer	3.00
RR2	Juwan Howard	.75
RR3	David Robinson	1.00
RR4	Gary Payton	1.00
RR5	Joe Smith	.25
RR6	Charles Barkley	1.00
RR7	Terrell Brandon	.50
RR8	John Stockton	.50
RR9	Adonal Foyle	.25
RR10	Tim Thomas	2.00
RR11	Tony Battie	1.00
RR12	Antonio McDyess	.75

1997-98 Ultra Star Power

Star Power was a 20-card insert that was inserted into packs of Ultra Series II. The insert arrived in three different versions, with regular versions seeded one per four packs. Star Power Plus and Star Power Supreme versions of each card also existed at more difficult odds and on a die-cut cut design.

		MT
Complete Set (20):		40.00
Common Player:		.50
SP1	Michael Jordan	8.00
SP2	Allen Iverson	3.00
SP3	Kobe Bryant	5.00
SP4	Shaquille O'Neal	2.50
SP5	Stephon Marbury	3.00
SP6	Shawn Kemp	2.00
SP7	Anfernee Hardaway	2.50
SP8	Kevin Garnett	4.00
SP9	Shareef Abdur-Rahim	2.00
SP10	Dennis Rodman	2.50
SP11	Grant Hill	4.00
SP12	Gary Payton	1.00
SP13	Antoine Walker	3.00
SP14	Scottie Pippen	2.00
SP15	Damon Stoudamire	1.00
SP16	Marcus Camby	.50
SP17	Hakeem Olajuwon	1.50
SP18	Tim Duncan	4.00
SP19	Keith Van Horn	4.00
SP20	Jerry Stackhouse	.75

1997-98 Ultra Star Power Plus

Star Power Plus was the second tier of the Star Power insert and was seeded one per 36 packs of Series II. These were die-cut and contained a holographic finish along with the words "Star Power Plus."

	MT
Plus Cards:	2x-4x

1997-98 Ultra Star Power Supreme

Star Power Supreme was the third and final tier of the Star Power insert. Each card was printed on a die-cut plastic stock and inserted one per 288 Series II packs.

	MT
Supreme Cards:	15x-30x

1997-98 Ultra Stars

Ultra Stars was a 20-card insert set that was seeded one per 144 packs of Ultra Series I. Fronts were embossed and printed on holographic silver foil, with the player's color image in placed over large silver stars. Gold versions were also available, with only 10 percent of the print run including gold foil.

		MT
Complete Set (20):		700.00
Common Player:		7.00
1	Michael Jordan	120.00
2	Allen Iverson	60.00
3	Kobe Bryant	80.00
4	Shaquille O'Neal	40.00
5	Stephon Marbury	50.00
6	Marcus Camby	15.00
7	Anfernee Hardaway	50.00
8	Kevin Garnett	60.00
9	Shareef Abdur-Rahim	35.00
10	Dennis Rodman	35.00
11	Ray Allen	15.00
12	Grant Hill	60.00
13	Kerry Kittles	7.00
14	Antoine Walker	50.00
15	Scottie Pippen	30.00
16	Damon Stoudamire	20.00
17	Shawn Kemp	30.00
18	Hakeem Olajuwon	25.00
19	Jerry Stackhouse	15.00
20	John Wallace	7.00

1997-98 Ultra Sweet Deal

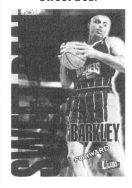

This 15-card insert set was seeded one per six packs of Ultra Series II. It included some of the top young players in the NBA and was numbered with a "SD" suffix.

		MT
Complete Set (12):		10.00
Common Player:		.50
SD1	Ray Allen	.75
SD2	Chauncey Billups	2.50
SD3	Ron Mercer	4.00
SD4	Hakeem Olajuwon	3.00
SD5	Jerry Stackhouse	.75
SD6	John Wallace	.50
SD7	Juwan Howard	.75
SD8	David Robinson	1.25
SD9	Bobby Jackson	1.75
SD10	Joe Smith	.75
SD11	Charles Barkley	1.25
SD12	Terrell Brandon	.50

1997-98 Ultra Ultrabilities

Ultrabilities was a 20-card insert set that was available in Ultra Series I packs. The insert was available in three different tiers - Starter (1:4 packs), All-Star (1:36) and Superstar (1:288). Starter versions had the word "Starter" running up the right side, All-Star versions had the word "All-Star" diagonal across a white background along with red and blue stars, while Superstar versions were die-cut and printed on holographic gold foil.

		MT
Complete Set (20):		50.00
Common Player:		.75
All-Star Cards:		3x-6x
Superstar Cards:		15x-30x
1	Michael Jordan	10.00
2	Allen Iverson	5.00
3	Kobe Bryant	7.00
4	Shaquille O'Neal	4.00
5	Stephon Marbury	4.00
6	Gary Payton	1.50
7	Anfernee Hardaway	4.00
8	Kevin Garnett	5.00
9	Scottie Pippen	2.50
10	Grant Hill	5.00
11	Marcus Camby	1.50
12	Ray Allen	.75
13	Kerry Kittles	.75
14	Antoine Walker	4.00
15	Shareef Abdur-Rahim	2.50
16	Damon Stoudamire	1.50
17	Shawn Kemp	2.50
18	Hakeem Olajuwon	1.50
19	Jerry Stackhouse	.75
20	Juwan Howard	.75

1997-98 Ultra View to a Thrill

This 15-card insert was seeded one per 18 packs of Ultra Series II. The card was printed on a black background, with the insert name printed across the top in yellow. The middle of the card features a film-like strip of the player in action. Cards are numbered with a "VT" suffix.

		MT
Complete Set (15):		80.00
Common Player:		1.50
ST1	Michael Jordan	20.00
ST2	Allen Iverson	10.00
ST3	Kobe Bryant	12.00
ST4	Tracy McGrady	6.00
ST5	Stephon Marbury	10.00
ST6	Shawn Kemp	5.00
ST7	Anfernee Hardaway	8.00
ST8	Kevin Garnett	10.00
ST9	Shareef Abdur-Rahim	5.00
ST10	Dennis Rodman	6.00
ST11	Grant Hill	10.00
ST12	Kerry Kittles	1.50
ST13	Antoine Walker	10.00
ST14	Scottie Pippen	5.00
ST15	Damon Stoudamire	3.00

1997-98 Upper Deck

Upper Deck was released in two, 180-card series in 1997- 1998. The first series had 135 base cards, 29 Jams '97 subset cards, 15 Court Perspective subset cards and one checklist. Series II had 120 current players, 29 Defining Moments subset cards, 15 Overtime subset cards and a checklist. Base cards featured an action shot of the player with a black border on the right side with silver lettering. A strip near the bottom contains the date of the photo and text about its significance. Inserts in Series I include: Game Jersey, Game-Dated, High Dimensions, Diamond Dimensions, Teammates, MJ Air Time and Ultimates. Inserts in Series II include: Jordan Power Deck, MJ Signed Jersey cards, Rookie Discovery I and II, NBA Records Collection, AIRLines, Great Eight and Jersey Cards.

		MT
Complete Set (360):		55.00
Complete Series 1 (180):		30.00
Complete Series 2 (180):		25.00
Common Player:		.10
MJ Air Time (10):		80.00
Common MJ Air Time:		8.00
Series 1 Wax Box:		60.00
Series 2 Wax Box:		60.00
1	Steve Smith	.10
2	Christian Laettner	.20
3	Alan Henderson	.10
4	Dikembe Mutumbo	.20
5	Dana Barros	.10
6	Antoine Walker	2.00
7	Dee Brown	.10
8	Eric Williams	.10
9	Muggsy Bogues	.10
10	Dell Curry	.10
11	Vlade Divac	.10
12	Anthony Mason	.10
13	Glen Rice	.20
14	Jason Caffey	.10
15	Steve Kerr	.10
16	Toni Kukoc	.10
17	Luc Longley	.10
18	Michael Jordan	4.00
19	Terrell Brandon	.10
20	Danny Ferry	.10
21	Tyrone Hill	.10
22	*Derek Anderson*	2.00
23	Bob Sura	.10
24	Shawn Bradley	.10
25	Michael Finley	.10
26	Ed O'Bannon	.10
27	Robert Pack	.10
28	Samaki Walker	.10
29	LaPhonso Ellis	.10
30	*Tony Battie*	2.00
31	Antonio McDyess	.30
32	Bryant Stith	.10
33	Randolph Childress	.10
34	Grant Hill	2.00
35	Lindsey Hunter	.10
36	Grant Long	.10
37	Theo Ratliff	.10
38	B.J. Armstrong	.10
39	*Adonal Foyle*	1.00
40	Mark Price	.10
41	Felton Spencer	.10
42	Latrell Sprewell	.30
43	Clyde Drexler	.30
44	Mario Elie	.10
45	Hakeem Olajuwon	.75
46	Brent Price	.10
47	Kevin Willis	.10
48	Erick Dampier	.10
49	Antonio Davis	.10
50	Dale Davis	.10
51	Mark Jackson	.10
52	Rik Smits	.10
53	Brent Barry	.10
54	Lamond Murray	.10
55	Eric Piatkowski	.10
56	Loy Vaught	.10
57	Lorenzen Wright	.10
58	Kobe Bryant	3.00
59	Elden Campbell	.10
60	Derek Fisher	.10
61	Eddie Jones	.50
62	Nick Van Exel	.20
63	Keith Askins	.10
64	Isaac Austin	.10
65	P.J. Brown	.10
66	Tim Hardaway	.20
67	Alonzo Mourning	.20
68	Ray Allen	.30
69	Vin Baker	.30
70	Sherman Douglas	.10
71	Armon Gilliam	.10
72	Elliott Perry	.10
73	Chris Carr	.10
74	Tom Gugliotta	.20
75	Kevin Garnett	2.00
76	Doug West	.10
77	*Keith Van Horn*	4.00
78	Chris Gatling	.10
79	Kendall Gill	.10
80	Kerry Kittles	.40
81	Jayson Williams	.10
82	Chris Childs	.10
83	Allan Houston	.20
84	Larry Johnson	.20
85	Charles Oakley	.10
86	John Starks	.10
87	Horace Grant	.10
88	Anfernee Hardaway	1.75
89	Dennis Scott	.10
90	Rony Seikaly	.10
91	Brian Shaw	.10
92	Derrick Coleman	.10
93	Allen Iverson	1.75
94	*Tim Thomas*	2.00
95	Scott Williams	.10
96	Cedric Ceballos	.10
97	Kevin Johnson	.20
98	Loren Meyer	.10
99	Steve Nash	.10
100	Wesley Person	.10
101	Kenny Anderson	.10
102	Jermaine O'Neal	.20
103	Isaiah Rider	.10
104	Arvydas Sabonis	.10
105	Gary Trent	.10
106	Mahmoud Abdul-Rauf	.10
107	Billy Owens	.10
108	Olden Polynice	.10
109	Mitch Richmond	.20
110	Michael Smith	.10
111	Cory Alexander	.10
112	Vinny Del Negro	.10
113	Carl Herrera	.10
114	*Tim Duncan*	6.00
115	Hersey Hawkins	.10
116	Shawn Kemp	1.00
117	Nate McMillan	.10
118	Sam Perkins	.10
119	Detlef Schrempf	.10
120	Doug Christie	.10
121	Popeye Jones	.10
122	Carlos Rogers	.10
123	Damon Stoudamire	.75
124	Adam Keefe	.10
125	Chris Morris	.10
126	Greg Ostertag	.10
127	John Stockton	.30
128	Shareef Abdur-Rahim	1.00
129	George Lynch	.10
130	Lee Mayberry	.10
131	Anthony Peeler	.10
132	Calbert Cheaney	.10
133	Tracy Murray	.10
134	Rod Strickland	.10
135	Chris Webber	.75
136	Christian Laettner	.10
137	Eric Williams	.10
138	Vlade Divac	.10
139	Michael Jordan	2.00
140	Tyrone Hill	.10
141	Michael Finley	.10
142	Tom Hammonds	.10
143	Theo Ratliff	.10
144	Latrell Sprewell	.10
145	Hakeem Olajuwon	.40
146	Reggie Miller	.10
147	Rodney Rogers	.10
148	Eddie Jones	.25
149	Jamal Mashburn	.10
150	Glenn Robinson	.10
151	Chris Carr	.10
152	Kendall Gill	.10
153	John Starks	.10
154	Anfernee Hardaway	.75
155	Derrick Coleman	.10
156	Cedric Ceballos	.10
157	Rasheed Wallace	.10
158	Corliss Williamson	.10
159	Sean Elliott	.10
160	Shawn Kemp	.50
161	Doug Christie	.10
162	Karl Malone	.10
163	Bryant Reeves	.10
164	Gheorghe Muresan	.10
165	Michael Jordan	2.00
166	Dikembe Mutombo	.10
167	Glen Rice	.10
168	Mitch Richmond	.10
169	Juwan Howard	.25
170	Clyde Drexler	.10
171	Terrell Brandon	.10
172	Jerry Stackhouse	.10
173	Damon Stoudamire	.10
174	Jayson Williams	.10
175	P.J. Brown	.10
176	Anfernee Hardaway	.75
177	Vin Baker	.10
178	LaPhonso Ellis	.10
179	Shawn Kemp	.50
180	Checklist	.10
181	Mookie Blaylock	.10
182	Tyrone Corbin	.10
183	Ken Norman	.10
184	*Ed Gray*	.50
185	*Chauncey Billups*	2.50
186	Tyus Edney	.10
187	Travis Knight	.10
188	*Ron Mercer*	3.00
189	Chris Mills	.10
190	Tony Delk	.10
191	Matt Geiger	.10
192	Bobby Phills	.10
193	David Wesley	.10
194	Keith Booth	.10
195	Randy Brown	.10
196	Ron Harper	.10
197	Scottie Pippen	1.25
198	Dennis Rodman	1.25
199	Zydrunas Ilgauskas	.50
200	*Brevin Knight*	1.25
201	Shawn Kemp	1.25
202	Vitaly Potapenko	.10
203	Donny Marshall	.10
204	Erick Strickland	.10
205	A.C. Green	.10
206	Khalid Reeves	.10
207	Kurt Thomas	.10
208	Dennis Scott	.10
209	*Danny Fortson*	.75
210	*Bobby Jackson*	1.25
211	Eric Williams	.10
212	Dean Garrett	.10
213	Priest Lauderdale	.10
214	Joe Dumars	.10
215	Aaron McKie	.10
216	Charles O'Bannon	.10
217	Brian Williams	.10
218	Malik Sealy	.10
219	Scott Burrell	.10
220	Erick Dampier	.10
221	Todd Fuller	.10
222	Donyell Marshall	.10
223	Joe Smith	.50
224	Charles Barkley	.75
225	Matt Bullard	.10
226	Othella Harrington	.10
227	*Rodrick Rhodes*	.50
228	Eddie Johnson	.10
229	Matt Maloney	.10
230	Travis Best	.10
231	Reggie Miller	.30
232	Chris Mullin	.20
233	Fred Hoiberg	.10
234	*Austin Croshere*	.50
235	Kevin Duckworth	.10
236	Darrick Martin	.10
237	Pooh Richardson	.10
238	Rodney Rogers	.10
239	*Maurice Taylor*	1.00
240	Robert Horry	.10
241	Rick Fox	.10
242	Shaquille O'Neal	2.00
243	Corie Blount	.10
244	Duane Causwell	.10
245	Voshon Lenard	.10
246	Todd Day	.10
247	Dan Majerle	.10
248	Terry Mills	.10
249	Terrell Brandon	.20
250	Tyrone Hill	.10
251	Ervin Johnson	.10
252	Glenn Robinson	.30
253	Terry Porter	.10
254	Paul Grant	.10
255	Stephon Marbury	2.00
256	Sam Mitchell	.10
257	Cherokee Parks	.10
258	Sam Cassell	.10
259	David Benoit	.10
260	Kevin Edwards	.10
261	Don MacLean	.10
262	Patrick Ewing	.30
263	Walter McCarty	.10
264	John Starks	.10
265	John Thomas	.10
266	Chris Dudley	.10
267	Darrell Armstrong	.10
268	Nick Anderson	.10
269	Derek Harper	.10
270	Johnny Taylor	.10
271	Gerald Wilkins	.10
272	Clarence Weatherspoon	.10
273	Jerry Stackhouse	.50
274	Eric Montross	.10
275	Anthony Parker	.10
276	Antonio McDyess	.30
277	Clifford Robinson	.10
278	Jason Kidd	.50
279	Danny Manning	.10
280	Rex Chapman	.10
281	Stacey Augmon	.10
282	*Kelvin Cato*	.50
283	Brian Grant	.10
284	Rasheed Wallace	.10
285	*Lawrence Funderburke*	.30
286	Kevin Gamble	.10
287	*Tariq Abdul-Wahad*	.50
288	Corliss Williamson	.10
289	Sean Elliott	.10
290	Avery Johnson	.10
291	David Robinson	.75
292	Will Perdue	.10
293	James Cotton	.10
294	Jim McIlvaine	.10
295	Dale Ellis	.10
296	Gary Payton	.50
297	Aaron Williams	.10
298	Marcus Camby	.50
299	John Wallace	.20
300	*Tracy McGrady*	2.50
301	Walt Williams	.10
302	Shandon Anderson	.10
303	Antoine Carr	.10
304	Jeff Hornacek	.10
305	Karl Malone	.30
306	Bryon Russell	.10
307	*Jacque Vaughn*	.50
308	*Antonio Daniels*	1.50
309	Lawrence Moten	.10
310	Bryant Reeves	.10
311	Otis Thorpe	.10
312	*God Shammgod*	.30
313	Tim Legler	.10
314	Juwan Howard	.30
315	Gheorghe Muresan	.10
316	Michael Jordan	2.50
317	Allen Iverson	1.00
318	Karl Malone	.10
319	Glen Rice	.10
320	Dikembe Mutombo	.10
321	Grant Hill	1.25
322	Hakeem Olajuwon	.50
323	Stephon Marbury	1.00
324	Anfernee Hardaway	1.00
325	Shawn Kemp	.25
326	Mitch Richmond	.10
327	Kevin Johnson	.10
328	Kevin Garnett	1.25
329	Shareef Abdur-Rahim	.50
330	Damon Stoudamire	.30
331	Multiple Players	.10
332	Multiple Players	.10
333	Multiple Players	.10
334	Multiple Players	.10
335	Multiple Players	.10
336	Multiple Players	.10
337	Multiple Players	.10
338	Multiple Players	.10
339	Multiple Players	.10
340	Multiple Players	.10
341	Multiple Players	.10
342	Multiple Players	.10
343	Multiple Players	.10
344	Multiple Players	.10
345	Multiple Players	.10
346	Multiple Players	.10
347	Multiple Players	.10
348	Multiple Players	.10
349	Multiple Players	.10
350	Multiple Players	.10
351	Multiple Players	.10
352	Multiple Players	.10
353	Multiple Players	.10
354	Multiple Players	.10
355	Multiple Players	.10
356	Multiple Players	.10
357	Multiple Players	.10
358	Multiple Players	.10
359	Multiple Players	.10
360	Checklist	.10
NNO	Michael Jordan Black Audio	25.00
NNO	Michael Jordan Red Audio	12.00

1997-98 Upper Deck Game Dated Memorable Moments

Game-Dated cards paralleled 30 cards in the base set, with the addition of special foil embossing. This insert was found in one per 1,500 packs of Series I.

		MT
Common Player:		25.00
4	Dikembe Mutombo	35.00
6	Antoine Walker	350.00
13	Glen Rice	50.00
18	Michael Jordan	1000.
23	Bob Sura	25.00
25	Michael Finley	40.00
31	Antonio McDyess	60.00
34	Grant Hill	450.00
42	Latrell Sprewell	35.00
43	Clyde Drexler	75.00
45	Hakeem Olajuwon	150.00
49	Antonio Davis	25.00
56	Loy Vaught	25.00
61	Eddie Jones	125.00
66	Tim Hardaway	70.00
69	Vin Baker	85.00
75	Kevin Garnett	450.00
79	Kendall Gill	35.00
83	Allan Houston	35.00
88	Anfernee Hardaway	350.00
93	Allen Iverson	350.00
97	Kevin Johnson	35.00
103	Isaiah Rider	25.00
109	Mitch Richmond	50.00
112	Vinny Del Negro	25.00
116	Shawn Kemp	200.00
123	Damon Stoudamire	125.00
127	John Stockton	50.00
128	Shareef Abdur-Rahim	200.00
135	Chris Webber	125.00

1997-98 Upper Deck AIRLines

This 12-card insert set chronicles each year in Michael Jordan's NBA career. AIRLines cards were die-cut and numbered with an "AL" prefix. They were inserted one per 230 packs in both hobby and retail.

		MT
Complete Set (12):		1000.
Common Player:		100.00
AL1	Michael Jordan	100.00
AL2	Michael Jordan	100.00
AL3	Michael Jordan	100.00
AL4	Michael Jordan	100.00
AL5	Michael Jordan	100.00
AL6	Michael Jordan	100.00
AL7	Michael Jordan	100.00
AL8	Michael Jordan	100.00
AL9	Michael Jordan	100.00
AL10	Michael Jordan	100.00
AL11	Michael Jordan	100.00
AL12	Michael Jordan	100.00

1997-98 Upper Deck Diamond Dimensions

This 30-card insert paralleled the High Dimensions inserts, but was distinguished by a diamond die-cut that made the shape of the card resemble an "X." Diamond Dimensions were also in Series I packs and sequentially numbered to 100 sets.

	MT
Common Player:	15.00
D1 Anfernee Hardaway	225.00
D2 Gary Payton	70.00
D3 Marcus Camby	50.00
D4 Charles Barkley	70.00
D5 Jason Kidd	90.00
D6 Alonzo Mourning	40.00
D7 Kenny Anderson	15.00
D8 Kobe Bryant	375.00
D9 Dennis Rodman	175.00
D10 Kerry Kittles	40.00
D11 Dikembe Mutombo	15.00
D12 Shaquille O'Neal	175.00
D13 Glenn Robinson	30.00
D14 Tony Delk	15.00
D15 Larry Johnson	30.00
D16 Brent Barry	15.00
D17 Scottie Pippen	125.00
D18 Shareef Abdur-Rahim	125.00
D19 David Robinson	50.00
D20 Damon Stoudamire	80.00
D21 Kevin Garnett	275.00
D22 Bob Sura	15.00
D23 Michael Jordan	700.00
D24 Joe Smith	30.00
D25 Karl Malone	50.00
D26 Antonio McDyess	40.00
D27 Allen Iverson	250.00
D28 Dale Davis	15.00
D29 Antoine Walker	225.00
D30 Chris Webber	100.00

1997-98 Upper Deck Game Jersey

Game Jerseys was a 22-card insert set that had 12 cards in Series I and 10 more in Series II, both with an insertion rate of one per 2,500 packs. The cards were numbered with a "GJ" prefix and were horizontal in design with a swatch of the player's game-used jersey included on the card. Series II packs included 23 serial numbered autographed Jordan Game Jersey cards.

	MT
Complete Set (22):	9200.
Complete Series 1 (12):	4200.
Complete Series 2 (10):	5000.
Common Player:	200.00
GJ1 Charles Barkley	375.00
GJ2 Clyde Drexler	300.00
GJ3 Kevin Garnett	650.00
GJ4 Anfernee Hardaway	600.00
GJ5 Grant Hill	650.00
GJ6 Allen Iverson	500.00
GJ7 Kerry Kittles	200.00
GJ8 Toni Kukoc	200.00
GJ9 Reggie Miller	200.00
GJ10 Hakeem Olajuwon	275.00
GJ11 Glen Rice	250.00
GJ12 David Robinson	275.00
GJ13 Michael Jordan	2700.
GJ13S Michael Jordan AUTO	13000.
GJ14 Alonzo Mourning	250.00
GJ15 Tim Hardaway	275.00
GJ16 Marcus Camby	225.00
GJ17 Antoine Walker	600.00
GJ18 Kevin Johnson	200.00
GJ19 Glenn Robinson	225.00
GJ20 Patrick Ewing	275.00
GJ21 Anfernee Hardaway	600.00
GJ22 Grant Hill	650.00

1997-98 Upper Deck Great Eight

This eight-card insert pays tribute to the some of the top

NBA veterans and was available only in Series II packs. These inserts are numbered with a "G" prefix and sequentially numbered to 800.

	MT
Complete Set (8):	275.00
Common Player:	10.00
G1 Charles Barkley	25.00
G2 Clyde Drexler	20.00
G3 Joe Dumars	10.00
G4 Patrick Ewing	15.00
G5 Michael Jordan	180.00
G6 Karl Malone	20.00
G7 Hakeem Olajuwon	35.00
G8 John Stockton	15.00

1997-98 Upper Deck High Dimensions

High Dimensions included 30 cards that were sequentially numbered to 2,000. Exclusive to Series I packs, these inserts are numbered with a "D" prefix.

	MT
Complete Set (30):	550.00
Common Player:	3.00
D1 Anfernee Hardaway	45.00
D2 Gary Payton	12.00
D3 Marcus Camby	10.00
D4 Charles Barkley	15.00
D5 Jason Kidd	12.00
D6 Alonzo Mourning	10.00
D7 Kenny Anderson	3.00
D8 Kobe Bryant	75.00
D9 Dennis Rodman	30.00
D10 Kerry Kittles	10.00
D11 Dikembe Mutombo	3.00
D12 Shaquille O'Neal	35.00
D13 Glenn Robinson	8.00
D14 Tony Delk	3.00
D15 Larry Johnson	6.00
D16 Brent Barry	3.00
D17 Scottie Pippen	30.00
D18 Shareef Abdur-Rahim	30.00
D19 David Robinson	10.00
D20 Damon Stoudamire	15.00
D21 Kevin Garnett	60.00
D22 Bob Sura	3.00
D23 Michael Jordan	110.00
D24 Joe Smith	10.00
D25 Karl Malone	10.00
D26 Antonio McDyess	10.00
D27 Allen Iverson	60.00
D28 Dale Davis	3.00
D29 Antoine Walker	45.00
D30 Chris Webber	25.00

1997-98 Upper Deck Records Collection

This Series II insert was found in one per 23 hobby and retail packs. Cards are numbered with a "RC" prefix, and resemble a vinyl record album on the front, with a red circle center that has a shot of the player.

	MT
Complete Set (30):	130.00
Common Player:	1.00
RC1 Dikembe Mutombo	1.00
RC2 Dana Barros	1.00
RC3 Glen Rice	2.00
RC4 Dennis Rodman	12.00
RC5 Shawn Kemp	10.00
RC6 A.C. Green	1.00
RC7 LaPhonso Ellis	1.00
RC8 Grant Hill	20.00
RC9 Joe Smith	4.00
RC10 Charles Barkley	5.00
RC11 Reggie Miller	3.00

	MT
RC12 Loy Vaught	1.00
RC13 Shaquille O'Neal	12.00
RC14 Tim Hardaway	4.00
RC15 Glenn Robinson	4.00
RC16 Stephon Marbury	20.00
RC17 Sam Cassell	1.00
RC18 Patrick Ewing	3.00
RC19 Anfernee Hardaway	15.00
RC20 Allen Iverson	20.00
RC21 Kevin Johnson	1.00
RC22 Kenny Anderson	1.00
RC23 Mitch Richmond	3.00
RC24 David Robinson	5.00
RC25 Gary Payton	4.00
RC26 Damon Stoudamire	5.00
RC27 John Stockton	3.00
RC28 Bryant Reeves	1.00
RC29 Chris Webber	7.00
RC30 Michael Jordan	40.00

1997-98 Upper Deck Rookie Discovery I

This 15-card insert showcases the top rookies from the 1997 NBA Draft. It was included in one per four packs of Series II and was numbered with a "R" prefix. Parallel versions also exist and are die-cut and numbered with a "D" prefix.

	MT
Complete Set (15):	40.00
Common Player:	.50
R1 Tim Duncan	10.00
R2 Keith Van Horn	10.00
R3 Chauncey Billups	4.00
R4 Antonio Daniels	3.00
R5 Tony Battie	3.00
R6 Ron Mercer	6.00
R7 Tim Thomas	5.00
R8 Adonal Foyle	1.00
R9 Tracy McGrady	5.00
R10 Danny Fortson	1.50
R11 Olivier Saint-Jean	1.50
R12 Austin Croshere	1.50
R13 Derek Anderson	3.00
R14 Maurice Taylor	2.00
R15 Kelvin Cato	.50

1997-98 Upper Deck Rookie Discovery II

Rookie Discovery II inserts were die-cut parallels of the Rookies Discovery I, but were numbered with a "D" prefix. These versions were seeded one per 108 packs of Series II.

	MT
Complete Set (15):	250.00
Common Player:	4.00
D1 Tim Duncan	60.00
D2 Keith Van Horn	60.00

	MT
D3 Chauncey Billups	25.00
D4 Antonio Daniels	15.00
D5 Tony Battie	15.00
D6 Ron Mercer	40.00
D7 Tim Thomas	30.00
D8 Adonal Foyle	8.00
D9 Tracy McGrady	30.00
D10 Danny Fortson	10.00
D11 Olivier Saint-Jean	8.00
D12 Austin Croshere	8.00
D13 Derek Anderson	15.00
D14 Maurice Taylor	12.00
D15 Kelvin Cato	4.00

1997-98 Upper Deck Teammates

Teammates was a 60-card insert that was exclusive to Series I packs and inserted at a rate of one per four packs. This insert matched up the top tandems for each team in the league, and included a special Jordan/ Hardaway card, on a die-cut format that fit together.

	MT
Complete Set (60):	100.00
Common Player:	.50
T1 Mookie Blaylock	.50
T2 Steve Smith	.50
T3 Antoine Walker	6.00
T4 Eric Williams	.50
T5 Anthony Mason	.50
T6 Glen Rice	1.00
T7 Michael Jordan	12.00
T8 Scottie Pippen	3.00
T9 Terrell Brandon	1.00
T10 Tyrone Hill	.50
T11 Shawn Bradley	.50
T12 Robert Pack	.50
T13 LaPhonso Ellis	.50
T14 Antonio McDyess	1.50
T15 Grant Hill	7.00
T16 Terry Mills	.50
T17 Joe Smith	1.00
T18 Latrell Sprewell	1.00
T19 Charles Barkley	2.00
T20 Hakeem Olajuwon	2.00
T21 Mark Jackson	.50
T22 Reggie Miller	1.00
T23 Brent Barry	.50
T24 Loy Vaught	.50
T25 Shaquille O'Neal	5.00
T26 Nick Van Exel	.50
T27 Tim Hardaway	1.00
T28 Alonzo Mourning	1.00
T29 Vin Baker	2.00
T30 Glenn Robinson	1.00
T31 Kevin Garnett	7.00
T32 Stephon Marbury	6.00
T33 Chris Gatling	.50
T34 Kerry Kittles	1.00
T35 Allan Houston	.50
T36 John Starks	.50
T37 Horace Grant	.50
T38 Anfernee Hardaway	5.00
T39 Allen Iverson	6.00
T40 Jerry Stackhouse	1.00
T41 Jason Kidd	1.50
T42 Wesley Person	.50
T43 Kenny Anderson	.50
T44 Isaiah Rider	.50
T45 Billy Owens	.50
T46 Mitch Richmond	1.00
T47 Sean Elliott	.50
T48 David Robinson	2.00
T49 Shawn Kemp	3.00
T50 Gary Payton	1.50
T51 Marcus Camby	1.00
T52 Damon Stoudamire	2.00
T53 Karl Malone	1.50
T54 John Stockton	1.50
T55 Shareef Abdur-Rahim	3.00
T56 Bryant Reeves	.50
T57 Juwan Howard	1.50
T58 Chris Webber	2.00
T59 Michael Jordan	12.00
T60 Anfernee Hardaway	5.00

1997-98 Upper Deck Ultimates

Ultimates was a 30-card insert set found in one per 23 packs of Series I. The cards are numbered with a "U" prefix and feature statistical information over a white background.

	MT
Complete Set (30):	160.00
Common Player:	1.50
U1 Michael Jordan	45.00
U2 Grant Hill	20.00
U3 Charles Barkley	6.00
U4 Tom Gugliotta	4.00
U5 Dennis Rodman	12.00
U6 Reggie Miller	4.00
U7 Jason Kidd	5.00
U8 Loy Vaught	1.50
U9 Mookie Blaylock	1.50
U10 Tim Hardaway	4.00
U11 Juwan Howard	4.00
U12 Shawn Kemp	10.00
U13 Mitch Richmond	4.00
U14 Larry Johnson	4.00
U15 Marcus Camby	4.00
U16 Bryant Stith	1.50
U17 Bryant Reeves	3.00
U18 Joe Smith	4.00
U19 Jerry Stackhouse	4.00
U20 Arvydas Sabonis	1.50
U21 John Stockton	3.00
U22 Eddie Jones	6.00
U23 Anfernee Hardaway	15.00
U24 Ray Allen	4.00
U25 Terrell Brandon	3.00
U26 David Robinson	6.00
U27 Anthony Mason	1.50
U28 Robert Pack	1.50
U29 Dana Barros	1.50
U30 Kendall Gill	1.50

1997-98 Collector's Choice

The 400-card, standard-size set features several inserts and subsets, including five Checklist Challenge card and 30 Game Night '97 cards. Inserts in Series I set are NBA SuperAction Stick-Ums (1:3), You Crash The Game (1:5) and the tiered StarQuest (90 cards with ranging odds from 1:1 to 1:145). Series II inserts included: MJ Bullseye, Star-Quest, and Mini-Standees. The base cards feature the player's name along the top edge within a team-colored stripe and his number and position in the upper right corner. Several of the cards have a horizontal design while all of the card backs have the horizontal design. Stats from the player's previous two seasons are on the back with a color photo and a brief descriptive highlight.

		MT
Complete Set (400):		30.00
Complete Series 1 (200):		15.00
Complete Series 2 (200):		15.00
Common Player:		.05
Series 1 Wax Box:		36.00
Series 2 Wax Box:		36.00
1	Mookie Blaylock	.05
2	Dikembe Mutombo	.10
3	Eldridge Recasner	.05
4	Christian Laettner	.10
5	Tyrone Corbin	.05
6	Antoine Walker	1.00
7	Eric Williams	.05
8	Dana Barros	.05
9	David Wesley	.05
10	Dino Radja	.05
11	Vlade Divac	.05
12	Dell Curry	.05
13	Muggsy Bogues	.05
14	Tony Smith	.05
15	Glen Rice	.10
16	Anthony Mason	.05
17	Dennis Rodman	.75
18	Brian Williams	.05
19	Toni Kukoc	.05
20	Jason Caffey	.05
21	Steve Kerr	.05
22	Luc Longley	.05
23	Michael Jordan	2.50
24	Chris Mills	.05
25	Tyrone Hill	.05
26	Vitaly Potapenko	.05
27	Bob Sura	.05
28	Robert Pack	.05
29	Ed O'Bannon	.05
30	Michael Finley	.05
31	Shawn Bradley	.05
32	Khalid Reeves	.05
33	Antonio McDyess	.10
34	Ervin Johnson	.05
35	Dale Ellis	.05
36	Bryant Stith	.05
37	Tom Hammonds	.05
38	Otis Thorpe	.05
39	Lindsey Hunter	.05
40	Grant Long	.05
41	Aaron McKie	.05
42	Randolph Childress	.05
43	Scott Burrell	.05
44	Bimbo Coles	.05
45	B.J. Armstrong	.05
46	Mark Price	.05
47	Latrell Sprewell	.10
48	Felton Spencer	.05
49	Charles Barkley	.25
50	Mario Elie	.05
51	Clyde Drexler	.20
52	Kevin Willis	.05
53	Antonio Davis	.05
54	Reggie Miller	.10
55	Dale Davis	.05
56	Mark Jackson	.05
57	Erick Dampier	.05
58	Pooh Richardson	.05
59	Terry Dehere	.05
60	Brent Barry	.05
61	Loy Vaught	.05
62	Lorenzen Wright	.05
63	Eddie Jones	.30
64	Kobe Bryant	1.50
65	Elden Campbell	.05
66	Corie Blount	.05
67	Shaquille O'Neal	.75
68	Dan Majerle	.05
69	P.J. Brown	.05
70	Tim Hardaway	.10
71	Isaac Austin	.05
72	Jamal Mashburn	.05
73	Ray Allen	.20
74	Glenn Robinson	.15
75	Armon Gilliam	.05
76	Johnny Newman	.05
77	Elliot Perry	.05
78	Sherman Douglas	.05
79	Doug West	.05
80	Kevin Garnett	1.25
81	Sam Mitchell	.05
82	Tom Gugliotta	.05
83	Terry Porter	.05
84	Chris Carr	.05
85	Kevin Edwards	.05
86	Jayson Williams	.05
87	Kendall Gill	.05
88	Kerry Kittles	.20
89	Chris Gatling	.05
90	John Starks	.05
91	Charlie Ward	.05
92	Larry Johnson	.10
93	Charles Oakley	.05
94	Chris Childs	.05
95	Allan Houston	.05
96	Horace Grant	.05
97	Darrell Armstrong	.05
98	Rony Seikaly	.05
99	Dennis Scott	.05
100	Anfernee Hardaway	1.00
101	Brian Shaw	.05
102	Jerry Stackhouse	.30
103	Rex Walters	.05
104	Don MacLean	.05
105	Derrick Coleman	.05
106	Lucious Harris	.05
107	Clarence Weatherspoon	.05
108	Cedric Ceballos	.05
109	Danny Manning	.05
110	Jason Kidd	.15
111	Loren Meyer	.05
112	Wesley Person	.05
113	Steve Nash	.05
114	Isaiah Rider	.05
115	Stacey Augmon	.05
116	Arvydas Sabonis	.05
117	Kenny Anderson	.05
118	Jermaine O'Neal	.15
119	Gary Trent	.05
120	Michael Smith	.05
121	Kevin Gamble	.05
122	Olden Polynice	.05
123	Billy Owens	.05
124	Corliss Williamson	.05
125	Cory Alexander	.05
126	Vinny Del Negro	.05
127	Sean Elliott	.05
128	Will Perdue	.05
129	Carl Herrera	.05
130	Shawn Kemp	.50
131	Hersey Hawkins	.05
132	Nate McMillan	.05
133	Craig Ehlo	.05
134	Detlef Schrempf	.05
135	Sam Perkins	.05
136	Sharone Wright	.05
137	Doug Christie	.05
138	Popeye Jones	.05
139	Shawn Respert	.05
140	Marcus Camby	.40
141	Adam Keefe	.05
142	Karl Malone	.20
143	John Stockton	.20
144	Greg Ostertag	.05
145	Chris Morris	.05
146	Shareef Abdur-Rahim	.50
147	Roy Rogers	.05
148	George Lynch	.05
149	Anthony Peeler	.05
150	Lee Mayberry	.05
151	Calbert Cheaney	.05
152	Harvey Grant	.05
153	Rod Strickland	.05
154	Tracy Murray	.05
155	Chris Webber	.30
156	Atlanta Hawks (Game Night '97)	.05
157	Boston Celtics (Game Night '97)	.05
158	Charlotte Hornets (Game Night '97)	.05
159	Chicago Bulls (Game Night '97)	.50
160	Cleveland Cavaliers (Game Night '97)	.05
161	Dallas Mavericks (Game Night '97)	.05
162	Denver Nuggets (Game Night '97)	.05
163	Detroit Pistons (Game Night '97)	.25
164	Golden State Warriors (Game Night '97)	.05
165	Houston Rockets (Game Night '97)	.05
166	Indiana Pacers (Game Night '97)	.05
167	Los Angeles Clippers (Game Night '97)	.05
168	Los Angeles Lakers (Game Night '97)	.05
169	Miami Heat (Game Night '97)	.05
170	Milwaukee Bucks (Game Night '97)	.05
171	Minnesota Timberwolves (Game Night '97)	.05
172	New Jersey Nets (Game Night '97)	.05
173	New York Knicks (Game Night '97)	.05
174	Orlando Magic (Game Night '97)	.05
175	Philadelphia 76ers (Game Night '97)	.05
176	Phoenix Suns (Game Night '97)	.05
177	Portland Trail Blazers (Game Night '97)	.05
178	Sacramento Kings (Game Night '97)	.05
179	San Antonio Spurs (Game Night '97)	.05
180	Seattle SuperSonics (Game Night '97)	.05
181	Toronto Raptors (Game Night '97)	.05
182	Utah Jazz (Game Night '97)	.05
183	Vancouver Grizzlies (Game Night '97)	.05
184	Washington Wizards (Game Night '97)	.05
185	1997 NBA Finals (Game Night '97)	.05
186	Michael Jordan (Catch 23)	.75
187	Michael Jordan (Catch 23)	.75
188	Michael Jordan (Catch 23)	.75
189	Michael Jordan (Catch 23)	.75
190	Michael Jordan (Catch 23)	.75
191	Michael Jordan (Catch 23)	.75
192	Michael Jordan (Catch 23)	.75
193	Michael Jordan (Catch 23)	.75
194	Michael Jordan (Catch 23)	.75
195	Michael Jordan (Catch 23)	.75
196	Checklist #1	.05
197	Checklist #2	.05
198	Checklist #3	.05
199	Checklist #4	.05
200	Checklist #5	.05
201	Steve Smith	.05
202	Chris Crawford	.05
203	Ed Gray	.05
204	Alan Henderson	.10
205	Walter McCarty	.05
206	Dee Brown	.05
207	*Chauncey Billups*	.75
208	*Ron Mercer*	1.50
209	Travis Knight	.05
210	Andrew DeClercq	.10
211	Tyus Edney	.05
212	Matt Geiger	.05
213	Tony Delk	.05
214	J.R. Reid	.05
215	Bobby Phills	.05
216	David Wesley	.05
217	Ron Harper	.05
218	Scottie Pippen	.60
219	Scott Burrell	.05
220	Keith Booth	.05
221	Bill Wennington	.05
222	Shawn Kemp	.60
223	*Zydrunas Ilgauskas*	.50
224	*Brevin Knight*	.75
225	Danny Ferry	.05
226	*Derek Anderson*	.75
227	Wesley Person	.05
228	A.C. Green	.05
229	Samaki Walker	.05
230	Hubert Davis	.05
231	Erick Strickland	.05
232	Dennis Scott	.05
233	*Tony Battie*	.50
234	LaPhonso Ellis	.05
235	Eric Williams	.05
236	*Bobby Jackson*	.50
237	Anthony Goldwire	.05
238	*Danny Fortson*	.25
239	Joe Dumars	.05
240	Grant Hill	1.25
241	Malik Sealy	.05
242	Brian Williams	.05
243	Theo Ratliff	.05
244	Scot Pollard	.05
245	Erick Dampier	.05
246	Duane Ferrell	.05
247	Joe Smith	.25
248	Todd Fuller	.05
249	*Adonal Foyle*	.25
250	Othella Harrington	.05
251	Matt Maloney	.10
252	Hakeem Olajuwon	.40
253	*Rodrick Rhodes*	.25
254	Eddie Johnson	.05
255	Brent Price	.05
256	*Austin Croshere*	.25
257	Derrick McKey	.05
258	Chris Mullin	.10
259	Rik Smits	.05
260	Jalen Rose	.05
261	Darrick Martin	.05
262	Lamond Murray	.05
263	*Maurice Taylor*	.40
264	Rodney Rogers	.05
265	James Robinson	.05
266	Rick Fox	.05
267	Nick Van Exel	.20
268	Sean Rooks	.05
269	Derek Fisher	.05
270	Jon Barry	.05
271	Robert Horry	.05
272	Terry Mills	.05
273	Charles Smith	.05
274	Alonzo Mourning	.10
275	Voshon Lenard	.05
276	Todd Day	.05
277	Ervin Johnson	.05
278	Terrell Brandon	.10
279	Michael Curry	.05
280	Andrew Lang	.05
281	Tyrone Hill	.05
282	Stephon Marbury	1.00
283	Cherokee Parks	.05
284	Stanley Roberts	.05
285	Paul Grant	.05
286	David Benoit	.05
287	Lucious Harris	.05
288	Don MacLean	.05
289	Sam Cassel	.05
290	*Keith Van Horn*	3.00
291	Patrick Ewing	.10
292	Walter McCarty	.05
293	Chris Dudley	.05
294	Chris Mills	.05
295	Buck Williams	.05
296	Nick Anderson	.05
297	Derek Strong	.05
298	Gerald Wilkins	.05
299	Johnny Taylor	.05
300	Derek Harper	.05
301	Anthony Parker	.05
302	Allen Iverson	1.00
303	Jim Jackson	.05
304	Eric Montross	.05
305	*Tim Thomas*	1.00
306	*Kebu Stewart*	.20
307	Rex Chapman	.05
308	Tom Chambers	.05
309	Kevin Johnson	.05
310	John Williams	.05
311	Clifford Robinson	.05
312	Antonio McDyess	.10
313	Rasheed Wallace	.05
314	Brian Grant	.05
315	Dontonio Wingfield	.05
316	*Kelvin Cato*	.10
317	Mahmoud Abdul-Rauf	.05
318	Lawrence Funderburke	.05
319	Mitch Richmond	.10
320	*Tariq Abdul-Wahad*	.25
321	Terry Dehere	.05
322	Michael Stewart	.05
323	*Tim Duncan*	3.50
324	Avery Johnson	.05
325	David Robinson	.30
326	Charles Smith	.05
327	Chuck Person	.05
328	Monty Williams	.05
329	Jim McIlvaine	.05
330	Gary Payton	.30
331	Eric Snow	.05
332	Dale Ellis	.05
333	Vin Baker	.20
334	Walt Williams	.05
335	*Tracy McGrady*	1.00
336	Damon Stoudamire	.30
337	Carlos Rogers	.05
338	John Wallace	.10
339	Shandon Anderson	.05
340	Jeff Hornacek	.05
341	Howard Eisley	.05
342	*Jacque Vaughn*	.25
343	Bryon Russell	.05
344	Antoine Carr	.05
345	*Antonio Daniels*	.50
346	Pete Chilcutt	.05
347	Blue Edwards	.05
348	Bryant Reeves	.05
349	*Chris Robinson*	.10
350	Otis Thorpe	.05
351	Tim Legler	.05
352	Juwan Howard	.25
353	*God Shammgod*	.10
354	Gheorghe Muresan	.05
355	Chris Whitney	.05
356	Dikembe Mutombo	.05
357	Antoine Walker	.50
358	Glen Rice	.05
359	Scottie Pippen	.30
360	Derek Anderson	.40
361	Michael Finley	.05
362	LaPhonso Ellis	.05
363	Grant Hill	.60
364	Joe Smith	.10
365	Charles Barkley	.10
366	Reggie Miller	.05
367	Loy Vaught	.05
368	Shaquille O'Neal	.40
369	Alonzo Mourning	.05
370	Glenn Robinson	.05
371	Kevin Garnett	.60
372	Kendall Gill	.05
373	Allan Houston	.05
374	Anfernee Hardaway	.50
375	Tim Thomas	.40
376	Jason Kidd	.10
377	Kenny Anderson	.05
378	Mitch Richmond	.05
379	Tim Duncan	1.25
380	Gary Payton	.10
381	Marcus Camby	.05
382	Karl Malone	.10
383	Shareef Abdur-Rahim	.25
384	Chris Webber	.20
385	Michael Jordan	1.50
386	Michael Jordan	.75
387	Michael Jordan	.75
388	Michael Jordan	.75
389	Michael Jordan	.75
390	Michael Jordan	.75
391	Michael Jordan	.75
392	Michael Jordan	.75
393	Michael Jordan	.75
394	Michael Jordan	.75
395	Michael Jordan	.75
396	Checklist #1	.05
397	Checklist #2	.05
398	Checklist #3	.05
399	Checklist #4	.05
400	Checklist #5	.05

1997-98 Collector's Choice You Crash the Game

This 30-card interactive insert gave collectors a chance to win if: A) either the player pictured scored 30 or more points during the week of the date shown on the front and you collected the full, 30-card set, or B) the player scored 30 or more points on the date shown on the front, or C) you redeemed 15 non-winning cards. Either scenerio could be redeemed for the 30-card redemption set. Crash the Game inserts were seeded one per five packs in Series I and the game ended 7/1/98.

		MT
Complete Set (30):		30.00
Common Player:		.50
C1	Dikembe Mutombo	.50
C2	Dana Barros	.50
C3	Glen Rice	1.00
C4	Scottie Pippen	3.00
C5	Terrell Brandon	.50
C6	Shawn Bradley	.50
C7	Antonio McDyess	1.00
C8	Lindsey Hunter	.50
C9	Joe Smith	1.50
C10	Hakeem Olajuwon	2.00
C11	Reggie Miller	1.00
C12	Rodney Rogers	.50
C13	Nick Van Exel	.50
C14	Tim Hardaway	.50
C15	Glenn Robinson	.50
C16	Kevin Garnett	5.00
C17	Kerry Kittles	1.00
C18	Larry Johnson	.50
C19	Anfernee Hardaway	5.00
C20	Allen Iverson	4.00
C21	Jason Kidd	1.50
C22	Arvydas Sabonis	.50
C23	Mitch Richmond	1.00
C24	David Robinson	2.00
C25	Gary Payton	1.50
C26	Marcus Camby	1.50
C27	Karl Malone	1.00
C28	Bryant Reeves	.50
C29	Chris Webber	2.00
C30	Michael Jordan	10.00

1997-98 Collector's Choice Draft Trade

Draft Trade cards were available to those collectors that filled in the checklist challenge cards correctly. Correct entries were redeemed for a 10-card set consisting of the top 10 picks from the 1997 NBA Draft.

		MT
Complete Set (10):		15.00
Common Player:		.50
1	Tim Duncan	5.00
2	Keith Van Horn	4.00
3	Chauncey Billups	1.50
4	Antonio Daniels	1.00
5	Tony Battie	.50
6	Ron Mercer	3.00
7	Tim Thomas	2.00
8	Adonal Foyle	.50
9	Tracy McGrady	2.00
10	Danny Fortson	.50

1997-98 Collector's Choice NBA Miniatures

NBA Miniatures was a 30-card insert that was seeded one per three packs of Series II. Each card, which was called a mini-standee, featured one player from each team in a special die-cut card that could be assembled into a tiny stand-up card.

		MT
Complete Set (30):		12.00
Common Player:		.10
M1	Mookie Blaylock	.10
M2	Chauncey Billups	.50
M3	Glen Rice	.20
M4	Scottie Pippen	.75
M5	Bob Sura	.10
M6	Erick Strickland	.10
M7	Tony Battie	.30
M8	Joe Dumars	.10
M9	Adonal Foyle	.20
M10	Charles Barkley	.30
M11	Dale Davis	.10
M12	Lamond Murray	.10
M13	Kobe Bryant	2.00
M14	Tim Hardaway	.20
M15	Glenn Robinson	.20
M16	Kevin Garnett	1.50
M17	Keith Van Horn	1.50
M18	Patrick Ewing	.20
M19	Anfernee Hardaway	1.00
M20	Tim Thomas	.75
M21	Jason Kidd	.40
M22	Isaiah Rider	.10
M23	Mahmoud Abdul-Rauf	.10
M24	Tim Duncan	1.75
M25	Detlef Schrempf	.10
M26	Damon Stoudamire	.50
M27	John Stockton	.30
M28	Bryant Reeves	.10
M29	Juwan Howard	.30
M30	Michael Jordan	3.00

1997-98 Collector's Choice MJ Bullseye

This 30-card insert was a variation of You Crash the Game, but featured Michael Jordan on each card. Collectors needed to match Jordan's point total to the numbers shown on the Bullseye targets in order to win. These inserts were found in one per five packs of Series II.

		MT
Complete Set (30):		60.00
Common Player:		2.00
B1	Michael Jordan	2.00
B2	Michael Jordan	2.00
B3	Michael Jordan	2.00
B4	Michael Jordan	2.00
B5	Michael Jordan	2.00
B6	Michael Jordan	2.00
B7	Michael Jordan	2.00
B8	Michael Jordan	2.00
B9	Michael Jordan	2.00
B10	Michael Jordan	2.00
B11	Michael Jordan	2.00
B12	Michael Jordan	2.00
B13	Michael Jordan	2.00
B14	Michael Jordan	2.00
B15	Michael Jordan	2.00
B16	Michael Jordan	2.00
B17	Michael Jordan	2.00
B18	Michael Jordan	2.00
B19	Michael Jordan	2.00
B20	Michael Jordan	2.00
B21	Michael Jordan	2.00
B22	Michael Jordan	2.00
B23	Michael Jordan	2.00
B24	Michael Jordan	2.00
B25	Michael Jordan	2.00
B26	Michael Jordan	2.00
B27	Michael Jordan	2.00
B28	Michael Jordan	2.00
B29	Michael Jordan	2.00
B30	Michael Jordan	2.00

1997-98 Collector's Choice MJ Rewind

This 13-card redemption set exclusively featured Michael Jordan and contained one card for each of Jordan's 13 years since he was drafted.

		MT
Complete Set (13):		60.00
Common Player:		5.00
R1	Michael Jordan	5.00
R2	Michael Jordan	5.00
R3	Michael Jordan	5.00
R4	Michael Jordan	5.00
R5	Michael Jordan	5.00
R6	Michael Jordan	5.00
R7	Michael Jordan	5.00
R8	Michael Jordan	5.00
R9	Michael Jordan	5.00
R10	Michael Jordan	5.00
R11	Michael Jordan	5.00
R12	Michael Jordan	5.00
R13	Michael Jordan	5.00

1997-98 Collector's Choice Star Attractions

Star Attractions was a 20-card insert found one per special retail pack of Collector's Choice. Both Series I and II had 10 cards each and the insert was numbered with a "SA" prefix. Gold versions were also available and seeded one per 20 packs.

		MT
Complete Set (20):		50.00
Complete Series 1 (10):		30.00
Complete Series 2 (10):		20.00
Common Player:		.50
Inserted 1:1 Special Retail Pack		
Gold Cards:		2x-4x
Inserted 1:20 Special Retail Pack		
1	Michael Jordan	25.00
2	Joe Smith	.50
3	Karl Malone	1.50
4	Chauncey Billups	1.50
5	Charles Barkley	1.50
6	Shaquille O'Neal	4.00
7	Jason Kidd	2.00
8	Chris Webber	2.00
9	Allen Iverson	4.00
10	Patrick Ewing	.50
11	Tim Duncan	6.00
12	Kevin Garnett	6.00
13	Tony Battie	.50
14	Gary Payton	1.00
15	Hakeem Olajuwon	2.00
16	Antonio Daniels	1.00
17	Grant Hill	6.00
18	Anfernee Hardaway	4.00
19	Scottie Pippen	3.00
20	Keith Van Horn	5.00

1997-98 Collector's Choice StarQuest

The 90-card, standard-size tiered insert set was seeded in Series I packs at varying ratios. The first 45 cards were found in each pack, while the next 20 (46-65) were inserted every 21 packs. The next 15 cards (66-80) were inserted every 71 packs with the final 10 cards (81-90) found every 145 packs. The card fronts feature the StarQuest logo in the center with the logo and name appearing in gold along the lower edge. The player's cut-out image appears over the center logo and the cards are numbered with the "SQ" prefix.

	MT
Complete Set (180):	1000.
Complete Series 1 (90):	500.00
Complete Series 2 (90):	500.00
Common Player (1-45/91-135):	.20
Common Player (46-65/136-155)	1.50
Common Player (66-80/156-170):	4.00
Common Player (81-90/171-180):	5.00
SQ1 Dale Davis	.20
SQ2 Jamal Mashburn	.20
SQ3 Christian Laettner	.20
SQ4 Billy Owens	.20
SQ5 Vlade Divac	.20
SQ6 Sean Elliott	.20
SQ7 Marcus Camby	.50
SQ8 Dana Barros	.20
SQ9 Rod Strickland	.20
SQ10Jim Jackson	.20
SQ11Tyrone Hill	.20
SQ12Ervin Johnson	.20
SQ13Antoine Walker	1.50
SQ14Lorenzen Wright	.20
SQ15Shawn Bradley	.20
SQ16John Starks	.20
SQ17Corliss Williamson	.20
SQ18Steve Smith	.20
SQ19Chris Mills	.20
SQ20Vinny Del Negro	.20
SQ21Jayson Williams	.20
SQ22Anthony Mason	.20
SQ23Dennis Scott	.20
SQ24Mark Jackson	.20
SQ25Dino Radja	.20
SQ26Greg Ostertag	.20
SQ27Anthony Peeler	.20
SQ28Toni Kukoc	.20
SQ29Michael Finley	.20
SQ30Brent Barry	.20
SQ31Wesley Person	.20
SQ32Horace Grant	.20
SQ33Walt Williams	.20
SQ34Bryant Stith	.20
SQ35Ray Allen	.30
SQ36Otis Thorpe	.20
SQ37Rasheed Wallace	.20
SQ38Charles Oakley	.20
SQ39Robert Pack	.20
SQ40Kendall Gill	.20
SQ41Lindsey Hunter	.20
SQ42Cedric Ceballos	.20
SQ43Allan Houston	.20
SQ44Bryant Reeves	.20
SQ45Derrick Coleman	.20
SQ46Isaiah Rider	1.50
SQ47Detlef Schrempf	1.50
SQ48Antonio McDyess	3.00
SQ49Glenn Robinson	3.00
SQ50Damon Stoudamire	5.00
SQ51Terrell Brandon	1.50
SQ52Joe Smith	4.00
SQ53Tom Gugliotta	1.50
SQ54Loy Vaught	1.50
SQ55Kenny Anderson	1.50
SQ56Dikembe Mutombo	1.50
SQ57Tim Hardaway	1.50
SQ58Chris Webber	6.00
SQ59Nick Van Exel	1.50
SQ60Kerry Kittles	5.00
SQ61Chris Mullin	1.50
SQ62Stephon Marbury	12.00
SQ63Juwan Howard	5.00
SQ64Larry Johnson	1.50
SQ65Shareef Abdur-Rahim	10.00
SQ66Dennis Rodman	25.00
SQ67Vin Baker	8.00
SQ68Clyde Drexler	10.00
SQ69Eddie Jones	12.00
SQ70Jerry Stackhouse	8.00
SQ71Karl Malone	8.00
SQ72Mitch Richmond	4.00
SQ73Glen Rice	4.00
SQ74Jason Kidd	4.00
SQ75Latrell Sprewell	4.00
SQ76David Robinson	10.00
SQ77Charles Barkley	10.00
SQ78Gary Payton	8.00
SQ79Scottie Pippen	20.00
SQ80Reggie Miller	4.00
SQ81Alonzo Mourning	5.00
SQ82Allen Iverson	30.00
SQ83Michael Jordan	75.00
SQ84Shawn Kemp	15.00
SQ85Kevin Garnett	35.00
SQ86Grant Hill	35.00
SQ87Anfernee Hardaway	30.00
SQ88Shaquille O'Neal	25.00
SQ89John Stockton	5.00
SQ90Hakeem Olajuwon	10.00
SQ91Billy Owens	.20
SQ92Derek Anderson	.75
SQ93Hersey Hawkins	.20
SQ94Bryon Russell	.20
SQ95Rik Smits	.20
SQ96Tracy McGrady	1.00
SQ97Kendall Gill	.20
SQ98Tim Thomas	.75
SQ99Robert Horry	.20
SQ100Marcus Camby	.40
SQ101Rodney Rogers	.20
SQ102Danny Manning	.20
SQ103John Starks	.20
SQ104Mahmoud Abdul-Rauf	.20
SQ105Chris Childs	.20
SQ106Antonio Davis	.20
SQ107Lamond Murray	.20
SQ108Nick Anderson	.20
SQ109Antoine Walker	1.50
SQ110Christian Laettner	.40
SQ111Gary Trent	.20
SQ112Tony Battie	.50
SQ113Vlade Divac	.20
SQ114Kevin Johnson	.20
SQ115Erick Strickland	.20
SQ116Ray Allen	.50
SQ117Antonio Daniels	.75
SQ118Sean Elliott	.20
SQ119Horace Grant	.20
SQ120Walt Williams	.20
SQ121Rony Seikaly	.20
SQ122Allan Houston	.20
SQ123Michael Finley	.20
SQ124Rasheed Wallace	.20
SQ125Doug Christie	.20
SQ126Danny Ferry	.20
SQ127Arvydas Sabonis	.20
SQ128Shandon Anderson	.20
SQ129Otis Thorpe	.20
SQ130Adonal Foyle	.30
SQ131Bryant Reeves	.20
SQ132Theo Ratliff	.20
SQ133Matt Maloney	.20
SQ134Voshon Lenard	.20
SQ135Danny Fortson	.20
SQ136Joe Smith	4.00
SQ137Mookie Blaylock	1.50
SQ138Loy Vaught	1.50
SQ139Tom Gugliotta	3.00
SQ140Damon Stoudamire	6.00
SQ141Antonio McDyess	4.00
SQ142Kobe Bryant	20.00
SQ143Juwan Howard	4.00
SQ144Tim Hardaway	1.50
SQ145Ron Mercer	10.00
SQ146Joe Dumars	1.50
SQ147Clyde Drexler	4.00
SQ148Shareef Abdur-Rahim	10.00
SQ149LaPhonso Ellis	1.50
SQ150Dikembe Mutombo	1.50
SQ151Chauncey Billups	8.00
SQ152Chris Webber	8.00
SQ153Glenn Robinson	3.00
SQ154Patrick Ewing	1.50
SQ155Stephon Marbury	15.00
SQ156Keith Van Horn	40.00
SQ157Karl Malone	6.00
SQ158Terrell Brandon	4.00
SQ159Sam Cassell	4.00
SQ160Jerry Stackhouse	6.00
SQ161Vin Baker	6.00
SQ162Jason Kidd	8.00
SQ163Charles Barkley	8.00
SQ164Reggie Miller	6.00
SQ165Alonzo Mourning	4.00
SQ166Scottie Pippen	15.00
SQ167Glen Rice	4.00
SQ168Allen Iverson	30.00
SQ169David Robinson	8.00
SQ170Shawn Kemp	15.00
SQ171Michael Jordan	75.00
SQ172Tim Duncan	50.00
SQ173Anfernee Hardaway	30.00
SQ174Shaquille O'Neal	30.00
SQ175John Stockton	5.00
SQ176Gary Payton	10.00
SQ177Mitch Richmond	5.00
SQ178Kevin Garnett	40.00
SQ179Hakeem Olajuwon	12.00
SQ180Grant Hill	40.00

1997-98 Collector's Choice Stick-Ums

The 30-card insert set, seeded every three packs, features some of the top players in the league on a peel-off sticker card.

		MT
Complete Set (30):		10.00
Common Player:		.15
S1	Steve Smith	.15
S2	Antoine Walker	1.50
S3	Anthony Mason	.15
S4	Dennis Rodman	1.00
S5	Terrell Brandon	.15
S6	Michael Finley	.15
S7	Antonio McDyess	.50
S8	Grant Hill	2.00
S9	Joe Smith	.50
S10	Hakeem Olajuwon	.75
S11	Reggie Miller	.30
S12	Loy Vaught	.15
S13	Shaquille O'Neal	1.50
S14	Alonzo Mourning	.30
S15	Vin Baker	.30
S16	Stephon Marbury	1.50
S17	Jim Jackson	.15
S18	John Starks	.15
S19	Anfernee Hardaway	1.50
S20	Allen Iverson	2.00
S21	Jason Kidd	.30
S22	Kenny Anderson	.15
S23	Mitch Richmond	.15
S24	David Robinson	.50
S25	Shawn Kemp	1.00
S26	Damon Stoudamire	.75
S27	Karl Malone	.40
S28	Bryant Reeves	.15
S29	Juwan Howard	.40
S30	Michael Jordan	4.00

1997-98 Collector's Choice The Jordan Dynasty

This five-card insert was found in Series I packs of Collector's Choice. All five cards featured Michael Jordan on the front and highlighted one of his five championships. The cards are sequentially numbered on the back to 23,000.

	MT
Complete Set (5):	60.00
Common Player:	12.00
Production 23,000 Sets	

1997-98 Upper Deck Diamond Vision

This 29-card set includes three inserts, including an all-Jordan set. The front shows game-action footage in a hologram view, with the player's name along the bottom. The back is a white background with text on the player.

		MT
Complete Set (29):		180.00
Common Player:		2.00
Wax Box:		100.00
1	Dikembe Mutombo	2.00
2	Dana Barros	2.00
3	Glen Rice	3.00
4	Michael Jordan	40.00
5	Terrell Brandon	2.00
6	Michael Finley	3.00
7	Antonio McDyess	4.00
8	Grant Hill	20.00
9	Latrell Sprewell	4.00
10	Hakeem Olajuwon	8.00
11	Reggie Miller	4.00
12	Loy Vaught	2.00
13	Shaquille O'Neal	16.00
14	Alonzo Mourning	3.00
15	Vin Baker	4.00
16	Kevin Garnett	20.00
17	Kerry Kittles	4.00
18	Patrick Ewing	4.00
19	Anfernee Hardaway	16.00
20	Allen Iverson	20.00
21	Jason Kidd	6.00
22	Isaiah Rider	2.00
23	Mitch Richmond	3.00
24	David Robinson	5.00
25	Gary Payton	5.00
26	Damon Stoudamire	6.00
27	Karl Malone	4.00
28	Shareef Abdur-Rahim	10.00
29	Chris Webber	8.00

1997-98 Upper Deck Diamond Vision Signature Moves

Signature Moves was a 29-card parallel set that was inserted one per five packs. They are identified by a facsimile signature of the player on the front.

	MT
Signature Move Cards:	2x

1997-98 Upper Deck Diamond Vision Reel Time

The one-card set is highlighted by Michael Jordan. The front has a photo of Jordan, with "Reel Time" along the bottom. The card is prefixed with the letter "R".

		MT
Complete Set (1):		400.00
Common Player:		400.00
R1	Michael Jordan	400.00

1997-98 Upper Deck Diamond Vision Dunk Vision

This six-card set features slam dunks by the superstars. Inserted at 1:40, the cards have a color action shot on the front, with the player's name in orange below the photo. The cards are numbered with the prefix "D".

		MT
Complete Set (6):		500.00
Common Player:		40.00
D1	Michael Jordan	175.00
D2	Anfernee Hardaway	85.00
D3	Shaquille O'Neal	85.00
D4	Grant Hill	100.00
D5	Kevin Garnett	100.00
D6	Hakeem Olajuwon	40.00

1997-98 Upper Deck UD3

A retail-only product, UD3 consists of 60 cards, with three sets of 20-card subsets. Also included are four sets of inserts, totaling 37 cards. The three main sets - Jam Masters, Starstruck and The Big Picture - have the title on the front, with a color action photo of the player. Inserts include: Awesome Action, Rookie Portfolio, Season Ticket Autographs and MJ3 Collection.

		MT
Complete Set (60):		60.00
Common Player:		.25
Wax Box:		70.00
1	Anfernee Hardaway	2.50
2	Alonzo Mourning	.50
3	Grant Hill	3.00
4	Kerry Kittles	.75
5	Latrell Sprewell	.50
6	Rasheed Wallace	.25
7	Jerry Stackhouse	.50
8	Glen Rice	.50
9	Marcus Camby	.75
10	Scottie Pippen	1.25
11	Patrick Ewing	.50
12	Michael Finley	.50
13	Karl Malone	.75
14	Antonio McDyess	.50
15	Michael Jordan	6.00
16	Clyde Drexler	.50
17	Brent Barry	.25
18	Glenn Robinson	.50
19	Kobe Bryant	4.00
20	Reggie Miller	.50
21	John Stockton	.50
22	Gary Payton	.50
23	Michael Jordan	6.00
24	Vin Baker	.50
25	Karl Malone	.50
26	Juwan Howard	.50
27	Charles Barkley	.75
28	Jason Kidd	.75
29	Joe Dumars	.25
30	Anfernee Hardaway	2.50
31	Mitch Richmond	.50
32	Alonzo Mourning	.50
33	Grant Hill	3.00
34	Shaquille O'Neal	2.00
35	Scottie Pippen	1.25
36	Reggie Miller	.50
37	Hakeem Olajuwon	1.00
38	Tim Hardaway	.25
39	David Robinson	.75
40	Shawn Kemp	1.25
41	Allen Iverson	3.50
42	Stephon Marbury	3.00
43	Dennis Rodman	2.50
44	Terrell Brandon	.25
45	Michael Jordan	8.00
46	Kerry Kittles	.75
47	Hakeem Olajuwon	1.75
48	Loy Vaught	.25
49	Antoine Walker	3.00
50	Gary Payton	1.00
51	Kevin Johnson	.25
52	Kevin Garnett	4.00
53	Shareef Abdur-Rahim	2.00
54	Larry Johnson	.50
55	Dikembe Mutombo	.25
56	Chris Webber	1.25
57	Joe Smith	.75
58	Kendall Gill	.25
59	Kenny Anderson	.25
60	Damon Stoudamire	1.00

1997-98 Upper Deck UD3 Awesome Action

A 20-card set, the front has a color action shot, with the featured player highlighted in a circle. The back has three sequence photos, and the numbers are prefixed with an "A". Insertion rate is 1:11.

		MT
Complete Set (20):		120.00
Common Player:		1.50
A1	Michael Jordan	30.00
A2	Kobe Bryant	20.00
A3	Jerry Stackhouse	4.00
A4	Shawn Kemp	8.00
A5	Hakeem Olajuwon	6.00
A6	Grant Hill	15.00
A7	Scottie Pippen	8.00
A8	Alonzo Mourning	1.50
A9	Damon Stoudamire	5.00
A10	Kevin Garnett	15.00
A11	Anfernee Hardaway	10.00
A12	Shareef Abdur-Rahim	8.00
A13	Allen Iverson	15.00
A14	Dennis Rodman	10.00
A15	Shaquille O'Neal	10.00
A16	Jason Kidd	3.00
A17	Gary Payton	3.00
A18	Dikembe Mutombo	1.50
A19	Karl Malone	3.00
A20	Stephon Marbury	12.00

1997-98 Upper Deck UD3 Michael Jordan MJ3

Just a three-card set, it's all Michael Jordan. The cards are rainbow-foiled, with red foil-stamping. The No.1 card is inserted 1:45, No.2 at 1:119 and No.3 at 1:167, prefixed "MJ".

		MT
Complete Set (3):		175.00
Common Player:		30.00
I	Michael Jordan	30.00
II	Michael Jordan	60.00
III	Michael Jordan	100.00

1997-98 Upper Deck UD3 Rookie Portfolio

The set features the first 10 players selected in the 1997 NBA Draft. The 10-card set has studio photos of the players on the front taken during Draft activities. The cards are inserted at 1:144.

		MT
Complete Set (10):		300.00
Common Player:		8.00
R1	Tim Duncan	80.00
R2	Keith Van Horn	70.00
R3	Chauncey Billups	30.00
R4	Antonio Daniels	30.00
R5	Tony Battie	25.00
R6	Ron Mercer	40.00
R7	Tim Thomas	25.00
R8	Adonal Foyle	8.00
R9	Tracy McGrady	40.00
R10	Danny Fortson	15.00

1997-98 Upper Deck UD3 Season Ticket Autographs

The four-card set is a replica of the "Season Ticket" set. The cards are simply autographed by four players and inserted at a rate of 1:1,800.

		MT
Complete Set (4):		3250.
Common Player:		200.00
MJ	Michael Jordan	2600.
AH	Anfernee Hardaway	500.00
TH	Tim Hardaway	200.00
JH	Juwan Howard	200.00

1997 Wheels Rookie Thunder

The 45-card set features picks from the 1997 NBA Draft. The fronts have a silhouted image, with a multi-colored background and the player's name in silver underneath. The backs have a partial photo with statistical data and text. The set was paralleled twice in Rising Storm (hobby) and Storm Front (retail) parallels. Insert sets include: Game Ball, Boomers, Lights Out, Double Trouble, Shooting Stars along with Stroke Autogaphs.

		MT
Complete Set (45):		15.00
Common Player:		.10
1	Tim Duncan	2.50
2	Keith Van Horn	2.00
3	Chauncey Billups	.75
4	Antonio Daniels	.75
5	Tony Battie	.75
6	Ron Mercer	1.50
7	Tim Thomas	.50
8	Adonal Foyle	.20
9	Tracy McGrady	1.00
10	Danny Fortson	.40
11	Olivier Saint-Jean	.10
12	Austin Croshere	.25
13	Derek Anderson	1.00
14	Maurice Taylor	.50
15	Kelvin Cato	.50
16	Brevin Knight	.75
17	Johnny Taylor	.10
18	Chris Anstey	.10
19	Scot Pollard	.10
20	Paul Grant	.10
21	Anthony Parker	.10
22	Ed Gray	.10
23	Bobby Jackson	.50
24	John Thomas	.10
25	Charles Smith	.10
26	Jacque Vaughn	.40
27	Keith Booth	.10
28	Serge Zwikker	.10
29	Charles O'Bannon	.10
30	Bubba Wells	.10
31	Kebu Stewart	.10
32	James Collins	.10
33	Eddie Elisma	.10
34	Ron Mercer	.40
35	Derek Anderson (Take Two)	.25
36	Scot Pollard (Take Two)	.10
37	Jacque Vaughn (Take Two)	.25
38	Bobby Jackson (Take Two)	.40
39	John Thomas (Take Two)	.10
40	Chauncey Billups (Young Guns)	.10
41	Ron Mercer (Young Guns)	.25
42	Tim Thomas (Young Guns)	.20
43	Tracy McGrady (Young Guns)	.20
44	Maurice Taylor (Young Guns)	.20
45	Checklist	.10

1997 Wheels Rookie Thunder Rising Storm/Storm Front

Rising Storm was the hobby parallel, while Storm Front was the retail parallel to Wheels Rookie Thunder. Each set contained all 45 cards in the base set and was seeded one per 12 packs.

	MT
Rising Storm Cards:	4x-8x
Inserted 1:12 Hobby	
Storm Front Cards:	4x-8x
Inserted 1:12 Retail	

1997 Wheels Rookie Thunder Game Ball

The highlight of this six-card set is the official basketball leather embedded in the background of a player image. The rest of the front is bordered in red. The backs have text on the player, and are numbered with the prefix "T". Insertion rate is 1:216.

	MT
Complete Set (10):	500.00
Common Player:	20.00
GB1 Tim Duncan	120.00
GB2 Keith Van Horn	100.00
GB3 Chauncey Billups	50.00
GB4 Antonio Daniels	40.00
GB5 Tony Battie	50.00
GB6 Ron Mercer	70.00
GB7 Tim Thomas	40.00
GB8 Adonal Foyle	20.00
GB9 Tracy McGrady	50.00
GB10 Danny Fortson	40.00

1997 Wheels Rookie Thunder Boomers

A 10-card set that highlights 10 draft picks from 1997. Inserted at 1:28, the background on the front is a red flame with a player image in the forefront. The backs have another image, and are numbered with the prefix "TB".

	MT
Complete Set (10):	75.00
Common Player:	4.00
TB1 Tim Duncan	25.00
TB2 Tony Battie	8.00
TB3 Tracy McGrady	10.00
TB4 Danny Fortson	8.00
TB5 Maurice Taylor	8.00
TB6 Serge Zwikker	4.00
TB7 Scot Pollard	4.00
TB8 Charles O'Bannon	4.00
TB9 Adonal Foyle	4.00
TB10 Keith Van Horn	20.00

1997 Wheels Rookie Thunder Double Trouble

A six-card set, the cards feature rookies from the 1997 draft. The cards are two-sided featuring embossed player images, with silver foil and micro-etching. The cards are inserted at 1:42, and numbered with the prefix "DT".

	MT
Complete Set (6):	60.00
Common Player:	6.00
DT1 Tim Duncan, Keith Van Horn	25.00
DT2 Chauncey Billups, Jacque Vaughn	8.00
DT3 Tracy McGrady, Ron Mercer	15.00
DT4 Bobby Jackson, Brevin Knight	8.00
DT5 Tim Duncan, Tony Battie	18.00
DT6 Danny Fortson, Tim Thomas	6.00

1997 Wheels Rookie Thunder Lights Out

This five-card set of rookies uses black light ink to glow in the dark. The fronts have two player images, with one in color. The cards were inserted at 1:96, and are numbered with the prefix "L".

	MT
Complete Set (5):	100.00
Common Player:	12.00
LO1 Chauncey Billups	18.00
LO2 Keith Van Horn	30.00
LO3 Tim Duncan	40.00
LO4 Ron Mercer	20.00
LO5 Antonio Daniels	12.00

1997 Wheels Rookie Thunder Shooting Stars

A 10-card set that highlights the rookies from the 1997-98 season. Numbered with the prefix "SS", the set was inserted at a rate of 1:11. The fronts have a color action shot, with a space background. The back says "Shooting Stars" across the top, followed by text.

	MT
Complete Set (10):	50.00
Common Player:	2.50
SS1 Chauncey Billups	5.00
SS2 Tracy McGrady	6.00
SS3 Brevin Knight	5.00
SS4 Austin Croshere	2.50
SS5 Derek Anderson	5.00
SS6 Jacque Vaughn	4.00
SS7 Bobby Jackson	5.00
SS8 Tim Duncan	15.00
SS9 Keith Van Horn	12.00
SS10 Ron Mercer	10.00

1998 Collector's Edge Impulse

This 100-card set featured top players eligible for the 1998 NBA Draft. Card fronts have a borderless design with the logo in the top right corner and the player's name across the bottom in gold foil. The set was paralled once and packs contained five different inserts, including: KB8, Pro Signatures Authentic, Memorable Moments, Swoosh and T3.

		MT
Complete Set (100):		20.00
Common Player:		.10
Wax Box:		70.00
1	Michael Olowokandi	2.50
2	Antawn Jamison	2.00
3	Vince Carter	1.50
4	Robert Traylor	1.50
5	Jason Williams	.50
6	Paul Pierce	1.25
7	Bonzi Wells	.50
8	Keon Clark	.50
9	Radoslav Nesterovic	.10
10	Pat Garrity	.20
11	Ricky Davis	.20
12	Tyrron Lue	.10
13	Felipe Lopez	.50
14	Al Harrington	.50
15	Corey Benjamin	.10
16	Rashard Lewis	.50
17	Jelani McCoy	.20
18	Shammond Williams	.50
19	DeMarco Johnson	.20
20	Korleone Young	.20
21	Miles Simon	.20
22	Toby Bailey	.20
23	J.R. Henderson	.20
24	Charles Jones	.10
25	Jeff Sheppard	.10
26	Kobe Bryant	2.00
27	Stephon Marbury	.50
28	Tracy McGrady	.20
29	Scottie Pippen	.40
30	Tim Thomas	.20
31	Checklist Michael Olowokandi	1.25
32	Checklist Antawn Jamison	1.00
33	Michael Olowokandi	1.25
34	Antawn Jamison	1.00
35	Vince Carter	.75
36	Robert Traylor	.75
37	Jason Williams	.25
38	Paul Pierce	.50
39	Bonzi Wells	.10
40	Keon Clark	.10
41	Radoslav Nesterovic	.10
42	Pat Garrity	.10
43	Michael Olowokandi	1.25
44	Antawn Jamison	1.00
45	Vince Carter	.50
46	Robert Traylor	.50
47	Jason Williams	.20
48	Paul Pierce	.50
49	Bonzi Wells	.10
50	Keon Clark	.10
51	Paul Pierce, Kobe Bryant	.75
52	Paul Pierce, Scottie Pippen	.50
53	Antawn Jamison, Stephon Marbury	.50
54	Antawn Jamison, Tracy McGrady	.50
55	Michael Olowokandi, Tim Thomas	.50
56	Michael Olowokandi, Kobe Bryant	1.25
57	Keon Clark, Scottie Pippen	.20
58	Keon Clark, Stephon Marbury	.20
59	Pat Garrity, Tracy McGrady	.20
60	Pat Garrity, Tim Thomas	.20
61	Corey Benjamin, Kobe Bryant	.75
62	Corey Benjamin, Scottie Pippen	.20
63	Robert Traylor, Stephon Marbury	.20
64	Robert Traylor, Tracy McGrady	.20
65	Rashard Lewis, Tim Thomas	.20
66	Rashard Lewis, Kobe Bryant	.75
67	Bonzi Wells, Scottie Pippen	.20
68	Bonzi Wells, Stephon Marbury	.20
69	J.R. Henderson, Tracy McGrady	.20
70	J.R. Henderson, Tim Thomas	.20
71	Toby Bailey, Kobe Bryant	.75
72	Toby Bailey, Scottie Pippen	.20
73	Tyrron Lue, Stephon Marbury	.20
74	Tyrron Lue, Tracy McGrady	.20
75	Radisav Nesterovic, Tim Thomas	.20
76	Radisav Nesterovic, Kobe Bryant	.75
77	Miles Simon, Scottie Pippen	.20
78	Miles Simon, Stephon Marbury	.20
79	Jeff Sheppard, Tracy McGrady	.20
80	Jeff Sheppard, Tim Thomas	.20
81	Felipe Lopez, Kobe Bryant	.75
82	Felipe Lopez, Scottie Pippen	.20
83	Shammond Williams, Stephon Marbury	.20
84	Shammond Williams, Tracy McGrady	.20
85	Charles Jones, Tim Thomas	.20
86	Charles Jones, Kobe Bryant	.75
87	Jason Williams, Scottie Pippen	.20
88	Jason Williams, Stephon Marbury	.20
89	Ricky Davis, Tracy McGrady	.20
90	Ricky Davis, Tim Thomas	.20
91	Korleone Young, Kobe Bryant	.75
92	Korleone Young, Scottie Pippen	.20
93	Vince Carter, Stephon Marbury	.20
94	Vince Carter, Tracy McGrady	.20
95	Al Harrington, Tim Thomas	.20
96	Al Harrington, Kobe Bryant	.75
97	Jelani McCoy, Scottie Pippen	.20
98	Jelani McCoy, Stephon Marbury	.20
99	DeMarco Johnson, Tracy McGrady	.20
100	DeMarco Johnson, Tim Thomas	.20

1998 Collector's Edge Impulse Parallel

This 100-card parallel reprinted each card on a thicker stock than used on the base cards. These were inserted one per pack.

	MT
Parallel Cards:	2x

1998 Collector's Edge Impulse Memorable Moments

This five-card set was available for exchange cards inserted into packs at a rate of one per 360 packs. Once redeemed, the cards featured pieces of game-used ball on the front. At press time, the cards hadn't been released yet. Therefore, only pricing of the redemption card is available.

	MT
1 Kobe Bryant	—
2 Stephon Marbury	—
3 Tracy McGrady	—
4 Scottie Pippen	—
5 Tim Thomas	—
NNO Memorable Moments	50.00

1998 Collector's Edge Impulse Pro Signatures

This 30-card set featured authentic signatures from 25 rookies and five veterans. Fourteen of these inserts were available exclusively through redempion cards, while three others were partially available through redemptions. Pro Signatures were seeded one per 18 packs.

	MT
Common Player:	10.00
Inserted 1:18	
Toby Bailey	12.00
Corey Benjamin	10.00
Kobe Bryant	350.00
Vince Carter	50.00
Keon Clark	15.00
Ricky Davis	10.00
Pat Garrity	10.00
Zendon Hamilton	10.00
Al Harrington	15.00
J.R. Henderson	12.00
Antawn Jamison	70.00
DeMarco Johnson	10.00
Rashard Lewis	12.00
Felipe Lopez	15.00
Tyrron Lue	10.00
Stephon Marbury	250.00
Jelani McCoy	10.00
Tracy McGrady	175.00
Michael Olowokandi	75.00
Paul Pierce	50.00
Scottie Pippen	275.00
Jeff Sheppard	12.00
Miles Simon	15.00
Tim Thomas	175.00
Robert Traylor	50.00
Bonzi Wells	10.00
Jason Williams	25.00
Shammond Williams	12.00
Korleone Young	12.00

1998 Collector's Edge Impluse KB8

This five-card insert features Lakers star Kobe Bryant and arrives in four different versions. Bronze cards are seeded 1:36, Silvers are 1:54, Golds are 1:72 and Holofoil versions are found one per 90 packs.

		MT
Complete Bronze Set (5):		30.00
Common Bronze Player:		6.00
Inserted 1:36		
Silver Cards:		2x
Inserted 1:54		
Gold Cards:		3x
Inserted 1:72		
Holofoil Cards:		4x
Inserted 1:90		
1	Kobe Bryant	6.00
2	Kobe Bryant	6.00
3	Kobe Bryant	6.00
4	Kobe Bryant	6.00
5	Kobe Bryant	6.00

1998 Collector's Edge Impulse Swoosh

Swoosh included 24 cards in total, with 12 different pairs of left and right cards that fit together. Printed on an acetate stock, these were inserted one per 72 packs.

		MT
Complete Set (26):		230.00
Common Player:		5.00
Inserted 1:72		
1	Michael Olowokandi	30.00
2	Antawn Jamison	25.00
3	Vince Carter	20.00
4	Robert Traylor	20.00
5	Jason Williams	10.00
6	Paul Pierce	15.00
7	Bonzi Wells	5.00
8	Keon Clark	5.00
9	Radisav Nesterovic	5.00
10	Pat Garrity	5.00
11	Ricky Davis	8.00
12	Tyrron Lue	5.00
13	Felipe Lopez	8.00
14	Al Harrington	8.00
15	Corey Benjamin	5.00
16	Rashard Lewis	5.00
17	Jelani McCoy	5.00
18	Shammond Williams	8.00
19	DeMarco Johnson	5.00
20	Korleone Young	5.00
21	Miles Simon	5.00
22	Kobe Bryant	30.00
23	Stephon Marbury	15.00
24	Tracy McGrady	10.00
25	Scottie Pippen	12.00
26	Tim Thomas	10.00

1998 Collector's Edge Impulse T3

This 15-card insert included 10 rookies and five veterans. Cards included a "T3" logo in the top right corner and arrived in three different versions. Bronze versions were seeded 1:12, Silver versions were seeded 1:18 and Gold versions were seeded 1:36 packs.

		MT
Complete Set (15):		50.00
Common Gold (1-5):		5.00
Inserted 1:36		
Common Silver (6-10):		2.00
Inserted 1:18		
Common Bronze (11-15):		1.00
Inserted 1:12		
1	Michael Olowokandi G	12.00
2	Antawn Jamison G	10.00
3	Kobe Bryant G	15.00
4	Scottie Pippen G	8.00
5	Robert Traylor G	5.00
6	Stephon Marbury S	5.00
7	Paul Pierce S	5.00
8	Vince Carter S	5.00
9	Shammond Williams S	2.00
10	Tim Thomas S	2.00
11	Bonzi Wells B	1.00
12	Tracy McGrady B	2.00
13	Rashard Lewis B	1.00
14	Keon Clark B	1.00
15	Corey Benjamin B	1.00

1998-99 Fleer

Fleer Tradition Series I contained 150 cardds, with 147 player cards and three checklists. This year's set featured players on a borderless design with a the player's name, team and position stamped across the bottom in gold foil. There were two hobby-only parallels: Vintage '61 and Classic '61, which featured the first 147 players on a 1961-62 card design. Insert sets in Series I include: Timeless Memories, Great Expectations, Rookie Rewind, Electrifying, Lucky 13 and Playmakers Theatre.

		MT
Complete Set (150):		20.00
Common Player:		.10
Wax Box:		45.00
1	Kobe Bryant	2.00
2	Corliss Williamson	.10
3	Allen Iverson	1.00
4	Michael Finley	.20
5	Juwan Howard	.20
6	Marcus Camby	.20
7	Toni Kukoc	.20
8	Antoine Walker	1.00
9	Stephon Marbury	1.00
10	Tim Hardaway	.25
11	Zydrunas Ilgauskas	.10
12	John Stockton	.25
13	Glenn Robinson	.20
14	Isaiah Rider	.20
15	Danny Fortson	.10
16	Donyell Marshall	.10
17	Chris Mullin	.20
18	Shareef Abdur-Rahim	.50
19	Bobby Phills	.10
20	Gary Payton	.30
21	Derrick Coleman	.10
22	Larry Johnson	.20
23	Michael Jordan	3.00
24	Danny Manning	.10
25	Nick Anderson	.10
26	Chris Gatling	.10
27	Steve Smith	.10
28	Chris Whitney	.10
29	Terrell Brandon	.20
30	Rasheed Wallace	.10
31	Reggie Miller	.25
32	Karl Malone	.25
33	Grant Hill	1.50
34	Hakeem Olajuwon	.50
35	Erick Dampier	.10
36	Vin Baker	.40
37	Tim Thomas	.75
38	Mark Price	.10
39	Shawn Bradley	.10
40	Calbert Cheaney	.10
41	Glen Rice	.20
42	Kevin Willis	.10
43	Chris Carr	.10
44	Keith Van Horn	1.25
45	Jamal Mashburn	.10
46	Eddie Jones	.40
47	Brevin Knight	.30
48	Olden Polynice	.10
49	Bobby Jackson	.20
50	David Robinson	.40
51	Patrick Ewing	.25
52	Samaki Walker	.10
53	Antonio Daniels	.20
54	Rodney Rogers	.10
55	Dikembe Mutombo	.20
56	Tracy McGrady	.75
57	Walt Williams	.10
58	Walter McCarty	.10
59	Detlef Schrempf	.10
60	Ervin Johnson	.10
61	Michael Smith	.10
62	Clifford Robinson	.10
63	Brian Williams	.10
64	Shandon Anderson	.10
65	P.J. Brown	.10
66	Scottie Pippen	.75
67	Anthony Peeler	.10
68	Tony Delk	.10
69	David Wesley	.10
70	John Starks	.10
71	Nick Van Exel	.20
72	Kerry Kittles	.20
73	Tony Battie	.20
74	Lamond Murray	.10
75	Anfernee Hardaway	1.00
76	Jalen Rose	.10
77	Derek Anderson	.30
78	Avery Johnson	.10
79	Michael Stewart	.10
80	Brian Shaw	.10
81	Chauncey Billups	.30
82	Kenny Anderson	.10
83	Bryon Russell	.10
84	Jason Kidd	.40
85	Tyrone Hill	.10
86	Jim McIlvaine	.10
87	Brian Grant	.10
88	Bryant Stith	.10
89	Brent Price	.10
90	John Wallace	.10
91	Dennis Rodman	1.00
92	Alonzo Mourning	.20
93	Bimbo Coles	.10
94	Chris Anstey	.10
95	Lindsey Hunter	.10
96	Ed Gray	.10
97	Chris Mills	.10
98	Rick Fox	.10
99	Lorenzen Wright	.10
100	Kevin Garnett	1.50
101	Shawn Kemp	.75
102	Mark Jackson	.10
103	Sam Cassell	.10
104	Monty Williams	.10
105	Ron Mercer	1.00
106	Bryant Reeves	.10
107	Tracy Murray	.10
108	Ray Allen	.25
109	Maurice Taylor	.25
110	Jerome Williams	.10
111	Horace Grant	.10
112	Tariq Abdul-Wahad	.10
113	Travis Knight	.10
114	Kendall Gill	.10
115	Aaron McKie	.10
116	Dean Garrett	.10
117	Jeff Hornacek	.10
118	Todd Fuller	.10
119	Arvydas Sabonis	.10
120	Voshon Lenard	.10
121	Steve Nash	.10
122	Cedric Henderson	.10
123	Rodrick Rhodes	.10
124	Mookie Blaylock	.10
125	Hersey Hawkins	.10
126	Doug Christie	.10
127	Eric Piatkowski	.10
128	Sean Elliott	.10
129	Anthony Mason	.10
130	Allan Houston	.10
131	Antonio Davis	.10
132	Hubert Davis	.10
133	Rod Strickland	.10
134	Jason Kidd	.20
135	Mark Jackson	.10
136	Marcus Camby	.10
137	Dikembe Mutombo	.10
138	Shawn Bradley	.10
139	Dennis Rodman	.50
140	Jayson Williams	.10
141	Tim Duncan	.75
142	Michael Jordan	1.50
143	Shaquille O'Neal	.50
144	Karl Malone	.10
145	Mookie Blaylock	.10
146	Brevin Knight	.10
147	Doug Christie	.10
148	Checklist	.10
149	Checklist	.10
150	Checklist	.10

1998-99 Fleer Vintage 61

Vintage 61 paralleled the first 147 cards (checklists not included) on 1961-62 Fleer card designs. These were exclusive to hobby packs and seeded one per hobby pack. Rarer Classic 61 versions exist and are sequentially numbered to 61.

	MT
Vintage 61 Cards:	2x-4x
Classic 61 Cards:	100x-200x

1998-99 Fleer Electrifying

This 10-card set features players over a gold prismatic foil background with embossing. These are numbered with an "E" suffix and inserted one per 72 Series I packs.

		MT
Complete Set (10):		200.00
Common Player:		7.00
1E	Kobe Bryant	45.00
2E	Kevin Garnett	30.00
3E	Anfernee Hardaway	20.00
4E	Grant Hill	30.00
5E	Allen Iverson	20.00
6E	Michael Jordan	60.00
7E	Shawn Kemp	15.00
8E	Stephon Marbury	20.00
9E	Gary Payton	7.00
10E	Dennis Rodman	20.00

1998-99 Fleer Great Expectations

Great Expectations was a 10-card insert that featured top players on a leather-like embossed card printed with team colors. These were numbered with a "GE" suffix and inserted one per 20 Series I packs.

		MT
Complete Set (10):		45.00
Common Player:		1.50
GE1	Shareef Abdur-Rahim	4.00
GE2	Ray Allen	1.50
GE3	Kobe Bryant	12.00
GE4	Tim Duncan	10.00
GE5	Kevin Garnett	10.00
GE6	Grant Hill	10.00
GE7	Allen Iverson	5.00
GE8	Stephon Marbury	6.00
GE9	Keith Van Horn	8.00
GE10	Antoine Walker	6.00

1998-99 Fleer Lucky 13

Lucky 13 was a draft redemption set that consisted of 13 different cards that a single digit 1-13. Each individual card was redeemable for the corresponding 1998 draft pick. These were seeded one per 96 Series I packs.

		MT
Complete Set (13):		150.00
Common Player:		5.00
Inserted 1:96		
1	Michael Olowokandi	35.00
2	Mike Bibby	25.00
3	Raef Lafrentz	15.00
4	Antawn Jamison	30.00
5	Vince Carter	15.00
6	Robert Traylor	15.00
7	Jason Williams	10.00
8	Larry Hughes	10.00
9	Dirk Nowitzki	5.00
10	Paul Pierce	12.00
11	Bonzi Wells	5.00
12	Michael Doleac	8.00
13	Keon Clark	5.00

1998-99 Fleer Playmakers Theatre

This insert included 15 players on gold holofoil stock with sculpted, debossed curtain-like backgrounds. The cards were numbered with a "PT" suffix, sequentially numbered to 100 on the back and only in Series I.

	MT
Complete Set (15):	2,500
Common Player:	25.00
PT1 Shareef Abdur-Rahim	100.00
PT2 Ray Allen	25.00
PT3 Kobe Bryant	400.00
PT4 Tim Duncan	300.00
PT5 Kevin Garnett	300.00
PT6 Anfernee Hardaway	175.00
PT7 Grant Hill	300.00
PT8 Allen Iverson	150.00
PT9 Michael Jordan	600.00
PT10 Karl Malone	50.00
PT11 Stephon Marbury	175.00
PT12 Shaquille O'Neal	175.00
PT13 Scottie Pippen	125.00
PT14 Keith Van Horn	200.00
PT15 Antoine Walker	200.00

1998-99 Fleer Rookie Rewind

Rookie Rewind featured the 1997-98 NBA All-Rookie Team on silver holofoil with accents and embossing. Cards are numbered with a "RR" suffix and inserted one per 36 Series I packs.

	MT
Complete Set (10):	45.00
Common Player:	1.50
RR1 Derek Anderson	3.00
RR2 Tim Duncan	15.00
RR3 Cedric Henderson	1.50
RR4 Zydrunas Ilgauskas	1.50
RR5 Bobby Jackson	2.00
RR6 Brevin Knight	3.00
RR7 Ron Mercer	10.00
RR8 Maurice Taylor	3.00
RR9 Tim Thomas	7.00
RR10 Keith Van Horn	12.00

1998-99 Fleer Timeless Memories

Timeless Memories was a 10-card insert featuring a large clock in the background with the player's face inside it. There is also an action shot of the player in the foreground.

These inserts are numbered with a "TM" suffix and inserted one per 12 Series I packs.

	MT
Complete Set (10):	15.00
Common Player:	.75
TM1 Shareef Abdur-Rahim	2.00
TM2 Ray Allen	.75
TM3 Vin Baker	1.25
TM4 Anfernee Hardaway	3.00
TM5 Tim Hardaway	1.25
TM6 Shaquille O'Neal	3.00
TM7 Scottie Pippen	2.00
TM8 David Robinson	1.25
TM9 Dennis Rodman	3.00
TM10 Antoine Walker	3.00

1998-99 Hoops

Hoops Series I featured 155 basic cards and 10 Steppin' Out subsets cards. Base cards featured an action shot of the player on the left, with a close-up shot of his face during the action shot in the background. This design faded into a white border around the card. The set was paralleled in a Starting Five set that was numbered to only five sets. Inserts sets in Series I included: Shout Outs, Pump Up the Jam, Rejectors, Freshman Flashback, Prime Twine, Bams, Slam Bams and Autographics.

		MT
Complete Set (165):		20.00
Common Player:		.10
Wax Box:		38.00
1	Kobe Bryant	2.00
2	Glenn Robinson	.20
3	Derek Anderson	.30
4	Terry Dehere	.10
5	Jalen Rose	.10
6	Zydrunas Ilgauskas	.10
7	Scott Williams	.10
8	Toni Kukoc	.20
9	John Stockton	.30
10	Kevin Garnett	1.50
11	Jerome Williams	.10
12	Anthony Mason	.10
13	Harvey Grant	.10
14	Mookie Blaylock	.10
15	Tyrone Hill	.10
16	Dale Davis	.10
17	Eric Washington	.10
18	Aaron McKie	.10
19	Jermaine O'Neal	.10
20	Anfernee Hardaway	1.00
21	Derrick Coleman	.10
22	Allan Houston	.20
23	Michael Jordan	3.00
24	Jason Kidd	.40
25	Tyrone Corbin	.10
26	Jacque Vaughn	.10
27	Bobby Jackson	.20
28	Chris Anstey	.10
29	Brent Barry	.10
30	Shareef Abdur-Rahim	.50
31	Jeff Hornacek	.10
32	Ed Gray	.10
33	Grant Hill	1.50
34	Steve Smith	.10
35	Rony Seikaly	.10
36	Mark Jackson	.10
37	Shawn Bradley	.10
38	Corie Blount	.10
39	Erick Dampier	.10
40	Kerry Kittles	.20
41	David Wesley	.10
42	Horace Grant	.10
43	Bobby Hurley	.10
44	Tariq Abdul-Wahad	.10
45	Brian Williams	.10
46	Ray Allen	.20
47	Kenny Anderson	.10
48	Rodrick Rhodes	.10
49	Greg Foster	.10
50	Tim Duncan	1.50
51	Steve Nash	.10
52	Kelvin Cato	.10
53	Donyell Marshall	.10
54	Marcus Camby	.20
55	Kevin Willis	.10
56	Michael Finley	.20
57	Muggsy Bogues	.10
58	Mark Price	.10
59	Larry Johnson	.20
60	Karl Malone	.30
61	Greg Ostertag	.10
62	Sean Elliott	.10
63	Johnny Taylor	.10
64	Howard Eisley	.10
65	Chris Childs	.10
66	Walt Williams	.10
67	Tracy Murray	.10
68	Patrick Ewing	.20
69	Olden Polynice	.10
70	Allen Iverson	1.00
71	David Robinson	.30
72	Calbert Cheaney	.10
73	Lamond Murray	.10
74	Scot Pollard	.10
75	Alonzo Mourning	.20
76	Tracy McGrady	.75
77	Jim McIlvaine	.10
78	Bob Sura	.10
79	Anthony Peeler	.10
80	Keith Van Horn	1.00
81	Maurice Taylor	.20
82	Charles Smith	.10
83	Dikembe Mutombo	.20
84	Nick Anderson	.10
85	Austin Croshere	.10
86	Armon Gilliam	.10
87	Eddie Jones	.50
88	Glen Rice	.20
89	Sam Cassell	.10
90	Stephon Marbury	1.00
91	Elliot Perry	.10
92	Jamal Mashburn	.20
93	Adonal Foyle	.10
94	Avery Johnson	.10
95	Michael Williams	.10
96	Danny Fortson	.10
97	Brevin Knight	.30
98	Ron Harper	.10
99	Chauncey Billups	.30
100	Shaquille O'Neal	1.00
101	Brent Price	.10
102	Tim Thomas	.75
103	Khalid Reeves	.10
104	Chris Gatling	.10
105	Terry Cummings	.10
106	Vin Baker	.30
107	Bryant Reeves	.10
108	John Starks	.10
109	Juwan Howard	.20
110	Antoine Walker	1.00
111	Rodney Rogers	.10
112	Nick Van Exel	.20
113	Chris Whitney	.10
114	Bobby Phills	.10
115	Travis Knight	.10
116	Robert Horry	.10
117	Erick Strickland	.10
118	Dontae Jones	.10
119	Tony Battie	.20
120	Lindsey Hunter	.10
121	Reggie Miller	.20
122	John Wallace	.10
123	Ron Mercer	1.00
124	Antonio Daniels	.20
125	Paul Grant	.10
126	Voshon Lenard	.10
127	Shawn Kemp	.75
128	Antonio Davis	.10
129	Hakeem Olajuwon	.50
130	Danny Manning	.10
131	Bimbo Coles	.10
132	Tim Hardaway	.30
133	Lorenzo Williams	.10
134	Dan Majerle	.10
135	Bryant Stith	.10
136	Randy Brown	.10
137	Hubert Davis	.10
138	Gary Payton	.30
139	Rasheed Wallace	.10
140	Chris Robinson	.10
141	Doug Christie	.10
142	Brian Grant	.10
143	Isaiah Rider	.10
144	Kendall Gill	.10
145	Lorenzen Wright	.10
146	Ervin Johnson	.10
147	Monty Williams	.10
148	Keith Closs	.10
149	Tony Delk	.10
150	Hersey Hawkins	.10
151	Dean Garrett	.10
152	Cedric Henderson	.10
153	Detlef Schrempf	.10
154	Dana Barros	.10
155	Dee Brown	.10
156	Jayson Williams	.10
157	Charles Barkley	.20
158	Damon Stoudamire	.10
159	Scottie Pippen	.40
160	Joe Smith	.10
161	Antonio McDyess	.10
162	Jerry Stackhouse	.10
163	Dennis Rodman	.50
164	Shaquille O'Neal	.50
165	Grant Hill	.75

1998-99 Hoops Promo Sheet

This six-card promo sheet was distributed with sales material previous to the release of Series I. Cards are perforated with set information across the top of the sheet.

	MT
Complete Set (1):	3.00
NNO Grant Hill, Kevin Garnett, Tim Duncan, Allen Iverson, Keith Van Horn, Shaquille O'Neal	3.00

1998-99 SkyBox Premium Autographics

The third season for NBA Autographics included over 120 veterans and 20 rookies. Cards were inserted into NBA Hoops I and II (1:144), Thunder I and II (1:112), Metal Universe I and II (1:68), SkyBox Premium (1:68) and E-X2001 (1:48).

	MT
Common Player:	10.00
Inserted 1:144 Hoops	
Inserted 1:68 Metal	
Inserted 1:68 SkyBox	
Inserted 1:112 Thunder	
Blue Century Marks:	4x
Production 50 Sets	
Iverson signed an equal amount in blue and black.	
Tariq Abdul-Wahad	20.00
Shareef Abdur-Rahim	120.00
Cory Alexander	10.00
Ray Allen	25.00
Kenny Anderson	20.00
Nick Anderson	15.00
Chris Anstey	10.00
Isaac Austin	10.00
Vin Baker	60.00
Dana Barros	10.00
Tony Battie	20.00
Cory Benjamin	—
Travis Best	10.00
Mike Bibby	125.00
Chauncey Billups	20.00
Corie Blount	10.00
Terrell Brandon	—
P.J. Brown	10.00
Scott Burrell	10.00
Jason Caffey	15.00
Marcus Camby	40.00
Elden Campbell	10.00
Chris Carr	10.00
Cory Carr	—
Vince Carter	75.00
Kelvin Cato	15.00
Calbert Cheaney	10.00
Keith Closs	15.00
Antonio Daniels	30.00
Dale Davis	10.00
Ricky Davis	40.00
Andrew DeClerq	10.00
Tony Delk	10.00
Michael Dickerson	50.00
Michael Doleac	30.00
Bryce Drew	30.00
Tim Duncan	300.00
Howard Eisley	10.00
Danny Ferry	10.00
Derek Fisher	15.00
Danny Fortson	10.00
Adonal Foyle	10.00
Todd Fuller	10.00
Pat Garrity	25.00
Brian Grant	10.00
Tom Gugliotta	40.00
Tom Hammonds	10.00
Tim Hardaway	60.00
Matt Harpring	20.00
Othella Harrington	10.00
Hersey Hawkins	10.00
Cedric Henderson	20.00
Grant Hill	250.00
Tyrone Hill	10.00
Allan Houston	30.00
Juwan Howard	60.00
Larry Hughes	85.00
Zydrunas Ilgauskas	25.00
Allen Iverson	200.00
Bobby Jackson	20.00
Antawn Jamison	150.00
Anthony Johnson	10.00
Ervin Johnson	10.00
Larry Johnson	30.00
Eddie Jones	100.00
Adam Keefe	10.00
Shawn Kemp	150.00
Steve Kerr	20.00
Jason Kidd	120.00
Kerry Kittles	20.00
Brevin Knight	40.00
Raef LaFrentz	100.00
Felipe Lopez	50.00
George Lynch	10.00
Karl Malone	200.00
Danny Manning	15.00
Stephon Marbury	—
Donyell Marshall	10.00
Tony Massenberg	10.00
Walter McCarty	10.00
Jelani McCoy	30.00
Antonio McDyess	50.00
Tracy McGrady	75.00
Ron Mercer	100.00
Sam Mitchell	10.00
Nazr Mohammed	20.00
Alonzo Mourning	75.00
Chris Mullin	15.00
Dikembe Mutumbo	40.00
Hakeem Olajuwon	200.00
Michael Olowokandi	200.00
Elliot Perry	10.00
Bobby Phills	10.00
Eric Piatkowski	10.00
Paul Pierce	70.00
Scottie Pippen	200.00
Scot Pollard	20.00
Vitaly Potapenko	10.00
Brent Price	10.00
Theo Ratliff	10.00
Eldridge Recasner	10.00
Bryant Reeves	30.00
Glen Rice	50.00
Chris Robinson	10.00
David Robinson	200.00
Glenn Robinson	—
Dennis Rodman	300.00
Bryon Russell	10.00
Danny Schayes	10.00
Detlef Schrempf	25.00
Rony Seikaly	—
Clayton Shields	—
Brian Skinner	20.00
Reggie Slater	10.00
Joe Smith	50.00
Steve Smith	25.00
Rik Smits	15.00
Jerry Stackhouse	40.00
John Starks	25.00
Bryant Stith	10.00
Damon Stoudamire	100.00
Mark Strickland	10.00
Rod Strickland	20.00
Bob Sura	10.00
Tim Thomas	100.00
Robert Traylor	100.00
Gary Trent	10.00
Keith Van Horn	120.00
Jacque Vaughn	10.00
Antoine Walker	125.00
Eric Washington	10.00
Clarence Weatherspoon	15.00
David Wesley	10.00
Erik Williams	10.00
Jason Williams	40.00
Jayson Williams	20.00
Monty Williams	10.00
Walt Williams	20.00
Corliss Williamson	—
Lorenzen Wright	10.00

1998-99 Hoops Bams

Bams displays 10 of the game's top dunkers on silver holofoil designs. These inserts are numbered with a "B" suffix, sequentially numbered to 250 sets and found in packs of Series I.

		MT
Complete Set (10):		850.00
Common Player:		40.00
Production 250 Sets		
B1	Michael Jordan	300.00
B2	Kobe Bryant	200.00
B3	Allen Iverson	100.00
B4	Shaquille O'Neal	100.00
B5	Tim Duncan	150.00
B6	Shareef Abdur-Rahim	40.00
B7	Keith Van Horn	120.00
B8	Grant Hill	150.00
B9	Anfernee Hardaway	100.00
B10	Kevin Garnett	150.00

1998-99 Hoops Slam Bams

Slam Bams was a parallel set to the Bams insert, but was sequentially numbered to only 100 and found only in Series I hobby packs.

	MT
Slam Bam Cards:	2x
Production 100 Sets	

1998-99 Hoops Freshman Flashback

Freshman Flashback features some of the top newcomers in 1997-98. Cards show a close-up shot of the player on in a black-and-white format with a bronze tint over it. This 10-card set was sequentially numbered to 1,000 sets, numbered with a "FF" suffix and inserted in Series I.

		MT
Complete Set (10):		275.00
Common Player:		10.00
Production 1,000 Sets		
FF1	Tim Duncan	80.00
FF2	Keith Van Horn	65.00
FF3	Tim Thomas	40.00
FF4	Antonio Daniels	15.00
FF5	Brevin Knight	25.00
FF6	Danny Fortson	10.00
FF7	Maurice Taylor	25.00
FF8	Chauncey Billups	25.00
FF9	Bobby Jackson	15.00
FF10	Derek Anderson	25.00

1998-99 Hoops Prime Twine

Prime Twine captures 10 top players on cards die-cut inside and outside and printed on gold foil. Cards are numbered with a "PT" suffix, sequentially numbered to 500 sets and inserted in Series I packs.

		MT
Complete Set (10):		375.00
Common Player:		20.00
Production 500 Sets		
PT1	Dennis Rodman	70.00
PT2	Allen Iverson	80.00
PT3	Karl Malone	30.00
PT4	Antonio McDyess	20.00
PT5	Damon Stoudamire	20.00
PT6	Eddie Jones	40.00
PT7	Scottie Pippen	60.00
PT8	Shawn Kemp	60.00
PT9	Antoine Walker	80.00
PT10	Stephon Marbury	80.00

1998-99 Hoops Pump Up The Jam

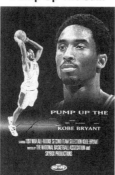

This 10-card insert was seeded every four packs of Series I. Cards show a close-up of the player on the right side, with an action shot on the left, all over a black background. Card backs are numbered with a "P" suffix.

		MT
Complete Set (10):		25.00
Common Player:		.50
Inserted 1:4		
BD1	Stephon Marbury	3.00
BD2	Allen Iverson	3.00
BD3	Grant Hill	4.00
BD4	Kobe Bryant	6.00
BD5	Michael Jordan	8.00
BD6	Antoine Walker	3.00
BD7	Shareef Abdur-Rahim	2.00
BD8	Shawn Kemp	2.00
BD9	Anfernee Hardaway	2.50
BD10	Antonio McDyess	.50

1998-99 Hoops Rejectors

Rejectors was a 10-card insert that featured top shot blockers on a horizontal format. Cards were numbered with a "R" suffix, sequentially numbered to 2,500 and inserted in Series I.

	MT
Complete Set (10):	100.00
Common Player:	3.00
Production 2,500 Sets	
R1	Dikembe Mutombo	3.00
R2	Marcus Camby	6.00
R3	Shaquille O'Neal	20.00
R4	Tim Duncan	30.00
R5	Shawn Bradley	3.00
R6	Chris Webber	10.00
R7	Patrick Ewing	3.00
R8	Kevin Garnett	30.00
R9	David Robinson	8.00
R10	Michael Stewart	3.00

1998-99 Hoops Shout Outs

Thirty Shout Outs inserts were inserted at a rate of one per pack in Series I. It showed emotional shots of the player and was numbered with a "SO" suffix.

		MT
Complete Set (30):		8.00
Common Player:		.10
Inserted 1:1		
SO1	Shareef Abdur-Rahim	.50
SO2	Chauncey Billups	.20
SO3	Terrell Brandon	.10
SO4	Patrick Ewing	.20
SO5	Michael Finley	.20
SO6	Adonal Foyle	.10
SO7	Kevin Garnett	1.00
SO8	Anfernee Hardaway	.60
SO9	Tim Hardaway	.25
SO10	Grant Hill	1.00
SO11	Tim Thomas	.50
SO12	Bobby Jackson	.10
SO13	Michael Jordan	2.00
SO14	Shawn Kemp	.50
SO15	Jason Kidd	.25
SO16	Karl Malone	.20
SO17	Stephon Marbury	.75
SO18	Anthony Mason	.10
SO19	Reggie Miller	.20
SO20	Dikembe Mutombo	.10
SO21	Kobe Bryant	1.25
SO22	Hakeem Olajuwon	.30
SO23	Gary Payton	.25
SO24	Michael Stewart	.10
SO25	David Robinson	.25
SO26	Maurice Taylor	.20
SO27	Keith Van Horn	.75
SO28	Antoine Walker	.75
SO29	Rasheed Wallace	.10
SO30	Juwan Howard	.20

1998 Pinnacle WNBA

Pinnacle WNBA returned for a second season with 85 cards, two parallel sets and three inserts. The set included 75 player cards and an eight-card Highlight subset along with two checklists. Cards featured a shot of the player with stats on the right side and the last name of the player in gold foil across the bottom. The two parallel sets were called Court Collection (1:3 packs) and Arena Collection (1:19). Insert sets in WNBA were: Coast to Coast, Number Ones and Planet Pinnacle.

		MT
Complete Set (85):		25.00
Common Player:		.10
Inserted 1:19		
1	Rhonda Blades	.50
2	Lisa Leslie	3.50
3	Jennifer Gillom	1.00
4	Ruthie Bolton-Holifield	1.75
5	Wendy Palmer	.75
6	Sophia Witherspoon	.30
7	Eva Nemcova	.30
8	Andrea Stinson	.75
9	Heidi Burge	.10
10	Cynthia Cooper	3.50
11	Christy Smith	.20
12	Penny Moore	.20
13	Penny Toler	.20
14	Bridget Pettis	.10
15	Tora Suber	.20
16	Elena Baranova	.75
17	Rebecca Lobo	3.00
18	Isabelle Fijalkowski	.10
19	Vicky Bullett	.20
20	Tina Thompson	.75
21	Andrea Kuklova	.10
22	Rita Williams	.50
23	Tamecka Dixon	.20
24	Michele Timms	1.00
25	Bridgette Gordon	.10
26	Tammi Reiss	.50
27	Kym Hampton	.20
28	Janice Braxton	.10
29	Rhonda Mapp	.10
30	Janeth Arcain	.10
31	Lynette Woodard	1.00
32	Tammy Jackson	.10
33	Haixia Zheng	.10
34	Toni Foster	.20
35	Chantel Tremitiere	.10
36	Vickie Johnson	.30
37	Michelle Edwards	.50
38	Wanda Guyton	.10
39	Kim Perrot	.30
40	Sheryl Swoopes	3.00
41	Merlakia Jones	.20
42	Teresa Weatherspoon	.40
43	Kim Williams	.10
44	Lady Hardmon	.10
45	Latasha Byears	.20
46	Umeki Webb	.10
47	Pamela McGee	.20
48	Nikki McCray	2.50
49	Cindy Brown	.10
50	Tiffany Woosley	.10
51	Andrea Congreaves	.10
52	Jamila Wideman	.20
53	Mwadi Mabika	.10
54	Murriel Page	.75
55	Mikiko Hagiwara	.10
56	Linda Burgess	.20
57	Olympia Scott	.10
58	Dena Head	.10
59	Quacy Barnes	.10
60	Suzie McConnell	.50
61	Trina Trice	.10
62	Rushia Brown	.10
63	Kisha Ford	.10
64	Sharon Manning	.10
65	Tangela Smith	.10
66	Jim Lewis	.10
67	Nancy Lieberman-Cline	1.50
68	Van Chancellor	.10
69	Denise Taylor	.10
70	Heidi VanDerveer	.10
71	Marynell Meadors	.10
72	Linda Hill-MacDonald	.10
73	Nancy Darsch	.10
74	Cheryl Miller	3.00
75	Julie Rousseau	.10
76	Rebecca Lobo (Highlights)	1.50
77	Jennifer Gillom (Highlights)	.50
78	Janeth Arcain (Highlights)	.10
79	Rhonda Mapp (Highlights)	.10
80	Cynthia Cooper (Highlights)	1.50
81	Tina Thompson (Highlights)	.30
82	Kym Hampton (Highlights)	.10
83	Cynthia Cooper (Highlights)	1.50
84	Checklist	.10
85	Checklist	.10

1998 Pinnacle WNBA Court

Court Collection was a parallel set of all 85 cards in Pinnacle WNBA. The cards featured a Court Collection logo and were seeded one per three packs.

	MT
Court Cards:	2x-4x

1998 Pinnacle WNBA Arena Collection

Arena Collection paralleled all 85 cards in Pinnacle WNBA. The cards included a prismatic foil and an Arena Collection logo and were seeded one per 19 packs.

	MT
Arena Cards:	8x-16x

1998 Pinnacle WNBA Coast to Coast

Coast to Coast displayed 10 of the top players in the WNBA that can take the ball up and down the court. These were seeded one per nine packs.

		MT
Complete Set (10):		35.00
Common Player:		1.00
Inserted 1:9		
1	Lynette Woodard	3.00
2	Nikki McCray	6.00
3	Lisa Leslie	12.00
4	Andrea Stinson	3.00
5	Eva Nemcova	1.00
6	Cynthia Cooper	12.00
7	Teresa Weatherspoon	1.00
8	Wendy Palmer	3.00
9	Ruthie Bolton-Holifield	6.00
10	Michele Timms	3.00

1998 Pinnacle WNBA Number Ones

This nine-card insert set highlighted some of the top picks for different WNBA franchises. Number Ones were were seeded every 19 packs.

		MT
Complete Set (9):		125.00
Common Player:		5.00
Inserted 1:19		
1	Margo Dydek	30.00
2	Ticia Penicheiro	10.00
3	Murriel Page	10.00
4	Korie Hlede	20.00
5	Allison Feaster	5.00
6	Cindy Blodgett	30.00
7	Tracy Reid	25.00
8	Alicia Thompson	5.00
9	Nyree Roberts	5.00

1998 Pinnacle WNBA Planet Pinnacle

Planet Pinnacle featured 10 top stars in a swirl design that featured the insert's name and a posed shot of the player inside. These were found every nine packs.

		MT
Complete Set (10):		25.00
Common Player:		.50
Inserted 1:9		
1	Korie Hlede	3.00
2	Eva Nemcova	.50
3	Haixia Zheng	.50
4	Michele Timms	3.00
5	Ticia Penicheiro	2.00
6	Elena Baranova	2.00
7	Rebecca Lobo	10.00
8	Isabelle Fijalkowski	.50
9	Andrea Congreaves	.50
10	Sheryl Swoopes	12.00

1998 Press Pass

One of the first sets to portray the 1998 NBA rookies, the set numbers 45 cards, with seven levels of inserts. The set also includes, in the base set, five cards featuring teammates, and a Mike Bibby checklist.

		MT
Complete Set (45):		15.00
Common Player:		.10
Wax Box:		60.00
1	Mike Bibby	2.00
2	Nazr Mohammed	.75
3	Raef Lafrentz	1.50
4	Vince Carter	1.50
5	Paul Pierce	1.00
6	Michael Olowokandi	2.50
7	Larry Hughes	1.00
8	Keon Clark	.50
9	Robert Traylor	1.25
10	Michael Doleac	.75
11	Pat Garrity	.20
12	Jason Williams	.75
13	Miles Simon	.20
14	Toby Bailey	.50
15	Bonzi Wells	.75
16	Tyrron Lue	.10
17	Matt Harpring	.10
18	J.R. Henderson	.20
19	Clayton Shields	.10
20	Michael Dickerson	.75
21	Saddi Washington	.10
22	Malcolm Johnson	.10
23	Cory Carr	.10
24	Brad Miller	.10
25	Mike Jones	.10
26	Brian Skinner	.10
27	Al Harrington	.50
28	Torraye Braggs	.10
29	Corey Louis	.10
30	DeMarco Johnson	.10
31	Anthony Carter	.10
32	Earl Boykins	.20
33	Roshown McCleod	.10
34	Casey Shaw	.10
35	Andrae Patterson	.10
36	Bryce Drew	.75
37	Jeff Sheppard	.20
38	Jahidi White	.20
39	Shammond Williams	.20
40	Ruben Patterson	.10
41	S. Williams, Carter	.75
42	Dickerson, Simon	.50
43	LaFrentz, Pierce	.75
44	Bailey, Henderson	.10
45	Checklist Bibby	1.00

1998 Press Pass In The Zone

In the Zone was a full 45-card parallel set in Press Pass that was seeded one per hobby pack. Cards featured silver foil instead of the gold foil used on regular-issue cards.

	MT
In The Zone Cards:	2x

1998 Press Pass Torquers

Torquers was a 45-card retail exclusive parallel set that featured red foil on each card instead of the blue foil used on regular-issue cards. These were inserted one per pack.

	MT
Torquer Cards:	2x

1998 Press Pass Reflectors

Reflectors was a 45-card parallel set to Press Pass. Cards had a protective plastic seal over the entire front that contained the insert name repeatedly. The cards were distinguished by the protective seal and a holographic finish and were seeded every 90 packs.

	MT
Reflector Cards:	20x-40x

1998 Press Pass Autographs

The 38-card set features the top rookies from the 1998 NBA Draft. As the first autographed cards of the rookies, the fronts have an action shot with the autograph across the

middle. The back has text congratulating the recipient. The cards are inserted at 1:36.

MIKE BIBBY

		MT
Common Player:		7.00
	Toby Bailey	10.00
	Mike Bibby	70.00
	Earl Boykins	10.00
	Torraye Braggs	7.00
	Cory Carr	7.00
	Anthony Carter	7.00
	Vince Carter	50.00
	Keon Clark	10.00
	Michael Dickerson	10.00
	Michael Doleac	20.00
	Bryce Drew	15.00
	Pat Garrity	7.00
	Matt Harpring	7.00
	Al Harrington	15.00
	J.R. Henderson	10.00
	Larry Hughes	30.00
	DeMarco Johnson	7.00
	Malcolm Johnson	7.00
	Mike Jones	7.00
	Raef Lafrentz	50.00
	Tyrron Lue	7.00
	Roshown McCleod	7.00
	Brad Miller	7.00
	Nazr Mohammed	15.00
	Michael Olowokandi	70.00
	Andrae Patterson	7.00
	Paul Pierce	20.00
	Casey Shaw	7.00
	Jeff Sheppard	7.00
	Clayton Shields	7.00
	Miles Simon	7.00
	Brian Skinner	7.00
	Robert Traylor	45.00
	Saddi Washington	7.00
	Bonzi Wells	7.00
	Jahidi White	7.00
	Jason Williams	20.00
	Shammond Williams	7.00

1998 Press Pass Fastbreak

PIERCE FASTBREAK

The 12-card set highlights 12 playmakers of the 1998 NBA Draft. Inserted at 1:12, the fronts have two player images, with the athlete's last name and the word "Fastbreak" on the lower half. The back has text on his collegiate career. The cards are numbered with the prefix "FB".

		MT
Complete Set (12):		45.00
Common Player:		2.00
1	Raef Lafrentz	7.00
2	Toby Bailey	2.00
3	Mike Bibby	12.00
4	Vince Carter	8.00
5	Paul Pierce	5.00
6	Michael Olowokandi	12.00
7	Keon Clark	3.00

8	Robert Traylor	7.00
9	Michael Doleac	4.00
10	Larry Hughes	5.00
11	Pat Garrity	2.00
12	Miles Simon	2.00

1998 Press Pass In Your Face

This set is made up of clear acetate cards, and number nine cards in all. Hobby only cards, the fronts hace a player ima This set features clear acetate cards that are hobby only. The nine-card set has a player image on the front silhouted against a clear background. The cards are inserted at 1:36, and are numbered with the prefix "IYF".

		MT
Complete Set (9):		75.00
Common Player:		2.50
1	Raef Lafrentz	15.00
2	Mike Bibby	20.00
3	Michael Dickerson	7.00
4	Paul Pierce	10.00
5	Pat Garrity	2.50
6	Matt Harpring	2.50
7	Robert Traylor	12.00
8	Brad Miller	2.50
9	Vince Carter	12.00

1998 Press Pass Jerseys

Authentic Game-Used Jersey

The five-card pack is prefixed with a "JC" in the numbering, and highlights five draft picks from the 1998 draft. The cards contain an actual piece of game-used jersey in the card. Insertion rate is 1:720.

		MT
Complete Set (5):		500.00
Common Player:		50.00
1	Michael Olowokandi	175.00
2	Vince Carter	125.00
3	Mike Bibby	150.00
4	Robert Traylor	100.00
5	Toby Bailey	50.00

1998 Press Pass Net Burners

The largest of Press Pass'98 basketball insert set at 36 cards, the set has a die-cut feature, with the player

portrayed in a net. The name appears in gold along the bottom. The back contains a quote on the player. The cards are inserted at 1:1.

MICHAEL OLOWOKANDI NET BURNERS

		MT
Complete Set (36):		25.00
Common Player:		.20
1	Mike Bibby	3.00
2	Nazr Mohammed	1.00
3	Raef Lafrentz	2.50
4	Vince Carter	2.50
5	Paul Pierce	1.75
6	Michael Olowokandi	4.00
7	Larry Hughes	2.00
8	Keon Clark	.75
9	Robert Traylor	2.00
10	Michael Doleac	1.00
11	Pat Garrity	.20
12	Saddi Washington	.20
13	Miles Simon	.20
14	Toby Bailey	.40
15	Bonzi Wells	1.00
16	Tyrron Lue	.20
17	Matt Harpring	.20
18	J.R. Henderson	.40
19	Clayton Shields	.20
20	Michael Dickerson	1.00
21	DeMarco Johnson	.20
22	Andrae Patterson	.20
23	Cory Carr	.20
24	Torraye Braggs	.20
25	Ruben Patterson	.20
26	Brian Skinner	.20
27	Bryce Drew	.75
28	Shammond Williams	.20
29	Corey Louis	.20
30	Tim Duncan	2.00
31	Keith Van Horn	1.50
32	Tim Thomas	1.00
33	Derek Anderson	.40
34	Brevin Knight	.40
35	Ron Mercer	1.25
36	Checklist Roshown McClood	.20

1998 Press Pass Real Deal Rookies

The nine-card set features the top rookies from the 1997 draft. The fronts have a color player image, with a black and white image in the background. The name of the player appears in silver foil along the side. The back has text and rookie season stats. The cards are numbered with the prefix "R", and inserted at 1:18.

		MT
Complete Set (9):		40.00
Common Player:		2.00
1	Tim Duncan	12.00
2	Keith Van Horn	10.00
3	Tim Thomas	6.00

4	Derek Anderson	3.00
5	Brevin Knight	3.00
6	Ron Mercer	8.00
7	Tracy McGrady	6.00
8	Danny Fortson	2.00
9	Maurice Taylor	3.00

1998 Press Pass Super Six

LARRY HUGHES SUPER SIX

The six-card set features the six players thought to excel right away. The set uses the holofoil inset cards, bordered in blue with the player's name in white along the left side. The back shows a color image, along with text. The cards are numbered with a prefix "S", and are inserted at 1:36.

		MT
Complete Set (6):		45.00
Common Player:		7.00
1	Raef Lafrentz	10.00
2	Larry Hughes	7.00
3	Mike Bibby	15.00
4	Vince Carter	10.00
5	Paul Pierce	7.00
6	Michael Olowokandi	15.00

1998 Press Pass Double Threat

Double Threat was the second Press Pass draft picks set of 1998, and contained 45 cards. The product added some new twists, with NBA veteran autographs, Game-used Jersey cards with a veteran and rookie and double-sided autographs. Double Threat was paralleled three times in an Alley Oop, Torquers and Foil set. Inserts included: Double Thread Jerseys, Dreammates, Jackpot, Player's Club Autographs, Rookie Jerseys, Rookie Script Autographs, Retros, Two-on-One and Veteran Approved Autographs.

		MT
Complete Set (45):		15.00
Common Player:		.10
Wax Box:		60.00
1	Michael Olowokandi	2.50
2	Mike Bibby	2.00
3	Raef LaFrentz	1.50
4	Vince Carter	1.50
5	Robert Traylor	1.25
6	Jason Williams	.75

7	Larry Hughes	1.00
8	Paul Pierce	1.00
9	Bonzi Wells	.75
10	Michael Doleac	.75
11	Keon Clark	.50
12	Michael Dickerson	.75
13	Matt Harpring	.10
14	Bryce Drew	.75
15	Pat Garrity	.20
16	Roshown McCleod	.10
17	Brian Skinner	.10
18	Tyron Lue	.10
19	Al Harrington	.50
20	Sam Jacobson	.10
21	Nazr Mohammed	.75
22	Ruben Patterson	.10
23	Shammond Williams	.20
24	Casey Shaw	.10
25	DeMarco Johnson	.10
26	Miles Simon	.20
27	Jahidi White	.20
28	Sean Marks	.10
29	Toby Bailey	.50
30	Andrae Patterson	.10
31	Tyson Wheeler	.10
32	Cory Carr	.10
33	J.R. Henderson	.20
34	Torraye Braggs	.10
35	Tim Duncan	2.00
36	Keith Van Horn	1.50
37	Ron Mercer	1.00
38	Stephon Marbury	.75
39	Ray Allen	.20
40	Glen Rice	.10
41	Tim Thomas	.75
42	Antoine Walker	.75
43	Kerry Kittles	.10
44	Shareef Abdur-Rahim	.10
45	Checklist Michael Olowokandi	1.25

1998 Press Pass Double Threat Alley-Oop

Alley-Oop was a 45-card hobby-only parallel set featuring each card printed with silver foil instead of the gold foil used on base cards. These parallel cards were inserted one per pack.

	MT
Alley-Oop Cards:	2x

1998 Press Pass Double Threat Torquers

Torquers was a 45-card parallel set to Double Threat and inserted one per retail pack. The cards featured blue foil instead of the gold foil used on regular-issue cards.

	MT
Torquer Cards:	2x

1998 Press Pass Double Threat Foils

Three Foils were issued in Double Threat and were inserted one per 180 packs. The cards, featuring the top three picks in the 1998 NBA Draft, were numbered with a "F" prefix.

	MT
Complete Set (3):	130.00
Common Player:	50.00
Inserted 1:180	
F1 Michael Olowokandi	70.00
F2 Mike Bibby	60.00
F3 Raef LaFrentz	50.00

1998 Press Pass Double Threat Double Thread Jerseys

This three card insert was numbered DD2-DD4, with no card DD1 ever issued. The cards featured a piece of game-used jersey from a draft pick and an NBA star on the same card. These were inserted one per 720 packs of Double Threat. Cards DD2 and DD4 were inserted into packs as redemption cards.

	MT
Complete Set (3):	550.00
Common Player:	100.00
Inserted 1:720	
DD2 Michael Olowokandi, Tim Duncan	300.00
DD3 Robert Traylor, Keith Van Horn	200.00
DD4 Vince Carter, Glen Rice	100.00

1998 Press Pass Double Threat Dreammates

Dreammates was a nine-card insert that matched an 1998 NBA Draft pick matched up with a NBA player. The cards were numbered with a "DM" prefix and inserted every 18 packs.

	MT
Complete Set (9):	45.00
Common Player:	2.50
Inserted 1:18	
DM1 Mike Bibby, Tim Duncan	15.00
DM2 Michael Olowokandi, Stephon Marbury	12.00
DM3 Larry Hughes, Tim Thomas	5.00
DM4 Vince Carter, Glen Rice	5.00
DM5 Robert Traylor, Ray Allen	5.00
DM6 Paul Pierce, Ron Mercer	5.00
DM7 Raef LaFrentz, Keith Van Horn	7.00
DM8 Michael Dickerson, Antoine Walker	2.50
DM9 Jason Williams, Shareef Abdur-Rahim	2.50

1998 Press Pass Double Threat Jackpot

Jackpot included eight top picks in the 1998 NBA Draft on foil-etched cards. Insert odds varied depending on the which pick the player was, with the highest picks being the most difficult to find. Ratios are as follows: J1A 1:720, J1B 1:360, J2A 1:180, J2B 1:90, J3A and J3B 1:45 and J4A and J4B 1:36.

	MT
Complete Set (8):	225.00
Common Player:	8.00
JP1A Michael Olowokandi	100.00
JP1B Mike Bibby	70.00
JP2A Raef LaFrentz	50.00
JP2B Vince Carter	25.00
JP3A Robert Traylor	15.00
JP3B Jason Williams	10.00
JP4A Larry Hughes	8.00
JP4B Paul Pierce	8.00

1998 Press Pass Double Threat Player's Club Autographs

Player's Club Autographs were sequentially numbered to 125 sets and inserted one per 360 hobby packs of Double Threat. This 13-card set was numbered with a "PC" prefix. Cards 1, 3, 5, 6, 8, 9, 11 and 12 were inserted as redemption cards.

	MT
Complete Set (13):	1000.00
Common Player:	30.00
PC1 Michael Olowokandi	175.00
PC2 Mike Bibby	175.00
PC3 Raef LaFrentz	125.00
PC4 Vince Carter	125.00
PC5 Robert Traylor	125.00
PC6 Jason Williams	75.00
PC7 Larry Hughes	100.00
PC8 Paul Pierce	100.00
PC9 Bonzi Wells	50.00
PC10 Michael Doleac	50.00
PC11 Keon Clark	50.00
PC12 Michael Dickerson	60.00
PC13 Matt Harpring	30.00

1998 Press Pass Double Threat Rookie Jerseys

Four different Rookie Jersey inserts were included in packs of Double Threat at a rate of one per 720 packs. The cards contained a piece of that player's game-used college jersey. Cards were numbered with a "JC" prefix and numbers 3 and 4 were included as redemptions.

	MT
Complete Set (4):	325.00
Common Player:	50.00
Inserted 1:720	
JC1 Raef LaFrentz	150.00
JC2 Pat Garrity	50.00
JC3 Paul Pierce	100.00
JC4 Michael Dickerson	75.00

1998 Press Pass Double Threat Rookie Script Autographs

Rookie Script Autographs were seeded one per 18 hobby packs and one per 36 retail packs. The cards are not numbered, but feature a white edge on the left side that the insert name is repeatedly printed in, with the player's signature.

	MT
Common Player:	7.00
Inserted 1:18 Hobby, 1:36 Retail	
Toby Bailey	10.00
Mike Bibby	60.00
Torraye Braggs	7.00
Cory Carr	7.00
Vince Carter	45.00
Keon Clark	10.00
Michael Dickerson	12.00
Michael Doleac	12.00
Bryce Drew	15.00
Pat Garrity	7.00
Matt Harpring	7.00
Al Harrington	12.00
J.R. Henderson	7.00
Larry Hughes	25.00
Sam Jacobson	7.00
DeMarco Johnson	7.00
Raef LaFrentz	45.00
Tyrron Lue	7.00
Sean Marks	7.00
Roshown McCleod	7.00
Nazr Mohammed	12.00
Michael Olowokandi	75.00
Andrae Patterson	7.00
Ruben Patterson	7.00
Paul Pierce	12.00
Casey Shaw	7.00
Miles Simon	7.00
Brian Skinner	7.00
Robert Traylor	45.00
Bonzi Wells	7.00
Tyson Wheeler	7.00
Jahidi White	7.00
Jason Williams	7.00
Shammond Williams	10.00

1998 Press Pass Double Threat Retros

mike bibby

Retros displayed 36 of the players in the base set on smaller, old-fashioned looking cards. The cards were numbered with a "R" prefix and inserted one per pack.

	MT
Complete Set (36):	25.00
Common Player:	.20
Inserted 1:1	
R1 Michael Olowokandi	4.00
R2 Mike Bibby	3.00
R3 Raef LaFrentz	2.00
R4 Vince Carter	2.00
R5 Robert Traylor	2.00
R6 Jason Williams	1.00
R7 Larry Hughes	1.50
R8 Paul Pierce	1.50
R9 Bonzi Wells	1.00
R10 Michael Doleac	.75
R11 Keon Clark	.40
R12 Michael Dickerson	.75
R13 Matt Harpring	.20
R14 Bryce Drew	.75
R15 Cory Carr	.20
R16 Andrae Patterson	.20
R17 Pat Garrity	.40
R18 Roshown McCleod	.20
R19 Brian Skinner	.20
R20 Tyrron Lue	.20
R21 Sam Jacobson	.20
R22 J.R. Henderson	.40
R23 Nazr Mohammed	.75
R24 Ruben Patterson	.20
R25 Shammond Williams	.40
R26 Toby Bailey	.40
R27 DeMarco Johnson	.20
R28 Miles Simon	.40
R29 Jahidi White	.40
R30 Tim Duncan	2.50
R31 Keith Van Horn	2.00
R32 Ron Mercer	1.50
R33 Stephon Marbury	1.00
R34 Ray Allen	.40
R35 Glen Rice	.20
R36 Checklist Mike Bibby	1.50

1998 Press Pass Double Threat Two-On-One

This 12-card insert featured plastic die-cut cards that fit together in threes. Numbered with a "TO" prefix, The card on each end features a single player, while the middle card features both players in the panel. Two-on-One inserts were seeded one per 12 packs.

	MT
Complete Set (12):	70.00
Common Player:	4.00
Inserted 1:12	
TO1 Raef LaFrentz	7.00
TO2 Raef LaFrentz, Keith Van Horn	5.00
TO3 Keith Van Horn	6.00
TO4 Michael Olowokandi	10.00
TO5 Michael Olowokandi, Tim Duncan	8.00
TO6 Tim Duncan	7.00
TO7 Mike Bibby	8.00
TO8 Mike Bibby, Stephon Marbury	7.00
TO9 Stephon Marbury	4.00
TO10 Vince Carter	6.00
TO11 Vince Carter, Antoine Walker	5.00
TO12 Antoine Walker	4.00

1998 Press Pass Double Threat Veteran Approved Autos.

This seven-card insert contained autographs from seven NBA players and were inserted one per 360 packs. The cards are not numbered, while Ray Allen, Kerry Kittles, Ron Mercer and Glen Rice were available through redemption cards.

	MT
Complete Set (7):	700.00
Common Player:	50.00
Inserted 1:360	
Ray Allen	75.00
Tim Duncan	150.00
Kerry Kittles	50.00
Stephon Marbury	125.00
Ron Mercer	100.00
Glen Rice	75.00
Antoine Walker	125.00

1998-99 SkyBox Thunder

This was the first year for the Thunder brand name, which replaced Z-Force. Series I had 125 cards, with the first 50 seeded four per pack, 51-100 seeded three per pack and 101-125 seeded one per pack. The set is paralleled in both Rave (numbered to 150) and Super Rave (numbered to

25) sets. Inserts in Series I include: Autographics, Boss, Bringin' It, Lift Off, Flight School and Noyz Boyz.

		MT
Complete Set (125):		30.00
Common Player (1-100):		.10
Common Player (101-125):		.25
#101-125 Inserted 1:1		
Wax Box:		50.00
1	Kerry Kittles	.20
2	Larry Johnson	.20
3	Hakeem Olajuwon	.50
4	Glenn Robinson	.20
5	Alonzo Mourning	.20
6	Reggie Miller	.20
7	Toni Kukoc	.20
8	Corliss Williamson	.10
9	Nick Van Exel	.20
10	Mookie Blaylock	.10
11	Michael Smith	.10
12	Avery Johnson	.10
13	Brian Williams	.10
14	Doug Christie	.10
15	Danny Fortson	.10
16	Michael Stewart	.10
17	Anthony Peeler	.10
18	Cedric Henderson	.10
19	Lamond Murray	.10
20	Walt Williams	.10
21	Samaki Walker	.10
22	David Wesley	.10
23	Maurice Taylor	.30
24	Todd Fuller	.10
25	Jeff Hornacek	.10
26	Danny Manning	.10
27	Detlef Schrempf	.10
28	Nick Anderson	.10
29	Ron Harper	.10
30	Brian Shaw	.10
31	Bryant Stith	.10
32	Chris Whitney	.10
33	Patrick Ewing	.20
34	Travis Knight	.10
35	Tracy McGrady	.75
36	Dan Majerle	.10
37	Dale Davis	.10
38	Kelvin Cato	.10
39	Zydrunas Ilgauskas	.20
40	Sean Elliott	.10
41	Tony Delk	.10
42	Bobby Phills	.10
43	Clifford Robinson	.10
44	Shawn Bradley	.10
45	Aaron McKie	.10
46	Mark Jackson	.10
47	P.J. Brown	.10
48	Armon Gilliam	.10
49	Ed Gray	.10
50	Olden Polynice	.10
51	Kendall Gill	.10
52	Bryon Russell	.10
53	Dale Ellis	.10
54	Mark Price	.10
55	Donyell Marshall	.10
56	John Starks	.10
57	Jerome Williams	.10
58	Rodney Rogers	.10
59	Michael Finley	.20
60	Marcus Camby	.20
61	Chris Anstey	.10
62	Rodrick Rhodes	.10
63	Derek Anderson	.30
64	Jermaine O'Neal	.10
65	Glen Rice	.20
66	Bryant Reeves	.10
67	Jalen Rose	.10
68	Calbert Cheaney	.10
69	Steve Smith	.10
70	Shandon Anderson	.10
71	Tony Battie	.10
72	Kenny Anderson	.10
73	Tim Hardaway	.30
74	Antonio Daniels	.20
75	Charles Barkley	.30
76	Chauncey Billups	.20
77	Lindsey Hunter	.10
78	Terrell Brandon	.20
79	Anthony Mason	.10
80	Elden Campbell	.10
81	Rasheed Wallace	.20
82	Erick Dampier	.10
83	Tracy Murray	.10
84	Sam Cassell	.10

85	Bobby Jackson	.20
86	Horace Grant	.10
87	Brent Price	.10
88	Allan Houston	.20
89	Brevin Knight	.30
90	Steve Nash	.10
91	Lorenzen Wright	.10
92	Hubert Davis	.10
93	Walter McCarty	.10
94	Jamal Mashburn	.20
95	Dikembe Mutombo	.20
96	Chris Carr	.10
97	Tariq Abdul-Wahad	.10
98	Chris Mullin	.20
99	Charlie Ward	.10
100	Tim Thomas	.75
101	Tim Duncan	2.25
102	Antoine Walker	1.50
103	Stephon Marbury	1.50
104	Ray Allen	.25
105	Shawn Kemp	1.00
106	Michael Jordan	4.50
107	Gary Payton	.50
108	Kobe Bryant	3.00
109	Karl Malone	.50
110	Kevin Garnett	2.25
111	Jason Kidd	.75
112	Dennis Rodman	1.50
113	Grant Hill	2.25
114	Keith Van Horn	1.75
115	Shareef Abdur-Rahim	1.00
116	Ron Mercer	1.50
117	Allen Iverson	1.00
118	Shaquille O'Neal	1.50
119	Anfernee Hardaway	1.50
120	Scottie Pippen	1.00
121	David Robinson	.50
122	Vin Baker	.75
123	John Stockton	.50
124	Eddie Jones	.75
125	Juwan Howard	.50

1998-99 SkyBox Thunder Rave

This 125-card parallel set was exclusively available in hobby packs and sequentially numbered to 150 sets. Cards feature prismatic silver foil on the front versus the gold foil used on base cards.

	MT
Rave Cards:	40x-80x

1998-99 SkyBox Thunder Super Rave

The 125-card set is also paralleled in Super Rave inserts, which are also hobby exclusive and sequentially numbered to 25 sets.

	MT
Super Rave Cards:	250x-500x

1998-99 SkyBox Thunder Boss

Boss was a 20-card insert that featured players on a sculpted card. These inserts were seeded one per 16 Series I packs and numbered with a "B" suffix.

		MT
Complete Set (20):		60.00
Common Player:		1.00
Inserted 1:16		
1	Shareef Abdur-Rahim	4.00
2	Vin Baker	3.00
3	Tim Duncan	8.00
4	Kevin Garnett	8.00
5	Tim Hardaway	2.00

6	Grant Hill	8.00
7	Michael Jordan	15.00
8	Shawn Kemp	4.00
9	Jason Kidd	3.00
10	Karl Malone	2.00
11	Stephon Marbury	5.00
12	Ron Mercer	5.00
13	Shaquille O'Neal	5.00
14	Gary Payton	2.00
15	Scottie Pippen	4.00
16	Glenn Robinson	1.00
17	John Stockton	2.00
18	Damon Stoudamire	2.00
19	Keith Van Horn	6.00
20	Antoine Walker	5.00

1998-99 SkyBox Thunder Bringin' It

Inserted into one per eight Series I packs, Bringin' It displays 10 top players. Cards arrived folded in half and can be opened to display a larger shot of the player over a multi-colored background.

		MT
Complete Set (10)		10.00
Common Player:		.50
Inserted 1:8		
1	Charles Barkley	.75
2	Anfernee Hardaway	2.50
3	Eddie Jones	1.25
4	Karl Malone	.75
5	Hakeem Olajuwon	1.00
6	Shaquille O'Neal	2.50
7	Scottie Pippen	1.75
8	Glen Rice	.50
9	David Robinson	.75
10	Dennis Rodman	2.50

1998-99 SkyBox Thunder Flight School

Flight School featured 12 players on cards that resembled viewfinders. Each had two magnified eyeholes that could be looked through to view a larger three-dimensional picture. This insert was seeded one per 96 packs of Series I and was numbered with a "FS" suffix.

		MT
Complete Set (12):		200.00
Common Player:		5.00
Inserted 1:96 Hobby		
1	Ray Allen	5.00
2	Kobe Bryant	35.00
3	Michael Finley	5.00
4	Kevin Garnett	25.00

5	Anfernee Hardaway	18.00
6	Grant Hill	25.00
7	Allen Iverson	18.00
8	Eddie Jones	10.00
9	Michael Jordan	50.00
10	Shawn Kemp	12.00
11	Antonio McDyess	5.00
12	Ron Mercer	18.00

1998-99 SkyBox Thunder Lift Off

Lift Off included 10 top players on a prismatic holofoil card. These were numbered with a "LO" suffix and inserted one per 56 packs of Series I.

		MT
Complete Set (10):		85.00
Common Player:		2.50
Inserted 1:56		
1	Shareef Abdur-Rahim	7.00
2	Ray Allen	2.50
3	Kobe Bryant	20.00
4	Tim Duncan	18.00
5	Allen Iverson	10.00
6	Kerry Kittles	2.50
7	Stephon Marbury	10.00
8	Ron Mercer	10.00
9	Keith Van Horn	14.00
10	Antoine Walker	10.00

1998-99 SkyBox Thunder Noyz Boyz

This 15-card insert is printed on a die-cut "Z" shape on an illusion stock with a material finish providing a 3-D effect. The cards are numbered with a "NB" suffix and inserted one per 300 packs of Series I.

		MT
Complete Set (15):		700.00
Common Player:		12.00
Inserted 1:300		
1	Shareef Abdur-Rahim	35.00
2	Ray Allen	12.00
3	Kobe Bryant	100.00
4	Tim Duncan	75.00
5	Kevin Garnett	75.00
6	Anfernee Hardaway	50.00
7	Grant Hill	75.00
8	Allen Iverson	50.00
9	Michael Jordan	150.00
10	Stephon Marbury	60.00
11	Shaquille O'Neal	50.00
12	Scottie Pippen	35.00
13	Dennis Rodman	50.00
14	Keith Van Horn	50.00
15	Antoine Walker	60.00

1998 SP

This 62-card set featured top college players available for the 1998 NBA Draft. The cards are printed on a foil-board stock that includes a framed picture of the player over a basketball background. The set was paralleled in a President's Edition parallel that is sequentially numbered to 10 sets. SP Top Prospects also utilizes Upper Deck's relationship with Michael Jordan to produce two Jordan-driven inserts - Phi Beta Jordan and Carolina Heroes. Others inserts include: Vital Signs autographs and Destination: Stardom.

		MT
Complete Set (62):		50.00
Common Player:		.20
Wax Box:		100.00
1	Antawn Jamison	4.00
2	Vince Carter	3.00
3	Michael Olowokandi	5.00
4	Paul Pierce	2.50
5	Korleone Young	.20
6	Rashard Lewis	.40
7	Miles Simon	.40
8	Al Harrington	1.25
9	Robert Traylor	3.00
10	Ansu Sesay	.40
11	DeMarco Johnson	.20
12	Earl Boykins	.40
13	Michael Doleac	1.25
14	Felipe Lopez	.40
15	Cory Carr	.20
16	J.R. Henderson	.40
17	Michael Dickerson	1.50
18	Jason Williams	2.00
19	Bonzi Wells	1.50
20	Matt Harpring	.20
21	Pat Garrity	.20
22	Ricky Davis	.20
23	Tyrron Lue	.20
24	Corey Benjamin	.20
25	Jelani McCoy	.40
26	Shammond Williams	.20
27	Toby Bailey	.20
28	Saddi Washington	.20
29	Zendon Hamilton	.20
30	Steve Wojciechowski	.20
31	Nazr Mohammed	.20
32	Andrae Patterson	.20
33	Ryan Bowen	.20
34	Anthony Carter	.20
35	Jarod Stevenson	.20
36	Casey Shaw	.20
37	Brad Miller	.20
38	Charles Jones	.20
39	Bryce Drew	.20
40	Jeff Sheppard	.20
41	Antawn Jamison	2.00
42	Vince Carter	1.50
43	Michael Olowokandi	2.50
44	Paul Pierce	1.25
45	Rashard Lewis	.20
46	Robert Traylor	1.50
47	Michael Doleac	.50
48	Felipe Lopez	.20
49	Michael Dickerson	.75
50	Jason Williams	1.00
51	Bonzi Wells	.75
52	Matt Harpring	.20
53	Ricky Davis	.20
54	Tyrron Lue	.20
55	Corey Benjamin	.20
56	Ansu Sesay	.20
57	Pat Garrity	.20
58	Shammond Williams	.40
59	Nazr Mohammed	.20
60	Bryce Drew	.20
61	Michael Olowokandi	2.50
62	Antawn Jamison	2.00

1998 SP Carolina Heroes

This 10-card insert show-cases top players that have played for North Carolina. It includes four Michael Jordan cards and two each of three other 1998 former North Carolina players drafted in 1998. Carolina Heroes are printed on etched foil, numbered with a "H" prefix and inserted one per 11 packs.

		MT
Complete Set (10):		85.00
Common Player:		2.50
Inserted 1:11		
H1	Michael Jordan	20.00
H2	Michael Jordan	20.00
H3	Michael Jordan	20.00
H4	Michael Jordan	20.00
H5	Antawn Jamison	10.00
H6	Antawn Jamison	10.00
H7	Vince Carter	7.00
H8	Vince Carter	7.00
H9	Shammond Williams	2.50
H10	Shammond Williams	2.50

1998 SP Destination: Stardom

Destination: Stardom featured 20 draft picks on a thick, wood-like background with a white frame. The cards were inserted one per 23 packs.

		MT
Complete Set (20):		150.00
Common Player:		5.00
Inserted 1:23		
1	Antawn Jamison	40.00
2	Vince Carter	30.00
3	Michael Olowokandi	50.00
4	Paul Pierce	12.50
5	Rashard Lewis	5.00
6	Robert Traylor	15.00
7	Michael Doleac	5.00
8	Felipe Lopez	5.00
9	Pat Garrity	5.00
10	Michael Dickerson	8.00
11	Jason Williams	10.00
12	Bonzi Wells	8.00
13	Matt Harpring	5.00
14	Ricky Davis	5.00
15	Corey Benjamin	5.00
16	Tyron Lue	5.00
17	Al Harrington	8.00
18	Ansu Sesay	5.00
19	Nazr Mohammed	5.00
20	Bryce Drew	5.00

1998 SP Phi Beta Jordan

Phi Beta Jordan displayed 23 cards of Michael Jordan in a North Carolina uniform on foil stock. The cards are numbered with a "J" prefix and inserted every two packs.

		MT
Complete Set (23):		40.00
Common Player:		2.00
Inserted 1:2		
J1	Michael Jordan	2.00
J2	Michael Jordan	2.00
J3	Michael Jordan	2.00
J4	Michael Jordan	2.00
J5	Michael Jordan	2.00
J6	Michael Jordan	2.00
J7	Michael Jordan	2.00
J8	Michael Jordan	2.00
J9	Michael Jordan	2.00
J10	Michael Jordan	2.00
J11	Michael Jordan	2.00
J12	Michael Jordan	2.00
J13	Michael Jordan	2.00
J14	Michael Jordan	2.00
J15	Michael Jordan	2.00
J16	Michael Jordan	2.00
J17	Michael Jordan	2.00
J18	Michael Jordan	2.00
J19	Michael Jordan	2.00
J20	Michael Jordan	2.00
J21	Michael Jordan	2.00
J22	Michael Jordan	2.00
J23	Michael Jordan	2.00

1998 SP Vital Signs

Vital Signs featured autographs from 19 top draft picks, as well as a Michael Jordan autograph numbered to 23. The cards look similar to base cards in design, but contain a closer shot of the player in the box and a white background within the photo box. These were inserted one per 12 packs.

		MT
Complete Set (20):		400.00
Common Player:		7.00
MJ	Michael Jordan	—
MO	Michael Olowokandi	70.00
AJ	Antawn Jamison	70.00
VC	Vince Carter	45.00
RT	Robert Traylor	45.00
JW	Jason Williams	25.00
PP	Paul Pierce	45.00
BW	Bonzi Wells	12.00
DO	Michael Doleac	12.00
MD	Michael Dickerson	20.00
MH	Matt Harpring	10.00
FL	Felipe Lopez	12.00
AH	Al Harrington	15.00

AS	Ansu Sesay	7.00
RL	Rashard Lewis	12.00
DJ	DeMarco Johnson	7.00
KY	Korleone Young	10.00
MS	Miles Simon	12.00
CC	Cory Carr	7.00
JR	J.R. Henderson	10.00
EB	Earl Boykins	7.00

1998-99 Topps

The 110-card set contain 109 player cards and one checklist. Cards featured a color action shot on the front with the name across the bottom in gold. Backs show a headshot and statistics. Inserts in Series I include: Apparitions, Autographs, Cornerstones, Draft Redemptions, Emissaries, Roundball Royalty, Roundball Royalty Refractors and Season's Best.

		MT
Complete Set (110):		10.00
Common Player:		.10
Wax Box:		40.00
1	Scottie Pippen	.75
2	Shareef Abdur-Rahim	.75
3	Rod Strickland	.20
4	Keith Van Horn	1.50
5	Ray Allen	.30
6	Chris Mullin	.20
7	Anthony Parker	.10
8	Lindsey Hunter	.10
9	Mario Elie	.10
10	Jerry Stackhouse	.20
11	Eldridge Recasner	.10
12	Jeff Hornacek	.10
13	Chris Webber	.40
14	Lee Mayberry	.10
15	Erick Strickland	.10
16	Arvydas Sabonis	.10
17	Tim Thomas	.75
18	Luc Longley	.10
19	Detlef Schrempf	.10
20	Alonzo Mourning	.20
21	Adonal Foyle	.10
22	Tony Battie	.20
23	Robert Horry	.10
24	Derek Harper	.10
25	Jamal Mashburn	.10
26	Elliott Perry	.10
27	Jalen Rose	.20
28	Joe Smith	.20
29	Henry James	.10
30	Travis Knight	.10
31	Tom Gugliotta	.20
32	Chris Anstey	.20
33	Antonio Daniels	.20
34	Elden Campbell	.10
35	Charlie Ward	.10
36	Eddie Johnson	.10
37	John Wallace	.10
38	Antonio Davis	.10
39	Antoine Walker	1.25
40	Patrick Ewing	.20
41	Doug Christie	.10
42	Andrew Lang	.10
43	Joe Dumars	.20
44	Jaren Jackson	.10
45	Loy Vaught	.10
46	Allan Houston	.20
47	Mark Jackson	.10
48	Tracy Murray	.10
49	Tim Duncan	2.00
50	Micheal Williams	.10
51	Steve Nash	.20
52	Clyde Drexler	.30
53	Sam Cassell	.10
54	Voshon Lenard	.10
55	Dikembe Mutombo	.20
56	Malik Sealy	.10
57	Dell Curry	.10
58	Stephon Marbury	1.25
59	Tariq Abdul-Wahad	.20
60	Isaiah Rider	.10
61	Kelvin Cato	.20
62	LaPhonso Ellis	.10
63	Jim Jackson	.20
64	Greg Ostertag	.10

65	Glenn Robinson	.20
66	Chris Carr	.10
67	Marcus Camby	.20
68	Kobe Bryant	1.75
69	Bobby Jackson	.20
70	B.J. Armstrong	.10
71	Alan Henderson	.10
72	Terry Davis	.10
73	John Stockton	.20
74	Lamond Murray	.10
75	Mark Price	.10
76	Rex Chapman	.10
77	Michael Jordan	3.00
78	Terry Cummings	.10
79	Dan Majerle	.10
80	Charles Outlaw	.10
81	Michael Finley	.20
82	Vin Baker	.30
83	Clifford Robinson	.10
84	Greg Anthony	.10
85	Brevin Knight	.30
86	Jacque Vaughn	.20
87	Bobby Phills	.10
88	Sherman Douglas	.10
89	Kevin Johnson	.10
90	Mahmoud Abdul-Rauf	.10
91	Lorenzen Wright	.10
92	Eric Williams	.10
93	Will Perdue	.10
94	Charles Barkley	.30
95	Kendall Gill	.10
96	Wesley Person	.10
97	Buck Williams	.10
98	Erick Dampier	.10
99	Nate McMillan	.10
100	Sean Elliott	.10
101	Rasheed Wallace	.10
102	Zydrunas Ilgauskas	.20
103	Eddie Jones	.40
104	Ron Mercer	1.00
105	Horace Grant	.10
106	Corliss Williamson	.10
107	Anthony Mason	.10
108	Mookie Blaylock	.10
109	Dennis Rodman	1.00
110	Checklist	.10

1998-99 Topps Promos

This six-card set was distributed to dealers and members of the media to promote the 1998-99 Topps Basketball set. Cards were identical to the base cards, but were distributed in a plastic sealed wrap with sales material.

		MT
Complete Set (6):		4.00
Common Player:		.25
2	Shareef Abdur-Rahim	1.00
13	Chris Webber	.50
39	Antoine Walker	1.50
40	Patrick Ewing	.25
82	Vin Baker	.50
103	Eddie Jones	.75

1998-99 Topps Apparitions

This 15-card insert set captured top NBA players on silver etched foil, with the insert name in large letters across the top. Cards are numbered with a "A" prefix and inserted one per 36 retail packs in Series I.

		MT
Complete Set (15):		120.00
Common Player:		1.50
Inserted 1:36 Retail		
A1	Kobe Bryant	25.00
A2	Stephon Marbury	12.00
A3	Brent Barry	1.50
A4	Karl Malone	4.00
A5	Shaquille O'Neal	10.00
A6	Chris Webber	5.00
A7	Shawn Kemp	8.00
A8	Hakeem Olajuwon	5.00
A9	Anfernee Hardaway	10.00
A10	Michael Finley	1.50
A11	Keith Van Horn	12.00
A12	Kevin Garnett	15.00
A13	Vin Baker	4.00
A14	Tim Duncan	15.00
A15	Michael Jordan	40.00

1998-99 Topps Autographs

These cards are hobby-exclusive featuring eight top players in the NBA. The eight-card set is inserted at 1:329, and include a stamp insuring its authenticity from the Topps company. The cards are pre-fixed with the letters "AG".

		MT
Complete Set (8):		475.00
Common Player:		25.00
AG1	Joe Smith	25.00
AG2	Kobe Bryant	150.00
AG3	Stephon Marbury	75.00
AG4	Dikembe Mutombo	25.00
AG5	Shareef Abdur-Rahim	60.00
AG6	Eddie Jones	60.00
AG7	Keith Van Horn	100.00
AG8	Glen Rice	35.00

1998-99 Topps Cornerstones

This 15-card set highlights the young players NBA teams build their futures around. Players with five years or less experience in the league are used. The cards are inserted at 1:36, and contain the prefix "C" in the numbering.

		MT
Complete Set (15):		100.00
Common Player:		1.50
C1	Keith Van Horn	12.00
C2	Kevin Garnett	15.00
C3	Shareef Abdur-Rahim	8.00
C4	Antoine Walker	12.00
C5	Allen Iverson	12.00
C6	Grant Hill	15.00
C7	Marcus Camby	1.50
C8	Stephon Marbury	12.00
C9	Kobe Bryant	20.00
C10	Bobby Jackson	1.50
C11	Kerry Kittles	1.50
C12	Ron Mercer	10.00
C13	Eddie Jones	4.00
C14	Tim Thomas	8.00
C15	Tim Duncan	20.00

1998-99 Topps Draft Redemption

This 29-card insert was seeded one per 18 Series I packs. Cards featured the words "1998 NBA Draft Redemption" in large white letters, with a Draft Pick 1-29 included. The cards could be redeemed for the corresponding draft choice before the deadline of 4/1/99.

		MT
Complete Set (29):		120.00
Common Player:		1.50
Inserted 1:18		
1	Michael Olowokandi	20.00
2	Mike Bibby	15.00
3	Raef LaFrentz	10.00
4	Antawn Jamison	15.00
5	Vince Carter	12.00
6	Robert Traylor	10.00
7	Jason Williams	6.00
8	Larry Hughes	8.00
9	Dirk Nowitzki	4.00
10	Paul Pierce	10.00
11	Bonzi Wells	4.00
12	Michael Doleac	3.00
13	Keon Clark	4.00
14	Michael Dickerson	5.00
15	Matt Harpring	3.00
16	Bryce Drew	3.00
17	Radoslav Nesterovic	1.50
18	Mirsad Turkcan	1.50
19	Pat Garrity	1.50
20	Roshown McLeod	1.50
21	Ricky Davis	4.00
22	Brian Skinner	3.00
23	Tyrron Lue	1.50
24	Felipe Lopez	4.00
25	Al Harrington	4.00
26	Cam Jacobson	1.50
27	Vladimir Stepania	1.50
28	Corey Benjamin	3.00
29	Nazr Mohammed	3.00

1998-99 Topps Emissaries

The Emissaries set features players who have represented their country in some form. The 20-card set has a gold map in the background on the front, with a color image of a player in the foreground. The backs contain text on their international experience. Cards are inserted at 1:24, and numbered with the prefix "E".

		MT
Complete Set (20):		90.00
Common Player:		1.50
E1	Scottie Pippen	10.00
E2	Karl Malone	4.00
E3	Chris Webber	6.00
E4	Anfernee Hardaway	15.00
E5	Detlef Schrempf	1.50
E6	Mitch Richmond	3.00
E7	Vlade Divac	1.50
E8	Shaquille O'Neal	15.00
E9	Luc Longley	1.50
E10	Grant Hill	20.00
E11	Christian Laettner	1.50
E12	Gary Payton	4.00
E13	Patrick Ewing	3.00
E14	Shawn Kemp	10.00
E15	Toni Kukoc	1.50
E16	David Robinson	5.00
E17	Hakeem Olajuwon	7.00
E18	Charles Barkley	5.00
E19	John Stockton	3.00
E20	Arvydas Sabonis	1.50

1998-99 Topps Roundball Royalty

The 20-card set highlights 20 of the best players in the NBA. The fronts have a gray diamond background, with the player in between the words "Roundball Royalty". The back has a picture frame around another player image, with text at the bottom. The cards are inserted at 1:36, and prefixed with a "R" in the numbering.

		MT
Complete Set (20):		150.00
Common Player:		2.00
Refractors:		3x
R1	Michael Jordan	40.00
R2	Kevin Garnett	20.00
R3	David Robinson	5.00
R4	Allen Iverson	12.00
R5	Hakeem Olajuwon	7.00
R6	Anfernee Hardaway	12.00
R7	Gary Payton	4.00
R8	Scottie Pippen	10.00
R9	Shaquille O'Neal	12.00
R10	Mitch Richmond	3.00
R11	John Stockton	3.00
R12	Grant Hill	20.00
R13	Charles Barkley	5.00
R14	Dikembe Mutombo	2.00
R15	Karl Malone	4.00
R16	Shawn Kemp	10.00
R17	Patrick Ewing	3.00
R18	Kobe Bryant	25.00
R19	Terrell Brandon	2.00
R20	Vin Baker	4.00

1998-99 Topps Season's Best

This 30-card set included the 25 best players by position, and five of the top rookies. Six themes range in the set, from Postmen to Navigators. The cards have the theme in writing along the top, with last season's numbers on the back. Insertion rate is 1:12, and have the prefix "SB" in the numbering.

		MT
Complete Set (30):		75.00
Common Player:		1.00
SB1	Rod Strickland	2.00
SB2	Gary Payton	3.00
SB3	Tim Hardaway	2.00
SB4	Stephon Marbury	8.00
SB5	Sam Cassell	1.00
SB6	Michael Jordan	20.00
SB7	Mitch Richmond	2.00
SB8	Steve Smith	1.00
SB9	Ray Allen	2.00
SB10	Isaiah Rider	1.00
SB11	Grant Hill	10.00
SB12	Kevin Garnett	10.00
SB13	Shareef Abdur-Rahim	5.00
SB14	Glenn Robinson	2.00
SB15	Michael Finley	2.00
SB16	Karl Malone	3.00
SB17	Tim Duncan	15.00
SB18	Antoine Walker	8.00
SB19	Chris Webber	3.00
SB20	Vin Baker	3.00
SB21	Shaquille O'Neal	6.00
SB22	David Robinson	3.00
SB23	Alonzo Mourning	2.00
SB24	Dikembe Mutombo	1.00
SB25	Hakeem Olajuwon	4.00
SB26	Tim Duncan	15.00
SB27	Keith Van Horn	8.00
SB28	Zydrunas Ilgauskas	2.00
SB29	Brevin Knight	3.00
SB30	Bobby Jackson	2.00

1998 Topps Golden Greats

Golden Greats included 18 of the greatest NBA players of all-time. The set utilized a combination of Kodamotion technology with Topps Super-Color color enhancement process to provide a finished product that allowed collectors to view three to four seconds of real game footage. Special laser-cut versions of each card were also randomly inserted one per 36 packs. Topps produced a very small quantity of Golden Greats due to limited orders. Each pack contained one card and carried a suggested retail price of $9.99.

		MT
Complete Set (18):		160.00
Common Player:		7.00
Laser Cut Cards:		2x-4x
Inserted 1:36		
Wax Box:		130.00
1	Kareem Abdul-Jabbar	12.00
2	Elgin Baylor	7.00
3	Larry Bird	16.00
4	Wilt Chamberlain	16.00
5	Bob Cousy	10.00
6	Julius Erving	14.00
7	Walt Frazier	7.00
8	George Gervin	7.00
9	John Havlicek	10.00
10	Magic Johnson	16.00
11	Kevin McHale	7.00
12	Earl Monroe	7.00
13	Willis Reed	7.00
14	Oscar Robertson	12.00
15	Bill Russell	16.00
16	Bill Walton	10.00
17	Jerry West	14.00
18	Rick Barry	7.00

1998-99 UD Choice Preview

This 55-card set contained a sampling of the 1998-99 UD Choice Series I set. The cards were identified by the word "PREVIEW" stamped in gold foil at the top of the card fronts. UD Choice Preview was distributed in seven-card packs before the release of the regular set. Each pack contained one Michael Jordan NBA Finals Shots insert and six Preview cards. While regular packs retailed for 79 cents, special retail-only ANCO packs arrived in six different can variations, each featuring Jordan on the outside and a Preview pack inside. These can-packs carried a suggested retail price of $1.97.

		MT
Complete Set (55):		10.00
Common Player:		.05
Wax Box:		12.00
1	Dikembe Mutombo	.10
3	Mookie Blaylock	.05
7	Ron Mercer	.75
9	Walter McCarty	.05
13	Anthony Mason	.05
14	Glen Rice	.20
18	Toni Kukoc	.10
23	Michael Jordan	2.50
26	Zydrunas Ilgauskas	.10
27	Cedric Henderson	.10
29	Michael Finley	.10
32	Hubert Davis	.05
34	Bobby Jackson	.10
37	Danny Fortson	.05
41	Grant Hill	1.25
43	Jerome Williams	.05
45	Erick Dampier	.05
48	Donyell Marshall	.05
50	Charles Barkley	.30
51	Hakeem Olajuwon	.40
56	Reggie Miller	.10
60	Chris Mullin	.10
64	Eric Piatkowski	.05
65	Maurice Taylor	.20
68	Shaquille O'Neal	.75
69	Kobe Bryant	1.50
74	Alonzo Mourning	.20
75	Tim Hardaway	.20
79	Ray Allen	.10
80	Terrell Brandon	.10
84	Stephon Marbury	.75
85	Kevin Garnett	1.25
89	Keith Van Horn	1.00
90	Sam Cassell	.05
95	Patrick Ewing	.20
97	John Starks	.05
100	Anfernee Hardaway	.75
101	Nick Anderson	.05
105	Allen Iverson	.50
110	Jason Kidd	.30
117	Isaiah Rider	.05
118	Rasheed Wallace	.05
121	Corliss Williamson	.05
123	Billy Owens	.05
126	Tim Duncan	1.25
127	Sean Elliott	.05
131	Vin Baker	.20
135	Gary Payton	.20
137	Chauncey Billups	.20
142	John Stockton	.10
143	Karl Malone	.20
148	Bryant Reeves	.05
149	Shareef Abdur-Rahim	.50
152	Chris Webber	.20
153	Juwan Howard	.10

1998-99 UD Choice Preview Michael Jordan NBA Finals Shots

This 10-card insert set was found exclusively in packs of UD Choice Preview. It features some of Jordan's most memorable shots during the NBA Finals.

	MT
Complete Set (10):	30.00
Common Player:	3.00
Inserted 1:1	

1998-99 UD Choice

Upper Deck changed its Collector's Choice brand name to UD Choice for 1998-99. Series I included 200 cards, with 30 NBA Flash Stats and 13 Year in Review subset cards. The set arrived with two parallel sets, including Choice Reserve and Prime Choice Reserve (100 numbered hobby sets). Inserts in Series I are: Mini Bobbing Heads, StarQuest and Draw Your Own Trading Card.

		MT
Complete Set (200):		15.00
Common Player:		.10
Wax Box:		40.00
1	Dikembe Mutombo	.20
2	Alan Henderson	.10
3	Mookie Blaylock	.10
4	Ed Gray	.10
5	Eldridge Recasner	.10
6	Kenny Anderson	.10
7	Ron Mercer	.75
8	Dana Barros	.10
9	Walter McCarty	.10
10	Travis Knight	.10
11	Andrew DeClercq	.10
12	David Wesley	.10
13	Anthony Mason	.10
14	Glen Rice	.20
15	J.R. Reid	.10
16	Bobby Phills	.10
17	Dell Curry	.10
18	Toni Kukoc	.20
19	Randy Brown	.10
20	Ron Harper	.10
21	Keith Booth	.10
22	Scott Burrell	.10
23	Michael Jordan	2.50
24	Derek Anderson	.30
25	Brevin Knight	.30
26	Zydrunas Ilgauskas	.20
27	Cedric Henderson	.20
28	Vitaly Potapenko	.10
29	Michael Finley	.20
30	Erick Strickland	.10
31	Shawn Bradley	.10
32	Hubert Davis	.10
33	Khalid Reeves	.10
34	Bobby Jackson	.20
35	Tony Battie	.20
36	Bryant Stith	.10
37	Danny Fortson	.20
38	Dean Garrett	.10
39	Eric Williams	.10
40	Brian Williams	.10
41	Grant Hill	1.25
42	Lindsey Hunter	.10
43	Jerome Williams	.10
44	Eric Montross	.10
45	Erick Dampier	.10
46	Muggsy Bogues	.10
47	Tony Delk	.10
48	Donyell Marshall	.10
49	Bimbo Coles	.10
50	Charles Barkley	.30
51	Hakeem Olajuwon	.40
52	Brent Price	.10
53	Mario Elie	.10
54	Rodrick Rhodes	.10
55	Kevin Willis	.10
56	Reggie Miller	.20
57	Jalen Rose	.10
58	Mark Jackson	.10
59	Dale Davis	.10
60	Chris Mullin	.10
61	Derrick McKey	.10
62	Lorenzen Wright	.10
63	Rodney Rogers	.10
64	Eric Piatkowski	.10
65	Maurice Taylor	.30
66	Isaac Austin	.10
67	Corie Blount	.10
68	Shaquille O'Neal	.75
69	Kobe Bryant	1.50
70	Robert Horry	.10
71	Sean Rooks	.10
72	Derek Fisher	.10
73	P.J. Brown	.10
74	Alonzo Mourning	.20
75	Tim Hardaway	.20
76	Voshon Lenard	.10
77	Dan Majerle	.10
78	Ervin Johnson	.10
79	Ray Allen	.20
80	Terrell Brandon	.20
81	Tyrone Hill	.10
82	Elliot Perry	.10
83	Anthony Peeler	.10
84	Stephon Marbury	1.00
85	Kevin Garnett	1.25
86	Paul Grant	.10
87	Chris Carr	.10
88	Michael Williams	.10
89	Keith Van Horn	1.00
90	Sam Cassell	.10
91	Kendall Gill	.10
92	Chris Gatling	.10
93	Kerry Kittles	.20
94	Allan Houston	.20
95	Patrick Ewing	.20
96	Charles Oakley	.10

#	Player	Price
97	John Starks	.10
98	Charlie Ward	.10
99	Chris Mills	.10
100	Anfernee Hardaway	.75
101	Nick Anderson	.10
102	Mark Price	.10
103	Horace Grant	.10
104	David Benoit	.10
105	Allen Iverson	1.00
106	Joe Smith	.20
107	Tim Thomas	.50
108	Brian Shaw	.10
109	Aaron McKie	.10
110	Jason Kidd	.40
111	Danny Manning	.10
112	Steve Nash	.20
113	Rex Chapman	.10
114	Dennis Scott	.10
115	Antonio McDyess	.20
116	Damon Stoudamire	.30
117	Isaiah Rider	.10
118	Rasheed Wallace	.10
119	Kelvin Cato	.10
120	Jermaine O'Neal	.10
121	Corliss Williamson	.10
122	Olden Polynice	.10
123	Billy Owens	.10
124	Lawrence Funderburke	.10
125	Anthony Johnson	.10
126	Tim Duncan	1.25
127	Sean Elliott	.10
128	Avery Johnson	.10
129	Vinny Del Negro	.10
130	Monty Williams	.10
131	Vin Baker	.20
132	Hersey Hawkins	.10
133	Nate McMillan	.10
134	Detlef Schrempf	.10
135	Gary Payton	.30
136	Jim McIlvaine	.10
137	Chauncey Billups	.30
138	Doug Christie	.10
139	John Wallace	.10
140	Tracy McGrady	.50
141	Dee Brown	.10
142	John Stockton	.20
143	Karl Malone	.30
144	Shandon Anderson	.10
145	Jacque Vaughn	.10
146	Bryon Russell	.10
147	Lee Mayberry	.10
148	Bryant Reeves	.10
149	Shareef Abdur-Rahim	.50
150	Michael Smith	.10
151	Pete Chilcutt	.10
152	Chris Webber	.30
153	Juwan Howard	.20
154	Calbert Cheaney	.10
155	Tracy Murray	.10
156	Dikembe Mutombo	.10
157	Antoine Walker	.50
158	Glen Rice	.10
159	Michael Jordan	1.25
160	Wesley Person	.10
161	Shawn Bradley	.10
162	Dean Garrett	.10
163	Jerry Stackhouse	.10
164	Donyell Marshall	.10
165	Hakeem Olajuwon	.20
166	Chris Mullin	.10
167	Isaac Austin	.10
168	Shaquille O'Neal	.40
169	Tim Hardaway	.10
170	Glenn Robinson	.10
171	Kevin Garnett	.50
172	Keith Van Horn	.50
173	Larry Johnson	.10
174	Horace Grant	.10
175	Derrick Coleman	.10
176	Steve Nash	.10
177	Arvydas Sabonis	.10
178	Corliss Williamson	.10
179	David Robinson	.10
180	Vin Baker	.10
181	Marcus Camby	.10
182	John Stockton	.10
183	Antonio Daniels	.10
184	Rod Strickland	.10
185	Michael Jordan	1.25
186	Kobe Bryant (All-Star debut)	.75
187	Clyde Drexler (final game 4/19)	.10
188	Gary Payton (Sea. wins 55th)	.10
189	Michael Jordan (10th scoring title)	1.25
190	Tim Duncan, David Robinson (T.T.)	.75
191	Hawks (largest crowd 62,046)	.10
192	Karl Malone (high scoring game)	.10
193	NBA Def. POY Dikembe Mutombo	.10
194	Nets Return to the Playoffs	.10
195	Ray Allen (hoop/movie star)	.10
196	Michael Jordan (NBA MVP)	1.25
197	Shaq and co. Shaquille O'Neal (Lake Show '98)	.40
198	Michael Jordan (Bulls 6th title)	1.25
199	Checklist #1	.10
200	Checklist #2	.10

1998-99 UD Choice Reserve

This 200-card parallel set reprints each card in the base set, but adds a unique foil treatment that includes the words "Choice Reserve." These parallel cards were inserted one per six packs.

	MT
Reserve Cards:	3x-6x

1998-99 UD Choice Premium Choice Reserve

This 200-card parallel set reprints each card in the base set, but adds a unique foil treatment that includes the words "Prime Choice Reserve." These parallel cards were inserted in hobby packs only and numbered to 100 sets.

	MT
PC Reserve Cards:	60x-120x

1998-99 UD Choice Mini Bobbing Heads

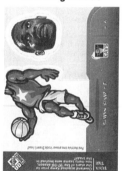

This 30-card insert set showcased miniature stand-up figures with removable bobbing heads of NBA players. These were inserted one per four packs of Series I.

	MT
Complete Set (30):	25.00
Common Player:	.50
M1	Dikembe Mutombo	.50
M2	Antoine Walker	2.00
M3	Anthony Mason	.50
M4	Toni Kukoc	.50
M5	Shawn Kemp	1.50
M6	Shawn Bradley	.50
M7	Danny Fortson	.50
M8	Brian Williams	.50
M9	Muggsy Bogues	.50
M10	Charles Barkley	1.00
M11	Mark Jackson	.50
M12	Rodney Rogers	.50
M13	Kobe Bryant	4.00
M14	Tim Hardaway	.50
M15	Ray Allen	1.00
M16	Kevin Garnett	3.00
M17	Sam Cassell	.50
M18	John Starks	.50
M19	Anfernee Hardaway	2.00
M20	Allen Iverson	2.00
M21	Danny Manning	.50
M22	Rasheed Wallace	.50
M23	Mitch Richmond	.50
M24	David Robinson	1.00
M25	Gary Payton	1.00
M26	Marcus Camby	.50
M27	John Stockton	.50
M28	Bryant Reeves	.50
M29	Juwan Howard	1.00
M30	Michael Jordan	6.00

1998-99 UD Choice StarQuest Blue

This 30-card insert included 30 top NBA players and arrived in four different foil versions. Numbered with a "SQ" prefix, Blue 1-Star versions were seeded one per pack, Green 2-Star versions were seeded 1:8, Red 3-Star versions were seeded 1:23 and Gold 4-Star versions were sequentially numbered to 100 sets.

	MT
Complete Set (30):	15.00
Common Player:	.25
Green Cards:	2x-4x
Red Cards:	5x-10x
Gold Cards:	40x-80x
SQ1	Steve Smith	.25
SQ2	Kenny Anderson	.25
SQ3	Glen Rice	.50
SQ4	Toni Kukoc	.25
SQ5	Shawn Kemp	.75
SQ6	Michael Finley	.50
SQ7	Bobby Jackson	.25
SQ8	Grant Hill	1.50
SQ9	Donyell Marshall	.25
SQ10	Hakeem Olajuwon	.75
SQ11	Reggie Miller	.50
SQ12	Maurice Taylor	.25
SQ13	Kobe Bryant	2.00
SQ14	Alonzo Mourning	.50
SQ15	Terrell Brandon	.25
SQ16	Stephon Marbury	1.25
SQ17	Keith Van Horn	1.25
SQ18	Patrick Ewing	.25
SQ19	Anfernee Hardaway	1.00
SQ20	Allen Iverson	1.00
SQ21	Jason Kidd	.50
SQ22	Damon Stoudamire	.25
SQ23	Mitch Richmond	.50
SQ24	Tim Duncan	1.50
SQ25	Gary Payton	.50
SQ26	Chauncey Billups	.50
SQ27	Karl Malone	.50
SQ28	Shareef Abdur-Rahim	.60
SQ29	Chris Webber	.50
SQ30	Michael Jordan	3.00

1998 Upper Deck Hardcourt

UD Hardcourt was a 90-card set that included 70 veterans and a 20-card Rookie Experience subset. The cards featured an image of the player and a circle in the background, both in etched foil. The rest of the background resembles the wood of a basketball court and also adds red stripes in a circular fashion. Hardcourt arrived with two parallels - Home Court Advantage and Home Court Advantage Plus - along with two inserts - High Court and Holding Court.

	MT
Complete Set (90):	90.00
Common Player:	.25
Jordan 5x7:	7.00
Wax Box:	100.00
1	Kobe Bryant	7.00
2	Donyell Marshall	.25
3	Bryant Reeves	.25
4	Keith Van Horn	10.00
5	David Robinson	1.00
6	Nick Anderson	.25
7	Nick Van Exel	.50
8	David Wesley	.25
9	Alonzo Mourning	.50
10	Shawn Kemp	2.00
11	Maurice Taylor	3.00
12	Kenny Anderson	.25
13	Jason Kidd	1.25
14	Marcus Camby	.50
15	Tim Hardaway	.75
16	Damon Stoudamire	1.00
17	Detlef Schrempf	.25
18	Dikembe Mutombo	.50
19	Charles Barkley	1.00
20	Ray Allen	.75
21	Ron Mercer	8.00
22	Shawn Bradley	.25
23	Michael Jordan	10.00
23a	Michael Jordan	20.00
24	Antonio McDyess	.75
25	Stephon Marbury	3.50
26	Rik Smits	.25
27	Michael Stewart	.25
28	Steve Smith	.25
29	Glenn Robinson	.50
30	Chris Webber	1.50
31	Antoine Walker	3.50
32	Eddie Jones	1.50
33	Mitch Richmond	.50
34	Kevin Garnett	4.00
35	Grant Hill	4.00
36	John Stockton	.50
37	Allan Houston	.50
38	Bobby Jackson	2.00
39	Sam Cassell	.25
40	Allen Iverson	3.50
41	LaPhonso Ellis	.25
42	Lorenzen Wright	.25
43	Gary Payton	1.00
44	Patrick Ewing	.50
45	Scottie Pippen	2.00
46	Hakeem Olajuwon	1.50
47	Glen Rice	.50
48	Antonio Daniels	2.50
49	Jayson Williams	.25
50	Juwan Howard	.75
51	Reggie Miller	.50
52	Joe Smith	.50
53	Shaquille O'Neal	3.00
54	Dennis Rodman	3.00
55	Vin Baker	1.00
56	Rod Strickland	.25
57	Anfernee Hardaway	3.00
58	Zydrunas Ilgauskas	.50
59	Chris Mullin	.25
60	Rasheed Wallace	.25
61	Shareef Abdur-Rahim	2.00
62	Tom Gugliotta	.25
63	Tim Duncan	20.00
64	Michael Finley	.50
65	Jim Jackson	.50
66	Chauncey Billups	4.00
67	Jerry Stackhouse	.50
68	Jeff Hornacek	.25
69	Clyde Drexler	.75
70	Karl Malone	1.00
71	Tim Duncan	10.00
72	Keith Van Horn	5.00
73	Chauncey Billups	2.00
74	Antonio Daniels	1.25
75	Tony Battie	2.50
76	Ron Mercer	4.00
77	Tim Thomas	6.00
78	Tracy McGrady	6.00
79	Danny Fortson	2.50
80	Derek Anderson	3.00
81	Maurice Taylor	1.50
82	Kelvin Cato	1.50
83	Brevin Knight	3.00
84	Bobby Jackson	1.00
85	Rodrick Rhodes	1.00
86	Anthony Johnson	1.00
87	Cedric Henderson	1.00
88	Alvin Williams	.25
89	Michael Stewart	.25
90	Zydrunas Ilgauskas	.25

1998 Upper Deck Hardcourt Home Court Advantage

This 90-card parallel reprinted each card and added the words "Home Court Advantage" across the middle and added blue foil stamping. These were inserted one per four packs.

	MT
HC Advantage Cards:	2x-3x

1998 Upper Deck Hardcourt Home Court Advantage Plus

Home Court Advantage Plus was a 90-card parallel that added gold foil to the front with the word "Plus" in large letters. Cards were sequentially numbered to 500.

	MT
HC Advantage Plus Cards:	8x-16x

1998 Upper Deck Hardcourt High Court

This 30-card insert was printed on wood paper stock and included gold and silver stamping. The cards featured the insert logo in the bottom right corner, with a basketball court look over the rest of the card. Cards were sequentially numbered on the back to 3,000 sets.

		MT
Complete Set (30):		600.00
Common Player:		10.00
H1	Dikembe Mutombo	10.00
H2	Ron Mercer	30.00
H3	Glen Rice	10.00
H4	Scottie Pippen	40.00
H5	Shawn Kemp	40.00
H6	Michael Finley	10.00
H7	LaPhonso Ellis	10.00
H8	Grant Hill	75.00
H9	Clarence Weatherspoon	10.00
H10	Hakeem Olajuwon	20.00
H11	Chris Mullin	10.00
H12	Lamond Murray	10.00
H13	Kobe Bryant	90.00
H14	Tim Hardaway	10.00
H15	Ray Allen	15.00
H16	Stephon Marbury	60.00
H17	Keith Van Horn	40.00
H18	Allan Houston	10.00
H19	Anfernee Hardaway	45.00
H20	Allen Iverson	60.00
H21	Antonio McDyess	15.00
H22	Rasheed Wallace	10.00
H23	Lawrence Funderburke	10.00
H24	Tim Duncan	75.00
H25	Gary Payton	18.00
H26	Chauncey Billups	18.00
H27	John Stockton	15.00
H28	Shareef Abdur-Rahim	40.00
H29	Juwan Howard	15.00
H30	Michael Jordan	150.00

1998 Upper Deck Hardcourt Jordan Holding Court

Jordan Holding Court features wood on wood cards that have Jordan on one side and one of 30 stars on the other. All double-fronted cards are done on 40-point stock, foil stamped and sequentially numbered. Red foil versions are numbered to 2,300, Bronze foil to 230, Silver foil to 23 and Gold foil versions are numbered 1 of 1.

		MT
Complete Set (30):		425.00
Common Player:		5.00
Bronze Cards:		3x-5x
J1	Steve Smith, Michael Jordan	5.00
J2	Antoine Walker, Michael Jordan	40.00
J3	Glen Rice, Michael Jordan	10.00
J4	Scottie Pippen, Michael Jordan	30.00
J5	Shawn Kemp, Michael Jordan	25.00
J6	Michael Finley, Michael Jordan	10.00
J7	Bobby Jackson, Michael Jordan	10.00
J8	Grant Hill, Michael Jordan	50.00
J9	Jim Jackson, Michael Jordan	5.00
J10	Charles Barkley, Michael Jordan	15.00
J11	Reggie Miller, Michael Jordan	10.00
J12	Lorenzen Wright, Michael Jordan	5.00
J13	Kobe Bryant, Michael Jordan	70.00
J14	Alonzo Mourning, Michael Jordan	10.00
J15	Glenn Robinson, Michael Jordan	10.00
J16	Kevin Garnett, Michael Jordan	50.00
J17	Keith Van Horn, Michael Jordan	30.00
J18	Patrick Ewing, Michael Jordan	10.00
J19	Anfernee Hardaway, Michael Jordan	35.00
J20	Allen Iverson, Michael Jordan	40.00
J21	Jason Kidd, Michael Jordan	15.00
J22	Damon Stoudamire, Michael Jordan	10.00
J23	Mitch Richmond, Michael Jordan	10.00
J24	Tim Duncan, Michael Jordan	60.00
J25	Gary Payton, Michael Jordan	15.00
J26	Chauncey Billups, Michael Jordan	20.00
J27	Karl Malone, Michael Jordan	15.00
J28	Shareef Abdur-Rahim, Michael Jordan	25.00
J29	Chris Webber, Michael Jordan	15.00
J30	Michael Jordan, Michael Jordan	100.00

Football Market Report

The Football Card Market Experiences Strong Third Quarter Sales Despite Fewer Releases In '98

See, there is truth to the rumor that less is more. The football card market has certainly proved that in 1998. Despite the loss of three licensees to bankruptcy – Pinnacle Brands, Donruss and Score Board – resulting in fewer brands, football card sales were up in the third quarter of 1998. Football was the only sport to experience an increase in card sales in this year's third quarter compared to 1997.

"Everyone has been very positive – from manufacturers to distributors to dealers to consumers – about football this year," said Dawn Ridley, assistant VP of trading cards and collectibles for Players Inc. "We started talking about the rookies a year ago, and they truly have had an impact on the game. But the game itself has been strong, too. The market is stable and that's something we've been hoping for. Generally, people have a positive attitude and are excited about football and football cards."

Ultra kicked off the season with a red-hot set that included seeded rookie cards. The seeded rookie card program continued in Upper Deck Football and Sky-Box Premium and now Topps Chrome is the hottest brand in the market thanks to the rookies. The successful history of Topps Chrome is carrying that brand, since the rookies weren't seeded in that set.

The good news for football card collectors is that more sets are on the way. Look for Bowman's Best and Bowman Chrome, both scheduled for late December releases, to be red-hot right out of the gate.

Collectors will also be happy to know that next year's rookie class could rival this year's talented crop. The '99 class of rookies could include Texas RB Ricky Williams, who passed Tony Dorsett for the all-time NCAA rushing record, UCLA QB Cade McNown and Kentucky QB Tim Couch. All three college stars would be top 10 picks next year if they decide to turn pro.

Ironically, Williams has already been featured on two card sets. The nation's leading rusher has played four seasons of minor league baseball with the Philadelphia Phillies organization after being selected in the eighth round of the 1995 draft. He saw limited action in 1998 at Class A Batavia and returned to college. He is pictured in the 1998 Team Batavia Muckdogs set ($12.50), while his 1996 Best Piedmont Boll Weevils card shows him in the Heisman Trophy pose with the heading "Heisman Hopeful?" That set is priced at $37.

Williams represents the future of the NFL and the football card market. But despite the loss of three licensees this year, the present looks pretty good for everyone involved.

FOOTBALL

1997 Bowman's Best

Bowman's Best Football is a 125-card set featuring 95 NFL veterans with a gold design and 30 rookies with a silver design. The base cards also come in Refractor (1:12) and Atomic Refractor (1:24) parallels. The insert sets include Bowman's Best Autographs, Laser Cuts and Mirror Image. Each of the insert cards has a Refractor and Atomic Refractor version. Bowman's Best Football was sold in six-card packs.

		MT
Complete Set (125):		100.00
Common Player:		.25
Wax Box:		100.00
1	Brett Favre	8.00
2	Larry Centers	.25
3	Trent Dilfer	.50
4	Rodney Hampton	.25
5	Wesley Walls	.25
6	Jerome Bettis	.50
7	Keyshawn Johnson	1.00
8	Keenan McCardell	.25
9	Terry Allen	.25
10	Troy Aikman	4.00
11	Tony Banks	1.50
12	Ty Detmer	.25
13	Chris Chandler	.25
14	Marshall Faulk	.50
15	Heath Shuler	.25
16	Stan Humphries	.25
17	Bryan Cox	.25
18	Chris Spielman	.25
19	Derrick Thomas	.25
20	Steve Young	2.50
21	Desmond Howard	.25
22	Jeff Blake	.50
23	Michael Jackson	.25
24	Cris Carter	.25
25	Joey Galloway	1.00
26	Simeon Rice	.25
27	Reggie White	.50
28	Dave Brown	.25
29	Mike Alstott	1.50
30	Emmitt Smith	7.00
31	Anthony Johnson	.25
32	Mark Brunell	4.00
33	Ricky Watters	.50
34	Terrell Davis	4.00
35	Ben Coates	.25
36	Gus Frerotte	.25
37	Andre Reed	.25
38	Isaac Bruce	.50
39	Junior Seau	.50
40	Eddie George	6.00
41	Adrian Murrell	.50
42	Jake Reed	.25
43	Karim Abdul-Jabbar	2.50
44	Scott Mitchell	.25
45	Ki-Jana Carter	.25
46	Curtis Conway	.50
47	Jim Harbaugh	.25
48	Tim Brown	.50
49	Mario Bates	.25
50	Jerry Rice	4.00
51	Byron Morris	.25
52	Marcus Allen	.50
53	Errict Rhett	.25
54	Steve McNair	3.00
55	Kerry Collins	3.00
56	Bert Emanuel	.25
57	Curtis Martin	4.00
58	Bryce Paup	.25
59	Brad Johnson	.50
60	John Elway	2.50
61	Natrone Means	.50
62	Deion Sanders	2.00
63	Tony Martin	.25
64	Michael Westbrook	.25
65	Chris Calloway	.25
66	Antonio Freeman	.50
67	Rick Mirer	.25
68	Kent Graham	.25
69	O.J. McDuffie	.25
70	Barry Sanders	4.00
71	Chris Warren	.25
72	Kordell Stewart	4.00
73	Thurman Thomas	.50
74	Marvin Harrison	1.00
75	Carl Pickens	.25
76	Brent Jones	.25
77	Irving Fryar	.25
78	Neil O'Donnell	.25
79	Elvis Grbac	.25
80	Drew Bledsoe	4.00
81	Shannon Sharpe	.25
82	Vinny Testaverde	.25
83	Chris Sanders	.25
84	Herman Moore	.50
85	Jeff George	.50
86	Bruce Smith	.25
87	Robert Smith	.25
88	Kevin Hardy	.25
89	Kevin Greene	.25
90	Dan Marino	7.00
91	Michael Irvin	.50
92	Garrison Hearst	.25
93	Lake Dawson	.25
94	Lawrence Phillips	.50
95	Terry Glenn	3.00
96	*Jake Plummer*	8.00
97	*Byron Hanspard*	2.00
98	*Bryant Westbrook*	.50
99	*Troy Davis*	1.00
100	*Danny Wuerffel*	3.00
101	*Tony Gonzalez*	2.00
102	*Jim Druckenmiller*	4.00
103	*Kevin Lockett*	.25
104	*Renaldo Wynn*	.25
105	*James Farrior*	.25
106	*Rae Carruth*	3.00
107	*Tom Knight*	.25
108	*Corey Dillon*	7.00
109	*Kenny Holmes*	.25
110	*Orlando Pace*	.25
111	*Reidel Anthony*	4.00
112	*Chad Scott*	.25
113	*Antowain Smith*	5.00
114	*David LaFleur*	2.00
115	*Yatil Green*	1.50
116	*Darrell Russell*	.25
117	*Joey Kent*	1.00
118	*Darnell Autry*	1.00
119	*Peter Boulware*	.50
120	*Shawn Springs*	.25
121	*Ike Hilliard*	3.00
122	*Dwayne Rudd*	.25
123	*Reinard Wilson*	.25
124	*Michael Booker*	.25
125	*Warrick Dunn*	8.00

1997 Bowman's Best Refractors

The entire 125-card Bowman's Best set was also available in Refractor versions. The cards contained a holofoil finish on the front and were inserted one per 12 packs.

	MT
Refractor Cards:	4x-8x
Refractor Rookies:	2x-4x

1997 Bowman's Best Atomic Refractors

The entire 125-card Bowman's Best set was reprinted in Atomic Refractor parallel versions. These were inserted one per 24 packs and featured a prismatic, reflective finish on the card front.

	MT
Atomic Refractor Stars:	8x-16x
Atomic Refractor Rookies:	4x-8x

1997 Bowman's Best Autographs

This 10-card set features autographed versions of 10 base set cards. The cards were inserted 1:131. Refractor (1:1578) and Atomic Refractor (1:4733) parallels are also available.

		MT
Complete Set (10):		500.00
Common Player:		20.00
22	Jeff Blake	20.00
44	Scott Mitchell	20.00
47	Jim Harbaugh	20.00
99	Troy Davis	20.00
102	Jim Druckenmiller	80.00
113	Antowain Smith	80.00
114	David LaFleur	30.00
120	Shawn Springs	20.00
121	Ike Hilliard	50.00
125	Warrick Dunn	150.00

1997 Bowman's Best Cuts

Best Cuts features 20 players on die-cut cards. The top of the cards says Best Cuts and the letters are die-cut. Best Cuts was inserted once per 24 packs. Refractor (1:48) and Atomic Refractor (1:96) parallels were also created.

		MT
Complete Set (20):		200.00
Common Player:		3.00
Refractors:		2x
Atomic Refractors:		2x-4x
BC1	Orlando Pace	3.00
BC2	Eddie George	16.00
BC3	John Elway	8.00
BC4	Tony Gonzalez	3.00
BC5	Brett Favre	25.00
BC6	Shawn Springs	3.00
BC7	Warrick Dunn	20.00
BC8	Troy Aikman	12.00
BC9	Terry Glenn	8.00
BC10	Dan Marino	20.00
BC11	Jake Plummer	8.00
BC12	Ike Hilliard	8.00
BC13	Emmitt Smith	20.00
BC14	Steve Young	8.00
BC15	Barry Sanders	18.00
BC16	Jim Druckenmiller	10.00
BC17	Drew Bledsoe	12.00
BC18	Antowain Smith	8.00
BC19	Mark Brunell	12.00
BC20	Jerry Rice	12.00

1997 Bowman's Best Mirror Images

The 10, double-sided card in Mirror Images showcases four top players from the same position. Two NFC players and two AFC players are fea-

tured on each card. The chromium cards (1:48) also had Refractor (1:96) and Atomic Refractor (1:192) parallels.

		MT
Complete Set (10):		180.00
Common Player:		5.00
Refractors:		2x
Atomic Refractors:		2x-4x
MI1	Brett Favre, Gus Frerotte, John Elway, Mark Brunell	40.00
MI2	Steve Young, Tony Banks, Dan Marino, Drew Bledsoe	35.00
MI3	Troy Aikman, Kerry Collins, Vinny Testaverde, Kordell Stewart	20.00
MI4	Emmitt Smith, Dorsey Levens, Marcus Allen, Eddie George	35.00
MI5	Barry Sanders, Errict Rhett, Thurman Thomas, Curtis Martin	25.00
MI6	Ricky Watters, Jamal Anderson, Chris Warren, Terrell Davis	20.00
MI7	Jerry Rice, Isaac Bruce, Tony Martin, Marvin Harrison	20.00
MI8	Herman Moore, Curtis Conway, Tim Brown, Terry Glenn	15.00
MI9	Michael Irvin, Eddie Kennison, Carl Pickens, Keyshawn Johnson	5.00
MI10	Wesley Walls, Jason Dunn, Shannon Sharpe, Rickey Dudley	5.00

1997 Collector's Edge Extreme

Extreme includes a 180-card base set. Three different parallel sets were made. Extreme Base Parallel 1 (1:2) parallels 108 base cards with a flat silver foil stamp. Extreme Base Parallel II (1:12) adds a gold foil stamp to 36 base cards redone on a silver card. Base Parallel III (1:36) parallels the other 36 base cards with a diamond etched foil stamp on a silver, die-cut card. The inserts include Force, Finesse, Fury, Forerunners and Gamegear Quads.

		MT
Complete Set (180):		30.00
Common Player:		.10
1	Larry Centers	.10
2	Leeland McElroy	.10
3	*Jake Plummer*	1.50
4	Simeon Rice	.10
5	Eric Swann	.10
6	Jamal Anderson	.20
7	Bert Emanuel	.10
8	*Byron Hanspard*	.75
9	Derrick Alexander	.10
10	Peter Boulware	.10
11	Michael Jackson	.10
12	Ray Lewis	.10
13	Vinny Testaverde	.10
14	Todd Collins	.10
15	Eric Moulds	.10
16	Bryce Paup	.10
17	Andre Reed	.10
18	Bruce Smith	.10
19	*Antowain Smith*	1.25
20	Chris Spielman	.10
21	Thurman Thomas	.20
22	Tim Biakabutuka	.10
23	*Rae Carruth*	.75
24	Kerry Collins	.75
25	Anthony Johnson	.10
26	Lamar Lathon	.10
27	Muhsin Muhammad	.10
28	*Darnell Autry*	.50
29	Curtis Conway	.20
30	Bryan Cox	.10
31	Bobby Engram	.10
32	Walt Harris	.10
33	Erik Kramer	.10
34	Rashaan Salaam	.10
35	Jeff Blake	.20
36	Ki-Jana Carter	.10
37	*Corey Dillon*	1.50
38	Carl Pickens	.20
39	Troy Aikman	1.00
40	Dexter Coakley	.10
41	Michael Irvin	.20
42	Daryl Johnston	.10
43	*David LaFleur*	.50
44	Anthony Miller	.10
45	Deion Sanders	.50
46	Emmitt Smith	2.00
47	Broderick Thomas	.10
48	Terrell Davis	1.00
49	John Elway	.75
50	John Mobley	.10
51	Shannon Sharpe	.10
52	Neil Smith	.10
53	Checklist	.10
54	Scott Mitchell	.10
55	Herman Moore	.20
56	Barry Sanders	1.25
57	Edgar Bennett	.10
58	Robert Brooks	.20
59	Mark Chmura	.20
60	Brett Favre	2.25
61	Antonio Freeman	.20
62	Dorsey Levens	.20
63	Reggie White	.20
64	Eddie George	1.50
65	Darryll Lewis	.10
66	Steve McNair	.75
67	Chris Sanders	.10
68	Marshall Faulk	.20
69	Jim Harbaugh	.10
70	Marvin Harrison	.20
71	Tony Brackens	.10
72	Mark Brunell	1.00
73	Kevin Hardy	.10
74	Rob Johnson	.20
75	Keenan McCardell	.10
76	Natrone Means	.20
77	Jimmy Smith	.10
78	Marcus Allen	.20
79	*Pat Barnes*	.50
80	*Tony Gonzalez*	.50
81	Elvis Grbac	.10

82	Brett Perriman	.10
83	Andre Rison	.10
84	Derrick Thomas	.10
85	Tamarick Vanover	.10
86	Karim Abdul-Jabbar	.50
87	Fred Barnett	.10
88	Terrell Buckley	.10
89	*Yatil Green*	.75
90	Dan Marino	2.00
91	O.J. McDuffie	.10
92	Jason Taylor	.10
93	Zach Thomas	.20
94	Cris Carter	.10
95	Brad Johnson	.20
96	John Randle	.10
97	Jake Reed	.10
98	Robert Smith	.10
99	Drew Bledsoe	1.00
100	Chris Canty	.10
101	Ben Coates	.10
102	Terry Glenn	.75
103	Ty Law	.10
104	Curtis Martin	1.00
105	Willie McGinest	.10
106	*Troy Davis*	.75
107	Wayne Martin	.10
108	Heath Shuler	.10
109	*Danny Wuerffel*	.75
110	Ray Zellars	.10
111	*Tiki Barber*	1.00
112	Dave Brown	.10
113	Checklist	.10
114	*Ike Hilliard*	.75
115	Jason Sehorn	.10
116	Amani Toomer	.10
117	Tyrone Wheatley	.10
118	Hugh Douglas	.10
119	Aaron Glenn	.10
120	Jeff Graham	.10
121	Keyshawn Johnson	.20
122	Adrian Murrell	.20
123	Neil O'Donnell	.10
124	Tim Brown	.10
125	Jeff George	.10
126	Desmond Howard	.10
127	Napoleon Kaufman	.20
128	Chester McGlockton	.10
129	Darrell Russell	.10
130	Ty Detmer	.10
131	Irving Fryar	.10
132	Chris T. Jones	.10
133	Ricky Watters	.20
134	Jerome Bettis	.20
135	Charles Johnson	.10
136	George Jones	.10
137	Greg Lloyd	.10
138	Kordell Stewart	.75
139	Yancey Thigpen	.10
140	Jim Everett	.10
141	Stan Humphries	.10
142	Tony Martin	.10
143	Eric Metcalf	.10
144	Junior Seau	.10
145	*Jim Druckenmiller*	1.50
146	Kevin Greene	.10
147	Garrison Hearst	.10
148	Terry Kirby	.10
149	Terrell Owens	.50
150	Jerry Rice	1.00
151	Dana Stubblefield	.10
152	Rod Woodson	.10
153	Bryant Young	.10
154	Steve Young	.50
155	Chad Brown	.10
156	John Friesz	.10
157	Joey Galloway	.20
158	Cortez Kennedy	.10
159	Warren Moon	.10
160	*Shawn Springs*	.20
161	Chris Warren	.10
162	Tony Banks	.50
163	Isaac Bruce	.20
164	Eddie Kennison	.20
165	Keith Lyle	.10
166	*Orlando Pace*	.20
167	Lawrence Phillips	.10
168	Checklist	.10
169	Mike Alstott	.50
170	*Reidel Anthony*	1.00
171	*Warrick Dunn*	2.50
172	Hardy Nickerson	.10
173	Errict Rhett	.10
174	Warren Sapp	.10
175	Terry Allen	.10
176	Gus Frerotte	.10
177	Sean Gilbert	.10
178	Ken Harvey	.10
179	Jeff Hostetler	.10
180	Michael Westbrook	.10

1997 Collector's Edge Extreme Foil

Collector's Edge ran three parallel sets to its Extreme set. The first parallel simply included a silver foil stripe up the left side and contained all 180 cards with an insert rate of one per two packs. The second parallel contained only 36 of the cards are featured a gold and silver strip on the left side, with the rest of the card done with a silver finish. These gold parallels are inserted every 12 packs. The third parallel level included a gold, silver and blue foil strip up the left side and was die-cut around the entire perimeter. The card fronts also featured a silver finish, with the cards inserted one per 36 packs. All three levels were numbered on the back with a "P" prefix.

	MT
Silver Cards:	2x
Gold Cards:	2x-4x
Die-Cut Stars:	8x-16x
Die-Cut Rookies:	4x-8x

1997 Collector's Edge Extreme Finesse

This 19-card insert is done on frosted, clear, foil-stamped cards. The cards were inesrted 1:60 packs of Extreme.

		MT
Complete Set (25):		400.00
Common Player:		5.00
1	Troy Aikman	30.00
2	Marcus Allen	10.00
3	Ben Coates	5.00
4	Tony Banks	10.00
5	Jeff Blake	10.00
6	Tim Brown	5.00
7	Mark Brunell	30.00
8	Todd Collins	5.00
9	Terrell Davis	30.00
10	Jim Druckenmiller	20.00
11	John Elway	25.00
12	Marshall Faulk	10.00
13	Brett Favre	60.00
14	Antonio Freeman	10.00
15	Joey Galloway	10.00
16	Eddie George	40.00
17	Terry Glenn	15.00
18	Marvin Harrison	10.00
19	Garrison Hearst	5.00
20	Warrick Dunn	35.00
21	Muhsin Muhammad	5.00
22	Jerry Rice	30.00
23	Barry Sanders	40.00
24	Emmitt Smith	55.00
25	Shawn Springs	5.00

1997 Collector's Edge Extreme Force

Force features 26 players on silver cards with flow etched designs. Force was inserted 1:8 packs of Extreme.

		MT
Complete Set (25):		75.00
Common Player:		.50
1	Marcus Allen	1.00
2	Chris Canty	.50
3	Jerome Bettis	1.00
4	Carl Pickens	.50
5	Drew Bledsoe	6.00
6	Robert Brooks	1.00
7	Shannon Sharpe	.50
8	Tim Brown	.50
9	Mark Brunell	6.00
10	Ben Coates	.50
11	Todd Collins	.50
12	Terrell Davis	6.00
13	John Elway	4.00
14	Brett Favre	12.00
15	Antonio Freeman	1.00
16	Joey Galloway	1.00
17	Warrick Dunn	6.00
18	Terry Glenn	3.00
19	Marvin Harrison	1.00
20	Dan Marino	10.00
21	Jerry Rice	6.00
22	Junior Seau	.50
23	Tony Banks	3.00
24	Emmitt Smith	10.00
25	Napoleon Kaufman	1.00

1997 Collector's Edge Extreme Forerunners

This 25-card redemption subset were made on clear 2-way view cards with a large head shot on the back visible from the front. Gold foil was also added to the cards. The cards were available by redemption through instant win cards, of which 250 were made.

		MT
Complete Set (25):		300.00
Common Player:		5.00
1	Karim Abdul-Jabbar	10.00
2	Marcus Allen	5.00
3	Jerome Bettis	10.00
4	Drew Bledsoe	20.00
5	Robert Brooks	5.00
6	Mark Brunell	20.00
7	Todd Collins	5.00
8	Terrell Davis	20.00
9	John Elway	15.00
10	Brett Favre	45.00
11	Joey Galloway	10.00
12	Eddie George	30.00
13	Terry Glenn	12.00
14	Marvin Harrison	10.00
15	Keyshawn Johnson	10.00
16	Rob Johnson	5.00
17	Eddie Kennison	10.00
18	Dorsey Levens	10.00
19	Dan Marino	40.00
20	Steve McNair	15.00
21	Terrell Owens	10.00
22	Carl Pickens	5.00
23	Jerry Rice	20.00
24	Emmitt Smith	40.00
25	Kordell Stewart	20.00

1997 Collector's Edge Extreme Fury

Fury is an 18-card insert with top players featured on a Deep Metal card with chromium finish. Fury was inserted 1:48 packs of Extreme.

		MT
Complete Set (18):		200.00
Common Player:		3.00
1	Jerome Bettis	6.00
2	Terry Glenn	12.00
3	Drew Bledsoe	20.00
4	Mark Brunell	20.00
5	Terrell Davis	20.00
6	Troy Davis	6.00
7	Marshall Faulk	6.00
8	Brett Favre	40.00
9	Antonio Freeman	6.00
10	Joey Galloway	6.00
11	Eddie George	30.00
12	Eddie Kennison	6.00
13	Errict Rhett	3.00
14	Rashaan Salaam	3.00
15	Emmitt Smith	35.00
16	Kordell Stewart	20.00
17	Danny Wuerffel	6.00
18	Steve Young	15.00

1997 Donruss Preferred

The inaugeral issue of Donruss Preferred Football contained 150 cards which were divided into four different tiers, with 80 Bronze, 40 Silver, 20 Gold and 10 Platinum cards. The cards are printed on all-foil, micro-etched surfaces and contain an action shot of the player, with his name and team across the bottom and "Donruss Preferred" and the word bronze, silver, gold or platinum across the top. There is also a white star in each corner of the card within the color border. Preferred also had a Cut to the Chase parallel set, as well as Chain Reaction, Staremaster and Precious Metals insert sets. Another interesting facet of this product is that it arrived in collectible tins, of which, there were 24 different players featured. The tins were packed into larger Hobby Master Tins for hobby accounts and came in boxes to retail accounts.

		MT
Complete Set (150):		800.00
Complete Bronze (80):		40.00
Common Bronze Player:		.25
Complete Silver (40):		110.00
Common Silver Player:		2.00
Complete Gold (20):		250.00
Common Gold Player:		4.00
Complete Platinum (10):		400.00
1	Emmitt Smith P	60.00
2	Steve Young G	15.00
3	Cris Carter S	2.00
4	Tim Biakabutuka B	.25
5	Brett Favre P	70.00
6	Troy Aikman G	20.00
7	Eddie Kennison S	4.00
8	Ben Coates B	.25
9	Dan Marino P	70.00
10	Deion Sanders G	10.00
11	Curtis Conway S	4.00
12	Jeff George S	2.00
13	Barry Sanders P	40.00
14	Kerry Collins G	15.00
15	Marvin Harrison S	4.00
16	Bobby Engram B	.50
17	Jerry Rice P	35.00
18	Kordell Stewart G	20.00
19	Tony Banks S	5.00
20	Jim Harbaugh B	.25
21	Mark Brunell P	35.00
22	Steve McNair G	15.00
23	Terrell Owens S	5.00
24	Raymont Harris B	.25
25	Curtis Martin P	35.00
26	Karim Abdul-Jabbar G	8.00
27	Joey Galloway S	4.00
28	Bobby Hoying B	.25
29	Terrell Davis P	35.00
30	Terry Glenn G	12.00
31	Antonio Freeman S	4.00
32	Brad Johnson B	.50
33	Drew Bledsoe P	35.00
34	John Elway G	20.00
35	Herman Moore G	8.00
36	Robert Brooks S	4.00
37	Rod Smith B	.25
38	Eddie George P	40.00
39	Keyshawn Johnson G	8.00
40	Greg Hill S	2.00
41	Scott Mitchell B	.25
42	Muhsin Muhammad B	.25
43	Isaac Bruce G	8.00
44	Jeff Blake S	4.00
45	Neil O'Donnell B	.25
46	Jimmy Smith B	.25
47	Jerome Bettis G	8.00
48	Terry Allen S	2.00
49	Andre Reed B	.25
50	Frank Sanders B	.25
51	Tim Brown G	4.00
52	Thurman Thomas S	4.00
53	Heath Shuler B	.25
54	Vinny Testaverde B	.25
55	Marcus Allen S	4.00
56	Napoleon Kaufman B	.50
57	Derrick Alexander B	.25
58	Carl Pickens G	4.00
59	Marshall Faulk S	4.00
60	Mike Alstott B	2.00
61	Jamal Anderson B	.50
62	Ricky Watters G	8.00
63	Dorsey Levens S	4.00
64	Todd Collins B	.25
65	Trent Dilfer B	.50
66	Natrone Means S	4.00
67	Gus Frerotte B	.25
68	Irving Fryar B	.25
69	Adrian Murrell S	4.00
70	Rodney Hampton B	.25
71	Garrison Hearst B	.25
72	Reggie White S	4.00
73	Anthony Johnson B	.25
74	Tony Martin B	.25
75	Chris Sanders S	2.00
76	O.J. McDuffie B	.25
77	Leeland McElroy B	.25
78	Ki-Jana Carter S	2.00
79	Anthony Miller B	.25
80	Johnnie Morton B	.25
81	Robert Smith S	2.00
82	Brett Perriman B	.25
83	Errict Rhett B	.25
84	Michael Irvin S	4.00
85	Darnay Scott B	.25
86	Shannon Sharpe B	.25
87	Lawrence Phillips S	2.00
88	Bruce Smith B	.25
89	James Stewart B	.25
90	J.J. Stokes B	.50
91	Chris Warren B	.25
92	Daryl Johnston B	.25
93	Andre Rison B	.25
94	Rashaan Salaam B	.50
95	Amani Toomer B	.25
96	*Warrick Dunn G*	50.00
97	*Tiki Barber S*	10.00
98	*Peter Boulware B*	.50
99	*Ike Hilliard G*	15.00
100	*Antowain Smith S*	10.00
101	*Yatil Green S*	6.00
102	*Tony Gonzalez B*	2.00
103	*Reidel Anthony G*	20.00
104	*Troy Davis S*	6.00
105	*Rae Carruth S*	6.00
106	*David LaFleur B*	2.00
107	*Jim Druckenmiller G*	30.00
108	*Joey Kent S*	4.00
109	*Byron Hanspard S*	6.00
110	*Darrell Russell B*	.50
111	*Danny Wuerffel S*	8.00
112	*Jake Plummer S*	12.00
113	*Jay Graham B*	1.00
114	*Corey Dillon S*	12.00
115	*Orlando Pace B*	.50
116	*Pat Barnes S*	5.00
117	*Shawn Springs B*	.50
118	Troy Aikman B (National Treasures)	2.00
119	Drew Bledsoe B (National Treasures)	2.00
120	Mark Brunell B (National Treasures)	2.00
121	Kerry Collins B (National Treasures)	1.50
122	Terrell Davis B (National Treasures)	2.00
123	Jerome Bettis B (National Treasures)	.25
124	Brett Favre B (National Treasures)	4.00
125	Eddie George B (National Treasures)	3.00

126	Terry Glenn B (National Treasures)	1.00
127	Karim Abdul-Jabbar B (National Treasures)	.50
128	Keyshawn Johnson B (National Treasures)	.25
129	Dan Marino B (National Treasures)	4.00
130	Curtis Martin B (National Treasures)	1.50
131	Natrone Means B (National Treasures)	.25
132	Herman Moore S (National Treasures)	2.00
133	Jerry Rice B (National Treasures)	2.00
134	Barry Sanders B (National Treasures)	2.50
135	Deion Sanders B (National Treasures)	.50
136	Emmitt Smith B (National Treasures)	3.00
137	Kordell Stewart B (National Treasures)	2.00
138	Steve Young B (National Treasures)	1.50
139	Carl Pickens S (National Treasures)	2.00
140	Isaac Bruce S (National Treasures)	2.00
141	Steve McNair S (National Treasures)	5.00
142	John Elway S (National Treasures)	6.00
143	Cris Carter B (National Treasures)	.25
144	Tim Brown B (National Treasures)	.25
145	Ricky Watters S (National Treasures)	.25
146	Robert Brooks B (National Treasures)	.25
147	Jeff Blake B (National Treasures)	.25
148	Tiki Barber CL B	.25
149	Jim Druckenmiller CL B	1.00
150	Warrick Dunn CL B	1.50

1997 Donruss Preferred Chain Reaction

This 24-card insert set captured 12 different offensive teammates on die-cut cards that linked together in order to display them side by side. The insert was printed on thick plastic stock with holographic treatments and sequentially numbered to 3,000.

		MT
Complete Set (24):		350.00
Common Player:		5.00
1a	Dan Marino	40.00
1b	Karim Abdul-Jabbar	10.00
2a	Troy Aikman	20.00
2b	Emmitt Smith	40.00
3a	Steve McNair	15.00
3b	Eddie George	30.00
4a	Brett Favre	45.00
4b	Robert Brooks	5.00
5a	John Elway	15.00
5b	Terrell Davis	20.00
6a	Drew Bledsoe	20.00
6b	Curtis Martin	15.00
7a	Steve Young	15.00
7b	Jerry Rice	20.00
8a	Mark Brunell	20.00
8b	Natrone Means	10.00
9a	Barry Sanders	30.00
9b	Herman Moore	10.00
10a	Kordell Stewart	20.00
10b	Jerome Bettis	10.00
11a	Jeff Blake	10.00
11b	Carl Pickens	5.00
12a	Lawrence Phillips	5.00
12b	Isaac Bruce	10.00

1997 Donruss Preferred Cut To The Chase

Cut to the Chase paralleled the full 150-card set from Donruss Preferred. Since the base set was fractured into different colors corresponding to the base set and was also die-cut around the perimeter. Cut to the Chase bronze cards are one per seven packs, silvers are one per 63, golds are one per 189 and platinums are one per 756.

	MT
Complete Set (150):	2500.
Complete Bronze (80)	300.00
Bronze Stars:	4x-8x
Bronze Rookies:	2x-4x
Complete Silver (40)	500.00
Silver Stars:	2x-4x
Silver Rookies:	1x-2x
Complete Gold (20)	600.00
Gold Cards:	1x-2x
Complete Platinum (10)	1100.
Platinum Cards:	2x-3x

1997 Donruss Preferred Double-Wide Tins

Twelve different players were available on Double-Wide Tins. These tins were available through retail locations and contained Donruss Preferred cards.

		MT
Complete Set (12):		15.00
Common Player:		.75
1	Emmitt Smith, Terrell Davis	2.00
2	Troy Aikman, Kerry Collins	1.00
3	Herman Moore, Carl Pickens	.75
4	Brett Favre, Mark Brunell	2.50
5	Deion Sanders, Kordell Stewart	1.00
6	Barry Sanders, Karim Abdul-Jabbar	1.50
7	Jerry Rice, Terry Glenn	1.25
8	Dan Marino, Drew Bledsoe	2.50
9	John Elway, Steve Young	1.25
10	Curtis Martin, Warrick Dunn	1.50
11	Eddie George, Tim Brown	1.50
12	Keyshawn Johnson, Ike Hilliard	.75

1997 Donruss Preferred Precious Metals

Precious Metals was a 15-card partial parallel set that was printed on actual silver, gold or platinum corresponding to which color subset the base card was from. Only 100 individually numbered Precious Metals sets were produced.

		MT
Complete Set (15):		4000.
Common Player:		100.00
1	Drew Bledsoe	250.00
2	Curtis Martin	225.00
3	Troy Aikman	250.00
4	Eddie George	300.00
5	Warrick Dunn	300.00
6	Brett Favre	500.00
7	John Elway	200.00
8	Barry Sanders	350.00
9	Emmitt Smith	400.00
10	Terrell Davis	250.00
11	Mark Brunell	250.00
12	Jerry Rice	250.00
13	Dan Marino	400.00
14	Terry Glenn	125.00
15	Tiki Barber	100.00

1997 Donruss Preferred Staremasters

These horizontal cards were printed on all-foil card stock with holographic foil stamping. Card fronts featured two close-up photos of the player, with one in full color and the other within the foil background. There were 1,500 sequentially numbered sets of Staremaster produced.

		MT
Complete Set (24):		750.00
Common Player:		6.00
1	Tim Brown	6.00
2	Mark Brunell	40.00
3	Kerry Collins	30.00
4	Brett Favre	80.00
5	Eddie George	60.00
6	Terry Glenn	25.00
7	Dan Marino	70.00
8	Curtis Martin	30.00
9	Jerry Rice	40.00
10	Barry Sanders	50.00
11	Deion Sanders	20.00
12	Emmitt Smith	70.00
13	Drew Bledsoe	40.00
14	Troy Aikman	40.00
15	Tiki Barber	12.00
16	Terrell Davis	40.00
17	Karim Abdul-Jabbar	12.00
18	Warrick Dunn	40.00
19	John Elway	30.00
20	Yatil Green	12.00
21	Ike Hilliard	12.00
22	Kordell Stewart	40.00
23	Ricky Watters	6.00
24	Steve Young	30.00

1997 Donruss Preferred Tins

Each pack of Donruss Preferred arrived for sale in collectible tin, with 24 different players each featured on their own tin. The 24 tins arrived in five different varieties: smaller blue pack tins were the "base" tins; silver pack tins were in hobby exclusive boxes and numbered to 1,200; gold pack tins were also available in hobby box tins and numbered to 300; blue box tins were hobby exclusive and contained 24 smaller tins - these were numbered to 1,200 and essentially the same as the smaller blue tins except in size; and gold box tins, which were parallel to the larger blue box tins, but printed in gold and numbered to 300. The larger box tins were only available to hobby accounts. Retail accounts received the tins packed in cardboard boxes.

		MT
Complete Blue Pack (24):		20.00
Common Pack:		.25
Complete Silver Pack (24):		200.00
Silver Pack Tins:		5x-10x
Complete Blue Box (24):		150.00
Blue Box Tins:		4x-8x
Complete Gold Pack (24):		400.00
Gold Pack Tins:		10x-20x
Complete Gold Box (24):		300.00
Gold Box Tins:		8x-16x
1	Mark Brunell	1.00
2	Karim Abdul-Jabbar	.50
3	Terry Glenn	.75
4	Brett Favre	2.00
5	Troy Aikman	1.00
6	Eddie George	1.50
7	John Elway	.75
8	Steve Young	.75
9	Terrell Davis	1.00
10	Kordell Stewart	1.00
11	Drew Bledsoe	1.00
12	Kerry Collins	.75
13	Dan Marino	2.00
14	Tim Brown	.25
15	Carl Pickens	.25
16	Warrick Dunn	1.50
17	Herman Moore	.25
18	Curtis Martin	.75
19	Ike Hilliard	.50
20	Barry Sanders	1.25
21	Deion Sanders	.50
22	Emmitt Smith	2.00
23	Keyshawn Johnson	.25
24	Jerry Rice	1.00

1997 Donruss Studio

1997 Studio Football is a special Quarterback Club edition. The 36-card base set features the NFL Quarterback Club stars on 8x10 cards. Each player is captured in full-color portrait photography. The base set features 24 Studio Portraits and 12 Class of Distinction cards. Class of Distinction highlights 12 of the stars in an action shot. The parallel sets include Silver Portrait Proof (individually numbered to 4,000) and Gold Portrait Proof (numbered to 1,000). The insert sets were Red Zone Masterpieces and Stained Glass Stars.

		MT
Complete Set (36):		50.00
Common Player:		.50
Wax Box:		55.00
1	Troy Aikman	3.00
2	Tony Banks	1.00
3	Jeff Blake	1.00
4	Drew Bledsoe	3.00
5	Mark Brunell	3.00
6	Kerry Collins	2.00
7	Trent Dilfer	1.00
8	John Elway	2.00
9	Brett Favre	6.00
10	Gus Frerotte	.50
11	Jeff George	.50
12	Neil O'Donnell	.50
13	Jim Harbaugh	.50
14	Michael Irvin	1.00
15	Dan Marino	5.00
16	Steve McNair	2.00
17	Rick Mirer	.50
18	Jerry Rice	3.00
19	Barry Sanders	3.00
20	Junior Seau	.50
21	Heath Shuler	.50
22	Emmitt Smith	5.00
23	Kordell Stewart	3.00
24	Steve Young	2.00
25	Troy Aikman (Class of Distinction)	1.50
26	Drew Bledsoe (Class of Distinction)	1.50
27	Mark Brunell (Class of Distinction)	1.50
28	Kerry Collins (Class of Distinction)	1.00
29	John Elway (Class of Distinction)	1.00
30	Brett Favre (Class of Distinction)	3.00
31	Dan Marino (Class of Distinction)	2.50
32	Jerry Rice (Class of Distinction)	1.50
33	Barry Sanders (Class of Distinction)	2.00
34	Emmitt Smith (Class of Distinction)	2.50
35	Kordell Stewart (Class of Distinction)	1.50
36	Steve Young (Class of Distinction)	1.00

1997 Donruss Studio Silver Press Proofs

This parallel set reprinted all 30 cards in Studio Football. Silver Press Proofs were distinguished by a silver holofoil strip running down each side of the card front. This parallel was limited to 3,500 sets.

	MT
Silver Press Proofs:	2x-4x

1997 Donruss Studio Gold Press Proofs

All 36 Studio 8" x 10" cards were reprinted in this parallel set. The cards were identified by a gold prismatic strip on the far right and left side of the cards. Gold Press Proofs were limited to 1,000 sets.

	MT
Gold Press Proofs:	5x-10x

1997 Donruss Studio Red Zone Masterpiece

Red Zone Masterpieces features the 24 players in the base set on a canvas material card. Each card is individually numbered to 3,500.

		MT
Complete Set (24):		300.00
Common Player:		5.00
1	Troy Aikman	20.00
2	Tony Banks	10.00
3	Jeff Blake	10.00
4	Drew Bledsoe	20.00
5	Mark Brunell	20.00
6	Kerry Collins	15.00
7	Trent Dilfer	10.00
8	John Elway	15.00
9	Brett Favre	40.00
10	Gus Frerotte	5.00
11	Jeff George	5.00
12	Elvis Grbac	5.00
13	Neil O'Donnell	5.00
14	Michael Irvin	10.00
15	Dan Marino	35.00
16	Steve McNair	15.00
17	Rick Mirer	5.00
18	Jerry Rice	20.00
19	Barry Sanders	25.00
20	Warren Moon	5.00
21	Heath Shuler	5.00
22	Emmitt Smith	35.00
23	Kordell Stewart	20.00
24	Steve Young	15.00

1997 Donruss Studio Stained Glass Stars

This 24-card insert features the QB Club stars on a die-cut plastic 8x10 card. Multi-color ink is used to give the appearance of stained glass. Stained Glass Stars are numbered to 1,000.

		MT
Complete Set (24):		650.00
Common Player:		10.00
1	Troy Aikman	40.00
2	Tony Banks	20.00
3	Jeff Blake	20.00
4	Drew Bledsoe	40.00
5	Mark Brunell	40.00
6	Kerry Collins	30.00
7	Trent Dilfer	20.00
8	John Elway	25.00
9	Brett Favre	100.00
10	Gus Frerotte	10.00
11	Jeff George	10.00
12	Elvis Grbac	10.00
13	Jim Harbaugh	10.00
14	Michael Irvin	20.00
15	Dan Marino	80.00
16	Steve McNair	30.00
17	Rick Mirer	10.00
18	Jerry Rice	40.00
19	Barry Sanders	60.00
20	Junior Seau	10.00
21	Vinny Testaverde	10.00
22	Emmitt Smith	80.00
23	Kordell Stewart	40.00
24	Steve Young	25.00

1997 Finest

The 175-card Series I set has a numbering format that features card Nos. 1-100 labeled as Common, cards Nos. 101-150 as Uncommon and Nos. 151-175 as Rare. Each card also has a different number corresponding to its theme. The Finest themes are Masters, Bulldozers, Hitmen, Dynamos and Field Generals. The numbering box on each card back indicates both sets of numbers, and which type of card it is, either Common, Uncommon or Rare. The card's theme is printed at the top of each card. Uncommon cards were seeded 1:4 packs, while Rare cards were inserted 1:24. Embossed Uncommon cards were seeded 1:16, while Embossed Die-Cut Rare cards were inserted 1:96. Embossed Die-Cut Rare cards were found 1:96. Series II was numbered 176-350. It consisted of 100 commons, 50 uncommons and 25 rares. The themes in Series II were Champions, Dominators, Impact, Masters and Stalwarts. Insertion rates for Series II were identical to Series I.

		MT
Comp. Bronze Ser.2 (100):		60.00
Common Bronze Player:		.25
Comp. Silver Ser.2 (50):		150.00
Common Silver Player:		2.00
Comp. Gold Ser.2 (25):		300.00
Common Gold Player:		7.50
Wax Box Series 2:		100.00
176	*Corey Dillon*	10.00
177	Tyrone Poole	.25
178	Anthony Pleasant	.25
179	Frank Sanders	.25
180	Troy Aikman	4.00
181	Bill Romanowski	.25
182	Ty Law	.25
183	Orlando Thomas	.25
184	Quentin Coryatt	.25
185	Kenny Holmes	.25
186	Bryant Young	.25
187	Michael Sinclair	.25
188	Mike Tomczak	.25
189	Bobby Taylor	.25
190	Brett Favre	7.00
191	Kent Graham	.25
192	Jessie Tuggle	.25
193	Jimmy Smith	.25
194	Greg Hill	.25
195	*Yatil Green*	2.00
196	Mark Fields	.25
197	Phillippi Sparks	.25
198	Aaron Glenn	.25
199	Pat Swilling	.25
200	Barry Sanders	7.00
201	Mark Chmura	.50
202	Marco Coleman	.25
203	Merton Hanks	.25
204	Brian Blades	.25
205	Errict Rhett	.50
206	Henry Ellard	.25
207	Andre Reed	.25
208	Bryan Cox	.25
209	Darnay Scott	.25
210	John Elway	3.00
211	Glyn Milburn	.25
212	Don Beebe	.25
213	Kevin Lockett	.25
214	Dorsey Levens	.50
215	Kordell Stewart	4.00
216	Larry Centers	.25
217	Cris Carter	.50
218	Willie McGinest	.25
219	Renaldo Wynn	.25
220	Jerry Rice	4.00
221	*Reidel Anthony*	5.00
222	Mark Carrier	.25
223	Quinn Early	.25
224	Chris Sanders	.25
225	*Shawn Springs*	.50
226	Kevin Smith	.25
227	Ben Coates	.25
228	Tyrone Wheatley	.25
229	Antonio Freeman	1.50
230	Dan Marino	6.00
231	Dwayne Rudd	.50
232	Leslie O'Neal	.25
233	Brent Jones	.25
234	*Jake Plummer*	15.00
235	Kerry Collins	2.00
236	Rashaan Salaam	.50
237	Tyrone Braxton	.25
238	Herman Moore	.50
239	Keyshawn Johnson	.50
240	Drew Bledsoe	4.00
241	Rickey Dudley	.25
242	*Antowain Smith*	6.00
243	Jeff Lageman	.25
244	Chris T. Jones	.25
245	Steve Young	3.00
246	Eddie Robinson	.25
247	Chad Cota	.25
248	Michael Jackson	.25
249	Robert Porcher	.25
250	Reggie White	.50
251	Carnell Lake	.25
252	Chris Calloway	.25
253	Terance Mathis	.25
254	Carl Pickens	.50
255	Curtis Martin	3.00
256	Jeff Graham	.25
257	Regan Upshaw	.25
258	Sean Gilbert	.25
259	*Will Blackwell*	1.00
260	Emmitt Smith	6.00
261	*Reinard Wilson*	.50
262	*Darrell Russell*	.50
263	Wayne Chrebet	.25
264	Kevin Hardy	.25
265	Shannon Sharpe	.25
266	Harvey Williams	.25
267	John Randle	.25
268	Tim Bowens	.25
269	*Tony Gonzalez*	3.00
270	*Warrick Dunn*	14.00
271	Sean Dawkins	.25
272	Darryll Lewis	.25
273	Alonzo Spellman	.25
274	Mark Collins	.25
275	Checklist 2	.25
276	*Pat Barnes S*	4.00
277	Dana Stubblefield S	2.00
278	Dan Wilkinson S	2.00
279	Bryce Paup S	2.00
280	Kerry Collins S	8.00
281	Derrick Brooks S	2.00
282	Walter Jones S	2.00
283	Terry McDaniel S	2.00
284	James Farrior S	2.00
285	Curtis Martin S	10.00
286	O.J. McDuffie S	2.00
287	Natrone Means S	3.00
288	*Bryant Westbrook S*	3.00
289	*Peter Boulware S*	3.00
290	Emmitt Smith S	15.00
291	*Joey Kent S*	4.00
292	Eddie Kennison S	4.00
293	LeRoy Butler S	2.00
294	Dale Carter S	2.00
295	*Jim Druckenmiller S*	15.00
296	*Byron Hanspard S*	8.00
297	Jeff Blake S	3.00
298	Levon Kirkland S	2.00
299	Michael Westbrook S	2.00
300	John Elway S	12.00
301	Lamar Lathon S	2.00
302	Ray Lewis S	2.00
303	Steve McNair S	7.00
304	*Shawn Springs S*	3.00
305	Karim Abdul-Jabbar S	4.00
306	*Orlando Pace S*	3.00
307	Scott Mitchell S	2.00
308	Walt Harris S	2.00
309	Bruce Smith S	2.00
310	Reggie White S	3.00
311	Eric Swann S	2.00
312	Derrick Thomas S	2.00
313	Tony Martin S	2.00
314	Darrell Russell S	2.00
315	Mark Brunell S	12.00
316	Trent Dilfer S	3.00
317	Irving Fryar S	2.00
318	Amani Toomer S	2.00
319	Jake Reed S	2.00
320	Steve Young S	8.00
321	*Troy Davis S*	4.00
322	Jim Harbaugh S	2.00
323	Neil O'Donnell S	2.00
324	Terry Glenn S	6.00
325	Deion Sanders S	6.00
326	Gus Frerotte G	7.50
327	Tom Knight G	7.50
328	*Peter Boulware G*	7.50
329	Jerome Bettis G	12.00
330	*Orlando Pace G*	12.00
331	*Darnell Autry G*	15.00
332	*Ike Hilliard G*	25.00
333	*David LaFleur G*	25.00
334	Jim Harbaugh G	7.50
335	Eddie George G	45.00
336	Vinny Testaverde G	7.50
337	Terry Allen G	7.50
338	*Jim Druckenmiller G*	30.00
339	Ricky Watters G	15.00
340	Brett Favre G	60.00
341	Simeon Rice G	7.50
342	Shannon Sharpe G	7.50
343	Kordell Stewart G	30.00
344	Isaac Bruce G	15.00
345	Drew Bledsoe G	30.00
346	Jeff Blake G	12.00
347	Herman Moore G	12.00
348	Junior Seau G	7.50
349	*Rae Carruth G*	20.00
350	Dan Marino G	50.00

1997 Finest Refractors

Each of the 350 base cards has a parallel Refractor. Refractor Common cards were inserted 1:12 packs, while Refractor Uncommon were seeded 1:48. Refractor Rare could be found 1:288 packs. In addition, Refractors of the Embossed and Embossed Die-Cut cards were also randomly seeded. An Embossed Uncommon Refractor was inserted 1:192 packs, while an Embossed Die-Cut Refractor was seeded 1:1,152 packs.

		MT
Comp. Bronze Ser.2 (100):		850.00
Common Bronze Player:		3.00
Comp. Silver Ser.2 (50):		900.00
Common Silver Player:		10.00
Comp. Gold Ser.2 (25):		2000.
Common Gold Player:		40.00
176	Corey Dillon	60.00
177	Tyrone Poole	3.00
178	Anthony Pleasant	3.00
179	Frank Sanders	3.00
180	Troy Aikman	30.00
181	Bill Romanowski	3.00
182	Ty Law	3.00
183	Orlando Thomas	3.00
184	Quentin Coryatt	3.00
185	Kenny Holmes	3.00
186	Bryant Young	3.00
187	Michael Sinclair	3.00
188	Mike Tomczak	3.00
189	Bobby Taylor	3.00
190	Brett Favre	60.00
191	Kent Graham	3.00
192	Jessie Tuggle	3.00
193	Jimmy Smith	3.00
194	Greg Hill	3.00
195	Yatil Green	10.00
196	Mark Fields	3.00
197	Phillippi Sparks	3.00
198	Aaron Glenn	3.00
199	Pat Swilling	3.00
200	Barry Sanders	60.00
201	Mark Chmura	6.00
202	Marco Coleman	3.00
203	Merton Hanks	3.00
204	Brian Blades	3.00
205	Errict Rhett	6.00
206	Henry Ellard	3.00
207	Andre Reed	3.00
208	Bryan Cox	3.00
209	Darnay Scott	3.00
210	John Elway	30.00
211	Glyn Milburn	3.00
212	Don Beebe	3.00
213	Kevin Lockett	3.00
214	Dorsey Levens	6.00
215	Kordell Stewart	30.00
216	Larry Centers	3.00
217	Cris Carter	6.00
218	Willie McGinest	3.00
219	Renaldo Wynn	3.00
220	Jerry Rice	20.00
221	Reidel Anthony	225.00
222	Mark Carrier	3.00
223	Quinn Early	3.00
224	Chris Sanders	3.00
225	Shawn Springs	6.00
226	Kevin Smith	3.00
227	Ben Coates	3.00
228	Tyrone Wheatley	3.00
229	Antonio Freeman	20.00
230	Dan Marino	50.00
231	Dwayne Rudd	6.00
232	Leslie O'Neal	3.00
233	Brent Jones	3.00
234	Jake Plummer	75.00
235	Kerry Collins	20.00
236	Rashaan Salaam	6.00
237	Tyrone Braxton	3.00
238	Herman Moore	6.00
239	Keyshawn Johnson	6.00
240	Drew Bledsoe	30.00
241	Rickey Dudley	3.00
242	Antowain Smith	35.00
243	Jeff Lageman	3.00
244	Chris T. Jones	3.00
245	Steve Young	20.00
246	Eddie Robinson	3.00
247	Chad Cota	3.00
248	Michael Jackson	3.00
249	Robert Porcher	3.00
250	Reggie White	6.00
251	Carnell Lake	3.00
252	Chris Galloway	3.00
253	Terance Mathis	3.00
254	Carl Pickens	6.00
255	Curtis Martin	25.00
256	Jeff Graham	3.00
257	Regan Upshaw	3.00
258	Sean Gilbert	3.00
259	Will Blackwell	8.00
260	Emmitt Smith	50.00
261	Reinard Wilson	6.00
262	Darrell Russell	6.00
263	Wayne Chrebet	3.00
264	Kevin Hardy	3.00
265	Shannon Sharpe	3.00
266	Harvey Williams	3.00
267	John Randle	3.00
268	Tim Bowens	3.00
269	Tony Gonzalez	20.00
270	Warrick Dunn	75.00
271	Sean Dawkins	3.00
272	Darryll Lewis	3.00
273	Alonzo Spellman	3.00
274	Mark Collins	3.00
275	Checklist 2	3.00
276	Pat Barnes S	20.00
277	Dana Stubblefield S	10.00
278	Dan Wilkinson S	10.00
279	Bryce Paup S	10.00
280	Kerry Collins S	30.00
281	Derrick Brooks S	10.00
282	Walter Jones S	10.00
283	Terry McDaniel S	10.00
284	James Farrior S	10.00
285	Curtis Martin S	40.00
286	O.J. McDuffie S	10.00
287	Natrone Means S	20.00
288	Bryant Westbrook S	20.00
289	Peter Boulware S	20.00
290	Emmitt Smith S	75.00
291	Joey Kent S	20.00
292	Eddie Kennison S	20.00
293	LeRoy Butler S	10.00
294	Dale Carter S	10.00
295	Jim Druckenmiller S	50.00
296	Byron Hanspard S	35.00
297	Jeff Blake S	20.00
298	Levon Kirkland S	10.00
299	Michael Westbrook S	10.00
300	John Elway S	50.00
301	Lamar Lathon S	10.00
302	Ray Lewis S	10.00
303	Steve McNair S	30.00
304	Shawn Springs S	20.00
305	Karim Abdul-Jabbar S	20.00
306	Orlando Pace S	20.00
307	Scott Mitchell S	10.00
308	Walt Harris S	10.00
309	Bruce Smith S	10.00
310	Reggie White S	20.00
311	Eric Swann S	10.00
312	Derrick Thomas S	10.00
313	Tony Martin S	10.00
314	Darrell Russell S	10.00
315	Mark Brunell S	60.00
316	Trent Dilfer S	20.00
317	Irving Fryar S	10.00
318	Amani Toomer S	10.00
319	Jake Reed S	10.00
320	Steve Young S	40.00
321	Troy Davis S	20.00
322	Jim Harbaugh S	10.00
323	Neil O'Donnell S	10.00
324	Terry Glenn S	25.00
325	Deion Sanders S	30.00
326	Gus Frerotte G	40.00
327	Tom Knight G	40.00
328	Peter Boulware G	40.00
329	Jerome Bettis G	60.00
330	Orlando Pace G	60.00
331	Darnell Autry G	60.00
332	Ike Hilliard G	75.00
333	David LaFleur G	60.00
334	Jim Harbaugh G	40.00
335	Eddie George G	150.00
336	Vinny Testaverde G	40.00
337	Terry Allen G	40.00
338	Jim Druckenmiller G	100.00
339	Ricky Watters G	80.00
340	Brett Favre G	300.00
341	Simeon Rice G	40.00
342	Shannon Sharpe G	40.00
343	Kordell Stewart G	150.00
344	Isaac Bruce G	80.00
345	Drew Bledsoe G	150.00
346	Jeff Blake G	60.00
347	Herman Moore G	60.00
348	Junior Seau G	40.00
349	Rae Carruth G	75.00
350	Dan Marino G	250.00

1997 Finest Embossed Silver

Each Silver or Uncommon card in Finest I and II was also available in an embossed version. This means that cards 101-150 in Series I and 276-325 in Series II featured embossing and a silver tint. Regular versions were seeded one per four packs, with Refractors every 192 packs.

	MT
Silver Cards:	1.5x
Silver Refractors:	4x-8x

1997 Finest Embossed Gold

Each Gold or Rare card in Finest Series I and II was also available in an Embossed/Die-cut version. This means that cards 151-175 in Series I and 326-350 in Series II featured a perimeter die-cut and added embossing on the card front. Regular versions of these were inserted one per 24 packs, with Refractors every 1,152 packs.

	MT
Gold Cards:	2x
Gold Refractors:	5x-10x

1997 Flair Showcase

Flair Showcase NFL is a 360-card set featuring 120 players. Each player has three base cards: Style, Grace and Showcase. The fronts feature distinct action and headshots with a holographic foil background on 24 pt card stock. The backs have another photo and complete career statistics. The basic card types have a tiered insertion ratio. Two parallel sets were issued: Legacy, with less than 100 cards per player, and the one-of-a-kind Legacy Masterpiece. Four inserts sets were included: Wave of the Future, Hot Hands, Midas Touch and Then & Now.

	MT
Complete Set (360):	1700.
Comp. Style Set (120):	75.00

Common Style (A1-A120): .25
Comp. Grace Set (120): 150.00
Common Grace (B1-B120): .50
Comp. Showcase Set (120): 1500.
Common Showcase (C1-C120): 2.00
Wax Box: 140.00
A1 Jerry Rice STY 4.00
A2 Mark Brunell STY 4.00
A3 Eddie Kennison STY .50
A4 Brett Favre STY 8.00
A5 Karim Abdul-Jabbar STY .75
A6 *David LaFleur STY* 1.50
A7 John Elway STY 3.00
A8 Troy Aikman STY 4.00
A9 Steve McNair STY 3.00
A10 Kordell Stewart STY 4.00
A11 Drew Bledsoe STY 4.00
A12 Kerry Collins STY .50
A13 Dan Marino STY 6.00
A14 Steve Young STY 3.00
A15 Marvin Harrison STY 1.00
A16 Lawrence Phillips STY .50
A17 Jeff Blake STY .50
A18 *Yatil Green STY* 1.50
A19 *Jake Plummer STY* 3.00
A20 Barry Sanders STY 4.00
A21 Deion Sanders STY 2.50
A22 Emmitt Smith STY 6.00
A23 *Rae Carruth STY* 2.00
A24 Chris Warren STY .25
A25 Terry Glenn STY 1.00
A26 *Jim Druckenmiller STY* 4.00
A27 Eddie George STY 5.00
A28 Curtis Martin STY 4.00
A29 *Warrick Dunn STY* 6.00
A30 Terrell Davis STY 4.00
A31 Rashaan Salaam STY .25
A32 Marcus Allen STY .50
A33 Jeff George STY .50
A34 Thurman Thomas STY .50
A35 Keyshawn Johnson STY 1.00
A36 Jerome Bettis STY .50
A37 Larry Centers STY .25
A38 Tony Banks STY 1.00
A39 Marshall Faulk STY .50
A40 Mike Alstott STY .50
A41 Elvis Grbac STY .25
A42 Errict Rhett STY .50
A43 Edgar Bennett STY .25
A44 Jim Harbaugh STY .25
A45 Antonio Freeman STY 1.00
A46 *Tiki Barber STY* 3.00
A47 Tim Biakabutuka STY .25
A48 Joey Galloway STY .50
A49 *Tony Gonzalez STY* 1.50
A50 Keenan McCardell STY .25
A51 Darnay Scott STY .25
A52 Brad Johnson STY .25
A53 Herman Moore STY .50
A54 *Reidel Anthony STY* 3.00
A55 Junior Seau STY .50
A56 Ricky Watters STY .50
A57 Amani Toomer STY .25
A58 Andre Reed STY .25
A59 *Antowain Smith STY* 5.00
A60 *Ike Hilliard STY* 2.50
A61 *Byron Hanspard STY* 1.50
A62 Robert Smith STY .25
A63 Gus Frerotte STY .25
A64 Charles Way STY .25
A65 Trent Dilfer STY .50
A66 Adrian Murrell STY .50
A67 Stan Humphries STY .25
A68 Robert Brooks STY .25
A69 Jamal Anderson STY .25
A70 Natrone Means STY .50
A71 John Friesz STY .25
A72 Ki-Jana Carter STY .25
A73 Marc Edwards STY .25
A74 Michael Westbrook STY .25
A75 Neil O'Donnell STY .25
A76 Scott Mitchell STY .25
A77 Wesley Walls STY .25
A78 Bruce Smith STY .25
A79 *Corey Dillon STY* 6.00
A80 Wayne Chrebet STY .25
A81 Tony Martin STY .25
A82 Jimmy Smith STY .25
A83 Terry Allen STY .25
A84 Shannon Sharpe STY .25
A85 Derrick Alexander STY .25
A86 Garrison Hearst STY .25
A87 Tamarick Vanover STY .25
A88 Michael Irvin STY .50
A89 Mark Chmura STY .50
A90 Bert Emanuel STY .25
A91 Eric Metcalf STY .25
A92 Reggie White STY .50
A93 Carl Pickens STY .25
A94 Chris Sanders STY .25
A95 Frank Sanders STY .25
A96 Desmond Howard STY .25
A97 Michael Jackson STY .25
A98 Tim Brown STY .50
A99 O.J. McDuffie STY .25
A100 Mario Bates STY .25
A101 Warren Moon STY .25
A102 Curtis Conway STY .25
A103 Irving Fryar STY .25
A104 Isaac Bruce STY .50
A105 Cris Carter STY .50
A106 Chris Chandler STY .25
A107 Charles Johnson STY .25
A108 Kevin Lockett STY .25
A109 Rob Moore STY .25
A110 Napoleon Kaufman STY .75
A111 Henry Ellard STY .25
A112 Vinny Testaverde STY .25
A113 Rick Mirer STY .25
A114 Ty Detmer STY .25
A115 Todd Collins STY .25
A116 Jake Reed STY .25
A117 Dave Brown STY .25
A118 Dedric Ward STY .25
A119 Heath Shuler STY .25
A120 Ben Coates STY .25
B1 Jerry Rice GRA 6.00
B2 Mark Brunell GRA 6.00
B3 Eddie Kennison GRA 1.00
B4 Brett Favre GRA 12.00
B5 Karim Abdul-Jabbar GRA 1.50
B6 David LaFleur GRA 2.00
B7 John Elway GRA 4.50
B8 Troy Aikman GRA 6.00
B9 Steve McNair GRA 4.50
B10 Kordell Stewart GRA 6.00
B11 Drew Bledsoe GRA 6.00
B12 Kerry Collins GRA 1.50
B13 Dan Marino GRA 9.00
B14 Steve Young GRA 4.50
B15 Marvin Harrison GRA 2.00
B16 Lawrence Phillips GRA .75
B17 Jeff Blake GRA .75
B18 Yatil Green GRA 2.50
B19 Jake Plummer GRA 5.00
B20 Barry Sanders GRA 6.00
B21 Deion Sanders GRA 4.00
B22 Emmitt Smith GRA 9.00
B23 Rae Carruth GRA 3.00
B24 Chris Warren GRA .50
B25 Terry Glenn GRA 2.50
B26 Jim Druckenmiller GRA 6.00
B27 Eddie George GRA 7.50
B28 Curtis Martin GRA 6.00
B29 Warrick Dunn GRA 9.00
B30 Terrell Davis GRA 6.00
B31 Rashaan Salaam GRA .50
B32 Marcus Allen GRA .75
B33 Jeff George GRA .75
B34 Thurman Thomas GRA .75
B35 Keyshawn Johnson GRA 2.00
B36 Jerome Bettis GRA .75
B37 Larry Centers GRA .50
B38 Tony Banks GRA 2.00
B39 Marshall Faulk GRA .75
B40 Mike Alstott GRA .75
B41 Elvis Grbac GRA .50
B42 Errict Rhett GRA .75
B43 Edgar Bennett GRA .50
B44 Jim Harbaugh GRA .50
B45 Antonio Freeman GRA 1.50
B46 Tiki Barber GRA 4.50
B47 Tim Biakabutuka GRA .50
B48 Joey Galloway GRA .75
B49 Tony Gonzalez GRA 2.00
B50 Keenan McCardell GRA .50
B51 Darnay Scott GRA .50
B52 Brad Johnson GRA .50
B53 Herman Moore GRA .75
B54 Reidel Anthony GRA 4.50
B55 Junior Seau GRA .75
B56 Ricky Watters GRA .75
B57 Amani Toomer GRA .50
B58 Andre Reed GRA .50
B59 Antowain Smith GRA 8.00
B60 Ike Hilliard GRA 4.00
B61 Byron Hanspard GRA 1.50
B62 Robert Smith GRA .50
B63 Gus Frerotte GRA .50
B64 Charles Way GRA .50
B65 Trent Dilfer GRA .75
B66 Adrian Murrell GRA .75
B67 Stan Humphries GRA .50
B68 Robert Brooks GRA .50
B69 Jamal Anderson GRA .75
B70 Natrone Means GRA .75
B71 John Friesz GRA .50
B72 Ki-Jana Carter GRA .50
B73 Marc Edwards GRA .50
B74 Michael Westbrook GRA .50
B75 Neil O'Donnell GRA .50
B76 Scott Mitchell GRA .50
B77 Wesley Walls GRA .50
B78 Bruce Smith GRA .50
B79 Corey Dillon GRA 8.00
B80 Wayne Chrebet GRA .50
B81 Tony Martin GRA .50
B82 Jimmy Smith GRA .50
B83 Terry Allen GRA .50
B84 Shannon Sharpe GRA .50
B85 Derrick Alexander GRA .50
B86 Garrison Hearst GRA .50
B87 Tamarick Vanover GRA .50
B88 Michael Irvin GRA .75
B89 Mark Chmura GRA .75
B90 Bert Emanuel GRA .50
B91 Eric Metcalf GRA .50
B92 Reggie White GRA .75
B93 Carl Pickens GRA .50
B94 Chris Sanders GRA .50
B95 Frank Sanders GRA .50
B96 Desmond Howard GRA .50
B97 Michael Jackson GRA .50
B98 Tim Brown GRA .75
B99 O.J. McDuffie GRA .50
B100 Mario Bates GRA .50
B101 Warren Moon GRA .50
B102 Curtis Conway GRA .50
B103 Irving Fryar GRA .50
B104 Isaac Bruce GRA .75
B105 Cris Carter GRA .75
B106 Chris Chandler GRA .50
B107 Charles Johnson GRA .50
B108 Kevin Lockett GRA .50
B109 Rob Moore GRA .50
B110 Napoleon Kaufman GRA 1.00
B111 Henry Ellard GRA .50
B112 Vinny Testaverde GRA .50
B113 Rick Mirer GRA .50
B114 Ty Detmer GRA .50
B115 Todd Collins GRA .50
B116 Jake Reed GRA .50
B117 Dave Brown GRA .50
B118 Dedric Ward GRA .50
B119 Heath Shuler GRA .50
B120 Ben Coates GRA .50
C1 Jerry Rice SHOW 60.00
C2 Mark Brunell SHOW 60.00
C3 Eddie Kennison SHOW 6.00
C4 Brett Favre SHOW 125.00
C5 Karim Abdul-Jabbar SHOW 6.00
C6 David LaFleur SHOW 15.00
C7 John Elway SHOW 50.00
C8 Troy Aikman SHOW 60.00
C9 Steve McNair SHOW 50.00
C10 Kordell Stewart SHOW 60.00
C11 Drew Bledsoe SHOW 60.00
C12 Kerry Collins SHOW 6.00
C13 Dan Marino SHOW 100.00
C14 Steve Young SHOW 50.00
C15 Marvin Harrison SHOW 8.00
C16 Lawrence Phillips SHOW 6.00
C17 Jeff Blake SHOW 4.00
C18 Yatil Green SHOW 6.00
C19 Jake Plummer SHOW 50.00
C20 Barry Sanders SHOW 70.00
C21 Deion Sanders SHOW 40.00
C22 Emmitt Smith SHOW 100.00
C23 Rae Carruth SHOW 25.00
C24 Chris Warren SHOW 2.00
C25 Terry Glenn SHOW 8.00
C26 Jim Druckenmiller SHOW 60.00
C27 Eddie George SHOW 75.00
C28 Curtis Martin SHOW 60.00
C29 Warrick Dunn SHOW 85.00
C30 Terrell Davis SHOW 60.00
C31 Rashaan Salaam SHOW 2.00
C32 Marcus Allen SHOW 6.00
C33 Jeff George SHOW 6.00
C34 Thurman Thomas SHOW 6.00
C35 Keyshawn Johnson SHOW 8.00
C36 Jerome Bettis SHOW 6.00
C37 Larry Centers SHOW 2.00
C38 Tony Banks SHOW 6.00
C39 Marshall Faulk SHOW 6.00
C40 Mike Alstott SHOW 7.50
C41 Elvis Grbac SHOW 2.00
C42 Errict Rhett SHOW 4.00
C43 Edgar Bennett SHOW 2.00
C44 Jim Harbaugh SHOW 2.00
C45 Antonio Freeman SHOW 8.00
C46 Tiki Barber SHOW 25.00
C47 Tim Biakabutuka SHOW 2.00
C48 Joey Galloway SHOW 7.50
C49 Tony Gonzalez SHOW 15.00
C50 Keenan McCardell SHOW 2.00
C51 Darnay Scott SHOW 2.00
C52 Brad Johnson SHOW 2.00
C53 Herman Moore SHOW 7.50
C54 Reidel Anthony SHOW 25.00
C55 Junior Seau SHOW 4.00
C56 Ricky Watters SHOW 4.00
C57 Amani Toomer SHOW 2.00
C58 Andre Reed SHOW 2.00
C59 Antowain Smith SHOW 25.00
C60 Ike Hilliard SHOW 25.00
C61 Byron Hanspard SHOW 6.00
C62 Robert Smith SHOW 2.00
C63 Gus Frerotte SHOW 2.00
C64 Charles Way SHOW 2.00
C65 Trent Dilfer SHOW 6.00
C66 Adrian Murrell SHOW 4.00
C67 Stan Humphries SHOW 2.00
C68 Robert Brooks SHOW 2.00
C69 Jamal Anderson SHOW 7.50
C70 Natrone Means SHOW 6.00
C71 John Friesz SHOW 2.00
C72 Ki-Jana Carter SHOW 2.00
C73 Marc Edwards SHOW 2.00
C74 Michael Westbrook SHOW 2.00
C75 Neil O'Donnell SHOW 2.00
C76 Scott Mitchell SHOW 2.00
C77 Wesley Walls SHOW 2.00
C78 Bruce Smith SHOW 2.00
C79 Corey Dillon SHOW 30.00
C80 Wayne Chrebet SHOW 2.00
C81 Tony Martin SHOW 2.00
C82 Jimmy Smith SHOW 2.00
C83 Terry Allen SHOW 2.00
C84 Shannon Sharpe SHOW 2.00
C85 Derrick Alexander SHOW 2.00
C86 Garrison Hearst SHOW 2.00
C87 Tamarick Vanover SHOW 2.00
C88 Michael Irvin SHOW 5.00
C89 Mark Chmura SHOW 4.00
C90 Bert Emanuel SHOW 2.00
C91 Eric Metcalf SHOW 2.00
C92 Reggie White SHOW 5.00
C93 Carl Pickens SHOW 2.00
C94 Chris Sanders SHOW 2.00
C95 Frank Sanders SHOW 2.00
C96 Desmond Howard SHOW 2.00
C97 Michael Jackson SHOW 2.00
C98 Tim Brown SHOW 4.00
C99 O.J. McDuffie SHOW 2.00
C100 Mario Bates SHOW 2.00
C101 Warren Moon SHOW 2.00
C102 Curtis Conway SHOW 2.00
C103 Irving Fryar SHOW 2.00
C104 Isaac Bruce SHOW 4.00
C105 Cris Carter SHOW 4.00
C106 Chris Chandler SHOW 2.00
C107 Charles Johnson SHOW 2.00
C108 Kevin Lockett SHOW 2.00
C109 Rob Moore SHOW 2.00
C110 Napoleon Kaufman SHOW 6.00
C111 Henry Ellard SHOW 2.00
C112 Vinny Testaverde SHOW 2.00
C113 Rick Mirer SHOW 2.00
C114 Ty Detmer SHOW 2.00
C115 Todd Collins SHOW 2.00
C116 Jake Reed SHOW 2.00
C117 Dave Brown SHOW 2.00
C118 Dedric Ward SHOW 2.00
C119 Heath Shuler SHOW 2.00
C120 Ben Coates SHOW 2.00

1997 Flair Showcase Legacy

Legacy parallels the 360-base cards in Flair Showcase. The cards feature blue-foil stamping and are sequentially numbered to 100. The backs are done in matte finish. The Legacy Masterpiece versions are a one-of-one parallel of each base card. The cards are stamped to signify their distinctness.

		MT
Common Player:		25.00
1	Jerry Rice	250.00
2	Mark Brunell	250.00
3	Eddie Kennison	125.00
4	Brett Favre	550.00
5	Karim Abdul-Jabbar	125.00
6	David LaFleur	50.00
7	John Elway	200.00
8	Troy Aikman	250.00
9	Steve McNair	200.00
10	Kordell Stewart	250.00
11	Drew Bledsoe	250.00
12	Kerry Collins	200.00
13	Dan Marino	500.00
14	Steve Young	200.00
15	Marvin Harrison	125.00
16	Lawrence Phillips	50.00
17	Jeff Blake	50.00
18	Yatil Green	100.00
19	Jake Plummer	100.00
20	Barry Sanders	300.00
21	Deion Sanders	125.00
22	Emmitt Smith	500.00
23	Rae Carruth	100.00
24	Chris Warren	25.00
25	Terry Glenn	200.00
26	Jim Druckenmiller	175.00
27	Eddie George	275.00
28	Curtis Martin	250.00
29	Warrick Dunn	250.00
30	Terrell Davis	250.00
31	Rashaan Salaam	25.00
32	Marcus Allen	50.00
33	Jeff George	50.00
34	Thurman Thomas	50.00
35	Keyshawn Johnson	100.00
36	Jerome Bettis	50.00
37	Larry Centers	25.00
38	Tony Banks	100.00
39	Marshall Faulk	50.00
40	Mike Alstott	50.00
41	Elvis Grbac	25.00
42	Errict Rhett	50.00
43	Edgar Bennett	25.00
44	Jim Harbaugh	25.00
45	Antonio Freeman	75.00
46	Tiki Barber	125.00
47	Tim Biakabutuka	25.00
48	Joey Galloway	50.00
49	Tony Gonzalez	75.00
50	Keenan McCardell	25.00
51	Darnay Scott	25.00
52	Brad Johnson	25.00
53	Herman Moore	50.00
54	Reidel Anthony	125.00
55	Junior Seau	50.00
56	Ricky Watters	50.00
57	Amani Toomer	25.00
58	Andre Reed	25.00
59	Antowain Smith	125.00
60	Ike Hilliard	125.00
61	Byron Hanspard	50.00
62	Robert Smith	25.00
63	Gus Frerotte	25.00
64	Charles Way	25.00
65	Trent Dilfer	50.00
66	Adrian Murrell	50.00
67	Stan Humphries	25.00
68	Robert Brooks	25.00
69	Jamal Anderson	50.00
70	Natrone Means	50.00
71	John Friesz	25.00
72	Ki-Jana Carter	25.00
73	Marc Edwards	25.00
74	Michael Westbrook	25.00
75	Neil O'Donnell	25.00
76	Scott Mitchell	25.00
77	Wesley Walls	25.00
78	Bruce Smith	25.00
79	Corey Dillon	125.00
80	Wayne Chrebet	25.00
81	Tony Martin	25.00
82	Jimmy Smith	25.00
83	Terry Allen	25.00
84	Shannon Sharpe	25.00
85	Derrick Alexander	25.00
86	Garrison Hearst	25.00
87	Tamarick Vanover	25.00
88	Michael Irvin	50.00
89	Mark Chmura	50.00
90	Bert Emanuel	25.00
91	Eric Metcalf	25.00
92	Reggie White	50.00
93	Carl Pickens	25.00
94	Chris Sanders	25.00
95	Frank Sanders	25.00
96	Desmond Howard	25.00
97	Michael Jackson	25.00
98	Tim Brown	50.00
99	O.J. McDuffie	25.00
100	Mario Bates	25.00
101	Warren Moon	25.00
102	Curtis Conway	25.00

103	Irving Fryar	25.00
104	Isaac Bruce	50.00
105	Cris Carter	50.00
106	Chris Chandler	25.00
107	Charles Johnson	25.00
108	Kevin Lockett	25.00
109	Rob Moore	25.00
110	Napoleon Kaufman	60.00
111	Henry Ellard	25.00
112	Vinny Testaverde	25.00
113	Rick Mirer	25.00
114	Ty Detmer	25.00
115	Todd Collins	25.00
116	Jake Reed	25.00
117	Dave Brown	25.00
118	Dedric Ward	25.00
119	Heath Shuler	25.00
120	Ben Coates	25.00

1997 Flair Showcase Hot Hands

Hot Hands is a 12-card insert featuring some of the top players in the NFL. The cards are die-cut in the shape of flames and have a fiery background. They are inserted once in every 90 packs.

	MT
Complete Set (12):	700.00
Common Player:	10.00
HH1 Kerry Collins	50.00
HH2 Emmitt Smith	100.00
HH3 Terrell Davis	60.00
HH4 Brett Favre	125.00
HH5 Eddie George	80.00
HH6 Marvin Harrison	10.00
HH7 Mark Brunell	60.00
HH8 Dan Marino	100.00
HH9 Curtis Martin	60.00
HH10Terry Glenn	45.00
HH11Keyshawn Johnson	10.00
HH12Jerry Rice	60.00

1997 Flair Showcase Midas Touch

Midas Touch is a 12-card insert featuring superstars with a "golden touch." The cards have a gold-colored background and were inserted once in every 20 packs.

	MT
Complete Set (12):	150.00
Common Player:	3.00
MT1 Troy Aikman	25.00
MT2 John Elway	20.00
MT3 Barry Sanders	25.00
MT4 Marshall Faulk	6.00
MT5 Karim Abdul-Jabbar	15.00
MT6 Drew Bledsoe	25.00
MT7 Ricky Watters	6.00
MT8 Kordell Stewart	25.00
MT9 Tony Martin	3.00
MT10Steve Young	20.00
MT11Joey Galloway	3.00
MT12Isaac Bruce	6.00

1997 Flair Showcase Now & Then

A four-card insert set, Then & Now features 12 NFL players as they looked when they entered the league. Each card highlights a particular draft year and three of the top players who were picked. The cards were inserted once in every 288 packs.

	MT
Complete Set (4):	800.00
Common Player:	175.00
NT1 Marino, Elway, D. Green (1983)	225.00
NT2 Aikman, B. Sanders, D. Sanders (1989)	175.00
NT3 E. Smith, C. Warren, J. Seau (1990)	225.00
NT4 Favre, H. Moore, R. Watters (1991)	275.00

1997 Flair Showcase Wave of the Future

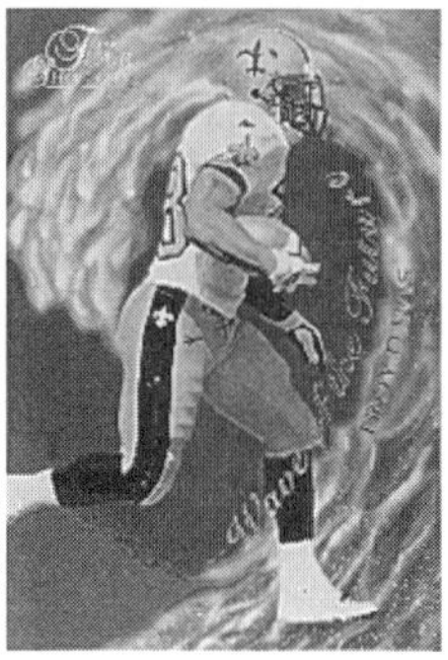

Wave of the Future showcases 25 top rookies entering the 1997 season. The fronts and backs feature a tidal wave design. Inserted once in per four packs.

	MT
Complete Set (25):	60.00
Common Player:	1.00
WF1 Mike Adams	1.00
WF2 John Allred	1.00
WF3 Pat Barnes	6.00
WF4 Kenny Bynum	1.00
WF5 Will Blackwell	2.00
WF6 Peter Boulware	2.00
WF7 Greg Clark	1.00
WF8 Troy Davis	8.00
WF9 Albert Connell	1.00
WF10Jay Graham	6.00
WF11Leon Johnson	1.00
WF12Damon Jones	1.00
WF13Freddie Jones	4.00
WF14George Jones	2.00
WF15Chad Levitt	1.00
WF16Joey Kent	6.00
WF17Danny Wuerffel	12.00
WF18Orlando Pace	2.00
WF19Darnell Autry	6.00
WF20Sedrick Shaw	4.00
WF21Shawn Springs	2.00
WF22Duce Staley	1.00
WF23Darrell Russell	1.00
WF24Bryant Westbrook	2.00
WF25Antowuan Wyatt	1.00

1997 Fleer Goudey II

Goudey Series II is a 150-card set. It contians 145 player cards, all of which feature "Gale Sayers Says" on the backs. There are also two checklist cards and a three card Gale Sayers subset (1:9). The parallel sets are Gridiron Greats (1:3) and Goudey Greats (numbered to 150). Sayers has autographed 40 of each subset card and each card #40 of the Goudey Greats parallel set. The insert sets included Rookie Classics, Glory Days, Vintage Goudey, Big Time Backs and Million Dollar Moments.

		MT
Complete Set (150):		25.00
Common Player:		.05
Wax Box:		45.00
1	Gale Sayers	1.25
2	Vinny Testaverde	.05
3	Jeff George	.10
4	Brett Favre	2.25
5	Eddie Kennison	.50
6	Ken Norton	.05
7	John Elway	.75
8	Troy Aikman	1.00
9	Steve McNair	.75
10	Kordell Stewart	1.00
11	Drew Bledsoe	1.00
12	Kerry Collins	.25
13	Dan Marino	2.00
14	Brad Johnson	.05
15	Todd Collins	.05
16	Ki-Jana Carter	.10
17	*Pat Barnes*	.50
18	Aeneas Williams	.05
19	Keyshawn Johnson	.20
20	Barry Sanders	1.25
21	*Tiki Barber*	1.00
22	Emmitt Smith	2.00
23	Kevin Hardy	.05
24	Mario Bates	.05
25	Ricky Watters	.10
26	Chris Canty	.05
27	Eddie George	1.50
28	Curtis Martin	1.00
29	Adrian Murrell	.10
30	Terrell Davis	1.00
31	Rashaan Salaam	.10
32	Marcus Allen	.10
33	Karim Abdul-Jabbar	.50
34	Thurman Thomas	.10
35	Marvin Harrison	.50
36	Jerome Bettis	.10
37	Larry Centers	.05
38	Stan Humphries	.05
39	Lawrence Phillips	.10
40	Gale Sayers	1.25
41	Henry Ellard	.05
42	Chris Warren	.05
43	Robert Brooks	.10
44	*Sedrick Shaw*	.50
45	Muhsin Muhammad	.05
46	Napoleon Kaufman	.20
47	*Reidel Anthony*	1.00
48	Jamal Anderson	.10
49	Scott Mitchell	.05
50	Mark Brunell	1.00
51	William Thomas	.05
52	Bryan Cox	.05
53	Carl Pickens	.10
54	Chris Spielman	.05
55	Junior Seau	.10
56	Hardy Nickerson	.05
57	*Dwayne Rudd*	.10
58	*Peter Boulware*	.10
59	*Jim Druckenmiller*	2.00
60	Michael Westbrook	.05
61	*Shawn Springs*	.25
62	Zach Thomas	.10
63	*David LaFleur*	.50
64	*Darrell Russell*	.10
65	*Jake Plummer*	1.50
66	Tim Biakabutuka	.10
67	Tyrone Wheatley	.05
68	Elvis Grbac	.05
69	Antonio Freeman	.30
70	Wayne Chrebet	.05
71	*Walter Jones*	.10
72	Marshall Faulk	.10
73	Jason Dunn	.05
74	Darnay Scott	.05
75	Errict Rhett	.10
76	*Orlando Pace*	.25
77	Natrone Means	.10
78	Bruce Smith	.05
79	Jamie Sharper	.05
80	Jerry Rice	1.00
81	Tim Brown	.10
82	Brian Mitchell	.05
83	Andre Reed	.05
84	Herman Moore	.10
85	Rob Moore	.05
86	*Rae Carruth*	.75
87	Bert Emanuel	.05
88	Michael Irvin	.10
89	Mark Chmura	.10
90	Tony Brackens	.05
91	Kevin Greene	.05
92	Reggie White	.10
93	Derrick Thomas	.05
94	*Troy Davis*	.25
95	Greg Lloyd	.05
96	Cortez Kennedy	.05
97	Simeon Rice	.05
98	Terrell Owens	.50
99	Hugh Douglas	.05
100	Terry Glenn	.25
101	Jim Harbaugh	.05
102	Shannon Sharpe	.05
103	*Joey Kent*	.30
104	Jeff Blake	.10
105	Terry Allen	.05
106	Cris Carter	.05
107	Amani Toomer	.05
108	Derrick Alexander	.05
109	*Darnell Autry*	.50
110	Irving Fryar	.05
111	*Bryant Westbrook*	.10
112	Tony Banks	.50
113	Michael Booker	.05
114	*Yatil Green*	.40
115	*James Farrior*	.10
116	*Warrick Dunn*	3.00
117	Greg Hill	.05
118	Tony Martin	.05
119	Chris Sanders	.05
120	Charles Johnson	.05
121	John Mobley	.05
122	Keenan McCardell	.05
123	Willie McGinest	.05
124	O.J. McDuffie	.05
125	Deion Sanders	.50
126	Curtis Conway	.05
127	Desmond Howard	.05
128	Johnnie Morton	.05
129	*Ike Hilliard*	1.00
130	Gus Frerotte	.05
131	*Tom Knight*	.10
132	Sean Dawkins	.05
133	Isaac Bruce	.10
134	Wesley Walls	.05
135	*Danny Wuerffel*	1.00
136	*Tony Gonzalez*	.50
137	Ben Coates	.05
138	Joey Galloway	.10
139	Michael Jackson	.05
140	Steve Young	.50
141	*Corey Dillon*	2.00
142	Jake Reed	.05
143	Edgar Bennett	.05
144	Ty Detmer	.05
145	Darrell Green	.05
146	*Antowain Smith*	1.50
147	Mike Alstott	.10
148	Checklist	.05
149	Checklist	.05
150	Gale Sayers (Commemorative Card)	1.25

1997 Fleer Goudey II Gridiron Greats

Gridiron Greats paralleled all 150 cards from Goudey II. They were inserted one per three packs.

	MT
Gridiron Greats Cards:	2x-4x

1997 Fleer Goudey II Greats

Greats paralleled all 150 cards in Goudey II. Cards from this parallel were sequentially numbered to 150 sets.

	MT
Greats Cards:	20x-40x
Greats Rookies:	10x-20x

1997 Fleer Goudey II Big Time Backs

This 10-card insert features top quarterbacks and running backs on a die-cut, embossed card designed as a clipboard. The cards were inserted 1:72.

		MT
Complete Set (10):		150.00
Common Player:		3.00
1	Karim Abdul-Jabbar	10.00
2	Marcus Allen	3.00
3	Jerome Bettis	3.00
4	Terrell Davis	15.00
5	Brett Favre	30.00
6	Eddie George	20.00
7	Dan Marino	25.00
8	Curtis Martin	15.00
9	Barry Sanders	30.00
10	Emmitt Smith	25.00

1997 Fleer Goudey II Glory Days

This 18-card insert features top players on an embossed card. Glory Days was inserted once per 18 retail packs.

		MT
Complete Set (15):		70.00
Common Player:		2.00
1	Troy Aikman	8.00
2	Isaac Bruce	2.00
3	Mark Brunell	8.00
4	Cris Carter	2.00
5	Joey Galloway	4.00
6	Terry Glenn	6.00
7	Marvin Harrison	4.00
8	Dan Marino	15.00
9	Deion Sanders	4.00
10	Shannon Sharpe	2.00
11	Emmitt Smith	15.00
12	Bruce Smith	2.00
13	Kordell Stewart	8.00
14	Ricky Watters	2.00
15	Reggie White	2.00

1997 Fleer Goudey II Rookie Classics

This 20-card insert features top 1997 rookies on a die-cut card. The first down marker is die-cut on the right side of the card. This set was inserted 1:3.

		MT
Complete Set (20):		18.00
Common Player:		.25
1	Reidel Anthony	2.50
2	Pat Barnes	1.00
3	Peter Boulware	.25
4	Rae Carruth	1.50
5	Troy Davis	1.50
6	Corey Dillon	1.50
7	Jim Druckenmiller	3.00
8	Warrick Dunn	5.00
9	Tony Gonzalez	1.00
10	Yatil Green	1.50
11	Ike Hilliard	2.00
12	Walter Jones	.25
13	David LaFleur	1.00
14	Orlando Pace	.50
15	Jake Plummer	1.00
16	Darrell Russell	.25
17	Antowain Smith	2.00
18	Shawn Springs	.25
19	Bryant Westbrook	.25
20	Danny Wuerffel	3.00

1997 Fleer Goudey II Vintage Goudey

This 15-card insert features players who are throwbacks to old-time football. The players are featured on cards die-cut into a football shape. This set also contained redemption cards for an original 1933 Sport Kings Football card of Red Grange, Jim Thorpe and Knute Rockne. This set was inserted 1:36 in hobby packs.

		MT
Complete Set (15):		120.00
Common Player:		4.00
1	Karim Abdul-Jabbar	8.00
2	Kerry Collins	10.00
3	Terrell Davis	12.00
4	John Elway	8.00
5	Brett Favre	25.00
6	Eddie George	18.00
7	Terry Glenn	10.00
8	Keyshawn Johnson	4.00
9	Curtis Martin	12.00
10	Herman Moore	4.00
11	Jerry Rice	12.00
12	Barry Sanders	20.00
13	Deion Sanders	6.00
14	Zach Thomas	4.00
15	Steve Young	8.00

1997 Leaf

Leaf Football is a 200-card set featuring a player action shot on the front and a close up on the back. The backs also include the past season's statistics. The Fractal Matrix chase set makes its Leaf Football debut. This base set parallel features three different colors schemes and three different die-cuts. The breakdown of die-cuts and colors is 100 X-Axis (5 gold/20 silver/75 bronze), 60 Y-Axis (10 gold/30 silver/20 bronze) and 40 Z-Axis (25 gold/10 silver/5 bronze). Inserts in this set include 1948 Leaf Reproductions, Lettermen, Run & Gun and Hardwear.

		MT
Complete Set (200):		35.00
Common Player:		.15
Wax Box:		60.00
1	Steve Young	1.00
2	Brett Favre	3.00
3	Barry Sanders	3.00
4	Drew Bledsoe	1.50
5	Troy Aikman	1.50
6	Kerry Collins	.30
7	Dan Marino	2.00
8	Jerry Rice	1.50
9	John Elway	1.50
10	Emmitt Smith	2.00
11	Tony Banks	.30
12	Gus Frerotte	.15
13	Elvis Grbac	.15
14	Neil O'Donnell	.15
15	Michael Irvin	.30
16	Marshall Faulk	.50
17	Todd Collins	.15
18	Scott Mitchell	.15
19	Trent Dilfer	.30
20	Rick Mirer	.15
21	Frank Sanders	.15
22	Larry Centers	.15
23	Brad Johnson	.30
24	Garrison Hearst	.30
25	Steve McNair	.75
26	Dorsey Levens	.30
27	Eric Metcalf	.15
28	Jeff George	.30
29	Rodney Hampton	.15
30	Michael Westbrook	.15
31	Cris Carter	.50
32	Heath Shuler	.15
33	Warren Moon	.30
34	Rod Woodson	.15
35	Ken Dilger	.15
36	Ben Coates	.15
37	Andre Reed	.15
38	Terrell Owens	.75
39	Jeff Blake	.30
40	Vinny Testaverde	.30
41	Robert Brooks	.15
42	Shannon Sharpe	.30
43	Terry Allen	.30
44	Terance Mathis	.15
45	Bobby Engram	.15
46	Rickey Dudley	.15
47	Alex Molden	.15
48	Lawrence Phillips	.15
49	Curtis Martin	.75
50	Jim Harbaugh	.30
51	Wayne Chrebet	.30
52	Quentin Coryatt	.15
53	Eddie George	1.50
54	Michael Jackson	.15
55	Greg Lloyd	.15
56	Natrone Means	.30
57	Marcus Allen	.30
58	Desmond Howard	.15
59	Stan Humphries	.15
60	Reggie White	.30
61	Brett Perriman	.15
62	Warren Sapp	.15
63	Adrian Murrell	.30
64	Mark Brunell	1.50
65	Carl Pickens	.30
66	Kordell Stewart	1.50
67	Ricky Watters	.30
68	Tyrone Wheatley	.15
69	Stanley Pritchett	.15
70	Kevin Greene	.15
71	Karim Abdul-Jabbar	.30
72	Ki-Jana Carter	.15
73	Rashaan Salaam	.15
74	Simeon Rice	.15
75	Napoleon Kaufman	.75
76	Muhsin Muhammad	.15
77	Bruce Smith	.15
78	Eric Moulds	.50
79	O.J. McDuffie	.15
80	Danny Kanell	.15
81	Harvey Williams	.15
82	Greg Hill	.15
83	Terrell Davis	1.50
84	Dan Wilkinson	.15
85	Yancey Thigpen	.15
86	Darrell Green	.15
87	Tamarick Vanover	.15
88	Mike Alstott	.30
89	Johnnie Morton	.15
90	Dale Carter	.15
91	Jerome Bettis	.30
92	James Stewart	.15
93	Irving Fryar	.15
94	Junior Seau	.15
95	Sean Dawkins	.15
96	J.J. Stokes	.15
97	Tim Biakabutuka	.15
98	Bert Emanuel	.15
99	Eddie Kennison	.75
100	Ray Zellars	.15
101	Dave Brown	.15
102	Leeland McElroy	.15
103	Chris Warren	.15
104	Bam Morris	.15
105	Thurman Thomas	.30
106	Kyle Brady	.15
107	Anthony Miller	.15
108	Derrick Thomas	.15
109	Mark Chmura	.15
110	Deion Sanders	.75
111	Eric Swann	.15
112	Amani Toomer	.15
113	Raymont Harris	.15
114	Jake Reed	.15
115	Bryant Young	.15
116	Keenan McCardell	.15
117	Herman Moore	.30
118	Errict Rhett	.15
119	Henry Ellard	.15
120	Bobby Hoying	.15
121	Robert Smith	.15
122	Keyshawn Johnson	.75
123	Zach Thomas	.30
124	Charlie Garner	.15
125	Terry Kirby	.15
126	Darren Woodson	.15
127	Darnay Scott	.15
128	Chris Sanders	.15
129	Charles Johnson	.15
130	Joey Galloway	.30
131	Curtis Conway	.15
132	Isaac Bruce	.30
133	Bobby Taylor	.15
134	Jamal Anderson	.15
135	Ken Norton	.15
136	Darick Holmes	.15
137	Tony Brackens	.15
138	Tony Martin	.15
139	Antonio Freeman	.50
140	Neil Smith	.15
141	Terry Glenn	1.25
142	Marvin Harrison	.75
143	Daryl Johnston	.15
144	Tim Brown	.15
145	Kimble Anders	.15
146	Derrick Alexander	.15
147	LeShon Johnson	.15
148	Anthony Johnson	.15
149	Leslie Shepherd	.15
150	Chris T. Jones	.15
151	Edgar Bennett	.15
152	Ty Detmer	.15
153	*Ike Hilliard*	1.25
154	*Jim Druckenmiller*	2.50
155	*Warrick Dunn*	4.00
156	*Yatil Green*	1.25
157	*Reidel Anthony*	1.75
158	*Antowain Smith*	2.00
159	*Rae Carruth*	1.25
160	*Tiki Barber*	1.50
161	*Byron Hanspard*	.50
162	*Jake Plummer*	3.00
163	*Joey Kent*	.50
164	*Corey Dillon*	2.50
165	*Kevin Lockett*	.15
166	*Will Blackwell*	.30
167	*Troy Davis*	.75
168	*James Farrior*	.15
169	*Danny Wuerffel*	1.50
170	*Pat Barnes*	.75
171	*Darnell Autry*	.30
172	*Tom Knight*	.15
173	*David LaFleur*	.75
174	*Tony Gonzalez*	.75
175	*Kenny Holmes*	.15
176	*Reinard Wilson*	.15
177	*Renaldo Wynn*	.15
178	*Bryant Westbrook*	.15
179	*Darrell Russell*	.15
180	*Orlando Pace*	.30
181	*Shawn Springs*	.15
182	*Peter Boulware*	.15
183	Dan Marino (Legacy)	1.25
184	Brett Favre (Legacy)	1.50
185	Emmitt Smith (Legacy)	1.25
186	Eddie George (Legacy)	1.00
187	Curtis Martin (Legacy)	.75
188	Tim Brown (Legacy)	.15
189	Mark Brunell (Legacy)	.75
190	Isaac Bruce (Legacy)	.15
191	Deion Sanders (Legacy)	.30
192	John Elway (Legacy)	.50
193	Jerry Rice (Legacy)	.75
194	Barry Sanders (Legacy)	.75
195	Herman Moore (Legacy)	.15
196	Carl Pickens (Legacy)	.15
197	Karim Abdul-Jabbar (Legacy)	.50
198	Checklist Drew Bledsoe	.75
199	Checklist Troy Aikman	.75
200	Checklist Terrell Davis	.75

1997 Leaf Signature Proofs

Leaf Signature Proofs paralleled all 200 cards in the Leaf Football set. The cards featured red and gold foil on the fronts, with the words "Signature Proofs" on the front. These were numbered to 200 sets.

	MT
Signature Proof Cards:	20x-40x
Signature Proof Rookies:	10x-20x
Production 200 Sets	

1997 Leaf Fractal Matrix

This 200-card parallel features multi-fractured technology. Each card is done in one of three colors: bronze (100 cards), silver (60 cards) or gold (40 cards).

		MT
Common Bronze X:		2.00
Common Bronze Y:		1.50
Common Bronze Z:		1.50
Common Silver X:		6.00
Common Silver Y:		5.00
Common Silver Z:		4.00
1	Steve Young GZ	70.00
2	Brett Favre GX	500.00
3	Barry Sanders GZ	100.00
4	Drew Bledsoe GZ	100.00
5	Troy Aikman GZ	100.00
6	Kerry Collins GZ	85.00
7	Dan Marino GX	450.00
8	Jerry Rice GZ	100.00
9	John Elway GZ	70.00
10	Emmitt Smith GX	450.00
11	Tony Banks GY	50.00
12	Gus Frerotte SX	6.00
13	Elvis Grbac SX	6.00
14	Neil O'Donnell BX	2.00
15	Michael Irvin SY	7.00
16	Marshall Faulk SY	7.00
17	Todd Collins SX	6.00
18	Scott Mitchell BX	2.00
19	Trent Dilfer SY	5.00
20	Rick Mirer SX	6.00
21	Frank Sanders SX	6.00
22	Larry Centers BX	2.00
23	Brad Johnson BX	2.00
24	Garrison Hearst SY	5.00
25	Steve McNair GZ	85.00
26	Dorsey Levens BX	4.00
27	Eric Metcalf BX	2.00
28	Jeff George SX	6.00
29	Rodney Hampton BX	2.00
30	Michael Westbrook SY	5.00
31	Cris Carter SY	5.00
32	Heath Shuler SX	6.00
33	Warren Moon BX	2.00
34	Rod Woodson SX	6.00
35	Ken Dilger BX	2.00
36	Ben Coates BX	2.00
37	Andre Reed BX	2.00
38	Terrell Owens SZ	25.00
39	Jeff Blake SY	5.00
40	Vinny Testaverde BX	2.00
41	Robert Brooks SY	5.00
42	Shannon Sharpe SX	6.00
43	Terry Allen SY	5.00
44	Terance Mathis BX	2.00
45	Bobby Engram BZ	3.00
46	Rickey Dudley BX	2.00
47	Alex Molden BX	2.00
48	Lawrence Phillips SY	5.00
49	Curtis Martin GZ	100.00
50	Jim Harbaugh BX	2.00
51	Wayne Chrebet BX	2.00
52	Quentin Coryatt BX	2.00
53	Eddie George GX	325.00
54	Michael Jackson BX	2.00
55	Greg Lloyd BX	2.00
56	Natrone Means SZ	7.00
57	Marcus Allen GY	30.00
58	Desmond Howard BX	2.00
59	Stan Humphries BX	2.00
60	Reggie White GY	30.00
61	Brett Perriman SY	5.00
62	Warren Sapp BX	2.00
63	Adrian Murrell SZ	4.00
64	Mark Brunell GZ	100.00
65	Carl Pickens GY	5.00
66	Kordell Stewart GZ	100.00
67	Ricky Watters GY	30.00
68	Tyrone Wheatley BX	2.00
69	Stanley Pritchett BX	2.00
70	Kevin Greene BX	2.00
71	Karim Abdul-Jabbar GZ	85.00
72	Ki-Jana Carter SY	5.00
73	Rashaan Salaam SY	5.00
74	Simeon Rice BX	2.00
75	Napoleon Kaufman SY	5.00
76	Muhsin Muhammad SZ	4.00
77	Bruce Smith GY	5.00
78	Eric Moulds SX	6.00
79	O.J. McDuffie BX	2.00
80	Danny Kanell BZ	1.50
81	Harvey Williams BX	2.00
82	Greg Hill SY	5.00
83	Terrell Davis GZ	100.00
84	Dan Wilkinson BX	2.00
85	Yancey Thigpen BX	2.00
86	Darrell Green SX	6.00
87	Tamarick Vanover SX	6.00
88	Mike Alstott BX	2.00
89	Johnnie Morton SX	6.00
90	Dale Carter BX	2.00
91	Jerome Bettis GY	30.00
92	James Stewart BX	2.00
93	Irving Fryar SX	6.00
94	Junior Seau SY	5.00
95	Sean Dawkins BX	2.00
96	J.J. Stokes BZ	1.50
97	Tim Biakabutuka SY	5.00
98	Bert Emanuel BX	2.00
99	Eddie Kennison GY	50.00
100	Ray Zellars BX	2.00
101	Dave Brown BX	2.00
102	Leeland McElroy SY	5.00
103	Chris Warren SY	5.00
104	Bam Morris BX	2.00
105	Thurman Thomas GY	30.00
106	Kyle Brady BX	2.00
107	Anthony Miller GY	10.00
108	Derrick Thomas SY	5.00
109	Mark Chmura BX	2.00
110	Deion Sanders GZ	50.00
111	Eric Swann BX	2.00
112	Amani Toomer SX	6.00
113	Raymont Harris BX	2.00
114	Jake Reed BX	2.00
115	Bryant Young BX	2.00
116	Keenan McCardell SX	6.00
117	Herman Moore GZ	20.00
118	Errict Rhett SZ	4.00
119	Henry Ellard BX	2.00
120	Bobby Hoying SX	6.00
121	Robert Smith BX	4.00
122	Keyshawn Johnson GZ	50.00
123	Zach Thomas BX	10.00
124	Charlie Garner BX	2.00
125	Terry Kirby BX	2.00
126	Darren Woodson BX	2.00
127	Darnay Scott SX	6.00
128	Chris Sanders SY	5.00
129	Charles Johnson SX	6.00
130	Joey Galloway SZ	8.00
131	Curtis Conway SY	5.00
132	Isaac Bruce GZ	20.00
133	Bobby Taylor BX	2.00
134	Jamal Anderson SY	5.00
135	Ken Norton BX	2.00
136	Darick Holmes BX	2.00
137	Tony Brackens BX	2.00
138	Tony Martin BX	2.00
139	Antonio Freeman SZ	15.00
140	Neil Smith BX	2.00
141	Terry Glenn GZ	85.00
142	Marvin Harrison SY	25.00
143	Daryl Johnston BX	2.00
144	Tim Brown GY	10.00
145	Kimble Anders BX	2.00
146	Derrick Alexander SX	6.00
147	LeShon Johnson BX	2.00
148	Anthony Johnson BX	2.00
149	Leslie Shepherd BX	2.00
150	Chris T. Jones BX	2.00
151	Edgar Bennett BX	2.00
152	Ty Detmer BX	2.00
153	*Ike Hilliard GX*	100.00
154	*Jim Druckenmiller SZ*	30.00
155	*Warrick Dunn GZ*	100.00
156	*Yatil Green GZ*	20.00
157	*Reidel Anthony GZ*	30.00
158	*Antowain Smith GZ*	40.00
159	*Rae Carruth SY*	10.00
160	*Tiki Barber GZ*	30.00
161	*Byron Hanspard SZ*	10.00
162	*Jake Plummer SY*	15.00
163	*Joey Kent SZ*	10.00
164	*Corey Dillon SY*	25.00
165	*Kevin Lockett BZ*	3.00
166	*Will Blackwell BY*	6.00
167	*Troy Davis GZ*	25.00
168	*James Farrior BX*	4.00
169	*Danny Wuerffel SY*	15.00
170	*Pat Barnes SY*	10.00
171	*Darnell Autry SY*	10.00
172	*Tom Knight BX*	4.00
173	*David LaFleur BY*	10.00
174	*Tony Gonzalez BY*	10.00
175	*Kenny Holmes BX*	4.00
176	*Reinard Wilson BX*	4.00
177	*Renaldo Wynn BX*	4.00
178	*Bryant Westbrook BX*	4.00
179	*Darrell Russell BX*	4.00
180	*Orlando Pace BX*	6.00
181	*Shawn Springs BX*	4.00
182	*Peter Boulware BX*	4.00
183	Dan Marino BY (Legacy)	20.00
184	Brett Favre BY (Legacy)	25.00
185	Emmitt Smith BY (Legacy)	20.00
186	Eddie George BY (Legacy)	18.00
187	Curtis Martin BY (Legacy)	15.00
188	Tim Brown BZ (Legacy)	3.00
189	Mark Brunell BY (Legacy)	15.00

190 Isaac Bruce BY (Legacy) 3.00
191 Deion Sanders BY (Legacy) 6.00
192 John Elway BY (Legacy) 10.00
193 Jerry Rice BY (Legacy) 15.00
194 Barry Sanders BY (Legacy) 20.00
195 Herman Moore BY (Legacy) 3.00
196 Carl Pickens BY (Legacy) 3.00
197 Karim Abdul-Jabbar BY (Legacy) 10.00
198 Checklist Drew Bledsoe BY 15.00
199 Checklist Troy Aikman BY 15.00
200 Checklist Terrell Davis BY 15.00

1997 Leaf Fractal Matrix Die-Cuts

This insert adds die-cutting to the Fractal Matrix parallel. The breakdown of cards is 100 X-Axis (5 gold/20 silver/75 bronze), 60 Y-Axis (10 gold/30 silver/20 bronze) and 40 Z-Axis (25 gold/10 silver/5 bronze).

		MT
	Common X-Axis:	5.00
	Common Y-Axis:	8.00
	Common Z-Axis:	12.00
1	Steve Young GZ	100.00
2	Brett Favre GX	120.00
3	Barry Sanders GZ	150.00
4	Drew Bledsoe GZ	150.00
5	Troy Aikman GZ	150.00
6	Kerry Collins GZ	125.00
7	Dan Marino GX	100.00
8	Jerry Rice GZ	150.00
9	John Elway GZ	100.00
10	Emmitt Smith GX	100.00
11	Tony Banks GY	60.00
12	Gus Frerotte SX	5.00
13	Elvis Grbac SX	5.00
14	Neil O'Donnell BX	5.00
15	Michael Irvin SY	15.00
16	Marshall Faulk SY	15.00
17	Todd Collins SX	5.00
18	Scott Mitchell BX	5.00
19	Trent Dilfer SY	8.00
20	Rick Mirer SX	5.00
21	Frank Sanders SX	5.00
22	Larry Centers BX	5.00
23	Brad Johnson BX	5.00
24	Garrison Hearst SY	8.00
25	Steve McNair GZ	125.00
26	Dorsey Levens BX	5.00
27	Eric Metcalf BX	5.00
28	Jeff George SX	5.00
29	Rodney Hampton BX	5.00
30	Michael Westbrook SY	8.00
31	Cris Carter SY	8.00
32	Heath Shuler SX	5.00
33	Warren Moon BX	5.00
34	Rod Woodson SX	5.00
35	Ken Dilger BX	5.00
36	Ben Coates BX	5.00
37	Andre Reed BX	5.00
38	Terrell Owens SZ	75.00
39	Jeff Blake SY	15.00
40	Vinny Testaverde BX	5.00
41	Robert Brooks SY	10.00
42	Shannon Sharpe SX	5.00
43	Terry Allen SY	8.00
44	Terance Mathis BX	5.00
45	Bobby Engram BZ	25.00
46	Rickey Dudley BX	5.00
47	Alex Molden BX	5.00
48	Lawrence Phillips SY	8.00
49	Curtis Martin GZ	150.00
50	Jim Harbaugh BX	5.00
51	Wayne Chrebet BX	5.00
52	Quentin Coryatt BX	5.00
53	Eddie George GX	75.00
54	Michael Jackson BX	5.00
55	Greg Lloyd BX	5.00
56	Natrone Means SZ	25.00
57	Marcus Allen GY	15.00
58	Desmond Howard BX	5.00
59	Stan Humphries BX	5.00
60	Reggie White GY	15.00
61	Brett Perriman SY	8.00
62	Warren Sapp BX	5.00
63	Adrian Murrell SZ	12.00
64	Mark Brunell GZ	150.00
65	Carl Pickens GY	8.00
66	Kordell Stewart GZ	150.00
67	Ricky Watters GY	15.00
68	Tyrone Wheatley BX	5.00
69	Stanley Pritchett BX	5.00
70	Kevin Greene BX	5.00
71	Karim Abdul-Jabbar GZ	100.00
72	Ki-Jana Carter SY	8.00
73	Rashaan Salaam SY	8.00
74	Simeon Rice BX	5.00
75	Napoleon Kaufman SY	15.00
76	Muhsin Muhammad SZ	12.00
77	Bruce Smith GY	8.00
78	Eric Moulds SX	5.00
79	O.J. McDuffie BX	5.00
80	Danny Kanell BZ	12.00
81	Harvey Williams BX	5.00
82	Greg Hill SY	8.00
83	Terrell Davis GZ	150.00
84	Dan Wilkinson BX	5.00
85	Yancey Thigpen BX	5.00
86	Darrell Green SX	5.00
87	Tamarick Vanover SX	5.00
88	Mike Alstott BX	5.00
89	Johnnie Morton SX	5.00
90	Dale Carter BX	5.00
91	Jerome Bettis GY	15.00
92	James Stewart BX	5.00
93	Irving Fryar SX	5.00
94	Junior Seau SY	8.00
95	Sean Dawkins BX	5.00
96	J.J. Stokes BZ	12.00
97	Tim Biakabutuka SY	8.00
98	Bert Emanuel BX	5.00
99	Eddie Kennison GY	60.00
100	Ray Zellars BX	5.00
101	Dave Brown BX	5.00
102	Leeland McElroy SY	8.00
103	Chris Warren SY	8.00
104	Bam Morris BX	5.00
105	Thurman Thomas GY	15.00
106	Kyle Brady BX	5.00
107	Anthony Miller GY	8.00
108	Derrick Thomas SY	8.00
109	Mark Chmura BX	5.00
110	Deion Sanders GZ	75.00
111	Eric Swann BX	5.00
112	Amani Toomer SX	5.00
113	Raymont Harris BX	5.00
114	Jake Reed BX	5.00
115	Bryant Young BX	5.00
116	Keenan McCardell SX	5.00
117	Herman Moore GZ	25.00
118	Errict Rhett SZ	25.00
119	Henry Ellard BX	5.00
120	Bobby Hoying SX	5.00
121	Robert Smith BX	5.00
122	Keyshawn Johnson GZ	75.00
123	Zach Thomas BZ	20.00
124	Charlie Garner BX	5.00
125	Terry Kirby BX	5.00
126	Darren Woodson BX	5.00
127	Darnay Scott SX	5.00
128	Chris Sanders SY	8.00
129	Charles Johnson SX	5.00
130	Joey Galloway SZ	25.00
131	Curtis Conway SY	8.00
132	Isaac Bruce GZ	25.00
133	Bobby Taylor BX	5.00
134	Jamal Anderson SY	8.00
135	Ken Norton BX	5.00
136	Darick Holmes BX	5.00
137	Tony Brackens BX	5.00
138	Tony Martin BX	5.00
139	Antonio Freeman SZ	60.00
140	Neil Smith BX	5.00
141	Terry Glenn GZ	130.00
142	Marvin Harrison SY	60.00
143	Daryl Johnston BX	5.00
144	Tim Brown GY	8.00
145	Kimble Anders BX	5.00
146	Derrick Alexander SX	5.00
147	LeShon Johnson BX	5.00
148	Anthony Johnson BX	5.00
149	Leslie Shepherd BX	5.00
150	Chris T. Jones BX	5.00
151	Edgar Bennett BX	5.00
152	Ty Detmer BX	5.00
153	*Ike Hilliard GX*	20.00
154	*Jim Druckenmiller SZ*	100.00
155	*Warrick Dunn GZ*	150.00
156	*Yatil Green GZ*	40.00
157	*Reidel Anthony GZ*	60.00
158	*Antowain Smith GZ*	70.00
159	*Rae Carruth SY*	30.00
160	*Tiki Barber GZ*	40.00
161	*Byron Hanspard SZ*	20.00
162	*Jake Plummer SY*	30.00
163	*Joey Kent SZ*	15.00
164	*Corey Dillon SY*	45.00
165	*Kevin Lockett BZ*	12.00
166	*Will Blackwell BY*	15.00
167	*Troy Davis GZ*	40.00
168	*James Farrior BX*	5.00
169	*Danny Wuerffel SY*	60.00
170	*Pat Barnes SY*	20.00
171	*Darnell Autry SY*	15.00
172	*Tom Knight BX*	5.00
173	*David LaFleur BY*	20.00
174	*Tony Gonzalez BY*	20.00
175	*Kenny Holmes BX*	5.00
176	*Reinard Wilson BX*	5.00
177	*Renaldo Wynn BX*	5.00
178	*Bryant Westbrook BX*	5.00
179	*Darrell Russell BX*	5.00
180	*Orlando Pace BX*	10.00
181	*Shawn Springs BX*	5.00
182	*Peter Boulware BX*	5.00
183	Dan Marino BY (Legacy)	100.00
184	Brett Favre BY (Legacy)	100.00
185	Emmitt Smith BY (Legacy)	100.00
186	Eddie George BY (Legacy)	75.00
187	Curtis Martin BY (Legacy)	50.00
188	Tim Brown BZ (Legacy)	12.00
189	Mark Brunell BY (Legacy)	50.00
190	Isaac Bruce BY (Legacy)	15.00
191	Deion Sanders BY (Legacy)	25.00
192	John Elway BY (Legacy)	35.00
193	Jerry Rice BY (Legacy)	50.00
194	Barry Sanders BY (Legacy)	50.00
195	Herman Moore BY (Legacy)	8.00
196	Carl Pickens BY (Legacy)	8.00
197	Karim Abdul-Jabbar BY (Legacy)	40.00
198	Checklist Drew Bledsoe BY	50.00
199	Checklist Troy Aikman BY	50.00
200	Checklist Terrell Davis BY	50.00

1997 Leaf Hardwear

Hardwear is a 20-card insert featuring top players on a plastic card. The cards are die-cut into a helmet-shaped design and sequentially numbered to 3,500.

		MT
	Complete Set (20):	300.00
	Common Player:	4.00
1	Dan Marino	35.00
2	Brett Favre	40.00
3	Emmitt Smith	35.00
4	Jerry Rice	20.00
5	Barry Sanders	25.00
6	Deion Sanders	12.00
7	Reggie White	8.00
8	Tim Brown	4.00
9	Steve McNair	15.00
10	Steve Young	15.00
11	Mark Brunell	20.00
12	Ricky Watters	4.00
13	Eddie Kennison	8.00
14	Kordell Stewart	20.00
15	Kerry Collins	15.00
16	Joey Galloway	8.00
17	Terrell Owens	10.00
18	Terry Glenn	20.00
19	Keyshawn Johnson	8.00
20	Eddie George	25.00

1997 Leaf Letterman

The cards in this 15-card insert look and feel like a college letter. The cards are also embossed and foil stamped. Each card is sequentially numbered to 1,000.

		MT
	Complete Set (15):	1000.
	Common Player:	20.00
1	Brett Favre	150.00
2	Emmitt Smith	125.00
3	Dan Marino	125.00
4	Jerry Rice	75.00
5	Mark Brunell	75.00
6	Barry Sanders	75.00
7	John Elway	60.00
8	Eddie George	100.00
9	Troy Aikman	75.00
10	Curtis Martin	75.00
11	Karim Abdul-Jabbar	50.00
12	Terrell Davis	40.00
13	Ike Hilliard	20.00
14	Yatil Green	20.00
15	Drew Bledsoe	75.00

1997 Leaf Reproductions

Twelve current and 12 former NFL stars are featured in this 24-card set. The cards are a reproduction of Leaf's 1948 set design. The first 500 cards of each former great are autographed. Each insert card is numbered to 1,948.

		MT
	Complete Set (24):	600.00
	Common Player:	10.00
1	Emmitt Smith	60.00
2	Brett Favre	75.00
3	Dan Marino	60.00
4	Barry Sanders	35.00
5	Jerry Rice	35.00
6	Terrell Davis	35.00
7	Curtis Martin	35.00
8	Troy Aikman	35.00
9	Drew Bledsoe	35.00
10	Herman Moore	10.00
11	Isaac Bruce	10.00
12	Carl Pickens	10.00
13	Len Dawson	20.00
14	Dan Fouts	20.00
15	Jim Plunkett	10.00
16	Ken Stabler	35.00
17	Joe Theismann	20.00
18	Billy Kilmer	20.00
19	Danny White	20.00
20	Archie Manning	10.00
21	Ron Jaworski	10.00
22	Y.A. Tittle	40.00
23	Sid Luckman	40.00
24	Sammy Baugh	40.00

1997 Leaf Run & Gun

This 18-card insert features a top quarterback/running back combo from the same team, one on each side of the card. One side features holographic foil stock adn the other is foil stamped. The cards are numbered to 3,500.

		MT
	Complete Set (18):	250.00
	Common Player:	5.00
1	Dan Marino, Karim Abdul-Jabbar	40.00
2	Troy Aikman, Emmitt Smith	40.00
3	John Elway, Terrell Davis	25.00
4	Drew Bledsoe, Curtis Martin	25.00
5	Kordell Stewart, Jerome Bettis	20.00
6	Mark Brunell, Natrone Means	20.00
7	Kerry Collins, Tim Biakabutuka	15.00
8	Rick Mirer, Rashaan Salaam	5.00
9	Scott Mitchell, Barry Sanders	25.00
10	Steve McNair, Eddie George	30.00
11	Trent Dilfer, Warrick Dunn	30.00
12	Jeff Blake, Ki-Jana Carter	5.00
13	Tony Banks, Lawrence Phillips	10.00
14	Steve Young, Garrison Hearst	15.00
15	Jim Harbaugh, Marshall Faulk	5.00
16	Elvis Grbac, Marcus Allen	5.00
17	Neil O'Donnell, Adrian Murrell	5.00
18	Gus Frerotte, Terry Allen	5.00

1997 Leaf Signature

Leaf Signature Football consisted of 118 8" x 10" cards that featured top established players and rookies. The card fronts feature a large color shot of the player, with and large off-color oval taking up the bottom portion. The player's name is stamped in silver foil above this oval, with a Leaf '97 Football logo in silver and black above that. The backs are horizontal and unnumbered and contain a large closeup shot of the player on the left side with a brief biography on the right. Most of the players also arrive in an autographed version, which have the words "Authentic Signature" printed in black across the bottom. Also included in packs were Old School Draft Autographs, which featured 11 retired quarterbacks.

		MT
	Complete Set (118):	150.00
	Common Player:	.50
1	Karim Abdul-Jabbar	2.00
2	Troy Aikman	5.00
3	Derrick Alexander	.50
4	Terry Allen	.50
5	Mike Alstott	2.00
6	Jamal Anderson	1.00
7	Reidel Anthony	4.00
8	Darnell Autry	2.00
9	Tony Banks	2.00
10	Tiki Barber	2.50
11	Pat Barnes	1.50
12	Jerome Bettis	1.00
13	Tim Biakabutuka	.50
14	Will Blackwell	1.00
15	Jeff Blake	1.00
16	Drew Bledsoe	5.00
17	Peter Boulware	.50
18	Robert Brooks	.50
19	Dave Brown	.50
20	Tim Brown	1.00
21	Isaac Bruce	1.00
22	Mark Brunell	5.00
23	Rae Carruth	3.00
24	Cris Carter	.50
25	Ki-Jana Carter	.50
26	Larry Centers	.50
27	Ben Coates	.50
28	Kerry Collins	3.00
29	Todd Collins	.50
30	Albert Connell	.50
31	Curtis Conway	.50
32	Terrell Davis	5.00
33	Troy Davis	2.00
34	Trent Dilfer	2.00
35	Corey Dillon	6.00
36	Jim Druckenmiller	5.00
37	Warrick Dunn	10.00
38	John Elway	3.00
39	Bert Emmanuel	.50
40	Bobby Engram	.50
41	Boomer Esiason	.50
42	Jim Everett	.50
43	Marshall Faulk	1.00
44	Brett Favre	12.00
45	Antonio Freeman	1.00
46	Gus Frerotte	.50
47	Irving Fryar	.50
48	Joey Galloway	1.00
49	Eddie George	7.50
50	Jeff George	.50
51	Tony Gonzalez	2.00
52	Jay Graham	1.00

53	Elvis Grbac	.50
54	Darrell Green	.50
55	Yatil Green	3.00
56	Rodney Hampton	.50
57	Byron Hanspard	3.00
58	Jim Harbaugh	.50
59	Marvin Harrison	1.00
60	Garrison Hearst	.50
61	Greg Hill	.50
62	Ike Hilliard	3.00
63	Jeff Hostetler	.50
64	Brad Johnson	.50
65	Keyshawn Johnson	1.00
66	Darryl Johnston	.50
67	Napoleon Kaufman	1.00
68	Jim Kelly	1.00
69	Eddie Kennison	1.00
70	Joey Kent	1.00
71	Bernie Kosar	.50
72	Eric Kramer	.50
73	Dorsey Levens	1.00
74	Kevin Lockett	.50
75	Dan Marino	10.00
76	Curtis Martin	5.00
77	Tony Martin	.50
78	Leeland McElroy	.50
79	Steve McNair	4.00
80	Natrone Means	1.00
81	Eric Metcalf	.50
82	Anthony Miller	.50
83	Rick Mirer	.50
84	Scott Mitchell	.50
85	Warren Moon	.50
86	Herman Moore	1.00
87	Muhsin Muhammad	.50
88	Adrian Murrell	1.00
89	Neil O'Donnell	.50
90	Terrell Owens	2.00
91	Brett Perriman	.50
92	Lawrence Phillips	.50
93	Jake Plummer	6.00
94	Andre Reed	.50
95	Jerry Rice	5.00
96	Darrell Russell	.50
97	Rashaan Salaam	.50
98	Barry Sanders	6.00
99	Deion Sanders	3.00
100	Frank Sanders	.50
101	Chris Sanders	.50
102	Junior Seau	.50
103	Darnay Scott	.50
104	Shannon Sharpe	.50
105	Sedrick Shaw	.50
106	Heath Shuler	.50
107	Antowain Smith	5.00
108	Bruce Smith	.50
109	Emmitt Smith	8.00
110	Kordell Stewart	5.00
111	J.J. Stokes	.50
112	Vinny Testaverde	.50
113	Thurman Thomas	1.00
114	Tamarick Vanover	.50
115	Herschel Walker	.50
116	Michael Westbrook	.50
117	Danny Wuerffel	3.00
118	Steve Young	3.00

1997 Leaf Signature Autographs

All but 11 of the players included in Leaf Signature Series Football signed cards for the product. Signature cards are identified by the player's autograph, usually found in the large, off-color oval part of the card and the words "Authentic Signature" in black letters across the bottom. Signature cards were inserted at a rate of one per pack. Included below with the player listing is the amount of cards that was reported that each player signed.

	MT
Common Player:	10.00
Karim Abdul-Jabbar 2500	30.00
Derrick Alexander 4000	10.00
Terry Allen 3000	20.00
Mike Alstott 4000	30.00
Jamal Anderson 4000	20.00
Reidel Anthony 2000	30.00
Darnell Autry 4000	20.00
Tony Banks 500	45.00
Tiki Barber 4000	30.00
Pat Barnes 4000	20.00
Jerome Bettis 500	60.00
Tim Biakabutuka 3000	20.00
Will Blackwell 2500	20.00
Jeff Blake 500	45.00
Drew Bledsoe 500	150.00
Peter Boulware 4000	10.00
Robert Brooks 1000	30.00
Dave Brown 500	40.00
Tim Brown 2500	30.00
Isaac Bruce 2500	30.00
Mark Brunell 500	150.00
Rae Carruth 5000	20.00
Cris Carter 2500	20.00
Larry Centers 4000	10.00
Ben Coates 4000	10.00
Todd Collins 4000	10.00
Albert Connell 4000	10.00
Curtis Conway 3000	20.00
Terrell Davis 2500	100.00
Troy Davis 4000	20.00
Trent Dilfer 500	60.00
Corey Dillon 4000	60.00
Jim Druckenmiller 5000	50.00
Warrick Dunn 2000	120.00
John Elway 500	150.00
Bert Emmanuel 4000	10.00
Bobby Engram 3000	10.00
Boomer Esiason 500	50.00
Jim Everett 500	40.00
Marshall Faulk 3000	30.00
Antonio Freeman 2000	30.00
Gus Frerotte 500	40.00
Irving Fryar 3000	10.00
Joey Galloway 3000	30.00
Eddie George 300	180.00
Jeff George 500	40.00
Tony Gonzalez 3500	20.00
Jay Graham 1000	30.00
Elvis Grbac 500	40.00
Darrell Green 2500	10.00
Yatil Green 5000	30.00
Rodney Hampton 4000	10.00
Byron Hanspard 4000	20.00
Jim Harbaugh 500	40.00
Marvin Harrison 3000	30.00
Garrison Hearst 4000	10.00
Greg Hill 4000	10.00
Ike Hilliard 2000	20.00
Jeff Hostetler 500	40.00
Brad Johnson 2000	20.00
Keyshawn Johnson 900	45.00
Darryl Johnston 3000	10.00
Jim Kelly 500	75.00
Eddie Kennison 3000	20.00
Joey Kent 4000	10.00
Bernie Kosar 500	40.00
Eric Kramer 500	40.00
Dorsey Levens 3000	30.00
Kevin Lockett 4000	10.00
Tony Martin 4000	10.00
Leeland McElroy 4000	10.00
Natrone Means 3000	20.00
Eric Metcalf 4000	10.00
Anthony Miller 3000	10.00
Rick Mirer 500	40.00
Scott Mitchell 500	40.00
Warren Moon 500	50.00
Herman Moore 2500	20.00
Muhsin Muhammad 3000	10.00
Adrian Murrell 3000	20.00
Neil O'Donnell 500	40.00
Terrell Owens 3000	30.00
Brett Perriman 700	40.00
Lawrence Phillips 750	40.00
Jake Plummer 5000	60.00
Andre Reed 3000	10.00
Darrell Russell 2000	20.00
Rashaan Salaam 3000	10.00
Frank Sanders 3000	10.00
Chris Sanders 3000	10.00
Junior Seau 500	40.00
Darnay Scott 2000	20.00
Shannon Sharpe 1000	30.00
Sedrick Shaw 4000	20.00
Heath Shuler 500	40.00
Antowain Smith 5000	50.00
Kordell Stewart 500	150.00
J.J. Stokes 3000	10.00
Vinny Testaverde 250	80.00
Thurman Thomas 2500	20.00
Tamarick Vanover 4000	10.00
Herschel Walker 3000	10.00
Michael Westbrook 3000	10.00
Danny Wuerffel 3000	20.00
Steve Young 500	150.00

1997 Leaf Signature First Down Marker Autographs

First Down Markers paralleled the entire Leaf Signature Autograph set. The first 100 cards signed by each player were given a special silver foil stamp and were sequentially numbered to 100.

	MT
First Down Markers:	2x

1997 Leaf Signature Old School Drafts Autographs

Old School Drafts Autographs included 11 former quarterbacks on 8" x 10" cards. The cards feature the insert name in large bold letters across the top and are individually numbered to 1,000. Card No. 10 is not available.

		MT
Complete Set (11):		500.00
Common Player:		25.00
Card #10 not included		
1	Joe Theismann	50.00
2	Archie Manning	50.00
3	Len Dawson	50.00
4	Sammy Baugh	120.00
5	Dan Fouts	75.00
6	Danny White	50.00
7	Ron Jaworski	25.00
8	Jim Plunkett	25.00
9	Y.A. Tittle	85.00
10	N/A	
11	Ken Stabler	85.00
12	Billy Kilmer	25.00

1997 Motion Vision

Motion Vision second year in football cards produced 28 cards, with 20 cards in Series I and eight in Series II. Packs consisted of compact disc-like cases that could be opened to expose the card, which is more like a video shown on thick plastic. The card is best viewed when held up to light and moved with the slightly with the hand. Each series had four insert cards, which were inserted one per 25, with Series I containing LDR1-4 and a Terrell Davis autograph version, while Series II had LDR5-6 and two redemption cards.

		MT
Complete Set (28):		150.00
Complete Series 1 (20):		90.00
Complete Series 2 (8):		60.00
Common Player:		3.00
Series 1 Wax Box:		45.00
Series 2 Wax Box:		45.00
1	Terrell Davis	10.00
2	Curtis Martin	7.00
3	Joey Galloway	3.00
4	Eddie George	10.00
5	Isaac Bruce	3.00
6	Antonio Freeman	3.00
7	Terry Glenn	4.00
8	Deion Sanders	5.00
9	Jerome Bettis	3.00
10	Reggie White	3.00
11	Brett Favre	15.00
12	Dan Marino	12.00
13	Emmitt Smith	12.00
14	Mark Brunell	8.00
15	John Elway	8.00
16	Drew Bledsoe	8.00
17	Barry Sanders	10.00
18	Jeff Blake	3.00
19	Kerry Collins	6.00
20	Jerry Rice	8.00
21	Dan Marino	12.00
22	Troy Aikman	8.00
23	Brett Favre	15.00
24	Emmitt Smith	12.00
25	Kordell Stewart	8.00
26	Terrell Davis	8.00
27	Eddie George	8.00
28	Drew Bledsoe	8.00

1997 Motion Vision Limited Digital Replays

Each Series of Motion Vision included four inserts at a rate of one per 25 packs. The Limited Digital Replays are numbered LDR1-6, with numbers 5 and 6 being trade cards for Warrick Dunn and Antoine Smith. Also included are Dunn and Smith XVRR cards. In addition, a autographed version of Terrell Davis' LDR was available.

		MT
Complete Set (8):		140.00
Complete Series 1 (4):		100.00
Complete Series 2 (4):		40.00
Common Player:		10.00
1	Terrell Davis	30.00
1A	Terrell Davis AUTO	200.00
2	Curtis Martin	25.00
3	Brett Favre	45.00
4	Barry Sanders	30.00
5	Warrick Dunn	15.00
6	Antowain Smith	10.00
XVRR	Warrick Dunn	15.00
XVRR	Antowain Smith	10.00

1997 Motion Vision Box Toppers

Five different box toppers were offered with boxes of Motion Vision Series II Football. The cards measure 4" x 6" and were included at a rate of one per box.

	MT
Complete Set (4):	50.00
Common Player:	7.00
John Elway	10.00
Brett Favre	20.00
Dan Marino	15.00
Steve Young	7.00

1997 Pacific Crown Royale

Crown Royale is a 144-card, all die-cut set. The base cards feature a player shot on a crown-shaped die-cut card. The two parallel sets are silver and holographic gold foil (4:25) and silver and holographic blue foil (1:25). Insert sets include NFL Cel-Fusions, Chalk Talk Laser Cuts, Pro Bowl Die-Cuts, Firestone on Football and Premium-sized Cramer's Choice Awards.

		MT
Complete Set (144):		150.00
Common Player:		.50
Wax Box:		100.00
1	Larry Centers	.50
2	Kent Graham	1.00
3	LeShon Johnson	.50
4	Leeland McElroy	.50
5	*Jake Plummer*	8.00
6	Jamal Anderson	1.00
7	Chris Chandler	.50
8	*Byron Hanspard*	1.50
9	Michael Haynes	.50
10	Derrick Alexander	.50
11	*Jay Graham*	1.50
12	Michael Jackson	.50
13	Vinny Testaverde	.50
14	Todd Collins	1.00
15	Jay Riemersma	.50
16	*Antowain Smith*	6.00
17	Steve Tasker	.50
18	Thurman Thomas	1.00
19	*Rae Carruth*	4.00
20	Kerry Collins	1.00
21	Anthony Johnson	.50
22	*Fred Lane*	3.00
23	Muhsin Muhammad	.50
24	Wesley Walls	.50
25	*Darnell Autry*	1.00
26	Raymont Harris	1.00
27	Erik Kramer	.50
28	Rick Mirer	.50
29	Rashaan Salaam	.50
30	Jeff Blake	1.00
31	Ki-Jana Carter	.50
32	*Corey Dillon*	8.00
33	Carl Pickens	.50
34	Troy Aikman	6.00
35	Michael Irvin	1.00
36	Daryl Johnston	.50
37	*David LaFleur*	2.00
38	Deion Sanders	3.00
39	Emmitt Smith	10.00
40	Terrell Davis	6.00
41	John Elway	4.00
42	Ed McCaffrey	.50
43	Shannon Sharpe	.50
44	Neil Smith	.50
45	Scott Mitchell	.50
46	Herman Moore	1.00
47	Johnnie Morton	.50
48	Barry Sanders	7.00
49	Robert Brooks	.50
50	Mark Chmura	.50
51	Brett Favre	12.00
52	Antonio Freeman	1.00
53	Dorsey Levens	1.00
54	Reggie White	1.00
55	Ken Dilger	.50
56	Marshall Faulk	1.00
57	Jim Harbaugh	.50
58	Marvin Harrison	2.00
59	Mark Brunell	6.00
60	Rob Johnson	.50
61	Keenan McCardell	.50
62	Natrone Means	1.00
63	Jimmy Smith	.50
64	Marcus Allen	1.00
65	*Tony Gonzalez*	3.00
66	Elvis Grbac	.50
67	Greg Hill	.50
68	Tamarick Vanover	.50
69	Karim Abdul-Jabbar	3.00
70	Fred Barnett	.50
71	Dan Marino	10.00
72	O.J. McDuffie	.50
73	Jerris McPhail	.50
74	Cris Carter	.50
75	Randall Cunningham	.50
76	Brad Johnson	1.00
77	Jake Reed	.50
78	Robert Smith	1.00
79	Drew Bledsoe	6.00
80	Ben Coates	.50
81	Terry Glenn	4.00
82	Curtis Martin	6.00
83	*Troy Davis*	1.50
84	Heath Shuler	.50
85	Irv Smith	.50
86	*Danny Wuerffel*	6.00
87	*Tiki Barber*	6.00
88	Dave Brown	.50
89	Rodney Hampton	.50
90	*Ike Hilliard*	5.00
91	Amani Toomer	.50
92	Wayne Chrebet	.50
93	Keyshawn Johnson	2.00

94	Adrian Murrell	1.00
95	Neil O'Donnell	.50
96	Dedric Ward	.50
97	Tim Brown	1.00
98	Jeff George	1.00
99	Desmond Howard	.50
100	Napoleon Kaufman	2.00
101	Ty Detmer	.50
102	Irving Fryar	.50
103	Bobby Hoying	.50
104	Ricky Watters	1.00
105	Jerome Bettis	1.00
106	*Will Blackwell*	2.00
107	Charles Johnson	.50
108	*George Jones*	1.00
109	Kordell Stewart	6.00
110	Tony Banks	2.00
111	Isaac Bruce	1.00
112	Eddie Kennison	2.00
113	Lawrence Phillips	1.00
114	Jim Everett	.50
115	Stan Humphries	.50
116	*Freddie Jones*	1.50
117	Tony Martin	.50
118	Junior Seau	1.00
119	*Jim Druckenmiller*	8.00
120	Garrison Hearst	.50
121	Brent Jones	.50
122	Terrell Owens	3.00
123	Jerry Rice	6.00
124	Steve Young	4.00
125	Chad Brown	.50
126	Joey Galloway	1.00
127	Jon Kitna	.50
128	Warren Moon	.50
129	Chris Warren	.50
130	Mike Alstott	3.00
131	*Reidel Anthony*	6.00
132	Trent Dilfer	1.00
133	*Warrick Dunn*	12.00
134	Karl Williams	.50
135	Willie Davis	.50
136	Eddie George	8.00
137	*Joey Kent*	1.50
138	Steve McNair	4.00
139	Chris Sanders	.50
140	Terry Allen	.50
141	Jamie Asher	.50
142	Stephen Davis	.50
143	Henry Ellard	.50
144	Gus Frerotte	.50

1997 Pacific Crown Royal Gold/Silver

Each card in the 144-card Crown Royale set was reprinted using gold or silver foil. Gold foil cards were inserted 4:25 packs, while silver foil cards were inserted in special retail packs..

	MT
Gold/Silver Cards:	2x-4x
Gold/Silver Rookies:	2x

1997 Pacific Crown Royale Blue

Each card in the 144-card Crown Royale set was reprinted with blue foil. Platinum Blue parallels were inserted one per 25 packs.

	MT
Blue Cards:	6x-12x
Blue Rookies:	3x-6x

1997 Pacific Crown Royale Cel-Fusions

This 20-card insert consists of a die-cut cel football fused to a trading card. The cards were inserted 1:49.

		MT
Complete Set (20):		700.00
Common Player:		12.00
1	Antowain Smith	30.00
2	Troy Aikman	50.00
3	Emmitt Smith	100.00
4	Terrell Davis	50.00
5	John Elway	35.00
6	Barry Sanders	50.00
7	Brett Favre	100.00
8	Mark Brunell	50.00
9	Elvis Grbac	12.00
10	Karim Abdul-Jabbar	20.00
11	Dan Marino	100.00
12	Drew Bledsoe	50.00
13	Curtis Martin	50.00
14	Danny Wuerffel	30.00
15	Tiki Barber	20.00
16	Jeff George	12.00
17	Kordell Stewart	50.00
18	Tony Banks	12.00
19	Jerry Rice	50.00
20	Steve Young	35.00

1997 Pacific Crown Royale Chalk Talk

This 20-card insert features a player action shot with a laser cut diagram of one of their signature plays. This set was inserted 1:73.

		MT
Complete Set (20):		900.00
Common Player:		25.00
1	Kerry Collins	40.00
2	Troy Aikman	60.00
3	Emmitt Smith	125.00
4	Terrell Davis	60.00
5	John Elway	40.00
6	Barry Sanders	80.00
7	Brett Favre	150.00
8	Mark Brunell	60.00
9	Marcus Allen	25.00
10	Dan Marino	125.00
11	Drew Bledsoe	60.00
12	Curtis Martin	60.00
13	Troy Davis	25.00
14	Napoleon Kaufman	25.00
15	Jerome Bettis	25.00
16	Jim Druckenmiller	45.00
17	Jerry Rice	60.00
18	Steve Young	40.00
19	Warrick Dunn	70.00
20	Eddie George	85.00

1997 Pacific Crown Royale Cramer's Choice Jumbos

Cramer's Choice is a jumbo-sized insert featuring 10 players on cards die-cut to look like trophies. This insert was found one card per box.

		MT
Complete Set (10):		85.00
Common Player:		4.00
1	Deion Sanders	4.00
2	Emmitt Smith	20.00
3	Terrell Davis	10.00
4	John Elway	7.00
5	Barry Sanders	15.00
6	Brett Favre	25.00
7	Mark Brunell	10.00
8	Drew Bledsoe	10.00
9	Jim Druckenmiller	12.00
10	Eddie George	15.00

1997 Pacific Crown Royale Firestone on Football

These 20 cards feature players on an etched-foil design. The backs have comments from Roy Firestone. A #21 card was made featuring Firestone with comments from a future Hall of Fame QB on the back. This set was inserted 1:25.

		MT
Complete Set (21):		600.00
Common Player:		7.00
1	Kerry Collins	25.00
2	Troy Aikman	30.00
3	Deion Sanders	18.00
4	Emmitt Smith	60.00
5	Terrell Davis	30.00
6	John Elway	25.00
7	Barry Sanders	40.00
8	Brett Favre	70.00
9	Reggie White	7.00
10	Mark Brunell	30.00
11	Marcus Allen	7.00
12	Dan Marino	60.00
13	Drew Bledsoe	30.00
14	Terry Glenn	25.00
15	Curtis Martin	30.00
16	Jerome Bettis	7.00
17	Jerry Rice	30.00
18	Steve Young	25.00
19	Eddie George	45.00
20	Gus Frerotte	7.00
21	Roy Firestone	7.00

1997 Pacific Crown Royale Pro Bowl Die-Cuts

These die-cut cards feature Pro Bowl players against an ocean background. The 20 cards were inserted 1:25.

		MT
Complete Set (20):		500.00
Common Player:		10.00
1	Kerry Collins	30.00
2	Troy Aikman	50.00
3	Deion Sanders	25.00
4	Terrell Davis	50.00
5	John Elway	30.00
6	Shannon Sharpe	10.00
7	Barry Sanders	50.00
8	Brett Favre	100.00
9	Reggie White	10.00
10	Mark Brunell	50.00
11	Derrick Thomas	10.00
12	Drew Bledsoe	50.00
13	Ben Coates	10.00
14	Curtis Martin	50.00
15	Jerome Bettis	10.00
16	Isaac Bruce	10.00
17	Jerry Rice	50.00
18	Steve Young	30.00
19	Terry Allen	10.00
20	Gus Frerotte	10.00

1997 Pacific Revolution

Revolution is a 150-card set. The base cards all feature holographic foil, etching and embossing. Three parallel sets were created: Silver & Holographic Gold (retail, 2:25), Copper & Holographic Silver (hobby, 2:25) and Platinum Blue & Holographic Gold (1:49). The inserts included Proteges, Air Mail Die-Cuts, Silks and Ring Bearer Laser-Cuts.

		MT
Complete Set (150):		120.00
Common Player:		.50
Wax Box:		80.00
1	Larry Centers	.50
2	Kent Graham	.50
3	Leeland McElroy	.50
4	Rob Moore	.50
5	*Jake Plummer*	7.00
6	Jamal Anderson	1.00
7	Bert Emanuel	.50
8	*Byron Hanspard*	1.50
9	Terance Mathis	.50
10	O.J. Santiago	.50
11	Derrick Alexander	.50
12	Peter Boulware	.50
13	*Jay Graham*	1.00
14	Michael Jackson	.50
15	Vinny Testaverde	.50
16	Todd Collins	1.00
17	Andre Reed	.50
18	Jay Riemersma	.50
19	*Antowain Smith*	5.00
20	Bruce Smith	.50
21	Thurman Thomas	1.00
22	*Rae Carruth*	2.00
23	Kerry Collins	1.00
24	Anthony Johnson	.50
25	Muhsin Muhammad	.50
26	Wesley Walls	.50
27	Curtis Conway	1.00
28	Bobby Engram	.50
29	Raymont Harris	.50
30	Rick Mirer	.50
31	Rashaan Salaam	.50
32	Jeff Blake	1.00
33	*Corey Dillon*	7.00
34	Carl Pickens	.50
35	Darnay Scott	.50
36	Troy Aikman	4.00
37	Michael Irvin	1.00
38	Daryl Johnston	.50
39	Deion Sanders	2.00
40	Emmitt Smith	8.00
41	Terrell Davis	4.00
42	John Elway	3.00
43	Ed McCaffrey	.50
44	Shannon Sharpe	.50
45	Neil Smith	.50
46	Scott Mitchell	.50
47	Herman Moore	1.00
48	Johnnie Morton	.50
49	Barry Sanders	7.00
50	Robert Brooks	.50
51	LeRoy Butler	.50
52	Brett Favre	10.00
53	Antonio Freeman	1.00
54	Dorsey Levens	1.00
55	Reggie White	1.00
56	Sean Dawkins	.50
57	Ken Dilger	.50
58	Marshall Faulk	1.00
59	Jim Harbaugh	.50
60	Marvin Harrison	2.00
61	Mark Brunell	4.00
62	Keenan McCardell	.50
63	Natrone Means	1.00
64	Jimmy Smith	.50
65	James Stewart	.50
66	Marcus Allen	1.00
67	*Tony Gonzalez*	2.00
68	Elvis Grbac	.50
69	Greg Hill	.50
70	Andre Rison	.50
71	Karim Abdul-Jabbar	2.00
72	Fred Barnett	.50
73	Dan Marino	8.00
74	O.J. McDuffie	.50
75	Irving Spikes	.50
76	Cris Carter	.50
77	Matthew Hatchette	.50
78	Brad Johnson	1.00
79	Jake Reed	.50
80	Robert Smith	1.00
81	Drew Bledsoe	4.00
82	Ben Coates	.50
83	Terry Glenn	3.00
84	Curtis Martin	4.00
85	Dave Meggett	.50
86	*Troy Davis*	1.50
87	Andre Hastings	.50
88	Heath Shuler	.50
89	Irv Smith	.50
90	*Danny Wuerffel*	4.00
91	Ray Zellars	.50
92	*Tiki Barber*	4.00
93	Dave Brown	.50
94	Chris Calloway	.50
95	Rodney Hampton	.50
96	Amani Toomer	.50
97	Wayne Chrebet	.50
98	Keyshawn Johnson	2.00
99	Adrian Murrell	1.00
100	Neil O'Donnell	.50
101	Dedric Ward	.50
102	Tim Brown	1.00
103	Rickey Dudley	.50
104	Jeff George	.50
105	Desmond Howard	.50
106	Napoleon Kaufman	1.00
107	Ty Detmer	.50
108	Jason Dunn	.50
109	Irving Fryar	.50
110	Rodney Peete	.50
111	Ricky Watters	1.00
112	Jerome Bettis	1.00
113	*Will Blackwell*	1.00
114	Charles Johnson	.50
115	Kordell Stewart	4.00
116	Tony Banks	2.00
117	Isaac Bruce	1.00
118	Ernie Conwell	.50
119	Eddie Kennison	1.00
120	Lawrence Phillips	.50
121	Stan Humphries	.50
122	Tony Martin	.50
123	Eric Metcalf	.50
124	Junior Seau	1.00
125	*Jim Druckenmiller*	7.00
126	Kevin Greene	.50
127	Garrison Hearst	.50
128	Terrell Owens	2.00
129	Jerry Rice	4.00
130	J.J. Stokes	.50
131	Rod Woodson	.50
132	Steve Young	3.00
133	Joey Galloway	1.00
134	Cortez Kennedy	.50
135	*Jon Kitna*	1.00
136	Warren Moon	.50
137	Chris Warren	.50
138	Mike Alstott	2.00
139	*Reidel Anthony*	5.00
140	Trent Dilfer	1.00
141	*Warrick Dunn*	10.00
142	Willie Davis	.50
143	Eddie George	6.00
144	Steve McNair	3.00
145	Chris Sanders	.50
146	Terry Allen	.50
147	Jamie Asher	.50
148	Henry Ellard	.50
149	Gus Frerotte	.50
150	Leslie Shepherd	.50

1997 Pacific Revolution Silver/Red/Copper

Revolution was reprinted using silver, red and copper foil instead of the gold foil used on base cards. These parallels were each inserted into different types of packs - silvers were inserted 2:25 retail, reds were inserted 2:25 into mass retail packs and coppers were inserted 2:25 into hobby packs.

	MT
Silver/Red/Copper Cards:	4x-8x
Silver/Red/Copper Rookies:	2x-4x

1997 Pacific Revolution Blue

All 150 cards in Revolution were reprinted using blue foil vs. the gold used on regular cards. These Platinum Blue parallels were inserted one per 49 packs.

	MT
Blue Cards:	10x-20x
Blue Rookies:	5x-10x

1997 Pacific Revolution Air Mail

The cards in this 36-card insert are die-cut to look like stamps. They were inserted once in every 25 packs.

		MT
Complete Set (36):		500.00
Common Player:		5.00
1	Vinny Testaverde	5.00
2	Andre Reed	5.00
3	Kerry Collins	20.00
4	Jeff Blake	10.00
5	Troy Aikman	25.00
6	Deion Sanders	15.00
7	Emmitt Smith	50.00
8	Michael Irvin	10.00
9	Terrell Davis	25.00
10	John Elway	18.00
11	Barry Sanders	45.00
12	Brett Favre	60.00
13	Antonio Freeman	10.00
14	Mark Brunell	25.00
15	Marcus Allen	10.00
16	Elvis Grbac	5.00
17	Dan Marino	50.00
18	Brad Johnson	10.00
19	Drew Bledsoe	25.00
20	Terry Glenn	20.00
21	Curtis Martin	25.00
22	Danny Wuerffel	20.00
23	Jeff George	5.00
24	Napoleon Kaufman	10.00
25	Kordell Stewart	25.00
26	Tony Banks	10.00
27	Isaac Bruce	10.00
28	Jim Druckenmiller	30.00
29	Jerry Rice	25.00
30	Steve Young	18.00
31	Warren Moon	5.00
32	Trent Dilfer	10.00
33	Warrick Dunn	40.00
34	Eddie George	40.00
35	Steve McNair	20.00
36	Gus Frerotte	5.00

1997 Pacific Revolution Proteges

These 20 insert cards feature a proven veteran alongside their young understudy. The foiled cards were inserted 2:25.

		MT
Complete Set (20):		200.00
Common Player:		3.00
1	Kent Graham, Jake Plummer	8.00
2	Jamal Anderson, Byron Hanspard	3.00
3	Thurman Thomas, Antowain Smith	8.00
4	Troy Aikman, Jason Garrett	15.00
5	Emmitt Smith, Sherman Williams	25.00
6	John Elway, Jeff Lewis	12.00
7	Barry Sanders, Ron Rivers	20.00
8	Brett Favre, Doug Pederson	30.00
9	Mark Brunell, Rob Johnson	15.00
10	Marcus Allen, Greg Hill	3.00
11	Dan Marino, Damon Huard	30.00
12	Curtis Martin, Marrio Grier	15.00
13	Heath Shuler, Danny Wuerffel	10.00
14	Rodney Hampton, Tiki Barber	8.00
15	Jerome Bettis, George Jones	3.00
16	Jerry Rice, Terrell Owens	15.00
17	Steve Young, Jim Druckenmiller	12.00
18	Warren Moon, Jon Kitna	3.00
19	Errict Rhett, Warrick Dunn	15.00
20	Terry Allen, Stephen Davis	3.00

1997 Pacific Revolution Ring Bearers

These 10 fully foiled and embossed cards are die-cut and laser-cut to look like a championship ring. The cards feature 10 of the NFL's best and were inserted 1:121.

		MT
Complete Set (10):		600.00
Common Player:		30.00
1	Emmitt Smith	100.00
2	John Elway	45.00
3	Barry Sanders	120.00
4	Brett Favre	120.00
5	Mark Brunell	60.00
6	Dan Marino	100.00
7	Drew Bledsoe	60.00
8	Steve Young	30.00
9	Warrick Dunn	70.00
10	Eddie George	80.00

1997 Pacific Revolution Silks

This 18-card, oversized insert features top NFL players on a silk-like material. The cards were inserted 1:49.

		MT
Complete Set (18):		400.00
Common Player:		8.00
1	Kerry Collins	20.00
2	Troy Aikman	25.00
3	Deion Sanders	15.00
4	Emmitt Smith	50.00
5	Terrell Davis	25.00
6	John Elway	18.00
7	Barry Sanders	40.00
8	Brett Favre	60.00
9	Mark Brunell	25.00
10	Marcus Allen	8.00
11	Dan Marino	50.00
12	Drew Bledsoe	25.00
13	Curtis Martin	25.00
14	Jerome Bettis	8.00
15	Jim Druckenmiller	30.00
16	Jerry Rice	25.00
17	Warrick Dunn	40.00
18	Eddie George	40.00

1997 Pinnacle

Pinnacle Football has a 200-card base set. Both sides feature a player action photo. Pinnacle Football also has two partial base set parallels (Artist's Proof and Trophy Collection) and three inserts. Trophy Collection utilizes Dufex technology. Artist's Proof parallels Trophy Collection by adding the Artist's Proof stamp. The parallel sets are re-numbered. The inserts include Epix (24 cards, 1:19), Scoring Core (24 cards, 1:89) and Team Pinnacle (10 cards, 1:240).

		MT
Complete Set (200):		25.00
Common Player:		.10
Wax Box:		45.00
1	Brett Favre	2.50
2	Dan Marino	2.00
3	Emmitt Smith	2.00
4	Steve Young	.75
5	Drew Bledsoe	1.00
6	Eddie George	1.50
7	Barry Sanders	1.25
8	Jerry Rice	1.00
9	John Elway	.75
10	Troy Aikman	1.00
11	Kerry Collins	.25
12	Rick Mirer	.10
13	Jim Harbaugh	.10
14	Elvis Grbac	.10
15	Gus Frerotte	.10
16	Neil O'Donnell	.10
17	Jeff George	.10
18	Kordell Stewart	1.00
19	Junior Seau	.20
20	Vinny Testaverde	.10
21	Terry Glenn	.75
22	Anthony Johnson	.10
23	Boomer Esiason	.10
24	Terrell Owens	.50
25	Natrone Means	.20
26	Marcus Allen	.20
27	James Jett	.10
28	Chris T. Jones	.10
29	Stan Humphries	.10
30	Keith Byars	.10
31	John Friesz	.10
32	Mike Alstott	.20
33	Eddie Kennison	.40
34	Eric Moulds	.10
35	Frank Sanders	.10
36	Daryl Johnston	.10
37	Cris Carter	.10
38	Errict Rhett	.20
39	Ben Coates	.10
40	Shannon Sharpe	.10
41	Jamal Anderson	.20
42	Tim Biakabutuka	.10
43	Jeff Blake	.20
44	Michael Irvin	.20
45	Terrell Davis	1.00
46	Bam Morris	.10
47	Rashaan Salaam	.10
48	Adrian Murrell	.20
49	Ty Detmer	.10
50	Terry Allen	.10
51	Mark Brunell	1.00
52	O.J. McDuffie	.10
53	Willie McGinest	.10
54	Chris Warren	.10
55	Trent Dilfer	.20
56	Jerome Bettis	.20
57	Tamarick Vanover	.10
58	Ki-Jana Carter	.10
59	Ray Zellars	.10
60	J.J. Stokes	.10
61	Cornelius Bennett	.10
62	Scott Mitchell	.10
63	Tyrone Wheatley	.10
64	Steve McNair	.75
65	Tony Banks	.40
66	James Stewart	.10
67	Robert Smith	.10
68	Thurman Thomas	.20
69	Mark Chmura	.10
70	Napoleon Kaufman	.20
71	Ken Norton	.10
72	Herschel Walker	.10
73	Joey Galloway	.20
74	Neil Smith	.10
75	Simeon Rice	.10
76	Michael Jackson	.10
77	Muhsin Muhammad	.10
78	Kevin Hardy	.10
79	Irving Fryar	.10
80	Eric Swann	.10
81	Yancey Thigpen	.10
82	Jim Everett	.10
83	Karim Abdul-Jabbar	.50
84	Garrison Hearst	.10
85	Lawrence Phillips	.20
86	Bryan Cox	.10
87	Larry Centers	.10
88	Wesley Walls	.10
89	Curtis Conway	.10
90	Darnay Scott	.10
91	Anthony Miller	.10
92	Edgar Bennett	.10
93	Willie Green	.10
94	Kent Graham	.10
95	Dave Brown	.10
96	Wayne Chrebet	.10
97	Ricky Watters	.20
98	Tony Martin	.10
99	Warren Moon	.10
100	Curtis Martin	1.00
101	Dorsey Levens	.30
102	Jim Pyne	.10
103	Antonio Freeman	.30
104	Leeland McElroy	.10
105	Isaac Bruce	.20
106	Chris Sanders	.10
107	Tim Brown	.10
108	Greg Lloyd	.10
109	Terrell Buckley	.10
110	Deion Sanders	.40
111	Carl Pickens	.10
112	Bobby Engram	.10
113	Andre Reed	.10
114	Terance Mathis	.10
115	Herman Moore	.20
116	Robert Brooks	.10
117	Ken Dilger	.10
118	Keenan McCardell	.10
119	Andre Hastings	.10
120	Willie Davis	.10
121	Bruce Smith	.10
122	Rob Moore	.10
123	Johnnie Morton	.10
124	Sean Dawkins	.10
125	Mario Bates	.10
126	Henry Ellard	.10
127	Derrick Alexander	.10
128	Kevin Green	.10
129	Derrick Thomas	.10
130	Rod Woodson	.10
131	Rodney Hampton	.10
132	Marshall Faulk	.20
133	Michael Westbrook	.10
134	Erik Kramer	.10
135	Todd Collins	.10
136	Bill Romanowski	.10
137	Jake Reed	.10
138	Heath Shuler	.10
139	Keyshawn Johnson	.40
140	Marvin Harrison	.40
141	Andre Rison	.10
142	Zach Thomas	.20
143	Eric Metcalf	.10
144	Amani Toomer	.10
145	Desmond Howard	.10
146	Jimmy Smith	.10
147	Brad Johnson	.10
148	Troy Vincent	.10
149	Bryce Paup	.10
150	Reggie White	.20
151	*Jake Plummer*	1.50
152	*Darnell Autry*	.25
153	*Tiki Barber*	1.50
154	*Pat Barnes*	.30
155	*Orlando Pace*	.20
156	*Peter Boulware*	.10
157	*Shawn Springs*	.20
158	*Troy Davis*	.50
159	*Ike Hilliard*	1.25
160	*Jim Druckenmiller*	3.00
161	*Warrick Dunn*	4.00
162	*James Farrior*	.10
163	*Tony Gonzalez*	.75
164	*Darrell Russell*	.10
165	*Byron Hanspard*	.50
166	*Corey Dillon*	2.00
167	*Kenny Holmes*	.10
168	*Walter Jones*	.10
169	*Danny Wuerffel*	3.00
170	*Tom Knight*	.10
171	*David LaFleur*	.75
172	*Kevin Lockett*	.10
173	*Will Blackwell*	.20
174	*Reidel Anthony*	1.50
175	*Dwayne Rudd*	.10
176	*Yatil Green*	.75
177	*Antowain Smith*	2.00
178	*Rae Carruth*	1.25
179	*Bryant Westbrook*	.10
180	*Reinard Wilson*	.10
181	*Joey Kent*	.30
182	*Renaldo Wynn*	.10
183	Brett Favre	1.25
184	Emmitt Smith	1.00
185	Dan Marino	1.00
186	Troy Aikman	.50
187	Jerry Rice	.50
188	Drew Bledsoe	.50
189	Eddie George	.75
190	Terry Glenn	.10
191	John Elway	.30
192	Steve Young	.30
193	Mark Brunell	.50
194	Barry Sanders	.50
195	Kerry Collins	.30
196	Curtis Martin	.50
197	Terrell Davis	.50
198	Checklist	.10
199	Checklist	.10
200	Checklist	.10

1997 Pinnacle Trophy Collection

Trophy Collection is a 100-card partial parallel of the base set. The cards were re-numbered and feature Dufex technology. They were inserted one per nine packs.

		MT
Complete Set (100):		250.00
Common Player:		1.00
P1	Brett Favre	25.00
P2	Dan Marino	20.00
P3	Emmitt Smith	20.00
P4	Steve Young	8.00
P5	Drew Bledsoe	12.00
P6	Eddie George	16.00
P7	Barry Sanders	12.00
P8	Jerry Rice	12.00
P9	John Elway	10.00
P10	Troy Aikman	12.00
P11	Kerry Collins	3.00
P12	Rick Mirer	1.00
P13	Jim Harbaugh	1.00
P14	Elvis Grbac	1.00
P15	Gus Frerotte	1.00
P16	Neil O'Donnell	1.00
P17	Jeff George	1.00
P18	Kordell Stewart	12.00
P19	Junior Seau	1.00
P20	Vinny Testaverde	1.00
P21	Terry Glenn	10.00
P22	Natrone Means	2.00
P23	Marcus Allen	2.00
P24	Stan Humphries	1.00

P25	John Friesz	1.00
P26	Cris Carter	1.00
P27	Shannon Sharpe	1.00
P28	Tim Biakabutuka	1.00
P29	Jeff Blake	2.00
P30	Michael Irvin	2.00
P31	Terrell Davis	12.00
P32	Rashaan Salaam	1.00
P33	Adrian Murrell	2.00
P34	Ty Detmer	1.00
P35	Mark Brunell	12.00
P36	Chris Warren	1.00
P37	Trent Dilfer	2.00
P38	Jerome Bettis	2.00
P39	Scott Mitchell	1.00
P40	Steve McNair	10.00
P41	Tony Banks	3.00
P42	Joey Galloway	2.00
P43	Karim Abdul-Jabbar	8.00
P44	Lawrence Phillips	2.00
P45	Dave Brown	1.00
P46	Warren Moon	1.00
P47	Curtis Martin	12.00
P48	Dorsey Levens	2.00
P49	Deion Sanders	5.00
P50	Herman Moore	2.00
P51	Bruce Smith	1.00
P52	Keyshawn Johnson	2.00
P53	Reggie White	2.00
P54	Jake Plummer	10.00
P55	Darnell Autry	4.00
P56	Tiki Barber	8.00
P57	Pat Barnes	4.00
P58	Orlando Pace	2.00
P59	Peter Boulware	1.00
P60	Shawn Springs	2.00
P61	Troy Davis	3.00
P62	Ike Hilliard	6.00
P63	Jim Druckenmiller	12.00
P64	Warrick Dunn	20.00
P65	James Farrior	1.00
P66	Tony Gonzalez	5.00
P67	Darrell Russell	1.00
P68	Byron Hanspard	3.00
P69	Corey Dillon	12.00
P70	Kenny Holmes	1.00
P71	Walter Jones	1.00
P72	Danny Wuerffel	10.00
P73	Tom Knight	1.00
P74	David LaFleur	5.00
P75	Kevin Lockett	1.00
P76	Will Blackwell	2.00
P77	Reidel Anthony	8.00
P78	Dwayne Rudd	1.00
P79	Yatil Green	6.00
P80	Antowain Smith	12.00
P81	Rae Carruth	6.00
P82	Bryant Westbrook	2.00
P83	Reinard Wilson	1.00
P84	Joey Kent	2.00
P85	Renaldo Wynn	1.00
P86	Brett Favre	12.00
P87	Emmitt Smith	10.00
P88	Dan Marino	10.00
P89	Troy Aikman	6.00
P90	Jerry Rice	6.00
P91	Drew Bledsoe	6.00
P92	Eddie George	8.00
P93	Terry Glenn	4.00
P94	John Elway	4.00
P95	Steve Young	4.00
P96	Mark Brunell	6.00
P97	Barry Sanders	6.00
P98	Kerry Collins	2.00
P99	Curtis Martin	6.00
P100	Terrell Davis	6.00

1997 Pinnacle Artist's Proof

Artist's Proof is a 100-card partial parallel of Pinnacle Football. The cards feature Dufex technology and the Artist's Proof stamp. The cards are re-numbered from one to 100.

		MT
Complete Set (100):		850.00
Common Player:		3.00
P1	Brett Favre	75.00
P2	Dan Marino	60.00
P3	Emmitt Smith	60.00
P4	Steve Young	20.00
P5	Drew Bledsoe	40.00
P6	Eddie George	50.00
P7	Barry Sanders	40.00
P8	Jerry Rice	40.00
P9	John Elway	30.00
P10	Troy Aikman	40.00
P11	Kerry Collins	8.00
P12	Rick Mirer	3.00
P13	Jim Harbaugh	3.00
P14	Elvis Grbac	3.00
P15	Gus Frerotte	3.00
P16	Neil O'Donnell	3.00
P17	Jeff George	3.00
P18	Kordell Stewart	40.00
P19	Junior Seau	3.00
P20	Vinny Testaverde	3.00
P21	Terry Glenn	30.00
P22	Natrone Means	6.00
P23	Marcus Allen	6.00
P24	Stan Humphries	3.00
P25	John Friesz	3.00
P26	Cris Carter	3.00
P27	Shannon Sharpe	3.00
P28	Tim Biakabutuka	3.00
P29	Jeff Blake	6.00
P30	Michael Irvin	6.00
P31	Terrell Davis	40.00
P32	Rashaan Salaam	3.00
P33	Adrian Murrell	6.00
P34	Ty Detmer	3.00
P35	Mark Brunell	40.00
P36	Chris Warren	3.00
P37	Trent Dilfer	6.00
P38	Jerome Bettis	6.00
P39	Scott Mitchell	3.00
P40	Steve McNair	30.00
P41	Tony Banks	8.00
P42	Joey Galloway	6.00
P43	Karim Abdul-Jabbar	20.00
P44	Lawrence Phillips	6.00
P45	Dave Brown	3.00
P46	Warren Moon	3.00
P47	Curtis Martin	40.00
P48	Dorsey Levens	6.00
P49	Deion Sanders	20.00
P50	Herman Moore	6.00
P51	Bruce Smith	3.00
P52	Keyshawn Johnson	6.00
P53	Reggie White	6.00
P54	Jake Plummer	25.00
P55	Darnell Autry	12.00
P56	Tiki Barber	20.00
P57	Pat Barnes	10.00
P58	Orlando Pace	6.00
P59	Peter Boulware	3.00
P60	Shawn Springs	6.00
P61	Troy Davis	8.00
P62	Ike Hilliard	15.00
P63	Jim Druckenmiller	30.00
P64	Warrick Dunn	50.00
P65	James Farrior	3.00
P66	Tony Gonzalez	12.00
P67	Darrell Russell	3.00
P68	Byron Hanspard	8.00
P69	Corey Dillon	30.00
P70	Kenny Holmes	3.00
P71	Walter Jones	3.00
P72	Danny Wuerffel	25.00
P73	Tom Knight	3.00
P74	David LaFleur	12.00
P75	Kevin Lockett	3.00
P76	Will Blackwell	6.00
P77	Reidel Anthony	20.00
P78	Dwayne Rudd	3.00
P79	Yatil Green	15.00
P80	Antowain Smith	25.00
P81	Rae Carruth	15.00
P82	Bryant Westbrook	6.00
P83	Reinard Wilson	3.00
P84	Joey Kent	6.00
P85	Renaldo Wynn	3.00
P86	Brett Favre	40.00
P87	Emmitt Smith	30.00
P88	Dan Marino	30.00
P89	Troy Aikman	20.00
P90	Jerry Rice	20.00
P91	Drew Bledsoe	20.00
P92	Eddie George	25.00
P93	Terry Glenn	15.00
P94	John Elway	15.00
P95	Steve Young	15.00
P96	Mark Brunell	20.00
P97	Barry Sanders	20.00
P98	Kerry Collins	8.00
P99	Curtis Martin	20.00
P100	Terrell Davis	20.00

1997 Pinnacle Epix

Epix is a 24-card insert which features holographic effects. The set consists of Game, Moment and Season cards which highlight each player's top performances. Orange, Purple and Emerald versions of each card were produced. The overall insertion rate for Epix was 1:19.

		MT
Complete Set (24):		400.00
Common Game (E1-E8):		4.00
Common Moment (E9-E16):		12.00
Common Season (E17-E24):		8.00
Purple Cards:		2x
Emerald Cards:		3x
1	Emmitt Smith	25.00
2	Troy Aikman	15.00
3	Terrell Davis	15.00
4	Drew Bledsoe	15.00
5	Jeff George	4.00
6	Kerry Collins	10.00
7	Antonio Freeman	4.00
8	Herman Moore	4.00
9	Barry Sanders	50.00
10	Brett Favre	80.00
11	Michael Irvin	12.00
12	Steve Young	30.00
13	Mark Brunell	40.00
14	Jerome Bettis	12.00
15	Deion Sanders	25.00
16	Jeff Blake	12.00
17	Dan Marino	50.00
18	Eddie George	35.00
19	Jerry Rice	25.00
20	John Elway	20.00
21	Curtis Martin	20.00
22	Kordell Stewart	25.00
23	Junior Seau	8.00
24	Reggie White	8.00

1997 Pinnacle Scoring Core

Scoring Core is a 24-card insert seeded 1:89 packs. Each card is specially die-cut and features foil-etching.

		MT
Complete Set (24):		375.00
Common Player:		4.00
1	Emmitt Smith	50.00
2	Troy Aikman	30.00
3	Michael Irvin	8.00
4	Robert Brooks	4.00
5	Brett Favre	60.00
6	Antonio Freeman	8.00
7	Curtis Martin	30.00
8	Drew Bledsoe	30.00
9	Terry Glenn	20.00
10	Tim Biakabutuka	4.00
11	Kerry Collins	20.00
12	Muhsin Muhammad	4.00
13	Karim Abdul-Jabbar	15.00
14	Dan Marino	50.00
15	O.J. McDuffie	4.00
16	Terrell Davis	30.00
17	John Elway	20.00
18	Shannon Sharpe	4.00
19	Garrison Hearst	4.00
20	Steve Young	20.00
21	Jerry Rice	30.00
22	Natrone Means	8.00
23	Mark Brunell	30.00
24	Keenan McCardell	4.00

1997 Pinnacle Team Pinnacle

Team Pinnacle is a 10-card insert consisting of double-sided foil cards. The cards feature two players from the same position, one from each conference. Team Pinnacle cards were inserted 1:240.

		MT
Complete Set (10):		400.00
Common Player:		25.00
1	Dan Marino, Troy Aikman	80.00
2	Drew Bledsoe, Brett Favre	100.00
3	Mark Brunell, Kerry Collins	50.00
4	John Elway, Steve Young	40.00
5	Terrell Davis, Emmitt Smith	80.00
6	Curtis Martin, Barry Sanders	50.00
7	Eddie George, Tim Biakabutuka	60.00
8	Karim Abdul-Jabbar, Lawrence Phillips	25.00
9	Terry Glenn, Jerry Rice	50.00
10	Joey Galloway, Michael Irvin	25.00

1997 Pinnacle Certified

Pinnacle Certified consists of a 150-card base set, four parallels and two inserts. The base cards were printed on silver mirror board. The parallel sets include Certified Red (1:5), Mirror Red (1:99), Mirror Blue (1:199) and Mirror Red (1:299). The inserts are Certified Team (20 cards, 1:19) and Epix (24 cards, 1:15). All cards in the set have a clear-coat protector.

		MT
Complete Set (150):		75.00
Common Player:		.25
Mirror Red Stars:		30x-60x
Mirror Red Rookies:		15x-30x
Mirror Blue Stars:		50x-100x
Mirror Blue Rookies:		25x-50x
Mirror Gold Stars:		100x-200x
Mirror Gold Rookies:		50-100x
Wax Box:		90.00
1	Emmitt Smith	5.00
2	Dan Marino	5.00
3	Brett Favre	6.00
4	Steve Young	2.00
5	Kerry Collins	.75
6	Troy Aikman	2.50
7	Drew Bledsoe	2.50
8	Eddie George	4.00
9	Jerry Rice	3.00
10	John Elway	2.00
11	Barry Sanders	4.00
12	Mark Brunell	2.50
13	Elvis Grbac	.25
14	Tony Banks	1.50
15	Vinny Testaverde	.25
16	Rick Mirer	.25
17	Carl Pickens	.25
18	Deion Sanders	1.50
19	Terry Glenn	2.50
20	Heath Shuler	.25
21	Dave Brown	.25
22	Keyshawn Johnson	1.00
23	Jeff George	.50
24	Ricky Watters	.50
25	Kordell Stewart	2.50
26	Junior Seau	.25
27	Terrell Owens	2.00
28	Warren Moon	.50
29	Isaac Bruce	.50
30	Steve McNair	2.00
31	Gus Frerotte	.25
32	Trent Dilfer	.50
33	Shannon Sharpe	.25
34	Scott Mitchell	.25
35	Antonio Freeman	.50
36	Jim Harbaugh	.25
37	Natrone Means	.50
38	Marcus Allen	.50
39	Karim Abdul-Jabbar	1.75
40	Tim Biakabutuka	.25
41	Jeff Blake	.50
42	Michael Irvin	.50
43	Herschel Walker	.25
44	Curtis Martin	2.50
45	Eddie Kennison	.50
46	Napoleon Kaufman	.75
47	Larry Centers	.25
48	Jamal Anderson	.50
49	Derrick Alexander	.25
50	Bruce Smith	.25
51	Wesley Walls	.25
52	Rod Smith	.25
53	Keenan McCardell	.25
54	Robert Brooks	.25
55	Willie Green	.25
56	Jake Reed	.25
57	Joey Galloway	.50
58	Eric Metcalf	.25
59	Chris Sanders	.25
60	Jeff Hostetler	.25
61	Kevin Greene	.25
62	Frank Sanders	.25
63	Dorsey Levens	.50
64	Sean Dawkins	.25
65	Cris Carter	.25
66	Andre Hastings	.25
67	Amani Toomer	.25
68	Adrian Murrell	.50
69	Ty Detmer	.25
70	Yancey Thigpen	.25
71	Jim Everett	.25
72	Todd Collins	.25
73	Curtis Conway	.50
74	Herman Moore	.50
75	Neil O'Donnell	.25
76	Rod Woodson	.25
77	Tony Martin	.25
78	Kent Graham	.25
79	Andre Reed	.25
80	Reggie White	.50
81	Thurman Thomas	.50
82	Garrison Hearst	.25
83	Chris Warren	.25
84	Wayne Chrebet	.25
85	Chris T. Jones	.25
86	Anthony Miller	.25
87	Chris Chandler	.25
88	Terrell Davis	3.00
89	Mike Alstott	1.50
90	Terry Allen	.25
91	Jerome Bettis	.50
92	Stan Humphries	.25
93	Andre Rison	.25
94	Marshall Faulk	.50
95	Erik Kramer	.25
96	O.J. McDuffie	.25
97	Robert Smith	.25
98	Keith Byars	.25
99	Rodney Hampton	.25
100	Desmond Howard	.25
101	Lawrence Phillips	.50
102	Michael Westbrook	.25
103	Johnnie Morton	.25
104	Ben Coates	.25
105	J.J. Stokes	.50
106	Terance Mathis	.25
107	Errict Rhett	.25
108	Tim Brown	.25
109	Marvin Harrison	1.00
110	Muhsin Muhammad	.25
111	Bam Morris	.25
112	Mario Bates	.25
113	Jimmy Smith	.25
114	Irving Fryar	.25
115	Tamarick Vanover	.25
116	Brad Johnson	.50
117	Rashaan Salaam	.25
118	Ki-Jana Carter	.25
119	Tyrone Wheatley	.25
120	John Friesz	.25
121	*Orlando Pace*	.50
122	*Jim Druckenmiller*	6.00
123	*Byron Hanspard*	.75
124	*David LaFleur*	1.50
125	*Reidel Anthony*	3.00
126	*Antowain Smith*	4.00
127	*Bryant Westbrook*	.50
128	*Fred Lane*	2.00
129	*Tiki Barber*	4.00
130	*Shawn Springs*	.50
131	*Ike Hilliard*	3.00
132	*James Farrior*	.25
133	*Darrell Russell*	.25
134	*Walter Jones*	.25
135	*Tom Knight*	.25
136	*Yatil Green*	1.00
137	*Joey Kent*	.50
138	*Kevin Lockett*	.50
139	*Troy Davis*	1.00
140	*Darnell Autry*	.50
141	*Pat Barnes*	.75
142	*Rae Carruth*	3.00
143	*Will Blackwell*	.50
144	*Warrick Dunn*	10.00
145	*Corey Dillon*	7.00
146	*Dwayne Rudd*	.25
147	*Reinard Wilson*	.25
148	*Peter Boulware*	.25
149	*Tony Gonzalez*	1.50
150	*Danny Wuerffel*	4.00

1997 Pinnacle Certified Red

Certified Red was a parallel to the Certified set. Inserted in one per five packs, the cards were printed on a red surface, with the words "Certified Red" printed down the side.

	MT
Certified Red Cards:	3x-6x
Certified Red Rookies:	2x-3x

1997 Pinnacle Certified Team

Certified Team is a 20-card insert that was seeded 1:19 in packs of Certified Football. The cards were printed on silver mirror board. Gold (inserted 1:119) and Mirror Gold (25 numbered sets) parallels were also issued.

		MT
Complete Set (20):		250.00
Common Player:		5.00
Inserted 1:19		
1	Brett Favre	30.00
2	Dan Marino	25.00
3	Emmitt Smith	25.00
4	Eddie George	20.00
5	Jerry Rice	15.00
6	Troy Aikman	15.00
7	Barry Sanders	18.00
8	Terrell Davis	15.00
9	Drew Bledsoe	15.00
10	Curtis Martin	15.00
11	Terry Glenn	10.00
12	Kerry Collins	10.00
13	John Elway	10.00
14	Kordell Stewart	15.00
15	Karim Abdul-Jabbar	8.00
16	Steve Young	10.00
17	Steve McNair	10.00
18	Terrell Owens	5.00
19	Keyshawn Johnson	5.00
20	Mark Brunell	15.00

1997 Pinnacle Certified Gold Team

Certified Gold Teams were a parallel set to the Certified Team inserts, but added a gold foil pattern to the card front. Gold Team included 20 cards and were inserted one per 19 packs. In addition, 25 of each card was also done in a Mirror Gold version.

	MT
Gold Cards:	2x-4x
Mirror Gold Cards:	20x-40x

1997 Pinnacle Inscriptions

Inscriptions consists of a 50-card base set, two parallel sets and two inserts. The base

set features a color player photo with a black and white background. The parallel sets are Challenge Collection (1:7) and Artist's Proof (1:35). Artist's Proof features Dufex technology and the Artist's Proof seal. The inserts are Autographs (30 cards, 1:23) and V2 (18 cards, 1:11). Each pack contained three cards and was packaged in a collectable box.

		MT
Complete Set (50):		75.00
Common Player:		.50
Wax Box:		150.00
1	Mark Brunell	4.00
2	Steve Young	3.00
3	Rick Mirer	.50
4	Brett Favre	10.00
5	Tony Banks	2.00
6	Elvis Grbac	.50
7	John Elway	3.00
8	Troy Aikman	4.00
9	Neil O'Donnell	.50
10	Kordell Stewart	4.00
11	Drew Bledsoe	4.00
12	Kerry Collins	3.00
13	Dan Marino	8.00
14	Jeff George	1.00
15	Scott Mitchell	.50
16	Jim Harbaugh	.50
17	Dave Brown	.50
18	Jeff Blake	1.00
19	Trent Dilfer	1.00
20	Barry Sanders	5.00
21	Jerry Rice	4.00
22	Emmitt Smith	8.00
23	Vinny Testaverde	.50
24	Warren Moon	.50
25	Junior Seau	.50
26	Gus Frerotte	.50
27	Heath Shuler	.50
28	Erik Kramer	.50
29	Boomer Esiason	.50
30	Jim Kelly	1.00
31	Mark Brunell	2.00
32	Steve Young	1.50
33	Brett Favre	5.00
34	Tony Banks	1.00
35	John Elway	1.50
36	Troy Aikman	2.00
37	Kordell Stewart	2.00
38	Drew Bledsoe	2.00
39	Kerry Collins	1.50
40	Dan Marino	4.00
41	Jim Harbaugh	.50
42	Jeff Blake	.50
43	Barry Sanders	2.50
44	Jerry Rice	2.00
45	Emmitt Smith	4.00
46	Rick Mirer	.50
47	Jeff George	.50
48	Neil O'Donnell	.50
49	Elvis Grbac	.50
50	Scott Mitchell	.50

1997 Pinnacle Inscriptions Challenge Collection

Challenge Collection was a 50-card parallel that featured each base card with printed on a red foil background with the player's signature appearing repeatedly in black. There is also a Challenge Collection logo in the lower right corner. These were inserted one per seven packs.

	MT
Challenge Collection Cards:	2x-4x

1997 Pinnacle Inscriptions Artist Proofs

This 50-card parallel set utilized a Dufex background to parallel the entire base set. Card fronts also added an Artist's Proof logo in the bottom right corner. These parallels were inserted into one per 35 packs of Inscriptions.

	MT
Artist Proof Cards:	8x-16x

1997 Pinnacle Inscriptions Autographs

Autographs is a 30-card insert which was seeded one per 23 packs. The cards are plastic, signed by the player and hand-numbered. Each player signed a different number of cards. individual player.

	MT
Common Player:	25.00
Tony Banks	50.00
Jeff Blake	50.00
Drew Bledsoe 1970	150.00
Dave Brown	25.00
Mark Brunell 2000	150.00
Kerry Collins 1300	100.00
Trent Dilfer	50.00
John Elway 1975	150.00
Boomer Esiason	25.00
Jim Everett	25.00
Brett Favre 215	700.00

Gus Frerotte	25.00
Jeff George	25.00
Elvis Grbac	25.00
Jim Harbaugh	25.00
Jeff Hostetler	25.00
Jim Kelly	50.00
Bernie Kosar	25.00
Eric Kramer	25.00
Dan Marino 440	500.00
Rick Mirer	25.00
Scott Mitchell	25.00
Warren Moon	25.00
Neil O'Donnell	25.00
Jerry Rice 950	300.00
Junior Seau	25.00
Heath Shuler	25.00
Emmitt Smith 220	600.00
Kordell Stewart 1495	150.00
Vinny Testaverde	25.00
Steve Young 1900	125.00

1997 Pinnacle Inscriptions V2

V2 is a 18-card insert consisting of plastic motion cards. Inserted 1:11, the cards came with a clear-coat protector.

		MT
Complete Set (18):		200.00
Common Player:		4.00
1	Mark Brunell	15.00
2	Steve Young	10.00
3	Brett Favre	35.00
4	Tony Banks	8.00
5	John Elway	10.00
6	Troy Aikman	15.00
7	Kordell Stewart	15.00
8	Drew Bledsoe	15.00
9	Kerry Collins	10.00
10	Dan Marino	30.00
11	Barry Sanders	20.00
12	Jerry Rice	15.00
13	Emmitt Smith	30.00
14	Neil O'Donnell	4.00
15	Scott Mitchell	4.00
16	Jim Harbaugh	4.00
17	Jeff Blake	8.00
18	Trent Dilfer	8.00

1997 Pinnacle Inside

Pinnacle Inside featured a 150-card base set and 28 collectible cans. The base cards include three different player shots. Silver Lining (1:7) and Gridiron Gold (1:63) were the parallel sets. The inserts are Fourth & Goal and Autographed Cards.

		MT
Complete Set (150):		40.00
Common Player:		.20
1	Troy Aikman	1.50
2	Dan Marino	3.00

3	Barry Sanders	1.50
4	Drew Bledsoe	1.50
5	Kerry Collins	.50
6	Emmitt Smith	3.00
7	Brett Favre	3.00
8	John Elway	1.00
9	Jerry Rice	1.50
10	Mark Brunell	1.50
11	Elvis Grbac	.20
12	Junior Seau	.20
13	Eddie George	1.75
14	Steve Young	1.00
15	Terrell Davis	1.50
16	Thurman Thomas	.40
17	Deion Sanders	.75
18	Terrell Owens	.75
19	Neil O'Donnell	.20
20	Carl Pickens	.20
21	Marcus Allen	.40
22	Ricky Watters	.40
23	Vinny Testaverde	.20
24	Kordell Stewart	1.25
25	Tony Banks	.75
26	Terry Glenn	1.25
27	Todd Collins	.20
28	Robert Brooks	.40
29	Heath Shuler	.20
30	Shannon Sharpe	.20
31	Michael Westbrook	.20
32	Reggie White	.40
33	Brad Johnson	.20
34	Tamarick Vanover	.20
35	Larry Centers	.20
36	Terance Mathis	.20
37	Hardy Nickerson	.20
38	Jamal Anderson	.40
39	Kevin Hardy	.20
40	Stan Humphries	.20
41	Chris Warren	.20
42	Tim Brown	.40
43	Joey Galloway	.60
44	Boomer Esiason	.20
45	Jake Reed	.20
46	Kent Graham	.20
47	Marshall Faulk	.40
48	Sean Dawkins	.20
49	Dave Brown	.20
50	Willie Green	.20
51	Andre Hastings	.20
52	Erik Kramer	.20
53	Michael Irvin	.40
54	Gus Frerotte	.20
55	Winslow Oliver	.20
56	Jimmy Smith	.20
57	Derrick Alexander	.20
58	Adrian Murrell	.20
59	Ki-Jana Carter	.20
60	Garrison Hearst	.20
61	Chris Sanders	.20
62	Johnnie Morton	.20
63	Lawrence Phillips	.40
64	Bobby Engram	.20
65	Tim Biakabutuka	.40
66	Anthony Johnson	.20
67	Keyshawn Johnson	.60
68	Jeff George	.20
69	Errict Rhett	.20
70	Cris Carter	.20
71	Chris T. Jones	.20
72	Eric Moulds	.20
73	Rick Mirer	.20
74	Keenan McCardell	.20
75	Simeon Rice	.20
76	Eddie Kennison	.75
77	Herman Moore	.40
78	Jim Harbaugh	.20
79	Robert Smith	.20
80	Bruce Smith	.20
81	John Friesz	.20
82	Irving Fryar	.20
83	Edgar Bennett	.20
84	Ty Detmer	.20
85	Curtis Conway	.20
86	Napoleon Kaufman	.20
87	Tony Martin	.20
88	Amani Toomer	.20
89	Willie McGinest	.20
90	Daryl Johnston	.20
91	Stanley Pritchett	.20
92	Chris Chandler	.20
93	Natrone Means	.20
94	Kimble Anders	.20
95	Steve McNair	1.00
96	Curtis Martin	1.50
97	O.J. McDuffie	.20
98	Ben Coates	.20
99	Jerome Bettis	.40
100	Andre Reed	.20
101	Jeff Blake	.40
102	Wesley Walls	.20
103	Warren Moon	.20
104	Isaac Bruce	.40
105	Terry Allen	.20
106	Rodney Hampton	.20
107	Karim Abdul-Jabbar	1.00
108	Marvin Harrison	.75
109	Dorsey Levens	.40
110	Rashaan Salaam	.40
111	Scott Mitchell	.20
112	Darnay Scott	.20
113	Aeneas Williams	.20
114	Trent Dilfer	.20
115	Antonio Freeman	.40
116	Jim Everett	.20
117	Muhsin Muhammad	.20
118	Rickey Dudley	.20
119	Mike Alstott	.20
120	*Jim Druckenmiller*	2.50

121	Tiki Barber	1.50
122	Ike Hilliard	1.25
123	Orlando Pace	.50
124	Jake Plummer	2.00
125	Yatil Green	.75
126	Byron Hanspard	.75
127	James Farrior	.20
128	Corey Dillon	2.50
129	Pat Barnes	.50
130	Kenny Holmes	.20
131	Rae Carruth	1.25
132	Danny Wuerffel	1.50
133	Darnell Autry	.75
134	Reidel Anthony	2.00
135	Darrell Russell	.20
136	Will Blackwell	.50
137	Peter Boulware	.20
138	Shawn Springs	.50
139	Joey Kent	.75
140	Troy Davis	.75
141	Antowain Smith	2.00
142	Walter Jones	.20
143	Tony Gonzalez	.75
144	David LaFleur	.75
145	Warrick Dunn	4.00
146	Bryant Westbrook	.20
147	Dwayne Rudd	.20
148	Tom Knight	.20
149	Kevin Lockett	.20
150	Checklist	.20

1997 Pinnacle Inside Silver

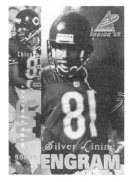

This 150-card parallel set features each base card printed with silver foil highlights. The lettering and words "Silver Lining" are printed in bronze foil. These parallels are inserted one per seven packs.

	MT
Silver Cards:	6x-12x
Silver Rookies:	3x-6x
Inserted 1:7	

1997 Pinnacle Inside Gridiron Gold

This 150-card parallel set featured each base card printed on a gold foil format that is die-cut on the right side. The logo, player's name and words "Gridiron Gold" are one per 63 hobby/retail packs. hobby/retail packs.

	MT
Gridiron Gold Cards:	20x-40x
Gridiron Gold Rookies:	10x-20x
Inserted 1:63	

1997 Pinnacle Inside Cans

Inside cards were available in 28 different cans. The first 25 cans featured a single player with the image of their Inside card on the outside of the can. Three special cans - Brett Favre MVP, Dan Marino passing record and Ice Bowl commemorative - were also issued. A Gold Can parallel set was also created. Gold Cans were found once per 47 cans.

		MT
Complete Set (28):		30.00
Common Can:		.50
Common Sealed Can:		3.00
Sealed Cans:		1x-2x
Gold Cans:		4x-8x
Gold Sealed Cans:		8x-16x
1	Brett Favre	3.00
2	Dan Marino	2.50
3	Emmitt Smith	2.50
4	Troy Aikman	1.50
5	Barry Sanders	1.50
6	Kerry Collins	1.50
7	Mark Brunell	1.50
8	John Elway	1.00
9	Steve Young	1.00
10	Jerry Rice	1.50
11	Terrell Davis	1.50
12	Curtis Martin	1.50
13	Terry Glenn	1.50
14	Eddie George	2.00
15	Jeff Blake	.50
16	Kordell Stewart	1.50
17	Rick Mirer	.50
18	Karim Abdul-Jabbar	1.00
19	Jeff George	.50
20	Keyshawn Johnson	.50
21	Jim Harbaugh	.50
22	Drew Bledsoe	1.50
23	Deion Sanders	1.00
24	Tony Banks	1.00
25	Jerome Bettis	.50
26	Brett Favre (MVP)	3.00
27	Dan Marino (Passing)	2.50
28	Ice Bowl	2.50

1997 Pinnacle Inside Fourth & Goal

This 20-card insert features clutch players on a foil card. These cards were inserted 1:23.

		MT
Complete Set (20):		500.00
Common Player:		10.00
1	Brett Favre	60.00
2	Drew Bledsoe	30.00
3	Troy Aikman	30.00
4	Mark Brunell	30.00

		MT
5	Steve Young	25.00
6	Vinny Testaverde	10.00
7	Dan Marino	50.00
8	Kerry Collins	30.00
9	John Elway	25.00
10	Emmitt Smith	50.00
11	Barry Sanders	30.00
12	Eddie George	40.00
13	Terrell Davis	30.00
14	Curtis Martin	30.00
15	Terry Glenn	25.00
16	Jerry Rice	30.00
17	Herman Moore	10.00
18	Jeff Blake	10.00
19	Warrick Dunn	35.00
20	Antowain Smith	20.00

1997 Pinnacle Mint Cards

This 30-card base set features a player photo and a foil stamped bronze medallion on the front. A die-cut parallel was created to hold the set's coins. The other parallels are Silver Team Pinnacle (silver foil printing, 1:15) and Gold Team Pinnacle (gold Dufex etched foil, 1:47). Inserts include Commemorative Collection, a six-card set capturing the top moments of 1996 with silver foil and inserted 1:31. Pinnacle Mint also includes Solid Gold Redemption Cards. The solid gold cards are a parallel of the regular set. One redemption card per player was issued and they were inserted 1:47,000.

		MT
Complete Die-Cut (30):		20.00
Common Player:		.20
Bronze Cards:		1x-2x
Silver Cards:		6x-12x
Gold Cards:		12x-24x
Wax Box:		60.00
1	Brett Favre	2.50
2	Drew Bledsoe	1.25
3	Mark Brunell	1.25
4	Kerry Collins	1.00
5	Troy Aikman	1.25
6	Steve Young	1.00
7	Dan Marino	2.00
8	Barry Sanders	1.25
9	John Elway	1.00
10	Emmitt Smith	2.00
11	Rick Mirer	.20
12	Kordell Stewart	1.25
13	Tony Banks	.75
14	Jeff George	.20
15	Jerry Rice	1.25
16	Jeff Blake	.40
17	Jim Harbaugh	.20
18	Heath Shuler	.20
19	Scott Mitchell	.20
20	Neil O'Donnell	.20
21	Brett Favre (Minted Highlights)	1.25
22	Drew Bledsoe (Minted Highlights)	.75
23	Mark Brunell (Minted Highlights)	.75
24	Kerry Collins (Minted Highlights)	.40
25	Troy Aikman (Minted Highlights)	.50
26	Dan Marino (Minted Highlights)	1.00
27	Barry Sanders (Minted Highlights)	.75
28	Emmitt Smith (Minted Highlights)	1.00
29	Tony Banks (Minted Highlights)	.20
30	John Elway (Minted Highlights)	.50

1997 Pinnacle Mint Coins

The 30-base coins feature each players face and match up with one of the base cards. Six parallels of the base coins were made. Nickel-Silver (1:20), Gold Plated (1:47), Brass Proof (numbered to 500), Silver Proof (numbered to 250), Gold Proof (numbered to 100) and Solid Silver (1:288) versions were all added to Pinnacle Mint. The only insert is Commemorative Collection.

		MT
Complete Brass (30):		60.00
Common Brass Coin:		.75
Nickel Coins:		2.5x-5x
Gold Plated Coins:		6x-12x
1	Brett Favre	8.00
2	Drew Bledsoe	4.00
3	Mark Brunell	4.00
4	Kerry Collins	3.00
5	Troy Aikman	4.00
6	Steve Young	3.00
7	Dan Marino	6.00
8	Barry Sanders	4.00
9	John Elway	3.00
10	Emmitt Smith	6.00
11	Rick Mirer	.75
12	Kordell Stewart	4.00
13	Tony Banks	2.50
14	Jeff George	.75
15	Jerry Rice	4.00
16	Jeff Blake	1.50
17	Jim Harbaugh	.75
18	Heath Shuler	.75
19	Scott Mitchell	.75
20	Neil O'Donnell	.75
21	Brett Favre (Minted Highlights)	4.00
22	Drew Bledsoe (Minted Highlights)	2.50
23	Mark Brunell (Minted Highlights)	2.50
24	Kerry Collins (Minted Highlights)	1.50
25	Troy Aikman (Minted Highlights)	1.75
26	Dan Marino (Minted Highlights)	3.00
27	Barry Sanders (Minted Highlights)	2.50
28	Emmitt Smith (Minted Highlights)	3.00
29	Tony Banks (Minted Highlights)	.75
30	John Elway (Minted Highlights)	1.75

1997 Pinnacle Mint Commemorative Cards

This six-card insert highlights six top moments of 1996. The cards feature silver foil and were inserted 1:31.

		MT
Complete Set (6):		60.00
Common Player:		8.00
1	Barry Sanders	25.00
2	Brett Favre	18.00
3	Mark Brunell	8.00
4	Emmitt Smith	16.00
5	Dan Marino	16.00
6	Jerry Rice	8.00

1997 Pinnacle Mint Commemorative Coins

These six coins are double-sized brass and match up with the Commemorative Collection cards. They also highlight top events of 1996 and were inserted 1:31.

		MT
Complete Set (6):		120.00
Common Player:		16.00
1	Barry Sanders	25.00
2	Brett Favre	35.00
3	Mark Brunell	16.00
4	Emmitt Smith	35.00
5	Dan Marino	35.00
6	Jerry Rice	16.00

1997 Pinnacle Totally Certified Platinum Red

Platinum Red is considered the "base set" for Totally Certified. Each card in the 150-card set is sequentially-numbered to 4,999. The cards feature a micro-etched holographic mylar finish. Platinum Blue (one per pack) and Platinum Gold (1:79) parallels were also included in this series.

		MT
Complete Set (150):		500.00
Common Player:		1.25
Reds Sequentially #'d to 4,999		
Complete Blue Set (150):		1000.
Blue Cards:		2x
Blues Sequentially #'d to 2,499		
Wax Box:		120.00
1	Emmitt Smith	25.00
2	Dan Marino	25.00
3	Brett Favre	30.00
4	Steve Young	10.00
5	Kerry Collins	3.00
6	Troy Aikman	15.00
7	Drew Bledsoe	15.00
8	Eddie George	20.00
9	Jerry Rice	15.00
10	John Elway	12.00
11	Barry Sanders	15.00
12	Mark Brunell	12.00
13	Elvis Grbac	1.25
14	Tony Banks	7.50
15	Vinny Testaverde	1.25
16	Rick Mirer	1.25
17	Carl Pickens	1.25
18	Deion Sanders	8.00
19	Terry Glenn	10.00
20	Heath Shuler	1.25
21	Dave Brown	1.25
22	Keyshawn Johnson	4.00
23	Jeff George	2.50
24	Ricky Watters	2.50
25	Kordell Stewart	15.00
26	Junior Seau	1.25
27	Terrell Owens	7.50
28	Warren Moon	1.25
29	Isaac Bruce	2.50
30	Steve McNair	12.00
31	Gus Frerotte	1.25
32	Trent Dilfer	2.50
33	Shannon Sharpe	1.25
34	Scott Mitchell	1.25
35	Antonio Freeman	4.00
36	Jim Harbaugh	1.25
37	Natrone Means	2.50
38	Marcus Allen	2.50
39	Karim Abdul-Jabbar	7.50
40	Tim Biakabutuka	1.25
41	Jeff Blake	2.50
42	Michael Irvin	2.50
43	Herschel Walker	1.25
44	Curtis Martin	12.00
45	Eddie Kennison	4.00
46	Napoleon Kaufman	4.00
47	Larry Centers	1.25
48	Jamal Anderson	2.50
49	Derrick Alexander	1.25
50	Bruce Smith	1.25
51	Wesley Walls	1.25
52	Rod Smith	1.25
53	Keenan McCardell	1.25
54	Robert Brooks	1.25
55	Willie Green	1.25
56	Jake Reed	1.25
57	Joey Galloway	2.50
58	Eric Metcalf	1.25

59	Chris Sanders	1.25
60	Jeff Hostetler	1.25
61	Kevin Greene	1.25
62	Frank Sanders	1.25
63	Dorsey Levens	4.00
64	Sean Dawkins	1.25
65	Cris Carter	1.25
66	Andre Hastings	1.25
67	Amani Toomer	1.25
68	Adrian Murrell	2.50
69	Ty Detmer	1.25
70	Yancey Thigpen	1.25
71	Jim Everett	1.25
72	Todd Collins	1.25
73	Curtis Conway	1.25
74	Herman Moore	2.50
75	Neil O'Donnell	1.25
76	Rod Woodson	1.25
77	Tony Martin	1.25
78	Kent Graham	1.25
79	Andre Reed	1.25
80	Reggie White	2.50
81	Thurman Thomas	2.50
82	Garrison Hearst	1.25
83	Chris Warren	1.25
84	Wayne Chrebet	1.25
85	Chris T. Jones	1.25
86	Anthony Miller	1.25
87	Chris Chandler	1.25
88	Terrell Davis	15.00
89	Mike Alstott	7.50
90	Terry Allen	1.25
91	Jerome Bettis	2.50
92	Stan Humphries	1.25
93	Andre Rison	1.25
94	Marshall Faulk	2.50
95	Erik Kramer	1.25
96	O.J. McDuffie	1.25
97	Robert Smith	1.25
98	Keith Byars	1.25
99	Rodney Hampton	1.25
100	Desmond Howard	1.25
101	Lawrence Phillips	2.50
102	Michael Westbrook	1.25
103	Johnnie Morton	1.25
104	Ben Coates	1.25
105	J.J. Stokes	1.25
106	Terance Mathis	1.25
107	Errict Rhett	1.25
108	Tim Brown	1.25
109	Marvin Harrison	4.00
110	Muhsin Muhammad	1.25
111	Bam Morris	1.25
112	Mario Bates	1.25
113	Jimmy Smith	1.25
114	Irving Fryar	1.25
115	Tamarick Vanover	1.25
116	Brad Johnson	2.50
117	Rashaan Salaam	1.25
118	Ki-Jana Carter	1.25
119	Tyrone Wheatley	1.25
120	John Friesz	1.25
121	*Orlando Pace*	2.50
122	*Jim Druckenmiller*	18.00
123	*Byron Hanspard*	5.00
124	*David LaFleur*	7.50
125	*Reidel Anthony*	12.00
126	*Antowain Smith*	18.00
127	*Bryant Westbrook*	2.50
128	*Fred Lane*	7.50
129	*Tiki Barber*	12.00
130	*Shawn Springs*	1.25
131	*Ike Hilliard*	10.00
132	*James Farrior*	1.25
133	*Darrell Russell*	1.25
134	*Walter Jones*	1.25
135	*Tom Knight*	1.25
136	*Yatil Green*	7.00
137	*Joey Kent*	2.50
138	*Kevin Lockett*	1.25
139	*Troy Davis*	7.00
140	*Darnell Autry*	3.00
141	*Pat Barnes*	4.00
142	*Rae Carruth*	10.00
143	*Will Blackwell*	2.50
144	*Warrick Dunn*	30.00
145	*Corey Dillon*	18.00
146	*Dwayne Rudd*	1.25
147	*Reinard Wilson*	1.25
148	*Peter Boulware*	1.25
149	*Tony Gonzalez*	7.50
150	*Danny Wuerffel*	12.00

1997 Pinnacle Totally Certified Platinum Gold

Platinum Gold cards feature a micro-etched holographic mylar finish. Each card is sequentially-numbered to 30 and they were inserted 1:79.

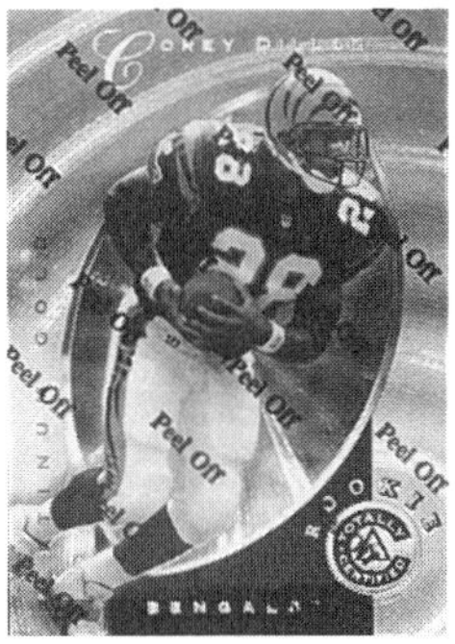

		MT
Common Player:		60.00
Golds Sequentially #'d to 30		
1	Emmitt Smith	1250.
2	Dan Marino	1250.
3	Brett Favre	1500.
4	Steve Young	500.00
5	Kerry Collins	175.00
6	Troy Aikman	750.00
7	Drew Bledsoe	750.00
8	Eddie George	1000.
9	Jerry Rice	750.00
10	John Elway	600.00
11	Barry Sanders	900.00
12	Mark Brunell	600.00
13	Elvis Grbac	60.00
14	Tony Banks	375.00
15	Vinny Testaverde	60.00
16	Rick Mirer	60.00
17	Carl Pickens	60.00
18	Deion Sanders	400.00
19	Terry Glenn	500.00
20	Heath Shuler	60.00
21	Dave Brown	60.00
22	Keyshawn Johnson	200.00
23	Jeff George	125.00
24	Ricky Watters	125.00
25	Kordell Stewart	750.00
26	Junior Seau	60.00
27	Terrell Owens	375.00
28	Warren Moon	60.00
29	Isaac Bruce	125.00
30	Steve McNair	600.00
31	Gus Frerotte	60.00
32	Trent Dilfer	125.00
33	Shannon Sharpe	60.00
34	Scott Mitchell	60.00
35	Antonio Freeman	200.00
36	Jim Harbaugh	60.00
37	Natrone Means	125.00
38	Marcus Allen	125.00
39	Karim Abdul-Jabbar	375.00
40	Tim Biakabutuka	60.00
41	Jeff Blake	125.00
42	Michael Irvin	125.00
43	Herschel Walker	60.00
44	Curtis Martin	600.00
45	Eddie Kennison	200.00
46	Napoleon Kaufman	200.00
47	Larry Centers	60.00
48	Jamal Anderson	125.00
49	Derrick Alexander	60.00
50	Bruce Smith	60.00
51	Wesley Walls	60.00
52	Rod Smith	60.00
53	Keenan McCardell	60.00
54	Robert Brooks	60.00
55	Willie Green	60.00
56	Jake Reed	60.00
57	Joey Galloway	125.00
58	Eric Metcalf	60.00
59	Chris Sanders	60.00
60	Jeff Hostetler	60.00
61	Kevin Greene	60.00
62	Frank Sanders	60.00
63	Dorsey Levens	200.00
64	Sean Dawkins	60.00
65	Cris Carter	60.00
66	Andre Hastings	60.00
67	Amani Toomer	60.00
68	Adrian Murrell	125.00
69	Ty Detmer	60.00
70	Yancey Thigpen	60.00
71	Jim Everett	60.00
72	Todd Collins	60.00
73	Curtis Conway	60.00
74	Herman Moore	125.00
75	Neil O'Donnell	60.00
76	Rod Woodson	60.00
77	Tony Martin	60.00
78	Kent Graham	60.00
79	Andre Reed	60.00
80	Reggie White	125.00
81	Thurman Thomas	125.00
82	Garrison Hearst	60.00
83	Chris Warren	60.00
84	Wayne Chrebet	60.00
85	Chris T. Jones	60.00
86	Anthony Miller	60.00
87	Chris Chandler	60.00
88	Terrell Davis	750.00
89	Mike Alstott	375.00
90	Terry Allen	60.00
91	Jerome Bettis	125.00
92	Stan Humphries	60.00
93	Andre Rison	60.00
94	Marshall Faulk	125.00
95	Erik Kramer	60.00
96	O.J. McDuffie	60.00
97	Robert Smith	60.00
98	Keith Byars	60.00
99	Rodney Hampton	60.00
100	Desmond Howard	60.00
101	Lawrence Phillips	125.00
102	Michael Westbrook	60.00
103	Johnnie Morton	60.00
104	Ben Coates	60.00
105	J.J. Stokes	60.00
106	Terance Mathis	60.00
107	Errict Rhett	60.00
108	Tim Brown	60.00
109	Marvin Harrison	200.00
110	Muhsin Muhammad	60.00
111	Bam Morris	60.00
112	Mario Bates	60.00
113	Jimmy Smith	60.00
114	Irving Fryar	60.00
115	Tamarick Vanover	60.00
116	Brad Johnson	125.00
117	Rashaan Salaam	60.00
118	Ki-Jana Carter	60.00
119	Tyrone Wheatley	60.00
120	John Friesz	60.00
121	*Orlando Pace*	75.00
122	*Jim Druckenmiller*	450.00
123	*Byron Hanspard*	150.00
124	*David LaFleur*	200.00
125	*Reidel Anthony*	300.00
126	*Antowain Smith*	450.00
127	*Bryant Westbrook*	75.00
128	*Fred Lane*	200.00
129	*Tiki Barber*	300.00
130	*Shawn Springs*	60.00
131	*Ike Hilliard*	250.00
132	*James Farrior*	60.00
133	*Darrell Russell*	60.00
134	*Walter Jones*	60.00
135	*Tom Knight*	60.00
136	*Yatil Green*	150.00
137	*Joey Kent*	75.00
138	*Kevin Lockett*	60.00
139	*Troy Davis*	150.00
140	*Darnell Autry*	125.00
141	*Pat Barnes*	150.00
142	*Rae Carruth*	250.00
143	*Will Blackwell*	75.00
144	*Warrick Dunn*	750.00
145	*Corey Dillon*	450.00
146	*Dwayne Rudd*	60.00
147	*Reinard Wilson*	60.00
148	*Peter Boulware*	60.00
149	*Tony Gonzalez*	200.00
150	*Danny Wuerffel*	300.00

1997 Pinnacle X-Press

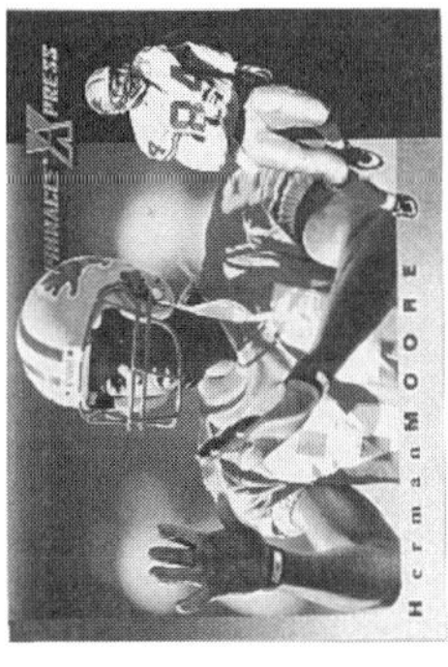

This 150-base card set features a 22-card Rookie subset, a 10-card Peak Performers subset and three checklist cards. The base cards are laid-out horizontally with two player photos on the front. The inserts included the Pursuit of Paydirt interactive game, Metal Works, Bombs Away and Divide & Conquer. Autumn Warriors is a base set parallel. The silver foil cards were inserted 1:7.

		MT
Complete Set (150):		25.00
Common Player:		.05
Wax Box:		20.00
1	Drew Bledsoe	1.00
2	Steve Young	.75
3	Brett Favre	2.25
4	John Elway	.75
5	Dan Marino	2.00
6	Jerry Rice	1.00
7	Tony Banks	.40
8	Kerry Collins	.25
9	Mark Brunell	1.00
10	Troy Aikman	1.00
11	Barry Sanders	1.25
12	Elvis Grbac	.05
13	Eddie George	1.50
14	Terry Glenn	.75
15	Kordell Stewart	1.00
16	Junior Seau	.10
17	Herman Moore	.10
18	Gus Frerotte	.05
19	Warren Moon	.05
20	Emmitt Smith	2.00
21	Chris Chandler	.05
22	Rashaan Salaam	.05
23	Sean Dawkins	.05
24	Tyrone Wheatley	.05
25	Lawrence Phillips	.05
26	Ty Detmer	.05
27	Vinny Testaverde	.05
28	Dorsey Levens	.10
29	Ricky Watters	.10
30	Natrone Means	.10
31	Curtis Conway	.05
32	Larry Centers	.05
33	Johnnie Morton	.05
34	Desmond Howard	.05
35	Marcus Allen	.10
36	Cris Carter	.05
37	James Stewart	.05
38	Frank Sanders	.05
39	Bruce Smith	.05
40	Carl Pickens	.05
41	Neil O'Donnell	.05
42	Trent Dilfer	.10
43	Rodney Peete	.05
44	Terance Mathis	.05
45	Muhsin Muhammad	.05
46	Jake Reed	.05
47	Jim Harbaugh	.05
48	Todd Collins	.05
49	Ki-Jana Carter	.05
50	Scott Mitchell	.05
51	Kevin Hardy	.05
52	Stanley Pritchett	.05
53	Dave Brown	.05
54	Jeff George	.05
55	Stan Humphries	.05
56	Isaac Bruce	.10
57	Eric Moulds	.05
58	Robert Brooks	.05
59	Steve McNair	.75
60	Adrian Murrell	.10
61	Mike Alstott	.10
62	Michael Jackson	.05
63	Tamarick Vanover	.05
64	Edgar Bennett	.05
65	Andre Hastings	.05
66	Robert Smith	.05
67	Thurman Thomas	.10
68	Tim Biakabutuka	.05
69	Rick Mirer	.05
70	Deion Sanders	.50
71	Curtis Martin	1.00
72	Garrison Hearst	.05
73	Kent Graham	.05
74	Anthony Johnson	.05
75	Antonio Freeman	.10
76	Marshall Faulk	.10
77	O.J. McDuffie	.05
78	Heath Shuler	.05
79	Napoleon Kaufman	.10
80	Aeneas Williams	.05
81	Hardy Nickerson	.05
82	Keenan McCardell	.05
83	Erik Kramer	.05
84	Ben Coates	.05
85	Shannon Sharpe	.05
86	Tony Martin	.05
87	Chris Sanders	.05
88	Jamal Anderson	.05
89	Karim Abdul-Jabbar	.50
90	Keyshawn Johnson	.40
91	Terrell Owens	.50
92	Michael Irvin	.10
93	John Friesz	.05
94	Chris Warren	.05
95	Errict Rhett	.05
96	Terry Allen	.10
97	Michael Westbrook	.05
98	Simeon Rice	.05
99	Willie Green	.05
100	Jerome Bettis	.10
101	Reggie White	.10
102	Bert Emanuel	.05
103	Zach Thomas	.10
104	Tim Brown	.05
105	Darnay Scott	.05
106	Terrell Davis	1.00
107	Andre Reed	.05
108	Amani Toomer	.05
109	Irving Fryar	.05
110	Joey Galloway	.10
111	Marvin Harrison	.40
112	Derrick Alexander	.05
113	Jeff Blake	.20
114	Brad Johnson	.05
115	Eddie Kennison	.40
116	*Rae Carruth*	.75
117	*Tony Gonzalez*	.50
118	*Joey Kent*	.10
119	*Peter Boulware*	.10
120	*Orlando Pace*	.20
121	*David LaFleur*	.50
122	*Darnell Autry*	.50
123	*Tiki Barber*	1.00
124	*Troy Davis*	.50
125	*Jim Druckenmiller*	1.50
126	*Corey Dillon*	1.50
127	*Ike Hilliard*	.75
128	*Reidel Anthony*	1.00
129	*Byron Hanspard*	.50
130	*Antowain Smith*	1.25
131	*Jake Plummer*	1.25
132	*Warrick Dunn*	2.50
133	*Bryant Westbrook*	.10
134	*Darrell Russell*	.10
135	*Yatil Green*	.50
136	*Shawn Springs*	.10
137	*Danny Wuerffel*	.75
138	Brett Favre (Peak Performer)	1.00
139	Emmitt Smith (Peak Performer)	1.00
140	Barry Sanders (Peak Performer)	.50
141	Troy Aikman (Peak Performer)	.50
142	Drew Bledsoe (Peak Performer)	.50
143	Jerry Rice (Peak Performer)	.50
144	Dan Marino (Peak Performer)	1.00
145	John Elway (Peak Performer)	.30
146	Kerry Collins (Peak Performer)	.30
147	Mark Brunell (Peak Performer)	.30
148	Checklist Brett Favre	.50
149	Checklist Dan Marino	.50
150	Checklist Troy Aikman	.25

1997 Pinnacle X-Press Autumn Warrior

This 150-card set paralleled each card in X-Press. They were found in one per seven packs.

	MT
Autumn Warrior Cards:	6x-12x
Autumn Warrior Rookies:	3x-6x
Inserted 1:7	

1997 Pinnacle X-Press Bombs Away

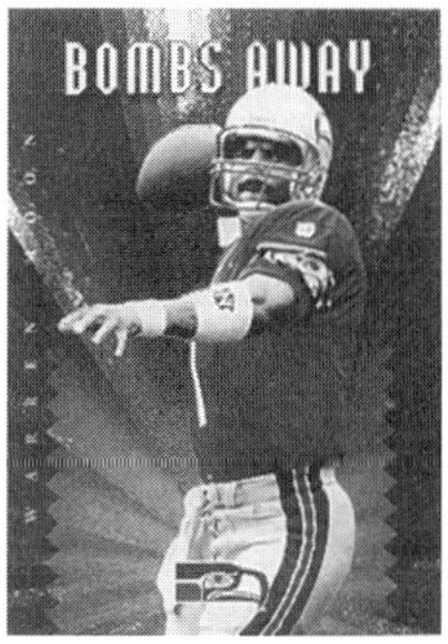

This 18-card insert features top quarterbacks on a full foil, microetched card. Bombs Away was inserted 1:19.

		MT
Complete Set (18):		100.00
Common Player:		2.00
1	Brett Favre	20.00
2	Dan Marino	18.00
3	Troy Aikman	10.00
4	Drew Bledsoe	10.00
5	Kerry Collins	8.00
6	Mark Brunell	10.00
7	John Elway	8.00
8	Steve Young	8.00
9	Jeff Blake	4.00
10	Kordell Stewart	10.00
11	Jeff George	2.00
12	Rick Mirer	2.00
13	Neil O'Donnell	2.00
14	Scott Mitchell	2.00
15	Jim Harbaugh	2.00
16	Warren Moon	2.00
17	Trent Dilfer	4.00
18	Jim Druckenmiller	8.00

1997 Pinnacle X-Press Divide & Conquer

Divide & Conquer is a 20-card insert on full foil, micro-etched card stock. The cards feature a player action shot and heliogram print technology. They are numbered to 500.

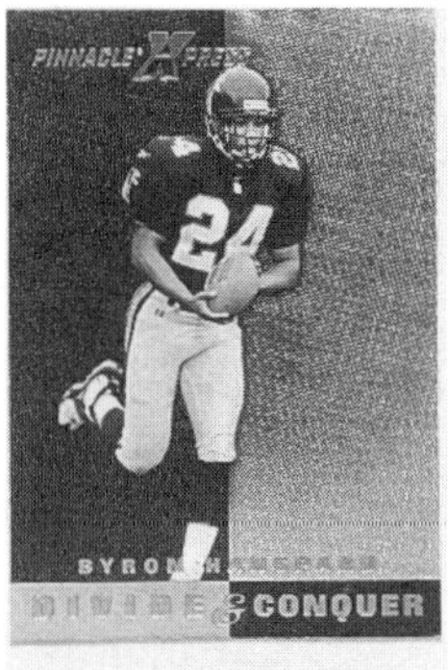

		MT
Complete Set (20):		750.00
Common Player:		7.00
1	Tim Biakabutuka	7.00
2	Karim Abdul-Jabbar	30.00
3	Jerome Bettis	14.00
4	Eddie George	80.00
5	Terrell Davis	60.00
6	Barry Sanders	60.00
7	Emmitt Smith	100.00
8	Brett Favre	120.00
9	Dan Marino	100.00
10	Troy Aikman	60.00
11	Jerry Rice	60.00
12	Drew Bledsoe	60.00
13	Kerry Collins	45.00
14	Mark Brunell	60.00
15	John Elway	45.00
16	Steve Young	45.00
17	Warrick Dunn	90.00
18	Byron Hanspard	25.00
19	Troy Davis	40.00
20	Jeff Blake	14.00

1997 Pinnacle X-Press Pursuit of Paydirt-Quarterbacks

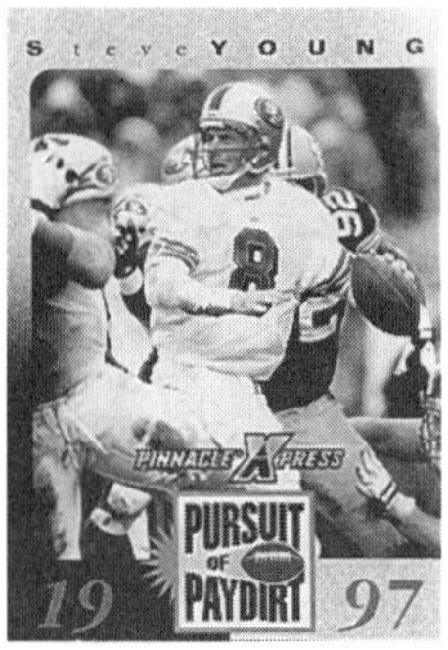

The Pursuit of Paydirt insert was an interactive game which ran during the 1997 season. This 30-card insert (found 1:2) featured quarterbacks and gave collectors the chance to win if they found the QB who led the league in touchdowns during the season.

		MT
Complete Set (30):		25.00
Common Player:		.25
1	Drew Bledsoe	2.00
2	Steve Young	1.50
3	Brett Favre	4.50
4	John Elway	1.50
5	Dan Marino	4.00
6	Tony Banks	1.00
7	Kerry Collins	1.50
8	Mark Brunell	2.00
9	Troy Aikman	2.00
10	Elvis Grbac	.25
11	Kordell Stewart	2.00
12	Gus Frerotte	.25
13	Warren Moon	.25
14	Chris Chandler	.25
15	Rick Mirer	.25
16	Vinny Testaverde	.25
17	Neil O'Donnell	.25
18	Trent Dilfer	.50
19	Rodney Peete	.25
20	Jim Harbaugh	.25
21	Todd Collins	.25
22	Scott Mitchell	.25
23	Dave Brown	.25
24	Jeff George	.25
25	Stan Humphries	.25
26	Steve McNair	1.50
27	Heath Shuler	.25
28	Jeff Blake	.50
29	Brad Johnson	.25
30	Jim Druckenmiller	2.00

1997 Pinnacle X-Press Pursuit of Paydirt-Running Backs

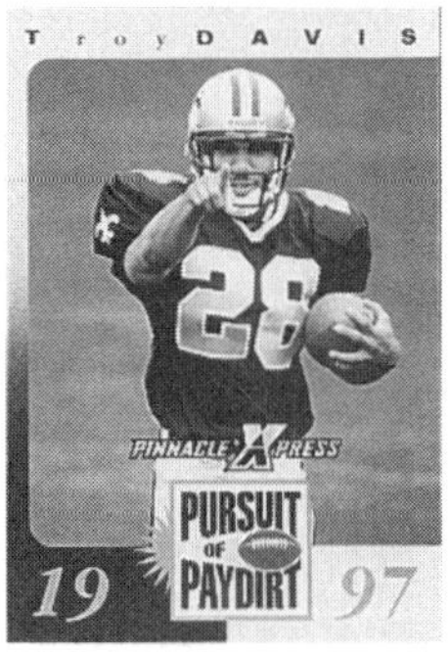

This 30-card insert featured running backs and gave collectors the chance to win prizes if they could match the leading TD scorer with the number of TDs he made. This insert was found 1:2.

		MT
Complete Set (30):		25.00
Common Player:		.25
1	Errict Rhett	.25
2	Terry Allen	.50
3	Jerome Bettis	.50
4	Terrell Davis	2.00
5	Tiki Barber	1.50
6	Troy Davis	1.25
7	Byron Hanspard	1.25
8	Greg Hill	.25
9	Barry Sanders	2.00
10	Eddie George	3.00
11	Emmitt Smith	4.00
12	Rashaan Salaam	.25
13	Tyrone Wheatley	.25
14	Lawrence Phillips	.25
15	Ricky Watters	.50
16	Natrone Means	.50
17	Marcus Allen	.50
18	James Stewart	.25
19	Ki-Jana Carter	.25
20	Dorsey Levens	.50
21	Robert Smith	.25
22	Thurman Thomas	.50
23	Tim Biakabutuka	.25
24	Curtis Martin	2.00
25	Garrison Hearst	.25
26	Marshall Faulk	.50
27	Napoleon Kaufman	1.00
28	Jamal Anderson	.25
29	Karim Abdul-Jabbar	1.50
30	Chris Warren	.25

1997 Playoff Contenders

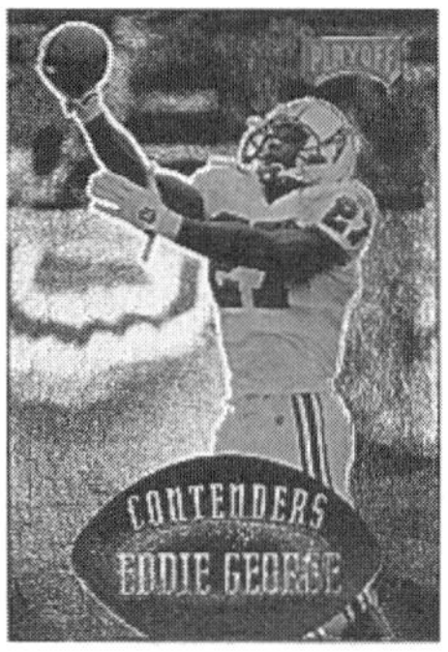

Playoff Contenders includes a 150-card base set. Printed on 30 pt. stock, these cards feature player shots on each side, with foil etching and holographic technology. The player's name is added in silver on each side. A Blue Level parallel version was included in 1:4 packs, while a Red Level version was sequentially numbered to 25. Inserts include Playoff Clash, Leather Die-Cut Helmets, Playoff Plaques, Playoff Pennants and Playoff Rookie Wave Pennants.

		MT
Complete Set (150):		140.00
Common Player:		.50
Wax Box:		85.00
1	Kent Graham	.50
2	Leeland McElroy	.50
3	Rob Moore	.50
4	Frank Sanders	.50
5	*Jake Plummer*	8.00
6	Chris Chandler	.50
7	Bert Emanuel	.50
8	O.J. Santiago	.50
9	*Byron Hanspard*	3.00
10	Vinny Testaverde	.50
11	Michael Jackson	.50
12	Ernest Byner	.50
13	Jermaine Lewis	.50
14	Derrick Alexander	.50
15	*Jay Graham*	1.00
16	Todd Collins	1.00
17	Thurman Thomas	1.00
18	Bruce Smith	.50
19	Andre Reed	.50
20	Quinn Early	.50
21	*Antowain Smith*	6.00
22	Kerry Collins	5.00
23	Tim Biakabutuka	.50
24	Anthony Johnson	.50
25	Wesley Johnson	.50
26	*Fred Lane*	3.00
27	*Rae Carruth*	4.00
28	Raymont Harris	.50
29	Rick Mirer	.50
30	*Darnell Autry*	3.00
31	Jeff Blake	1.00
32	Ki-Jana Carter	1.00
33	Carl Pickens	.50
34	Darnay Scott	.50
35	*Corey Dillon*	6.00
36	Troy Aikman	6.00
37	Emmitt Smith	10.00
38	Michael Irvin	1.00
39	Deion Sanders	3.00
40	Anthony Miller	.50
41	Eric Bjornson	.50
42	*David LaFleur*	3.00
43	John Elway	4.00
44	Terrell Davis	6.00
45	Shannon Sharpe	.50
46	Ed McCaffrey	.50
47	Rod Smith	.50
48	Scott Mitchell	.50
49	Barry Sanders	7.00
50	Herman Moore	2.00
51	Brett Favre	12.00
52	Dorsey Levens	1.00
53	William Henderson	.50
54	Derrick Mayes	.50
55	Antonio Freeman	1.00
56	Robert Brooks	.50
57	Mark Chmura	.50
58	Reggie White	1.00
59	Darren Sharper	.50
60	Jim Harbaugh	.50
61	Marshall Faulk	1.00
62	Marvin Harrison	2.00
63	Mark Brunell	6.00
64	Natrone Means	1.00
65	Jimmy Smith	.50
66	Keenan McCardell	.50
67	Elvis Grbac	.50
68	Greg Hill	.50
69	Marcus Allen	1.00
70	Andre Rison	.50
71	Kimble Anders	.50
72	*Tony Gonzalez*	3.00
73	*Pat Barnes*	2.00
74	Dan Marino	10.00
75	Karim Abdul-Jabbar	3.00
76	Zach Thomas	1.00
77	O.J. McDuffie	.50
78	*Brian Manning*	1.00
79	Brad Johnson	1.00
80	Cris Carter	1.00
81	Jake Reed	.50
82	Robert Smith	1.00
83	Drew Bledsoe	6.00
84	Curtis Martin	6.00
85	Ben Coates	.50
86	Terry Glenn	3.00
87	Shawn Jefferson	.50
88	Heath Shuler	.50
89	Mario Bates	.50
90	Andre Hastings	.50
91	*Troy Davis*	3.00
92	*Danny Wuerffel*	4.00
93	Dave Brown	.50
94	Chris Calloway	.50
95	*Tiki Barber*	6.00
96	Mike Cherry	.50
97	Neil O'Donnell	.50
98	Keyshawn Johnson	2.00
99	Adrian Murrell	1.00
100	Wayne Chrebet	.50
101	Dedric Ward	.50
102	Leon Johnson	.50
103	Jeff George	1.00
104	Napoleon Kaufman	2.00
105	Tim Brown	1.00
106	James Jett	.50
107	Ty Detmer	.50
108	Ricky Watters	1.00
109	Irving Fryar	.50
110	Michael Timpson	.50
111	Chad Lewis	.50
112	Kordell Stewart	6.00
113	Jerome Bettis	1.00
114	Charles Johnson	.50
115	*George Jones*	1.00
116	*Will Blackwell*	1.00
117	Stan Humphries	.50
118	Junior Seau	1.00
119	*Freddie Jones*	1.00
120	Steve Young	4.00
121	Jerry Rice	6.00
122	Garrison Hearst	.50
123	William Floyd	.50
124	Terrell Owens	3.00
125	J.J. Stokes	.50
126	Marc Edwards	.50
127	*Jim Druckenmiller*	8.00
128	Warren Moon	.50
129	Chris Warren	.50
130	Joey Galloway	1.00
131	*Shawn Springs*	1.00
132	Tony Banks	3.00
133	Lawrence Phillips	1.00
134	Isaac Bruce	1.00
135	Eddie Kennison	2.00
136	*Orlando Pace*	1.00
137	Trent Dilfer	1.00
138	Mike Alstott	3.00
139	Horace Copeland	.50
140	Jackie Harris	.50
141	*Warrick Dunn*	12.00
142	*Reidel Anthony*	6.00
143	Steve McNair	5.00
144	Eddie George	8.00
145	Chris Sanders	.50
146	Gus Frerotte	.50
147	Terry Allen	.50
148	Henry Ellard	.50
149	Leslie Shepherd	.50
150	Michael Westbrook	.50

1997 Playoff Contenders Blue

All 150 cards in Contenders were printed on blue foil for this parallel set. Blue versions were seeded one per four packs. Red foil versions also exist and are numbered to 25.

	MT
Blue Cards:	2x-4x
Blue Rookies:	2x
Inserted 1:4	

1997 Playoff Contenders Red

This 150-card parallel set features each card from Contenders printed on a red foil surface. Red parallel cards are sequentially numbered to 25 sets.

	MT
Red Cards:	40x-80x
Red Rookies:	20x-40x
Production 25 Sets	

1997 Playoff Contenders Clash

Clash is a 12-card insert highlighting some of the NFL's top match-ups. The cards feature two players with their team helmets die-cut in the background. Silver Level cards were inserted 1:48 and Blue Level cards were found 1:192.

		MT
Complete Set (12):		500.00
Common Player:		20.00
Blue Cards:		3x
1	Brett Favre, Troy Aikman	100.00
2	Barry Sanders, Brad Johnson	75.00
3	Curtis Martin, Warrick Dunn	50.00
4	Steve Young, John Elway	40.00
5	Jerry Rice, Marcus Allen	50.00
6	Dan Marino, Drew Bledsoe	85.00
7	Terrell Davis, Napoleon Kaufman	50.00
8	Eddie George, Emmitt Smith	85.00
9	Mark Brunell, Tim Brown	40.00
10	Kerry Collins, Reggie White	40.00
11	Deion Sanders, Carl Pickens	20.00
12	Mike Alstott, Keyshawn Johnson	20.00

1997 Playoff Contenders Leather Helmets

This 18-card insert features a die-cut leather helmet. The Silver Level was found 1:24, Blue Level 1:216 and the Red Parallel was numbered to 25.

		MT
Complete Set (18):		600.00
Common Player:		8.00
Blue Cards:		4x-8x
1	Dan Marino	60.00
2	Troy Aikman	30.00
3	Brett Favre	75.00
4	Barry Sanders	50.00
5	Drew Bledsoe	30.00
6	Deion Sanders	15.00
7	Curtis Martin	30.00
8	Warrick Dunn	45.00
9	Napoleon Kaufman	8.00
10	Eddie George	45.00
11	Antowain Smith	15.00
12	Emmitt Smith	60.00
13	John Elway	25.00
14	Steve Young	25.00
15	Mark Brunell	30.00
16	Terrell Davis	30.00
17	Terry Glenn	20.00
18	Terrell Owens	15.00

1997 Playoff Contenders Pennants

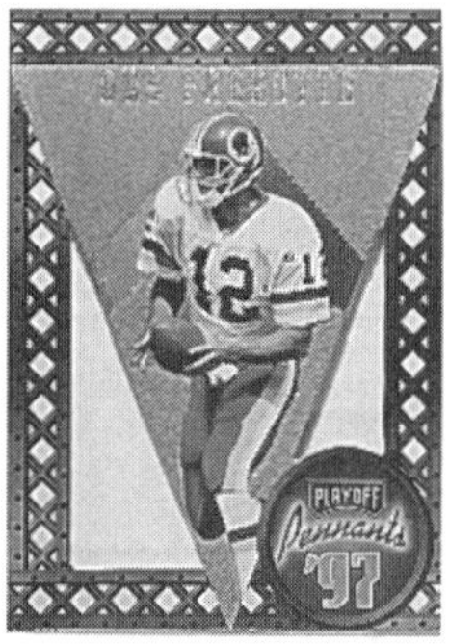

Pennants features player shots on a fuzzy pennant. The 36 cards came in Silver Level (1:12) and Blue Parallel (1:72) versions.

		MT
Complete Set (36):		600.00
Common Player:		4.00
Blue Carrds		4x
1	Dan Marino	40.00
2	Kordell Stewart	25.00
3	Drew Bledsoe	25.00
4	Kerry Collins	20.00
5	John Elway	20.00
6	Trent Dilfer	8.00
7	Jerry Rice	25.00
8	Emmitt Smith	40.00
9	Jeff George	4.00
10	Eddie George	30.00
11	Terrell Davis	25.00
12	Mike Alstott	10.00
13	Jim Druckenmiller	20.00
14	Antowain Smith	15.00
15	Marcus Allen	8.00
16	Jerome Bettis	8.00
17	Terrell Owens	8.00
18	Gus Frerotte	4.00
19	Troy Aikman	25.00
20	Andre Rison	4.00
21	Mark Brunell	25.00
22	Antonio Freeman	8.00
23	Brett Favre	50.00
24	Steve McNair	20.00
25	Barry Sanders	40.00
26	Steve Young	20.00
27	Curtis Martin	25.00
28	Napoleon Kaufman	8.00
29	Deion Sanders	12.00
30	Terry Glenn	18.00
31	Warrick Dunn	25.00

32	Danny Wuerffel	10.00
33	Elvis Grbac	4.00
34	Cris Carter	4.00
35	Joey Galloway	8.00
36	Corey Dillon	20.00

1997 Playoff Contenders Plaques

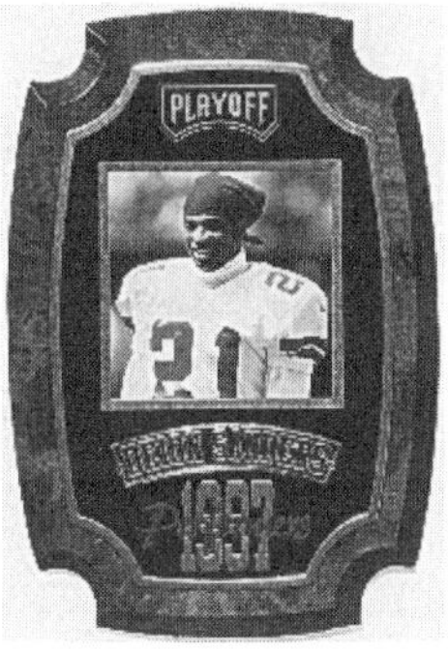

These 45 die-cut cards feature a player shot on a card designed to resemble a plaque. Plaques were made in Silver Level (1:12) and Blue Parallel (1:36) versions.

		MT
Complete Set (45):		600.00
Common Player:		4.00
Blue Cards:		3x
1	Jim Druckenmiller	20.00
2	Danny Wuerffel	10.00
3	Antowain Smith	15.00
4	Warrick Dunn	30.00
5	Terrell Owens	8.00
6	Elvis Grbac	4.00
7	Andre Rison	4.00
8	Tim Brown	4.00
9	Trent Dilfer	8.00
10	Brad Johnson	4.00
11	Deion Sanders	12.00
12	Dan Marino	50.00
13	Kerry Collins	20.00
14	Steve McNair	20.00
15	Eddie George	30.00
16	Ricky Watters	8.00
17	Jerome Bettis	8.00
18	Robert Brooks	4.00
19	Keyshawn Johnson	8.00
20	Antonio Freeman	8.00
21	Eddie Kennison	8.00
22	Mike Alstott	10.00
23	Brett Favre	60.00
24	Troy Aikman	25.00
25	Emmitt Smith	50.00
26	Terrell Davis	25.00
27	John Elway	20.00
28	Barry Sanders	35.00
29	Steve Young	20.00
30	Curtis Martin	25.00
31	Cris Carter	4.00
32	Drew Bledsoe	25.00
33	Mark Brunell	25.00
34	Kordell Stewart	25.00
35	Tony Banks	10.00
36	Napoleon Kaufman	8.00
37	Marcus Allen	8.00
38	Terry Glenn	18.00
39	Herman Moore	8.00
40	Michael Irvin	8.00
41	Joey Galloway	8.00
42	Karim Abdul-Jabbar	15.00
43	Reggie White	8.00
44	Jerry Rice	25.00
45	Gus Frerotte	4.00

1997 Playoff Contenders Rookie Wave

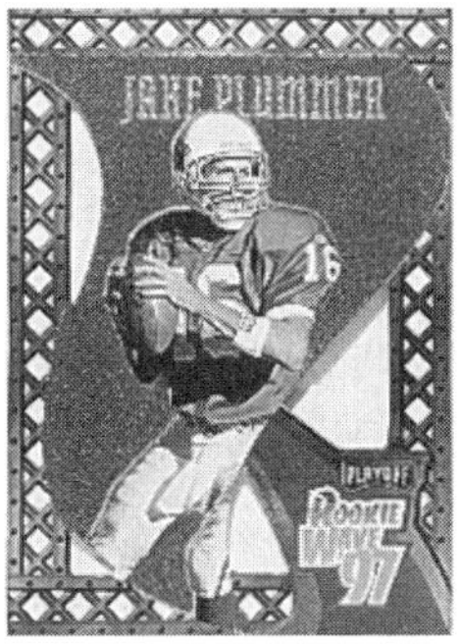

Similar to the Pennants, except with a wavy design, this 27-card insert was only available in Silver Level (1:6).

		MT
Complete Set (27):		150.00
Common Player:		1.50
1	Jim Druckenmiller	12.00
2	Antowain Smith	10.00
3	Will Blackwell	3.00
4	Tiki Barber	8.00
5	Rae Carruth	6.00
6	Jay Graham	3.00
7	Darnell Autry	4.00
8	David LaFleur	4.00
9	Tony Gonzalez	4.00
10	Chad Lewis	1.50
11	Freddie Jones	3.00
12	Shawn Springs	3.00
13	Danny Wuerffel	8.00
14	Warrick Dunn	20.00
15	Troy Davis	5.00
16	Reidel Anthony	8.00
17	Jake Plummer	18.00
18	Byron Hanspard	5.00
19	Fred Lane	4.00
20	Corey Dillon	12.00
21	Darren Sharper	3.00
22	Pat Barnes	5.00
23	Mike Cherry	1.50
24	Leon Johnson	1.50
25	George Jones	3.00
26	Marc Edwards	1.50
27	Orlando Pace	3.00

1997 Playoff Zone

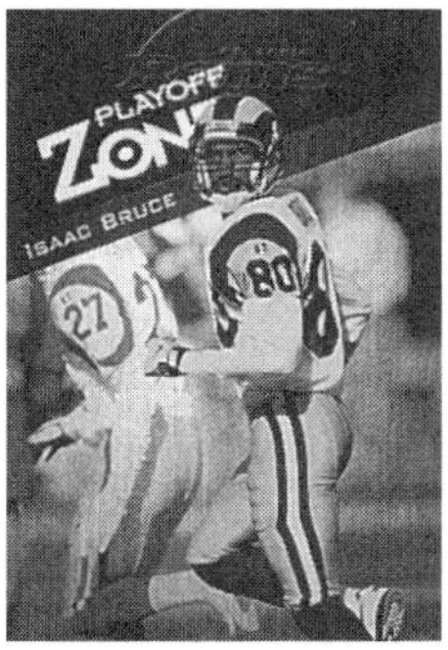

Playoff Zone consist of a 150-card base set done on 24 pt. Tekchrome and 14 insert sets. The inserts include Prime Target, Prime Target Parallel, Sharp Shooters, Sharp Shooters Parallel, Rookies, Close-Ups, Frenzy and Treasures as well as a "1 of 5" parallel set of each insert. The parallels are limited to five each and are sequentially numbered.

		MT
Complete Set (150):		40.00
Common Player:		.10
Wax Box:		40.00
1	Brett Favre	3.00
2	Dorsey Levens	.20
3	William Henderson	.10
4	Derrick Mayes	.10
5	Antonio Freeman	.20
6	Robert Brooks	.10
7	Mark Chmura	.10
8	Reggie White	.20
9	Randall Cunningham	.10
10	Brad Johnson	.20
11	Robert Smith	.10
12	Cris Carter	.10
13	Jake Reed	.10
14	Trent Dilfer	.20
15	Errict Rhett	.10
16	Mike Alstott	.20
17	Scott Mitchell	.10
18	Barry Sanders	2.00
19	Herman Moore	.20
20	Erik Kramer	.10
21	Rick Mirer	.10
22	Rashaan Salaam	.10
23	Troy Aikman	1.50
24	Deion Sanders	.75
25	Emmitt Smith	2.50
26	Daryl Johnston	.10
27	Anthony Miller	.10
28	Eric Bjornson	.10
29	Michael Irvin	.20
30	Chris Jones	.10
31	Ty Detmer	.10
32	Ricky Watters	.20
33	Irving Fryar	.10
34	Rodney Peete	.10
35	Jeff Hostetler	.10
36	Terry Allen	.20
37	Michael Westbrook	.10
38	Gus Frerotte	.10
39	Frank Sanders	.10
40	Larry Centers	.10
41	Kent Graham	.10
42	Dave Brown	.10
43	Rodney Hampton	.10
44	Tyrone Wheatley	.10
45	Chris Calloway	.10
46	Ernie Mills	.10
47	Tim Biakabutuka	.10
48	Anthony Johnson	.10
49	Wesley Walls	.10
50	Muhsin Muhammad	.10
51	Kerry Collins	1.00
52	Terrell Owens	1.00
53	Garrison Hearst	.10
54	Jerry Rice	1.50
55	Steve Young	1.00
56	Lawrence Phillips	.10
57	Isaac Bruce	.20
58	Eddie Kennison	.50
59	Tony Banks	.75
60	Heath Shuler	.10
61	Andre Hastings	.10
62	Mario Bates	.10
63	Chris Chandler	.10
64	Jamal Anderson	.10
65	Bert Emanuel	.10
66	Drew Bledsoe	1.50
67	Curtis Martin	1.50
68	Ben Coates	.10
69	Terry Glenn	1.25
70	Dan Marino	2.50
71	Karim Abdul-Jabbar	1.00
72	Fred Barnett	.10
73	O.J. McDuffie	.10
74	Jim Harbaugh	.10
75	Marshall Faulk	.20
76	Zack Crockett	.10
77	Ken Dilger	.10
78	Marvin Harrison	.50
79	Keyshawn Johnson	.50
80	Neil O'Donnell	.10
81	Adrian Murrell	.20
82	Wayne Chrebet	.10
83	Todd Collins	.10
84	Thurman Thomas	.20
85	Bruce Smith	.10
86	Eric Moulds	.10
87	Rob Johnson	.10
88	Mark Brunell	1.50
89	Natrone Means	.20
90	Jimmy Smith	.10
91	Keenan McCardell	.10
92	Kordell Stewart	1.50
93	Jerome Bettis	.20
94	Charles Johnson	.10
95	Courtney Hawkins	.10
96	Greg Lloyd	.10
97	Ki-Jana Carter	.10
98	Carl Pickens	.10
99	Jeff Blake	.20
100	Steve McNair	1.00
101	Chris Sanders	.10
102	Eddie George	2.00
103	Vinny Testaverde	.10
104	Michael Jackson	.10
105	Derrick Alexander	.10
106	Willie Green	.10
107	Shannon Sharpe	.10
108	Rod Smith	.10
109	Terrell Davis	1.50
110	John Elway	1.00
111	Elvis Grbac	.10
112	Greg Hill	.10
113	Marcus Allen	.20
114	Derrick Thomas	.10
115	Brett Perriman	.10
116	Andre Rison	.10
117	Rickey Dudley	.10
118	Tim Brown	.10
119	Desmond Howard	.10
120	Napoleon Kaufman	.30
121	Jeff George	.10
122	Warren Moon	.10
123	John Friesz	.10
124	Chris Warren	.10
125	Joey Galloway	.20
126	Stan Humphries	.10
127	Tony Martin	.10
128	Eric Metcalf	.10
129	Jim Everett	.10
130	*Warrick Dunn*	5.00
131	*Reidel Anthony*	2.50
132	*Derrick Mason*	.10
133	*Joey Kent*	.20
134	*Will Blackwell*	.20
135	*Jim Druckenmiller*	3.00
136	*Byron Hanspard*	1.25
137	*John Allred*	.10
138	*David LaFleur*	1.00
139	*Danny Wuerffel*	2.00
140	*Tiki Barber*	2.00
141	*Ike Hilliard*	1.50
142	*Troy Davis*	1.50
143	*Sedrick Shaw*	.10
144	*Tony Gonzalez*	1.00
145	*Jake Plummer*	4.00
146	*Antowain Smith*	2.50
147	*Rae Carruth*	1.75
148	*Darnell Autry*	1.00
149	*Corey Dillon*	3.00
150	*Orlando Pace*	.20

1997 Playoff Zone Close-Up

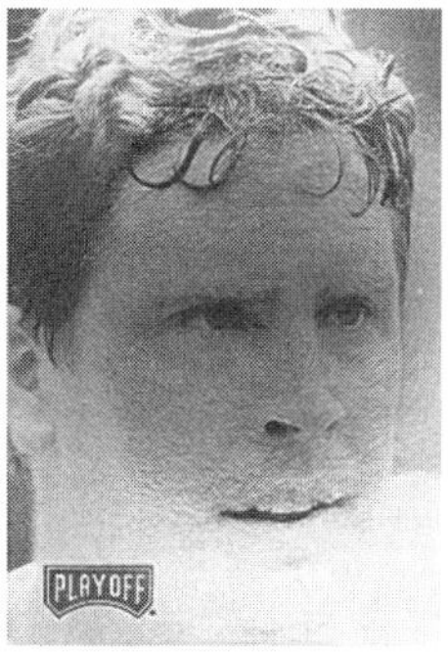

This 32-card insert features helmetless close-ups of top NFL playes. The cards were inserted 1:6.

		MT
Complete Set (32):		100.00
Common Player:		.75
1	Brett Favre	12.00
2	Mark Brunell	5.00
3	Dan Marino	10.00
4	Kerry Collins	4.00
5	Troy Aikman	5.00
6	Drew Bledsoe	5.00
7	John Elway	4.00
8	Kordell Stewart	5.00
9	Steve Young	4.00
10	Steve McNair	4.00
11	Tony Banks	3.00
12	Emmitt Smith	10.00
13	Barry Sanders	8.00
14	Jerry Rice	5.00
15	Deion Sanders	3.00
16	Terrell Davis	5.00
17	Curtis Martin	5.00
18	Karim Abdul-Jabbar	3.00
19	Terry Glenn	4.00
20	Eddie George	8.00
21	Keyshawn Johnson	1.50
22	Marvin Harrison	2.00
23	Muhsin Muhammad	.75
24	Joey Galloway	1.50
25	Terrell Owens	3.00
26	Antonio Freeman	1.50
27	Ricky Watters	1.50
28	Jeff Blake	1.50
29	Reggie White	1.50
30	Michael Irvin	1.50
31	Eddie Kennison	2.00
32	Robert Brooks	.75

1997 Playoff Zone Frenzy

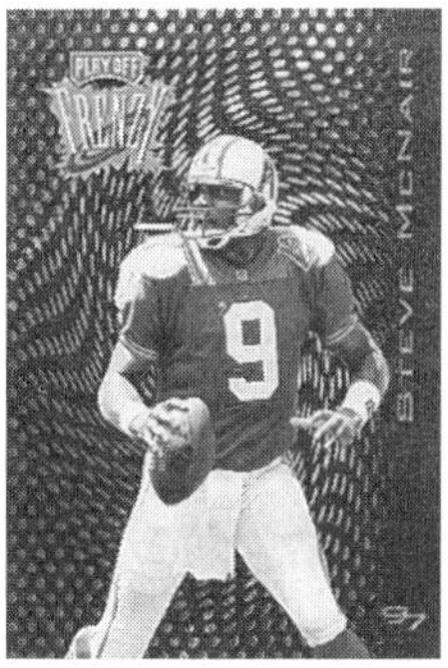

This 26-card insert set was done on etched foil cards and inserted 1:12.

		MT
Complete Set (26):		175.00
Common Player:		1.00
1	Brett Favre	25.00
2	Dan Marino	20.00
3	Troy Aikman	10.00
4	Drew Bledsoe	10.00
5	John Elway	10.00
6	Kordell Stewart	10.00
7	Steve Young	6.00
8	Steve McNair	6.00
9	Tony Banks	4.00
10	Emmitt Smith	20.00
11	Barry Sanders	15.00
12	Deion Sanders	4.00
13	Terrell Davis	10.00
14	Curtis Martin	8.00
15	Karim Abdul-Jabbar	4.00
16	Terry Glenn	2.00
17	Eddie George	10.00
18	Keyshawn Johnson	2.00
19	Marvin Harrison	2.00
20	Joey Galloway	2.00
21	Antonio Freeman	2.00
22	Jeff Blake	2.00
23	Michael Irvin	2.00
24	Eddie Kennison	2.00
25	Reggie White	2.00
26	Robert Brooks	1.00

1997 Playoff Zone Prime Target

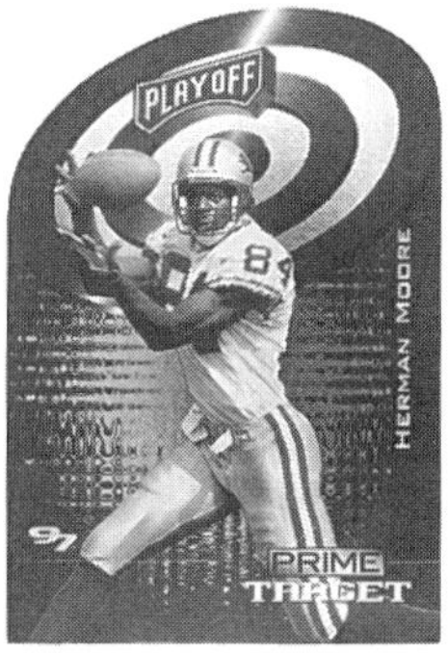

This 20-card insert features the NFL's top pass catchers backed by a blue and silver die-cut target design. This set had an insert rate of 1:24.

		MT
Complete Set (20):		170.00
Common Player:		4.00
Red Cards:		3x
1	Emmitt Smith	25.00
2	Barry Sanders	20.00
3	Jerry Rice	15.00
4	Terrell Davis	15.00
5	Curtis Martin	15.00
6	Karim Abdul-Jabbar	10.00
7	Terry Glenn	12.00
8	Eddie George	20.00
9	Keyshawn Johnson	8.00
10	Joey Galloway	8.00
11	Antonio Freeman	8.00
12	Herman Moore	8.00
13	Tim Brown	4.00
14	Michael Irvin	8.00
15	Isaac Bruce	8.00
16	Eddie Kennison	8.00
17	Shannon Sharpe	4.00
18	Cris Carter	4.00
19	Napoleon Kaufman	8.00
20	Carl Pickens	4.00

1997 Playoff Zone Rookies

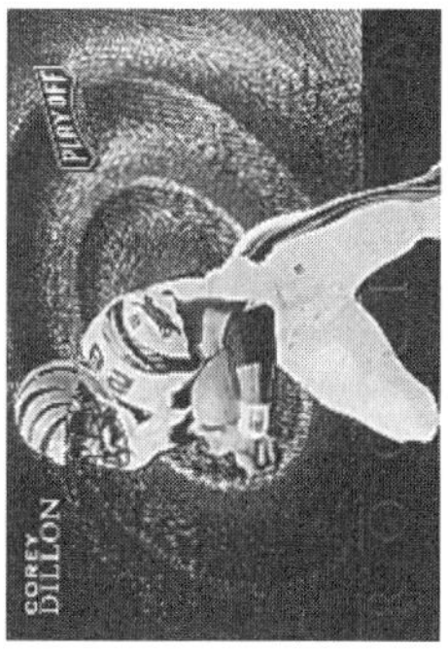

This insert features 24 rookies on etched foil cards. The cards were inserted 1:8.

		MT
Complete Set (24):		100.00
Common Player:		1.00
1	Jake Plummer	10.00
2	George Jones	1.00
3	Pat Barnes	4.00
4	Brian Manning	1.00
5	O.J. Santiago	1.00
6	Byron Hanspard	4.00
7	Antowain Smith	8.00
8	Rae Carruth	6.00
9	Darnell Autry	4.00
10	Corey Dillon	10.00
11	David LaFleur	4.00

12	Tony Gonzalez	4.00
13	Sedrick Shaw	4.00
14	Danny Wuerffel	6.00
15	Troy Davis	6.00
16	Ike Hilliard	6.00
17	Tiki Barber	7.00
18	Will Blackwell	1.00
19	Jim Druckenmiller	10.00
20	Orlando Pace	2.00
21	Warrick Dunn	15.00
22	Reidel Anthony	7.00
23	Derrick Mason	1.00
24	Joey Kent	2.00

1997 Playoff Zone Sharpshooters

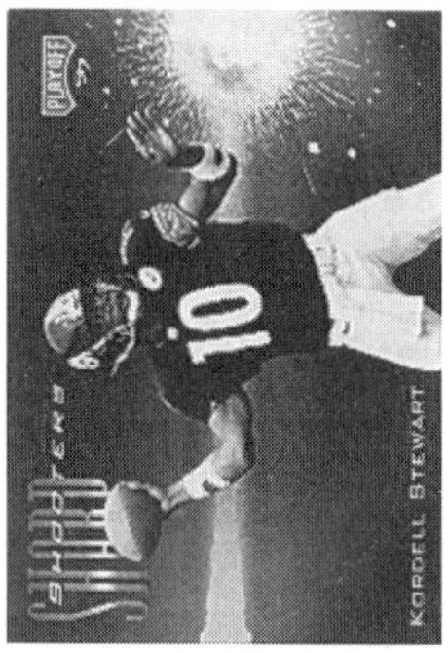

The top NFL QBs are highlighted in this 18-card set with flaming graphics in the background. The cards were inserted 1:72.

		MT
Complete Set (18):		160.00
Common Player:		3.00
Red Cards:		2x
1	Brett Favre	35.00
2	Dan Marino	30.00
3	John Elway	12.00
4	Troy Aikman	15.00
5	Drew Bledsoe	15.00
6	Todd Collins	3.00
7	Brad Johnson	6.00
8	Stan Humphries	3.00
9	John Friesz	3.00
10	Tony Banks	8.00
11	Ty Detmer	3.00
12	Steve McNair	12.00
13	Rob Johnson	3.00
14	Kordell Stewart	15.00
15	Danny Wuerffel	12.00
16	Jim Druckenmiller	12.00
17	Jake Plummer	10.00
18	Kerry Collins	12.00

1997 Playoff Zone Treasures

This 12-card insert features the top collectible NFL players. The cards were inserted 1:196.

		MT
Complete Set (12):		700.00
Common Players:		25.00
1	Brett Favre	120.00
2	Dan Marino	100.00
3	Troy Aikman	50.00
4	Drew Bledsoe	50.00
5	Emmitt Smith	100.00
6	Barry Sanders	75.00
7	Warrick Dunn	60.00
8	Deion Sanders	25.00
9	Terrell Davis	50.00
10	Curtis Martin	40.00
11	Tiki Barber	25.00
12	Eddie George	50.00

1997 Pro Line Gems

The 100-card base set consists of three subsets. Veterans is a 60-card set on blue foil-stamped cards, Rookies features 30 black foil-stamped cards and Leaders is a 10-card set with black and blue foil-stamping. The insert sets include Gems of the NFL, Championship Ring and Through the Years.

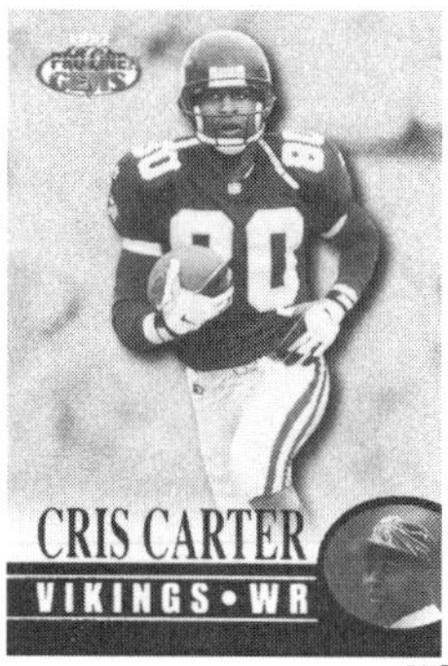

		MT
Complete Set (100):		35.00
Common Player:		.10
Wax Box:		35.00
1	Brett Favre	3.50
2	Robert Brooks	.10
3	Reggie White	.20
4	Drew Bledsoe	1.50
5	Curtis Martin	1.50
6	Terry Glenn	1.25
7	Kerry Collins	1.25
8	Kevin Greene	.10
9	Troy Aikman	1.50
10	Emmitt Smith	3.00
11	Deion Sanders	.75
12	John Elway	1.00
13	Terrell Davis	1.50
14	Kordell Stewart	1.50
15	Jerome Bettis	.20
16	Steve Young	1.00
17	Jerry Rice	1.50
18	Bruce Smith	.10
19	Thurman Thomas	.20
20	Jim Harbaugh	.10
21	Marshall Faulk	.20
22	Marvin Harrison	.50
23	Ricky Watters	.20
24	Seth Joyner	.10
25	Mark Brunell	1.50
26	Natrone Means	.20
27	Dan Marino	3.00
28	Zach Thomas	.50
29	Karim Abdul-Jabbar	1.00
30	Isaac Bruce	.20
31	Eddie Kennison	.50
32	Tony Banks	.50
33	Tony Martin	.10
34	Junior Seau	.20
35	Barry Sanders	1.50
36	Herman Moore	.20
37	Leeland McElroy	.10
38	Jamal Anderson	.20
39	Rick Mirer	.10
40	Rashaan Salaam	.20
41	Vinny Testaverde	.10
42	Elvis Grbac	.10
43	Cris Carter	.10
44	Brad Johnson	.20
45	Keyshawn Johnson	.50
46	Adrian Murrell	.10
47	Joey Galloway	.30
48	Trent Dilfer	.20
49	Gus Frerotte	.10
50	Terry Allen	.10
51	Tim Brown	.10
52	Desmond Howard	.10
53	Jeff George	.10
54	Heath Shuler	.10
55	Steve McNair	1.25
56	Eddie George	2.00
57	Jeff Blake	.20
58	Carl Pickens	.10
59	Dave Brown	.10
60	Brett Favre	1.50
61	Antowain Smith	1.50
62	Emmitt Smith	1.25
63	Terry Glenn	.50
64	Herman Moore	.10
65	Barry Sanders	.50
66	Derrick Thomas	.10
67	Brett Favre	1.50
68	Warrick Dunn	2.50
69	Emmitt Smith	1.25
70	Brett Favre	1.50
71	Orlando Pace	.10
72	Darrell Russell	.10
73	Shawn Springs	.10
74	Warrick Dunn	3.00
75	Tiki Barber	1.50
76	Tom Knight	.10
77	Peter Boulware	.10
78	David LaFleur	.50
79	Tony Gonzalez	.50
80	Yatil Green	1.00
81	Ike Hilliard	1.00
82	James Farrior	.10
83	Jim Druckenmiller	2.00
84	Jon Harris	.10
85	Walter Jones	.10
86	Reidel Anthony	1.25
87	Jake Plummer	1.50
88	Reinard Wilson	.10
89	Kevin Lockett	.10
90	Rae Carruth	1.00
91	Byron Hanspard	.50
92	Renaldo Wynn	.10
93	Troy Davis	.75
94	Duce Staley	.10
95	Kenard Lang	.10
96	Freddie Jones	.75
97	Corey Dillon	2.00
98	Antowain Smith	1.50
99	Dwayne Rudd	.10
100	Warrick Dunn	.75

1997 Pro Line Gems Championship Ring

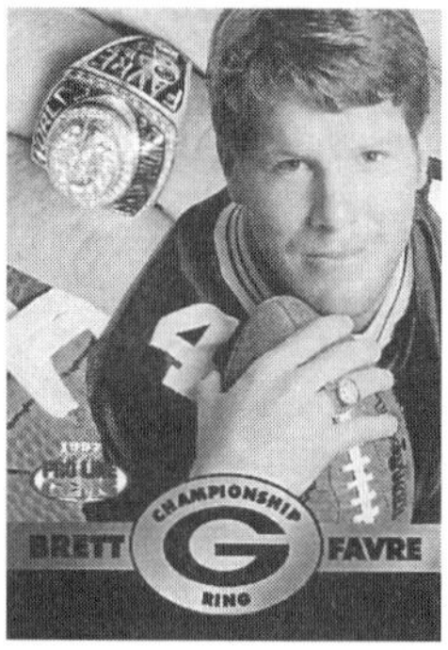

This card featured Brett Favre and his Super Bowl XXXI championship ring. The card contains a real diamond and was inserted one per case (10 boxes per case, 24 packs per box).

		MT
Complete Set (1):		100.00
Common Player:		100.00
CR1	Brett Favre	100.00

1997 Pro Line Gems of the NFL

This 15-card insert features either a sapphire or emerald gemstone on a 23-karat gold card. These cards were seeded one per box (24 packs per box).

		MT
Complete Set (15):		400.00
Common Player:		5.00
G1	Kerry Collins	25.00
G2	Troy Aikman	25.00
G3	Emmitt Smith	45.00
G4	Terrell Davis	25.00
G5	Barry Sanders	60.00
G6	Brett Favre	50.00
G7	Eddie George	35.00
G8	Mark Brunell	25.00
G9	Dan Marino	45.00
G10	Curtis Martin	25.00
G11	Terry Glenn	20.00
G12	Jerome Bettis	5.00
G13	Steve Young	15.00
G14	Jerry Rice	25.00
G15	Warrick Dunn	40.00

1997 Pro Line Gems Through the Years

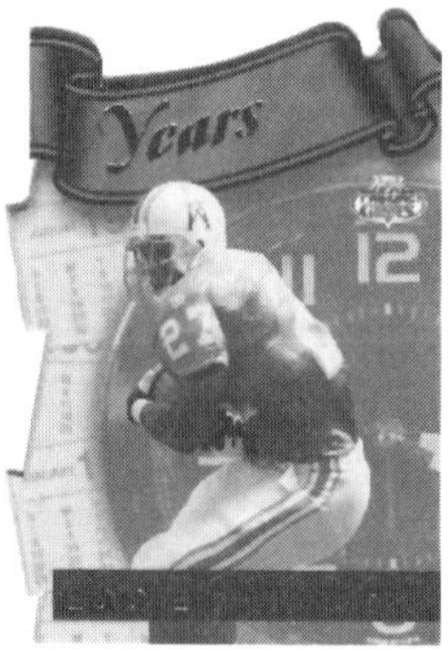

This 20-card insert features 10 veterans and 10 rookies. The cards are die-cut to fit one of the rookies' cards with one of the veterans'. The cards were inserted 1:12.

		MT
Complete Set (20):		150.00
Common Player:		2.50
TY1	Emmitt Smith	20.00
TY2	Brett Favre	25.00
TY3	Deion Sanders	8.00
TY4	Dan Marino	20.00
TY5	Barry Sanders	15.00
TY6	Herman Moore	5.00
TY7	Curtis Martin	10.00
TY8	Jerome Bettis	5.00
TY9	Mark Brunell	10.00
TY10	Jerry Rice	10.00
TY11	Warrick Dunn	15.00
TY12	Jim Druckenmiller	10.00
TY13	Shawn Springs	2.50
TY14	Tony Banks	5.00
TY15	Byron Hanspard	5.00
TY16	Ike Hilliard	5.00
TY17	Antowain Smith	10.00
TY18	Eddie George	15.00
TY19	Jake Plummer	15.00
TY20	Terry Glenn	5.00

1997 SkyBox

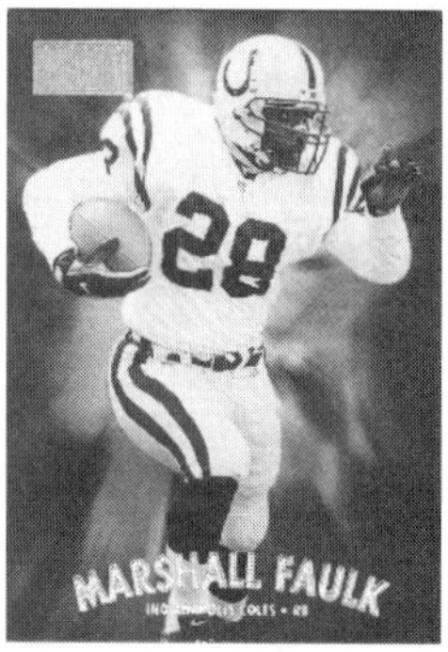

This 250-card base set features 208 veterans, 40 rookies and two checklists. The base cards have a holographic foil design on 20 pt. card stock. The inserts for the set include Rookie Preview, Close Ups, PrimeTime Rookies, Premium Players, Larger Than Life, Autographics and Star Rubies.

		MT
Complete Set (250):		35.00
Common Player:		.10
Wax Box:		45.00
1	Brett Favre	3.00
2	Michael Bates	.10
3	Jeff Graham	.10
4	Terry Glenn	1.00
5	Stephen Davis	.10
6	Wesley Walls	.10
7	Barry Sanders	1.50
8	Chris Sanders	.10
9	O.J. McDuffie	.10
10	Ken Dilger	.10
11	Kimble Anders	.10
12	Keenan McCardell	.10
13	Ki-Jana Carter	.10
14	Gary Brown	.10
15	Andre Rison	.10
16	Edgar Bennett	.10
17	Jerome Bettis	.20
18	Ted Johnson	.10
19	John Friez	.10
20	Tony Brackens	.10
21	Bryan Cox	.10
22	Eric Moulds	.10
23	Johnnie Morton	.10
24	Brad Johnson	.10
25	Bam Morris	.10
26	Anthony Johnson	.10
27	Jim Harbaugh	.10
28	Keyshawn Johnson	.20
29	Cary Blanchard	.10
30	Curtis Conway	.10
31	Herschel Walker	.10
32	Thurman Thomas	.20
33	Frank Sanders	.10
34	Lawrence Phillips	.20
35	Scottie Graham	.10
36	Jim Everett	.10
37	Dale Carter	.10
38	Ashley Ambrose	.10
39	Mark Chmura	.20
40	James Stewart	.10
41	John Mobley	.10
42	Terrell Davis	1.25
43	Ben Coates	.10
44	Jeff George	.10
45	Ty Detmer	.10
46	Isaac Bruce	.20
47	Chris Warren	.10
48	Steve Walsh	.10
49	Bruce Smith	.10
50	Cris Carter	.10
51	Jamal Anderson	.10
52	Tim Biakabutuka	.10
53	Steve Young	.75
54	Eric Turner	.10
55	Jessie Tuggle	.10
56	Chris T. Jones	.10
57	Daryl Johnston	.10
58	Randall Cunningham	.10
59	Trent Dilfer	.20
60	Mark Brunell	1.25
61	Warren Moon	.10
62	Terry Kirby	.10
63	Eddie George	1.75
64	Neil Smith	.10
65	Gilbert Brown	.10
66	Emmitt Smith	2.50
67	Chad Brown	.10
68	Jamie Asher	.10
69	Willie McGinest	.10
70	Tim Brown	.10
71	Quentin Coryatt	.10
72	Mario Bates	.10
73	Fred Barnett	.10
74	Hugh Douglas	.10
75	Eric Swann	.10
76	Chris Chandler	.10
77	Larry Centers	.10
78	Vinny Testaverde	.10
79	Jermaine Lewis	.10
80	Junior Seau	.10
81	Kevin Greene	.10
82	Ricky Watters	.20
83	Anthony Miller	.10
84	Michael Westbrook	.10
85	Charles Way	.10
86	Andre Reed	.10
87	Darrell Green	.10
88	Troy Aikman	1.25
89	Jim Pyne	.10
90	Dan Marino	2.50
91	Elvis Grbac	.10
92	Mel Gray	.10
93	Marcus Allen	.20
94	Terry Allen	.10
95	Karim Abdul-Jabbar	.75
96	Rick Mirer	.10
97	Bert Emanuel	.10
98	John Elway	.75
99	Tony Martin	.10
100	Zach Thomas	.20
101	Harvey Williams	.10
102	Jason Sehorn	.10
103	Lawyer Milloy	.10
104	Thomas Lewis	.10
105	Michael Irvin	.20
106	James Hundon	.10
107	Willie Green	.10
108	Bobby Engram	.10
109	Mike Alstott	.20
110	Greg Lloyd	.10
111	Shannon Sharpe	.10
112	Desmond Howard	.10
113	Jason Elam	.10
114	Qadry Ismail	.10
115	William Thomas	.10
116	Marshall Faulk	.20
117	Tyrone Wheatley	.10
118	Tommy Vardell	.10
119	Rashaan Salaam	.20
120	Brian Mitchell	.10
121	Terance Mathis	.10
122	Dorsey Levens	.20
123	Todd Collins	.20
124	Derrick Alexander	.10
125	Stan Humphries	.10
126	Kordell Stewart	1.25
127	Kent Graham	.10
128	Yancey Thigpen	.10
129	Bryan Still	.10
130	Carl Pickens	.10
131	Ray Lewis	.10
132	Curtis Martin	1.25
133	Kerry Collins	1.00
134	Ed McCaffrey	.10
135	Darick Holmes	.10
136	Glyn Milburn	.10
137	Rickey Dudley	.10
138	Terrell Owens	.75
139	Kevin Williams	.10
140	Reggie White	.20
141	Darnay Scott	.10
142	Brett Perriman	.10
143	Neil O'Donnell	.10
144	Natrone Means	.20
145	Jerris McPhail	.10
146	Lamar Lathon	.10
147	Michael Jackson	.10
148	Simeon Rice	.10
149	Greg Hill	.10
150	Erik Kramer	.10
151	Quinn Early	.10
152	Tamarick Vanover	.10
153	Derrick Thomas	.10
154	Nilo Silvan	.10
155	Deion Sanders	.50
156	Lorenzo Neal	.10
157	Steve McNair	1.00
158	Levon Kirkland	.10
159	Bobby Hebert	.10
160	William Floyd	.20
161	Leeland McElroy	.10
162	Chester McGlockton	.10
163	Michael Haynes	.10
164	Aeneas Williams	.10
165	Hardy Nickerson	.10
166	Rodney Woodson	.10
167	Iheanyi Uwaezuoke	.10
168	Chris Slade	.10

169	Herman Moore	.20
170	Rob Moore	.10
171	Andre Hastings	.10
172	Antonio Freeman	.40
173	Tony Boselli	.10
174	Drew Bledsoe	1.25
175	Sam Mills	.10
176	Robert Smith	.10
177	Jimmy Smith	.10
178	Alex Molden	.10
179	Joey Galloway	.20
180	Irving Fryar	.10
181	Wayne Chrebet	.10
182	Dave Brown	.10
183	Robert Brooks	.20
184	Tony Banks	.75
185	Eric Metcalf	.10
186	Napoleon Kaufman	.20
187	Frank Wycheck	.10
188	Donnell Woolford	.10
189	Kevin Turner	.10
190	Eddie Kennison	.40
191	Cortez Kennedy	.10
192	Raymont Harris	.10
193	Ronnie Harmon	.10
194	Kevin Hardy	.10
195	Gus Frerotte	.10
196	Marvin Harrison	.40
197	Jeff Blake	.20
198	Mike Tomczak	.10
199	William Roaf	.10
200	Jerry Rice	1.25
201	Jake Reed	.10
202	Ken Norton	.10
203	Errict Rhett	.20
204	Adrian Murrell	.20
205	Rodney Hampton	.10
206	Scott Mitchell	.10
207	Jason Dunn	.10
208	Ray Zellars	.10
209	Michael Adams	.10
210	John Allred	.10
211	Reidel Anthony	1.50
212	Darnell Autry	.75
213	Tiki Barber	1.50
214	Will Blackwell	.20
215	Peter Boulware	.10
216	Macey Brooks	.10
217	Rae Carruth	1.50
218	Troy Davis	1.00
219	Corey Dillon	2.50
220	Jim Druckenmiller	2.50
221	Warrick Dunn	4.00
222	Marc Edwards	.10
223	James Farrior	.10
224	Tony Gonzalez	.75
225	Jay Graham	.50
226	Yatil Green	.30
227	Byron Hanspard	.75
228	Ike Hilliard	1.25
229	Leon Johnson	.10
230	Damon Jones	.10
231	Freddie Jones	.50
232	Joey Kent	.50
233	David LaFleur	.75
234	Kevin Lockett	.10
235	Sam Madison	.10
236	Brian Manning	.10
237	Ronnie McAda	.10
238	Orlando Pace	.50
239	Jake Plummer	2.00
240	Keith Poole	.10
241	Darrell Russell	.10
242	Sedrick Shaw	1.00
243	Antowain Smith	2.00
244	Shawn Springs	.50
245	Duce Staley	.10
246	Dedric Ward	.10
247	Bryant Westbrook	.20
248	Danny Wuerffel	1.50
249	Checklist	.10
250	Checklist	.10

1997 SkyBox Rubies

Rubies paralleled all 250 cards in SkyBox, but contained Ruby colored foil on the front. Rubies were sequentially numbered to 50 sets on the back.

	MT
Ruby Cards:	50x-100x
Ruby Rookies:	25x-50x
Production 50 Sets	

1997 SkyBox Autographics

Inserted 1:240 packs, the cards featured signed fronts. In addition, an Autographics Century Marks parallel set was also randomly seeded.

	MT
Common Player:	15.00
Century Marks:	2x
Karim Abdul-Jabbar	80.00
Larry Allen	15.00
Terry Allen	30.00
Mike Alstott	75.00
Darnell Autry	45.00
Tony Banks	75.00
Pat Barnes	30.00
Jeff Blake	30.00
Michael Booker	15.00
Reuben Brown	15.00
Rae Carruth	60.00
Cris Carter	30.00
Ben Coates	30.00
Ernie Conwell	15.00
Terrell Davis	150.00
Ty Detmer	15.00
Ken Dilger	15.00
Corey Dillon	80.00
Jim Druckenmiller	125.00
Rick Dudley	30.00
Brett Favre CM	700.00
Antonio Freeman	50.00
Daryl Gardner	15.00
Chris Gedney	15.00
Eddie George	200.00
Hunter Goodwin	15.00
Marvin Harrison	60.00
Garrison Hearst	30.00
William Henderson	30.00
Michael Jackson	30.00
Tory James	15.00
Rob Johnson	30.00
Chris T. Jones	15.00
Pete Kendall	15.00
Eddie Kennison	60.00
David LaFleur	40.00
Jeff Lewis	30.00
Thomas Lewis	15.00
Keith Lockett	30.00
Brian Manning	15.00
Dan Marino	400.00
Ed McCaffrey	15.00
Keenan McCardell	30.00
Glyn Milburn	15.00
Alex Molden	15.00
Johnnie Morton	15.00
Winslow Oliver	15.00
Jerry Rice	350.00
Rashaan Salaam	30.00
Frank Sanders	15.00
Shannon Sharpe	30.00
Sedrick Shaw	40.00
Alex Smith	15.00
Antowain Smith	80.00
Emmitt Smith	350.00
Jimmy Smith	30.00
Shawn Springs	15.00
James Stewart	15.00
Kordell Stewart	150.00
Rodney Thomas	15.00
Amani Toomer	15.00
Floyd Turner	15.00
Alex Van Dyke	15.00
Mike Vrabel	15.00
Chris Warren	15.00
Charles Way	15.00
Reggie White (Century)	100.00
Rickey Whittle	15.00
Sherman Williams	15.00
John Wittman	15.00

1997 SkyBox Close Ups

This 18-card insert features head shots of young NFL players. Four more pictures are included on the card. Close Ups were inserted 1:18.

	MT
Complete Set (10):	100.00
Common Player:	3.00
1 Terrell Davis	15.00
2 Troy Aikman	15.00
3 Drew Bledsoe	15.00
4 Steve McNair	10.00
5 Jerry Rice	15.00
6 Kordell Stewart	15.00
7 Kerry Collins	10.00
8 John Elway	10.00
9 Deion Sanders	8.00
10 Joey Galloway	3.00

1997 SkyBox Larger Than Life

Larger Than Life is a 10-card insert featuring the legends of today. Larger Than Life cards were inserted one per 360 packs.

	MT
Complete Set (10):	550.00
Common Player:	15.00
1 Emmitt Smith	100.00
2 Barry Sanders	90.00
3 Curtis Martin	60.00
4 Dan Marino	100.00
5 Keyshawn Johnson	15.00
6 Marvin Harrison	15.00
7 Terry Glenn	50.00
8 Eddie George	80.00
9 Brett Favre	125.00
10 Karim Abdul-Jabbar	40.00

1997 SkyBox Premium Players

Premium Players is a 15-card insert set which was seeded one per 192 packs.

	MT
Complete Set (15):	800.00
Common Player:	8.00
1 Eddie George	85.00
2 Terry Glenn	50.00
3 Karim Abdul-Jabbar	40.00
4 Emmitt Smith	100.00
5 Dan Marino	100.00
6 Brett Favre	120.00
7 Keyshawn Johnson	8.00
8 Curtis Martin	60.00
9 Marvin Harrison	8.00
10 Barry Sanders	75.00
11 Jerry Rice	60.00
12 Terrell Davis	60.00
13 Troy Aikman	60.00
14 Drew Bledsoe	60.00
15 John Elway	40.00

1997 SkyBox PrimeTime Rookies

PrimeTime Rookies is a 10-card insert featuring the top rookies of 1997. This set was inserted one per 96 packs.

	MT
Complete Set (10):	175.00
Common Player:	7.00
1 Jim Druckenmiller	35.00
2 Antowain Smith	25.00
3 Rae Carruth	15.00
4 Yatil Green	15.00
5 Ike Hilliard	15.00
6 Reidel Anthony	20.00
7 Orlando Pace	7.00
8 Peter Boulware	7.00
9 Warrick Dunn	45.00
10 Troy Davis	15.00

1997 SkyBox Reebok

The Reebok Value Added set came in bronze, silver, gold, ruby and emerald versions. The overall insertion rate for the Reebok Value Added set was one per pack.

	MT
Complete Set (15):	4.00
Common Player:	.10
Gold:	4x
Green:	25x-50x
Red:	10x-20x
Silver:	2x
12 Keenan McCardell	.10
37 Dale Carter	.10
38 Ashley Ambrose	.10
43 Ben Coates	.10
66 Emmitt Smith	1.50
95 Karim Abdul-Jabbar	.50
98 John Elway	.75
110 Greg Lloyd	.10
123 Todd Collins	.10
161 Leeland McElroy	.10
169 Herman Moore	.10
175 Sam Mills	.10
180 Irving Fryar	.10
202 Ken Norton	.10
205 Rodney Hampton	.10

1997 SkyBox Rookie Preview

These 15 embossed insert cards feature some of the top rookies of 1997. Rookie Preview cards were inserted 1:6.

	MT
Complete Set (15):	30.00
Common Player:	1.00
1 Reidel Anthony	3.00
2 Tiki Barber	3.00
3 Peter Boulware	1.00
4 Rae Carruth	2.50
5 Jim Druckenmiller	4.50
6 Warrick Dunn	6.00
7 James Farrior	1.00
8 Yatil Green	2.50
9 Byron Hanspard	2.00
10 Ike Hilliard	2.50

11	Orlando Pace	1.50
12	Darrell Russell	1.00
13	Antowain Smith	3.00
14	Shawn Springs	1.50
15	Bryant Westbrook	1.00

1997 SkyBox E-X2000

E-X2000 consists of a 60-card base set with one parallel and four inserts. The base cards feature "SkyView" technology, with a die-cut image over a transparent window. The Essential Credentials parallel set consists of less than 100 numbered sets. The inserts include A Cut Above, Fleet of Foot, Star Date 2000 and Autographics.

	MT
Complete Set (60):	100.00
Common Player:	.40
Credential Cards:	10x-20x
Credential Rookies:	5x-10x
Wax Box:	100.00
1 Jake Plummer	20.00
2 Jamal Anderson	.75
3 Rae Carruth	5.00
4 Kerry Collins	3.00
5 Darnell Autry	3.00
6 Rashaan Salaam	.75
7 Troy Aikman	5.00
8 Deion Sanders	2.50
9 Emmitt Smith	8.00
10 Herman Moore	.75
11 Barry Sanders	5.00
12 Mark Chmura	.75
13 Brett Favre	12.00
14 Antonio Freeman	.75
15 Reggie White	.75
16 Cris Carter	.40
17 Brad Johnson	.40
18 Troy Davis	3.00
19 Danny Wuerffel	4.00
20 Dave Brown	.40
21 Ike Hilliard	5.00
22 Ty Detmer	.40
23 Ricky Watters	.75
24 Tony Banks	3.00
25 Eddie Kennison	2.50
26 Jim Druckenmiller	8.00
27 Jerry Rice	5.00
28 Steve Young	3.00
29 Trent Dilfer	.75
30 Warrick Dunn	20.00
31 Terry Allen	.40
32 Gus Frerotte	.40
33 Vinny Testaverde	.40
34 Antowain Smith	10.00
35 Thurman Thomas	.75
36 Jeff Blake	.75
37 Carl Pickens	.40
38 Terrell Davis	5.00
39 John Elway	3.00
40 Eddie George	7.00
41 Steve McNair	4.00
42 Marshall Faulk	.75
43 Marvin Harrison	2.50
44 Mark Brunell	5.00
45 Marcus Allen	.75
46 Elvis Grbac	.40
47 Karim Abdul-Jabbar	3.50
48 Dan Marino	10.00
49 Drew Bledsoe	5.00
50 Terry Glenn	4.00
51 Curtis Martin	5.00
52 Keyshawn Johnson	1.00
53 Tim Brown	.40
54 Jeff George	.40
55 Jerome Bettis	.75
56 Kordell Stewart	5.00
57 Stan Humphries	.40
58 Junior Seau	.75
59 Joey Galloway	.75
60 Chris Warren	.40

1997 SkyBox E-X2000 Essential Credentials

Essential Credentials paralleled the 60-card E-X2000 set, but was reprinted with silver holofoil around the border. The cards contained the words "Essential Credentials" across the top and were numbered to 100 sets on the back.

	MT
Essential Credential Cards:	10x-20x
Essential Credential Rookies:	5x-10x
Production 100 Sets	

1997 SkyBox E-X2000 A Cut Above

This 10-card insert features players on cards die-cut to look like saw blades. A Cut Above cards were inserted 1:288.

		MT
Complete Set (10):		600.00
Common Player:		15.00
1	Barry Sanders	75.00
2	Brett Favre	120.00
3	Dan Marino	100.00
4	Eddie George	80.00
5	Emmitt Smith	100.00
6	Jerry Rice	60.00
7	Joey Galloway	15.00
8	John Elway	40.00
9	Mark Brunell	60.00
10	Terrell Davis	60.00

1997 SkyBox E-X2000 Fleet of Foot

The cards in this 20-card insert are die-cut to look like football cleats. They were inserted 1:20.

		MT
Complete Set (20):		220.00
Common Player:		3.00
1	Antonio Freeman	8.00
2	Barry Sanders	25.00
3	Carl Pickens	3.00
4	Chris Warren	3.00
5	Curtis Martin	20.00
6	Deion Sanders	12.00
7	Emmitt Smith	40.00
8	Jerry Rice	20.00
9	Joey Galloway	6.00
10	Karim Abdul-Jabbar	15.00
11	Kordell Stewart	20.00
12	Lawrence Phillips	3.00
13	Mark Brunell	20.00
14	Marvin Harrison	8.00
15	Rae Carruth	10.00
16	Ricky Watters	3.00
17	Steve Young	15.00
18	Terrell Davis	20.00
19	Terry Glenn	18.00
20	Shawn Springs	3.00

1997 SkyBox E-X2000 Star Date 2000

This 15-card insert features young stars of the NFL. The cards were inserted 1:9.

		MT
Complete Set (15):		60.00
Common Player:		1.50
1	Curtis Martin	6.00
2	Darnell Autry	3.00
3	Darrell Russell	1.50
4	Eddie Kennison	3.00
5	Jim Druckenmiller	8.00
6	Karim Abdul-Jabbar	6.00
7	Kerry Collins	8.00
8	Keyshawn Johnson	3.00
9	Marvin Harrison	3.00
10	Orlando Pace	1.50
11	Pat Barnes	1.50
12	Reidel Anthony	5.00
13	Tim Biakabutuka	1.50
14	Warrick Dunn	12.00
15	Yatil Green	4.00

1997 SP Authentic

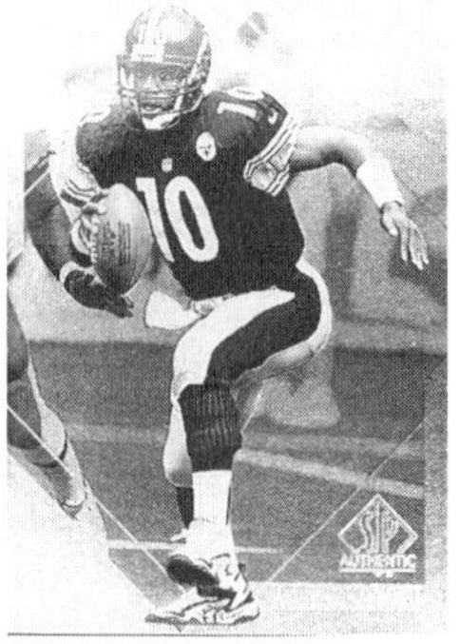

SP Authentic Football is a 198-card set featuring 168 veterans and a subset called Future Watch which contains 30 of the year's top rookies. The front of the cards features an action shot with the player's name in the bottom right corner and team name in the upper left. The card backs feature another action shot and career stats. The inserts include Aikman PowerDeck Audio Cards, ProFiles, Sign of the TImes, Mark of a Legend, Tradition, SP Authentic s, and SP Authentics Collection.

		MT
Complete Set (198):		75.00
Common Player:		.30
Wax Box:		150.00
1	*Orlando Pace*	.75
2	*Darrell Russell*	.60
3	*Shawn Springs*	.75
4	*Peter Boulware*	.75
5	*Bryant Westbrook*	.60
6	*Walter Jones*	.30
7	*Ike Hilliard*	3.00
8	*James Farrior*	.30
9	*Tom Knight*	.30
10	*Warrick Dunn*	15.00
11	*Tony Gonzalez*	2.00
12	*Reinard Wilson*	.30
13	*Yatil Green*	3.00
14	*Reidel Anthony*	4.00
15	*Kenny Holmes*	.30
16	*Dwayne Rudd*	.30
17	*Renaldo Wynn*	.30
18	*David LaFleur*	2.00
19	*Antowain Smith*	7.00
20	*Jim Druckenmiller*	7.00
21	*Rae Carruth*	3.00
22	*Byron Hanspard*	3.00
23	*Jake Plummer*	15.00
24	*Joey Kent*	.75
25	*Corey Dillon*	10.00
26	*Danny Wuerffel*	4.50
27	*Will Blackwell*	.75
28	*Troy Davis*	3.00
29	*Darnell Autry*	3.00
30	*Pat Barnes*	3.00
31	Kent Graham	.30
32	Simeon Rice	.30
33	Frank Sanders	.30
34	Rob Moore	.30
35	Eric Swann	.30
36	Chris Chandler	.30
37	Jamal Anderson	.60
38	Terance Mathis	.30
39	Bert Emanuel	.30
40	Michael Booker	.30
41	Vinny Testaverde	.30
42	Bam Morris	.30
43	Michael Jackson	.30
44	Derrick Alexander	.30
45	Jamie Sharper	.30
46	Kim Herring	.30
47	Todd Collins	.30
48	Thurman Thomas	.60
49	Andre Reed	.30
50	Quinn Early	.30
51	Bryce Paup	.30
52	Marcelius Wiley	.30
53	Kerry Collins	2.00
54	Anthony Johnson	.30
55	Tshimanga Biakabutuka	.30
56	Muhsin Muhammad	.30
57	Sam Mills	.30
58	Wesley Walls	.30
59	Rick Mirer	.30
60	Raymont Harris	.30
61	Curtis Conway	.60
62	Bobby Engram	.30
63	Bryan Cox	.30
64	John Allred	.30
65	Jeff Blake	.60
66	Ki-Jana Carter	.30
67	Darnay Scott	.30
68	Carl Pickens	.30
69	Dan Wilkerson	.30
70	Troy Aikman	3.00
71	Emmitt Smith	5.00
72	Michael Irvin	.60
73	Deion Sanders	1.50
74	Anthony Miller	.30
75	Antonio Anderson	.30
76	John Elway	1.75
77	Terrell Davis	3.00
78	Rod Smith	.30
79	Shannon Sharpe	.30
80	Neil Smith	.30
81	Trevor Pryce	.30
82	Scott Mitchell	.30
83	Barry Sanders	3.00
84	Herman Moore	.60
85	Johnnie Morton	.30
86	Matt Russell	.30
87	Brett Favre	6.00
88	Edgar Bennett	.30
89	Robert Brooks	.30
90	Antonio Freeman	.60
91	Reggie White	.60
92	Craig Newsome	.30
93	Jim Harbaugh	.30
94	Marshall Faulk	.60
95	Sean Dawkins	.30
96	Marvin Harrison	.60
97	Quentin Coryatt	.30
98	Tarik Glenn	.30
99	Mark Brunell	3.00
100	Natrone Means	.30
101	Keenan McCardell	.30
102	Jimmy Smith	.30
103	Tony Brackens	.30
104	Kevin Hardy	.30
105	Elvis Grbac	.30
106	Marcus Allen	.60
107	Greg Hill	.30
108	Derrick Thomas	.30
109	Dale Carter	.30
110	Dan Marino	5.00
111	Karim Abdul-Jabbar	1.75
112	Brian Manning	.30
113	Quadry Ismail	.30
114	Troy Drayton	.30
115	Zach Thomas	.60
116	Jason Taylor	.30
117	Brad Johnson	.60
118	Robert Smith	.30
119	John Randle	.30
120	Cris Carter	.30
121	Jake Reed	.30
122	Randall Cunningham	.30
123	Drew Bledsoe	3.00
124	Curtis Martin	3.00
125	Terry Glenn	2.50
126	Willie McGinest	.30
127	Chris Canty	.30
128	Sedrick Shaw	.30
129	Heath Shuler	.30
130	Mario Bates	.30
131	Ray Zellars	.30
132	Andre Hastings	.30
133	Dave Brown	.30
134	Tyrone Wheatley	.30
135	Rodney Hampton	.30
136	Chris Calloway	.30
137	*Tiki Barber*	5.00
138	Neil O'Donnell	.30
139	Adrian Murrell	.60
140	Wayne Chrebet	.30
141	Keyshawn Johnson	.60
142	Hugh Douglas	.30
143	Jeff George	.30
144	Napoleon Kaufman	.60
145	Tim Brown	.30
146	Desmond Howard	.30
147	Rickey Dudley	.30
148	Terry McDaniel	.30
149	Ty Detmer	.30
150	Ricky Watters	.60
151	Chris T. Jones	.30
152	Irving Fryar	.30
153	Mike Mamula	.30
154	Jon Harris	.30
155	Kordell Stewart	3.00
156	Jerome Bettis	.60
157	Charles Johnson	.30
158	Greg Lloyd	.30
159	George Jones	.30
160	Terrell Fletcher	.30
161	Stan Humphries	.30
162	Tony Martin	.30
163	Eric Metcalf	.30
164	Junior Seau	.30
165	Rod Woodson	.30
166	Steve Young	1.75
167	Terry Kirby	.30
168	Garrison Hearst	.30
169	Jerry Rice	3.00
170	Ken Norton	.30
171	Kevin Greene	.30
172	Lamar Smith	.30
173	Warren Moon	.30
174	Chris Warren	.30
175	Cortez Kennedy	.30
176	Joey Galloway	.60
177	Tony Banks	1.25
178	Isaac Bruce	.60
179	Eddie Kennison	.60
180	Kevin Carter	.30
181	Craig Heyward	.30
182	Trent Dilfer	.60
183	Errict Rhett	.30
184	Mike Alstott	.60
185	Hardy Nickerson	.30
186	Ronde Barber	.30
187	Steve McNair	2.00
188	Eddie George	4.50
189	Chris Sanders	.30
190	Blaine Bishop	.30
191	Derrick Mason	.30
192	Gus Frerotte	.30
193	Terry Allen	.30
194	Brian Mitchell	.30
195	Alvin Harper	.30
196	Jeff Hostetler	.30
197	Lesley Sheppard	.30
198	Stephen Davis	.30

1997 SP Authentic Aikman PowerDeck

Aikman PowerDeck was a three-card insert that contained a mini-compact disc within a trading card. Regular Blue versions were seeded every 22 packs, Pro Bowl versions were seeded every 130 and White versions were numbered to 500.

		MT
Common Player:		5.00
A1	Aikman Audio Blue	5.00
A2	Aikman Audio Pro Bowl	15.00
A3	Aikman Audio White/500	50.00

1997 SP Authentic Authentics

This 30-card insert was found in packs of SP Authentic. It allowed the collector to redeem the card for the specific piece of autographed memorabilia noted. Cards SPA1-SPA10 were for Dan Marino autograhped memorabilia, SPA11-SPA20 were for Joe Montana autographed memorabilia and SPA21-SPA26 were for Troy Aikman autographed memorabilia. SPC27 was for a two-card Dan Marino set. The final three cards were numbered with a "SPC" prefix and entitled the collector to get either a Marino, Montana or Aikman collection of autographed memorabilia.

	MT
Complete Set (26):	—
Common Player:	—
SPA1Dan Marino (Signed Helmet)	—
SPA2Dan Marino (Signed Jersey)	—
SPA3Dan Marino (Signed NFL Football)	—
SPA4Dan Marino (Replica Signed Helmet)	—
SPA5Dan Marino (Collector's Choice Football)	—
SPA6Dan Marino(Signed Mini Football)	—
SPA7Dan Marino (Signed Sports Illustrated Cover)	—
SPA8Dan Marino (Signed Mini Helmet)	—
SPA9Dan Marino (Signed Photo, 8X10)	—
SPA10Dan Marino (C-Card)	—
SPA11Joe Montana (Signed Jersey)	—
SPA12Joe Montana (Signed NFL Football)	—
SPA13Joe Montana (Collector's Choice Football)	—
SPA14Joe Montana (Signed Sports Illustrated Cover)	—
SPA15Joe Montana (Signed Mini Helmet)	—
SPA16Joe Montana (Signed Photo, 8X10)	—
SPA17Joe Montana (C-Card)	—
SPA18Joe Montana (Signed Helmet)	—
SPA19Joe Montana (Collector's Choice Helmet)	—
SPA20Joe Montana (Signed Two-Card Set)	—
SPA21Troy Aikman (Signed NFL Football)	—
SPA22Troy Aikman (Signed Mini Football)	—
SPA23Troy Aikman (Signed Sports Illustrated Cover)	—
SPA25Troy Aikman (Signed Photo, 8X10)	—
SPA26Troy Aikman (Signed Two-Card Set)	—
SPA27Dan Marino (Signed Two-Card Set)	—

1997 SP Authentic Mark of a Legend

This seven-card collection features autographs from some of the NFL's greatest playes. The inserts were seeded 1:168 packs.

		MT
Complete Set (7):		600.00
Common Player:		50.00
ML1	Bob Griese	50.00
ML2	Roger Staubach	150.00
ML3	Joe Montana	200.00
ML4	Franco Harris	50.00
ML5	Gale Sayers	75.00
ML6	Steve Largent	50.00
ML7	Tony Dorsett	50.00

1997 SP Authentic ProFiles

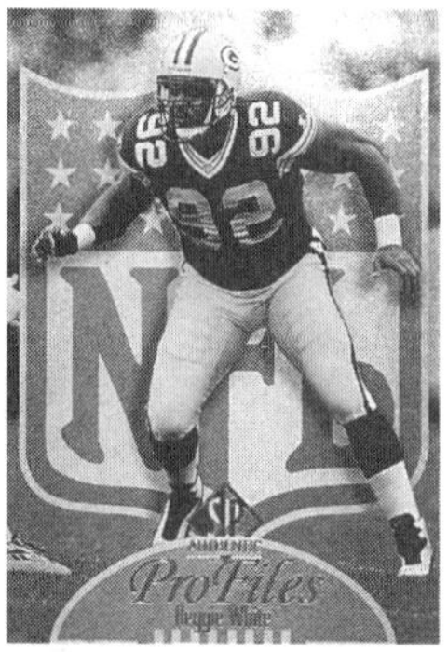

ProFiles is a three-tiered, 40-card insert. The first tier has an action shot of the player with the NFL logo in the background and is inserted 1:5. The second tier card is a die-cut version of tier one and is inserted 1:12. Tier three cards are sequentially numbered to 100.

		MT
Complete Set (40):		150.00
Common Player:		1.50
P1	Dan Marino	10.00
P2	Kordell Stewart	6.00
P3	Emmitt Smith	10.00
P4	Brett Favre	12.00
P5	Marcus Allen	1.50
P6	Jerry Rice	6.00
P7	Jeff George	1.50
P8	Mark Brunell	6.00
P9	Eddie George	8.00
P10	Cris Carter	1.50
P11	Tshimanga Biakabutuka	1.50
P12	Ike Hilliard	4.00
P13	Darrell Russell	1.50
P14	Jim Druckenmiller	8.00
P15	Rae Carruth	4.00
P16	Warrick Dunn	12.00
P17	Herman Moore	1.50
P18	Deion Sanders	3.00
P19	Drew Bledsoe	6.00
P20	Jeff Blake	1.50
P21	Keyshawn Johnson	1.50
P22	Curtis Martin	6.00
P23	Michael Irvin	1.50
P24	Barry Sanders	10.00
P25	Carl Pickens	1.50
P26	Steve McNair	5.00
P27	Terry Allen	1.50
P28	Terrell Davis	6.00
P29	Lawrence Phillips	1.50
P30	Marshall Faulk	1.50
P31	Karim Abdul-Jabbar	4.00
P32	Steve Young	5.00
P33	Tim Brown	1.50
P34	Antowain Smith	6.00
P35	Kerry Collins	5.00
P36	Reggie White	1.50
P37	John Elway	5.00
P38	Jerome Bettis	1.50
P39	Troy Aikman	6.00
P40	Junior Seau	1.50

1997 SP Authentic ProFiles Die-Cuts

This 40-card insert paralleled the Profiles insert, but featured each card on a die-cut design. Die-cut versions were sequentially numbered to 100.

	MT
Die-Cut Cards:	2x
Inserted 1:12	
Die-Cut 100's:	7x-14x
Production 100 Sets	

1997 SP Authentic Sign of the Times

This 30-card insert consists of cards autographed by current NFL players. They were inserted once in 24 packs.

	MT
CompleteSet (28)	1800.00
Common Player:	15.00
Jeff Blake	15.00
Kerry Collins	30.00
Warrick Dunn	100.00
Rae Carruth	15.00
Karim Abdul-Jabbar	30.00
Reidel Anthony	30.00
Terrell Davis	250.00
Joey Galloway	40.00
Marshall Faulk	40.00
Robert Brooks	15.00
Will Blackwell	15.00
Emmitt Smith	300.00
Herman Moore	30.00
Napoleon Kaufman	75.00
Antowain Smith	50.00
Terry Allen	30.00
Tim Brown	30.00
Jerome Bettis	30.00
Rashaan Salaam	30.00
Jim Druckenmiller	50.00
George Jones	15.00
Isaac Bruce	30.00
Tony Gonzalez	30.00
Troy Aikman	200.00
Dan Marino	300.00
Jerry Rice	275.00
Curtis Martin	80.00
Eddie George	100.00

1997 SP Authentic Traditions

Tradition is a six-card insert. The cards feature two autographs, one from an NFL legend and the other from a proven superstar, both from the same team. Tradition was inserted once per 1,440 packs.

		MT
Complete Set (6):		2500.00
Common Player:		125.00
TD1	Dan Marino, Bob Griese	600.00
TD2	Troy Aikman, Roger Staubach	450.00
TD3	Jerry Rice, Joe Montana	1000.
TD4	Jerome Bettis, Franco Harris	125.00
TD5	Emmitt Smith, Tony Dorsett	500.00
TD6	Joey Galloway, Steve Largent	125.00

1997 Stadium Club

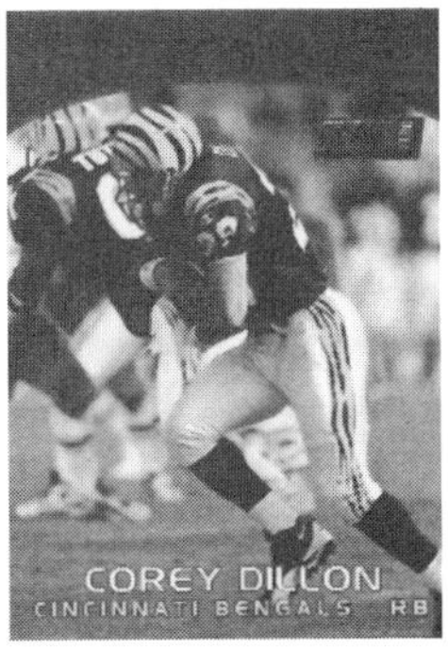
COREY DILLON
CINCINNATI BENGALS RB

The 170-card Series I set included a full-bleed photo on the front, with the Stadium Club logo at the top and a "wave" on the bottom that included the player's name and position. The backs included an action shot, with the player's name, bio and highlights on the left side in a "ripped out" area. The stats appear in a box in the lower right, along with one highlight. There are three parallel sets. Printing Plates (cyan, yellow, magenta and black plates of each card for a total of 640 cards) were inserted in Home Team Advantage packs. One-of-a-Kind parallel cards were seeded 1:48 packs, while First Day Issue parallel cards were found 1:24 retail packs. Series II also had 170 cards and the same three parallel sets. The base set did include a 20-card Transaction subset, featuring important offseason moves.

		MT
Complete Series 2 (170):		30.00
Common Player:		.10
Series 2 Wax Box:		40.00
171	Mark Carrier	.10
172	Greg Hill	.10
173	Erik Kramer	.10
174	Chris Spielman	.10
175	Tom Knight	.10
176	Sam Mills	.10
177	Robert Smith	.10
178	Dorsey Levens	.20
179	Chris Slade	.10
180	Troy Vincent	.10
181	Mario Bates	.10
182	Ed McCaffrey	.10
183	Mike Mamula	.10
184	Chad Hennings	.10
185	Stan Humphries	.10
186	Reinard Wilson	.10
187	Kevin Carter	.10
188	Qadry Ismail	.10
189	Cortez Kennedy	.10
190	Eric Swann	.10
191	*Corey Dillon*	3.00
192	Renaldo Wynn	.10
193	Bobby Hebert	.10
194	Fred Barnett	.10
195	Ray Lewis	.10
196	Robert Jones	.10
197	Brian Williams	.10
198	Willie McGinest	.10
199	*Jake Plummer*	3.00
200	Aeneas Williams	.10
201	Ashley Ambrose	.10
202	Cornelius Bennett	.10
203	Mo Lewis	.10
204	James Hasty	.10
205	Carnell Lake	.10
206	Heath Shuler	.10
207	Dana Stubblefield	.10
208	Corey Miller	.10
209	*Ike Hilliard*	1.50
210	Bryant Young	.10
211	Hardy Nickerson	.10
212	Blaine Bishop	.10
213	Marcus Robertson	.10
214	Tony Bennett	.10
215	Kent Graham	.10
216	Steve Bono	.10
217	*Will Blackwell*	.50
218	Tyrone Braxton	.10
219	Eric Moulds	.20
220	Rod Woodson	.10
221	Anthony Johnson	.10
222	Willie Davis	.10
223	Darrin Smith	.10
224	Rick Mirer	.10
225	Marvin Harrison	.50
226	Dixon Edwards	.10
227	Joe Aska	.10
228	*Yatil Green*	1.50
229	William Fuller	.10
230	Eddie Robinson	.10
231	Brian Blades	.10
232	Michael Sinclair	.10
233	Ken Harvey	.10
234	Harvey Williams	.10
235	Simeon Rice	.10
236	Chris T. Jones	.10
237	Bert Emanuel	.10
238	Corey Sawyer	.10
239	Chris Calloway	.10
240	Jeff Blake	.20
241	Alonzo Spellman	.10
242	Bryan Cox	.10
243	*Antowain Smith*	2.50
244	Tim Biakabutuka	.20
245	Ray Crockett	.10
246	Dwayne Rudd	.10
247	Glyn Milburn	.10
248	Gary Plummer	.10
249	O.J. McDuffie	.10
250	Willie Clay	.10
251	Jim Everett	.10
252	Eugene Daniel	.10
253	Jessie Armstead	.10
254	Mel Gray	.10
255	Ken Norton	.10
256	Johnnie Morton	.10
257	Courtney Hawkins	.10
258	Ricardo McDonald	.10
259	Todd Lyght	.10
260	Michael Barrow	.10
261	Aaron Glenn	.10
262	Clay Matthews	.10
263	*Troy Davis*	1.00
264	Eric Hill	.10
265	Darrien Gordon	.10
266	Lake Dawson	.10
267	John Randle	.10
268	Lamar Thomas	.10
269	Mickey Washington	.10
270	Amani Toomer	.10
271	Steve Grant	.10
272	Adrian Murrell	.20
273	Derrick Witherspoon	.10
274	Michael Zordich	.10
275	Ben Coates	.10
277	Jim Schwantz	.10
278	Aaron Hayden	.10
279	Ryan McNeil	.10
280	LeRoy Butler	.10
281	Craig Newsome	.10
282	Bill Romanowski	.10
283	Michael Bankston	.10
284	Kevin Smith	.10
285	Byron Morris	.10
286	Darnay Scott	.10
287	*David LaFleur*	1.00
288	Randall Cunningham	.10
289	Eric Davis	.10
290	Todd Collins	.10
291	Steve Tovar	.10
292	Jermaine Lewis	.10
293	Alfred Williams	.10
294	Brad Johnson	.20
295	Charles Johnson	.10
296	Ted Johnson	.10
297	Merton Hanks	.10
298	Andre Coleman	.10
299	Keith Jackson	.10
300	Terry Kirby	.10
301	Tony Banks	.30
302	Terrance Shaw	.10
303	Bobby Engram	.10
304	Hugh Douglas	.10
305	Lawyer Milloy	.10
306	James Jett	.10
307	*Joey Kent*	.50
308	Rodney Hampton	.10
309	DeWayne Washington	.10
310	Kevin Lockett	.10
311	Ki-Jana Carter	.10
312	Jeff Lageman	.10
313	Don Beebe	.10
314	Willie Williams	.10
315	Tyrone Wheatley	.10
316	Leslie O'Neal	.10
317	Quinn Early	.10
318	Sean Gilbert	.10
319	Tim Bowens	.10
320	Sean Dawkins	.10
321	Ken Dilger	.10
322	George Koonce	.10
323	Jevon Langford	.10
324	Mike Caldwell	.10
325	*Orlando Pace*	.75
326	Garrison Hearst	.10
327	Mike Tomczak	.10
328	Rob Moore	.10
329	Andre Reed	.10
330	Kimble Anders	.10
331	Qadry Ismail	.10
333	Dave Brown	.10
334	Bonnie Blades	.10
335	Jamal Anderson	.20
336	John Lynch	.10
337	Tyrone Hughes	.10
338	Ronnie Harmon	.10
339	*Rae Carruth*	1.25
340	Robert Brooks	.10

1997 Stadium Club First Day

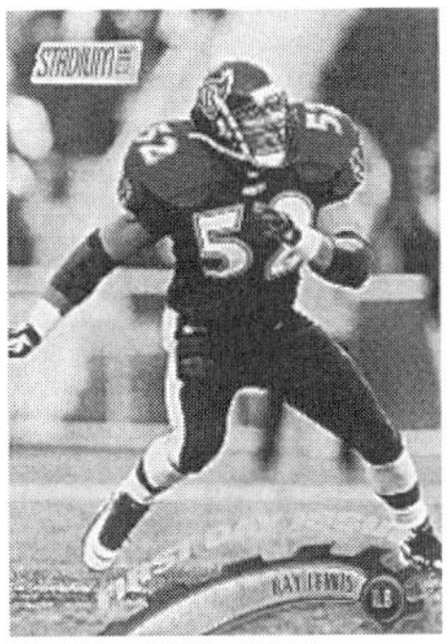

First Day Issue is a retail-only parallel of the Stadium Club Series base set which was inserted one per 24 packs. Each card was marked with a gold foil logo with the parallel name on the front of the card.

	MT
First Day Stars:	20x-40x
First Day Rookies:	10x-20x

1997 Stadium Club One of a Kind

One of a Kind is a hobby-only parallel which was seeded one per 48 packs. Each card is marked with a special security stamp. All 340 cards from Series I and II are paralleled.

	MT
One of a Kind Stars:	30x-60x
One of a Kind Rookies:	15x-30x

1997 Stadium Club Bowman's Best Rookie Preview

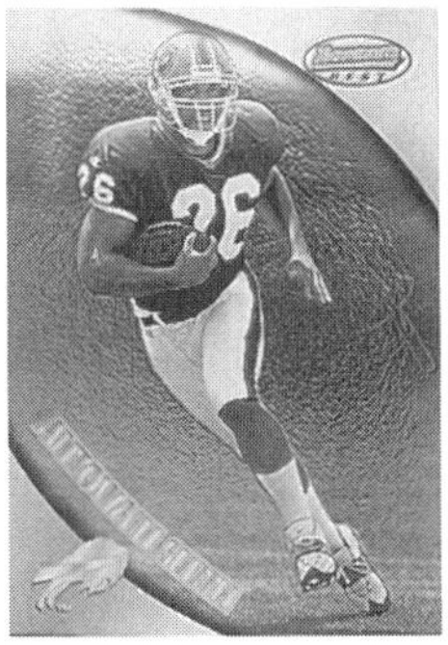

These 15 chromium cards feature top rookies from 1997. The cards were inserted 1:24, with Refractor (1:96) and Atomic Refractor (1:192) versions also available.

	MT
Complete Set (15):	100.00
Common Player:	3.00
Refractors:	2x-3x
Atomic Refractors:	3x-6x
BBP1Orlando Pace	3.00
BBP2David LaFleur	6.00
BBP3James Farrior	3.00
BBP4Tony Gonzalez	6.00
BBP5Ike Hilliard	12.00
BBP6Antowain Smith	15.00
BBP7Tom Knight	3.00
BBP8Troy Davis	15.00
BBP9Yatil Green	12.00
BBP10Jim Druckenmiller	20.00
BBP11Bryant Westbrook	3.00
BBP12Darrell Russell	3.00
BBP13Rae Carruth	10.00
BBP14Shawn Springs	3.00
BBP15Peter Boulware	3.00

1997 Stadium Club Co-Signers

Seventy-two NFL players autographed these two-sided cards. There are 108 Co-Signers matchups. Co-Signers were found one per 63 Series I packs and one per 68 Series II packs.

		MT
Common Player (1-36):		75.00
Common Player (37-72):		50.00
Common Player (73-108):		25.00
1	Karim Abdul-Jabbar, Eddie George	400.00
2	Trace Armstrong, Alonzo Spellman	75.00
3	Steve Atwater, Kevin Hardy	75.00
4	Fred Barnett, Lake Dawson	75.00
5	Blaine Bishop, Darrell Green	75.00
6	Jeff Blake, Gus Frerotte	150.00
7	Steve Bono, Cris Carter	125.00
8	Tim Brown, Isaac Bruce	150.00
9	Wayne Chrebet, Mickey Washington	75.00
10	Curtis Conway, Eddie Kennison	150.00
11	Eric Davis, Jason Sehorn	75.00
12	Terrell Davis, Thurman Thomas	180.00
13	Ken Dilger, Kent Graham	75.00
14	Stephen Grant, Marvcus Patton	75.00
15	Keith Hamilton, Mike Tomczak	75.00
16	Rodney Hampton, David Meggett	75.00
17	Merton Hanks, Aeneas Williams	75.00
18	No Card	
19	Brent Jones, Wesley Walls	75.00
20	Carnell Lake, Tim McDonald	75.00
21	Thomas Lewis, Keith Lyle	75.00
22	Leeland McElroy, Jeff Lageman	75.00
23	Ray Mickens, Willie Davis	75.00
24	Herman Moore, Desmond Howard	150.00
25	Stevon Moore, William Thomas	75.00
26	Adrian Murrell, Levon Kirkland	125.00
27	Simeon Rice, Winslow Oliver	75.00
28	Bill Romanowski, Gary Plummer	75.00
29	Junior Seau, Chris Spielman	75.00
30	Chris Slade, Kevin Greene	75.00
31	Derrick Thomas, Chris T. Jones	75.00
32	Orlando Thomas, Bobby Engram	75.00
33	Amani Toomer, Thomas Randolph	75.00
34	Steve Tovar, Ellis Johnson	75.00
35	Herschel Walker, Anthony Johnson	75.00
36	Darren Woodson, Aaron Glenn	75.00
37	Karim Abdul-Jabbar, Thurman Thomas	125.00
38	Blaine Bishop, Tim McDonald	50.00
39	Jeff Blake, Derrick Thomas	80.00
40	No Card	
41	Cris Carter, Marvin Harrison	125.00
42	Curtis Conway, Wesley Walls	50.00
43	Willie Davis, Amani Toomer	50.00
44	Lake Dawson, Ray Mickens	50.00
45	Ken Dilger, Ellis Johnson	50.00
46	Bobby Engram, Thomas Lewis	50.00
47	Gus Frerotte, Chris T. Jones	75.00
48	Eddie George, Terrell Davis	250.00
49	Aaron Glenn, Eric Davis	50.00
50	Kent Graham, Steve Tovar	50.00
51	Darrell Green, Carnell Lake	50.00
52	Kevin Greene, Steve Atwater	50.00
53	Rodney Hampton, Anthony Johnson	50.00
54	Kevin Hardy, Merton Hanks	50.00
55	Desmond Howard, Tim Brown	80.00
56	Eddie Kennison, Brent Jones	100.00
57	Levon Kirkland, Simeon Rice	50.00
58	Jeff Lageman, Adrian Murrell	75.00
59	Keith Lyle, Wayne Chrebet	50.00
60	David Meggett, Herschel Walker	50.00
61	Herman Moore, Isaac Bruce	125.00
62	Winslow Oliver, Leeland McElroy	50.00
63	Marvcus Patton, Keith Hamilton	50.00
64	Gary Plummer, Junior Seau	50.00
65	Thomas Randolph, Fred Barnett	50.00
66	Alonzo Spellman, Stephen Grant	50.00
67	Chris Spielman, Stevon Moore	50.00
68	William Thomas, Bill Romanowski	50.00
69	Mike Tomczak, Trace Armstrong	50.00
70	Mickey Washington, Orlando Thomas	50.00
71	Aeneas Williams, Chris Slade	50.00
72	Darren Woodson, Jason Sehorn	50.00

73	Trace Armstrong, Keith Hamilton	25.00
74	Isaac Bruce, Desmond Howard	75.00
75	Terrell Davis, Karim Abdul-Jabbar	250.00
76	Tim Brown, Herman Moore	100.00
77	Derrick Thomas, Gus Frerotte	40.00
78	Thurman Thomas, Eddie George	150.00
79	Steve Atwater, Chris Slade	25.00
80	Merton Hanks, Kevin Greene	25.00
81	Marvin Harrison, Steve Bono	75.00
82	Anthony Johnson, David Meggett	25.00
83	Stephen Grant, Mike Tomczak	25.00
84	Herschel Walker, Rodney Hampton	25.00
85	Aeneas Williams, Kevin Hardy	25.00
86	Anthony Johnson, David Meggett	25.00
87	Brent Jones, Curtis Conway	25.00
88	Carnell Lake, Blaine Bishop	25.00
89	Tim McDonald, Darrell Green	25.00
90	Trace Armstrong, Keith Hamilton	25.00
91	Winslow Oliver, Levon Kirkland	25.00
92	Simeon Rice, Jeff Lageman	25.00
93	Wesley Walls, Eddie Kennison	40.00
94	Adrian Murrell, Leeland McElroy	40.00
95	Winslow Oliver, Levon Kirkland	25.00
96	Marvcus Patton, Alonzo Spellman	25.00
97	No Card	
98	Ray Mickens, Thomas Randolph	25.00
99	Junior Seau, Bill Romanowski	25.00
100	Marvcus Patton, Alonzo Spellman	25.00
101	Derrick Thomas, Gus Frerotte	40.00
102	Orlando Thomas, Keith Lyle	25.00
103	Thurman Thomas, Eddie George	150.00
104	Wayne Chrebet, Thomas Lewis	25.00
105	Steve Tovar, Ken Dilger	25.00
106	Ellis Johnson, Kent Graham	25.00
107	Wesley Walls, Eddie Kennison	40.00
108	Aeneas Williams, Kevin Hardy	25.00

1997 Stadium Club Never Compromise

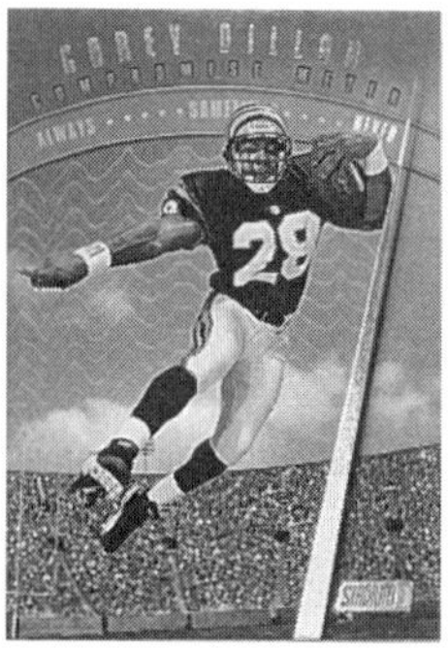

This 40-card insert features 10 veterans and 30 rookies. The cards could be found every 12 packs.

		MT
Complete Set (40):		225.00
Common Player:		1.50
NC1	Orlando Pace	3.00
NC2	Corey Dillon	15.00
NC3	Tony Gonzalez	8.00
NC4	Tom Knight	1.50
NC5	Deion Sanders	10.00
NC6	Dwayne Rudd	1.50
NC7	Warrick Dunn	25.00
NC8	Kenny Holmes	1.50
NC9	Will Blackwell	1.50
NC10	Shawn Springs	1.50
NC11	Rae Carruth	8.00
NC12	Edgar Bennett	1.50
NC13	Walter Jones	1.50
NC14	Reidel Anthony	8.00
NC15	Troy Davis	8.00
NC16	Mark Brunell	15.00
NC17	Pat Barnes	6.00
NC18	Reggie White	3.00
NC19	Darrell Russell	1.50
NC20	Ike Hilliard	8.00
NC21	Emmitt Smith	30.00
NC22	David LaFleur	6.00
NC23	Yatil Green	8.00
NC24	Barry Sanders	20.00
NC25	Bryant Westbrook	1.50
NC26	Lawrence Phillips	1.50
NC27	Peter Boulware	1.50
NC28	Joey Kent	3.00
NC29	Kevin Lockett	1.50
NC30	Derrick Thomas	1.50
NC31	Antowain Smith	15.00
NC32	James Farrior	1.50
NC33	Kordell Stewart	15.00
NC34	Byron Hanspard	6.00
NC35	Jim Druckenmiller	15.00
NC36	Reinard Wilson	1.50
NC37	Darnell Autry	6.00
NC38	Steve Young	10.00
NC39	Renaldo Wynn	1.50
NC40	Jake Plummer	15.00

1997 Stadium Club Triumvirate II

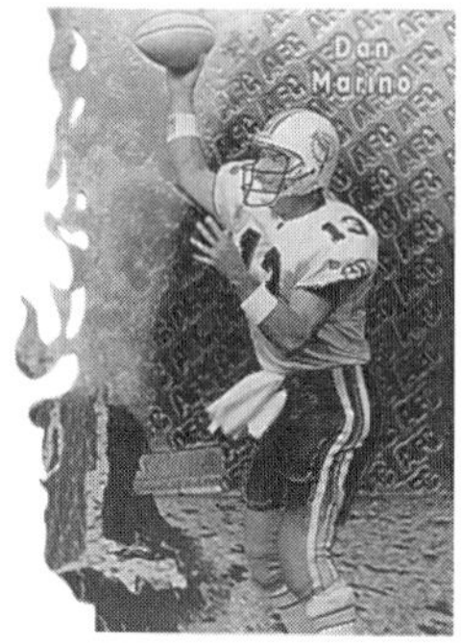

This 18-card, laser-cut insert consists of six trios of players, whose cards can be fit together. Triumvirate was seeded 1:36, with Refractor (1:144) and Atomic Refractor (1:288) also created.

		MT
Complete Set (18):		200.00
Common Player:		5.00
Refractors:		2x-3x
Atomic Refractors:		3x-6x
T1A	John Elway	10.00
T1B	Drew Bledsoe	15.00
T1C	Dan Marino	25.00
T2A	Troy Aikman	15.00
T2B	Brett Favre	30.00
T2C	Steve Young	10.00
T3A	Terrell Davis	15.00
T3B	Eddie George	20.00
T3C	Curtis Martin	15.00
T4A	Emmitt Smith	25.00
T4B	Ricky Watters	5.00
T4C	Barry Sanders	20.00
T5A	Shannon Sharpe	5.00
T5B	Terry Glenn	5.00
T5C	Carl Pickens	5.00
T6A	Jake Plummer	10.00
T6B	Orlando Pace	5.00
T6C	Jim Druckenmiller	15.00

1997 Topps Chrome

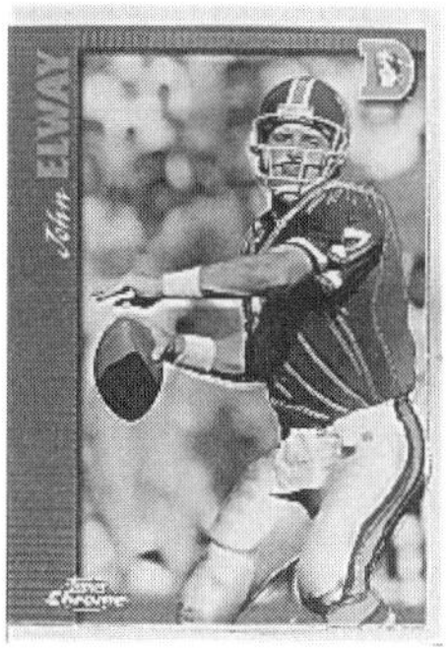

Chrome Football is a 165-card set created with Topps' chromium technology and a Topps Chrome logo added to regular Topps cards. Chrome arrived with a full parallel set of Refractors and four inserts also from Topps: Draft Year, Underclassmen, Season's Best and Career Best.

		MT
Complete Set (165):		180.00
Common Player:		.40
Common Player (143-163):		1.00
Wax Box:		220.00
1	Brett Favre	6.00
2	Tim Biakabutuka	.40
3	Deion Sanders	1.50
4	Marshall Faulk	1.00
5	John Randle	.40
6	Stan Humphries	.40
7	Ki-Jana Carter	.75
8	Rashaan Salaam	.40
9	Rickey Dudley	.75
10	Isaac Bruce	1.00
11	Keyshawn Johnson	1.00
12	Ben Coates	.40
13	Ty Detmer	.40
14	Gus Frerotte	.40
15	Mario Bates	.40
16	Chris Calloway	.40
17	Frank Sanders	.40
18	Bruce Smith	.40
19	Jeff Graham	.40
20	Trent Dilfer	1.00
21	Tyrone Wheatley	.40
22	Chris Warren	.40
23	Terry Kirby	.40
24	*Tony Gonzalez*	5.00
25	Ricky Watters	.75
26	Tamarick Vanover	.40
27	Kerry Collins	2.00
28	Bobby Engram	.40
29	Derrick Alexander	.40
30	Hugh Douglas	.40
31	Thurman Thomas	.75
32	Drew Bledsoe	3.00
33	LeShon Johnson	.40
34	Byron Morris	.40
35	Herman Moore	1.00
36	Troy Aikman	3.00
37	Mel Gray	.40
38	Adrian Murrell	.75
39	Carl Pickens	.40
40	Tony Brackens	.40
41	O.J. McDuffie	.40
42	Napoleon Kaufman	1.00
43	Chris T. Jones	.40
44	Kordell Stewart	3.00
45	Steve Young	2.00
46	Shannon Sharpe	.40
47	Leeland McElroy	.40
48	Eric Moulds	.40
49	Eddie George	4.00
50	Jamal Anderson	.75
51	Robert Smith	.75
52	Mike Alstott	1.50
53	Darrell Green	.40
54	Irving Fryar	.40
55	Derrick Thomas	.40
56	Antonio Freeman	1.00
57	Terrell Davis	3.00
58	Henry Ellard	.40
59	Daryl Johnston	.40
60	Bryan Cox	.40
61	Vinny Testaverde	.40
62	Andre Reed	.40
63	Larry Centers	.40
64	Hardy Nickerson	.40
65	Tony Banks	1.50
66	David Meggett	.40
67	Simeon Rice	.40
68	*Warrick Dunn*	40.00
69	Michael Irvin	.75
70	John Elway	3.00
71	Jake Reed	.40
72	Rodney Hampton	.40
73	Aaron Glenn	.40
74	Terry Allen	.40
75	Blaine Bishop	.40
76	Bert Emanuel	.40
77	Mark Carrier	.40
78	Jimmy Smith	.40
79	Jim Harbaugh	.40
80	Brent Jones	.40
81	Emmitt Smith	5.00
82	Fred Barnett	.40
83	Errict Rhett	.40
84	Michael Sinclair	.40
85	Jerome Bettis	1.00
86	Chris Sanders	.40
87	Kent Graham	.40
88	Cris Carter	.40
89	Harvey Williams	.40
90	Eric Allen	.40
91	Bryant Young	.40
92	Marcus Allen	1.00
93	Michael Jackson	.40
94	Mark Chmura	.75
95	Keenan McCardell	.40
96	Joey Galloway	1.00
97	Eddie Kennison	1.00
98	Steve Atwater	.40
99	Dorsey Levens	1.00
100	Rob Moore	.40
101	Steve McNair	3.00
102	Sean Dawkins	.40
103	Don Beebe	.40
104	Willie McGinest	.40
105	Tony Martin	.40
106	Mark Brunell	3.00
107	Karim Abdul-Jabbar	1.00
108	Michael Westbrook	.40
109	Lawrence Phillips	.75
110	Barry Sanders	6.00
111	Willie Davis	.40
112	Wesley Walls	.40
113	Todd Collins	.40
114	Jerry Rice	3.00
115	Scott Mitchell	.40
116	Terance Mathis	.40
117	Chris Spielman	.40
118	Curtis Conway	.40
119	Marvin Harrison	1.00
120	Terry Glenn	2.00
121	Dave Brown	.40
122	Neil O'Donnell	.40
123	Junior Seau	.75
124	Reggie White	.75
125	Lamar Lathon	.40
126	Natrone Means	.75
127	Tim Brown	.40
128	Eric Swann	.40
129	Dan Marino	6.00
130	Anthony Johnson	.40
131	Edgar Bennett	.40
132	Kevin Hardy	.40
133	Brian Blades	.40
134	Curtis Martin	3.00
135	Zach Thomas	.75
136	Darnay Scott	.40
137	Desmond Howard	.40
138	Aeneas Williams	.40
139	Bryce Paup	.40
140	Brad Johnson	.75
141	Jeff Blake	1.00
142	Wayne Chrebet	.40
143	*Will Blackwell*	2.00
144	*Tom Knight*	1.00
145	*Darnell Autry*	2.00
146	*Bryant Westbrook*	2.00
147	*David LaFleur*	5.00
148	*Antowain Smith*	20.00
149	*Rae Carruth*	8.00
150	*Jim Druckenmiller*	15.00
151	*Shawn Springs*	1.00
152	*Troy Davis*	3.00
153	*Orlando Pace*	2.00
154	*Byron Hanspard*	5.00
155	*Corey Dillon*	30.00
156	*Reidel Anthony*	10.00
157	*Peter Boulware*	2.00
158	*Reinard Wilson*	1.00
159	*Pat Barnes*	3.00
160	*Joey Kent*	2.00
161	*Ike Hilliard*	8.00
162	*Jake Plummer*	40.00
163	*Darrell Russell*	1.00
164	Checklist 1	.40
165	Checklist 2	.40

1997 Topps Chrome Refractors

Refractors are a parallel of the Topps Chrome base set. They were inserted one per 12 packs.

		MT
Complete Set (165):		2400.
Common Player:		4.00
Common Player (143-163):		6.00
1	Brett Favre	90.00
2	Tim Biakabutuka	4.00
3	Deion Sanders	20.00
4	Marshall Faulk	8.00
5	John Randle	4.00
6	Stan Humphries	4.00
7	Ki-Jana Carter	8.00
8	Rashaan Salaam	4.00
9	Rickey Dudley	8.00
10	Isaac Bruce	8.00
11	Keyshawn Johnson	8.00
12	Ben Coates	4.00
13	Ty Detmer	4.00
14	Gus Frerotte	4.00
15	Mario Bates	4.00
16	Chris Calloway	4.00
17	Frank Sanders	4.00
18	Bruce Smith	4.00
19	Jeff Graham	4.00
20	Trent Dilfer	8.00
21	Tyrone Wheatley	4.00
22	Chris Warren	4.00
23	Terry Kirby	4.00
24	*Tony Gonzalez*	25.00
25	Ricky Watters	8.00
26	Tamarick Vanover	4.00
27	Kerry Collins	8.00
28	Bobby Engram	4.00
29	Derrick Alexander	4.00
30	Hugh Douglas	4.00
31	Thurman Thomas	8.00
32	Drew Bledsoe	45.00
33	LeShon Johnson	4.00
34	Byron Morris	4.00
35	Herman Moore	8.00
36	Troy Aikman	45.00
37	Mel Gray	4.00
38	Adrian Murrell	8.00
39	Carl Pickens	4.00
40	Tony Brackens	4.00
41	O.J. McDuffie	4.00
42	Napoleon Kaufman	15.00
43	Chris T. Jones	4.00
44	Kordell Stewart	40.00
45	Steve Young	30.00
46	Shannon Sharpe	4.00
47	Leeland McElroy	4.00
48	Eric Moulds	4.00
49	Eddie George	50.00
50	Jamal Anderson	8.00
51	Robert Smith	8.00
52	Mike Alstott	20.00
53	Darrell Green	4.00
54	Irving Fryar	4.00
55	Derrick Thomas	4.00
56	Antonio Freeman	20.00
57	Terrell Davis	50.00
58	Henry Ellard	4.00
59	Daryl Johnston	4.00
60	Bryan Cox	4.00
61	Vinny Testaverde	4.00
62	Andre Reed	4.00
63	Larry Centers	4.00
64	Hardy Nickerson	4.00
65	Tony Banks	8.00
66	David Meggett	4.00
67	Simeon Rice	4.00
68	*Warrick Dunn*	200.00
69	Michael Irvin	8.00
70	John Elway	45.00
71	Jake Reed	4.00
72	Rodney Hampton	4.00
73	Aaron Glenn	4.00
74	Terry Allen	4.00
75	Blaine Bishop	4.00
76	Bert Emanuel	4.00
77	Mark Carrier	4.00
78	Jimmy Smith	4.00
79	Jim Harbaugh	4.00
80	Brent Jones	4.00
81	Emmitt Smith	75.00
82	Fred Barnett	4.00
83	Errict Rhett	4.00
84	Michael Sinclair	4.00
85	Jerome Bettis	8.00
86	Chris Sanders	4.00
87	Kent Graham	4.00
88	Cris Carter	4.00
89	Harvey Williams	4.00
90	Eric Allen	4.00
91	Bryant Young	4.00
92	Marcus Allen	8.00
93	Michael Jackson	4.00
94	Mark Chmura	8.00
95	Keenan McCardell	4.00
96	Joey Galloway	8.00
97	Eddie Kennison	8.00
98	Steve Atwater	4.00
99	Dorsey Levens	8.00
100	Rob Moore	4.00
101	Steve McNair	25.00
102	Sean Dawkins	4.00
103	Don Beebe	4.00
104	Willie McGinest	4.00
105	Tony Martin	4.00
106	Mark Brunell	40.00
107	Karim Abdul-Jabbar	8.00
108	Michael Westbrook	4.00
109	Lawrence Phillips	4.00
110	Barry Sanders	90.00
111	Willie Davis	4.00
112	Wesley Walls	4.00
113	Todd Collins	4.00
114	Jerry Rice	45.00
115	Scott Mitchell	4.00
116	Terance Mathis	4.00
117	Chris Spielman	4.00
118	Curtis Conway	4.00
119	Marvin Harrison	8.00
120	Terry Glenn	10.00
121	Dave Brown	4.00
122	Neil O'Donnell	4.00
123	Junior Seau	8.00
124	Reggie White	8.00
125	Lamar Lathon	4.00
126	Natrone Means	8.00
127	Tim Brown	4.00
128	Eric Swann	4.00
129	Dan Marino	75.00
130	Anthony Johnson	4.00
131	Edgar Bennett	4.00
132	Kevin Hardy	4.00
133	Brian Blades	4.00
134	Curtis Martin	25.00
135	Zach Thomas	8.00
136	Darnay Scott	4.00
137	Desmond Howard	4.00
138	Aeneas Williams	4.00
139	Bryce Paup	4.00
140	Brad Johnson	8.00
141	Jeff Blake	8.00
142	Wayne Chrebet	4.00
143	Will Blackwell	8.00
144	Tom Knight	6.00
145	Darnell Autry	8.00
146	Bryant Westbrook	8.00
147	David LaFleur	20.00
148	Antowain Smith	100.00
149	Rae Carruth	35.00
150	Jim Druckenmiller	70.00
151	Shawn Springs	6.00
152	Troy Davis	12.00
153	Orlando Pace	10.00
154	Byron Hanspard	30.00
155	Corey Dillon	175.00

156	Reidel Anthony	50.00
157	Peter Boulware	6.00
158	Reinard Wilson	6.00
159	Pat Barnes	10.00
160	Joey Kent	6.00
161	Ike Hilliard	30.00
162	Jake Plummer	200.00
163	Darrell Russell	6.00
164	Checklist 1	4.00
165	Checklist 2	4.00

1997 Topps Chrome Career Best

This five-card set was reprinted from Topps with chromium technology added and randomly inserted into packs. Refractor versions also exist, but no insert rates were given for either.

		MT
Complete Set (5):		60.00
Common Player:		10.00
Refractors:		2x
1	Dan Marino	30.00
2	Marcus Allen	10.00
3	Marcus Allen	10.00
4	Reggie White	10.00
5	Jerry Rice	15.00

1997 Topps Chrome Draft Year

Draft Year is a 15-card insert highlighting two players from the last 15 draft classes. Each side features one of the best players to emerge from that particular draft. Draft Year was inserted 1:48. The Refractor versions were found once in every 144 packs.

		MT
Complete Set (15):		250.00
Common Player:		5.00
Refractors:		2x
DR1	Dan Marino, John Elway (1983)	40.00
DR2	Reggie White, Steve Young (1984)	15.00
DR3	Bruce Smith, Jerry Rice (1985)	20.00
DR4	Ronnie Harmon, Pat Swilling (1986)	5.00
DR5	Jim Harbaugh, Vinny Testaverde (1987)	5.00
DR6	Michael Irvin, Tim Brown (1988)	10.00
DR7	Troy Aikman, Barry Sanders (1989)	30.00
DR8	Emmitt Smith, Junior Seau (1990)	40.00
DR9	Brett Favre, Ricky Watters (1991)	45.00
DR10	Carl Pickens, Desmond Howard (1992)	5.00
DR11	Mark Brunell, Drew Bledsoe (1993)	30.00
DR12	Marshall Faulk, Isaac Bruce (1994)	10.00
DR13	Terrell Davis, Curtis Martin (1995)	30.00
DR14	Eddie George, Terry Glenn (1996)	35.00
DR15	Ike Hilliard, Shawn Springs (1997)	15.00

1997 Topps Chrome Season's Best

The 25-card Season's Best insert has five different subsets. Each of the five subsets consists of five cards fea-

turing the season's top performers. Air Command features top quarterbacks, Thunder & Lightning has the top rushers, Magicians showcases the top total yardage gainers, Demolition Men highlights the top sack artists and Special Delivery has the top wide receivers. There are also five Career best cards for each category. Season's Best was inserted 1:12 with Refractors found 1:36.

		MT
Complete Set (25):		80.00
Common Player:		1.00
Refractors:		2x-3x
1	Mark Brunell (Air Command)	10.00
2	Vinny Testaverde (Air Command)	1.00
3	Drew Bledsoe (Air Command)	10.00
4	Brett Favre (Air Command)	20.00
5	Jeff Blake (Air Command)	2.00
6	Barry Sanders (Thunder & Lightning)	12.00
7	Terrell Davis (Thunder & Lightning)	10.00
8	Jerome Bettis (Thunder & Lightning)	2.00
9	Ricky Watters (Thunder & Lightning)	2.00
10	Eddie George (Thunder & Lightning)	15.00
11	Brian Mitchell (Magicians)	1.00
12	Tyrone Hughes (Magicians)	1.00
13	Eric Metcalf (Magicians)	1.00
14	Glyn Milburn (Magicians)	1.00
15	Ricky Watters (Magicians)	2.00
16	Kevin Greene (Demolition Men)	1.00
17	Lamar Lathon (Demolition Men)	1.00
18	Bruce Smith (Demolition Men)	1.00
19	Michael Sinclair (Demolition Men)	1.00
20	Derrick Thomas (Demolition Men)	1.00
21	Jerry Rice (Special Delivery)	10.00
22	Herman Moore (Special Delivery)	4.00
23	Carl Pickens (Special Delivery)	1.00
24	Cris Carter (Special Delivery)	1.00
25	Brett Perriman (Special Delivery)	1.00

1997 Topps Chrome Underclassmen

Underclassmen is a 10-card insert highlighting the top second and third year players. The set is inserted 1:8, with Refractor versions found 1:36.

		MT
Complete Set (10):		50.00
Common Player:		2.00
Refractors:		2x-3x
U1	Kerry Collins	8.00
U2	Karim Abdul-Jabbar	5.00
U3	Simeon Rice	2.00
U4	Keyshawn Johnson	3.00
U5	Eddie George	14.00
U6	Eddie Kennison	4.00
U7	Terry Glenn	6.00
U8	Kevin Hardy	2.00
U9	Steve McNair	8.00
U10	Kordell Stewart	10.00

1997 Topps Gallery

This 135-card base set features top player photos framed by a foil design. The Players Private Issue parallel set includes foil stamping and was inserted 1:12. Insert sets included Photo Gallery, Gallery of Heroes, Critics Choice and Peter Max Serigraphs.

		MT
Complete Set (135):		55.00
Common Player:		.20
Wax Box:		60.00
1	Orlando Pace	.50
2	Darrell Russell	.20
3	Shawn Springs	.50
4	Peter Boulware	.20
5	Bryant Westbrook	.40
6	Walter Jones	.20
7	Ike Hilliard	2.00
8	James Farrior	.20
9	Tom Knight	.20
10	Warrick Dunn	8.00
11	Tony Gonzalez	2.00
12	Reinard Wilson	.20
13	Yatil Green	1.00
14	Reidel Anthony	3.00
15	Kenny Holmes	.20
16	Dwayne Rudd	.20
17	Renaldo Wynn	.20
18	David LaFleur	1.50
19	Antowain Smith	4.00
20	Jim Druckenmiller	4.00
21	Rae Carruth	2.00
22	Byron Hanspard	1.00
23	Jake Plummer	8.00
24	Corey Dillon	6.00
25	Darnell Autry	.50
26	Kevin Lockett	.20
27	Troy Davis	.75
28	Mike Alstott	.40
29	Napoleon Kaufman	.40
30	Terrell Davis	2.50
31	Byron Morris	.20
32	Dana Stubblefield	.20
33	Ki-Jana Carter	.40
34	Hugh Douglas	.20
35	Natrone Means	.40
36	Marshall Faulk	.40
37	Tyrone Wheatley	.20
38	Tony Banks	1.50
39	Marvin Harrison	1.50
40	Eddie George	3.50
41	Eddie Kennison	1.50
42	Ray Mickens	.20
43	Mike Mamula	.20
44	Tamarick Vanover	.20
45	Rashaan Salaam	.40
46	Trent Dilfer	.40
47	John Mobley	.20
48	Gus Frerotte	.20
49	Isaac Bruce	.50
50	Mark Brunell	2.50
51	Jamal Anderson	.40
52	Keyshawn Johnson	1.50
53	Curtis Conway	.40
54	Zach Thomas	.75
55	Simeon Rice	.20
56	Lawrence Phillips	.40
57	Ty Detmer	.20
58	Bobby Engram	.20
59	Joey Galloway	.75
60	Curtis Martin	2.50
61	Kevin Hardy	.20
62	Eric Moulds	.20
63	Michael Westbrook	.20
64	Robert Smith	.20
65	Karim Abdul-Jabbar	1.75
66	Errict Rhett	.40
67	Ray Lewis	.20
68	Terry Glenn	2.25
69	Leeland McElroy	.20
70	Kerry Collins	2.00
71	Steve McNair	2.00
72	Kordell Stewart	2.00
73	Terry Allen	.20
74	Michael Irvin	.40
75	John Elway	1.50
76	Lamar Lathon	.20
77	Rob Moore	.20
78	Irving Fryar	.20
79	Jim Everett	.20
80	Steve Young	1.50
81	Bryan Cox	.20
82	Dale Carter	.20
83	Chris Warren	.20
84	Shannon Sharpe	.20
85	Reggie White	.40
86	Deion Sanders	1.00
87	Hardy Nickerson	.20
88	Edgar Bennett	.20
89	Kent Graham	.20
90	Dan Marino	4.00
91	Kevin Greene	.20
92	Derrick Thomas	.20
93	Carl Pickens	.20
94	Neil O'Donnell	.20
95	Drew Bledsoe	2.50
96	Michael Haynes	.20
97	Tony Martin	.20
98	Scott Mitchell	.20
99	Rodney Hampton	.20
100	Brett Favre	5.00
101	Darrell Green	.20
102	Rod Woodson	.20
103	Chris Spielman	.20
104	Jake Reed	.20
105	Jerry Rice	2.50
106	Jeff Hostetler	.20
107	Anthony Johnson	.20
108	Keenan McCardell	.20
109	Ben Coates	.20
110	Emmitt Smith	4.00
111	LeRoy Butler	.20
112	Steve Atwater	.20
113	Ricky Watters	.40
114	Jim Harbaugh	.20
115	Marcus Allen	.40
116	Levon Kirkland	.20
117	Jessie Tuggle	.20
118	Ken Norton	.20
119	Thurman Thomas	.40
120	Junior Seau	.40
121	Tim Brown	.20
122	Michael Jackson	.20
123	Eric Metcalf	.20
124	Herman Moore	.40
125	Bruce Smith	.20
126	Cris Carter	.20
127	Dave Brown	.20
128	Jeff Blake	.40
129	Robert Blackmon	.20
130	Barry Sanders	2.50
131	Blaine Bishop	.20
132	Jerome Bettis	.40
133	Stan Humphries	.20
134	Vinny Testaverde	.20
135	Troy Aikman	2.50

1997 Topps Gallery Player's Private Issue

Player's Private Issue was a 135-card parallel set to Gallery. Cards were inserted one per 12 packs and featured black strips down each side and a Player's Private Issue logo.

	MT
Private Issue Cards:	20x-40x
Private Issue Rookies:	10x-20x
Inserted 1:12	

1997 Topps Gallery Critics Choice

Critics Choice is a 20-card insert featuring player action shots. The cards were inserted 1:24.

		MT
Complete Set (20):		230.00
Common Player:		4.00
CC1	Barry Sanders	25.00
CC2	Jeff Blake	4.00
CC3	Vinny Testaverde	4.00
CC4	Ricky Watters	4.00
CC5	John Elway	15.00
CC6	Drew Bledsoe	20.00
CC7	Kordell Stewart	20.00
CC8	Mark Brunell	20.00
CC9	Troy Aikman	20.00
CC10	Brett Favre	40.00
CC11	Kevin Hardy	4.00
CC12	Shannon Sharpe	4.00
CC13	Emmitt Smith	35.00
CC14	Rob Moore	4.00
CC15	Eddie George	30.00
CC16	Herman Moore	4.00
CC17	Terry Glenn	15.00
CC18	Jim Harbaugh	4.00
CC19	Terrell Davis	20.00
CC20	Junior Seau	4.00

1997 Topps Gallery Gallery of Heroes

This 15-card insert features a player shot on a transparent, luminous card that looks like a stained glass window. They were inserted 1:36.

		MT
Complete Set (15):		240.00
Common Player:		12.00
GH1	Desmond Howard	12.00
GH2	Marcus Allen	12.00
GH3	Kerry Collins	20.00
GH4	Troy Aikman	25.00
GH5	Jerry Rice	25.00
GH6	Drew Bledsoe	25.00
GH7	John Elway	18.00
GH8	Mark Brunell	25.00
GH9	Junior Seau	12.00
GH10	Brett Favre	45.00
GH11	Dan Marino	40.00
GH12	Barry Sanders	30.00
GH13	Reggie White	12.00
GH14	Emmitt Smith	40.00
GH15	Steve Young	18.00

1997 Topps Gallery Peter Max

This 10-card insert combines player pictures with colorful art. This insert can be found 1:24. A limited number of the cards were autographed by the artist, Peter Nax.

in the upper left. The player's name is written in script at the bottom center, while the team and his position are printed beneath the name. The backs include two photos, with his name, bio and stats beginning in the center and continuing to the bottom. The Gold Medallion parallel cards were inserted one per pack, while the Platinum Medallion parallel cards were exclusive in hobby packs and found 1:100 packs. Inserts in Series I include Blitzkrieg, Play of the Game, Rookies, Starring Role, Sunday School and Talent Show. Inserts in Series II include First Rounders, Rising Stars, Specialists, Comeback Kids, The Main Event, Ultra All-Rookie Team, Ultra Specialists, Ultra Stars, Million Dollar Moments, Memorabilia Offer Card, Lucky 13 Redemption Cards and REEBOK Chase Promotion.

	MT
Complete Set (10):	125.00
Common Player:	4.00
Autographs:	10x-20x
PM1 Brett Favre	25.00
PM2 Jerry Rice	15.00
PM3 Emmitt Smith	20.00
PM4 John Elway	10.00
PM5 Barry Sanders	18.00
PM6 Reggie White	4.00
PM7 Steve Young	10.00
PM8 Troy Aikman	15.00
PM9 Drew Bledsoe	15.00
PM10 Dan Marino	20.00

1997 Topps Gallery Photo Gallery

Photo Gallery features top players and double foil stamping. The 15-card set was inserted 1:24.

	MT
Complete Set (15):	200.00
Common Player:	3.00
PG1 Eddie George	25.00
PG2 Drew Bledsoe	20.00
PG3 Brett Favre	35.00
PG4 Emmitt Smith	30.00
PG5 Dan Marino	30.00
PG6 Terrell Davis	20.00
PG7 Kevin Greene	3.00
PG8 Troy Aikman	20.00
PG9 Curtis Martin	20.00
PG10 Barry Sanders	20.00
PG11 Junior Seau	3.00
PG12 Deion Sanders	10.00
PG13 Steve Young	15.00
PG14 Reggie White	3.00
PG15 Jerry Rice	20.00

1997 Ultra

The 350-card set featured 346 cards and four checklists. The fronts showcase a full-bleed photo with the Ultra logo

	MT
Complete Series 2 (150):	20.00
Common Player:	.10
Series 2 Wax Box:	55.00
201 Rick Mirer	.10
202 Torrance Small	.10
203 Ricky Proehl	.10
204 Will Blackwell	.30
205 Warrick Dunn	2.50
206 Rob Johnson	.20
207 Jim Schwantz	.10
208 Ike Hilliard	1.00
209 Chris Canty	.10
210 Chris Boniol	.10
211 Jim Druckenmiller	1.50
212 Tony Gonzalez	1.00
213 Scottie Graham	.10
214 Byron Hanspard	1.00
215 Gary Brown	.10
216 Darrell Russell	.10
217 Sedrick Shaw	.50
218 Boomer Esiason	.10
219 Peter Boulware	.10
220 Willie Green	.10
221 Dietrich Jells	.10
222 Freddie Jones	.30
223 Eric Metcalf	.10
224 John Henry Mills	.10
225 Michael Timpson	.10
226 Danny Wuerffel	1.00
227 Daimon Shelton	.10
228 Henry Ellard	.10
229 Flipper Anderson	.10
230 Hunter Goodwin	.10
231 Jay Graham	.50
232 Duce Staley	.10
233 Lamar Thomas	.10
234 Rod Woodson	.10
235 Zack Crockett	.10
236 Ernie Mills	.10
237 Kyle Brady	.10
238 Jesse Campbell	.10
239 Anthony Miller	.10
240 Michael Haynes	.10
241 Qadry Ismail	.10
242 Tom Knight	.10
243 Brian Manning	.10
244 Derrick Mayes	.10
245 Jamie Sharper	.10
246 Sherman Williams	.10
247 Yatil Green	1.00
248 Howard Griffith	.10
249 Brian Blades	.10
250 Mark Chmura	.20
251 Chris Darkins	.10
252 Willie Davis	.10
253 Quinn Early	.10
254 Marc Edwards	.10
255 Charlie Jones	.10
256 Jake Plummer	1.00
257 Heath Shuler	.10
258 Fred Barnett	.10
259 Koy Detmer	.20
260 Michael Booker	.10
261 Chad Brown	.10
262 Garrison Hearst	.20
263 Leon Johnson	.10
264 Antowain Smith	2.00
265 Darnell Autry	1.00
266 Craig Heyward	.10
267 Walter Jones	.10
268 Dexter Coakley	.30
269 Mercury Hayes	.10
270 Brett Perriman	.10
271 Chris Spielman	.10
272 Kevin Greene	.10
273 Kevin Lockett	.10
274 Troy Davis	.75
275 Brent Jones	.10
276 Chris Chandler	.10
277 Bryant Westbrook	.20
278 Desmond Howard	.10
279 Tyrone Hughes	.10
280 Kez McCorvey	.10

281	Stephen Davis	.10
282	Steve Everitt	.10
283	Andre Hastings	.10
284	Marcus Robinson	.10
285	Donnell Woolford	.10
286	Mario Bates	.10
287	Corey Dillon	1.25
288	Jackie Harris	.10
289	Lorenzo Neal	.10
290	Anthony Pleasant	.10
291	Andre Rison	.10
292	Amani Toomer	.10
293	Eric Turner	.10
294	Elvis Grbac	.10
295	Cris Dishman	.10
296	Tom Carter	.10
297	Mark Carrier	.20
298	Orlando Pace	.10
299	Jay Riemersma	.10
300	Daryl Johnston	.10
301	Joey Kent	.30
302	Ronnie Harmon	.10
303	Raghib Ismail	.10
304	Terrell Davis	1.25
305	Sean Dawkins	.10
306	Jeff George	.20
307	David Palmer	.10
308	Dwayne Rudd	.10
309	J.J. Stokes	.20
310	James Farrior	.10
311	William Fuller	.10
312	George Jones	.20
313	John Allred	.10
314	Tony Graziani	.10
315	Jeff Hostetler	.10
316	Keith Poole	.10
317	Neil Smith	.10
318	Steve Tasker	.10
319	Mike Vrabel	.10
320	Pat Barnes	.75
321	James Hundon	.10
322	O.J. Santiago	.10
323	Billy Davis	.10
324	Shawn Springs	.20
325	Reinard Wilson	.10
326	Charles Johnson	.10
327	Michael Barrow	.10
328	Derrick Mason	.10
329	Muhsin Muhammad	.10
330	David LaFleur	.75
331	Reidel Anthony	.75
332	Tiki Barber	1.00
333	Ray Buchanan	.10
334	John Elway	.75
335	Alvin Harper	.10
336	Damon Jones	.10
337	Dedric Ward	.10
338	Jim Everett	.10
339	Jon Harris	.10
340	Warren Moon	.10
341	Rae Carruth	.75
342	John Mobley	.10
343	Tyrone Poole	.10
344	Mike Cherry	.10
345	Horace Copeland	.10
346	Deon Figures	.10
347	Antowuan Wyatt	.10
348	Tommy Vardell	.10
349	Checklist	.10
350	Checklist	.10

1997 Ultra Gold

Gold Medallions ran parallel to the Ultra Football set, and included 198 cards from Series I and 148 cards from Series II (the two checklist cards in each series were not issued in Gold Medallion versions). The foil on the front of the card was printed in gold versus the silver foil used on regular-issue cards. In addition, the words "Gold Medallion Edition" were printed across the front bottom right of the card, while card backs carried a "G" prefix on the card number. Gold Medallion parallels were issued at a rate of one per pack in both Series.

	MT
Gold Stars:	2x-4x
Gold Rookies:	2x

1997 Ultra Platinum

Platinum Medallions were a parallel set to the Ultra Football set and included 198 cards from Series I and 148 from Series II (the two checklist cards in each series were not issued in Platinum Medallion versions). A prismatic foil is used on the front of the card versus the silver foil used on regular-issue cards. In addition, the words "Platinum Medallion Edition" were printed across the front bottom right of the cards, while card backs carried a "P" prefix on the card number. Platinum Medallion parallels were issued at a rate of one per 100 hobby packs in both Series.

	MT
Platinum Stars:	40x-80x
Platinum Rookies:	20x-40x

1997 Ultra All-Rookie Team

This 12-card insert features the top rookies of 1997. An action shot of the players is set on a golden plaque. The cards were inserted once per 18 packs in Series II.

		MT
Complete Set (12):		70.00
Common Player:		3.00
1	Antowain Smith	10.00
2	Jay Graham	3.00
3	Ike Hilliard	6.00
4	Warrick Dunn	18.00
5	Tony Gonzalez	3.00
6	David LaFleur	3.00
7	Reidel Anthony	8.00
8	Rae Carruth	6.00
9	Byron Hanspard	3.00
10	Joey Kent	3.00
11	Kevin Lockett	3.00
12	Jake Plummer	8.00

1997 Ultra Comeback Kids

Comeback Kids contains 10 cards featuring the NFL's top go-to players. The cards

are designed as die-cut wanted posters. They were inserted 1:8 in Series II.

		MT
Complete Set (10):		35.00
Common Player:		1.25
1	Dan Marino	10.00
2	Barry Sanders	7.00
3	Jerry Rice	5.00
4	John Elway	4.00
5	Steve Young	3.00
6	Deion Sanders	2.00
7	Mark Brunell	5.00
8	Tim Biakabutuka	1.25
9	Tony Banks	2.00
10	Terry Allen	1.25

1997 Ultra First Rounders

This 12-card insert features first-round draft picks who made an immediate impression in 1997. The card fronts feature an action shot of the player against a gridiron background. The insertion rate was 1:4 in Series II.

		MT
Complete Set (12):		18.00
Common Player:		.50
1	Antowain Smith	3.00
2	Rae Carruth	2.00
3	Peter Boulware	.50
4	Shawn Springs	1.00
5	Bryant Westbrook	.50
6	Orlando Pace	1.00
7	Jim Druckenmiller	5.00
8	Yatil Green	2.00
9	Reidel Anthony	2.00
10	Ike Hilliard	2.00
11	Darrell Russell	.50
12	Warrick Dunn	6.00

1997 Ultra Reebok

The Reebok Chase Promotion consisted of parallel versions of 15 basic cards. The parallels featured a Reebok logo on the back and came in three tiers of scarcity (bronze, silver, and gold). The cards were inserted one per pack in Series II.

	MT
Complete Bronze Set (15):	3.00
Common Bronze Player:	.20
Gold Cards:	3x
Green Cards:	15x-30x
Red Cards:	8x-16x
Silver Cards:	1x
Torrance Small	.20
Jim Schwantz	.20

	Chris Boniol	.20
	Eric Metcalf	.20
	Jesse Campbell	.20
	Qadry Ismail	.20
	Brett Perriman	.20
	Chris Spielman	.20
	Desmond Howard	.20
	Steve Everitt	.20
	Lorenzo Neal	.20
	Neil Smith	.20
	Steve Tasker	.20
	John Elway	.75
	Tyrone Poole	.20

1997 Ultra Rising Stars

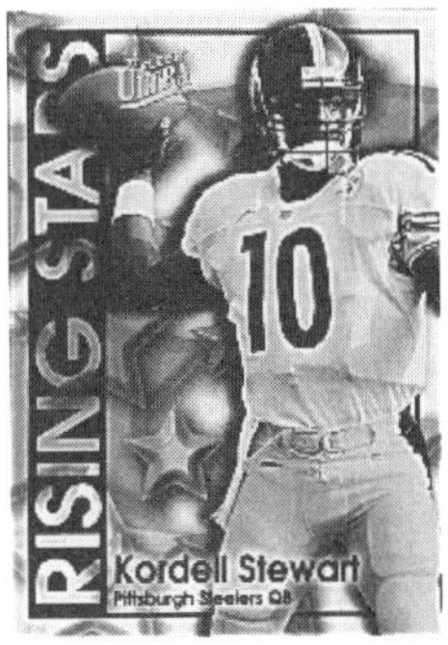

Rising Stars were inserted 1:4 in Series II. The 10 cards feature a soon-to-be star player. The front has an action shot with a star-filled background.

		MT
Complete Set (10):		10.00
Common Player:		.50
1	Keyshawn Johnson	1.00
2	Terrell Davis	3.00
3	Kordell Stewart	3.00
4	Kerry Collins	2.00
5	Joey Galloway	1.00
6	Steve McNair	2.00
7	Jamal Anderson	.50
8	Michael Westbrook	.50
9	Marshall Faulk	.50
10	Isaac Bruce	1.00

1997 Ultra Specialists

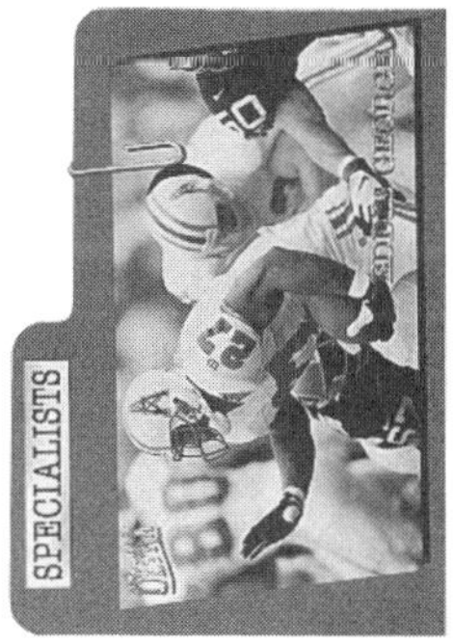

This 18-card insert features top players on a die-cut card that looks like a manilla file folder. The cards were inserted 1:6 in Series II. Ultra Specialists parallels the regular insert. Inserted 1:36, the die-cut folders open up to reveal an oversized photo. Ultra Specialists also appeared only in Series II.

		MT
Complete Set (18):		80.00
Common Player:		2.00
Ultra Specialists:		3x
1	Eddie George	8.00
2	Terry Glenn	4.00
3	Karim Abdul-Jabbar	3.00
4	Emmitt Smith	10.00
5	Brett Favre	12.00
6	Mark Brunell	6.00
7	Curtis Martin	6.00
8	Kerry Collins	4.00
9	Marvin Harrison	2.00
10	Jerry Rice	6.00
11	Tony Martin	2.00
12	Terrell Davis	6.00
13	Troy Aikman	6.00
14	Drew Bledsoe	6.00
15	John Elway	4.00
16	Kordell Stewart	6.00
17	Keyshawn Johnson	2.00
18	Steve Young	4.00

1997 Upper Deck Collector's Choice

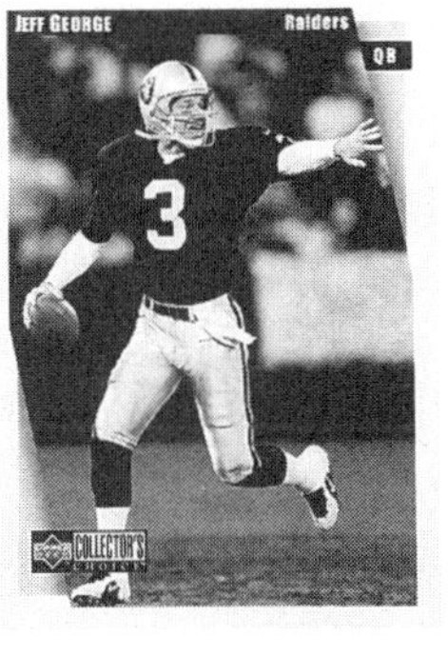

The 565-card set features white borders on the front. The player's name and team are printed inside a stripe at the top, while his position is located inside a rectangle at the upper right. The Collector's Choice logo is printed in the lower left of the front. The backs have a photo on the left, with the player's bio, "Did you know?" and stats along the right side. The cards feature a dual numbering system that helps collectors put players from their favorite team together. Series I also features a 45-card Rookie Class subset and a 40-card Names of the Game subset. Series II includes Checklist/Collector Info cards, 30 NFL Mini Standees and the StarQuest insert.

		MT
Complete Series 2 (255):		15.00
Common Player:		.05
Series 2 Wax Box:		40.00
311	Jim Druckenmiller	1.00
312	Greg Clark	.05
313	Darnell Autry	.30
314	Reinard Wilson	.05
315	Corey Dillon	1.50
316	Antowain Smith	.75
317	Trevor Pryce	.05
318	Warrick Dunn	1.75
319	Reidel Anthony	.75
320	Jake Plummer	1.75
321	Tom Knight	.05
322	Freddie Jones	.10
323	Tony Gonzalez	.30
324	Pat Barnes	.30
325	Kevin Lockett	.05
326	Tarik Glenn	.05
327	David LaFleur	.30
328	Antonio Anderson	.05
329	Yatil Green	.40
330	Jason Taylor	.05
331	Brian Manning	.05
332	Michael Booker	.05
333	Byron Hanspard	.40
334	Ike Hilliard	.40
335	Tiki Barber	.50
336	Renaldo Wynn	.05
337	Damon Jones	.05
338	James Farrior	.05
339	Dedric Ward	.05
340	Bryant Westbrook	.05
341	Matt Russell	.05
342	Joey Kent	.05
343	Kenny Holmes	.05
344	Darren Sharper	.05
345	Rae Carruth	.40
346	Chris Canty	.05
347	Darrell Russell	.05
348	Orlando Pace	.05
349	Peter Boulware	.05
350	*Danny Wuerffel*	.75
351	Troy Davis	.40
352	Shawn Springs	.05
353	Walter Jones	.05
354	Will Blackwell	.05
355	Dwayne Rudd	.05
356	Cardinals	.05
357	Falcons	.05
358	Ravens	.05
359	Bills	.05
360	Panthers	.05
361	Bears	.05
362	Bengals	.05
363	Cowboys	.05
364	Broncos	.05
365	Lions	.05
366	Packers	.05
367	Oilers	.05
368	Colts	.05
369	Jaguars	.05
370	Chiefs	.05
371	Dolphins	.05
372	Vikings	.05
373	Patriots	.05
374	Saints	.05
375	Jets	.05
376	Giants	.05
377	Raiders	.05
378	Eagles	.05
379	Steelers	.05
380	Chargers	.05
381	49ers	.05
382	Seahawks	.05
383	Rams	.05
384	Buccaneers	.05
385	Redskins	.05
386	William Floyd	.05
387	Steve Young	.75
388	Lee Woodall	.05
389	J.J. Stokes	.05
390	Marc Edwards	.05
391	Rod Woodson	.05
392	Jim Schwantz	.05
393	Garrison Hearst	.05
394	Rick Mirer	.05
395	Alonzo Spellman	.05
396	Tom Carter	.05
397	Bryan Cox	.05
398	John Allred	.05
399	Ricky Proehl	.05
400	Tyrone Hughes	.05
401	Carl Pickens	.05
402	Tremain Mack	.05
403	Boomer Esiason	.05
404	Ki-Jana Carter	.05
405	Steve Tovar	.05
406	Billy Joe Hobert	.05
407	Andre Reed	.05
408	Marcelius Wiley	.05
409	Steve Tasker	.05
410	Chris Spielman	.05
411	Alfred Williams	.05
412	John Elway	.75
413	Shannon Sharpe	.05
414	Steve Atwater	.05
415	Neil Smith	.05
416	Darrien Gordon	.05
417	Jeff Lewis	.05
418	Flipper Anderson	.05
419	Willie Green	.05
420	Jackie Harris	.05
421	Steve Walsh	.05
422	Anthony Parker	.05
423	Ronde Barber	.05
424	Warren Sapp	.05
425	Aeneas Williams	.05
426	Larry Centers	.05
427	Eric Swann	.05
428	Kevin Williams	.05
429	Darren Bennett	.05
430	Tony Martin	.05
431	John Carney	.05
432	Jim Everett	.05
433	William Fuller	.05
434	Latario Rachel	.05
435	Erric Pegram	.05
436	Eric Metcalf	.05
437	Jerome Woods	.05
438	Derrick Thomas	.05
439	Elvis Grbac	.05
440	Terry Wooden	.05
441	Andre Rison	.05
442	Brett Perriman	.05
443	Roosevelt Potts	.05
444	Robert Blackman	.05
445	Carlton Gray	.05
446	Chris Gardocki	.05
447	Marshall Faulk	.10
448	Sammie Burroughs	.05
449	Quentin Coryatt	.05
450	Troy Aikman	1.00
451	Daryl Johnston	.05
452	Tony Tolbert	.05
453	Brock Marion	.05
454	Billy Davis	.05
455	Dexter Coakley	.05
456	Anthony Miller	.05
457	Dan Marino	2.00
458	Jerris McPhail	.05
459	Terrell Buckley	.05
460	Daryl Gardener	.05
461	George Teague	.05
462	Qadry Ismail	.05
463	Fred Barnett	.05
464	Darrin Smith	.05
465	Michael Timpson	.05
466	Jon Harris	.05
467	Jason Dunn	.05
468	Bobby Hoying	.05
469	Ricky Watters	.10
470	Derrick Witherspoon	.05
471	Chris Chandler	.05
472	Ray Buchanan	.05
473	Michael Haynes	.05
474	Nathan Davis	.05
475	Morten Andersen	.05
476	Bert Emanuel	.05
477	Chris Calloway	.05
478	Jason Sehorn	.05
479	John Jurkovic	.05
480	Keenan McCardell	.05
481	James O. Stewart	.05
482	Rob Johnson	.05
483	Mike Logan	.05
484	Deon Figures	.05
485	Kyle Brady	.05
486	Alex Van Dyke	.05
487	Jeff Graham	.05
488	Jason Hanson	.05
489	Herman Moore	.10
490	Scott Mitchell	.05
491	Tommy Vardell	.05
492	Derrick Mason	.05
493	Rodney Thomas	.05
494	Ronnie Harmon	.05
495	Eddie George	1.50
496	Edgar Bennett	.05
497	William Henderson	.05
498	Dorsey Levens	.10
499	Gilbert Brown	.05
500	Steve Bono	.05
501	Derrick Mayes	.05
502	*Fred Lane*	.50
503	Ernie Mills	.05
504	Tshimanga Biakabutuka	.05
505	Michael Bates	.05
506	Winslow Oliver	.05
507	Ty Law	.05
508	Shawn Jefferson	.05
509	Vincent Brisby	.05
510	Henry Thomas	.05
511	Tedy Bruschi	.05
512	Curtis Martin	.75
513	Jeff George	.05
514	Desmond Howard	.05
515	Napoleon Kaufman	.10
516	Kenny Shedd	.05
517	Russell Maryland	.05
518	Lance Johnstone	.05
519	Chad Levitt	.05
520	Dexter McLeon	.05
521	Craig Heyward	.05
522	Ryan McNeil	.05
523	Mark Rypien	.05
524	Mike Jones	.05
525	Jamie Sharper	.05
526	Tony Siragusa	.05
527	Michael Jackson	.05
528	Floyd Turner	.05
529	Eric Green	.05
530	Michael McCrary	.05
531	Jay Graham	.05
532	Terry Allen	.05
533	Sean Gilbert	.05
534	Scott Turner	.05
535	Cris Dishman	.05
536	Jeff Hostetler	.05
537	Chris Mims	.05
538	Alvin Harper	.05
539	Daryl Hobbs	.05
540	Wayne Martin	.05
541	Heath Shuler	.05
542	Andre Hastings	.05
543	Jared Tomich	.05
544	Nicky Savoie	.05
545	Cortez Kennedy	.05
546	Warren Moon	.05
547	Chad Brown	.05
548	Willie Williams	.05
549	Bennie Blades	.05
550	Darren Perry	.05
551	Mark Bruener	.05
552	Yancey Thigpen	.05
553	Courtney Hawkins	.05
554	Chad Scott	.05
555	George Jones	.05
556	Robert Tate	.05
557	Torrian Gray	.05
558	Robert Griffith	.05
559	Leroy Hoard	.05
560	Robert Smith	.05
561	Randall Cunningham	.05
562	Darrell Russell CL	.05
563	Troy Aikman CL	.25
564	Dan Marino CL	.40
565	Jim Druckenmiller CL	.25

1997 Upper Deck Collector's Choice Mini-Standee

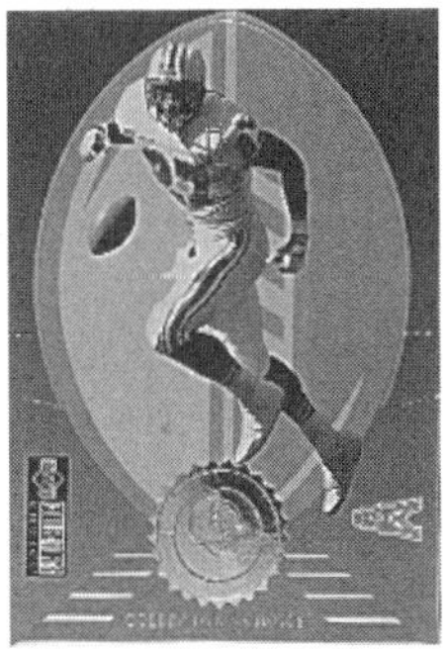

Inserted 1:5, the 30-card Mini Standee insert appeared in Series II. The cards can be folded into a football shaped stand up card.

		MT
Complete Set (30):		25.00
Common Player:		.25
ST1	Jerry Rice	1.50
ST2	Rashaan Salaam	.25
ST3	Jeff Blake	.50
ST4	Antowain Smith	1.25
ST5	John Elway	1.25
ST6	Errict Rhett	.25
ST7	Jake Plummer	1.25
ST8	Junior Seau	.25
ST9	Marcus Allen	.50
ST10	Marvin Harrison	.50
ST11	Emmitt Smith	3.00
ST12	Dan Marino	3.00
ST13	Ricky Watters	.50
ST14	Jamal Anderson	.25
ST15	Rodney Hampton	.25
ST16	Mark Brunell	1.50
ST17	Keyshawn Johnson	.50
ST18	Barry Sanders	2.00
ST19	Eddie George	2.00
ST20	Brett Favre	3.50
ST21	Kerry Collins	1.00
ST22	Drew Bledsoe	1.50
ST23	Napoleon Kaufman	.50
ST24	Tony Banks	.50
ST25	Vinny Testaverde	.25
ST26	Terry Allen	.25
ST27	Mario Bates	.25
ST28	Joey Galloway	.50
ST29	Jerome Bettis	.50
ST30	Robert Smith	.25

1997 Upper Deck Collector's Choice Star Quest

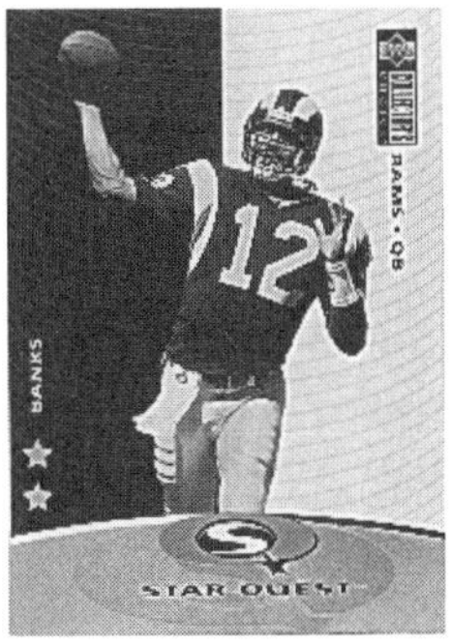

StarQuest is a four-tiered insert available in Series II. The tiers are indicated by the number of stars on the card - one per tier. Tier one includes 45 cards and were inserted 1:1. Tier two includes 20 cards inserted 1:21. The 15 tier three cards were inserted 1:71. TIer four had 10 cards and was inserted 1:145. The insert totaled 90 cards, featuring the top players in the game.

		MT
Complete Set (90):		500.00
Common Player (1-45):		.25
Common Player (46-65):		2.00
Common Player (66-80):		5.00
Common Player (81-90):		10.00
SQ1	Frank Sanders	.25
SQ2	Jamal Anderson	.50
SQ3	Bam Morris	.25
SQ4	Thurman Thomas	.50
SQ5	Muhsin Muhammad	.25
SQ6	Bobby Engram	.25
SQ7	Carl Pickens	.25
SQ8	Deion Sanders	.75
SQ9	Shannon Sharpe	.25
SQ10	Herman Moore	.50
SQ11	Robert Brooks	.25
SQ12	Steve McNair	1.50
SQ13	Marshall Faulk	.50
SQ14	Keenan McCardell	.25
SQ15	Tamarick Vanover	.25
SQ16	Fred Barnett	.25
SQ17	Orlanda Thomas	.25
SQ18	Drew Bledsoe	1.50
SQ19	Mario Bates	.25
SQ20	Keyshawn Johnson	.50
SQ21	Rodney Hampton	.25
SQ22	Darrell Russell	.25
SQ23	Irving Fryar	.25
SQ24	Charles Johnson	.25
SQ25	Stan Humphries	.25

SQ26	Terrell Owens	.50
SQ27	Chris Warren	.25
SQ28	Isaac Bruce	.50
SQ29	Warrick Dunn	2.50
SQ30	Gus Frerotte	.25
SQ31	Raghib Ismail	.25
SQ32	Natrone Means	.50
SQ33	Chris Sanders	.25
SQ34	Vinny Testaverde	.25
SQ35	Ken Norton	.25
SQ36	Kevin Greene	.25
SQ37	Marcus Allen	.50
SQ38	Zach Thomas	.25
SQ39	Derrick Thomas	.25
SQ40	Tyrone Wheatley	.25
SQ41	Dorsey Levens	.50
SQ42	Darnay Scott	.25
SQ43	Scott Mitchell	.25
SQ44	Marvin Harrison	.50
SQ45	Eddie Kennison	.50
SQ46	Jake Reed	2.00
SQ47	Andre Reed	2.00
SQ48	Neil Smith	2.00
SQ49	Anthony Johnson	2.00
SQ50	Napoleon Kaufman	4.00
SQ51	Terance Mathis	2.00
SQ52	Tony Martin	2.00
SQ53	Adrian Murrell	4.00
SQ54	Bryant Westbrook	2.00
SQ55	Errict Rhett	2.00
SQ56	Kerry Collins	10.00
SQ57	Curtis Conway	2.00
SQ58	Eric Swann	2.00
SQ59	Michael Jackson	2.00
SQ60	Ty Detmer	2.00
SQ61	Michael Irvin	4.00
SQ62	Andre Coleman	2.00
SQ63	Brian Mitchell	2.00
SQ64	Tony Banks	4.00
SQ65	Eddie George	20.00
SQ66	Kordell Stewart	20.00
SQ67	Greg Hill	5.00
SQ68	Karim Abdul-Jabbar	12.00
SQ69	Cris Carter	5.00
SQ70	Terry Glenn	15.00
SQ71	Emmitt Smith	60.00
SQ72	Jim Harbaugh	5.00
SQ73	Jeff Blake	8.00
SQ74	Rashaan Salaam	5.00
SQ75	Ricky Watters	5.00
SQ76	Joey Galloway	8.00
SQ77	Junior Seau	5.00
SQ78	Dave Brown	5.00
SQ79	Tim Brown	5.00
SQ80	Troy Aikman	25.00
SQ81	Dan Marino	70.00
SQ82	Brett Favre	75.00
SQ83	John Elway	30.00
SQ84	Steve Young	25.00
SQ85	Mark Brunell	35.00
SQ86	Barry Sanders	40.00
SQ87	Jerome Bettis	10.00
SQ88	Terrell Davis	35.00
SQ89	Curtis Martin	30.00
SQ90	Jerry Rice	35.00

1997 Upper Deck UD3

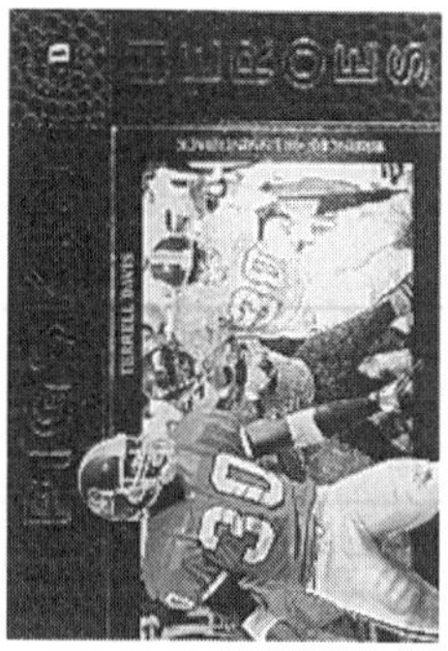

UD3 consists of a 90-card base set made up of three unique subsets. The first 30 cards are Prime Choice Rookies. The rookies are all featured with Light F/X technology. Cards 31-60 are Eye of a Champion. This subset features Cel-Chrome technology. The final subset is Pigskin Heroes. These cards feature two player shots on the front with an embossed, pigskin feel to the card. The inserts for UD3 are Generation eXcitement, Marquee Attraction and Signature Performers.

		MT
Complete Set (90):		75.00
Common Player:		.20
Wax Box:		75.00
1	*Orlando Pace*	.50
2	*Walter Jones*	.20
3	*Tony Gonzalez*	1.00
4	*David LaFleur*	1.00
5	*Jim Druckenmiller*	4.00
6	*Jake Plummer*	7.00
7	*Pat Barnes*	1.00
8	*Ike Hilliard*	1.50
9	*Reidel Anthony*	2.00
10	*Rae Carruth*	1.50
11	*Yatil Green*	.50
12	*Joey Kent*	.50
13	*Will Blackwell*	.50
14	*Kevin Lockett*	.50
15	*Warrick Dunn*	7.00
16	*Antowain Smith*	4.00
17	*Troy Davis*	.50
18	*Byron Hanspard*	1.50
19	*Corey Dillon*	5.00
20	*Darnell Autry*	1.00
21	*Peter Boulware*	.20
22	*Darrell Russell*	.20
23	*Kenny Holmes*	.20
24	*Reinard Wilson*	.20
25	*Renaldo Wynn*	.20
26	*Dwayne Rudd*	.20
27	*James Farrior*	.20
28	*Shawn Springs*	.40
29	*Bryant Westbrook*	.20
30	*Tom Knight*	.20
31	Barry Sanders	6.00
32	Brett Favre	6.00
33	Brian Mitchell	.20
34	Curtis Martin	2.00
35	Dan Marino	5.00
36	Deion Sanders	1.50
37	Drew Bledsoe	3.00
38	Eddie George	4.00
39	Edgar Bennett	.20
40	Emmitt Smith	5.00
41	Isaac Bruce	.40
42	Jerome Bettis	.40
43	Jerry Rice	3.00
44	John Elway	3.00
45	Junior Seau	.20
46	Karim Abdul-Jabbar	.50
47	Kerry Collins	.50
48	Marshall Faulk	.50
49	Marvin Harrison	.50
50	Michael Irvin	.40
51	Natrone Means	.40
52	Reggie White	.40
53	Ricky Watters	.40
54	Stan Humphries	.20
55	Steve Young	2.00
56	Terry Glenn	.50
57	Thurman Thomas	.40
58	Tony Martin	.20
59	Troy Aikman	3.00
60	Vinny Testaverde	.20
61	Anthony Johnson	.20
62	Bobby Engram	.20
63	Carl Pickens	.20
64	Cris Carter	.20
65	Derrick Witherspoon	.20
66	Eddie Kennison	.50
67	Eric Swann	.20
68	Gus Frerotte	.20
69	Herman Moore	.40
70	Irving Fryar	.20
71	Jamal Anderson	.40
72	Jeff Blake	.40
73	Jim Harbaugh	.20
74	Joey Galloway	.40
75	Keenan McCardell	.20
76	Kevin Greene	.20
77	Keyshawn Johnson	.50
78	Kordell Stewart	3.00
79	Marcus Allen	.40
80	Mario Bates	.20
81	Mark Brunell	3.00
82	Michael Jackson	.20
83	Mike Alstott	.40
84	Scott Mitchell	.20
85	Shannon Sharpe	.20
86	Steve McNair	2.50
87	Terrell Davis	3.00
88	Tim Brown	.20
89	Ty Detmer	.20
90	Tyrone Wheatley	.20

1997 Upper Deck UD3 Generation Excitement

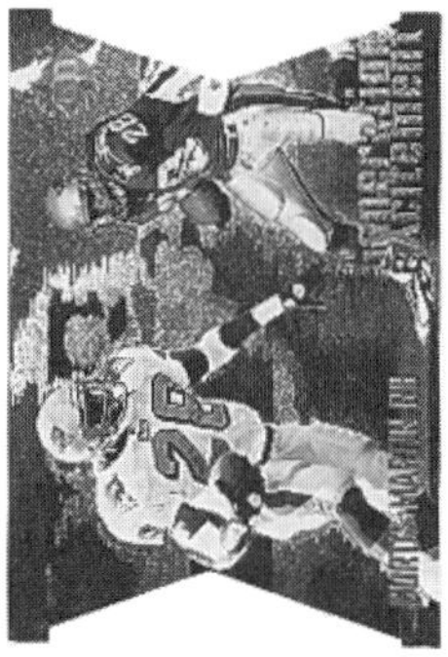

This 15-card insert features the NFL's most spectacular players. Each card has a die-cut, Light F/X design and features two action shots of the player on the front. The cards were inserted 1:11.

		MT
Complete Set (15):		130.00
Common Player:		3.00
GE1	Jerry Rice	15.00
GE2	Carl Pickens	3.00
GE3	Curtis Conway	3.00
GE4	John Elway	15.00
GE5	Ike Hilliard	8.00
GE6	Marvin Harrison	5.00
GE7	Emmitt Smith	25.00
GE8	Barry Sanders	20.00
GE9	Deion Sanders	7.00
GE10	Rae Carruth	7.00
GE11	Curtis Martin	12.00
GE12	Terry Glenn	10.00
GE13	Napoleon Kaufman	5.00
GE14	Kordell Stewart	15.00
GE15	Jake Plummer	10.00

1997 Upper Deck UD3 Marquee Attraction

Marquee Attraction features the most collectible NFL players in a 15-card insert set. The cards are die-cut and feature Cel-Chrome technology. They were inserted 1:144 in UD3.

		MT
Complete Set (15):		600.00
Common Player:		10.00
MA1	Steve Young	35.00
MA2	Troy Aikman	50.00
MA3	Keyshawn Johnson	10.00
MA4	Marcus Allen	10.00
MA5	Dan Marino	100.00
MA6	Mark Brunell	50.00
MA7	Eddie George	75.00
MA8	Brett Favre	110.00
MA9	Drew Bledsoe	50.00
MA10	Eddie Kennison	25.00
MA11	Terrell Davis	50.00
MA12	Warrick Dunn	60.00
MA13	Yatil Green	20.00
MA14	Troy Davis	30.00
MA15	Shawn Springs	10.00

1997 Upper Deck UD3 Signature Performers

Signature Performers is a four-card insert featuring special electric technology. The cards were autographed by the players in the set: Curtis Martin, Troy Aikman, Marcus Allen and Eddie George. The cards were inserted 1:1,500.

		MT
Complete Set (4):		1100.
Common Player:		125.00
PF1	Curtis Martin	250.00
PF2	Troy Aikman	350.00
PF3	Marcus Allen	125.00
PF4	Eddie George	450.00

1997 Upper Deck Legends

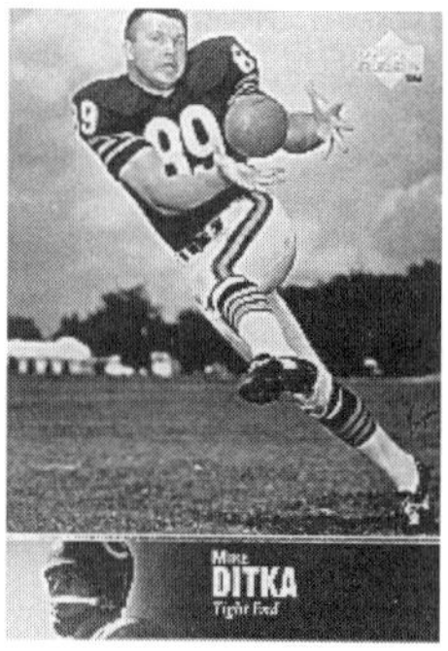

Legends is a 208-card set featuring the greatest players from the NFL's past. Besides the 168 regular cards, a 30-card Super Bowl Memories by Walter Iooss, Jr. subset and a 10-card Legendary Leaders subset were added. A parallel of the 168 regular cards featuring player autographs was inserted 1:5. The insert sets are Sign of the Times, Big Game Hunters and Marquee Matchups.

		MT
Complete Set (208):		45.00
Common Player:		.10
Wax Box:		125.00
1	Bart Starr	1.50
2	Jim Brown	2.50
3	Joe Namath	2.50
4	Walter Payton	2.50
5	Terry Bradshaw	2.50
6	Franco Harris	.50
7	Dan Fouts	.20
8	Steve Largent	.20
9	Johnny Unitas	1.50
10	Gale Sayers	1.00
11	Roger Staubach	2.50
12	Tony Dorsett	.50
13	Fran Tarkenton	1.00
14	Charley Taylor	.10
15	Ray Nitschke	.20
16	Jim Ringo	.10
17	Dick Butkus	1.00
18	Fred Biletnikoff	.20
19	Lenny Moore	.10
20	Len Dawson	.10
21	Lance Alworth	.10
22	Chuck Bednarik	.10
23	Raymond Berry	.10
24	Donnie Shell	.10
25	Mel Blount	.10
26	Willie Brown	.10
27	Ken Houston	.10
28	Larry Csonka	.50
29	Mike Ditka	.75
30	Art Donovan	.50
31	Sam Huff	.10
32	Lem Barney	.10
33	Hugh McElhenny	.10
34	Otto Graham	.75
35	Joe Greene	.50
36	Mike Rozier	.10
37	Lou Groza	.10
38	Ted Hendricks	.10
39	Elroy Hirsch	.10
40	Paul Hornung	.75
41	Charlie Joiner	.10
42	Deacon Jones	.20
43	Bill Bradley	.10
44	Floyd Little	.10
45	Willie Lanier	.10
46	Bob Lilly	.10
47	Sid Luckman	.10
48	John Mackey	.10
49	Don Maynard	.10
50	Mike McCormack	.10
51	Bobby Mitchell	.10
52	Ron Mix	.10
53	Marion Motley	.10
54	Leo Nomellini	.10
55	Mark Duper	.10
56	Mel Renfro	.10
57	Jim Otto	.10
58	Alan Page	.10
59	Joe Perry	.10
60	Andy Robustelli	.10
61	Lee Roy Selmon	.10
62	Jackie Smith	.10
63	Art Shell	.10
64	Jan Stenerud	.10
65	Gene Upshaw	.10
66	Y.A. Tittle	.10
67	Paul Warfield	.10
68	Kellen Winslow	.20
69	Randy White	.10
70	Larry Wilson	.10
71	Willie Wood	.10
72	Jack Ham	.10
73	Jack Youngblood	.10
74	Dan Abramowicz	.10
75	Dick Anderson	.10
76	Ken Anderson	.10
77	Steve Bartkowski	.10
78	Bill Bergey	.10
79	Rocky Bleier	.10
80	Cliff Branch	.10
81	John Brodie	.10
90	Bobby Bell	.10
83	Billy Cannon	.10
84	Gino Capelletti	.10
85	Harold Carmichael	.10
86	Dave Casper	.10
87	Wes Chandler	.10
88	Todd Christensen	.10
89	Dwight Clark	.10
90	Mark Clayton	.10
91	Cris Collinsworth	.10
92	Roger Craig	.10
93	Randy Cross	.10
94	Isaac Curtis	.10
95	Mike Curtis	.10
96	Ben Davidson	.10
97	Fred Dean	.10
98	Tom Dempsey	.10
99	Eric Dickerson	.10
100	Lynn Dickey	.10
101	John McKay	.10
102	Carl Eller	.10
103	Chuck Foreman	.10
104	Russ Francis	.10
105	Joe Gibbs	.10
106	Gary Garrison	.10
107	Randy Gradishar	.10
108	L.C. Greenwood	.10
109	Roosevelt Grier	.10
110	Steve Grogan	.10
111	Ray Guy	.10
112	John Hadl	.10
113	Jim Hart	.10
114	George Halas	.10
115	Mike Haynes	.10
116	Charlie Hennigan	.10
117	Chuck Howley	.10
118	Harold Jackson	.10
119	Tom Jackson	.10
120	Ron Jaworski	.10
121	John Jefferson	.10
122	Billy Johnson	.10
123	Ed "Too Tall" Jones	.10
124	Jack Kemp	1.50
125	Jim Kiick	.10
126	Billy Kilmer	.10
127	Jerry Kramer	.10
128	Paul Krause	.10
129	Daryle Lamonica	.10
130	Bill Walsh	.10
131	James Lofton	.10
132	Hank Stram	.10
133	Archie Manning	.10
134	Jim Marshall	.10
135	Harvey Martin	.10
136	Tommy McDonald	.10
137	Max McGee	.10
138	Reggie McKenzie	.10
139	Karl Mecklenberg	.10
140	Tom Landry	.20
141	Terry Metcalf	.10
142	Matt Millen	.10
143	Earl Morrall	.10
144	Mercury Morris	.10
145	Chuck Noll	.10
146	Joe Morris	.10
147	Mark Moseley	.10
148	Haven Moses	.10
149	Chuck Muncie	.10
150	Anthony Munoz	.10
151	Tommy Nobis	.10
152	Babe Parilli	.10
153	Drew Pearson	.10
154	Ozzie Newsome	.10
155	Jim Plunkett	.20
156	William Perry	.10
157	Johnny Robinson	.10
158	Ahmad Rashad	.30
159	George Rogers	.10
160	Sterling Sharpe	.10
161	Billy Sims	.10
162	Sid Gillman	.10
163	Mike Singletary	.10
164	Charlie Sanders	.10
165	Bubba Smith	.10
166	Ken Stabler	1.50
167	Freddie Soloman	.10
168	John Stallworth	.10
169	Dwight Stephenson	.10
170	Vince Lombardi	.30
171	Weeb Ewbank	.10
172	Lionel Taylor	.10
173	Otis Taylor	.10
174	Joe Theismann	.20
175	Bob Trumpy	.10
176	Mike Webster	.10
177	Jim Zorn	.10
178	Joe Montana	3.00
179	Packer Defense	.10
180	Bart Starr	.75
181	Max McGee	.10
182	Joe Namath	1.25
183	Johnny Unitas	.75
184	Len Dawson	.10
185	Chuck Howley	.10
186	Roger Staubach	.75
187	Paul Warfield	.10
188	Larry Csonka	.20
189	Fran Tarkenton	.20
190	Joe Green	.10
191	Ken Stabler	.10
192	Fred Biletnikoff	.10
193	Dick Anderson	.10
194	Harvey Martin	.10
195	Tony Dorsett	.20
196	Terry Bradshaw	1.00
197	John Stallworth	.10
198	Franco Harris	.20
199	Ken Anderson	.10
200	Joe Theismann	.10
201	Jim Plunkett	.10
202	Roger Craig	.10
203	William Perry	.10
204	Joe Morris	.10
205	Karl Mecklenberg	.10
206	Joe Montana	1.50
207	Joe Montana	1.50
208	Joe Montana	1.50

1997 Upper Deck Legends Autographs

Many players from the Legends base set signed a number of their cards. The autograph set consists of 162 cards which were inserted one per five packs.

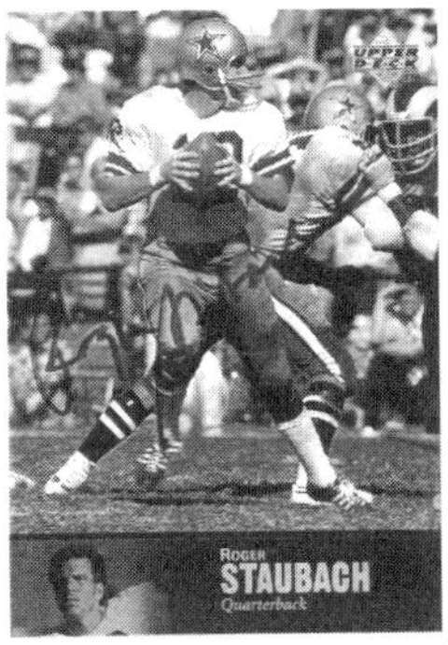

	MT
Complete Set (162):	8000.
Common Player:	12.50
Inserted 1:5 Hobby	
Inserted 1:10 Retail	
Inserted 1:7 Special Retail	

1	Bart Starr	500.00
2	Jim Brown	500.00
3	Joe Namath	500.00
4	Walter Payton	500.00
5	Terry Bradshaw	500.00
6	Franco Harris	375.00
7	Dan Fouts	50.00
8	Steve Largent	50.00
9	Johnny Unitas	375.00
10	Gale Sayers	50.00
11	Roger Staubach	200.00
12	Tony Dorsett	300.00
13	Fran Tarkenton	50.00
14	Charley Taylor	12.50
15	Ray Nitschke	75.00
16	Jim Ringo	35.00
17	Dick Butkus	200.00
18	Fred Biletnikoff	35.00
19	Lenny Moore	12.50
20	Len Dawson	75.00
21	Lance Alworth	50.00
22	Chuck Bednarik	25.00
23	Raymond Berry	25.00
24	Donnie Shell	25.00
25	Mel Blount	25.00
26	Willie Brown	12.50
27	Ken Houston	12.50
28	Larry Csonka	175.00
29	Mike Ditka	75.00
30	Art Donovan	25.00
31	Sam Huff	12.50
32	Lem Barney	12.50
33	Hugh McElhenny	12.50
34	Otto Graham	50.00
35	Joe Greene	175.00
36	Mike Rozler	35.00
37	Lou Groza	12.50
38	Ted Hendricks	25.00
39	Elroy Hirsch	12.50
40	Paul Hornung	35.00
41	Charlie Joiner	25.00
42	Deacon Jones	25.00
43	Bill Bradley	12.50
44	Floyd Little	12.50
45	Willie Lanier	12.50
46	Bob Lilly	12.50
48	John Mackey	12.50
49	Don Maynard	25.00
50	Mike McCormack	35.00
51	Bobby Mitchell	12.50
52	Ron Mix	12.50
53	Marion Motley	12.50
54	Leo Nomellini	12.50
55	Mark Duper	25.00
56	Mel Renfro	12.50
57	Jim Otto	12.50
58	Alan Page	25.00
59	Joe Perry	12.50
60	Andy Robustelli	12.50
61	Lee Roy Selmon	12.50
62	Jackie Smith	12.50
63	Art Shell	50.00
64	Jan Stenerud	12.50
65	Gene Upshaw	12.50
66	Y.A. Tittle	35.00
67	Paul Warfield	35.00
68	Kellen Winslow	50.00
69	Randy White	25.00
70	Larry Wilson	12.50
72	Jack Ham	12.50
73	Jack Youngblood	12.50
74	Dan Abramowicz	12.50
75	Dick Anderson	12.50
76	Ken Anderson	25.00
77	Steve Bartkowski	25.00
78	Bill Bergey	12.50
79	Rocky Bleier	12.50
80	Cliff Branch	12.50
81	John Brodie	12.50
82	Bobby Bell	12.50
83	Billy Cannon	75.00
84	Gino Capelletti	12.50
85	Harold Carmichael	12.50
86	Dave Casper	12.50
87	Wes Chandler	12.50
88	Todd Christensen	12.50
89	Dwight Clark	25.00
90	Mark Clayton	12.50
91	Cris Collinsworth	25.00
92	Roger Craig	25.00
93	Randy Cross	12.50
94	Isaac Curtis	12.50
95	Mike Curtis	12.50
96	Ben Davidson	12.50
98	Tom Dempsey	12.50
99	Eric Dickerson	25.00
100	Lynn Dickey	12.50
102	Carl Eller	35.00
103	Chuck Foreman	12.50
106	Gary Garrison	25.00
107	Randy Gradishar	12.50
108	L.C. Greenwood	12.50
109	Roosevelt Grier	25.00
110	Steve Grogan	12.50
111	Ray Guy	12.50
112	John Hadl	12.50
113	Jim Hart	12.50
115	Mike Haynes	25.00
116	Charlie Hennigan	12.50
117	Chuck Howley	12.50
118	Harold Jackson	12.50
119	Tom Jackson	25.00
120	Ron Jaworski	25.00
121	John Jefferson	25.00
123	Ed "Too Tall" Jones	25.00
124	Jack Kemp	100.00
125	Jim Klick	12.50
126	Billy Kilmer	12.50
127	Jerry Kramer	12.50
128	Paul Krause	12.50
129	Daryle Lamonica	12.50
131	James Lofton	25.00
133	Archie Manning	35.00
134	Jim Marshall	35.00
135	Harvey Martin	35.00
136	Tommy McDonald	12.50
137	Max McGee	12.50
138	Reggie McKenzie	12.50
139	Karl Mecklenburg	12.50
141	Terry Metcalf	12.50
142	Matt Millen	35.00
143	Earl Morrall	12.50
144	Mercury Morris	25.00
146	Joe Morris	12.50
147	Mark Moseley	12.50
148	Haven Moses	12.50
149	Chuck Muncie	12.50
150	Anthony Munoz	35.00
151	Tommy Nobis	12.50
152	Babe Parilli	12.50
153	Drew Pearson	25.00
154	Ozzie Newsome	12.50
155	Jim Plunkett	35.00
156	William Perry	25.00
157	Johnny Robinson	12.50
158	Ahmad Rashad	50.00
159	George Rogers	25.00
160	Sterling Sharpe	25.00
161	Billy Sims	12.50
163	Mike Singletary	25.00
164	Charlie Sanders	12.50
165	Bubba Smith	50.00
166	Ken Stabler	100.00
167	Freddie Solomon	12.50
168	John Stallworth	12.50
169	Dwight Stephenson	12.50
172	Lionel Taylor	12.50
173	Otis Taylor	50.00
174	Joe Theismann	50.00
177	Jim Zorn	12.50
178	Joe Montana	500.00

1997 Upper Deck Legends Big Game Hunters

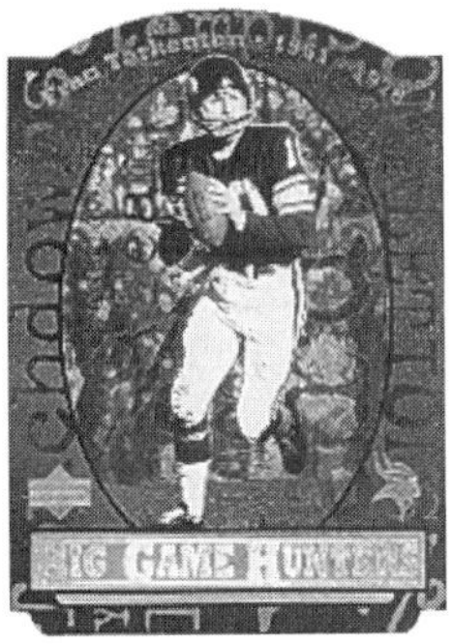

This 20-card insert features the top 20 clutch QBs on a die-cut card. They were inserted 1:75.

		MT
Complete Set (20):		800.00
Common Player:		20.00
BG1	Joe Montana	100.00
BG2	Bart Starr	50.00
BG3	Roger Staubach	75.00
BG4	Johnny Unitas	50.00
BG5	Terry Bradshaw	75.00
BG6	Ken Stabler	50.00
BG7	Jim Plunkett	40.00
BG8	Len Dawson	20.00
BG9	Fran Tarkenton	50.00
BG10	Dan Fouts	40.00
BG11	Daryle Lamonica	20.00
BG12	Y.A. Tittle	20.00
BG13	Joe Namath	80.00
BG14	Kenny Anderson	20.00
BG15	John Brodie	20.00
BG16	Billy Kilmer	20.00
BG17	Earl Morrall	20.00
BG18	Jack Kemp	50.00
BG19	Steve Grogan	20.00
BG20	Joe Theismann	40.00

1997 Upper Deck Legends Marquee Matchups

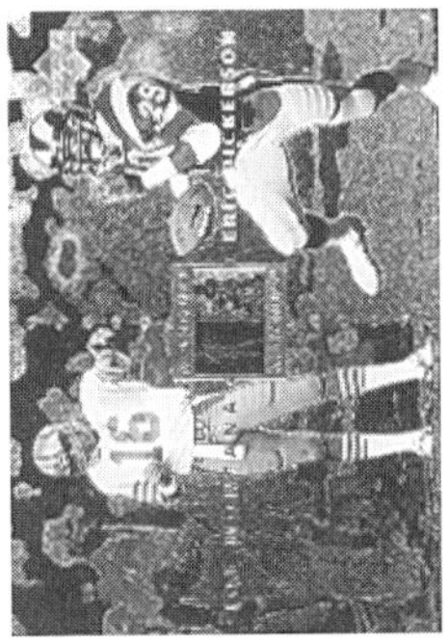

This 30-card insert features two of the NFL's greatest and creates a classic matchup. The cards use Light F/X technology and were inserted 1:17.

		MT
Complete Set (30):		500.00
Common Player:		7.00
MM1	Joe Namath, Dan Fouts	30.00
MM2	Johnny Unitas, Joe Namath	40.00
MM3	Len Dawson, Bart Starr	25.00
MM4	Roger Staubach, Fran Tarkenton	30.00
MM5	Terry Bradshaw, Ken Stabler	30.00
MM6	Joe Montana, Kenny Anderson	45.00
MM7	Bart Starr, Johnny Unitas	30.00
MM8	Joe Greene, Jim Kiick	7.00
MM9	Franco Harris, Walter Payton	35.00
MM10	Ken Stabler, Dan Fouts	20.00
MM11	Charlie Joiner, Steve Largent	14.00
MM12	James Lofton, Drew Pearson	7.00
MM13	John Brodie, Deacon Jones	7.00
MM14	Fred Biletnikoff, Don Maynard	7.00
MM15	Jim Brown, Chuck Bednarik	30.00
MM16	Ray Nitschke, Gale Sayers	25.00
MM17	Paul Hornung, Dick Butkus	20.00
MM18	Joe Montana, Eric Dickerson	45.00
MM19	Tony Dorsett, Mike Singletary	14.00
MM20	Billy Sims, Chuck Foreman	7.00
MM21	Len Dawson, Willie Brown	7.00
MM22	Johnny Robinson, Larry Wilson	7.00
MM23	Marion Motley, Raymond Berry	7.00
MM24	Ron Mix, Jim Otto	7.00
MM25	Roger Staubach, Terry Bradshaw	35.00
MM26	Bob Lilly, Billy Kilmer	7.00
MM27	Ted Hendricks, Russ Francis	7.00
MM28	Babe Parilli, Jack Kemp	14.00
MM29	Deacon Jones, Alan Page	7.00
MM30	Dick Butkus, Ray Nitschke	25.00

1997 Upper Deck Legend Sign of the Times

This 10-card insert features autographs from some of the greatest players ever. The set was limited to less than 1,000 total cards.

		MT
Complete Set (10):		2500.00
Common Player:		125.00
ST1	Joe Montana	450.00
ST2	Fran Tarkenton	200.00
ST3	Johnny Unitas	225.00
ST4	Joe Namath	300.00
ST5	Terry Bradshaw	225.00
ST6	Jim Brown	300.00
ST7	Franco Harris	125.00
ST8	Walter Payton	250.00
ST9	Steve Largent	125.00
ST10	Bart Starr	250.00

1998 Bowman

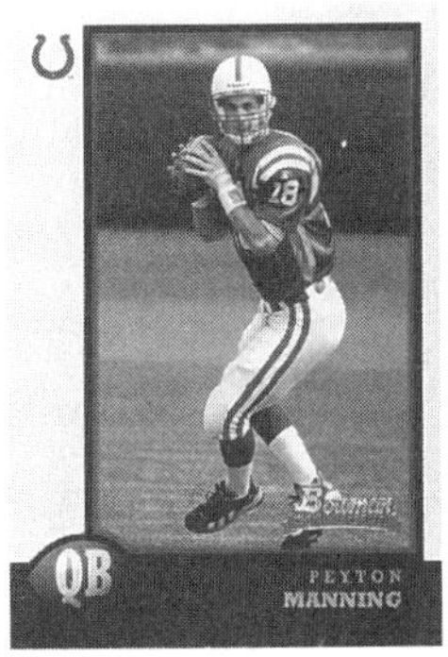

Bowman contained 220 cards, including 150 veterans and 70 rookies. Prospects were featured on a silver and blue design while veterans are shown on a silver and red design. Rookies contain a "Bowman Rookie Card" gold foil stamp. The set is paralleled in Inter-State and Golden Anniversary sets. Three insert sets are inclued in packs: Bowman Autographs, which come in blue, silver and gold foil versions, Scout's Choice and Bowman Chrome Preview.

		MT
Complete Set (220):		100.00
Common Player:		.25
Common Rookie:		.50
Golden Ann. Stars:		50x-100x
Golden Ann. Rookies:		10x-20x
Inserted 1:180		
Production 50 Sets		
Wax Box:		75.00
1	*Peyton Manning*	15.00
2	*Keith Brooking*	.50
3	*Duane Starks*	.50
4	*Takeo Spikes*	.50
5	*Andre Wadsworth*	2.00
6	*Greg Ellis*	1.00
7	*Brian Griese*	4.00
8	*Germane Crowell*	3.00
9	*Jerome Pathon*	2.00
10	*Ryan Leaf*	10.00
11	*Fred Taylor*	10.00
12	*Robert Edwards*	7.00
13	*Grant Wistrom*	.50
14	*Robert Holcombe*	4.00
15	*Tim Dwight*	3.00
16	*Jacquez Green*	4.00
17	*Marcus Nash*	3.00
18	*Jason Peter*	.50
19	*Anthony Simmons*	.50
20	*Curtis Enis*	5.00
21	*John Avery*	3.00
22	*Patrick Johnson*	.50
23	*Joe Jurevicius*	2.00
24	*Brian Simmons*	.50
25	*Kevin Dyson*	3.00
26	*Skip Hicks*	3.00
27	*Hines Ward*	3.00
28	*Tavian Banks*	3.00
29	*Ahman Green*	4.00
30	*Tony Simmons*	.50
31	Charles Johnson	.25
32	Freddie Jones	.25
33	Joey Galloway	.75
34	Tony Banks	.50
35	Jake Plummer	1.50
36	Reidel Anthony	.25
37	Steve McNair	.75
38	Michael Westbrook	.50
39	Chris Sanders	.25
40	Isaac Bruce	.50
41	Charlie Garner	.25
42	Wayne Chrebet	.25
43	Michael Strahan	.25
44	Brad Johnson	.50
45	Mike Alstott	.50
46	Tony Gonzalez	.50
47	Johnnie Morton	.25
48	Darnay Scott	.25
49	Rae Carruth	.25
50	Terrell Davis	2.50
51	Jermaine Lewis	.25
52	Frank Sanders	.25
53	Byron Hanspard	.25
54	Gus Frerotte	.25
55	Terry Glenn	.50
56	J.J. Stokes	.25
57	Will Blackwell	.25
58	Keyshawn Johnson	.50
59	Tiki Barber	.50
60	Dorsey Levens	.50
61	Zach Thomas	.25
62	Corey Dillon	1.25
63	Antowain Smith	1.00
64	Michael Sinclair	.25
65	Rod Smith	.25
66	Trent Dilfer	.50
67	Warren Sapp	.25
68	Charles Way	.25
69	Tamarick Vanover	.25
70	Drew Bledsoe	1.50
71	John Mobley	.25
72	Kerry Collins	.50
73	Peter Boulware	.25
74	Simeon Rice	.25
75	Eddie George	1.50
76	Fred Lane	.50
77	Jamal Anderson	.50
78	Antonio Freeman	.75
79	Jason Sehorn	.25
80	Curtis Martin	.75
81	Bobby Hoying	.25
82	Garrison Hearst	.25
83	Glenn Foley	.25
84	Danny Kanell	.25
85	Kordell Stewart	1.50
86	O.J. McDuffie	.25
87	Marvin Harrison	.75
88	Bobby Engram	.25
89	Chris Slade	.25
90	Warrick Dunn	1.50
91	Ricky Watters	.50
92	Rickey Dudley	.25
93	Terrell Owens	.50
94	Karim Abdul-Jabbar	.50
95	Napoleon Kaufman	.75
96	Darrell Green	.25
97	Levon Kirkland	.25
98	Jeff George	.50
99	Andre Hastings	.25
100	John Elway	2.00
101	John Randle	.25
102	Andre Rison	.25
103	Keenan McCardell	.25
104	Marshall Faulk	.75
105	Emmitt Smith	3.00
106	Robert Brooks	.25
107	Scott Mitchell	.25
108	Shannon Sharpe	.50
109	Deion Sanders	.75
110	Jerry Rice	2.00
111	Erik Kramer	.25
112	Michael Jackson	.25
113	Aeneas Williams	.25
114	Terry Allen	.25
115	Steve Young	1.25
116	Warren Moon	.50
117	Junior Seau	.50
118	Jerome Bettis	.50
119	Irving Fryar	.25
120	Barry Sanders	4.00
121	Tim Brown	.50
122	Chad Brown	.25
123	Ben Coates	.25
124	Robert Smith	.50
125	Brett Favre	4.00
126	Derrick Thomas	.25
127	Reggie White	.50
128	Troy Aikman	2.00
129	Jeff Blake	.50
130	Mark Brunell	1.50
131	Curtis Conway	.50
132	Wesley Walls	.25
133	Thurman Thomas	.50
134	Chris Chandler	.25
135	Dan Marino	3.00
136	Larry Centers	.25
137	Shawn Jefferson	.25
138	Andre Reed	.25
139	Jake Reed	.25
140	Cris Carter	.50
141	Elvis Grbac	.25
142	Mark Chmura	.50
143	Michael Irvin	.50
144	Carl Pickens	.50
145	Herman Moore	.50
146	Marvin Jones	.25
147	Terance Mathis	.25
148	Rob Moore	.25
149	Bruce Smith	.25
150	Checklist	.25
151	Leslie Shepherd	.25
152	Chris Spielman	.25
153	Tony McGee	.25
154	Kevin Smith	.25
155	Bill Romanowski	.25

156	Stephen Boyd	.25
157	James Stewart	.25
158	Jason Taylor	.25
159	Troy Drayton	.25
160	Mark Fields	.25
161	Jessie Armstead	.25
162	James Jett	.25
163	Bobby Taylor	.25
164	Kimble Anders	.25
165	Jimmy Smith	.25
166	Quentin Coryatt	.25
167	Bryant Westbrook	.25
168	Neil Smith	.25
169	Darren Woodson	.25
170	Ray Buchanan	.25
171	Earl Holmes	.25
172	Ray Lewis	.25
173	Steve Broussard	.25
174	Derrick Brooks	.25
175	Ken Harvey	.25
176	Darryll Lewis	.25
177	Derrick Rodgers	.25
178	James McKnight	.25
179	Cris Dishman	.25
180	Hardy Nickerson	.25
181	*Charles Woodson*	5.00
182	*Randy Moss*	25.00
183	*Stephen Alexander*	.50
184	*Samari Rolle*	.50
185	*Jamie Duncan*	.50
186	*Lance Schulters*	.50
187	*Tony Parrish*	.50
188	*Corey Chavous*	.50
189	*Jammi German*	.50
190	*Sam Cowart*	.50
191	*Donald Hayes*	.50
192	*R.W. McQuarters*	1.00
193	*Az-Zahir Hakim*	2.00
194	*Chris Fuamatu-Ma'afala*	2.00
195	*Allen Rossum*	.50
196	*Jon Ritchie*	.50
197	*Blake Spence*	.50
198	*Brian Alford*	.50
199	*Fred Weary*	.50
200	*Rod Rutledge*	.50
201	*Michael Myers*	.50
202	*Rashaan Shehee*	2.00
203	*Donovin Darius*	.50
204	*E.G. Green*	.50
205	*Vonnie Holliday*	2.00
206	*Charlie Batch*	8.00
207	*Michael Pittman*	.50
208	*Artrell Hawkins*	.50
209	*Jonathan Quinn*	.50
210	*Kailee Wong*	.50
211	*Deshea Townsend*	1.00
212	*Patrick Surtain*	.50
213	*Brian Kelly*	.50
214	*Tebucky Jones*	.50
215	*Pete Gonzalez*	1.00
216	*Shaun Williams*	.50
217	*Scott Frost*	.50
218	*Leonard Little*	.50
219	*Alonzo Mayes*	1.00
220	*Cordell Taylor*	.50

1998 Bowman Inter-State

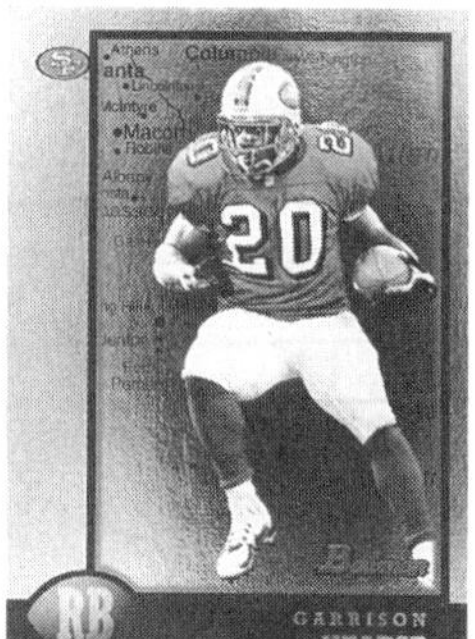

All 220 cards were reprinted in Inter-State parallel versions and seeded one per pack. These are printed on silver foil and included a background map of where the player was born on the front and a vanity plate on the back.

	MT
Inter-State Cards:	3x
Inter-State Rookies:	2x

1998 Bowman Blue Autographs

Eleven different players signed cards to be inserted into packs of Bowman. Card rarity was differentiated by blue (1:360 packs), silver (2,401) or gold foil Topps Certified Autograph Issue stamps (1:7,202).

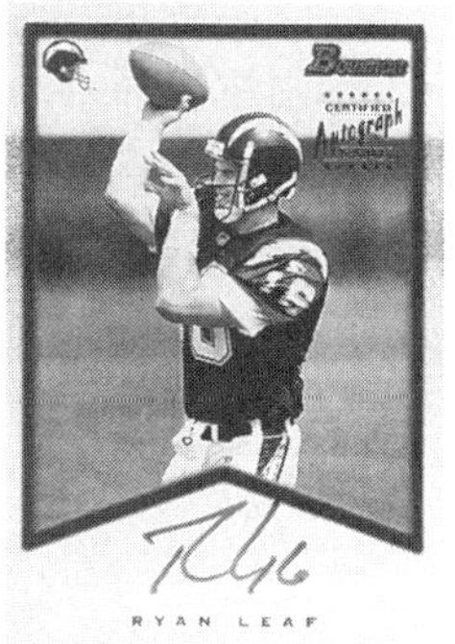

		MT
Complete Set (11):		700.00
Common Player:		20.00
Inserted 1:360		
Silver Cards:		2x
Inserted 1:2,401		
Gold Cards:		4x
Inserted 1:7,202		
1	Peyton Manning	140.00
2	Andre Wadsworth	20.00
3	Brian Griese	50.00
4	Ryan Leaf	100.00
5	Fred Taylor	100.00
6	Robert Edwards	75.00
7	Randy Moss	250.00
8	Curtis Enis	60.00
9	Kevin Dyson	40.00
10	Charles Woodson	60.00
11	Tim Dwight	40.00

1998 Bowman Chrome Preview

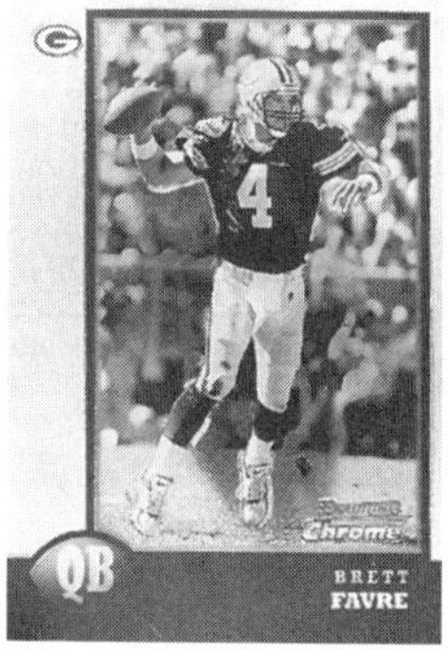

This 10-card insert set previewed the upcoming Bowman Chrome set. It included five veterans and five rookies, with regular versions seeded one per 12 packs and Refractors every 48 packs.

		MT
Complete Set (10):		50.00
Common Player:		4.00
Inserted 1:12		
Refractors:		2x
Inserted 1:48		
1	Peyton Manning	10.00
2	Curtis Enis	5.00
3	Charles Woodson	4.00
4	Robert Edwards	6.00
5	Ryan Leaf	8.00
6	Brett Favre	12.00
7	John Elway	6.00
8	Barry Sanders	12.00
9	Kordell Stewart	4.00
10	Terrell Davis	8.00

1998 Bowman Scout's Choice

This 14-card insert set showcased the top rookies according to the Bowman Scouts. Cards featured a borderless, double-etched foil design and were inserted one per 12 packs.

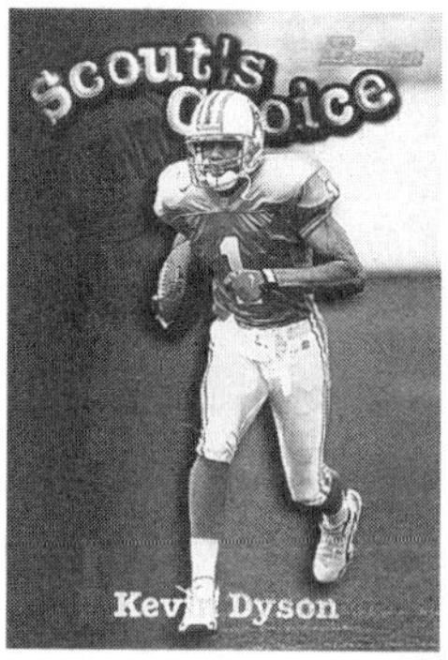

		MT
Complete Set (14):		60.00
Common Player:		2.00
Inserted 1:12		
SC1	Peyton Manning	15.00
SC2	John Avery	3.00
SC3	Grant Wistrom	2.00
SC4	Kevin Dyson	3.00
SC5	Andre Wadsworth	3.00
SC6	Joe Jurevicius	2.00
SC7	Charles Woodson	6.00
SC8	Takeo Spikes	2.00
SC9	Fred Taylor	10.00
SC10	Ryan Leaf	10.00
SC11	Robert Edwards	8.00
SC12	Randy Moss	20.00
SC13	Patrick Johnson	2.00
SC14	Curtis Enis	6.00

1998 Collector's Edge Advantage

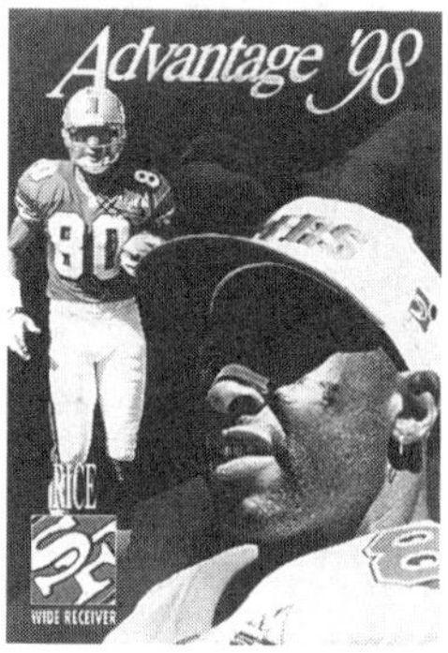

Edge Advantage was a 180-card set that included three different parallel sets and five insert sets. The base cards contain the words "Advantage '98" written in script across the top, with the player's name, team logo and position in the bottom left corner. An action shot of the player is on the left part of the card with a close-up head shot on the right side, with all of this over another closer shot of the player in the background. Advantage also has a silver parallel (one per two packs) that has the front in a silver foil, a gold parallel (one per six) that has the front printed on gold foil and a 50-point stock parallel (one per pack) with the words "Advantage '98" printed in gold foil. Advantage Football included five insert sets: Livin' Large, Memorable Moments, Personal Victory, Prime Connection and Showtime.

		MT
Complete Set (180):		60.00
Common Player:		.25
Wax Box:		85.00
1	Larry Centers	.25
2	Kent Graham	.25
3	LaShon Johnson	.25
4	Leeland McElroy	.25
5	Jake Plummer	2.50
6	Jamal Anderson	.50
7	Chris Chandler	.25
8	Bert Emanuel	.25
9	Byron Hanspard	.50
10	O.J. Santiago	.25
11	Derrick Alexander	.25
12	Peter Boulware	.25
13	Eric Green	.25
14	Michael Jackson	.25
15	Bam Morris	.25
16	Vinny Testaverde	.25
17	Todd Collins	.25
18	Quinn Early	.25
19	Jim Kelly	.50
20	Andre Reed	.25
21	Antowain Smith	1.75
22	Steve Tasker	.25
23	Thurman Thomas	.50
24	Steve Beuerlein	.25
25	Rae Carruth	.50
26	Kerry Collins	.50
27	Anthony Johnson	.25
28	Ernie Mills	.25
29	Wesley Walls	.25
30	Curtis Conway	.50
31	Bobby Engram	.25
32	Raymont Harris	.25
33	Erik Kramer	.25
34	Rick Mirer	.25
35	Darnay Scott	.25
36	Tony McGee	.25
37	Jeff Blake	.50
38	Corey Dillon	2.00
39	Carl Pickens	.25
40	Troy Aikman	2.50
41	Billy Davis	.25
42	David LaFleur	.50
43	Anthony Miller	.25
44	Emmitt Smith	4.00
45	Herschel Walker	.25
46	Sherman Williams	.25
47	Flipper Anderson	.25
48	Terrell Davis	2.50
49	Jason Elam	.25
50	John Elway	2.00
51	Darrien Gordon	.25
52	Ed McCaffrey	.25
53	Shannon Sharpe	.25
54	Neil Smith	.25
55	Rod Smith	.25
56	Maa Tanuvasa	.25
57	Glyn Milburn	.25
58	Scott Mitchell	.25
59	Herman Moore	.50
60	Johnnie Morton	.25
61	Barry Sanders	3.00
62	Tommy Vardell	.25
63	Bryant Westbrook	.25
64	Robert Brooks	.25
65	Mark Chmura	.50
66	Brett Favre	5.00
67	Antonio Freeman	.50
68	Dorsey Levens	.50
69	Bill Schroeder	.25
70	Marshall Faulk	.50
71	Jim Harbaugh	.25
72	Marvin Harrison	.50
73	Derek Brown	.25
74	Mark Brunell	2.00
75	Rob Johnson	.50
76	Keenan McCardell	.25
77	Natrone Means	.50
78	Jimmy Smith	.25
79	James Stewart	.25
80	Marcus Allen	.50
81	Pat Barnes	.50
82	Tony Gonzalez	.50
83	Elvis Grbac	.25
84	Greg Hill	.25
85	Kevin Lockett	.25
86	Andre Rison	.25
87	Karim Abdul-Jabbar	.50
88	Fred Barnett	.25
89	Troy Drayton	.25
90	Dan Marino	4.00
91	Irving Spikes	.25
92	Cris Carter	.25
93	Matthew Hatchette	.25
94	Brad Johnson	.50
95	Jake Reed	.25
96	Robert Smith	.50
97	Drew Bledsoe	2.50
98	Keith Byars	.25
99	Ben Coates	.25
100	Terry Glenn	1.00
101	Shawn Jefferson	.25
102	Curtis Martin	2.00
103	Dave Meggett	.25
104	Troy Davis	.50
105	Danny Wuerffel	.50
106	Ray Zellers	.25
107	Tiki Barber	1.25
108	Rodney Hampton	.25
109	Ike Hilliard	.50
110	Danny Kanell	.25
111	Tyrone Wheatley	.25
112	Kyle Brady	.25
113	Wayne Chrebet	.25
114	Aaron Glenn	.25
115	Jeff Graham	.25
116	Keyshawn Johnson	.50
117	Adrian Murrell	.50
118	Neil O'Donnell	.25
119	Heath Shuler	.25
120	Tim Brown	.50
121	Rickey Dudley	.25
122	Jeff George	.50
123	Desmond Howard	.25
124	James Jett	.25
125	Napoleon Kaufman	.50
126	Chad Levitt	.25
127	Darrell Russell	.25
128	Ty Detmer	.25
129	Irving Fryar	.25
130	Charlie Garner	.25
131	Kevin Turner	.25
132	Ricky Watters	.50
133	Jerome Bettis	.50
134	Will Blackwell	.25
135	Mark Bruener	.25
136	Charles Johnson	.25
137	George Jones	.25
138	Kordell Stewart	2.50
139	Yancey Thigpen	.25
140	Gary Brown	.25
141	Jim Everett	.25
142	Terrell Fletcher	.25
143	Stan Humphries	.25
144	Freddie Jones	.25
145	Tony Martin	.25
146	Jim Druckenmiller	1.50
147	Garrison Hearst	.25
148	Brent Jones	.25
149	Terrell Owens	.50
150	Jerry Rice	2.50
151	J.J. Stokes	.25
152	Steve Young	1.50
153	Steve Broussard	.25
154	Joey Galloway	.50
155	Jon Kitna	.25
156	Warren Moon	.50
157	Shawn Springs	.25
158	Chris Warren	.25
159	Tony Banks	.50
160	Isaac Bruce	.50
161	Eddie Kennison	.50
162	Orlando Pace	.25
163	Lawrence Phillips	.25
164	Mike Alstott	.50
165	Reidel Anthony	1.25
166	Horace Copeland	.25
167	Trent Dilfer	.50
168	Warrick Dunn	3.00
169	Hardy Nickerson	.25
170	Karl Williams	.25
171	Eddie George	2.50
172	Ronnie Harmon	.25
173	Joey Kent	.25
174	Steve McNair	2.00
175	Chris Sanders	.25
176	Terry Allen	.25
177	Jamie Asher	.25
178	Stephen Davis	.25
179	Gus Frerotte	.25
180	Leslie Shepherd	.25

1998 Collector's Edge Advantage Gold

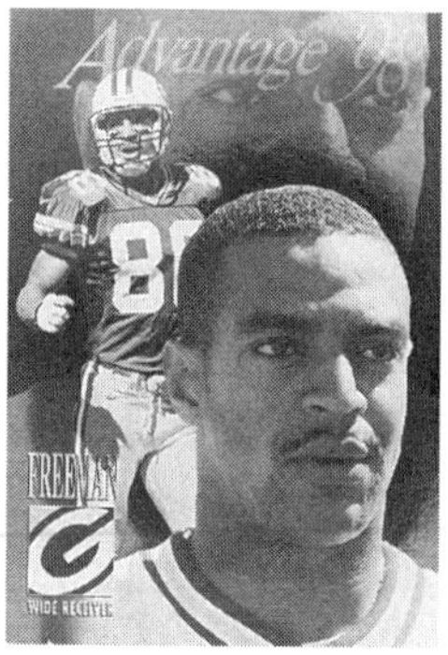

The 180-card Advantage base set has a lacquered gold parallel version. The cards were inserted one per six packs.

	MT
Gold Cards:	5x

1998 Collector's Edge Advantage Silver

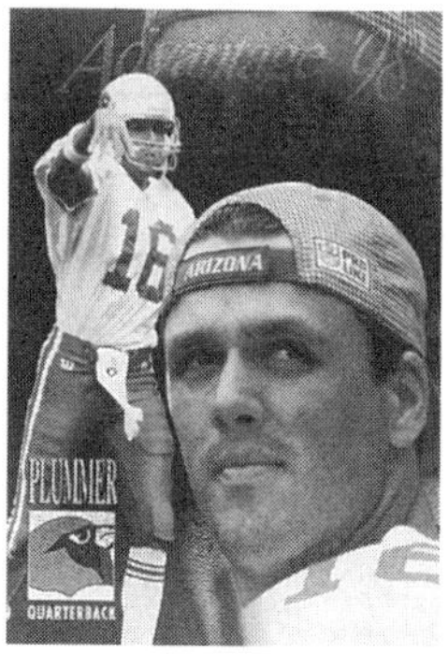

A parallel of the 180-card Advantage base set was printed on embossed silver stock and inserted 1:2.

	MT
Silver Cards:	4x

1998 Collector's Edge Advantage 50-Point

This parallel of the 180-card Advantage base set was printed on 50-point card stock and seeded one per pack.

	MT
50-Point Cards:	3x

1998 Collector's Edge Advantage Livin' Large

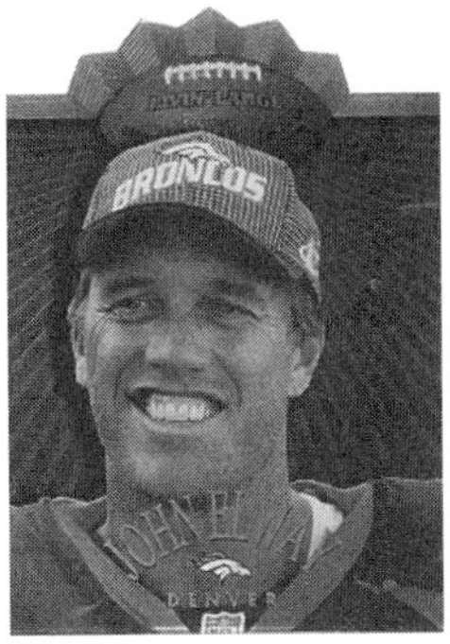

Livin' Large was a 22-card insert that was printed on plastic with a die-cut out of the top of the card. Inserted every 12 packs, these inserts featured a head shot of the player, with a football over his head with the insert name inside. The player's name, position and team logo was printed across the bottom, with the background colors related to that team. Holofoil versions of each card were also printed with a stated prind run of 100 sets.

		MT
Complete Set (22):		150.00
Common Player:		2.00
Holofoil Cards:		5x-10x
1	Leeland McElroy	2.00
2	Jamal Anderson	4.00
3	Antowain Smith	8.00
4	Emmitt Smith	20.00
5	John Elway	12.00
6	Barry Sanders	20.00
7	Elvis Grbac	2.00
8	Dan Marino	20.00
9	Cris Carter	2.00
10	Drew Bledsoe	12.00
11	Curtis Martin	12.00
12	Troy Davis	4.00
13	Ike Hilliard	4.00
14	Adrian Murrell	2.00
15	Tim Brown	2.00
16	Kordell Stewart	12.00
17	Jerry Rice	12.00
18	Tony Banks	4.00
19	Mike Alstott	5.00
20	Trent Dilfer	4.00
21	Eddie George	12.00
22	Steve McNair	8.00

1998 Collector's Edge Advantage Personal Victory

This six-card set was also individually numbered to 200 on the back and contained a piece of a game-used ball on the front. The front has three shots of the player - one on each side of a large gold foil "V" and another inside the "V." The player's name is stamped across the bottom, with the piece of game ball above it with the words "Personal Victory" over the game ball. A dull finish is used on the back of the card along with a shot of the game in which the featured player achieved his personal victory.

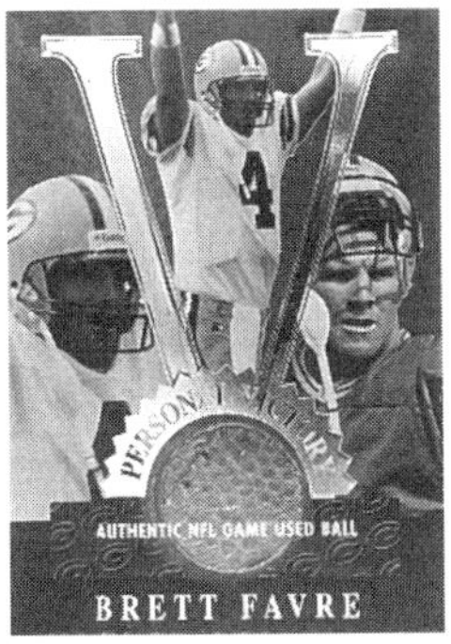

		MT
Complete Set (6):		1100.00
Common Player:		150.00
1	John Elway	200.00
2	Barry Sanders	300.00
3	Brett Favre	400.00
4	Mark Brunell	150.00
5	Drew Bledsoe	150.00
6	Jerry Rice	200.00

1998 Collector's Edge Advantage Prime Connection

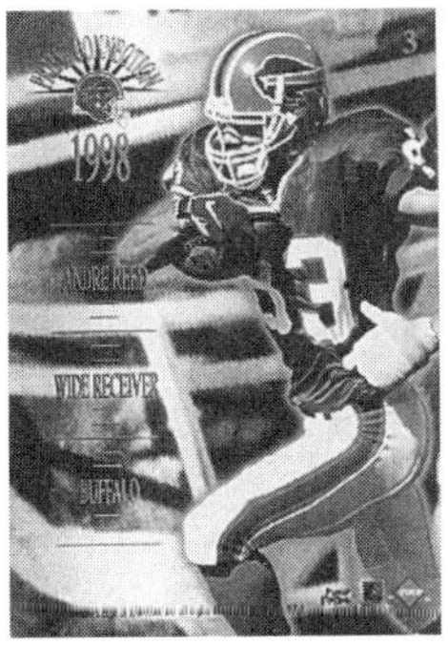

Prime Connections spotlights the top tandems of 25 NFL teams on a double-sided, metallic looking card. Each side has an action shot of a player on the right side, with the player's name, position and team on the left side, along with the Prime Connections logo in the upper left corner. The cards are numbered on both sides in the upper right corner and were inserted every 36 packs of Advantage.

		MT
Complete Set (25):		500.00
Common Player:		5.00
1	LeShon Johnson, Leeland McElroy	5.00
2	Peter Boulware, Michael Jackson	5.00
3	Andre Reed, Antowain Smith	20.00
4	Rae Carruth, Anthony Johnson	10.00
5	Herschel Walker, Emmitt Smith	50.00
6	Terrell Davis, John Elway	40.00
7	Ed McCaffrey, Shannon Sharpe	5.00
8	Herman Moore, Barry Sanders	40.00
9	Brett Favre, Antonio Freeman	60.00
10	Mark Brunell, James Stewart	25.00
11	Marcus Allen, Elvis Grbac	10.00
12	Karim Abdul-Jabbar, Dan Marino	50.00
13	Drew Bledsoe, Ben Coates	25.00
14	Terry Glenn, Curtis Martin	25.00
15	Troy Davis, Danny Wuerffel	10.00
16	Ike Hilliard, Danny Kanell	10.00
17	Aaron Glenn, Adrian Murrell	5.00
18	Tim Brown, Napoleon Kaufman	10.00
19	Mark Bruener, Jerome Bettis	10.00
20	Jim Druckenmiller, Terrell Owens	20.00
21	Garrison Hearst, Steve Young	20.00
22	Tony Banks, Eddie Kennison	15.00
23	Mike Alstott, Reidel Anthony	15.00
24	Hardy Nickerson, Warrick Dunn	30.00
25	Eddie George, Steve McNair	30.00

1998 Collector's Edge Advantage Showtime

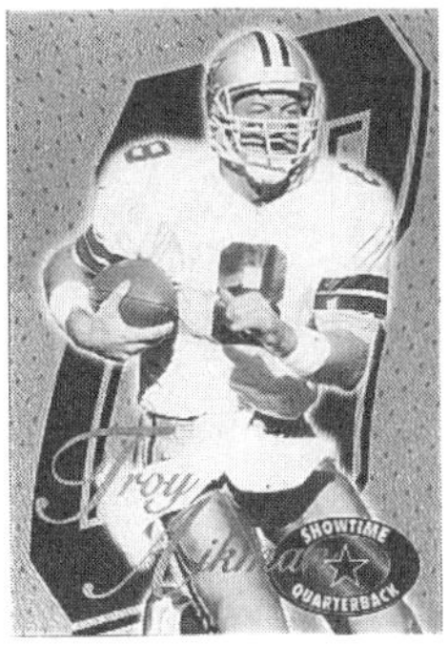

This 23-card insert set was seeded one per 18 packs of Advantage Football. Card fronts featured an action shot of the player, with his name written across the bottom. The background was printed in team colors and was supposed to look like jersey material, with the player's position in large letters behind him. Holofoil versions of these cards also exist and were limited in print run to 100 sets.

		MT
Complete Set (23):		250.00
Common Player:		3.00
Holofoils:		3x-6x
1	LeShon Johnson	3.00
2	Peter Boulware	3.00
3	Jim Kelly	6.00
4	Rae Carruth	6.00
5	Kerry Collins	10.00
6	Troy Aikman	20.00
7	Terrell Davis	20.00
8	Shannon Sharpe	3.00
9	Brett Favre	40.00
10	Mark Brunell	20.00
11	Keenan McCardell	3.00
12	Marcus Allen	6.00
13	Terry Glenn	8.00
14	Danny Wuerffel	6.00
15	Danny Kanell	3.00
16	Aaron Glenn	3.00
17	Napoleon Kaufman	8.00
18	Mark Bruener	3.00
19	Jim Druckenmiller	10.00
20	Terrell Owens	8.00
21	Steve Young	12.00
22	Reidel Anthony	8.00
23	Warrick Dunn	20.00

1998 Collector's Edge Supreme

Supreme Season Review consists of a 200-card base set, with 170 veterans and 30 redmeption cards for the top draft pick from each NFL team. The player's name and Collector's Edge logo are printed in gold foil on the front. The base set is paralleled by Gold Ingots. Inserts include Markers, T-3 Triple Threat and Pro Signatures Authentic. Two 1-of-1 inserts were also created: Memorable Moments and the 200-card Personal Collection, which features photos from Super Bowl XXXII.

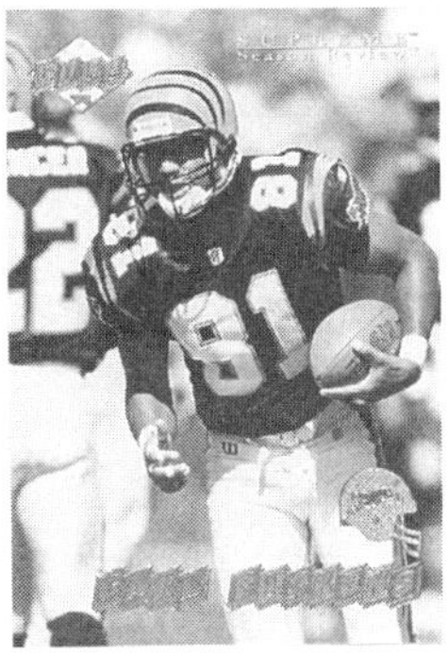

		MT
Complete Set (200):		75.00
Common Player:		.20
Wax Box:		60.00
1	Larry Centers	.20
2	Jake Plummer	2.00
3	Simeon Rice	.20
4	Arizona Draft Pick	2.00
5	Jamal Anderson	.40
6	Bert Emanuel	.20
7	Byron Hanspard	.40
8	Atlanta Draft Pick	1.00
9	Derrick Alexander	.20
10	Peter Boulware	.20
11	Michael Jackson	.20
12	Ray Lewis	.20
13	Vinny Testaverde	.40
14	Baltimore Draft Pick	1.00
15	Todd Collins	.20
16	Jim Kelly	.40
17	Andre Reed	.20
18	Antowain Smith	1.00
19	Bruce Smith	.20
20	Thurman Thomas	.40
21	Buffalo Draft Pick	1.00
22	Tim Biakabutuka	.20
23	Rae Carruth	.40
24	Kerry Collins	1.00
25	Anthony Johnson	.20
26	Lamar Lathon	.20
27	Carolina Draft Pick	1.00
28	Curtis Conway	.40
29	Bryan Cox	.20
30	Bobby Engram	.20
31	Erik Kramer	.20
32	Rick Mirer	.20
33	Rashaan Salaam	.40
34	Chicago Draft Pick	3.00
35	Jeff Blake	.40
36	Ki-Jana Carter	.20
37	Corey Dillon	1.50
38	Carl Pickens	.40
39	Cincinnati Draft Pick	1.00
40	Troy Aikman	2.00
41	Daryl Johnston	.20
42	David LaFleur	.40
43	Anthony Miller	.20
44	Deion Sanders	1.00
45	Emmitt Smith	3.00
46	Broderick Thomas	.20
47	Dallas Draft Pick	1.00
48	Terrell Davis	2.00
49	John Elway	2.00
50	Ed McCaffrey	.20
51	John Mobley	.20
52	Bill Romanowski	.20
53	Shannon Sharpe	.20
54	Neil Smith	.20
55	Rod Smith	.20
56	Maa Tanuvasa	.20
57	Denver Draft Pick	2.00
58	Scott Mitchell	.20
59	Herman Moore	.40
60	Barry Sanders	3.00
61	Detroit Draft Pick	1.00
62	Robert Brooks	.40
63	Mark Chmura	.20
64	Brett Favre	4.00
65	Antonio Freeman	.40
66	Dorsey Levens	.40
67	Derrick Mayes	.20
68	Ross Verba	.20
69	Reggie White	.40
70	Green Bay Draft Pick	1.00
71	Marshall Faulk	.40
72	Jim Harbaugh	.40
73	Marvin Harrison	.40
74	Indianapolis Draft Pick	6.00
75	Tony Brackens	.20
76	Mark Brunell	2.00
77	Rob Johnson	.40
78	Keenan McCardell	.20
79	Natrone Means	.40
80	Jimmy Smith	.20
81	Jacksonville Draft Pick	4.00
82	Marcus Allen	.40
83	Tony Gonzalez	.40
84	Elvis Grbac	.20
85	Derrick Thomas	.20
86	Tamarick Vanover	.20
87	Kansas City Draft Pick	1.00
88	Karim Abdul-Jabbar	.40
89	Fred Barnett	.20
90	Dan Marino	3.00
91	O.J. McDuffie	.20
92	Brett Perriman	.20
93	Irving Spikes	.20
94	Zach Thomas	.20
95	Miami Draft Pick	2.00
96	Cris Carter	.20
97	Brad Johnson	.40
98	John Randle	.20
99	Jake Reed	.20
100	Robert Smith	.20
101	Minnesota Draft Pick	10.00
102	Drew Bledsoe	2.00
103	Chris Canty	.20
104	Ben Coates	.20
105	Terry Glenn	.40
106	Curtis Martin	1.50
107	Willie McGinest	.20
108	Sedrick Shaw	.20
109	New England Draft Pick	3.00
110	Mario Bates	.20
111	Heath Shuler	.20
112	Danny Wuerffel	.40
113	New Orleans Draft Pick	1.00
114	Ray Zellars	.20
115	Tiki Barber	.40
116	Dave Brown	.20
117	Ike Hilliard	.40
118	Danny Kanell	.20
119	Jason Sehorn	.20
120	Amani Toomer	.20
121	New York Giants Draft Pick	1.00
122	Wayne Chrebet	.20
123	Hugh Douglas	.20
124	Jeff Graham	.20
125	Keyshawn Johnson	.40
126	Adrian Murrell	.40
127	Neil O'Donnell	.20
128	New York Jets Draft Pick	1.00
129	Tim Brown	.40
130	Jeff George	.40
131	Desmond Howard	.20
132	Napoleon Kaufman	.40
133	Darrell Russell	.20
134	Oakland Draft Pick	3.00
135	Ty Detmer	.20
136	Irving Fryar	.20
137	Bobby Hoying	.40
138	Chris T. Jones	.20
139	Ricky Watters	.40
140	Philadelphia Draft Pick	1.00
141	Jerome Bettis	.40
142	Charles Johnson	.20
143	George Jones	.20
144	Greg Lloyd	.20
145	Kordell Stewart	2.00
146	Yancey Thigpen	.20
147	Pittsburgh Draft Pick	1.00
148	Stan Humphries	.20
149	Tony Martin	.20
150	Eric Metcalf	.20
151	Junior Seau	.40
152	San Diego Draft Pick	5.00
153	Jim Druckenmiller	.40
154	William Floyd	.40
155	Kevin Greene	.20
156	Garrison Hearst	.20
157	Ken Norton	.20
158	Terrell Owens	.40
159	Jerry Rice	2.00
160	J.J. Stokes	.20
161	Dana Stubblefield	.20
162	Rod Woodson	.20
163	Bryant Young	.20
164	Steve Young	1.00
165	San Francisco Draft Pick	1.00
166	Steve Broussard	.20
167	Chad Brown	.20
168	Joey Galloway	.40
169	Jon Kitna	.20
170	Warren Moon	.40
171	Chris Warren	.20
172	Seattle Draft Pick	2.00
173	Tony Banks	.40
174	Isaac Bruce	.40
175	Eddie Kennison	.40
176	Keith Lyle	.20
177	Lawrence Phillips	.20
178	St. Louis Draft Pick	2.00
179	Mike Alstott	.40
180	Anthony Reidel	.40
181	Trent Dilfer	.40
182	Warrick Dunn	2.00
183	Hardy Nickerson	.20
184	Errict Rhett	.20
185	Warren Sapp	.20
186	Tampa Bay Draft Pick	2.00
187	Eddie George	2.00
188	Darryll Lewis	.20
189	Steve McNair	1.00
190	Chris Sanders	.20
191	Tennessee Draft Pick	1.00
192	Terry Allen	.40
193	Jamie Asher	.20
194	Stephen Davis	.20

195	Gus Frerotte	.40
196	Sean Gilbert	.20
197	Ken Harvey	.20
198	Jeff Hostetler	.20
199	Michael Westbrook	.20
200	Washington Draft Pick	1.00

1998 Collector's Edge Supreme Gold Ingots

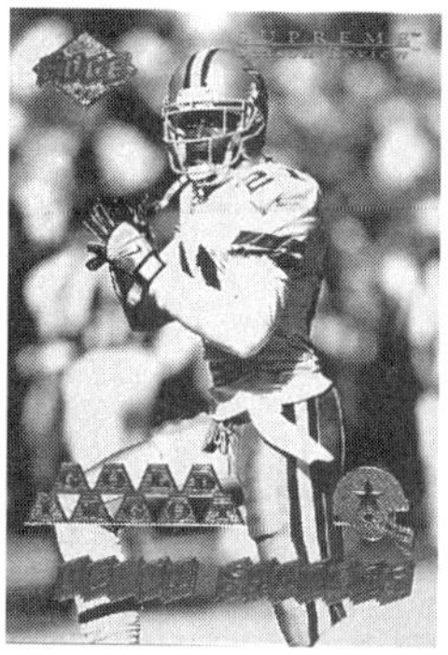

Gold Ingots is a full parallel of the Supreme Season Review base set. The cards are printed on 48-point card stock and have "Gold Ingots" printed in gold foil on the front.

	MT
Gold Ingots Cards:	2x-4x
Gold Ingots Rookies:	2x

1998 Collector's Edge Supreme Markers

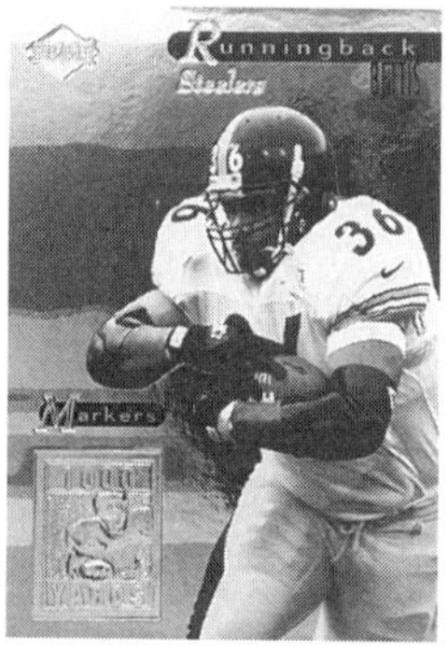

Markers is a 30-card insert seeded one per 24 packs. The cards are printed on 48-point stock. The player's last name, position and team are listed at the top. An embossed gold-foil logo denotes which statistical "marker" the player has acheived.

		MT
Complete Set (30):		375.00
Common Player:		5.00
1	Jamal Anderson	5.00
2	Corey Dillon	20.00
3	Emmitt Smith	40.00
4	Terrell Davis	25.00
5	John Elway	25.00
6	Rod Smith	5.00
7	Herman Moore	10.00
8	Barry Sanders	40.00
9	Robert Brooks	5.00
10	Brett Favre	50.00
11	Antonio Freeman	10.00
12	Dorsey Levens	10.00
13	Marshall Faulk	10.00
14	Mark Brunell	20.00
15	Karim Abdul-Jabbar	10.00
16	Dan Marino	40.00
17	Cris Carter	5.00
18	Drew Bledsoe	20.00
19	Curtis Martin	15.00
20	Adrian Murrell	5.00
21	Tim Brown	5.00
22	Jeff George	5.00
23	Napoleon Kaufman	10.00
24	Jerome Bettis	10.00
25	Kordell Stewart	20.00
26	Yancey Thigpen	5.00
27	Garrison Hearst	5.00
28	Steve Young	15.00
29	Joey Galloway	10.00
30	Eddie George	25.00

1998 Collector's Edge Supreme Pro Signatures Authentic

Seven players signed cards for the Pro Signatures Authentic insert (1:800). Collector's Edge also obtained rookie draft-day jerseys and put swatches on Draft Day Jersey cards.

		MT
Common Player:		125.00
TA	Troy Aikman	450.00
DH	Desmond Howard	150.00
JR	Jerry Rice	500.00
MA	Marcus Allen	200.00
TD	Terrell Davis	500.00
RL	Ryan Leaf	150.00
PM	Peyton Manning	150.00

1998 Collector's Edge Supreme T-3 Triple Threat

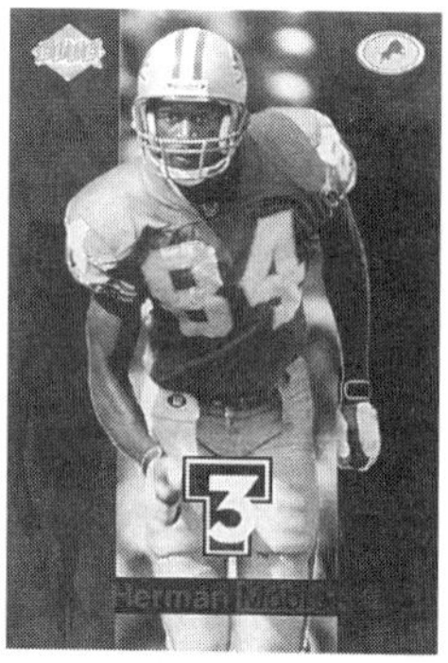

T-3 Triple Threat is a 30-card insert. The set features 10 quarterbacks (1:36), 10 running backs (1:24) and 10 wide receivers (1:12). The front has a color player image which is repeated on the left and right. The team's logo is in the upper right and the player's name and T-3 logo are at the bottom.

		MT
Complete Set (29):		225.00
Common WR:		2.50
Common RB:		4.00
Common QB:		6.00
Card #18 Never Issued		
1	Rae Carruth	2.50
2	Carl Pickens	2.50
3	Troy Aikman	15.00
4	Emmitt Smith	20.00
5	Terrell Davis	12.00
6	John Elway	15.00
7	Herman Moore	5.00
8	Barry Sanders	20.00
9	Robert Brooks	2.50
10	Brett Favre	30.00
11	Antonio Freeman	5.00
12	Dorsey Levens	4.00
13	Rob Johnson	6.00
14	Jerry Rice	10.00
15	Dan Marino	25.00
16	Cris Carter	2.50
17	Drew Bledsoe	15.00
19	Adrian Murrell	4.00
20	Tim Brown	2.50
21	Napoleon Kaufman	4.00
22	Jerome Bettis	4.00
23	Kordell Stewart	15.00
24	Joey Galloway	5.00
25	Jim Druckenmiller	6.00
26	Terrell Owens	2.50
27	Jake Plummer	12.00
28	Warrick Dunn	12.00
29	Eddie George	12.00
30	Steve McNair	8.00

1998 Finest

Finest was issued in two, 150-card series in 1998,with 150 in Series I and 120 in Series II. Each card was available in a Protector (base cards), No-Protector (1:2 packs), Protector Refractor (1:12) and No-Protector Refractor (1:24) version. An interesting twist to the releases was that the 30 rookies (121-150) were available in Protector and No-Protector Refractor versions in Series I, but the No-Protector and Protector Refractor versions were only issued in Series II packs. Series I inserts were: Double-Sided Mystery Finest, Centurions, Undergrads and Jumbos, while Series II inserts included Mystery Finest, Stadium Stars, Future's Finest, Jumbos (base cards), Jumbo Stadium Stars and Jumbo Mystery

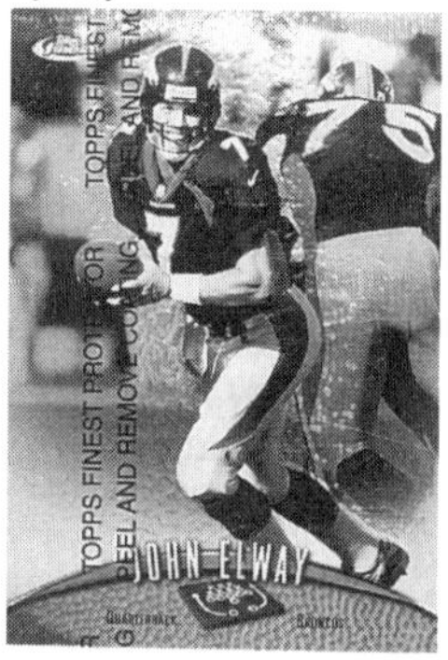

		MT
Complete Set (150):		150.00
Common Player:		.25
Wax Box:		120.00
1	John Elway	2.50
2	Terance Mathis	.25
3	Jermaine Lewis	.25
4	Fred Lane	.50
5	Bryan Cox	.25
6	David Dunn	.25
7	Dexter Coakley	.25
8	Carl Pickens	.50
9	Antonio Freeman	.75
10	Herman Moore	.75
11	Kevin Hardy	.25
12	Tony Gonzalez	.50
13	O.J. McDuffie	.25
14	David Palmer	.25
15	Lawyer Milloy	.25
16	Danny Kanell	.25
17	Randal Hill	.25
18	Keyshawn Johnson	.50
19	Charlie Garner	.25
20	Mark Brunell	2.00
21	Donnell Woolford	.25
22	Freddie Jones	.25
23	Ken Norton	.25
24	Tony Banks	.50
25	Isaac Bruce	.50
26	Willie Davis	.25
27	Cris Dishman	.25
28	Aeneas Williams	.25
29	Michael Booker	.25
30	Cris Carter	.50
31	Michael McCrary	.25
32	Eric Moulds	.25
33	Rae Carruth	.25
34	Bobby Engram	.25
35	Jeff Blake	.50
36	Deion Sanders	1.00
37	Rod Smith	.50
38	Bryant Westbrook	.25
39	Mark Chmura	.50
40	Tim Brown	.50
41	Bobby Taylor	.25
42	James Stewart	.25
43	Kimble Anders	.25
44	Karim Abdul-Jabbar	.75
45	Willie McGinest	.25
46	Jessie Armstead	.25
47	Aaron Glenn	.25
48	Greg Lloyd	.25
49	Stephen Davis	.25
50	Jerome Bettis	.50
51	Warren Sapp	.25
52	Horace Copeland	.25
53	Chad Brown	.25
54	Chris Canty	.25
55	Robert Smith	.50
56	Pete Mitchell	.25
57	Aaron Bailey	.25
58	Robert Porcher	.25
59	John Mobley	.25
60	Tony Martin	.25
61	Michael Irvin	.50
62	Charles Way	.25
63	Raymont Harris	.25
64	Chuck Smith	.25
65	Larry Centers	.25
66	Greg Hill	.25
67	Kenny Holmes	.25
68	John Lynch	.25
69	Michael Sinclair	.25
70	Steve Young	1.50
71	Michael Strahan	.25
72	Levon Kirkland	.25
73	Rickey Dudley	.25
74	Marcus Allen	.50
75	John Randle	.25
76	Erik Kramer	.25
77	Neil Smith	.25
78	Byron Hanspard	.50
79	Quinn Early	.25
80	Warren Moon	.50
81	William Thomas	.25
82	Ben Coates	.25
83	Lake Dawson	.25
84	Steve McNair	1.50
85	Gus Frerotte	.25
86	Rodney Harrison	.25
87	Reggie White	.50
88	Derrick Thomas	.25
89	Dale Carter	.25
90	Warrick Dunn	3.00
91	Will Blackwell	.25
92	Troy Vincent	.25
93	Johnnie Morton	.25
94	David LaFleur	.25
95	Tony McGee	.25
96	Lonnie Johnson	.25
97	Thurman Thomas	.50
98	Chris Chandler	.25
99	Jamal Anderson	.50
100	Emmitt Smith	4.00
101	Marshall Faulk	.75
102	Chris Calloway	.25
103	Chris Spielman	.25
104	Zach Thomas	.25
105	Jeff George	.50
106	Darrell Russell	.25
107	Darryll Lewis	.25
108	Reidel Anthony	.50
109	Terrell Owens	.75
110	Rob Moore	.25
111	Darrell Green	.25
112	Merton Hanks	.25
113	Shawn Jefferson	.25
114	Chris Sanders	.25
115	Scott Mitchell	.25
116	Vaughn Hebron	.25
117	Ed McCaffrey	.25
118	Bruce Smith	.25
119	Peter Boulware	.25
120	Brett Favre	5.00
121	*Peyton Manning*	25.00
122	*Brian Griese*	8.00
123	*Tavian Banks*	8.00
124	*Duane Starks*	2.00
125	*Robert Holcombe*	5.00
126	*Brian Simmons*	1.50
127	*Skip Hicks*	6.00
128	*Keith Brooking*	3.00
129	*Ahman Green*	7.00
130	*Jerome Pathon*	3.00
131	*Curtis Enis*	10.00
132	*Grant Wistrom*	2.00
133	*Germane Crowell*	6.00
134	*Jacquez Green*	7.00
135	*Randy Moss*	40.00
136	*Jason Peter*	4.00
137	*John Avery*	6.00
138	*Takeo Spikes*	4.00
139	*Patrick Johnson*	2.00
140	*Andre Wadsworth*	4.00
141	*Fred Taylor*	15.00
142	*Charles Woodson*	10.00
143	*Marcus Nash*	5.00
144	*Robert Edwards*	12.00
145	*Kevin Dyson*	5.00
146	*Joe Jurevicius*	3.00
147	*Anthony Simmons*	2.00
148	*Hines Ward*	5.00
149	*Greg Ellis*	2.00
150	*Ryan Leaf*	15.00

1998 Finest Refractors

Both Protector and No-Protector versions had parallel Refractor versions for all 270 cards. Protector Refractors were inserted one per 12 packs and had only the front of the card with a Refractor finish, while No-Protector Refractors were inserted one per 24 packs and were basically a double-sided Refractor. No-Protector Refractor versions of the 30 rookies (121-150) were inserted into Series I packs, while Protector Refractor versions were only in Series II packs.

	MT
Refractor Set (120):	300.00
Refractors:	6x-12x
Rookies Not Included	
No-Protector Set (120):	100.00
No-Protector Cards:	2x-4x
Rookies Not Included	
NP Refractor Set (150):	1500.
NP Ref. Stars:	12x-25x
NP Ref. Rookies:	4x-8x

1998 Finest Centurions

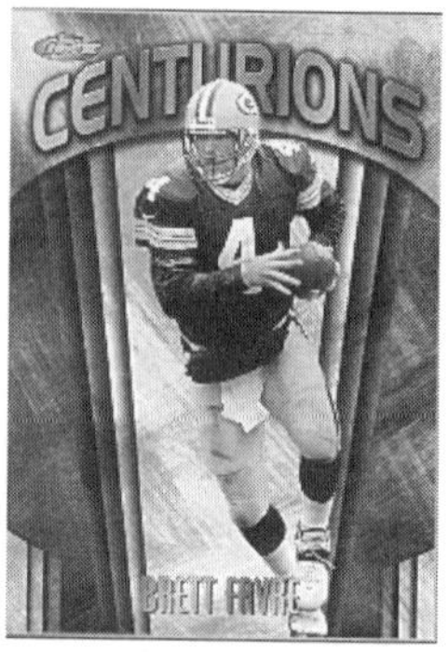

This 20-card insert set was found in packs of Series I. Regular versions were numbered to 500, while Refractors were numbered to only 75. Centurions inserts were numbered with a "C" prefix.

		MT
Complete Set (20):		550.00
Common Player:		12.00
Comp. Ref. Set (20):		2000.
Refractors:		2x-4x
C1	Brett Favre	100.00
C2	Eddie George	50.00
C3	Antonio Freeman	24.00
C4	Napoleon Kaufman	25.00
C5	Terrell Davis	60.00
C6	Keyshawn Johnson	12.00
C7	Peter Boulware	12.00
C8	Mike Alstott	24.00
C9	Jake Plummer	50.00
C10	Mark Brunell	50.00
C11	Marvin Harrison	12.00
C12	Antowain Smith	30.00
C13	Dorsey Levens	24.00
C14	Terry Glenn	24.00
C15	Warrick Dunn	50.00
C16	Joey Galloway	12.00
C17	Steve McNair	40.00
C18	Corey Dillon	40.00
C19	Drew Bledsoe	50.00
C20	Kordell Stewart	50.00

1998 Finest Mystery Finest

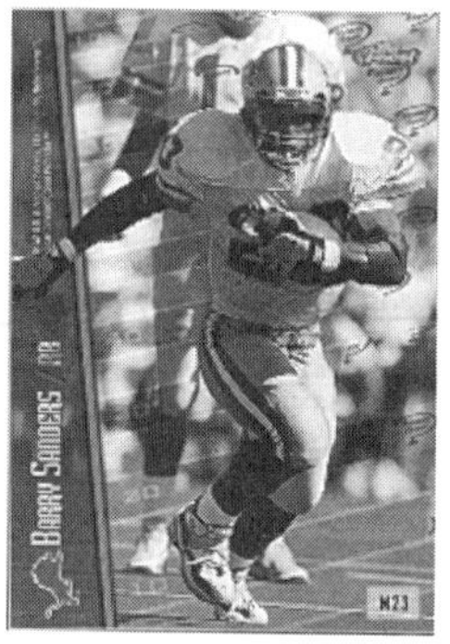

Twenty different players were displayed either with one of three other players on the back, or by themselves on both sides in Mystery Finest. Each side has a Finest Opaque protector and is numbered with a "M" prefix. Regular versions are seeded one per 36 packs, while Refractors are found every 144 packs.

		MT
Complete Set (50):		1200.
Common Player:		12.00
Comp. Ref. Set (50):		2400.
Refractors:		2x
M1	Brett Favre, Mark Brunell	50.00
M2	Brett Favre, Jake Plummer	50.00
M3	Brett Favre, Steve Young	50.00
M4	Brett Favre, Brett Favre	60.00
M5	Mark Brunell, Steve Young	20.00

M6	Mark Brunell, Mark Brunell	20.00
M7	Jake Plummer, Mark Brunell	20.00
M8	Jake Plummer, Jake Plummer	30.00
M9	Steve Young, Jake Plummer	20.00
M10	Steve Young, Steve Young	20.00
M11	John Elway, Drew Bledsoe	30.00
M12	John Elway, Troy Aikman	30.00
M13	John Elway, Dan Marino	50.00
M14	John Elway, John Elway	30.00
M15	Drew Bledsoe, Troy Aikman	30.00
M16	Drew Bledsoe, Drew Bledsoe	30.00
M17	Troy Aikman, Dan Marino	50.00
M18	Troy Aikman, Troy Aikman	30.00
M19	Dan Marino, Drew Bledsoe	50.00
M20	Dan Marino, Dan Marino	60.00
M21	Kordell Stewart, Corey Dillon	30.00
M22	Kordell Stewart, Tim Brown	30.00
M23	Kordell Stewart, Barry Sanders	50.00
M24	Kordell Stewart, Kordell Stewart	30.00
M25	Corey Dillon, Tim Brown	20.00
M26	Corey Dillon, Corey Dillon	20.00
M27	Tim Brown, Barry Sanders	40.00
M28	Tim Brown, Tim Brown	12.00
M29	Barry Sanders, Corey Dillon	50.00
M30	Barry Sanders, Barry Sanders	60.00
M31	Terrell Davis, Emmitt Smith	40.00
M32	Terrell Davis, Jerome Bettis	30.00
M33	Terrell Davis, Eddie George	30.00
M34	Terrell Davis, Terrell Davis	40.00
M35	Emmitt Smith, Eddie George	40.00
M36	Emmitt Smith, Emmitt Smith	50.00
M37	Jerome Bettis, Emmitt Smith	40.00
M38	Jerome Bettis, Jerome Bettis	12.00
M39	Eddie George, Jerome Bettis	25.00
M40	Eddie George, Eddie George	30.00
M41	Herman Moore, Jerry Rice	30.00
M42	Herman Moore, Herman Moore	12.00
M43	Warrick Dunn, Herman Moore	25.00
M44	Warrick Dunn, Jerry Rice	40.00
M45	Warrick Dunn, Dorsey Levens	25.00
M46	Warrick Dunn, Warrick Dunn	40.00
M47	Jerry Rice, Dorsey Levens	30.00
M48	Jerry Rice, Jerry Rice	40.00
M49	Dorsey Levens, Herman Moore	12.00
M50	Dorsey Levens, Dorsey Levens	12.00

1998 Finest Jumbos

Eight different Jumbo Finest cards were inserted as box toppers in both Series I and II. The 16-card set was inserted 1:3 boxes (1:2 hobby collector boxes), with Refractors every 12 boxes (1:6 hobby collector boxes).

		MT
Complete Set (8):		125.00
Common Player:		5.00
Inserted 1:3 Boxes		
Refractors:		2x
Inserted 1:12 Boxes		
1	John Elway	20.00
2	Peyton Manning	35.00
3	Mark Brunell	15.00
4	Curtis Enis	15.00
5	Jerome Bettis	5.00
6	Ryan Leaf	35.00
7	Warrick Dunn	15.00
8	Brett Favre	30.00

1998 Finest Undergrads

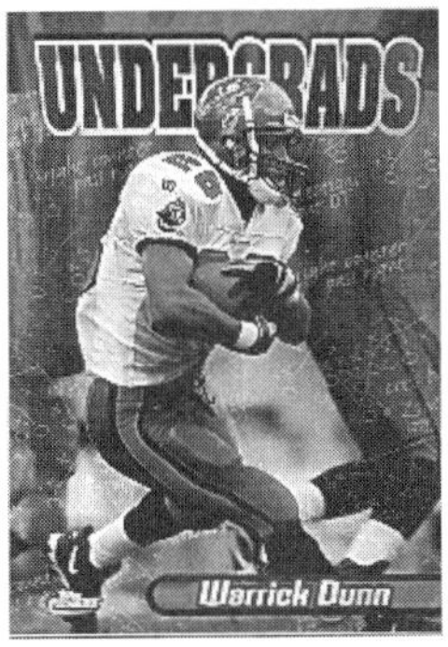

This 20-card insert showcased top rookies and second-year players. Undergrads were numbered with a "U" prefix and inserted one per 72 packs, with Refractor versions one per 216 packs.

		MT
Complete Set (20):		250.00
Common Player:		8.00
Com. Ref. Set (20):		500.00
Refractors:		2x
U1	Warrick Dunn	30.00
U2	Tony Gonzalez	8.00
U3	Antowain Smith	15.00
U4	Jake Plummer	30.00
U5	Peter Boulware	8.00
U6	Derrick Rodgers	8.00
U7	Freddie Jones	8.00
U8	Reidel Anthony	10.00
U9	Bryant Westbrook	8.00
U10	Corey Dillon	20.00
U11	Curtis Enis	20.00
U12	Andre Wadsworth	8.00
U13	Fred Taylor	30.00
U14	Greg Ellis	8.00
U15	Ryan Leaf	40.00
U16	Robert Edwards	25.00
U17	Germane Crowell	10.00
U18	Brian Griese	12.00
U19	Kevin Dyson	10.00
U20	Peyton Manning	50.00

1998 Fleer

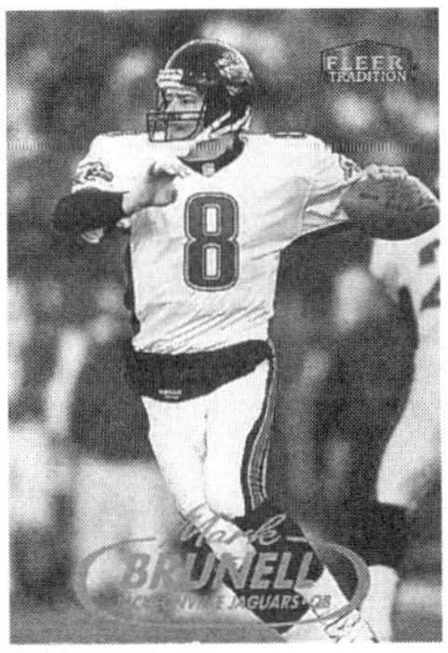

Fleer scrapped its matte finish and produced Tradition in 1998. This 250-card set, including 247 player cards and three checklists, is printed on a borderless design with the player's name, position and team printed across the bottom in gold foil. Tradition arrived with a parallel set called Heritage, which was numbered to 125 sets, and four different inserts, including Big Numbers, Rookie Sensations, Red Zone Rockers and Playmakers Theatre.

		MT
Complete Set (250):		45.00
Common Player:		.15
Wax Box:		50.00
1	Brett Favre	3.00
2	Barry Sanders	2.50
3	John Elway	1.50
4	Emmitt Smith	2.50
5	Dan Marino	2.50
6	Eddie George	1.50
7	Jerry Rice	1.50
8	Jake Plummer	1.50
9	Joey Galloway	.30
10	Mike Alstott	.50
11	Brian Mitchell	.15
12	Keyshawn Johnson	.30
13	Jerald Moore	.15
14	Randal Hill	.15
15	Byron Hanspard	.15
16	Jeff George	.30
17	Terry Glenn	.30
18	Jerome Bettis	.30
19	Curtis Conway	.30
20	Fred Lane	.30
21	Isaac Bruce	.30
22	Tiki Barber	.30
23	Bobby Hoying	.15
24	Marcus Allen	.30
25	Dana Stubblefield	.15
26	Peter Boulware	.15
27	John Randle	.15
28	Jason Sehorn	.15
29	Rod Smith	.30
30	Michael Sinclair	.15
31	Marshall Faulk	.30
32	Karl Williams	.15
33	Kordell Stewart	1.50
34	Corey Dillon	1.00
35	Bryant Young	.15
36	Charlie Garner	.15
37	Andre Reed	.15
38	Ray Buchanan	.15
39	Brett Perriman	.15
40	Leon Lett	.15
41	Keenan McCardell	.15
42	Eric Swann	.15
43	Leslie Shepherd	.15
44	Curtis Martin	1.00
45	Andre Rison	.30
46	Keith Lyle	.15
47	Rae Carruth	.15
48	William Henderson	.15
49	Sean Dawkins	.15
50	Terrell Davis	1.50
51	Tim Brown	.30
52	Willie McGinest	.15
53	Jermaine Lewis	.15
54	Ricky Watters	.30
55	Freddie Jones	.15
56	Robert Smith	.30
57	Reidel Anthony	.15
58	James Stewart	.15
59	Earl Holmes	.15
60	Dale Carter	.15
61	Michael Irvin	.30
62	Jason Taylor	.15
63	Eric Metcalf	.15
64	LeRoy Butler	.15
65	Jamal Anderson	.30
66	Jamie Asher	.15
67	Chris Sanders	.15
68	Warren Sapp	.15
69	Ray Zellars	.15
70	Carl Pickens	.30
71	Garrison Hearst	.15
72	Eddie Kennison	.30
73	John Mobley	.15
74	Rob Johnson	.30
75	William Thomas	.15
76	Drew Bledsoe	1.50
77	Michael Barrow	.15
78	Jim Harbaugh	.30
79	Terry McDaniel	.15
80	Johnnie Morton	.15
81	Danny Kanell	.15
82	Larry Centers	.15
83	Courtney Hawkins	.15
84	Tony Brackens	.15
85	Tony Gonzalez	.15
86	Aaron Glenn	.15
87	Cris Carter	.30
88	Chuck Smith	.15
89	Tamarick Vanover	.15
90	Karim Abdul-Jabbar	.30
91	Bryant Westbrook	.15
92	Mike Pritchard	.15
93	Darren Woodson	.15
94	Wesley Walls	.15
95	Tony Banks	.30
96	Michael Westbrook	.15
97	Shannon Sharpe	.30
98	Jeff Blake	.30
99	Terrell Owens	.30
100	Warrick Dunn	1.50
101	Levon Kirkland	.15
102	Frank Wycheck	.15
103	Gus Frerotte	.15
104	Simeon Rice	.15
105	Shawn Jefferson	.15
106	Irving Fryar	.15
107	Michael McCrary	.15
108	Robert Brooks	.15
109	Chris Chandler	.15
110	Junior Seau	.30
111	O.J. McDuffie	.15
112	Glenn Foley	.15
113	Darryl Williams	.15
114	Elvis Grbac	.15
115	Napoleon Kaufman	.50
116	Anthony Miller	.15
117	Troy Davis	.15
118	Charles Way	.15
119	Scott Mitchell	.15
120	Ken Harvey	.15
121	Tyrone Hughes	.15
122	Mark Brunell	1.25
123	David Palmer	.15
124	Rob Moore	.15
125	Kerry Collins	.75
126	Will Blackwell	.15
127	Ray Crockett	.15
128	Leslie O'Neal	.15
129	Antowain Smith	.75
130	Carlester Crumpler	.15
131	Michael Jackson	.15
132	Trent Dilfer	.30
133	Dan Williams	.15
134	Dorsey Levens	.30
135	Ty Law	.15
136	Rickey Dudley	.15
137	Jessie Tuggle	.15
138	Darrien Gordon	.15
139	Kevin Turner	.15
140	Willie Davis	.15
141	Zach Thomas	.15
142	Tony McGee	.15
143	Dexter Coakley	.15
144	Troy Brown	.15
145	Leeland McElroy	.15
146	Michael Strahan	.15
147	Ken Dilger	.15
148	Bryce Paup	.15
149	Herman Moore	.30
150	Reggie White	.30
151	DeWayne Washington	.15
152	Natrone Means	.30
153	Ben Coates	.15
154	Bert Emanuel	.15
155	Steve Young	1.00
156	Jimmy Smith	.15
157	Darrell Green	.15
158	Troy Aikman	1.50
159	Greg Hill	.15
160	Raymont Harris	.15
161	Troy Drayton	.15
162	Stevon Moore	.15
163	Warren Moon	.30
164	Wayne Martin	.15
165	Jason Gildon	.15
166	Chris Calloway	.15
167	Aeneas Williams	.15
168	Michael Bates	.15
169	Hugh Douglas	.15
170	Brad Johnson	.30
171	Bruce Smith	.15
172	Neil Smith	.15
173	James McKnight	.15
174	Robert Porcher	.15
175	Merton Hanks	.15
176	Ki-Jana Carter	.15
177	Mo Lewis	.15
178	Chester McGlockton	.15
179	Zack Crockett	.15
180	Derrick Thomas	.15
181	J.J. Stokes	.15
182	Derrick Rodgers	.15
183	Daryl Johnston	.15
184	Chris Penn	.15
185	Steve Atwater	.15
186	Amp Lee	.15
187	Frank Sanders	.15
188	Chris Slade	.15
189	Mark Chmura	.30
190	Kimble Anders	.15
191	Charles Johnson	.15
192	William Floyd	.15
193	Jay Graham	.15
194	Hardy Nickerson	.15
195	Terry Allen	.15
196	James Jett	.15
197	Jessie Armstead	.15
198	Yancey Thigpen	.15
199	Terance Mathis	.15
200	Steve McNair	.75
201	Wayne Chrebet	.15
202	Jamir Miller	.15
203	Duce Staley	.15
204	Deion Sanders	.75
205	Carnell Lake	.15
206	Ed McCaffrey	.15
207	Shawn Springs	.15
208	Tony Martin	.15
209	Jerris McPhail	.15
210	Darnay Scott	.15
211	Jake Reed	.15
212	Adrian Murrell	.30
213	Quinn Early	.15
214	Marvin Harrison	.30
215	Ryan McNeil	.15
216	Derrick Alexander	.15
217	Ray Lewis	.15
218	Antonio Freeman	.30
219	Dwayne Rudd	.15
220	Muhsin Muhammad	.15
221	Kevin Hardy	.15
222	Andre Hastings	.15
223	*John Avery*	2.00
224	*Keith Brooking*	1.00
225	*Kevin Dyson*	1.50
226	*Robert Edwards*	2.50
227	*Greg Ellis*	.15
228	*Curtis Enis*	3.00
229	*Terry Fair*	1.00
230	*Ahman Green*	2.00
231	*Jacquez Green*	2.00
232	*Brian Griese*	2.00
233	*Skip Hicks*	2.00
234	*Ryan Leaf*	8.00
235	*Peyton Manning*	8.00
236	*R.W. McQuarters*	.15
237	*Randy Moss*	15.00
238	*Marcus Nash*	2.00
239	*Anthony Simmons*	.50
240	*Brian Simmons*	.50
241	*Takeo Spikes*	1.00
242	*Duane Starks*	.15
243	*Fred Taylor*	4.00
244	*Andre Wadsworth*	1.00
245	*Shaun Williams*	.15
246	*Grant Wistrom*	1.00
247	*Charles Woodson*	2.50
248	Checklist	.15
249	Checklist	.15
250	Checklist	.15

1998 Fleer Heritage

This parallel set was exclusive to hobby packs and was sequentially numbered to 125 sets. Heritage cards added a special foil treatment on the front and sequential numbering on the back.

	MT
Heritage Cards:	30x-60x
Heritage Rookies:	10x-20x

1998 Fleer Big Numbers

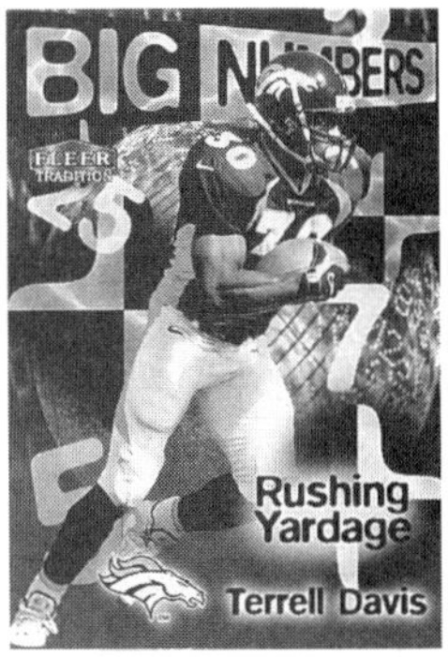

Big Numbers was a nine-card interactive set featuring top players at each skill position, with nine total players each featured on 11 different versions (0-9 and a wild card). The goal was to collect four cards, whereby the overprinted numbers, when combined, make out the players total yards through all games of Dec. 1, 1998. Winners were eligible to enter a contest for a chance to win a trip to the 2000 Pro Bowl. Big Numbers inserts were seeded one per four packs.

		MT
Common Player:		.25
BN1	Tim Brown	.25
BN2	Cris Carter	.25
BN3	Terrell Davis	1.00
BN4	John Elway	1.00
BN5	Brett Favre	2.00
BN6	Eddie George	1.00
BN7	Dorsey Levens	.50
BN8	Herman Moore	.50
BN9	Steve Young	.75

1998 Fleer Playmakers Theatre

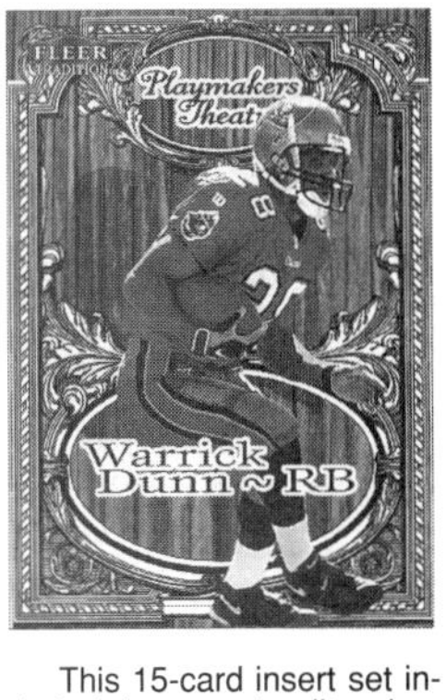

This 15-card insert set included the game's elite players on silver holofoil and sculpture embossing. Playmakers Theatre cards were sequentially numbered to 100 sets.

	MT
Complete Set (15):	1000.
Common Player:	30.00
Production 100 Sets	
PT1 Terrell Davis	100.00
PT2 Corey Dillon	60.00
PT3 Warrick Dunn	85.00
PT4 John Elway	100.00
PT5 Brett Favre	200.00
PT6 Antonio Freeman	30.00
PT7 Joey Galloway	30.00
PT8 Eddie George	85.00
PT9 Terry Glenn	30.00
PT10 Dan Marino	175.00
PT11 Curtis Martin	60.00
PT12 Jake Plummer	85.00
PT13 Barry Sanders	200.00
PT14 Deion Sanders	50.00
PT15 Kordell Stewart	85.00

1998 Fleer Red Zone Rockers

Red Zone Rockers were printed on a horizontal red laser holofoil and inserted one per 32 packs. The insert included 10 players who are best in the clutch.

	MT
Complete Set (10):	70.00
Common Player:	2.00
RZ1 Jerome Bettis	2.00
RZ2 Drew Bledsoe	10.00
RZ3 Mark Brunell	8.00
RZ4 Corey Dillon	6.00
RZ5 Joey Galloway	2.00
RZ6 Keyshawn Johnson	2.00
RZ7 Dorsey Levens	2.00
RZ8 Dan Marino	15.00
RZ9 Barry Sanders	20.00
RZ10 Emmitt Smith	15.00

1998 Fleer Rookie Sensations

This 15-card insert displayed the top rookies in 1998. Cards were embossed with spot UV coating and inserted one per 16 packs.

	MT
Complete Set (15):	60.00
Common Player:	2.00
RS1 John Avery	4.00
RS2 Keith Brooking	2.00
RS3 Kevin Dyson	4.00
RS4 Robert Edwards	7.00
RS5 Greg Ellis	2.00
RS6 Curtis Enis	7.00
RS7 Terry Fair	2.00
RS8 Ryan Leaf	10.00
RS9 Peyton Manning	15.00
RS10 Randy Moss	25.00
RS11 Marcus Nash	4.00
RS12 Fred Taylor	7.00

RS13 Andre Wadsworth	2.00
RS14 Grant Wistrom	2.00
RS15 Charles Woodson	5.00

1998 Fleer Metal Universe

Metal Universe was released in a single series, 200-card set for 1998. The cards featured foil-etched designs in the background pertaining to the player or the city they play in. The set was paralleled in a Precious Metal Gems set. Inserts in Metal Universe include: Decided Edge, E-X2001 Previews, Planet Football, Quasars and Titanium.

	MT
Complete Set (200):	35.00
Common Player:	.10
Wax Box:	60.00
1 Jerry Rice	1.00
2 Muhsin Muhammad	.10
3 Ed McCaffrey	.10
4 Brett Favre	2.50
5 Troy Brown	.10
6 Brad Johnson	.20
7 John Elway	1.00
8 Herman Moore	.20
9 O.J. McDuffie	.10
10 Tim Brown	.20
11 Byron Hanspard	.10
12 Rae Carruth	.10
13 Rod Smith	.10
14 John Randle	.10
15 Karim Abdul-Jabbar	.20
16 Bobby Hoying	.10
17 Steve Young	.50
18 Andre Hastings	.10
19 Chidi Ahanotu	.10
20 Barry Sanders	2.00
21 Bruce Smith	.10
22 Kimble Anders	.10
23 Troy Davis	.10
24 Jamal Anderson	.10
25 Curtis Conway	.20
26 Mark Chmura	.20
27 Reggie White	.20
28 Jake Reed	.10
29 Willie McGinest	.10
30 Terrell Davis	1.00
31 Joey Galloway	.20
32 Leslie Shepherd	.10
33 Peter Boulware	.10
34 Chad Lewis	.10
35 Marcus Allen	.20
36 Randal Hill	.10
37 Jerome Bettis	.20
38 William Floyd	.10
39 Warren Moon	.20
40 Mike Alstott	.40
41 Jay Graham	.10
42 Emmitt Smith	2.00
43 James Stewart	.10
44 Charlie Garner	.10
45 Merton Hanks	.10
46 Shawn Springs	.10
47 Chris Calloway	.10
48 Larry Centers	.10
49 Michael Jackson	.10
50 Deion Sanders	.50
51 Jimmy Smith	.10
52 Jason Sehorn	.10
53 Charles Johnson	.10
54 Garrison Hearst	.10
55 Chris Warren	.10
56 Warren Sapp	.10
57 Corey Dillon	.75
58 Marvin Harrison	.20
59 Chris Sanders	.10
60 Jamie Asher	.10
61 Yancey Thigpen	.10
62 Freddie Jones	.10
63 Rob Moore	.10
64 Jermaine Lewis	.10
65 Michael Irvin	.20
66 Natrone Means	.20
67 Charles Way	.10
68 Terry Kirby	.10

69 Tony Banks	.20
70 Steve McNair	.50
71 Vinny Testaverde	.10
72 Dexter Coakley	.10
73 Keenan McCardell	.10
74 Glenn Foley	.10
75 Isaac Bruce	.10
76 Terry Allen	.10
77 Todd Collins	.10
78 Troy Aikman	1.00
79 Damon Jones	.10
80 Leon Johnson	.10
81 James Jett	.10
82 Frank Wycheck	.10
83 Andre Reed	.10
84 Derrick Alexander	.10
85 Jason Taylor	.10
86 Wayne Chrebet	.10
87 Napoleon Kaufman	.50
88 Eddie George	1.00
89 Ernie Conwell	.10
90 Antowain Smith	.50
91 Johnnie Morton	.10
92 Jerris McPhail	.10
93 Cris Carter	.10
94 Danny Kanell	.10
95 Stan Humphries	.10
96 Terrell Owens	.10
97 Willie Davis	.10
98 David Dunn	.10
99 Tony Brackens	.10
100 Kordell Stewart	1.00
101 Rodney Thomas	.10
102 Keyshawn Johnson	.20
103 Carl Pickens	.10
104 Mark Brunell	.75
105 Jeff George	.20
106 Bert Emanuel	.10
107 Wesley Walls	.10
108 Bryant Westbrook	.10
109 Dorsey Levens	.20
110 Drew Bledsoe	1.00
111 Adrian Murrell	.20
112 Aeneas Williams	.10
113 Raymont Harris	.10
114 Tony Gonzalez	.20
115 Sean Dawkins	.10
116 Billy Joe Hobert	.10
117 James McKnight	.10
118 Reidel Anthony	.10
119 Terance Mathis	.10
120 Darrien Gordon	.10
121 Dale Carter	.10
122 Duce Staley	.10
123 Jerald Moore	.10
124 Eric Swann	.10
125 Antonio Freeman	.20
126 Chris Penn	.10
127 Ken Dilger	.10
128 Robert Smith	.20
129 Tiki Barber	.30
130 Mark Bruener	.10
131 Junior Seau	.20
132 Trent Dilfer	.20
133 Gus Frerotte	.10
134 Jake Plummer	1.00
135 Jeff Blake	.20
136 Jim Harbaugh	.20
137 Michael Strahan	.10
138 Gary Brown	.10
139 Tony Martin	.10
140 Stephen Davis	.10
141 Thurman Thomas	.20
142 Scott Mitchell	.10
143 Dan Marino	2.00
144 David Palmer	.10
145 J.J. Stokes	.10
146 Chris Chandler	.10
147 Darnell Autry	.20
148 Robert Brooks	.10
149 Derrick Mayes	.10
150 Curtis Martin	.75
151 Steve Broussard	.10
152 Eddie Kennison	.20
153 Kerry Collins	.30
154 Shannon Sharpe	.20
155 Andre Rison	.20
156 Dwayne Rudd	.10
157 Orlando Pace	.10
158 Terry Glenn	.20
159 Frank Sanders	.10
160 Ricky Proehl	.10
161 Marshall Faulk	.20
162 Irving Fryar	.10
163 Courtney Hawkins	.10
164 Eric Metcalf	.10
165 Warrick Dunn	1.00
166 Cris Dishman	.10
167 Fred Lane	.10
168 John Mobley	.10
169 Elvis Grbac	.10
170 Ben Coates	.10
171 Rickey Dudley	.10
172 Ricky Watters	.20
173 Alonzo Mayes	.30
174 Andre Wadsworth	.50
175 Brian Simmons	.10
176 Charles Woodson	3.00
177 Curtis Enis	4.00
178 Fred Taylor	4.00
179 Germane Crowell	1.50
180 Greg Ellis	.30
181 Jacquez Green	3.00
182 Jason Peter	.30
183 John Dutton	.30
184 Kevin Dyson	2.00
185 Kivuusama Mays	.10
186 Marcus Nash	2.00

187 Michael Myers	.10
188 Ahman Green	3.00
189 Peyton Manning	8.00
190 Randy Moss	15.00
191 Robert Edwards	4.00
192 Robert Holcombe	2.50
193 Ryan Leaf	8.00
194 Takeo Spikes	.50
195 Tavian Banks	3.00
196 Tim Dwight	1.25
197 Vonnie Holliday	.50
198 Dorsey Levens	.10
199 Jerry Rice	.50
200 Dan Marino	1.00

1998 Fleer Metal Universe Precious Metal Gems

Precious Metal Gems was a 200-card parallel set found only in hobby packs. Cards were sequentially numbered to 50 sets on the back.

	MT
Metal Gem Cards:	100x-200x
Metal Gem Rookies:	15x-30x

1998 Fleer Metal Universe Decided Edge

Decided Edge was a 10-card insert that was seeded one per 288 packs. The outside of these cards was silver foil with the player's image etched into it, while the inside could be pulled out to reveal another card of the player. Three circles were cut into the outside of the front, and one circle was on the back - each allowed you to see the inner card. When lined up, the player's face could be seen through each of the circles. Decided Edge inserts were numbered "of 10" on the inside card.

	MT
Complete Set (10):	450.00
Common Player:	20.00
CE1 Terrell Davis	45.00
CE2 Brett Favre	90.00
CE3 John Elway	45.00
CE4 Barry Sanders	80.00
CE5 Eddie George	45.00
CE6 Jerry Rice	45.00
CE7 Emmitt Smith	75.00
CE8 Dan Marino	75.00
CE9 Troy Aikman	45.00
CE10 Marcus Allen	20.00

1998 Fleer Metal Universe E-X2001 Previews

This 15-card insert previewed the upcoming E-X2001 set. Cards featured the two layered, plastic design, but added the word "Preview" in gold foil under the E-X2001 logo. The Metal Universe logo does not appear anywhere on the card. Preview inserts were seeded one per 144 packs.

	MT
Complete Set (15):	300.00
Common Player:	6.00
EX1 Barry Sanders	50.00
EX2 Brett Favre	60.00
EX3 Corey Dillon	15.00
EX4 John Elway	30.00
EX5 Drew Bledsoe	30.00
EX6 Eddie George	30.00
EX7 Emmitt Smith	50.00
EX8 Joey Galloway	6.00
EX9 Karim Abdul-Jabbar	12.00
EX10 Kordell Stewart	30.00
EX11 Mark Brunell	20.00
EX12 Mike Alstott	15.00
EX13 Warrick Dunn	30.00
EX14 Antonio Freeman	6.00
EX15 Terrell Davis	30.00

1998 Fleer Metal Universe Planet Football

Planet Football was a 15-card insert that was seeded one per eight packs. The player's color image was shown over a foil etched background that contained a large football in space.

	MT
Complete Set (15):	50.00
Common Player:	1.00
PF1 Barry Sanders	8.00
PF2 Corey Dillon	3.00
PF3 Warrick Dunn	5.00
PF4 Jake Plummer	5.00
PF5 John Elway	5.00
PF6 Kordell Stewart	5.00
PF7 Curtis Martin	3.00
PF8 Mark Brunell	4.00
PF9 Dorsey Levens	1.00
PF10 Troy Aikman	5.00
PF11 Terry Glenn	1.00
PF12 Eddie George	5.00
PF13 Keyshawn Johnson	1.00
PF14 Steve McNair	3.00
PF15 Jerry Rice	5.00

1998 Fleer Metal Universe Quasars

This 15-card set showcased the top rookies from the 1998 NFL Draft. Cards had a color shot of the player in his college uniform over a etched foil background. These were inserted one per 20 packs.

MT
Complete Set (15): 100.00
Common Player: 2.00
QS1 Peyton Manning 20.00
QS2 Ryan Leaf 20.00
QS3 Charles Woodson 10.00
QS4 Randy Moss 30.00
QS5 Curtis Enis 10.00
QS6 Tavian Banks 6.00
QS7 Germane Crowell 2.00
QS8 Kevin Dyson 6.00
QS9 Robert Edwards 10.00
QS10 Jacquez Green 8.00
QS11 Alonzo Mayes 3.00
QS12 Brian Simmons 2.00
QS13 Takeo Spikes 2.00
QS14 Andre Wadsworth 3.00
QS15 Ahman Green 8.00

1998 Fleer Metal Universe Titanium

Titanium was a 10-card insert printed on a silver holofoil background. The insert name runs up the left side with the letters in circles. These were inserted one per 96 packs.

MT
Complete Set (10): 120.00
Common Player: 6.00
TM1 Corey Dillon 6.00
TM2 Emmitt Smith 30.00
TM3 Terrell Davis 20.00
TM4 Brett Favre 40.00
TM5 Mark Brunell 15.00
TM6 Dan Marino 30.00
TM7 Curtis Martin 12.00
TM8 Kordell Stewart 20.00
TM9 Warrick Dunn 20.00
TM10 Steve McNair 6.00

1998 Pacific Omega

Omega football consists of a 250-card base set and five inserts. The base cards have a horizontal layout. The fronts feature three photos separated by a football stitching pattern. The color center photo is duplicated in silver foil on the right. Another color photo is on the left.

MT
Complete Set (250): 50.00
Common Player: .10
Wax Box: 60.00
1 Larry Centers .10
2 Rob Moore .10
3 Michael Pittman .10
4 Jake Plummer 2.00
5 Simeon Rice .10
6 Frank Sanders .10
7 Eric Swann .10
8 Morten Anderson .10
9 Jamal Anderson .20
10 Chris Chandler .10
11 Harold Green .10
12 Byron Hanspard .10
13 Terance Mathis .10
14 O.J. Santiago .10
15 Peter Boulware .10
16 Jay Graham .10
17 Eric Green .10
18 Michael Jackson .10
19 Jermaine Lewis .10
20 Ray Lewis .10
21 Jonathan Ogden .10
22 Eric Zeier .10
23 Steve Christie .10
24 Todd Collins .10
25 Quinn Early .10
26 Eric Moulds .20
27 Andre Reed .10
28 Antowain Smith 1.00
29 Bruce Smith .10
30 Thurman Thomas .20
31 Ted Washington .10
32 Michael Bates .10
33 Tim Biakabutuka .10
34 Mark Carrier .10
35 Rae Carruth .20
36 Kerry Collins .30
37 Kevin Greene .10
38 Fred Lane .20
39 Muhsin Muhammad .10
40 Wesley Walls .10
41 Curtis Conway .20
42 Bobby Engram .10
43 *Curtis Enis* 5.00
44 Raymont Harris .10
45 Erik Kramer .10
46 Chris Penn .10
47 Ryan Wetnight .10
48 Jeff Blake .20
49 Ki-Jana Carter .10
50 John Copeland .10
51 Corey Dillon 1.00
52 Tony McGee .10
53 Carl Pickens .20
54 Darnay Scott .10
55 Takeo Spikes .10
56 Troy Aikman 1.50
57 Eric Bjornson .10
58 *Greg Ellis* .20
59 Michael Irwin .20
60 Daryl Johnston .10
61 David LaFleur .10
62 Deion Sanders .50
63 Emmitt Smith 2.50
64 Jason Garrett .10
65 Nicky Sualua .10
66 Steve Atwater .10
67 Terrell Davis 1.50
68 John Elway 1.50
69 *Brian Griese* 3.00
70 Ed McCaffrey .10
71 John Mobley .10
72 *Marcus Nash* 2.00
73 Shannon Sharpe .20
74 Neil Smith .10
75 Rod Smith .20
76 *Charlie Batch* 6.00
77 *Germane Crowell* 1.50
78 Jason Hanson .10
79 Scott Mitchell .10
80 Herman Moore .20
81 Johnnie Morton .10
82 Barry Sanders 3.00
83 Tommy Vardell .10
84 Robert Brooks .10
85 Gilbert Brown .10
86 Leroy Butler .10
87 Mark Chmura .20
88 Brett Favre 3.00
89 Antonio Freeman .20
90 William Henderson .10
91 *Vonnie Holliday* .20
92 Dorsey Levens .20
93 Reggie White .20
94 Aaron Bailey .10
95 Quentin Coryatt .10
96 Zack Crockett .10
97 Ken Dilger .10
98 Marshall Faulk .20
99 *E.G. Green* .20
100 Marvin Harrison .20
101 *Peyton Manning* 10.00

102 Jerome Pathon .10
103 *Tavian Banks* 3.00
104 Tony Boselli .10
105 Tony Brackens .10
106 Mark Brunell 1.25
107 Kevin Hardy .10
108 Keenan McCardell .10
109 Pete Mitchell .10
110 Jimmy Smith .20
111 James Stewart .20
112 *Fred Taylor* 4.00
113 Kimble Anders .10
114 Dale Carter .10
115 Tony Gonzalez .10
116 Elvis Grbac .10
117 Donnell Bennett .10
118 Andre Rison .10
119 *Rashaan Shehee* .50
120 Derrick Thomas .20
121 Tamarick Vanover .10
122 Karim Abdul-Jabbar .30
123 *John Avery* 2.50
124 Troy Drayton .10
125 John Dutton .10
126 Craig Erickson .10
127 Dan Marino 2.50
128 O.J. McDuffie .10
129 Jerris McPhail .10
130 Stanley Pritchett .10
131 Larry Shannon .10
132 Zach Thomas .20
133 Cris Carter .20
134 Randall Cunningham .20
135 Andrew Glover .10
136 Brad Johnson .20
137 Randall McDaniel .10
138 David Palmer .10
139 John Randle .10
140 Jake Reed .10
141 Robert Smith .20
142 Drew Bledsoe 1.25
143 Ben Coates .10
144 *Robert Edwards* 4.00
145 Terry Glenn .30
146 Shawn Jefferson .10
147 Willie McGinest .10
148 Tony Simmons .10
149 Chris Slade .10
150 Troy Davis .10
151 Mark Fields .10
152 Andre Hastings .10
153 Billy Joe Hobert .10
154 William Roaf .10
155 Heath Shuler .10
156 Danny Wuerffel .10
157 Ray Zellars .10
158 Jessie Armstead .10
159 Tiki Barber .20
160 Chris Calloway .10
161 Mike Cherry .10
162 Danny Kanell .10
163 Amani Toomer .10
164 Charles Way .10
165 Tyrone Wheatley .10
166 Kyle Brady .10
167 Wayne Chrebet .10
168 Glenn Foley .20
169 *Scott Frost* .20
170 Keyshawn Johnson .20
171 Leon Johnson .10
172 Alex Van Dyke .10
173 Dedric Ward .10
174 Tim Brown .20
175 Rickey Dudley .10
176 Jeff George .20
177 Desmond Howard .10
178 James Jett .10
179 Napoleon Kaufman .50
180 Darrell Russell .10
181 *Charles Woodson* 4.00
182 Jason Dunn .10
183 Irving Fryar .10
184 Charlie Garner .20
185 Bobby Hoying .10
186 Chris T. Jones .10
187 Michael Timpson .10
188 Kevin Turner .10
189 Jerome Bettis .20
190 Will Blackwell .10
191 Mark Bruener .10
192 Charles Johnson .10
193 George Jones .10
194 Levon Kirkland .10
195 Kordell Stewart 1.25
196 *Hines Ward* 2.00
197 Tony Banks .20
198 Isaac Bruce .20
199 Ernie Conwell .10
200 *Robert Holcombe* 3.00
201 Eddie Kennison .20
202 Amp Lee .10
203 Orlando Pace .10
204 Charlie Jones .10
205 Freddie Jones .10
206 *Ryan Leaf* 8.00
207 Natrone Means .20
208 Junior Seau .20
209 Bryan Still .10
210 Greg Clark .10
211 Jim Druckenmiller .20
212 Marc Edwards .10
213 Garrison Hearst .20
214 Terrell Owens .20
215 Jerry Rice 1.50
216 J.J. Stokes .10
217 Bryant Young .10
218 Steve Young 1.00
219 Chad Brown .10

220 Joey Galloway .30
221 Cortez Kennedy .10
222 Jon Kitna .10
223 James McKnight .10
224 Warren Moon .20
225 Michael Sinclair .10
226 Ricky Watters .20
227 Mike Alstott .30
228 Reidel Anthony .20
229 Derrick Brooks .10
230 Trent Dilfer .20
231 Warrick Dunn 2.00
232 Dave Moore .10
233 Hardy Nickerson .10
234 Warren Sapp .10
235 Karl Williams .10
236 Willie Davis .10
237 *Kevin Dyson* 2.00
238 Eddie George 1.25
239 Derrick Mason .10
240 Steve McNair .75
241 Chris Sanders .10
242 Frank Wycheck .10
243 Terry Allen .10
244 Jamie Asher .10
245 Gus Frerotte .10
246 Darrell Green .10
247 *Skip Hicks* 1.50
248 Brian Mitchell .10
249 Leslie Shepherd .10
250 Michael Westbrook .10

1998 Pacific Omega EO Portraits

EO Portraits is a 20-card insert seeded 1:73. The cards feature a color player photo with a closeup photo of the player's face laser-cut into the card. A hoobby-only parallel version is numbered to one.

MT
Complete Set (20): 350.00
Common Player: 10.00
Inserted 1:73
1 Jake Plummer 25.00
2 Corey Dillon 15.00
3 Troy Aikman 25.00
4 Emmitt Smith 40.00
5 Terrell Davis 25.00
6 John Elway 25.00
7 Barry Sanders 50.00
8 Brett Favre 50.00
9 Dorsey Levens 10.00
10 Peyton Manning 40.00
11 Mark Brunell 20.00
12 Dan Marino 40.00
13 Drew Bledsoe 20.00
14 Jerome Bettis 10.00
15 Kordell Stewart 20.00
16 Ryan Leaf 30.00
17 Jerry Rice 25.00
18 Steve Young 15.00
19 Warrick Dunn 25.00
20 Eddie George 20.00

1998 Pacific Omega Face To Face

Face To Face is a 10-card insert seeded 1:145. The cards have a horizontal layout and feature two NFL stars on the front.

MT
Complete Set (10): 300.00
Common Player: 20.00
Inserted 1:145
1 Peyton Manning, Ryan Leaf 40.00
2 Barry Sanders, Warrick Dunn 50.00
3 Dan Marino, John Elway 40.00
4 Jerry Rice, Antonio Freeman 25.00
5 Jake Plummer, Drew Bledsoe 25.00
6 Corey Dillon, Eddie George 20.00
7 Emmitt Smith, Terrell Davis 40.00
8 Steve Young, Mark Brunell 25.00
9 Kordell Stewart, Steve McNair 25.00
10 Troy Aikman, Brett Favre 50.00

1998 Pacific Omega Online

Online is a 36-card insert seeded 4:37. The card is designed to resemble a computer, with the color player photo on the monitor. The player's name, position, team logo and team web page appear on the keyboard at the bottom.

MT
Complete Set (36): 200.00
Common Player: 2.00
Inserted 4:37
1 Jake Plummer 10.00
2 Antowain Smith 5.00
3 Curtis Enis 10.00
4 Corey Dillon 6.00
5 Troy Aikman 10.00
6 Emmitt Smith 15.00
7 Terrell Davis 10.00
8 John Elway 10.00
9 Shannon Sharpe 2.00
10 Herman Moore 2.00
11 Barry Sanders 20.00
12 Brett Favre 20.00
13 Antonio Freeman 2.00
14 Dorsey Levens 2.00
15 Peyton Manning 20.00
16 Marshall Faulk 2.00
17 Mark Brunell 8.00
18 Fred Taylor 6.00
19 Dan Marino 15.00
20 Robert Smith 2.00
21 Drew Bledsoe 8.00
22 Tiki Barber 2.00
23 Danny Kanell 2.00
24 Tim Brown 2.00
25 Napoleon Kaufman 5.00
26 Charles Woodson 10.00
27 Jerome Bettis 2.00
28 Kordell Stewart 8.00
29 Ryan Leaf 15.00
30 Jerry Rice 10.00
31 Steve Young 6.00
32 Joey Galloway 2.00
33 Trent Dilfer 2.00
34 Warrick Dunn 10.00
35 Eddie George 8.00
36 Steve McNair 5.00

1998 Pacific Omega Prisms

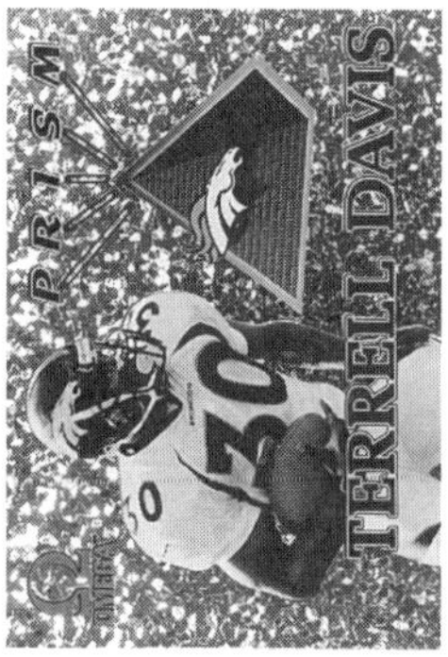

Prism is a 20-card insert seeded one per 37 packs. The cards have a horizontal layout on prismatic foil. A color player photo is on the left with a pyramid and team logo on the right.

		MT
Complete Set (20):		200.00
Common Player:		1.50
Inserted 1:37		
1	Jake Plummer	12.00
2	Corey Dillon	8.00
3	Troy Aikman	12.00
4	Emmitt Smith	20.00
5	Terrell Davis	12.00
6	John Elway	12.00
7	Barry Sanders	25.00
8	Brett Favre	25.00
9	Peyton Manning	25.00
10	Mark Brunell	10.00
11	Dan Marino	20.00
12	Drew Bledsoe	10.00
13	Napoleon Kaufman	6.00
14	Jerome Bettis	1.50
15	Kordell Stewart	10.00
16	Ryan Leaf	20.00
17	Jerry Rice	12.00
18	Steve Young	8.00
19	Warrick Dunn	12.00
20	Eddie George	10.00

1998 Pacific Omega Rising Stars

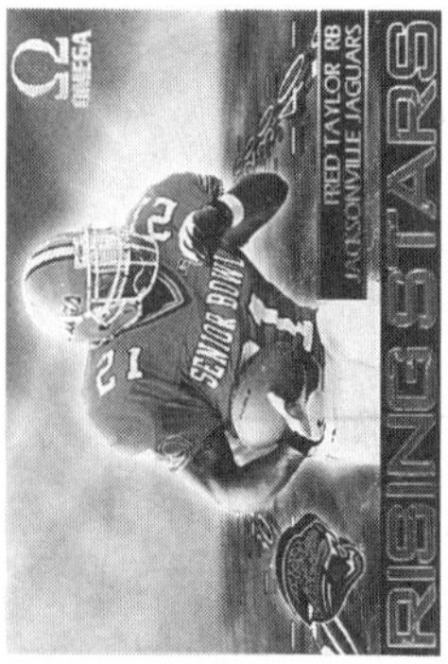

Rising Stars is a 30-card insert seeded 4:37. The set features NFL rookies from 1998. The insert is paralleled five times, each with a different foil color. The blue foil parallel is numbered to 100, red to 75, green to 50, purple to 25 and gold to one.

		MT
Complete Set (30):		90.00
Common Player:		2.00
Inserted 4:37 Hobby		
1	Michael Pittman	2.00
2	Keith Brooking	2.00
3	Duane Starks	2.00
4	Curtis Enis	10.00
5	Marcus Nash	5.00
6	Brian Griese	6.00
7	Terry Fair	2.00
8	Germane Crowell	5.00
9	Charlie Batch	5.00
10	E.G. Green	2.00
11	Peyton Manning	20.00
12	Jerome Pathon	2.00
13	Fred Taylor	8.00
14	Tavian Banks	6.00
15	Rashaan Shehee	4.00
16	John Avery	5.00
17	John Dutton	2.00
18	Robert Edwards	8.00
19	Tony Simmons	4.00
20	Joe Jurevicius	4.00
21	Scott Frost	2.00
22	Charles Woodson	8.00
23	Hines Ward	5.00
24	Robert Holcombe	6.00
25	Az-Zahir Hakim	2.00
26	Ryan Leaf	15.00
27	Ahman Green	6.00
28	Kevin Dyson	5.00
29	Stephen Alexander	2.00
30	Skip Hicks	5.00

1998 Pacific Paramount

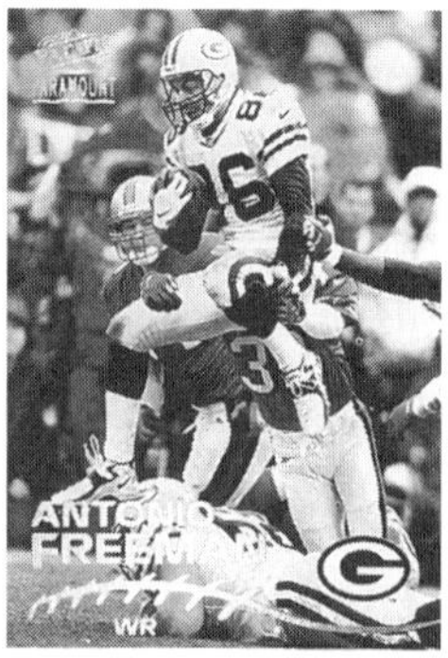

Paramount Football consists of a 250-card base set with three parallels and four inserts. The base cards feature full-bleed photos with the player's name, position and team logo at the bottom. The regular cards have Copper, Silver and Platinum Blue parallels. Inserts include Pro Bowl Die-Cuts, Super Bowl XXXII Highlights, Personal Bests and Kings of the NFL.

		MT
Complete Set (250):		25.00
Common Player:		.10
Wax Box:		45.00
1	Larry Centers	.10
2	Chris Gedney	.10
3	Rob Moore	.10
4	Jake Plummer	1.00
5	Simeon Rice	.10
6	Frank Sanders	.10
7	Mark Smith	.10
8	Eric Swann	.10
9	Jamal Anderson	.20
10	Chris Chandler	.10
11	Bert Emanuel	.10
12	Tony Graziani	.10
13	Byron Hanspard	.20
14	Terance Mathis	.10
15	O.J. Santiago	.10
16	Chuck Smith	.10
17	Derrick Alexander	.10
18	Peter Boulware	.10
19	Jay Graham	.10
20	Priest Holmes	.10
21	Michael Jackson	.10
22	Bam Morris	.10
23	Vinny Testaverde	.20
24	Eric Zeier	.10
25	Todd Collins	.10
26	Quinn Early	.10
27	Bryce Paup	.10
28	Andre Reed	.10
29	Jay Riemersma	.10
30	Antowain Smith	.50
31	Bruce Smith	.10
32	Thurman Thomas	.20
33	Michael Bates	.10
34	Mark Carrier	.10
35	Rae Carruth	.20
36	Kerry Collins	.30
37	Fred Lane	.10
38	Lamar Lathon	.10
39	Muhsin Muhammad	.10
40	Wesley Walls	.10
41	Darnell Autry	.20
42	Curtis Conway	.20
43	Raymont Harris	.20
44	Tyrone Hughes	.10
45	Chris Penn	.10
46	Ricky Proehl	.10
47	Steve Stenstrom	.10
48	Ryan Wetnight	.10
49	Jeff Blake	.20
50	Ki-Jana Carter	.10
51	Corey Dillon	.75
52	David Dunn	.10
53	Boomer Esiason	.10
54	Brian Milne	.10
55	Carl Pickens	.20
56	Darnay Scott	.10
57	Troy Aikman	1.00
58	Eric Bjornson	.10
59	Michael Irvin	.20
60	Daryl Johnston	.10
61	Anthony Miller	.10
62	Deion Sanders	.40
63	Emmitt Smith	1.50
64	Omar Stoutmire	.10
65	Sherman Williams	.10
66	Terrell Davis	1.25
67	John Elway	1.00
68	Darrien Gordon	.10
69	Ed McCaffrey	.10
70	Bill Romanowski	.10
71	Shannon Sharpe	.20
72	Neil Smith	.10
73	Rod Smith	.20
74	Maa Tanuvasa	.10
75	Tommie Boyd	.10
76	Glyn Milburn	.10
77	Scott Mitchell	.10
78	Herman Moore	.20
79	Johnnie Morton	.10
80	Robert Porcher	.10
81	Barry Sanders	1.50
82	Bryant Westbrook	.10
83	Robert Brooks	.10
84	LeRoy Butler	.10
85	Mark Chmura	.20
86	Brett Favre	2.00
87	Antonio Freeman	.20
88	Dorsey Levens	.20
89	Eugene Robinson	.10
90	Bill Schroeder	.10
91	Reggie White	.20
92	Aaron Bailey	.10
93	Quentin Coryatt	.10
94	Zack Crockett	.10
95	Sean Dawkins	.10
96	Ken Dilger	.10
97	Marshall Faulk	.20
98	Jim Harbaugh	.20
99	Marvin Harrison	.20
100	Bryan Barker	.10
101	Tony Boselli	.10
102	Tony Brackens	.10
103	Mark Brunell	1.00
104	Mike Hollis	.10
105	Keenan McCardell	.10
106	Natrone Means	.20
107	Jimmy Smith	.10
108	James Stewart	.10
109	Marcus Allen	.20
110	Kimble Anders	.10
111	Dale Carter	.10
112	Tony Gonzalez	.20
113	Elvis Grbac	.20
114	Greg Hill	.10
115	Andre Rison	.10
116	Will Shields	.10
117	Derrick Thomas	.10
118	Karim Abdul-Jabbar	.30
119	Trace Armstrong	.10
120	Damon Huard	.10
121	Charles Jordan	.10
122	Dan Marino	1.50
123	O.J. McDuffie	.10
124	Irving Spikes	.10
125	Zach Thomas	.10
126	Cris Carter	.10
127	*Charles Woodson*	1.25
128	Brad Johnson	.20
129	Randall McDaniel	.10
130	John Randle	.10
131	Jake Reed	.10
132	Robert Smith	.10
133	Todd Steussie	.10
134	Bruce Armstrong	.10
135	Drew Bledsoe	1.00
136	Ben Coates	.10
137	Derrick Cullors	.10
138	Terry Glenn	.30
139	Shawn Jefferson	.10
140	Curtis Martin	.75
141	Chris Slade	.10
142	Larry Whigham	.10
143	Troy Davis	.20
144	Andre Hastings	.10
145	Randal Hill	.10
146	Sammy Knight	.10
147	William Roaf	.10
148	Heath Shuler	.10
149	Danny Wuerffel	.20
150	Ray Zellars	.10
151	Jessie Armstead	.10
152	Tiki Barber	.40
153	Chris Calloway	.10
154	Danny Kanell	.10
155	David Patten	.10
156	Michael Strahan	.10
157	Charles Way	.10
158	Tyrone Wheatley	.10
159	Kyle Brady	.10
160	Wayne Chrebet	.10
161	Glenn Foley	.10
162	Aaron Glenn	.10
163	Leon Johnson	.10
164	Adrian Murrell	.20
165	Neil O'Donnell	.10
166	Dedric Ward	.10
167	Tim Brown	.20
168	Rickey Dudley	.10
169	Jeff George	.20
170	Desmond Howard	.10
171	James Jett	.10
172	Napoleon Kaufman	.20
173	Chester McGlockton	.10
174	Darrell Russell	.10
175	Ty Detmer	.10
176	Irving Fryar	.10
177	Charlie Garner	.10
178	Bobby Hoying	.10
179	Chad Lewis	.10
180	Duce Staley	.10
181	Kevin Turner	.10
182	Ricky Watters	.20
183	Jerome Bettis	.20
184	Will Blackwell	.10
185	Charles Johnson	.10
186	George Jones	.10
187	Levon Kirkland	.10
188	Carnell Lake	.10
189	Kordell Stewart	1.00
190	Yancey Thigpen	.10
191	Tony Banks	.30
192	Isaac Bruce	.20
193	Ernie Conwell	.10
194	Craig Heyward	.10
195	Eddie Kennison	.20
196	Amp Lee	.10
197	Orlando Pace	.10
198	Torrance Small	.10
199	Gary Brown	.10
200	Kenny Bynum	.10
201	Freddie Jones	.10
202	Tony Martin	.10
203	Eric Metcalf	.10
204	Junior Seau	.20
205	Craig Whelihan	.10
206	William Floyd	.20
207	Merton Hanks	.10
208	Garrison Hearst	.10
209	Brent Jones	.10
210	Terrell Owens	.20
211	Jerry Rice	1.00
212	J.J. Stokes	.10
213	Rod Woodson	.10
214	Steve Young	.50
215	Steve Broussard	.10
216	Joey Galloway	.20
217	Cortez Kennedy	.10
218	Jon Kitna	.10
219	James McKnight	.10
220	Warren Moon	.20
221	Michael Sinclair	.10
222	*Ryan Leaf*	2.00
223	Darryl Williams	.10
224	Mike Alstott	.30
225	Reidel Anthony	.20
226	Derrick Brooks	.10
227	Horace Copeland	.10
228	Trent Dilfer	.20
229	Warrick Dunn	1.00
230	Hardy Nickerson	.10
231	Warren Sapp	.10
232	Karl Williams	.10
233	Blaine Bishop	.10
234	Willie Davis	.10
235	Eddie George	1.25
236	Derrick Mason	.10
237	Bruce Matthews	.10
238	Steve McNair	.75
239	Chris Sanders	.10
240	Rodney Thomas	.10
241	Frank Wycheck	.10
242	Terry Allen	.10
243	Jamie Asher	.10
244	Larry Bowie	.10
245	Albert Connell	.10
246	Stephen Davis	.10
247	Gus Frerotte	.10
248	Ken Harvey	.10
249	Leslie Shepherd	.10
250	Michael Westbrook	.10

1998 Pacific Paramount Copper/Silver

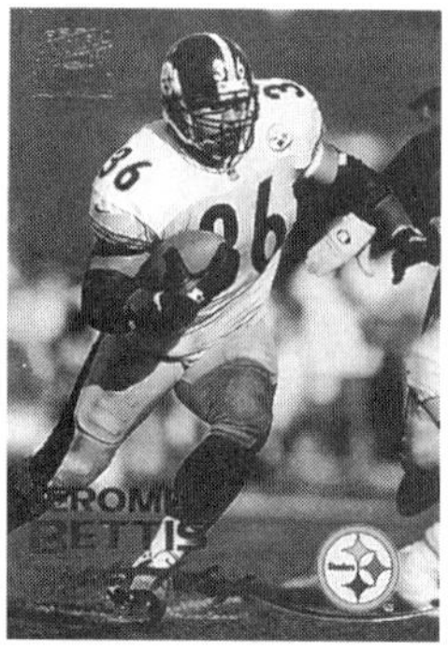

The 250-card base set is paralleled in the Copper hobby-only and Silver retail-only sets (1:1).

	MT
Copper/Silver Cards:	2x-4x

1998 Pacific Paramount Platinum Blue

Platinum Blue is a full parallel of the Paramount base set, seeded one per 73 packs.

	MT
Platinum Blue Cards:	40x-80x

1998 Pacific Paramount Kings of the NFL

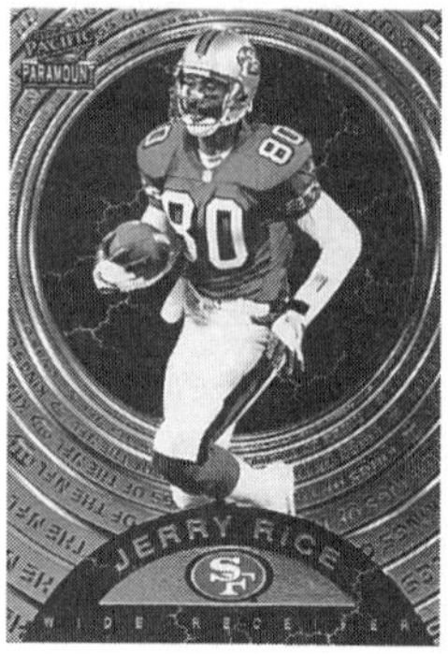

Kings of the NFL is a fully-foiled 20-card insert seeded one per 73 packs. The cards have a color photo with the player's name, position and team logo at the bottom.

		MT
Complete Set (20):		450.00
Common Player:		7.00
1	Antowain Smith	15.00
2	Corey Dillon	20.00
3	Troy Aikman	30.00
4	Emmitt Smith	50.00
5	Terrell Davis	30.00
6	John Elway	30.00
7	Barry Sanders	50.00
8	Brett Favre	60.00
9	Dorsey Levens	7.00
10	Reggie White	7.00
11	Mark Brunell	30.00
12	Dan Marino	50.00
13	Curtis Martin	20.00
14	Drew Bledsoe	30.00
15	Jerome Bettis	7.00
16	Kordell Stewart	30.00
17	Jerry Rice	30.00
18	Steve Young	20.00
19	Warrick Dunn	30.00
20	Eddie George	30.00

1998 Pacific Paramount Personal Bests

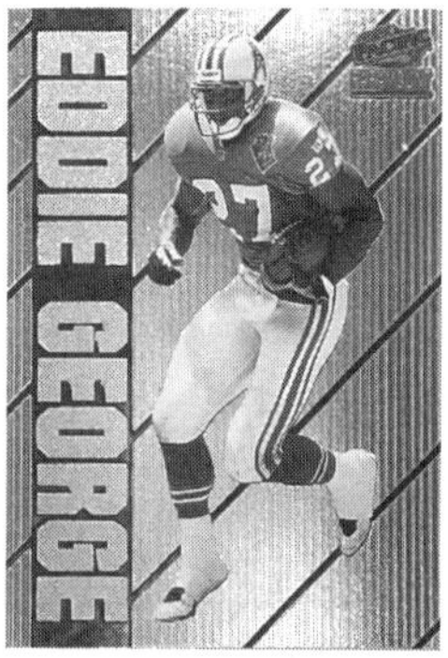

Personal Bests is a 36-card insert seeded 4:37. The cards have a color player photo on holographic silver foil. The player's name is printed vertically on the left.

		MT
Complete Set (36):		100.00
Common Player:		1.50
1	Jake Plummer	8.00
2	Antowain Smith	5.00
3	Kerry Collins	4.00
4	Raymont Harris	1.50

5	Corey Dillon	6.00
6	Troy Aikman	8.00
7	Deion Sanders	4.00
8	Emmitt Smith	10.00
9	Terrell Davis	8.00
10	John Elway	8.00
11	Shannon Sharpe	1.50
12	Herman Moore	1.50
13	Barry Sanders	12.00
14	Brett Favre	16.00
15	Antonio Freeman	1.50
16	Dorsey Levens	1.50
17	Marshall Faulk	1.50
18	Mark Brunell	8.00
19	Dan Marino	10.00
20	Robert Smith	1.50
21	Curtis Martin	6.00
22	Drew Bledsoe	8.00
23	Danny Kanell	1.50
24	Adrian Murrell	1.50
25	Napoleon Kaufman	4.00
26	Jerome Bettis	1.50
27	Kordell Stewart	8.00
28	Terrell Owens	1.50
29	Jerry Rice	8.00
30	Steve Young	5.00
31	Warren Moon	1.50
32	Mike Alstott	4.00
33	Trent Dilfer	1.50
34	Warrick Dunn	8.00
35	Eddie George	8.00
36	Steve McNair	6.00

1998 Pacific Paramount Pro Bowl Die-Cuts

Pro Bowl Die-Cuts is a 20-card insert featuring players in their uniforms from the 1998 Pro Bowl. The background has a Hawaiian theme and the left side of the card features a die-cut outrigger. This set was inserted 1:37.

		MT
Complete Set (20):		200.00
Common Player:		4.00
1	Terrell Davis	20.00
2	John Elway	20.00
3	Shannon Sharpe	4.00
4	Herman Moore	4.00
5	Barry Sanders	30.00
6	Mark Chmura	4.00
7	Brett Favre	40.00
8	Dorsey Levens	4.00
9	Mark Brunell	20.00
10	Andre Rison	4.00
11	Cris Carter	4.00
12	Drew Bledsoe	20.00
13	Ben Coates	4.00
14	Jerome Bettis	4.00
15	Steve Young	10.00
16	Warren Moon	4.00
17	Mike Alstott	10.00
18	Trent Dilfer	4.00
19	Warrick Dunn	20.00
20	Eddie George	20.00

1998 Pacific Paramount Super Bowl XXXII Highlights

Super Bowl XXXII Highlights is a 10-card insert seeded two per 37 packs. The cards feature photography from the Super Bowl.

		MT
Complete Set (10):		40.00
Common Player:		2.00
1	Terrell Davis	8.00
2	John Elway	8.00
3	John Elway	8.00
4	Brett Favre	12.00
5	Antonio Freeman	4.00
6	Dorsey Levens	4.00
7	Ed McCaffrey	2.00
8	Eugene Robinson	2.00
9	Bill Romanowski	2.00
10	Darren Sharper	2.00

1998 Pacific Revolution

Pacific Revolution Football consists of a 150-card base set with one parallel and five inserts. The base cards feature a color player photo with a swirled foil background. The cards are etched and embossed. The player's name and his team helmet are featured on a black bar on the bottom. The base set is paralleled by Shadow Series. The inserts include Icons, Prime Time Performers, Rookies & Stars, Showstoppers and Touchdown Laser-Cuts.

		MT
Complete Set (150):		140.00
Common Player:		.25
Wax Box:		80.00
1	Larry Centers	.25
2	Leeland McElroy	.25
3	Rob Moore	.25
4	Jake Plummer	5.00
5	Frank Sanders	.25
6	Jamal Anderson	.25
7	Chris Chandler	.25
8	Byron Hanspard	.25
9	Jay Graham	.25
10	Michael Jackson	.25
11	Vinny Testaverde	.25
12	Eric Zeier	.25
13	Todd Collins	.25
14	Quinn Early	.25
15	Andre Reed	.25
16	Antowain Smith	2.00
17	Bruce Smith	.25
18	Thurman Thomas	.50
19	Rae Carruth	.25
20	Kerry Collins	.50
21	Wesley Walls	.25
22	Darnell Autry	.50
23	Curtis Conway	.50
24	Bobby Engram	.25
25	*Curtis Enis*	8.00
26	Raymont Harris	.25
27	Jeff Blake	.50
28	Corey Dillon	3.00
29	Carl Pickens	.25
30	Darnay Scott	.25
31	Troy Aikman	5.00

32	Michael Irvin	.50
33	Deion Sanders	2.00
34	Emmitt Smith	8.00
35	Steve Atwater	.25
36	Terrell Davis	5.00
37	John Elway	4.00
38	*Brian Griese*	6.00
39	Ed McCaffrey	.25
40	*Marcus Nash*	3.00
41	Shannon Sharpe	.25
42	Neil Smith	.25
43	Rod Smith	.25
44	*Charlie Batch*	10.00
45	*Germane Crowell*	.25
46	Scott Mitchell	.25
47	Herman Moore	.50
48	Barry Sanders	7.00
49	Robert Brooks	.25
50	Mark Chmura	.25
51	Brett Favre	10.00
52	Antonio Freeman	.50
53	Dorsey Levens	.50
54	Sean Dawkins	.25
55	Ken Dilger	.25
56	Marshall Faulk	.50
57	Marvin Harrison	.50
58	*Peyton Manning*	16.00
59	*Tavian Banks*	5.00
60	Tony Brackens	.25
61	Mark Brunell	4.00
62	Keenan McCardell	.25
63	Natrone Means	.50
64	Jimmy Smith	.25
65	James Stewart	.25
66	*Fred Taylor*	10.00
67	Tony Gonzalez	.50
68	Elvis Grbac	.25
69	Greg Hill	.25
70	Andre Rison	.25
71	Derrick Thomas	.50
72	Karim Abdul-Jabbar	.50
73	*John Avery*	4.00
74	Troy Drayton	.25
75	Dan Marino	8.00
76	O.J. McDuffie	.25
77	Cris Carter	.50
78	Brad Johnson	.50
79	John Randle	.25
80	Jake Reed	.25
81	Robert Smith	.50
82	Drew Bledsoe	5.00
83	Ben Coates	.25
84	*Robert Edwards*	7.00
85	Terry Glenn	.50
86	*Tony Simmons*	.25
87	Troy Davis	.50
88	Heath Shuler	.25
89	Danny Wuerffel	.25
90	Ray Zellars	.25
91	Tiki Barber	1.00
92	*Joe Jurevicius*	1.50
93	Danny Kanell	.25
94	Charles Way	.25
95	Tyrone Wheatley	.25
96	Wayne Chrebet	.25
97	Glenn Foley	.25
98	Keyshawn Johnson	.50
99	Curtis Martin	3.00
100	Tim Brown	.50
101	Rickey Dudley	.25
102	Jeff George	.50
103	Desmond Howard	.25
104	Napoleon Kaufman	1.50
105	*Charles Woodson*	7.00
106	Jason Dunn	.25
107	Irving Fryar	.25
108	Charlie Garner	.25
109	Bobby Hoying	.50
110	Jerome Bettis	.50
111	Mark Bruener	.25
112	Charles Johnson	.25
113	Levon Kirkland	.25
114	Kordell Stewart	5.00
115	*Hines Ward*	3.00
116	Tony Banks	.50
117	Isaac Bruce	.50
118	*Robert Holcombe*	5.00
119	Eddie Kennison	.50
120	Freddie Jones	.25
121	*Ryan Leaf*	12.00
122	Tony Martin	.25
123	Junior Seau	.50
124	Jim Druckenmiller	.50
125	Garrison Hearst	.25
126	Terrell Owens	.50
127	Jerry Rice	5.00
128	J.J. Stokes	.25
129	Steve Young	2.00
130	Joey Galloway	.50
131	*Ahman Green*	6.00
132	Cortez Kennedy	.25
133	Jon Kitna	.25
134	James McKnight	.25
135	Warren Moon	.50
136	Mike Alstott	2.00
137	Reidel Anthony	.50
138	Trent Dilfer	.50
139	Warrick Dunn	5.00
140	Warren Sapp	.25
141	*Kevin Dyson*	3.00
142	Eddie George	5.00
143	Steve McNair	2.00
144	Chris Sanders	.25
145	Frank Wycheck	.25
146	Stephen Alexander	.25
147	Terry Allen	.25
148	Gus Frerotte	.25
149	*Skip Hicks*	3.00
150	Michael Westbrook	.25

1998 Pacific Revolution Shadows

Shadows are a full parallel of the Revolution base set. The parallel cards are numbered to 99.

	MT
Shadow Cards:	10x-20x
Shadow Rookies:	5x-10x

1998 Pacific Revolution Icons

Icons is a 10-card insert seeded one per 121 packs. The cards have a die-cut design resembling the NFL's shield logo.

		MT
Complete Set (10):		500.00
Common Player:		30.00
1	Emmitt Smith	85.00
2	Terrell Davis	50.00
3	John Elway	40.00
4	Barry Sanders	80.00
5	Brett Favre	100.00
6	Mark Brunell	30.00
7	Dan Marino	85.00
8	Jerry Rice	50.00
9	Warrick Dunn	50.00
10	Eddie George	50.00

1998 Pacific Revolution Prime Time Performers

Prime Time Performers is a 20-card insert seeded 1:25. The cards feature a small player photo on the left and a football with the team's logo laser-cut on the right. The cards have a horizontal layout.

		MT
Complete Set (20):		275.00
Common Player:		7.00
1	Jake Plummer	16.00
2	Corey Dillon	12.00
3	Troy Aikman	16.00
4	Deion Sanders	10.00
5	Emmitt Smith	25.00
6	Terrell Davis	16.00
7	John Elway	16.00
8	Barry Sanders	30.00
9	Brett Favre	30.00
10	Peyton Manning	25.00
11	Mark Brunell	16.00
12	Dan Marino	30.00
13	Drew Bledsoe	16.00
14	Jerome Bettis	7.00
15	Kordell Stewart	16.00

16	Jerry Rice	16.00
17	Steve Young	10.00
18	Warrick Dunn	16.00
19	Eddie George	16.00
20	Steve McNair	10.00

1998 Pacific Revolution Rookies and Stars

Rookies & Stars is a 30-card hobby-only insert. Seeded 4:25, the set features 20 rookies and 10 established stars. A gold parallel version was also produced. The parallel cards are numbered to 50.

		MT
Complete Set (30):		150.00
Common Player:		1.50
Inserted 4:25 Hobby		
Gold Cards:		8x-16x
Production 50 Sets		
1	Michael Pittman	1.50
2	Curtis Enis	5.00
3	Takeo Spikes	1.50
4	Greg Ellis	3.00
5	Emmitt Smith	10.00
6	Terrell Davis	8.00
7	John Elway	8.00
8	Brian Griese	4.00
9	Marcus Nash	3.00
10	Charlie Batch	6.00
11	Barry Sanders	15.00
12	Brett Favre	15.00
13	Vonnie Holliday	3.00
14	E.G. Green	1.50
15	Peyton Manning	12.00
16	Fred Taylor	6.00
17	John Avery	3.00
18	Dan Marino	10.00
19	Drew Bledsoe	6.00
20	Robert Edwards	0.00
21	Joe Jurevicius	1.50
22	Charles Woodson	6.00
23	Kordell Stewart	6.00
24	Robert Holcombe	4.00
25	Ryan Leaf	12.00
26	Warrick Dunn	6.00
27	Jacquez Green	4.00
28	Kevin Dyson	3.00
29	Eddie George	6.00
30	Stephen Alexander	1.50

1998 Pacific Revolution Showstoppers

Showstoppers is a 36-card insert seeded two per 25 packs. The background features the player's name and team name printed in holographic silver foil.

		MT
Complete Set (36):		250.00
Common Player:		2.00
1	Jake Plummer	15.00
2	Antowain Smith	7.00
3	Kerry Collins	4.00
4	Corey Dillon	10.00
5	Troy Aikman	15.00
6	Deion Sanders	7.00
7	Emmitt Smith	30.00
8	Terrell Davis	15.00
9	John Elway	12.00
10	Shannon Sharpe	2.00
11	Herman Moore	4.00
12	Barry Sanders	25.00
13	Brett Favre	35.00
14	Antonio Freeman	4.00
15	Dorsey Levens	4.00
16	Peyton Manning	15.00
17	Mark Brunell	12.00
18	Dan Marino	30.00
19	Robert Smith	2.00
20	Drew Bledsoe	15.00
21	Danny Kanell	2.00
22	Curtis Martin	12.00
23	Tim Brown	2.00
24	Napoleon Kaufman	6.00
25	Jerome Bettis	4.00
26	Kordell Stewart	15.00
27	Ryan Leaf	12.00
28	Terrell Owens	2.00
29	Jerry Rice	15.00
30	Steve Young	10.00
31	Ricky Watters	2.00
32	Mike Alstott	6.00
33	Trent Dilfer	2.00
34	Warrick Dunn	15.00
35	Eddie George	15.00
36	Steve McNair	8.00

1998 Pacific Revolution Touchdown

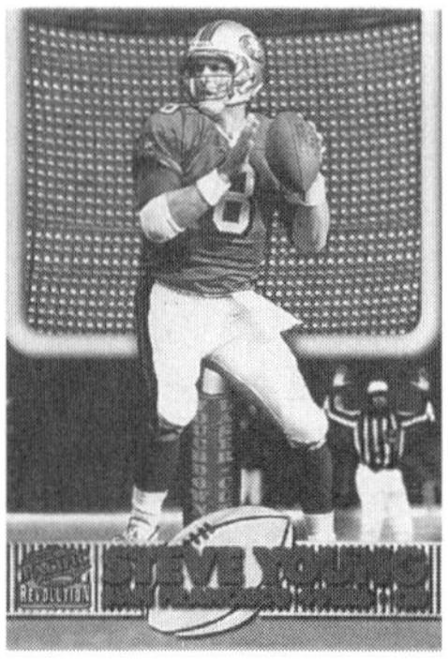

Touchdown Laser-Cuts is a 20-card insert seeded one per 49 packs. The cards have a color player photo in the foreground with a set of goal posts in the background. The netting behind the goal posts is laser-cut.

		MT
Complete Set (20):		250.00
Common Player:		7.00
1	Jake Plummer	15.00
2	Corey Dillon	10.00
3	Troy Aikman	15.00
4	Emmitt Smith	25.00
5	Terrell Davis	15.00
6	John Elway	12.50
7	Barry Sanders	25.00
8	Brett Favre	30.00
9	Dorsey Levens	7.00
10	Peyton Manning	25.00
11	Mark Brunell	12.50
12	Marcus Allen	7.00
13	Dan Marino	25.00
14	Drew Bledsoe	15.00
15	Jerome Bettis	7.00
16	Kordell Stewart	15.00
17	Jerry Rice	15.00
18	Steve Young	10.00
19	Warrick Dunn	15.00
20	Eddie George	15.00

1998 Playoff Absolute Hobby

Absolute SSD was made for the hobby-only and contained 200 cards on super-thick 24-point stock. The horizontal cards featured brushed silver foil with a celluloid player image laminated between the front and back. Playoff also produced a retail version, called Absolute, which included all 200 cards, but on a thinner stock with a different twist to some of the inserts. The set was paralleled twice, in a Silver foil version and a Gold foil version numbered to 25 sets. Inserts include: Checklists, Draft Picks, Honors, Marino Milestones, Platinum Quads, Shields, Red Zone and Statistically Speaking.

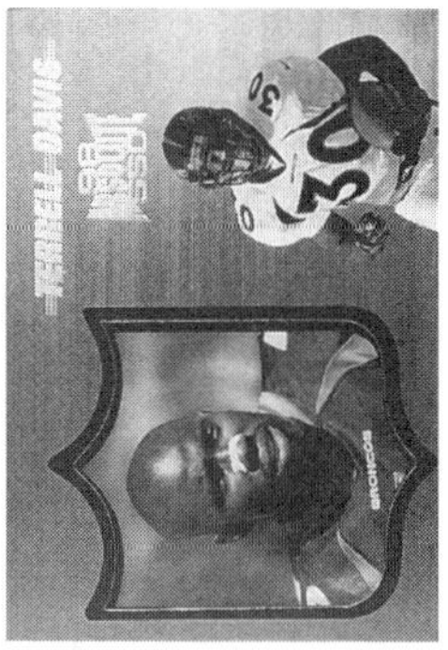

		MT
Complete Set (200):		275.00
Common Player:		.50
Wax Box:		100.00
1	John Elway	6.00
2	*Marcus Nash*	8.00
3	*Brian Griese*	12.00
4	Terrell Davis	8.00
5	Rod Smith	1.00
6	Shannon Sharpe	1.00
7	Ed McCaffrey	.50
8	Brett Favre	12.00
9	Dorsey Levens	1.00
10	Derrick Mayes	.50
11	Antonio Freeman	1.00
12	Robert Brooks	.50
13	Mark Chmura	1.00
14	Reggie White	1.00
15	Kordell Stewart	5.00
16	*Hines Ward*	8.00
17	Jerome Bettis	1.00
18	Charles Johnson	.50
19	Courtney Hawkins	.50
20	Will Blackwell	.50
21	Mark Bruener	.50
22	Steve Young	4.00
23	Jim Druckenmiller	1.00
24	Garrison Hearst	1.00
25	*R.W. McQuarters*	2.00
26	Marc Edwards	.50
27	Irv Smith	.50
28	Jerry Rice	6.00
29	Terrell Owens	1.00
30	J.J. Stokes	1.00
31	Elvis Grbac	1.00
32	*Rashaan Shehee*	2.00
33	Donnell Bennett	.50
34	Kimble Anders	.50
35	Ted Popson	.50
36	Derrick Alexander	.50
37	Tony Gonzalez	1.00
38	Andre Rison	1.00
39	Brad Johnson	1.00
40	*Randy Moss*	75.00
41	Robert Smith	1.00
42	Leroy Hoard	.50
43	Cris Carter	1.00
44	Jake Reed	.50
45	Drew Bledsoe	6.00
46	*Tony Simmons*	1.00
47	*Chris Floyd*	1.00
48	*Robert Edwards*	15.00
49	Shawn Jefferson	.50
50	Ben Coates	.50
51	Terry Glenn	1.00
52	Trent Dilfer	1.00
53	*Jacquez Green*	12.00
54	Warrick Dunn	6.00
55	Mike Alstott	1.00
56	Reidel Anthony	1.00
57	Bert Emanuel	.50
58	Warren Sapp	.50
59	*Charlie Batch*	20.00
60	*Germane Crowell*	8.00
61	Scott Mitchell	.50
62	Barry Sanders	12.00
63	Tommy Vardell	.50
64	Herman Moore	1.00
65	Johnnie Morton	.50
66	Mark Brunell	5.00
67	*Jonathan Quinn*	1.00
68	*Fred Taylor*	20.00
69	James Stewart	.50
70	Jimmy Smith	1.00
71	Damon Jones	.50
72	Keenan McCardell	.50
73	Dan Marino	10.00
74	*Larry Shannon*	1.00
75	*John Avery*	8.00
76	Troy Drayton	.50
77	Stanley Pritchett	.50
78	Karim Abdul-Jabbar	1.00
79	O.J. McDuffie	1.00
80	Yatil Green	1.00
81	Danny Kanell	.50
82	Tiki Barber	1.00
83	Tyrone Wheatley	.50
84	Charles Way	.50
85	Gary Brown	.50
86	*Brian Alford*	1.00
87	*Joe Jurevicius*	2.00
88	Ike Hilliard	1.00
89	Troy Aikman	6.00
90	Deion Sanders	3.00
91	Emmitt Smith	10.00
92	Chris Warren	1.00
93	Daryl Johnston	.50
94	Michael Irvin	1.00
95	David LaFleur	.50
96	*Kevin Dyson*	8.00
97	Steve McNair	5.00
98	Eddie George	5.00
99	Yancey Thigpen	.50
100	Frank Wycheck	.50
101	Glenn Foley	1.00
102	Vinny Testaverde	1.00
103	Keyshawn Johnson	1.00
104	Curtis Martin	3.00
105	Keith Byars	.50
106	*Scott Frost*	1.00
107	Wayne Chrebet	.50
108	Warren Moon	1.00
109	*Ahman Green*	10.00
110	Steve Broussard	.50
111	Ricky Watters	1.00
112	Joey Galloway	1.00
113	Mike Pritchard	.50
114	Brian Blades	.50
115	Gus Frerotte	.50
116	*Skip Hicks*	6.00
117	Terry Allen	.50
118	Michael Westbrook	1.00
119	Jamie Asher	.50
120	Leslie Shepherd	.50
121	Jeff Blake	1.00
122	Corey Dillon	4.00
123	Carl Pickens	1.00
124	Tony McGee	.50
125	Darnay Scott	.50
126	Kerry Collins	1.00
127	Fred Lane	1.00
128	William Floyd	.50
129	Rae Carruth	.50
130	Wesley Walls	.50
131	Muhsin Muhammad	.50
132	Jake Plummer	6.00
133	Adrian Murrell	1.00
134	*Michael Pittman*	1.00
135	Larry Centers	.50
136	Frank Sanders	.50
137	Rob Moore	.50
138	*Andre Wadsworth*	3.00
139	Mario Bates	.50
140	Chris Chandler	.50
141	Byron Hanspard	1.00
142	Jamal Anderson	1.00
143	Terance Mathis	.50
144	O.J. Santiago	.50
145	Tony Martin	.50
146	*Jammi German*	1.00
147	Jim Harbaugh	.50
148	Errict Rhett	.50
149	Michael Jackson	.50
150	*Patrick Johnson*	1.00
151	Eric Green	.50
152	Doug Flutie	4.00
153	Rob Johnson	1.00
154	Antowain Smith	3.00
155	Bruce Smith	.50
156	Eric Moulds	.50
157	Andre Reed	.50
158	Erik Kramer	.50
159	Darnell Autry	.50
160	Edgar Bennett	.50
161	*Curtis Enis*	12.00
162	Curtis Conway	1.00
163	*E.G. Green*	1.00
164	*Jerome Pathon*	2.00
165	*Peyton Manning*	35.00
166	Marshall Faulk	1.00
167	Zack Crockett	.50
168	Ken Dilger	.50
169	Marvin Harrison	1.00
170	Danny Wuerffel	.50
171	Lamar Smith	.50
172	Ray Zellars	.50
173	Qadry Ismail	.50
174	Sean Dawkins	.50
175	Andre Hastings	.50
176	Jeff George	1.00
177	*Charles Woodson*	15.00
178	Napoleon Kaufman	3.00
179	*Jon Ritchie*	1.00
180	Desmond Howard	.50
181	Tim Brown	.50
182	James Jett	.50
183	Rickey Dudley	.50
184	Bobby Hoying	.50
185	Rodney Peete	.50
186	Charlie Garner	.50
187	Irving Fryar	.50
188	Chris T. Jones	.50
189	Jason Dunn	.50
190	Tony Banks	1.00
191	*Robert Holcombe*	12.00
192	Craig Heyward	.50
193	Isaac Bruce	1.00
194	*Az-Zahir Hakim*	1.00
195	Eddie Kennison	1.00
196	*Mikhael Ricks*	1.00
197	*Ryan Leaf*	25.00
198	Natrone Means	1.00
199	Junior Seau	1.00
200	Freddie Jones	.50

1998 Playoff Absolute Hobby Silver/Gold

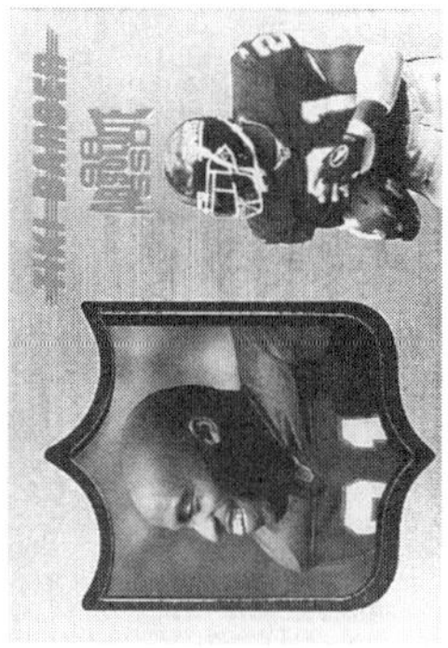

Two parallel versions of the 200-card Absolute SSD set exist. Silver foil versions were printed on a silver foil versus the team colored foil used on base cards. These were inserted one per three packs. Gold versions were printed on gold foil and sequentially numbered to 25 on the back.

	MT
Silver Cards:	3x
Silver Rookies:	2x
Gold Cards:	50x-100x
Gold Rookies:	7x-14x

1998 Playoff Absolute Hobby Checklist

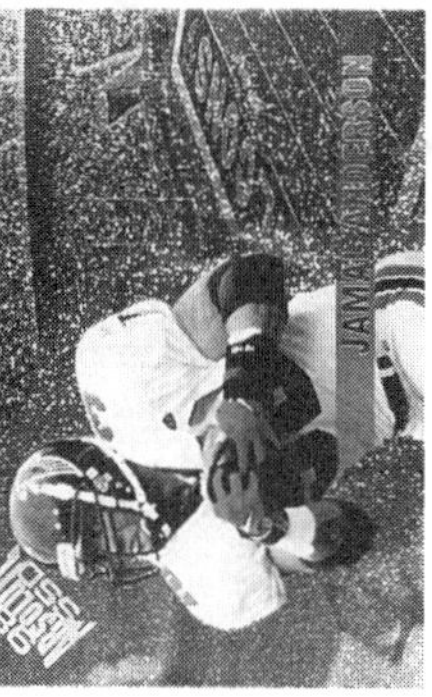

This 30-card insert featured a horizontal shot of a key player from one of the NFL teams, with that team's home stadium in the background. On the back, each player card from that team is listed. Checklists were inserted one per 19 packs.

		MT
Complete Set (30):		300.00
Common Player:		5.00
Inserted 1:19		
1	Jake Plummer	15.00
2	Jamal Anderson	5.00
3	Jim Harbaugh	5.00
4	Rob Johnson	5.00
5	Fred Lane	5.00
6	Curtis Enis	15.00
7	Corey Dillon	12.00
8	Troy Aikman	20.00
9	Terrell Davis	20.00
10	Barry Sanders	30.00
11	Brett Favre	30.00
12	Peyton Manning	30.00
13	Mark Brunell	12.00
14	Elvis Grbac	5.00
15	Dan Marino	25.00
16	Cris Carter	5.00
17	Drew Bledsoe	15.00
18	Ray Zellars	5.00
19	Charles Way	5.00
20	Curtis Martin	8.00
21	Napoleon Kaufman	8.00
22	Irving Fryar	5.00
23	Kordell Stewart	15.00
24	Tony Banks	5.00
25	Ryan Leaf	20.00
26	Jerry Rice	20.00
27	Warren Moon	5.00
28	Warrick Dunn	15.00
29	Eddie George	15.00
30	Terry Allen	5.00

1998 Playoff Absolute Hobby Draft Picks

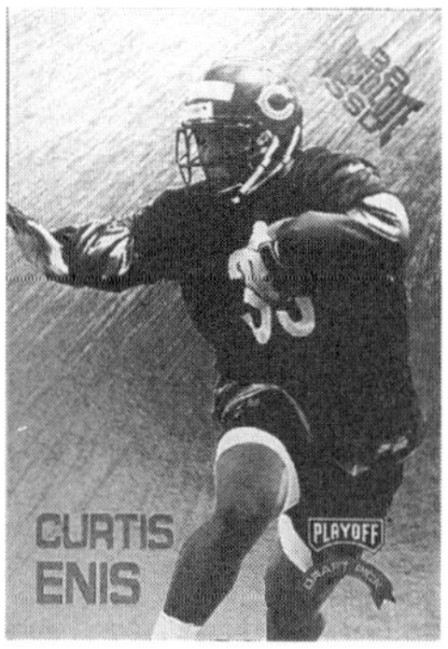

This 36-card insert set featured top players from the 1998 NFL Draft over a foil background. These were inserted one per 10 packs. In addition, Bronze versions of each card were available only through special three-card packs that contained only these Bronze versions. Those packs were inserted one per four boxes.

		MT
Complete Set (36):		300.00
Common Player:		4.00
Inserted 1:10		
1	Peyton Manning	30.00
2	Ryan Leaf	20.00
3	Andre Wadsworth	6.00
4	Charles Woodson	15.00
5	Curtis Enis	12.00
6	Fred Taylor	20.00
7	Kevin Dyson	10.00
8	Robert Edwards	15.00
9	Randy Moss	40.00
10	R.W. McQuarters	4.00
11	John Avery	10.00
12	Marcus Nash	10.00
13	Jerome Pathon	4.00
14	Jacquez Green	12.00
15	Robert Holcombe	10.00
16	Patrick Johnson	4.00
17	Germane Crowell	8.00
18	Tony Simmons	4.00
19	Joe Jurevicius	6.00
20	Mikhael Ricks	4.00
21	Charlie Batch	20.00
22	Jon Ritchie	4.00
23	Scott Frost	4.00
24	Skip Hicks	6.00
25	Brian Alford	4.00
26	E.G. Green	4.00
27	Jammi German	4.00
28	Ahman Green	12.00
29	Chris Floyd	4.00
30	Larry Shannon	4.00
31	Jonathan Quinn	4.00
32	Rashaan Shehee	6.00
33	Brian Griese	12.00
34	Hines Ward	8.00
35	Michael Pittman	4.00
36	Az-Zahir Hakim	4.00

1998 Playoff Absolute Hobby Marino Milestones

Playoff continued its 15-card Marino Milestones insert, with cards 6-10 inserted one per 397 packs of Absolute. Cards 1-5 were found in Prestige SSD and 11-15 were inserted into Momentum SSD. All versions were signed and featured a different record of Dan Marino's.

		MT
Complete Set (5):		1500.
Common Player:		300.00
Inserted 1:397		
6	Dan Marino	300.00
7	Dan Marino	300.00
8	Dan Marino	300.00
9	Dan Marino	300.00
10	Dan Marino	300.00

1998 Playoff Absolute Hobby Platinum Quads

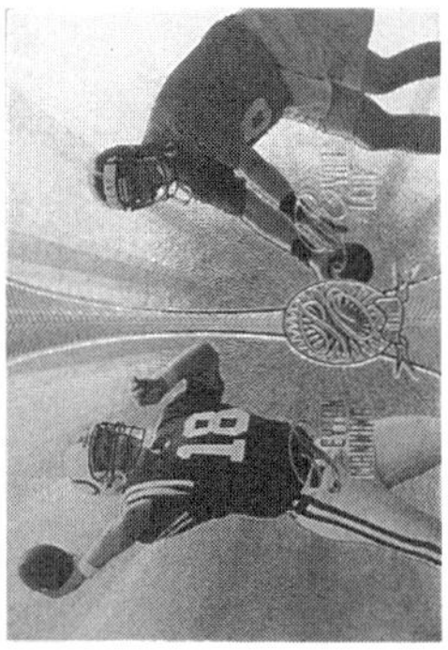

Platinum Quads was an 18-card insert that captured four players on a single card, with two per side. Cards were printed horizontally with the player's image appearing over foil with a "sunburst" etch. These were inserted one per 73 packs of Absolute SSD.

		MT
Complete Set (18):		1100.
Common Player:		30.00
Inserted 1:73		
1	Brett Favre, John Elway, Barry Sanders, Warrick Dunn	150.00
2	Dan Marino, Terrell Davis, Napoleon Kaufman, Jerome Bettis	125.00
3	Jerry Rice, Brad Johnson, Marshall Faulk, Jimmy Smith	80.00
4	Troy Aikman, Herman Moore, Mark Chmura, Gus Frerotte	80.00
5	Steve Young, Mike Alstott, Tiki Barber, Keyshawn Johnson	50.00
6	Kordell Stewart, Robert Brooks, Karim Abdul-Jabbar, Shannon Sharpe	60.00
7	Mark Brunell, Dorsey Levens, Carl Pickens, Rob Moore	60.00
8	Drew Bledsoe, Joey Galloway, Tim Brown, Fred Lane	60.00
9	Eddie George, Rob Johnson, Irving Fryar, Andre Rison	50.00
10	Jake Plummer, Antonio Freeman, Steve McNair, Warren Moon	50.00
11	Emmitt Smith, Cris Carter, Junior Seau, Danny Kanell	125.00
12	Corey Dillon, Jake Reed, Curtis Martin, Bobby Hoying	50.00
13	Deion Sanders, Jim Druckenmiller, Reidel Anthony, Terry Allen	30.00
14	Antowain Smith, Wesley Walls, Isaac Bruce, Terry Glenn	30.00
15	Charlie Batch, Scott Frost, Jonathan Quinn, Brian Griese	50.00
16	Kevin Dyson, Randy Moss, Marcus Nash, Jerome Pathon	125.00
17	Curtis Enis, Fred Taylor, Robert Edwards, John Avery	80.00
18	Peyton Manning, Ryan Leaf, Andre Wadsworth, Charles Woodson	100.00

1998 Playoff Absolute Hobby Playoff Honors

This three-card insert continued Playoff's Honors insert through all of its products, and was numbered PH13-PH15. These die-cut cards showed the player's image over a large black Playoff logo with white letters. Honors were inserted one per 3,970 packs of Absolute SSD.

		MT
Complete Set (3):		600.00
Common Player:		100.00
Inserted 1:3,970		
13	John Elway	300.00
14	Jerome Bettis	100.00
15	Steve Young	200.00

1998 Playoff Absolute Hobby Red Zone

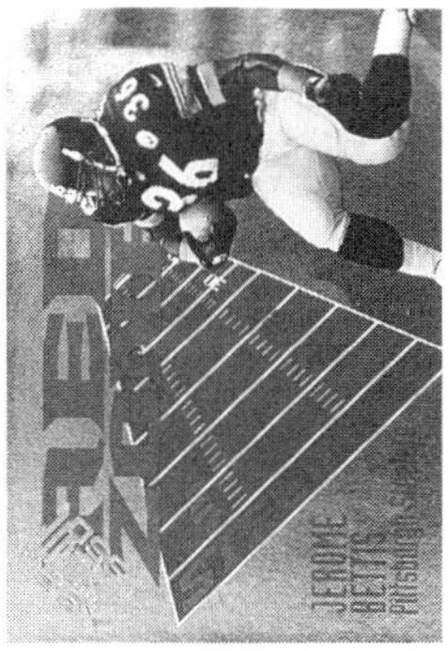

Red Zone featured 26 different players on a horizontal card with a mock-football field across the background. The insert name was printed in large letters in red foil, with his photo off to the right side. These were inserted one per 19 packs.

		MT
Complete Set (26):		250.00
Common Player:		4.00
Inserted 1:19		
1	Terrell Davis	20.00
2	Jerome Bettis	4.00
3	Mike Alstott	4.00
4	Brett Favre	35.00
5	Mark Brunell	15.00
6	Jeff George	4.00
7	John Elway	20.00
8	Troy Aikman	20.00
9	Steve Young	15.00
10	Kordell Stewart	15.00
11	Drew Bledsoe	20.00
12	James Jett	4.00
13	Dan Marino	25.00
14	Brad Johnson	4.00
15	Jake Plummer	15.00
16	Karim Abdul-Jabbar	4.00
17	Eddie George	15.00
18	Warrick Dunn	15.00
19	Cris Carter	4.00
20	Barry Sanders	35.00
21	Corey Dillon	10.00
22	Steve McNair	10.00
23	Herman Moore	4.00
24	Antonio Freeman	4.00
25	Dorsey Levens	4.00
26	James Stewart	4.00

1998 Playoff Absolute Hobby Shields

Shields was a 20-card insert that featured the player over a die-cut football with the Playoff logo cut across the top. These were inserted one per 37 packs.

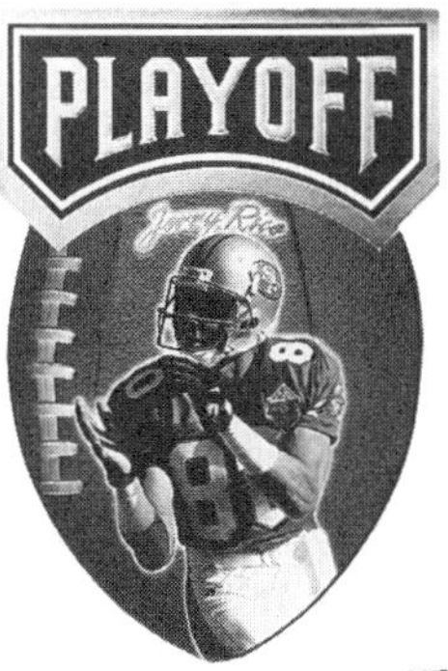

		MT
Complete Set (20):		350.00
Common Player:		10.00
Inserted 1:37		
1	Terrell Davis	25.00
2	Corey Dillon	15.00
3	Dorsey Levens	10.00
4	Brett Favre	50.00
5	Warrick Dunn	20.00
6	Jerome Bettis	10.00
7	John Elway	25.00
8	Troy Aikman	25.00
9	Mark Brunell	20.00
10	Kordell Stewart	20.00
11	Eddie George	20.00
12	Jerry Rice	25.00
13	Dan Marino	40.00
14	Emmitt Smith	40.00
15	Napoleon Kaufman	10.00
16	Ryan Leaf	30.00
17	Curtis Martin	15.00
18	Peyton Manning	40.00
19	Cris Carter	10.00
20	Barry Sanders	50.00

1998 Playoff Absolute Hobby Statistically Speaking

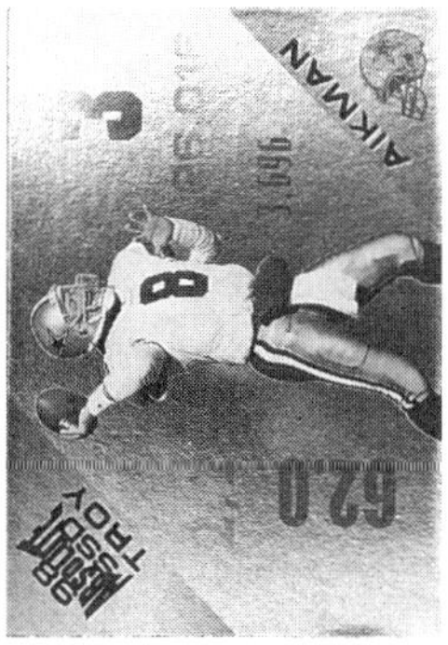

Statistically Speaking features 18 cards, with the player shown over a brushed foil background that highlights individual numbers of the featured player. These were inserted one per 55 packs.

		MT
Complete Set (18):		350.00
Common Player:		7.00
Inserted 1:55		
1	Jerry Rice	25.00
2	Barry Sanders	50.00
3	Deion Sanders	12.00
4	Brett Favre	50.00
5	Curtis Martin	12.00
6	Warrick Dunn	20.00
7	John Elway	25.00
8	Steve Young	15.00
9	Cris Carter	7.00
10	Kordell Stewart	20.00
11	Terrell Davis	25.00
12	Irving Fryar	7.00
13	Dan Marino	40.00
14	Tim Brown	7.00
15	Jerome Bettis	7.00
16	Troy Aikman	25.00
17	Napoleon Kaufman	15.00
18	Emmitt Smith	40.00

1998 Playoff Prestige

Prestige was a 200-card set that arrived with two different looks - one in hobby and one in retail. Prestige SSD cards are printed on 30-point etched silver foil stock. Retail versions are printed on thinner stock, with a foil strip across the bottom. While hobby cards are paralleled in red and gold versions, retail cards are paralleled in red and green foil versus the silver foil used on base cards. Inserts include: Alma Mater (both retail and hobby), Award Winning Performers (both), Best of the NFL (both), Checklists (both), Draft Picks (both), Honors (hobby), Inside the Numbers (both) and Marino Milestones (hobby).

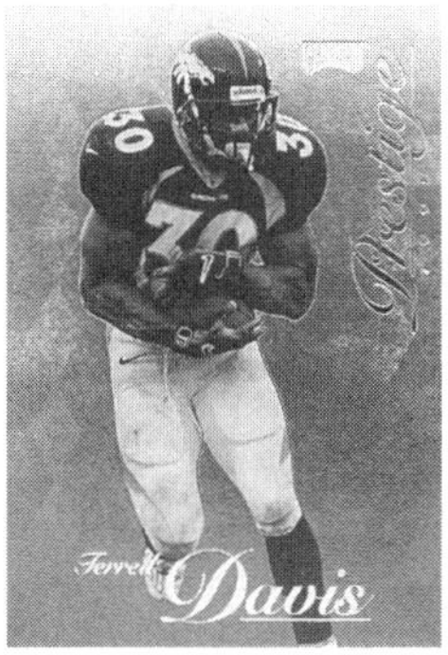

		MT
Complete Set (200):		170.00
Common Player:		.30
Common Rookie (165-200):		1.50
Wax Box:		100.00
1	John Elway	4.00
2	Steve Atwater	.30
3	Terrell Davis	5.00
4	Bill Romanowski	.30
5	Rod Smith	.30
6	Shannon Sharpe	.60
7	Ed McCaffrey	.30
8	Neil Smith	.30
9	Brett Favre	8.00
10	Dorsey Levens	.60
11	LeRoy Butler	.30
12	Antonio Freeman	.60
13	Robert Brooks	.30
14	Mark Chmura	.60
15	Gilbert Brown	.30
16	Kordell Stewart	3.00
17	Jerome Bettis	.60
18	Carnell Lake	.30
19	Dermontti Dawson	.30
20	Charles Johnson	.30
21	Greg Lloyd	.30
22	Levon Kirkland	.30
23	Steve Young	3.00
24	Jim Druckenmiller	.60
25	Garrison Hearst	.30
26	Merton Hanks	.30
27	Ken Norton	.30
28	Jerry Rice	5.00
29	Terrell Owens	.60
30	J.J. Stokes	.30
31	Trent Dilfer	.60
32	Warrick Dunn	4.00
33	Mike Alstott	.75
34	Reidel Anthony	.60
35	Warren Sapp	.30
36	Elvis Grbac	.30
37	Kimble Anders	.30
38	Ted Popson	.30
39	Derrick Thomas	.30
40	Tony Gonzalez	.60
41	Andre Rison	.30
42	Derrick Alexander	.30
43	Brad Johnson	.60
44	Robert Smith	.30
45	Randall McDaniel	.30
46	Cris Carter	.30
47	Jake Reed	.30
48	John Randle	.30
49	Drew Bledsoe	4.00
50	Willie Clay	.30
51	Chris Slade	.30
52	Willie McGinest	.30
53	Shawn Jefferson	.30
54	Ben Coates	.30
55	Terry Glenn	.60
56	Jason Hanson	.30
57	Scott Mitchell	.30
58	Barry Sanders	10.00
59	Herman Moore	.60
60	Johnnie Morton	.30
61	Mark Brunell	4.00
62	James Stewart	.30
63	Tony Boselli	.30
64	Jimmy Smith	.30
65	Keenan McCardell	.30
66	Dan Marino	8.00
67	Troy Drayton	.30
68	Bernie Parmalee	.30
69	Karim Abdul-Jabbar	.75
70	Zach Thomas	.30
71	O.J. McDuffie	.30
72	Tim Bowens	.30
73	Danny Kanell	.30
74	Tiki Barber	.60
75	Tyrone Wheatley	.30
76	Charles Way	.30
77	Jason Sehorn	.30
78	Ike Hilliard	.60
79	Michael Strahan	.30
80	Troy Aikman	4.00
81	Deion Sanders	2.00
82	Emmitt Smith	7.00
83	Darren Woodson	.30
84	Daryl Johnston	.30
85	Michael Irvin	.60
86	David LaFleur	.60
87	Glenn Foley	.30
88	Neil O'Donnell	.30
89	Keyshawn Johnson	.60
90	Aaron Glenn	.30
91	Wayne Chrebet	.30
92	Curtis Martin	2.00
93	Steve McNair	2.00
94	Eddie George	3.00
95	Bruce Matthews	.30
96	Frank Wycheck	.30
97	Yancey Thigpen	.30
98	Gus Frerotte	.30
99	Terry Allen	.30
100	Michael Westbrook	.30
101	Jamie Asher	.30
102	Marshall Faulk	.60
103	Zack Crockett	.30
104	Ken Dilger	.30
105	Marvin Harrison	.60
106	Chris Chandler	.30
107	Byron Hanspard	.60
108	Jamal Anderson	.60
109	Terance Mathis	.30
110	Peter Boulware	.30
111	Michael Jackson	.30
112	Jim Harbaugh	.60
113	Errict Rhett	.30
114	Antowain Smith	3.00
115	Thurman Thomas	.60
116	Bruce Smith	.30
117	Doug Flutie	3.00
118	Rob Johnson	.60
119	Kerry Collins	.75
120	Fred Lane	.30
121	Wesley Walls	.30
122	William Floyd	.30
123	Kevin Greene	.30
124	Erik Kramer	.30
125	Darnell Autry	.60
126	Curtis Conway	.30
127	Edgar Bennett	.30
128	Jeff Blake	.60
129	Corey Dillon	4.00
130	Carl Pickens	.30
131	Darnay Scott	.30
132	Jake Plummer	4.00
133	Larry Centers	.30
134	Frank Sanders	.30
135	Rob Moore	.30
136	Adrian Murrell	.60
137	Troy Davis	.60
138	Ray Zellars	.30
139	Willie Roaf	.30
140	Andre Hastings	.30
141	Jeff George	.60
142	Napoleon Kaufman	.75
143	Desmond Howard	.30
144	Tim Brown	.30
145	James Jett	.30
146	Rickey Dudley	.30
147	Bobby Hoying	.30
148	Duce Staley	.30
149	Charlie Garner	.30
150	Irving Fryar	.30
151	Chris T. Jones	.30
152	Tony Banks	.60
153	Craig Heyward	.30
154	Isaac Bruce	.60
155	Eddie Kennison	.60
156	Junior Seau	.30
157	Tony Martin	.30
158	Freddie Jones	.30
159	Natrone Means	.60
160	Warren Moon	.60
161	Steve Broussard	.30
162	Joey Galloway	.60
163	Brian Blades	.30
164	Ricky Watters	.60
165	*Peyton Manning*	20.00
166	*Ryan Leaf*	15.00
167	*Andre Wadsworth*	3.00
168	*Charles Woodson*	8.00
169	*Curtis Enis*	7.00
170	*Fred Taylor*	15.00
171	*Kevin Dyson*	5.00
172	*Robert Edwards*	12.00
173	*Randy Moss*	30.00
174	*R.W. McQuarters*	1.50
175	*John Avery*	5.00
176	*Marcus Nash*	5.00
177	*Jerome Pathon*	3.00
178	*Jacquez Green*	6.00
179	*Robert Holcombe*	6.00
180	*Patrick Johnson*	1.50
181	*Germane Crowell*	4.00
182	*Tony Simmons*	3.00
183	*Joe Jurevicius*	3.00
184	*Mikhael Ricks*	1.50
185	*Charlie Batch*	15.00
186	*Jon Ritchie*	1.50
187	*Scott Frost*	1.50
188	*Skip Hicks*	5.00
189	*Brian Alford*	1.50

190	E.G. Green	3.00
191	Jammi German	1.50
192	Ahman Green	7.00
193	Chris Floyd	1.50
194	Larry Shannon	1.50
195	Jonathan Quinn	2.00
196	Rashaan Shehee	3.00
197	Brian Griese	6.00
198	Hines Ward	5.00
199	Michael Pittman	1.50
200	Az-Zahir Hakim	1.50

1998 Playoff Prestige Red Hobby

All 200 cards in Prestige SSD were paralleled in this red foil version. Red parallels were seeded one per three packs.

	MT
Red Cards:	3x
Red Rookies:	2x

1998 Playoff Prestige Red/Green Retail

Each card in the Prestige retail set was paralleled in both red and green foil versions. The 200-card set contained either red foil (retail) or green foil (special retail) across the bottom instead of the silver used on base cards. Red foil versions were seeded one per three packs, while green foil versions were seeded one per Jumbo retail pack.

	MT
Red/Green Cards:	1.5x
Red/Green Rookies:	1x

1998 Playoff Prestige Gold

All 200 cards in Prestige were available in a gold foil parallel version. These were sequentially numbered to 25 on the card back.

	MT
Gold Cards:	50x-100x
Gold Rookies:	12x-25x

1998 Playoff Prestige Alma Maters

This 28-card set featured three players from the same college on the silver foilboard. The back showed the same three players are gave a "Did you Know?" statistic about each. Silver versions were seeded one per 17 hobby packs, while Blue versions were seeded one per 25 retail packs.

		MT
Complete Set (28):		375.00
Common Player:		6.00
1	Favre, Jackson, P. Carter	45.00
2	Irvin, Maryland, Testaverde	6.00
3	Dunn, Wadsworth, Boulware	20.00
4	D. Sanders, Bennett, B. Johnson	12.00
5	E. Smith, F. Taylor, Anthony	30.00
6	A. Smith, Anders, Lathon	12.00
7	Barry Sanders, R.J. McQuarters, Thurman Thomas	40.00
8	Leaf, Bledsoe, Hansen	25.00
9	Brunell, Moon, Shehee	20.00
10	Kaufman, Dillon, Pathon	15.00
11	Manning, Pickens, R. White	40.00
12	K. Stewart, Carruth, Westbrook	20.00
13	Enis, Collins, McDuffie	20.00
14	George, Hoying, Dudley	20.00
15	C. Carter, Glenn, Galloway	6.00
16	Grbac, Harbaugh, Woodson	15.00
17	Elway, McCaffrey, Milburn	20.00
18	T. Davis, Hearst, Edwards	25.00
19	Walker, Hastings, Ward	6.00
20	Marino, C. Martin, Heyward	40.00
21	Aikman, Stokes, Hicks	25.00
22	Seau, K. Johnson, Morton	6.00
23	Bettis, T. Brown, Watters	6.00
24	Faulk, Scott, Hakim	6.00
25	B. Smith, Druckenmiller, Freeman	6.00
26	Plummer, Woodson, Bates	20.00
27	H. Moore, Barber, Way	6.00
28	Avery, Walls, Bowens	6.00

1998 Playoff Prestige Award Winning Performers

This 22-card insert showcased top players on a large trophy, with the record they achieved and the Playoff logo near the top of the trophy. Hobby versions of this insert were printed on silver foil, die-cut around the trophy and inserted one per 65 packs, while retail versions were printed on blue foil, not die-cut and inserted one per 97 packs.

		MT
Complete Set (22):		750.00
Common Player:		15.00
1	Terrell Davis	60.00
2	Troy Aikman	50.00
3	Brett Favre	90.00
4	Barry Sanders	90.00
5	Warrick Dunn	45.00
6	John Elway	50.00
7	Jerome Bettis	15.00
8	Jake Plummer	45.00
9	Corey Dillon	25.00
10	Jerry Rice	50.00
11	Steve Young	30.00
12	Mark Brunell	35.00
13	Drew Bledsoe	45.00
14	Dan Marino	75.00
15	Kordell Stewart	45.00
16	Emmitt Smith	75.00
17	Deion Sanders	20.00
18	Mike Alstott	15.00
19	Herman Moore	15.00
20	Cris Carter	15.00
21	Eddie George	35.00
22	Dorsey Levens	15.00

1998 Playoff Prestige Best of the NFL

Best in the NFL features 24 top players over a large NFL logo. Hobby versions of this insert were die-cut around the top of the NFL shield and inserted one per 33 hobby packs, while retail versions were not die-cut and inserted one per 49 retail packs.

		MT
Complete Set (24):		400.00
Common Player:		6.00
1	Terrell Davis	25.00
2	Troy Aikman	25.00
3	Brett Favre	50.00
4	Barry Sanders	40.00
5	Warrick Dunn	20.00
6	John Elway	25.00
7	Jerome Bettis	6.00
8	Jake Plummer	20.00
9	Corey Dillon	15.00
10	Jerry Rice	25.00
11	Steve Young	15.00
12	Mark Brunell	20.00
13	Drew Bledsoe	25.00
14	Dan Marino	40.00
15	Kordell Stewart	25.00
16	Emmitt Smith	40.00
17	Deion Sanders	15.00
18	Mike Alstott	6.00
19	Herman Moore	6.00
20	Cris Carter	6.00
21	Eddie George	25.00
22	Dorsey Levens	6.00
23	Peyton Manning	35.00
24	Ryan Leaf	25.00

1998 Playoff Prestige Checklist

This 30-card insert arrived in both retail and hobby packs, and contained a star player from each NFL team on the front and shots of each player on that team's cards on the back. Silver hobby versions were seeded one per 17 hobby packs, while gold retail versions were seeded one per 17 retail packs.

		MT
Complete Set (30):		350.00
Common Player:		4.00
1	Jake Plummer	20.00
2	Byron Hanspard	4.00
3	Michael Jackson	4.00
4	Antowain Smith	10.00
5	Wesley Walls	4.00
6	Erik Kramer	4.00
7	Corey Dillon	15.00
8	Troy Aikman	25.00
9	John Elway	20.00
10	Barry Sanders	35.00
11	Brett Favre	40.00
12	Peyton Manning	35.00
13	Mark Brunell	20.00
14	Andre Rison	4.00
15	Dan Marino	35.00
16	Cris Carter	4.00
17	Drew Bledsoe	25.00
18	Troy Davis	4.00
19	Danny Kanell	4.00
20	Glenn Foley	4.00
21	Napoleon Kaufman	6.00
22	Bobby Hoying	4.00
23	Kordell Stewart	25.00
24	Isaac Bruce	6.00
25	Ryan Leaf	25.00
26	Jerry Rice	25.00
27	Joey Galloway	6.00
28	Warrick Dunn	20.00
29	Eddie George	25.00
30	Gus Frerotte	4.00

1998 Playoff Prestige Draft Picks

This 30-card insert featured the top draft picks from 1998. Silver versions were seeded one per nine hobby packs, while Silver Jumbos were inserted one per hobby box. Bronze standard sized cards were seeded one per nine retail packs, while Bronze Jumbos were inserted one per retail box. Green standard sized cards and Green Jum-

bos were also available, but only in special retail boxes, and both seeded one per box.

		MT
Complete Set (33):		250.00
Common Player:		3.00
Jumbos:		1x
1	Peyton Manning	30.00
2	Ryan Leaf	20.00
3	Andre Wadsworth	6.00
4	Charles Woodson	12.00
5	Curtis Enis	12.00
6	Fred Taylor	15.00
7	Kevin Dyson	10.00
8	Robert Edwards	15.00
9	Randy Moss	40.00
10	R.W. McQuarters	3.00
11	John Avery	10.00
12	Marcus Nash	10.00
13	Jerome Pathon	3.00
14	Jacquez Green	10.00
15	Robert Holcombe	10.00
16	Patrick Johnson	3.00
17	Germane Crowell	3.00
18	Tony Simmons	6.00
19	Joe Jurevicius	6.00
20	Mikhael Ricks	3.00
21	Charlie Batch	12.00
22	Jon Ritchie	3.00
23	Scott Frost	3.00
24	Skip Hicks	10.00
25	Brian Alford	3.00
26	E.G. Green	3.00
27	Jammi German	3.00
28	Ahman Green	12.00
29	Chris Floyd	3.00
30	Larry Shannon	3.00
31	Jonathan Quinn	3.00
32	Rashaan Shehee	6.00
33	Brian Griese	12.00

1998 Playoff Prestige Inside the Numbers

This 18-card insert set featured a player over some statistic that he has achieved. Hobby versions were die-cut and inserted one per 49 hobby packs, while retail were not die-cut and inserted one per 72 retail packs.

		MT
Complete Set (18):		450.00
Common Player:		10.00
1	Barry Sanders	75.00
2	Terrell Davis	45.00
3	Jerry Rice	30.00
4	Kordell Stewart	30.00
5	Dan Marino	60.00
6	Warrick Dunn	30.00
7	Corey Dillon	20.00
8	Drew Bledsoe	30.00
9	Herman Moore	10.00
10	Troy Aikman	30.00
11	Brett Favre	75.00
12	Mark Brunell	25.00
13	Tim Brown	10.00
14	Jerome Bettis	10.00
15	Eddie George	30.00
16	Dorsey Levens	10.00
17	Napoleon Kaufman	10.00
18	John Elway	40.00

1998 Playoff Prestige Marino Milestones

The first five Marino Milestones cards were inserted into Prestige SSD at a rate of one per 321 packs. Each card highlighted a different record held by Marino, and no unautographed versions were available. Cards 6-10 were inserted into Absolute SSD and 11-15 were in Momentum SSD.

		MT
Complete Set (5):		1250.
Common Player:		250.00
1	Dan Marino	250.00
2	Dan Marino	250.00
3	Dan Marino	250.00
4	Dan Marino	250.00
5	Dan Marino	250.00

1998 Playoff Prestige Playoff Honors

This three-card insert was found only in hobby packs of Pretige. The cards were un-numbered and are listed al-phabetically. The were inserted one per 3,200 packs.

		MT
Complete Set (3):		800.00
Common Player:		200.00
10	Terrell Davis	275.00
11	Barry Sanders	375.00
12	Warrick Dunn	200.00

1998 Press Pass

Press Pass Draft Picks Football contained 50 cards in 1998, with 45 players eligible for the 1998 NFL Draft, four coaches and a checklist card featuring Peyton Manning. Cards featured a black strip across the bottom identifying the player, with his position and several logo above over the bottom of the player photo-graph. The set was paralleled in Paydirt (hobby), Pickoffs (retail), Reflectors and Reflec-tor Solos sets. Inserts include: Fields of Fury, Head Butt, Jer-seys, Kick-off, Triple Threat and Trophy Case.

		MT
Complete Set (50):		18.00
Common Player:		.10
Wax Box:		60.00
1	Peyton Manning	3.50
2	Ryan Leaf	2.50
3	Charles Woodson	1.50
4	Andre Wadsworth	.75
5	Randy Moss	5.00
6	Curtis Enis	1.50
7	T. Thomas	.10
8	Flozell Adams	.10
9	Jason Peter	.10
10	Brian Simmons	.10
11	Takeo Spikes	.10
12	Michael Myers	.10
13	Kevin Dyson	.75
14	Grant Wistrom	.10
15	Fred Taylor	2.00

16	Germane Crowell	.75
17	Sam Cowart	.10
18	Anthony Simmons	.10
19	Robert Edwards	1.50
20	Shaun Williams	.10
21	Phil Savoy	.10
22	Leonard Little	.10
23	Saladin McCullough	.10
24	Duane Starks	.10
25	John Avery	.75
26	Vonnie Holliday	.50
27	Tim Dwight	.50
28	Donovin Darius	.10
29	Alonzo Mayes	.30
30	Jerome Pathon	.30
31	Brian Kelly	.10
32	Hines Ward	.50
33	Jacquez Green	.75
34	Marcus Nash	.75
35	Ahman Green	.75
36	Joe Jurevicius	.50
37	Tavian Banks	1.00
38	Donald Hayes	.30
39	Robert Holcombe	.75
40	Eric Green	.50
41	John Dutton	.30
42	Skip Hicks	.75
43	Patrick Johnson	.10
44	Keith Brooking	.10
45	Alan Faneca	.10
46	Steve Spurrier	1.00
47	Mike Price	.10
48	Bobby Bowden	.75
49	Tom Osborne	1.00
50	Manning - Checklist	1.50

1998 Press Pass Paydirt

Paydirt included all 50 cards, but were distinguised by red foil stamping versus the gold used on base cards. These were found in hobby packs only and inserted one per pack.

	MT
Paydirt Cards:	2x

1998 Press Pass Pickoff

Pickoff included parallel versions of all 50 cards, but were distinguished by silver foil stamping on the front ver-sus the gold foil used on base cards. These were retail ex-clusive and inserted one per pack.

	MT
Pickoff Cards:	2x

1998 Press Pass Reflectors

This 50-card parallel set was seeded one per 180 packs and arrived with a pro-tective covering over the card. This covering could be peeled back to reveal a holofoil finish. Reflectors were numbered with a "R" prefix. In addition, Solos versions of Reflectors were also available, with only one existing set. These were distinguished by a "Solos 1 of 1" stamp on the card back.

	MT
Reflector Cards:	25x-50x

1998 Press Pass Autographs

Autographed versions of Press Pass cards were seed-ed one per 18 hobby packs and one per 36 retail packs. They were similar to base cards, except for a faded area across the bottom of the pho-tograph that included the play-er's signature. Backs were green, with the word "Auto-graph" in large white letters and a paragraph that congrat-ulated the collector and certi-fied the card. Autographs were unnumbered and are list-ed in alphabetical order.

		MT
Complete Set (38):		300.00
Common Player:		8.00
1	John Avery	12.00
2	Tavian Banks	20.00
3	Bobby Bowden	20.00
4	Germane Crowell	20.00
5	Donovin Darius	8.00
6	Tim Dwight	15.00
7	Kevin Dyson	20.00
8	Robert Edwards	40.00
9	Curtis Enis	30.00
10	Alan Faneca	8.00
11	Ahman Green	20.00
12	Jacquez Green	25.00
13	Donald Hayes	12.00
14	Skip Hicks	15.00
15	Robert Holcombe	12.00
16	Vonnie Holliday	15.00
17	Patrick Johnson	8.00
18	Joe Jurevicius	15.00
19	Brian Kelly	8.00
20	Ryan Leaf	70.00
21	Peyton Manning	100.00
22	Alonzo Mayes	12.00
23	Randy Moss	150.00
24	Michael Myers	8.00
25	Marcus Nash	15.00
26	Tom Osborne	25.00
27	Jason Peter	8.00
28	Mike Price	8.00
29	Phil Savoy	12.00
30	Anthony Simmons	8.00
31	Brian Simmons	8.00
32	Takeo Spikes	12.00
33	Steve Spurrier	25.00
34	Fred Taylor	40.00
35	Andre Wadsworth	15.00
36	Hines Ward	15.00
37	Shaun Williams	8.00
38	Grant Wistrom	8.00

1998 Press Pass Fields of Fury

This horizontal, nine-card set featured the player off to the right side, with a game highlight of him roughly bor-dered in black along the ma-jority of the card. Fields of Fury were numbered with a "FF" prefix and inserted one per 36 packs.

	MT
Complete Set (9):	90.00
Common Player:	7.00
FF 1/9Peyton Manning	30.00
FF 2/9Marcus Nash	10.00
FF 3/9Ryan Leaf	20.00
FF 4/9Randy Moss	40.00
FF 5/9Robert Edwards	12.00
FF 6/9Curtis Enis	10.00
FF 7/9Kevin Dyson	10.00
FF 8/9Fred Taylor	12.00
FF 9/9Jacquez Green	7.00

1998 Press Pass Head Butt

Head Butt was a nine-card insert that included a film-like shot of the player over a black background, with his em-bossed college team helmet at the bottom center. These were numbered with a "HB" prefix and inserted one per 18 packs. Die-cut versions were seeded one per 36 packs.

	MT
Complete Set (9):	50.00
Common Player:	3.00
Die-Cut Cards:	2x
HB 1/9Peyton Manning	18.00
HB 2/9Charles Woodson	8.00
HB 3/9Ryan Leaf	12.00
HB 4/9Curtis Enis	8.00
HB 5/9Jacquez Green	3.00
HB 6/9Ahman Green	3.00
HB 7/9Randy Moss	25.00
HB 8/9Tavian Banks	6.00
HB 9/9Robert Edwards	8.00

1998 Press Pass Jerseys

Jerseys was a four-card insert that featured a swatch of the player's game-used col-lege jersey embedded in the front. These were sequentially numbered to 425 sets, num-bered with a "JC" prefix and in-serted one per 720 packs.

	MT
Complete Set (4):	500.00
Common Player:	70.00
JC PMPeyton Manning	200.00
JC RLRyan Leaf	175.00
JC KDKevin Dyson	70.00
JC TBTavian Banks	70.00

1998 Press Pass Kick-Off

Kick-Off included 36 of the players from the base set on a die-cut, football-shaped card. The player's image and the football were both embossed. These were numbered with a "KO" prefix and inserted one per pack in both hobby and re-tail.

	MT
Complete Set (36):	30.00
Common Player:	.20
KO 1 Peyton Manning	6.00
KO 2 Ryan Leaf	5.00
KO 3 Charles Woodson	3.00
KO 4 Andre Wadsworth	1.50
KO 5 Randy Moss	12.00
KO 6 Curtis Enis	3.00
KO 7 Donald Hayes	.20
KO 8 Flozell Adams	.20
KO 9 Jason Peter	.20
KO 10Brian Simmons	.20
KO 11Takeo Spikes	.20
KO 12Germane Crowell	.20
KO 13Donovin Darius	.20
KO 14Grant Wistrom	.20
KO 15Alonzo Mayes	.20
KO 16Kevin Dyson	1.50
KO 17John Avery	1.50
KO 18Anthony Simmons	.20
KO 19Robert Edwards	1.50
KO 20Shaun Williams	.20
KO 21Leonard Little	.20
KO 22Skip Hicks	1.50
NO 23Phil Savoy	.20
KO 24Tavian Banks	2.00
KO 25Robert Holcombe	1.00
KO 26Eric Green	1.00
KO 27Tim Dwight	.20
KO 28Saladin McCullough	.20
KO 29Fred Taylor	1.50
KO 30Jerome Pathon	.20
KO 31Brian Kelly	.20
KO 32Hines Ward	1.00
KO 33Jacquez Green	1.00
KO 34Marcus Nash	1.50
KO 35Ahman Green	1.50
KO 36Joe Jurevicius	.20

1998 Press Pass Triple Threat

This nine-card insert fea-tured three different players, with each having three differ-ent fit-together cards to form a three-card panel. They were numbered with a "TT" prefix and inserted one per 12 packs.

	MT
Complete Set (9):	40.00
Common Player:	3.00
TT 1/9Peyton Manning	8.00
TT 2/9Peyton Manning	8.00
TT 3/9Peyton Manning	8.00
TT 4/9Ryan Leaf	6.00
TT 5/9Ryan Leaf	6.00
TT 6/9Ryan Leaf	6.00
TT 7/9Charles Woodson	3.00
TT 8/9Charles Woodson	3.00
TT 9/9Charles Woodson	3.00

1998 Press Pass Trophy Case

This 12-card insert was printed on silver foilboard, with the player's name across the top and the insert name across the bottom. Trophy Case cards are numbered with a "TC" prefix and inserted one per nine packs.

	MT
Complete Set (12):	40.00
Common Player:	2.00
TC 1/12 Peyton Manning	12.00
TC 2/12 Ryan Leaf	10.00
TC 3/12 Charles Woodson	6.00
TC 4/12 Randy Moss	16.00
TC 5/12 Curtis Enis	6.00
TC 6/12 Grant Wistrom	2.00
TC 7/12 Kevin Dyson	4.00
TC 8/12 Fred Taylor	6.00
TC 9/12 Tavian Banks	4.00
TC10/12 Ahman Green	2.00
TC11/12 Skip Hicks	4.00
TC12/12 Andre Wadsworth	4.00

1998 Pro Line DC III

Pro Line DC III was a 100-card, all die-cut set that included 20 DC Rewind subset cards and 10 Rookie Uprising subset cards. The primary base cards feature the player in an oval shot with gold foil extended and squared off on all four corners, with the Pro Line DC logo in the upper right corner. Inserts in the product included: Clear Cuts, X-Tra Effort, Decade Draft, SB Team Totals and Choice Cuts. Each card and insert was also included in a Perfect Cut 1 of 1 set that was encapsulated in a PSA container and graded Mint. This included 170 total cards and these were available through redemptions.

	MT
Complete Set (100):	50.00
Common Player:	.30
Wax Box:	80.00
1 Drew Bledsoe	2.00
2 Emmitt Smith	3.00
3 Dana Stubblefield	.30
4 Brett Favre	4.00
5 Derrick Alexander	.30
6 Bert Emanuel	.30
7 Joey Galloway	.60
8 Terrell Davis	2.00
9 Mark Brunell	2.00
10 Marshall Faulk	.60

11 Jake Reed	.30
12 Terry Allen	.30
13 Kordell Stewart	2.00
14 Reggie White	.60
15 Michael Irvin	.60
16 Tony Martin	.30
17 Barry Sanders	3.00
18 Carl Pickens	.30
19 Bobby Hoying	.30
20 Adrian Murrell	.60
21 Jeff George	.60
22 Tim Brown	.30
23 Karim Abdul-Jabbar	.60
24 Robert Smith	.30
25 Eddie George	2.50
26 Corey Dillon	1.50
27 Keyshawn Johnson	.60
28 Ricky Watters	.60
29 Robert Brooks	.30
30 Antonio Freeman	.60
31 Danny Kanell	.30
32 Steve McNair	1.50
33 Antowain Smith	1.50
34 Warrick Dunn	3.00
35 Napoleon Kaufman	.60
36 Trent Dilfer	.60
37 Herman Moore	.60
38 Brad Johnson	.30
39 Deion Sanders	1.00
40 Kerry Collins	1.25
41 Shannon Sharpe	.30
42 Irving Fryar	.30
43 Dorsey Levens	.60
44 Jerry Rice	2.00
45 Curtis Martin	2.00
46 Jerome Bettis	.60
47 Raymont Harris	.30
48 Vinny Testaverde	.30
49 Dan Marino	3.00
50 Junior Seau	.30
51 Steve Young	1.50
52 Troy Aikman	2.00
53 Jimmy Smith	.30
54 Ben Coates	.30
55 Gus Frerotte	.30
56 Marcus Allen	.60
57 Bruce Smith	.30
58 Jeff Blake	.60
59 John Elway	1.50
60 Rod Smith	.30
61 Andre Rison	.30
62 Isaac Bruce	.60
63 Cris Carter	.30
64 Danny Wuerffel	1.00
65 Rob Moore	.30
66 Garrison Hearst	.30
67 Warren Moon	.30
68 Checklist Jerome Bettis	.30
69 Marcus Allen (DC Rewind)	.30
70 James Stewart (DC Rewind)	.30
71 Karim Abdul-Jabbar (DC Rewind)	.30
72 Joey Galloway (DC Rewind)	.30
73 Corey Dillon (DC Rewind)	1.50
74 Andre Rison (DC Rewind)	.30
75 Napoleon Kaufman (DC Rewind)	.30
76 Dorsey Levens (DC Rewind)	.30
77 Irving Fryar (DC Rewind)	.30
78 Eric Metcalf (DC Rewind)	.30
79 Darrien Gordon (DC Rewind)	.30
80 Neil O'Donnell (DC Rewind)	.30
81 Rod Woodson (DC Rewind)	.30
82 Rob Johnson (DC Rewind)	.30
83 Michael Westbrook (DC Rewind)	.30
84 Jake Plummer (DC Rewind)	1.50
85 Bobby Hoying (DC Rewind)	.30
86 Adrian Murrell (DC Rewind)	.30
87 Jim Druckenmiller (DC Rewind)	1.50
88 Warren Moon (DC Rewind)	.30
89 Checklist Dorsey Levens (DC Rewind)	.30
90 *Tony Gonzalez* (Rookie Uprising)	.30
91 *Jim Druckenmiller* (Rookie Uprising)	1.50
92 *Corey Dillon* (Rookie Uprising)	1.50
93 *Darrell Russell* (Rookie Uprising)	.30
94 *Byron Hanspard* (Rookie Uprising)	1.00
95 *Rae Carruth* (Rookie Uprising)	1.00
96 *Peter Boulware* (Rookie Uprising)	.30
97 *Troy Davis* (Rookie Uprising)	1.00
98 *Reidel Anthony* (Rookie Uprising)	1.25
99 *Tiki Barber* (Rookie Uprising)	1.25
100 Checklist *Jake Plummer* (Rookie Uprising)	.30

1998 Pro Line DC III Choice Cuts

Choice Cuts were randomly inserted into packs of Pro Line DC III. The cards are horizontal and die-cut in design, with the player featured on the left side, with a large blue "C" die-cut out of the right side. The insert name is included in the blue "C" with "Choice" on the top and "Cuts" across the bottom. Choice Cuts are numbered on the back with a "CHC" prefix, with 10 cards in the set.

	MT
Complete Set (10):	90.00
Common Player:	5.00
CC1 Deion Sanders	7.00
CC2 Jerome Bettis	5.00
CC3 Troy Aikman	15.00
CC4 Jerry Rice	15.00
CC5 Mark Brunell	12.00
CC6 Curtis Martin	10.00
CC7 Cris Carter	7.00
CC8 Steve Young	10.00
CC9 Reggie White	7.00
CC10 Dan Marino	30.00

1998 Pro Line DC III Clear Cuts

This 10-card set was prined on horizontal plastic that was hobby exclusive. Clear Cuts were hobby exclusive, inserted in one per 95 packs and sequentially numbered to 500. Cards featured the insert name printed across the top, with a gold foil finish. A color shot of the player was centered on the card, with his name and team logo off to the right. Clear Cuts inserts were numbered on the back with a "CLC" prefix.

	MT
Complete Set (10):	475.00
Common Player:	20.00
CC1 John Elway	40.00
CC2 Drew Bledsoe	50.00
CC3 Terrell Davis	50.00
CC4 Brett Favre	100.00
CC5 Cris Carter	20.00
CC6 Eddie George	75.00
CC7 Kordell Stewart	50.00
CC8 Warrick Dunn	75.00
CC9 Tim Brown	20.00
CC10 Barry Sanders	85.00

1998 Pro Line DC III Decade Draft

Decade Draft was a 10-card insert that was inserted at a rate of one per 24 packs in Pro Line DC III. The cards are die-cut in the shape of a "D" with foil etched around the edge. An action shot of the player is shown on the right side of the card with a closer shot on the left. Decade Draft inserts are numbered with a "DD" prefix on the back.

	MT
Complete Set (10):	120.00
Common Player:	2.50
DD1 T. Aikman, B. Sanders	25.00
DD2 J. George, E. Smith	20.00
DD3 R. Maryland, B. Favre	30.00
DD4 S. Emtman, C. Pickens	2.50
DD5 D. Bledsoe, D. Bledsoe	12.00
DD6 D. Wilkinson, M. Faulk	5.00
DD7 K. Carter, T. Davis	20.00
DD8 K. Johnson, E. George	15.00
DD9 O. Pace, W. Dunn	15.00
DD10 1998 Top Draft Pick	8.00

1998 Pro Line DC III Team Totals

Team Totals was a 30-card insert that was found in packs of Pro Line DC III at a rate of one per eight packs. The cards were die-cut in the shape of a crystal ball, with the insert name across the bottom in gold foil and two shots of the player in the ball part - an action shot on the right and a closeup on the left. Team Totals inserts are numbered on the back with a "TT" prefix.

	MT
Complete Set (30):	100.00
Common Player:	2.00
SB1 Ben Coates, Willie McGinest	2.00
SB2 Michael Irvin, Deion Sanders	6.00
SB3 Carl Pickens, Dan Wilkinson	2.00
SB4 LeRoy Butler, Antonio Freeman	6.00
SB5 Adrian Murrell, Hugh Douglas	3.00
SB6 Raymont Harris, Bryan Cox	2.00
SB7 Ricky Watters, William Thomas	4.00
SB8 Neil Smith, Shannon Sharpe	3.00
SB9 Dana Stubblefield, Garrison Hearst	3.00
SB10 Keenan McCardell, Jeff Lageman	2.00
SB11 Rae Carruth, Lamar Lathon	4.00
SB12 Yancey Thigpen, Greg Lloyd	2.00
SB13 Chris Calloway, Michael Strahan	2.00
SB14 Troy Davis, Wayne Martin	3.00
SB15 Warren Moon, Cortez Kennedy	3.00
SB16 Rob Moore, Simeon Rice	2.00
SB17 O.J. McDuffie, Zach Thomas	3.00
SB18 John Randle, Robert Smith	3.00
SB19 Derrick Thomas, Elvis Grbac	3.00
SB20 Antowain Smith, Bruce Smith	10.00
SB21 Jeff George, Darrell Russell	2.00
SB22 Steve McNair, Darryll Lewis	10.00
SB23 Isaac Bruce, Leslie O'Neal	4.00
SB24 Junior Seau, Tony Martin	3.00
SB25 Warren Sapp, Mike Alstott	4.00
SB26 Jessie Tuggle, Jamal Anderson	2.00
SB27 Michael Jackson, Peter Boulware	2.00
SB28 Quentin Coryatt, Marvin Harrison	4.00
SB29 Bryant Westbrook, Scott Mitchell	2.00
SB30 Michael Westbrook, Darrell Green	3.00

1998 Pro Line DC III X-Tra Effort

X-Tra Effort inserts are die-cut in the shape of an "X" on a horizontal format. Card fronts have the player's first name in the top left corner, his last name in the top right corner, a Pro Line DC logo in the bottom left and the insert name in the bottom right corner. The player is centered in the card with lightning bolts coming out on all sides. In addition, the front bears gold foil on all sides of the "X" as if a gold oval was set in back of the card to form a second layer. X-Tra Effort was a 20-card insert that was found one per 24 hobby packs and sequentially numbered to 1,000 sets. Cards carried a "XE" prefix on the back card number.

	MT
Complete Set (20):	325.00
Common Player:	5.00
XE1 Reggie White	8.00
XE2 Emmitt Smith	40.00

XE3	Junior Seau	5.00
XE4	Brett Favre	50.00
XE5	Warrick Dunn	30.00
XE6	Keyshawn Johnson	8.00
XE7	Dan Marino	40.00
XE8	Thurman Thomas	5.00
XE9	Steve Young	15.00
XE10	Curtis Martin	20.00
XE11	Karim Abdul-Jabbar	10.00
XE12	John Elway	20.00
XE13	Marcus Allen	8.00
XE14	Napoleon Kaufman	8.00
XE15	Irving Fryar	5.00
XE16	Mark Brunell	20.00
XE17	Andre Rison	5.00
XE18	Herman Moore	8.00
XE19	Jerry Rice	20.00
XE20	Kordell Stewart	20.00

1998 SkyBox

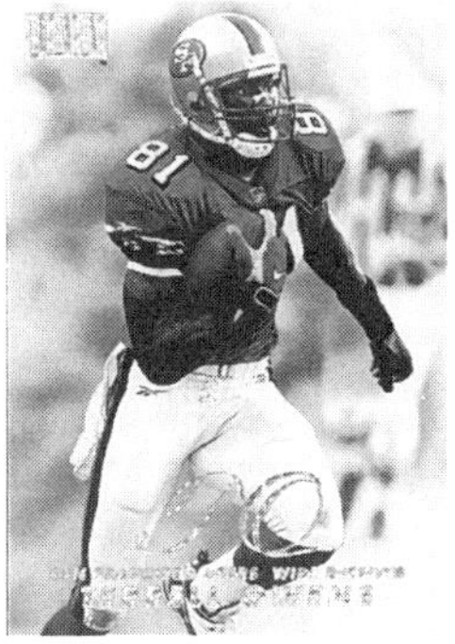

This 250-card included 195 veteran stars, 15 One for the Ages subset cards and 40 rookies seeded one per four packs. Each card featured a borderless design on the front, with the player's name, team, position and SkyBox logo printed in a prismatic gold foil. Backs contain a closeup of the player over a black background. Each card was paralleled in a Star Rubies parallel which was numbered to 50 sets. Insert sets include: Autographics, D'Stroyers, Intimidation Nation, Prime Time Rookies, Rap Show and Soul of the Game.

		MT
Complete Set (250):		250.00
Common Player:		.10
Common Rookie (211-250):		1.50
Inserted 1:4		
Wax Box:		80.00
1	John Elway	1.25
2	Drew Bledsoe	1.25
3	Antonio Freeman	.50
4	Merton Hanks	.10
5	James Jett	.10
6	Ricky Proehl	.10
7	Deion Sanders	.50
8	Frank Sanders	.10
9	Bruce Smith	.10
10	Tiki Barber	.20
11	Isaac Bruce	.20
12	Mark Brunell	1.00
13	Quinn Early	.10
14	Terry Glenn	.20
15	Darrien Gordon	.10
16	Keith Byars	.10
17	Terrell Davis	1.25
18	Charlie Garner	.10
19	Eddie Kennison	.20
20	Keenan McCardell	.10
21	Eric Moulds	.10
22	Jimmy Smith	.20
23	Reidel Anthony	.20
24	Rae Carruth	.10
25	Michael Irvin	.50
26	Dorsey Levens	.20
27	Derrick Mayes	.10
28	Adrian Murrell	.20
29	Dwayne Rudd	.10
30	Leslie Shepherd	.10
31	Jamal Anderson	.20
32	Robert Brooks	.10
33	Sean Dawkins	.10
34	Cris Dishman	.10
35	Rickey Dudley	.10
36	Bobby Engram	.10
37	Chester McGlockton	.10
38	Terrell Owens	.20
39	Wayne Chrebet	.10
40	Dexter Coakley	.10
41	Kerry Collins	.20
42	Trent Dilfer	.20
43	Bobby Hoying	.10
44	Glyn Milburn	.10
45	Rob Moore	.10
46	Jake Reed	.10
47	Dana Stubblefield	.10
48	Reggie White	.20
49	Natrone Means	.20
50	Troy Aikman	1.25
51	Aaron Bailey	.10
52	William Floyd	.10
53	Eric Metcalf	.10
54	Warrick Dunn	1.00
55	Chad Lewis	.10
56	Curtis Martin	.75
57	Tony Martin	.10
58	John Randle	.10
59	Jeff Burris	.10
60	Larry Centers	.10
61	Bert Emanuel	.10
62	Sean Gilbert	.10
63	David Palmer	.10
64	Eric Bieniemy	.10
65	Peter Boulware	.10
66	Charles Johnson	.10
67	Jerris McPhail	.10
68	Scott Mitchell	.10
69	Chris Sanders	.10
70	Ken Dilger	.10
71	Brad Johnson	.20
72	Danny Kanell	.10
73	Fred Lane	.20
74	Warren Sapp	.10
75	Carl Pickens	.20
76	Cris Carter	.20
77	Marshall Faulk	.20
78	Keyshawn Johnson	.20
79	Tony McGee	.10
80	Muhsin Muhammad	.10
81	Kordell Stewart	1.00
82	Karl Williams	.10
83	Willie Davis	.10
84	David Dunn	.10
85	Marvin Harrison	.20
86	Michael Jackson	.10
87	John Mobley	.10
88	Shawn Springs	.10
89	Wesley Walls	.10
90	Jermaine Lewis	.10
91	Ed McCaffrey	.10
92	Chris Calloway	.10
93	Lamont Warren	.10
94	Ricky Watters	.20
95	Tony Banks	.20
96	Tony Brackens	.10
97	Gary Brown	.10
98	Howard Griffith	.10
99	Ray Lewis	.10
100	Jeff Blake	.20
101	Charlie Jones	.10
102	Glenn Foley	.20
103	Jay Graham	.10
104	James McKnight	.10
105	Steve McNair	.75
106	Chad Scott	.10
107	Rod Smith	.20
108	Jason Taylor	.10
109	Corey Dillon	1.00
110	Eddie George	1.00
111	Jim Harbaugh	.20
112	Warren Moon	.20
113	Shannon Sharpe	.20
114	Darnell Autry	.10
115	Brett Favre	2.50
116	Jeff George	.20
117	Tony Gonzalez	.20
118	Garrison Hearst	.20
119	Randal Hill	.10
120	Eric Swann	.10
121	Jamie Asher	.10
122	Tim Brown	.20
123	Stephen Davis	.10
124	Chris Chandler	.10
125	Jerry Rice	1.25
126	Troy Davis	.10
127	Ronnie Harmon	.10
128	Andre Rison	.10
129	Duce Staley	.10
130	Charles Way	.10
131	Bryant Westbrook	.10
132	Mike Alstott	.50
133	Gus Frerotte	.10
134	Travis Jervey	.10
135	Daryl Johnston	.10
136	Jake Plummer	1.00
137	Junior Seau	.20
138	Robert Smith	.20
139	Thurman Thomas	.20
140	Karim Abdul-Jabbar	.20
141	Jerome Bettis	.20
142	Byron Hanspard	.10
143	Raymont Harris	.10
144	Willie McGinest	.10
145	Barry Sanders	2.50
146	Irv Smith	.10
147	Michael Strahan	.10
148	Frank Wycheck	.10
149	Steve Broussard	.10
150	Joey Galloway	.50
151	Courtney Hawkins	.10
152	O.J. McDuffie	.10
153	Herman Moore	.20
154	Chris Penn	.10
155	O.J. Santiago	.10
156	Yancey Thigpen	.10
157	Jason Sehorn	.10
158	Ben Coates	.10
159	Ernie Conwell	.10
160	Dale Carter	.10
161	Jeff Graham	.10
162	Rob Johnson	.20
163	Damon Jones	.10
164	Mark Chmura	.20
165	Curtis Conway	.20
166	Elvis Grbac	.10
167	Andre Hastings	.10
168	Terry Kirby	.10
169	Aeneas Williams	.10
170	Derrick Alexander	.10
171	Troy Brown	.10
172	Irving Fryar	.10
173	Jerald Moore	.10
174	Andre Reed	.10
175	James Stewart	.20
176	Chris Warren	.10
177	Will Blackwell	.10
178	Erik Kramer	.10
179	Dan Marino	2.00
180	Terance Mathis	.10
181	Johnnie Morton	.10
182	J.J. Stokes	.20
183	Rodney Thomas	.10
184	Steve Young	.75
185	Kimble Anders	.10
186	Napoleon Kaufman	.50
187	Orlando Pace	.10
188	Antowain Smith	.75
189	Emmitt Smith	2.00
190	Terry Allen	.10
191	Mark Bruener	.10
191	Mark Bruener	.10
192	Rodney Harrison	.10
193	Billy Joe Hobert	.10
194	Leon Johnson	.10
195	Freddie Jones	.10
196	Super Bowl	.10
197	Super Bowl	.10
198	Super Bowl	.10
199	Super Bowl	.10
200	Super Bowl	.10
201	Super Bowl	.10
202	Super Bowl	.10
203	Super Bowl	.10
204	Super Bowl	.10
205	Super Bowl	.10
206	Super Bowl	.10
207	Super Bowl	.10
208	Super Bowl	.10
209	Super Bowl	.10
210	Super Bowl	.10
211	*Robert Edwards*	20.00
212	*Roland Williams*	1.50
213	*Joe Jurevicius*	3.00
214	*Wilmont Perry*	1.50
215	*Robert Holcombe*	10.00
216	*Larry Shannon*	1.50
217	*Skip Hicks*	4.00
218	*Patrick Johnson*	1.50
219	*Pat Palmer*	1.50
220	*John Dutton*	1.50
221	*Az-Zahir Hakim*	3.00
222	*Mikhael Ricks*	3.00
223	*Rashaan Shehee*	3.00
224	*Ryan Leaf*	25.00
225	*Alvis Whitted*	1.50
226	*Marcus Nash*	6.00
227	*Fred Taylor*	25.00
228	*Hines Ward*	6.00
229	*Chris Fuamatu-Ma'afala*	5.00
230	*Jerome Pathon*	3.00
231	*Peyton Manning*	45.00
232	*Charles Woodson*	15.00
233	*Jon Ritchie*	1.50
234	*Scott Frost*	1.50
235	*John Avery*	6.00
236	*Jonathon Linton*	1.50
237	*Jacquez Green*	8.00
238	*Andre Wadsworth*	3.00
239	*Cam Quayle*	1.50
240	*Randy Moss*	75.00
241	*Raymond Priester*	1.50
242	*Donald Hayes*	1.50
243	*Brian Griese*	8.00
244	*Brian Alford*	1.50
245	*Kevin Dyson*	8.00
246	*Jammi German*	1.50
247	*Cameron Cleeland*	4.00
248	*Curtis Enis*	15.00
249	*Terry Hardy*	1.50
250	*Tony Simmons*	4.00

1998 SkyBox Star Rubies

Star Rubies paralleled all 250 cards in SkyBox. The gold foil stamps of the regular cards were replaced by red foil and backs were numbered to 50.

	MT
Star Ruby Cards:	75x-150x
Star Ruby Rookies:	4x-8x

1998 SkyBox Autographics

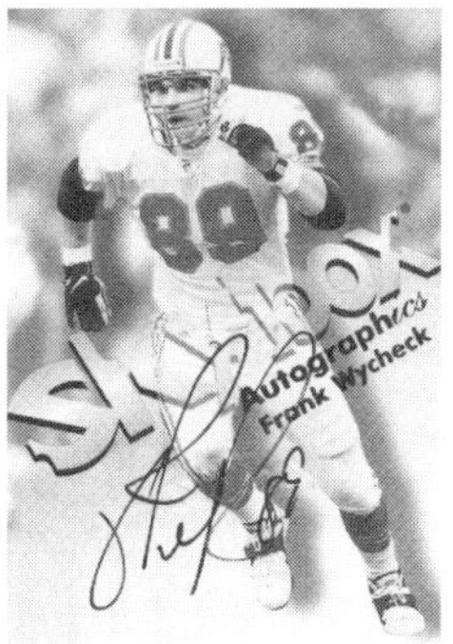

A total of 73 different NFL players signed cards for Autographics in 1998. The program ran through Thunder, Metal Universe, SkyBox and E-X2001 products. Regular versions are signed in black ink, while Blue versions are individually numbered to 50. Cards were inserted 1:112 in Thunder, 1:68 in Metal Universe and Premium and 1:48 packs of E-X2001.

	MT
Common Player:	10.00
Inserted 1:48 E-X2001	
Inserted 1:68 Metal Universe	
Inserted 1:68 SkyBox Premium	
Inserted 1:112 Thunder	
Blue Signatures:	4x
Production 50 Sets	
Kevin Abrams	10.00
Mike Alstott	35.00
Jamie Asher	10.00
Jon Avery	40.00
Tavian Banks	45.00
Pat Barnes	10.00
Jerome Bettis	30.00
Eric Bjornson	10.00
Peter Boulware	10.00
Troy Brown	10.00
Mark Breunner	10.00
Mark Brunell	85.00
Rae Carruth	10.00
Ray Crockett	10.00
Germane Crowell	40.00
Stephen Davis	15.00
Troy Davis	10.00
Sean Dawkins	10.00
Trent Dilfer	30.00
Corey Dillon	60.00
Jim Druckenmiller	30.00
Kevin Dyson	35.00
Marc Edwards	10.00
Robert Edwards	90.00
Bobby Engram	10.00
Curtis Enis	75.00
William Floyd	15.00
Glenn Foley	15.00
Chris Fuamatu-Ma'afal	25.00
Joey Galloway	35.00
Jeff George	30.00
Ahman Green	50.00
Jacquez Green	50.00
Yatil Green	10.00
Byron Hanspard	25.00
Marvin Harrison	30.00
Skip Hicks	35.00
Robert Holcombe	45.00
Bobby Hoying	25.00
Travis Jervey	10.00
Rob Johnson	30.00
Freddie Jones	10.00
Eddie Kennison	10.00
Fred Lane	20.00
Ryan Leaf	150.00
Dorsey Levens	25.00
Jeff Lewis	10.00
Jermaine Lewis	10.00
Dan Marino	220.00
Curtis Martin	60.00
Steve Matthews	10.00
Alonzo Mayes	15.00
Keenan McCardell	20.00
Willie McGinnest	10.00
James McKnight	10.00
Glyn Milburn	10.00
Warren Moon	20.00
Randy Moss	250.00
Marcus Nash	35.00
Terrell Owens	50.00
Jason Peter	10.00
Jake Plummer	90.00
John Randle	15.00
Shannon Sharpe	40.00
Jimmy Smith	25.00
Lamar Smith	10.00
Robert Smith	20.00
Duce Staley	10.00
Kordell Stewart	90.00
Fred Taylor	100.00
Rodney Thomas	10.00
Kevin Turner	10.00
Hines Ward	40.00
Charles Way	10.00
Frank Wycheck	10.00

1998 SkyBox D'stroyers

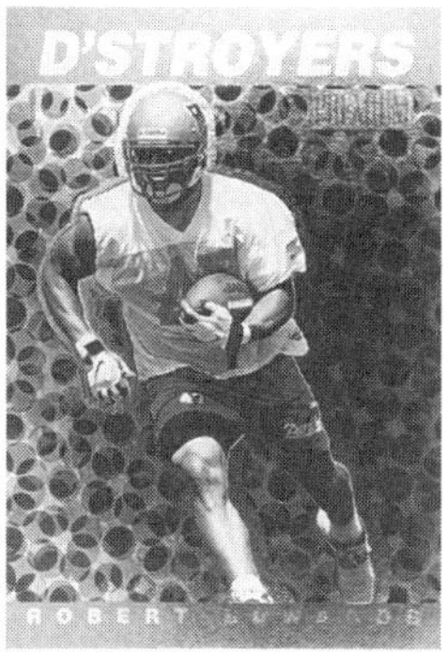

D'Stroyers was a 15-card insert that highlighted top young players in the league. The players were featured over a prismatic foil background and inserted one per six packs.

		MT
Complete Set (15):		35.00
Common Player:		.75
Inserted 1:6		
1	Antowain Smith	3.00
2	Corey Dillon	4.00
3	Charles Woodson	4.00
4	Randy Moss	12.00
5	Deion Sanders	1.50
6	Robert Edwards	6.00
7	Herman Moore	1.50
8	Mark Brunell	6.00
9	Dorsey Levens	.75
10	Curtis Enis	4.00
11	Drew Bledsoe	6.00
12	Steve McNair	3.00
13	Keyshawn Johnson	.75
14	Bobby Hoying	.75
15	Trent Dilfer	1.50

1998 SkyBox Intimidation Nation

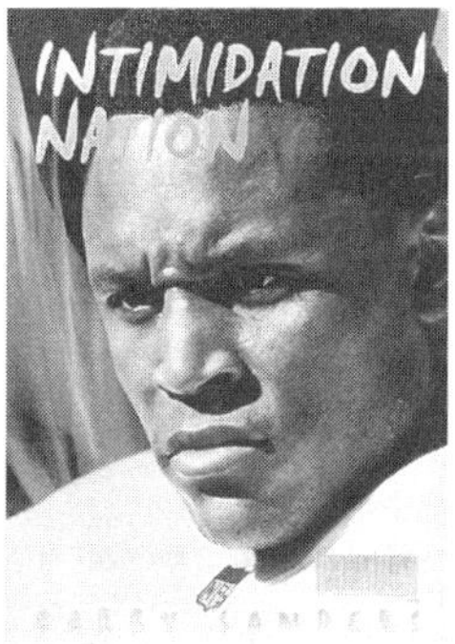

Intimidation Nation captured 15 of the top players in the league over a flaming background. This insert was the toughest to find in SkyBox and inserted one per 360 packs.

		MT
Complete Set (15):		750.00
Common Player:		20.00
Inserted 1:360		
1	Terrell Davis	75.00
2	Emmitt Smith	100.00
3	Barry Sanders	120.00
4	Brett Favre	120.00
5	Eddie George	45.00
6	Jerry Rice	60.00
7	John Elway	60.00
8	Mark Brunell	50.00
9	Troy Aikman	60.00
10	Peyton Manning	100.00
11	Ryan Leaf	80.00

12	Curtis Martin	20.00
13	Dan Marino	100.00
14	Warrick Dunn	45.00
15	Jake Plummer	45.00

1998 SkyBox Prime Time Rookies

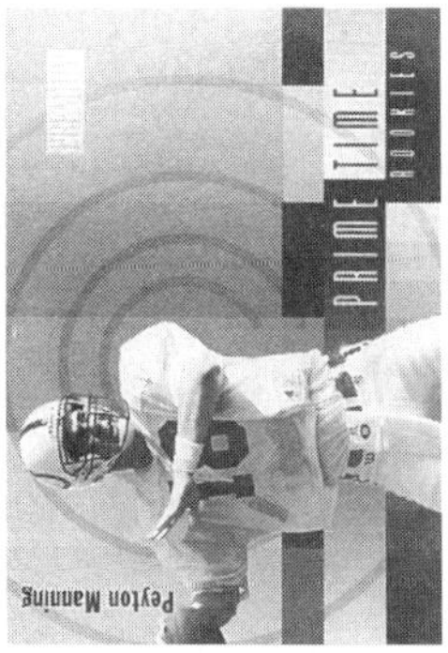

Ten rookies were featured on this horizontal, multi-colored background insert set. The cards featured the rookie on the left side with a bullseye over the background. Prime Time Rookies were seeded one per 96 packs.

		MT
Complete Set (10):		200.00
Common Player:		6.00
Inserted 1:96		
1	Curtis Enis	15.00
2	Robert Edwards	20.00
3	Fred Taylor	25.00
4	Robert Holcombe	12.00
5	Ryan Leaf	25.00
6	Peyton Manning	40.00
7	Randy Moss	60.00
8	Charles Woodson	20.00
9	Andre Wadsworth	6.00
10	Kevin Dyson	6.00

1998 SkyBox Rap Show

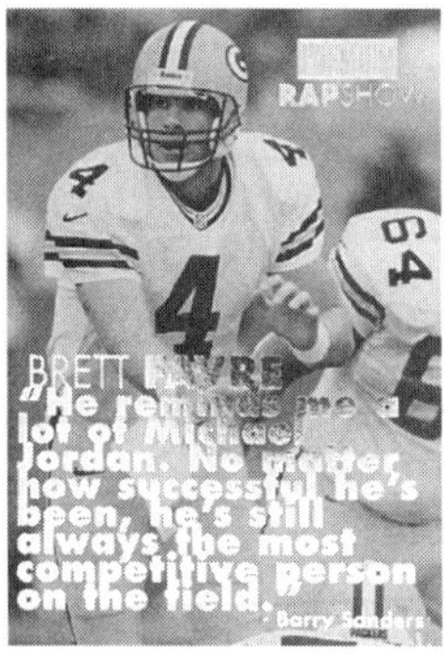

This 15-card insert featured an action shot of the player with a silver foil-stamped quote from one of his peers on the front. Rap Show inserts were seeded per 36 packs.

		MT
Complete Set (15):		150.00
Common Player:		5.00
Inserted 1:36		
1	John Elway	20.00
2	Drew Bledsoe	20.00
3	Corey Dillon	12.00
4	Brett Favre	40.00
5	Barry Sanders	40.00
6	Eddie George	15.00
7	Emmitt Smith	30.00
8	Jake Plummer	15.00
9	Joey Galloway	8.00
10	Ricky Watters	5.00
11	Mike Alstott	8.00
12	Kordell Stewart	15.00
13	Antonio Freeman	8.00
14	Terrell Davis	20.00
15	Warrick Dunn	15.00

1998 SkyBox Soul of the Game

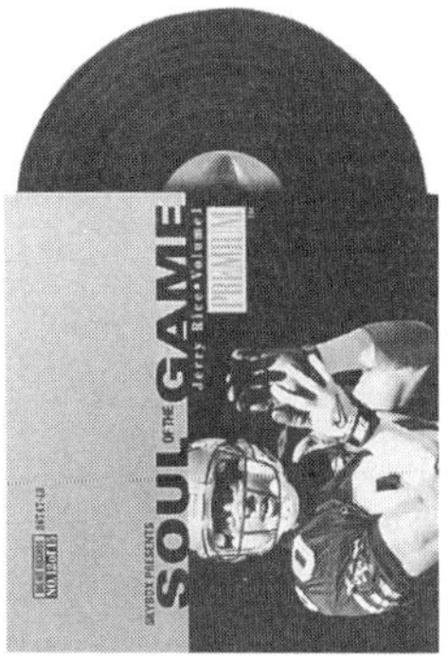

Soul of the Game were horizontal inserts that resembled a record sleeve with the album half out. The cards were one solid piece of plastic and inserted one per 18 packs.

		MT
Complete Set (15):		80.00
Common Player:		3.00
Inserted 1:18		
1	Troy Aikman	15.00
2	Dorsey Levens	3.00
3	Deion Sanders	7.00
4	Antonio Freeman	5.00
5	Dan Marino	20.00
6	Keyshawn Johnson	3.00
7	Terry Glenn	5.00
8	Tim Brown	3.00
9	Curtis Martin	10.00
10	Bobby Hoying	3.00
11	Kordell Stewart	12.00
12	Jerry Rice	15.00
13	Steve McNair	10.00
14	Joey Galloway	5.00
15	Steve Young	10.00

1998 SkyBox Thunder

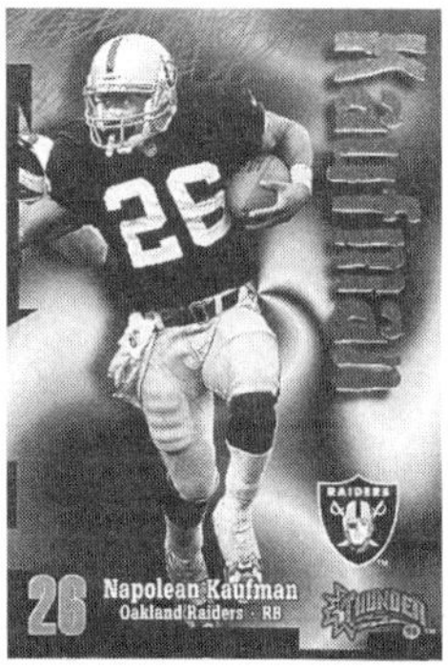

This 250-card set replaced Thunder in 1998 and arrived with 225 veterans and 25 rookies. Thunder was tiered, with 1-100 seeded 4:1 packs, 101-200 seeded 3:1 and 201-250 seeded 1:1. Cards featured a borderless artsy design with the color image of the player over it. The player's last name was foil stamped in large letters down either side. Each card was reprinted in both Rave and Super Rave parallel sets. Thunder also included five insert sets: Boss, Destination: End Zone, Number Crushers, Quick Strike, Autographics and StarBurst.

		MT
Complete Set (250):		50.00
Common Player (1-200):		.10
Common Player (201-250):		.20
Wax Box:		48.00
1	Reggie White	.20
2	Elvis Grbac	.10
3	Ed McCaffrey	.10
4	O.J. McDuffie	.10
5	Scott Mitchell	.10
6	Byron Hanspard	.20
7	John Randle	.10
8	Shawn Jefferson	.10
9	Peter Boulware	.10
10	Karl Williams	.10
11	Napoleon Kaufman	.50
12	Barry Minter	.10
13	Cris Dishman	.10
14	James Stewart	.10
15	Marcus Robertson	.10
16	Rodney Harrison	.10
17	Micheal Barrow	.10
18	Michael Sinclair	.10
19	DeWayne Washington	.10
20	Phillippi Sparks	.10
21	Ernie Conwell	.10
22	Ken Dilger	.10
23	Johnnie Morton	.10
24	Eric Swann	.10
25	Curtis Conway	.20
26	Duce Staley	.10
27	Darrell Green	.10
28	Quinn Early	.10
29	LeRoy Butler	.10
30	Winfred Tubbs	.10
31	Darren Woodson	.10
32	Marcus Allen	.20
33	Glenn Foley	.10
34	Tom Knight	.10
35	Sam Shade	.10
36	James McKnight	.10
37	Leeland McElroy	.10
38	Earl Holmes	.10
39	Ryan McNeil	.10
40	Cris Carter	.20
41	Jessie Armstead	.10
42	Bryce Paup	.10
43	Chris Slade	.10
44	Eric Metcalf	.10
45	Jim Harbaugh	.20
46	Terry Kirby	.10
47	Donnie Edwards	.10
48	Darryl Williams	.10
49	Neil Smith	.10
50	Warren Sapp	.10
51	Jason Taylor	.10
52	Irving Fryar	.10
53	Jeff George	.20
54	Yancey Thigpen	.10
55	Ricky Proehl	.10
56	Kevin Greene	.10
57	Joel Steed	.10
58	Larry Allen	.10
59	Thurman Thomas	.20
60	Aaron Glenn	.10
61	Natrone Means	.20
62	Chris Calloway	.10
63	Chuck Smith	.10
64	Chidi Ahanotu	.10
65	Mario Bates	.10
66	Jonathan Ogden	.10
67	Drew Bledsoe	1.00
68	John Mobley	.10
69	Antowain Smith	.60
70	Aeneas Williams	.10
71	Brian Williams	.10
72	Derrick Thomas	.10
73	Ted Johnson	.10
74	Troy Drayton	.10
75	Mike Pritchard	.10
76	Darnay Scott	.10
77	James Jett	.10
78	Dwayne Rudd	.10
79	Marvin Harrison	.20
80	Dermontti Dawson	.10
81	Keith Lyle	.10
82	Steve Atwater	.10
83	Tyrone Wheatley	.10
84	Tony Brackens	.10
85	Dale Carter	.10
86	Robert Porcher	.10
87	Merton Hanks	.10
88	Leon Johnson	.10
89	Simeon Rice	.10
90	Robert Brooks	.10
91	William Thomas	.10
92	Wesley Walls	.10
93	Chester McGlockton	.10
94	Chris Chandler	.10
95	Michael Strahan	.10
96	Ray Zellars	.10
97	Dexter Coakley	.10
98	Rob Johnson	.20
99	Eric Green	.10
100	Darrien Gordon	.10
101	Gary Brown	.10
102	Reidel Anthony	.20
103	Keenan McCardell	.10
104	Leslie O'Neal	.10
105	Bryant Westbrook	.10
106	Derrick Alexander	.10
107	Jeff Blake	.20
108	Ben Coates	.10
109	Shawn Springs	.10
110	Robert Smith	.20
111	Karim Abdul-Jabbar	.20
112	Willie Davis	.10
113	Mark Chmura	.20
114	Terry Allen	.10
115	Will Blackwell	.10
116	Jamal Anderson	.10
117	Dana Stubblefield	.10
118	Trent Dilfer	.20
119	Jermaine Lewis	.10
120	Chad Brown	.10
121	Tamarick Vanover	.10
122	Tony Martin	.10
123	Larry Centers	.10
124	J.J. Stokes	.10
125	Danny Kanell	.10
126	Wayne Chrebet	.10
127	Kerry Collins	.20
128	Tony Banks	.30
129	Randal Hill	.10
130	Jimmy Smith	.10
131	Tim Brown	.20
132	Zach Thomas	.10
133	Rod Smith	.20
134	Frank Wycheck	.10
135	Garrison Hearst	.20
136	Bruce Smith	.10
137	Hardy Nickerson	.10
138	Sean Dawkins	.10
139	Willie McGinest	.10
140	Kimble Anders	.10
141	Michael Westbrook	.10
142	Chris Doleman	.10
143	Ricky Watters	.20
144	Levon Kirkland	.10
145	Rob Moore	.20
146	Eddie Kennison	.20
147	Rickey Dudley	.10
148	Jay Graham	.10
149	Brad Johnson	.30
150	Bobby Hoying	.10
151	Sherman Williams	.10
152	Charles Way	.10
153	Adrian Murrell	.20
154	Chris Sanders	.10
155	Greg Hill	.10
156	Rae Carruth	.20
157	Mike Alstott	.50
158	Terance Mathis	.10
159	Antonio Freeman	.30
160	Junior Seau	.20
161	Chris Warren	.10
162	Shannon Sharpe	.20
163	Derrick Rodgers	.10
164	Charles Johnson	.10
165	Marshall Faulk	.20
166	Jamie Asher	.10
167	Michael Jackson	.10
168	Terrell Owens	.30
169	Jason Sehorn	.10
170	Raymont Harris	.10
171	Jake Reed	.10
172	Kevin Hardy	.10
173	Jerald Moore	.10
174	Michael Irvin	.20
175	Freddie Jones	.10
176	Steve McNair	.50
177	Carnell Lake	.10
178	Troy Brown	.10
179	Hugh Douglas	.10
180	Andre Rison	.20
181	Leslie Shepherd	.10
182	Andre Hastings	.10
183	Fred Lane	.20
184	Andre Reed	.10
185	Darrell Russell	.10
186	Frank Sanders	.10
187	Derrick Brooks	.10
188	Charlie Garner	.10
189	Bert Emanuel	.10
190	Terrell Buckley	.10
191	Carl Pickens	.20
192	Tiki Barber	.30
193	Pete Mitchell	.10
194	Gilbert Brown	.10
195	Isaac Bruce	.30
196	Ray Lewis	.10
197	Warren Moon	.20
198	Tony Gonzalez	.20
199	John Mobley	.10
200	Gus Frerotte	.10
201	Brett Favre	4.00
202	Terrell Davis	2.50
203	Dan Marino	3.50
204	Barry Sanders	4.00
205	Steve Young	1.00
206	Deion Sanders	1.00
207	Kordell Stewart	2.00
208	Eddie George	2.50
209	Jake Plummer	2.00
210	Warrick Dunn	2.00
211	John Elway	2.00
212	Terry Glenn	.40
213	Mark Brunell	2.00
214	Corey Dillon	1.50
215	Joey Galloway	.40
216	Dorsey Levens	.40
217	Troy Aikman	2.00
218	Keyshawn Johnson	.40
219	Jerome Bettis	.40
220	Curtis Martin	1.25
221	Herman Moore	.40
222	Emmitt Smith	3.50
223	Jerry Rice	2.00
224	Drew Bledsoe	2.00
225	Antowain Smith	1.25
226	*Stephen Alexander*	.20
227	*John Avery*	1.50
228	*Kevin Dyson*	1.50
229	*Robert Edwards*	4.00
230	*Greg Ellis*	.20
231	*Curtis Enis*	4.00
232	*Chris Fuamatu-Ma'afal*	1.00
233	*Ahman Green*	2.00
234	*Jacquez Green*	2.00
235	*Az-Zahir Hakim*	.20
236	*Skip Hicks*	2.00
237	*Joe Jurevicius*	.50
238	*Ryan Leaf*	10.00
239	*Peyton Manning*	10.00
240	*Alonzo Mayes*	.50
241	*R.W. McQuarters*	.20
242	*Randy Moss*	20.00
243	*Marcus Nash*	2.00
244	*Jerome Pathon*	.20
245	*Jason Peter*	1.00
246	*Brian Simmons*	.30
247	*Takeo Spikes*	1.00
248	*Fred Taylor*	4.00
249	*Andre Wadsworth*	1.00
250	*Charles Woodson*	4.00

1998 SkyBox Thunder Rave

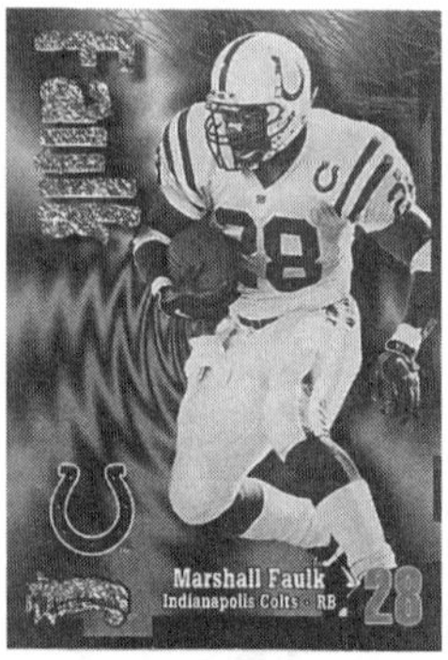

Rave was a 250-card parallel set to Thunder, and featured prismatic silver foil on the front to distinguish them from the base cards. Rave parallels were sequentially numbered to 150 on the back in silver foil and were found only in hobby packs.

	MT
Rave Cards (1-200):	40x-80x
Rave Stars (201-250):	20x-40x
Rave Rookies (201-250):	10x-20x

1998 SkyBox Thunder Super Rave

Super Rave was a 250-card parallel set that was found only in hobby packs. Cards were sequentially numbered to 25 sets.

	MT
Super Rave Cards (1-200):	125x-250x
Super Rave Stars (201-250):	100x-200x
Super Rave Rookies (201-250):	20x-40x

1998 SkyBoxThunder Boss

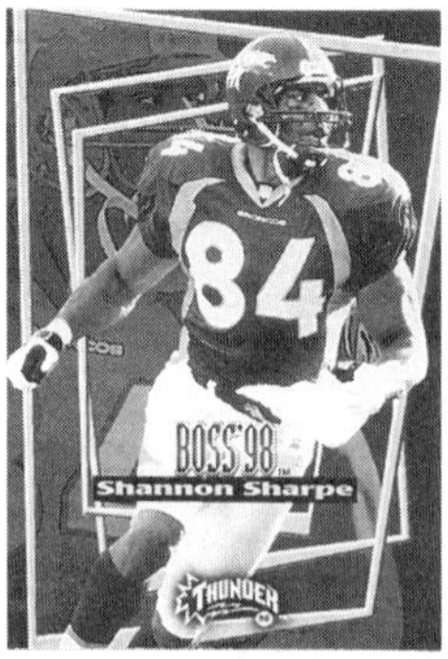

This insert featured 20 players on an embossed design. Backgrounds on the front were done in team colors with several quardrilaterals added. Boss cards were inserted one per eight packs and numbered with a "B" suffix.

		MT
Complete Set (20):		35.00
Common Player:		.75
B1	Troy Aikman	6.00
B2	Drew Bledsoe	6.00
B3	Tim Brown	.75
B4	Antonio Freeman	1.50
B5	Joey Galloway	1.50
B6	Terry Glenn	1.50

		MT
B7	Bobby Hoying	.75
B8	Michael Irvin	1.50
B9	Keyshawn Johnson	.75
B10	Dorsey Levens	1.50
B11	Curtis Martin	5.00
B12	John Mobley	.75
B13	Jake Plummer	6.00
B14	John Randle	.75
B15	Deion Sanders	3.00
B16	Junior Seau	.75
B17	Shannon Sharpe	.75
B18	Bruce Smith	.75
B19	Robert Smith	.75
B20	Dana Stubblefield	.75

1998 SkyBox Thunder Destination End Zone

This 15-card insert captured top scorers in the league on a green background. A small image of the player is placed in a bottom corner with his name in silver letters, and the insert name in red foil. These were inserted one per 96 packs and numbered with a "DE" suffix.

		MT
Complete Set (15):		200.00
Common Player:		5.00
D1	Jerome Bettis	5.00
D2	Mark Brunell	20.00
D3	Terrell Davis	25.00
D4	Corey Dillon	15.00
D5	Warrick Dunn	20.00
D6	John Elway	20.00
D7	Brett Favre	50.00
D8	Eddie George	20.00
D9	Dorsey Levens	5.00
D10	Curtis Martin	15.00
D11	Herman Moore	5.00
D12	Barry Sanders	50.00
D13	Emmitt Smith	40.00
D14	Kordell Stewart	25.00
D15	Steve Young	15.00

1998 SkyBox Thunder Number Crushers

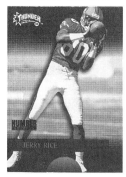

Number Crushers was a 10-card insert that featured the player on the front over a gridlike background. Backs were numbered with a "NC" suffix and included a Q&A section with a pull-out card that contained the answers. These were inserted one per 16 packs.

		MT
Complete Set (10):		45.00
Common Player:		2.00
NC1	Troy Aikman	6.00

		MT
NC2	Jerome Bettis	4.00
NC3	Tim Brown	2.00
NC4	Mark Brunell	6.00
NC5	Dan Marino	12.00
NC6	Herman Moore	4.00
NC7	Rob Moore	2.00
NC8	Jerry Rice	6.00
NC9	Shannon Sharpe	2.00
NC10	Emmitt Smith	12.00

1998 SkyBox Thunder Quick Strike

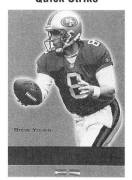

This 12-card, matchbook-like insert featured players over an olive background, with a black strip across the bottom resembling a match strike area. The card opened up to reveal another card of the player, while the back of the matchbook contained only the insert logo. Cards were inserted one per 300 packs and numbered with a "QS" suffix.

		MT
Complete Set (12):		550.00
Common Player:		25.00
QS1	Terrell Davis	50.00
QS2	John Elway	50.00
QS3	Brett Favre	80.00
QS4	Joey Galloway	25.00
QS5	Eddie George	50.00
QS6	Keyshawn Johnson	25.00
QS7	Dan Marino	70.00
QS8	Jerry Rice	50.00
QS9	Barry Sanders	80.00
QS10	Deion Sanders	30.00
QS11	Kordell Stewart	50.00
QS12	Steve Young	40.00

1998 SkyBox Thunder Star Burst

StarBurst was a 10-card insert featuring the player over a gold holofoil background that "bursts" against a regular background tinted in team colors. These were inserted one per 32 packs and numbered with a "SB" suffix.

		MT
Complete Set (10):		100.00
Common Player:		3.00
SB1	Tiki Barber	3.00
SB2	Corey Dillon	8.00
SB3	Warrick Dunn	10.00
SB4	Curtis Enis	8.00
SB5	Ryan Leaf	20.00
SB6	Peyton Manning	20.00
SB7	Randy Moss	30.00
SB8	Jake Plummer	10.00
SB9	Antowain Smith	6.00
SB10	Charles Woodson	8.00

1998 SPx

SPx Football features Holoview cards. The 50-card base set utilizes decorative foil and Light F/X on 32-point card stock. Each card features three player photos on the front. SPx Football also has five parallel sets and three inserts. The parallels are Steel Parallel Universe (1:1), Bronze Parallel Universe (1:3), Silver Parallel Universe (1:6), Gold Parallel Universe (1:17) and Grand Finale Parallel Universe (50 total sets). The insert sets are HoloFame (1:54), ProMotion (1:252) and Piece of History (500 total cards). Piece of History cards could be redeemed for a framed, un-cut, numbered HoloFame Holoview sheet.

		MT
Complete Set (50):		70.00
Common Player:		.50
Wax Box:		75.00
1	Jake Plummer	4.00
2	Byron Hanspard	1.00
3	Vinny Testaverde	.50
4	Antowain Smith	2.50
5	Kerry Collins	2.00
6	Rae Carruth	1.00
7	Darnell Autry	1.00
8	Rick Mirer	.50
9	Jeff Blake	1.00
10	Carl Pickens	.50
11	Troy Aikman	3.50
12	Emmitt Smith	5.00
13	Deion Sanders	1.50
14	John Elway	3.00
15	Terrell Davis	3.50
16	Herman Moore	1.00
17	Barry Sanders	5.00
18	Brett Favre	7.00
19	Reggie White	1.00
20	Marshall Faulk	1.00
21	Mark Brunell	2.50
22	Elvis Grbac	.50
23	Marcus Allen	1.00
24	Karim Abdul-Jabbar	1.00
25	Dan Marino	6.00
26	Cris Carter	.50
27	Drew Bledsoe	3.00
28	Curtis Martin	2.50
29	Heath Shuler	.50
30	Ike Hilliard	1.00
31	Keyshawn Johnson	1.00
32	Jeff George	.50
33	Napoleon Kaufman	1.00
34	Darrell Russell	.50
35	Ricky Watters	1.00
36	Kordell Stewart	3.00
37	Jerome Bettis	1.00
38	Junior Seau	.50
39	Steve Young	2.00
40	Jerry Rice	3.00
41	Joey Galloway	1.00
42	Chris Warren	.50
43	Orlando Pace	1.00
44	Isaac Bruce	1.00
45	Tony Banks	1.00
46	Trent Dilfer	1.00
47	Warrick Dunn	5.00
48	Steve McNair	2.50
49	Eddie George	3.50
50	Terry Allen	.50

1998 SPx Bronze/Gold/ Silver/Steel

The SPx base set had five parallels, including Steel (1:1), Bronze (1:3), Silver (1:6) and Gold (1:17).

	MT
Bronze Cards:	2x
Gold Cards:	4x-8x
Silver Cards:	2x-4x
Steel Cards:	1.5x

1998 SPx Grand Finale

Grand Finale parallels the SPx base set. The all-gold Holoview cards commemorate the final SPx Holoview set. Only 50 sets were produced.

		MT
Common Player:		25.00
1	Jake Plummer	175.00
2	Byron Hanspard	100.00
3	Vinny Testaverde	25.00
4	Antowain Smith	125.00
5	Kerry Collins	175.00
6	Rae Carruth	50.00
7	Darnell Autry	50.00
8	Rick Mirer	25.00
9	Jeff Blake	50.00
10	Carl Pickens	25.00
11	Troy Aikman	200.00
12	Emmitt Smith	350.00
13	Deion Sanders	125.00
14	John Elway	200.00
15	Terrell Davis	225.00
16	Herman Moore	50.00
17	Barry Sanders	325.00
18	Brett Favre	450.00
19	Reggie White	50.00
20	Marshall Faulk	50.00
21	Mark Brunell	175.00
22	Elvis Grbac	25.00
23	Marcus Allen	50.00
24	Karim Abdul-Jabbar	100.00
25	Dan Marino	400.00
26	Cris Carter	25.00
27	Drew Bledsoe	200.00
28	Curtis Martin	175.00
29	Heath Shuler	25.00
30	Ike Hilliard	100.00
31	Keyshawn Johnson	50.00
32	Jeff George	25.00
33	Napoleon Kaufman	50.00
34	Darrell Russell	25.00
35	Ricky Watters	50.00
36	Kordell Stewart	200.00
37	Jerome Bettis	50.00
38	Junior Seau	25.00
39	Steve Young	175.00
40	Jerry Rice	225.00
41	Joey Galloway	50.00
42	Chris Warren	25.00
43	Orlando Pace	50.00
44	Isaac Bruce	50.00
45	Tony Banks	100.00
46	Trent Dilfer	50.00
47	Warrick Dunn	250.00
48	Steve McNair	150.00
49	Eddie George	200.00
50	Terry Allen	25.00

1998 SPx HoloFame

HoloFame is a 20-card insert, seeded one per 54 packs. The cards feature top players embossed on Holoview cards with silver decorative foil.

		MT
Complete Set (20):		325.00
Common Player:		10.00
HF1	Troy Aikman	30.00
HF2	Emmitt Smith	50.00
HF3	John Elway	25.00
HF4	Terrell Davis	30.00
HF5	Herman Moore	10.00
HF6	Reggie White	10.00
HF7	Brett Favre	60.00
HF8	Napoleon Kaufman	10.00
HF9	Dan Marino	50.00
HF10	Karim Abdul-Jabbar	10.00
HF11	Cris Carter	10.00
HF12	Drew Bledsoe	30.00
HF13	Curtis Martin	25.00
HF14	Kordell Stewart	30.00
HF15	Junior Seau	10.00
HF16	Steve Young	20.00
HF17	Jerry Rice	30.00
HF18	Marshall Faulk	10.00
HF19	Eddie George	30.00
HF20	Terry Allen	10.00

1998 SPx ProMotion

ProMotion is a 10-card insert (1:252) produced on copper and silver Holoview cards.

		MT
Complete Set (10):		600.00
Common Player:		30.00
P1	Troy Aikman	60.00
P2	Emmitt Smith	85.00
P3	Terrell Davis	60.00
P4	Brett Favre	100.00
P5	Marcus Allen	30.00
P6	Dan Marino	100.00
P7	Drew Bledsoe	60.00
P8	Ike Hilliard	30.00
P9	Warrick Dunn	60.00
P10	Eddie George	60.00

1998 SPx Finite

SPx Finite Series One consists of a 190-card base set built from five subsets. The base cards feature silver foil. The set consists of 90 regular cards (numbered to 7,600), 30 Playmakers (5,500), 30 Youth Movement (3,000), 20 Pure Energy (2,500) and 10 Heroes of the Game (1,250). Ten rookie cards were also added to SPx Finite, numbered to 1,998.

		MT
Complete Set (190):		1250.
Common Player (1-90):		1.00
Production 7,600 Sets		
Common Player (91-120):		1.50
Production 5,500 Sets		
Common Player (121-150):		2.00
Production 3,000 Sets		
Common Player (151-170):		2.50
Production 2,500 Sets		
Common Player (171-180):		6.00
Production 1,250 Sets		
Common Player (181-190):		12.00
Production 1,998 Sets		
Wax Box:		100.00
1	Jake Plummer	5.00
2	Eric Swann	1.00
3	Rob Moore	1.00
4	Jamal Anderson	2.00
5	Byron Hanspard	1.00
6	Cornelius Bennett	1.00
7	Michael Jackson	1.00
8	Peter Boulware	1.00
9	Jermaine Lewis	1.00
10	Antowain Smith	3.00
11	Bruce Smith	1.00
12	Bryce Paup	1.00
13	Rae Carruth	1.00
14	Michael Bates	1.00
15	Fred Lane	2.00
16	Darnell Autry	1.00
17	Curtis Conway	2.00
18	Erik Kramer	1.00
19	Corey Dillon	4.00
20	Darnay Scott	1.00
21	Reinard Wilson	1.00
22	Troy Aikman	6.00
23	David LaFleur	1.00
24	Emmitt Smith	8.00
25	John Elway	5.00
26	John Mobley	1.00
27	Terrell Davis	6.00
28	Rod Smith	2.00
29	Bryant Westbrook	1.00
30	Scott Mitchell	1.00

31	Barry Sanders	12.00
32	Dorsey Levens	2.00
33	Antonio Freeman	2.00
34	Reggie White	2.00
35	Marshall Faulk	2.00
36	Marvin Harrison	2.00
37	Ken Dilger	1.00
38	Mark Brunell	5.00
39	Keenan McCardell	1.00
40	Renaldo Wynn	1.00
41	Marcus Allen	2.00
42	Elvis Grbac	1.00
43	Andre Rison	1.00
44	Yatil Green	1.00
45	Zach Thomas	1.00
46	Karim Abdul-Jabbar	2.00
47	John Randle	1.00
48	Brad Johnson	2.00
49	Jake Reed	1.00
50	Danny Wuerffel	1.00
51	Andre Hastings	1.00
52	Drew Bledsoe	5.00
53	Terry Glenn	2.00
54	Ty Law	1.00
55	Danny Kanell	1.00
56	Tiki Barber	2.00
57	Jesse Armstead	1.00
58	Glenn Foley	1.00
59	James Farrior	1.00
60	Wayne Chrebet	1.00
61	Tim Brown	2.00
62	Napoleon Kaufman	3.00
63	Darrell Russell	1.00
64	Bobby Hoying	1.00
65	Irving Fryar	1.00
66	Charlie Garner	1.00
67	Will Blackwell	1.00
68	Kordell Stewart	5.00
69	Levon Kirkland	1.00
70	Tony Banks	2.00
71	Ryan McNeil	1.00
72	Isaac Bruce	2.00
73	Tony Martin	1.00
74	Junior Seau	2.00
75	Natrone Means	2.00
76	Jerry Rice	6.00
77	Garrison Hearst	2.00
78	Terrell Owens	2.00
79	Warren Moon	2.00
80	Joey Galloway	2.00
81	Chad Brown	1.00
82	Warrick Dunn	5.00
83	Mike Alstott	2.00
84	Hardy Nickerson	1.00
85	Steve McNair	3.00
86	Chris Sanders	1.00
87	Darryll Lewis	1.00
88	Gus Frerotte	1.00
89	Terry Allen	1.00
90	Chris Dishman	1.00
91	Kordell Stewart	7.00
92	Jerry Rice	8.00
93	Michael Irvin	3.00
94	Brett Favre	15.00
95	Jeff George	3.00
96	Joey Galloway	3.00
97	John Elway	7.00
98	Troy Aikman	8.00
99	Steve Young	5.00
100	Andre Rison	1.50
101	Ben Coates	1.50
102	Robert Brooks	1.50
103	Dan Marino	12.00
104	Isaac Bruce	3.00
105	Junior Seau	3.00
106	Jake Plummer	7.00
107	Curtis Conway	3.00
108	Jeff Blake	3.00
109	Rod Smith	3.00
110	Barry Sanders	15.00
111	Deion Sanders	4.00
112	Drew Bledsoe	7.00
113	Emmitt Smith	12.00
114	Herman Moore	3.00
115	Dorsey Levens	3.00
116	Jimmy Smith	1.50
117	Tony Martin	1.50
118	Carl Pickens	1.50
119	Keyshawn Johnson	1.50
120	Cris Carter	1.50
121	Warrick Dunn	10.00
122	Marshall Faulk	4.00
123	Trent Dilfer	4.00
124	Napoleon Kaufman	5.00
125	Corey Dillon	8.00
126	Darrell Russell	2.00
127	Danny Kanell	2.00
128	Reidel Anthony	2.00
129	Steve McNair	6.00
130	Ike Hilliard	2.00
131	Tony Banks	4.00
132	Yatil Green	2.00
133	J.J. Stokes	2.00
134	Fred Lane	4.00
135	Bryant Westbrook	2.00
136	Jake Plummer	10.00
137	Byron Hanspard	2.00
138	Rae Carruth	2.00
139	Keyshawn Johnson	2.00
140	Jim Druckenmiller	4.00
141	Amani Toomer	2.00
142	Troy Davis	2.00
143	Antowain Smith	6.00
144	Shawn Springs	2.00
145	Rickey Dudley	2.00
146	Terry Glenn	4.00
147	Johnnie Morton	2.00
148	David LaFleur	2.00
149	Eddie Kennison	4.00
150	Bobby Hoying	2.00
151	Junior Seau	5.00
152	Shannon Sharpe	2.50
153	Bruce Smith	2.50
154	Brett Favre	25.00
155	Emmitt Smith	15.00
156	Keenan McCardell	2.50
157	Kordell Stewart	10.00
158	Troy Aikman	12.00
159	Steve Young	8.00
160	Tim Brown	5.00
161	Eddie George	10.00
162	Herman Moore	5.00
163	Dan Marino	15.00
164	Dorsey Levens	5.00
165	Jerry Rice	12.00
166	Warren Sapp	2.50
167	Robert Smith	5.00
168	Mark Brunell	10.00
169	Terrell Davis	12.00
170	Jerome Bettis	5.00
171	Dan Marino	30.00
172	Barry Sanders	40.00
173	Marcus Allen	6.00
174	Brett Favre	40.00
175	Warrick Dunn	20.00
176	Eddie George	20.00
177	John Elway	20.00
178	Troy Aikman	20.00
179	Cris Carter	6.00
180	Terrell Davis	20.00
181	*Peyton Manning*	100.00
182	*Ryan Leaf*	75.00
183	*Andre Wadsworth*	20.00
184	*Charles Woodson*	40.00
185	*Curtis Enis*	35.00
186	*Grant Wistrom*	12.00
187	*Fred Taylor*	60.00
188	*Takeo Spikes*	25.00
189	*Kevin Dyson*	25.00
190	*Robert Edwards*	50.00

1998 SPx Finite Radiance

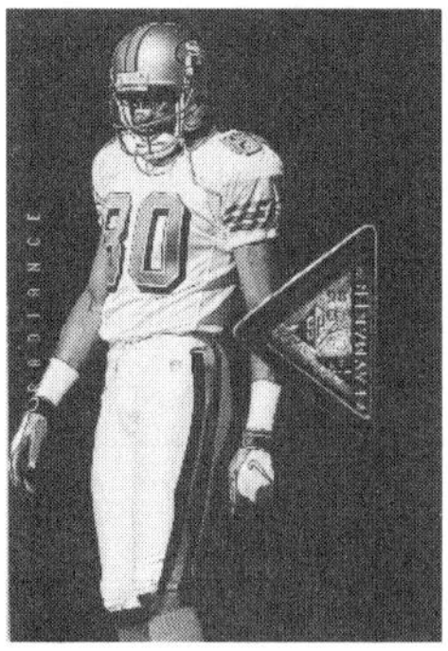

Radiance is a gold-foil parallel of the SPx Finite base set. Regular cards are numbered to 3,800, Playmakers to 2,750, Youth Movement to 1,500, Pure Energy to 1,000 and Heroes of the Game to 100. The ten rookie cards are numbered to 50 in this set.

	MT
Cards (1-90):	2x
Production 3,800 Sets	
Cards (91-120):	2x
Production 2,750 Sets	
Cards (121-150):	2x
Production 1,500 Sets	
Cards (151-170):	2x
Production 1,000 Sets	
Cards (171-180):	5x
Production 100 Sets	
Cards (181-190):	4x
Production 50 Sets	

1998 SPx Finite Spectrum

Spectrum is a rainbow foil version of the SPx Finite base set. Regular cards are numbered to 1,900, Playmakers to 1,375, Youth Movement to 750, Pure Energy to 50 and Heroes of the Game is a 1-of-1 set. The ten rookie cards are also 1-of-1 in this parallel.

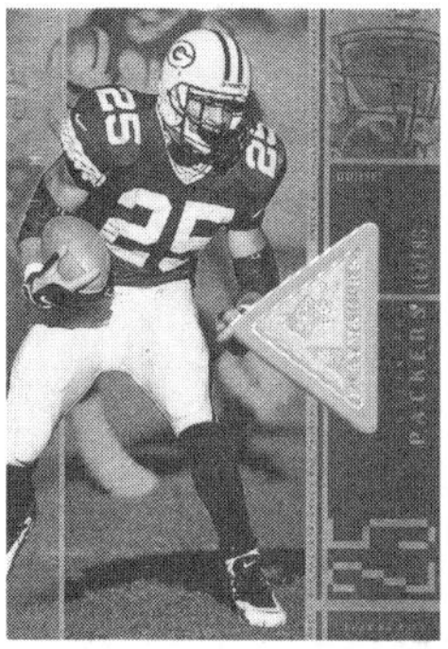

	MT
Cards (1-90):	3x
Production 1,900 Sets	
Cards (91-120):	3x
Production 1,375 Sets	
Cards (121-150):	4x
Production 750 Sets	
Cards (151-170):	15x-20x
Production 50 Sets	

1998 Stadium Club

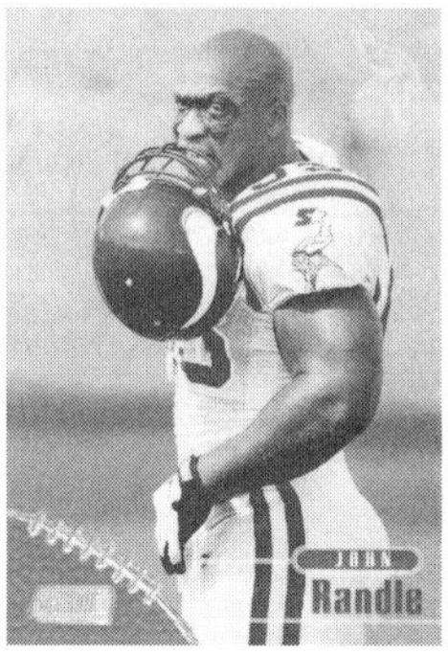

Stadium Club was issued in a single-series, 195-card set in 1998, with a 30-card Star Rookies subset seeded one per two packs (1:1 jumbo pack). Cards featured a borderless design with embossed, holographic foil on 20-point stock. Stadium Club was paralleled in three different sets, with each exclusive to specific packs: First Day Issue (retail), One of a Kind (hobby) and Printing Plates (Home Team Advantage). Inserts include: Chrome, Chrome Refractors, Co-Signers (hobby), Double Threat, Leading Legends (retail), Prime Rookies, Triumvirates (hobby) and SuperChrome Oversized cards.

		MT
Complete Set (195):		110.00
Common Player:		.15
Common Rookie (166-195):		1.50
Inserted 1:2		
Wax Box:		65.00
1	Barry Sanders	3.00
2	Tony Martin	.15
3	Fred Lane	.30
4	Darren Woodson	.15
5	Andre Reed	.30
6	Blaine Bishop	.15
7	Robert Brooks	.30
8	Tony Banks	.30
9	Charles Way	.15
10	Mark Brunell	1.25
11	Darrell Green	.15
12	Aeneas Williams	.15
13	Rob Johnson	.30
14	Deion Sanders	.50
15	Marshall Faulk	.30
16	Stephen Boyd	.15
17	Adrian Murrell	.30
18	Wayne Chrebet	.15
19	Michael Sinclair	.15
20	Dan Marino	2.00
21	Willie Davis	.15
22	Chris Warren	.30
23	John Mobley	.15
24	Shannon Sharpe	.30
25	Thurman Thomas	.30
26	Corey Dillon	1.00
27	Zach Thomas	.30
28	James Jett	.15
29	Eric Metcalf	.15
30	Drew Bledsoe	1.25
31	Scott Greene	.15
32	Simeon Rice	.15
33	Robert Smith	.30
34	Keenan McCardell	.15
35	Jessie Armstead	.15
36	Jerry Rice	1.50
37	Eric Green	.15
38	Terrell Owens	.50
39	Tim Brown	.30
40	Vinny Testaverde	.15
41	Brian Stablein	.15
42	Bert Emanuel	.15
43	Terry Glenn	.30
44	Chad Cota	.15
45	Jermaine Lewis	.15
46	Derrick Thomas	.15
47	O.J. McDuffie	.15
48	Frank Wycheck	.15
49	Steve Broussard	.15
50	Terrell Davis	2.00
52	Napoleon Kaufman	.50
53	Dan Wilkinson	.15
54	Kerry Collins	.30
55	Frank Sanders	.15
56	Jeff Burris	.15
57	Michael Westbrook	.15
58	Michael McCrary	.15
59	Bobby Hoying	.15
60	Jerome Bettis	.30
61	Amp Lee	.15
62	Levon Kirkland	.15
63	Dana Stubblefield	.15
64	Terance Mathis	.15
65	Mark Chmura	.30
66	Bryant Westbrook	.15
67	Rod Smith	.30
68	Derrick Alexander	.15
69	Jason Taylor	.15
70	Eddie George	1.25
71	Elvis Grbac	.15
72	Junior Seau	.30
73	Marvin Harrison	.30
74	Neil O'Donnell	.15
75	Johnnie Morton	.15
76	John Randle	.15
77	Danny Kanell	.15
78	Charlie Garner	.15
79	J.J. Stokes	.30
80	Troy Aikman	1.50
81	Gus Frerotte	.15
82	Jake Plummer	1.25
83	Andre Hastings	.15
84	Steve Atwater	.15
85	Larry Centers	.15
86	Kevin Hardy	.15
87	Willie McGinest	.15
88	Joey Galloway	.30
89	Charles Johnson	.15
90	Warrick Dunn	1.25
91	Derrick Rodgers	.15
92	Aaron Glenn	.15
93	Shawn Jefferson	.15
94	Antonio Freeman	.30
95	Jake Reed	.15
96	Reidel Anthony	.30
97	Cris Dishman	.15
98	Jason Sehorn	.15
99	Herman Moore	.30
100	John Elway	1.50
101	Brad Johnson	.30
102	Jeff George	.30
103	Emmitt Smith	2.00
104	Steve McNair	.75
105	Ed McCaffrey	.15
106	Errict Rhett	.15
107	Dorsey Levens	.30
108	Michael Jackson	.15
109	Carl Pickens	.15
110	James Stewart	.30
111	Karim Abdul-Jabbar	.30
112	Jim Harbaugh	.15
113	Yancey Thigpen	.15
114	Chad Brown	.15
115	Chris Sanders	.15
116	Cris Carter	.30
117	Glenn Foley	.30
118	Ben Coates	.15
119	Jamal Anderson	.30
120	Steve Young	.75
121	Scott Mitchell	.15
122	Rob Moore	.15
123	Bobby Engram	.15
124	Rod Woodson	.15
125	Terry Allen	.15
126	Warren Sapp	.15
127	Irving Fryar	.15
128	Isaac Bruce	.30
129	Rae Carruth	.15
130	Sean Dawkins	.15
131	Andre Rison	.15
132	Kevin Greene	.15
133	Warren Moon	.30
134	Keyshawn Johnson	.30
135	Jay Graham	.15
136	Mike Alstott	.50
137	Peter Boulware	.15
138	Doug Evans	.15
139	Jimmy Smith	.30
140	Kordell Stewart	1.25
141	Tamarick Vanover	.15
142	Chris Slade	.15
143	Freddie Jones	.15
144	Erik Kramer	.15
145	Ricky Watters	.30
146	Chris Chandler	.15
147	Garrison Hearst	.30
148	Trent Dilfer	.30
149	Bruce Smith	.15
150	Brett Favre	3.00
151	Will Blackwell	.15
152	Rickey Dudley	.15
153	Natrone Means	.30
154	Curtis Conway	.30
155	Tony Gonzalez	.15
156	Jeff Blake	.30
157	Michael Irvin	.30
158	Curtis Martin	.75
159	Tim McDonald	.15
160	Wesley Walls	.15
161	Michael Strahan	.15
162	Reggie White	.30
163	Jeff Graham	.15
164	Ray Lewis	.15
165	Antowain Smith	.75
166	*Ryan Leaf*	15.00
167	*Jerome Pathon*	1.50
168	*Duane Starks*	1.50
169	*Brian Simmons*	1.50
170	*Patrick Johnson*	1.50
171	*Keith Brooking*	1.50
172	*Kevin Dyson*	4.00
173	*Robert Edwards*	10.00
174	*Grant Wistrom*	1.50
175	*Curtis Enis*	6.00
176	*John Avery*	4.00
177	*Jason Peter*	1.50
178	*Brian Griese*	6.00
179	*Tavian Banks*	4.00
180	*Andre Wadsworth*	2.50
181	*Skip Hicks*	4.00
182	*Hines Ward*	4.00
183	*Greg Ellis*	2.00
184	*Robert Holcombe*	4.00
185	*Joe Jurevicius*	2.00
186	*Takeo Spikes*	2.00
187	*Ahman Green*	4.00
188	*Jacquez Green*	4.00
189	*Randy Moss*	30.00
190	*Charles Woodson*	7.00
191	*Fred Taylor*	8.00
192	*Marcus Nash*	4.00
193	*Germane Crowell*	4.00
194	*Tim Dwight*	2.50
195	*Peyton Manning*	15.00

1998 Stadium Club First Day Issue

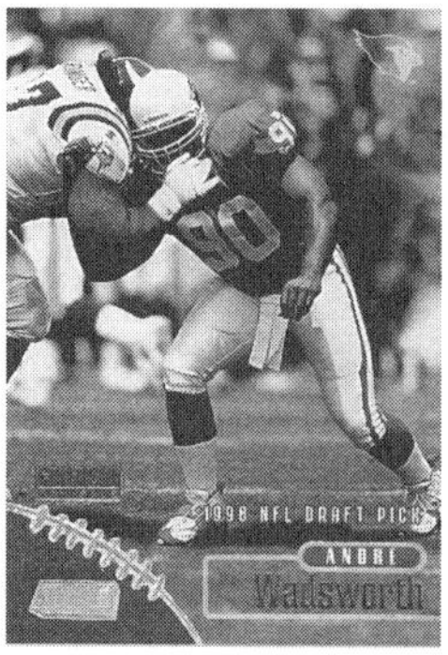

First Day Issue cards parallel the 195-card regular-issue set, but are distinguished by a gold foil "First Day Issue" stamp on the front. These parallels were exclusive to retail packs, are numbered to 200 in gold foil on the back and inserted one per 47 packs.

	MT
First Day Issue Cards:	20x-40x
First Day Issue Rookies:	2x-4x

1998 Stadium Club One of a Kind

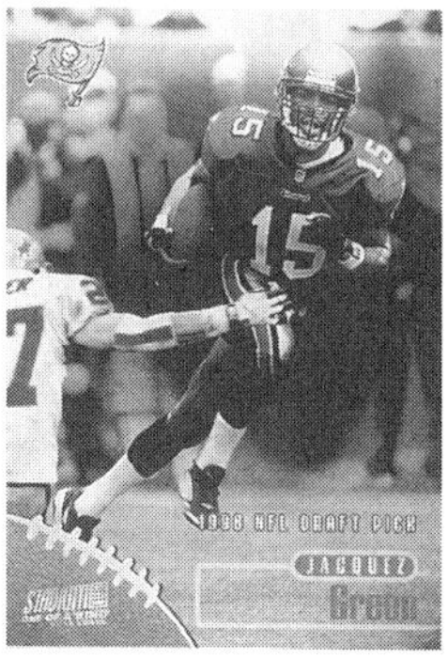

One of a Kind cards paralleled the 195-card base set in Stadium Club, but added a darkened, foil finish the the front, with the insert name below the Stadium Club logo in the lower left corner. These parallel cards were exclusive to hobby packs, numbered on the back to 150 in gold foil and inserted one per 32 packs.

	MT
One of a Kind Cards:	30x-60x
One of a Kind Rookies:	3x-6x

1998 Stadium Club Chrome

This 20-card insert was seeded one per 12 packs of Stadium Club. Cards previewed the upcoming Chrome set, however with a different design. While normal Chrome cards were patterned after Topps cards, these inserts were chromium versions of the Stadium Club base cards. Chrome inserts were numbered with a "SCC" prefix and also had Refractor versions seeded one per 48 packs.

		MT
Complete Set (20):		100.00
Common Player:		2.00
Inserted 1:12		
Refractors:		2x
Inserted 1:48		
1	John Elway	6.00
2	Mark Brunell	6.00
3	Jerome Bettis	4.00
4	Steve Young	5.00
5	Herman Moore	4.00
6	Emmitt Smith	10.00
7	Warrick Dunn	6.00
8	Dan Marino	10.00
9	Kordell Stewart	8.00
10	Barry Sanders	15.00
11	Tim Brown	2.00
12	Dorsey Levens	4.00
13	Eddie George	6.00
14	Jerry Rice	8.00
15	Terrell Davis	8.00
16	Napoleon Kaufman	5.00
17	Troy Aikman	8.00
18	Drew Bledsoe	8.00
19	Antonio Freeman	4.00
20	Brett Favre	15.00

1998 Stadium Club Co-Signers

This 12-card hobby exclusive insert featured eight total players with both autographs on the same side of the card. Each arrived with a gold foil Topps "Certified Autograph Issue" stamp. Cards 1-4 were inserted 1:9,400 hobby and 1:5,640 jumbos, 5-8 were inserted 1:3,133 hobby and 1:1,880 jumbos 9-12 were inserted one per 261 hobby and 1:141 jumbo packs. Co-Signers were numbered with a "CO" prefix.

		MT
Complete Set (12):		3000.00
Common Player:		50.00
CO1	Peyton Manning, Ryan Leaf	500.00
CO2	Dan Marino, Kordell Stewart	500.00
CO3	Eddie George, Corey Dillon	350.00
CO4	Dorsey Levens, Mike Alstott	250.00
CO5	Ryan Leaf, Dan Marino	350.00
CO6	Peyton Manning, Kordell Stewart	300.00
CO7	Eddie George, Mike Alstott	200.00
CO8	Dorsey Levens, Corey Dillon	130.00
CO9	Peyton Manning, Dan Marino	225.00
CO10	Ryan Leaf, Kordell Stewart	130.00
CO11	Eddie George, Dorsey Levens	75.00
CO12	Mike Alstott, Corey Dillon	50.00

1998 Stadium Club Double Threat

This 10-card insert features two top tandems from 10 different NFL teams. Each player takes up half the card and contains the insert name printed repeatedly across the background along with the team logo. Double Threat inserts are seeded one per eight packs and are numbered with a "DT" prefix.

		MT
Complete Set (10):		50.00
Common Player:		1.50
Inserted 1:8		
1	Marshall Faulk, Peyton Manning	15.00
2	Curtis Conway, Curtis Enis	6.00
3	Drew Bledsoe, Robert Edwards	8.00
4	Warrick Dunn, Jacquez Green	6.00
5	John Elway, Marcus Nash	7.00
6	Mark Brunell, Fred Taylor	8.00
7	Eddie George, Kevin Dyson	6.00
8	Michael Jackson, Patrick Johnson	1.50
9	Terry Glenn, Tony Simmons	1.50
10	Natrone Means, Ryan Leaf	15.00

1998 Stadium Club Leading Legends

Leading Legends was a retail-exclusive insert that displayed the NFL's current record-holders among quarterbacks, wide receivers and running backs. The cards are printed on plastic with a gold foil background and card back. These were inserted one per 12 packs and unnumbered.

		MT
Complete Set (10):		40.00
Common Player:		2.00
Inserted 1:12 Retail		
1	Jerry Rice	5.00
2	Bruce Smith	2.00
3	Reggie White	3.00
4	Warren Moon	2.00
5	Dan Marino	7.00
6	John Elway	5.00
7	Emmitt Smith	7.00
8	Brett Favre	10.00
9	Steve Young	4.00
10	Barry Sanders	10.00

1998 Stadium Club Prime Rookies

This 10-card insert displayed the top draft picks in 1998 on a silver foil finish, with the insert name running up the right side. Prime Rookies were inserted one per eight packs and numbered with a "PR" prefix.

		MT
Complete Set (10):		50.00
Common Player:		1.50
Inserted 1:8		
1	Ryan Leaf	15.00
2	Andre Wadsworth	3.00
3	Fred Taylor	8.00
4	Kevin Dyson	4.00
5	Charles Woodson	6.00
6	Robert Edwards	8.00
7	Grant Wistrom	1.50
8	Curtis Enis	6.00
9	Randy Moss	20.00
10	Peyton Manning	15.00

1998 Stadium Club Super Chrome

SuperChrome featured 3-1/4" x 4-9/16" versions of the 20-card Chrome set. These were inserted one per hobby box, with Refractor versions every 12 Home Team Advantage/ Hobby Collector Pack boxes.

		MT
Complete Set (20):		100.00
Common Player:		2.00
Refractors:		2x
1	John Elway	6.00
2	Mark Brunell	6.00
3	Jerome Bettis	4.00
4	Steve Young	5.00
5	Herman Moore	4.00
6	Emmitt Smith	10.00
7	Warrick Dunn	6.00
8	Dan Marino	10.00
9	Kordell Stewart	8.00
10	Barry Sanders	15.00
11	Tim Brown	2.00
12	Dorsey Levens	4.00
13	Eddie George	6.00
14	Jerry Rice	8.00
15	Terrell Davis	8.00
16	Napoleon Kaufman	5.00
17	Troy Aikman	8.00
18	Drew Bledsoe	8.00
19	Antonio Freeman	4.00
20	Brett Favre	15.00

1998 Stadium Club Triumvirate Luminous

Triumvirate was a 15-card, hobby-only insert in 1998. It featured three teammates on die-cut, fit-together cards numbered with a "T" prefix and either an A, B or C suffix. Regular, Luminous versions were seeded one per 24 packs, Luminescent versions were one per 96 and Illuminators were one per 192 packs.

		MT
Complete Set (15):		100.00
Common Player:		3.00
Inserted 1:24 Hobby		
Luminescent Cards:		2x
Inserted 1:96 Hobby		
Illuminator Cards:		5x
Inserted 1:192 Hobby		
T1A	Terrell Davis	10.00
T1B	John Elway	10.00
T1C	Shannon Sharpe	3.00
T2A	Barry Sanders	20.00
T2B	Scott Mitchell	3.00
T2C	Herman Moore	6.00
T3A	Dorsey Levens	6.00
T3B	Brett Favre	20.00
T3C	Antonio Freeman	6.00
T4A	Emmitt Smith	15.00
T4B	Troy Aikman	10.00
T4C	Michael Irvin	6.00
T5A	Napoleon Kaufman	6.00
T5B	Jeff George	3.00
T5C	Tim Brown	3.00

1998 Topps

Topps was issued in a single-series 360-card set in 1998. It contained a 30-card 1998 NFL Draft Picks subset that was seeded one per three packs. Cards utilize a gold border around the color shot of the player, with the Topps logo in the upper right, team logo in the lower left and the player's name and team printed up the right side. Backs are horizontal and add another shot of the player, along with statistics and bio information. Inserts in Topps include: Season's Best, Measures of Greatness, Myster Finest, Gridiron Gods (hobby), Hidden Gems (retail), Autographs (hobby) and Generation 2000.

		MT
Complete Set (360):		75.00
Common Player:		.10
Wax Box:		50.00
1	Barry Sanders	2.00
2	Derrick Rodgers	.10
3	Chris Calloway	.10
4	Bruce Armstrong	.10
5	Horace Copeland	.10
6	Chad Brown	.10
7	Ken Harvey	.10
8	Levon Kirkland	.10
9	Glenn Foley	.10
10	Corey Dillon	.50
11	Sean Dawkins	.10
12	Curtis Conway	.20
13	Chris Chandler	.10
14	Kerry Collins	.20
15	Jonathan Ogden	.10
16	Sam Shade	.10
17	Vaughn Hebron	.10
18	Quentin Coryatt	.10
19	Jerris McPhail	.10
20	Warrick Dunn	1.00
21	Wayne Martin	.10
22	Chad Lewis	.10
23	Danny Kanell	.10
24	Shawn Springs	.10
25	Emmitt Smith	1.75
26	Todd Lyght	.10
27	Donnie Edwards	.10
28	Charlie Jones	.10
29	Willie McGinest	.10
30	Steve Young	.75
31	Darrell Russell	.10
32	Gary Anderson	.10
33	Stanley Richard	.10
34	Leslie O'Neal	.10
35	Dermontti Dawson	.10
36	Jeff Brady	.10
37	Kimble Anders	.10
38	Glyn Milburn	.10
39	Greg Hill	.10
40	Freddie Jones	.10
41	Bobby Engram	.10
42	Aeneas Williams	.10
43	Antowain Smith	.75
44	Reggie White	.20
45	Rae Carruth	.10
46	Leon Johnson	.10
47	Bryant Young	.10
48	Jamie Asher	.10
49	Hardy Nickerson	.10
50	Jerome Bettis	.20
51	Michael Strahan	.10
52	John Randle	.10
53	Kevin Hardy	.10
54	Eric Bjornson	.10
55	Morten Andersen	.10
56	Larry Centers	.10
57	Bryce Paup	.10
58	John Mobley	.10
59	Michael Bates	.10
60	Tim Brown	.20
61	Doug Evans	.10
62	Will Shields	.10
63	Jeff Graham	.10
64	Henry Jones	.10
65	Steve Broussard	.10
66	Blaine Bishop	.10
67	Ernie Conwell	.10
68	Heath Shuler	.10
69	Eric Metcalf	.10
70	Terry Glenn	.20
71	James Hasty	.10
72	Robert Porcher	.10
73	Keenan McCardell	.10
74	Tyrone Hughes	.10
75	Troy Aikman	1.00
76	Peter Boulware	.10
77	Rob Johnson	.20
78	Erik Kramer	.10
79	Kevin Smith	.10
80	Andre Rison	.10
81	Jim Harbaugh	.20
82	Chris Hudson	.10
83	Ray Zellars	.10
84	Jeff George	.20
85	Willie Davis	.10
86	Jason Gildon	.10
87	Robert Brooks	.10
88	Chad Cota	.10
89	Simeon Rice	.10
90	Mark Brunell	.75
91	Jay Graham	.10
92	Scott Greene	.10
93	Jeff Blake	.20
94	Jason Belser	.10
95	Derrick Alexander	.10
96	Ty Law	.10
97	Charles Johnson	.10
98	James Jett	.10
99	Darrell Green	.10
100	Brett Favre	2.00
101	George Jones	.10
102	Derrick Mason	.10
103	Sam Adams	.10
104	Lawrence Phillips	.10
105	Randal Hill	.10
106	John Mangum	.10
107	Natrone Means	.20
108	Bill Romanowski	.10
109	Terance Mathis	.10
110	Bruce Smith	.10
111	Pete Mitchell	.10
112	Duane Clemons	.10
113	Willie Clay	.10
114	Eric Allen	.10

115	Troy Drayton	.10
116	Derrick Thomas	.10
117	Charles Way	.10
118	Wayne Chrebet	.10
119	Bobby Hoying	.10
120	Michael Jackson	.10
121	Gary Zimmerman	.10
122	Yancey Thigpen	.10
123	Dana Stubblefield	.10
124	Keith Lyle	.10
125	Marco Coleman	.10
126	Karl Williams	.10
127	Stephen Davis	.10
128	Chris Sanders	.10
129	Cris Dishman	.10
130	Jake Plummer	1.00
131	Darryl Williams	.10
132	Merton Hanks	.10
133	Torrance Small	.10
134	Aaron Glenn	.10
135	Chester McGlockton	.10
136	William Thomas	.10
137	Kordell Stewart	1.00
138	Jason Taylor	.10
139	Lake Dawson	.10
140	Carl Pickens	.10
141	Eugene Robinson	.10
142	Ed McCaffrey	.10
143	Lamar Lathon	.10
144	Ray Buchanan	.10
145	Thurman Thomas	.20
146	Andre Reed	.10
147	Wesley Walls	.10
148	Rob Moore	.10
149	Darren Woodson	.10
150	Eddie George	1.00
151	Michael Irvin	.20
152	Johnnie Morton	.10
153	Ken Dilger	.10
154	Tony Boselli	.10
155	Randall McDaniel	.10
156	Mark Fields	.10
157	Phillippi Sparks	.10
158	William Roaf	.10
159	Troy Vincent	.10
160	Cris Carter	.10
161	Amp Lee	.10
162	Will Blackwell	.10
163	Chad Scott	.10
164	Henry Ellard	.10
165	Robert Jones	.10
166	Garrison Hearst	.10
167	James McKnight	.10
168	Rodney Harrison	.10
169	Adrian Murrell	.20
170	Rod Smith	.10
171	Desmond Howard	.10
172	Ben Coates	.10
173	David Palmer	.10
174	Zach Thomas	.10
175	Dale Carter	.10
176	Mark Chmura	.10
177	Elvis Grbac	.10
178	Jason Hanson	.10
179	Walt Harris	.10
180	Ricky Watters	.20
181	Ray Lewis	.10
182	Lonnie Johnson	.10
183	Marvin Harrison	.20
184	Dorsey Levens	.20
185	Tony Gonzalez	.10
186	Andre Hastings	.10
187	Kevin Turner	.10
188	Mo Lewis	.10
189	Jason Sehorn	.10
190	Drew Bledsoe	1.00
191	Michael Sinclair	.10
192	William Floyd	.10
193	Kenny Holmes	.10
194	Marvcus Patton	.10
195	Warren Sapp	.10
196	Junior Seau	.20
197	Ryan McNeil	.10
198	Tyrone Wheatley	.10
199	Robert Smith	.10
200	Terrell Davis	1.50
201	Brett Perriman	.10
202	Tamarick Vanover	.10
203	Stephen Boyd	.10
204	Zack Crockett	.10
205	Sherman Williams	.10
206	Neil Smith	.10
207	Jermaine Lewis	.10
208	Kevin Williams	.10
209	Byron Hanspard	.20
210	Warren Moon	.20
211	Tony McGee	.10
212	Raymont Harris	.10
213	Eric Davis	.10
214	Darrien Gordon	.10
215	James Stewart	.10
216	Derrick Mayes	.10
217	Brad Johnson	.10
218	Karim Abdul-Jabbar	.20
219	Hugh Douglas	.10
220	Terry Allen	.10
221	Rhett Hall	.10
222	Terrell Fletcher	.10
223	Carnell Lake	.10
224	Darryll Lewis	.10
225	Chris Slade	.10
226	Michael Westbrook	.10
227	Willie Williams	.10
228	Tony Banks	.20
229	Keyshawn Johnson	.20
230	Mike Alstott	.20
231	Tiki Barber	.20
232	Jake Reed	.10
233	Eric Swann	.10
234	Eric Moulds	.10
235	Vinny Testaverde	.10
236	Jessie Tuggle	.10
237	Ryan Wetnight	.10
238	Tyrone Poole	.10
239	Bryant Westbrook	.10
240	Steve McNair	.75
241	Jimmy Smith	.10
242	DeWayne Washington	.10
243	Robert Harris	.10
244	Rod Woodson	.10
245	Reidel Anthony	.20
246	Jessie Armstead	.10
247	O.J. McDuffie	.10
248	Carlton Gray	.10
249	LeRoy Butler	.10
250	Jerry Rice	1.00
251	Frank Sanders	.10
252	Todd Collins	.10
253	Fred Lane	.10
254	David Dunn	.10
255	Micheal Barrow	.10
256	Luther Ellis	.10
257	Scott Mitchell	.10
258	David Meggett	.10
259	Rickey Dudley	.10
260	Isaac Bruce	.20
261	Tony Martin	.10
262	Leslie Shepherd	.10
263	Derrick Thomas	.10
264	Greg Lloyd	.10
265	Terrell Buckley	.10
266	Antonio Freeman	.20
267	Tony Brackens	.10
268	Mark McMillian	.10
269	Dexter Coakley	.10
270	Dan Marino	1.75
271	Bryan Cox	.10
272	Leeland McElroy	.10
273	Jeff Burris	.10
274	Eric Green	.10
275	Darnay Scott	.10
276	Greg Clark	.10
277	Mario Bates	.10
278	Eric Turner	.10
279	Neil O'Donnell	.10
280	Herman Moore	.20
281	Gary Brown	.10
282	Terrell Owens	.20
283	Frank Wycheck	.10
284	Trent Dilfer	.20
285	Curtis Martin	.75
286	Ricky Proehl	.10
287	Steve Atwater	.10
288	Aaron Bailey	.10
289	William Henderson	.10
290	Marcus Allen	.20
291	Tom Knight	.10
292	Quinn Early	.10
293	Michael McCrary	.10
294	Bert Emanuel	.10
295	Tom Carter	.10
296	Kevin Glover	.10
297	Marshall Faulk	.20
298	Harvey Williams	.10
299	Chris Warren	.10
300	John Elway	.75
301	Eddie Kennison	.20
302	Gus Frerotte	.10
303	Regan Upshaw	.10
304	Kevin Gogan	.10
305	Napoleon Kaufman	.30
306	Charlie Garner	.10
307	Shawn Jefferson	.10
308	Tommy Vardell	.10
309	Mike Hollis	.10
310	Irving Fryar	.10
311	Shannon Sharpe	.10
312	Byron Morris	.10
313	Jamal Anderson	.10
314	Chris Gedney	.10
315	Chris Spielman	.10
316	Derrick Alexander	.10
317	O.J. Santiago	.10
318	Anthony Miller	.10
319	Ki-Jana Carter	.10
320	Deion Sanders	.40
321	Joey Galloway	.20
322	J.J. Stokes	.10
323	Rodney Thomas	.10
324	John Lynch	.10
325	Mike Pritchard	.10
326	Terrance Shaw	.10
327	Ted Johnson	.10
328	Ashley Ambrose	.10
329	Checklist	.10
330	Checklist	.10
331	*Jerome Pathon*	2.00
332	*Ryan Leaf*	10.00
333	*Duane Starks*	1.50
334	*Brian Simmons*	1.00
335	*Keith Brooking*	2.00
336	*Robert Edwards*	8.00
337	*Curtis Enis*	6.00
338	*John Avery*	3.00
339	*Fred Taylor*	8.00
340	*Germane Crowell*	2.00
341	*Hines Ward*	3.00
342	*Marcus Nash*	3.00
343	*Jacquez Green*	4.00
344	*Joe Jurevicius*	2.00
345	*Greg Ellis*	1.00
346	*Brian Griese*	4.00
347	*Tavian Banks*	4.00
348	*Robert Holcombe*	4.00
349	*Skip Hicks*	3.00
350	Ahman Green	4.00
351	*Takeo Spikes*	2.00
352	*Randy Moss*	20.00
353	*Andre Wadsworth*	1.50
354	*Jason Peter*	2.00
355	*Grant Wistrom*	2.00
356	*Charles Woodson*	5.00
357	*Kevin Dyson*	3.00
358	*Patrick Johnson*	2.00
359	*Tim Dwight*	2.00
360	*Peyton Manning*	15.00

1998 Topps Season Opener

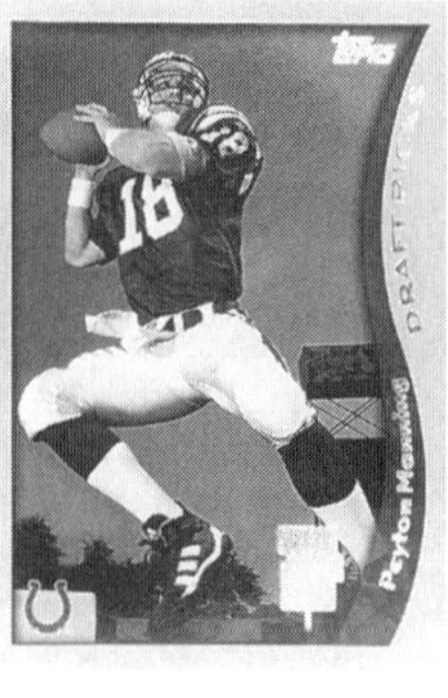

Topps Season Opener was a retail exclusive product comprised of 165 cards that paralleled Topps. While Topps cards were printed with a gold border, Season Opener cards used a silver border and a silver "Season Opener '98" stamp on a goal post to distinguish them. Packs contained seven cards and one Season Opener Sweepstakes card, with which collectors could win a trip to the Pro Bowl in Honolulu, Hawaii.

		MT
Complete Set (165):		50.00
Common Player:		.10
Wax Box:		25.00
1	*Peyton Manning*	8.00
2	*Jerome Pathon*	.10
3	*Duane Starks*	.10
4	*Brian Simmons*	.10
5	*Keith Brooking*	.10
6	*Robert Edwards*	5.00
7	*Curtis Enis*	3.00
8	*John Avery*	1.50
9	*Fred Taylor*	5.00
10	*Germane Crowell*	2.00
11	*Hines Ward*	1.50
12	*Marcus Nash*	2.00
13	*Jacquez Green*	3.00
14	*Joe Jurevicius*	.50
15	*Greg Ellis*	.50
16	*Brian Griese*	3.00
17	*Tavian Banks*	2.00
18	*Robert Holcombe*	2.50
19	*Skip Hicks*	2.00
20	*Ahman Green*	2.50
21	*Takeo Spikes*	.20
22	*Randy Moss*	20.00
23	*Andre Wadsworth*	.50
24	*Jason Peter*	.20
25	*Grant Wistrom*	.10
26	*Charles Woodson*	3.00
27	*Kevin Dyson*	2.00
28	*Patrick Johnson*	.10
29	*Tim Dwight*	2.00
30	*Ryan Leaf*	8.00
31	Chad Brown	.10
32	Levon Kirkland	.10
33	Corey Dillon	.50
34	Curtis Conway	.20
35	Chris Chandler	.10
36	Warrick Dunn	1.00
37	Danny Kanell	.10
38	Emmitt Smith	2.00
39	Steve Young	.75
40	Kimble Anders	.10
41	Freddie Jones	.10
42	Bobby Engram	.10
43	Aeneas Williams	.10
44	Antowain Smith	.75
45	Reggie White	.20
46	Rae Carruth	.10
47	Jamie Asher	.10
48	Hardy Nickerson	.10
49	Jerome Bettis	.20
50	Michael Strahan	.10
51	John Randle	.10
52	Larry Centers	.10
53	Tim Brown	.20
54	Terry Glenn	.20
55	Keenan McCardell	.10
56	Troy Aikman	1.00
57	Peter Boulware	.10
58	Erik Kramer	.10
59	Andre Rison	.10
60	Jeff George	.20
61	Robert Brooks	.10
62	Simeon Rice	.10
63	Mark Brunell	1.00
64	Jeff Blake	.20
65	Brett Favre	2.00
66	Lawrence Phillips	.10
67	Randal Hill	.10
68	Terance Mathis	.10
69	Bruce Smith	.10
70	Troy Drayton	.10
71	Derrick Thomas	.10
72	Charles Way	.10
73	Bobby Hoying	.10
74	Michael Jackson	.10
75	Chris Sanders	.10
76	Cris Dishman	.10
77	Jake Plummer	1.00
78	Kordell Stewart	1.00
79	Carl Pickens	.10
80	Ed McCaffrey	.10
81	Ray Buchanan	.10
82	Thurman Thomas	.10
83	Andre Reed	.10
84	Wesley Walls	.10
85	Rob Moore	.10
86	Eddie George	1.00
87	Michael Irvin	.20
88	Johnnie Morton	.10
89	Cris Carter	.20
90	Garrison Hearst	.20
91	Rod Smith	.20
92	Ben Coates	.10
93	Zach Thomas	.20
94	Dale Carter	.10
95	Mark Chmura	.20
96	Elvis Grbac	.10
97	Ray Lewis	.10
98	Lonnie Johnson	.10
99	Darrell Green	.10
100	Marvin Harrison	.20
101	Dorsey Levens	.20
102	Tony Gonzalez	.10
103	Andre Hastings	.10
104	Jason Sehorn	.10
105	Drew Bledsoe	1.00
106	Junior Seau	.20
107	Robert Smith	.20
108	Terrell Davis	1.50
109	Neil Smith	.10
110	Jermaine Lewis	.10
111	Warren Moon	.20
112	Brad Johnson	.20
113	Karim Abdul-Jabbar	.20
114	Terry Allen	.10
115	Chris Slade	.10
116	Michael Westbrook	.10
117	Tony Banks	.20
118	Mike Alstott	.20
119	Jake Reed	.10
120	Bryant Westbrook	.10
121	Steve McNair	.75
122	Jimmy Smith	.20
123	Reidel Anthony	.10
124	Jessie Armstead	.10
125	O.J. McDuffie	.10
126	Jerry Rice	1.00
127	Frank Sanders	.10
128	Fred Lane	.20
129	Scott Mitchell	.10
130	Rickey Dudley	.10
131	Isaac Bruce	.20
132	Tony Martin	.10
133	Leslie Shepherd	.10
134	Derrick Thomas	.10
135	Antonio Freeman	.20
136	Dan Marino	2.00
137	Eric Green	.10
138	Darnay Scott	.10
139	Herman Moore	.20
140	Terrell Owens	.20
141	Trent Dilfer	.20
142	Marshall Faulk	.20
143	John Elway	1.00
144	Gus Frerotte	.10
145	Napoleon Kaufman	.40
146	Charlie Garner	.10
147	Irving Fryar	.10
148	Shannon Sharpe	.10
149	Jamal Anderson	.10
150	Chris Spielman	.10
151	Deion Sanders	.40
152	Joey Galloway	.20
153	J.J. Stokes	.10
154	Quinn Early	.10
155	Michael McCrary	.10
156	Willie McGinest	.10
157	Kevin Hardy	.10
158	Michael Barrow	.10
159	John Mobley	.10
160	Michael Sinclair	.10
161	Warren Sapp	.10
162	Michael Bates	.10
163	Pete Mitchell	.10
164	Barry Sanders	2.00
165	Checklist	.10

1998 Topps Autographs

This hobby-only insert featured autographs from 15 top players, with eight veterans, two rookies and the five 1997 NFL Hall of Fame inductees. Each card has a gold foil "Topps Certified Autograph Issue" stamp and was inserted one per 260 hobby packs.

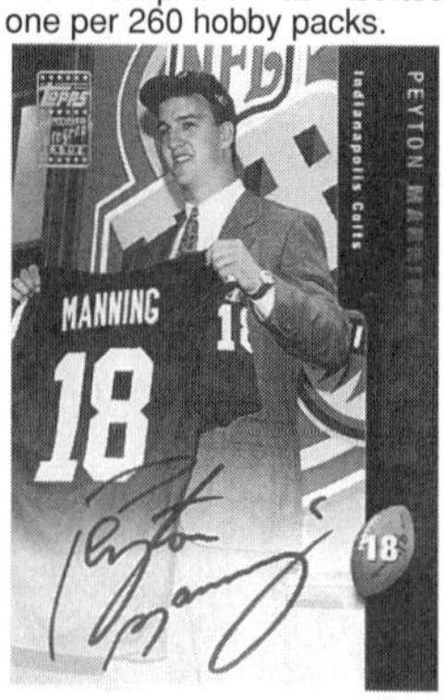

		MT
Complete Set (15):		650.00
Common Player:		30.00
A1	Randy Moss	250.00
A2	Mike Alstott	40.00
A3	Jake Plummer	70.00
A4	Corey Dillon	50.00
A5	Kordell Stewart	70.00
A6	Eddie George	60.00
A7	Jason Sehorn	30.00
A8	Joey Galloway	30.00
A9	Ryan Leaf	100.00
A10	Peyton Manning	120.00
A11	Dwight Stephenson	30.00
A12	Anthony Munoz	30.00
A13	Mike Singletary	30.00
A14	Tommy McDonald	30.00
A15	Paul Krause	30.00

1998 Topps Generation 2000

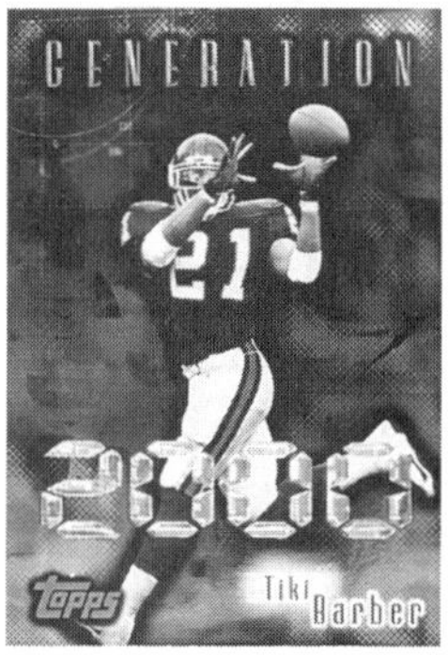

Generation 2000 showcases 15 of football's top young players who should lead the game into the year 2000. The inserts have the word "Generation" across the top and "2000" printed in silver, embossed foil across the bottom. These were numbered with a "GE" prefix and inserted one per 18 packs.

		MT
Complete Set (15):		60.00
Common Player:		2.00
GE1	Warrick Dunn	10.00
GE2	Tony Gonzalez	2.00
GE3	Corey Dillon	8.00
GE4	Antowain Smith	6.00
GE5	Mike Alstott	4.00
GE6	Kordell Stewart	8.00
GE7	Peter Boulware	2.00
GE8	Jake Plummer	10.00
GE9	Tiki Barber	4.00
GE10	Terrell Davis	12.00
GE11	Steve McNair	6.00
GE12	Curtis Martin	8.00
GE13	Napoleon Kaufman	6.00
GE14	Terrell Owens	2.00
GE15	Eddie George	8.00

1998 Topps Gridiron Gods

This hobby exclusive insert captures 15 players on uniluster technology, which is a silver etched, holofoil looking background. Cards are numbered with a "G" prefix and inserted one per 36 packs.

		MT
Complete Set (15):		100.00
Common Player:		2.00
G1	Barry Sanders	15.00
G2	Jerry Rice	10.00
G3	Herman Moore	4.00
G4	Drew Bledsoe	10.00
G5	Kordell Stewart	10.00
G6	Tim Brown	2.00
G7	Eddie George	8.00
G8	Dorsey Levens	4.00
G9	Warrick Dunn	8.00
G10	Brett Favre	15.00
G11	Terrell Davis	12.00
G12	Steve Young	7.00
G13	Jerome Bettis	4.00
G14	Mark Brunell	8.00
G15	John Elway	8.00

1998 Topps Hidden Gems

Hidden Gems were exclusive to retail packs and inserted one per 15. This 15-card set is printed on a plastic-like surface and numbered with a "HG" prefix.

		MT
Complete Set (15):		25.00
Common Player:		.50
HG1	Andre Reed	.50
HG2	Kevin Greene	.50
HG3	Tony Martin	.50
HG4	Shannon Sharpe	1.00
HG5	Terry Allen	1.00
HG6	Brett Favre	8.00
HG7	Ben Coates	1.00
HG8	Michael Sinclair	.50
HG9	Keenan McCardell	1.00
HG10	Brad Johnson	1.00
HG11	Mark Brunell	4.00
HG12	Dorsey Levens	1.00
HG13	Terrell Davis	8.00
HG14	Curtis Martin	2.00
HG15	Derrick Rodgers	.50

1998 Topps Measures Of Greatness

Fifteen different players that are bound for the Hall of Fame are featured in this insert printed on micro dyna-etch technology. The silver foil fronts that feature markings of a football field includes the in-

sert name up the left side, with the player's name in a banner below it. Cards are numbered with a "MG" prefix and inserted one per 36 packs.

		MT
Complete Set (15):		70.00
Common Player:		2.00
MG1	John Elway	8.00
MG2	Marcus Allen	4.00
MG3	Jerry Rice	10.00
MG4	Tim Brown	2.00
MG5	Warren Moon	2.00
MG6	Bruce Smith	2.00
MG7	Troy Aikman	10.00
MG8	Reggie White	4.00
MG9	Irving Fryar	2.00
MG10	Barry Sanders	15.00
MG11	Cris Carter	2.00
MG12	Emmitt Smith	12.00
MG13	Dan Marino	12.00
MG14	Rod Woodson	2.00
MG15	Brett Favre	15.00

1998 Topps Mystery Finest

This 20-card insert arrives with black opaque protectors over the front and four different players on the back. Collectors needed to peel the fronts in order to determine which of the four players it was. Mystery Finest cards are numbered with a "M" prefix and inserted one per 36 packs. Refractor versions were also available and seeded one per 144 packs.

		MT
Complete Set (20):		125.00
Common Player:		2.00
Refractors:		3x
M1	Steve Young	7.00
M2	Dan Marino	17.00
M3	Brett Favre	20.00
M4	Drew Bledsoe	10.00
M5	Mark Brunell	8.00
M6	Troy Aikman	10.00
M7	Kordell Stewart	10.00
M8	John Elway	10.00
M9	Barry Sanders	20.00
M10	Jerome Bettis	4.00
M11	Eddie George	10.00
M12	Emmitt Smith	17.00
M13	Curtis Martin	5.00
M14	Warrick Dunn	10.00
M15	Dorsey Levens	4.00
M16	Terrell Davis	12.00
M17	Herman Moore	4.00
M18	Jerry Rice	10.00
M19	Tim Brown	2.00
M20	Yancey Thigpen	2.00

1998 Topps Season's Best

Season's Best includes 30 of the NFL's statistical leaders in six differerent categories on prismatic foilboard. Power & Speed are rushing leaders, Gunslingers are quarterbacks, Prime Targets are receiving leaders, Heavy Hitters are sack leaders, Quick Six are all-purpose yardage and Career Best are all-time leaders. These are numbered with a "SB" prefix and inserted one per 12 packs.

		MT
Complete Set (30):		90.00
Common Player:		1.00
1	Terrell Davis	8.00
2	Barry Sanders	10.00
3	Jerome Bettis	2.00
4	Dorsey Levens	2.00
5	Eddie George	5.00
6	Brett Favre	10.00
7	Mark Brunell	6.00
8	Jeff George	1.00
9	Steve Young	4.00
10	John Elway	6.00
11	Herman Moore	2.00
12	Rob Moore	1.00
13	Yancey Thigpen	1.00
14	Cris Carter	1.00
15	Tim Brown	1.00
16	Bruce Smith	1.00
17	Michael Sinclair	1.00
18	John Randle	1.00
19	Dana Stubblefield	1.00
20	Michael Strahan	1.00
21	Tamarick Vanover	1.00
22	Darrien Gordon	1.00
23	Michael Bates	1.00
24	David Meggett	1.00
25	Jermaine Lewis	1.00
26	Terrell Davis	8.00
27	Jerry Rice	8.00
28	Barry Sanders	10.00
29	John Randle	1.00
30	John Elway	6.00

1998 Topps Chrome

Topps Chrome includes 165 cards from Topps reprinted with a chromium finish. The Topps logo is replaced on both the front and the back by a Topps Chrome logo. Cards are renumbered and reordered within the checklist for the mostpart. Each card was also available in a Refractor versions, while the three inserts - Hidden Gems, Measures of Greatness and

Season's Best - are also reprinted from Topps and available in both regular and Refractor versions.

		MT
Complete Set (165):		300.00
Common Player:		.40
Common Rookie:		3.00
Refractor Cards:		6x-12x
Refractor Rookies:		2x-4x
Wax Box:		170.00
1	Barry Sanders	6.00
2	Duane Starks	.40
3	J.J. Stokes	.40
4	Joey Galloway	.75
5	Deion Sanders	1.50
6	Anthony Miller	.40
7	Jamal Anderson	.75
8	Shannon Sharpe	.40
9	Irving Fryar	.40
10	Curtis Martin	1.50
11	Shawn Jefferson	.40
12	Charlie Garner	.75
13	*Robert Edwards*	20.00
14	Napoleon Kaufman	1.50
15	Gus Frerotte	.40
16	John Elway	3.00
17	Jerome Pathon	.40
18	Marshall Faulk	.75
19	Michael McCrary	.40
20	Marcus Allen	.75
21	Trent Dilfer	.75
22	Frank Wycheck	.40
23	Terrell Owens	.75
24	Herman Moore	.40
25	Neil O'Donnell	.40
26	Darnay Scott	.40
27	Keith Brooking	.40
28	Eric Green	.40
29	Dan Marino	5.00
30	Antonio Freeman	.75
31	Tony Martin	.40
32	Isaac Bruce	.75
33	Rickey Dudley	.40
34	Scott Mitchell	.40
35	*Randy Moss*	100.00
36	Fred Lane	.75
37	Frank Sanders	.40
38	Jerry Rice	3.00
39	O.J. McDuffie	.40
40	Jessie Armstead	.40
41	Reidel Anthony	.40
42	Steve McNair	2.00
43	Jake Reed	.40
44	*Charles Woodson*	20.00
45	Tiki Barber	.40
46	Mike Alstott	.75
47	Keyshawn Johnson	.75
48	Tony Banks	.75
49	Michael Westbrook	.40
50	Chris Slade	.40
51	Terry Allen	.40
52	Karim Abdul-Jabbar	.75
53	Brad Johnson	.75
54	Tony McGee	.40
55	*Kevin Dyson*	10.00
56	Warren Moon	.75
57	Byron Hanspard	.40
58	Jermaine Lewis	.40
59	Neil Smith	.40
60	Tamarick Vanover	.40
61	Terrell Davis	3.00
62	Robert Smith	.75
63	Junior Seau	.40
64	Warren Sapp	.40
65	Michael Sinclair	.40
66	*Ryan Leaf*	30.00
67	Drew Bledsoe	3.00
68	Jason Sehorn	.40
69	Andre Hastings	.40
70	Tony Gonzalez	.75
71	Dorsey Levens	.75
72	Ray Lewis	.40
73	Grant Wistrom	.40
74	Elvis Grbac	.40
75	Mark Chmura	.75
76	Zach Thomas	.40
77	Ben Coates	.40
78	Rod Smith	.40
79	*Andre Wadsworth*	6.00
80	Garrison Hearst	.40
81	Will Blackwell	.40
82	Cris Carter	.40
83	Mark Fields	.40
84	Ken Dilger	.40
85	Johnnie Morton	.40
86	Michael Irvin	.75
87	Eddie George	3.00
88	Rob Moore	.40
89	Takeo Spikes	.40
90	Wesley Walls	.40
91	Andre Reed	.40
92	Thurman Thomas	.75
93	Ed McCaffrey	.40
94	Carl Pickens	.40
95	Jason Taylor	.40
96	Kordell Stewart	3.00
97	*Greg Ellis*	1.00
98	Aaron Glenn	.40
99	Jake Plummer	3.00
100	Checklist	.40
101	Chris Sanders	.40
102	Michael Jackson	.40
103	Bobby Hoying	.40
104	Wayne Chrebet	.40
105	Charles Way	.40
106	Derrick Thomas	.40
107	Troy Drayton	.40
108	*Robert Holcombe*	8.00
109	Pete Mitchell	.40
110	Bruce Smith	.40
111	Terance Mathis	.40
112	Lawrence Phillips	.40
113	Brett Favre	6.00
114	Darrell Green	.40
115	Charles Johnson	.40
116	Jeff Blake	.75
117	Mark Brunell	3.00
118	Simeon Rice	.40
119	Robert Brooks	.40
120	*Jacquez Green*	10.00
121	Willie Davis	.40
122	Jeff George	.75
123	Andre Rison	.40
124	Erik Kramer	.40
125	Peter Boulware	.40
126	*Marcus Nash*	10.00
127	Troy Aikman	3.00
128	Keenan McCardell	.40
129	Bryant Westbrook	.40
130	Terry Glenn	.75
131	Blaine Bishop	.40
132	Tim Brown	.75
133	*Brian Griese*	12.00
134	John Mobley	.40
135	Larry Centers	.40
136	Eric Bjornson	.40
137	Kevin Hardy	.40
138	John Randle	.40
139	Michael Strahan	.40
140	Jerome Bettis	.75
141	Rae Carruth	.40
142	Reggie White	.75
143	Antowain Smith	1.50
144	Aeneas Williams	.40
145	Bobby Engram	.40
146	*Germane Crowell*	10.00
147	Freddie Jones	.40
148	Kimble Anders	.40
149	Steve Young	2.00
150	Willie McGinest	.40
151	Emmitt Smith	5.00
152	*Fred Taylor*	30.00
153	Danny Kanell	.40
154	Warrick Dunn	3.00
155	Kerry Collins	.75
156	Chris Chandler	.40
157	Curtis Conway	.75
158	*Curtis Enis*	15.00
159	Corey Dillon	2.00
160	Glenn Foley	.75
161	Marvin Harrison	.75
162	Chad Brown	.40
163	Derrick Rodgers	.40
164	Levon Kirkland	.40
165	*Peyton Manning*	50.00

1998 Topps Chrome Refractors

All 165 cards in Topps Chrome were reprinted in Refractor versions and inserted one per 12 packs.

	MT
Refractor Cards:	6x-12x
Refractor Rookies:	2x-4x

1998 Topps Chrome Hidden Gems

This 15-card set was reprinted from Topps in a chromium version and inserted one per 12 packs. Cards are numbered with "HG" prefix, while Refractors are seeded one per 24 packs.

		MT
Complete Set (15):		40.00
Common Player:		1.50
Refractors:		2x
HG1	Andre Reed	1.50
HG2	Kevin Greene	1.50

HG3	Tony Martin	1.50
HG4	Shannon Sharpe	1.50
HG5	Terry Allen	1.50
HG6	Brett Favre	15.00
HG7	Ben Coates	1.50
HG8	Michael Sinclair	1.50
HG9	Keenan McCardell	1.50
HG10	Brad Johnson	3.00
HG11	Mark Brunell	7.00
HG12	Dorsey Levens	3.00
HG13	Terrell Davis	10.00
HG14	Curtis Martin	4.00
HG15	Derrick Rodgers	1.50

1998 Topps Chrome Measures of Greatness

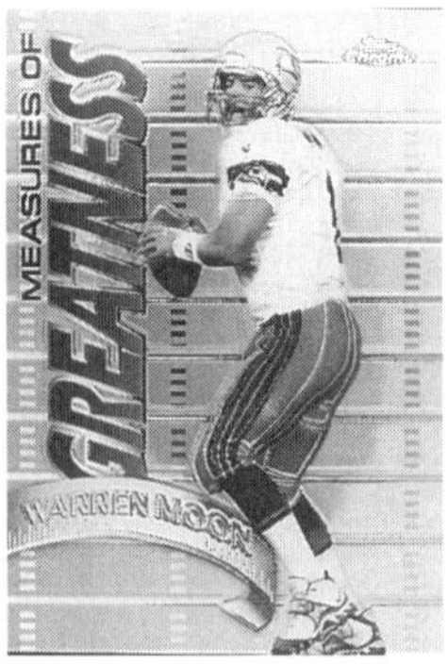

This 15-card set is reprinted from Topps in a chromium version and seeded one per 12 packs. The cards are numbered with a "HG" prefix, while Refractor versions are seeded one per 48 packs.

		MT
Complete Set (15):		80.00
Common Player:		1.50
Refractors:		3x
MG1	John Elway	7.00
MG2	Marcus Allen	3.00
MG3	Jerry Rice	8.00
MG4	Tim Brown	1.50
MG5	Warren Moon	1.50
MG6	Bruce Smith	1.50
MG7	Troy Aikman	8.00
MG8	Reggie White	3.00
MG9	Irving Fryar	1.50
MG10	Barry Sanders	15.00
MG11	Cris Carter	1.50
MG12	Emmitt Smith	12.00
MG13	Dan Marino	12.00
MG14	Rod Woodson	1.50
MG15	Brett Favre	15.00

1998 Topps Chrome Season's Best

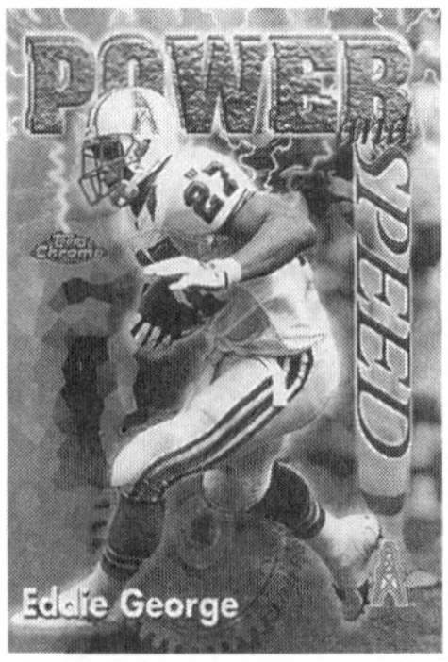

This 30-card insert was reprinted from Topps in a chromium version and inserted one per eight packs. The set is broken up with five cards in six different categories, including Power & Speed, Gunslingers, Prime Targets, Heavy Hitters, Quick Six and Career Best. Season's Best cards are numbered with a "SB" prefix and Refractor versions are seeded one per 24 packs.

		MT
Complete Set (30):		90.00
Common Player:		.50
Refractors:		2x
1	Terrell Davis	10.00
2	Barry Sanders	15.00
3	Jerome Bettis	1.00
4	Dorsey Levens	1.00
5	Eddie George	6.00
6	Brett Favre	15.00
7	Mark Brunell	5.00
8	Jeff George	1.00
9	Steve Young	4.00
10	John Elway	7.00
11	Herman Moore	1.00
12	Rob Moore	.50
13	Yancey Thigpen	.50
14	Cris Carter	1.00
15	Tim Brown	1.00
16	Bruce Smith	.50
17	Michael Smith	.50
18	John Randle	.50
19	Dana Stubblefield	.50
20	Michael Strahan	.50
21	Tamarick Vanover	.50
22	Darrien Gordon	.50
23	Michael Bates	.50
24	David Meggett	.50
25	Jermaine Lewis	.50
26	Terrell Davis	10.00
27	Jerry Rice	6.00
28	Barry Sanders	15.00
29	John Randle	.50
30	John Elway	7.00

1998 Ultra

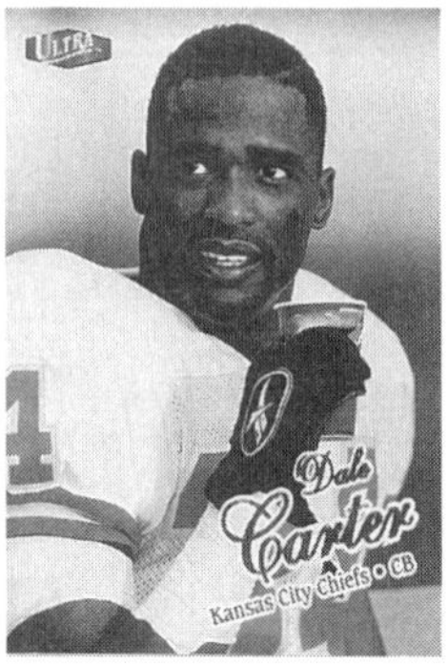

Ultra Football was released in two series in 1998 and contained a total of 425 cards. Series I had 197 veterans, three checklists and a 25-card 1998 Rookies subset seeded one per three packs. Series II had 132 player cards, 25 '98 Greats, three checklists and 40 rookies seeded one per three packs. Cards featured a full color shot of the player, with his name embossed foil writing in the lower right corner. Every card appears in three different parallels - Gold Medallion, Platinum Medallion and Masterpieces. Inserts in Series I include: Canton Classics, Flair Showcase Preview, Next Century, Sensational Sixty, Shots and Touchdown Kings. Inserts in Series II include: Rush Hour, Damage, Inc., Caught in the Draft, Indefensible and Exclamation Points.

		MT
Complete Series 1 (225):		200.00
Common Player:		.15
Common Rookie (201-225):		2.00
Inserted 1:3		
Wax Box Series 1:		125.00
1	Barry Sanders	2.50
2	Brett Favre	2.50
3	Napoleon Kaufman	.50
4	Robert Smith	.30
5	Terry Allen	.15
6	Vinny Testaverde	.15
7	William Floyd	.15
8	Carl Pickens	.15
9	Antonio Freeman	.30
10	Ben Coates	.15
11	Elvis Grbac	.15
12	Kerry Collins	.30
13	Orlando Pace	.15
14	Steve Broussard	.15
15	Terance Mathis	.15
16	Tiki Barber	.30
17	Cris Carter	.15
18	Derrick Alexander	.15
19	Eric Metcalf	.15
20	Jeff George	.30
21	Leslie Shepherd	.15
22	Natrone Means	.30
23	Scott Mitchell	.15
24	Adrian Murrell	.15
25	Gilbert Brown	.15
26	Jimmy Smith	.15
27	Mark Bruener	.15
28	Troy Aikman	1.00
29	Warrick Dunn	1.50
30	Jay Graham	.15
31	Craig Whelihan	.15
32	Ed McCaffrey	.15
33	Jamie Asher	.15
34	John Randle	.15
35	Michael Jackson	.15
36	Rickey Dudley	.15
37	Sean Dawkins	.15
38	Andre Rison	.15
39	Bert Emanuel	.15
40	Jeff Blake	.30
41	Curtis Conway	.15
42	Eddie Kennison	.30
43	James McKnight	.15
44	Rae Carruth	.15
45	Tito Wooten	.15
46	Cris Dishman	.15
47	Ernie Conwell	.15
48	Fred Lane	.15
49	Jamal Anderson	.15
50	Lake Dawson	.15
51	Michael Strahan	.15
52	Reggie White	.30
53	Trent Dilfer	.30
54	Troy Brown	.15
55	Wesley Walls	.15
56	Chidi Ahanotu	.15
57	Dwayne Rudd	.15
58	Jerry Rice	1.25
59	Johnnie Morton	.15
60	Sherman Williams	.15
61	Steve McNair	.75
62	Yancey Thigpen	.15
63	Chris Chandler	.15
64	Dexter Coakley	.15
65	Horace Copeland	.15
66	Jerald Moore	.15
67	Leon Johnson	.15
68	Mark Chmura	.30
69	Michael Barrow	.15
70	Muhsin Muhammad	.15
71	Terry Glenn	.30
72	Tony Brackens	.15
73	Chad Scott	.15
74	Glenn Foley	.15
75	Keenan McCardell	.15
76	Peter Boulware	.15
77	Reidel Anthony	.30
78	William Henderson	.15
79	Tony Martin	.15
80	Tony Gonzalez	.15
81	Charlie Jones	.15
82	Chris Gedney	.15
83	Chris Calloway	.15
84	Dale Carter	.15
85	Ki-Jana Carter	.15
86	Shawn Springs	.15
87	Antowain Smith	.75
88	Eric Turner	.15
89	John Mobley	.15
90	Ken Dilger	.15
91	Bobby Hoying	.15
92	Curtis Martin	1.00
93	Drew Bledsoe	1.00
94	Gary Brown	.15
95	Marvin Harrison	.30
96	Todd Collins	.15
97	Chris Warren	.15
98	Danny Kanell	.15
99	Tony McGee	.15
100	Rod Smith	.15
101	Frank Sanders	.15
102	Irving Fryar	.15
103	Marcus Allen	.30
104	Marshall Faulk	.30
105	Bruce Smith	.15
106	Charlie Garner	.15
107	Jim Harbaugh	.30
108	Randal Hill	.15
109	Ricky Proehl	.15
110	Rob Moore	.15
111	Shannon Sharpe	.15
112	Warren Moon	.15
113	Zach Thomas	.15
114	Dan Marino	2.00
115	Duce Staley	.15
116	Eric Swann	.15
117	Kenny Holmes	.15
118	Merton Hanks	.15
119	Raymont Harris	.15
120	Terrell Davis	1.25
121	Thurman Thomas	.30
122	Wayne Martin	.15
123	Charles Way	.15
124	Chuck Smith	.15
125	Corey Dillon	1.00
126	Darnell Autry	.15
127	Isaac Bruce	.30
128	Joey Galloway	.30
129	Kimble Anders	.15
130	Aeneas Williams	.15
131	Andre Hastings	.15
132	Chad Lewis	.15
133	J.J. Stokes	.15
134	John Elway	1.00
135	Karim Abdul-Jabbar	.30
136	Ken Harvey	.15
137	Robert Brooks	.15
138	Rodney Thomas	.15
139	James Stewart	.15
140	Billy Joe Hobert	.15
141	Frank Wycheck	.15
142	Jake Plummer	1.50
143	Jerris McPhail	.15
144	Kordell Stewart	1.25
145	Terrell Owens	.30
146	Willie Green	.15
147	Anthony Miller	.15
148	Courtney Hawkins	.15
149	Larry Centers	.15
150	Gus Frerotte	.15
151	O.J. McDuffie	.15
152	Ray Zellars	.15
153	Terry Kirby	.15
154	Tommy Vardell	.15
155	Willie Davis	.15
156	Chris Canty	.15
157	Byron Hanspard	.15
158	Chris Penn	.15
159	Damon Jones	.15
160	Derrick Mayes	.15
161	Emmitt Smith	2.00
162	Keyshawn Johnson	.15
163	Mike Alstott	.50
164	Tom Carter	.15
165	Tony Banks	.30
166	Bryant Westbrook	.15
167	Chris Sanders	.15
168	Deion Sanders	.50
169	Garrison Hearst	.15
170	Jason Taylor	.15
171	Jerome Bettis	.30
172	John Lynch	.15
173	Troy Davis	.15
174	Freddie Jones	.15
175	Herman Moore	.30
176	Jake Reed	.15
177	Mark Brunell	1.00
178	Ray Lewis	.15
179	Stephen Davis	.15
180	Tim Brown	.15
181	Willie McGinest	.15
182	Andre Reed	.15
183	Darrien Gordon	.15
184	David Palmer	.15
185	James Jett	.15
186	Junior Seau	.15
187	Zack Crockett	.15
188	Brad Johnson	.30
189	Charles Johnson	.15
190	Eddie George	1.25
191	Jermaine Lewis	.15
192	Michael Irvin	.30
193	Reggie Brown	.15
194	Steve Young	.50
195	Warren Sapp	.15
196	Wayne Chrebet	.15
197	David Dunn	.15
198	Dorsey Levens CL	.15
199	Troy Aikman CL	.30
200	John Elway CL	.30
201	*Peyton Manning*	40.00
202	*Ryan Leaf*	25.00
203	*Charles Woodson*	15.00
204	*Andre Wadsworth*	5.00
205	*Brian Simmons*	2.00
206	*Curtis Enis*	12.00
207	*Randy Moss*	70.00
208	*Germane Crowell*	6.00
209	*Greg Ellis*	2.00
210	*Kevin Dyson*	8.00
211	*Skip Hicks*	6.00
212	*Alonzo Mayes*	2.00
213	*Robert Edwards*	20.00
214	*Fred Taylor*	25.00
215	*Robert Holcombe*	8.00
216	*John Dutton*	2.00
217	*Vonnie Holliday*	4.00
218	*Tim Dwight*	5.00
219	*Tavian Banks*	8.00
220	*Marcus Nash*	6.00
221	*Jason Peter*	2.00
222	*Michael Myers*	2.00
223	*Takeo Spikes*	4.00
224	*Kivuusama Mays*	2.00
225	*Jacquez Green*	7.00

1998 Ultra Gold Medallion

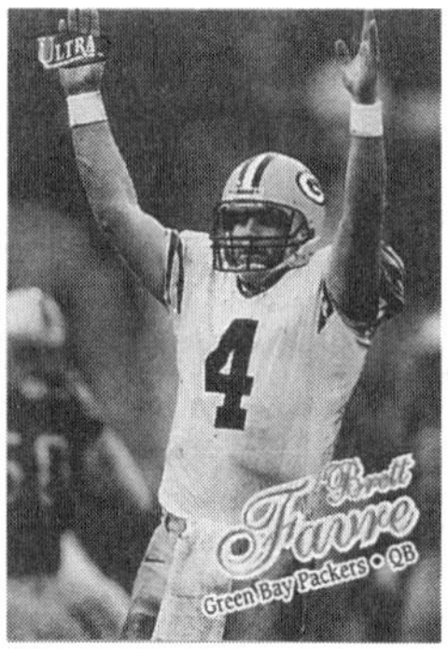

All 425 cards in Ultra Series I and II were paralleled in Gold Medallion versions. The cards featured a gold tint to the front and were numbered with a "G" suffix. Throughout both series, they were inserted in hobby packs only at a rate of one per pack, except for the rookie subsets in both series which were seeded one per 24 packs.

	MT
Gold Medallion Cards:	2x-4x
Gold Medallion Rookies:	1.5x

1998 Ultra Platinum Medallion

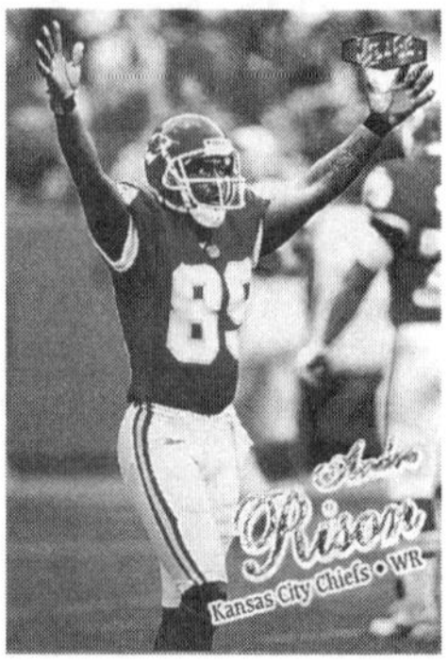

All 425 cards in Ultra Series I and II were also available in Platinum Medallion versions. These cards added a platinum tint to the background, showed the player image in black and white and added silver prismatic writing to the player's name. All cards were hobby-only with cards all regular cards sequentially numbered to 98, while the 25-card rookie subset in Series I and the 40-card rookie subset in Series II are numbered to only 66.

	MT
Platinum Medallion Cards:	50x-100x
Platinum Medallion Rookies:	4x-8x

1998 Ultra Canton Classics

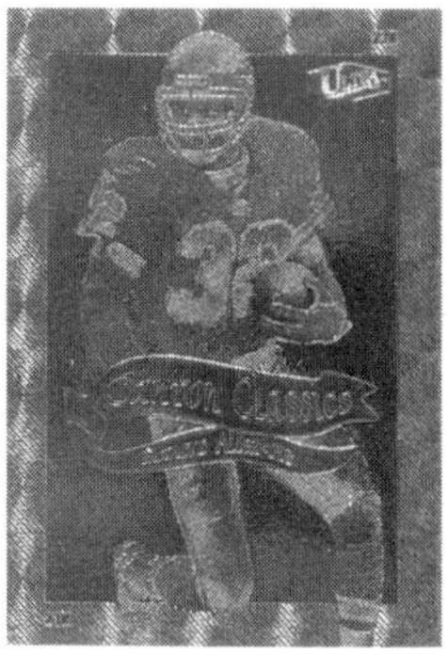

Canton Classics features 10 future Hall of Famers on cards enhanced with 23 karat gold coating and embossing, with an etched border. Backs are numbered with a "CC" suffix and feature an off-color shot of the player again along with some career highlights. These were inserted one per 288 packs.

		MT
Complete Set (10):		375.00
Common Player:		20.00
1	Terrell Davis	50.00
2	Brett Favre	70.00
3	John Elway	35.00
4	Barry Sanders	70.00
5	Eddie George	30.00
6	Jerry Rice	35.00
7	Emmitt Smith	50.00
8	Dan Marino	50.00
9	Troy Aikman	35.00
10	Marcus Allen	25.00

1998 Ultra Flair Showcase Preview

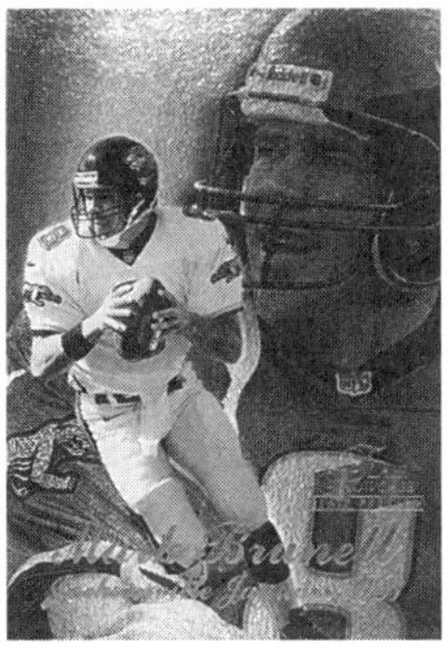

This 10-card insert previewed the upcoming Flair Showcase set. Cards featured the designs of 1998 Flair Showcase and included the logo. They were inserted one per 144 packs of Series I.

		MT
Complete Set (10):		250.00
Common Player:		10.00
1	Kordell Stewart	30.00
2	Mark Brunell	20.00
3	Terrell Davis	30.00
4	Brett Favre	60.00
5	Steve McNair	10.00
6	Curtis Martin	10.00
7	Warrick Dunn	30.00
8	Emmitt Smith	45.00
9	Dan Marino	45.00
10	Corey Dillon	20.00

1998 Ultra Next Century

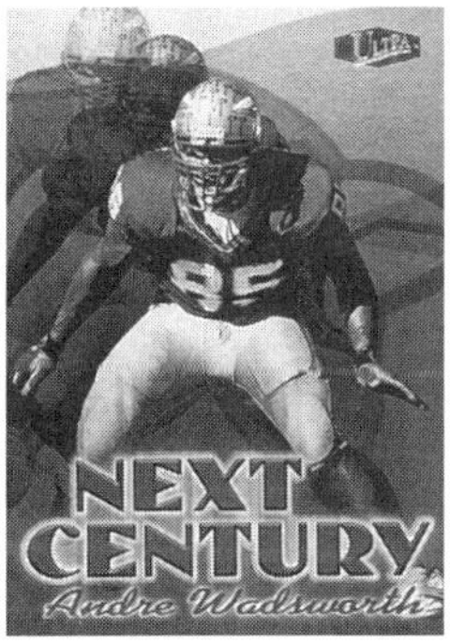

This 15-card insert featured top rookies from 1998 on cards printed on 100 percent gold foil and sculpture embossing. Next Century inserts were numbered with a "NC" suffix and inserted one per 72 packs.

		MT
Complete Set (15):		200.00
Common Player:		5.00
1	Ryan Leaf	30.00
2	Peyton Manning	40.00
3	Charles Woodson	20.00
4	Randy Moss	50.00
5	Curtis Enis	20.00
6	Ahman Green	10.00
7	Peter Warrick	5.00
8	Andre Wadsworth	10.00
9	Germane Crowell	5.00
10	Robert Edwards	20.00
11	Tavian Banks	12.00
12	Takeo Spikes	5.00
13	Jacquez Green	12.00
14	Brian Simmons	5.00
15	Alonzo Mayes	5.00

1998 Ultra Sensational Sixty

This 60-card insert was available only in retail packs at a rate of one per pack. These were numbered with a "SS" suffix and found in Series I.

		MT
Complete Set (60):		45.00
Common Player:		.50
Inserted 1:1 Retail		
1	Karim Abdul-Jabbar	1.00
2	Troy Aikman	2.00
3	Terry Allen	.50
4	Mike Alstott	1.00
5	Tony Banks	1.00
6	Jerome Bettis	1.00
7	Drew Bledsoe	1.50
8	Peter Boulware	.50
9	Robert Brooks	.50
10	Tim Brown	.50
11	Isaac Bruce	1.00
12	Mark Brunell	1.50
13	Cris Carter	1.00
14	Kerry Collins	1.00
15	Curtis Conway	.50
16	Terrell Davis	3.00
17	Troy Davis	.50
18	Trent Dilfer	1.00
19	Corey Dillon	1.25
20	Warrick Dunn	1.50
21	John Elway	2.00
22	Bert Emanuel	.50
23	Brett Favre	4.00
24	Antonio Freeman	1.00
25	Gus Frerotte	.50
26	Joey Galloway	1.00
27	Eddie George	1.50
28	Jeff George	1.00
29	Elvis Grbac	.50
30	Marvin Harrison	1.00
31	Bobby Hoying	.50
32	Michael Irvin	1.00
33	Brad Johnson	1.00
34	Keyshawn Johnson	1.00
35	Dan Marino	3.00
36	Curtis Martin	1.00
37	Tony Martin	.50
38	Keenan McCardell	.50
39	Steve McNair	1.00
40	Warren Moon	1.00
41	Herman Moore	1.00
42	Johnnie Morton	.50
43	Terrell Owens	1.00
44	Carl Pickens	.50
45	Jake Plummer	1.50
46	Jerry Rice	2.00
47	Andre Rison	.50
48	Barry Sanders	4.00
49	Deion Sanders	1.00
50	Junior Seau	.50
51	Shannon Sharpe	1.00
52	Antowain Smith	1.00
53	Emmitt Smith	3.00
54	Jimmy Smith	.50
55	Robert Smith	1.00
56	Kordell Stewart	1.50
57	Jeff Blake	.50
58	Charles Way	.50
59	Reggie White	1.00
60	Steve Young	1.25

1998 Ultra Shots

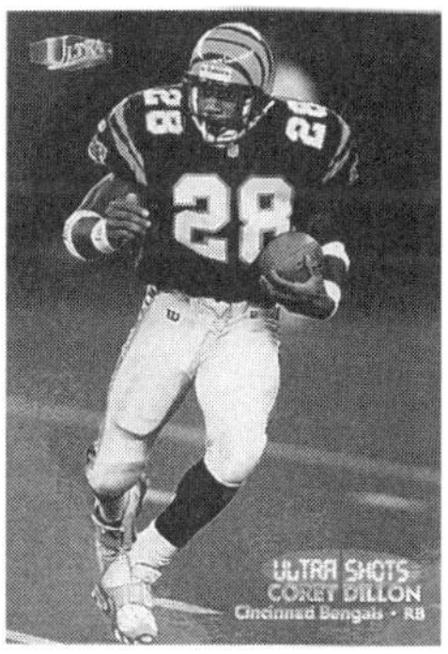

Shots was a 20-card insert that allowed photographers to discuss the shot that is captured on the card front. These were numbered with a "US" suffix and inserted one per six packs of Series I.

		MT
Complete Set (20):		45.00
Common Player:		1.50
1	Deion Sanders	3.00
2	Corey Dillon	4.00
3	Mike Alstott	3.00
4	Jake Plummer	4.00
5	Antowain Smith	3.00
6	Kordell Stewart	4.00
7	Curtis Martin	3.00
8	Bobby Hoying	1.50
9	Kerry Collins	3.00
10	Herman Moore	3.00
11	Terry Glenn	3.00
12	Eddie George	4.00
13	Drew Bledsoe	4.00
14	Steve McNair	3.00
15	Jerry Rice	4.00
16	Trent Dilfer	1.50
17	Joey Galloway	3.00
18	Dan Marino	8.00
19	Barry Sanders	10.00
20	Warrick Dunn	4.00

1998 Ultra Touchdown Kings

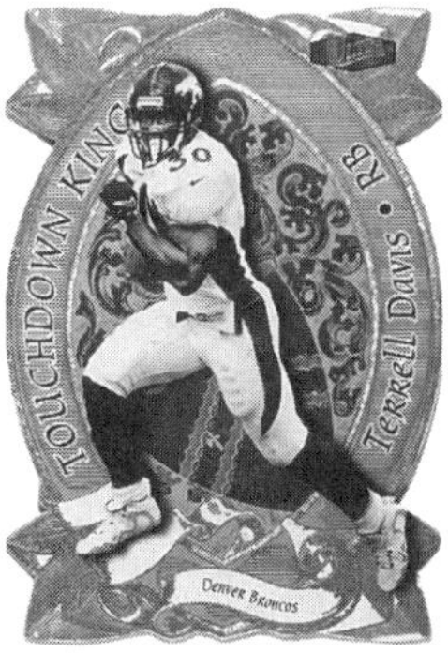

This die-cut insert showcased 15 players on an embossed design. Cards were numbered on the back with a "TK" suffix and inserted one per 24 packs of Series I.

		MT
Complete Set (15):		100.00
Common Player:		3.00
1	Terrell Davis	12.00
2	Joey Galloway	6.00
3	Kordell Stewart	10.00
4	Corey Dillon	8.00
5	Barry Sanders	20.00
6	Cris Carter	3.00
7	Antonio Freeman	6.00
8	Mike Alstott	6.00
9	Eddie George	10.00
10	Warrick Dunn	10.00
11	Drew Bledsoe	10.00
12	Karim Abdul-Jabbar	6.00
13	Mark Brunell	10.00
14	Brett Favre	20.00
15	Emmitt Smith	15.00

1998 Upper Deck

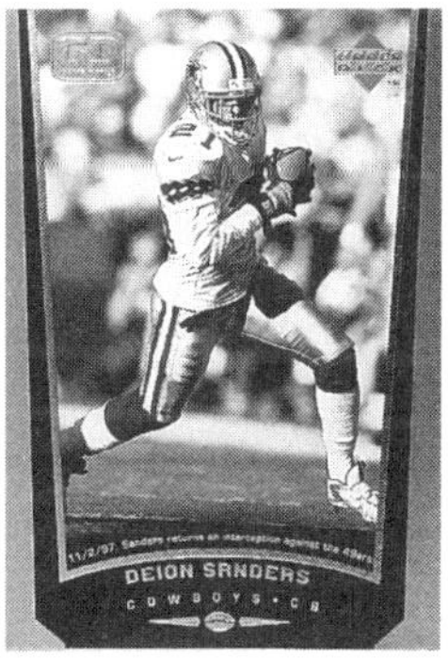

Upper Deck Series One Football consists of a 255-card base set. The base cards have a color photo bordered on three sides, with the player's name, team and position printed at the bottom. The set consists of 210 regular cards, 42 Star Rookie subset cards (1:4) and three checklists. The set is paralleled in UD Exclusives. Inserts include Super-Powers, Constant Threat, Define the Game (each with a tiered Quantum parallel), Game Jerseys and Hobby-Exclusive Game Jerseys.

		MT
Complete Set (255):		225.00
Common Player:		.15
Common Rookie (1-42):		2.50
Wax Box:		120.00
1	*Peyton Manning*	45.00
2	*Ryan Leaf*	25.00
3	*Andre Wadsworth*	5.00
4	*Charles Woodson*	20.00
5	*Curtis Enis*	15.00
6	*Grant Wistrom*	2.50
7	*Greg Ellis*	2.50
8	*Fred Taylor*	25.00
9	*Duane Starks*	2.50
10	*Keith Brooking*	2.50
11	*Takeo Spikes*	4.00
12	*Jason Peter*	4.00
13	*Anthony Simmons*	2.50
14	*Kevin Dyson*	8.00
15	*Brian Simmons*	2.50
16	*Robert Edwards*	20.00
17	*Randy Moss*	70.00
18	*John Avery*	6.00
19	*Marcus Nash*	6.00
20	*Jerome Pathon*	4.00
21	*Jacquez Green*	8.00
22	*Robert Holcombe*	12.00
23	*Patrick Johnson*	2.50
24	*Germane Crowell*	7.00
25	*Joe Jurevicius*	4.00
26	*Skip Hicks*	6.00
27	*Ahman Green*	8.00
28	*Brian Griese*	8.00
29	*Hines Ward*	6.00
30	*Tavian Banks*	10.00
31	*Tony Simmons*	4.00
32	*Victor Riley*	2.50
33	*Rashaan Shehee*	4.00
34	*R.W. McQuarters*	2.50
35	*Flozell Adams*	2.50
36	*Tre Thomas*	2.50
37	*Greg Favors*	2.50
38	*Jon Ritchie*	2.50
39	*Jessie Haynes*	2.50
40	*Ryan Sutter*	2.50
41	*Mo Collins*	2.50
42	*Tim Dwight*	6.00
43	Chris Chandler	.15
44	Byron Hanspard	.15
45	Jessie Tuggle	.15
46	Jamal Anderson	.30
47	Terance Mathis	.15
48	Morten Andersen	.15
49	Jake Plummer	2.00
50	Mario Bates	.15
51	Frank Sanders	.15
52	Adrian Murrell	.30
53	Simeon Rice	.15
54	Aeneas Williams	.15
55	Eric Swann	.15
56	Jim Harbaugh	.15
57	Michael Jackson	.15
58	Peter Boulware	.15
59	Errict Rhett	.15
60	Jermaine Lewis	.15
61	Eric Zeier	.15
62	Rod Woodson	.15
63	Rob Johnson	.30
64	Antowain Smith	1.00
65	Bruce Smith	.15
66	Eric Moulds	.15
67	Andre Reed	.15
68	Thurman Thomas	.30
69	Lonnie Johnson	.15
70	Kerry Collins	.50
71	Kevin Greene	.15
72	Fred Lane	.30
73	Rae Carruth	.15
74	Michael Bates	.15
75	William Floyd	.15
76	Sean Gilbert	.15
77	Erik Kramer	.15
78	Edgar Bennett	.15
79	Curtis Conway	.30
80	Darnell Autry	.15
81	Ryan Wetnight	.15
82	Walt Harris	.15
83	Bobby Engram	.15
84	Jeff Blake	.30
85	Carl Pickens	.30
86	Darnay Scott	.15
87	Corey Dillon	1.25
88	Reinard Wilson	.15
89	Ashley Ambrose	.15
90	Troy Aikman	1.50
91	Michael Irvin	.30
92	Emmitt Smith	2.50
93	Deion Sanders	.50
94	David LaFleur	.15
95	Chris Warren	.15
96	Darren Woodson	.15
97	John Elway	1.50
98	Terrell Davis	1.50
99	Rod Smith	.30
100	Shannon Sharpe	.30
101	Ed McCaffrey	.15
102	Steve Atwater	.15
103	John Mobley	.15
104	Darrian Gordon	.15
105	Barry Sanders	3.00
106	Scott Mitchell	.15
107	Herman Moore	.30
108	Johnnie Morton	.15
109	Robert Porcher	.15
110	Bryant Westbrook	.15
111	Tommy Vardell	.15
112	Brett Favre	3.00
113	Dorsey Levens	.30
114	Reggie White	.30
115	Antonio Freeman	.30
116	Robert Brooks	.15
117	Mark Chmura	.30
118	Derrick Mayes	.15
119	Gilbert Brown	.15
120	Marshall Faulk	.30
121	Torrance Small	.15
122	Marvin Harrison	.30
123	Quentin Coryatt	.15
124	Ken Dilger	.15
125	Zack Crockett	.15
126	Mark Brunell	1.25
127	Bryce Paup	.15
128	Tony Brackens	.15
129	Renaldo Wynn	.15
130	Keenan McCardell	.15
131	Jimmy Smith	.30
132	Kevin Hardy	.15
133	Elvis Grbac	.15
134	Tamarick Vanover	.15
135	Chester McGlockton	.15
136	Andre Rison	.15
137	Derrick Alexander	.15
138	Tony Gonzalez	.15
139	Derrick Thomas	.15
140	Dan Marino	2.50
141	Karim Abdul-Jabbar	.30
142	O.J. McDuffie	.15
143	Yatil Green	.15
144	Charles Jordan	.15
145	Brock Marion	.15
146	Zach Thomas	.15
147	Brad Johnson	.30
148	Cris Carter	.30
149	Jake Reed	.15
150	Robert Smith	.30
151	John Randle	.15
152	Dwayne Rudd	.15
153	Randall Cunningham	.15
154	Drew Bledsoe	1.25
155	Terry Glenn	.30
156	Ben Coates	.15
157	Willie Clay	.15
158	Chris Slade	.15
159	Derrick Cullors	.15
160	Ty Law	.15
161	Danny Wuerffel	.30
162	Andre Hastings	.15
163	Troy Davis	.30
164	Billy Joe Hobert	.15
165	Eric Guliford	.15
166	Mark Fields	.15
167	Alex Molden	.15
168	Danny Kanell	.15
169	Tiki Barber	.30
170	Charles Way	.15
171	Amani Toomer	.15
172	Michael Strahan	.15
173	Jesse Armstead	.15
174	Jason Sehorn	.15
175	Glenn Foley	.30
176	Curtis Martin	1.00
177	Aaron Glenn	.15
178	Keyshawn Johnson	.30
179	James Farrior	.15
180	Wayne Chrebet	.15
181	Keith Byars	.15
182	Jeff George	.30
183	Napoleon Kaufman	.50
184	Tim Brown	.30
185	Darrell Russell	.15
186	Rickey Dudley	.15
187	James Jett	.15
188	Desmond Howard	.15
189	Bobby Hoying	.15
190	Charlie Garner	.15
191	Irving Fryar	.15
192	Chris T. Jones	.15
193	Mike Mamula	.15
194	Troy Vincent	.15
195	Kordell Stewart	1.50
196	Jerome Bettis	.30
197	Will Blackwell	.15
198	Levon Kirkland	.15
199	Carnell Lake	.15
200	Charles Johnson	.15
201	Greg Lloyd	.15
202	Donnell Woolford	.15
203	Tony Banks	.30
204	Amp Lee	.15
205	Isaac Bruce	.30
206	Eddie Kennison	.30
207	Ryan McNeil	.15
208	Craig Heyward	.15
209	Ernie Conwell	.15
210	Natrone Means	.30
211	Junior Seau	.30
212	Tony Martin	.15
213	Freddie Jones	.15
214	Bryan Still	.15
215	Rodney Harrison	.15
216	Steve Young	1.00
217	Jerry Rice	1.50
218	Garrison Hearst	.15
219	J.J. Stokes	.15
220	Ken Norton	.15
221	Greg Clark	.15
222	Bryant Young	.15
223	Gabe Wilkins	.15
224	Warren Moon	.30
225	Jon Kitna	.15
226	Ricky Watters	.30
227	Chad Brown	.15
228	Joey Galloway	.30
229	Shawn Springs	.15
230	Cortez Kennedy	.15
231	Trent Dilfer	.30
232	Warrick Dunn	2.00
233	Mike Alstott	.30
234	Warren Sapp	.15
235	Bert Emanuel	.15
236	Reidel Anthony	.15
237	Hardy Nickerson	.15
238	Derrick Brooks	.15
239	Steve McNair	.50
240	Yancey Thigpen	.15
241	Anthony Dorsett	.15
242	Blaine Bishop	.15

243	Kenny Holmes	.15
244	Eddie George	1.25
245	Chris Sanders	.15
246	Gus Frerotte	.15
247	Terry Allen	.15
248	Dana Stubblefield	.15
249	Michael Westbrook	.15
250	Darrell Green	.15
251	Brian Mitchell	.15
252	Ken Harvey	.15
253	Checklist A	.75
	Troy Aikman	
254	Checklist B	1.25
	Dan Marino	
255	Checklist C	.15
	Herman Moore	

1998 Upper Deck Bronze

The UD Exclusives set parallels the Upper Deck Series One base set. One level is numbered to 100 and the other is a 1-of-1 set.

	MT
Bronze Cards:	40x-80x
Bronze Rookies:	2x-4x

1998 Upper Deck Constant Threat

Constant Threat is a 30-card insert seeded one per 12 packs. The cards have a horizontal layout and two player photos. The color player photo is on the left and a negative exposure is on the right. The cards also feature blue foil highlights.

		MT
Complete Set (30):		150.00
Common Player:		1.50
CT1	Dan Marino	12.00
CT2	Peyton Manning	18.00
CT3	Randy Moss	20.00
CT4	Brett Favre	15.00
CT5	Mark Brunell	6.00
CT6	Keyshawn Johnson	1.50
CT7	John Elway	6.00
CT8	Troy Aikman	7.00
CT9	Steve Young	5.00
CT10	Kordell Stewart	6.00
CT11	Drew Bledsoe	7.00
CT12	Joey Galloway	3.00
CT13	Elvis Grbac	1.50
CT14	Marvin Harrison	3.00
CT15	Napoleon Kaufman	4.00
CT16	Ryan Leaf	18.00
CT17	Jake Plummer	7.00
CT18	Terrell Davis	10.00
CT19	Steve McNair	5.00
CT20	Barry Sanders	15.00
CT21	Deion Sanders	4.00
CT22	Emmitt Smith	12.00
CT23	Antowain Smith	4.00
CT24	Herman Moore	3.00
CT25	Curtis Martin	6.00
CT26	Jerry Rice	7.00
CT27	Eddie George	6.00
CT28	Warrick Dunn	7.00
CT29	Curtis Enis	8.00
CT30	Michael Irvin	3.00

1998 Upper Deck Constant Threat Bronze/Silver

The Constant Threat insert has a three-tiered Quantum parallel. The cards are die-cut and sequentially numbered. Tier One features silver foil and is numbered to 1,000, Tier Two has bronze foil and numbering to 25 and Tier Three has gold foil and is a 1-of-1 set.

	MT
Bronze Cards:	20x-40x
Silver Cards:	2x-4x

1998 Upper Deck Define the Game

Define the Game is a 30-card insert seeded one per eight packs. The cards feature a small color photo of the player with a larger black-and-white photo in the background. The front of each card has a word that describes the player and the definition.

		MT
Complete Set (30):		100.00
Common Player:		1.00
DG1	Dan Marino	10.00
DG2	Curtis Enis	6.00
DG3	Dorsey Levens	2.00
DG4	Charles Woodson	4.00
DG5	Junior Seau	1.00
DG6	Tiki Barber	1.00
DG7	Randy Moss	12.00
DG8	Troy Aikman	6.00
DG9	Jake Plummer	6.00
DG10	Corey Dillon	4.00
DG11	Jerry Rice	6.00
DG12	Emmitt Smith	10.00
DG13	Herman Moore	2.00
DG14	Brad Johnson	2.00
DG15	Gus Frerotte	1.00
DG16	Ryan Leaf	10.00
DG17	Shannon Sharpe	1.00
DG18	Jermaine Lewis	1.00
DG19	Jerome Bettis	2.00
DG20	Barry Sanders	12.00
DG21	Terry Allen	1.00
DG22	Reidel Anthony	1.00
DG23	Isaac Bruce	2.00
DG24	Mike Alstott	3.00
DG25	Rae Carruth	1.00
DG26	Tamarick Vanover	1.00
DG27	Eddie George	5.00
DG28	Warrick Dunn	6.00
DG29	Tony Gonzalez	1.00
DG30	Keenan McCardell	1.00

1998 Upper Deck Define the Game Bronze/Silver

Define the Game has a three-tiered Quantum parallel. The cards are die-cut and sequentially numbered. Tier One is numbered to 1,500, Tier Two to 50 and Tier Three to 1.

	MT
Bronze Cards:	15x-30x
Silver Cards:	2x

1998 Upper Deck Hobby Exclusive Game Jerseys

The Hobby-Exclusive Game Jersey insert features 10-cards inserted 1:288. The set features veterans and rookies. The veteran cards have a piece of game-worn jersey and the rookie cards have a piece of jersey from the NFL rookie photo shoot.

		MT
Complete Set (10):		900.00
Common Player:		70.00
GJ11	Dan Marino	250.00
GJ12	Deion Sanders	100.00
GJ13	Steve Young	110.00
GJ14	Terrell Davis	140.00
GJ15	Tim Brown	70.00
GJ16	Peyton Manning	200.00
GJ17	Takeo Spikes	70.00
GJ18	Curtis Enis	100.00
GJ19	Fred Taylor	125.00
GJ20	John Avery	85.00

1998 Upper Deck Game Jersey

The Game Jersey insert features 10 cards inserted 1:2,500. The set contains both veterans and rookies. The veteran cards feature a piece of game-used jersey and the rookie cards have a piece of jersey worn during the NFL rookie photo shoot. Dan Marino signed 13 of his cards.

	MT
Complete Set (10):	3000.
Common Player:	150.00
GJ1	Brett Favre	600.00
GJ2	Reggie White	150.00
GJ3	Barry Sanders	625.00
GJ4	John Elway	425.00
GJ5	Mark Brunell	300.00
GJ6	Mike Alstott	200.00
GJ7	Ryan Leaf	425.00
GJ8	Andre Wadsworth	150.00
GJ9	Robert Edwards	250.00
GJ10	Kevin Dyson	150.00

1998 Upper Deck SuperPowers

SuperPowers is a 30-card insert seeded one per four packs. The cards have a horizontal layout and feature a color photo on the left with a black-and-white photo on the right.

		MT
Complete Set (30):		45.00
Common Player:		.50
S1	Dan Marino	5.00
S2	Jerry Rice	3.00
S3	Napoleon Kaufman	1.50
S4	Brett Favre	6.00
S5	Andre Rison	.50
S6	Jerome Bettis	1.00
S7	John Elway	2.00
S8	Troy Aikman	3.00
S9	Steve Young	1.50
S10	Kordell Stewart	3.00
S11	Drew Bledsoe	3.00
S12	Antonio Freeman	1.00
S13	Mark Brunell	2.00
S14	Shannon Sharpe	.50
S15	Trent Dilfer	1.00
S16	Peyton Manning	6.00
S17	Cris Carter	.50
S18	Michael Irvin	1.00
S19	Terry Glenn	1.00
S20	Keyshawn Johnson	1.00
S21	Deion Sanders	1.50
S22	Emmitt Smith	5.00
S23	Marcus Allen	1.00
S24	Dorsey Levens	1.00
S25	Jake Plummer	3.00
S26	Eddie George	3.00
S27	Tim Brown	.50
S28	Warrick Dunn	3.00
S29	Reggie White	1.00
S30	Terrell Davis	3.00

1998 Upper Deck SuperPowers Bronze/Silver

The SuperPowers insert has a three-tiered Quantum parallel. The cards are die-cut and sequentially numbered. Tier One is numbered to 2,000, Tier Two to 100 and Tier Three is a 1-of-1 set.

	MT
Bronze Cards:	10x-20x
Silver Cards:	2x

1998 Upper Deck Black Diamond

The Black Diamond Football base set consists of 150 cards designated by the Black Diamond logo and a single Black Diamond in the lower right corner. Three parallel versions were produced. Dou-

ble Black Diamond cards (inserted 1:1) have two diamonds and red Light F/X backgrounds. Triple Black Diamonds (1:5) have gold Light F/X backgrounds and Quadruple Black Diamonds (50 total sets) have black Light F/X backgrounds. The Premium Cuts insert (30 cards) features the same four diamond levels of scarcity and a special die-cut. Single Diamond (1:7), Double Diamond (1:15), Triple Diamond (1:30) and Quadruple Diamond (1:180) versions were created. Upper Deck also included a hobby-only "Mystery Premium Cut" insert in Black Diamond. The 30 cards feature Black Light F/X backgrounds, embossing and a horizontal die-cut design. The cards in the "Mystery" insert have different insertion rates.

		MT
Complete Set (150):		50.00
Common Player:		.25
Doubles:		2x
Triples:		3x-6x
Quadruples:		40x-80x
Wax Box:		80.00
1	Kent Graham	.25
2	Darrell Russell	.25
3	Jim Harbaugh	.25
4	Cornelius Bennett	.25
5	Troy Vincent	.25
6	Natrone Means	.50
7	Michael Jackson	.25
8	Will Blackwell	.25
9	Greg Hill	.25
10	Andre Reed	.25
11	Darren Bennett	.25
12	Dan Marino	5.00
13	Tshimanga	.25
	Biakabutuka	
14	Terrell Owens	.75
15	Cris Carter	.25
16	Darnell Autry	.50
17	Joey Galloway	.50
18	Terry Glenn	1.00
19	Ki-Jana Carter	.25
20	Isaac Bruce	.50
21	Shawn Jefferson	.25
22	Michael Irvin	.50
23	Warren Sapp	.25
24	Dave Brown	.25
25	Terrell Davis	2.50
26	Frank Wycheck	.25
27	Neil O'Donnell	.25
28	Scott Mitchell	.25
29	Michael Westbrook	.25
30	Tim Brown	.50
31	Antonio Freeman	.75
32	Jake Plummer	2.00
33	Irving Fryar	.25
34	Quentin Coryatt	.25
35	Jamal Anderson	.50
36	Jerome Bettis	.50
37	Keenan McCardell	.25
38	Derrick Alexander	.25
39	Stan Humphries	.25
40	Andre Rison	.25
41	Bruce Smith	.25
42	Garrison Hearst	.25
43	Zach Thomas	.50
44	Rae Carruth	.50
45	Kevin Greene	.25
46	Robert Smith	.25
47	Curtis Conway	.50
48	Christian Fauria	.25
49	Curtis Martin	2.00
50	Dan Wilkinson	.25
51	Eddie Kennison	.75
52	Mark Fields	.25
53	Anthony Miller	.25
54	Mike Alstott	1.00
55	Tiki Barber	.75
56	Neil Smith	.25
57	Gus Frerotte	.25
58	Adrian Murrell	.50
59	Johnnie Morton	.25
60	O.J. McDuffie	.25
61	Napoleon Kaufman	.50
62	Robert Brooks	.25
63	Byron Hanspard	.75
64	Ty Detmer	.25
65	Mark Brunell	2.00
66	Bam Morris	.25
67	Kordell Stewart	2.50
68	Elvis Grbac	.25
69	Antowain Smith	1.50
70	Junior Seau	.50
71	Tony Gonzalez	.50
72	Anthony Johnson	.25
73	Steve Young	1.50
74	Brian Manning	.25
75	Rick Mirer	.25
76	Warren Moon	.50
77	Torrian Gray	.25
78	Carl Pickens	.25

79	Tony Banks	1.00
80	Willie McGinest	.25
81	Deion Sanders	1.25
82	Warrick Dunn	3.00
83	Danny Wuerffel	.75
84	Rod Smith	.25
85	Steve McNair	1.75
86	Danny Kanell	.25
87	Herman Moore	.50
88	Brian Mitchell	.25
89	James Farrior	.25
90	Reggie White	.50
91	Simeon Rice	.25
92	James Jett	.25
93	Marshall Faulk	.50
94	Chris Chandler	.25
95	Mike Mamula	.25
96	Jimmy Smith	.25
97	Jamie Sharper	.25
98	Carnell Lake	.25
99	Marcus Allen	.50
100	Thurman Thomas	.50
101	Freddie Jones	.25
102	Karim Abdul-Jabbar	1.00
103	Kerry Collins	.50
104	Jerry Rice	2.50
105	Brad Johnson	.50
106	Raymont Harris	.25
107	Lamar Smith	.25
108	Drew Bledsoe	2.00
109	Corey Dillon	2.00
110	Lawrence Phillips	.25
111	Heath Shuler	.25
112	Emmitt Smith	4.00
113	Reidel Anthony	1.00
114	Ike Hilliard	.75
115	Shannon Sharpe	.25
116	Chris Sanders	.25
117	Keyshawn Johnson	.75
118	Barry Sanders	3.00
119	Cris Dishman	.25
120	Jeff George	.50
121	Dorsey Levens	.50
122	Rob Moore	.25
123	Ricky Watters	.50
124	Marvin Harrison	.75
125	Vinny Testaverde	.25
126	Charles Johnson	.25
127	Renaldo Wynn	.25
128	Todd Collins	.25
129	Tony Martin	.25
130	Derrick Thomas	.25
131	Wesley Walls	.25
132	Rod Woodson	.25
133	Troy Drayton	.25
134	Bryan Cox	.25
135	Shawn Springs	.25
136	Jake Reed	.25
137	Jeff Blake	.50
138	Craig Heyward	.25
139	Ben Coates	.25
140	Troy Aikman	2.50
141	Trent Dilfer	1.00
142	Troy Davis	.75
143	John Elway	2.00
144	Eddie George	2.50
145	Rodney Hampton	.25
146	Ed McCaffrey	.25
147	Terry Allen	.25
148	Wayne Chrebet	.25
149	Brett Favre	5.00
150	Daryl Johnston	.25

1998 Upper Deck Black Diamond Premium Cut

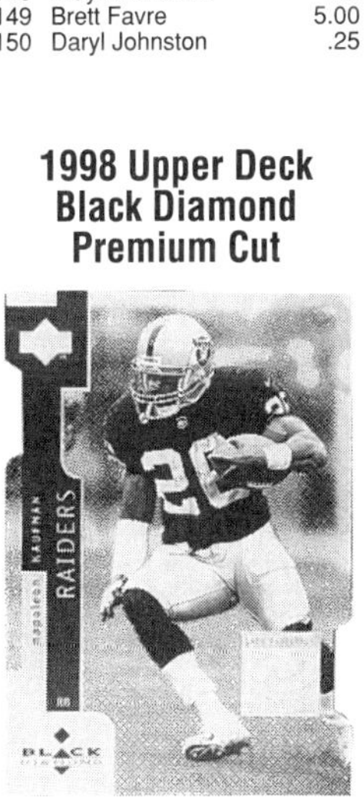

Premium Cut is a 30-card insert with four diamond versions. The cards have a special die-cut and Light F/X technology. Single Diamond (inserted 1:7), Double Diamond (1:15), Triple Diamond (1:30) and Quadruple Diamond (1:180) versions were produced.

	MT
Complete Set (30):	225.00
Common Player:	3.00
Doubles:	2x
Triples:	2x-4x
Quad Horizontals:	2x-4x
Quad Verticals:	5x-10x
PC1 Karim Abdul-Jabbar	6.00
PC2 Troy Aikman	12.00
PC3 Kerry Collins	6.00
PC4 Drew Bledsoe	12.00
PC5 Barry Sanders	20.00
PC6 Marcus Allen	6.00
PC7 John Elway	12.00
PC8 Adrian Murrell	3.00
PC9 Junior Seau	3.00
PC10Eddie George	12.00
PC11Antowain Smith	8.00
PC12Reggie White	6.00
PC13Dan Marino	24.00
PC14Joey Galloway	6.00
PC15Kordell Stewart	12.00
PC16Terry Allen	3.00
PC17Napoleon Kaufman	6.00
PC18Curtis Martin	12.00
PC19Steve Young	10.00
PC20Rod Smith	3.00
PC21Mark Brunell	12.00
PC22Emmitt Smith	24.00
PC23Rae Carruth	6.00
PC24Brett Favre	30.00
PC25Jeff George	6.00
PC26Terry Glenn	6.00
PC27Warrick Dunn	12.00
PC28Herman Moore	6.00
PC29Cris Carter	3.00
PC30Terrell Davis	12.00

1998 UD Choice Preview

Upper Deck released a 55-card UD Choice Preview set at retail outlets. The set consists of cards from the regular 1998 UD Choice set.

		MT
Complete Set (55):		10.00
Common Player:		.10
Wax Box:		10.00
2	Rob Moore	.10
4	Larry Centers	.10
7	Jamal Anderson	.50
12	Byron Hanspard	.10
15	Jermaine Lewis	.10
20	Eric Moulds	.20
22	Bruce Smith	.10
26	Rae Carruth	.10
28	Winslow Oliver	.10
32	Bryan Cox	.10
35	Curtis Conway	.20
39	Jeff Blake	.10
40	Carl Pickens	.20
49	Deion Sanders	.30
53	Ed McCaffrey	.20
55	John Mobley	.10
58	Scott Mitchell	.10
62	Bryant Westbrook	.10
67	Reggie White	.20
70	LeRoy Butler	.10
72	Marshall Faulk	.50
76	Quentin Coryatt	.10
77	Keenan McCardell	.10
80	Jimmy Smith	.20
84	Andre Rison	.10
86	Tony Gonzalez	.10
92	Yatil Green	.10
96	Brad Johnson	.30
98	Jake Reed	.10
103	Troy Davis	.10
104	Andre Hastings	.10
110	Terry Glenn	.20
111	Ben Coates	.20
115	Danny Kanell	.10
119	Tiki Barber	.20
122	Glenn Foley	.20
124	Adrian Murrell	.20
129	Jeff George	.20
131	Darrell Russell	.10
136	Irving Fryar	.10
137	Mike Mamula	.10
143	Levon Kirkland	.10
147	Greg Lloyd	.10
150	Orlando Pace	.20
151	Isaac Bruce	.20
155	Eric Metcalf	.10
157	Tony Martin	.10
161	Merton Hanks	.10
165	J.J. Stokes	.20
168	Chad Brown	.10
173	Trent Dilfer	.30
175	Warren Sapp	.10
180	Steve McNair	.50
186	Gus Frerotte	.10
191	Chris Dishman	.10

1998 UD Choice

UD Choice was released in two series. Series One consists of a 255-card base set. The set has 165 regular cards featuring white borders and 27 full-bleed regular cards. Subsets include 30 Rookie Class cards and 30 Draw Your Own Trading Card contest winners. Three checklists round out the set. The base set is paralleled in Choice Reserve and Prime Choice Reserve. Inserts include StarQuest and Mini Bobbing Head cards. A Draw Your Own Trading Card entry was inserted in each pack. UD Choice Series Two consists of a 183-card base set, featuring the 30-card Domination Next subset (1:4). Series Two also has Choice Reserve and Prime Choice Reserve parallels. Inserts include NFL GameDay '99, StarQuest-RookQuest and Domination Next SE.

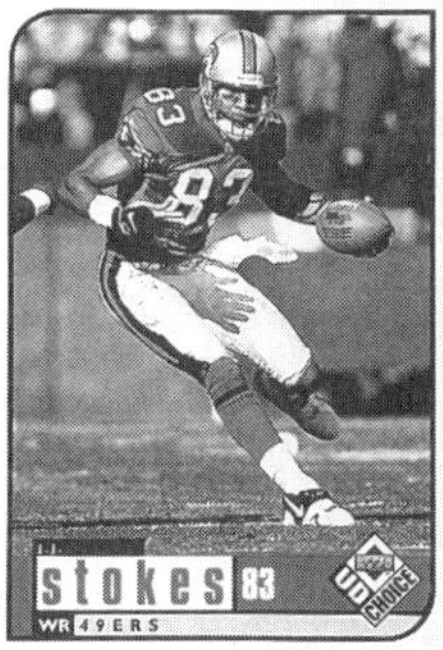

		MT
Complete Series 1 (255):		35.00
Common Player:		.10
Series 1 Wax Box:		40.00
1	Jake Plummer	.75
2	Rob Moore	.10
3	Simeon Rice	.10
4	Larry Centers	.10
5	Aeneas Williams	.10
6	Chris Gedney	.10
7	Jamal Anderson	.20
8	Michael Booker	.10
9	Ronnie Bradford	.10
10	Cornelius Bennett	.10
11	Terance Mathis	.10
12	Byron Hanspard	.20
13	Peter Boulware	.10
14	Jonathan Ogden	.10
15	Jermaine Lewis	.10
16	Tony Siragusa	.10
17	Brian Kinchen	.10
18	Michael Jackson	.10
19	Doug Flutie	.50
20	Eric Moulds	.10
21	Antowain Smith	.40
22	Bruce Smith	.10
23	Jay Riemersma	.10
24	Ruben Brown	.10
25	Fred Lane	.20
26	Rae Carruth	.10
27	Wesley Walls	.10
28	Winslow Oliver	.10
29	Tyrone Poole	.10
30	Lamar Lathon	.10
31	Anthony Johnson	.10
32	Erik Kramer	.10
33	Darnell Autry	.20
34	Bobby Engram	.10
35	Curtis Conway	.20
36	Jeff Jaeger	.10
37	Chris Penn	.10
38	Corey Dillon	.50
39	Jeff Blake	.20
40	Carl Pickens	.10
41	Ki-Jana Carter	.10
42	Reinard Wilson	.10
43	Tremain Mack	.10
44	Troy Aikman	1.00
45	Larry Allen	.10
46	Darren Woodson	.10
47	Anthony Miller	.10
48	Erik Williams	.10
49	Deion Sanders	.50
50	Rick Cunningham	.10
51	John Elway	1.00
52	Steve Atwater	.10
53	Ed McCaffrey	.10
54	Maa Tanuvasa	.10
55	John Mobley	.10
56	Bill Romanowski	.10
57	Shannon Sharpe	.20
58	Scott Mitchell	.10
59	Jason Hansen	.10
60	Herman Moore	.20
61	Luther Elliss	.10
62	Bryant Westbrook	.10
63	Kevin Abrams	.10
64	Brett Favre	2.00
65	Gilbert Brown	.10
66	Antonio Freeman	.20
67	Reggie White	.20
68	Mark Chmura	.10
69	Seth Joyner	.10
70	LeRoy Butler	.10
71	Marvin Harrison	.20
72	Marshall Faulk	.20
73	Ken Dilger	.10
74	Steve Morrison	.10
75	Zack Crockett	.10
76	Quentin Coryatt	.10
77	Keenan McCardell	.10
78	Mark Brunell	.75
79	Renaldo Wynn	.10
80	Jimmy Smith	.10
81	James O. Stewart	.10
82	Kevin Hardy	.10
83	Marcus Allen	.20
84	Andre Rison	.10
85	Pete Stoyanovich	.10
86	Tony Gonzalez	.20
87	Derrick Thomas	.10
88	Rich Gannon	.10
89	Elvis Grbac	.10
90	Dan Marino	1.50
91	Lawrence Phillips	.10
92	Yatil Green	.20
93	Zach Thomas	.10
94	Olindo Mare	.10
95	Charles Jordan	.10
96	Brad Johnson	.20
97	Cris Carter	.20
98	Jake Reed	.10
99	Ed McDaniel	.10
100	Dwayne Rudd	.10
101	Leroy Hoard	.10
102	Danny Wuerffel	.10
103	Troy Davis	.10
104	Andre Hastings	.10
105	Nicky Savoie	.10
106	Willie Roaf	.10
107	Ray Zellars	.10
108	Tedy Bruschi	.10
109	Drew Bledsoe	1.00
110	Terry Glenn	.20
111	Ben Coates	.10
112	Willie Clay	.10
113	Chris Slade	.10
114	Larry Whigham	.10
115	Danny Kanell	.10
116	Jessie Armstead	.10
117	Phillipi Sparks	.10
118	Michael Strahan	.10
119	Tiki Barber	.20
120	Charles Way	.10
121	Chris Calloway	.10
122	Glenn Foley	.10
123	Wayne Chrebet	.10
124	Kyle Brady	.10
125	Keyshawn Johnson	.20
126	Aaron Glenn	.10
127	James Farrior	.10
128	Victor Green	.10
129	Jeff George	.20
130	Rickey Dudley	.10
131	Darrell Russell	.10
132	Tim Brown	.10
133	James Trapp	.10
134	Napoleon Kaufman	.40
135	Bobby Hoying	.10
136	Irving Fryar	.10
137	Mike Mamula	.10
138	Troy Vincent	.10
139	Bobby Taylor	.10
140	Chris Boniol	.10
141	Jerome Bettis	.20
142	Charles Johnson	.10
143	Levon Kirkland	.10
144	Carnell Lake	.10
145	Will Blackwell	.10
146	Tim Lester	.10
147	Greg Lloyd	.10
148	Tony Banks	.20
149	Ryan McNeil	.10
150	Orlando Pace	.10
151	Isaac Bruce	.20
152	Eddie Kennison	.20
153	Leslie O'Neal	.10
154	Darren Bennett	.10
155	Natrone Means	.20
156	Junior Seau	.20
157	Tony Martin	.10
158	Rodney Harrison	.10
159	Freddie Jones	.10
160	Terrell Owens	.20
161	Merton Hanks	.10
162	Chris Doleman	.10
163	Steve Young	.50
164	Chuck Levy	.10
165	J.J. Stokes	.20
166	Ken Norton	.10
167	Bennie Blades	.10
168	Chad Brown	.10
169	Warren Moon	.20
170	Cortez Kennedy	.10
171	Darryl Williams	.10
172	Michael Sinclair	.10
173	Trent Dilfer	.20
174	Mike Alstott	.40
175	Warren Sapp	.10
176	Reidel Anthony	.20
177	Derrick Brooks	.10
178	Horace Copeland	.10
179	Hardy Nickerson	.10
180	Steve McNair	.50
181	Anthony Dorsett	.10
182	Chris Sanders	.10
183	Derrick Mason	.10
184	Eddie George	1.00
185	Blaine Bishop	.10
186	Gus Frerotte	.10
187	Terry Allen	.10
188	Darrell Green	.10
189	Ken Harvey	.10
190	Matt Turk	.10
191	Chris Dishman	.10
192	Keith Thibodeaux	.10
193	*Peyton Manning*	5.00
194	*Ryan Leaf*	5.00
195	*Charles Woodson*	2.50
196	*Andre Wadsworth*	.30
197	*Keith Brooking*	.10
198	*Jason Peter*	.30
199	*Curtis Enis*	2.50
200	*Randy Moss*	12.00
201	*Tre Thomas*	.10
202	*Robert Edwards*	2.50
203	*Kevin Dyson*	1.00
204	*Fred Taylor*	2.50
205	*Corey Chavous*	.10
206	*Grant Wistrom*	.10
207	*Vonnie Holliday*	.40
208	*Brian Simmons*	.10
209	*Jeremy Staat*	.10
210	*Alonzo Mayes*	.10
211	*Anthony Simmons*	.10
212	*Sam Cowart*	.10
213	*Flozell Adams*	.10
214	*Terry Fair*	.10
215	*Germane Crowell*	.40
216	*Robert Holcombe*	2.00
217	*Jacquez Green*	2.00
218	*Skip Hicks*	.50
219	*Takeo Spikes*	.40
220	*Az-Zahir Hakim*	.10
221	*Ahman Green*	2.00
222	*Chris Fuamatu-Ma'afal*	.10
223	Darnell Autry	.10
224	John Randle	.10
225	Scott Mitchell	.10
226	Troy Aikman	.30
227	Terrell Davis	.30
228	Kordell Stewart	.30
229	Warrick Dunn	.20
230	Craig Newsome	.10
231	Brett Favre	.60
232	Kordell Stewart	.30
233	Barry Sanders	.50
234	Dan Marino	.50
235	Dan Marino	.50
236	Tamarick Vanover	.10
237	Warrick Dunn	.20
238	Andre Rison	.10
239	Dan Marino	.50
240	Reggie White	.10
241	Tim Brown	.10
242	Joe Montana	.30
243	Robert Brooks	.10
244	Danny Kanell	.10
245	Emmitt Smith	.50
246	Barry Sanders	.50
247	Brett Favre	.60
248	Brett Favre	.60
249	Jerome Bettis	.10
250	Kordell Stewart	.30
251	Terrell Davis	.30
252	Drew Bledsoe	.30
253	Troy Aikman	.30
254	Dan Marino	.50
255	Warrick Dunn	.30

1998 UD Choice Choice Reserve

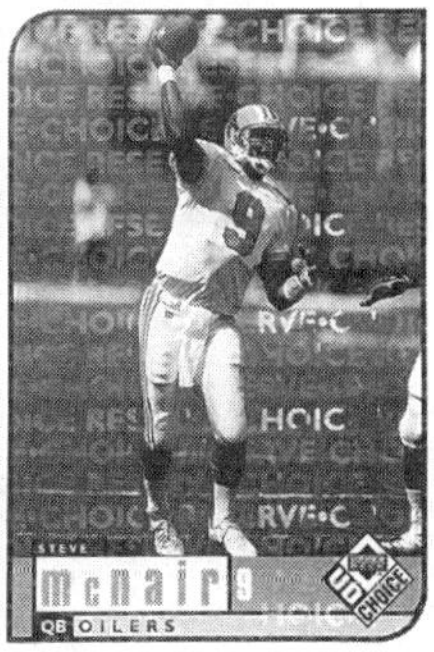

Choice Reserve is a parallel of the entire 438-card UD Choice set (255 cards from Series One and 183 from Series Two). The parallel was inserted one per six packs in each series.

	MT
Choice Reserve Cards:	5x-10x
Choice Reserve Rookies:	3x

1998 UD Choice Prime Choice Reserve

Prime Choice Reserve is a parallel of the complete 438-card UD Choice base set (255 cards from Series One and 183 from Series Two). This hobby-only set has "Prime Choice Reserve" foil-stamped on the card fronts and is numbered to 100.

	MT
PC Reserve Cards:	40x-80x
PC Reserve Rookies:	12x-25x

1998 UD Choice Mini Bobbing Head

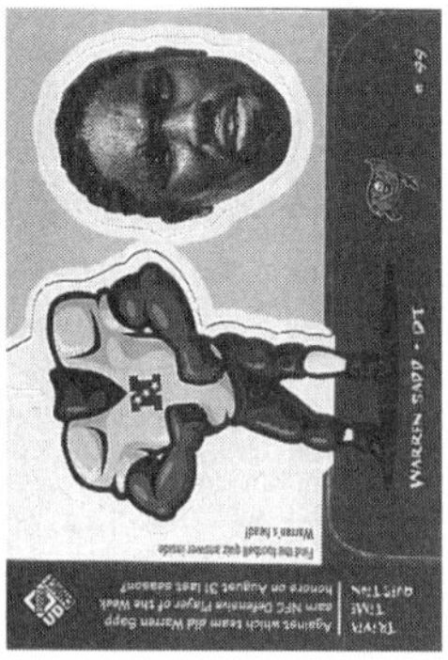

Mini Bobbing Head cards were an insert in Series One. The 30-card set consists of cards that can be folded into a stand-up figure with a removable bobbing head. The cards were inserted one per four packs.

		MT
Complete Set (30):		15.00
Common Player:		.25
M1	Jake Plummer	1.25
M2	Jamal Anderson	.25
M3	Michael Jackson	.25
M4	Bruce Smith	.25
M5	Rae Carruth	.25
M6	Curtis Conway	.25
M7	Jeff Blake	.50
M8	Troy Aikman	1.50
M9	Michael Irvin	.50
M10	Terrell Davis	1.50
M11	Barry Sanders	3.00
M12	Herman Moore	.50
M13	Reggie White	.50
M14	Dorsey Levens	.50
M15	Marvin Harrison	.25
M16	Keenan McCardell	.25
M17	Andre Rison	.25
M18	Dan Marino	3.00
M19	Curtis Martin	1.00
M20	Keyshawn Johnson	.25
M21	Tim Brown	.25
M22	Kordell Stewart	1.50
M23	Greg Lloyd	.25
M24	Junior Seau	.25
M25	Jerry Rice	1.50
M26	Merton Hanks	.25
M27	Joey Galloway	.50
M28	Warrick Dunn	1.25
M29	Warren Sapp	.25
M30	Darrell Green	.25

1998 UD Choice Starquest Blue

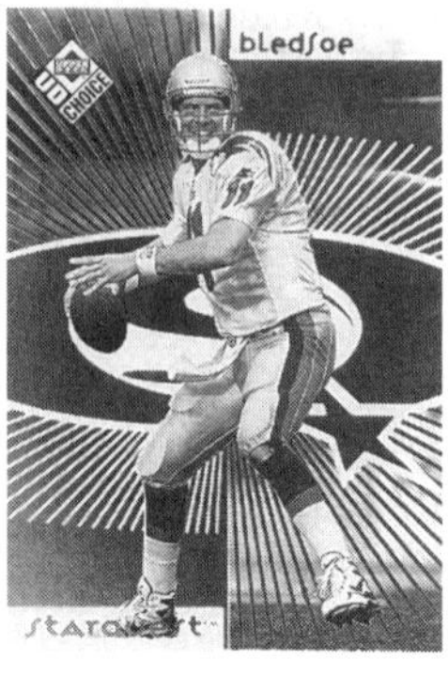

StarQuest is a 30-card, four-tiered insert in UD Choice Series One. Each tier has a different insertion rate and foil color. StarQuest 1-Star cards were seeded 1:1, 2-Star cards were found 1:7, 3-Stars were inserted 1:23 and 4-Star cards are numbered to 100.

		MT
Complete Set (30):		15.00
Common Player:		.25
Green Cards:		2x-4x
Red Cards:		5x-10x
Gold Cards:		40x-80x
W1	Warren Moon	.25
W2	Jerry Rice	1.00
W3	Jeff George	.25
W4	Brett Favre	2.00
W5	Junior Seau	.25
W6	Cris Carter	.25
W7	John Elway	1.00
W8	Troy Aikman	1.00
W9	Steve Young	.75
W10	Kordell Stewart	1.00
W11	Drew Bledsoe	1.00
W12	Dorsey Levens	.50
W13	Dan Marino	1.75
W14	Joey Galloway	.50
W15	Antonio Freeman	.50
W16	Jake Plummer	1.00
W17	Corey Dillon	.75
W18	Mark Brunell	.75
W19	Andre Rison	.25
W20	Barry Sanders	1.50
W21	Deion Sanders	.60
W22	Emmitt Smith	1.75
W23	Antowain Smith	.60
W24	Herman Moore	.50
W25	Napoleon Kaufman	.60
W26	Jerome Bettis	.50
W27	Eddie George	1.00
W28	Warrick Dunn	1.00
W29	Adrian Murrell	.25
W30	Terrell Davis	1.00

1998 UD3

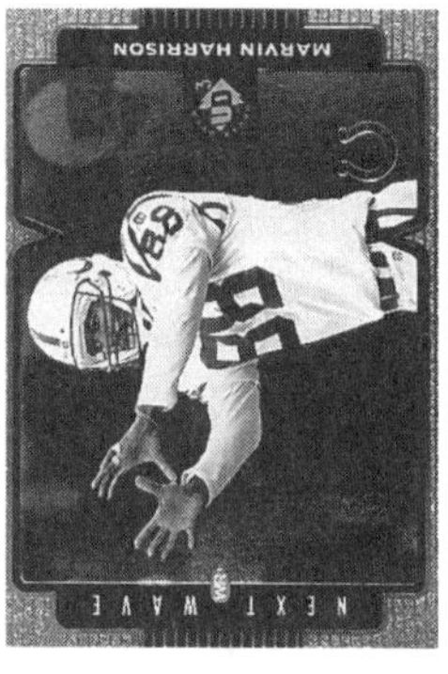

UD Cubed Football consists of a 270-card base set built from three 30-card subsets. Each subset is printed on three different technologies. Future Shock features rookies, Next Wave has young stars and Upper Realm highlights the established stars. Future Shock Embossed cards are inserted 1:6, Light F/X is seeded 1:12 and Rainbow Foil cards are found 1:1.33. Next Wave Embossed are seeded 1:4, Light F/X are found 1:1.5 and Rainbow Foil cards are inserted 1:12. Upper Realm Embossed cards are seeded 1:1.25, Light F/X are found 1:6 and Rainbow Foil cards are inserted 1:24. Die-cut versions of each card were also produced.

		MT
Complete Set (270):		750.00
Common Player (1-30):		2.50
#1-30 Inserted 1:6		
Common Player (31-60):		1.25
#31-60 Inserted 1:4		
Common Player (61-90):		.50
#61-90 Inserted 1:1.25		
Common Player (91-120):		5.00
#91-120 Inserted 1:12		
Common Player (121-150):		.50
#121-150 Inserted 1:1.5		
Common Player (151-180):		2.50
#151-180 Inserted 1:6		
Common Player (181-210):		.75
#181-210 Inserted 1:1.33		
Common Player (211-240):		5.00
#211-240 Inserted 1:12		
Common Player (241-270):		7.00
#241-270 Inserted 1:24		
Wax Box:		75.00
1	Peyton Manning	25.00
2	Ryan Leaf	25.00
3	Andre Wadsworth	5.00
4	Charles Woodson	12.00
5	Curtis Enis	12.00
6	Grant Wistrom	2.50
7	Greg Ellis	2.50
8	Fred Taylor	12.00
9	Duane Starks	5.00
10	Keith Brooking	2.50
11	Takeo Spikes	5.00
12	Jason Peter	5.00
13	Anthony Simmons	5.00
14	Kevin Dyson	8.00
15	Brian Simmons	5.00
16	Robert Edwards	15.00
17	Randy Moss	40.00
18	John Avery	8.00
19	Marcus Nash	8.00
20	Jerome Pathon	5.00
21	Jacquez Green	8.00
22	Robert Holcombe	8.00
23	Patrick Johnson	5.00
24	Germane Crowell	5.00
25	Joe Jurevicius	5.00
26	Skip Hicks	5.00
27	Ahman Green	8.00
28	Brian Griese	8.00
29	Hines Ward	8.00
30	Tavian Banks	10.00
31	Warrick Dunn	8.00
32	Jake Plummer	8.00
33	Derrick Mayes	1.25
34	Napoleon Kaufman	2.50
35	Jamal Anderson	1.25
36	Marvin Harrison	1.25
37	Jermaine Lewis	1.25
38	Corey Dillon	6.00
39	Keyshawn Johnson	2.50
40	Mike Alstott	2.50
41	Bobby Hoying	2.50
42	Keenan McCardell	1.25
43	Will Blackwell	1.25
44	Peter Boulware	1.25
45	Tony Banks	2.50
46	Rod Smith	1.25
47	Tony Gonzalez	1.25
48	Antowain Smith	4.00
49	Rae Carruth	1.25
50	J.J. Stokes	1.25
51	Brad Johnson	2.50
52	Shawn Springs	1.25
53	Elvis Grbac	1.25
54	Jimmy Smith	2.50
55	Terry Glenn	2.50
56	Tiki Barber	1.25
57	Gus Frerotte	1.25
58	Danny Wuerffel	1.25
59	Fred Lane	2.50
60	Todd Collins	1.25
61	Barry Sanders	8.00
62	Troy Aikman	4.00
63	Dan Marino	6.00
64	Drew Bledsoe	4.00
65	Dorsey Levens	1.00
66	Jerome Bettis	1.00
67	John Elway	4.00
68	Steve Young	3.00
69	Terrell Davis	4.00
70	Kordell Stewart	3.00
71	Jeff George	1.00
72	Emmitt Smith	6.00
73	Irving Fryar	.50
74	Brett Favre	8.00
75	Eddie George	3.00
76	Terry Allen	.50
77	Warren Moon	1.00
78	Mark Brunell	3.00
79	Robert Smith	1.00
80	Jerry Rice	4.00
81	Tim Brown	1.00
82	Carl Pickens	1.00
83	Joey Galloway	1.00
84	Herman Moore	1.00
85	Adrian Murrell	1.00
86	Thurman Thomas	1.00
87	Robert Brooks	.50
88	Michael Irvin	1.00
89	Andre Rison	1.00
90	Marshall Faulk	1.00
91	Peyton Manning	45.00
92	Ryan Leaf	45.00
93	Andre Wadsworth	8.00
94	Charles Woodson	20.00
95	Curtis Enis	20.00
96	Grant Wistrom	5.00
97	Greg Ellis	5.00
98	Fred Taylor	20.00
99	Duane Starks	8.00
100	Keith Brooking	8.00
101	Takeo Spikes	8.00
102	Jason Peter	8.00
103	Anthony Simmons	8.00
104	Kevin Dyson	12.00
105	Brian Simmons	5.00
106	Robert Edwards	25.00
107	Randy Moss	60.00
108	John Avery	12.00
109	Marcus Nash	12.00
110	Jerome Pathon	8.00
111	Jacquez Green	12.00
112	Robert Holcombe	12.00
113	Patrick Johnson	8.00
114	Germane Crowell	8.00
115	Joe Jurevicius	8.00
116	Skip Hicks	8.00
117	Ahman Green	12.00
118	Brian Griese	12.00
119	Hines Ward	12.00
120	Tavian Banks	15.00
121	Warrick Dunn	4.00
122	Jake Plummer	4.00
123	Derrick Mayes	.50
124	Napoleon Kaufman	1.00
125	Jamal Anderson	1.00
126	Marvin Harrison	1.00
127	Jermaine Lewis	.50
128	Corey Dillon	3.00
129	Keyshawn Johnson	1.00
130	Mike Alstott	1.00
131	Bobby Hoying	1.00
132	Keenan McCardell	.50
133	Will Blackwell	.50
134	Peter Boulware	.50
135	Tony Banks	1.00
136	Rod Smith	.50
137	Tony Gonzalez	.50
138	Antowain Smith	2.00
139	Rae Carruth	.50
140	J.J. Stokes	.50
141	Brad Johnson	1.00
142	Shawn Springs	.50
143	Elvis Grbac	.50
144	Jimmy Smith	1.00
145	Terry Glenn	1.00
146	Tiki Barber	1.00
147	Gus Frerotte	.50
148	Danny Wuerffel	.50
149	Fred Lane	1.00
150	Todd Collins	.50
151	Barry Sanders	20.00
152	Troy Aikman	10.00
153	Dan Marino	15.00
154	Drew Bledsoe	10.00
155	Dorsey Levens	5.00
156	Jerome Bettis	5.00
157	John Elway	10.00
158	Steve Young	8.00
159	Terrell Davis	10.00
160	Kordell Stewart	8.00
161	Jeff George	5.00
162	Emmitt Smith	15.00
163	Irving Fryar	2.50
164	Brett Favre	20.00
165	Eddie George	10.00
166	Terry Allen	2.50
167	Warren Moon	5.00
168	Mark Brunell	8.00
169	Robert Smith	5.00
170	Jerry Rice	10.00
171	Tim Brown	5.00
172	Carl Pickens	5.00
173	Joey Galloway	5.00
174	Herman Moore	5.00
175	Adrian Murrell	5.00
176	Thurman Thomas	5.00
177	Robert Brooks	2.50
178	Michael Irvin	5.00
179	Andre Rison	2.50
180	Marshall Faulk	5.00
181	*Peyton Manning*	10.00
182	*Ryan Leaf*	10.00
183	*Andre Wadsworth*	1.50
184	*Charles Woodson*	5.00
185	*Curtis Enis*	5.00
186	*Grant Wistrom*	.75
187	*Greg Ellis*	1.50
188	*Fred Taylor*	5.00
189	*Duane Starks*	1.50
190	*Keith Brooking*	1.50
191	*Takeo Spikes*	1.50
192	*Jason Peter*	1.50
193	*Anthony Simmons*	1.50
194	*Kevin Dyson*	3.00
195	*Brian Simmons*	.75
196	*Robert Edwards*	6.00
197	*Randy Moss*	15.00
198	*John Avery*	3.00
199	*Marcus Nash*	3.00
200	*Jerome Pathon*	1.50
201	*Jacquez Green*	3.00
202	*Robert Holcombe*	3.00
203	*Patrick Johnson*	1.50
204	*Germane Crowell*	1.50
205	*Joe Jurevicius*	1.50
206	*Skip Hicks*	1.50
207	*Ahman Green*	3.00
208	*Brian Griese*	3.00
209	*Hines Ward*	3.00
210	*Tavian Banks*	4.00
211	Warrick Dunn	18.00
212	Jake Plummer	18.00
213	Derrick Mayes	4.00
214	Napoleon Kaufman	6.00
215	Jamal Anderson	6.00
216	Marvin Harrison	6.00
217	Jermaine Lewis	4.00
218	Corey Dillon	12.00
219	Keyshawn Johnson	6.00
220	Mike Alstott	6.00
221	Bobby Hoying	6.00
222	Keenan McCardell	4.00
223	Will Blackwell	4.00
224	Peter Boulware	4.00
225	Tony Banks	6.00
226	Rod Smith	6.00
227	Tony Gonzalez	4.00
228	Antowain Smith	10.00
229	Rae Carruth	4.00
230	J.J. Stokes	4.00
231	Brad Johnson	6.00
232	Shawn Springs	4.00
233	Elvis Grbac	4.00
234	Jimmy Smith	6.00
235	Terry Glenn	6.00
236	Tiki Barber	6.00
237	Gus Frerotte	4.00
238	Danny Wuerffel	4.00
239	Fred Lane	6.00
240	Todd Collins	4.00
241	Barry Sanders	50.00
242	Troy Aikman	25.00
243	Dan Marino	40.00
244	Drew Bledsoe	25.00
245	Dorsey Levens	10.00
246	Jerome Bettis	10.00
247	John Elway	25.00
248	Steve Young	18.00
249	Terrell Davis	25.00
250	Kordell Stewart	20.00
251	Jeff George	10.00
252	Emmitt Smith	40.00
253	Irving Fryar	7.00
254	Brett Favre	50.00
255	Eddie George	20.00
256	Terry Allen	7.00
257	Warren Moon	10.00
258	Mark Brunell	20.00
259	Robert Smith	10.00
260	Jerry Rice	25.00
261	Tim Brown	7.00
262	Carl Pickens	7.00
263	Joey Galloway	10.00
264	Herman Moore	10.00
265	Adrian Murrell	7.00
266	Thurman Thomas	7.00
267	Robert Brooks	7.00
268	Michael Irvin	10.00
269	Andre Rison	7.00
270	Marshall Faulk	10.00

1998 UD3 Die Cuts

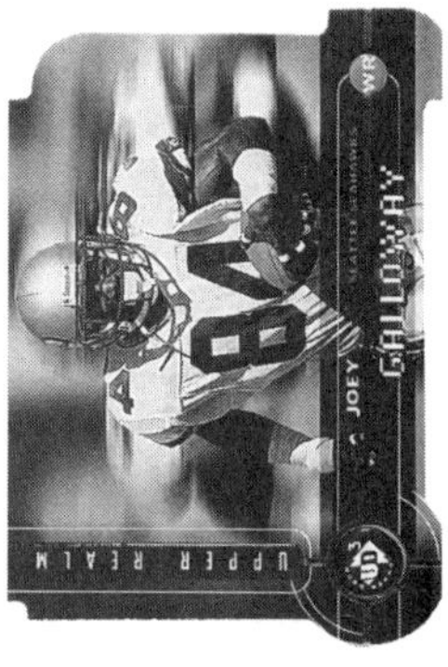

Die-cut versions were produced of each UD Cubed base card. The Embossed Die-Cut parallel is numbered to 2,000, Light F/X Die-Cut parallel cards are numbered to 1,000 and Rainbow Foil Die-Cuts are numbered to 100.

		MT
Common Player (1-90):		3.00
Production 2,000 Sets		
Common Player (91-180):		5.00
Production 1,000 Sets		
Common Player (181-270):		20.00
Production 100 Sets		
1	Peyton Manning	35.00
2	Ryan Leaf	35.00
3	Andre Wadsworth	6.00
4	Charles Woodson	15.00
5	Curtis Enis	15.00
6	Grant Wistrom	3.00
7	Greg Ellis	3.00
8	Fred Taylor	15.00
9	Duane Starks	6.00
10	Keith Brooking	3.00
11	Takeo Spikes	6.00
12	Jason Peter	6.00
13	Anthony Simmons	6.00
14	Kevin Dyson	10.00
15	Brian Simmons	6.00
16	Robert Edwards	20.00
17	Randy Moss	40.00
18	John Avery	10.00
19	Marcus Nash	10.00
20	Jerome Pathon	6.00
21	Jacquez Green	10.00
22	Robert Holcombe	10.00
23	Patrick Johnson	6.00
24	Germane Crowell	6.00
25	Joe Jurevicius	6.00
26	Skip Hicks	6.00
27	Ahman Green	10.00
28	Brian Griese	10.00
29	Hines Ward	10.00
30	Tavian Banks	12.00
31	Warrick Dunn	12.00
32	Jake Plummer	12.00
33	Derrick Mayes	3.00
34	Napoleon Kaufman	6.00
35	Jamal Anderson	3.00

36	Marvin Harrison	3.00	83	Joey Galloway	6.00	130	Mike Alstott	8.00	177	Robert Brooks	5.00	224	Peter Boulware	20.00

No.	Player	Price
36	Marvin Harrison	3.00
37	Jermaine Lewis	3.00
38	Corey Dillon	10.00
39	Keyshawn Johnson	6.00
40	Mike Alstott	6.00
41	Bobby Hoying	6.00
42	Keenan McCardell	3.00
43	Will Blackwell	3.00
44	Peter Boulware	3.00
45	Tony Banks	6.00
46	Rod Smith	3.00
47	Tony Gonzalez	3.00
48	Antowain Smith	8.00
49	Rae Carruth	3.00
50	J.J. Stokes	3.00
51	Brad Johnson	6.00
52	Shawn Springs	3.00
53	Elvis Grbac	3.00
54	Jimmy Smith	6.00
55	Terry Glenn	6.00
56	Tiki Barber	3.00
57	Gus Frerotte	3.00
58	Danny Wuerffel	3.00
59	Fred Lane	6.00
60	Todd Collins	3.00
61	Barry Sanders	25.00
62	Troy Aikman	12.00
63	Dan Marino	20.00
64	Drew Bledsoe	12.00
65	Dorsey Levens	6.00
66	Jerome Bettis	6.00
67	John Elway	12.00
68	Steve Young	10.00
69	Terrell Davis	12.00
70	Kordell Stewart	10.00
71	Jeff George	6.00
72	Emmitt Smith	20.00
73	Irving Fryar	3.00
74	Brett Favre	25.00
75	Eddie George	10.00
76	Terry Allen	3.00
77	Warren Moon	6.00
78	Mark Brunell	10.00
79	Robert Smith	6.00
80	Jerry Rice	12.00
81	Tim Brown	6.00
82	Carl Pickens	6.00
83	Joey Galloway	6.00
84	Herman Moore	6.00
85	Adrian Murrell	6.00
86	Thurman Thomas	6.00
87	Robert Brooks	3.00
88	Michael Irvin	6.00
89	Andre Rison	3.00
90	Marshall Faulk	6.00
91	Peyton Manning	50.00
92	Ryan Leaf	50.00
93	Andre Wadsworth	10.00
94	Charles Woodson	20.00
95	Curtis Enis	20.00
96	Grant Wistrom	5.00
97	Greg Ellis	10.00
98	Fred Taylor	20.00
99	Duane Starks	10.00
100	Keith Brooking	10.00
101	Takeo Spikes	10.00
102	Jason Peter	10.00
103	Anthony Simmons	10.00
104	Kevin Dyson	12.00
105	Brian Simmons	5.00
106	Robert Edwards	25.00
107	Randy Moss	55.00
108	John Avery	12.00
109	Marcus Nash	12.00
110	Jerome Pathon	10.00
111	Jacquez Green	15.00
112	Robert Holcombe	15.00
113	Patrick Johnson	10.00
114	Germane Crowell	10.00
115	Joe Jurevicius	10.00
116	Skip Hicks	10.00
117	Ahman Green	15.00
118	Brian Griese	15.00
119	Hines Ward	12.00
120	Tavian Banks	15.00
121	Warrick Dunn	20.00
122	Jake Plummer	20.00
123	Derrick Mayes	5.00
124	Napoleon Kaufman	10.00
125	Jamal Anderson	8.00
126	Marvin Harrison	8.00
127	Jermaine Lewis	5.00
128	Corey Dillon	15.00
129	Keyshawn Johnson	8.00
130	Mike Alstott	8.00
131	Bobby Hoying	8.00
132	Keenan McCardell	5.00
133	Will Blackwell	5.00
134	Peter Boulware	5.00
135	Tony Banks	8.00
136	Rod Smith	5.00
137	Tony Gonzalez	5.00
138	Antowain Smith	12.00
139	Rae Carruth	5.00
140	J.J. Stokes	5.00
141	Brad Johnson	8.00
142	Shawn Springs	5.00
143	Elvis Grbac	5.00
144	Jimmy Smith	8.00
145	Terry Glenn	8.00
146	Tiki Barber	8.00
147	Gus Frerotte	5.00
148	Danny Wuerffel	5.00
149	Fred Lane	8.00
150	Todd Collins	5.00
151	Barry Sanders	50.00
152	Troy Aikman	25.00
153	Dan Marino	40.00
154	Drew Bledsoe	25.00
155	Dorsey Levens	8.00
156	Jerome Bettis	8.00
157	John Elway	25.00
158	Steve Young	20.00
159	Terrell Davis	25.00
160	Kordell Stewart	20.00
161	Jeff George	8.00
162	Emmitt Smith	40.00
163	Irving Fryar	5.00
164	Brett Favre	50.00
165	Eddie George	20.00
166	Terry Allen	5.00
167	Warren Moon	8.00
168	Mark Brunell	20.00
169	Robert Smith	8.00
170	Jerry Rice	25.00
171	Tim Brown	8.00
172	Carl Pickens	8.00
173	Joey Galloway	8.00
174	Herman Moore	8.00
175	Adrian Murrell	8.00
176	Thurman Thomas	8.00
177	Robert Brooks	5.00
178	Michael Irvin	8.00
179	Andre Rison	5.00
180	Marshall Faulk	8.00
181	Peyton Manning	200.00
182	Ryan Leaf	200.00
183	Andre Wadsworth	40.00
184	Charles Woodson	60.00
185	Curtis Enis	75.00
186	Grant Wistrom	20.00
187	Greg Ellis	20.00
188	Fred Taylor	75.00
189	Duane Starks	20.00
190	Keith Brooking	20.00
191	Takeo Spikes	20.00
192	Jason Peter	20.00
193	Anthony Simmons	20.00
194	Kevin Dyson	50.00
195	Brian Simmons	20.00
196	Robert Edwards	100.00
197	Randy Moss	300.00
198	John Avery	50.00
199	Marcus Nash	50.00
200	Jerome Pathon	20.00
201	Jacquez Green	50.00
202	Robert Holcombe	60.00
203	Patrick Johnson	20.00
204	Germane Crowell	40.00
205	Joe Jurevicius	20.00
206	Skip Hicks	40.00
207	Ahman Green	50.00
208	Brian Griese	50.00
209	Hines Ward	50.00
210	Tavian Banks	50.00
211	Warrick Dunn	85.00
212	Jake Plummer	85.00
213	Derrick Mayes	20.00
214	Napoleon Kaufman	40.00
215	Jamal Anderson	30.00
216	Marvin Harrison	30.00
217	Jermaine Lewis	20.00
218	Corey Dillon	60.00
219	Keyshawn Johnson	30.00
220	Mike Alstott	30.00
221	Bobby Hoying	30.00
222	Keenan McCardell	20.00
223	Will Blackwell	20.00
224	Peter Boulware	20.00
225	Tony Banks	30.00
226	Rod Smith	20.00
227	Tony Gonzalez	20.00
228	Antowain Smith	50.00
229	Rae Carruth	20.00
230	J.J. Stokes	20.00
231	Brad Johnson	30.00
232	Shawn Springs	20.00
233	Elvis Grbac	20.00
234	Jimmy Smith	30.00
235	Terry Glenn	30.00
236	Tiki Barber	30.00
237	Gus Frerotte	20.00
238	Danny Wuerffel	20.00
239	Fred Lane	30.00
240	Todd Collins	20.00
241	Barry Sanders	200.00
242	Troy Aikman	100.00
243	Dan Marino	175.00
244	Drew Bledsoe	100.00
245	Dorsey Levens	30.00
246	Jerome Bettis	30.00
247	John Elway	100.00
248	Steve Young	85.00
249	Terrell Davis	100.00
250	Kordell Stewart	100.00
251	Jeff George	30.00
252	Emmitt Smith	175.00
253	Irving Fryar	20.00
254	Brett Favre	200.00
255	Eddie George	85.00
256	Terry Allen	20.00
257	Warren Moon	30.00
258	Mark Brunell	100.00
259	Robert Smith	30.00
260	Jerry Rice	100.00
261	Tim Brown	30.00
262	Carl Pickens	30.00
263	Joey Galloway	30.00
264	Herman Moore	30.00
265	Adrian Murrell	30.00
266	Thurman Thomas	30.00
267	Robert Brooks	20.00
268	Michael Irvin	30.00
269	Andre Rison	20.00
270	Marshall Faulk	30.00

Hockey Market Report

Pacific, Topps And Upper Deck Will Remain The Three Manufacturers Of Hockey Cards This Season

When Pinnacle Brands — and its Donruss subsidiary — filed for bankruptcy in August, two of the four companies that produced hockey cards last season were suddenly out of business. That fueled speculation among hockey card collectors that companies such as Fleer/SkyBox, Playoff or Collector's Edge would scramble to fill the void left by these two long-time manufacturers. While some of those companies may have expressed an interest in becoming hockey card manufacturers, it appears as if hockey is content, for the time being at least, with its three primary licensees, They consist of Pacific, Upper Deck and Topps, which returned to the hockey card market this season after a two-year absence.

"After the bankruptcy filing of Pinnacle and Donruss, we had a lot of interest expressed about obtaining licensing, but our view was that it made sense to see what happens this year in the hockey card market and not rush into anything," said Ted Saskin, senior director of licensing and business affairs for the NHL Players Association. "We'll make an assessment at the end of this season, I think the fact that there are fewer products out there really bodes well for hockey collectors and the market as a whole."

One brand that will be returning this year is the Be A Player, but it will be produced by a new company. In the Game, based out of Toronto, has been granted the license to produce this autograph-driven set.

Be A Player was produced by Pinnacle the last two seasons, and by Upper Deck for two season before that. Sales of BAP had slipped the last two years, primarily because Pinnacle did not have access to autographs from Wayne Gretzky, an Upper Deck spokesman. This year, however, Gretzky's autograph will again be part of the Be A Player product, along with game used stick and jersey insert cards.

So this year's lineup of hockey card manufacturers is finalized — Upper Deck, Pacific and Topps will produce multiple brands, while In The Game will issue the Be A Player set. Does that mean Playoff or Fleer/SkyBox has a shot to get a license next year?

"We've really only had the most preliminary discussions with Fleer and Playoff," said Saskin. "It's inevitable that we'll have more discussions with them in the future.

With the NBA lockout wiping out most of the first two months of the season, the NHL is currently in the pro sports spotlight. The league is hoping that the increased attention will help boost hockey card sales in '98-99.

HOCKEY

1997-98 Donruss

Donruss Hockey consists of a 230-card base set with two parallels and five inserts. The base cards feature a full-bleed player photo with a darkened bar on the left and bottom to give the appearance of a border. The parallels are Press Proofs Gold and Silver. The inserts include Line to Line, Elite, Between the Pipes, Red Alert and Rated Rookies.

		MT
Complete Set (230):		25.00
Common Player:		.10
Wax Box:		45.00
1	Peter Forsberg	1.25
2	Steve Yzerman	1.25
3	Eric Lindros	1.50
4	Mark Messier	.40
5	Patrick Roy	2.00
6	Jeremy Roenick	.25
7	Paul Kariya	1.50
8	Valeri Bure	.10
9	Dominik Hasek	.75
10	Doug Gilmour	.20
11	Garth Snow	.10
12	Todd Bertuzzi	.10
13	Chris Osgood	.40
14	Jarome Iginla	.20
15	Lonny Bohonos	.10
16	Jeff O'Neill	.10
17	Daniel Alfredsson	.20
18	Daymond Langkow	.20
19	Alexei Yashin	.20
20	Byron Dafoe	.10
21	Mike Peca	.10
22	Jim Carey	.30
23	Pat Verbeek	.10
24	Terry Ryan	.10
25	Adam Oates	.20
26	Kevin Hatcher	.10
27	Ken Wregget	.10
28	Pierre Turgeon	.20
29	John LeClair	.50
30	Jere Lehtinen	.10
31	Jamie Storr	.10
32	Doug Weight	.20
33	Tommy Salo	.20
34	Bernie Nicholls	.10
35	Jocelyn Thibault	.20
36	Dale Hawerchuk	.20
37	Chris Chelios	.20
38	Kirk Muller	.10
39	Steve Sullivan	.10
40	Andy Moog	.20
41	Martin Gelinas	.10
42	Shayne Corson	.10
43	Curtis Joseph	.30
44	Donald Audette	.10
45	Rick Tocchet	.10
46	Craig Janney	.10
47	Geoff Courtnall	.10
48	Wade Redden	.10
49	Steve Rucchin	.10
50	Ethan Moreau	.10
51	Steve Shields	.10
52	Jamie Pushor	.10
53	Saku Koivu	.40
54	Oleg Tverdovsky	.10
55	Jeff Friesen	.10
56	Chris Gratton	.20
57	Wendel Clark	.10
58	John Vanbiesbrouck	.75
59	Trevor Kidd	.20
60	Sandis Ozolinsh	.10
61	Dave Andreychuk	.10
62	Travis Green	.20
63	Paul Coffey	.20
64	Roman Turek	.10
65	Vladimir Konstantinov	.20
66	Ray Bourque	.20
67	Wayne Primeau	.10
68	Todd Harvey	.10
69	Derek King	.10
70	Adam Graves	.10
71	Brett Hull	.40
72	Scott Niedermayer	.10
73	Mike Vernon	.20
74	Brian Holzinger	.10
75	Dainius Zubrus	.25
76	Patrick Lalime	.20
77	Corey Schwab	.10
78	Alexandre Daigle	.10
79	Geoff Sanderson	.10
80	Dave Gagner	.10
81	Jose Theodore	.20
82	Sergei Fedorov	.75
83	Keith Tkachuk	.40
84	Owen Nolan	.20
85	Brandon Convery	.10
86	Trevor Linden	.10
87	Landon Wilson	.10
88	Claude Lemieux	.10
89	Dimitri Khristich	.10
90	Luc Robitaille	.10
91	Todd Warriner	.10
92	Kelly Hrudey	.10
93	Mike Dunham	.10
94	Mike Grier	.20
95	Joe Juneau	.10
96	Alexei Zhamnov	.10
97	Jamie Langenbrunner	.10
98	Sean Pronger	.10
99	Janne Niinimaa	.20
100	Chris Pronger	.10
101	Ray Sheppard	.10
102	Tony Amonte	.20
103	Ron Tugnutt	.10
104	Mike Modano	.30
105	Dan Trebil	.10
106	Alexander Mogilny	.20
107	Darren McCarty	.10
108	Ted Donato	.10
109	Brian Savage	.10
110	Mike Gartner	.10
111	Jim Campbell	.10
112	Roman Hamrlik	.10
113	Andreas Dackell	.10
114	Ron Hextall	.20
115	Steve Washburn	.10
116	Jeff Hackett	.20
117	Joe Sakic	1.00
118	Anson Carter	.10
119	Vyacheslav Kozlov	.10
120	Nikolai Khabibulin	.20
121	Tony Granato	.10
122	Al MacInnis	.10
123	Daren Puppa	.10
124	Mike Richter	.20
125	Zigmund Palffy	.40
126	Martin Brodeur	.75
127	Rem Murray	.10
128	Sean Burke	.20
129	Aki Berg	.10
130	Dmitri Mironov	.10
131	Jamie Allison	.10
132	Valeri Kamensky	.10
133	Pat LaFontaine	.20
134	Jozef Stumpel	.10
135	Peter Bondra	.20
136	Mark Recchi	.10
137	Ron Francis	.20
138	Harry York	.10
139	Mats Sundin	.25
140	Bobby Holik	.10
141	Eric Desjardins	.10
142	Scott Lachance	.10
143	Wayne Gretzky	2.50
144	Ed Jovanovski	.10
145	Jason Arnott	.20
146	Andrew Cassels	.10
147	Roman Vopat	.10
148	Dwayne Roloson	.10
149	Derek Plante	.10
150	Phil Housley	.10
151	Mikael Renberg	.10
152	Petr Nedved	.10
153	Grant Fuhr	.20
154	Felix Potvin	.30
155	John MacLean	.10
156	Brian Leetch	.20
157	Rod Brind'Amour	.10
158	Ryan Smyth	.25
159	Teemu Selanne	.75
160	Theoren Fleury	.20
161	Adam Deadmarsh	.10
162	Corey Hirsch	.10
163	Bryan Berard	.20
164	Ed Belfour	.25
165	Sergei Berezin	.20
166	Damian Rhodes	.20
167	Guy Hebert	.20
168	Derian Hatcher	.10
169	Jonas Hoglund	.10
170	Matthew Barnaby	.10
171	Scott Mellanby	.10
172	Bill Ranford	.10
173	Vincent Damphousse	.10
174	Anders Eriksson	.10
175	Chad Kilger	.10
176	Darren Turcotte	.10
177	Dino Ciccarelli	.10
178	Niklas Sundstrom	.10
179	Stephane Fiset	.10
180	Mike Ricci	.10
181	Brendan Shanahan	.75
182	Darcy Tucker	.10
183	Eric Fichaud	.20
184	Todd Marchant	.10
185	Keith Primeau	.10
186	Joe Nieuwendyk	.10
187	Pavel Bure	.75
188	Jaromir Jagr	1.50
189	Kirk McLean	.20
190	Daniel Goneau	.10
191	Rob Niedermayer	.10
192	Eric Daze	.20
193	Richard Matvichuk	.10
194	Scott Stevens	.10
195	Dale Hunter	.10
196	Hnat Domenichelli	.10
197	Philippe Derouville	.10
198	Marcel Cousineau	.10
199	Kevin Hodson	.25
200	Jean-Sebastien Giguere	.10
201	Paxton Schafer	.10
202	Marc Denis	.10
203	*Frank Banham*	.10
204	Vadim Sharifijanov	.10
205	Paul Healey	.10
206	*D.J. Smith*	.10
207	*Christian Matte*	.20
208	Sean Brown	.10
209	*Tomas Vokoun*	.10
210	Vladimir Vorobiev	.10
211	*Jean-Yves Leroux*	.10
212	Domenic Pittis	.10
213	Derek Wilkinson	.10
214	Jason Holland	.10
215	Pascal Rheaume	.10
216	Steve Kelly	.10
217	Vaclav Varada	.10
218	Mike Fountain	.10
219	*Vaclav Prospal*	.50
220	Jaroslav Svejkovsky	.40
221	Marty Murray	.10
222	*Wade Belak*	.10
223	Jamal Mayers	.10
224	Shayne Toporowski	.10
225	*Mike Knuble*	.10
226	Jarome Iginla	.10
227	Keith Tkachuk CL	.25
228	Adam Oates CL	.15
229	John LeClair CL	.25
230	Brian Leetch CL	.15

1997-98 Donruss Press Proofs Silver

Press Proofs Silver is a full parallel of the Donruss Hockey base set. The cards have silver foil and are numbered 1 of 1,500.

	MT
Silver Stars:	15x to 30x
Yng Stars & RCs:	8x to 15x
Production 2,000 sets	

1997-98 Donruss Press Proofs Gold

Press Proofs is a full parallel of the Donruss Hockey base set. A stated total of 2,000 cards were produced. The first 500 cards, Press Proofs Gold, are numbered 1 of 500 and feature die-cutting and gold foil.

	MT
Gold Stars:	40x to 75x
Yng Stars & RCs:	25x to 50x
Production 500 sets	

1997-98 Donruss Between the Pipes

Between the Pipes is a 10-card insert numbered to 3,000. The set features goalies on horizontal cards which are embossed with red foil.

		MT
Complete Set (10):		200.00
Common Player:		10.00
1	Patrick Roy	60.00
2	Martin Brodeur	30.00
3	John Vanbiesbrouck	25.00
4	Dominik Hasek	30.00
5	Chris Osgood	18.00
6	Jose Theodore	10.00
7	Garth Snow	10.00
8	Curtis Joseph	12.00
9	Felix Potvin	15.00
10	Jocelyn Thibault	10.00

1997-98 Donruss Elite Inserts

Elite is a 12-card insert sequentially numbered to 2,500. The cards feature gold and holographic gold foil. The color player photo appears inside a thick gold border.

		MT
Complete Set (12):		500.00
Common Player:		25.00
1	Wayne Gretzky	100.00
2	Jaromir Jagr	60.00
3	Eric Lindros	60.00
4	Paul Kariya	60.00
5	Patrick Roy	80.00
6	Steve Yzerman	50.00
7	Peter Forsberg	50.00
8	John Vanbiesbrouck	30.00
9	Brendan Shanahan	30.00
10	Martin Brodeur	35.00
11	Dominik Hasek	35.00
12	Teemu Selanne	30.00

1997-98 Donruss Line to Line

Line to Line is a 24-card insert. The set is broken into 12 "Red Line", eight "Blue Line" and four "Gold Line" cards. The foil cards have a horizontal layout with two photos of the player on the front. Red cards are sequentially numbered to 4,000, Blues are numbered to 2,000 and Golds are numbered to 1,000. The first 250 of each card are die-cut.

		MT
Complete Set (24):		600.00
Common Red & Blue:		8.00
Common Gold:		25.00
1st 250 of each level will be die-cut		
Red Die-cut Stars:		3x to 5x
Red Young Stars:		1.5x to 3x
Blue Die-cut:		1.5x to 3x
Gold Die-cut:		1.5x to 2x
1	Wayne Gretzky G	150.00
2	Teemu Selanne R	20.00
3	Brian Leetch B	12.00
4	Peter Forsberg R	30.00
5	Steve Yzerman R	40.00
6	Oleg Tverdovsky B	8.00
7	Doug Gilmour R	8.00
8	Eric Lindros G	90.00
9	Bryan Berard B	15.00
10	Brendan Shanahan R	20.00
11	Pavel Bure R	20.00
12	Joe Sakic R	25.00
13	Chris Chelios B	15.00
14	Mike Modano R	8.00
15	Paul Coffey B	8.00
16	Jaromir Jagr G	90.00
17	Jarome Iginla R	12.00
18	Brett Hull R	12.00
19	Wade Redden B	8.00
20	Paul Kariya G	90.00
21	Ray Bourque B	12.00
22	Ryan Smyth R	8.00
23	Mark Messier R	15.00
24	Sandis Ozolinsh B	10.00

1997-98 Donruss Rated Rookie

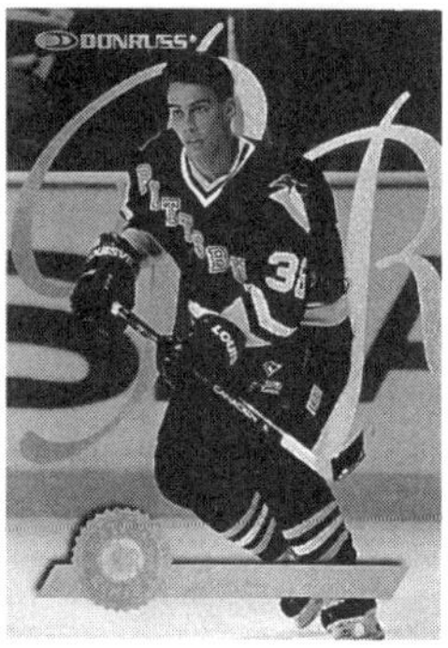

Rated Rookies is a 10-card insert randomly inserted in Donruss Hockey packs. The cards feature full-bleed photos with a large script "RR" in the background. The cards were created using micro-etched holographic foil. Medalist is a parallel of Rated Rookies. The cards feature both gold and silver holographic foil.

		MT
Complete Set (10):		40.00
Common Player:		3.00
Medalists:		8x to 12x
1	Tomas Vokoun	4.00
2	Paxton Schafer	4.00
3	Vaclav Prospal	10.00
4	Marc Denis	8.00
5	Domenic Pittis	3.00
6	Christian Matte	3.00
7	Marcel Cousineau	3.00
8	Steve Kelly	5.00
9	Jaroslav Svejkovsky	8.00
10	Jean-Sebastien Giguere	5.00

1997-98 Donruss Red Alert

Red Alert is a 10-card retail-only insert. Printed on plastic, the cards are die-cut to resemble the red scoring lamp. The set is sequentially numbered to 5,000.

		MT
Complete Set (10):		160.00
Common Player:		10.00
1	Adam Deadmarsh	10.00
2	Ryan Smyth	10.00
3	Sergei Fedorov	25.00
4	Keith Tkachuk	20.00
5	Brett Hull	20.00
6	Pavel Bure	30.00
7	John LeClair	25.00
8	Zigmund Palffy	20.00
9	Mats Sundin	15.00
10	Peter Bondra	15.00

1997-98 Donruss Elite

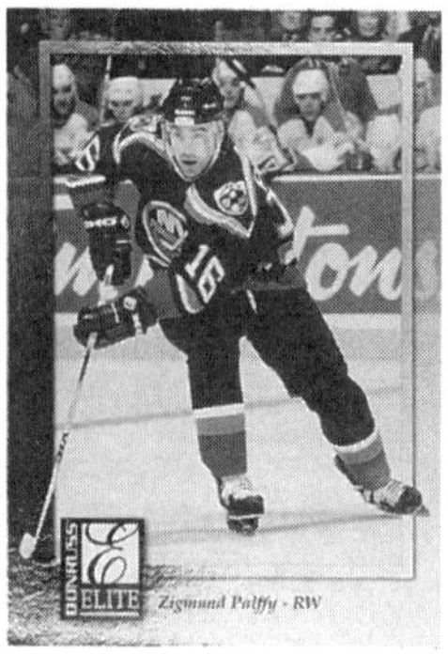

Donruss Elite Hockey consists of a 150-card base set. The base cards have a color photo inside a silver border, with the player's name, position, team name and Elite logo at the bottom. The base set is paralleled by the Status and Aspirations sets. Inserts include Back to the Future, Craftsmen and Prime Numbers.

		MT
Complete Set (150):		40.00
Common Player:		.15
1	Peter Forsberg	2.00
2	Mike Modano	.50
3	John Vanbiesbrouck	1.00
4	Pavel Bure	1.25
5	Mark Messier	.75
6	Joe Thornton	2.00
7	Paul Kariya	2.50
8	Martin Brodeur	1.50
9	Wayne Gretzky	4.00
10	Eric Lindros	2.50
11	Jaromir Jagr	2.50
12	Brett Hull	.60
13	Jarome Iginla	.15
14	Patrick Roy	3.00
15	Steve Yzerman	2.00
16	Sergei Samsonov	.75
17	Teemu Selanne	1.25
18	Brendan Shanahan	1.25
19	Curtis Joseph	.50
20	Saku Koivu	.60
21	Ray Bourque	.40
22	Jaroslav Svejkovsky	.15
23	Keith Primeau	.15
24	Alexandre Daigle	.15
25	Vyacheslav Kozlov	.15
26	Jozef Stumpel	.25
27	Alexei Yashin	.30
28	*Marian Hossa*	1.50
29	Bryan Berard	.30
30	Dominik Hasek	1.25
31	Chris Chelios	.40
32	Derian Hatcher	.15
33	Ed Jovanovski	.15
34	Zigmund Palffy	.75
35	Ron Hextall	.40
36	Daymond Langkow	.15
37	Daniel Cleary	.15
38	Alyn McCauley	.15
39	Sean Burke	.30
40	Brian Leetch	.30
41	Joe Juneau	.15
42	Damian Rhodes	.15
43	Dino Ciccarelli	.15
44	Valeri Kamensky	.15
45	Guy Hebert	.30
46	Brad Isbister	.15
47	Adam Graves	.15
48	Andrew Cassels	.15
49	Joe Sakic	1.50
50	Dainius Zubrus	.40
51	*Roberto Luongo*	5.00
52	Ethan Moreau	.15
53	Chris Osgood	.60
54	Stephane Fiset	.30
55	Sergei Berezin	.30
56	Mike Richter	.40
57	Valeri Bure	.15
58	Mats Sundin	.50
59	Mike Dunham	.15
60	Byron Dafoe	.40
61	Joe Nieuwendyk	.30
62	Mike Grier	.15
63	Paul Coffey	.30
64	Chris Phillips	.15
65	*Patrik Elias*	1.00
66	Andy Moog	.40
67	Geoff Sanderson	.15
68	Jere Lehtinen	.15
69	Alexander Mogilny	.40
70	Ryan Smyth	.15
71	John LeClair	1.00
72	*Olli Jokinen*	.75
73	Doug Gilmour	.40
74	Theoren Fleury	.30
75	Adam Deadmarsh	.30
76	Scott Mellanby	.15
77	Jeremy Roenick	.50
78	Jim Campbell	.15
79	Daren Puppa	.15
80	*Vaclav Prospal*	.75
81	Vincent Damphousse	.15
82	Derek Plante	.15
83	Sandis Ozolinsh	.15
84	Darren McCarty	.15
85	Luc Robitaille	.30
86	Wade Redden	.15
87	Eric Fichaud	.15
88	Jocelyn Thibault	.40
89	Trevor Linden	.15
90	Boyd Devereaux	.15
91	Chris Gratton	.15
92	Janne Niinimaa	.15
93	Jeff Friesen	.15
94	Roman Hamrlik	.15
95	Jason Arnott	.15
96	Sergei Fedorov	1.00
97	Tony Amonte	.40
98	Mattias Ohlund	.15
99	Patrick Marleau	1.25
100	Felix Potvin	.50
101	Tommy Salo	.40
102	Ed Belfour	.50
103	Doug Weight	.30
104	Daniel Alfredsson	.30
105	Pierre Turgeon	.30
106	*Espen Knutsen*	.15
107	Trevor Kidd	.30
108	Alexei Morozov	.15
109	Oleg Tverdovsky	.30
110	Grant Fuhr	.50
111	Pat LaFontaine	.30
112	Keith Tkachuk	.75
113	Ron Francis	.40
114	*Derek Morris*	.15
115	Joe Sakic (Elite Generations)	.75
116	Brian Leetch (Elite Generations)	.15
117	Alyn McCauley (Elite Generations)	.15
118	Pavel Bure (Elite Generations)	.60
119	Eric Lindros (Elite Generations)	1.25
120	Teemu Selanne (Elite Generations)	.60
121	Jarome Iginla (Elite Generations)	.15
122	Steve Yzerman (Elite Generations)	1.00
123	Daniel Cleary (Elite Generations)	.15
124	Bryan Berard (Elite Generations)	.15
125	Jaromir Jagr (Elite Generations)	1.25
126	John Vanbiesbrouck (Elite Generations)	.50
127	Mark Messier (Elite Generations)	.40
128	Patrick Marleau (Elite Generations)	.60
129	Mike Modano (Elite Generations)	.30
130	Zigmund Palffy (Elite Generations)	.40
131	Felix Potvin (Elite Generations)	.30
132	Derek Morris (Elite Generations)	.15
133	Brendan Shanahan (Elite Generations)	.50
134	Sergei Samsonov (Elite Generations)	.30
135	Dainius Zubrus (Elite Generations)	.25
136	Paul Kariya (Elite Generations)	1.25
137	Martin Brodeur (Elite Generations)	.60
138	Joe Thornton (Elite Generations)	1.00
139	Mattias Ohlund (Elite Generations)	.15
140	Ryan Smyth (Elite Generations)	.15
141	Jaroslav Svejkovsky (Elite Generations)	.15
142	Patrick Roy (Elite Generations)	1.50
143	Wayne Gretzky (Elite Generations)	2.00
144	Espen Knutsen (Elite Generations)	.15
145	Checklist Patrick Marleau	.30
146	Checklist Pat LaFontaine	.15
147	Checklist Mike Gartner	.15
148	Checklist Joe Thornton	.75
149	Checklist Teemu Selanne	.50
150	Checklist Mark Messier	.40

1997-98 Donruss Elite Aspirations

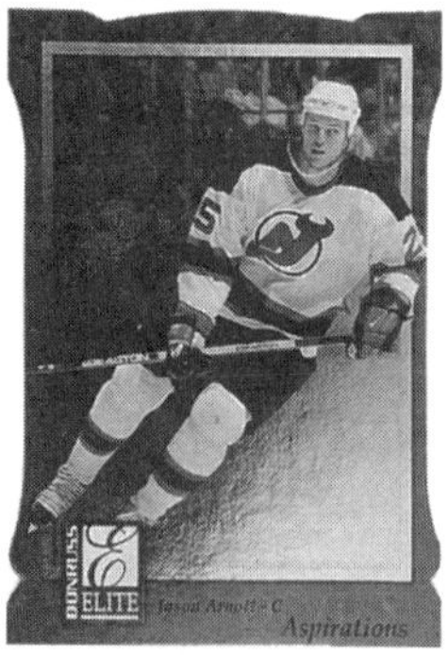

Aspirations is a full parallel of the Elite base set. The cards are die-cut and numbered "1 of 750" on the back.

	MT
Aspirations Stars:	8x to 15x
Yng Stars & RCs:	5x to 10x
Production 750 sets	

1997-98 Donruss Elite Status

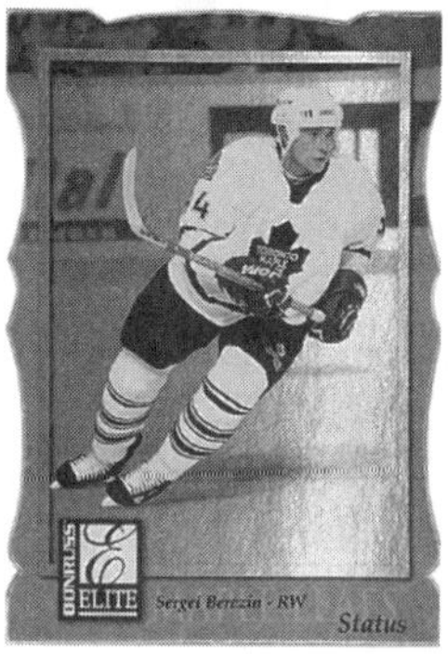

Status is a full parallel of the Elite base set. The cards are die-cut and sequentially numbered to 100.

		MT
Common Player:		15.00
1	Peter Forsberg	200.00
2	Mike Modano	50.00
3	John Vanbiesbrouck	90.00
4	Pavel Bure	120.00
5	Mark Messier	70.00
6	Joe Thornton	60.00
7	Paul Kariya	200.00
8	Martin Brodeur	120.00
9	Wayne Gretzky	450.00
10	Eric Lindros	250.00
11	Jaromir Jagr	250.00
12	Brett Hull	70.00
13	Jarome Iginla	30.00
14	Patrick Roy	300.00
15	Steve Yzerman	250.00
16	Sergei Samsonov	40.00
17	Teemu Selanne	120.00
18	Brendan Shanahan	100.00
19	Curtis Joseph	40.00
20	Saku Koivu	70.00
21	Ray Bourque	40.00
22	Jaroslav Svejkovsky	15.00
23	Keith Primeau	30.00
24	Alexandre Daigle	15.00
25	Vyacheslav Kozlov	15.00
26	Jozef Stumpel	30.00
27	Alexei Yashin	30.00
28	Marian Hossa	15.00
29	Bryan Berard	30.00
30	Dominik Hasek	120.00
31	Chris Chelios	40.00
32	Derian Hatcher	15.00
33	Ed Jovanovski	15.00
34	Zigmund Palffy	70.00
35	Ron Hextall	30.00
36	Daymond Langkow	15.00
37	Daniel Cleary	15.00
38	Alyn McCauley	15.00
39	Sean Burke	30.00
40	Brian Leetch	30.00
41	Joe Juneau	15.00
42	Damian Rhodes	15.00
43	Dino Ciccarelli	15.00
44	Valeri Kamensky	15.00
45	Guy Hebert	40.00
46	Brad Isbister	15.00
47	Adam Graves	15.00
48	Andrew Cassels	15.00
49	Joe Sakic	140.00
50	Dainius Zubrus	40.00
51	Roberto Luongo	75.00
52	Ethan Moreau	15.00
53	Chris Osgood	50.00
54	Stephane Fiset	15.00
55	Sergei Berezin	30.00
56	Mike Richter	40.00
57	Valeri Bure	15.00
58	Mats Sundin	50.00
59	Mike Dunham	15.00
60	Byron Dafoe	30.00
61	Joe Nieuwendyk	30.00
62	Mike Grier	15.00
63	Paul Coffey	30.00
64	Chris Phillips	30.00
65	Patrik Elias	40.00
66	Andy Moog	40.00
67	Geoff Sanderson	15.00
68	Jere Lehtinen	15.00
69	Alexander Mogilny	40.00
70	Ryan Smyth	15.00
71	John LeClair	60.00
72	Olli Jokinen	40.00
73	Doug Gilmour	40.00
74	Theoren Fleury	30.00
75	Adam Deadmarsh	30.00
76	Scott Mellanby	15.00
77	Jeremy Roenick	50.00
78	Jim Campbell	15.00
79	Daren Puppa	15.00
80	Vaclav Prospal	40.00
81	Vincent Damphousse	15.00
82	Derek Plante	15.00
83	Sandis Ozolinsh	15.00
84	Darren McCarty	15.00
85	Luc Robitaille	30.00
86	Wade Redden	15.00
87	Eric Fichaud	30.00
88	Jocelyn Thibault	40.00
89	Trevor Linden	30.00
90	Boyd Devereaux	15.00
91	Chris Gratton	30.00
92	Janne Niinimaa	30.00
93	Jeff Friesen	15.00
94	Roman Hamrlik	15.00
95	Jason Arnott	15.00
96	Sergei Fedorov	90.00
97	Tony Amonte	40.00
98	Mattias Ohlund	30.00
99	Patrick Marleau	40.00
100	Felix Potvin	40.00
101	Tommy Salo	30.00
102	Ed Belfour	40.00
103	Doug Weight	30.00
104	Daniel Alfredsson	30.00
105	Pierre Turgeon	30.00
106	Espen Knutsen	15.00
107	Trevor Kidd	30.00
108	Alexei Morozov	15.00
109	Oleg Tverdovsky	30.00
110	Grant Fuhr	40.00
111	Pat LaFontaine	30.00
112	Keith Tkachuk	60.00
113	Ron Francis	30.00
114	Derek Morris	15.00
115	Joe Sakic (Elite Generations)	70.00
116	Brian Leetch (Elite Generations)	15.00
117	Alyn McCauley (Elite Generations)	15.00
118	Pavel Bure (Elite Generations)	50.00
119	Eric Lindros (Elite Generations)	100.00
120	Teemu Selanne (Elite Generations)	50.00
121	Jarome Iginla (Elite Generations)	15.00
122	Steve Yzerman (Elite Generations)	80.00
123	Daniel Cleary (Elite Generations)	15.00
124	Bryan Berard (Elite Generations)	15.00
125	Jaromir Jagr (Elite Generations)	100.00
126	John Vanbiesbrouck (Elite Generations)	40.00
127	Mark Messier (Elite Generations)	35.00
128	Patrick Marleau (Elite Generations)	25.00
129	Mike Modano (Elite Generations)	25.00
130	Zigmund Palffy (Elite Generations)	30.00
131	Felix Potvin (Elite Generations)	25.00
132	Derek Morris (Elite Generations)	15.00
133	Brendan Shanahan (Elite Generations)	50.00
134	Sergei Samsonov (Elite Generations)	25.00
135	Dainius Zubrus (Elite Generations)	25.00
136	Paul Kariya (Elite Generations)	100.00
137	Martin Brodeur (Elite Generations)	60.00
138	Joe Thornton (Elite Generations)	30.00
139	Mattias Ohlund (Elite Generations)	25.00
140	Ryan Smyth (Elite Generations)	15.00
141	Jaroslav Svejkovsky (Elite Generations)	15.00
142	Patrick Roy (Elite Generations)	125.00
143	Wayne Gretzky (Elite Generations)	175.00
144	Espen Knutsen (Elite Generations)	15.00
145	Checklist Patrick Marleau	25.00
146	Checklist Pat LaFontaine	15.00
147	Checklist Mike Gartner	15.00
148	Checklist Joe Thornton	30.00
149	Checklist Teemu Selanne	40.00
150	Checklist Mark Messier	30.00

1997-98 Donruss Elite Back to the Future

Back to the Future is an eight-card insert numbered to 1,500. The double-front cards feature a veteran star on one side and a young player on the other. Some of the cards feature an NHL legend on one side with an established current star on the other.

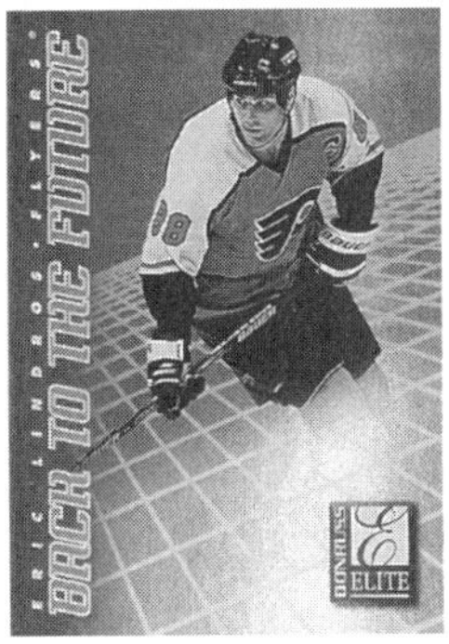

		MT
Complete Set (8):		300.00
Common Player:		20.00
1	Eric Lindros, Joe Thornton	60.00
2	Jocelyn Thibault, Marc Denis	20.00
3	Teemu Selanne, Patrick Marleau	40.00
4	Jaromir Jagr, Daniel Cleary	60.00
5	Sergei Fedorov, Peter Forsberg	50.00
6	Bobby Hull, Brett Hull	40.00
7	Martin Brodeur, Roberto Luongo	40.00
8	Gordie Howe, Steve Yzerman	60.00

1997-98 Donruss Elite Back to the Future Autographs

The first 100 of each Back to the Future card was signed by both players.

		MT
Complete Set (8):		2000.
Common Player:		125.00
1	Eric Lindros, Joe Thornton	400.00
2	Jocelyn Thibault, Marc Denis	125.00
3	Teemu Selanne, Patrick Marleau	300.00
4	Jaromir Jagr, Daniel Cleary	300.00
5	Sergei Fedorov, Peter Forsberg	400.00
6	Bobby Hull, Brett Hull	250.00
7	Martin Brodeur, Roberto Luongo	300.00
8	Gordie Howe, Steve Yzerman	700.00

1997-98 Donruss Elite Craftsmen

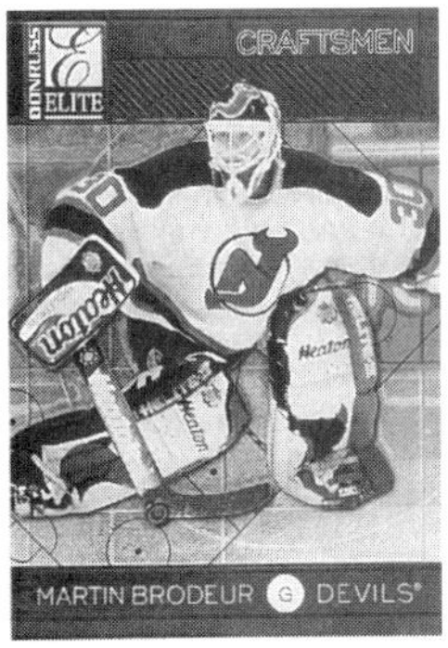

Craftsmen is a 30-card insert sequentially numbered to 2,500. The etched foil cards feature a color photo with a blue border on the top and bottom.

		MT
Complete Set (30):		220.00
Common Player:		2.50
1	John Vanbiesbrouck	6.00
2	Eric Lindros	15.00
3	Richard Sako	2.50
4	Mark Messier	5.00
5	Jaroslav Svejkovsky	2.50
6	Dominik Hasek	8.00
7	Chris Osgood	5.00
8	Martin Brodeur	8.00
9	Sergei Fedorov	6.00
10	Daniel Cleary	2.50
11	Patrick Marleau	5.00
12	Sergei Samsonov	6.00
13	Felix Potvin	4.00
14	Patrick Roy	20.00
15	Teemu Selanne	6.00
16	Steve Yzerman	12.00
17	Jarome Iginla	2.50
18	Mike Modano	6.00
19	Wayne Gretzky	25.00
20	Pavel Bure	6.00
21	Ryan Smyth	2.50
22	Paul Kariya	15.00
23	Peter Forsberg	12.00
24	Joe Thornton	6.00
25	Jaromir Jagr	15.00
26	Bryan Berard	2.50
27	Brendan Shanahan	6.00
28	Keith Tkachuk	5.00
29	Curtis Joseph	4.00
30	Brian Leetch	2.50

1997-98 Donruss Elite Master Craftsmen

Master Craftsmen is a parallel of the Craftsmen insert. Printed on holofoil board, the cards are numbered to 100.

	MT
Master Craftsmen:	10x to 20x
Production 100 sets	

1997-98 Donruss Elite Prime Numbers

Prime Numbers is a 36-card base set, with three cards for each of the 12 players. The cards are based on a statistic for each player. For example, Patrick Roy's cards are based on his career win total - 349. Roy has a "3" card, a "4" and a "9" card, with 349 cards produced for each. Die-cut versions were also produced. Of the 349 cards, 300 of the "3" cards are die-cut, 40 of the "4s" and nine of the "9s". The same pattern follows for each player's cards.

		MT
Common Player:		30.00
1a	Peter Forsberg (54)	200.00
1b	Peter Forsberg (204)	80.00
1c	Peter Forsberg (250)	70.00
2a	Patrick Roy (49)	350.00
2b	Patrick Roy (309)	100.00
2c	Patrick Roy (340)	90.00
3a	Mark Messier (95)	90.00
3b	Mark Messier (205)	40.00
3c	Mark Messier (290)	40.00
4a	Eric Lindros (36)	375.00
4b	Eric Lindros (406)	60.00
4c	Eric Lindros (430)	60.00
5a	Paul Kariya (46)	300.00
5b	Paul Kariya (206)	100.00
5c	Paul Kariya (240)	90.00
6a	Jaromir Jagr (66)	250.00
6b	Jaromir Jagr (206)	90.00
6c	Jaromir Jagr (260)	75.00
7a	Teemu Selanne (37)	170.00
7b	Teemu Selanne (207)	50.00
7c	Teemu Selanne (230)	50.00
8a	John Vanbiesbrouck (88)	100.00
8b	John Vanbiesbrouck (208)	50.00
8c	John Vanbiesbrouck (280)	40.00
9a	Brendan Shanahan (35)	160.00
9b	Brendan Shanahan (305)	40.00
9c	Brendan Shanahan (330)	40.00
10a	Steve Yzerman (39)	275.00
10b	Steve Yzerman (509)	40.00
10c	Steve Yzerman (530)	40.00
11a	Joe Sakic (7)	25.00
11c	Joe Sakic (300)	50.00
12a	Pavel Bure (88)	100.00
12b	Pavel Bure (308)	40.00
12c	Pavel Bure (380)	40.00

1997-98 Donruss Elite Prime Numbers Die-Cuts

Prime Numbers is a 36-card base set, with three cards for each of the 12 players. The cards are based on a statistic for each player. For example, Patrick Roy's cards are based on his career win total - 349. Roy has a "3" card, a "4" card and a "9" card, with 349 cards produced for each. Of the 349 cards, 300 of the "3s" are die-cut, 40 of the "4s" and nine of the "9s". This pattern follows for each player's cards.

		MT
Common Player:		30.00
1a	Peter Forsberg (200)	80.00
1b	Peter Forsberg (50)	200.00
1c	Peter Forsberg (4)	30.00
2a	Patrick Roy (300)	100.00
2b	Patrick Roy (40)	350.00
2c	Patrick Roy (9)	30.00
3a	Mark Messier (200)	40.00
3b	Mark Messier (90)	90.00
3c	Mark Messier (5)	30.00
4a	Eric Lindros (400)	60.00
4b	Eric Lindros (30)	375.00
4c	Eric Lindros (6)	30.00
5a	Paul Kariya (200)	100.00
5b	Paul Kariya (40)	300.00
5c	Paul Kariya (6)	30.00
6a	Jaromir Jagr (200)	90.00
6b	Jaromir Jagr (60)	250.00
6c	Jaromir Jagr (6)	30.00
7a	Teemu Selanne (200)	50.00
7b	Teemu Selanne (30)	170.00
7c	Teemu Selanne (7)	30.00
8a	John Vanbiesbrouck (200)	50.00
8b	John Vanbiesbrouck (80)	100.00
8c	John Vanbiesbrouck (8)	30.00
9a	Brendan Shanahan (300)	40.00
9b	Brendan Shanahan (30)	160.00
9c	Brendan Shanahan (5)	30.00
10a	Steve Yzerman (500)	40.00
10b	Steve Yzerman (30)	275.00
10c	Steve Yzerman (9)	30.00
11a	Joe Sakic (300)	50.00
11c	Joe Sakic (7)	30.00
12a	Pavel Bure (300)	40.00
12b	Pavel Bure (80)	100.00
12c	Pavel Bure (8)	30.00

1997-98 Donruss Limited

Donruss Limited consists of a 200-card base set made up of four subsets. Each base card is a double front card. Counterparts is a 100-card subset featuring players who play similar positions. The cards have a hockey puck in the background, with the player's name, position and a career highlight at the bottom. Double Team features 40 pairs of superstar teammates. Star Factor is another 40-card subset with the same player on both sides. Pictured against a "sunburst" design, the player's name and a statistic are printed at the bottom. The final subset is Unlimited Potential/Talent. One side features a star veteran and the other highlights a young player on these horizontal cards. Donruss stated that less than 600 sets were produced. Limited Exposure is the only parallel and Fabric of the Game is the lone insert.

		MT
Common Counterpart:		.25
Common Double Team:		1.50
Common Unlimited Potential/Talent:		3.00
Common Star Factor:		5.00
1	Brendan Shanahan, Harry York C	1.50
2	Peter Forsberg, Mike Knuble C	2.50
3	Chris Osgood, Kirk McLean C	.75
4	Wayne Gretzky SF	100.00
5	John Vanbiesbrouck, Ed Jovanovski DT	12.00
6	Paul Coffey, Darryl Sydor C	.40
7	Pavel Bure, Valeri Bure C	1.50
8	Sergei Berezin, Jaromir Jagr U	40.00
9	Saku Koivu, Mats Sundin C	1.50
10	Trevor Kidd, Corey Hirsch C	.25
11	Teemu Selanne SF	30.00
12	Zigmund Palffy, Radek Bonk C	.75
13	Mats Sundin, Sergei Berezin DT	2.00
14	Jim Carey, Bill Ranford C	.40
15	John LeClair, Claude Lemieux C	1.00
16	Janne Niinimaa, Chris Chelios U	3.00
17	Kevin Hodson, Mike Knuble DT	1.50
18	Adam Graves, Keith Jones C	.25
19	Mike Modano, Trevor Linden C	.75
20	Brett Hull SF	20.00
21	Derian Hatcher, Kevin Hatcher C	.25
22	Daniel Alfredsson, Dave Andreychuk C	.25
23	Steve Shields, Vaclav Varada DT	1.50
24	Theoren Fleury, Geoff Courtnall C	.50
25	Mark Messier, Dino Ciccarelli C	1.00
26	Ryan Smyth SF	5.00
27	Mike Grier, Jason Arnott DT	1.50
28	Ed Belfour, Andy Moog C	.50
29	Jean-Sebastien Giguere, Felix Potvin U	6.00
30	Eric Lindros, Todd Bertuzzi C	3.00
31	Daymond Langkow, David Roberts C	.25
32	Mike Richter, Grant Fuhr C	.75
33	Adam Oates, Jaroslav Svejkovsky DT	5.00
34	Saku Koivu, Darcy Tucker DT	10.00
35	Paul Kariya SF	50.00
36	Joe Sakic, Bernie Nicholls C	2.00
37	Ed Jovanovski, D.J. Smith C	.25
38	Vaclav Prospal, Brendan Shanahan U	35.00
39	Mike Peca, Marty Murray C	.25
40	Mike Gartner, Wendel Clark C	.25
41	Steve Yzerman SF	50.00
42	Mike Modano, Roman Turek DT	2.50
43	Joe Nieuwendyk, Jarome Iginla C	.50
44	Patrick Roy, Jocelyn Thibault C	4.00
45	Hnat Domenichelli, Andrew Cassels C	.25
46	Christian Dube, Steve Sullivan C	.25
47	Marc Denis, Valeri Kamensky DT	1.50
48	Peter Forsberg SF	50.00
49	Derek Plante, Todd Harvey C	.25
50	Mike Grier, Eric Lindros U	50.00
51	Brett Hull, Jim Campbell DT	5.00
52	Mark Recchi, Landon Wilson C	.25
53	Darcy Tucker, Pascal Rheaume C	.25
54	Chris O'Sullivan, Anders Eriksson C	.25
55	Jaromir Jagr SF	60.00
56	Paul Kariya, Teemu Selanne DT	25.00
57	Felix Potvin, Damian Rhodes C	.75
58	Brian Holzinger, Mike Ricci C	.25
59	Eric Fichaud, Travis Green DT	1.50
60	Ethan Moreau, John MacLean C	.25
61	Joe Juneau, Jeff O'Neill C	.25
62	John Vanbiesbrouck SF	40.00
63	Byron Dafoe, Steve Shields C	.25
64	Mikael Renberg, Niklas Sundstrom C	.25
65	Ryan Smyth, Eric Daze C	.25
66	Doug Gilmour, Pascal Rheaume DT	2.00
67	Jim Campbell, Craig Janney C	.25
68	Alexander Mogilny, Matthew Barnaby C	.50
69	Alexei Yashin SF	8.00
70	Bryan Berard, Brian Leetch U	4.00
71	Alexei Yashin, Brian Savage C	.50
72	Jeff Friesen, Darren McCarty C	.25
73	Dimitri Khristich, Chad Kilger C	.25
74	Martin Brodeur, Dave Andreychuk DT	12.00
75	Luc Robitaille, Pat Verbeek C	.25
76	Dominik Hasek, Jamie Storr C	1.50
77	Felix Potvin SF	20.00
78	Mike Dunham, Vadim Sharifijanov DT	1.50
79	Jason Arnott, Rob Niedermayer C	.25
80	Eric Desjardins, Chris Phillips C	.25
81	Curtis Joseph, Jose Theodore C	.50
82	Doug Gilmour, Rod Brind'Amour C	.50
83	Keith Tkachuk, Rick Tocchet C	1.00
84	Mark Messier SF	25.00
85	Chris Pronger, Aki Berg C	.25
86	Marcel Cousineau, Dominik Hasek U	25.00
87	Ethan Moreau, Chris Chelios DT	2.50
88	Jonas Hoglund, Rob Zamuner C	.25
89	Ron Hextall, Kevin Hodson C	.50
90	John LeClair SF	20.00
91	Vaclav Prospal, Vyacheslav Kozlov C	.75
92	Ray Bourque, Joe Thornton DT	20.00
93	Oleg Tverdovsky, Sergei Zubov C	.25
94	Ethan Moreau, John LeClair U	20.00
95	Adam Deadmarsh SF	5.00
96	Jaroslav Svejkovsky, Jozef Stumpel C	1.00
97	Wayne Gretzky, Vladimir Vorobiev DT	30.00
98	Sergei Fedorov SF	30.00
99	Jim Campbell, Ryan Smyth U	3.00
100	Vaclav Prospal, Paul Coffey DT	2.00
101	Wayne Primeau, Sean Pronger C	.25
102	Jean-Sebastien Giguere, Guy Hebert C	.25
103	Curtis Joseph SF	10.00
104	Pavel Bure, Alexander Mogilny DT	10.00
105	Jeremy Roenick, Tony Amonte C	.75
106	Sandis Ozolinsh, Kyle McLaren C	.25
107	Anson Carter, Steve Kelly C	.25
108	Paul Coffey SF	8.00
109	Dainius Zubrus, Peter Forsberg U	40.00
110	Travis Green, Scott Mellanby C	.25
111	Pat LaFontaine, Valeri Kamensky C	.50
112	Adam Oates SF	10.00
113	John Vanbiesbrouck, Roman Turek C	2.00
114	Jarome Iginla, Paul Kariya U	50.00
115	Steve Yzerman, Chris Osgood DT	15.00
116	Marcel Cousineau, Steve Sullivan DT	1.50
117	Owen Nolan, Steve Rucchin C	.25
118	Donald Audette, Ted Donato C	.25
119	Geoff Sanderson, Sean Burke DT	1.50
120	Jeremy Roenick SF	10.00
121	Vladimir Vorobiev, Andreas Johansson C	.25
122	Alexander Mogilny SF	10.00
123	Jocelyn Thibault, Terry Ryan DT	2.50
124	Eric Fichaud, Nikolai Khabibulin C	.50

125 Ray Bourque, Eric Messier C .75
126 Sergei Fedorov, Keith Primeau C 1.50
127 Marc Denis, Martin Brodeur U 35.00
128 Mats Sundin SF 10.00
129 Peter Bondra, Roman Vopat C .40
130 Tommy Salo, Corey Schwab C .25
131 Sergei Samsonov, Jim Carey DT 6.00
132 Adam Deadmarsh, Joe Sakic DT 10.00
133 Daymond Langkow, Keith Tkachuk U 12.00
134 Mike Richter SF 8.00
135 Geoff Sanderson, Jere Lehtinen C .25
136 Janne Niinimaa, Jamie Pushor C .25
137 Andreas Dackell, Vincent Damphousse C .25
138 Keith Tkachuk SF 20.00
139 Ray Bourque SF 10.00
140 Keith Tkachuk, Jeremy Roenick DT 5.00
141 Rem Murray, Ray Sheppard C .25
142 Paxton Schafer, Patrick Lalime C .25
143 Jaroslav Svejkovsky, Teemu Selanne U 25.00
144 Todd Marchant, Tony Granato C .25
145 Sandis Ozolinsh SF 5.00
146 Roman Hamrlik, Nicklas Lidstrom C .40
147 Dominik Hasek SF 35.00
148 Chris Gratton, Daniel Goneau C .25
149 Martin Brodeur SF 40.00
150 Martin Brodeur, Stephane Fiset C 2.00
151 Jose Theodore, Patrick Roy U 50.00
152 Jose Theodore, Mark Recchi DT 1.50
153 Pavel Bure SF 35.00
154 Sergei Berezin, Denis Pederson C .25
155 Doug Gilmour SF 10.00
156 Petr Nedved, Kirk Muller C .25
157 Theoren Fleury SF 8.00
158 Harry York, Pierre Turgeon DT 1.50
159 Andreas Johansson, Patrick Lalime DT 1.50
160 Marcel Cousineau, Jeff Hackett C .25
161 Adam Deadmarsh, Alexandre Daigle C .25
162 Adam Oates, Todd Warriner C .50
163 Zigmund Palffy SF 20.00
164 Ed Belfour SF 8.00
165 Saku Koivu, Steve Yzerman U 40.00
166 Chris Chelios, Scott Lachance C .50
167 Jamie Langenbrunner, Brandon Convery C .25
168 Janne Niinimaa, John LeClair DT 6.00
169 Brendan Shanahan SF 30.00
170 Daren Puppa, Garth Snow C .25
171 Chris Osgood SF 15.00
172 Pierre Turgeon, Shayne Corson C .40
173 Doug Weight, Rem Murray DT 2.00
174 Eric Fichaud, Curtis Joseph U 4.00
175 Chris Chelios SF 10.00
176 Wade Redden, Scott Stevens C .25
177 Jarome Iginla, Theoren Fleury DT 2.50
178 Vaclav Varada, Igor Larionov C .25
179 Brian Leetch SF 10.00
180 Stephane Fiset, Roman Vopat DT 1.50
181 Zigmund Palffy, Bryan Berard DT 5.00
182 Bryan Berard, Brian Leetch C .50
183 Eric Lindros SF 60.00
184 Derek Plante, Brian Holzinger DT 1.50
185 Brett Hull, Martin Gelinas C 1.50
186 Daniel Alfredsson, Damian Rhodes DT 1.50
187 Joe Thornton, Mark Messier U 40.00
188 Mike Vernon, Ken Wregget C .25
189 Alexei Yashin, Wade Redden DT 2.00
190 Joe Sakic SF 40.00
191 Doug Weight, Darren Turcotte C .40
192 Daymond Langkow, Daren Puppa DT 1.50
193 Mike Modano SF 12.00
194 Sean Burke, Mike Dunham C .25
195 Dainius Zubrus, Sebastian Bordeleau C .50
196 Owen Nolan, Jeff Friesen DT 1.50
197 Vladimir Vorobiev, Sergei Fedorov U 25.00
198 Patrick Roy SF 75.00
199 Mike Grier, Ron Francis C .25
200 Patrick Marleau, Wayne Gretzky U 80.00

1997-98 Donruss Limited Exposure

Limited Exposure is a complete parallel of the Limited Hockey base set. The cards feature holographic poly-chromium technology on both sides. Donruss stated that less than 25 complete sets were produced.

MT
Common Counterpart: 4.00
Common Double Team: 12.00
Common Unlimited Potential/Talent: 25.00
Common Star Factor: 60.00
1 Brendan Shanahan, Harry York C 25.00
2 Peter Forsberg, Mike Knuble C 40.00
3 Chris Osgood, Kirk McLean C 10.00
4 Wayne Gretzky SF 1200.
5 John Vanbiesbrouck, Ed Jovanovski DT 80.00
6 Paul Coffey, Darryl Sydor C 6.00
7 Pavel Bure, Valeri Bure C 25.00
8 Sergei Berezin, Jaromir Jagr U 500.00
9 Saku Koivu, Mats Sundin C 20.00
10 Trevor Kidd, Corey Hirsch C 4.00
11 Teemu Selanne SF 400.00
12 Zigmund Palffy, Radek Bonk C 15.00
13 Mats Sundin, Sergei Berezin DT 20.00
14 Jim Carey, Bill Ranford C 8.00
15 John LeClair, Claude Lemieux C 20.00
16 Janne Niinimaa, Chris Chelios U 35.00
17 Kevin Hodson, Mike Knuble DT 12.00
18 Adam Graves, Keith Jones C 4.00
19 Mike Modano, Trevor Linden C 12.00
20 Brett Hull SF 250.00
21 Derian Hatcher, Kevin Hatcher C 4.00
22 Daniel Alfredsson, Dave Andreychuk C 4.00
23 Steve Shields, Vaclav Varada DT 12.00
24 Theoren Fleury, Geoff Courtnall C 6.00
25 Mark Messier, Dino Ciccarelli C 15.00
26 Ryan Smyth SF 60.00
27 Mike Grier, Jason Arnott DT 12.00
28 Ed Belfour, Andy Moog C 10.00
29 Jean-Sebastien Giguere, Felix Potvin U 40.00
30 Eric Lindros, Todd Bertuzzi C 60.00
31 Daymond Langkow, David Roberts C 4.00
32 Mike Richter, Grant Fuhr C 12.00
33 Adam Oates, Jaroslav Svejkovsky DT 25.00
34 Saku Koivu, Darcy Tucker DT 50.00
35 Paul Kariya SF 750.00
36 Joe Sakic, Bernie Nicholls C 35.00
37 Ed Jovanovski, D.J. Smith C 4.00
38 Vaclav Prospal, Brendan Shanahan U 275.00
39 Mike Peca, Marty Murray C 4.00
40 Mike Gartner, Wendel Clark C 4.00
41 Steve Yzerman SF 600.00
42 Mike Modano, Roman Turek DT 25.00
43 Joe Nieuwendyk, Jarome Iginla C 8.00
44 Patrick Roy, Jocelyn Thibault C 60.00
45 Hnat Domenichelli, Andrew Cassels C 4.00
46 Christian Dube, Steve Sullivan C 4.00
47 Marc Denis, Valeri Kamensky DT 12.00
48 Peter Forsberg SF 600.00
49 Derek Plante, Todd Harvey C 4.00
50 Mike Grier, Eric Lindros U 500.00
51 Brett Hull, Jim Campbell DT 50.00
52 Mark Recchi, Landon Wilson C 4.00
53 Darcy Tucker, Pascal Rheaume C 4.00
54 Chris O'Sullivan, Anders Eriksson C 4.00
55 Jaromir Jagr SF 750.00
56 Paul Kariya, Teemu Selanne DT 175.00
57 Felix Potvin, Damian Rhodes C 10.00
58 Brian Holzinger, Mike Ricci C 4.00
59 Eric Fichaud, Travis Green DT 12.00
60 Ethan Moreau, John MacLean C 4.00
61 Joe Juneau, Jeff O'Neill C 4.00
62 John Vanbiesbrouck SF 450.00
63 Byron Dafoe, Steve Shields C 4.00
64 Mikael Renberg, Niklas Sundstrom C 4.00
65 Ryan Smyth, Eric Daze C 4.00
66 Doug Gilmour, Pascal Rheaume DT 20.00
67 Jim Campbell, Craig Janney C 4.00
68 Alexander Mogilny, Matthew Barnaby C 10.00
69 Alexei Yashin SF 60.00
70 Bryan Berard, Brian Leetch U 40.00
71 Alexei Yashin, Brian Savage C 8.00
72 Jeff Friesen, Darren McCarty C 4.00
73 Dimitri Khristich, Chad Kilger C 4.00
74 Martin Brodeur, Dave Andreychuk DT 100.00
75 Luc Robitaille, Pat Verbeek C 4.00
76 Dominik Hasek, Jamie Storr C 30.00
77 Felix Potvin SF 125.00
78 Mike Dunham, Vadim Sharifijanov DT 12.00
79 Jason Arnott, Rob Niedermayer C 4.00
80 Eric Desjardins, Chris Phillips C 4.00
81 Curtis Joseph, Jose Theodore C 10.00
82 Doug Gilmour, Rod Brind'Amour C 10.00
83 Keith Tkachuk, Rick Tocchet C 20.00
84 Mark Messier SF 250.00
85 Chris Pronger, Aki Berg C 4.00
86 Marcel Cousineau, Dominik Hasek U 160.00
87 Ethan Moreau, Chris Chelios DT 20.00
88 Jonas Hoglund, Rob Zamuner C 4.00
89 Ron Hextall, Kevin Hodson C 8.00
90 John LeClair SF 200.00
91 Vaclav Prospal, Vyacheslav Kozlov C 8.00
92 Ray Bourque, Joe Thornton DT 100.00
93 Oleg Tverdovsky, Sergei Zubov C 4.00
94 Ethan Moreau, John LeClair U 150.00
95 Adam Deadmarsh SF 50.00
96 Jaroslav Svejkovsky, Jozef Stumpel C 15.00
97 Wayne Gretzky, Vladimir Vorobiev DT 250.00
98 Sergei Fedorov SF 300.00
99 Jim Campbell, Ryan Smyth U 25.00
100 Vaclav Prospal, Paul Coffey DT 18.00
101 Wayne Primeau, Sean Pronger C 4.00
102 Jean-Sebastien Giguere, Guy Hebert C 4.00
103 Curtis Joseph SF 100.00
104 Pavel Bure, Alexander Mogilny DT 100.00
105 Jeremy Roenick, Tony Amonte C 15.00
106 Sandis Ozolinsh, Kyle McLaren C 4.00
107 Anson Carter, Steve Kelly C 4.00
108 Paul Coffey SF 75.00
109 Dainius Zubrus, Peter Forsberg U 350.00
110 Travis Green, Scott Mellanby C 4.00
111 Pat LaFontaine, Valeri Kamensky C 8.00
112 Adam Oates SF 100.00
113 John Vanbiesbrouck, Roman Turek C 30.00
114 Jarome Iginla, Paul Kariya U 450.00
115 Steve Yzerman, Chris Osgood DT 120.00
116 Marcel Cousineau, Steve Sullivan DT 12.00
117 Owen Nolan, Steve Rucchin C 4.00
118 Donald Audette, Ted Donato C 4.00
119 Geoff Sanderson, Sean Burke DT 12.00
120 Jeremy Roenick SF 125.00
121 Vladimir Vorobiev, Andreas Johansson C 4.00
122 Alexander Mogilny SF 100.00
123 Jocelyn Thibault, Terry Ryan DT 20.00
124 Eric Fichaud, Nikolai Khabibulin C 8.00
125 Ray Bourque, Eric Messier C 12.00
126 Sergei Fedorov, Keith Primeau C 20.00
127 Marc Denis, Martin Brodeur U 250.00
128 Mats Sundin SF 120.00
129 Peter Bondra, Roman Vopat C 8.00
130 Tommy Salo, Corey Schwab C 4.00
131 Sergei Samsonov, Jim Carey DT 35.00
132 Adam Deadmarsh, Joe Sakic DT 90.00
133 Daymond Langkow, Keith Tkachuk U 100.00
134 Mike Richter SF 75.00
135 Geoff Sanderson, Jere Lehtinen C 4.00
136 Janne Niinimaa, Jamie Pushor C 4.00
137 Andreas Dackell, Vincent Damphousse C 4.00
138 Keith Tkachuk SF 200.00
139 Ray Bourque SF 150.00
140 Keith Tkachuk, Jeremy Roenick DT 40.00
141 Rem Murray, Ray Sheppard C 4.00
142 Paxton Schafer, Patrick Lalime C 4.00
143 Jaroslav Svejkovsky, Teemu Selanne U 250.00
144 Todd Marchant, Tony Granato C 4.00
145 Sandis Ozolinsh SF 50.00
146 Roman Hamrlik, Nicklas Lidstrom C 8.00
147 Dominik Hasek SF 400.00
148 Chris Gratton, Daniel Goneau C 4.00
149 Martin Brodeur SF 400.00
150 Martin Brodeur, Stephane Fiset C 30.00
151 Jose Theodore, Patrick Roy U 600.00
152 Jose Theodore, Mark Recchi DT 12.00
153 Pavel Bure SF 350.00
154 Sergei Berezin, Denis Pederson C 4.00
155 Doug Gilmour SF 90.00
156 Petr Nedved, Kirk Muller C 4.00
157 Theoren Fleury SF 75.00
158 Harry York, Pierre Turgeon DT 12.00
159 Andreas Johansson, Patrick Lalime DT 12.00
160 Marcel Cousineau, Jeff Hackett C 4.00
161 Adam Deadmarsh, Alexandre Daigle C 4.00
162 Adam Oates, Todd Warriner C 8.00
163 Zigmund Palffy SF 175.00
164 Ed Belfour SF 75.00
165 Saku Koivu, Steve Yzerman U 400.00
166 Chris Chelios, Scott Lachance C 8.00
167 Jamie Langenbrunner, Brandon Convery C 4.00
168 Janne Niinimaa, John LeClair DT 50.00
169 Brendan Shanahan SF 300.00
170 Daren Puppa, Garth Snow C 4.00
171 Chris Osgood SF 125.00
172 Pierre Turgeon, Shayne Corson C 8.00
173 Doug Weight, Rem Murray DT 15.00
174 Eric Fichaud, Curtis Joseph U 35.00
175 Chris Chelios SF 100.00
176 Wade Redden, Scott Stevens C 4.00
177 Jarome Iginla, Theoren Fleury DT 20.00
178 Vaclav Varada, Igor Larionov C 4.00
179 Brian Leetch SF 90.00
180 Stephane Fiset, Roman Vopat DT 12.00
181 Zigmund Palffy, Bryan Berard DT 40.00
182 Bryan Berard, Brian Leetch C 10.00
183 Eric Lindros SF 700.00
184 Derek Plante, Brian Holzinger DT 12.00
185 Brett Hull, Martin Gelinas C 12.00
186 Daniel Alfredsson, Damian Rhodes DT 12.00
187 Joe Thornton, Mark Messier U 200.00
188 Mike Vernon, Ken Wregget C 4.00
189 Alexei Yashin, Wade Redden DT 15.00
190 Joe Sakic SF 450.00
191 Doug Weight, Darren Turcotte C 6.00
192 Daymond Langkow, Daren Puppa DT 12.00
193 Mike Modano SF 150.00
194 Sean Burke, Mike Dunham C 4.00
195 Dainius Zubrus, Sebastian Bordeleau C 8.00
196 Owen Nolan, Jeff Friesen DT 12.00
197 Vladimir Vorobiev, Sergei Fedorov U 175.00
198 Patrick Roy SF 750.00
199 Mike Grier, Ron Francis C 4.00
200 Patrick Marleau, Wayne Gretzky U 750.00

1997-98 Donruss Limited Fabric of the Game

Fabric of the Game is a 72-card, five-tiered insert. The set is broken down into three 24-card sets, each printed on a different material. Players in the 24-card Goals category have cards printed on nylon, Wins cards are printed on canvas and Assists are printed on wood. Each category has five different tiers: Major Material (numbered to 1,000), Star Material (750), Superstar Material (500), Hall of Fame Material (250) and Legendary Material (100). Players are placed in a tier based on their career numbers in each statistic.

MT
Complete Nylon Set (24): 1000.
Wayne Gretzky (100) 600.00
Steve Yzerman (100) 300.00
Brett Hull (100) 140.00
Mark Messier (250) 75.00
Joe Sakic (250) 100.00
Alexander Mogilny (250) 25.00
Brendan Shanahan (250) 70.00
Jeremy Roenick (500) 20.00
Pavel Bure (500) 35.00
Teemu Selanne (500) 35.00
Mats Sundin (500) 20.00
Eric Lindros (750) 60.00
Paul Kariya (750) 60.00
Keith Tkachuk (750) 15.00
John LeClair (750) 25.00
Zigmund Palffy (750) 15.00
Ryan Smyth (750) 6.00
Dainius Zubrus (1,000) 8.00

Daniel Alfredsson (1,000)	4.00
Joe Thornton (1,000)	20.00
Sergei Samsonov (1,000)	25.00
Sergei Berezin (1,000)	4.00
Jaroslav Svejkovsky (1,000)	6.00
Daymond Langkow (1,000)	4.00
Complete Canvas Set (24):	700.00
Patrick Roy (100)	400.00
Andy Moog (100)	75.00
Grant Fuhr (100)	75.00
John Vanbiesbrouck (250)	80.00
Mike Vernon (250)	25.00
Ron Hextall (250)	25.00
Kelly Hrudey (250)	25.00
Ed Belfour (500)	15.00
Mike Richter (500)	15.00
Curtis Joseph (500)	15.00
Felix Potvin (500)	15.00
Martin Brodeur (750)	40.00
Dominik Hasek (750)	40.00
Chris Osgood (750)	15.00
Jim Carey (750)	8.00
Nikolai Khabibulin (750)	8.00
Jocelyn Thibault (750)	8.00
Marc Denis (1,000)	4.00
Jose Theodore (1,000)	8.00
Jean-Sebastien Giguere (1,000)	4.00
Eric Fichaud (1,000)	4.00
Marcel Cousineau (1,000)	4.00
Damian Rhodes (1,000)	4.00
Mike Dunham (1,000)	4.00
Complete Wood Set (24):	900.00
Wayne Gretzky (250)	300.00
Paul Coffey (100)	75.00
Mark Messier (100)	175.00
Steve Yzerman (250)	125.00
Doug Gilmour (250)	30.00
Chris Chelios (250)	30.00
Ray Bourque (250)	30.00
Joe Sakic (500)	40.00
Brian Leetch (500)	15.00
Brett Hull (500)	20.00
Jaromir Jagr (500)	60.00
Mats Sundin (750)	10.00
Mike Modano (750)	12.00
Sergei Fedorov (750)	20.00
Brendan Shanahan (750)	25.00
Peter Forsberg (750)	50.00
Eric Lindros (750)	60.00
Saku Koivu (1,000)	20.00
Jarome Iginla (1,000)	10.00
Janne Niinimaa (1,000)	4.00
Bryan Berard (1,000)	8.00
Mike Grier (1,000)	4.00
Paul Kariya (1,000)	50.00
Chris Phillips (1,000)	4.00

1997-98 Donruss Preferred

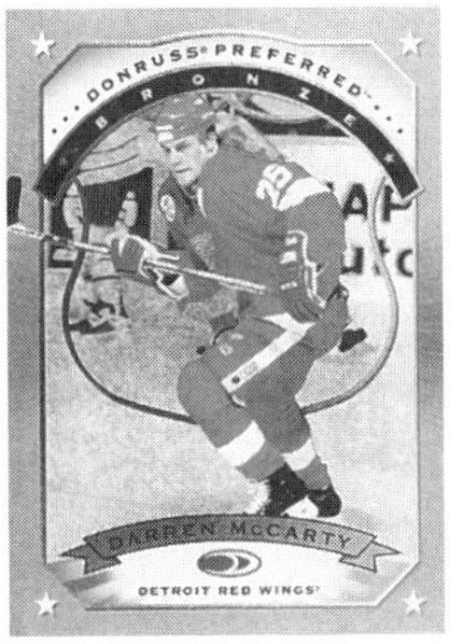

Donruss Preferred consists of a 200-card base set. The set was broken down into 100 Bronze, 60 Silver, 30 Gold and 10 Platinum cards. The borders were colored according to the level, with the player's name and team at the bottom and "Donruss Preferred" and the level at the top. The base set is paralleled in Cut to the Chase. Inserts include Color Guard, Line of the Times and Precious Metals. The cards were packaged in collectible tins which were in turn packaged in large box tins.

		MT
	Complete Set (200):	1000.
	Common Bronze:	.25
	Common Silver:	1.50
	Common Gold:	3.00
	Common Platinum:	20.00
1	Dominik Hasek G	25.00
2	Peter Forsberg G	30.00
3	Brendan Shanahan P	30.00
4	Wayne Gretzky P	100.00
5	Eric Lindros P	60.00
6	Keith Tkachuk G	15.00
7	Mark Messier P	20.00
8	Mike Modano G	10.00
9	John Vanbiesbrouck P	30.00
10	Paul Kariya P	60.00
11	Saku Koivu G	15.00
12	Paul Coffey B	.50
13	Joe Juneau B	.25
14	Jeff Friesen S	1.50
15	Brett Hull G	15.00
16	Martin Brodeur G	25.00
17	Jarome Iginla G	4.00
18	Keith Primeau S	2.00
19	Ed Jovanovski B	.25
20	Jamie Langenbrunner B	.50
21	Derian Hatcher S	1.50
22	Brian Leetch G	6.00
23	Daymond Langkow S	1.50
24	Ray Bourque S	5.00
25	Pavel Bure G	20.00
26	Janne Niinimaa S	2.00
27	Jamie Storr S	2.00
28	Darcy Tucker B	.25
29	Anson Carter B	.25
30	Jeff O'Neill B	.25
31	Jason Arnott G	4.00
32	Tommy Salo B	.50
33	Petr Nedved B	.25
34	Mike Peca B	.25
35	Ethan Moreau S	2.00
36	Ray Sheppard B	.25
37	Damian Rhodes B	.50
38	Mats Sundin S	6.00
39	Alexander Mogilny G	6.00
40	Mike Dunham S	1.50
41	Steve Yzerman P	50.00
42	Alexei Yashin S	3.00
43	Jim Carey S	1.50
44	Mike Grier S	1.50
45	Steve Rucchin B	.25
46	Mark Recchi S	1.50
47	Mike Gartner B	.25
48	Alexandre Daigle S	1.50
49	Eric Fichaud B	.50
50	Harry York B	.25
51	Dino Ciccarelli B	.25
52	Bill Ranford B	.25
53	Adam Deadmarsh G	5.00
54	Ed Belfour B	.75
55	Jozef Stumpel S	3.00
56	Rem Murray B	.25
57	Pat Verbeek B	.25
58	Pat LaFontaine S	3.00
59	Dainius Zubrus S	5.00
60	Grant Fuhr B	.75
61	Rob Niedermayer B	.25
62	Brian Savage B	.25
63	Gary Roberts B	.25
64	Tony Amonte B	.75
65	Jere Lehtinen B	.25
66	Dave Andreychuk B	.25
67	Rod Brind'Amour B	.50
68	Mikael Renberg B	.25
69	Doug Gilmour S	4.00
70	Kevin Hatcher B	.25
71	Byron Dafoe B	.50
72	Derek Plante S	1.50
73	Trevor Kidd B	.25
74	Doug Weight S	3.00
75	Valeri Bure B	.50
76	John LeClair G	15.00
77	Sergei Berezin B	.50
78	Peter Bondra S	4.00
79	Bryan Berard G	6.00
80	Steve Shields B	.75
81	Chris Osgood G	10.00
82	Mike Vernon B	.50
83	Martin Gelinas B	.25
84	Curtis Joseph S	5.00
85	Geoff Sanderson S	1.50
86	Patrick Roy P	75.00
87	Jocelyn Thibault G	6.00
88	Jeremy Roenick S	4.00
89	Trevor Linden B	.25
90	Daniel Alfredsson S	3.00
91	Sergei Zubov B	.25
92	Dimitri Khristich S	1.50
93	Brian Holzinger B	.25
94	Andrew Cassels B	.25
95	Teemu Selanne G	20.00
96	Ron Hextall B	.50
97	Wade Redden B	.25
98	Jim Campbell B	.25
99	Felix Potvin G	8.00
100	Adam Oates S	4.00
101	Nikolai Khabibulin B	.50
102	Jose Theodore S	3.00
103	Sandis Ozolinsh S	2.50
104	Sean Burke B	.50
105	Vaclav Prospal G	12.00
106	Zigmund Palffy G	12.00
107	Kyle McLaren B	.25
108	Owen Nolan S	3.00
109	Chris Pronger S	3.00
110	Daren Puppa B	.25
111	Garth Snow B	.50
112	Aki Berg B	.25
113	Andy Moog B	.75
114	Darren McCarty B	.25
115	Joe Nieuwendyk B	.50
116	Eric Daze S	3.00
117	Pierre Turgeon S	3.00
118	Ken Wregget B	.25
119	Ryan Smyth G	5.00
120	Kirk Muller B	.25
121	Luc Robitaille B	.50
122	Sergei Fedorov G	20.00
123	Sean Pronger B	.25
124	Mike Richter S	5.00
125	Jaromir Jagr P	60.00
126	Claude Lemieux B	.25
127	Chris Chelios S	4.00
128	Joe Sakic P	40.00
129	Guy Hebert S	4.00
130	Chris Gratton S	3.00
131	Steve Sullivan B	.25
132	Al MacInnis B	.50
133	Adam Graves S	2.50
134	Vyacheslav Kozlov B	.25
135	Scott Mellanby S	1.50
136	Stephane Fiset B	.25
137	Oleg Tverdovsky S	2.50
138	Theoren Fleury S	4.00
139	Jeff Hackett B	.75
140	Vincent Damphousse B	.25
141	Roman Hamrlik S	1.50
142	Ron Francis S	5.00
143	Scott Lachance B	.25
144	Todd Harvey B	.25
145	Marc Denis S	3.00
146	Jaroslav Svejkovsky G	3.00
147	Olli Jokinen S	8.00
148	Sergei Samsonov G	15.00
149	Chris Phillips G	3.00
150	Patrick Marleau G	20.00
151	Joe Thornton G	30.00
152	Daniel Cleary S	3.00
153	Alyn McCauley G	3.00
154	Brad Isbister S	3.00
155	Alexei Morozov S	5.00
156	Shawn Bates B	.25
157	Jean-Yves Leroux B	.25
158	Marcel Cousineau B	.25
159	Vaclav Varada B	1.50
160	Jean-Sebastien Giguere S	1.50
161	Espen Knutsen B	.25
162	Marian Hossa B	10.00
163	Robert Dome B	.25
164	Juha Lind B	.25
165	Sergei Fedorov B (National Treasures)	6.00
166	Jarome Iginla B (National Treasures)	.50
167	Jaroslav Svejkovsky B (National Treasures)	.25
168	Patrick Roy S (National Treasures)	20.00
169	Dominik Hasek B (National Treasures)	2.00
170	Alexander Mogilny B (National Treasures)	.75
171	Chris Chelios B (National Treasures)	.50
172	Wayne Gretzky S (National Treasures)	25.00
173	Peter Forsberg B (National Treasures)	5.00
174	Ray Bourque B (National Treasures)	.50
175	Joe Sakic S (National Treasures)	10.00
176	Mike Modano B (National Treasures)	1.00
177	Mark Messier B (National Treasures)	1.50
178	Teemu Selanne B (National Treasures)	2.00
179	Steve Yzerman S (National Treasures)	12.00
180	Eric Lindros S (National Treasures)	15.00
181	Doug Weight B (National Treasures)	.50
182	John Vanbiesbrouck B (National Treasures)	1.50
183	Paul Kariya S (National Treasures)	15.00
184	Brendan Shanahan S (National Treasures)	8.00
185	Martin Brodeur B (National Treasures)	2.00
186	Bryan Berard B (National Treasures)	.25
187	Marc Denis B (National Treasures)	.25
188	Brian Leetch B (National Treasures)	.40
189	Ryan Smyth S (National Treasures)	1.50
190	Dainius Zubrus B (National Treasures)	.75
191	Keith Tkachuk B (National Treasures)	1.00
192	Jaromir Jagr S (National Treasures)	12.00
193	Brett Hull B (National Treasures)	1.00
194	Pavel Bure B (National Treasures)	1.50
195	Checklist Sergei Samsonov B	1.00
196	Checklist Olli Jokinen B	.50
197	Checklist Chris Phillips B	.25
198	Checklist Patrick Marleau B	1.50
199	Checklist Daniel Cleary B	.25
200	Checklist Joe Thornton B	2.50

1997-98 Donruss Preferred Cut to the Chase

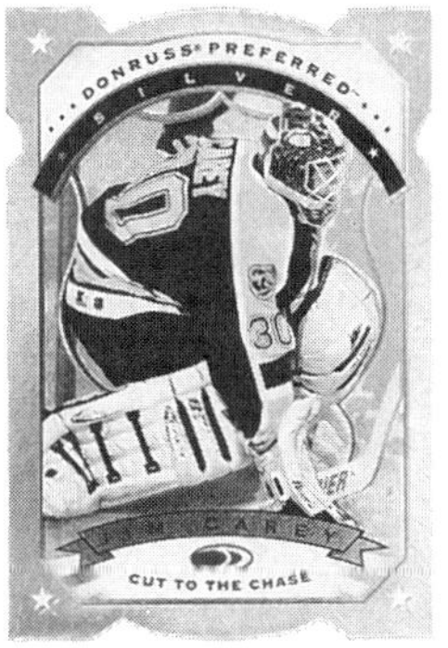

Cut to the Chase is a full parallel of the Preferred base set. The cards have a die-cut design.

		MT
	Common Bronze:	1.50
	Common Silver:	5.00
	Common Gold:	10.00
	Common Platinum:	75.00
1	Dominik Hasek G	60.00
2	Peter Forsberg G	100.00
3	Brendan Shanahan P	100.00
4	Wayne Gretzky P	300.00
5	Eric Lindros P	175.00
6	Keith Tkachuk G	40.00
7	Mark Messier P	75.00
8	Mike Modano G	25.00
9	John Vanbiesbrouck P	80.00
10	Paul Kariya P	175.00
11	Saku Koivu G	50.00
12	Paul Coffey B	2.50
13	Joe Juneau B	1.50
14	Jeff Friesen S	5.00
15	Brett Hull G	40.00
16	Martin Brodeur G	80.00
17	Jarome Iginla G	10.00
18	Keith Primeau S	5.00
19	Ed Jovanovski B	1.50
20	Jamie Langenbrunner B	2.50
21	Derian Hatcher S	5.00
22	Brian Leetch G	15.00
23	Daymond Langkow S	5.00
24	Ray Bourque S	10.00
25	Pavel Bure G	60.00
26	Janne Niinimaa S	5.00
27	Jamie Storr S	8.00
28	Darcy Tucker B	1.50
29	Anson Carter B	1.50
30	Jeff O'Neill B	1.50
31	Jason Arnott G	10.00
32	Tommy Salo B	3.00
33	Petr Nedved B	1.50
34	Mike Peca B	1.50
35	Ethan Moreau S	5.00
36	Ray Sheppard B	1.50
37	Damian Rhodes B	3.00
38	Mats Sundin S	12.00
39	Alexander Mogilny G	15.00
40	Mike Dunham S	5.00
41	Steve Yzerman P	150.00
42	Alexei Yashin S	10.00
43	Jim Carey S	5.00
44	Mike Grier S	5.00
45	Steve Rucchin B	1.50
46	Mark Recchi S	5.00
47	Mike Gartner B	1.50
48	Alexandre Daigle S	5.00
49	Eric Fichaud B	1.50
50	Harry York B	1.50
51	Dino Ciccarelli B	1.50
52	Bill Ranford B	1.50
53	Adam Deadmarsh G	10.00
54	Ed Belfour B	4.00
55	Jozef Stumpel S	8.00
56	Rem Murray B	1.50
57	Pat Verbeek B	1.50
58	Pat LaFontaine S	10.00
59	Dainius Zubrus S	10.00
60	Grant Fuhr B	4.00
61	Rob Niedermayer B	1.50
62	Brian Savage B	1.50
63	Gary Roberts B	1.50
64	Tony Amonte B	4.00
65	Jere Lehtinen B	1.50
66	Dave Andreychuk B	1.50
67	Rod Brind'Amour B	3.00
68	Mikael Renberg B	1.50
69	Doug Gilmour S	10.00
70	Kevin Hatcher B	1.50
71	Byron Dafoe B	1.50
72	Derek Plante S	5.00
73	Trevor Kidd B	1.50
74	Doug Weight S	8.00
75	Valeri Bure B	1.50
76	John LeClair G	45.00
77	Sergei Berezin B	1.50
78	Peter Bondra S	10.00
79	Bryan Berard G	15.00
80	Steve Shields B	3.00
81	Chris Osgood G	25.00
82	Mike Vernon B	3.00
83	Martin Gelinas B	1.50
84	Curtis Joseph S	10.00
85	Geoff Sanderson S	5.00
86	Patrick Roy P	225.00
87	Jocelyn Thibault G	20.00
88	Jeremy Roenick S	12.00
89	Trevor Linden B	1.50
90	Daniel Alfredsson S	8.00
91	Sergei Zubov B	1.50
92	Dimitri Khristich S	5.00
93	Brian Holzinger B	1.50
94	Andrew Cassels B	1.50
95	Teemu Selanne G	60.00
96	Ron Hextall B	3.00
97	Wade Redden B	1.50
98	Jim Campbell B	1.50
99	Felix Potvin G	20.00
100	Adam Oates S	10.00
101	Nikolai Khabibulin B	3.00
102	Jose Theodore S	8.00
103	Sandis Ozolinsh S	5.00
104	Sean Burke B	3.00
105	Vaclav Prospal G	20.00
106	Zigmund Palffy G	35.00
107	Kyle McLaren B	1.50
108	Owen Nolan S	8.00
109	Chris Pronger S	8.00
110	Daren Puppa B	1.50
111	Garth Snow B	3.00
112	Aki Berg B	1.50
113	Andy Moog B	3.00
114	Darren McCarty B	1.50
115	Joe Nieuwendyk B	3.00
116	Eric Daze S	8.00
117	Pierre Turgeon S	10.00
118	Ken Wregget B	1.50
119	Ryan Smyth G	10.00
120	Kirk Muller B	1.50
121	Luc Robitaille B	2.50
122	Sergei Fedorov G	50.00
123	Sean Pronger B	1.50
124	Mike Richter S	10.00
125	Jaromir Jagr P	175.00
126	Claude Lemieux B	1.50
127	Chris Chelios S	10.00
128	Joe Sakic P	120.00
129	Guy Hebert S	10.00
130	Chris Gratton S	8.00
131	Steve Sullivan B	1.50
132	Al MacInnis B	3.00
133	Adam Graves S	5.00
134	Vyacheslav Kozlov B	1.50
135	Scott Mellanby S	5.00
136	Stephane Fiset B	1.50
137	Oleg Tverdovsky S	5.00
138	Theoren Fleury S	10.00
139	Jeff Hackett B	3.00
140	Vincent Damphousse B	1.50
141	Roman Hamrlik S	5.00
142	Ron Francis S	10.00
143	Scott Lachance B	1.50
144	Todd Harvey B	1.50
145	Marc Denis S	5.00
146	Jaroslav Svejkovsky G	10.00
147	Olli Jokinen S	20.00

148	Sergei Samsonov G	20.00
149	Chris Phillips G	1.50
150	Patrick Marleau G	35.00
151	Joe Thornton G	50.00
152	Daniel Cleary S	5.00
153	Alyn McCauley G	10.00
154	Brad Isbister S	5.00
155	Alexei Morozov S	8.00
156	Shawn Bates B	1.50
157	Jean-Yves Leroux B	1.50
158	Marcel Cousineau B	1.50
159	Vackav Varada B	1.50
160	Jean-Sebastien Giguere S	5.00
161	Espen Knutsen B	1.50
162	Marian Hossa B	20.00
163	Robert Dome B	1.50
164	Juha Lind B	1.50
165	Sergei Fedorov B (National Treasures)	10.00
166	Jarome Iginla B (National Treasures)	1.50
167	Jaroslav Svejkovsky B (National Treasures)	1.50
168	Patrick Roy S (National Treasures)	90.00
169	Dominik Hasek B (National Treasures)	15.00
170	Alexander Mogilny B (National Treasures)	3.00
171	Chris Chelios B (National Treasures)	3.00
172	Wayne Gretzky S (National Treasures)	120.00
173	Peter Forsberg B (National Treasures)	20.00
174	Ray Bourque B (National Treasures)	4.00
175	Joe Sakic S (National Treasures)	50.00
176	Mike Modano B (National Treasures)	5.00
177	Mark Messier B (National Treasures)	8.00
178	Teemu Selanne B (National Treasures)	12.00
179	Steve Yzerman S (National Treasures)	60.00
180	Eric Lindros S (National Treasures)	75.00
181	Doug Weight B (National Treasures)	3.00
182	John Vanbiesbrouck B (National Treasures)	10.00
183	Paul Kariya S (National Treasures)	75.00
184	Brendan Shanahan S (National Treasures)	40.00
185	Martin Brodeur B (National Treasures)	15.00
186	Bryan Berard B (National Treasures)	3.00
187	Marc Denis B (National Treasures)	1.50
188	Brian Leetch B (National Treasures)	3.00
189	Ryan Smyth S (National Treasures)	5.00
190	Dainius Zubrus B (National Treasures)	2.50
191	Keith Tkachuk B (National Treasures)	8.00
192	Jaromir Jagr S (National Treasures)	75.00
193	Brett Hull B (National Treasures)	4.00
194	Pavel Bure B (National Treasures)	12.00
195	Checklist Sergei Samsonov B	6.00
196	Checklist Olli Jokinen B	4.00
197	Checklist Chris Phillips B	1.50
198	Checklist Patrick Marleau B	8.00
199	Checklist Daniel Cleary B	1.50
200	Checklist Joe Thornton B	12.00

1997-98 Donruss Preferred Color Guard

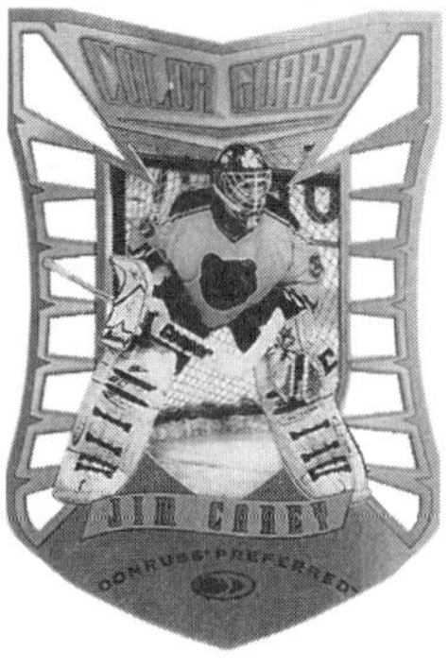

Color Guard is an 18-card insert numbered to 1,500. Printed on plastic, the cards have a die-cut shield design. "Color Guard" is printed at the top and the player's name is at the bottom.

		MT
Complete Set (18):		300.00
Common Player:		10.00
1	Patrick Roy	75.00
2	Martin Brodeur	40.00
3	Curtis Joseph	20.00
4	John Vanbiesbrouck	30.00
5	Felix Potvin	20.00
6	Dominik Hasek	40.00
7	Chris Osgood	20.00
8	Eric Fichaud	10.00
9	Jocelyn Thibault	15.00
10	Marc Denis	10.00
11	Jose Theodore	15.00
12	Mike Vernon	10.00
13	Jim Carey	10.00
14	Ron Hextall	10.00
15	Mike Richter	18.00
16	Ed Belfour	20.00
17	Mike Dunham	10.00
18	Damian Rhodes	10.00

1997-98 Donruss Preferred Line of the Times

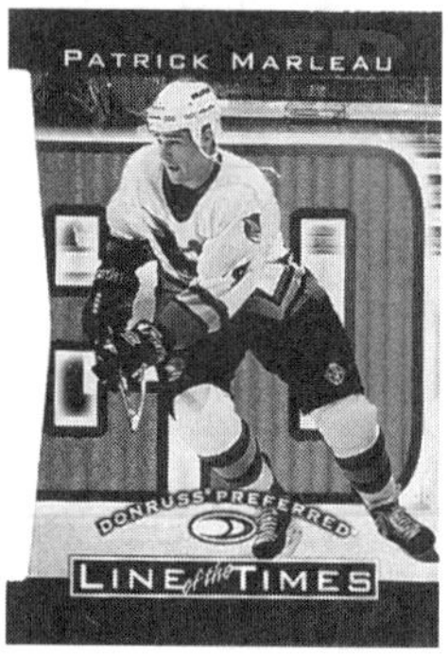

Line of the Times is a 24-card insert numbered to 2,500. The die-cut cards are assembled in eight three-card sets. Each group of three cards can be fit together to form a line of NHL players.

		MT
Complete Set (24):		500.00
Common Player:		8.00
1A	Ryan Smyth	8.00
1B	Sergei Fedorov	25.00
1C	Jaromir Jagr	50.00
2A	Eric Lindros	50.00
2B	Joe Thornton	25.00
2C	Brendan Shanahan	25.00
3A	John LeClair	20.00
3B	Keith Tkachuk	15.00
3C	Brett Hull	15.00
4A	Pavel Bure	25.00
4B	Sergei Samsonov	10.00
4C	Paul Kariya	50.00
5A	Mike Modano	12.00
5B	Teemu Selanne	25.00
5C	Patrick Marleau	15.00
6A	Wayne Gretzky	75.00
6B	Steve Yzerman	40.00
6C	Daniel Cleary	8.00
7A	Jarome Iginla	8.00
7B	Peter Forsberg	40.00
7C	Mark Messier	15.00
8A	Joe Sakic	30.00
8B	Jaroslav Svejkovsky	8.00
8C	Dainius Zubrus	12.00

1997-98 Donruss Preferred Precious Metals

Precious Metals is a 15-card, renumbered partial parallel of the Preferred Hockey base set. Each card is printed on a metal surface which corresponds to the color of the player's base card. For example, Paul Kariya's card includes one gram of platinum. Only 100 sets were produced.

		MT
Complete Set (15):		4500.
Common Player:		100.00
1	Brendan Shanahan	250.00
2	Joe Thornton	200.00
3	Wayne Gretzky	750.00
4	Mark Messier	200.00
5	Patrick Roy	600.00
6	Martin Brodeur	300.00
7	Eric Lindros	450.00
8	Paul Kariya	450.00
9	Teemu Selanne	250.00
10	Jaromir Jagr	450.00
11	Joe Sakic	300.00
12	Peter Forsberg	375.00
13	John Vanbiesbrouck	250.00
14	Steve Yzerman	375.00
15	Sergei Samsonov	100.00

1997-98 Donruss Preferred Tins

Donruss Preferred Hockey was packaged in collectible tins. Each of the 24 tins contained five cards. Gold parallel versions of the tins are sequentially numbered to 499. The pack tins were packaged in larger box-sized tins. Each of the 24 box tins had a blue (U.S. Hobby) and red (Canada) parallel version numbered to 499.

		MT
Complete Set (24):		20.00
Common Tin:		.25
1	Eric Lindros	1.25
2	Paul Kariya	1.25
3	Wayne Gretzky	2.00
4	Teemu Selanne	.75
5	Patrick Roy	1.50
6	John Vanbiesbrouck	.50
7	Mike Modano	.50
8	Joe Sakic	.75
9	Peter Forsberg	1.00
10	Martin Brodeur	.75
11	Sergei Samsonov	.50
12	Brendan Shanahan	.75
13	Steve Yzerman	1.00
14	Jaromir Jagr	1.25
15	Mark Messier	.50
16	Joe Thornton	1.00
17	Pavel Bure	.75
18	Brett Hull	.50
19	Brendan Shanahan	.75
20	Jaromir Jagr	1.25
21	Eric Lindros	1.25
22	Paul Kariya	1.25
23	Wayne Gretzky	2.00
24	Patrick Roy	1.50

1997-98 Donruss Preferred Double-Wide Tins

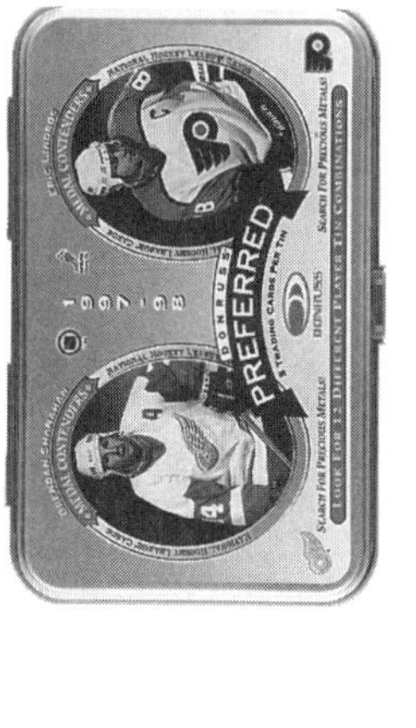

Double-wide tins contained a pack of five cards and featured two NHL players on the front. Twelve different double-wide tins were available as retail packs.

		MT
Complete Set (12):		15.00
Common Tin:		.75
1	Wayne Gretzky, Joe Thornton	2.50
2	Paul Kariya, Brett Hull	1.50
3	Eric Lindros, Joe Sakic	1.50
4	Teemu Selanne, Peter Forsberg	1.25
5	Pavel Bure, Mike Modano	.75
6	Sergei Samsonov, Steve Yzerman	1.25
7	Jaromir Jagr, Brendan Shanahan	1.50
8	Mark Messier, John Vanbiesbrouck	.75
9	Patrick Roy, Martin Brodeur	2.00
10	Brendan Shanahan, Eric Lindros	1.50
11	Jaromir Jagr, Paul Kariya	2.00
12	Wayne Gretzky, Patrick Roy	3.00

1997-98 Donruss Priority

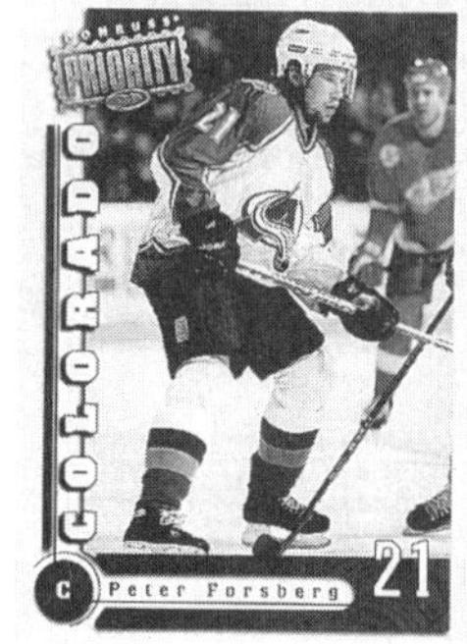

Donruss Priority Hockey consists of a 220-card base set. The product is based around a "postal" theme, with postcards and stamps being the main items. Of the 15 packs in each box, 10 contained a 4-x-6 postcard and some regular cards and five packs held a stamp and cards. Even-numbered cards were in the postcard packs and odd-numbered cards were inserted in the stamp packs. The stamps are paralleled three times (bronze, silver and gold). The base cards are paralleled in Stamp of Approval. The inserts include Direct Deposit, Opening Day Issue and Postmaster Generals. Also included in Priority Hockey is Lindros Locker Collection. Redmeption cards for 750 autographed pucks, 15 signed jerseys and 15 signed game-used sticks.

		MT
Complete Set (220):		50.00
Common Player:		.20
1	Patrick Roy	3.00
2	Eric Lindros	2.50
3	Keith Tkachuk	.75
4	Steve Yzerman	2.00
5	John Vanbiesbrouck	1.00
6	Teemu Selanne	1.00
7	Martin Brodeur	1.00
8	Peter Forsberg	2.00
9	Brett Hull	.75
10	Wayne Gretzky	4.00
11	Mike Modano	.60
12	Sergei Fedorov	1.00
13	Paul Kariya	2.50
14	Saku Koivu	.75
15	Pavel Bure	1.00
16	Mark Messier	1.00
17	Joe Sakic	1.50
18	Jaromir Jagr	2.50
19	Brendan Shanahan	1.00
20	Ray Bourque	.60
21	Daymond Langkow	.20
22	Alexandre Daigle	.20
23	Dainius Zubrus	.40
24	Ryan Smyth	.20
25	Derek Plante	.20
26	Eric Daze	.20
27	Ed Jovanovski	.20
28	Sergei Berezin	.20
29	Roman Turek	.20
30	Derian Hatcher	.20
31	Jarome Iginla	.20
32	Luc Robitaille	.40
33	Rod Brind'Amour	.40
34	Mathieu Schneider	.20
35	Olaf Kolzig	.75
36	Nikolai Khabibulin	.50
37	Scott Niedermayer	.20
38	Keith Primeau	.40
39	Dimitri Khristich	.20
40	Eric Fichaud	.40
41	Pierre Turgeon	.40
42	Kevin Stevens	.20
43	Nicklas Lidstrom	.50
44	Sean Burke	.50
45	Sandis Ozolinsh	.20
46	Owen Nolan	.20
47	Peter Bondra	.60
48	Ron Hextall	.50
49	Rob Blake	.20
50	Geoff Sanderson	.20
51	Sergei Zubov	.20
52	Doug Gilmour	.50
53	Oleg Tverdovsky	.20
54	Bryan Berard	.40
55	Bill Ranford	.50
56	Mats Sundin	.60
57	Damian Rhodes	.20
58	Zigmund Palffy	.75
59	Mike Grier	.20
60	Jozef Stumpel	.40
61	Mark Recchi	.20
62	Alexei Zhamnov	.20
63	Jere Lehtinen	.20
64	Andrew Cassels	.20
65	Kevin Hodson	.50
66	Dino Ciccarelli	.20
67	Niklas Sundstrom	.20
68	Jeff Hackett	.50
69	Brian Holzinger	.20
70	Jeff Friesen	.20
71	Ed Belfour	.75
72	Wayne Primeau	.20
73	Sami Kapanen	.20
74	Brian Leetch	.40
75	Mikael Renberg	.20
76	Ron Tugnutt	.40
77	Ron Francis	.50
78	Jocelyn Thibault	.50
79	Jamie Langenbrunner	.20
80	Dominik Hasek	1.50
81	Chris Osgood	.75
82	Grant Fuhr	.75
83	Adam Graves	.20
84	Janne Niinimaa	.20
85	Kelly Hrudey	.40
86	Mike Dunham	.20
87	Valeri Kamensky	.20
88	Cory Stillman	.20
89	Anson Carter	.20
90	Igor Larionov	.20
91	Chris Pronger	.50
92	Steve Sullivan	.20
93	Mike Gardner	.20
94	Jim Campbell	.20
95	Valeri Bure	.20
96	Stephane Fiset	.40
97	Jason Arnott	.20
98	Trevor Kidd	.50
99	Chris Chelios	.50
100	Kevin Hatcher	.20
101	Felix Potvin	.75
102	Travis Green	.20
103	Dave Gagner	.20
104	Byron Dafoe	.50
105	Rick Tabaracci	.20
106	Gary Roberts	.20
107	Mike Ricci	.20
108	Andy Moog	.50
109	Sean Pronger	.20
110	Paul Coffey	.40
111	Trevor Linden	.20
112	Rob Zamuner	.20
113	Daniel Alfredsson	.40
114	Ray Sheppard	.20
115	Steve Shields	.40
116	Ethan Moreau	.20
117	Tomas Sandstrom	.20
118	Chris Gratton	.20
119	Alexander Mogilny	.50
120	Roman Hamrlik	.20
121	Tommy Salo	.50
122	Jason Allison	.40
123	Curtis Joseph	.75
124	Guy Hebert	.50
125	Jeff O'Neill	.20
126	Donald Audette	.20
127	Claude Lemieux	.40
128	Brian Savage	.20
129	Scott Mellanby	.20
130	Vyacheslav Kozlov	.20
131	Wade Redden	.20
132	John LeClair	1.00
133	Jeremy Roenick	.75
134	Andreas Johansson	.20
135	Nelson Emerson	.20
136	Daren Puppa	.40

137	Joe Juneau	.20
138	Garth Snow	.50
139	Tom Barrasso	.50
140	Joe Nieuwendyk	.50
141	Theoren Fleury	.50
142	Yanic Perreault	.20
143	Mike Richter	.75
144	Al MacInnis	.40
145	Mike Peca	.20
146	Darren McCarty	.20
147	Alexei Yashin	.50
148	Rick Tocchet	.20
149	Adam Oates	.50
150	Wendel Clark	.20
151	Tony Amonte	.50
152	Dave Andreychuk	.20
153	Jamie Storr	.50
154	Craig Janney	.20
155	Todd Bertuzzi	.20
156	Harry York	.20
157	Todd Harvey	.20
158	Bobby Holik	.20
159	Mike Vernon	.50
160	Pat LaFontaine	.40
161	Doug Weight	.40
162	Kirk McLean	.50
163	Adam Deadmarsh	.40
164	Vincent Damphousse	.20
165	Vaclav Prospal	1.00
166	Daniel Cleary	.20
167	Jaroslav Svejkovsky	.20
168	*Marco Sturm*	1.00
169	Robert Dome	.20
170	*Patrik Elias*	1.00
171	Mattias Ohlund	.20
172	Espen Knutsen	.20
173	Joe Thornton	2.00
174	*Jan Bulis*	.50
175	Patrick Marleau	1.00
176	Brad Isbister	.20
177	*Kevin Weekes*	.50
178	Sergei Samsonov	.75
179	*Tyler Moss*	.20
180	Chris Phillips	.20
181	Alyn McCauley	.20
182	*Derek Morris*	.40
183	Alexei Morozov	.20
184	Boyd Devereaux	.20
185	Peter Forsberg (1st Class Package)	1.00
186	Brendan Shanahan (1st Class Package)	.50
187	Teemu Selanne (1st Class Package)	.50
188	Eric Lindros (1st Class Package)	1.25
189	Mark Messier (1st Class Package)	.50
190	Vaclav Prospal (1st Class Package)	.50
191	Jarome Iginla (1st Class Package)	.20
192	Mike Modano (1st Class Package)	.40
193	John Vanbiesbrouck (1st Class Package)	.50
194	Bryan Berard (1st Class Package)	.20
195	Patrick Marleau (1st Class Package)	.50
196	Martin Brodeur (1st Class Package)	.60
197	Patrick Roy (1st Class Package)	1.50
198	Felix Potvin (1st Class Package)	.40
199	Wayne Gretzky (1st Class Package)	2.00
200	Sergei Samsonov (1st Class Package)	.40
201	Ryan Smyth (1st Class Package)	.20
202	Keith Tkachuk (1st Class Package)	.40
203	Chris Osgood (1st Class Package)	.40
204	Paul Kariya (1st Class Package)	1.25
205	John LeClair (1st Class Package)	.50
206	Alyn McCauley (1st Class Package)	.20
207	Joe Thornton (1st Class Package)	1.00
208	Joe Sakic (1st Class Package)	.75
209	Steve Yzerman (1st Class Package)	1.00
210	Saku Koivu (1st Class Package)	.40
211	Pavel Bure (1st Class Package)	.50
212	Zigmund Palffy (1st Class Package)	.40
213	Alexei Yashin (1st Class Package)	.20
214	Sergei Fedorov (1st Class Package)	.50
215	Checklist Joe Thornton	.50
216	Checklist Patrick Marleau	.40
217	Checklist Daniel Cleary	.20
218	Checklist Sergei Samsonov	.40
219	Checklist Jaroslav Svejkovsky	.20
220	Checklist Alyn McCauley	.20

1997-98 Donruss Priority Direct Deposit

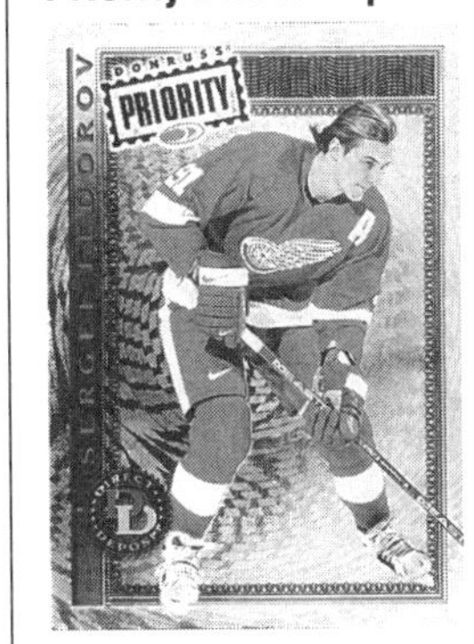

Direct Deposit is a 30-card insert featuring swirled foil. The cards are numbered to 3,000.

		MT
Complete Set (30):		250.00
Common Player:		4.00
1	Brendan Shanahan	10.00
2	Steve Yzerman	20.00
3	Pavel Bure	10.00
4	Jaromir Jagr	25.00
5	Ryan Smyth	4.00
6	Sergei Samsonov	6.00
7	Mark Messier	10.00
8	Wayne Gretzky	40.00
9	Jarome Iginla	4.00
10	Peter Forsberg	20.00
11	Joe Sakic	15.00
12	Sergei Fedorov	10.00
13	Mike Modano	8.00
14	Paul Kariya	25.00
15	Teemu Selanne	10.00
16	Eric Lindros	25.00
17	Keith Tkachuk	8.00
18	Patrick Marleau	8.00
19	Jaroslav Svejkovsky	4.00
20	Alyn McCauley	4.00
21	Saku Koivu	8.00
22	Zigmund Palffy	8.00
23	Brett Hull	8.00
24	Patrik Elias	4.00
25	Joe Thornton	12.00
26	Espen Knutsen	4.00
27	Daniel Alfredsson	4.00
28	John LeClair	10.00
29	Dainius Zubrus	4.00
30	Jason Arnott	4.00

1997-98 Donruss Priority Opening Day Issues

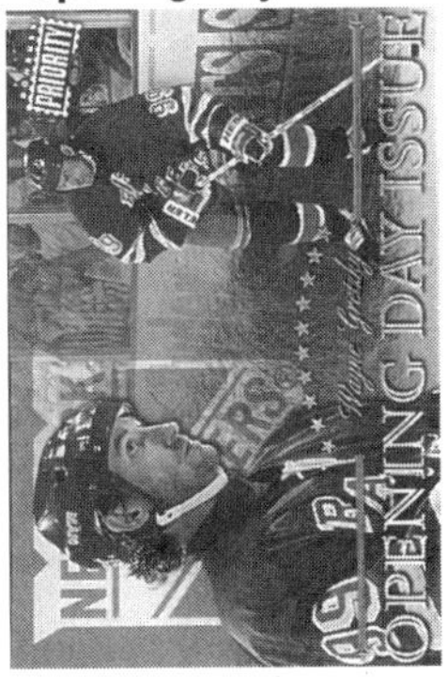

Opening Day Issue is an insert consisting of 30 postcards. The all-foil cards feature gold-foil stamping with a commemorative canceled stamp. Each card also has a spot for a corresponding player stamp or trading card. The postcards had a production run of 1,000.

		MT
Complete Set (30):		375.00
Common Player:		6.00
1	Patrick Roy	40.00
2	Eric Lindros	30.00
3	Keith Tkachuk	10.00
4	Steve Yzerman	25.00
5	John Vanbiesbrouck	12.00
6	Teemu Selanne	12.00
7	Martin Brodeur	15.00
8	Peter Forsberg	25.00
9	Brett Hull	10.00
10	Wayne Gretzky	50.00
11	Mike Modano	8.00
12	Paul Kariya	30.00
13	Pavel Bure	12.00
14	Mark Messier	12.00
15	Joe Sakic	20.00
16	Jaromir Jagr	30.00
17	Brendan Shanahan	12.00
18	Ryan Smyth	6.00
19	Jarome Iginla	6.00
20	Bryan Berard	6.00
21	Jocelyn Thibault	6.00
22	Dominik Hasek	15.00
23	Chris Osgood	8.00
24	Chris Chelios	6.00
25	Felix Potvin	8.00
26	John LeClair	12.00
27	Saku Koivu	10.00
28	Joe Thornton	15.00
29	Patrick Marleau	12.00
30	Sergei Samsonov	8.00

1997-98 Donruss Priority Postcards

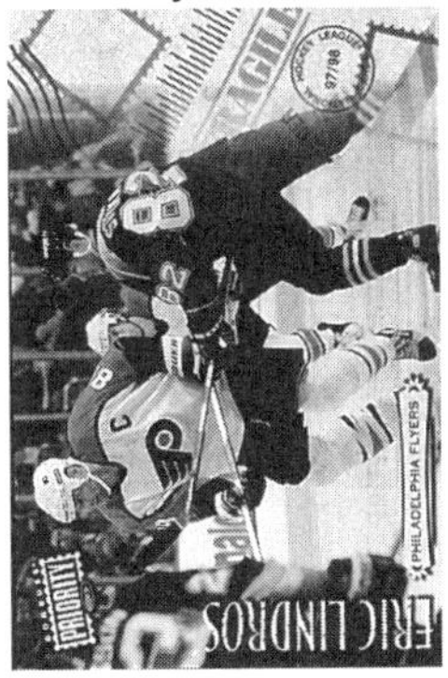

Thirty-six NHL players are featured on postcards. Each card measures 4-x-6 and features a player photo on the left and a spot to place the matching stamp on the right. Ten postcard packs were included in each box of Priority Hockey, with one postcard in each pack.

		MT
Complete Set (36):		30.00
Common Player:		.50
1	Patrick Roy	3.00
2	Brendan Shanahan	1.00
3	Steve Yzerman	2.00
4	Jaromir Jagr	2.50
5	Pavel Bure	1.00
6	Mark Messier	1.00
7	Wayne Gretzky	4.00
8	Eric Lindros	2.50
9	Joe Sakic	1.50
10	Peter Forsberg	2.00
11	John Vanbiesbrouck	1.00
12	Mike Modano	.75
13	Paul Kariya	2.50
14	Teemu Selanne	1.00
15	Sergei Fedorov	1.00
16	Joe Thornton	1.50
17	Sergei Samsonov	.75
18	Patrick Marleau	1.00
19	Ryan Smyth	.50
20	Jarome Iginla	.50
21	John LeClair	1.00
22	Brian Leetch	.50
23	Chris Chelios	.50
24	Martin Brodeur	1.25
25	Bryan Berard	.50
26	Keith Tkachuk	.75
27	Saku Koivu	.75
28	Brett Hull	.75
29	Felix Potvin	.50
30	Chris Osgood	.50
31	Dominik Hasek	1.50
32	Zigmund Palffy	.75
33	Jeremy Roenick	.75
34	Dainius Zubrus	.50
35	Ray Bourque	.50
36	Jocelyn Thibault	.50

1997-98 Donruss Priority Postmaster General

Postmaster Generals is a 20-card insert featuring the league's top goalies. The full-foil cards are numbered to 1,500.

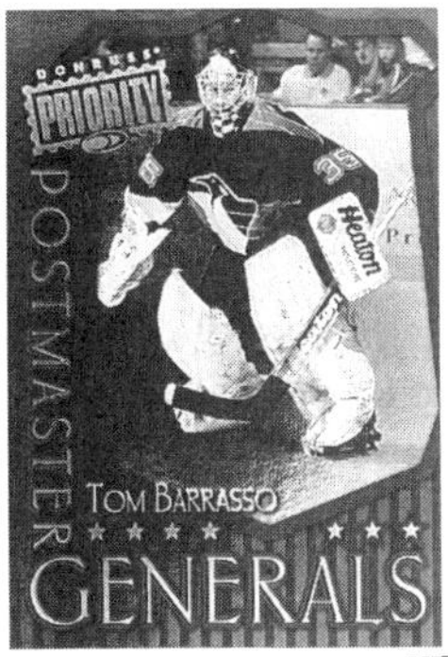

		MT
Complete Set (20):		275.00
Common Player:		8.00
1	Patrick Roy	65.00
2	John Vanbiesbrouck	25.00
3	Felix Potvin	15.00
4	Curtis Joseph	15.00
5	Mike Richter	12.00
6	Jocelyn Thibault	8.00
7	Ed Belfour	15.00
8	Chris Osgood	15.00
9	Ron Hextall	8.00
10	Martin Brodeur	40.00
11	Mike Vernon	12.00
12	Eric Fichaud	8.00
13	Dominik Hasek	40.00
14	Byron Dafoe	12.00
15	Tommy Salo	10.00
16	Garth Snow	8.00
17	Tom Barrasso	12.00
18	Marc Denis	8.00
19	Grant Fuhr	15.00
20	Guy Hebert	8.00

1997-98 Donruss Priority Stamp of Approval

Stamp of Approval is a parallel of the 220-card base set. The cards are printed on holo-foil, die-cut like the edges of a stamp and numbered to 100.

		MT
Common Player:		20.00
Semistars & Goalies:		40.00
1	Patrick Roy	350.00
2	Eric Lindros	300.00
3	Keith Tkachuk	100.00
4	Steve Yzerman	250.00
5	John Vanbiesbrouck	125.00
6	Teemu Selanne	140.00
7	Martin Brodeur	160.00
8	Peter Forsberg	250.00
9	Brett Hull	100.00
10	Wayne Gretzky	500.00
11	Mike Modano	75.00
12	Sergei Fedorov	125.00
13	Paul Kariya	300.00
14	Saku Koivu	75.00
15	Pavel Bure	125.00
16	Mark Messier	125.00
17	Joe Sakic	200.00
18	Jaromir Jagr	300.00
19	Brendan Shanahan	125.00
20	Ray Bourque	75.00
21	Daymond Langkow	20.00
22	Alexandre Daigle	20.00
23	Dainius Zubrus	30.00
24	Ryan Smyth	20.00
25	Derek Plante	20.00
26	Eric Daze	20.00
27	Ed Jovanovski	20.00
28	Sergei Berezin	20.00
29	Roman Turek	20.00
30	Derian Hatcher	20.00
31	Jarome Iginla	20.00
32	Luc Robitaille	30.00
33	Rod Brind'Amour	40.00
34	Mathieu Schneider	20.00
35	Olaf Kolzig	60.00
36	Nikolai Khabibulin	40.00
37	Scott Niedermayer	20.00
38	Keith Primeau	40.00
39	Dimitri Khristich	20.00
40	Eric Fichaud	30.00
41	Pierre Turgeon	40.00
42	Kevin Stevens	20.00
43	Nicklas Lidstrom	50.00
44	Sean Burke	40.00
45	Sandis Ozolinsh	20.00
46	Owen Nolan	20.00
47	Peter Bondra	50.00
48	Ron Hextall	40.00
49	Rob Blake	20.00
50	Geoff Sanderson	20.00
51	Sergei Zubov	20.00
52	Doug Gilmour	40.00
53	Oleg Tverdovsky	20.00
54	Bryan Berard	40.00
55	Bill Ranford	40.00
56	Mats Sundin	60.00
57	Damian Rhodes	20.00
58	Zigmund Palffy	75.00
59	Mike Grier	20.00
60	Jozef Stumpel	20.00
61	Mark Recchi	20.00
62	Alexei Zhamnov	20.00
63	Jere Lehtinen	20.00
64	Andrew Cassels	20.00
65	Kevin Hodson	40.00
66	Dino Ciccarelli	20.00
67	Niklas Sundstrom	20.00
68	Jeff Hackett	50.00
69	Brian Holzinger	20.00
70	Jeff Friesen	20.00
71	Ed Belfour	60.00
72	Wayne Primeau	20.00
73	Sami Kapanen	20.00
74	Brian Leetch	40.00
75	Mikael Renberg	20.00
76	Ron Tugnutt	40.00
77	Ron Francis	50.00
78	Jocelyn Thibault	40.00
79	Jamie Langenbrunner	20.00
80	Dominik Hasek	180.00
81	Chris Osgood	60.00
82	Grant Fuhr	60.00
83	Adam Graves	20.00
84	Janne Niinimaa	20.00
85	Kelly Hrudey	20.00
86	Mike Dunham	20.00
87	Valeri Kamensky	20.00
88	Cory Stillman	20.00
89	Anson Carter	20.00
90	Igor Larionov	20.00
91	Chris Pronger	40.00
92	Steve Sullivan	20.00
93	Mike Gardner	20.00
94	Jim Campbell	20.00
95	Valeri Bure	20.00
96	Stephane Fiset	40.00
97	Jason Arnott	20.00
98	Trevor Kidd	40.00
99	Chris Chelios	50.00
100	Kevin Hatcher	20.00
101	Felix Potvin	60.00
102	Travis Green	20.00
103	Dave Gagner	20.00
104	Byron Dafoe	40.00
105	Rick Tabaracci	20.00
106	Gary Roberts	20.00
107	Mike Ricci	20.00
108	Andy Moog	40.00
109	Sean Pronger	20.00
110	Paul Coffey	40.00
111	Trevor Linden	20.00
112	Rob Zamuner	20.00
113	Daniel Alfredsson	40.00
114	Ray Sheppard	20.00
115	Steve Shields	40.00
116	Ethan Moreau	20.00
117	Tomas Sandstrom	20.00
118	Chris Gratton	20.00
119	Alexander Mogilny	50.00
120	Roman Hamrlik	20.00
121	Tommy Salo	40.00
122	Jason Allison	40.00
123	Curtis Joseph	60.00
124	Guy Hebert	40.00
125	Jeff O'Neill	20.00
126	Donald Audette	20.00
127	Claude Lemieux	40.00
128	Brian Savage	20.00
129	Scott Mellanby	20.00
130	Vyacheslav Kozlov	20.00
131	Wade Redden	20.00
132	John LeClair	100.00
133	Jeremy Roenick	75.00
134	Andreas Johansson	20.00
135	Nelson Emerson	20.00
136	Daren Puppa	40.00
137	Joe Juneau	20.00
138	Garth Snow	40.00
139	Tom Barrasso	50.00
140	Joe Nieuwendyk	40.00
141	Theoren Fleury	40.00
142	Yanic Perreault	20.00
143	Mike Richter	60.00
144	Al MacInnis	40.00
145	Mike Peca	20.00
146	Darren McCarty	20.00
147	Alexei Yashin	40.00
148	Rick Tocchet	20.00
149	Adam Oates	50.00
150	Wendel Clark	20.00
151	Tony Amonte	40.00
152	Dave Andreychuk	20.00
153	Jamie Storr	40.00
154	Craig Janney	20.00
155	Todd Bertuzzi	20.00
156	Harry York	20.00
157	Todd Harvey	20.00
158	Bobby Holik	20.00
159	Mike Vernon	50.00
160	Pat LaFontaine	40.00
161	Doug Weight	40.00
162	Kirk McLean	40.00
163	Adam Deadmarsh	40.00
164	Vincent Damphousse	20.00
165	Vaclav Prospal	60.00
166	Daniel Cleary	20.00
167	Jaroslav Svejkovsky	20.00
168	*Marco Sturm*	75.00
169	Robert Dome	20.00
170	*Patrik Elias*	60.00
171	Mattias Ohlund	20.00

172	Espen Knutsen	20.00
173	Joe Thornton	150.00
174	*Jan Bulis*	20.00
175	Patrick Marleau	100.00
176	Brad Isbister	20.00
177	*Kevin Weekes*	40.00
178	Sergei Samsonov	75.00
179	*Tyler Moss*	20.00
180	Chris Phillips	20.00
181	Alyn McCauley	20.00
182	*Derek Morris*	20.00
183	Alexei Morozov	20.00
184	Boyd Devereaux	20.00
185	Peter Forsberg (1st Class Package)	125.00
186	Brendan Shanahan (1st Class Package)	60.00
187	Teemu Selanne (1st Class Package)	60.00
188	Eric Lindros (1st Class Package)	150.00
189	Mark Messier (1st Class Package)	60.00
190	Vaclav Prospal (1st Class Package)	20.00
191	Jarome Iginla (1st Class Package)	20.00
192	Mike Modano (1st Class Package)	40.00
193	John Vanbiesbrouck (1st Class Package)	60.00
194	Bryan Berard (1st Class Package)	20.00
195	Patrick Marleau (1st Class Package)	50.00
196	Martin Brodeur (1st Class Package)	80.00
197	Patrick Roy (1st Class Package)	175.00
198	Felix Potvin (1st Class Package)	40.00
199	Wayne Gretzky (1st Class Package)	250.00
200	Sergei Samsonov (1st Class Package)	40.00
201	Ryan Smyth (1st Class Package)	20.00
202	Keith Tkachuk (1st Class Package)	40.00
203	Chris Osgood (1st Class Package)	40.00
204	Paul Kariya (1st Class Package)	150.00
205	John LeClair (1st Class Package)	50.00
206	Alyn McCauley (1st Class Package)	20.00
207	Joe Thornton (1st Class Package)	75.00
208	Joe Sakic (1st Class Package)	90.00
209	Steve Yzerman (1st Class Package)	125.00
210	Saku Koivu (1st Class Package)	40.00
211	Pavel Bure (1st Class Package)	60.00
212	Zigmund Palffy (1st Class Package)	40.00
213	Alexei Yashin (1st Class Package)	20.00
214	Sergei Fedorov (1st Class Package)	60.00
215	Checklist Joe Thornton	75.00
216	Checklist Patrick Marleau	50.00
217	Checklist Daniel Cleary	20.00
218	Checklist Sergei Samsonov	40.00
219	Checklist Jaroslav Svejkovsky	20.00
220	Checklist Alyn McCauley	20.00

1997-98 Donruss Priority Stamps

Thirty-six NHL players are featured on postage stamps issued by Grenada. Three stamp parallels were created: Bronze (1:5 stamp packs), silver (1:9) and gold (1:18). Five stamp packs were included in each box of Priority Hockey, with one stamp per pack.

		MT
Complete Set (36):		40.00
Common Player:		.40
Bronze Stamps:		1x to 2x
Silver Stamps:		2x to 4x
Gold Stamps:		3x to 6x
1	Patrick Roy	4.00
2	Brendan Shanahan	1.25
3	Steve Yzerman	2.50
4	Jaromir Jagr	3.00
5	Pavel Bure	1.25
6	Mark Messier	1.00
7	Wayne Gretzky	5.00
8	Eric Lindros	3.00
9	Joe Sakic	2.00
10	Peter Forsberg	2.50
11	John Vanbiesbrouck	1.25
12	Mike Modano	1.25
13	Paul Kariya	3.00
14	Teemu Selanne	1.25
15	Sergei Fedorov	1.25
16	Joe Thornton	1.25
17	Sergei Samsonov	1.25
18	Patrick Marleau	1.00
19	Ryan Smyth	.40
20	Jarome Iginla	.40
21	John LeClair	1.00
22	Brian Leetch	.40
23	Chris Chelios	.50
24	Martin Brodeur	1.50
25	Bryan Berard	.40
26	Keith Tkachuk	1.00
27	Saku Koivu	.75
28	Brett Hull	1.00
29	Felix Potvin	.50
30	Chris Osgood	.75
31	Dominik Hasek	1.50
32	Zigmund Palffy	.75
33	Jeremy Roenick	1.00
34	Dainius Zubrus	.40
35	Ray Bourque	.50
36	Jocelyn Thibault	.60

1997-98 Donruss Studio

Donruss Studio Hockey consists of a 110-card base set. The cards have portrait photography of the NHL players on the front. Thirty-six players were paralleled in the 8-x-10 Studio Portraits set. Each pack of Studio had one 8-x-10 and five regular cards. Three players signed 8-x-10s: Martin Brodeur (total of 700), Jarome Iginla (1,000) and Ryan Smyth (1,000). The regular cards are paralleled by Silver Press Proofs (1,000 sets) and Gold Press Proofs (250). Inserts included Hard Hats and Silhouettes.

		MT
Complete Set (110):		25.00
Common Player:		.10
M. Brodeur Auto. (700):		100.00
R. Smyth Auto. (1,000):		30.00
J. Iginla Auto. (1,000):		40.00
Wax Box:		65.00
1	Wayne Gretzky	2.50
2	Dominik Hasek	.75
3	Eric Lindros	2.00
4	Paul Kariya	1.50
5	Jaromir Jagr	1.50
6	Brendan Shanahan	.75
7	Patrick Roy	2.00
8	Keith Tkachuk	.50
9	Mark Messier	.40
10	Steve Yzerman	1.25
11	Brett Hull	.40
12	Jarome Iginla	.20
13	Mike Modano	.30
14	Pavel Bure	.75
15	Peter Forsberg	1.25
16	Ryan Smyth	.10
17	John Vanbiesbrouck	.75
18	Teemu Selanne	.75
19	Saku Koivu	.50
20	Martin Brodeur	.75
21	Sergei Fedorov	.60
22	John LeClair	.50
23	Joe Sakic	1.00
24	Jose Theodore	.10
25	Marc Denis	.10
26	Dainius Zubrus	.20
27	Bryan Berard	.25
28	Ray Bourque	.25
29	Curtis Joseph	.25
30	Chris Chelios	.25
31	Alexei Yashin	.20
32	Adam Oates	.20
33	Anson Carter	.10
34	Jim Campbell	.10
35	Jason Arnott	.10
36	Derek Plante	.10
37	Guy Hebert	.20
38	Oleg Tverdovski	.10
39	Ed Jovanovski	.10
40	Jeremy Roenick	.30
41	Scott Mellanby	.10
42	Keith Primeau	.10
43	Ron Hextall	.20
44	Daren Puppa	.10
45	Jim Carey	.20
46	Zigmund Palffy	.50
47	Jaroslav Svejkovsky	.10
48	Daymond Langkow	.10
49	Mikael Renberg	.10
50	Pat LaFontaine	.20
51	Mike Grier	.10
52	Stephane Fiset	.10
53	Luc Robitaille	.10
54	Joe Thornton	1.00
55	Joe Nieuwendyk	.20
56	Mike Dunham	.10
57	Mark Recchi	.10
58	Ed Belfour	.25
59	Mike Richter	.25
60	Peter Bondra	.20
61	Trevor Kidd	.10
62	Sean Burke	.20
63	Nikolai Khabibulin	.20
64	Pierre Turgeon	.20
65	Dino Ciccarelli	.10
66	Felix Potvin	.40
67	Mats Sundin	.25
68	Joe Juneau	.10
69	Mike Vernon	.20
70	Adam Deadmarsh	.10
71	Damian Rhodes	.10
72	Mike Peca	.10
73	Jean-Sebastien Giguere	.10
74	Ron Francis	.20
75	Roman Hamrlik	.10
76	Vincent Damphousse	.10
77	Jocelyn Thibault	.25
78	Claude Lemieux	.10
79	Steve Shields	.10
80	Dimitri Khristich	.10
81	Theo Fleury	.20
82	Sandis Ozolinsh	.20
83	Ethan Moreau	.10
84	Geoff Sanderson	.10
85	Paul Coffey	.20
86	Brian Leetch	.20
87	Chris Osgood	.50
88	Kirk McLean	.10
89	Mike Gartner	.10
90	Chris Gratton	.20
91	Eric Fichaud	.10
92	Alexandre Daigle	.10
93	Doug Gilmour	.25
94	Daniel Alfredsson	.10
95	Doug Weight	.20
96	Derian Hatcher	.10
97	Wade Redden	.10
98	Jeff Friesen	.10
99	Tony Amonte	.10
100	Janne Niinimaa	.10
101	Trevor Linden	.10
102	Grant Fuhr	.25
103	Chris Phillips	.10
104	Sergei Berezin	.10
105	Brendan Shanahan CL	.40
106	Steve Yzerman CL	.60
107	Teemu Selanne CL	.40
108	Eric Lindros CL	1.00
109	Wayne Gretzky CL	1.25
110	Patrick Roy CL	1.00

1997-98 Donruss Studio Silver Press Proofs

Silver Press Proofs is a parallel of the 110-card regular set with a production run of 1,500.

	MT
Silver Stars:	15x to 30x
Yng Stars & RCs:	10x to 20x
Production 1,000 sets	

1997-98 Donruss Studio Gold Press Proofs

Gold Press Proofs is a parallel of the regular-size Studio base cards. Only 250 total sets were produced.

	MT
Gold Stars:	40x to 75x
Yng Stars & RCs:	25x to 50x
Production 250 sets	

1997-98 Donruss Studio Hard Hats

Hard Hats is a 24-card insert numbered to 3,000. Printed on plastic card stock, the cards are die-cut around a helmet that is pictured in the background.

		MT
Complete Set (24):		260.00
Common Player:		6.00
1	Wayne Gretzky	40.00
2	Eric Lindros	25.00
3	Paul Kariya	25.00
4	Bryan Berard	8.00
5	Dainius Zubrus	8.00
6	Daymond Langkow	6.00
7	Keith Tkachuk	10.00
8	Ryan Smyth	6.00
9	Brendan Shanahan	15.00
10	Steve Yzerman	20.00
11	Teemu Selanne	15.00
12	Jarome Iginla	8.00
13	Zigmund Palffy	10.00
14	Sergei Berezin	6.00
15	Saku Koivu	10.00
16	Peter Forsberg	20.00
17	Joe Sakic	18.00
18	Pavel Bure	15.00
19	Jaromir Jagr	25.00
20	Brett Hull	10.00
21	Sergei Fedorov	12.00
22	Mike Grier	6.00
23	Ethan Moreau	6.00
24	Mats Sundin	8.00

1997-98 Donruss Studio Portraits

The 8-x-10 Portraits set is a partial parallel of the base set. Thirty-six players are featured in this larger format, with one card in each pack. Three players signed a number of their portraits: Martin Brodeur (signed 700 cards), Ryan Smyth (1,000) and Jarome Iginla (1,000).

		MT
Complete Set (36):		40.00
Common Player:		.50
1	Wayne Gretzky	5.00
2	Dominik Hasek	1.75
3	Eric Lindros	3.00
4	Paul Kariya	3.00
5	Jaromir Jagr	3.00
6	Brendan Shanahan	1.50
7	Patrick Roy	4.00
8	Keith Tkachuk	1.00
9	Mark Messier	1.00
10	Steve Yzerman	3.00
11	Brett Hull	1.00
12	Jarome Iginla	.50
13	Mike Modano	.75
14	Pavel Bure	1.50
15	Peter Forsberg	2.50
16	Ryan Smyth	.50
17	John Vanbiesbrouck	1.50
18	Teemu Selanne	1.50
19	Saku Koivu	1.00
20	Martin Brodeur	1.75
21	Sergei Fedorov	1.25
22	Joe Thornton	2.00
23	Joe Sakic	2.00
24	Bryan Berard	.50
25	John LeClair	1.25
26	Marc Denis	.50
27	Dainius Zubrus	.50
28	Chris Chelios	.75
29	Jason Arnott	.50
30	Jeremy Roenick	.75
31	Zigmund Palffy	.75
32	Jaroslav Svejkovsky	.50
33	Mike Richter	.75
34	Felix Potvin	.75
35	Brian Leetch	.50
36	Chris Osgood	.75

1997-98 Donruss Studio Silhouettes

Silhouettes is a 24-card insert produced in both the regular and 8-x-10 formats. The cards were produced using laser die-cut technology to enhance the player's facial features.

		MT
Complete Set (24):		450.00
Common Player:		10.00
8x10's:		.3x to .5x
1	Wayne Gretzky	60.00
2	Eric Lindros	40.00
3	Patrick Roy	50.00
4	Martin Brodeur	20.00
5	Paul Kariya	40.00
6	Mark Messier	15.00
7	Dominik Hasek	25.00
8	Brett Hull	15.00
9	Pavel Bure	20.00
10	Steve Yzerman	30.00
11	Brendan Shanahan	20.00
12	Joe Sakic	25.00
13	Peter Forsberg	30.00
14	Sergei Fedorov	15.00
15	John LeClair	15.00
16	John Vanbiesbrouck	20.00
17	Teemu Selanne	20.00
18	Keith Tkachuk	15.00
19	Mike Modano	15.00
20	Felix Potvin	12.00
21	Ryan Smyth	10.00
22	Jaromir Jagr	40.00
23	Brian Leetch	10.00
24	Jarome Iginla	10.00

1997-98 Leaf

Leaf Hockey consists of a 200-card base set. The base cards have full-bleed photos with a thin white interior border. The player's name and Leaf logo appear in the bottom center with the team logo in one of the upper corners. The inserts include Banner Season, Lindros Collection, Fire on Ice, Fractal Matrix and Pipe Dreams. The base set includes the 10-card Day in the Life subset, featuring the daily exploits of Trevor Linden. Linden also signed a total of 500 cards.

		MT
Complete Set (200):		20.00
Common Player:		.10
Wax Box:		65.00
1	Eric Lindros	2.00
2	Dominik Hasek	1.00
3	Peter Forsberg	1.50
4	Steve Yzerman	1.50
5	John Vanbiesbrouck	1.00
6	Paul Kariya	2.00
7	Martin Brodeur	1.00
8	Wayne Gretzky	3.00
9	Mark Messier	.50
10	Jaromir Jagr	2.00
11	Brett Hull	.50
12	Brendan Shanahan	1.00
13	Ray Bourque	.20
14	Jarome Iginla	.20
15	Mike Modano	.30
16	Curtis Joseph	.20
17	Ed Jovanovski	.10
18	Teemu Selanne	1.00
19	Saku Koivu	.75
20	Eric Fichaud	.10
21	Paul Coffey	.20
22	Jeremy Roenick	.30
23	Owen Nolan	.10
24	Felix Potvin	.25
25	Alexander Mogilny	.25
26	Alexandre Daigle	.10
27	Chris Gratton	.20
28	Geoff Sanderson	.10
29	Dimitri Khristich	.10
30	Bryan Berard	.25
31	Vyacheslav Kozlov	.10
32	Jeff Hackett	.20
33	Bill Ranford	.10
34	Pat LaFontaine	.20
35	Joe Sakic	1.25
36	Niklas Sundstrom	.10
37	Martin Gelinas	.10
38	Mikael Renberg	.10
39	Trevor Linden	.10
40	Jozef Stumpel	.10
41	Joe Thornton	1.00
42	Jocelyn Thibault	.25
43	Pierre Turgeon	.20
44	Ron Francis	.20
45	Damian Rhodes	.10
46	Jamie Langenbrunner	.10
47	Chris Osgood	.40
48	Vaclav Varada	.10
49	Ryan Smyth	.10
50	Daren Puppa	.10
51	Petr Nedved	.10
52	Ron Hextall	.20
53	Joe Juneau	.10
54	Jim Campbell	.10
55	Zigmund Palffy	.60
56	Roman Turek	.10
57	Adam Deadmarsh	.10
58	Rob Niedermayer	.10
59	Alexei Yashin	.20
60	Pavel Bure	1.00
61	Jason Arnott	.10
62	Nikolai Khabibulin	.20
63	Sean Burke	.10

64 Chris Chelios .25
65 Mike Ricci .10
66 Sergei Berezin .20
67 Jaroslav Svejkovsky .25
68 Brian Savage .10
69 Roman Vopat .10
70 Mike Richter .25
71 Jim Carey .10
72 Guy Hebert .20
73 Keith Tkachuk .50
74 Kirk McLean .10
75 Janne Niinimaa .10
76 Roman Hamrlik .10
77 Darcy Tucker .10
78 Pat Verbeek .10
79 Hnat Domenichelli .10
80 Doug Gilmour .25
81 Mike Grier .10
82 Ken Wregget .10
83 Dino Ciccarelli .10
84 Steve Sullivan .10
85 Anson Carter .10
86 Steve Shields .10
87 Ed Belfour .25
88 Darren McCarty .10
89 Adam Graves .10
90 Chris Pronger .10
91 Peter Bondra .25
92 Oleg Tverdovsky .10
93 Stephane Fiset .10
94 Mike Vernon .20
95 Scott Lachance .10
96 Corey Schwab .10
97 Eric Daze .10
98 Jere Lehtinen .10
99 Donald Audette .10
100 John LeClair .50
101 Steve Rucchin .10
102 Jeff Friesen .10
103 Daymond Langkow .10
104 Mike Dunham .10
105 Marc Denis .10
106 Andrew Cassels .10
107 Mike Peca .10
108 Joe Nieuwendyk .25
109 Vincent Damphousse .10
110 Scott Mellanby .10
111 Patrick Lalime .10
112 Derek Plante .10
113 Wade Redden .10
114 Marcel Cousineau .10
115 Ray Sheppard .10
116 Dave Andreychuk .20
117 Brian Leetch .25
118 Sandis Ozolinsh .20
119 Keith Primeau .10
120 Brian Holzinger .10
121 Luc Robitaille .20
122 Jose Theodore .20
123 Grant Fuhr .30
124 Dainius Zubrus .25
125 Rod Brind'Amour .20
126 Trevor Kidd .10
127 Mark Recchi .20
128 Patrick Roy 2.50
129 Kevin Hatcher .10
130 Adam Oates .25
131 Doug Weight .20
132 *Vaclav Prospal* .60
133 Harry York .10
134 Todd Bertuzzi .10
135 Sergei Fedorov .75
136 Theoren Fleury .25
137 Chad Kilger .10
138 Jamie Storr .10
139 Tony Amonte .20
140 Rem Murray .10
141 Chris O'Sullivan .10
142 Mats Sundin .25
143 Ethan Moreau .10
144 Derian Hatcher .10
145 Daniel Alfredsson .20
146 Corey Hirsch .10
147 Landon Wilson .10
148 Marc Denis (Gold Leaf Rookie) .20
149 Boyd Devereaux (Gold Leaf Rookie) 2.00
150 Joe Thornton (Gold Leaf Rookie) 4.00
151 Sergei Samsonov (Gold Leaf Rookie) 2.00
152 Alyn McCauley (Gold Leaf Rookie) .40
153 Erik Rasmussen (Gold Leaf Rookie) .40
154 Patrick Marleau (Gold Leaf Rookie) 3.00
155 *Olli Jokinen* (Gold Leaf Rookie) 2.00
156 Chris Phillips (Gold Leaf Rookie) .40
157 *Tomas Vokoun* (Gold Leaf Rookie) .25
158 *Chris Dingman* (Gold Leaf Rookie) .25
159 Daniel Cleary (Gold Leaf Rookie) 2.00
160 *Juha Lind* (Gold Leaf Rookie) .25
161 *Jean-Yves Leroux* (Gold Leaf Rookie) 2.00
162 Brad Isbister (Gold Leaf Rookie) .25
163 Vadim Sharifijanov (Gold Leaf Rookie) .25
164 Alexei Morozov (Gold Leaf Rookie) .25
165 Vaclav Prospal (Gold Leaf Rookie) 1.50
166 Vaclav Varada (Gold Leaf Rookie) .50
167 Jaroslav Svejkovsky (Gold Leaf Rookie) .50
168 Eric Lindros (Gamers) 8.00
169 Dominik Hasek (Gamers) 5.00
170 Peter Forsberg (Gamers) 6.00
171 Steve Yzerman (Gamers) 8.00
172 John Vanbiesbrouck (Gamers) 3.00
173 Paul Kariya (Gamers) 8.00
174 Martin Brodeur (Gamers) 4.00
175 Wayne Gretzky (Gamers) 15.00
176 Mark Messier (Gamers) 2.00
177 Jaromir Jagr (Gamers) 8.00
178 Brett Hull (Gamers) 2.50
179 Brendan Shanahan (Gamers) 4.00
180 Jarome Iginla (Gamers) .25
181 Mike Modano (Gamers) .75
182 Teemu Selanne (Gamers) 4.00
183 Bryan Berard (Gamers) .25
184 Ryan Smyth (Gamers) .25
185 Keith Tkachuk (Gamers) 1.00
186 Dainius Zubrus (Gamers) .50
187 Patrick Roy (Gamers) 10.00
188 Trevor Linden (Day In The Life) .10
189 Trevor Linden (Day In The Life) .10
190 Trevor Linden (Day In The Life) .10
191 Trevor Linden (Day In The Life) .10
192 Trevor Linden (Day In The Life) .10
193 Trevor Linden (Day In The Life) .10
194 Trevor Linden (Day In The Life) .10
195 Trevor Linden (Day In The Life) .10
196 Trevor Linden (Day In The Life) .10
197 Trevor Linden (Day In The Life) .10
198 Checklist Chris Phillips .25
199 Checklist Sergei Samsonov .75
200 Checklist Daniel Cleary .25

1997-98 Leaf Banner Season

Banner Season is a 24-card insert sequentially numbered to 3,500. The die-cut canvas cards are designed to look like a banner, with a color player photo in front of a multi-colored background filled with stars.

	MT
Complete Set (24):	450.00
Common Player:	8.00

1 Paul Kariya 40.00
2 Eric Lindros 40.00
3 Wayne Gretzky 60.00
4 Jaromir Jagr 40.00
5 Steve Yzerman 30.00
6 Brendan Shanahan 20.00
7 John LeClair 15.00
8 Teemu Selanne 20.00
9 Mike Modano 12.00
10 Ryan Smyth 8.00
11 Brett Hull 15.00
12 Zigmund Palffy 15.00
13 Peter Forsberg 30.00
14 Keith Tkachuk 15.00
15 Saku Koivu 15.00
16 Sergei Fedorov 15.00
17 Brian Leetch 12.00
18 Bryan Berard 8.00
19 Mats Sundin 12.00
20 Jarome Iginla 8.00
21 Sergei Berezin 8.00
22 Dainius Zubrus 8.00
23 Mike Grier 8.00
24 Joe Sakic 25.00

1997-98 Leaf Eric Lindros Collection

Lindros Collection is a five-card insert numbered to 100. Each card features a piece of game-used equipment. The cards feature pieces of home and road jerseys, stirrups, gloves and sticks used by Eric Lindros in an NHL game.

	MT
Complete Set (5):	1700.
Common Lindros:	300.00

1 Home Jersey 450.00
2 Away Jersey 450.00
3 Stick 350.00
4 Glove 350.00
5 Stirrup 300.00

1997-98 Leaf Fire On Ice

Fire on Ice is a 16-card insert numbered to 1,000. The cards feature dot matrix hologram technology.

	MT
Complete Set (16):	700.00
Common Player:	20.00

1 Wayne Gretzky 120.00
2 Eric Lindros 80.00
3 Jaromir Jagr 80.00
4 Steve Yzerman 60.00
5 Brendan Shanahan 40.00
6 Mike Modano 25.00
7 Joe Sakic 30.00
8 Pavel Bure 40.00
9 Ryan Smyth 20.00
10 Teemu Selanne 40.00
11 Mark Messier 30.00
12 Peter Forsberg 60.00
13 Dainius Zubrus 20.00
14 Joe Thornton 40.00
15 Sergei Samsonov 30.00
16 Paul Kariya 80.00

1997-98 Leaf Fractal Matrix

Fractal Matrix is a parallel of the Leaf Hockey base set. The cards come in three different colors and three different patterns, making nine combinations. Each base card has only one parallel combination. Of the 200 cards, 100 are Bronze (75 X-Axis, 20 Y-Axis and five Z-Axis), 60 are Silver (20 X-Axis, 30 Y-Axis and 10 Z-Axis) and 40 are Gold (five X-Axis, 10 Y-Axis and 25 Z-Axis). Each combination had a different print run: Bronze X-Axis (1,400 sets), Bronze Y-Axis (1,600), Bronze Z-Axis (1,700), Silver X-Axis (500), Silver Y-Axis (700), Silver Z-Axis (800), Gold X-Axis (50), Gold Y-Axis (250) and Gold Z-Axis (350). A die-cut parallel version was also created.

	MT
Common Bronze:	2.00
Common Silver:	4.00
Common Gold:	15.00
Common Gold X-Axis:	30.00

1 Eric Lindros G/X 220.00
2 Dominik Hasek G/Z 50.00
3 Peter Forsberg G/Z 75.00
4 Steve Yzerman G/Z 80.00
5 John Vanbiesbrouck G/Z 50.00
6 Paul Kariya G/X 220.00
7 Martin Brodeur G/Z 60.00
8 Wayne Gretzky G/X 300.00
9 Mark Messier G/Y 40.00
10 Jaromir Jagr G/Z 100.00
11 Brett Hull G/Y 40.00
12 Brendan Shanahan G/Z 50.00
13 Ray Bourque G/Y 30.00
14 Jarome Iginla G/Y 30.00
15 Mike Modano G/Y 40.00
16 Curtis Joseph G/Y 25.00
17 Ed Jovanovski S/X 4.00
18 Teemu Selanne G/Z 50.00
19 Saku Koivu G/Y 40.00
20 Eric Fichaud S/Z 4.00
21 Paul Coffey S/X 8.00
22 Jeremy Roenick S/X 12.00
23 Owen Nolan B/X 2.00
24 Felix Potvin G/Y 35.00
25 Alexander Mogilny S/Z 6.00
26 Alexandre Daigle S/X 4.00
27 Chris Gratton S/X 6.00
28 Geoff Sanderson S/X 4.00
29 Dimitri Khristich S/X 4.00
30 Bryan Berard G/Y 30.00
31 Vyacheslav Kozlov B/X 2.00
32 Jeff Hackett B/Y 4.00
33 Bill Ranford B/Y 2.00
34 Pat LaFontaine S/Y 8.00
35 Joe Sakic G/Y 60.00
36 Niklas Sundstrom B/X 2.00
37 Martin Gelinas B/X 2.00
38 Mikael Renberg B/X 2.00
39 Trevor Linden B/X 2.00
40 Jozef Stumpel B/Y 2.00
41 Joe Thornton G/Y 30.00
42 Jocelyn Thibault G/Y 30.00
43 Pierre Turgeon B/X 4.00
44 Ron Francis B/X 5.00
45 Damian Rhodes S/Y 4.00
46 Jamie Langenbrunner S/Y 4.00
47 Chris Osgood S/Z 8.00
48 Vaclav Varada S/X 4.00
49 Ryan Smyth G/Z 10.00
50 Daren Puppa B/X 2.00
51 Petr Nedved B/X 2.00
52 Ron Hextall B/X 4.00
53 Joe Juneau B/X 2.00
54 Jim Campbell S/Y 4.00
55 Zigmund Palffy S/Z 15.00
56 Roman Turek B/X 4.00
57 Adam Deadmarsh G/Y 20.00
58 Rob Niedermayer B/X 2.00
59 Alexei Yashin G/Y 25.00
60 Pavel Bure G/Y 60.00
61 Jason Arnott G/Y 20.00
62 Nikolai Khabibulin S/Y 6.00
63 Sean Burke S/Y 6.00
64 Chris Chelios S/X 10.00
65 Mike Ricci B/X 2.00
66 Sergei Berezin S/Y 6.00
67 Jaroslav Svejkovsky G/Y 30.00
68 Brian Savage B/X 2.00
69 Roman Vopat B/X 2.00
70 Mike Richter S/X 8.00
71 Jim Carey S/Y 6.00
72 Guy Hebert B/Y 4.00
73 Keith Tkachuk G/Y 40.00
74 Kirk McLean B/X 2.00
75 Janne Niinimaa S/Y 6.00
76 Roman Hamrlik S/Y 4.00
77 Darcy Tucker S/Y 4.00
78 Pat Verbeek B/X 2.00
79 Hnat Domenichelli B/X 2.00
80 Doug Gilmour S/Y 10.00
81 Mike Grier G/Y 20.00
82 Ken Wregget B/X 2.00
83 Dino Ciccarelli B/X 2.00
84 Steve Sullivan B/X 2.00
85 Anson Carter S/X 4.00
86 Steve Shields B/Y 5.00
87 Ed Belfour S/Y 8.00
88 Darren McCarty B/X 2.00
89 Adam Graves B/X 2.00
90 Chris Pronger B/X 2.00
91 Peter Bondra S/Y 6.00
92 Oleg Tverdovsky S/Y 4.00
93 Stephane Fiset B/X 4.00
94 Mike Vernon B/Y 2.00
95 Scott Lachance B/X 2.00
96 Corey Schwab B/X 2.00
97 Eric Daze B/Y 2.00
98 Jere Lehtinen B/X 2.00
99 Donald Audette B/X 2.00
100 John LeClair G/Y 40.00
101 Steve Rucchin B/X 2.00
102 Jeff Friesen S/X 4.00
103 Daymond Langkow S/X 4.00
104 Mike Dunham S/Y 6.00
105 Marc Denis B/Z 2.00
106 Andrew Cassels B/X 2.00
107 Mike Peca B/X 2.00
108 Joe Nieuwendyk B/X 5.00
109 Vincent Damphousse B/X 2.00
110 Scott Mellanby B/X 2.00
111 Patrick Lalime B/X 2.00
112 Derek Plante S/Y 4.00
113 Wade Redden S/Y 4.00
114 Marcel Cousineau B/Y 2.00
115 Ray Sheppard B/X 2.00
116 Dave Andreychuk B/X 3.00
117 Brian Leetch G/Y 30.00
118 Sandis Ozolinsh B/Y 2.00
119 Keith Primeau B/X 2.00
120 Brian Holzinger B/X 2.00
121 Luc Robitaille B/X 4.00
122 Jose Theodore S/X 6.00
123 Grant Fuhr S/Y 8.00
124 Dainius Zubrus G/Y 20.00
125 Rod Brind'Amour B/X 4.00
126 Trevor Kidd S/Y 6.00
127 Mark Recchi B/X 4.00
128 Patrick Roy G/Y 125.00
129 Kevin Hatcher B/X 2.00
130 Adam Oates S/Y 8.00
131 Doug Weight S/X 6.00
132 Vaclav Prospal S/X 6.00
133 Harry York S/Y 4.00
134 Todd Bertuzzi B/X 2.00
135 Sergei Fedorov G/Y 40.00
136 Theoren Fleury S/X 8.00
137 Chad Kilger B/Y 2.00
138 Jamie Storr S/X 4.00
139 Tony Amonte B/Y 5.00
140 Rem Murray B/Y 2.00
141 Chris O'Sullivan B/X 2.00
142 Mats Sundin S/Z 10.00
143 Ethan Moreau S/Z 4.00
144 Derian Hatcher S/Y 4.00
145 Daniel Alfredsson S/Y 8.00
146 Corey Hirsch B/X 2.00
147 Landon Wilson B/X 2.00
148 Marc Denis G/Y (Gold Leaf Rookie) 20.00
149 Boyd Devereaux B/Z (Gold Leaf Rookie) 2.00
150 Joe Thornton G/X (Gold Leaf Rookie) 150.00
151 Sergei Samsonov G/Z (Gold Leaf Rookie) 30.00
152 Alyn McCauley S/Z (Gold Leaf Rookie) 2.00
153 Erik Rasmussen S/Z (Gold Leaf Rookie) 2.00
154 Patrick Marleau S/X (Gold Leaf Rookie) 25.00
155 Olli Jokinen B/X (Gold Leaf Rookie) 2.00
156 Chris Phillips G/Y (Gold Leaf Rookie) 20.00
157 Tomas Vokoun B/X (Gold Leaf Rookie) 2.00
158 Chris Dingman S/Z (Gold Leaf Rookie) 2.00
159 Daniel Cleary G/Y (Gold Leaf Rookie) 30.00
160 Juha Lind B/X (Gold Leaf Rookie) 2.00
161 Jean-Yves Leroux B/Y (Gold Leaf Rookie) 2.00
162 Brad Isbister S/Y (Gold Leaf Rookie) 2.00
163 Vadim Sharifijanov B/X (Gold Leaf Rookie) 2.00
164 Alexei Morozov S/X (Gold Leaf Rookie) 2.00
165 Vaclav Prospal B/X (Gold Leaf Rookie) 2.00
166 Vaclav Varada B/Y (Gold Leaf Rookie) 2.00
167 Jaroslav Svejkovsky B/Z (Gold Leaf Rookie) 2.00
168 Eric Lindros S/Y (Gamers) 40.00
169 Dominik Hasek B/Y (Gamers) 12.00
170 Peter Forsberg B/Y (Gamers) 20.00
171 Steve Yzerman S/Y (Gamers) 30.00
172 John Vanbiesbrouck B/X (Gamers) 12.00
173 Paul Kariya S/Y (Gamers) 40.00
174 Martin Brodeur B/Z (Gamers) 15.00
175 Wayne Gretzky S/Y (Gamers) 60.00
176 Mark Messier B/X (Gamers) 8.00
177 Jaromir Jagr B/Z (Gamers) 25.00
178 Brett Hull B/X (Gamers) 8.00
179 Brendan Shanahan B/Y (Gamers) 12.00
180 Jarome Iginla B/X (Gamers) 4.00
181 Mike Modano B/Y (Gamers) 5.00
182 Teemu Selanne B/Y (Gamers) 12.00
183 Bryan Berard B/Y (Gamers) 5.00
184 Ryan Smyth S/Y (Gamers) 4.00
185 Keith Tkachuk B/X (Gamers) 8.00
186 Dainius Zubrus B/X (Gamers) 4.00
187 Patrick Roy B/X (Gamers) 30.00
188 Trevor Linden B/X (Day In The Life) 2.00
189 Trevor Linden B/X (Day In The Life) 2.00
190 Trevor Linden B/X (Day In The Life) 2.00
191 Trevor Linden B/X (Day In The Life) 2.00
192 Trevor Linden B/X (Day In The Life) 2.00
193 Trevor Linden B/X (Day In The Life) 2.00
194 Trevor Linden B/X (Day In The Life) 2.00
195 Trevor Linden B/X (Day In The Life) 2.00

196 Trevor Linden B/X (Day In The Life) 2.00
197 Trevor Linden B/X (Day In The Life) 2.00
198 Checklist Chris Phillips B/X 2.00
199 Checklist Sergei Samsonov B/X 12.00
200 Checklist Daniel Cleary B/X 6.00

1997-98 Leaf Fractal Matrix Die-Cuts

The Fractal Matrix Die-Cuts parallel has a different die-cut for each of the three axis patterns. Leaf stated the print runs at 400 sets for X-Axis, 200 sets for Y-Axis and 100 sets for Z-Axis cards.

	MT
Common X-Axis:	8.00
Common Y-Axis:	12.00
Y-Axis Unlisted Stars:	20.00
Common Z-Axis:	20.00
Z-Axis Unlisted Stars:	30.00

1 Eric Lindros G/X 100.00
2 Dominik Hasek G/Z 100.00
3 Peter Forsberg G/Z 150.00
4 Steve Yzerman G/Z 150.00
5 John Vanbiesbrouck G/Z 100.00
6 Paul Kariya G/X 100.00
7 Martin Brodeur G/Z 120.00
8 Wayne Gretzky G/X 150.00
9 Mark Messier G/Y 40.00
10 Jaromir Jagr G/Z 200.00
11 Brett Hull G/Y 40.00
12 Brendan Shanahan G/Z 100.00
13 Ray Bourque G/Y 30.00
14 Jarome Iginla G/Y 30.00
15 Mike Modano G/Y 40.00
16 Curtis Joseph G/Y 25.00
17 Ed Jovanovski S/X 8.00
18 Teemu Selanne G/Z 100.00
19 Saku Koivu G/Y 40.00
20 Eric Fichaud S/Z 20.00
21 Paul Coffey S/X 12.00
22 Jeremy Roenick S/X 15.00
23 Owen Nolan B/X 8.00
24 Felix Potvin G/Y 35.00
25 Alexander Mogilny S/Z 30.00
26 Alexandre Daigle S/X 8.00
27 Chris Gratton S/X 10.00
28 Geoff Sanderson S/X 8.00
29 Dimitri Khristich S/X 8.00
30 Bryan Berard G/Y 30.00
31 Vyacheslav Kozlov B/X 8.00
32 Jeff Hackett B/Y 20.00
33 Bill Ranford B/Y 15.00
34 Pat LaFontaine S/Y 20.00
35 Joe Sakic G/Y 60.00
36 Niklas Sundstrom B/X 8.00
37 Martin Gelinas B/X 8.00
38 Mikael Renberg B/X 8.00
39 Trevor Linden B/X 8.00
40 Jozef Stumpel B/Y 12.00
41 Joe Thornton S/Z 100.00
42 Jocelyn Thibault G/Y 30.00
43 Pierre Turgeon B/X 15.00
44 Ron Francis B/X 15.00
45 Damian Rhodes S/Y 12.00
46 Jamie Langenbrunner S/Y 12.00
47 Chris Osgood S/Z 35.00
48 Vaclav Varada S/X 8.00
49 Ryan Smyth G/Z 20.00
50 Daren Puppa B/X 8.00
51 Petr Nedved B/X 8.00
52 Ron Hextall B/X 15.00
53 Joe Juneau B/X 8.00
54 Jim Campbell S/Y 12.00
55 Zigmund Palffy S/Z 60.00
56 Roman Turek B/X 12.00
57 Adam Deadmarsh G/Y 20.00
58 Rob Niedermayer B/X 8.00
59 Alexei Yashin G/Y 25.00
60 Pavel Bure G/Y 60.00
61 Jason Arnott G/Y 20.00
62 Nikolai Khabibulin S/Y 20.00
63 Sean Burke S/Y 15.00
64 Chris Chelios S/X 15.00
65 Mike Ricci B/X 8.00
66 Sergei Berezin S/Y 15.00
67 Jaroslav Svejkovsky G/Y 30.00
68 Brian Savage B/X 8.00
69 Roman Vopat B/X 8.00
70 Mike Richter S/X 15.00
71 Jim Carey S/Y 15.00
72 Guy Hebert B/Y 15.00
73 Keith Tkachuk G/Y 40.00
74 Kirk McLean B/X 8.00
75 Janne Niinimaa S/Y 15.00
76 Roman Hamrlik S/Y 12.00
77 Darcy Tucker S/Y 12.00
78 Pat Verbeek B/X 8.00
79 Hnat Domenichelli B/X 8.00
80 Doug Gilmour S/Y 25.00
81 Mike Grier G/Y 20.00
82 Ken Wregget B/X 8.00
83 Dino Ciccarelli B/X 10.00
84 Steve Sullivan B/X 8.00
85 Anson Carter S/X 8.00
86 Steve Shields B/Y 20.00
87 Ed Belfour S/Y 25.00
88 Darren McCarty B/X 8.00
89 Adam Graves B/X 8.00
90 Chris Pronger B/X 8.00
91 Peter Bondra S/Y 20.00
92 Oleg Tverdovsky S/Y 12.00
93 Stephane Fiset B/X 8.00
94 Mike Vernon B/Y 20.00
95 Scott Lachance B/X 8.00
96 Corey Schwab B/X 8.00
97 Eric Daze B/Y 15.00
98 Jere Lehtinen B/X 8.00
99 Donald Audette B/X 8.00
100 John LeClair G/Y 40.00
101 Steve Rucchin B/X 8.00
102 Jeff Friesen S/X 8.00
103 Daymond Langkow S/X 8.00
104 Mike Dunham S/Y 15.00
105 Marc Denis B/Z 20.00
106 Andrew Cassels B/X 8.00
107 Mike Peca B/X 8.00
108 Joe Nieuwendyk B/X 15.00
109 Vincent Damphousse B/X 8.00
110 Scott Mellanby B/X 8.00
111 Patrick Lalime B/X 8.00
112 Derek Plante S/Y 12.00
113 Wade Redden S/Y 12.00
114 Marcel Cousineau B/Y 12.00
115 Ray Sheppard B/X 8.00
116 Dave Andreychuk B/X 12.00
117 Brian Leetch G/Y 30.00
118 Sandis Ozolinsh B/Y 15.00
119 Keith Primeau B/X 8.00
120 Brian Holzinger B/X 8.00
121 Luc Robitaille B/X 15.00
122 Jose Theodore S/X 12.00
123 Grant Fuhr S/Y 20.00
124 Dainius Zubrus G/Y 20.00
125 Rod Brind'Amour B/X 12.00
126 Trevor Kidd S/Y 15.00
127 Mark Recchi B/X 15.00
128 Patrick Roy G/Y 125.00
129 Kevin Hatcher B/X 8.00
130 Adam Oates S/Y 20.00
131 Doug Weight S/X 12.00
132 Vaclav Prospal S/X 8.00
133 Harry York S/Y 12.00
134 Todd Bertuzzi B/X 8.00
135 Sergei Fedorov G/Y 40.00
136 Theoren Fleury S/X 15.00
137 Chad Kilger B/Y 12.00
138 Jamie Storr S/X 8.00
139 Tony Amonte B/Y 20.00
140 Rem Murray B/Y 12.00
141 Chris O'Sullivan B/X 8.00
142 Mats Sundin S/Z 40.00
143 Ethan Moreau S/Z 20.00
144 Derian Hatcher S/Y 12.00
145 Daniel Alfredsson S/Y 20.00
146 Corey Hirsch B/X 8.00
147 Landon Wilson B/X 8.00
148 Marc Denis G/Y (Gold Leaf Rookie) 20.00
149 Boyd Devereaux B/Z (Gold Leaf Rookie) 20.00
150 Joe Thornton G/X (Gold Leaf Rookie) 30.00
151 Sergei Samsonov G/Z (Gold Leaf Rookie) 50.00
152 Alyn McCauley S/Z (Gold Leaf Rookie) 20.00
153 Erik Rasmussen S/Z (Gold Leaf Rookie) 20.00
154 Patrick Marleau S/X (Gold Leaf Rookie) 30.00
155 Olli Jokinen B/X (Gold Leaf Rookie) 12.00
156 Chris Phillips G/Y (Gold Leaf Rookie) 20.00
157 Tomas Vokoun B/X (Gold Leaf Rookie) 8.00
158 Chris Dingman S/Z (Gold Leaf Rookie) 20.00
159 Daniel Cleary G/Y (Gold Leaf Rookie) 30.00
160 Juha Lind B/X (Gold Leaf Rookie) 8.00
161 Jean-Yves Leroux B/Y (Gold Leaf Rookie) 12.00
162 Brad Isbister S/Y (Gold Leaf Rookie) 12.00
163 Vadim Sharifijanov B/X (Gold Leaf Rookie) 8.00
164 Alexei Morozov S/X (Gold Leaf Rookie) 8.00
165 Vaclav Prospal B/X (Gold Leaf Rookie) 8.00
166 Vaclav Varada B/Y (Gold Leaf Rookie) 12.00
167 Jaroslav Svejkovsky B/Z (Gold Leaf Rookie) 30.00
168 Eric Lindros S/Y (Gamers) 100.00
169 Dominik Hasek B/Y (Gamers) 60.00
170 Peter Forsberg B/Y (Gamers) 75.00
171 Steve Yzerman S/Y (Gamers) 75.00
172 John Vanbiesbrouck B/X (Gamers) 25.00
173 Paul Kariya S/Y (Gamers) 100.00
174 Martin Brodeur B/Z (Gamers) 120.00
175 Wayne Gretzky S/Y (Gamers) 150.00
176 Mark Messier B/X (Gamers) 15.00
177 Jaromir Jagr B/Z (Gamers) 150.00
178 Brett Hull B/X (Gamers) 15.00
179 Brendan Shanahan B/Y (Gamers) 50.00
180 Jarome Iginla B/X (Gamers) 8.00
181 Mike Modano B/Y (Gamers) 20.00
182 Teemu Selanne B/Y (Gamers) 50.00
183 Bryan Berard B/Y (Gamers) 20.00
184 Ryan Smyth S/Y (Gamers) 12.00
185 Keith Tkachuk B/X (Gamers) 15.00
186 Dainius Zubrus B/X (Gamers) 12.00
187 Patrick Roy B/X (Gamers) 60.00
188 Trevor Linden B/X (Day In The Life) 8.00
189 Trevor Linden B/X (Day In The Life) 8.00
190 Trevor Linden B/X (Day In The Life) 8.00
191 Trevor Linden B/X (Day In The Life) 8.00
192 Trevor Linden B/X (Day In The Life) 8.00
193 Trevor Linden B/X (Day In The Life) 8.00
194 Trevor Linden B/X (Day In The Life) 8.00
195 Trevor Linden B/X (Day In The Life) 8.00
196 Trevor Linden B/X (Day In The Life) 8.00
197 Trevor Linden B/X (Day In The Life) 8.00
198 Checklist Chris Phillips B/X 8.00
199 Checklist Sergei Samsonov B/X 25.00
200 Checklist Daniel Cleary B/X 12.00

1997-98 Leaf International Stars

Leaf International is a 150-card product that had the same checklist as Leaf Hockey minus the subsets. The base cards feature a color photo with the name of the player's home country on one side and a map section in the background. The set was paralleled in Universal Ice.

	MT
Complete Set (150):	50.00
Common Player:	.25
Universal Stars:	40x to 60x
Yng Stars & RCs:	25x to 50x
Production 250 sets	

1 Eric Lindros 2.50
2 Dominik Hasek 1.50
3 Peter Forsberg 2.00
4 Steve Yzerman 2.00
5 John Vanbiesbrouck 1.25
6 Paul Kariya 2.50
7 Martin Brodeur 1.50
8 Wayne Gretzky 4.00
9 Mark Messier .75
10 Jaromir Jagr 2.50
11 Brett Hull .75
12 Brendan Shanahan 1.25
13 Ray Bourque .40
14 Jarome Iginla .25
15 Mike Modano .50
16 Curtis Joseph .40
17 Ed Jovanovski .25
18 Teemu Selanne 1.25
19 Saku Koivu .75
20 Eric Fichaud .25
21 Paul Coffey .25
22 Jeremy Roenick .40
23 Owen Nolan .25
24 Felix Potvin .40
25 Alexander Mogilny .40
26 Alexandre Daigle .25
27 Chris Gratton .25
28 Geoff Sanderson .25
29 Dimitri Khristich .25
30 Bryan Berard .25
31 Vyacheslav Kozlov .25
32 Jeff Hackett .25
33 Bill Ranford .25
34 Pat LaFontaine .25
35 Joe Sakic 1.50
36 Niklas Sundstrom .25
37 Martin Gelinas .25
38 Mikael Renberg .25
39 Trevor Linden .25
40 Jozef Stumpel .25
41 Joe Thornton 2.00
42 Jocelyn Thibault .40
43 Pierre Turgeon .40
44 Ron Francis .40
45 Damian Rhodes .25
46 Jamie Langenbrunner .25
47 Chris Osgood .50
48 Vaclav Varada .50
49 Ryan Smyth .25
50 Daren Puppa .25
51 Petr Nedved .25
52 Ron Hextall .40
53 Joe Juneau .25
54 Jim Campbell .25
55 Zigmund Palffy .75
56 Roman Turek .25
57 Adam Deadmarsh .25
58 Rob Niedermayer .25
59 Alexei Yashin .25
60 Pavel Bure 1.25
61 Jason Arnott .25
62 Nikolai Khabibulin .40
63 Sean Burke .40
64 Chris Chelios .40
65 Mike Ricci .25
66 Sergei Berezin .25
67 Jaroslav Svejkovsky .25
68 Brian Savage .25
69 Roman Vopat .25
70 Mike Richter .40
71 Jim Carey .25
72 Guy Hebert .40
73 Keith Tkachuk .75
74 Kirk McLean .25
75 Janne Niinimaa .25
76 Roman Hamrlik .25
77 Darcy Tucker .25
78 Pat Verbeek .25
79 Hnat Domenichelli .25
80 Doug Gilmour .50
81 Mike Grier .25
82 Ken Wregget .25
83 Dino Ciccarelli .25
84 Steve Sullivan .25
85 Anson Carter .25
86 Steve Shields .40
87 Ed Belfour .50
88 Darren McCarty .25
89 Adam Graves .25
90 Chris Pronger .25
91 Peter Bondra .40
92 Oleg Tverdovsky .25
93 Stephane Fiset .25
94 Mike Vernon .40
95 Scott Lachance .25
96 Corey Schwab .25
97 Eric Daze .25
98 Jere Lehtinen .25
99 Donald Audette .25
100 John LeClair 1.00
101 Steve Rucchin .25
102 Jeff Friesen .25
103 Daymond Langkow .25
104 Mike Dunham .25
105 Marc Denis .25
106 Andrew Cassels .25
107 Mike Peca .25
108 Joe Nieuwendyk .40
109 Vincent Damphousse .25
110 Scott Mellanby .25
111 Patrick Lalime .25
112 Derek Plante .25
113 Wade Redden .25
114 Marcel Cousineau .25
115 Ray Sheppard .25
116 Dave Andreychuk .25
117 Brian Leetch .40
118 Sandis Ozolinsh .25
119 Keith Primeau .40
120 Brian Holzinger .25
121 Luc Robitaille .25
122 Jose Theodore .25
123 Grant Fuhr .50
124 Dainius Zubrus .75
125 Rod Brind'Amour .25
126 Trevor Kidd .25
127 Mark Recchi .25
128 Patrick Roy 3.00
129 Kevin Hatcher .25
130 Adam Oates .40
131 Doug Weight .40
132 Vaclav Prospal 1.00
133 Harry York .25
134 Todd Bertuzzi .25
135 Sergei Fedorov 1.00
136 Theoren Fleury .40
137 Chad Kilger .25
138 Jamie Storr .25
139 Tony Amonte .40
140 Rem Murray .25
141 Chris O'Sullivan .25
142 Mats Sundin .50
143 Ethan Moreau .25
144 Derian Hatcher .25
145 Daniel Alfredsson .25
146 Corey Hirsch .25
147 Landon Wilson .25
148 Chris Phillips .25
149 Sergei Samsonov .75
150 Daniel Cleary .25

1997-98 Leaf Pipe Dreams

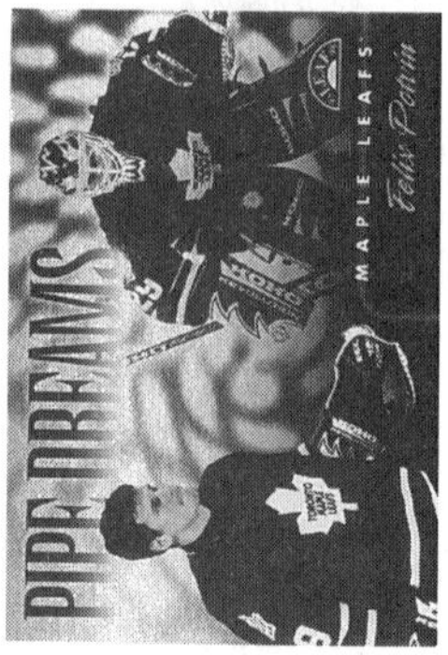

Pipe Dreams is a 16-card insert sequentially numbered to 2,500. The cards are printed on micro-etched silver foil board and have a horizontal layout. The set features top NHL goalies.

	MT
Complete Set (16):	220.00
Common Goalie:	8.00

1 Dominik Hasek 30.00
2 John Vanbiesbrouck 30.00
3 Patrick Roy 60.00
4 Curtis Joseph 12.00
5 Felix Potvin 15.00
6 Martin Brodeur 40.00
7 Guy Hebert 8.00
8 Mike Richter 12.00
9 Jose Theodore 8.00
10 Jim Carey 8.00
11 Damian Rhodes 8.00
12 Jocelyn Thibault 12.00
13 Nikolai Khabibulin 8.00
14 Chris Osgood 18.00
15 Eric Fichaud 8.00
16 Mike Dunham 8.00

1997-98 Pacific Crown Royale

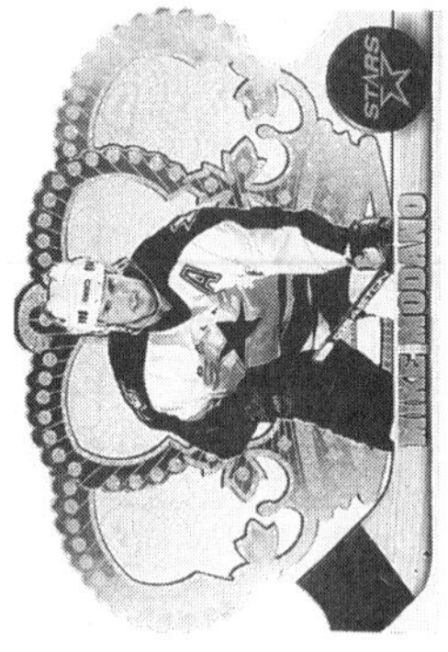

Crown Royale consists of a 144-card base set with three parallels and five inserts. The base cards have a horizontal layout and are die-cut in the shape of a crown. The parallels include silver (U.S., 4:25), emerald green (Canada, 4:25) and Ice Blue (1:25). The inserts include Blades of Steel, Hat Tricks, Freeze Out, Lamplighters and Premium-Sized Cramer's Choice Awards.

	MT
Complete Set: (144)	120.00
Common Player:	.50
Wax Box:	120.00

1 Guy Hebert 1.00
2 Paul Kariya 6.00
3 Steve Rucchin .50
4 Tomas Sandstrom .50

5	Teemu Selanne	3.00
6	Jason Allison	.50
7	Ray Bourque	1.00
8	Anson Carter	.50
9	Byron Dafoe	1.00
10	Ted Donato	.50
11	Joe Thornton	6.00
12	Jason Dawe	.50
13	Michal Grosek	.50
14	Dominik Hasek	4.00
15	Mike Peca	.50
16	Miroslav Satan	.50
17	*Chris Dingman*	.50
18	Theoren Fleury	1.00
19	Jarome Iginla	.75
20	*Tyler Moss*	1.00
21	Cory Stillman	.50
22	Kevin Dineen	.50
23	Nelson Emerson	.50
24	Trevor Kidd	1.00
25	Keith Primeau	.75
26	Geoff Sanderson	.50
27	Tony Amonte	1.00
28	Chris Chelios	1.00
29	Eric Daze	.50
30	Jeff Hackett	1.00
31	Chris Terreri	.50
32	Adam Deadmarsh	.50
33	Peter Forsberg	5.00
34	Valeri Kamensky	.75
35	Jari Kurri	.75
36	Claude Lemieux	.50
37	Patrick Roy	8.00
38	Joe Sakic	4.00
39	Ed Belfour	1.00
40	Derian Hatcher	.50
41	Mike Modano	1.50
42	Joe Nieuwendyk	1.00
43	Pat Verbeek	.50
44	Sergei Zubov	.50
45	Sergei Fedorov	2.50
46	Vyacheslav Kozlov	.50
47	Nicklas Lidstrom	1.00
48	Darren McCarty	.50
49	Chris Osgood	1.50
50	Brendan Shanahan	2.50
51	Steve Yzerman	5.00
52	Jason Arnott	.50
53	Curtis Joseph	1.00
54	Ryan Smyth	.50
55	Doug Weight	1.00
56	Dave Gagner	.50
57	Ed Jovanovski	.50
58	Viktor Kozlov	.50
59	Scott Mellanby	.50
60	John Vanbiesbrouck	3.00
61	*Kevin Weekes*	1.00
62	Rob Blake	.50
63	*Donald MacLean*	.50
64	Yanic Perreault	.50
65	Luc Robitaille	.75
66	Jozef Stumpel	.75
67	Shayne Corson	.50
68	Vincent Damphousse	.50
69	Saku Koivu	2.00
70	Andy Moog	1.00
71	Mark Recchi	.50
72	Stephane Richer	.50
73	Martin Brodeur	3.00
74	*Patrik Elias*	1.50
75	Doug Gilmour	1.00
76	Bobby Holik	.50
77	Scott Stevens	.50
78	Bryan Berard	1.00
79	Zigmund Palffy	1.50
80	Robert Reichel	.50
82	Bryan Smolinski	.50
81	Tommy Salo	.75
83	Adam Graves	.50
84	Wayne Gretzky	10.00
85	Pat LaFontaine	.75
86	Brian Leetch	1.00
87	Mike Richter	1.00
88	Niklas Sundstrom	.50
89	Daniel Alfredsson	.75
90	Alexandre Daigle	.50
91	Shawn McEachern	.50
92	Chris Phillips	.50
93	Ron Tugnutt	.50
94	Alexei Yashin	.75
95	Rod Brind'Amour	.75
96	Chris Gratton	.75
97	Ron Hextall	1.00
98	John LeClair	2.00
99	Eric Lindros	6.00
100	*Vaclav Prospal*	2.00
101	Dainius Zubrus	.50
102	Mike Gartner	.50
103	Brad Isbister	.50
104	Nikolai Khabibulin	1.00
105	Jeremy Roenick	1.25
106	Cliff Ronning	.50
107	Keith Tkachuk	2.00
108	Tom Barrasso	.75
109	Ron Francis	1.00
110	Jaromir Jagr	6.00
111	Alexei Morozov	.50
112	Ed Olczyk	.50
113	Jim Campbell	.50
114	Pavol Demitra	.50
115	Steve Duchesne	.75
116	Grant Fuhr	1.00
117	Brett Hull	2.00
118	Pierre Turgeon	1.00
119	Jeff Friesen	.50
120	Patrick Marleau	3.00
121	Owen Nolan	.75
122	*Marco Sturm*	1.50
123	Mike Vernon	1.00
124	Dino Ciccarelli	.50
125	Roman Hamrlik	.75
126	Darren Puppa	.50
127	Paul Ysebaert	.50
128	Sergei Berezin	.75
129	Wendel Clark	.50
130	Alyn McCauley	.50
131	Felix Potvin	1.50
132	Mats Sundin	1.50
133	Pavel Bure	3.00
134	Martin Gelinas	.50
135	Trevor Linden	.50
136	Mark Messier	2.00
137	Alexander Mogilny	1.00
138	Peter Bondra	1.00
139	Dale Hunter	.50
140	Joe Juneau	.50
141	Olaf Kolzig	.50
142	Adam Oates	1.00
143	Jaroslav Svejkovsky	.50
144	Richard Zednik	.50

1997-98 Pacific Crown Royale Emerald/Silver

Three parallels of the Crown Royale base set were produced. Emerald (Canada, 4:25) and Silver (U.S., 4:25) parallels were produced, as well as the Ice Blue parallel.

	MT
Emeralds:	2x to 4x
Silvers:	2x to 4x

1997-98 Pacific Crown Royale Ice Blue

Ice Blue is a full parallel of the Crown Royale base set. The set was inserted in packs for all outlets at a rate of 1:25.

	MT
Ice Blue Stars:	10x to 20x
Yng Stars & RCs:	8x to 15x

1997-98 Pacific Crown Royale Blades of Steel

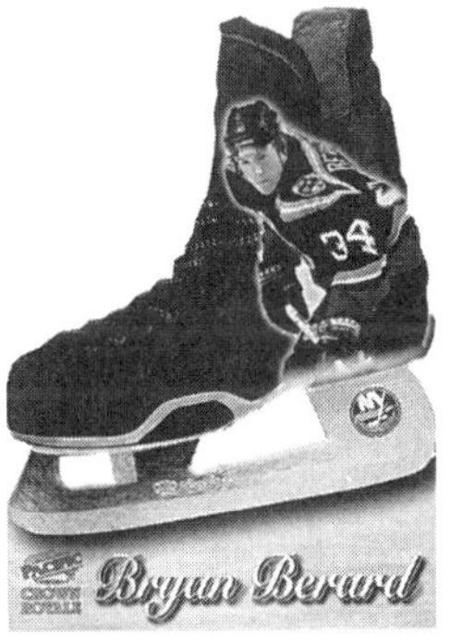

Blades of Steel is a 20-card insert seeded one per 49 packs. The cards are die-cut in the shape of a hockey skate with the player's image on the boot.

		MT
	Complete Set (20):	475.00
	Common Player:	10.00
1	Paul Kariya	45.00
2	Teemu Selanne	25.00
3	Joe Thornton	30.00
4	Chris Chelios	10.00
5	Peter Forsberg	35.00
6	Patrick Roy	60.00
7	Mike Modano	15.00
8	Sergei Fedorov	20.00
9	Brendan Shanahan	25.00
10	Steve Yzerman	35.00
11	Ryan Smyth	10.00
12	Saku Koivu	18.00
13	Bryan Berard	10.00
14	Wayne Gretzky	75.00
15	Brian Leetch	10.00
16	Eric Lindros	45.00
17	Jaromir Jagr	45.00
18	Brett Hull	18.00
19	Pavel Bure	25.00
20	Mark Messier	20.00

1997-98 Pacific Crown Royale Cramer's Choice Jumbos

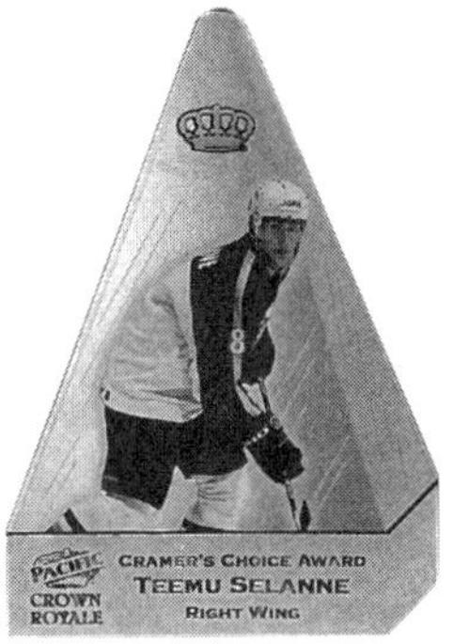

Premium-Sized Cramer's Choice Awards were seeded one per box. The ten-card set has a die-cut trophy design and the players were selected by Pacific CEO Mike Cramer.

		MT
	Complete Set (10):	90.00
	Common Player:	4.00
1	Paul Kariya	12.00
2	Teemu Selanne	8.00
3	Joe Thornton	8.00
4	Peter Forsberg	10.00
5	Patrick Roy	15.00
6	Steve Yzerman	10.00
7	Wayne Gretzky	20.00
8	Eric Lindros	12.00
9	Jaromir Jagr	12.00
10	Pavel Bure	8.00

1997-98 Pacific Crown Royale Freeze Out

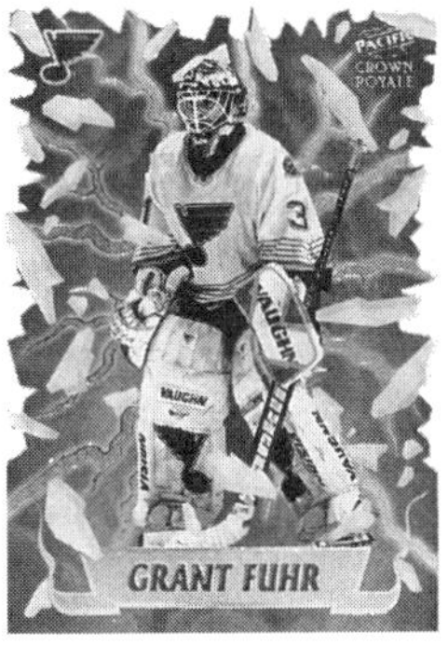

Freeze Out is a 20-card insert seeded 1:25. The cards feature top goalies and are die-cut on three sides. The background has flying ice chunks and lightning.

		MT
	Complete Set (20):	220.00
	Common Player:	5.00
1	Guy Hebert	5.00
2	Byron Dafoe	5.00
3	Dominik Hasek	30.00
4	Tyler Moss	10.00
5	Patrick Roy	50.00
6	Ed Belfour	10.00
7	Chris Osgood	15.00
8	Curtis Joseph	10.00
9	John Vanbiesbrouck	25.00
10	Andy Moog	10.00
11	Martin Brodeur	30.00
12	Mike Richter	12.00
13	Ron Hextall	5.00
14	Garth Snow	5.00
15	Nikolai Khabibulin	8.00
16	Tom Barrasso	5.00
17	Grant Fuhr	10.00
18	Mike Vernon	8.00
19	Felix Potvin	12.00
20	Olaf Kolzig	5.00

1997-98 Pacific Crown Royale Hat Tricks

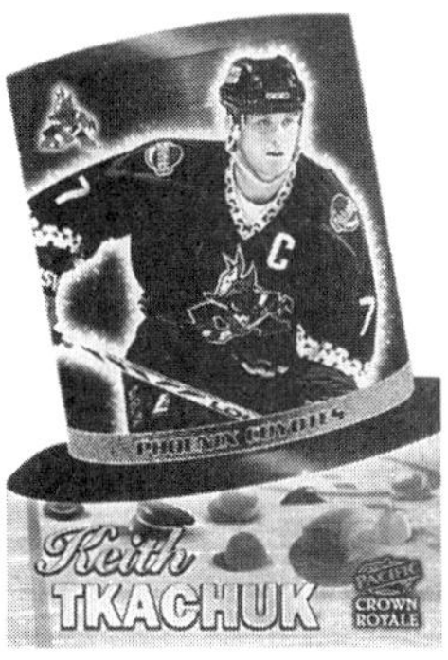

Hat Tricks is a 20-card insert seeded one per 25 packs. The top of each card features a player image on a die-cut top hat. The bottom has a computer-generated image of a hockey rink covered in hats, with the player's name and Crown Royale logo also featured.

		MT
	Complete Set (20):	375.00
	Common Player:	5.00
1	Paul Kariya	40.00
2	Teemu Selanne	20.00
3	Joe Thornton	25.00
4	Peter Forsberg	30.00
5	Joe Sakic	25.00
6	Mike Modano	10.00
7	Brendan Shanahan	20.00
8	Steve Yzerman	30.00
9	Ryan Smyth	5.00
10	Zigmund Palffy	10.00
11	Wayne Gretzky	60.00
12	John LeClair	15.00
13	Eric Lindros	40.00
14	Keith Tkachuk	15.00
15	Jaromir Jagr	40.00
16	Brett Hull	15.00
17	Mats Sundin	10.00
18	Pavel Bure	20.00
19	Mark Messier	15.00
20	Peter Bondra	8.00

1997-98 Pacific Crown Royale Lamplighters

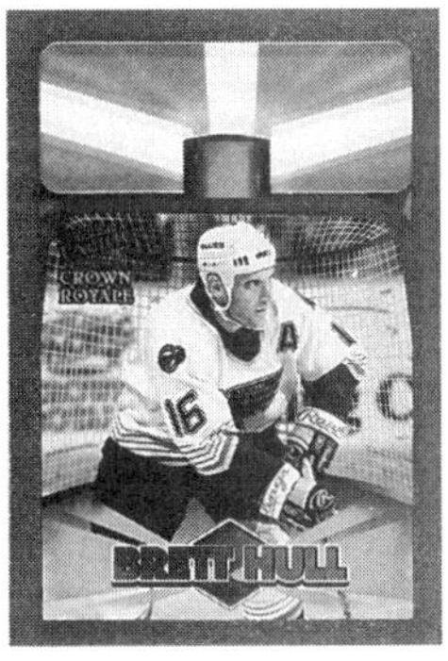

Lamplighters is a 20-card insert seeded 1:73. Each card features a color player image in front of a hockey net. The top of the card features a fused cel window for the red goal light.

		MT
	Complete Set (20):	775.00
	Common Player:	20.00
1	Paul Kariya	80.00
2	Teemu Selanne	40.00
3	Joe Thornton	35.00
4	Mike Peca	20.00
5	Peter Forsberg	60.00
6	Joe Sakic	50.00
7	Mike Modano	25.00
8	Brendan Shanahan	35.00
9	Steve Yzerman	60.00
10	Saku Koivu	25.00
11	Wayne Gretzky	125.00
12	Pat LaFontaine	20.00
13	John LeClair	30.00
14	Eric Lindros	80.00
15	Dainius Zubrus	20.00
16	Keith Tkachuk	30.00
17	Jaromir Jagr	80.00
18	Brett Hull	30.00
19	Pavel Bure	35.00
20	Mark Messier	25.00

1997-98 Pacific Dynagon

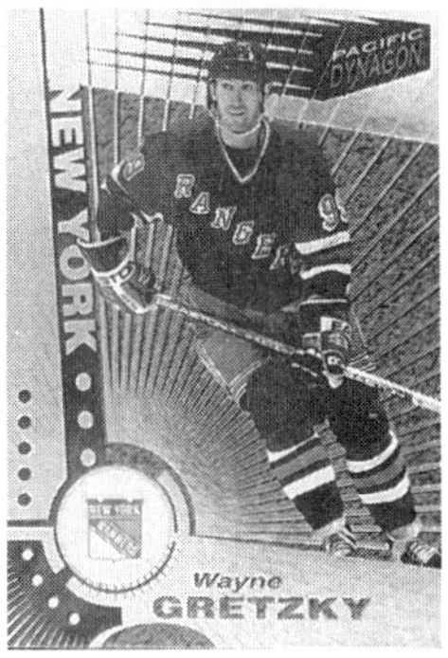

Dynagon Hockey consists of a 144-card base set with six parallels and five inserts. The base cards are fully foiled and double-etched. The fronts have a color player shot, with his name at the bottom, his team name and logo on the left and the Dynagon logo in the upper right. The parallels are Copper, Silver, Dark Grey, Red, Emerald and Ice Blue. The inserts include Best-Kept Secrets, Tandems, Dynamic Duos, Kings of the NHL and Stonewallers.

		MT
	Complete Set (156):	140.00
	Common Player:	.50
	Wax Box:	70.00
1	Brian Bellows	.50
2	Guy Hebert	.75
3	Paul Kariya	6.00
4	Steve Rucchin	.50
5	Teemu Selanne	3.00
6	Jason Allison	.50
7	Ray Bourque	.75
8	Jim Carey	.75
9	Jozef Stumpel	.50
10	Dominik Hasek	3.50
11	Brian Holzinger	.50
12	Mike Peca	.50
13	Derek Plante	.50
14	Miroslav Satan	.50
15	Theoren Fleury	.75
16	Jonas Hoglund	.50
17	Jarome Iginla	1.00
18	Trevor Kidd	.50
19	German Titov	.50
20	Sean Burke	.75
21	Andrew Cassels	.50
22	Keith Primeau	.50
23	Geoff Sanderson	.50
24	Tony Amonte	.75
25	Chris Chelios	1.00
26	Eric Daze	.75
27	Jeff Hackett	.75
28	Ethan Moreau	.50
29	Peter Forsberg	5.00
30	Valeri Kamensky	.50
31	Claude Lemieux	.50
32	Sandis Ozolinsh	.50
33	Patrick Roy	8.00
34	Joe Sakic	4.00
35	Derian Hatcher	.50
36	Jamie Langenbrunner	.50
37	Mike Modano	1.00
38	Joe Nieuwendyk	.50
39	Darryl Sydor	.50
40	Sergei Zubov	.50
41	Sergei Fedorov	2.50
42	Vladimir Konstantinov	.50
43	Chris Osgood	2.00
44	Brendan Shanahan	4.00
45	Mike Vernon	.50
46	Steve Yzerman	5.00
47	Kelly Buchberger	.50
48	Mike Grier	.50
49	Curtis Joseph	1.00
50	Rem Murray	.50
51	Ryan Smyth	.75
52	Doug Weight	.75
53	Ed Jovanovski	.50
54	Scott Mellanby	.50
55	Ray Sheppard	.50
56	Robert Svehla	.50
57	John Vanbiesbrouck	3.50

58 Rob Blake .50
59 Ray Ferraro .50
60 Dimitri Khristich .50
61 Vladimir Tsyplakov .50
62 Vincent Damphousse .50
63 Saku Koivu 3.00
64 Mark Recchi .75
65 Stephane Richer .50
66 Jocelyn Thibault 1.00
67 Dave Andreychuk .50
68 Martin Brodeur 3.00
69 Doug Gilmour .75
70 Bobby Holik .50
71 John MacLean .50
72 Bryan Berard .75
73 Travis Green .50
74 Zigmund Palffy 1.50
75 Tommy Salo .75
76 Bryan Smolinski .50
77 Adam Graves .50
78 Wayne Gretzky 10.00
79 Alexei Kovalev .50
80 Brian Leetch .75
81 Mark Messier 2.00
82 Mike Richter 1.00
83 Daniel Alfredsson .75
84 Alexandre Daigle .50
85 Wade Redden .50
86 Damian Rhodes .50
87 Alexei Yashin .75
88 Rod Brind'Amour .75
89 Ron Hextall .75
90 John LeClair 2.00
91 Eric Lindros 6.00
92 Janne Niinimaa .75
93 Garth Snow .50
94 Dainius Zubrus 1.50
95 Mike Gartner .50
96 Nikolai Khabibulin .75
97 Jeremy Roenick 1.00
98 Keith Tkachuk 1.50
99 Oleg Tverdovsky .50
100 Ron Francis .75
101 Kevin Hatcher .50
102 Jaromir Jagr 6.00
103 Patrick Lalime .50
104 Petr Nedved .50
105 Jim Campbell .50
106 Grant Fuhr 1.00
107 Brett Hull 1.50
108 Pierre Turgeon .75
109 Harry York .50
110 Jeff Friesen .50
111 Tony Granato .50
112 Stephen Guolla .50
113 Viktor Kozlov .50
114 Owen Nolan .50
115 Dino Ciccarelli .50
116 John Cullen .50
117 Chris Gratton .75
118 Roman Hamrlik .50
119 Daymond Langkow .50
120 Sergei Berezin .75
121 Wendel Clark .50
122 Felix Potvin 1.50
123 Steve Sullivan .50
124 Mats Sundin 1.00
125 Pavel Bure 3.00
126 Martin Gelinas .50
127 Trevor Linden .50
128 Kirk McLean .50
129 Alexander Mogilny 1.00
130 Peter Bondra .75
131 Joe Juneau .50
132 Steve Konowalchuk .50
133 Adam Oates .75
134 Bill Ranford .50
135 Paul Kariya, Teemu Selanne 2.00
136 Dominik Hasek, Mike Peca 1.50
137 Theoren Fleury, Jarome Iginla .50
138 Peter Forsberg, Patrick Roy 3.00
139 Brendan Shanahan, Steve Yzerman 2.00
140 Wayne Gretzky, Mark Messier 5.00
141 John LeClair, Eric Lindros 2.50
142 Jaromir Jagr, Patrick Lalime 2.00
143 Jim Campbell, Brett Hull .75
144 Sergei Berezin, Mats Sundin .50
— Shawn Bates 1.00
— Daniel Cleary 1.50
— *Marian Hossa* 2.50
— *Olli Jokinen* 2.50
— Espen Knutsen .75
— Mattias Ohlund 1.50
— Patrick Marleau 4.00
— Alyn McCauley 1.00
— Chris Phillips 1.00
— Erik Rasmussen .75
— Sergei Samsonov 2.50
— Joe Thornton 5.00

1997-98 Pacific Dynagon Copper

Five base set parallels were each exclusive to packs for a certain outlet. Copper (U.S. hobby), Silver (U.S. retail), Dark Grey (Canada retail), Emerald (Canada hobby) and Red (Treat) parallels all had an insertion rate of 2:37.

	MT
Coppers:	3x to 6x
Silvers:	3x to 6x
Dark Grey:	4x to 8x
Reds:	8x to 15x
Emeralds:	3x to 6x

1997-98 Pacific Dynagon Ice Blue

The Ice Blue parallel was not exclusive to any outlet, unlike the other parallels in this set. The cards were inserted one per 73 packs.

	MT
Ice Blue Stars:	15x to 25x
Yng Stars & RCs:	10x to 15x

1997-98 Pacific Dynagon Best Kept Secrets

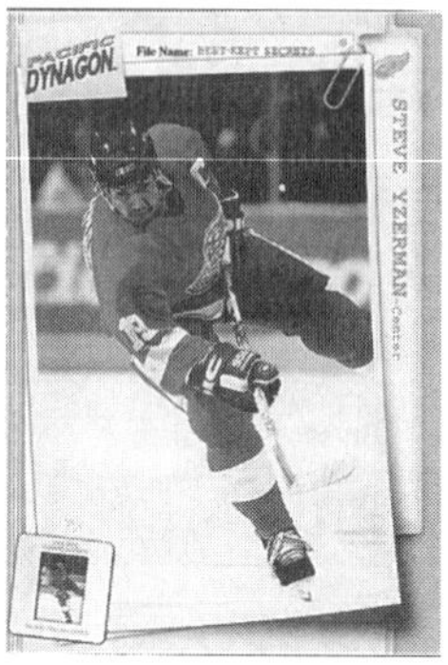

Best-Kept Secrets is a 110-card insert seeded one per pack. The card fronts are designed to look like a file folder holding top secret information on the player. The cards have a horizontal layout. The color player photo appears to be held to the file by a paper clip. The Dynagon logo looks like a post-it note.

		MT
	Complete Set (110):	20.00
	Common Player:	.10
1	J.J. Daigneault	.10
2	Paul Kariya	1.50
3	Dave Karpa	.10
4	Teemu Selanne	.75
5	Ray Bourque	.20
6	Jim Carey	.20
7	Davis Payne	.10
8	Paxton Schafer	.10
9	Bob Boughner	.10
10	Dominik Hasek	.75
11	Brad May	.10
12	Cale Hulse	.10
13	Jarome Iginla	.20
14	James Patrick	.10
15	Zarley Zalapski	.10
16	Jeff Brown	.10
17	Keith Primeau	.10
18	Steven Rice	.10
19	James Black	.10
20	Chris Chelios	.20
21	Steve Dubinsky	.10
22	Steve Smith	.10
23	Craig Billington	.10
24	Peter Forsberg	1.25
25	Jon Klemm	.10
26	Patrick Roy	2.00
27	Joe Sakic	1.00
28	Neal Broten	.10
29	Richard Matvichuk	.10
30	Mike Modano	.30
31	Andy Moog	.20
32	Sergei Fedorov	.60
33	Kirk Maltby	.10
34	Brendan Shanahan	.75
35	Tim Taylor	.10
36	Steve Yzerman	1.25
37	Louie DeBrusk	.10
38	Joe Hulbig	.10
39	Ryan Smyth	.20
40	Mike Hough	.10
41	Jody Hull	.10
42	Paul Laus	.10
43	John Vanbiesbrouck	1.00
44	Aki Berg	.10
45	Ray Ferraro	.10
46	Craig Johnson	.10
47	Ian Laperriere	.10
48	Vincent Damphousse	.10
49	Dave Manson	.10
50	Stephane Richer	.10
51	Craig Rivet	.10
52	Martin Brodeur	.75
53	Jay Pandolfo	.10
54	Brian Rolston	.10
55	Doug Houda	.10
56	Brent Hughes	.10
57	Zigmund Palffy	.30
58	Adam Graves	.10
59	Wayne Gretzky	2.50
60	Chris Ferraro	.10
61	Glenn Healy	.10
62	Brian Leetch	.20
63	Mark Messier	.30
64	Radim Bicanek	.10
65	Phil Crowe	.10
66	Christer Olsson	.10
67	Jason York	.10
68	Rod Brind'Amour	.10
69	John Druce	.10
70	Daniel Lacroix	.10
71	John Leclair	.30
72	Eric Lindros	1.50
73	Murray Baron	.10
74	Mike Gartner	.10
75	Brad McCrimmon	.10
76	Keith Tkachuk	.40
77	Jaromir Jagr	1.50
78	Patrick Lalime	.10
79	Ian Moran	.10
80	Petr Nedved	.10
81	Brett Hull	.30
82	Robert Petrovicky	.10
83	Pierre Turgeon	.20
84	Trent Yawney	.10
85	Tim Hunter	.10
86	Marcus Ragnarsson	.10
87	Dody Wood	.10
88	Dino Ciccarelli	.10
89	Alexander Selivanov	.10
90	Jason Wiemer	.10
91	Sergei Berezin	.10
92	Felix Potvin	.40
93	Mats Sundin	.25
94	Craig Wolanin	.10
95	Pavel Bure	.75
96	Troy Crowder	.10
97	Dana Murzyn	.10
98	Gino Odjick	.10
99	Craig Berube	.10
100	Peter Bondra	.20
101	Mike Eagles	.10
102	Andrei Nikolishin	.10
103	Paul Kariya	1.50
104	Dominik Hasek	.75
105	Mike Peca	.10
106	Brodeur, M. Dunham	.10
107	Bryan Berard	.20
108	Brian Leetch	.20
109	Tony Granato	.10
110	Trevor Linden	.10

1997-98 Pacific Dynagon Dynamic Duos

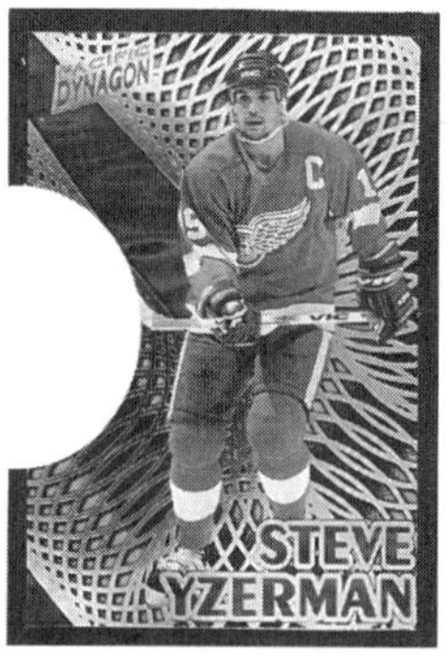

Dynamic Duos is a 30-card insert featuring 15 pairs of cards. Each pair features two teammates. The cards are die-cut, with one having a full team logo and the other having an indent so the two cards can be put together. The card fronts have a color player photo with a gold spring design in the background and black borders.

		MT
	Complete Set (30):	350.00
	Common Player:	6.00
1A	Paul Kariya	30.00
1B	Teemu Selanne	15.00
2A	Ray Bourque	6.00
2B	Jim Carey	6.00
3A	Dominik Hasek	15.00
3B	Mike Peca	6.00
4A	Theoren Fleury	6.00
4B	Jarome Iginla	6.00
5A	Peter Forsberg	25.00
5B	Claude Lemieux	6.00
6A	Patrick Roy	40.00
6B	Joe Sakic	20.00
7A	Sergei Fedorov	15.00
7B	Vladimir Konstantinov	6.00
8A	Brendan Shanahan	15.00
8B	Steve Yzerman	25.00
9A	Bryan Berard	6.00
9B	Zigmund Palffy	10.00
10A	Wayne Gretzky	50.00
10B	Mark Messier	10.00
11A	Eric Lindros	30.00
11B	Dainius Zubrus	8.00
12A	Jeremy Roenick	8.00
12B	Keith Tkachuk	10.00
13A	Jaromir Jagr	30.00
13B	Patrick Lalime	6.00
14A	Jim Campbell	6.00
14B	Brett Hull	10.00
15A	Pavel Bure	15.00
15B	Alexander Mogilny	8.00

1997-98 Pacific Dynagon Kings of the NHL

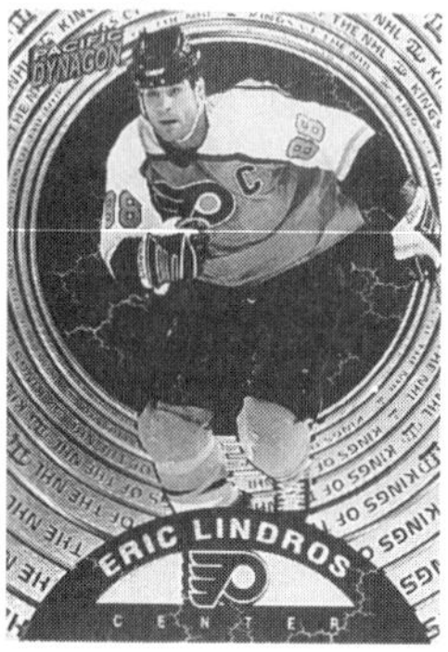

Kings of the NHL is a 10-card insert seeded one per 361 packs. The cards have a color player photo in front of a circular foiled design.

		MT
	Complete Set (10):	650.00
	Common Player:	30.00
1	Paul Kariya	80.00
2	Peter Forsberg	80.00
3	Patrick Roy	120.00
4	Joe Sakic	60.00
5	John Vanbiesbrouck	60.00
6	Wayne Gretzky	150.00
7	Mark Messier	30.00
8	Eric Lindros	90.00
9	Jaromir Jagr	90.00
10	Pavel Bure	40.00

1997-98 Pacific Dynagon Stonewallers

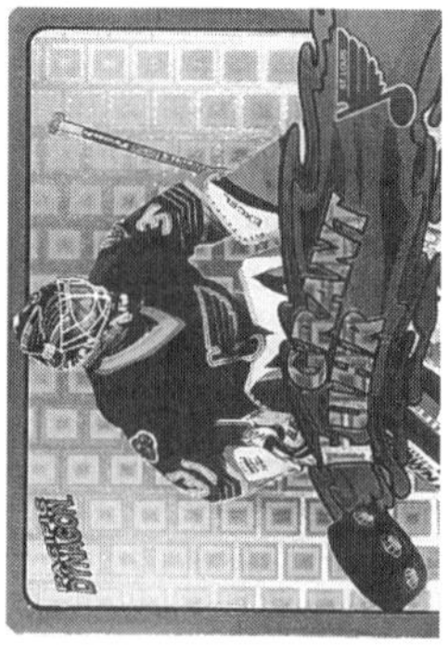

Stonewallers is a 20-card insert seeded one per 73 packs. The horizontal cards feature the NHL's top goalies with red and silver foil.

		MT
	Complete Set (20):	250.00
	Common Goalie:	10.00
1	Guy Hebert	10.00
2	Jim Carey	10.00
3	Dominik Hasek	35.00
4	Trevor Kidd	10.00
5	Jeff Hackett	10.00
6	Patrick Roy	60.00
7	Chris Osgood	20.00
8	Mike Vernon	10.00
9	Curtis Joseph	15.00
10	John Vanbiesbrouck	30.00
11	Jocelyn Thibault	10.00
12	Martin Brodeur	30.00
13	Tommy Salo	10.00
14	Mike Richter	15.00
15	Ron Hextall	10.00
16	Garth Snow	10.00
17	Nikolai Khabibulin	10.00
18	Patrick Lalime	10.00
19	Grant Fuhr	15.00
20	Felix Potvin	20.00

1997-98 Pacific Dynagon Tandems

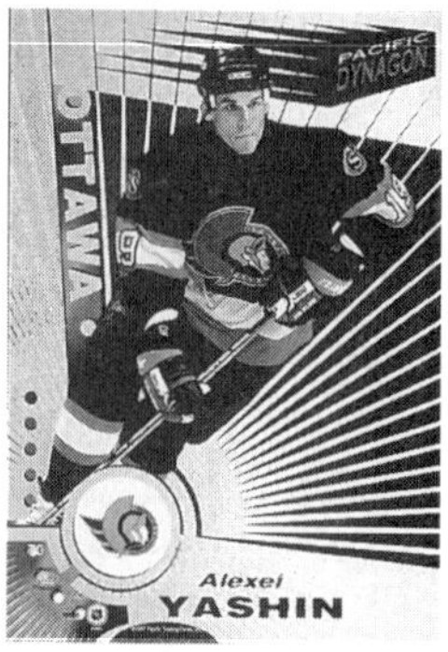

Tandems is a 72-card insert seeded one per 37 packs. The double-front cards feature two NHL stars. The cards have the same design as the base set and holographic foil.

		MT
	Complete Set (72):	1000.
	Common Player:	8.00
1	Wayne Gretzky, Eric Lindros	140.00
2	Joe Sakic, Paul Kariya	75.00
3	Jarome Iginla, Mark Messier	20.00
4	Patrick Roy, Dominik Hasek	100.00
5	Peter Forsberg, Jaromir Jagr	75.00
6	Brendan Shanahan, Keith Tkachuk	35.00
7	Steve Yzerman, Teemu Selanne	70.00
8	Sergei Fedorov, Brett Hull	35.00
9	Dainius Zubrus, Patrick Lalime	12.00
10	Sergei Berezin, Mike Grier	8.00
11	Zigmund Palffy, Curtis Joseph	15.00
12	Chris Osgood, Martin Brodeur	35.00
13	John Vanbiesbrouck, Jocelyn Thibault	35.00
14	Saku Koivu, Pavel Bure	35.00
15	John LeClair, Peter Bondra	20.00
16	Mats Sundin, Janne Niinimaa	12.00
17	Felix Potvin, Jim Carey	15.00
18	Grant Fuhr, Brett Hull, Jim Campbell	12.00
19	Wayne Gretzky, Alexei Kovalev, Brian Leetch	90.00
20	Eric Lindros, John LeClair, Rod Brind'Amour	50.00
21	Dominik Hasek, Mike Peca, Miroslav Satan	25.00
22	Jaromir Jagr, Patrick Lalime, Petr Nedved	40.00
23	Jarome Iginla, Theoren Fleury, Trevor Kidd	8.00
24	Paul Kariya, Teemu Selanne, Guy Hebert	40.00
25	Peter Forsberg, Patrick Roy, Claude Lemieux	50.00
26	S. Yzerman, B. Shanahan, V. Konstantinov	35.00
27	Mats Sundin, Sergei Berezin, Wendel Clark	12.00
28	Ray Bourque, Derek Plante	8.00

29	Brian Bellows, Jason Allison	8.00
30	Steve Rucchin, Keith Primeau	8.00
31	Jozef Stumpel, Eric Daze	8.00
32	Brian Holzinger, Jamie Langenbrunner	8.00
33	Mike Peca, Tony Amonte	8.00
34	German Titov, Darryl Sydor	8.00
35	Theoren Fleury, Chris Chelios	10.00
36	Jonas Hoglund, Dimitri Khristich	8.00
37	Sean Burke, Dale Andreychuck	8.00
38	Geoff Sanderson, Derian Hatcher	8.00
39	Andrew Cassels, Jeff Hackett	8.00
40	Ethan Moreau, Ray Ferraro	8.00
41	Sandis Ozolinsh, Doug Gilmour	12.00
42	Valeri Kamensky, Mike Modano	15.00
43	Joe Nieuwendyk, Vladimir Tsyplakov	8.00
44	Sergei Zubov, Mike Vernon	8.00
45	Rob Blake, Bobby Holik	8.00
46	Vincent Damphousse, Doug Weight	8.00
47	Mark Recchi, Ryan Smyth	8.00
48	Stephane Richer, John MacLean	8.00
49	Kelly Buchberger, Ed Jovanovski	8.00
50	Rem Murray, Owen Nolan	8.00
51	Robert Svehla, Bill Ranford	8.00
52	Ray Sheppard, Steve Sullivan	8.00
53	Scott Mellanby, John Cullen	8.00
54	Garth Snow, Alexandre Daigle	8.00
55	Ron Hextall, Alexander Mogilny	10.00
56	Kirk McLean, Adam Oates	8.00
57	Joe Juneau, Dino Ciccarelli	8.00
58	Steve Konowalchuk, Jim Campbell	8.00
59	Trevor Linden, Pierre Turgeon	8.00
60	Martin Gelinas, Jeff Friesen	8.00
61	Roman Hamrlik, Harry York	8.00
62	Kevin Hatcher, Chris Gratton	8.00
63	Ron Francis, Jeremy Roenick	15.00
64	Nikolai Khabibulin, Viktor Kozlov	8.00
65	Daymond Langkow, Mike Gartner	8.00
66	Oleg Tverdovsky, Stephen Guolla	8.00
67	Tony Granato, Tommy Salo	8.00
68	Bryan Smolinski, Wade Redden	8.00
69	Adam Graves, Damian Rhodes	8.00
70	Mike Richter, Alexei Yashin	12.00
71	Daniel Alfredsson, Bryan Berard	8.00
72	Travis Green, Alexei Kovalev	8.00

1997-98 Pacific Invincible

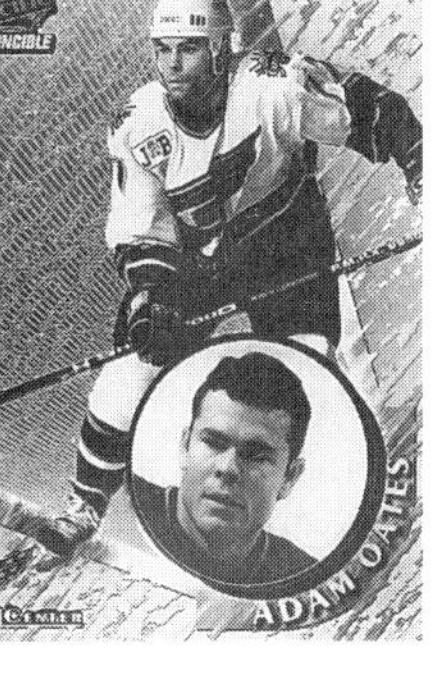

Invincible Hockey consists of a 150-card base set. The base cards feature a color player photo with a gold background. A cel window is located in the bottom right corner and features a headshot of the player. The base set is paralleled five times and four inserts were also included.

		MT
Complete Set (150):		140.00
Common Player:		.75
Wax Box:		70.00
1	Brian Bellows	.75
2	Guy Hebert	1.25
3	Paul Kariya	8.00
4	Teemu Selanne	4.00
5	Darren Van Impe	.75
6	Jason Allison	.75
7	Ray Bourque	1.25
8	Jim Carey	2.00
9	Ted Donato	.75
10	Jozef Stumpel	.75
11	Jason Dawe	.75
12	Dominik Hasek	4.00
13	Mike Peca	.75
14	Derek Plante	.75
15	Miroslav Satan	.75
16	Theoren Fleury	1.25
17	Dave Gagner	.75
18	Jonas Hoglund	.75
19	Jarome Iginla	1.50
20	Trevor Kidd	.75
21	German Titov	.75
22	Sean Burke	1.25
23	Andrew Cassels	.75
24	Derek King	.75
25	Keith Primeau	.75
26	Geoff Sanderson	.75
27	Tony Amonte	.75
28	Chris Chelios	1.50
29	Eric Daze	.75
30	Jeff Hackett	.75
31	Ethan Moreau	.75
32	Alexei Zhamnov	.75
33	Adam Deadmarsh	.75
34	Peter Forsberg	6.00
35	Valeri Kamensky	.75
36	Claude Lemieux	.75
37	Sandis Ozolinsh	.75
38	Patrick Roy	10.00
39	Joe Sakic	5.00
40	Jamie Langenbrunner	.75
41	Mike Modano	2.00
42	Andy Moog	1.25
43	Joe Nieuwendyk	.75
44	Pat Verbeek	.75
45	Sergei Zubov	.75
46	Sergei Fedorov	4.00
47	Vladimir Konstantinov	.75
48	Vyacheslav Kozlov	.75
49	Nicklas Lidstrom	.75
50	Chris Osgood	2.00
51	Brendan Shanahan	4.00
52	Mike Vernon	1.25
53	Steve Yzerman	6.00
54	Jason Arnott	.75
55	Mike Grier	1.25
56	Curtis Joseph	1.50
57	Rem Murray	.75
58	Ryan Smyth	1.50
59	Doug Weight	1.25
60	Ed Jovanovski	.75
61	Scott Mellanby	.75
62	Kirk Muller	.75
63	Ray Sheppard	.75
64	John Vanbiesbrouck	5.00
65	Rob Blake	.75
66	Ray Ferraro	.75
67	Stephane Fiset	.75
68	Dimitri Khristich	.75
69	Vladimir Tsyplakov	.75
70	Vincent Damphousse	.75
71	Saku Koivu	2.50
72	Mark Recchi	.75
73	Stephane Richer	.75
74	Jocelyn Thibault	1.25
75	Dave Andreychuk	.75
76	Martin Brodeur	4.00
77	Doug Gilmour	1.50
78	Bobby Holik	.75
79	Denis Pederson	.75
80	Bryan Berard	1.50
81	Travis Green	.75
82	Zigmund Palffy	2.00
83	Tommy Salo	1.25
84	Bryan Smolinski	.75
85	Adam Graves	.75
86	Wayne Gretzky	12.00
87	Alexei Kovalev	.75
88	Brian Leetch	1.50
89	Mark Messier	2.00
90	Mike Richter	1.50
91	Luc Robitaille	1.25
92	Daniel Alfredsson	1.25
93	Alexandre Daigle	.75
94	Steve Duchesne	.75
95	Wade Redden	.75
96	Ron Tugnutt	.75
97	Alexei Yashin	1.50
98	Rod Brind'Amour	.75
99	Paul Coffey	1.25
100	Ron Hextall	1.00
101	John LeClair	2.00
102	Eric Lindros	8.00
103	Janne Niinimaa	1.25
104	Mikael Renberg	.75
105	Dainius Zubrus	1.50
106	Mike Gartner	.75
107	Nikolai Khabibulin	1.25
108	Jeremy Roenick	1.50
109	Keith Tkachuk	2.00
110	Oleg Tverdovsky	.75
111	Ron Francis	1.25
112	Kevin Hatcher	.75
113	Jaromir Jagr	8.00
114	Patrick Lalime	1.50
115	Petr Nedved	.75
116	Ed Olczyk	.75
117	Jim Campbell	.75
118	Geoff Courtnall	.75
119	Grant Fuhr	1.50
120	Brett Hull	2.00
121	Sergio Momesso	.75
122	Pierre Turgeon	.75
123	Ed Belfour	1.50
124	Jeff Friesen	.75
125	Tony Granato	.75
126	Stephen Guolla	.75
127	Bernie Nicholls	.75
128	Owen Nolan	.75
129	Dino Ciccarelli	.75
130	John Cullen	.75
131	Chris Gratton	.75
132	Roman Hamrlik	.75
133	Daymond Langkow	.75
134	Paul Ysebaert	.75
135	Sergei Berezin	1.25
136	Wendel Clark	.75
137	Felix Potvin	2.00
138	Steve Sullivan	.75
139	Mats Sundin	1.50
140	Pavel Bure	4.00
141	Martin Gelinas	.75
142	Trevor Linden	.75
143	Kirk McLean	.75
144	Alexander Mogilny	1.50
145	Peter Bondra	1.25
146	Dale Hunter	.75
147	Joe Juneau	.75
148	Steve Konowalchuk	.75
149	Adam Oates	1.50
150	Bill Ranford	.75

1997-98 Pacific Invincible Copper

The Invincible base set had four different parallels seeded two per 37 packs: Copper (U.S. hobby), Silver (U.S. retail), Emerald (Canada hobby) and Red (Canada retail).

	MT
Copper Stars:	4x to 8x
Yng Stars & RCs:	3x to 6x
Emerald Stars:	5x to 10x
Yng Stars & RCs:	4x to 8x
Silver Stars:	5x to 10x
Yng Stars & RCs:	4x to 8x
Reds:	8x to 15x

1997-98 Pacific Invincible Ice Blue

The Ice Blue parallel of the Invincible base set was seeded one per 73 packs.

	MT
Ice Blue Stars:	12x to 25x
Yng Stars & RCs:	8x to 15x

1997-98 Pacific Invincible Attack Zone

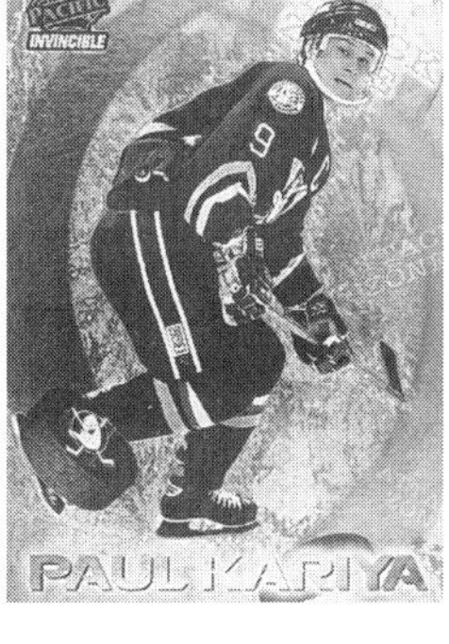

Attack Zone is a 24-card insert seeded one per 37 packs. The player's name is at the bottom, the Invincible logo is in the upper left corner and "Attack Zone" is in the upper right.

		MT
Complete Set (24):		250.00
Common Player:		4.00
1	Paul Kariya	25.00
2	Teemu Selanne	12.00
3	Mike Peca	4.00
4	Jarome Iginla	6.00
5	Peter Forsberg	20.00
6	Claude Lemieux	4.00
7	Joe Sakic	15.00
8	Mike Modano	8.00
9	Sergei Fedorov	12.00
10	Brendan Shanahan	12.00
11	Steve Yzerman	20.00
12	Bryan Berard	6.00
13	Zigmund Palffy	10.00
14	Wayne Gretzky	40.00
15	Brian Leetch	6.00
16	Mark Messier	8.00
17	John LeClair	8.00
18	Eric Lindros	25.00
19	Ron Francis	4.00
20	Jaromir Jagr	25.00
21	Brett Hull	8.00
22	Dino Ciccarelli	4.00
23	Pavel Bure	12.00
24	Alexander Mogilny	6.00

1997-98 Pacific Invincible Feature Performers

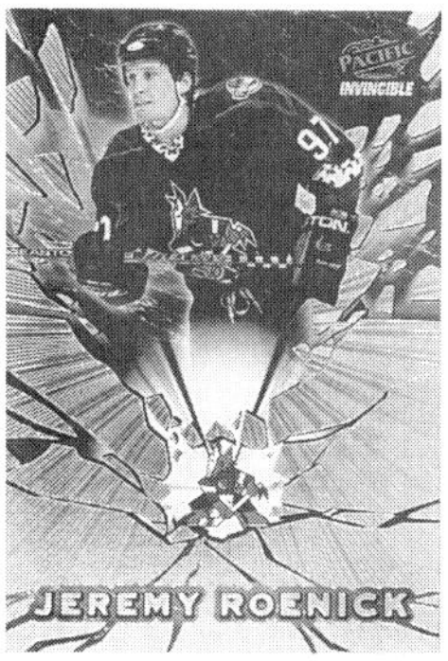

Feature Performers is a 36-card insert seeded 2:37. The card front features a "shattering glass" design that reveals a star player.

		MT
Complete Set (36):		250.00
Common Player:		3.00
1	Paul Kariya	20.00
2	Teemu Selanne	10.00
3	Ray Bourque	4.00
4	Dominik Hasek	10.00
5	Jarome Iginla	5.00
6	Chris Chelios	4.00
7	Peter Forsberg	15.00
8	Claude Lemieux	3.00
9	Patrick Roy	25.00
10	Joe Sakic	12.00
11	Mike Modano	5.00
12	Sergei Fedorov	10.00
13	Vladimir Konstantinov	3.00
14	Brendan Shanahan	10.00
15	Mike Vernon	3.00
16	Steve Yzerman	15.00
17	John Vanbiesbrouck	12.00
18	Saku Koivu	8.00
19	Martin Brodeur	10.00
20	Zigmund Palffy	6.00
21	Wayne Gretzky	30.00
22	Mark Messier	8.00
23	Alexandre Daigle	3.00
24	John LeClair	8.00
25	Eric Lindros	20.00
26	Janne Niinimaa	3.00
27	Jeremy Roenick	5.00
28	Jaromir Jagr	20.00
29	Patrick Lalime	3.00
30	Jim Campbell	3.00
31	Brett Hull	6.00
32	Sergei Berezin	3.00
33	Felix Potvin	6.00
34	Mats Sundin	4.00
35	Alexander Mogilny	4.00
36	Peter Bondra	3.00

1997-98 Pacific Invincible Off the Glass

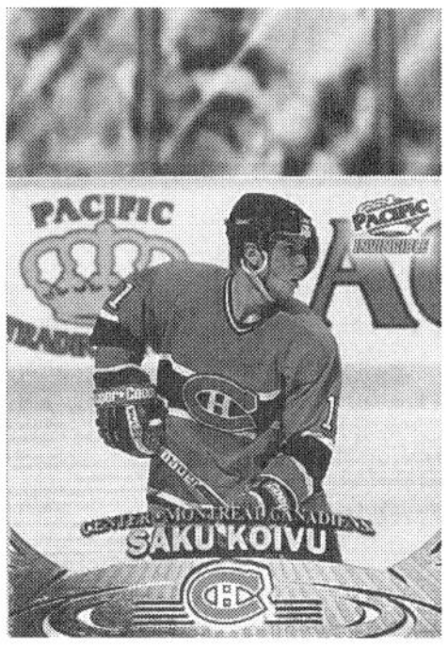

Off The Glass is a 20-card insert seeded one per 73 packs. The cards have a cel window fused to the top to give the appearance of the plexiglass attached to the boards of a hockey rink.

		MT
Complete Set (20):		500.00
Common Player:		8.00
1	Paul Kariya	50.00
2	Teemu Selanne	25.00
3	Mike Peca	8.00
4	Jarome Iginla	12.00
5	Peter Forsberg	40.00
6	Joe Sakic	30.00
7	Sergei Fedorov	25.00
8	Brendan Shanahan	25.00
8	Steve Yzerman	40.00
10	Mike Grier	12.00
11	Saku Koivu	20.00
12	Wayne Gretzky	80.00
13	Mark Messier	20.00
14	Eric Lindros	60.00
15	Dainius Zubrus	12.00
16	Keith Tkachuk	15.00
17	Jaromir Jagr	50.00
18	Brett Hull	15.00
19	Sergei Berezin	8.00
20	Pavel Bure	25.00

1997-98 Pacific Invincible NHL Regime

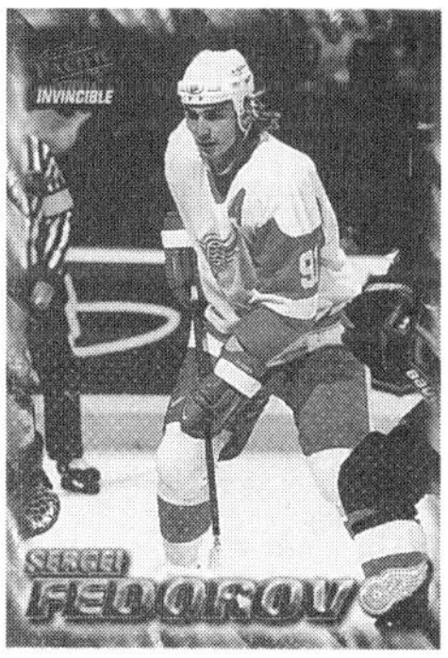

NHL Regime is a 220-card bonus set included in packs of Pacific Invincible Hockey. The cards feature a color player photo with a "frosted" border. The player's name is in the bottom left, the team logo is in the bottom right and the Invincible logo is in the top left.

		MT
Complete Set (220):		20.00
Common Player:		.10
1	Ken Baumgartner	.10
2	Mark Jenssens	.10
3	Jean-Francois Jomphe	.10
4	Paul Kariya	1.25
5	Jason Marshall	.10
6	Richard Park	.10
7	Teemu Selanne	.50
8	Mikhail Shtalenkov	.20
9	Bob Beers	.10
10	Ray Bourque	.25
11	Jim Carey	.15
12	Brett Harkins	.10

13 Sheldon Kennedy .10
14 Troy Meallette .10
15 Sandy Moger .10
16 Jon Rohloff .10
17 Don Sweeney .10
18 Randy Burridge .10
19 Michal Grosek .10
20 Dominik Hasek .75
21 Rob Ray .10
22 Steve Shields .25
23 Richard Smehlik .10
24 Dixon Ward .10
25 Mike Wilson .10
26 Tommy Albelin .10
27 Aaron Gavey .10
28 Todd Hlushko .10
29 Jarome Iginla .20
30 Yves Racine .10
31 Dwayne Roloson .10
32 Mike Sullivan .10
33 Ed Ward .10
34 Adam Burt .10
35 Nelson Emerson .10
36 Kevin Haller .10
37 Derek King .10
38 Curtis Leschyshyn .10
39 Chris Murray .10
40 Jason Muzzatti .10
41 Keith Carney .10
42 Chris Chelios .25
43 Enrico Chiccone .10
44 Jim Cummins .10
45 Cam Russell .10
46 Jeff Shantz .10
47 Michal Sykora .10
48 Chris Terreri .10
49 Eric Weinrich .10
50 Rene Corbet .10
51 Peter Forsberg 1.00
52 Alexei Gusarov .10
53 Uwe Krupp .10
54 Sylvain Lefebrve .10
55 Eric Messier .10
56 Patrick Roy 1.50
57 Joe Sakic .75
58 Brent Severyn .10
59 Greg Adams .10
60 Todd Harvey .10
61 Jere Lehtinen .10
62 Craig Ludwig .10
63 Mike Modano .50
64 Andy Moog .20
65 Dave Reid .10
66 Roman Turek .20
67 Doug Brown .10
68 Kris Draper .10
69 Sergei Fedorov .50
70 Joey Kocur .10
71 Kirk Maltby .10
72 Bob Rouse .10
73 Brendan Shanahan .50
74 Aaron Ward .10
75 Steve Yzerman 1.00
76 Greg DeVries .10
77 Bob Essensa .20
78 Kevin Lowe .10
79 Bryan Marchment .10
80 Dean McAmmond .10
81 Boris Mironov .10
82 Luke Richardson .10
83 Ryan Smyth .10
84 Terry Carkner .10
85 Ed Jovanovski .10
86 Bill Lindsay .10
87 Dave Lowry .10
88 Gord Murphy .10
89 John Vanbiesbrouck .50
90 Steve Washburn .10
91 Chris Wells .10
92 Philippe Boucher .10
93 Steven Finn .10
94 Mattias Norstrom .10
95 Kai Nurminen .10
96 Sean O'Donnell .10
97 Yanic Perreault .10
98 Jeff Shevalier .10
99 Brad Smyth .10
100 Brad Brown .10
101 Jassen Cullimore .10
102 Vincent Damphousse .20
103 Vladimir Malakhov .10
104 Peter Popovic .10
105 Stephane Richer .10
106 Turner Stevenson .10
107 Jose Theodore .25
108 Martin Brodeur .60
109 Bob Carpenter .10
110 Mike Dunham .50
111 Patrik Elias .25
112 Dave Ellett .10
113 Doug Gilmour .25
114 Randy McKay .10
115 Todd Bertuzzi .20
116 Kenny Jonsson .10
117 Paul Kruse .10
118 Claude Lapointe .10
119 Zigmund Palffy .40
120 Richard Pilon .10
121 Dan Plante .10
122 Dennis Vaske .10
123 Shane Churla .10
124 Bruce Driver .10
125 Mike Eastwood .10
126 Patrick Flatley .10
127 Adam Graves .10
128 Wayne Gretzky 2.00
129 Brian Leetch .25
130 Doug Lidster .10
131 Mark Messier .40
132 Tom Chorske .10
133 Sean Hill .10
134 Denny Lambert .10
135 Janne Laukkanen .10
136 Frank Musil .10
137 Lance Pitlick .10
138 Shaun Van Allen .10
139 Rod Brind'Amour .20
140 Paul Coffey .20
141 Karl Dykhuis .10
142 Dan Kordic .10
143 Daniel Lacroix .10
144 John LeClair .50
145 Eric Lindros 1.25
146 Joel Otto .10
147 Shjon Podein .10
148 Chris Therien .10
149 Shane Doan .10
150 Dallas Drake .10
151 Jeff Finley .10
152 Mike Gartner .10
153 Nikolai Khabibulin .25
154 Darrin Shannon .10
155 Mike Stapleton .10
156 Keith Tkachuk .40
157 Tom Barrasso .25
158 Josef Beranek .10
159 Alex Hicks .10
160 Jaromir Jagr 1.25
161 Patrick Lalime .10
162 Francois Leroux .10
163 Petr Nedved .10
164 Roman Oksiuta .10
165 Chris Tamer .10
166 Marc Bergevin .10
167 Jon Casey .10
168 Craig Conroy .10
169 Brett Hull .40
170 Igor Kravchuck .10
171 Stephen Leach .10
172 Ricard Persson .10
173 Pierre Turgeon .20
174 Ed Belfour .30
175 Doug Bodger .10
176 Shean Donovan .10
177 Bob Errey .10
178 Todd Ewen .10
179 Wade Flaherty .10
180 Mike Rathje .10
181 Ron Sutter .10
182 Mikael Andersson .10
183 Dino Ciccarelli .10
184 Cory Cross .10
185 Jamie Huscroft .10
186 Rudy Poeschek .10
187 Daren Puppa .10
188 David Shaw .10
189 Jay Wells .10
190 Jamie Baker .10
191 Sergei Berezin .10
192 Brandon Convery .10
193 Darby Hendrickson .10
194 Matt Martin .10
195 Felix Potvin .25
196 Jason Smith .10
197 Craig Wolanin .10
198 Adrian Aucoin .10
199 Dave Babych .10
200 Donald Brashear .10
201 Pavel Bure .50
202 Chris Joseph .30
203 Alexander Mogilny .25
204 David Roberts .10
205 Scott Walker .10
206 Peter Bondra .30
207 Andrew Brunette .10
208 Calle Johanson .10
209 Ken Klee .10
210 Olaf Kolzig .40
211 Kelly Miller .10
212 Joe Reekie .10
213 Chris Simon .10
214 Brendan Witt .10
215 Paul Kariya .75
216 Peter Forsberg .50
217 Patrick Roy .75
218 Wayne Gretzky 1.00
219 Eric Lindros .75
220 Jaromir Jagr .75

1997-98 Pacific Omega

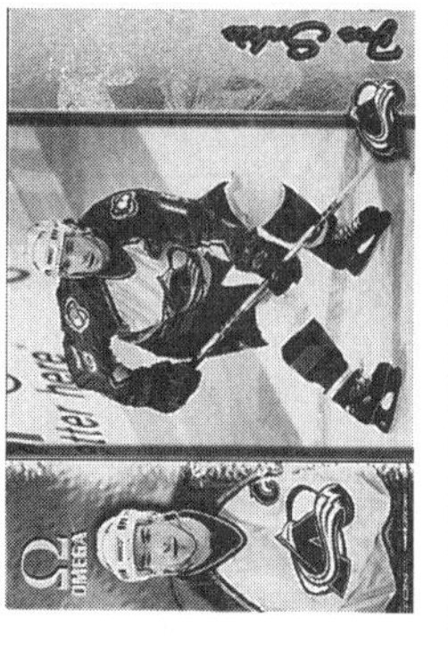

Omega consists of a 250-card base set. The horizontal cards feature a color player image in the center that is duplicated in foil on the right. A different photo is on the left. The base set has four parallels: Copper (U.S. Hobby, 1:1), Emerald (Canada, 1:1), Gold (U.S. Retail, 1:1) and Ice Blue (1:73). Inserts include Silks, Stick Handle Laser-Cuts, Game Face Cel-Fusions, No Scoring Zone and Team Leaders.

		MT
Complete Set (250):		20.00
Common Player:		.10
1	Matt Cullen	.10
2	Guy Hebert	.20
3	Paul Kariya	1.50
4	Dmitri Mironov	.10
5	Steve Rucchin	.10
6	Tomas Sandstrom	.10
7	Teemu Selanne	.75
8	Mikhail Shtalenkov	.10
9	*Pavel Trnka*	.20
10	Jason Allison	.20
11	*Per Axelsson*	.10
12	Ray Bourque	.25
13	Anson Carter	.10
14	Byron Dafoe	.20
15	Ted Donato	.10
16	Hal Gill	.10
17	Dmitri Khristich	.10
18	Sergei Samsonov	.60
19	Joe Thornton	1.50
20	Jason Dawe	.10
21	Michal Grosek	.10
22	Dominik Hasek	1.00
23	Brian Holzinger	.10
24	Mike Peca	.10
25	Derek Plante	.10
26	Miroslav Satan	.10
27	Steve Shields	.10
28	Andrew Cassels	.10
29	Theoren Fleury	.20
30	Jarome Iginla	.20
31	*Derek Morris*	.10
32	*Tyler Moss*	.10
33	Michael Nylander	.10
34	Dwayne Roloson	.10
35	Cory Stillman	.10
36	Rick Tabaracci	.10
37	German Titov	.10
38	Jon Battaglia	.10
39	Nelson Emerson	.10
40	Martin Gelinas	.10
41	Sami Kapanen	.20
42	Trevor Kidd	.20
43	Kirk McLean	.20
44	Keith Primeau	.20
45	Gary Roberts	.10
46	Tony Amonte	.25
47	Keith Carney	.10
48	Chris Chelios	.25
49	Eric Daze	.20
50	Brian Felsner	.10
51	Jeff Hackett	.25
52	Christian LaFlamme	.10
53	Alexei Zhamnov	.10
54	Craig Billington	.20
55	Adam Deadmarsh	.20
56	Peter Forsberg	1.25
57	Valeri Kamensky	.20
58	Uwe Krupp	.10
59	Jari Kurri	.10
60	Claude Lemieux	.20
61	*Eric Messier*	.10
62	Jeff Odgers	.10
63	Sandis Ozolinsh	.20
64	Patrick Roy	2.00
65	Joe Sakic	1.00
66	Greg Adams	.10
67	Ed Belfour	.30
68	Manny Fernandez	.10
69	Derian Hatcher	.20
70	Jamie Langenbrunner	.20
71	Jere Lehtinen	.10
72	Juha Lind	.10
73	Mike Modano	.40
74	Joe Nieuwendyk	.25
75	Darryl Sydor	.10
76	Pat Verbeek	.10
77	Sergei Zubov	.10
78	Viacheslav Fetisov	.10
79	Brent Gilchrist	.10
80	Kevin Hodson	.25
81	Vyacheslav Kozlov	.10
82	Igor Larionov	.10
83	Nicklas Lidstrom	.20
84	Darren McCarty	.10
85	Larry Murphy	.10
86	Chris Osgood	.40
87	Brendan Shanahan	.75
88	Steve Yzerman	1.25
89	Kelly Buchberger	.10
90	Mike Grier	.10
91	Bill Guerin	.10
92	Roman Hamrlik	.10
93	Curtis Joseph	.30
94	Boris Mironov	.10
95	Ryan Smyth	.10
96	Doug Weight	.20
97	Dino Ciccarelli	.10
98	Dave Gagner	.10
99	Ed Jovanovski	.10
100	Scott Mellanby	.10
101	Robert Svehla	.10
102	John Vanbiesbrouck	.75
103	Steve Washburn	.10
104	*Kevin Weekes*	.25
105	Ray Whitney	.10
106	Rob Blake	.10
107	Stephane Fiset	.20
108	Garry Galley	.10
109	Steve McKenna	.10
110	Glen Murray	.10
111	Yanic Perreault	.10
112	Luc Robitaille	.20
113	Jamie Storr	.20
114	Jozef Stumpel	.10
115	Vladimir Tsyplakov	.10
116	Shayne Corson	.10
117	Vincent Damphousse	.10
118	Saku Koivu	.50
119	Vladimir Malakhov	.10
120	Andy Moog	.25
121	Mark Recchi	.20
122	Martin Rucinsky	.10
123	Brian Savage	.10
124	Jocelyn Thibault	.25
125	Jason Arnott	.10
126	Brad Bombardir	.10
127	Martin Brodeur	1.00
128	*Patrik Elias*	.50
129	Doug Gilmour	.25
130	Bobby Holik	.10
131	Randy McKay	.10
132	Scott Niedermayer	.10
133	Krzysztof Oliwa	.10
134	Scott Stevens	.10
135	Petr Sykora	.10
136	Bryan Berard	.20
137	Travis Green	.10
138	Bryan McCabe	.10
139	Sergei Nemchinov	.10
140	Zigmund Palffy	.50
141	Robert Reichel	.10
142	Tommy Salo	.20
143	Bryan Smolinski	.10
144	Adam Graves	.10
145	Wayne Gretzky	2.50
146	Pat LaFontaine	.20
147	Brian Leetch	.20
148	Mike Richter	.30
149	Kevin Stevens	.10
150	Niklas Sundstrom	.10
151	Tim Sweeney	.10
152	Daniel Alfredsson	.20
153	Magnus Arvedson	.10
154	Andreas Dackell	.10
155	Igor Kraychuk	.10
156	Shawn McEachern	.10
157	Damian Rhodes	.20
158	Ron Tugnutt	.20
159	Alexei Yashin	.20
160	Rod Brind'Amour	.20
161	Paul Coffey	.20
162	Eric Desjardins	.10
163	*Colin Forbes*	.20
164	Chris Gratton	.20
165	Ron Hextall	.25
166	Trent Klatt	.10
167	John LeClair	.60
168	Eric Lindros	1.50
169	Joel Otto	.10
170	Garth Snow	.20
171	Dainius Zubrus	.10
172	Dallas Drake	.10
173	Mike Gartner	.10
174	Nikolai Khabibulin	.25
175	Teppo Numminen	.10
176	Jeremy Roenick	.40
177	Keith Tkachuk	.50
178	Rick Tocchet	.10
179	Oleg Tverdovsky	.20
180	Juha Ylonen	.10
181	Stu Barnes	.10
182	Tom Barrasso	.25
183	Rob Brown	.10
184	Ron Francis	.25
185	Kevin Hatcher	.10
186	Jaromir Jagr	1.50
187	Alexei Morozov	.10
188	Ed Olczyk	.10
189	Jim Campbell	.10
190	Geoff Courtnall	.10
191	Pavol Demitra	.10
192	Steve Duchesne	.10
193	Grant Fuhr	.25
194	Brett Hull	.50
195	Al MacInnis	.20
196	Chris Pronger	.20
197	Pascal Rheaume	.10
198	Jamie Rivers	.10
199	Pierre Turgeon	.20
200	Jeff Friesen	.10
201	Tony Granato	.10
202	John MacLean	.10
203	Patrick Marleau	.10
204	Marty McSorley	.10
205	Owen Nolan	.10
206	*Marco Sturm*	.40
207	Mike Vernon	.25
208	*Andrei Zyuzin*	.25
209	Karl Dykhuis	.10
210	Daymond Langkow	.10
211	Bryan Marchment	.10
212	Daren Puppa	.10
213	Mikael Renberg	.10
214	Alexander Selivanov	.10
215	Paul Ysebaert	.10
216	Rob Zamuner	.10
217	Sergei Berezin	.10
218	Wendel Clark	.10
219	Marcel Cousineau	.10
220	Tie Domi	.10
221	*Mike Johnson*	.40
222	Igor Korolev	.10
223	Felix Potvin	.30
224	Mathieu Schneider	.10
225	Mats Sundin	.40
226	Yannick Tremblay	.10
227	Donald Brashear	.10
228	Pavel Bure	.75
229	Sean Burke	.20
230	Trevor Linden	.10
231	Mark Messier	.40
232	Alexander Mogilny	.25
233	Markus Naslund	.10
234	Mattias Ohlund	.10
235	Dave Scatchard	.10
236	Peter Bondra	.25
237	Andrew Brunette	.10
238	Phil Housley	.10
239	Dale Hunter	.10
240	Calle Johansson	.10
241	Joe Juneau	.10
242	Olaf Kolzig	.20
243	Adam Oates	.25
244	Richard Zednik	.10
245	Chris Chelios, Keith Tkachuk	.25
246	Mike Modano, Ed Belfour	.25
247	Teemu Selanne, Saku Koivu	.50
248	Eric Lindros, Shayne Corson	.75
249	Patrick Roy, Martin Brodeur	1.00
250	Wayne Gretzky, Mark Messier	1.50

1997-98 Pacific Omega Copper

The Copper parallel was inserted in U.S. hobby packs, Gold was found in U.S Retail packs and the Emerald parallel was exclusive to Canada. Each parallel was inserted one per pack.

	MT
Coppers:	2x to 4x
Emeralds:	2x to 4x
Golds:	2x to 4x

1997-98 Pacific Omega Ice Blue

Ice Blue is a full parallel of the Omega base set that was seeded 1:73 in packs for all outlets.

	MT
Ice Blue Stars:	40x to 75x
Yng Stars & RCs:	25x to 50x

1997-98 Pacific Omega Game Face

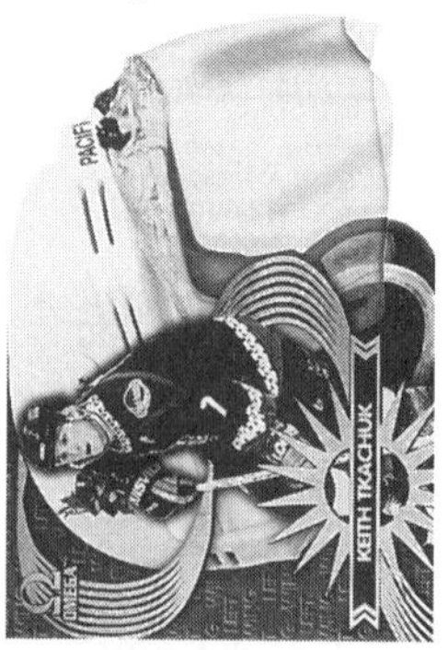

Game Face Die-Cut Cel-Fusions is a 20-card insert seeded 1:37. The cards have a horizontal layout with a cel facemask attached to a die-cut helmet.

		MT
Complete Set (20):		180.00
Common Player:		4.00
1	Paul Kariya	20.00
2	Teemu Selanne	10.00

3	Peter Forsberg	15.00
4	Joe Sakic	12.00
5	Mike Modano	6.00
6	Nicklas Lidstrom	4.00
7	Brendan Shanahan	10.00
8	Steve Yzerman	15.00
9	Ryan Smyth	4.00
10	Saku Koivu	8.00
11	Wayne Gretzky	30.00
12	John LeClair	8.00
13	Eric Lindros	20.00
14	Dainius Zubrus	4.00
15	Keith Tkachuk	8.00
16	Jaromir Jagr	20.00
17	Brett Hull	6.00
18	Pavel Bure	10.00
19	Mark Messier	6.00
20	Peter Bondra	5.00

1997-98 Pacific Omega No Scoring Zone

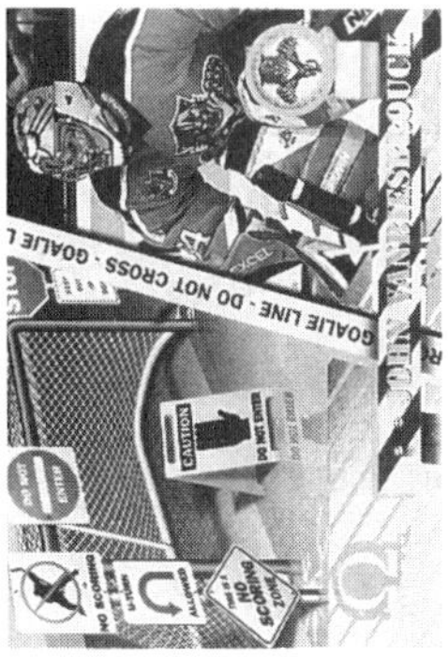

No Scoring Zone is a 10-card insert featuring top goalies. Seeded 2:37, the cards have a horizontal layout, with a photo of the goalie on the right and a graphic of a blocked-off goal on the left.

		MT
Complete Set (10):		40.00
Common Player:		2.50
1	Dominik Hasek	8.00
2	Patrick Roy	12.00
3	Ed Belfour	4.00
4	Chris Osgood	5.00
5	John Vanbiesbrouck	6.00
6	Andy Moog	3.00
7	Martin Brodeur	8.00
8	Mike Richter	4.00
9	Ron Hextall	2.50
10	Felix Potvin	4.00

1997-98 Pacific Omega Silks

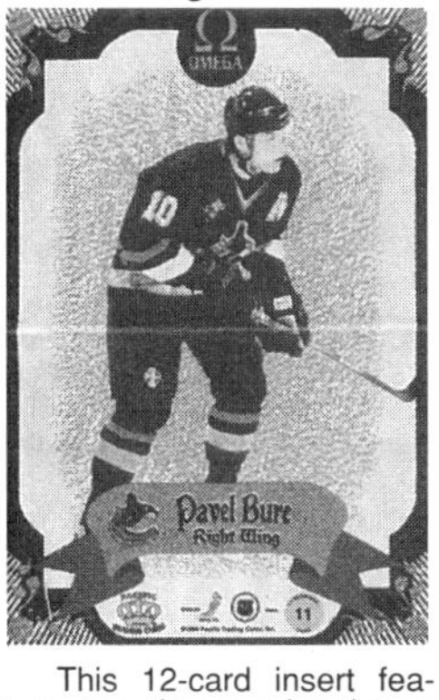

This 12-card insert features top players printed on a silk-like fabric. Inserted 1:73, the cards are approximately twice the size of regular cards.

		MT
Complete Set (12):		120.00
Common Player:		4.00
1	Paul Kariya	15.00
2	Teemu Selanne	8.00
3	Peter Forsberg	12.00
4	Patrick Roy	20.00
5	Joe Sakic	10.00
6	Steve Yzerman	12.00
7	Martin Brodeur	8.00
8	Wayne Gretzky	25.00
9	Eric Lindros	15.00
10	Jaromir Jagr	15.00
11	Pavel Bure	8.00
12	Mark Messier	6.00

1997-98 Pacific Omega Stick Handle

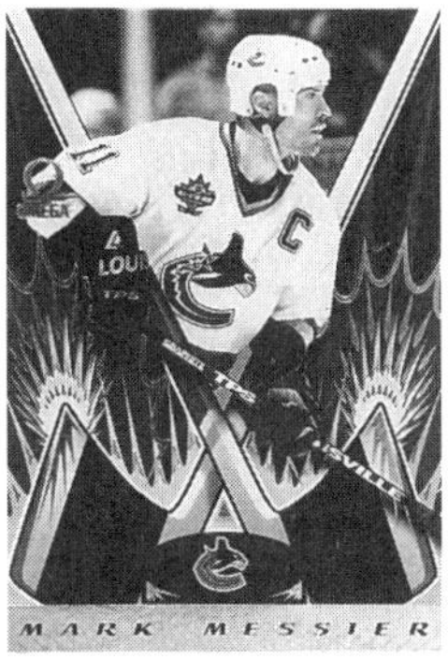

Stick Handle Laser-Cuts is a 20-card insert seeded 1:145. The card fronts feature a player photo and crossing hockey sticks which are laser-cut.

		MT
Complete Set (20):		600.00
Common Player:		10.00
1	Paul Kariya	60.00
2	Teemu Selanne	30.00
3	Theoren Fleury	10.00
4	Chris Chelios	15.00
5	Peter Forsberg	50.00
6	Joe Sakic	40.00
7	Mike Modano	20.00
8	Brendan Shanahan	30.00
9	Steve Yzerman	50.00
10	Saku Koivu	25.00
11	Doug Gilmour	15.00
12	Zigmund Palffy	20.00
13	Wayne Gretzky	100.00
14	Pat LaFontaine	10.00
15	John LeClair	25.00
16	Eric Lindros	60.00
17	Jaromir Jagr	60.00
18	Mats Sundin	20.00
19	Pavel Bure	30.00
20	Mark Messier	25.00

1997-98 Pacific Omega Hockey Team Leaders

Team Leaders is a 20-card insert seeded one per 24 packs. The full-foil cards were exclusive to Canadian retail outlets.

		MT
Complete Set (20):		200.00
Common Player:		4.00
Inserted 1:24 Can.		
1	Paul Kariya	25.00
2	Ray Bourque	6.00
3	Theo Fleury	4.00
4	Patrick Roy	30.00
5	Joe Sakic	15.00
6	Ed Belfour	8.00
7	Joe Nieuwendyk	6.00
8	Brendan Shanahan	10.00
9	Steve Yzerman	20.00
10	Ryan Smyth	4.00
11	Shayne Corson	4.00
12	Mark Recchi	4.00
13	Martin Brodeur	12.00
14	Wayne Gretzky	40.00
15	Rod Brind'Amour	4.00
16	Eric Lindros	25.00
17	Chris Pronger	4.00
18	Felix Potvin	6.00
19	Pavel Bure	10.00
20	Mark Messier	8.00

1997-98 Pacific Paramount

Paramount Hockey consists of a 200-card base set with six parallels and four inserts. The base cards feature full-bleed photos. The parallels include copper, dark grey, emerald, red, silver and ice blue. Inserts include Big Numbers, Canadian Greats, Glove Side Laser_Cuts and Photoengravings.

		MT
Complete Set (200):		20.00
Common Player:		.10
Wax Box:		50.00
1	Guy Hebert	.20
2	Paul Kariya	1.50
3	*Espen Knutsen*	.20
4	Dmitri Mironov	.10
5	Steve Rucchin	.10
6	Tomas Sandstrom	.10
7	Teemu Selanne	.75
8	Scott Young	.10
9	Ray Bourque	.20
10	Jim Carey	.20
11	Anson Carter	.10
12	Ted Donato	.10
13	Dave Ellett	.10
14	Dimitri Khristich	.10
15	Sergei Samsonov	.60
16	Joe Thornton	1.50
17	Matthew Barnaby	.10
18	Jason Dawe	.10
19	Dominik Hasek	.75
20	Brian Holzinger	.10
21	Mike Peca	.10
22	Derek Plante	.10
23	Erik Rasmussen	.10
24	Miroslav Satan	.10
25	*Steve Begin*	.25
26	Andrew Cassels	.10
27	*Chris Dingman*	.10
28	Theoren Fleury	.20
29	Jonas Hoglund	.10
30	Jarome Iginla	.20
31	Rick Tabaracci	.10
32	German Titov	.10
33	Kevin Dineen	.10
34	Nelson Emerson	.10
35	Trevor Kidd	.10
36	Stephen Leach	.10
37	Keith Primeau	.10
38	Steven Rice	.10
39	Gary Roberts	.10
40	Tony Amonte	.10
41	Chris Chelios	.20
42	*Daniel Cleary*	.50
43	Eric Daze	.10
44	Jeff Hackett	.20
45	Sergei Krivokrasov	.10
46	Ethan Moreau	.10
47	Alexei Zhamnov	.10
48	Adam Deadmarsh	.10
49	Peter Forsberg	1.25
50	Valeri Kamensky	.10
51	Jari Kurri	.10
52	Claude Lemieux	.10
53	Sandis Ozolinsh	.10
54	Patrick Roy	2.00
55	Joe Sakic	1.00
56	Ed Belfour	.25
57	Derian Hatcher	.10
58	Jamie Langenbrunner	.10
59	Jere Lehtinen	.10
60	Mike Modano	.25
61	Joe Nieuwendyk	.20
62	Darryl Sydor	.10
63	Pat Verbeek	.10
64	Anders Eriksson	.10
65	Sergei Fedorov	.50
66	Vyacheslav Kozlov	.10
67	Nicklas Lidstrom	.20
68	Darren McCarty	.10
69	Chris Osgood	.40
70	Brendan Shanahan	.75
71	Steve Yzerman	1.25
72	Jason Arnott	.10
73	Boyd Devereaux	.10
74	Mike Grier	.10
75	Curtis Joseph	.20
76	Andrei Kovalenko	.10
77	Ryan Smyth	.10
78	Doug Weight	.20
79	Dave Gagner	.10
80	Ed Jovanovski	.10
81	Scott Mellanby	.10
82	Kirk Muller	.10
83	Rob Niedermayer	.10
84	Ray Sheppard	.10
85	Esa Tikkanen	.10
86	John Vanbiesbrouck	1.00
87	Rob Blake	.10
88	Stephane Fiset	.15
89	Garry Galley	.10
90	*Olli Jokinen*	.60
91	Luc Robitaille	.15
92	Jozef Stumpel	.10
93	Shayne Corson	.10
94	Vincent Damphousse	.10
95	Saku Koivu	.75
96	Andy Moog	.20
97	Mark Recchi	.10
98	Stephane Richer	.10
99	Brian Savage	.10
100	Dave Andreychuk	.10
101	Martin Brodeur	.75
102	Doug Gilmour	.20
103	Bobby Holik	.10
104	John MacLean	.10
105	Brian Rolston	.10
106	Bryan Berard	.20
107	Todd Bertuzzi	.10
108	Travis Green	.10
109	Zigmund Palffy	.40
110	Robert Reichel	.10
111	Tommy Salo	.20
112	Bryan Smolinski	.10
113	Christian Dube	.10
114	Adam Graves	.10
115	Wayne Gretzky	2.50
116	Alexei Kovalev	.10
117	Pat LaFontaine	.20
118	Brian Leetch	.20
119	Mike Richter	.25
120	Brian Skrudland	.10
121	Kevin Stevens	.10
122	Daniel Alfredsson	.20
123	Radek Bonk	.10
124	Alexandre Daigle	.10
125	*Marian Hossa*	.60
126	Igor Kravchuk	.10
127	Chris Phillips	.10
128	Damian Rhodes	.10
129	Alexei Yashin	.20
130	Rod Brind'Amour	.20
131	Chris Gratton	.20
132	Ron Hextall	.20
133	John LeClair	.40
134	Eric Lindros	2.00
135	Janne Niinimaa	.10
136	*Vaclav Prospal*	.40
137	Garth Snow	.10
138	Dainius Zubrus	.30
139	Mike Gartner	.10
140	Brad Isbister	.10
141	Nikolai Khabibulin	.20
142	Jeremy Roenick	.25
143	Cliff Ronning	.10
144	Keith Tkachuk	.40
145	Rick Tocchet	.10
146	Oleg Tverdovsky	.10
147	Tom Barrasso	.20
148	Ron Francis	.20
149	Kevin Hatcher	.10
150	Jaromir Jagr	1.50
151	Darius Kasparaitis	.10
152	Alexei Morozov	.10
153	Petr Nedved	.10
154	Ed Olczyk	.10
155	Jim Campbell	.10
156	Kelly Chase	.10
157	Geoff Courtnall	.10
158	Grant Fuhr	.20
159	Brett Hull	.30
160	Joe Murphy	.10
161	Pierre Turgeon	.20
162	Tony Twist	.10
163	Shawn Burr	.10
164	Jeff Friesen	.10
165	Tony Granato	.10
166	Viktor Kozlov	.10
167	Patrick Marleau	1.00
168	Stephane Matteau	.10
169	Owen Nolan	.10
170	Mike Vernon	.20
171	Dino Cicarelli	.10
172	Karl Dykhuis	.10
173	Roman Hamrlik	.10
174	Daymond Langkow	.10
175	Mikael Renberg	.10
176	Alexander Selivanov	.10
177	Paul Ysebaert	.10
178	Sergei Berezin	.10
179	Wendel Clark	.10
180	Glenn Healy	.10
181	Derek King	.10
182	Alyn McCauley	.10
183	Felix Potvin	.30
184	*Martin Prochazka*	.10
185	Mats Sundin	.30
186	Pavel Bure	.75
187	Martin Gelinas	.10
188	Trevor Linden	.10
189	Kirk McLean	.10
190	Mark Messier	.30
191	Markus Naslund	.10
192	Mattias Ohlund	.10
193	Peter Bondra	.20
194	Dale Hunter	.10
195	Joe Juneau	.10
196	Olaf Kolzig	.10
197	Steve Konowalchuk	.10
198	Adam Oates	.20
199	Bill Ranford	.10
200	Jaroslav Svejkovsky	.30

1997-98 Pacific Paramount Copper

Five base set parallels were created exclusively for certain outlets and inserted one per pack. The parallel sets include copper (U.S. hobby), silver (U.S. retail), emerald (Canada hobby), dark grey (Canada retail) and red (Treat).

	MT
Coppers:	2x to 4x
Reds:	5x to 10x
Dark Greys:	2x to 4x
Silvers:	2x to 4x
Emeralds:	2x to 4x

1997-98 Pacific Paramount Ice Blue

Ice Blue is a full parallel of the Paramount base set, seeded one per 73 packs.

	MT
Ice Blue Stars:	40x to 75x
Yng Stars & RCs:	30x to 50x

1997-98 Pacific Paramount Big Numbers

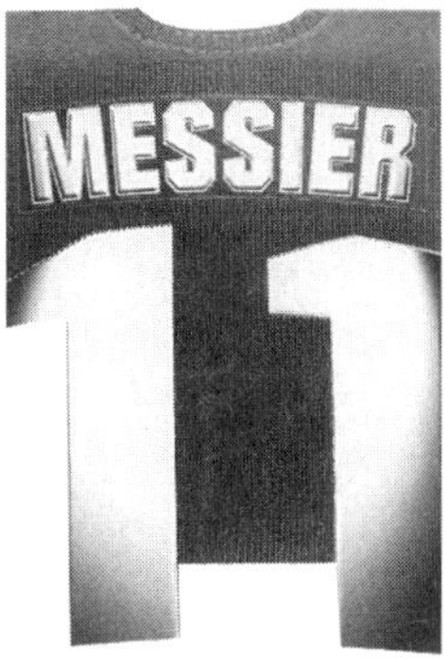

Big Numbers Die-Cuts is a 20-card insert seeded one per 37 packs.

		MT
Complete Set (20):		160.00
Common Player:		3.00
1	Paul Kariya	15.00
2	Teemu Selanne	8.00
3	Joe Thornton	6.00
4	Dominik Hasek	8.00
5	Peter Forsberg	12.00
6	Patrick Roy	20.00
7	Joe Sakic	10.00
8	Sergei Fedorov	6.00
9	Brendan Shanahan	8.00
10	Steve Yzerman	12.00
11	John Vanbiesbrouck	8.00
12	Martin Brodeur	10.00
13	Doug Gilmour	4.00
14	Wayne Gretzky	25.00
15	Eric Lindros	18.00
16	Keith Tkachuk	6.00
17	Jaromir Jagr	15.00
18	Brett Hull	5.00
19	Pavel Bure	8.00
20	Mark Messier	5.00

1997-98 Pacific Paramount Canadian Greats

Canadian Greats is a 12-card insert featuring top players from Canada. The cards were inserted one per 24 Canadian retail packs.

		MT
Complete Set (12):		100.00
Common Player:		3.00
1	Paul Kariya	15.00
2	Joe Thornton	6.00
3	Jarome Iginla	4.00
4	Patrick Roy	20.00
5	Joe Sakic	8.00
6	Brendan Shanahan	6.00
7	Steve Yzerman	12.00
8	Ryan Smyth	3.00
9	Martin Brodeur	8.00
10	Wayne Gretzky	25.00
11	Eric Lindros	15.00
12	Mark Messier	5.00

1997-98 Pacific Paramount Glove Side

Glove Side Laser-Cuts is a 20-card insert seeded one per 73 packs. The set features top goalies. The cards are die-cut around a goalie glove in the background with laser-cut webbing.

		MT
Complete Set (20):		160.00
Common Goalie:		6.00
1	Guy Hebert	6.00
2	Dominik Hasek	20.00
3	Trevor Kidd	6.00
4	Jeff Hackett	6.00
5	Patrick Roy	35.00
6	Ed Belfour	10.00
7	Chris Osgood	12.00
8	Curtis Joseph	8.00
9	John Vanbiesbrouck	20.00
10	Andy Moog	6.00
11	Martin Brodeur	20.00
12	Tommy Salo	6.00
13	Mike Richter	8.00
14	Ron Hextall	6.00
15	Garth Snow	6.00
16	Nikolai Khabibulin	6.00
17	Tom Barrasso	6.00
18	Grant Fuhr	8.00
19	Mike Vernon	6.00
20	Felix Potvin	10.00

1997-98 Pacific Paramount Photoengravings

Photoengravings is a 20-card insert seeded two per 37 packs. Printed on parchment paper, each card features a different "old-time" design on the front. The cards have rounded corners.

		MT
Complete Set (20):		80.00
Common Player:		1.50
1	Paul Kariya	8.00
2	Teemu Selanne	4.00
3	Joe Thornton	4.00
4	Dominik Hasek	4.00
5	Peter Forsberg	6.00
6	Patrick Roy	10.00
7	Joe Sakic	5.00
8	Mike Modano	1.50
9	Brendan Shanahan	4.00
10	Steve Yzerman	6.00
11	John Vanbiesbrouck	4.00
12	Saku Koivu	4.00
13	Wayne Gretzky	12.00
14	John LeClair	3.00
15	Eric Lindros	8.00
16	Keith Tkachuk	3.00
17	Jaromir Jagr	8.00
18	Brett Hull	2.50
19	Pavel Bure	4.00
20	Mark Messier	2.50

1997-98 Pacific Revolution

Revolution consists of a 150-card base set with four parallels and four inserts. The embossed base cards feature

gold and holographic silver foils. The parallel sets include Copper (U.S. Hobby, 2:25), Silver (U.S. Retail, 2:25), Emerald (Canada, 2:25) and Ice Blue (1:49). The insert sets are NHL Icons, Return to Sender, Team Checklists and '98 All-Star Game.

		MT
Complete Set (150):		120.00
Common Player:		.40
1	Guy Hebert	.75
2	Paul Kariya	6.00
3	Dmitri Mironov	.40
4	Ruslan Salei	.40
5	Teemu Selanne	3.00
6	Jason Allison	.40
7	Ray Bourque	1.00
8	Byron Dafoe	.75
9	Ted Donato	.40
10	Dimitri Khristich	.40
11	Joe Thornton	6.00
12	Matthew Barnaby	.40
13	Jason Dawe	.40
14	Dominik Hasek	3.00
15	Mike Peca	.40
16	Miroslav Satan	.40
17	Theoren Fleury	.75
18	Jarome Iginla	.50
19	Marty McInnis	.40
20	Cory Stillman	.40
21	Rick Tabaracci	.40
22	Martin Gelinas	.40
23	Sami Kapanen	.75
24	Trevor Kidd	.75
25	Keith Primeau	.75
26	Gary Roberts	.40
27	Tony Amonte	.75
28	Chris Chelios	1.00
29	Eric Daze	.75
30	Jeff Hackett	.75
31	Dmitri Nabokov	.40
32	Peter Forsberg	5.00
33	Valeri Kamensky	.75
34	Jari Kurri	.75
35	Claude Lemieux	.75
36	*Eric Messier*	.40
37	Sandis Ozolinsh	.75
38	Patrick Roy	8.00
39	Joe Sakic	4.00
40	Ed Belfour	1.00
41	Jamie Langenbrunner	.75
42	Jere Lehtinen	.40
43	Mike Modano	1.50
44	Joe Nieuwendyk	.75
45	Sergei Zubov	.75
46	Viacheslav Fetisov	.75
47	Nicklas Lidstrom	.75
48	Darren McCarty	.40
49	Larry Murphy	.40
50	Chris Osgood	1.50
51	Brendan Shanahan	2.50
52	Steve Yzerman	5.00
53	Roman Hamrlik	.40
54	Bill Guerin	.40
55	Curtis Joseph	1.00
56	Ryan Smyth	.75
57	Doug Weight	.75
58	Dino Ciccarelli	.40
59	Dave Gagner	.40
60	Ed Jovanovski	.40
61	Paul Laus	.40
62	John Vanbiesbrouck	2.50
63	Ray Whitney	.40
64	Russ Courtnall	.40
65	Yanic Perreault	.40
66	Luc Robitaille	.75
67	Jozef Stumpel	.75
68	Vladimir Tsyplakov	.40
69	Shayne Corson	.40
70	Vincent Damphousse	.40
71	Saku Koivu	2.00
72	Andy Moog	1.00
73	Mark Recchi	.40
74	Jocelyn Thibault	.75
75	Martin Brodeur	3.00
76	*Patrik Elias*	1.00
77	Doug Gilmour	1.00
78	Bobby Holik	.40
79	Scott Niedermayer	.40
80	Bryan Berard	.75

		MT
81	Travis Green	.40
82	Zigmund Palffy	1.50
83	Robert Reichel	.75
84	Tommy Salo	.75
85	Dan Cloutier	.40
86	Adam Graves	.40
87	Wayne Gretzky	10.00
88	Pat LaFontaine	.75
89	Brian Leetch	.75
90	Mike Richter	1.00
91	Kevin Stevens	.40
92	Daniel Alfredsson	.75
93	Shawn McEachern	.40
94	Damian Rhodes	.75
95	Ron Tugnutt	.60
96	Alexei Yashin	.75
97	Rod Brind'Amour	.75
98	Paul Coffey	.75
99	Alexandre Daigle	.40
100	Chris Gratton	.40
101	Ron Hextall	.75
102	John LeClair	2.00
103	Eric Lindros	8.00
104	Dainius Zubrus	.40
105	Mike Gartner	.40
106	Craig Janney	.40
107	Nikolai Khabibulin	1.00
108	Jeremy Roenick	1.25
109	Keith Tkachuk	2.00
110	Stu Barnes	.40
111	Tom Barrasso	.75
112	Ron Francis	1.00
113	Jaromir Jagr	6.00
114	*Peter Skudra*	.75
115	Martin Straka	.40
116	*Blair Atcheynum*	.75
117	Jim Campbell	.40
118	Geoff Courtnall	.40
119	Steve Duchesne	.75
120	Grant Fuhr	1.00
121	Brett Hull	2.00
122	Pierre Turgeon	.75
123	Jeff Friesen	.40
124	John MacLean	.40
125	Patrick Marleau	3.00
126	Owen Nolan	.40
127	*Marco Sturm*	1.50
128	Mike Vernon	1.00
129	Daren Puppa	.40
130	Mikael Renberg	.40
131	Paul Ysebaert	.40
132	Rob Zamuner	.40
133	Wendel Clark	.40
134	Tie Domi	.40
135	Igor Korolev	.40
136	Felix Potvin	1.50
137	Mats Sundin	1.50
138	Donald Brashear	.40
139	Pavel Bure	2.50
140	Sean Burke	.75
141	Trevor Linden	.40
142	Mark Messier	2.00
143	Alexander Mogilny	1.00
144	Mattias Ohlund	.40
145	Peter Bondra	.75
146	Phil Housley	.40
147	Dale Hunter	.40
148	Joe Juneau	.40
149	Olaf Kolzig	.75
150	Adam Oates	1.00

1997-98 Pacific Revolution Copper

The Revolution base set had three outlet exclusive parallels. Copper (U.S. hobby), Silver (U.S. retail) and Emerald (Canada) parallels were all inserted 2:25.

	MT
Copper Stars:	4x to 8x
Yng Stars & RCs:	2.5x to 5x
Emerald Stars:	4x to 8x
Yng Stars & RCs:	2.5x to 5x
Silver Stars:	4x to 8x
Young Stars & RCs:	2.5x to 5x
Reds:	5x to 10x

1997-98 Pacific Revolution Ice Blue

Ice Blue is a full parallel of the Revolution base set that was included in packs for all outlets at a rate of one per 49 packs.

	MT
Ice Blue Stars:	10x to 20x
Yng Stars & RCs:	6x to 12x

1997-98 Pacific Revolution NHL Icons

NHL Icons is a 10-card set seeded 1:121. The die-cut cards are shaped like the NHL shield logo.

		MT
Complete Set (10):		475.00
Common Player:		30.00
1	Paul Kariya	60.00
2	Teemu Selanne	30.00
3	Peter Forsberg	50.00
4	Patrick Roy	80.00
5	Steve Yzerman	50.00
6	Martin Brodeur	35.00
7	Wayne Gretzky	100.00
8	Eric Lindros	60.00
9	Jaromir Jagr	60.00
10	Pavel Bure	30.00

1997-98 Pacific Revolution Return to Sender

Return to Sender Die-Cuts (20 cards, 1:25) features the NHL's top goaltenders. The cards are die-cut like a stamp and feature three photos of the player on the front. The backs are designed like a postcard, with player info and another photo.

		MT
Complete Set (20):		180.00
Common Player:		4.00
1	Guy Hebert	4.00
2	Byron Dafoe	4.00
3	Dominik Hasek	30.00
4	Jeff Hackett	6.00
5	Patrick Roy	45.00
6	Ed Belfour	10.00
7	Chris Osgood	15.00
8	Curtis Joseph	10.00
9	John Vanbiesbrouck	20.00
10	Andy Moog	4.00
11	Martin Brodeur	30.00
12	Tommy Salo	8.00
13	Mike Richter	10.00
14	Ron Hextall	8.00
15	Nikolai Khabibulin	4.00
16	Tom Barrasso	4.00
17	Grant Fuhr	10.00
18	Mike Vernon	8.00
19	Felix Potvin	12.00
20	Olaf Kolzig	4.00

1997-98 Pacific Revolution Team Checklist

Team Checklist Laser-Cuts (26 cards, 1:25) have a horizontal layout. The fronts have a player photo on the left and the team logo is laser-cut on the right side.

		MT
Complete Set (26):		300.00
Common Player:		4.00
1	Paul Kariya	30.00
2	Joe Thornton	20.00
3	Mike Peca	4.00
4	Theoren Fleury	4.00
5	Keith Primeau	6.00
6	Chris Chelios	8.00
7	Patrick Roy	40.00
8	Mike Modano	10.00
9	Steve Yzerman	25.00
10	Ryan Smyth	4.00
11	John Vanbiesbrouck	12.00
12	Jozef Stumpel	4.00
13	Saku Koivu	10.00
14	Martin Brodeur	15.00
15	Zigmund Palffy	10.00
16	Wayne Gretzky	50.00
17	Daniel Alfredsson	4.00
18	Eric Lindros	30.00
19	Keith Tkachuk	10.00
20	Jaromir Jagr	30.00
21	Brett Hull	10.00
22	Mike Vernon	4.00
23	Rob Zamuner	4.00
24	Mats Sundin	8.00
25	Pavel Bure	12.00
26	Peter Bondra	6.00

1997-98 Pacific Revolution 1998 All-Star Game

All-Star Game Die-Cuts (20 cards, 1:49) feature players from the North America vs. The World All-Star Game. The top of each card is die-cut and the players are featured in their All-Star Game uniform.

		MT
Complete Set (20):		375.00
Common Player:		6.00
1	Teemu Selanne	20.00
2	Ray Bourque	10.00
3	Dominik Hasek	25.00
4	Theoren Fleury	6.00
5	Chris Chelios	10.00
6	Peter Forsberg	35.00
7	Patrick Roy	50.00
8	Joe Sakic	30.00
9	Ed Belfour	10.00
10	Mike Modano	12.00
11	Brendan Shanahan	20.00
12	Saku Koivu	12.00
13	Martin Brodeur	25.00
14	Wayne Gretzky	70.00
15	John LeClair	15.00
16	Eric Lindros	40.00
17	Jaromir Jagr	40.00
18	Pavel Bure	20.00
19	Mark Messier	15.00
20	Peter Bondra	6.00

1997-98 Pinnacle

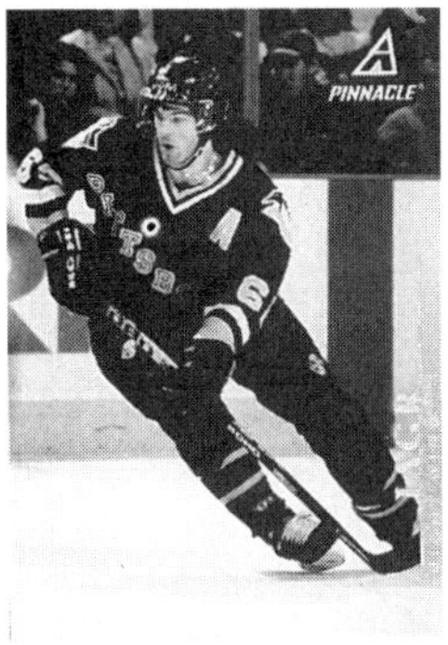

The Pinnacle Hockey base set consists of 200 cards. The cards feature full-bleed photos with the player's last name and position printed in silver foil on the right side. The set is paralleled by Rink Collection and Artist's Proofs. Inserts include Masks, Epix and Team Pinnacle.

		MT
Complete Set (200):		20.00
Common Player:		.10
Wax Box:		50.00
1	*Espen Knutsen*	.25
2	*Juha Lind*	.15
3	Erik Rasmussen	.10
4	*Olli Jokinen*	.75
5	Chris Phillips	.10
6	Alexei Morozov	.10
7	*Chris Dingman*	.10
8	Mattias Ohlund	.10
9	Sergei Samsonov	.75
10	*Daniel Cleary*	.50
11	Terry Ryan	.10
12	Patrick Marleau	1.25
13	Boyd Devereaux	.10
14	*Donald MacLean*	.10
15	Marc Savard	.10
16	*Magnus Arvedson*	.20
17	*Marian Hossa*	.75
18	Alyn McCauley	.10
19	*Vaclav Prospal*	.75
20	Brad Isbister	.10
21	*Robert Dome*	.20
22	Kevyn Adams	.10
23	Joe Thornton	2.00
24	*Jan Bulis*	.40
25	Jaroslav Svejkovsky	.10
26	Saku Koivu	.75
27	Mark Messier	.60
28	Dominik Hasek	1.00
29	Patrick Roy	2.50
30	Jaromir Jagr	2.00
31	Jarome Iginla	.20
32	Joe Sakic	1.00
33	Jeremy Roenick	.25
34	Chris Osgood	.35
35	Brett Hull	.50
36	Mike Vernon	.20
37	John Vanbiesbrouck	1.00
38	Ray Bourque	.25
39	Doug Gilmour	.20
40	Keith Tkachuk	.50
41	Pavel Bure	.75
42	Sean Burke	.20
43	Martin Brodeur	1.00
44	Damian Rhodes	.10
45	Geoff Sanderson	.10
46	Bill Ranford	.10
47	Kevin Hodson	.20
48	Eric Lindros	2.00
49	Owen Nolan	.10
50	Mats Sundin	.25
51	Ed Belfour	.25
52	Stephane Fiset	.10
53	Paul Kariya	2.00
54	Doug Weight	.20
55	Mike Richter	.25
56	Zigmund Palffy	.40
57	John LeClair	.50
58	Alexander Mogilny	.25
59	Tommy Salo	.20
60	Trevor Kidd	.20
61	Jason Arnott	.10
62	Adam Oates	.25
63	Garth Snow	.10
64	Rob Blake	.10
65	Chris Chelios	.25
66	Eric Fichaud	.10
67	Wayne Gretzky	3.00
68	Dino Ciccarelli	.10
69	Pat LaFontaine	.20
70	Andy Moog	.25
71	Steve Yzerman	1.50
72	Jeff Hackett	.20
73	Peter Forsberg	1.50
74	Arturs Irbe	.10
75	Pierre Turgeon	.20
76	Tom Barrasso	.20
77	Sergei Fedorov	.50
78	Ron Francis	.20
79	Mike Dunham	.10
80	Brendan Shanahan	.75
81	Grant Fuhr	.25
82	Jamie Storr	.10
83	Jim Carey	.20
84	Daren Puppa	.10
85	Vincent Damphousse	.10
86	Teemu Selanne	1.00
87	Dwayne Roloson	.10
88	Kirk McLean	.10
89	Olaf Kolzig	.20
90	Guy Hebert	.20
91	Mike Modano	.35
92	Brian Leetch	.20
93	Curtis Joseph	.20
94	Nikolai Khabibulin	.20
95	Felix Potvin	.40
96	Ken Wregget	.10
97	Steve Shields	.10
98	Jocelyn Thibault	.20
99	Ron Tugnutt	.10
100	Ron Hextall	.20
101	Mike Peca	.10
102	Donald Audette	.10
103	Theoren Fleury	.20
104	Mark Recchi	.10
105	Dainius Zubrus	.10
106	Trevor Linden	.10
107	Joe Juneau	.10
108	Matthew Barnaby	.10
109	Keith Primeau	.10
110	Joe Nieuwendyk	.20
111	Rod Brind'Amour	.20
112	Daymond Langkow	.10
113	Ed Jovanovski	.10
114	Adam Deadmarsh	.10
115	Scott Niedermayer	.10
116	Al MacInnis	.20
117	Slava Kozlov	.10
118	Jere Lehtinen	.10
119	Jeff Friesen	.10
120	Alexei Kovalev	.10
121	Eric Daze	.10
122	Mariusz Czerkawski	.10
123	Alexei Zhamnov	.10
124	Petr Nedved	.10
125	Dmitri Mironov	.10
126	Alexei Yashin	.20
127	Todd Marchant	.10
128	Sandis Ozolinsh	.20
129	Igor Larionov	.10
130	Jim Campbell	.10
131	Dave Andreychuk	.10
132	Glen Wesley	.10
133	Rem Murray	.10
134	Steve Sullivan	.10
135	Miroslav Satan	.10
136	Bill Guerin	.10
137	Mike Gartner	.10
138	Jozef Stumpel	.10
139	Darryl Sydor	.10
140	Darcy Tucker	.10
141	Robert Svehla	.10
142	Steve Duchesne	.10
143	Kevin Stevens	.10
144	Mikael Renberg	.10
145	Bryan Berard	.25
146	Ray Ferraro	.10
147	Jason Allison	.10
148	Tony Amonte	.20
149	Luc Robitaille	.20
150	Mathieu Schneider	.10
151	Steve Rucchin	.10
152	Brian Savage	.10
153	Paul Coffey	.25
154	Jeff O'Neill	.10
155	Daniel Alfredsson	.20
156	Dave Gagner	.10
157	Rob Niedermayer	.10
158	Scott Stevens	.10
159	Alexandre Daigle	.10
160	Stephane Richer	.10
161	Harry York	.10
162	Sergei Berezin	.25
163	Claude Lemieux	.10
164	Ray Sheppard	.10
165	Bernie Nicholls	.10
166	Oleg Tverdovsky	.10
167	Travis Green	.20
168	Martin Gelinas	.10
169	Derek Plante	.10
170	Gary Roberts	.10
171	Kevin Hatcher	.10
172	Martin Rucinsky	.10
173	Pat Verbeek	.10
174	Adam Graves	.10
175	Roman Hamrlik	.10
176	Darren McCarty	.10
177	Mike Grier	.10
178	Andrew Cassels	.10
179	Dimitri Khristich	.10
180	Tomas Sandstrom	.10
181	Peter Bondra	.20
182	Derian Hatcher	.10
183	Chris Gratton	.20
184	John MacLean	.10
185	Wendel Clark	.10
186	Valeri Kamensky	.10
187	Tony Granato	.10
188	Vladimir Vorobiev	.10
189	Ethan Moreau	.10
190	Kirk Muller	.10
191	Peter Forsberg	.75
192	Wayne Gretzky	1.50
193	Jaromir Jagr	1.00
194	Mark Messier	.25
195	Brian Leetch	.15
196	John LeClair	.25
197	Jeremy Roenick	.20
198	Checklist	.10
199	Checklist	.10
200	Checklist	.10

1997-98 Pinnacle Rink Collection

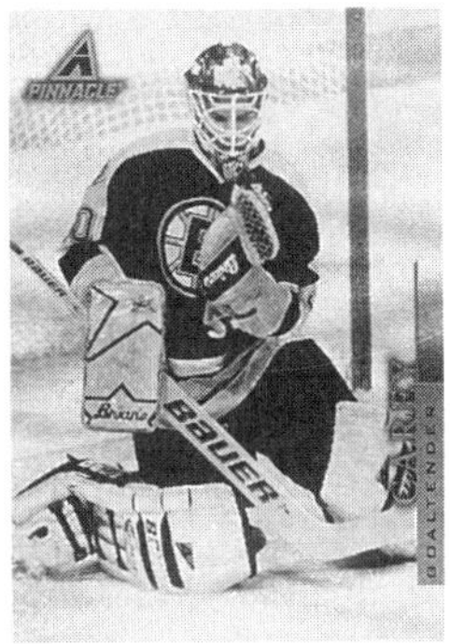

Rink Collection is a full parallel of the Pinnacle Hockey base set. The cards feature dufex technology and were inserted 1:7.

	MT
Rink Collection Stars:	6x to 10x
Yng Stars & RCs:	3x to 6x

1997-98 Pinnacle Artist's Proofs

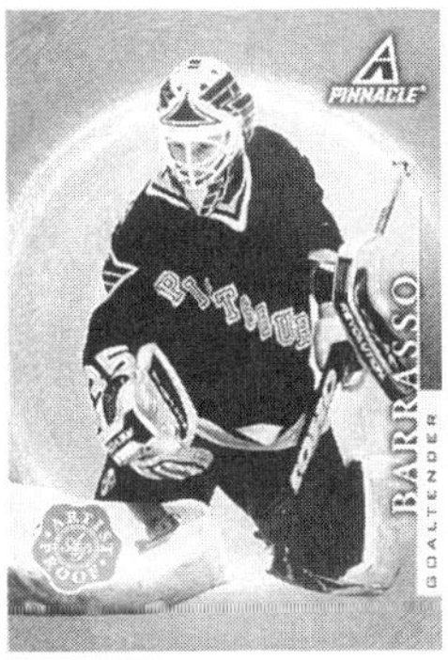

Artist's Proofs is a full parallel of the Pinnacle Hockey base set. The cards feature dufex technology and the Artist's Proof stamp.

		MT
Complete Set (100):		750.00
Common Player:		3.00
1	*Espen Knutsen*	4.00
2	*Juha Lind*	4.00
3	Erik Rasmussen	3.00
4	*Olli Jokinen*	15.00
5	Chris Phillips	3.00
6	Alexei Morozov	3.00
7	*Chris Dingman*	4.00
8	Mattias Ohlund	5.00
9	Sergei Samsonov	15.00
10	*Daniel Cleary*	8.00
11	Terry Ryan	3.00
12	Patrick Marleau	30.00
13	Boyd Devereaux	3.00
14	*Donald MacLean*	3.00
15	Marc Savard	3.00
16	*Magnus Arvedson*	5.00
17	Marian Hossa	5.00
18	Alyn McCauley	3.00
19	Vaclav Prospal	12.00
20	Brad Isbister	8.00
21	Robert Dome	3.00
22	Kevyn Adams	3.00
23	Joe Thornton	35.00
24	Jan Bulis	8.00
25	Jaroslav Svejkovsky	5.00
26	Saku Koivu	18.00
27	Mark Messier	15.00
28	Dominik Hasek	25.00
29	Patrick Roy	60.00
30	Jaromir Jagr	50.00
31	Jarome Iginla	5.00
32	Joe Sakic	30.00
33	Jeremy Roenick	8.00
34	Chris Osgood	12.00
35	Brett Hull	15.00
36	Mike Vernon	5.00
37	John Vanbiesbrouck	20.00
38	Ray Bourque	6.00
39	Doug Gilmour	6.00
40	Keith Tkachuk	15.00
41	Pavel Bure	25.00
42	Sean Burke	5.00
43	Martin Brodeur	25.00
44	Damian Rhodes	3.00
45	Geoff Sanderson	3.00
46	Bill Ranford	5.00
47	Kevin Hodson	5.00
48	Eric Lindros	50.00
49	Owen Nolan	3.00
50	Mats Sundin	10.00
51	Ed Belfour	8.00
52	Stephane Fiset	3.00
53	Paul Kariya	50.00
54	Doug Weight	5.00
55	Mike Richter	8.00
56	Zigmund Palffy	12.00
57	John LeClair	15.00
58	Alexander Mogilny	8.00
59	Tommy Salo	6.00
60	Trevor Kidd	5.00
61	Jason Arnott	3.00
62	Adam Oates	8.00
63	Garth Snow	5.00
64	Rob Blake	3.00
65	Chris Chelios	8.00
66	Eric Fichaud	3.00
67	Wayne Gretzky	80.00
68	Dino Ciccarelli	3.00
69	Pat LaFontaine	6.00
70	Andy Moog	6.00
71	Steve Yzerman	40.00
72	Jeff Hackett	6.00
73	Peter Forsberg	40.00
74	Arturs Irbe	3.00
75	Pierre Turgeon	6.00
76	Tom Barrasso	5.00
77	Sergei Fedorov	15.00
78	Ron Francis	6.00
79	Mike Dunham	3.00
80	Brendan Shanahan	20.00
81	Grant Fuhr	8.00
82	Jamie Storr	3.00
83	Jim Carey	3.00
84	Daren Puppa	3.00
85	Vincent Damphousse	3.00
86	Teemu Selanne	25.00
87	Dwayne Roloson	3.00
88	Kirk McLean	3.00
89	Olaf Kolzig	5.00
90	Guy Hebert	5.00
91	Mike Modano	8.00
92	Brian Leetch	6.00
93	Curtis Joseph	6.00
94	Nikolai Khabibulin	5.00
95	Felix Potvin	8.00
96	Ken Wregget	3.00
97	Steve Shields	3.00
98	Jocelyn Thibault	6.00
99	Ron Tugnutt	3.00
100	Ron Hextall	6.00

1997-98 Pinnacle Epix

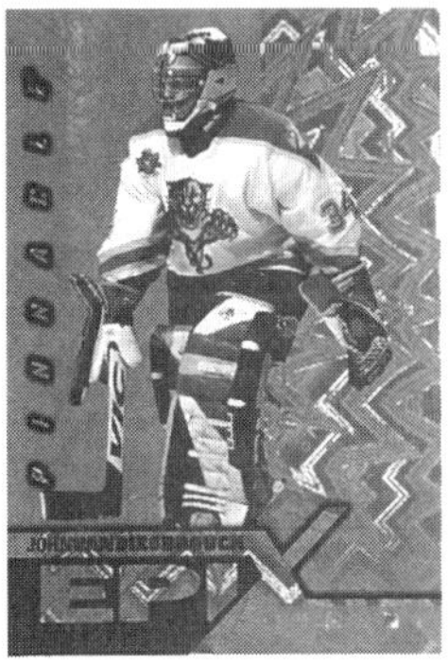

Epix is a multi-tiered, cross-brand insert. This insert was included in packs of Pinnacle, Score, Certified and Zenith hockey products. Twenty-four players each have an Epix Game, Moment, Play and Season card. Of the four tiers, Moments are the rarest, followed by Season, Game and Play cards. The base Epix cards were printed on holographic foil and featured Orange coloring. Each card also had a Purple and Emerald version.

		MT
Common Game & Play:		6.00
Common Season:		15.00
Common Moment:		30.00
Purples:		1.5x
Emeralds:		2x to 3x
1	Wayne Gretzky S	100.00
2	John Vanbiesbrouck S	30.00
3	Joe Sakic S	30.00
4	Alexei Yashin S	15.00
5	Sergei Fedorov S	25.00
6	Keith Tkachuk S	25.00
7	Patrick Roy M	125.00
8	Martin Brodeur M	50.00
9	Steve Yzerman M	80.00
10	Saku Koivu M	40.00
11	Felix Potvin M	30.00
12	Mark Messier M	40.00
13	Eric Lindros P	25.00
14	Peter Forsberg P	20.00
15	Teemu Selanne P	15.00
16	Brendan Shanahan P	12.00
17	Curtis Joseph P	6.00
18	Brett Hull P	8.00
19	Paul Kariya G	25.00
20	Jaromir Jagr G	25.00
21	Pavel Bure G	15.00
22	Dominik Hasek G	12.00
23	John LeClair G	10.00
24	Doug Gilmour G	8.00

1997-98 Pinnacle Masks

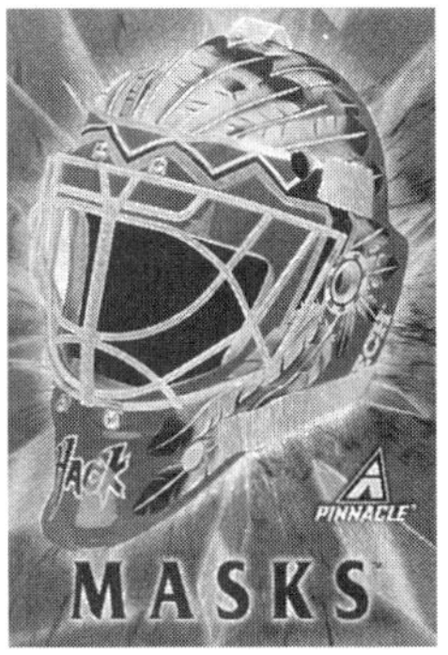

Masks is a 10-card insert seeded one per 89 packs. The card fronts have a painting of an NHL goalie's distinctive mask. The backs have a photo of the player and some info on his mask. Die-cut versions of the cards were also produced.

		MT
Complete Set (10):		275.00
Common Goalie:		20.00
1	John Vanbiesbrouck	50.00
2	Mike Richter	25.00
3	Martin Brodeur	50.00
4	Curtis Joseph	25.00
5	Patrick Roy	100.00
6	Guy Hebert	20.00
7	Jeff Hackett	20.00
8	Garth Snow	20.00
9	Nikolai Khabibulin	20.00
10	Grant Fuhr	30.00

1997-98 Pinnacle Masks Die-Cut

A die-cut parallel of the Masks insert was produced and inserted one per 299 packs.

	MT
Die-Cut Masks:	1.5x to 2x

1997-98 Pinnacle Team Pinnacle

Team Pinnacle is a 10-card insert seeded one per 99 packs. The card fronts feature two photos of the player; one action shot and one closeup.

		MT
Complete Set (10):		250.00
Common Player:		8.00
1	Martin Brodeur, Patrick Roy	45.00
2	Dominik Hasek, Curtis Joseph	20.00
3	Brian Leetch, Chris Chelios	8.00
4	Wayne Gretzky, Paul Kariya	60.00
5	Eric Lindros, Mark Messier	40.00
6	Jaromir Jagr, Keith Tkachuk	35.00

7	Saku Koivu, Peter Forsberg	30.00
8	John LeClair, Brendan Shanahan	20.00
9	Doug Gilmour, Steve Yzerman	30.00
10	John Vanbiesbrouck, Chris Osgood	20.00

1997-98 Pinnacle Be a Player

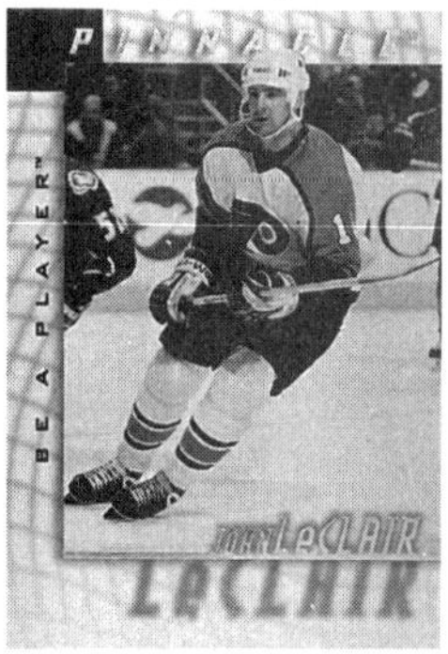

Be A Player Hockey was released in two 125-card series. The numbering of the two series was intermingled, so certain low number cards were in Series Two and some high numbers were in Series One. Many players signed cards for this product. The base autographs were printed on gold foil stock, with die-cut and prismatic die-cut versions available for most players. One autographed card was inserted in each pack. Inserts included One Timers, Take A Number and Stacking the Pads.

		MT
Complete Set (250):		30.00
Common Player:		.20
1	Eric Lindros	2.50
2	Martin Brodeur	1.50
3	Saku Koivu	1.00
4	Felix Potvin	.50
5	Adam Oates	.50
6	Rob DiMaio	.20
7	Jari Kurri	.40
8	Andrew Cassels	.20
9	Trevor Linden	.20
10	Jocelyn Thibault	.50
11	Chris Chelios	.50
12	Paul Coffey	.40
13	Nikolai Khabibulin	.50
14	Robert Lang	.20
15	Brett Hull	.75
16	Mike Sillinger	.20
17	Lyle Odelein	.20
18	Bryan Berard	.40
19	Craig Muni	.20
20	Kris Draper	.20
21	Ed Jovanovski	.20
22	Keith Tkachuk	.75
23	Dean Malkoc	.20
24	Cory Stillman	.20
25	Chris Osgood	.75
26	Dainius Zubrus	.40
27	Yves Racine	.20
28	Eric Cairns	.20
29	Dan Bylsma	.20
30	Chris Terreri	.20
31	Bill Huard	.20
32	Warren Rychel	.20
33	Scott Walker	.20
34	Brian Holzinger	.20
35	Roman Turek	.20
36	Ron Tugnutt	.40
37	Mike Richter	.60
38	Mattias Norstrom	.20
39	Joe Sacco	.20
40	Derrick King	.20
41	Brad Werenka	.20
42	Paul Kruse	.20
43	Mike Knuble	.20
44	Mike Peca	.20
45	Jean-Yves Leroux	.20
46	Ray Sheppard	.20
47	Reid Simpson	.20
48	Rob Brown	.20
49	Dave Babych	.20
50	Scott Pellerin	.20
51	Bruce Gardiner	.20
52	Adam Deadmarsh	.40
53	Curtis Brown	.20
54	Jason Marshall	.20
55	Gerald Diduck	.20
56	Mick Vukota	.20
57	Kevin Dean	.20
58	Adam Graves	.20
59	Craig Conroy	.20
60	Cale Hulse	.20
61	Dimitri Khristich	.20
62	Chris Wells	.20
63	Travis Green	.20
64	Tyler Wright	.20
65	Chris Simon	.20
66	Mikhail Shtalenkov	.20
67	Anson Carter	.20
68	Zarley Zalapski	.20
69	Per Gustafsson	.20
70	Jayson More	.20
71	Steve Thomas	.20
72	Todd Marchant	.20
73	Gary Roberts	.20
74	Richard Smehlik	.20
75	Aaron Miller	.20
76	Daren Puppa	.20
77	Garth Snow	.40
78	Greg DeVries	.20
79	Randy Burridge	.20
80	Jim Cummins	.20
81	Richard Pilon	.20
82	Chris McAlpine	.20
83	Joe Sakic	1.50
84	Ted Drury	.20
85	Brent Gilchrist	.20
86	Dallas Eakins	.20
87	Bruce Driver	.20
88	Jamie Huscroft	.20
89	Jeff Brown	.20
90	Janne Laukkanen	.20
91	Ken Klee	.20
92	Peter Bondra	.50
93	Ian Moran	.20
94	Stephane Quintal	.20
95	Jason York	.20
96	Todd Harvey	.20
97	Slava Kozlov	.40
98	Kevin Haller	.20
99	Alexei Zhamnov	.20
100	Craig Johnson	.20
101	Mike Keane	.20
102	Craig Rivet	.20
103	Roman Vopat	.20
104	Jim Johnson	.20
105	Ray Whitney	.20
106	Ron Sutter	.20
107	Jamie McLennan	.20
108	Kris King	.20
109	Lance Pitlick	.20
110	Mike Dunham	.20
111	Jim Dowd	.20
112	Geoff Sanderson	.20
113	Vladimir Vujtek	.20
114	Tim Taylor	.20
115	Sandis Ozolinsh	.40
116	Scott Daniels	.20
117	Bob Corkum	.20
118	Kirk McLean	.20
119	Darcy Tucker	.20
120	Dennis Vaske	.20
121	Kirk Muller	.20
122	Jay McKee	.20
123	Jere Lehtinen	.20
124	Ruslan Salei	.20
125	Al MacInnis	.20
126	Ulf Samuelsson	.20
127	Rick Tocchet	.20
128	Nick Kypreos	.20
129	Joel Bouchard	.20
130	Jeff O'Neill	.20
131	Daniel McGillis	.20
132	Sean Pronger	.20
133	Vladimir Malakhov	.20
134	Petr Sykora	.20
135	Zigmund Palffy	.75
136	Joe Reekie	.20
137	Chris Gratton	.20
138	Craig Billington	.20
139	Steve Washburn	.20
140	Robert Kron	.20
141	Larry Murphy	.40
142	Shean Donovan	.20
143	Scott Young	.20
144	Janne Niinimaa	.40
145	Ken Belanger	.20
146	Pavol Demitra	.20
147	Roman Hamrlik	.40
148	Lonny Bohonos	.20
149	Mike Eagles	.20
150	Kelly Buchberger	.20
151	Mattias Timander	.20
152	Benoit Hogue	.20
153	Joey Kocur	.20
154	Mats Lindgren	.20
155	Aki Berg	.20
156	Tim Sweeney	.20
157	Vincent Damphousse	.20
158	Dan Kordic	.20
159	Darius Kasparaitis	.20
160	Randy McKay	.20
161	Steve Staios	.20
162	Brendan Witt	.20
163	Paul Ysebaert	.20
164	Greg Adams	.20
165	Kent Manderville	.20
166	Steve Dubinsky	.20
167	David Nemirovsky	.20
168	Todd Bertuzzi	.20
169	Frederic Chabot	.20
170	Dmitri Mironov	.20
171	Pat Peake	.20
172	Ed Ward	.20
173	Jeff Shantz	.20
174	Dave Gagner	.20
175	Randy Cunneyworth	.20
176	Daymond Langkow	.20
177	Alex Hicks	.20
178	Darby Hendrickson	.20
179	Mike Sullivan	.20
180	Anders Ericksson	.20
181	Turner Stevenson	.20
182	Shane Churla	.20
183	Dave Lowry	.20
184	Joe Juneau	.20
185	Bob Essensa	.20
186	James Black	.20
187	Michal Grosek	.20
188	Tomas Holmstrom	.20
189	Ian Laperriere	.20
190	Terry Yake	.20
191	Jason Smith	.20
192	Sergei Zholtok	.20
193	Doug Houda	.20
194	Guy Carbonneau	.20
195	Terry Carkner	.20
196	Alexei Gusarov	.20
197	Vladimir Tsyplakov	.20
198	Jarrod Skalde	.20
199	Marty Murray	.20
200	Aaron Ward	.20
201	Bobby Holik	.20
202	Steve Chiasson	.20
203	Brantt Myhres	.20
204	Eric Messier	.20
205	Rene Corbet	.20
206	Mathieu Schneider	.20
207	Tom Chorske	.20
208	Doug Lidster	.20
209	Igor Ulanov	.20
210	Blair Atcheynum	.20
211	Sebastian Bordeleau	.20
212	Alexei Morozov	.60
213	*Vaclav Prospal*	1.00
214	Brad Bombardir	.20
215	Mattias Ohlund	.60
216	Chris Dingman	.20
217	Erik Rasmussen	.20
218	Mike Johnson	.40
219	Chris Phillips	.20
220	Sergei Samsonov	2.00
221	Patrick Marleau	1.25
222	Alyn McCauley	.20
223	Ryan Vandenbussche	.20
224	Daniel Cleary	.20
225	Magnus Arvedson	.20
226	Brad Isbister	.20
227	Pascal Rheaume	.20
228	Patrik Elias	.40
229	Krzysztof Oliwa	.20
230	Tyler Moss	.20
231	Jamie Rivers	.20
232	Joe Thornton	1.50
233	Steve Shields	.20
234	Dave Scatchard	.20
235	Patrick Cote	.20
236	Rich Brennan	.20
237	Boyd Devereaux	.20
238	*Per Axelsson*	.20
239	Craig Millar	.20
240	Juha Ylonen	.20
241	Donald MacLean	.20
242	Jaroslav Svejkovsky	.20
243	*Marco Sturm*	1.00
244	Steve McKenna	.20
245	Derek Morris	.20
246	Dean Chynoweth	.20
247	Alexander Mogilny	.20
248	Ray Bourque	.50
249	Ed Belfour	.50
250	John LeClair	1.00

1997-98 Pinnacle Be a Player Autographs

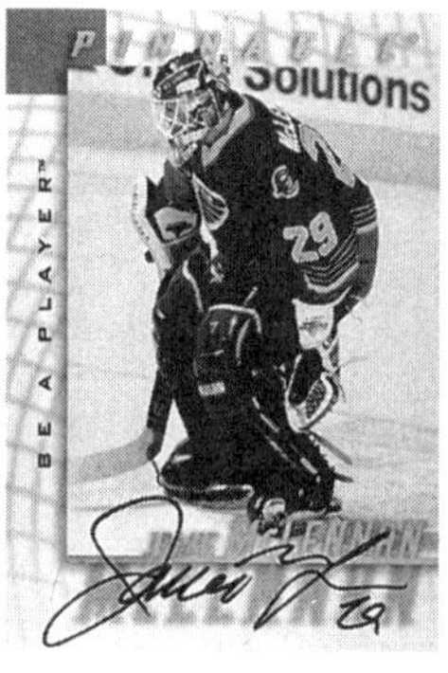

Many of the 250 players in Be A Player signed cards for the product. The base autographed cards feature gold foil. Die-cut autographed cards were inserted one per seven packs and prismatic die-cut autographs were limited to no more than 100 per player. One autograph card was inserted in each pack.

		MT
Complete Set (249):		2000.
Common Player:		5.00
2	Martin Brodeur SP	180.00
3	Saku Koivu	40.00
4	Felix Potvin	25.00
5	Adam Oates	30.00
6	Rob DiMaio	5.00
7	Jari Kurri	20.00
8	Andrew Cassels	5.00
9	Trevor Linden	10.00
10	Jocelyn Thibault	20.00
11	Chris Chelios	30.00
12	Paul Coffey	25.00
13	Nikolai Khabibulin	15.00
14	Robert Lang	5.00
15	Brett Hull SP	100.00
16	Mike Sillinger	5.00
17	Lyle Odelein	5.00
18	Bryan Berard	5.00
19	Craig Muni	5.00
20	Kris Draper	5.00
21	Ed Jovanovski	5.00
22	Keith Tkachuk	30.00
23	Dean Malkoc	5.00
24	Cory Stillman	5.00
25	Chris Osgood	30.00
26	Dainius Zubrus	20.00
27	Yves Racine	5.00
28	Eric Cairns	5.00
29	Dan Bylsma	5.00
30	Chris Terreri	5.00
31	Bill Huard	5.00
32	Warren Rychel	5.00
33	Scott Walker	5.00
34	Brian Holzinger	5.00
35	Roman Turek	5.00
36	Ron Tugnutt	10.00
37	Mike Richter	30.00
38	Mattias Norstrom	5.00
39	Joe Sacco	5.00
40	Derrick King	5.00
41	Brad Werenka	5.00
42	Paul Kruse	5.00
43	Mike Knuble	5.00
44	Mike Peca	5.00
45	Jean-Yves Leroux	5.00
46	Ray Sheppard	5.00
47	Reid Simpson	5.00
48	Rob Brown	5.00
49	Dave Babych	5.00
50	Scott Pellerin	5.00
51	Bruce Gardiner	5.00
52	Adam Deadmarsh	10.00
53	Curtis Brown	5.00
54	Jason Marshall	5.00
55	Gerald Diduck	5.00
56	Mick Vukota	5.00
57	Kevin Dean	5.00
58	Adam Graves	5.00
59	Craig Conroy	5.00
60	Cale Hulse	5.00
61	Dimitri Khristich	5.00
62	Chris Wells	5.00
63	Travis Green	5.00
64	Tyler Wright	5.00
65	Chris Simon	5.00
66	Mikhail Shtalenkov	5.00
67	Anson Carter	5.00
68	Zarley Zalapski	5.00
69	Per Gustafsson	5.00
70	Jayson More	5.00
71	Steve Thomas	5.00
72	Todd Marchant	5.00
73	Gary Roberts	5.00
74	Richard Smehlik	5.00
75	Aaron Miller	5.00
76	Daren Puppa	5.00
77	Garth Snow	10.00
78	Greg DeVries	5.00
79	Randy Burridge	5.00
80	Jim Cummins	5.00
81	Richard Pilon	5.00
82	Chris McAlpine	5.00
83	Joe Sakic SP	200.00
84	Ted Drury	5.00
85	Brent Gilchrist	5.00
86	Dallas Eakins	5.00
87	Bruce Driver	5.00
88	Jamie Huscroft	5.00
89	Jeff Brown	5.00
90	Janne Laukkanen	5.00
91	Ken Klee	5.00
92	Peter Bondra	25.00
93	Ian Moran	5.00
94	Stephane Quintal	5.00
95	Jason York	5.00
96	Todd Harvey	5.00
97	Slava Kozlov	15.00
98	Kevin Haller	5.00
99	Alexei Zhamnov	5.00
100	Craig Johnson	5.00
101	Mike Keane	5.00
102	Craig Rivet	5.00
103	Roman Vopat	5.00
104	Jim Johnson	5.00
105	Ray Whitney	5.00
106	Ron Sutter	5.00
107	Jamie McLennan	5.00
108	Kris King	5.00
109	Lance Pitlick	5.00
110	Mike Dunham	5.00
111	Jim Dowd	5.00
112	Geoff Sanderson	5.00
113	Vladimir Vujtek	5.00
114	Tim Taylor	5.00
115	Sandis Ozolinsh	15.00
116	Scott Daniels	5.00
117	Bob Corkum	5.00
118	Kirk McLean	5.00
119	Darcy Tucker	5.00
120	Dennis Vaske	5.00
121	Kirk Muller	5.00
122	Jay McKee	5.00
123	Jere Lehtinen	5.00
124	Ruslan Salei	5.00
125	Al MacInnis SP	50.00
126	Ulf Samuelsson	5.00
127	Rick Tocchet	5.00
128	Nick Kypreos	5.00
129	Joel Bouchard	5.00
130	Jeff O'Neill	5.00
131	Daniel McGillis	5.00
132	Sean Pronger	5.00
133	Vladimir Malakhov	5.00
134	Petr Sykora	5.00
135	Zigmund Palffy	35.00
136	Joe Reekie	5.00
137	Chris Gratton	15.00
138	Craig Billington	5.00
139	Steve Washburn	5.00
140	Robert Kron	5.00
141	Larry Murphy	15.00
142	Shean Donovan	5.00
143	Scott Young	5.00
144	Janne Niinimaa	15.00
145	Ken Belanger	5.00
146	Pavol Demitra	5.00
147	Roman Hamrlik	10.00
148	Lonny Bohonos	5.00
149	Mike Eagles	5.00
150	Kelly Buchberger	5.00
151	Mattias Timander	5.00
152	Benoit Hogue	5.00
153	Joey Kocur	5.00
154	Mats Lindgren	5.00
155	Aki Berg	5.00
156	Tim Sweeney	5.00
157	Vincent Damphousse	5.00
158	Dan Kordic	5.00
159	Darius Kasparaitis	5.00
160	Randy McKay	5.00
161	Steve Staios	5.00
162	Brendan Witt	5.00
163	Paul Ysebaert	5.00
164	Greg Adams	5.00
165	Kent Manderville	5.00
166	Steve Dubinsky	5.00
167	David Nemirovsky	5.00
168	Todd Bertuzzi	5.00
169	Frederic Chabot	5.00
170	Dmitri Mironov	10.00
171	Pat Peake	5.00
172	Ed Ward	5.00
173	Jeff Shantz	5.00
174	Dave Gagner	5.00
175	Randy Cunneyworth	5.00
176	Daymond Langkow	5.00
177	Alex Hicks	5.00
178	Darby Hendrickson	5.00
179	Mike Sullivan	5.00
180	Anders Ericksson	5.00
181	Turner Stevenson	5.00
182	Shane Churla	5.00
183	Dave Lowry	5.00
184	Joe Juneau	5.00
185	Bob Essensa	5.00
186	James Black	5.00
187	Michal Grosek	5.00
188	Tomas Holmstrom	5.00
189	Ian Laperriere	5.00
190	Terry Yake	5.00
191	Jason Smith	5.00
192	Sergei Zholtok	5.00
193	Doug Houda	5.00
194	Guy Carbonneau	5.00
195	Terry Carkner	5.00
196	Alexei Gusarov	5.00
197	Vladimir Tsyplakov	5.00
198	Jarrod Skalde	5.00
199	Marty Murray	5.00
200	Aaron Ward	5.00
201	Bobby Holik	5.00
202	Steve Chiasson	5.00
203	Brantt Myhres	5.00
204	Eric Messier	5.00
205	Rene Corbet	5.00
206	Mathieu Schneider	5.00
207	Tom Chorske	5.00
208	Doug Lidster	5.00
209	Igor Ulanov	5.00
210	Blair Atcheynum	5.00
211	Sebastian Bordeleau	5.00
212	Alexei Morozov	15.00
213	Vaclav Prospal	20.00
214	Brad Bombardir	5.00
215	Mattias Ohlund	15.00
216	Chris Dingman	5.00
217	Erik Rasmussen	5.00
218	Mike Johnson	20.00
219	Chris Phillips	5.00
220	Sergei Samsonov	70.00
221	Patrick Marleau	40.00
222	Alyn McCauley	5.00
223	Ryan Vandenbussche	5.00
224	Daniel Cleary	5.00
225	Magnus Arvedson	5.00
226	Brad Isbister	5.00
227	Pascal Rheaume	5.00
228	Patrik Elias	15.00

229	Krzysztof Oliwa	5.00
230	Tyler Moss	5.00
231	Jamie Rivers	5.00
232	Joe Thornton	40.00
233	Steve Shields	5.00
234	Dave Scatchard	5.00
235	Patrick Cote	5.00
236	Rich Brennan	5.00
237	Boyd Devereaux	5.00
238	Per Axelsson	5.00
239	Craig Millar	5.00
240	Juha Ylonen	5.00
241	Donald MacLean	5.00
242	Jaroslav Svejkovsky	5.00
243	Marco Sturm	15.00
244	Steve McKenna	5.00
245	Derek Morris	5.00
246	Dean Chynoweth	5.00
247	Alexander Mogilny SP	60.00
248	Ray Bourque SP	80.00
249	Ed Belfour SP	90.00
250	John LeClair SP	160.00

1997-98 Pinnacle Be A Player Die-Cut Autographs

Die-cut Autographed cards were inserted at a rate of 1:7.

	MT
Die-Cuts:	1x to 2x

1997-98 Pinnacle Be A Player Prismatic Autographs

Printed on prismatic foil board, Prismatic Autographs were limited to 100 sets.

	MT
Common Prismatic Autograph:	25.00
Prismatics:	3x to 5x

1997-98 Pinnacle Be a Player One Timers

One Timers is a 20-card insert seeded one per seven packs.

		MT
Complete Set (20):		75.00
Common Player:		1.00
1	Wayne Gretzky	15.00
2	Keith Tkachuk	2.50
3	Eric Lindros	8.00
4	Brendan Shanahan	4.00
5	Paul Kariya	8.00
6	Brett Hull	2.50

7	Jaromir Jagr	8.00
8	Teemu Selanne	4.00
9	John LeClair	4.00
10	Mike Modano	3.00
11	Peter Forsberg	7.00
12	Pavel Bure	4.00
13	Peter Bondra	2.50
14	Saku Koivu	3.00
15	Pat LaFontaine	1.00
16	Patrik Elias	1.00
17	Richard Zednik	1.00
18	Mike Johnson	1.00
19	Marco Sturm	1.00
20	Joe Thornton	4.00

1997-98 Pinnacle Be a Player Stacking the Pads

Stacking the Pads features the NHL's top goalies and dufex technology. The 15-card insert was seeded 1:15.

		MT
Complete Set (15):		150.00
Common Player:		6.00
1	Guy Hebert	6.00
2	Dominik Hasek	25.00
3	Felix Potvin	12.00
4	Patrick Roy	40.00
5	Ed Belfour	12.00
6	Chris Osgood	12.00
7	Curtis Joseph	10.00
8	John Vanbiesbrouck	15.00
9	Jocelyn Thibault	6.00
10	Mike Richter	10.00
11	Martin Brodeur	25.00
12	Garth Snow	6.00
13	Nikolai Khabibulin	6.00
14	Tommy Salo	6.00
15	Byron Dafoe	6.00

1997-98 Pinnacle Be a Player Take a Number

Take a Number is a 20-card insert seeded 1:15. The die-cut cards utilize dufex technology and explain why the players wear their number.

		MT
Complete Set (20):		200.00
Common Player:		2.00
1	Ray Bourque	5.00
2	Eric Daze	2.00
3	Ed Belfour	5.00
4	Patrick Roy	30.00
5	Sergei Fedorov	12.00
6	John Vanbiesbrouck	10.00
7	Doug Gilmour	5.00
8	Wayne Gretzky	40.00
9	Bryan Berard	2.00
10	Eric Lindros	25.00
11	Paul Coffey	4.00
12	Jeremy Roenick	6.00

13	Brett Hull	8.00
14	Pierre Turgeon	2.00
15	Keith Primeau	2.00
16	Daren Puppa	2.00
17	Mark Messier	8.00
18	Alexander Mogilny	2.00
19	Joe Sakic	15.00
20	Jaromir Jagr	25.00

1997-98 Pinnacle Beehive

BeeHive Hockey consists of a 75-card base set. The 5-x-7 base cards have a color photo with a tan honeycomb-patterned border. The backs have stats and a brief bio printed in both English and French. The base set is paralleled by Golden Portraits (1:3). Inserts include BeeHive Team, Golden Originals Autographs and Authentic Autographs. Redemption cards for original BeeHive photos were inserted 1:89.

		MT
Complete Set (75):		60.00
Common Player:		.25
Golden Portraits:		2x to 5x
1	Eric Lindros	3.00
2	Teemu Selanne	1.50
3	Brendan Shanahan	1.50
4	Joe Sakic	2.00
5	John LeClair	1.25
6	Brett Hull	1.00
7	Jaromir Jagr	3.00
8	Bryan Berard	.50
9	Peter Forsberg	2.50
10	Ed Belfour	.60
11	Steve Yzerman	2.50
12	Curtis Joseph	.75
13	Saku Koivu	.75
14	Keith Tkachuk	1.00
15	Pavel Bure	1.50
16	Felix Potvin	.75
17	Ray Bourque	.60
18	Theoren Fleury	.40
19	Patrick Roy	4.00
20	Joe Nieuwendyk	.40
21	Alexei Yashin	.40
22	Owen Nolan	.25
23	Mark Recchi	.25
24	Dominik Hasek	2.00
25	Chris Chelios	.60
26	Mike Modano	.75
27	John Vanbiesbrouck	1.50
28	Brian Leetch	.50
29	Dino Ciccarelli	.25
30	Mark Messier	1.25
31	Paul Kariya	3.00
32	Jocelyn Thibault	.50
33	Wayne Gretzky	5.00
34	Doug Weight	.40
35	Yanic Perreault	.25
36	Luc Robitaille	.40
37	Chris Osgood	.75
38	Adam Oates	.50
39	Mats Sundin	.75
40	Trevor Linden	.25
41	Mike Richter	.60
42	Zigmund Palffy	.75
43	Pat LaFontaine	.40
44	Grant Fuhr	.75
45	Martin Brodeur	2.00
46	Sergei Fedorov	1.50
47	Doug Gilmour	.50
48	Daniel Alfredsson	.40
49	Ron Francis	.40
50	Geoff Sanderson	.25
51	Joe Thornton	2.00
52	*Vaclav Prospal*	1.00
53	*Patrik Elias*	.75
54	*Mike Johnson*	1.00
55	Alyn McCauley	.25
56	*Brendan Morrison*	1.00
57	Johnny Bower (Golden Originals)	1.00
58	John Bucyk (Golden Originals)	1.00

59	Stan Mikita (Golden Originals)	1.50
60	Ted Lindsay (Golden Originals)	1.00
61	Maurice Richard (Golden Originals)	3.00
62	Andy Bathgate (Golden Originals)	.75
63	*Stefan Cherneski* (CHL Stars)	.75
64	*Craig Hillier* (CHL Stars)	.75
65	Daniel Tkaczuk (CHL Stars)	.25
66	*Josh Holden* (CHL Stars)	.25
67	Marian Cisar (CHL Stars)	.25
68	*J.P. Dumont* (CHL Stars)	1.00
69	*Roberto Luongo* (CHL Stars)	2.50
70	Aren Miller (CHL Stars)	.25
71	Mathieu Garon (CHL Stars)	.25
72	Charlie Stephens (CHL Stars)	.25
73	*Sergei Varlamov* (CHL Stars)	.75
74	*Pierre Dagenais* (CHL Stars)	1.00
75	Willie O'Ree (Commemorative)	2.00

1997-98 Pinnacle Beehive Golden Portraits

Golden Portraits is a full parallel of the 75-card Beehive base set. Printed on foil board, the cards were inserted one per three packs.

	MT
Golden Portraits:	2x to 5x

1997-98 Pinnacle Beehive Autographs

Seventeen players signed versions of their base cards. The signers consisted of NHL rookies, CHL players and Willie O'Ree. The autographed cards were inserted 1:12.

		MT
Complete Set (17):		350.00
Common Autograph:		15.00
51	Joe Thornton	50.00
52	Vaclav Prospal	25.00
53	Patrik Elias	25.00
56	Brendan Morrison	20.00
63	Stefan Cherneski	15.00
64	Craig Hillier	15.00
65	Daniel Tkaczuk	25.00
66	Josh Holden	15.00
67	Marian Cisar	15.00
68	J.P. Dumont	25.00
69	Roberto Luongo	40.00
70	Aren Miller	15.00
71	Mathieu Garon	15.00
72	Charlie Stephens	15.00
73	Sergei Varlamov	20.00
74	Pierre Dagenais	25.00
75	Willie O'Ree	25.00

1997-98 Pinnacle Beehive Golden Originals Autographs

Six NHL Hall of Famers signed cards for this insert which was seeded 1:36.

		MT
Complete Set (6):		200.00
Common Autograph:		25.00
57	Johnny Bower	25.00
58	John Bucyk	40.00
59	Stan Mikita	50.00
60	Ted Lindsay	25.00
61	Maurice Richard	75.00
62	Andy Bathgate	25.00

1997-98 Pinnacle Beehive Team

BeeHive Team is a 25-card insert. The cards were seeded 1:11, with Gold Bee-Hive Team parallel cards found 1:49.

		MT
Complete Set (25):		300.00
Common Player:		4.00
1	Paul Kariya	25.00
2	Mark Messier	10.00
3	Mike Modano	6.00
4	Brendan Shanahan	12.00
5	John Vanbiesbrouck	12.00
6	Martin Brodeur	15.00
7	Wayne Gretzky	40.00
8	Eric Lindros	25.00
9	Peter Forsberg	20.00
10	Jaromir Jagr	25.00
11	Teemu Selanne	12.00
12	John LeClair	10.00
13	Saku Koivu	8.00
14	Brett Hull	10.00
15	Patrick Roy	30.00
16	Steve Yzerman	20.00
17	Keith Tkachuk	8.00
18	Pat LaFontaine	4.00
19	Joe Sakic	15.00
20	Patrik Elias	4.00
21	Vaclav Prospal	4.00
22	Joe Thornton	15.00
23	Sergei Samsonov	8.00
24	Alexei Morozov	4.00
25	Marco Sturm	4.00

1997-98 Pinnacle Beehive Team Gold

Gold Beehive Team cards parallel the Beehive Team insert. They were inserted one per 49 packs.

	MT
Golds:	1.5x to 2.5x

1997-98 Pinnacle Certified

Certified Hockey consists of a 130-card base set. The card fronts give the appearance that the player is standing in a spotlight. The base set is paralleled four times in the Certified Red, Mirror Red, Mirror Blue and Mirror Gold sets. Inserts include Epix, Summit Silver Anniversary, Certified Rookie Redemption and Certified Team.

		MT
Complete Set (130):		40.00
Common Player:		.25
Wax Box:		90.00
1	Dominik Hasek	1.50
2	Patrick Roy	4.00
3	Martin Brodeur	1.50
4	Chris Osgood	.75
5	Andy Moog	.40
6	John Vanbiesbrouck	2.00
7	Steve Shields	.25
8	Mike Vernon	.25
9	Ed Belfour	.40
10	Grant Fuhr	.50
11	Felix Potvin	.75
12	Bill Ranford	.25
13	Mike Richter	.60
14	Stephane Fiset	.25
15	Jim Carey	.75
16	Nikolai Khabibulin	.40
17	Ken Wreggett	.25
18	Curtis Joseph	.50
19	Guy Hebert	.40
20	Damian Rhodes	.25
21	Trevor Kidd	.25
22	Daren Puppa	.25
23	Patrick Lalime	.40
24	Tommy Salo	.25
25	Sean Burke	.40
26	Jocelyn Thibault	.40
27	Kirk McLean	.40
28	Garth Snow	.25
29	Ron Tugnutt	.25
30	Jeff Hackett	.40
31	Eric Lindros	3.50
32	Peter Forsberg	2.50
33	Mike Modano	.75
34	Paul Kariya	3.00
35	Jaromir Jagr	3.00
36	Brian Leetch	.40
37	Keith Tkachuk	.75
38	Steve Yzerman	2.50
39	Teemu Selanne	1.50
40	Bryan Berard	.40
41	Ray Bourque	.40
42	Theoren Fleury	.25
43	Mark Messier	.75
44	Saku Koivu	1.00
45	Pavel Bure	1.50
46	Peter Bondra	.40
47	Dave Gagner	.25
48	Ed Jovanovski	.25
49	Adam Oates	.50
50	Joe Sakic	1.75
51	Doug Gilmour	.50
52	Jim Campbell	.25
53	Mats Sundin	.50
54	Derian Hatcher	.25
55	Jarome Iginla	.40
56	Sergei Fedorov	1.50
57	Keith Primeau	.25
58	Mark Recchi	.25
59	Owen Nolan	.25
60	Alexander Mogilny	.50
61	Brendan Shanahan	1.50
62	Pierre Turgeon	.40
63	Joe Juneau	.25
64	Steve Rucchin	.25
65	Jeremy Roenick	.50
66	Doug Weight	.40
67	Valeri Kamensky	.25
68	Tony Amonte	.40
69	Dave Andreychuk	.25
70	Brett Hull	.75
71	Wendel Clark	.25
72	Vincent Damphousse	.25
73	Mike Grier	.40
74	Chris Chelios	.40
75	Nicklas Lidstrom	.25
76	Joe Nieuwendyk	.25
77	Rob Blake	.25
78	Alexei Yashin	.40
79	Ryan Smyth	.50
80	Pat LaFontaine	.40
81	Jeff Friesen	.25
82	Ray Ferraro	.25

83	Steve Sullivan	.25
84	Chris Gratton	.40
85	Mike Gartner	.25
86	Kevin Hatcher	.25
87	Ted Donato	.25
88	German Titov	.25
89	Sandis Ozolinsh	.25
90	Ray Sheppard	.25
91	John MacLean	.25
92	Luc Robitaille	.25
93	Rod Brind'Amour	.25
84	Zigmund Palffy	.75
95	Petr Nedved	.25
96	Adam Graves	.25
97	Jozef Stumpel	.25
98	Alexandre Daigle	.25
99	Mike Peca	.25
100	Wayne Gretzky	5.00
101	Alexei Zhamnov	.25
102	Paul Coffey	.40
103	Oleg Tverdovsky	.25
104	Trevor Linden	.25
105	Dino Ciccarelli	.25
106	Andrei Kovalenko	.25
107	Scott Mellanby	.25
108	Bryan Smolinski	.25
109	Bernie Nicholls	.25
110	Derek Plante	.25
111	Pat Verbeek	.25
112	Adam Deadmarsh	.25
113	Martin Gelinas	.25
114	Daniel Alfredsson	.40
115	Scott Stevens	.25
116	Dainius Zubrus	.50
117	Kirk Muller	.25
118	Brian Holzinger	.25
119	John LeClair	.75
120	Al MacInnis	.25
121	Ron Francis	.40
122	Eric Daze	.25
123	Travis Green	.25
124	Jason Arnott	.25
125	Geoff Sanderson	.25
126	Dimitri Khristich	.25
127	Sergei Berezin	.25
128	Jeff O'Neill	.25
129	Claude Lemieux	.25
130	Andrew Cassels	.25

1997-98 Pinnacle Certified Red

The Certified Red parallel was inserted one per five packs. The full foil cards were printed on mirror mylar.

	MT
Red Stars:	4x to 8x
Yng Stars & RCs:	3x to 6x

1997-98 Pinnacle Certified Mirror Red/Blue

Mirror Red and Blue cards parallel the Certified base set. Mirror Reds are printed on red-tinted holographic board and seeded one per 99 packs. Mirror Blues are printed on blue-tinted holographic board and inserted 1:199.

	MT
Mirror Red Stars:	40x to 80x
Yng Stars & RCs:	30x to 50x
Mirror Blue Stars:	100x to 150x
Yng Stars & RCs:	50x to 100x

1997-98 Pinnacle Certified Mirror Gold

Mirror Gold cards parallel the Certified base set on golden holographic mirror mylar. Mirror Golds were inserted 1:299.

	MT
Mirror Gold Stars:	200x to 350x
Yng Stars & RCs:	150x to 250x

1997-98 Pinnacle Certified Rookie Redemption

Cards of 12 NHL rookies were available via redemption. Redemption cards were inserted one per 19 packs. The rookie cards were printed on 24-point board and featured Pinnacle's authenticator bar.

		MT
Complete Set (12):		65.00
Common Player:		3.00
A	Joe Thornton	15.00
B	Chris Phillips	6.00
C	Patrick Marleau	12.00
D	Sergei Samsonov	20.00
E	Daniel Cleary	6.00
F	Olli Jokinen	8.00
G	Alyn McCauley	5.00
H	Alexei Morozov	6.00
I	Brad Isbister	3.00
J	Boyd Devereaux	5.00
K	Espen Knutsen	3.00
L	Marc Savard	3.00

1997-98 Pinnacle Certified Summit Silver Anniversary

Summit Silver Anniversary is a four-card insert honoring Paul Henderson's dramatic goal in the 1972 Canada-Russia Summit Series. The card fronts feature artistic renderings of the moment drawn by Daniel Parry. Printed on mirror mylar, the cards were inserted 1:29. Henderson autographed 1,000 of card #4 (700 in black ink, 200 in silver and 100 in gold).

		MT
Complete Set (4):		30.00
Common Henderson:		8.00
Henderson Black Auto (700):60.00		
Henderson Silver Auto (200):		
		100.00
Henderson Gold Auto (100):		
		250.00
1	Paul Henderson	8.00
2	Paul Henderson	8.00
3	Paul Henderson	8.00
4	Paul Henderson	8.00

1997-98 Pinnacle Certified Team

Certified Team is a 20-card insert seeded 1:19. The cards are printed on mirror mylar.

		MT
Complete Set (20):		250.00
Common Player:		5.00
1	Martin Brodeur	12.00
2	Patrick Roy	30.00
3	John Vanbiesbrouck	15.00
4	Dominik Hasek	12.00
5	Chris Chelios	5.00
6	Brian Leetch	5.00
7	Wayne Gretzky	40.00
8	Eric Lindros	25.00
9	Paul Kariya	25.00
10	Peter Forsberg	20.00
11	Keith Tkachuk	8.00
12	Mark Messier	8.00
13	Steve Yzerman	20.00
14	Jaromir Jagr	25.00
15	Mats Sundin	5.00
16	Teemu Selanne	12.00
17	Brendan Shanahan	12.00
18	Saku Koivu	10.00
19	Brett Hull	8.00
20	John LeClair	8.00

1997-98 Pinnacle Certified Team Gold

Certified Gold Team is a parallel of the Certified Team insert. This 20-card set is printed on micro-etched mirror mylar with gold accents and foil stamping. Only 300 total sets were produced.

	MT
Gold Teams:	3x to 4x

1997-98 Pinnacle Inside

Pinnacle Inside Hockey was the company's "cards in a can" product. The base set consisted of 190 cards. The card fronts featured two images of the player. The base set was paralleled in Coach's Collection and Executive Collection. Card inserts included Inside Track, Stoppers and Stand Up Guys. Twenty-four different cans were produced, with gold parallel versions seeded one per hobby box. Also inserted in cans were 200 redemption cards for a game-used puck from an NHL game (1:64,800).

		MT
Complete Set (190):		40.00
Common Player:		.15
Common Executive Collection:		
1	Brendan Shanahan	1.25
2	Dominik Hasek	1.25
3	Wayne Gretzky	4.00
4	Eric Lindros	2.50
5	Keith Tkachuk	.75
6	Jaromir Jagr	2.50
7	Martin Brodeur	1.50
8	Peter Forsberg	2.00
9	Chris Osgood	.50
10	Paul Kariya	2.50
11	Pavel Bure	1.25
12	Brett Hull	.60
13	Saku Koivu	.75
14	Zigmund Palffy	.75
15	Mike Modano	.40
16	Ray Bourque	.35
17	Jarome Iginla	.25
18	Chris Chelios	.35
19	John Vanbiesbrouck	1.25
20	Brian Leetch	.25
21	Mats Sundin	.35
22	Ron Hextall	.25
23	Stephane Fiset	.15
24	Steve Yzerman	2.00
25	Curtis Joseph	.40
26	Daniel Alfredsson	.15
27	Owen Nolan	.40
28	Adam Oates	.40
29	Corey Hirsch	.15
30	Sean Burke	.25
31	Eric Fichaud	.15
32	Ken Wregget	.15
33	Dainius Zubrus	.40
34	Alexander Mogilny	.40
35	Bill Ranford	.15
36	Vincent Damphousse	.15
37	Patrick Roy	3.00
38	Teemu Selanne	1.25
39	Pat LaFontaine	.35
40	Theoren Fleury	.25
41	Jeff Hackett	.25
42	Sergei Fedorov	1.00
43	Jocelyn Thibault	.40
44	Nikolai Khabibulin	.25
45	Daren Puppa	.15
46	Felix Potvin	.40
47	Andy Moog	.35
48	Doug Weight	.25
49	Tommy Salo	.25
50	Mark Messier	.75
51	Grant Fuhr	.40
52	Ron Francis	.40
53	Tony Amonte	.25
54	Joe Sakic	1.50
55	Jason Arnott	.15
56	Jose Theodore	.25
57	Alexei Yashin	.25
58	John LeClair	.75
59	Jeremy Roenick	.40
60	Kirk McLean	.25
61	Arturs Irbe	.25
62	Jim Carey	.15
63	J.S. Giguere	.15
64	Marc Denis	.15
65	Damian Rhodes	.15
66	Jim Campbell	.15
67	Patrick Lalime	.15
68	Garth Snow	.25
69	Marcel Cousineau	.15
70	Guy Hebert	.25
71	Rob Blake	.15
72	*Tomas Vokoun*	.15
73	Doug Gilmour	.50
74	Ed Belfour	.40
75	Parris Duffus	.15
76	Mike Fountain	.15
77	Steve Shields	.15
78	Geoff Sanderson	.15
79	Roman Turek	.15
80	Bryan Berard	.40
81	Mike Richter	.50
82	Ron Tugnutt	.25
83	Peter Bondra	.40
84	Mike Vernon	.40
85	Mike Grier	.15
86	Ed Jovanovski	.25
87	Trevor Kidd	.25
88	Eric Daze	.25
89	Wendel Clark	.25
90	Checklist	.15
91	Nicklas Lidstrom	.25
92	Rod Brind'Amour	.25

93	Hnat Domenichelli	.15
94	Rem Murray	.15
95	Scott Niedermayer	.15
96	Martin Rucinsky	.15
97	Mike Gartner	.15
98	Kevin Hatcher	.15
99	Daymond Langkow	.15
100	Jamie Langenbrunner	.15
101	Ted Donato	.15
102	Steve Sullivan	.15
103	Martin Gelinas	.15
104	Adam Graves	.25
105	Donald Audette	.15
106	Andrew Cassels	.15
107	Alexei Zhamnov	.15
108	Kirk Muller	.15
109	Alexandre Daigle	.15
110	Chris Gratton	.25
111	Andrew Brunette	.15
112	Mark Recchi	.25
113	Jari Kurri	.25
114	Valeri Kamensky	.15
115	Joe Nieuwendyk	.25
116	Slava Kozlov	.15
117	Steve Kelly	.15
118	Dave Andreychuk	.25
119	Mikael Renberg	.15
120	Sergei Berezin	.25
121	Jeff Friesen	.15
122	Pierre Turgeon	.25
123	*Vladimir Vorobiev*	.15
124	Dimitri Khristich	.15
125	Jaroslav Svejkovsky	.60
126	Vladimir Konstantinov	.15
127	Jozef Stumpel	.15
128	Mike Peca	.15
129	Jonas Hoglund	.15
130	Travis Green	.15
131	Bill Guerin	.15
132	Oleg Tverdovsky	.15
133	Petr Nedved	.15
134	Dino Ciccarelli	.15
135	Brian Savage	.15
136	Steve Duchesne	.25
137	Sandis Ozolinsh	.15
138	Derian Hatcher	.15
139	Ray Sheppard	.15
140	Brian Bellows	.15
141	Paul Brousseau	.15
142	Tony Granato	.15
143	*Vaclav Prospal*	1.25
144	Vitali Yachmenev	.15
145	John MacLean	.15
146	Igor Larionov	.15
147	Jason Allison	.25
148	Derek Plante	.15
149	Jeff O'Neill	.15
150	Trevor Linden	.15
151	Joe Juneau	.15
152	Brandon Convery	.15
153	Kevin Stevens	.15
154	Scott Stevens	.15
155	Niklas Sundstrom	.15
156	Claude Lemieux	.15
157	Pat Verbeek	.15
158	Mariusz Czerkawski	.15
159	Robert Svehla	.15
160	Paul Coffey	.25
161	Al MacInnis	.25
162	Roman Hamrlik	.15
163	Brian Holzinger	.15
164	Cory Stillman	.15
165	Scott Mellanby	.15
166	Todd Warriner	.15
167	Terry Ryan	.15
168	Luc Robitaille	.25
169	Ed Olczyk	.15
170	Adam Deadmarsh	.15
171	Anson Carter	.15
172	*Mike Knuble*	.40
173	Cliff Ronning	.15
174	Rick Tocchet	.15
175	Chris Pronger	.15
176	Matthew Barnaby	.15
177	Andrei Kovalenko	.15
178	Bryan Smolinski	.15
179	Janne Niinimaa	.25
180	Ray Ferraro	.15
181	Dave Gagner	.15
182	Rob Niedermayer	.15
183	*Vadim Sharifijanov*	.15
184	Ethan Moreau	.15
185	Bernie Nicholls	.15
186	*Jean-Yves Leroux*	.15
187	Jere Lehtinen	.15
188	Steve Rucchin	.15
189	Keith Primeau	.15
190	Checklist	.15

1997-98 Pinnacle Inside Executive Collection

Executive Collection is a 90-card partial parallel of the Inside base set. The cards were die-cut, printed on prismatic foil and seeded one per 57 cans.

	MT
Executive Collection Stars:	60x to 90x
Yng Stars & RCs:	40x to 60x

1997-98 Pinnacle Inside Coaches Collection

Coach's Collection is a 90-card partial parallel of the Inside base set. The cards were printed on silver foil and inserted one per seven cans.

	MT
Coaches Coll. Stars:	5x to 10x
Yng Stars & RCs:	3x to 6x

1997-98 Pinnacle Inside Cans

Pinnacle Inside cards were packaged in collectible cans. Twenty-four different cans were produced with reprints of the featured player's card on the can. Gold parallel versions of the cans were also created and inserted one per hobby box.

		MT
Complete Set (24):		20.00
Common Can:		.50
Opened Gold Cans:		3x to 5x
Sealed Gold Cans:		6x to 12x
1	Patrick Roy	2.50
2	Martin Brodeur	1.25
3	John Vanbiesbrouck	1.00
4	Curtis Joseph	.50
5	Mike Richter	.50
6	Jocelyn Thibault	.50
7	Guy Hebert	.50
8	Mike Vernon	.50
9	Wayne Gretzky	3.00
10	Paul Kariya	2.00
11	Peter Forsberg	1.50
12	Eric Lindros	2.00
13	Jaromir Jagr	2.00
14	Steve Yzerman	1.50
15	Joe Sakic	1.25
16	Saku Koivu	.75
17	John LeClair	.75
18	Keith Tkachuk	.75
19	Teemu Selanne	1.00
20	Pavel Bure	1.00
21	Brendan Shanahan	1.00
22	Mark Messier	.75
23	Mats Sundin	.50
24	Brett Hull	.75

1997-98 Pinnacle Inside Stand Up Guys

Stand Up Guys were inserted one per special jumbo can. The 20-card set consisted of 10 pairs of cards which could be fit together to form a four-sided stand up card.

		MT
Complete Set (20):		15.00
Common Player:		1.00
C/D cards equal value to A/B cards
1A/B	Mike Vernon, Tom Barasso	1.00
2A/B	John Vanbiesbrouck, Martin Brodeur	3.00
3A/B	Jocelyn Thibault, Jim Carey	1.00
4A/B	Garth Snow, Marcel Cousineau	1.00
5A/B	Patrick Roy, Eric Fichaud	8.00
6A/B	Patrick Lalime, Grant Fuhr	1.00
7A/B	Olaf Kolzig, Jeff Hackett	1.00
8A/B	Trevor Kidd, Guy Hebert	1.00
9A/B	Nicolai Khabibulin, Corey Hirsch	1.00
10A/B	Curtis Joseph, Kelly Hrudey	2.00

1997-98 Pinnacle Inside Stoppers

Stoppers is a 24-card insert seeded one per seven cans. The circular cards feature NHL goaltenders with a 3-D effect.

		MT
Complete Set (24):		120.00
Common Player:		3.00
1	Patrick Roy	25.00
2	John Vanbiesbrouck	10.00
3	Dominik Hasek	10.00
4	Martin Brodeur	12.00
5	Mike Richter	6.00
6	Guy Hebert	3.00
7	Jim Carey	3.00
8	Jeff Hackett	3.00
9	Roman Turek	5.00
10	Kevin Hodson	5.00
11	Mike Vernon	5.00
12	Curtis Joseph	5.00
13	J.S. Giguere	3.00
14	Jose Theodore	5.00
15	Jocelyn Thibault	6.00
16	Nikolai Khabibulin	5.00
17	Garth Snow	3.00
18	Ron Hextall	3.00
19	Steve Shields	3.00
20	Grant Fuhr	6.00
21	Felix Potvin	6.00
22	Marcel Cousineau	3.00
23	Bill Ranford	3.00
24	Ed Belfour	6.00

1997-98 Pinnacle Inside Track

Inside Track is a 30-card insert seeded one per 19 cans.

		MT
Complete Set (30):		650.00
Common Player:		8.00
1	Wayne Gretzky	75.00
2	Patrick Roy	60.00
3	Eric Lindros	45.00
4	Paul Kariya	45.00
5	Peter Forsberg	40.00
6	Martin Brodeur	30.00
7	John Vanbiesbrouck	25.00
8	Joe Sakic	35.00
9	Steve Yzerman	40.00
10	Jaromir Jagr	45.00
11	Teemu Selanne	25.00
12	Pavel Bure	25.00
13	Sergei Fedorov	20.00
14	Brendan Shanahan	25.00
15	Dominik Hasek	25.00
16	Saku Koivu	20.00
17	Jocelyn Thibault	12.00
18	Mark Messier	20.00
19	Brett Hull	15.00
20	Felix Potvin	10.00
21	Curtis Joseph	8.00
22	Zigmund Palffy	15.00
23	Mats Sundin	15.00
24	Keith Tkachuk	15.00
25	John LeClair	20.00
26	Mike Richter	12.00
27	Alexander Mogilny	10.00
28	Jarome Iginla	8.00
29	Mike Grier	8.00
30	Dainius Zubrus	12.00

1997-98 Pinnacle Mint Collection

Mint Collection Hockey combines collectible cards and coins. The 30 horizontal base cards feature a player photo on the left and a circular foil emblem on the right. The emblem features the team logo and basic player info. The base cards are inserted one per pack, with Die-Cut versions found two per pack. Die-Cut cards have a hole instead of the emblem. Silver Mint Team (1:15) and Gold Mint Team (1:47) are the other parallels, printed on silver-foil or gold-foil board, respectively. The coins can fit in the hole of the die-cut cards. The base coins are paralleled six times. The only insert is Minternational, which included both cards and coins.

		MT
Complete Set (30):		15.00
Common Die-Cut:		.25
1	Eric Lindros	1.50
2	Paul Kariya	1.50
3	Peter Forsberg	1.25
4	John Vanbiesbrouck	.75
5	Steve Yzerman	1.25
6	Brendan Shanahan	.75
7	Teemu Selanne	.75
8	Dominik Hasek	1.00
9	Jarome Iginla	.25
10	Mats Sundin	.40
11	Patrick Roy	2.00
12	Joe Sakic	1.00
13	Mark Messier	.50
14	Sergei Fedorov	.60
15	Saku Koivu	.50
16	Martin Brodeur	.75
17	Pavel Bure	.75
18	Wayne Gretzky	2.50
19	Brian Leetch	.25
20	John LeClair	.50
21	Keith Tkachuk	.50

22	Jaromir Jagr	1.50
23	Brett Hull	.50
24	Curtis Joseph	.40
25	Jaroslav Svejkovsky	.25
26	Sergei Samsonov	.50
27	Alexei Morozov	.25
28	Alyn McCauley	.25
29	Joe Thornton	1.00
30	Vaclav Prospal	.25

1997-98 Pinnacle Mint Collection Bronze

	MT
Bronze:	1.5x to 2x
Silver:	2x to 4x
Gold:	8x to 15x

1997-98 Pinnacle Mint Collection Coins

Mint Collection coins are designed to fit in the hole of the Die-Cut cards. Two coins were inserted in each pack. The fronts feature the player's face and basic info, while the backs contain the Mint Collection logo. The 30 coins are paralleled six times: Nickel-Silver (1:41), Bronze Proof Coins (1:79), Silver-Plated Proof (1:170), Gold-Plated Proof (1:425), Solid Silver (1:288) and Solid Gold (1:47,000).

		MT
Complete Set (30):		40.00
Common Coin:		.75
Silver Coins:		4x to 8x
Gold Coins:		20x to 30x
1	Eric Lindros	4.00
2	Paul Kariya	4.00
3	Peter Forsberg	3.00
4	John Vanbiesbrouck	1.50
5	Steve Yzerman	3.00
6	Brendan Shanahan	1.50
7	Teemu Selanne	2.00
8	Dominik Hasek	2.00
9	Jarome Iginla	.75
10	Mats Sundin	1.00
11	Patrick Roy	5.00
12	Joe Sakic	2.50
13	Mark Messier	1.25
14	Sergei Fedorov	1.25
15	Saku Koivu	1.00
16	Martin Brodeur	1.50
17	Pavel Bure	1.50
18	Wayne Gretzky	6.00
19	Brian Leetch	.75
20	John LeClair	1.00
21	Keith Tkachuk	1.00
22	Jaromir Jagr	4.00
23	Brett Hull	1.00
24	Curtis Joseph	.75
25	Jaroslav Svejkovsky	.75
26	Sergei Samsonov	1.00
27	Alexei Morozov	.75
28	Alyn McCauley	.75
29	Joe Thornton	2.00
30	Vaclav Prospal	.75

1997-98 Pinnacle Mint Collection Minternational

Minternational is a six-card and six-coin insert. The card set features one player from each of the major nations in the 1998 Winter Olympics. The oversized Minternational coins feature the same players. Both cards and coins were inserted 1:31.

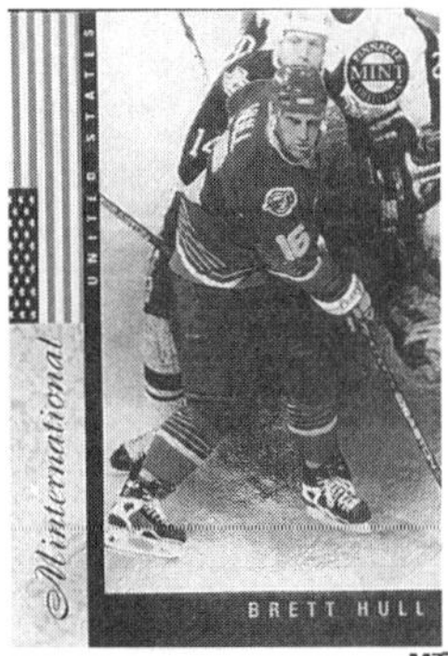

		MT
Complete Set (6):		50.00
Common Player:		4.00
Coins:		.5x to 1x
1	Eric Lindros	15.00
2	Peter Forsberg	12.00
3	Brett Hull	6.00
4	Teemu Selanne	8.00
5	Dominik Hasek	10.00
6	Pavel Bure	8.00

1997-98 Pinnacle Totally Certified Platinum Red

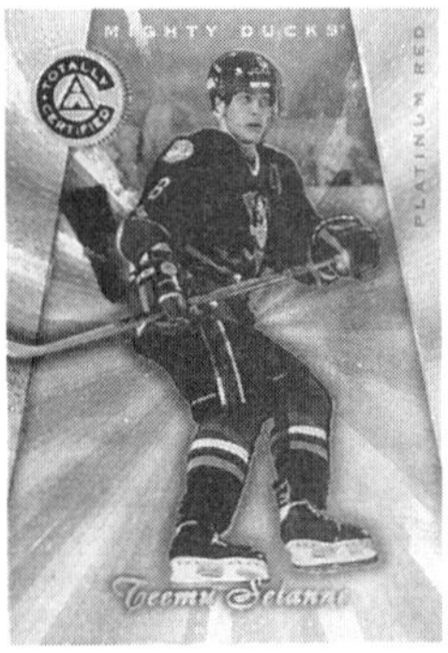

Totally Certified has the same 130-card checklist as the Certified product. Platinum Reds act as the "base set" for Totally Certified. Every card in the product is serially numbered, with Platinum Reds being numbered to 6,199. Platinum Red goalie cards are numbered to 4,299. Platinum Red cards are printed on mirror mylar with red foil etching and were inserted two per pack.

		MT
Complete Set (130):		400.00
Common Goalie (1-30): 4,299 of each		2.00
Common Skater (31-130): 6,199 of each		1.50
Wax Box:		105.00
1	Dominik Hasek	10.00
2	Patrick Roy	25.00
3	Martin Brodeur	10.00
4	Chris Osgood	5.00
5	Andy Moog	3.00
6	John Vanbiesbrouck	12.00
7	Steve Shields	2.00
8	Mike Vernon	2.00
9	Ed Belfour	3.00
10	Grant Fuhr	3.00
11	Felix Potvin	5.00
12	Bill Ranford	2.00
13	Mike Richter	3.00
14	Stephane Fiset	2.00
15	Jim Carey	3.00
16	Nikolai Khabibulin	2.00
17	Ken Wreggett	2.00
18	Curtis Joseph	3.00
19	Guy Hebert	2.00
20	Damian Rhodes	2.00
21	Trevor Kidd	2.00
22	Daren Puppa	2.00
23	Patrick Lalime	2.00
24	Tommy Salo	2.00
25	Sean Burke	2.00
26	Jocelyn Thibault	3.00
27	Kirk McLean	2.00
28	Garth Snow	2.00
29	Ron Tugnutt	2.00
30	Jeff Hackett	2.00
31	Eric Lindros	15.00
32	Peter Forsberg	12.00
33	Mike Modano	4.00
34	Paul Kariya	15.00
35	Jaromir Jagr	15.00
36	Brian Leetch	2.00
37	Keith Tkachuk	4.00
38	Steve Yzerman	15.00
39	Teemu Selanne	8.00
40	Bryan Berard	2.00
41	Ray Bourque	2.50
42	Theoren Fleury	1.50
43	Mark Messier	5.00
44	Saku Koivu	6.00
45	Pavel Bure	8.00
46	Peter Bondra	2.00
47	Dave Gagner	1.50
48	Ed Jovanovski	1.50
49	Adam Oates	2.50
50	Joe Sakic	10.00
51	Doug Gilmour	3.00
52	Jim Campbell	1.50
53	Mats Sundin	2.50
54	Derian Hatcher	1.50
55	Jarome Iginla	2.00
56	Sergei Fedorov	8.00
57	Keith Primeau	1.50
58	Mark Recchi	1.50
59	Owen Nolan	2.00
60	Alexander Mogilny	3.00
61	Brendan Shanahan	8.00
62	Pierre Turgeon	2.00
63	Joe Juneau	1.50
64	Steve Rucchin	1.50
65	Jeremy Roenick	2.50
66	Doug Weight	2.00
67	Valeri Kamensky	1.50
68	Tony Amonte	1.50
69	Dave Andreychuk	1.50
70	Brett Hull	5.00
71	Wendel Clark	1.50
72	Vincent Damphousse	1.50
73	Mike Grier	1.50
74	Chris Chelios	2.50
75	Nicklas Lidstrom	2.00
76	Joe Nieuwendyk	1.50
77	Rob Blake	1.50
78	Alexei Yashin	2.00
79	Ryan Smyth	2.50
80	Pat LaFontaine	2.50
81	Jeff Friesen	1.50
82	Ray Ferraro	1.50
83	Steve Sullivan	1.50
84	Chris Gratton	2.00
85	Mike Gartner	2.00
86	Kevin Hatcher	1.50
87	Ted Donato	1.50
88	German Titov	1.50
89	Sandis Ozolinsh	2.00
90	Ray Sheppard	1.50
91	John MacLean	1.50
92	Luc Robitaille	2.00
93	Rod Brind'Amour	2.00
84	Zigmund Palffy	4.00
95	Petr Nedved	1.50
96	Adam Graves	1.50
97	Jozef Stumpel	1.50
98	Alexandre Daigle	1.50
99	Mike Peca	1.50
100	Wayne Gretzky	30.00
101	Alexei Zhamnov	1.50
102	Paul Coffey	2.50
103	Oleg Tverdovsky	1.50
104	Trevor Linden	1.50
105	Dino Ciccarelli	1.50
106	Andrei Kovalenko	1.50
107	Scott Mellanby	1.50
108	Bryan Smolinski	1.50
109	Bernie Nicholls	1.50
110	Derek Plante	1.50
111	Pat Verbeek	1.50
112	Adam Deadmarsh	1.50
113	Martin Gelinas	1.50
114	Daniel Alfredsson	2.00
115	Scott Stevens	1.50
116	Dainius Zubrus	4.00
117	Kirk Muller	1.50
118	Brian Holzinger	1.50
119	John LeClair	8.00
120	Al MacInnis	2.50
121	Ron Francis	2.50
122	Eric Daze	1.50
123	Travis Green	2.00
124	Jason Arnott	1.50
125	Geoff Sanderson	1.50
126	Dimitri Khristich	1.50
127	Sergei Berezin	2.00
128	Jeff O'Neill	1.50
129	Claude Lemieux	1.50
130	Andrew Cassels	1.50

1997-98 Pinnacle Totally Certified Platinum Blue

Platinum Blue is the second level of cards in Totally Certified. Featuring blue foil etching, the cards are numbered to 3,099, with goalies numbered to 2,599. The 130-card set was inserted one per pack.

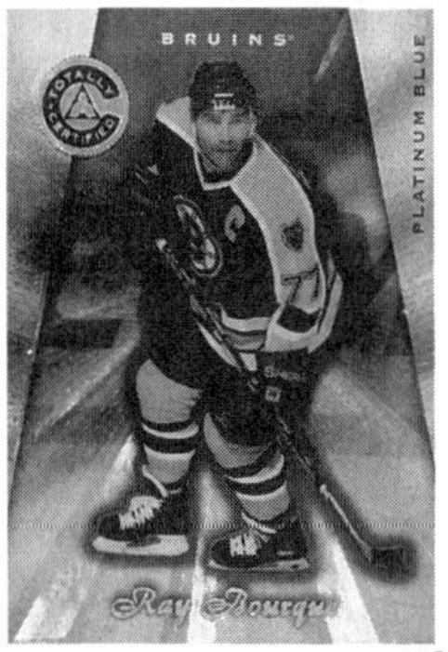

		MT
Complete Set (130):		750.00
Common Goalie (1-30): 2,599 of each		4.00
Common Skater (31-130): 3,099 of each		3.00
1	Dominik Hasek	20.00
2	Patrick Roy	40.00
3	Martin Brodeur	18.00
4	Chris Osgood	10.00
5	Andy Moog	6.00
6	John Vanbiesbrouck	20.00
7	Steve Shields	4.00
8	Mike Vernon	4.00
9	Ed Belfour	6.00
10	Grant Fuhr	6.00
11	Felix Potvin	10.00
12	Bill Ranford	4.00
13	Mike Richter	6.00
14	Stephane Fiset	4.00
15	Jim Carey	5.00
16	Nikolai Khabibulin	4.00
17	Ken Wreggett	4.00
18	Curtis Joseph	6.00
19	Guy Hebert	4.00
20	Damian Rhodes	4.00
21	Trevor Kidd	4.00
22	Daren Puppa	4.00
23	Patrick Lalime	4.00
24	Tommy Salo	4.00
25	Sean Burke	4.00
26	Jocelyn Thibault	6.00
27	Kirk McLean	4.00
28	Garth Snow	4.00
29	Ron Tugnutt	4.00
30	Jeff Hackett	4.00
31	Eric Lindros	30.00
32	Peter Forsberg	25.00
33	Mike Modano	8.00
34	Paul Kariya	25.00
35	Jaromir Jagr	30.00
36	Brian Leetch	4.00
37	Keith Tkachuk	8.00
38	Steve Yzerman	25.00
39	Teemu Selanne	15.00
40	Bryan Berard	4.00
41	Ray Bourque	5.00
42	Theoren Fleury	4.00
43	Mark Messier	10.00
44	Saku Koivu	12.00
45	Pavel Bure	15.00
46	Peter Bondra	4.00
47	Dave Gagner	3.00
48	Ed Jovanovski	3.00
49	Adam Oates	5.00
50	Joe Sakic	20.00
51	Doug Gilmour	6.00
52	Jim Campbell	3.00
53	Mats Sundin	5.00
54	Derian Hatcher	3.00
55	Jarome Iginla	4.00
56	Sergei Fedorov	15.00
57	Keith Primeau	3.00
58	Mark Recchi	3.00
59	Owen Nolan	4.00
60	Alexander Mogilny	6.00
61	Brendan Shanahan	18.00
62	Pierre Turgeon	4.00
63	Joe Juneau	3.00
64	Steve Rucchin	3.00
65	Jeremy Roenick	5.00
66	Doug Weight	4.00
67	Valeri Kamensky	3.00
68	Tony Amonte	3.00
69	Dave Andreychuk	3.00
70	Brett Hull	10.00
71	Wendel Clark	3.00
72	Vincent Damphousse	3.00
73	Mike Grier	3.00
74	Chris Chelios	5.00
75	Nicklas Lidstrom	4.00
76	Joe Nieuwendyk	3.00
77	Rob Blake	3.00
78	Alexei Yashin	4.00
79	Ryan Smyth	5.00
80	Pat LaFontaine	5.00
81	Jeff Friesen	3.00
82	Ray Ferraro	3.00
83	Steve Sullivan	3.00
84	Chris Gratton	4.00
85	Mike Gartner	4.00
86	Kevin Hatcher	3.00
87	Ted Donato	3.00
88	German Titov	3.00
89	Sandis Ozolinsh	3.00
90	Ray Sheppard	3.00
91	John MacLean	3.00
92	Luc Robitaille	4.00
93	Rod Brind'Amour	4.00
84	Zigmund Palffy	8.00
95	Petr Nedved	3.00
96	Adam Graves	3.00
97	Jozef Stumpel	3.00
98	Alexandre Daigle	3.00
99	Mike Peca	3.00
100	Wayne Gretzky	50.00
101	Alexei Zhamnov	3.00
102	Paul Coffey	5.00
103	Oleg Tverdovsky	3.00
104	Trevor Linden	3.00
105	Dino Ciccarelli	3.00
106	Andrei Kovalenko	3.00
107	Scott Mellanby	3.00
108	Bryan Smolinski	3.00
109	Bernie Nicholls	3.00
110	Derek Plante	3.00
111	Pat Verbeek	3.00
112	Adam Deadmarsh	3.00
113	Martin Gelinas	3.00
114	Daniel Alfredsson	4.00
115	Scott Stevens	3.00
116	Dainius Zubrus	8.00
117	Kirk Muller	3.00
118	Brian Holzinger	3.00
119	John LeClair	15.00
120	Al MacInnis	5.00
121	Ron Francis	5.00
122	Eric Daze	3.00
123	Travis Green	4.00
124	Jason Arnott	3.00
125	Geoff Sanderson	3.00
126	Dimitri Khristich	3.00
127	Sergei Berezin	4.00
128	Jeff O'Neill	3.00
129	Claude Lemieux	3.00
130	Andrew Cassels	3.00

1997-98 Pinnacle Totally Certified Platinum Gold

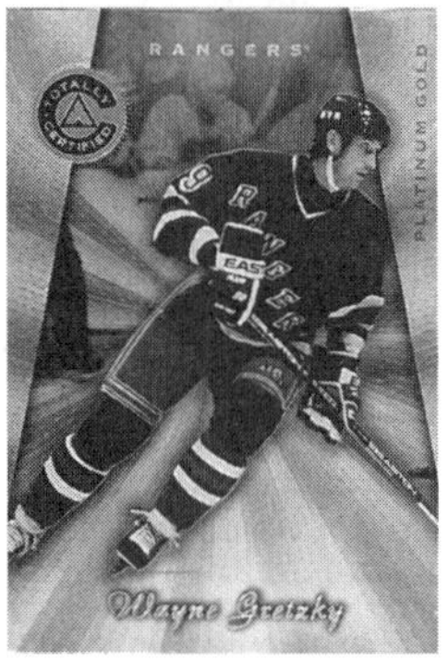

Platinum Golds are the third level in Totally Certified. The 130 cards feature gold foil etching, with skaters numbered to 69 and goalies to 59. Pinnacle stated the odds of finding a Platinum Gold at 1:79.

		MT
Common Goalie (1-30): 59 of each		50.00
Common Skater (31-130): 69 of each		40.00
1	Dominik Hasek	275.00
2	Patrick Roy	700.00
3	Martin Brodeur	200.00
4	Chris Osgood	100.00
5	Andy Moog	60.00
6	John Vanbiesbrouck	250.00
7	Steve Shields	50.00
8	Mike Vernon	50.00
9	Ed Belfour	75.00
10	Grant Fuhr	75.00
11	Felix Potvin	150.00
12	Bill Ranford	50.00
13	Mike Richter	75.00
14	Stephane Fiset	50.00
15	Jim Carey	60.00
16	Nikolai Khabibulin	50.00
17	Ken Wreggett	50.00
18	Curtis Joseph	75.00
19	Guy Hebert	50.00
20	Damian Rhodes	50.00
21	Trevor Kidd	50.00
22	Daren Puppa	50.00
23	Patrick Lalime	50.00
24	Tommy Salo	50.00
25	Sean Burke	50.00
26	Jocelyn Thibault	60.00
27	Kirk McLean	50.00
28	Garth Snow	50.00
29	Ron Tugnutt	50.00
30	Jeff Hackett	50.00
31	Eric Lindros	450.00
32	Peter Forsberg	350.00
33	Mike Modano	100.00
34	Paul Kariya	400.00
35	Jaromir Jagr	450.00
36	Brian Leetch	60.00
37	Keith Tkachuk	150.00
38	Steve Yzerman	400.00
39	Teemu Selanne	250.00
40	Bryan Berard	60.00
41	Ray Bourque	75.00
42	Theoren Fleury	60.00
43	Mark Messier	200.00
44	Saku Koivu	200.00
45	Pavel Bure	200.00
46	Peter Bondra	75.00
47	Dave Gagner	40.00
48	Ed Jovanovski	40.00
49	Adam Oates	75.00
50	Joe Sakic	300.00
51	Doug Gilmour	100.00
52	Jim Campbell	40.00
53	Mats Sundin	75.00
54	Derian Hatcher	40.00
55	Jarome Iginla	60.00
56	Sergei Fedorov	200.00
57	Keith Primeau	40.00
58	Mark Recchi	40.00
59	Owen Nolan	40.00
60	Alexander Mogilny	75.00
61	Brendan Shanahan	200.00
62	Pierre Turgeon	60.00
63	Joe Juneau	40.00
64	Steve Rucchin	40.00
65	Jeremy Roenick	75.00
66	Doug Weight	60.00
67	Valeri Kamensky	40.00
68	Tony Amonte	40.00
69	Dave Andreychuk	40.00
70	Brett Hull	150.00
71	Wendel Clark	40.00
72	Vincent Damphousse	40.00
73	Mike Grier	40.00
74	Chris Chelios	75.00
75	Nicklas Lidstrom	60.00
76	Joe Nieuwendyk	40.00
77	Rob Blake	40.00
78	Alexei Yashin	60.00
79	Ryan Smyth	75.00
80	Pat LaFontaine	60.00
81	Jeff Friesen	40.00
82	Ray Ferraro	40.00
83	Steve Sullivan	40.00
84	Chris Gratton	60.00
85	Mike Gartner	50.00
86	Kevin Hatcher	40.00
87	Ted Donato	40.00
88	German Titov	40.00
89	Sandis Ozolinsh	40.00
90	Ray Sheppard	40.00
91	John MacLean	40.00
92	Luc Robitaille	60.00
93	Rod Brind'Amour	60.00
84	Zigmund Palffy	125.00
95	Petr Nedved	40.00
96	Adam Graves	40.00
97	Jozef Stumpel	40.00
98	Alexandre Daigle	40.00
99	Mike Peca	40.00
100	Wayne Gretzky	1000.
101	Alexei Zhamnov	40.00
102	Paul Coffey	75.00
103	Oleg Tverdovsky	40.00
104	Trevor Linden	40.00
105	Dino Ciccarelli	40.00
106	Andrei Kovalenko	40.00
107	Scott Mellanby	40.00
108	Bryan Smolinski	40.00
109	Bernie Nicholls	40.00
110	Derek Plante	40.00
111	Pat Verbeek	40.00
112	Adam Deadmarsh	40.00
113	Martin Gelinas	40.00
114	Daniel Alfredsson	50.00
115	Scott Stevens	40.00
116	Dainius Zubrus	125.00
117	Kirk Muller	40.00
118	Brian Holzinger	40.00
119	John LeClair	175.00
120	Al MacInnis	60.00
121	Ron Francis	60.00
122	Eric Daze	40.00
123	Travis Green	40.00
124	Jason Arnott	50.00
125	Geoff Sanderson	40.00
126	Dimitri Khristich	40.00
127	Sergei Berezin	60.00
128	Jeff O'Neill	40.00
129	Claude Lemieux	40.00
130	Andrew Cassels	40.00

1997-98 Pinnacle Zenith

Zenith Hockey was part of Pinnacle's "Dare to Tear" promotion. The set consisted of 80 5-x-7 cards which had a regular-size card inside. Collectors could keep the larger card or tear it open to get the smaller card. The smaller Z2 cards were paralleled in Z-Silver (1:7) and Z-Gold (numbered to 100). The 5-x-7s were paralleled in Silver Impulse (1:7) and Gold Impulse (numbered to 100). Inserts include Chasing the Cup, Rookie Reign, Epix, Z Team, Z Team Gold and 5-x-7 Z Team.

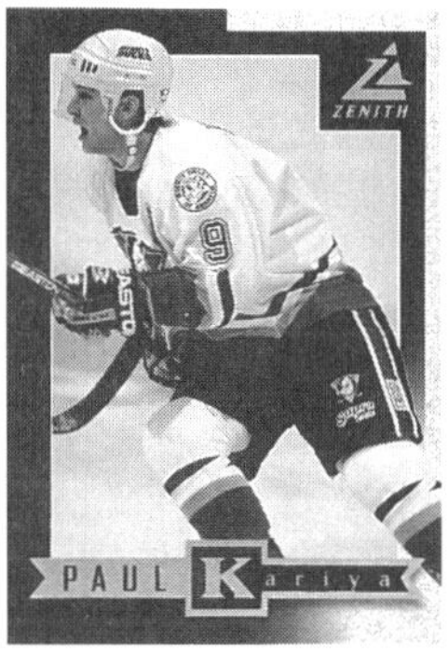
ZENITH
PAUL
K a r i y a

		MT
Complete Set (100):		90.00
Common Player:		.15
Silvers:		2x to 4x
1	Jarome Iginla	.15
2	Peter Forsberg	3.00
3	Brendan Shanahan	1.50
4	Wayne Gretzky	6.00
5	Steve Yzerman	3.00
6	Eric Lindros	4.00
7	Keith Tkachuk	1.00
8	John LeClair	1.25
9	John Vanbiesbrouck	1.50
10	Patrick Roy	5.00
11	Ray Bourque	.60
12	Theoren Fleury	.15
13	Brian Leetch	.40
14	Chris Chelios	.60
15	Paul Kariya	4.00
16	Mark Messier	1.25
17	Curtis Joseph	.75
18	Mike Richter	.60
19	Jeremy Roenick	.75
20	Dominik Hasek	2.00
21	Martin Brodeur	1.50
22	Sergei Fedorov	1.50
23	Pierre Turgeon	.40
24	Teemu Selanne	1.50
25	Brett Hull	1.00
26	Saku Koivu	.75
27	Owen Nolan	.15
28	Jozef Stumpel	.15
29	Joe Sakic	2.00
30	Zigmund Palffy	.75
31	Jaromir Jagr	4.00
32	Adam Oates	.50
33	Jeff Friesen	.15
34	Pavel Bure	1.50
35	Chris Osgood	.75
36	Mark Recchi	.15
37	Mike Modano	.75
38	Felix Potvin	.60
39	Vincent Damphousse	.15
40	Byron Dafoe	.40
41	Luc Robitaille	.40
42	Peter Bondra	.40
43	Daniel Alfredsson	.15
44	Pat LaFontaine	.15
45	Mikael Renberg	.15
46	Doug Gilmour	.50
47	Dino Ciccarelli	.15
48	Mats Sundin	.50
49	Ed Belfour	.75
50	Ron Francis	.40
51	Miroslav Satan	.15
52	Cory Stillman	.15
53	Bryan Berard	.40
54	Keith Primeau	.40
55	Eric Daze	.15
56	Chris Gratton	.15
57	Claude Lemieux	.15
58	Nicklas Lidstrom	.50
59	Olaf Kolzig	.15
60	Grant Fuhr	.75
61	Jamie Langenbrunner	.15
62	Doug Weight	.40
63	Joe Nieuwendyk	.40
64	Yanic Perreault	.15
65	Jocelyn Thibault	.40
66	Guy Hebert	.40
67	Shayne Corson	.15
68	Bobby Holik	.15
69	Sami Kapanen	.15
70	Robert Reichel	.15
71	Ryan Smyth	.15
72	Alexei Yashin	.40
73	Trevor Linden	.15
74	Rod Brind'Amour	.40
75	Dave Gagner	.15
76	Nikolai Khabibulin	.40
77	Tom Barrasso	.50
78	Tony Amonte	.40
79	Alexander Mogilny	.40
80	Jason Allison	.15
81	*Patrik Elias*	1.00
82	*Mike Johnson*	1.00
83	Richard Zednik	.15
84	Patrick Marleau	3.00
85	Mattias Ohlund	.15
86	Sergei Samsonov	3.00
87	*Marco Sturm*	2.00
88	Alyn McCauley	.15
89	Chris Phillips	.15
90	*Brendan Morrison*	1.50
91	*Vaclav Prospal*	2.00
92	Joe Thornton	3.00
93	Boyd Devereaux	.15
94	Alexei Morozov	.15
95	Vincent Lecavalier	10.00
96	*Manny Maholtra*	3.00
97	*Roberto Luongo*	5.00
98	Mathieu Garon	.15
99	*Alex Tanguay*	2.50
100	*Josh Holden*	.15

1997-98 Pinnacle Zenith Silver

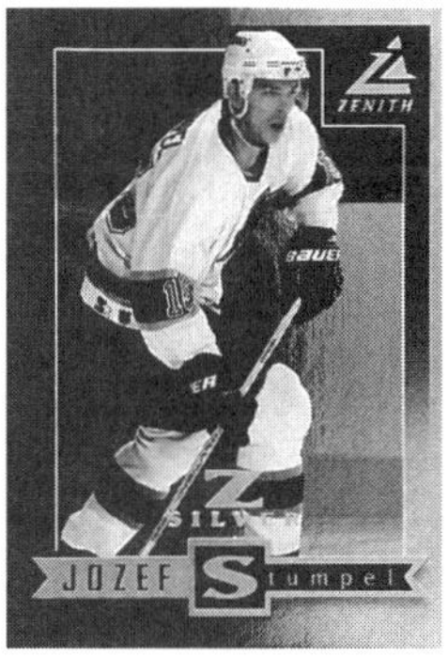
ZENITH
SILV
JOZEF
S t u m p e l

Z-Silver is a full parallel of the Z2 set. The silver foil cards were inserted one per seven packs.

	MT
Silvers:	2x to 4x

1997-98 Pinnacle Zenith Gold

Z-Gold is a parallel of the 100-card Z2 base set. The cards are sequentially numbered to 100 and printed on gold-foil stock.

		MT
Common Player:		25.00
Semistars/Goalies:		50.00
1	Jaromo Iginla	25.00
2	Peter Forsberg	250.00
3	Brendan Shanahan	150.00
4	Wayne Gretzky	500.00
5	Steve Yzerman	250.00
6	Eric Lindros	300.00
7	Keith Tkachuk	100.00
8	John LeClair	125.00
9	John Vanbiesbrouck	125.00
10	Patrick Roy	350.00
11	Ray Bourque	80.00
12	Theoren Fleury	50.00
13	Brian Leetch	40.00
14	Chris Chelios	60.00
15	Paul Kariya	300.00
16	Mark Messier	125.00
17	Curtis Joseph	75.00
18	Mike Richter	50.00
19	Jeremy Roenick	75.00
20	Dominik Hasek	200.00
21	Martin Brodeur	175.00
22	Sergei Fedorov	150.00
23	Pierre Turgeon	40.00
24	Teemu Selanne	150.00
25	Brett Hull	125.00
26	Saku Koivu	75.00
27	Owen Nolan	25.00
28	Jozef Stumpel	25.00
29	Joe Sakic	200.00
30	Zigmund Palffy	75.00
31	Jaromir Jagr	275.00
32	Adam Oates	50.00
33	Jeff Friesen	25.00
34	Pavel Bure	150.00
35	Chris Osgood	75.00
36	Mark Recchi	25.00
37	Mike Modano	75.00
38	Felix Potvin	60.00
39	Vincent Damphousse	25.00
40	Byron Dafoe	40.00
41	Luc Robitaille	40.00
42	Peter Bondra	40.00
43	Daniel Alfredsson	25.00
44	Pat LaFontaine	25.00
45	Mikael Renberg	25.00
46	Doug Gilmour	50.00
47	Dino Ciccarelli	25.00
48	Mats Sundin	60.00
49	Ed Belfour	75.00
50	Ron Francis	50.00
51	Miroslav Satan	25.00
52	Cory Stillman	25.00
53	Bryan Berard	40.00
54	Keith Primeau	40.00
55	Eric Daze	25.00
56	Chris Gratton	25.00
57	Claude Lemieux	25.00
58	Nicklas Lidstrom	50.00
59	Olaf Kolzig	25.00
60	Grant Fuhr	75.00
61	Jamie Langenbrunner	25.00
62	Doug Weight	40.00
63	Joe Nieuwendyk	40.00
64	Yanic Perreault	25.00
65	Jocelyn Thibault	40.00
66	Guy Hebert	40.00
67	Shayne Corson	25.00
68	Bobby Holik	25.00
69	Sami Kapanen	25.00
70	Robert Reichel	25.00
71	Ryan Smyth	25.00
72	Alexei Yashin	50.00
73	Trevor Linden	25.00
74	Rod Brind'Amour	50.00
75	Dave Gagner	25.00
76	Nikolai Khabibulin	50.00
77	Tom Barrasso	50.00
78	Tony Amonte	50.00
79	Alexander Mogilny	50.00
80	Jason Allison	25.00
81	*Patrik Elias*	50.00
82	*Mike Johnson*	50.00
83	Richard Zednik	25.00
84	Patrick Marleau	100.00
85	Mattias Ohlund	25.00
86	Sergei Samsonov	80.00
87	*Marco Sturm*	80.00
88	Alyn McCauley	25.00
89	Chris Phillips	25.00
90	*Brendan Morrison*	25.00
91	*Vaclav Prospal*	80.00
92	Joe Thornton	150.00
93	Boyd Devereaux	25.00
94	Alexei Morozov	25.00
95	Vincent Lecavalier	150.00
96	*Manny Maholtra*	25.00
97	*Roberto Luongo*	100.00
98	Mathieu Garon	25.00
99	*Alex Tanguay*	25.00
100	*Josh Holden*	25.00

1997-98 Pinnacle Zenith 5x7

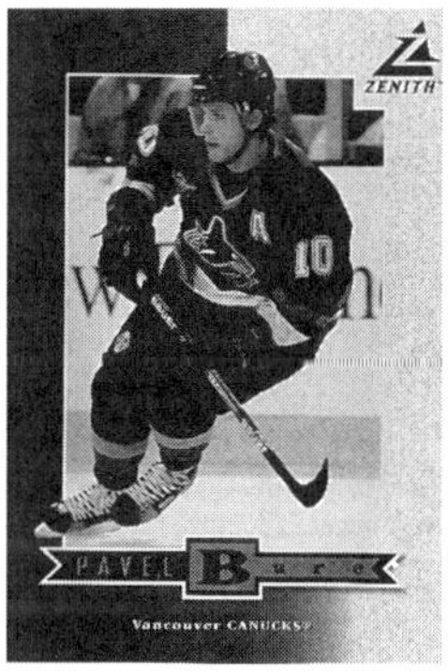
ZENITH
PAVEL
B u r e
Vancouver CANUCKS

The Zenith 5-x-7 cards contained a regular-size Z2 card. Eighty 5-x-7 base cards were included in the set.

		MT
Complete Set (80):		60.00
Common Player:		.25
1	Wayne Gretzky	5.00
2	Eric Lindros	3.00
3	Patrick Roy	4.00
4	John Vanbiesbrouck	1.50
5	Martin Brodeur	1.50
6	Teemu Selanne	1.50
7	Joe Sakic	2.00
8	Jaromir Jagr	3.00
9	Brendan Shanahan	1.50
10	Ed Belfour	.60
11	Guy Hebert	.50
12	Doug Gilmour	.50
13	Keith Primeau	.40
14	Grant Fuhr	.75
15	Joe Nieuwendyk	.50
16	Ryan Smyth	.25
17	Chris Osgood	.75
18	Keith Tkachuk	1.00
19	Peter Forsberg	2.50
20	Jarome Iginla	.25
21	Steve Yzerman	2.50
22	Jeremy Roenick	.60
23	Jozef Stumpel	.40
24	Mark Recchi	.25
25	Daniel Alfredsson	.50
26	Pat LaFontaine	.40
27	Zigmund Palffy	.75
28	Jason Allison	.40
29	Yanic Perreault	.25
30	Olaf Kolzig	.50
31	Mikael Renberg	.25
32	Bryan Berard	.40
33	Jocelyn Thibault	.50
34	Shayne Corson	.25
35	Dave Gagner	.25
36	Claude Lemieux	.40
37	Saku Koivu	.75
38	Curtis Joseph	.75
39	Chris Chelios	.60
40	Ray Bourque	.60
41	Adam Oates	.50
42	Felix Potvin	.75
43	Peter Bondra	.75
44	Sergei Fedorov	1.50
45	Paul Kariya	3.00
46	Theoren Fleury	.40
47	John LeClair	1.25
48	Brett Hull	1.00
49	Rod Brind'Amour	.50
50	Doug Weight	.50
51	Jamie Langenbrunner	.40
52	Mats Sundin	.75
53	Ron Francis	.50
54	Eric Daze	.40
55	Nicklas Lidstrom	.40
56	Luc Robitaille	.40
57	Vincent Damphousse	.25
58	Mike Modano	.75
59	Pavel Bure	1.50
60	Owen Nolan	.25
61	Pierre Turgeon	.50
62	Dominik Hasek	2.00
63	Mike Richter	.75
64	Mark Messier	1.00
65	Brian Leetch	.40
66	Sergei Samsonov	.75
67	Alexei Morozov	.25
68	Marco Sturm	1.25
69	Patrik Elias	1.00
70	Alyn McCauley	.25
71	Mike Johnson	1.00
72	Richard Zednik	.25
73	Mattias Ohlund	.25
74	Joe Thornton	2.00
75	Vincent Lecavalier	8.00
76	Manny Maholtra	1.00
77	Roberto Luongo	4.00
78	Mathieu Garon	.25
79	Alex Tanguay	2.50
80	Josh Holden	.25

1997-98 Pinnacle Zenith 5x7 Silver

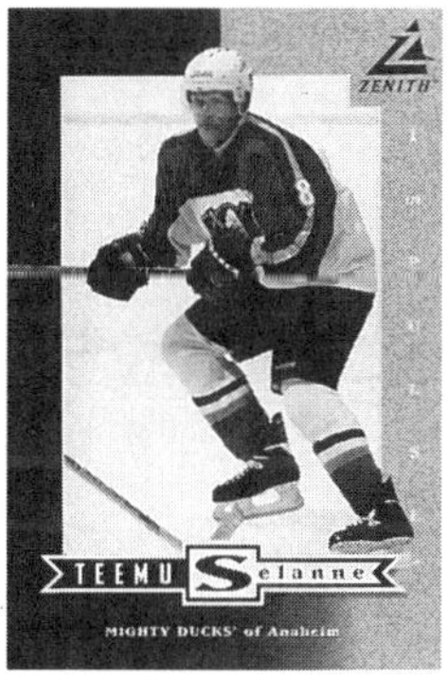
ZENITH
TEEMU
S e l a n n e
MIGHTY DUCKS of Anaheim

Silver Impulse is a parallel of the 80-card 5-x-7 base set. The silver foil cards were inserted 1:7.

	MT
Silvers:	2x to 4x

1997-98 Pinnacle Zenith 5x7 Gold

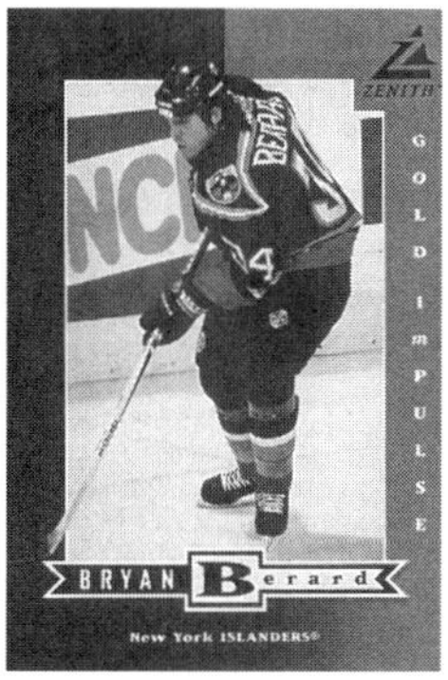
ZENITH
GOLD IMPULSE
BRYAN
B e r a r d
New York ISLANDERS

Gold Impulse is a full parallel of the 80-card 5x7 Zenith base set. The cards have a gold tint and are sequentially numbered to 100.

	MT
Gold Stars:	40x to 75x
Yng Stars & RCs:	25x to 50x

1997-98 Pinnacle Zenith Chasing the Cup

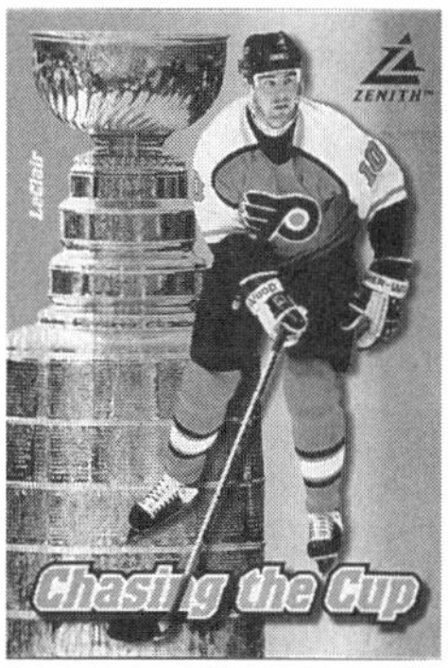
ZENITH
LeClair
Chasing the Cup

Chasing the Cup is a 15-card insert in the Z2 format. The cards have rainbow foil and feature a player and the Stanley Cup on the front. The set was inserted one per 25 packs.

		MT
Complete Set (15):		250.00
Common Player:		6.00
1	Patrick Roy	40.00
2	Wayne Gretzky	50.00
3	Jaromir Jagr	30.00
4	Eric Lindros	30.00
5	Mike Modano	10.00
6	Brendan Shanahan	15.00
7	Brett Hull	12.00
8	John LeClair	15.00
9	Jocelyn Thibault	6.00
10	Ed Belfour	8.00
11	Martin Brodeur	15.00
12	Peter Forsberg	25.00
13	Saku Koivu	10.00
14	Pat LaFontaine	6.00
15	Steve Yzerman	25.00

1997-98 Pinnacle Zenith Rookie Reign

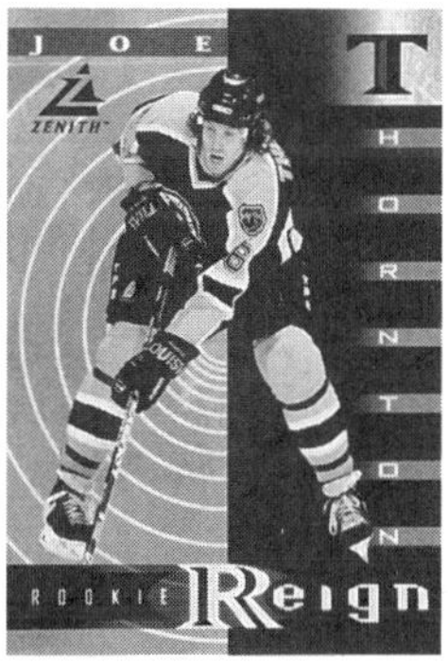
J O E
T H O R N T O N
ZENITH
ROOKIE
Reign

Rookie Reign is a 15-card insert produced in the regular-sized Z2 format. The foil cards feature top young players and were inserted one per 25 packs.

		MT
Complete Set (15):		125.00
Common Player:		5.00
1	Sergei Samsonov	30.00
2	Joe Thornton	30.00
3	Erik Rasmussen	5.00
4	Brendan Morrison	15.00
5	Magnus Arvedson	5.00
6	Vaclav Prospal	12.00
7	Brad Isbister	5.00
8	Alexei Morozov	5.00
9	Marco Sturm	15.00
10	Patrick Marleau	20.00
11	Alyn McCauley	5.00
12	Mike Johnson	10.00
13	Mattias Ohlund	10.00
14	Patrik Elias	15.00
15	Richard Zednik	5.00

1997-98 Pinnacle Zenith Z-Team

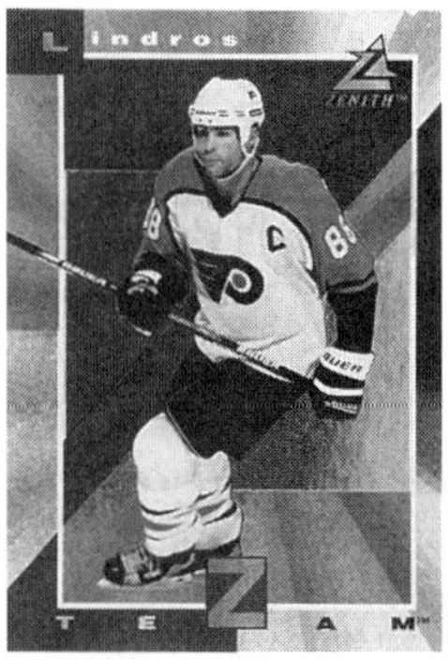

Z Team cards were produced in both Zenith card formats. The Z2 set consisted of 18 cards - nine veterans and nine rookies. The veterans were seeded 1:35 and the rookies were found 1:58. Gold parallel versions of the 18 cards were inserted 1:175. The 5-x-7 Z Team set consisted of the nine veterans from the Z2 set, inserted 1:35.

		MT
Complete Set (18):		500.00
Common Player:		15.00
Golds:		1.5x to 3x
1	Teemu Selanne	30.00
2	Wayne Gretzky	100.00
3	Patrick Roy	80.00
4	Eric Lindros	60.00
5	Peter Forsberg	50.00
6	Paul Kariya	60.00
7	John LeClair	25.00
8	Martin Brodeur	30.00
9	Brendan Shanahan	30.00
10	Joe Thornton	35.00
11	Mattias Ohlund	15.00
12	Mike Johnson	15.00
13	Vaclav Prospal	20.00
14	Sergei Samsonov	20.00
15	Marco Sturm	20.00
16	Patrik Elias	20.00
17	Richard Zednik	15.00
18	Alexei Morozov	15.00

1997-98 Pinnacle Zenith 5x7 Z-Team

The 5-x-7 Z Team insert features nine NHL veterans. The cards were inserted 1:35.

		MT
Complete Set (9):		160.00
Common Player:		6.00
1	Teemu Selanne	15.00
2	Wayne Gretzky	40.00
3	Patrick Roy	30.00
4	Eric Lindros	25.00
5	Peter Forsberg	20.00
6	Paul Kariya	25.00
7	John LeClair	12.00
8	Martin Brodeur	15.00
9	Brendan Shanahan	15.00

1997-98 Score

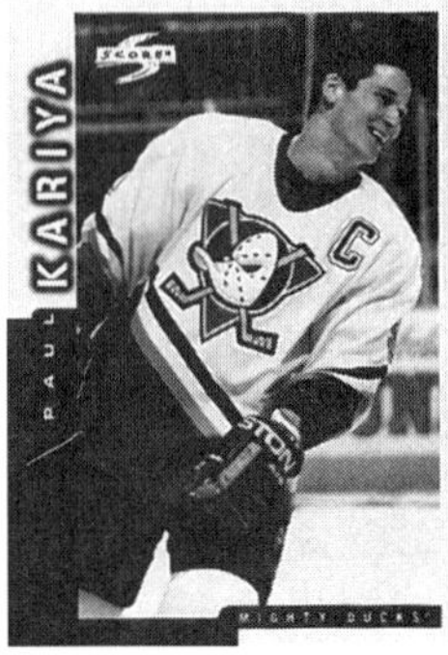

Score Hockey consists of a 270-card base set. The base cards have a color photo, with the player's name in the left border and team name in the bottom border. The base set has two partial parallels: Golden Blades and Artist's Proof. The inserts include Net Worth, Check-It and Epix.

		MT
Complete Set (270):		15.00
Common Player:		.05
Wax Box:		32.00
1	Sean Burke	.10
2	Chris Osgood	.50
3	Garth Snow	.05
4	Mike Vernon	.15
5	Grant Fuhr	.20
6	Guy Hebert	.10
7	Arturs Irbe	.05
8	Andy Moog	.10
9	Tommy Salo	.10
10	Nikolai Khabibulin	.10
11	Mike Richter	.20
12	Corey Hirsch	.05
13	Bill Ranford	.05
14	Jim Carey	.10
15	Jeff Hackett	.10
16	Damian Rhodes	.05
17	Tom Barrasso	.10
18	Daren Puppa	.05
19	Craig Billington	.05
20	Ed Belfour	.20
21	Mikhail Shtalenkov	.05
22	Glenn Healy	.05
23	Marcel Cousineau	.05
24	Kevin Hodson	.15
25	Olaf Kolzig	.10
26	Eric Fichaud	.10
27	Ron Hextall	.15
28	Rick Tabaracci	.05
29	Felix Potvin	.35
30	Martin Brodeur	.60
31	Curtis Joseph	.15
32	Ken Wregget	.05
33	Patrick Roy	1.50
34	John Vanbiesbrouck	.75
35	Stephane Fiset	.05
36	Roman Turek	.05
37	Trevor Kidd	.05
38	Dwayne Roloson	.05
39	Dominik Hasek	.60
40	Patrick Lalime	.15
41	Jocelyn Thibault	.15
42	Jose Theodore	.15
43	Kirk McLean	.10
44	Steve Shields	.05
45	Mike Dunham	.05
46	Jamie Storr	.10
47	Byron Dafoe	.15
48	Chris Terreri	.05
49	Ron Tugnutt	.05
50	Kelly Hrudey	.05
51	*Vaclav Prospal*	.40
52	Alyn McCauley	.05
53	Jaroslav Svejkovsky	.20
54	Joe Thornton	1.00
55	*Chris Dingman*	.05
56	*Vadim Sharifijanov*	.05
57	*Larry Courville*	.05
58	Erik Rasmussen	.05
59	Sergei Samsonov	.40
60	Kevyn Adams	.05
61	*Daniel Cleary*	.30
62	*Martin Prochazka*	.05
63	Mattias Ohlund	.05
64	*Juha Lind*	.05
65	*Olli Jokinen*	.40
66	*Espen Knutsen*	.15
67	Marc Savard	.05
68	*Hnat Domenichelli*	.05
69	*Warren Luhning*	.05
70	*Magnus Arvedson*	.10
71	Chris Phillips	.05
72	Brad Isbister	.05
73	Boyd Devereaux	.05
74	Alexei Morozov	.05
75	Vladimir Vorobiev	.05
76	Steven Rice	.05
77	Tony Granato	.05
78	Lonny Bohonos	.05
79	Dave Gagner	.05
80	Brendan Shanahan	.75
81	Brett Hull	.35
82	Jaromir Jagr	1.25
83	Peter Forsberg	1.00
84	Paul Kariya	1.25
85	Mark Messier	.35
86	Steve Yzerman	1.00
87	Keith Tkachuk	.35
88	Eric Lindros	1.50
89	Ray Bourque	.20
90	Chris Chelios	.20
91	Sergei Fedorov	.40
92	Mike Modano	.25
93	Doug Gilmour	.20
94	Saku Koivu	.60
95	Mats Sundin	.20
96	Pavel Bure	.75
97	Theoren Fleury	.15
98	Keith Primeau	.05
99	Wayne Gretzky	2.00
100	Doug Weight	.15
101	Alexandre Daigle	.05
102	Owen Nolan	.10
103	Peter Bondra	.15
104	Pat LaFontaine	.20
105	Kirk Muller	.05
106	Zigmund Palffy	.35
107	Jeremy Roenick	.25
108	John LeClair	.40
109	Derek Plante	.05
110	Geoff Sanderson	.05
111	Dimitri Khristich	.05
112	Vincent Damphousse	.05
113	Teemu Selanne	.75
114	Tony Amonte	.15
115	Dave Andreychuk	.10
116	Alexei Yashin	.15
117	Adam Oates	.15
118	Pierre Turgeon	.15
119	Dino Ciccarelli	.05
120	Ryan Smyth	.15
121	Ray Sheppard	.05
122	Jozef Stumpel	.05
123	Jarome Iginla	.15
124	Pat Verbeek	.05
125	Joe Sakic	.75
126	Brian Leetch	.20
127	Rod Brind'Amour	.15
128	Wendel Clark	.05
129	Alexander Mogilny	.20
130	Mark Recchi	.15
131	Daniel Alfredsson	.15
132	Ron Francis	.15
133	Martin Gelinas	.05
134	Andrew Cassels	.05
135	Joe Nieuwendyk	.15
136	Jason Arnott	.05
137	Bryan Berard	.15
138	Mikael Renberg	.05
139	Mike Gartner	.05
140	Joe Juneau	.05
141	John MacLean	.05
142	Adam Graves	.05
143	Petr Nedved	.05
144	Trevor Linden	.05
145	Sergei Berezin	.15
146	Adam Deadmarsh	.05
147	Jeff O'Neill	.05
148	Rob Blake	.05
149	Luc Robitaille	.15
150	Markus Naslund	.05
151	Ethan Moreau	.05
152	Martin Rucinsky	.05
153	Mike Grier	.05
154	Craig Janney	.05
155	John Cullen	.05
156	Alexei Kovalev	.05
157	Tony Twist	.05
158	Claude Lemieux	.05
159	Kevin Stevens	.05
160	Mathieu Schneider	.05
161	Randy Cunneyworth	.05
162	Darius Kasparaitis	.05
163	Joe Murphy	.05
164	Brandon Convery	.05
165	Janne Niinimaa	.05
166	Paul Coffey	.15
167	Daymond Langkow	.05
168	Chris Gratton	.15
169	Ray Ferraro	.05
170	Jeff Friesen	.05
171	Ted Donato	.05
172	Brian Holzinger	.05
173	Travis Green	.15
174	Sandis Ozolinsh	.15
175	Alexei Zhamnov	.05
176	Steve Rucchin	.05
177	Scott Mellanby	.05
178	Andrei Kovalenko	.05
179	Donald Audette	.05
180	Bernie Nicholls	.05
181	Jonas Hoglund	.05
182	Nicklas Lidstrom	.20
183	Bobby Holik	.05
184	Geoff Courtnall	.05
185	Steve Sullivan	.05
186	Valeri Kamensky	.05
187	Mike Peca	.05
188	Jere Lehtinen	.05
189	Robert Svehla	.05
190	Darren McCarty	.05
191	Brian Savage	.05
192	Harry York	.05
193	Eric Daze	.05
194	Niklas Sundstrom	.05
195	Oleg Tverdovsky	.05
196	Eric Desjardins	.05
197	German Titov	.05
198	Derian Hatcher	.05
199	Bill Guerin	.05
200	Rob Zamuner	.05
201	Dale Hunter	.05
202	Darcy Tucker	.05
203	Andreas Dackell	.05
204	Jason Dawe	.05
205	Brian Rolston	.05
206	Ed Olczyk	.05
207	Todd Warriner	.05
208	Mariusz Czerkawski	.05
209	Slava Kozlov	.05
210	Marty McInnis	.05
211	Jamie Langenbrunner	.05
212	Vitali Yachmenev	.05
213	Stephane Richer	.05
214	Roman Hamrlik	.05
215	Jim Campbell	.05
216	Matthew Barnaby	.05
217	Benoit Hogue	.05
218	Robert Reichel	.05
219	Tie Domi	.05
220	Steve Konowalchuk	.05
221	Radek Dvorak	.05
222	Kevin Hatcher	.05
223	Viktor Kozlov	.05
224	Scott Stevens	.05
225	Cory Stillman	.05
226	Anson Carter	.05
227	Rem Murray	.05
228	Vladimir Konstantinov	.05
229	Scott Niedermayer	.05
230	Steve Duchesne	.15
231	Valeri Bure	.05
232	Miroslav Satan	.05
233	Jason Allison	.05
234	Mark Fitzpatrick	.05
235	Ed Jovanovski	.05
236	Esa Tikkanen	.05
237	Stu Barnes	.05
238	Darryl Sydor	.05
239	Ulf Samuelsson	.05
240	Dmitri Mironov	.05
241	Bryan Smolinski	.05
242	Rob Ray	.05
243	Todd Marchant	.05
244	Cliff Ronning	.05
245	Alexander Selivanov	.05
246	Rick Tocchet	.05
247	Vladimir Malakhov	.05
248	Al MacInnis	.05
249	Dainius Zubrus	.15
250	Keith Jones	.05
251	Darren Turcotte	.05
252	Ulf Dahlen	.05
253	Rob Niedermayer	.05
254	J.J. Daigneault	.05
255	Michal Grosek	.05
256	Chris Therien	.05
257	Adam Foote	.05
258	Tomas Sandstrom	.05
259	Scott Lachance	.05
260	Paul Kariya (EA)	.60
261	Pavel Bure (EA)	.40
262	Mike Modano (EA)	.10
263	Steve Yzerman (EA)	.40
264	Sergei Fedorov (EA)	.20
265	Eric Lindros (EA)	.75
266	Checklist Dominik Hasek	.30
267	Checklist Bryan Berard	.05
268	Checklist Mike Peca	.05
269	Checklist M. Brodeur, M. Dunham	.05
270	Checklist Paul Kariya	.40

1997-98 Score Golden Blades

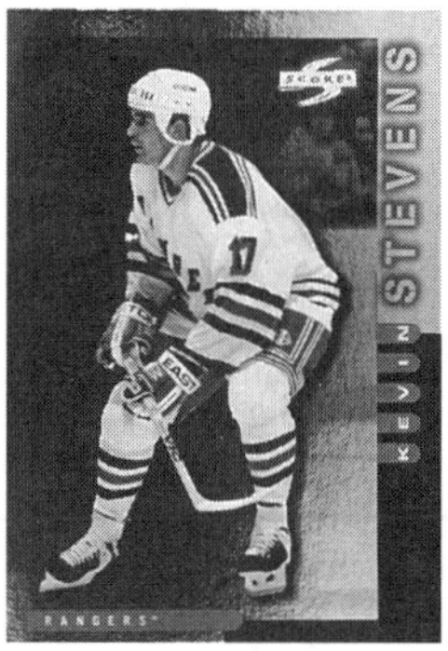

Golden Blades is a 165-card partial parallel of the Score base set. The cards were printed on foil board and inserted one per seven packs.

	MT
Golden Blades:	4x to 8x

1997-98 Score Artist's Proofs

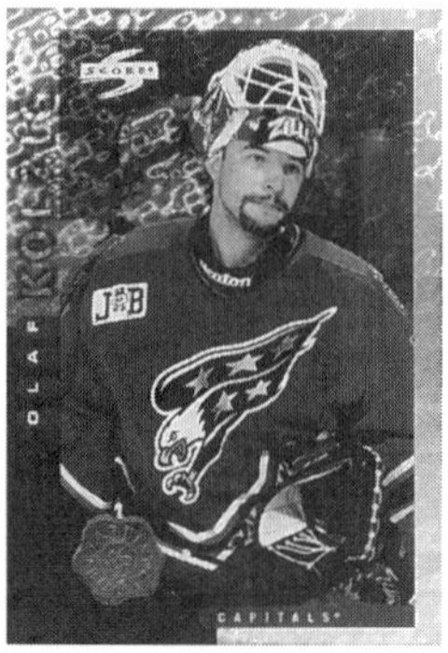

Artist's Proofs is a 165-card partial parallel of the Score base set. The cards were printed on prismatic foil board and inserted 1:35.

	MT
Artist's Proofs:	25x to 35x

1997-98 Score Check-It

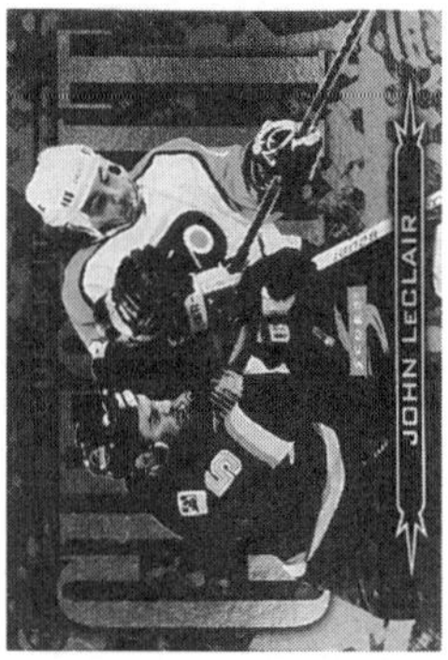

Check-It is an 18-card insert seeded one per 19 packs. The set features the most physical players in the NHL. The cards have a horizontal layout with a large "Check-It" logo in the background.

		MT
Complete Set (18):		100.00
Common Player:		3.00
1	Eric Lindros	25.00
2	Mark Messier	10.00
3	Brendan Shanahan	12.00
4	Keith Tkachuk	8.00
5	John LeClair	10.00
6	Doug Gilmour	6.00
7	Jarome Iginla	6.00
8	Ryan Smyth	3.00
9	Chris Chelios	5.00
10	Mike Grier	3.00
11	Vincent Damphousse	3.00
12	Bryan Berard	5.00
13	Jaromir Jagr	20.00
14	Mike Peca	3.00
15	Dino Ciccarelli	3.00
16	Rod Brind'Amour	3.00
17	Owen Nolan	3.00
18	Pat Verbeek	3.00

1997-98 Score Net Worth

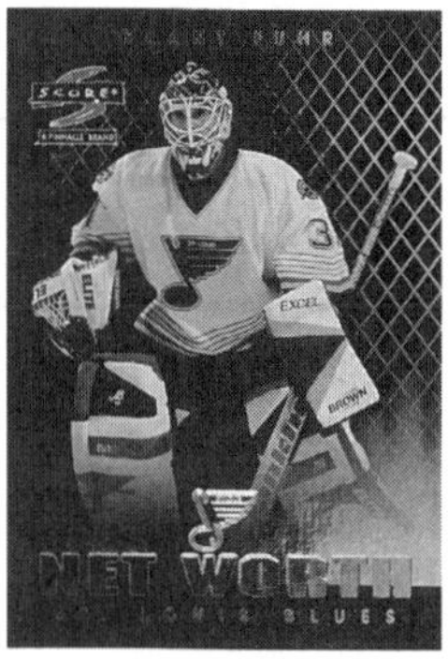

Net Worth is a 12-card insert featuring the leagues top goalies. The cards were inserted one per 35 packs.

		MT
Complete Set (18):		160.00
Common Player:		6.00
1	Guy Hebert	6.00
2	Jim Carey	6.00
3	Trevor Kidd	6.00
4	Chris Osgood	12.00
5	Curtis Joseph	8.00
6	Mike Richter	10.00
7	Damian Rhodes	6.00
8	Garth Snow	6.00
9	Nikolai Khabibulin	6.00
10	Grant Fuhr	6.00
11	Jocelyn Thibault	8.00
12	Tommy Salo	6.00
13	Patrick Roy	40.00

14	Martin Brodeur	20.00
15	John Vanbiesbrouck	20.00
16	Felix Potvin	10.00
17	Dominik Hasek	20.00
18	Ed Belfour	10.00

1997-98 SP Authentic

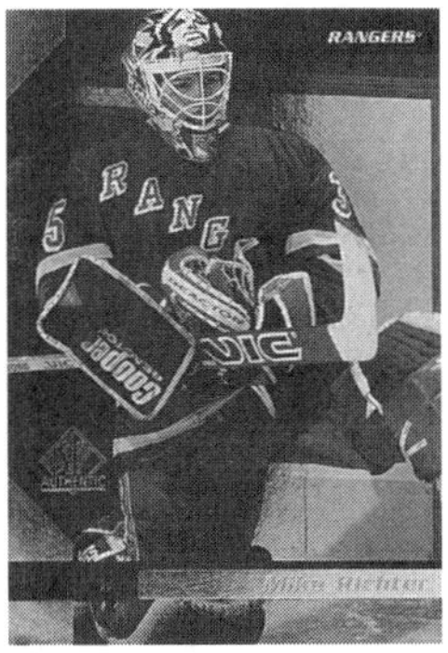

SP Authentic Hockey consists of a 198-card base set. The set features 168 veterans and 30 rookies in the Future Watch subset. Inserts in the set include Icons, Mark of a Legend, Sign of the Times and Tradition. Redemption cards for Wayne Gretzky-autographed memorabilia were also included, but too many jersey redemption cards were produced. Thirty-nine total jerseys were supposed to be available, but almost 400 redemption cards found their way into packs. Upper Deck offered all collectors who found a card a Gretzky-signed stick and entrance into a drawing for one of the jerseys.

		MT
Complete Set (198):		50.00
Common Player:		.20
1	Teemu Selanne	1.00
2	Sean Pronger	.20
3	Joe Sacco	.20
4	Tomas Sandstrom	.20
5	Steve Rucchin	.20
6	Paul Kariya	2.50
7	Ted Donato	.20
8	Ray Bourque	.50
9	Tim Taylor	.20
10	Jason Allison	.40
11	Kyle McLaren	.20
12	Dimitri Khristich	.20
13	Jason Dawe	.20
14	Dominik Hasek	1.50
15	Miroslav Satan	.20
16	Brian Holzinger	.20
17	Alexei Zhitnik	.20
18	Theoren Fleury	.40
19	Cory Stillman	.20
20	Jarome Iginla	.20
21	Sandy McCarthy	.20
22	German Titov	.20
23	Glen Wesley	.20
24	Keith Primeau	.40
25	Geoff Sanderson	.20
26	Gary Roberts	.20
27	Sami Kapanen	.40
28	Jeff O'Neill	.40
29	Tony Amonte	.50
30	Chris Chelios	.50
31	Eric Daze	.40
32	Alexei Zhamnov	.20
33	Chris Terreri	.20
34	Sergei Krivokrasov	.20
35	Joe Sakic	1.50
36	Peter Forsberg	2.00
37	Patrick Roy	3.00
38	Claude Lemieux	.20
39	Valeri Kamensky	.20
40	Adam Deadmarsh	.40
41	Sandis Ozolinsh	.20
42	Jari Kurri	.20
43	Mike Modano	.75
44	Ed Belfour	.60
45	Derian Hatcher	.20
46	Sergei Zubov	.20
47	Jamie Langenbrunner	.40
48	Jere Lehtinen	.20
49	Joe Nieuwendyk	.40
50	Vyacheslav Kozlov	.20
51	Chris Osgood	.75
52	Steve Yzerman	2.00
53	Nicklas Lidstrom	.40
54	Igor Larionov	.20
55	Brendan Shanahan	1.00
56	Anders Eriksson	.20
57	Darren McCarty	.20
58	Doug Weight	.40
59	Jason Arnott	.20
60	Curtis Joseph	.50
61	Ryan Smyth	.20
62	Dean McAmmond	.20
63	Mike Grier	.20
64	Kelly Buchberger	.20
65	Ed Jovanovski	.20
66	Ray Whitney	.20
67	Rob Niedermayer	.20
68	Scott Mellanby	.20
69	John Vanbiesbrouck	1.00
70	Viktor Kozlov	.20
71	Jozef Stumpel	.40
72	Rob Blake	.20
73	Garry Galley	.20
74	Vladimir Tsyplakov	.20
75	Yanic Perreault	.20
76	Stephane Fiset	.40
77	Luc Robitaille	.40
78	Valeri Bure	.20
79	Mark Recchi	.40
80	Saku Koivu	.75
81	Andy Moog	.50
82	Vincent Damphousse	.20
83	Vladimir Malakhov	.20
84	Shayne Corson	.20
85	Scott Stevens	.20
86	Bill Guerin	.20
87	Martin Brodeur	1.00
88	Doug Gilmour	.50
89	Bobby Holik	.20
90	Petr Sykora	.20
91	Zigmund Palffy	.75
92	Bryan Berard	.40
93	Tommy Salo	.50
94	Travis Green	.20
95	Kenny Jonsson	.20
96	Todd Bertuzzi	.20
97	Robert Reichel	.20
98	Pat LaFontaine	.40
99	Wayne Gretzky	4.00
100	Brian Leetch	.40
101	Mike Richter	.60
102	Alexei Kovalev	.20
103	Adam Graves	.20
104	Niklas Sundstrom	.20
105	Alexei Yashin	.50
106	Daniel Alfredsson	.50
107	Alexandre Daigle	.20
108	Wade Redden	.20
109	Andreas Dackell	.20
110	Shawn McEachern	.20
111	Eric Lindros	2.50
112	Chris Gratton	.40
113	Paul Coffey	.40
114	John LeClair	1.00
115	Rod Brind'Amour	.50
116	Ron Hextall	.50
117	Dainius Zubrus	.20
118	Jeremy Roenick	.60
119	Keith Tkachuk	.75
120	Nikolai Khabibulin	.50
121	Rick Tocchet	.20
122	Teppo Numminen	.20
123	Craig Janney	.20
124	Mike Gartner	.20
125	Jaromir Jagr	2.50
126	Ron Francis	.50
127	Kevin Hatcher	.20
128	Robert Dome	.20
129	Martin Straka	.20
130	*Peter Skudra*	.60
131	Owen Nolan	.40
132	Bernie Nicholls	.20
133	Mike Vernon	.50
134	Jeff Friesen	.40
135	Tony Granato	.20
136	Mike Ricci	.20
137	Jim Campbell	.20
138	Brett Hull	.75
139	Chris Pronger	.50
140	Al MacInnis	.50
141	Pierre Turgeon	.50
142	Pavol Demitra	.20
143	Grant Fuhr	.60
144	Steve Duchesne	.20
145	Daymond Langkow	.20
146	Alexander Selivanov	.20
147	Daren Puppa	.20
148	Dino Ciccarelli	.20
149	Roman Hamrlik	.20
150	Mats Sundin	.75
151	Felix Potvin	.60
152	Wendel Clark	.20
153	Sergei Berezin	.20
154	Steve Sullivan	.20
155	Alexander Mogilny	.50
156	Pavel Bure	1.00
157	Mark Messier	.75
158	Bret Hedican	.20
159	Kirk McLean	.40
160	Trevor Linden	.40
161	Dave Scatchard	.20
162	Adam Oates	.50
163	Joe Juneau	.20
164	Peter Bondra	.75
165	Bill Ranford	.20
166	Sergei Gonchar	.20
167	Calle Johansson	.20
168	Phil Housley	.20
169	Espen Knutsen (Future Watch)	.20
170	*Pavel Trnka* (Future Watch)	.50
171	Joe Thornton (Future Watch)	1.50
172	Sergei Samsonov (Future Watch)	.75
173	Erik Rasmussen (Future Watch)	.20
174	*Tyler Moss* (Future Watch)	.20
175	*Derek Morris* (Future Watch)	.40
176	Craig Mills (Future Watch)	.20
177	Daniel Cleary (Future Watch)	.20
178	*Eric Messier* (Future Watch)	.20
179	Kevin Hodson (Future Watch)	.50
180	*Mike Knuble* (Future Watch)	.20
181	Boyd Devereaux (Future Watch)	.20
182	*Craig Millar* (Future Watch)	.50
183	*Kevin Weekes* (Future Watch)	.50
184	*Donald MacLean* (Future Watch)	.50
185	*Patrik Elias* (Future Watch)	1.00
186	*Zdeno Chara* (Future Watch)	.75
187	Chris Phillips (Future Watch)	.20
188	*Vaclav Prospal* (Future Watch)	2.00
189	Brad Isbister (Future Watch)	.20
190	Alexei Morozov (Future Watch)	.20
191	Patrick Marleau (Future Watch)	1.50
192	*Marco Sturm* (Future Watch)	1.00
193	*Brendan Morrison* (Future Watch)	1.50
194	*Mike Johnson* (Future Watch)	1.00
195	Alyn McCauley (Future Watch)	.20
196	Mattias Ohlund (Future Watch)	.20
197	Richard Zednik (Future Watch)	.20
198	*Jan Bulis* (Future Watch)	.50

1997-98 SP Authentic Icons

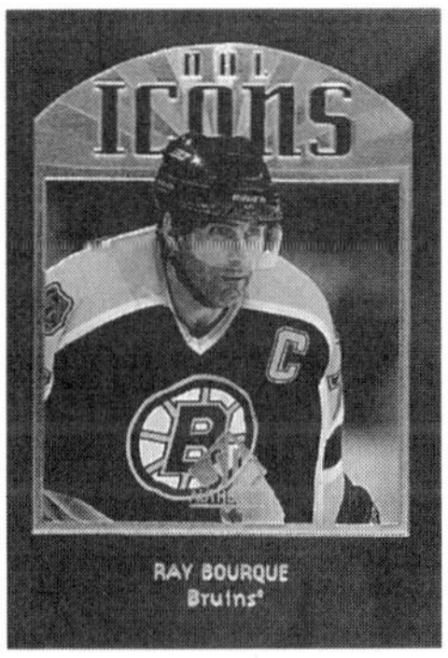

Icons is a 40-card, three-tiered insert. The regular Icons cards feature a color player photo with a thick green border. Icons were inserted 1:5, embossed Icons cards were seeded 1:12 and die-cut versions were numbered to 100.

		MT
Complete Set (40):		150.00
Common Player:		1.00
Embossed:		1.5x to 2x
I1	Pat LaFontaine	1.00
I2	Brett Hull	4.00
I3	Chris Chelios	2.00
I4	Joe Sakic	6.00
I5	John Vanbiesbrouck	4.00
I6	Patrik Elias	1.00
I7	Eric Lindros	10.00
I8	Jaromir Jagr	10.00
I9	Joe Thornton	4.00
I10	Brendan Shanahan	4.00
I11	Paul Kariya	10.00
I12	Peter Forsberg	8.00
I13	Ed Belfour	2.00
I14	Martin Brodeur	5.00
I15	Alexei Morozov	1.00
I16	Mark Messier	3.00
I17	John LeClair	3.00
I18	Luc Robitaille	1.00
I19	Teemu Selanne	4.00
I20	Theoren Fleury	1.00
I21	Steve Yzerman	8.00
I22	Chris Phillips	1.00
I23	Keith Tkachuk	3.00
I24	Patrick Roy	12.00
I25	Mark Recchi	1.00
I26	Wayne Gretzky	15.00
I27	Dino Ciccarelli	1.00
I28	Ray Bourque	2.00
I29	Tony Amonte	1.50
I30	Daniel Alfredsson	1.50
I31	Saku Koivu	3.00
I32	Doug Weight	1.00
I33	Mats Sundin	3.00
I34	Dominik Hasek	5.00
I35	Scott Stevens	1.00
I36	Pavel Bure	4.00
I37	Mike Modano	4.00
I38	Zigmund Palffy	2.50
I39	Brian Leetch	1.50
I40	Marco Sturm	1.00

1997-98 SP Authentic Hockey Die-Cut Icons

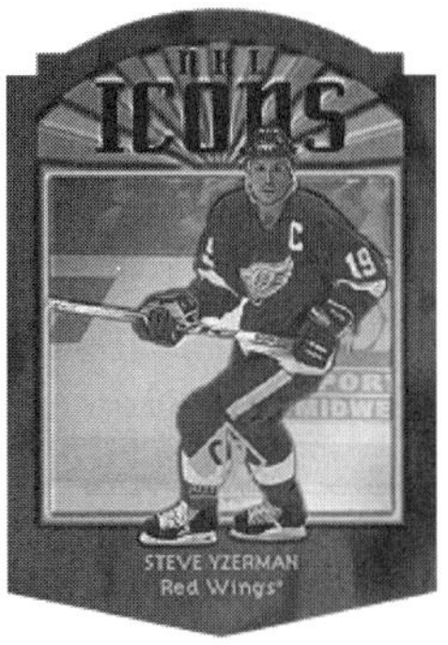

Icons is a 40-card, three-tieredinsert. The third tier consists of die-cut versions of the regular Icons cards and are numbered to 100.

	MT
Die-Cut Stars:	15x to 25x
Yng Stars:	10x to 20x

1997-98 SP Authentic Mark of a Legend

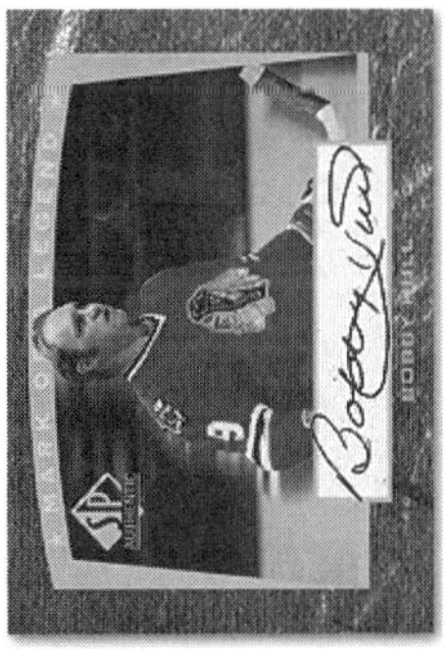

Mark of a Legend is a six-card insert featuring autographs from some of the game's legendary players. Seeded one per 198 packs, the cards have a horizontal layout.

		MT
Complete Set (6):		
Common Player:		60.00
M1	Gordie Howe	450.00
M2	Billy Smith	75.00
M3	Cam Neely	80.00
M4	Bryan Trottier	60.00
M5	Bobby Hull	125.00
M6	Wayne Gretzky	500.00

1997-98 SP Authentic Sign of the Times

Sign of the Times features autographs from 29 top NHL players. The signature is placed in a white box below the player's photo. Cards were inserted one per 23 packs.

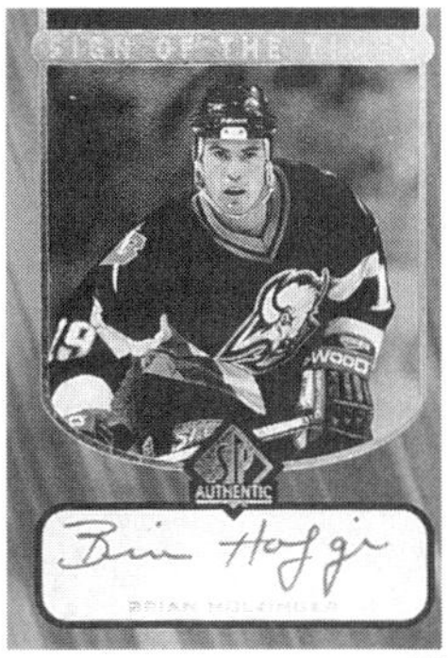

		MT
Common Player:		20.00
S1	Wayne Gretzky	400.00
S2	Patrick Roy	250.00
S3	Steve Yzerman	200.00
S4	Sergei Samsonov	90.00
S5	Brett Hull	80.00
S6	Ray Bourque	80.00
S7	Joe Thornton	20.00
S8	Yanic Perreault	20.00
S9	Chris Chelios	50.00
S10	Tony Amonte	40.00
S11	Jamie Langenbrunner	20.00
S12	Mats Sundin	50.00
S13	Grant Fuhr	40.00
S14	Doug Weight	30.00
S15	Martin Brodeur	125.00
S16	Bryan Berard	20.00
S17	Peter Bondra	35.00
S18	Nicklas Lidstrom	30.00
S19	Rob Niedermayer	20.00
S20	Nikolai Khabibulin	30.00
S21	Jose Theodore	20.00
S22	Darren McCarty	20.00
S23	Guy Hebert	30.00
S24	Jarome Iginla	20.00
S25	Dainius Zubrus	30.00
S26	Jaroslav Svejkovsky	20.00
S27	Sergei Berezin	20.00
S28	Mike Grier	20.00
S29	Brian Holzinger	20.00

1997-98 SP Authentics

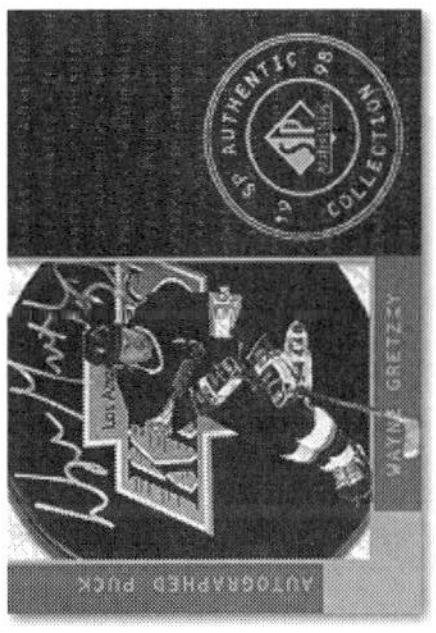

SP Authentics is an 11-card insert consisting of redemption cards for signed Wayne Gretzky memorabilia. Jerseys, sticks, pucks and photos were among the items available, with a different number of each produced. Two different jerseys were available with a total production of 39. An error resulted in almost 400 jersey redemption cards being inserted in packs. Upper Deck offered to give collectors with jersey redemption cards an autographed stick and entry into a drawing for the jerseys.

		MT
Commons:		50.00
1	Gretzky Jersey (19)	1500.
2	Gretzky 802 Jersey (20)	1500.
3	Gretzky Stick (40)	500.00
4	Gretzky Rangers Puck (399)	120.00
5	Gretzky Kings Puck (200)	160.00
6	Gretzky Photo (250)	100.00
7	Gretzky 802 Photo (249)	100.00
8	Gretzky Blues Puck (200)	160.00
9	Gretzky Standee (249)	60.00

10	Gretzky 802 card (184)	50.00
11	Gretzky Motiv. Photo (185)	60.00

1997-98 SP Authentic Tradition

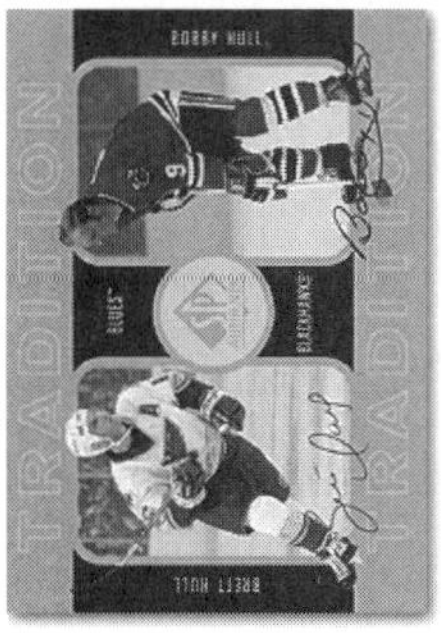

The six Tradition cards each feature an autograph from a current player and an NHL legend. Tradition cards were inserted 1:340.

		MT
Complete Set (6):		
Common Player:		75.00
T1	Wayne Gretzky, Gordie Howe	1200.
T2	Patrick Roy, Billy Smith	400.00
T3	Joe Thornton, Cam Neely	200.00
T4	Bryan Berard, Bryan Trottier	75.00
T5	Brett Hull, Bobby Hull	500.00
T6	Ray Bourque, Cam Neely	250.00

1997-98 SPx

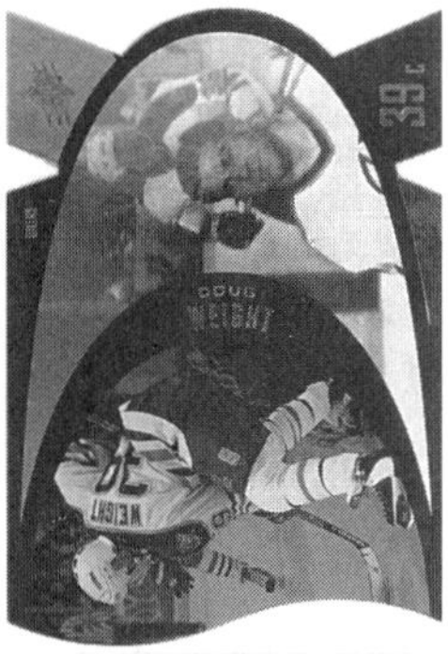

SPx Hockey consists of a 50-card base set with five parallels and three inserts. The die-cut base card design vaguely resembles an "SPx." A color player photo is on the left side of the horizontal card. The right side features two Holoview images. The parallels include Steel, Bronze, Silver, Gold and Grand Finale. The inserts are DuoView, DuoView Autographs and SPx Dimension.

		MT
Complete Set (50):		40.00
Common Player:		.50
Bronzes: 2x to 3x		
Silvers: 3x to 4x		
Golds: 5x to 10x		
Wax Box:		80.00
1	Paul Kariya	4.00
2	Teemu Selanne	2.00
3	Ray Bourque	.75
4	Dominik Hasek	2.00
5	Pat LaFontaine	.75
6	Theoren Fleury	.75
7	Jarome Iginla	.50
8	Tony Amonte	.50
9	Chris Chelios	.75
10	Patrick Roy	5.00
11	Peter Forsberg	3.00
12	Joe Sakic	2.50
13	Mike Modano	1.00
14	Steve Yzerman	3.00
15	Sergei Fedorov	1.50
16	Brendan Shanahan	2.00
17	Doug Weight	.50
18	Jason Arnott	.50
19	Curtis Joseph	.75
20	John Vanbiesbrouck	2.50
21	Ed Jovanovski	.50
22	Geoff Sanderson	.50
23	Rob Blake	.50
24	Saku Koivu	1.50
25	Doug Gilmour	.75
26	Scott Stevens	.50
27	Martin Brodeur	2.00
28	Zigmund Palffy	1.50
29	Bryan Berard	.75
30	Wayne Gretzky	6.00
31	Mike Richter	.75
32	Mark Messier	1.25
33	Brian Leetch	.75
34	Daniel Alfredsson	.50
35	Alexei Yashin	.50
36	Eric Lindros	4.00
37	Janne Niinimaa	.50
38	John LeClair	1.50
39	Jeremy Roenick	1.00
40	Keith Tkachuk	1.50
41	Ron Francis	.75
42	Jaromir Jagr	4.00
43	Brett Hull	1.50
44	Owen Nolan	.50
45	Chris Gratton	.50
46	Mats Sundin	.75
47	Pavel Bure	2.00
48	Adam Oates	.75
49	Joe Juneau	.50
50	Peter Bondra	.75

1997-98 SPx Steel

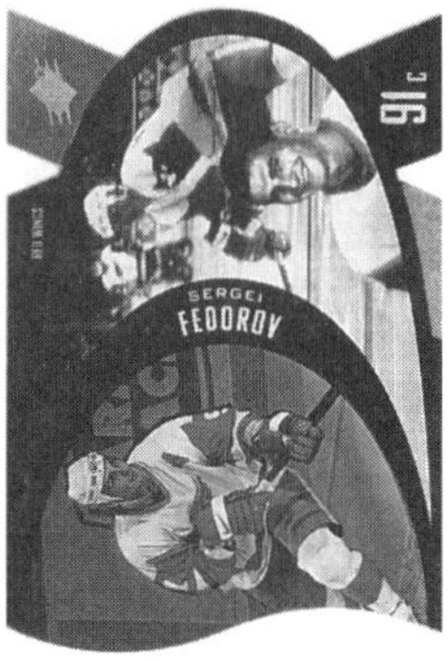

SPx Hockey included five parallels of the base set. Steel (inserted one per pack), Bronze (1:3), Silver (1:6) and Gold (1:17) parallels were produced, as well as the Grand Finale parallel.

	MT
Steels:	1.5x to 2x
Bronzes:	2x to 3x
Silvers:	3x to 4x
Golds:	5x to 10x

1997-98 SPx Dimension

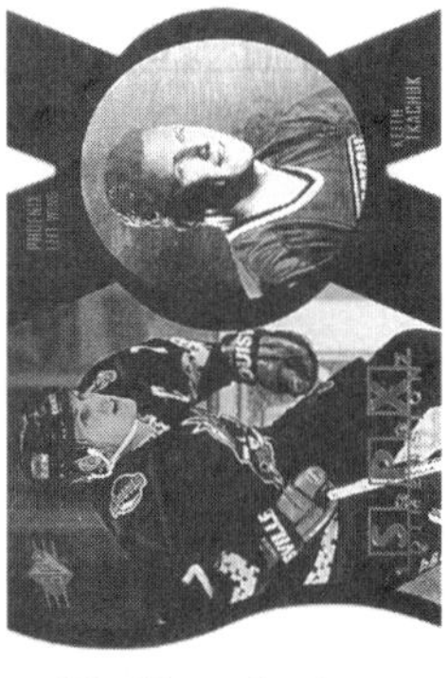

SPx Dimension is a 20-card insert seeded one per 54 packs. The cards have the same die-cut design as the base cards but feature a larger color image on the left and a circular Holoview closeup of the player in his All-Star jersey on the right.

	MT
Complete Set (20):	
Common Player:	15.00
SPX1Wayne Gretzky	125.00
SPX2Jeremy Roenick	20.00
SPX3Mark Messier	35.00
SPX4Eric Lindros	75.00
SPX5Doug Gilmour	20.00
SPX6Pavel Bure	40.00
SPX7Brendan Shanahan	40.00
SPX8Bryan Berard	15.00
SPX9Curtis Joseph	15.00
SPX10Chris Chelios	25.00
SPX11Sergei Fedorov	35.00
SPX12Adam Oates	20.00
SPX13Zigmund Palffy	30.00
SPX14Theoren Fleury	15.00
SPX15Keith Tkachuk	30.00
SPX16Peter Forsberg	65.00
SPX17Mats Sundin	25.00
SPX18Teemu Selanne	50.00
SPX19Paul Kariya	75.00
SPX20Brett Hull	30.00

1997-98 SPx DuoView

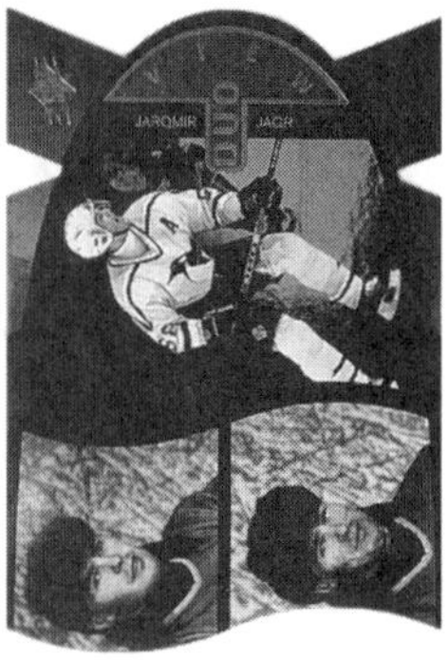

DuoView is a 10-card insert seeded one per 252 packs. The cards have the same die-cut design as the base cards but feature a color photo on the right and two Holoview images on the left.

		MT
Complete Set (10):		1000.
Common Player:		30.00
DV	Wayne Gretzky	275.00
DV	Jaromir Jagr	160.00
DV	Martin Brodeur	90.00
DV	Jarome Iginla	30.00
DV	Steve Yzerman	140.00
DV	Patrick Roy	220.00
DV	Doug Weight	30.00
DV	John Vanbiesbrouck	90.00
DV	Dominik Hasek	100.00
DV	Joe Sakic	120.00

1997-98 SPx DuoView Autographs

Six players signed and hand-numbered 100 of their DuoView cards.

		MT
Complete Set (6):		2800.
Common Autograph:		100.00
1	Wayne Gretzky	1200.
2	Jaromir Jagr	500.00
3	Martin Brodeur	300.00
4	Jarome Iginla	150.00
5	Patrick Roy	800.00
6	Doug Weight	100.00

1997-98 SPx Grand Finale

Grand Finale is a parallel of the SPx base set. A total of 50 sets were produced.

		MT
Common Player:		75.00
Semistars:		125.00
1	Paul Kariya	450.00
2	Teemu Selanne	250.00
3	Ray Bourque	100.00
4	Dominik Hasek	250.00
5	Pat LaFontaine	75.00
6	Theoren Fleury	75.00
7	Jarome Iginla	75.00
8	Tony Amonte	75.00
9	Chris Chelios	100.00
10	Patrick Roy	600.00
11	Peter Forsberg	375.00
12	Joe Sakic	300.00
13	Mike Modano	125.00
14	Steve Yzerman	400.00
15	Sergei Fedorov	175.00
16	Brendan Shanahan	200.00
17	Doug Weight	75.00
18	Jason Arnott	75.00
19	Curtis Joseph	100.00
20	John Vanbiesbrouck	175.00
21	Ed Jovanovski	75.00
22	Geoff Sanderson	75.00
23	Rob Blake	75.00
24	Saku Koivu	150.00
25	Doug Gilmour	125.00
26	Scott Stevens	75.00
27	Martin Brodeur	275.00
28	Zigmund Palffy	150.00
29	Bryan Berard	75.00
30	Wayne Gretzky	750.00
31	Mike Richter	100.00
32	Mark Messier	150.00
33	Brian Leetch	75.00
34	Daniel Alfredsson	75.00
35	Alexei Yashin	75.00
36	Eric Lindros	450.00
37	Janne Niinimaa	75.00
38	John LeClair	175.00
39	Jeremy Roenick	125.00
40	Keith Tkachuk	150.00
41	Ron Francis	75.00
42	Jaromir Jagr	450.00
43	Brett Hull	150.00
44	Owen Nolan	75.00
45	Chris Gratton	75.00
46	Mats Sundin	125.00
47	Pavel Bure	250.00
48	Adam Oates	100.00
49	Joe Juneau	75.00
50	Peter Bondra	75.00

1997-98 Upper Deck

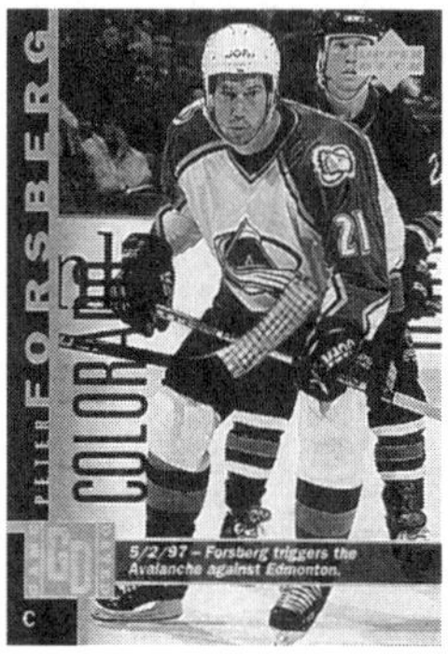

The 420-card Upper Deck Hockey base set was released in two 210-card series. The base cards are bordered on the left, with the player's name, position and Upper Deck logo in the border. The Series One base set contains 180 regular cards, 15 Star Rookie subset cards, 13 Fan Favorites cards and two checklists. Inserts in Series One included Game Jersey, The Specialists, Three Star Selects and Game Dated Moments. Series Two featured a 10-card Physical Force subset. Inserts in Series Two included Game Jersey, Sixth Sense, Smooth Grooves and Game Dated Moments.

		MT
Complete Set (420):		40.00
Complete Series 1 Set (210):		20.00
Complete Series 2 Set (210):		20.00
Common Player:		.10
Series I & II Box:		55.00
1	Teemu Selanne	1.00
2	Steve Rucchin	.10
3	Kevin Todd	.10
4	Darren Van Impe	.10
5	Mark Janssens	.10
6	Guy Hebert	.10
7	Sean Pronger	.10
8	Jason Allison	.10
9	Ray Bourque	.25
10	Landon Wilson	.10
11	Anson Carter	.10
12	Jean-Yves Roy	.10
13	Kyle McLaren	.10
14	Don Sweeney	.10
15	Brian Holzinger	.10
16	Matthew Barnaby	.10
17	Wayne Primeau	.10
18	Steve Shields	.10
19	Jason Dawe	.10
20	Donald Audette	.10
21	Dixon Ward	.10
22	Hnat Domenichelli	.10
23	Trevor Kidd	.10
24	Jarome Iginla	.25
25	Sandy McCarthy	.10
26	Marty McInnis	.10
27	Jonas Hoglund	.10
28	Aaron Gavey	.10
29	Keith Primeau	.10
30	Geoff Sanderson	.10
31	Sean Burke	.20
32	Steve Rice	.10
33	Stu Grimson	.10
34	Jeff O'Neil	.10
35	Curtis Leschyshyn	.10
36	Chris Chelios	.25
37	Sergei Krivokrasov	.10
38	Jeff Hackett	.20
39	Bob Probert	.10
40	Chris Terreri	.10
41	Eric Daze	.10
42	Alexei Zhamnov	.10
43	Patrick Roy	2.50
44	Sandis Ozolinsh	.10
45	*Eric Messier*	.60
46	Adam Deadmarsh	.10
47	Claude Lemieux	.10
48	Mike Ricci	.10
49	Stephane Yelle	.10
50	Joe Nieuwendyk	.20
51	Derian Hatcher	.10
52	Jere Lehtinen	.10
53	Roman Turek	.10
54	Darryl Sydor	.10
55	Todd Harvey	.10
56	Mike Modano	.40
57	Steve Yzerman	2.00
58	Martin Lapointe	.10
59	Darren McCarty	.10
60	Mike Vernon	.20
61	Kirk Maltby	.10
62	Kris Draper	.10
63	Vladimir Konstantinov	.10
64	Todd Marchant	.10
65	Doug Weight	.20
66	Jason Arnott	.20
67	Mike Grier	.20
68	Mats Lindgren	.10
69	Bryan Marchment	.10
70	Rem Murray	.10
71	Radek Dvorak	.10
72	John Vanbiesbrouck	1.25
73	Robert Svehla	.10
74	Bill Lindsay	.10
75	Paul Laus	.10
76	Kirk Muller	.10
77	David Nemirovsky	.10
78	Roman Vopat	.10
79	Jan Vopat	.10
80	Dimitri Khristich	.10
81	Glen Murray	.10
82	Mattias Norstrom	.10
83	Ian Laperriere	.10
84	Mark Recchi	.20
85	Jose Theodore	.20
86	Vincent Damphousse	.10
87	Sebastian Bordeleau	.10
88	Darcy Tucker	.10
89	Martin Rucinsky	.10
90	Jocelyn Thibault	.25
91	Doug Gilmour	.25
92	Brian Rolston	.10
93	Jay Pandolfo	.10
94	John MacLean	.10
95	Scott Stevens	.10
96	Dave Andreychuk	.10
97	Denis Pederson	.10
98	Bryan Berard	.25
99	Zigmund Palffy	.50
100	Bryan McCabe	.10
101	Rich Pilon	.10
102	Eric Fichaud	.20
103	Todd Bertuzzi	.10
104	Robert Reichel	.10
105	Christian Dube	.10
106	Niklas Sundstrom	.10
107	Mike Richter	.30
108	Adam Graves	.10
109	Wayne Gretzky	3.00
110	Bruce Driver	.10
111	Esa Tikkanen	.10
112	Daniel Alfredsson	.20
113	Ron Tugnutt	.10
114	Steve Duchesne	.10
115	Bruce Gardiner	.10
116	Sergei Zholtok	.10
117	Alexandre Daigle	.10
118	Wade Redden	.10
119	Mikael Renberg	.10
120	Trent Klatt	.10
121	Rod Brind'Amour	.20
122	Dainius Zubrus	.40
123	John LeClair	.50
124	Janne Niinimaa	.20
125	*Vaclav Prospal*	.75
126	Keith Tkachuk	.50
127	Jeremy Roenick	.25
128	Mike Gartner	.10
129	Nikolai Khabibulin	.20
130	Chad Kilger	.10
131	Shane Doan	.10
132	Cliff Ronning	.10
133	Patrick Lalime	.10
134	Greg Johnson	.10
135	Ron Francis	.20
136	Darius Kasparaitis	.10
137	Petr Nedved	.10
138	Jason Wooley	.10
139	Frederik Olausson	.10
140	Harry York	.10
141	Brett Hull	.50
142	Chris Pronger	.10
143	Jim Campbell	.10
144	Libor Zabransky	.10

145	Grant Fuhr	.25
146	Pavol Demitra	.10
147	Owen Nolan	.20
148	Stephen Guolla	.10
149	Marcus Ragnarsson	.10
150	Bernie Nicholls	.10
151	Todd Gill	.10
152	Shean Donovan	.10
153	Corey Schwab	.10
154	Dino Ciccarelli	.10
155	Chris Gratton	.20
156	Alexander Selivanov	.10
157	Roman Hamrlik	.10
158	Daymond Langkow	.10
159	Paul Ysebaert	.10
160	Steve Sullivan	.10
161	Sergei Berezin	.20
162	Fredrik Modin	.10
163	Todd Warriner	.10
164	Wendel Clark	.10
165	Jason Podollan	.10
166	Darby Hendrickson	.10
167	Martin Gelinas	.10
168	Pavel Bure	1.00
169	Trevor Linden	.10
170	Mike Sillinger	.10
171	Corey Hirsch	.10
172	Lonny Bohonos	.10
173	Markus Naslund	.10
174	Steve Konowalchuk	.10
175	Dale Hunter	.10
176	Joe Juneau	.10
177	Adam Oates	.25
178	Bill Ranford	.10
179	Pat Peake	.10
180	Sergei Gonchar	.10
181	*Mike Leclerc* (Star Rookie)	.25
182	*Randy Robitaille* (Star Rookie)	.25
183	Paxton Schafer (Star Rookie)	.10
184	*Rumun Ndur* (Star Rookie)	.10
185	*Christian Laflamme* (Star Rookie)	.10
186	*Wade Belak* (Star Rookie)	.10
187	*Mike Knuble* (Star Rookie)	.10
188	Steve Kelly (Star Rookie)	.10
189	*Patrik Elias* (Star Rookie)	.75
190	*Ken Belanger* (Star Rookie)	.10
191	*Colin Forbes* (Star Rookie)	.20
192	Juha Ylonen (Star Rookie)	.10
193	David Cooper (Star Rookie)	.10
194	*D.J. Smith* (Star Rookie)	.10
195	Jaroslav Svejkovsky (Star Rookie)	.50
196	Tie Domi (Fan Favorites)	.10
197	Bob Probert (Fan Favorites)	.10
198	Doug Gilmour (Fan Favorites)	.20
199	Dino Ciccarelli (Fan Favorites)	.10
200	Martin Gelinas (Fan Favorites)	.10
201	Tony Twist (Fan Favorites)	.10
202	Claude Lemieux (Fan Favorites)	.10
203	Vladimir Konstantinov (Fan Favorites)	.10
204	Ulf Samuelsson (Fan Favorites)	.10
205	Chris Simon (Fan Favorites)	.10
206	Gino Odjick (Fan Favorites)	.10
207	Mike Grier (Fan Favorites)	.10
208	Tony Amonte (Fan Favorites)	.10
209	Checklist Wayne Gretzky	1.50
210	Checklist Patrick Roy	1.00
211	Paul Kariya	2.00
212	J.J. Daigneault	.10
213	Dmitri Mironov	.10
214	Joe Sacco	.10
215	Richard Park	.10
216	*Espen Knutsen*	.25
217	Dave Karpa	.10
218	Joe Thornton	1.50
219	Sergei Samsonov	.75
220	*P.J. Axelsson*	.25
221	Ted Donato	.10
222	Dean Chynoweth	.10
223	*Rob Tallas*	.20
224	Mattias Timander	.10
225	Dominik Hasek	1.25
226	Erik Rasmussen	.10
227	Mike Peca	.10
228	Rob Ray	.10
229	Vaclav Varada	.10
230	Curtis Brown	.10
231	Jay McKee	.10
232	Theoren Fleury	.20
233	*Derek Morris*	.10
234	Chris Dingman	.10
235	Chris O'Sullivan	.10
236	Rick Tabaracci	.10
237	Tommy Albelin	.10
238	Todd Simpson	.10
239	Sami Kapanen	.10
240	Gary Roberts	.10
241	Kevin Dineen	.10
242	Kevin Haller	.10
243	Nelson Emerson	.10
244	Glen Wesley	.10
245	Tony Amonte	.10
246	Eric Weinrich	.10
247	*Daniel Cleary*	.60
248	Jeff Shantz	.10
249	Jean-Yves Leroux	.10
250	Ethan Moreau	.10
251	Craig Mills	.10
252	Peter Forsberg	1.50
253	Joe Sakic	1.25
254	Valeri Kamensky	.10
255	Adam Foote	.10
256	Josef Marha	.10
257	*Christian Matte*	.20
258	*Aaron Miller*	.10
259	Ed Belfour	.30
260	Jamie Langenbrunner	.10
261	*Juha Lind*	.10
262	Pat Verbeek	.10
263	Sergei Zubov	.10
264	Dave Reid	.10
265	Greg Adams	.10
266	Sergei Fedorov	.75
267	Nicklas Lidstrom	.25
268	Brendan Shanahan	.75
269	Chris Osgood	.40
270	Aaron Ward	.10
271	Vyacheslav Kozlov	.10
272	Kevin Hodson	.25
273	Curtis Joseph	.25
274	Ryan Smyth	.10
275	Dean McAmmond	.10
276	Boris Mironov	.10
277	Dennis Bonvie	.10
278	Kelly Buchberger	.10
279	Kevin Lowe	.10
280	Ray Sheppard	.10
281	Rob Niedermayer	.10
282	Scott Mallanby	.10
283	Terry Carkner	.10
284	Ed Jovanovski	.10
285	Gord Murphy	.10
286	Tom Fitzgerald	.10
287	Jamie Storr	.20
288	*Olli Jokinen*	.75
289	Vladimir Tsyplakov	.10
290	Luc Robitaille	.25
291	Vitali Yachmenev	.10
292	*Donald MacLean*	.10
293	Saku Koivu	.75
294	Andy Moog	.25
295	Patrice Brisebois	.10
296	Brad Brown	.10
297	Turner Stevenson	.10
298	Shayne Corson	.10
299	Brian Savage	.10
300	Martin Brodeur	1.00
301	Scott Niedermayer	.10
302	*Krzysztof Oliwa*	.25
303	Valeri Zelepukin	.10
304	Bobby Holik	.10
305	Ken Daneyko	.10
306	Lyle Odelein	.10
307	Travis Green	.10
308	*Steve Webb*	.20
309	Dan Plante	.10
310	Bryan Smolinski	.10
311	Claude Lapointe	.10
312	Kenny Jonsson	.10
313	Ulf Samuelsson	.10
314	Jeff Beukeboom	.10
315	Mike Keane	.10
316	Brian Leetch	.25
317	Shane Chrula	.10
318	Pat LaFontaine	.20
319	Alexei Kovalev	.10
320	Radek Bonk	.10
321	Alexei Yashin	.25
322	Damian Rhodes	.10
323	Andreas Dackell	.10
324	*Magnus Arvedson*	.20
325	Chris Phillips	.10
326	*Marian Hossa*	1.00
327	Chris Gratton	.20
328	Shjon Podein	.10
329	Paul Coffey	.25
330	Luke Richardson	.10
331	Eric Lindros	2.00
332	Eric Desjardins	.10
333	Joel Otto	.10
334	Craig Janney	.10
335	Oleg Tverdovsky	.10
336	Teppo Numminen	.10
337	Jim McKenzie	.10
338	Dallas Drake	.10
339	Rick Tocchet	.10
340	Brad Isbister	.10
341	Alexei Morozov	.10
342	Jaromir Jagr	2.00
343	Kevin Hatcher	.10
344	Ken Wregget	.10
345	Chris Tamer	.10
346	*Robert Dome*	.20
347	Neil Wilkinson	.10
348	Chris McAlpine	.10
349	Joe Murphy	.10
350	Robert Petrovicky	.10
351	Marc Bergevin	.10
352	Al MacInnis	.20
353	Pierre Turgeon	.20
354	Patrick Marleau	1.25
355	*Marco Sturm*	.50
356	Mike Vernon	.25
357	Al Iafrate	.10
358	Jeff Friesen	.10
359	Viktor Kozlov	.10
360	Tony Granato	.10
361	Mikael Renberg	.10
362	Daren Puppa	.10
363	Roman Hamrlik	.20
364	Rob Zamuner	.10
365	Cory Cross	.10
366	Patrick Poulin	.10
367	Felix Potvin	.40
368	Tie Domi	.10
369	Mats Sundin	.40
370	Jeff Ware	.10
371	Alyn McCauley	.10
372	Mathieu Schneider	.10
373	Craig Wolanin	.10
374	Mark Messier	.60
375	Kirk McLean	.20
376	Donald Brashear	.10
377	Adrian Aucoin	.10
378	Jyrki Lumme	.10
379	Gino Odjick	.10
380	Mattias Ohlund	.10
381	*Jan Bulis*	.40
382	Andrew Brunette	.10
383	Calle Johansson	.10
384	Brendan Witt	.10
385	Mark Tinordi	.10
386	Ken Klee	.10
387	Chris Simon	.10
388	Richard Zednik	.10
389	Ed Jovanovski (Physical Force)	.10
390	Darren McCarty (Physical Force)	.10
391	Darius Kasparaitis (Physical Force)	.10
392	Bryan Marchment (Physical Force)	.10
393	Matthew Barnaby (Physical Force)	.10
394	Chris Chelios (Physical Force)	.25
395	Ulf Samuelsson (Physical Force)	.10
396	Scott Stevens (Physical Force)	.10
397	Derian Hatcher (Physical Force)	.10
398	Chris Pronger (Physical Force)	.10
399	*Mathieu Chouinard* (Program of Excellence)	.25
400	*Jake McCracken* (Program of Excellence)	.25
401	*Bryan Allen* (Program of Excellence)	.75
402	*Christian Chartier* (Program of Excellence)	.25
403	*Jonathan Girard* (Program of Excellence)	.25
404	*Abe Herbst* (Program of Excellence)	.25
405	*Stephen Peat* (Program of Excellence)	.25
406	*Robyn Regehr* (Program of Excellence)	.25
407	*Blair Betts* (Program of Excellence)	.25
408	*Eric Chouinard* (Program of Excellence)	.25
409	*Brett DeCecco* (Program of Excellence)	.25
410	*Rico Fata* (Program of Excellence)	1.00
411	*Simon Gagne* (Program of Excellence)	.25
412	*Vincent Lecavalier* (Program of Excellence)	6.00
413	*Manny Malhotra* (Program of Excellence)	1.00
414	*Norm Milley* (Program of Excellence)	.75
415	*Justin Papineau* (Program of Excellence)	.25
416	*Garrett Prosofsky* (Program of Excellence)	.25
417	*Mike Ribeiro* (Program of Excellence)	.50
418	*Brad Richards* (Program of Excellence)	.10
419	Checklist Wayne Gretzky	1.50
420	Checklist Patrick Roy	1.00

1997-98 Upper Deck Game Dated Moments

A total of 60 cards (30 from each series) were included in the Game Dated Moments insert. The cards were seeded one per 1,500 packs.

		MT
Common Player:		30.00
1	Teemu Selanne	200.00
9	Ray Bourque	100.00
30	Geoff Sanderson	30.00
43	Patrick Roy	500.00
47	Claude Lemieux	30.00
57	Steve Yzerman	350.00
59	Darren McCarty	30.00
60	Mike Vernon	60.00
63	Vladimir Konstantinov	30.00
64	Todd Marchant	30.00
72	John Vanbiesbrouck	200.00
84	Mark Recchi	30.00
85	Jose Theodore	60.00
91	Doug Gilmour	75.00
98	Bryan Berard	60.00
105	Christian Dube	30.00
107	Mike Richter	75.00
109	Wayne Gretzky	700.00
112	Daniel Alfredsson	60.00
118	Wade Redden	30.00
121	Rod Brind'Amour	60.00
124	Janne Niinimaa	30.00
126	Keith Tkachuk	125.00
133	Patrick Lalime	30.00
135	Ron Francis	60.00
141	Brett Hull	125.00
143	Jim Campbell	30.00
147	Owen Nolan	30.00
154	Dino Ciccarelli	30.00
168	Pavel Bure	200.00
211	Paul Kariya	400.00
218	Joe Thornton	200.00
219	Sergei Samsonov	100.00
225	Dominik Hasek	300.00
227	Mike Peca	30.00
232	Theo Fleury	75.00
240	Gary Roberts	30.00
245	Tony Amonte	60.00
252	Peter Forsberg	350.00
253	Joe Sakic	300.00
266	Sergei Fedorov	200.00
267	Nicklas Lidstrom	60.00
268	Brendan Shanahan	200.00
271	Vyacheslav Kozlov	30.00
273	Curtis Joseph	60.00
274	Ryan Smyth	30.00
282	Scott Mellanby	30.00
290	Luc Robitaille	60.00
300	Martin Brodeur	250.00
316	Brian Leetch	60.00
325	Chris Phillips	30.00
329	Paul Coffey	60.00
331	Eric Lindros	400.00
335	Oleg Tverdovsky	60.00
342	Jaromir Jagr	500.00
353	Pierre Turgeon	60.00
354	Patrick Marleau	150.00
360	Tony Granato	30.00
369	Mats Sundin	80.00
374	Mark Messier	100.00

1997-98 Upper Deck Game Jersey

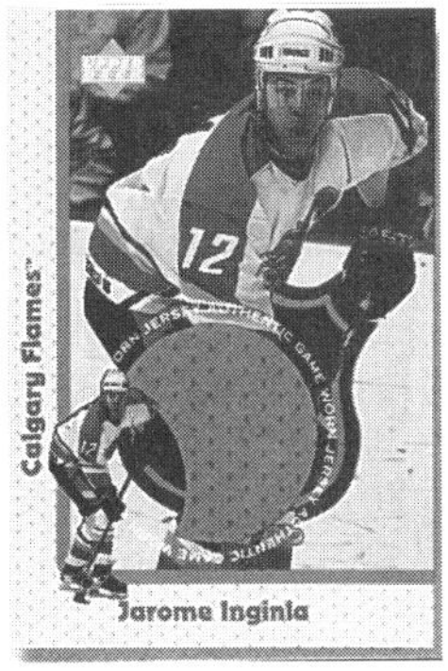

Seven Game Jersey cards were inserted in Series One, while six were included in Series Two. Each card contains a piece of game-worn jersey. Series One featured a Patrick Roy autographed Game Jersey card, hand-numbered to 33. Series Two had signed Wayne Gretzky Game Jersey cards, numbered to 99.

	MT
Complete Set (13):	3400.
Complete Series 1 Set (7):	1800.
Complete Series 2 Set (6):	1600.
Common Player:	150.00
Patrick Roy Autograph:	1800.
W. Gretzky Autograph (99):	2500.
GJ1 Patrick Roy (Home)	600.00
GJ2 Patrick Roy (Road)	600.00
GJ3 Dominik Hasek	350.00
GJ4 Jarome Iginla	150.00
GJ5 Sergei Fedorov	300.00
GJ6 Tony Amonte	150.00
GJ7 Joe Sakic	350.00
GJ8 Wayne Gretzky	1200.
GJ9 Saku Koivu	250.00
GJ11 Mike Richter	200.00
GJ12 Doug Weight	150.00
GJ13 Brendan Shanahan	300.00
GJ14 Brian Leetch	200.00

1997-98 Upper Deck Sixth Sense Masters

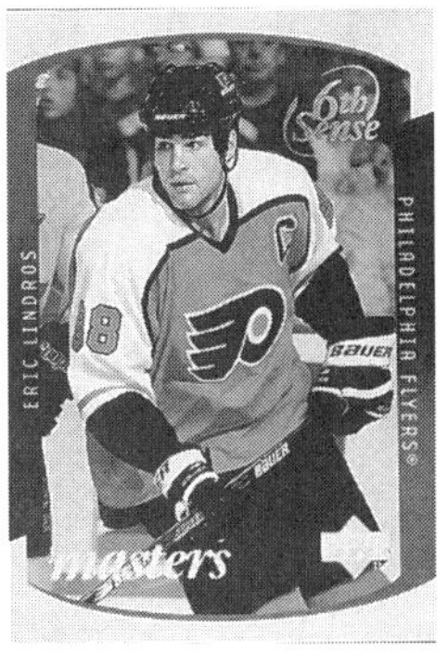

Sixth Sense Masters is a 30-card insert, numbered to 2,000. This insert was seeded in Series Two packs.

	MT
Complete Set (30):	500.00
Common Player:	8.00
SS1 Wayne Gretzky	60.00
SS2 Jaromir Jagr	40.00
SS3 Sergei Fedorov	15.00
SS4 Brett Hull	12.00
SS5 Brian Leetch	8.00
SS6 Joe Thornton	20.00
SS7 Ray Bourque	12.00
SS8 Teemu Selanne	20.00
SS9 Paul Kariya	40.00
SS10 Doug Weight	8.00
SS11 Mark Messier	15.00
SS12 Adam Oates	8.00
SS13 Mats Sundin	12.00
SS14 Brendan Shanahan	20.00
SS15 Saku Koivu	15.00
SS16 Doug Gilmour	10.00
SS17 Eric Lindros	40.00
SS18 Tony Amonte	8.00
SS19 Joe Sakic	25.00
SS20 Steve Yzerman	30.00
SS21 Peter Forsberg	30.00
SS22 Geoff Sanderson	8.00
SS23 Keith Tkachuk	12.00
SS24 Pavel Bure	15.00
SS25 Ron Francis	8.00
SS26 Zigmund Palffy	12.00
SS27 Daniel Alfredsson	8.00
SS28 Bryan Berard	8.00
SS29 Mike Modano	12.00
SS30 Patrick Roy	50.00

1997-98 Upper Deck Sixth Sense Wizards

Sixth Sense Wizards is a 30-card insert which parallels the Sixth Sense Masters insert. Inserted in Series Two packs, the die-cut cards are numbered to 100.

	MT
Common Player:	100.00
SS1 Wayne Gretzky	800.00
SS2 Jaromir Jagr	500.00
SS3 Sergei Fedorov	200.00
SS4 Brett Hull	150.00
SS5 Brian Leetch	100.00
SS6 Joe Thornton	150.00
SS7 Ray Bourque	150.00
SS8 Teemu Selanne	300.00
SS9 Paul Kariya	500.00
SS10 Doug Weight	100.00
SS11 Mark Messier	175.00
SS12 Adam Oates	100.00
SS13 Mats Sundin	150.00
SS14 Brendan Shanahan	250.00
SS15 Saku Koivu	150.00
SS16 Doug Gilmour	100.00
SS17 Eric Lindros	500.00

SS18	Tony Amonte	100.00
SS19	Joe Sakic	350.00
SS20	Steve Yzerman	400.00
SS21	Peter Forsberg	400.00
SS22	Geoff Sanderson	100.00
SS23	Keith Tkachuk	150.00
SS24	Pavel Bure	300.00
SS25	Ron Francis	100.00
SS26	Zigmund Palffy	150.00
SS27	Daniel Alfredsson	100.00
SS28	Bryan Berard	100.00
SS29	Mike Modano	150.00
SS30	Patrick Roy	600.00

1997-98 Upper Deck Smooth Grooves

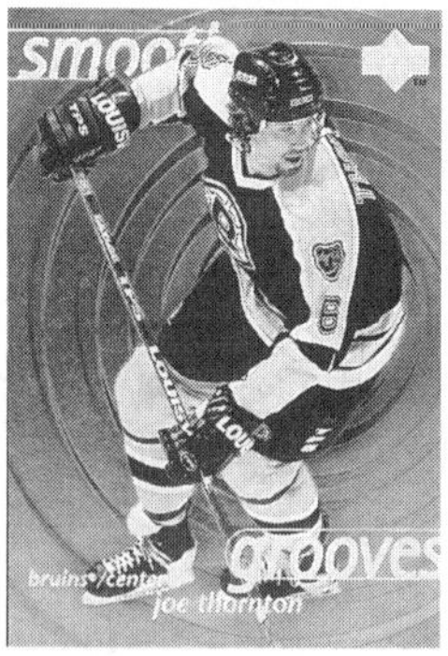

Smooth Grooves is a 60-card insert seeded one per four Series Two packs.

		MT
Complete Set (60):		75.00
Common Player:		.50
SG1	Wayne Gretzky	10.00
SG2	Patrick Roy	8.00
SG3	Patrick Marleau	3.00
SG4	Martin Brodeur	3.00
SG5	Zigmund Palffy	1.50
SG6	Joe Thornton	5.00
SG7	Chris Chelios	.75
SG8	Teemu Selanne	3.00
SG9	Paul Kariya	6.00
SG10	Tony Amonte	.50
SG11	Mark Messier	2.00
SG12	Jarome Iginla	.50
SG13	Mats Sundin	1.00
SG14	Brendan Shanahan	2.50
SG15	Ed Jovanovski	.50
SG16	Brett Hull	2.00
SG17	Brian Rolston	.50
SG18	Saku Koivu	2.00
SG19	Steve Yzerman	5.00
SG20	Doug Weight	.50
SG21	Peter Forsberg	5.00
SG22	Brian Leetch	.75
SG23	Alexei Yashin	.50
SG24	Owen Nolan	.50
SG25	Mike Grier	.50
SG26	Jere Lehtinen	.50
SG27	Vaclav Prospal	1.50
SG28	Sandis Ozolinsh	.50
SG29	Mike Modano	1.25
SG30	Sergei Samsonov	2.50
SG31	Curtis Joseph	.75
SG32	Daymond Langkow	.50
SG33	Doug Gilmour	.75
SG34	Bryan Berard	.50
SG35	Joe Sakic	4.00
SG36	Wade Redden	.50
SG37	Keith Tkachuk	1.50
SG38	Jaromir Jagr	6.00
SG39	Dominik Hasek	4.00
SG40	Patrick Lalime	.50
SG41	Janne Niinimaa	.50
SG42	Oleg Tverdovsky	.50
SG43	Vitali Yachmenev	.50
SG44	Rob Niedermayer	.50
SG45	Nicklas Lidstrom	.50
SG46	Jim Campbell	.50
SG47	Roman Hamrlik	.50
SG48	Eric Lindros	6.00
SG49	Brian Holzinger	.50
SG50	John LeClair	1.50
SG51	Sergei Berezin	.50
SG52	Jaroslav Svejkovsky	.50
SG53	Mike Richter	1.00
SG54	John Vanbiesbrouck	3.00
SG55	Keith Primeau	.50
SG56	Adam Oates	.75
SG57	Jeremy Roenick	.75
SG58	Pavel Bure	3.00
SG59	Dainius Zubrus	.50
SG60	Jose Theodore	.50

1997-98 Upper Deck The Specialists

The Specialists is a 30-card insert that was featured in Series Two. The cards are numbered to 4,000.

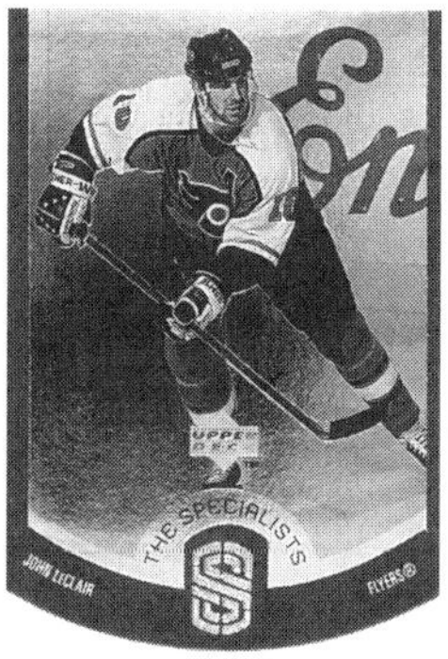

		MT
Complete Set (30):		325.00
Common Player:		6.00
S1	Wayne Gretzky	40.00
S2	Patrick Roy	30.00
S3	Jaromir Jagr	25.00
S4	Joe Sakic	15.00
S5	Mark Messier	10.00
S6	Eric Lindros	25.00
S7	John Vanbiesbrouck	12.00
S8	Teemu Selanne	15.00
S9	Paul Kariya	25.00
S10	Pavel Bure	15.00
S11	Sergei Fedorov	12.00
S12	Peter Bondra	6.00
S13	Mats Sundin	6.00
S14	Brendan Shanahan	15.00
S15	Keith Tkachuk	10.00
S16	Brett Hull	10.00
S17	Jeremy Roenick	6.00
S18	Dominik Hasek	15.00
S19	Steve Yzerman	20.00
S20	John LeClair	12.00
S21	Peter Forsberg	20.00
S22	Zigmund Palffy	10.00
S23	Tony Amonte	6.00
S24	Jarome Iginla	6.00
S25	Curtis Joseph	6.00
S26	Mike Modano	8.00
S27	Ray Bourque	6.00
S28	Brian Leetch	6.00
S29	Bryan Berard	8.00
S30	Martin Brodeur	15.00

1997-98 Upper Deck The Specialists Level 2

The Specialists Level Two parallels the Level One cards. Level Two cards are die-cut and numbered to 100.

		MT
Common Player:		100.00
S1	Wayne Gretzky	800.00
S2	Patrick Roy	600.00
S3	Jaromir Jagr	500.00
S4	Joe Sakic	350.00
S5	Mark Messier	180.00
S6	Eric Lindros	500.00
S7	John Vanbiesbrouck	250.00
S8	Teemu Selanne	300.00
S9	Paul Kariya	500.00
S10	Pavel Bure	300.00
S11	Sergei Fedorov	200.00
S12	Peter Bondra	100.00
S13	Mats Sundin	100.00
S14	Brendan Shanahan	250.00
S15	Keith Tkachuk	150.00
S16	Brett Hull	150.00
S17	Jeremy Roenick	125.00
S18	Dominik Hasek	300.00
S19	Steve Yzerman	450.00
S20	John LeClair	150.00
S21	Peter Forsberg	400.00
S22	Zigmund Palffy	150.00
S23	Tony Amonte	100.00
S24	Jarome Iginla	100.00
S25	Curtis Joseph	100.00
S26	Mike Modano	150.00
S27	Ray Bourque	150.00
S28	Brian Leetch	100.00
S29	Bryan Berard	100.00
S30	Martin Brodeur	300.00

1997-98 Upper Deck Three Star Selects

Inserted one per four Series One packs, these 60 interlocking die-cut cards allow collectors to put a line of three players together.

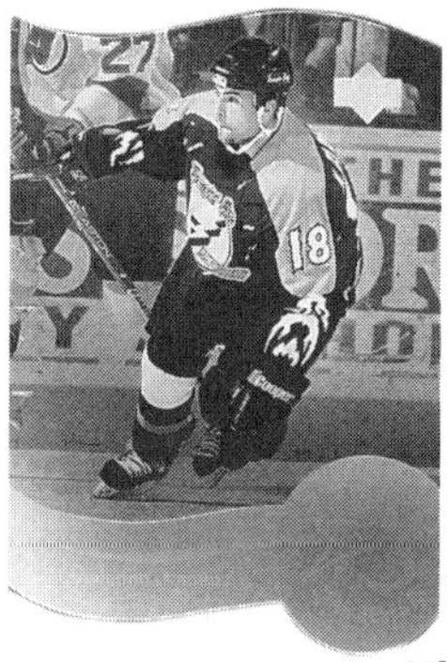

		MT
Complete Set (60):		75.00
Common Player:		.50
T1-A	Eric Lindros	6.00
T1-B	Wayne Gretzky	10.00
T1-C	Peter Forsberg	5.00
T2-A	Dominik Hasek	3.00
T2-B	Patrick Roy	8.00
T2-C	John Vanbiesbrouck	4.00
T3-A	Joe Sakic	4.00
T3-B	Steve Yzerman	5.00
T3-C	Paul Kariya	6.00
T4-A	Bryan Berard	1.00
T4-B	Brian Leetch	.75
T4-C	Chris Chelios	.75
T5-A	Teemu Selanne	2.50
T5-B	Jaromir Jagr	6.00
T5-C	Pavel Bure	2.50
T6-A	Owen Nolan	.50
T6-B	Brendan Shanahan	2.50
T6-C	Keith Tkachuk	1.50
T7-A	Sergei Fedorov	2.50
T7-B	Niklas Sundstrom	.50
T7-C	Mike Peca	.50
T8-A	Janne Niinimaa	.75
T8-B	Saku Koivu	2.00
T8-C	Jere Lehtinen	.50
T9-A	Tony Amonte	.50
T9-B	John LeClair	2.00
T9-C	Brett Hull	1.50
T10-A	Martin Brodeur	2.50
T10-B	Curtis Joseph	.75
T10-C	Mike Richter	1.00
T11-A	Ray Bourque	1.00
T11-B	Mark Messier	1.50
T11-C	Scott Stevens	.50
T12-A	Patrick Lalime	.50
T12-B	Marc Denis	.50
T12-C	Jose Theodore	.75
T13-A	Adam Deadmarsh	.50
T13-B	Doug Weight	.75
T13-C	Bill Guerin	.50
T14-A	Daniel Alfredsson	.50
T14-B	Mats Sundin	.75
T14-C	Nicklas Lidstrom	.50
T15-A	Jim Campbell	.50
T15-B	Dainius Zubrus	1.00
T15-C	Daymond Langkow	.50
T16-A	Mike Grier	.50
T16-B	Mike Modano	1.25
T16-C	Jeremy Roenick	1.00
T17-A	Jason Arnott	.50
T17-B	Trevor Linden	.50
T17-C	Rod Brind'Amour	.75
T18-A	Adam Oates	.75
T18-B	Doug Gilmour	.75
T18-C	Joe Juneau	.50
T19-A	Sergei Berezin	.75
T19-B	Alexander Mogilny	1.00
T19-C	Alexei Zhamnov	.50
T20-A	Derian Hatcher	.50
T20-B	Wade Redden	.50
T20-C	Sandis Ozolinsh	.50

1997-98 Upper Deck Black Diamond

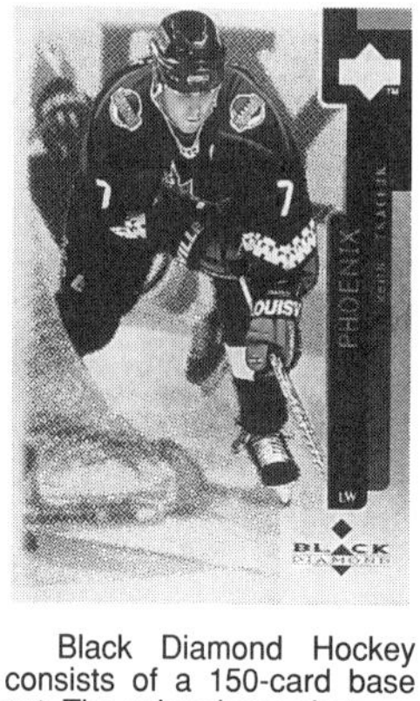

Black Diamond Hockey consists of a 150-card base set. The color player photo on the front of each card is bordered on the right. The bottom-right of the card features the Black Diamond logo and a single black diamond, designating the cards as part of the base set. The base set is paralleled three times. Double Black Diamond (1:1), Triple Black Diamond (1:5) and Quadruple Black Diamond (50 total sets) cards all feature the appropriate number of black diamonds at the bottom-right, designating the cards' level. The only insert is the tiered Premium Cuts.

		MT
Complete Set (150):		100.00
Common Player:		.20
1	Alexei Zhitnik	
2	Adam Graves	.20
3	Keith Primeau	.40
4	Mike Richter	.60
5	Felix Potvin	.60
6	Valeri Bure	.20
7	Mark Messier	.75
8	Dainius Zubrus	.50
9	Owen Nolan	.20
10	Kenny Jonsson	.20
11	Ron Francis	.40
12	Bryan Berard	.40
13	*Eric Messier*	.20
14	Paul Kariya	2.50
15	*Teemu Elomo*	1.00
16	Joe Nieuwendyk	.40
17	Scott Stevens	.20
18	Zigmund Palffy	.75
19	Brett Hull	.75
20	Dominik Hasek	1.50
21	Dino Cicarelli	.20
22	Rob Niedermayer	.20
23	Mark Recchi	.20
24	Brad Isbister	.20
25	*Timo Vertala*	.50
26	*Mika Noronen*	3.00
27	Sandis Ozolinsh	.30
28	Chris Phillips	.20
29	Chris Chelios	.50
30	Jason Dawe	.20
31	Geoff Sanderson	.20
32	Jason Allison	.40
33	Brian Leetch	.40
34	Guy Hebert	.40
35	*David Legwand*	10.00
36	*Josef Boumedienne*	.50
37	Sergei Samsonov	1.00
38	Jason Arnott	.20
39	Chris Osgood	.75
40	Jere Lehtinen	.20
41	Patrick Roy	3.00
42	John Vanbiesbrouck	1.00
43	*Maxim Afinogenov*	.50
44	*Patrik Elias*	.75
45	*Josh Holden*	.20
46	Saku Koivu	.75
47	*Maxim Balmockhnykh*	.40
48	Pasi Petrilainen	.20
49	Robert Reichel	.40
50	Wade Redden	.20
51	Richard Zednik	.20
52	*Ty Jones*	.50
53	Nikolai Khabibulin	.50
54	Kyle McLaren	.20
55	*Daniel Tkaczuk*	2.50
56	Alexei Zhamnov	.20
57	*Donald MacLean*	.20
58	Dave Gagner	.20
59	Jeremy Roenick	.60
60	Ray Bourque	.50
61	Rod Brind'Amour	.40
62	Miroslav Satan	.20
63	Eric Daze	.40
64	Mike Ricci	.20
65	John LeClair	1.00
66	Roman Hamrlik	.20
67	*Kristian Huselius*	.50
68	John MacLean	.20
69	*Roman Lyashenko*	.50
70	Doug Gilmour	.50
71	*Marco Sturm*	2.00
72	Jaromir Jagr	2.50
73	Daniel Alfredsson	.40
74	Daren Puppa	.20
75	Adam Deadmarsh	.40
76	Luc Robitaille	.40
77	Mats Sundin	.60
78	Trevor Linden	.20
79	*Manny Malhotra*	5.00
80	Mike Modano	.75
81	Espen Knutsen	.20
82	Sergei Fedorov	1.00
83	Chris Pronger	.20
84	Doug Weight	.40
85	Bill Ranford	.20
86	Gary Roberts	.20
87	Peter Bondra	.50
88	Robert Dome	.20
89	Jan Bulis	.20
90	Eric Brewer	.20
91	*Nikos Tselios*	.50
92	Scott Mellanby	.20
93	*Vitali Vishnevsky*	.40
94	Derian Hatcher	.20
95	Teemu Selanne	1.00
96	Joe Sakic	1.50
97	Alexander Mogilny	.50
98	*Jesse Boulerice*	.50
99	*Johan Forsander*	.20
100	Pierre Turgeon	.40
101	Tony Amonte	.40
102	*Timo Ahmaoja*	.40
103	Rob Blake	.20
104	*Derek Morris*	.50
105	*Vaclav Prospal*	4.00
106	Peter Forsberg	2.00
107	Shayne Corson	.20
108	*Tyler Moss*	.75
109	Adam Oates	.50
110	Keith Tkachuk	.75
111	Alexei Yashin	.50
112	Joe Thornton	1.50
113	Andy Moog	.50
114	*Daniel Sedin*	4.00
115	Pavel Bure	1.00
116	*Denis Shvidky*	3.00
117	Scott Niedermayer	.20
118	*Mike Johnson*	1.00
119	Nicklas Lidstrom	.40
120	Mattias Ohlund	.20
121	Alexander Selivanov	.20
122	Martin Brodeur	1.50
123	Steve Yzerman	2.00
124	*Yuri Butsayev*	.50
125	*Jeff Farkas*	.40
126	Curtis Joseph	.60
127	Stephane Fiset	.40
128	Alyn McCauley	.20
129	Vyacheslav Kozlov	.20
130	Alexei Morozov	.20
131	*Roberto Luongo*	5.00
132	Jarome Iginla	.20
133	Pat LaFontaine	.40
134	Ed Belfour	.60
135	*Toby Peterson*	.50
136	*Henrik Sedin*	3.00
137	Markus Nilsson	.20
138	Cameron Mann	.20
139	*Ero Somervuori*	.40
140	Patrick Marleau	1.25
141	Ed Jovanovski	.20
142	Yanic Perreault	.20
143	Theoren Fleury	.40
144	Wayne Gretzky	4.00
145	Eric Lindros	2.50
146	Boyd Devereaux	.20
147	Sami Kapanen	.20
148	Grant Fuhr	.75
149	Brendan Shanahan	1.00
150	*Vincent Lecavalier*	12.00

1997-98 Upper Deck Black Diamond Double

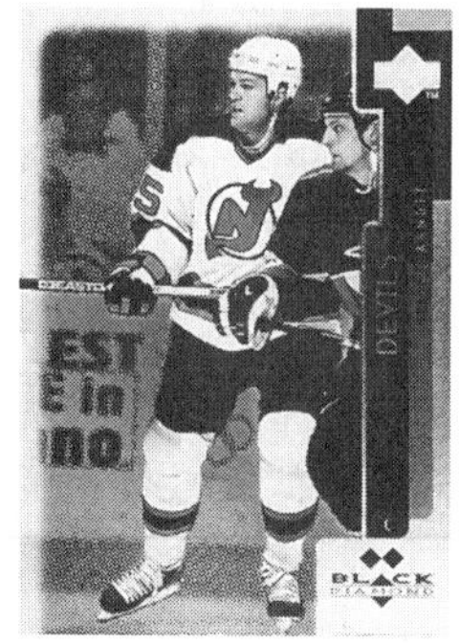

Double Black Diamond cards are designated by two black diamonds in the bottom right corner. This parallel of the Single Black Diamond set was inserted one per pack.

	MT
Doubles:	1x to 2x

1997-98 Upper Deck Black Diamond Triple

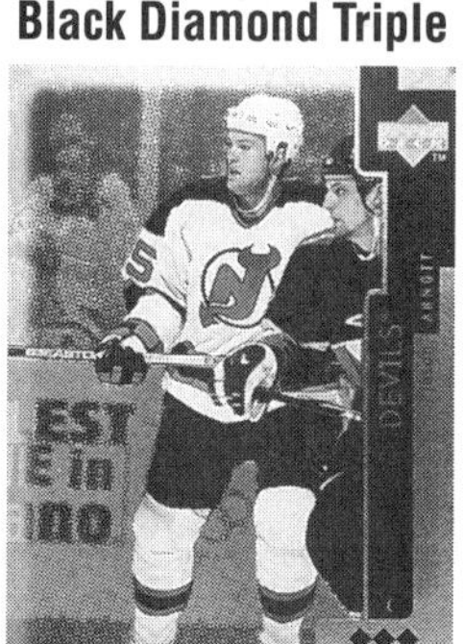

Triple Black Diamond cards are designated by three black diamonds in the bottom right corner. Triple Black Diamond cards were inserted one per five packs.

	MT
Triple Stars:	4x to 8x
Yng Stars & RCs:	2x to 4x

1997-98 Upper Deck Black Diamond Quadruple Diamond

Quadruple Black Diamond cards featured four black diamonds in the lower-right corner. Only 50 total sets were produced.

		MT
Common Player:		25.00
1	Alexei Zhitnik	25.00
2	Adam Graves	25.00
3	Keith Primeau	40.00
4	Mike Richter	50.00
5	Felix Potvin	75.00
6	Valeri Bure	25.00
7	Mark Messier	100.00
8	Dainius Zubrus	50.00
9	Owen Nolan	25.00
10	Kenny Jonsson	25.00
11	Ron Francis	50.00
12	Bryan Berard	40.00
13	Eric Messier	25.00
14	Paul Kariya	250.00
15	*Teemu Elomo*	25.00
16	Joe Nieuwendyk	40.00
17	Scott Stevens	25.00
18	Zigmund Palffy	80.00
19	Brett Hull	100.00
20	Dominik Hasek	125.00
21	Dino Cicarelli	40.00
22	Rob Niedermayer	25.00
23	Mark Recchi	25.00
24	Brad Isbister	25.00
25	*Timo Vertala*	25.00
26	Mika Noronen	25.00
27	Sandis Ozolinsh	25.00
28	Chris Phillips	25.00
29	Chris Chelios	50.00
30	Jason Dawe	25.00
31	Geoff Sanderson	25.00
32	Jason Allison	40.00
33	Brian Leetch	50.00
34	Guy Hebert	50.00
35	*David Legwand*	25.00
36	*Josef Boumedienne*	25.00
37	Sergei Samsonov	75.00
38	Jason Arnott	25.00
39	Chris Osgood	75.00
40	Jere Lehtinen	25.00
41	Patrick Roy	300.00
42	John Vanbiesbrouck	100.00
43	*Maxim Afinogenov*	25.00
44	Patrik Elias	25.00
45	Josh Holden	25.00
46	Saku Koivu	75.00
47	*Maxim Balmockhnykh*	25.00
48	Pasi Petrilainen	25.00
49	Robert Reichel	25.00
50	Wade Redden	25.00
51	Richard Zednik	25.00
52	*Ty Jones*	25.00
53	Nikolai Khabibulin	50.00
54	Kyle McLaren	25.00
55	*Daniel Tkaczuk*	100.00
56	Alexei Zhamnov	25.00
57	Donald MacLean	25.00
58	Dave Gagner	25.00
59	Jeremy Roenick	60.00
60	Ray Bourque	60.00
61	Rod Brind'Amour	50.00
62	Miroslav Satan	25.00
63	Eric Daze	40.00
64	Mike Ricci	25.00
65	John LeClair	100.00
66	Roman Hamrlik	25.00
67	*Kristian Huselius*	25.00
68	John MacLean	25.00
69	*Roman Lyashenko*	25.00
70	Doug Gilmour	50.00
71	*Marco Sturm*	60.00
72	Jaromir Jagr	250.00
73	Daniel Alfredsson	40.00
74	Daren Puppa	25.00
75	Adam Deadmarsh	40.00
76	Luc Robitaille	50.00
77	Mats Sundin	60.00
78	Trevor Linden	25.00
79	*Manny Malhotra*	50.00
80	Mike Modano	75.00
81	Espen Knutsen	25.00
82	Sergei Fedorov	100.00
83	Chris Pronger	40.00
84	Doug Weight	40.00
85	Bill Ranford	25.00
86	Gary Roberts	25.00
87	Peter Bondra	50.00
88	Robert Dome	25.00
89	Jan Bulis	25.00
90	Eric Brewer	25.00
91	*Nikos Tselios*	25.00
92	Scott Mellanby	25.00
93	*Vitali Vishnevsky*	25.00
94	Derian Hatcher	25.00
95	Teemu Selanne	100.00
96	Joe Sakic	150.00
97	Alexander Mogilny	50.00
98	*Jesse Boulerice*	25.00
99	*Johan Forsander*	25.00
100	Pierre Turgeon	40.00
101	Tony Amonte	50.00
102	*Timo Ahmaoja*	25.00
103	Rob Blake	25.00
104	*Derek Morris*	25.00
105	*Vaclav Prospal*	50.00
106	Peter Forsberg	200.00
107	Shayne Corson	25.00
108	*Tyler Moss*	40.00
109	Adam Oates	50.00
110	Keith Tkachuk	80.00
111	Alexei Yashin	50.00
112	Joe Thornton	80.00
113	Andy Moog	60.00
114	*Daniel Sedin*	25.00
115	Pavel Bure	100.00
116	*Denis Shvidry*	25.00
117	Scott Niedermayer	25.00
118	*Mike Johnson*	50.00
119	Nicklas Lidstrom	50.00
120	Mattias Ohlund	25.00
121	Alexander Selivanov	25.00
122	Martin Brodeur	125.00
123	Steve Yzerman	200.00
124	*Yuri Butsayev*	25.00
125	*Jeff Farkas*	25.00
126	Curtis Joseph	60.00
127	Stephane Fiset	25.00
128	Alyn McCauley	25.00
129	Vyacheslav Kozlov	25.00
130	Alexei Morozov	25.00
131	*Roberto Luongo*	150.00
132	Jarome Iginla	25.00
133	Pat LaFontaine	40.00
134	Ed Belfour	60.00
135	*Toby Peterson*	25.00
136	*Henrik Sedin*	25.00
137	Markus Nilsson	25.00
138	Cameron Mann	25.00
139	*Ero Somervuori*	25.00
140	Patrick Marleau	50.00
141	Ed Jovanovski	25.00
142	Yanic Perreault	25.00
143	Theoren Fleury	50.00
144	Wayne Gretzky	400.00
145	Eric Lindros	250.00
146	Boyd Devereaux	25.00
147	Sami Kapanen	25.00
148	Grant Fuhr	75.00
149	Brendan Shanahan	100.00
150	*Vincent Lecavalier*	150.00

1997-98 Upper Deck Black Diamond Premium Cut

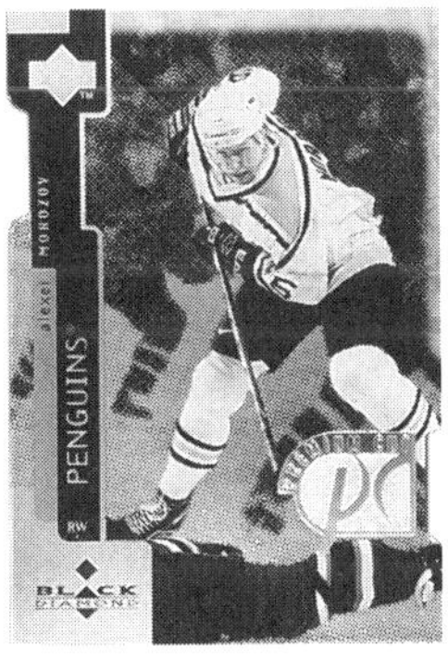

Premium Cuts is a 30-card, four-tiered insert. The designs are identical to the regular Black Diamond cards except the border is on the left side and the cards are die-cut. Single Black Diamond Premium Cut cards are inserted 1:7, Doubles 1:15, Triples 1:30 and Quadruples 1:180. Mystery Premium Cut cards are a hobby-only insert and feature a horizontal layout and die-cutting.

		MT
Complete Set (30):		200.00
Common Player:		4.00
Double Diamonds:		1x to 1.5x
Triple Diamonds:		1.5x to 2x
Quadruple Diamonds:		5x to 10x
PC1	Wayne Gretzky	25.00
PC2	Patrick Roy	20.00
PC3	Brendan Shanahan	8.00
PC4	Ray Bourque	5.00
PC5	Alexei Morozov	4.00
PC6	John LeClair	8.00
PC7	Steve Yzerman	12.00
PC8	Patrik Elias	4.00
PC9	Pavel Bure	8.00
PC10	Brian Leetch	5.00
PC11	Peter Forsberg	12.00
PC12	Marco Sturm	4.00
PC13	Eric Lindros	15.00
PC14	Keith Tkachuk	6.00
PC15	Teemu Selanne	8.00
PC16	Bryan Berard	4.00
PC17	Joe Thornton	8.00
PC18	Brett Hull	6.00
PC19	Nicklas Lidstrom	4.00
PC20	Jaromir Jagr	15.00
PC21	Vaclav Prospal	6.00
PC22	Pat LaFontaine	4.00
PC23	Mark Messier	6.00
PC24	Martin Brodeur	10.00
PC25	Mike Modano	6.00
PC26	Paul Kariya	15.00
PC27	Mike Johnson	6.00
PC28	Sergei Samsonov	6.00
PC29	Joe Sakic	10.00
PC30	Mats Sundin	6.00

1997-98 Upper Deck Diamond Vision

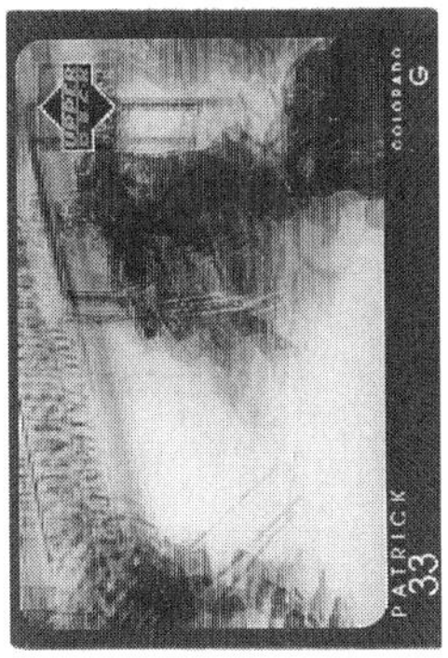

Diamond Vision is a motion card product. The base set consists of 25 horizontal cards, each with an action sequence of the featured player. The base set is paralleled in the Signature Moves set. Inserts include Defining Moments and REEL Time.

		MT
Complete Set (25):		200.00
Common Player:		4.00
1	Wayne Gretzky	25.00
2	Patrick Roy	20.00
3	Jaromir Jagr	15.00
4	Steve Yzerman	12.00
5	Martin Brodeur	10.00
6	Paul Kariya	15.00
7	John Vanbiesbrouck	8.00
8	Ray Bourque	4.00
9	Theoren Fleury	4.00
10	Pavel Bure	10.00
11	Brendan Shanahan	8.00
12	Brian Leetch	4.00
13	Owen Nolan	4.00
14	Peter Forsberg	12.00
15	Doug Weight	4.00
16	Teemu Selanne	10.00
17	Mats Sundin	4.00
18	Keith Tkachuk	6.00
19	Tony Amonte	4.00
20	Joe Sakic	10.00
21	Zigmund Palffy	6.00
22	Eric Lindros	15.00
23	Sergei Fedorov	8.00
24	Dominik Hasek	10.00
25	Brett Hull	6.00

1997-98 Upper Deck Diamond Vision Signature Moves

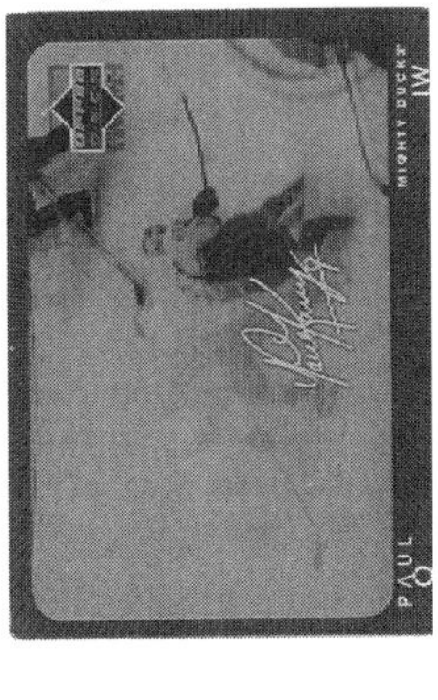

Signature Moves is a parallel of the Diamond Vision base set. Each of the 25 cards includes the pictured player's autograph. Signature Moves were inserted one per five packs.

	MT
Signature Moves:	1x to 2x

1997-98 Upper Deck Diamond Vision Reel Time

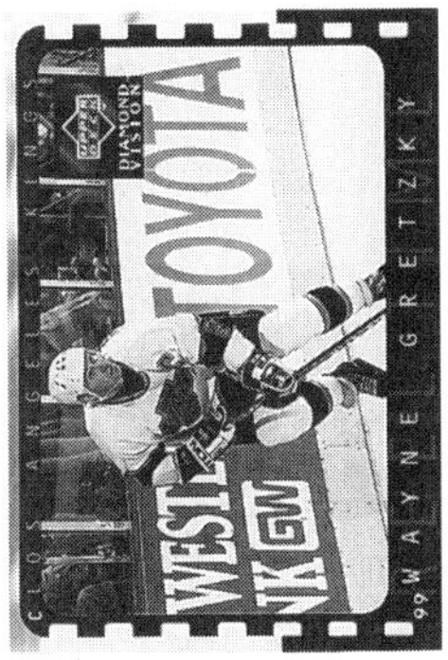

REEL Time is a one-card insert (1:500). This motion card features one of the greatest moments in Wayne Gretzky's career.

	MT
Wayne Gretzky (RT1):	200.00

1997-98 Upper Deck Diamond Vision Defining Moments

Defining Moments is a six-card insert that uses lenticular motion technology to show a "defining moment" in the player's career. Defining Moment cards were inserted one per 40 packs.

		MT
Complete Set (6):		300.00
Common Player:		30.00
DM1	Wayne Gretzky	100.00
DM2	Patrick Roy	75.00
DM3	Steve Yzerman	50.00
DM4	Jaromir Jagr	60.00
DM5	Joe Sakic	40.00
DM6	Brendan Shanahan	30.00

1997-98 Upper Deck Ice

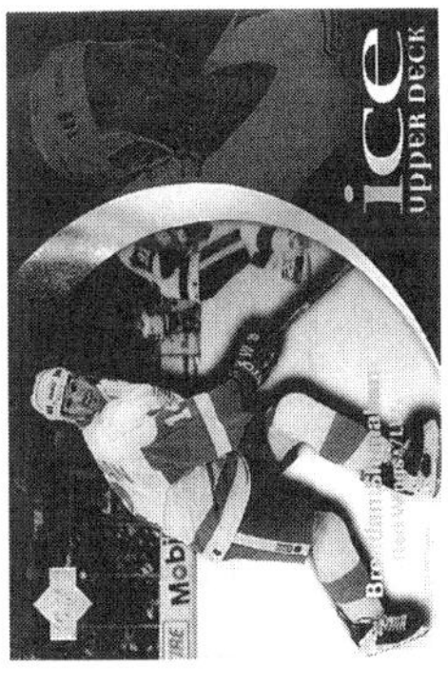

Upper Deck ICE consists of a 90-card base set with three partial parallels, one full parallel and two inserts. The base set is printed on acetate and features two photos of the player on the front. The Power Shift parallel adds gold foil to the 90 cards (1:23). The three 30-card partial parallels are ICE Performers (1:2), ICE Phenoms (1:5) and ICE Legends (1:11). The inserts are ICE Champions and Lethal Lines. Each insert has a Level 2.

		MT
Complete Set (90):		75.00
Common Player:		.50
Power Shift (1-90):		5x to 10x
1	Nelson Emerson	.50
2	Derian Hatcher	.50
3	Mike Richter	1.00
4	Sergei Berezin	.75
5	Nicklas Lidstrom	.75
6	Ryan Smyth	.75
7	Martin Brodeur	3.00
8	Geoff Sanderson	.50
9	Doug Weight	.75
10	Owen Nolan	.75
11	Daniel Alfredsson	.75
12	Peter Bondra	1.00
13	Jim Campbell	.50
14	Rob Niedermayer	.50
15	Daymond Langkow	.50
16	Zigmund Palffy	2.00
17	Adam Oates	.75
18	Adam Deadmarsh	.50
19	Brian Holzinger	.50
20	Jarome Iginla	.75
21	Janne Niinimaa	.50
22	Dino Ciccarelli	.50
23	Mark Recchi	.50
24	Sandis Ozolinsh	.75
25	Keith Primeau	.75
26	Ed Jovanovski	.50
27	Jeremy Roenick	1.50
28	Alexei Yashin	.75
29	Felix Potvin	1.00
30	Chris Osgood	1.50
31	Marc Denis	.50
32	*Tyler Moss*	1.00
33	Kevin Hodson	.75
34	Jamie Storr	.75
35	Roman Turek	.75
36	Jose Theodore	1.00
37	Magnus Arvedson	.50
38	Daniel Cleary	1.00
39	*Mike Knuble*	.50
40	Jaroslav Svejkovsky	.50
41	Patrick Marleau	3.00
42	Mattias Ohlund	.50
43	Sergei Samsonov	1.50
44	*Espen Knutsen*	1.00
45	*Vaclav Prospal*	2.00
46	Joe Thornton	4.00
47	Chris Phillips	.50
48	*Mike Johnson*	2.00
49	Dainius Zubrus	1.00
50	Wade Redden	.50
51	*Derek Morris*	1.00
52	*Marco Sturm*	1.50
53	Don MacLean	.50
54	Bryan Berard	.75
55	Richard Zednik	.50
56	Alexei Morozov	.50
57	Erik Rasmussen	.50
58	*Olli Jokinen*	2.50
59	*Jan Bulis*	1.00
60	*Patrik Elias*	1.00
61	Peter Forsberg	5.00
62	Mike Modano	1.50
63	Tony Amonte	1.00
64	Theoren Fleury	.75
65	Ron Francis	1.00
66	Brett Hull	2.00
67	Chris Chelios	1.00
68	Jaromir Jagr	6.00
69	Sergei Fedorov	2.50
70	Keith Tkachuk	1.50
71	Mark Messier	2.50
72	Pat LaFontaine	.75
73	Mats Sundin	1.00
74	John Vanbiesbrouck	2.50
75	John LeClair	2.00
76	Brian Leetch	.75
77	Ray Bourque	1.00
78	Saku Koivu	1.50
79	Joe Sakic	4.00
80	Teemu Selanne	2.50
81	Curtis Joseph	1.00
82	Doug Gilmour	.75
83	Patrick Roy	8.00
84	Brendan Shanahan	2.50
85	Paul Kariya	6.00
86	Pavel Bure	2.50
87	Dominik Hasek	3.00
88	Eric Lindros	6.00
89	Steve Yzerman	5.00
90	Wayne Gretzky	10.00

1997-98 Upper Deck Ice Power Shift

Power Shift is a parallel of the 90-card ICE base set. Inserted 1:23, the cards feature gold foil.

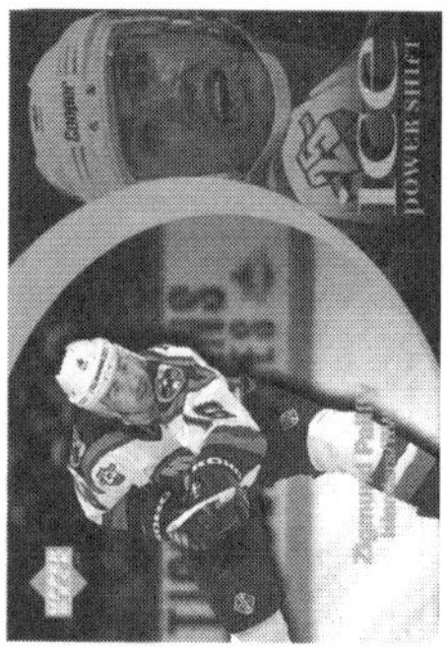

	MT
Power Shift Stars:	5x to 10x
Yng Stars & RCs:	4x to 8x

1997-98 Upper Deck Ice Parallel

Three 30-card partial parallels of the ICE base set were produced: ICE Performers (1:2), ICE Phenoms (1:5) and ICE Legends (1:11).

	MT
Performers (1-30):	1x to 2x
Phenoms (31-60):	1.5x to 2x
Legends (61-90):	4x to 6x

1997-98 Upper Deck Ice Champions

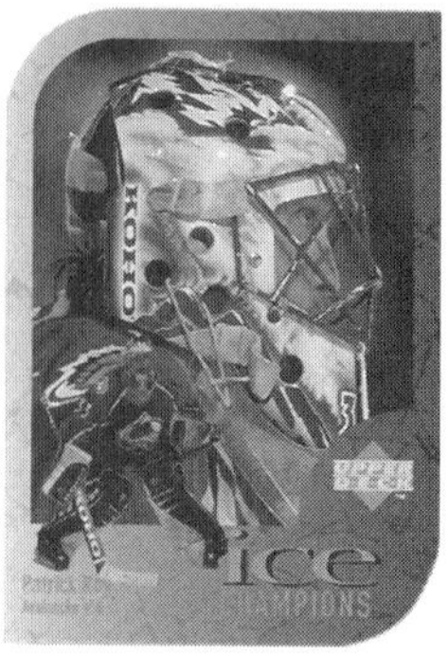

This 20-card insert is printed on a combination Light FX/ litho/acetate card. The cards have two photos of the player on the front. The insertion rate was 1:47. ICE Champions Level 2 is die-cut and numbered to 100.

		MT
Complete Set (20):		675.00
Common Player:		15.00
Level 2 (100 sets):		5x to 8x
IC1	Wayne Gretzky	100.00
IC2	Patrick Roy	75.00
IC3	Eric Lindros	60.00
IC4	Saku Koivu	20.00
IC5	Dominik Hasek	30.00
IC6	Joe Thornton	25.00
IC7	Martin Brodeur	30.00
IC8	Teemu Selanne	25.00
IC9	Paul Kariya	60.00
IC10	Joe Sakic	40.00
IC11	Mark Messier	25.00
IC12	Peter Forsberg	50.00
IC13	Mats Sundin	20.00
IC14	Brendan Shanahan	25.00
IC15	Keith Tkachuk	20.00
IC16	Brett Hull	20.00
IC17	John Vanbiesbrouck	25.00
IC18	Jaromir Jagr	60.00
IC19	Steve Yzerman	50.00
IC20	Sergei Samsonov	15.00

1997-98 Upper Deck Ice Lethal Lines

Lethal Lines is a 30-card insert seeded one per 11 packs. The die-cut cards can fit together to form a line of three superstar players. Lethal Lines Level 2 (1:120) adds a special foil treatment to the cards.

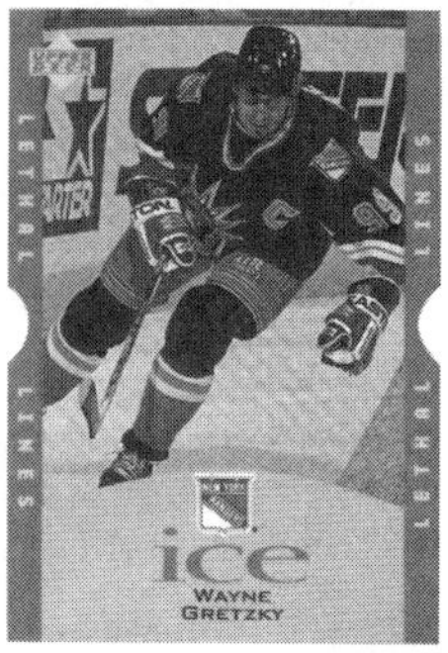

		MT
Complete Set (30):		325.00
Common Player:		4.00
Level 2:		4x to 6x
L1A	Paul Kariya	30.00
L1B	Wayne Gretzky	50.00
L1C	Joe Thornton	15.00
L2A	Brendan Shanahan	15.00
L2B	Eric Lindros	30.00
L2C	Jaromir Jagr	30.00
L3A	Keith Tkachuk	12.00
L3B	Mark Messier	12.00
L3C	Owen Nolan	4.00
L4A	Daniel Alfredsson	4.00
L4B	Peter Forsberg	25.00
L4C	Mats Sundin	8.00
L5A	Ryan Smyth	4.00
L5B	Steve Yzerman	25.00
L5C	Jarome Iginla	4.00
L6A	Sergei Samsonov	8.00
L6B	Igor Larionov	4.00
L6C	Sergei Fedorov	15.00
L7A	Patrik Elias	6.00
L7B	Alexei Morozov	4.00
L7C	Vaclav Prospal	6.00
L8A	John LeClair	15.00
L8B	Mike Modano	8.00
L8C	Brett Hull	10.00
L9A	Olli Jokinen	8.00
L9B	Saku Koivu	10.00
L9C	Teemu Selanne	15.00
L10A	Brian Leetch	4.00
L10B	Patrick Roy	40.00
L10C	Nicklas Lidstrom	4.00

1998 Bowman CHL

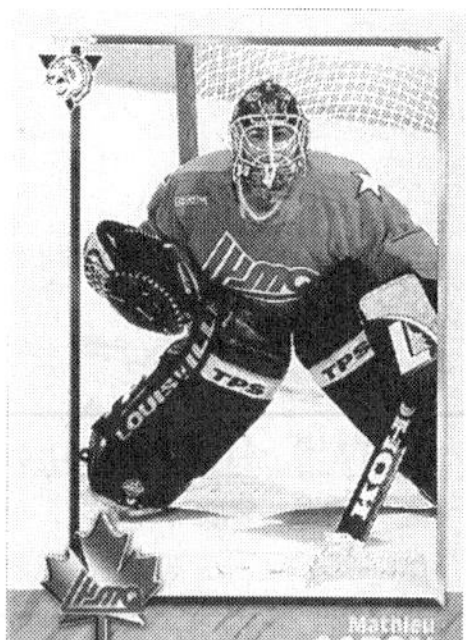

Bowman CHL Hockey consists of a 165-card base set featuring the top players from the Canadian Hockey League. The set has 120 cards of CHL players, 40 cards of 1998 NHL draft picks, four CHL game MVP cards and one checklist. The set is paralleled in O-Pee-Chee International and Bowman Golden Anniversary. The inserts include Autographs and Scout's Choice.

		MT
Complete Set (165)		40.00
Common Player:		.20
1	Robert Esche	.40
2	Chris Hajt	.20
3	Mark McMahon	.20
4	Jeff Brown	.20
5	Richard Jackman	.50
6	Greg Labenski	.20
7	Marek Posmyk	.40
8	Brian Willsie	.40
9	Jason Ward	1.00
10	Manny Malhotra	4.00
11	Matt Cooke	.40
12	Mike Gorman	.40
13	Rodney Richard	.20
14	David Legwand	5.00
15	Jonathan Sim	.20
16	Peter Sarno	.50
17	Andrew Long	.20
18	Peter Cava	.40
19	Colin Pepperall	.20
20	Jay Legault	.50
21	Brian Finley	1.25
22	Martin Skoula	.50
23	Brian Campbell	.20
24	Sean Blanchard	.40
25	Bryan Allen	.50
26	Peter Hogan	.20
27	Nick Boynton	.40
28	Matt Bradley	.40
29	Jeremy Adduono	.40
30	Mike Henrich	1.00
31	Justin Papineau	1.50
32	Bujar Amidovski	.75
33	Robert Mailloux	.20
34	Daniel Tkaczuk	2.00
35	Sean Avery	.20
36	Mark Bell	1.00
37	Kevin Colley	.20
38	Norm Milley	1.50
39	Scott Barney	.40
40	Joel Trottier	.20
41	Brent Belecki	.40
42	Randy Petruk	.40
43	Brad Ference	1.50
44	Perry Johnson	.20
45	Joel Kwiatkowski	.20
46	Zenith Komarniski	.20
47	Greg Kuznik	.20
48	Andrew Ference	.20
49	Jason Deleurme	.20
50	Trent Whitfield	.40
51	Dylan Gyori	.20
52	Todd Robinson	.20
53	Marian Hossa	2.50
54	Mike Hurley	.20
55	Greg Leeb	.20
56	Andrej Podkonicky	.20
57	Quinn Hancock	.20
58	Marian Cisar	.75
59	Brett DeCecco	.20
60	Brenden Morrow	.50
61	Evan Lindsay	.50
62	Terry Friesen	.50
63	Ryan Shannon	.20
64	Michal Rozsival	.50
65	Luc Theoret	.20
66	Brad Stuart	.50
67	Burke Henry	.20
68	Cory Sarich	.20
69	Martin Sonnenberg	.20
70	Mark Smith	.40
71	Shawn McNeil	.20
72	Brad Moran	.20
73	Josh Holden	.40
74	Cory Cyrenne	.75
75	Shane Willis	.20
76	Stefan Cherneski	1.00
77	Jay Henderson	.20
78	Ronald Petrovicky	.20
79	Sergei Varlamov	1.50
80	Chad Hinz	.20
81	Mathieu Garon	1.50
82	Mathieu Chouinard	2.00
83	Dominic Perna	.20
84	Didier Tremblay	.20
85	Mike Ribiero	1.50
86	Marty Johnston	.20
87	Remi Royer	.50
88	Patrick Pelchat	.20
89	Daniel Corso	.20
90	Francois Fortier	.50
91	Marc-Andre Gaudet	.20
92	Francois Beauchemin	.20
93	Michel Tremblay	.20
94	Jean-Philippe Pare	.20
95	Francois Methot	.40
96	David Thibeault	.20
97	Jonathan Girard	.50
98	Karol Bartanus	.40
99	Peter Ratchuk	.20
100	Pierre Dagenais	.50
101	Philippe Sauve	1.50
102	Remi Bergeron	.40
103	Vincent Lecavalier	5.00
104	Eric Chouinard	1.50
105	Oleg Timchenko	.20
106	Sebastien Roger	.20
107	Simon Gagne	.75
108	Alex Tanguay	2.00
109	David Gosselin	.20
110	Ramzi Abid	1.00
111	Eric Drouin	.20
112	Dominic Auger	.20
113	Martin Moise	.20
114	Randy Copley	.50
115	Alexandre Mathieu	.20
116	Brad Richards	.50
117	Dmitri Tolkunov	.20
118	Alexei Tezikov	.20
119	Derrick Walser	.20
120	Adam Borzecki	.20
121	Ramzi Abid	1.50
122	Brett Allan	.50
123	Mark Bell	1.00
124	Blair Betts	.40
125	Randy Copley	.50
126	Simon Gagne	.75
127	Mike Henrich	1.00
128	Vincent Lecavalier	5.00
129	Norm Milley	1.50
130	Chris Neilsen	.20
131	Rico Fata	2.50
132	Mike Ribeiro	1.50
133	Bryan Allen	.50
134	John Erskine	.20
135	Jonathan Girard	.50
136	Stephen Peat	.20
137	Robyn Regehr	.40
138	Brad Stuart	.50
139	Patrick Desrochers	1.50
140	Jason Labarbera	.40
141	David Cameron	.50
142	Jonathan Cheechoo	.75
143	Eric Chouinard	1.50
144	Brent Gauvreau	.50
145	Scott Gomez	.75
146	Jeff Heerema	.50
147	David Legwand	4.00
148	Manny Malhotra	1.00
149	Justin Papineau	.75
150	Andrew Peters	.40
151	Michael Rupp	.75
152	Alex Tanguay	2.00
153	Francois Beauchemin	.20
154	Mathieu Biron	.40
155	Jiri Fischer	.40
156	Alex Henry	.20
157	Kyle Rossiter	.20
158	Martin Skoula	.75
159	Mathieu Chouinard	2.00
160	Philippe Sauve	1.50
161	Brian Finley	.75
162	Brent Belecki	.40
163	Dominic Perna	.20
164	Jonathan Cheechoo	.75
165	Checklist	.20

1998 Bowman CHL Gold Anniversary

Bowman Golden Anniversary is a parallel of the 165-card base set. The set is sequentially numbered to 50, with an insertion rate of 1:57.

	MT
Gold Anniversary:	15x to 25x

1998 Bowman CHL OPC Internationals

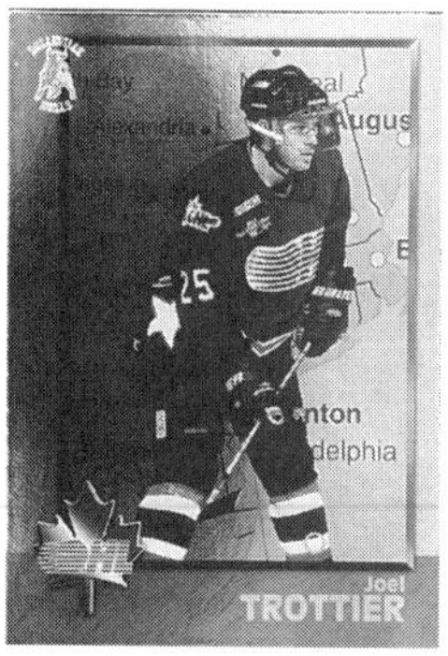

O-Pee-Chee International is a parallel of the 165-card base set. Inserted one per pack, the card backgrounds feature a map portion from the player's home country. The backs have text written in the player's native language. The cards were printed on mirror board.

	MT
OPC Internationals:	1x to 2x

1998 Bowman CHL Autographs

Forty players signed cards for Bowman CHL Hockey. Three different levels of rarity are designated by the "Topps Certified Issue" stamp. Cards with a blue stamp were inserted 1:59, silver stamps were found 1:157 and cards with a gold stamp were seeded 1:470.

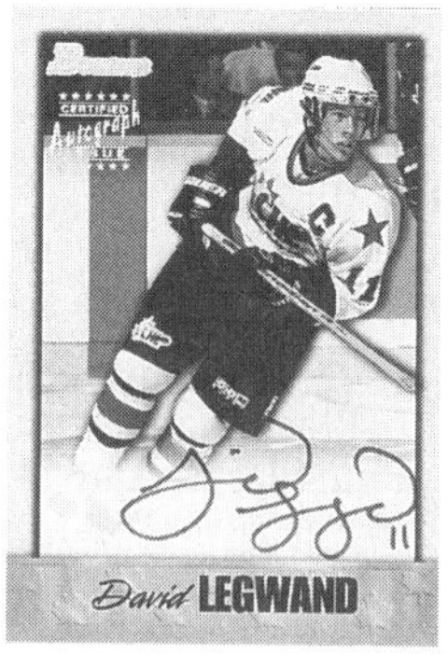

		MT
Complete Set (40):		500.00
Common Autograph:		6.00
Silvers:		1.5x to 2x
Golds:		3x to 4x
A1	Justin Papineau	15.00
A2	Jason Labarbera	10.00
A3	Michael Rupp	12.00
A4	Stephen Peat	6.00
A5	Manny Malhotra	30.00
A6	Mike Henrich	15.00
A7	Kyle Rossiter	6.00
A8	Mark Bell	15.00
A9	Mathieu Chouinard	20.00
A10	Vincent Lecavalier	60.00
A11	David Legwand	40.00
A12	Bryan Allen	10.00
A13	Francois Beauchemin	6.00
A14	Robyn Regehr	6.00
A15	Eric Chouinard	15.00
A16	Norm Milley	15.00
A17	Alex Henry	6.00
A18	Ramzi Abid	12.00
A19	Jiri Fischer	6.00
A20	Patrick Desrochers	25.00
A21	Mathieu Biron	10.00
A22	Brad Stuart	10.00
A23	Philippe Sauve	20.00
A24	John Erskine	6.00
A25	Jonathan Cheechoo	12.00
A26	Brett Allan	10.00
A27	Scott Gomez	12.00
A28	Chris Neilsen	6.00
A29	David Cameron	10.00
A30	Jonathan Girard	10.00
A31	Jeff Heerema	6.00
A32	Blair Betts	6.00
A33	Andrew Peters	6.00
A34	Randy Copley	12.00
A35	Alex Tanguay	25.00
A36	Simon Gagne	10.00
A37	Brent Gauvreau	10.00
A38	Mike Ribeiro	15.00
A39	Martin Skoula	10.00
A40	Rico Fata	35.00

1998 Bowman CHL Scout's Choice

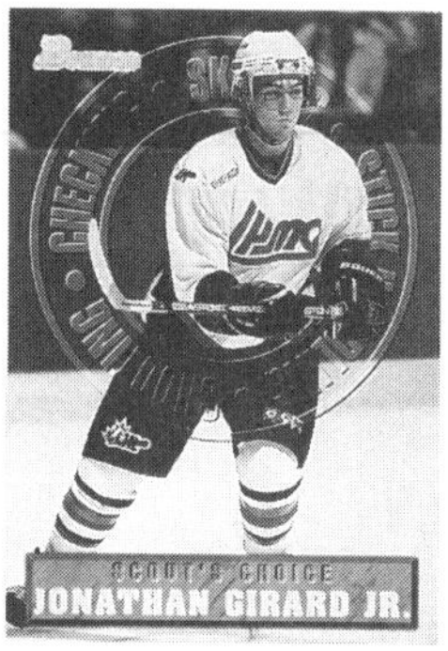

Scout's Choice is a 21-card inserted printed on double-etched foil board. The borderless cards were inserted 1:12.

		MT
Complete Set (21):		80.00
Common Player:		1.50
SC1	Bryan Allen	2.50
SC2	Manny Molhatra	8.00
SC3	Daniel Tkaczuk	3.00
SC4	Bujar Amidovski	2.50
SC5	Patrick Desrochers	5.00
SC6	Brad Ference	3.00
SC7	Marian Hossa	6.00
SC8	Brad Stuart	3.00
SC9	Sergei Varlamov	2.50
SC10	Randy Petruk	3.00
SC11	Karol Bartanus	1.50
SC12	Vincent Lecavalier	15.00
SC13	Jonathan Girard	1.50

SC14 Peter Ratchuk 1.50
SC15 Alex Tanguay 5.00
SC16 Rico Fata 8.00
SC17 Brian Finley 2.50
SC18 Jonathan Cheechoo 4.00
SC19 Scott Gomez 5.00
SC20 Michal Rozsival 1.50
SC21 Mathieu Garon 6.00

1998-99 Pacific

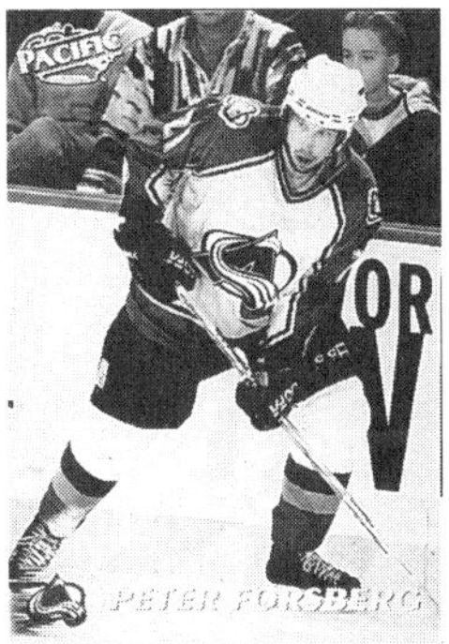

Pacific Hockey consists of a huge 450-card base set. The cards have full-bleed photos with the player's name and team logo on the bottom and the Pacific logo in the upper left. The set is paralleled in the Platinum Blue set (1:73). Inserts include Cramer's Choice, Dynagon Ice, Gold Crown Die-Cuts, Team Checklists, Trophy Winners and Timelines.

	MT
Complete Set (451):	35.00
Common Player:	.10
Ice Blues:	60x to 120x
Inserted 1:73	

1 Damian Rhodes .25
2 Mattias Ohlund .25
3 Craig Ludwig .10
4 Rob Blake .10
5 Nicklas Lidstrom .25
6 Calle Johansson .10
7 Chris Chelios .40
8 Teemu Selanne .75
9 Paul Kariya 2.00
10 Pavel Bure .75
11 Mark Messier .50
12 Peter Bondra .40
13 Mats Sundin .40
14 Brendan Shanahan .75
15 Jamie Langenbrunner .10
16 Brett Hull .50
17 Rod Brind'Amour .25
18 Adam Deadmarsh .20
19 Steve Yzerman 1.50
20 Ed Belfour .40
21 Peter Forsberg 1.50
22 Dino Ciccarelli .10
23 Brian Bellows .10
24 Janne Niinimaa .20
25 Joe Nieuwendyk .25
26 Patrik Elias .25
27 Mike Peca .10
28 Tie Domi .10
29 Felix Potvin .40
30 Martin Brodeur .75
31 Grant Fuhr .40
32 Trevor Linden .10
33 Patrick Roy 2.50
34 John Vanbiesbrouck .75
35 Tom Barrasso .25
36 Matthew Barnaby .10
37 Olaf Kolzig .25
38 Pavol Demitra .10
39 Dominik Hasek 1.00
40 Chris Terreri .10
41 Jason Allison .25
42 Richard Smehlik .10
43 Frank Banham .10
44 Chris Pronger .25
45 Matt Cullen .10
46 Mike Rucinski .10
47 *Mike Crowley* .25
48 Scott Young .10
49 Brian Savage .10
50 Travis Green .10
51 John LeClair .75
52 Adam Foote .10
53 Derek Morris .10
54 Guy Hebert .25
55 Chris Gratton .10
56 Sergei Zubov .10
57 Dave Karpa .10
58 Sergei Varlamov .40
59 Josef Marha .10
60 Jason Marshall .10
61 *Jeff Nielsen* .20
62 Steve Rucchin .10
63 Tomas Sandstrom .10
64 Jason Bonsignore .10
65 Mikhail Shtalenkov .25
67 *Tom Askey* .25
68 Jaromir Jagr 2.00
69 Per Axelsson .10
70 Ken Baumgartner .10
71 Jiri Slegr .10
72 Mathieu Schneider .10
73 Anson Carter .10
74 Byron Dafoe .40
75 Rob DiMaio .10
76 Ted Donato .10
77 Ray Bourque .40
78 Dave Ellett .10
79 Steve Heinze .10
80 Geoff Sanderson .10
81 Miroslav Satan .10
82 Martin Straka .10
83 Dmitri Khristich .10
84 Grant Ledyard .10
85 Cameron Mann .10
86 Kyle McLaren .10
87 Sergei Samsonov .75
88 Eric Lindros 2.00
89 Alexander Mogilny .30
90 Joe Juneau .10
91 Sergei Fedorov .75
92 Rick Tocchet .10
93 Doug Gilmour .30
94 Ryan Smyth .10
95 Alexei Morozov .20
96 Phil Housley .10
97 Jeremy Roenick .40
98 Jayson More .10
99 Wayne Gretzky 3.00
100 Rob Tallas .10
101 Tim Taylor .10
102 Joe Thornton .50
103 Donald Audette .10
104 Curtis Brown .10
105 Michal Grosek .10
106 Brian Holzinger .10
107 Derek Plante .10
108 Rob Ray .10
109 Darryl Shannon .10
110 Steve Shields .25
111 Vaclav Varada .10
112 Dixon Ward .10
113 Jason Woolley .10
114 Alexei Zhitnik .10
115 Andrew Cassels .10
116 Hnat Domenichelli .10
117 Theoren Fleury .25
118 Denis Gauthier .10
119 Cale Hulse .10
120 Jarome Iginla .10
121 Marty McInnis .10
122 Tyler Moss .10
123 Michael Nylander .10
124 Dwayne Roloson .10
125 Cory Stillman .10
126 Rick Tabaracci .10
127 German Titov .10
128 Jason Wiemer .10
129 Steve Chiasson .10
130 Kevin Dineen .10
131 Nelson Emerson .10
132 Martin Gelinas .10
133 Stu Grimson .10
134 Sami Kapanen .10
135 Trevor Kidd .25
136 Robert Kron .10
137 Jeff O'Neill .10
138 Keith Primeau .25
139 Paul Ranheim .10
140 Gary Roberts .10
141 Glen Wesley .10
142 Tony Amonte .40
143 Eric Daze .10
144 Jeff Hackett .40
145 Greg Johnson .10
146 Chad Kilger .10
147 Sergei Krivokrasov .10
148 Christian LaFlamme .10
149 Jean-Yves Leroux .10
150 Dmitri Nabokov .10
151 Jeff Shantz .10
152 Gary Suter .10
153 Eric Weinrich .10
154 Todd White .10
155 Alexei Zhamnov .10
156 Wade Belak .10
157 Craig Billington .10
158 Rene Corbet .10
159 Shean Donovan .10
160 Valeri Kamensky .10
161 Uwe Krupp .10
162 Jari Kurri .10
163 Eric Lacroix .10
164 Claude Lemieux .10
165 Eric Messier .10
166 Jeff Odgers .10
167 Sandis Ozolinsh .10
168 Warren Rychel .10
169 Joe Sakic 1.00
170 Stephane Yelle .10
171 Greg Adams .10
172 Jason Botterill .10
173 Guy Carbonneau .10
174 Shawn Chambers .10
175 Manny Fernandez .10
176 Derian Hatcher .10
177 Benoit Hogue .10
178 Mike Keane .10
179 Jere Lehtinen .10
180 Juha Lind .10
181 Mike Modano .50
182 Brian Skrudland .10
183 Darryl Sydor .10
184 Roman Turek .25
185 Pat Verbeek .10
186 Jamie Wright .10
187 Doug Brown .10
188 Kris Draper .10
189 Anders Eriksson .10
190 Viacheslav Fetisov .10
191 Brent Gilchrist .10
192 Kevin Hodson .25
193 Tomas Holmstrom .10
194 Mike Knuble .10
195 Joey Kocur .10
196 Vlacheslav Kozlov .10
197 Martin Lapointe .10
198 Igor Larionov .10
199 Kirk Maltby .10
200 *Norm Maracle* .25
201 Darren McCarty .10
202 Dmitri Mironov .10
203 Larry Murphy .10
204 Chris Osgood .50
205 Kelly Buchberger .10
206 Bob Essensa .10
207 Scott Fraser .10
208 Mike Grier .10
209 Bill Guerin .10
210 Tony Hrkac .10
211 Curtis Joseph .50
212 Mats Lindgren .10
213 Todd Marchant .10
214 Dean McAmmond .10
215 Craig Millar .10
216 Boris Mironov .10
217 Doug Weight .25
218 Valeri Zelepukin .10
219 Roman Hamrlik .10
220 Radek Dvorak .10
221 Dave Gagner .10
222 Ed Jovanovski .10
223 Viktor Kozlov .10
224 Paul Laus .10
225 Kirk McLean .20
226 Scott Mellanby .10
227 Kirk Muller .10
228 Robert Svehla .10
229 Steve Washburn .10
230 Kevin Weekes .10
231 Ray Whitney .10
232 *Peter Worrell* .25
233 Russ Courtnall .10
234 Stephane Fiset .25
235 Garry Galley .10
236 Craig Johnson .10
237 Ian Laperriere .10
238 Donald MacLean .10
239 Steve McKenna .10
240 Sandy Moger .10
241 Glen Murray .10
242 Sean O'Donnell .10
243 Yanic Perreault .10
244 Luc Robitaille .25
245 Jamie Storr .25
246 Jozef Stumpel .10
247 Vladimir Tsyplakov .10
248 Benoit Brunet .10
249 Shayne Corson .10
250 Vincent Damphousse .10
251 *Eric Houde* .20
252 Saku Koivu .50
253 Vladimir Malakhov .10
254 Dave Manson .10
255 Andy Moog .25
256 Mark Recchi .10
257 Martin Rucinsky .10
258 Jocelyn Thibault .25
259 Mick Vukota .10
260 Dave Andreychuk .20
261 Jason Arnott .10
262 Mike Dunham .40
263 Bobby Holik .10
264 Randy McKay .10
265 Brendan Morrison .25
266 Scott Niedermayer .10
267 Lyle Odelein .10
268 Krzysztof Oliwa .10
269 Denis Pederson .10
270 Brian Rolston .10
271 *Sheldon Souray* .25
272 Scott Stevens .10
273 Petr Sykora .10
274 Steve Thomas .10
275 Bryan Berard .10
276 Zdeno Chara .25
277 *Vladimir Chebaturkin* .25
278 Tom Chorske .10
279 Mariusz Czerkawski .10
280 Jason Dawe .10
281 Wade Flaherty .10
282 Kenny Jonsson .10
283 Sergei Nemchinov .10
284 Zigmund Palffy .50
285 Richard Pilon .10
286 Robert Reichel .10
287 Joe Sacco .10
288 Tommy Salo .25
289 Bryan Smolinski .10
290 Jeff Beukeboom .10
291 Dan Cloutier .10
292 Bruce Driver .10
293 Adam Graves .10
294 Alexei Kovalev .10
295 Pat LaFontaine .25
296 Darren Langdon .10
297 Brian Leetch .25
298 Mike Richter .40
299 Ulf Samuelsson .10
300 Marc Savard .10
301 Kevin Stevens .10
302 Niklas Sundstrom .10
303 Tim Sweeney .10
304 Vladimir Vorobiev .10
305 Daniel Alfredsson .25
306 Magnus Arvedson .10
307 Radek Bonk .10
308 Andreas Dackell .10
309 Bruce Gardiner .10
310 Igor Kravchuk .10
311 Denny Lambert .10
312 Janne Laukkanen .10
313 Shawn McEachern .10
314 Chris Phillips .10
315 Wade Redden .10
316 Ron Tugnutt .25
317 Shaun Van Allen .10
318 Alexei Yashin .30
319 Jason York .10
320 Sergei Zholtok .10
321 Sean Burke .25
322 Paul Coffey .25
323 Alexandre Daigle .10
324 Eric Desjardins .10
325 Colin Forbes .10
326 Ron Hextall .25
327 Trent Klatt .10
328 Daniel McGillis .10
329 Joel Otto .10
330 Shjon Podein .10
331 Mike Sillinger .10
332 Chris Therien .10
333 Dainius Zubrus .10
334 Bob Corkum .10
335 Jim Cummins .10
336 Jason Doig .10
337 Dallas Drake .10
338 Mike Gartner .10
339 Brad Isbister .10
340 Craig Janney .10
341 Nikolai Khabibulin .25
342 Teppo Numminen .10
343 Cliff Ronning .10
344 Keith Tkachuk .50
345 Oleg Tverdovsky .10
346 Jim Waite .10
347 Juha Ylonen .10
348 Stu Barnes .10
349 Rob Brown .10
350 Robert Dome .10
351 Ron Francis .25
352 Kevin Hatcher .10
353 Alex Hicks .10
354 Darius Kasparaitis .10
355 Robert Lang .10
356 Fredrik Olausson .10
357 Ed Olczyk .10
358 Peter Skudra .10
359 Chris Tamer .10
360 Ken Wregget .25
361 Blair Atcheynum .10
362 Jim Campbell .10
363 Kelly Chase .10
364 Craig Conroy .10
365 Geoff Courtnall .10
366 Steve Duchesne .10
367 Todd Gill .10
368 Al MacInnis .30
369 Jamie McLennan .25
370 Scott Pellerin .10
371 Pascal Rheaume .10
372 Jamie Rivers .10
373 Darren Turcotte .10
374 Pierre Turgeon .25
375 Tony Twist .10
376 Terry Yake .10
377 Rich Brennan .10
378 Murray Craven .10
379 Jeff Friesen .10
380 Tony Granato .10
381 Bill Houlder .10
382 Kelly Hrudey .10
383 Alexander Korolyuk .10
384 John MacLean .10
385 Bryan Marchment .10
386 Patrick Marleau .75
387 Stephane Matteau .10
388 Marty McSorley .10
389 Bernie Nichols .10
390 Owen Nolan .10
391 Mike Ricci .10
392 Marco Sturm .10
393 Mike Vernon .25
394 Andrei Zyuzin .10
395 Mikael Andersson .10
396 *Zac Bierk* .25
397 Enrico Ciccone .10
398 Louie DeBrusk .10
399 Karl Dykhuis .10
400 Daymond Langkow .10
401 Mike McBain .10
402 Sandy McCarthy .10
403 Daren Puppa .10
404 Mikael Renberg .10
405 Stephane Richer .10
406 Alexander Selivanov .10
407 Darcy Tucker .10
408 Paul Ysebaert .10
409 Rob Zamuner .10
410 Sergei Berezin .10
411 Wendel Clark .10
412 Sylvain Cote .10
413 Mike Johnson .25
414 Derek King .10
415 Kris King .10
416 Igor Korolev .10
417 *Daniil Markov* .25
418 Alyn McCauley .10
419 Fredrik Modin .10
420 Martin Prochazka .10
421 Jason Smith .10
422 Steve Sullivan .10
423 Yannick Tremblay .10
424 Todd Bertuzzi .10
425 Donald Brashear .10
426 Bret Hedican .10
427 Arturs Irbe .25
428 Jyrki Lumme .10
429 Brad May .10
430 Bryan McCabe .10
431 Markus Naslund .10
432 Brian Noonan .10
433 Dave Scatchard .10
434 Garth Snow .25
435 *Lubomir Vaic* .25
436 Peter Zezel .10
437 Craig Berube .10
438 Jeff Brown .10
439 Andrew Brunette .10
440 Jan Bulis .10
441 Sergei Gonchar .10
442 Dale Hunter .10
443 Steve Konowalchuk .10
444 Kelly Miller .10
445 Adam Oates .40
446 Bill Ranford .10
447 Jaroslav Svejkovsky .10
448 Esa Tikkanen .10
449 Mark Tinordi .10
450 Brendan Witt .10
451 Richard Zednik .10

1998-99 Pacific Cramer's Choice

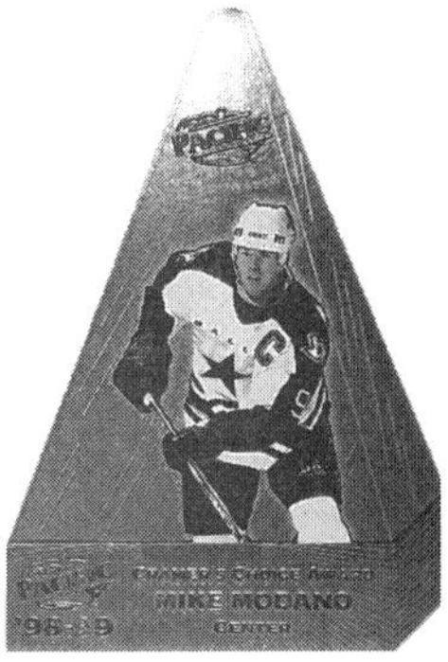

This 10-card insert was seeded one per 721 packs of Pacific Hockey. The cards have a die-cut trophy design and feature the league's best players as chosen by Pacific CEO Mike Cramer.

	MT
Complete Set (10):	800.00
Common Player:	40.00

1 Sergei Samsonov 60.00
2 Dominik Hasek 75.00
3 Peter Forsberg 100.00
4 Patrick Roy 175.00
5 Mike Modano 50.00
6 Martin Brodeur 60.00
7 Wayne Gretzky 225.00
8 Eric Lindros 150.00
9 Jaromir Jagr 150.00
10 Pavel Bure 60.00

1998-99 Pacific Dynagon Ice

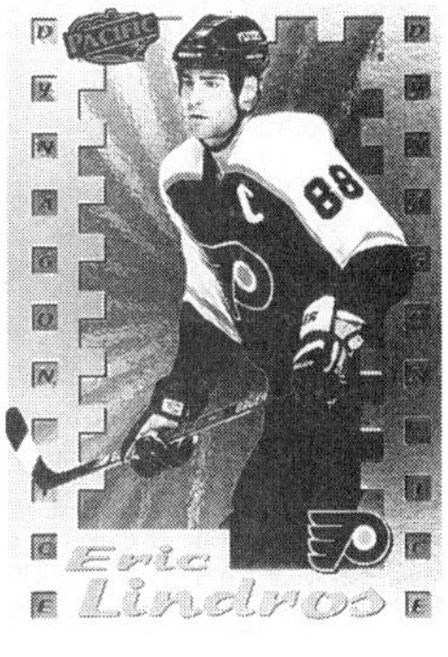

These 20 mirror-patterned, full-foil cards were inserted four per 37 packs. The hobby-only Dynagon Titanium Ice parallel is sequentially numbered to 99.

		MT
Complete Set (20):		75.00
Common Player:		1.00
1	Paul Kariya	10.00
2	Teemu Selanne	4.00
3	Sergei Samsonov	3.00
4	Dominik Hasek	4.00
5	Peter Forsberg	8.00
6	Patrick Roy	12.00
7	Joe Sakic	5.00
8	Mike Modano	3.00
9	Sergei Fedorov	4.00
10	Steve Yzerman	8.00
11	Saku Koivu	3.00
12	Martin Brodeur	4.00
13	Wayne Gretzky	15.00
14	John LeClair	3.00
15	Eric Lindros	10.00
16	Jaromir Jagr	10.00
17	Pavel Bure	4.00
18	Mark Messier	3.00
19	Peter Bondra	3.00
20	Olaf Kolzig	1.00

1998-99 Pacific Gold Crown

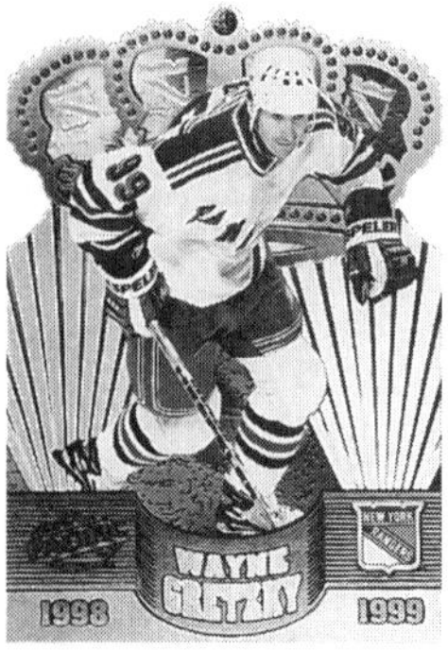

Gold Crown Die-Cuts is a 36-card insert seeded one per 37 packs. Printed on 24-point stock, the cards feature dual-foil and laser-cutting.

		MT
Complete Set (36):		300.00
Common Player:		4.00
1	Paul Kariya	25.00
2	Teemu Selanne	10.00
3	Sergei Samsonov	10.00
4	Dominik Hasek	15.00
5	Mike Peca	4.00
6	Theoren Fleury	4.00
7	Chris Chelios	6.00
8	Peter Forsberg	20.00
9	Patrick Roy	25.00
10	Joe Sakic	12.00
11	Ed Belfour	6.00
12	Mike Modano	8.00
13	Sergei Fedorov	10.00
14	Chris Osgood	6.00
15	Brendan Shanahan	10.00
16	Steve Yzerman	20.00
17	Saku Koivu	8.00
18	Martin Brodeur	10.00
19	Patrik Elias	4.00
20	Doug Gilmour	6.00
21	Trevor Linden	4.00
22	Zigmund Palffy	8.00
23	Wayne Gretzky	40.00
24	John LeClair	10.00
25	Eric Lindros	25.00
26	Dainius Zubrus	4.00
27	Keith Tkachuk	8.00
28	Tom Barrasso	4.00
29	Jaromir Jagr	25.00
30	Brett Hull	8.00
31	Felix Potvin	6.00
32	Mats Sundin	6.00
33	Pavel Bure	10.00
34	Mark Messier	8.00
35	Peter Bondra	6.00
36	Olaf Kolzig	6.00

1998-99 Pacific Team Checklists

One Team Checklist card was produced for each of the 27 NHL teams. The card fronts have a color player photo and the team's logo. The embossed logo is printed on holographic silver foil. The cards were inserted 2:37.

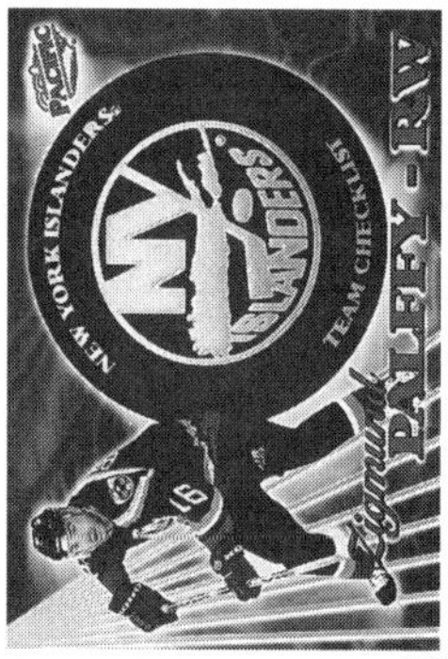

		MT
Complete Set (27):		175.00
Common Player:		2.00
1	Paul Kariya	20.00
2	Sergei Samsonov	6.00
3	Dominik Hasek	10.00
4	Theoren Fleury	2.00
5	Keith Primeau	3.00
6	Chris Chelios	4.00
7	Patrick Roy	25.00
8	Mike Modano	6.00
9	Steve Yzerman	15.00
10	Ryan Smyth	2.00
11	John Vanbiesbrouck	8.00
12	Jozef Stumpel	2.00
13	Saku Koivu	6.00
14	TBD	2.00
15	Martin Brodeur	8.00
16	Zigmund Palffy	6.00
17	Wayne Gretzky	30.00
18	Alexei Yashin	3.00
19	Eric Lindros	20.00
20	Keith Tkachuk	6.00
21	Jaromir Jagr	20.00
22	Brett Hull	6.00
23	Patrick Marleau	8.00
24	Rob Zamuner	2.00
25	Mats Sundin	5.00
26	Pavel Bure	8.00
27	Olaf Kolzig	3.00

1998-99 Pacific Trophy Winners

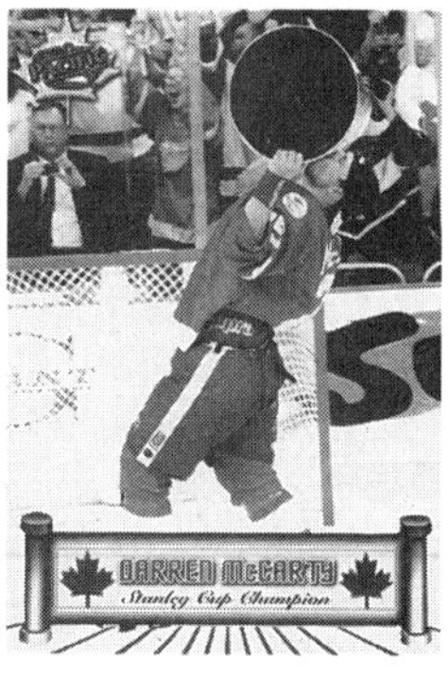

The 10-card Trophy Winners insert was seeded one per 37 packs. A Canada-only insert, the set features players who won awards at the NHL awards banquet.

		MT
Complete Set (10):		75.00
Common Player:		2.50
Inserted 1:37 Can.		
1	Martin Brodeur	12.00
2	Dominik Hasek	12.00
3	Jaromir Jagr	20.00
4	Sergei Samsonov	8.00
5	Sergei Fedorov	10.00
6	Nicklas Lidstrom	4.00
7	Darren McCarty	2.50
8	Chris Osgood	5.00
9	Brendan Shanahan	10.00
10	Steve Yzerman	20.00

1998-99 Pacific Timelines

Timelines is a 20-card hobby-only insert seeded 1:181. The set honors NHL players at various stages of their career with three color photos on the card fronts.

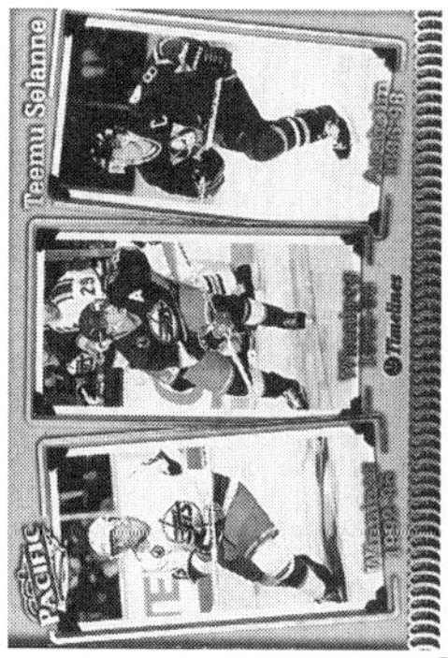

		MT
Complete Set (20):		900.00
Common Player:		20.00
Inserted 1:181		
1	Teemu Selanne	40.00
2	Dominik Hasek	60.00
3	Peter Forsberg	80.00
4	Patrick Roy	120.00
5	Joe Sakic	60.00
6	Ed Belfour	30.00
7	Brendan Shanahan	40.00
8	Steve Yzerman	80.00
9	Mike Modano	35.00
10	Doug Gilmour	20.00
11	Wayne Gretzky	160.00
12	Pat LaFontaine	20.00
13	John LeClair	30.00
14	Eric Lindros	100.00
15	Keith Tkachuk	30.00
16	Jaromir Jagr	100.00
17	Brett Hull	30.00
18	Mats Sundin	25.00
19	Pavel Bure	40.00
20	Mark Messier	35.00

1998-99 UD Choice

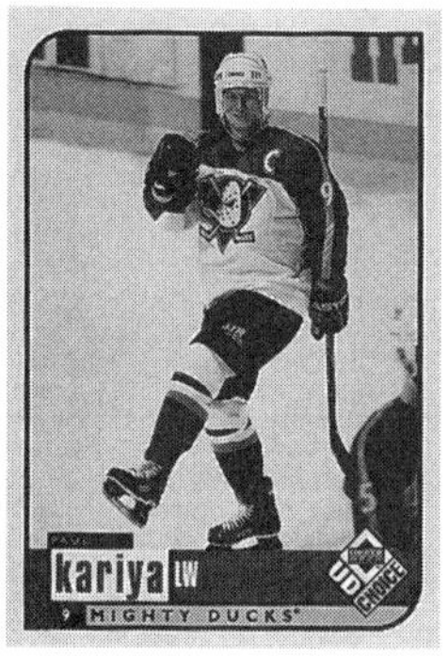

UD Choice Hockey consists of a 310-card base set. The set has 220 regular cards, three checklists and three subsets. GM's Choice is a 22-card subset featuring players selected by Patrick Roy and Steve Yzerman. Crease Lightning (10 cards) is a subset featuring goalies and World Junior Showcase (55 cards) features NHL prospects. Each pack contains an entry card for the "Draw Your Own Trading Card" contest. The entire base set is paralleled in Choice Reserve and Prime Choice Reserve. The inserts are StarQuest and Mini Bobbing-Head cards.

		MT
Complete Set (310):		20.00
Common Player:		.10
1	Guy Hebert	.25
2	Mikhail Shtalenkov	.10
3	Josef Marha	.10
4	Paul Kariya	1.25
5	Travis Green	.10
6	Steve Rucchin	.10
7	Matt Cullen	.10
8	Teemu Selanne	.50
9	Antti Aalto	.10
10	Byron Dafoe	.25
11	Ted Donato	.10
12	Dmitri Khristich	.10
13	Sergei Samsonov	.75
14	Jason Allison	.20
15	Ray Bourque	.25
16	Kyle McLaren	.10
17	Cameron Mann	.10
18	Shawn Bates	.10
19	Joe Thornton	.50
20	Vaclav Varada	.10
21	Brian Holzinger	.10
22	Miroslav Satan	.10
23	Dominik Hasek	.75
24	Mike Peca	.10
25	Erik Rasmussen	.10
26	Alexei Zhitnik	.10
27	Geoff Sanderson	.10
28	Donald Audette	.10
29	Derek Morris	.10
30	German Titov	.10
31	Valeri Bure	.10
32	Michael Nylander	.10
33	Cory Stillman	.10
34	Theoren Fleury	.20
35	Jarome Iginla	.10
36	Gary Roberts	.10
37	Jeff O'Neill	.10
38	Bates Battaglia	.10
39	Keith Primeau	.20
40	Sami Kapanen	.20
41	Glen Wesley	.10
42	Trevor Kidd	.25
43	Nelson Emerson	.10
44	Daniel Cleary	.10
45	Eric Daze	.20
46	Chris Chelios	.25
47	Gary Suter	.10
48	Alexei Zhamnov	.10
49	Jeff Hackett	.25
50	Dmitri Nabokov	.10
51	Tony Amonte	.20
52	Jean-Yves Leroux	.10
53	Eric Messier	.10
54	Patrick Roy	1.50
55	Claude Lemieux	.10
56	Peter Forsberg	1.00
57	Adam Deadmarsh	.10
58	Valeri Kamensky	.10
59	Joe Sakic	.75
60	Sandis Ozolinsh	.20
61	Jamie Langenbrunner	.10
62	Joe Nieuwendyk	.20
63	Ed Belfour	.30
64	Juha Lind	.10
65	Derian Hatcher	.10
66	Sergei Zubov	.10
67	Darryl Sydor	.10
68	Jere Lehtinen	.10
69	Mike Modano	.50
70	Larry Murphy	.10
71	Igor Larionov	.10
72	Darren McCarty	.10
73	Steve Yzerman	1.00
74	Chris Osgood	.30
75	Sergei Fedorov	.50
76	Brendan Shanahan	.50
77	Nicklas Lidstrom	.20
78	Vyacheslav Kozlov	.10
79	Dean McAmmond	.10
80	Roman Hamrlik	.10
81	Curtis Joseph	.30
82	Ryan Smyth	.10
83	Boris Mironov	.10
84	Bill Guerin	.10
85	Doug Weight	.20
86	Janne Niinimaa	.10
87	Ray Whitney	.10
88	Robert Svehla	.10
89	John Vanbiesbrouck	.50
90	Scott Mellanby	.10
91	Ed Jovanovski	.10
92	Dave Gagner	.10
93	Dino Ciccarelli	.10
94	Rob Niedermayer	.10
95	Rob Blake	.10
96	Yanic Perreault	.10
97	Stephane Fiset	.20
98	Luc Robitaille	.20
99	Glen Murray	.10
100	Jozef Stumpel	.10
101	Vladimir Tsyplakov	.10
102	Donald MacLean	.10
103	Shayne Corson	.10
104	Vladimir Malakhov	.10
105	Saku Koivu	.40
106	Andy Moog	.25
107	Matt Higgins	.10
108	Dave Manson	.10
109	Mark Recchi	.10
110	Vincent Damphousse	.10
111	Brian Savage	.10
112	Petr Sykora	.10
113	Scott Stevens	.10
114	Patrik Elias	.20
115	Bobby Holik	.10
116	Martin Brodeur	.60
117	Doug Gilmour	.25
118	Jason Arnott	.10
119	Scott Niedermayer	.10
120	Brendan Morrison	.25
121	Zigmund Palffy	.40
122	Trevor Linden	.10
123	Bryan Berard	.20
124	Zdeno Chara	.20
125	Kenny Jonsson	.10
126	Robert Reichel	.10
127	Bryan Smolinski	.10
128	Wayne Gretzky	2.00
129	Brian Leetch	.20
130	Pat LaFontaine	.20
131	Dan Cloutier	.10
132	Niklas Sundstrom	.10
133	Marc Savard	.10
134	Adam Graves	.10
135	Mike Richter	.30
136	Jeff Beukeboom	.10
137	Daniel Goneau	.10
138	Shawn McEachern	.10
139	Damian Rhodes	.20
140	Wade Redden	.10
141	Alexei Yashin	.20
142	Marian Hossa	.10
143	Chris Phillips	.10
144	Daniel Alfredsson	.20
145	Vaclav Prospal	.10
146	Andreas Dackell	.10
147	Sean Burke	.20
148	Alexandre Daigle	.10
149	Rod Brind'Amour	.20
150	Chris Gratton	.10
151	Paul Coffey	.20
152	Eric Lindros	1.25
153	John LeClair	.40
154	Chris Therien	.10
155	Keith Carney	.10
156	Craig Janney	.10
157	Teppo Numminen	.10
158	Jeremy Roenick	.30
159	Oleg Tverdovsky	.10
160	Keith Tkachuk	.40
161	Brad Isbister	.10
162	Nikolai Khabibulin	.25
163	Daniel Briere	.10
164	Juha Ylonen	.10
165	Tom Barrasso	.25
166	Alexei Morozov	.10
167	Stu Barnes	.10
168	Jaromir Jagr	1.25
169	Ron Francis	.20
170	Peter Skudra	.10
171	Robert Dome	.10
172	Kevin Hatcher	.10
173	Patrick Marleau	.50
174	Jeff Friesen	.10
175	Owen Nolan	.10
176	John MacLean	.10
177	Mike Vernon	.25
178	Marcus Ragnarsson	.10
179	Andrei Zyuzin	.10
180	Mike Ricci	.10
181	Marco Sturm	.20
182	Steve Duchesne	.20
183	Brett Hull	.40
184	Pierre Turgeon	.20
185	Chris Pronger	.20
186	Pavol Demitra	.10
187	Jamie McLennan	.20
188	Al MacInnis	.20
189	Jim Campbell	.10
190	Geoff Courtnall	.10
191	Daren Puppa	.10
192	Daymond Langkow	.10
193	Stephane Richer	.10
194	Paul Ysebaert	.10
195	Alexander Selivanov	.10
196	Rob Zamuner	.10
197	Mikael Renberg	.10
198	Mathieu Schneider	.10
199	Mike Johnson	.20
200	Alyn McCauley	.10
201	Sergei Berezin	.10
202	Wendel Clark	.10
203	Mats Sundin	.40
204	Tie Domi	.10
205	Jyrki Lumme	.10
206	Mattias Ohlund	.10
207	Garth Snow	.20
208	Pavel Bure	.50
209	Dave Scatchard	.10
210	Alexander Mogilny	.25
211	Mark Messier	.50
212	Todd Bertuzzi	.10
213	Peter Bondra	.40
214	Joe Juneau	.10
215	Olaf Kolzig	.30
216	Jan Bulis	.10
217	Adam Oates	.25
218	Richard Zednik	.10
219	Calle Johansson	.10
220	Phil Housley	.10
221	Dominik Hasek (GM's Choice)	.40
222	Ray Bourque (GM's Choice)	.20
223	Chris Chelios (GM's Choice)	.20
224	Paul Kariya (GM's Choice)	.60
225	Wayne Gretzky (GM's Choice)	1.00
226	Jaromir Jagr (GM's Choice)	.60
227	Rob Blake (GM's Choice)	.10
228	Adam Foote (GM's Choice)	.10
229	Peter Forsberg (GM's Choice)	.50
230	Joe Sakic (GM's Choice)	.40
231	Mark Recchi (GM's Choice)	.10
232	Patrick Roy (GM's Choice)	.75
233	Nicklas Lidstrom (GM's Choice)	.10
234	Rob Blake (GM's Choice)	.10
235	John LeClair (GM's Choice)	.25
236	Wayne Gretzky (GM's Choice)	1.00

237	Eric Lindros (GM's Choice)	.60
238	Brian Leetch (GM's Choice)	.20
239	Scott Stevens (GM's Choice)	.10
240	Paul Kariya (GM's Choice)	.60
241	Peter Forsberg (GM's Choice)	.50
242	Teemu Selanne (GM's Choice)	.30
243	Patrick Roy (Crease Lightning)	.75
244	Dominik Hasek (Crease Lightning)	.40
245	Martin Brodeur (Crease Lightning)	.40
246	Mike Richter (Crease Lightning)	.20
247	John Vanbiesbrouck (Crease Lightning)	.25
248	Chris Osgood (Crease Lightning)	.20
249	Ed Belfour (Crease Lightning)	.20
250	Tom Barrasso (Crease Lightning)	.10
251	Curtis Joseph (Crease Lightning)	.20
252	Sean Burke (Crease Lightning)	.10
253	Josh Holden (Jr. Showcase)	.10
254	Daniel Tkaczuk (Jr. Showcase)	.10
255	Manny Malhotra (Jr. Showcase)	.25
256	Eric Brewer (Jr. Showcase)	.10
257	Alex Tanguay (Jr. Showcase)	.25
258	Roberto Luongo (Jr. Showcase)	.75
259	Vincent Lecavalier (Jr. Showcase)	1.50
260	Mathieu Garon (Jr. Showcase)	.10
261	*Brad Ference* (Jr. Showcase)	.75
262	Jesse Wallin (Jr. Showcase)	.10
263	*Zenith Komarniski* (Jr. Showcase)	.20
264	*Sean Blanchard* (Jr. Showcase)	.20
265	Cory Sarich (Jr. Showcase)	.10
266	Mike Van Ryn (Jr. Showcase)	.10
267	Steve Begin (Jr. Showcase)	.10
268	Matt Cooke (Jr. Showcase)	.20
269	*Daniel Corso* (Jr. Showcase)	.20
270	*Brett McLean* (Jr. Showcase)	.25
271	*Jean-Pierre Dumont* (Jr. Showcase)	.25
272	Jason Ward (Jr. Showcase)	.10
273	*Brian Willsie* (Jr. Showcase)	.20

274	*Matt Bradley* (Jr. Showcase)	.25
275	Olli Jokinen (Jr. Showcase)	.20
276	Teemu Elomo (Jr. Showcase)	.20
277	Timo Vertala (Jr. Showcase)	.10
278	Mika Noronen (Jr. Showcase)	.40
279	Pasi Petrilainen (Jr. Showcase)	.10
280	Timo Ahmaoja (Jr. Showcase)	.10
281	Ero Somervuori (Jr. Showcase)	.10
282	Maxim Afinogenov (Jr. Showcase)	.20
283	Maxim Balmockhnykh (Jr. Showcase)	.10
284	*Artem Chubarov* (Jr. Showcase)	.40
285	Vitali Vishnevsky (Jr. Showcase)	.10
286	Denis Shvidky (Jr. Showcase)	.40
287	*Dmitri Vlassenkov* (Jr. Showcase)	.30
288	*Magnus Nilsson* (Jr. Showcase)	.25
289	*Mikael Holmqvist* (Jr. Showcase)	.25
290	*Mattias Karlin* (Jr. Showcase)	.25
291	*Pierre Hedin* (Jr. Showcase)	.25
292	*Henrik Petre* (Jr. Showcase)	.25
293	Johan Forsander (Jr. Showcase)	.10
294	Daniel Sedin (Jr. Showcase)	.50
295	Henrik Sedin (Jr. Showcase)	.50
296	Markus Nilsson (Jr. Showcase)	.10
297	Paul Mara (Jr. Showcase)	.10
298	*Brian Gionta* (Jr. Showcase)	.25
299	Chris Hajt (Jr. Showcase)	.10
300	*Mike Mattau* (Jr. Showcase)	.25
301	*Jean-Marc Pelletier* (Jr. Showcase)	.25
302	David Legwand (Jr. Showcase)	1.00
303	Ty Jones (Jr. Showcase)	.25
304	Nikos Tselios (Jr. Showcase)	.20
305	Jesse Boulerice (Jr. Showcase)	.10
306	Jeff Farkas (Jr. Showcase)	.10
307	Toby Peterson (Jr. Showcase)	.10
308	Checklist Wayne Gretzky	1.00
309	Checklist Patrick Roy	.75
310	Checklist Steve Yzerman	.50

1998-99 UD Choice Reserve

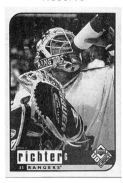

Choice Reserve is a full parallel of the UD Choice base set. The cards have a foil treatment and were inserted 1:6.

	MT
Choice Reserve Stars:	3x to 6x
Yng Stars & RCs:	2x to 4x

1998-99 UD Choice Prime Choice Reserve

This full parallel of the base set was sequentially numbered to 100. The words "Prime Choice Reserve" were foil stamped on the cards.

	MT
Prime Choice Stars:	60x to 100x
Yng Stars & RCs:	20x to 50x

1998-99 UD Choice Bobbing Head

Mini Bobbing-Head cards (30 cards) were inserted one per four packs. Each card could be folded into a mini standup with a removable bobbing head.

	MT
Complete Set (30):	20.00
Common Player:	.25
Inserted 1:4	
BH1 Wayne Gretzky	3.00
BH2 Keith Tkachuk	.50
BH3 Ray Bourque	.40
BH4 Brett Hull	.50
BH5 Jaromir Jagr	2.00
BH6 John LeClair	.50
BH7 Martin Brodeur	1.00
BH8 Eric Lindros	2.00
BH9 Mark Messier	.75
BH10 John Vanbiesbrouck	.75
BH11 Paul Kariya	2.00
BH12 Luc Robitaille	.25
BH13 Zigmund Palffy	.50
BH14 Peter Forsberg	1.50
BH15 Teemu Selanne	.75
BH16 Mike Modano	.50
BH17 Mats Sundin	.40
BH18 Dominik Hasek	1.00
BH19 Joe Sakic	1.00
BH20 Rob Blake	.25
BH21 Patrick Roy	2.00
BH22 Sergei Samsonov	1.00
BH23 Chris Chelios	.40
BH24 Brendan Shanahan	.75
BH25 Theoren Fleury	.25
BH26 Ed Belfour	.40
BH27 Steve Yzerman	1.50
BH28 Saku Koivu	.50
BH29 Brian Leetch	.35
BH30 Pavel Bure	.75

1998-99 UD Choice StarQuest

StarQuest is a 30-card, four-tiered insert. The "One-Star" tier has blue borders and was inserted 1:1. "Two-Star" cards (1:7) have green borders, "Three-Stars" (1:23) have red borders and "Four-Star" cards (numbered to 100) have gold borders.

	MT
Complete Set (30):	12.00
Common Player:	.25
Inserted 1:1	
Doubles:	2x to 3x
Inserted 1:7	
Triples:	5x to 10x
Inserted 1:23	
4-Stars:	60x to 100x
Production 100 sets	
SQ1 Wayne Gretzky	2.00
SQ2 Pavel Bure	.50
SQ3 Patrick Roy	1.50
SQ4 Dominik Hasek	.75
SQ5 Teemu Selanne	.50
SQ6 Sergei Samsonov	.75
SQ7 Brian Leetch	.25
SQ8 Saku Koivu	.40
SQ9 Brendan Shanahan	.50
SQ10 Alexei Yashin	.25
SQ11 Joe Sakic	.75
SQ12 Patrik Elias	.25
SQ13 Theoren Fleury	.25
SQ14 Peter Bondra	.40
SQ15 John LeClair	.50
SQ16 Jaromir Jagr	1.25
SQ17 Ed Belfour	.40
SQ18 Steve Yzerman	1.00
SQ19 Mats Sundin	.40
SQ20 Peter Forsberg	1.00
SQ21 Ray Bourque	.35
SQ22 Brett Hull	.40
SQ23 Martin Brodeur	.75
SQ24 Mike Modano	.40
SQ25 Paul Kariya	1.25
SQ26 Tony Amonte	.25
SQ27 Mike Johnson	.25
SQ28 Eric Lindros	1.25
SQ29 Mark Messier	.50
SQ30 Keith Tkachuk	.40

RACING

1997 Pinnacle Certified

This 100-card set incorporates silver foil across the card front, with a photo of the driver or car and a black oval simulating a racing track in the background. The cards consist of 24-point card stock with the driver's name and/or car along with Pinnacle Certified stamped in gold foil along with a protective peel. The card backs give miscellaneous career information along with the names of each member of the driver's pit crew and a photo on the top third, of the driver or car.

		MT
Complete Set (100):		35.00
Common Driver:		.25
1	Kyle Petty	.30
2	Rusty Wallace	2.00
3	Dale Earnhardt	4.00
4	Sterling Marlin	.30
5	Terry Labonte	2.00
6	Mark Martin	2.00
7	Bill Elliott	2.00
8	Jeremy Mayfield	.25
9	Ted Musgrave	.25
10	Ricky Rudd	.25
11	Robby Gordon	.25
12	Johnny Benson	.40
13	Bobby Hamilton	.25
14	Mike Skinner	.25
15	Dale Jarrett	1.50
16	Steve Grissom	.25
17	Darrell Waltrip	.25
18	Bobby Labonte	.40
19	Ernie Irvan	1.50
20	Jeff Green	.25
21	Michael Waltrip	.25
22	Ward Burton	.25
23	Geoff Bodine	.25
24	Jeff Gordon	4.00
25	Ricky Craven	.25
26	Jimmy Spencer	.25
27	Brett Bodine	.25
28	David Green	.25
29	John Andretti	.25
30	Ken Schrader	.25
31	Chad Little	.25
32	Joe Nemechek	.25
33	Hut Stricklin	.25
34	Kenny Wallace	.25
35	PE2	.25
36	R. Wallace Car	1.00
37	D. Earnhardt Car	2.00
38	S. Marlin Car	.25
39	T. Labonte Car	1.00
40	M. Martin Car	1.00
41	B. Elliott Car	1.00
42	T. Musgrave Car	.25
43	T. Musgrave Car	.25
44	R. Rudd Car	.25
45	R. Gordon Car	.25
46	J. Benson Car	.30
47	B. Hamilton Car	.25
48	M. Skinner Car	.25
49	Robert Yates Racing	.25
50	S. Grissom Car	.25
51	D. Waltrip Car	.25
52	B. Labonte Car	.30
53	E. Irvan Car	.75
54	J. Green Car	.25

55	M. Waltrip Car	.25
56	W. Burton Car	.25
57	G. Bodine Car	.25
58	J. Gordon Car	2.00
59	R. Craven Car	.25
60	J. Spencer Car	.25
61	B. Bodine Car	.25
62	D. Green Car	.25
63	J. Andretti Car	.25
64	K. Schrader Car	.25
65	C. Little Car	.25
66	J. Nemechek Car	.25
67	H. Stricklin Car	.25
68	K. Wallace Car	.25
69	D. Waltrip Motorsports	.25
70	D. Waltrip Motorsports	.25
71	D. Waltrip Motorsports	.25
72	J. Mayfield Car	.25
73	J. Mayfield Car	.25
74	J. Gordon Car	2.00
75	Ward Burton Car	.25
76	D. Earnhardt Car	2.00
77	B. Labonte Car	.30
78	M. Waltrip Car	.25
79	R. Gordon Car	.25
80	T. Labonte Car	1.00
81	B. Elliott Car	1.00
82	B. Hamilton Car	.25
83	C. Little Car	.25
84	J. Green Car	.25
85	J. Green Car	.25
86	R. Mast Car	.25
87	E. Irvan Car	.75
88	G. Bodine Car	.25
89	Jeff Gordon	2.50
90	Terry Labonte	1.25
91	Mark Martin	1.25
92	Dale Jarrett	1.00
93	Dale Earnhardt	2.50
94	Ricky Rudd	.25
95	Rusty Wallace	1.25
96	Bobby Hamilton	.25
97	Bobby Labonte	.30
98	Kyle Petty	.30
99	Checklist	.25
100	Checklist	.25

1997 Pinnacle Certified Red

Like the Mirror inserts these 1:5 pack parallel inserts feature the same photo and card design as the base cards. Red replaces silver foil with certified red stamped over the Pinnacle Certified stamping.

	MT
Certified Reds:	3x to 5x

1997 Pinnacle Certified Mirror Red/Blue

Both of these 100-card parallel sets have either a holographic red or blue front, with either mirror red or mirror blue written over the Pinnacle Certified stamping in the upper left corner. Mirror Blues are found on the average of

1:199 packs, while Mirror Reds are found 1:99 packs.

	MT
Mirror Reds:	20x to 40x
Mirror Blues:	40x to 80x

1997 Pinnacle Certified Mirror Gold

These Holographic inserts are tinted Gold to give them their desired "mirror effect". The most difficult insert to pull from the product, these parallel inserts are found on the average of 1:299 packs.

	MT
Mirror Golds:	70x to 140x

1997 Pinnacle Certified Team

Twenty of the hottest drivers in NASCAR were selected for this insert set. Card fronts have a silver mirror mylar finish, with the driver's name and Certified Team stamped in blue foil stamping, encircling the driver. These are found 1:19 packs. A Gold Team variation also exists, that features the same photos and replaces the silver mirror mylar finish with gold accents and blue foil stamping with gold foil stamping. Gold Teams are found 1:119 packs.

		MT
Complete Set (10):		90.00
Common Driver:		5.00
	Golds:	3x
1	Dale Earnhardt	25.00
2	Jeff Gordon	25.00
3	Ricky Rudd	5.00
4	Bobby Labonte	5.00
5	Terry Labonte	12.00
6	Rusty Wallace	12.00
7	Mark Martin	12.00
8	Bill Elliott	12.00
9	Dale Jarrett	10.00
10	Jeremy Mayfield	5.00

1997 Pinnacle Certified Epix

The 10-card Epix insert set, takes a look back at the "epic" moments of each driver. The set is fractured into three different colors: Orange, purple and aqua. These are found on the average of 1:15 packs.

		MT
Complete Set (10):		75.00
Common Driver:		4.00
1	Dale Earnhardt	20.00
2	Jeff Gordon	20.00
3	Ricky Rudd	4.00
4	Bobby Labonte	4.00
5	Terry Labonte	10.00
6	Rusty Wallace	10.00
7	Mark Martin	10.00
8	Darrell Waltrip	4.00
9	Dale Jarrett	8.00
10	Ernie Irvan	8.00

1997 Upper Deck SPx

This 25-card base set utilizes Holoview technology with each card featuring a perimeter die-cut design and a 3-D holoview photo of each driver on the right hand side of the horizontal card. The left-half of each card has a photo of the drivers' car. The card backs feature stats from the prior five years and highlights of the prior season along with a photo of the driver and car.

		MT
Complete Set (25):		30.00
Common Driver:		1.00
1	Bobby Gordon	.75
2	Rusty Wallace	3.00
3	Dale Earnhardt	6.00
4	Sterling Marlin	1.00
5	Terry Labonte	3.00
6	Mark Martin	3.00
7	Geoff Bodine	.75
8	Dale Jarrett	2.00
9	Ernie Irvan	2.00
10	Ricky Rudd	.75
11	Mike Skinner	.75
12	Johnny Benson	.75
13	Kyle Petty	1.00
14	John Andretti	.75
15	Jeff Burton	.75
16	Ted Musgrave	.75
17	Darrell Waltrip	.75
18	Bobby Labonte	.75
19	Bobby Hamilton	.75
20	Bill Elliott	3.00
21	Michael Waltrip	.75
22	Ken Schrader	.75
23	Jimmy Spencer	.75
24	Jeff Gordon	6.00
25	Ricky Craven	.75

1997 Upper Deck SPx Blue/Silver/Gold

All of these inserts are parallels of the base set that only differ by the color foil treatment of the car number and SPx logo. Blues are seeded one per pack, Silvers 1:5 packs and Golds 1:72 packs.

	MT
Blues:	1x to 2x
Silvers:	2x to 3x
Golds:	12x to 20x

1997 Upper Deck SPx Speedview Autographs

This 10-card autographed insert set features many of the top drivers in the Winston Cup Circuit including Jeff Gordon and have a die-cut design. Speedview Autographs are seeded 1:175 packs.

		MT
Complete Set (10):		1100.
Common Driver:		75.00
1	Jeff Gordon	300.00
2	Rusty Wallace	150.00
3	Bill Elliott	150.00
4	Sterling Marlin	75.00
5	Terry Labonte	150.00
6	Mark Martin	150.00
7	Dale Jarrett	125.00
8	Ernie Irvan	125.00
9	Bobby Labonte	75.00
10	Ricky Rudd	75.00

1997 Upper Deck SPx Tag-Team

These dual inserts feature two drivers on the left-hand side of the horizontal format along with a photo of each of their respective cars on the right-hand side. The five-card set pairs drivers who are on the same racing team, including Gordon and Terry Labonte. These are found at a rate of 1:55 packs.

		MT
Complete Set (5):		120.00
Common Card:		15.00
1	Terry Labonte, Jeff Gordon	50.00
2	Dale Jarrett, Ernie Irvan	25.00
3	Mark Martin, Jeff Burton	25.00
4	Richard Petty, Kyle Petty	15.00
5	Jeff Gordon, Ricky Craven	40.00

1997 Upper Deck SPx Tag-Team Autographed

Identical to the regular Tag-Team inserts besides the autographs. These scarce autographed inserts are found on the average of 1:2,500 packs.

		MT
Complete Set (5):		900.00
Common Player:		150.00
1	Terry Labonte, Jeff Gordon	300.00
2	Dale Jarrett, Ernie Irvan	150.00
3	Mark Martin, Jeff Burton	200.00
4	Richard Petty, Kyle Petty	150.00
5	Jeff Gordon, Ricky Craven	250.00

1997 Wheels Jurassic Park

Wheels teamed up with Universal Studios to produce this dinosaur-themed racing set. The 61-card base set features a photo of the driver with the drivers last name and the Jurassic Park logo enhanced by silver foil stamping. The card backs feature the drivers career statistics along with a photo of his/her car.

		MT
Complete Set (61):		20.00
Common Driver:		.15
Triceratops: 2x to 4x		
1	Jeff Gordon	3.00
2	Dale Jarrett	1.00
3	Terry Labonte	1.50
4	Mark Martin	1.50
5	Rusty Wallace	1.50
6	Bobby Labonte	.25
7	Sterling Marlin	.25
8	Jeff Burton	.25
9	Ted Musgrave	.15
10	Michael Waltrip	.15
11	David Green	.15
12	Ricky Craven	.15
13	Johnny Benson	.15
14	Jeremy Mayfield	.15
15	Bobby Hamilton	.15
16	Kyle Petty	.15
17	Darrell Waltrip	.15
18	Wally Dallenbach	.15
19	Bill Elliott	1.50
20	Jeff Green	.15
21	Joe Nemechek	.15
22	Derrick Cope	.15
23	Ward Burton	.15
24	Chad Little	.15
25	Mike Skinner	.15
26	Brett Bodine	.15
27	Hut Stricklin	.15
28	Ken Schrader	.15
29	Steve Grissom	.15
30	Robby Gordon	.15
31	Kenny Wallace	.15
32	Bobby Hillin, Jr.	.15
33	Jimmy Spencer	.15
34	John Andretti	.15
35	Steve Park	.15
36	Michael Waltrip	.15
37	Dale Jarrett	.75
38	Mike McLaughlin	.15
39	Todd Bodine	.15
40	Bobby Labonte	.15
41	Jeff Fuller	.15
42	Phil Parsons	.15
43	Jason Keller	.15
44	Mark Martin	1.00
45	Randy LaJoie	.15
46	Glenn Allen	.15
47	Glenn Allen	.15
48	Jeff Gordon	2.00
49	Mark Martin	1.00
50	Mark Martin	1.00
51	Jeff Gordon	2.00
52	John Andretti	.15
53	Jimmy Makar	.15
54	Charlie Pressley	.15
55	Donnie Wingo	.15
56	Richard Childress	.15
57	Andy Petree	.15
58	Travis Carter	.15
59	Joe Gibbs	.15
60	Checklist	.15
61	Checklist	.15

1997 Wheels Jurassic Park Triceratops

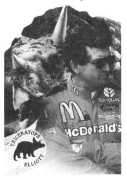

This 61-card set parallels the base set and features a die-cut design. An image of a Triceratops is in the background, with a gold foil medallion featuring the drivers name in the bottom left corner of the card. These parallel inserts are seeded 1:2 packs.

	MT
Triceratops: 2x to 4x	

1997 Wheels Jurassic Park Carnivore

This 12-card set features the top Winston Cup drivers. The inserts feature metallic, micro-etched design enhanced by gold holographic foil. They are seeded 1:15 packs.

		MT
Complete Set (12):		60.00
Common Driver:		2.50
C1	Dale Earnhardt	15.00
C2	Jeff Gordon	15.00
C3	Dale Jarrett	5.00
C4	Bobby Labonte	3.00
C5	Jimmy Spencer	2.50
C6	Bill Elliott	8.00
C7	Terry Labonte	8.00
C8	Rusty Wallace	8.00
C9	Jeff Burton	3.00
C10	Mark Martin	8.00
C11	Brett Bodine	2.50
C12	Sterling Marlin	2.50

1997 Wheels Jurassic Park Pteranodon

These inserts are printed on plastic exhibiting sleek black and gold foil stamping. There are 10-cards in the set, which are seeded 1:30 packs.

		MT
Complete Set (10):		100.00
Common Driver:		5.00
P1	Dale Earnhardt	30.00
P2	Jeff Gordon	30.00
P3	Bobby Labonte	8.00
P4	Terry Labonte	15.00
P5	Rusty Wallace	15.00
P6	Jeff Burton	5.00
P7	Sterling Marlin	5.00
P8	Mark Martin	15.00
P9	Dale Jarrett	10.00
P10	Kyle Petty	5.00

1997 Wheels Jurassic Park Raptors

These 1:6 pack inserts feature a Raptor in the background with the drivers last name and Raptors stamped with silver foil stamping. The card front is also enhanced with a holographic shimmer.

		MT
Complete Set (16):		25.00
Common Driver:		1.50
R1	Terry Labonte	4.00
R2	Jeff Gordon	8.00
R3	Johnny Benson	1.50
R4	Ward Burton	1.50
R5	Bobby Hamilton	1.50
R6	Ricky Craven	1.50
R7	Michael Waltrip	1.50
R8	Bobby Labonte	1.50
R9	Dale Jarrett	2.50
R10	Bill Elliott	4.00
R11	Rusty Wallace	4.00
R12	Jimmy Spencer	1.50
R13	Sterling Marlin	1.50
R14	Kyle Petty	1.50
R15	Ken Schrader	1.50
R16	Robby Gordon	1.50

1997 Wheels Jurassic Park Thunder Lizard

Each card in this 10-card set is imprinted with micro-lining covered with an electrifying array of silver, gold, and black foils, and brought to life with actual lizard skin encased in each card. Thunder Lizards are inserted 1:90 packs.

		MT
Complete Set (10):		350.00
Common Driver:		20.00
TL1	Jeff Gordon	90.00
TL2	Dale Jarrett	30.00
TL3	Bobby Labonte	20.00
TL4	Rusty Wallace	40.00
TL5	Bill Elliott	40.00
TL6	Jeff Burton	20.00
TL7	Mark Martin	40.00
TL8	Dale Earnhardt	90.00
TL9	Mike Skinner	20.00
TL10	Robby Gordon	20.00

1997 Wheels Jurassic Park T-Rex

The card fronts feature foil stamping, metallic micro-etching and embossed design. Inserts in this 10-card set are seeded in every 60 packs.

		MT
Complete Set (10):		180.00
Common Driver:		10.00
TR1	Terry Labonte	25.00
TR2	Jeff Gordon	50.00
TR3	Dale Jarrett	15.00
TR4	Bobby Labonte	10.00
TR5	Dale Earnhardt	50.00
TR6	Rusty Wallace	25.00
TR7	Mike Skinner	10.00
TR8	Joe Nemechek	10.00
TR9	Jeremy Mayfield	10.00
TR10	Bill Elliott	25.00

1998 Maxx

This 105-card set includes 60 regular car and driver cards, along with three subsets: "Home Cookin", "License to Drive" and "Front Runners". Inserts included in '98 Maxx are Swappin' Paint, Signed, Sealed and Delivered Autographs, Focus on a Champion and a 1-of-1 Richard Petty card, which enables the lucky recipient to a free visit to the Richard Petty Driving Experience as well as all expenses paid. Packs sell for a suggested retail of $1.99.

		MT
Complete Set (105):		25.00
Common Driver:		.10
1	Jeremy Mayfield	.25
2	Rusty Wallace	1.50
3	Dale Earnhardt	3.00
4	Bobby Hamilton	.10
5	Terry Labonte	1.50
6	Mark Martin	1.50
7	Geoff Bodine	.10
8	Ernie Irvan	.50
9	Jeff Burton	.40
10	Ricky Rudd	.20
11	Johnny Benson	.40
12	Dale Jarrett	.75
13	Jerry Nadeau	.10
14	Steve Park	.10
15	Bill Elliott	1.50
16	Ted Musgrave	.10
17	Darrell Waltrip	.10
18	Bobby Labonte	.25
19	Todd Bodine	.10
20	Kyle Petty	.25
21	Michael Waltrip	.10
22	Ken Schrader	.10
23	Jimmy Spencer	.10
24	Jeff Gordon	3.00
25	Ricky Craven	.40
26	John Andretti	.25
27	Sterling Marlin	.25
28	Kenny Irwin	.10
29	Mike Skinner	.10
30	Derrick Cope	.10
31	Jeremy Mayfield	.40
32	Rusty Wallace	1.50
33	Dale Earnhardt	1.50
34	Bobby Hamilton	.10
35	Terry Labonte	.75
36	Mark Martin	.75
37	Geoff Bodine	.10
38	Ernie Irvan	.40
39	Jeff Burton	.10
40	Ricky Rudd	.20
41	Johnny Benson	.25
42	Dale Jarrett	.25
43	Jerry Nadeau	.10
44	Steve Park	.10
45	Bill Elliott	.40
46	Ted Musgrave	.10
47	Darrell Waltrip	.10
48	Bobby Labonte	.20
49	Todd Bodine	.10
50	Kyle Petty	.20
51	Michael Waltrip	.10
52	Ken Schrader	.10
53	Jimmy Spencer	.10
54	Jeff Gordon	1.50
55	Ricky Craven	.25
56	John Andretti	.10
57	Sterling Marlin	.20
58	Kenny Irwin	.10
59	Mike Skinner	.10
60	Derrike Cope	.10
61	Jimmy Spencer (Home Cookin')	.10
62	Bill Elliott (Home Cookin')	.75
63	Darrell Waltrip (Home Cookin')	.10
64	Jeff Gordon (Home Cookin')	1.50
65	John Andretti (Home Cookin')	.10
66	Johnny Benson (Home Cookin')	.25
67	Jeff Burton (Home Cookin')	.25
68	Bobby Hamilton (Home Cookin')	.10
69	Ernie Irvan (Home Cookin')	.40
70	Dale Jarrett (Home Cookin')	.40
71	Bobby Labonte (Home Cookin')	.25
72	Terry Labonte (Home Cookin')	.75
73	Kyle Petty (Home Cookin')	.25
74	Ricky Rudd (Home Cookin')	.10
75	Morgan Shepherd (Home Cookin')	.10
76	Kenny Irwin (License to Drive)	.10
77	Steve Park (License to Drive)	.10
78	Jerry Nadeau (License to Drive)	.10
79	Todd Bodine (License to Drive)	.10
80	Mike Skinner (License to Drive)	.10
81	Jeremy Mayfield (License to Drive)	.25
82	Ricky Craven (License to Drive)	.25
83	Steve Grissom (License to Drive)	.10
84	Brett Bodine (License to Drive)	.10
85	Jeff Burton (License to Drive)	.25
86	Ward Burton (License to Drive)	.10
87	Chad Little (License to Drive)	.10
88	David Green (License to Drive)	.10
89	John Andretti (License to Drive)	.25
90	Bobby Labonte (License to Drive)	.25
91	Jeff Gordon (Front Runners)	1.50
92	Dale Jarrett (Front Runners)	.40

93	Mark Martin (Front Runners)	.75
94	Jeff Burton (Front Runners)	.25
95	Dale Earnhardt (Front Runners)	1.50
96	Terry Labonte (Front Runners)	.75
97	Bobby Labonte (Front Runners)	.25
98	Bill Elliott (Front Runners)	.75
99	Rusty Wallace (Front Runners)	.75
100	Ken Schrader (Front Runners)	.10
101	Johnny Benson (Front Runners)	.10
102	Ted Musgrave (Front Runners)	.10
103	Ernie Irvan (Front Runners)	.40
104	Steve Park (Front Runners)	.10
105	Kenny Irwin (Front Runners)	.10

1998 Maxx Focus on a Champion

This 15-card set consists of those drivers Maxx felt would contend for the Winston Cup Championship in '98. They are inserted 1:24 packs with the checklist including Gordon, Earnhardt and Mark Martin. A die-cut parallel version also exists. These are seeded 1:96 packs with each insert sporting a special die-cut design.

	MT
Complete Set (15):	100.00
Common Driver:	2.00
Cel Cards:	1.5x to 2.5x
FC1 Jeff Gordon	25.00
FC2 Dale Jarrett	10.00
FC3 Dale Earnhardt	25.00
FC4 Mark Martin	12.00
FC5 Jeff Burton	5.00
FC6 Kyle Petty	2.00
FC7 Terry Labonte	12.00
FC8 Bobby Labonte	4.00
FC9 Bill Elliott	12.00
FC10Rusty Wallace	12.00
FC11Ken Schrader	2.00
FC12Johnny Benson	4.00
FC13Ted Musgrave	2.00
FC14Ernie Irvan	6.00
FC15Kenny Irwin	2.00

1998 Maxx Swappin' Paint

These specially designed inserts showcase the new 1998 paint schemes and uniforms of all the top cars and drivers in NASCAR. The 25-card set features many of the top drivers and are seeded 1:3 packs.

	MT
Complete Set (25):	25.00
Common Driver:	.50
S1 Steve Park	4.00
S2 Terry Labonte	4.00
S3 Ernie Irvan	1.50
S4 Bobby Hamilton	.50
S5 Derrike Cope	.50
S6 John Andretti	.50
S7 Geoff Bodine	.50
S8 Hut Stricklin	.50
S9 Jeff Burton	2.00
S10 Robert Pressley	.50
S11 Brett Bodine	.50
S12 Rick Mast	.50
S13 Jerry Nadeau	.50
S14 Sterling Marlin	1.00
S15 Johnny Benson	1.50
S16 Ted Musgrave	.50
S17 Todd Bodine	.50
S18 Jeremy Mayfield	4.00
S19 Mark Martin	4.00
S20 Chad Little	.50
S21 Joe Nemechek	.50
S22 Dick Trickle	.50
S23 Jimmy Spencer	1.00
S24 Kenny Irwin	.50
S25 Ricky Craven	1.00

1998 Maxx Teamwork

Drivers who make up multiple car teams, for example, Gordon and Labonte are highlighted in this 10-card set. These inserts can be found at a rate of 1:11 packs.

	MT
Complete Set (10):	20.00
Common Driver:	.75
TW1 Jeff Gordon	8.00
TW2 Terry Labonte	4.00
TW3 Ricky Craven	2.00
TW4 Mark Martin	4.00
TW5 Jeff Burton	2.00
TW6 Ted Musgrave	.75
TW7 Chad Little	.75
TW8 Johnny Benson	1.50
TW9 Dale Jarrett	3.00
TW10Kenny Irwin	.75

1998 Maxx Signed, Sealed, Delivered Autographs

This five-card set features the actual signatures of top NASCAR drivers including Gordon and Rusty Wallace. Each card is hand numbered and limited to 250.

	MT
Complete Set (5):	550.00
Common Driver:	50.00
S1 Richard Petty	50.00
S2 Rusty Wallace	125.00
S3 Jeff Gordon	300.00
S4 Dale Jarrett	90.00
S5 Jeff Burton	75.00

1998 Maxx '97 Year in Review

This 175-card set was released in a specially designed boxed set imitating a car hauler. Each card is printed on 20-point stock with a number of different subsets, including Pole Sitter, Memorable Moments, In The Pits, Top 10 Point Leaders and Award Winners. A limited number of 50 hand- numbered autographs of Dale Earnhardt were also randomly inserted into the sets.

		MT
Complete Set (175):		40.00
Common Driver:		.10
Dale Earnhardt Auto.		350.00
1	Jeff Gordon	2.00
2	Mike Skinner	.10
3	Ricky Craven	.25
4	Ward Burton	.10
5	Hendrick Sweep	.10
6	Jeff Gordon	1.00
7	Mark Martin	.50
8	Ernie Irvan	.25
9	Dale Earnhardt	1.00
10	Ricky Craven	.20
11	Rusty Wallace	1.00
12	Terry Labonte	.50
13	Kyle Petty	.20
14	Ricky Rudd	.20
15	Ernie Irvan	.25
16	Dale Jarrett	.60
17	Robby Gordon	.10
18	Johnny Benson	.25
19	Geoff Bodine	.10
20	Steve Grissom	.10
21	Dale Jarrett	.60
22	Dale Jarrett	.25
23	Darrell Waltrip	.10
24	Michael Waltrip	.10
25	Ted Musgrave	.10
26	Jeff Burton	.25
27	Dale Jarrett	.25
28	Steve Grissom	.10
29	Jeff Gordon	1.00
30	Darrell Waltrip	.10
31	Jeff Gordon	1.00
32	Rusty Wallace	.50
33	Dale Earnhardt	1.00
34	Jeremy Mayfield	.25
35	Ted Musgrave	.10
36	Jeff Gordon	1.00
37	Kenny Wallace	.10
38	Mark Martin	1.00
39	Rusty Wallace	1.00
40	Ricky Craven	.20
41	Mark Martin	1.00
42	John Andretti	.10
43	Jeff Burton	.25
44	Bill Elliott	1.00
45	Dale Jarrett	.25
46	Mark Martin	1.00
47	Mark Martin	.50
48	Darrell Waltrip	.10
49	Ernie Irvan	.25
50	Golden Gate Shot	.10
51	Jeff Gordon	1.00
52	Jeff Gordon	2.00
53	Dale Earnhardt	1.00
54	Jeff Burton	.25
55	Darrell Waltrip	.10
56	Ricky Rudd	.10
57	Bobby Labonte	.20
58	Jeff Burton	.20
59	Bobby Labonte	.20
60	Dave Marcis	.10
61	Jeff Gordon	2.00
62	Bobby Hamilton	.10
63	Derrick Cope	.10
64	Morgan Shepherd	.10
65	Ward Burton	.10
66	Ernie Irvan	.40
67	Dale Jarrett	.60
68	Derrick Cope	.10
69	Ted Musgrave	.10
70	Bill Elliott	.50
71	Jeff Gordon	2.00
72	Joe Nemechek	.10
73	Ricky Rudd	.20
74	Jimmy Spencer	.10
75	Ted Musgrave	.10
76	John Andretti	.10
77	Mike Skinner	.10
78	Terry Labonte	.50
79	Kyle Petty	.20
80	Ward Burton	.10
81	Jeff Burton	.25
82	Ken Schrader	.10
83	Hut Stricklin	.10
84	Rusty Wallace	1.00
85	Dale Jarrett	.60
86	Dale Jarrett	.25
87	Joe Nemechek	.10
88	Johnny Benson	.25
89	Ted Musgrave	.10
90	Bill Elliott	.50
91	Ricky Rudd	.20
92	Ernie Irvan	.25
93	Kyle Petty	.10
94	Michael Waltrip	.10
95	Darrell Waltrip	.10
96	Jeff Gordon	1.00
97	Todd Bodine	.10
98	Steve Grissom	.10
99	Ricky Rudd	.20
100	Robby Gordon	.10
101	Mark Martin	1.00
102	Johnny Benson	.20
103	Rusty Wallace	.50
104	Bill Elliott	.50
105	Jeff Burton	.20
106	Dale Jarrett	.25
107	Kenny Wallace	.10
108	Steve Grissom	.10
109	Geoff Bodine	.10
110	David Green	.10
111	Jeff Gordon	2.00
112	Bobby Labonte	.20
113	Chad Little	.10
114	Dick Trickle	.10
115	Jeff Burton	.20
116	Dale Jarrett	.60
117	Bill Elliott	.50
118	Ted Musgrave	.10
119	Joe Nemechek	.10
120	Kenny Irwin	.10
121	Jeff Gordon	2.00
122	Ken Schrader	.10
123	Ernie Irvan	.25
124	John Andretti	.10
125	Geoff Bodine	.10
126	Mark Martin	1.00
127	Mark Martin	.50
128	Dale Earnhardt	1.00
129	Robby Gordon	.10
130	Jeff Gordon	1.00
131	Jeff Burton	.20
132	Ward Burton	.10
133	Ricky Craven	.20
134	Bobby Hamilton	.10
135	Rusty Wallace	.50
136	Dale Jarrett	.50
137	Geoff Bodine	.10
138	Terry Labonte	.50
139	Bobby Labonte	.20
140	Darrell Waltrip	.10
141	Terry Labonte	1.00
142	Ernie Irvan	.25
143	Kyle Petty	.20
144	Mark Martin	.50
145	Ken Schrader	.10
146	Bobby Hamilton	.10
147	Bobby Labonte	.20
148	Sterling Martin	.10
149	Bill Elliott	1.00
150	Bobby Hamilton	.10
151	Dale Jarrett	.50
152	Bobby Hamilton	.10
153	Kyle Petty	.10
154	Dale Jarrett	.25
155	Darrell Waltrip	.10
156	Bobby Labonte	.20
157	Geoff Bodine	.10
158	Bobby Hamilton	.10
159	Mark Martin	.50
160	Chad Little	.10
161	Checklist	.10
P1	Jeff Gordon	2.00
P2	Dale Jarrett	.75
P3	Mark Martin	1.00
P4	Jeff Burton	.25
P5	Dale Earnhardt	2.00
P6	Terry Labonte	1.00
P7	Bobby Labonte	.20
P8	Bill Elliott	1.00
P9	Rusty Wallace	1.00
P10	Ken Schrader	.10
AW1	Jeff Gordon	2.00
AW2	Mike Skinner	.10
AW3	Dale Jarrett	.75
AW4	Bill Elliott	1.00

1998 Pinnacle Mint Collection

Mint Collection features two coins and three cards per pack. Die-Cut cards are included to provide the perfect fit for the coin to fit into the card. The 30-card set features coins that come in brass, nickel-silver, solid silver and solid gold as well as bronze-plated proof coins, silver- plated proof coins and gold-plated proof coins.

		MT
Complete Set (30):		15.00
Common Die-Cut:		.25
Bronze:		1.5x to 2x
Silver:		4x to 8x
Gold:		8x to 15x
1	Jeff Gordon	2.50
2	Mark Martin	1.00
3	Dale Earnhardt	2.50
4	Terry Labonte	1.00
5	Dale Jarrett	.75
6	Bobby Labonte	.25
7	Bill Elliott	1.00
8	Ted Musgrave	.25
9	Ricky Rudd	.25
10	Rusty Wallace	1.00
11	Jeremy Mayfield	.25
12	Michael Waltrip	.25
13	J Gordon Car	1.00
14	M Martin Car	.50
15	D Jarrett Car	.50
16	T Labonte Car	.50
17	D Earnhardt Car	1.00
18	B Labonte Car	.25
19	B Elliott Car	.50
20	T Musgrave Car	.25
21	R Rudd Car	.25
22	R Wallace Car	.50
23	J Mayfield Car	.25
24	M Waltrip Car	.25
25	Mark Martin	.75
26	Rusty Wallace	.75
27	Jeff Gordon	1.50
28	Dale Jarrett	.50
29	Ricky Rudd	.25
30	Ernie Irvan	.50

1998 Pinnacle Mint Collection Bronze/Silver/Gold

In addition to Bronze, Gold and Silver Mint Team parallel versions also exist. Each of the versions is printed on full Bronze, Silver or Gold foil card stock respectively with identical photos and design of the base cards. Silvers are found 1:23 retail and 1:15 hobby packs. Golds are seeded 1:47 in all packs.

	MT
Bronze:	1.5x to 2x
Silver:	4x to 8x
Gold:	8x to 15x

1998 Pinnacle Mint Collection Coins

Each pack of Mint Collection has two coins, the most common being Brass, replacing Brass coins on a randon basis are Nickel-Silver, Gold Plated and Solid Silver coins. Nickel-Silver coins are seeded 1:41 packs, Gold-Plated 1:199 and Solid Silver are found 1:960 retail and 1:288 hobby packs. In addition Proof coins are also available. Bronze, Silver and Gold Proof versions exist for each coin in the 30-card set. Each is individually numbered with Bronze limited to 500, Silver 250 and Gold 100.

		MT
Complete Set (30):		45.00
Common Coin:		.75
Silver:		4x to 8x
Gold:		20x to 30x
1	Jeff Gordon	6.00
2	Mark Martin	3.00
3	Dale Earnhardt	6.00
4	Terry Labonte	3.00
5	Dale Jarrett	2.00
6	Bobby Labonte	.75
7	Bill Elliott	3.00
8	Ted Musgrave	.75
9	Ricky Rudd	.75
10	Rusty Wallace	3.00
11	Jeremy Mayfield	.75
12	Michael Waltrip	.75
13	J Gordon Car	3.00
14	M Martin Car	1.50
15	D Jarrett Car	1.00
16	T Labonte Car	1.50
17	D Earnhardt Car	3.00
18	B Labonte Car	.75
19	B Elliott Car	1.50
20	T Musgrave Car	.75
21	R Rudd Car	.75
22	R Wallace Car	1.50
23	J Mayfield Car	.75
24	M Waltrip Car	.75
25	Mark Martin	2.00
26	Rusty Wallace	2.00
27	Jeff Gordon	4.00
28	Dale Jarrett	1.50
29	Ricky Rudd	.75
30	Ernie Irvan	1.50

1998 Pinnacle Mint Collection Championship Mint

This special two-card commemorative set honors 1997 Winston Cup champion Jeff Gordon. The set features one card with a close-up photo of Gordon while the other card has a photo of his car. These are found at a rate of 1:71 in retail packs and 1:41 hobby packs.

	MT
Complete Set (2):	40.00
Common Gordon:	20.00

1998 Pinnacle Mint Collection Championship Mint Coins

This three-card insert set offers racing fans the opportunity to own coins from the actual hood of Jeff Gordon's car. The odds of finding one of these coins are 1:129 retail and 1:89 hobby packs. The hobby version of these coins is printed on an oversized version.

		MT
Complete Set (3):		225.00
Common Coin:		60.00
1	Jeff Gordon's Car	60.00
2	Jeff Gordon (Standard Size)	100.00
3	Jeff Gordon (Oversized)	75.00

1998 Press Pass

The card fronts feature a full-size photo with silver foil stamping. Backs have a photo along with personal information, with stats and a brief highlight from the driver's career. There are eight cards per pack with 100 cards in the set. There also is a #0 Jeff Gordon Championship card showcased on an all-foil card, found exclusively in hobby packs at a 1:480 pack ratio. Press Pass also created a "set within a set" named Retros that help celebrate NASCAR's 50th Anniversary with 50 of the greatest drivers of all time. They are seeded one per pack. Retros are mini cards that are numbered 101-150.

		MT
Complete Set (150):		18.00
Common Driver:		.10
J. Gordon Winston Cup Champ.		
:		80.00
1	Jeff Gordon	2.00
2	Mark Martin	1.00
3	Dale Jarrett	.75
4	Dale Earnhardt	2.00
5	Terry Labonte	1.00
6	Ricky Rudd	.20
7	Rusty Wallace	1.00
8	Sterling Marlin	.20
9	Bobby Hamilton	.20
10	Ernie Irvan	.75
11	Bobby Labonte	.25
12	Ken Schrader	.20
13	Jeff Burton	.20
14	Michael Waltrip	.20
15	Ted Musgrave	.20
16	Geoff Bodine	.20
17	Ward Burton	.20
18	Ricky Craven	.20
19	Johnny Benson	.20
20	Jeremy Mayfield	.20
21	Kyle Petty	.25
22	Darrell Waltrip	.20
23	Bill Elliott	1.00
24	Mike Skinner	.20
25	David Green	.20
26	Joe Nemechek	.20
27	Wally Dallenbach	.20
28	R. Wallace Car	.50
29	D. Earnhardt Car	1.00
30	T. Labonte Car	.50
31	M. Martin Car	.50
32	R. Rudd Car	.10
33	#18 Interstate Batteries	.10
34	#24 DuPont Automotive Finishes J. Gordon Car	1.00
35	#88 Quality Care D. Jarrett Car	.40
36	#94 McDonald's B. Elliott Car	.50
37	Randy LaJoie	.10
38	Todd Bodine	.10
39	Tim Fedewa	.10
40	Kevin LePage	.10
41	Mark Martin	1.00
42	Mike McLaughlin	.10
43	Jason Keller	.10
44	Steve Park	.10
45	Dale Jarrett	.40
46	Dale Earnhardt Jr.	2.00
47	Ricky Craven	.10
48	Elliott Sadler	.10
49	Hermie Sadler	.10
50	Rich Bickle	.10
51	Jack Sprague	.10
52	Joe Ruttman	.10
53	Mike Bliss	.10
54	Ron Hornaday	.10
55	Ernie Irvan	.40
56	Kenny Irwin	.10
57	Sterling Marlin	.10
58	Steve Park	.10
59	Johnny Benson	.10
60	Todd Bodine	.10
61	Bobby Hamilton	.10
62	Ted Musgrave	.10
63	Jimmy Spencer	.10
64	Darren Jolly	.10
65	Jeff Knight	.10
66	Barry Muse	.10
67	Mike Belden	.10
68	Mike Trower	.10
69	Chris Anderson	.10
70	Patrick Donahue	.10
71	Brian Whitesell	.10
72	Ray Evernham (#6 Valvoline)	.10
73	J.J. Clodfelter	.10
74	Ben Leslie	.10
75	Dennis Ritchie	.10
76	Mitch Williams	.10
77	Lonnie Dubay	.10

78	Luke Shimp	.10
79	Butch Hylton	.10
80	Steve Spahr	.10
81	Jimmy Fennig	.10
82	Randy LaJoie	.10
83	Jack Sprague	.10
84	Mike Stefanik	.10
85	Butch Gilliland	.10
86	Mike Swaim Jr.	.10
87	Hal Goodson	.10
88	Bryan Germone	.10
89	Joe Kosiski	.10
90	Kelly Tanner	.10
91	Gary Scelzi	.10
92	Mark Martin	1.00
93	Andy Green	.10
94	Jimmy Makar	.10
95	Ray Evernham	.10
96	Jimmy Fennig	.10
97	Larry McReynolds	.10
98	Todd Parrott	.10
99	Robin Pemberton	.10
100	Checklist (1998 NASCAR Winston Cup Schedule)	.10
101	Jeff Gordon	3.00
102	Mark Martin	1.50
103	Dale Jarrett	.75
104	Dale Earnhardt	3.00
105	Rusty Wallace	1.50
106	Ricky Rudd	.20
107	Bill Elliott	1.00
108	Terry Labonte	1.50
109	Ralph Earnhardt	.10
110	Richie Evans	.10
111	Red Farmer	.10
112	Ray Hendrick	.10
113	Darrell Waltrip	.10
114	Tiny Lund	.10
115	Jerry Cook	.10
116	Geoff Bodine	.10
117	Bob Welborn	.10
118	Fred Lorenzen	.10
119	Herb Thomas	.10
120	Tim Flock	.10
121	Lee Petty	.10
122	Buck Baker	.10
123	Rex White	.10
124	Ned Jarrett	.25
125	Benny Parsons	.10
126	Joe Weatherly	.10
127	David Pearson	.25
128	Bobby Isaac	.10
129	Tim Richmond	.10
130	Curtis Turner	.10
131	Alan Kulwicki	.50
132	Bobby Allison	.50
133	Cale Yarborough	.25
134	Richard Petty	.75
135	Davey Allison	.50
136	Glen Wood	.10
137	Harry Gant	.10
138	Junior Johnson	.10
139	Fireball Roberts	.10
140	Neil Bonnett	.25
141	Lee Roy Yarbrough	.10
142	Buddy Baker	.10
143	A.J. Foyt	.25
144	Red Byron	.10
145	Cotton Owens	.10
146	Hershel McGriff	.10
147	Marvin Panch	.10
148	Jack Ingram	.10
149	Marshall Teague	.10
150	Checklist Ernie Irvan	.25

1998 Press Pass Oil Slicks

These inserts are a parallel to the 100-card base set and feature blue-foil stamping with each card individually numbered to 100. They are found exclusively in hobby packs at a rate of 1:48 packs.

	MT
Oil Slicks:	25x to 40x

1998 Press Pass Autographs

This set features certified authentic autographs of NASCAR Winston Cup top drivers including Gordon and Earnhardt. Autographs are found exclusively in hobby packs at a rate of 1:240 packs.

		MT
Complete Set (14):		850.00
Common Autograph:		15.00
1	Dale Earnhardt	250.00
2	Jeff Gordon	250.00
3	Dale Jarrett	70.00
4	Terry Labonte	100.00
5	Mark Martin	90.00
6	Bobby Labonte	30.00
7	Jeff Burton	20.00
8	Rusty Wallace	100.00
9	Michael Waltrip	15.00
10	Ricky Craven	20.00
11	Ricky Rudd	20.00
12	Mike Skinner	15.00
13	Darrell Waltrip	20.00
14	Johnny Benson	20.00

1998 Press Pass Cup Chase '98

This interactive insert set features 20 drivers, race winners cards are redeemable for an all-foil die-cut version of the set. These inserts are seeded 1:24 packs.

		MT
Complete Set (20):		125.00
Common Driver:		3.00
CC1	Johnny Benson	3.00
CC2	Jeff Burton	3.00
CC3	Ward Burton	3.00
CC4	Ricky Craven	3.00
CC5	D. Earnhardt Car	30.00
CC6	Bill Elliott	15.00
CC7	Jeff Gordon	35.00
CC8	Bobby Hamilton	3.00
CC9	Ernie Irvan	10.00
CC10	Dale Jarrett	10.00
CC11	Bobby Labonte	3.00
CC12	Terry Labonte	15.00
CC13	Sterling Marlin	3.00
CC14	Mark Martin	15.00
CC15	Kyle Petty	3.00
CC16	Ricky Rudd	3.00
CC17	Ken Schrader	3.00
CC18	Rusty Wallace	15.00
CC19	Michael Waltrip	3.00
CC20	Field Card	3.00

1998 Press Pass Oil Cans

This nine-card embossed set features an all-foil front, shaped like an oil can. Card fronts have a photo of the driver with a brief description of the driver's career on the card backs. They are seeded 1:18 packs.

		MT
Complete Set (9):		60.00
Common Driver:		2.50
OC1	Jeff Burton	2.50
OC2	D. Earnhardt Car	15.00
OC3	Jeff Gordon	20.00
OC4	Dale Jarrett	8.00
OC5	Bobby Labonte	2.50
OC6	Terry Labonte	10.00
OC7	Mark Martin	10.00
OC8	Ricky Rudd	2.50
OC9	Rusty Wallace	10.00

1998 Press Pass Pit Stop

This 18-card set captures the hottest Winston Cup pit crews in action during their record pit stip. They are die-cut in the shape of a stop sign with a photo of the car during a pit stop. The bottom right has the record time the pit crew did the pit stop. Backs have a date, track and race finish from the record pit stop. They are seeded 1:12 packs.

		MT
Complete Set (18):		60.00
Common Driver:		2.00
PS1	Rusty Wallace	10.00
PS2	D. Earnhardt Car	15.00
PS3	Kodak	2.00
PS4	Terry Labonte	10.00
PS5	Mark Martin	10.00
PS6	Ricky Rudd	2.00
PS7	Ted Musgrave	2.00
PS8	Darrell Waltrip	2.00
PS9	Bobby Labonte	2.00
PS10	Michael Waltrip	2.00
PS11	Ward Burton	2.00
PS12	Jeff Gordon	20.00
PS13	E. Irvan Car	2.00
PS14	STP	2.00
PS15	Kyle Petty	2.00
PS16	Dale Jarrett	8.00
PS17	Bill Elliott	10.00
PS18	Jeff Burton	2.00

1998 Press Pass Shockers

Shockers is a 15-card set die-cut in the shape of a shock. Card fronts have gold-

foil stamping with a photo of the driver surrounded by two shocks. Card backs give a brief personal history of the driver. They are seeded 1:12 hobby packs.

		MT
Complete Set (15):		60.00
Common Driver:		1.50
ST1A	Terry Labonte	8.00
ST2A	Jeff Gordon	15.00
ST3A	Dale Earnhardt	15.00
ST4A	Dale Jarrett	6.00
ST5A	Mark Martin	8.00
ST6A	Ricky Rudd	1.50
ST7A	Rusty Wallace	8.00
ST8A	Bill Elliott	8.00
ST9A	Bobby Labonte	2.50
ST10A	Kyle Petty	2.50
ST11A	Jeff Burton	1.50
ST12A	Michael Waltrip	1.50
ST13A	Ted Musgrave	1.50
ST14A	Mike Skinner	1.50
ST15A	Ward Burton	1.50

1998 Press Pass Torpedoes

This 15-card set is a sort of parallel of the Shockers, only these have photos of the corresponding driver's car from the Shockers insert set. These are found only in retail packs at an insert ratio of 1:12 packs.

		MT
Complete Set (15):		60.00
Common Driver:		1.50
ST1B	T. Labonte Car	8.00
ST2B	J. Gordon Car	15.00
ST3B	D. Earnhardt Car	15.00
ST4B	D. Jarrett Car	6.00
ST5B	M. Martin Car	8.00
ST6B	Tide	1.50
ST7B	R. Wallace Car	8.00
ST8B	B. Elliott Car	8.00
ST9B	Interstate Batteries	1.50
ST11B	Exide	1.50
ST12B	Citgo	1.50
ST13B	Family Channel	1.50
ST14B	Loew's	1.50
ST15B	MBNA	1.50

1998 Press Pass Triple Gear "Burning Rubber"

Nine different "Burning Rubber" tire cards feature a piece of race-used tires from NASCAR Winston Cup drivers, including Gordon and Earnhardt, complete with a certificate of authenticity with each card individually numbered. These are seeded 1:480 packs.

		MT
Complete Set (9):		800.00
Common Driver:		50.00
TG1	Rusty Wallace	100.00
TG2	Dale Earnhardt	200.00
TG3	Terry Labonte	100.00
TG4	Mark Martin	100.00
TG5	Bobby Labonte	50.00
TG6	Jeff Gordon	200.00
TG7	Mike Skinner	50.00
TG8	Dale Jarrett	80.00
TG9	Jeff Burton	50.00

1998 Press Pass Triple Gear "3 in 1"

These scarce redemption inserts were evenly allocated across three Press Pass brands: VIP, Premium and Press Pass. A total of 33 numbered versions for each driver exist, with 11 redemptions for each driver seeded into each of the three products. The inserts have all three race-used materials on it, which include tire, sheet metal and firesuit. Press Pass and Premium stated odds were 1:5,500 packs.

	MT
Common Driver:	125.00
Redemption, 11 of each card inserted into Press Pass, VIP & Premium	
STG1Rusty Wallace	400.00
STG2Dale Earnhardt	600.00
STG3Terry Labonte	400.00
STG4Mark Martin	400.00
STG5Bobby Labonte	250.00
STG6Jeff Gordon	600.00
STG7Mike Skinner	125.00
STG8Dale Jarrett	300.00
STG9Jeff Burton	250.00

1998 Press Pass Premium

The 54-card base set features gold foil stamping with driver's cards done in a horizontal format and car cards done in a vertical format. Each regular-sized card is UV coated, on 24 point card stock. Card backs highlight the driver's sponsor, car-make, s historical highlight and career stats.

		MT
Complete Set (54):		20.00
Common Driver:		.25
1	Randy LaJoie	.25
2	Todd Bodine	.25
3	Mike McLaughlin	.25
4	Elliott Sadler	.25
5	TBD	.25
6	Terry Labonte	1.50
7	Bobby Labonte	.40
8	Jeff Burton	.40
9	Michael Waltrip	.25
10	Dale Jarrett	1.00
11	Mark Martin	1.50
12	Jimmy Spencer	.25
13	Hermie Sadler	.25
14	Dale Earnhardt Jr.	3.00
15	Kevin LePage	.25
16	R. Wallace Car	.75
17	D. Earnhardt Car	1.50
18	T. Labonte Car	.75
19	M. Martin Car	.75
20	R. Rudd Car	.25
21	#18 Interstate Batteries	.25
22	J. Gordon Car	1.50
23	#26 Cheerios	.25
24	#28 Texaco Havoline E. Irvan Car	.50
25	D. Jarrett Car	.50
26	B. Elliott Car	.75
27	#99 Exide Batteries	.25
28	Jeff Gordon	3.00
29	Dale Jarrett	1.00
30	Mark Martin	1.50
31	Jeff Burton	.25
32	Dale Earnhardt	3.00
33	Terry Labonte	1.50
34	Bobby Labonte	.40
35	Bill Elliott	1.50

36	Rusty Wallace	1.50
37	Ken Schrader	.25
38	Johnny Benson	.25
39	Ted Musgrave	.25
40	Jeremy Mayfield	.25
41	Ernie Irvan	1.00
42	Kyle Petty	.40
43	Bobby Hamilton	.25
44	Ricky Rudd	.25
45	Michael Waltrip	.25
46	Ricky Craven	.25
47	Jimmy Spencer	.25
48	Geoff Bodine	.25
49	Ward Burton	.25
50	Sterling Marlin	.40
51	Darrell Waltrip	.25
52	Joe Nemechek	.25
53	Mike Skinner	.25
54	Kenny Irwin	.25

1998 Press Pass Premium Reflectors

This 81-card set parallels the 54-card base set as well as the 27-card Flag Chasers insert set. Odds of finding a Reflector from the base set are 1:8 packs, while the odds of finding a Flag Chaser Reflector are 1:24 packs. Reflectors are easy to identify by the protective Reflector Shield, which easily peels off and their mirror-like appearance.

	MT
Reflectors:	2x to 4x

1998 Press Pass Signings

These autographs are randomly seeded across two products, Press Pass VIP and Press Pass Premium. Some autographs are found in both products while some signatures are exclusive to one or the other. Odds of finding a Signings in Premium are 1:48 packs while VIP stated odds are 1:60.

		MT
Common Autograph		10.00
VIP inserted 1:60		
Premium inserted 1:48		
1	Jeff Gordon	200.00
2	Dale Jarrett	75.00
3	Dale Earnhardt	200.00
4	Terry Labonte	100.00
5	Ricky Rudd	10.00
6	John Andretti	20.00
7	Sterling Marlin	20.00
8	Bobby Hamilton	10.00

9	Ernie Irvan	40.00
10	Bobby Labonte	30.00
11	Ken Schrader	10.00
12	Jeff Burton	30.00
13	Michael Waltrip	20.00
14	Ted Musgrave	10.00
15	Geoff Bodine	10.00
16	Ward Burton	10.00
17	Ricky Craven	20.00
18	Johnny Benson	30.00
20	Wally Dallenbach	10.00
22	Bill Elliott	80.00
23	Mike Skinner	10.00
24	David Green	10.00
25	Joe Nemechek	10.00
27	Steve Park	10.00
28	Robin Pemberton	10.00
29	Larry McReynolds	10.00
30	Jimmy Makar	10.00
31	Ray Evernham	10.00
32	Todd Parrott	10.00
33	Randy Lajoie	10.00
34	Robert Pressley	10.00
35	Tim Fedewa	10.00
36	Kevin LePage	10.00
37	Mike McLaughlin	10.00
38	Jason Keller	10.00
39	Dale Earnhardt Jr.	125.00
40	Jimmy Spencer	20.00

1998 Press Pass Premium Flag Chasers

This 27-card set features multi-dimensional die-cutting, with micro-etched foil stamping. The set includes the top Winston Cup drivers and cars. These inserts are seeded 1:2 packs.

		MT
Complete Set (27):		30.00
Common Driver:		.50
Reflectors:		5x to 10x
FC1	Jeff Gordon	5.00
FC2	Dale Earnhardt	5.00
FC3	Dale Jarrett	2.00
FC4	Mark Martin	3.00
FC5	Jeff Burton	.50
FC6	Rusty Wallace	3.00
FC7	Ricky Rudd	.50
FC8	Terry Labonte	3.00
FC9	Bobby Labonte	.50
FC10	Ernie Irvan	2.00
FC11	Johnny Benson	.50
FC12	Michael Waltrip	.50
FC13	Bill Elliott	3.00
FC14	Ken Schrader	.50
FC15	Kyle Petty	.75
FC16	Steve Park	.50
FC17	Kenny Irwin	.50
FC18	Ricky Craven	.50
FC19	Mike Skinner	.50
FC20	#2 Miller Lite	1.50
FC21	#3 Goodwrench Service Plus	2.50
FC22	#5 Kellogg's	1.50
FC23	#18 Interstate Batteries	.50
FC24	#24 DuPont Automotive Finishes	2.50
FC25	#88 Quality Care	1.00
FC26	#94 McDonald's	1.50
FC27	#99 Exide Batteries	.50

1998 Press Pass Premium Rivalries

Celebrating NASCAR's 50th Anniversary, these 12 interlocking die-cut cards depict the top six driver duels from the Winston Cup circuit. These are seeded one per six packs.

		MT
Complete Set (12):		25.00
Common Player:		1.50
R1A	Jeff Burton	1.50
R1B	Jeff Gordon	8.00
R2A	David Pearson	1.50
R2B	Richard Petty	1.50
R3A	Dale Earnhardt	8.00
R3B	Rusty Wallace	4.00
R4A	Cale Yarborough	2.00
R4B	Bobby Allison	1.50
R5A	Mark Martin	4.00
R5B	Dale Jarrett	3.00
R6A	Ernie Irvan	3.00
R6B	Jimmy Spencer	1.50

1998 Press Pass Premium Steel Horses

Steel Horses feature a die-cut design in the shape of a horse head, with silver foil etching and embossing. The driver's car is featured in the foreground with his last name underneath. This is a 12-card set, with the approximate odds of finding one at 1:12 packs.

		MT
Complete Set (12):		60.00
Common Car:		3.00
SH1	R. Wallace Car	8.00
SH2	D. Earnhardt Car	15.00
SH3	T. Labonte Car	8.00
SH4	M. Martin Car	8.00
SH5	#10 Tide	3.00
SH6	#18 Interstate Batteries	3.00
SH7	J. Gordon Car	15.00
SH8	#40 Coors Light	3.00
SH9	#44 Hot Wheels	3.00
SH10	D. Jarrett Car	6.00
SH11	B. Elliott Car	8.00
SH12	#99 Exide Batteries	3.00

1998 Press Pass Premium Triple Gear

This nine-card set gives the racing collector an opportunity to own an authentic piece of the top drivers' race-used firesuits. The overall odds of finding a Triple Gear race-used firesuit insert are 1:432, with Press Pass stating a total number of 150 numbered sets exist.

	MT
Complete Set (9):	800.00
Common Driver:	50.00
TGF1Rusty Wallace	120.00
TGF2Dale Earnhardt	200.00
TGF3Terry Labonte	120.00
TGF4Mark Martin	120.00
TGF5Bobby Labonte	50.00
TGF6Jeff Gordon	200.00
TGF7Mike Skinner	50.00
TGF8Dale Jarrett	80.00
TGF9Jeff Burton	50.00

1998 Press Pass VIP

The regular-sized 50-card set features gold-foil stamping with a photo of the driver and a shadow image of the driver in the background. The Press Pass VIP logo along with the facsimile driver signature are gold-foil stamped. The top-half of the card backs have another photo of the driver along with stats on the bottom half.

		MT
Complete Set (50):		25.00
Common Driver:		.15
Explosives:		1.5x to 2.5x
1	John Andretti	.15
2	Johnny Benson	.25
3	Geoff Bodine	.25
4	Jeff Burton	.40
5	Ward Burton	.25
6	Dale Earnhardt	3.00
7	Bill Elliott	1.50
8	Jeff Gordon	3.00
9	Bobby Hamilton	.15
10	Ernie Irvan	.75
11	Kenny Irwin	.15
12	Dale Jarrett	1.00
13	Bobby Labonte	.40
14	Terry Labonte	1.50
15	Sterling Marlin	.40
16	Mark Martin	1.50
17	Jeremy Mayfield	.75
18	Ted Musgrave	.25
19	Joe Nemechek	.15
20	Steve Park	.15
21	Robert Pressley	.15
22	Ricky Rudd	.25
23	Ken Schrader	.15
24	Mike Skinner	.15
25	Jimmy Spencer	.15
26	Rusty Wallace	1.50
27	Michael Waltrip	.25
28	Dale Earnhardt Jr.	3.00
29	Tim Fedewa	.15
30	Jason Keller	.15
31	Randy LaJoie	.15
32	Mark Martin	1.50
33	Mike McLaughlin	.15
34	Elliott Sadler	.15
35	Hermie Sadler	.15
36	Tony Stewart	.15
37	Jeff Burton	.40
38	Dale Earnhardt	1.50
39	Bill Elliott	.75

40	Jeff Gordon	1.50
41	Dale Jarrett	.50
42	Bobby Labonte	.40
43	Terry Labonte	.75
44	Chad Little	.15
45	Mark Martin	.75
46	Rusty Wallace	.75
47	Mark Martin	.75
48	Dale Jarrett	.50
49	Roush Racing	.15
50	Checklist	.15

1998 Press Pass VIP Explosives

Each of the 50 base cards is meticulously etched using a custom die and printed on a unifoil board creating an almost rainbow effect. These parallel inserts have Explosives written beneath the driver's name or car. They are found one per pack.

	MT
Explosives:	1.5x to 2.5x

1998 Press Pass VIP Driving Force

This 18-card all-foil insert set features the driver's car encircled by a whirlwind of red-tinted colors. The card backs give a brief overview of the drivers' 1998 track success. These are seeded one per 10 packs. A die-cut version also exists, which are found every 30 packs.

		MT
Complete Set (18):		40.00
Common Driver:		1.00
Die-Cuts:		1.5x to 2x
DF1	John Andretti	1.00
DF2	Johnny Benson	1.00
DF3	Jeff Burton	1.50
DF4	Ward Burton	1.00
DF5	Earnhardt	8.00
DF6	Bill Elliott	4.00
DF7	Jeff Gordon	8.00
DF8	Bobby Hamilton	1.00
DF9	Kenny Irwin	1.00
DF10	Dale Jarrett	3.00
DF11	Bobby Labonte	2.00
DF12	Terry Labonte	2.00
DF13	Sterling Marlin	2.00
DF14	Mark Martin	4.00
DF15	Jeremy Mayfield	2.50
DF16	Ricky Rudd	1.00
DF17	Ken Schrader	1.00
DF18	Rusty Wallace	4.00

1998 Press Pass VIP Head Gear

This nine-card set features drivers' helmets and the artwork that adorns them. The card design features all-foil etching. These are seeded one per 16 packs with special die-cut parallel versions seeded one per 40 packs.

		MT
Complete Set (9):		30.00
Common Driver:		1.50
Die-Cuts:		1.5x to 2x
HG1	Jeff Burton	2.00
HG2	Dale Earnhardt	8.00
HG3	Bill Elliott	4.00
HG4	Jeff Gordon	8.00
HG5	Dale Jarrett	3.00
HG6	Bobby Labonte	2.00
HG7	Terry Labonte	4.00
HG8	Mark Martin	4.00
HG9	Rusty Wallace	4.00

1998 Press Pass VIP Lap Leader

This nine-card set features the cars of the top NASCAR drivers, which are micro-embossed on a thick all-foil card stock. These are seeded one per 20 packs. A parallel version featuring an all acetate clear card stock with double etched foil stamping also exists, they are seeded one per 60 packs.

		MT
Complete Set (9):		35.00
Common Driver:		2.00
Acetates:		1.5x to 2x
LL1	Jeff Burton	2.00
LL2	Dale Earnhardt	10.00
LL3	Jeff Gordon	10.00
LL4	Dale Jarrett	4.00
LL5	Bobby Labonte	2.00
LL6	Terry Labonte	5.00
LL7	Mark Martin	5.00
LL8	Jeremy Mayfield	3.00
LL9	Rusty Wallace	5.00

1998 Press Pass VIP NASCAR Country

This nine-card set helps celebrate NASCAR's 50th anniversary. The top nine winston cup drivers team up with country music as collectors can expect to find one of these

inserts in every 10 packs. A special die-cut version also exists which are seeded 1:30 packs.

		MT
Complete Set (9):		30.00
Common Driver:		2.00
Die-Cuts:		1.5x to 2x
NC1	Dale Earnhardt	8.00
NC2	Bill Elliott	4.00
NC3	Jeff Gordon	8.00
NC4	Dale Jarrett	3.00
NC5	Bobby Labonte	2.00
NC6	Terry Labonte	4.00
NC7	Mark Martin	4.00
NC8	Ricky Rudd	2.00
NC9	Rusty Wallace	4.00

1998 Press Pass VIP Triple Gear

These Triple Gear inserts feature race-used pieces of sheet metal from the drivers' Winston Cup car. The odds of finding one of these race-used inserts are 1:384 packs, there are only 225 serial numbered sets produced.

		MT
Common Driver:		50.00
TGS1	Rusty Wallace	120.00
TGS2	Dale Earnhardt	200.00
TGS3	Terry Labonte	100.00
TGS4	Mark Martin	120.00
TGS5	Bobby Labonte	75.00
TGS6	Jeff Gordon	220.00
TGS7	Mike Skinner	50.00
TGS8	Dale Jarrett	90.00
TGS9	Jeff Burton	75.00

1998 SP Authentic

The complete 84-card set boasts 34 driver cards, 34 car cards, and 16 "Victory Lap" subset cards. The base card design features close-up photo of the driver with the drivers' name and SP Authentic logo in gold foil stamping. The card backs have a photo of the driver on the right-half with the driver's career stats listed on the left-half. There are five-cards per pack with an SRP of $4.99 per pack.

		MT
Complete Set (84):		35.00
Common Driver:		.25
1	Jeremy Mayfield	1.50

2	Rusty Wallace	2.50
3	Dale Earnhardt	5.00
4	Bobby Hamilton	.25
5	Terry Labonte	2.50
6	Mark Martin	2.50
7	Geoff Bodine	.40
8	Hut Stricklin	.25
9	Jeff Burton	.50
10	Ricky Rudd	.40
11	Johnny Benson	.40
12	Dale Jarrett	1.50
13	Jerry Nadeau	.25
14	Steve Park	.25
15	Bill Elliott	2.50
16	Ted Musgrave	.25
17	Darrell Waltrip	.40
18	Bobby Labonte	.50
19	Todd Bodine	.25
20	Kyle Petty	.50
21	Michael Waltrip	.40
22	Ken Schrader	.25
23	Jimmy Spencer	.25
24	Jeff Gordon	5.00
25	Ricky Craven	.50
26	John Andretti	.40
27	Sterling Marlin	.50
28	Kenny Irwin	.25
29	Mike Skinner	.25
30	Derrike Cope	.25
31	Ernie Irvan	1.00
32	Joe Nemechek	.25
33	Kenny Wallace	.25
34	Ward Burton	.40
35	Jeremy Mayfield	1.00
36	Rusty Wallace	1.00
37	Dale Earnhardt	2.00
38	Bobby Hamilton	.25
39	Terry Labonte	1.00
40	Mark Martin	1.00
41	Geoff Bodine	.25
42	Hut Stricklin	.25
43	Jeff Burton	.50
44	Ricky Rudd	.25
45	Johnny Benson	.25
46	Dale Jarrett	.50
47	Jerry Nadeau	.25
48	Steve Park	.25
49	Bill Elliott	1.00
50	Ted Musgrave	.25
51	Darrell Waltrip	.25
52	Bobby Labonte	.40
53	Todd Bodine	.25
54	Kyle Petty	.40
55	Michael Waltrip	.25
56	Ken Schrader	.25
57	Jimmy Spencer	.25
58	Jeff Gordon	1.00
59	Ricky Craven	.25
60	John Andretti	.25
61	Sterling Marlin	.25
62	Kenny Irwin	.25
63	Mike Skinner	.25
64	Derrike Cope	.25
65	Ernie Irvan	.75
66	Joe Nemechek	.25
67	Kenny Wallace	.25
68	Ward Burton	.25
69	Darrell Waltrip	.25
70	Rusty Wallace	1.50
71	Bill Elliott	1.50
72	Jeff Gordon	3.00
73	Geoff Bodine	.25
74	Terry Labonte	1.50
75	Mark Martin	1.50
76	Ricky Rudd	.40
77	Ernie Irvan	.75
78	Dale Jarrett	1.00
79	Kyle Petty	.50
80	Sterling Marlin	.40
81	Dave Marcis	.25
82	Bobby Labonte	.40
83	Ken Schrader	.25
84	Jimmy Spencer	.25

1998 Sp Authentic Behind the Wheel

This is a three-tiered insert set featuring 20 cards of the top Winston Cup drivers. Each level has its own insert ratio

and foil treatment. Level one has a silver foil treatment and are seeded 1:4 packs. Level two has a gold foil treatment are inserted 1:12 packs. Level three is the scarcest and are die-cut and treated with gold foil. Only 100 numbered level three sets exist.

		MT
Complete Set (20):		40.00
Common Driver:		1.00
Golds:		1.5x to 2x
Die-Cuts:		15x to 25x
BW1	Jeff Gordon	8.00
BW2	Dale Jarrett	3.00
BW3	Mark Martin	4.00
BW4	Jeff Burton	1.50
BW5	Terry Labonte	4.00
BW6	Bobby Labonte	2.00
BW7	Bill Elliott	4.00
BW8	Rusty Wallace	4.00
BW9	Ken Schrader	1.00
BW10	Johnny Benson	1.00
BW11	Ted Musgrave	1.00
BW12	Jeremy Mayfield	2.50
BW13	Ernie Irvan	2.00
BW14	Kyle Petty	1.50
BW15	Bobby Hamilton	1.00
BW16	Ricky Rudd	1.00
BW17	Michael Waltrip	1.50
BW18	Ricky Craven	1.50
BW19	Kenny Irwin Jr.	1.00
BW20	Steve Park	1.00

1998 SP Authentic Mark of a Legend

This five-card autographed insert set includes five all-time NASCAR greats including Richard Petty, Ned Jarrett and Cale Yarborough. Card fronts include the drivers autograph along with a photo of a career milestone and the drivers photo. These are seeded 1:168 packs.

		MT
Complete Set (5):		200.00
Common Driver:		40.00
M1	Richard Petty	60.00
M2	David Pearson	40.00
M3	Benny Parsons	40.00
M4	Ned Jarrett	40.00
M5	Cale Yarborough	50.00

1998 SP Authentic Sign of the Times Level 1

This two-tiered insert set contains autographs from today's top NASCAR stars including Jeff Gordon, Mark Martin and Rusty Wallace. The autographs are put into a license plate shaped box, with a photo of the drivers car behind it. Level ones are seeded 1:24 packs and are highlighted with blue foil. Level two's are seeded 1:96 packs and are highlighted with red foil.

		MT
Complete Set (10):		200.00
Common Driver:		10.00
S1	Rusty Wallace	50.00
S2	Ted Musgrave	10.00
S3	Ricky Craven	20.00
S4	Sterling Marlin	20.00
S5	John Andretti	10.00
S6	Michael Waltrip	10.00
S7	Darrell Waltrip	20.00
S8	Jeremy Mayfield	30.00
S9	Kenny Irwin	25.00
S10	Bobby Hamilton	10.00

1998 SP Authentic Tradition

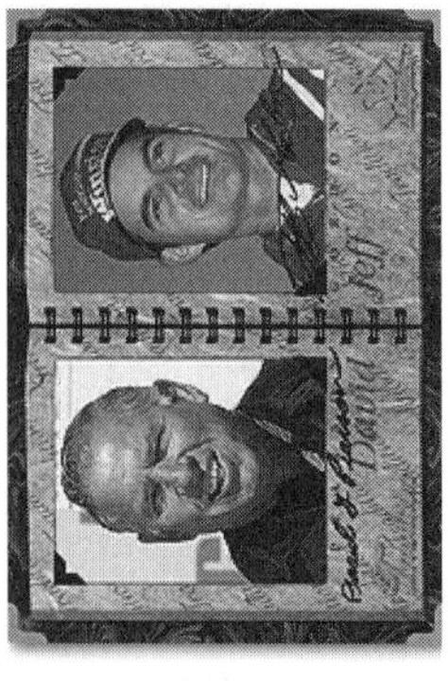

This five-card dual signature set features one autograph from a NASCAR legend and one autograph from a current NASCAR superstar. The first two cards in the set, Richard Petty/Dale Earnhardt and Pearson/Jeff Gordon were redemptions which expire 7-15-99. The odds of finding one of these rare autographed inserts are 1:288 packs.

		MT
Complete Set (5):		850.00
Common Driver:		100.00
T1	Richard Petty, Dale Earnhardt	300.00
T2	David Pearson, Jeff Gordon	250.00
T3	Benny Parsons, Terry Labonte	150.00
T4	Ned Jarrett, Dale Jarrett	125.00
T5	Cale Yarborough, Rusty Wallace	125.00

1998 Collector's Choice

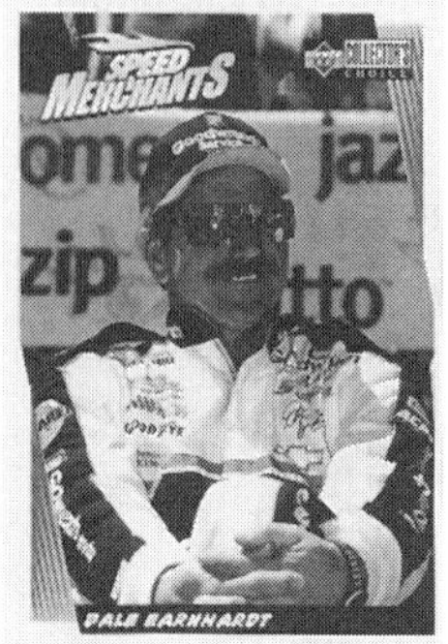

This 117-card set features a number of exciting subsets and a simple card design. The fronts have a white border encasing a photo of the driver or car, with the Collector's Choice logo in the top right corner. Card backs have one or two small photos depending on the subset along with some career information.

		MT
Complete Set (117):		12.00
Common Driver:		.05
1	Morgan Shepherd	.05
2	Rusty Wallace	.75
3	Dale Earnhardt	1.50
4	Sterling Marlin	.15
5	Terry Labonte	.75
6	Mark Martin	.75
7	Geoff Bodine	.05
8	Hut Stricklin	.05
9	Lake Speed	.05
10	Ricky Rudd	.05
11	Brett Bodine	.05
12	Dale Jarrett	.60
13	Bill Elliott	.75
14	Bobby Hamilton	.05
15	Wally Dallenbach	.05
16	Ted Musgrave	.05
17	Darrell Waltrip	.05
18	Bobby Labonte	.15
19	Steve Grissom	.05
20	Rick Mast	.05
21	Michael Waltrip	.05
22	Ward Burton	.05
23	Jimmy Spencer	.05
24	Jeff Gordon	1.50
25	Ricky Craven	.05
26	Kyle Petty	.15
27	Kenny Wallace	.05
28	Ernie Irvan	.60
29	David Green	.05
30	Johnny Benson	.15
31	Mike Skinner	.05
32	Jeremy Mayfield	.05
33	Ken Schrader	.05
34	Jeff Burton	.05
35	Robby Gordon	.05
36	Derrike Cope	.05
37	Morgan Shepherd	.05
38	R Wallace Car	.40
39	D Earnhardt Car	.75
40	Sterling Marlin	.05
41	T Labonte Car	.40
42	M Martin Car	.40
43	Geoff Bodine	.05
44	Hut Stricklin	.05
45	Lake Speed	.05
46	Ricky Rudd	.05
47	Brett Bodine	.05
48	D Jarrett Car	.30
49	B Elliott Car	.30
50	Bobby Hamilton	.05
51	Wally Dallenbach	.05
52	Ted Musgrave	.05
53	Darrell Waltrip	.05
54	Bobby Labonte	.05
55	Steve Grissom	.05
56	Rick Mast	.05
57	Michael Waltrip	.05
58	Ward Burton	.05
59	Jimmy Spencer	.05
60	J Gordon Car	.75
61	Ricky Craven	.05
62	Kyle Petty	.10
63	Kenny Wallace	.05
64	E Irvan Car	.30
65	David Green	.05
66	Johnny Benson	.05
67	Mike Skinner	.05
68	Jeremy Mayfield	.05
69	Ken Schrader	.05
70	Jeff Burton	.05
71	Robby Gordon	.05
72	Derrike Cope	.05
73	Jeff Burton	.05
74	Robby Gordon	.05
75	Mike Skinner	.05
76	Johnny Benson	.05
77	Ricky Craven	.05
78	Ward Burton	.05
79	Jeremy Mayfield	.05
80	Steve Grissom	.05
81	John Andretti	.05
82	David Green	.05
83	Bobby Labonte	.10
84	Kenny Wallace	.05
85	Mike Wallace	.05
86	Joe Nemechek	.05
87	Chad Little	.05
88	J Gordon Car	.75
89	T Labonte Car	.40
90	Ricky Craven	.05
91	Kyle Petty	.05
92	D Jarrett Car	.30
93	R Wallace Car	.40
94	Ricky Rudd	.05
95	Bobby Labonte	.05
96	Bobby Hamilton	.05
97	M Martin Car	.40
98	J Gordon Car	.75
99	M Martin Car	.40
100	T Labonte Car	.40
101	D Jarrett Car	.30
102	Jeff Burton	.05
103	D Earnhardt Car	.75
104	Bobby Labonte	.05
105	Ricky Rudd	.05
106	Michael Waltrip	.05
107	Jeremy Mayfield	.05
108	Ted Musgrave	.05
109	B Elliott Car	.40
110	Johnny Benson	.05
111	R Wallace Car	.40
112	Darrell Waltrip	.05
113	Checklist	.05
114	Checklist	.05
115	Checklist	.05
116	Checklist	.05
117	Checklist	.05

1998 Collector's Choice StarQuest

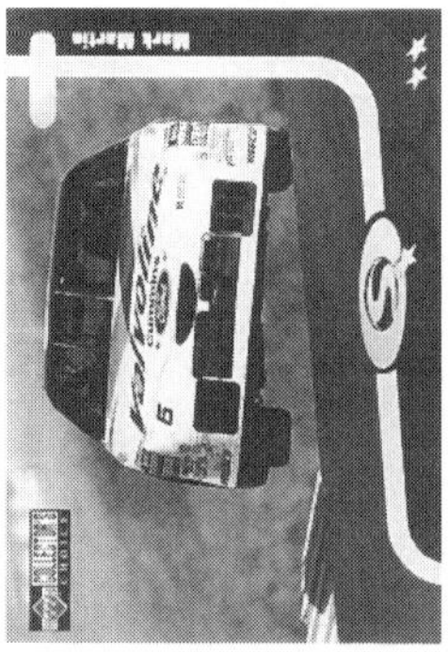

This 50-card set is broken into four different sets, with the first level cards numbered SQ1-SQ20 and found at a rate of one per three packs. The two-star level has cards numbered SQ21-SQ30 and are seeded 1:11 packs. The three-star level cards are numbered SQ31-SQ40 and are found 1:71 packs. The final level cards are numbered SQ41-SQ50 and are distinctive because they are all autographed by the drivers themselves. These are seeded 1:250 packs.

	MT
Common Star Quest 1 (1-20):	.25
Common Star Quest 2 (21-30):	.75
Common Star Quest 3 (31-40):	4.00
Common Star Quest 4 (41-50):	15.00
SQ1 Brett Bodine	.25
SQ2 Jimmy Spencer	.25
SQ3 Mike Wallace	.25
SQ4 Bobby Labonte	.40
SQ5 Morgan Shepherd	.25
SQ6 Derrike Cope	.25
SQ7 Kenny Wallace	.25
SQ8 Chad Little	.25
SQ9 Hut Stricklin	.25
SQ10Lake Speed	.25
SQ11Ricky Craven	.25
SQ12Steve Grissom	.25
SQ13Dick Trickle	.25
SQ14Rick Mast	.25
SQ15David Green	.25
SQ16Wally Dallenbach	.25
SQ17Joe Nemechek	.25
SQ18Ken Schrader	.25
SQ19Geoff Bodine	.25
SQ20Bobby Hamilton	.25
SQ21Mike Skinner	.75
SQ22Michael Waltrip	.75
SQ23Johnny Benson	.75
SQ24Ward Burton	.75
SQ25Robby Gordon	.75
SQ26Dale Earnhardt	6.00
SQ27Ted Musgrave	.75
SQ28Jeremy Mayfield	.75
SQ29Mark Martin	3.00
SQ30Sterling Marlin	.75
SQ31Ernie Irvan	10.00
SQ32Ricky Rudd	.25
SQ33Jeff Burton	.25
SQ34Rusty Wallace	15.00
SQ35Darrell Waltrip	.25
SQ36Jeff Gordon	30.00
SQ37Terry Labonte	15.00
SQ38Bill Elliott	15.00
SQ39Dale Jarrett	10.00
SQ40Kyle Petty	5.00
SQ41Jeff Gordon	125.00
SQ42Bill Elliott	60.00
SQ43Dale Jarrett	50.00
SQ44Kyle Petty	20.00
SQ45Bobby Labonte	20.00
SQ46Mark Martin	60.00
SQ47Geoff Bodine	15.00
SQ58Rusty Wallace	60.00
SQ49Robby Gordon	15.00
SQ50Ted Musgrave	15.00

1998 Collector's Choice CC600

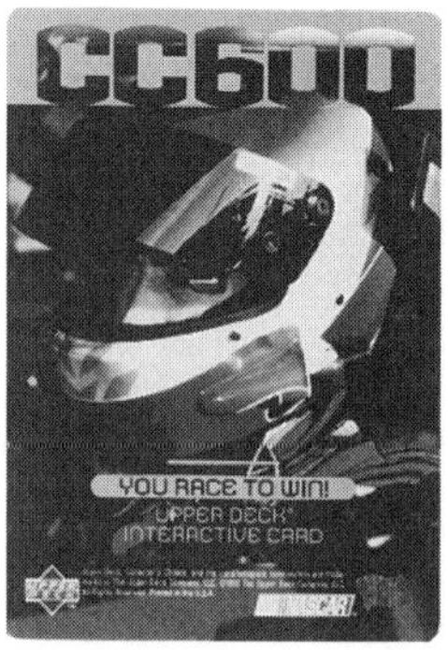

This 90-card set was intended to be a game where players need to finish 600 laps in order to win. Each game card has the same front but each has different results on the back pertaining to the game. These are found one per pack.

	MT
Complete Set (90):	15.00
Common Driver:	.15
CC6 Morgan Shepherd	.15
CC7 Rusty Wallace	.75
CC8 Sterling Marlin	.15
CC9 Terry Labonte	.75
CC10Mark Martin	.75
CC11Geoff Bodine	.15
CC12Hut Sticklin	.15
CC13Lake Speed	.15
CC14Ricky Rudd	.15
CC15Brett Bodine	.15
CC16Dale Jarrett	.50
CC17Bill Elliott	.75
CC18Bobby Hamilton	.15
CC19Wally Dallenbach	.15
CC20Ted Musgrave	.15
CC21Darrell Waltrip	.15
CC22Bobby Labonte	.25
CC23Steve Grissom	.15
CC24Rick Mast	.15
CC25Michael Waltrip	.15
CC26Ward Burton	.15
CC27Jimmy Spencer	.15
CC28Ricky Craven	.15
CC29Kyle Petty	.25
CC30Kenny Wallace	.15
CC31Ernie Irvan	.50
CC32David Green	.15
CC33Johnny Benson	.25
CC34Mike Skinner	.15
CC35Jeremy Mayfield	.15
CC36Ken Schrader	.15
CC37Jeff Burton	.15
CC38Robby Gordon	.15
CC39Derrike Cope	.15
CC40Morgan Shepherd	.15
CC41Rusty Wallace	.75
CC42Sterling Marlin	.15
CC43Mark Martin	.75
CC44Geoff Bodine	.15
CC45Hut Stricklin	.15
CC46Lake Speed	.15
CC47Ricky Rudd	.15
CC48Brett Bodine	.15
CC49Dale Jarrett	.50
CC50Bill Elliott	.75
CC51Bobby Hamilton	.15
CC52Wally Dallenbach	.15
CC53Ted Musgrave	.15
CC54Darrell Waltrip	.15
CC55Bobby Labonte	.15
CC56Steve Grissom	.15
CC57Rick Mast	.15
CC58Michael Waltrip	.15
CC59Ward Burton	.15
CC60Jimmy Spencer	.15
CC61Ricky Craven	.15
CC62Kyle Petty	.25
CC63Kenny Wallace	.15
CC64Ernie Irvan	.50
CC65David Green	.15
CC66Johnny Benson	.20
CC67Mike Skinner	.15
CC68Jeremy Mayfield	.15
CC69Ken Schrader	.15
CC70Jeff Burton	.25
CC71Robby Gordon	.15
CC72Derrike Cope	.15
CC73Morgan Shepherd	.15
CC74Rusty Wallace	.75
CC75Sterling Marlin	.15
CC76Mark Martin	.75
CC77Geoff Bodine	.15
CC78Hut Stricklin	.15
CC79Lake Speed	.15
CC80Ricky Rudd	.15
CC81Brett Bodine	.15
CC82Dale Jarrett	.50
CC83Bill Elliott	.75
CC84Bobby Hamilton	.15
CC85Wally Dallenbach	.15
CC86Ted Musgrave	.15
CC87Darrell Waltrip	.15
CC88Bobby Labonte	.15
CC89Steve Grissom	.15
CC90Rick Mast	.15

1998 Upper Deck Diamond Vision

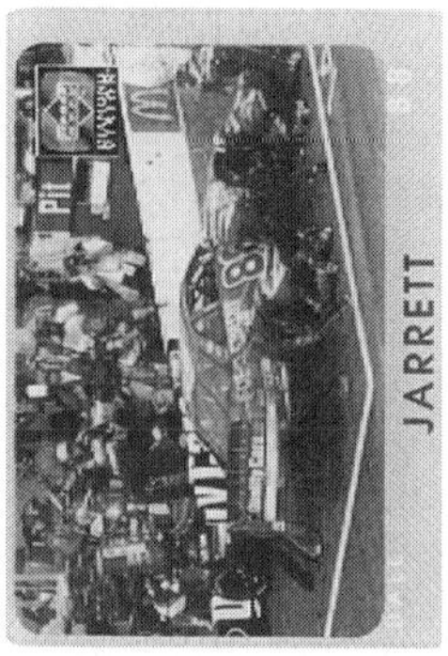

This 15-card set features actual race footage of the top drivers in action during the '97 Winston Cup season. The set incorporates Diamond Vision technology, by tipping the card the collector can watch the many frames of motion, reliving a moment from the prior season. They were packaged one card per pack with a SRP of $7.99 per pack.

		MT
Complete Set (15):		75.00
Common Driver:		4.00
1	Jeff Gordon	12.00
2	Rusty Wallace	8.00
3	Dale Earnhardt	12.00
4	Sterling Marlin	4.00
5	Terry Labonte	8.00
6	Mark Martin	8.00
7	Dale Jarrett	6.00
8	Bill Elliott	8.00
9	Ernie Irvan	5.00
10	Ricky Rudd	4.00
11	Jeff Burton	5.00
12	Ricky Craven	5.00
13	Bobby Labonte	5.00
14	Kyle Petty	5.00
15	Robby Gordon	4.00

1998 Upper Deck Diamond Vision Signature Moves

This 15-card parallel set is identical to the base cards besides the gold facsimile gold signatures across the card fronts. These are seeded one per five packs.

	MT
Sig. Moves:	1.5x to 2.5x

1998 Upper Deck Diamond Vision of a Champion

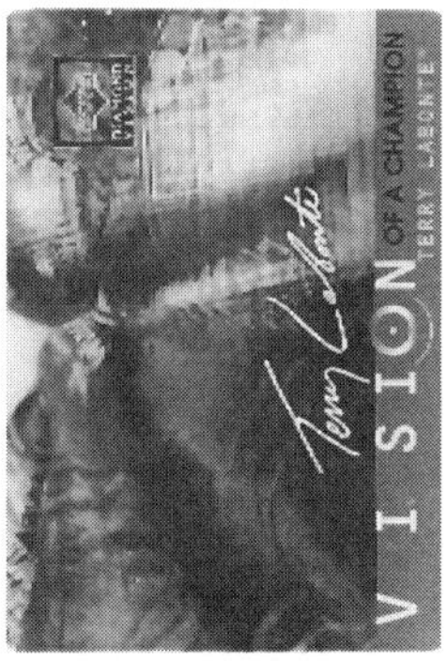

This four-card set salutes prior Winston Cup points champions, with each card capturing the driver receiving his championship cup after winning a race. These are seeded one per forty packs.

		MT
Complete Set (4):		150.00
Common Driver:		30.00
VC1	Rusty Wallace	30.00
VC2	Dale Earnhardt	50.00
VC3	Jeff Gordon	50.00
VC4	Terry Labonte	30.00

1998 Upper Deck "Road to the Cup"

The regular-sized base set is comprised of 45 driver cards, five checklist cards and five special subsets: "Days of Daytona", "Viva Las Vegas", "Taurus Time", "Double Barrel" and "Young Guns". The card fronts feature one photo with the Upper Deck logo, drivers last name and Road to the Cup logo all stamped with silver foil. Card backs have one photo along with a caption of a career highlight. There are 10 cards per pack at a SRP of $2.49 per pack.

		MT
Complete Set (120):		25.00
Common Driver:		.10
1	Kevin LePage	.10
2	Rusty Wallace	1.50
3	Dale Earnhardt	3.00
4	Bobby Hamilton	.10
5	Terry Labonte	.50
6	Mark Martin	1.50
7	Geoff Bodine	.10
8	Hut Stricklin	.10
9	Jeff Burton	.25
10	Ricky Rudd	.10
11	Brett Bodine	.10
12	Jeremy Mayfield	.50
13	Jerry Nadeau	.10
14	Loy Allen	.10
15	Bill Elliott	1.50
16	Jeff Green	.10
17	Darrell Waltrip	.10
18	Bobby Labonte	.40
19	David Green	.10
20	Dale Jarrett	.75
21	Michael Waltrip	.10
22	Ward Burton	.10
23	Jimmy Spencer	.10
24	Jeff Gordon	3.00
25	Randy LaJoie	.10
26	Johnny Benson	.25
27	Gary Bradberry	.10
28	Kenny Irwin	.10
29	Dave Marcis	.10
30	Derrike Cope	.10
31	Mike Skinner	.10
32	Ron Hornaday	.10
33	Ken Schrader	.10
34	Rick Mast	.10
35	Todd Bodine	.10
36	Ernie Irvan	.40
37	Dick Trickle	.10
38	Robert Pressley	.10
39	Wally Dallenbach	.10
40	Sterling Marlin	.25
41	Steve Grissom	.10
42	Joe Nemechek	.10
43	John Andretti	.10
44	Kyle Petty	.25
45	Kenny Wallace	.10
46	Rusty Wallace	.75
47	Mark Martin	.75
48	Geoff Bodine	.10
49	Ricky Rudd	.25
50	Jeremy Mayfield	.40
51	Jerry Nadeau	.10

52	Chad Little	.10
53	Michael Waltrip	.10
54	Jimmy Spencer	.10
55	Johnny Benson	.25
56	Kenny Irwin	.10
57	Kenny Wallace	.10
58	Dale Jarrett	.50
59	Bill Elliott	.75
60	Jeff Burton	.25
61	NASCAR Gold Car	.10
62	Jimmy Spencer	.10
63	Rusty Wallace	.75
64	Jeremy Mayfield, Rusty Wallace	.50
65	Geoff Bodine	.10
66	Jeff Gordon	3.00
67	John Andretti	.10
68	Bros. on the Pole	.10
69	Terry Labonte	.50
70	Bobby Labonte	.25
71	Chad Little	.10
72	Sterling Marlin	.25
73	Dave Marcis	.10
74	Jerry Nadeau	.10
75	Dale Earnhardt	3.00
76	Kenny Irwin	.10
77	Jerry Nadeau	.10
78	Todd Bodine	.10
79	Johnny Benson	.25
80	John Andretti	.10
81	Jeremy Mayfield	.25
82	Kevin LePage	.10
83	Dale Earnhardt	1.50
84	Randy LaJoie	.10
85	Mike Skinner	.10
86	Rusty Wallace	.75
87	Ernie Irvan	.25
88	Jeff Gordon	1.50
89	Jeff Burton	1.50
90	Dale Jarrett	.50
91	Bill Elliott	.75
92	Jeremy Mayfield	.25
93	Johnny Benson	.25
94	Dale Earnhardt	1.50
95	Kyle Petty	.20
96	Rick Mast	.10
97	Terry Labonte	.25
98	Ricky Rudd	.20
99	Chad Little	.10
100	Mark Martin	.75
101	Mark Martin	1.50
102	Dale Jarrett	1.00
103	Joe Nemechek	.10
104	Bobby Labonte	.40
105	Elliott Sadler	.10
106	Michael Waltrip	.10
107	Dick Trickle	.10
108	Jeff Burton	.40
109	Derrike Cope	.10
110	John Andretti	.10
111	Mike Wallace	.10
112	Robert Pressley	.10
113	Hermie Sadler	.10
114	Randy LaJoie	.10
115	Tony Stewart	.25
116	First Logo	.10
117	Second Logo	.10
118	25th Anniversary	.10
119	Current Logo	.10
120	50th Anniversary	.10

1998 Upper Deck "Road to the Cup" 50th Anniversary

This 50-card set commemorates the most memorable moments from NASCAR's last 50 years, saluting it's 50th Anniversary. The card fronts feature blue foil with a 50th Anniversary logo and a nostalgic photo. The card backs have a brief description of the NASCAR moment pictured on the front as well as a small photo. They were seeded 1:4 packs.

		MT
Complete Set (50):		40.00
Common Driver:		.25
AN1	Bill France Sr (NASCAR Founding Father)	.75
AN2	Daytona Beach Races (Late 1940's)	.25
AN3	1st stock car race (1st Sanctioned Stickly Stock Race 1949)	.25
AN4	Tim Flock (1952 NASCAR Champion)	1.50
AN5	Hudson Hornet (Engine of Choice in early NASCAR events)	.25
AN6	Fireball Roberts (A Star of NASCAR)	1.50
AN7	Smokey Yunick (Chevy's Motor Genius)	.75
AN8	Buck Baker (1st of 2 consecutive Championships '56-'57)	.50
AN9	Ned Jarrett (1st Championship/Star and spokesman 1961)	.75
AN10	Richard Petty (1st Championship 1964)	2.00
AN11	Junior Johnson (13 Wins in 1965)	1.00
AN12	David Pearson (1st Championship 1966)	1.00
AN13	Ned Jarrett (Autograph) (Last Championship on to the booth 1967)	.75
AN14	Richard Petty (Autograph) (Incredible year in 1967)	2.00
AN15	Donnie Allison (Car that debuted at Daytona)	.25
AN16	Bobby Allison (Car that debuted at Talledega)	.25
AN17	Richard Petty (Hot aerodynamic car)	1.00
AN18	David Pearson (Autograph) (Ties record with 3rd Championship 1969)	.75
AN19	Winston Cup Series (RJR enters NASCAR and creates Winston Cup '71)	.25
AN20	Bobby Allison (Star in NASCAR)	.75
AN21	Richard Petty (Breaks record with 4th Championship 1972)	2.00
AN22	Benny Parsons (1st Championship 1973)	.75
AN23	Silver Anniversary (NASCAR celebrates 25 years in 1973)	.25
AN24	Junior Johnson (130+ Wins as a Driver/ Owner)	1.50
AN25	Cale Yarborough (Autograph) (3rd Straight Championship 1978)	.75
AN26	David Pearson (100th Grand National Win 1978)	1.00
AN27	Richard Petty (Wins 7th and final Championship 1979)	2.00
AN28	AMC Matador Bobby Allison (Cars of NASCAR)	.25
AN29	Ford Thunderbird Bill Elliott (Cars of NASCAR)	1.50
AN30	Chevy Monte Carlo Darrell Waltrip (Cars of NASCAR)	.75
AN31	Buick Regal Bobby Jr. Hillin (Cars of NASCAR)	.25
AN32	Olds Cutlass Richard Petty (Cars of NASCAR)	.25
AN33	Pontiac Grand Prix Richard Petty (Cars of NASCAR)	.25
AN34	Chevy Lumina Ernie Irvan (Cars of NASCAR)	.75

AN35	Darrell Waltrip (Autograph) (Back to Back Championships 1981-1983)	.75
AN36	Richard Petty (Records 200th and last Grand National wi n 1984)	2.00
AN37	Bill Elliott (Winner of the 1st Winston Million 1985)	1.50
AN38	Davey Allison (Star of Winston Cup)	2.00
AN39	Bobby Allison (Autograph) (Wins '88 Daytona At Age 50, Son Davey Fi nished 2nd)	2.00
AN40	Rusty Wallace (Autograph) (1st Championship 1989)	3.00
AN41	Richard Petty (The King Retires in 1992)	2.00
AN42	Alan Kulwicki (1st Championship 1992)	2.50
AN43	Jeff Gordon (Wins the Inaugural Brickyard 400 1994)	6.00
AN44	Terry Labonte (Autograph) (Sets "Iron Man" record for Consecutive S tarts '96)	3.00
AN45	Terry Labonte (Captures 1996 Winston Cup Championship)	3.00
AN46	Suzuka, Japan (Demostration Race run in Japan 1996)	.25
AN47	Jeff Gordon (Autograph) (2nd Championship 1997)	6.00
AN48	Ford Taurus Rusty Wallace (Cars of NASCAR)	1.50
AN49	Dale Earnhardt (Autograph) (Earnhardt Takes Daytona 500 1998)	6.00
AN50	Mark Martin (Martin Takes Inaugural Las Vegas 400)	3.00

1998 Upper Deck "Road to the Cup" Autographs

This autographed 10-card set helps commemorate NASCAR's 50th Anniversary with autographs from current stars as well as past legends, including Richard Petty. These are hobby exclusive inserts and are hand numbered to 50 sets.

		MT
Complete Set (10):		900.00
Common Driver:		40.00
AN13	Ned Jarrett	40.00
AN14	Richard Petty	70.00
AN18	David Pearson	40.00
AN25	Cale Yarborough	40.00
AN35	Darrell Waltrip	50.00
AN39	Bobby Allison	40.00
AN40	Rusty Wallace	125.00
AN44	Terry Labonte	125.00
AN47	Jeff Gordon	300.00
AN49	Dale Earnhardt	300.00

1998 Upper Deck "Road to the Cup" Cover Story

This 16-card set features hand picked photos from the editors of Tuff Stuff magazine and Winston Cup Scene. The card fronts feature previous covers from each of the two magazines mentioned above. Card backs have a written summary about the cover and driver from each of the magazine's editors. These are inserted 1:11 packs.

		MT
Complete Set (16):		30.00
Common Driver:		.50
CS1	Ernie Irvan	1.00
CS2	Terry Labonte	3.00

CS3	Darrell Waltrip	.75
CS4	Kyle Petty	.75
CS5	Rusty Wallace	3.00
CS6	Alan Kulwicki	1.00
CS7	Bill Elliott	3.00
CS8	Jeff Gordon	6.00
CS9	Grand National Scene	.50
CS10	Dale Earnhardt	6.00
CS11	Ernie Irvan	1.00
CS12	Rusty Wallace	3.00
CS13	Jeff Gordon	6.00
CS14	Indianapolis Motor Speedway	.50
CS15	Gordon/Labonte/ Craven	1.50
CS16	Gordon/Waltrip	3.00

1998 Upper Deck "Road to the Cup" Cup Quest Turn #1

This insert set features Silver Light F/X technology, and features the top ten drivers who should contend for the Winston Cup title. The set is broken down into four tiers. Turn one inserts are sequentially numbered to 4,000, Turn two's are numbered to 2,000, Turn three's are numbered to 1,000 while Turn four's are numbered to 100.

	MT
Complete Set (10):	50.00
Common Driver:	3.00
Production 4,000 sets	
Turn 2:	1x to 1.5x
Production 2,000 sets	
Turn 3:	1.5x to 2.5x
Production 1,000 sets	
Turn 4:	4x to 8x
Production 100 sets	

CQ1	Jeff Gordon	15.00
CQ2	Rusty Wallace	8.00
CQ3	Kenny Irwin	3.00
CQ4	Jeremy Mayfield	5.00
CQ5	Terry Labonte	8.00
CQ6	Mark Martin	8.00
CQ7	Bobby Labonte	4.00
CQ8	Dale Jarrett	5.00
CQ9	Jeff Burton	3.00
CQ10	Ernie Irvan	4.00

1998 Upper Deck Victory Circle

The 150-card regular-sized set is comprised of 45 driver cards, 45 car cards, and three subsets: Season Highlights, Freeze Frame, and Hard Chargers. Card fronts feature a photo of the driver or car with the driver's name, Upper Deck logo and Victory Circle stamped in silver foil. Packs consist of 10 cards with a SRP of $2.49.

		MT
Complete Set (150):		25.00
Common Driver:		.10
1	Morgan Shepherd	.10
2	Rusty Wallace	1.00
3	Dale Earnhardt	2.50
4	Sterling Marlin	.20
5	Terry Labonte	1.00
6	Mark Martin	1.00
7	Geoff Bodine	.10
8	Hut Sticklin	.10
9	Lake Speed	.10
10	Ricky Rudd	.10
11	Brett Bodine	.10
12	Dale Jarrett	.75
13	Bill Elliott	1.00
14	Dick Trickle	.10
15	Wally Dallenbach	.10
16	Ted Musgrave	.10
17	Darrell Waltrip	.10
18	Bobby Labonte	.25
19	Gary Bradberry	.10
20	Rick Mast	.10
21	Michael Waltrip	.10
22	Ward Burton	.10
23	Jimmy Spencer	.10
24	Jeff Gordon	2.50
25	Ricky Craven	.25
26	Chad Little	.10
27	Kenny Wallace	.10
28	Ernie Irvan	.75
29	Steve Park	.10
30	Johnny Benson	.25
31	Mike Skinner	.10
32	Mike Wallace	.10
33	Ken Schrader	.10
34	Jeff Burton	.25
35	David Green	.10
36	Derrike Cope	.10
37	Jeremy Mayfield	.10
38	Dave Marcis	.10
39	John Andretti	.10
40	Robby Gordon	.25
41	Steve Grissom	.10
42	Joe Nemechek	.10
43	Bobby Hamilton	.10
44	Kyle Petty	.25
45	Kenny Irwin Jr.	.10
46	Morgan Shepherd	.10
47	Rusty Wallace	.50
48	Dale Earnhardt	1.25
49	Sterling Marlin	.10
50	Terry Labonte	.50
51	Mark Martin	.50
52	Geoff Bodine	.10
53	Hut Sticklin	.10
54	Lake Speed	.10
55	Ricky Rudd	.10
56	Brett Bodine	.10
57	Dale Jarrett	.40
58	Bill Elliott	.50
59	Dick Trickle	.10
60	Wally Dallenbach	.10
61	Ted Musgrave	.10
62	Darrell Waltrip	.10
63	Bobby Labonte	.20
64	Gary Bradberry	.10
65	Rick Mast	.10
66	Michael Waltrip	.10
67	Ward Burton	.10
68	Jimmy Spencer	.10
69	Jeff Gordon	1.25
70	Ricky Craven	.10
71	Chad Little	.10
72	Kenny Wallace	.10
73	Ernie Irvan	.40
74	Steve Park	.10
75	Johnny Benson	.20
76	Mike Skinner	.10
77	Mike Wallace	.10
78	Ken Schrader	.10
79	Jeff Burton	.20
80	David Green	.10
81	Derrike Cope	.10
82	Jeremy Mayfield	.10
83	Dave Marcis	.10
84	John Andretti	.10
85	Robby Gordon	.10
86	Steve Grissom	.10
87	Joe Nemechek	.10
88	Bobby Hamilton	.10
89	Kyle Petty	.20
90	Kenny Irwin Jr.	.10
91	Mike Skinner	.10
92	Gordon, Labonte, Craven	.50
93	Jeff Gordon	1.00
94	Robby Gordon	.10
95	Dale Jarrett	.40
96	Jeff Burton	.20
97	Mark Martin	.50
98	Mark Martin	.50
99	Joe Nemechek	.10
100	Jeff Gordon	1.00
101	Mike Skinner	.10
102	John Andretti	.10
103	Ricky Rudd	.10
104	Todd Bodine	.10
105	Jeff Gordon	1.00
106	Mark Martin	.50
107	Geoff Bodine	.10
108	Kenny Irwin Jr.	.10
109	Dave Marcis	.10
110	Rusty Wallace	.50
111	Ricky Rudd	.10
112	Bobby Labonte	.20
113	Ernie Irvan	.40
114	Kenny Wallace	.10
115	Mike Skinner	.10
116	Dale Jarrett	.40
117	Mark Martin	.50
118	Terry Labonte	.50
119	Jeff Gordon	1.00
120	Jeff Gordon	1.00
121	Derrike Cope	.10
122	Jeremy Mayfield	.10
123	Robby Gordon	.10
124	Ricky Craven	.10
125	Ernie Irvan	.40
126	Terry Labonte	.50
127	Johnny Benson	.20
128	Mike Skinner	.10
129	Kyle Petty	.20
130	Wally Dallenbach	.10
131	Rick Mast	.10
132	Morgan Shepherd	.10
133	Michael Waltrip	.10
134	Ted Musgrave	.10
135	Ricky Rudd	.10
136	Ricky Craven	.10
137	Geoff Bodine	.10
138	Morgan Shepherd	.10
139	Ted Musgrave	.10
140	Mark Martin	.50
141	Darrell Waltrip	.10
142	Rusty Wallace	.50
143	Jeff Burton	.10
144	Bill Elliott	.50
145	Ricky Rudd	.10
146	Terry Labonte	.50
147	Bobby Labonte	.20
148	Steve Grissom	.10
149	Dale Jarrett	.40
150	Ernie Irvan	.40

1998 Upper Deck Victory Circle 32 Days of Speed

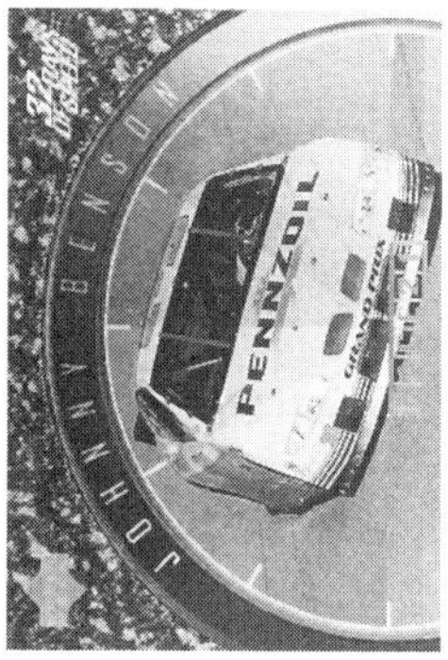

Each week of the 1997 NASCAR season is chronicled in this 32-card set. Highlighting some of the memorable races from the Winston Cup circuit. These were seeded 1:3 packs.

		MT
Complete Set (32):		25.00
Common Driver:		.25
DS1	Mike Skinner	.25
DS2	Jeff Gordon	5.00
DS3	Rusty Wallace	2.00
DS4	Robby Gordon	.25
DS5	Dale Jarrett	1.50
DS6	Jeff Burton	.50
DS7	Rusty Wallace	2.00
DS8	Kenny Wallace	.25
DS9	Mark Martin	2.00
DS10	Mark Martin	2.00
DS11	Jeff Gordon	5.00
DS12	Ricky Rudd	.25
DS13	Bobby Hamilton	.25
DS14	Ernie Irvan	1.50
DS15	Joe Nemechek	.25
DS16	John Andretti	.25
DS17	Ken Schrader	.25
DS18	Dale Jarrett	1.50
DS19	Ricky Rudd	.25
DS20	Todd Bodine	.25
DS21	Johnny Benson	.50
DS22	Kenny Wallace	.25
DS23	Bobby Labonte	.50
DS24	Bill Elliott	2.00
DS25	Ken Schrader	.25
DS26	Mark Martin	2.00
DS27	Ward Burton	.25
DS28	Bobby Labonte	.50
DS29	Terry Labonte	2.00
DS30	Bobby Hamilton	.25
DS31	Bobby Hamilton	.25
DS32	Geoff Bodine	.25

1998 Upper Deck Victory Circle Auto-Graphs

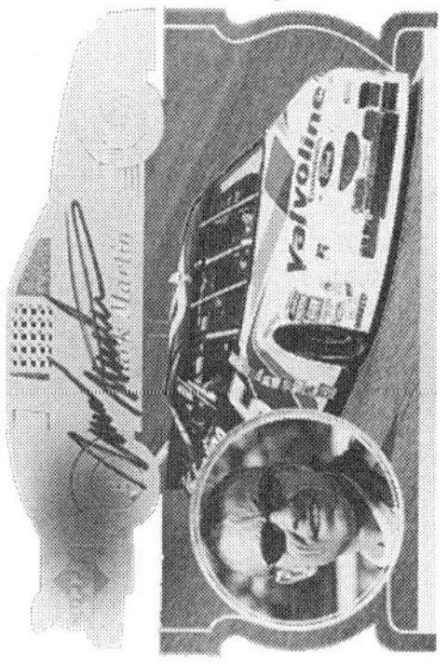

This five-card set features a die-cut design with authentic autographs from today's top Winston Cup drivers. Each card is individually hand-numbered to 250.

		MT
Complete Set (5):		
Common Driver:		40.00
AG1	Jeff Gordon	250.00
AG2	Jeff Burton	40.00
AG3	Dale Jarrett	75.00
AG4	Mark Martin	100.00
AG5	Terry Labonte	100.00

1998 Upper Deck Victory Circle Piece of the Engine

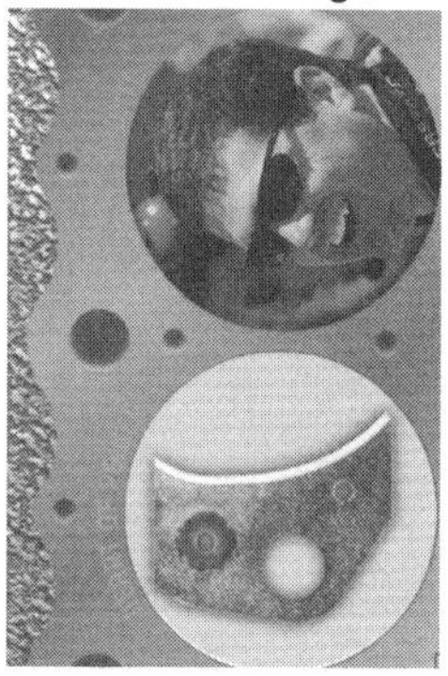

Each card in this five-card set contains an actual race-used engine piece (fragments of head gasket) from five of NASCAR's top drivers, including Rusty Wallace and Dale Jarrett. The card fronts have one rounded corner on the bottom right with two large circles, one containing the race-used engine piece and the other a photo of the driver. The date of the race when the engine fragment was taken from is also stamped on the bottom right. These are found 1:999 packs.

		MT
Complete Set (5):		600.00
Common Driver:		100.00
PE1	Darrell Waltrip	100.00
PE2	Rusty Wallace	200.00
PE3	Dale Jarrett	150.00
PE4	Ernie Irvan	125.00
PE5	Bobby Labonte	125.00

1998 Upper Deck Victory Circle Point Leaders

This 20-card set showcases those drivers who finished among the top 20 in NASCAR's overall point standings. The card fronts feature silver foil stamping, a photo of the driver in a circle with his car above the photo. Card backs have the driver's last three year's of stats, along with a photo of his car and a brief description of the driver's 1997 highlights. They are seeded 1:13 packs.

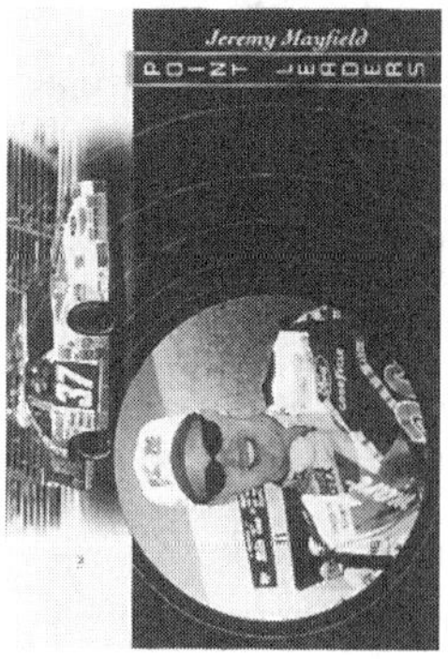

		MT
Complete Set (20):		50.00
Common Driver:		1.00
PL1	Jeff Gordon	12.00
PL2	Dale Jarrett	4.00
PL3	Mark Martin	6.00
PL4	Jeff Burton	1.00
PL5	Dale Earnhardt	12.00
PL6	Terry Labonte	6.00
PL7	Bobby Labonte	1.50
PL8	Bill Elliott	6.00
PL9	Rusty Wallace	6.00
PL10	Ken Schrader	1.00
PL11	Johnny Benson	1.00
PL12	Ted Musgrave	1.00
PL13	Jeremy Mayfield	1.00
PL14	Ernie Irvan	4.00
PL15	Kyle Petty	1.50
PL16	Bobby Hamilton	1.00
PL17	Ricky Rudd	1.00
PL18	Michael Waltrip	1.00
PL19	Ricky Craven	1.00
PL20	Jimmy Spencer	1.00

1998 Upper Deck Victory Circle Predictor +

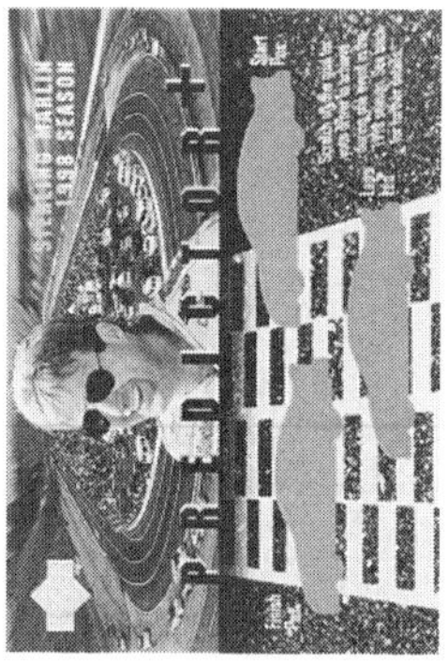

These scratch-off game cards give collectors two ways to win: scratch-off and instant win. For the scratch-off portion, there are three categories revealed: Start position, Laps Led and Finish Position. Collectors can scratch off one of these three categories and if the featured driver achieves the revealed goal, the collector will win a redemption cel card of that driver. For the instant win portion, if you scratch one space and reveal the words "Instant Win," the collector wins a complete set of the cel card redemption collection. These are seeded 1:23 packs.

		MT
Complete Set (20):		50.00
Common Driver:		2.00
Prices for Unscratched cards		
P+1	Ernie Irvan	8.00
P+2	Rusty Wallace	10.00
P+3	Dale Jarrett	8.00
P+4	Sterling Marlin	2.00
P+5	Terry Labonte	10.00
P+6	Mark Martin	10.00
P+7	Geoff Bodine	2.00
P+8	Hut Sticklin	2.00
P+9	Lake Speed	2.00
P+10	Ricky Rudd	2.00
P+11	Brett Bodine	2.00
P+12	Bill Elliott	10.00
P+13	Kyle Petty	2.00
P+14	Jeff Burton	2.00
P+15	Jeremy Mayfield	2.00
P+16	Ricky Craven	2.00
P+17	Ted Musgrave	2.00
P+18	Bobby Labonte	3.00
P+19	Mike Skinner	2.00
P+20	Johnny Benson	2.00

1998 Upper Deck Victory Circle Sparks of Brilliance

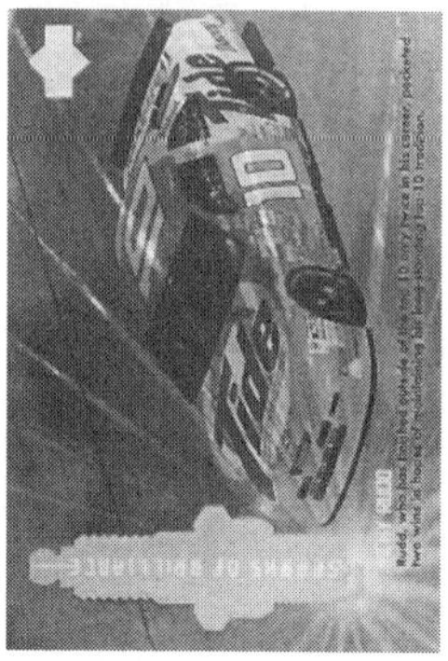

This 10-card set pays tribute to the top ten drivers who accomplished outstanding feats, such as back-to-back wins, during the 1997 Winston Cup season. The card fronts have a photo of the driver's car that has a mirror-like, reflective sheen to it. Sparks of Brilliance is stamped on the left-hand side of the horizontal card encased in a bronze spark plug shape. The driver's name is silver foil stamped beneath. The backs have a photo of the driver with a brief description of his '97 highlights.

		MT
Complete Set (10):		150.00
Common Driver:		8.00
SB1	Jeff Gordon	40.00
SB2	Rusty Wallace	20.00
SB3	Dale Earnhardt	40.00
SB4	Ernie Irvan	15.00
SB5	Terry Labonte	20.00
SB6	Mark Martin	20.00
SB7	Bobby Labonte	10.00
SB8	Ricky Rudd	8.00
SB9	Dale Jarrett	15.00
SB10	Jeff Burton	8.00

1998 Wheels

This 100-card base set, features full bleed photography, gold foil stamping with UV coating. The product is highlighted by the innovataive build-your-own "Custom Shop" inserts and certified authentic autographs.

		MT
Complete Set (100):		20.00
Common Driver:		.10
1	John Andretti	.20
2	Johnny Benson	.25
3	Geoff Bodine	.10
4	Todd Bodine	.10
5	Jeff Burton	.25
6	Ward Burton	.10
7	Ricky Craven	.20
8	Wally Dallenbach	.10
9	Dale Earnhardt	2.00
10	Bill Elliott	1.00
11	Jeff Gordon	2.00
12	David Green	.10
13	Bobby Hamilton	.10
14	Ernie Irvan	.40
15	Kenny Irwin	.10
16	Dale Jarrett	.60
17	Bobby Labonte	.20
18	Terry Labonte	1.00
19	Sterling Marlin	.25

20	Mark Martin	1.00
21	Jeremy Mayfield	.50
22	Ted Musgrave	.10
23	Joe Nemechek	.10
24	Steve Park	.10
25	Ricky Rudd	.20
26	Ken Schrader	.10
27	Mike Skinner	.10
28	Jimmy Spencer	.10
29	Rusty Wallace	1.00
30	Michael Waltrip	.20
31	John Andretti	.25
32	Johnny Benson	.25
33	Jeff Burton	.25
34	Dale Earnhardt	1.00
35	Bill Elliott	.50
36	Jeff Gordon	1.00
37	Kenny Irwin	.10
38	Dale Jarrett	.30
39	Bobby Labonte	.25
40	Terry Labonte	.50
41	Sterling Marlin	.25
42	Mark Martin	.50
43	Jeremy Mayfield	.10
44	Ricky Rudd	.10
45	Rusty Wallace	.50
46	Jeff Burton	.10
47	Dale Earnhardt Jr.	1.50
48	Tim Fedewa	.10
49	Dale Jarrett	.75
50	Jason Jarrett	.10
51	Jason Keller	.10
52	Randy LaJoie	.10
53	Mark Martin	1.00
54	Mike McLauglin	.10
55	Joe Nemechek	.10
56	Elliott Sadler	.10
57	Hermie Sadler	.10
58	Tony Stewart	.25
59	Michael Waltrip	.10
60	Dale Earnhardt Jr.	.75
61	Randy LaJoie	.10
62	Elliott Sadler	.10
63	Tony Stewart	.25
64	Rich Bickle	.10
65	Mike Bliss	.10
66	Ron Hornaday	.10
67	Joe Ruttman	.10
68	Jack Sprague	.10
69	Ray Evernham	.10
70	Jimmy Fennig	.10
71	Andy Graves	.10
72	Jimmy Makar	.10
73	Larry McReynolds	.10
74	Todd Parrott	.10
75	Robin Pemberton	.10
76	Richard Childress	.10
77	Bill Elliott	1.00
78	Joe Gibbs	.10
79	John Hendrick	.10
80	Jack Roush	.10
81	Ricky Rudd	.10
82	Geoff Bodine	.10
83	Dale Earnhardt	2.00
84	Bill Elliott	1.00
85	Jeff Gordon	2.00
86	Ernie Irvan	.50
87	Dale Jarrett	.75
88	Fred Lorenzen	.10
89	Dale Jarrett	.10
90	Richard Petty	.40
91	Jeff Burton	.10
92	Danny Myers	.10
93	Jack Lewis	.10
94	Steve Muse	.10
95	Jerry Hailey	.10
96	Mike Moore	.10
97	David Rogers	.10
98	Larry McReynolds	.10
99	Goodwrench Service Plus	.25
100	Checklist	.10

1998 Wheels Golden

This is a parallel to the 100-card base set, which feature custom NASCAR 50th Anniversary logo foil treatment and individually numbered and limited to 50. Goldens are exclusive to hobby packs and inserted 1:68 packs.

	MT
Golden:	20x to 50x

1998 Wheels 50th Anniversary

Celebrating NASCAR's 50th anniversary, this set shows off the most talented drivers and their cars in Winston Cup racing. Each is card is intricately die-cut and includes a customized micro-etched foil treatment and are seeded 1:2 packs.

		MT
Complete Set (27):		15.00
Common Driver:		.15
A1	Johnny Benson	.40
A2	Jeff Burton	.25
A3	Dale Earnhardt	3.00
A4	Bill Elliott	1.50
A5	Jeff Gordon	3.00
A6	Kenny Irwin	.15
A7	Dale Jarrett	.75
A8	Bobby Labonte	.30
A9	Terry Labonte	1.50
A10	Sterling Marlin	.25
A11	Mark Martin	1.50
A12	Ricky Rudd	.15
A13	Jimmy Spencer	.15
A14	Rusty Wallace	1.50
A15	Michael Waltrip	.15
A16	Johnny Benson	.25
A17	Jeff Burton	.25
A18	Dale Earnhardt	1.50
A19	Bill Elliott	.75
A20	Jeff Gordon	1.50
A21	Kenny Irwin	.15
A22	Dale Jarrett	.40
A23	Bobby Labonte	.25
A24	Terry Labonte	.75
A25	Sterling Marlin	.20
A26	Mark Martin	.75
A27	Rusty Wallace	.75

1998 Wheels Autographs

This certified autographed insert set features autographs of the top drivers in NASCAR, including Gordon and Earnhardt. Fewer than 200 individually numbered autographed cards per driver exist, they are seeded 1:240 packs.

		MT
Common Driver:		10.00
1	Dale Earnhardt	200.00
2	Jeff Gordon	200.00
3	Dale Jarrett	75.00
4	Terry Labonte	90.00
5	Bobby Labonte	25.00
6	Jimmy Spencer	10.00
7	Jeff Burton	25.00
8	Geoff Bodine	10.00
9	Michael Waltrip	10.00
10	Ricky Craven	25.00
11	Ricky Rudd	25.00
12	Mike Skinner	10.00
13	Kenny Irwin	25.00
14	Johnny Benson	10.00

1998 Wheels Custom Shop

The Custom Shop inserts seeded 1:192 packs give collectors a choice of building their own insert. Each card has three different card fronts and card backs that the collector gets to choose from. The collector then sends in the interactive redemption card to Wheels, who in turn sends back the custom card to the collector.

	MT
Complete Set (3):	200.00
Common Driver:	40.00
CS RWRusty Wallace	60.00
CS JGJeff Gordon	120.00
CS DJDale Jarrett	40.00

1998 Wheels Double Take

This nine-card insert set features a technology that allows the collector to the change the exposure of the card front by tilting the card. Watch your favorite driver magically transform into his NASCAR ride, they are seeded 1:72 packs.

		MT
Complete Set (9):		300.00
Common Driver:		10.00
DT1	Jeff Burton	10.00
DT2	Dale Earnhardt	75.00
DT3	Bill Elliott	40.00
DT4	Jeff Gordon	75.00
DT5	Dale Jarrett	25.00
DT6	Bobby Labonte	10.00
DT7	Terry Labonte	40.00
DT8	Mark Martin	40.00
DT9	Rusty Wallace	40.00

1998 Wheels Green Flags

This 18-card set features the top cars in Winston Cup action. The set is all foil with emerald green foil stamping and are seeded 1:8 packs.

		MT
Complete Set (18):		40.00
Common Driver:		1.00
GF1	John Andretti	1.00
GF2	Johnny Benson	1.50
GF3	Jeff Burton	1.00
GF4	D. Earnhardt	10.00
GF5	Bill Elliott	5.00
GF6	Jeff Gordon	10.00
GF7	Bobby Hamilton	1.00
GF8	Kenny Irwin	1.00
GF9	Dale Jarrett	3.00
GF10	Bobby Labonte	2.00
GF11	Terry Labonte	5.00
GF12	Sterling Marlin	1.50
GF13	Mark Martin	5.00
GF14	Ricky Rudd	1.50
GF15	Mike Skinner	1.00
GF16	Jimmy Spencer	1.00
GF17	Rusty Wallace	5.00
GF18	Michael Waltrip	1.00

1998 Wheels Jackpot

This nine-card insert set features embossing, NitroKrome technology with all-foil fronts. The set showcases NASCAR Winton Cup's biggest winners over the past five years and are inserted 1:12 packs.

		MT
Complete Set (9):		35.00
Common Driver:		2.00
J1	Dale Earnhardt	10.00
J2	Bill Elliott	5.00
J3	Jeff Gordon	10.00
J4	Dale Jarrett	3.00
J5	Bobby Labonte	2.00
J6	Terry Labonte	5.00
J7	Jeremy Mayfield	2.50
J8	Ricky Rudd	2.00
J9	Rusty Wallace	5.00

1998 Wheels High Gear

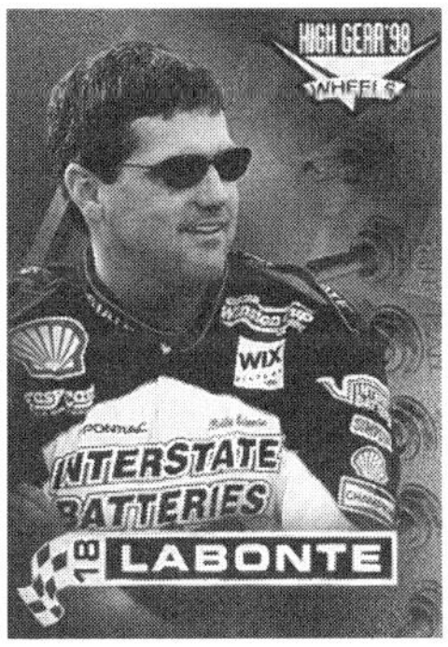

This 72-card base set is printed on an extra thick, 24 point card stock. The card fronts feature silver foil stamping, while the backs have career and 1997 stats along with a photo of the driver. Each pack contains six-cards and sells for a suggested retail of $2.29.

		MT
Complete Set (72):		25.00
Common Driver:		.20
First Gears:		1.5x to 2x
MPH's:		25x to 40x
1	Jeff Gordon	3.00
2	Mark Martin	1.50
3	Dale Jarrett	1.00
4	Dale Earnhardt	3.00
5	Terry Labonte	1.50
6	Ricky Rudd	.20
7	Rusty Wallace	1.50
8	Sterling Marlin	.20
9	Bobby Hamilton	.20
10	Jimmy Spencer	.20
11	Bobby Labonte	.40
12	Ken Schrader	.20
13	Jeff Burton	.40
14	Michael Waltrip	.20
15	Ted Musgrave	.20
16	Ward Burton	.20
17	Ricky Craven	.20
18	Johnny Benson	.20
19	Jeremy Mayfield	.20
20	Kyle Petty	.40
21	Darrell Waltrip	.20
22	Bill Elliott	1.50
23	Mike Skinner	.20
24	David Green	.20
25	Joe Nemechek	.20
26	Wally Dallenbach	.20
27	Ernie Irvan	1.00
28	R. Wallace Car	.75
29	D. Earnhardt Car	1.50
30	T. Labonte Car	.75
31	M. Martin Car	.75
32	B. Labonte Car	.20
33	J. Gordon Car	1.50
34	D. Jarrett Car	.50
35	B. Elliott Car	.75
36	#99 Exide Batteries	.20
37	Randy LaJoie	.20
38	Todd Bodine	.20
39	Steve Park	.20
40	Buckshot Jones	.20
41	Elliott Sadler	.20
42	Rich Bickle	.20
43	Jack Sprague	.20
44	Joe Ruttman	.20
45	Ron Hornaday Jr.	.20
46	Busch Pole Award	.20
47	Mechanic of the Year	.20
48	Unocal 76 Point Fund Standings	.20
49	Rookie of the Year	.20
50	Gatorade Front Runner Award	.20
51	Exide All Charged Up Award	.20
52	Plasti-Kote Quality Finish Award	.20
53	Engine Builder of the Year Award	.20
54	MCI Fast Pace Award	.20
55	Johnny Benson	.20
56	Todd Bodine	.20
57	Derrike Cope	.20
58	Bobby Hamilton	.20
59	Ernie Irvan	1.00
60	Kenny Irwin Jr.	.20
61	Sterling Marlin	.30
62	Steve Park	.20
63	John Andretti	.20
64	#3 Earnhardt Car	1.50
65	#5 T. Labonte Car	.75
66	#10	.20
67	#18 B. Labonte Car	.30
68	#21	.20
69	#24 J. Gordon Car	1.50
70	#29	.20
71	#94 B. Elliott Car	.75
72	Checklist	.20

1998 Wheels High Gear First Gear

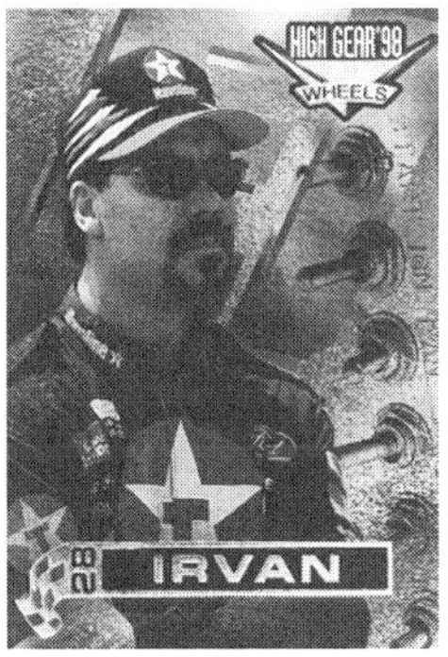

This 72-card parallel set is identical to High Gear except instead of silver foil stamping the card fronts are stamped with gold foil. They are seeded one per pack.

	MT
First Gears:	1.5x to 2x

1998 Wheels High Gear MPH

This 72-card parallel set features special foil stamping and are limited to 100 numbered sets. These are hobby exclusive.

	MT
Complete Set (72):	500.00
Common Driver:	4.00
MPH's:	15x to 25x

1998 Wheels High Gear Autographs

Autographs of 20 top Winston Cup drivers with each autograph individually numbered and limited to a maximum of 250 cards of each driver, accompanied by a certificate of authenticity. The insertion ratio is 1:192 packs.

	MT
Common Driver:	15.00
Dale Earnhardt	200.00
Jeff Gordon	200.00
Dale Jarrett	60.00
Terry Labonte	80.00
Mark Martin	80.00
Bobby Labonte	25.00
Jeff Burton	20.00
Rusty Wallace	80.00
Bill Elliott	70.00
Michael Waltrip	15.00
Ricky Craven	15.00
Ricky Rudd	15.00
Darrell Waltrip	15.00
Ernie Irvan	60.00
Jeremy Mayfield	15.00
Bobby Hamilton	15.00
Ted Musgrave	15.00
Jimmy Spencer	15.00
Kyle Petty	20.00
Ken Schrader	15.00

1998 Wheels High Gear Custom Shop

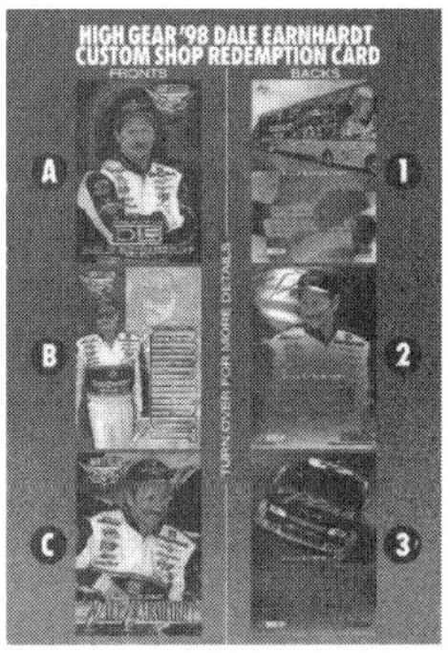

The card fronts present a choice of three different card front designs and three different backs for the collector to choose from. While there is a maximum of 800 Custom Shop redemption cards for each driver, the exact amount of cards of each driver version will only be decided after all collectors redeem their cards. Odds of finding a redemption card are 1:192 packs.

		MT
Complete Set (5):		800.00
Common Driver:		40.00
CS1	Dale Earnhardt	100.00
CS2	Jeff Gordon	100.00
CS3	Mark Martin	60.00
CS4	Terry Labonte	60.00
CS5	Dale Jarrett	40.00

1998 Wheels High Gear Gear Jammers

These 1:2 pack inserts feature an intricate die-cut design with silver foil stamping. Card fronts feature a photo of the driver while backs have a small caption of a historical highlight of the driver. There are 27 cards in the set.

	MT
Complete Set (27):	10.00
Common Driver:	.25
GJ1 Rusty Wallace	1.50
GJ2 #3 Goodwrench Service Plus	2.50
GJ3 Sterling Marlin	.25
GJ4 Terry Labonte	1.50
GJ5 Mark Martin	1.50
GJ6 Ricky Rudd	.25
GJ7 Ted Musgrave	.25
GJ8 Darrell Waltrip	.25
GJ9 Bobby Labonte	.40
GJ10 Michael Waltrip	.25
GJ11 Ward Burton	.25
GJ12 Jeff Gordon	3.00
GJ13 Bobby Hamilton	.25
GJ14 Kyle Petty	.25
GJ15 Dale Jarrett	1.00
GJ16 Bill Elliott	1.50
GJ17 Jeff Burton	.25
GJ18 Wally Dallenbach	.25
GJ19 Jimmy Spencer	.25
GJ20 Ken Schrader	.25
GJ21 Johnny Benson	.25
GJ22 David Green	.25
GJ23 Mike Skinner	.25
GJ24 Joe Nemechek	.25
GJ25 Jeremy Mayfield	.25
GJ26 Ricky Craven	.25
GJ27 Morgan Shepherd	.25

1998 Wheels High Gear High Groove

This set highlights nine of NASCAR Winston Cup's hardest charging cars on a die-cut, foil stamped card. They are seeded 1:10 packs.

	MT
Complete Set (9):	35.00
Common Driver:	2.00
HG1 #2 Wallace	5.00
HG2 #3 - Goodwrench Service Plus	10.00
HG3 #5 Labonte	5.00
HG4 #6 Martin	5.00
HG5 #24 Gordon	10.00
HG6 #29 Green	2.00
HG7 #88 Jarrett	4.00
HG8 #94 Elliott	5.00
HG9 #99 Burton	2.00

1998 Wheels High Gear Man and Machine

This 18-card set matches up nine drivers in a two-piece interlocking design with their cars, on an all-foil card. The nine drivers are found exclusively in hobby packs, while the car inserts are found only in retail. These can be found on the average of 1:20 packs.

	MT
Complete Set (9):	75.00
Common Driver:	3.00
MM1 Jeff Gordon (#24)	20.00
MM2 Mark Martin (#6)	10.00
MM3 Dale Jarrett (#88)	8.00
MM4 Jeff Burton (#99)	3.00
MM5 Terry Labonte (#5)	10.00
MM6 Bobby Labonte (#18)	3.00
MM7 Dale Earnhardt (#3)	20.00
MM8 Bill Elliott (#94)	10.00
MM9 Rusty Wallace (#2)	10.00

1998 Wheels High Gear Pure Gold

This nine-card all-foil set commemorates NASCAR's 50th anniversary with some of NASCAR's best drivers of all-time. They are seeded 1:6 packs.

	MT
Complete Set (9):	12.00
Common Driver:	.75
PG1 Dale Earnhardt	6.00
PG2 Richard Petty	1.50
PG3 Jeff Gordon	6.00
PG4 David Pearson	.75
PG5 Bobby Allison	.75
PG6 Darrell Waltrip	.75
PG7 Ned Jarrett	.75
PG8 Bill Elliott	3.00
PG9 Rusty Wallace	3.00

1998 Wheels High Gear Top Tier

This eight card set features an all foil card front and progressive insert ratios. Card number one is seeded 1:384 packs, number two 1:192, number three 1:100, number four 1:60, number five and six 1:40 and seven and eight 1:20. The set represents the top eight NASCAR Winston Cup finishers from 1997.

	MT
Complete Set (8):	180.00
TT1 Jeff Gordon	125.00
TT2 Mark Martin	30.00
TT3 Dale Jarrett	15.00
TT4 Jeff Burton	5.00
TT5 Dale Earnhardt	20.00
TT6 Terry Labonte	10.00
TT7 Bobby Labonte	5.00
TT8 Bill Elliott	8.00

FIGURINES

1998 Kenner Starting Lineup Baseball

The figures in this 39-piece set are packaged with a standard-size trading card. The set includes first figures of Nomar Garciaparra, Darin Erstad and Mariano Rivera.

	MT
Complete Set (40):	450.00
Albert Belle	10.00
Craig Biggio	10.00
Barry Bonds	10.00
Kevin Brown	8.00
Jose Canseco	8.00
Will Clark	8.00
Darin Erstad	20.00
Andres Galarraga	8.00
Nomar Garciaparra	40.00
Tom Glavine	8.00
Juan Gonzalez	10.00
Mark Grace	8.00
Mark Grace Special	12.00
Ken Griffey Jr.	20.00
Mark Grudzielanek	12.00
Tony Gwynn	12.00
Bobby Higginson	12.00
Glenallen Hill	10.00
Derek Jeter	14.00
Chipper Jones	18.00
David Justice	10.00
Chuck Knoblauch	10.00
Ray Lankford	8.00
Barry Larkin	8.00
Mickey Morandini	8.00
Marc Newfield	8.00
Hideo Nomo	12.00
Rafael Palmeiro	8.00
Mike Piazza	12.00
Cal Ripken Jr.	18.00
Mariano Rivera	20.00
Alex Rodriguez	18.00
Deion Sanders	8.00
Gary Sheffield	8.00
Ed Sprague	8.00
Frank Thomas	14.00
Jim Thome	10.00
Mo Vaughn	10.00
Larry Walker	10.00
Bernie Williams	8.00

1998 Kenner Starting Lineup Baseball Extended

This 14-figure set features the first SLUs of Scott Rolen and Hideki Irabu as well as the first piece portraying Mark McGwire in a St. Louis Cardinals' uniform. Each piece comes with a standard-size trading card.

	MT
Complete Set (14):	300.00
Sandy Alomar	15.00
Moises Alou	20.00
Jay Bell	15.00
Jim Edmonds	15.00
Ken Griffey Jr.	20.00
Hideki Irabu	25.00
Greg Maddux	25.00
Fred McGriff	15.00
Mark McGwire	125.00
Dean Palmer	15.00

Scott Rolen	30.00
Sammy Sosa	85.00
Larry Walker	15.00
Tony Womack	15.00

1998 Kenner Starting Lineup Baseball Classic Doubles

This set consists of 10 pairs of figures. Five of the sets feature legendary players and the other five portray current stars. Each set comes with two trading cards, one for each player.

	MT
Complete Set (10):	200.00
Albert Belle, Frank Thomas	25.00
Johnny Bench, Joe Morgan	25.00
Yogi Berra, Thurman Munson	25.00
Jose Canseco, Mark McGwire	50.00
Reggie Jackson, Catfish Hunter	25.00
Derek Jeter, Rey Ordonez	25.00
Mike Piazza, Ivan Rodriguez	25.00
Alex Rodriguez, Ken Griffey Jr.	30.00
Babe Ruth, Roger Maris	25.00
Nolan Ryan, Walter Johnson	25.00

1998 Kenner Baseball Cooperstown Collection

This 11-figure set features Hall of Fame players. The standard-size SLUs come with a trading card of the player.

	MT
Complete Set (11):	100.00
Yogi Berra	10.00
Lou Brock	10.00
Roy Campanella	15.00
Roberto Clemente	15.00
Buck Leonard	10.00
Phil Niekro	10.00
Jim Palmer	12.00
Frank Robinson	12.00

Tom Seaver	12.00
Warren Spahn	10.00
Tris Speaker	10.00

1998 Kenner Starting Lineup Baseball Freeze Frame

	MT
Complete Set (6):	140.00
Jeff Bagwell	20.00
Barry Bonds	20.00
Derek Jeter	25.00
Greg Maddux	35.00
Cal Ripken	35.00
Alex Rodriguez	30.00

1998 Kenner Starting Lineup Baseball Stadium Stars

This seven-figure set featured star players standing on top of a replica of their home stadium.

	MT
Complete Set (7):	150.00
Albert Belle	25.00
Ken Griffey Jr.	30.00
Mike Piazza	25.00
Cal Ripken Jr.	30.00
Ivan Rodriguez	25.00
John Smoltz	25.00
Bernie Williams	25.00

1998 Kenner Starting Lineup Baseball 12" Figures

	MT
Complete Set (4):	100.00
Derek Jeter	30.00
Chipper Jones	30.00
Hideo Nomo	25.00
Alex Rodriguez	30.00

1997 Kenner Starting Lineup Basketball

	MT
Complete Set (39):	425.00
Shareef Abdur-Rahim	25.00
Ray Allen	18.00
Kenny Anderson	10.00
Vin Baker	10.00
Charles Barkley	10.00
Terrell Brandon	18.00
Marcus Camby	18.00
Vlade Divac	10.00
Patrick Ewing	10.00
Michael Finley	18.00
Kevin Garnett	20.00
Horace Grant	10.00
Tim Hardaway	10.00
Grant Hill	15.00
Allan Houston	15.00
Juwan Howard	12.00
Allen Iverson	15.00
Mark Jackson	10.00
Shawn Kemp	12.00
Jason Kidd	15.00
Kerry Kittles	20.00
Stephon Marbury	30.00
Reggie Miller	10.00
Alonzo Mourning	10.00
Hakeem Olajuwon	12.00
Shaquille O'Neal	15.00
Gary Payton	15.00
Scottie Pippen	15.00
Mitch Richmond	10.00
David Robinson	12.00
Dennis Rodman (Special)	25.00
Steve Smith	10.00
Latrell Sprewell	12.00
Damon Stoudamire	10.00
John Stockton	12.00

	MT
Loy Vaught	10.00
Nick Van Exel	10.00
Antoine Walker	50.00
Chris Webber	12.00

1997-98 Kenner Starting Lineup Basketball Extended

	MT
Complete Set (8):	150.00
Clyde Drexler	10.00
Tim Duncan	50.00
Anfernee Hardaway	12.00
Eddie Jones	15.00
Luc Longley	12.00
Anthony Mason	10.00
Antonio McDyess	10.00
Keith Van Horn	45.00

1997 Kenner Starting Lineup Basketball Backboard Kings

	MT
Complete Set (6):	150.00
Charles Barkley	25.00
Grant Hill	30.00
Karl Malone	25.00
Shaquille O'Neal	25.00
Scottie Pippen	25.00
Damon Stoudamire	25.00

1997 Kenner Starting Lineup Basketball Classic Doubles

	MT
Complete Set (7):	130.00
L. Bird, K. McHale	20.00
W. Chamberlain, B. Russell	20.00
J. Dumars, G. Hill	30.00
P. Ewing, W. Reed	20.00
S. O'Neal, K. Abdul-Jabbar	30.00
B. Russell, H. Olajuwon	25.00
J. Stockton, K. Malone	25.00

1997 Kenner Starting Lineup Basketball 14" Figures

	MT
Complete Set (5):	180.00
Charles Barkley	40.00
Grant Hill	50.00
Shawn Kemp	40.00
Shaquille O'Neal	40.00
Dennis Rodman	45.00

1998 Kenner Starting Lineup Basketball

	MT
Complete Set (16):	180.00
Vin Baker	12.00
Terrell Brandon	10.00

	MT
Kobe Bryant	20.00
Patrick Ewing	10.00
Kevin Garnett	15.00
Grant Hill	15.00
Allen Iverson	15.00
Magic Johnson	15.00
Shawn Kemp	12.00
Jason Kidd	12.00
Karl Malone	12.00
Stephon Marbury	15.00
Alonzo Mourning	10.00
Shaquille O'Neal	15.00
Dennis Rodman	15.00
Rik Smits	10.00

1998 Kenner Starting Lineup Football

	MT
Complete Set (42):	450.00
Troy Aikman	15.00
Terry Allen	10.00
Jerome Bettis	15.00
Drew Bledsoe	15.00
Tony Boselli	10.00
Derrick Brooks	10.00
Mark Brunell	15.00
Kerry Collins	10.00
Terrell Davis	25.00
Trent Dilfer	20.00
Corey Dillon	30.00
John Elway	15.00
Brett Favre	20.00
Antonio Freeman	20.00
Gus Frerotte	12.00
Joey Galloway	12.00
Eddie George	15.00
Terry Glenn	15.00
Elvis Grbac	10.00
Raymont Harris	12.00
Bobby Hoying	12.00
Carnell Lake	12.00
Lamar Lathon	12.00
Dan Marino	15.00
Randall McDaniel	12.00
Chester McGlockton	12.00
Scott Mitchell	10.00
Adrian Murrell	20.00
Nate Newton	12.00
Jonathan Ogden	12.00
Orlando Pace	12.00
Carl Pickens	10.00
Jerry Rice	15.00
Simeon Rice	12.00
Barry Sanders Special	20.00
Deion Sanders	12.00
Antowain Smith	25.00
Emmitt Smith	15.00
Kordell Stewart Special	20.00
Dana Stubblefield	15.00
Vinny Testaverde	10.00
Tyrone Wheatley	12.00
Reggie White	12.00
Steve Young	12.00

1998 Kenner Starting Lineup Football Classic Doubles

	MT
Complete Set (8):	170.00
Troy Aikman, Emmitt Smith	30.00
Marcus Allen, Mike Garrett	25.00

John Elway, Dan Marino	35.00
Joe Namath, Don Maynard	25.00
Jerry Rice, Steve Young	30.00
Deion Sanders, Herb Adderly	25.00
Junior Seau, Dick Butkus	25.00
Y.A. Tittle, Sam Huff	25.00

1998 Kenner Starting Lineup Football Gridiron Greats

	MT
Complete Set (7):	175.00
Troy Aikman	30.00
Drew Bledsoe	30.00
Mark Brunell	30.00
John Elway	30.00
Barry Sanders	40.00
Junior Seau	25.00
Steve Young	30.00

1998 Kenner Starting Lineup Football Hall of Fame

	MT
Complete Set (11):	100.00
Dick Butkus	10.00
Larry Csonka	12.00
Joe Greene	12.00
Deacon Jones	10.00
Bob Lilly	10.00
Vince Lombardi	15.00
Ray Nitschke	10.00
Gale Sayers	10.00
Bart Starr	12.00
Y.A. Tittle	10.00
Gene Upshaw	10.00

1998 Kenner Starting Lineup Football Heisman Contenders

	MT
Complete Set (10):	100.00
Marcus Allen	12.00
Earl Campbell	12.00
John Cappelletti	10.00
Glenn Davis	10.00
Paul Hornung	12.00
Desmond Howard	10.00
Rashaan Salaam	10.00
Roger Staubach	12.00
Herschel Walker	10.00
Charles Woodson	20.00

1998 Kenner Starting Lineup Football 12" Figures

	MT
Complete Set (5):	140.00
Drew Bledsoe	30.00
John Elway	30.00
Brett Favre	45.00
Dan Marino	40.00
Jerry Rice	30.00

1997 Kenner Starting Lineup Hockey American

	MT
Complete Set (21):	250.00

Daniel Alfredsson	15.00
Jason Arnott	10.00
Peter Bondra	15.00
Martin Brodeur	20.00
Paul Coffey (BOSCOV Spec.)	18.00
Chris Chelios	10.00
Peter Forsberg	18.00
Wayne Gretzky	35.00
Ron Hextall	18.00
Jaromir Jagr	15.00
Patrick LaLime (Pit. Spec.)	20.00
Eric Lindros	15.00
Mark Messier	15.00
Chris Osgood	20.00
Sandis Ozolinsh	10.00
Zigmund Palffy	10.00
Daren Puppa	20.00
Mark Recchi	15.00
Teemu Selanne	10.00
Keith Tkachuk	15.00
John Vanbiesbrouck	20.00

1997 Kenner Starting Lineup Hockey Canadian

	MT
Complete Set (19):	220.00
Daniel Alfredsson	15.00
Jason Arnott	10.00
Peter Bondra	15.00
Martin Brodeur	20.00
Chris Chelios	10.00
Peter Forsberg	18.00
Wayne Gretzky	35.00
Ron Hextall	18.00
Jaromir Jagr	15.00
Eric Lindros	15.00
Mark Messier	15.00
Chris Osgood	20.00
Sandis Ozolinsh	10.00
Zigmund Palffy	10.00
Daren Puppa	20.00
Mark Recchi	15.00
Teemu Selanne	10.00
Keith Tkachuk	15.00
John Vanbiesbrouck	20.00

1997 Kenner Starting Lineup Hockey One on One

	MT
Complete Set (7):	200.00
Eric Lindros, Paul Kariya	30.00
Jaromir Jagr, Patrick Roy	30.00
Jeremy Roenick, Steve Yzerman	30.00
Joe Sakic, Mike Richter	30.00
Mats Sundin, Ray Bourque	30.00
Owen Nolan, Chris Osgood	30.00
Wayne Gretzky, Dominik Hasek	70.00

1998 Kenner Starting Lineup Hockey American

	MT
Complete Set (23):	225.00
Tony Amonte	12.00
Ed Belfour	15.00
Brian Berard	12.00
Martin Brodeur	12.00
Jim Campbell	12.00
Vincent Damphousse	12.00
Wayne Gretzky	20.00
Dominik Hasek	15.00
Jaromir Jagr	12.00
Paul Kariya	15.00
Brian Leetch	12.00

Eric Lindros	15.00
Kirk McLean	12.00
Mark Messier	15.00
Rob Neidermayer	15.00
Chris Osgood	15.00
Felix Potvin	15.00
Jeremy Roenick	12.00
Patrick Roy	15.00
Joe Sakic	10.00
Joe Thornton	15.00
Alexei Yashin	15.00
Steve Yzerman	12.00

1997 Racing Winners Circle

	MT
Complete Set (8):	75.00
Ward Burton	10.00
Dale Earnhardt (Black Glasses)	30.00
Dale Earnhardt (Gold Glasses)	25.00
John Force	12.00
Jeff Gordon	20.00
Dale Jarrett	10.00
Bobby Labonte	10.00
Darrell Waltrip	10.00

1997 Timeless Legends

	MT
Complete Set (9):	75.00
Len Dawson	12.00
Tony Esposito	12.00
Walt Frazier	12.00
Michael Johnson	12.00
Sugar Ray Leonard	12.00
Maurice Richard	12.00
Sam Snead	12.00
Joe Theismann	12.00
Bill Walton	14.00

1997 Canadian Timeless Legends

	MT
Complete Set (6):	100.00
Jean Beliveau	20.00
Mike Bossy	20.00
Marcel Dionne	20.00
Phil Esposito	20.00
Glenn Hall	20.00
Bernie Parent	20.00

1998 Corinthian Headliners Baseball

	MT
Complete Set (41):	200.00
Common Player:	6.00
Roberto Alomar	6.00
Wade Boggs	6.00
Barry Bonds	6.00
Jay Buhner	6.00
Ken Caminiti	6.00
Roger Clemens	10.00
Dennis Eckersley	6.00
Jim Edmonds	6.00
Juan Gonzalez	8.00
Ken Griffey Jr.	10.00
Tony Gwynn	6.00
Orel Hershiser Giants	6.00
Orel Hershiser Indians	6.00
Derek Jeter	8.00
Charles Johnson	6.00
Randy Johnson	6.00
Chipper Jones	8.00
David Justice	6.00
Eric Karros	6.00
Barry Larkin	6.00
Kenny Lofton Braves	6.00
Kenny Lofton Indians	6.00
Fred McGriff	6.00
Raul Mondesi	6.00
Hideo Nomo	6.00

Paul O'Neill	6.00
Rey Ordonez	6.00
Chan Ho Park	6.00
Mike Piazza	7.00
Cal Ripken Jr.	8.00
Alex Rodriguez	10.00
Ivan Rodriguez	6.00
Tim Salmon	6.00
Deion Sanders	6.00
Gary Sheffield	6.00
Sammy Sosa	10.00
Jim Thome	6.00
Frank Thomas	7.00
Bernie Williams	7.00
Matt Williams D'backs	6.00
Matt Williams Indians	6.00

1998 Corinthian Headliners Baseball XL

	MT
Complete Set (12):	200.00
Common Player:	20.00
Set price doesn't include blue versions	
Barry Bonds	20.00
Andres Galarraga	20.00
Ken Griffey Jr. Blue	25.00
Ken Griffey Jr. White	25.00
Derek Jeter	20.00
Chipper Jones	20.00
David Justice	20.00
Mark McGwire Blue	50.00
Mark McGwire White	85.00
Hideo Nomo	20.00
Mike Piazza	20.00
Cal Ripken Jr.	20.00
Alex Rodriguez	20.00
Frank Thomas	20.00

1997-98 Corinthian Headliners Basketball

	MT
Complete Set (36):	160.00
Common Player:	5.00
Special Packs Not Included In Set Price	
Charles Barkley	5.00
Muggsy Bogues	5.00
Cedric Ceballos	5.00
Clyde Drexler	6.00
Patrick Ewing	5.00
Kevin Garnett	10.00
Horace Grant	5.00
Anfernee Hardaway	6.00
Grant Hill	8.00
Allen Iverson	10.00
Larry Johnson	5.00
Shawn Kemp	5.00
Jason Kidd	8.00
Toni Kukoc	6.00
Karl Malone	5.00
Jamal Mashburn	5.00
Reggie Miller	5.00
Alonzo Mourning	5.00
Dikembe Mutombo	5.00
Scottie Pippen	6.00
Bryant Reeves	5.00
Mitch Richmond	5.00
Clifford Robinson	5.00
David Robinson	5.00
Glenn Robinson	5.00
Dennis Rodman	8.00
Detlef Schrempf	6.00
Joe Smith	5.00
Rik Smits	5.00
Latrell Sprewell	6.00
Jerry Stackhouse	6.00
John Stockton	8.00
Damon Stoudamire	5.00

Nick Van Exel	8.00
Chris Webber	7.00
Centers 4-Pack Patrick Ewing, Hakeem Olajuwon, Bryant Reeves, Rik Smits	20.00
Forwards 4-Pack Charles Barkley, Horace Grant, Grant Hill, Scottie Pippen	20.00
Future 4-Pack Kevin Garnett, Allen Iverson, Joe Smith, Damon Stoudamire	20.00
Guards 4-Pack Clyde Drexler, Reggie Miller, Latrell Sprewell, Nick Van Exel	20.00

1997 Corinthian Headliners Football

	MT
Complete Set (40):	220.00
Common Player:	5.00
Special Packs Not Included In Set Price	
Troy Aikman	6.00
Marcus Allen	5.00
Bill Bates	5.00
Jerome Bettis	8.00
Drew Bledsoe	6.00
Robert Brooks	6.00
Tim Brown	5.00
Isaac Bruce	6.00
Mark Brunell	8.00
Cris Carter	6.00
Mark Chmura	6.00
Kerry Collins	5.00
Brett Favre	8.00
Gus Frerotte	5.00
Eddie George	8.00
Jeff George	5.00
Kevin Greene	5.00
Jim Harbaugh	5.00
Jeff Hostetler	5.00
Michael Irvin	6.00
Keyshawn Johnson	6.00
Greg Lloyd	5.00
Dan Marino Away	7.00
Dan Marino Home	7.00
Curtis Martin	10.00
Steve McNair	8.00
Natrone Means	5.00
Ken Norton Jr.	5.00
Neil O'Donnell	5.00
Jerry Rice	6.00
Rashaan Salaam	5.00
Deion Sanders	5.00
Junior Seau	5.00
Bruce Smith	5.00
Emmitt Smith	7.00
Kordell Stewart	10.00
Vinny Testaverde	5.00
Ricky Watters	5.00
Reggie White	5.00
Steve Young	5.00
AFC QB 4-Pack Drew Bledsoe, John Elway, Jim Harbaugh, Dan Marino	20.00
NFC QB 4-Pack Troy Aikman, Kerry Collins, Brett Favre, Steve Young	20.00
RB's 4-Pack Terry Allen, Marshall Faulk, Rashaan Salaam, Emmitt Smith	20.00
WR's 4-Pack Cris Carter, Keyshawn Johnson, Jerry Rice, Deion Sanders	20.00
Heroes/Gridiron Set Kerry Collins, Kevin Greene, Deion Sanders, Reggie White	20.00

1998 Corinthian Headliners Hockey in the Crease

	MT
Complete Set (5):	50.00
Common Player:	12.00
Martin Brodeur	12.00
Grant Fuhr	12.00
Mike Richter	12.00
Patrick Roy	12.00
John Vanbiesbrouck	12.00

Michael Jordan Card Checklist

Card	Card #	Price
1984-85 Star	101	2700.00
1984-85 Star	195	425.00
1984-85 Star	288	425.00
1984-85 Star Court Kings	26	225.00
1985 Bulls Interlake	—	75.00
1985-86 Bulls Team Issue	1	50.00
1985 Nike Poster Cards	—	35.00
1985 Prism/Jewel Stickers	—	275.00
1985-86 Star	117	900.00
1985-86 Star All-Rookie Team	2	325.00
1985 Star Crunch 'n Munch	4	300.00
1985 Star Gatorade Slam Dunk	7	250.00
1985 Star Last 11 R.O.Y	1	250.00
1985 Star Lite All-Stars	4	250.00
1985 Star Slam Dunk	5	225.00
1985 Star Super Teams	1	200.00
1986-87 Fleer	57	1150.00
1986-87 Fleer Stickers	8	100.00
1986 Star Best of the Best	9	200.00
1986 Star Best of the New	2	400.00
1986 Star Court Kings	18	225.00
1986 Star Michael Jordan	1	80.00
1986 Star Michael Jordan	2	80.00
1986 Star Michael Jordan	3	80.00
1986 Star Michael Jordan	4	80.00
1986 Star Michael Jordan	5	80.00
1986 Star Michael Jordan	6	80.00
1986 Star Michael Jordan	7	80.00
1986 Star Michael Jordan	8	80.00
1986 Star Michael Jordan	9	80.00
1986 Star Michael Jordan	10	80.00
1987-88 Bulls Entenmann's	23	100.00
1987-88 Fleer	59	185.00
1987-88 Fleer Stickers	2	45.00
1988-89 Bulls Entenmann's	23	70.00
1988-89 Fleer	17	55.00
1988-89 Fleer	120	20.00
1988-89 Fleer Stickers	7	18.00
1988 Fournier NBA Estrellas Stickers	—	20.00
1988 Fournier NBA Estrellas	22	8.00
1988-89 Kenner Slam Dunk White Box	—	150.00
1988-89 Kenner Slam Dunk Red Box	—	250.00
1988 Kenner Starting Lineup Basketball	—	100.00
1988-89 Panini European Stickers	76	35.00
1988-89 Panini European Stickers	261	15.00
1988-89 Panini European Stickers	285	15.00
1989-90 Bulls Dairy Council	—	70.00
1989-90 Bulls Equal	—	30.00
1989-90 Fleer	21	10.00
1989-90 Fleer Stickers	3	5.00
1989-90 Hoops	21	1.50
1989-90 Hoops	200	3.00
1989-90 Hoops All-Star Panels	4	5.00
1989 Magnetables	—	4.00
1989-90 North Carolina Collegiate Collection	13	1.50
1989-90 North Carolina Collegiate Collection	14	1.50
1989-90 North Carolina Collegiate Collection	15	1.50
1989-90 North Carolina Collegiate Collection	16	1.50
1989-90 North Carolina Collegiate Collection	17	1.50
1989-90 North Carolina Collegiate Collection	18	1.50
1989-90 North Carolina Collegiate Collection	65	1.50
1989-90 Panini European Stickers	67	20.00
1989-90 Panini European Stickers	254	15.00
1990 Action Packed Promos	—	200.00
1990-91 Bulls Equal/Star	—	15.00
1990-91 Fleer	26	2.50
1990-91 Fleer All-Stars	5	5.00
1990-91 Hoops	5	2.50
1990-91 Hoops	65	2.50
1990-91 Hoops	358	1.25
1990-91 Hoops	382	1.25
1990-91 Hoops	385	1.00
1990 Hoops Action Photos	—	2.00
1990-91 Hoops All-Star Panels	—	6.00
1990-91 Hoops All-Star Panels	—	8.00
1990-91 Hoops CollectABooks	4	4.00
1990 Hoops Superstars	12	4.00
1990-91 Hoops Team Night Sheets	4	10.00
1990 Kenner Starting Lineup Basketball	—	125.00
1990-91 North Carolina Collegiate Collection	3	1.50
1990-91 North Carolina Collegiate Collection	44	1.50
1990-91 North Carolina Collegiate Collection	61	1.50
1990-91 North Carolina Collegiate Collection	89	1.50
1990-91 North Carolina Collegiate Collection	93	1.50
1990-91 Panini Stickers	91	1.00
1990-91 Panini Stickers	G	.75
1990-91 Panini Stickers	K	.75
1990-91 SkyBox	41	4.00
1990 SkyBox Promo Cards	41	135.00
1990 SCD BCPG Pocket Price Guides	51	12.00
1990-92 Baseball Cards Presents Repli-cards	19	3.00
1991 Cardboard Dreams	8	1.00
1991 Farley's Fruit Snacks	1	2.50
1991 Farley's Fruit Snacks	2	2.50
1991 Farley's Fruit Snacks	3	2.50
1991 Farley's Fruit Snacks	4	2.50
1991-92 Fleer	29	2.00
1991-92 Fleer	211	1.00
1991-92 Fleer	220	1.00
1991-92 Fleer	375	1.00
1991-92 Fleer Pro Visions	2	3.00
1991-92 Fleer Tony's Pizza	33	45.00
1991-92 Fleer Wheaties Sheets	6	12.00
1991-92 Hoops	30	2.50
1991-92 Hoops	253	1.25
1991-92 Hoops	306	1.00
1991-92 Hoops	317	1.25
1991-92 Hoops	455	1.25
1991-92 Hoops	536	1.25
1991-92 Hoops	579	5.00
1991 Hoops McDonald's	5	3.00
1991 Hoops McDonald's	55	2.00
1991-92 Hoops MVP All-Stars	9	20.00
1991 Hoops Prototypes 00	004	75.00
1991-92 Hoops Slam Dunk	4	20.00
1991 Hoops Superstars	13	5.00
1991-92 Hoops Team Night Sheets	—	10.00

'90-91 Fleer No. 26 $2.50

Card	Card #	Price
1991-92 Hoops Team Night Sheets	—	10.00
1991 Kenner Starting Lineup Basketball	—	120.00
1991 Kenner Starting Lineup Basketball	—	120.00
1991 Little Basketball Big Leaguers	19	6.00
1991-92 Panini Stickers	96	1.50
1991-92 Panini Stickers	116	5.00
1991-92 Panini Stickers	190	1.50
1991-92 Pro Set Prototypes	4	600.00
1991-92 SkyBox	39	4.00
1991-92 SkyBox	307	2.00
1991-92 SkyBox	333	1.25
1991-92 SkyBox	334	2.00
1991-92 SkyBox	408	2.00
1991-92 SkyBox	462	1.50
1991-92 SkyBox	534	10.00
1991-92 SkyBox	572	2.00
1991-92 SkyBox	583	2.00
1991-92 SkyBox Mark and See Minis	534	12.00
1991-92 SkyBox Mark and See Minis	545	3.00
1991 SkyBox Mini	7	5.00
1991-92 Tuff Stuff jr.	28	4.00
1991-92 Upper Deck	22	1.00
1991-92 Upper Deck	34	1.25
1991-92 Upper Deck	44	3.00
1991-92 Upper Deck	48	2.00
1991-92 Upper Deck	69	2.00
1991-92 Upper Deck	75	2.00
1991-92 Upper Deck	452	3.00
1991 Upper Deck	SP1	15.00
1991-92 Upper Deck Holograms	1AW	12.00
1991-92 Upper Deck Holograms	4AW	12.00
1991 Upper Deck Promos	1	20.00
1991-92 Upper Deck Sheets	6	20.00
1991-92 Upper Deck Sheets	14	20.00
1991 Wooden Award Winners	13	5.00
1991-93 5 Majeur	—	35.00
1992 ACC Tournament Champs	29	20.00
1992-93 Fleer	32	2.50
1992-93 Fleer	238	1.25
1992-93 Fleer	246	1.25
1992-93 Fleer	273	1.25
1992-93 Fleer All-Stars	6	50.00
1992-93 Fleer Drake's	7	7.50
1992-93 Fleer Team Leaders	4	175.00
1992-93 Fleer Team Night Sheets	—	6.00
1992-93 Fleer Tony's Pizza	S33	5.00
1992-93 Fleer Total D	5	75.00
1992-93 Hoops	30	3.00
1992-93 Hoops	298	1.50
1992-93 Hoops	320	.75
1992-93 Hoops	341	1.50
1992-93 Hoops Supreme Court	1SC	20.00
1992 Hoops 100 Superstars	14	20.00
1992 John McClean	—	1.00
1992 Kenner Starting Lineup BK Headline Collection	—	125.00
1992 Kenner Starting Lineup Basketball Olympic	—	40.00
1992 Kenner Starting Lineup Basketball	—	120.00
1992 Kenner Starting Lineup Basketball	—	120.00
1992-93 Panini Stickers	12	1.50
1992-93 Panini Stickers	16	.50
1992-93 Panini Stickers	17	.50
1992-93 Panini Stickers	18	.50
1992-93 Panini Stickers	19	.50
1992-93 Panini Stickers	20	1.50
1992-93 Panini Stickers	102	2.00
1992-93 Panini Stickers	128	2.50
1992-93 SkyBox	31	4.50
1992-93 SkyBox	314	2.50
1992-93 SkyBox Olympic Team	11	25.00
1992-93 SkyBox School Ties	ST16	8.00
1992 SkyBox USA Basketball	37	2.00
1992 SkyBox USA Basketball	38	2.00
1992 SkyBox USA Basketball	39	2.00
1992 SkyBox USA Basketball	40	2.00
1992 SkyBox USA Basketball	42	2.00
1992 SkyBox USA Basketball	43	2.00
1992 SkyBox USA Basketball	44	2.00
1992 SkyBox USA Basketball	45	2.00
1992-99 Sports Illustrated For Kids	270	7.50
1992-99 Sports Illustrated For Kids	349	6.00
1992 Sports Report	8	.50
1992-93 Stadium Club	1	7.00
1992-93 Stadium Club	210	3.00
1992-93 Stadium Club Beam Team	1	90.00
1992-93 Stadium Club Members Only	1	30.00
1992-93 Stadium Club Members Only	210	14.00
1992-93 Stadium Club Members Only	BT1	50.00
1992-93 Topps	3	.75
1992-93 Topps	115	.75
1992-93 Topps	141	1.50
1992-93 Topps	205	.75
1992-93 Topps Archives	52	4.00
1992-93 Topps Beam Team	3	4.00
1992-93 Ultra	27	6.00
1992-93 Ultra	216	1.50
1992-93 Ultra All-NBA Team	4	25.00
1992-93 Ultra NBA Award Winners	1	40.00
1992-93 Upper Deck	23	3.00
1992-93 Upper Deck	62	1.00
1992-93 Upper Deck	67	1.50
1992-93 Upper Deck	425	1.50
1992-93 Upper Deck	453a	1.50
1992-93 Upper Deck Error	453b	30.00
1992-93 Upper Deck	488	1.50
1992-93 Upper Deck	506	1.50
1992-93 Upper Deck	510	1.00
1992-93 Upper Deck	SP2	7.00
1992-93 Upper Deck All-Division Team	AD9	8.00
1992-93 Upper Deck All-NBA	AN1	50.00
1992-93 Upper Deck All-Star Weekend	15	4.00
1992 UD European Award Winner Holograms	—	17.00
1992 UD European Award Winner Holograms	—	17.00
1992 Upper Deck European	4	3.00
1992 Upper Deck European	38	6.00
1992 Upper Deck European	107	3.00
1992 Upper Deck European	158	3.00
1992 Upper Deck European	172	6.00

Michael Jordan Card Checklist

Set	No.	Value
1992 Upper Deck European	174	3.00
1992 Upper Deck European	176	6.00
1992 Upper Deck European	177	6.00
1992 Upper Deck European	178	6.00
1992 Upper Deck European	181	6.00
1992-93 Upper Deck Holograms	AW1	12.00
1992-93 Upper Deck Holograms	AW9	12.00
1992-93 Upper Deck Jerry West Selects	1JW	20.00
1992-93 Upper Deck Jerry West Selects	4JW	20.00
1992-93 Upper Deck Jerry West Selects	8JW	20.00
1992-93 Upper Deck Jerry West Selects	9JW	20.00
1992-93 Upper Deck McDonald's	P5	3.00
1992-93 Upper Deck McDonald's	CH4	10.00
1992-93 Upper Deck McDonald's	NNO	10.00
1992-93 Upper Deck MVP Holograms	4	10.00
1992-93 Upper Deck Sheets	—	25.00
1992-93 Upper Deck Team MVP's	TM1	40.00
1992-93 Upper Deck Team MVP's	TM5	40.00
1992-93 Upper Deck 15000-Point Club	PC4	60.00
1993 Fax Pax World of Sport	7	4.00
1993-94 Finest	1	20.00
1993-94 Finest Refractors	1	300.00
1993-94 Fleer	28	2.50
1993-94 Fleer	224	1.00

'91 Upper Deck No. SP1 $15

Set	No.	Value
1993-94 Fleer All-Stars	5	40.00
1993-94 Fleer Living Legends	4	14.00
1993-94 Fleer NBA Superstars	7	8.00
1993-94 Fleer Sharpshooters	3	20.00
1993-94 Hoops	28	2.00
1993-94 Hoops	257	1.00
1993-94 Hoops	283	.50
1993-94 Hoops	289	.50
1993-94 Hoops Face to Face	10	12.00
1993-94 Hoops Supreme Court	SC11	5.00
1993-94 Jam Session	33	5.00
1993 Kenner Starting Lineup Basketball	—	225.00
1993 Nike/Warner Brothers Michael Jordan	—	1.50
1993 Nike/Warner Brothers Michael Jordan	—	1.50
1993-94 SkyBox	14	2.00
1993-94 SkyBox	45	3.00
1993-94 SkyBox Center Stage	CS1	25.00
1993-94 SkyBox Dynamic Dunks	D4	20.00
1993 SkyBox Promos	—	10.00
1993-94 SkyBox Showdown Series	SS11	2.00
1993-94 Stadium Club	1	2.50
1993-94 Stadium Club	169	5.00
1993-94 Stadium Club	181	1.50
1993-94 Stadium Club Beam Team	4	30.00
1993-94 Stadium Club First Day Cards	1	100.00
1993-94 Stadium Club First Day Cards	169	200.00
1993-94 Stadium Club First Day Cards	181	100.00
1993-94 Stadium Club Members Only	1	12.00
1993-94 Stadium Club Members Only 59	6	8.00
1993-94 Stadium Club Members Only	169	25.00
1993-94 Stadium Club Members Only	181	12.00
1993-94 Stadium Club Members Only	BT4	25.00
1993-94 Topps	23	2.00
1993-94 Topps	64	1.00
1993-94 Topps	101	1.00
1993-94 Topps	199	1.00
1993-94 Topps	384	1.00
1993-94 Ultra	30	3.00
1993-94 Ultra All-Defensive Team	2	90.00
1993-94 Ultra All-NBA Team	2	25.00
1993-94 Ultra Famous Nicknames	7	20.00
1993-94 Ultra Inside Outside	4	10.00
1993-94 Ultra Power in the Key	2	35.00
1993-94 Ultra Scoring Kings	5	120.00
1993-94 Upper Deck	23	3.00
1993-94 Upper Deck	166	1.50
1993-94 Upper Deck	171	1.50
1993-94 Upper Deck	180	.75
1993-94 Upper Deck	187	.75
1993-94 Upper Deck	193	1.50
1993-94 Upper Deck	198	1.50
1993-94 Upper Deck	201	1.50
1993-94 Upper Deck	204	1.50
1993-94 Upper Deck	213	.75
1993-94 Upper Deck	237	1.50
1993-94 Upper Deck	438	1.50
1993-94 Upper Deck	466	1.50
1993-94 Upper Deck	SP3	7.00
1993-94 Upper Deck All-NBA	AN4	10.00
1993-94 Upper Deck All-NBA	AN15	5.00
1993-94 Upper Deck Box Bottoms	—	1.00
1993 UD European Award Winner Holograms	—	14.00
1993 Upper Deck European	5	3.00
1993 UD European Award Winner Holograms	—	14.00
1993 Upper Deck European	33	3.00
1993 Upper Deck European	43	3.00
1993 Upper Deck European	86	3.00
1993 Upper Deck European	90	6.00
1993 Upper Deck European	118	6.00
1993 Upper Deck European	254	1.00
1993 Upper Deck European	255	1.00
1993 Upper Deck French McDonald's	15	15.00
1993-94 Upper Deck Holojams	H4	12.00
1993-94 Upper Deck Locker Talk	LT1	40.00
1993-94 Upper Deck M.J. Mr. June	MJ1	18.00
1993-94 Upper Deck M.J. Mr. June	MJ2	18.00
1993-94 Upper Deck M.J. Mr. June	MJ9	18.00
1993-94 Upper Deck Pro View	23	3.00
1993-94 Upper Deck Pro View	91	1.50
1993-94 Upper Deck Sheets	1	10.00
1993-94 Upper Deck SE	MJRI	10.00
1993-94 Upper Deck SE Behind the Glass	11	25.00
1993-94 Upper Deck SE USA Trade	USA5	25.00
1993-94 Upper Deck Triple Double	TD2	18.00
1994 Action Packed Scouting Report	23	10.00
1994-97 Bleachers 23 Karat Gold	6	50.00
1994-97 Bleachers 23 Karat Gold	7	50.00
1994-97 Bleachers 23 Karat Gold	8	40.00
1994-97 Bleachers 23 Karat Gold	9	50.00
1994-97 Bleachers 23 Karat Gold	10	65.00
1994 Classic Birmingham Barons (Set)	23	15.00
1994-95 Collector's Choice	23	3.00
1994-95 Collector's Choice	204	1.50
1994-95 Collector's Choice	240	1.50
1994-95 Collector's Choice	402	1.50
1994-95 Collector's Choice	420	1.00
1994 Collector's Choice	635	3.00
1994 Collector's Choice	661	7.50
1994-95 Collector's Choice Gold Signature	23	100.00
1994-95 Collector's Choice Gold Signature	204	60.00
1994-95 Collector's Choice Gold Signature	240	60.00
1994-95 Collector's Choice Gold Signature	402	60.00
1994-95 Collector's Choice Gold Signature	420	30.00
1994-95 Collector's Choice Hobby Blowups	23	7.00
1994-95 Collector's Choice Hobby Blowups	A23	5000.00
1994-95 E-Motion	100	13.00
1994-95 E-Motion N-Tense	N3	50.00
1994-95 Embossed	121	10.00
1994-95 Finest	331	25.00
1994-95 Finest Refractors	331	400.00
1994-95 Flair	326	15.00
1994 Fleer/ProCards Birmingham Barons	633	15.00
1994-95 Highland Mint	3	75.00
1994 McDonald's Nothing But Net MVPs	4	4.00
1994-95 SP	MJIR	10.00
1994-95 SP	MJIS	35.00
1994-95 SP Championship Playoff Heroes	P2	30.00
1994 SP Holoview Blue	16	30.00
1994 SP Holoview Red	16	250.00
1994 Ted Williams Co. Dan Gardiner	1DG	8.00
1994 Upper Deck	19	12.00
1994-95 Upper Deck	359	2.00
1994 Upper Deck Diamond Collection	1C	50.00
1994 Upper Deck European Triple Double	TD2	15.00
1994 Upper Deck European	23	6.00
1994 Upper Deck European	176	10.00
1994-95 Upper Deck Jordan He's Back	23	2.00
1994-95 Upper Deck Jordan He's Back	23	2.00
1994-95 Upper Deck Jordan He's Back	41	2.00
1994-95 Upper Deck Jordan He's Back	44	2.00
1994-95 Upper Deck Jordan He's Back	204	2.00
1994-95 Upper Deck Jordan He's Back	237	2.00
1994-95 Upper Deck Jordan He's Back	402	2.00
1994-95 Upper Deck Jordan He's Back	425	2.00
1994-95 Upper Deck Jordan He's Back	453	2.00
1994 Upper Deck Jordan Rare Air	1	1.00
1994 Upper Deck Jordan Rare Air	2	1.00
1994 Upper Deck Jordan Rare Air	3	.50
1994 Upper Deck Jordan Rare Air	4	.25
1994 Upper Deck Jordan Rare Air	5	.50
1994 Upper Deck Jordan Rare Air	6	.50
1994 Upper Deck Jordan Rare Air	7	.50
1994 Upper Deck Jordan Rare Air	8	.50
1994 Upper Deck Jordan Rare Air	9	.50
1994 Upper Deck Jordan Rare Air	10	.50
1994 Upper Deck Jordan Rare Air	11	.50
1994 Upper Deck Jordan Rare Air	12	.50
1994 Upper Deck Jordan Rare Air	13	.25
1994 Upper Deck Jordan Rare Air	14	.50
1994 Upper Deck Jordan Rare Air	15	.25
1994 Upper Deck Jordan Rare Air	16	1.00
1994 Upper Deck Jordan Rare Air	17	.50
1994 Upper Deck Jordan Rare Air	18	1.00
1994 Upper Deck Jordan Rare Air	19	.50
1994 Upper Deck Jordan Rare Air	20	.50
1994 Upper Deck Jordan Rare Air	21	.25
1994 Upper Deck Jordan Rare Air	22	1.00
1994 Upper Deck Jordan Rare Air	23	1.00
1994 Upper Deck Jordan Rare Air	24	.50
1994 Upper Deck Jordan Rare Air	25	.50
1994 Upper Deck Jordan Rare Air	26	.50
1994 Upper Deck Jordan Rare Air	27	.25
1994 Upper Deck Jordan Rare Air	28	.50
1994 Upper Deck Jordan Rare Air	29	.50
1994 Upper Deck Jordan Rare Air	30	.50
1994 Upper Deck Jordan Rare Air	31	.50
1994 Upper Deck Jordan Rare Air	32	.50
1994 Upper Deck Jordan Rare Air	33	1.00
1994 Upper Deck Jordan Rare Air	34	1.00
1994 Upper Deck Jordan Rare Air	35	.25
1994 Upper Deck Jordan Rare Air	36	.50
1994 Upper Deck Jordan Rare Air	37	1.00
1994 Upper Deck Jordan Rare Air	38	1.00
1994 Upper Deck Jordan Rare Air	39	.50
1994 Upper Deck Jordan Rare Air	40	.50
1994 Upper Deck Jordan Rare Air	41	.50
1994 Upper Deck Jordan Rare Air	42	.50
1994 Upper Deck Jordan Rare Air	43	.50
1994 Upper Deck Jordan Rare Air	44	.50
1994 Upper Deck Jordan Rare Air	45	.50
1994 Upper Deck Jordan Rare Air	46	1.00
1994 Upper Deck Jordan Rare Air	47	.50
1994 Upper Deck Jordan Rare Air	48	1.00
1994 Upper Deck Jordan Rare Air	49	.25
1994 Upper Deck Jordan Rare Air	50	1.00
1994 Upper Deck Jordan Rare Air	51	.25
1994 Upper Deck Jordan Rare Air	52	.25
1994 Upper Deck Jordan Rare Air	53	.50
1994 Upper Deck Jordan Rare Air	54	.50
1994 Upper Deck Jordan Rare Air	55	.50
1994 Upper Deck Jordan Rare Air	56	.50
1994 Upper Deck Jordan Rare Air	57	.50
1994 Upper Deck Jordan Rare Air	58	.50
1994 Upper Deck Jordan Rare Air	59	.50
1994 Upper Deck Jordan Rare Air	60	.50
1994 Upper Deck Jordan Rare Air	61	1.00
1994 Upper Deck Jordan Rare Air	62	1.00
1994 Upper Deck Jordan Rare Air	63	1.00
1994 Upper Deck Jordan Rare Air	64	1.00
1994 Upper Deck Jordan Rare Air	65	1.00
1994 Upper Deck Jordan Rare Air	66	.50
1994 Upper Deck Jordan Rare Air	67	.50
1994 Upper Deck Jordan Rare Air	68	.50
1994 Upper Deck Jordan Rare Air	69	.50
1994 Upper Deck Jordan Rare Air	70	.50
1994 Upper Deck Jordan Rare Air	71	.50
1994 Upper Deck Jordan Rare Air	72	1.00
1994 Upper Deck Jordan Rare Air	73	.50
1994 Upper Deck Jordan Rare Air	74	.50
1994 Upper Deck Jordan Rare Air	75	1.00
1994 Upper Deck Jordan Rare Air	76	1.00
1994 Upper Deck Jordan Rare Air	77	.50
1994 Upper Deck Jordan Rare Air	78	1.00

Michael Jordan Card Checklist

Card	#	Price
1994 Upper Deck Jordan Rare Air	79	.50
1994 Upper Deck Jordan Rare Air	80	.50
1994 Upper Deck Jordan Rare Air	81	.50
1994 Upper Deck Jordan Rare Air	82	.50
1994 Upper Deck Jordan Rare Air	83	1.00
1994 Upper Deck Jordan Rare Air	84	.50
1994 Upper Deck Jordan Rare Air	85	1.00
1994 Upper Deck Jordan Rare Air	86	.50
1994 Upper Deck Jordan Rare Air	87	.50
1994 Upper Deck Jordan Rare Air	88	.50
1994 Upper Deck Jordan Rare Air	89	1.00
1994 Upper Deck Jordan Rare Air	90	.50
1994 Upper Deck Scouting Report Supers	SR1	3.00
1994 Upper Deck Scouting Report Supers	SR2	3.00
1994 Upper Deck Scouting Report Supers	SR3	3.00
1994 Upper Deck Scouting Report Supers	SR4	3.00
1994 Upper Deck Scouting Report Supers	SR5	3.00
1994 Upper Deck Scouting Report Supers	MJ23	5.00
1994 Upper Deck Minor League	MJ23	20.00
1994 Upper Deck Minor League	MJ23	70.00
1994 Upper Deck Next Generation	8	35.00
1994 Upper Deck Nothing But Net	5	1.50
1994 Upper Deck Nothing But Net	7	1.00
1994 Upper Deck Nothing But Net	9	1.00
1994 Upper Deck Nothing But Net	13	1.50
1994 Upper Deck SP Insert	2	25.00
1994 Upper Deck USA Basketball	85	4.00
1994 Upper Deck USA Jordan's Highlights	JH1	10.00
1994 Upper Deck USA Jordan's Highlights	JH2	10.00
1994 Upper Deck USA Jordan's Highlights	JH3	10.00
1994 Upper Deck USA Jordan's Highlights	JH4	10.00
1994 Upper Deck USA Jordan's Highlights	JH5	10.00
1994 Upper Deck World Cup Contenders	3	.15
1994 Upper Deck/American Epic Inserts	2BC	4.00
1994 Upper Deck/Fun Packs	170	9.00
1995-96 Bulls Jewel/Nabisco	1	3.00
1995 Cardtoons	95	3.75
1995-96 Collector's Choice	45	2.25
1995-96 Collector's Choice	169	1.25
1995-96 Collector's Choice	195	1.25
1995-96 Collector's Choice	324	1.00
1995-96 Collector's Choice	410	.50
1995 Collector's Choice	500	2.50
1995-96 Collector's Choice Crash The Game	C1A	12.00
1995-96 Collector's Choice Crash The Game II	C1A	8.00
1995-96 Collector's Choice Crash The Game	C1B	12.00
1995-96 Collector's Choice Crash The Game II	C1B	8.00
1995-96 Collector's Choice Crash The Game	C1C	12.00
1995-96 Collector's Choice Crash The Game II	C1C	8.00
1995-96 Collector's Choice European Sticker	MJ1	4.00
1995-96 Collector's Choice European Sticker	MJ2	4.00
1995-96 Collector's Choice European Sticker	MJ3	4.00
1995-96 Collector's Choice European Sticker	MJ4	4.00
1995-96 Collector's Choice European Sticker	MJ5	4.00
1995-96 Collector's Choice European Sticker	MJ6	4.00
1995-96 Collector's Choice European Sticker	MJ7	4.00
1995-96 Collector's Choice European Sticker	MJ8	4.00
1995-96 Collector's Choice European Sticker	MJ9	4.00
1995-96 Collector's Choice European Stickers	120	12.00
1995 Collector's Choice Gold Signature	500	80.00
1995 Collector's Choice Int. Decade of Dominance	J1	15.00
1995 Collector's Choice Int. Decade of Dominance	J2	15.00
1995 Collector's Choice Int. Decade of Dominance	J3	15.00
1995 Collector's Choice Int. Decade of Dominance	J4	15.00
1995 Collector's Choice Int. Decade of Dominance	J5	15.00
1995 Collector's Choice Int. Decade of Dominance	J6	15.00
1995 Collector's Choice Int. Decade of Dominance	J7	15.00
1995 Collector's Choice Int. Decade of Dominance	J8	15.00
1995 Collector's Choice Int. Decade of Dominance	J9	15.00
1995 Collector's Choice Int. Decade of Dominance	J10	15.00
1995 Collector's Choice Int. Spanish II	21	2.50
1995 Collector's Choice Int. Japanese I	23	10.00
1995 Collector's Choice Int. Spanish I	23	5.00
1995 Collector's Choice Int. Japanese Gold Sig. II	402	50.00
1995 Collector's Choice Int. Japanese II	240	5.00
1995 Collector's Choice Int. European Gold Sig.	402	50.00
1995 Collector's Choice Int. Spanish II	183	2.50

Card	#	Price
1995 Collector's Choice Int. Japanese II	402	5.00
1995 Collector's Choice Int. Spanish II	201	1.25
1995 Collector's Choice Int. Japanese II	420	2.00
1995 Collector's Choice Int. European	204	5.00
1995 Collector's Choice Int. Japanese I	204	5.00
1995 Collector's Choice Int. Spanish I	204	2.50
1995 Collector's Choice Int. European	211	15.00
1995 Collector's Choice Int. Japanese I	211	15.00
1995 Collector's Choice Int. Spanish I	211	10.00
1995 Collector's Choice Int. European	212	15.00
1995 Collector's Choice Int. Japanese I	212	15.00
1995 Collector's Choice Int. Japanese II	T1	20.00
1995 Collector's Choice Int. Spanish I	212	10.00
1995 Collector's Choice Int. European	213	15.00
1995 Collector's Choice Int. Japanese I	213	15.00
1995 Collector's Choice Int. Spanish I	213	10.00
1995 Collector's Choice Int. European	214	15.00
1995 Collector's Choice Int. Japanese I	214	15.00
1995 Collector's Choice Int. Spanish I	214	10.00
1995 Collector's Choice Int. European	215	15.00
1995 Collector's Choice Int. Japanese I	215	15.00
1995 Collector's Choice Int. Spanish I	215	10.00
1995 Collector's Choice Int. European	216	15.00
1995 Collector's Choice Int. Japanese I	216	15.00
1995 Collector's Choice Int. Spanish I	216	10.00
1995 Collector's Choice Int. Japanese I	217	15.00
1995 Collector's Choice Int. Spanish I	217	10.00
1995 Collector's Choice Int. European	218	15.00
1995 Collector's Choice Int. Japanese I	218	15.00
1995 Collector's Choice Int. Spanish I	218	10.00
1995 Collector's Choice Int. European	219	15.00
1995 Collector's Choice Int. Japanese I	219	15.00
1995 Collector's Choice Int. Spanish I	219	10.00
1995 Collector's Choice Int. European	240	5.00
1995 Collector's Choice Int. European	402	5.00
1995 Collector's Choice Int. European	420	2.00
1995-96 Collector's Choice Jordan He's Back	M1	1.50
1995-96 Collector's Choice Jordan He's Back	M2	1.50
1995-96 Collector's Choice Jordan He's Back	M3	1.50
1995-96 Collector's Choice Jordan He's Back	M4	1.50
1995-96 Collector's Choice Jordan He's Back	M5	1.50
1995 Collector's Choice Michael Jordan Jumbo	661	25.00
1995 Collector's Choice Silver Signature	500	10.00
1995 Collector's Choice/SE Gold	238	140.00
1995 Collector's Choice/SE Silver	238	20.00
1995 Collector's Choice/SE	238	3.50
1995-96 Finest	229	14.00
1995-96 Finest Dish and Swish	DS4	150.00
1995-96 Finest Hot Stuff	HS1	25.00
1995-96 Finest Mystery	M1	15.00
1995-96 Finest Mystery Borderless Refractors/Gold	M1	400.00
1995-96 Finest Refractors	229	425.00
1995-96 Finest Veteran/Rookie	RV20	120.00
1995-96 Flair	15	12.00
1995-96 Flair	235	5.00
1995-96 Flair Anticipation	2	80.00
1995-96 Flair Hardwood Leaders	4	8.00
1995-96 Flair Hot Numbers	4	80.00
1995-96 Flair New Heights	4	50.00
1995-96 Fleer	22	2.00
1995-96 Fleer	323	1.00
1995-96 Fleer End 2 End	9	10.00
1995-96 Fleer Total D	3	10.00
1995-96 Fleer Total O	2	20.00
1995 Highland Mint Medallions	2	10.00
1995 Highland Mint Mint-Cards	38b	55.00
1995 Highland Mint Mint-Cards	38s	225.00
1995 Highland Mint Mint-Cards	38g	600.00
1995-96 Hoop Magazine/Mother's Cookies	4	25.00
1995-96 Hoops	21	2.00
1995-96 Hoops	358	1.00
1995-96 Hoops Hot List	1	30.00
1995-96 Hoops Number Crunchers	1	5.00
1995-96 Hoops Power Palette	1	30.00
1995-96 Hoops Skyview	SV1	70.00
1995-96 Hoops Top Ten	AR7	20.00
1995-96 Jam Session	13	3.00
1995-96 Jam Session Show Stoppers	S3	120.00
1995-96 Metal	13	6.00
1995-96 Metal	212	3.00
1995-96 Metal Maximum Metal	4	40.00
1995-96 Metal Scoring Magnets	4	70.00
1995-96 Metal Slick Silver	3	28.00
1995-96 Panini Stickers	83	5.00
1995-96 SkyBox	15	2.00
1995-96 SkyBox	278	1.50
1995-96 SkyBox E-XL	10	10.00
1995-96 SkyBox E-XL Natural Born Thrillers	1	100.00
1995-96 SkyBox E-XL No Boundaries	1	60.00
1995-96 SkyBox Larger Than Life	L1	65.00
1995-96 SkyBox Meltdown	M1	50.00

Card	#	Price
1995-96 SkyBox Standouts Hobby	SH1	40.00
1995-96 Stadium Club	1	3.00
1995-96 Stadium Club Beam Team	14	60.00
1995-96 Stadium Club Members Only I	1	12.00
1995 Stadium Club Members Only 50	20	5.00
1995-96 Stadium Club Members Only II	B14	50.00
1995-96 Stadium Club Members Only II	RM2	50.00
1995-96 Stadium Club Members Only II	SS1	12.00
1995-96 Stadium Club Members Only I	WS1	25.00
1995-96 Stadium Club Nemeses	N10	25.00
1995-96 Stadium Club Reign Men	RM2	65.00
1995-96 Stadium Club Spike Says	SS1	25.00
1995-96 Stadium Club Warp Speed	1	50.00
1995-96 SP	23	6.00
1995-96 SP All-Stars	AS2	25.00

'93-94 Finest No. 1 $20

Card	#	Price
1995-96 SP Championship	17	5.00
1995-96 SP Championship	121	2.00
1995-96 SP Champ. Champions of the Court	C30	30.00
1995-96 SP Champ. Champ. of the Court Die-Cut	C30	250.00
1995-96 SP Championship Jordan Collection	JC17	10.00
1995-96 SP Championship Jordan Collection	JC18	10.00
1995-96 SP Championship Jordan Collection	JC19	10.00
1995-96 SP Championship Jordan Collection	JC20	10.00
1995-96 SP Championship Shots	S16	12.00
1995-96 SP Holoviews	PC5	40.00
1995-96 SP Holoviews Die-Cuts	PC5	225.00
1995-96 SP The Jordan Collection	JC17	15.00
1995-96 SP The Jordan Collection	JC18	15.00
1995-96 SP The Jordan Collection	JC19	15.00
1995-96 SP The Jordan Collection	JC20	15.00
1995-96 SP The Jordan Collection	JC21	15.00
1995-96 SP The Jordan Collection	JC22	15.00
1995-96 SP The Jordan Collection	JC23	15.00
1995-96 SP The Jordan Collection	JC24	15.00
1995-96 Topps	1	1.25
1995-96 Topps	4	1.25
1995-96 Topps	277	1.50
1995-96 Topps Gallery	10	5.00
1995-96 Topps Gallery Expressionists	EX2	50.00
1995-96 Topps Mystery Finest	M1	60.00
1995-96 Topps Power Boosters	1	70.00
1995-96 Topps Power Boosters	4	70.00
1995-96 Topps Power Boosters	277	70.00
1995-96 Topps Show Stoppers	1	30.00
1995-96 Topps Spark Plugs	SP2	12.00
1995-96 Topps Top Flight	1	30.00
1995-96 Topps World Class	WC1	25.00
1995-96 Ultra	25	4.00
1995-96 Ultra Double Trouble	3	7.00
1995-96 Ultra Fabulous Fifties	5	13.00
1995-96 Ultra Jam City	3	30.00
1995-96 Ultra Scoring Kings	4	50.00
1995-96 Upper Deck	23	3.00
1995 Upper Deck	133	3.00
1995 Upper Deck	137	1.50
1995 Upper Deck	200	4.00
1995 Upper Deck	335	1.50
1995 Upper Deck	337	.75
1995 Upper Deck	339	.75
1995 Upper Deck	341	.75

Michael Jordan Card Checklist

1995-96 Upper Deck	352	1.50
1995-96 Upper Deck Ball Park Jordan	BP1	10.00
1995-96 Upper Deck Ball Park Jordan	BP2	10.00
1995-96 Upper Deck Ball Park Jordan	BP3	10.00
1995-96 Upper Deck Ball Park Jordan	BP4	10.00
1995-96 Upper Deck Ball Park Jordan	BP5	10.00
1995 Upper Deck Minor League Highlights	MJ-1	5.00
1995 UD Minor League Jordan One-On-One	1	.50
1995 UD Minor League Jordan's Scrapbook	1	15.00
1995 UD Minor League Jordan Highlights	MJ-2	5.00
1995 UD Minor League Jordan One-On-One	2	.50
1995 UD Minor League Jordan's Scrapbook	2	15.00
1995 UD Minor League Jordan Highlights	MJ-3	5.00
1995 UD Minor Leagu Jordan One-On-One	3	.50
1995 UD Minor League Jordan's Scrapbook	3	15.00
1995 UD Minor League Jordan Highlights	MJ-4	5.00
1995 UD Minor League Jordan One-On-One	4	.50
1995 UD Minor League Jordan's Scrapbook	4	15.00
1995 UD Minor League Jordan Highlights	MJ-5	5.00
1995 UDMinor League Jordan One-On-One	5	.50
1995 UD Minor League Jordan's Scrapbook	5	15.00
1995 UD Minor League Jordan One-On-One	6	.50
1995 UD Minor League Organizational Pro-Files	OP6	25.00
1995 UD Minor League Jordan's Scrapbook	6	15.00
1995 UD Minor League Jordan One-On-One	7	.50
1995 UD Minor League Jordan's Scrapbook	7	15.00
1995 UD Minor League Jordan One-On-One	8	.50
1995 UD Minor League Jordan's Scrapbook	8	15.00
1995 UD Minor League Jordan One-On-One	9	.50
1995 UD Minor League Jordan's Scrapbook	9	15.00
1995 UD Minor League Jordan One-On-One	10	.50
1995 UD Minor League Jordan's Scrapbook	10	15.00
1995 Upper Deck Minor League	45	6.00
1995-96 UD Predictor Hobby Player of the Week	H1	10.00
1995-96 UD Predictor Retail Player of the Month	R1	10.00
1995-96 Upper Deck Predictor Hobby Scoring	H1	10.00
1995-96 Upper Deck Predictor Retail MVP	R1	10.00
1995-96 UD Predictor Hobby Player of the Week	H2	10.00
1995-96 UD Predictor Retail Player of the Month	R2	10.00
1995-96 Upper Deck Predictor Hobby Scoring	H2	10.00
1995-96 Upper Deck Predictor Retail MVP	R2	10.00
1995-96 UD Predictor Hobby Player of the Week	H3	10.00
1995-96 UD Predictor Retail Player of the Month	R3	10.00
1995-96 Upper Deck Predictor Hobby Scoring	H3	10.00
1995-96 Upper Deck Predictor Retail MVP	R3	10.00
1995-96 UD Predictor Hobby Player of the Week	H4	10.00
1995-96 UD Predictor Retail Player of the Month	R4	10.00
1995-96 Upper Deck Predictor Hobby Scoring	H4	10.00
1995-96 Upper Deck Predictor Retail MVP	R4	10.00
1995-96 UD Predictor Hobby Player of the Week	H5	10.00
1995-96 UD Predictor Retail Player of the Month	R5	10.00

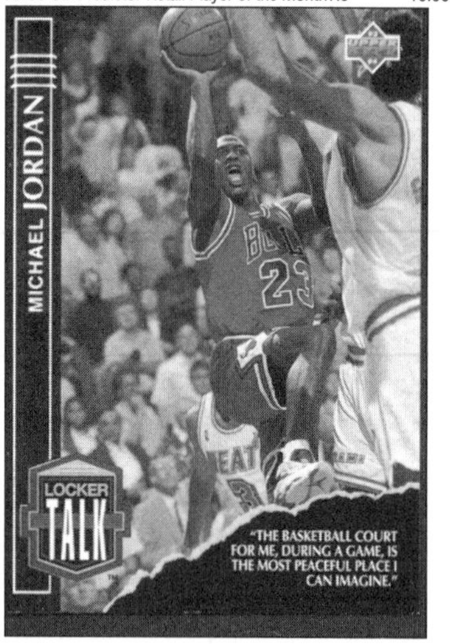
MICHAEL JORDAN
LOCKER TALK
"THE BASKETBALL COURT FOR ME, DURING A GAME, IS THE MOST PEACEFUL PLACE I CAN IMAGINE."

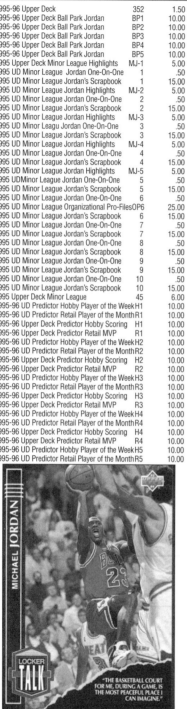

'93-94 Upper Deck Locker Talk No. LT1 $40

1995-96 Upper Deck Predictor Hobby Scoring	H5	10.00
1995-96 Upper Deck Predictor Retail MVP	R5	10.00
1995-96 Upper Deck Special Edition	SE100	12.00
1995 Upper Deck Steal of a Deal	SD15	40.00
1995 UD/Metallic Impressions Michael Jordan	JT1	4.00
1995 UD/Metallic Impressions Michael Jordan	JT2	4.00
1995 UD/Metallic Impressions Michael Jordan	JT3	4.00
1995 UD/Metallic Impressions Michael Jordan	JT4	4.00
1995 UD/Metallic Impressions Michael Jordan	JT5	4.00
1995 UD/SP Top Prospects Jordan Time Capsule	TC1	10.00
1995 UD/SP Top Prospects Jordan Time Capsule	TC2	10.00
1995 UD/SP Top Prospects Jordan Time Capsule	TC3	10.00
1995 UD/SP Top Prospects Jordan Time Capsule	TC4	10.00
1995 UD/SP Top Prospects Autographs	—	4750.00
1996-97 Bowman's Best	80	10.00
1996-97 Bowman's Best Cuts	BC2	45.00
1996-97 Bowman's Best Honor Roll	HR2	60.00
1996-97 Bowman's Best Shots	BS6	20.00
1996-97 Collector's Choice	23	3.00
1996-97 Collector's Choice	25	1.00
1996-97 Collector's Choice	26	1.00
1996-97 Collector's Choice	195	1.00
1996-97 Collector's Choice	362	.50
1996-97 Collector's Choice	363	.50
1996-97 Collector's Choice	364	.50
1996-97 Collector's Choice	365	.50
1996-97 Collector's Choice	366	.50
1996-97 Collector's Choice Chicago Bulls Team Set	B1	2.00
1996-97 Collector's Choice Chicago Bulls Team Set	CH3	3.00
1996-97 Collector's Choice Crash the Game	C30	10.00
1996-97 Collector's Choice Crash the Game II	C30	10.00
1996-97 Collector's Choice Factory Blow-Ups	1	4.00
1996-97 Collector's Choice Factory Blow-Ups	4	4.00
1996-97 Collector's Choice Game Face	GF2	7.00
1996 Collector's Choice Int. Jordan Collection	JC1	10.00
1996 Collector's Choice Int. Jordan Collection	JC2	10.00
1996 Collector's Choice Int. Jordan Collection	JC3	10.00
1996 Collector's Choice Int. Jordan Collection	JC4	10.00
1996 Collector's Choice International I	45	6.00
1996 Collector's Choice International Japanese	45	6.00
1996 Collector's Choice International II	114	3.00
1996 Collector's Choice International II	143	3.00
1996 Collector's Choice International I	169	3.00
1996 Collector's Choice International Japanese	169	3.00
1996 Collector's Choice International I	195	3.00
1996 Collector's Choice International Japanese	195	3.00
1996 Collector's Choice International II	200	1.50
1996 Collector's Choice International I	210	1.50
1996 Collector's Choice International Japanese	210	1.50
1996 Collector's Choice International Japanese	324	3.00
1996 Collector's Choice International Japanese	353	3.00
1996 Collector's Choice International Japanese	410	1.50
1996-97 Collector's Choice Jordan A Cut Above	CA1	2.50
1996-97 Collector's Choice Jordan A Cut Above	CA2	2.50
1996-97 Collector's Choice Jordan A Cut Above	CA3	2.50
1996-97 Collector's Choice Jordan A Cut Above	CA4	2.50
1996-97 Collector's Choice Jordan A Cut Above	CA5	2.50
1996-97 Collector's Choice Jordan A Cut Above	CA6	2.50
1996-97 Collector's Choice Jordan A Cut Above	CA7	2.50
1996-97 Collector's Choice Jordan A Cut Above	CA8	2.50
1996-97 Collector's Choice Jordan A Cut Above	CA9	2.50
1996-97 Collector's Choice Jordan A Cut Above	CA10	2.50
1996-97 Collector's Choice Mini-Cards	1	5.00
1996-97 Collector's Choice Memorable Moments	1	10.00
1996-97 Collector's Choice Stick-Ums	S30	6.00
1996-97 Collector's Choice Stick-Ums II	S30	6.00
1996-97 Finest	50	12.00
1996-97 Finest	127	30.00
1996-97 Finest	291	125.00
1996-97 Finest Refractors	50	150.00
1996-97 Finest Refractors	127	200.00
1996-97 Finest Refractors	291	900.00
1996-97 Flair Showcase Hot Shots	1	175.00
1996-97 Flair Showcase Legacy	23	550.00
1996-97 Flair Showcase Row 0	23	125.00
1996-97 Flair Showcase Row 1	23	15.00
1996-97 Flair Showcase Row 2	23	10.00
1996-97 Fleer	13	2.50
1996-97 Fleer	123	1.25
1996-97 Fleer	282	1.50
1996-97 Fleer Decade of Excellence	4	130.00
1996-97 Fleer Game Breakers	1	100.00
1996-97 Fleer Stackhouse's All-Fleer	4	14.00
1996-97 Fleer Thrill Seekers	6	175.00
1996-97 Fleer Total "O"	4	50.00
1996-97 Hoops	20	3.00
1996-97 Hoops	176	1.25
1996-97 Hoops	335	1.25
1996-97 Hoops Head to Head	HH2	25.00
1996-97 Hoops Hot List	8	60.00
1996-97 Hoops Starting Five	4	15.00
1996-97 Hoops Superfeats	1	60.00
1996-97 Metal	11	5.00
1996-97 Metal	128	2.50
1996-97 Metal	241	2.50
1996-97 Metal Decade of Excellence	4	50.00
1996-97 Metal Maximum Metal	4	150.00
1996-97 Metal Molten Metal	18	120.00
1996-97 Metal Net-Rageous	NR5	200.00
1996-97 Metal Platinum Portraits	PP5	80.00
1996-97 Metal Steel Slammin	6	90.00
1996-97 SkyBox	16	4.00
1996-97 SkyBox	247	2.00
1996-97 SkyBox Bulls Triple Threat	TT11	75.00
1996-97 SkyBox E-X2000	9	15.00
1996-97 SkyBox E-X2000 A Cut Above	8	225.00
1996-97 SkyBox E-X2000 Net Assets	8	50.00
1996-97 SkyBox Golden Touch	5	160.00
1996-97 SkyBox Larger Than Life	L7	175.00
1996-97 SkyBox Net Set	8	80.00
1996-97 SkyBox Rubies	16	200.00
1996-97 SkyBox Rubies	247	100.00
1996-97 SkyBox Thunder and Lightning	1	100.00
1996-97 SkyBox Z-Force	11	5.00
1996-97 SkyBox Z-Force	179	2.00
1996-97 SkyBox Z-Force Big Men On The Court	4	200.00
1996-97 SkyBox Z-Force BMOC Z-Peat	4	600.00
1996-97 SkyBox Z-Force Slam Cam	SC5	200.00
1996-97 SkyBox Z-Force Vortex	V5	60.00
1996-97 Stadium Club	101	4.00
1996-97 Stadium Club Class Acts	CA1	20.00
1996-97 Stadium Club Finest Reprints	24	45.00
1996-97 Stadium Club Fusion	F1	60.00
1996-97 Stadium Club High Risers	HR14	60.00
1996-97 Stadium Club Members Only II	101	25.00
1996-97 Stadium Club Members Only 55	41	6.00
1996 Stadium Club Members Only I	F1	25.00
1996-97 Stadium Club Members Only II	CA1	15.00
1996 Stadium Club Members Only I	GM3	2.00
1996 Stadium Club Members Only I	SF4	15.00
1996 Stadium Club Members Only I	SM2	2.50
1996-97 Stadium Club Members Only II	HR14	25.00
1996 Stadium Club Members Only I	TC9	12.00
1996-97 Stadium Club Moments	GM3	3.50
1996-97 Stadium Club Moments	SM2	4.00
1996-97 Stadium Club Player's Private Issue	10	300.00
1996-97 Stadium Club Special Forces	SF4	40.00
1996-97 Stadium Club Top Crop	TC9	40.00
1996-97 SP	16	5.00
1996-97 SP Game Film	GF1	120.00
1996-97 SP Holoviews	PC5	35.00
1996-97 SP Inside Info	25K	60.00
1996-97 SP SPx Force	F1	200.00
1996-97 SP SPx Force	F5	200.00
1996-97 SP SPx Force	F5A	2000.00
1996 SPx	8	20.00
1996 SPx Holoview Heroes	H1	60.00
1996 SPx Record Breaker Card	R1	25.00
1996-97 Topps	139	2.50
1996-97 Topps Chrome	139	40.00
1996-97 Topps Chrome Pro Files	PF3	20.00
1996-97 Topps Chrome Refractors	139	425.00
1996-97 Topps Chrome Season's Best	SB1	20.00
1996-97 Topps Chrome Season's Best	SB18	20.00
1996-97 Topps Holding Court	HC2	50.00
1996-97 Topps Mystery Finest Bordered	M14	50.00
1996 Topps NBA Stars	24	4.00
1996 Topps NBA Stars	74	4.00
1996 Topps NBA Stars	124	4.00
1996 Topps NBA Stars Imagine	I6	40.00
1996 Topps NBA Stars Reprints	24	60.00
1996-97 Topps Pro Files	PF3	15.00
1996-97 Topps Season's Best	SB1	25.00
1996-97 Topps Season's Best	SB18	25.00
1996-97 Ultra	16	4.00
1996-97 Ultra	143	2.00
1996-97 Ultra	280	2.00
1996-97 Ultra Board Game	7	30.00
1996-97 Ultra Court Masters	2	140.00
1996-97 Ultra Decade of Excellence	U4	75.00
1996-97 Ultra Full Court Trap	1	20.00
1996-97 Ultra Give and Take	5	30.00
1996-97 Ultra Platinum	16	500.00
1996-97 Ultra Platinum	143	250.00
1996-97 Ultra Platinum	280	200.00
1996-97 Ultra Scoring Kings	4	50.00
1996-97 Ultra Starring Role	4	160.00
1996-97 Upper Deck	16	4.00
1996-97 Upper Deck	165	2.00
1996-97 Upper Deck Ball Park Jordan	1	10.00
1996-97 Upper Deck Ball Park Jordan	2	10.00
1996-97 Upper Deck Ball Park Jordan	3	10.00
1996-97 Upper Deck Ball Park Jordan	4	10.00
1996-97 Upper Deck Ball Park Jordan	5	10.00
1996-97 Upper Deck Fast Break	FB23	30.00

Michael Jordan Card Checklist

1996-97 Upper Deck Italian Stickers	88	2.50
1996-97 Upper Deck Italian Stickers	89	2.50
1996-97 Upper Deck Italian Stickers	90	2.50
1996-97 Upper Deck Italian Stickers	91	2.50
1996-97 Upper Deck Italian Stickers	114	5.00
1996-97 Upper Deck Jordan-Greater Heights	GH1	20.00
1996-97 Upper Deck Jordan-Greater Heights	GH2	20.00
1996-97 Upper Deck Jordan-Greater Heights	GH3	20.00
1996-97 Upper Deck Jordan-Greater Heights	GH4	20.00
1996-97 Upper Deck Jordan-Greater Heights	GH5	20.00
1996-97 Upper Deckl Jordan-Greater Heights	GH6	20.00
1996-97 Upper Deckl Jordan-Greater Heights	GH7	20.00
1996-97 Upper Deckl Jordan-Greater Heights	GH8	20.00
1996-97 Upper Deck Jordan-Greater Heights	GH9	20.00
1996-97 Upper Deck Jordan-Greater Heights	GH10	20.00
1996-97 Upper Deck Michael's Viewpoints	VP1	16.00
1996-97 Upper Deck Michael's Viewpoints	VP2	16.00
1996-97 Upper Deck Michael's Viewpoints	VP3	16.00
1996-97 Upper Deck Michael's Viewpoints	VP4	16.00
1996-97 Upper Deck Michael's Viewpoints	VP5	16.00
1996-97 Upper Deck Michael's Viewpoints	VP6	16.00
1996-97 Upper Deck Michael's Viewpoints	VP7	16.00
1996-97 Upper Deck Michael's Viewpoints	VP8	16.00
1996-97 Upper Deck Michael's Viewpoints	VP9	16.00
1996-97 Upper Deck Michael's Viewpoints	VP10	16.00
1996-97 Upper Deck Predictor II	P2	30.00
1996-97 Upper Deck Predictor	P3	30.00
1996-97 Upper Deck Rookie of the Year	RC13	120.00
1996-97 Upper Deck Smooth Grooves	SG8	90.00
1996-97 Upper Deck UD3	23	8.00
1996-97 Upper Deck UD3 Court Comm. Autographs	C1	2500.00
1996-97 Upper Deck UD3 SuperStar Spotlight	S5	150.00
1996-97 Upper Deck UD3 Winning Edge	W1	40.00
1996 Upper Deck USA Michael Jordan	M1	25.00
1996 Upper Deck USA Michael Jordan	M2	25.00
1996 Upper Deck USA Michael Jordan	M3	25.00
1996 Upper Deck USA Michael Jordan	M4	25.00
1996 Upper Deck 23 Nights Jordan Experience	1	1.50
1996 Upper Deck 23 Nights Jordan Experience	2	1.50
1996 Upper Deck 23 Nights Jordan Experience	3	1.50
1996 Upper Deck 23 Nights Jordan Experience	4	1.50
1996 Upper Deck 23 Nights Jordan Experience	5	1.50
1996 Upper Deck 23 Nights Jordan Experience	6	1.50
1996 Upper Deck 23 Nights Jordan Experience	7	1.50
1996 Upper Deck 23 Nights Jordan Experience	8	1.50
1996 Upper Deck 23 Nights Jordan Experience	9	1.50
1996 Upper Deck 23 Nights Jordan Experience	10	1.50
1996 Upper Deck 23 Nights Jordan Experience	11	1.50
1996 Upper Deck 23 Nights Jordan Experience	12	1.50
1996 Upper Deck 23 Nights Jordan Experience	13	1.50
1996 Upper Deck 23 Nights Jordan Experience	14	1.50
1996 Upper Deck 23 Nights Jordan Experience	15	1.50
1996 Upper Deck 23 Nights Jordan Experience	16	1.50
1996 Upper Deck 23 Nights Jordan Experience	17	1.50
1996 Upper Deck 23 Nights Jordan Experience	18	1.50
1996 Upper Deck 23 Nights Jordan Experience	19	1.50
1996 Upper Deck 23 Nights Jordan Experience	20	1.50
1996 Upper Deck 23 Nights Jordan Experience	21	1.50
1996 Upper Deck 23 Nights Jordan Experience	22	1.50
1996 Upper Deck 23 Nights Jordan Experience	23	1.50
1996 Upper Deck 23 Nights Jordan Experience	NNO	1.50
1997-98 Bowman's Best	60	6.00
1997-98 Bowman's Best	96	3.00
1997-98 Bowman's Best Mirror Image	M1	50.00
1997-98 Bowman's Best Techniques	T2	20.00
1997 Coll. Choice Int'l Ital. Crash the Game Scoring	C30A	30.00
1997 Coll. Choice Int'l Ital. Crash the Game Scoring	C30B	30.00
1997-98 Collector's Choice	23	2.50
1997-98 Collector's Choice	186	.75
1997-98 Collector's Choice	187	.75
1997-98 Collector's Choice	188	.75
1997-98 Collector's Choice	189	.75
1997-98 Collector's Choice	190	.75
1997-98 Collector's Choice	191	.75
1997-98 Collector's Choice	192	.75
1997-98 Collector's Choice	193	.75
1997-98 Collector's Choice	194	.75
1997-98 Collector's Choice	195	.75
1997-98 Collector's Choice	385	1.50
1997-98 Collector's Choice	386	.75
1997-98 Collector's Choice	387	.75
1997-98 Collector's Choice	388	.75
1997-98 Collector's Choice	389	.75
1997-98 Collector's Choice	390	.75
1997-98 Collector's Choice	391	.75
1997-98 Collector's Choice	392	.75
1997-98 Collector's Choice	393	.75
1997-98 Collector's Choice	394	.75
1997-98 Collector's Choice	395	.75
1997 Collector's Choice Catch 23	1	—
1997 Collector's Choice Catch 23 Blow-Ups	C1	—
1997 Collector's Choice Catch 23	2	—
1997 Collector's Choice Catch 23 Blow-Ups	C2	—
1997 Collector's Choice Catch 23	3	—
1997 Collector's Choice Catch 23 Blow-Ups	C3	—
1997 Collector's Choice Catch 23	4	—
1997 Collector's Choice Catch 23 Blow-Ups	C4	—
1997 Collector's Choice Catch 23	5	—
1997 Collector's Choice Catch 23 Blow-Ups	C5	—
1997 Collector's Choice Catch 23	6	—
1997 Collector's Choice Catch 23 Blow-Ups	C6	—
1997 Collector's Choice Catch 23	7	—
1997 Collector's Choice Catch 23 Blow-Ups	C7	—
1997 Collector's Choice Catch 23	8	—
1997 Collector's Choice Catch 23 Blow-Ups	C8	—
1997 Collector's Choice Catch 23	9	—
1997 Collector's Choice Catch 23 Blow-Ups	C9	—
1997 Collector's Choice Catch 23	10	—
1997 Collector's Choice Catch 23 Blow-Ups	C10	—
1997 Collector's Choice Int'l Italian Jordan's Journal	J1	10.00
1997 Collector's Choice Int'l Italian Jordan's Journal	J2	10.00
1997 Collector's Choice Int'l Italian Jordan's Journal	J3	10.00
1997 Collector's Choice Int'l Italian Jordan's Journal	J4	10.00
1997 Collector's Choice Int'l Italian Jordan's Journal	J5	10.00
1997 Collector's Choice Int'l Italian Jordan's Journal	J6	10.00
1997 Collector's Choice Int'l Italian 1	23	8.00
1997 Collector's Choice Int'l Italian 1	25	4.00
1997 Collector's Choice Int'l Italian Mini-Cards	M78	10.00
1997 Collector's Choice Int'l Italian 1	26	4.00
1997 Collector's Choice Int'l Italian Stick Ums	S30	10.00

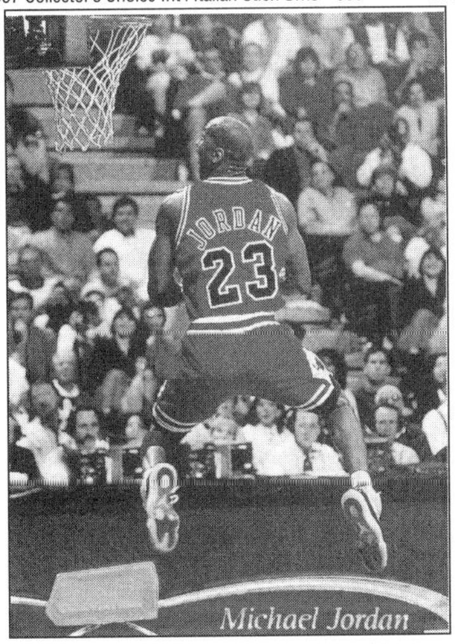

'97-98 Stadium Club No. 118 $5

1997 Collector's Choice Int'l Italian 1	195	4.00
1997-98 Collector's Choice MJ Bullseye	B1	4.00
1997-98 Collector's Choice MJ Rewind	R1	3.00
1997-98 Collector's Choice MJ Bullseye	B2	4.00
1997-98 Collector's Choice MJ Rewind	R2	3.00
1997-98 Collector's Choice MJ Bullseye	B3	4.00
1997-98 Collector's Choice MJ Rewind	R3	3.00
1997-98 Collector's Choice MJ Bullseye	B4	4.00
1997-98 Collector's Choice MJ Rewind	R4	3.00
1997-98 Collector's Choice MJ Bullseye	B5	4.00
1997-98 Collector's Choice MJ Rewind	R5	3.00
1997-98 Collector's Choice MJ Bullseye	B6	4.00
1997-98 Collector's Choice MJ Rewind	R6	3.00
1997-98 Collector's Choice MJ Bullseye	B7	4.00
1997-98 Collector's Choice MJ Rewind	R7	3.00
1997-98 Collector's Choice MJ Bullseye	B8	4.00
1997-98 Collector's Choice MJ Rewind	R8	3.00
1997-98 Collector's Choice MJ Bullseye	B9	4.00
1997-98 Collector's Choice MJ Rewind	R9	3.00
1997-98 Collector's Choice MJ Bullseye	B10	4.00
1997-98 Collector's Choice MJ Rewind	R10	3.00
1997-98 Collector's Choice MJ Bullseye	B11	4.00
1997-98 Collector's Choice MJ Rewind	R11	3.00
1997-98 Collector's Choice MJ Bullseye	B12	4.00
1997-98 Collector's Choice MJ Rewind	R12	3.00
1997-98 Collector's Choice MJ Bullseye	B13	4.00
1997-98 Collector's Choice MJ Rewind	R13	3.00
1997-98 Collector's Choice MJ Bullseye	B14	4.00
1997-98 Collector's Choice MJ Bullseye	B15	4.00
1997-98 Collector's Choice MJ Bullseye	B16	4.00
1997-98 Collector's Choice MJ Bullseye	B17	4.00
1997-98 Collector's Choice MJ Bullseye	B18	4.00
1997-98 Collector's Choice MJ Bullseye	B19	4.00
1997-98 Collector's Choice MJ Bullseye	B20	4.00
1997-98 Collector's Choice MJ Bullseye	B21	4.00
1997-98 Collector's Choice MJ Bullseye	B22	4.00
1997-98 Collector's Choice MJ Bullseye	B23	4.00
1997-98 Collector's Choice MJ Bullseye	B24	4.00
1997-98 Collector's Choice MJ Bullseye	B25	4.00
1997-98 Collector's Choice MJ Bullseye	B26	4.00
1997-98 Collector's Choice MJ Bullseye	B27	4.00
1997-98 Collector's Choice MJ Bullseye	B28	4.00
1997-98 Collector's Choice MJ Bullseye	B29	4.00
1997-98 Collector's Choice MJ Bullseye	B30	4.00
1997-98 Collector's Choice NBA Miniatures	M30	3.00
1997-98 Collector's Choice Star Attractions	1	25.00
1997-98 Collector's Choice Stick-Ums	S30	4.00
1997-98 Collector's Choice StarQuest	SQ83	75.00
1997-98 Collector's Choice StarQuest	SQ171	75.00
1997-98 Collector's Choice You Crash the Game	C30	10.00
1997-98 Finest	39	8.00
1997-98 Finest	154	90.00
1997-98 Finest	271	6.00
1997-98 Finest	287	25.00
1997-98 Finest Refractors	39	90.00
1997-98 Finest Refractors	154	700.00
1997-98 Finest Refractors	271	90.00
1997-98 Finest Refractors	287	100.00
1997-98 Flair Showcase Legacy	1	600.00
1997-98 Flair Showcase Row 0	1	300.00
1997-98 Flair Showcase Row 1	1	80.00
1997-98 Flair Showcase Row 2	1	15.00
1997-98 Flair Showcase Row 3	1	10.00
1997-98 Fleer	23	3.00
1997-98 Fleer Decade of Excellence	5	50.00
1997-98 Fleer Flair Hardwood Leaders	4	15.00
1997-98 Fleer Game Breakers	1	150.00
1997-98 Fleer High Flying Soaring Stars	9	20.00
1997-98 Fleer Soaring Stars	9	4.00
1997-98 Fleer Thrill Seekers	7	120.00
1997-98 Fleer Total "O"	5	30.00
1997-98 Fleer Zone	10	30.00
1997-98 Hoops	1	1.50
1997-98 Hoops	220	3.00
1997-98 Hoops Dish N Swish	DS5	20.00
1997-98 Hoops Frequent Flyer Club	FF4	40.00
1997-98 Hoops High Voltage	HV14	30.00
1997-98 Hoops HOOPerstars	H1	100.00
1997-98 Hoops Rock the House	RH6	30.00
1997-98 Hoops 911	N1	125.00
1997-98 Metal Universe	23	4.00
1997-98 Metal Universe Champ. Champ. Galaxy	1	120.00
1997-98 Metal Universe Champ. All-Millenium Team	5	12.00
1997-98 Metal Universe Championship Hardware	5	180.00
1997-98 Metal Universe Championship	23	4.00
1997-98 Metal Universe Planet Metal	1	30.00
1997-98 Metal Universe Platinum Portraits	1	180.00
1997-98 Metal Universe Titanium	1	100.00
1997-98 SkyBox	29	4.00
1997-98 SkyBox	235	8.00
1997-98 SkyBox and One	10	70.00
1997-98 SkyBox Competitive Advantage	CA3	70.00
1997-98 SkyBox E-X2001	9	15.00
1997-98 SkyBox E-X2001 Essential Creden. Future	9	1000.00
1997-98 SkyBox E-X2001 Gravity Denied	9	70.00
1997-98 SkyBox E-X2001 Jam-Balaya	6	400.00
1997-98 SkyBox Golden Touch	GT1	250.00
1997-98 SkyBox Premium Players	1	120.00
1997-98 SkyBox Silky Smooth	1	175.00
1997-98 SkyBox Thunder & Lightning	TL5	100.00
1997-98 SkyBox Z-Force	23	3.50
1997-98 SkyBox Z-Force	190	1.50
1997-98 SkyBox Z-Force B.M.O.C.	B9	140.00
1997-98 SkyBox Z-Force Boss	10	12.00
1997-98 SkyBox Z-Force Limited Access	6	20.00
1997-98 SkyBox Z-Force Quick Strike	QS5	70.00
1997-98 SkyBox Z-Force Rave Reviews	6	150.00
1997-98 SkyBox Z-Force Slam Cam	SC5	25.00
1997-98 Stadium Club	118	5.00
1997-98 Stadium Club Hardcourt Heroics	H1	20.00
1997-98 Stadium Club Hoop Screams	HS10	20.00
1997-98 Stadium Club Never Compromise	NC1	40.00
1997-98 Stadium Club Royal Court	RC6	20.00
1997-98 Stadium Club Triumvirate	T1B	60.00
1997-98 Stadium Club Triumvirate	T9B	50.00
1997-98 SP Authentic	23	6.00
1997-98 SP Authentic Authentics	MJ1	2500.00
1997-98 SP Authentic Authentics	MJ2	750.00
1997-98 SP Authentic Authentics	MJ3	75.00
1997-98 SP Authentic Authentics	MJ4	75.00
1997-98 SP Authentic Authentics	MJ5	85.00
1997-98 SP Authentic Authentics	MJ6	500.00
1997-98 SP Authentic Authentics	MJ6	100.00
1997-98 SP Authentic Authentics	MJ8	8500.00
1997-98 SP Authentic BuyBack	21	4000.00

Michael Jordan Card Checklist

Card	#	Price
1997-98 SP Authentic Profiles	P1	16.00
1997-98 SP Authentic Sign of the Times	MJ	—
1997 SPx	5	16.00
1997 SPx Holoview Heroes	H1	100.00
1997 SPx NBA Pro-Motion	1	150.00
1997 SPx PROmotion Autographs	1	2500.00
1997-98 Topps1	23	3.00
1997-98 Topps Bound for Glory	BG10	40.00
1997-98 Topps Chrome	123	25.00

'97-98 Topps Topps 40 No. 5 $15

Card	#	Price
1997-98 Topps Chrome Season's Best	SB6	25.00
1997-98 Topps Chrome Topps 40	T40-5	25.00
1997-98 Topps Clutch Time	CT1	40.00
1997-98 Topps Generations	G2	50.00
1997-98 Topps Inside Stuff	IS1	25.00
1997-98 Topps Rock Stars	RS1	50.00
1997-98 Topps Season's Best	SB6	30.00
1997-98 Topps 40	5	15.00
1997-98 Ultra	23	5.00
1997-98 Ultra	259	10.00
1997-98 Ultra Big Shots	1	10.00
1997-98 Ultra Court Masters	CM1	100.00
1997-98 Ultra Platinum	23	625.00
1997-98 Ultra Platinum	259	300.00
1997-98 Ultra Star Power	SP1	8.00
1997-98 Ultra Stars	1	120.00
1997-98 Ultra Ultrabilities	1	10.00
1997-98 Ultra View to a Thrill	ST1	20.00
1997-98 Upper Deck	18	4.00
1997-98 Upper Deck	139	2.00
1997-98 Upper Deck	165	2.00
1997-98 Upper Deck	316	2.50
1997-98 Upper Deck	NNO	25.00
1997-98 Upper Deck	NNO	12.00
1997-98 Upper Deck AIRLines	AL1	100.00
1997-98 Upper Deck AIRLines	AL2	100.00
1997-98 Upper Deck AIRLines	AL3	100.00
1997-98 Upper Deck AIRLines	AL4	100.00
1997-98 Upper Deck AIRLines	AL5	100.00
1997-98 Upper Deck AIRLines	AL6	100.00
1997-98 Upper Deck AIRLines	AL7	100.00
1997-98 Upper Deck AIRLines	AL8	100.00
1997-98 Upper Deck AIRLines	AL9	100.00
1997-98 Upper Deck AIRLines	AL10	100.00
1997-98 Upper Deck AIRLines	AL11	100.00
1997-98 Upper Deck AIRLines	AL12	100.00
1997-98 Upper Deck Diamond Dimensions	D23	700.00
1997-98 Upper Deck Diamond Vision Dunk Vision	D1	175.00
1997-98 Upper Deck Diamond Vision Reel Time	R1	400.00
1997-98 Upper Deck Diamond Vision	4	40.00
1997-98 UD Game Dated Memorable Moments	18	1000.00
1997-98 Upper Deck Game Jersey	GJ13	2700.00
1997-98 Upper Deck Game Jersey	GJ13S	13000.00
1997-98 Upper Deck Great Eight	G5	180.00
1997-98 Upper Deck High Dimensions	D23	110.00
1997 Upper Deck Holojam	1	30.00
1997-98 Upper Deck Records Collection	RC30	40.00
1997-98 Upper Deck Slam Dunk	22	20.00
1997-98 Upper Deck Teammates	T7	12.00
1997-98 Upper Deck Teammates	T59	12.00
1997-98 Upper Deck Ultimates	U1	45.00
1997-98 Upper Deck UD3	15	6.00
1997-98 Upper Deck UD3	23	6.00
1997-98 Upper Deck UD3	45	8.00
1997-98 Upper Deck UD3 Awesome Action	A1	30.00

Card	#	Price
1997-98 Upper Deck UD3 Michael Jordan MJ3	I	30.00
1997-98 Upper Deck UD3 Michael Jordan MJ3	II	60.00
1997-98 Upper Deck UD3 Michael Jordan MJ3	III	100.00
1997-98 UD UD3 Season Ticket Autographs	MJ	2600.00
1998-99 Finest	81	6.00
1998-99 Finest Mystery Finest	M1	50.00
1998-99 Finest Mystery Finest	M20	40.00
1998-99 Finest Hardwood Honors	H1	50.00
1998-99 Fleer	23	3.00
1998-99 Fleer	142	1.50
1998-99 Fleer Electrifying	6E	60.00
1998-99 Fleer Playmakers Theatre	PT9	500.00
1998-99 Hoops	23	3.00
1998-99 Hoops Bams	B1	300.00
1998-99 Hoops Pump Up The Jam	BD5	8.00
1998-99 Hoops Shout Outs	SO13	2.00
1998-99 Metal Universe	1	5.00
1998-99 Metal Universe Linchpins	8	120.00
1998-99 Metal Universe Planet Metal	1	45.00
1998-99 Metal Universe Two for Me	4	60.00
1998-99 SkyBox Premium	23	5.00
1998-99 SkyBox Premium Intimidation Nation	IN8	125.00
1998-99 SkyBox Premium Soul of the Game	SG1	20.00
1998-99 SkyBox Premium 3 D's	DDD4	60.00
1998-99 SkyBox Thunder	106	4.50
1998-99 SkyBox Thunder Boss	7	15.00
1998-99 SkyBox Thunder Flight School	9	50.00
1998-99 SkyBox Thunder Noyz Boyz	9	150.00
1998-99 Stadium Club	62	5.00
1998-99 Stadium Club Never Compromise	NC1	15.00
1998-99 Stadium Club Statliners	S2	30.00
1998 SP Carolina Heroes	H1	20.00
1998 SP Carolina Heroes	H2	20.00
1998 SP Carolina Heroes	H3	20.00
1998 SP Carolina Heroes	H4	20.00
1998 SP Phi Beta Jordan	J1	2.00
1998 SP Phi Beta Jordan	J2	2.00
1998 SP Phi Beta Jordan	J3	2.00
1998 SP Phi Beta Jordan	J4	2.00
1998 SP Phi Beta Jordan	J5	2.00
1998 SP Phi Beta Jordan	J6	2.00
1998 SP Phi Beta Jordan	J7	2.00
1998 SP Phi Beta Jordan	J8	2.00
1998 SP Phi Beta Jordan	J9	2.00
1998 SP Phi Beta Jordan	J10	2.00
1998 SP Phi Beta Jordan	J11	2.00
1998 SP Phi Beta Jordan	J12	2.00
1998 SP Phi Beta Jordan	J13	2.00
1998 SP Phi Beta Jordan	J14	2.00
1998 SP Phi Beta Jordan	J15	2.00
1998 SP Phi Beta Jordan	J16	2.00
1998 SP Phi Beta Jordan	J17	2.00
1998 SP Phi Beta Jordan	J18	2.00
1998 SP Phi Beta Jordan	J19	2.00
1998 SP Phi Beta Jordan	J20	2.00
1998 SP Phi Beta Jordan	J21	2.00
1998 SP Phi Beta Jordan	J22	2.00
1998 SP Phi Beta Jordan	J23	2.00
1998 SP Vital Signs	MJ	—
1997-98 SPx	6	12.00
1998-99 SPx Finite	1	16.00
1998-99 SPx Finite	100	30.00
1998-99 SPx Finite	181	40.00
1998-99 SPx Finite	201	85.00
1997-98 SPx Grand Finale	6	500.00
1997-98 SPx Hardcourt Holoview	HH1	60.00
1997-98 SPx Pro-Motion	PM1	120.00
1998-99 Topps	77	3.00
1998-99 Topps Apparitions	A15	40.00
1998-99 Topps Roundball Royalty	R1	40.00
1998-99 Topps Season's Best	SB6	20.00
1998 Topps Tip Off	77	—
1998-99 Upper Deck	23	5.00
1998-99 Upper Deck	25	10.00
1998-99 Upper Deck	26	12.00
1998-99 Upper Deck	169	10.00
1998-99 Upper Deck	174	2.00
1998-99 Upper Deck	175	2.00
1998-99 Upper Deck AeroDynamics	A1	15.00
1998-99 Upper Deck Forces	F1	40.00
1998 Upper Deck Hardcourt Jordan Holding Court	J1	5.00
1998 Upper Deck Hardcourt Jordan Holding Court	J2	40.00
1998 Upper Deck Hardcourt Jordan Holding Court	J3	10.00
1998 Upper Deck Hardcourt Jordan Holding Court	J4	30.00
1998 Upper Deck Hardcourt Jordan Holding Court	J5	25.00
1998 Upper Deck Hardcourt Jordan Holding Court	J6	10.00
1998 Upper Deck Hardcourt Jordan Holding Court	J7	10.00
1998 Upper Deck Hardcourt Jordan Holding Court	J8	50.00
1998 Upper Deck Hardcourt Jordan Holding Court	J9	5.00

Card	#	Price
1998 Upper Deck Hardcourt Jordan Holding Court	J10	15.00
1998 Upper Deck Hardcourt Jordan Holding Court	J11	10.00
1998 Upper Deck Hardcourt Jordan Holding Court	J12	5.00
1998 Upper Deck Hardcourt Jordan Holding Court	J13	70.00
1998 Upper Deck Hardcourt Jordan Holding Court	J14	10.00
1998 Upper Deck Hardcourt Jordan Holding Court	J15	10.00
1998 Upper Deck Hardcourt Jordan Holding Court	J16	50.00
1998 Upper Deck Hardcourt Jordan Holding Court	J17	30.00
1998 Upper Deck Hardcourt Jordan Holding Court	J18	10.00
1998 Upper Deck Hardcourt Jordan Holding Court	J19	35.00
1998 Upper Deck Hardcourt Jordan Holding Court	J20	40.00
1998 Upper Deck Hardcourt Jordan Holding Court	J21	15.00
1998 Upper Deck Hardcourt Jordan Holding Court	J22	10.00
1998 Upper Deck Hardcourt	23	10.00
1998 Upper Deck Hardcourt Jordan Holding Court	J23	10.00
1998 Upper Deck Hardcourt	23a	20.00
1998 Upper Deck Hardcourt Jordan Holding Court	J24	60.00
1998 Upper Deck Hardcourt	J25	15.00
1998 Upper Deck Hardcourt Jordan Holding Court	J26	20.00
1998 Upper Deck Hardcourt Jordan Holding Court	J27	15.00
1998 Upper Deck Hardcourt Jordan Holding Court	J28	25.00
1998 Upper Deck Hardcourt Jordan Holding Court	J29	15.00
1998 Upper Deck Hardcourt High Court	H30	150.00
1998 Upper Deck Hardcourt Jordan Holding Court	J30	100.00
1998-99 UD Hobby Exclusive Game Jerseys	GJ20	1200.00
1998-99 UD Hobby Exclusive Game Jerseys	GJA2	10000.00
1998-99 Upper Deck Intensity	I1	25.00
1998-99 Upper Deck Jordan Living Legend	1-165	1.00
1998 UD Jordan Living Leg. Jordan-In-Flight	IF1-IF15	2.00
1998 UD Jordan Living Legend Cover Story	C1-8	5.00
1998 UD Jordan Living Leg. Game Action Tiered	G1-30	15.00
1998 UD Jordan Living Leg. A Sign of Greatness	MJ1	5,000
1998 UD Jordan Living Leg. Signed Jersey Card	LL-MJGJ	—
1998 UD Jordan Special Issue Autograph Card	A1	—
1998 Upper Deck M.J. Game Commemoratives	GC1	—
1998 Upper Deck M.J. Game Commemoratives	GC2	—
1998 Upper Deck M.J. Live!	L1-L30	100.00
1998 Upper Deck M.J. Timepieces	T1-T90	5.00
1998 Upper Deck MJx	1-45	.50
1998 Upper Deck MJx	46-55	15.00
1998 Upper Deck MJx	56-65	10.00
1998 Upper Deck MJx	66-110	.50
1998 Upper Deck MJx	111-120	5.00
1998 Upper Deck MJx	121-130	1.00
1998 Upper Deck MJx	131-135	15.00
1998-99 Upper Deck Nestle Crunch	5	20.00
1998-99 Upper Deck Ovation	7	10.00
1998-99 Upper Deck Ovation Jordan Rules	J1	15.00
1998-99 Upper Deck Ovation Jordan Rules	J2	15.00
1998-99 Upper Deck Ovation Jordan Rules	J3	15.00
1998-99 Upper Deck Ovation Jordan Rules	J4	15.00
1998-99 Upper Deck Ovation Jordan Rules	J5	15.00
1998-99 Upper Deck Ovation Jordan Rules	J6	25.00
1998-99 Upper Deck Ovation Jordan Rules	J7	25.00
1998-99 Upper Deck Ovation Jordan Rules	J8	25.00
1998-99 Upper Deck Ovation Jordan Rules	J9	25.00
1998-99 Upper Deck Ovation Jordan Rules	J10	25.00
1998-99 Upper Deck Ovation Jordan Rules	J11	50.00
1998-99 Upper Deck Ovation Jordan Rules	J12	50.00
1998-99 Upper Deck Ovation Jordan Rules	J13	50.00
1998-99 Upper Deck Ovation Jordan Rules	J14	50.00
1998-99 Upper Deck Ovation Jordan Rules	J15	50.00
1998-99 UD Ovation Superstars of the Court	C1	15.00
1998-99 UD Choice	23	2.50
1998-99 UD Choice	159	1.25
1998-99 UD Choice	185	1.25
1998-99 UD Choice	189	1.25
1998-99 UD Choice	196	1.25
1998-99 UD Choice	198	1.25
1998-99 UD Choice Mini Bobbing Heads	M30	6.00
1998-99 UD Choice Preview	23	2.50
1998-99 UD Choice StarQuest Blue	SQ30	3.00

Michael Jordan Memorabilia Checklist

1993 Ballpark Franks ad sheet. ($12)

1993 Ballpark Franks lunch bag and cooler. ($75)

1995 Ballpark Franks ad sheet with coupon, Jordan with wife, Juanita. ($2)

Ball Park Franks

93	Ad Sheet, "Ball Park Franks. The Hot dogs Hot Dogs Love." Actmedia Inc., MJ + package	$12
93	Ad Sheet, Fun Franks, "Honey, I Shrunk the Ball Park.," voided $.35 coupon on sheet	3
93	Ad Sheet, Lunch Bag & Clik Cooler, with "Official Order Form"	3
93	Bag/Cooler, MJ black Lunch Bag and yellow hard plastic Clik! Cooler, bag with MJ picture, cooler with autograph, mail in offer	75
93	Order Card, Lunch Bag/Clik Cooler	6
95	Coupon, $.40 Off Fat Free Classic Franks, "The Perfect Marriage of Taste & Greatness." MJ & Juanita, Look for Juanita Jordan's Healthy Recipes & Coupons	2
95	Coupon, $.40 Off Fat Free Classic Franks, "The Taste of Greatness," Introducing BP Fat Free Classics	2
95	Coupon, $.40 Off Fat Free Classic Franks, "Only BP Can Make Fat Free Taste This Good, Great BP Taste, None of the Fat, white signature	2
96	Coupons-2, $.40 Off Any Fat Free Product, $.50 Off Any 2 BP Products, "Michael's Family Values Enjoy BP Franks, Fat Free	
96	Coupon, $.50 Off Any 2 Packages of Fat Free or Lite Franks (or any BP Product), "Jordan's Trademark Move Off the Court," white signature (1.33)	2
96	Coupon, $.25 Off Any BP Product, Jordan's Trademark Move Off the Court., "Here's the best part: it's a move anyone can do. BP Franks..."	2
96	Coupon, $.50 Off Any 2 Ball Park Fat Free Products, Coupon for Go For The Gold! card set, BP Franks & Michael's Trading Cards Both Worth Shooting For!	2
96	Coupons-2, $.50 Off Any 2 BP Fat Fee Product, $.50 Off Any 2 BP Product, different pages, "How Michael Looks Cool All Summer," Micro Magic coupons above	2
96	Coupons-2, $.50 Off Any 2 BP Fat Fee Product, $.50 Off Any 2 BP Product, different pages, "How Michael Looks Cool All Summer," Nabisco Granola Bars coupons above	2
96	Boxes, Fun Franks, Michael's Magic Mania, 6 Microwaveable Fun Franks, 12 different magic tricks on box bottoms	
	—Magically Make a Playing Card Rise Out of a Cup!	3
	—Make a Penny Mysteriously Disappear From a Cup!	3
	—Baffle Your Audience as You Magically Levitate a Piece of Rope	3
96	Booklet, "Commemorative Stickers" from Atlanta Olympic Games, "Izzy & Michael Stick Together"	35
97	Coupon, $.50 Off Any Two BP Products, "It's not really summer 'til you have your BP"	2
97	Coupons-2, $1.00 Off a Bag of Halloween Candy, $.40 Any Package of BP Fat Free or Lite Franks Treat Yourself to the Monster Taste of Ball Park	2
97	Coupon, $.40 Off Any BP Product, "Monster Space Jam Video $5.00 Rebate!,"	2
97	Box, Fun Franks, red 23, holding hot dog in right hand, Free Funtoos inside box, MJ, Corn Doggie & Fun Frank cutouts on bottom	6

Banners, Pennants

80s	MJ, black signature, dunking, folded	12
92	Back to Back	10
	—MJ Banner/Flag, cartoon-like MJ picture, large size, 13 basketballs	5
94	Banner with MJ photo, top says, "Michael Jordan Day, the People of Chicago Salute You,"bottom says, "City of Chicago, Richard M. Daley, Mayor"	450
98	Banner, 1998 Chicago Bulls 6 Time NBAChampions Pennants, 1998 Chicago Bulls 6 Time Standard Pennants	4

Basketballs

96	Mini, Best Team Ever 72-10, Mini Litho, clear case SCCA Produced, Sportacular Art,	45
96	Mini, Best Team Ever 72-10, cardboard case, TSC Members Only Club-SCCA Produced	35

Birmingham Barons

94	Souvenir Program, 93 Baseball Southern League Championship Ring,	15
94	Book Collectors Edition	7
95	Merchandise Brochure-8 sided foldout, MJ full front cover, hats back cover	8
95	Group Planner, schedule, ticket brochure	15

Bradford Exchange Platcs

95-96	MJ Collection-12 flat plates, Artist-Chuck Gillies, 95 non consecutive firing days	
	1st Championship-84-B10-244.1	35
	The Comeback-84-B10-244.2	35
	'92 Champions-84-B10-244.3	35
	'82 NCAA Championship-84-B10-244.4	35
	'93 Champions-84-B10-244.5	35
	'88 Slam Dunk Champion-84-B10-244.6	35
	'86 Playoffs-84-B10-244.7	35
	Rookie Year-84-B10-244.8	35
	Returns to Greatness-12 flat plates, Artist-Glen Greast, 95 non consecutive firing days	
	Record 72 Wins-84-B10-700.1	40
	MVP-84-B10-700.1	40
	The 4th Title-84-B10-700.1	40
	The Sweep-84-B10-700.1	40
	Return to Greatness	40
	New York Knockout-84-B10-700.1	40
	Soaring Star, 84-B10-268.1, 7,200 produced	60
	Rim Rockers, 84-B10-268.2	75
	Soaring Above the Rest-5 plates	
	Taking It Higher	40

Cachets

87	Gateway Stamp Company, MJ 3000 points in a season, Autograph, 1000 issued in 96	125
91	Wild Horse, Heir Jordan, 100th Anniversary of Basketball, 150 produced	25
91	Wild Horse, R. Seikaly & MJ, Chicago vs. Miami 55 produced	25
91	Wild Horse, Magic & MJ, Best of Best, 125 produced	25
91	Colorado "Silk" Cachet, 1000 produced	10
92	Triumph, Barcelona Olympic Basketball Team Picture & Flag, #10 envelope	10
92	Triumph, Barcelona Olympics Michael Jordan, dunking, white #9, #10 envelope	10
93	Wild Horse, MJ No Peat	54
93	Wild Horse, Playoff Finals Set, 4 different	121
93	MJ & Barkley, 85 produced	
94	SA Sports Covers, Windy City Classic, MJ First Appearance at Wrigley Field, C of A, 50 produced, White Sox 4, Cubs 4, hand painted	.30
95	Gateway Stamp Company, MJ Returns to NBA MJ Autograph, 500 issued in 96	125
96	SA Sports Covers, 1996 MVP All-Star Game, C of A, 50 signed, East 129, West 118	30
96	Bevil, Bulls 70 Game Win, MJ, SP & Rodman, hand painted, C of A, #10 envelope, 550 signed by artist	40
96	Bulls Win No 70!, MJ & SP photo, 200 produced	10

Michael Jordan Memorabilia Checklist

Wheaties Cereal Boxes

The backs of many boxes have the same information and photos. These will be noted as: Common backs. Prices for factory flat are 25 percent more than full box price. For viewing of actual inserts and send-in items offered, check poster section for posters, games, basketball cards, etc.

Year	Description	Price
1988	12oz. 1st edition Basketball offering Photo and Story	100
1988	18oz. Same as 12oz	100
1989	8oz. Jumpshot Photo and Story #2	45
1989	12oz. Same as 8oz	45
1989	18oz. Same as 12oz	45
1989	24oz. Same as 18oz	100
1989	12oz. Holding spoon and bowl. "Made with 100% whole grain" Is common	55
1989	12oz. Same as series 73	50
1989	18oz. Free blue color poster included on the front of this box. States it is a special bonus poster Part A. MJ is breaking out of box. Is common	45
1989	18oz. Free green color poster included on the front of this box. States it is a special bonus poster Part B. MJ is breaking out of box Is common	45
1989	18oz. Free purple color poster included on the front of this box. States it is a special bonus poster Part C. MJ is breaking out of box. Is common	45
1989	18oz. "Box without" Free poster on the front of box. Same as series 73, 73Z 12oz.	30
1989	18oz. Air Jordan Flight Club calendar MJ "Quotes"	30
1989	18oz. Same as series 82.	30
1989	18oz. Same as series 82, 82Z	30
1989	18oz. Box without free calendar on the front.	25
1990	18oz. Pouring Wheaties into bowl Photo and story #3	50
1990	18oz. Four poses of MJ "Shoot Hoops" Pull down Action Game flap	30
1990	18oz. Four poses of MJ "Shoot Hoops" Pull down Action Game flap	30
1990	12oz. Pouring Wheaties into bowl Common	45
1990	18oz. Pouring Wheaties into bowl Common	35
1990	24oz. Pouring Wheaties into bowl Common	100
1990	12oz. Pouring Wheaties into bowl Common	35
1990	18oz. Pouring Wheaties into bowl Common	40
1990	24oz. Pouring Wheaties into bowl Common	75
1990	12oz. Pouring Wheaties into bowl Common	40
1990	12oz. Pouring Wheaties into bowl Common	40
1990	12oz. Holding spoon and bowl."Now made with 25% less sodium" Common	50
1990	12oz. Holding spoon and bowl Common	35
1990	18oz. Same as 12oz	25
1990	18oz. Pouring Cereal Common	35
1990	12oz. Pouring Cereal Common	35
1990	18oz. Pouring Cereal Common	40
1990	18oz. Pouring Cereal Common	25
1990	1oz. Holding spoon and bowl in hands; with hair Back same as front	8
1991	1oz. Holding spoon and bowl, carrying bag Back same as front	6
1991	1oz. Holding spoon and bowl. "Sample not for resale" on white background Back same as front	10
1991	1oz. Holding spoon and bowl; with hair Back same as front	10
1991	3/4oz. Holding spoon and bowl; with hair Back same as front	6
1991	1oz. Holding spoon and bowl. "Sample not for resale" Not on white background Back same as front	10
1991	3/4oz. Holding spoon and bowl, carrying bag Save $.50 coupon	15
1991	12oz. Holding spoon and bowl, carrying bag Common	40
1991	18oz. Holding spoon and bowl, carrying bag Common	40
1991	12oz. Holding spoon and bowl, carrying bag Common	30
1991	12oz. Pouring cereal. $5.00 refund offer Save $530	15
1991	18oz. Holding spoon and bowl, carrying bag 2 of 8	25
1991	18oz. Holding spoon and bowl, carrying bag 3 of 8	25
1991	18oz. Holding spoon and bowl, carrying bag 6 of 8 with MJ Card	40
1991	18oz. Holding spoon and bowl, carrying bag 7 of 8 with Larry Bird card	30
1991	18oz. Holding spoon and bowl, carrying bag 8 of 8	25
1991	18oz. Front and back same as above, but a different series number. Prices are also the same by series number	20
1993	18oz. MJ golfing Golf course picture	35
1993	500g Canadian version - Silver Collection Edition Three MJ photos	35
1993	18oz. Silver Collection Edition Three MJ photos Two ways to get your own MJ basketball	25
1997	18oz. Purple Box, Jump shot different than series 91-21. Win an autographed MJ basketball.Two ways to get your own MJ basketball	25

Chevrolet & General Motors

84-85	Garbage Bag, "When I drive, I drive a Chevy.," MJ dribbling right hand, USA uniform, white bag; blue writing, sig., & pictures	60
87	Chart, Growth Chart Chicagoland & NW Indiana Chevy.Dealers.	20
93	Mask, Chevy & Restaurant, & Bulls Logo on back 7 x 10.	12
98	Sticker, "The Greatest," MJ & Ali, Chicago Auto Show Handout.	3
90s	Sticker, Chevrolet/Geo, MJ head in a basketball, "Drives A Blazer Just Like You Do" 4 x 4	3

Chicago Tribune Newspaper

5/28/91	Sports Section, Bulls end Pistons' reign of terror cover	10
5/29/91	Sports Section, Bulls not relaxing just yet cover	10
6/1/91	Sports Section, Dream one a nightmare cover	10
6/2/91	Newspaper, Michael: City's most valuable imagemaker cover	10
6/3/91	Newspaper, Lakers gore Bulls, 93-91 cover	10
6/4/91	Newspaper, Bull's good old days were mostly just old cover	10
6/5/91	Newspaper, Jordan keeps a vow, We're going to hit it cover	10
6/6/91	Newspaper, Blowout! Bulls roar right back in it cover	10
6/7/91	Newspaper, Jackson turned Bulls in potential champions cover	10
6/8/91	Newspaper, Bulls win in OT cover	10
6/9/91	Newspaper, Bulls get up off the floor, KO Lakers cover	10
6/10/91	Newspaper, Bulls storm to the brink of title cover	10
6/12/91	Newpaper, 911? I'm dying! But wait until half time cover	10
6/13/91	Newspaper, Five High! Bulls Are Champs! cover	10
6/13/91	Paper Weight, High Five! Bulls Are Champs front	10
6/13/91	Plaque, High Five! Bulls Are Champs.	10
6/14/91	Newspaper, A champion city opens up its arms cover	10
6/15/91	Newspaper, Hundreds of thousands reach out touch Bulls cover	10

1995 Gateway Stamp Co. autographed cachet. ($125)

1996 Crispy Wheaties 'n Raisins box. ($20)

1990 Wheaties (pouring cereal) box. ($75)

Michael Jordan Memorabilia Checklist

1996 Fasson items "Class for all Seasons" sticker. ($35).

Wilson basketball with handpainted portrait of Jordan ($110).1995 Wilson Michael Jordan Cologne black basketball ($35).

1982 Carolina Tar Heels championship soda can. ($125). Ball Corp. soda can ($25)

6/16/91	Newspaper, Bulls bring out the champion in everyone cover	10
6/17/91	Section 7, Champions cover	10
91	Book, Stampede, soft cover book	15
92	Book, DaBull, soft cover book	10
92	Book, DaBull, hard cover book	20
6/15/92	Newspaper, Two for Two: Bulls Still Champs! cover	8
6/15/92	Newspaper, Sports Section, Twice as Nice cover	8
6/15/92	Paper Weight, Two For Two, Still Champs	8
6/15/92	Plaque, Two for Two, Still Champs	8
93	Book, Three Peat, soft cover book	10
6/21/93	Newspaper, Three-Mendous! cover	8
6/21/93	Paper Weight, Three Mendous	8
6/21/93	Plaque, Three Mendous	8
6/24/93	Commemorative Section	8
10/6/93	Newspaper, Jordan Retires from Basketball cover	8
10/7/93	Newspaper, So Long Michael It's Been Great cover	8
3/19/95	Newspaper, The Jordan Comeback cover	6
3/20/96	Newspaper, Relaunched	5
4/17/96	Newspaper, 70 Bookit	5
6/17/96	Newspaper, Ring Masters	5
6/17/96	Paper Weight, Ring Masters	5
6/17/96	Plaque, Ring Masters	5
6/18/96	Newspaper, Commemorating Championship Year	5
10/27/96	TV Week, Bulls' Eyes, Megaviews of Jordan & Co. cover	5
4/24/97	Newspaper, A Day in the Life of the World Champions cover	15
6/12/97	Newspaper, Heart of a Champion front	4
6/13/97	Newspaper front	4
6/14/97	Newspaper, Enough Said front	4
4/19/98	Newspaper cover	3
6/4/98	Newspaper, Breathless in Utah front	3
6/6/98	Newspaper, May we cut in? front	3
6/8/98	Newspaper, Utah sits on out front	3
6/11/98	Newspaper, The fat lady warms up front	3
6/12/98	Newspaper, O, we of little faith front	3
6/14/98	Newspaper, The band takes a break front	3
6/14/98	Newspaper, Relax, take a deep breath, Final Edition front	3
6/15/98	Newspaper, The Joy of Six front	3
6/16/98	Newspaper, And then there were 6 front	3
6/17/98	Newspaper, Bulls leave them Cheering front	3

Chris Martin Enterprises Magnets
94-95	Pro Magnets, Rodman/MJ, Chris Martin Enterprises on front NNO	5

Coca Cola
89-90	Sticker, Chevy Blazer, Hot Tops 5 x 7	20
89-90	Sticker, Chevy Blazer, Hot Tops 5 x 12	30

Coins-miscellaneous
87-88	Chicago Bulls, MJ picture name, 86-87 Scoring Champ, 3,041 Season Point, & stars on front, silver, 1987 & 1988, NBA, Don't Foul Out on back NNO	30
91	MVP top, 1992 middle, NBA bottom on back, silver, MJ name, picture & No. 23 on front 1,117	30
92	USA Basketball on back, silver, MJ name, picture & No. 9 on front 2,889	30
92	MVP top, 1992 middle, NBA bottom on back, silver, MJ name, picture & No. 23 on front 13,918	30

Cologne
96	Spray 3.4 oz	35
96	Box, Spray	23
96	Travel Size Spray 5 oz	12
96	Travel Kit	25
96	Water Bottle	6
96	Sticker	2
97	Coupon, Free MJ Basketball Magazine	1
97	Pin	20
97	Splash, Royal Selections No.33, "Our Alternative to Michael Jordan for Men," black box with MJ dunking, clear bottle with red "Michael Jordan" writing 3.3 oz	15
97	Ad sheet, Macy's, Collector's Icon, Pin Offer	1
98	Basketball, Wilson, black with MJ silhouette, free with $35.00 purchase	35
	Spray, M Jam, Cologne for Men, 2.7 o	20
	Spray, Slam, MJ Deodorant Body Spray 3 oz	8

Enviromint
94	Medallion Set 2 coins	35
	— MJ name, picture in baseball cap, No. 45 & Birmingham Barons on front,silver, MJ in BB uniform & batting helmet, mintage 25,000	
	— Birmingham Barons Baseball on front, silver, "B" on back, mintage 5,000	
94	Medallion, MJ name, picture in baseball cap, No. 45 & Birmingham Barons on front, silver, MJ in BB uniform & batting helmet, mintage 25,000 4,956	35
95-96	Card & Medallion Set, 500 sets produced	225
	— Silver Coin with gold trim	
	— #45 He's Back Metal Card, nickel/silver etched, 24kt gold trim	1
95-96	Ad Sheet, Card & Medallion Set	1
95-96	Ad Sheet, Commemorative Proof Set	1
95-96	Medallions, MJ 95-96 Commemorative Proof Set, black case, 500 sets produced	160
	— 24kt Gold Select Medallion, MJ dunking, #23	
	— Silver Medallion, Chicago Bulls, logo, & stats	
	— Bronze Medallion, MJ on back95-96 Medallion, Most Wins in an NBA Season, 72-10, Chicago Bulls, Logo, front, silver, 1966 Chicago Bulls 1996, 30 Years and Running, XXX, 15,000 sets produced 6,181	35
96	Ad Sheet, #45 He's Back Medallion & Card	1
96	MVP Scoring Champion, silver, 10,000 mintage coin	
96	MVP Scoring Champion, 24kt select, 1,996 mintage coin	

Michael Jordan Memorabilia Checklist

96	MVP Scoring Champion 3 piece set, 500 mintage 3 coins	
96	MVP Scoring Champion, gold, 96 mintage coin	
96	Coin/Card, Scoring Champion & MVP, silver, 500 mintage	
96	Coin/Card, Scoring Champion & MVP, 24kt select, 23 mintage	
96	Bulls Team Set, silver, 1,000 mintage 6 coins	
96	Bulls Team Set, 24kt select, 196 mintage 6 coins	
96	Chicago Bulls "Best Record in NBA, History" silver, 500 mintage 5 coins	
96	8 Time Scoring Champion, silver, 10,000 mintage coin	
96	Scoring & MVP silver, 2,500 mintage card	
96	Scoring & MVP, 24kt select, 1,996 mintage coin	
93-94	Phone card, World Com, WS swinging bat, "Batman Mike" 5616	35
93-94	Phone card, World Com, red 23, ball in hands, jumping, "Flying Mike" 5317	35
	—Sheet, "Basket" stamps, "The Face 2 Face Chicago Bulls"	25
	—Sheet, "Basket" stickers, white 23, "Dunk Machine"	25
	—Tattoos, "Air Michael," jumping with ball over head, black 23	25

Fuji basketball shaped disc holder with Jordan and four other Bulls players. ($20)

Games-miscellaneous

87	Interactive VCR Games, The VCR Basketball Game, MJ on VCR tape	60
88	Cadaco, NBA Real Basketball in Miniature Game, MJ on cover and backboards, NBA Bas-Ket court, balls, net and levers to shoot balls.	45
91	Sports World Game Company, Hornet Mania, MJ listed on team sheet, dice, game board, team sheets, 2 chips	45
91-92	Sports Adventure Let The Games Begin, box, book, 5-5" floppies, MS Dos Version	40
93	Wall Ball UD Sticker Sheet, 4 players	4
96	Display board, "NBA Pick-Up Game, Pick Three and Win Big," send in coupons, MJ on board	2

Gatorade

89	Calendar, Slam Dunk Championship, Day Dreams Manufacturer	20
90	Pin, "It's All You're Thirsting For"	30
91	Ad Display, "It's All You're Thirsting For.,"3D or die-cut	30
92	Can, Thirst Quencher, 14 quarts, Lemon Lime Figure, Life Size Cardboard, "Its All You're Thirsting For,"	75
92	Label, aqua, MJ dribbling right hand, looking right, red 23, 1988 Defensive Player of the Year, Tropical Fruit Flavor, red arm band left forearm, blue signature 32 oz	15
92	Label, black, MJ dribbling right hand, looking front, red 23, Mike's #1 Flavor top front, Citrus Cooler Flavor, 32 oz	15
92	Label, black, MJ dribbling right hand, looking front, red 23, Mike's Favorite Flavor top front, Citrus Cooler Flavor, 32 oz	15
92	Label, blue, MJ jump shot, red 23, Hold NBA playoff record points scored Citrus Cooler Flavor, blue signature, red arm band l left forearm 63 against Boston in 1986 32 oz	15
92	Label, blue, glass bottle, MJ jump shot, red 23, Hold NBA playoff record points scored 63 against Boston in 1986, Citrus Cooler Flavor, blue signature, red arm band left forearm 32 oz	15
92	Label, green, glass bottle, MJ dribbling right hand, looking left, red 23, Lemon Lime Flavor 32 oz	15
92	Label, orange, MJ holding ball in USA #9, Member 92 Dream Team, Orange Flavor 32 oz	15
92	Label, red, MJ dribbling right hand, looking left, white 23, Named 91 NBA Finals MVP, Fruit Punch Flavor, black signature, black arm band left elbow 32 oz	15
92	Label, red, glass bottle, MJ dribbling right hand, looking left, white 23, Named 91 NBA Finals MVP, Fruit Punch Flavor, black signature, black arm band left elbow 32 oz	15
92	Label, yellow, glass bottle, MJ right hand dunk, red 23, Lemonade Flavor 32 oz	15
92	Label, yellow, MJ right hand dunk, red 23, 87 & 88 Gatorade Slam Dunk Champ, 88 All Lemonade Flavor, 32 oz	15
92	Window Ad, "Be Like Mike, Drink Gatorade," sticky clear background, red 23, ball in RH, layup, black signature	45
93	Ad, "Nothing Beats Gatorade, Works 30% Faster Than Water," cardboard, MJ holding plastic bottle, white/red shirt 28" x 20"	25
93	Label, black, MJ dribbling right hand, looking front, red 23, Citrus Cooler Flavor, Mike's Favorite Flavor top front 4 oz	15
93	Label, black, plastic jug, red 23, MJ dribbling right hand, looking front, Citrus Cooler Flavor, Mike's Favorite Flavor top front 64 oz	15
93	Magazine Sheet, "Gatorade Quenchology" Ad, #23, red undershirt, 6.5 x 7.5	10
94	Sticker, "Quench It," 3D, towel on shoulders, 6.5 x 7	10
95	Book Cover, "Drive+Skills+Guts+Passion+Life"	5
95	Book Cover, "Life is Sport, Drink it Up, What's on Your Mind," MJ walking on his own head	6
95	Label, green with light green border, plastic jug, "The Big Grip," MJ hand print, Lemon Lime, blue & white signature 1 gallon	5
95	Label, green with blue border, plastic jug, "The Big Grip," MJ hand print, Tropical Burst, blue & white signature 1 gallon	5
95	Label, green with orange border, plastic jug, "The Big Grip," MJ hand print, Orange, blue & white signature 1 gallon	5
95	Label, green with yellow border, plastic jug, "The Big Grip," MJ hand print, Lemon Ice, blue & white signature 1 gallon	5
95	Label, blue with black border, plastic jug, "The Big Grip," MJ hand print, Cool Blue Raspberry, blue & white signature 1 gallon	5
95	Mask, "Life is Sport, Drink it Up, What's on Your Mind," MJ walking on his own head	6
95	Shelf Insert, "Life is Sport, Drink It Up," blue t-shirt, holding bottle right hand, t-handle top, MJ picture bottom	3
96	Magazine Sheet, "Life is Sport," closeup head view	2
96	Magazine Sheet, "Life is Sport," back "Buzz Beamer"	2
97	UD/Gatorade Send In Card, "MJ Four Time NBA Champions 1991, 1992, 1993, 1996," envelope, backing, MJ holding ball on front with Harper in background, MJ pointing on back, 3 x 5	3
97	Window Ad, acetate sticker, dribbling ball RH, white 23, "Life is a Sport Drink it UP" in upper left, 7 Eleven logo in bottom left, Lemon Lime 32 oz and Fruit Punch 20 oz in lower right 14 inches x 3 feet	35

14 quart can lemon lime flavor Gatorade. ($40)

Hanes Underwear

93	Display Board, Briefs Rebate Coupon, Fathers Day, 2 MJ views holding underwear/Air Time Video 9" x 12"	15

Orange flavor Gatorade label. ($15)

Michael Jordan Memorabilia Checklist

Packet of Hang Time grape flavored shredded bubble gum. ($10)

93	Display Board, MJ Air Time Video, Rebate Offer, $5 17" x 12"	15
93	Magnet, red signature, brown coat, closeup, smiling, white t-shirt #1	15
93	Magnet, red signature, brown coat, closeup mouth open with ball, white t-shirt)#2	15
97	Package, Knit Boxers, large, no boxers	15

Hang Time Gum

92	Ad Sheet, Free Life Size Poster	5
92	Order form, Life Size Michael Jordan Poster	2

Highland Mint Cards & Medallion

95	Card, bronze, baseball	75
	Card, silver, baseball	275
	Card, gold, baseball	700
95-96	Coin, bronze, MJ picture, name, 23, & signature, on front, Hardcourt Heroes, dates, back, 25,000 produced	10
95-96	Coin, silver, MJ picture, name, 23, & signature, on front, Hardcourt Heroes, dates, back, 7,500 produced	25
95-96	Coin, gold, MJ picture, name, 23, & signature, on front, Hardcourt Heroes, dates, back, 100 produced	80
95-96	Coin, silver, First 70 Win Season, Chicago Bulls, Logo, 1995-1996, 1966 Chicago Bulls 1996, XXX	35
95-96	Coin, silver with gold picture & signature on front, Signature Series, gold Hardcourt Heroes, MJ & number on back 770	100

Jump, Gibson & Cleo

89	Button pin, Gibson, ball in right hand, red 23, white signature	10
89	Button pin, Gibson, dribbling right hand, white #23, black signature	10
89	Button pin, Gibson, looking, red 23, black signature	10
89	Magnet Button, Gibson, dribbling, tongue out, black signature	15
89	Magnet Button, Gibson, closeup, gold signature	10
89	Magnet Button, Gibson, closeup, black signature	2
90	Greeting Card, Gibson, red front, dribbling, white signature, It's impossible to keep up with you! What's New?	8
90	Magnet, Jump Inc., 2 pictures on one magnet NNO	10
91	Stickers, Cleo, Self Adhesive Basketball, 4 sheets #314 0115, orange BBs on border, 9 MJ pictures, 36 stickers	15
92	Calendar, Cleo, MJ + Giant MJ Action Photo, red 23, Slam Dunk Contest photo,	25
92	Calendar, Cleo, Dream Team, 92 USA Basketball Team, #260-7040	25
92	Greeting Card, MJ shooting ball right hand, back view, red 23, "You're 16," tan background, red stripes top and bottom, inside "and you're simply the best! Happy Birthday"	10
92	Greeting Card, MJ shooting ball, white 23, gold background, 6 black BBs, black stripes, white signature, "When it comes to being a Great Son...," inside "You never miss! Happy Birthday"	10
92	Puzzle, Greeting Card Valentine, Cleo, one handed jump shot, slam dunk contest, "Have a High Flying Valentine's Day," 5-7/8 x 7-3/8	9
92	Tags, Cleo, Self Stick, 6 tags of MJ dribbling in top & bottom, sections, 6 tags	12
92	Tags, Cleo, Self Stick, 3 tags of MJ dribbling in bottom section3 tags MJ's name in top section	12
92	Tags, Cleo, Self Stick, 3 tags of MJ dribbling in top section 3 tags MJ's name in bottom section	12
93	Wrapping Paper, Gibson, MJ shooting, red background, 8.33 sq. ft., 2 sheets,sealed package	15
96	Greeting Card, Space Jam, front "MJ" and drawing like color picture, green inside, blue "MJ" and "What's Up Doc,"	4

MAGAZINES AND BOOKS

Basketball Annual Magazine

91-92	Guide, Roster, Schedules, Statistics cover	3
91-92	Special NBA Preview, NBA Champion Chicago Bulls	6
92-93	NCAA Hoop Fever, The Road to the Final Four	6
92-93	Guide, MJ Eyes a Third Title	3

Basketball Digest Magazine

7/85	MJ Rookie of the Year	20
86-87	NBA BB Yearbook, Teams to Beat	10
1/87	MJ Chicago's Raging Bull Challenges the NBA	15
4/88	The New and Improved MJ	12
6/89	MJ Player of the Year	12
88/89	NBA BB Yearbook, Teams to Beat, MJ, Bird, Thomas, Magic	12
1/90	The NBA Zone Trap	10
6/91	No 1! MJ is our Player of the Year	7
92	Annual, MJ Cover with inserts of Malone, Mullin, & Ewing	7
6/92	Barcelona Bound, 92 Player of the Year, MJ	7
87-88	Scene, 9th Big Year, Roundup of all NBA Teams cover	20
88-89	Dick Vitale's, Mega Talents Light Up NBA's Toughest Division cover	18
89-90	Dick Vitale's, To 'Air' is Not Human! cover	16
90-91	Dick Vitale's, Looking for A Title! cover	16
90	Super Stars, B. Allison, dribbling left hand, paperback book cover	10
91	Awesome Guards by BJ Arneson, paperback book cover	2
91-92	Dick Vitale's, Bravo!, MJ & Bulls 2nd Title cover	15
92-93	Action, Mike Warren's, Incredi-Bull cover	15
92-93	Dick Vitale's, Colossal Collegians cover	15
93	Greats, by M. Teitelbaum, book cover	13
91	Basketball Guide Premiere Edition	5
5/91	Basketball-MJ on cover	5
9/91	Basketball-MJ on cover	5
7/92	Basketball-Olympics, MJ on back cover	4
8/92	Basketball-MJ on cover	4
2/93	Basketball-MJ on cover	3
9/93	Basketball-MJ on cover	3
12/93	Basketball-MJ on cover	3
94	Tribute-Michael Jordan, cover	5
4/94	Baseball-MJ on cover	3
1/95	Basketball-MJ on back cover	3
5/95	Basketball-MJ on cover, MJ red 45 uniform	3
5/95	Baseball-MJ on back cover	2
95	Sports Heroes-Michael Jordan	9
95	Great Sport Heroes-Michael Jordan, hard cover	15
2/96	Basketball-MJ on cover	3
4/96	Basketball-MJ on cover	3
5/96	Bulls Tribute 72 Wins-MJ on cover	5
6/96	Championship Commemorative-cover, 17th NSCC-Fantastic Four	5

Jump Inc., poster sticker ($15)

June/July issue of Basketball Digest. ($7)

Michael Jordan Memorabilia Checklist

6/96	Basketball Card Price Guide-cover, 1st large size	18
9/96	Basketball-MJ on cover	4
96-97	Pro Basketball-MJ on cover	5
97	Basketball Alphabetical Checklist	14
8/97	Five High	4

Bulls Media Guides

87/88	All-Star Game, 2/7/88, Chicago, 38th Annual cover	35
88/89	West Side Story, Directed by Doug Collins cover	30
89/90	The Adventures of Chicago Bulls cover	25
90/91	Chicago Bulls cover	20
93/94	CB NBA World Champions 91-92-93, 3 Trophy Cover	15
94-95	Chicago Bulls-United Center cover	5
95-96	30th Anniversary Bulls Logo Cover	10
96-97	NBA 50th (5.74) cover	20

Bulls Playoff Guides & Magazine

94-95	NBA Eastern Finals, Bulls vs. Magic, "MJ He's Back #45" cover	20
95	Official Playoff Guide, MJ, SP, Jackson, TK, BJA cover	20
95-96	NBA Finals, Bulls vs. Seattle cover	20
96	Official Playoff Guide, shot from above center court	15
96	Official Playoff Program, MJ, SP, DR on cover cover	15
96	Official NBA Finals Guide, Bulls Team Art	15
97	Official Playoff Guide, MJ Action Art cover	10
97	Official NBA Finals Guide, Bulls Team glossy cover	10

Bulls Tip Off Magazine

94	HOOP, MJ in SP Ameritech Uniform, tongue out, Michael's Back, No. 23, Send CS...,holding ball cover	8
96	HOOP, MJ holding trophy, P. Jackson Strangely Successful (article) cover	7
96	HOOP, MJ in 3 pictures, P. Jackson Strangely Successful (article) cover	7
97	HOOP, Scottie Pippen dunking on cover, MJ name on cover & inside inside	5

Bulls Yearbooks

84/85	MJ and Woolridge cover	40
88-89	Players huddled in warmups, CB & logo upper left side cover	30
89-90	MJ layup, white 23, drawing like cover	25
90-91	25th Anniversary	20
91-92	MJ holding trophy, cheering crowd cover	20
92-93	MJ holding ball with hat, 6 picture	15
93-94	World Champions Chicago Bulls	15
95-96	MJ & SP shooting cover	10
96-97	MJ shooting in crowd cover	10

Comic Books

3/92	Personality Comics Presents, Slam Dunk Kings #1 Featuring MJ, blue front cover with 2 MJs, Joe DiMaggio back cover	15
4/92	Revolutionary Comics Sports Superstars Comics, 3 views, red #23, white #23, closeup, blue and blue cover	15
4/94	Revolutionary Comics MJ Tribute Special	8
93	Shaquille O'Neal vs. Michael Jordan in red letters, Shaq on front cover, MJ on back cover, red shirt, illustrations by Deborah Max, Script by John DiMeola Part 1	15
93	Shaquille O'Neal vs. Michael Jordan in blue letters, MJ on front cover, red shirt, Shaq back cover, illustrations by Deborah Max, Script by John DiMeola Part 2	15

Ebony Magazine

8/91	How Black Creativity Is Changing America cover	18
11/91	MJ & Juanita cover	18
8/92	Winning, From J. Robinson to MJ cover	15
12/93	The MJ Nobody Knows cover	
5/97	Michael's Mom: We Didn't Set Out To Raise A Superstar cover	12

Inside Sports Magazine

11/85	NBA Preview, Laker Repeat, Ewing & MJ Showtime in NBA	40
11/86	Annual NBA Preview, MJ Air Awesome, MJ cover	35
6/87	NBA Playoffs, MJ cover	30
12/87	Pro/College Basketball Ratings, MJ Raging Bull at Crunch Time	30
5/88	Playoffs, NBA, MJ his Bulls are a Long Shot	25
11/88	NBA Preview, Chicago's MJ	25
5/89	NBA Playoffs Preview, MJ tongue out	20
10/89	Slam, Slam, Slam, Dunk cover	20
11/89	Bad Boys vs. the NBA, Preseason Predictions	20
2/90	Sports Salaries cover	18
5/90	MJ Three Part Special Section cover	18
10/90	In Your Face cover	18
11/90	Basketball Preview cover	18
12/90	Who's Better Than MJ? cover	18
4/91	Sports Salaries	18
5/91	NBA Playoffs Preview cover	15
10/91	MJ World Champions cover	15
11/91	91-92 NBA & College Preview	15
5/92	Malone: This is Our Year! cover	14
6/92	US Olympic Team is Out to Conquer the World cover	14
10/92	3 Peat! cover	14
11/92	NBA and College Preview cover	14
12/92	How good are the Bulls?, MJ & Wilt cover	14
2/93	NBA Insiders Poll Tells All) cover	12
5/93	NBA Playoffs Preview cover	12
11/93	Head to Head, sealed with NBA Guide cover	12
93	End of an Era cover	12

Jet Magazine

6/12/89	Michael Jordan Leaps to Success cover	20
10/9/89	Michael Jordan Takes a Bride: Juanita Vaney cover	20
4/29/91	MJ: The Most Exciting Pro BB Player Ever cover	18

1994-95 Chicago Bulls media guide. ($15)

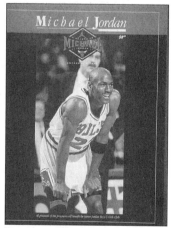

November 1994 tribute program to benefit James Jordan Boys & Girls Clubs ($15)

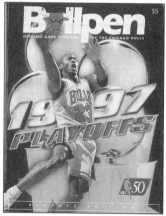

1997 Chicago Bulls playoff program. ($7)

Michael Jordan Memorabilia Checklist

July 6, 1992 issue of *Newsweek* magazine (Jordan with Larry Bird and Magic Johnson). ($15)

July 6, 1992 Jet magazine . ($15)

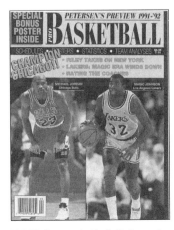

1991-92 Peterson's Basketball preview magazine. ($15)

7/1/91	MJ Leads Chicago To NBA Crown cover	18
7/6/92	MJ Leads Chicago Bulls to #2 NBA Title cover	15
8/12/92	Blacks Who are Best Bets to Win Gold in Olympics cover	15
7/12/93	MJ Takes Chicago Bulls to 3rd NBA Championship cover	12
8/30/93	James Jordan: Shock & Sadness follow shooting of dad inside	12
10/25/93	MJ Says: The Thrill... is Gone and Retires cover	12
4/10/95	MJ Says: I'm Back For the Love of the Game cover	10
3/18/96	The Awesome Threesome, DR, MJ, SP cover	7
7/8/96	Chicago Rocks with Joy as Bulls Celebrate Champions cover	7
5/6/96	Chicago Bulls Make NBA History Win 70 Games/Season cover	7
5/13/96	Deloris Jordan Tells How to Win at Parenting cover	7
4/14/97	Why Bald Heads Have Become So Popular cover	3
6/30/97	Jordan, Pippen, & Kerr Lead Chicago To 5th NBA Champions cover	3

Life Magazine
11/92	Facing The Wall, Hang Time With MJ, by B. Greene cover	15
1/94	Year in Pictures 93 A Legend Retires cover	10
96	Special Issue, The Baby Boom Turns 50	6

Newsweek Magazine
7/6/92	Team Dream	15
10/93	Greatest Ever	4
3/20/95	Hoop Dreams	3

People Magazine
12/18/89	The Sexiest Man Alive Sexiest Athlete	20
Sum 91	50 Most Beautiful People in the World 1991	15
8/30/93	Richest Women in Show Biz cover	10
10/10/93	The Sexiest Couple Alive cover	10

Peterson's Magazine
89	Preview 89-90, Michael's Bulls for a Title	20
90-91	Preview 90-91 & poster cover	15
91	Preview 91-92, Champion Chicago cover	15
93-94	Pro Basketball, Shaq Attack, Shaq hologram, Sports Series, blue cover, sealed cover	10
9/96	Pro Basketball cover	6
96	Pro Basketball Action, Are the Bulls da Bomb?	6
96	Pro Basketball, Bulls, the Best Team Ever	6
97	Pro Basketball, The Bulls, Back for Another	4

Pro Basketball Magazine
90-91	Annual, Basketball Today, MJ overhead shot cover	12
92	Complete Handbook, Celebrating a Century of Hoop cover	12
91-92	Illustrated, NBA Champion Chicago, Bulls One More Time cover	10
92-93	Illustrated, NBA Scoring Champ & MVP cover	8
93-94	Illustrated, NBA's Top Gun!, 7 Time Scoring cover	6
94	Illustrated, MJ 85-93 A Final Tribute cover	12
95	Illustrated cover	10
	—18 MJ 8.5 x 11 sheets	
	— 4 MJ posters	
90-91	Scene Annual, MJ close up cover	20
91-92	Scene Annual, MJ & Ewing, Barkley Robinson	15
92-93	Scene Annual, Jordan How He Rates With All cover	12
93-94	Scene Season Preview, In-Depth Analysis of 27 Teams cover	10
90	Today cover	25

Rare Air Book
| 93 | Soft cover | 15 |
| 93 | Hard cover | 30 |

Sport Magazine
3/82	The Fight Holmes vs. Cooney, NC Tar Heels: Can They Win the Title inside	45
3/87	Spring Training Warm-Up, cover	35
6/87	Who Makes What In Sports, 5th 100 Best Salary Survey cover	35
11/88	Jordan of the Chicago Bulls Changing of the Guard	25
11/89	89-90 Pro Basketball Preview cover	20
6/90	Top 100 Earners in All of Sports cover	15
10/90	100 Best in Sports cover	15
1/91	Air to the Throne cover	12
11/91	NBA Preview cover	12
12/91	"Michael, The Price of Fame"	12
91	Ad Flyer, "MJ Prince of Fame" cover	3
6/92	Can Bulls be Beaten? cover	12
1/93	Top 40 cover	10
11/93	NBA Preview cover	10
12/93	Ten Years of MJ	10
1/94	Top 40 The Best in Sports cover	8
11/94	NBA Preview Issue 94-95 cover	8
4/95	Baseball's Future? cover	8
6/95	Jordan's Back cover	8
7/95	Slam	8
11/95	Pro Basketball Preview Issue cover	8
1/96	Jordan's Next Jump cover	6
9/96	MJ Player of the Half Century	6
11/96	America's Teams	10
85-86	Pro & College Yearbook, MJ & David Rivers cover	50
87-88	Pro Basketball Yearbook, High & Mighty Series	40
87/88	Official NBA Register cover	30
88/89	Official NBA Guide cover	20
89-90	Official NBA Register cover	25
90-91	Official NBA Guide cover	15

Michael Jordan Memorabilia Checklist

92/93	Official NBA Guide, SP & MJ vs. Drexler cover	12
89/90	Pro Basketball Yearbook, Thriller cover	12
92-93	Pro Basketball Yearbook, Three Peat cover	10
93-94	Pro Basketball Yearbook, Bull Run cover	10

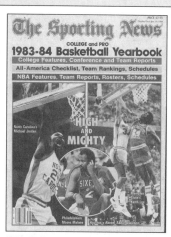

1983-84 Sporting News college and pro Basketball Yearbook. ($60)

The Sporting News Newspaper

3/28/83	Player of the year, NC's MJ cover	75
2/13/84	NC...Nothin' Could Be Finer cover	50
3/26/84	Player of the Year, MJ is Head & Shoulders Above the Rest cover	50
10/29/84	The Next Dr. J, MJ is Ready to Operate in the NBA cover	50
12/8/86	Making Point cover	45
3/23/87	(Show) Business As Usual, MJ & Dr. J cover	40
5/18/87	Manager Pete Rose, MJ TSN All-Star cover	35
5/23/88	The Last Hurrah?, MJ Player of Year cover	30
3/20/89	One Man Gangs, Barkley & MJ cover	25
5/28/90	Taking Bulls by Their Horns cover	20
3/4/91	Keep the DH, AL to Fay cover	15
5/6/91	It's In the Stars cover	15
6/10/91	Michael & Magic A Dream Matchup cover	15
6/24/91	Bulls! Jordan & Co. Bury Lakers cover	15
7/22/91	Power of Appeal cover	15
1/6/92	Man of the Year cover	15
6/15/92	Rising to the Occasion cover	15
10/18/9	What Now? Report on MJ Retirement cover	10
10/18/93	The Next Dr. J	10
3/20/95	The One and Only cover	8
5/15/95	Knockout Round cover	8
9/96	Mike the Magnificent, 96/97 Yearbook cover	5

Sports Illustrated Magazine

11/28/83	No 1 UNC, MJ/Perkins cover	70
7/23/84	Up For LA Olympics cover	65
12/10/84	A Star is Born cover	60
11/17/86	One Man Gang cover	55
11/9/87	Special NBA Preview cover	40
12/28/87	Year In Pictures cover	40
5/16/88	Sky High vs. Cavs. cover	35
6/16/88	MJ/Bulls cover	35
3/13/89	How High Can He Fly cover	30
5/15/89	Raging Bull cover	30
8/14/89	Jordan's My Name, Golf's My Game cover	30
11/6/89	Can Anyone Shut Michael Down?, MJ/Joe Dumars cover	30
5/21/90	Show Time cover	25
12/17/90	Another Bull Run cover	25
2/18/91	Dream Team cover	20
5/21/91	MJ 1st Cover Track cover	20
6/3/91	Finally, NBA Finals cover	20
6/10/91	Magic and Michael cover	20
6/17/91	Air Power, NBA Finals cover	20
6/24/91	Insert MJ's Crowning Glory cover	20
8/5/91	The Black Athlete cover	20
11/11/91	Man in the Middle cover	20
12/23/91	Sportsman of the Year Hologram	20
1991	Sportsman of the Year Hologram Proof Card, larger than the hologram on the magazine	
91	Order Form, video offer "Come Fly with Me" cover	20
5/11/92	On Collision Course vs. Drexler cover	18
5/25/92	Busting Loose vs. Knicks cover	18
6/15/92	Yesss! cover	18
6/22/92	How Sweet It Is To Repeat cover	18
6/7/93	Hanging Tough, NBA Finals cover	15
6/21/93	Head To Head vs. Barkley cover	15
6/28/93	3!. with cover cover	15
6/28/93	Collector Edition-3 Seasons to Savor cover	15
10/18/93	Why, MJ Retires cover	15
93	Sports Almanac	20
3/14/94	Bag It Michael! cover	12
9/19/94	40 For the Ages cover	12
3/20/95	It's Super Michael cover	10
3/27/95	I'm Back, #45 Jersey vs. Pacers cover	10
5/22/95	Battle of Titans vs. Shaq cover	10
10/23/95	Air & Space, Rodman cover	10
95	The Year in Pictures cover	10
95/96	Presents Pro Basketball Premier Edition, Presents "Eyes On the Prize," Regional Issue cover	10
5/27/96	The Running of the Bulls cover	8
6/3/96	Chicago Fires vs. Orlando cover	8
6/17/96	Bulls Whipped, NBA Finals cover	8
6/19/	The Best	8
11/96	"The Best"-Chicago Bulls 95-96 A Special Collector's Edition, sent to SI subscribers	8
12/96-97	"Presents Pro Basketball 96-97," Drive for Five cover	10
3/10/97	Are The Bulls So Good They're Bad for the NBA cover	6
3/17/97	Family Portrait, "BB-A History of the Game" cover	6
5/19/97	Guarding Jordan cover	6
6/9/97	Gimme Five cover	5
6/23/97	Is the Jordan Dynasty the NBA's cover	5
6/25/97	Presents Chicago Bulls 96-97 Champs cover	5
9/97	SI Presents The Fantastic 5, Gatorade Cap Mail In Offer inside	5
97	SI Order Form, Save Up to 80% with Educational Discount folder	5
97	Presents Pro Basketball: One More Time	5
2/16/98	Don't Bag It, Michael	4
6/8/98	The Last Stand	4

March 14, 1994 Sports Illustrated magazine. ($12)

November 11, 1991 Sports Illustrated magazine (Jordan with Phil Jackson and Scottie Pippen). ($20)

Michael Jordan Memorabilia Checklist

1986-87 Street and Smith's college and pro basketball guide. ($35)

1989 Jump, Gibson &Cleo magnet button. ($12)

1996 McDonald's Space Jam French Fry holder. ($7)

Street and Smith Magazine

86-87	College, Pro, Prep Basketball, Can MJ & Bulls Bounce Back cover	35
88	Pro BB, Who's The Greatest?, Inaugural Issue cover	35
89	MVP Michael Jordan cover	30
90/91	Michael's Too Much! Bulls Star Still on the Rise cover	25
91/92	Michael Jordan NBA's MVP cover	20
92/93	Olympic Uniform cover	15
93/94	Jordan Soars Bulls Drive for 4 cover	10
95/96	Rare Air cover	6
9/96	Unstoppabul! MJ's Drive for 5 cover	6
97	The Last Dance? cover	4

NBA Inside Stuff Magazine

11/93	1,2,3,4, Michael? cover	6
	— Commemorative Sheet, 8.5 x 11, UD Issue, World Championship of Basketball, 8/4/94-8/14/94 nno	2
12/96	Rising Stars, different cover	2
	—MJ UD "Still The Best" Commemorative Sheet, 8.5 x 11, 95-96 UD MJ #23 card on sheet nno	
12/96	Jordan Rules Again, different cover	8
	— MJ UD "Still The Best" Commemorative Sheet, 8.5 x 11, 95-96 UD MJ #23 card on sheet nno	
5/97	Drive for 5 cover	3
	— MJ Poster nno	

Magnets-miscellaneous

90's	Waist high closeup, red 23, hands on hips, hair NNO	10
90's	Jump shot on Dumars #4, red #23 NNO	10
90's	Layup, white #23 NNO	10

Magnetables

89	Bulls MJ, red #23,"Bull" top right, dunking, side view	25

McDonald's & Upper Deck Related Items

80's	Ad display, Help McDonald's Fight Muscular Dystrophy, MJ with a lot of hair	20
85-86	School Folder, MJ & Bulls, 20th Bulls Season, D.L. Strouse Business card on front, group ticket sales packet, layup on front & dunk on back, white 23, schedule inside McD-14084	100
	— Bumper Sticker, "Chicago Bulls" & Bulls Logo, white background9" x 3"	
	— Entry Blank, 1985-86 McDonald's Discount Night— Schedule, Bulls	
	— Order form, Group Ticket Sales & schedule	
	— Photo, 20th Season Chicago Bulls, "Group A whole new breed of entertainment,"	
5/6-90	Crew Pages-2, MJ pictures, folded brochure	15
	— MJ on cover	
	— MJ on page 3	
90	Sheet, "Catch Michael's Best Moves" 8 cds	6
	—The Layup	
	— The Blocked Shot	
	— The Chest Pass	
	— The Drive	
	— The Speed Dribble	
	— The Backup Dribble	
	— The Jump Shot	
	— The Free Throw	
90	Window Ad, MJ dunking, red color, 2' x 3'	45
91	Ad Poster, Sport Fitness Fun Happy Meal, Collect all 8 toys! While Supplies Last, rcd to yellow background, 14 x 14	25
91	Bag, Sport Fitness Fun Happy Meal, quiz on back	2
91	Disc, It'll Be Sweet 2 Repeat, Free when you buy a McJordan Combo-back, Not Intended for children under 8.	15
91	Pin, "It'll Be Sweet 2 Repeat," MJ sitting on bb, red shirt, black shorts, free with McJordan Combo 3"	2
91	Sticker, It'll Be Sweet 2 Repeat, Free when Buying McJordan Combo, 2 discs joined 4"	8
91	Sticker, It'll Be Sweet 2 Repeat, Only __cents Off With Any Purchase, 2 discs joined 5"	15
91-92	Ad poster, Collect all 62! NBA Hoops Limited Edition BB Cards, Get 4 Cards Free!, 4 x 14BB background, yellow bottom,	15
91-92	Card, Hoops '92 USA Basketball Team, back #55 in orange basketball 55	2
91-92	Card, Hoops MVP, back #5 in orange basketball 5	1
91-92	Card Strip, Hoops MVP Factory, uncut10 cards	20
	— 5 MJ cards with #5, numbers in basketball	
	— 5 Wilkins cards with #1, numbers in basketball	
91-92	Card, Upper Deck French Issue, number in arches 15	15
91-92	Set, McJordan Special Items	75
	— Pin, MJ head view, "Try A McJordan Special" head view 3"	35
	— BB Hoop & Backboard, "Try A McJordan Special"	40
9/92	Kemper Lakes Country Club, Ronald McDonald's Children's Charities Celebrity Golf Championship, September 5-7,	
1992	— Pin, 1992 Event Pass, red border 3"	15
	— Placement with photo 14 x 11	10
	— Brochure	2
	— Luggage Tag	15
	— Pairing guide, 9/7/92, foldout 4.5 x 11	15
	— Color photo, MJ swinging club, Chicago Tribune 8 x 10	5
	— Envelope with invite	10
	—Poster 21 x 30	40
92	Ad Display, Free McDonald's NBA Fantasy Pack When You Buy an Extra Value Meal, MJ with ball in RH over head on left side; pack, MJ, Stockton & Ewing cards on 26 x 44 right side, blue and red background, American Airline plane bottom	35
92	Ad Poster, Gold Metal Meal, MJ on cup, triple cheeseburger, large fries, $4.33, gold background & coin 15 x 17	15
92	Ad Poster, McJordan Special Meal Includes: only $3.19 pictured, 22 x 22	15
92	Ad Sheet, "Burger of the Month McJordan Special Meal"	20
92	Cup, USA Basketball5 of 10	4
92	Drink container, MJ handprint & signature, Bulls Logo, black bottle with green cap	25
92	Drink container, MJ handprint & signature, Bulls Logo, red with black top & straw	25
92	Pin, "It'll Be Sweet 2 Repeat," MJ sitting on BB, red shirt, black shorts, free with McJordan Combo 3"	2
92-93	Ad poster, Fantasy Pack, "Free pack with Extra Value Meal," American Airlines plane, MJ jumping, MJ card, red & blue, white bottom 9 x 10	15
92-93	Ad poster, Fantasy Pack, "Free pack with Extra Value Meal," American Airlines plane, MJ jumping, MJ card,	10
92-93	Ad poster, "Win An NBA Fantasy Instantly, One-on-One with MJ, NBA European	

Michael Jordan Memorabilia Checklist

NBA Jam Session Items, Slam Dunk
92	Puzzle, NBA Inside Stuff Slam Dunk, Sky Jams, MJ, Shawn Kemp, Tom Champers, 200 piece puzzle with Magazine Coupon	75
92-93	Book, Photo Salute of the NBA Dunk, Intro-D Stern, Drakes Offer	15
94	Calendar, 16 month, Day Dream Calendar	10
94	Sticker Book, purple cover, Golden Pub.	15
94	Book, Fleer Mark & See, Pen, Golden Pub., yellow cover	20
94	Marker Book, tear out pages, Golden Pub., blue cover	20

NBA Jam Session Items, Slam Dunk
92	Puzzle, NBA Inside Stuff Slam Dunk, Sky Jams, MJ, Shawn Kemp, Tom Champers, 200 piece puzzle with Magazine Coupon Offer, listed in the Golden Puzzle Section Book, Photo Salute of the NBA Dunk, Intro-D Stern, Drakes Offer	15
94	Calendar, 16 month, Day Dream Calendar	10
	Sticker Book, purple cover, Golden Pub.	15
	Book, Fleer Mark & See, Pen, Golden Pub., yellow cover	20
	Marker Book, tear out pages, Golden Pub., blue cover	20

Posters

Poster-Amoco Oil Company
97	Posters, United Way, Mounted, MJ/SP/DR on cover 40 x 30	75

Poster-Boy Scouts of America
90-91	BSA Poster, Chicago Area Council, MJ Says Stay in School, It's Your Best Move 14 x 18	20

Poster-Bull's Eye Barbecue Sauce
87	Poster, "Big Bold Stuff," 8 photos, MJ in bottom left, Paxson, Oakley, Sellers, Pippen, Corzine, Grant, MJ, Vincent, tan background, bottle in lower right, 16 x 25 Techtron Imaging Network, Ridges Finer Foods Inc.	60

Poster- Chevy Dealers
98	Poster, "The Greatest," MJ & Ali, Chevy Dealers handout 37 x 23	10

Posters-Chicago Sun Times Newspaper
85-87	Poster, "Your Hometown Sports Authority, Catch it Today, Just $.35," MJ going for layup, "CST It's a Smart Move to Make"	60
91	Poster, "Bulls Win It," front page cover	15
92	Poster, "Champs!" front page cover	15
93	Poster, "3 Fest!" front page cover	12
95	Poster, "I'm Back!" front page cover	4

Posters-Chicago Tribune Newspaper
87	Poster, Slam Dunk Contest , April 8, 1987 11 x 17	60
80s	Poster, MJ flying to basket, red 23, like	
93	Posters, front page, Thanks for the Memories	8
96	Posters, front page, Relaunched	5
96	Posters, front page, 70 Booklet	5
96	Posters, front page, Ring Masters	5

Posters-Coca Cola
86-87	Poster, Chevy Blazer, Hot Tops, 23 jersey)18 x 26	50
89	Poster, "Share The Dream" top, "Lifelong Careers Begin With Education, Dr. J, I. Thomas, MJ, Classic, Coke, diet Coke, cherry Coke, Sprite, Minute Maid logo on bottom 18 x 20	50
90	Poster, "No Brain No Gain," "Stay in School," MJ in white shirt & gray tie, sitting at desk, books in background Coke logo bottom right 18 x 24	45
90	Poster, "The Coca Cola Company 1990," MJ dunking 6 pack of coke, white 23, Chicago skyline in background 18 x 24	45

Posters-Costacos Brothers
93	Poster, "Invincibulls" top center, "Back-to-Back NBA World Champions," Team in warmups, lined up near foul line 30 x 12	30
95	Poster, "Space 2," door size, shooting overhead, red 23 26 x 74"	15
96	Poster, "Year of the Bull," 1996 NBA Champions, MJ in 4 pictures, 12 pictures on poster 23 x 35	10
97	Poster, "The Eighth Wonder of the World, 11 MJ pictures, black 23, From 1985 through 1996 23 x 35	6
-	Poster, "Dream" 23 x 35	3
-	Poster, "Count Down" 23 x 35	3
-	Poster, "Enter the Zone" 23 x 35	3
-	Poster, "Return Flight" 23 x 35	3
-	Poster, "Out of the World" 23 x 35	3
-	Poster, "Space" 23 x 35	3
-	Poster, "Great Chicago Flyer" 23 x 35	3
-	Poster, "Pure Energy" 23 x 35	3

Posters-Gatorade
91	Display, It's All You Thirst For, two sided and top and bottom half,for 3-D book 24 x 36	40
92	Poster, "Be Like Mike," white 23, dunking, NBA Property 17 x 25	20
92	Poster, "Be Like Mike," USA BB #9, dunking, USA BB Inc. 17 x 25	15
92	Poster"Dream Team" 12 x 18	20
93	Poster, "Michael Jordan" on left vertical, "Gatorade. For That Deep,Down Body Thirst" on bottom, white 23, layup, Stokely-Van Camp, Inc. 18 x 26	15
93	Poster, "MJ Ready to Slam," promotional poster18 x 24	30
93	Poster, "Nothing Beats Gatorade" left side, MJ layup, white 23, on front side of poster, back side of poster MJ dribbling waist up view, red 23 17 x 24	20
93	Poster, "Nothing Beats Gatorade" bottom, MJ reverse layup, red 23, on front side poster, back side of poster MJ dribbling waist down view, red 23 17 x 24	20
94	Poster, "Quench It," towel on shoulder	10
95	Poster, "45," MJ dunking, red 45, Gatorade logo lower right, Starline Inc. 22 x 34	20
95	Poster, "I'm Back." "Reaching for More," black signature March 24, 1995, MJ in black t-shirt, arm stretched out with Gatorade cup 30 x 11	15
95	Poster, "Drive, Skills, Guts, Passion= Life" 14 x 22	15
95	Poster, "Life is Sport," MJ head view, promotional 15 x 23	10
97	Poster, "It's a Sport, Drink it Up," 7/Eleven Stores 14 x 37	45

Posters-Hanes
93	Store Display, MJ holding BB in street clothes, sport coat, white t-shirt, Hanes logo upper right, black signature & "Michael Jordan for Hanes" lower right, blue background 31 x 39	60
97	Store Display, MJ in sport coat and white t-shirt, Hanes logo upper left, "Unconditionally Guaranteed" lower left, earring in left ear, brown stripe background	60

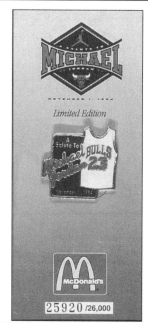

1994 McDonald's numbered pin. ($15)

1993 Chevrolet dealers and Jordan's restaurant cardboard mask. ($12)

1991 NBC Toys R Us Shopping Spree ad sheet. ($2)

Michael Jordan Memorabilia Checklist

1993 Hanes store poster (31 x 39). ($60)

1985-86 Nike (29 x 24) poster. ($65)

1990 Costacos Brothers postcard "Space the Final Frontier." ($10)

Poster-Hang Time Gum
92   Poster, Life Size Michael Jordan 35

Posters-Miscellanous
85   Midas Muffler Poster-MJ vs. Bucks, coupons on bottom 60
85-86   Poster, "Chicago Bulls 20th Season, 1 MJ photo out of 8 pictured, orange color, Sports Phone 976-1313 on bottom 65
85-86   Poster, "Chicago's Newest Generation of Winners!, Sports Vision, "Ed Olczyk-Blackhawks, MJ, Kar Heinz
       Granitza-Sting pictured,"Chicago's Winners on Cable" schedule listed for each sport, Odyssey Productions, Chicago, Bradley Printing
       12 x 28 65
86   Bill Clark Litho, 5 player set, NBA licensed, SFI Tampa, FL Magic,Bird, Dr. J, Kareem 16" x 20
87   MJ Personality Poster, 17 x 2, 2 sided...45
90   "Air Michael Jordan" foldout, Publications Intl. 25
90-91   Poster, Focus on Sports, two sided, "Michael Jordan" top left in white and yellow letters, hands on knees, white 23, closeup;
       back cartoon like MJ in red 23 slam dunking with hand on rim, head bigger hand body, way above court, ball through net,
       "Michael Jordan" lower right, white & yellow letters 16 x 21 50
90-91   Ron Dumas' Serigraph & Nike, 723 autographed by artist, 23 signed by MJ, Nike's Certificate of Authenticity 24" x 30" ....
91   Nobody Does BB Like UD, MJ jumping hold ball, white 23, shiny on gray background with letters.............................15
91   Michael 'n' Magic Poster Book, Kids Books Inc. 10
91   Break Away Slam Dunk, 91 Finals vs. Lakers 16 x 20 25
92   MJ Poster Book, A Book of 12 Tear Out Posters, sealed packet 12 posters...30
92-93   Poster, MarketCom, "Chicago Bulls," SP, MJ JP, HG, SK & BC, 20 x 16 six individual pictures with white signature 40
93   Basketball Superstars Album, by R. Brenner 16 posters 25

Posters-Nike
85-86   Poster, red "Air Jordan" bottom left, jumping to basket in playground with red and black clothes, night shot of Chicago skyline,
       metal BB net and poles, red "Nike" logo bottom right 29 x 24 65
86-87   Poster, Air Jordan 4 Frame Slam Dunk, getting ready to dunk, dunking wearing, 23 on jersey, in early Air Jordans with red body,
       black trim 2 x 36 60
86-87   Poster, Nike Air Jordan, 5 action photos of running, jumping and dunking, wearing white top and bottom sweatsuit 21 x 36................60
88-89   Poster, "A High Flying 360 Slam Dunk, Death Defying," MJ and Spike Lee 36 x 24 45
88-89   Poster, "Slam Dunk Championship," MJ flying to dunk, red 23, gray stripe on bottom with "1988 NBA MVP, Defensive Player of
       the Year, Slam Dunk Champion, All-Star MVP Leading Scorer," crowd in the background,35 x 23 3:51 on clock, red "Nike" logo
       bottom right 45
90   Poster, "Nice Shoes as Seen On TV," 'I've never ever seen anything like it,' pictures of Gretzky, McEnroe, Strange, Jordan, & Bo;
       bottom of poster has Albert, Michaels, Caray, Heinsohn, Summerall, Vitale, Enberg in purple strip, "Holy cow!" Four shoes
       pictured Air Jordan, Air Trainer SC, Air Max, Air Tech Challenge II 24 x 32 40
91   Poster, MJ kneeling on left knee, white AJFC t-shirt, black shorts, left hand on Wilson BB, right hand on right knee,
       "Nike" red in upper right corner 24 x 36 40
91   Poster, "Evolution, A Process of Change from a Lower Simpler Form to a More Complex or Better State," jumping ball in RH 24 x 24....20
92   Poster, "Slam Dunk Championship," MJ flying to dunk, red 23 crowd in the background, 3:51 on clock 35 x 23....................12
92   Poster, "Art of the Dunk," MJ going to dunk with light lines, red 23, black background, red "Nike" logo upper right 35 x 23....................12
93   Poster, Warner/MJ Sticker Set CD 20
93   Poster, Spike Lee/MJ, "Mars, Blackman," black & white 32 x 22 30
93   Poster, "In the unlikely event of a water landing, this poster can be used as a Flotation Device," white 23, MJ dunking the ball,
       "Nike Inc."and logo bottom center 23 x 35 35
93   Poster Book, Aerospace, 8 images 35
93   Poster, "Great Moments in Flight," 4 MJ pictures, other astronauts 23 x 35 and pilots, black background, white "Nike" logo bottom 12
93   Posters, Aerospace, 6 different kinds
       —"Earth The Best on Mars," MJ holding Martian & BB, Bugs next to MJ, red "Nike" logo upper left 23 x 35 35
       —"Aerospace," BB in LH, flying in air, white t-shirt, black shorts, white "Nike" logo upper left 23 x 35................................35
97   Poster, "The Master," MJ dribbling ball on white background, black chirt and gray chorts, lines from center circle 23 x 35....................6
90s   Poster, slide strip with 4 shots of MJ, red "Nike" logo bottom left, red "Chicago Bulls" logo bottom right 36 x 17 30
80s   Poster, slide strip with 4 shots of MJ, red "Nike" logo bottom left, red "Air Jordan" logo bottom right, 36 x 22 45
90s   Poster, "Commemorative"...20
90s   Poster, "Earth to Mars," 22 x 36 20
90s   Poster, "Earth to Orbit," 22 x 36 20
90s   Poster, "Imagination," 5 pictures of MJ dunking, white sweatsuit, white "Air Jordan" logo bottom right 38 x 21 45
90s   Poster, "Is It the Shoes?" 24 x 36 20
90s   Poster, "Reverse Jam," 24 x 24 20
90s   Poster, "Sky Jordan" 20
90s   Poster, "Super Jordan," 24 x 36 20
90s   Poster, "Wings," door size, horizontal, 75 x 24 35
90s   Poster Sample Book-Reverse Dunk, Orbit, Wings, Playground, MVP, Shirts & Skins, Is It The Shoes-white, Is It The Shoes-black,
       High Flying 360, Earth & Mars, Jam & Slam, brown cover with hole and "poster" spelled out.....................................25

Posters-Sports Illustrated For Kids
90   Set of 4 Posters Distributed over 4 issues 21 x 32..55
       —2/90 Issue, Part 1, MJ's right hand with basketball 10.5 x 16..12
       —3/90 Issue, Part 2, MJ's right foot with crowd in background 10.5 x 16..12
       —4/90 Issue, Part 3, MJ from waist down jumping in air 10.5 x 16..12
       —5/90 Issue, Part 4, MJ from waist up jumping in air 10.5 x 16...12

Posters-Starline
88   Poster, MJ layup right hand, red 23, crowd in background, "Michael Jordan" top center, photo by Noren Trotman 16 x 20 35
90   Poster, "Jordan," 5 MJ pictures, "CB" & logo center 41 x 58 40
90   Poster, "Jordan," on left vertical, white 23, red & black striped on left vertical and bottom dunking, 16 x 20 40
90   Poster, "Michael Jordan" in red 7 black flag on bottom, red 23, dunking, tongue out, vs. Clippers # 20 8 x 24 25
92   Poster, "America's Team," team players with flag in background, .MJ in white USA #9 dunking 16 x 20 20
92   Poster, "America's Team," USA BB logo lower left, team players with flag in background 25
95   "1995," poster 5
96   "1996," poster 4
       —"Home-Red Uniform," poster 3
       —"Home-White Uniform," poster 3
       —"Soaring," poster 3

Posters-Starting Lineups
92   Poster-Walking with basketball 11 x 14 25
92   Poster-Soaring to Jam (7.136) 11 x 14 25

Posters-Wheaties Cereal Box
86   Poster, Slam Dunk Contest Action photos 16 x 23...60

Michael Jordan Memorabilia Checklist

89	Nike posters were attached to Wheaties boxes with series numbers 43, 56, 57, 18 oz. There were four different 2 sided posters. The back of the posters show a photo of all four posters and has the following quote, "Collect All Four"8' x 12'45	
	—Poster, Nike, jump shot next to brick wall, red shirt and black shorts, shooting with six kids, graffiti on white part of wall16 x 24"	10
	—Poster, Nike, dribbling next to brick wall, white shirt and black shorts,dribbling alone, graffiti on brick wall,16 x 24"	10
	—Poster, Nike, dunk shot in air, red #23 uniform, 1 camera man on floor,2 referees on floor, side view, 16 x 24"	10
	—Poster, Nike, flying through air to dunk shot, front-side view, 3:51 on clock, side view 16 x 24"	10
89	Wheaties attached 3 different, 4 sided posters, to cereal boxes with series numbers 73z. When the backs are assembled they made one large action photo of MJ dunking 24 x 48	15
	—Poster, MJ Bursting Out of Box, blue strip on cover, top poster section with head shot dunking on inside poster 8 x 12	5
	—Poster, MJ Bursting Out of Box, green strip on cover, middle poster section with chest and hip section on inside poster 8 x 12	5
	—Poster, MJ Bursting Out of Box, purple strip on cover, bottom section with knees and feet section on inside poster 8 x 12	5
89	Poster, MJ Bursting Out of Box, blue strip on cover, proof poster, top poster section with head shot dunking on inside poster	100
89	Poster, MJ Bursting Out of Box, green strip on cover, proof poster, middle poster section with chest and hip section	100
89	Poster, MJ Bursting Out of Box, purple strip on cover, proof poster, bottom section with knees and feet section on inside poster	100

Salvino Figurines

95	Baseball #2004, facsimile signature, certificate, original generation, 8 issued, black uniform master mold	1200
95	Baseball #2004, facsimile signature, swinging bat black uniform, 2500 issued	175
95	Baseball #2005 SP, facsimile signature, certificate, original generation, 8 issued, pinstripe uniformmaster mold	1200
95	Baseball #2005 SP, facsimile signature, swinging bat, pinstripe uniform, 343 issued	250
95	Baseball #2005 SP, hand signature, swinging bat, pinstripe uniform, 25 issued	1300
95	Basketball #1074 UDA, facsimile signature, 2 poles, knees straight,8 issued, red uniform,master mold	1200
95	Basketball #1074 UDA, facsimile signature, 2 poles, knees straight,	
95	Basketball #1074 UDA, facsimile signature, 2 poles, knees straight, ed uniform	175
95	Basketball #1074 UDA, facsimile signature, 2 poles, knees straight, 8 issued, original generation .master mold	1200
95	Basketball #1074 UDA, facsimile signature, 2 poles, knees straight,	
95	Basketball #1074 UDA, facsimile signature, 2 poles, knees straight, white uniform, 2500 issued	175
95	Basketball 700 UDA, facsimile signature, 1 pole, knees bend, certificate, original generationmaster mold	1200
95	Basketball 700 UDA, facsimile signature, 1 pole, knees bend, 16-20 issued,	
95	Basketball 700 UDA, facsimile signature, 1 pole, knees bend white uniform, jumping, 318 issued	325
95	Basketball 700 UDA, hand signature, 1 pole, knees bent, white uniform, jumping, 50 issued	1300
95	Basketball 700 UDA, facsimile signature, 1 pole, knees bent, 8 issued, red uniform, certificate, original generation master mold	1200
95	Basketball 700 UDA, facsimile signature, 1 pole, knees bent, 16-20 issued,	
95	Basketball 700 UDA, hand signature, 1 pole, knees bent, red uniform, jumping, 368 issued	225

School Folder

89	School Folder, "Introducing Chicago Bulls Sponsorship Opportunities," inside Bulls vs. Celtics on scoreboard, team in warmups huddled together front, back crowd shots, inside MJ, Jackson, SP, Bull-et, Mascot & full court view fold out	15

Sega Genesis

92	NBC Sports Barcelona 92 Olympic Games	40
92	Game, Team USA Basketball, MJ cover, made by Electronic Arts	40
92	Jordan vs. Bird, made by Electronic Arts (8.5)	40
92	Box & directions, Bulls vs. Lakers and the NBA Playoffs, MJ on box, made by Electronic Arts	40
93	Bulls vs. Blazers, no MJ on box, MJ in game	20

Starline

88	Photo, MJ vs. Celtics #20 8x10	6
88	Puzzle with poster, "Jordan" mouth open, New York #8 dunking, white #23,	20
88	Puzzle with poster, "Michael Jordan" tongue out, red #23, dunking, red border top/sides	20
88	Puzzle with poster, "Licensed to Jam Bucs #21," dunking, yellow strip, tongue out, red #23,	20
89	Book Cover, MJ front and back, red border, inside schedule for week and eight classroom periods, "Bulls" inside	5
89	Greeting card, MJ dunking vs. #20 Clippers, view behind the basket, red border, scoreboard in background, red 23, inside "Happy Birthday Michael Jordan" NBA-1	8
89	Greeting card, MJ layup vs. New York #33 Ewing, red border, red 23, inside "Michael Jordan NBA-1 NM	8
89	Greeting card, MJ waist up pose, red 23, red border, inside "Happy Birthday Michael Jordan" NBA-5	8
89	Greeting card, MJ waist up pose, red 23, red border, inside "Michael Jordan" NBA-5 NM	8
89	School folder, MJ front and back, red border, inside schedule for week and eight classroom periods, "Bulls" inside	3
	—Ad card, "Michael Jordan," red border, MJ dunking front view from side of basket, old red #2 3 x 5	10
	—Ad card, "Michael Jordan Star Series," gray background, 2 MJ pictures,red and white #23, Bulls logo 3 x 5	10
	—Ad card, "Michael Jordan, Chicago Bulls," ad card, white 23,hook shot layup, SP & crowd in background 3 x 5	10
	—Ad card, "Jordan Chicago Bulls," MJ dunking from side of basket,MJ front view, red 23, both hands overhead 3 x 5	10
	—Ad card, "Chicago Bulls," SP, DR & MJ, all jumping in air & shooting ball with right hand, Bulls logo 3 x 5	10
	—Ad card, "Jordan Out of this World," Bulls logo, MJ jumping with two hands on ball, world in background 3 x 5	10

Starting Lineup

88	Figure in box—blue card	35
89	One on One	150
89	White Box Slam Dunk Set, offered before Red Boxes, numbers and letters on mailing labels 6 units	
	—Michael Jordan, #32 Bulls, #1327 615 0029 07 on box mailing label	200
90	Red Box Slam Dunk, labels attached with numbers for individual players, all boxes produced with same number #96500, left over White Boxes were then sold as Red Boxes	200
90	Figure in box, All-Star	80
91	Palming ball, jumping	70
91	Shooting on floor	90
92	Dribbling poster,	75
92	Jump shot, in warm ups	75
92	USA	125
92	Headliner	70
93	Figure in box	80

Statues and Figurines

87	NBA Yalada from Spain, like SLU, white 23, feet flat, right hand out to side, holding basketball in left hand above head, red wrist band on left hand	125
87	MJ Horse Figure	25
92	USA #9 white, car window suction cup doll, suction cups on hands, cloth doll, plastic head with tongue out, black feet, 12"	60
95	Bank, statue, MJ holding basketball in RH, red 23, Bugs in white #23, holding carrot in left hand, Made in Mexico	50
96	MJ by Renaissance Company, bronze	250
97	MJ by Susan Wagner, bronze 23"	11,000
	—Celebrity Spoofs Dolls, 6," holding BB with right hand, cape, white #23, big brown eyes, Christhomas Corp, Irvine CA	50

1996 Space Jam movie poster with Warner Brothers characters (27 x 40). ($20)

Nike ad card with Mars Blackmon (Spike Lee). ($25)

1990 Starting Lineup figure in box. ($80)

Michael Jordan Memorabilia Checklist

1997 Christhomas Corp. Celebrity Spoofs doll. ($50)

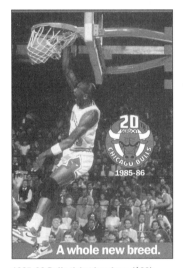

1985-86 Bulls ticket brochure ($60)

Ticket stubs from Bulls/Bucks ($20) and Jordan tribute game ($30)

Stickers: American Pro Basketball USA
95-96	Album and Stickers Service line, Modena Italy 190 stickers	100

STS Telephone Card
96	NBA Commemorative Yearbook Sets	175

Taco Bell
93	Untouch-A-Bull in '91, WIN!, MJ behind trophy	6
93	Unbelieve-A-Bull in '92, MJ behind hand	6

Team Schedules
84-85	Team Schedule Pamphlet-cover, in USA #9 red, slam dunk	90
84-85	Bulls Schedule-insid	35
85-86	NBA Schedule Pamphlet with MJ & Jabbar cover	35
85-86	Team Schedule Pamphlet 20th Anniversary cover, white 23, slam dunk	30
85-86	Bulls Schedule-front	30
86-87	Bulls Schedule-back	25
86-87	Individual/Group Ticket Order Form and Schedule,	
87-88	Bulls Schedule-front	20
88-89	Bulls Schedule-front	15
89-90	Illinois Basketball-MJ on back with Chevy	10
89-90	TNT & NBA Schedule-front	10
91-92	UD & NBA TV Schedule-front & inside, Catch All the Moves	6
91-92	Bulls Schedule, proof sheet, "Sky Man," MJ layup vs. Lakers, red 23, 39x55	75
91-92	Bulls Schedule-round disc, "World Champs," Cameo All-Stars	25
92-93	Bulls Schedule-front	5
92-93	Bulls Schedule-front, uncut double schedule, special insert in Chicago Sun Times Sports	15
92-93	NBA Schedule-inside, Includes, Broadcast & Cable	5
92-93	Bulls Schedule-round disc, "3 Peat A Bull? 28"	25
93-94	Bulls Schedule-round disc, "3 Time World Champ" 28"	25
94-95	Bulls Schedule-United front, No MJ	3
94-95	Birmingham Barons Schedule-front	5
95-96	Bulls Schedule-Logo front, MJ's shirt and shoes on back	2
96-97	Bulls Schedule Display with schedule, MJ on Display only, no MJ on schedule 2 items	15
96-97	NBA Schedule Book-MJ 3 pictures, NBA at 50	20

Ticket Stubs and Pamphlets
84-85	Season Ticket Pamphlet, red #9, '84 USA/Converse cover	100
84-85	Group/Individual Ticket Pamphlet, water damage, MJ in USA #9 & O. Woolridge #0 Bulls, b&w photos cover	75
85-86	Season/Group/Individual Ticket Brochure, "20th Season Chicago Bulls, A Whole New Breed," MJ reverse RH dunk under basket, white 23, 4 MJ photos in pamphlet	60
86-87	Season Ticket Pamphlet, 4 MJ pictures cover	50
87/88	Washington Bullets Ticket Pamphlet, MJ rebounding, Paxson cover	20
12/21/88	Milwaukee Bucks Ticket Stub, MJ waiting for rebound from #34 Bucks, Game 11 red 23, aqua ticket, game 114 x 2	20
12/29/88	Bulls Ticket Stub, MJ back view & SP front view slapping one hand, New York Knicks, white 23, red ticket 4.25 x 2	60
4/4/89	Bulls Ticket Stub, MJ layup with left hand, 2 Cavs. Players, Charlotte Hornets,gray ticket, True Value banner background	45
4/21/89	Bulls Ticket Stub, MJ in background from #34 Bucks, aqua background, Game 4 1Milwaukee Bucks, 2 x 4	25
11/21/89	Portland Trail Blazers Ticket Stub, MJ dribbling, Chicago Bulls, Game 7 red 23 with hair, not used 2 x 5.75	30
12/19/89	Bulls Ticket Stub, MJ back view slapping both hands with SP front view, Los Angeles Lakers, white 23, red ticket 4.25 x 2	45
1/12/90	Charlotte Hornets Ticket Stub, MJ left hand layup Game 18,aqua ticket, game 18 4.25 x 2	25
2/27/90	Bulls Ticket Stub, MJ layup with right hand, 2 New York & 1 Bulls players, Milwaukee Bucks, white 23,4.25 x 2	40
4/9/91	Bulls Ticket Stub, MJ slam dunk with right hand in front of basket, New York Knicks, white 23, blue ticket 4 x 2	35
4/19/91	Charlotte Hornets Ticket Stub, MJ blocking #3 Charlotte with right Game 41 arm, aqua ticket, red 23 4 x 2	25
11/5/91	Bulls Ticket Stub, MJ slam dunk with 2 players, Golden State Warriors, white 23, yellow ticket 4.25 x 2	45
12/10/91	Bulls Ticket Stub, MJ dunking, white 23, gray background, Seattle Supersonics 1.75 x 4	30
1/22/92	Bulls Ticket Stub, Bulls #23 jersey & Charlotte #50 jersey, vs. Game 19 Charlotte Hornets, white background 4 x 2	10
12/12/92	Bulls Ticket Stub, MJ & Scottie right fists in air, MJ holding BB, gray background, New Jersey Nets, MJ in white hat, SP in Game 9 black hat, 3rd guy holding trophy 6.25 x 3	25
92	NBA Playoff Ticket-Chicago Stadium, Home Game "O," No MJ, Trophy & Logo, 91 NBA World Champions 5.5 x 2	25
12/9/92	Bulls Ticket Stub, MJ in huddle in warmups Cleveland Cavaliers, Game 7 green ticket 7 x 3	20
1/22/93	Bulls Ticket Stub, MJ slam dunk with right hand, Charlotte Hornets, Game 21 gold ticket, white 23 6.25 x 3	65
2/17/93	Bulls Ticket Stub, MJ with hand in air and one with BB, Utah Jazz, Game 25 green ticket, white 23 7 x 3	40
3/5/93	Bulls Ticket Stub, MJ dunking, white 23, red background, Game 29 San Antonio Spurs, 6.25 x 3	25
3/12/93	Bulls Ticket Stub, MJ & team in huddle, gray background, Game 31 Charlotte Hornets, team in warm-ups (9.24) x 3	25
12/18/93	Bulls Ticket Stub, MJ in locker room getting champagne on head Game 8, San Antonio Spurs, yellow ticket, 6.25 x 3	35
12/20/93	Bulls Ticket Stub, MJ in team huddle, Charlotte Hornets, Game 9 yellow ticket, white 236.25 x 3	25
2/16/94	Bulls Ticket Stub, MJ and Phil Jackson hugging, Game 21 Miami Heat, black ticket, red 23 6.25 x 3	30
2/23/94	Bulls Ticket Stub, SP pouring champagne over, Golden State Warriors, Game 24 MJ & Team in locker room 6.25 x 3	25
2/26/94	Bulls Ticket Stub, team huddle in white uniform, blue background, Game 25 Indiana Pacers 6.25x3	25
3/8/94	Bulls Ticket Stub, MJ and Phil Jackson hugging, red 23, yellow background, Atlanta Hawks, locker room 5 x 3	25
3/25/94	Nets vs. Chicago, MJ layup RH, black background, gold "Michael," Game 33 Michael Jordan 3-Peat 7.5 x 2	20
3/24/95	Bulls Ticket Stub, MJ layup shot, Orlando Magic Game 1	20
11/2/96	Bulls Ticket Stub, Team Picture with Trophy, 76ers, yellow ticket 5 x 3	25
12/5/96	Bulls Ticket Stub, Court Pictures from stands yellow & gold ticket Game 7 5 x 3	15
96	NBA Eastern Conference Finals Media Pass for all Games, postcard size with MJ & Scottie	30
1/25/97	Bulls Ticket Stub, #23 blue NBA All-Star, MJ slam dunk, vs. Raptors Game 22 6.25 x 3	30
5/97	NBA Playoffs vs. Atlanta, Game C, MJ hand on trophy Game	15
5/97	NBA Playoff Game Ticket, SP & MJ pouring champagne, blue border, Game game not played, tickets not used 3 x 7	15
5/97	NBA Playoff Game Ticket, SP & MJ pouring champagne, gold border, Game game not played, tickets not used seat 1 3 x 7	15
97	Media Pass NBA Playoffs, blank, Eastern Conference 1st Round	15
97	Media Pass NBA Playoffs, blank, Eastern Conference Semi Finals	20
97	Media Pass NBA Playoffs, blank, All Games, no clipped corners, Eastern Conference Finals 1623	25

Time Jordan Watches
85-86	Time Jordan Slam Dunk Champion, Excelsior International Corp., Kids Watches, 8 different versions-white band with white buckle and end loop, "Time Jordan" on buckle side above and through red lines, round white bezel, white face, blue number dots #6, 2 baskets 1 ball, red & white hands, "Time Jordan" on face	50
	—black band with black buckle and end loop, "Time Jordan" on buckle side of band above and through white line, round black bezel, white face with black BB courts at 12, 3, 6 & 9, black and white hands,"Time Jordan" on face	50

Michael Jordan Memorabilia Checklist

—red & black band with red buckle and end loop, "Time Jordan" on buckle side of band below black line, round red bezel, 1/2 white 1/2 red face, BB & hoop, bouncing ball, black/white hands "Time Jordan" on face 50
—red & black band with red buckle and end loop, "Time Jordan" onbuckle side of band above and through black line, round black bezel/ white face with red-black circle, BB & hoop, black/white hands and "Time Jordan" on face 50
—red & black link band, round black bezel/red-black face, "Time Jordan" on face 50
—white band with red buckle & bezel band ends, white band end loop, rectangle orange BB court face with 2 red/white lines, ...50
—black band with red buckle & bezel band ends, black band end loop, rectangle black BB court face with 2 red/white lines, ...50
—black band with white buckle & bezel band ends, black band end loop, rectangle gray BB court face with 2 red/white lines, ...50

True Value
91-92 Coin & Package, MJ name on package, Back 2 Back wins Highlighting a Championship Year bronze...15
92-93 Coin & MJ name on package, Back to Back to Back, bronze...10

TV Sports Calendar Pamphlets
91 NBA Action on TBS, Ads not completed proto 10
92 NBA Action on TBS, Hass Pub at Dominick cover...8
93 Slam into the New Season, Longs Pharmacy cover..6
93 Slam into the New Season, Haas Pub. at Jewel 5

UD & UDA
91-92 Ad Folder with 6 sides & 6 Sheets 20
—Nobody Does Basketball Like UD, 7 MJ pictures on folder, folder
—We're Keeping the Best Players, in the NBA Under Wraps, MJ on sheet, sheet 1
—On the Courts & in the Locker Room, A New Way to Get ..., MJ on sheet, sheet 2
—All Pro. All Season., MJ on sheet, sheet 3
—Inaugural NBA BB 91-92 Season, b & w, MJ on sheet, sheet 4
—Low # Case Information, MJ on sheet, sheet 5
—Dear Hobby Customer Letter, MJ on sheet, sheet 6
91-92 Ad Folder with 6 sides & 4 sheets high # 25
—Nobody Does Basketball Like UD, 7 MJ pictures on folder, folder
—"We're Keeping the Best Players in the NBA Under Wraps," MJ on sheet, sheet 1
—"On the Courts & in the Locker Room, A New Way to Get ...," MJ on sheet, sheet 2
—"Make a High Percentage Shot With the UD High Series," MJ on sheet, sheet 3
—All Pro All Season. MJ on sheet, sheet 4
92 Magazine, Upper Deck Direct Dealer Program, box, 15,000 produced 35
92-93 Ad Folder, 4 sided folder 20
91-92 Ad Sheet, magazine, Rise Above the Rest folded 1
91-92 Sheet, Orlando All-Star Weekend, 1 MJ picture Gatorade, blank back, 22,000 produced 10
91-92 Sheet, Hologram Scoring Leader, uncut, non perforated 75
—8 full MJ cards AW-1
—4 top half MJ cards AW-
—4 bottom half MJ cards AW-1
92 Sheet, '92 USA BB Team, 1 MJ picture, Team Picture, blank back, 80,000 produced 10
92 Game, All-Stars, restickable items to cover walls, MJ & Mullin in USA Basketball Olympic Uniforms, #8082 20x20.........................10
92-93 Sheet, The Ultimate Hoop It Up 3 on 3 Matchup, 1 MJ picture, East vs. West, no perforations NNO 10
92-93 Sheet, 1992-93 Bulls, 4/20/93, 1 MJ picture, Jewel & Nabisco, blank back, 22,500 produced 15
93 Ad Sheet, Pro View; MJ holding card, MJ on card and glasses 5
93 Ad Sheet, Pro View; card, pack and box on sheet 1
93 Sheet, Adventures in 'Toon World, 2 MJ pictures, movie ad sheet 2
93 Sheet, 1993 National, Chicago July 20-25, 2 MJ pictures, UD Five Year Anniversary, blank back NNO..15
93 Sheet, NBA Jam Session, Sydney 8/31/93, Melbourne 9/3/93, 1 MJ picture, 48,500 issued 10
93 Standee, MJ waist up view, red 23, holding his own ....
93-94 Sheet, 1993-94 Chicago Bulls, 11/13/93, blank back, 52,000 produced, no MJ on sheet 4
94 Ad Sheet, Pro View; card, pack and box on sheet 4
94 Golf balls, UDA CC, 3 pack, black picture & signature 80012 15
94 Magazine, Introducing MJ Memorabilia, UDA Catalog Ed-8 8
94 Magazine, Amazing Michael, UDA Catalog Ed-11 8
94 Magazine, Holiday Issue Ed-12 8
94 Magazine, Holiday Issue Ed-13 8
94 Magazine, UDA Catalog, "Can Mike Save Baseball" 8
94 Pins, Baseball Set, 2,500 sets issued 3 pins...30
—swinging, white #23
—running, black and white
—swinging, red and white
94 Pins, CC Collector Series Edition. Set 3 pins 15
—MJ Retirement
—Bull Logo
—Team MVP
94 Sheet, Father's Day, MJ, Montana, Gretzky, Williams, non perforated sheet, 7,500 issued 15
94 Sheet, From Slam Dunk to Grand Slam Set, Salute to MJ Minor League Debut
—MJ Baseball Sheet, Salute to MJ, blank back, 50,000 produced 12
—8/1994 Minor League Packs 97 cards
94 Sheet, Salutes MJ-9 Sensational NBA Seasons, sitting, 7 pictures, blank back, 40,000 produced 6
94 Sheet, Salutes MJ-9 Sensational NBA Seasons, flying, 7 pictures, blank back, 40,000 produced 6
94 Sheet, Salutes NBA Standouts During NBA All-Star Weekend, MJ's name on Flight Team card, 30,000 produced 4
94 Sheet, USA Basketball High Lights, World Championship of Basketball, MJ in USA #9, hands on knees, 8/4 to 14/94, Toronto Canada, taken from magazine NNO..10
94 Statue, Sam, Inc. Bobbing Head Doll & Box, Bulls Basketball, 10,000 produced, model #2300 75
94 Statue, Sam, Inc. Bobbing Head Doll & Box, Barons Baseball, 10,000 produced, ...75
94-95 Ad Sheet, Collectors Choice Series 2 foil 1
94-95 Card, Soccer, Spanish World Cup USA ....
94-95 Sheet, Salutes MJ/Jewel, 3 MJ pictures, blank back, 50,000 produced 10
95 Ad Sheet, CC NBA Series One 1
95 Ad Sheet, MJ Bleacher Medal Card 1
95 Ad Sheet, MJ Tribute Medal Card Set Baseball 1
—Basketball with Signature, Air Slammin' Exclusive 6..2

Time Jordan wrist watch (white). ($50)

Game worn Bulls or Olympic uniform jerseys. ($10,000-$20,000)

1980s "MVP" 6-inch pin/button. ($25)

Michael Jordan Memorabilia Checklist

1996 Upper Deck Authenticated cardboard "Standee" display. ($25)

1994 Upper Deck commemorative baseball sheet. ($12)

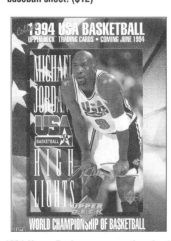

1994 Upper Deck commemorative sheet from magazine. ($10)

UDA Items

Baseball, Autographed	360
Basketball, MJ Autographed	600
Basketball, MJ Autographed "I'm Back," laser, 1,995 issued	650
Basketball, Wilson, "Jordan Portrait Basketball" Painting, autographed, 200 issues	1600
Basketball/Baseball, MJ Autographed, Nike, with Display, 1,000 issued	350
Bat, Autographed, Baseball, 500 issued	800
Book, "Rare Air," Linen Sleeve, autographed	500
Book, "Rare Air," Linen Sleeve, 2,500 issued	100
Book, "Rare Air," with black cover, slipcase, autographed, #12917, 2,500 issued	500
Book, "Rare Air," with black cover, slipcase, unsigned, 2,500 issued	100
Cap, Autographed, White Sox, 500 issued	200
Card, NC, "10 Time All-Star," die cut, commemorative, 3.5 x 5	15
Sports Illustrated, 7/84, "USA," framed, 2,500 issued	100
Sports Illustrated, '84 "A Star is Born," framed, 2,500 issued	100
Floor, Autographed Chicago Stadium, with Gatorade 8 x 10,	800
Jersey, Autographed, #23 Red, unframed	950
Jersey, Autographed, #23 White, unframed	950
Jersey, Autographed, #23 Black, unframed	950
Jersey, Autographed, #45 Red, N/A, unframed	950
Jersey, Autographed, #45 White, N/A, unframed	950
Jersey, Autographed Barons, white, unframed, 500 issued	700
Newspaper, MJ Chicago Tribune Retirement, 2,500 issued, 10/13/93, framed 6	100
Newspaper, MJ Chicago Tribune Cover, "Thanks for the Memories," 1000 issued	100
Photo, Autographed "Returns," unframed Josten, 8 x 10	300
Photo, Autographed "Gatorade Slam, Dunk," framed, 8 x 10	300
Photo, Autographed "Crying Trophy," framed, 16 x 20	600
Photo, Autographed "Crying Trophy," unframed, 16 x 20	500
Photo, Autographed "Slam Dunk," unframed, 16 x 20	500
Photo, Autographed "Slam Dunk," framed, 16 x 20	600
Photo, Autographed "Jordan Flying," 16 x 20, framed	600
Photo, Autographed "Jordan Flying," 16 x 20, unframed	500
Photo, Autographed "Trophy," 16 x 20, framed	600
Photo, Autographed "Trophy," 16 x 20, unframed	500
Photo, Unsigned "Trophy," 16 x 20, frame	150
Photo, MJ/Magic/Bird Autographs, 16 x 20, USA, framed	1200
Photo, MJ/Magic/Bird Autographs, 16 x 20, USA	1200
Photo, MJ/Magic Autographs, 91 Finals, 16 x 20, 1,991 issued	900
Photo, MJ/Magic Autographs, 91 Finals, 16 x 20, 1,991 issued	800
Photo, MJ/Magic Autographs, At Net, 16 x 20, framed	900
Photo, MJ/Magic Autographs, At Net, 16 x 20, unframed	800
Photo, NC, Autographed "17 Seconds," 8 x 10, unframed Josten	300
Photo, NC, Autographed, "UNC Dunk," 16 x 20, framed	600
Photo, NC, Autographed, "UNC Dunk," 16 x 20, unframed	500
Photo, NC, Autographed "17 Seconds," 16 x 20, unframed, 750 issued	500
Photo & Spring Training Ticket, matted & framed	100
Pins, MJ Individual, 12 Pack	135

USA Today Newspapers

6/13/91	Bulls Capture 1st NBA Title cover	12
6/15/91	Chicago Bulls to 2nd Title cover	12
6/21/91	Bulls' Three-Peat Thriller cover	12
6/4/93	Weekend Newspaper Insert-Is This the New National Past Time cover	8
10/7/93	Goodbye To The Game cover	8
4/19/94	Baseball Weekly, Michael Mania cover	5
10/11/94	Baseball Weekly, Is Arizona Out of Jordan's League cover	5
4/24/97	Who can beat the Bulls cover	4
6/2/97	MJ Stops Jazz at Buzzer cover	4
6/3/97	MJ Knows Malone's Agony inside	4
6/4/97	Round 2 for Utah, Chicago inside	4
6/5/97	Bulls Silence Jazz front	4
6/6-8/97	Can Jazz Stay Alive front	4
6/9/97	Utah Ties Bulls 2-2 front	4
6/10/97	Jordan Hopes Tie front	4
6/11/97	Sloan Has Jazz Rocking inside	4
6/12/97	Bulls Beat Jazz front	4

1994 Kid's Wilson bat and ball set. ($60)

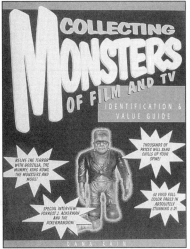

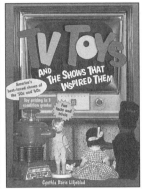